EUROPE

ON A SHOESTRING

Janet Austin
Carolyn Bain
Neal Bedford
Glenda Bendure
Lou Callan
Verity Campbell
Peter Carney
Geert Cole
Joyce Connolly
Graeme Cornwallis
Fionn Davenport
Paul Dawson
Matt Fletcher
Susan Forsythe
Ned Friary
Kate Galbraith
Jeremy Gray
Anthony Haywood
Paul Hellander
Mark Honan
Patrick Horton
Keti Japaridze
John King
Steve Kokker
Leanne Logan
Clay Lucas

Sarah Mathers
Emma Miller
Richard Nebeský
John Noble
Tim Nollen
Oda O'Carroll
Jeanne Oliver
Nick Ray
Daniel Robinson
Miles Roddis
David Rowson
Andrea Schulte-
Peevers
Tom Smallman
Rachel Suddart
Bryn Thomas
Rebecca Turner
Ryan Ver Berkmoes
Mara Vorhees
Kim Wildman
Julia Wilkinson
David Willett
Nicola Williams
Neil Wilson
Pat Yale

LONELY PLANET PUBLICATIONS
Melbourne | Oakland | London | Paris

EUROPE

58°N   32°W   66°N   16°W   8°W   0°

40°W

ATLANTIC OCEAN

Faxaflói

GREENLAND SEA

Ísafjörður

Akureyri

Reykjavík ⭑ ICELAND   Egilsstðir

Vestmannaeyjar   Þórsmörk   Seðisfjöður

Heimaey   Vík

ARCTIC CIRCLE

NORWEGIAN SEA

FAROE ISLANDS
Denmark
⭑ **Tórshavn**

Ålesund

NORWAY

Bergen

Shetland Islands

Stavanger

32°W

Kristiansand

Orkney Islands

50°N

Outer Hebrides

Inverness

Aberdeen

Aalborg

NORTH SEA

Oban   Scotland   Dundee

Derry   **Glasgow**   **Edinburgh**

DENMARK

Árhus

24°W

Odense

Galway   NI   **Belfast**   **Newcastle-upon-Tyne**

Isle of Man   Middlesborough

IRELAND   Irish Sea

Lübeck

Dublin   Liverpool   York

Killarney   Cork   Manchester

BRITAIN

Frisian Islands

Hamburg

Rosslare   Wales   **Birmingham**

St George's Ch   Swansea   England   NETHERLANDS

Amsterdam   Hanover

Cardiff   Oxford   **London**   The Hague

Bristol   Rotterdam   Düsseldorf

GERMANY

42°N

Plymouth   Portsmouth   Cologne

English Channel   Le Havre   **Brussels**

Channel Is   Rouen   BELGIUM

Brest   St Malo   Caen   Rheims   Frankfurt/Main

Quimper   Rennes   **Paris**   LUXEMBOURG

St Nazaire   **Nantes**   Blois   Nancy   **Luxembourg**   Stuttgart

Tours   Dijon   **Strasbourg**   Munich

La Rochelle   F R A N C E   Freiburg   Liechtenstein

Limoges   **Bern**   Zürich

Bay of Biscay   Bordeaux   Lausanne   SWITZERLAND

La Coruña   Geneva   Venice

Vigo   Santiago de Compostela   Gijón   Santander   Clermont-Ferrand   Mt Blanc 4807m   **Lyon**   Milan

Léon   **Bilbao**   Bayonne   **Turin**   Genoa   Bologna

Porto   San Sebastián   Toulouse   Avignon   San Marino

Coimbra   Pamplona   Nîmes   Nice   Florence

PORTUGAL   Andorra la Vella   ANDORRA   Monaco   Pisa

Duero   **Marseille**

Lisbon   **Zaragoza**   Corsica   Elba

Badajoz   **Madrid**   **Barcelona**   Ajaccio   **Rome**

Évora   Toledo   Tarragona

16°W   S P A I N   **Valencia**

Córdoba   Majorca

34°N

Faro   **Seville**   Granada   Alicante   Palma   Sassari

Cádiz   **Málaga**   Murcia   Balearic Islands   Sardinia   Tyrrhenian Sea

Tangier   Gibraltar Br   Almería   Cagliari

Str of Gibraltar   Ceuta Sp   MEDITERRANEAN SEA   Palermo

Tetouan   Melilla Sp   **Algiers**

Rabat   Fès   Oran   Annaba   Bizerte   Italy

Casablanca   Meknès   Oujda   Constantine   **Tunis**   Pantelleria

CANARY ISLANDS Sp   MOROCCO   Sousse

Marrakesh   Isole Pelagie

Agadir   A L G E R I A   TUNISIA

El Aaiun   **8°W**   **0°**   **8°E**   **Tripoli** LIBYA

0   250   500 km
0   150   300 mi

GERMANY 487

GREECE 567

HUNGARY 613

8 Contents – Text

Contents – Maps

The Authors

Janet Austin

Janet worked on the Italy chapter. Her taste for travel was fostered at an early age with two child-hood ocean voyages from Australia to the UK. She was lured back in her teenage years by a love for all things European and the London punk rock explosion, remaining for over 10 years. Janet edits Lonely Planet's travel literature series, Journeys, which allows her to vicariously clock up some kilometres while sitting in front of a computer screen. She is married and lives in Melbourne with two grey cats.

Carolyn Bain

Carolyn worked on the Greece chapter. She was born in Melbourne, Australia (the third-largest Greek city in the world) and first visited Greece as a teenager (on a package tour from Scandi-navia, no less). She was therefore eminently qualified to ferry-hop around two dozen Greek islands in search of the perfect beach, best calamari and any unattached shipping magnates. Due to an unfortunate shortage of shipping magnates, she returned to her job as an editor at Lonely Planet's Melbourne office.

Neal Bedford

Neal worked on the Spain and Britain chapters. Born in Papakura, New Zealand, Neal gave up an exciting career in accounting after university to experience the mundane life of a traveller. With the urge to move, travel led him through a number of countries and jobs, ranging from an au pair in Vienna, lifeguard in the USA, fruit picker in Israel and lettuce washer at rock concerts. De-ciding to give his life some direction, he well and truly got his foot stuck in the door by landing the lucrative job of packing books in Lonely Planet's London office. One thing led to another and he managed to cross over to the mystic world of authoring. Neal currently resides in London.

Lou Callan

Lou worked on the Britain chapter. After four years at LP as an editor, she packed up and fol-lowed her husband to the red dunes of the United Arab Emirates for a very long, hot 2½ years. Here she wrote LP's *Dubai* city guide and, with Gordon Robison, *Oman & UAE* as well as an update for *Middle East* (3rd edition). Lou is now very nicely wedged between beaches and wineries on the Mornington Peninsula in Victoria with Tony the husband and Ziggy the cat.

Verity Campbell

Verity worked on the Turkey chapter. Born with a ticket in her hand, Verity was on a mission to have a full passport by the age of seven. Struggling to fight the travel bug, she went to Uni and studied Landscape Architecture. It was in vain – a year later she quit her graduate job and wrestled Tony Wheeler to the ground to land a job at Lonely Planet (Melbourne). She jumped (literally) at the chance to return to Turkey where she lived in 1990-91. Lured by Turkish Delight and misdemeanours, İstanbul nightlife and with a belly to dance she all too willingly abandoned her hairy companion Max.

Peter Carney

Peter updated the Bulgaria chapter. Born into a military family, his wanderlust has led him to mag-azine writing in Japan, ski-bumming in Aspen and training US Peace Corps volunteers in Ukraine. Bulgaria has been home since 1991 when he arrived in the midst of heady post-communist revelry to train Bulgarian teachers of English. Three years later he traded in academia for a rucksack full of writing paraphernalia and set off, like a latter-day ronin, to roam the country in endless search of unusual and captivating stories. The result is four self-published regional guidebooks to Bulgaria and numerous print and online articles.

Joyce Connolly

Joyce Connolly worked on the Morocco chapter. Born in Edinburgh, Scotland, she has been on the move since an early age, including time in Germany and the Netherlands where she developed an appreciation of fine beers. Fuelled by the travel bug, she studied to become a professional tourist but instead stumbled into publishing in Oxford. In 1995 she set off to Australia in pursuit of Jason Donovan who obligingly moved in round the corner from her in Bondi. Having satisfied that urge she moved to Melbourne to woo LP; she became an editor and was entrusted with updating the Gippsland chapter of the *Victoria* guide. Since then she's flown the editorial coop to update the Zimbabwe chapter of *Southern Africa* and *Morocco*. She's now back in the UK trying to come with terms with the British weather.

Graeme Cornwallis

Graeme updated the Iceland and Sweden chapters in this book. Born and raised in Edinburgh, Graeme later wandered around Scotland before coming to rest in Glasgow. While studying astronomy at Glasgow University, he developed a passion for peaks – particularly the Scottish Munros – and eventually bagged all 284 summits over 3000ft in Scotland at least once. Graeme has travelled extensively throughout Scandinavia, Asia, North & South America and the Pacific. Mountaineering successes include trips to the Bolivian Andes, arctic Greenland and Norway. When he's not hiking, climbing or travelling, Graeme teaches mathematics and physics at home in Glasgow.

Fionn Davenport

Fionn worked on the Britain and Italy chapters. He was born in and spent most of his youth in Dublin – that is, when his family wasn't moving him to Buenos Aires or Geneva or New York (all thanks to his Dad, whose job took him far and wide). Infected with the travel disease, he became a nomad in his own right after graduating from Trinity College, moving first to Paris and then to New York, where he spent five years as a travel editor and sometime writer. The call of home was too much to resist, however, so armed with his portable computer, his record collection and an empty wallet he returned to Dublin. When he's not DJing in pubs and clubs throughout the city he's writing and updating travel guides. He has worked on Lonely Planet guides to *Spain*, *Dublin*, *Ireland*, *Sicily*, *England* and *Britain*.

Paul Dawson

Paul updated the Ireland chapter. He was born in Melbourne, and after a lengthy degree in architecture he studied literature, travelled, then ended up drawing maps and laying out pages for Lonely Planet's European guidebooks.

Matt Fletcher

Matt worked on the Morocco chapter. After travelling on and off since leaving Art College, Matt got the inspiration for a writing career while travelling down through Southern Africa. A brief incarnation as a staff writer on an adventure sports magazine soon passed on and Matt has been freelancing ever since, travelling and trekking in the UK, Europe and East Africa. Matt is a contributor to Lonely Planet's *Walking in Spain* and *Walking in Australia, Kenya* and *East Africa* guides. When not working he plays at playing football and studies libel law.

Ned Friary & Glenda Bendure
Ned and Glenda updated the Denmark and Norway chapters. Ned grew up near Boston, studied Social Thought and Political Economy at the University of Massachusetts in Amherst and upon graduating headed west. Glenda grew up in California's Mojave Desert and first travelled overseas as a high school AFS exchange student to India. She graduated from the University of California, Santa Cruz.

Glenda and Ned met in Santa Cruz, California. They spent several years travelling throughout Asia and the Pacific, including stints in Japan where Ned taught English and Glenda edited a monthly magazine. Their first book was Lonely Planet's *Micronesia* and since then they have authored LP's guides to *Denmark*, *Hawaii*, *Oahu*, *Bermuda* and the *Eastern Caribbean*. They live on Cape Cod in Massachusetts.

Kate Galbraith
Kate updated the Albania and Macedonia chapters (and, perhaps a bit crazed from Macedonian rakija, she flew home to run the London marathon in between). Born in Washington, DC, Kate first heard the call of the Balkans in 1996, when she spent the summer before her final year at Harvard University working for a local news agency in Sarajevo. Two years later she updated the Bosnia-Hercegovina chapter for *Eastern Europe 5*, her first LP assignment; subsequent LP sojourns include *Latvia* and *Micronesia*. Kate recently finished a Masters degree at the London School of Economics in Eastern European political economy. She currently works for Economist.com, the Web site of *The Economist* magazine, in New York and London.

Jeremy Gray
Jeremy worked on the France chapter. A Louisiana native, he studied literature and business in the wilds of Texas before moving to Germany on a scholarship in 1984. Infatuated with Europe, he chucked his MBA plans and stayed on to teach English, translate and best of all, file plumbing orders for the US Air Force. In the meantime he grew to appreciate many things French, such as the wonderful way the *pâtisseries* wrap takeaway cakes like baby gifts.

A master's degree in international relations from Canterbury led Jeremy back to Germany, where he spent the 1990s chasing politicians and CEOs for news agencies, newspapers and television. While freelancing for the *Financial Times* he discovered Lonely Planet, and since 1998 has contributed to or written *Germany*, *The Netherlands* and city guides for *Munich* and *Montreal*. He lives in Amsterdam, a mere three-hour drive from the French border.

Anthony Haywood
Anthony worked on the Germany chapter. Born in the port town of Fremantle, Australia, Anthony first pulled anchor at 18 to spend two years travelling through Europe and the USA. He studied literature and then Russian language at university, and worked as a technical writer, editor and trainer in Melbourne before taking up residence in Germany in 1992. Since then he has worked on a number of Lonely Planet guidebooks, including *Germany* and *Russia, Ukraine & Belarus*, while also contributing to Lonely Planet's travel literature and restaurant guides series. He is based in Frankfurt am Main, where he works as a journalist, author and translator.

Paul Hellander
Paul worked on the France chapter. He has never really stopped travelling since he first looked at a map in his native England. He graduated from Birmingham University with a degree in Greek before heading for Australia. He taught Modern Greek and trained interpreters and translators for thirteen years before throwing it all away for a life as a travel writer. Paul has contributed to over 20 LP titles including guides to *Greece*, *Cyprus*, *Israel*, *Eastern Europe*, *Singapore* and *Central*

America. When not travelling with his PC and Nikon, he lives in Adelaide, South Australia. He was last spotted heading once more for Greece to write a guide to *Rhodes & the Dodecanese*.

Mark Honan

Mark worked on the Austria, Liechtenstein, Switzerland and Getting Around chapters. After a university degree in philosophy opened up a glittering career as an office clerk, Mark decided that there was more to life than data entry. He set off on a two-year trip round the world, armed with a backpack and an intent to sell travel stories and pictures upon his return. Astonishingly, this barely-formed plan succeeded and Mark has since contributed regularly to magazine travel pages. He started writing for Lonely Planet in 1991 and has worked on guides to *Vienna, Austria, Switzerland, India, Mexico, Central America* and *Solomon Islands* – next up are *Vienna* and *Austria* again.

Patrick Horton

Patrick updated the Yugoslavia chapter. Patrick, a writer and photographer, was born with restless feet. He travelled extensively in his native Britain before hitting the around-the-world trail as a Thatcher refugee in 1985. Since bringing his old British bikes out to Australia, he now calls Melbourne home. He prefers the more arcane areas of travel such as North Korea, Eritrea or Tonga, or riding a motorcycle over the Himalaya. He lives with his long-suffering partner Christine, another ardent traveller he met in Paris. Patrick has had photographs published in many Lonely Planet guides and contributed to Lonely Planet's *Australia* guide.

Keti Japaridze

Keti worked on the Bosnia-Hercegovina chapter. Born in Tbilisi, Georgia, Keti is an art historian by profession. The writing of the Georgia section of the Lonely Planet guide to *Georgia, Armenia & Azerbaijan* with her husband David introduced her to the world of travel writing, a development unlikely to have occurred when her country was part of the USSR. She was fascinated to compare the culture and recent history of Bosnia-Hercegovina, another former communist republic in the south-east of Europe, with that of her homeland, and impressed by the sense of a country bursting with vitality again after the terrible years of war.

Steve Kokker

Steve Kokker worked on the St Petersburg, Estonia, Latvia and Lithuania chapters. Steve is a writer from Montreal, Canada, who used his degrees in psychology to work as a counsellor before taking up film criticism. He later quit his position as editor and critic to be true to his peripatetic soul (24 countries and counting!). After a 1992 visit to his father's homeland, Estonia, he fell in love with the Baltic region, eventually moving to Tallinn and St Petersburg and travelling through Russia. He now works as a writer and independent videomaker whose documentaries have been screened in international film festivals. He's currently based in Tallinn.

Leanne Logan & Geert Cole

Leanne and Geert worked on the Belgium, Luxembourg and Netherlands chapters. Leanne has long been lured by travel. Bitten by the bug before even reaching her teens, she has spent much of the past 10 years travelling and writing for Lonely Planet. A journalist by trade, Leanne was conducting research into Belgium's multitude of beers when she met local connoisseur, Geert Cole, in 1991. The pair have been a team ever since.

Born in Antwerp in Belgium, Geert swapped university and art studies in the 1970s to discover broader horizons and other cultures. Each trip resulted in an extra diary being put on the shelf and another job experience being added to life's list. A spark of destiny saw this artist, cook, writer, traveller and landscaper linked to partner/colleague, Leanne, with whom he lives in Australia on the fertile slopes of an extinct volcano.

Clay Lucas

Clay worked on the Finland chapter. After a puzzling degree in public relations at Melbourne's RMIT, Clay found he was not up to writing press releases and instead launched his career in television at local station GTV9, dubbing videotapes and chatting to *Sale of the Century's* Pete Smith each morning. Realising after six months he was as ill-suited to the strange world of TV as he was PR, Clay landed a job sub-editing on *The Jakarta Post* newspaper during the dying days of the Suharto regime in 1997-98. He returned to Australia to work for Lonely Planet, as an editor and then on the Web site. He now lives in London, writing content for youth website lifebyte.com, and also working on Lonely Planet's CitySync Palm Pilot guides.

Emma Miller

Emma worked on the Hungary chapter. Born and bred in the 'burbs of Melbourne, Emma always knew there was a bigger and weirder world out there, courtesy of her Polish, Lithuanian, British and Dutch heritage. She complicated matters by studying Indonesian and French, then got a BA in Journalism, with dangerously small doses of German and Japanese thrown in for good measure. After working as a reporter for Melbourne's *Herald Sun*, Emma joined Lonely Planet as an editor, going on to join the gang of LP authors.

Emma is a now a freelance writer and editor in London; she has updated the Sumatra chapter of Lonely Planet's *Indonesia* guide and played restaurant critic for Lonely Planet's *Out to Eat – Melbourne*.

Richard Nebeský

Richard worked on the Czech Republic chapter. Born one snowy evening in the grungy Praha suburb of Žižkov, Richard got his taste for travelling early in his life, when his parents dragged him away from the 'pretentious socialist paradise' of Czechoslovakia after it was invaded by the 'brotherly' Soviet troops. A stint on campus was followed by a working trek around the ski resorts of the northern hemisphere and an overland odyssey across south Asia. Since joining Lonely Planet in 1987, he has co-authored I P's *Eastern Europe* and *Central Europe* phrasebooks, *Czech & Slovak Republics* and *Prague* city guide, and has helped to update the travel guides to *Australia; Victoria; Indonesia; Thailand; Russia, Ukraine & Belarus; France; Central Europe; Eastern Europe;* and *Europe on a shoestring*.

John Noble & Susan Forsyth

John and Susan worked on the Spain chapter. John comes from the Ribblesdale, England, Susan from Melbourne, Australia. After studies, John worked in Fleet Street journalism and Susan taught secondary and adult students. But travel distracted them both and one year they found themselves simultaneously in Sri Lanka – Susan working as a volunteer teacher and John carrying out his first commission for Lonely Planet. They married three years later and have since been kept extremely busy rearing two children, Isabella and Jack, as well as coauthoring heaps of Lonely Planet titles such as *Mexico, Spain, Andalucía, Indonesia, Russia, Ukraine & Belarus* and *Baltic States*. Current home base is an Andalucian hill village.

Oda O'Carol

Oda worked on the Britain chapter – her first assignment with Lonely Planet. Born in Roscommon, in the windy mid-west of Ireland, she packed her knapsack for the big smoke of Dublin where she studied communications until 1990. Since graduating she has worked as a television researcher and writer for the independent sector in Ireland. Oda also spent some time donkey-working on film sets and made her own short film in 1998. She has travelled extensively in Europe and last summer, chugged between America's coasts, with friends, in a clapped-out 1967 Cadillac (without air-con) and hopes to return soon for the northern route. She still lives happily in Dublin with her husband Eoin.

Jeanne Oliver

Jeanne Oliver updated the Croatia and Slovenia chapters. Born in New Jersey, she spent her childhood mulling over the *New York Times* travel section and plotting her future voyages. After a BA in English and a stint at the *Village Voice* newspaper, Jeanne got a law degree. Her legal practice was interrupted by ever-more-frequent trips to far-flung destinations and eventually she set off on a round-the-world trip that landed her in Paris. A job in the tourist business led to freelance writing assignments for magazines and guidebooks. She started working for Lonely Planet in 1996 and has written first editions of Lonely Planet's *Croatia, Crete* and *Crete Condensed* guides as well as updating chapters in *Greece, Mediterranean Europe* and *Eastern Europe*.

Nick Ray

Nick worked on the Britain chapter. A Londoner of sorts, he comes from Watford, the sort of town that makes you want to travel. For once he didn't have to travel too far, darting about the green fields of England, not to mention a few pubs along the way. Usually, he is to be found in the more obscure parts of Africa or Asia, Cambodia in particular, a country he thinks of as a second home. If you are heading that way, you might well run into him in Phnom Penh or Siem Reap.

Daniel Robinson

Daniel Robinson, who updated the Getting There & Away, Getting Around, Alsace & Lorraine, South-Western France, Dordogne, Quercy and Burgundy sections of the France chapter, was raised in the USA (the San Francisco Bay Area and Glen Ellyn, Illinois) and Israel. His passion for shoestring travel was kindled at age 17 with a trip to Cyprus, and since then he has spent several years on the road exploring some of the more remote parts of Asia, the Middle East and Europe. Daniel's work for Lonely Planet has included the first editions of the award-winning *Vietnam* and (with Tony Wheeler) *Cambodia*, and all four editions of *France*. Daniel has a BA in Near Eastern Studies from Princeton University and is currently finishing up an MA in Israeli history at Tel Aviv University.

Miles Roddis

Miles worked on the Andorra, France and Spain chapters. Miles and his partner Ingrid live in a shoe-box sized apartment in the Barrio del Carmen, the oldest and most vibrant quarter of Valencia, Spain. His involvement with France began when, 15 and spotty, he noisily threw up the night's red wine in a Paris cafe. Undeterred, he mainlined in French at university, became seriously hooked and later bought an equally tiny place in a hamlet in the Jura that will never feature in any guidebook.

Miles has contributed to Lonely Planet's *Africa on a Shoestring, West Africa, Read This First: Africa, Lonely Planet Unpacked, France, Spain, Walking in Britain, Walking in France* and *Walking in Spain*.

David Rowson

David worked on the Bosnia-Hercegovina chapter. Brought up in the suburbs of London, David graduated in English Literature and then hit on the time-honoured idea of teaching English as a good way to get out and see something of the world. This profession has taken him to Spain,

Egypt and Georgia. He was recently surprised to realise that he had spent a quarter of his life in Tbilisi, which came in handy when he wrote the Georgia part of the Lonely Planet guide to *Georgia, Armenia & Azerbaijan* with his wife Keti. He is now adapting to life in Kingston upon Thames again, but doesn't rule out future moves.

Andrea Schulte-Peevers

Andrea worked on the Spain chapter. She is a Los Angeles-based writer, editor and translator who caught the travel bug early and had been to all continents but Antarctica by the age of 18. After finishing high school in Germany, she decided the world was too big to stay in one place and moved first to London, then to Los Angeles. Armed with a degree from UCLA, she managed to turn her wanderlust into a professional career as a travel writer and may still chase penguins around the South Pole one of these days. Since joining the LP team in 1995 Andrea has updated and/or authored the guides to *Los Angeles, Berlin, Germany, California & Nevada* and *Spain*.

Tom Smallman

Tom worked on the Britain chapter. He lives in Melbourne, Australia, and had a number of jobs before joining Lonely Planet as an editor. He now works full time as an author and has worked on Lonely Planet guides to *Britain, Scotland, Edinburgh, Australia, New South Wales, Sydney, Canada, Ireland, Dublin* and *Pennsylvania*.

Rachel Suddart

Rachel updated the Cyprus Chapter. Born and raised in Cumbria, she escaped to the city to study English at Manchester University. After being eyeballed by the sphinx at the age of 15, she knew she wanted more and funded her subsequent travels by pulling endless pints, waiting tables and soldering circuit boards. Despite her dire navigational skills she has travelled round many countries and hopes to continue until she's too old to carry her ever-expanding rucksack. In January 2000, she got her first taste of Lonely Planet authorship by taking part in a BBC documentary. She currently lives in London where she thrives on paperback fiction, soap operas and copious amounts of salad cream.

Bryn Thomas

Bryn worked on the Britain chapter. Born in Zimbabwe, where he grew up on a farm, Bryn contracted an incurable case of wanderlust during camping holidays by the Indian Ocean in Mozambique. An anthropology degree at Durham University in England earned him a job polishing the leaves of pot plants in London. He also has been a ski-lift operator, encyclopedia seller, and an English teacher in Cairo, Singapore and Tokyo. Travel on six continents has included a 2500km Andean cycling trip. Bryn's first guide, the *Trans-Siberia Handbook*, was shortlisted for the Thomas Cook Guidebook of the Year awards. He is also coauthor of Lonely Planet's *Britain, India* and *Goa*, and has contributed to *Walking in Britain*.

Rebecca Turner

Rebecca worked on the Germany chapter and found that years of torturing the German language finally paid off during her research trip there, her first authoring job for LP. Rebecca grew up in Perth, Western Australia. After her studies, a journalism cadetship in lovely south-west WA (where she excelled in giant vegetable stories) and some overseas travel, poverty drove her into the Australian desert to write for the *Kalgoorlie Miner*. Later she moved to Melbourne to work for Lonely Planet as an editor and senior editor, and now lives in Sydney.

Ryan Ver Berkmoes

Ryan worked on the Britain chapter. He grew up in Santa Cruz, California and has held a number of jobs in journalism that have taken him far from the fog-drenched land of his youth. Among his work for Lonely Planet, he is the author of *Chicago* and *Moscow*, co-wrote *Texas* and *Canada* and co-ordinated *Russia, Ukraine & Belarus*; *Great Lakes*; *Out to Eat London*; *Netherlands*; *Britain* and *England*. In the future, Ryan hopes to add more warm weather destinations to the list above. He and his journalist wife Sara Marley reside in London near the point of inspiration for noted musician Nigel Tufnel.

Mara Vorhees

Mara updated the Poland chapter. She was born in St Clair Shores, Michigan. Her fascination with world cultures and her penchant for good deeds led her into the field of international development. She joined the ranks of the Circumnavigators Club upon completing a round-the-world investigation of foreign aid programs. After graduating from Georgetown University, she set off to assist Russia in its economic transition, although she claims no responsibility for the outcome. Having travelled extensively in Scandinavia and the former Soviet Union, she is trying to work her way to warmer climes. She now lives in Cambridge, Massachusetts with her cat and her husband.

Kim Wildman

Kim worked on the Romania chapter. She grew up in Toowoomba, Queensland, with parents who unwittingly instilled her desire to travel at a very young age by extending the immediate family to include 11 exchange students. After graduating from Queensland College of Art, having studied photography, Kim packed a backpack and headed to the USA and Bermuda. Her next adventure was Southern Africa. It was there she decided to combine her three loves: photography, writing and travelling. Kim has also studied journalism full-time and worked as a feature writer for *The Chronicle* in Toowoomba.

Julia Wilkinson & John King

Julia and John worked on the Portugal chapter. After leaving university, Julia set off from England for a jaunt round the world and immediately got sidetracked in Hong Kong, where she stayed for some 20 years, exploring Asia as a freelance travel writer and photographer. A frequent PATA award winner, she has contributed to numerous international publications. She is also author of Lonely Planet's *Lisbon* guide and coauthor, with her husband John King, of LP's *Portugal* and *South-West France*.

John grew up in the USA, and in earlier incarnations has been a physics teacher and an environmental consultant. In 1984 he headed off to China and ended up living there for half a year. He and Julia met in Lhasa. John took up travel writing with the 1st edition of LP's *Karakoram Highway*. He has also coauthored LP's *Pakistan*; *Central Asia*; *Russia, Ukraine & Belarus*; *Czech & Slovak Republics*; and the *Prague* city guide.

David Willett

David worked on the Greece chapter. He is a freelance journalist based near Bellingen on the north coast of New South Wales, Australia. He grew up in Hampshire, England, and wound up in Australia in 1980 after stints working on newspapers in Iran (1975-78) and Bahrain. He spent two years working as a sub-editor on the Melbourne *Sun* before trading a steady job for a warmer climate. Between jobs, David has travelled extensively in Europe, the Middle East and Asia. He is also the author of Lonely Planet's guide to *Tunisia* and coordinating author of *Greece*. He has contributed to various other guides, including *Africa*, *Australia*, *New South Wales*, *Indonesia* and *South-East Asia*.

Nicola Williams

Nicola worked on the France and Romania chapters. Since her first trip to Romania in 1991 with 10 Welsh policemen as part of an international aid convoy, her work as a journalist has taken her to most corners of Eastern Europe. Following 12 months in Latvia as features editor of the *Baltic Times* newspaper, she moved to Lithuania to bus it around the Baltics as editor-in-chief of the *In Your Pocket* city-guide series. In 1996 she traded in Lithuanian *cepelinai* for Lyonnais *andouillette*. Nicola has authored or updated several Lonely Planet titles, including *Romania & Moldova; Estonia, Latvia & Lithuania;* and *Russia, Ukraine & Belarus.*

Neil Wilson

Neil updated the Malta chapter. After working as a geologist in Australia and the North Sea and doing geological research at Oxford University, Neil gave up the rock business for the more precarious life of a freelance writer and photographer. Since 1988 he has travelled in five continents and written some 27 travel and walking guides for various publishers. He has worked on Lonely Planet's *Georgia, Armenia & Azerbaijan; Malta; Czech & Slovak Republics; Prague* and *Slovenia* guides. Although he was born in Glasgow, Neil defected to the east at the age of 18 and still lives in Edinburgh.

Pat Yale

Pat Yale worked on the Turkey chapter. Pat first went to Turkey in 1974 in an old van that didn't look as if it would make it past Dover. After graduating she spent several years selling holidays before throwing away sensible careerdom to head overland from Egypt to Zimbabwe. Returning home, she mixed teaching with extensive travelling in Europe, Asia, and Central and South America. A full-time writer now, she has worked on Lonely Planet *Britain, Ireland, London, Dublin, Middle East* and assorted other titles. She currently lives in an old pasha's house in Göreme, Cappadocia.

This Book

Europe on a shoestring is part of Lonely Planet's Europe series, which includes *Western Europe*, *Eastern Europe*, *Mediterranean Europe*, *Central Europe* and *Scandinavian & Baltic Europe*. Lonely Planet also publishes phrasebooks to these regions.

The first edition of this book was compiled and edited by Scott McNeely, based on chapters that were originally researched for the other books in the series.

This second edition of *Europe on a shoestring* was updated by the small army of authors whose names are listed on the previous pages.

From the Publisher

The editing of this edition of *Europe on a shoestring* was coordinated by Kalya Ryan and the cartography by Mark Germanchis. They were assisted by Susie Ashworth, Caroline Bain, Yvonne Bischofberger, Lisa Borg, Simon Bracken, Yvonne Byron, Csanád Csutoros, Hunor Csutoros, Melanie Dankel, Tony Davidson, Janine Eberle, Tony Fankhauser, Susannah Farfor, Liz Filleul, Quentin Frayne, Cris Gibcus, Gabrielle Green, Mark Griffiths, Rachel Imeson, Birgit Jordan, Kate Kiely, Joelene Kowalski, Dan Levin, Craig MacKenzie, Sarah Mathers, Fiona Meiers, Lara Morcombe, Sally Morgan, Shelley Muir, Anne Mulvaney, Sarah Mathers, Tim Nollen, Darren O'Connell, Brett Pascoe, Paul Piaia, Adrian Persoglia, Agustín Poó y Balbontin, Jacqui Saunders, Tom Smallman, Ray Thompson, Celia Wood and Chris Wyness.

Acknowledgements

THANKS

Many thanks to the travellers who used the last edition and wrote to us with helpful hints, useful advice and interesting anecdotes:

Adina McCarthy, Aileen & Terry Wilson, Alen Kursar, Alex Grenero, Amanda Jefferies, Andrew Hill, Aned Muniz, Anthony Everard, Ashley Coon, Barbara Morrison, Bruno Geoffrion, Catherine Matzig, Cathy Constable, Cheryl Roberston, Chris Phillips, Christine Valentine, Clare Carmody, Cornelia Ionescu, Daniel McCormack, David Clarke, David Dramountains, David Holzer, David Smale, David Woods, Dineke De Groot, Dirk de Man, Doug Lewin, Dr Thomas Rapp, Dylan Brown, Elizabeth Evatt, Emily Lo, Enda Nolan, Eng Seng, Evangelos Photi, Felicity McGrath, Frank Bovelander, Fred Borman, Geoff Caflisch, Graham Giaame, Graham Phollips, Helen Pavlinovich, Horia Ionutiu, James Felece, Jan Matou, Jenny Virtue, Jessica Glazer, Jo Aitken, John Moore, John Robertson, Jolie Low, Julie Venning, Justin Barrass, Kaevan Gazdar, Kara Cornish, Karin A Goeman, Kristen Bartram, Lauren Smith, Leila & Stuart, Christie Leon Macdonald, Louis So, M Bowler, M CJ Fletcher, Maciek Starosolski, Mara Fremgen, Marc Harsman, Maria Losada, Marianne Kuiper Milks, Mark Hanrath, Mark Kennedy, Martha R Matthews, Martin & Phyllis Schulmeister, Martin Gluckman, Matt Wheeland, Michael Kirby, Mike Ingham, Molly Brunkow, N P Padalino, Nadiya Schneider, Neil Rooney, Nick Penn, Norma Schneider, Pam Brandt, Patricia Champion, Paulo Dutra, Phil Roberts, Piran Montford, Rey delRosario, Richard Joel, Richard Runcie, Sara Cohen, Sarah Jones, Scott Carveth, Serge & Lise Lavoie, Sharon Kaye, Snezana Savic, Sonia H McVormick, Stacey Kerns, Stacey Lucas, Stephen Revucky, Steve Bailey, Sue Moss, Summer Li, Sundar G, Susana Goncalves, Suzie Bogve, Thomas Summerhayes, Tiffany Kemp, Tom Hawking, Tom Sawyer, Tracy Augustin, Tracy Buschen, Veronica W Rogers, Wyn Hawker, Xavier Gros, Yong Gyun Ghim.

Foreword

ABOUT LONELY PLANET GUIDEBOOKS

The story begins with a classic travel adventure: Tony and Maureen Wheeler's 1972 journey across Europe and Asia to Australia. Useful information about the overland trail did not exist at that time, so Tony and Maureen published the first Lonely Planet guidebook to meet a growing need.

From a kitchen table, then from a tiny office in Melbourne (Australia), Lonely Planet has become the largest independent travel publisher in the world, an international company with offices in Melbourne, Oakland (USA), London (UK) and Paris (France).

Today Lonely Planet guidebooks cover the globe. There is an ever-growing list of books and there's information in a variety of forms and media. Some things haven't changed. The main aim is still to help make it possible for adventurous travellers to get out there – to explore and better understand the world.

At Lonely Planet we believe travellers can make a positive contribution to the countries they visit – if they respect their host communities and spend their money wisely. Since 1986 a percentage of the income from each book has been donated to aid projects and human rights campaigns.

Updates Lonely Planet thoroughly updates each guidebook as often as possible. This usually means there are around two years between editions, although for more unusual or more stable destinations the gap can be longer. Check the imprint page (following the colour map at the beginning of the book) for publication dates.

Between editions up-to-date information is available in two free newsletters – the paper *Planet Talk* and email *Comet* (to subscribe, contact any Lonely Planet office) – and on our Web site at www.lonelyplanet.com. The *Upgrades* section of the Web site covers a number of important and volatile destinations and is regularly updated by Lonely Planet authors. *Scoop* covers news and current affairs relevant to travellers. And, lastly, the *Thorn Tree* bulletin board and *Postcards* section of the site carry unverified, but fascinating, reports from travellers.

Correspondence The process of creating new editions begins with the letters, postcards and emails received from travellers. This correspondence often includes suggestions, criticisms and comments about the current editions. Interesting excerpts are immediately passed on via newsletters and the Web site, and everything goes to our authors to be verified when they're researching on the road. We're keen to get more feedback from organisations or individuals who represent communities visited by travellers.

> Lonely Planet gathers information for everyone who's curious about the planet – and especially for those who explore it first-hand. Through guidebooks, phrasebooks, activity guides, maps, literature, newsletters, image library, TV series and Web site we act as an information exchange for a worldwide community of travellers.

Research Authors aim to gather sufficient practical information to enable travellers to make informed choices and to make the mechanics of a journey run smoothly. They also research historical and cultural background to help enrich the travel experience and allow travellers to understand and respond appropriately to cultural and environmental issues.

Authors don't stay in every hotel because that would mean spending a couple of months in each medium-sized city and, no, they don't eat at every restaurant because that would mean stretching belts beyond capacity. They do visit hotels and restaurants to check standards and prices, but feedback based on readers' direct experiences can be very helpful.

Many of our authors work undercover, others aren't so secretive. None of them accept freebies in exchange for positive write-ups. And none of our guidebooks contain any advertising.

Production Authors submit their raw manuscripts and maps to offices in Australia, USA, UK or France. Editors and cartographers – all experienced travellers themselves – then begin the process of assembling the pieces. When the book finally hits the shops, some things are already out of date, we start getting feedback from readers and the process begins again ...

WARNING & REQUEST

Things change – prices go up, schedules change, good places go bad and bad places go bankrupt – nothing stays the same. So, if you find things better or worse, recently opened or long since closed, please tell us and help make the next edition even more accurate and useful. We genuinely value all the feedback we receive. Julie Young coordinates a well travelled team that reads and acknowledges every letter, postcard and email and ensures that every morsel of information finds its way to the appropriate authors, editors and cartographers for verification.

Everyone who writes to us will find their name in the next edition of the appropriate guidebook. They will also receive the latest issue of *Planet Talk*, our quarterly printed newsletter, or *Comet*, our monthly email newsletter. Subscriptions to both newsletters are free. The very best contributions will be rewarded with a free guidebook.

Excerpts from your correspondence may appear in new editions of Lonely Planet guidebooks, the Lonely Planet Web site, *Planet Talk* or *Comet*, so please let us know if you *don't* want your letter published or your name acknowledged.

Send all correspondence to the Lonely Planet office closest to you:

Australia: Locked Bag 1, Footscray, Victoria 3011
USA: 150 Linden St, Oakland, CA 94607
UK: 10A Spring Place, London NW5 3BH
France: 1 rue du Dahomey, 75011 Paris

Or email us at: talk2us@lonelyplanet.com.au

For news, views and updates see our Web site: www.lonelyplanet.com

HOW TO USE A LONELY PLANET GUIDEBOOK

The best way to use a Lonely Planet guidebook is any way you choose. At Lonely Planet we believe the most memorable travel experiences are often those that are unexpected, and the finest discoveries are those you make yourself. Guidebooks are not intended to be used as if they provide a detailed set of infallible instructions!

Contents All Lonely Planet guidebooks follow roughly the same format. The Facts about the Destination chapters or sections give background information ranging from history to weather. Facts for the Visitor gives practical information on issues like visas and health. Getting There & Away gives a brief starting point for re-searching travel to and from the destination. Getting Around gives an overview of the transport options when you arrive.

The peculiar demands of each destination determine how sub-sequent chapters are broken up, but some things remain constant. We always start with background, then proceed to sights, places to stay, places to eat, entertainment, getting there and away, and getting around information – in that order.

Heading Hierarchy Lonely Planet headings are used in a strict hierarchical structure that can be visualised as a set of Russian dolls. Each heading (and its following text) is encompassed by any preceding heading that is higher on the hierarchical ladder.

Entry Points We do not assume guidebooks will be read from beginning to end, but that people will dip into them. The tradi-tional entry points are the list of contents and the index. In addition, however, some books have a complete list of maps and an index map illustrating map coverage.

There may also be a colour map that shows highlights. These highlights are dealt with in greater detail in the Facts for the Visitor chapter, along with planning questions and suggested itin-eraries. Each chapter covering a geographical region usually begins with a locator map and another list of highlights. Once you find something of interest in a list of highlights, turn to the index.

Maps Maps play a crucial role in Lonely Planet guidebooks and include a huge amount of information. A legend is printed on the back page. We seek to have complete consistency between maps and text, and to have every important place in the text captured on a map. Map key numbers usually start in the top left corner.

Although inclusion in a guidebook usually implies a recommen-dation we cannot list every good place. Exclusion does not necessarily imply criticism. In fact there are a number of reasons why we might exclude a place – sometimes it is simply inappropriate to encourage an influx of travellers.

Introduction

Europe is many things to many people. Some marvel at the diversity of cultures and languages crammed into its relatively small area, the wealth of the region's museums and architecture, the seemingly endless restaurants and nightlife on offer. Others are attracted to Europe's varied scenery, from its sun-drenched beaches and dense forests to its august mountain peaks. Most visitors are impressed by the minimal amount of bureaucracy, the well-developed tourist facilities and the efficient transport that make it possible to explore most of Europe with little fuss.

Western Europe is often looked upon as the hub of the developed world – at least historically. Though its growth rate is not what it was in the heady days of the 1950s and 60s, Western Europe remains an economic powerhouse and a leader in art, literature and music. There are magnificent museums and galleries such as the British Museum in London, the Louvre in Paris and the Prado in Madrid. There are superb natural features – the soaring Swiss Alps and Pyrenees mountains, magnificent stretches of rugged coastline in western Ireland and Portugal. And there are places that are simply fun, whether it's clubbing in London or Berlin, pub-crawling through Dublin or watching the world go by from a street cafe in Paris or Barcelona.

Central and Eastern Europe have been the source of much of what we know as 'western' culture, not just in literature and music (Mozart, Dvořák, Liszt, Chopin, Goethe, Kafka etc) but in so many other disciplines. Since 1989 these regions have undergone changes of historic proportions – in 1990 the communist regimes of Poland, Czechoslovakia, Hungary and Romania collapsed and East Germany ceased to exist altogether. The regions' major cities – Prague, Vienna, Budapest, Warsaw, Kraków – have, at various times, been major centres of European culture, and their museums, theatres, concert halls and historical sites are world-class. For travellers, prices almost everywhere in Eastern Europe are much lower than those in Western Europe.

Mediterranean Europe evokes images of beautiful beaches, the brilliant blue of the Mediterranean Sea, spectacular landscapes dotted with olive and citrus groves, outdoor cafes, wonderful food, friendly local people, exuberant festivals and a relaxed way of life. Some of Europe's earliest and most powerful civilisations flourished around the Mediterranean, and traces of them remain in the many monuments they created – the Parthenon in Athens, the Hagia Sofia in İstanbul, Fès el-Bali in Morocco. When museums and churches begin to overwhelm you, turn to the many active pursuits Mediterranean Europe has to offer, from island-hopping in Greece to lounging on a Turkish beach or climbing a volcano in Sicily.

Scandinavian Europe has everything to offer from dramatic fjords and glaciers to the treeless Arctic tundra. Scandinavia's cities range from cosmopolitan Copenhagen to the resurgent capitals of the Baltic states – Rīga, Tallinn and Vilnius – as well as St Petersburg, Russia's most enchanting and European city. Outdoor enthusiasts will get their fill of activities in Scandinavia, be it ski-touring in Sweden, dog sledding in Finland or fjord-trekking in Norway.

Lonely Planet's *Europe on a shoestring* covers this diverse collection of countries with an insight into their history, people and culture. Whether you're a first-time traveller or a seasoned veteran, it offers practical information to help make the most of your time and money. There's information on how to get to Europe and how to get around once you've arrived. There are extensive details on what to see, when to see it and how much it all costs. The thousands of recommendations about places to stay range from Czech camping grounds and French hostels to Turkish pensions and Irish B&Bs. Cafes, restaurants and bars are covered in equally exhaustive detail with suggestions ranging from the cheapest of cheap eats to the ideal place for a splurge.

Europe is an awesome region to visit and *Europe on a shoestring* will guide you – all you have to do is go.

Facts for First-Time Visitors

This chapter covers the questions that can seem most daunting to first-time travellers – where to go, when to go, is it safe and, inevitably, how much will it all cost?

Good preparation is important to the success of any trip and you'll find more detailed information in the following Facts for the Visitor, Getting There & Away and Getting Around chapters.

THE ESSENTIALS

To paraphrase George Orwell, all items are essential but some are more essential than others. Clean socks and underwear are certainly important, but in the early planning stages you should focus on the must-have, can't-live-without items listed below. They are the crucial first steps in planning a successful trip to Europe.

Passport A passport is your most important travel document. It contains a photo, an ID number (which is required on all sorts of travel documents) and blank pages for foreign customs officials to stamp when you enter (and sometimes leave) their country. In countries that require a pre-arranged travel visa (see below), a visa will be stapled or stamped into your passport and later validated when you arrive at that country's borders.

For more information see Passports in the Facts for the Visitor chapter.

Visas Citizens of the USA, Canada and the UK need only a valid passport to enter many European countries (Australians and New Zealanders are not so lucky). See Visas in the Facts for the Visitor chapter for which countries, if any, require pre-arranged travel visas. The Web is another good place to search for up-to-date visa requirements.

Insurance A travel insurance policy – one that covers theft, medical treatment, emergency evacuation and personal liability – is *must*. See Visas & Documents and Health in the Facts for the Visitor chapter.

Money The first step is to calculate a realistic budget that suits both your bank account and your desired style of travel. The second step is to establish safe, dependable methods of accessing your cash while abroad (bank card, credit card, travellers cheques etc). Lastly, have a secure method of transporting your money and valuables (eg in a money belt, neck pouch or belt pouch).

For further information see the following Costs & Money and Safety & Security sections, as well as Money in the Facts for the Visitor chapter.

Other Useful Documents

The following passes and ID cards may not be 'essential', but in many cases they will save you heaps of money when travelling in Europe. Deciding which, if any, you need is an important pre-trip exercise, as they're mostly cheaper (and often easier) to purchase before leaving home.

Rail Passes These offer a flexible, low-cost way of getting around Europe. If you plan to visit more than a few countries on a single trip, you will definitely save money with a rail pass. The most common passes are Inter-Rail (for European citizens) and Eurail (for non-Europeans), both of which offer unlimited travel within a set number of days in many (but not all) European countries. Both passes also cover some bus and ferry services.

For a complete rundown see Rail Passes & Cheap Train Tickets in the Getting Around chapter.

Hostelling & Camping Cards A hostelling card is useful, if not always mandatory, for staying at Europe's 'official' hostels, ie, ones that belong to an international network such as Hostelling International (HI). Since many hostels give discounts to cardholders, a hostelling card will soon pay for itself. There are similar benefits with a Camping Card International, which gives discounts at many camping grounds.

For more information see Accommodation in the Facts for the Visitor chapter.

Student Cards Registered students can save a pile of money with an International

Student Identification Card (ISIC). Discounts vary from country to country – at best you'll save up to 50% on museum entry fees and 10% to 30% on some buses, trains and ferries.

For details see Student & Youth Cards in the Facts for the Visitor chapter.

WHEN & WHERE TO GO

Most first-time travellers visit Europe in summer (roughly mid-June to late August). On the plus side summer is packed with cultural events, the weather is warm and the days are long. In summer most public transport networks are in full operation, a definite plus in places like Scotland, Ireland, Greece and the Scandinavian countries.

The bad news is that, in summer, you will battle heavy crowds in major cities, prices will be higher and the weather can be sweltering, especially in southern Europe. The worst month of all is August, when millions of European families and holiday-makers hit the road, clogging beach towns, ferries and trains like sardines. Avoid travelling during this month if at all possible, or bypass the over-crowded tourist haunts and head instead for the semi-somnolent towns and cities.

When it comes to crowds and high prices, the general rule of thumb is that June is better than July, and July is better than August. Depending on your itinerary the best times to visit Europe are late May/early June and September, when the crowds thin, prices drop and the weather is still good.

And don't forget about winter. Except at Christmas and New Year winter crowds are much thinner – a big plus in places like Prague and Paris – and prices are dramatically lower. Winter is a time for skiing some of the world's finest slopes (Switzerland, France, Austria, Italy, etc) and some of the world's cheapest slopes (Romania, Poland, Slovakia, etc).

For more details see When to Go in the Facts for the Visitor chapter and in the appropriate country chapters.

What Kind of Trip?

Travelling Companions If you decide to travel with others, keep in mind that travel can put relationships to the test like few other experiences can. Many a long-term friendship has collapsed under the strains of constant negotiations about where to stay and eat, what to see and where to go next. But many friendships have also become closer than ever before. You won't find out until you try, but make sure you agree on itineraries and routines beforehand and try to remain flexible about everything – even in the heat of an August afternoon in Paris or Berlin. Travelling with someone else also has financial benefits as single rooms are more expensive per person than a double in most countries.

If travel is a good way of testing established friendships, it's also a great way of making new ones. Hostels and camping grounds are good places to meet fellow travellers, so even if you're travelling alone you need never be lonely.

Move or Stay? Though often ridiculed, the mad dash that crams eight or nine countries into a month does have its merits. If you've never visited Europe before, you won't know which areas you'll like, and a quick 'scouting' tour will give an overview of the options. A rail pass that offers unlimited travel within a set period of time is the best way to do this.

But if you know where you want to go or find a place you like, the best advice is to stay put for a while, discover some of the lesser known sights, make a few local friends and settle in. It's also cheaper in the long run.

If you're daunted by the thought of planning an actual itinerary, we offer a few planning tips later in this chapter.

Planning an Itinerary

There is no shame in carefully planning a first trip to Europe. We're not talking about a minute-by-minute itinerary, because all travellers to Europe – veterans and first-timers alike – need to be flexible.

Wherever you go, don't make the mistake of trying to see too much in too little time. With a Eurail or Inter-Rail train pass it's perhaps a bit too easy to hop from city to city at a dizzying pace, which often leads to travel burnout. Statistically speaking, if you visit Europe once there is a very good chance that you will visit again at some later point in your life. So pick a handful of countries to explore in-depth and leave the rest for a second, third or fourth trip.

If you have a rail pass, make sure your itinerary meshes with its restrictions and requirements. For example, if you visit 12 countries on a 10-day Eurail pass, you may have to cover some additional travel costs. It's much the same with an Inter-Rail pass, which is divided into zones and may not cover all the countries you intend to visit.

Sample Itineraries When you're ready to plot an actual itinerary, consider the following simple strategies for a month-long trip to Europe – but don't forget that flexibility is the key to a stress-free, enjoyable trip. So once you've crafted the perfect itinerary, stuff it in your backpack and do your best to ignore it. Dozens (if not hundreds) of fellow travellers will proffer tips and suggestions during your travels, and there is no substitute for their first-hand advice.

• Pick a few major cities that you absolutely, positively must visit – for example London, Paris, Munich, Venice, Florence and Madrid. Budget at least 2½ days in each city, and add a day each for travelling between them. So far that's 20 days. Now spend a few hours researching day trips from your chosen cities. If you budget one day-trip per city, you're at 26 days. Now add three days for impromptu sidetrips and/or sleeping late and relaxing, and three days for travel-related delays (slow trains, bus strikes and random acts of road congestion), for a total of 32 days.

The main problem with a city-to-city itinerary is that you will spend large chunks of time on trains and buses, especially if you include far-flung cities (ie İstanbul and Helsinki). Another problem is that city-to-city itineraries mostly preclude small towns and villages.

• Pick four to six countries that you want to visit, and budget a week or so each for the larger countries, four to five days for the smaller countries. Within each country budget two or three days in the capital city, the remaining days for lesser-known towns, villages and regions covered in this book. A sample trip might include Britain (five days), Holland (three days), Germany (six days), Czech Republic (three days), Italy (six days), France (six days) and Spain (five days), plus a day or two back to Britain, for a total of 35 days. If you can, budget a few days en route between your chosen countries – for example, between the Czech Republic and Italy you could add two days each in Vienna and Lubljana (Slovenia's capital).

Planning Aids You're holding one of the very best pre-trip planning aids. Get your money's worth by reading as much as possible before leaving home, especially this book's Facts for the Visitor, Getting There & Away and Getting Around chapters. Better still, get Lonely Planet's *Read This First: Europe*. It profiles 36 countries in the region and includes suggested itineraries, advice on visas, the lowdown on train and bus passes, tips on saving money, and everything you need to know to stay healthy on the road.

In addition to Lonely Planet's numerous European titles, there are hundreds of other useful guidebooks to Europe. Many cater to specific interests and special needs – vegetarians, hard-core hikers, architecture enthusiasts, history buffs, nudists, gays and lesbians and more. The best starting point is your local bookstore's travel section.

Lonely Planet has a comprehensive Web site at www.lonelyplanet.com; and there are other sites dedicated to each and every country in Europe. Ignore the overtly commercial sites (the ones selling high-end hotel packages, etc) and focus on sites that offer photos, travel tips, up-to-date political news, and notes or comments from fellow travellers. See Internet Resources in the Facts for the Visitor chapter, and the Internet Resources section of each country chapter, for more information.

WHAT TO PACK

A backpack is still the most popular method of carrying gear as it is convenient, especially for walking. For most travellers, a sturdy backpack with adjustable and padded straps, lower-back support and plenty of zipper compartments is an essential pre-trip purchase. On the down side, a backpack doesn't offer much protection for your valuables, the straps tend to get caught on things and some airlines may refuse to accept responsibility if the pack is damaged or tampered with.

Travelpacks, a combination backpack/shoulder bag, are very popular. The backpack straps zip away inside the pack when they are not needed, so you almost have the best of both worlds. Some packs have sophisticated shoulder-strap adjustment systems and can be used comfortably even on long hikes. Backpacks or travelpacks can be made reasonably theft-proof with small padlocks. Do not skimp on a backpack, because there's nothing worse than having a strap or harness break when you're 100km from the nearest city. Moreover, replacement packs are not always easy to find on the road – can you say 'high-quality backpack with adjustable straps' in Croatian?

Forget suitcases unless you're travelling in style, but if you do take one, make sure it has wheels.

It's best to bring two pairs of shoes to Europe. For day-to-day walking bring a sturdy pair of lightweight shoes. Also bring a pair of waterproof sandals for showers, beaches and sightseeing. Hiking boots are essential for serious trekkers. Avoid blisters by wearing new shoes and sandals at least two hours a day for two weeks before leaving home.

Even if you spend most of your trip on a Greek beach, bring at least one pair of long pants. Some churches and mosques require visitors to wear long pants or a full-length skirt and refuse entry to people in shorts. Lightweight cotton pants are best. Blue jeans are bulky, get dirty quickly and take forever to dry.

Even if you don't camp, sleeping bags make handy blankets on trains and buses (though they are bulky to carry in your pack). If you stay in hostels you will need a sleeping bag or a sleep sheet with a built-in pillow case (cover). Otherwise you must rent one each night for US$1 to US$2.50.

There's nothing worse than being a backpacker who brought a suitcase, especially if that suitcase contains seven pairs of shoes, five sweaters and the complete works of William Shakespeare. Bearing in mind that you can buy virtually anything on the spot, a minimum packing list could include:

- underwear, socks
- lightweight towel and swimming gear
- a pair (or two) of lightweight cotton pants (jeans are bulky and hard to launder)
- a pair of shorts or a skirt
- a few T-shirts and shirts
- a warm sweater
- a solid pair of walking shoes
- sturdy sandals for showers and beaches
- a coat or jacket
- a raincoat, waterproof jacket or umbrella
- a medical kit and sewing kit
- a padlock
- a Swiss Army knife
- a small flashlight (torch)
- sunglasses
- toothpaste, toothbrush, soap and other toiletries
- a few plastic bags (to store wet/dirty clothes)

COSTS & MONEY

Europe can be monstrously expensive or dirt-cheap, depending on how and where you travel. The best advice is to calculate a budget before leaving home, and try to stick to it. Do some pre-trip research and weigh the costs and benefits of the countries you most want to visit. For example, beer drinkers will enjoy the Czech republic and most of Eastern Europe, where beer averages less than US$1.50 for 500ml. In Scandinavia the same beer could cost a whopping US$6.

All travellers should save room in their budgets for emergencies. A credit card is useful for unexpected expenses. We also recommend setting aside US$125 to US$165 in cash for the 'worst-case scenario', which goes something like this: taxi to embassy (US$10) to replace lost passport (US$30 to US$50), taxi to airport (US$15) to replace lost airline ticket (US$10 to US$30) and to catch flight back home, taxi back to town (US$10) because you missed the flight, dinner and much-needed drink (US$15), fleabag hotel for one night (US$25), and taxi back to the airport (US$10).

For a complete run-down on travellers cheques, wire transfers, bank cards, ATMs and more, see Money in the Facts for the Visitor chapter.

Sample Costs

The following chart gives a rough estimate of per-person daily expenses (US$). Even with a rail pass you must pay for some private trains, buses, ferries and local transport – we've given a rough daily average in the 'local transport' category. In the 'supermarket' section we've calculated the average cost of a one-day supply of basic eats (bread, cheese, fruit, dried pasta and sauce, etc).

The cost of a return airfare is your first major expense and will vary greatly depending on where you fly from, what time of year and what special deals, if any, are available. Fares from the US range from US$500 to $1000; see the Getting There & Away chapter for more information.

Be sure to add a bit of padding when calculating the grand total for a 30-day trip, as you will probably sleep in both hostels and hotels, eat some meals at restaurants and cook some meals for yourself, etc. In general, the cheapest per-day budget is US$35

Average Costs in Europe (US$)

	Western	Mediterranean	Scandinavian	Eastern
Camping	$8 to $13	$4 to $8	$6 to $20	$2 to $6
Hostel	$10 to $28	$6 to $9	$12 to $23	$4 to $8
Budget hotel (double)	$35 to $70	$20 to $40	$60 to $80	$14 to $40
Cheap restaurant meal	$7 to $10	$5 to $9	$9 to $18	$2 to $10
Local Transport (one day)	$3 to $5	$2 to $4	$5 to $8	$1 to $3
Museum fees	$4 to $11	$2.50 to $5	$5 to $10	$1 to $3
One beer (500ml)	$2.50 to $4	$1.50 to $3	$3 to $9	$0.50 to $2.50
Three-minute call to USA	$2 to $5	$1.50 to $6	$2 to $4.50	$1.50 to $10
15-day rail pass	$380 to $554 (Eurail; all areas)			

to US$40, and that's for a bare-bones trip with few luxuries. With airfare and a rail pass, the grand total is US$2200 to US$2350. A more realistic budget is US$50 per day, for a grand total of about US$2700.

Daily budgets will be US$5 to $10 less if you spend more time in Eastern Europe, Turkey and Morocco. Add US$10 to $15 per day in Scandinavian countries.

10 Tips to Stay on Budget

If you're serious about staying on budget, for every splurge expense there must be an equal and opposite money-saver. There are many free things to do in Europe, from hiking to beach bumming to loitering on a piazza. The following tips can also save you money.

- Always ask to see a menu with prices at restaurants and cafes. Also ask if there's a surcharge for sitting inside, on the patio, at a table, etc.
- Buy food at open-air markets and supermarkets. Remember that a tube of mustard or garlic spread can transform dull bread and cheese into a tasty meal.
- Wash your clothes in hotel and hostel sinks if facilities are available.
- Spread lodging costs among a few trustworthy travelling companions. At many hotels and hostels, quads (four-person rooms) are cheaper than triples and triples are cheaper than doubles.
- Take overnight trains on long trips to save the cost of a night in a hostel or hotel.
- Concerts and cultural events are often free in summer – ask at tourist offices and check around town for fliers and posters.
- Buy alcohol at supermarkets and drink with the locals on main squares, gardens and beaches (where it's legal and acceptable to do so).

- Many museums are free one day a month and sometimes one evening per week – be sure to ask. Also ask about joint-entry tickets and discount passes for tourists.
- Use a phonecard (instead of coins or tokens) to make phone calls within Europe. If dialling home you may save money with a 'Home Direct' service offered by your local telephone company.
- Don't spend all your time in big cities. Prices are generally lower in towns and villages.

Smart Ways to Blow your Budget

Successful budgets strike a balance between low cost and high value. Europe on US$10 a day is a low cost, low value strategy – you may save a heap of money, but you will see absolutely nothing. Aim instead to get the maximum value for your money, even if that means occasionally going over budget.

- If you don't make an effort to sample local cuisines, you are denying yourself one of travelling's great pleasures. Self-service and budget restaurants are OK, but every now and again try an upper-end spot. Most restaurants – even the 'fancy' ones – offer set-priced meals and lunch specials that are good value.
- Don't assume that the cheapest hostel or hotel is also the best-value. A hostel may charge only US$20 for a double, but factor in the incidentals: you and a friend arrive by bus (US$0.50 each), pay extra for showers (US$1 each), rent sheets (US$1), take a bus back to town (US$0.50) and then catch an early bus back (US$0.50) in order to make the 11 pm curfew. Grand total: US$13.50 per person. If you stay at a central hotel with US$35 doubles and free showers, the cost is US$17.50 per person. That extra US$4 per person saves you three bus rides and an early evening staring at a hostel TV.

- Renting a car can be good value in the right circumstances, especially if you're travelling in a small group and do not already have a rail pass. In remote or rural regions that are poorly served by buses and trains, a rental car will save you time and trouble. It may also enable you to sleep at a far-flung (but cheap) camping ground instead of a (more expensive) hostel or hotel.
- You spent 12 hours on an overnight train to reach a small town in the Swiss Alps/Moroccan desert/French wine country. You booked into a cheap hostel for two nights and saved a bundle shopping at the local supermarket. You've done a good job keeping costs down, so don't balk at splashing out on a skiing/trekking/chateau tour, even if the cost exceeds your daily budget.

SAFETY & SECURITY

Travelling in Europe is generally quite safe. Violent crime is rare and the threat from terrorists and religious fanatics is virtually nil. The main threats facing travellers are pickpockets and scam artists. Specific perils are covered in the Dangers & Annoyances section in this book's individual country chapters. The following are general guidelines that all travellers should keep in mind.

General Security

You can deter most thieves by wearing a money belt (see below) and never letting your bags out of sight. Small zipper locks are handy (but not fool-proof) for securing backpacks and daypacks. On trains and buses it's wise to lock your bags to a luggage rack, preferably with a sturdy combination cable.

Sadly, some travellers finance their wanderlust by taking advantage of fellow travellers. Never leave bags unattended in a hostel or hotel, not even for five seconds. If you are concerned, store your luggage in a locker (found at many train and bus stations). You should always carry passports, money and airline tickets on your person – never leave them in a hotel room, even if it seems 'safe'. Luggage-storage rooms are OK, but there's no guarantee that hotel or hostel staff, or even fellow travellers, won't help themselves to your belongings.

Flaunting cameras, portable CD players and other expensive electronic goods is only asking for trouble. Remember that a US$500 camera represents two months' wages in some countries. Keep all valuables in a locked daypack or backpack when they're not being used. Don't leave them sitting in the open on trains or buses, just in case you doze off.

Last but not least, don't be cavalier in so-called 'safe' countries. Crime is a worldwide phenomenon.

Carrying cash Most travellers would not walk around their hometown with large wads of cash, and there's no reason to do so on the streets of Europe. Carry no more than 10% to 15% of your total trip money in cash. The remainder should be in travellers cheques, which can be replaced in case of loss or theft. Equally useful are ATM cards linked to a cheque or savings account back home. Bank-issued ATM cards (at least those linked to the Visa/Plus, Master-Card/Cirrus and Eurocard networks) are widely accepted in European countries, and they allow you to draw small amounts of local currency every few days.

Some credit cards also allow you to draw cash at foreign ATMs and banks for a fee (plus interest if you don't pay the balance within a month or so).

Photocopies Make two sets of photocopies of your passport, airline ticket, travellers cheques, insurance papers and credit cards. Keep one set safely separated from the original documents and leave the other set at home.

Money belts Carrying a wallet or purse is like wearing a flashing neon billboard that says 'there is money here – please take some'. It is much safer to keep travellers cheques, passports, airline tickets etc close to your skin in a money belt. It's useful to carry day-to-day money in an easily accessible wallet or purse (preferably kept in a front pocket rather than a back pocket), but keep the bulk of your cash and all important documents in a money belt. These are sold at luggage stores and even some bookshops. Neck pouches are OK, but not if you wear them (as many travellers inexplicably do) on the *outside* of your clothes.

Have at least one contingency plan in the unlikely event that your money belt is stolen. Some travellers walk around with US$100 in their shoe (risky), others stash US$50 in their aspirin bottle. We recommend sewing US$50 in cash into hard-to-reach corners of your backpack (preferably) or daypack.

Daypacks Small daypacks are useful for carrying guidebooks, cameras, portable stereos and the like. This makes them a favourite target for thieves – it only takes a few seconds for a practised hand to unzip your bag and rifle its contents. Small zipper locks may deter a novice thief, but they will not stop an expert pickpocket from slashing your bag in the blink of an eye. The best advice is to keep your daypack in front of you when in crowded areas and keep an eye on it at all times.

Scams & Swindles
Each year Lonely Planet receives hundreds of letters from travellers who have been duped by predatory scam-artists. As new swindles constantly appear, there is no single way to protect yourself. The best advice is to keep your wits about you, and to approach all situations with a healthy dose of scepticism.

We try to list specific scams in particular individual country chapters. The following is a general list of deceits common throughout Europe.

Druggings Though it may run counter to your generous nature, it is unwise to accept food and drinks from strangers (do we sound like your mother, or what?). Travellers are especially vulnerable on trains and buses. The typical ploy involves someone you've just met offering to buy or share a drink or snack. Your new 'friend' may seem offended if you do not accept their small token of friendship; if you acquiesce, you may wake 10 hours later with a throbbing headache and a missing backpack.

Gassings have also been reported on a handful of overnight international trains. The usual scenario involves the release of a sleep-inducing gas into a sleeping compartment in the middle of the night. Once the gas takes effect, the perpetrator searches the victims for money belts and whatever valuables are lurking in their luggage. The best protection against gassings is to lock the door of your sleeping compartment (use your own lock if there isn't one) and to lock your bags to luggage racks. Most important, never sleep alone in a train compartment.

Hello my friend! After a few months in Europe you will recognise the type – a nice man (rarely a woman) who speaks good English, is very friendly, and goes out of his way to be helpful. The actual scam varies from country to country, but all share one common feature – lulling you into a false sense of trust. At some point your new friend will gently suggest something that, under normal circumstances, you would not do. Maybe you need to visit the toilet – your new friend will kindly offer to watch your bags. Maybe you're tired and need help lifting your bags – your new friend (or perhaps an accomplice) will create a diversion and grab a camera or a daypack.

In some cases your new friend is less a thief and more a hustler. It's late and you don't have a hostel or hotel reservation. Coincidentally your new friend knows this great hotel just across town. This ploy could involve an exorbitant taxi fare and an inflated hotel price, with your new friend scoring hefty commissions from the taxi driver and hotel owner.

There is no limit to the number of scams out there. Don't be paranoid, and don't cut yourself off from the people you meet on the road, 99% of whom are honestly interested in striking up a friendship. Yet it pays to be suspicious of overly friendly people, especially on long-distance trains and buses (after all, most people are less than friendly after 10 hours on a train). Never allow strangers to watch your bags and never allow a situation to evolve in ways that make you feel uncomfortable. If your new friend is genuine, they will certainly understand if you say 'no' to taking a taxi at 1 am in a strange town to an unfamiliar hotel.

Black markets The black market is a thing of the past in most European countries. With the passing of communism most countries have begun the transition to free-market economics. In the process currencies have been freed from government controls (the main reason that black markets exist) and are now fully convertible.

Black markets still exist in some countries, but the rates on offer are only marginally better than bank rates. Moreover, many black-market money changers will not hesitate to dupe foreign travellers. Each year Lonely Planet warns travellers not to change money on the black market, and each year we receive letters from travellers who wish they had heeded our warnings.

Can I see some ID? In some countries, especially Eastern European countries, you may encounter people claiming to be from the tourist police, the special police, the super-secret police, whatever. Unless they're wearing a uniform and have good reason for accosting you (ie you're robbing a bank), treat their claims with suspicion.

One common scam runs like this: a random person asks you to change money. You say no, and seconds later an 'undercover' police officer 'arrests' the money changer. The undercover agent then asks to check your passport and money, in case it's counterfeit.

Needless to say, never show your passport or cash to anyone on the street. Simply walk away. If they flash a badge, politely offer to accompany them to the nearest police station.

CULTURAL SENSITIVITY

This section is about so-called 'ugly' tourists. In Europe you will instantly recognise the type. They tend to shout at people, always loudly and in English, about how things are so much better/more efficient/cheaper in their home country. Whether the 'ugly' tourist is drunk, ignorant or simply rude, witnessing such an outburst is thoroughly embarrassing. It's even worse if the 'ugly' tourist is from your own country.

Embarrassing situations can arise from simple misunderstandings – for example, Bulgarians and Albanians tend to shake their head side to side to say 'yes', up and down to say 'no'. We discuss such issues in the Culture & Conduct section in individual country chapters. Also keep in mind the following general guidelines.

- English may be the world's most widely understood language, but do not assume that everyone in Europe speaks English.
- If you ask a question in English and are met with blank stares, don't repeat the question slowly and loudly *in English*. This is extremely rude.
- Learn a few phrases in the local language, such as 'please', 'thank you' 'excuse me' and 'do you speak English?'. We include language guides at the back of this book to help with the basics.
- It's always best to blend in rather than stand out. For example, aggressive queue-jumping is a way of life in some European countries. If you're involved in a queue skirmish don't make a scene, don't get into a huff and don't lecture an old lady on the etiquette of queuing as it's practised in your home country. As the saying goes, when in Rome do as the Romans.

There are countless other examples. The best advice is to keep an open mind, observe your surroundings and learn from the locals themselves what is appropriate and inappropriate behaviour. Don't impose your views on a foreign culture.

Facts for the Visitor

There are those who say that Europe – especially Western Europe – is so well developed and organised that you don't have to plan a thing before your trip; anything can be arranged on the spot. As any experienced traveller knows, the problems you thought about at home often turn out to be irrelevant or will sort themselves out once you're on the move.

This is fine if you've decided to blow the massive inheritance sitting in your bank account. However, if your financial status is somewhat more modest, a bit of prior knowledge and careful planning can make your travel budget stretch further than you ever thought possible. You'll also want to make sure that the things you plan to see and do will be possible at the particular time of year when you'll be travelling.

First-time travellers to Europe should also see the previous Facts for First-time Visitors chapter or Lonely Planet's *Read This First: Europe*, which covers some key planning issues that experienced travellers may take for granted.

PLANNING
When to Go

Any time can be the best time to visit Europe, depending on what you want to see and do. Summer lasts roughly from June to September and offers the best weather for most outdoor pursuits in the northern half of Europe. In the southern half (Mediterranean coast, Iberian Peninsula, Morocco, southern Italy, Greece and Turkey), where the summers tend to be hotter, you can extend that period by one or perhaps even two months either way, when temperatures may also be more agreeable.

You won't be the only tourist in Europe during summer – all of France and Italy, for instance, goes on holiday in August. Prices can be high, accommodation fully booked and the sights packed. No matter how you approach it, August is a difficult month for European travel – avoid the beach resorts if possible, and branch out into eastern or Scandinavian Europe until the crowds in Western and southern Europe start to thin in early September.

You'll find much better deals – and far fewer crowds – in the shoulder seasons on either side of summer. In April and May, for instance, flowers are in bloom and the weather can be surprisingly mild. Indian summers are common in September and October.

If you're keen on winter sports, resorts in the Alps and the Pyrenees begin operating in late November and move into full swing after the New Year, closing down when the snows begin to melt in March or even April.

The Climate & When to Go sections in the individual country chapters explain what to expect and when to expect it, and the Climate Charts in Appendix I at the back of the book will help you compare the weather in different destinations.

As a rule, spring and autumn tend to be wetter and windier than summer and winter. The temperate maritime climate along the Atlantic is relatively wet all year, with moderate extremes in temperature. The Mediterranean coast is hotter and drier, with most rainfall occurring during the mild winter. The continental climate in central and eastern Europe and the Alps tends to show much stronger extremes in weather between summer and winter.

Books & Maps

Lonely Planet produces a wide range of travel guides and other books to complement and expand on the information provided in this book. As well as more detailed regional titles to Western, Mediterranean, Eastern, Central and Scandinavian Europe, there are individual guides to most of the countries in this book, as well as to regions within some countries, including Scotland, Andalucia, Tuscany, Provence & the Côte D'Azur, etc. Lonely Planet also publishes city guides to some of Europe's great capitals (London, Paris, Rome, Berlin, Amsterdam, Dublin etc) and walking guides to Britain, Italy, Turkey, Switzerland and more. If you're a cyclist there are cycling guides to Britain and France, and for foodies the Lonely Planet World Food series covers Ireland, Italy, Morocco, Spain and Turkey. Budding photographers can improve their prints with Lonely

Planet's new *Travel Photography: A Guide to Taking Better Pictures.*

Good maps are easy to come by once you're in Europe, but you might want to buy a few beforehand to plan your route. The maps in this book will help you get an idea of where you might want to go and will be a useful first reference when you arrive in a city. Lonely Planet also publishes plastic-coated full-colour maps to some of Europe's greatest cities – Amsterdam, Barcelona, Berlin, Brussels, Budapest, Dublin, İstanbul, London, Paris, Prague and Rome – with a full index of streets and sights plus transit routes and walking tours.

Proper road maps are essential if you're driving or cycling. You can't go wrong with Michelin maps and they fold up easily so you can stick them in your pocket. Some people prefer the maps meticulously produced by Freytag & Berndt, Kümmerly & Frey and Hallwag. As a rule, maps published by European automobile associations (the AA in Britain, the ADAC and AvD in Germany etc) are excellent and sometimes free if membership of your local association gives you reciprocal rights. Tourist offices are often another good source for (usually free and fairly basic) maps.

What to Bring

It's very easy to find almost anything you need in most European countries and, since you'll probably buy things as you go along, it's better to start with too little rather than too much.

As for clothing, the climate will have a bearing on what you take along. Remember that insulation works on the principle of trapped air, so several layers of thin clothing are warmer than a single thick one (and will be easier to dry). You'll also be much more flexible if the weather suddenly turns warm. Just be prepared for rain at any time of year.

A padlock is useful to lock your bag to a luggage rack in a bus or train; it may also be needed to secure your hostel locker. During city sightseeing, a small daypack is better than a shoulder bag at deterring thieves (see Theft in the Dangers & Annoyances section of this chapter).

A Swiss Army knife comes in handy for all sorts of things. *Any* pocketknife is fine, but make sure it includes such essentials as a bottle opener and strong corkscrew! Toiletries are readily available almost anywhere, but you will need your own supply of paper in many public toilets and those at camping grounds. Tampons are available at pharmacies and supermarkets in all but the most remote places. Condoms, both locally made and imported, are widely available throughout Europe. That said, it's easier to find condoms and the like in France than it is in, say, Turkey or Albania.

A tent and sleeping bag are vital if you want to save money by camping. Even if you're not camping, a sleeping bag is still very useful. A sleeping sheet with pillow cover (case) is necessary if you plan to stay in hostels – otherwise you may have to hire or purchase one.

Other optional items may include a compass, a torch (flashlight), a calculator for currency conversions, an adapter plug for electrical appliances, a universal bath/sink plug (an empty film canister will sometimes work), a few clothes pegs and a large cotton handkerchief that you can soak in water fountains and use to cool yourself off while touring cities during the hot European summer months.

RESPONSIBLE TOURISM

As a visitor, you have a responsibility to the local people and to the environment. For guidelines on how to avoid offending the people you meet, read the following Appearances & Conduct section. When it comes to the environment, the key rules are to preserve natural resources and to leave the countryside as you find it. Those Alpine flowers look much better on the mountainside than squashed in your pocket (many species are protected anyway).

Wherever you are, littering is irresponsible and offensive. Mountain areas have fragile ecosystems, so stick to prepared paths wherever possible, and always carry your rubbish away with you. Don't use detergents or toothpaste in or near watercourses, even if they are biodegradable. If you just gotta go when you're out in the wilderness somewhere, bury human waste in holes at least 15cm deep and at least 100m from any watercourse.

Recycling is a way of local life in countries such as Austria, Germany and Switzerland, and you will be encouraged to follow suit. Traffic congestion on the roads is a

HIGHLIGHTS

The Top 10

There is so much to see in Europe that compiling top 10 lists is next to impossible. But we asked the authors involved in this book to list their personal highlights. The results (in no particular order) are as follows:

Western & Mediterranean Europe
1. Paris
2. Venice, Rome & Florence
3. London
4. The Alps (France, Italy & Switzerland)
5. Greek island-hopping
6. Berlin
7. Amsterdam
8. İstanbul
9. Scotland's highlands & islands
10. High Atlas Mountains (Morocco)

Eastern Europe
1. Budapest
2. Prague
3. Kraków (Poland)
4. St Petersburg
5. Dalmatian Coast (Croatia)
6. Lake Ohrid (Macedonia)

7. High Tatra Mountains (Poland and Slovakia)
8. Rila Mountains (Bulgaria)
9. Škocjan Caves (Slovenia)
10. Painted churches of Bucovina (Romania)

Scandinavian & Baltic Europe
1. Geirangerfjord, Norway's western fjords
2. Frederiksborg Castle, Hillerød (Denmark)
3. Lapland (Finland)
4. Gamla Stan, Stockholm
5. Bygdøy Viking Ship Museum, Oslo (Norway)
6. Lofoten islands (Norway)
7. Ride on a working icebreaker ship, Finland
8. The historic old towns of Tallinn (Estonia), Vilnius (Lithuania) and Rīga (Latvia)
9. The Hurtigruten coastal steamer trip from Bergen to Kirkenes (Norway)
10. The Hermitage, St Petersburg

Other nominations included Barcelona, Munich, the Algarve, western Ireland, Hamburg (Germany), Umbria (Italy), Provence (France), the Pyrenees (France and Spain), Corsica, Bruges (Belgium), Languedoc-Roussillon (France), Lisbon (Portugal), Yorkshire Dales (England), Cappadocia (Turkey) and Edinburgh (Scotland).

---

major problem, and visitors will do themselves and residents a favour if they forgo driving and use public transport.

Appearances & Conduct

Although dress standards are fairly informal in northern Europe, your clothes may well have some bearing on how you're treated in southern Europe (especially in Spain, Portugal, Italy and Greece).

Dress casually, but keep your clothes clean, and ensure sufficient body cover (trousers or a knee-length dress) if your sightseeing includes churches, monasteries, synagogues or mosques. In most Muslim countries, including Morocco and Turkey, western women or men in shorts or sleeveless shirts are virtually in their underwear in the eyes of the more conservative locals. Even in non-Muslim countries, wearing shorts away from the beach or camping

ground is not very common among men. Some nightclubs and fancy restaurants may refuse entry to people wearing jeans, a tracksuit or sneakers (trainers).

While nude bathing is usually restricted to certain beaches, topless bathing is very common in many parts of Europe. Nevertheless, women should be wary of taking their tops off as a matter of course. The rule is: if nobody else seems to be doing it, you shouldn't either.

Most border guards and immigration officials are too professional to judge people entirely on their appearance, but first impressions do count. You may find life easier if you're well presented when dealing with officialdom. Most Europeans have a 'been there, done that' opinion of hair length. Nevertheless, the 'long hair equals despicable hippie' syndrome still survives in some places (Morocco, for example).

LOWLIGHTS

The Bottom 10

The writers were also asked to list the 10 worst or most overrated 'attractions' in Europe and offered the following:

Western & Mediterranean Europe

1. Spanish coastal resorts
2. Paris
3. Dog turds on the streets of Amsterdam and Paris
4. Traffic jams in Paris, London and Rome
5. The Sound of Music tour in Salzburg (Austria)
6. France's northern coast
7. Munich Bierfest
8. The Monte Carlo casino (Monaco)
9. British coastal resorts
10. Bullfights in Spain

Eastern Europe

1. Banja Luka (Bosnia-Hercegovina)
2. Bucharest (Romania)
3. Nowa Huta industrial complex near Kraków (Poland)
4. National Museum of History in Sofia (Bulgaria)
5. Prague at the height of the tourist season

6. Siófok on Lake Balaton (Hungary)
7. U Fleků beer hall in Prague
8. Much of Bulgaria
9. Schmaltzy Hungarian Gypsy music
10. Service staff at most train and bus stations

Scandinavian & Baltic Europe

1. Drottningholm (Stockholm)
2. Santa Claus' house, Rovaniemi (Finland)
3. Seal clubbing display at the Polar Museum, Tromsø (Norway)
4. Endless Swedish forests with swarming mosquitoes
5. Danish cafes thick with cigar smoke
6. The Little Mermaid, Copenhagen (Denmark)
7. Legoland (Denmark)
8. Blue Lagoon (Iceland)
9. The Soviet-era suburbs of any sizeable town in Estonia, Latvia or Lithuania
10. Scandinavian tourists bingeing on duty-free booze

Other nominations included Britain's weather, rising racism, Madame Tussaud's in London, the Scottish east coast, Milan (Italy), Rotterdam (Netherlands), Disneyland Paris, the Greek island of Kos and Palma de Mallorca (Spain). A visit to any of these places could leave you feeling that you've wasted your time. Note that Paris is almost as good at repelling our authors as attracting them.

You'll soon notice that Europeans are heavily into shaking hands and even kissing when they greet one another. Don't worry about the latter with those you don't know too well, but get into the habit of shaking hands with virtually everyone you meet. In many parts of Europe, it's also customary to greet the proprietor when entering a shop, cafe or quiet bar, and to say goodbye when you leave.

VISAS & DOCUMENTS
Passport

Your most important travel document is your passport, which should remain valid until well after you return home. If it's just about to expire, renew it before you go. This may not be easy to do overseas, and some countries insist that your passport remains valid for a specified period (usually

three months beyond the date of your departure from that country).

Applying for or renewing a passport can take anything from an hour to several months, so don't leave it till the last minute. Bureaucratic wheels usually turn faster if you do everything in person rather than relying on the post or agents, but check first what you need to take with you: photos of a certain size, birth certificate, population register extract, signed statements, exact payment in cash, etc.

Australian citizens can apply at a post office or the passport office in their state capital; Britons can pick up application forms from major post offices, and the passport is issued by the regional passport office; Canadians can apply at regional passport offices; New Zealanders can apply at any district office of the Department of Internal

Affairs; US citizens must apply in person (but may usually renew by mail) at a US Passport Agency office or at some courthouses and post offices.

Once you start travelling, carry your passport at all times and guard it carefully. Camping grounds and hotels sometimes insist that you hand over your passport for the duration of your stay, which is very inconvenient, but a driving licence or Camping Card International usually solves the problem.

Citizens of the European Union (EU) and those from certain other European countries (eg Switzerland) don't need a valid passport to travel to another EU country or even some non-EU countries; a national identity card is sufficient. If you want to exercise this option, check with your travel agent or the embassies of the countries you plan to visit.

Visas

A visa is a stamp in your passport or on a separate piece of paper permitting you to enter the country in question and stay for a specified period of time. Often you can get the visa at the border or at the airport on arrival, but not always – check first with the embassies or consulates of the countries you plan to visit – and seldom on trains.

There's a wide variety of visas, including tourist, transit and business ones. Transit visas are usually cheaper than tourist or

Visa Requirements

	Aust	Can	Ire	NZ	SA	UK	US
Albania	−	+	−	−	✓	−	−
Bosnia-Hercegovina	✓	−	−	✓	✓	−	−
Bulgaria	+	+	+	+	✓	+	+
Croatia	−	−	−	−	✓	−	−
Czech Republic	✓	−	−	−	✓	−	+
Denmark	−	−	−	−	✓	−	−
Estonia	−	✓	−	−	✓	−	−
Finland	−	−	−	−	✓	−	−
Greece	−	−	−	−	✓	−	−
Hungary	✓	−	−	−	+	−	−
Iceland	−	−	−	−	✓	−	−
Latvia	✓	✓	−	✓	✓	−	−
Lithuania	−	−	−	−	✓	−	−
Macedonia	✓	✓	−	−	✓	−	✓
Morocco	−	−	−	−	✓	−	−
Norway	−	−	−	−	✓	−	−
Poland	✓	−	−	✓	✓	−	−
Portugal	✓	*	−	*	✓	−	*
Romania	✓	✓	✓	✓	✓	✓	+
Slovakia	#	+	−	#	+	−	+
Slovenia	−	−	−	−	✓	−	−
St Petersberg	✓	✓	✓	✓	✓	✓	✓
Sweden	−	−	−	−	✓	−	−
Turkey	−	−	✓	−	+	✓	✓
Yugoslavia	✓	✓	✓	✓	✓	✓	✓

✓	tourist visa required
+	30-day maximum stay without visa
*	60-day maximum stay without visa
#	90-day maximum stay without visa
−	no visa required

Note: Countries involved in the Schengen Agreement are not included in this table.

business visas, but they only allow a very short stay (one or two days) and can be difficult to extend. Most readers of this book, however, will have very little to do with visas. With a valid passport they'll be able to visit most European countries for up to three (sometimes even six) months, provided they have some sort of onward or return ticket and/or 'sufficient means of support' (money).

In line with the Schengen Agreement there are no passport controls at the borders between Germany, France, Spain, Portugal, the Benelux countries (Belgium, Netherlands and Luxembourg), Italy and Austria; an identity card should suffice, but it's always safest to carry your passport. The other EU countries (Britain, Denmark, Finland, Greece, Ireland and Sweden) are not yet full members of Schengen and still maintain low-key border controls over traffic from other EU countries.

Border procedures between EU and non-EU countries can still be fairly thorough, though citizens of Australia, Canada, Israel, Japan, New Zealand, Norway, Switzerland and the USA do not need visas for tourist visits to any Schengen country.

All non-EU citizens visiting a Schengen country and intending to stay for longer than three days or to visit another Schengen country are supposed to obtain an official entry stamp in their passport either at the point of entry or from the local police within 72 hours. This is very loosely enforced, however, and in general registering at a hotel will be sufficient.

For those who do require visas, it's important to remember that these will have a 'use-by' date, and you'll be refused entry after that period has elapsed. It may not be checked when entering these countries overland, but major problems can arise if it is requested during your stay or on departure and you can't produce it.

Visa requirements can change, and you should always check with the individual embassies or a reputable travel agent before travelling. In some cases it's easier to get your visas as you go along, rather than arranging them all beforehand – notable exceptions include Russia (for St Petersburg) and the Baltic states. Carry spare passport photos (you may need from one to four every time you apply for a visa). The ac-

companying table lists visa requirements for some nationalities.

Eastern Europe Visas are *usually* issued immediately by consulates in Eastern Europe, although some may levy a 50% to 100% surcharge for 'express service'. Nationals requiring visas – everyone needs one for Russia – are strongly advised to get them at a consulate beforehand and not to rely on it being available at every border crossing. They're often cheaper in your home country anyway.

Consulates are generally open weekday mornings (if there's both an embassy and a consulate, you want the consulate). Consulates in countries not neighbouring the one you want to visit are far less crowded (for example, get your Polish visa in Bucharest, your Hungarian visa in Sofia or Warsaw, your Slovakian visa in Zagreb etc). Take your own pen and be sure to have a good supply of passport photos that actually look like you.

Travel Insurance

A travel insurance policy to cover theft, loss and medical problems is a good idea. The policies handled by STA Travel and other student travel organisations are usually good value. Some policies offer lower and higher medical expense options; the higher ones are chiefly for countries such as the USA that have extremely high medical costs. There is a wide variety of policies available so check the small print.

Some policies specifically exclude 'dangerous activities', which can include scuba diving, motorcycling and even trekking. A locally acquired motorcycle licence is not valid under some policies.

You may prefer a policy that pays doctors or hospitals directly rather than you having to pay on the spot and claim later. If you have to claim later, make sure you keep all documentation. Some policies ask you to call back (reverse charges) to a centre in your home country where an immediate assessment of your problem is made. Check that the policy covers ambulances or an emergency flight home.

International Driving Permit

Many non-European drivers licences are valid in Europe, but it's still a good idea to get an International Driving Permit, which can make life much simpler, especially when hiring cars and motorcycles. Basically a multilingual translation of the vehicle class and personal details noted on your local driver's licence, an IDP is not valid unless accompanied by your original licence. An IDP can be obtained for a small fee from your local automobile association – bring along a passport photo and a valid licence.

Hostel Cards

A hostelling card is useful – if not always mandatory – for those staying at hostels (particularly HI hostels). Some hostels in Europe don't require that you be a hostelling association member, but they often charge less if you have a card. Many hostels will issue one on the spot or after a few stays, though this might cost a bit more than getting it in your home country. See Hostels in the Accommodation section later in this chapter.

Camping Card International

The Camping Card International (CCI; formerly the Camping Carnet) is a camping ground ID that can be used instead of a passport when checking into a camp site and includes third-party insurance. As a result, many camping grounds offer a small discount if you sign in with one. CCIs are issued by automobile associations, camping federations and, sometimes, on the spot at camping grounds. In the UK, the AA issues them to its members for UK£4.50.

Student & Youth Cards

The most useful of these is the International Student Identity Card (ISIC), a plastic ID-style card with your photograph, which provides substantial discounts on many forms of transport (including airlines and local public transport), cheap or free admission to museums and sights, and inexpensive meals in some student cafeterias and restaurants.

If you're under 26 but not a student, you can apply for a GO25 card issued by the Federation of International Youth Travel Organisations (FIYTO) or the Euro26 card, both of which go under different names in various countries. Both give much the same discounts and benefits as an ISIC. All these cards are issued by student unions, hostelling organisations or youth-oriented

travel agencies such as STA and Council Travel. You can also get information on the Web (www.istc.org/p_ab_isic.asp).

Seniors Cards

Museums and other sights, public swimming pools and spas and transport companies frequently offer discounts to retired people/old age pensioners/those over 60 (slightly younger for women). Make sure you bring proof of age – that suave *signore* in Italy or that polite Parisian *mademoiselle* is not going to believe you're a day over 39.

European nationals aged over 60 can get a Railplus (formerly Rail Europe Senior) Card. For more information see Rail Passes & Cheap Train Tickets in the Getting Around chapter.

International Health Certificate

You'll need this yellow booklet only if you're arriving in Europe from certain parts of Asia, Africa and South America, where diseases such as yellow fever are prevalent. See Immunisations in the Health section for more information on jabs.

CUSTOMS

Duty-free goods are no longer sold to those travelling from one EU country to another. For goods purchased at airports or on ferries *outside* the EU, the usual allowances apply for tobacco (200 cigarettes, 50 cigars or 250g of loose tobacco), alcohol (1L of spirits or 2L of liquor with less than 22% alcohol by volume; 2L of wine) and perfume (50g of perfume and 0.25L of toilet water).

Do not confuse these with *duty-paid* items (including alcohol and tobacco) bought at normal shops and supermarkets in another EU country, where certain goods might be more expensive. (Cigarettes in France, for example, are half the price they are in the UK.) Then the allowances are more than generous: 800 cigarettes, 200 cigars or 1kg of loose tobacco; 10L of spirits (more than 22% alcohol by volume), 20L of fortified wine or aperitif, 90L of wine or 110L of beer; unlimited quantities of perfume.

MONEY
Exchanging Money

By the year 2002, some countries within the EU will have a single currency called the euro (see boxed text). Until then francs, marks, pesetas and pounds remain in place or share equal status with the euro.

In general, US dollars, Deutschmarks, pounds sterling, and French and Swiss francs are the most easily exchanged currencies in Europe. You lose out through commissions and customer exchange rates every time you change money, so if you only visit Portugal, for example, you may be better off buying escudos straight away if your bank at home can provide them.

Nearly all European currencies are fully convertible, but you may have trouble exchanging some of the lesser known ones at small banks. The importation and exportation of certain currencies (eg Moroccan dirham and Cypriot pounds) is restricted or banned entirely so get rid of any local currency before you leave the country. Also try not to have too many leftover Portuguese escudos, Spanish pesetas, Bulgarian leva, Estonian kroons, Yugoslav dinar etc, as it can be difficult to change them back into hard currency. Get rid of Scottish and Northern Irish pounds before leaving the UK; nobody outside Britain will touch them.

Most airports, central train stations, big hotels and many border posts have banking facilities outside normal office hours, sometimes on a 24-hour basis. You'll often find

The Euro

Don't be surprised if you come across two sets of prices for goods and services in parts of Europe. Since 1 January 1999 Europe's new currency – the euro – has been legal tender here along with the local monetary unit.

While Britain, Denmark, Sweden and Greece have not yet joined, the other 11 EU countries (Austria, Belgium, Finland, France, Germany, Ireland, Italy, Luxembourg, Netherlands, Portugal, Spain) are all counting down the days when venerable currencies like the franc and escudo will be no longer be legal tender – 1 July 2002, to be precise. Between now and that date the countries in Euroland operate two currencies – running their old currencies alongside the euro.

No actual coins or banknotes will be issued until 1 January 2002; until then, the euro is, in effect, 'paperless'. Prices are quoted in euros, but there aren't actually any euros in circulation. Companies use the new currency for their accounting, banks offer euro accounts and travellers cheques in euros, credit-card companies bill in euros. Essentially, the euro is used any time it is not necessary to hand over hard cash.

This can lead to confusion – a restaurant might list prices in both francs and euros or escudos and euros. Check your bill carefully – the total might have the amount in francs or escudos, your credit card may bill you in the euro equivalent. In practice, however, the total is usually listed in both currencies. Things could be more complicated during the first half of 2002 when countries can use both their old currencies and the newly issued euro notes and coins.

The euro has the same value in all member countries of the EU; the E5 note in France is the same E5 note you will use in Italy and Portugal. The official exchange rates were set on 1 January 1999.

Coins and notes have already been designed. There are seven euro notes (five, 10, 20, 50, 100, 200 and 500 euros), and eight euro coins (one and two euros, then one, two, five, 10, 20 and 50 cents). Each country is permitted to design coins with one side standard for all euro coins and the other bearing a national emblem.

Rates of exchange of the euro and foreign currencies against local currencies are given in the country chapters.

country	unit		euro	country	unit		euro
Australia	A$1	=	€0.64	Canada	C$1	=	€0.75
France	1FF	=	€0.15	Germany	DM1	=	€0.51
Ireland	IR£1	=	€1.26	Italy	L1000	=	€0.52
Japan	¥100	=	€1.02	Netherlands	f1	=	€0.45
New Zealand	NZ$1	=	€0.50	Spain	100 ptas	=	€0.60
South Africa	R1	=	€0.16	UK	UK£1	=	€1.66
USA	US$1	=	€1.11				

automatic exchange machines outside banks or tourist offices that accept the currencies of up to two dozen countries. Post offices in Europe often perform banking tasks, tend to be open longer hours, and outnumber banks in remote places. Be aware, though, that while they always exchange cash, they might balk at handling travellers cheques unless they're denominated in the local currency.

The best exchange rates are usually at banks. *Bureaux de change* usually – but not always by any means – offer worse rates or charge higher commissions. Hotels are almost always the worst places to change money. American Express and Thomas Cook offices usually do not charge commission for changing their own cheques, but may offer a less favourable exchange rate than banks.

Cash Nothing beats cash for convenience ...or risk. If you lose it, it's gone forever and very few travel insurers will come to your rescue. Those that do, limit the amount to somewhere around US$300/UK£200. For tips on carrying your money safely, see Theft in the Dangers & Annoyances section later in this chapter.

It's still a good idea, though, to bring some local currency in cash, if only to tide you over until you get to an exchange facility or find an automatic teller machine (ATM). The equivalent of, say, US$50 or US$100 should usually be enough. Some extra cash in an easily exchanged currency (eg US dollars or German marks) is also a good idea, especially in Eastern Europe.

Travellers Cheques In most European countries these days, the exchange rate for travellers cheques is slightly better than the exchange rate for cash.

The main idea of carrying travellers cheques rather than cash is the protection they offer from theft, though they are losing their popularity as more travellers – including those on tight budgets – deposit their money in their bank at home and withdraw it as they go along using ATMs.

American Express, Visa and Thomas Cook travellers cheques are widely accepted and have efficient replacement policies. If you're going to remote places, it's worth sticking to American Express, since small local banks may not always accept other brands.

When you change cheques, don't look at just the exchange rate; ask about fees and commissions as well. There may be a service fee per cheque, a flat transaction fee or a percentage of the total amount irrespective of the number of cheques. Some banks charge fees (often exorbitant) to cash cheques and not cash; others do the reverse.

Cheques are available in various currencies, but ones denominated in US dollars, British pounds and German marks are the easiest to cash. Still, you may not be comfortable using a currency you're not familiar with and watching it converted into still another (for example an Australian cashing German mark cheques into Finnish markka).

Keeping a record of the cheque numbers and those you have used is vital when it comes to replacing lost travellers cheques. You should keep this separate from the cheques themselves.

Credit Cards & ATMs If you're not familiar with the many options, ask your bank to explain the workings and relative merits of credit, credit/debit, debit, charge and cash cards.

A major advantage of credit cards is that they allow you to pay for expensive items (eg airline tickets) without your having to carry great wads of cash around. They also allow you to withdraw cash at selected banks or from the many ATMs that are linked up internationally. However, if an ATM in Europe swallows a card that was issued outside Europe, it can be a major headache. Also, some credit cards aren't hooked up to ATM networks unless you specifically ask your bank to do this.

Cash cards, which you use at home to withdraw money directly from your bank account or savings account, can be used throughout Europe at ATMs linked to international networks like Cirrus and Maestro.

Credit and credit/debit cards like Visa and MasterCard are widely accepted. MasterCard is linked to Europe's extensive Eurocard system, and Visa (sometimes called Carte Bleue) is particularly strong in France and Spain. However, these cards often have a credit limit that is too low to cover major expenses like long-term car rental or airline tickets and can be difficult to replace if lost abroad. Also, when you get a cash advance against your Visa or MasterCard credit card account, your issuer charges a transaction fee and/or finance charge. With some issuers, the fees can reach as high as US$10 *plus* interest per transaction so it's best to check with your card issuer before leaving home and compare rates.

Charge cards like American Express and Diners Club have offices in the major cities of most countries that will replace a lost card within 24 hours. However, charge cards are not widely accepted off the beaten track.

The best advice is not to put all your eggs in one basket. If you want to rely heavily on bits of plastic, go for two different cards, an American Express or Diners Club, for instance, along with a Visa or MasterCard. Better still is a combination of credit or cash card and travellers cheques so you have something to fall back on if an ATM swallows your card or the banks in the area are closed.

A word of warning: fraudulent shopkeepers have been known to quickly make several charge slip imprints with your credit card when you're not looking, and then simply copy your signature from the one that you authorise. Try not to let your card out of sight, and always check your statements upon your return.

International Transfers Telegraphic transfers are not very expensive but, despite their name, can be quite slow. Be sure to specify the name of the bank and the name and address of the branch where you'd like to pick it up.

It's quicker and easier to have money wired via an American Express office (US$60 for US$1000). Western Union's Money Transfer system (available at post offices in some countries) and Thomas Cook's MoneyGram service are also popular.

Black Market A 'black market' exists whenever a government puts restrictions on free currency trading through regulations that prohibit banks and licensed foreign exchange dealers from changing the national currency into western hard currency. A black market is eliminated overnight when a currency is made internally convertible, the way that most Eastern European currencies have gone or are going – the days when you could get five times the official rate for cash on the streets of Warsaw and Bucharest are gone for good.

Changing money on the street is extremely risky, not because it is illegal but because many of the people offering to change are professional thieves with years of experience in cheating tourists. Lonely Planet does not recommend that you use the black market – these days it is simply too risky, and the rates on offer are usually no more than 1% to 5% higher than bank rates.

Guaranteed Cheques Guaranteed personal cheques are another way of carrying money or obtaining cash. Eurocheques, available if you have a European bank account, are guaranteed up to a certain limit. When cashing them (eg at post offices), you will be asked to show your Eurocheque card bearing your signature and registration number, and perhaps a passport or ID card. Your Eurocheque card should be kept separately from the cheques. Many hotels and merchants refuse to accept eurocheques because of the relatively large commissions.

Costs

The secret to budget travel in Europe is cheap accommodation. Europe has a highly developed network of camping grounds and hostels, some of them quite luxurious, and they're great places to meet people.

Other money-saving strategies include preparing your own meals and avoiding alcohol, using a student card (see the earlier Other Useful Documents section) and buying any of the various rail and public transport passes (see the Getting Around chapter). Also remember that the more time you spend in any one place, the lower your daily expenses are likely to be as you get to know your way around.

Including transport but not private motorised transport, your daily expenses could work out to around US$35 to US$40 a day if you're operating on a rock-bottom budget. This means camping or staying in hostels, eating economically and using a transport pass. Travelling on a moderate budget, you would be able to manage on US$60 to US$80 a day. This would allow you to stay at cheap hotels, guesthouses or B&Bs, eat at cheap restaurants and savour the occasional beer.

Be warned that these budgets are rough estimates. Daily expenses will be much higher (US$10 to US$15 extra per day) if you spend all your time in Paris and London, or travel exclusively in Scandinavian countries. Conversely, you will spend less per day in Eastern Europe (though not in Prague or Budapest), Greece, Portugal, Turkey and Morocco.

For more information on budgeting, see Costs & Money in the Facts for First-Time Visitors chapter.

A general warning about the prices we list in this book – they're likely to change, usually moving upward, but if last season was particularly slow they may remain the same or even come down a bit. Nevertheless, relative price levels should stay fairly constant – if hotel A costs twice as much as hotel B, it's likely to stay that way.

Tipping & Bargaining

In many European countries it's common (and the law in France) for a service charge to be added onto restaurant bills, in which case no tipping is necessary. In others, simply rounding up the bill is often sufficient. See the individual country chapters for more details.

Taxes & Refunds

A kind of sales tax called value-added tax (VAT) applies to most goods and services in many European countries; it's 20.6% in France, 20% in Italy and Slovenia, 18% in Greece and 16% in Spain. In most countries, visitors can claim back the VAT on purchases that are being taken out of the country. Those actually *residing* in one EU country are not entitled to a refund on VAT paid on goods bought in another EU country. Thus an American citizen living in London is not entitled to a VAT rebate on items bought in Paris while an EU passport holder residing in New York is.

The procedure for making the claim is fairly straightforward, though it may vary somewhat from country to country, and there are minimum-purchase amounts imposed. First of all make sure the shop offers duty-free sales (often identified with a sign reading 'Tax-Free for Tourists'). When making your purchase, ask the shop attendant for a VAT-refund voucher (sometimes called a Tax-Free Shopping Cheque) filled in with the correct amount and the date. This can either be refunded directly at international airports on departure or stamped at ferry ports or border crossings and mailed back for refund.

POST & COMMUNICATIONS
Post

From major European centres, air mail typically takes about five days to North America and a week to Australasian destinations, though mail from the UK can be much faster and from Greece much slower. Postage costs vary from country to country as does post office efficiency – for details see the relevant country chapters.

You can collect mail from poste restante sections at major post offices. Ask people writing to you to print your name clearly and underline your surname. When collecting mail, your passport may be required for identification and you may have to pay a small fee. If an expected letter is not awaiting you, ask to check under your given name; letters commonly get misfiled. Post offices usually hold mail for about a month, but sometimes less (in Germany, for instance, they only hold mail for two weeks). Unless the sender specifies otherwise, mail will always be sent to the city's main post office.

You can also have mail (but not parcels) sent to you at American Express offices so long as you have an American Express card or are carrying American Express travellers cheques. When you buy the cheques, ask for a booklet listing all the American Express offices worldwide.

Telephone

You can ring abroad from almost any phone box in Europe. Public telephones accepting stored value phonecards (available from post offices, telephone centres, newsstands or retail outlets) are virtually the norm now; in some countries, France, for example, coin-operated phones are almost impossible to find.

Lonely Planet's eKno global communication service provides low cost international calls, a range of innovative messaging services, an online travel vault where you can securely store all your important documents, free email and travel information, all in one easy service. You can join online at www.ekno.lonelyplanet.com, where you can also find the best local access numbers to connect to the 24-hour customer service centre to join or find out more. Once you have joined always check the eKno website for the latest access numbers for each country and updates on new features.

For local calls, you're usually better off with a local card.

Without a phonecard, you can ring from a booth inside a post office or telephone centre and settle your bill at the counter. Reverse-charge (collect) calls are often possible, but not always. From many countries, however, the Country Direct system lets you phone home by billing the long-distance carrier you use at home. The numbers can often be dialled from public phones without even inserting a phone card.

Fax
You can send faxes and telexes from most main post offices.

Email & Internet Access
Travelling with a portable computer is a great way to stay in touch with life back home but, unless you know what you're doing, it's fraught with potential problems. A good investment is a universal AC adaptor for your appliance, so you can plug it in anywhere without frying the innards if the power supply voltage varies. You'll also need a plug adaptor for each country you visit, often easiest bought before you leave home.

Secondly, your PC-card modem may or may not work once you leave your home country – and you won't know for sure until you try. The safest option is to buy a reputable 'global' or 'world' modem before you leave home, or buy a local PC-card modem if you're spending an extended time in any one country.

Keep in mind that the telephone socket in each country you visit will probably be different from that at home, so ensure that you have at least a US RJ-11 telephone adaptor that works with your modem. You can almost always find an adaptor that will convert from RJ-11 to the local variety. For more information on travelling with a portable computer, see www.teleadapt.com or www.warrior.com.

Major Internet service providers (ISPs) such as AOL (www.aol.com), CompuServe (www.compuserve.com) and IBM Net (www.ibm.net) have dial-in nodes throughout Europe; it's best to download a list of the dial-in numbers before you leave home. If you access your Internet email account at home through a smaller ISP or your office or school network, your best option is either to open an account with a global ISP, like those mentioned above, or to rely on cybercafes and other public access points to collect your mail.

If you do intend to rely on cybercafes, you'll need to carry three pieces of information with you so you can access your Internet mail account: your incoming (POP or IMAP) mail server name, your account name, and your password. Your ISP or network supervisor will give you these. Armed with this information, you should be able to access your Internet mail account from any Internet-connected machine in the world, provided it runs some kind of email software. It pays to become familiar with the process for doing this before you leave home. A final option to collect mail through cybercafes is to open a free eKno Web-based email account on-line at www.ekno.lonelyplanet.com. You can then access your mail from anywhere in the world from any net-connected machine running a standard Web browser.

You'll find cybercafes throughout Europe: check out the country chapters in this book, and see www.netcafeguide.com for an up-to-date list. You may also find public Internet access in post offices, libraries, hostels, hotels, universities and so on.

INTERNET RESOURCES
The World Wide Web is a rich resource for travellers. You can research your trip, hunt for bargain air fares, book hotels, check on weather conditions or chat with locals and other travellers about the best places to visit (or avoid!).

The following Web sites offer useful general information about Europe, its cities, transport systems, currencies etc. Country-specific Web sites are listed in the relevant country chapters.

Lonely Planet
There's no better place to start your Web explorations than the Lonely Planet Web site. Here you'll find succinct summaries on travelling to most places on earth, postcards from other travellers and the Thorn Tree bulletin board, where you can ask questions before you go or dispense advice when you get back. You can also find travel news and updates to many of our most popular guidebooks, and the sub-WWWay section links you to the most useful travel resources elsewhere on the Web. www.lonelyplanet.com

Tourist Offices
Lists tourist offices at home and around the world for most countries.
www.mbnet.mb.ca/lucas/travel

Rail Information
Train fares and schedules on the most popular routes in Europe, including information on rail and youth passes.
www.raileurope.com

Airline Information
What airlines fly where, when and for how much.
www.travelocity.com

Airline Tickets
Name the price you're willing to pay for an airline seat and if an airline has an empty seat for which it would rather get something than nothing, US-based Priceline lets you know.
www.priceline.com

Currency Conversions
Exchange rates of hundreds of currencies worldwide.
www.xe.net/ucc

NEWSPAPERS & MAGAZINES

Keeping up with the news in English is obviously no problem in the UK or Ireland. In larger European towns you can buy the excellent *International Herald Tribune* on the day of publication, as well as the colourful but superficial *USA Today*. Among other English-language newspapers widely available are the *Guardian*, the *Financial Times* and the *Times*. The *European* weekly newspaper is also readily available, as are *Newsweek*, *Time* and the *Economist*.

VIDEO SYSTEMS

If you want to record or buy video tapes to play back home, you won't get a picture if the image registration systems are different. Europe generally uses PAL (SECAM in France), which is incompatible with the North American and Japanese NTSC system. Australia also uses PAL.

PHOTOGRAPHY

Both where you'll be travelling and the weather will dictate what film to take or buy locally. In places like Ireland and Britain, where the sky is often overcast, photographers should bring high-speed film (eg 200 to 400 ASA). For southern Europe (or northern Europe under a blanket of snow and sunny skies) slower film is the answer (eg 50 to 100 ASA).

Film and camera equipment is available everywhere in Europe, but obviously shops in the larger cities and towns have a wider selection. One of the best (and most widely available) slide films around is Fuji Velvia. Unlike Kodachrome, whose developing is easy to mishandle and must usually be sent out by developers, Velvia is developed using the standard E6 process, and it's virtually idiot-proof.

Avoid buying film at tourist sites in Europe – eg at kiosks below the Eiffel Tower in Paris or at the Tower of London. It may have been stored badly or reached its sell-by date. It certainly will be expensive.

TIME

The standard international time measurements – GMT and UTC – are identical, and both are calibrated to the prime meridian (which famously passes through Greenwich in England). For the sake of comparison, if it's noon in Britain (GMT/UTC) it is 4 am on the USA's West Coast (GMT/UTC minus eight hours), 7 am on the USA's East Coast (GMT/UTC minus five hours), 1 pm in Paris (GMT/UTC plus one hour; also called Central European Time), 2 pm in Greece (GMT/UTC plus two hours) and 10 pm in Sydney (GMT/UTC plus 10 hours).

In most European countries, clocks are turned one hour ahead for daylight-saving time on the last Sunday in March, and turned back again on the last Sunday in October. During daylight-saving time, Britain and Ireland are GMT/UTC plus one hour, Central European Time is GMT/UTC plus two hours and Greece is GMT/UTC plus three hours.

ELECTRICITY
Voltage & Cycle

Most of Europe runs on 220V, 50Hz AC. The exceptions are the UK, which has 240V, and Spain, which runs at 220V and sometimes at 125V, depending on the network (some houses can have both). Some old buildings and hotels in Italy (including Rome) might also have 125V. All EU countries were supposed to have been standardised at 230V by now, but like everything else in the EU, this is taking longer than anticipated.

Check the voltage and cycle (usually 50Hz) used in your home country. Most appliances that are set up for 220V will handle 240V without modifications (and vice versa); the same goes for 110 and 125V combinations. Just don't mix 110/125V with 220/240V without a transformer.

Several countries outside Europe (such as the USA and Canada) have 60Hz AC, which will affect the speed of electric motors even after the voltage has been adjusted to European values, so CD and tape players (where motor speed is all-important) will be useless. But things like electric razors, hair dryers, irons and radios will be fine.

Plugs & Sockets
The UK and Ireland use a design with three flat pins – two for current and one for earth/grounding. Most of Continental Europe uses the 'europlug' with two round pins. Many europlugs and some sockets don't have provision for earth since most local home appliances are double-insulated; when provided, earth usually consists of two contact points along the edge, although Italy, Greece and Switzerland use a third round pin in such a way that the standard two-pin plug still fits the sockets (though not always in Italy and Switzerland).

If your plugs are of a different design, you'll need an adapter. Get one before you leave, since the adapters available in Europe usually go the other way. If you find yourself without one, however, a specialist electrical-supply shop should be able to help.

HEALTH
Travel health depends on your predeparture preparations, your day-to-day health care while travelling and how you handle any medical problem that does develop. Fortunately Europe is a fairly healthy place in which to travel. Your main risks are sunburn, insect bites, foot blisters and an upset stomach from overeating or drinking.

Predeparture Planning
Immunisations Jabs are not really necessary for Europe, but they may be an entry requirement if you're coming from an infected area – yellow fever is the most likely requirement. If you're going to Europe with stopovers in Asia, Africa or South America, check with your travel agent or with the embassies of the countries you plan to visit.

There are, however, a few routine vaccinations that are recommended whether you're travelling or not, and this Health section assumes that you've had them: polio (usually administered during childhood), tetanus and diphtheria (usually administered together during childhood, with a booster shot every 10 years) and measles. See your physician or nearest health agency about these. You might also consider having an immunoglobulin or hepatitis A (Havrix) vaccine before extensive travels in southern Europe; a tetanus booster; an immunisation against hepatitis B before travelling to Malta; or a rabies (pre-exposure) vaccination.

All vaccinations should be recorded on an International Health Certificate (see that entry in the Visas & Documents section). Don't leave this till the last minute, as the vaccinations may have to be staggered over a period of time.

Health Insurance Make sure you have adequate health insurance. See Travel Insurance under Visa & Documents earlier in this chapter for details.

Other Preparations Make sure you're healthy before you start travelling. If you are going on a long trip make sure your teeth are OK. If you wear glasses take a spare pair and your prescription.

If you require a particular medication take an adequate supply, as it may not be available locally. Take part of the packaging showing the generic name, rather than the brand, which will make getting replacements easier. It's a good idea to have a legible prescription or letter from your doctor to show that you legally use the medication.

Basic Rules
Food Salads and fruit should be safe throughout Europe, though care should be taken in Morocco, the more remote parts of Turkey and southern Europe. If you're at all unsure, wash fruits and vegies with purified water and peel foods where possible.

Ice cream is usually OK, but not if it has melted and been refrozen. Take great care with fish or shellfish (cooked mussels that haven't opened properly can be dangerous, for instance), and avoid undercooked meat.

If a place looks clean and well run and if the vendor also looks clean and healthy, then the food is probably safe. In general, places that are packed with travellers or locals will be fine. Be careful with food that has been cooked and left to go cold.

Picking mushrooms is a favourite pastime in some parts of Europe as autumn approaches, but make sure you don't eat any that haven't first been positively identified as safe. Many cities and towns have set up inspection tables at markets or at entrances to national parks to separate the good from the deadly.

Water Tap water is safe to drink in most parts of Europe. In countries where it is unsafe (we list such warnings in the relevant country chapters) bottled water is usually widely available and reasonably priced. Where tap water is unsafe to drink, don't use it to brush your teeth or wash your face. Try not to splash your mouth or face in showers, and avoid foods that may have been washed in tainted water (eg salad, peeled fruits and vegetables). Also avoid ice cubes and the like.

Throughout Europe be wary of natural water unless you can be sure that there are no people or cattle upstream; run-off from fertilised fields is also a concern. If you are planning extended hikes where you have to rely on natural water, it may be useful to know about water purification.

The simplest way of purifying water is to boil it thoroughly. Technically this means boiling for 10 minutes, something that happens very rarely. Remember that at high altitude water boils at a lower temperature, so germs are less likely to be killed.

Simple filtering will not remove all dangerous organisms, so if you cannot boil water it should be treated chemically. Chlorine tablets (Puritabs, Steritabs or other brand names) will kill many – but not all – pathogens. Iodine is very effective in purifying water and is available in tablet form (such as Potable Aqua), but follow the directions carefully and remember that too much iodine can be harmful.

Medical Problems & Treatment

Local pharmacies or neighbourhood medical centres are good places to visit if you have a small medical problem and can explain what the problem is. Hospital casualty wards will help if it's more serious. Major hospitals and emergency numbers are mentioned in the various individual country chapters of this book. Tourist offices and hotels can put you on to a doctor or dentist, and your embassy or consulate will probably know one who speaks your language.

Environmental Hazards

Altitude Sickness Lack of oxygen at high altitudes (over 2500m) affects most people to some extent. The affect may be mild or severe and occurs because less oxygen reaches the muscles and the brain, requiring the heart and lungs to compensate by working harder. Symptoms of Acute Mountain Sickness (AMS) usually develop during the first 24 hours at high altitude but may be delayed up to three weeks. Mild symptoms include headache, lethargy, dizziness, difficulty sleeping and loss of appetite. AMS may become more severe without warning and can be fatal. Severe symptoms include breathlessness, a dry, irritating cough (which may progress to the production of pink, frothy sputum), severe headache, lack of coordination and balance, confusion, irrational behaviour, vomiting, drowsiness and unconsciousness. There is no hard-and-fast rule as to what is too high: AMS has been fatal at 3000m, although 3500m to 4500m is the usual range.

Treat mild symptoms by resting at the same altitude until recovery, usually a day or two. Paracetamol or aspirin can be taken for headaches. If symptoms persist or become worse, however, immediate descent is necessary; even 500m can help. Drug treatments should never be used to avoid descent or to enable further ascent.

Heat Exhaustion Dehydration and salt deficiency can cause heat exhaustion. Take time to acclimatise to high temperatures, drink sufficient liquids and do not do anything too physically demanding.

Salt deficiency is characterised by fatigue, lethargy, headaches, giddiness and muscle cramps; salt tablets may help, but adding extra salt to your food is better.

Heat Stroke This serious, occasionally fatal, condition can occur if the body's heat-regulating mechanism breaks down and the body temperature rises to dangerous levels. Long, continuous periods of exposure to high temperatures and insufficient fluids can leave you vulnerable to heat stroke.

The symptoms are feeling unwell, not sweating very much (or at all) and a high body temperature (39°C to 41°C or 102°F to 106°F). Where sweating has ceased the skin becomes flushed and red. Severe, throbbing headaches and lack of coordination will also occur, and the sufferer may be confused or aggressive. Eventually the victim will become delirious or convulse. Hospitalisation is essential, but in the interim get victims out of the sun, remove their clothing, cover them with a wet sheet or towel and then fan continually. Give fluids if they are conscious.

Hypothermia Too much cold can be just as dangerous as too much heat. Be prepared for cold, wet or windy conditions even if you're just out walking.

Hypothermia occurs when the body loses heat faster than it can produce it and the core temperature of the body falls. It is surprisingly easy to progress from very cold to dangerously cold due to a combination of wind, wet clothing, fatigue and hunger, even if the air temperature is above freezing. It is best to dress in layers; silk, wool and some of the new artificial fibres are all good insulating materials. A hat is important, as a lot of heat is lost through the head. A strong, waterproof outer layer (and a 'space' blanket for emergencies) are essential. Carry basic supplies, including food containing simple sugars to generate heat quickly and fluid to drink.

Symptoms of hypothermia are exhaustion, numb skin (particularly toes and fingers), shivering, slurred speech, irrational or violent behaviour, lethargy, stumbling, dizzy spells, muscle cramps and violent bursts of energy. Irrationality may take the form of sufferers claiming they are warm and trying to take off their clothes.

To treat mild hypothermia, first get the person out of the wind and/or rain, remove their clothing if it's wet and replace it with dry, warm clothing. Give them hot liquids – not alcohol – and some high-kilojoule (calorie) easily digestible food. Do not rub victims; instead allow them to warm themselves slowly. This should be enough to treat the early stages of hypothermia. The early recognition and treatment of mild hypothermia is the only way to prevent severe hypothermia, which is a critical condition.

Jet Lag A person experiences jet lag when travelling by air across more than three time zones (each time zone usually represents a

---

Medical Kit Check List

Following is a list of items you should consider including in your medical kit – consult your pharmacist for brands available in your country.

- ☐ **Aspirin or paracetamol (acetaminophen in the USA)** – for pain or fever
- ☐ **Antihistamine** – for allergies, eg, hay fever; to ease the itch from insect bites or stings; and to prevent motion sickness
- ☐ **Cold and flu tablets, throat lozenges and nasal decongestant**
- ☐ **Multivitamins** – consider for long trips, when dietary vitamin intake may be inadequate
- ☐ **Antibiotics** – consider including these if you're travelling well off the beaten track; see your doctor, as they must be prescribed, and carry the prescription with you
- ☐ **Loperamide or diphenoxylate** –'blockers' for diarrhoea
- ☐ **Prochlorperazine or metaclopramide** – for nausea and vomiting
- ☐ **Rehydration mixture** – to prevent dehydration, which may occur, for example, during bouts of diarrhoea; particularly important when travelling with children
- ☐ **Insect repellent, sunscreen, lip balm and eye drops**
- ☐ **Calamine lotion, sting relief spray or aloe vera** – to ease irritation from sunburn and insect bites or stings
- ☐ **Antifungal cream or powder** – for fungal skin infections and thrush
- ☐ **Antiseptic (such as povidone-iodine)** – for cuts and grazes
- ☐ **Bandages, Band-Aids (plasters) and other wound dressings**
- ☐ **Water purification tablets or iodine**
- ☐ **Scissors, tweezers and a thermometer** – note that mercury thermometers are prohibited by airlines

---

one-hour time difference. It occurs because many of the functions of the human body (such as temperature, pulse rate and emptying of the bladder and bowels) are regulated by internal 24-hour cycles. When we travel long distances rapidly, our bodies take time to adjust to the 'new time' of our destination, and we may experience fatigue, disorientation, insomnia, anxiety, impaired concentration and loss of appetite. These effects will usually be gone within three days of arrival, but to minimise the impact of jet lag:

• Rest for a few days prior to departure.
• Try to select flight schedules that minimise sleep deprivation; arriving late in the day means you can go to sleep soon after you arrive. For very long flights, try to organise a stopover.
• Avoid excessive eating (which bloats the stomach) and alcohol (which causes dehydration) during the flight. Instead, drink plenty of non-carbonated, non-alcoholic drinks such as fruit juice or water.
• Avoid smoking.
• Make yourself comfortable by wearing loose-fitting clothes and perhaps bringing an eye mask and earplugs to help you sleep.
• Try to sleep at the appropriate time for the time zone you are travelling to.

Motion Sickness Eating lightly before and during a trip will reduce the chances of motion sickness. If you are prone to motion sickness try to find a place that minimises movement – near the wing on aircraft, close to midships on boats, near the centre on buses. Fresh air usually helps; reading and cigarette smoke do not. Commercial motion-sickness preparations, which can cause drowsiness, have to be taken *before* the trip commences. Ginger (available in capsule form) and peppermint (including mint-flavoured sweets) are natural preventatives.

Prickly Heat Prickly heat is an itchy rash caused by excessive perspiration trapped under the skin. It usually strikes people who have just arrived in a hot climate. Keeping cool, bathing often, drying the skin and using a mild talcum or prickly heat powder or resorting to air-conditioning may help.

Sunburn You can get sunburned very quickly, even through cloud cover. Use a sunscreen, hat, and barrier cream for your nose and lips. Calamine lotion or a sting relief spray are good for mild sunburn. Protect your eyes with good quality sunglasses, particularly if you will be near water, sand or snow.

Infectious Diseases

Diarrhoea Simple things like a change of water, food or climate can all cause a mild bout of diarrhoea, but a few rushed toilet trips with no other symptoms is not indicative of a major problem.

Dehydration is the main danger with any diarrhoea, particularly in children or the elderly, as dehydration can occur quite quickly. Under all circumstances fluid replacement (at least equal to the volume being lost) is the most important thing to remember. Weak black tea with a little sugar, soda water, or soft drinks allowed to go flat and diluted 50% with clean water are all good.

With severe diarrhoea a rehydrating solution is preferable to replace minerals and salts lost. Commercially available oral rehydration salts (ORS) are very useful; add them to boiled or bottled water. In an emergency you can make up a solution of six teaspoons of sugar and half a teaspoon of salt to a litre of boiled or bottled water. You need to drink at least the same volume of fluid that you are losing in bowel movements and vomiting. Urine is the best guide to the adequacy of replacement – if you have small amounts of concentrated urine, you need to drink more. Keep drinking small amounts often. Stick to a bland diet as you recover.

Lomotil or Imodium can be used to bring relief from the symptoms, but they do not actually cure the problem. Only use these drugs if you do not have access to toilets (eg if you *must* travel). For children under 12 years Lomotil and Imodium are not recommended. Do not use these drugs if the person has a high fever or is severely dehydrated.

Viral Gastroenteritis This is caused not by bacteria but, as the name suggests, by a virus. It is characterised by stomach cramps, diarrhoea, and sometimes by vomiting and/or a slight fever. All you can do is rest and drink lots of fluids.

Fungal Infections Fungal infections occur more commonly in hot weather and are usually found on the scalp, between the toes or fingers, in the groin and on the body (ringworm). You get ringworm (which is a fungal infection, not a worm) from infected animals or other people. Moisture encourages these infections.

To prevent fungal infections wear loose, comfortable clothes, avoid artificial fibres, wash frequently and dry carefully. If you do get an infection, wash the infected area at least daily with a disinfectant or medicated soap and water, and rinse and dry well. Apply an antifungal cream or powder like tolnifate

(Tinaderm). Try to expose the infected area to air or sunlight as much as possible and wash all towels and underwear in hot water, change them often and let them dry in the sun.

Hepatitis Hepatitis is a general term for inflammation of the liver. It is a common disease worldwide. The symptoms are fever, chills, headache, fatigue, feelings of weakness and aches and pains, followed by loss of appetite, nausea, vomiting, abdominal pain, dark urine, light-coloured faeces, jaundiced (yellow) skin and the whites of the eyes may turn yellow. **Hepatitis A** is transmitted by contaminated food and drinking water. You should seek medical advice, but there is not much you can do apart from resting, drinking lots of fluids, eating lightly and avoiding fatty foods. People who have had hepatitis should avoid alcohol for some time after the illness, as the liver needs time to recover.

There are almost 300 million chronic carriers of **Hepatitis B** in the world. It is spread through contact with infected blood, blood products or body fluids, for example through sexual contact, unsterilised needles and blood transfusions, or contact with blood via small breaks in the skin. Other risk situations include having a shave, tattoo, or having your body pierced with contaminated equipment. The symptoms of type B may be more severe and may lead to long-term problems.

HIV & AIDS HIV, the Human Immunodeficiency Virus, develops into AIDS (Acquired Immune Deficiency Syndrome), which is a fatal disease. HIV is a major problem in many European countries, especially France. Any exposure to blood, blood products or body fluids may put the individual at risk. The disease is often transmitted through sexual contact or dirty needles; vaccinations, acupuncture, tattooing and body piercing can be potentially as dangerous as intravenous drug use. HIV/AIDS can also be spread through infected blood transfusions; some developing countries do not screen blood used for transfusions. Fear of HIV infection should never preclude treatment for serious medical conditions.

Sexually Transmitted Diseases Gonorrhoea, herpes and syphilis are among these

---

Everyday Health

Normal body temperature is up to 37°C or 98.6°F; more than 2°C (4°F) higher indicates a high fever. The normal adult pulse rate is 60 to 100 per minute (children 80 to 100, babies 100 to 140). As a general rule the pulse increases about 20 beats per minute for each 1°C (2°F) rise in fever.

Respiration (or breathing) rate is also an indicator of illness. Count the number of breaths per minute: between 12 and 20 is normal for adults and older children (up to 30 for younger children, 40 for babies). People with a high fever or serious respiratory illness breathe more rapidly than normal. More than 40 shallow breaths a minute may indicate pneumonia.

---

diseases; sores, blisters or rashes around the genitals, discharges or pain when urinating are common symptoms. With some STDs, such as wart virus or chlamydia, symptoms may be less marked or not observed at all – especially in women. Syphilis symptoms eventually disappear completely, but the disease continues and can cause severe problems in later years. While abstinence from sexual contact is the only 100% effective prevention, using condoms is also effective. The treatment of gonorrhoea and syphilis is with antibiotics. The different sexually transmitted diseases each require specific antibiotics. There is no cure for herpes.

Cuts, Bites & Stings
Bedbugs & Lice Bedbugs live in various places, but particularly in dirty mattresses and bedding, evidenced by spots of blood on bedclothes or on the wall. Bedbugs leave itchy bites in neat rows. Calamine lotion or a sting relief spray may help.

All lice cause itching and discomfort. They will live in your hair (head lice), your clothing (body lice) or in your pubic hair (crabs). You catch lice through direct contact with infected people or by sharing combs, clothing and the like. Powder or shampoo treatment will kill the lice, and infected clothing should then be washed in very hot, soapy water and left in the sun to dry.

Bites & Stings Bee and wasp stings are often more painful than they are dangerous. However, in people who are allergic to them severe breathing difficulties may occur and require urgent medical care. Calamine lotion or a sting relief spray will give relief and ice packs will reduce the pain and swelling.

Mosquitoes can be a nuisance in southern and Eastern Europe, but can almost drive you insane during the summer months in northern Europe, particularly around lakes and rivers. They also cause sleepless nights in a swampy country like the Netherlands. Fortunately, mosquito-borne diseases like malaria are for the most part unknown in Western Europe. Most people get used to mosquito bites after a few days as their bodies adjust, and the itching and swelling will become less severe. An antihistamine cream may help alleviate the symptoms. For some people, a daily dose of vitamin B will keep mosquitoes at bay.

Midges – small, blood-sucking flies related to mosquitoes – are a major problem in some parts of Europe (eg Scotland and parts of England) during summer.

Ticks You should always check all over your body if you have been walking through a potentially tick-infested area as ticks can cause skin infections and other more serious diseases. If a tick is found attached, press down around the tick's head with tweezers, grab the head and gently pull upwards. Avoid pulling the rear of the body as this may squeeze the tick's gut contents through the attached mouth parts into the skin, increasing the risk of infection and disease. Smearing chemicals on the tick will not make it let go and is not recommended.

Lyme disease is a tick-transmitted infection that may be acquired in parts of southern Europe. The illness usually begins with a spreading rash at the site of the tick bite and is accompanied by fever, headache, extreme fatigue, aching joints and muscles and mild neck stiffness. If untreated, these symptoms usually resolve over several weeks but over subsequent weeks or months disorders of the nervous system, heart and joints may develop. Treatment works best early in the illness. Medical help should be sought.

Another tick that can bring on more than just an itch is the forest tick, which burrows under the skin, causing inflammation and even encephalitis. It has become a common problem in parts of central and Eastern Eur-

ope, especially eastern Austria, Germany, Hungary and the Czech Republic. You might consider getting an FSME (meningo-encephalitis) vaccination if you plan to do extensive hiking and camping between May and September.

Rabies Rabies is a fatal viral infection but is rare in most countries in Western Europe. Rabies is nonexistent in the UK, Ireland, Portugal, Monaco and Malta. Many animals can be infected (such as dogs, cats, foxes and bats) and it is their saliva which is infectious. Any bite, scratch or even lick from a warm-blooded, furry animal should be cleaned immediately and thoroughly. Scrub with soap and running water, and then apply alcohol or iodine solution. Medical help should be sought promptly to receive a course of injections to prevent the onset of symptoms and death.

Snakes To minimise your chances of being bitten always wear boots, socks and long trousers when walking through undergrowth where snakes may be present. Don't put your hands into holes and crevices, and be careful when collecting firewood.

Snake bites do not cause instantaneous death and antivenenes are usually available. Immediately wrap the bitten limb tightly, as you would for a sprained ankle, and then attach a splint to immobilise it. Keep the victim still and seek medical help, if possible with the dead snake for identification. Don't attempt to catch the snake if there is a possibility of being bitten again. Tourniquets and sucking out the poison are now comprehensively discredited.

Women's Health

Antibiotic use, synthetic underwear, sweating and contraceptive pills can lead to fungal vaginal infections when travelling in hot climates. Maintaining good personal hygiene and wearing loose-fitting clothes and cotton underwear will help to prevent these infections. Fungal infections, characterised by a rash, itch and discharge, can be treated with a vinegar or lemon-juice douche, or with yogurt. Nystatin, miconazole or clotrimazole pessaries or vaginal cream are the usual treatment.

Sexually transmitted diseases are a major cause of vaginal problems. Symptoms include a smelly discharge, painful intercourse and sometimes a burning sensation when urinating. Male sexual partners must also be treated. Medical attention should be sought and remember, in addition to these diseases, HIV or hepatitis B may also be acquired during exposure. Besides abstinence, the best thing is to practise safer sex using condoms.

WOMEN TRAVELLERS

Women are more likely to attract unwanted attention in rural Spain and southern Italy, particularly Sicily, where many men still think that staring suavely at or calling out to a passing woman is to pay her a flattering compliment. This behaviour is not confined to these areas, however, and the potential is, sadly, everywhere. Slightly conservative dress can help to deter lascivious gazes and wolf whistles, dark sunglasses help avoid unwanted eye contact. Marriage is highly respected in southern Europe, and a wedding ring (on the left ring finger) sometimes helps, along with talk about 'my husband'. Hitchhiking alone in these areas is asking for trouble. For more information see the relevant country chapters.

GAY & LESBIAN TRAVELLERS

The *Spartacus International Gay Guide* (Bruno Gmünder, Berlin; US$39.95) is a good male-only international directory of gay entertainment venues in Europe and elsewhere. It's best when used in conjunction with listings in local gay papers, usually distributed for free at gay bars and clubs. For lesbians, *Women's Travel in Your Pocket* (Ferrari Publications, London; UK£8.99) is a good international guide.

See the following individual country chapters for contact addresses and gay and lesbian venues.

DISABLED TRAVELLERS

If you have a physical disability, get in touch with your national support organisation (preferably the 'travel officer' if there is one) and ask about the countries you plan to visit. They often have complete libraries devoted to travel, and they can put you in touch with travel agents who specialise in tours for the disabled.

The British-based Royal Association for Disability & Rehabilitation (RADAR) pub-

lishes a useful guide entitled *European Holidays & Travel Abroad: A Guide for Disabled People* (UK£5), which gives a good overview of facilities available to disabled travellers in Western Europe (published in even-numbered years) and one to places farther afield called *Long-Haul Holidays* (in odd-numbered years). The *Accessible Holidays in the British Isles* (£7.50) includes Ireland. Contact RADAR (☎ 020-7250 3222, fax 020-7250 0212) at 12 City Forum, 250 City Rd, London EC1V 8AF.

SENIOR TRAVELLERS

Senior citizens are entitled to many discounts in Europe on things like public transport, museum admission fees etc, provided they show proof of their age. In some cases they might need a special pass. The minimum qualifying age is generally 60 or 65 for men and slightly younger for women.

In your home country, a lower age may already entitle you to all sorts of interesting travel packages and discounts (on car hire, for instance) through organisations and travel agents that cater for senior travellers. Start hunting at your local senior citizens advice bureau.

DANGERS & ANNOYANCES

On the whole, you should experience few problems travelling in most European countries – even alone – as the region is well developed and relatively safe. But do exercise common sense. Whatever you do, don't leave friends and relatives back home worrying about how to get in touch with you in case of emergency. Work out a list of places where they can contact you or, best of all, phone or email home now and then.

For more information on dangers, scams and travel precautions see Safety & Security in the Facts for First-Time Visitors chapter.

Precautions

The hassles created by losing your passport can be considerably reduced if you have a record of its number and issue date or, even better, photocopies of the relevant data pages. A photocopy of your birth certificate can also be useful.

Also add the serial numbers of your travellers cheques (cross them off as you cash them) and photocopies of your credit cards, airline ticket and other travel documents.

Keep all this emergency material separate from your passport, cheques and cash, and leave extra copies with someone you can rely on back home. If you do lose your passport, notify the police immediately to get a statement, and contact your nearest consulate.

Theft

Theft is definitely a problem in Europe, and nowadays you also have to be wary of other travellers. The most important things to guard are your passport, papers, tickets and money – in that order. It's always best to carry these next to your skin in a sturdy money belt or pouch hooked to your belt.

Train station lockers or luggage storage counters are useful places to store your bags (but *never* valuables) while you get your bearings in a new town. Be very suspicious about people who offer to help you operate your locker. Carry your own padlock for hostel lockers.

You can lessen the risks further by being careful of snatch thieves. Cameras or shoulder bags are an open invitation for these people, who sometimes operate from motorcycles or scooters and expertly slash the strap before you have a chance to react. A small daypack is better, but watch your rear. Be very careful at cafes and bars – loop the strap around your leg while seated.

Pickpockets are most active in dense crowds, especially in busy train stations and on public transport during peak hours. A common ploy is for one person to distract you while another zips through your pockets. Beware of gangs of kids – dishevelled-looking *and* well dressed – waving newspapers and demanding attention. In the blink of an eye, a wallet or camera can go missing.

Be careful even in hotels; don't leave valuables lying around in your room. Parked cars containing luggage and other bags are prime targets for petty criminals in most cities.

Drugs

Always treat drugs with a great deal of caution. There are a lot of drugs available in Europe, sometimes quite openly (eg in the Netherlands), but that doesn't mean it's legal. Even a little harmless hashish can cause a great deal of trouble in some places. Don't even think about bringing drugs home with you either. With what they may

consider 'suspect' stamps in your passport (eg Amsterdam's Schiphol airport), energetic customs officials could well decide to take a closer look.

ACTIVITIES

Europe offers countless opportunities to indulge in more active pursuits than sightseeing. The varied geography and climate supports the full range of outdoor pursuits: windsurfing, skiing, fishing, trekking, cycling and mountaineering. For local information see the individual country chapters.

Cycling

Much of Europe is ideally suited to cycling. In the north-west, the flat terrain ensures that bicycles are a popular form of everyday transport, though rampant headwinds often spoil the fun. In the rest of the region, hills and mountains can make for heavy going, but this is offset by the dense concentration of things to see. Cycling is a great way to explore many of the Mediterranean islands, though the heat can get to you after a while (make sure you drink enough fluids).

Popular cycling areas among holiday-makers include the Belgian Ardennes, the west of Ireland, the upper reaches of the Danube in southern Germany, anywhere in the Alps (for those fit enough) and the south of France.

If you are arriving from outside Europe, you can often bring your own bicycle along on the plane (see Bicycle in the Getting Around chapter). Alternatively, this book lists many places where you can hire one (make sure it has plenty of gears if you plan anything serious), though apart from in Ireland they might take a dim view of rentals lasting more than a week.

Skiing

In winter, Europeans flock to the hundreds of resorts in the Alps and Pyrenees for downhill skiing and snowboarding, though cross-country is very popular in some areas.

A skiing holiday can be an expensive one due to the costs of ski lifts, accommodation and the inevitable après-ski drinking sessions. Equipment hire (or even purchase), on the other hand, can be relatively cheap if you follow the tips in this book, and the hassle of bringing your own skis may not be worth it. As a rule, a skiing holiday in Europe will work out twice as expensive as a summer holiday of the same length; the exceptions are Romania, Slovakia, Czech Republic and Poland, where skiing is still cheap compared with Western Europe. Cross-country skiing costs less than downhill since you don't rely as much on ski lifts.

The skiing season generally lasts from early December to late March, though at higher altitudes it may extend an extra month either way. Snow conditions can vary greatly from one year to the next and from region to region, but January and February tend to be the best (and busiest) months. During the snow season, the Thursday and Friday editions of the *International Herald Tribune* have a weekend ski report on snow conditions at every major ski resort in Europe.

Ski resorts in the French and Swiss Alps offer great skiing and facilities, but are also the most expensive. Expect high prices, too, in the German Alps, though Germany has cheaper (but far less spectacular) options in the Black Forest and Harz Mountains. Austria is generally slightly cheaper than France and Switzerland. Prices in the Italian Alps are similar to Austria (with some up-market exceptions like Cortina d'Ampezzo), and can work out relatively cheaply with the right package.

Possibly the cheapest skiing in Western Europe is to be found in the Pyrenees in Spain and Andorra, and in the Sierra Nevada range in the south of Spain.

Hiking

Keen hikers can spend a lifetime exploring Europe's many exciting trails. Probably the most spectacular are to be found in the Alps and Italian Dolomites, which are criss-crossed with well-marked trails; food and accommodation are available along the way in season. The equally sensational Pyrenees are less developed, which can add to the experience as you often rely on remote mountain villages for rest and sustenance. Hiking areas that are less well known but nothing short of stunning are Sardinia, northern Portugal, Turkey, Morocco, Slovakia, Poland, Romania and Bulgaria. The Picos de Europa range in Spain is also rewarding.

The Ramblers' Association (☎ 020-7339 8500) is a London charity that promotes long-distance walking in the UK and can help with maps and information.

The British-based Ramblers Holidays (☎ 01707-331133) offers hiking-oriented trips in Europe and elsewhere.

Windsurfing & Surfing

After swimming and fishing, windsurfing could well be the most popular of the many water sports on offer in Europe. It's easy to rent sailboards in many tourist centres, and courses are usually available for beginners.

Believe it or not, you can also go surfing in Europe. Forget the shallow North Sea and Mediterranean and the calm Baltic. But there can be excellent surf, and an accompanying surfer scene, in south-west England and west Scotland (wetsuit advisable!), along Ireland's north-west coast, the Atlantic coast of France and Portugal, and along the north and south-west coasts of Spain.

COURSES

If your interests are more cerebral, you can enrol in courses in Europe on anything from language to alternative medicine. Language courses are available to foreigners through universities or private schools, and are justifiably popular since the best way to learn a language is to study in the country where it's spoken. But you can also take courses in art, literature, architecture, drama, music, cooking, alternative energy, photography and organic farming, among other subjects.

The best sources of information are the cultural institutes maintained by many European countries around the world; failing that, try their national tourist offices or embassies. Student exchange organisations, student travel agencies such as STA and Council Travel, and organisations like the YMCA/YWCA and Hostelling International (HI) can also put you on the right track. Ask about special holiday packages that include a course.

WORK

European countries aren't keen on handing out jobs to foreigners with unemployment rates what they are in some areas. Officially, an EU citizen is allowed to work in any other EU country, but the paperwork isn't always straightforward for long-term employment. Other country/nationality combinations require special work permits that can be almost impossible to arrange, especially for temporary work. That doesn't prevent enterprising travellers from topping up their funds occasionally by working in the hotel or restaurant trades at beach or ski resorts or teaching a little English, and they don't always have to do this illegally either.

The UK, for example, issues special 'working holiday' visas to Commonwealth citizens aged between 17 and 27 valid for two years. Your national student exchange organisation may be able to arrange temporary work permits to several countries through special programs.

If you have a parent or grandparent who was born in an EU country, you may have certain rights you never knew about. Get in touch with that country's embassy and ask about dual citizenship and work permits – if you go for citizenship, also ask about any obligations, such as military service and residency. Ireland is particularly easy-going about granting citizenship to people with an Irish parent or grandparent, and with an Irish passport, the EU is your oyster. Be aware that your home country may not recognise dual citizenship.

If you do find a temporary job, the pay may be less than that offered to local people. The one big exception is teaching English, but these jobs are hard to come by – at least officially. Other typical tourist jobs (picking grapes in France, washing dishes in Alpine resorts, working at a bar in Greece) often come with board and lodging, and the pay is little more than pocket money, but you'll have a good time partying with other travellers.

Work Your Way Around the World by Susan Griffith gives good, practical advice on a wide range of issues. Its publisher, Vacation Work, has many other useful titles, including *Summer Jobs Abroad*, edited by David Woodworth. *Working Holidays*, published by the Central Bureau for Educational Visits & Exchanges in London, is another good source.

If you play an instrument or have other artistic talents, you could try working the streets. As every Peruvian pipe player (and his fifth cousin) knows, busking is fairly common in major European cities like Amsterdam and Paris, but is illegal in some parts of Switzerland and Austria; in Belgium and Germany, where it has been more or less tolerated in the past, crackdowns are not unknown. Most other countries require municipal permits that can be hard to obtain. Talk to other buskers first.

Selling goods on the street is generally frowned upon and can be tantamount to vagrancy, apart from at flea markets. It's also a hard way to make money if you're not selling something special. Most countries require permits for this sort of thing. It's fairly common, though officially illegal, in the UK, Germany and Spain.

ACCOMMODATION

The cheapest places to stay in Europe are camping grounds, followed by hostels and accommodation in student dormitories. Cheap hotels are virtually unknown in the northern half of Europe, but guesthouses, pensions, private rooms and B&Bs often offer good value. Self-catering flats and cottages are worth considering with a group, especially if you plan to stay somewhere for a while.

See the Facts for the Visitor sections in the individual country chapters for an overview of the local accommodation options. During peak holiday periods, accommodation can be hard to find and it's advisable to book ahead. Even camping grounds can fill up, especially in or around big cities.

Reservations

Cheap hotels in popular destinations (eg Paris, London, Rome) – especially the well-run ones in desirable or central neighbourhoods – fill up quickly. It's a good idea to make reservations as far ahead as possible – at least for the first night or two. A three-minute international phone call to reserve a room (followed, if necessary, by written confirmation and/or deposit) is a lot cheaper than wasting your first day in a city looking for a place to stay.

If you arrive in a country by air and without a reservation, there is often an airport accommodation-booking desk, although it rarely covers the lower strata of hotels. Tourist offices often have extensive accommodation lists, and the more helpful ones will go out of their way to find you something suitable. In most countries the fee for this service is very low, and if accommodation is tight, it can save you a lot of running around. This is also an easy way to get around any language problems. Agencies offering private rooms can be good value.

Staying with a local family doesn't always mean that you'll lack privacy, but you'll probably have less freedom than in a hotel.

Sometimes people will come up to you on the street offering a private room or a hostel bed. This can be good or bad, there's no hard-and-fast rule – just make sure it's not way out in a dingy suburb and that you negotiate a clear price. As always, be careful when someone offers to carry your luggage: they might carry it away altogether.

Camping

Camping is immensely popular in Europe (especially among Germans, Dutch, Czechs and Poles) and provides the cheapest accommodation. There's usually a charge per tent or site, per person and per vehicle. National tourist offices should have booklets or brochures listing camping grounds all over their country. See the earlier Other Useful Documents section for information on the Camping Card International.

In large cities, most camp sites will be some distance from the centre. For this reason, camping is most popular with people who have their own transport. If you're on foot, the money you save by camping can quickly be eaten up by the bus or train fares spent on commuting to/from a town centre. You may also need a tent, sleeping bag and cooking equipment, though not always: many camp sites hire bungalows or cottages accommodating from two to eight people.

Camping other than on designated camping grounds is difficult because the population density of Western Europe makes it hard to find a suitable spot to pitch a tent away from prying eyes. It is also illegal without permission from the local authorities (the police or local council office) or from the owner of the land (don't be shy about asking – you may be pleasantly surprised by the response).

In some countries, such as Austria, the UK, France and Germany, free camping is illegal on all but private land, and in Greece it's illegal altogether. This doesn't prevent hikers from occasionally pitching their tent, and they'll usually get away with it if they have only a small tent, are discreet, stay only one or two nights, take the tent down during the day and do not light a campfire or leave rubbish. At worst, they'll be woken up by the police and asked to move on.

Hostels

Hostels offer the cheapest (secure) roof over your head in Europe, and you don't have to be a youngster to use them. Bavaria in Germany is one of the few places with a strict age limit (27 years old) for hostelling members. Most hostels are part of the national youth hostel association (YHA), which is affiliated with what was formerly called the IYHF (International Youth Hostel Federation) and has been renamed Hostelling International (HI) in order to attract a wider clientele and move away from the emphasis on youth. The situation remains slightly confused, however. Some countries, such as the USA and Canada, immediately adopted the new name, but many European countries will take a few years to change their logos. In practice it makes no difference: IYHF and HI are the same thing and the domestic YHA almost always belongs to the parent group.

Technically, you're supposed to be a YHA or HI member to use affiliated hostels, but you can often stay by paying an extra charge and this will usually be set against future membership. Stay enough nights as a nonmember and you're automatically a member.

To join the HI, ask at any hostel or contact your local or national hostelling office. There's a useful Web site at www.iyhf.org with links to most HI sites. There are many hostel guides with listings available, including the HI *Europe* (UK£7.50) and the England & Wales *YHA Accommodation Guide* (UK£2.99). The offices for English-speaking countries appear below. Otherwise, check the individual country chapters for addresses.

Australia
Australian Youth Hostels Association
(☎ 02-9565 1699, fax 9565 1325,
❸ yha@yha.org.au), Level 3, 10 Mallett St, Camperdown, NSW 2050
Canada
Hostelling International Canada
(☎ 613-237 7884, fax 237 7868,
❸ info@hostellingintl.ca), 205 Catherine St, Suite 400, Ottawa, Ontario K2P 1C3
England & Wales
Youth Hostels Association (☎ 01727-855215, fax 844126, ❸ customerservices@yha.org.uk), Trevelyan House, 8 St Stephen's Hill, St Albans, Herts AL1 2DY
Ireland
An Óige (Irish Youth Hostel Association; ☎ 01-830 4555, fax 830 5808, ❸ mailbox@anoige.ie), 61 Mountjoy St, Dublin 7

New Zealand
  Youth Hostels Association of New Zealand
  (☎ 03-379 9970, fax 365 4476,
  📧 info@yha.org.nz), 193 Cashel St, 3rd floor,
  Union House, Christchurch
Northern Ireland
  Hostelling International Northern Ireland
  (☎ 0128-9031 5435, fax 9043 9699,
  📧 info@hini.org.uk), 22-32 Donegall Rd,
  Belfast BT12 5JN
Scotland
  Scottish Youth Hostels Association (☎ 01786-
  891400, fax 891333, 📧 info@syha.org.uk),
  7 Glebe Crescent, Stirling FK8 2JA
South Africa
  Hostelling International South Africa (☎ 021-
  424 2511, fax 424 4119, 📧 info@hisa.org.za),
  PO Box 4402, St George's House, 73 St
  George's Mall, Cape Town 8001
USA
  Hostelling International/American Youth
  Hostels (☎ 202-783 6161, fax 783 6171,
  📧 hiayhserv@hiayh.org), 733 15th St NW,
  Suite 840, Washington DC 20005

Private Hostels There are some privately
run hostelling organisations in Europe, not
to mention hundreds of unaffiliated hostels.
Unlike HI hostels, private hostels have
fewer rules (eg no curfew, no daytime lock-
out) and are often booked by small groups
of independent travellers rather than large
and noisy groups of European school children. The main drawback of private hostels
is that the facilities will often vary greatly
(unlike HI hostels, which must meet minimum safety and cleanliness standards).

University Accommodation
Some university towns rent out student accommodation during the holiday periods.
This is a very popular practice in France,
the UK and in many Eastern European
countries (see those individual country
chapters for more details), as universities
become more accountable financially.

University accommodation will sometimes be in single rooms (although it's more
commonly in doubles or triples) and may
have cooking facilities. For details inquire
at the college or university itself, at the student information services or at the local
tourist offices.

B&Bs, Guesthouses & Hotels
There's a huge range of accommodation
above the hostel level. In the UK and Ireland the myriad B&Bs are the real bargains
in this field, where you get a room (a bed)
and breakfast in a private home. In some
areas every other house will have a B&B
sign out front. In other countries similar private accommodation – though often without
breakfast – may go under the name of pension, guesthouse, *Gasthaus*, *Zimmer frei*,
chambre d'hôte and so on. Although the
majority of guesthouses are simple affairs,
there are more expensive ones where you'll
find en suite bathrooms and other luxuries.

Above this level are hotels, which at the
bottom of the bracket may be no more expensive than B&Bs or guesthouses, while at
the other extreme extend to luxury five-star
properties with price tags to match. Although
categorisation depends on the country, the
hotels recommended in this book will generally range from no stars to one or two stars.
You'll often find inexpensive hotels clustered around the bus and train station areas –
always good places to start hunting.

Check your hotel room and the bathroom
before you agree to take it, and make sure you
know what it's going to cost – discounts are
often available for groups or for longer stays.
Ask about breakfast: sometimes it's included,
but other times it may be obligatory and
you'll have to pay extra for it. If the sheets
don't look clean, ask to have them changed
right away. Check where the fire exits are
located.

If you think a hotel room is too expensive,
ask if there's anything cheaper – often, hotel
owners may have tried to steer you into
more expensive rooms. In southern Europe
in particular, hotel owners may be open to a
little bargaining if times are slack. In France
and the UK it is common practice for business hotels (usually more than two stars) to
slash their rates by up to 40% on Friday and
Saturday nights when business is dead. Save
your big hotel splurge for the weekend.

FOOD
Few regions in the world offer such a variety of cuisines in such a small area as Europe. The Facts for the Visitor sections in the
individual country chapters contain details
of local cuisines, and the Places to Eat sections list many suggestions.

Restaurant prices vary enormously. The
cheapest places for a decent meal are often
the self-service restaurants in department

stores. University restaurants are dirt cheap, but the food tends to be bland and you may not be allowed in if you're not a local student. Kiosks often sell cheap snacks that can be as much a part of the national cuisine as the fancy dishes.

Self-catering – buying your ingredients at a shop or market and preparing them yourself – can be a cheap and wholesome way of eating. Even if you don't cook, a lunch on a park bench with a half a loaf of fresh bread, some local cheese and salami and a tomato or two, washed down with a bottle of local wine, can be one of the recurring highlights of your trip. It also makes a nice change from restaurant food.

If you have dietary restrictions – you're a vegetarian or you keep kosher, for example – tourist organisations may be able to advise you about suitable restaurants. We list some vegetarian and kosher restaurants in this book.

In general, vegetarians needn't worry about going hungry in Europe; many restaurants have at least one vegetarian dish, and southern European menus in particular tend to contain many vegetable dishes and salads. Some restaurants will prepare dishes on request, but you should ask about this in advance. Vegetarians will have a harder time in Eastern Europe and meat-heavy countries such as Spain, where even so-called 'vegetable soup' is often made with meat stock.

Getting There & Away

Step one of your trip is actually getting to Europe and, in these days of severe competition among airlines, there are plenty of opportunities to find cheap tickets to a variety of gateway cities.

Forget shipping – only a handful of ships still carry passengers across the Atlantic; they don't sail often and are very expensive, even compared with full-fare air tickets. Some travellers still arrive or leave overland – the options being Africa, the Middle East and Asia via Russia on the Trans-Siberian railway from China.

AIR

Remember always to reconfirm your onward or return bookings by the specified time – at least 72 hours before departure on international flights. Otherwise there's a real risk that you'll turn up at the airport only to find that you've missed your flight because it was rescheduled, or that you've been reclassified as a 'no show' and 'bumped' (see the Air Travel Glossary in this chapter).

Buying Tickets

An air ticket alone can gouge a great slice out of anyone's budget, but you can reduce the cost by finding discounted fares. Stiff competition has resulted in widespread discounting – good news for travellers! The only people likely to be paying full fare these days are travellers flying in 1st or business class. Passengers flying in economy can usually manage some sort of discount. But unless you buy carefully and flexibly, it is still possible to end up paying exorbitant amounts for a journey.

For long-term travel there are plenty of discount tickets which are valid for 12 months, allowing multiple stopovers with open dates. For short-term travel cheaper fares are available by travelling mid-week, staying away at least one Saturday night or taking advantage of promotional offers.

When you're looking for bargain air fares, go to a travel agent rather than directly to the airline. From time to time, airlines do have promotional fares and special offers, but generally they only sell fares at the official listed price. One exception to

this rule is the expanding number of 'no-frills' carriers operating in the United States and north-west Europe, which mostly sell direct to travellers. Unlike the 'full service' airlines, no-frills carriers often make one-way tickets available at around half the return fare, meaning that it is easy to put together a return ticket when you fly to one place but leave from another.

The other exception is booking on the Internet. Many airlines, full-service and no-frills, offer some excellent fares to Web surfers. They may sell seats by auction or simply cut prices to reflect the reduced cost of electronic selling. Many travel agents around the world have Web sites, which can make the Internet a quick and easy way to compare prices, a good start for when you're ready to begin negotiating with your favourite travel agency. On-line ticket sales work well if you are doing a simple one-way or return trip on specified dates. However, on-line superfast fare generators are no substitute for a travel agent who knows all about special deals, has strategies for avoiding layovers and can offer advice on everything from which airline has the best vegetarian food to the best travel insurance to bundle with your ticket.

The days when some travel agents would routinely fleece travellers by running off with their money are, happily, almost over, though it's generally not advisable to send money (even cheques) through the post unless the agent is very well established. Paying by credit card generally offers protection, as most card issuers provide refunds if you can prove you didn't get what you paid for. Similar protection can be obtained by buying a ticket from a bonded agent, such as one covered by the Air Transport Operators Licence (ATOL) scheme in the UK. Agents who only accept cash should hand over the tickets straight away and not tell you to 'come back tomorrow'. After you've made a booking or paid your deposit, call the airline and confirm that the booking was made.

You may decide to pay more than the rock-bottom fare by opting for the safety of a better known travel agent. Firms such as STA Travel, which has offices worldwide, Council Travel in the USA and Usit Campus (formerly Campus Travel) in the UK are not going to disappear overnight and they do offer good prices to most destinations.

If you purchase a ticket and later want to make changes to your route or get a refund, you need to contact the original travel agent. Airlines only issue refunds to the purchaser of a ticket – usually the travel agent who bought the ticket on your behalf. Many travellers change their routes halfway through their trips, so think carefully before you buy a ticket which is not easily refunded.

Student & Youth Fares Full-time students and people under 26 have access to better deals than other travellers. The better deals may not always be cheaper fares but can include more flexibility to change flights and/or routes. You have to show a document proving your date of birth or a valid International Student Identity Card (ISIC) when buying your ticket and boarding the plane. There are plenty of places around the world where nonstudents can get fake student cards, but if you get caught using a fake card you could have your ticket confiscated.

Frequent Flyers Most airlines offer frequent flyer deals that can earn you a free air ticket or other goodies. To qualify, you have to accumulate sufficient mileage with the same airline or airline alliance. Many airlines have 'blackout periods', or times when you cannot fly for free on your frequent-flyer points (Christmas and Chinese New Year, for example). The worst thing about frequent-flyer programs is that they tend to lock you into one airline, and that airline may not always have the cheapest fares or most convenient flight schedule.

Courier Flights Courier flights are a great bargain if you're lucky enough to find one. Air-freight companies expedite delivery of urgent items by sending them with you as your baggage allowance. You are permitted to bring along a carry-on bag, but that's all. In return, you get a steeply discounted ticket.

There are other restrictions: courier tickets are sold for a fixed date and schedule changes can be difficult to make. If you buy a return ticket, your schedule will be even more rigid. You need to clarify before you fly what restrictions apply to your ticket, and don't expect a refund once you've paid.

Booking a courier ticket takes some effort. They are not readily available and arrangements have to be made a month or more in advance. You won't find courier flights on all routes either – just on the major air routes.

Courier flights are occasionally advertised in the newspapers, or you could contact air-freight companies listed in the phone book. You may even have to go to the air-freight company to get an answer – the companies aren't always keen to give out information over the phone. *Travel Unlimited* (PO Box 1058, Allston, MA 02134, USA) is a monthly travel newsletter based in the USA that publishes many courier flight deals from destinations worldwide. A 12-month subscription to the newsletter costs US$25, or US$35 for readers outside the USA. Another possibility (at least for US residents) is to join the International Association of Air Travel Couriers (IAATC). The membership fee of US$45 gets members a bimonthly update of air-courier offerings, access to a fax-on-demand service with daily updates of last minute specials and the bimonthly newsletter *The Shoestring Traveler*. For more information, contact IAATC (☎ 561-582-8320) or visit its

Web site, www.courier.org. However, be aware that joining this organisation does not guarantee that you'll get a courier flight.

Second-Hand Tickets You'll occasionally see advertisements on youth hostel bulletin boards and in newspapers for 'second-hand tickets'. That is, somebody purchased a return ticket or a ticket with multiple stopovers and now wants to sell the unused portion of the ticket. Unfortunately, these tickets, if used for international travel, are usually worthless, as the name on the ticket must match the name on the passport of the person checking in. Some people reason that the seller of the ticket can check you in with his or her passport, and then give you the boarding pass – wrong again! Usually the immigration people want to see your boarding pass, and if it doesn't match the name in your passport, then you won't be able to board your flight.

Round-the-World (RTW) Tickets RTW tickets can work out to be no more expensive or even cheaper than an ordinary return ticket. Official RTW tickets are usually put together by a combination of two or more airlines, and permit you to fly anywhere you want on their route systems as long as you don't backtrack. Other restrictions are that you (usually) must book the first sector in advance and cancellation penalties apply. There may be restrictions on how many stops (or kilometres/miles) you are permitted. Prices start at about UK£900, A$1700 or US$1300, depending on the season and length of ticket validity. An alternative type of RTW ticket is one put together by a travel agent using a combination of discounted tickets. These can be much cheaper than the official ones, but usually carry a lot of restrictions. For more details contact your travel agent or an airline.

Travellers with Special Needs
Most international airlines can cater to people with special needs – travellers with disabilities, people with young children and even children travelling alone.

Travellers with special dietary preferences (vegetarian, kosher etc) can request appropriate meals with advance notice. If you are travelling in a wheelchair, most international airports can provide an escort from check-in desk to plane where needed, and ramps, lifts, toilets and phones are generally available.

Airlines usually allow babies up to two years of age to fly for 10% of the adult fare, although a few may allow them free of charge. Reputable international airlines usually provide nappies (diapers), tissues, talcum and all the other paraphernalia needed to keep babies clean, dry and half-happy. For children between the ages of two and 12, the fare on international flights is usually 50% of the regular fare or 67% of a discounted fare.

The USA
Discount travel agents in the USA are known as consolidators. San Francisco is the ticket consolidator capital of America, although some good deals can be found in Los Angeles, New York and other big cities. Consolidators can be found through the Yellow Pages or the major daily newspapers. Ticket Planet is a leading ticket consolidator and is recommended. Visit its Web site at www.ticketplanet.com.

The *New York Times*, *LA Times*, *Chicago Tribune* and *San Francisco Chronicle* all have weekly travel sections in which you'll find any number of travel agents' ads. Council Travel, America's largest student travel organisation, has around 60 offices in the USA; its head office (☎ 800-226-8624) is at 205 E 42 St, New York, NY 10017. Call to find out the office nearest you or visit its Web site at www.ciee.org. STA Travel (☎ 800-777-0112) has offices in major cities. Call for office locations or visit its Web site at www.statravel.com.

You should be able to fly from New York to London or Paris and back for US$400 to US$500 in the low season and US$550 to US$800 in the high season. Equivalent fares from the west coast are US$100 to US$300 higher.

On a stand-by basis, one-way fares can work out to be remarkably cheap. New York-based Airhitch (☎ 212-864 2000) can get you to/from Europe for US$185/235/265/215 each way from the east coast/midwest/west coast/southeast. Visit its Web site at www.airhitch.org.

Another option is a courier flight. A New York-London return ticket can cost as little as US$210 in the low season. See Courier

Air Travel Glossary

Cancellation Penalties If you have to cancel or change a discounted ticket, there are often heavy penalties involved; insurance can sometimes be taken out against these penalties. Some airlines impose penalties on regular tickets as well, particularly against 'no-show' passengers.

Courier Fares Businesses often need to send urgent documents or freight securely and quickly. Courier companies hire people to accompany the package through customs and, in return, offer a discount ticket which is sometimes a phenomenal bargain. However, you may have to surrender all your baggage allowance and take only carry-on luggage.

Full Fares Airlines traditionally offer 1st class (coded F), business class (coded J) and economy class (coded Y) tickets. These days there are so many promotional and discounted fares available that few passengers pay full economy fare.

Lost Tickets If you lose your airline ticket an airline will usually treat it like a travellers cheque and, after inquiries, issue you with another one. Legally, however, an airline is entitled to treat it like cash and if you lose it then it's gone forever. Take good care of your tickets.

Onward Tickets An entry requirement for many countries is that you have a ticket out of the country. If you're unsure of your next move, the easiest solution is to buy the cheapest onward ticket to a neighbouring country or a ticket from a reliable airline which can later be refunded if you do not use it.

Open-Jaw Tickets These are return tickets where you fly out to one place but return from another. If available, this can save you backtracking to your arrival point.

Overbooking Since every flight has some passengers who fail to show up, airlines often book more passengers than they have seats. Usually excess passengers make up for the no-shows, but occasionally somebody gets 'bumped' onto the next available flight. Guess who it is most likely to be? The passengers who check in late.

Promotional Fares These are officially discounted fares, available from travel agencies or direct from the airline.

Reconfirmation If you don't reconfirm your flight at least 72 hours prior to departure, the airline may delete your name from the passenger list. Ring to find out if your airline requires reconfirmation.

Restrictions Discounted tickets often have various restrictions on them – such as needing to be paid for in advance and incurring a penalty to be altered. Others are restrictions on the minimum and maximum period you must be away.

Round-the-World Tickets RTW tickets give you a limited period (usually a year) in which to circumnavigate the globe. You can go anywhere the carrying airlines go, as long as you don't backtrack. The number of stopovers or total number of separate flights is decided before you set off and they usually cost a bit more than a basic return flight.

Transferred Tickets Airline tickets cannot be transferred from one person to another. Travellers sometimes try to sell the return half of their ticket, but officials can ask you to prove that you are the person named on the ticket. On an international flight tickets are compared with passports.

Travel Periods Ticket prices vary with the time of year. There is a low (off-peak) season and a high (peak) season, and often a low-shoulder season and a high-shoulder season as well. Usually the fare depends on your outward flight – if you depart in the high season and return in the low season, you pay the high-season fare.

Flights in the Buying a Ticket section earlier or try As You Like It Travel (☎ 212-216 0644), Now Voyager Travel (☎ 212-431 1616). Web sites at www.asulikeit.com and www.nowvoyagertravel.com.

Eastern Europe Long-haul air fares to/from Eastern Europe are not the continent's biggest bargains. Your best bet is to buy the cheapest possible ticket to somewhere in Western or Central Europe and proceed by surface (ie bus or train) from there. Look for a ticket to London, Amsterdam, Athens, İstanbul or anywhere in Germany. Vienna is a useful gateway as the Czech Republic, Slovakia, Hungary and Slovenia are all just a few hours away.

Scandinava You should be able to fly return from New York or Boston to Copenhagen, Oslo or Stockholm for around US$600 in the low season and US$800 in the high season.

Icelandair (☎ 800-223-5500) has expanded its routes and now flies from New York, Boston, Baltimore, Fort Lauderdale and Orlando via Reykjavík to Oslo, Stockholm and Copenhagen. On all of its transatlantic flights it allows a free stopover in Reykjavík – making it an great way to spend a few days in Iceland.

On the other hand, if you're planning on flying within Scandinavian and Baltic Europe, SAS (☎ 800-221-2350) has regional air passes available to passengers who also fly on their transatlantic flights.

Canada

Canadian discount air ticket sellers are also known as consolidators and their air fares tend to be about 10% higher than those sold in the USA. The *Globe & Mail*, the *Toronto Star*, the *Montreal Gazette* and the *Vancouver Sun* carry travel agents' ads and are a good place to look for cheap fares.

Travel CUTS (☎ 800-667-2887) is Canada's national student travel agency and has offices in all major cities. Its Web address is www.travelcuts.com.

Airhitch (see the USA section) has standby fares to/from Toronto, Montreal and Vancouver.

If you're travelling to Scandinavia or Baltic Europe, Icelandair (☎ 800-223 5500) has low-cost seasonal flights from Halifax

in Nova Scotia to Oslo, Stockholm and Copenhagen via Reykjavík.

Australia

Cheap flights from Australia to Europe generally go via South-East Asian capitals, involving stopovers at Kuala Lumpur, Bangkok or Singapore. If a long stopover between connections is necessary, transit accommodation is sometimes included in the price of the ticket. If it's at your own expense, it may be worth considering a more expensive ticket.

Quite a few travel offices specialise in discount air tickets. Some travel agents, particularly smaller ones, advertise cheap air fares in the travel sections of weekend newspapers, such as the *Age* in Melbourne and the *Sydney Morning Herald*. And with Australia's large and well organised ethnic populations, it pays to check special deals in the ethnic press – Olympic Airways sometimes has good deals to Athens, for example.

Two well-known agents for cheap fares are STA Travel and Flight Centre. STA Travel (☎ 03-9349 2411) has its main office at 224 Faraday St, Carlton, VIC 3053, and offices in all major cities and on many university campuses. Call ☎ 131 776 Australia-wide for the location of your nearest branch or check out its Web site at www.statravel.com.au. Flight Centre (☎ 131 600 Australia-wide) has a central office at 82 Elizabeth St, Sydney, and there are dozens of offices throughout Australia. Web address is www.flightcentre.com.au.

Flights from Australia to a European destination on Thai, Malaysian, Qantas and Singapore airlines start from about A$1700 (low season) up to A$2500. All have frequent promotional fares so it pays to check daily newspapers.

Flights to/from Perth are a couple of hundred dollars cheaper. Another option for travellers wanting to go to Britain between November and February is to hook up with a charter flight returning to Britain. These low-season, one-way fares do have restrictions, but may work out to be considerably cheaper. Ask your travel agent for details.

New Zealand

As in Australia, STA and Flight Centres International are popular travel agents in New

Zealand. The cheapest fares to Europe are routed through Asia. A discounted return flight to London from Auckland costs around NZ$2100. A RTW ticket with Air New Zealand or Lufthansa via the USA is around NZ$2400 in the low season.

The UK

Discount air travel is big business in London. Advertisements for many travel agents appear in the travel pages of the weekend broadsheets, such as the *Independent on Saturday* and the *Sunday Times*. Look out for the free magazines, such as *TNT*, which are widely available in London – often outside the main railway and underground stations.

For students or travellers under 26, popular travel agencies in the UK include STA Travel (☎ 020-7361 6144), which has an office at 86 Old Brompton Rd, London SW7 3LQ, and other offices in London and Manchester. Web site at www.statravel.co.uk. Usit Campus (☎ 0870-240 1010), 52 Grosvenor Gardens, London SW1WOAG, has branches throughout the UK. Web address is www.usitcampus.com. Both of these agencies sell tickets to all travellers but cater especially to young people and students. Charter flights can work out as a cheaper alternative to scheduled flights, especially if you do not qualify for the under-26 and student discounts.

Other recommended travel agencies include: Trailfinders (☎ 020-7938 3939), 194 Kensington High St, London W8 7RG; Bridge the World (☎ 020-7734 7447), 4 Regent Place, London W1R 5FB; and Flightbookers (☎ 020-7757 2000), 177-178 Tottenham Court Rd, London W1P 9LF.

Africa

Nairobi and Johannesburg are probably the best places in Africa to buy tickets to Europe, thanks to the many bucket shops and the lively competition between them. Student Travel Centre (☎ 011-716 3945) in Johannesburg and the Africa Travel Centre (☎ 021-235 555) in Cape Town are worth trying for cheap tickets.

Several West African countries such as Senegal and The Gambia offer cheap charter flights to France and London. Charter fares to Morocco and Tunisia can be quite cheap if you're lucky enough to find a seat.

Asia

Singapore and Bangkok are the discount airfare capitals of Asia. Shop around and ask the advice of other travellers before handing over any money. STA has branches in Hong Kong, Tokyo, Singapore, Bangkok, Jakarta and Kuala Lumpur.

In India, tickets may be slightly cheaper from the bucket shops around Delhi's Connaught Place. Check with other travellers about their current trustworthiness.

LAND
The UK

Bus Eurolines, Europe's largest network of buses, has seven circular explorer routes, always starting and ending in London. For further details, see the Bus section in the Getting Around chapter.

Train The Channel Tunnel allows for a land link between Britain and France. Eurostar is the passenger train service which travels between London and Paris and London and Brussels; cars travel on the Eurotunnel vehicle service.

Eurostar The highly civilised Eurostar passenger train service takes three hours (not including the one-hour time change) to get from London's Waterloo station to the Gare du Nord in Paris. Passport and customs checks take place on board or very cursorily on arrival.

There's quite a wide range of tickets. Cheapest is the non-refundable Leisure Apex return which must include a Saturday night away; booked at least 14 days in advance it costs £69/119 in standard/1st class; booked at least seven days in advance it costs £85/160. Flexi Tickets can be refunded and cost £140/220. Regular one-way tickets cost £155/190.

The Youth Return ticket (£75) available to those under 26 can be booked at any time. Changes can be made only once in each direction and the ticket is non-refundable.

Children's return fares, available for those aged four to 11 years, are £58/90 in standard/first class. There are often special deals on offer (eg day returns, weekend trips, etc), so it pays to phone Eurostar or its agents for the latest information.

Eurostar tickets are available direct from Eurostar (☎ 0870-518 6186 in the UK or

☎ 08 36 35 35 39 in France), from some travel agents, at Waterloo station, from international ticket offices at many of the UK's mainline train stations, and from Rail Europe (☎ 0870-530 0003) which also sell other European rail tickets. Eurostar's Web site is at www.eurostar.com.

You can take a bicycle on Eurostar as part of your luggage only if it is in a bike bag.

Eurotunnel The Eurotunnel vehicle service (☎ 0870-535 3535 in the UK, or ☎ 03 21 00 61 00 in France) travels between terminals in Folkestone and Calais. Its Web address is www.eurotunnel.com. This train carries cars, motorcycles and bicycles with their passengers/riders.

You can just drive into the terminal, buy your ticket and get on the next train but you'll almost always make a saving by buying your ticket in advance. Fares vary with the time of year and there are peak (6.30 am to 10 pm) and off-peak (10 pm to 6.30 am) periods. The one-way/return fare for a car with driver and all passengers is £169.50/369 or £134.50/269 off-peak. A five-day return costs £159 off-peak or £229 peak. A day return is £69, and for the same price you can get an overnight return as long as you leave after 12 noon on the 1st day and are back by 4 pm on the 2nd day.

A motorcycle and rider costs from £89 return. Bicycles can be taken but only on two trips per day and they must be booked 24 hours in advance on ☎ 01303-288680. The cost is £15 for bicycle and rider.

Trains run 24 hours a day, every day of the year, with up to four departures an hour during peak periods. During the 35-minute crossing, passengers can sit in their cars or walk around the air-conditioned, sound-proofed rail carriage. The entire process, including loading and unloading, should take about an hour.

Train-Boat-Train There are train-boat-train combos in association with Hoverspeed (☎ 0870-524 0241) and others from London's Charing Cross station to Paris' Gare du Nord that take between seven and eight hours and cost £44/59 one way/return. Check out the Hoverspeed Web site at www.hoverspeed.co.uk. It's obviously cheaper than Eurostar but takes a lot longer, and you've got to mess around transferring

by bus between the train station and the ferry terminal on both sides.

Africa & Asia

Morocco and most of Turkey lie outside Europe, but the rail systems of both countries are still covered by Inter-Rail (Zone F and Zone G respectively). The price of a cheap return train ticket from London to Morocco compares favourably with equivalent bus fares.

It *is* possible to get to Western Europe by rail from central and eastern Asia, though count on spending at least eight days doing it. You can choose from four different routes to Moscow: the Trans-Siberian (9297km from Vladivostok), the Trans-Mongolian (7860km from Beijing) and the Trans-Manchurian (9001km from Beijing), which all use the same tracks across Siberia but have different routes east of Lake Baikal; and the Trans-Kazakhstan, which runs between Moscow and Urumqi in north-western China. Prices vary enormously, depending on where you buy the ticket and what is included – advertised 2nd-class fares cost around US$330 from Beijing to Moscow. Web sites worth consulting for trans-Siberian packages include: www.monkeyshrine.com, www.finnsov.fi, www.trans-siberian.co.uk and www.regent-holidays.co.uk.

There are countless travel options between Moscow and the rest of Europe. Most people will opt for the train, usually to/from Berlin, Helsinki, Munich, Budapest or Vienna. The *Trans-Siberian Handbook* (Trailblazer) by Bryn Thomas is a comprehensive guide to the route, as is the *Trans-Siberian Rail Guide* (Compass Star) by Robert Strauss & Tamsin Turnbull. Lonely Planet's *Russia, Ukraine & Belarus* has a separate chapter on trans-Siberian travel.

Overland Trails

In the early 1980s, the overland trail to/from Asia lost much of its popularity as the Islamic regime in Iran made life difficult for most independent travellers, and the war in Afghanistan closed that country off to all but the foolhardy. Now that Iran seems to be rediscovering the merits of tourism, the Asia route has begun to pick up again, though unsettled conditions in Afghanistan, southern Pakistan and north-west India could prevent the trickle of travellers turning into a flood for the time being.

Discounting the complicated Middle East route via Egypt, Jordan, Syria, Turkey and Eastern Europe, going to/from Africa involves a Mediterranean ferry crossing (see the following Sea section). Due to the unrest in Africa, the most feasible overland routes through the continent have all but closed down.

Travelling by private transport beyond Europe requires plenty of paperwork and other preparations. A detailed description is beyond the scope of this book, but the following Getting Around chapter tells you what's required within Europe.

SEA
Channel Ferries
Several different ferry companies compete on all the main Channel ferry routes. The resulting service is comprehensive but very complicated. The same ferry company can have a host of different prices for the same route depending upon the time of day or year, the validity of the ticket, or the length of your vehicle. Vehicle tickets include the driver and often up to five passengers free of charge. It is worth planning (and booking) ahead where possible as there may be special reductions on off-peak crossings and advance purchase tickets. On Channel routes, apart from one-day or short-term excursion returns, there is little price advantage in buying a return ticket as against two singles.

The shortest cross-Channel routes between England and France (Dover to Calais or Folkestone to Boulogne) are also the busiest, though there is now great competition from the Channel Tunnel. P&O Stena handle the short-hop Dover-Calais routes. P&O Ferries and Brittany Ferries also sail direct between England and northern Spain, taking 24 to 35 hours, and between France and Ireland.

Rail-pass holders are entitled to discounts or free travel on some lines, and most ferry companies give discounts to disabled drivers.

Useful Web sites include Brittany Ferries: www.brittany-ferries.com, P&O European Ferries: www.poef.com, and P&O Stena Line: www.posl.com.

Baltic & North Sea Ferries
Central Europe can be reached from the north, west and east by ferry via the North or Baltic seas. There are direct links from Newcastle and Harwich in the UK to Hamburg a couple of times a week, and a slew of other seacraft transport cars and people between Germany and Scandinavia. Regularly scheduled services include a 2½-hour crossing from Kiel to Bagenkop (on the Danish island of Langeland), to Gothenburg in Sweden (14 hours) and all the way to Oslo (19½ hours). There are also ferries to Denmark, Sweden and/or Finland from the eastern German ports of Travemünde and, on Rügen Island, Sassnitz.

Poland also has a ferry service – year-round for the most part – to/from Scandinavia. Routings include Gdynia-Karlskrona and Gdańsk-Oxelösund in Sweden; and Świnoujście to Copenhagen. See Getting There & Away in the Germany and Poland chapters for more details.

Mediterranean Ferries
There are many ferries across the Mediterranean between Africa and Europe. The ferry you take will depend on where you plan to travel in Africa, but options include: Spain-Morocco, Italy-Tunisia and France-Morocco and France-Tunisia. There are also ferries between Greece and Israel via Cyprus. Ferries are often filled to capacity in summer, especially to/from Tunisia, so book well in advance if you're taking a vehicle across. See the relevant country chapters.

Passenger Ships & Freighters
Regular, long-distance passenger ships disappeared with the advent of cheap air travel and were replaced by a small number of luxury cruise ships. Cunard's *Queen Elizabeth 2* sails between New York and Southampton 20 times a year; the trip takes six nights each way and costs around UK£1500 for the return trip, though there are also one-way and 'fly one-way' deals. The bible for passenger ships and sea travel is the *OAG Cruise & Ferry Guide* published by the UK-based Reed Travel Group (☎ 01582-600 111), but it costs UK£50 per issue so you may want to consult it at your library.

A slightly more adventurous alternative is as a paying passenger on a freighter. Freighters are far more numerous than cruise ships and there are many more routes from which to choose. The previously mentioned *OAG Cruise & Ferry Guide* is the most comprehensive source of information, though *Travel by Cargo Ship* (Cadogan) is also a good source. Passenger freighters typically carry six to 12 passengers (more than 12 would require a doctor on board) and, though less luxurious than dedicated cruise ships, give you a real taste of life at sea. Schedules tend to be flexible and costs vary, but seem to hover around US$100 a day; vehicles can often be included for an additional fee.

DEPARTURE TAX

Some countries charge you a fee for the privilege of leaving from their airports. Some also charge port fees when departing by ship. Such fees are *usually* included in the price of your ticket, but it pays to check this when purchasing it. If not, you'll have to have the fee ready when leaving. Details of departure taxes are given at the end of the Getting There & Away sections of individual country chapters.

Getting Around

Travel within most of the EU, whether by air, rail or car, has been made easier following the Schengen Agreement. This abolished border controls between signed-up states. Britain and Ireland are the only EU countries currently outside the agreement.

AIR

Air travel is best viewed as a means to get you to the starting point of your itinerary rather than as your main means of travel, since it lacks the flexibility of ground transport. Using air travel for short hops can be extremely expensive, though for longer trips the air option might be cheaper than going by bus or train.

Since 1997 air travel within the EU has been deregulated. This 'open skies' policy allows greater flexibility in routing, wider competition and lower prices. Air travel is still dominated by the large state-run and private carriers, but these have been joined by several no-frills small airlines which sell budget tickets directly to the customer. They operate routes from the UK to most countries in Europe, though note they sometimes use smaller, less convenient airports.

Refer to the Air Travel Glossary in the previous Getting There & Away chapter for information on types of air tickets. London is a good centre for picking up cheap, restricted-validity tickets through bucket shops. Some airlines, such as the UK-based easyJet (Web site: www.easyJet.com), give discounts for tickets purchased via the Internet; its one-way fares from the UK to Barcelona, Madrid or Nice start at UK£50. Amsterdam and Athens are other good places for bucket-shop tickets in Europe.

So-called open-jaw returns, by which you can travel into one city and exit from another, are worth considering, though they sometimes work out more expensive than simple returns. In the UK, Trailfinders (☎ 020-7937 5400) and STA Travel (☎ 020-7361 6161) can give you tailor-made versions of these tickets. Your chosen cities don't necessarily have to be in the same country. STA sells Young Europe Special (YES) flights, which allow travel around Europe using Lufthansa German Airlines at UK£39, UK£59 or UK£79 per flight (minimum four flights, maximum 10). Britain is the starting point, and the offer is open to students under 31 years of age and anybody under 26.

BUS
International Buses

International bus travel tends to take second place to train travel. The bus has the edge in terms of cost, sometimes quite substantially, but is generally slower and less comfortable.

Eurolines Europe's biggest network of international buses is provided by a group of companies operating under the name Eurolines. Web site: www.eurolines.com.

Eurolines representatives include:

Eurolines UK (☎ 0870-514 3219),
   52 Grosvenor Gardens, London SW1, Britain
Eurolines Nederland (☎ 020-560 87 87),
   Rokin 10, 1012 KR Amsterdam
Eurolines Belgium (☎ 02-203 07 07),
   Coach Station, CCN North Station, Brussels
Eurolines France (☎ 08-36 69 52 52),
   Gare Routière Internationale, 28 Ave du
   Général de Gaulle, 75020 Paris
Deutsche-Touring (☎ 069-790 30),
   Am Römerhof 17, Frankfurt
Eurolines Italy (☎ 055-35 71 10),
   Via Mercadante 2b, 50144 Florence
Eurolines Austria (☎ 01-712 04 53),
   Autobusbahnhof Wien-Mitte, Landstrasser
   Hauptstrasse, 1030 Vienna
Eurolines Czech Republic (☎ 02-2421 3420),
   Opletalova 37, Prague 1
Volánbusz (☎ 1-117 2562),
   Erzsébet tér, V Budapest, Hungary
Eurolines Peninsular (☎ 93-490 4000),
   Estació d'Autobuses de Sants, Calle Viriato,
   Barcelona, Spain

These may also be able to advise you on other bus companies and deals.

Eurolines has nine circular explorer routes, always starting and ending in London (no youth/senior reductions). The popular London-Amsterdam-Brussels-Paris route costs UK£59, as does London-Dublin-Galway-Kilarney-Cork-London. London-Vienna-Budapest-Prague-London is UK£116. Eurolines also offers passes. Compared to rail passes, they're cheaper but not as extensive or as flexible. They cover 48 European cities as far afield as Dublin, Glasgow, Stockholm, Tallinn, Bucharest, Rome and Madrid. The cost is UK£245 for 30 days (UK£195 for youths and senior citizens) or UK£283 for 60 days (UK£227). The passes are cheaper off-season.

On ordinary return trips, youths under 26 and seniors over 60 pay less; eg, a London-Munich return ticket costs UK£91 for adults or UK£85 for youths/seniors. Explorer or return tickets are valid for six months.

Busabout Busabout (☎ 020-7950 1661), 258 Vauxhall Bridge Rd, Victoria, London SW1, England, operates buses that complete set circuits round Europe, stopping at major cities. You get unlimited travel per sector, and can 'hop-on, hop-off' at any scheduled stop, then resume with a later bus. Buses are often oversubscribed, so prebook each sector to avoid being stranded. Departures are every two days from April to October, or May to September for Spain and Portugal. The circuits cover all countries in continental Western Europe, and you can pay to 'add-on' Greece, Scandinavia and/or a London-Paris link. See the Web site: www.busabout.com.

Busabout's Consecutive Pass allows unlimited travel within the given time period. For 15/21 days the cost is UK£155/219 for adults or UK£139/199 for students and those under 26. Passes are also available for one, two or three months, or for the whole season (UK£659 for adults, UK£589 for students/youths). The Flexipass allows you to select travel days within the given time period. Ten or 15 days in two months costs UK£235 or UK£335; 21 days in three months costs UK£445 and 30 days in four months is UK£609. Student/youth prices are about 10% lower than these adult prices.

National Buses

Domestic buses provide a viable alternative to the rail network in most countries. Again, compared to trains they are usually slightly cheaper and somewhat slower. Buses tend to be best for shorter hops such as getting around cities and reaching remote villages. They are often the only option in mountainous regions. Advance reservations are rarely necessary. On many city buses you usually buy your ticket in advance from a kiosk or machine and cancel it on entering.

See the individual country chapters for more details on local buses.

TRAIN

Trains are a popular way of getting around: they are comfortable, frequent, and generally on time. The Channel Tunnel makes it possible to get from Britain to continental Europe using the Eurostar service (see the Getting There & Away chapter). In some countries, such as Italy, Spain and Portugal, fares are subsidised; in others, European rail passes make travel more affordable.

If you plan to travel extensively by train, it might be worth getting hold of the *Thomas Cook European Timetable*, which gives a complete listing of train schedules and indicates where supplements apply or where reservations are necessary. It is updated monthly and is available from Thomas Cook outlets in the UK, or in the USA from Forsyth Travel Library (☎ 800-367 7984). In Australia, contact Mercury Travel Books (☎ 02-9344 8877).

If you are planning to do a lot of train travel in one or a handful of countries it might be worthwhile getting hold of the national timetables published by the state railways. The *European Planning & Rail Guide* is an informative annual magazine. To get a copy, call the toll-free USA number ☎ 877-441 2387, or visit the Web site (www.budgeteuropetravel.com). It's free within the USA; send US$3 if you want it posted anywhere else.

Paris, Milan and Vienna are all important hubs for international rail connections. See the relevant city sections for details and budget-ticket agents. Note that European trains sometimes split en route in order to service two destinations, so even if you know you're on the right train, make sure you're also in the correct carriage.

Express Trains

Fast trains or those that make few stops are identified by the symbols EC (EuroCity) or IC (InterCity). The French TGV, Spanish AVE and German ICE trains are even faster. Supplements can apply on fast trains, and it is a good idea (sometimes obligatory) to make seat reservations at peak times and on certain lines.

Overnight Trains

Overnight trains will usually offer a choice of couchette or sleeper if you don't fancy sleeping in your seat with somebody else's elbow in your ear. Again, reservations are advisable as sleeping options are allocated on a first-come, first-served basis.

Couchette bunks are comfortable enough, if lacking a bit in privacy. There are four per compartment in 1st class or six in 2nd class. A bunk costs a fixed price of around US$28 for most international trains, irrespective of the length of the journey.

Sleepers are the most comfortable option, offering beds for one or two passengers in 1st class, and two or three passengers in 2nd class. Charges vary depending upon the journey, but they are significantly more expensive than couchettes. Most long-distance trains have a dining (buffet) car or an attendant who wheels a snack trolley through carriages. Prices tend to be steep.

Security

Stories sometimes surface about passengers being gassed or drugged and then robbed, though bag-snatching is more of a worry. Sensible security measures include not letting your bags out of your sight (especially at stations), chaining them to the luggage rack, and locking compartment doors overnight. For more information see Safety & Security in the Facts for First-time Visitors chapter.

Rail Passes

European rail passes are only worth buying if you plan to do a reasonable amount of inter-country travelling within a short space of time. If you decide to purchase a rail pass, shop around for the best price, as they can vary between different outlets. Once purchased, take care of your pass, as it cannot be replaced or refunded if lost or stolen.

Note that supplements (eg for some express and overnights trains) and seat reservation fees (mandatory on some trains, merely a good idea on others) are not covered by rail passes – always ask. European passes get reductions on Eurostar through the Channel Tunnel and on certain ferries.

Pass holders must always carry their passport for identification purposes.

Eurail These passes can only be bought by residents of non-European countries, and are supposed to be purchased before arriving in Europe. However, Eurail passes *can* be purchased within Europe, so long as your passport proves you've been there for less than six months, but the outlets where you can do this are limited, and the passes will be more expensive than getting them outside Europe. If you've lived in Europe for more than six months, you are eligible for an Inter-Rail pass, which is a better buy.

Eurail passes are valid for unlimited travel on national railways and some private lines in Austria, Belgium, Denmark, Finland, France (including Monaco), Germany, Greece, Hungary, Ireland, Italy, Luxembourg, the Netherlands, Norway, Portugal, Spain, Sweden and Switzerland (including Liechtenstein). The UK is not covered.

Eurail is also valid on some ferries between Italy and Greece and between Sweden and Finland. Reductions are given on some other ferry routes and on river/lake steamer services in various countries.

Eurail passes offer reasonable value to people aged under 26. A Youthpass gives unlimited 2nd-class travel within a choice of five validity periods: 15/21 days (US$388/499) or one/two/three months (US$623/882/1089). The Youth Flexipass, also for 2nd class, is valid for freely chosen days within a two-month period: 10 days for US$458 or 15 days for US$599. Overnight journeys commencing after 7 pm count as the following day's travel. The traveller must fill out in ink the relevant box in the calendar before starting a day's travel.

For those aged over 26, the equivalent passes provide 1st-class travel. The standard Eurail pass costs US$554/718 for 15/21 days or US$890/1260/1558 for one/two/three months. The Flexipass costs US$654/862 for 10/15 days within two months. Two people travelling together can get a 'saver' version of either pass, saving about 15%. Eurail passes for children are also available.

Europass Also for non-Europeans, the Europass gives unlimited travel on freely chosen days within a two-month period. Youth (aged under 26) and adult (solo, or two sharing) versions are available, and purchasing requirements and sales outlets are as for Eurail passes. They are cheaper than Eurail passes as they cover only France, Germany,

Italy, Spain and Switzerland. The youth/adult price is US$296/348 for a minimum five travel days, or US$620/728 for a maximum 15 days. 'Associate countries' can be added on to the basic pass. The charge to add any one/two countries is US$52/86 for youths or US$60/100 for adults. These associate countries are Austria (including Hungary), Belgium (including Luxembourg and the Netherlands), Greece (including ferries from Italy) and Portugal.

Other Passes Other Eurail passes include the Benelux Tour Rail Pass (for travel in Belgium, the Netherlands and Luxembourg), which costs US$258/173 adult/youth and is valid for 2nd-class travel over any five days in a one-month period.

There are similar deals with the Balkan Rail Pass (Bulgaria, Greece, Macedonia, Turkey and Yugoslavia), Iberic Pass (Spain and Portugal), European East Pass (Austria, Czech Republic, Hungary, Poland and Slovakia) and the ScanRail Pass (Denmark, Finland, Norway and Sweden).

Inter-Rail Inter-Rail passes are available to European residents of at least six months standing (passport identification is required). Terms and conditions vary slightly from country to country, but in the country of origin there is a discount of around 50% on normal fares.

The Inter-Rail pass is split into zones. Zone A is Ireland (and Britain if purchased in continental Europe); B is Sweden, Norway and Finland; C is Denmark, Germany, Switzerland and Austria; D is the Czech Republic, Slovakia, Poland, Hungary and Croatia; E is France, Belgium, the Netherlands and Luxembourg; F is Spain, Portugal and Morocco; G is Italy, Greece, Turkey, Slovenia and Italy-Greece ferries; and H is Bulgaria, Romania, Yugoslavia and Macedonia.

The normal Inter-Rail pass is for people under 26, though travellers over 26 can get the Inter-Rail 26+ version. The price for any one zone is UK£129 (UK£179 for 26+) for 22 days. Multizone passes are valid for one month: two zones cost UK£169 (UK£235), three zones UK£195 (UK£269) and the all-zone global pass is UK£219 (UK£309).

Euro Domino There is a Euro Domino pass for each of the countries covered in the Inter-Rail pass, and they're worth considering if you're homing in on a particular region. Adults (travelling 1st or 2nd class) and youths under 26 can opt for three to eight days valid travel within one month. Examples of adult/youth prices for eight days in 2nd class are UK£108/48 for Greece and UK£196/£122 for Spain.

National Rail Passes

If you intend to travel extensively within one country, check which national rail passes are available; these can sometimes save you a lot of money. Details can be found in the Getting Around sections in the individual country chapters. You need to plan ahead if you intend to take this option, as some passes can only be purchased prior to arrival in the country concerned.

Cheap Tickets

European rail passes are only worth buying if you plan to do a reasonable amount of inter-country travelling within a short space of time. Some people tend to overdo it and spend every night they can on the train, ending up too tired to enjoy sightseeing the next day.

When weighing up options, consider the cost of other cheap ticket deals, including advance purchase reductions, one-off promotions or special circular-route tickets. Normal international tickets are valid for two months, and you can make as many stops as you like en route; make your intentions known when purchasing, and inform the train conductor how far you're going before they punch your ticket.

Travellers aged under 26 can pick up BIJ (Billet International de Jeunesse) tickets which can cut fares by up to about 30%. The BIJ Paris to Madrid return for UK£142 saves UK£36 on the normal fare, though on some other routes the reduction may be much less. Various agents issue BIJ tickets in Europe, eg Voyages Wasteels (☎ 01-43 43 46 10), 2 Rue Michel Chasles, Paris. There are over 60 branches of Wasteels across France, visit its Web site at www.voyages-wasteels.fr. Rail Europe (☎ 0990-848 848), 179 Piccadilly, London, sells BIJ tickets, Eurail and Inter-Rail passes. Web site: www.raileurope.co.uk.

For a small fee, European residents aged 60 and over can get a Rail Plus (formerly

Rail Europe Senior) card as an add-on to their national rail senior pass. It entitles the holder to reduced European fares. The percentage saving varies according to the route – it's usually similar to the BIJ reduction.

TAXI

Taxis in Europe are metered and rates are usually high. There might also be supplements (depending on the country) for things like luggage, the time of day, the location from where you were picked up, and extra passengers. Good bus, rail and underground/subway railway networks make the use of taxis all but unnecessary, but if you need one in a hurry they can usually be found idling near train stations or outside big hotels. Lower fares make taxis more viable in some countries, such as Spain, Greece, Portugal and Turkey.

CAR & MOTORCYCLE

Travelling with your own vehicle is the best way to get to remote places and it gives you the most flexibility. Unfortunately, the independence you enjoy does tend to isolate you from the local people. Also, cars are usually inconvenient in city centres, where it is generally worth ditching your vehicle and relying on public transport. Various car-carrying trains can help you avoid long, tiring drives. Le Shuttle through the Channel Tunnel transports cars: see the Getting There & Away chapter.

Paperwork & Preparations

Proof of ownership of a private vehicle should always be carried (Vehicle Registration Document for British-registered cars) when touring Europe. An EU driving licence is acceptable for driving throughout Europe, as are North American and Australian ones (however, old-style green UK licences are no good for Spain or Italy and should be backed up by a German translation in Austria). Even so, it is a good idea (and in some countries necessary) to obtain an International Driving Permit (IDP) from your motoring organisation (see Other Useful Documents in the Facts for the Visitor chapter). An IDP is recommended for Turkey even if you have a European licence.

Third-party motor insurance is a minimum requirement in Europe. Most UK motor insurance policies will automatically provide this for EU countries and some others. Get your insurer to issue a Green Card (which may cost extra), an internationally recognised proof of insurance, and check that it lists all the countries you intend to visit. You'll need this in the event of an accident outside the country where the vehicle is insured. Also ask your insurer for a European Accident Statement form, which can simplify things if worse comes to worst. Never sign statements you can't read or understand – insist on a translation and sign that only if it's acceptable.

If you want to insure a vehicle you've just purchased (see the following Purchase section) and have a good insurance record, you might be eligible for considerable discounts if you can show a letter to this effect from your insurance company back home.

Taking out a European motoring assistance policy – such as the AA Five Star Service or the Royal Automobile Club (RAC) Eurocover Motoring Assistance – is a good investment. Expect to pay about UK£54 for 14 days cover with a small discount for association members. With the Five Star Service you can request a bail bond for Spain, which is less necessary nowadays than in the past, but could be worth having. Non-Europeans might find it cheaper to arrange international coverage with their national motoring organisation before leaving home. Ask your motoring organisation for details about free services offered by affiliated organisations around Europe.

Every vehicle travelling across an international border should display a sticker showing its country of registration (see the International Country Abbreviations appendix). A warning triangle, to be used in the event of breakdown, is compulsory almost everywhere. Recommended accessories are a first-aid kit (compulsory in Austria, Slovenia, Croatia, Yugoslavia and Greece), a spare bulb kit (compulsory in Spain), and a fire extinguisher (compulsory in Greece and Turkey). In the UK, contact the RAC (☎ 0800-550055) or the AA (☎ 0990-500600) for more information.

Road Rules

With the exception of Britain and Ireland, driving is on the right. Vehicles brought over from either of these countries should have their headlights adjusted to avoid blinding oncoming traffic at night (a simple solution on older headlight lenses is to cover up a triangular section of the lens with tape). Priority is usually given to traffic approaching from the right in countries that drive on the right-hand side.

The RAC publishes an annual *European Motoring Guide* (UK£4.99), which gives the visiting motorist an excellent summary of regulations in each country, including parking rules. Motoring organisations in other countries have similar publications.

Take care with speed limits, as they vary from country to country. You may be surprised at the apparent disregard for traffic regulations in some places (particularly in Italy and Greece), but as a visitor it is always best to be on the cautious side. Many driving infringements are subject to an on-the-spot fine in all countries except Britain and Ireland. Always ask for a receipt. European drink-driving laws are particularly strict. The blood-alcohol concentration (BAC) limit when driving is between 0.05% and 0.08%, but in certain areas – Gibraltar and some Eastern European countries – it can be 0%.

Roads

Conditions and types of roads vary across Europe, but it is possible to make some generalisations. The fastest routes are four or six-lane dual carriageways/highways (ie two or three lanes either side) – called *autoroutes*, *autostrade* etc. These tend to skirt cities and plough through the countryside in straight lines, often avoiding the most scenic bits. Some of these roads incur tolls, which are often quite hefty (eg in Italy, France and Spain), but there will always be an alternative route you can take. Motorways and other primary routes are generally in good condition.

Road surfaces on minor routes are not so reliable in some countries (eg Romania, Ireland, Morocco and Greece) although normally they will be more than adequate. These roads are narrower and progress is generally much slower. To compensate, you can expect much better scenery and plenty of interesting villages along the way.

Rental

The big international rental firms will give you reliable service and a good standard of vehicle. Usually you will have the option of returning the car to a different outlet at the end of the rental period. Prebook for the lowest rates – if you walk into an office and ask for a car on the spot, you will pay over the odds, even allowing for special weekend deals. Fly-drive combinations and other programs are worth looking into. You should be able to make advance reservations online. Check the Web sites:

Hertz	www.hertz.com
Avis	www.avis.com
Budget	budget.com
Europcar	www.europcar.com

Brokers can cut hire costs. Holiday Autos (UK ☎ 0990-300400) has low rates and offices or representatives in over 20 countries. Its Web site is at www.holidayautos.com. In the USA call Kemwel Holiday Autos (☎ 800-576 1590). In the UK, a competitor with even lower prices is Autos Abroad (☎ 020-7287 6000). Check out its Web site at www.autosabroad.co.uk.

If you want to rent a car and haven't prebooked, look for national or local firms, which can often undercut the big companies by up to 40%. Nevertheless, you need to be wary of dodgy deals where they take your money and point you towards some clapped-out wreck, or where the rental agreement is bad news if you have an accident or the car is stolen – a cause for concern if you can't even read what you sign.

No matter where you rent, make sure you understand what is included in the price (unlimited or paid kilometres, tax, injury insurance, collision damage waiver etc) and what your liabilities are. We recommend taking the collision damage waiver, though you can probably skip the injury insurance if you and your passengers have decent travel insurance. Ask in advance if you can drive a rented car across borders from a country where hire prices are low to another where they're high.

The minimum rental age is usually 21 or even 23, and you'll probably need a credit card. Note that prices at airport rental offices are usually higher than at branches in the city centre.

Motorcycle and moped rental is common in some countries, such as Italy, Spain, Greece and the south of France. Sadly, it's also common to see inexperienced riders leap on rented bikes and very quickly fall off them again, leaving a layer or two of skin on the road in the process.

Purchase

The purchase of vehicles in some European countries is illegal for non-nationals or non-EU residents. Britain is probably the best place to buy: second-hand prices are good and, whether buying privately or from a dealer, the absence of language difficulties will help you establish exactly what you are getting and what guarantees you can expect if you break down. See the Britain Getting Around section for information on purchase paperwork and European insurance.

Bear in mind that you will be getting a car with the steering wheel on the right in Britain. If you want left-hand drive and can afford to buy new, prices are usually reasonable in Greece, France, Germany, Belgium, Luxembourg the Netherlands. Paperwork can be tricky wherever you buy, and many countries have compulsory roadworthiness checks on older vehicles.

Leasing

Leasing a vehicle has none of the hassles of purchasing and can work out considerably cheaper than hiring over longer periods. The Renault Eurodrive scheme provides new cars for non-EU residents for a period of between 17 and 170 days. Under this arrangement, a Renault Clio 1.2 for 30 days, for example, would cost 4710FF (if picked up/dropped off in France), including insurance and roadside assistance. Other companies with comparable leasing programs include Peugeot and Citroen. Check out the options before leaving home. In the US, Kemwel Holiday Autos (see under Rental earlier) arranges European leasing deals.

Camper Van

One popular way to tour Europe is for a group of three or four people to band together to buy or rent a camper van. London is the usual embarkation point. Look at the advertisements in London's free *TNT* magazine if you wish to form or join a group. *TNT* is also a good source for purchasing a van, as is the *Loot* newspaper and the Van Market in Market Rd, London N7 (near the Caledonian Rd tube station), where private vendors congregate on a daily basis. Some second-hand dealers offer a 'buy-back' scheme for when you return from the Continent, but we've received warnings that some dealers don't fully honour their refund commitments. Anyway, buying and re-selling privately should be more advantageous if you have the time. A reader recommended Down Under Insurance (☎ 020-7402 9211) for European cover. Check out the Web site at www.downunderinsurance.co.uk.

Camper vans usually feature a fixed high-top or elevating roof and two to five bunk beds. Apart from the essential camping gas cooker, professional conversions may include a sink, fridge and built-in cupboards. You will need to spend at least UK£2000 (US$3200) for something reliable enough to get you around Europe for any length of time. Getting a mechanical check (from UK£30) is a good idea before you buy. Once on the road you should be able to keep budgets lower than backpackers using trains, but don't forget to set some money aside for emergency repairs.

The main advantage of going by camper van is flexibility: with transport, eating and sleeping requirements all taken care of in one unit, you are tied to nobody's timetable but your own. It's also easier to set up at night than if you rely on a car and tent.

A disadvantage of camper vans is that you are in a confined space for much of the time. Four adults in a small van can soon get on each other's nerves, particularly if the group has been formed at short notice. You might also become too self-contained, and miss out on experiences in the world outside your van.

Other negatives are that vans are not very manoeuvrable around town, and you'll often have to leave your gear unattended inside (many people bolt extra locks onto the van). They're also expensive to buy in spring and hard to sell in autumn.

Motorcycle Touring

Europe is made for motorcycle touring, with good-quality winding roads, stunning scenery, and an active motorcycling scene. Just make sure your wet-weather gear is up to scratch.

From Britain to Bulgaria, the wearing of crash helmets for rider and passenger is compulsory everywhere in Europe. Austria,

Belgium, France, Germany, Luxembourg, Portugal and Spain also require that motorcyclists use headlights during the day; in other countries it is recommended.

On ferries, motorcyclists rarely have to book ahead as they can generally be squeezed in. Take note of the local custom about parking motorcycles on pavements (sidewalks). Though this is illegal in some countries, the police usually turn a blind eye so long as the vehicle doesn't obstruct pedestrians. Don't try this in Britain, however.

Fuel

Fuel prices can vary enormously from country to country (though it's always more expensive than in North America or Australia). Refuelling in Luxembourg or Andorra will save about 30% compared to prices in neighbouring countries. The Netherlands, France and Italy have Europe's most expensive petrol; Gibraltar and Andorra are by far the cheapest in Western Europe. Greece, Spain and Switzerland are also reasonably cheap. Motoring organisations such as the RAC can supply more details.

Unleaded petrol is widely available throughout Europe (though not always in Romania, Albania, Slovakia and Yugoslavia) and is usually slightly cheaper than super (premium grade, the only 'leaded' choice in some countries). Diesel is usually significantly cheaper, though the difference is only marginal in Britain, Ireland and Switzerland.

BICYCLE

A tour of Europe by bike may seem a daunting prospect, but one organisation that can help in the UK is the Cyclists' Touring Club (CTC; ☎ 01483-417 217, ✉ cycling@ctc.org.uk), Cotterell House, 69 Meadrow, Godalming, Surrey GU7 3HS. It can supply information to members on cycling conditions in Europe as well as detailed routes, itineraries and maps. Membership includes specialised insurance and costs UK£25 per annum, or UK£12.50 for people aged under 27 or over 65. Web site: www.ctc.org.uk.

A primary consideration on a cycling tour is to travel light, but you should take a few tools and spare parts, including a puncture repair kit and an extra inner tube. Panniers are essential to balance your possessions on either side of the bike frame.

A bike helmet is also a very good idea. Take a good lock and always use it when you leave your bike unattended.

Michelin maps indicate scenic routes, which can help you construct good cycling itineraries. Seasoned cyclists can average 80km a day, but there's no point in overdoing it. The slower you travel, the more local people you are likely to meet. If you get tired of pedalling or simply want to skip a boring transport section, you can put your feet up on the train. On slower trains, bikes can usually be transported as luggage, subject to a small supplementary fee. Fast trains can rarely accommodate bikes: they might need to be sent as registered luggage and may end up on a different train from the one you take. This is often the case in France and Spain. Eurostar (the train service through the Channel Tunnel) charges UK£20 to send a bike as registered luggage on its routes. You can also transport your bicycle with you on Eurotunnel through the Channel Tunnel. With a bit of tinkering and dismantling (eg removing wheels), you might be able to get your bike into a bag or sack and take it on a train as hand luggage.

The European Bike Express is a coach service where cyclists can travel with their bicycles. It runs in the summer from northeast England to France, Italy and Spain, with pick-up/drop-off points en route. The maximum return fare is UK£169 (£10 off for CTC members); phone ☎ 01642-251 440 in the UK for details or visit the Web site at www.bike-express.co.uk.

Rental

It is easy to hire bikes throughout most of Europe on an hourly, half-day, daily or weekly basis. Many train stations have bike-rental counters. See the country chapters for more details. It is sometimes possible to return the bike at a different outlet so you don't have to retrace your route.

Purchase

There are plenty of places to buy in Europe (shops sell new and second-hand bicycles or you can check local papers for private vendors) but you'll need a specialist bicycle shop for a bike capable of withstanding a European tour. CTC can provide a leaflet on purchasing. Cycling is very popular in the Netherlands and Germany, and they are good places to pick up a well-equipped touring bicycle. European prices are quite high (certainly higher than in North America), but non-Europeans should be able to claim back VAT on the purchase.

Bringing Your Own

For major cycling tours, it's best to have a bike you're familiar with, so consider bringing your own rather than buying on arrival. You should be able to take it along with you on the plane relatively easily. You can either take it apart and pack everything in a bike bag or box, or simply wheel it to the check-in desk, where it should be treated as a piece of luggage. You may have to remove the pedals and turn the handlebars sideways so that it takes up less space in the aircraft's hold; check all this with the airline well in advance, preferably before you pay for your ticket. If your bicycle and other luggage exceed your weight allowance, ask about alternatives or you may suddenly find yourself being charged a fortune for excess baggage.

HITCHING

Hitching is never entirely safe in any country in the world, and we don't recommend it. Travellers who decide to hitch should understand that they are taking a small but potentially serious risk. People who do choose to hitch will be safer if they travel in pairs and let someone know where they plan to go.

Hitching can be the most rewarding and frustrating way of getting around. Rewarding, because you get to meet and interact with local people and are forced into unplanned detours that may yield unexpected highlights off the beaten track. Frustrating, because you may get stuck on the side of the road to nowhere with nowhere (or nowhere cheap) to stay. Then it begins to rain.

That said, hitchers can end up making good time, but obviously your plans need to be flexible in case a trick of the light makes you appear invisible to passing motorists. A man and woman travelling together is probably the best combination. Two or more men must expect some delays; two women together will make good time and should be relatively safe. A woman hitching on her own is taking a big risk, particularly in parts of southern Europe.

Don't try to hitch from city centres: take public transport to suburban exit routes. Hitching is usually illegal on motorways (freeways) – stand on the slip roads, or approach drivers at petrol stations and truck stops. Look presentable and cheerful and make a cardboard sign indicating your intended destination in the local language. Never hitch where drivers can't stop in good time or without causing an obstruction. At dusk, give up and think about finding somewhere to stay. If your itinerary includes a ferry crossing (for instance, across the Channel), it might be worth trying to score a ride before the ferry rather than after, since vehicle tickets sometimes include a number of passengers free of charge. This also applies to Le Shuttle via the Channel Tunnel.

It is sometimes possible to arrange a lift in advance: scan student notice boards in colleges, or contact car-sharing agencies. Such agencies are particularly popular in France (Allostop Provoya, Auto-Partage) and Germany (Mitfahrzentralen). See the relevant country chapters.

BOAT

Several different ferry companies compete on all the main ferry routes. The resulting service is comprehensive but complicated. The same ferry company can have a host of different prices for the same route, depending on the time of day or year, the validity of the ticket, or the length of your vehicle. Vehicle tickets include the driver and often up to five passengers free of charge. It is worth planning (and booking) ahead where possible as there may be special reductions on off-peak crossings and advance purchase tickets. On English Channel routes, apart from one-day or short-term excursion returns, there is little price advantage in buying a return ticket as against two singles.

Stena Line is one of the largest ferry companies in the world. It serves British, Irish and Scandinavian routes (but from England to/from Norway, contact Color Line). P&O and Brittany Ferries sail direct between England and northern Spain, taking 24 to 35 hours. The shortest cross-Channel routes (Dover to Calais, or Folkestone to Boulogne) are also the busiest, though there is now great competition from the Channel Tunnel. Stena and P&O recently combined forces on the

Newhaven-Dieppe and Dover-Calais routes. Italy (Brindisi or Bari) to Greece (Corfu, Igoumenitsa and Patras) is also a popular route. The Greek islands are connected to the mainland and each other by a spider's web of routings; Lonely Planet's *Greek Islands* gives details.

Rail-pass holders are entitled to discounts or free travel on some lines (see the earlier Rail Passes & Cheap Train Tickets section), and most ferry companies give discounts to disabled drivers. Food on ferries is often expensive (and lousy), so it is worth bringing your own when possible. It is also worth knowing that if you take your vehicle on board, you are usually denied access to it during the voyage.

ORGANISED TOURS

Tailor-made tours abound; see your travel agent or look in the small ads in newspaper travel pages. Specialists include Ramblers Holidays (☎ 01707-331 133) in Britain and CBT Tours (☎ 800-736 2453) in the USA for bicycle trips.

Young revellers can party on Europewide bus tours. Contiki and Top Deck offer camping or hotel-based bus tours for the 18 to 35 age group. The duration of Contiki's tours are from 10 to 46 days, and prices start at around UK£25 per day including 'food fund'. Contiki (☎ 020-7290 6422) and Top Deck (☎ 020-7370 4555) have London offices, as well as offices or company representatives in Europe, North America, Australasia and South Africa. Check the Web sites at www.contiki.com and www.topdecktravel.co.uk.

New Millennium Holidays (☎ 01564-770 750), 1665 High St, Knowle, Solihull, West Midlands B93 OLL, England, runs inexpensive bus or air tours year-round from the UK to Central and Eastern Europe, including Russia. Packages vary from 10 to 17 days, some combining two or three countries, with half-board or B&B accommodation. Another British company highly experienced in booking travel to Eastern Europe is Regent Holidays (☎ 0117-921 1711, fax 925 4866), 15 John St, Bristol BS1 2HR. Check the Web site: www.regent-holidays.co.uk.

In Australia you can obtain a detailed brochure outlining dozens of upmarket tours (including to Russia) from the Eastern Europe Travel Bureau (☎ 02-9262 1144), Level 5, 75 King St, Sydney, NSW 2000. The office in Victoria (☎ 03-9600 0299) is at Suite 313, Level 3, 343 Little Collins St, Melbourne, Vic 3000.

For people aged over 50, Saga Holidays (☎ 0800-300 500), Saga Building, Middelburg Square, Folkestone, Kent CT20 1AZ, England, offers holidays ranging from cheap coach tours to luxury cruises (and has cheap travel insurance). In the USA, Saga Holidays (☎ 800-343 0273) is at 222 Berkeley St, Boston, MA 02116.

National tourist offices in most countries offer organised trips to points of interest. These may range from one-hour city tours to several-day circular excursions. They often work out more expensive than going it alone, but are sometimes worth it if you are pressed for time. A short city tour will give you a quick overview of the place and can be a good way to begin your visit.

Albania

Albania, the 'Land of the Eagle', is Europe's last unknown, a mix of enchanting classical ruins and majestic mountain landscapes. Politically, however, the country has ridden waves of chaos since Communism's demise in 1992. The situation came to a head in 1996, when so-called pyramid investment schemes – widely thought to have been supported by the government – collapsed spectacularly, sparking nationwide violence. However, while dangers of banditry and violence remain, the situation is slowly improving: Albania weathered the influx of 450,000 ethnic-Albanian refugees from Kosovo in spring 1999, and the country now boasts an 8% economic growth rate, among the highest in Europe.

Facts about Albania

GEOGRAPHY
Albania is strategically positioned between Greece, Macedonia, Yugoslavia and Italy. Over three-quarters of Albania (28,748 sq km) consists of mountains and hills, the highest being Mt Korab (2751m), on the border with Macedonia. Forests cover 40% of the land, and the many olive trees, citrus plantations and vineyards give Albania a true Mediterranean air.

CLIMATE
Albania has a warm Mediterranean climate. The summers are hot, clear and dry, and the winters, when 40% of the rain falls, are cool, cloudy and moist. In winter the high interior plateau can be very cold.

POPULATION & PEOPLE
Approximately 3.3 million Albanians live in Albania. Traditionally, Albania has been 70% Sunni Muslim, 20% Albanian Orthodox (mostly in the south) and 10% Roman Catholic (mostly in the north).

AT A GLANCE

Capital:	Tirana
Population:	3.3 million
Official Language:	Albanian (Tosk)
Currency:	1 lekë (L) = 100 qintars

SOCIETY & CONDUCT
The *Kanun* is an ancient social law outlining most aspects of social behaviour, including the treatment of guests. This has meant that Albanians can be hospitable in the extreme. Travellers must be wary of exploiting this tradition – offering a small gift such as a book or memento from home is a good return.

Observe respect when visiting mosques – remove your shoes and avoid visits during prayer times.

Albanians, like Bulgarians, shake their heads to say 'yes' and will generally nod to say 'no'.

LANGUAGE
Albanian (Shqip) is an Indo-European dialect with many Latin, Slavonic and (modern) Greek words. In 1909 a standardised form of the Gheg dialect of Elbasan was adopted as the official language, but since WWII a modified version of the Tosk dialect of southern Albania has been used. See the Language Guide at the back of this book for pronunciation guidelines and useful words and phrases.

Italian is the most useful foreign language to know in Albania, with English a strong second.

Facts for the Visitor

PLANNING
Maps
A topographical/road map of Albania is produced by Cartographia in Budapest and sold for 800 lekë in bookshops in Tirana.

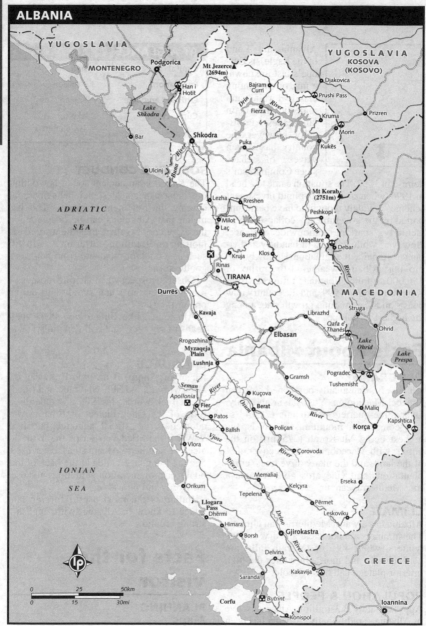

Warning

! For this edition of *Europe on a shoe-string*, the Lonely Planet author decided, for security reasons, to visit only Tirana and Durrës. Any traveller wanting more travel information should make inquiries around Tirana.

It is essential that travellers check the current situation in Albania before they make their decision to go, as criminal activity remains prevalent throughout the country, and travel outside the major cities was not recommended at the time of writing. Travellers should check with their foreign office or their embassy in Tirana to monitor the current situation, as the political climate in Albania can change at flash-flood speed. In mid-2000, the US Department of State still warned against all travel to Albania, considering the overall security situation unstable.

Once in Albania, general caution can be observed by never travelling at night and avoiding the northern part of the country, where banditry is particularly widespread. It is also wise to have someone, preferably Albanian, to accompany you – or, at least, to meet you at your first port of entry.

TOURIST OFFICES

There are no tourist information offices in Albania, but hotel receptionists will sometimes give you directions.

VISAS & DOCUMENTS

No visa is required from citizens of EU countries or of Australia, New Zealand, the United States, or Great Britain. However, you must pay an 'entry tax' at the border. For US/UK/Australian citizens it's US$45/57/40.

Keep the departure card you fill in upon arrival with your passport and present it when you leave.

EMBASSIES & CONSULATES
Albanian Embassies Abroad
UK (☎ 0207-730 5709, fax 730 5747) 38 Grosvenor Gardens, London SW1 0EB
USA (☎ 202-223 4942, fax 628 7342) 1511 K Street NW, Washington, DC 20005

Foreign Embassies in Albania
UK (☎/fax 349 73) Rruga Skënderbeg 12, Tirana
USA (☎ 278 52 or 335 20, fax 322 22) Rruga Elbasanit 103, Tirana

MONEY

Albanian banknotes come in denominations of 100 lekë, 200 lekë, 500 lekë and 1000 lekë. There are five lekë, 10 lekë, 20 lekë and 50 lekë coins.

In 1964 the currency was revalued 10 times and prices are sometimes still quoted at the old rate. Though prices in this chapter are usually quoted in US dollars (US$), you can always pay in lekë. Banks and large hotels will change travellers cheques and may do credit card cash advances. Otherwise credit cards are only accepted in larger hotels and travel agencies. There are no ATMs in Albania.

Every town has a currency market, which usually operates in front of the main post office or state bank – look for the men holding calculators or wads of money. Such transactions are not dangerous, but count their money twice before tendering yours. The advantage is you'll avoid commission and get a good rate.

Exchange Rates

country	unit		lekë
Australia	A$1	=	83.5 lekë
Canada	C$1	=	95.2 lekë
euro	€1	=	127.5 lekë
France	10FF	=	194.4 lekë
Germany	DM1	=	65.2 lekë
Japan	¥100	=	129.6 lekë
New Zealand	NZ$1	=	63.7 lekë
UK	UK£1	=	210.6 lekë
US	US$1	=	140.5 lekë

Tipping
Albania is a tip-conscious society. Round up the bill in restaurants and for taxi rides.

POST & COMMUNICATIONS
Post
Postage is inexpensive and the service surprisingly reliable. There are no public mailboxes in Albania; you must hand in your letters at a post office. Letters to the USA, Australia and Canada cost 90 lekë and within Europe 50 lekë.

Telephone, Fax & Email
Albania's country code is ☎ 355, though a few towns still lack direct-dial access from abroad.

In Albania, long-distance calls made from main post offices are cheap, costing

ALBANIA

about 90 lekë a minute to Italy and 230 lekë per minute to the USA. The international access code is ☎ 00. Phone cards are available from the post office and street kiosks in versions of 50 units (560 lekë), 100 units (980 lekë) and 200 units (1800 lekë).

Send faxes from the main post office in Tirana or from major hotels at slightly higher prices.

Tirana bursts with inexpensive Internet cafes, and Durrës may soon follow.

INTERNET RESOURCES

The Albanian Home Page (www.albanian .com) has country news and links, as does the United Nations Development Project (www.tirana.al).

BOOKS

The Accursed Mountains: Journeys in Albania by Robert Carver is a lively, colourful narrative of one journalist's 1996 journey through Albania, while *Albania: From Anarchy to Balkan Identity* (1997), by Miranda Vickers and James Pettifer, provides useful historical background.

An excellent source of rare books on Albania is Eastern Books (☎/fax 0208-871 0880, ☺ info@easternbooks.com), 81 Replingham Rd, Southfields, London SW18 5LU, England, UK. Check its Web page at www.easternbooks.com.

WOMEN TRAVELLERS

While women are not likely to encounter any particular problems, it is recommended that you travel in pairs or with male companions, in order to avoid unwanted attention – particularly outside of Tirana. Bear in mind that Albania is a predominantly Muslim country. Dress should be conservative.

GAY & LESBIAN TRAVELLERS

Homosexuality was legalised in 1995, but attitudes are still highly conservative.

DANGERS & ANNOYANCES

Beware of pickpockets on crowded city buses and don't flash money around! Walking around the towns is safe during the day, but at night you must beware of falling into deep potholes in the unlit streets, and occasional gangs of youths.

If you are accosted by Roma women and children begging, do not respond and avoid eye contact. Just keep walking or head to the nearest hotel and they will soon give up.

Resist paying money to the police without an official receipt. Always keep at least a copy of your passport on you.

Before you travel, do some research into the current political situation, as hotspots in Albania can appear at flash-flood pace. At the time of writing, the north was particularly unsafe for travel because of banditry and violence.

Albania's tap water is not drinkable, but bottled water is available and cheap.

BUSINESS HOURS

Most shops open Monday to Saturday at 8 am and may close for a siesta from noon to 4 pm, opening again until 7 pm. Banks tend to close early in the afternoon (around 2 pm).

PUBLIC HOLIDAYS & SPECIAL EVENTS

Public holidays in Albania include New Year's Day, Easter Monday, 1 May (Labour Day), 28 November (Independence & Liberation Day) and Christmas Day.

Ramadan and Bajram, variable Muslim holidays, are also celebrated.

ACCOMMODATION

Accommodation is undergoing a rapid transformation in Albania with the opening of new, custom-built, private hotels (US$40 to US$50 per person, per night), and the conversion of homes or villas into so-called private hotels. For budget travellers, these are without doubt the best way to go. State-owned hotels by contrast are in poor shape and you may not feel as safe there.

For security reasons it's not a good idea to camp.

FOOD & DRINKS

Albanian cuisine, like that of Serbia, has been strongly influenced by Turkey. Look for grilled meats such as *shishqebap* (shish kebab), *romstek* (minced meat patties) and *qofte* (meat balls). Some local dishes include *çomlek* (meat and onion stew), *fërges* (a rich beef stew), and *rosto me salcë kosi* (roast beef with sour cream).

Albanians take their coffee both as *kafe turke* (Turkish coffee) and *kafe ekspres* (espresso). If you ask for *kafe surogato* you will get something close to filter coffee.

Raki (a clear brandy distilled from grapes; ask your host for the home-made variety) is taken as an aperitif. There's also *konjak* (cognac), *uzo* (a colourless aniseed-flavoured liqueur like Greek ouzo) and various fruit liqueurs.

Getting There & Away

Airport departure tax is US$10. Departure tax from Albanian ports is US$4.

AIR

Rinas airport, 26km north-west of Tirana, is served by Ada Air (Athens, Bari, Prishtina, Skopje, and Ioannina); Adria Airways (Ljubljana); Albanian Airlines (Bologna, Frankfurt, Istanbul, Prishtina, Rome and Zürich); Austrian Airlines (Vienna); Hemus Air (Sofia); Lufthansa (Frankfurt and Munich); Malév Hungarian Airlines (Budapest); Olympic Airlines (Athens via Ioannina or Thessaloniki); Swissair (Zürich); and Turkish Airlines (Istanbul).

LAND

Buses to Thessaloniki (US$20, 10 hours) and Athens (US$35, 24 hours) leave at 5.30 each morning from in front of Skënderbeg Travel (☎ 321 71), Rruga Durrësit 5/11, in Tirana. They stop in El Basan and Korça.

Buses to Prishtina, the capital of Kosovo, leave every day from beside the Tirana International Hotel at 6 pm. The 12-hour ride costs DM50.

If you're Macedonia-bound, take the daily bus to Tetovo (five to six hours, two per day) from the Axhensi bus office. From Tetovo you can take a frequent local bus to Skopje.

Buses for İstanbul and Sofia leave from Albtransport (☎ 230 26) on Rruga Mine Peza in Tirana. The Sofia bus (US$26 one-way, return US$47, 15 hours) departs every Wednesday at 10 am. Two buses for İstanbul (US$40 one-way, US$70 return, 24 hours) depart on Monday, at 10 am and 1 pm. These go through Sofia.

There are no international trains.

SEA

The Italian company Adriatica di Navigazione offers ferry services to Durrës from Bari (nine hours, 220km) daily and from Ancona (20 hours, 550km) four times a week.

Deck fares per passenger are US$60 Bari-Durrës and US$80 Ancona-Durrës; cabin fares cost more. Bicycles are carried free. From Ancona you can catch a ferry to Split, Croatia.

A ferry runs every Tuesday and Saturday from Trieste to Durrës (and back on Wednesday and Sunday). A deck ride costs US$37.

In Trieste ferry tickets are available from Agenzia Marittima 'Agemar' (☎ 040-363 737). In Bari the agent is 'Agestea' (☎ 080-5531 555, @ agestea.bari02@interbusiness .it), Via Liside 4. In Ancona the people to see are Maritime Agency Srl (☎ 071-204 915, @ tickets.adn@maritime.it), Via XXIX Settembre 10. In Albania tickets are sold at any number of travel agencies in both Durrës or Tirana.

The fastest ferry connections between Bari and Durrës are the passenger catermans operated by the line La Vikinga (US$100, 3½ hours). These high-speed vessels departs Durrës daily at 5.30 pm and 9.30 am and Bari at 11 am and 5 pm and travel at speeds of up to 90km/h. The ticket office of La Vikinga (☎ 225 55, fax 242 68) in Durrës is on Rruga Durrah, the street from the port to the mosque. The Bari agent is at ☎ 080-523 2429.

From Vlora, Albania Travel & Tours (☎/fax 063-249 01 in Vlora) can arrange tickets for the ferry *Niobe 1*, which runs three times a week to Brindisi and three times a week to Otronto. The price to both is 60,000 lire (plus 10,000 in port taxes). Two other ferries, the *Vlora 5* and the *Europa Skënderbeg*, run to Brindisi; it should not be a problem to find a travel agent to book your ticket on either end.

Approximately three ferries run from Corfu to Saranda.

Getting Around

Most Albanians travel in private minibuses or state-owned buses. These run fairly frequently throughout the day between Tirana and Durrës (38km) and other towns north and south. Tickets are sold by a conductor on board, and the fares are low (approximately 100 lekë).

Train travel is really only useful between Tirana and Durrës (60 lekë, 90 minutes), but Albanians avoid the trains, even though they are slightly cheaper than the minibuses, because the carriages can be quite decrepit.

Albania has only recently acquired an official road traffic code and most motorists have only learned to drive in the last five years. The roads are terrible and banditry targets private cars, particularly in the north. There is currently no place to rent a car in Albania.

Tirana

☎ 042

Tirana (Tiranë), a bustling city of 444,000, still revolves around the larger-than-life 'palaces of the people' that the Communists built around Skënderbeg Square and along Bulevardi Dëshmorët e Kombit (Martyrs of the Nation Blvd). The city also displays Italian parks and a Turkish mosque, and ever-growing clumps of trendy cafe-bars.

Orientation

Tirana revolves around Skënderbeg Square. Running south from the square is Bulevardi Dëshmorët e Kombit, which leads to the three-arched university building. Running north the same street leads to the train station.

Information

Money A free currency market operates directly in front of the post office.

The Rogner Europapark Hotel has a currency exchange booth (near the Swissair offices) that does Mastercard advances and cashes travellers cheques (1% commission) and exchanges cash; it's open 10.30 am to 5 pm weekdays. World Travel, the American Express representative on Mine Peza 2, cashes travellers cheques for 2% commission.

Post & Communications The post office and telephone centre are adjacent on a street jutting west from Skënderbeg Square.

Email & Internet Access Access the Internet on the top floor in the Palace of Culture, on Skënderbeg Square (380 lekë per hour), or at the Internet Center on Rruga Brigada VIII 8/1 (300 lekë per hour).

Travel Agencies Albania Travel & Tours (☎ 329 83, fax 339 81), Rruga Durrësit 102, books plane and ferry tickets and can arrange private rooms.

Medical & Emergency Services Most foreigners use the ABC Health Foundation, 260 Rruga Quemal Stafa (☎ 341 05, @ ABC@maf.org), staffed by Western-trained doctors; watch carefully for the small sign. Regular/emergency consultations are US$60/90. Appointments are weekdays from 9 am to 1 pm.

The emergency phone number for an ambulance is ☎ 222 35 and for the police it's ☎ 19.

Things to See

Most visits to Tirana begin at **Skënderbeg Square**, a great open space in the heart of the city. On the square's northern side, beside the 15-storey Tirana International hotel (the tallest building in Albania), the **National Museum of History** is the country's largest and best museum (open 8 am to 1 pm Monday to Saturday; 300 lekë). Free temporary exhibits are shown in the gallery on the side of the building facing the Tirana International Hotel.

To the east is another massive building, the **Palace of Culture** (completed in 1966), which houses a theatre, shops and travel agencies. The entrance to the **National Library** is on the south side of the building. Opposite this is the cupola and minaret of the **Mosque of Ethem Bey** (1793), one of the most distinctive buildings in the city. Enter to see the beautifully painted dome. Tirana's **clock tower** (1830) stands beside the mosque.

From the square, Bulevardi Dëshmorët e Kombit leads south to the three arches of **Tirana University** (1957).

Follow Rruga Ismail Qemali to the **former residence of Enver Hoxha**. When the area was first opened to the general public in 1991, crowds of Albanians flocked to see the style in which their 'proletarian' leaders lived.

On the left, farther east on Bulevardi Dëshmorët e Kombit, is the ultramodern **Palace of Congresses** (1986).

Beyond the university is **Parku Kombëtar** (National Park), a large park with an open-air theatre (Teatri Veror) and an artificial

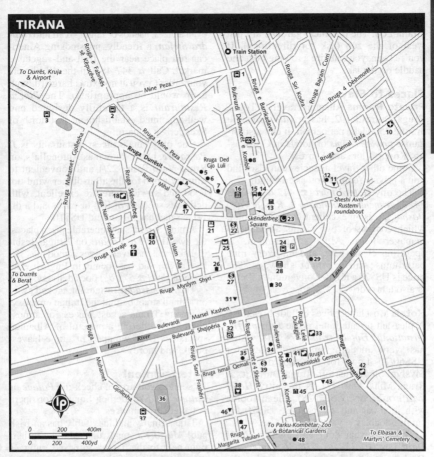

TIRANA

PLACES TO STAY
14 Tirana International Hotel
17 Hotel California
26 Europa International Hotel
30 Hotel Dajti
40 Europapark Rogner Hotel
47 Hotel Endri

PLACES TO EAT
11 Qendra Stefan
31 La Voglia
43 Ambassador
46 Il Passatore

OTHER
1 Bus Station
2 Kruja Bus Station
3 Northern Bus Station
4 World Travel

5 Skënderbeg Travel
6 Albtransport
7 Albania Travel & Tours
8 Ve-ve Business Centre
9 Telephone Centre
10 ABC Health Foundation
12 Fruit & Vegetable Market
13 Palace of Culture
15 Bus departure point for
   Prishtina
16 National Museum of History
18 UK Embassy
19 Orthodox Church
20 Cathedral of St Anthony
21 Kinema Millennium
22 State Bank of Albania
23 Mosque of Ethem Bey;
   Clock tower
24 Axhensi Bus Office

25 Post Office; Telephone Centre
27 Unioni Financiar Tiranë Exchange
28 Art Gallery
29 Parliament
32 Internet Centre
33 Macedonian Embassy
34 Former Central Committee
   Building
35 Former Residence of
   Enver Hoxha
36 Selman Stërmasi Stadium
37 Southern Bus Station
38 Murphy's
39 American Bank of Albania
41 Italian Embassy
42 US Embassy
44 Qemal Stafa Stadium
45 Palace of Congresses
48 Tirana University

lake. Cross the dam retaining the lake to Tirana Zoo. The **botanical gardens** are just west of the zoo (ask for directions). If you're keen, you can hire a rowing boat and paddle on the lake.

Places to Stay

Private Rooms Albania Travel & Tours, Rruga Durrësit 102, has *private rooms* at around 2500 lekë per person. It can also organise *private rooms* or hotels in Gjirokastra, Korça, Vlora and Durrës.

Some other travel agencies can also find you a private room if you ask around.

The tiny *Hotel Endri (☎ 442 68 or 293 34, apartment 30, building 3, Rruga Vaso Pasha 37)*, is an excellent deal. The hotel, which consists of two rooms adjacent to manager Petrit Alikaj's apartment, is sparkling clean, new, and has very nice bathrooms with excellent showers. The price is US$20 a night. Conveniently, Petrit is also a taxi driver.

Hotels Most hotel prices include breakfast. A pleasant private hotel is the *Europa International Hotel (☎/fax 274 03)*, which has very modern singles/doubles for US$60/70. Look for the sign on Rruga Myslym Shyri. Just off Rruga Durrësit, at Rruga Mihal Duri 2/7, is the nifty *Hotel California (☎/fax 322 28)*. Clean rooms with mini-bar and TV cost US$50/70 for singles/doubles.

The somewhat dour and ageing *Hotel Dajti (☎ 510 35, fax 510 36, Bulevardi Dëshmorët e Kombit 6)*, was erected in the 1930s by the Italians. The 90 rooms with bath are US$50-60/80 for singles/doubles.

Major splurges include the high-rise *Tirana International Hotel (☎ 341 85, fax 341 88)*, on Skënderbeg Square, with well-appointed singles/doubles costing US$140/190, and the *Rogner Europapark Hotel (☎ 350 35, in the USA 1-800-650 8018, fax 35 050)*, on Bulevardi Dëshmorët e Kombit. The latter, run by the Rogner Group, is Tirana's top choice and has excellent rooms for US$200/230 per night.

Places to Eat

There is no shortage of small restaurants, cafes and snack bars to be found on and around Skënderbeg Square and Bulevardi Dëshmorët e Kombit.

If you fancy a cuppa and a sandwich – or even a pizza, nachos or fajitas – call into *Qendra Stefan*, a friendly, nonsmoking American-run place near the fruit-and-vegetable market. Call ☎ 347 48 and they'll bicycle your order to you at no extra charge (though a tip would be appropriate). The *Piazza Restaurant* is a tastefully designed and well-appointed establishment just north of Skënderbeg Square.

One of Tirana's nicest restaurants is *Il Passatore*, better known as Antonella's, on Rruga Vaso Pasha 22/1 and convenient to Murphy's pub for the after-dinner wind-up. Food and service here are excellent, with delicious specials of fish or pasta and a diverse salad bar for around US$10.

Among Tirana's innumerable pizza places, the two-floor *La Voglia*, on Rruga Reshit Çollaku near the river, serves a good pie (350 lekë or so) and has menus in English. The pizzeria *Era (☎ 578 05)* does delivery.

The *Ambassador* restaurant, tucked away on a small street behind the Italian embassy, is among Tirana's best places for atmosphere. Try ordering a plateful of Albanian specialties (rice wrapped in grape leaves, burek, and more).

Entertainment

As soon as you arrive, check the *Palace of Culture*, on Skënderbeg Square, for opera or ballet performances.

Tirana finally and inevitably has an Irish pub! *Murphy's*, on Rruga Abdyl Frashëri right next to the Tirana Fitness Center, is the new darling of the expat community. It's open until the last person leaves. The bathroom is clean.

Tirana's biggest hit is the new *Kinema Millennium (☎ 486 47)*, on Rruga Kavaje near Skënderbeg Square, which shows recent box-office hits for 200 lekë or 300 lekë.

Spectator Sports

Behind the Palace of Congresses is the **Qemal Stafa Stadium** where football matches are held every Saturday and Sunday afternoon, except during July and August.

Getting There & Away

Both private and state-owned buses operate between Tirana and most towns. There's no central station in Tirana and pick-up venues may change, so always check for the latest departure points. Service to/from Durrës (100 lekë, 38km) is fairly frequent, leaving from the block adjacent to the train station.

The train station is at the north end of Bulevardi Dëshmorët e Kombit. Seven trains a day go to Durrës (60 lekë, one hour).

Getting Around

Tirana's local taxis cost about 300 lekë per ride in the city during the day, 500 lekë at night (flat fee). Radio Taxi (☎ 777 77) is the most reliable cab company.

Durrës

☎ 052

Only 38km west of Tirana, Durrës (Durazzo in Italian) is a major industrial city and commercial port, with a population of 85,000. On the bay south-east of the city are long, sandy beaches where all the tourist hotels are concentrated. In 1991 the city saw desperate mobs attempting to escape by ship to Italy and there's now a heavy Italian military presence in the area.

Unlike Tirana, Durrës is an ancient city. In 627 BC the Greeks founded Epidamnos (Durrës), whose name the Romans changed to Dyrrhachium. The famous Via Appia (Appian Way) to Rome began 150km south-west of Durrës at Brindisi, Italy. Durrës changed hands frequently before being taken by the Turks in 1501. A slow revival began in the 17th century, and from 1914 to 1920 Durrës was the capital of Albania. Today the city is best known for its Roman and Byzantine ruins.

Orientation & Information

Ferries from Italy dock on the east side of the port; follow road signs to the ferry quay when departing.

The Savings Bank of Albania, across the bus parking lot from the train station, changes travellers cheques and does Mastercard advances for a 1% commission. It's open until 2 pm weekdays.

The post office and phone centre are located one block west of the train and bus stations.

Things to See

Behind the former archaeological museum that faces the waterfront are the 6th-century Byzantine **city walls**, built after the Visigoth invasion of AD 481 and supplemented by round Venetian towers in the 14th century.

The town's impressive **Roman amphitheatre**, built between the 1st and 2nd centuries AD, is on the hillside just inside the walls. Much of the amphitheatre has now been excavated. Follow the road just inside the walls down towards the port to the **Sultan Fatih Mosque** (1502) and the **Moisiut Ekspozita e Kulturës Popullore**. It features ethnographic displays housed in the former home of actor Alexander Moisiu (1879-1935). The latter is open in the morning only.

The former **palace of King Ahmet Zog** is on a hilltop west of the amphitheatre. Soldiers guarding the palace will expect you to buy a ticket from them to wander around. In front of the palace is a statue of Skënderbeg and huge radar disks set up by the Italian army. On the next hill there's a **lighthouse** with splendid views of Durrës and the entire coast.

Places to Stay

Albanian Tours (☎ 242 76, ☎/fax 254 50), on Rruga Tregtare near the waterfront, may be able to help arrange a private room with advance notice; the office is open 8 am to 8 pm daily.

An excellent choice is the *bed & breakfast* (☎ 243 43, ✉ ipmcrsp@icc.al.eu.org) in the gracious 19th-century house of a personable Italian-Albanian couple, Alma Tedeschini and her husband, Josef. It's just US$15 for a bed; add US$10 for lunch and dinner. The place, at Dom Nikoll Kaçorri 5, is a bit hard to find: from the square fronting the mosque, walk towards the restaurant Il Costello. Take the first right, then a quick left, then a quick right. The house is about 10m down a narrow alleyway and has a red iron gate.

Good choices for private hotels include *Hotel Lido* (☎/fax 279 41), on Rruga A. Goga, in the centre of town, (singles/doubles US$35/42), and the cheery *Hotel Pepeto* (☎ 241 90, ☎/fax 263 46), just east of the square fronting the mosque (US$40/60, laundry and breakfast included).

The *Hotel Ceka* (☎/fax 244 12), on Rruga Currila on a hill above the former archaeological museum, provides simple rooms at a good price – US$25 for one or two persons.

ALBANIA

Places to Eat

By far the best place to grab a meal in town is the restaurant *Il Castello* (☎ *268 87, Rruga H Troplini 3*), which has, among other culinary delights, outstanding pastas (be sure to try the delicious seafood pasta, at 450 lekë); there's also an interesting selection of fish dishes.

For a meal of fresh shrimp or fish try *Arragosta*; enjoy your meal while sitting on the patio overlooking the water. It's on the point about an 800m walk west from town centre. Also worth trying is the *café-bar* on Rruga A. Goga inside the tower by the entrance to the port.

Getting There & Away

Albania's 720km railway network centres on Durrës. There are seven trains a day to Tirana (60 lekë, 1½ hours) from the station beside the Tirana Highway, conveniently close to central Durrës.

Minibuses to Tirana and beyond leave from in front of the train station whenever they're full (100 lekë, one hour).

Ferries travel several times a week between Durrës and the Italian cities of Bari, Ancona and Trieste (see the Getting There & Away section at the beginning of this chapter). Allow plenty of time to board ferries in Durrës.

Andorra

The principality of Andorra, nestled in the Pyrenees mountains between France and Spain, covers just 464 sq km. Although tiny, this political anomaly is at the heart of some of the range's most dramatic scenery. It's also a skiing venue and duty-free shopping haven. These activities, together with great summer walking, attract over eight million visitors a year and bring not only wealth but also some unsightly development around the capital, Andorra la Vella.

From the Middle Ages until 1993, Andorra was headed by two 'princes': the Catholic bishop of the Spanish town of La Seu d'Urgell and the French president (who inherited the job from France's pre-Revolutionary kings). Nowadays, democratic Andorra is a 'parliamentary co-princedom', its 'princes' little more than nominal heads of state. Andorra is a member of the United Nations and the Council of Europe, but not a full member of the EU.

Andorrans form only about a quarter of the total population of 66,000 and are outnumbered by Spaniards. The official language is Catalan, which is related to both Spanish and French. Most people speak at least two of these languages.

AT A GLANCE

Capital:	Andorra la Vella
Population:	66,000
Official Language:	Catalan
Currency:	1 French franc (FF) = 100 centimes; 1 Paseta = 100 centimos

Facts for the Visitor

EMBASSIES & CONSULATES
Andorra has embassies in France and Spain, both of whom have reciprocal diplomatic missions in Andorra.

MONEY
Andorra uses the Spanish peseta (ptas) and the French franc (FF) and, like both countries, will use the euro from 2002. It's best to buy in pesetas: the exchange rate for francs in shops and restaurants is seldom in your favour. See the France and Spain chapters for exchange rates.

POST & COMMUNICATIONS
Post
Andorra has no postal system of its own; France and Spain each operate separate systems with their own Andorran stamps, which are needed only for international mail – letters within the country are delivered free. Regular French and Spanish stamps can't be used in Andorra.

It's usually swifter to route international mail (except letters to Spain) through the French postal system.

Telephone
Andorra's country code is ☎ 376. The cheapest way to make an international call is to buy a *teletarja* (phonecard, sold for 500 ptas, 900 ptas and 1350 ptas) and ring off-peak (9 pm to 7 am plus all day Sunday), when a three-minute call to Europe costs 210 ptas (306 ptas to the USA or Australia). You can't make a reverse-charge (collect) call from Andorra.

Email & Internet Access
Log on at Punt Internet on the 5th floor of Carrer Bonaventura 39 in Andorra La Vella, very near the bus station (open to 9 pm weekdays plus 4 to 8 pm Saturday, August and September, 1000 ptas per hour).

BUSINESS HOURS
Shops in Andorra la Vella are generally open 9.30 am to 1 pm and 3.30 to 8 pm daily, except (usually) Sunday afternoon.

ACTIVITIES
Above the main valleys, there's attractive, lake-dotted mountain country, good for skiing in winter and walking in summer. Largest and best of Andorra's ski resorts are

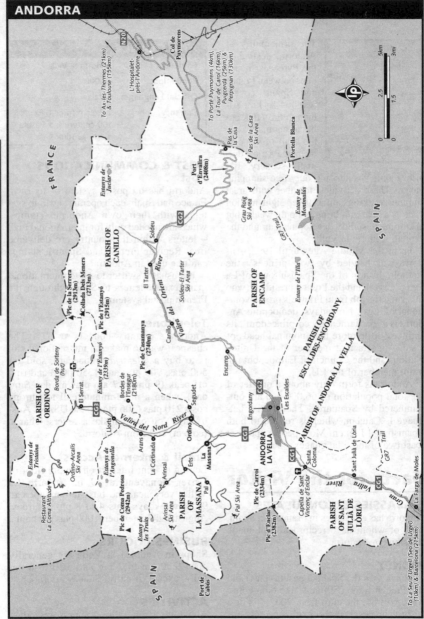

ANDORRA

To Ax-les-Thermes (21km)
& Toulouse (155km)

N20

Col de
Puymorens

To Porté Puymorens (4km),
La Tour de Carol (25km) &
Puigcerdà (130km)

L'Hospitalet-
près-l'Andorre

Pas de
la Casa

Port
d'Envalira (2408m)

Pas de la Casa Ski Area

Portella Blanca

FRANCE

SPAIN

5km
3mi

2.5

1.5

0   0

Estanys de
Juclar

Grau Roig
Ski Area

Estany de
Montmalús

GR7 Trail

Soldeu

PARISH OF
CANILLO

El Tarter

Soldeu-El Tarter
Ski Area

Canillo

Oriente
River

Valira
del
Oriente

PARISH OF
ENCAMP

Estany de l'Illa

Pic de la Serrera
(2915m)

Collada Dels Meners
(2713m)

Pic de l'Estanyó
(2915m)

Pic de Casamanya
(2740m)

Borda de Sorteny
(hut)

Estany de l'Estanyó
(2339m)

Bordes de
l'Ensegur
(2180m)

PARISH OF
ORDINO

El Serrat

Llorts

Valira del Nord River

Arans

La Cortinada

Encamp

PARISH OF
ESCALDES-ENGORDANY

Segudet

Ordino

Arinsal

Les Escaldes

Engordany

PARISH OF ANDORRA LA VELLA

Estanys de
Tristaina

Ordino-Arcalís
Ski Area

Restaurant
La Coma Altitude

Pic de Coma Pedrosa
(2942m)

Estany de
l'Angonella

La Massana

ANDORRA
LA VELLA

CG3

CG2

CG2

CG3

CG1

Estany de
les Truits

Arinsal
Ski Area

Pal

Pal Ski Area

Pic de Carroi
(2334m)

Santa
Coloma

Capella de Sant
Vincenç d'Enclar

Pic d'Enclar
(2382m)

PARISH
OF
LA MASSANA

Erts

Sant Julià de Lòria

Gran
Valira
River

GR7 Trail

PARISH OF SANT
JULIÀ DE LÒRIA

SPAIN

Port de
Cabús

La Farga de Moles

To La Seu d'Urgell (Seo de Urgel)
(10km) & Barcelona (215km)

Soldeu-El Tarter and Pas de la Casa-Grau Roig. Ski passes cost 2800 ptas to 4200 ptas a day, depending on location and season; downhill ski-gear is 1200 ptas to 1600 ptas a day, snowboards 2500 ptas to 3000 ptas.

Tourist offices stock a useful free English-language booklet, *Sport Activities*, describing numerous hiking and mountain bike routes. In summer, bikes can be rented in some resorts for around 2800 ptas a day.

ACCOMMODATION

Tourist offices have a comprehensive free brochure, *Hotels, Restaurants, Apartaments i Cámpings*.

Outside Andorra la Vella and Canillo, there are few budget options for independent travellers. In compensation, there are plenty of camping grounds, many beautifully situated. In the high season (December to March, July and August), some hotels put prices up substantially and others don't take in independent travellers.

For walkers, Andorra has 26 off-the-beaten-track *refugis* (mountain refuges); all except one are unstaffed and free. Invest 200 ptas in the *Mapa de Refugis i Grans Recorreguts*, which pinpoints them all.

Getting There & Away

The only way to reach Andorra, unless you trek across the mountains, is by road.

FRANCE

Autocars Nadal (☎ 821138) has two buses a day (2750 ptas, four hours) on Monday, Wednesday, Friday and Sunday, linking Toulouse's Gare Routière (bus station) and Andorra la Vella.

By rail, take a train from Toulouse to either L'Hospitalet (2¼ to 2¾ hours, four daily) or Latour-de-Carol (2½ to three hours). Two daily connecting buses link Andorra la Vella with both L'Hospitalet (960 ptas) and Latour-de-Carol (1125 ptas). On Saturdays, up to five buses run from L'Hospitalet to Pas de la Casa, just in Andorra.

SPAIN

Alsina Graells (☎ 827379) runs up to seven buses daily between Barcelona's Estació

del Nord and Andorra la Vella's bus station (2435 ptas to 2715 ptas, according to the time of day at which they depart; four hours). Eurolines (☎ 860010) has four services daily (2800 ptas) between Andorra (departing from the car park of Hotel Diplomátic, opposite the bus station) and Barcelona's Sants bus station.

The rail journey from Barcelona via Latour-de-Carol or Puigcerdà on the French side, then onward by bus, is possible but longer and no cheaper.

Samar/Andor-Inter (☎ 826289) runs three times weekly between Andorra and Madrid (4700 ptas, nine hours) via Zaragoza (2300 ptas).

La Hispano Andorrana (☎ 821372) has five to eight buses daily between La Seu d'Urgell, across the border, and Carrer Doctor Nequi in Andorra la Vella (345 ptas, 30 minutes).

Getting Around

BUS

Ask at a tourist office for a current timetable of the eight bus routes, run by Cooperativa Interurbana (☎ 820412), which follow Andorra's three main highways.

Destinations from the Avinguda de Príncep Benlloch stop in Andorra la Vella include Ordino (130 ptas, every half-hour), Arinsal (185 ptas, three daily), Soldeu (375 ptas, hourly) and Pas de la Casa (620 ptas, at 9 am daily).

CAR & MOTORCYCLE

The speed limit is 40km/h in populated areas and 90km/h elsewhere. Two problems are the recklessness of local drivers on the tight, winding roads and Andorra la Vella's horrendous traffic jams.

Petrol in Andorra is about 25% cheaper than in Spain or France.

Andorra la Vella

Andorra la Vella (population 23,000), squeezed within the Riu Gran Valira valley, is mainly engaged in retailing electronic and luxury goods. With the constant din of jackhammers and shopping-mall architecture, you may well be in Hong Kong – but

ANDORRA LA VELLA

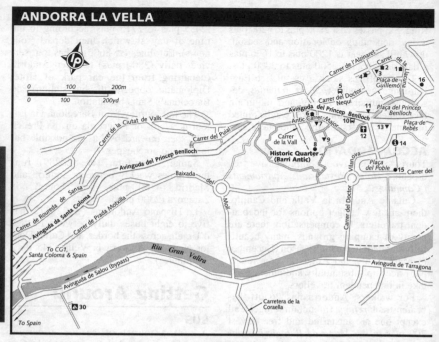

ANDORRA LA VELLA

PLACES TO STAY
1 Hotel Florida
2 Residència Benazet
4 Hostal del Sol
6 Pensió La Rosa
18 Hotel Costa
20 Hotel Residència Albert
30 Càmping Valira

PLACES TO EAT
3 Forn de l'Avinew name
7 Restaurant Can Benet

9 Restaurant Ca La Conxita
11 Papanico
13 Pans & Company
21 McDonald's
23 Pans & Company
29 McDonald's

OTHER
5 Bus for Seu d'Urgell
8 Casa de la Vall
10 Bus for Ordino, Arinsal, Canillo, Soldeu & Pas de la Casa

12 Església de Sant Esteve
14 National Tourist Office
15 Public Lift to Plaça del Poble
16 Viatges Relax
17 Pyrénées Department Store
19 Municipal Tourist Office
22 Telephones
24 Spanish Post Office
25 French Post Office
26 Servei de Policía
27 Bus Station
28 Punt Internet (Cybercafe)

for the snowcapped peaks and absence of noodle shops!

Orientation

Andorra la Vella is strung out along the main drag, whose name changes from Avinguda de Príncep Benlloch to Avinguda de Meritxell to Avinguda Carlemany. The tiny historic quarter (Barri Antic) is split by this heavily trafficked artery. The town merges with the once-separate villages of Escaldes and Engordany to the east and Santa Coloma to the south-west.

Information

Tourist Offices The municipal tourist office (☎ 827117), Plaça de la Rotonda, is open 9 am to 1 pm and 4 to 8 pm daily (to 7 pm Sunday, to 9 pm July and August).

The national tourist office (☎ 820214), off Plaça Rebés, is open 10 am (9 am July to September) to 1 pm and 3 to 7 pm Monday to Saturday plus Sunday morning.

Money Crèdit Andorrà, Avinguda de Meritxell 80, has a 24-hour banknote exchange machine that accepts 15 currencies.

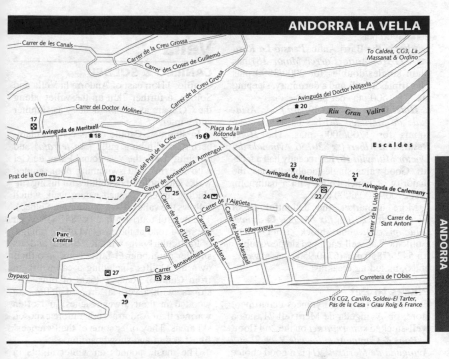

ANDORRA LA VELLA

Banks open 9 am to 1 pm and 3 to 5 pm weekdays and to noon Saturday, and can be found everywhere.

American Express is represented by Viatges Relax (☎ 822044), Carrer de Mossén Tremosa 2.

Post & Communications La Poste, the French post office, Carrer de Pere d'Urg 1, takes only French francs. Conversely, the Spanish post office, Correus i Telègrafs, Carrer de Joan Maragall 10, accepts only pesetas. Both are open 8.30 am to 2.30 pm weekdays and 9 am to noon Saturday.

You can make international calls from pay phones or from the Servei de Telecomunicacions d'Andorra (STA), Avinguda de Meritxell 110, which also has a fax service. It's open 9 am to 9 pm daily.

Things to See & Do
Built in 1580 as a private home, **Casa de la Vall** in the Barri Antic has served as Andorra's parliament building since 1702. Downstairs is **El Tribunal de Corts**, the country's only courtroom. Free guided tours (available in English) are given 9.30

am to 1 pm and 3 to 7 pm Monday to Saturday (daily in August).

Pamper yourself at **Caldea** (☎ 800995) in Escaldes, a 10-minute walk upstream from Plaça de la Rotonda. Enclosed in what looks like a futuristic cathedral is Europe's largest spa complex of lagoons, hot tubs and saunas, fed by thermal springs. It's open 10 am to 11 pm daily; three-hour tickets cost 2950 ptas.

If you've enough left in the kitty for a little **shopping**, you can make savings on things like sports gear, photographic equipment, shoes and clothing, with prices around 25% less than in Spain or France.

Places to Stay
Camping *Camping Valira* on Avinguda de Salou, charges 1575 ptas for two people and a tent. Open year round, it has a small indoor swimming pool.

Hotels *Residència Benazet* (☎ 820698, *Carrer de la Llacuna 21*) has large rooms with washbasin for up to four people at 1400 ptas a person. Nearby on Plaça Guillemó, spruce singles/doubles, with shower, at friendly *Hostal del Sol* (☎ *823701)* cost 2000/3900 ptas.

Also in the Barri Antic, *Pensió La Rosa* (☎ *821810, Antic Carrer Major 18)* has plain singles/doubles for 2000/3500 ptas plus triples, quads and a dormitory, sleeping six, for 1500 ptas per person.

Hotel Costa (☎ *821439, 3rd floor, Avinguda de Meritxell 44)* has basic but clean rooms for 1700/3000 ptas. The *Hotel Residència Albert* (☎ *820156, Avinguda del Doctor Mitjavila 16)* has recently had a facelift. Good-value singles/doubles/triples, the majority of which come with a bathroom, cost 2700/4500/6000 ptas.

More upmarket, the delightful *Hotel Florida* (☎ *820105, fax 861925,* ✉ *aran@ solucions.ad),* one block from Plaça Guillemó, has well-equipped singles/doubles for 5425/7850 ptas (6750/9500 ptas at weekends), including breakfast.

Places to Eat

For self-caterers, the Pyrénées department store, on Avinguda de Meritxell 21, has a well-stocked *supermarket* on the 2nd floor.

Pans & Company (Plaça de Rebés 2 and Avinguda de Meritxell 91) is a good choice for baguettes with a range of fillings (350 ptas to 500 ptas). Just off Plaça Guillemó, *Forn de l'Aví* has an excellent *menú* for 850 ptas and does good *platos combinados* (plentiful mixed dishes; costing from 725 ptas to 850 ptas).

In the Barri Antic, *Papanico*, on Avinguda de Príncep Benlloch, is fun for morning coffee all the way through to late-night snacks. It has tasty *tapas* from 250 ptas each and does a range of yummy sandwiches and substantial platos combinados. *Restaurant Ca La Conxita (Placeta de Monjó 3)* is a bustling, family place where you can eat a satisfying meal for around 2500 ptas. Around the corner, *Restaurant Can Benet* (*Carrer Major 9*) has main dishes that cost between 1600 ptas and 2300 ptas, and is equally as delightful.

There are a couple of *McDonald's* – opposite the bus station and at Avinguda de Meritxell 105.

Getting There & Around

See the Getting There & Away and Getting Around sections earlier in this chapter for transport options.

Around Andorra la Vella

CANILLO & SOLDEU

Canillo, 11km east of Andorra la Vella and Soldeu, a further 7km up the valley along the CG2, are as complementary as summer and winter.

In summer, **Canillo** offers canyon clambering, a climbing gully *(vía ferrata)* and climbing wall, the year-round Palau de Gel with ice rink and swimming pool, guided walks and endless possibilities for hiking (including an easy signed nature walk which follows the valley downstream from Soldeu). The helpful tourist office (☎ 851002) is on the main road at the east end of the village.

Particularly in winter, **Soldeu** and its smaller neighbour **El Tarter** come into their own as 23 lifts (including a cabin lift up from Canillo) connect 86km of runs. The slopes, with a vertical drop of 850m, are wooded in their lower reaches, and often warmer than Andorra's other more exposed ski areas. They offer some of the Pyrenees' finest skiing and snowboarding.

The music pounds on winter nights in Soldeu. *Pussy Cat* and its neighbour, *Fat Albert*, both one block from the main drag, rock until far too late for impressive skiing the next day. *Capital Discoteca*, with free entry on Tuesday, Wednesday and weekends, is a busy dance hang-out.

Places to Stay

Year-round, accommodation in Canillo, with five camping grounds, is markedly less expensive than higher up in the valley. *Hotel Casa Nostra* (☎ *851023)* has simple rooms for 2500 ptas (3250 ptas with shower, 3750 ptas with full bathroom). *Hotel Pellissé* (☎ *851205, fax 851875),* just east of town, has decent singles/doubles for 2750/4400 ptas, while *Hotel Canigó* (☎ *851024, fax 851824)* has comfortable rooms at 3000/5000 ptas.

On Soldeu's main drag, the cheerful restaurant of *Hotel Bruxelles* does well-filled sandwiches (450 ptas to 575 ptas), whopping burgers and a tasty *menú* at 1175 ptas.

Getting There & Around

Buses run from Andorra la Vella to El Tarter and Soldeu (375 ptas, 40 minutes)

9 am to 8 pm hourly. In winter, there are free hourly shuttle buses (just flash your ski pass) between Canillo and Soldeu.

ORDINO & AROUND
Despite recent development, Ordino (population 1000), on highway CG3 8km north of Andorra la Vella, retains its rural Andorran character. At 1000m, it's a good starting point for summer activity holidays. The tourist office (☎ 737080), beside the CG3, is open 9 am to 1 pm and 3 to 7 pm daily (closed Sunday afternoon).

Things to See & Do
The **Museu d'Areny i Plandolit** (☎ 836908) is a 17th-century manor house with a richly furnished interior. Within the same grounds is the **Museo Postal de Andorra**. Give it a try. It has an interesting 15-minute audiovisual program (available in English) and stamps by the thousand, issued by France and Spain specifically for Andorra (see Post & Communications earlier in this chapter). Both are open 9.30 am to 1.30 pm and 3 to 6.30 pm Tuesday to Saturday plus Sunday morning. Admission to each costs 300 ptas.

Walking From the hamlet of Segudet, 500m east of Ordino, a path goes up through fir woods to the **Coll d'Ordino** (1980m), reached in about 1½ hours. **Pic de Casamanya** (2740m), with knock-me-down views, is some two hours north from the Coll.

Other trails lead off from the tiny settlements beside the CG3 north of Ordino.

A track (three hours one way) heads west from **Llorts** (1413m), up the Riu de l'Angonella Valley, to a group of lakes, the **Estanys de l'Angonella** at about 2300m.

Just north of **El Serrat** (1600m), a secondary road leads 4km east to the Borda de Sorteny mountain refuge (1969m), from where more trails lead on into the high mountain area.

From **Arans** (1385m), a trail goes northeastward to **Bordes de l'Ensegur** (2180m), where there's an old shepherd's hut.

Places to Stay & Eat
The cheapest option in Ordino is the cavernous *Hotel Casamanya* (☎ *835011)* with singles/doubles for 4000/7000 ptas. *Bar Restaurant Quim* on the Plaça Major has a basic *menú* at 1350 ptas. Next door, *Restaurant Armengol* offers a *menú* for 1500 ptas and a good range of meat dishes.

Up the valley and some 200m north of Llorts, *Camping Els Pardassos* (☎ *850022)* is one of Andorra's most beautiful camp sites. Open mid-June to mid-September it charges 975 ptas for two people and a tent. *Hotel Vilaró* (☎ *850225)*, 200m south of the village, has rooms for 2200/2400 ptas.

Getting There & Away
Buses between Andorra la Vella and Ordino (130 ptas) run about every half-hour daily from 7 am to 9 pm. Buses to El Serrat (240 ptas) via Ordino leave Andorra la Vella at 1 and 8.30 pm. The valley is also served by four buses daily (10 in the ski season) linking Ordino and Arcalís.

ANDORRA

Austria

Austria (Österreich) thrives on tourism, and is one of the most popular destinations in Europe. Its rich cultural heritage, historic cities, winter sports and stunning scenery are a hard combination to beat. Vienna is one of the world's great cities; Salzburg is a living baroque museum; and Innsbruck is dramatically situated in a perfect panorama of peaks. And everywhere you go, the country moves to the rhythm of its unrivalled musical tradition.

Facts about Austria

HISTORY

In its early years, the land that became Austria was invaded by the Celts, Romans, Vandals, Visigoths, Huns, Avars and Slavs. In 803 Charlemagne established a territory in the Danube Valley known as the Ostmark. In 962 the leader of the Ostmark, Otto I, was crowned as Holy Roman Emperor by Pope John XII.

After a spell under the control of the Babenbergs, Austria fell into the hands of the Habsburgs in 1278. They ruled the country until WWI and greatly expanded its territory. In 1477, Maximilian gained control of Burgundy and the Netherlands and later married his son, Philip, to the infanta of Spain. In 1516 Philip's son became Charles I of Spain. Three years later, he also became Charles V of the Holy Roman Empire. In 1521 Charles handed over the Austrian territories to his younger brother, Ferdinand, the first Habsburg ruler to live in Vienna.

In 1740 Maria Theresa ascended the throne, despite the fact that as a woman she was supposedly ineligible to do so. A war followed to ensure that she stayed there. Her rule lasted 40 years, during which Maria Theresa centralised control, reformed the army and the economy, and introduced a public education system. This period is

AT A GLANCE	
Capital:	Vienna
Population:	8.1 million
Official Language:	German
Currency:	1 Austrian Schilling = 100 Groschen

generally acknowledged as the era in which Austria developed as a modern state.

Progress was halted when Napoleon defeated Austria at Austerlitz in 1805 and forced the abolition of the title of Holy Roman Emperor. In 1867 the dual monarchy of Austria-Hungary was formed under emperor Franz Josef. A period of prosperity followed and Vienna, in particular, flourished.

The situation changed on 28 June 1914 when the emperor's nephew, Archduke Franz Ferdinand, was assassinated in Sarajevo. A month later WWI began, with Austria-Hungary declaring war on Serbia.

Franz Josef died in 1916. His successor abdicated in 1918 and the Republic of Austria was created on 12 November. In 1919 the new state was forced to recognise the independent states of Czechoslovakia, Poland, Hungary and Yugoslavia, which, along with Transylvania, had previously been under the control of the Habsburgs.

In the run-up to WWII, Hitler manipulated the chancellor of Austria so successfully that German troops met little resistance when they invaded in 1938. A national referendum by Austrians in April 1938 supported the *Anschluss* (annexation).

Austria was bombed heavily in WWII, and in 1945 the victorious Allies restored Austria to its 1937 frontiers. Occupation by the Allies (including Russia) lasted till 1955, and there was much cloak-and-dagger activity by cold-war spies. In 1972 Austria established a free-trade treaty with the EU (then known as the EC), and full EU membership followed in 1995.

In 2000, Austria became politically isolated when a coalition government was formed that contained far-right politicians from the Freedom Party. The resignation of the Freedom Party's leader, Jörg Haider,

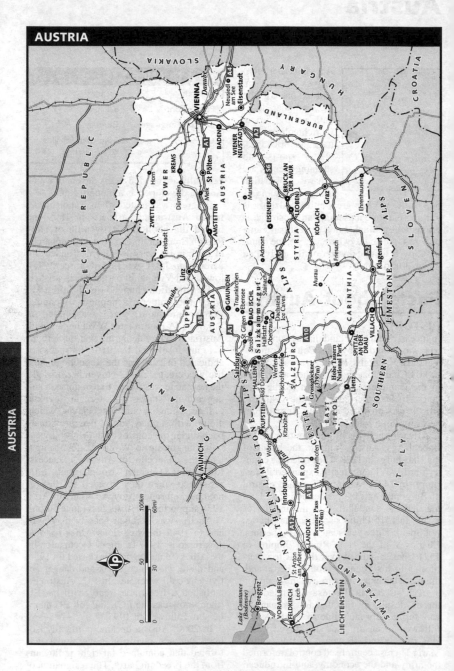

AUSTRIA

who is notorious for making pro-Nazi statements, failed to stem international criticism.

GEOGRAPHY

Two-thirds of Austria (83,855 sq km) is mountainous, with three chains running west to east. The Grossglockner (3797m) is Austria's highest peak. Forming a natural barrier along the border with Italy are the Southern Limestone Alps. The most fertile land is in the Danube Valley. North of Linz is an area of forested hills; the only other relatively flat area is south-east of Graz.

CLIMATE

Average rainfall is 71cm per year. Maximum temperatures in Vienna are: January 1°C, April 15°C, July 25°C and October 14°C. Salzburg and Innsbruck match the maximum temperatures of Vienna, but are colder at night.

POPULATION & PEOPLE

Austria has a population of around 8.1 million, of whom 80% are Catholic. Vienna is the largest city (population 1.6 million), followed by Graz (242,000), Linz (190,000), Salzburg (145,000) and Innsbruck (111,000).

SOCIETY & CONDUCT

Traditional costumes are still worn in rural areas of Tirol. The best known form of dress for women is the *Dirndl*: pleated skirt, apron, and white, pleated corsage with full sleeves.

It is customary to greet people, even shop assistants, with the salute *Grüss Gott*, and to say *Auf Wiedersehen* before leaving. When you are introduced to someone, shake hands.

LANGUAGE

Austrians speak German, with pockets of Croatian speakers in Burgenland and Slovene speakers in Carinthia. English is widely understood in the main cities and tourist resorts. Knowledge of some German phrases is an asset; see the Language Guide at the back of the book for pronunciation guidelines and useful words and phrases.

Facts for the Visitor

HIGHLIGHTS

Vienna is the Habsburgs' legacy to the world, offering awe-inspiring public buildings, art treasures and music – don't miss a trip to the opera. Salzburg is another shrine to music, and its baroque skyline is breathtaking. Enjoy the beautiful scenery and sightseeing in Innsbruck.

SUGGESTED ITINERARIES

Three days
  Explore Vienna.
One week
  Spend four days in Vienna, two days in Salzburg and one day visiting the Salzkammergut.
Two weeks
  Spend five days in Vienna, including a day trip by train or boat to Melk's monastery; three days in Salzburg, two days in Salzkammergut, two days in Innsbruck and two days at one of the Alpine resorts.

PLANNING
When to Go

Summer sightseeing and winter sports make Austria a favoured year-round destination, though Alpine resorts are pretty dead in May and November. High season is in July and August and (in ski resorts) Christmas to late February.

Maps

Freytag & Berndt of Vienna publishes good maps in varying scales. Its 1:100,000 series and 1:50,000 blue series have proved popular with hikers.

TOURIST OFFICES
Local Tourist Offices

Helpful local tourist offices – usually called *Kurverein* or *Verkehrsamt* – are found in most towns and villages. At least one of the staff will speak English. Many offices have a room-finding service. Maps are always available and usually free.

Tourist Offices Abroad

Austrian National Tourist Office (ANTO) branches include:

Australia (☎ 02-9299 3621, fax 9299 3808,
  ℮ oewsyd@world.net) 1st floor,
  36 Carrington St, Sydney, NSW 2000
UK (☎ 020-7629 0461, fax 7499 6038,
  ℮ info@anto.co.uk) 14 Cork St,
  London W1A 2QB
USA (☎ 212-944 6880, fax 730 4568,
  ℮ info@oewnyc.com) PO Box 1142,
  New York, NY 10108-1142

AUSTRIA

EMBASSIES & CONSULATES
Austrian Embassies Abroad
Australia (☎ 02-6295 1533, fax 6239 6751) 12 Talbot St, Forrest, Canberra, ACT 2603

Canada (☎ 613-789 1444, fax 789 3431) 445 Wilbrod St, Ottawa, Ontario KIN 6M7

New Zealand (☎ 04-499 6393, fax 499 6392) Austrian Consulate, Level 2, Willbank House, 587 Willis St, Wellington – does not issue visas or passports; contact the Australian office for these services

UK (☎ 020-7235 3731, fax 7235 8025) 18 Belgrave Mews West, London SW1X 8HU

USA (☎ 202-895 6700, fax 895 6750) 3524 International Court NW, Washington, DC 20008

Embassies in Austria
The following embassies are in Vienna (area code ☎ 01):

Australia (☎ 512 85 80-0) 04, Mattiellistrasse 2-4

Canada (☎ 531 38-3000) 01, Laurenzerberg 2

UK (☎ 716 13-0) 03, Jaurèsgasse 12

USA (☎ 313 39) 09, Boltzmanngasse 16

MONEY
The Austrian Schilling (AS, or ÖS in German) is divided into 100 Groschen. There are coins to the value of one, five, 10, 25, 50, 100 and 500 Schillings, and for two, five, 10 and 50 Groschen. Banknotes come in denominations of AS20, AS50, AS100, AS500, AS1000 and AS5000. Austria is part of the EU monetary union, and dual pricing (in Schillings and euros) is the norm.

Exchange rates can vary between banks, so it pays to shop around. Always check commission rates first – they're usually high, but some are extortionate. Many banks give cash advances with a Visa card, Eurocard or MasterCard. Austria is well stocked with Bankomats (ATMs).

Exchange Rates

country	unit		Schilling
Australia	A$1	=	AS8.83
Canada	C$1	=	AS10.27
euro	€1	=	AS13.76
France	1FF	=	AS2.10
Germany	DM1	=	AS7.04
Japan	¥100	=	AS14.02
New Zealand	NZ$1	=	AS6.85
UK	UK£1	=	AS22.90
USA	US$1	=	AS15.23

Costs
Expenses are average for Western Europe, with the highest prices in big cities and ski resorts. Budget travellers can get by on AS450 a day, after rail-card costs. *Minimum* prices are around AS140/250 for a hostel/hotel and AS60/100 for a lunch/dinner, excluding drinks.

Tipping
It is customary to tip 5% in restaurants (make sure to pay the server direct, don't leave it on the table). Taxi drivers will expect tips of 10%.

POST & COMMUNICATIONS
Post
Postcards/letters within Austria cost AS6.50/7. Letters (up to 20g) cost AS6.50/7 nonpriority/priority to the rest of Europe and AS7.50/13 to the rest of the world. Stamps are sold at post offices and at some *Tabak* (tobacco) shops.

Telephone & Fax
Telekom Austria has two zones for national calls – Regional-Zone (up to 50km) and Österreich-Zone (over 50km), which is about 300% more expensive. The minimum tariff in phone boxes is AS2. A three-minute call to the USA is AS24. The national and international cheap rate is available from 6 pm to 8 am, and at weekends. Look out for cut-price telephone call centres in cities.

Most post offices have telephones outside. You'll save money with a *Telefon-Wertkarte* (phonecard) – for AS95/190 you get AS100/200 worth of calls.

Phone Quirks A peculiar complication of Austrian phone numbers is that telephone extensions (DW) are often tacked onto the main telephone number, and it's necessary to dial these to get through. Often this extension will be for a fax number. In this chapter, any telephone extensions are separated from the main number by a hyphen, and fax extensions are shown only by a hyphen and the extension number (ie, you'd have to dial the main number first to reach it). Sometimes the fax number is a completely different number, but still with an extension, in which case the whole number is shown.

INTERNET RESOURCES

There is public Internet access in most towns – see the city sections.

The Austrian National Tourist Office Web site (www.austria-tourism.at) has plenty of useful stuff, while the Austrian Press & Information Service (www.austria.org) offers weekly news and visa information.

BOOKS

For more detailed information see Lonely Planet's *Austria* and *Vienna* guides. *The Xenophobe's Guide to the Austrians* by Louis James is amusing. Graham Greene's famous spy story *The Third Man*, and John Irving's *Setting Free the Bears*, are both set in Austria.

WOMEN TRAVELLERS

Women should experience no special problems. Physical violations and verbal harassment are less common than in many other countries. Vienna has a Rape Crisis Hotline: ☎ 01-717 19.

GAY & LESBIAN TRAVELLERS

Public attitudes to homosexuality are less tolerant than in most other Western European countries, except perhaps in Vienna. A good information centre in Vienna is Rosa Lila (☎ 01-586 8150), 06, Linke Wienziele 102. The age of consent for gay men is 18; for everyone else it's 14. Vienna has a Pride march, the Rainbow Parade, on the last Saturday in June.

DISABLED TRAVELLERS

Many sights and venues have wheelchair ramps. Local tourist offices usually have information for the disabled; the Vienna office, for example, has a free 90-page booklet.

DANGERS & ANNOYANCES

Dial ☎ 133 for the police, ☎ 144 for an ambulance, or ☎ 122 in the event of fire.

BUSINESS HOURS

Shops usually open at 8 am and close between 6 and 7.30 pm on weekdays, between 1 and 5 pm on Saturday; they generally close for up to two hours at noon, except in big cities. Banking hours can vary but are commonly 9 am to 12.30 pm and 1.30 to 3 pm weekdays, with late closing on Thursday.

PUBLIC HOLIDAYS & SPECIAL EVENTS

Public holidays are 1 and 6 January, Easter Monday, 1 May, Ascension Day, Whit Monday, Corpus Christi, 15 August, 26 October, 1 November, and 8, 25 and 26 December.

Vienna and Salzburg have almost continuous music festivals (see their Special Events entries). Linz has the Bruckner Festival in September. Religious holidays are noted for colourful processions. Look out for *Fasching* (Shrovetide carnival) in early February, maypoles on 1 May, Midsummer Night's celebrations on 21 June, the autumn cattle roundup at the end of October, and St Nicholas Day parades on 5 and 6 December.

ACCOMMODATION

It's wise to book ahead in July and August and at Christmas and Easter. Unless otherwise noted, the price of breakfast is *included* in places listed in this chapter.

Austria has over 400 camping grounds, but most close in winter. They charge AS40 to AS70 per person, plus from AS40 for a tent. The Austrian Camping Club (☎ 01-711 99) is at Schubertring 1-3, A-1010 Vienna.

A cheap and widely available option is a private room for AS160 to AS280 per person – look for 'Zimmer frei' signs.

Most *Jugendherbergen* (hostels) are part of the Hostelling International (HI) network, and charge AS140 to AS240 for dorms. Except in a few private hostels, non-HI members pay a surcharge of AS40 per night for a guest card; after six nights you get full HI membership. Some hostels accept reservations by telephone. For hostel information contact Österreichischer Jugendherbergswerk (☎ 01-533 18 33, ✉ oejhw@oejhw.or.at), 01, Helferstorferstrasse 4, Vienna. Web site: www.oejhw.or.at.

Hotel prices in major cities (especially Vienna) are significantly higher than in rural areas. In many resorts (rarely in towns) a guest card is issued to people who stay overnight. They offer useful discounts and are well worth having.

FOOD & DRINKS

The main meal is taken at midday. Most restaurants offer a *Tagesteller* or *Tagesmenu* (menu of the day), which gives the best value for money. The cheapest deals around are at *mensas* (university cafeterias); these

AUSTRIA

are listed only if they are open to all. Almost as cheap are lunch menus at numerous Chinese restaurants. For a fast snack, head for a *Würstel Stand* (sausage stand).

Austrian soups are good, often with *Knödel* (dumplings) and pasta added. *Wiener Schnitzel* is a veal or pork cutlet coated in breadcrumbs. *Huhn* (chicken) is also popular. Paprika is used to flavour several dishes including *Gulasch* (beef stew). Look out for regional dishes such as *Tiroler Bauernschmaus*, a selection of meats served with sauerkraut, potatoes and dumplings. Austrians eat a lot of meat; vegetarians will have a fairly tough time finding suitable or varied dishes.

Famous Austrian desserts include *Strudel* (baked dough filled with a variety of fruits) and *Salzburger Nockerl* (egg, flour and sugar pudding).

Be sure to visit a coffee house. A *Kaffeehaus*, traditionally preferred by men, offers games such as chess and billiards and serves wine, beer and light meals. A *Café Konditorei* attracts more women and typically has a salon look.

Austria is famous for its lager beer; some well-known brands include Gösser, Schwechater, Stiegl and Zipfer. Also try *Weizenbier* (wheat beer). Beer is usually served in 0.5L or 0.3L glasses; in eastern Austria these are respectively called a *Krügerl* and a *Seidel*.

Getting There & Away

The airports at Vienna, Linz, Graz, Salzburg, Innsbruck and Klagenfurt all receive international flights. Vienna is the busiest airport, with several daily, nonstop flights to major transport hubs such as Amsterdam, Berlin, Frankfurt, London, Paris and Zürich.

Buses depart from London's Victoria Station five days a week (daily in summer), arriving in Vienna 22 hours later (UK£111 return). See the Vienna Getting There & Away section for services to Eastern Europe. Vienna and Salzburg are stops on Busabout routes (see the Getting Around chapter).

Austria has excellent rail connections to all important destinations. Vienna is the main hub (see its Getting There & Away section for details). Salzburg has at least hourly trains to Munich (AS298, two hours) with onward connections north. Express services to Italy go via Innsbruck or Villach; trains to Slovenia are routed through Graz. Generally, reserving 2nd-class train seats in Austria costs AS40. Supplements sometimes apply on international trains.

Getting Around

BUS
Efficient yellow or orange/red buses are run by the post office or Austrian Railways. Either way, they're called *Bundesbus*. Advance reservations are possible, but sometimes you can only buy tickets from the drivers. Fares are comparable to train fares.

TRAIN
Eurail and Inter-Rail passes are valid on the vast state rail network, but generally not on private rail lines. Trains are expensive (eg, AS178 for 100km, AS300 for 200km). Austria has withdrawn most of its rail passes. You could consider buying a Domino Pass (see the Getting Around chapter) – the Austrian version costs UK£68/108 for three/eight days. The VORTEILS card (AS1290, valid one year) reduces fares by 50% – fine if you stay a while, but forget it for short stays. Two or more people travelling together can get fare reductions with the 1 Plus-Ticket.

In this chapter, fares quoted are for 2nd class. Buy tickets at a *Bahnhof* (train station) or *Hauptbahnhof* (main train station), or on the train for an extra AS30. Austrian stations usually close overnight to stop people sleeping in the waiting rooms; an exception is Salzburg Hauptbahnhof.

CAR & MOTORCYCLE
Austria charges an annual fee for using its motorways, though tourists can opt to buy a weekly pass (AS70) or two-month pass (AS150).

Austrians drive on the right (it's best if you do likewise). Roads are generally good, but take it carefully on difficult mountain routes. In addition to the motorway tax, there are hefty toll charges for some mountain tunnels. The penalty for drink-driving

AUSTRIA

(over 0.05% BAC) is a substantial on-the-spot fine and confiscation of your licence. Speed limits are 50km/h in towns, 130km/h on motorways and 100km/h on other roads. Snow chains are highly recommended in winter. Many city streets have restricted parking (called blue zones); parking is free and unrestricted outside the specified times.

Dial ☎ 120 for emergency assistance. The Austrian Automobile Club (ÖAMTC; ☎ 01-711 99-0) is at Schubertring 1-3, A-1010 Vienna.

BICYCLE

Bicycles can be hired from most train stations for AS180 per day, or AS120 with a train ticket valid for that day or after 3 pm the previous day. There's a surcharge of AS90 to return bikes to a different station. You can take bikes on slow trains (AS40/90 for a day/week ticket); on fast trains they might have to go as registered luggage (AS90).

Vienna

☎ 01

Vienna (Wien) has jaw-dropping architecture, world-renowned museums and an enviable musical tradition. The city that invented the waltz is hardly staid – in Vienna you can party all night if you want to.

The Habsburgs settled in Vienna in 1278 and made it the capital of the Austrian empire. The city flourished under their strong leadership, despite being dragged into various European conflicts and withstanding attacks by the Turks in 1529 and 1683. Vienna's 'golden years' as the cultural heart of Europe were the 18th and 19th centuries, when Strauss, Mozart, Beethoven, Brahms and Schubert made their homes here. Numerous be-wigged Mozart lookalikes, touting overpriced concert tickets, will remind you of this glorious past.

Orientation

Many of the historic sights are in the old city, the *Innere Stadt*, which is encircled by a series of boulevards known as the Ring or Ringstrasse. Stephansdom (St Stephen's Cathedral) is the Innere Stadt's principal landmark.

The main train stations are Franz Josefs Bahnhof to the north, Westbahnhof to the

west and Südbahnhof to the south; transferring between them is easy.

In Vienna, a number *before* a street name denotes the district, of which there are 23. District 1 (the Innere Stadt) is mostly within the Ring. Generally speaking, the higher the district number, the farther it is from the city centre.

Information

Tourist Offices The main tourist office is at 01, Am Albertinaplatz, and there is extensive free literature on hand, including good maps and the youth-oriented *10 good reasons for Vienna*. The office is open 9 am to 7 pm daily. The tourist office at the airport is open 8.30 am to 9 pm daily. Telephone and postal inquiries are best addressed to the Vienna Tourist Board (☎ 211 14, fax 216 84 92, ✉ inquiries@info.wien.at), Obere Augartenstrasse 40, A-1025 Wien.

Information and room reservations (AS40 commission) are available in Westbahnhof and Südbahnhof, from 6.30 or 7 am until 9 or 10 pm daily.

Tourist offices and hotels sell the Vienna Card (AS210), which gives museum discounts and 72 hours of free local transport.

Money Bankomat ATMs allow cash advances with Visa, Eurocard and MasterCard, and train stations have extended hours for exchanging money. American Express (☎ 515 40-777), 01, Kärntner Strasse 21-23, is open 9 am to 5.30 pm weekdays, to noon Saturday.

Post & Telephone The main post office (Hauptpost 1010) is at 01, Fleischmarkt 19. Additional post offices are at Südbahnhof and Franz Josefs Bahnhof.

For information on hyphenated phone numbers see the Telephone & Fax section earlier in this chapter.

Email & Internet Access Jugend-Info (☎ 17 79), a youth information centre at 01, Babenbergerstrasse 1, can supply a full listing. Some places are free, like Haus Wien Energie (☎ 581 05 00), 06, Mariahilfer Strasse 63, open shop hours. Café Stein (☎ 319 72 411), 09, Währinger Strasse 6, charges AS65 for 30 minutes (10 am to 11 pm daily).

AUSTRIA

VIENNA (WIEN)

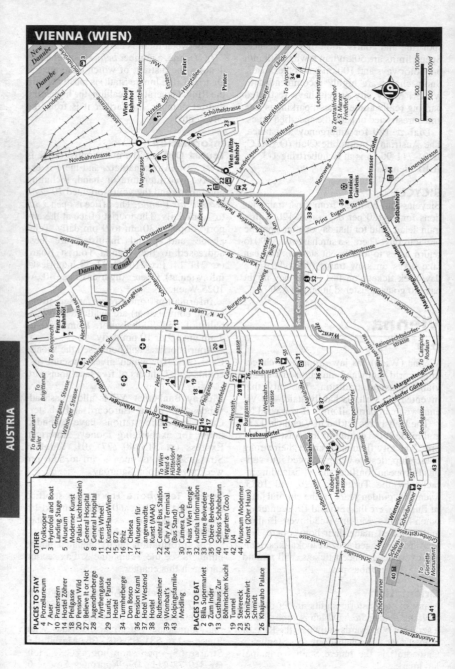

1000m
500
0
1000yd
500
0

See Central Vienna Map

PLACES TO STAY
4 Porzellaneum
7 Auer
10 Praterstern
14 Hostel Zöhrer
18 Pfeilgasse
20 Pension Wild
27 Believe It or Not Jugendherberge
28 Myrthengasse
29 Lauria; Panda Hostel
34 Turmherberge Don Bosco
36 Pension Kraml
37 Hotel Westend
38 Hostel Ruthensteiner
39 Wombat's
43 Kolpingsfamilie Meidling

PLACES TO EAT
9 Billa Supermarket
13 Zum Inder
19 Gasthaus Zur Böhmischen Kuchl
23 Tunnel
25 Steiereck Schmidt
26 Schnitzelwirt Schmidt
26 Khajuraho Palace

OTHER
1 Volksoper
3 Hydrofoil and Boat Landing Stage
5 Museum Moderner Kunst (Palais Liechtenstein)
6 General Hospital
8 General Hospital
11 Ferris Wheel
12 KunstHausWien
15 B72
16 Rhiz
17 Chelsea
21 Museum für angewandte Kunst (MAK)
22 Central Bus Station
24 City Air Terminal (Bus Stand)
30 Camera Club
31 Haus Wien Energie
32 Austria Information
33 Untere Belvedere
35 Obere Belvedere
40 Schloss Schönbrunn
41 Tiergarten (Zoo)
42 U4
44 Museum Moderner Kunst (20er Haus)

Travel Agencies ÖKISTA (☎ 401 48-0, 🖃 info@oekista.co.at) 09, Garnisongasse 7, is a specialist in student and budget fares. It's open 9 am to 6.30 pm weekdays. Other offices are at 09, Türkenstrasse 6 (☎ 401 48-7000) and 04, Karlsgasse 3 (☎ 502 43-0).

Bookshops The British Bookshop (☎ 512 19 45), 01, Weihburggasse 24-6, has the most English-language titles. Shakespeare & Co Booksellers (☎ 535 50 53), 01, Sterngasse 2, has new and second-hand books. Freytag & Berndt (☎ 533 85 85), 01, Kohlmarkt 9, stocks a vast selection of maps. Reisebuchladen (☎ 317 33 84), 09, Kolingasse 6, has many Lonely Planet guides.

Things to See & Do

Stephansdom From the State Opera, walk north up the pedestrian-only Kärntner Strasse, a walkway of plush shops, trees and cafes. It leads directly to Stephansplatz and Stephansdom (St Stephen's Cathedral). The latticework spire of this 13th-century Gothic masterpiece rises high above the city. Take the lift up the north tower (AS40) or the stairs up the higher south tower (AS30) for an impressive view.

Hofburg The Hofburg (Imperial Palace) has been periodically enlarged since the 13th century, resulting in the current mixture of architectural styles. The Spanish Riding School office is to the left within the entrance. Opposite are the **Kaiserappartements**, which cost AS80/60 to visit. Walk into the large courtyard, and go left into the Swiss Courtyard. Here you'll find the **Burgkapelle** (Royal Chapel) and the **Schatzkammer** (Imperial Treasury), which contains treasures spanning 1000 years, including the crown jewels. Entry is AS80/50, and it's closed Tuesday.

Schloss Schönbrunn This sumptuous 1440-room palace is open daily and can be reached by U-Bahn No 4. Self-guided tours of 22/40 rooms are AS95/125 (students under 26 AS80/105), including a personal audio guide in English. The interior is suitably majestic, with frescoed ceilings and crystal chandeliers. Mozart played his first royal concert in the Mirror Room at the ripe age of six. You can enjoy excellent views from the **Gloriette monument**, or visit the

maze (AS30 each; open April to October). The attractive **Tiergarten** (zoo) is also worth a look (AS120).

Schloss Belvedere This baroque palace is within walking distance of the Ring and has good views of the city. It houses the **Österreichische Galerie** (Austrian Gallery) in the two buildings that flank the spacious gardens. Untere (Lower) Belvedere (enter at Rennweg 6A) contains some elaborate baroque pieces, but the more important art collection is in Obere (Upper) Belvedere (enter at Prinz Eugen Strasse 27), with prime works by Gustav Klimt, Egon Schiele and other Austrian artists from the 19th and 20th centuries. It is open 10 am to 5 pm Tuesday to Sunday; combined entry is AS90/60.

Kunsthistorisches Museum The must-see Museum of Fine Arts, on Maria Theresien Platz, houses a vast collection of 16th- and 17th-century paintings, ornaments and glassware, and Greek, Roman and Egyptian antiquities. Rubens was appointed to the service of a Habsburg governor in Brussels, so it's not surprising that the Kunsthistorisches has one of the world's best collections of his works. There is also an unrivalled collection of paintings by Peter Brueghel the Elder.

The museum is open 10 am to 6 pm Tuesday to Sunday. The picture gallery closes at 9 pm on Thursday. Entry costs AS100/70.

Secession Building This 1898 Art Nouveau 'temple of art' at Friedrichstrasse 12 bears a delicate golden dome that deserves a better sobriquet than the description 'golden cabbage' accorded it by some Viennese. The 1902 exhibition here featured the famous 34m-long *Beethoven Frieze* by Klimt, which is in the basement. The rest of the building is devoted to contemporary art. It's open 10 am to 6 pm Tuesday to Sunday (to 8 pm Thursday). Entry is AS60/40.

KunstHausWien This extraordinary gallery at 03, Untere Weissgerberstrasse 13, was designed by Friedensreich Hundertwasser to house his own works of art. It features coloured ceramics, uneven floors, irregular corners and grass on the roof. His vivid paintings are equally distinctive. It is

AUSTRIA

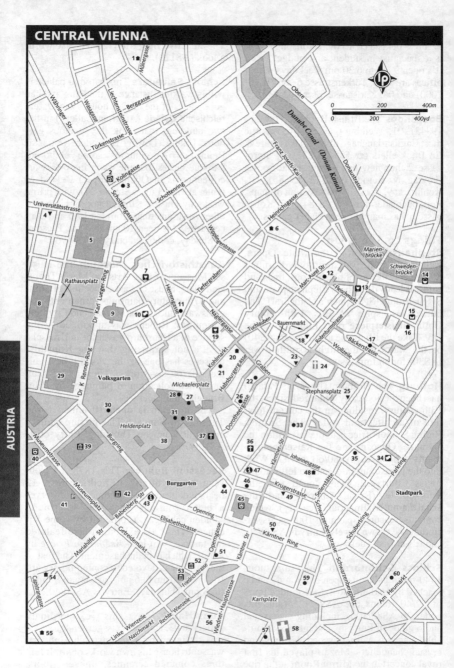

CENTRAL VIENNA

CENTRAL VIENNA

open 10 am to 7 pm daily. Entry is AS95/70 or AS160/120 including temporary exhibitions. Monday is half-price.

Other Museums For a bizarre take on anatomy check out the **Josephinium** at 09, Währinger Strasse 25 (closed weekends; AS20/10).

During the ongoing renovations to its usual premises, temporary exhibitions from the **Albertina** graphic arts collection are sited at the Akademiehof, at 01, Markatgasse 3 (closed Monday; AS70). The **Museum für angewandte Kunst** (MAK) is an impressive collection of applied arts at 01, Stubenring 5 (closed Monday; AS90/45).

The **Museum Moderner Kunst** displays modern art in two locations: Palais Liechtenstein, 09, Fürstengasse 1, and 20er Haus, 03, Arsenalstrasse 1 (closed Monday). Combined tickets are available but they're closed till December 2001.

Cemeteries Beethoven, Schubert, Brahms and Schönberg have memorial tombs in the **Zentralfriedhof** (Central Cemetery), 11, Simmeringer Hauptstrasse 232-244. Mozart also has a monument here, though he is buried in an unmarked grave in the **St Marxer Friedhof** (Cemetery of St Mark), 03, Leberstrasse 6-8.

Naschmarkt The Naschmarkt consists mainly of fruit, vegetable and meat stalls, plus a few clothing and curios stalls. Visit on Saturday, for the flea market. The market is at 06, Linke Wienzeile, and is open Monday to Saturday from 6 am to 6 pm.

Prater This large amusement park, a short walk from the Wien Nord train station, is dominated by a giant Ferris wheel, built in 1897, which featured prominently in *The Third Man* movie. Rides in the park cost AS15 to AS55, but it is also a great place to just have a wander. On Rondeau and Calafatti Platz there are colourful metal sculptures depicting humans caught up in strange hallucinogenic happenings.

Special Events

The cycle of musical events is unceasing. The Vienna Festival, from mid-May to mid-June, has a wide-ranging program of the arts. Contact Wiener Festwochen (☎ 589 22-22, fax -49), 06, Lehárgasse 11. Web site: www.festwochen.or.at.

Vienna's Summer of Music runs from mid-July to mid-September; contact Klang-Bogen (☎ 4000-8410), 01, Stadiongasse 9. Web site: www.klangbogen.at. Reduced student tickets go on sale at the venue 10 minutes before the performance.

AUSTRIA

At the end of June there are free rock, jazz and folk concerts in the Donauinselfest. The free open-air Opera Film Festival on Rathausplatz runs in July and August.

Vienna's traditional Christmas market, Christkindlmarkt, takes place out the front of the city hall between mid-November and 24 December.

Places to Stay

Vienna can be a nightmare for backpackers. Budget places are often full, especially in summer. Reserve ahead when possible. Tourist offices have lists of private rooms and camping grounds.

Camping *Wien West* (☎ 914 23 14; 14, Hüttelbergstrasse 80), is open all year except February. It costs AS68/40 per adult/tent, or AS75/45 in July and August. Two-/four-person bungalows are AS300/440. To get there, take U4 or the S-Bahn to Hütteldorf, then bus No 148 or 152. *Camping Rodaun* (☎ 888 41 54; 23, An der Au 2) is open from late March to mid-November and charges AS73/60 per adult/tent. Take S1 or S2 to Liesing then bus No 60A.

Hostels No hostels have invaded the imperial elegance of the Innere Stadt. One of the nearest is the HI *Jugendherberge Myrthengasse* (☎ 523 63 16, fax 523 58 49, ✉ hostel@chello.at; 07, Myrthengasse 7). Based in two buildings, it's efficiently run and has daytime check-in. All rooms have a private shower and bedside lights. Beds are AS170 in six- or four-bed dorms or AS200 in double rooms. Lunch or dinner is AS65 and laundry is AS50 per load. Curfew is at 1 am. Telephone reservations are accepted and strongly advised.

Friendly *Believe it or Not* (☎ 526 46 58; 07, Apartment 14, Myrthengasse 10) is a small private hostel. There are no signs outside, except on the doorbell. There's no breakfast; use the kitchen facilities instead. Beds are AS160 (AS110 November to Easter). There's no curfew.

Panda Hostel (☎ 522 53 53; 07, 3rd floor, Kaiserstrasse 77) also charges AS160 for hostel beds. There's a TV in every room, no breakfast but use of a kitchen. It's linked to *Lauria* (see Pensions & Hotels – Budget).

Hostel Zöhrer (☎ 406 07 30, fax 408 04 09, ✉ zoehrer@compuserve.com; 08,

Skodagasse 26) is a private hostel close to the Ring. Six- to eight-bed dorms are AS170 and doubles (bunk beds) are AS460, all with private shower. There's a kitchen; reception is open from 7.30 am to 10 pm. *Turmherberge Don Bosco* (☎ 713 14 94; 03, Lechnerstrasse 12), south-east of the Ring, is unrenovated but has a kitchen and the cheapest beds in town – AS80 without breakfast. Sheets are AS25. Reception is closed between noon and 5 pm and the hostel is open from March to November.

Two hostels, both of which open 24 hours, are near Westbahnhof. *Hostel Ruthensteiner* (☎ 893 42 02, fax 893 27 96, ✉ hostel.ruthensteiner@telecom.at; 15, Robert Hamerling Gasse 24) has large dorms for AS130 or AS145 (without sheets). Sheets are provided in the smaller dorms (AS169) and the singles/doubles (AS245/470). Breakfast costs AS29 and there's a kitchen. *Wombat's* (☎ 897 23 36, fax 897 25 77, ✉ wombats@chello.at; 15, Grangasse 6) is a new non-HI hostel, with a pub. Dorms/doubles are AS175/490 and breakfast is AS35.

Kolpingsfamilie Meidling (☎ 813 54 87, fax 812 21 30, ✉ office@wien12.kolping.at; 12, Bendlgasse 10-12) is near the Niederhofstrasse U6 stop. Dorm beds are AS130 to AS180. Non-HI members pay AS40 extra and don't get the guest stamp. Curfew is at midnight, though reception is open 24 hours.

Two large HI hostels lie in the suburbs. *Brigittenau* (☎ 332 82 94, fax 330 83 79, ✉ jgh1200@chello.at; 20, Friedrich Engels Platz 24), to the north (tram No, 31 or 33), has 24-hour reception. Dorms/doubles are AS170/400. *Hütteldorf-Hacking* (☎ 877 02 63, fax -2, ✉ jgh@wigast.com; 13, Schlossberggasse 8) has 307 beds and charges AS158/376 for dorms/doubles. The doors are locked from 9.30 am to 3 pm; take the U4 west from the city centre.

Student Residences These are available to travellers from July to September. The cheapest is *Porzellaneum* (☎ 317 72 82, fax -30; 09, Porzellangasse 30), with singles/doubles for AS190/380, without breakfast. Other *Studentenheime* to try are: *Pfeilgasse* (☎ 401 74, fax 401 76-20; 08, Pfeilgasse 4-6) and *Music Academy* (☎ 514 84 48; 01, Johannesgasse 8).

Pensions & Hotels – Budget *Lauria* (☎ 522 25 55, ✉ *lauria.apartments@ chello.at; 07, 3rd floor, Kaiserstrasse 77)* is in a residential building, close to transport and shops. It has friendly staff, kitchen facilities and TVs. Doubles cost from AS480, triples/quads are AS750/880.

Pension Wild (☎ 406 51 74, fax 402 21 68; 08, Langegasse 10) is central. 'Wild' is the family name, not a description. Singles/ doubles are AS490/590 and singles/ doubles/triples with private shower are AS590/790/1050. There are kitchens and reception is open 24 hours.

Kolping-Gästehaus (☎ 587 56 31-0, fax 586 36 30, ✉ reservierung@wien-zentral .kolping.at; 06, Gumpendorfer Strasse 39) has single rooms without/with shower for AS300/720. Doubles with shower are AS980. This is partially a student residence and feels like it. Book well ahead.

Auer (☎ 406 21 21, fax -4; 09, Lazarett- gasse 3) is friendly, pleasant and more Viennese in style. Singles/doubles start at AS370/560; doubles with shower are AS630.

Hotel Westend (☎ 597 67 29-0, fax -27; 06, Fügergasse 3) is close to Westbahnhof and has reasonable singles/doubles for AS355/625, or AS405/745 with shower. Reception is open 24 hours.

Pension Kraml (☎ 587 85 88, fax 586 75 73; 06, Brauergasse 5) is nearby. Small, friendly and family-run, it has singles/ doubles for AS340/640 and large doubles with private shower for AS700.

Quisisana (☎ 587 33 41, fax -33; 06, Windmühlgasse 6) is conveniently situated, with variable but good-value rooms. Singles/doubles are AS390/640 with shower, AS330/540 without.

Pension Falstaff (☎ 317 91 86, fax -4; 09, Müllnergasse 5) charges AS420/660 (AS30 to use the hall shower) or AS500/760 with private shower. It's convenient for tram D to the Ring and Nussdorf.

Praterstern (☎ 214 01 23, fax 214 78 80, ✉ hotelpraterstern@aon.at; 02, Mayer- gasse 6), east of the Ring, has a garden. Singles/doubles are AS330/585, or AS395/ 740 with shower.

Pensions & Hotels – Mid-Range The following are in the Innere Stadt. *Pension Nossek* (☎ 533 70 41, fax 535 36 46; 01,

Graben 17) has baroque-style singles (AS650 to AS850) and doubles (AS1250 to AS1600). *Schweizer Pension Solderer* (☎ 533 81 56, fax 535 64 69, ✉ schweizer .pension@gmx.at; 01, Heinrichsgasse 2) has clean singles/doubles from AS480/780 with hall shower, AS700/900 with private shower. *Hotel Post* (☎ 515 83-0, fax -808; 01, Fleischmarkt 24) has bright, renovated singles/doubles for AS880/1260, or AS490/ 840 without shower.

Places to Eat

Budget If you're self-catering, head to the train stations for Sunday or late-night shopping. The best value is the *Billa* supermarket at Franz Josefs Bahnhof, open 7 am to 7.30 pm daily.

Meals for AS35 to AS60 are offered at mensas. They're open to the public 11 am to 2 pm weekdays. The *University Mensa* (01, Universitätsstrasse 7) has an adjoining cafe open 8 am to 6 pm weekdays. The *Technical University Mensa* (04, Ressel- gasse 7-9) is also convenient. The *Music Academy Mensa* (01, Johannesgasse 8) is the only one inside the Ring.

Tunnel (08, Florianigasse 39) is another student haunt, open 9 am to 2 am daily. The food is satisfying and easy on the pocket (lunch specials AS45, big pizzas from AS60, salads from AS20). Its cellar bar has live music nightly from 9 pm (entry AS30).

Nearby is *Gasthaus Zur Böhmischen Kuchl* (08, Schlösselgasse 18), an atmospheric place for Czech and Slovak food from AS62 (closed weekends).

Restaurant Marché Movenpick (Ring- strassen Galerien, 01, Kärntner Ring 5-7) has help-yourself small salad/vegie plates from AS22, and self-select pizzas for AS65. It's open till 8 pm daily (7 pm Sunday).

Chinese restaurants are numerous and inexpensive. *Restaurant Siam* (01, Kruger- strasse 6) has Chinese lunches from AS59, and an all-you-can-eat lunch buffet for AS78. There are a few Indian restaurants about; *Zum Inder* (02, Praterstrasse 57) and *Khajuraho Palace* (07, Burggasse 64) have cheap lunch buffets.

Schnitzelwirt Schmidt (07, Neubaugasse 52) is a good place for a range of schnitzels (from AS65, plus garnishes). Service is sloppy but portions are ridiculously large. It's closed Sunday.

AUSTRIA

Mid-Range & Top End *Wrenkh* (☎ *533 15 26; 01, Bauernmarkt 10)* is a fairly up-market specialist vegetarian restaurant. Meticulously prepared dishes are AS95 to AS130 and it's open daily till midnight.

The creatively decorated *La Crêperie* (☎ *512 56 87; 01, Grünangergasse 10)* has meat and fish dishes (AS145 and up) and tasty savoury crepes (AS82 to AS225). It's closed weekday lunchtimes. *Restaurant Sailer* (☎ *479 21 21-0; 18, Gersthofer Strasse 14)* serves traditional Viennese dishes for around AS180. The quality and service are exceptional for the price.

The busy *DO & CO* (☎ *535 39 69; 01, Haas Haus, Stephansplatz 12)* has top views and superb international and oriental dishes (AS250 and up); book well ahead.

Coffee Houses *Café Museum* (01, Friedrichstrasse 6) is open 8 am to midnight daily and has chess, many newspapers and outside tables. *Café Bräunerhof* (01, Stallburggasse 2) offers free classical music from 3 to 6 pm on weekends and holidays. *Alt Wien* (01, Bäckerstrasse 9) is a rather dark coffee house by day and a good drinking venue by night. It's famed for its goulash (AS90 large, AS60 small).

Café Central (01, Herrengasse 14) has a fine ceiling and pillars, and piano music from 4 to 7 pm. Trotsky came here to play chess. The *Hotel Sacher Café* (01, Philharmonikerstrasse 4), behind the Staatsoper (State Opera), is a picture of opulence, and famous for its *Sacher Torte* (chocolate apricot cake; AS55). More arty and down to earth is *Café Hawelka* (01, Dorotheergasse 6). It's closed Tuesday.

Heurigen Identified by a green wreath or branch hanging over the door, *Heurigen* are wine taverns that only sell 'new' wine produced on the premises – usually for around AS28 per Viertel (0.25L). Many have inexpensive hot and cold buffets. Opening times are approximately 4 to 11 pm. Heurigen, concentrated in Vienna's wine-growing suburbs, are close together – it's best to pick a region and explore.

Heurigen in Nussdorf and Heiligenstadt are near the terminus of tram D. Down the road (bus No 38A from Heiligenstadt or tram No 38 from the Ring) is Grinzing, a large, lively area favoured by tour groups.

There are several good Heurigen where Cobenzlgasse and Sandgasse meet, notably *Reinprecht (19, Cobenzlgasse 22)*.

Stammersdorf (tram No 31) and Strebersdorf (tram No 32) are cheaper, quieter regions. In the city centre try *Esterházykeller (01, Haarhof 1)*, off Naglergasse.

Entertainment

The tourist office has copies of *Vienna Scene* and produces a monthly listing of events. Weekly magazines with extensive listings include *Wienside* (free), *City* (AS10) and *Falter* (AS28).

Cheap *Stehplatz* (standing-room) tickets are sold in the **Staatsoper**, **Volksoper**, **Burgtheater** and **Akademietheater**. Queue up for up to three hours in advance for major productions. These four venues also sell discount tickets (from AS50) to students aged under 27 (university ID necessary, plus ISIC card) one hour before performance time. The state ticket office, Bundestheaterverkassen (☎ 514 44-7880), 01, Goethegasse 1, charges no commission. Also try Wien Ticket (☎ 588 85) in the hut by the Staatsoper.

The famous Lipizzaner stallions strut their stuff in the **Spanish Riding School** in the Hofburg. Performances are sold out months in advance, so write to the Spanische Reitschule, Michaelerplatz 1, A-1010 Wien, or ask in the office about unclaimed tickets (sold 45 minutes before performances). You need to be pretty keen on horses to fork out AS250 to AS900 for a seat or AS200 for standing room. Tickets to watch moderately interesting training sessions (AS100) can be bought the same day; training is held 10 am to noon Tuesday to Friday, from mid-February to June and September to mid-December.

Classical Music Productions in the *Staatsoper* (State Opera) are lavish affairs. Seats cost from AS70 (restricted view) to AS2450. The Viennese take opera very seriously and dress accordingly (hint: leave your clown costume at home). There are no performances in July and August. The Vienna Philharmonic Orchestra performs in the *Musikverein*.

The Wiener Sängerknaben (Vienna Boys' Choir) sings Mass every Sunday (except in July and August) at 9.15 am in the

Hofburg's *Burgkapelle*. Seats are AS70 to AS380, but standing room is free. Join the queue by 8.30 am. The choir also performs in the *Konzerthaus*.

Bars & Nightclubs The following are in the Innere Stadt. *Krah Krah (Rabensteig 8)* has 50 different beers (from AS39) and is open daily from 11 am until late. *Volksgarten (Burgring 1)*, is three linked venues: a cafe with DJs, a disco with theme evenings, and a more formal 'Walzer Dancing' place. *Molly Darcy's Irish Pub (Teinfaltstrasse 6)* is one of several Irish bars.

Late-night bars are not limited to the Innere Stadt. *Chelsea (08, Lerchenfelder Gürtel 29-31)* has DJs, occasional indie bands, and English football via satellite. Bars within the same U-Bahn arches, heading north, are *Rhiz (08, Lerchenfelder Gürtel 37-38)*, favouring modern electronic music, and *B72 (08, Lerchenfelder Gürtel 72)*, featuring varied bands and DJs. *Camera Club (07, Neubaugasse)*, by Mariahilfer Strasse, is a dope-smoker's bar and disco with a modest cover charge.

One of the best-known discos in Vienna is *U4 (12, Schönbrunner Strasse 222)*, open daily from around 10 pm to 5 am. Each night has a different theme – Sunday is 1960s and 1970s music (AS60); Thursday is gay night.

Getting There & Away

Air There are daily nonstop flights to all major European destinations. Austrian Airlines (☎ 1789) has a city office at 01, Kärntner Ring 18.

Bus Most international departures go from the central bus station at Wien Mitte, including several daily buses to Budapest, starting at 7 am (AS350, 3½ hours). Buses to Prague depart at 7 am daily (2 pm on Friday and Sunday) from 01, Rathausplatz 5 (AS325, five hours). The Eurolines counter (☎ 712 04 53) at Wien Mitte, open noon to 9 pm daily, sells all tickets.

Train Not all destinations are exclusively serviced by one station, so check at the train stations or call ☎ 1717.

Westbahnhof has trains to Western and northern Europe and western Austria. Hourly services head to Salzburg, and some continue to Munich and terminate in Paris (14½ hours total). To Zürich, there are two day trains (AS1122, nine hours) and one night train that departs at 9.15 pm (AS1102, plus charge for fold-down seat/couchette). A direct overnight train goes to Bucharest (18 hours, departs 8.05 pm). Eight trains a day go to Budapest (AS440, 3½ hours).

Südbahnhof has trains to Italy (eg, Rome, via Venice and Florence), Slovakia, the Czech Republic, Hungary and Poland, and southern Austria.

Franz Josefs Bahnhof and Wien Mitte Bahnhof handle local trains only.

Hitching Mitzfahrzentrale Josefstadt (☎ 408 22 10), 08, Daungasse 1a, links hitchhikers and drivers. It's open 7 to 8 pm daily but telephone ahead to check availability before going to the office. There are usually lots of cars going into Germany. Examples of fares include: Salzburg AS250, Innsbruck AS370, Frankfurt AS500 and Munich AS350.

Boat Fast hydrofoils travel eastward in summer to Bratislava (1½ hours, Wednesday to Sunday) for AS240/370 one way/return; and Budapest (5½ hours, daily), AS780/1100. Make bookings at G Glaser (☎ 726 08 201), 02, Handelskai 265, or DDSG Blue Danube (☎ 588 80-0, fax -440), 01, Friedrichstrasse 7.

Getting Around

To/From the Airport Wien Schwechat airport (☎ 7007-2233) is 19km from the city centre. There are buses every 20 or 30 minutes to/from the city air terminal at the Hotel Hilton. Buses also run every 30 or 60 minutes from Westbahnhof and Südbahnhof (AS70; not from midnight to 5.30 am). It's cheaper to take the S7 line (every 30 minutes; AS38) from Wien Mitte. A taxi should cost about AS430.

Public Transport Tickets are valid for trains, trams, buses, the underground (U-Bahn) and S-Bahn trains. Single tickets cost AS22 at machines on buses and trams or AS19 at ticket machines in U-Bahn stations. All advance-purchase tickets must be validated before use, and you may change lines on the same trip. Fare dodgers pay an on-the-spot fine of AS560, plus the fare.

AUSTRIA

Stunden-Netzkarte (daily passes) are a better deal: AS60 for 24 hours or AS150 for 72 hours. A Monday to Sunday pass costs AS155 (buy from Tabak shops). Austrian and European rail passes are valid on the S-Bahn only.

Public transport finishes around midnight, but there's also an excellent night bus service around the Ring and to the suburbs. Tickets are AS15 (day tickets/passes not valid). There are plans for the city to offer free bike loans – inquire at the tourist office.

The Danube Valley

The Wachau section of the Danube (Donau), between Krems and Melk, is the river's most scenic stretch, with idyllic wine-growing villages and imposing fortresses at nearly every bend. DDSG Blue Danube (☎ 01-588 80-0, fax -440), 01 Friedrichstrasse 7 in Vienna, offers various trips along the Wachau. A short single/return trip costs AS100/140; the full trip from Melk to Krems (1¾ hours) or Krems to Melk (2¾ hours) costs AS200 one way or AS270 return. Boats sail from early April to late October. DDSG carries bicycles free of charge.

Ardagger (☎ 07479-64 64) connects Linz and Krems three times a week in summer. G Glaser (☎ 01-726 08 201), 02 Handelskai 265 in Vienna, does all the above trips, and its prices for Wachau tours slightly undercut DDSG's rates: Krems to Melk is AS190 one way or AS260 return.

KREMS
☎ 02732
The historic town of Krems reclines on the north bank of the Danube, surrounded by terraced vineyards. Wander the connecting cobbled streets of Landstrasse in Krems and Steiner Landstrasse in the suburb of Stein, 2km west. Krems' **Dominikanerkirche** (Dominican church) displays religious and modern art plus wine-making artefacts.

Midway between Krems and Stein is the tourist office (☎ 826 76, ✉ austropa.krems@netway.at), Undstrasse 6).

Places to Stay
Camping Donau (☎ 844 55, *Wiedengasse 7*) is near the boat station. The HI *Jugendherberge* (☎ 834 52, *Ringstrasse 77*) has

excellent facilities for cyclists. Both are open around April to October. In Stein, try *Gästehaus Einzinger* (☎ 823 16, *Steiner Landstrasser 82*). Singles/doubles with bathroom are AS350/700.

Getting There & Away
Infrequent buses to Melk (AS74, 65 minutes) leave from outside the train station. Trains to Vienna (AS133, one hour) arrive at Franz Josefs Bahnhof.

DÜRNSTEIN
☎ 02711
West of Krems, reached by boat or rail, lies picturesque Dürnstein. Ascend to the Kuenringerburg ruins for a sweeping view of the river. This castle is where King Richard the Lionheart of England was imprisoned in 1192. Dürnstein offers cheap accommodation, restaurants and good wine taverns. Find out more at the tourist office (☎ 200) or the Rathaus (☎ 219).

MELK
☎ 02752
Melk and its imposing monastery-fortress are essential stops on the Wachau. **Stift Melk** (AS70/35), the hill-top monastery, dominates the town and offers excellent views. A guided tour (an extra AS20) is well worth taking. In the high season (the Saturday before Palm Sunday to All Saints' Day) it's open 9 am to 5 or 6 pm daily. In winter the monastery can only be visited by guided tour (☎ 555-232 for information).

Orientation & Information
From the train station, walk 50m down Bahnhofstrasse to the post office (you can change money here). Turn right for the HI hostel or carry straight on, taking the Bahngasse path, for the central Rathausplatz. To the right is the tourist office (☎ 23 07-32), Babenbergerstrasse 1 (closed from November to March).

Places to Stay & Eat
Camping Melk, open from March to October, is on the west bank of the canal that joins the Danube. It's AS45 per adult plus AS35 per tent. Reception is in the restaurant *Melker Fährhaus* (☎ 32 91, *Kolomaniau 3*).

The HI *Jugendherberge* (☎ 526 81, fax 542 57, *Abt Karl Strasse 42*) has four-bed dorms for AS144 (AS119 for those aged under 19), plus a AS25 surcharge for single-night stays. Reception is closed from 10 am to 5 pm, and the hostel is closed from November to mid-March.

Gasthof Weisses Lamm (☎ *540 85, Linzer Strasse 7*) has a few singles/doubles for AS350/550. On the premises is Pizzeria Venezia (open daily), with many tasty pizzas starting at AS60. *Gasthof Goldener Stern* (☎ *522 14, fax -4, Sterngasse 17*) provides slightly cheaper accommodation, and has a restaurant serving affordable Austrian food.

Getting There & Away
Trains to Vienna Westbahnhof (AS150, 70 minutes) are direct or via St Pölten. There's bicycle hire in the train station. Boats leave from the canal by Pionierstrasse, 400m to the rear of the monastery.

LINZ
☎ 0732
The provincial capital of Upper Austria has a picturesque old-town centre. It's a shame about the belching smokestacks on the outskirts of town.

Orientation & Information
The tourist office (☎ 7070-1777) on Hauptplatz (the main square) has a free room-finding service and is open to 6 or 7 pm daily. From the train station (which is on the main Vienna-Salzburg line) walk right (east), then turn left at the far side of the park and continue along Landstrasse for 10 minutes; alternatively, save your legs and catch tram No 3.

Things to See & Do
From Hauptplatz, turn into Hofgasse and climb the hill to **Schloss Linz**. The castle, dating from AD 799, provides a good view of Linz's many church spires and houses a museum (closed Monday; AS50).

The neo-Gothic **Neuer Dom** (New Cathedral), built in 1855, features a graceless exterior and exceptional stained-glass windows, including one depicting the history of the town.

The **Neue Galerie**, Blütenstrasse 15, on the Danube's north bank, exhibits modern German and Austrian art (closed Sunday; AS60/30). Nearby, the **Ars Electronica Center** reveals interactive computer wizardry and

provides free Internet access. Opening hours are 10 am to 7 pm Wednesday to Sunday (AS80, students AS40).

Places to Stay
There is a camping ground south-east of town at *Pichlinger See* (☎ *30 53 14, Wiener Bundesstrasse 937*), or another at *Pleschinger See* (☎ *24 78 70*), which is a protected area (no motor vehicles allowed), on the north bank.

The HI *Jugendgästehaus* (☎ *66 44 34, fax -75, Stanglhofweg 3*), near the Linz Stadium, has singles/doubles for AS343/486, and four-bed dorms for AS173 per person. Morning check-in is possible during the week; on the weekend it's from 6 pm.

The HI *Landesjugendherberge* (☎ *73 70 78, fax -15, Blütenstrasse 19-23*), on the north bank, has two- to five-bed rooms and charges AS130 per person, plus an extra AS25 for breakfast. Take the lift within the multistorey car park. There's daytime check-in on weekdays. The HI *Jugendherberge* (☎ *77 87 77, fax 78 17 28 94, Kapuzinerstrasse 14*) is small, near the centre of town, and is a more personal experience. Beds are AS190 for people over 19 and AS160 for those under 19. Check-in is from 5 to 8 pm daily, and it's closed from November to March.

Goldenes Dachl (☎ *77 58 97, Hafnerstrasse 27*), one block away from the Neuer Dom, has basic singles/doubles for AS260/460, without breakfast and using the hall showers. Doubles with shower are AS520. Reception is closed till 5 pm on Saturday, all day on Sunday and from 2 to 5 pm on weekdays.

Places to Eat
For self-caterers there is a *Mondo supermarket* at Blumauerplatz, by the start of Landstrasse. One of the cheapest sit-down places is *Schnitzel Express* on Hauptstrasse, open to 10 pm daily. *Mangolds* (*Hauptplatz 3*) is a self-service vegetarian restaurant, open 11 am to 8 pm (to 5 pm Saturday; closed Sunday). *Josef Stadtbräu* (*Landstrasse 49*) occupies several rooms and has a big beer garden. The all-you-can-eat weekday brunches cost AS88. *Café Ex-Blatt* (*Waltherstrasse 15*) is a drinking joint favoured by the student population (closed weekends till 6 pm).

AUSTRIA

The South

GRAZ
☎ 0316

Graz is the capital of Styria, a province characterised by mountains and dense forests. In former times Graz was an important bulwark against invading Turks; today, it is fast becoming an essential stop on the tourist trail.

Orientation & Information

Graz is dominated by the Schlossberg, the castle hill that rises over the medieval town centre. The river Mur cuts a north-south path west of the hill, dividing the old centre from the main train station. Tram Nos 3, 6 and 14 run from the station to Hauptplatz. The bus station is at Andreas Hofer Platz.

The tourist office in the main train station is open 9 am to 6 pm Monday to Friday, March to December and till 6 pm Saturday in July and August . The station also has bike rental and currency exchange. The main tourist office (☎ 80 75-0, ✉ info@graztourismus.at), Herrengasse 16, is open till 6 pm weekdays, 3 pm weekends.

Café Zentral, Andreas Hofer Platz, has Internet access (AS60 for one hour), as does the Jugendgästehaus (AS1 for two minutes).

Things to See & Do

Paths wind up the **Schlossberg** from all sides. The climb takes less than 30 minutes and repays the effort with excellent views. Otherwise public-transport tickets (AS20) are valid on the Schlossbergbahn, a train that runs from Sackstrasse up the Schlossberg. Running beneath the hill is a pedestrian tunnel showing WWII shelters (free).

The nearby **Stadtpark** (city park) is a relaxing place to sit or wander. The **cathedral**, on the corner of Hofgasse and Bürgergasse, is worth a look, as is the impressive baroque **Mausoleum** next door, resting place of Ferdinand II and several other Habsburgs (AS10/5; closed Sunday).

The **Landeszeughaus** (armoury), Herrengasse 16, houses an incredible array of gleaming armour and crude weapons, enough to equip about 30,000 soldiers (AS80/60; closed Monday and January/February).

Schloss Eggenberg is 4km west of the centre (take tram No 1). The **Prunkräume** (state rooms) of this opulent 17th-century residence can be visited by guided tour. The palace is closed Monday and from November to March. Tickets (AS80/60) include two on-site museums.

Places to Stay

Camping Central (☎ 28 18 31, *Martinhofstrasse 3*) is open from April to October, and costs AS295 for a two-person site, including swimming pool entry. It's about 6km south-west of the city centre; take bus No 32 from Jakominiplatz.

The HI *Jugendgästehaus* (☎ 71 48 76, *fax -88, Idlhofgasse 74*) has four-bed dorms for AS230, and singles/doubles for AS325/550. These all have private shower/toilet, but the larger dorms in the basement (AS155) don't. Reception is open from 7 am to 10 pm (closed 10 am to 5 pm on weekends and holidays), and there's always daytime access.

Five minutes from the station is *Hotel Strasser* (☎ 71 39 77, *fax 71 68 56*, ✉ *hotel.strasser@noten.com, Eggenberger Gürtel 11*). It has pleasant singles/doubles for AS480/690 with private shower, or AS380/590 without. Reach *Gasthof Kokol* (☎/*fax 68 43 20, Thalstrasse 3*) by bus No 40 from Jakominiplatz or No 85 from the train station. Rooms cost AS390/640 with bathroom, or AS240/480 without (reservations advised). On weekends, reception closes from 1 to 6 pm.

Places to Eat

The *University Mensa* (*Schubertstrasse 2-4*) offers main meals for AS39 to AS61. It's open 8.30 am to 2.30 pm Monday to Friday, and has breakfasts for AS29.

Girardikeller (*Leonhardstrasse 28*) is a cellar bar with cheap food – the weekday special is just AS50, and pizzas with seven toppings are AS65. It's open daily from 5 pm (6 pm on weekends) till 2 am. Vegetarians can eat for a similarly low price at both *Salateria* (*Leonhardstrasse 18*), which closes at 7 pm (5 pm Friday) and over the weekend, and at *Mangolds Vollwert Restaurant* (*Griesgasse 11*), which closes at 8 pm weekdays, 4 pm on Saturday and all day Sunday.

Mohrenwirt (*Mariahilfer Strasse 16*) is a typical small Gasthof with snacks and meals from AS20 to AS90 (open Saturday

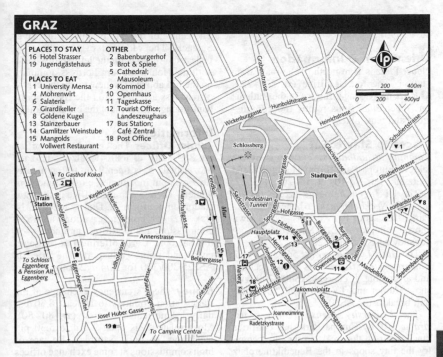

GRAZ

PLACES TO STAY
16 Hotel Strasser
19 Jugendgästehaus

PLACES TO EAT
1 University Mensa
4 Mohrenwirt
6 Salateria
7 Girardikeller
8 Goldene Kugel
13 Stainzerbauer
14 Gamlitzer Weinstube
15 Mangolds
   Vollwert Restaurant

OTHER
2 Babenburgerhof
3 Brot & Spiele
5 Cathedral;
   Mausoleum
9 Kommod
10 Opernhaus
11 Tageskasse
12 Tourist Office;
   Landeszeughaus
17 Bus Station;
   Café Zentral
18 Post Office

to Wednesday). A little more expensive but also with authentic Styrian cooking is *Gamlitzer Weinstube (Mehlplatz 4)*; it's closed weekends. To sample numerous varieties of beer and affordable Austrian food (under AS100), go to *Goldene Kugel (Leonhardstrasse 32)*. It's closed Saturday.

For a splurge, head to the traditional *Stainzerbauer (☎ 82 11 06, Bürgergasse 4)*. Styrian and Austrian specialities are mostly AS100 to AS235, though the weekday two-course lunch is a mere AS80 (closed Sunday).

Entertainment

The **Tageskasse** (☎ 8000), Kaiser Josef Platz 10, sells tickets without commission for the *Schauspielhaus* (theatre) and *Opernhaus* (opera). An hour before performances, students can buy remaining tickets at the door for AS80, and anybody can buy standing room tickets for AS40 or AS45.

Kommod (Burggasse 15) is a bar that's often packed with students. *Brot & Spiele (Mariahilfer Strasse 17)* offers beer, inexpensive food, chess and pool tables. *Babenburgerhof (Babenburgerstrasse 39)* is a

friendly bar with free live jazz on Wednesday (closed weekends).

Getting There & Away

Every two hours there are direct trains to Vienna's Südbahnhof (AS320, 2¾ hours) and Salzburg (AS430, 4¼ hours). Trains to Klagenfurt go via Bruck.

International train services include Zagreb (AS364, four hours, two daily) and Budapest (change at Szentgotthard and Szombathely; AS598, 6½ hours).

KLAGENFURT
☎ 0463

Klagenfurt, the capital of Carinthia (Kärnten) since 1518, merits a brief visit. The **Wörther See**, 4km west of the city, is one of the warmer lakes in the region thanks to subterranean thermal springs. You can swim or go boating in summer at the lakeside **Strandbad**. Nearby is the boat station; get further details of summer boat tours from STW (☎ 211 55). The adjoining **Europa Park** has various attractions, including the touristy Minimundus, which displays 150 models of famous international buildings on a scale of

1:25 (closed November to mid-April; AS120/90).

Orientation & Information

Neuer Platz is 1km north of the main train station. The tourist office (☎ 537 223, 🖃 tourismus@klagenfurt.at) in the Rathaus on Neuer Platz finds rooms (no commission) and rents bikes.

Places to Stay & Eat

Camping Strandbad (☎ 211 69) is by the lake in Europa Park. From Heiligen Geist Platz take bus No 10, 11, 12, 20, 21 or 22.

The HI *Jugendherberge* (☎ 23 00 20, fax -20, Neckheimgasse 6), near Europa Park, has four-bed dorms with own shower/toilet for AS210. Single/double occupancy costs AS310/520.

The *Hotel Liebetegger* (☎ 569 35, fax -6, Völkermarkter Strasse 8) is stylish, central and affordable. It charges AS400/700 with shower/toilet and TV or AS250/500 without; breakfast is AS80.

The *University Mensa* (*Universitäts-strasse 90*), by Europa Park, has cut-price lunches during the week. In the city centre, try the tiny shops in the Benediktinerplatz market where you can have a hot meal for only about AS50. *Gasthaus Pirker*, straddling Adlergasse and Lidmanskygasse, has traditional Austrian fare from AS70 to AS150 (closed weekends).

Getting There & Away

There are frequent trains to Graz (AS340, three hours) and (via Villach) to west Austria, Italy and Germany.

Salzburg

☎ 0662

The city that delivered Mozart to the world has much to recommend it, despite the fact that *The Sound of Music* (which was partly filmed here) has spawned tacky tours and a crush of tourists in summer.

The influence of Mozart is everywhere. There is Mozartplatz, the Mozarteum, Mozart's birthplace, Mozart's residence – even chocolate bars and liqueurs named after him. The old town, impossibly quaint and picturesque, is deservedly a Unesco World Heritage site.

Orientation

The centre of the city is split by the River Salzach. The old part of town (mostly pedestrian-only) is on the left (south) bank, with the Hohensalzburg Fortress dominant on the hill above. The new town, the centre of business activity, is on the right (north) bank, along most of the cheaper hotels.

Information

Tourist Offices The central tourist office (☎ 889 87-0, 🖃 tourist@salzburginfo.at), Mozartplatz 5, is open 9 am to 6 pm daily (to 7 or 8 pm in summer; closed Sunday in winter). There's a branch office in the train station on platform 2a. Dial ☎ 889 87-314 (fax -32) for hotel reservations at AS30 commission. Tourist offices and hotels sell the Salzburg Card, offering free museum entry and public transport. The price is AS225/300/390 for 24/48/72 hours.

Money There's currency exchange at the train station counters to at least 8.30 pm daily. American Express (☎ 80 80), Mozartplatz 5, is open 9 am to 5.30 pm weekdays, to noon Saturday. Beware of high commissions at some exchange offices in the city centre.

Post The post office at the train station has money-exchange and is open until at least 8 pm daily. In the town centre, the main post office (Hauptpostamt 5010) is at Residenzplatz 9 (closed Sunday).

Email & Internet Access Cybercafe, Gstättengasse 27, is open daily from 2 to 11 pm or later. Surfing costs AS40 for 30 minutes. International Telephone Discount, Kaiserschützenstrasse 8, is AS1.70 per minute (9 am to midnight daily).

Travel Agencies ÖKISTA (☎ 45 87 33), at Fanny-von-Lehnert Strasse 1, is closed on weekends. Young Austria (☎ 62 57 58-0), at Alpenstrasse 108a, is another recommended budget travel agency.

Things to See & Do

Start at the vast **Dom** (cathedral) on Domplatz, which has three bronze doors symbolising faith, hope and charity. Head west along Franziskanergasse and turn left into a courtyard for **St Peter's Abbey**, dating from

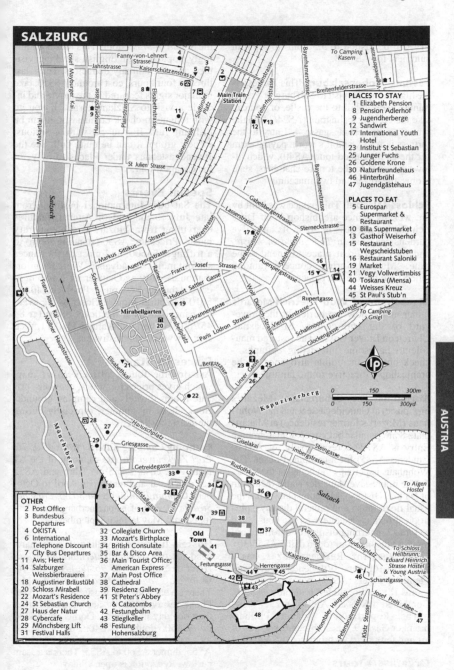

SALZBURG

PLACES TO STAY
1 Elizabeth Pension
8 Pension Adlerhof
9 Jugendherberge
12 Sandwirt
17 International Youth Hotel
23 Institut St Sebastian
25 Junger Fuchs
26 Goldene Krone
30 Naturfreundehaus
46 Hinterbrühl
47 Jugendgästehaus

PLACES TO EAT
5 Eurospar Supermarket & Restaurant
10 Billa Supermarket
13 Gasthof Weiserhof
15 Restaurant Wegscheidstuben
16 Restaurant Saloniki
19 Market
21 Vegy Vollwertimbiss
40 Toskana (Mensa)
44 Weisses Kreuz
45 St Paul's Stub'n

OTHER
2 Post Office
3 Bundesbus Departures
4 ÖKISTA
6 International Telephone Discount
7 City Bus Departures
11 Avis; Hertz
14 Salzburger Weissbierbrauerei
18 Augustiner Bräustübl
20 Schloss Mirabell
22 Mozart's Residence
24 St Sebastian Church
27 Haus der Natur
28 Cybercafe
29 Mönchsberg Lift
31 Festival Halls
32 Collegiate Church
33 Mozart's Birthplace
34 British Consulate
35 Bar & Disco Area
36 Main Tourist Office; American Express
37 Main Post Office
38 Cathedral
39 Residenz Gallery
41 St Peter's Abbey & Catacombs
42 Festungbahn
43 Stieglkeller
48 Festung Hohensalzburg

AUSTRIA

AD 847. Its graveyard contains **catacombs** that can be visited to 3.30 pm (to 5 pm in summer) for AS12/8.

Festung Hohensalzburg This fortress is the high point of a visit to Salzburg. It's a 15-minute walk uphill to the castle, or you can take the Festungsbahn train (AS24/34 single/return) from Festungsgasse 4. Entry to the fortress is AS42, and it's worth paying extra for the audio guided tour (AS40), which allows entrance to the torture chambers, state rooms, the tower and two museums.

Schloss Mirabell This palace was built by the worldly prince-archbishop Wolf Dietrich for his mistress in 1606. Its attractive gardens featured in *The Sound of Music*, and they're a great place to spend some time. 'Musical Spring' concerts (among others) are held in the palace.

Mausoleum of Wolf Dietrich Mozart's father and widow are buried in the graveyard of the 16th-century St Sebastian Church on Linzer Gasse. The restored mausoleum has some interesting epitaphs – check out the incredible arrogance of the archbishop's directive to the faithful.

Museums The **Geburtshaus** (Mozart's birthplace) at Getreidegasse 9 and the **Wohnhaus** (Mozart's former residence) at Makartplatz 8 are popular but cover similar ground. Entry is AS70/65 respectively, or AS110 (students AS85) for a combined ticket. The Wohnhaus is perhaps the better of the two.

The impressive **Haus der Natur** (Museum of Natural History), Museumsplatz 5, has the usual flora, fauna and mineral displays, plus tropical fish, an excellent reptile house, and a stomach-churning display of deformed animals on the 4th floor (open daily; AS55/30).

The **Residenz**, Residenzplatz 1, has a gallery of 16th- and 17th-century Dutch and Flemish painters (AS70), plus baroque state rooms (by audio guided tour only, AS50). Combined tickets are AS91/70.

The **Rupertinium**, Wiener Philharmoniker Gasse 9, has 20th-century works of art and temporary exhibitions (AS40/20).

Organised Tours

One-hour walking tours (AS100) leave from the main tourist office. Other city tours mostly leave from Mirabellplatz, including the *Sound of Music* tour. This tour is enduringly popular with English-speaking visitors, despite its many detractors. Tours last three to four hours, cost around AS350, take in major sights featured in the movie and include a visit to Salzkammergut. If you go with tongue-in-cheek enthusiasm, it can be brilliant fun. If you go with a serious, earnest group, it can be quite dull. See the Jugendgästehaus under Places to Stay for the cheapest tour.

Special Events

The Salzburg International Festival, from late July to the end of August, features everything from Mozart to contemporary music. Prices are AS50 (standing room) to a trifling AS4600, and most performances sell out months in advance. Write for information as early as October to: Kartenbüro der Salzburger Festspiele, Postfach 140, A-5010 Salzburg. Inquire closer to the event for cancellations at the ticket office (☎ 84 45 760), Herbert von Karajan Platz 11. Web site: www.salzburgfestival.at

Places to Stay

Ask for the tourist office's *Hotel* map, which gives prices for hotels, pensions, private rooms, hostels and camping grounds. Book ahead in summer, especially during the music festival.

Camping *Camping Kasern* (☎/fax 45 05 76, Carl Zuckmayer Strasse 4), north of the A1 Nord exit, costs AS65 per adult and AS35 each for a car and tent (open April to October). *Camping Gnigl* (☎ 64 30 60, Parscher Strasse 4), east of Kapuzinerberg, costs less (open mid-May to mid-September).

Hostels If you're travelling to party hard, head for the sociable *International Youth Hotel* or YoHo (☎ 87 96 49, fax 87 88 10, ✉ office@yoho.at, Paracelsusstrasse 9). There's a bar with loud music and cheap beer. Phone reservations are accepted no earlier than one day in advance. Dorms are AS130 or AS150, doubles AS400. Showers and lockers are AS10 each. Breakfast is AS30 to AS55, dinner AS60 to AS75. There's a 1 am curfew. Reception is open all day.

HI's modern *Jugendgästehaus* (☎ 84 26 70-0, fax 84 11 01, Josef Preis Allee 18) is probably the most comfortable hostel. Beds are AS162 to AS212, and doubles cost AS524, plus a surcharge of AS10 for the first night's stay. Phone reservations are accepted. Check-in from 11 am, though reception is closed for periods during the day. It has free lockers, a bar, small kitchen, and bike rental (AS90 per day). Daily *Sound of Music* tours are AS300 for anybody who shows up by 8.45 am or 1.30 pm.

The HI *Jugendherberge* (☎ *87 50 30, fax 88 34 77, Haunspergstrasse 27*) near the train station is only open around July and August, and costs AS170. *Institut St Sebastian* (☎ *87 13 86, fax -85, Linzer Gasse 41*) has a roof terrace and kitchens, and dorms for AS190 plus AS30 for sheets. Singles/doubles cost AS360/600 or AS400/700 with shower.

The *Naturfreundehaus* (☎ *84 17 29, Mönchsberg 19*), also called Gasthaus Bürgerwehr, is clearly visible on the hill between the fortress and Café Winkler (great views). Take the footpath up from near Max Reinhardt Platz, or the Mönchsberg lift (AS16/27 single/return) from A Neumayr Platz. It's AS120 for a dorm bed, AS10 for a shower. Reception is open all day, but there's a 1 am curfew. The restaurant serves breakfast (from AS30) and meals (AS65 to AS110). Beds are available from about May to September (phone ahead).

If everywhere is full in town, try two *HI hostels* in the south: at Aignerstrasse 34, Aigen (☎ *62 32 48*), and at Eduard Heinrich Strasse 2 (☎ *62 59 76*); beds in both hostels cost AS186.

Pensions & Hotels – Budget *Sandwirt* (☎/*fax 87 43 51, Lastenstrasse 6a*) is near the rail tracks. Singles/doubles are AS300/480 using hall shower; doubles/triples/quads cost AS508/720/880 with a private shower and TV. The rooms are clean, reasonably large and quiet, and the staff are helpful.

Rooms at *Elizabeth Pension* (☎/*fax 87 16 64, Vogelweiderstrasse 5*) are smallish but pleasant. Singles/doubles are AS300/480 or AS350/540 with private shower.

Convenient *Junger Fuchs* (☎ *87 54 96, Linzer Gasse 54*) has singles/doubles/triples for AS280/380/480, not including breakfast. *Hinterbrühl* (☎ *84 67 98, Schanzlgasse 12*) has singles/doubles without bath

for AS420/520. Breakfast is AS50; reception is in the restaurant downstairs.

Pensions & Hotels – Mid-Range *Pension Adlerhof* (☎ *87 52 36, fax 87 36 636, Elisabethstrasse 25*), near the train station, offers modern or rustic rooms from AS590/790 with private shower and toilet.

Goldene Krone (☎ *87 23 00, fax -66, Linzer Gasse 48*) is more central and has singles/doubles with private facilities for AS570/970.

Places to Eat

There's a fruit and vegetable *market* at Mirabellplatz on Thursday mornings. The large *Eurospar supermarket* by the train station has a self-service restaurant that's half-price after 6 pm; it's open to 7 pm weekdays, to 5 pm Saturday.

University mensas are open to the public from 11.30 am to 2 pm on weekdays, with meals from AS40. The most convenient is *Toskana* (*Sigmund Haffner Gasse 11*).

The vegetarian *Vegy Vollwertimbiss* (*Schwarzstrasse 21*) has a salad buffet (from AS38) and daily lunch menu (AS89) and is open 11 am to 5 pm weekdays.

Gasthof Weiserhof (*Weiserhofstrasse 4*) is a friendly, typical Austrian tavern, with two-course menus for lunch and evening meals from just AS70. *Restaurant Wegscheidstuben* (*Lasserstrasse 1*) is similar, albeit a little more expensive. Both places are closed Sunday evening and Saturday. Opposite Wegscheidstuben is *Restaurant Saloniki*, for affordable Greek food (closed Monday).

St Paul's Stub'n (*Herrengasse 16*), on the 1st floor, has a low-key entrance and terrace tables. Pasta and tasty pizzas from AS72 are served until late (open from 6 pm; closed Sunday).

Weisses Kreuz (*Bierjodlgasse 6*) serves Balkan specialities such as *djuvec* (rice, succulent pork and paprika; AS82), as well as Austrian fare from AS100. It's closed Tuesday in the low season.

Entertainment

The atmospheric *Augustiner Bräustübl* (*Augustinergasse 4-6*) proves that monks can make beer – served by the litre (AS60) or half-litre (AS30) – as well as anybody. It's open from 3 pm to 11 pm daily.

AUSTRIA

Stieglkeller (Festungsgasse 10), a beer hall, is open April to October only. Ignore the touristy *Sound of Music* show here, and head for the garden overlooking the town.

For wheat beer made on the premises try *Salzburger Weissbierbrauerei*, on the corner of Rupertgasse and Virgilgasse.

The liveliest area for bars, clubs and discos is the area near the Radisson Hotel on Rudolfskai. There's a range of (often packed) places, including a couple of *Irish pubs* with live music.

Getting There & Away

Bundesbuses depart from Südtiroler Platz (where there's a timetable board), across from the train station post office. There's a bus information office in the train station. To Kitzbühel (2¼ hours), change at Lofer. Numerous buses leave for Salzkammergut towns like Bad Ischl (AS100, 1¾ hours), St Gilgen (AS60, 50 minutes) and St Wolfgang (AS90, 1½ hours).

Fast trains leave for Vienna via Linz every hour (AS110 to Linz, AS215 to Vienna, 3¼ hours). The quickest way to get to Innsbruck is by the 'corridor' train through Germany, via Kufstein; trains depart at least every two hours and the fare is AS360 (two hours). There are trains departing every 30 to 60 minutes to Munich (AS298, approximately two hours).

Getting Around

Bus drivers sell single tickets (AS20). Get day passes (AS40) and multiple tickets from Tabak shops or the tourist office.

AROUND SALZBURG
Hellbrunn

The popular **Schloss Hellbrunn**, built in the 17th century by bishop Marcus Sitticus, is 4km south of Salzburg's old town. The main attractions here are the ingenious trick fountains and water-powered figures installed by the bishop and activated today by tour guides. Be prepared to get wet! This section of the gardens is open daily from April to October, with the last tour at 4.30 pm (5.30 pm in summer). Tickets are AS80/60. There is no charge to stroll around the lovely palace gardens.

From the Salzburg Hauptbahnhof, city bus No 55 runs to the palace every half-hour via Rudolfskai.

Hallein
☎ 06245

Hallein is primarily visited for the **Salzbergwerk** (salt mine) at Bad Dürrnberg, on the hill above the town. Much of Salzburg's past prosperity was dependent upon salt mines, and this one is the closest and easiest to visit from the city. The mine stopped production in 1989 to concentrate on guided tours. Some people rave about the experience, others find the one-hour tour disappointing and overpriced (AS200/180 per adult/child). Careering down the wooden slides in the caves is fun, and you get to take a brief raft trip on the salt lake, but there's little else to see. It is open 9 am to 5 pm daily (from 11 am to 3 pm in winter). Note that saltmine tours in the Salzkammergut are cheaper – see that section later.

The tourist office in Hallein (☎ 853 94, ✉ info-tg@eunet.at), on Mauttorpromenade, is on the narrow island that adjoins the Stadtbrücke.

Getting There & Away Hallein is 30 minutes or less from Salzburg by bus or train (AS40). There are several ways to reach Bad Dürrnberg. The easiest option is to take the cable car, which is a signposted 10-minute walk from the train station. The AS275/245 return fare includes entry to the mines. It's cheaper to take the bus (AS19, 10 minutes, hourly) from outside the station, but departures are less frequent on weekends.

Werfen
☎ 06468

Werfen is a rewarding day trip from Salzburg. The 16th-century **Hohenwerfen Fortress**, on a hill above the village, is open daily from April to November. Entry costs AS110/100 and includes a guided tour and a dramatic falconry show. The walk up from the village takes 20 minutes.

The **Eisriesenwelt Höhle** in the mountains are the largest accessible ice caves in the world. The ice formations inside are vast, elaborate and beautiful. The 70-minute tour costs AS100. The caves are open from May to early October. Take warm clothes because it can get cold inside.

Both attractions can be fitted into the same day if you start early (visit the caves first, and be at the castle by 3 pm for the falconry show). The tourist office (☎ 5388,

@ info@werfen.at), Markt 24, is in the village's main street.

Getting There & Away Take a train from Salzburg to Werfen (AS80, 50 minutes). The village is a five-minute walk from Werfen station. To reach the caves from Werfen station, take a minibus to the caves' car park (AS70 return), walk 15 minutes to the cable car (AS120 return), and then another 15 minutes to the caves' entrance. Allow four hours return from Werfen station (peak-season queues may add an hour).

Salzkammergut

Salzkammergut, named after its salt mines, is a region of mountains and lakes to the east of Salzburg. The main season is summer, when hiking and water sports are popular. In winter, 80 cable cars and lifts serve 145km of ski runs; a general ski pass costs AS625 for a minimum two days.

Bad Ischl, the geographical centre of Salzkammergut, is a spa resort with an imperial aura – Emperor Franz Josef used to holiday here in the Kaiservilla, which can be visited. There's also a salt mine tour and some skiing. West of Bad Ischl, the **Wolfgangsee** is a scenic lake bordered by photogenic villages. On the lake's northern shore the main resort is **St Wolfgang**, with a fabulous church that's awash with altars. It's adjacent to the Schafberg peak (1783m), with phenomenal views (AS150/260 single/return by cog-wheel train; 15% off with rail passes).

Hallstatt is set in idyllic scenery, wedged between steep mountains and its namesake lake. It is continually invaded by crowds of day-trippers; fortunately they only stay a few hours and then the village returns to its natural calm. This Unesco World Heritage site also has salt mine tours.

Information

Bad Ischl has a tourist office (☎ 277 57-0), Bahnhofstrasse 6, and the Salzkammergut Info-Center (☎ 240 00-0), Götzstrasse 12, which is open till at least 8 pm daily. Both are close to the train station.

St Wolfgang's tourist office (☎ 2239) is at the entrance to the road tunnel. Turn left from Hallstatt's ferry dock to reach its tourist office (☎ 8208).

Your resort accommodation provides a *Gästekarte* (guest card) that offers useful benefits. If you plan to spend a while here, buy the Salzkammergut Card for AS65. It is valid between May and October for the duration of your stay, and earns a 25% discount on sights, ferries, cable cars and some Bundesbuses.

The phone code for Bad Ischl is ☎ 06132; St Wolfgang ☎ 06138; and Hallstatt ☎ 06134.

Places to Stay

Tourist offices can supply lists of private rooms, and will sometimes make free hotel bookings. Some pensions and private rooms close in winter.

Bad Ischl The HI *Jugendgästehaus (☎ 265 77, Am Rechensteg 5)* is in the town centre behind Kreuzplatz. Dorms are AS155, singles/doubles are AS255/370. Reception is open 8 am to 1 pm and 5 to 7 pm. *Haus Rothauer (☎ 236 28, Kaltenbachstrasse 12)* has singles from AS180 (hall shower) and doubles with shower for AS200 per person.

St Wolfgang *Camping Appesbach (☎ 06138-2206, Au 99)* is on the lakefront, 1km from St Wolfgang in the direction of Strobl. It's open from Easter to October and costs AS63 per adult and from AS65 for a tent and car. Across the lake is St Gilgen, where there's a HI *Jugendgästehaus (☎ 06227-2365, Mondseestrasse 7)*. Prices are from AS135 to AS285 per person, in anything from 10-bed dorms to singles. Check-in is from 5 to 7 pm.

The chalet-style *Gästehaus Raudaschl (☎ 06138-2329, Pilgerstrasse 4)*, in the centre of St Wolfgang, has homy singles/doubles for AS370/700 with shower and toilet; doubles using hall shower are AS440.

Hallstatt *Campingplatz Höll (☎ 8329, Lahnstrasse 6)* costs AS55 per adult, AS45 per tent and is open 15 April to 15 October. The HI *Jugendherberge (☎ 8212, Salzbergstrasse 50)* is open from around May to September; in July and August it's reserved for groups only. Beds are AS112 excluding breakfast (AS35) and sheets (AS45). Check-in from 5 pm, but phone ahead as hours are irregular. *TVN Naturfreunde Herberge (☎/fax 8318, Kirchenweg*

36), run by Zur Mühle Gasthaus, has dorm beds for AS115, plus AS40 each for sheets and breakfast (if required).

Getting There & Away
Bad Ischl From outside Bad Ischl's train station there are Bundesbuses to/from Salzburg (via St Gilgen; AS100) and to Hallstatt (AS50, 50 minutes). To St Wolfgang (AS40) change at Strobl (the bus will be waiting, and the same ticket is valid). By train it's AS208 to/from Salzburg (two hours, via Attnang Puchheim) and AS38 to Hallstatt.

Wolfgangsee An hourly ferry goes between St Gilgen and St Wolfgang from May to late October. The journey takes 40 minutes and costs AS52 (15% discount with rail passes). Buses from Salzburg go to St Gilgen (AS60, 50 minutes) and via Strobl to St Wolfgang.

Hallstatt Get off the Bundesbus at the Parkterrasse stop for the centre and the tourist office, or at Lahn (at the southern end of the tunnel) for the hostel. The train station is across the lake; the boat service from there to the village (AS23) coincides with train arrivals, but the last is at 6.46 pm.

Tirol

The province of Tirol (sometimes spelled Tyrol) has some of the best mountain scenery in Austria and is an ideal playground for skiers and hikers. Trains and buses within Tirol are cheaper using VVT tickets, which can only be bought within Tirol (from train stations, etc). Innsbruck's IVB Kundenbüro (☎ 0512-53 07-103), Stainerstrasse 2, has full details.

INNSBRUCK
☎ 0512

Innsbruck, scenically squeezed between the northern chain of the Alps and the Tuxer mountain range to the south, has been an important trading post since the 12th century, thanks in part to the Brenner Pass, the gateway to the south. It wasn't long before the city found favour with the Habsburgs, particularly Maximilian I and Maria Theresa, who built many of the important buildings that survive in the well-preserved old town.

More recently, the capital of Tirol has become an important winter sports centre. The Winter Olympics were held here in 1964 and 1976.

Orientation
The main train station is a 10-minute walk from the pedestrian-only *Altstadt* (old town). The main street in the Altstadt is Herzog Friedrich Strasse.

Information
Tourist Offices The main tourist office (☎ 598 50, fax -7, 🖂 info@innsbruck .tvb.co.at), Burggraben 3, books accommodation (AS40 commission) and sells ski passes and public transport tickets (24-hour pass AS35). It's open 8 am to 7 pm Monday to Saturday, 9 am to 6 pm Sunday and holidays. The hotel reservation centre in the train station is open daily from 9 am to at least 9 pm. The Tirol Information office (☎ 72 72, fax -7, 🖂 tirol.info@tirolwerbung .at), Maria Theresien Strasse 55, is open 8 am to 6 pm weekdays.

Ask your hotel for 'Club Innsbruck' membership; it's free and provides various discounts and benefits. The Innsbruck Card, available at the main tourist office, gives free entry to museums and free use of public transport. It costs AS230/300/370 for 24/48/72 hours.

Money The train station has money-exchange and a Bankomat. The tourist office also exchanges money.

American Express (☎ 58 24 91-0), Brixnerstrasse 3, is open 9 am to 5.30 pm weekdays, to noon Saturday.

Post The main post office (Hauptpostamt 6010) is at Maximilianstrasse 2, it's open 7 am to 11 pm on weekdays and 8 am to 9 pm on weekends.

Email & Internet Access Free Internet access is available in the bar at Utopia (see Entertainment, later in this section), though you won't have to queue at International Telephone Discount, Brunecker Strasse 12 (AS1.70 per minute).

Travel Agency ÖKISTA (☎ 58 89 97), Wilhelm Greil Strasse 17, is open 9 am to 5.30 pm weekdays.

AUSTRIA

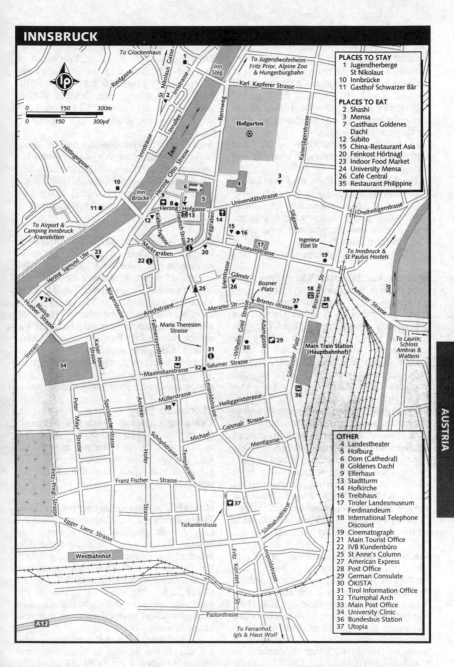

INNSBRUCK

PLACES TO STAY
1 Jugendherberge St Nikolaus
10 Innbrücke
11 Gasthof Schwarzer Bär

PLACES TO EAT
2 Shashi
3 Mensa
7 Gasthaus Goldenes Dachl
12 Subito
15 China-Restaurant Asia
20 Feinkost Hörtnagl
23 Indoor Food Market
24 University Mensa
26 Café Central
35 Restaurant Philippine

OTHER
4 Landestheater
5 Hofburg
6 Dom (Cathedral)
8 Goldenes Dachl
9 Elferhaus
13 Stadtturm
14 Hofkirche
16 Treibhaus
17 Tiroler Landesmuseum Ferdinandeum
18 International Telephone Discount
19 Cinematograph
21 Main Tourist Office
22 IVB Kundenbüro
25 St Anne's Column
27 American Express
28 Post Office
29 German Consulate
30 ÖKISTA
31 Tirol Information Office
32 Triumphal Arch
33 Main Post Office
34 University Clinic
36 Bundesbus Station
37 Utopia

AUSTRIA

Things to See & Do

For an overview climb the 14th-century **Stadtturm** tower on Herzog Friedrich Strasse. It's open daily (AS27/15). Across the square is the famous **Goldenes Dachl** (Golden Roof); it comprises 2657 gilded copper tiles dating from the 16th century. Inside the building is a museum devoted to Maximilian I (AS50/20).

Behind the Golden Roof is the **Dom** (cathedral), with a typically over-the-top baroque interior.

The **Alpine Zoo**, north of the River Inn on Weiherburggasse, features a comprehensive collection of Alpine animals (AS70/35; open daily). Either walk up the hill to get here or take the Hungerburgbahn train, which is free if you buy your zoo ticket at the Hungerburgbahn station.

Hofburg The Imperial Palace dates from 1397, but has been rebuilt and restyled several times since. The grand rooms are decorated with paintings of Maria Theresa and family. It's worth seeing, but if you're going to Vienna, save your money for Schönbrunn instead. The palace is open 9 am to 5 pm daily for AS70/45. Guided tours are in German (AS25), or buy the English booklet (AS25).

The **Hofkirche** (Imperial Church) opposite the palace contains the massive but empty sarcophagus of Maximilian I. The twin rows of 28 giant bronze figures of the Habsburgs are memorable (AS30/20). The dull bronze has been polished in parts by the sheer number of hands that have touched them; a certain private part of Kaiser Rudolf is very shiny indeed! On Sunday and holidays you can get in free. Combined tickets (AS75/55) are available for the adjoining folk art museum.

Schloss Ambras Located east of the city centre (take tram No 3 or 6, or bus K), this medieval castle was greatly extended by Archduke Ferdinand II in the 16th century. It features the Renaissance Spanish Hall, fine gardens, exhaustive portraits of Habsburgs and other dignitaries, and collections of weapons, armour and oddities. Opening hours are 10 am to 5 pm Wednesday to Monday, April to October (AS60/30). From December to March, interior visits are by guided tour at 2 pm only (AS25 extra).

Tiroler Landesmuseum Ferdinandeum This museum at Museumstrasse 15 (AS50/30) houses a good collection of art and artefacts, including Gothic statues and altarpieces. It's open 10 am to 5 pm daily, May to September. From October to April hours are 10 am to noon and 2 to 5 pm Tuesday to Saturday, 10 am to 1 pm Sunday.

Swarovski Kristallwelten The Swarovski Kristallwelten (Crystal Worlds) is a well-presented series of caverns featuring the famous Swarovski crystals (AS75). It's open 9 am to 6 pm daily and is in Wattens, 20 minutes east of town by Bundesbus or train.

Skiing A one-day ski pass is AS240 to AS330, depending on the area. Downhill equipment rental starts at AS200. With 'Club Innsbruck' membership, ski buses are free.

You can ski all year at the **Stubai Glacier**; a one-day pass is AS420. The journey there takes 80 minutes by the white IVB Stubaltalbahn bus, departing hourly from the bus station (buy tickets from the driver; AS163 return). Complete packages to the glacier are good value: the tourist office package for AS599 (AS540 in winter) includes transport, passes and equipment rental.

Places to Stay

Camping *Camping Innsbruck Kranebitten* (☎/fax 28 41 80, Kranebitter Allee 214) is 5km west of the town centre (take bus LK) and open year-round. Prices are AS75 per adult and AS40 for a tent. There is a restaurant on site.

Hostels The convenient backpacker hostel *Jugendherberge St Nikolaus* (☎ 28 65 15, fax -14, ✉ yhnikolaus@tirol.com, Innstrasse 95) has a (noisy) cellar bar and an attached restaurant. Dorm beds are AS180 the first night and AS165 for additional nights. Singles/doubles cost AS265/430. Check-in is from 5 to 10 pm, though you can usually leave bags during the day. Some travellers have complained that staff are rude here.

Two HI hostels down Reichenauerstrasse are accessible by bus O from Museumstrasse. *Innsbruck* (☎ 34 61 79, fax -12) at No 147 costs AS155 the first night, AS125 thereafter. Curfew is at 11 pm, and the place is closed from 10 am to 5 pm (3 pm in summer). It has a kitchen, double rooms (AS440) and slow washing machines (AS45). At No 72, *St Paulus* (☎ *34 42 91*), open mid-June to early September, charges AS170, and has a kitchen. The doors are locked from 10 am until 5 pm.

Open July and August, the *Jugendwohnheim Fritz Prior* (☎ *58 58 14, fax -4, Rennweg 17b*), north of the centre, charges AS120 for beds, AS20 for sheets and AS45 for breakfast.

Pensions & Hotels Check in at the Jugendherberge St Nikolaus hostel for the *Glockenhaus* pension, up the hill at Weiherburggasse 3. It charges AS345/470 for singles/doubles with shower.

Ferrarihof (☎/fax *57 88 98, Brennerstrasse 8*) is south of town. Ageing (but soon to be renovated) singles/doubles are AS250/500 with either private or hall shower. Reception is in the bar downstairs, open from 10 am to midnight, and breakfast is extra. It's 500m from tram No 1.

Laurin (☎ *34 11 04, Gumppstrasse 19*) is behind the station, near tram No 3. Singles/doubles are AS350/520, or AS430/680 with private shower.

Innbrücke (☎ *28 19 34, fax 27 84 10, ✉ innbrueke@magnet.at, Innstrasse 1*) is nearer the Altstadt. Simple, sometimes noisy rooms are AS450/800 with shower/toilet or AS350/600 without. Along the road, *Gasthof Schwarzer Bär* (☎ *29 49 00, fax -4, Mariahilfstrasse 16*) is an old house but has big, modern doubles with shower, toilet and TV for AS840.

Places to Eat
Feinkost Hörtnagl on Burggraben is a supermarket with a cafe and a self-service section for hot meals. *Subito* (*Kiebachgasse 2*) has cheap pizza-slice deals and Italian ice cream; it's open 11 am to 1 am daily. The large indoor *food market* by the river in Markthalle, Herzog Siegmund Ufer, is closed Sunday.

The *University Mensa* (*Herzog Siegmund Ufer 15*), on the 1st floor, serves good lunches between 11 am and 1.30 pm Monday to Thursday, 11 am to 2 pm Friday and Saturday. For less than AS75 you can get a main dish, soup and salad. Another *Mensa* is at Universitätsstrasse 15.

Restaurant Philippine (*Müllerstrasse 9*) has an extensive range of vegetarian dishes from AS88 to AS140, and an excellent salad buffet for AS32/98 for a small/big plate (closed Sunday).

China-Restaurant Asia (*Angerzellgasse 10*) has good three-course weekday lunch specials (AS69). *Shashi* (*Innstrasse 81*) has big pizzas from AS60; excellent Indian meals for around AS95 include rice, poppadoms and bread (closed Monday).

Café Central (*Gilmstrasse 5*) is a good example of a typical Austrian coffee house. It has English newspapers, daily specials from around AS95, and piano music from 8 to 10 pm on Sunday.

In the centre, *Gasthaus Goldenes Dachl* (*Hofgasse 1*) provides a civilised environment for Tirolean specialities such as *Bauerngröstl* (a pork, bacon, potato and egg concoction; AS124).

Entertainment
The tourist office sells tickets for 'Tirolean evenings' (AS220 gets you some Alpine music, folk dancing, yodelling and one drink), classical concerts and performances in the *Landestheater*.

Utopia (☎ *58 85 87, Tschamlerstrasse 3*) stages theatre, art, parties and live music in the cellar downstairs; entry is free or up to AS200. There's also a cafe/bar, open 6 pm to 1 am Monday to Saturday. Web site: www.utopia.or.at

Treibhaus (☎ *58 68 74, Angerzellgasse 8*) has live music most nights (AS100 to AS250) and affordable food. It's closed Sunday, except for the once-monthly Tango night (free).

Cinemas around town are cheaper on Monday, when seats are AS70 or AS80. *Cinematograph* (☎ *57 85 00, Museumstrasse 31*) shows independent films in their original language. Nearby is Ingenieur Etzel Strasse, where there are lively bars within the railway arches. Or try *Elferhaus* (*Herzog Friedrich Strasse 11*) for a huge choice of beers.

Getting There & Away
Bundesbuses leave from next to the train station. The bus ticket office is in the smaller of the station's two halls.

Fast trains depart every two hours for Bregenz (3¾ hours) and Salzburg (two

AUSTRIA

hours). Regular express trains head north to Munich (via Kufstein; two hours) and south to Verona (3½ hours). Connections are hourly to Kitzbühel (AS142). Four daily trains (three on Sunday) go to Lienz via Italy (3½ hours). At 1.53 pm there is an international train (AS290), for which Austrian Domino pass-holders must pay for the Italian section (AS132). The other trains (AS165) are Austrian 'corridor' trains, and you can disembark in Italy. For train information, call ☎ 05-1717.

KITZBÜHEL
☎ 05356

Kitzbühel is a fashionable winter resort, with good intermediate skiing on **Kitzbüheler Horn** to the north and **Hahnenkamm** to the south. A one-day ski pass is AS420, though some pensions and hotels can offer 'Ski Hit' reductions before mid-December or after mid-March. A day's ski rental is around AS180.

In summer there are dozens of nearby hiking trails; enthusiasts should consider buying the three-day cable car pass (AS390). The tourist office has free maps and free guided hikes.

From the main train station it's 1km to the town centre – turn left from Bahnhofstrasse into Josef Pirchl Strasse, take the right fork and continue past the post office (Postamt 6370). The tourist office (☎ 62155-0, ✉ info@kitzbuehel.com) is in the centre at Hinterstadt 18.

Places to Stay & Eat

Room prices are highest at Christmas and in February, July and August. The prices quoted here are peak-season rates.

Campingplatz Schwarzsee (☎ 628 06), by the Schwarzsee lake, is open year-round. Despite its three stars, *Hotel Kaiser* (☎ 647 08, fax 662 13, Bahnhofstrasse 2) courts backpackers with four-bed rooms (AS260 to AS320 per person) and singles/doubles (AS420/640). It's closed between seasons.

Pension Hörl (☎/fax 631 44, Josef Pirchl Strasse 60) has rooms for AS270/500, or AS300/560 with shower. The *Pension Schmidinger* (☎ 631 34, Ehrenbachgasse 13) has rooms for AS300 per person with shower/toilet, or AS250 without (young people might get a discount).

On Bichlstrasse there's a *Spar supermarket* and a self-service *Prima* restaurant. *Huberbräu Stüberl* (*Vorderstadt 18*) offers good Austrian food, an AS85 menu and plentiful beer (AS34 for 0.5L). *La Fonda* (*Hinterstadt 13*) is a cheap Tex-Mex place, with a bar.

Getting There & Away

There are hourly trains from Kitzbühel to Innsbruck (AS142, 1¼ hours) and Salzburg (AS260, 2½ hours). Slower trains stop at Kitzbühel-Hahnenkamm, which is more central than the main Kitzbühel stop.

Getting to/from Lienz is awkward by train – the bus is much easier, albeit infrequent (AS153, two hours).

LIENZ
☎ 04852

The capital of East Tirol combines winter sports and summer hiking with a relaxed, small-town ambience. The jagged Dolomite mountain range crowds the southern skyline. **Schloss Bruck** overlooks the town and contains folklore displays and the work of local artist Albin Egger (closed Monday and in winter; AS70/45).

The tourist office (☎ 652 65, ✉ lienz@netway.at) is at Europaplatz 1, off Hauptplatz near the train station. Staff book rooms free of charge.

Places to Stay & Eat

Camping Falken (☎ 640 22, Eichholz 7), south of the town, is closed from November to mid-December. *Haus Egger* (☎ 720 98, Alleestrasse 3) has private rooms for AS200 per person. *Haus Wille* (☎ 629 25, Drahtzuggasse 6) is an excellent deal at only AS140 per person, though there's a three-night minimum stay. There's a *Spar supermarket* on Tiroler Strasse. *Imbissstube* (Albin Egger Strasse 5) has mouth-watering rotisserie chicken for AS32. *China-Restaurant Sechuan* (Beda Weber Gasse 13) has weekday lunch specials for AS55.

Getting There & Away

There are trains to Innsbruck and Salzburg (AS310, three hours) and, via Spittal Millstättersee, to destinations in eastern Austria. Villach, between Spittal and Klagenfurt, is a main junction for rail routes to the south.

AUSTRIA

The state-of-the-art reconstructed Reichstag, Berlin, Germany

View from the Golden Gallery, St Paul's, London

St Peter's Basilica, Rome, Italy

The stunning Louvre, Paris, France

RICHARD I'ANSON

British pub sign

DAVID PEEVERS

Happy hour! Oktoberfest, Munich, Germany

DOUG McKINLAY

Dublin, Ireland

TOM SMALLMAN

Jameson whiskey distillery, Cork, Ireland

HOHE TAUERN NATIONAL PARK

Europe's largest national park contains the **Grossglockner** (3797m), Austria's highest mountain, which towers over the 10km-long **Pasterze Glacier**. The best viewing point is Franz Josefs Höhe, reached from Lienz by Bundesbus from mid-June to late September (AS103 each way, but inquire about day passes). By car, you can reach Franz Josefs Höhe from May to November, but there's a AS350/230 car/motorcycle toll. Cyclists and hikers can enter the park for free.

En route you pass **Heiligenblut**, with its HI *Jugendherberge* (☎ 04824-2259, *Hof 36*). The hostel is closed from mid-October to mid-December.

The north-south road through the park (Highway 107, the Grossglockner Hochalpenstrasse) is extremely scenic. At the northern end of the park, turn west along Highway 165 to reach the beautiful triple-level **Krimml Falls**. It takes 1½ hours to walk to the top.

Vorarlberg

The small state of Vorarlberg encompasses plains by Lake Constance (Bodensee) and mighty Alpine ranges. It provides skiing, dramatic landscapes and access to Liechtenstein, Switzerland and Germany. To get around the province you can buy VVV tickets, which work like VVT tickets (see the Tirol introduction earlier).

BREGENZ
☎ 05574

Bregenz, on the eastern shore of Lake Constance, is the provincial capital of Vorarlberg.

Orientation & Information

To reach the town centre from the train station, walk left along Bahnhofstrasse for 10 minutes. The train station rents bikes to 9.40 pm daily; Bundesbuses leave from outside.

The tourist office (☎ 4959-0, fax -59, @ tourismus@bregenz.at), Bahnhofstrasse 14, is open 9 am to noon Monday to Saturday and 1 to 5 pm Monday to Friday. Staff book rooms for a commission (AS30).

Things to See & Do

The old town merits a stroll. Its centrepiece and the town emblem is the bulbous, baroque **St Martin's Tower**, built in 1599.

The **Pfänder** mountain offers an impressive panorama over the lake and beyond. A cable car operates from 9 am to 6 pm (to 7 pm in summer). Fares are AS70 each way, AS125 return.

The Bregenz Festival is held from late July to late August. Operas and classical works are performed from a vast floating stage on the edge of the lake. For information and tickets (reserve at least nine months in advance) contact the Kartenbüro (☎ 407-6), Postfach 311, A-6901. Web site: www.bregenzerfestspiele.com

Places to Stay

Camping Lamm (☎ 717 01, *Mehrerauerstrasse 51*), 1.5km west of the station, is open from May to mid-October, and charges AS50 for adults, AS35 for tents.

The HI *Jugendgästehaus* (☎ 7083-0, *fax-88, Mehrerauerstrasse 3-5*), across from the swimming pool, is open year-round and all day. There's a cafe, lift, and dorms from AS180 (AS230 in summer).

Pension Gunz (☎/*fax 436 57, Anton Schneider Strasse 38*) has simple singles/doubles for AS380/680 with shower, AS340/600 without. Reception is in the cafe downstairs (closed Tuesday).

Getting There & Away

Trains to/from Munich (AS474, 2½ hours) go via Lindau; trains to/from Constance (AS172, 1½ hours) go via the Swiss shore of the lake. There are also regular departures to/from St Gallen and Zürich as well as Feldkirch and Innsbruck.

Bregenz to Constance by boat (via Lindau) takes about 3½ hours. Inquire about special boat passes giving free or half-price travel. Boats operate from late May to late October. For information call ☎ 428 68.

FELDKIRCH
☎ 05522

Feldkirch is a gateway to neighbouring Liechtenstein, and most travellers pass through merely for practical, transport-related reasons. If you find yourself with a few hours to spare, there are some good views from Feldkirch's 12th-century **Schattenburg** castle (closed Monday and November; AS25/10). A free **Wildpark** (animal park), with 200 species, is only 1km from the town centre.

The tourist office (☎ 734 67), Herrengasse 12, is open weekdays and Saturday morning, and reserves rooms free of charge.

Places to Stay

The HI *Jugendherberge* (☎ *731 81, fax 793 99, Reichsstrasse 111)* is 1.5km north of the train station. Beds are AS142 (dorms) or AS193 (rooms) and dinners are AS82. There's a AS25 heating surcharge in winter, subtract AS20 if you don't need sheets. Reception is open 7 am to 10 pm. The hostel is closed for two weeks in early December.

Gasthof Engel (☎*/fax 720 56, Liechtensteiner Strasse, Tisis),* on the bus route to Liechtenstein, has rooms for AS340/520 using hall shower (closed Monday).

Getting There & Away

Two buses an hour (one on weekends) depart for Liechtenstein from outside the train station. Some buses to Liechtenstein's capital, Vaduz (AS32, 40 minutes), require a change in Schaans. There are trains to Buchs on the Swiss border, with onward connections to major destinations in Switzerland, including Zürich and Chur.

ARLBERG REGION

The Arlberg region, shared by Vorarlberg and neighbouring Tirol, is considered to have some of the best skiing in Austria. Summer is less busy.

St Anton is the largest resort, enjoying an easy-going atmosphere and a vigorous nightlife (except in the summer months,

when it's quieter). It has good medium-to-advanced runs, as well as nursery slopes on Gampen and Kapall. Get information from the tourist office (☎ 05446-226 90, ✉ st.anton@netway.at), on the main street.

Lech, a more upmarket resort, is a favourite with royalty and film stars. Runs are predominantly medium to advanced. For details, contact the Lech tourist office (☎ 05583-2161-0).

A ski pass valid for 85 ski lifts in Lech, Zürs, Stuben, St Anton and St Christoph costs AS475/2670 per day/week. Daily rental starts at AS190/90 for skis/boots.

Places to Stay

Accommodation is mainly in small B&Bs – there are nearly 200 in St Anton alone. Tourist office brochures have full listings. Bottom-end prices start at around AS350 per person in winter, about 30% to 50% less in the low season and summer. Try *Tiroler Frieden* (☎ *05446-2247,* ✉ *tiroler.frieden@ski-arlberg.com)* in St Anton's main street, or the cheaper *Franz Schuler* (☎ *05446-3108)* in nearby St Jakob.

Despite its sophisticated profile, Lech has a *hostel* (☎ *05583-2419, Stubenbach 244),* 2km north-east from the main resort. It is closed between seasons.

Getting There & Away

From St Anton there are daily buses to Lech (AS46, 40 minutes). St Anton is on the main rail line from Bregenz to Innsbruck, under 1½ hours from either place.

Belgium

Think of Belgium (België in Flemish, Belgique in French) and it's Bruges, beer and chocolate that generally spring to mind. Surprisingly little else is commonly known about this often-embattled country which gave rise to Western Europe's first great towns, and whose early artists are credited with inventing oil painting.

Perhaps it's a lack of fervent nationalism – the result of many dominant cultures integrating here over the centuries – which has kept Belgium's spotlight dim on the European stage. Rarely boastful, the country has in fact plenty to fascinate the visitor – from historically rich towns to the serenity of the hilly Ardennes, and everywhere wonderful bars and cafes where Belgians feel at home.

Facts about Belgium

HISTORY

Belgium's position between France, Germany and, across the North Sea, England, has long made it one of Europe's main battlegrounds. Prosperous throughout the 13th and 14th centuries, the Flemish towns of Ypres, Bruges and Ghent were the first major cities, booming on the manufacture and trade of cloth. Trade later moved to Antwerp, which soon became the greatest port in Europe.

When Protestantism swept Europe in the 16th century, the Low Countries (present-day Belgium, the Netherlands and Luxembourg, often referred to as the Benelux) embraced it, to the chagrin of their ruler, the fanatically Catholic Philip II of Spain. He sent the cruel Inquisition to enforce Catholicism, thus inflaming the smouldering religious tensions. The eruption came with the Iconoclastic Fury, in which Protestants ran riot, ransacking the

churches. Philip retaliated with a force of 10,000 soldiers, and thousands of citizens were imprisoned or executed before war broke out in 1568. The Revolt of the Netherlands lasted 80 years, and in the end roughly laid the region's present-day borders – Holland and its allied provinces victoriously expelling the Spaniards while Belgium and Luxembourg stayed under their rule.

For the next 200 years Belgium remained a battlefield for successive foreign powers. After the Spaniards, the Austrians came, and then the French. The largely unpopular French occupation ended in 1814 with the creation of the United Kingdom of the Netherlands, which incorporated Belgium and Luxembourg. Napoleon was finally trounced the following year at the Battle of Waterloo near Brussels. In 1830, the Catholic Belgians revolted, winning independence from the Netherlands and forming their own kingdom.

The ensuing years saw the start of Flemish nationalism, with tension growing between Flemish (Dutch) and French speakers which would eventually lead to a language partition dividing the country (see the following Population & People section).

In 1885 the then king, Léopold II, personally acquired the Congo in Africa. He was later disgraced over the continuing slave trade there. In the early 1900s the Congo was made a Belgian colony; much-disputed independence was granted in 1960.

Despite Belgium's neutral policy, the Germans invaded in 1914. Used as a bloody battleground throughout WWI, the town of Ypres was wiped off the map. In WWII the whole country was taken over within three weeks of the surprise German attack in May

BELGIUM

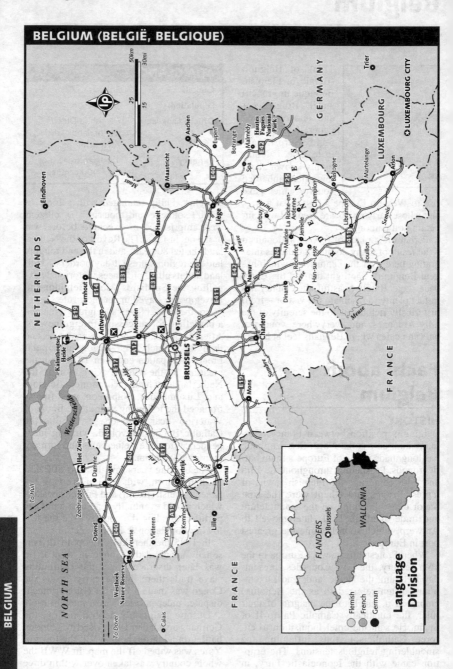

BELGIUM (BELGIË, BELGIQUE)

1940. Controversy over the questionably early capitulation by the then king, Léopold III, led to his abdication in 1950 in favour of his son, King Baudouin, whose popular reign ended with his death (at age 62) in 1993. Childless, Baudouin was succeeded by his brother, the present King Albert II.

Postwar Belgium was characterised by an economic boom, later accentuated by Brussels' appointment as the headquarters of the EU and the North Atlantic Treaty Organisation (NATO).

GEOGRAPHY

Belgium (30,510 sq km) is one of Europe's smallest nations. The north is flat, the south dominated by the hilly, forested Ardennes, and the 66km North Sea coastline monopolised by resorts, save for a few patches of windswept dunes and nature reserves.

CLIMATE

The country has a generally mild, maritime climate. July and August are the warmest months. They are also the wettest, although precipitation is spread pretty evenly over the year. The Ardennes are often a few degrees colder than the rest of the country, with snow from November to March.

POPULATION & PEOPLE

Belgium's population is basically split in two: the Flemish and the Walloons. Language is the dividing factor, made official in 1962 when an invisible line – or Linguistic Divide as it's called – was drawn across the country, cutting it almost equally in half.

To the north lies Flanders, whose Flemish speakers make up 60% of the population. To the south lies Wallonia where French-speaking Walloons make up most of the remainder. There's also a tiny German-speaking enclave in the far east.

ARTS

The arts first flourished in Belgium as early as the 15th century, starting with the realist paintings of the Flemish Primitives, whose leading figure, Jan van Eyck, is said to have invented oil painting.

The mid-16th century gave way to Pieter Brueghel the Elder with his famous scenes of peasant life and grotesque religious allegories. Pieter Paul Rubens dominated the

start of the 17th century, spending much of his early career in Italy where he was heavily influenced by baroque painting.

The turn of the 20th century saw the beginnings of sinuous Art Nouveau architecture in Brussels, led by architect, Victor Horta. Later, Brussels painter René Magritte became one of the world's most prominent Surrealist artists. Hergé, the creator of Tintin, is the best internationally known Belgian cartoonist.

LANGUAGE

For a run-down of the Flemish (Dutch), French and German languages, see the Language Guide at the back of this book. English is widely spoken, although less frequently in Wallonia and the Ardennes.

For travellers, the Linguistic Divide will cause few problems. The most confusing part will be on the road, when the sign you're following to Bergen (as it's known in Flemish) disappears and the town of Mons (the French name) appears.

Facts for the Visitor

HIGHLIGHTS

Some of Belgium's finest museums and sights include the Musée Horta in Brussels, Begijnhof in Bruges, the In Flanders Fields Museum in Ypres and Rubenshuis in Antwerp.

Good places to sample Belgium's famous beers – including Duvel and Westmalle Triple – are Falstaff and Le Greenwich cafes in Brussels and 't Brugs Beertje in Bruges. Hikers will be impressed by the La Roche and Hautes Fagnes areas of the Ardennes.

SUGGESTED ITINERARIES

Three days
Spend one day each in Brussels, Bruges and Antwerp.
One week
Spend two days each in Brussels and the Ardennes, and one day each in Antwerp, Bruges and Ypres.
Two weeks
Spend three days in and around Brussels, two days each in Antwerp and the Ardennes, two days in Bruges and Ypres, two days in Ostend and other coastal resorts, and one day each in Ghent, Namur and Liège.

BELGIUM

PLANNING
Maps
Michelin's map No 909 (scale: 1:350,000) covers both Belgium and Luxembourg. The Institut Géographique National (IGN) publishes topographical maps (scale: 1:25,000) which are good for hikers.

TOURIST OFFICES
The Flemish and Walloon tourist authorities (Toerisme Vlaanderen and Office de Promotion du Tourisme respectively) have their head office (☎ 02-504 03 90, fax 02-504 02 70) at Rue du Marché aux Herbes 63, B-1000 Brussels. Much of the tourist literature they supply is free.

Tourist Offices Abroad
Canada (☎ 514-484 3594, fax 489 8965) PO Box 760, Succursale NDG, Montreal, Quebec H4A 3S2
UK (☎ 0906 3020 245, brochures ☎ 0800 0345 245, fax 020-7531 0393, ✉ info@belgium-tourism.org) 225 Marsh Wall, London E14 9FW
USA (☎ 212-758 8130, fax 355 7675, ✉ info@visitbelgium.com) 780 Third Ave, Suite 1501, New York, NY 10017

EMBASSIES & CONSULATES
Belgian Embassies Abroad
Australia (☎ 02-6273 2501) 19 Arkana St, Yarralumla, Canberra, ACT 2600
Canada (☎ 613-236 7267/7269) 4th floor, 80 Elgin St, Ottawa, Ontario K1P 1B7
New Zealand (☎ 04-472 9558) 1-3 Willeston St, Wellington
UK (☎ 020-7470 3700) 103-105 Eaton Square, London SW1W 9AB
USA (☎ 202-333 6900) 3330 Garfield St, NW Washington DC 20008

Foreign Embassies in Belgium
All the following embassies are in Brussels (area code ☎ 02):

Australia (☎ 231 05 00) Rue Guimard 6, B-1040
Canada (☎ 741 06 11) Ave de Tervueren 2, B-1040
New Zealand (☎ 512 10 40) Blvd du Régent 47, B-1000
UK (☎ 287 62 11) Rue Arlon 85, B-1040
USA (☎ 508 21 11) Blvd du Régent 27, B-1000

MONEY
The Belgian franc (f or BF) has f1, f5, f20 and f50 coins, and notes in f100, f200, f500, f1000, f2000 and f10,000 denominations. Belgian francs are equal to Luxembourg francs and are widely used there, but the reverse does not apply.

Banks are the best place to change money; most charge a commission of 1.25% on cash for EU currencies, f50 on other currencies, and f225 on travellers cheques. Exchange bureaus mostly have lower rates and longer hours. All the major credit cards are widely accepted. You'll find ATMs in major cities and at Zaventem (Brussels) airport.

Travelling modestly – hostels and cheap restaurants – you can get by on about f900 to f1000 a day. Tipping is not obligatory.

Exchange Rates

country	unit		franc
Australia	A$1	=	f25.87
Canada	C$1	=	f30.10
euro	€1	=	f40.33
France	1FF	=	f6.15
Germany	DM1	=	f20.63
Japan	¥100	=	f41.10
New Zealand	NZ$1	=	f20.09
UK	UK£1	=	f67.13
USA	US$1	=	f44.65

POST & COMMUNICATIONS
Post
Post offices open 8 or 9 am to 5 or 6 pm weekdays and Saturday mornings. Letters (under 20g) cost f17 within Belgium, f21 in the EU, f23 in the rest of Europe or f34 elsewhere.

Telephone, Fax & Email
Belgium's international country code is ☎ 32.

Telephone numbers in Belgium have recently changed. Under the new system, you must dial the full area code when phoning anywhere in the country, including within the city you're in. For example, if you're in Brussels and phoning a Brussels number, you must use the ☎ 02 area code.

Local phone calls are metered and cost a minimum of f10. Most numbers prefixed with 0900 or 070 cost f18 per minute.

Call boxes take f5 and f10 coins as well as f200, f500 and f1000 Telecards (Belgacom phonecards), available from post offices and newsagents. A three-minute phone call to the USA from a phonebox costs f120.

Faxes can be sent and received from Belgacom shops (known as *teleboetieks/*

téléboutiques) and cost f85/f350 for the first page to the UK and USA/Australia, plus f75/150 for consecutive pages. Receiving a fax costs f10 per page.

Internet cafes are plentiful; expect to pay f200 to f250 per hour.

INTERNET RESOURCES

The Belgian Tourism site (www.visitbel gium.com) has transport and accommodation information, plus links to other Belgium-related sites. For an overview of Brussels, go to www.bruxelles.irisnet.be.

BOOKS

Lonely Planet publishes a detailed *Brussels, Bruges & Antwerp* city guide. For an affectionate look at Belgium's many idiosyncrasies, pick up *A Tall Man in a Low Land* by Harry Pearson.

WOMEN TRAVELLERS

Women should encounter few problems travelling around Belgium. However, in the event of rape or attack, contact SOS Viol (☎ 02-534 36 36) or Helpline (☎ 02-648 40 14).

GAY & LESBIAN TRAVELLERS

Attitudes to homosexuality are becoming less conservative and same-sex marriages are now legal in Belgium. The age of consent is 16.

Flanders' biggest gay/lesbian organisation is Federatie Werkgroepen Homoseksualiteit (FWH; ☎ 09-223 69 29, fax 09-223 58 21, ✉ info@fwh.be), Kammerstraat 22, 9000 Ghent. It has an information/help hotline called Holebifoon (☎ 09-238 26 26), and a Web site at www.fwh.be on the Web.

The main French-speaking gay/lesbian group is Tels Quels (☎ 02-512 45 87, fax 02-511 31 48, ✉ telsquels@skynet.be), Rue du Marché au Charbon 81 in Brussels.

DISABLED TRAVELLERS

Some government buildings, museums, hotels and restaurants have lifts and/or ramps, but not the majority. Wheelchair users will be up against rough, uneven pavements, and will need to give an hours' notice when travelling by train.

For more information, contact Mobility International (☎ 02-201 56 08, fax 02-201 57 63, ✉ mobint@acradis.be), 18 Blvd Baudouin, 1000 Brussels.

DANGERS & ANNOYANCES

The only danger you're likely to encounter is a big night out on Belgian beer. The national emergency numbers are police ☎ 101 and fire/ambulance ☎ 100.

BUSINESS HOURS

Shops are open 8.30 or 9 am to 6 pm weekdays (often closing for lunch) with similar hours on Saturday. Shops in some cities also open on Sunday. Banks are open 9 am to noon or 1 pm, and 2 to 4 or 5 pm weekdays, and Saturday mornings; in large cities, they often don't close for lunch.

PUBLIC HOLIDAYS & SPECIAL EVENTS

Public holidays are: New Year's Day, Easter Monday, Labour Day (1 May), Ascension Day, Whit Monday, National Day (21 July), Assumption (15 August), All Saints' Day (1 November), Armistice Day (11 November) and Christmas Day.

The religious festival of Carnival is celebrated throughout Belgium. There's a swarm of local and national, artistic or religious festivals – pick up the tourist office's free brochure. The Belgian Pride gay and lesbian parade is held on the first weekend of May.

ACCOMMODATION

The national tourist office will reserve accommodation for free and has camping and hotel leaflets, as well as booklets on guesthouses (*gastenkamers* in Flemish; *chambres d'hôtes* in French). You can also book hotels via Belgian Tourist Reservations (☎ 02-513 74 84, fax 02-513 92 77), Blvd Anspach 111 bte 4, B-1000 Brussels.

Camping rates vary widely – from f260 to f500 for two adults, a tent and vehicle in a basic ground.

There are private hostels in some cities. Otherwise, Belgium has two HI hostelling groups. Les Auberges de Jeunesse (☎ 02-219 56 76, fax 02-219 14 51, ✉ info@ laj.be), Rue de la Sablonnière 28, B-1000 Brussels, runs hostels in Wallonia; its Flemish counterpart is the Vlaamse Jeugdherbergcentrale (☎ 03-232 72 18, fax 03-231 81 26, ✉ info@vjh.be), Van Stralenstraat 40, 2060 Antwerp. Rates range from f420 to f475 per night in a dorm, including breakfast. Some of the hostels also have

BELGIUM

single/double rooms for f800/1170. Most charge f125 extra for sheets.

B&Bs and guesthouses are rapidly gaining ground in Belgium – prices range from f800 to f1200 for singles, f1200 to f1800 for doubles and f1500 to f2700 for triples.

The cheapest hotels charge about f1000/1500 for singles/doubles without bathroom facilities but with breakfast. Some mid-range and top-end hotels in Brussels drop their rates dramatically at weekends when the EU quarter is dead – great deals can be had.

FOOD & DRINKS

Belgian cuisine is highly regarded throughout Europe – combining French style with German portions, you'll rarely have reason to complain. Meat and seafood are abundantly consumed, as are *wafels* or *gaufres* (waffles) and *frites* (chips or fries) which the Belgians swear they invented.

The popularity of frites cannot be understated. Every village has at least one *frituur/friture* where frites are served up in a paper cone or dish, smothered until almost unrecognisable with mayonnaise. A *belegd broodje* or *sandwich garni* (half a baguette filled with an array of garnishings) is another popular snack.

The national dish is *mosselen/moules* (mussels) cooked in white wine and served with a mountain of frites. The rule of thumb for mussels is to eat them during the months with an 'r' and don't touch the ones that haven't opened properly when cooked.

When dining out, the *dagschotel/plat du jour* (dish of the day) is often the cheapest option. Vegetarians will find many cafes and brasseries have at least one suitable option.

The quality of Belgian beer is excellent and the variety incomparable – somewhere upwards of 400 types. The most noted are the abbey-brewed Trappist beers, dark in colour, grainy in taste and dangerously strong (from 6% to 11.5% alcohol by volume).

Then there's *lambiek/lambic*, a spontaneously fermented beer which comes sweet or sour depending on what's added during fermentation – *gueuze*, a sour variety, is the most famous.

Getting There & Away

AIR

Belgium's national airline is Sabena and the main international airport is Zaventem (also known as Brussels National), 14km northeast of Brussels.

LAND

Bus

Eurolines operates international bus services to and from Belgium. Depending on the destination and the time of year, its buses stop in Brussels, Antwerp, Bruges, Ghent, and Liège. To most major destinations there's just one price whether you depart from Brussels or, for example, Antwerp. Given Belgium's small size, there's not much difference in journey times – Brussels-Paris is 3¾ hours, or 4¾ hours from Antwerp. As an indication, services from Brussels include Amsterdam (f600, four hours, eight per day), Cologne (f700, four hours, two per day), London (f1690, 8½ hours, seven per day) and Paris (f790, 3¾ hours, eight per day).

Train

The train network is run by the Belgische Spoorwegen/Société National des Chemins de Fer Belges, whose logo is a 'B' in an oval. For all international inquiries – including Eurostar and Thalys trains – call ☎ 0900-10366 (f18 per minute).

Brussels, Belgium's international train hub, has three main train stations: Gare du Nord, Gare du Midi, and Gare Centrale. Gare du Midi is the main station for international connections: the Eurostar and Thalys fast trains stop here only. All other international trains stop at Gare du Nord and Gare du Midi.

Eurostar trains between Brussels and London (2¾ hours, 10 trains per day) operate through the Channel Tunnel. Standard 2nd-class fares are f6500/13,000 one-way/return, but cheaper weekend and midweek fares are available (conditions apply). For more, check the Web site at www. eurostar.com.

Thalys fast trains connect Brussels with Paris (f2180, 1½ hours, hourly), Cologne (f1230, 2½ hours, seven trains per day) and Amsterdam (f1310, 2¾ hours, five per day).

Thalys prices are generally reduced on weekends and those under 26 years get a 50% discount. For more details see www.thalys.com.

Examples of one-way, 2nd-class adult fares and journey times with ordinary trains from Brussels to some neighbouring countries include: Amsterdam (f1150, three hours, hourly trains), Cologne (f1150, three hours, every two hours), and Luxembourg City (f920, 2¾ hours, hourly). To London's Charing Cross station (five hours), there's a train-boat-train combo which costs f1440/2160 one-way/return. At weekends, all return train fares are reduced by 40%.

SEA
Hover-speed's highspeed Seacat sails from Ostend to Dover (England) in two hours (two to five services per day). One-way fares for cars plus one adult range from f4792 to f9274, depending on the season. Passengers are charged f1642. P&O/North Sea Ferries sails overnight from Zeebrugge to Hull (England; 14 hours) and charges f3700/7660 for a car in the low/high season and f2300/4900 for adult passengers. Cabins start at f888 per person.

Getting Around

BUS
Buses are used to connect towns and villages in more remote areas, particularly throughout the Ardennes. Local tourist offices will generally have details.

TRAIN
Belgium's transport system is dominated by its efficient rail network. There are four levels of service: InterCity (IC) trains (which are the fastest), InterRegional (IR), local (L) and peak-hour (P) commuter trains. Depending on the line, there will be an IC and an IR train every half-hour or hour. For all national train information call ☎ 02-555 25 55.

On weekends, return tickets within Belgium are reduced by 40% for the first passenger, 60% for the rest of the group (to a maximum of six people). Discount excursion tickets, known as B-Excursions, to a huge number of destinations around the country are also available. Purchase these from ticket counters at train stations.

Several rail passes are available. The Benelux Tourrail – which gives five days travel in one month in Belgium, the Netherlands and Luxembourg – costs f4400 (2nd class) for adults and f3400 for those aged under 26. This pass can no longer be bought in the Netherlands, but passes bought in either Belgium or Luxembourg are valid for all three countries.

The Belgian Tourrail pass (f2100) gives five-days travel in one month within Belgium. A Fixed Price Reduction Card (f650) gives up to 50% off all train tickets for a month. The Go Pass (f1490; under 26 only), valid for six months, gives 10 one-way journeys anywhere in Belgium.

CAR & MOTORCYCLE
Drive on the right and give way to the right. The speed limit is 50km/h in towns, 90km/h outside and 120km/h on motorways. The blood alcohol limit is 0.05%. Fuel prices per litre are f44 for super, f42 for lead-free and f30 for diesel. More motoring information can be obtained from the Touring Club de Belgique (☎ 02-233 22 11), Rue de la Loi 44, 1040 Brussels.

BICYCLE
Normal/mountain bikes can be hired from some train stations for f365/680 per day (plus a f500/1500 deposit). They must be returned to the same station. Bikes can be taken on trains (only from stations in cities and major towns) for f150.

Brussels

☎ 02

Brussels (Brussel in Flemish, Bruxelles in French) is an unpretentious mix of grand edifices and modern skyscrapers. Its character largely follows that of the nation it governs: modest, confident, but rarely striving to overtly impress. Having grown from a 6th-century marshy village on the banks of the River Senne (filled in long ago for sanitary reasons), this bilingual city is now headquarters of the EU and NATO, and home to Europe's most impressive central square.

Orientation
The Grand Place, Brussels' imposing 15th-century market square, sits dead centre in

BELGIUM

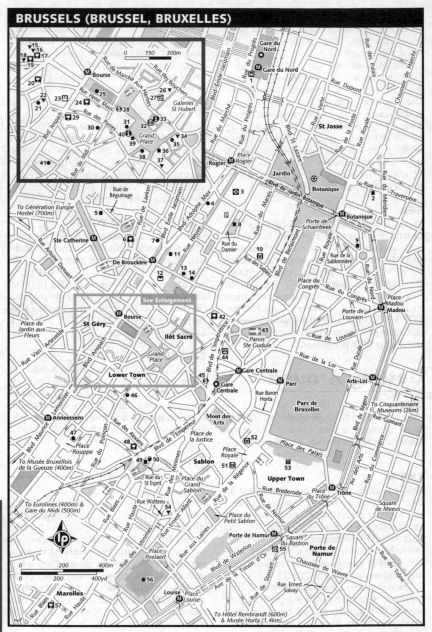

BRUSSELS (BRUSSEL, BRUXELLES)

BELGIUM

BRUSSELS (BRUSSEL, BRUXELLES)

PLACES TO STAY		4	Waterstones	38	Art-Nouveau	
2	Centre Vincent van Gogh		(Bookshop)		Plaque	
5	Hôtel Noga	6	Le Wings	39	Hôtel de Ville	
8	Sleep Well Hostel	7	Eurolines		(City Hall)	
9	Jacques Brel Hostel	10	Centre Belge de la	40	Tourist Information	
11	Hôtel Métropole		Bande Dessinée		Brussels (TIB)	
36	Hôtel Saint Michel	12	Main Post Office	41	Tels Quels	
47	Hôtel à la Grande Cloche	13	AirStop/TaxiStop	42	À la Mort Subite	
49	Bruegel Hostel	14	Sterling Books	43	Cathédrale Sts Michel	
		17	L'Archiduc		& Gudule	
PLACES TO EAT		19	Le Greenwich	44	Belgacom	
15	Kasbash	20	Mappa Mundo		Téléboutique	
16	Le Pain Quotidien	21	Wash Club	45	Citibank	
18	Fin de Siècle	23	Kladaradatch! Palace	46	Manneken Pis	
22	Sushi Factory	24	Falstaff	48	La Fleur en	
26	Aux Armes de Bruxelles	25	Bourse (Stock Exchange)		Papier Doré	
34	Panos	27	Point Net Surf	50	Lavoir Friza	
37	Frites/Pitta Bread Places	28	Basle	51	Musées Royaux des	
54	Le Perroquet	29	Ancienne Belgique		Beaux-Arts	
		30	usit/CONNECTIONS	52	Musée des Instruments	
OTHER		31	Thomas Cook		de Musique	
1	Eurolines Bus Station/	32	Musée de la Ville de	53	Palais Royal	
	Main Office		Bruxelles	55	CyberTheatre	
3	City 2 Shopping Centre;	33	National Tourist Office	56	Palais de Justice	
	GB Supermarket	35	De Boeck (Bus Tours)	57	La Démence	

the Petit Ring, a pentagon of boulevards enclosing central Brussels. Many of the main sights are within the Ring, but there's also plenty to see outside. Gare Centrale, Brussels' most central train station, is about five minutes' walk from the Grand Place; Gare du Midi, where most international trains arrive, is 2.5km from the famous square.

Brussels' street and station names are written in both French and Flemish – we have used the French versions.

Information

Tourist Offices Tourist Information Brussels (TIB; ☎ 02-513 89 40, fax 02-514 45 38, ⓔ tourism.brussels@tib.be), in the city hall on the Grand Place, has city information and is open 9 am to 6 pm daily (10 am to 2 pm on Sunday from October to December). It sells two passes – the Must of Brussels (f600) and the Brussels Passport (f300) which give discounts to museums, restaurants etc.

For country-wide information head to the national tourist office (☎ 02-504 03 90, fax 02-504 02 70), Rue du Marché aux Herbes 63. It's open 9 am to 6 pm daily (until 1 pm on Sunday from November to April).

Money Outside banking hours, there are exchange bureaus at the airport and at all

three train stations. ATMs are located at the airport and at Citibank, Carrefour de l'Europe 13, immediately opposite Gare Centrale. A good central exchange agency (cash only) is Basle, Rue au Beurre 23. Thomas Cook (☎ 02-513 28 45) is at Grand Place 4.

Post & Communications The main post office is in the Centre Monnaie (1st floor) on Blvd Anspach. The Belgacom Téléboutique (fax 02-540 67 85) on Blvd de l'Impératrice is open 9 am to 6 pm Monday to Saturday. The city's premier cybercafe is CyberTheatre (☎ 02-500 78 78, ⓔ info@cybertheatre.net), Ave de la Toison d'Or 4. A more central cybercafe is Point Net Surf (☎ 02-513 14 15, ⓔ info@pointnet.be), Petite Rue des Bouchers 16.

Travel Agencies AirStop/TaxiStop (☎ 070-23 31 88 for AirStop, ☎ 02-223 23 10 for TaxiStop), Rue du Fossé aux Loups 28, offers cheap charter flights and paid rides (f1.3 per km) in cars going to other European cities. Usit/Connections (☎ 02-550 01 30), Rue du Midi 19, is a good general travel agency.

Bookshops Waterstones (☎ 02-219 27 08), Blvd Adolphe Max 71, and Sterling

Books (☎ 02-223 62 23), Rue du Fossé aux Loups 38, are specialist English-language bookshops.

Laundry Lavoir Friza on Rue Haute, and Wash Club, Place St Géry 25, are self-service laundries.

Medical & Emergency Services For 24-hour medical emergencies including ambulance services, dial ☎ 100. Helpline (☎ 02-648 40 14) is a Brussels-based, 24-hour English-speaking crisis line and information service. Several hospitals provide 24-hour emergency assistance. Hospital St Pierre (☎ 02-218 74 35), on the corner of Rue Haute and Rue de l'Abricotier, is one of the most central.

Things to See & Do

Grand Place & Around The Grand Place is the obvious start for exploring the Petit Ring. It was formerly home to the craft guilds, whose rich guildhalls line the square.

To the south on Rue Charles Buls is one of the earliest works of the city's once-famous Art Nouveau cult: an 1899 **gilded plaque** dedicated to the city from its appreciative artists. Beside it is a **statue of Everard t'Serclaes**, a 14th-century hero whose gleaming torso passers-by rub for good luck. A few blocks farther, on the corner of Rue du Chêne and Rue de l'Étuve, is **Manneken Pis**, the famous statue of a small boy weeing.

One block north-east of the Grand Place is the **Galeries St Hubert**, Europe's oldest glass-covered shopping arcade (and home to Neuhaus, one of the city's finest chocolate shops).

Atomium The space-age leftover from the 1958 World Fair, Atomium, Blvd du Centenaire in the suburb of Laeken, has virtually become a symbol of the city. It's open 9 am to 8 pm daily (10 am to 6 pm from 1 September to 31 March); entry is f200. Take tram No 81 to Heysel.

Museums The Grand Place is home to several museums, the most interesting of which is the **Musée de la Ville de Bruxelles** in the Maison du Roi. It gives a historical rundown on the city and exhibits every piece of clothing ever worn by Manneken Pis (closed Friday; f100).

The **Musées Royaux des Beaux-Arts**, Rue de la Régence 3, houses Belgium's premier collections of ancient and modern art. The Flemish Primitives, Brueghel and Rubens are well represented (closed Monday; f150). Its Web site is at www.fine-arts-museum.be.

The nearby **Musée des Instruments de Musique**, Place Royale, boasts the world's biggest collection of musical instruments and is newly housed in the stunning Old England building – check with the TIB for new opening times and prices.

Tintin fans must not miss the **Centre Belge de la Bande Dessinée**, Rue des Sables 20, which houses the nation's best ensemble of comic-strip art (closed Monday; f200).

There are several museums to draw you out of the Petit Ring. The **Musée Horta**, Rue Américaine 25 in St Gilles, was Horta's house and is an excellent introduction to his architectural movement (f150/200 on weekdays/weekends). To the east, **Cinquantenaire** is a large museum conglomerate – art, history, military and motor vehicles together in a huge complex.

About 500m north-west of Gare du Midi is the **Musée Bruxellois de la Gueuze**, Rue Gheude 56 in Anderlecht – a working brewery where you can sample Brussels' unique gueuze beer (closed Sunday; f100).

Organised Tours

Three-hour bus tours of Brussels are run by De Boeck (☎ 02-513 77 44), Rue de la Colline 8 (just off the Grand Place).

For specialised tours – Horta and Art Nouveau, or Brussels in the Art Deco era, for example – contact ARAU (☎ 02-219 33 45), Blvd Adolphe Max 55.

Special Events

The annual Ommegang is a 16th-century-style procession staged within the illuminated Grand Place in early July. Just as popular is the biennial flower carpet that colours the square in mid-August in even-numbered years.

Places to Stay

Visitors can find good accommodation deals on weekends – Friday to Sunday – when many hotels cut prices because of the absence of business people.

BELGIUM

Camping Heading south, *Beersel* (☎ *02-331 05 61, fax 02-378 19 77, Steenweg op Ukkel 75)* is a small ground which charges f100/80 for an adult/child and f80/50 tent/car, and is open all year. Tram No 55 (direction: Uccle) stops 3km away, but you can take bus UB the rest of the way to Beersel.

Hostels Brussels' three HI-affiliated hostels charge the same prices – singles/doubles for f800/1170 and dorm beds from f420 to f495. The most central is *Bruegel* (☎ *02-511 04 36, ✆ jeugdherberg.bruegel@ping.be, Rue du St Esprit 2)*. *Jacques Brel* (☎ *02-218 01 87, fax 02-219 14 51, ✆ brussels.brel@ laj.be, Rue de la Sablonnière 30)* is 15 minutes' walk from the city centre. *Génération Europe* (☎ *02-410 38 58, fax 02-410 39 05, ✆ gener.europe@infonie.be, Rue de l'Éléphant 4)* is a 20-minute walk north-west of the Grand Place.

Centrally located and very popular is *Sleep Well* (☎ *02-218 50 50, fax 02-218 13 13, ✆ info@sleepwell.be, Rue du Damier 23)*. Single/double rooms go for f695/1140, and there are six/eight-bed dorms for f410/350 per person.

The *Centre Vincent van Gogh* (☎ *02-217 01 58, fax 02-219 79 95, ✆ chab@ping.be, Rue Traversière 8)* is more laid-back but just as likeable. Singles/doubles cost f700/1160, four/six-bed dorms go for f480/410 and beds in a larger dorm are f340. It's 1.25km uphill from Gare Centrale or take the metro to Botanique.

Guesthouses For B&B accommodation contact Bed & Brussels (☎ 02-646 07 37, fax 02-644 01 14), Rue Gustave Biot 2, 1050 Brussels, or visit www.BnB-Brussels.be. Prices start at f1200/2000 for a single/double room, and rise to f1800/3000 (there's a 30% surcharge for bookings of just one night).

Hotels The *Hôtel à la Grande Cloche* (☎ *02-512 61 40, fax 02-512 65 91, ✆ info@hotelgrandecloche.com, Place Rouppe 10)* has well-kept doubles without private bathroom for f1750, or f2350 with.

The charming *Hôtel Noga* (☎ *02-218 67 63, fax 02-218 16 03, ✆ info@nogaho tel.com, Rue du Béguinage 38)* in the Ste Catherine quarter has rooms from f2950/3300 (discounted to f2600 on the

weekends). If you'd prefer to be dead centre, head to *Hôtel Saint Michel* (☎ *02-511 09 56, fax 02-511 46 00, Grand Place 11)*. It's overpriced (rooms from f4250/5100) but that's to be expected with such a unique location.

For *belle époque* luxury there's the *Hôtel Métropole* (☎ *02-217 23 00, fax 02-218 02 20, ✆ info@metropolehotel.be, Place de Brouckère 31)*. Rooms start at f10,500/ 12,500 but on weekends drop to f4500 (email bookings only) or f6500/8500 for other bookings.

Places to Eat

Restaurants Brussels' dining heart is Rue des Bouchers (Butcher's Street), near the Grand Place. Most of the seafood restaurants here are tourist traps – *Aux Armes de Bruxelles* (☎ *02-511 55 98, Rue des Bouchers 13)* is a notable exception. Expect efficient service, Belgian classics, and main courses for about f500.

Fin de Siècle (☎ *513 51 23, Rue des Chartreux 9)* is a popular bistro with a blackboard menu and meals in the f350 to f450 bracket.

Kasbash (☎ *02-502 40 26, Rue Antoine Dansaert 20)* is a lovely, lantern-lit restaurant on one of the city's trendiest streets. Moroccan dishes – couscous (f400 to f500) and *tajines* (meat-based stews) – are the order of the day.

Cafes For wholesome savoury pies and filled sandwiches in a pleasant non-smoking environment head to *Le Pain Quotidien* (☎ *02-502 23 61, Rue Antoine Dansaert 16)*.

In the Sablon, *Le Perroquet* (☎ *02-512 99 22, Rue Watteeu 31)* is a lovely Art Nouveau cafe with a great range of salads (f175 to f375), exotic stuffed pitta bread (from f170) and vegetarian fare.

Fast Food Rue Marché aux Fromages near the Grand Place is stacked with *frites/pitta bread places*. For a half-baguette sandwich, head to *Panos (Rue du Marché aux Herbes 85)*. Japanese snacks are available from the *Sushi Factory (Place St Géry 28)*.

Self-Catering There's a *GB supermarket* in the basement of the City 2 shopping centre on Rue Neuve (closed Sunday).

BELGIUM

Entertainment

Among Brussels' bars, *Falstaff (Rue Henri Maus 17)* is an Art Nouveau showpiece. *Mappa Mundo (Rue du Pont de la Carpe 2)* is where the young and trendy flock. Those into Art Deco and live jazz shouldn't go past the *L'Archiduc (Rue Antoine Dansaert 6)*. *Le Greenwich (Rue des Chartreux 7)*, *À la Mort Subite (Rue Mont aux Herbes Potagères 7)* and *La Fleur en Papier Doré (Rue des Alexiens 53)* are three wonderful ancient cafes each with a unique ambience.

The biggest gay rave is *La Démence (Rue Blaes 208)* held one Sunday per month at the Fuse, a techno/house club. *Le Wings (Rue du Cyprès 3)* is a lesbian disco (Saturday only).

For local and international bands, check out the line-up at the *Ancienne Belgique (☎ 02-548 24 24, Blvd Anspach 110)*. A good central cinema is *Kladaradatch! Palace (☎ 02-501 67 76, Blvd Anspach 85)*.

Getting There & Away

Bus Eurolines has three offices in Brussels. The main office (☎ 02-274 13 50), Rue du Progrès 80, is next to Gare du Nord and most of its buses depart from here. Other offices are at Place de Brouckère 50 (☎ 02-217 00 25) and Ave Fonsny 9 near Gare du Midi (☎ 02-538 20 49). For details on fares and schedules, see the Getting There & Away section earlier in this chapter.

Train For prices and journey times from Brussels to other Belgian cities and towns, check the Getting There & Away section in those places. For international services, see the Getting There & Away section at the beginning of this chapter.

Getting Around

Brussels' efficient bus, tram and metro network is operated by the Société des Transports Intercommunaux de Bruxelles (STIB in French, MIVB in Flemish). Single-journey tickets cost f50, five/10-journey cards f240/350 and a one-day card f140. Tickets valid on all transport can be bought from metro stations or bus drivers; the one-day card is also available from the TIB. Public transport runs until about midnight.

AROUND BRUSSELS

A huge stone lion and nearly a million visitors a year look out over the plains where Napoleon was defeated and European history changed course at the Battle of **Waterloo**, south of Brussels. At the base of the **Butte du Lion** is a **Visitor's Centre** (☎ 02-385 19 12) at Route du Lion 254 – take bus W from Place Rouppe in Brussels. Those interested in the British version of events should head to the **Musée Wellington**, Chaussée de Bruxelles 147, 5km away from Butte du Lion in the village of Waterloo – bus W also passes here.

Flanders

ANTWERP
☎ 03

Antwerp (Antwerpen in Flemish, Anvers in French) is perhaps Belgium's most underrated tourist city. Second in size to the capital and often more likeable, it's compact and beautifully endowed with baroque buildings. As a world port, its atmosphere is international (though at times seedy). From behind the discreet facades of Antwerp's Jewish quarter runs the world's largest diamond-cutting industry.

With a prime spot on the Scheldt (Flemish: Schelde) River, Antwerp came to the fore as Western Europe's greatest economic centre in the early 16th century. In the 17th century it was home to the artist Pieter Paul Rubens.

Orientation

Antwerp is bordered by the Scheldt and the Ring, a highway built on a moat that once encircled the city. Many of the sights are concentrated between the impressive Centraal Station and the old centre – a 20-minute walk away, based around the Grote Markt. Others are spread around Het Zuid, the city's trendiest area (about 1.25km south of the Grote Markt).

Information

Tourist Office The tourist office (☎ 03-232 01 03, fax 03-231 19 37, ✉ toerisme@antwerpen.be), Grote Markt 15, is open 9 am to 6 pm daily (until 5 pm on Sunday).

Money You get a good rate (cash only) at Leo Stevens exchange bureau, De Keyserlei 64 near Centraal Station (9 am to 5 pm weekdays, 1 pm Saturday). Thomas Cook (☎ 03-226 29 53) is at Koningin Astridplein 33.

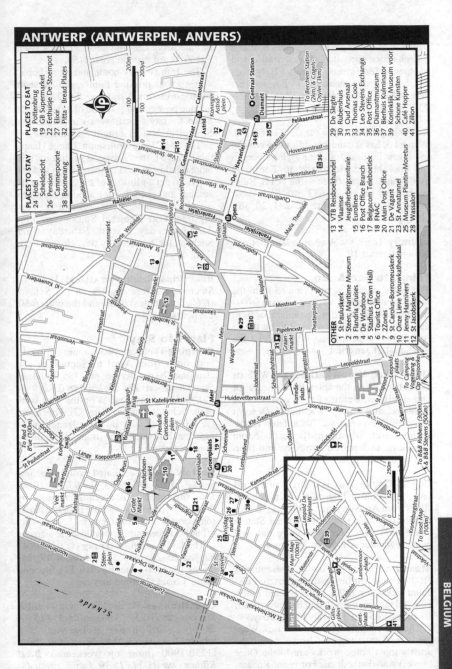

ANTWERP (ANTWERPEN, ANVERS)

PLACES TO STAY
24 Hotel
26 Scheldezicht
26 Pension
27 Cammerpoorte
38 Boomerang

PLACES TO EAT
8 Pottenbrug
19 GB Supermarket
22 Eethuisje De Stoempot
27 Elixir
32 Pitta - Bread Places

OTHER
1 St Pauluskerk
2 Steen; Maritime Museum
3 Flandria Cruises
4 De Windroos
5 Stadhuis (Town Hall)
6 Tourist Office
9 ZZones
9 St Carolus-Borromeuskerk
10 Onze Lieve Vrouwkathedraal
11 Jenny Hanivers
12 St Jacobskerk
13 VTB Reisboekhandel
14 Vlaamse Jeugdherbergcentrale
15 Eurolines
16 Post Office Branch
17 Belgacom Telebæetiek
18 FNAC
20 Main Post Office
21 De Vagant
23 St Anntunnel
25 Museum Plantin-Moretus
28 Wassalon
29 De Slegte
30 Rubenshuis
31 Oud Arsenaal
33 Thomas Cook
34 Leo Stevens Exchange
35 Post Office
36 Diamantmuseum
37 Bierhuis Kulminator
39 Koninklijk Museum voor Schone Kunsten
40 Café Hopper
41 Zillion

BELGIUM

Post & Communications The main post office is at Groenplaats 43; there's also a branch office opposite Centraal Station and another on Jezusstraat. There's a Belgacom Teleboetiek at Jezusstraat 1. For Internet access, head to the cybercafe 2Zones (☎ 03-232 24 00), Wolstraat 15.

Bookshops De Slegte (☎ 03-231 66 27), Wapper 5, has second-hand English novels; more can be found at Jenny Hannivers, a tiny bookshop at Melkmarkt 30. For travel guides and maps, there's the VTB Reisboekhandel (☎ 03-220 33 66), St Jakobsmarkt 45, or FNAC (☎ 03-231 20 56), Groenplaats 31.

Laundry There's a Wassalon laundrette at Nationalestraat 18.

Things to See & Do

The city's skyline is best viewed from the raised **promenades**, known as *wandelterrassen*, leading off from Steenplein, or from the river's west bank, accessible by the St Annatunnel, a pedestrian tunnel under the Scheldt at St Jansvliet.

Onze Lieve Vrouwkathedraal With its 120m-high spire, the splendid Cathedral of Our Lady is Belgium's largest Gothic cathedral and home to Rubens' *Descent from the Cross*. Entry (f70) is from Handschoenmarkt; it's open 10 am to 5 pm weekdays, to 3 pm on Saturday, and from 1 to 4 pm Sunday.

Cogels-Osylei This is a street of radical late 19th-century houses built in eclectic styles from Art Nouveau to classical or neo-Renaissance. It's south of Centraal Station and a little way from the centre but well worth a wander – tram No 11 runs along it.

Museums Entry to major museums is f100, or you can buy a three-museum discount ticket for f200. Unless noted otherwise, all the museums listed below are open 10 am to 4.45 pm Tuesday to Saturday.

The **Rubenshuis** (Rubens' House), Wapper 9, tops most visitors' lists although the artist's most noted works are in the Onze Lieve Vrouwkathedraal. For more Rubens, as well as Flemish Primitives and contemporary art works, there's the **Koninklijk Museum voor Schone Kunsten** (Royal Museum of Fine Arts), Leopold de Waelplaats 1-9 in Het Zuid. Admission costs f150.

The 16th-century home and workshop of a prosperous printing family, the **Museum Plantin-Moretus**, Vrijdagmarkt 22, displays antique presses and splendid old globes. The **Steen**, the city's medieval riverside castle at Steenplein, houses a **maritime museum**.

The free **Diamantmuseum**, Lange Herentalsestraat 31, traces aspects of the city's diamond industry, and is open 10 am to 5 pm daily. To get a glimpse of the amount of diamonds and gold being traded in Antwerp, just wander along Pelikaanstraat or Vestingstraat near Centraal Station any time during the day (except Saturday when Shabbat, the Jewish holy day, closes everything down).

Boat Trips Flandria (☎ 03-231 31 00) on Steenplein offers cruises on the Scheldt (f260, 50 minutes) or around the port (f450, 2½ hours).

Places to Stay

Camping There are two camping grounds, both open from April to September and charging f70 per person, plus f35 for a tent, caravan or car. *De Molen* (☎ 03-219 81 79), on St Annastrand, is on the west bank of the Scheldt (bus No 81 or 82). *Vogelzang* (☎ 03-238 57 17), on Vogelzanglaan, is near the Bouwcentrum (tram No 2, direction: Hoboken).

Hostels The HI-affiliated hostel, *Op Sinjoorke* (☎ 03-238 02 73, fax 03-248 19 32, Eric Sasselaan 2) is about 10 minutes by tram No 2 (direction: Hoboken) or bus No 27 (direction: Zuid) from Centraal Station – get off at Bouwcentrum and follow the signs.

The laid-back *Boomerang* (☎ 03-238 47 82, fax 03-288 66 67, Volkstraat 49) has dorms for f360 – get bus No 23 (direction 'Zuid') from Centraal Station.

Guesthouses Particularly nice is *B&B Stevens* (☎ 03-259 15 90, fax 03-259 15 99, ✉ fdj.greta@wol.be, Molenstraat 35), which has single/double rooms from f1250/1900 (more on weekends). *B&B Ribbens* (☎ 03-248 15 39, Justitiestraat 43) is wonderfully spacious and charges f1250/1700.

Hotels The new *Hotel Scheldezicht* (☎ *03-231 66 02, fax 03-231 90 02, St Jansvliet 2*) has spacious, well-priced rooms for f1250/1850. A sage mid-range choice is *Pension Cammerpoorte* (☎ *03-231 28 36, fax 03-226 28 43,* ❻ *jactoe@net4all.be, Steenhouwersvest 55*). Tucked away on a quiet street in the heart of town, it has 16 bright rooms for f1950/2450.

Places to Eat

For authentic Flemish *stoemp* (mashed potatoes), go no further than *Eethuisje De Stoempot* (☎ *03-231 36 86, Vlasmarkt 12*). This down-to-earth eatery offers meals the way mum made them, at prices to match.

Vegetarians should head to *Elixir* (☎ *03-231 73 21, Steenhouwersvest 57*), a 1st-floor restaurant with a good dagschotel for f345. It's open mainly for lunch (also 6 to 8 pm Saturday).

Pottenbrug (☎ *03-231 51 47, Minder-broedersrui 38*) is a wonderful old bistro with mains for f520 to f650.

Pitta bread places reign in the streets in front of Centraal Station. Self-caterers will find a *GB supermarket* in the basement of the Grand Bazaar shopping centre at Groenplaats.

Entertainment

With some 4000 bars and cafes, you'll be hard-pressed to find a better place to pub crawl. For terrace cafes, head to Groenplaats or the more intimate Handschoenmarkt. The *Oud Arsenaal* (*Pijpelinckxstraat 4*) is a popular local haunt (and the beers are among the cheapest in town). *De Vagant* (*Reynderssstraat 21*) serves more than 200 *jenevers* (Belgian gins). *Bierhuis Kulminator* (*Vleminckveld 32*) is the place to sink a host of Belgian brews – there's more than 600 on the menu.

The big name on the club scene is *Zillion* (*Jan Van Gentstraat 4*) in Het Zuid. *Red & Blue* (*Lange Schipperskapelstraat 11*), north of the Grote Markt, bills itself as the biggest gay disco in the country. For live jazz, head to *Café Hopper* (*Leopold De Waelstraat 2*) in Het Zuid.

Getting There & Away

Eurolines (☎ *03-233 86 62*) has an office at Van Stralenstraat 8 – all buses depart from here.

Antwerp's main train station, Centraal Station, is about 1.5km east of the old city centre. National connections from Antwerp include IC trains to Brussels (f200, 35 minutes), Bruges (f405, 70 minutes) and Ghent (f260, 45 minutes). The Thalys trains go to Amsterdam (f1110, two hours).

Getting Around

A good network of buses, trams and a premetro (a tram that runs underground for part of its journey) is run by De Lijn. Public transport information kiosks are located at premetro station Diamant (in front of Centraal Station) and Groenplaats. The main bus hubs are Koningin Astridplein next to Centraal Station and Franklin Rooseveltplaats two blocks west. Bikes can be hired from De Windroos (☎ 03-480 93 88), Steenplein 1a.

GHENT
☎ 09

In the Middle Ages, Ghent (Gent in Flemish, Gand in French) was the second-largest city in Europe (after Paris) and the continent's largest cloth producer. Modern Ghent's attractions are largely medieval, its most noted sight being the Van Eyck brothers' *Adoration of the Mystic Lamb* at St Baafskathedraal. Though not picturesque like Bruges, Ghent is home to many students and plenty of lively bars.

Orientation

Ghent does not have one central square. Instead, the medieval core is a row of large open areas connected by two imposing churches and a belfry – their line of towers has long been the trademark of Ghent's skyline. The Korenmarkt is the westernmost square, and is technically the city's centre – it's a 25-minute walk from the main train station, St Pietersstation, but is regularly connected with it by tram Nos 1, 10 and 11. Halfway between the two is the university quarter, based along St Pietersnieuwstraat.

Information

The tourist office (☎ 09-266 52 32, fax 09-225 62 88, ❻ voorlichting@gent.be), Botermarkt 17, is open 9 am to 8 pm daily from April to early November, and 9.30 am to 6 pm the rest of the year.

BELGIUM

The Europabank inside St Pietersstation and the Goffin Change at Mageleinstraat 36 are both open daily. The post office is at Lange Kruisstraat 55. Internet users should head to Globetrotter (☎ 09-269 08 60), Kortrijkse Poortstraat 180, south of the centre. There's a laundrette at Oudburg 25.

Things to See
The 15th-century *Adoration of the Mystic Lamb* in **St Baafskathedraal** is a lavish representation of medieval religious thinking and one of the earliest known oil paintings. The entrance to the cathedral is on St Baafsplein; it's open 8.30 am to 6 pm daily. The crypt with the Mystic Lamb is open 9.30 am to 5 pm Monday to Saturday and from 1 to 5 pm Sunday (in winter it's open 10.30 am to noon and 2.30 to 4 pm daily, and 2 to 5 pm Sunday). Entry to the cathedral is free but it costs f100 to see the Mystic Lamb.

Rising from the old Cloth Hall, the 14th-century **belfort** (belfry) on Botermarkt affords spectacular views of the city. Entry costs f100. With moat, turrets and arrow slits, the fearsome 12th-century **Gravensteen**, St Veerleplein, is the quintessential

castle. It was built to protect the townsfolk as well as intimidate them into law-abiding submission. It's open 9 am to 5 or 6 pm daily and costs f200.

The **Museum voor Schone Kunsten** in Citadelpark is home to some Flemish Primitives and a couple of typically nightmarish works by Hieronymus Bosch. Across the road is **SMAK**, the city's new contemporary art museum. Both museums are open 10 am to 5 or 6 pm (closed Monday), and admission to each is f100.

Organised Tours
City canal cruises (f170, 35 minutes) depart from the Graslei and Korenlei, west of Korenmarkt.

Places to Stay
Camping The *Camping Blaarmeersen* (☎ 09-221 53 99, Zuiderlaan 12), to the west of the city, charges f130/60 per adult/child, plus f140/70 for a tent/car. Take bus No 9 from the station then bus No 38.

Hostel Ghent's attractive hostel, *De Draecke* (☎ 09-233 70 50, fax 09-233 80 01,

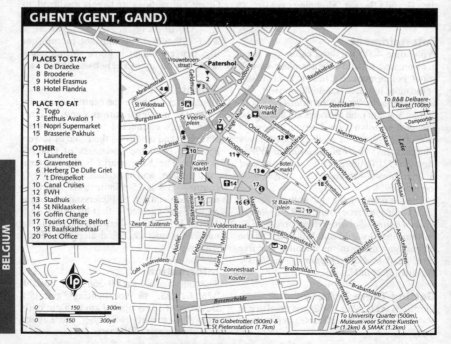

GHENT (GENT, GAND)

PLACES TO STAY
4 De Draecke
8 Brooderie
9 Hotel Erasmus
18 Hotel Flandria

PLACE TO EAT
2 Togo
3 Eethuis Avalon 1
11 Nopri Supermarket
15 Brasserie Pakhuis

OTHER
1 Laundrette
5 Gravensteen
6 Herberg De Dulle Griet
7 't Dreupelkot
10 Canal Cruises
12 FWH
13 Stadhuis
14 St Niklaaskerk
16 Goffin Change
17 Tourist Office; Belfort
19 St Baafskathedraal
20 Post Office

BELGIUM

0   150   300m
0   150   300yd

To Globetrotter (500m) & St Pietersstation (1.7km)

To University Quarter (500m), Museum voor Schone Kunsten (1.2km) & SMAK (1.2km)

@ *youthhostel.gent@skynet.be, St Widos-traat 11)*, occupies a renovated warehouse close to the heart of town. A bunk in a six-bed room, all with private facilities, costs f385; singles/doubles go for f625/950. From the train station, take tram No 1, 10 or 11 to St Veerleplein.

Guesthouses The Gilde der Gentse Gas-tenkamers (☎ 09-233 30 99), Tentoon-stellingslaan 69, 9000 Ghent, is a guild organising the city's B&Bs. It publishes a free booklet (in English) detailing guesthouses.

One excellent option is *B&B Delbaere-Ravet (☎/fax 09-233 43 52,* @ *sderavet@ worldonline.be, Hagelandkaai 38)*, east of the centre, which is run by a young couple and has three fantastically spacious rooms for f1000/1600, or f2100/2600 for three/four people. Take bus No 70 from St Pietersstation.

Hotels The *Hotel Flandria (☎ 09-223 06 26, fax 09-233 77 89,* @ *gent@flandria-centrum.be, Barrestraat 3)* is a rabbit warren of cheap but decent rooms – rates are f1300/1400 for single/double. Much more at-mospheric is *Brooderie (☎ 09-225 06 23, Jan Breydelstraat 8)*. This place is principally a bakery-cum-tearoom but it also has four lovely rooms located upstairs. Each has a sink but shared bathroom; rooms cost f1500/2300.

Hotel Erasmus (☎ 09-224 21 95, fax 09-233 42 41, Poel 25) is a renovated, 16th-century house with 12 rooms, some with stained-glass windows and oak beam ceil-ings. Prices start at f2500/3650.

Places to Eat

The student ghetto around St Pietersnieuw-straat and its continuation, Overpoortstraat, is the best place for cheap eats. Here you'll find plenty of cafes and pubs including the *Overpoort mensa (Overpoortstraat 49)*, a self-service student cafeteria.

Eethuis Avalon 1 (☎ 09-224 37 24, Geldmunt 32) is a delightful vegetarian restaurant with a small outdoor terrace. It's open for lunch only (closed Sunday). *Brooderie (☎ 09-225 06 23, Jan Breydel-straat 8)* is a rustic tearoom and a great spot for a snack (in a non-smoking environment).

Trendy restaurants are dotted around the Patershol quarter, a thicket of cobbled lanes with an old-world ambience just north of

the city centre. *Togo (☎ 09-223 65 51, Vrouwebroersstraat 21)* is a sage choice and specialises in African cuisine.

Brasserie Pakhuis (☎ 09-223 55 55, Schuurkenstraat 4) is a huge new brasserie-cum-restaurant in a beautifully restored tex-tile warehouse. The cuisine is eclectic and mains range from f600 to f950.

Self-caterers can find a *Nopri supermar-ket* at Hoogpoort 42.

Entertainment

The *Herberg De Dulle Griet (Vrijdagmarkt 50)* is one of the city's best known beer pubs. For *jenevers* try *'t Dreupelkot (Groentenmarkt 12)* which also has a pleas-ant waterfront terrace.

Getting There & Away

The Eurolines office (☎ 09-220 90 24), Koningin Elisabethlaan 73, is 100m from St Pietersstation. Buses leave from this office to destinations all over Europe. See the Get-ting There & Away chapter for more details.

The train station information office (☎ 09-241 44 44) is open 7 am to 9 pm daily. There are IC trains to Antwerp (f250, 45 minutes), Bruges (f175, 20 minutes), Brussels (f235, 45 minutes) and Ypres (f315, one hour).

BRUGES
☎ 050

Bruges (Brugge in Flemish) is one of Eur-ope's best-preserved medieval cities and, hardly surprisingly, Belgium's most visited. Its richly ornate 13th-century centre has changed little in the five centuries since the silting of the Zwin River. At that time, Bruges was a prosperous cloth manufacturing town and the centre of Flemish Primitive art. When the river silted, Bruges died, its wealthy mer-chants abandoning it for Antwerp.

Today, particularly in summer, this 'living museum' is smothered with people. Go out of season or stay around late on summer evenings, when the carillon chimes seep through the cobbled streets and local boys (illegally) cast their fishing rods into willow-lined canals, and Bruges shows its age-old beauty.

Orientation

Bruges, neatly encased by an oval-shaped series of canals, has two central squares:

BELGIUM

the Markt and the Burg. Many local buses stop at the former, while the more impressive latter is home to the tourist office. The train station is 1.5km south of the Markt – buses shuttle regularly between the two.

Information
The main tourist office (☎ 050-44 86 86, fax 050-44 86 00, 📧 toerisme@brugge.be), Burg 11, is open 9.30 am to 6.30 pm weekdays and 10 am to noon and 2 to 6.30 pm at weekends from 1 April to 30 September. From October to March, it's open 9.30 am to 5 pm weekdays and 9.30 am to 1 pm and 2 to 5.30 pm on Saturday. There's also a tiny branch office (☎ 050-38 80 83) open daily at the train station.

There's a BBL Bank at Markt 19. Alternatively, you can change cash, albeit usually at lower rates, at the train station ticket counters from 5 am to 10.30 pm daily.

The post office is at Markt 5. For Internet access, head to The Coffee Link (☎ 050-34 93 52, 📧 info@thecoffeelink .com), Mariastraat 38 in Oud St Jan (a former hospital).

Things to See & Do
Rising from the Markt is the 83m-high **belfort** (belfry) with its 47-bell carillon. The view from the top of the 366 steps is breathtaking; entry is f100. The Burg, connected to the Markt by an alley lined with lace shops, features Belgium's oldest **Stadhuis** as well as the **Heilig Bloed Basiliek** (Basilica of the Holy Blood) where a few coagulated drops of Christ's blood are said to be stored.

From the Burg, go through the archway marking Blinde Ezelstraat (Blind Donkey St) to the **Vismarkt** (fish market).

Immediately west of the Vismarkt is **Huidenvettersplein**, a charming square lined with restaurants. This is the start of the **Dijver**, along which you'll find departure points for **canal cruises**. Here too are the town's premier museums. The **Groeninge-museum**, Dijver 12, is home to a prized collection of Flemish Primitives paintings. The **Arentshuis**, Dijver 16, features lace and the artwork of Frank Brangwyn, a Bruges-born artist. An excellent collection of applied and decorative arts is displayed in the rambling **Gruuthusemuseum**, Dijver 17.

The nearby **Onze Lieve Vrouwekerk** (Our Lady's Church) is home to Michelangelo's delicate *Madonna and Child*. Across from the church on Mariastraat is the prestigious **Memlingmuseum**, with works by Hans Memling, one of the early Flemish Primitives. Farther down Mariastraat, signs lead to the **Begijnhof** which was home to a 13th-century religious community of unmarried and widowed women. From here you can easily cross to the **Minnewater** (Lake of Love), once an inner-city port.

The **Brouwerij De Halve Maan**, Walplein 26, will show you the workings of one of Belgium's many little breweries (f140; hourly tours).

Note that a f400 discount ticket is available from the tourist office if you're visiting the Groeninge, Memling, Gruuthuse and Arentshuis museums, all of which are open from 9.30 am to 5 pm daily (closed Tuesday and at lunchtime in winter).

Organised Tours
Bruges by boat, bike, bus, foot or horse-drawn carriage – name it and you can tour by it. The tourist office has copious details.

Quasimodo (☎ 050-37 04 70, fax 050-37 49 60, 📧 info@quasimodo.be), Leen-hoofweg 7, offers day tours either to Ypres and around the battlefields of Flanders or on a 'Triple Treat' tour to indulge in waffles, beers and chocolate – prices are f1400/1100 for those over/under 26 years, and include a picnic lunch. Quasimodo also does mountain bike tours through the villages around Bruges (daily from Easter to September). The cost is f650/550 for those aged over/under 26.

Places to Stay
Bruges' popularity has resulted in a mass of accommodation – all heavily booked in summer.

Camping The nicest camping ground is *Memling (☎ 050-35 58 45, Veltemweg 109)*. It's open all year and charges f110/100/130 per adult/tent/car. Get bus No 11 from the station.

Hostels Several hostels compete for Bruges' backpacker market. *Passage (☎ 050-34 02 32, fax 050-34 01 40, Dweersstraat 26-28)* has modern dorms as well as a hotel section next door. A bed in a six/four-bed room costs f380/480 per person (breakfast f100 extra), or there are doubles

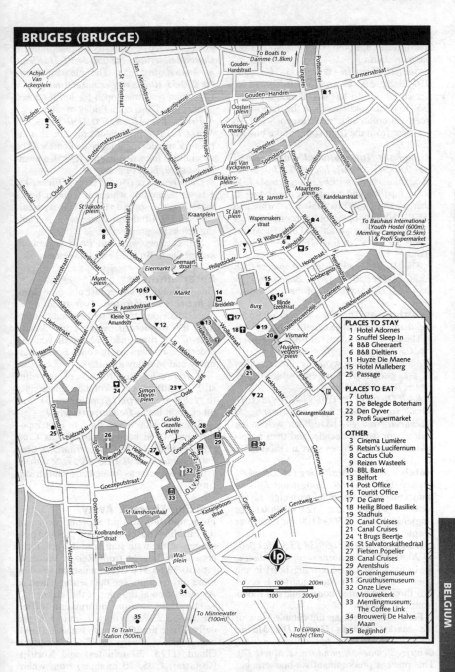

BRUGES (BRUGGE)

PLACES TO STAY
1 Hotel Adornes
2 Snuffel Sleep In
4 B&B Gheeraert
6 B&B Dieltiens
11 Huyze Die Maene
15 Hotel Malleberg
25 Passage

PLACES TO EAT
7 Lotus
12 De Belegde Boterham
22 Den Dyver
23 Profi Supermarket

OTHER
3 Cinema Lumière
5 Retsin's Lucifernum
8 Cactus Club
9 Reizen Wasteels
10 BBL Bank
13 Belfort
14 Post Office
16 Tourist Office
17 De Garre
18 Heilig Bloed Basiliek
19 Stadhuis
20 Canal Cruises
21 Canal Cruises
24 't Brugs Beertje
26 St Salvatorskathedraal
27 Fietsen Popelier
28 Canal Cruises
29 Arentshuis
30 Groeningemuseum
31 Gruuthusemuseum
32 Onze Lieve
   Vrouwekerk
33 Memlingmuseum;
   The Coffee Link
34 Brouwerij De Halve
   Maan
35 Begijnhof

BELGIUM

including breakfast for f1400/1600 without/ with private bathroom. Take bus No 16 from the train station.

Snuffel Sleep In (☎ *050-33 31 33, fax 050-33 32 50,* **@** *snuffel@freegates.be, Ezelstraat 47-49)* has dorms ranging from f350 to f490. A kitchen is at the disposal of guests; alternatively, breakfast costs f80. To get there from the train station take bus No 3 or 13.

Bauhaus International Youth Hotel (☎ *050-34 10 93, fax 050-33 41 80,* **@** *bauhaus@bauhaus.be, Langestraat 135)* is big, bustling and constantly expanding. It charges from f380 to f450 for dorms and f550/1050 for single/double rooms; there's also a popular restaurant and bar. Breakfast is f60. Get bus No 6 or 16 from the train station.

The HI-affiliated hostel ***Europa*** (☎ *050-35 26 79, fax 050-35 37 32, Baron Ruzette-laan 143)* is 500m south of the city walls.

Guesthouses There's a swarm of B&Bs and many represent excellent value.

The three lofty rooms at ***B&B Gheeraert*** (☎ *050-33 56 27, fax 050-34 52 01,* **@** *paul.gheeraert@skynet.be, Riddersstraat 9)* are gorgeous. Singles/doubles/triples cost f1700/1900/2400.

B&B Dieltiens (☎ *050-33 42 94, fax 050-33 52 30,* **@** *koen.dieltiens@skynet.be, St Walburgastraat 14)* have been welcoming visitors for over a decade, and their hospitality still shines. Prices start at f1300/1600.

Hotels The ***Hotel Malleberg*** (☎ *050-34 41 11, fax 050-34 67 69, Hoogstraat 7)* is an immaculate two-star hotel with eight lovely rooms. Prices are f2100/2900 for single/double, or f3500/4100 for three/four people.

Hotel Adornes (☎ *050-34 13 36, fax 050-34 20 85,* **@** *hotel.adornes@proximedia.be, St Annarei 26)* is a charming hotel in the often overlooked St Anna quarter. It occupies three old gabled houses and has rooms from f2700/2900.

For a room with an unbeatable view of the Markt head to ***Huyze Die Maene*** (☎ *050-33 39 59, fax 050-33 44 60,* **@** *huyzediemaene@pandora.be, Markt 17).* This place is predominantly a brasserie but it has three fabulous upstairs rooms starting at f3950.

Places to Eat

For a sandwich or snack, try the rustic little ***De Belegde Boterham*** (☎ *050-34 91 31, Kleine St Amandsstraat 5).* The pleasant ***Lotus*** (☎ *050-33 10 78, Wapenmakerstraat 5)* is a vegetarian restaurant open for lunch (closed Sunday), and also open Friday evening.

Huyze Die Maene (☎ *050-33 39 59, Markt 17)* is a proficient brasserie that attracts a mixed local/tourist clientele. The speciality *Vlaamse hutsepot* (f525), a meat-based stew, is very good.

Den Dyver (☎ *050-33 60 69, Dijver 5)* is a large restaurant which uses the nation's many beers to spice up traditional-style cuisine. The f1400 three-course *menu* (including drinks) is great value.

Self-caterers will find ***Profi supermarkets*** at Oude Burg 22 and Langestraat 55.

Entertainment

One of Belgium's wierdest places to drink is ***Retsin's Lucifernum*** *(Twijnstraat 8).* A huge mansion strewn with moody paintings, it's frequented by those who love a shot of hot rum (that's about all you can order) and modern art. It's open Friday, Saturday and Monday evenings.

If you're hanging for a beer, or better still, 300 different types of them, go directly to ***'t Brugs Beertje*** *(Kemelstraat 5).* Another great bar is ***De Garre*** *(Garre 1).*

Bruges' main venue for live contemporary and world music is the ***Cactus Club*** (☎ *050-33 20 14, St Jakobsstraat 33).* ***Cinema Lumière*** (☎ *050-33 48 57, St Jakobsstraat 36a)* screens foreign and mainstream films.

Getting There & Away

From mid-July to mid-September, one of the Eurolines buses to London picks up passengers at the train station in Bruges. Tickets can be bought from Reizen Wasteels (☎ 050-33 65 31), Geldmuntstraat 30a. For more information, see the Getting There & Away section at the start of this chapter.

The train station information office (☎ 050-38 23 82) is open 7 am to 8.30 pm daily. There are IC trains to Brussels (f390, one hour), Antwerp (f405, 70 minutes), Ghent (f175, 20 minutes) and Kortrijk (Courtrai; f205, 40 minutes) from where there are hourly connections to Ypres and Tournai.

Getting Around

Fietsen Popelier (☎ 050-34 32 62), Mariastraat 26, rents 40cc mopeds (f500/1000/1500 for one/three/five hours) and bicycles (f110 per hour, or f250/325 per half-day/day).

YPRES

☎ 057

Stories have long been told about the WWI battlefields of Flanders. There were the tall red poppies that rose over the flat, flat fields; the 300,000 Allied soldiers who disappeared forever in the quagmire of battle; and the little town of Ypres (Ieper in Flemish), which was wiped off the map.

Though Ypres and its medieval core were obliterated in WWI, they have since been convincingly rebuilt. Today, the town's outlying farmlands are dotted with cemeteries and, in early summer, the poppies still flower.

Orientation & Information

The town's hub is the Grote Markt, a leisurely 10-minute walk from the train station – head straight up Stationsstraat and, at the end, turn left into Tempelstraat and then right into Boterstraat. Three blocks on, at the beginning of the Markt, rises the Renaissance-style Lakenhalle (cloth hall) which houses the Ieper Visitors Centre (☎ 057-22 85 84, fax 057-22 85 89). It's open 9 am to 5 or 6 pm daily.

Things to See

The excellent **In Flanders Fields Museum** (☎ 057-22 85 84), on the 1st floor of the Lakenhalle, focuses on the stories of ordinary people and is a moving testament to the horrors of war. It's open 10 am to 5 or 6 pm daily (closed Monday from October to March). Admission costs f250; check out the Web site at www.inflandersfields.be.

One of the saddest reminders of the Great War is Ypres' **Meensepoort** (Menin Gate), inscribed with the names of 55,000 British and Commonwealth troops who were lost in the quagmire of the trenches and who have no graves. A bugler sounds the last post here at 8 pm every evening. It's about 300m from the tourist office.

Around Ypres, in outlying fields and hamlets, there are 170 **cemeteries** and row upon row of crosses. The tourist office sells maps of car and bike routes that wind through the old battlefields.

Organised Tours

It's worth taking a tour of the cemeteries and battlefields. Salient Tours (☎ 057-91 02 23) charges f650/950 for 2½- to four-hour tours. Alternatively, join Quasimodo's tour (see the Organised Tours section in Bruges for details).

Places to Stay & Eat

The **Jeugdstadion** camping ground (☎ 057-21 72 82, Leopold III laan 16) is 900m south-east of the town centre. The closest private hostel is **De Iep** (☎/fax 057-20 88 11, Poperingseweg 34), 2km west of town. Beds are f510/540 for students/adults.

B&B Brouwers (☎ 057-20 27 23, Adjudant Masscheleinlaan 18), 500m north of the Grote Markt, is homy and has rooms for f800/1500.

An affordable central hotel is the newly renovated **Gasthof 't Zweerd** (☎ 057-20 04 75, fax 057-21 78 96, Grote Markt 2) with single/double rooms for f2000/2500.

Cafes and restaurants line the Grote Markt – a good choice is **In het Klein Stadhuis**, a cosy brasserie next to the town hall. **Pita Farao** (☎ 057-20 65 72, Tempelstraat 7), halfway to the train station, serves excellent stuffed pitta breads.

For picnic supplies, there's a **Spar** supermarket on Rijselstraat.

Getting There & Away

There are direct hourly trains to Kortrijk (f145, 30 minutes), Ghent (f315, one hour) and Brussels (f480, 1½ hours). For Antwerp and Bruges, you have to change in Kortrijk.

Wallonia

Belgium's southern half, Wallonia, is best known for the Ardennes – a region of deep river valleys, tall forests and tranquil villages. Historically, the Ardennes is where the Battle of the Bulge once raged. The city of Liège and town of Namur are the main gateways to this region.

LIÈGE

☎ 04

Liège (Luik in Flemish) is a city people tend to love or loathe. Sprawled along the Meuse River in the eastern part of Wallonia, it's busy and gritty and is the sort of place

BELGIUM

that takes time to know. It's worth a stop if you're passing, particularly for the rich showcase of local and religious art in its many museums.

Orientation & Information

The main train station, Gare Guillemins, is 2km south of Place St Lambert, the city's nominal heart. Bus Nos 1 and 4 run between the station and Place St Lambert. A few hundred metres east of Place St Lambert, two bridges cross the Meuse River to the island of Outremeuse.

The Office du Tourisme (☎ 04-221 92 21), Féronstfe 92, has local information, as does a small bureau inside the train station. The Fédération du Tourisme de la Province de Liège (☎ 04-232 65 10), Blvd de la Sauvenière 77, has regional information.

Things to See & Do

Excellent views of the city can be had from the top of the **Montagne de Bueren** – an impressive flight of 373 stairs which lead up from Hors Château. On Sunday mornings there's **La Batte**, a street market that stretches along 1.5km of riverfront quays.

The area around the tourist office is home to three of the city's best museums: the **Musée d'Art Religieux et d'Art Mosan** (Museum of Religious Art and Art from the Meuse Valley), Rue Mère Dieu (f100); the nearby **Musée de la Vie Wallonne** (Walloon Life Museum), Cours des Mineurs (f80); and the **Musée d'Ansembourg**, Féronstrée 114, a rich, Regency-styled mansion (f50).

Places to Stay & Eat

The big HI-affiliated *Auberge de Jeunesse* (☎ 04-344 56 89, fax 04-344 56 87, @ ajliege@gate71.be, Rue Georges Simenon 2) in Outremeuse, charges f495 for a bed in a dorm and has singles/doubles for f800/1170 – take bus No 4 from Gare Guillemins.

The *Hôtel Le Berger* (☎ 04-223 00 80, fax 04-221 19 48, Rue des Urbanistes 10) is simple but well-kept and charges f1000/1400 for rooms (breakfast is f200). Bus No 1 or 4 stops a block away.

En Roture is a cobbled street in Outremeuse that's lined with little restaurants. In the centre, Rue St-Jean-en-Isle is also filled with restaurants and brasseries.

Nearby, *La Feuille de Vigne* (☎ 04-222 20 10, Rue Sœurs de Hasque 12) is a vegetarian restaurant open from noon to 3 pm weekdays. *As Ouhès* (☎ 04-223 32 25, Place du Marché 21) specialises in rich Wallonian cuisine – the servings are extra generous and the prices reasonable.

Self-caterers will find a *Delhaize* supermarket on Place de la Cathédrale.

Getting There & Away

Eurolines (☎ 04-222 36 18) has an office at Blvd de la Sauvenière 26, from where buses depart to destinations all over Europe. More details are given in the Belgium Getting There & Away section earlier.

From Gare Guillemins, Thalys trains connect Liège with Cologne (f840, 1½ hours, seven trains per day). Other train services include: Brussels (f405, 1¼ hours, two per hour), Maastricht (f270, 30 minutes, hourly) and Luxembourg City (f900, 2½ hours, seven per day). Locally there are hourly trains to Namur (f245, 50 minutes) and Spa (f145, 50 minutes).

AROUND LIÈGE
Spa

Spa was for centuries the luxurious retreat for royalty and the wealthy who came to drink, bathe and cure themselves in the mineral-rich waters which bubble forth here. These days it's a rather run-down reminder of what was, but is pleasant enough for a day trip. The surrounding hills offer enjoyable walks along well-marked paths.

The town is about 35km south-east of Liège, connected by regular trains. The local Office du Tourisme (☎ 087-79 53 53) is at Place Royale 41.

Hautes Fagnes National Park

Bordering the Eifel hills in Germany, the Hautes Fagnes park is a region of swampy heath and woods. Within the park is the Botrange Centre Nature (☎ 080-44 03 00, fax 080-44 44 29, @ botrange.centrenature@ skynet.be), located close to the highest point in Belgium – the Signal de Botrange (694m). This area is a popular base for serious hikers, cyclists and, in winter, cross-country skiers. Those wanting just a short walk (1½ hours) through this bleak but interesting landscape should head to the boardwalk at Fagne de Polleur, nearby at Mt Rigi.

The Botrange Centre Nature is about 50km east of Liège. It can be reached in 1¼ hours by public transport from Liège – take the train to Verviers and then bus No 390 in the direction 'Rocherath'.

TOURNAI
☎ 069

Just 10km from the French border and 80km south-west of Brussels, Tournai (Doornik in Flemish) is one of Belgium's oldest cities. Tournai's skyline is dominated by the five towers of its austere 12th-century **cathedral** and the more ornate 13th-century **belfry**.

Its most interesting museums are the **Musée des Beaux-Arts** (Fine Arts Museum), on Enclos St Martin, in a building designed by Victor Horta; and the **Musée de la Tapisserie et des Arts du Tissu** (Museum of Tapestry and Cloth Arts), Place Reine Astrid. Both are closed Tuesday.

Orientation & Information
The train station is a 10-minute walk from the centre of town – head straight up Rue Royale until you reach the cathedral. The tourist office (☎ 069-22 20 45, fax 069-21 62 21, ⊜ tourisme@tournai.be), Vieux Marché aux Poteries 14, is uphill to the left, near the base of the belfry.

Places to Stay & Eat
Camping de l'Orient (☎ 069-22 26 35, *Vieux Chemin de Mons*) is 4km south-east of town near the Aqua Tournai (an indoor swimming complex). From the station take bus W.

The HI-affiliated *Auberge de Jeunesse* (☎ 069-21 61 36, fax 069-21 61 40, *Rue St Martin 64*) is a 20-minute walk from the station – take bus No 4 (direction Baisieux).

As for hotels, if price is a problem head to *Tour Saint-Georges* (☎ 069-22 53 00, *Rue St Georges 2*). Rooms start at f765/1050 for single/double – it's passable if you don't expect much.

The *Pita Pyramide* (☎ 069-84 35 83, *Rue Tête d'Or 7*) has large stuffed pitta breads for f210. Picnic supplies can be obtained from the *GB* supermarket across the road. A good mid-range French restaurant is *L'Écurie d'Ennetières* (☎ 069-21 56 89, *Ruelle d'Ennetières*).

Getting There & Away
There are regular trains to Kortrijk (Courtrai; f145, 40 minutes), Brussels (f250, one hour) and Ypres via Kortrijk (f250, one hour).

NAMUR
☎ 081

Just 50km south-east of Brussels, Namur (Namen in Flemish) is the capital of Wallonia. It's the best base for exploring the Ardennes – well positioned on the railway line to Luxembourg and with rail and bus connections to some of the region's less accessible spots.

Namur is a picturesque town, dominated by its 15th-century **citadel**, which can be reached either on foot, by car along the Route Merveilleuse, or by a shuttle bus (f40) which departs half-hourly from the tourist office.

Of the handful of museums, the most intriguing are the **Félicien Rops**, Rue Fumal 12, which has works by the 19th-century Namur-born artist who fondly illustrated erotic lifestyles, and the tiny **Musée du Prieuré d'Oignies**, Rue Julie Billiart 17, a one-roomed hoard of exquisite Gothic treasures.

The tourist office (☎ 081-24 64 49), Square Léopold, is 200m to the left out of the station, and is open 9.30 am to 6 pm daily.

Places to Stay & Eat
Camping Les 4 Fils Aymon (☎ 081-58 02 94, *Chaussée de Liège*) is 8km east of town – get bus No 12 from the bus station.

The riverfront *Auberge de Jeunesse* (☎ 081-22 36 88, fax 081-22 44 12, ⊜ ajna mur@skynet.be, *Ave F Rops 8*) is 3km from the train station, or jump on bus No 3 or 4.

Grand Hôtel de Flandre (☎ 081-23 18 68, fax 081-22 80 60, *Place de la Gare 14*) has no-nonsense rooms starting at f1700/2100. For considerably more charm head to *Hôtel Les Tanneurs* (☎ 081-24 00 24, fax 081-24 00 25, ⊜ info@tanneurs.com, *Rue des Tanneries 13*) which has individually-styled rooms from f1250 to f8000 for a single, and f2000 to f8500 for a double.

Tea Time Café (☎ 081-23 10 75, *35 Rue St Jean*) is a stylish tearoom which does excellent filled multigrain baguettes (f120), as well as *crêpes* (pancakes) and waffles. A delicious range of international meals is served at *Brasserie Henry* (☎ 081-22 02 04, *3 Place St Aubain*).

BELGIUM

Getting There & Away

Local and regional buses are operated by TEC (☎ 081-25 35 55) which has an office (open 7 am to 7 pm daily) opposite the train station. Regional buses leave from the bus station near the C&A department store (to the left out of the train station).

From Namur there are trains to Brussels (f245, one hour, half-hourly), Luxembourg City (f820, 1¾ hours, hourly) and Liège (f245, 50 minutes, hourly). For information on regional trains see the Getting There & Away section in each of the following towns: Dinant, Han-sur-Lesse, Rochefort, La Roche-en-Ardenne and Bastogne.

DINANT
☎ 082

This heavy, distinctive town, 28km south of Namur, is one of the Ardennes' tourist hot spots. Its bulbous cathedral competes for attention with the cliff-front **citadel**, open year-round and accessible by cable car (f195 return). Below the citadel, a hive of agencies offer sedate **boat tours** on the Meuse River – from the 45-minute trip to Anseremme (f180) to the nine-hour round-trip to Givet in France (f520). For schedules contact Bayard (☎ 082-22 30 42), Quai de Meuse 1.

Several companies – including Kayaks Ansiaux (☎ 082-22 23 25), Rue du Vélodrome 15 in Anseremme, offer **kayaking** trips that leave in the morning upriver from Houyet and finish later in the day at Anseremme. The tourist office (☎ 082-22 28 70, fax 082-22 77 88) is at Rue Grande 37.

Places to Stay

There is no hostel in Dinant. *Le Rouge et Noir* (☎ 082-22 69 44, fax 082-64 64 01, Rue Grande 26) has rudimentary rooms without/with private bathroom for f1500/2000. Much nicer is *Hôtel de la Couronne* (☎ 082-22 24 41, fax 082-22 70 31, Rue Sax 1) which has pleasant singles/doubles for f2200/2300.

Getting There & Away

There are hourly trains between Namur and Dinant (f135, 30 minutes). Every two hours bus No 433 (50 minutes) also connects the two.

HAN-SUR-LESSE & ROCHEFORT
☎ 084

The millennium-old **limestone grottoes** are the drawing card of these two villages, which

sit just 8km apart on the Lesse and Lomme rivers respectively. The impressive Han-sur-Lesse caves are situated a little way out of town – a tram takes you to the entrance and a boat brings you back. The caves are open 10 am to noon and 1 to 4.30 pm from April to October (from 11.30 am the rest of the year and closed January). Entry is f360.

Rochefort's cave, the Grotte de Lorette, is much smaller. From April to mid-November, hour-long tours (f220) start at 10 am.

There are tourist offices in both towns: in Han-sur-Lesse (☎ 084-37 75 96) at Place Théo Lannoy, and in Rochefort (☎ 084-21 25 37) at Rue de Behogne 5.

Places to Stay

In Han-sur-Less, *Camping de la Lesse* (☎ 084-37 72 90, Rue du Grand Hy) is open all year. So too is the *Gîte d'Étape* hostel (☎/fax 084-37 74 41, Rue du Gîte d'Étape 10) which charges f385. Alternatively, the *Hôtel Le Central* (☎ 084-37 72 61, Rue des Grottes 20) has basic singles/doubles for f1250/2500.

In Rochefort, the *Gîte d'Étape* hostel (☎/fax 084-21 46 04, Rue du Hableau 25) charges f385. Just up the same road is *Camping Communal* (☎ 084-21 19 00), open from Easter to 31 October. *Hotel La Fayette* (☎ 084-21 42 73, fax 084-22 11 63, Rue Jacquet 87) has bright, attractive rooms starting at f1220/1520.

Getting There & Away

To reach either town, take the Namur-Luxembourg train to Jemelle and transfer to bus No 29, which runs hourly.

LA ROCHE-EN-ARDENNE
☎ 084

Hugging a bend in the Ourthe River, La Roche is a vibrant little town, hidden in a deep valley, crowned by a ruined castle, and surrounded by verdant hills much enjoyed by hikers. The tourist office (☎ 084-41 13 42, fax 084-41 23 43) is at Place du Marché 15.

Places to Stay

The *Camping Le Vieux Moulin* (☎ 084-41 13 80, Petite Strument 62) is beautifully located and open Easter to 31 October. *Hôtel Les Olivettes* (☎ 084-41 16 52, fax 084-41 21 69, ✉ olivettes@ping.be, Chemin de Soeret 12) has an auberge with dormitory-style accommodation (four to eight beds) for f500 per person (excluding breakfast). *Le Vieux La Roche* (☎ *084-41 25 86,* 🖂 *levieuxlaroche@online.be, Rue du Chalet 45)* is a quaint B&B with rooms for f1400. The charming *Moulin de la Strument* (☎ *084-41 15 07, fax 084-41 10 80, Petite Strument 62)* is a hotel/restaurant with eight rooms for f2350/2550.

Getting There & Away
From Namur, take a Luxembourg-bound train to Marloie, then bus No 15 to La Roche (35 minutes, four per day).

BASTOGNE
☎ 061

It was here, north of Arlon and close to the Luxembourg border, that thousands of soldiers and civilians died during the Battle of the Bulge in the winter of 1944-45. Testament to these events is a huge, star-shaped **American memorial**, on a hill 2km from Bastogne, and the neighbouring **Bastogne Historical Centre**, open daily 1 March to 31 October. The tourist office (☎ 061-21 27 11) is at Place McAuliffe.

Places to Stay
Camping de Renval (☎ *061-21 29 85, Rue du Marché 148)* is 1km from the tourist office and open all year. *Hôtel du Sud* (☎ *061-21 11 14, fax 061-21 79 08,* 🖂 *hotel.du.sud@ping.be, Rue du Marché 39)* has basic rooms starting at f1635/1960. The new *Hôtel Collin* (☎ *061-21 43 58, fax 061-21 80 83, Place McAuliffe 8)* has pleasant modern rooms from f2500/3000.

Getting There & Away
From Namur, take a Luxembourg-bound train to the rail junction of Libramont, from where bus No 163b departs every two hours for Bastogne's defunct train station (35 minutes).

Bosnia-Hercegovina

Sandwiched between Croatia and Yugoslavia, the mountainous country of Bosnia-Hercegovina has been a meeting point of east and west – Orthodox Byzantium mingled with Catholic Rome, Turkish peoples with Slavs – for nearly two millennia.

Bosnia-Hercegovina's status as the third-largest republic in Yugoslavia ended soon after independence was declared in October 1991. Six months later Bosnian Serb ultra-nationalists, assisted by Yugoslavia's federal army, began a ruthless campaign of ethnic cleansing intended to bring Bosnia-Hercegovina into Belgrade's orbit.

When the three-way war ended in 1995, it left the country physically devastated and ethnically divided. Out of a pre-war population of five million, over two million people fled their former homes. Peace is currently being enforced by more than 34,000 NATO-led troops, and a large international civilian presence is working towards rebuilding the country. Progress has been substantial, and Sarajevo, Mostar, Travnik, Međugorje and Banja Luka are now safe to visit.

AT A GLANCE

Capital:	Sarajevo
Population:	2.8 million
Official Language:	Bosnian (Serbo-Croatian)
Currency:	1 convertible mark (KM) = 100 convertible pfennigs

The agreement also emphasised the rights of refugees to return to their pre-war homes. This was relevant for both the 1.2 million people who sought refuge in other countries, and the one million people who were displaced within Bosnia by ethnic cleansing.

A NATO-led peace implementation force, IFOR, was installed as the military force behind the accords. IFOR's 60,000 international troops gave way in January 1997 to the 30,000-strong Stabilization Force (SFOR), whose current mandate has no definite time limit.

The hopes of the west got a boost in January 1998 when a new, relatively liberal Bosnian Serb prime minister, Milorad Dodik, came to power. Dodik quickly pushed several measures through the RS parliament aimed at compliance with Dayton, including a common vehicle licence plate (that would no longer be entity-specific), common passports and a new common currency called the convertible mark. A new national flag was approved just in time for the Winter Olympic Games in 1998.

Bosnia-Hercegovina today remains divided along ethnic lines. However, Muslim-Croat tensions have ebbed, and more people are now crossing between the RS and the Federation. Many of the country's towns are physically destroyed, although a US$5.1 billion reconstruction program is underway.

Facts about Bosnia-Hercegovina

HISTORY

Fighting in Bosnia was suspended following the peace conference in Dayton, Ohio, USA, in November 1995. The Dayton agreement stated that Bosnia would retain its pre-war external boundaries, but would be composed of two parts or 'entities'. The Federation of Bosnia-Hercegovina (the Muslim and Croat portion) would administer 51% of the country, including Sarajevo, and the Serb Republic of Bosnia-Hercegovina 49%. The latter is commonly referred to as Republika Srpska (RS).

GEOGRAPHY

Bosnia-Hercegovina (51,129 sq km) is a mountainous country on the west side of the Balkan Peninsula. Most of the country's rivers flow north into the Sava. Bosnia-Hercegovina contains over 30 mountain peaks ranging from 1700m to 2386m high.

BOSNIA-HERCEGOVINA

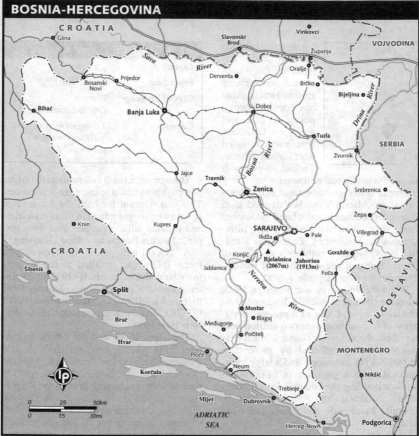

POPULATION & PEOPLE

Before the war, Bosnia-Hercegovina's population of four million was 43% Muslim Slavs, 31% Orthodox Serbs and 17% Catholic Croats. Ethnic cleansing has since concentrated Croats in Hercegovina (to the south), Muslims in Sarajevo and central Bosnia, and Serbs in areas adjacent to Yugoslavia. Of the current population of 2.8 million, approximately 42% are Muslim, 37% Serb and 15% Croat.

SOCIETY & CONDUCT

Removing one's shoes is customary in Muslim households; usually the host family will provide slippers. The Bosnian people are incredibly friendly, but when the subject turns to politics, the best strategy is to listen.

LANGUAGE

Dialects notwithstanding, the people of Bosnia-Hercegovina speak the same language. However, that language is referred to as 'Bosnian' in the Muslim part of the Federation, 'Croatian' in Croat-controlled parts, and 'Serbian' in the RS. The Federation uses the Latin alphabet but the RS uses Cyrillic (see the Croatian, Serbian & Bosnian section of the Language Guide at the back of this book).

Facts for the Visitor

PLANNING

In mountainous Bosnia-Hercegovina it is hot in summer but chilly in winter, and snowfall can last until April. The best time to visit is spring or summer. Don't worry about a seasonal crush of tourists just yet.

VISAS & DOCUMENTS

No visas are required for citizens of the USA, Canada, Ireland, the UK and most other EU countries. Citizens of other countries can obtain a tourist visa in advance by sending a personal cheque or money order for US$35, your passport, a copy of a round-trip plane ticket, an invitation letter and an application to the nearest embassy.

Tourists in Bosnia are required to register with the local police. A hotel or accommodation agency will do this for you, but foreigners staying in privately arranged houses must do this themselves (in Sarajevo, go to Zmaja od Bosne 9, room 3).

EMBASSIES & CONSULATES
Bosnian Embassies Abroad
Australia (☎ 02-6239 5955, fax 6239 5793) 15 State Circle, Canberra ACT 2603
UK (☎ 071-255 3758, fax 255 2760) 320 Regent St, London W1R 5AB
USA
Embassy: (☎ 202-833 3612, fax 833 2061) 2109 E St NW, Washington DC 20037
Consulate: (☎ 212-751 9015, fax 751 9019) 866 UN Plaza, Suite 580, New York NY 10017

Foreign Embassies in Bosnia-Hercegovina
The following embassies are in Sarajevo (area code ☎ 071):

Canada (☎ 447 900, fax 447 901) Logavina 7
UK (☎ 444 429, fax 666 131) Tina Ujevića 8
USA (☎ 659 992 or 445 700, fax 659 722) Alipašina 43

MONEY
The 'convertible mark' (KM) is, at the time of writing, tied to the German mark (DM) at a rate of 1KM to DM1, or around 2KM to the US dollar. At present Deutschmarks are accepted everywhere except in official institutions such as post offices.

In Croat-controlled parts of the Federation, Croatian kuna are widely used, as are Serbian dinars in the Republika Srpska, but this may change soon. You may receive these in change, but there is no problem paying in KM anywhere.

Exchange Rates

country	unit		convertible mark
Australia	A$1	=	1.28KM
Canada	C$1	=	1.46KM
euro	€1	=	1.96KM
France	10FF	=	2.98KM
Germany	DM1	=	1KM
Japan	¥100	=	1.99KM
NZ	NZ$1	=	0.98KM
UK	UK£1	=	3.23KM
US	US$1	=	2.15KM

Costs
Staying in pansions and eating in inexpensive restaurants, you can expect to get by on around 70-80KM a day, which would include about 30KM for accommodation and 30KM for meals. Hotel stays will bump the costs up considerably, as a single room is likely to cost over 100KM.

POST & COMMUNICATIONS
Bosnia's postal system works, but poste restante is available only at the post office in west Mostar.

Bosnia-Hercegovina's international country code is ☎ 387. Drop the initial zero on area codes when dialling in from abroad. If you are calling to the Republika Srpska, you may have more luck dialling through Belgrade (country code ☎ 381, then the city code, etc).

International calls from Bosnia-Hercegovina are cheapest at post offices. Dial the international access number (☎ 00), then the country code and number. A three minute call to the USA costs 6KM.

INTERNET RESOURCES
For general background try Bosnia Virtual Fieldtrip (geog.gmu.edu/projects/bosnia). For the latest political news visit the Office of the High Representative (www.ohr.int).

DANGERS & ANNOYANCES
Always look into local political conditions before undertaking a journey. In the Republika Srpska anti-western sentiments have been reputed to run higher than in the Federation, but it is not likely that you will be made to feel at all unwelcome.

Mines
Over one million land mines are estimated to be in Bosnia-Hercegovina. These were

laid mostly, but not exclusively, in zones of conflict. All of Sarajevo's suburbs are heavily mined, as are areas around Travnik and Mostar.

The golden rule for mines is to stick to asphalt surfaces. Do not drive off the shoulder of roads, do not poke around in abandoned villages or damaged houses, and regard every centimetre of ground as suspicious.

ACCOMMODATION

The year-round presence of international officials has jump-started Bosnia's hotel industry. Sarajevo and Mostar have some pleasant new hotels, but in general prices are high. Except in a few hotels in west Mostar and Međugorje, payment is in cash only.

Pansions (pensions) and private accommodation agencies have sprouted in Sarajevo. People at the market or at a local shop may also be able to help you out; don't hesitate to ask. Staying in private accommodation can be a very pleasant experience.

Most places charge tax (2KM to 5KM), which is included in the prices listed in this chapter.

FOOD & DRINKS

Bosnia's Turkish heritage is savoured in its grilled meats such as *bosanski lonac* (Bosnian stew of cabbage and meat). When confronted with the ubiquitous *burek* (a layered meat pie sold by weight), vegetarians can opt for *sirnica* (cheese pie) or *zeljanica* (spinach pie). *Čevapčići*, another favourite, is lamb and beef rolls tucked into a half-loaf of spongy *somun* bread.

Good wines from Hercegovina include *Žilavka* (white) and *Blatina* (red). A meal can always be washed down with a shot of *šlivovica* (plum brandy) or *loza* (grape brandy).

Getting There & Away

Airlines serving Sarajevo include Croatia Airlines, Crossair (the partner of Swissair), Lufthansa and Austrian Airlines. Air Bosna flies to Belgrade, İstanbul, Vienna, and several destinations in Germany.

In the absence of international train lines, buses are an excellent, safe way to enter Bosnia-Hercegovina. Stowing luggage costs up to 5KM, depending on the route. Bus travel between Croatia and the Federation of Bosnia-Hercegovina is routine. Two daily buses travel between Sarajevo and Zagreb (417km) and Sarajevo and Split. The Sarajevo-Dubrovnik bus makes one trip each day via Mostar, and buses from Sarajevo go to Germany several times a week.

The Republika Srpska is closely connected by bus to Yugoslavia. Buses run every hour between Banja Luka and Belgrade. Several buses a day go between Zagreb and Banja Luka, though you change buses at the border (the other bus will be waiting).

Getting Around

Trains are generally useless, as they run only from Sarajevo to Zenica and a few other small cities. The exception is the beautiful trip from Sarajevo down to Ploče on the Croatian coast.

Bosnia's bus network is quite comprehensive. Inter-entity travel has become less of a problem since the 1998 introduction of daily buses between Sarajevo and Banja Luka.

Plenty of car rental places have sprung up, particularly in Sarajevo, Mostar and Međugorje. The new common licence plates mean that there is no problem crossing from one entity to another.

Bosnia

SARAJEVO
☎ 071

Sarajevo, tucked in a valley beside the Miljacka River, is the capital of Bosnia-Hercegovina. Before the war, Sarajevo was an ethnic microcosm of Yugoslavia, a place where Muslims, Serbs, Croats, Turks, Jews and others could peacefully coexist. During the war, Sarajevo was pounded into rubble by Bosnian-Serb artillery during the siege of 1992 to 1995, when Sarajevo's only access to the outside world was via a 1km tunnel under the airport. Over 10,500 Sarajevans died and 50,000 were wounded by Bosnian-Serb sniper fire and shelling.

Despite the highly visible scars of war, Sarajevo is again bursting with energy.

SALLY DILLON

Biking the Bordeaux way, France

JOHN HAY

Scooting!

NEIL SETCHFIELD

Piccadilly Circus, London

MARTIN MOOS

Express train, Frankfurt/Main

VERONICA GARBUTT

On a Palma-Seller train, Spain

Florence, Italy

Coffee break, Dutch-style, Amsterdam

Street cafe near the Louvre, Paris, France

Piazza Navona, Rome, Italy

Colourful trams run down the road once called 'Sniper's Alley', innumerable cafes blast pop music into the streets, and locals spend leisurely evenings strolling down the main pedestrian street, Ferhadija. A large international presence made up of government officials and humanitarian aid workers is also altering the face of the city. The energy poured into Bosnia-Hercegovina's recovery has rendered Sarajevo the fastest-changing city in Europe.

Information

The Tourist Information Bureau (☎ 532 606, fax 532 281), ul Zelenih Beretki 22, has a good supply of books and maps and is open 8 am to 5 pm weekdays, 9 am to 5 pm Saturday.

The Central Profit Banka (☎ 533 688), ul Zelenih Beretki 24, with other branches around town, changes travellers cheques for 3% commission.

A post office just behind the eternal flame on Ferhadija sends letters and faxes and sells phonecards. There is another inside the bus station, by the train station. The big post office at Obala Kulina Bana 8 is currently being restored.

Šahinpašić, ul Mula Mustafe Bašekije 1, near the eternal flame, sells English-language newspapers, magazines and books.

Things to See

In the city centre itself, the **eternal flame** commemorates WWII. Places of worship for four different religions – Catholic, Orthodox, Muslim and Jewish – lie in close vicinity to one another, as Sarajevans still very proudly point out.

The cobbled **Baščaršija** (Turkish Quarter), where artisans working in bronze ply their trade, is the heart of Sarajevo.

The graceful Austro-Hungarian **National Library** lies along the river at the end of Baščaršija. The building was destroyed by an incendiary shell on 25 August 1992, 100 years after construction began. It has since received a new dome, courtesy of Austria, but is still not open to visitors.

Austrian Archduke Franz Ferdinand and his wife Sophie paused at the National Library (then the town hall) on 28 June, 1914, then rode west along the riverside in an open car to the second bridge. It was here that they were shot by a Serb assassin, Gavrilo

Princip, an event that led to WWI. The one-room **City Museum** (currently being restored), where ul Zelenih Beretki meets the river, now stands on 'Princip's corner'.

The three-year siege made Sarajevo itself a stunning sight. The road into the city from the airport (now Zmaja od Bosne) was dubbed **Sniper's Alley** during the war because Serb snipers picked off civilians crossing the road. Along the road, across from the Holiday Inn, is the **National Museum**, with good archaeology and ethnology collections. A nearby **history museum** shows some old photographs of Bosnia-Hercegovina and has rotating exhibits.

Places to Stay

Ask about the water situation wherever you stay – parts of the city have running water only at certain times of the day.

Private Rooms Bosnia Tours (☎ 202 207, fax 202 206) at ul Maršala Tita 54, has single/double *rooms* near the centre for 40/70KM. The agency is closed on Sundays.

Turistička Agencija Ljubačica (☎/fax 232 109), ul Mula Mustafa Bašekije 65, in Baščaršija, has a handful of *rooms* near the centre for 30KM to 65KM per person. If you arrive after 10 pm call ☎ 090 121 813. Unis Tours (☎ 205 074, ☎/fax 232 109), Ferhadija 16, has *rooms* for rates between 40KM and 70KM.

Pensions The cheapest place in town is the bizarre *Pansion Train* (☎ 615 653, Halida Kajtaza 11), where beds in a stationary train sleeper car cost 33/40KM. It's a bit cramped, but a good bargain option if there aren't too many guests using the bathroom facilities. From the bus station, take the road to Hotel Grand, turn left at the petrol station and follow the big sign.

The cosy *Pansion Hondo* (☎ 666 564, fax 469 375, ul Zaima Šarca 23) is a 20-minute walk uphill from the centre. Rooms cost 80/120KM with breakfast. Head straight up ul Pehlivanuša, behind the cathedral; it turns into ul Zaima Šarca.

Pansion Čobanija (☎ 441 749, fax 203 937, ul Čobanija 29), just past Pizzeria Galija, has rooms with private baths and cable TV for 80/120KM. The central *Pansion Konak* (☎ 533 506, Mustafe Bašeskije 48) charges 40/60KM.

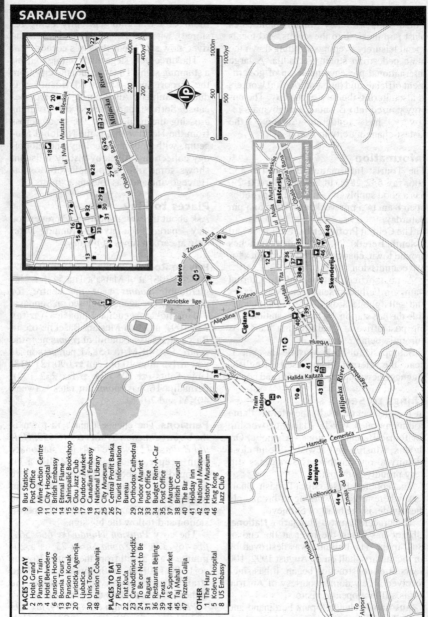

SARAJEVO

PLACES TO STAY
2 Hotel Grand
3 Pansion Train
4 Hotel Belvedere
6 Pansion Hondo
13 Bosnia Tours
19 Pansion Konak
20 Turistička Agencija Ljubačica
30 Unis Tours
48 Pansion Cobanija

PLACES TO EAT
7 Pizzeria Indi
22 Inat Kuća
23 Cevabdžinica Hodžić
24 To Be or Not to Be
31 Ragusa
36 Restaurant Beijing
39 Texas
44 As Supermarket
45 Taj Mahal
47 Pizzeria Galija

OTHER
1 The Harp
5 Koševo Hospital
8 US Embassy
9 Bus Station;
  Post Office
10 Mine Action Centre
11 City Hospital
12 British Embassy
14 Eternal Flame
15 Šahinpašić Bookshop
16 Clou Jazz Club
17 Outdoor Market
18 Canadian Embassy
21 National Library
25 City Museum
26 Central Profit Banka
27 Tourist Information
   Bureau
29 Orthodox Cathedral
32 Indoor Market
33 Post Office
34 Budget Rent-A-Car
35 Post Office
37 Marquee
38 British Council
40 The Bar
41 Holiday Inn
42 National Museum
43 History Museum
46 King Kong
   Jazz Club

Places to Eat
Most restaurant menus are in English, and main meals usually cost 10KM to 15KM.

As is a sizeable supermarket, four tram stops beyond the Holiday Inn, along Zmaja od Bosne. *Ćevabdžinica Hodžić (ul Bravadžiluk 34),* near the National Library, is good for a cheap, quick meal.

Ragusa (Ferhadija 10b) serves tasty Bosnian cuisine. *To Be or Not to Be (5 Čizmedžiluk),* in Baščaršija, has colourful salads in a candle-lit setting. Vegetarians can opt for an omelette or spaghetti. *Inat Kuća,* on the opposite side of the river to the National Library, offers good food in an old Turkish setting. *Restaurant Beijing (Maršala Tita 38)* actually dares to offer tofu. Main meals are 13KM to 20KM. Spicy Indian dishes at *Taj Mahal (ul Hamdije Kreševljakovića 6)* are slightly less expensive. Or fill up on hearty burritos at *Texas (ul Vladmira Perića 4).*

The most popular pizza spots are *Pizzeria Galija (ul Čobanija 20)* and *Pizzeria Indi,* at the corner of ul Gabelina and ul Koševo.

Entertainment
Sarajevo's best-known bar is *The Bar (ul Maršala Tita 5).* It has live music some weekends. *The Harp,* on Patriotske lige, is an Irish bar that serves Guinness. The crowded *Marquee (Obala Kulina Bana 5)* plays rock music. For occasional live jazz try *Clou (ul Mula Mustafe Bašekija 5)* and *King Kong (Hamdije Kreševljakovića 17).*

Getting There & Away
To Sarajevo there are four daily buses from Zagreb, four from Split and one from Dubrovnik. Two daily buses also go to/from Banja Luka.

Buses run from the Serb-controlled Sarajevo suburb of Lukavica to various parts of the RS and Belgrade – explain to a taxi driver that you want to go to the bus station in Lukavica, and he will take you to a spot on the RS border near the airport, where you can switch cabs or walk 150m to the bus station and buy a ticket.

Getting Around
An efficient but often crowded tram network runs east-west between Baščaršija and Illidža. Buy tram tickets (1KM) at kiosks near tram stations. Buy bus and trolleybus tickets (1KM) from the driver.

Taxis all have meters that begin at 2KM and cost 1KM per kilometre. Call ☎ 970 for a Radio Taxi.

Budget (☎/fax 206 640), ul Branilaca Sarajeva 21, also has an office at the airport (☎ 463 598). ASA Rent has offices at ul Branilaca Sarajeva 20 (☎/fax 445 209) and at the airport (☎ 463 598).

TRAVNIK
Tucked into a narrow valley only 90km northwest of Sarajevo, Travnik served as the seat of Turkish viziers who ruled Bosnia from 1699 to 1851. The town grew into a diplomatic crossroads, and earned fame more recently as the birthplace of Bosnia's best-known writer Ivo Andrić.

Though Muslims and Croats fought in the surrounding hills, Travnik was mostly spared. The town itself, which today is in Muslim hands, has a lovely medieval castle and pristine natural springs, and is well worth a day trip from Sarajevo.

Travnik's main street, ul Bosanska, runs east to west. The bus station is on the west end of town, within sight of the post office. Buses go almost hourly to Sarajevo and twice daily to Banja Luka.

BANJA LUKA
☎ 078 (☎ 058 from Sarajevo)
Banja Luka, the capital of Republika Srpska, was never much of a tourist centre and in 1993 local Serbs made sure it never would be by blowing up all 16 of the city's mosques. While not otherwise damaged during the war, the city is economically depressed and flooded with Serb refugees. Even as the RS leadership in Banja Luka opens slowly to the west, the city's transportation, banking and communication networks remain closely tied to Belgrade.

The Turistički Savez (☎/fax 12 323), ul Kralja Petra 175, sells maps and can give advice. At present no banks change travellers cheques or give credit card cash advances. Currency can be exchanged at Bank Kristal, on Franje Jukića 4 near the town hall, or Vojvodjanska Banka, ul Kralja Petra 87. The train and bus stations lie roughly 3km north of the centre; a taxi should cost 5KM. Buses run twice daily to Zagreb, five times daily to Sarajevo, and hourly to Belgrade (seven hours).

Hercegovina

MOSTAR
☎ 088

Mostar, the main city in Hercegovina, is a medieval town set in the valley of the aqua-green Neretva River. Sadly, Mostar was the scene of intense Muslim-Croat fighting during the war, which left many buildings destroyed. Nonetheless, visitors are slowly drifting back to enjoy Mostar's old medieval buildings, cobbled streets and Turkish souvenir shops.

Orientation & Information

Stari Most (Old Bridge), now being rebuilt, is still the heart of the old town, which is called Kujundžiluk. The dramatic 'front line', which essentially divides the town into Muslim (east of the river) and Croat (west of the river) sections, runs along the street behind Hotel Ero, then jogs one street west to the main boulevard.

Atlas Travel Agency (☎/fax 318 771), in the same building as Hotel Ero, has useful suggestions and a rough map of the west side. The staff at the tourist office by the east side bus station are also helpful.

Hrvatska Banka, adjacent to Hotel Ero, changes travellers cheques to any currency for 1.5% commission.

Places to Stay

The 12-bed *Pansion Zlatni Liljan* (☎ 551 353, ul Sehovina 8) costs 20KM or 25KM with breakfast. Head left past the Pavarotti Music Centre and follow the cobblestone road that starts by the mosque. The 10-bed *Vila Ossa* (☎ 578 532, Gojka Vokovića 40), on the other side of the river, costs 30/40KM or 35/50KM with breakfast.

Getting There & Away

Six buses per day run to Sarajevo, two to Split, one to Dubrovnik, and one to Zagreb. Two bus stops on the west side send buses to Međugorje and other parts of Hercegovina.

MEĐUGORJE
☎ 088

On 24 June 1981, six teenagers in this dirt-poor mountain village saw a miraculous apparition of the Virgin Mary. A decade later Međugorje, 30km south of Mostar, was awash with tour buses, souvenir stands, travel agencies and hundreds of pansions. Today these facilities are intact and open for business.

Though the Catholic Church has not officially acknowledged the apparitions, 'religious tourism' has been developed as if this were a beach resort. Crowds are especially heavy around Easter, the anniversary of the first apparition (24 June), the Assumption of the Virgin (15 August) and the Nativity of the Virgin (8 September).

Apparition Hill, where the Virgin was first spotted, is near the hamlet of Podbrdo – take the road curving left (east) from the centre of Međugorje, and follow the signs to Podbrdo (about 3km).

Orientation & Information

The streets have no names or numbers, but most tourist offices and hotels sell town maps (10 kuna). Taxis cost a flat fee of US$4 to anywhere in town.

Tourist information centres are a dime a dozen, but Globtour (☎/fax 651 393), 50m from the post office toward the church, arranges accommodation, and the staff speak English. Make international phone calls at the post office, which is next to the bus stop.

Places to Stay

With 17,000 rooms, Međugorje has more accommodation space than the rest of Bosnia combined. The 49-bed *Pansion Ostojić* (☎ 651 562, fax 651 095), not far from the post office, has rooms for 20KM to 45KM. Inquire in the Café Santa Fe, just in front of the pansion.

About 100m behind Ostojić, the white-washed *Pansion Santa Maria* (☎ 651 523, fax 651 723) charges 26KM to 45KM for bed and breakfast. Book early, as it is often filled with groups.

Getting There & Away

Two buses run daily from Split (3½ hours), one from Dubrovnik (three hours), and one from Zagreb (nine hours). Many international bus lines are run by Globtour; ask there for a schedule. A handful of buses run daily between Međugorje and Mostar; inquire at the post office about times.

Britain

At one stage of its history this small island ruled half the world's population and had a major impact on much of the rest. For those whose countries once lay in the shadow of its great empire a visit may almost be a cliche, but it's also essential – a peculiar mixture of homecoming and confrontation.

To the surprise of many, Britain remains one of the most beautiful islands in the world. In summer it can feel as if the whole world has come to Britain, so don't spend all your time in the big, tourist-ridden towns; rather, pick a small area and spend a week or so wandering around the country lanes and villages. Covering it all in one trip is impossible – and that's before you even start thinking of Scotland and Wales.

The United Kingdom comprises Britain (England, Wales and Scotland) and Northern Ireland. For reasons of geographical coherence, Northern Ireland is covered in the Ireland chapter.

Facts about Britain

HISTORY
England had long been settled by small bands of hunters when, around BC 4000, the Celts arrived from Europe. They brought two forms of the Celtic language – Gaelic, which is still spoken in parts of Ireland and Scotland, and Brythonic, which is still spoken in parts of Wales. Around 3000 BC the Celts began the construction of the great ceremonial complexes at Avebury and Stonehenge.

In AD 43 the Romans arrived in force, and paved roads later radiated from London to important Roman regional centres. The mountains of Wales and Scotland remained Celtic strongholds, but England was a part of the Roman Empire for 350 years.

During the 5th century the heathen Angles, Jutes and Saxons – Teutonic tribes

AT A GLANCE	
Capital:	London
Population:	56.7 million
Official Language:	English, Welsh, Scottish Gaelic
Currency:	1 British pound (£) = 100 pence

originating from north of the Rhine – advanced across what had been Roman England, and by the 7th century they had come to think of themselves collectively as English. The next wave of invaders were the Norwegian Vikings and the Danes. They were finally stopped by Alfred the Great, and he and his successors created a tenuously unified country.

After a brief period of Danish rule, Edward the Confessor was made king. He had been brought up in Normandy – a Viking duchy in France – alongside his cousin Duke William, the future Conqueror. After Edward's death, William landed with 12,000 men and defeated the Saxons at the Battle of Hastings in 1066. The conquest of England by the Normans was completed rapidly: English aristocrats were replaced by French-speaking Normans, dominating castles were built and the feudal system was imposed.

The 16th century was a golden age for Britain. Greek learning was rediscovered, trade boomed, Shakespeare wrote his plays, and Francis Bacon laid the foundations for modern science.

An age of religious intolerance was beginning, however, and after Elizabeth I the relationship between Parliament and the autocratic Stuart kings deteriorated. In 1642 the conflict became a civil war. Catholics and the old gentry supported Charles I, while the Protestant Puritans supported the Parliament, which had found a brilliant leader in Oliver Cromwell. The royalists were soon defeated – in 1649 Charles I was executed and Cromwell assumed dictatorial powers.

Two years after Cromwell's death in 1658, a reconstituted Parliament recalled Charles II from exile. The so-called Restoration was a period of expansion:

BRITAIN

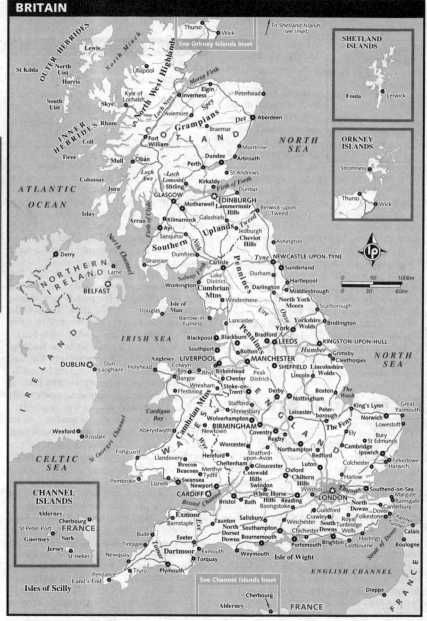

BRITAIN

To Shetland Islands
(see inset)

SHETLAND ISLANDS
Foula   Lerwick

ORKNEY ISLANDS
Stromness
Thurso   Wick

Thurso   Wick
See Orkney Islands Inset

OUTER HEBRIDES
Lewis
St Kilda   North Uist
Harris
South Uist

Ullapool
North West Highlands
Moray Firth
Kyle of Lochalsh   Inverness   Elgin
Skye   Peterhead
Aviemore   Spey
Loch Ness
Grampians   Dee   Aberdeen
Rhum   Braemar
INNER HEBRIDES
Coll   Fort William
Tiree   Montrose
Mull   Oban   Dundee   Arbroath
Loch Awe   Perth
Colonsay   Loch Lomond   St Andrews
Jura   Stirling   Kirkcaldy   Dunbar
Islay   GLASGOW   Firth of Forth
Motherwell   EDINBURGH
Lammermuir Hills
Arran   Kilmarnock   Berwick-upon-Tweed
Galashiels
Ayr   Tweed
Sanquhar   Jedburgh
Southern   Uplands   Cheviot Hills
Derry   Dumfries   Ashington
Stranraer   Nith   Tyne   NEWCASTLE-UPON-TYNE
Larne   Solway Firth   Sunderland
NORTHERN IRELAND   Carlisle   Durham
BELFAST   Lake District   Hartlepool
Workington   Cumbrian Mtns   Darlington   Middlesbrough
Douglas   Windermere   North York Moors   Scarborough
Isle of Man
Barrow-in-Furness   Ure
Lancaster   Yorkshire Wolds   Bridlington
IRISH SEA   Blackpool   Blackburn   Bradford   York
DUBLIN   Dun Laoghaire   Southport   Bolton's   LEEDS   KINGSTON-UPON-HULL
Holyhead   LIVERPOOL   MANCHESTER   Humber   Grimsby
Anglesey   Colwyn Bay   Birkenhead   SHEFFIELD   Cleethorpes
Rhyl   Chester   Peak District   Lincolnshire Wolds
Bangor   Lincoln
IRELAND   Wrexham   Stoke-on-Trent   Boston
Ffestiniog   Derby   The Wash
Cardigan Bay   Stafford   Nottingham
Aberystwyth   Cambrian Mtns   Shrewsbury   Leicester   Peterborough   King's Lynn
Wolverhampton   Great Yarmouth
Wexford   Newtown   BIRMINGHAM   Norwich
Rosslare   Coventry   Rugby   The Fens   Lowestoft
Fishguard   Wye   Worcester   Northampton   Bury St Edmunds
Llandovery   Hereford   Stratford-upon-Avon   Bedford   Cambridge   Ipswich
CELTIC SEA   Brecon Beacons   Cheltenham   Gloucester   Oxford   Luton   Colchester   Felixstowe
Pembroke   Merthyr Tydfil   Cotswold Hills   Chiltern Hills   Harwich
Llanelli   Swansea   Newport   Swindon   Harlow
WALES   CARDIFF   White Horse   Windsor   Thames   Southend-on-Sea
Bristol Channel   Bristol   Bath   Reading   LONDON   Margate
Exmoor   Basingstoke   North Downs   Ramsgate
Barnstaple   Taunton   Salisbury   Guildford   Crawley   Canterbury   Dover
Bude   North Dorset Downs   Winchester   Royal Tunbridge Wells   Folkestone
Tintagel   Exeter   Southampton   Chichester   South Downs   Calais
Newquay   Dartmoor   Exmouth   Bournemouth   Portsmouth   Brighton   Eastbourne   Hastings   Boulogne
Truro   Plymouth   Torquay   Weymouth   Isle of Wight
Penzance
Land's End
Isles of Scilly

CHANNEL ISLANDS
Alderney
Cherbourg
St Peter Port   FRANCE
Guernsey   Sark
Jersey   St Helier

See Channel Islands Inset
Cherbourg
Alderney   FRANCE

ENGLISH CHANNEL
Dieppe
FRANCE
Channel Tunnel
Strait of Dover

ATLANTIC OCEAN

NORTH SEA

SCOTLAND

ENGLAND

North Minch

St Georges Channel

0   50   100km
0   30   60mi

colonies stretched down the American coast and the East India Company established its headquarters in Bombay. France ceded all of Canada to Britain in 1770, and Captain Cook claimed Australia for Britain in 1778. The empire's first major reverse came when the American colonies won their independence in 1783.

The 1780s witnessed the birth of the Industrial Revolution in Britain as canals, trains, coal, water and steam power transformed the means of production and transport. By the time Queen Victoria took the throne in 1837, Britain's fleets dominated the seas and its factories dominated world trade. Under prime ministers Disraeli and Gladstone, the worst excesses of the Industrial Revolution were addressed, education became universal and the right to vote was extended to most men (women did not get equal voting rights until 1928).

Queen Victoria died at the very beginning of the 20th century, and the old order was shattered by the Great War (WWI). By the war's end in 1918 a million British men had died and 15% of the country's accumulated capital had been spent.

In 1939 Hitler provoked a new war by invading Poland. By mid-1940, most of Europe was under the direct influence of the Nazis, Stalin had negotiated a peace deal, the USA was neutral, and Britain, under the extraordinary leadership of Winston Churchill, was virtually isolated. Between July and October 1940 the Royal Air Force fought and won the Battle of Britain and Hitler's invasion plans were blocked. Forty-three thousand Britons died in the bombing raids of 1940-41.

The postwar years have been challenging. The last of the empire has gained independence (India in 1947, Malaya in 1957, Kenya in 1963), many traditional industries have collapsed and the nation has had to accept a new role as a partner in the European Union (EU). Britain is still a wealthy and influential country, but it's no longer a superpower.

Britain suffered many setbacks in the 1990s – a disastrous fire at Windsor Castle, the tragic death of Princess Diana, and a distinct lack of success in international sport. Yet the landslide victory of Tony Blair's Labour Party in the 1997 elections gave the country a boost that reverberated around the world. This has dimmed with time and the Labour government seems to be digging itself almost as many holes as the previous Conservative administrations. But politics aside, Britain remains a happening place to be in the new millennium.

GEOGRAPHY

Britain (240,000 sq km), about the same size as New Zealand, or half the size of France, is less than 1000km from south to north and under 500km at its widest point. The Grampians form the mountainous barrier between the Scottish Lowlands and Highlands, and include Ben Nevis (1343m), the highest mountain on the island.

CLIMATE

The seas surrounding the British Isles are shallow, and relatively warm because of the influence of the warm North Atlantic Current (the Gulf Stream). This creates a temperate maritime climate with few extremes of temperature but few cloudless, sunny days. Although in relative terms the climate is mild and the rainfall not spectacular (912mm), grey skies can make for an utterly depressing atmosphere.

The average July temperature in London is 17.6°C (64°F), and the average January temperature is 4°C (39°F).

POPULATION & PEOPLE

Britain has a population of about 57 million. Since WWII there has been significant immigration from the ex-colonies, especially the West Indies, Bangladesh, Pakistan and India. Outside the big cities of the Midlands and Northern England, however, the population is overwhelmingly white.

SOCIETY & CONDUCT

The most common British stereotype is of a reserved, anally retentive politeness and conservatism. Yet the phrases 'cold' and 'inhibited' don't generally leap to mind when you're mixing with the working classes, the northern English, the Welsh or the Scots. Visit a nightclub in one of the big cities, a football match or a good local pub and you might more readily describe the Brits as uninhibited, passionate, humorous and sentimental.

LANGUAGE

English may be one of the world's most widely spoken languages but the language as

BRITAIN

it's spoken in some parts of Britain is sometimes incomprehensible to overseas visitors – even those who assume they've spoken it all their lives. You may also hear Gaelic spoken in Scotland and Welsh in Wales.

Facts for the Visitor

HIGHLIGHTS

Islands
  Orkney, Skye, Lewis and Harris (Scotland)
Museums & Galleries
  British Museum, Victoria & Albert Museum, Science Museum, Natural History Museum, National Gallery, Tate Galleries (London), HMS Victory (Portsmouth), Castle Museum (York), Burrell Collection (Glasgow)
Historic Towns
  Salisbury, Winchester, Bath, Oxford, Cambridge, St David's, York, Durham, Edinburgh, St Andrews
Cathedrals
  Canterbury, Salisbury, Winchester, Wells, York, Durham

SUGGESTED ITINERARIES

Three days
  Visit London, possibly with a day trip to Windsor and Eton.
One week
  Visit London, Canterbury, Oxford and Bath; or London, Oxford, York and Edinburgh.
Two weeks
  Visit London, Salisbury, Avebury, Bath, Wells, Oxford, York and Edinburgh. If Scotland is a priority, visit London, York, Edinburgh, Inverness, Isle of Skye, Fort William, Oban and Glasgow. If rural countryside is a priority, visit London then the Lake District or Peak District, Snowdonia (North Wales) and the Cotswolds.

PLANNING
When to Go

July and August are the busiest months and should be avoided if possible – the crowds in London and popular towns such as Oxford, Bath and York have to be seen to be believed. May/June and September/October are the best times to visit, although October is a bit late for the Scottish Highlands.

Maps

The best introductory map to Britain is published by the British Tourist Authority (BTA), and is widely available. The Ordnance Survey caters to walkers, with a wide variety of maps at different scales. Its Landranger maps (1:50,000) are ideal. Look out for Harveys hiking maps, which can sometimes be more user-friendly and up-to-date than Ordnance Survey maps.

Passes & Discounts

Entry to English Heritage (EH; ☎ 020-7973 3000) properties – comprising castles, palaces and prehistoric sites throughout England – costs nonmembers around £2.30. EH membership is £28 and gives free entry to all EH properties, half-price entry to Historic Scotland and Cadw (Wales) properties. You can join at most EH sites.

Entry to National Trust (NT; ☎ 020 7222 9251) properties is £1 to £6. NT membership is £30 (£15 under age 26) and gives free entry to all English, Welsh, Scottish and Northern Irish properties. You can join at most NT sites.

The Great British Heritage Pass gives free access to NT and EH properties and some of the expensive private properties. A seven-day pass is £25, 15 days is £36 or one month is £60. It's available overseas (contact a travel agent or Thomas Cook office) or at the British Travel Centre in London.

TOURIST OFFICES

The British Tourist Authority (BTA) has extensive information on England, Scotland and Wales, quite a lot of it free and relevant to budget travellers. Contact BTA before leaving home, because some of the material and discounts are only available outside Britain.

Tourist Information Centres (TICs) can be found even in small towns. They give invaluable advice on accommodation and cheap ways of seeing the area.

Tourist Offices Abroad

BTA offices abroad include:

Australia (☎ 02-9377 4400, fax 02-9377 4499) Level 16, The Gateway, 1 Macquarie Place, Circular Quay, Sydney, NSW 2000
Canada (☎ 905-405 1840, fax 905-405 1835) 5915 Airport Road, Suite 120, Mississauga, Ontario L4V 1T1
New Zealand (☎ 09-303 1446, fax 09-776 965) 3rd floor, Dilworth Building, corner Queen & Customs Sts, Auckland 1
USA (☎ 1-800-462 2748) 551 Fifth Avenue, Suite 701, New York, NY 10176;
(no ☎) 625 N Michigan Avenue, Suite 1510, Chicago IL 60611

EMBASSIES & CONSULATES
UK Embassies Abroad
British diplomatic missions abroad include:

Australia (☎ 02-6270 6666) Commonwealth Ave, Yarralumla, Canberra, ACT 2600
Canada (☎ 613-237 1530) 80 Elgin St, Ottawa K1P 5K7
New Zealand (☎ 04-472 6049) 44 Hill St, Wellington 1
USA (☎ 202-462 1340) 3100 Massachusetts Ave NW, Washington DC 20008

Foreign Embassies in the UK
The following diplomatic missions are in London:

Australian High Commission (☎ 020-7379 4334) Australia House, The Strand, London WC2 (tube: Temple)
Canadian High Commission (☎ 020-7258 6600) 1 Grosvenor Square, London W1 (tube: Bond St)
New Zealand High Commission (☎ 020-7930 8422) New Zealand House, 80 Haymarket, London SW1 (tube: Piccadilly Circus)
US (☎ 020-7499 9000) 24 Grosvenor Square, London W1 (tube: Bond St)

MONEY
The currency is the pound sterling (£), made up of 100 pence (p). One and 2p coins are copper; 5p, 10p, 20p and 50p coins are silver; the bulky £1 coin is gold-coloured; and the £2 coin is coloured gold and silver. Notes come in £5, £10, £20 and £50 denominations and vary in colour and size.

Notes issued by several Scottish banks, including a £1 note, are legal tender on both sides of the border, though shopkeepers in England and Wales may be reluctant to accept them.

Banks and ATMs (called cashpoints in Britain) are everywhere. Travellers cheques are easy to cash at banks (though not at shops and hotels), as are notes in most major currencies. ATMs usually accept major credit cards and foreign bank cards (Plus, Cirrus, Eurocard etc). Be careful using bureaux de change – they frequently levy outrageous commissions and fees.

American Express and Thomas Cook travellers cheques are widely recognised, and don't charge for cashing their own cheques. Thomas Cook has an office in every decent-sized town, and American Express has representation in most cities.

Exchange Rates

country	unit		pound
Australia	A$1	=	£0.39
Canada	C$1	=	£0.45
euro	€1	=	£0.60
France	1FF	=	£0.09
Germany	DM1	=	£0.31
Ireland	IR£1	=	£0.76
Japan	¥100	=	£0.61
New Zealand	NZ$1	=	£0.30
USA	US$1	=	£0.67

Costs
Britain can be extremely expensive and London is horrendous. In London budget £25 to £30 a day for bare survival. Any sightseeing, restaurant meals or nightlife will be on top of that. Costs will obviously be even higher if you choose to stay in a central hotel and eat well.

Costs drop outside London – though you'll still need around £15 to £20 per day (staying in hostels), not including long-distance transport.

Tipping
Taxi drivers and waiters expect 10% tips. Some restaurants automatically include a service charge (tip) of 10% to 15%, and no extra tip is required.

POST & COMMUNICATIONS
Post
Post-office hours can vary, but most are open 9 am to 5 pm weekdays, to noon Saturday. Within the UK, first-class mail is quicker and more expensive (27p per letter) than 2nd-class mail (19p). Air-mail letters to Europe are 30p, to the Americas and Australasia 43p (up to 10g) to 63p (up to 20g).

Telephone, Fax & Email
Britain's country code is ☎ 44. When dialling in from abroad drop the initial zero from area codes.

Public phones are easy to find and easy to use. Many accept phonecards sold at newsstands, post offices and shops. You can buy numerous cheap phonecards, which massively undercut British Telecom (BT) rates on international calls. Check the posters in newsagents' windows for the best rates for the country you are dialling.

Dial ☎ 100 for a BT operator. Local calls are charged by time, and national calls

BRITAIN

(including Scotland, Wales and Northern Ireland) are charged by time and distance. Cheap rates apply 6 pm to 8 am weekdays, and midnight Friday to midnight Sunday. For an international operator dial ☎ 155. In larger towns look for independently operated telecom centres – international rates at these places are generally the lowest available. Note that any number that begins with the code 0870- is charged at the national rate; a number that begins with the code 0845- is charged at the (cheaper) local rate.

Most hotels now have fax machines. Some shops also offer fax services, advertised by a sign in the window. To collect your email visit one of the growing number of cybercafes and cyberpubs.

INTERNET RESOURCES

The About Britain site, www.aboutbritain .com, has useful information and links. The BTA also has an excellent Web site at www.bta.org.uk. There is an official Wales site at www.tourism.wales.gov.uk.

TIME

Time worldwide is measured according to Greenwich near London – Greenwich Mean Time (GMT). Daylight-saving time is from late March to late October.

WOMEN TRAVELLERS

Women will find Britain a reasonably enlightened country. Lone travellers should have no problems, although common-sense caution should be observed in big cities, especially when walking alone at night. Some pubs still retain a heavy masculine atmosphere but on the whole they're becoming increasingly family-friendly.

The London Rape Crisis Centre (☎ 020-7837 1600) is run by women and gives confidential advice and support to women who have been sexually assaulted.

GAY & LESBIAN TRAVELLERS

London, Manchester and Brighton are Britain's main gay and lesbian centres. You'll also find gay and lesbian information centres in most cities and large towns. Check listings in *Gay Times*, available from newsagents.

DISABLED TRAVELLERS

The Royal Association for Disability and Rehabilitation (RADAR) publishes a useful guide: *Holidays and Travel Abroad: A Guide for Disabled People*. Contact RADAR (☎ 020-7250 3222) at 12 City Forum, 250 City Rd, London EC1V 8AF.

DANGERS & ANNOYANCES

Britain is remarkably safe considering its size and the disparities in wealth. However, city crime is certainly not unknown so caution is necessary, especially at night. Pickpockets and bag snatchers operate in crowded public places. Avoid large groups of young lads after the pubs shut (11 pm), as violence is not uncommon on High Sts across Britain.

Drugs of every description are widely available, especially in nightclubs. Nonetheless, marijuana, hash, ecstasy and the other usual suspects are illegal.

Throughout Britain dial ☎ 999 for fire, police or ambulance.

BUSINESS HOURS

Offices are open 9 am to 5 pm weekdays. Shops may be open longer hours, and 9 am to 5 pm on Saturday. Except in rural areas some shops also open 10 am to 4 pm on Sunday. In country towns, particularly in Scotland and Wales, there may be an early closing day for shops – usually Tuesday or Wednesday afternoon.

PUBLIC HOLIDAYS & SPECIAL EVENTS

Most banks, businesses and a number of museums are closed on the following days: New Year's Day, 2 January (bank holiday in Scotland), Good Friday, Easter Monday (not in Scotland), May Day (first Monday in May), Spring Bank Holiday (last Monday in May), Summer Bank Holiday (last Monday in August, first Monday in August in Scotland) and 25 and 26 December.

The main festivals include: the New Year's Hogmanay festival in Edinburgh, the Edinburgh Folk Festival in late March, the Oxford/Cambridge boat race (London) in late March, the two-week Bath International Festival in late May, the Chelsea Flower Show (London) in late May, Trooping the Colour (Queen's birthday parade) in mid-June, the Royal Ascot horse races in mid-June, the Wimbledon tennis tournament in mid-June, the Glastonbury music festival in late June, the Edinburgh

International and Fringe festivals in late August, and the Royal Braemar Gathering (Highland Games) in early September.

ACCOMMODATION

This will almost certainly be your single largest daily expense. Local TICs provide free lists of nearby possibilities (from camping grounds to upmarket B&Bs) and make bookings (sometimes free, often £2.75, £5 in London).

Camping

Free camping is rarely possible, except in Scotland. Most camping grounds have reasonable facilities, although they're often inaccessible unless you have a car or bike. For an extensive listing buy *Camping & Caravanning in Britain* (£7.99) published by the Automobile Association. Local TICs also have listings.

YHA/HI Hostels

Hostelling International (known as Youth Hostel Association, or YHA, in Britain) membership gives you access to a huge network of hostels throughout England, Wales and Scotland.

There are separate local associations for England/Wales, Scotland, and Northern Ireland, and each publishes its own individual listings. Membership cards (£10, £5 for under 18s) are available at the YHA Adventure Shop (☎ 020-7836 1036), 14 Southampton St, London WC2 (tube: Covent Garden).

All hostels have facilities for self-catering and some have cheap meals; many also have curfews and daytime closing. Advance booking is advisable, especially on weekends, bank holidays and at any time in summer. Overnight prices are in two tiers: under 18 (£5 to £18, averaging £7) and adult (£7 to £23, averaging £11). Bear in mind that when you add £3 for breakfast, you come close to cheap B&B prices.

Independent Hostels

The growing network of independent hostels are more laid-back, and rarely have curfews or daytime lockouts. Dorm beds average £10 per night. The *Independent Hostel Guide* (£3.95) covers England, Scotland, Wales and the whole of Ireland. TICs also have listings.

University Accommodation

Many British universities offer accommodation to travellers from late June to late September, although some universities have rooms early in June and over Easter and Christmas. Most rooms are comfortable, functional, and cost £18 to £25 per person. For more information contact the British Universities Accommodation Consortium (BUAC), Box No 967, University Park, Nottingham NG7 2RD (☎ 0115-950 4571, fax 0115-942 2505).

B&Bs & Guesthouses

B&Bs are a great British institution and the cheapest private accommodation you can find. At the bottom end (£13 to £18 per person) you get a bedroom in a normal house, a shared bathroom and an enormous cooked breakfast. More upmarket B&Bs have bathrooms and TVs in each room. Guesthouses, which are often just large converted houses, charge from £15 to £50 a night.

FOOD & DRINKS

In the main towns and cities a cosmopolitan range of cuisines is available for £4 to £10. Chain restaurants like Café Rouge have also brought 'French' cuisine to most touristed towns, again at moderate prices.

Vegetarians should buy a copy of *The Vegetarian Travel Guide*, published annually by the UK Vegetarian Society and covering hundreds of places to eat and stay.

If you're on a tight budget, pubs are often the best sources of cheap nutrition. At the bottom end they're not much different from cafes, while at the expensive end they're closer to restaurants.

English pubs serve an impressive range of beers – lagers, bitters, ales and stouts. The drink most people from the New World know as beer is actually lager. Fortunately the traditional English bitter – lukewarm and flat – has made a comeback, thanks to the Campaign for Real Ale (CAMRA) organisation. Look for their endorsement sticker on pub windows. Ale is similar to bitter – it's more a regional difference in name. Stout is a dark, rich, foamy drink; Guinness is the most famous brand. Beers are usually served in pints (£1.50 to £2.50), but you can also ask for a 'half' (a half-pint).

Pubs are allowed to open daily from 11 am to 11 pm, but beware: the bell for last

BRITAIN

drinks rings out at about 10.45 pm. In bigger cities, many pubs and bars have late licences until 2 am. Takeaway alcoholic drinks are sold from 'off-licence' shops, but rarely from pubs. Every neighbourhood has one. Most restaurants are licensed and their alcoholic drinks, particularly good wines, are always expensive.

Getting There & Away

AIR

There are international air links with London, Manchester, Newcastle, Edinburgh and Glasgow, but most travellers arrive/depart from one of the five main London airports: Heathrow, Gatwick, Stansted, Luton or London City.

London is a major centre for cheap tickets. Local travel agents – STA, Council Travel and Campus Travel are reputable – book discounted student and youth fares to destinations worldwide. Also check travel ads in *TNT Magazine* and London's Sunday papers. The largest discounts are for full-time students aged under 30 and all travellers aged under 26 (you need an ISIC or youth card).

Low season one-way/return flights from London bucket shops (discount travel agents) start at: Amsterdam £45/65, Athens £69/99, Frankfurt £55/75, İstanbul £79/129, Madrid £79/99, Paris £40/59 and Rome £69/89. Discount carriers including Easyjet, Ryanair and Go have some very good offers to a range of destinations.

LAND

It's possible to travel to/from Britain by bus and train either via the rail-only Channel Tunnel or car-and-passenger ferries. The cost of crossing the English Channel is usually included in ticket prices.

Bus

Eurolines (☎ 0870-514 3219), at 52 Grosvenor Gardens, Victoria, London SW1, a division of National Express (the largest UK bus line), has an enormous network of European destinations, including Ireland and Eastern Europe.

You can book through any National Express office, including the Victoria coach station in London (which is where Eurolines' buses arrive and depart), and at many travel agents. Sample single/return prices and journey times include: Amsterdam £33/39 (12 hours), Athens £128/207 (56 hours), Frankfurt £42/69 (18½ hours), Madrid £77/89 (27 hours), Paris £31/33 (10 hours) and Rome £69/79 (36 hours).

Eurolines also has some good-value explorer tickets that are valid up to six months and allow travel between a number of major cities. For example, you can visit Amsterdam, Brussels and Paris and return to London for £59.

Train

Trains that connect with European ferries leave from London's Victoria or Liverpool St stations. The prices given here are for adults; youth tickets and passes are considerably lower. For inquiries concerning European trains contact the following: International Rail Centre (☎ 020-7834 2345) and Wasteels (☎ 020-7834 7066), both at Platform 2, Victoria Station, London SW1; and Rail Europe (☎ 0870-584 8848), 179 Piccadilly, London W1.

Non-tunnel rail options depend on whether you cross the Channel on a catamaran or ferry, and whether you cross from Folkestone, Harwich or Newhaven. For example, 2nd class to Paris via Newhaven and the Sealink ferry costs £39/65 (nine hours); you can book onward rail connections to anywhere in Europe. London to Amsterdam via Harwich and the Stena high speed catamaran costs £49/79 (8¾ hours).

Travellers aged under 26 can pick up Billet International de Jeunesse (BIJ) tickets (also known as Eurotrain tickets) that cut fares by up to 50%. BIJ/Eurotrain options include circular Explorer tickets, allowing a different route for the return trip: eg, London to Madrid takes in Barcelona, Paris and numerous other cities.

Channel Tunnel Two services operate through the tunnel: Eurotunnel operates a rail shuttle service for motorbikes, cars, buses and freight vehicles between terminals at Folkestone in the UK and Calais (Coquelles) in France (one hour); and the railway companies of Britain, France and Belgium operate a high-speed passenger service, known as Eurostar, from London to

Paris (£45 to £120 one way, three hours) and Brussels (2¾ hours). Get tickets from travel agents and major train stations. Holders of Britrail, Eurail and Euro passes are entitled to discounted fares on Eurostar trains.

SEA

There is a bewildering array of alternatives between Britain and mainland Europe. It's impossible to list all the services because of space limitations. See the Ireland chapter for details on links between Britain and Ireland.

Contact details for services are as follows:

Scandinavian Seaways	(☎ 0870-533 3000)
P&O Stena Line	(☎ 0870-598 0980)
Hoverspeed	(☎ 01304-240241)
P&O	(☎ 0870-598 0555)
Brittany Ferries	(☎ 0870-536 0360)
Color Line	(☎ 0191-296 1313)

France

Dover & Folkestone The shortest ferry link to Europe is from Dover and Folkestone to Calais and Boulogne. Dover is the most convenient port for those who plan onward travel (in Britain) by bus or train. Between Dover and Calais, P&O Stena and Hoverspeed operate every one to two hours.

On its 75-minute ferry service P&O Stena Line charges one-way foot passengers £24; car plus driver and up to nine passengers £129 to £255; motorcycles and riders £75 to £132. Special offers make a big difference.

Hoverspeed's catamarans take only 35 minutes to cross the Channel. It charges £24 for a one-way passenger, £58 for a five-day return.

Portsmouth P&O operates three to four ferries a day to/from Cherbourg and Le Havre. The day ferries take five to six hours and the night ferries take seven to eight hours. One-way foot passenger fare is £9 to £30, and a car costs from a bargain £21 to a steep £138. Brittany Ferries has at least one sailing a day to/from Caen and St Malo.

Spain

From Plymouth, Brittany Ferries operates at least one ferry a week to Santander on Spain's north coast (£47 to £98 single, £112 to £317 for a vehicle; 24 hours). Brittany also operates a service between Santander

and Portsmouth that takes 30 hours. P&O operates a service between Portsmouth and Bilbao at similar rates.

Scandinavia

Newcastle Norway's Color Line operates ferries all year to Stavanger, Haugesund and Bergen in Norway. These are overnight trips, and the high-season fare for a reclining chair is £80; a car and five people costs £315. Bicycles are free.

Scandinavian Seaways runs ferries to Gothenburg, Sweden (£187 and up, 22 hours) on Friday from June to mid-August.

Harwich Scandinavian Seaways has ferries to Esbjerg in Denmark (£134 and up, 20 hours) and Gothenburg in Sweden (£187 and up, 24 hours).

Belgium, the Netherlands & Germany

Harwich Scandinavian Seaways has ferries to Hamburg (Germany) every two days for most of the year (£135 to £225 return in a four-berth couchette, 19 hours).

Stena Line has two ferries a day to the Hook of Holland in the Netherlands (£22 one way, 7½ to 9½ hours).

Newcastle Scandinavian Seaways has a twice-weekly ferry to Hamburg from late May to early September, taking 20 hours. The fare is the same as from Harwich.

Getting Around

AIR

Most regional centres and islands are linked to London. However, unless you're going to the outer reaches of Britain, in particular northern Scotland, planes (including the time it takes to get to/from airports) are only marginally quicker than trains. Prices are generally higher than 1st-class rail, but see the Scotland Getting There & Away section for details of no-frills flights from London to Scotland (from £29). Note that there is now a £10 Air Passenger Duty added to the quoted price of tickets.

BUS

National Express is affiliated with Eurolines and runs the UK's largest national network; for information nationwide call ☎ 0870-580 8080. There are smaller, better-value competitors on many major routes. A number of counties operate telephone inquiry lines which try to explain the fast-changing and often chaotic situation with timetables; wherever possible, these numbers have been given.

Passes & Discounts

The National Express Discount Coach Card (£8) gives 30% off standard adult fares. It is available to full-time students and those aged 16 to 25 and 50 or over. The cards are available from all National Express agents and require a passport photo.

The National Express Explorer Pass allows unlimited coach travel within a specified period. It is available to all overseas visitors but it must be bought *outside* Britain. You will be given a travel voucher that can be exchanged for the pass at Heathrow or Gatwick airports, or at any of the larger National Express agencies. Passes cost £59 for three days' travel within five consecutive days, £110 for seven days in a 21-day period, and £170 for 14 days in a 30-day period. Students and youth receive discounts.

National Express Tourist Trail Passes are available to UK and overseas citizens. They provide unlimited travel on all services for two days within three consecutive days (£49/39 for adults/students and youth), any five days within 10 consecutive days (£85/69), any seven days within 21 consecutive days (£120/94) and any 14 days within 30 consecutive days (£187/143). The passes can be bought overseas, or at National Express in the UK.

Hop-on Hop-off Buses

The Stray Travel Network (Slowcoach; ☎ 020-7373 7737) is an excellent bus service designed especially for those staying in hostels, but useful for all budget travellers. Buses run on a regular circuit between London, Windsor, Bath, Manchester, Howarth, the Lake District, Glasgow, Stirling, Edinburgh, York, Nottingham, Cambridge and London, calling at hostels.

You can get on and off the bus where you like, and the £129 ticket is valid for the whole circuit for six months. Buses leave London three times a week throughout the year; the price includes some activities and

visits en route. Tickets are available from branches of STA.

TRAIN

Inter-Rail passes are valid, but Eurail passes are *not* recognised in Britain. There are UK rail passes, but these aren't normally recognised in Europe.

British Rail is no more. Services are provided by 25 train operating companies (TOCs). A separate company, Railtrack, owns and maintains the track and the stations. For the sake of convenience the British Rail logo and name are still used on direction signs. Passengers can travel only on services provided by the company who issued their ticket and each company is able to set whatever fare it chooses.

If you do not have one of the passes listed below, the cheapest tickets must be purchased at least one week in advance. Phone the general inquiry line (☎ 0845-748 4950) for timetables, fares and the numbers to ring for credit card bookings. For short journeys, it's not really necessary to purchase tickets or make seat reservations in advance.

BritRail Passes

BritRail passes are the most interesting possibility for visitors, but they are *not available in Britain* and must be bought in your country of origin. Contact the BTA in your country for details.

A BritRail pass, which allows unlimited travel, can be bought for eight, 15, 22 or 30 days. An eight-day pass for an adult/youth is US$259/205, a 15-day pass is US$395/318, a 22-day pass is US$510/410 and a 30-day pass is US$590/475.

A BritRail plus Ireland pass costs US$359 for five days in a month or US$511 for 10 days in a month and includes unlimited rail travel in both countries and the ferry trip from one to the other and back.

The Flexipass allows four days' unlimited travel in a month (US$219/175), eight days in one month (US$315/253), 15 days in one month for adults (US$480) and 15 days in two months for youth (US$385).

Rail Rovers

BritRail Rovers are valid on most UK trains. A seven-day All Line Rover is £300/198, and 14 days is £440/198. There are also regional Rovers and some Flexi

Rovers to Wales, north and mid-Wales, the North Country, the north-west coast and Peaks, the south-west, and Scotland.

Railcards

Various railcards, available from major stations, give a third off most tickets and are valid for a year. The Young Person's Railcard (£18) is for people aged 16 to 25, or for those studying full time. You'll need two passport photos and proof of age (birth certificate or passport) or student status.

CAR & MOTORCYCLE

Anyone using the roads should get hold of the *Highway Code* (99p), which is often available at TICs. Americans and Australians will find petrol expensive.

Briefly, vehicles should be driven on the left-hand side of the road; front seat belts are compulsory and belts must be worn if they are fitted in the back; the speed limit is 30mph (50kmh) in built-up areas, 60mph (100kmh) on single carriageways and 70mph (110kmh) on dual carriageways and motorways; you give way to your right at roundabouts (that is, traffic already on the roundabout has the right of way); and motorcyclists must wear helmets.

A yellow line painted along the edge of the road indicates there are parking restrictions. The only way to establish the exact restrictions is to find the nearby sign that spells them out.

London

☎ 020

At times Europe's largest city is more grand, beautiful and stimulating than you could have imagined; at others it is colder, greyer, dirtier and more expensive than you believed possible.

London is a cosmopolitan mix of the developed and developing worlds, of chauffeurs and beggars, of the establishment and the avant-garde, with seven to 12 million inhabitants (depending on where you stop counting) and 26 million visitors a year.

For the budget traveller, London is a challenge. Money has a way of mysteriously evaporating every time you move. With limited funds it's necessary to plan, book ahead and prioritise. And remember – there's little point in putting up with London's crowds, the pollution and the often dreary weather if you can't take advantage of at least some of London's theatres, exhibitions, pubs, clubs, cafes and restaurants. Fortunately, some of the very best – including most of the major museums – remain free or very cheap.

Orientation

'London' is an imprecise term used loosely to describe over 2000 sq km of Greater London enclosed by the M25 ring road. The city's main geographical feature is the Thames, a tidal river that flows from west to east and divides the city into northern and southern halves.

Though London sprawls over an enormous area, the Underground system (the 'tube') makes most of it easily accessible. All the international airports lie some distance from the city centre but transport is easy.

Maps A decent map is vital. The single-sheet Lonely Planet *London City Map* (£3.99) has three separate maps at different scales as well as an inset map of Theatreland and an index. The bound *Mini London A-Z Street Atlas & Index* (£3.75) provides comprehensive coverage of London in a discreet size.

Terminology London is divided into boroughs, which are further subdivided into districts. Postal code letters correspond to compass directions from the centre of London: EC means East Central, WC means West Central, NW means North West etc.

To further confuse visitors, many streets change name – Holland Park Ave becomes Notting Hill Gate, which becomes Bayswater Rd, which becomes Oxford St. Street numbering can also bewilder (315 might be opposite 520).

Information

Lonely Planet has several publications with more detailed coverage of London. For comprehensive coverage, see *London* (£9.99). For colourful coverage in a handy pocket size, try *London Condensed* (£5.99), while *Out to Eat – London* (£7.99) describes an enormous selection of London's best eateries.

Time Out magazine (issued every Tuesday, £1.95) is a complete listing of everything

BRITAIN

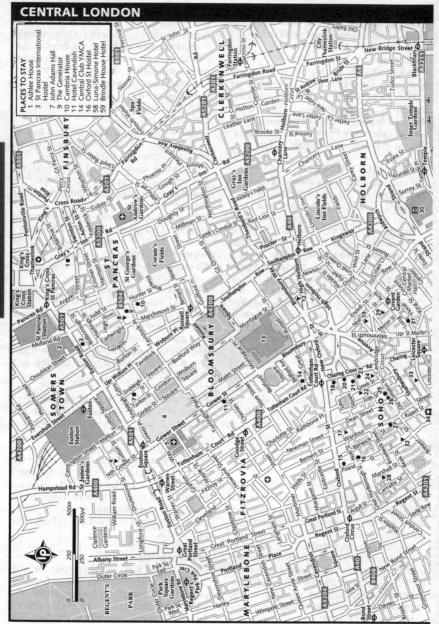

CENTRAL LONDON

PLACES TO STAY
1 Ashlee House
3 St Pancras International Hostel
7 John Adams Hall
9 The Generator
10 Cambria House
11 Hotel Cavendish
14 Central Club YMCA
16 Oxford St Hostel
58 Luna-Simone Hotel
59 Brindle House Hotel

CENTRAL LONDON

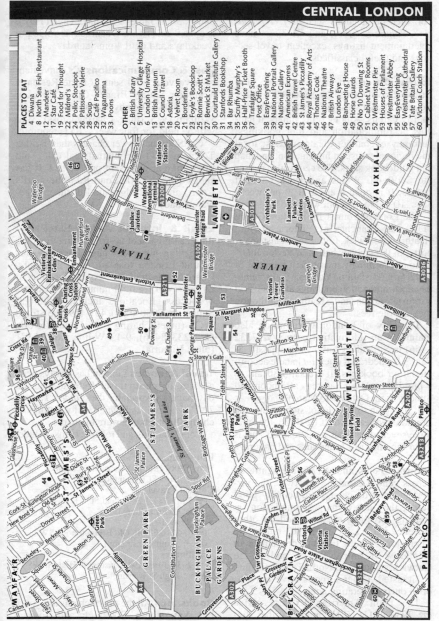

BRITAIN

happening and is recommended for every visitor. Free publications such as *TNT Magazine*, *Southern Cross*, and *SA Times* have entertainment listings, excellent travel sections and useful classifieds.

Tourist Offices The massive, always busy British Travel Centre (☎ 8846 9000) is at 1 Regent St, a two-minute walk from Piccadilly Circus. Among other things, it handles accommodation and tour bookings; currency exchange; theatre tickets; local and regional transport information; and map and guidebook sales. The centre also houses the Scotland, Wales and Ireland tourist boards. It is open 9 am to 6.30 pm weekdays, 10 am to 4.30 pm weekends.

The London Tourist Information Centre (TIC) has branches at Victoria station; Heathrow, Gatwick, Luton and Stansted airports; in the arrivals hall at Waterloo International Terminal; and at the Liverpool St underground station. You can make same-day accommodation bookings at the TICs at Victoria station and Heathrow, although they charge fees.

The City of London Corporation also maintains an information centre (☎ 7332 1456) in St Paul's Churchyard, opposite St Paul's Cathedral. It does *not* handle accommodation bookings. It's open 9.30 am to 5 pm daily (closed Saturday afternoon and Sunday from October to March).

If you plan to do a lot of sightseeing, the London GoSee card (£10/16/26 for one/three/seven days) can be purchased and is valid for entry to 17 museums and galleries.

Money Banks and ATMs are scattered across central London. Otherwise the airport bureaux de change are actually good value; they don't charge commission on sterling travellers cheques, and on other currencies it's 1.5% with a £3 minimum. There are 24-hour bureaux de change in Heathrow Terminals 1, 3 and 4; in Gatwick's South and North Terminals; and at Stansted. Other airports have bureaus open during operating hours.

The main American Express office (☎ 7930 4411), 6 Haymarket (tube: Piccadilly Circus), is open for currency exchange 9 am to 5.30 pm Monday to Friday, 9 am to 4 pm Saturday and Sunday. There are slightly longer hours June to September.

The main Thomas Cook office (☎ 7853 6400), 30 St James's St (tube: Green Park), is open 9 am (10 am Wednesday) to 5.30 pm weekdays and until 4 pm Saturday.

Post & Communications It's convenient to have your mail sent to Poste Restante, Trafalgar Square Branch Office, London WC2N 4DL. The physical address is 24-28 William IV St (tube: Charing Cross). Mail will be held for four weeks; ID is required.

CallShop has lower charges than British Telecom (BT) for international calls, and faxes may also be sent or received. It has shops at 181a Earls Court Rd (tube: Earl's Court) and 189 Edgeware Rd (tube: Edgeware Road).

Email & Internet Access EasyEverything, a division of no-frills airline EasyJet, is opening numerous huge Internet cafes around London that are open 24 hours. Charges vary by how busy the location is: £1 buys you from 40 minutes to six hours of access. Locations include Trafalgar Square (☎ 7930 4094), 457-459 The Strand WC2 (tube: Charing Cross) and Victoria (☎ 7233 8456), 9-13 Wilton Road SW1 (tube: Victoria).

Travel Agencies London has always been a centre for cheap travel. Refer to the Sunday papers (especially the *Sunday Times*), *TNT Magazine* and *Time Out* for listings of cheap flights, but beware of sharks.

Long-standing and reliable firms include:

Usit Campus
  (☎ 7938 2188) 174 Kensington High St W8
  (tube: High St Kensington)
Council Travel
  (☎ 7287 3337) 28 Poland St W1
  (tube: Oxford Circus)
STA Travel
  (☎ 7361 6262) 86 Old Brompton Rd SW7
  (tube: South Kensington)
Trailfinders
  (☎ 7938 3939) 194 Kensington High St W8
  (tube: High St Kensington)

Bookshops All the major chains are good, but Waterstones, Books etc and Borders have particularly strong travel sections. Also try one of the following bookshops: Daunt Books (☎ 7224 2295), 83 Marylebone High St W1 (tube: Baker St); Foyles

(☎ 7437 5660), 119 Charing Cross Rd WC2 (tube: Leicester Square); and Stanfords (☎ 7836 1321), 12 Long Acre WC2 (tube: Covent Garden).

Medical & Emergency Services The following hospitals have 24-hour accident and emergency (A&E) departments: Guy's Hospital (☎ 7955 5000), St Thomas St SE1 (tube: London Bridge); University College Hospital (☎ 7387 9300), Grafton Way WC1 (tube: Euston Square); and the Royal Free Hospital (☎ 7794 0500), Pond St NW3 (tube: Belsize Park).

To find an emergency dentist you can phone the Dental Emergency Care Service (☎ 7955 2186).

Things to See & Do

Walking Tour The centre of London can easily be explored on foot. The following tour could be covered in a day but doesn't allow time to explore the individual sights in detail; it will, however, introduce you to the West End, the South Bank and Westminster.

Start at **St Paul's Cathedral**, Christopher Wren's masterpiece completed in 1710 (tube: St Paul's). Entry costs £5, which gains you access to the cathedral plus the dome and crypt.

From the cathedral, walk down to the Thames. Here you should be able to cross on the new **Millennium Bridge** directly to the **Tate Modern**. Housed in the huge old Bankside Power Station, this is the new home for the Tate's collection of modern art.

Walk west along the river past the many attractions of the **South Bank Centre** and stop when you reach the **British Airways London Eye**. At 135m it is the world's tallest observation wheel and on on a rare clear day you can see 40 miles. It's very popular whatever the weather and you best book your ride in advance (☎ 0870-500 0600). Tickets cost £7.45 and some are held back for same-day sale, but beware of the crowds.

Cross the **Hungerford Bridge**, which is getting new walkways, cut through Charing Cross Station and walk east along the Strand to Southhampton St and head north to **Covent Garden piazza**. Once London's fruit and vegetable market, these days it has been turned into a bustling tourist attraction. It's one of the few places in London where pedestrians rule, and you can

watch the buskers for a few coins and the tourists for free.

Leave the piazza walking west on Long Acre (look for Stanfords bookshop on your left). Continue across Charing Cross Rd to **Leicester Square** with its cinemas and franchise food. Note the Leicester Square Half-Price Ticket Booth, which sells half-price theatre tickets on the day of performance.

Continue along Coventry St to **Piccadilly Circus**. On the north-eastern corner a cluster of cheap kebab/pizza counters herald the junction with Shaftesbury Ave. This theatre-lined street runs back into **Soho**, with its myriad restaurants.

Continue west along Piccadilly to the **Royal Academy of Arts**, which often has special shows, and Wren's **St James's Piccadilly**. Detour into the timeless **Burlington Arcade**, just after the academy, and see the many smart shops.

Return to Piccadilly and continue until you get to St James's St on your left. This runs down to **St James's Palace**, the royal home from 1660 to 1837 until it was judged insufficiently impressive. Skirt around its eastern side to the Mall.

Trafalgar Square is to the east, **Buckingham Palace** (☎ 7799 2331) to the west. The palace is open 9.30 am to 4.15 pm daily from early August to early October. Admission costs £10.50. Don't be surprised if the palace reminds you of a series of ornate hotel lobbies.

From mid-April to late July the changing of the guard happens outside Buckingham Palace at 11.30 am daily; the rest of the year it's at 11.30 am on alternate days. The best place to be is by the gates of Buckingham House, but the crowds are awesome.

Cross back into St James's Park, the most beautiful in London, and follow the lake to its eastern end. Turn right onto Horse Guards Rd. This takes you past the **Cabinet War Rooms** (£4.80), which give an extraordinary insight into the dark days of WWII. They're open 10 am to 6 pm daily.

Continue south along Horse Guards Rd and then turn left onto Great George St, which takes you through to beautiful Westminster Abbey, the Houses of Parliament and Westminster Bridge.

Westminster Abbey is so rich in history you really need a few hours to do it justice. The coronation chair, where all but two monarchs since 1066 have been crowned, is behind the altar, and many greats – from Darwin to Chaucer – have been buried here. Unfortunately the crowds are now so dense that an admission fee of £5 is charged to go into any part of the cathedral. The best way to soak in the atmosphere is to attend evensong, which takes place at 5 pm weekdays and 3 pm weekends.

The **Houses of Parliament** and the clock tower (actually its bell), **Big Ben**, were built in the 19th century in neo-Gothic style. The best way to get into the building is to attend the Commons or Lords visitors' galleries during a Parliamentary debate. Phone ☎ 7219 4272 for information.

Walking away from Westminster Bridge, turn right into Parliament St, which becomes Whitehall. On your left, the hard-to-see but ordinary-looking house at **No 10 Downing St** offers accommodation to prime ministers. Farther along on the right is the Inigo Jones-designed **Banqueting House** (£3.60), outside which Charles I was beheaded. Continue past the **Horse Guards**, where you can see a less crowded changing of the guard at 11 am Monday to Saturday, and 10 am on Sunday.

Finally, you reach **Trafalgar Square** and Nelson's Column. The National Gallery and National Portrait Gallery, both free, are on the northern side.

River Tour Consider catching a boat from Westminster Pier (beside Westminster Bridge) down the river to Greenwich (every half-hour from 10 am, single/return costs £6.30/7.60). You'll pass the site of Shakespeare's Globe Theatre, stop at the Tower of London, continue under Tower Bridge and past many famous docks.

Greenwich can absorb the best part of a day. Start with the *Cutty Sark* (£3.50), the only surviving clipper and arguably one of the most beautiful ships ever built. Britain's famous naval traditions are covered in fascinating fashion at the expanded **National Maritime Museum** (£7.50).

Climb the hill behind the museum to the **Royal Observatory**. A brass strip in the courtyard marks the prime meridian that divides the world into eastern and western hemispheres. There are great views over the Docklands. Admission is £6.

Walk back down the hill and through the historic Greenwich foot tunnel (near the *Cutty Sark*) to Island Gardens. The Docklands Light Railway runs above ground from Island Gardens back to Tower Gateway, offering good views of the Docklands developments. Alternatively, you can catch the DLR at the Cutty Sark stop and avoid the tunnel.

The **Tower of London** is one of London's most popular attractions and dates from 1078, when William the Conqueror began to construct the White Tower. It was turned into an enormous concentric fortress by Henry III and has been a fortress, royal residence and prison. This is where you come to whisk past the crown jewels on a moving sidewalk. There are inevitably big crowds even during the week. It's usually open from 9 am to 5 pm daily and admission is £10.50. **Tower Bridge**, built in 1894, is often wrongly called 'London Bridge'. A tour covering its history costs £6.25.

Museums The **British Museum**, Great Russell St WC1 (tube: Tottenham Court Rd), has the world's greatest collection of Egyptian, Mesopotamian, Greek and Roman antiquities. This is a must-see, though there's far too much to cover in a single day (10 am to 5 pm, noon to 6 pm Sunday; free).

The **Victoria & Albert Museum**, Cromwell Rd SW7 (tube: South Kensington), has the world's greatest collection of decorative arts, including clothes; it also has an excellent cafe (10 am to 5.45 pm daily; £5).

The **Science Museum**, Exhibition Rd SW7 (tube: South Kensington) has a huge new wing that covers the latest science and technological developments (10 am to 6 pm daily; £6.50).

The **Natural History Museum**, Cromwell Rd SW7 (tube: South Kensington) features the wonderful Life and Earth Galleries, which look at natural history and geology (10 am to 5.50 pm, from 11 am Sunday; £6/3).

The **Museum of London**, 150 London Wall EC2 (tube: St Paul's), showcases London's history, from the Romans to the Dome (10 am to 5.50 pm, from noon Sunday; £5).

The **Imperial War Museum**, Lambeth Rd SE1 (tube: Lambeth North), houses many thoughtful exhibits; the new Holocaust Museum is especially recommended (10 am to 6 pm daily; £5.20).

Galleries The **National Gallery**, Trafalgar Square WC2 (tube: Charing Cross), has masterpieces from the leading European schools from the 13th to 20th centuries (10 am to 6 pm, until 9 pm Wednesday; free).

Around the corner, the **National Portrait Gallery**, 2 St Martin's Place WC2 (tube: Charing Cross), has received a major makeover that opens up the fascinating galleries of images from British political life and popular culture.

The **Courtauld Institute Gallery**, Somerset House, the Strand WC2 (tube: Temple), has a mind-blowing collection of Post-Impressionists (Cézanne, Gauguin, Van Gogh). Its amazing building has reopened after a long restoration (10 am to 6 pm, from noon Sunday; £4).

The **Tate Modern**, 25 Sumner St SE1 (tube: Southwark), is the new big deal on the London cultural scene. Housed in a huge old power station on the Thames, it has a huge collection of modern art dating from 1900 to the present (10 am to 6 pm, until 10 pm Friday to Sunday; free).

The **Tate Britain**, Millbank SW11 (tube: Pimlico), majors in the history of British art, especially Turner (10 am to 5.50 pm, free).

Markets Bustling, interesting and full of character(s), the markets are where you see London life at its best. Most are in full swing by 9 am and fold up by mid-afternoon.

Camden (tube: Camden Town) attracts huge crowds all weekend. It's a lot of fun but the litter and clutter can make it feel pretty tacky. Start at Camden Lock and follow the crowds.

Supposed home of the cockney barrow-boy, **Petticoat Lane**, Middlesex St (tube: Aldgate), is open Sunday and sells a wide variety of clothing and odds and ends.

Brick Lane (tube: Aldgate East) is open Sunday. It's cheap, chaotic and dominated by Bengalis.

Portobello Rd (tube: Ladbroke Grove) has fruit and vegetables daily (closed Thursday afternoon and Sunday) and general goods on Friday and Saturday. There are reasonable second-hand stalls at the Westway end, expensive antiques at the Notting Hill end.

Other Attractions All visitors, especially budget travellers, should make the most of London's glorious parks – in particular

Hyde Park, central London's largest. You can heckle the soapbox orators every Sunday at the park's **Speakers' Corner** (tube: Marble Arch).

Kensington Palace, Kensington Gardens W8 (tube: High St Kensington), was home to the late Princess Diana. The State Apartments are open 10 am to 4 pm daily and cost £9.50.

Kew Gardens, Richmond (tube: Kew Gardens), the Royal Botanic Gardens, are a haven of tranquillity amid the urban sprawl. Entry costs £5. As an alternative to the tube, ferries sail from Westminster Pier from 10.15 am to 2 pm (April to October). They take 1¾ hours and cost £7.

Hampton Court Palace is Britain's grandest Tudor house, built by Cardinal Wolsey in 1514 and later 'adopted' by Henry VIII. The superb palace grounds, near the Thames, include a deer park and a 300-year-old maze. It's open 9.30 am to 6 pm daily (4.30 pm in winter) and admission is £10.50; the grounds are free, the maze alone £2.50. There are trains every half-hour from Waterloo (£4.40 return), or you can catch a ferry from Westminster Pier. Ferries sail from April to late-September at 10.30 and 11.15 am, and noon; they take 3½ hours and cost £10.

Organised Tours

The Original London Sightseeing Tour (☎ 8877 1722), the Big Bus Company (☎ 7233 9533) and London Pride Sightseeing (☎ 7520 2050) offer tours of the main sights in double-decker buses. You can hop on and off at your leisure. They're all expensive (around £12). Most companies sell advance tickets to the biggest attractions to save wasting time in queues.

Convenient starting points are Trafalgar Square in front of the National Gallery; in front of the Trocadero on Coventry St, between Leicester Square and Piccadilly Circus; and in Wilton Gardens opposite Victoria Station.

Places to Stay

However you look at it, accommodation in London is ridiculously expensive no matter what your budget. Expect less than you've received elsewhere and you won't be so disappointed.

It's always wise to book a night or two's accommodation in advance, especially in

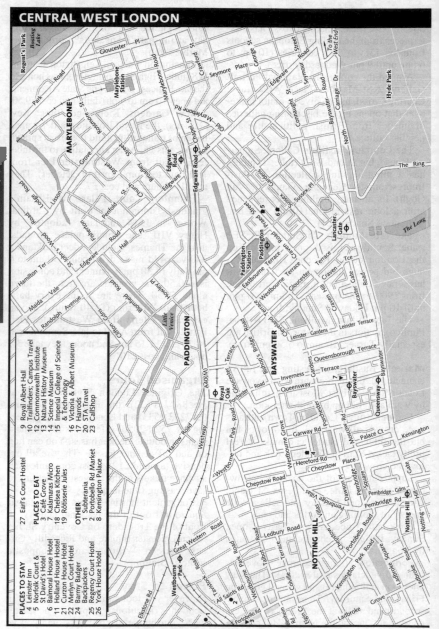

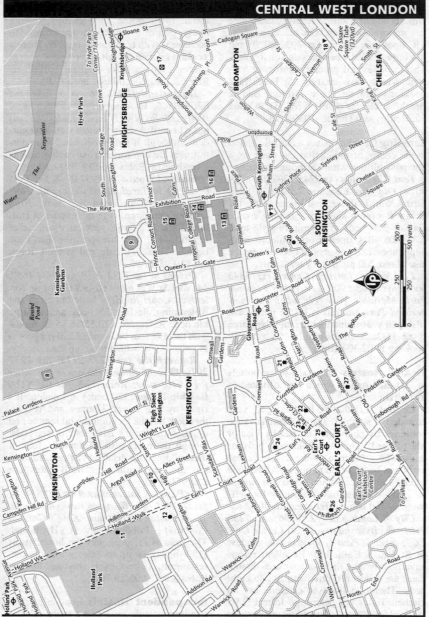

July and August. The official TICs at the airports and at Victoria station can arrange last-minute bookings. You can also try the TIC bookings hotline (☎ 7932 2020), but it is only staffed weekdays and charges £5. There are several private services at Victoria which also charge £5. Free B&B bookings can be made through Bed & Breakfast GB (☎ 01491-578803), PO Box 66, Henley-on-Thames RG9 1XS.

Camping Camping is not a realistic option in the centre of the capital but there are a few possibilities within striking distance.

Tent City Acton (☎ 8743 5708, fax 8749 9074, Old Oak Common Lane W3; tube: East Acton) is in far west London. It is the cheapest option short of camping rough. One of 320 beds in dormitory-style tents costs £6. It's open from June to mid-September, and you should book. There are also about 200 pitches for tents only.

Lee Valley Leisure Centre (☎ 8345 6666, fax 8803 6900, Lee Valley Regional Park, Meridian Way N9; tube: Northumberland Park station) is to the north-east. It's open year round and the nightly charge is £5.35/2.25 adults/children; electricity hook-up is £2.30 extra.

YHA/HI Hostels There are seven hostels in central London which are affiliated to YHA/HI.

Central London's hostels get very crowded in summer. They all take advance bookings by phone (if you pay by Visa or MasterCard). They also hold some beds for those who wander in on the day, but come early and be prepared to queue. All but one offer 24-hour access and all have a *bureau de change*. Most have facilities for self-catering and some offer cheap meals.

City of London (☎ 7236 4965, fax 7236 7681, ✉ city@yha.org.uk, 36 Carter Lane EC4; tube: St Paul's) stands in the shadow of St Paul's Cathedral. Excellent rooms have mainly two, three or four beds though there are a dozen rooms with five to eight beds. There's a licensed cafeteria but no kitchen. Rates per person go from £22.95 (£19.70 for juniors), depending on the room type. Remember: this part of town is pretty quiet outside working hours.

Earl's Court (☎ 7373 7083, fax 7835 2034, ✉ earlscourt@yha.org.uk, 38 Bolton Gardens SW5; tube: Earl's Court) is a Victorian town house in a shabby, though lively, part of town. Rooms are mainly 10-bed dorms with communal showers. There's a cafe, a kitchen for self-catering and a small garden courtyard for summer barbecues. Rates for adults/children are £19.95/17.95.

Hampstead Heath (☎ 8458 9054, fax 8209 0546, ✉ hampstead@yha.org.uk, 4 Wellgarth Rd NW11; tube: Golders Green) has a beautiful setting with a well-kept garden, although it's rather isolated. The dormitories are comfortable and each room has a washbasin. Rates are £19.70/17.30.

Holland House (☎ 7937 0748, fax 7376 0667, ✉ hollandhouse@yha.org.uk, Holland Walk, Kensington W8; tube: High Street Kensington) is in the middle of Holland Park. It's large, very busy and rather institutional, but the position can't be beaten. There's a cafe and kitchen. Rates are £19.95/17.95.

Oxford St (☎ 7734 1618, fax 7734 1657, 14 Noel St W1; tube: Oxford Circus or Tottenham Court Road) is basic but clean and welcoming. It has 75 beds and a large kitchen. Rates are £20.55/16.85 in rooms with three or four beds and £22.20 per person in twin rooms, which make up the majority.

Rotherhithe (☎ 7232 2114, fax 7237 2919, ✉ rotherhithe@yha.org.uk, 20 Salter Rd SE16; tube: Rotherhithe) is the YHA flagship hostel (320 beds) in London. It's right by the River Thames and recommended, but the location is a bit remote and quiet. Most rooms have four or six beds, though there are also 22 doubles (four of them adapted for disabled visitors); all have an attached bathroom. B&B rates are £22.95/19.70.

St Pancras International (☎ 7388 9998, fax 7388 6766, ✉ stpancras@yha.org.uk, 79-81 Euston Rd N1; tube: King's Cross St Pancras) is London's newest YHA hostel. The area isn't great, but the hostel itself (153 beds) is up-to-date, with kitchen, restaurant, lockers, cycle shed and lounge. Rates are £22.95/19.70.

Independent Hostels London's independent hostels tend to be more relaxed and cheaper than the YHA ones though standards can be pretty low; some of the places are downright grotty. Expect to pay a minimum of £10 per night in a basic dormitory. Check that fire escapes and stairwells are accessible.

Ashlee House (☎ *7833 9400, fax 7833 9677,* @ *ashleehouse@tsnxt.co.uk, 261-265 Gray's Inn Rd WC1; tube: King's Cross St Pancras)* is clean and well maintained on three floors close to King's Cross station. Dorm rooms can be very cramped, but there's double-glazing on the windows, a laundry and a decent-sized kitchen. Rooms with between four and 16 beds cost between £13 and £17 per person in the low season and between £15 and £19 in the high season. There are a few twins for £44 (£48 in high season).

Barmy Badger Backpackers (☎*/fax 7370 5213,* @ *barmy-badger.b@virgin.net, 17 Longridge Rd SW5; tube: Earl's Court)* is a basic dormitory with dorm beds from £13 per person, including breakfast. Twins without/with facilities cost £28/31. There's a big kitchen and safe-deposit boxes.

Curzon House Hotel (☎ *7581 2116, fax 7835 1319, 58 Courtfield Gardens SW5; tube: Gloucester Road)* is a relaxed, friendly place in Earl's Court. Dorm beds are £16 per person, singles/doubles with facilities £26/36. Rates include breakfast.

The Generator (☎ *7388 7666, fax 7388 7644,* @ *generator@lhdr.demon.co.uk, Compton Place, 37 Tavistock Place WC1; tube: Russell Square)* is one of the grooviest budget places in central London. Along with 207 rooms (830 beds), it has a bar open to 2 am, a large lounge for eating, watching TV or playing pool, a room with Internet kiosks, safe-deposit boxes and a large eating area, but no kitchen. Depending on the season, a place in a dorm with seven or eight beds costs from £18 to £19.50 and with three to six beds £19 to £21. Singles are £36, while twins are £46. All prices include breakfast.

Leinster Inn (☎ *7229 9641, fax 7229 5255,* @ *astorhotels@msn.com, 7-12 Leinster Square W2; tube: Bayswater),* in a large old house north-west of Bayswater tube station and close to Portobello Market, has 100 beds. Rates in dorms with up to 10 beds are £14, doubles are £28 to £42 per person.

Student Accommodation University halls of residence are let to nonstudents during the holidays, usually from the end of June to mid-September and sometimes over the Easter break. They're a bit more expensive than the hostels, but you usually get a single room (there are a few doubles) with shared facilities, plus breakfast.

London School of Economics and Political Science (☎ *7955 7531),* Room B508, Page Building, Houghton St, London WC2A 2AE, lets half a dozen of its halls in summer and sometimes during the Easter break. The buildings are all over London and rates average £25/45 per single/double.

John Adams Hall (☎ *7387 4086, fax 7383 0164,* @ *jah@ioe.ac.uk, 15-23 Endsleigh St WC1; tube: Euston)* is quite a grand residence in a row of Georgian houses. It's open at Easter and from July to September. B&B costs from £23/39 for a single/double, depending on the time of year.

University of Westminster (☎ *7911 5000, fax 7911 5141, 35 Marylebone Rd NW1; tube: Baker Street)* has singles or doubles for £20/130 per night/week for people under 26, £25/165 for those over 26.

YMCAs YMCA England (☎ 8520 5599), 640 Forest Rd, London E17 3DZ, can supply you with a list of all its hostels in the Greater London area.

Barbican YMCA (☎ *7628 0697, fax 7638 2420,* @ *admin@barbican.ymca .org.uk, 2 Fann St EC2; tube: Barbican)* has 240 beds with singles/doubles costing £23/41 with breakfast.

Central Club YMCA (☎ *7636 7512, fax 7636 5278, 16-22 Great Russell St WC1; tube: Tottenham Court Road)* also has 240 beds. Singles/doubles cost £38/69.

London City YMCA (☎ *7628 8832, fax 7628 4080, 8 Errol St EC1; tube: Barbican)* has 111 beds. B&B costs £25 per person.

B&Bs & Hotels This may come as a shock, but anything below £30/50 for a single/double with shared facilities and below £40/60 with private bathroom is considered 'budget' in London.

Don't be afraid to ask for the 'best' price or a discount if you're staying out of season or for more than a couple of nights, or if you don't want a cooked breakfast. In July, August and September prices can jump by 25% or more, and it's advisable to book ahead. Be warned: some places don't accept credit cards.

The following listings are arranged by neighbourhood and listed in order of price.

BRITAIN

Victoria Victoria may not be the most attractive part of London, but you'll be very close to the action and the budget hotels are better value than those in Earl's Court.

Luna-Simone Hotel (☎ *7834 5897, fax 7828 2474, 47 Belgrave Rd SW1; tube: Victoria)* is central, spotlessly clean and comfortable. Singles/doubles without bathroom start at £30/50. There are free storage facilities if you want to leave bags while travelling. If the Luna-Simone is full, there are a lot more B&Bs on Belgrave Rd.

Brindle House Hotel (☎ *7828 0057, fax 7931 8805, 1 Warwick Place North SW1; tube: Victoria)* is a recently renovated place in an old building on a quiet street. The rooms are small but clean. Singles/doubles/triples are £34/48/69.

Bloomsbury Bloomsbury is very convenient, especially for the West End. There are lots of places on Gower and North Gower Sts.

Hotel Cavendish (☎ *7636 9079, fax 7580 3609, 75 Gower St WC1; tube: Goodge Street)* is a clean and pleasant family-run place, with singles/doubles without bath for £32/47 including breakfast.

Cambria House (☎ *7837 1654, fax 7837 1229, 37 Hunter St WC1; tube: Russell Square)* is run by the Salvation Army and is one of the best deals around. Singles/doubles with shared bathroom are £29/47 a night or £196/308 a week. Prices include breakfast.

Earl's Court Earl's Court is not really within walking distance of many places of interest, but the tube station is a busy interchange, so getting around is easy.

Regency Court Hotel (☎ *7244 6615, 14 Penywern Rd SW5; tube: Earl's Court)* has undergone a much needed renovation. Its 20 bright rooms, all with en suite facilities, cost £30 to £35 for singles and £40 to £45 for doubles.

York House Hotel (☎ *7373 7519, fax 7370 4641, 27-28 Philbeach Gardens SW5; tube: Earl's Court)* is good value for what and where it is – on a quiet crescent – and the welcome is warm. The rooms are basic, although some have showers. Singles/doubles without facilities are £34/55.

The *Merlyn Court Hotel* (☎ *7370 1640, fax 7370 4986, 2 Barkston Gardens SW5; tube: Earl's Court)* is an unpretentious

place with a nice atmosphere and a lovely location close to the tube. Small but clean singles/doubles/triples without bathroom are £35/50/65.

Paddington Paddington can be a bit seedy, especially right around the station, but there are lots of cheap hotels and it's a good transit location.

Norfolk Court & St David's Hotel (☎ *7723 4963, fax 7402 9061, 16-20 Norfolk Square W2; tube: Paddington)* is right in the centre of the action and is clean, comfortable and friendly with the usual out-of-control decor. Basic singles/doubles have washbasin, colour TV and phone and cost £36/45 including a huge breakfast.

Balmoral House Hotel (☎ *7723 7445, fax 7402 0118, 156 & 157 Sussex Gardens W2; tube: Paddington)* is immaculate and very comfortable. It is one of the better places to stay along Sussex Gardens, a street lined with small hotels but unfortunately a major traffic artery. Singles without bathroom cost £38, doubles with facilities are £67.

Places to Eat

The West End The liveliest streets tend to be Greek, Frith, Old Compton and Dean Sts. Gerrard and Lisle Sts are chock-a-block with Chinese eateries of every description.

Pâtisserie Valerie (44 Old Compton St W1; tube: Leicester Square or Tottenham Court Road) is a Soho institution for coffee or tea and something sweet.

Stockpot (18 Old Compton St W1; tube: Leicester Square) does a long list of basic dishes (including some vegetarian options) for £3 to £5.

Star Café (22 Great Chapel St W1; tube: Tottenham Court Road) is a reliable cheapie dating from the 1930s. It serves up bangers and mash, fried breakfasts and pastas for under £5.

Soup (1 Newburgh St W1; tube: Oxford Circus) has a wide variety of choices – from pea and mushroom claret to Indonesian crab laksa. Prices start at £2.95 for a small cup.

Pollo (20 Old Compton St W1; tube: Leicester Square) attracts a student crowd with its pastas, risottos, pizzas and chicken dishes for under £4.

Poons (27 Lisle St WC2; tube: Leicester Square) offers OK food at very good prices and specialises in dried duck and pork (£4.20 per plate). Be prepared to queue at busy times.

Wagamama (10A Lexington St W1; tube: Piccadilly Circus) is a brash and spartan place that does great Japanese food. Main dishes range from £5 to £7.50.

Mildred's (58 Greek St W1; tube: Tottenham Court Road) is so small (and popular) that you may have to share a table. The chaos is worth it, however, because the vegetarian food is both good and well priced (from £5 to £7 for a large main course).

Covent Garden The *Food for Thought* restaurant *(31 Neal St WC2; tube: Covent Garden)* features dishes like West Indian curry for £3.80 and stir-fried vegetables with brown rice for £3.30.

Café Pacifico (5 Langley St; tube: Covent Garden) serves Mexican food in a cheerful dining room, with main courses for £6.25 to £8.95 and great margaritas.

Bloomsbury The *Mandeer (8 Bloomsbury Way WC1; tube: Tottenham Court Road)* serves vegetarian Indian, with main dishes from £3.75 to £5.25.

North Sea Fish Restaurant (7-8 Leigh St WC1; tube: Russell Square) cooks great fresh fish and chips for £7.

The City Convenient to St Paul's and the City of London YHA hostel, *Dim Sum (5-6 Deans Court EC4; tube: St Paul's)* is a budget traveller's delight. It serves Peking and Szechuan dishes for £3 to £6.

Café Spice Namaste (16 Prescot St E1; tube: Tower Hill) is an excellent Indian restaurant. A memorable emal will cost under £15.

Southwark The oldest pie shop still trading in London is *Manze's (87 Tower Bridge Rd SE1; tube: London Bridge)*. In its pleasantly tiled interior jellied eels cost £1.80, pie and mash £2.05, and pie and liquor £1.40.

Fish! (Cathedral St SE1; tube: London Bridge) serves fresher-than-fresh fish and seafood. Expect to pay anything from £8.50 to £15.95 for a main course.

Chelsea, South Kensington & Earl's Court Some of the cheapest food in London can be had at *Chelsea Kitchen (98*

King's Rd SW3; tube: Sloane Square), with a set meal costing under £5.

Rôtisserie Jules (6-8 Bute St SW3; tube: South Kensington) is a simple French-style cafeteria with dishes from £4.95 to £9.75.

New Culture Revolution (305 King's Rd SW3; tube: Sloane Square) is a good-value dumpling and noodle bar with main dishes at around £6.

Notting Hill & Bayswater For a gigantic and imaginative breakfast head to *Café Grove (253A Portobello Rd; tube: Ladbroke Grove)*. There's also cheap and cheerful vegetarian food at around £5.

Kalamaras Micro (66 Inverness Mews W2; tube: Bayswater) is a small but fine Greek spot in a quiet mews off Queensway. Main courses average £7.50 and it's BYO.

Euston Drummond St (tube: Euston Square or Euston) has a number of good South Indian vegetarian restaurants. *Diwana* at No 121 specialises in Bombay-style bel poori (a kind of 'party mix' snack) and dosas and has an all-you-can-eat lunchtime buffet for £3.95.

Camden The granddaddy of French-style brasseries in London, *Café Delancey (3 Delancey St NW1; tube: Camden Town)*, has main dishes from £8 to £13.

Lemon Grass (243 Royal College St; tube: Camden Town) has authentic food and charming decor and staff. Main dishes are around £6.

Lemonia (89 Regent's Park Rd NW1; tube: Chalk Farm) is an upmarket and very popular Greek restaurant that offers good-value food and a lively atmosphere. The moussakas for £7.50 are particularly tasty.

Islington Islington is an excellent place for a night out with many good choices on Upper St.

Le Sacré Coeur Bistro (18 Theberton St N1; tube: Angel) is a cramped little restaurant with reliable French food for under £7.

Inter Mezzo (207 Liverpool Rd N1; tube: Angel) is a Turkish eatery that's one of the best value and friendliest in town. Set dinners are about £10.

East End A good 24-hour delicatessen is *Brick Lane Beigel Bake (159 Brick Lane*

E2; tube: Shoreditch). You won't find fresher or cheaper bagels anywhere in London.

Brick Lane *(tube: Shoreditch or Aldgate East)* is lined wall-to-wall with cheap Indian and Bangladeshi restaurants. *Aladin* at No 132, a favourite of Prince Charles, and *Nazrul* at No 130 are worth a try; both are unlicensed but you can BYO and should eat for around £8.

Entertainment

The essential events guide is *Time Out* (£1.95), published every Tuesday. Though most pubs close at a puritanical 11 pm, there are plenty of late-night clubs (many charge a £5 to £10 cover). Note that the last underground trains leave between 11.30 pm and 12.30 am, after which you must figure out the night-bus system or take a taxi.

Pubs London is awash with pubs. Unfortunately many are uninspired boozers or charmless chain outlets. However there are many gems to be found.

Scruffy Murphy's (15 Denman St W1; tube: Piccadilly Circus) is the most authentic – snugs, brogues, Guinness and drunks – of the Irish pubs in Soho.

Ye Olde Mitre (1 Ely Court EC1; tube: Chancery Lane) is one of London's oldest and most historic pubs, although the 18th-century-sized rooms can be a bit tight.

The Angel (101 Bermondsey Wall East SE16; tube: Rotherhithe) is a riverside pub dating from the 15th century (though the present building is early 17th century). Captain Cook supposedly prepared for his trip to Australia from here.

Music & Clubs Major venues for live contemporary music include *Brixton Academy* (☎ 7924 9999, 211 Stockwell Rd SW9; tube: Brixton), *Hackney Empire* (☎ 8985 242, 291 Mare St E8; tube: Bethnal Green) and *Wembley Arena* (☎ 8900 1234, Empire Way, Middlesex, tube: Wembley Park).

Smaller places with a more club-like atmosphere that are worth checking for interesting bands include *Borderline* (☎ 7734 2095, Orange Yard, off Manette St WC2; tube: Tottenham Court Rd), *Barfly at the Falcon* (☎ 7485 3834, 234 Royal College St NW1; tube: Camden Town), *Subterania* (☎ 8960 4590, 12 Acklam Rd W10; tube: Ladbroke Grove) and *Garage* (☎ 7607

1818, 20-22 Highbury Corner N5; tube: Highbury & Islington). Ring ahead to find out what kind of band you'll get.

Venues that are usually reliable for club nights and recorded music include *Fabric* (☎ 7490 0444, 77a Charterhouse St EC1; tube: Farringdon), which has three floors; *Astoria* (☎ 7434 9592, 157-165 Charing Cross Rd WC2; tube: Tottenham Court Rd), which is popular with gays; the multi-faceted *Fridge* (☎ 7326 5100, Town Hall Parade SW2; tube: Brixton); the friendly *Velvet Room* (☎ 7439 4655, 143 Charing Cross Rd WC2; tube: Tottenham Court Rd) and the famous *Ministry of Sound* (☎ 7378 6528, 103 Gaunt St SE1; tube: Elephant & Castle).

If you're a jazz fan, keep your eye on *Ronnie Scott's* (☎ 7439 0747, 47 Frith St W1; tube: Leicester Square) and the *Jazz Café* (☎ 7344 0044, 5 Parkway NW1; tube: Camden Town).

Theatre Even if you don't normally go to the theatre, you really should look at the reviews and organise cheap tickets for one of the better productions. The South Bank's *National Theatre* (☎ 7452 3000), actually three theatres in one – the Olivier, Lyttleton and Cottesloe – puts on consistently good performances.

The Half Price Theatre Ticket Booth (tube: Leicester Square), on the southern side of Leicester Square, sells half-price tickets (plus £2 commission) on the day of performance. It opens daily from noon to 6.30 pm, but the queues can be very long.

Make sure you catch a performance at *Shakespeare's Globe Theatre* (☎ 7401 9919, 21 New Globe Walk; tube: London Bridge), the replica of Shakespeare's 'wooden O'. With no roof, the Globe is open to the elements – wrap up warmly (no umbrellas allowed). Performances are staged from May to September only. Tickets cost £10 to £25, or £5 for standing room.

Getting There & Away

See Getting There & Away information in the earlier transport sections of this chapter.

Bus Bus travellers will arrive at Victoria coach station, Buckingham Palace Rd, about 10 minutes' walk south of Victoria station (or there's a shuttle bus if you're carrying loads of luggage).

Train London's eight major train stations are all connected by tube. For those with a combined rail/ferry ticket, Victoria is your station for getting to/from Dover and Folkestone, Liverpool St for getting to/from Harwich, and King's Cross for getting to/from Newcastle. The international terminal at Waterloo services Eurostar trains.

For national rail inquiries, fares and timetables phone ☎ 0845-748 4950.

Getting Around
To/From the Airports Transport to and from London's five airports is as follows:

Heathrow The airport (☎ 0870 000 0123) is accessible by bus, underground (between 5 am and 11 pm) and main-line train.

The Heathrow Express rail link whisks people from Paddington station to Heathrow in 15 minutes. Tickets cost an exorbitant £12 each way. Trains leave every 15 minutes from 5 am to 10.30 pm. Many airlines have check-in desks at Paddington.

The underground station for Terminals 1, 2 and 3 is directly linked to the terminus buildings; there's a separate station for Terminal 4. Check which terminal your flight uses when you reconfirm. The adult single fare is £3.50, or you can use an All Zone travelcard which is £4.70. The journey time from central London to Heathrow is about 50 minutes – allow an hour.

Airbus (☎ 7222 1234) services are prone to traffic congestion. There are two routes: the A1, which runs along Cromwell Rd to Victoria; and the A2, which runs along Notting Hill Gate and Bayswater Rd to Russell Square. Buses run every half-hour and cost £7.

Gatwick The Gatwick Express train (☎ 0870-530 1530) runs nonstop between the main terminal and Victoria railway station 24 hours daily. Singles are £10.20 and the journey takes about 30 minutes. The Connex SouthCentral service takes a little longer and costs £8.20. Jetlink 777 buses (☎ 8668 7261) from Victoria coach station cost £8, but the trip takes 90 minutes.

Gatwick's north and south terminals (☎ 01293-535353) are linked by a monorail; check which terminal your flight uses.

London City The airport (☎ 7646 0000) is two minutes' walk from the Silvertown & City Airport train station which is linked by train to Stratford. A frequent shuttle bus also connects the airport with the Canning Town tube, DLR and train station. The Airbus connects the airport with Liverpool St station (£5, 30 minutes) and Canary Wharf (£2, 10 minutes).

Luton The airport (☎ 01582 405100) is connected by frequent shuttle bus to the Luton Airport Parkway station. Several trains (☎ 0845-748 4950) an hour go to/from London through the Kings Cross Thameslink station. Fares cost £9 and the journey takes about 35 minutes.

Stansted The airport (☎ 01279 680500) is served by the Stansted Express (☎ 0845-748 4950) from Liverpool St station which costs £11 and takes 45 minutes. Trains depart every 15 to 30 minutes.

Bus & Underground London Regional Transport is responsible for buses and the tube. It has several information centres where you can get free maps, tickets and information on night buses. There are centres in each Heathrow terminal and at Victoria, Piccadilly and King's Cross stations; or phone ☎ 7222 1234. It's well worth asking for one of the free bus maps.

Buses are much more interesting and pleasant to use than the tube, although they can be frustratingly slow. Prices depend on how many geographic zones your journey covers. Central London is covered by Zone 1. A ticket good for Zones 1 & 2 should suffice for most visitors. Single journeys on the bus cost 70p/£1 for Zone 1/Zones 1 & 2 and by tube £1.50/£1.80.

Travelcards are the easiest and cheapest option, and they can be used on all forms of transport (trains in London, buses and the tube) after 9.30 am. A Zones 1 & 2 card costs £3.90. Weekly travelcards are also available; they require an ID card with a passport photo (Zones 1 & 2 cost £18.20). A 'Carnet' of Zone 1 tube tickets good for 10 rides costs £11.

Times of the last tube trains vary from 11.30 pm to 12.30 am, depending on the station and line. A reasonably comprehensive network of night buses runs from or through Trafalgar Square. London Regional Transport has a free brochure listing all the services. One-day travelcards can't be used on night buses, but weekly travelcards can.

AROUND LONDON
Windsor & Eton
Home to British royalty for over 900 years, **Windsor Castle** is one of the world's greatest surviving medieval castles. It was built in stages between 1165 and the 16th century on chalk bluffs overlooking the Thames.

Inside the castle, **St George's Chapel** (closed Sunday) is a masterpiece of Perpendicular Gothic architecture. You can also examine Queen Mary's Dolls' House and the recently restored State Apartments. The castle is open from 10 am daily but can be closed at short notice when members of the royal family are in residence; for schedule phone ☎ 01753-831118. In summer, the changing of the guard takes place at 11 am Monday to Saturday, weather permitting. Entry to the castle is £10 (£8.50 on Sunday).

A short walk along Thames St and across the river brings you to another enduring symbol of Britain's class system, **Eton College**, a famous public (meaning private) school that has educated no fewer than 18 prime ministers. It's open to visitors 2 to 4.30 pm during term, and from 10.30 am during Easter and summer holidays (£2.50).

Easily accessible from London, Windsor crawls with tourists. If possible, avoid weekends. There are numerous trains direct from London's Waterloo station to Windsor & Eton Riverside station (£5.90 return).

South-East England

Due to their proximity to London the counties of Kent, East and West Sussex and Hampshire are home to a large chunk of the capital's workforce. For this reason there are plenty of fast, regular rail and bus services making it possible to see the main sights on day trips, though you are advised to avoid weekends and school holidays. Compared to the rest of England, prices in the south-east tend to be high for accommodation and food.

CANTERBURY
☎ 01227
Canterbury's greatest treasure is its magnificent **cathedral** (☎ 762862), the successor to the church St Augustine built after he began converting the English to Christianity in AD 597. In 1170 Archbishop Thomas à Becket was murdered in the cathedral by four of Henry II's knights; the cult that grew up around his martyrdom made Canterbury the centre of one of the most important medieval pilgrimages in Europe, immortalised by Geoffrey Chaucer in the *Canterbury Tales*.

A guided tour is recommended. They take place at 10.30 am, noon and 2 pm for £3.50, or there's a Walkman tour for £2.95 (30 minutes). Admission is £3/2. The cathedral is open 9 am to 7 pm on weekdays and Saturday (to 5 pm from October to Easter); shorter hours on Sunday.

Orientation & Information
The centre of Canterbury is enclosed by a medieval city wall and a modern ring road. It's easily covered on foot. The two train stations are a few minutes' walk from the centre. The bus station is just within the city walls at the eastern end of High St.

TIC (☎ 766567, fax 459840, ℮ canterburyinformation@canterbury.gov.uk), 34 St Margaret's St, has a free booking service for B&Bs (open 9.30 am to 5 pm daily).

The Library at the Royal Museum on High St has free Internet access for up to one hour but you'll need to book ahead on ☎ 463608. There's a laundrette at 36 St Peter's St.

Places to Stay & Eat
Head to London Rd or New Dover Rd for good value B&Bs. To camp, try *Yew Tree Park* (☎ 700306, Stone St, Petham), 5 miles (8km) south of Canterbury off the B2068. It's £4 for one adult plus tent; £6 for two. A bus from Canterbury to Petham village (a half mile walk to the camp site) leaves hourly.

The *Youth Hostel* (☎ 462911, 54 New Dover Rd) is about a mile east of the centre. The nightly charge is £9.75 and there is one twin room for £28.

Let's Stay (☎ 463628, 26 New Dover Rd) is homey and good value. It costs £10 per person with breakfast. Men and women are accommodated separately.

The University of Kent (☎ 828000, Tanglewood) is a 20-minute walk from the centre and is open in April and from July to September. B&B costs from £14.50.

There's a *Safeway* supermarket on the corner of New Dover Rd and Lower Chantry Rd, south-east of the centre.

Canterbury Grill & Kebab (☎ 765458, *66 Castle St*) has chip butties for £1.30. Kebabs cost from £3 and burgers from £2.20.

The *Three Tuns Hotel* (☎ 456391, *24 Watling St*) serves traditional pub meals for around £4.

The Custard Tart (☎ 785178, *35a St Margaret's St*) charges around £2.30 for delicious baguettes and sandwiches and £1 for sausage rolls.

Entertainment

What & Where When is a free leaflet to what's on in Canterbury, available from the TIC. *The Miller's Arms* (☎ 456057, *Mill Lane*) is a cosy student hang-out and *Caseys* (☎ 463252, *5 Butchery Lane*), near the main gate to the cathedral, has a selection of Irish ales and stouts.

Getting There & Away

Bus National Express buses leave every half hour from London Victoria (£7/9 one way/day return, two hours). Stagecoach East Kent (☎ 472082) has 100 buses which run hourly (less on Sunday) from Canterbury to Dover, Deal, Sandwich, Ramsgate, Broadstairs, Margate, Herne Bay, Whitstable and back to Canterbury. Canterbury to Dover costs £2.50/3.50 (30 minutes).

Train Canterbury East station (for the YHA hostel) is accessible from London's Victoria station, and Canterbury West is accessible from London's Charing Cross and Waterloo stations (£14.80 day return, £19.99 for two adults; 1½ hours). There are regular trains between Canterbury East and Dover Priory (£4.50, 45 minutes).

DOVER
☎ 01304

Dover may be England's 'Gateway to Europe' but the place has just two things going for it: the famous white cliffs and the spectacular **Dover Castle** (☎ 211067), open daily 10 am to 6 pm. Entry is £6.90/5.20 adults/concession, including a tour of **Hellfire Corner** which is a series of underground tunnels used in WWII. Stagecoach bus No 90 goes to the castle from Dover Priory station.

Orientation & Information

Ferry departures are from the Eastern Docks (accessible by bus) below the castle, but the Hoverport is below the Western Heights. Dover Priory train station is a short walk to the west of the town centre.

The TIC (☎ 205108, fax 225498, ✉ tic@doveruk.com) is on Townwall St near the seafront and is open 9 am to 6 pm daily. It has an accommodation and ferry-booking service. Mangle laundrette is on Worthington St.

Places to Stay & Eat

Book well ahead if you intend to be here in July and August. The cheaper B&Bs are on Castle St and Maison Dieu Rd.

Martin Mill Caravan Park (☎ 852658) is at Hawthorn Farm, three miles (4.8km) north-east of Dover, off the A258. It's open from March to November and costs £6 for one person with tent (£7 for two).

Dover Central Youth Hostel (☎ 201314, *306 London Rd*) is five minutes' walk from Market Square. It costs £10.50 per night.

The *YMCA* (☎ 225500, *4 Leyburne Rd*) was closed for refurbishment at the time of writing but may well be open by now for overnight accommodation.

Unfortunately, Dover is short on decent places to eat. *Jermain's* (☎ 205956, *Beaconsfield Rd*) is near the hostel and has good value traditional lunches like roast beef for £5 and pudding for £1.

Curry Garden (☎ 206357, *24 High St*) is a cheap Indian restaurant with plush decor where prawn korma costs £4.20 and daal is £1.95.

Riveria Coffee House (☎ 201766, *9311 Worthington St*) is basic and good with cream teas for £1.80, or sandwiches and light meals from £1.20.

Getting There & Away

See the Getting There & Away section at the beginning of this chapter for details on ferries to mainland Europe.

Bus National Express coaches leave hourly from London Victoria (£9/11 one way/day return, 2½ hours). Stagecoach East Kent has an office on Pencester Rd (☎ 240024). Canterbury to Dover (30 minutes) costs £2.50. There's an hourly bus to Brighton but you'll need to change at Eastbourne (four hours). Later in the evenings it's a direct service. An Explorer ticket for £6 is better value on this route.

Train There are over 40 trains a day from London Victoria and Charing Cross stations to Dover Priory via Ashford and Sevenoaks (£18.20 one way/day return, 1½ hours). The ferry companies run complimentary buses between the docks and train stations.

LEEDS CASTLE
Near Maidstone in Kent, Leeds Castle (☎ 01622-765400) is one of the most famous in the world. It stands on two small islands in a lake, and is surrounded by a park with an aviary, a maze and a grotto. Unfortunately, it's usually overrun by families and school groups. Also, some of the rooms are closed from time to time for conferences and functions. If you want to be sure of getting your money's worth, call ahead.

It's open 10 am to 5 pm daily (to 3 pm from November to February). Entry is £9.50/7.50 adults/concession. National Express has a bus from Victoria coach station, leaving at 9 am and returning at 3.50 pm (1¼ hrs). It must be prebooked and combined admission/travel is £12.50. Greenline Buses (☎ 020-8668 7261) have the same deal costing £13/7 (leave London Victoria at 9.35 am, return 4 pm).

BRIGHTON
☎ 01273
Brighton is deservedly Britain's number one seaside town – a fascinating mixture of seediness and sophistication. It has a reputation as the club and party capital of the south. Fat Boy Slim hails from here and he DJs regularly around town. There's a vibrant population of students and travellers, excellent shopping, a terrific arts scene and countless restaurants, pubs and cafes.

In May Brighton hosts the largest arts festival outside Edinburgh (☎ 292961). Web site: www.brighton-festival.org.uk

Orientation & Information
Brighton train station is a 15-minute walk north of the beach. The interesting part of Brighton is a series of streets north of North St, including Bond, Gardner, Kensington and Sydney Sts. The bus station is tucked away in Poole Valley.

The TIC (☎ 292599, ✉ tourism@ brighton.co.uk), 10 Bartholomew Square, has maps and copies of events magazines. Bubbles Laundrette (☎ 738556) is at 75 Preston St. For internet access go to Riki Tik (☎ 683844) at 18a Bond St.

Things to See & Do
The **Royal Pavilion** is an extraordinary fantasy: an Indian palace on the outside, a

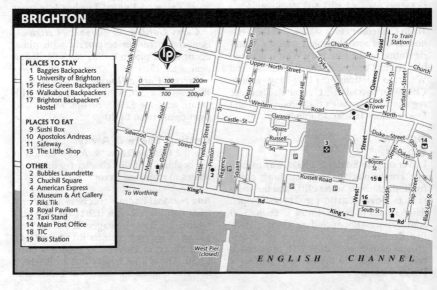

BRIGHTON

PLACES TO STAY
1 Baggies Backpackers
5 University of Brighton
15 Friese Green Backpackers
16 Walkabout Backpackers
17 Brighton Backpackers'
   Hostel

PLACES TO EAT
9 Sushi Box
10 Apostolos Andreas
11 Safeway
13 The Little Shop

OTHER
2 Bubbles Laundrette
3 Chuchill Square
4 American Express
6 Museum & Art Gallery
7 Riki Tik
8 Royal Pavilion
12 Taxi Stand
14 Main Post Office
18 TIC
19 Bus Station

ENGLISH   CHANNEL

Chinese brothel on the inside, all built between 1815 and 1822 for George IV. The whole edifice is way over the top and is not to be missed. It's open 10 am to 6 pm (until 5 pm from October to May); admission is £4.50/3.25 adult/concession.

The **Brighton Museum & Art Gallery** (☎ 290900) houses Art Deco and Art Nouveau furniture, archaeological finds and surrealist paintings (including Salvador Dali's sofa in the shape of lips). The nearby **Palace Pier** is the very image of Brighton. **The Lanes** is a maze of alleyways crammed with shops, restaurants and bars.

Places to Stay & Eat
There's plenty of accommodation in Brighton. The main cluster of cheap B&Bs is to the east of the Palace Pier, off St James'.

Baggies Backpackers (☎ 733740, 33 Oriental Place) has beds for £10 (plus £5 deposit for the room key) and double rooms for £25. It's more friendly and homey than the other hostels.

The **Brighton Backpackers' Hostel** (☎ 777717, fax 887778, @ stay@brighton backpackers.com, 75-6 Middle St) is also £10 per night (or £11 in the seafront annexe). Weekly rates are £55/60.

Friese Green – The Backpacker's Rest (☎ 747551, 20 Middle St) is a comfortable

place and charges £9 for a bed and £30 for a double room.

Walkabout Backpackers (☎ 770232, 79-81 West St) is not exclusively for Australians and New Zealanders but it might seem that way. Beds in bland rooms cost £10 (£12 in a double room). They don't take reservations.

The **University of Brighton** (☎ 643167, fax 642610) has flats for two to eight people from July to September. Prices start at £60 per person per week.

For self-caterers there's a **Safeway** on St James St. **Apostolos Andreas** (☎ 687935), on George St, is a Greek coffeehouse with English-style food. It's extremely good value and, if you can get a seat in this tiny place, you'll pay about 65p for a coffee, 95p to £1.45 for a sandwich and from £1.35 for a hot meal.

Sushi Box (☎ 818040, 181 Edward St) is close to the university and charges £3 to £4 for a takeaway lunch box of sashimi and/or california rolls.

The Little Shop (☎ 325594, 48a Market St, The Lanes) has delicious and chunky sandwiches from £2.25.

Entertainment
Pubs, bars and clubs are constantly opening and closing – check *The Brighton Latest*, *New Insight* and bar and cafe walls for what's on. Most of the gay bars and clubs can be found around St James' St and the Old Steine.

Getting There & Away
National Express coaches leave hourly from London's Victoria station (£7 one way, £5 off-peak). Stagecoach East Kent bus No 711 runs between Brighton and Dover via Hastings and Rye. There are twice hourly train services from London's Victoria and King's Cross stations (£13.70/14.60 one way/day return, 50 mins). Trains leave from Brighton hourly for Portsmouth (£11.70 one way, 1½ hours), and there are frequent services to Canterbury and Dover.

PORTSMOUTH
☎ 023
For much of British history, Portsmouth has been the home of the Royal Navy. After 437 years underwater, Henry VIII's favourite ship, the *Mary Rose*, and its time-capsule

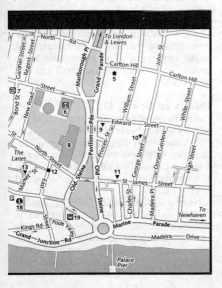

BRITAIN

contents can now be seen. And you can walk the decks of the magnificent 1765 HMS *Victory*, Lord Nelson's flagship at the Battle of Trafalgar. Entry is around £6 for each ship, or £11.90 for an All-Ships ticket which includes the Royal Naval Museum and the Mary Rose Museum.

Unfortunately, Portsmouth is not a particularly attractive city, largely due to WWII bombing.

Orientation & Information

The train and bus stations are a stone's throw from the Naval Heritage Area and the TIC (☎ 9282 6722, The Hard). It's worth having a wander around atmospheric Old Portsmouth, just south of the Naval Heritage Area. Southsea, where the beaches are, as well as most of the cheap accommodation and restaurants, is about 2 miles (3.2km) south of Portsmouth Harbour.

There's Internet access at Southsea Backpackers Lodge (see Places to Stay).

Places to Stay & Eat

Most budget accommodation is in Southsea. One exception is the *Youth Hostel* (☎ *9237 5661, Old Wymering Lane, Cosham*), about 4 miles (6.5km) from the main sights. It's £8.80/5.95 adults/juniors and bus Nos 12 and 12a operate to Cosham from the harbour bus station.

Southsea Backpackers Lodge (☎ *9283 2495, 4 Florence Rd, Southsea*) is far more convenient and charges £10 for a bed in a dorm and £15/22-25 for singles/doubles.

The University of Portsmouth (☎ *9284 3178, Nuffield Centre, St Michael's Rd*) offers B&B accommodation from June to September from £16.75 per person.

Osborne Rd and Palmerston Rd are the main restaurant strips in Southsea. The *snack bar* near the bus station on The Hard has tasty, greasy morsels from 80p.

Lady Hamilton (☎ *9287 0505, 21 The Hard*) is a large pub which charges £4.95 for a roast lunch.

Twigs (☎ *9282 8316, 39 High St*) is a small coffee shop with sandwiches, baguettes and baps from £1.80 to £3.30.

Getting There & Away

Some National Express buses from London go via Heathrow (£9/11 one way/day return, 2½ hrs). Stagecoach Coastline (☎ 01903-

237661) No 700 runs between Brighton and Portsmouth every 30 minutes (£3.20) and Stagecoach No 69 runs to/from Winchester hourly from Monday to Saturday.

There are over 40 trains a day from London's Victoria and Waterloo stations (£17.80, 1½ hours). There are plenty of trains to/from Brighton (£11.70 one way, 1½ hours) and Winchester (£6.70 one way, one hour).

Wightlink (☎ 0870-582 7744) operates passenger ferries from The Hard to the Isle of Wight about every half hour. A day return is £7.40.

P&O Ferries (☎ 0870-242 4999) sail twice a week to Bilbao in Spain and daily to Cherbourg and Le Havre in France. Brittany Ferries (☎ 0870-901 2400) have overnight services to St Malo, Caen and Cherbourg in France. The Continental Ferryport is north of Flagship Portsmouth.

WINCHESTER
☎ 01962

Winchester is a beautiful cathedral city, interspersed with water meadows, on the River Itchen. It has played an important role in the history of England, being both the capital of Saxon England and the seat of the powerful Bishops of Winchester from AD 670. Much of the present-day city dates from the 18th century.

Orientation & Information

The city centre is easily covered on foot. From the train station it's a 10-minute walk to the city centre. The bus station is on Broadway, opposite the Guildhall and TIC (☎ 840500).

Things to See & Do

One of the most beautiful cathedrals in the country is **Winchester Cathedral**, a mixture of Norman, Early English and Perpendicular styles, with some modern sculptures and paintings thrown in. Cathedral tours are run by enthusiastic local volunteers. Suggested entry is £2.50.

Nearby is **Winchester College**, founded in 1382 and the model for the great public schools of England. Guided tours operate several times daily and cost £2.50.

In town it's also worth visiting the **Great Hall**, begun by William the Conqueror and the site of the trial of Sir Walter Raleigh in

1603. It houses **King Arthur's Round Table**, now known to be a fake at *only* 600 years of age.

Places to Stay & Eat
Morn Hill Caravan Club Site (☎ *869877, Morn Hill*) is three miles (4.8km) east of the city centre off the A31. Tent sites are £6.40 per person.

The *Youth Hostel* (☎ *853723, City Mill, 1 Water Lane*) is in a beautiful 18th-century water mill. The nightly cost is £8.80/5.95 for adults/juniors.

There's a *Sainsbury's* supermarket on Middle Brook St. At *Granny Pastries* (☎ *878370, The Square*) try a Thai green curry chicken pie or a Stilton and celery pastie. Huge baguettes are around £2.

The Refectory, near the entrance to the cathedral, has sandwiches from £1.70 and a cream tea costs £3.45.

Blue Dolphin Restaurant (☎ *853804*) on Broadway has pretty good fish and chips for £3.10.

Getting There & Away
National Express bus No 32 leaves every two hours from London's Victoria station via Heathrow (£7, two hours). Stagecoach Hampshire Bus (☎ 01256-464501) has a good network of services linking Salisbury, Southampton, Portsmouth and Brighton. Trains depart about every 15 minutes from London's Waterloo station (£17.30 one way, one hour), Southampton (£3.60; 18 minutes) and Portsmouth (£6.70; one hour).

South-West England

SALISBURY
☎ 01722
Salisbury is justly famous for the cathedral and its close, but its appeal also lies in the fact that it is still a bustling market town, not just a tourist trap. Markets have been held in the town centre every Tuesday and Saturday since 1361, and the jumble of stalls still draws a large crowd.

Orientation & Information
The town centre is a 10-minute walk from the train station – walk down the hill and turn right at the T-junction onto Fisherton St. It's another 15 minutes to the YHA hostel. The bus station is just north of the centre of town; just two minutes down Endless St and you'll be in the thick of things.

The helpful TIC (☎ 334956), Fish Row, is behind the impressive 18th-century Guildhall on the south-eastern corner of Market Square.

Things to See & Do
Beautiful **St Mary's Cathedral** is built in a uniform style known as Early English (or Early Pointed). This period is characterised by the first pointed arches and flying buttresses, and has a rather austere feel. The spire, at 123m, is the highest in Britain. Suggested entry is £3.

The adjacent **chapter house** is one of the most perfect achievements of Gothic architecture. There is plenty more to see in the **cathedral close**, including two houses that have been restored and two museums. The **Salisbury & South Wiltshire Museum** (£3) is also worth visiting.

Places to Stay & Eat
Salisbury Youth Hostel (☎ *327572, Milford Hill*), in an attractive old building, is an easy walk from the centre – from the TIC, turn left onto Fish Row, then immediately right onto Queen St, first left onto Milford St, and go straight for 400m, under the overpass.

Matt & Tiggy's (☎ *327443, 51 Salt Lane*), close to the bus station, is an independent hostel-like guesthouse with dorm beds (£10), but no curfew.

Fisherton St, running from the centre to the train station, has Chinese, Thai, Indian and other restaurants. *Le Hérisson* (*Crane St*) has tasty vegetarian meals and a deli. The *Haunch of Venison* (*1 Minster St*), is a great pub that dates from the 16th century.

Getting There & Away
National Express has three buses a day from London via Heathrow to Salisbury (£12, three hours), and one daily bus from Portsmouth, Bath (£6.25) and Bristol – Bath is cheaper with Badgerline/Wiltshire buses (£5, two hours).

Salisbury is linked by rail to Portsmouth (1¼ hours), Bath (£9.80, two hours) and Exeter (two hours). There are numerous daily trains from London's Waterloo station (£21.80, 1½ hours).

AROUND SALISBURY
Stonehenge
Stonehenge is the most famous prehistoric site in Europe – a ring of enormous stones (some of which were brought from Wales), built in stages beginning 5000 years ago. Reactions vary; some find that the car park, gift shop and crowds of tourists swamp the monument. Avebury, 29km north, is much more impressive in scale and recommended for those who would like to commune with the ley lines in relative peace.

Stonehenge is 3.2km west of Amesbury at the junction of the A303 and A344/A360, and 14.5km from Salisbury (the nearest station); entry is £4 including audio tour. Some feel it's unnecessary to pay the entry fee, because you can get a good view from the road. There are four buses a day from Salisbury – consider a Wilts & Dorset Explorer ticket for £5. For details phone ☎ 01722-336855.

Avebury
☎ 01672
Avebury, just off the A4, stands at the hub of a prehistoric complex of ceremonial sites, ancient avenues and burial chambers dating from 3500 BC.

In addition to an enormous stone circle, there's Silbury Hill (the largest constructed mound in Europe), West Kennet Long Barrow (a burial chamber) and a pretty village with an ancient church. The **Avebury Museum** is a good place to start an exploration.

Avebury's TIC (☎ 539425) can help with finding accommodation. The **Red Lion** pub (☎ 539266) has doubles for £40. Avebury can be easily reached by bus from Salisbury (Wiltshire Bus No 5 or 6) or Swindon. To travel to and from Bath you'll have to change buses at Devizes; to check connections phone ☎ 0845-709 0899.

EXETER
☎ 01392
Exeter is the heart of the West Country, with a population of 102,000. It was devastated during WWII and as a result first impressions are not particularly inspiring; if you get over these, you'll find a lively university city with a thriving nightlife. It's a good starting point for Dartmoor and Cornwall.

The **cathedral** is one of the most attractive in England, with two massive Norman towers surviving from the 11th century. There are a number of recommended free tours, covering both the cathedral and town.

Orientation & Information
There are two train stations, but most Inter-City trains use St David's, a 20-minute walk west of the centre – cross the station forecourt and Bonhay Rd, climb some steps to St David's Hill and turn right up the hill, go for 1.2km and turn left up High St.

The TIC (☎ 265700), in the Civic Centre on Paris St, is just across the road from the bus station, a short walk north-east of the cathedral (closed Sunday).

Places to Stay & Eat
Exeter Youth Hostel (☎ 873329, 47 Countess Wear Rd) is 3.2km south-east of the city towards Topsham. It's open year round except over Christmas/New Year. From High St, catch minibus J, K or T (10 minutes) and ask for the Countess Wear post office.

The best value accommodation in central Exeter is the university's *St Luke's Hall* (☎ 211500) – from just £13.50 per person, including breakfast. It's available only during college vacations.

There are several B&Bs on St David's Hill. The *Highbury* (☎ 434737) at No 89 has singles/doubles for £15/25.

Coolings is a busy wine bar on medieval Gandy St, which is signposted off High St. *Herbies*, on North St, is an excellent vegetarian restaurant. Carnivores should be satisfied by the steaks at *Mad Meg's*, on Fore St. The *Ship Inn*, near the cathedral, was Sir Francis Drake's local.

Getting There & Away
There are nine buses a day to/from London via Heathrow airport (£16.50, four hours). There are direct buses to Brighton, but it's actually quicker to go via Heathrow. Other buses run to Dorchester and Penzance (£16, 4½ hours).

Exeter is at the hub of rail lines running from Bristol (1½ hours), Salisbury (two hours) and Penzance (three hours). There are hourly trains from London's Waterloo and Paddington stations (£38.30, three hours).

DARTMOOR NATIONAL PARK
Although the park is only about 40km from north to south and east to west, it encloses

some of the wildest, bleakest country in England – suitable terrain for the Hound of the Baskervilles (one of Sherlock Holmes' most notorious foes). This is hiking country par excellence. The only village of any size on the moor is Princetown, which is not a particularly attractive place.

Information
The National Park Authority (NPA) has eight information centres in and around the park, but it is also possible to get information at Exeter's TIC before setting off. There's also the High Moorland Visitor Centre (☎ 01822-890414) in Princetown, which is open all year.

Places to Stay
The owners of unenclosed moorland don't usually object to free campers who keep to a simple code: don't camp on moorland enclosed by walls or within sight of roads or houses; don't stay on one site for more than two nights; and leave the site as you found it.

The *Bellever Youth Hostel* (☎ 01822-880227, Postbridge) is very popular. It closes from November to mid-March and on Sunday, except in July and August. The *Steps Bridge Youth Hostel* (☎ 01647-252435) is closed from October to March. *Plume of Feathers Inn Bunkhouse* (☎ 01822-890240, Princetown) has 42 beds for £3.50 to £5.50, but three months advance booking is wise for summer weekends. Beds cost £6 at *Dartmoor Expedition Centre* (☎ 01364-621249, Widecombe-in-the-Moor).

Getting There & Away
Exeter is a good starting point for the park. Public transport in and around the park is lousy, so consider hiring a bike (about £7 a day) from Flash Gordon (☎ 01392-213141) in Exeter.

From Exeter, DevonBus 359 follows a circular route through Steps Bridge, Moretonhampstead and Chagford (Monday to Saturday). The most important bus that actually crosses Dartmoor is DevonBus 82, the Transmoor Link (☎ 01752-222666), running between Exeter and Plymouth via Moretonhampstead and Princetown. Unfortunately, it only runs daily from late May to late September.

THE CORNWALL COAST
Penzance
☎ 01736
At the end of the rail line from London, Penzance is a busy little town that has not yet completely sold its soul to tourists. You may want to stay here if you're walking the section of the Coast Path around Land's End to or from St Ives. This dramatic 40km section can be broken at the YHA hostel at St Just (near Land's End), and there are many cheap farm B&Bs along the way.

The TIC (☎ 362207) is just outside the train station.

Places to Stay The *Penzance Youth Hostel* (☎ 362666, Castle Horneck, Alverton) is an 18th-century mansion on the outskirts of town. Walk west through town on the Land's End road (Market Jew St) until you get to a thatched cottage opposite the Pirate Inn, turn right and cross the A30 bypass road until you get to the signposted lane.

Closer to the town centre is the *Penzance Backpackers* (☎ 363836, Alexander Rd), which charges £9.

Getting There & Away There are four buses a day from Penzance to Bristol via Truro and Plymouth; one direct bus a day to Exeter (five hours); and five buses a day from London and Heathrow (£27.50, 7½ hours). There are seven trains a day from London's Paddington station (£54, five hours) and frequent trains from Penzance to St Ives (£2.90, 20 minutes).

Land's End
☎ 01736
The coastal scenery on either side of Land's End is some of the finest in Britain, although the development at Land's End itself is shameful. However, the *Youth Hostel* (☎ 788437, St Just), 13km from Penzance, is highly recommended. It's open from April to October. You can also stay at the *Whitesand's Lodge* (☎ 871776), a backpackers hostel in Sennen village, with dorm beds for £9. Even cheaper is the tiny *Kelynack Bunkbarn* (☎ 787633), 1.6km south of St Just, with beds for £6.

The coastal hills between St Just and St Ives, with their dry stone walling, form one of the oldest, most fascinating agricultural landscapes in Britain.

BRITAIN

St Ives
☎ 01736

St Ives is the ideal to which all seaside towns aspire. Artists have long been attracted to St Ives, and in 1993 a branch of London's Tate Gallery was opened here. The omnipresent sea, the harbour, the beaches, the narrow alleyways, steep slopes and hidden corners are captivating, but it gets very busy in summer. It's easily accessible by train from Penzance and London via St Erth. There are numerous B&Bs in the £14 to £16 bracket.

The TIC (☎ 796297), in the Guildhall on Street-an-Pol, a short walk from the train station, is open all year. There are several surf shops on the Wharf (the street edging the harbour) where it is possible to rent boards.

Newquay
☎ 01637

Newquay, the original 'Costa del Cornwall', was drawing them in long before the British learnt to say Torremolinos. There are numerous sandy beaches, several of them right in town (including Fistral Beach for board riders).

The TIC (☎ 871345) is near the bus station in the centre of town. There are several surf shops on Fore St and they all hire boards and wetsuits, each around £6 per day.

Popular *Newquay Cornwall Backpackers (☎ 874668)*, in an excellent central position overlooking Towan Beach in Beachfield Ave, has dorm beds for £7 a night. *Home Surf Lodge (☎ 873387, 18 Tower Rd)*, has beds from £10 and free internet access.

There are four trains a day between Par, on the main London to Penzance line, and Newquay, and numerous buses to Truro.

Tintagel
☎ 01840

Even the summer crowds and the grossly commercialised village can't destroy the surf-battered grandeur of **Tintagel Head**. According to legend the scanty ruins mark the birthplace of King Arthur, hence the plethora of King Arthur tea shops etc. Entry to the ruins is £2.90. It's also worth visiting the picturesque 14th-century **Old Post Office** (£2.20).

Tintagel Youth Hostel (☎ 770334, Dunderhole Point) is open April to September.

Alternatively *Boscastle Youth Hostel (☎ 250287)*, overlooking the harbour, is open mid-May to September.

For information on the irregular bus services phone ☎ 01872-322142.

BATH
☎ 01225

For more than 2000 years Bath's fortune has been linked to its hot springs and tourism. The Romans developed a complex of baths and a temple to Sulis-Minerva. Today, Bath's Georgian architecture is an equally important attraction.

Like Italy's Florence, Bath is an architectural jewel, with a much-photographed, shop-lined bridge. In high summer the town can seem little more than an exotic shopping mall for wealthy tourists. However, when sunlight brightens the honey-coloured stone, no-one can deny Bath's exceptional beauty.

The TIC (☎ 462831), Abbey Chambers, Abbey Churchyard, is open daily year round.

Things to See & Do

Bath was designed for wandering around – it takes at least a full day. Don't miss the **covered market** next to the Guildhall, or the maze of passageways just north of the **Abbey Churchyard**. Free walking tours (recommended) leave from the Churchyard at 10.30 am (except Saturday).

On the southern side of the Abbey Churchyard, the **Pump Room** houses an opulent restaurant exemplifying the elegant style that once drew the aristocrats. Nearby, the **Roman Baths Museum** is a series of excavated passages and chambers beneath street level, taking in the sulphurous mineral springs, the ancient central-heating system and the bath itself. This is Bath's top attraction. Entry is £6.30, or £8.40 including the worthwhile **Museum of Costume** in the Assembly Rooms, a 20-minute walk uphill. The museum contains an enormous collection of clothing from 1590 to the present day.

The **Circus** is an architectural masterpiece by John Wood the Elder, designed so that a true crescent faces each of its three approaches. Continue to **Royal Crescent**, designed by John Wood the Younger and even more highly regarded than his father's effort. The house at **No 1** has been restored to its 1770 glory; entry is certainly worth £4/3.

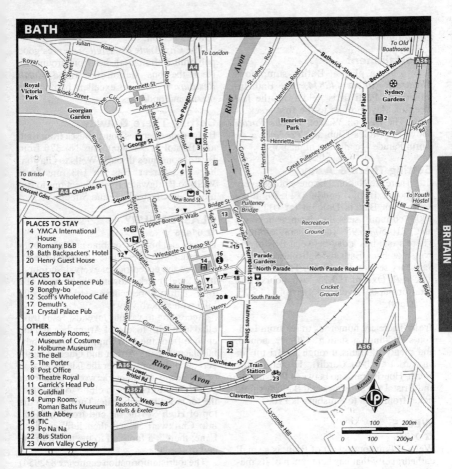

BATH

BRITAIN

PLACES TO STAY
4 YMCA International House
7 Romany B&B
18 Bath Backpackers' Hotel
20 Henry Guest House

PLACES TO EAT
6 Moon & Sixpence Pub
9 Bonghy-bo
12 Scoff's Wholefood Café
17 Demuth's
21 Crystal Palace Pub

OTHER
1 Assembly Rooms; Museum of Costume
2 Holburne Museum
3 The Bell
5 The Porter
8 Post Office
10 Theatre Royal
11 Garrick's Head Pub
13 Guildhall
14 Pump Room; Roman Baths Museum
15 Bath Abbey
16 TIC
19 Po Na Na
22 Bus Station
23 Avon Valley Cyclery

Places to Stay

Advance booking of accommodation is essential over Easter, during the Bath International Festival, on summer weekends and throughout July and August.

The cheerful *Bath Backpackers Hotel* (☎ 446787), on Pierrepont St, is a five-minute walk from the bus and train stations, with dorm beds for £12. *YMCA International House* (☎ 460471), on Broad St Place, is central, unisex, and has no curfew. Singles/doubles with light breakfast are £15/28, and dorms are £11. *Bath Youth Hostel* (☎ 465674) is out towards the University of Bath, a good 25-minute walk, or catch Badgerline bus No 18 from the bus station. There are compensatory views and the building is magnificent. Beds are £10.85.

Considering its central location, *Henry Guest House* (☎ 424052, 6 Henry St) is good value at £20 per person. *Romany* (☎ 424193, 9 Charlotte St) is also dead central, and charges £38 for a double.

Places to Eat

Scoff's Wholefood Café, on Kingsmead Square, has excellent filled rolls and light lunches. The *Moon & Sixpence (6 Broad St)* is a pleasant pub with all-you-can-eat lunches for £5. The *Crystal Palace* pub, Abbey Green, has a beer garden, traditional ale and cheap pub meals. *Demuth's*, on North Parade Passage, is a popular vegetarian restaurant with food to die for at around £5. *Bonghy-bo*, on Upper Borough Walls, has an eclectic mix of Asian dishes.

The finest cream teas (£5.75) are at the *Pump Room*.

Entertainment

Try to see a play at Bath's sumptuous *Theatre Royal* (☎ 448844). The Bath International Festival is held from the last week of May through to the first week of June. The *Bell* on Walcot St, *The Porter* above the Moles Club and *Po Na Na* on North Parade are all cool nightspots.

Getting There & Away

Bus There are National Express buses every two hours from London (£11.50, three hours), but Bakers Dolphin (☎ 0117-961 4000) currently sells the cheapest tickets – just £10.50/16.95 for a single/return. There's one bus a day between Bristol and Portsmouth via Bath and Salisbury – see the Salisbury section for details. There's also a link with Oxford (£9.75, two hours) and Stratford-upon-Avon via Bristol (£15.75, 2½ hours).

Train There are numerous trains from London's Paddington station (£30, 1½ hours), and plenty of trains through to Bristol for onward travel to Cardiff, Exeter or the North. Hourly trains go between Portsmouth and Bristol via Salisbury and Bath. A single ticket from Bath to Salisbury is £10.

WELLS
☎ 01749

Wells, 34km south-west of Bath, is a small cathedral city that has kept much of its medieval character; many claim that the **cathedral** is England's most beautiful. Try and join one of the free tours. Beyond the cathedral is the moated **Bishop's Palace**, with its beautiful gardens. It's open Tuesday, Thursday and Sunday summer afternoons only; daily in August (£3).

The TIC (☎ 672552) is in the town hall on the picturesque Market Place. The Bicycle Company (☎ 675096), 80 High St, has bikes for hire from £10/5 for the first/second day.

Places to Stay & Eat

The nearest YHA *hostel* is at Street near Glastonbury (see the following section).

Opposite St Cuthbert's church is *19 St Cuthbert St* (☎ 673166) with rooms from £16 per person. The *B&B* (☎ 672270) at 9 Chamberlain St is very central and charges £18 per person.

The *City Arms* (*69 High St*) serves good pub grub with main dishes from around £5. Near the bus station the *Good Earth Restaurant* produces excellent home-made pizzas and puddings.

Getting There & Away

Badgerline operates hourly buses from Bath and Bristol (1¼ hours). Bus No 376 from Bristol continues through Wells to Glastonbury and Street. Bus No 163 runs from Wells to Bridgwater (for connections to Exmoor) via Glastonbury and Street.

GLASTONBURY
☎ 01458

Legend and history combine at Glastonbury to produce an irresistible attraction for romantics and eccentrics of every description. It's a small market town with the ruins of a 14th-century abbey, and a nearby tor (rocky hill) with superb views.

According to various legends, Jesus travelled here with Joseph of Arimathea and the chalice from the Last Supper; it is the burial place of King Arthur and Queen Guinevere; and the tor is either the Isle of Avalon or a gateway to the underworld. Whatever you choose to believe, a climb to the top of the tor is well worthwhile. Turn right at the top of High St (the far end from the TIC) into Chilkwell St and then left into Dod Lane; there's a footpath to the tor from the end of the lane.

The tourist information centre (☎ 832954) can supply maps and details about accommodation; there are plenty of B&Bs for around £15. At *Glastonbury Backpackers Hostel* (☎ 833353, *Crown Hotel, 4 Market Place*), dorm beds are £9. The nearest hostel is *Street Youth Hostel* (☎ 442961), 6.5km south.

The **Glastonbury Festival**, a three-day epic of theatre, music, circus, mime, natural healing etc, is a massive affair with over 1000 acts. It takes place at Pilton, 13km from Glastonbury; admission is by advance ticket only (around £90 for the whole festival; bring a tent). Phone ☎ 832020 for details.

There are Badgerline buses from Bristol to Wells, Glastonbury and Street. Glastonbury is only six miles from Wells, so walking or hitching is feasible.

Central England

OXFORD
☎ 01865

Oxford is famous for its spires, and like all great cliches it's strikingly apt – looking across the meadows or rooftops to Oxford's golden spires is certainly an experience to inspire purple prose.

These days, however, Oxford battles against a flood of tourists and some typical Midlands social problems. It is not just a university city, but the home of Morris cars with a bustling centre and some sprawling industrial suburbs.

Oxford University is the oldest university in Britain. The colleges began to appear from the mid-13th century onwards. There are now about 14,500 undergraduates and 36 colleges.

Orientation & Information
The train station is west of the centre, with frequent buses to Carfax Tower, a central landmark at the intersection of Queen St and Cornmarket St/St Aldate's. Alternatively, turn left off the station concourse into Park End St and it's a 15-minute walk. The bus station is nearer the centre, on Gloucester Green.

The hectic TIC (☎ 726871) on Gloucester Green charges a hefty £2.75 (plus 10% deposit) for local B&B bookings. It's imperative to pick up a few brochures at the TIC – you need more information than this guide can give. The *Welcome to Oxford* brochure (£1) has a walking tour with college opening times. The TIC has daily two-hour walking tours of the colleges for £4/2.50.

Things to See & Do
You need more than a day to 'do' Oxford, but, at a bare minimum, make sure you visit Christ Church (with the Oxford Cathedral), Merton and Magdalen (pronounced 'maudlen') colleges and the Ashmolean Museum. The colleges remain open throughout the year (unlike Cambridge) but their hours vary.

Colleges Starting at the **Carfax Tower**, which you can climb for £1.20, cross Cornmarket St and walk down the hill, along St Aldate's, to **Christ Church**, perhaps the most famous college in Oxford. The main

entrance is beneath Tom Tower, which was built by Wren in 1680, but the usual visitors' entrance is farther down the hill via the wrought-iron gates facing out over Christ Church Meadow. Entry is £3.

Return to the Broad Walk, follow the stone wall, then turn left up Merton Grove, through wrought-iron gates, then right into Merton St. **Merton College** was founded in 1264 and its buildings are among the oldest in Oxford. The present buildings mostly date from the 15th to the 17th centuries.

Turn left into Merton St, then take the first right into Magpie Lane, which will take you through to High St with its fascinating mix of architectural styles. Turn right down the hill until you come to **Magdalen** just before the river on your left. Magdalen is one of the richest Oxford colleges and has the most extensive and beautiful grounds.

Walk back up High St until you come to the **University Church of St Mary the Virgin** on your right (there's a good view from the tower), turn right up Cattle St to the distinctive, circular **Radcliffe Camera**, a reading room for the **Bodleian Library**. Continue up Cattle St passing the **Bridge of Sighs** on your right, then turn left into Broad St. On your left you pass Wren's **Sheldonian Theatre**, and on your right **Trinity** and **Balliol** colleges. Turn left at Cornmarket St and you'll be back where you started.

Museums Established in 1683, the free **Ashmolean** in Beaumont St is the country's oldest museum and houses extensive displays of European art and Middle Eastern antiquities (closed Monday and Sunday morning).

Housed in a superb Victorian Gothic building on Parks Rd, the **University Museum** is devoted to natural science. You reach the **Pitt Rivers Museum** through the University Museum. The glass cases here are crammed with everything from a sailing boat to a gory collection of shrunken South American heads. Both museums are free and closed Sunday.

Punts From Easter to September, punts and boats can be hired at Magdalen Bridge and Follybridge (£9 per hour, £25 deposit). There's no better way of letting the atmosphere of Oxford seep in. Go left for peace

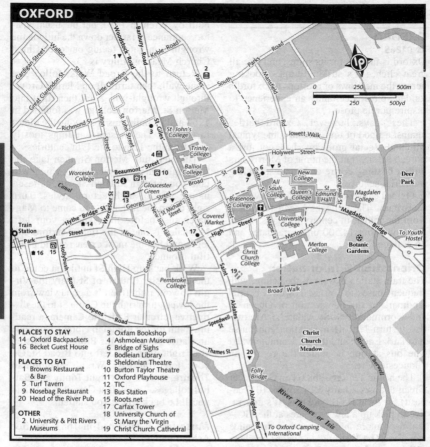

OXFORD

0   250   500m
0   250   500yd

To Youth Hostel

To Oxford Camping International

PLACES TO STAY
14 Oxford Backpackers & Bar
16 Becket Guest House

PLACES TO EAT
1 Browns Restaurant & Bar
5 Turf Tavern
9 Nosebag Restaurant
20 Head of the River Pub

OTHER
2 University & Pitt Rivers Museums

3 Oxfam Bookshop
4 Ashmolean Museum
6 Bridge of Sighs
7 Bodleian Library
8 Sheldonian Theatre
10 Burton Taylor Theatre
11 Oxford Playhouse
12 TIC
13 Bus Station
15 Roots.net
17 Carfax Tower
18 University Church of St Mary the Virgin
19 Christ Church Cathedral

and quiet, and right for views back to the colleges across the Botanic Gardens and Christ Church Meadow.

Places to Stay

Oxford Camping International (☎ 246551, *426 Abingdon Rd*) is about 5km south of the centre. Sites are £2.50/2 per tent/person, plus temporary membership.

Oxford Backpackers (☎ 721761, *9A Hythe Bridge St*) is close to the train station. Beds are £11. The less convenient *Oxford Youth Hostel* (☎ 62997, *32 Jack Straw's Lane*) has beds for £10.85. From the post office on St Aldate's take bus No 13, 14 or 14A to the hostel.

Athena Guest House (☎ 243124, *253 Cowley Rd*) is within walking distance of

shops and restaurants and has singles/ doubles for £18/36. Near the train station, *Becket* (☎ 724675, *5 Becket St*) is a large and basic B&B with rooms for £25/36.

Places to Eat

There's excellent pub grub at *Turf Tavern*, Bath Place, a recommended watering hole hidden away down an alley. *Head of the River*, ideally situated by Folly Bridge, is very popular. Self-caterers should visit the *covered market*, on the northern side of High St near Carfax Tower, for fruit and vegetables. *Nosebag Restaurant*, St Michael's St, has filling soups and a good range of vegetarian choices. *Browns Restaurant & Bar* (*5 Woodstock Rd*) is a stylish brasserie with mains for around £7.

Getting There & Away

Bus The Oxford Tube (☎ 772250) starts at London's Victoria coach station (stopping at Marble Arch, Notting Hill Gate and Shepherd's Bush) and runs daily to Oxford (£5 to £8, 1½ hours).

National Express has numerous buses to/from London via Heathrow airport (£5 to £8, 1¾ hours). There are two or three services a day to and from Bath (£9.75, two hours) and Bristol (£12.75, 2¼ hours). Buses to Shrewsbury, North Wales, York and Durham go via Birmingham.

Oxford Citylink (☎ 711312), the third major operator, has frequent departures to London, Heathrow, Gatwick, Birmingham and Stratford. Stagecoach (☎ 772250) runs six buses a day to Cambridge.

Train There are frequent trains to Oxford from London's Paddington station (£13 single, 1½ hours). Regular trains go north to Coventry and Birmingham, and north-west to Worcester and Hereford. Birmingham is the main hub for transport farther north.

To connect with trains to the south-west you have to change at Didcot Parkway (15 minutes). There are plenty of connections to Bath. Phone ☎ 0845-748 4950 for train inquiries.

BLENHEIM PALACE

Blenheim Palace (☎ 01993-811325), the birthplace of Winston Churchill and one of the largest palaces in Europe, was a gift to John Churchill from Queen Anne and Parliament as a reward for his role in defeating Louis XIV. Designed and built by Vanbrugh and Hawksmoor between 1704 and 1722 with gardens by Capability Brown, Blenheim is an enormous baroque fantasy and is definitely worth visiting.

The house is open 10.30 am to 5.30 pm mid-March to October (£8.50/6). Catch Thames Transit Minibus No 20A, 20B or 20C from Gloucester Green in Oxford (£2.75 return, 30 minutes) to the palace's entrance.

STRATFORD-UPON-AVON

☎ 01789

Thanks to the pen of William Shakespeare, Stratford has found itself transformed from a quiet market town into one of England's busiest tourist attractions. Fans can visit several buildings associated with his life –

including Shakespeare's Birthplace, New Place, Nash's House, Hall's Croft, Anne Hathaway's Cottage and Mary Arden's House. A passport ticket to all the Shakespearean properties costs £12.

As it's just beyond the northern edge of the Cotswolds, Stratford makes a handy stopover en route to and from the North. The Royal Shakespeare Company (☎ 295623) has three theatres here, in addition to its London venues, and there's nearly always something on. Tickets are often available on the day of performance, but queue early; the box office opens at 9.30 am. Stand-by tickets are made available to students immediately before performances (£11 or £14) and there are almost always standing room tickets (£5).

The TIC (☎ 293127), Bridgefoot, has plenty of information about local B&Bs.

Places to Stay & Eat

Backpackers Hostel (☎ 263838, 33 Greenhill St) has beds for £11. It is centrally located on the road between the train station and the town centre. The YHA *Stratford Youth Hostel* (☎ 297093, Hemmingford House, Alveston) is 2.5km out of town – from the TIC, cross Clopton Bridge and follow the B4086, or take bus No 18 from Wood St near the TIC. Bed and breakfast costs £14.90.

Prices for B&Bs can lurch skywards in summer but there are plenty of places at around £18 on Evesham Place, Grove Rd and Broad Walk, just west of the centre. Try the cheerful *Grosvenor Villa* (☎ 266192) at 9 Evesham Place, the *Dylan* (☎ 204819) at No 10 or the good-value *Clomendy* (☎ 266957) at No 157. Alcester Rd, by the train station, also has several options.

Sheep St has a fine selection of dining possibilities, or try the stylish *Edward Moon's* (9 Chapel St), where you'll pay around £8.50 for a meal. *Dirty Duck* on Waterside is good for an ale.

Getting There & Away

Bus National Express (☎ 0870-580 8080) buses link Birmingham, Stratford, Warwick, Oxford, Heathrow and London.

Phone ☎ 01788-535555 for local bus information. The X20 operates regularly to Birmingham (£3.05, one hour), the X16 runs to Warwick (£2.10, 20 minutes) and

Coventry (£2.75, 1¼ hours), and the X50 to Oxford (£4.25, 1½ hours).

Train Direct services to/from London's Paddington station cost £20. There are trains to Warwick (£2.50) and Birmingham (£3.50). Phone ☎ 0845-748 4950 for information.

COTSWOLDS

The Cotswolds, more than any other region, embody the popular image of English countryside. The prettiness can be forced, and the villages are certainly no strangers to mass tourism, but the combination of golden stone, flower-draped cottages, church spires, towering chestnuts and oaks and rolling hills is extraordinarily picturesque.

Many of the villages are extremely popular with tourists; it's difficult to escape commercialism unless you have your own transport or are walking. The best advice is to take your time and wander off the beaten track in search of your own ideal Cotswold village.

Orientation & Information

There are train stations at Cheltenham, Kemble (serving Cirencester), Moreton-in-Marsh (serving Stow-on-the-Wold) and Stroud. Bath, Cheltenham, Stratford-upon-Avon and Oxford are the best starting points for the Cotswolds. Cirencester likes to think of itself as the region's capital.

The TICs in surrounding towns all stock information on the Cotswolds, but the TICs dealing specifically with the region are at Market Place, Cirencester (☎ 01285-654180) and The Square, Stow-on-the-Wold (☎ 01451-831082).

Things to See & Do

Stow-on-the-Wold Stow, as it is known, is one of the most impressive (and visited) towns in the Cotswolds. It's a terrific base if you don't have a vehicle, because several particularly beautiful villages, including the famous Upper and Lower Slaughters, are within a day's walk or cycle ride.

Stow can be reached by bus from Moreton-in-Marsh, which is on the main Cotswolds line between Worcester and Oxford. Regular buses leave from the town hall, a five-minute walk from the station, and take between 10 and 30 minutes to

reach Stow. Contact Pulhams' Coaches (☎ 820369) for a timetable.

Cheltenham Cheltenham is a large and elegant spa town easily accessible by bus and train. The TIC (☎ 01242-522878) is helpful. Cheltenham is on the main Bristol to Birmingham rail line, and can be reached easily by train from South Wales, Bath and south-west England, and Oxford (changing at Didcot and Swindon).

Places to Stay

The Cotswolds area is not particularly well served by YHA hostels – the exception being Stow's pleasant *Youth Hostel* (☎ 01451-830497), open Monday to Saturday from March to September, and Sunday from April to August. There are other *hostels* in Slimbridge, Charlbury and Duntisbourne Abbots (near Cirencester).

BIRMINGHAM
☎ 0121

Birmingham is the most southerly of the great Midlands industrial cities and the second-largest city in Britain, with over one million inhabitants. Traditionally it has been thought of as a drab and dreary city with no essential sights and not particularly accessible to the short-term visitor. Recently, however, things have started looking up, with the restoration of the old canal network and the opening of numerous popular restaurants and bars in the Brindleyplace area.

The **Museum & Art Gallery** has a fine collection of Pre-Raphaelite paintings and overlooks **Victoria** and **Chamberlain Squares**, both full of interesting statuary. The old **Jewellery Quarter**, where (surprise, surprise) jewellery was made is also looking much smarter and houses a couple of interesting small museums.

It's unlikely that you'll want to stay long in Birmingham even now, and a dearth of cheap accommodation in the city centre hardly helps (there's no hostel). However, New St station and Digbeth St coach station are both major transport hubs. If you're passing through it might be worth stepping out to explore for a few hours.

You'll find the tourist information centre (☎ 693 6300) on Victoria Square, and it's open daily.

PEAK DISTRICT

Squeezed between the industrial Midlands to the south, Manchester to the west and Sheffield to the east, the Peak District seems an unlikely site for one of England's most beautiful regions. Even the name is misleading – being derived from the tribes who once lived here, not from the existence of any significant peaks. Nonetheless, the Peak District National Park is a delight, particularly for walkers and cyclists.

The Peak District divides into the green fields and steep-sided dales of the southern White Peak and the bleak, gloomy moors of the northern Dark Peak. Buxton, to the west, and Matlock, to the east, are good bases for exploring the park, or you can stay right in the centre at Bakewell, Castleton or nearby Edale.

From Edale, the **Pennine Way** starts its 400km meander northwards. From Castleton, the 40km **Limestone Way** is a superb day walk covering the length of the White Peak to Matlock. In addition, a number of disused railway lines in the White Peak have been redeveloped as walking and cycling routes, with strategically situated bicycle-rental outlets at old station sites.

There are information centres at Edale (☎ 01433-670207), Castleton (☎ 01433-620679), and Bakewell (☎ 01629-813227). The Peak District is packed with B&Bs, YHA hostels and a collection of camping barns (☎ 01629-825850), together with plenty of convivial pubs and good restaurants. And nearby are the excellent cities of Nottingham, Sheffield and Manchester with superb nightlife.

The regular Transpeak bus service cuts right across the Peak District from Nottingham and Derby to Manchester via Matlock, Bakewell and Buxton.

Eastern England

CAMBRIDGE
☎ 01223

Cambridge (population 100,000), 87km north of London, can hardly be spoken of without reference to Oxford – so much so that the term Oxbridge is used to cover them both. The two cities are not just ancient and beautiful university towns; they embody preconceptions and prejudices that are almost mythical in dimension. An Oxbridge graduate is popularly characterised as male, public-school educated, intelligent and upper class. It can be both abusive and admiring: for some it means academic excellence, for others it denotes an elitist club whose members unfairly dominate many aspects of British life.

Cambridge University is the newer of the two, probably beginning some time early in the 13th century, perhaps a century later than Oxford. There is a fierce rivalry between the two cities and the two universities, and a futile debate over which is best and most beautiful. Oxford draws many more tourists than Cambridge. Partly because of this, if you only have time for one and the colleges are open, choose Cambridge. If the colleges are closed, choose Oxford.

Cambridge can easily be visited as a day trip from London or en route to the North. If you are seriously interested in architecture, however, you will need considerably more than a day.

Orientation & Information

The bus station is in the centre of town, which lies on a wide bend of the River Cam. The train station is a 20-minute walk to the south. Sidney St is the main shopping street. The most important group of colleges (including King's) and the Backs (the meadows adjoining the Cam) are to the west of Sidney St, which changes its name many times.

The TIC (☎ 322640), Wheeler St, organises walking tours daily at 1.30 pm, with more in summer. Buy your ticket in advance (£7 including King's College, £6 including St John's). The TIC is closed on Sunday in the off season.

CB1 (☎ 576306), an Internet cafe on Mill Rd, is open to 8 pm daily.

College Opening Times The university has three eight-week terms: Michaelmas (October to December), Lent (mid-January to mid-March) and Easter (mid-April to mid-June). Exams are held from mid-May to mid-June. Most colleges are closed to visitors for the Easter term, and all are closed for exams. Contact the TIC for up-to-date information.

Things to See & Do

Starting at Magdalene Bridge walk south down Bridge St until you can see the

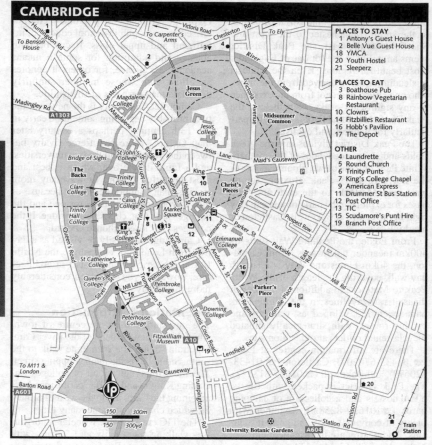

CAMBRIDGE

PLACES TO STAY
1 Antony's Guest House
2 Belle Vue Guest House
18 YMCA
20 Youth Hostel
21 Sleeperz

PLACES TO EAT
3 Boathouse Pub
8 Rainbow Vegetarian Restaurant
10 Clowns
14 Fitzbillies Restaurant
16 Hobb's Pavilion
17 The Depot

OTHER
4 Laundrette
5 Round Church
6 Trinity Punts
7 King's College Chapel
9 American Express
11 Drummer St Bus Station
12 Post Office
13 TIC
15 Scudamore's Punt Hire
19 Branch Post Office

BRITAIN

unmistakable **Round Church**, one of only four surviving medieval round churches. Turn right down St John's St, which is named in honour of **St John's College**.

Next door, **Trinity College** is one of the largest and most attractive. It was established in 1546 by Henry VIII. Its Great Court, Cambridge's largest enclosed court, incorporates buildings from the 15th century. Beyond Great Court is **Nevile's Court**, with one of Cambridge's most important buildings on its western side: Sir Christopher Wren's library, built in the 1680s.

Next comes **Caius College** (pronounced 'keys'), and then **King's College** (☎ 331100) and its famous **chapel**, one of Europe's greatest buildings. The chapel was begun in 1446 by Henry VI, but was not completed

until 1545. It comes alive when the choir sings; even the most pagan heavy-metal fan will find choral evensong an extraordinary experience. Entry is £3.50/2.25.

Continue south on what is now King's Parade and turn right into Silver St (**St Catherine's College** is on the corner) which takes you down to the Cam and the hiring point for punts. **Punting** along the Backs is sublime, but it can also be a wet and hectic experience, especially on a busy weekend. Cheapest is Trinity Punts (£6 per hour); Scudamore's rents punts for £11 from the Silver St branch, £9 from the Magdalene Bridge branch. Punting the 4.8km upriver to the idyllic village of **Grantchester** makes a great day out. Punts hold up to six people; deposits of £50 are required.

Places to Stay

Cambridge Youth Hostel (☎ *354601, 97 Tenison Rd*) has small dormitories and a restaurant near the train station. It's very popular – book ahead. Adult/junior rates are £11.70/8.50.

Right outside the train station is *Sleeperz* (☎ *304050,* @ *info@sleeperz.com, Station Rd*), an attractively converted railway warehouse with single/twin rooms for £35/45 with a shower. Rooms with a double bed are larger and cost £55.

YMCA (☎ *356998, Gonville Place*) charges £22.65/37 and is good value for weekly stays (£127.50/224). Breakfast is included.

The other B&B area is in the north of the city around Chesterton Rd. *Antony's Guest House* (☎ *357444, 4 Huntingdon Rd*) is spacious and comfortable, with four singles, four doubles and three triples at £15 to £22 per person. Similarly priced but a bit farther out, *Benson House* (☎ *311594, 24 Huntingdon Rd*) has well-equipped doubles with showers.

Closer to the city centre, *Belle Vue Guest House* (☎ *351859, 33 Chesterton Rd*) has comfortable doubles for £40.

Places to Eat

Across the road from King's College is *Rainbow* (*9 King's Parade*), a good vegetarian restaurant. *Clowns* (*54 King St*) is popular with students, and serves good-value light meals. *Hobb's Pavilion* (*Park Terrace*) occupies the old cricket pavilion and specialises in filled pancakes (closed Sunday and Monday). *The Depot* (*Regent St*) is stylish yet good value, offering an interesting international menu based around starters. *Fitzbillies* (*52 Trumpington St*) is a brilliant bakery/restaurant – try the Chelsea buns or the chocolate cake. The *Boathouse* (*14 Chesterton Rd*) is a good riverside pub.

Getting There & Away

Bus National Express has hourly buses to London (£8.50, two hours). There are four buses a day to and from Bristol (two stop at Bath). Unfortunately, links to the North aren't very straightforward. To reach Lincoln or York you must change at Peterborough or Nottingham, respectively. For more detailed bus information phone ☎ 317740.

Cambridge Coach Services (☎ 423900) runs the Inter-Varsity Link via London's Stansted airport to Oxford (£7/13 single/return, three hours). It also runs buses to Heathrow (£13) and Gatwick (£17) airports.

Train There are trains every half-hour from London's King's Cross and Liverpool St stations (one hour). If you catch the train at King's Cross you travel via Hatfield (see Hatfield House in the Around London section) and Stevenage. There are also regular train connections to Bury St Edmunds (£5.30), Ely (£2.90) and King's Lynn (£6.70). There are connections at Peterborough with the main northbound trains to Lincoln, York and Edinburgh. If you want to head west to Oxford or Bath, you'll have to return to London first. For more information, phone ☎ 0845-748 4950.

Getting Around

Cambus (☎ 423554) runs numerous free buses around town from Drummer St, including bus No 1 from the train station to the town centre. Rent bikes at Geoff's Bike Hire (☎ 365629), 65 Devonshire Rd, near the youth hostel.

AROUND CAMBRIDGE
Ely
☎ 01353

Ely is a small city set on a low hill that was once an island deep in a watery world of the fens. It is dominated by the overwhelming bulk of **Ely Cathedral**, a superb example of the Norman Romanesque style, built between 1081 and 1200. This is an easy, rewarding day trip by train from Cambridge (20 minutes, £2.90). Phone the TIC (☎ 662062) for places to stay.

Harwich
☎ 01255

The only reason to visit this ugly shipping terminal is to catch a ferry to mainland Europe; see the Getting There & Away section at the beginning of this chapter for ferry details.

Contact the TIC (☎ 506139) if you need a B&B. There are numerous trains from Harwich (International Port) to London (Liverpool St station); on some services you will have to change trains at Manningtree or Colchester. Alternatively, you could go north to Norwich, or change for Bury St Edmunds and Cambridge at Ipswich.

North-East England

North-east England is quite different from the rest of the country – as a rule, the countryside is more rugged than in the south and it's as if the history reflects this, because every inch has been fought over. The central conflict was the long struggle between north and south, with the battle lines shifting over the centuries. The Romans were the first to attempt to delineate a border with Hadrian's Wall.

There is a very useful bus information service (☎ 0970-608 2608) that covers the whole region.

YORK
☎ 01904

For nearly 2000 years York has been the capital of the north. It existed before the Romans, but entered the world stage under their rule. In AD 306, Constantine, the first Christian emperor and founder of Constantinople (now İstanbul), was probably proclaimed emperor on the site of the cathedral. In Saxon times York became an important centre for Christianity and learning – the first church on the site of the current cathedral was built in AD 627.

York's city walls were built during the 13th century and are among the most impressive surviving medieval fortifications in Europe. They enclose a thriving, fascinating centre with medieval streets, Georgian town houses and riverside pubs. The crowning glory is the Minster, the largest Gothic cathedral in England. York attracts millions of visitors and the crowds can get you down, especially in July and August. But it's too old and too impressive to be overwhelmed by mere tourists.

Orientation & Information

There are five major landmarks: the 4km wall that encloses the city centre; the Minster at the northern corner; Clifford's Tower, a 13th-century castle and mound at the southern end; the River Ouse that cuts the centre in two; and the train station just outside the western corner. The main bus terminal is on Rougier St (off Station Rd), but some local buses also leave from the train station.

Bear in mind that in York, 'gate' means street and 'bar' means gate.

The main TIC (☎ 621756, fax 551801, ✉ tic@york-tourism.co.uk) is in De Grey Rooms, Exhibition Square, north of the river near Bootham Bar. It opens 9 am to 6 pm daily (10 am to 4 pm Sunday). There's also a small TIC at the train station.

Things to See & Do

Starting at the main TIC, climb the city wall at **Bootham Bar** (on the site of a Roman gate) and walk north-east along the wall to Monk Bar, from where there are beautiful views of the Minster.

York Minster took over 250 years to complete (from 1220 to 1480), so it incorporates a number of architectural styles. The cathedral is most famous for its extensive medieval stained glass, particularly the enormous Great Eastern Window (1405-08), which depicts the beginning and end of the world. To see everything could easily absorb the best part of a day. The cathedral is open 7 am to 6 pm daily. It is free, but a £2 donation is requested and areas such as the tower cost extra. There are worthwhile free guided tours.

Monk Bar is York's best-preserved medieval gate, with a working portcullis. Leave the walls here, walk along Goodramgate and take the first right onto Ogleforth, then left into Chapter House St. The **Treasurer's House** (open April to October, £3.50) on the right, has been restored by the National Trust. Turn left again into College St and pass a 15th-century timber-framed building, **St William's College**.

The **Shambles**, a much-touristed medieval butcher's street, is off King's Square. Walk down the Shambles, then turn left and immediately right into Fossgate for the **Merchant Adventurers' Hall** (£2), which was built in the 14th century by a guild of merchants who controlled the cloth export trade.

Continue down Walmgate (the continuation of Fossgate) to **Walmgate Bar**. This is the only city gate in England with an intact barbican – an extended gateway designed to make life difficult for uninvited guests. Follow the wall around to the right and across the River Foss to **Clifford's Tower** and the popular **York Castle Museum**, which contains displays of everyday life and is one of the best in Britain. It's open 9.30 to 5 pm daily and admission is £5.25.

One of York's most popular attractions is the smells-and-all **Jorvik Viking Centre**, a

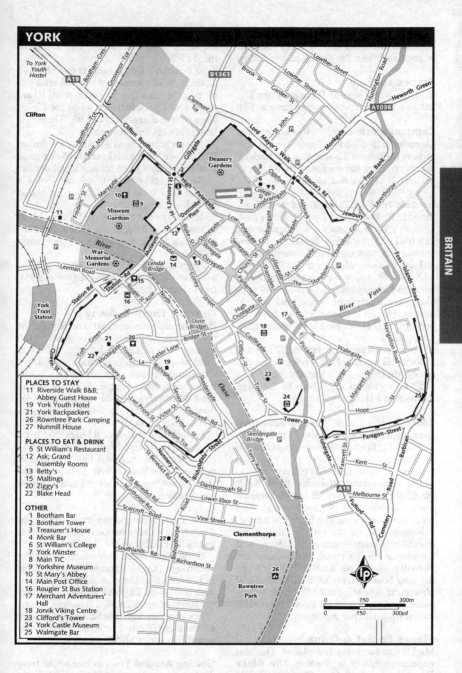

recreation of Viking York (£45.65). The **Yorkshire Museum** has the best collection of remnants from the Roman past (£3.95).

Places to Stay

York gets very crowded. Fortunately, the TIC has an accommodation-booking service (£4).

Camping Pitch a tent at *Rowntree Park Camping* (☎ 658997, *Terry Ave*), a 20-minute walk from the station in the park by the river. They have a few sites for backpackers at £10 for two adults.

Hostels The *York Youth Hostel* (☎ 653147, *fax 651230,* ☻ *york@yha.org.uk, Water End, Clifton)* is open all year. Seniors/juniors pay £15.05/11.25, including breakfast. Follow the riverside footpath from the station.

York Youth Hotel (☎ 625904, *fax 612494,* ☻ *info@yorkyouthhotel.demon .co.uk, 11 Bishophill Senior)* is equally popular, particularly with school and student parties. There's a range of rooms, from 20-bed dorms (£11) to twin bunk rooms (£15 per person).

York Backpackers (☎ 627720, *fax 339350,* ☻ *yorkbackpackers@cwcom.net, 88-90 Micklegate)* is a friendly place in a 1752 Georgian building. Beds in the large dorms cost £11; doubles are £30.

B&Bs With a central position beside the river, the *Abbey Guest House* (☎ 627782, *fax 671743,* ☻ *abbey@rsummers.cix.co.uk, 14 Earlsborough Terrace)* is a standard B&B with rooms from £20 per person.

The comfortable *Riverside Walk B&B* (☎ 620769, *fax 646249,* ☻ *julie@riverside walkbb.demon.co.uk, 9 Earlsborough Terrace)* has rooms with bath from £24 a head.

Running along the railway line, both Bootham Terrace (south of Bootham) and Grosvenor Terrace (north of Bootham) are virtually lined with B&Bs. Bishopthorpe Rd also boasts plenty of B&Bs; *Nunmill House* (☎ 634047, *fax 655879,* ☻ *b&b@ nunmill.co.uk)* at No 85 is a good place with rooms from £25 per person.

Places to Eat & Drink

Micklegate has many fine places. The best vegetarian eatery in York is *The Blake Head Bookshop & Café* (☎ 623767, *104 Micklegate)*. The emphasis is on simple but imaginative cooking. It's open daily for lunch; soup costs £2.50, a three-course meal £7.50.

St William's Restaurant (☎ 634830), off College St, is a great spot to relax after exploring the cathedral. It's open from 10 am to 10 pm. Lunch includes soups for £3.25. Two course dinners are £12.95. There is a beautiful cobbled courtyard.

The gorgeous Grand Assembly Rooms on Blake St are home to *Ask* (☎ 637254), a good moderate Italian place for lunch and dinner.

Betty's (☎ 659142), on St Helen's Square, is a local institution for tea and it has a fine bakery.

Maltings (☎ 655387), on Tanners Moat below Lendal Bridge, has a great beer selection, a fine atmosphere and good lunch specials.

Ziggy's (☎ 620602, *53-55 Micklegate)* is a relaxed club with theme nights ranging from Goth to disco.

Getting There & Away

Bus The main bus terminal is on Rougier St (off Station Rd, inside the city walls on the western side of Lendal Bridge), but some local buses leave from the train station.

National Express (☎ 0870-580 8080) buses leave from Rougier St. There are at least three services a day to London (4½ hours), two a day to Birmingham (2½ hours) and one to Edinburgh (5½ hours).

For information on local buses (to Castle Howard, Helmsley, Scarborough, Whitby etc), contact the regional bus information number or in York call ☎ 551400. Yorkshire Coastliner has buses to Leeds, Malton and Scarborough.

Train There are numerous trains from London's King's Cross station (£59, two hours) and on to Edinburgh (£47, 2¾ hours).

North-south trains also connect with Peterborough (£33, 1½ hours) for Cambridge and East Anglia. There are good connections with south-west England including Oxford, via Birmingham (£25.50, 2¼ hours).

Local trains to/from Scarborough take 45 minutes (£9.10). For Whitby it's necessary to change at Middlesbrough.

Getting Around You can hire a bike from the Europcar office (☎ 656161) in the train station for £7.50 per day.

AROUND YORK
Castle Howard
There are few buildings in the world that are so perfect their visual impact is almost a physical blow. Castle Howard (☎ 01653-648333), of *Brideshead Revisited* fame, is one. The house has a picturesque setting in the rolling Howardian Hills and is surrounded by 400 hectares of superb terraces and landscaped grounds dotted with monumental follies.

Castle Howard is 15 miles north of York off the A64. It's open at 10 am (last admission 4.30 pm) daily mid-March to early-October (£7). The castle can be reached by several tours from York. Check with the York TIC for up-to-date schedules. Yorkshire Coastliner has a morning bus from York linking Castle Howard and Pickering.

NORTH YORK MOORS NATIONAL PARK
The North York Moors National Park (☎ 01439-770657) is less crowded than the Lake District and more expansive than Exmoor. The coast is superb, with high cliffs and long, sandy beaches backing onto beautiful countryside. From the ridge-top roads and open moors there are wonderful views, and the dales shelter abbeys, castles and small stone villages.

The Cleveland Way long-distance footpath (174km) curves around the edge of the park from Helmsley to Saltburn-by-the-Sea, then down the coast to Scarborough. Maps and accommodation information are available from TICs. The North Yorkshire Moors Railway (NYMR; ☎ 01751-472508), a privately owned steam train, runs up the beautiful wooded Newtondale from Pickering to Grosmont. It operates from April to October. The excellent free brochure *Moors Connections*, available from TICs, is a must for public-transport users.

Pickering
☎ 01751
Pickering is a terminus for the NYMR. The helpful TIC (☎ 473791) can suggest one of the numerous B&Bs. The nearest YHA hostel is the *Old School Youth Hostel (☎/fax 460376, Lockton)*, about 4 miles north. It's another good walking base, and is open from Monday to Saturday from mid-April to late-September (daily in July and August).

Pickering can be reached by bus from York and Whitby on Yorkshire Coastliner, Helmsley and Scarborough on Scarborough & District.

Helmsley & Around
☎ 01493
Helmsley is an attractive market town (Friday is market day) with excellent short walks in the surrounding countryside, including a short stretch of the Cumberland Way. There's the picturesque ruined **Helmsley Castle** on the edge of town, and 5.6km uphill along the Cleveland Way are the remains of 13th-century **Rievaulx Abbey**, arguably the most beautiful monastic ruins in England (£2.90).

The TIC (☎ 770173) can book B&Bs. There are several camping grounds in the area; the nearest is *Foxholme Caravan Park (☎ 770416, Harome)*, 3km south-east of town. At *Helmsley Youth Hostel (☎/fax 770433)* the nightly rate is £9. Opening times vary so phone ahead.

Stephenson's bus No 57 runs once daily between York and Helmsley (one hour). Scarborough & District has daily buses between Helmsley and Scarborough via Pickering (1½ hours).

Scarborough
☎ 01723
Scarborough is a traditional seaside resort with a spectacular location. It's jam-packed with arcades, boarding houses and B&Bs. The coastline to the north, especially around Robin Hood's Bay, is beautiful.

If you need to stay, contact the TIC (☎ 373333). The YHA *White House Youth Hostel (☎ 361176, fax 500054, @ scarborough@yha.org.uk, Burniston Rd)* is 2 miles north of town. It has complex opening times, so ring ahead.

Scarborough is connected by rail to York and Kingston-upon-Hull. There are reasonably frequent buses west along the A170 to Pickering and Helmsley.

DURHAM
☎ 0191
Durham is the most dramatic cathedral city in Britain and also home to the third-oldest university in England (founded in 1832). The massive Norman cathedral stands on a high, wooded promontory above a bend in

BRITAIN

the River Wear. Other cathedrals are more refined, but none has more impact.

Orientation & Information

The marketplace, TIC (☎ 384 3720), castle and cathedral are all on a teardrop-shaped peninsula surrounded by the River Wear. The train station is above and north-west of the cathedral, on the other side of the river. The bus station is also on the western side. Internet access is available at Reality X, west of the marketplace on your way to the bus station.

Things to See & Do

The World Heritage-listed **Durham Cathedral** is Britain's most complete Norman cathedral, with characteristic round arches, enormous columns and zigzagged chevron ornament. Don't miss the beautiful Galilee Chapel at the western end. There are tours (£3) at 10.30 am and 2 pm Monday to Saturday, late May to September.

Durham Castle dates from 1093 and served as the home for Durham's prince-bishops. These bishops had powers and responsibilities more normally associated with a warrior king than a priest. It's now a residential college for the university.

There are superb views back to the cathedral and castle from the outer bank of the river; walk around the bend between Elvet and Framwelgate bridges.

Places to Stay

Several colleges rent their rooms during the university vacations (particularly July to September); inquire at the TIC. The most exciting possibility is *University College* (☎ 374 3863), in Durham Castle, which has B&B at £20.50 per person.

There are a number of B&Bs for around £16 per person on Gilesgate – leave the market square from its northern end and go over the freeway onto Claypath (which becomes Gilesgate). *Mrs Koltai* (☎ 386 2026) is at No 10 and *Mr Nimmins* (☎ 384 6485) at No 14.

Getting There & Away

There are six National Express buses a day to London (£20, 6½ hours), one to Edinburgh (4½ hours), and numerous to Birmingham (5¾ hours) and to/from Newcastle (30 minutes). Primrose Coaches (☎ 232

5567) run daily via Durham between Newcastle upon Tyne and Blackpool.

There are plenty of trains to York (£13.90, one hour), a good number of which head on to London (£68, three hours) via Peterborough (for Cambridge). Frequent trains also run to Edinburgh (two hours).

NEWCASTLE-UPON-TYNE
☎ 0191

Newcastle is the largest city in the northeast. It grew famous as a coal-exporting port and in the 19th century became an important industrial centre, before falling into decline after WWII. Newcastle's city centre retains some 19th-century grandeur, and has gained new impetus through the redevelopment of the Quayside area.

The new **Life Interactive World** (☎ 243 8210) is a hands-on experience delving into all aspects of life. Both **St Nicholas Cathedral** and **Castle Garth Keep** are also worth visiting. There are river cruises in summer and in nearby Jarrow, **Bede's World** (☎ 489 2106) is a park with many reconstructed medieval buildings. **Segedunum** (☎ 295 5757), in Wallsend, is the last outpost of Hadrians Wall.

Orientation & Information

The city centre is easy to get around on foot, and the metro (for the YHA hostel and B&Bs) is cheap and easy to use. The Central train station is just south of the city centre, and the bus station is just east.

There's a TIC at the train station (closed Sunday in the off season). The main TIC (☎ 277 8000) is on Grainger St. Both have free maps, city guides and accommodation lists. Surf the Net at McNulty's Internet Café on Market St, behind the main TIC.

Places to Stay

Newcastle Youth Hostel (☎ 281 2570, 107 Jesmond Rd) mainly opens February to November. Take the metro to Jesmond station (55p), turn left from the station, cross Osborne Rd and continue for five minutes. A bed costs £10.85. Call in advance, as it can be busy.

North East YWCA (☎ 281 1233, Jesmond House), on Clayton Rd, accepts male and female guests at £16 per person. Turn left on Osborne Rd from Jesmond station and take the second street on the right.

There are quite a number of B&Bs within easy walking distance of West Jesmond station, mostly along Jesmond and Osborne Rds. *Minerva Hotel* (☎ *281 0190*), at No 105, is a small place with rooms for £22.50/35. *Portland Guest House* (☎ *232 7868, 134 Sandyford Rd*) is close to the town centre with rooms starting at £18/36.

Places to Eat

For interesting restaurants and nightlife walk south down Grey St, which becomes Dean St and takes you down to Quayside and the River Tyne. On Grey St itself, *Marco Polo* (☎ *232 5533*) at No 33 has pizzas and pastas for as little as £2.95. *Shikara* (☎ *233 0005, 52 St Andrew's St*) serves excellent Indian food and is cheap for lunch, with mains in the evening costing £6 to £10. *Flynns Bar* (*Quayside*) has a beer garden and cheap food and drink. Also check out *Bob Trollop* and *Red House*, both with pub meals for about £3.

Getting There & Away

There are numerous National Express bus connections to virtually every major city in the country. For local buses around the northeast, don't forget the excellent-value Explorer North East ticket (£5.25), valid on most services. Arriva Buses (☎ 212 3000) has details on services to Berwick-upon-Tweed (bus No 505) and along Hadrian's Wall (bus No 685). There are numerous trains to Edinburgh (1¾ hours), London (three hours) and York (one hour). Berwick-upon-Tweed and Alnmouth (for Alnwick) are farther north on this line. Ferries run regularly to Stavanger and Bergen (Norway) and in summer to Gothenburg (Sweden). See this chapter's introductory Getting There & Away section for details.

Getting Around

There's an excellent metro with fares from 55p. Bus No 327 links the ferry (at Tyne Commission Quay) and the Central train station. The fare is £3, and it leaves the station 2½ hours and 1¼ hours before ferry departure times.

BERWICK-UPON-TWEED
☎ 01289
Berwick, beautifully sited at the mouth of the River Tweed, changed hands between the Scots and the English 13 times from the 12th to the 15th centuries. This to-and-fro ceased after the construction of the massive ramparts that still enclose the town centre. The TIC (☎ 330733) should help you find a B&B for around £17; there's no hostel.

There are two superb castles between Newcastle and Berwick: **Alnwick Castle** (☎ 01665-510777) is particularly fascinating (inside and out), while **Bamburgh Castle** (☎ 01668-214515) is dramatic-looking, but not so interesting inside.

Berwick is on the main London to Edinburgh line, so it is easy to get to by train. Arriva Buses (☎ 0191-212 3000) has services linking Newcastle and Berwick. Monday to Saturday, bus No 501 runs several times to/from Alnwick via Bamburgh.

HADRIAN'S WALL

Hadrian's Wall stretches 118km from Newcastle-upon-Tyne, past Carlisle to Bowness-on-Solway. It follows a naturally defensible line and peaks at the bleak and windy Winshields Crags. The most spectacular section is between Hexham and Brampton. It's possible to walk the entire length (allow at least five days), but the first section through Newcastle is fairly dull.

The **Chesters Roman Fort & Museum** (☎ 01434-681379) is in a pleasant valley by the River Tyne (£2.80). There's an interesting museum, an extraordinary bath house and the remains of a massive bridge. **Housesteads Fort** (☎ 01434-344363), the most dramatic of the ruins, has a famous latrine and is perched on a ridge overlooking the Northumbrian countryside (£2.80). The **Vindolanda Fort & Museum** (☎ 01434-344277), 4km south, is an excavated fort (excavations continue) and civil settlement with a museum (£3.80). The **Birdoswald Roman Fort** (☎ 016977-47602) overlooks the picturesque Irthing Gorge, and is less inundated with visitors than some of the other sites (£2.50).

Places to Stay

Cheap, basic accommodation is available at *Bankshead Camping Barn* (☎ *01200-420102*), close to Banks East Turret. It costs £3.60 per person. Bus No 682 drops you outside.

Starting in the east, the *Acomb Youth Hostel* (☎ *01434-602864*) is about 4km north of Hexham and 3.5km south of the wall; beds are £6.65. Hexham can be reached by bus or train.

Once Brewed Youth Hostel (*01434-344360)* is central for both Housesteads Fort (4.8km) and Vindolanda (1.5km). Arriva bus No 685 (from Hexham or Haltwhistle stations) stops at Henshaw, 3.2km south; bus Nos 682 and 890 will drop you at the front door. The nearest train station is at Bardon Mill, 4km south-east.

Greenhead Youth Hostel (*016977-47401)* is three miles west of Haltwhistle station, but is also served by the trusty bus No 685.

Getting There & Away

West of Hexham the wall parallels the A69. Bus No 685, operated jointly by Arriva (☎ 0191-212 3000) and Stagecoach Cumberland (☎ 0870-608 2608), runs between Carlisle and Newcastle hourly. The Newcastle to Carlisle railway line (☎ 0845-748 4950) has stations at Hexham, Haydon Bridge, Bardon Mill, Haltwhistle and Brampton, but not all trains stop at all stations.

Late May to September the special hail-and-ride Hadrian's Wall Bus (No 682) runs between Hexham and Haltwhistle train stations along the B6318, connecting with trains and calling at the main sites and the Once Brewed Youth Hostel. For further information contact Hexham's TIC (☎ 01434-605225).

Explorer tickets on all the bus services cost £5.

North-West England

MANCHESTER
☎ 0161

Probably best known for the Manchester United football team, the city that produced Oasis, New Order and The Smiths is also a monument to England's industrial history. The 1990s saw a gradual transformation of parts of the city centre, a process given added impetus by the IRA bomb blast of 1996 that devastated much of the area round the Arndale Shopping Centre. The bombing has allowed the city to create some wonderful public spaces and stunning modern

architecture but there are still areas where empty warehouses and factories rub shoulders with stunning Victorian Gothic buildings, rusting train tracks and motorway overpasses with flashy bars and nightclubs. The longer you stay, the more you'll like Manchester. Not many cities in England can rival its vibrancy and nightlife, its gay scene and fantastic sports facilities.

Orientation & Information

The University of Manchester lies to the south of the centre (on Oxford St/Rd). Continue south on Oxford St/Rd for Rusholme, *the* place for cheap Indian restaurants. To the east of the university is Moss Side, a ghetto with high unemployment and a thriving drug trade – keep well clear.

The TIC (☎ 234 3157) is in the town hall extension, off St Peter Square. *City Life* is the local 'what's on' magazine – a compulsory purchase. Internet cafe Cyberia is at the north end of Oxford St.

Things to See & Do

City Centre Dominating Albert Square is the enormous Victorian Gothic **town hall** with its 84m tower. The free **City Art Gallery** on the corner of Princess and Mosley Sts was designed by Sir Charles Barry (architect for London's Houses of Parliament) in 1824. Its impressive collection covers everything from early Italian, Dutch and Flemish painters to Gainsborough, Blake and Constable (closed Sunday morning).

Castlefield Urban Heritage Park This extraordinary landscape is littered with industrial relics that have been tumbled together like pieces of Lego. Unpromising as this may sound, the result is fascinating. Attractions include the excellent **Museum of Science & Industry**, a reconstruction of a Roman fort, as well as footpaths, pubs and a YHA hostel. Manchester's latest, **The Lowry**, is an eye-catching complex on Salford Quay encapsulating two theatres and a number of galleries. Take the Metrolink to either Broadway or Harbour City.

Places to Stay

The ***Youth Hostel (*** *839 9960)*, across the road from the Museum of Science & Industry in the Castlefield area, has comfortable four-bed rooms for £17.40 per person.

From mid-June to mid-September, the University of Manchester lets students' rooms to visitors from around £12.25 per person. Contact **St Anselm Hall** (☎ 224 7327) or **Woolaton Hall** (☎ 224 7244).

Newly opened **Woodies Backpackers** (☎ 228 3456, 19 Blossom St), 10 minutes walk north-east of Piccadilly Gardens, is comfortable and offers Internet access; dorm beds are £12 per night.

Commercial Hotel (☎ 834 3504, 125 Liverpool Rd, Castlefield) is a smartly renovated traditional pub close to the museum. Singles/doubles are £25/40. Otherwise the TIC books B&Bs (£2.50).

Places to Eat
The most distinctive restaurant zones are Chinatown in the city centre and Rusholme in the south. Chinatown is bounded by Charlotte, Portland, Oxford and Mosley Sts; the most acclaimed spot is the semi-pricey **Little Yang Sing** (17 George St). Rusholme is to the south of the university on Wilmslow Rd, the extension of Oxford St/Rd, and has numerous popular, cheap and good Indian/Pakistani places. **Darbar** (☎ 224 4392, 65-67 Wilmslow Rd) is not only cheap (student discounts) but exceptionally good; most mains are between £6.50 and £6.90. Bring your own booze.

Cafe-bars have taken off in a big way in Manchester. **Dry 201** (28 Oldham St) and **Manto** (46 Canal St) are among the best.

Entertainment
One of the best venues for live music is **Band on the Wall** (☎ 832 6625), Swan St, which has an eclectic variety of acts from jazz, blues and folk to pop. The **Lass O'Gowrie**, on Charles St, off Oxford St, is a popular student hang-out, with an excellent small brewery on the premises. Two historic pubs are the **Old Wellington Inn** and **Sinclairs Oyster Bar** at the top of New Cathedral St.

Canal St is the centre of Manchester's enormous gay nightlife scene – there are over 20 bars and clubs in the so-called 'Gay Village'. **Paradise Factory** (☎ 273 5422, 112 Princess St) is a cutting edge club, with gay nights at the weekend.

Getting There & Away
There are numerous coach links with the rest of the country. National Express operates out of Chorlton St station in the city centre to pretty well anywhere you'll want to go. Piccadilly is the main train station, though Victoria serves Halifax and Bradford. The two stations are linked by Metrolink. Phone ☎ 0845-748 4950 for information.

Getting Around
For general inquiries about local transport, phone ☎ 228 7811. Frequent Metrolink light-railway trams link Victoria and Piccadilly train stations and G-Mex (for Castlefield). Buy tickets from machines on the platforms.

CHESTER
☎ 01244
Despite steady streams of tourists Chester remains a beautiful town, built in a bow formed by the River Dee and ringed by an unbroken, red sandstone **city wall** that dates back to the Romans. The 3.2km walk along the top of the wall is the best way to see the town – allow a few hours to include detours down to the river and a visit to the **cathedral**, built between 1250 and 1540 (£2). The **Dewa Roman Experience**, Pierpoint Lane, off Bridge St, aims to show what life was like in Roman times (£3.95/2.25).

Orientation & Information
The train station is a 15-minute walk from the town centre – go up City Rd and turn right onto Foregate at the large roundabout. From the bus station, turn left onto Northgate St.

The TIC (☎ 402111) is in the town hall opposite the cathedral. There's a second TIC just outside Newgate opposite the Roman amphitheatre, and another at the train station. There are excellent guided walks around the city every day at 10.30 and 10.45 am (£3).

Places to Stay
The **Youth Hostel** (☎ 680056, 40 Hough Green) is over 1.5km from the centre and on the opposite side from the train station. Leave by Grosvenor Rd past the castle on your left, cross the river and turn right at the roundabout. Beds cost £10.85.

There are numerous good-value B&Bs along Hoole Rd, the road into the city from the M53/M56. **Bawn Park Hotel** (☎ 324971) at No 10 is typical. **Aplas Guest House**

(☎ *312401, 106 Brook St*) is a five-minute walk from the train station. Both have rooms starting at £17.

Places to Eat

Chester's pubs have good, basic food at reasonable prices. Try *Watergates* on Watergate or *Pied Bull* on Northgate. The fine Edwardian *Albion Inn* serves reliable English food without chips or fry-ups. The atmospheric *cathedral refectory* serves soup for £1.95, and another good place for a light lunch is *Katie's Tea Rooms*, spread over three floors of a historic building in Watergate St. *Alexander's Jazz Theatre*, Rufus Court by Northgate, is a wine, coffee and tapas bar with great music.

Getting There & Away

Bus National Express has numerous connections to/from Birmingham (£8.25, 2½ hours), London (£15, 5½ hours), Manchester (£4.50, 1¼ hours), Glasgow (£22.50, six hours), Liverpool (£5, one hour) and Llandudno (£5.50, 1¾ hours). For many destinations in the south or east it will be necessary to change at Birmingham; for the north, change at Manchester.

For information on local bus services ring Chester City Transport (☎ 602666). Local buses leave from Market Square behind the town hall.

Train There are numerous trains to Shrewsbury (£5.80, one hour), Manchester (£8.50, one hour), Liverpool (£3), Holyhead (£16.50, two hours) and London's Euston station (£44, three hours). Phone ☎ 0845-748 4950 for details.

LIVERPOOL
☎ 0151

Liverpool's strong sense of identity is closely tied up with the Beatles, the Liverpool and Everton football teams, and the Grand National horse race, run at Aintree since 1839.

Liverpool's contrast between grandeur and decay – decrepit streets and boarded-up windows, massive cathedrals and imperious buildings – creates some of the most arresting sights in Britain. On weekends the centre vibrates to music from countless pubs and clubs, a vivid testimony to the perverse exhilaration of the city's decline.

Orientation

Lime St, the main train station, is just to the east of the city centre. The National Express coach station is on the corner of Norton and Islington Sts in the north of the city. The bus station is in the centre on Paradise St. Although the main hazard is likely to be over-friendly drunks, it's best to avoid dark side streets even in the city centre.

Information

The main TIC (☎ 709 5111) is in Queen Square Centre. There's also a branch at Albert Dock (☎ 708 8854). Both can book accommodation.

The NMGM Eight Pass (£3) covers admission to six central attractions – Liverpool Museum, Walker Art Gallery, Merseyside Maritime Museum, HM Customs & Excise National Museum, Museum of Liverpool Life and the new Conservation Centre. It's valid for 12 months and is on sale at all the museums.

Things to See & Do

In the 1980s the derelict **Albert Dock** was restored. It has since become a deservedly popular tourist attraction housing several outstanding modern museums – the **Merseyside Maritime Museum**, **Museum of Liverpool Life** and the **Tate Gallery Liverpool**, as well as shops and restaurants. The tacky **Beatles Story** is disappointing.

The **Western Approaches Museum**, the secret command centre for the Battle of the Atlantic, was buried under yards of concrete behind the town hall in Rumford Square. At the end of the war the bunker was abandoned, with virtually everything left intact (£4.75, closed Friday and Sunday).

Organised Tours

There are numerous sites around Liverpool associated with the Beatles, all of whom grew up here. Both TICs sell tickets to the Magical Mystery Tour (£10.95), a 2¼-hour bus trip taking in homes, schools, venues, Penny Lane, Strawberry Fields and more. It departs daily from the Albert Dock TIC at 2.20 pm, and from the main TIC at 2.30 pm.

The ferry across the Mersey (£1.05), made famous by Gerry & the Pacemakers, offers one of the best views of Liverpool. Boats depart from the Pier Head ferry terminal, to the north of Albert Dock and next to the Liver Building. One-hour cruises run daily year round (£3.50). Phone ☎ 639 0609 for schedules.

Places to Stay

The new *Youth Hostel* (☎ 248 5647, 25 Tabley St) is right across the road from Albert Dock. Beds cost £17.40.

The excellent *Embassie Youth Hostel* (☎ 707 1089, 1 Falkner Square), to the west of the Anglican Cathedral, has dorm beds from £11.50.

The *University of Liverpool* (☎ 794 3298, Mulberry Court), on Oxford St, near the Metropolitan Cathedral, has self-catering rooms for £16 a head.

The *Aachen Hotel* (☎ 709 3477, 89 Mount Pleasant), between the city centre and the Metropolitan Cathedral, has rooms, mostly with showers, for £34/40. The smaller and more basic *Belvedere* (☎ 709 2356, 83 Mount Pleasant) has beds from £18.50.

Places to Eat

There are lots of places to eat down Bold St in the city centre. At the eastern end of this street is *Cafe Tabac*, No 124, a relaxed wine bar that attracts a young crowd. *Everyman Bistro* (5 Hope St), underneath the famous Everyman Theatre, is recommended for its good cheap food and its atmosphere. The *refectory* at the Anglican Cathedral serves hot lunches for around £4.

Entertainment

Get hold of *In Touch*, a free monthly entertainment guide. *Everyman Theatre* (☎ 709 4776) is one of the best repertory theatres in the country. Wander around Mathew St and south-west to Bold, Seel and Slater Sts and you'll stumble on an amazing array of clubs and pubs catering to every style you can imagine. A re-creation of the Beatles-era *Cavern Club* (☎ 236 1964) on Mathew St attracts a big crowd. Phone for opening times.

Getting There & Away

There are National Express services linking Liverpool to most major towns. Numerous InterCity rail services run to Lime St station.

LAKE DISTRICT

The Lake District is arguably the most beautiful corner of England – a combination of green dales, rocky mountains and lakes that multiply the scenery with their reflections. The Cumbrian Mountains are not particularly high – none reach 1000m – but they're much more dramatic than their height would suggest.

Unfortunately, there are over 10 million visitors a year. The crowds are so intense it's questionable whether it's worth visiting on any weekend between May and October, or any time at all from mid-July to the end of August. Good times to visit are weekdays in May, June, September and October.

The two main bases for the Lake District are Keswick in the north (particularly for walkers) and the tourist conurbation of Bowness/Windermere in the south. Kendal and Coniston are less hectic alternatives. All these towns have hostels, numerous B&Bs and places to eat.

The Lake District is William Wordsworth country, and his houses at Grasmere (Dove Cottage; ☎ 015394-35544) and Rydal (☎ 015394-33002) are literary shrines.

Information

Both Windermere and Keswick have decent TICs with free booking services. The free paper, *Explorer*, available from TICs, gives bus and boat timetable details for Cumbria and the lakes. If you're staying more than a day or so, buy a copy of *A Walk Round the Lakes* by Hunter Davies. There are almost 30 YHA hostels in the region, many of which can be linked by foot. Look for the *Lake District Youth Hostellers' Walking Guide*.

George Fisher (☎ 017687-72178), Lake Rd, Keswick, is a great hiking-walking shop with equipment and information.

Getting There & Away

There are two National Express buses a day from Manchester via Preston (three hours) and on to Keswick. There's also a service from London via Birmingham and on to Keswick (seven hours), and a train service from Manchester airport to Windermere (two hours).

Stagecoach Cumberland (☎ 0870-608 2608) runs bus No 555, which links Lancaster with Carlisle via Kendal, Windermere, Ambleside, Grasmere and Keswick. Bus No 505/506 (the Coniston Rambler) runs from Bowness Pier to Coniston via the Steamboat Museum, Brockhole, Ambleside and Hawkshead. Ask about Day Ranger and Explorer tickets.

Windermere is at the end of a spur off the main railway line between London's Euston station and Glasgow. For Windermere, change at Oxenholme.

Windermere & Bowness
☎ 015394

Thanks to the railway, the Windermere/Bowness conglomerate is the largest tourist town in the Lake District. The town is quite strung out, with Windermere a 30-minute uphill walk from Bowness on the lakeside. The excellent TIC (☎ 46499), Victoria St, is conveniently near the train station at the northern end of town.

Within spitting distance of the train station, *Lake District Backpackers Lodge* (☎ 46374), on High St, has dorm beds for £11. *Windermere Youth Hostel* (☎ 43543, *High Cross, Bridge Lane, Troutbeck*) is 3.2km from the station. Numerous buses run past Troutbeck Bridge and in summer the hostel sends a minibus to meet trains.

Windermere is wall-to-wall B&Bs, most of them costing about £16 a night. Most of the restaurants are in Bowness near the lake. *Miller Howe Café*, in the Lakeland Limited factory shop behind the train station, serves surprisingly nice cakes. *Millers* (☎ 43877, *31 Crescent Rd*) offers a standard, cheapish tourist menu while *Gibby's*, a few doors down, is cheap and filling.

Keswick
☎ 017687

Keswick is an important walking centre, with a beautiful lake. The *Youth Hostel* (☎ 72484), open most of the year, has beds for £10.85 and is a short walk down Station Rd from the TIC (☎ 72645).

Coniston
☎ 015394

Though still a tourist town, Coniston is decidedly less busy than Keswick or Windermere, probably because it's slightly less accessible by public transport. The TIC (☎ 41533) is open daily in summer and weekends in winter.

There are two excellent YHA hostels near the town. *Holly How Youth Hostel* (☎ 41323), just north of Coniston on the Ambleside Rd, is open daily over Easter and from late June to mid-September; phone for other opening times. The marginally cheaper *Coppermines* (☎ 41261) is 1.6km along the minor road between the Black Bull Hotel and the Co-op, but is often closed on Sunday and Monday.

Kendal
☎ 01539

On the eastern outskirts of the Lake District National Park, Kendal is a lively town with several interesting museums. The TIC (☎ 725758) is in the Town Hall in Highgate.

To the south of town on the banks of the River Kent are the excellent **Museum of Lakeland Life** and the **Abbot Hall Art Gallery**. The museum has reconstructed period shops and rooms, a model of a local mine and information on lost local industries. Entry to each is £3.

Kendal Youth Hostel (☎ 724066, 118 *Highgate*) is open daily from mid-April to August, closing on Sunday and Monday at other times. Beds are £12.80/9.65. Next door is the *Brewery*, an arts complex with a theatre, cinema and bar-bistro. Soup of the day is £2.95 and dishes such as seared tuna with salsa verde go for £8.25.

CARLISLE
☎ 01228

The unsettled history of Carlisle (it changed hands between England and Scotland 13 times) is well represented in its 11th-century **Castle** and **Tullie House Museum** (☎ 534781) which reveals much on the Border Reivers, bandits who rampaged around the border areas during the Middle Ages. The TIC in the old town hall (☎ 625600) offers a free accommodation booking service for Cumbria.

The University halls double as the *Carlisle Youth Hostel* (☎ 597352) from early July to early September in the Old Brewery Residences on Bridge Lane. A bed costs £12.50. There are plenty of comfortable and accessible B&Bs for around £16, especially along Warwick Rd; from the station, cross Butchergate, walk around the crescent and it's on your right.

There are numerous National Express (☎ 0870-580 8080) services, including buses to London, Glasgow and Manchester. Carlisle is the terminus for five famous scenic railways; phone ☎ 0845-748 4950 for information. There are 15 trains a day to Carlisle from London's Euston station.

Scotland

Despite its official union with England in 1707, Scotland maintains an independent national identity that extends considerably further than the occasional kilt and bagpipes. With few exceptions the country is beautiful and the Highlands are exceptional. It's hardly a secret, but for a region that has some of the world's most dramatic scenery, it's curiously under-appreciated.

FACTS ABOUT SCOTLAND
History
It's believed that the earliest settlement of Scotland was undertaken by hunters and fishers 6000 years ago. They were followed by the Celtic Picts, whose loose tribal organisation survived to the 18th century in the clan structure of the Highlands. They never bowed to the Romans, who retreated and built Hadrian's Wall. Another Celtic tribe, the Gaels (Scotti), arrived from northern Ireland (Scotia) in the 6th century. By the time the Normans arrived, most of Scotland was loosely united under the Canmore dynasty.

Despite almost continuous border warfare, it wasn't until a dispute over the Canmore succession that England's Edward I attempted the conquest of Scotland. Beginning with the siege of Berwick in 1296, fighting finally ended in 1328 with the Treaty of Northampton, which recognised Robert the Bruce as king of an independent Scotland. Robert, more Norman than Scottish in his ancestry, cemented an alliance with France that would complicate the political map for almost 400 years.

In 1371 the Scottish kingship passed to the Fitzalan family. The Fitzalans had served William the Conqueror and his descendants as High Stewards, and Stewart (changed to Stuart following Mary's accession) became the dynasty's name.

In 1542 Scotland's James V died, leaving his two-week-old daughter Mary to be proclaimed queen. Henry VIII of England decided she would make a suitable daughter-in-law, and his armies ravaged the Borders and sacked Edinburgh in a failed attempt to force agreement from the Scots (the 'Rough Wooing').

At 15, Mary married the French dauphin and duly became Queen of France as well as Scotland. Mary was later forced to abdicate in favour of her son, James VI. Mary was imprisoned but escaped and fled to England's Queen Elizabeth (her cousin), who locked her in the Tower of London. Nineteen years later, at the age of 44, Mary was beheaded for allegedly plotting Elizabeth's death. When the childless Elizabeth died in 1603, Mary's son united the two crowns for the first time as James VI of Scotland and James I of England.

In 1707, after complex bargaining (and buying a few critical votes), England's government persuaded the Scottish Parliament to agree to the union of the two countries under a single parliament. The Scots received trading privileges and retained their independent church and legal system. The decision was unpopular from the start, and the exiled Stuarts promised to repeal it.

Jacobites (Stuart supporters) led two major rebellions, first in 1715 then in 1745, when Bonnie Prince Charlie failed to extend his support beyond the Catholic Highland clans. The Jacobite cause was finally buried at the Battle of Culloden (1746), after which the English set out to destroy the clans, prohibiting Highland dress, weapons and military service.

In the mid-19th century overpopulation, the collapse of the kelp industry, the 1840s potato famine and the increased grazing of sheep by the lairds (landowning aristocrats) led to the Highland Clearances. After WWI Scotland's ship, steel, coal, cotton and jute industries began to fail, and, though there was a recovery during the Second World War, since the 1960s they have been in terminal decline.

In the 1970s and 80s, North Sea oil — Scottish oil, as many will tell you — gave the economy a boost. Despite the bonanza, Thatcherism failed to impress the Scots. From 1979 to 1997, Scotland was ruled by a Conservative government for which the majority of Scots didn't vote. Following the Labour Party's May 1997 electoral victory, voters in a referendum chose overwhelmingly in favour of the creation of a Scottish Parliament, which began sitting in Edinburgh in 1999.

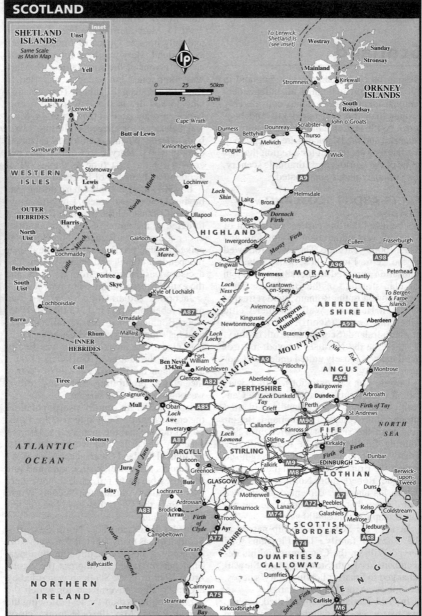

SCOTLAND

SHETLAND ISLANDS
Same Scale as Main Map
Inset

Unst
Yell
Mainland
Lerwick
Sumburgh

To Lerwick, Shetland Is (see inset)

Westray
Mainland
Stromness
Kirkwall
Sanday
Stronsay
ORKNEY ISLANDS
South Ronaldsay
John o'Groats

Cape Wrath
Durness
Bettyhill
Dounreay
Scrabster
Thurso
Butt of Lewis
Kinlochbervie
Melvich
Tongue
Wick

WESTERN ISLES
Stornoway
Lewis
Lochinver
Loch Shin
Lairg
Brora
Helmsdale
A9

Tarbert
OUTER HEBRIDES
Harris
Ullapool
Bonar Bridge
Dornoch Firth

North Uist
Gairloch
Loch Maree
HIGHLAND
Invergordon
Cullen
Fraserburgh

Benbecula
Uig
Dingwall
Moray Firth
Forres Elgin
A96
A98

South Uist
Portree
Skye
Kyle of Lochalsh
Inverness
MORAY
Huntly
Peterhead

Lochboisdale
Loch Ness
Grantown-on-Spey
To Bergen & Faroe Islands

Barra
Armadale
A87
Aviemore
Spey
ABERDEEN SHIRE
Aberdeen
A93

RHUM
INNER HEBRIDES
Mallaig
Loch Lochy
Kingussie
Newtonmore
Cairngorm Mountains
Braemar

Coll
Ben Nevis 1343m
Fort William
Kinlochleven
Glencoe
A82
MOUNTAINS
Pitlochry
ANGUS
Montrose

Tiree
Lismore
A85
Oban
Loch Awe
Aberfeldy
Blairgowrie
A94
Arbroath

Craignure
Mull
Inveraray
A83
Loch Dunkeld Tay
Crieff
Dundee
Firth of Tay
St Andrews

Colonsay
Callander
Kinross
Perth
NORTH SEA

ATLANTIC OCEAN
Loch Lomond
Stirling
FIFE
Kirkaldy

Dunoon
Greenock
M90
Firth of Forth
Dunbar

ARGYLL
STIRLING
Falkirk
M9
EDINBURGH
M8
LOTHIAN
Berwick-upon-Tweed

Jura
Lochranza
GLASGOW
Motherwell
A7
Duns

Islay
Bute
Ardrossan
Brodick
Arran
Kilmarnock
Lanark
A72
Peebles
Kelso
Coldstream

Campbeltown
Firth of Clyde
Troon
Ayr
SCOTTISH BORDERS
Galashiels
Melrose
Jedburgh
A68

Girvan
AYRSHIRE
A77
DUMFRIES & GALLOWAY
A74

Ballycastle
Cairnryan
Dumfries

NORTHERN IRELAND
Larne
Stranraer
Luce Bay
Kirkcudbright
A75
Solway Firth
Carlisle
M6

ENGLAND

North Minch
Little Minch
Sound of Jura
North Channel
GREAT GLEN
GRAMPIAN
A9
Nith Est.

0 25 50km
0 15 30mi

Language

Scotland's five-million-plus people speak three main languages. Gaelic is spoken by some 80,000 people, mainly in the Highlands and Islands, and is undergoing a revival. Lallans or Lowland Scots is spoken in the south. Then there's English, which the Scottish accent can make almost impenetrable to the *Sassenach* (the English or Lowland Scots) and other foreigners.

FACTS FOR THE VISITOR
Planning

When to Go Whenever you visit Scotland, you're likely to see both sun and rain. The best time to visit is May to September. April and October are also acceptable weather risks, although many businesses close in October. In winter the weather's cold and daylight hours are short but Edinburgh and Glasgow are still worth visiting. Travel in the islands can be a problem in winter because high winds easily disrupt ferries.

Tourist Offices

The Scottish Tourist Board (STB; ☎ 0131-332 2433, fax 0131-315 4545) has its headquarters at 23 Ravelston Terrace (PO Box 705), Edinburgh EH4 3EU; their Web site is at www.visitscotland.com. In London, the STB (☎ 020-7930 8661), 19 Cockspur St, London SW1 5BL, off Trafalgar Square, can suggest routes and make reservations.

In small places, particularly in the Highlands, TICs only open Easter to September.

Money

The same currency is valid both sides of the border; however, the Clydesdale Bank, the Royal Bank of Scotland and the Bank of Scotland print their own pound notes. You won't have any trouble changing Scottish notes immediately south of the Scotland-England border, but elsewhere it's best to change them at banks.

Useful Organisations

Historic Scotland (HS; ☎ 0131-668 8800), Longmore House, Salisbury Place, Edinburgh EH9 1SH, offers short-term 'Explorer' membership – three/seven/14 days for £10/15/20. Check out their Web site at www.historic-scotland.gov.uk.

The National Trust for Scotland (NTS; ☎ 0131-226 5922), 28 Charlotte Square,

Edinburgh EH2 4ET, cares for more than 100 historic buildings. YHA/SYHA members and student-card-holders get half-price entry to its properties. Their Web site is at www.nts.org.uk.

Accommodation

You can camp free on all public land (unless it's specifically protected). Commercial camping grounds are geared to caravans and vary widely in quality, but usually have tent sites for £5 to £10.

The Scottish Youth Hostel Association (SYHA; ☎ 01786-891400, fax 01786-891333, ℮ syha@syha.org.uk), 7 Glebe Crescent, Stirling FK8 2JA, produces a handbook (£1.50) that gives details on over 70 hostels it operates, including transport links. SYHA hostels are supplemented by independent hostels and bunkhouses. The *Independent Hostel Guide Budget Accommodation* is available from some TICs.

B&Bs and small hotels are generally cheaper than their English counterparts; you're unlikely to pay more than £20 a head. TICs have local booking services (usually £1 or £2) and a Book-a-Bed-Ahead scheme (£3).

GETTING THERE & AWAY
Air

There are direct services from many European cities to Edinburgh, Glasgow, Dundee, Aberdeen and Inverness, and from North America to Glasgow. Coming from overseas it's often more economical to buy a cheap fare to London then take a train to Scotland. The standard return airfare from London to Glasgow or Edinburgh is around £275, but discount return flights can be as low as £70 and there are often no-frills special deals from companies like Easyjet (☎ 0870-600 0000) and Go (☎ 0845-605 4321).

Bus

Long-distance buses are usually the cheapest method of getting to Scotland. The main operator is Scottish Citylink (☎ 0870-550 5050), part of National Express, with services from London and cities throughout England and Wales. From London to Glasgow or Edinburgh, advance-purchase tickets cost from £19/24 single/return with Silver Choice (☎ 020-7730 3466).

Train

InterCity services (☎ 0845-748 4950) can take you from London's King's Cross to Edinburgh in as little as 4½ hours or to Glasgow in 5½ hours. With Virgin Trains the cheapest adult return ticket between London and Edinburgh or Glasgow is the Virgin Value seven-day advance ticket, which costs only £29. This compares with the standard open return fare of £175.

Boat

For more details on ferry services see the Getting There & Away section at the start of this chapter.

Northern Ireland P&O (☎ 0870-242 4666 for Irish services) has ferry links from Cairnryan to Larne, near Belfast. Seacat (☎ 0870-552 3523) runs a high-speed catamaran between Belfast, Stranraer and Troon; see the Web site at www.steam-packet .com. The Argyll & Antrim Steam Packet Company (☎ 0870-552 3523) also runs a ferry from Campbeltown in Argyll to Ballycastle in County Antrim.

Scandinavia From mid May to early September, P&O/Smyril Line (☎ 01224-572615) operates between Lerwick (Shetland Islands), Bergen (Norway), Tórshavn (Faroe Islands) and Seydisfjördur (Iceland) calling at Lerwick twice weekly; check out their Web site at www.smyril-line.fo. To make a fascinating northern sea route, you could link this ferry service with P&O services to Stromness (Orkney Islands), Scrabster (near Thurso) or Aberdeen.

GETTING AROUND

If you're not a student, it's worth considering ScotRail's Freedom of Scotland Travelpass, available from the British Travel Centre in Regent St, London, and most staffed train stations in Scotland.

The pass gives unlimited travel on Scot-Rail trains; Caledonia MacBrayne (Cal-Mac) ferries and Strathclyde Public Transport (SPT) ferries; a 33% discount on postbuses and selected regional bus routes with Scottish Citylink, Fife Scottish and First Edinburgh; a 33% discount on P&O Orkney (Stromness) to Scrabster ferry; and a 20% discount on P&O Aberdeen to Shetland and Aberdeen to Orkney.

The Travelpass costs £79 for four days' travel out of eight consecutive days, £109 for 8 days out of 15, and £119 for 12 days out of 15.

Bus

Scotland's major player is Scottish Citylink (☎ 0870-550 5050), part of the National Express group; their Web site is at www.citylink.co.uk. There are also smaller regional operators many of which form part of the Stagecoach or First networks. On most Citylink lines discounts of up to 30% are available to full-time students and people under the age of 26 with the so-called Smart Card (£5), sold at most ticket counters; you'll need proof of age or student status and a passport photo.

From June to September, Haggis Backpackers (☎ 0131-557 9393 ⓔ haggis@ radicaltravel.com), 60 High St, Edinburgh, operates a daily service between hostels in Edinburgh, Pitlochry, Inverness, Loch Ness, Ullapool, Isle of Skye, Fort William, Glencoe, Oban, Loch Lomond and Glasgow, finishing back in Edinburgh. You can hop on and off the minibus wherever and whenever you like. There's no compulsion to stay in hostels either. Bus fares start at £85.

Go Blue Banana (☎ 0131-220 6868), Suite 8, North Bridge House, 28 North Bridge, Edinburgh, also runs a jump-on, jump-off service on a similar circuit for the same price. Both offer excellent three-day Highlands tours (£79) from Edinburgh.

Train

ScotRail (☎ 0845-748 4950) operates Scotland's trains, which travel on some incredibly scenic routes – from Stirling to Inverness, Inverness to Thurso and Inverness to Kyle of Lochalsh – but they're limited and expensive; see their Web site at www.scotrail.co.uk.

Inter-Rail passes (but not Eurail) are valid in Scotland. The BritRail pass, which includes Scotland, must be bought outside Britain. ScotRail's Freedom of Scotland Travelpass and its regional Rover tickets can be bought in England and at staffed train stations in Scotland. The Highland Rover ticket covers the West Highlands and Aberdeen-Inverness-Kyle line (£49 for four out of eight days).

Boat

Caledonian MacBrayne (CalMac; ☎ 0870-565 0000) is the most important ferry operator on the west coast, with services from Ullapool to the Outer Hebrides, from Mallaig to Skye and on to the Outer Hebrides. Its main west-coast port is Oban, with ferries to the Inner Hebridean islands of Barra, South Uist, Coll, Tiree, Lismore, Mull and Colonsay. CalMac's Island Hopscotch tickets are usually the best deal, with ferry combinations over 20 set routes. CalMac also has Island Rover tickets, offering unlimited travel for eight and 15 days (£42/61). Their useful Web site is at www.calmac.co.uk.

P&O (☎ 01224-574411) has ferries from Aberdeen and Scrabster to Orkney and from Aberdeen to Shetland. There's a 10% student discount; see their Web site at www.poscottishferries.co.uk.

EDINBURGH

☎ 0131

Edinburgh (population 409,000) has an incomparable location, superb architecture (16,000 of the city's buildings are listed as architecturally or historically important), excellent pubs and one of Britain's most dramatic castles. In some ways, however, Edinburgh is the least Scottish of Scotland's cities – partly because of the impact of tourism, partly because of its closeness to England, and partly because of its multicultural and sophisticated population.

The royal capital since the 11th century, all the great dramas of Scottish history played at least one act in Edinburgh. Even after the union of 1707 it remained the centre for government administration (now the Scottish Executive). With devolution and the location of the new Scottish Parliament in Edinburgh, the city once again wields real political power.

Orientation

The most important landmark is Arthur's Seat, the 251m rocky peak south-east of the city. The Old and New Towns are separated by the Princes St Gardens and Waverley train station. The bus station is in the New Town, just off the north-eastern corner of St Andrew Square. Princes St runs west from Calton Hill, which is crowned by several monuments. The Royal Mile (Lawnmarket, High St and Canongate) is the parallel equivalent in the Old Town.

Information

The busy main TIC (☎ 557 1700), Waverley Market, 3 Princes St, opens daily year round. There's also a branch at Edinburgh airport (☎ 338 2167). Both have Scotland-wide information, and sell the useful *Essential Guide to Edinburgh* (£1). Accommodation brochures are free, but it costs £3 to make a booking. Check out the Tourist Board's Web site at www.edinburgh.org.

American Express (☎ 225 7881) is at 139 Princes St. Thomas Cook (☎ 465 7700) is at 26-28 Frederick St. Both close Sunday.

Web 13 Internet Café (☎ 229 8883), 13 Bread St, offers online access for £5 per hour as does Cyberia (☎ 220 4403), 88 Hanover St. Both open daily.

Things to See & Do

Stunning **Edinburgh Castle** (☎ 225 9846) has excellent views of central Edinburgh. The castle is the headquarters of the British army's Scottish Division. The smallest, oldest building is **St Margaret's Chapel**, built in the 12th century. The castle was the seat of Scottish kings, and the royal apartments include the tiny room where Mary Queen of Scots gave birth to the boy who became King James VI of Scotland and James I of England. You can also see the **Stone of Destiny**, returned to Scotland in 1996. It's open 9.30 am to 6 pm daily (to 5 pm October to March); admission is £7.

The castle is at the west end of the **Royal Mile**, which runs down to the Palace of Holyroodhouse (see later in this section). The streetscape is an extraordinary collage of 16th- and 17th-century architecture. On the left, **Gladstone's Land** (closed November to March) and **The Writers' Museum** (Lady Stair's House) are town houses that give insights into urban life of the past.

Turn right onto the George IV Bridge, which crosses Cowgate (an ancient street). **Grassmarket**, below and to the right, has a number of pubs and restaurants. Continue to the angled intersection with Candlemaker Row and **Greyfriars Kirk** (where the National Covenant was signed) with its beautiful old churchyard.

Return to the Royal Mile and turn right past the 15th-century **St Giles' Cathedral**. At the cathedral's rear is **Parliament House**, now the seat of Scotland's supreme law courts. Immediately east of St Giles stands

BRITAIN

CENTRAL EDINBURGH

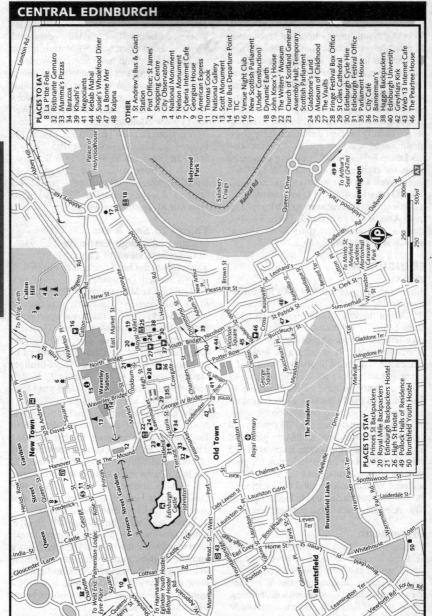

PLACES TO EAT
8 La P'tite Folie
32 Ristorante Gennaro
33 Mamma's Pizzas
34 Baracoa
39 Khushi's
41 Negociants
44 Kebab Mahal
45 Susie's Wholefood Diner
47 La Bonne Mer
48 Kalpna

OTHER
1 St Andrew's Bus & Coach Station
2 Post Office; St James' Shopping Centre
3 City Observatory
4 Nelson Monument
5 National Monument
9 Cyberia Internet Cafe
9 Georgian House
10 American Express
11 Thomas Cook
12 National Gallery
13 Scott Monument
14 Tour Bus Departure Point
15 TIC
16 Venue Night Club
17 New Scottish Parliament (Under Construction)
18 Dynamic Earth
19 John Knox's House
21 The Writers' Museum
22 Church of Scotland General Assembly Hall; Temporary Scottish Parliament
24 Gladstone's Land
25 Museum of Childhood
27 The Vaults
28 Fringe Festival Box Office
29 St Giles Cathedral
30 Edinburgh Cycle Hire
31 Edinburgh Festival Office
35 Parliament House
36 City Café
37 Bannerman's
38 Haggis Backpackers
40 Edinburgh University
42 Greyfriars Kirk
43 Web 13 Internet Cafe
46 The Peartree House

PLACES TO STAY
6 Princes St Backpackers
20 Royal Mile Backpackers
21 Edinburgh Backpackers Hostel
26 High St Hostel
49 Pollock Halls of Residence
50 Bruntsfield Youth Hostel

BRITAIN

the **Mercat Cross**, where public proclamations were once made.

Continue down the Royal Mile over North/South Bridge to the free **Museum of Childhood**, with a fascinating collection of toys, and **John Knox's House** (closed Sunday, £2.25), home to the fiery leader of the Scottish Reformation.

At the eastern end of the Royal Mile, the **Palace of Holyroodhouse** is a Stuart palace mostly dating from 1671. Holyroodhouse is the official Scottish residence of the British royal family. Although you're carefully shepherded through a limited part of the palace, it has a certain fascination. It's open daily April to October except when the Queen is in residence (usually around mid-May or mid-June). Admission is £6.

Close to Holyroodhouse, the new **Scottish Parliament** is under construction. Opposite is the **Dynamic Earth** exhibition on the planet's geology and natural history, open daily Easter to October, Wednesday to Sunday the rest of the year (£6.95).

From the palace, turn right and climb Abbey Hill (under the railway overpass). Turn left into Regent Rd, which leads back to Princes St. On the right you pass **Calton Hill** – worth climbing for its superb views across to the castle.

If you're a little thirsty at this stage, **Rose St** to the west is famous for its pubs. From there, continue west to Charlotte Square; on its northern side at No 7 is Robert Adam's masterpiece, the **Georgian House**, restored to its full 18th-century glory. It's open April to October daily (closed Sunday morning, £5).

Special Events

The Edinburgh International Festival, held each year in mid-August, is the world's largest, most important arts festival. The Fringe Festival grew alongside it, presenting would-be future stars. Just to make sure that every bed within 50km is full, the Edinburgh Military Tattoo is held at the same time.

To attend the International Festival you must book ahead. The program, published in April, is available from the Edinburgh Festival Office (☎ 473 2000), The Hub, Castlehill, Royal Mile, EH1 2NE, or on their Web site at www.eif.co.uk. The Fringe Festival is less formal, and many performances have seats available at the last minute. Programs are available from the

Festival Fringe Society (☎ 226 5257), 180 High St EH1 1QS, or on the Web site at www.edfringe.com.

Hogmanay, the Scottish celebration of the New Year, is another major Edinburgh fixture – book accommodation well ahead if you want to be part of the fun.

Places to Stay

Edinburgh has numerous accommodation options, but the city fills quickly at New Year and Easter, and from mid-May to mid-September (particularly August). Book in advance if possible, or use the accommodation services that are run by the TIC or Thomas Cook.

Other than hostels, the best budget choice is a private room in a suburban family home. Get the TIC's free accommodation guide and make some phone calls. The going rate (outside festival time) is £20 per person.

Camping The *Mortonhall Caravan Park (☎ 664 1533, 38 Mortonhall Gate)*, off Frogston Rd East, 5 miles south-east of the centre, opens March to October. Sites are £8.25 to £12.75.

SYHA Hostels The *Eglinton Youth Hostel (☎ 337 1120, 18 Eglinton Crescent)* is less than 2km west of the city near the Haymarket train station; beds cost £12.75/11.25 for seniors/juniors. Walk down Princes St and continue on Shandwick Place (which becomes West Maitland St), veer right at Haymarket along Haymarket Terrace, and turn right onto Coates Gardens (which runs into Eglinton Crescent).

Bruntsfield Youth Hostel (☎ 447 2994, 7 Bruntsfield Crescent), about 4km south of Waverley train station, is trickier to find. Catch bus No 11 or 16 from the garden side of Princes St and alight at Forbes Rd, just after the gardens on the left. Beds are £11.75/10.50.

Independent Hostels Edinburgh's most popular hostel is the friendly, central *High St Hostel (☎ 557 3984, 8 Blackfriars St)*, where beds are £10.50. Nearby is the *Royal Mile Backpackers (☎ 557 6120, 105 High St)* and *Edinburgh Backpackers Hostel (☎ 220 1717, 65 Cockburn St)*, both £11.50.

Princes St Backpackers (☎ 556 6894, 5 West Register St) has an equally good location

BRITAIN

– behind Princes St and close to the bus station – but 77 exhausting steps to reach reception. Dorm beds are £9.50, doubles £24 (Sunday dinner is free!).

Belford Hostel (☎ *225 6209, 6 Douglas Gardens*) is a well-run, cheerful hostel in a converted church. Dorm beds are £11.50, doubles £33.

Quiet *Palmerston Lodge* (☎ *220 5141, 25 Palmerston Place*), on the corner of Chester St, is a former boarding school with dorm beds for £12 and up, singles/doubles with bath for £30/40.

During university vacations the *Pollock Halls of Residence* (☎ *667 0662, 18 Holyrood Park Rd*) has modern (often noisy) singles/doubles for £25/48, including breakfast.

B&Bs The *Ardenlee Guest House* (☎ *556 2838, 9 Eyre Place*), north of the New Town 1.6km from the centre, has rooms from £26 per person, while *Dene Guest House* (☎ *556 2700, 7 Eyre Place*) does B&B from £19.50.

Pilrig St, left off Leith Walk (veer left at the eastern end of Princes St), is a happy hunting ground for guesthouses. *Balmoral Guest House* (☎ *554 1857*), at No 32, has easy access to the city and rooms from £20 to £30 per person. *Barrosa* (☎ *554 3700*), at No 21, charges £22/32 per person without/with bath. At No 94, the attractive *Balquhidder Guest House* (☎ *554 3377*) has rooms with bath from £20 to £40 a head.

There are numerous guesthouses on and around Minto St/Mayfield Gardens in Newington, south of the centre, accessed by plenty of buses. This is the main traffic artery from the south and carries traffic from the A7 and A68 (both routes are signposted). Nonsmoking *Salisbury Guest House* (☎ *667 1264, 45 Salisbury Rd*), east of Newington and 10 minutes from the centre by bus, is quiet and comfortable. Singles/doubles with bath cost £25 to £48 per person. *Casa Buzzo* (☎ *667 8998, 8 Kilmaurs Rd*), east of Dalkeith Rd, has doubles for £20 per person.

Places to Eat

The pubs and restaurants on the northern side of Grassmarket cater to a mixed crowd. *Ristorante Gennaro*, No 64, has standard Italian fare, with pizzas and pastas from £4.80 to £7. Nearby, *Mamma's*, No 30, is an informal, extremely popular pizzeria (£3.95 to £9.95). Exotic *Baracoa* (☎ *225 5846, 7 Victoria St*) is a Cuban restaurant and bar, serving tasty, filling mains for under £10.

La P'tite Folie (*61 Frederick St*) offers reasonably priced, good-quality French food. Most mains are under £10. *La Bonne Mer* (*113 Beccleuch St*) specialises in seafood with a French twist. A three-course meal costs £17.95.

The university area – between Nicolson St and Bristo Place at the end of the George IV Bridge – has a few budget favourites. Legendary *Kebab Mahal* (*7 Nicolson Square*) has kebabs from £2.95, curries from £3.25. *Susie's Wholefood Diner* (*51 West Nicolson St*) serves good, inexpensive, healthy (mostly vegetarian) food – and has a belly dancer in the evenings. *Negociants* (*45-7 Lothian St*) is a cool cafe and music venue, with good-value food (mains from £6.75). It opens 9 am until late daily.

Kalpna (☎ *667 9890, 2 St Patrick's Square*), a highly acclaimed, reasonably priced Gujarati (Indian) vegetarian restaurant, offers filling lunch buffets for £5. A cheap, eccentric possibility is *Khushi's* (*16 Drummond St*), Edinburgh's original curry house. Lamb bhuna (£4.95) is the local favourite, and you can bring your own booze. It takes cash only and is closed Sunday.

Entertainment

The *List* (£1.95) is a fortnightly guide to films, theatre, cabaret and music in Edinburgh and Glasgow.

There are several busy pubs on Grassmarket's northern side, often with live music. Turn up Cowgate, off Grassmarket's southeast, for the more relaxed *Bannerman's*. For the long summer evenings *The Peartree House*, on West Nicolson St, has a large outdoor courtyard. There are some interesting music/club venues in old vaults under the George IV and South bridges – try the *Vaults* (*15 Niddry St*) under South Bridge.

City Café (*19 Blair St*) is a cool, 1950s US-style bar and diner. *Venue Night Club* (*17 Calton Rd*) has dance music and is worth checking out.

Getting There & Away

See also the Getting There & Away and Getting Around sections earlier in this chapter.

Bus Fares from London are competitive, so shop around. National Express (☎ 0870-580 8080) and Scottish Citylink (☎ 0870-550 5050) are the main operators. The journey time is 9½ to 11¼ hours depending on the route, and the cheapest fare with National Express is £22 one way. There are links to cities throughout England and Wales, including Newcastle (2¾ hours) and York (5½ hours).

Scottish Citylink has buses to virtually every major town in Scotland. Most west-coast buses travel via Glasgow (£5 return).

Train There are 20 trains a day from London's King's Cross station (4½ to 5½ hours).

ScotRail has two northern lines from Edinburgh: one cuts north across the Grampians to Inverness (3½ hours) and on to Thurso, and the other follows the coast around to Aberdeen (three hours) and on to Inverness. There are trains every 15 to 20 minutes to Glasgow (£7.30, 50 minutes).

For rail inquiries, call ☎ 0845-748 4950.

Getting Around
Bus The two main companies, Lothian Regional Transport (LRT; ☎ 555 6363) and First Edinburgh (☎ 663 9233) provide frequent, cheap services. For short trips in the city, fares are 50p to £1. After midnight there are special night buses. The free *Edinburgh Travelmap* is available from the TIC, or on weekdays contact Traveline (☎ 225 3858 or 0800-232323), 2 Cockburn St.

Bicycle Edinburgh Cycle Hire (☎ 556 5560, ✉ info@cyclescotland.co.uk), 29 Blackfriars St, hires out mountain and hybrid bikes for £10 to £15 a day.

GLASGOW
☎ 0141
Glasgow, with a population of nearly 620,000, is one of Britain's largest, most interesting cities. Though it's not as instantly attractive as Edinburgh, Glasgow has some fine Georgian and Victorian architecture, and a vibrancy and energy that's lacking in more staid Edinburgh.

Glasgow is the most Scottish of cities – a unique blend of friendliness, urban chaos and black humour. There are some excellent art galleries and museums (most free), good-value restaurants, countless pubs and a lively arts scene.

Orientation
The city centre is built on a grid system on the northern side of the River Clyde. The two train stations (Central and Queen St) and Buchanan bus station are within a few blocks of George Square, the main city square. The TIC is on George Square.

Sauchiehall St, running east-west along a ridge in the northern part of the city, has a pedestrian mall with shops at its eastern end, and pubs and restaurants to the west.

Information
Tourist Offices The main TIC (☎ 204 4400), 11 George Square, has an accommodation-booking service (£2) and a bureau de change. It's open 9 am to 6 pm Monday to Saturday, to 7 pm in June and September and 9 am to 8 pm in July and August (plus 10 am to 6 pm Sunday from May to September). The Glasgow Tourist Board has a Web site at www.seeglasgow.com.

Email & Internet Access You can access the Web at the Internet Café (☎ 564 1052), 569 Sauchiehall St, for £3 for 30 minutes. There's also the 24-hour Surfin' Internet Café (☎ 332 0404) at 81 St George's Rd.

Things to See & Do
Most of Glasgow's museums are free and open 10 am to 5 pm daily.

George Square is surrounded by imposing Victorian architecture, including the post office, the Bank of Scotland and, along its eastern side, the extravagant 19th-century **City Chambers**, which offers free tours at 10.30 am and 2.30 pm weekdays.

Glasgow Cathedral, begun in 1238, is regarded as a perfect example of pre-Reformation Gothic architecture. St Mungo, Glasgow's 6th-century founder, is buried here. Beside the cathedral, the excellent **St Mungo Museum of Religious Life & Art** has Dali's *Christ of St John of the Cross*, statues of the Buddha and Hindu deities, and Britain's only Zen garden.

Glasgow has some superb Art Nouveau buildings designed by Scottish architect Charles Rennie Mackintosh. In particular, check out the **Glasgow School of Art** at 167 Renfrew St, which has guided tours from Monday to Saturday (£5/3). At 217 Sauchiehall St is the Mackintosh-designed **Willow Tearoom**.

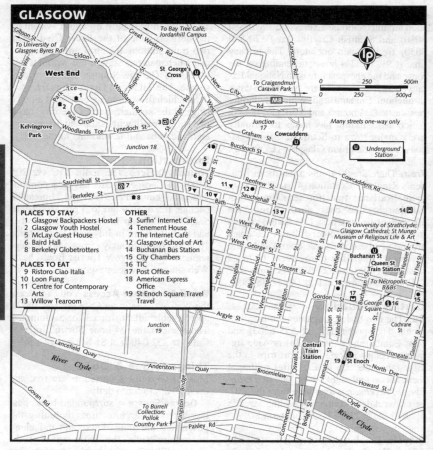

GLASGOW

PLACES TO STAY
1 Glasgow Backpackers Hostel
2 Glasgow Youth Hostel
5 McLay Guest House
6 Baird Hall
8 Berkeley Globetrotters

PLACES TO EAT
9 Ristoro Ciao Italia
10 Loon Fung
11 Centre for Contemporary
 Arts
13 Willow Tearoom

OTHER
3 Surfin' Internet Café
4 Tenement House
7 The Internet Café
12 Glasgow School of Art
14 Buchanan Bus Station
15 City Chambers
16 TIC
17 Post Office
18 American Express
 Office
19 St Enoch Square Travel
 Travel

Tenement House, 145 Buccleuch St,
gives an insight into middle-class life 100
years ago (open March to October, £3.50).

The **Burrell Collection** – from medieval
furniture to paintings by Renoir and
Cézanne – was amassed by a wealthy local
before it was given to the city and housed
in a superb museum in Pollok Country
Park, 5km south of the centre. Catch a train
to Pollokshaws West from Central station,
then walk for 10 minutes through the park.

Special Events
The West End Festival (☎ 341 0844) of
music and the arts runs for two weeks in
June and is Glasgow's biggest festival. The
excellent International Jazz Festival (☎ 400
5000) is held in July.

Places to Stay
Camping The nearest camping ground is
Craigendmuir Caravan Park (☎ 779 4159,
Campsie View, Stepps), 10km north-east of
Glasgow, but it's still a 15-minute walk
from Stepps station. Two-person tent sites
are £8.50.

Hostels The excellent SYHA *Glasgow
Youth Hostel* (☎ 332 3004, 7 Park Terrace)
has four-bed rooms and a few doubles.
Seniors/juniors pay £13.25/11.75 per night;
book ahead in summer. From Central station
take bus No 44 or 59 to the first stop on
Woodlands Rd.

Berkeley Globetrotters (☎ 221 7880, 63
Berkeley St), just past the Mitchell Library,
has dorm beds from £8.50, doubles from

£12.50 per person; book ahead. Berkeley St is a western continuation of Bath St (one block south of Sauchiehall St).

The popular *Glasgow Backpackers Hostel* (☎ 332 5412, *Maclay Hall, 17 Park Terrace*) is in a university residence hall that's open July to September only. Beds start at £10.

Mid-March to mid-April and July to September, the *University of Glasgow* (☎ 330 5385, 3 The Square) has a range of rooms at £13/81 a day/week and B&B accommodation from £30 per head.

The University of Strathclyde (☎ 553 4148, *Cathedral St*) has two popular residence halls: the year-round *Baird Hall* (*460 Sauchiehall St*) has £19/33 singles/doubles with breakfast; and the summer-only *Jordanhill Campus* (*76 Southbrae Drive*) has rooms for £20.50/30, with breakfast. For the latter, take bus No 44 from Central station to the college's gates.

B&Bs Central Renfrew St, to the north of Sauchiehall St, has several places. *McLay Guest House* (☎ 332 4796), No 264, is labyrinthine, but considering the location you can't quibble at £21/27 for a single without/with bathroom, doubles £38/46.

There's a batch of reasonable-value B&Bs east of the Necropolis. *Campsie Guest House* (☎ 554 6797, *2 Onslow Drive*) has decent rooms from £18 per person. *Craigpark Guest House* (☎ 554 4160, 33 Circus Drive) does singles/doubles from £16/28.

Places to Eat

Sauchiehall St has some interesting choices. The *Centre for Contemporary Arts*, No 346, is a performing-arts venue with a well-regarded cafe. *Ristoro Ciao Italia* (*441 Sauchiehall St*) is an efficient Italian restaurant where filling three-course lunches cost only £6.50. *Loon Fung*, at No 417, is one of Glasgow's best Cantonese spots, with set lunches for £6.30.

Willow Tearoom, No 217, has long queues for lunch (last orders at 4.15 pm), but is less busy when it first opens at 9.30 am (noon Sunday). A superior breakfast (served all day) costs £5.30.

The vegetarian *Bay Tree Café* (*403 Great Western Rd*), in the Kelvingrove Park area, serves filling mains (mostly Middle Eastern) for less than £5.

Entertainment

The *List* (£1.95) is an invaluable fortnightly entertainment magazine. There's no shortage of fun places. The centre is where the club action is focused; West Regent and Bath Sts have a plethora of small, subterranean hang outs; and Merchant City is full of larger, hip joints. The West End offers a cool nightlife alternative.

Getting There & Away

Bus Fares from London are competitive. Silver Choice (☎ 333 7133) offers the best deal at £19/24 a single/return to London's Victoria coach station (eight hours). National Express (☎ 0870-580 8080) runs the same route for £20/30, has direct links to Heathrow and Gatwick airports, and serves English cities such as Birmingham (5½ hours), Cambridge (nine hours), Carlisle (two hours), Newcastle (four hours) and York (6½ hours).

Scottish Citylink (☎ 0870-550 5050) has buses to most major towns in Scotland. Most east coast buses travel via Edinburgh (£5, one hour). Other destinations include Stirling (45 minutes), Inverness (3½ hours), Oban (three hours), Aberdeen (four hours), Fort William (three hours) and Skye (6¼ hours). There's a twice-daily service to Stranraer from mid-May to mid-October, connecting with the ferry to Larne in Northern Ireland.

Stagecoach Fife (☎ 01592-642394) operates buses to St Andrews (2¼ hours) and Dundee (2½ hours) via Glenrothes. The return fare to both is £12.50.

First Edinburgh (☎ 01324-613777) runs hourly buses to Milngavie (30 minutes), the start of the West Highland Way.

Train As a general rule, Central Station serves southern Scotland, England and Wales, and Queen St station serves north and east Scotland. There are buses every 10 minutes between the two stations (50p, or free with a through train ticket).

From Central Station there are direct trains to London's Euston and King's Cross stations (five to six hours); see also the Getting There & Away section to Scotland.

ScotRail operates the West Highland line north to Oban and Fort William, and direct links to Dundee, Aberdeen and Inverness. There are trains every 15 minutes to Edinburgh (£7.30 one way, 50 minutes).

For rail inquiries call ☎ 0845-748 4950.

Getting Around

At the St Enoch Square Travel Centre (☎ 226 4826, St Enoch Square), Strathclyde Passenger Transport (STP) provides information on transport in the Glasgow region.

The Roundabout Glasgow ticket (£3.50/ 1.75) covers all public transport for a day; it also entitles you to a £1.50 discount on city bus tours.

There's an extensive suburban rail network – buy tickets at staffed stations or from conductors. There's also an Underground line serving 15 stations in the centre and west (north and south of the river) for 80p one way – a Discovery Pass (£2.50) gives unlimited travel for a day.

SOUTH-WEST SCOTLAND

Billed as Scotland's 'surprising southwest', it's only surprising if you expect magnificent mountain and coastal scenery to be confined to the Highlands.

National Express has coaches from London and Birmingham (via Manchester and Carlisle), and Glasgow/Edinburgh to Stranraer. Stagecoach Western (☎ 01387-253496) provides local bus services. Glasgow to Stranraer by rail is 2½ hours.

Isle of Arran
☎ 01770

Described as 'Scotland in miniature' because of its varied scenery, Arran is an hour's ferry ride from Ardrossan, conveniently accessible from Glasgow.

With 10 peaks over 600m, this is good walking country. A coastal road around the island provides good cycling (watch out for heavy traffic on summer weekends). The TIC (☎ 302140) in **Brodick** (the main town), has details of accommodation on the island. There's little to see here, although **Brodick Castle** is worth visiting. The best base is the peaceful village of **Lochranza**, 22.5km north. *Lochranza Youth Hostel (☎ 830631)* is a great place to stay, with beds for £9.25.

Stranraer & Cairnryan
☎ 01776

Stranraer is more pleasant than the average ferry port, but there's no reason to stay. The bus and train stations, accommodation and TIC are close to the Stena and SeaCat terminals. The TIC (☎ 702595) has regional information and books accommodation. Cairnryan is 8km north of Stranraer on the eastern side of the loch (accessed by bus from Stranraer).

The **Southern Upland Way** starts at Portpatrick about 14.5km south of Stranraer and runs for 340km to Cockburnspath near Berwick-upon-Tweed. It offers varied walking country, but includes some long, demanding stretches. TICs stock guides and maps.

Frequent car and passenger ferries operate between Stranraer and nearby Cairnryan to Larne in Northern Ireland; Stena Line (☎ 0870-570 7070) runs to/from Stranraer and P&O (☎ 08702-424666) to/from Cairnryan. The fastest option is a SeaCat (☎ 0870-552 3523) between Stranraer and Belfast. See Northern Ireland in the Ireland chapter for details.

SOUTH-EAST SCOTLAND

There's a tendency to think that the real Scotland doesn't start until you're north of Perth but the castles, forests and glens of the Scottish Borders have a romance of their own. The region survived centuries of war and plunder and was romantically portrayed by Robert Burns and Sir Walter Scott.

First Edinburgh (☎ 01896-752237), in Galashiels, has numerous buses between Galashiels, Melrose and Edinburgh. First Edinburgh buses also run regularly between Berwick-upon-Tweed and Galashiels via Melrose. Another useful, frequent service links Jedburgh, Melrose and Galashiels. First Edinburgh's Waverley Wanderer ticket allows a day's unlimited travel around the Borders, and includes Edinburgh (£11.50). National Express (☎ 0870-580 8080) bus No 383 runs once a day between Chester and Edinburgh via Manchester, Leeds, Newcastle, Jedburgh and Melrose.

Jedburgh & Around
☎ 01835

The most complete of the ruined Border abbeys is **Jedburgh Abbey**. After a famous ride to visit her lover, the Earl of Bothwell, at Hermitage Castle, Mary Queen of Scots was nursed back to health in a Jedburgh house (now a museum) that bears her name. The TIC (☎ 863435) opens year round.

Hermitage Castle, off the B6399 from Hawick, is only accessible if you have transport, but it's well worth a detour.

Melrose
☎ 01896

Melrose is an attractive small town 6.5km east of Galashiels, and is a popular base for exploring the Borders. This is the only Borders town with a convenient *Youth Hostel* (☎ 822521), open Easter to September, and overlooking ruined **Melrose Abbey**.

Sir Walter Scott's house, **Abbotsford** (☎ 752043), in a beautiful spot 3km west of Melrose on the banks of the Tweed, has an extraordinary collection of the great man's possessions.

Thirlestane Castle (☎ 01578-722430), 16km north, near Lauder off the A68, is one of Scotland's most fascinating castles and still a family home. The original keep, built in the 13th century, was refashioned and added to in the 16th century with fairytale turrets and towers. It opens 11 am to 4.15 pm Sunday to Friday, Easter to October.

STIRLING
☎ 01786

More than 40km north of Glasgow and occupying the most strategically important location in Scotland, Stirling (population 37,000) has witnessed many of the struggles of the Scots against the English. The cobbled streets of Stirling's attractive old town surround the castle. The TIC (☎ 475019), 41 Dumbarton Rd, opens all year.

The town is dominated by **Stirling Castle** (☎ 450000), perched dramatically on a rock. Mary Queen of Scots was crowned here and it was a favourite royal residence. Open daily, it's one of Scotland's most interesting castles.

Stirling Youth Hostel (☎ 473442, St John St) is central and an excellent place to stay. There are regular buses to Edinburgh, Glasgow and Aberdeen.

ST ANDREWS
☎ 01334

St Andrews is a beautiful, unusual seaside town – a concoction of medieval ruins, obsessive golfers, windy coastal scenery, tourist glitz and a big university. Although St Andrews was once the ecclesiastical capital of Scotland, both its cathedral and castle are now in ruins. For most people, the town is the home of golf – St Andrews is the headquarters of the game's governing body, the Royal & Ancient Golf Club, and home of the world's most famous golf course, the 16th-century Old Course.

The most important parts of old St Andrews, lying to the east of the bus station, are easily explored on foot. The TIC (☎ 472021), 70 Market St, opens year round. Pick up a copy of *Getting Around Fife*, a free guide to regional transport.

St Andrews Cathedral, at the eastern end of North St, is the ruined west end of what was once the largest cathedral in Scotland. Many of the town's buildings are constructed from its stones. **St Andrews Castle**, not far from the cathedral, has a spectacular clifftop location. Near the Old Course is the **British Golf Museum** (☎ 478880), open daily April to October (Thursday to Monday mid-October to March).

Places to Stay & Eat

There's no SYHA hostel, but two of the cheaper B&Bs are *Cairnsden* (☎ 476326, 2 King St), south of the centre, with singles/doubles for £20/36; and in the centre, *Fairnie House* (☎ 474094, 10 Abbey St) for £15 to £30 per person. The B&Bs and hotels that line Murray Park and Murray Place in the centre are expensive, charging around £22 per person.

PM, on the corner of Market and Union Sts, does breakfast, burgers, and fish and chips from £1.95. The nearby *Fisher & Donaldson* sells Selkirk bannocks (rich fruit bread) and a wonderful range of pastries. *Brambles (5 College St)* has excellent soups, salads and vegetarian choices. *Ogston's (116 South St)* is a good-value bar and bistro.

Getting There & Away

Stagecoach Fife (☎ 01592-642394) runs half-hourly buses from Edinburgh's St Andrew Square to St Andrews (£5.70, two hours) and on to Dundee (£2.40, 30 minutes).

The nearest train station is Leuchars (one hour from Edinburgh), 8km away, on the Edinburgh, Dundee, Aberdeen, Inverness coastal line. Bus Nos X59 and X60 leave every half-hour Monday to Saturday to St Andrews, hourly on Sunday.

EASTERN HIGHLANDS

A great elbow of land juts into the North Sea between Perth and the Firth of Tay in the south and Inverness and Moray Firth in the north. The valley of the River Dee – the Royal Dee thanks to the Queen's residence at Balmoral – has sublime scenery.

The main bus and train routes from Edinburgh to Inverness run directly north through Perth, or around the coast to Aberdeen and then north-west and inland back to Inverness. Scottish Citylink (☎ 0870-550 5050) links the main towns by bus. There are also regular buses from Glasgow.

The train journey from Perth to Inverness (2¼ hours) is one of the most spectacular in Scotland. Otherwise, there are frequent trains from Edinburgh and Glasgow to Aberdeen (2½ hours) and from Aberdeen to Inverness (2¼ hours).

Grampian Country – Inland

The region between Braemar and Huntly and east to the coast is castle country, and includes the Queen's residence at Balmoral. The TICs have information on a Castle Trail, but you really need private transport. **Balmoral Castle** (☎ 013397-42334) opens Easter to early August and attracts large numbers of visitors; it can be reached by the Aberdeen to Braemar bus (see below).

Braemar is an attractive, small town surrounded by mountains. There's a helpful year-round TIC (☎ 013397-41600), and the town makes a fine walking base. On the first Saturday in September the town is invaded by 20,000 people, led by the royal family, for the Braemar Gathering (Highland Games); accommodation bookings are essential at this time. There are several B&Bs, or try *Braemar Youth Hostel* (☎ 01339-741659) or *Braemar Bunkhouse* (☎ 01339-741242), both of which have cheap dorm beds.

It's a beautiful drive between Perth and Braemar but unfortunately public transport is limited. From Aberdeen to Braemar there are several buses a day operated by Stagecoach Bluebird (☎ 01224-212266), which travel along the beautiful valley of the River Dee.

The direct inland route from Aberdeen to Inverness, serviced by bus and train, cuts across malt whisky country. Aficionados might be tempted by the Malt Whisky Trail (information from TICs), which gives you an inside look and complimentary tastings at a number of famous distilleries, including Cardhu, Glenfiddich and Glenlivet.

Aberdeen
☎ 01224

Aberdeen is an extraordinary symphony in grey. Almost everything is built of granite. In the sun, especially after a shower of rain, the stone turns silver and shines like a fairytale, but with low grey clouds and rain it can be a bit depressing. The good news is that Aberdeen has a thriving nightlife.

Orientation & Information The train and bus stations are next to each other off Guild St, near the ferry quay. The TIC (☎ 632727), in St Nicholas House, Broad St, opens all year.

Places to Stay The year-round *Aberdeen Youth Hostel* (☎ 646988, 8 Queen's Rd) is 1.6km west of the train station – walk east along Union St and take the right fork along Albyn Place until you reach a roundabout; Queen's Rd continues on the western side.

Clusters of B&Bs line Bon Accord St and Springbank Terrace (both close to the centre). *Nicoll's Guest House* (☎ 572867, 63 Springbank Terrace) is a friendly place with singles/doubles from £20/32.

Places to Eat The *Ashvale Fish Restaurant (42 Great Western Rd)* is a well-known fish and chip shop. *Lemon Tree (5 West North St)* is an excellent cafe attached to the theatre of the same name. It's open noon to 3 pm Wednesday to Sunday. For a classier ambience and delicious cakes, try *Wild Boar (19 Belmont St)*. *Prince of Wales (7 St Nicholas Lane)* is a good, traditional pub.

Getting There & Away Scottish Citylink (☎ 0870-550 5050) has daily buses from London (12 hours). Stagecoach Bluebird (☎ 212266) is the major local bus operator, with reasonable coverage of the Aberdeenshire region. By train it's seven hours to/from London's King's Cross station.

From Aberdeen, P&O (☎ 572615) has weekday ferries to Lerwick on Shetland (£52/58 low/high season, 14 hours, or 20 hours via Orkney). June to August there are departures Tuesday and Saturday to Stromness on Orkney (£39/42, 10 hours).

WESTERN HIGHLANDS

This is the Highlands of the tour bus, but there are also some unspoilt peninsulas and serious mountains where you can be very isolated. The scenery is dramatic – Ben Nevis (1343m) is Britain's highest mountain; brooding Glencoe still seems haunted by the massacre of the MacDonalds; the Cowal and Kintyre peninsulas have a magic of their own; and Loch Lomond, though it's a tourist cliche, is beautiful.

Fort William, at the southern end of the Great Glen, is a major tourist centre, easily reached by bus and train. Oban, on the west coast, is the most important ferry port to the Inner and Outer Hebrides Islands.

Getting There & Away

Bus From Glasgow, Scottish Citylink (☎ 0870-550 5050) and its subsidiary, Skyeways Travel (☎ 01599-534328), are the main operators, with daily connections to Oban (£10, three hours), Fort William (£10.50, three hours) and Inverness (£12, from 3½ hours). Highland Country Buses (☎ 01397-702373) runs buses along these routes for similar prices.

Train The spectacular West Highland line runs from Glasgow north to Fort William and Mallaig, with a spur to Oban from Crianlarich. The Highland Rover ticket (£49) gives unlimited travel for four days in an eight-day period.

Fort William
☎ 01397

Fort William is a pleasant little town and an excellent base for the mountains, but don't plan on hanging around. The town meanders along the edge of Loch Linnhe for several kilometres. The centre with its small selection of shops, takeaways and pubs is easy to cover on foot. The TIC (☎ 703781), Cameron Square, opens year round.

Fort William is at the northern end of the **West Highland Way**, an excellent 153km walk through some of Scotland's finest scenery. TICs have a free brochure listing accommodation.

Popular *Fort William Backpackers' Guest House* (☎ *700711, Alma Rd*) is a short walk from the train station and costs £10 per night. About 5km from Fort William, up magical Glen Nevis, are the *Glen Nevis Youth Hostel* (☎ *702336*) which costs £12.25, and, across the river, the *Ben Nevis Bunkhouse* (☎ *702240, Achintee Farm*) for £9.

You can hire bikes from Off-Beat Bikes (☎ 704008), 117 High St, for £12.50 per day.

Oban
☎ 01631

Though there isn't much to see or do, Oban gets inundated with visitors, mostly because it's the most important ferry port on the west coast. By Highland standards it's a large town, but you can easily get around on foot.

The bus, train and ferry terminals are grouped together beside the harbour. The TIC (☎ 563122), Argyll Square, one block behind the harbour, opens year round.

The popular *Oban Backpackers Lodge* (☎ *562107)*, on Breadalbane St, charges £9.50. There are numerous B&Bs in this area. *Oban Youth Hostel* (☎ *562025*), on Corran Esplanade, north of town, on the other side of the bay from the terminals, opens year round.

Numerous CalMac (☎ 566688) boats link Oban with the Inner and Outer Hebrides (Lochboisdale). Up to seven ferries sail daily to Craignure on Mull (£3.45, 45 minutes).

NORTHERN HIGHLANDS & ISLANDS

This is one of Europe's last great wildernesses, and it's more beautiful than you can imagine. The east coast is dramatic, but it's the north and west, where the mountains and sea collide, that exhaust superlatives.

This is a remote and scarcely populated region, so you need to be organised and/or have plenty of time if you're relying on public transport. Transport services are drastically reduced after September. Car rentals are available in Inverness, Oban and Stornoway; if you can get a group together, this can be a worthwhile option.

Getting There & Away

Bus Wick, Thurso, Ullapool and Kyle of Lochalsh can all be reached by bus from Inverness, or from Edinburgh and Glasgow via Inverness or Fort William; contact Scottish Citylink (☎ 0870-550 5050) or Highland Country Buses (☎ 01463-233371) in Inverness. In remote areas Royal Mail postbuses are the main option.

Train The Highland lines are justly famous. There are two routes from Inverness: up the

BRITAIN

east coast to Thurso, and west to Kyle of Lochalsh. There's also a regular train from Glasgow to Oban, Fort William and Mallaig (for Skye and the Inner Hebrides). Call ☎ 0845-748 4950.

Ferry CalMac (☎ 01475-650000) sails car and passenger ferries to all the major islands. The ferries can be expensive, so consider Island Rover tickets for unlimited travel between islands for eight or 15 days, and Island Hopscotch tickets that offer various route combinations at reduced rates. Ferry timetables depend on tides and weather, so check departures with TICs.

Inverness
☎ 01463
Inverness is the capital of the Highlands, and the hub for Highlands transport. It's a pleasant place to while away a few days, though it lacks major attractions. In summer it's packed with visitors. Fortunately, most are intrepid monster hunters and their next stops are Loch Ness and Fort William.

Orientation & Information The bus and train stations, the TIC and the hostels are east of the River Ness, within 10 minutes' walk of each other. The TIC (☎ 234353), beside the museum on Castle Wynd, just off Bridge St, opens daily. The Laundrette, 17 Young St over the bridge, opens daily.

Places to Stay & Eat Three hostels are clustered together, just past the castle. Beds are £9 at the friendly *Inverness Student Hostel* (☎ 236556, 8 Culduthel Rd), which has the same owner as Edinburgh's High St Hostel – you can make phone bookings from there. *Bazpackers Backpackers Hotel* (☎ 717663, 4 Culduthel Rd) charges from £7.50, with linen. The excellent *Inverness Millburn Youth Hostel* (☎ 231771, 1 Old Edinburgh Rd) charges £12.75.

Ivybank Guest House (☎ 232796, 28 Old Edinburgh Rd) charges £20 per person for B&B as does the graceful *Ardconnel House* (☎ 240455, 21 Ardconnel St). On Kenneth St west of the river, and adjoining Fairfield Rd, there are several B&Bs, including *Mardon* (☎ 231005), at No 37, which charges £15/28 a single/double.

Near the hostels, *Castle Restaurant* (41 Castle St) is a traditional cafe with plentiful food at low prices. *Littlejohn's* (28-30 Church St) has a pasta-Mexican-burger menu. The busy *CHSS Coffee Shop* (5 Mealmarket Close) offers nourishing, healthy food in a relaxed atmosphere.

Getting There & Away From Inverness' bus station (☎ 233371), Scottish Citylink (☎ 0870-550 5050) has bus connections with major centres in England, as well as numerous buses to/from Glasgow (£12, 3½ hours) and Edinburgh (via Perth; £12.50, four hours). Two buses run daily to Ullapool (£5, 1½ hours), connecting with the CalMac ferry to Stornoway on Lewis (except Sunday). The 3½-hour ferry trip costs £12.70.

There are three or four daily Scottish Citylink services via Wick to Thurso and Scrabster (£9, three hours) for ferries to Orkney. Citylink/Skyeways (☎ 01599-534328) operate three buses a day (two on Sunday) from Inverness to Kyle of Lochalsh and Portree (£7.50, three hours) on Skye.

Stagecoach Inverness (☎ 239292) has a Monday to Saturday service to Lairg (plus Sunday in summer). In summer, daily buses run through to Durness. There's also a postbus service (☎ 01246-546329) travelling Lairg-Tongue-Durness.

Trains to/from Glasgow or Edinburgh cost £29.90. The onward line from Inverness to Kyle of Lochalsh (£14.70, 2½ hours) offers one of the greatest scenic journeys in Britain and leaves you within walking distance of the pier for buses across the Skye Bridge. The line to Thurso (£12.50, 3½ hours) connects with the ferry to Orkney. There are three trains a day Monday to Saturday on both lines.

Getting Around The TIC has a handy *Car Hire* leaflet. As well as the big boys there's Sharp's Car Rental (☎ 236694), 1st floor, Highland Rail House, Station Square. Inverness Student Hostel rents out bikes for £6/12 for a half/full day.

East Coast
The coast starts to get really interesting when you leave behind Invergordon's industrial development. Great, heather-covered hills heave themselves out of the wild North Sea, with towns like Dornoch and Helmsdale moored precariously at its edge.

There are SYHA hostels at *Carbisdale Castle* (☎ *01549-421232*) and *Helmsdale* (☎ *01431-821577*). Don't miss **Wick**'s superb heritage centre (open June to September) but otherwise keep going to John o'Groats and beyond.

John o'Groats The coast at the island's north-eastern tip isn't particularly dramatic, and John o'Groats is little more than a ramshackle tourist trap – but there's something inviting about the view across to Orkney. *John o'Groats Youth Hostel* (☎ *01955-611424*), Canisbay, is 4.8km west of John o'Groats and opens late March to September. There are up to seven buses Monday to Saturday from Wick (£2.30) and Thurso (£2.50). May to September, MV *Pentland Venture* (☎ 01955-611353) shuttles across to Burwick (Orkney).

Thurso & Scrabster Thurso (population 9000) is a fairly large, bleak place looking across Pentland Firth to Hoy, in Orkney. It's the end of the line, both for the east-coast railway and the big bus lines. The TIC (☎ 01847-892371), Riverside Rd, opens April to October.

The nearby coast has arguably the best, most regular **surf** in Britain. On the eastern side of town, in front of Lord Caithness' castle, there's a right-hand reef break. There's another shallow reef break 8km west at Brimms Ness.

Thurso Hostel (☎ *01847-896888, Ormlie Rd*), also called Ormlie Lodge, charges £6 to £8 for dorm beds. In July and August *Thurso Youth Club Hostel* (☎ *01847-892964, Old Mill, Millbank)* has basic dorm beds for £8. There are plenty of B&Bs around town. For a cheap bar meal, try the *Central Hotel (Traill St)*.

Scrabster, from where car ferries run to Orkney, is a 3.2km walk or a £1 bus ride from Thurso. Wheels Shop (☎ 01847-896124), The Arcade, 34 High St, rents mountain bikes for £10 a day.

Orkney Islands
☎ 01856

This magical group of islands, 10km off Scotland's north coast, is known for its dramatic coastal scenery (which ranges from 300m-tall cliffs to white, sandy beaches) and abundant marine-bird life, and for its prehistoric sites, including an entire 4500-year-old village at Skara Brae. If you're in the area around mid-June, don't miss the St Magnus Arts Festival.

Sixteen of the 70 islands are inhabited. Kirkwall (population 6100) is the main town, and Stromness the major port; both are on the largest island, which is known as Mainland. The land is virtually treeless, but is lush and level rather than rugged. The climate, warmed by the Gulf Stream, is surprisingly moderate, with April and May being the driest months. Contact the TIC (☎ 872856), 6 Broad St, Kirkwall, for more information.

Places to Stay There's a good selection of cheap B&Bs, six SYHA hostels and three independent hostels.

In Stromness, *Stromness Youth Hostel* (☎ *850589, Hellihole Rd*), a 10-minute walk from the ferry, charges £8.25, while *Brown's Hostel* (☎ *850661, 45 Victoria St)* is popular, and charges £8. On beautiful Papa Westray, the most northerly island, the excellent *Papa Westray Hostel* (☎ *01857-644267, Beltane)* opens year round; beds are £8.

Getting There & Away P&O (☎ 850655) operates a car ferry from Scrabster, near Thurso, to Stromness (£16). There's at least one departure a day year round. P&O also sails from Aberdeen (see the Aberdeen section for details).

From May to September, John o'Groats Ferries (☎ 01955-611353) has a passenger ferry from John o'Groats to Burwick on South Ronaldsay. One-way tickets are £16, or £27 return if you leave John o'Groats in the afternoon and Orkney in the morning. In Thurso, a free bus meets the afternoon train from Inverness, and a bus for Kirkwall meets the ferry in Burwick (32km away).

Shetland Islands
☎ 01595

Almost 100km north of Orkney, the Shetland Islands remained under Norse rule until 1469, when they were given to Scotland as part of a Danish princess' dowry. Even today, these remote, windswept, treeless islands are almost as much a part of Scandinavia as of Britain. Lerwick, the capital, is only about 370km from Bergen, Norway.

BRITAIN

Much bleaker than Orkney, Shetland is famous for its varied bird life, its rugged coastline and a 4000-year-old archaeological heritage. There are 15 inhabited islands and a population of 23,000. Lerwick is the largest town on Mainland Shetland, which is used as a base for the North Sea oilfields. Oil has brought a certain amount of prosperity to the islands – there are well-equipped leisure centres in many villages.

Small ferries travel between a handful of the smaller islands. Contact the TIC (☎ 693434, ☒ shetland.tourism@zetnet .co.uk) in Lerwick for information on B&Bs and camping *böds* (barns). *Lerwick Youth Hostel* (☎ 692114, *King Harald St*), open mid-April to October, charges £9.25.

Getting There & Away British Airways/ Loganair (☎ 0845-773 3377) and Business Air (☎ 0500-341046) operate low-flying turboprop aircraft (with great views of the islands) daily between Orkney and Shetland. The standard fare is around £135 return.

Lerwick can be reached by P&O (☎ 01224-572615) ferries from Aberdeen, or from Orkney, leaving Stromness on Tuesday morning and Sunday evening (£39/78 single/return, eight hours). See Scotland's introductory Getting There & Away section for ferry links to Scandinavia.

North Coast

The coast from Dounreay, with its nuclear power station, west around to Ullapool is mind-blowing. Everything is on a massive scale: vast emptiness, enormous lochs and snowcapped mountains. The unreliable weather and inadequate public transport are the only drawbacks.

Getting to Thurso by bus or train is no problem, but from there your troubles start. In July and August, Highland Country (☎ 01463-222244) runs a once-daily bus from Thurso to Durness. At other times of year, Highland Country and Rapson's (☎ same) have Monday to Saturday services from Thurso to Bettyhill. There's also a postbus (☎ 01246-546329) from Tongue to Cape Wrath once daily Monday to Saturday.

The alternative is to come up from Inverness via Lairg. There are trains daily to Lairg, from where Highland Country bus No 64 runs north to Durness daily from Monday to Saturday.

Monday to Saturday postbus services operate the Lairg-Tongue-Talmine and Lairg-Kinlochbervie-Durness routes. There are also services around the coast from Elphin to Scourie, Drumbeg to Lochinver, Shieldaig to Kishorn via Applecross, and Shieldaig to Torridon and Strathcarron, but often with gaps between towns.

The *Tongue Youth Hostel* (☎ 01847-611301) has a spectacular lochside location, while the *Durness Youth Hostel* (☎ 01971-511244) is backed by the rocky Sutherland hills.

West Coast

Ullapool The small fishing village of Ullapool attracts the crowds because it's easily accessible along beautiful Loch Broom from Inverness. The TIC (☎ 01854-612135), 6 Argyle St, is one block inland, but most places are strung along the harbourfront, including *Ullapool Youth Hostel* (☎ 01854-612254), open February to December with beds for £9.25. There are a great many B&Bs. *Arch Inn* (☎ 01854-612454) has rooms from £18.

See the Inverness Getting There & Away section for details on the ferry to Stornoway on the Isle of Lewis, and bus connections.

Mallaig This fishing village makes a pleasant stopover between Fort William and Skye. From Mallaig the beautiful West Highland line train runs south four times daily Monday to Saturday to Fort William (£7.40, 1¼ hours), Oban and Glasgow.

Kyle of Lochalsh Kyle, as it's known, is a small village overlooking the lovely island of Skye across Loch Alsh. There's a TIC (☎ 01599-534276) beside the seafront car park. The nearest hostels are on Skye.

Kyle can be reached by bus and train from Inverness (see the Inverness section), and by direct Scottish Citylink buses from Glasgow (£15.30, five hours), which continue across to Kyleakin on Skye and on to Uig (£7.20, 6½ hours) for ferries to Tarbert on Harris and Lochmaddy on North Uist.

Isle of Skye

Skye is a large, rugged island, 80km north to south and east to west. It's ringed by beautiful coastline and dominated by the Cuillin Hills, immensely popular for the sport of 'Munro bagging' – climbing Scottish mountains that top 3000 feet (914m). Tourism is a mainstay of the island economy, so you won't escape the crowds until you get off the main roads. Contact the Portree TIC (☎ 01478-612137) for more information. Bicycles can be hired from Island Cycles (☎ 01478-613121) in Portree and at Fairwinds Cycle Hire (☎ 01471-822270) in Broadford.

Places to Stay & Eat There are more than a dozen SYHA and independent hostels on the island and numerous B&Bs. The SYHA hostels most relevant to ferry users are at *Kyleakin* (☎ 01599-534585) for Kyle of Lochalsh, open year round; *Uig* (☎ 01470-542211) for the Outer Hebrides (Western Isles), open April to October; and *Armadale* (☎ 01471-844260) for Mallaig, open April to September.

The pick of the independents is the friendly *Skye Backpackers* (☎ 01599-534510, Kyleakin), a short walk from the Skye Bridge; beds cost £10 and there are some double rooms. There's also the nearby *Fossil Bothy* (☎ 01471-822644, Lower Breakish) and on the west coast there's *Croft Bunkhouse* (☎ 01478-640254).

Portree is the main centre on the island. *Ben Tianavaig Vegetarian Bistro (5 Bosville Terrace)* has an extensive vegetarian and seafood menu.

Getting There & Away There are two ferries from the mainland to Skye. Mid-July to August, CalMac (☎ 01678-462403) operates between Mallaig and Armadale (30 minutes; £2.70). There's also a private Glenelg to Kylerhea service (☎ 01599-511302) from mid-April to late October (not always on Sunday), costing 70p and taking 10 minutes.

From Uig on Skye, CalMac has daily services to Lochmaddy on North Uist and (except Sunday) to Tarbert on Harris; both trips cost £8.30 and take 1¾ hours.

Outer Hebrides

The Outer Hebrides (Western Isles) are bleak, remote and treeless. The climate is fierce: the islands are completely exposed to the gales that sweep in from the Atlantic, and it rains on more than 250 days of the year. Some people find the landscape mournful, but others find the stark beauty and isolated world of the crofters strangely unique and captivating.

The islands are much bigger than might be imagined (stretching in a 210km arc); those who do fall under the islands' spell will need plenty of time to explore. The Sabbath is strictly observed: nothing moves on a Sunday and it can be hard finding anything to eat. Tarbert (Harris) and Lochmaddy (North Uist) are reasonably pleasant villages, but the real attraction lies in the landscape.

See the Skye and Kyle of Lochalsh sections for details of CalMac ferries to Tarbert and Lochmaddy, and the Oban section for ferries to Lochboisdale. All the TICs open for late ferry arrivals in summer but close between mid-October and early April.

Lewis & Harris Lewis (main town Stornoway, reached by ferry from Ullapool) and Harris (Tarbert, by ferry from Uig on Skye) are actually one island with a border of high hills between them. Lewis has low, rolling hills and miles of untouched moorland and freshwater lochs. Harris is rugged, with stony mountains bordered by meadows and sweeping, sandy beaches.

Stornoway (population 8100) is the largest town, but it's not particularly attractive. It does have a reasonable range of facilities, including a TIC (☎ 01851-703088) and several banks. It's also possible to rent cars, but they can't be taken off the islands: contact Arnol Motors (☎ 01851-710548) or Mackinnon Self-Drive (☎ 01851-702984).

Ring around for a B&B, or stay at the *Stornoway Backpackers Hostel* (☎ 01851-703628) for £9. There's also the year-round *Garenin Crofters' Hostel (no ☎)*, 29km from Stornoway (buses twice daily). There's at least one bus a day between Tarbert and Stornoway (except Sunday). Alex Dan's Cycle Centre (☎ 01851-704025) hires bikes.

Tarbert has a TIC (☎ 01859-502011), open April to October only, a bank (no ATM) and two general stores. The nearest SYHA hostel is about 11km south at *Stockinish* (☎ 01859-530373); there's one bus a day from Tarbert. At **Rhenigidale**, there's the SYHA *Rhenigidale Crofters' Hostel (no ☎)*, 16km north of Tarbert; a bus can take you to the end of the road at Maraig, but it's a two-hour walk from there; alternatively, walk the whole way – it's a great hike.

North & South Uist North Uist (Loch-maddy, by ferry from Uig on Skye, or Tar-bert or Leverburgh on Harris), Benbecula (by air from Inverness and Glasgow) and South Uist (Lochboisdale, by ferry from Oban or Mallaig) are joined by bridge and causeway. These are low, flat, green islands half-drowned by sinuous lochs and open to the sea and sky.

Barra (Castlebay, by ferry from Loch-boisdale and, for passengers only, Ludag on South Uist) lies at the southern tip of the is-land chain and is famous for its wild flow-ers and glorious white, sandy beaches.

Lochmaddy has a TIC (☎ 01876-500321), bank and hotel. *Uist Outdoor Centre (☎ 01876-500480)* opens all year and has dorm accommodation from £7.

There's one postbus a day between Lochmaddy and Lochboisdale, which also has a bank and TIC (☎ 01878-700286). In Howmore, 24km north on the west coast, *Howmore Youth Hostel (no ☎)* opens all year. There's a bus from Lochboisdale.

Barra has a TIC (☎ 01871-810336) in Castlebay and about 20 B&Bs, but there's no hostel.

Wales

Wales (Cymru) has had the misfortune of being so close to England that it could not be allowed its independence, and yet far enough away to be conveniently forgotten. It sometimes feels rather like England's unloved back yard – a suitable place for coal mines and nuclear power stations. It is almost miraculous that anything Welsh should have survived the onslaught of its dominating neighbour. However, Welsh culture has proved to be remarkably endur-ing and the language stubbornly refuses to die. The Welsh also got a boost in 1997 with the passage of a 'home rule' referen-dum; the first National Assembly was put in place in May 1999.

Wales' appeal lies in its countryside. In general, the towns and cities are not partic-ularly inspiring. The best way to appreciate the Great Welsh Outdoors is by walking, bicycling, canal boating or hitching. Simply catching buses or trains from one regional hub to another is not recommended. In-stead, base yourself in a small town and

explore the surrounding countryside for a few days. Hay-on-Wye, Brecon, St David's, Dolgellau, Llanberis and Betws-y-Coed are good possibilities.

Wales also has an unsurpassed legacy of magnificent medieval castles. All of the fol-lowing are within 2km of a train station: Caerphilly, north of Cardiff; Kidwelly, north of Llanelli; Harlech, south of Porth-madog; Caernarfon, in the north-west; and Conwy, near Llandudno in the north.

FACTS ABOUT WALES
Language
Of Wales' 2.9 million people, some 20% speak Welsh, mainly in the north. Although almost everyone speaks English, there is Welsh TV and radio, and most signs are bilingual. At first sight, Welsh looks impos-sibly difficult to get your tongue around. Once you know that 'dd' is pronounced 'th', that 'w' can also be a vowel pronounced 'oo', that 'f' is 'v' and 'ff' is 'f', and you've had a native speaker teach you how to pro-nounce 'll' (roughly 'cl'), you'll be able to say (pronunciation in parentheses): *bore da* (bora-da) good morning, *shw'mae* (shoo-my) hello, *peint o gwrw* (paint-o-guru) pint of beer, *diolch* (diolkh) thank you, *da boch* (da bokh) goodbye.

FACTS FOR THE VISITOR
Tourist Offices
Contact the BTA for information outside the UK (see Tourist Offices in the Facts for the Visitor section at the start of this chap-ter). The Wales Tourist Board (☎ 029-2049 9909) has its headquarters at Brunel House, 2 Fitzalan Rd, Cardiff CF2 1UY, and also operates a branch on the drop-in Britain Vis-itor Centre, 1 Regent St, Piccadilly Circus, London SW1Y 4NS.

GETTING THERE & AWAY
There are ferry links with Ireland from four Welsh towns: Holyhead to Dublin (Irish Fer-ries) and Dun Laoghaire (Stena Line); Pem-broke to Rosslare (Irish Ferries); Fishguard to Rosslare (Stena Line); and, from March to November, Swansea to Cork (Swansea Cork Ferries). See the Ireland chapter for details.

GETTING AROUND
Distances in Wales are small but, with the exception of links around the coast,

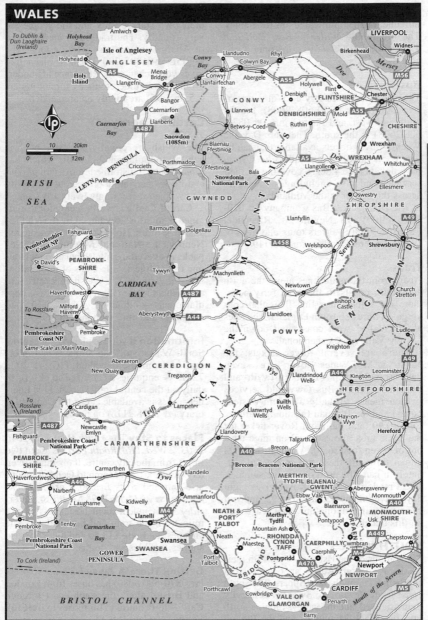

BRITAIN

public transport users have to fall back on infrequent and complicated bus timetables. The invaluable *Wales – Bus, Rail and Tourist Map & Guide* is sometimes available from TICs.

Bus

The major operators serving Wales are Arriva Cymru (☎ 0870-608 2608), for the north and west, and First Cymru (☎ 0870-608 2608) in the south. There are Day and Weekly Saver tickets available that can be very good value. For example, First Cymru have tickets for £4.80/16 covering all their services and also including some buses across the border in the Midlands.

The Backpacker Bus Company (☎ 029-2066 6900), 98 Neville St, Riverside, Cardiff CF1 8LS, offers tours and treks of Wales for three/six days for £99/119.

Train

Apart from the main lines along the north and south coasts to the Irish ferry ports, there are some interesting lines that converge on Shrewsbury in England. The lines along Wales' west coast, and down the Conwy Valley, are exceptional.

There are several Rover tickets: the North & Mid-Wales Rover gives seven days travel north of Aberystwyth and Shrewsbury plus Bus Gwynedd services (which means virtually all north-western buses) and the Blaenau Ffestiniog Railway for £40.90; and the Flexi Rover ticket for the same area allows travel on three days out of seven for £26.30. A railcard will get you a third off these prices but unfortunately it can't be used during the summer. The Freedom of Wales Rover gives eight days travel in any 15 days for £92, and you can use a railcard (one-third off) year round on this ticket.

SOUTH WALES

The valleys of the Usk and Wye, with their castles and **Tintern Abbey**, are beautiful, but can be packed with day-trippers. The south coast from Newport to Swansea is heavily industrialised, and the valleys running north into the Black Mountains and the Brecon Beacons National Park are still struggling to come to grips with the loss of the coal-mining industry.

Even so, the little villages that form a continuous chain along the valleys have their own stark beauty and the people are very friendly. The traditional market town of Abergavenny is also worth a look. The **Big Pit** (☎ 01495-790311), near Blaenafon, gives you a chance to experience life underground, and guided tours by former miners (£5.75/3.95) are highly recommended.

Cardiff (Caerdydd)
☎ 029

The Welsh are proudly defensive of their capital (population 285,000), which has rapidly been transformed from a dull provincial backwater into a prosperous university city with an increasingly lively arts scene.

Cardiff Castle is worth seeing for its outrageous interior. Revamped by the Victorians, it's more Hollywood than medieval. Nearby, the **National Museum of Wales** packs in everything Welsh but also includes one of the finest collections of impressionist art in Britain. The **Welsh Folk Museum**, at St Fagan's, 8km from the centre, is a popular open-air attraction with reconstructed buildings and craft demonstrations.

Information If you are planning to explore South Wales, stock up on maps and information from the excellent TIC (☎ 2022 7281, @ enquiries@cardifftic.co.uk), open daily, at the central train station. Free Internet access is available at Cardiff Central Library (☎ 2038 2116) on Frederick St.

Places to Stay The *Youth Hostel* (☎ *2046 2303, 2 Wedal Rd, Roath Park*) is about two miles from the city centre. It operates seven days a week from March to October, opens at 3 pm and costs £13.50. *Cardiff Backpacker* (☎ *2034 5577, 98 Neville St, Riverside*) is an independent hostel less than a mile from the train and bus stations. The cheapest beds are £13.50 and there are also singles, doubles and dorms.

Getting There & Away National Express (☎ 0870-580 8080) has buses from London and Bristol along the south coast through Cardiff to Pembroke (for ferries to Ireland). London to Cardiff is £14.

InterCity trains can travel from London's Paddington station to Cardiff in as little as 1¾ hours (from £36/47 single/return). There's also a line to/from London's

Waterloo station but journey time is almost three hours. For rail inquiries phone ☎ 0845-748 4950.

Swansea
☎ 01792

Swansea is the second-largest town (it would be stretching the definition to call it a city), and the gateway to the **Gower Peninsula** and its superb coastal scenery (crowded in summer). Dylan Thomas grew up in Swansea and later called it an 'ugly, lovely town'. The town's position is certainly lovely, but there's no pressing reason to stay.

For more information, contact the TIC (☎ 468321, ✉ swantrsm@cableol.co.uk). Internet access is available at Swansea public library (☎ 516757) on Alexandra Rd.

Moving on west to the Gower Peninsula, the *Youth Hostel* (☎ *390706*) is a converted lifeboat house, superbly situated right on the beach at Port Eynon. Bus No 18/A covers the 26km from Swansea.

Brecon Beacons National Park
The Brecon Beacons National Park covers 1352 sq km of high bare hills, surrounded on the northern flanks by a number of attractive market towns; Llandovery, Brecon, Crickhowell, Talgarth and Hay-on-Wye make good bases. The railhead is at Abergavenny. A 124km cycleway/footpath, the Taff Trail, connects Cardiff with Brecon. The Monmouthshire & Brecon Canal, which runs south-east from Brecon, is popular both with hikers (especially the 53km between Brecon and Pontypool) and canal boaters, and cuts through beautiful country.

There are three mountain ridges in the park: Brecon Beacons in the centre, the Black Mountains in the east and (confusingly) Black Mountain in the west.

You'll find the National Park Visitor Centre (☎ 01874-623366) in open countryside near Libanus, 8km south-west of Brecon. Other information offices are in Brecon (☎ 01874-623156) at the Cattle Market Car Park and in Llandovery (☎ 01550-720693) on Kings Rd. Both make B&B bookings.

Brecon Brecon is an attractive, historic market town, with a cathedral dating from the 13th century. The market is held on Tuesday and Friday. There's a highly acclaimed jazz festival in August. The TIC (☎ 01874-622485, ✉ Brectic@powys.gov.uk) can organise B&Bs. *Tymn-y-Caeau Youth Hostel* (☎ *01874-665270*) is about 5km from town; ask directions from the TIC.

Brecon has no train station, but Stagecoach Red & White (☎ 01633-266336) has regular buses to Swansea, Abergavenny and Hereford via Hay-on-Wye.

Hay-on-Wye At the north-eastern tip of the Black Mountains, Hay-on-Wye is an eccentric market village that is now known as the world centre for second-hand books – there are over 26 shops and two million books, everything from first editions costing £1000 to books by the yard (literally).

The TIC (☎ 01497-820144) has lists of the excellent restaurants and B&Bs in the neighbourhood. *Capel-y-Ffin Youth Hostel* (☎ *01873-890650*) is 13km south of Hay on the road to Abergavenny. The walk here from Hay follows part of Offa's Dyke and is highly recommended.

SOUTH-WEST WALES
The coast from St David's to Cardigan is particularly beautiful and, as it is protected by the national park, remains unspoilt.

Carmarthen Bay is often referred to as Dylan Thomas Country; in fact, the **Dylan Thomas boathouse** at Laugharne (☎ 01994-427420), where he wrote *Under Milk Wood*, has been preserved exactly as he left it (£2.75/1). Llanstephan has a beautiful Norman castle overlooking sandy beaches. On west-facing beaches, the surf is usually good; the Newgale filling station (☎ 01437-721398), Newgale, hires the necessary equipment and has daily surf reports.

Irish Ferries (☎ 0870-532 9129) leave Pembroke Dock for Rosslare in Ireland; ferries connect with buses from Cardiff and destinations east. Stena Line (☎ 0870-570 7070) has ferries to Rosslare from Fishguard; these connect with buses and trains. See the Ireland chapter for more details.

Pembrokeshire Coast National Park
The national park protects a narrow band of magnificent coastline, broken only by the denser development around Pembroke and Milford Haven. The only significant inland portion is the Preseli Hills to the south-east

BRITAIN

of Fishguard. There are National Park Information Centres and TICs at Tenby (☎ 01834-842402), St David's (☎ 01437-720392) and Fishguard (☎ 01348-873484), among others. Get a copy of the free paper, *Coast to Coast*, which has detailed local information. Apart from hostels, there are loads of B&Bs from around £15 per head.

Around Pembroke the main bus operator is Silcox Coaches (☎ 01646-683143), with buses from Pembroke and Pembroke Dock to Tenby. Richards Bros (☎ 01239-613756) is the main operator from St David's to Cardigan.

St David's The linchpin for the south-west is beautiful St David's, one of Europe's smallest cities. There's a web of interesting streets and, concealed in the Vale of Roses, beautiful **St David's Cathedral**. There is something particularly magical about this isolated 12th-century building. Unfortunately, it's often packed with day-trippers.

Contact the TIC (☎ 01437-720392, e enquiries@stdavids.pembrokeshirecoast .org.uk) for more information. There are regular Richards Bros buses to/from Fishguard (except on Sunday).

There are four handy youth hostels: near *St David's* (☎ 720345), open from May to October except Thursday (daily mid-July to August); near *Newgale and Solva* (☎ 720959); at *Trevine* (☎ 01348-831414), 17.5km from St David's; and at *Pwll Deri* (☎ 01348-891233), 13km from Trevine and just over 7km from Fishguard.

Fishguard Fishguard stands out like a jewel among the depressing ranks of ugly ferry ports. It is on a beautiful bay, and the old part of town – Lower Fishguard – was the location for the 1971 film version of *Under Milk Wood*, which starred Richard Burton and Elizabeth Taylor. The train station and harbour (for Stena Line ferries to Rosslare in Ireland) are at Goodwick, a 20-minute walk from the town proper.

The TIC (☎ 873484) is open daily in summer. *Hamilton Guest House & Backpackers Lodge* (☎ 874797, 21 Hamilton St) is near the TIC. It's a very friendly place, open 24 hours, with 20 beds in dormitories for £10 per person; £12 in a double room. By rail, Fishguard to London is £44 for a SuperSaver single or £27 Apex.

NORTH WALES

North Wales is dominated by the Snowdonia Mountains, which loom over the beautiful coastline. Unfortunately, this is the holiday playground for many of England's Midlands dwellers, and the coast is marred by tacky holiday villages and caravan parks.

Heading east from Chester, the country is flat, industrialised and uninteresting until you reach Llandudno, which is virtually contiguous with Conwy. From Llandudno and Conwy you can catch buses or trains to Betws-y-Coed or Llanberis, the main centres for exploring Snowdonia National Park. From Betws-y-Coed there's a train to the bleak but strangely beautiful mining town of Blaenau Ffestiniog. One of Wales' most spectacular steam railways runs from Blaenau to the coastal market town of Porthmadog. From Porthmadog you can loop back to Shrewsbury, via Harlech and its castle.

The remote Lleyn Peninsula in the west escapes the crowds to a large extent; start from Caernarfon, with its magnificent castle, or Pwllheli. Near Porthmadog is whimsical Portmeirion, a holiday village built in the Italianate style and the backdrop to the trippy 1960s show *The Prisoner* – it's very attractive, but crowded in summer.

The Red Rover day ticket (£4.60) covers most of the region. For more information phone ☎ 01286-679535.

Holyhead
☎ 01407

Holyhead is a grey and daunting ferry port. Both Irish Ferries (☎ 0870-532 9129) and Stena Line (☎ 0870-570 7070) run ferries to Ireland. Irish Ferries runs direct to Dublin, Stena Line goes to Dun Laoghaire, just outside Dublin.

The TIC (☎ 762622) is in ferry terminal 1. Nearby there's a batch of B&Bs that are used to dealing with late ferry arrivals. The *Min-y-Don* (☎ 762718) is pleasant, with rooms for £15 per person. The TIC has a 24-hour information terminal in the train station. There are hourly trains east to Llandudno, Chester, Birmingham and London.

Llandudno
☎ 01492

Llandudno seethes with tourists, which in this instance seems entirely fitting. It was developed as a Victorian holiday town and has retained most of its 19th-century architecture and antiquated atmosphere. There's a wonderful pier and promenade – and donkeys on the beach.

Llandudno is on its own peninsula between two sweeping beaches, and is dominated by the spectacular limestone headland – the Great Orme – with the mountains of Snowdonia as a backdrop. The Great Orme, with its tramway, chair lift, superb views and Bronze-Age mine, is fascinating.

Though there are hundreds of guesthouses, it can be difficult to find a bed in the busy months of July and August. Contact the TIC (☎ 876413) for B&B information.

Getting There & Away There are numerous trains and buses between Llandudno and Chester, and Llandudno and Holyhead.

Buses and trains run between Llandudno Junction, Betws-y-Coed (for the Snowdonia National Park) and Blaenau Ffestiniog (for the brilliant narrow-gauge railway to Porthmadog). There are six trains a day from Monday to Saturday and the journey takes just over an hour. A North & Mid Wales Rover ticket (£26.30) gives three days travel over one week and covers buses as well as trains.

Arriva Cymru's bus Nos 5 and 5B run between Llandudno, Bangor and Caernarfon; there are plenty of buses from Bangor to Holyhead for the ferry.

Conwy

Conwy has been revitalised since the through traffic on the busy A55 was consigned to a tunnel that burrows under the town. It is now a picturesque and interesting little town, dominated by superb **Conwy Castle** (£3.50/2.50), one of the grandest of Edward I's castles.

The TIC (☎ 01492-592248) is in the Conwy Castle Visitor Centre. Conwy is linked to Llandudno (8km east) by several buses an hour and a few trains. There are also numerous trains from Llandudno to Llandudno Junction, a 15-minute walk from Conwy.

Snowdonia National Park

Although the Snowdonia Mountains are fairly compact, they loom over the coast and are quite spectacular. The most popular region is in the north around Mt Snowdon (1085m), the highest peak in Britain south of the Scottish Highlands. Hikers must be prepared for hostile conditions at any time of year.

There are National Park Information Centres at Betws-y-Coed (☎ 01690-710665), Blaenau Ffestiniog (☎ 01766-830360) and Harlech (☎ 01766-780658), among others; they all have a wealth of information, and all make B&B bookings.

Betws-y-Coed Betus (as it is known and pronounced) is a tourist village in the middle of the Snowdonia National Park. Despite bus loads of tourists it just can't help being beautiful. There's nothing to do except go for walks and take afternoon tea, which in this case is enough.

The TIC (☎ 01690-710426) is useful, but the National Park Information Centre is better. Both are near the train station. There are plenty of B&Bs, and the two hostels are both about 8km away. *Capel Curig Youth Hostel (☎ 01690-720225)* is to the west on the A5; the *Ledr Valley Youth Hostel (☎ 01690-750202, Pont-y-Pant)* is on the A470. There are other hostels in the Snowdon area.

Snowdon Sherpa Buses, which is part of Bus Gwynedd, runs from Llandudno to Conwy, Betws-y-Coed, Capel Curig and Pen-y-Pas (for the hostels), and then on to Llanberis and Caernarfon. There are regular services daily from mid-May to late September. A Red Rover ticket (£4.40) can be bought on the bus.

Llanberis This tourist town lies at the foot of Mt Snowdon and is packed with walkers and climbers. If you're neither, for a mere £14.80 you can take the Snowdon Mountain Railway (☎ 01286-870223) for the ride to the top and back. The TIC (☎ 01286-870765) is on High St.

The area's best hostel is *Pen-y-Pas Youth Hostel (☎ 01286-870428)*, about 10km up the valley at the start of one of the paths up Snowdon. Back in Llanberis there are numerous B&Bs.

Pete's Eats is a warm cafe where hikers swap information and stories over large portions of healthy food. In the evenings climbers hang out in *Heights (☎ 01286-871179)*, a hotel with a pub that even has its own climbing wall.

BRITAIN

Llangollen

☎ 01978

In the north-east, about 13km from the border with England, Llangollen is famous for its **International Musical Eisteddfod**. This six-day music and dance festival, held in July, attracts folk groups from around the world. Phone ☎ 860236 for details. The TIC (☎ 860828, ☻ croeso@nwt.co.uk) is open daily in summer.

The town is an excellent base for outdoor activities – walks to ruined **Valle Crucis**

Abbey and the Horseshoe Pass, horse-drawn canal-boat trips, and canoeing on the River Dee. **Plas Newydd** was the 'stately cottage' of the eccentric Ladies of Llangollen, fascinating as much for their unorthodox (for those days – 1780-1831) lifestyle as for the building's black-and-white decoration.

Llangollen Youth Hostel & Activity Centre is 2.5km from the centre. Contact the TIC (☎ 860828) for B&Bs. There are frequent buses from Wrexham, but public transport to Snowdonia is limited.

Bulgaria (България)

Bulgaria comes as a pleasant surprise to visitors, with its pristine hiking trails, handsome historical towns and sunny, sandy beaches. It doesn't get nearly as many Western tourists as it deserves, but those who do come are assured of a warm welcome.

Now that visas are no longer required for citizens of the UK, Australia, New Zealand, North America and most of Europe, independent tourism (as opposed to package tourism at the major resorts) is much easier. Bulgarian bureaucracy can be very frustrating, but scores of new private hotels, restaurants and tourist agencies have smoothed the path for independent travellers.

Facts about Bulgaria

HISTORY

In antiquity, Bulgaria, the land of Orpheus and Spartacus, belonged to the Kingdom of Macedonia and its inhabitants were Thracians. Slavic tribes arrived in the mid-6th century, followed in 679 by the Bulgars (the so-called 'Proto-Bulgarians'), a fierce Turkic tribe from between the Ural Mountains and the Volga River. In 681 the Proto-Bulgars founded the First Bulgarian Empire (681-1018).

In 1185, with much of Bulgaria under Byzantine rule, two brothers named Asen and Peter led a general uprising and founded the Second Bulgarian Empire (1185-1396), with Veliko Târnovo as its capital.

Turkish incursions began in 1340 and by 1371 the Bulgarian tsar Ivan Shishman had become a vassal of the Turks, beginning five centuries of Ottoman rule. In the early 19th century, popular customs and folklore blossomed in the National Revival of Bulgarian Culture (*vuzrazhdane*), when books were first printed in the Bulgarian language.

Following an anti-Turkish revolt at Koprivshtitsa in April 1876, the Turks responded with unprecedented brutality – thousands of Bulgarians were massacred and 58 villages were destroyed. This led Russia to declare war on Turkey. When the Russian army and its Bulgarian volunteers advanced to within 50km of Istanbul, Turkey ceded 60% of the Balkan Peninsula to Bulgaria. The modern history of Bulgaria dates from this 1878 liberation. Complete independence from Turkey was declared on 22 September 1908.

Bulgarian claims to neighbouring Macedonia led the country into the two Balkan Wars (1912 and 1914) and an alliance with Germany during both world wars.

In 1941 Bulgaria joined the Nazi invasion of Yugoslavia, hoping to gain control of Macedonia. In August 1944, with the Soviet army advancing across Romania, Bulgaria declared itself neutral and disarmed the German troops. Soviet soldiers entered Bulgaria unopposed, and the Bulgarian monarchy was overthrown by communists led by Todor Zhivkov, Bulgaria's leader from 1962 to 1989.

On 9 November 1989 the Berlin Wall fell, and the next day in Sofia an internal Communist Party coup put an end to the 27-year reign of the ageing Zhivkov. In February 1991, he became the first ex-communist leader in Eastern Europe to stand trial for corruption. (Zhivkov was sentenced to seven years in prison but wangled a hasty release and lived comfortably in an affluent suburb of Sofia until his death in August 1998.)

The country's first post-Communist elections in 1990 were won by the 'new' Communist Party, renamed the Bulgarian Socialist Party (BSP). Over the next seven years, seven successive governments proved unable to implement the reforms needed to regulate the money supply, curb inflation and privatise the economy.

BULGARIA

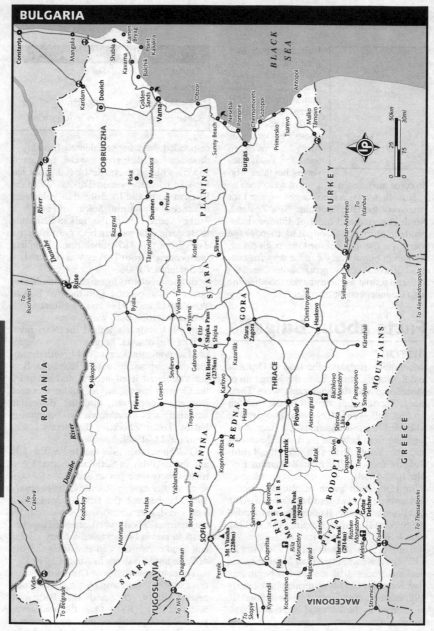

BULGARIA

The current democratic government, under president Petâr Stoyanov and premier Ivan Kostov, took office in April 1997 promising to clamp down on rampant corruption, enact fiscal reforms and attract much-needed foreign investment. Their efforts have not gone unnoticed by the West. Recent official negotiations put Bulgaria on the timetable to join the EU as early as 2008.

GEOGRAPHY

Bulgaria (110,912 sq km) has an amazing variety of landforms. Musala Peak (2925m) in the Rila Mountains south of Sofia is the highest mountain between the Alps and Transcaucasia. The Rodopi Mountains stretch east along the Greek border from Rila and Pirin. Central Bulgaria's Thracian Plain opens onto the Black Sea coast and its long sandy beaches.

POPULATION & PEOPLE

About 8.2 million people live in Bulgaria. The major cities and their population figures are Sofia (population 1.14 million), Plovdiv (400,000), Varna (315,000), Burgas (210,000), Ruse (190,000), Stara Zagora (162,000) and Pleven (140,000).

The Bulgarians, like the Serbs, are South Slavs. The largest national minorities are Turks (8.5%), Roma (2.6%) and Macedonians (2.5%). About 85% of the population is Orthodox, and 13% is Sunni Muslim.

SOCIETY & CONDUCT

As with other cultures in the region, when Bulgarians wag their head it means 'yes' and when they nod their head it means 'no'. This can be confusing, especially when they reverse it to accommodate foreigners unfamiliar with the custom. If in doubt, ask 'da ili ne?' (yes or no?). When entering an establishment it's polite to say 'dobar den' (good day).

LANGUAGE

Almost everything in Bulgaria is written in Cyrillic, so it's essential to learn this alphabet. See the Language guide at the back of this book for a basic rundown on Bulgarian pronunciation and some useful words and phrases.

To complicate and confuse matters, the lower-case script is quite different from printed Cyrillic.

Many older Bulgarians speak Russian as a second language. Young people, tourism workers and business types are more likely to speak English.

Facts for the Visitor

SUGGESTED ITINERARIES

Three days
  Sofia, Rila Monastery, and either Old Plovdiv or Koprivshtitsa.
One week
  Sofia, Rila Monastery, Veliko Târnovo, and either Old Plovdiv or Koprivshtitsa.
Two weeks
  Sofia, Rila Monastery, Bansko, Koprivshtitsa, Old Plovdiv, Veliko Târnovo, Varna and Nesebâr.

PLANNING
When to Go

Bulgaria has a temperate climate with cold, damp winters and hot, dry summers. The Black Sea moderates temperatures in the east of the country. Rainfall is highest in the mountains. Bulgaria's well-developed tourism infrastructure means lots of vacant hotel rooms and restaurant tables, except during high season at the Black Sea resorts (mid-July through August) and at the mountain ski resorts (Christmas/New Year and February through mid-March). Shoulder season (June and September) is best for the coastal resorts; off-season everything is dead. The ski resorts are also active in July and August and are a great way to beat the city heat.

TOURIST OFFICES

In a concerted effort to boost regional tourism and business investment opportunities, the Bulgarian government has recently opened a number of autonomous local tourist information and business development centres around the country.

The old Balkantourist monopoly has been broken up and now operates domestically under a myriad different names. Abroad it goes by either the old name or Balkan Holidays. It's a good source of information though staff may try to sign you up for one of their package tours.

Tourist Offices Abroad

Germany (☎ 4969-290755, ✉ bhf.mail@to nline.de) 1-3 Stephanstrasse, Frankfurt 6000

UK (☎ 020-7543 5550,
📧 bhlond@btinternet.com) 19 Conduit St,
London W1R 9TD

VISAS & DOCUMENTS

Bulgaria's once rigid border controls have
eased considerably in keeping with international reciprocity agreements. Nationals
of some 30 countries, including the USA,
UK, Australia, Canada, and the EU are admitted without a visa for stays of less than
30 days.

For visitors of most other nationalities
visas are issued based on a sliding fee scale
depending on whether the visa is transit,
tourist or business. These must be obtained
in advance as no visas are issued at the borders. A transit visa is US$40, a single-entry
tourist visa is US$50, a three-month multi-
entry visa is US$60.

The nefarious 'statistical card' is a thing
of the past except for visitors from some
former Soviet-bloc nations. Also officially
abolished are border and transit taxes.

In Sofia the main passport office (☎ 982
3316), bul Maria Luiza 48, is open 8.30 am
to noon and 1.30 to 5.30 pm weekdays.

EMBASSIES & CONSULATES
Bulgarian Embassies Abroad
Bulgarian embassies abroad include:

Australia (☎ 02-9327 7581, fax 9327 8067)
4 Carlotta Rd, Double Bay, NSW 2028
Canada (☎ 613-789 3215, fax 789-3524,
📧 mailmn@storm.ca) 325 Stewart St, Ottawa,
Ontario K1N 6K5
UK (☎ 020-7584 9400, fax 7584 4948)
187 Queen's Gate, London SW7 5HL
USA (☎ 202-387 7679, fax 234 7973)
1621 22nd St NW, Washington, DC 20008

Foreign Embassies in Bulgaria
The following are in Sofia (area code ☎ 02):

UK (☎ 980 1220) bul Vasil Levski 38
USA (☎ 963 2022) Kapitan Andreev 1

MONEY
The Bulgarian lev (plural 'leva') comes in
banknotes of 1, 2, 5, 10, 20 and 50 leva. There
are coins of 1, 2, 5, 10, 20 and 50 stotinki.

Since 1997 the lev has been officially
pegged to the Deutschmark. When the euro
is introduced in 2002, the lev will automatically follow suit and be tied to the euro.

In this chapter, accommodation prices
and international travel tickets are quoted in
US dollars. Local transport, food and
sundry expenses are given in leva.

Many banks and some exchange offices
change travellers cheques but fees vary
widely so shop around. ATMs are much in
evidence in the larger cities and resort areas
and are linked to the Visa, MasterCard,
Plus, JCB, Cirrus and Maestro networks.
Cash advances on credit cards are also increasingly available. Still, it's a good idea
to bring along some extra cash to Bulgaria.

The lev is a freely convertible currency
and there are no problems changing excess
leva back into dollars. There is no black
market as such, though street hustlers may
offer better rates. If you use this method,
count on the fact that you will be ripped
off.

Exchange Rates

country	unit		leva
Australia	A$1	=	1.25 leva
Canada	C$1	=	1.47 leva
euro	€1	=	1.94 leva
France	10FF	=	2.96 leva
Germany	DM1	=	1.00 leva
Japan	¥100	=	2.05 leva
NZ	NZ$1	=	0.93 leva
UK	UK£1	=	3.17 leva
USA	US$1	=	2.18 leva

Costs
Anything you can get for the same price as
a Bulgarian will be cheap, but if it's a tourist
price it can get expensive. You can get by on
a budget of US$20 to US$40 a day, depending on the level of comfort you're after.

Tipping
Waiters expect the bill to be rounded up;
give a bit more if the service was efficient
(a rarity) and honest. Some places already
include a service charge, usually 10%.

POST & COMMUNICATIONS
It costs 50 stotinki to send postcards
abroad, and 80 stotinki for air-mail letters.
Stamps are available at post office windows and at lobby kiosks

Telephone, Fax & Email
Bulgaria's country code is ☎ 359. Drop the
initial zero on area codes when dialling

BULGARIA

from overseas. Bulgarian phone numbers are slowly adding digits, especially in Sofia – some five or six-digit numbers in this chapter may have changed by the time you read this.

Most post offices have international pay phones – simply enter the booth, dial ☎ 00 (Bulgaria's international access code) and then the country code and number. Pay the clerk as you leave. A one-minute call to the USA from Bulgaria costs 3 leva.

Phones throughout the country accept BulFon and Betkom phone cards, which come in various denominations and are sold at kiosks.

Faxes can be sent from most post offices but are expensive. Internet access is available at cybercafes in Sofia.

INTERNET RESOURCES

Bulgaria Online at www.online.bg has links to dozens of Bulgaria-related Web sites as well as current news summaries and entertainment listings. For an excellent virtual tour of Bulgaria, go to 'sights and sounds' at bg.orientation.com.

WOMEN TRAVELLERS

Women travelling alone will definitely attract interest from both sexes, but it's unlikely to lead to trouble. In this family-oriented culture, people are simply amazed by solo journeying. Stick close to family groups on trains, especially if travelling overnight. 'Omâzhena sâm' means 'I am married' and gives a pretty firm message.

GAY & LESBIAN TRAVELLERS

Homosexual sex is legal in Bulgaria (from the age of 21) provided it does not cause 'public scandal or entice others to perversity'. As you might deduce from this, the official line in Bulgaria is far from gay-friendly. The local gay organisation is Erotic Centre 'Flamingo' (mobile/cellphone ☎ 048 97 46 47) at 208 Tsar Simeon, Sofia, 1303.

DANGERS & ANNOYANCES

The perception that all westerners are wealthy has led to various scams. As a foreigner you will stand out as a target for pickpockets so take precautions, especially around train and bus stations and on crowded public transport.

While the situation is improving (slowly), official corruption is still rampant in Bulgaria and occasionally foreigners have been targeted on international trains and while driving. Sometimes all it takes is insistence on an official *smetka* (receipt) to sidestep these hustlers in uniform.

Emergency numbers (in Bulgarian only) within Bulgaria are: police ☎ 166, ambulance ☎ 150, fire ☎ 160.

PUBLIC HOLIDAYS & SPECIAL EVENTS

Public holidays include New Year (1 and 2 January), 1878 Liberation Day (3 March), Easter Monday (March/April), Labour Day (1 May), Cyrillic Alphabet Day (24 May), 1885 Unification Day (6 September), 1908 Independence Day (22 September), National Revival Day (1 November) and Christmas (25 and 26 December). The Bulgarian Orthodox Easter falls at a different time to the Catholic Easter.

At the Koprivshtitsa Folk Festival, which is held every five years (the next in 2005), some 4000 finalists compete for awards in various fields. Almost as big is Pirin Sings, a biennial (next in 2001) folk festival held near Bansko in mid-August. The Festival of Roses is celebrated with folk songs and dances at Kazanlâk and Karlovo on the first weekend in June. The March Musical Days are held annually at Ruse, followed by the two-month Sofia Music Weeks beginning on 24 May.

ACCOMMODATION

Most camping grounds are reliably open only from late May to early September. Tent sites cost about US$4 per person; small bungalows or villas are often available for not much more than that.

In Bulgaria, hostels are not called 'student' hostels as they are open to all. There are some 320 mountain hostels, hotels, huts and dorms. The hostels are of two kinds. A *Turisticheski dom* is a fairly comfortable hotel-type facility with double and triple rooms; a *Turisticheska spalnya* is a more basic dorm. Both types are usually located in or near a town. A *hizha* is a mountain hut with dorm beds. Many hostels are currently undergoing privatisation and their status is in flux. Though they are not listed in the Hostelling International (HI) handbook, some display the HI

BULGARIA

symbol and may (or may not) honour the membership card. Prices range from US$5 to US$20 per person.

Since November 1989, privately owned pensions and family-run hotels have opened in Bulgaria, especially in the mountain and beach resorts. All are fairly small with less than a dozen rooms. Expect to pay US$20 to US$50 for a double.

Hotels are classified from one to five stars. The most expensive are called Interhotels. Many two and three-star former Balkantourist hotels are run-down and overpriced.

In Sofia, Balkantour, Tourist Information & Reservations (TIR) and Odysseia-In can book hotel rooms and private lodgings throughout the country (see Information under Sofia for contact details).

FOOD & DRINKS

Food is inexpensive in Bulgaria, even in restaurants; but waiters sometimes overcharge foreigners, so insist on seeing a menu.

Taverns that serve traditional Bulgarian dishes are known as *mehanas*. Popular dishes include *kebabcheta* or *kebapche* (grilled meat patties), *kavarma* (meat and vegetable casserole), *drob sarma* (chopped liver with rice and eggs), *sarmi* (stuffed vine or cabbage leaves) and *kebab* (meat on a spit). *Topcheta supa* is a creamy soup with meatballs. *Plakiya* and *gyuvech* are rich fish and meat stews, respectively.

Vegetarians will find several dishes based on *sirene* (cheese). *Sirene po shopski* is cheese, eggs and tomatoes baked in an earthenware pot. *Kashkaval pane* is breaded cheese. *Banitsa* is a baked cheese pastry. A *shopska* salad is made from fresh diced tomatoes, cucumbers, onions and peppers covered with grated sheep's cheese. *Tarator* is a refreshing cold soup of yoghurt, diced cucumber and onions. *Bop*, bean soup, is ubiquitous.

Bulgaria is one of the world's leading exporters of wine, both red and white. Bulgarians also swear by *slivova* or *rakiya* (plum brandy). Bulgaria's finest beers are Zagorka, Astika and Kamenitsa and have been acquired through privatisation by Dutch and Belgian breweries. All alcoholic drinks are cheap. 'Na zdrave!' is 'cheers!' in Bulgarian.

Getting There & Away

BUS

Most buses to the Balkan countries depart from Sofia's now-privatised international bus station (☎ 952 50 04) on Damen Gruev. There are buses for Niš in Yugoslavia (US$8, four hours, three daily) with the 9 pm bus continuing on to Belgrade (US$16, seven hours); to Skopje (US$9, six hours, two daily) and Ohrid (US$13, 11 hours, twice daily) in Macedonia; to Tirana in Albania (US$26, 18 hours, four weekly); to İstanbul (US$25, 18 hours, daily except Friday); and to Thessaloniki (US$18, six hours, three daily) with the 9 am bus continuing on to Athens (US$41, 12 hours).

International and domestic destinations are served by a host of competing private firms from the large staging areas on either side of Sofia's Princess Hotel (just south of the Central train station) and head off on a regular basis to destinations throughout Europe, as well as to Ukraine, Turkey, Greece and other Balkan countries. Sample destinations and fares include Frankfurt (US$95, 30 hours), Brussels (US$90, 36 hours), Munich (US$60, 26 hours), Prague (US$50, 24 hours), Budapest (US$40, 18 hours), Bratislava (US$48, 20 hours), Vienna (US$45, 21 hours), Thessaloniki (US$16, six hours) and Athens (US$37, 12 hours).

Unfortunately, no buses operate between Romania and Bulgaria due to long delays at the border. However, there are buses from Bucharest to İstanbul via Bulgaria, and you could simply get off after clearing Bulgarian customs.

TRAIN

Bus travel is cheaper, faster and more comfortable to/from Greece, Turkey and Macedonia. Only to/from Yugoslavia is it as good to take the train.

The main rail routes into Bulgaria are from Bucharest (Romania), Niš (Yugoslavia), Thessaloniki and Alexandroupolis (Greece) and Edirne (Turkey). All lines are served at least once a day with through trains to/from İstanbul, Athens, Belgrade, Budapest, Kyiv, Moscow, Vilnius and St Petersburg.

Train travel between Romania and Bulgaria is much simpler than it once was. The

Bulgaria Express originates in Moscow, picks up connections from Ukraine and St Petersburg and runs to/from Bucharest and Sofia (US$17, 10 hours).

The *Balkan Express* departs daily from Sofia at 10.50 am and arrives in Belgrade at 6.30 pm (US$18, 7½ hours). There is also an overnight train (US$28 sleeper) which departs at 9.50 pm and arrives the next morning at 6.30 am.

The *Maritza Express* leaves Sofia at 8.15 am and arrives in Istanbul at 6.45 pm.

The *Bosphorus Express* between Bucharest and Istanbul passes through Ruse at 5.25 pm and arrives in Istanbul at 7.20 am (US$25 sleeper). In the other direction it leaves Ruse at 2.55 pm, arriving in Bucharest at 5.35 pm.

International train tickets should be purchased at Rila train ticket offices, found in the city centres. Do so well ahead, as most Rila offices are open only on weekdays. You pay for international train tickets in leva.

CAR & MOTORCYCLE

When entering Bulgaria by car you must state which border crossing you'll be using to leave the country and pay a road tax accordingly. If your plans change and you leave by a crossing with a higher tax, you must pay the difference.

Getting Around

BUS

Overnight buses and all buses to the coast should be booked the day before, as they usually fill up. Otherwise, it's important to arrive at the *avtogara* (bus station) early in order to purchase tickets, which are usually sold at counters rather than from the driver. At way stations, tickets for long-distance buses can be purchased only after the bus arrives and the driver tells the ticket clerk how many seats are available.

Private buses now operate on long-distance routes in competition with the railways, especially from Sofia and Plovdiv to the Black Sea resorts.

TRAIN

Bulgarian State Railways (BDŽ) classifies trains as *ekspresen* (express), *bârz* (fast) or *putnichki* (slow). Sleepers and couchettes are available between Sofia and Burgas or Varna for between 4 leva and 9 leva on top of the normal fare, but you'll need to book well ahead to get one. Seat reservations are recommended on express trains to the Black Sea. Buy tickets at Sofia's Rila office.

Most domestic ticket prices included throughout this chapter are 1st-class fares on fast trains (express trains cost an additional 1 leva) during the designated 'calendar' period (Friday to Monday plus holidays). Fares during the less-frequented 'regular' period (Tuesday to Thursday) average 20% less. First-class compartments seat six, as opposed to eight in 2nd class, and fares are around 25% higher.

CAR & MOTORCYCLE

Travelling around Bulgaria by private car or motorcycle is quite feasible, though drivers must cope with poor and sometimes non-existent signposting, slow moving vehicles, horses and carts and sometimes erratic driving. Signs to minor destinations are usually in Cyrillic only. Vehicle theft – especially of foreign-registered cars – is another concern. Renting a low-cost, Bulgarian-registered car for as little as US$20 a day is a better option.

Speed limits are 40 or 50km/h in built-up areas, 90km/h on the open road and 120km/h on highways. People riding in the front seat of a car must (supposedly) wear seat belts and everyone on a motorcycle must wear a helmet.

Fuel is available in normal (86 octane), unleaded (93 octane) and super (93 to 98 octane). Normal petrol has an octane rating that is too low for Western cars. Petrol costs around 1.50 leva for 1L of unleaded.

Shipka, the travel agency of the Union of Bulgarian Motorists, has offices at all major border crossings and in Sofia (☎ 02-88 38 56) at Lavele 18. The national road assistance number in Bulgaria is ☎ 146 (mobile/cellphone ☎ 048 146).

Sofia (София)

☎ 02

Sofia sits on a 545m-high plateau at the foot of Mt Vitosha (2290m), and is the highest capital in Europe. The city centre is a mix of the old, the new and the recently renovated, thanks in large part to international assistance such as the EU's 'Beautiful Bulgaria' program which has been sprucing up historic buildings in the central area.

As the government and commercial hub, Sofia is not truly representative of the country as a whole, so after getting your bearings, re-pack your bags and head off to discover the 'real' Bulgaria.

Orientation

Sofia's central train station is in the northern part of the city. From the station, bul Maria Luiza runs south through ploshtad Sveta Nedelya. Beyond Sveta Nedelya Cathedral this thoroughfare becomes bul Vitosha, the fashionable avenue of modern Sofia. The narrow Graf Ignatiev, Sofia's liveliest shopping precinct, runs south-east from near the beginning of bul Vitosha (take tram No 2, 12 or 19).

Information

Tourist Offices & Travel Agencies The
National Information and Advertising Centre (☎ 987 9778, ✉ infctr@tir.ttm.bg), Sveta

Sofia 1, has helpful English-speaking staff and excellent printed material for travellers.

The equally helpful Odysseia-In (☎ 989 0538, ✉ odysseia@omega.bg), bul Stamboliyski 20 (enter from Lavele), organises hiking trips (plus a variety of other adventure sports activities), sells outdoor gear, stocks maps and countrywide brochures, and books accommodation around the country. It's a great resource for do-it-yourselfers; see the Web site at www.newtravel.com.

Balkantour (☎ 986 5691, ✉ balkantour@hotmail.com), bul Stamboliyski 27, books private lodgings and hotel rooms (at discounts of up to 50%) and sightseeing tours.

The Orbita Youth Travel Agency (☎ 987 9128), bul Hristo Botev 48, sells ISIC cards (US$4) and books accommodation. It's open 9 am to 6.30 pm weekdays.

Tourist Information & Reservations (TIR; ☎ 980 3314), Lavele 22, books double rooms at two-star hotels around Bulgaria from US$20 to US$50. Prices are about 20% off the walk-in rates.

Money The First East International Bank, Lege 15, gives the best cash rates. ATMs

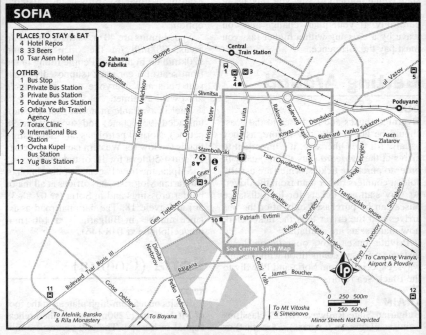

SOFIA

PLACES TO STAY & EAT
4 Hotel Repos
8 33 Beers
10 Tsar Asen Hotel

OTHER
1 Bus Stop
2 Private Bus Station
3 Private Bus Station
5 Poduyane Bus Station
6 Orbita Youth Travel Agency
7 Torax Clinic
9 International Bus Station
11 Ovcha Kupel Bus Station
12 Yug Bus Station

See Central Sofia Map

0   250   500m
0   250   500yd

Minor Streets Not Depicted

To Camping Vranya, Airport & Plovdiv

To Melnik, Bansko & Rila Monastery

To Boyana

To Mt Vitosha & Simeonovo

are in Halite shopping centre and scattered across town.

Post & Communications Sofia's main post office is on Vasil Levski. Around the corner on Stefan Karadzha is the main 24-hour telephone centre.

Email & Internet Access The Internet Agency (☎ 9166 2213) on the lower floor of the NDK Palace of Culture has 12 terminals with fast satellite connections (4 leva per hour). It's open 9 am to 7 pm daily. The Euro-Bulgarian Cultural Centre (☎ 988 0084) at Stamboliyski 17 has five new terminals (3 leva per hour; 20% student discount) and an adjacent cafe. It's open 9 am to 8 pm weekdays, 10 am to 7 pm Saturday.

Bookshops The newsstand in the basement of the Sheraton Balkan Hotel sells foreign periodicals. Arbat, on bul Vitosha next to McDonald's, and Book World, Graf Ignatiev 15, sell English-language books.

Medical Services In an emergency contact Torax Clinic (☎ 988 5259) at Stamboliyski 57. There is a 24-hour pharmacy on ploshtad Sveta Nedelya.

Things to See & Do
The neo-Byzantine **Aleksander Nevski Church** (1912) is a memorial to the 200,000 Russian soldiers who died for Bulgaria's independence. In the crypt is a museum of icons (closed Tuesday). Nearby is the 6th-century basilica **Church of Sveta Sophia**, who gave her name to the city. The square is the site of a daily flea market.

The street that runs south from Aleksander Nevski empties into ploshtad Narodno Sabranie, where you'll find the **National Assembly** (1884) and an equestrian statue (1905) of Aleksander II, the Russian tsar who freed Bulgaria from the Turks.

Ploshtad Batenberg, former site of the Georgi Dimitrov Mausoleum until its demolition in 1999, is now dominated by the former Royal Palace which houses the **National Art Gallery**, with Bulgarian paintings, and the **Ethnographical Museum**. Both are closed on Monday.

To the west are the nine lead-covered domes of the Buyuk Djami, or Great Mosque (1496), now the recently-restored **National**

Archaeological Museum (closed Monday). Across from the museum in the courtyard behind the Presidency is Sofia's oldest building, the 4th-century **Rotunda of St George**.

On the east side of Largo is the former Communist Party headquarters. The pedestrian underpass in front contains the ruins of ancient Serdika's fortress walls (2nd to 14th centuries).

Behind **TsUM** (1955), the former all-in-one central department store where the toiling masses had no choice but to shop, is the **Banya Bashi Mosque** (1576). Nearby is the colourful **Central Mineral Baths** (1913), currently in the process of being renovated, and, opposite, the recently renovated **Halite**, the city's central marketplace since 1911.

South of Largo is **Sveta Nedelya Cathedral** (1863), restored after a 1924 bomb attempt on Tsar Boris III in which 124 people (including most of the Cabinet) were killed.

Vitosha, Sofia's main shopping street, intersects the monstrous **NDK Palace of Culture** (1981), often used for concerts and conferences. On the square in front is a huge monument celebrating Bulgaria's 1300th anniversary.

Eight kilometres south in the mountain suburb of Boyana are two of Bulgaria's most noteworthy sights: the excellent **National Museum of History**, with fabulous Thracian gold treasures, and the 13th-century **Boyana Church**.

Places to Stay
Camping The year-round *Camping Vranya* (☎ 973 6213) is 9km east of Sofia on the Plovdiv Highway. From the train station, take bus No 213 to bul Tsarigradsko Shose, then change to bus No 5 or 6. Camping costs US$3/4 per tent/person; bungalows are US$28.

Private Rooms Several accommodation offices in the train station organise private rooms from US$10 to US$14 per person.

Odysseia-In charges US$10 per person, Balkantour charges US$16/20/27 a single/double/triple with a 25% youth (under 21) discount (see Tourist Offices & Travel Agencies earlier).

Hotels The *Sofia Hostel* (☎/fax 989 1504, ✉ hostelsofia@usa.net, Pozitano 16), above a Chinese restaurant, has basic dorm-type

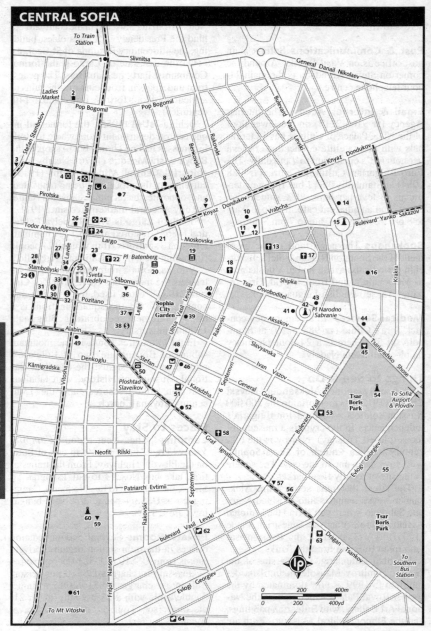

CENTRAL SOFIA

CENTRAL SOFIA

PLACES TO STAY
2 Hotel Enny
8 Hotel Iskâr
26 Hotel Maya
31 Sofia Hostel

PLACES TO EAT
3 Asia
9 Birhale Gambrinus
11 Luciano
12 Mayor's Club
36 Trops Kâshta
37 Bonjour Supermarket
56 Mimas
57 Mimas
59 El Cabana

OTHER
1 Lions Bridge
4 Synagogue
5 Halite
6 Banya Bashi Mosque
7 Central Mineral Baths (closed)
10 National Opera
13 Church of Sveta Sofia
14 State Musical Theatre
15 Vasil Levski Monument
16 National Library & Bibliotekata Nightclub

17 Aleksander Nevski Church
18 St Nicholas Russian Church
19 National Art Gallery & Ethnographical Museum
20 National Archaeological Museum
21 Former Communist Party Headquarters
22 Church of St George Rotunda
23 Sheraton Balkan Hotel
24 Sveta Petka Samardjiiska Church
25 Central Department Store (TsUM)
27 Odysseia-In Travel Agency
28 Stateside
29 Balkantour
30 Shipka Travel Agency; Tourist Information & Reservations
32 National Information & Advertising Centre
33 Euro-Bulgarian Cultural Centre
34 24-hour Pharmacy
35 Sveta Nedelya Cathedral
38 First East International Bank

39 Ivan Vazov National Academic Theatre
40 Zala Bâlgaria
41 Balkan Bulgarian Airlines
42 Monument to the Liberators
43 National Assembly
44 Sofia University
45 Pleven Beer Hall
46 Puppet Theatre
47 Main Post Office
48 Rila Train Ticket Office
49 Arbat Bookshop
50 24-Hour Telephone Centre
51 Mr Punch
52 Book World Bookshop
53 Baba Yaga
54 Soviet Army Monument
55 Vasil Levski Stadium
58 Sveti Sedmotchislenitsi Church
60 1300th Anniversary Monument
61 NDK Palace of Culture & Internet Agency
62 UK Embassy
63 Swinging Hall
64 US Consulate

accommodation with 10 beds in two rooms for US$10 per person with breakfast.

Hotel Enny (☎ 833 002, *Pop Bogomil 46*) has reasonably decent singles/double/ triples with shared bath for US$15/20/30; doubles with bathroom cost US$30. *Hotel Maya* (☎ 89 4611, *Trapezitsa 4*) is a welcoming, family-run place directly opposite TsUM. Bright clean singles/doubles with bath are US$20/30.

The tiny, four-room *Tsar Asen Hotel* (☎ 547 801, ☻ elena@mbox.infotel.bg, *Tsar Asen 68*), on the 2nd floor of a small residential block, has good, clean rooms with bath for US$28/34.

Hotel Repos (☎ 317 785, ☻ repo@npc .omega.bg, *Klokotnitsa 1*), in a multi-purpose block directly opposite the Hotel Princess, has 10 large, clean singles/ doubles/triples, some with private bath, for US$20/30/45.

The newly built *Hotel Iskâr* (☎ 986 6750, ul Iskâr 11b) may well be the best deal in Sofia with eight squeaky clean rooms, with bath and breakfast, for US$25/44 a double/apartment (there are no singles).

Places to Eat

Two modern supermarkets, *Bonjour* on Lege and *Oasis* in TsUM, stock picnic supplies, as does *Halite*. The *Ladies Market* on bul Stefan Stambolov is the best place for fresh fruit and vegetables.

Forget the Western mega-franchises. *Mimas*, with two locations at Graf Ignatiev and Vasil Levski, has tasty doner kebab and falafel pockets for 1 leva.

The *Trops Kâshta* cafeteria chain (several locations, including Sâborna 5 and in Halite), has Bulgarian dishes; the priciest item costs 3 leva. *33 Beers* is a lively pub-cum-restaurant on ploshtad Vâzrazhdane.

Of Sofia's zillion Chinese restaurants, *Asia (Chiprovtsi 1)* arguably has the hugest portions at the cheapest prices. *Birhale Gambrinus (Knyaz Dondukov 17)* has grilled meats and other national dishes washed down with draught Czech beer. The *Mayors' Club*, opposite Sveta Sophia off Moskovska, has good and cheap pub-type nosh and one of the most congenial atmospheres in town.

A romantic place for coffee and cakes is *Luciano*, on the corner of Rakovski and

BULGARIA

Moskovska. For insomniacs, *El Cabana* in NDK park is open 24 hours.

Entertainment

Opera and most classical music performances take place at the *National Opera* on Vrabcha and at *Zala Bâlgaria* on Aksakov, respectively.

During July and August, when these and other venues close for the holidays, NDK has a near-daily program of events. Check at the box office (north-eastern corner of the building) for specifics. The *Puppet Theatre (General Gurko 14)* never fails to please kids of all ages. Weekend performances start at 10.30 am and noon.

Bars & Nightclubs Not so long ago, an oft-heard complaint was that, culturally speaking, Sofia was 'dead from the waist down'. Well, no longer. *Stateside (Stamboliyski 34)* is a friendly American-theme beer hall with nachos, burgers and brownies at Bulgarian prices and good live bands most nights from 10 pm. *Mr Punch (Stefan Karadzha 20)* has live music nightly from 11 pm and a magnetic swipe-card system to keep tabs on how much you imbibe at their three bars. *Bibliotekata*, in the basement of the National Library, rocks nightly with loud live music to clear the residue of boring lectures from the noggins of party-hearty students. *Swinging Hall (bul Dragan Tsankov 8)* picks up when other places close for the night, rocking into the wee hours with bands on two opposing stages.

During the dog days of summer, city parks are filled with makeshift beer halls serving up heady Bulgarian draught and munchies. In the wooded confines of Tsar Boris Park, the *Pleven Beer Hall* and *Baba Yaga* are popular hang-outs for nature-loving beer drinkers.

Getting There & Away

Bus For international routes and fares see the Getting There & Away section earlier in this chapter.

Direct services to Rila Monastery and Melnik depart from the Ovcha Kupel bus station in the town's south-west (tram No 5 or 11). Buses and vans to Samokov (with connections to Complex Malyovitsa) leave frequently from the bus station beyond the Park-Hotel Moskva (tram No 14 or 19).

Private buses chug off to almost every corner of Bulgaria from near Hotel Princess, opposite Hotel Repos. Buy tickets in advance at nearby kiosks.

Train For international routes and fares see Getting There & Away earlier in this chapter. International train tickets are also sold at the main Rila office at General Gurko 5, open 7 am to 7 pm weekdays, and at the Rila office at the train station, downstairs opposite the regular ticket windows.

Important domestic routes include: Ruse (via Pleven, 15 leva, seven hours), Vidin (direct or via Lom, 10 leva, 5½ hours), Varna (via Pleven or Karlovo, 20 leva, 8½ hours), and Burgas (via Karlovo or Plovdiv, 15 leva, seven hours). For Veliko Târnovo change at Gorna Oryahovitsa (12 leva, 4½ hours). Plovdiv is only two hours from Sofia by frequent fast (6 leva) or occasional express (7 leva) trains. A local line east to Kazanlâk serves Koprivshtitsa (4 leva, two hours), Karlovo and Kazanlâk (for Shipka, 9 leva, three hours). Sleepers (9 leva) and couchettes (4 leva) are available to Burgas and Varna.

Sofia's central train station can be confusing. In addition to the Cyrillic destination signs, the platforms *(peron)* are numbered in Roman numerals and the tracks *(kolovoz)* in Arabic numerals.

Same-day tickets to Vidin, Ruse and Varna are sold at street level, same-day tickets to southern destinations are sold downstairs. Advanced tickets, seat reservations and sleepers are available downstairs opposite and down the hall from the regular ticket windows (6 am to 7.30 pm Monday to Friday, 7 am to 2.30 pm Saturday). The left-luggage office is also on the lower level (open 5.30 am to midnight), as is the entrance to most tracks. It's wise to buy international tickets and book sleepers/couchettes to the Black Sea coast in advance.

Getting Around

Sofia's public transport system includes trams, buses, trolleybuses and, since 1998, an underground metro. Tickets (25 stotinki) and passes valid on all vehicles are sold at kiosks but these are poorly marked so stock up. Most drivers also sell tickets. Roaming inspectors often check and on-the-spot fines are 3 leva. Remember to have an extra ticket for each piece of oversized luggage. Once punched, tickets are non-transferable.

Public transit passes *(abonamentna karta)* are available for one day (1.50 leva) and five days (5 leva).

Minibus taxis depart from many bus and tram stops. Destinations are posted on the windscreen. The fare is about three times that of buses and trams (pay the driver).

The metro has six stops but is of little value to tourists as it mainly shuttles commuters from the western Lyulin residential district to the city centre.

AROUND SOFIA
Rila Monastery (Рилски Манастир)
Rila, Bulgaria's largest and most famous monastery, is 119km south of Sofia. Rila was founded by Ivan Rilski in 927 as a colony of hermits, and in 1335 the monastery was moved 3km to its present location. Rila Monastery helped keep Bulgarian culture alive during the long dark age of Turkish rule from the 15th to the 19th centuries. In 1833 a fire destroyed the monastery but it was soon rebuilt on an even grander scale in the National Revival style.

The monastery's forbidding exterior contrasts with the warmth of the arcades inside. Four levels of balconies surround the large, irregular courtyard and three **museums** occupy some of the 300 rooms. The magnificent **church**, with its three great domes, was built between 1834 and 1837.

The monastery is open daily. People wearing shorts may not be admitted and backpacks must be left in a cloakroom outside.

Places to Stay & Eat *Rooms* with attached bath (but no hot water) are available at the monastery for US$10 per person; reception is near the museum. Behind the monastery there are several restaurants. Dorm beds (with grungy shared bath) at the *Turisticheski spalnya*, near the monastery's snack bars, cost US$5. *Camping Bor* (☎ *073-25 654)*, 1km up the valley, is open from June to September. Nearby *Zodiak Camping* (☎ *22 340)* has bungalows for about US$4 per person.

Getting There & Away Just two buses a day (10.20 am and 6.20 pm) depart from Sofia's Ovcha Kupel bus station for Rila village (two hours), from where five daily buses shuttle to the monastery (30 minutes). Get to Ovcha Kupel early as no advance tickets are sold.

In summer and on Sunday and holidays, the afternoon bus from Rila to Sofia may be booked, in which event take one of the hourly buses to Blagoevgrad and catch the train to Sofia from there. For a day's outing, it's a lot less hassle to take a guided excursion with the likes of Balkantour (US$25 per person).

Hiking in the Rila Mountains
Complex Malyovitsa is a small mountain resort (elevation 1750m) at the foot of the Rila Mountains and is an ideal starting point for anyone wishing to hike in the area. The classic trip is across the mountains from Complex Malyovitsa to Rila Monastery, which can be done in one day, or two days if you visit the Seven Lakes. Buy a Rila Mountains hiking map in Sofia before setting out. In winter the complex is a no-frills ski resort.

The *hotel* (☎ *07125-22 22)* at Complex Malyovitsa charges US$14 per person, including breakfast, and there's a pretty good restaurant. Make reservations through Odysseia-In in Sofia.

In the mountains, *hizhas* (huts) provide basic dormitory accommodation. Though many serve meals, it's best to bring some food. For current information on hizhas, contact Odysseia-In.

To Rila via Malyovitsa About an hour's hike above Complex Malyovitsa is the year-round *Hizha Malyovitsa* (2050m), where a dorm bed (US$4) and a bowl of soup are usually available. From Hizha Malyovitsa you can hike up to *Hizha Sedemte ezera* in about seven hours. This hizha is right beside one of the legendary Seven Lakes. From Hizha Sedemte ezera you can hike down to Rila Monastery (1147m) in six hours.

Thrace

KOPRIVSHTITSA
(КОПРИВЩИЦА)
☎ 07184
This picturesque village in the Sredna Gora Mountains, 113km east of Sofia, has been carefully preserved as an open-air museum of the Bulgarian National Revival style.

Even without its 388 registered architectural monuments, Koprivshtitsa would merit a visit for its cobblestone streets, redtile houses and photogenic stone bridges.

It was here, on 20 April 1876, that Todor Kableshkov proclaimed the uprising against the Turks that eventually led to the Russo-Turkish War of 1877-78.

Information

The Tourist Information Centre (TIC; ☎ 21 91) in the park provides information and books lodgings.

The ticket office next to the April 20 Mehana sells a joint ticket (1.50 leva) to six museum houses. If it's closed, buy the ticket at Oslekov House.

The State Savings Bank is one block south of the TIC.

Things to See

Half of Koprivshtitsa's house-museums are closed Monday, the others Tuesday. Working hours are 8 am to noon and 1 to 5.30 pm all year.

Just uphill from the ticket office is **Oslekov House** (1856), formerly a rich merchant's home. Its spacious interior and stylish furnishings are outstanding. Just beyond is the **Assumption Church** (1817), which you pass to reach **Kableshov House**, former home of the revolutionary Todor Kableshkov, now a museum of the 1876 uprising (all labels are in Bulgarian).

Continue south to the small stone bridge over the Byala stream, where the first shot of the 1876 uprising was fired.

Next to the bus station, the **Sts Cyril & Methodius School** (1837) was the second primary school to teach in Bulgarian.

Other museums of note include **Debelyanov House** (1832), not far from Oslekov House; **Lyutov House** (1854), with a resplendent salon; the **House of Lyuben Karavelov** (1834-79), now a museum portraying the life of this ideologist of the uprising; and **Benkovski House** (1831), which is on the hillside in the south-eastern part of town.

Georgi Benkovski led the Bulgarian cavalry on legendary exploits until he fell in a Turkish ambush. Above the house is a huge **equestrian statue** of the man and a view of the entire valley.

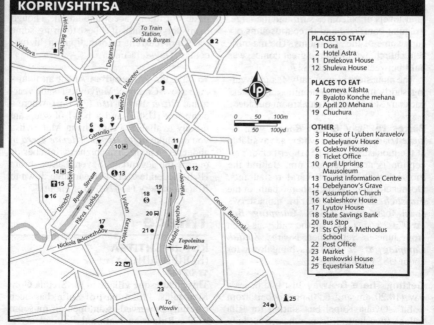

KOPRIVSHTITSA

BULGARIA

PLACES TO STAY
1 Dora
2 Hotel Astra
11 Drelekova House
12 Shuleva House

PLACES TO EAT
4 Lomeva Kâshta
7 Byaloto Konche mehana
9 April 20 Mehana
19 Chuchura

OTHER
3 House of Lyuben Karavelov
5 Debelyanov House
6 Oslekov House
8 Ticket Office
10 April Uprising Mausoleum
13 Tourist Information Centre
14 Debelyanov's Grave
15 Assumption Church
16 Kableshkov House
17 Lyutov House
18 State Savings Bank
20 Bus Stop
21 Sts Cyril & Methodius School
22 Post Office
23 Market
24 Benkovski House
25 Equestrian Statue

Places to Stay

The TIC organises *private rooms* for US$7. Two authentic period houses, *Shuleva House* and *Drelekova House*, both located due east of the TIC, have rooms with shared bath for US$10 per person.

Dora (☎ 25 16, Hristo Belchev 4) has a dozen double and triple rooms with shared bath in two adjacent wooden buildings for US$6 per person.

Hotel Astra (☎ 23 64, Hadzhi Nencho Palaveev 9) is a friendly place with four double rooms and shared bath at US$10 per person.

Places to Eat

Watch out for possible overcharging, especially at the heavily touristed *April 20 Complex*.

Lomeva Kâshta, hard to miss with its striking blue exterior, specialises in Bulgarian fare. *Chuchura*, near the bus station, serves up tasty national cuisine. One of the nicest places in town is *Byaloto Konche*. It's located directly opposite Oslekov House.

Getting There & Away

The train station is about 10km north of town, but there are connecting buses to Koprivshtitsa. Trains run to/from Sofia (4 leva, two hours) every few hours. If you're heading east from Koprivshtitsa, change trains at Karlovo for Plovdiv and Burgas, or at Tulovo for Veliko Târnovo.

A daily bus from Sofia to Koprivshtitsa (4 leva, 2½ hours) departs at 4 pm Monday to Saturday (5 pm Sunday) from the western end of the main staging area behind the Princess Hotel. From Koprivshtitsa to Sofia, the bus departs at 6.45 am (2 pm Sunday) from the town bus station.

PLOVDIV (ПЛОВДИВ)
☎ 032

Plovdiv is Bulgaria's second-largest city, occupying both banks of the Maritsa River. Two main trans-European corridors converge here: one from Asia Minor to Europe, the other from Central Asia to Greece via Ukraine. This strategic position accounts for Plovdiv's pre-eminence, beginning in 341 BC when Philip II of Macedonia conquered Philipoupolis (Plovdiv). The Romans left extensive remains in the city, which they called Trimontium (Three Hills), as did the Turks, who called it Philibe.

Yet it was the Bulgarian National Revival that gave Plovdiv its 19th-century 'baroque' houses. Many of these ornate buildings are now open to the public as museums, galleries or restaurants and make a visit to Old Plovdiv well worthwhile.

Orientation & Information

The train station is south-west of the old town. From the station head north-east along ul Ivan Vazov to Central Square. Knyaz Aleksandre, Plovdiv's pedestrian mall, runs north from the square; the old town is accessed from the narrow streets to the right.

Balkan VIP Tours (☎ 56 24 30) is at bul Tsar Boris III in the fairgrounds north of the river.

The Foreign Trade Bank on Knyaz Aleksandre will change travellers cheques for a 1% commission, and there is an ATM out the front. There's a telephone centre at the main post office on Central Square.

Things to See

The excavated remains of the **Roman Forum** are in front of the post office. Knyaz Aleksandre, a bustling pedestrian mall, runs north from here to the 15th-century **Djoumaya Mosque**, which is still used for religious services.

Go east on Sâborna into the old town. The national landmark **Church of Constantin & Elena** (1832) has been beautifully restored, and next to it is a good icon gallery. The **Ethnographical Museum**, in a photogenic baroque 1847 mansion on Doctor Tchomakov, has a collection of folk costumes (closed Monday).

Downhill from the museum are two of the finest examples of Revival architecture and period furnishings, the **Balabanov and Hindlian houses** (open daily April through September).

Retracing your steps, the street beside the Ethnographical Museum leads down through **Hisar Kapiya**, the Roman eastern city gate, to Georgiadi House (1848), another fine example of Plovdiv baroque, and now the fascinating **National Revival Museum** (closed Sunday).

To the south of the museum is a quaint cobblestone quarter with more colourful 19th-century houses, courtyard restaurants

BULGARIA

and church ensembles crowding the winding streets. Nearby to the west, the restored 3000-seat **Roman theatre** (2nd century), uncovered by a freak landslide in 1972, is used at festival time.

Places to Stay

Camping *Camping Gorski Kat* (☎ 55 13 60), open year-round, is 4km west of Plovdiv on the Sofia Highway. Bus No 222 leaves hourly from the train station and stops here. Camping costs US$5 per person; bungalow beds are US$15.

Private Rooms The Prima Vista Accommodation Agency (☎/fax 27 27 78), Vassil Aprilov 61, arranges rooms at US$5 to US$10 per person. Esperantsa (☎ 26 51 27), Ivan Vazov 14, charges US$8 to $US10.

Hotels The delightful if musty *Turisticheski dom* (☎ 23 32 11, Slaveikov 5), in the old town, has hostel-style rooms with shared facilities for US$15 per person.

Plovdiv's most affordable former state-owned hotels include the 10-storey *Hotel Leipzig* (☎ 23 22 51, bul Ruski 20), four blocks from the train station, and the four-storey *Hotel Bâlgaria* (☎ 22 60 64) in the centre of town. The former has rooms for US$28/40, the latter for US$30/50. All prices include breakfast.

Places to Eat

Restaurant Puldin (*Knjaz Tseretelev 6*) has several unique dining rooms, one of them in the basement amid Byzantine walls and Roman artefacts, another in a 200-year-old hall where dervishes once whirled themselves into exhaustion.

One block over is the *Alafrangite Restaurant* (*Cyril Nektariev 17*) an authentic 19-th century house with excellent Bulgarian cuisine. *Chevermeto Mehana* (*Dondukov 4*) occupies a labyrinth of WWII bomb shelters dug into Sahat Tepe hill. Its spit-roasted lamb (*chevermeto*) goes well with live Balkan folk-pop music and rollicking plate-smash dancing.

Entertainment

Opera and gala performances at the restored Roman theatre are a summer highlight; check posters around town for starting times. The underground *Midas Taverna* (*Otets Paisii 14*) is Plovdiv's hottest disco, bumping and grinding until 4 am.

Getting There & Away

Buses to Sofia, Burgas, Nesebâr and Sozopol depart from the Yug bus station opposite the train station. For İstanbul, Athens, Thessaloniki, and Western Europe check with Eurobus and the City Local Transport Company, located side by side at Central Square 1.

For international train tickets and couchettes, go to the Rila office at Hristo Botev 31. For advance tickets on domestic trains, go to Byuro at Nezavisimost 29 (closed weekends).

All trains between Istanbul and Belgrade pass through Plovdiv. Other trains run to Sofia (6 leva, two hours) and Burgas (9 leva, 4½ hours).

Black Sea Coast

Every summer Bulgaria's Black Sea beaches lure masses of sun seekers on holiday. Burgas and Varna take on a carnival atmosphere as camping grounds and hotels fill up. In the off season, from around mid-September to the end of May, the resorts are dead.

Though it's convenient to come from Sofia by train, travel up and down the coast is almost exclusively by bus.

BURGAS (БУРГАС)

☎ 056

Smaller and less crowded than Varna, Burgas also has less to offer. The northern side of the city is crowded with concrete apartment blocks, and there's a big oil refinery to the west. The old town by the port is still pretty, however, and Burgas makes a convenient base from which to explore the towns along the coast.

The **Archaeological Museum** at Bogoridi 21 has a small collection of antiquities plus a new live reptile exhibit (to boost sagging interest in antiquities). The **National Science Museum**, Fotinov 30, has an informative display of regional flora and fauna. The most illuminating museum is the **City History Museum** at Lermontov 31; especially good are the old photos of turn-of-the-century Burgas town and beach life. The museum is open 9 am to 5 pm weekdays.

But it's the **Maritime Park** which is the town's showpiece. This extensive swath of greenery runs alongside the sea from the port area north to the salt-pan shores of Lake Atanasovsko and features manicured flower beds, spouting fountains, Soviet-era war memorials and modern sculptures.

Orientation & Information

The train, bus and boat terminals are all adjacent. Aleksandrovska and Bogoridi, the inter-connected pedestrian malls, run north to the Soviet soldier monument on ploshtad Troikata and east to the Maritime Park, respectively

There's a tourist information office in the lobby of the Hotel Bâlgaria at Alexandrovska 21. Orbita Student Travel (☎ 42 380) is at Filip Kutev 2a. There are private exchange offices around the central pedestrian malls, plus an ATM at the Bulbank on Aleksandrovska opposite the Hotel Bâlgaria.

Places to Stay & Eat

Primorets Travel (☎ 84 27 27; open 9.30 am to 5.30 pm weekdays) directly opposite the train station and Balkanov Tourist Bureau (☎ 84 04 01; open 8 am to 8 pm daily) at Bogoridi 14 all book *rooms* with local families for US$5 to US$6 per person

A good private hotel is *Mirazh Hotel (☎ 38 177, Lermontov 48)*. Rooms are US$15 per person. There are two private hotels near Hotel Kosmos, north of the centre. Try *Hotel Biela Rosa (☎ 36 686, Batak 42a)*, with pleasant singles/doubles for US$22/30.

A delightful garden restaurant tucked midway along the Bogoridi promenade is *Kaminata*. The folksy *National Mehana (Filip Kutev 6)* serves tasty national cuisine 24 hours a day.

Getting There & Away

Bus service all along the coast is much easier now thanks to Minibus Express (☎ 40 484). The staging area is near the state bus terminal.

Vans to Sozopol, Sunny Beach and Nesebâr depart about every 40 minutes. More distant points such as Varna (two hours) and Ahtopol (1½ hours) are per demand or as scheduled (6.30 pm and 8 am respectively).

Group, Etap and other companies run several daily coaches to Sofia, Plovdiv and other main cities from near the major hotels.

Omega 3 (☎ 49 432) at ploshtad Garov 12 has daily buses departing at 4 pm for Istanbul (US$15, 16 hours). Balkanov Tourist Bureau (☎ 84 04 01), Bogoridi 14, has services to Greece, Turkey and Western Europe.

The historic train station (1902) has been beautifully restored inside and out and is the most attractive such facility in Bulgaria. For all train tickets go to the train station as the Rila office is defunct. Express trains run between Sofia and Burgas seven times a day, via Plovdiv or Karlovo. For Veliko Târnovo change trains at Stara Zagora or Tulovo.

SOZOPOL (СОЗОПОЛ)
☎ 05514

In this picturesque little town, sturdy wooden dwellings choke narrow cobblestone streets on which women sell lace to visitors. On the western side of the peninsula, a naval base flanks the local fishing port; on the eastern side there are two fairly good beaches (although the best beach is at **Dyuni**, 6km south). Sozopol is very relaxed and is one of the few coastal resorts that caters to individual travellers.

You can hire one of the water taxis bobbing at the harbour for an excursion to the **Ropotamo River nature reserve** for a negotiable fee.

The telephone centre is in the post office in the middle of the old town. There are plenty of private exchange offices and an ATM at the Bâlgarska Banka.

Places to Stay

Camping *Zlatna Ribka Camping(☎ 24 27)* is 2km before Sozopol on the road north from Burgas. No bungalows are available but there's plenty of camping space (US$2 per person) above a small beach from where small boats shuttle to Sozopol.

Private Rooms Lotos Agency (☎/fax 24 29), Apollonia 22, organises *private rooms* at US$8 to US$12 per person. It's open 8 am to 9 pm daily April through October.

Two small *guesthouses* at Milet 24 and Morski Skali 33 have rooms so close to the sea you can hear the waves lapping. Rooms with shared bath cost US$8 per person.

Hotels The *Hotel Sozopol (☎ 23 62)*, next to the bus station, charges US$10 per person. There are small private hotels along

BULGARIA

Republikanska, the street running south towards the new town. Try *Hotel Radik* (☎ 37 06) at No 4 which charges US$15 a double. The new *Hotel Orion* (☎ 31 93, Vihren 28) has very pleasant rooms for US$15 per person with breakfast and sweeping views of Sozopol Bay at no extra charge.

Getting There & Away The small bus station is next to the market but private vans offer much better service to Burgas for the same price (1.50 leva, 30 minutes). There's just one scheduled bus a day south to Tsarevo (1.15 pm) and Ahtopol (4 pm), with intermediary stops, but vans will go there per demand.

NESEBÂR (НЕСЕБЬР)
☎ 0554
Nesebâr sits on a small, rocky island connected to the mainland by a narrow man-made isthmus. Remnants of the 2nd-century city walls and towers flank the entrance, and along the winding cobblestone streets are handsome stone-and-timber houses.

Scattered through the town are more than a dozen medieval churches, most of them now in ruins. Of special interest is the 11th-century **St Stefan Church** above the maritime terminal, almost completely covered inside with 16th-century frescoes. The superb collection of the **Archaeological Museum** is in the modern building just inside the city walls.

Nesebâr has become highly commercialised with plenty of twee souvenir shops and restaurants advertising roast beef and Yorkshire pudding, but it's a must-see for travellers.

Places to Stay & Eat
Gama Tours (☎ 44 280) at Hristo Botev 10 in the new town can arrange *private rooms* for US$6 to US$10 per person. It's open 9 am to 9 pm daily. *Guesthouses* along sea-facing Kraibrezhna at Nos 16 and 20 rent double rooms with shared facilities for US$20.

For fresh seafood (opt for the *lefer* or bluefish) try *Neptun Restaurant (Neptun 1)*. Nearby is *Lozarska Kâshta*, a typical tavern serving meat dishes.

Getting There & Away
The bus stop is behind the museum next to the harbour. Buses to Burgas and Sunny Beach depart at regular intervals, or you can hop one of the nearby sea taxis to Sunny Beach and make connections from there.

Etap and Bimet have daily overnight coaches to Sofia (17 leva, 6½ hours), by way of Burgas, departing at 10.30 pm. Ask at Gama Tours (see Places to Stay & Eat) about buses to other destinations.

VARNA (ВАРНА)
☎ 052
Varna, Bulgaria's largest Black Sea city and its second-busiest port, is the country's summer capital, with beaches, extensive parks, museums, restaurants, theatres and teeming pedestrian malls. The excellent **Museum of History & Art** at Maria Luiza 41 is dedicated to archaeology and features a collection of 6000-year-old worked gold and copper objects. The **Ethnographical Museum** is also superb, housed in an authentic (1860) National Revival house compound at Panagyurishte 22. Also visit the 2nd-century **Roman Baths** on Khan Krum, the most extensive Roman ruins in Bulgaria.

The focus of summer activity is the verdant **Seaside Gardens**, in Primorski Park, with myriad outdoor cafes, beachside beer halls and late-night discos.

The Varna Summer Festival (June through August) features outstanding musical events. Information and tickets are available at the kiosk across from Assumption Cathedral.

Orientation
The bus and train stations are on opposite sides of the city; bus Nos 1, 22 and 41 run between them. The maritime terminal is within walking distance of the train station. From the train station, walk north on Tsar Simeon to Nezavisimost, the centre of town. A broad pedestrian mall, Knyaz Boris-I, runs east from here into Slivnitsa, which heads south into the Seaside Gardens.

Information
Staff at Varnenski Bryag (☎ 22 55 24), Musala 3, provide maps and information and can book rooms and international and domestic bus tickets. The office is open 8.30 am to 7 pm weekdays.

Tourist Agency George (☎/fax 60 74 74, ✉ georgesm@revolta.com), Tsar Simeon 36b, is a helpful information and bookings

BULGARIA

office open 8 am to 8 pm daily (closed Sunday in winter).

Megatours at the Hotel Chernomorets is the local American Express representative.

Varna's oversupply of exchange bureaus means that you can convert cash at decent rates. The bureau at Sheinovo 6 changes travellers cheques at no commission, albeit at lower rates. The Post Bank, on Knyaz Boris-I near the Opera House, charges US$5 to change travellers cheques; it's open 8 am to 5 pm weekdays, 8.30 am to noon Saturday. Opposite, the Dresden Bank has an ATM.

You can place long-distance telephone calls at the main post office, Sâborna 36; it's open 7 am to 11 pm daily.

Places to Stay

Private Rooms Two tourist services in the train station rent *private rooms* from US$5 US$7 per person. They're open 6 am to 10 pm daily in summer.

Tourist Agency George (see Information earlier) organises *private rooms* at US$8/12 for a single/double.

Hotels The cheapest hotel right in town is the seedy *Hotel Musala* (☎ *22 39 25, Musala 3*), with dorm-like rooms and shared baths for US$14/20 a single/ double.

The three-star *Hotel Odesa* (☎ *22 53 12, Slivnitsa 1*) overlooks the Seaside Gardens and has singles at US$30/35, doubles at US$36/46 for park/sea views, respectively.

The modern new *Hotel Akropolis* (☎ *60 31 07/08, Tsar Shishman 13*) has clean singles/doubles with bath, air con, TV and phone for US$27/32.

Places to Eat

Paraklisa (The Monastery; Primorski 47) is Varna's most distinctive restaurant, with a menu featuring old Bulgarian recipes.

El Taco, next door to McDonald's on Nezavisimost and open 24 hours, has good Tex-Mex fare and live music in the evening.

The unassuming *Mustang Food Bar*, on Preslav near Hotel Musala, is a great place for a drink or a quick snack. Next door is the Revival-era Union of Architects building with a *mehana* and a pleasant garden patio.

Getting There & Away

Etap (☎ 23 04 87), at the Hotel Chernomorets, runs six daily coaches to Sofia (15 leva, 6½ hours). Kaly (☎ 60 08 85), Tsar Simeon 33, has two daily buses to Burgas and Plovdiv.

The state bus station at bul Vladislav Varnencik 159 has services to most major cities. There is also a daily bus to Durankulak on the Romanian border.

City bus Nos 109 and 209 run as far as Camping Panorama at Golden Sands from the south side of Hristo Botev, west of Assumption Cathedral. Vans to Albena (the last one around 7.30 pm), Golden Sands (No 9) and Sveti Konstantin (No 8) also leave from here. Purchase tickets at the kiosk.

Seven daily trains go to Sofia (20 leva, 8½ hours), most via Pleven, though two go via either Plovdiv or Karlovo. For Veliko Târnovo change trains at Gorna Oryahovitsa. Two trains a day go direct to Ruse. Daily service to Burgas takes five hours on a roundabout route.

Northern Bulgaria

SHUMEN (ШУМЕН)
☎ 054

Shumen sits at the base of a low flat spur of the Stara Planina, halfway from the Black Sea to the Danube. Shumen is a transportation hub and there are several things worth stopping off to see.

From the bus station, take bus No 10 west to the end of the line. It passes the **Tombul Mosque** (1744), Bulgaria's largest and most beautifully decorated mosque, before terminating at the town's famous **brewery**, Shumensko pivo. From here, head uphill 3km to the partially restored **Shumen Fortress** which is open 9 am to 5 pm all year.

The **Madara Horseman**, 10km east of Shumen, is a large 8th-century rock carving of a mounted figure spearing a lion.

Orientation & Information

The adjacent bus and train stations are on the eastern side of town; follow bul Slavianski west to the centre. The old Turkish town is to the west of Hotel Madara; the 19th-century National Revival area is to the north.

Places to Stay & Eat

Camping Madara (☎ 05313-99 53 13) is a pleasant wooded spot 500m from the horseman with tent sites (US$3 per person) and bungalows (US$10). There is a *hostel* (☎ *20 91)* with dorm beds for US$7 near the horseman parking area.

The rather run-down *Orbita Hotel (☎ 52 398)* in Kyoshkovete Park, beyond the brewery, offers doubles for US$20. *Hotel Stariyagrad (☎ 55 376)*, up near the Shumen Fortress in a serene wooded locale, costs US$16 a double.

Three authentic *mehanas* occupy a complex of traditional wooden buildings just east of Hotel Shumen.

Getting There & Away
Shumen is on the main line from Sofia to Varna via Pleven. Madara (18km) is accessible by local train on the line to Kaspichan and Varna.

Buses include three a day to Madara and one every hour to Preslav.

Etap and Group run private coaches to Sofia (12 leva, 5½ hours), Varna (3 leva, one hour) and other destinations; their kiosks are between the bus and train stations.

PRESLAV (ПРЕСЛАВ)
☎ 0538

Preslav, 20km south-west of Shumen, was founded in 821 by Khan Omourtag.

Tsar Simeon moved the court here in 893 from Pliska and Preslav remained the capital of the First Bulgarian Empire until it was conquered by the Byzantines in 971.

The extensive ruins of Veliki Preslav are 2km south of the present town of Preslav. The 5-sq-km outer city was protected by a high stone wall and contained churches, monasteries and the residences of the nobles. The most famous building was the **Round Gold Church**, built by Simeon in 908 and partially restored in recent times. The modern **Archaeological Museum** at the ruins has architectural fragments and a model of the original buildings.

Buses run to/from Preslav and Shumen. If you want to stay, the grubby two-star *Hotel Preslav (☎ 25 08)* in the centre has singles/doubles for US$18/24.

RUSE (РУСЕ)
☎ 082

Ruse, the largest Bulgarian port on the Danube, is a gateway to the country and a parade of riverboats stops here. In AD 70 a Roman fortress, Sexaginta Prista (60 ships),

defended the empire's northern border. Under the Ottomans, Ruse was modernised and its eclectic architecture reflects Western European influences. Today, the 'Beautiful Bulgaria' project is restoring these edifices to their former glory.

Orientation & Information
The adjacent bus and train stations are on the southern side of town. Head north up Borisova to ploshtad Svoboda, the town's centre. Among the 18 streets that meet on this square is Aleksandrovska, Ruse's pedestrian mall.

Dunav Tours (☎ 22 30 88) at ploshtad Khan Kubrat 5, just off Aleksandrovska, provides useful city information. Opening hours are 9 am to noon and 1 to 5.30 pm weekdays.

Places to Stay
The *Ribarska Koliba Campground (☎ 22 40 68)*, open May to mid-October, is 6km south of Ruse on the road to Sofia. It's US$3 per person to camp or US$7 for a two-person cabin. It's best to take a taxi out there (4 leva). A kilometre beyond the camping ground is a hostel, *Hizha Prista (☎ 23 41 67)*, with dorm beds at US$5 per person (30% less with a HI card). It's open all year.

Dunav Tours (see Orientation & Information) has *private rooms* at US$12/20 a single/double. The concrete *Hotel Helios (☎ 22 56 61, Nikolaevska 1)* will do in a pinch with marginal-quality rooms at US$15 per person with shared bath, US$22/33 a single/double with private bath.

Getting There & Away
Express coaches run to Varna, Shumen, Sofia and other destinations from the bus station and Hotel Dunav.

Two trains a day go from Ruse to Varna (four hours), while others stop short at Kaspichan (three hours) near Madara. Fast trains run to Sofia (seven hours) via Pleven, including one overnight train. For Veliko Târnovo (three hours) change trains at Gorna Oryahovitsa. There are six trains a day to Romania, three of them going through to Bucharest, the others terminating in Giurgiu.

It's possible to hitch (walking is not allowed) across the border on the Friendship Bridge (Dunav Most), 6km downstream. Cars pay a US$7 toll and long delays are common. The chaos means there's no bus direct from Ruse to Romania.

VELIKO TÂRNOVO
(ВЕЛИКО ТЪРНОВО)
☎ 062

The Yantra River winds through a gorge in the centre of Veliko Târnovo, and picturesque houses cling to the cliffs. This is one town you won't want to miss.

Almost encircled by the river, the ruined Tsarevets Citadel recalls the Second Bulgarian Empire (1185-1393), with Veliko Târnovo as its capital.

North-west, across the abyss, is the now overgrown Trapezitsa Hill, former residence of nobles and courtiers. In the valley below, the artisans' and merchants' quarter – known as Asenova – is marked by medieval churches.

Orientation & Information

The train station is by the river, far below the centre of town (catch bus Nos 4 or 13). The bus station is on Nikola Gabrovski, at the western edge of town (bus Nos 7, 10, 11 or 12). Many buses arriving in Veliko Târnovo stop near the market before terminating at the bus station, so ask.

The new Tourist Information Centre (☎ 22 148) at Hristo Botev 13A is a font of useful information; its hours are 7.30 am to 6 pm weekdays.

United Bulgarian Bank, across the road from Hotel Yantra, changes travellers cheques for a 1.5% commission.

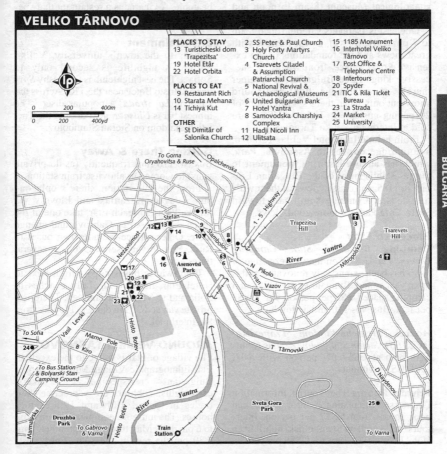

VELIKO TÂRNOVO

PLACES TO STAY	2 SS Peter & Paul Church	15 1185 Monument
13 Turisticheski dom 'Trapezitsa'	3 Holy Forty Martyrs Church	16 Interhotel Veliko Târnovo
19 Hotel Etâr	4 Tsarevets Citadel & Assumption Patriarchal Church	17 Post Office & Telephone Centre
22 Hotel Orbita		18 Intertours
	5 National Revival & Archaeological Museums	20 Spyder
PLACES TO EAT		21 TIC & Rila Ticket Bureau
9 Restaurant Rich	6 United Bulgarian Bank	
10 Starata Mehana	7 Hotel Yantra	23 La Strada
14 Tichiya Kut	8 Samovodska Charshiya Complex	24 Market
		25 University
OTHER	11 Hadji Nicoli Inn	
1 St Dimitâr of Salonika Church	12 Ulitsata	

0   200   400m
0   200   400yd

To Gorna Oryahovitsa & Ruse

Opalchenska

Nezavisimost

Stefan

To Gabrovo & Varna

To Sofia

Vasil Levski

Marno Pole

B Kiro

To Bus Station & Bolyarski Stan Camping Ground

Marmalijka

Druzhba Park

Hristo Botev

River   Yantra

Train Station

1 - 5 Highway

Stambolov

N Pikolo

Ivan Vazov

Asenovtsi Park

Trapezitsa Hill

River   Yantra

Mitropolska

Tsarevets Hill

T Târnovski

Sveta Gora Park

D Naydenov

To Varna

BULGARIA

The telephone centre in the main post office, at Hristo Botev 1, is open from 7 am to 10 pm daily.

Things to See & Do

Opposite Hotel Yantra on Stefan Stambolov, a stairway leads up to the colourful neighbourhood of Varosha. Veer left down the stone-surfaced Rakovski, where Bulgarian artisans keep small shops. The **Hadji Nicoli Inn** (1858) at No 17 is one of the best known National Revival buildings in Bulgaria.

Return to the Hotel Yantra and head south to scenic Gurko, then east to the **Bulgarian National Revival Museum** in the old Turkish town hall (8 am to 6 pm, daily, June through September). The arched stone building next door houses the excellent **Archaeological Museum** (8 am to noon and 1 to 6 pm, closed Monday in summer).

Due east is **Tsarevets Citadel** (open 8 am to 7 pm daily; 3 leva), a vast fortress with great views and the foundations of the extensive **Royal Palace**, from where 22 successive kings ruled Bulgaria. In summer there's an impressive **light-and-sound show** but only when there's a minimum of 20 paying customers. Tickets (US$7) are sold at Interhotel Veliko Târnovo.

From behind Interhotel Veliko Târnovo, a footbridge crosses to **Asenovtsi Park**, which has an awe-inspiring **monument** to the re-establishment of the Bulgarian Empire in 1185, and classic views of the town's tier houses. Continue south-east toward **Sveta Gora Park** for more good views.

Places to Stay

Camping *Bolyarski Stan Camping Ground* (☎ *41 859*) on the western edge of town has been extensively renovated and is open year-round. Bungalows are US$8 and camping space US$3 per person plus US$3 per tent. Bus Nos 110 and 5 stop here.

Hostel *Turisticheski dom 'Trapezitsa'* (☎ *22 061, Stefan Stambolov 79*) has rooms with bath at US$7 per person with a HI card, US$9 without.

Private Rooms The Tourist Information Centre (see Orientation & Information) can book rooms from US$7 per person. Intertours (☎ *28 669*) on Stamboliiski uphill from Hotel Etâr books rooms for US$9 per person.

Hotels The dodgy *Hotel Orbita* (☎ *62 20 41, Hristo Botev 15*) charges US$8 per person for rooms with shared bath; reception is on the 4th floor.

The two-star *Hotel Etâr* (☎ *62 18 38, Ivailo 1*), is directly behind Hotel Orbita. Rooms are US$15/30 for a single/double with shared bath, US$20/40 with private bath.

Places to Eat

Starata Mehana is a friendly little place on the cliff-side of Stefan Stambolov. The food is good and cheap and the terrace views are spectacular. If it's full, one block up the street is the equally good *Restaurant Rich* with a larger terrace offering the same killer views. For honest-to-goodness folksiness the *Tichya Kut vinarna (Gurko 5)* is unbeatable. A vinarna is a restaurant that specialises in wine.

Entertainment

Thanks to the town's university, Veliko Târnovo's nightlife is second only to Sofia's. The best nightclub is the flashy *Spyder* on Hristo Botev near the TIC. Across the street is *La Strada*, a popular disco. The hippest bar is *Ulitsata*, next door to the Turisticheski dom on Stefan Stambolov.

Getting There & Away

Bus No 110 runs frequently (as do private vans) to Gorna Oryahovitsa train station.

From the bus station, there's only one bus a day to Kazanlâk and Plovdiv via Shipka Pass. To reach Etâr, take one of the seven daily buses to Gabrovo and change there. Other service includes two buses to Ruse. Private vans serve Gabrovo several times a day.

Etap, whose buses depart from next to Hotel Etâr, has several daily coaches to Sofia and to Varna via Shumen. There is a private van at 8.30 am daily to Plovdiv from the Interhotel.

AROUND VELIKO TÂRNOVO

The village of **Etâr** is home to the excellent Etâr Ethnographic Village Museum, where Bulgarian craftspeople – bakers, cartwrights, cobblers etc – practice their trades in typical 18th and 19th-century houses. The museum complex is open 8 am to 6 pm daily May through September, until 4.30 pm the rest of the year. Entry costs

5 leva. Take the bus from Veliko Târnovo to Gabrovo (49km), then catch a bus to Etâr (9km).

KAZANLÂK (КАЗАНЛЪК)
☎ 0431

Kazanlâk, an important stop on the railway line from Burgas to Sofia, is tucked between the Stara Planina and Sredna Gora mountains in the Valley of Roses. This is not a particularly attractive town, but it is a useful base for visiting nearby attractions.

The **Valley of Roses** was, until just recently, the source of 70% of the world's supply of rose attar (essential oil). The roses bloom from late May to early June and must be picked before sunrise when still wet with dew if the fragrance is to be preserved. Two thousand petals are required for a single gram of attar. The Festival of Roses, held during the first week in June, features a carnival atmosphere and parades in Kazanlâk and Karlovo.

In Tjulbeto Park, 2km north-east of Kazanlâk's train and bus stations, is a 4th-century BC **Thracian tomb** with delicate frescos discovered during the construction of a bomb shelter in 1944. The original brick tomb cannot be visited without official permission, but a full-scale replica has been created nearby. It's open 8 am to noon and 1.30 to 6 pm daily.

The most atmospheric place to eat and stay is *Hadji Eminova Kâshta* (☎ *42 095, Nikola Petkov 22*), an authentic 19th-century walled compound with a good mehana and a couple of traditionally furnished rooms for an unbeatable US$10 a double.

Croatia

With almost 6000km of Adriatic coastline speckled with Roman ruins, Venetian ports and innumerable bays and inlets, it's not surprising that Croatia (Hrvatska) became a major tourist destination for German, Italians, Austrians and Brits in the 1970s and 1980s. When Yugoslavia split in 1991, Croatia's brief but violent struggle for independence brought tourism to a standstill.

Nowadays Croatia is regaining its balance and tourists are once again flocking to its shores. It's easy to binge on the sunny skies and clear seas but take time to appreciate the cultural contrasts as well. Zagreb retains the serene elegance of an Austro-Hungarian city while the Italian-influenced coast has a distinctively Mediterranean exhuberance. Above all, there's the magnificent walled city of Dubrovnik, justifiably known as the 'Pearl of the Adriatic'.

Facts about Croatia

HISTORY

In 229 BC the Romans began their conquest of the indigenous Illyrians, establishing a colony at Salona (near Split) in Dalmatia. Around AD 625, Croatian tribes moved into what is now Croatia. In 925 the Dalmatian duke Tomislav united the Croats in a single kingdom that prospered for nearly 200 years.

In the 14th century the Turks began pushing into the Balkans. Northern Croatia in 1527 turned to the Habsburgs of Austria for protection and remained under their influence until 1918. The coast fell under the control of Venice in the early 15th century and remained part of *La Serenissima* until the Napoleonic invasion of 1797.

With the defeat of the Austro-Hungarian empire in WWI, Croatia became part of the Kingdom of Serbs, Croats and Slovenes (called Yugoslavia after 1929) – a move strongly resisted by Croatian nationalists.

After the German invasion of Yugoslavia in March 1941, a puppet government dominated by the fascist Ustaša movement was set up in Croatia under Ante Pavelić. The Ustaša launched an extermination campaign that surpassed even that of the Nazis in scale, brutally murdering some 350,000 ethnic Serbs, Jews and Roma (Gypsies), although the exact number is controversial. The Ustaša program called for 'one-third of Serbs killed, one-third expelled and one-third converted to Catholicism'.

Postwar Croatia was granted republic status within the Yugoslav Federation. During the 1960s Croatia and Slovenia moved far ahead of the southern republics economically, leading to demands for greater autonomy. In 1989, following severe repression of the Albanian majority in Serbia's Kosovo province, Croats felt the time had come to end more than four decades of communist rule and attain complete autonomy.

In the free elections of April 1990, Franjo Tudjman's Croatian Democratic Union (Hrvatska Demokratska Zajednica) easily defeated the old Communist Party. When Croatia declared independence on 25 June 1991, the Serbian enclave of Krajina proclaimed its independence from Croatia. Heavy fighting broke out in Krajina, Baranja and Slavonia. The 180,000-member Yugoslav People's Army, dominated by Serbian communists, began to intervene under the pretext of halting ethnic violence. After EC mediation, Croatia agreed to freeze its independence declaration for three months to avoid bloodshed. Yet the violence continued – during six months of fighting in Croatia 10,000 people died, hundreds of thousands fled and tens of thousands of homes were deliberately destroyed.

CROATIA

CROATIA (HRVATSKA)

In early December 1991 the United Nations successfully negotiated with Serbia over the deployment of a 14,000-member UN Protection Force. A 15th cease-fire beginning on 3 January 1992 generally held, and the Yugoslav federal army was allowed to withdraw from its bases inside Croatia. In January 1992 the EC recognised Croatia. This was followed three months later by US recognition and in May 1992 Croatia was admitted to the United Nations.

On 1 May 1995, the Croatian army and police entered occupied western Slavonia, east of Zagreb, and seized control of the region within days. As the Croatian military consolidated its hold in western Slavonia, the Serb army, outnumbered by two to one, fled towards northern Bosnia, along with 150,000 civilians whose roots in the Krajina stretched back centuries.

The Dayton agreement signed in Paris in December 1995 recognised Croatia's traditional borders and provided for the return of eastern Slavonia, a transition that was completed in January 1998. Although stability has returned to the country, a key provision of the agreement was the promise by the Croatian government to allow the return of Serbian refugees – a promise that remains unfulfilled although Croatia's new government headed by Stipe Mesic is promising to expedite matters.

GEOGRAPHY

The narrow Croatian coastal belt at the foot of the Dinaric Alps is only about 600km long as the crow flies, but it's so indented that the actual length is 1778km. Most of the 'beaches' along this jagged coast consist of slabs of rock sprinkled with nudists (naturists). Croatia's 1185 islands – 66 of them inhabited – are every bit as beautiful as those in Greece.

CLIMATE
Croatia's high coastal mountains shield the coast from cold northerly winds. The sunny coastal areas experience hot, dry summers and mild, rainy winters – temperatures rarely fall below 10°C in winter and are as high as 26°C in August. The interior regions are cold in winter and warm in summer.

POPULATION & PEOPLE
Before the war Croatia had a population of nearly five million, of which 78% were Croats and 12% were Serbs. Reliable statistics since the war are difficult to compile, but it's estimated that only 5% of the Serbian population remains. Croats are overwhelmingly Roman Catholic, while virtually all Serbs belong to the Eastern Orthodox Church. Muslims make up 1.2% of the population.

SOCIETY & CONDUCT
Croats take pride in keeping up appearances. The tidy streets and stylish clothes are rooted in the Croats' image of themselves as Western Europeans, not Yugoslavs, a word that makes Croats wince. Dressing neatly will go a long way toward winning a traveller acceptance. Because of the intense propaganda surrounding the recent war, Croats are inclined to see themselves as wholly right and the other side as wholly wrong. Comments questioning this assumption are not particularly appreciated.

LANGUAGE
Prior to 1991 both Croatian and Serbian were considered dialects of a single language known as Serbo-Croatian. The most obvious difference is that Serbian is written in Cyrillic script and Croatian in Roman script. See the Language Guide at the back of this book for a basic rundown on Croatian.

German is the most commonly spoken foreign language in Croatia. Many people in Istria speak Italian, and English is popular among young people.

Terms worth knowing are *aleja* (walkway), *cesta* (road), *donji* (lower), *gora* (hill), *grad* (town), *jezero* (lake), *luka* (harbour), *malo* (little), *novo* (new), *otok* (island), *planina* (mountain), *polje* (valley), *prolaz* (strait), *rijeka* (river), *selo* (village), *šetalište* (way), *stanica* (station, stop), *stari* (old), *šuma* (forest), *trg* (square), *ulica* (street; abbreviated as *ul*), *veliko* (big) and *zaljev* (bay). Two words everyone should know are *ima* (there is) and *nema* (there isn't).

Facts for the Visitor

HIGHLIGHTS
All along the Adriatic coast are white-stone towns with narrow, winding streets enclosed by defensive walls, though none can quite match the exquisite harmony of Dubrovnik. Both Dubrovnik and the palace of the Roman emperor Diocletian in Split have been named world heritage sites by Unesco.

SUGGESTED ITINERARIES
Three days
  Visit Dubrovnik
One week
  Visit Zagreb, Dubrovnik and Korčula
Two weeks
  Visit Zagreb and most of Dalmatia and Istria

PLANNING
When to Go
May, June and September have good weather and few tourists. In July and August all Europe arrives on the coast and prices soar. In April and October it may be too cool for camping but the weather should still be fine along the coast.

Books & Maps
Lonely Planet's *Croatia* provides comprehensive coverage of Croatian culture and destinations. *The Death of Yugoslavia* by Laura Silber and Allan Little is a superb, comprehensive account of the collapse of ex-Yugoslavia. *Café Europa* is a series of post-independence essays by the Croatian journalist Slavenka Drakulić.

Kúmmerley & Frey's map *Croatia & Slovenia* (1:500,000) is detailed and depicts the latest borders. Most tourist offices have local maps.

CROATIA

TOURIST OFFICES

In addition to municipal tourist offices which have free brochures and information on local events, there are commercial travel agencies such as Atlas, Croatia Express and Kompas that arrange private rooms, sightseeing tours, etc.

The Croatian Ministry of Tourism has few offices abroad; there is a USA branch (☎ 212-279 8672) at 350 Fifth Ave, Suite 4003, New York, NY 10118. In the UK try the helpful private agency Phoenix Holidays (☎ 0208-563 7979), 2 The Lanchesters, 162-164 Fulham Palace Rd, London W6 9ER.

EMBASSIES & CONSULATES
Croatian Embassies & Consulates

Croatian diplomatic missions abroad include:

Australia (☎ 02-6286 6988) 6 Bulwarra Close, O'Malley, Canberra, ACT 2606
(☎ 03-9699 2633) 9-24 Albert Rd, South Melbourne, Victoria 3205
(☎ 02-9299 8899) 379 Kent St, Level 4, Sydney, NSW 2000
(☎ 08-9321 6044) 68 St George's Terrace, Perth, WA 6832
Canada (☎ 613-230 7351) 130 Albert St, Suite 1700, Ottawa, ON K1P 5G4
(☎ 905-277 9051) 918 Dundas St E, Suite 302, Mississauga, ON L4Y 2B8
New Zealand (☎ 09-836 5581) 131 Lincoln Rd, Henderson, Box 83200, Edmonton, Auckland
UK (☎ 0171-387 0022) 21 Conway St, London W1P 5HL
USA (☎ 202-588 5899) 2343 Massachusetts Ave NW, Washington, DC 20008

Embassies & Consulates in Croatia

The following embassies and consulates are in Zagreb (area code ☎ 01):

Australia (☎ 48 36 600) Kršnjavoga 1
Canada (☎ 48 81 200) Prilas Gjure Deželića 4
UK (☎ 45 55 310) Vlaška 121
USA (☎ 45 55 500) Andrije Hebranga 2
Yugoslavia (☎ 46 80 552) Mesićeva 19

MONEY

In May 1994 the Croatian dinar was replaced by the kuna (KN). Within Croatia there are numerous places to change money, all of which offer similar rates. Kuna can be converted into hard currency only at a bank and if you submit a receipt of a previous transaction. Hungarian currency is difficult to change in Croatia.

American Express, MasterCard, Visa and Diners Club cards are widely accepted. ATMs accepting Mastercard, Maestro, Cirrus, Plus and Visa are available in most bus and train stations, airports, all major cities and most small towns.

To stay ahead of inflation many hotel prices are in German marks – though you pay in kuna calculated at the official daily rate.

Exchange Rates

country	unit		kuna
Australia	A$1	=	4.75KN
Canada	C$1	=	5.59KN
euro	€1	=	7.46KN
France	10FF	=	11.37KN
Germany	DM1	=	3.81KN
Japan	¥100	=	7.77KN
New Zealand	NZ$1	=	3.57KN
UK	UK£1	=	12.32KN
USA	US$1	=	8.32KN

Costs

Transport and food are reasonably priced for Europe, though budget accommodation is in short supply. Accommodation costs rise substantially in July and August. You can get by on US$30 per day off-season (US$40 in summer) if you eat at simple restaurants and stay in hostels or private rooms; you'll spend less if you camp and self-cater.

Tipping

At restaurants round up the bill as you're paying (don't leave money on the table). Bar bills and taxi fares can also be rounded up.

POST & COMMUNICATIONS

Poste-restante mail (Poste Restante, 10000 Zagreb) is held at the post office next to the Zagreb train station. On the coast, a good address is c/o Poste Restante, Main Post Office, 21000 Split.

The international country code for Croatia is ☎ 385. When dialling in from abroad drop the initial zero from city area codes. To make a call within Croatia, go to the main post office or use a pay phone (tokens and phonecards only). Phonecards are sold at newsstands, post offices and tobacco shops in denominations of 50, 100, 200 and 500 *impulsa* (units). A three-minute call from Croatia to the USA is about 20KN. The international access code is ☎ 00.

INTERNET RESOURCES

Croatia Tourist is the official government Web site at www.htz.hr. The Institute for Culture & Information's site at www.croatia .hr has useful news and travel information.

WOMEN TRAVELLERS

Women face no special danger in Croatia, though women on their own may be harassed in large coastal cities. Some bars and cafes seem like private men's clubs; a woman alone is likely to be greeted with silence and cold stares. Topless sunbathing is considered acceptable.

GAY & LESBIAN TRAVELLERS

Homosexuality has been legal in Croatia since 1977 and is generally tolerated. However, public displays of affection may meet with hostility, especially outside major cities. Check out the web site www.crogay .com for up-to-date information on gay venues.

DANGERS & ANNOYANCES

Although the government moved with lightning speed to remove land mines from areas even remotely interesting to tourists, remote areas are still undergoing de-mining operations. It is unwise to stray into fields or abandoned villages.

Personal security and theft are not major worries in Croatia. Useful numbers are ☎ 92 for the police, ☎ 93 for the fire department and ☎ 94 for emergency medical assistance.

BUSINESS HOURS

Most bank and shops are open 7.30 am to 7 pm weekdays, 8 am to noon Saturday. Along the coast, shops and offices frequently close around 1 pm for an afternoon break.

PUBLIC HOLIDAYS & SPECIAL EVENTS

Public holidays in Croatia are 1 January, Easter Monday, 1 May (Labour Day), 15 May (Bleiburg and Way of the Cross Victims Day), 30 May (Statehood Day), 22 June (Day of Antifascist Struggle), 5 August (Homeland Thanksgiving Day), 15 August (Feast of the Assumption), 1 November (All Saints' Day) and 25 and 26 December.

In July and August there are summer festivals in Dubrovnik, Opatija, Split and Zagreb.

ACCOMMODATION

Prices along the coast vary according to the seasons. April, May and October are the cheapest months; prices jump in June and September and skyrocket in July and August. Prices quoted in this chapter are for the peak period and don't include 'residence taxes' (4.30KN to 7.60KN).

Nearly 100 camping grounds are scattered along the Croatian coast. Most of these operate from mid-May to September only. Many are expensive because prices are set in US dollars or German marks. Nudist camping grounds (marked FKK) are among the best because of their secluded locations.

The Croatian Youth Hostel Association (☎ 01-48 47 953, fax 01-48 41 269), Dežmanova 9, 10000 Zagreb, operates summer hostels in Dubrovnik and Zadar and year-round hostels in Zagreb and Pula available to members only. Membership costs 40KN for adults over 26, 30KN for those under 26 and 10KN for children up to 14. See their Web site at www.nncomp.com/hfhs.

Croatia is well stocked with private rooms – look for 'Sobe' or 'Zimmer frei' signs. Rooms can be arranged at travel agencies, though by dealing direct with proprietors you'll avoid residence taxes and may not be charged extra (20% to 30%) for stays of less than four nights. Renting an unofficial room is common practice along the Adriatic coast, but be discreet. Technically you're breaking the law by not registering with the police.

There are few cheap hotels in Croatia. Prices average around 350KN for doubles in summer along the coast, dropping to around 250KN in late spring or early autumn.

FOOD & DRINKS

Always ask for a menu with prices at a restauracija or gostionica (restaurant) and at kavana (cafes). If you don't ask, you will automatically be charged the 'tourist price'. At most places vegetables, salads and bread cost extra and some deluxe restaurants add a 10% service charge.

Throughout ex-Yugoslavia the breakfast of the people is burek, a greasy layered pie made with *mesa* (meat) or *sira* (cheese). The Adriatic coast excels in seafood, including *prstaci* (shellfish) and *brodet* (mixed fish stewed with rice), cooked in olive oil and served with boiled vegetables or *tartufe* (mushrooms). In the interior, look for *manistra od bobića* (beans and fresh maize soup) and *štrukle* (cottage cheese rolls). A Zagreb speciality is *štrukli* (boiled cheesecake).

It's customary to have a small glass of brandy before a meal and to accompany the food with one of Croatia's fine wines. *Pivo* (beer) is also popular – try the Ožujsko or Karlovačko labels. Croatia is also famous for its *šljivovica* (plum brandies) and *vinjak* (cognacs).

Getting There & Away

AIR

Croatia Airlines has flights from Zagreb to Amsterdam, Berlin, Düsseldorf, Frankfurt, İstanbul, London, Madrid, Manchester, Milan, Mostar, Munich, Paris, Prague, Rome, Sarajevo, Skopje, Tel Aviv, Vienna and Zürich.

BUS

From Vienna there are Eurolines buses to Zagreb (190KN) and Rijeka, Split and Zadar (330KN), which run weekly off-season and twice weekly in summer. Croatia is a prime destination for Germans, and Deutsche Touring/Eurolines services are cheap and frequent to Zagreb, Zadar and Split from Berlin, Cologne, Frankfurt/Main, Munich, Nuremberg, Stuttgart and other cities.

Other Eurolines buses run to Zagreb (and other major Croatian cities) from throughout Western Europe. To/from Hungary there are local buses between Zagreb and Nagykanizsa (71KN, 145km), with onward connections to Budapest. To Yugoslavia, there are three buses each morning from Zagreb to Belgrade (185KN, six hours); at Bajakovo, on the border, a Yugoslav bus takes you on to Belgrade. There are five daily buses to Ljubljana in Slovenia (71KN, 135km).

TRAIN

Between Zagreb and Venice (279KN, seven hours), there's an overnight direct train and a daily train via Trieste and Ljubljana. There are three daily trains to Zagreb from Munich (500KN, nine hours) via Salzburg and Ljubljana. The *Ljubljana* express travels from Vienna to Rijeka (eight hours, daily) via Ljubljana. The EuroCity train *Croatia* connects Zagreb and Vienna (374KN, 6½ hours). To/from Zagreb and Budapest (156KN to 168KN, 6½ hours) there are four daily express trains. Four trains a day connect Zagreb with Belgrade (128KN, 6½ hours); and there's a daily train to Bucharest (580KN, 25 hours).

BOAT

Ferries connect Croatia with Italy. The main carriers are Jadrolinija and Lošinjska Plovidba (Croatia), SEM and Adriatica Navigazione (Italy).

There are year-round ferries (up to six per week) between Split and Ancona (311KN, 10 hours), stopping June to September at Stari Grad on Hvar Island. In summer Jadrolinija runs ferries between Ancona and Zadar (288KN), with stops at Vela Luka on Korčula Island. Lošinjska Plovidba runs summer-only ferries between Venice and Zadar (L90,000, 14½ hours). From May to September Adriatica Navigazione runs the *Marconi* between Trieste and Rovinj (L30,000, 3½ hours), stopping at the Brijuni Islands six times a week and stopping three times a week in July and August at Poreč (L27,000) and once a week in Pula (L45,000, 5½ hours).

From Bari there are weekly year-round ferries to Dubrovnik (311KN, nine hours).

Getting Around

BUS

Bus services in Croatia are excellent. At large stations, tickets must be purchased at the office, not from drivers; book ahead to be sure of a seat. Tickets for buses that arrive from somewhere else are usually purchased from the driver. On Croatian bus schedules, *vozi svaki dan* means 'every day', *ne vozi nedjeljom ni praznikom* means 'not Sunday or public holidays'.

TRAIN

Domestic train travel is about 15% cheaper than bus travel and often more comfortable, if slower. Local trains usually have only un-reserved 2nd-class seats but they're rarely crowded. Reservations may be required on express trains. *Poslovni* (executive) trains have only 1st-class seats and are 40% more expensive than local trains.

On posted timetables in Croatia the word for arrivals is *dolazak*, and for departures it's *odlazak* or *polazak*. Other terms you may encounter include *brzi* or *ubrazni* (fast train), *putnički* (local train), *rezerviranje mjesta obvezatno* (compulsory seat reservation), *presjedanje* (change of trains), *ne vozi nedjeljom i blagdanom* (no service Sunday or holidays) and *svakodnevno* (daily).

Inter-Rail passes (Zone D) are valid in Croatia, but Eurail is not.

CAR & MOTORCYCLE

Unless otherwise posted, the speed limits for cars and motorcycles are 50km/h in built-up areas, 80km/h on main highways and 130km/h on motorways. On any of Croatia's winding two-lane highways, it's illegal to pass long military convoys or a whole line of cars caught behind a slow-moving truck.

Petrol is either leaded super, unleaded *(bezolovni)* or diesel. You have to pay tolls on the motorways around Zagreb and to use the Učka tunnel between Rijeka and Istria.

The Croatian Auto Club (HAK) has a main office in Zagreb (☎ 01-46 40 800) at Dcrenčinova 20. HAK's nationwide road assistance number is ☎ 987.

BOAT

Jadrolinija car ferries operate year-round along the Bari-Rijeka-Dubrovnik coastal route, stopping at Zadar, Split and the islands Hvar, Korčula and Mljet. The most scenic section is Split to Dubrovnik. Rijeka to Split (13 hours) is usually an overnight trip.

Ferries are more comfortable than buses, though considerably more expensive. From Rijeka to Dubrovnik the deck fare is 192KN one way. *Poltrone* (reclining seats) are about 26KN extra. With a through ticket, passengers can stop at any port for up to a week, provided you notify the purser beforehand and have your ticket validated. This is much cheaper than buying individual tickets. There are also local ferries that connect the bigger offshore islands with each other and the mainland.

Zagreb

☎ 01

Zagreb (population 810,000) has been the capital of Croatia since 1557. Much of medieval Zagreb remains today, along with the stately 19th-century commercial centre between the old town and the train station. There are many fine parks, galleries and museums in both the upper and lower towns. Finding a place to stay at a reasonable price is Zagreb's only serious drawback.

Orientation

The main square, Trg Jelačića, is a short walk north of the train station. To reach the bus station, which is 1km east of the train station, take tram No 2, 3 or 6. Tram No 6 continues to Trg Jelačića.

Most of the city's highlights lie within the Upper Town (Gornji Grad), which includes Gradec and Kaptol, and the Lower Town (Donji Grad), which runs between the Upper Town and the train station.

Information

Tourist Offices The main tourist office (☎ 48 14 051), Trg Jelačića 11, is open 8.30 am to 8 pm weekdays, 9 am to 5 pm Saturday and 10 am to 2 pm Sunday.

Plitvice National Park has an information office (☎ 46 13 586) at Trg Tomislava 19. It also has information on other national parks around Croatia.

Money There are ATMs at the bus and train stations and in numerous locations around town. Exchange offices at the bus and train stations change money with 1% commission. The banks in the train station (open 7 am to 9 pm) and the bus station (open 6 am to 8 pm) accept travellers cheques. Croatia Express at the train station is open 24-hours and changes cash and travellers cheques.

The American Express representative is Atlas travel agency (☎ 48 13 933), Trg Zrinjskoga 17.

Post & Communications The post office, on the eastern side of the train station, is open 24 hours a day. This is the best place to make long-distance phone calls.

Email & Internet Access Zagreb's flashiest cybercafe is the Art Net Cafe (☎ 45 58 471)

CROATIA

ZAGREB

PLACES TO STAY
32 Hotel Jadran
46 Omladinski Hotel (Youth Hostel)
53 Central Hotel

PLACES TO EAT
22 Biovega
23 Market
24 Delikatese
25 Pizzicato
31 Mimiće

OTHER
1 Polish Embassy
2 City Museum
3 Natural History Museum
4 Meštrović Studio
5 Historical Museum of Croatia
6 Banski Dvori Palace
7 St Mark's Church
8 Sabor (Parliament)
9 Gallerija Fortezza
10 Stone Gate
11 Komedija Theatre
12 Gallery of Naive Art
13 Muzejski Prostor
14 Lotrščak Tower
15 St Catherine's Church
16 Dolac (Market)
17 St Stephen's Cathedral
18 Funicular Railway
19 Nama Department Store
20 British Council
21 Croatian YHA/ Dali Travel
26 Academy of Music
27 Oktogon
28 Hotel Dubrornik; Algoritam
29 Tourist Office
30 Post Office/Telephone Centre
33 Archaeological Museum; Rock Forum Café
34 Art Café Thalia; BP Club
35 Canadian Embassy
36 Embassy of Slovakia
37 Croatian National Theatre
38 Art Net Cafe
39 US Embassy
40 Atlas Travel Agency; Antikrarijat
41 Strossmayer Gallery
42 Police Station
43 Emergency Centar
44 Predom
45 Hotel Sheraton
47 Exhibition Pavilion; Paviljon Restaurant
48 Plitvice National Park Office
49 Pivnica Tomaslav
50 Ethnographic Museum
51 Museum Mimara
52 National Library
54 Evistas
55 Post Office
56 City Hall
57 Vatroslav Lisinski Concert Hall

at Peradovićeva 25. It's open 9 am to 11 pm daily and hosts frequent concerts and performances.

Travel Agencies Dali Travel (☎ 48 47 4872), Dežmanova 9, a branch of Croatia's hostelling association, has hostel information and makes bookings (closed weekends).

Bookshops Algoritam, in the Hotel Dubrovnik on Trg Jelačića, has a wide selection of English-language books. Antikvarijat, next to the Atlas travel agency, has excellent (though expensive) maps and paperbacks in English.

Laundry Predom, across the street from HAK at Draškovićeva 31, is open Saturday mornings and 7 am to 7 pm weekdays. Jeans and shirts cost 6KN each to wash, underwear 3KN each.

Medical Services The Emergency Centar (☎ 46 10 011), at Draskovića 19, is open 24 hours a day. An examination will set you back 200KN.

Things to See

Kaptol Zagreb's daily **Dolac** (vegetable market) is just up the steps from Trg Jelačića and continues north along Opatovina. The twin neo-Gothic spires of **St Stephen's Cathedral** (1899), now renamed the Cathedral of the Assumption of the Blessed Virgin Mary, are nearby. The 13th-century frescoes inside the cathedral are worth a look. The baroque **Archiepiscopal Palace** surrounds the cathedral, as do impressive 16th-century fortifications.

Gradec The upper and lower towns are connected by a funicular railway (2KN). The nearby **Lotršćak Tower** can be climbed for sweeping 360-degree views of the city (closed Sunday).

The **Gallerija Fortezza**, Jezuitski trg 4, is Zagreb's premier exhibition hall (closed Monday). Farther north is the 13th-century **Stone Gate**, with a painting of the Virgin that escaped a devastating fire of 1731.

The colourful painted-tile roof of the Gothic **St Mark's Church** on Markov trg marks the centre of Gradec. Inside are works by Ivan Meštrović, Croatia's most famous modern sculptor. On the eastern side of St Mark's is the **Sabor** (1908), Croatia's National Assembly. To the west of St Mark's is the 18th-century **Banski Dvori Palace**, the presidential palace. From April to September there is a guard-changing ceremony on weekends at noon.

Museums in this area include the **Historical Museum of Croatia** (open only for temporary exhibitions), Matoševa 9; the **Gallery of Naive Art**, Ćirilometodska 3; and the **Natural History Museum**, Demetrova 1. More interesting is the renovated **City Museum**, Opatićka 20, with a scale model of old Gradec. Most of the museums are closed Monday.

Lower Town There are three museums in the parks between the train station and Trg Jelačića. The yellow **exhibition pavilion** (1897) has rotating contemporary art exhibitions. The **Strossmayer Gallery** displays art by old masters (closed Monday).

The **Archaeological Museum**, Trg Nikole Zrinjskog 19, is currently open only for temporary exhibitions. Behind the museum is a garden of Roman sculpture that's home to a pleasant open-air cafe in summer.

Other Attractions The **Museum Mimara**, Rooseveltov trg 5, has a diverse collection of icons, glassware, sculpture and Oriental art. The Spanish, Italian and Dutch paintings are the highlight. The **Ethnographic Museum**, Trg Mažuranića 14, has a large collection of Croatian folk costumes (closed Monday).

Special Events
In April of every odd-numbered year, Zagreb hosts the Biennial of Contemporary Music, Croatia's most important music event. In July and August the Zagreb Summer Festival presents a cycle of concerts and theatre performances on open stages in the upper town.

Places to Stay
Budget accommodation is in short supply in Zagreb. Arrive early and/or book ahead.

Camping *Motel Plitvice (☎ 65 30 444)* has a camping area (18/30KN per tent/person) but is far from and south-west of town. Take tram No 7 or 14 to Savski Most, then catch a bus to Lučko village, from which the motel-camp is a 10-minute walk. The motel sometimes runs a minibus service from Savski Most – call for details.

Hostels The noisy 215-bed *Omladinski Hotel (☎ 48 41 261, fax 48 41 269, Petrinjska 77)*, is open year-round, though its six-bed dorms (80KN per person) may still be occupied by war refugees. Otherwise doubles without/with bath are 204/274KN.

From mid-July to late September *Studenthotel Cvjetno Naselje (☎ 61 91 239)*, part of the university, has comfy singles/doubles for 240/360KN, breakfast included. There's a self service restaurant here. From Savska cesta (west of the Botanical Garden) take tram No 4, 5, 14, 16 or 17 southwest to 'Vjesnik'. The complex is behind the building marked 'Vjesnik'.

Rooms are 150/300KN at the huge *Studentski dom Stjepan Radić (☎ 36 34 255, Jarunska ul 3)*, off Horvaćanska near the Sava River (take tram No 5 or 17 south from Savska cesta). It's open in July and August only.

Private Rooms Evistas (☎ 48 39 546, fax 48 39 543) at Šenoina 28, between the bus and train stations, rents out *private rooms* (182/254KN, less for people under 25) and apartments (365KN and up). It's open 9 am to 8 pm weekdays, 9.30 am to 5 pm Saturday. Otherwise, try Lacio (☎/fax 65 21 523, Trnsko 15e) or Di Prom (☎ 65 50 039, Trnsko 25a). Lina Gabino (☎ 39 21 27) at Bartolići 33 near Lake Jarun is the only agency open on Sunday.

Hotels The best deal is *Hotel Ilica* (☎ *37 77 622, fax 37 77 722, Ilica 102)*, two tram stops west from Trg Jelačića. Quiet singles/ doubles with bath and breakfast are 299/399KN. The 110-room *Central Hotel* (☎ *484 11 22, fax 48 41 304, Branimirova 3)* opposite the train station, is blandly modern and charges 327/474KN. The six-storey *Hotel Jadran* (☎ *45 53 777, fax 46 12 151, Vlaška 50)*, charges 360/436KN.

Places to Eat

Delikatese (Ilica 39) is a good place to pick up cheese, fruit, bread and cold meats. The adjacent *grocery store* sells whole roasted chicken and pre-prepared salads. Farther along Ilica at Trg Britanski a daily fruit and vegetable *market* is open to 3 pm daily.

For regional dishes and local colour, dine in summer at one of the *outdoor restaurants* along ul Tkalčićeva, up from Trg Jelačića. The popular *Mimiće (Jurišićeva 21)* turns out plates of fried fish – ten sardines and a hunk of bread is 9KN. Vegetarians should try *Biovega (Petrinjska 9)*, which offers a two-course vegetarian meal for 60KN. *Pizzicato (Gundilićeva 4)*, near the Academy of Music, serves delicious pizzas starting at 18KN.

The best restaurant for meaty Croatian specialties is *Baltazar (Nova Ves 4)*. The most elegant place in town is the *Paviljon*, in the Lower Town's yellow exhibition pavilion. Main courses with an Italian flavour start at 70KN.

Entertainment

The *Croatian National Theatre (Trg Maršala Tita 15)*, stages opera and ballet. The *Komedija Theatre (Kaptol 9)*, near the cathedral, stages operettas and musicals. The *Vatroslav Lisinski Concert Hall* is just south of the train station. Concerts also take place at the *Academy of Music (Gundulićeva 6a)*, off Ilica.

Bars & Clubs The liveliest scene is along Tkalčićeva, north of Trg Jelačića, where crowds spill out of cafes, drinks in hand. Farther up on Kozarska ul the city's young people cluster shoulder to shoulder.

The summer-only *Rock Forum Café (Gajeva ul 13)* is in the Archaeological Museum's rear sculpture garden. Across the street and back from the Hard Rock Café,

the *Art Café Thalia* really tries to live up to its name. In the basement, the *BP Club* hosts jazz, blues and rock bands. *Pivnica Tomislav (Trg Tomislava 18)*, in front of the train station, is a good local bar.

Kulušić (Hrvojeva 6) near the Hotel Sheraton, is a casual, funky rock club with occasional live bands; entry 30KN. Zagreb's only exclusively gay and lesbian club is *Badboy (Ksaver 210)*, in the north of the city on the way to Miragoj cemetery. It's open 5 pm to 1 am during the week but stays open until 4 am Friday, Saturday and Sunday. *Sokol klub*, across the street from the Ethnographic Museum, is upscale and admits women free before midnight. It's open Wednesday to Sunday from 10 pm, and entry is 30KN.

Getting There & Away

Bus Buy an advance ticket at the station if you're travelling far; international tickets are sold at window Nos 11 and 12. For information on international buses see the earlier Getting There & Away section.

Major domestic destinations include: Dubrovnik (135KN to 165KN, 713km), Plitvice (35KN to 55KN, 140km), Poreč (95KN to 128KN, 264km), Pula (90KN to 110KN, 283km), Rijeka (68KN to 101KN, 173km), Rovinj (105KN to 130KN, 278km), Split (90KN to 110KN, 478km) and Zadar (80KN to 95KN, 320km).

Train For information on international trains to/from Zagreb, see the earlier Getting There & Away section.

Domestic trains run from Zagreb to Koprivnica (31KN, two hours, daily), Rijeka (55KN, five hours), Pula (145KN, 5½ hours) and Split (91KN, nine hours). Both daily trains to Zadar (53KN, 11 hours) stop at Knin. Reservations are required on some trains, so check.

Getting Around

Public transport is based on an efficient but overcrowded network of trams. Buy tickets at newspaper kiosks (5.50KN) or from the driver (6KN). You can use your ticket for transfers within 90 minutes but only in one direction. A 15KN *dnevna karta* (day ticket), valid on all public transport until 4 am the next morning, is available at most Vjesnik or Tisak newsstands.

AROUND ZAGREB
Plitvice Lakes National Park
☎ 053

The Plitvice Lakes National Park is 140km from Zagreb towards Zadar. The extraordinary natural beauty of the site merits at least a three-day visit, but you can experience a lot simply on a day trip from either town.

Its 19.5 hectares of wooded hills enclose 16 turquoise lakes which are linked together by a series of waterfalls and cascades. The mineral-rich waters carve new paths through the rock, depositing tufa (calcium carbonate) in continually changing formations. Wooden footbridges follow the lakes and streams over, under and across the rumbling water for an exhilaratingly damp 18km. Swimming is allowed in several lakes.

Park admission is 60/80KN low/high season (40/48KN for students). There are park information centres in Zagreb (see Zagreb's Information section) and at the park's first entrance (☎ 751 048; open 8 am to 6.30 pm daily). Both have information about *private rooms* (these will obviously be outside the park and therefore inconvenient unless you have your own car).

Buses run hourly from Zagreb to Plitvice, and then continue to Zadar or Split. It is possible to visit Plitvice on a day trip on the way to/from the coast, though buses that are already full will not pick up extra passengers in Plitvice.

Istria

Istria (Istra to Croatians) is a 3600-sq-km peninsula just south of the Italian port of Trieste. The scenery gets better the farther south you go – cleaner water, fewer visitors and less industry. Rovinj is a perfect base from which to explore Poreč and Pula.

ROVINJ
☎ 052

Relaxed Rovinj (Rovigno in Italian), its high peninsula topped by the 57-metre tower of the St Euphemia Cathedral, is perhaps the best place to visit in the whole of Istria. Wooded hills punctuated by low-rise luxury hotels surround this active fishing port and its cobbled, picturesque streets. Offshore are the 13 green islands of the Rovinj archipelago.

Orientation & Information

From the bus station it's an easy walk to the old town – go north-east on Carera to Trg Maršala Tita, the main square.

The tourist office (☎ 811 566) is at Obala Pina Budicina 12, just off Trg Maršala Tita. The American Express representative is Atlas (☎ 811 241) in the Hotel Park, Ronjgova bb. Make long-distance phone calls from the post office behind the bus station.

Things to See & Do

The **Cathedral of St Euphemia** (1736), which completely dominates the town from its hill-top location, is the largest baroque building in Istria. It was built when Rovinj was the bulwark of the Venetian fleet. Take a wander along the narrow backstreets below the cathedral – try ul Grisia – where local artists sell their work.

The **Rovinj Aquarium** at Obala Giordano Paliaga 5, a few hundred metres north-east from the main square, has a good collection of local marine life, from poisonous scorpion fish to colourful anemones (closed mid-October to Easter; 10KN).

When you've seen enough of the town, follow the waterfront southwards past the Park Hotel to **Punta Corrente Forest Park**. Here you can go swimming off the rocks, climb a cliff or just sit and admire the offshore islands.

Cruises Delfin Agency (☎ 813 266) near the ferry dock runs half-day cruises to the Lim Channel (80KN). There are also hourly ferries to Crveni otok (Red Island; 20KN return) and Katarina Island (10KN); get tickets on board or from the nearby kiosk. These boats operate May to mid-October only.

Places to Stay

For camping, *Porton Biondi* (☎ 813 557) is less than 1km from town (on the Monsena bus) and charges 28KN per person and 16KN for a tent. *Polari Camping* (☎ 813 441), 5km south-east of Rovinj, is open from April to mid-October and is slightly cheaper. Get there on the Villas Rubin bus.

The going rate for *private rooms* is 108/160KN for a single/double in summer, with a 50% surcharge for stays of less than four nights and 100% for one-night stays. Pula and Poreč are within easy commuting

CROATIA

distance of Rovinj, so staying four nights is not out of the question. Try Lokva-Natale (☎ 813 365, Via Carducci 4) or Marco Polo (☎ 816 955), both opposite the bus station; Futura Travel (☎ 817 281, M.Benussi 2) or Integrale (☎ 814 022, Trg na Lokvi 3), which all have rooms at the same price. Most agencies close from 2 to 6 pm.

The 192-room *Hotel Monte Mulin* (☎ *811 512, fax 815 882*) is on a wooded hillside overlooking the bay just beyond Hotel Park – a 15-minute walk south of the bus station. It's open year-round and charges 260/400KN with half-board.

Places to Eat
Most of the fish and spaghetti places along the harbour cater to well-heeled tourists. An exception is *Kantinon (Obala Alzo Rismondo 18)*, with fresh grilled fish from 20KN. The mid-range *Veli Jože (Svetoga Križa 1)*, is a good place to try Istrian dishes. There's a *supermarket* next to the bus station.

Getting There & Away
There are hourly buses from Rovinj to Pula (34km) and up to eight a day to Poreč (38km), Rijeka (84km) and Zagreb (278km). Other buses run to Split (509km), Dubrovnik (744km) and Ljubljana in Slovenia (190km, summer only).

Eurostar Travel (☎ 813 144), Obala Pina Budicina 1, has Rovinj-Trieste ferry information and may have tickets (payable in Italian lire only).

PULA
☎ 052
Pula is a large regional centre with some industry, a big naval base and a busy commercial harbour. The old town – with its museums and well-preserved Roman ruins – is certainly worth a visit, perhaps as a day trip from Rovinj. During the summer there are concerts with major international stars at the amphitheatre.

Orientation & Information
The bus station is on ul Carrarina in the centre of town. One block south is Giardini, the central hub, while the harbour is just north of the bus station. The train station is near the water about 1km north of town.

The Tourist Association of Pula (☎ 219 197) at Forum 2 has city maps and is open

9 am to 1 pm and 5 to 8 pm weekdays. The American Express representative is Atlas (☎ 214 172) at Starih Statuta 1. Jadroagent (☎ 211 878), Riva 14, sells ferry tickets and books private rooms.

Things to See
Pula's most imposing sight is the 1st-century **Roman amphitheatre**, which overlooks the harbour north-east of the old town (16KN).

The **Archaeological Museum** is on the hill opposite the bus station (closed weekends in winter; 10KN). Be sure to visit the large sculpture garden around it and the **Roman theatre** behind. Along the street facing the bus station are **Roman walls** that mark the eastern boundary of old Pula. Follow the walls to the south and continue down Giardini to the **Triumphal Arch of Sergius** (27 BC). The street beyond the arch winds around old Pula, changing names several times, to the **Temple of Augustus** and the **old town hall** (1296).

The 17th-century Venetian **citadel** on a high hill in the centre of the old town has good views and a meagre history museum.

Places to Stay & Eat
The year-round *Ljetovalište Ferijalnog Saveza Youth Hostel* (☎ *391 133, fax 391 106)* is 3km south of Pula overlooking a clean pebble beach. Take bus No 2 or 7 (direction: Verudela) to the 'Piramida' stop, walk back to the first street, turn left, and look for the sign. Bed and breakfast is 71KN per person and camping is 40KN including breakfast. You can sip cold beer on the terrace.

If the youth hostel is full and you have a tent, it's only a 10-minute walk to *Autocamp Ribarska Koliba* (☎ *214 410*), open from May to mid-September. Otherwise *Autocamp Stoja* (☎ *387 144*), open mid-April to mid-October, is 3km south-west of the centre (take bus No 1 to the terminus at Stoja). The two restaurants at Stoja are good.

Private rooms start at 108KN per person. Try Arenatours (☎ 218 696), Giardini 4 and Atlas (see Information earlier) or Kompas (☎ 212 511), Narodni trg 10.

Delfin (Kandlerova 17) has a pleasant terrace and an excellent selection of seafood. Locals rave about the home cooking at *Vodnjanka* – it's cheap, casual but open for lunch only. Walk south on Radićeva to Vitežića 4.

Getting There & Away

There are two daily trains to Zagreb (90KN, 6½ hours) and Ljubljana (90KN, four hours) but you must board a bus for part of the trip.

The 20 daily buses to Rijeka (1½ hours) are sometimes crowded, especially the eight that continue to Zagreb (292km) – reserve a day in advance. Other buses run to Zadar (333km), Split (514km), Dubrovnik (749km) and Trieste in Italy (124km). Buses to/from Rovinj (42km) and Poreč (56km) are frequent.

In summer the fast boat *Marina* connects Pula with Zadar and Venice (Italy); see the Getting There & Away section at the beginning of this chapter. Jadroagent sells tickets.

POREČ
☎ 052

Poreč (Parenzo in Italian) sits on a low, narrow peninsula about halfway down Istria's west coast. Though busy tourist resorts line the nearby beaches, vestiges of earlier times and a quiet, small-town atmosphere make Poreč well worth a day trip from Rovinj.

Orientation & Information

The bus station is directly opposite the small-boat harbour just outside the old town. Dekumanus, the old town's main street, runs between Trg Slobode and Trg Marafor.

The tourist office (☎ 451 293) is at Zagrebačka 8. The Atlas travel agency (☎ 434 983) at Eufrazijeva 63 represents American Express.

Things to See

Poreč's historic sites include the ruins of two **Roman temples** between Trg Marafor and the western end of the peninsula. Archaeology and history are featured in the four-floor **Regional Museum**, in an old baroque palace at Dekumanus 9.

The main reason to visit Poreč, however, is to see the 6th-century **Euphrasian basilica**, a Unesco world heritage site featuring well-preserved Byzantine gold mosaics. Entry to the church is free; for a small fee you can visit the adjacent early Christian basilica and its 4th-century mosaic floor.

Places to Stay & Eat

From April to mid-October there are two *camping grounds* at Zelena Laguna, 6km south of Poreč. From the bus station take the hourly 'Plava Laguna' bus direct to Zelena Laguna; both sites are within a short walk.

There are few *private rooms* in Poreč and almost none outside the main summer season. Near the vegetable market at Partizanska there is Istra-Line (☎ 432 339, fax 432 116) in a pink building. If you follow Nikole Tesle until it becomes Kalčića you'll come to Mate Vašića and at No 6 is Fiore tours (☎/fax 431 397) which also finds private accommodation. There are no single rooms. Expect to pay 200KN for a double with a private shower and 168KN for a double with shared facilities.

The *Peškera Self-Service Restaurant*, just outside the north-western corner of the old city wall is a good deal. *Pizzeria Nono (Zagrebac 4)* is a local favorite.

Getting There & Away

Buses run six times daily to Rovinj (38km), 12 times daily to Pula (56km) and eight times daily to Zagreb (264km). Between Poreč and Rovinj the bus runs along the scenic Lim Channel – make sure you see the view on the right-hand side southbound, the left-hand side northbound. Other bus destinations include Trieste (89km) and Ljubljana (176km).

For information on ferries to/from Trieste inquire at the Sunny Way agency (☎ 452 021), Alda Negrija 1, and see Getting There & Away at the beginning of this chapter.

Dalmatia

ZADAR
☎ 023

After suffering bombing raids in WWII, Zadar relived history when Yugoslav rockets ploughed into its old city in November 1991, damaging the cathedral. For the next three months the city's inhabitants were under siege. Today few war wounds are visible and Zadar's narrow, traffic-free stone streets are again full of life. The main city of northern Dalmatia, Zadar is a fascinating place to explore.

Orientation & Information

The adjacent train and bus stations are a 15-minute walk south-east of the harbour and old town – take Zrinsko-Frankopanska ul

CROATIA

north-west past the main post office. Buses marked 'Poluotok' run from the bus station to the harbour. Narodni trg is the heart of Zadar.

The tourist office, Turistička Zajednica (☎ 212 412), is at Smiljanića 4 but you'll get more information at Miatours (☎/fax 212 788, ✉ miatrade@zd.tel.hr) at Vrata Sveti Krševana or Kompas (☎/fax 433 380) on Široka. The American Express representative is Atlas (☎ 314 206), Branimirova Obala 12, across the footbridge north-east of Narodni trg.

Things to See & Do
The main sights are near the circular **St Donatus Church**, a 9th-century Byzantine structure built over a Roman forum. In summer, ask about musical evenings here. The outstanding **Museum of Church Art** in the Benedictine monastery opposite has a substantial collection of reliquaries and religious paintings. The most interesting museum is the **Archaeological Museum** across from St Donatus, with an extensive collection of artifacts from the neolithic period through the Roman occupation to the development of Croatian culture under the Byzantines.

There's a swimming area with diving boards and a cafe on the coastal promenade east of the old town off Zvonimira.

Travel agencies around town have information on cruises to the beautiful **Kornati Islands** for 250KN, including lunch and a swim. As this is about the only way to see these 101 barren, uninhabited islands it's worthwhile if you can spare the cash.

Places to Stay & Eat
Staying in the old town is nearly impossible – most travellers head out to the 'tourist settlement' at Borik, 3km north-west of Zadar, where there are hotels, a hostel, camping grounds and numerous '*Sobe*' signs. From the bus station take one of the frequent buses to Puntamika (6KN).

Autocamp Borik (☎ 332 074) is only steps away from Borik beach. The nearby *Borik Youth Hostel* (☎ 331 145, fax 331 190, Obala Kneza Trpimira 76), is open May to September and charges 80KN for a bed and breakfast, 120KN for full board.

For *private rooms* try Kompas, Miatours or Marlin Tours (☎/fax 313 194), around the corner from Atlas at Jeretova 3. Expect to pay around 120/200KN for a single/double with a 30% surcharge for stays of less than three nights.

Dalmacija at the end of Kraljice Elizabete Kotromanić is a good place for pizza, spaghetti, fish and local specialities. *Jure (Matafara 9)* a self-service restaurant in the passage at Nikole, has hot dishes starting at 25KN. There's a *supermarket* on the corner of Široka and Sabora that keeps long hours and you'll find a number of *burek stands* around the vegetable market.

Getting There & Away
The bus to Zagreb (85KN) is quicker than the train. There are also buses to Rijeka (228km), Split (158km), Mostar (301km), Dubrovnik (138KN, 393km) and Sarajevo (208KN). Croatia Express sells bus tickets to many German cities, including Munich (400KN), Frankfurt (624KN) and Berlin (800KN).

There are two daily trains to Zagreb (53KN, 11 hours), with a change at Knin.

From late June to September the fast boat *Marina* runs from Venice to Zadar twice a week and from Pula to Zadar four times a week, stopping at Mali Lošinj. There are weekly local ferries all year between Pula and Zadar (66KN, eight hours). The Jadrolinija coastal ferry from Rijeka to Dubrovnik calls at Zadar four times a week (144KN). Buy tickets at Jadrolinija (☎ 212 003), on the harbour at Liburnska obala 7. For more information on ferries to Italy, see Getting There & Away at the beginning of this chapter.

SPLIT
☎ 021
Split (Spalato in Italian), the largest Croatian city on the Adriatic coast, is the heart of Dalmatia. The old town is built around the harbour, on the southern side of a high peninsula sheltered from the open sea by numerous islands. High coastal mountains set against the blue Adriatic provide a striking frame to the scene. Split is one of Croatia's most fascinating cities, so settle in for a few days.

Split achieved fame when Roman emperor Diocletian (AD 245-313) had his retirement palace built here. When the nearby colony of Salona was abandoned in the 7th century, many of the Romanised inhabitants fled to Split and barricaded themselves behind the high palace walls, where their descendants live to this day.

Orientation & Information

The bus, train and ferry terminals are adjacent on the east side of the harbour, a short walk from the old town. Obala hrvatskog narodnog preporoda, the waterfront promenade, is your best central orientation point in Split.

The Turistički Biro (☎/fax 342 142) is at Obala hrvatskog narodnog preporoda 12. The main post office at Kralja Tomislava 9 also has a telephone office. The American Express representative, Atlas (☎ 343 055), is on Trg Braće Radića. Algoritam at Bajamontijeva 2 is a well-stocked bookstore with English-language titles.

Things to See & Do

Split has dozens of sights, so pick up a local guidebook if you're staying more than a day or two. **Diocletian's Palace**, facing the harbour, is one of the most imposing Roman ruins in existence. Enter at Obala hrvatskog narodnog preporoda 22. Continue through the passage to the **Peristyle**, a picturesque colonnaded square with a neo-Romanesque cathedral tower rising above. The **vestibule**, an open dome above the ground-floor passageway, is stunning. A lane off the Peristyle opposite the cathedral leads to the **Temple of Jupiter**, now a baptistry.

On the eastern side of the Peristyle is the **cathedral**, originally Diocletian's mausoleum. You can climb its **tower** for a small fee. The palace's west gate opens onto medieval Narodni trg, dominated by the 15th-century Venetian Gothic **old town hall**. Trg Braće Radića, between Narodni trg and the harbour, contains the surviving north tower of the 15th-century Venetian garrison castle, which once extended to the water's edge.

The palace's east gate leads into the market area.

Museums & Galleries Most of Split's museums have been closed for the last ten years awaiting money for renovation.

In the Middle Ages the nobility and rich merchants built residences within the old palace walls, one of which, the Papalic Palace, Papalićeva ul 5, is now the **town museum** (open 10 am to 5 pm Tuesday to Friday, 10 am to noon weekends). It has a well-displayed collection of artefacts, paintings, furniture and clothes from Split – captions are in Croatian only.

Split's finest art museum is the **Meštrović Gallery**, Šetalište Ivana Meštrovića 46 (closed Monday). Croatia's premier modern sculptor, Ivan Meštrović, built the gallery as a personal residence in 1931-39. Bus No 12 passes the gate infrequently. There are beaches on the southern side of the peninsula below the gallery. From the gallery it's also possible to hike straight up **Marjan Hill**, with lookouts, old chapels and the local **zoo**.

Special Events

The Split Summer Festival from mid-July to mid-August features opera, drama, ballet and concerts on open-air stages.

Places to Stay & Eat

The closest camping ground to Split is *Lisičina* (☎ 861 332), 20km south-east of Split near Omiš.

The Turistički Biro has *private rooms* starting at 78/92KN, plus the usual 30% surcharge for stays of less than four nights.

The 32-room *Slavija* hotel (☎ 47 053, Buvinova 3), has the cheapest rooms in town: 170/220KN or 220/260KN with bath.

Galija, on Tončićeva, serves the best pizzas in town (22KN and up). Also try *Pizzeria Bakra* (Radovanova 2), off ul Sv Petra Starog just down from the *vegetable market*.

The vegetarian salad bar at *Ponoćno Sunce (Teutina 15)*, is excellent value at 40KN. It also serves pastas and grilled meats. The spiffy *Burek Bar (Domaldova 13)*, serves burek and yoghurt for about 12KN. There's a large *supermarket* at Svačićeva 1.

Entertainment

During the winter months, opera and ballet are presented at the *Croatian National Theatre* on Trg Gaje Bulata. The best seats are about 60KN.

In summer everyone starts the evening at one of the cafes along Obala hrvatskog narodnog preporoda and then heads to the *Bačvice* complex on the beach. This former public baths offers restaurants, cafes, discos and venues for live rock and salsa.

Getting There & Away

Bus Advance bus tickets with seat reservations are recommended. There are return buses from the main station beside the harbour to Zadar (158km), Zagreb (478km), Rijeka (404km), Pula (514km, three daily) and Dubrovnik (84KN, 235km). There are also buses to Sarajevo (271km) in Bosnia.

City bus No 37 to Split's airport and Trogir leaves from a local bus station on Domovinskog, 1km north-east of the city centre.

Croatia Express (☎ 342 645), near the bus station, has buses to many German cities, including Munich (400KN, 912km) and Berlin (840KN). Agencija Touring (☎ 338 503), at the bus station, also has buses to Germany and a weekly bus to Amsterdam (900KN).

Train There are three or four trains daily between Split and Zagreb (60KN, nine hours) and two trains daily between Split and Šibenik (26KN, 74km).

Boat Jadrolinija (☎ 355 399), in the large ferry terminal opposite the bus station, handles year-round services to Hvar Island. The local ferry is cheaper (26KN) and calls at Vela Luka on Korčula Island (29KN).

For information on connections to Italy see Getting There & Away at the beginning of this chapter.

TROGIR
☎ 021
Trogir (formerly Trau), a lovely medieval town on the coast and just 20km west of Split, is well worth a stop if you're coming south from Zadar. A day trip to Trogir from Split can easily be combined with a visit to the Roman ruins of Salona.

The old town of Trogir occupies a tiny island in the narrow channel between Čiovo Island and the mainland, and is just off the coastal highway. There's many sights on the 15-minute walk around this island.

Orientation & Information
The heart of the old town is a few minutes' walk from the bus station. After crossing the small bridge near the station, go through the North Gate. Trogir's finest sights are around Narodni trg, slightly left and ahead.

The tourist office (☎ 881 554), opposite the cathedral, sells a map of the area. There's no left-luggage office in Trogir bus station, so you'll end up toting your bags around town if you only visit on a stopover.

Things to See
The glory of the three-naved Venetian **Cathedral of St Lovro** on Narodni trg is the Romanesque portal of Adam and Eve (1240) by Master Radovan, which you can admire for free, any time. Enter the building through an obscure back door to see the perfect Renaissance Chapel of St Ivan and the choir, pulpit, ciborium and treasury. You can even climb the cathedral tower, if it's open, for a delightful view. Also on Narodni trg is the **town hall**, with an excellent Gothic staircase and Renaissance loggia.

Getting There & Away
In Split bus No 37 leaves from the local bus station. If you're making a day trip to Trogir buy your ticket back to Split, as the ticket window at Trogir bus station is often closed. Drivers also sell tickets if you're stuck. City bus No 37 runs between Trogir and Split (28km) every 20 minutes throughout the day with a stop at Split airport en route.

There's also a ferry once a week between Trogir and Split.

Southbound buses from Zadar (130km) will drop you off in Trogir. Getting buses north can be more difficult, as they often arrive full from Split.

HVAR ISLAND
☎ 021
Called the 'Croatian Madeira', Hvar is said to receive more sunshine than anywhere else in the country: 2724 hours each year. Hvar is luxuriantly green, with brilliant patches of lavender, rosemary and heather. The fine weather is so reliable that hotels give a discount on cloudy days and a free stay if you ever see snow. After Korčula Island, Hvar is one of the all-around finest islands in Dalmatia.

The main attraction is medieval **Hvar Town**, nestled between pine-covered slopes overlooking the azure Adriatic. Its Gothic palaces are hidden among narrow backstreets below the 13th-century city walls. The traffic-free marble avenues of Hvar Town have an air of Venice; under Venetian rule Hvar grew rich exporting wine, figs and fish. **Stari Grad**, 20km east of Hvar Town on the island's northern coast, is rather picturesque, though somewhat of a disappointment after Hvar Town.

Orientation & Information

A curious feature of Hvar Town is its lack of street names. Jadrolinija ferries dock in the centre of town.

Hvar Town's tourist office (☎ 741 059) is in the arsenal building on the corner of Trg Sv Stjepana. Atlas (☎ 741 670), facing the harbour, represents American Express. Public telephones are in the post office on the waterfront.

Things to See & Do

The **Dominican monastery** at the head of Hvar Town's bay was destroyed by Turks in the 16th century. The local **Archaeological Museum** is now housed among the ruins. If the museum is closed (as it usually is), the road just above leads up to a stone cross offering picture-postcard views of Hvar.

At the south-eastern end of Hvar Town is the 15th-century **Franciscan monastery**, with a fine collection of Venetian paintings in the church and adjacent museum.

Smack in the middle of town is the imposing Gothic **arsenal**, its great arch visible from afar. Upstairs off the arsenal's terrace is the **municipal theatre** (1612), the first ever built in Europe.

On a hill high above Hvar Town, the 16th-century **Venetian fortress** is well worth the climb for the sweeping views. The best **beach** in Hvar is in front of the Hotel Amphora, around the western corner of the cove, though most people take a launch to the nudist islands of **Jerolim** and **Stipanska**, just offshore.

Places to Stay & Eat

Accommodation in Hvar is extremely tight in July and August and expensive at all times. Making a prior reservation is highly recommended.

There's a camp site at *Jurjevac (☎ 765 555)* near Stari Grad and there are frequent buses to Jelsa, where you can pitch a tent at *Grebišće (☎ 761 191)* or *Mina (☎ 761 227)*.

For *private accommodation*, try Mengola Travel (☎/fax 742 099), a right-hand turn from Sv Stjepana along the harbour, or Pelegrini (☎/fax 742 250), next to where the Jadrolinija ferries tie up. Expect to pay from 92/140KN a single/double for a room with private bathroom.

There are cheap *pizzerias* along the harbour. For fish, pastas and grilled meats (main dishes 45KN to 65KN) try *Bounty* next to the Mengola travel agency; *Hannibal* on the southern side of Trg Sv Stjepana or *Paradise Garden*, up some stairs on the northern side of the cathedral. There's a *grocery store* on Trg Sv Stjepana.

Getting There & Away

The Jadrolinija ferries between Rijeka and Dubrovnik stop in Stari Grad before continuing to Korčula. The Jadrolinija agency (☎ 741 132) beside the landing sells tickets.

The local ferry from Split calls at Stari Grad (26KN) three times daily (five in July and August) and connects Hvar town with Vela Luka on Korčula Island in the afternoon. See the Getting There & Away section of this chapter for information on international connections. Buses meet all ferries that dock at Stari Grad.

KORČULA ISLAND

☎ 020

Korčula, the largest island in an archipelago of 48 islets, is rich in vineyards and olive trees. The southern coast is dotted with quiet coves and small beaches linked to the interior by winding, scenic roads. **Vela Luka**, at the western end of Korčula, is the centre of the island's fishing industry. There isn't a lot to see and no real beaches, so if you're arriving by ferry from Split or Hvar jump on the waiting bus to **Korčula Town** (population 3000), a typical medieval Dalmatian town with round defensive towers and red-roofed houses. Just 15 minutes from Korčula Town by bus, **Lumbarda** is a picturesque small settlement known for its wine. A good ocean beach, **Plaža Pržina**, is on the other side of Lumbarda's vineyards.

Orientation & Information

The Jadrolinija car ferry docks below the walls of Korčula Town.

The Turistička Agencija (☎/fax 711 710) is on the west harbour as you enter the old town. Atlas travel agency (☎ 711 231) is the local American Express representative and there's a Jadrolinija office (☎ 711 101) about 25m up from the west harbour.

The post office (with public telephones) is rather hidden next to the stairs up to the old town. There are no ATMs on the island but you can change money at the post office or any of the travel agencies listed above.

CROATIA

Things to See

Other than following the circuit of the former city walls or walking along the shore, sightseeing in Korčula Town centres on **Cathedral Square**. The Gothic **Cathedral of St Mark** features two paintings by Tintoretto – *Three Saints* on the altar and *Annunciation* to one side.

The treasury in the 14th-century **Abbey Palace**, next to the cathedral, is worth a look, as is the **town museum** in the 15th-century Gabriellis Palace opposite.

It's said that Marco Polo was born in Korčula in 1254; for a small fee, you can climb the tower of what is believed to have been his house.

Organised Tours

In the high summer season, water taxis at the Jadrolinija port head to various points on the island as well as to Badija Island, which features a 15th-century Franciscan monastery (now a hotel) and a nudist beach.

Travel agencies offer tours to Mljet Island (145KN) and half-day boat trips to surrounding islands (70KN).

Places to Stay & Eat

Autocamp Kalac (☎ 711 182), near the beach behind Hotel Bon Repos, charges 14/21KN per tent/person.

The Turistička Agencija and Marko Polo Tours arrange *private rooms* starting at 120/184KN.

Hotel Bon Repos (☎ 711 102), overlooking a small beach outside of town, and *Hotel Park (☎ 726 004)* in town have the same rates: 330/480KN with bath and breakfast.

Just around the corner from Marco Polo's house, *Adio Mare* serves a variety of fresh fish. *Planjak*, between the *supermarket* and the Jadrolinija ferry office, has tasty Dalmatian dishes at low prices. A 20-minute walk from town on the road to Lumbarda leads to another local favourite, the inexpensive *Gastrionica Hajuk*. The shady terrace at *Hotel Korčula* is a lovely spot for coffee.

Entertainment

From May to September there's moreška sword dancing by the old town gate at 9 pm on Thursday. Buy tickets (35KN) at any travel agency.

Getting There & Away

There are daily bus services to/from Dubrovnik (50KN) and Zagreb (180KN), twice weekly to Sarajevo (145KN).

Once a week from June to September, Jadrolinija runs a car ferry between Korčula Town and Ancona, Italy (311KN, 16 hours), with stops at Split and Vis. Buy tickets at the Jadrolinija office (☎ 715 410 or 711 101) about 25m up from the harbour.

Some ferries from Split land at Vela Luka (buses to Korčula Town meet all arrivals) on the way to/from Hvar Island.

Getting Around

Six daily buses link Korčula Town to Vela Luka at the western end of the island (18KN, 1½ hours). Buses to Lumbarda run hourly in the morning (7KN, 7km). No bus runs to Lumbarda on Sunday and service to Vela Luka is sharply reduced on weekends.

Dubrovnik

☎ 020

The eight-month siege by the Yugoslav federal army in late 1991 tore through Dubrovnik's distinctive honey-coloured clay roofs, but otherwise the city escaped the war largely intact. The most severe blow to Dubrovnik was the catastrophic decline of tourism following the war. The city has begun to climb back and in July and August the streets are again crowded with visitors.

Whatever the time of year, Dubrovnik is completely enchanting. Stari Grad, the well-preserved old town, is unique for its marble-paved squares, steep cobbled streets, tall houses, churches, palaces, fountains and museums, all cut from the same light-coloured stone. The intact city walls, Dubrovnik's major claim to fame, keep motorists at bay.

Orientation & Information

The Jadrolinija ferry terminal and the bus station are a few hundred metres apart at Gruž, several kilometres north-west of the old town. The camping ground and most of the tourist hotels are on the leafy Lapad Peninsula, west of the bus station. The main street of the old town is Placa, also called Stradun.

The tourist office (☎ 426 354) is on Placa, opposite the Franciscan monastery in the old town.

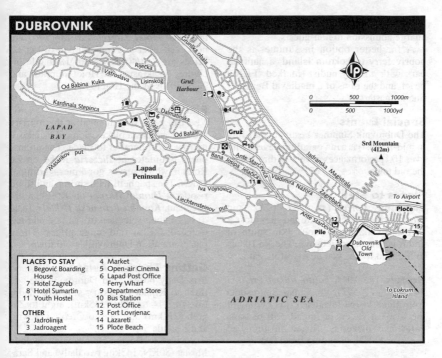

DUBROVNIK

LAPAD BAY

Rijecka
Vatroslava
Od Babina Kuka
Lisinskog
Kardinala Stepinca
Gruž Harbour
Dalmatinska
Kralja Tomislava
Od Batale
Gruž
LAPAD BAY
Mazankov put
Lapad Peninsula
Bana Josipa Jelačića
Ante Starčevića
Iva Vojnovića
Vladimira Nazora
Jadranska Magistrala
Zagrebačka
Liechtensteinov put
Srd Mountain (412m)
Ante Starčevića
To Airport
Ploče
Pile
Dubrovnik Old Town
Fort Lovrjenac
To Lokrum Island

ADRIATIC SEA

0   500   1000m
0   500   1000yd

PLACES TO STAY		4 Market
1	Begović Boarding House	5 Open-air Cinema
7	Hotel Zagreb	6 Lapad Post Office Ferry Wharf
8	Hotel Sumartin	9 Department Store
11	Youth Hostel	10 Bus Station
		12 Post Office
OTHER		13 Fort Lovrjenac
2	Jadrolinija	14 Lazareti
3	Jadroagent	15 Ploče Beach

Atlas (☎ 442 222, fax 411 100), Brsalje 17, next to the old town's Pile Gate, is the American Express agent.

You can make international phone calls at the main post office, Ante Starčevića 2, a block up from Pile Gate. There's another post office/telephone centre on Lapad near Hotel Kompas.

Algoritam, on Placa in Dubrovnik's old town, has a good range of English-language books and guidebooks.

Things to See & Do

Most travellers begin their visit at the city bus stop outside **Pile Gate**. As you enter the city, Dubrovnik's pleasant pedestrian promenade, Placa, extends all the way to the clock tower at the other end of town. The **Franciscan monastery** just inside Pile Gate has the third-oldest functioning pharmacy in Europe. **Orlando Column**, in front of the clock tower at the eastern end of Placa, is a favourite meeting place. On opposite sides of Orlando are the 16th-century **Sponza Palace** (now the State Archives) and **St Blaise's Church**, a lovely Italian baroque building.

Next to the church, a broad street leads to Dubrovnik's baroque **cathedral** and the Gothic **Rector's Palace** (1441), now a museum with furnished rooms, baroque paintings and historical exhibits. The narrow street opposite the palace opens onto **Gundulićeva Poljana**, a bustling morning market. Up the stairway at the southern end of the square is the imposing **Jesuit monastery** (1725).

Don't leave without taking a walk along Dubrovnik's brawny, perfectly intact **city walls**, built between the 13th and 16th centuries. They enclose the entire city in a curtain of stone over 2km long and up to 25m high, with two round towers, 14 square towers, two corner fortifications and a large fortress. The views over the town and sea are tremendous.

Whichever way you walk, you'll notice the large **Dominican monastery** in the north-eastern corner of the city. It houses Dubrovnik's best religious museum – don't miss it.

Beaches The closest beach, Ploče, is just beyond the 17th-century Lazareti (a former quarantine station) outside Ploče Gate.

CROATIA

Hotel beaches on the Lapad Peninsula charge admission to non-guests.

A far better option in summer is the hourly ferry to **Lokrum Island**, a national park with a rocky nudist (marked 'FKK') beach and the ruins of a medieval Benedictine monastery.

Special Events
The Dubrovnik Summer Festival (mid-July to mid-August) is a major cultural event with over 100 performances at venues throughout the old town.

Places to Stay
Camping *Porto* (☎ *487 078*) and *Matkovica* (☎ *486 096*) are the sites closest to Dubrovnik, lying about 8km south of Dubrovnik near a quiet cove. The No 10 bus to Srebeno leaves you nearly at its gate.

Hostels The YHA *youth hostel* (☎ *423 241, fax 412 592*), up Vinka Sagrestana from Bana Josipa Jelačića 17, is on one of the liveliest streets in Lapad, full of bars, cafes and pizzerias. Space in four-bed rooms is 88KN, including breakfast.

Private Rooms Locals with spare rooms meet arriving ferries; their prices may be lower than those charged by room-finding agencies. There are no singles, and doubles run from 124KN for rooms with shared bath to 220KN for rooms with private bath. Try Atlas, the tourist office or Globtour (☎ 428 144, fax 426 322) on Placa.

Hotels Most of the cheaper hotels are on the Lapad Peninsula. The *Begović Boarding House* (☎ *435 191, Primorska 17*), a few blocks up from the Lapad post office (bus No 6), has three rooms with shared bath at 75KN per person and three small apartments for 90KN per person. There's a nice terrace out the back with a good view.

Hotel Sumratin (☎ *436 333, fax 436 006*) and *Hotel Zagreb* (☎ *436 146*) are near each other in a tranquil part of Lapad. Prices are 248/400KN a single/double including breakfast at the Hotel Sumratin and 272/440KN at the Hotel Zagreb.

Places to Eat
You can get a decent meal at the touristy seafood and pasta places along ul Prijeko, a narrow street parallel to Placa. The atmosphere is quieter at *Pizzeria Roko* on Za Rokum, which serves good pies starting at 28KN. The spaghetti with shrimp and squid risotto at *Dundo Maroje* on Kovačka are excellent. *Konoba Primorka* (*Nikole Tesle 8*) has a good selection of seafood and national dishes at mid-range prices. These places are all in Dubrovnik's old town.

Getting There & Away
Bus Daily buses from Dubrovnik include three to Rijeka (639km), seven to Zadar (393km), 14 to Split (235km), eight to Zagreb (713km) and one to Orebić (113km) and Korčula.

Sevices to Bosnia-Hercegovina include Mostar (80KN, 143km, two daily) and Sarajevo (161KN, 278km, daily). There's a bus to the Montenegrijan border Monday, Wednesday and Friday (20KN, 30 minutes) from which a Montenegro bus takes you to Merceg-Novi (10KN, two hours) and on to Bar (65KN, five hours). For further information ask at Globtour on Placa. In a busy summer season and on weekends, buses out of Dubrovnik can be crowded, so book a ticket well before the scheduled departure time.

Boat Jadrolinija ferries run north to Hvar, Split, Zadar, and Rijeka. Buy tickets at the Jadrolinija office (☎ 418 000) at Obala S Radića 40. For information on international ferries see Getting There & Away at the beginning of this chapter.

Cyprus

Two high mountain ranges tower above Cyprus, the third largest island in the Mediterranean. Ancient Greek and Roman ruins, Orthodox monasteries and crusader castles are dotted across its fertile landscape. The island's lifestyle is easy-going, the crime rate is low and the sun shines a lot. All of this makes Cyprus sound like a paradise – and perhaps it would be, were it not for the long-running dispute between the Greeks and the Turks resulting in the partition of the island.

AT A GLANCE

Capital:	Lefkosia (formerly Nicosia)
Population:	926,000 (185,000 in Northern Cyprus)
Official Language:	Greek, Turkish in North Cyprus
Currency:	1 Cypriot pound (CY£) = 100 cents; 1 Turkish lira (TL) = 100 kurus

Facts about Cyprus

HISTORY

Cyprus has been inhabited since the Neolithic period and was later colonised by the Mycenaeans, Phoenicians, Assyrians, Persians, Hellenistic Egyptians and Romans.

In 1191, during the Third Crusade, Richard the Lionheart conquered the island and later sold it to the Knights Templar, a military religious order, who then sold it to Guy de Lusignan, the deposed king of Jerusalem. The Venetians ruled from 1489 to 1570, followed by the 300 year reign of the Ottoman Turks.

In 1878 the Turks ceded the island to Britain, and in 1925 Cyprus became a Crown colony of the UK. By now Cypriots were deeply frustrated by their own lack of self-determination, and the first stirrings of *enosis* (union with Greece) were felt. The island's Turkish population (18%) opposed enosis, believing it would lead to greater oppression.

In 1954 Britain prepared a new constitution for Cyprus that was accepted by the Turkish population but opposed by Greek extremists in the National Organisation of Cypriot Freedom Fighters (EOKA).

In August 1960 the UK granted independence to Cyprus with a Greek president, Archbishop Makarios, and a Turkish vice president, Fasal Kükük. This arrangement did little to quell intercommunal violence on Cyprus, and in 1964 the United Nations (UN) sent in a peacekeeping force.

In 1967 a military junta seized power in Greece, and on 15 July 1974 it mounted a coup d'etat in Cyprus, installing ex-guerilla leader Nicos Samson as president. Turkey reacted by invading and occupying the northern third of the island.

Since 1974 Cyprus has been divided by the so-called Green Line. Turkey essentially controls the Turkish Republic of Northern Cyprus (TRNC; also called North Cyprus), while Greece calls most of the shots in the Republic of Cyprus (the Republic), which comprises 63% of the island.

There is hope of reunification, as both sides want to join the EU, however despite pressure from major world powers the outcome of the talks remain undecided.

POPULATION & PEOPLE

Cyprus' total population is 926,000, with some 185,000 people living in the TRNC.

LANGUAGE

Most Cypriots in the Republic speak English and many road signs are in Greek and English. In North Cyprus you'll have to brush up on your Turkish. In both areas, the spelling of place and street names varies enormously. See the Turkish and Greek sections of the Language Guide at the back of this book for pronunciation guidelines and useful words and phrases.

CYPRUS

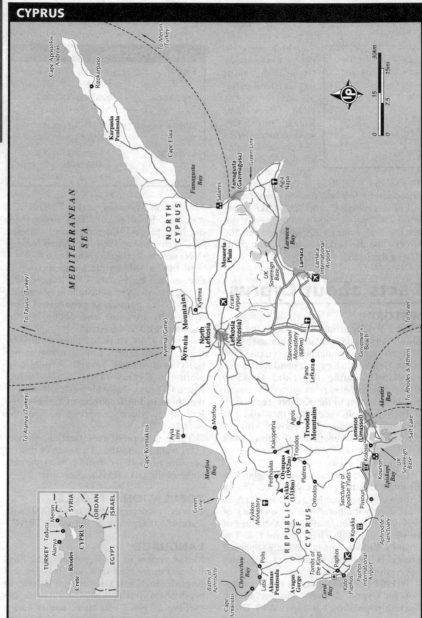

To Mersin (Turkey)

Cape Apostolos
Andreas

Rizokarpaso

**Karpasia
Peninsula**

Cape Elaia

*MEDITERRANEAN
SEA*

Famagusta
Bay

**N O R T H
C Y P R U S**

Famagusta
(Gazimagusa)

Green Line

Salamis

Agia
Napa

To Tasucu (Turkey)

**Mesaoria
Plain**

Larnaca
Bay

Larnaca

Larnaca
International
Airport

To Israel

Kyrenia
Mountains

Kythrea

Ercan
Airport

UK
Sovereign
Base

To Alanya (Turkey)

Kyrenia (Girne)

Kyrenia North
Lefkosa

**North
Lefkosa**

**Lefkosia
(Nicosia)**

Stavrovouni
Monastery
(689m)

Pano
Lefkara

Governor's
Beach

Cape Kormakitis

Ayia
Irini

Morfou

Agros

Kakopetria

**Troodos
Mountains**

Akrotiri
Bay

To Rhodes & Athens

*Morfou
Bay*

Pedhoulas Olympus
Troodos (1952m)▲

Kykko
(1318m)▲

Platres

Salt Lake

**Lemesos
(Limassol)**

Kolossi

UK
Sovereign
Base

Green
Line

Kyikkos
Monastery

Omodos

Sanctuary of
Apollon Ylatis

Kourion

Pissouri

*Episkopi
Bay*

Polis

**R E P U B L I C
O F   C Y P R U S**

Koukila

Aphrodite's
sanctuary

*Chrysochou
Bay*

Latsi

**Akamas
Peninsula**

*Baths of
Aphrodite*

Avagas
Gorge

Tombs of
the Kings

Paphos

Kato
Paphos

Paphos
International
Airport

Cape
Arnaouti

*Coral
Bay*

0   15   30km
0   7.5   15mi

TURKEY Tasucu
Mersin
Alanya

SYRIA

JORDAN

ISRAEL

Crete   Rhodes   CYPRUS

EGYPT

Since 1995 the Republic has converted all Greek place names into Latin characters. Throughout this chapter the new names are used because the old ones are being phased out on all tourist maps and road signs. In the North Cyprus section, Greek place names are used with the Turkish in parentheses.

Facts for the Visitor

TOURIST OFFICES
The Cyprus Tourism Organisation (CTO) has offices in major towns in the Republic, as well as in most EU countries and the USA.

There are North Cyprus tourist offices in North Nicosia, Famagusta and Kyrenia, and in Turkey, the UK and the USA.

VISAS & DOCUMENTS
In both the Republic and North Cyprus, nationals of the USA, Australia, Canada, New Zealand and EU countries can stay for up to three months without a visa.

Legally, you can only cross from the Republic to the TRNC for a few hours at a time (see the following Getting There & Away section). Though you can visit the Republic of Cyprus and mainland Greece with a North Cyprus stamp in your passport, it's best to ask for a stamp on a separate piece of paper when entering North Cyprus.

MONEY
The unit of currency in the Republic is the Cyprus pound (CY£), which is divided into 100 cents (c). The unit of currency in North Cyprus is the Turkish lira (TL).

Banks throughout Cyprus exchange cash or travellers cheques in all major currencies. Most shops, hotels, etc, in North Cyprus accept CY£ and other hard currencies.

In the Republic you can get a cash advance on Visa, MasterCard, Diners Club, Eurocard and American Express at major banks; ATMs are plentiful. In North Cyprus cash advances are given on Visa cards at the Vakiflar and Kooperatif Banks in North Nicosia and Kyrenia. Major banks have ATMs.

In the Republic, during summer, banks are open 8.15 am to 12.30 pm Monday to Friday and from 3.15 to 4.45 pm on Monday afternoons; some large banks offer a tourist service other afternoons. In North Cyprus they are open 8 am to noon weekdays and in winter 2 to 4 pm also.

Exchange Rates
Due to the severe, perennial inflation of the Turkish lira, all prices quoted in the North Cyprus section are in British pounds (UK£). Exchange rates for the Cyprus pound are:

country	unit	lira
Australia	$A1	CY£0.36
Canada	C$1	CY£0.41
euro	€1	CY£0.58
Germany	DM1	CY£0.29
Greece	100dr	CY£0.17
New Zealand	NZ$1	CY£0.29
UK	UK£1	CY£0.92
USA	US$1	CY£0.60

Costs
Cyprus is cheaper to visit than most European countries, and in North Cyprus costs are slightly lower still. You could get by on CY£14 a day, or live well on CY£30. Accommodation costs rise between April and November, peaking during July and August.

If not free, admission costs to all museums and sites are between CY£0.50 and CY£2.

Tipping & Bargaining
In both parts of the island a 10% service charge is sometimes added to a restaurant bill, but if not, offer a similar tip. Taxi drivers and hotel porters appreciate a small tip. It's not normal to bargain for goods in markets.

POST & COMMUNICATIONS
Post
In the Republic, postal rates for cards and letters are between 25c and 41c. In North Cyprus, postal rates are between UK£0.39 and UK£0.45.

Telephone
The Republic of Cyprus' country code is ☎ 357. To call North Cyprus from abroad, dial ☎ 90 (Turkey's country code), ☎ 392 (North Cyprus) and then the phone number.

In the Republic, you can make overseas calls from all telephone boxes but they only accept phonecards bought from newsagents, some banks or the Republic's telephone company (CYTA). A three-minute call to the USA costs CY£1.83 (peak times) or CY£1.53 (off-peak; 10 pm to 8 am and on Sunday). In North Cyprus most public telephones only accept phonecards bought at a Turkish Telecom office. From the north a three-minute call to the USA costs UK£1.35 (peak times) or UK£0.90 (off-peak).

Note that in North Cyprus area codes must be used at all times, even when calling locally. For this reason, area codes have been incorporated into all phone numbers in the North Cyprus section.

ACCOMMODATION

There are seven licensed camping grounds in the Republic, mostly with limited opening times. The Republic's four hostels are slightly cheaper if you are a member of Hostelling International (HI). The Cyprus Youth Hostel Association (☎ 02-670027) is at PO Box 1328, 1506 Lefkosia. There are no HI hostels in North Cyprus.

Hotels in the Republic are classified from one to five stars, and prices for a double room range from CY£17 up to CY£210. Guesthouses cost from CY£10 to CY£32. In North Cyprus these prices are slightly lower.

Getting There & Away

The Republic's airports are at Larnaka and Paphos. There are scheduled and charter flights from most European cities and the Middle East (around UK£230 return from London, including tax), with discounts for students. North Cyprus' Ercan airport is not recognised by international airline authorities, so all connections are via Turkey.

The Republic's passenger ferry port is in Lemesos. In summer there are regular boats to Greece (CY£52), Rhodes (CY£49), and Israel (CY£44). Student reductions are available. See the Lemesos Getting There & Away section for details. From North Cyprus there are two routes to mainland Turkey: Famagusta-Mersin (UK£10) and Kyrenia-Taşucu (from UK£15).

North Cyprus

Depending on diplomatic relations, it is possible to visit North Nicosia on a day trip

from Lefkosia – but check first at Lefkosia's CTO tourist office. It is impossible to travel in the opposite direction. The UN-monitored border crossing is in Lefkosia at the Ledra Palace Hotel, and you are allowed to walk or drive (no rental cars) across the border from 8 am to 1 pm, returning by 5 pm. There is no limit to the number of times you can cross into North Cyprus, but you *must* return by 5 pm, as officials keep track of how many people cross the border each day. To spend more than a few hours at a time in North Cyprus, you must enter the country from Turkey.

In theory, it is possible to travel to North Cyprus from Lefkosia and continue on to Turkey without returning to the south, however, Greek Cypriot authorities will not let you travel across the border with luggage and you will be placed on the Greek Cypriot 'black list'. So, unless you are prepared to part with your worldly goods for good, it's more trouble than it's worth.

The Republic of Cyprus

LEFKOSIA
☎ 02

Lefkosia (formerly Nicosia), is the capital, bisected by the Green Line separating the Republic from North Cyprus. According to the sign at UN-patrolled barrier at Lidras St, this is 'the last divided capital', and a visit is essential to appreciate the island's plight. Being inland, it attracts far fewer visitors, and so is much more genuinely Cypriot than the coastal towns.

Orientation & Information

Lefkosia's old town is surrounded by a 16th-century Venetian wall and divided by the Green Line. It's possible to go to/from North Cyprus at the UN-controlled Ledra Palace Hotel checkpoint, which is just outside the city wall on the old town's western side. For more information on crossing to/from North Cyprus, see the Getting There & Away section earlier in this chapter.

The CTO tourist office (☎ 674264), on Laïki Yitonia in the old town, is open 8.30 am to 4 pm weekdays, to 2 pm Saturday. Close by, is the Hellenic Bank, 5 Leoforos

Konstantinou Palaiologou, which changes money from 8.15 am to 12.30 pm.

The main post office is on Leoforos Konstantinou Palaiologou. The CYTA telephone office on Leoforos Aigyptou is open 7.30 am to 1.30 pm daily (3 to 5.30 pm Tuesday). Check email and surf the Web at the Nicosia Palace Arcade (✉ n.palace@cytanet.cy), situated just near the city walls.

Things to See

Just north of Plateia Archiepiskopou Kyprianou, a busy square in the old town, are the **Byzantine Museum** with its superb collection of icons, and the 17th-century **St John's Cathedral**, with some stunning frescoes dating from 1736. Both are closed on Sunday.

Next door is the **Cyprus Folk Art Museum** (closed Sunday).

Continue north along Agiou Ioannou St and turn right onto Thiseos St, which leads to Leoforos N Foka. Turn left here for the imposing **Famagusta Gate**, which was once the main entrance to the city.

The **Cyprus Museum**, near the CYTA telephone office, has an extraordinary collection of 7th-century BC terracotta figurines found at the sanctuary of Ayia Irini, as well as the original *Leda and the Swan* mosaic from Aphrodite's sanctuary near Kouklia. It's open 9 am to 5 pm Monday to Saturday, 10 am to 1 pm Sunday.

If you fancy a change from the museums then check out the **Ledra Observatory**. Situated in the Woolworths building (Shacolas Tower), the observatory boasts amazing views of the city.

Places to Stay

The pleasant HI *hostel* (✆ 674808, *Hadjidakis 5*) is in a quiet part of the new town, about six blocks south-west of Plateia Eleftherias. Beds are CY£4/5 per night.

Solonos Street is a good bet for fairly inexpensive accommodation. The best choice is *Tony's Bed & Breakfast* (✆ 466752, fax 454225, Solonos 13) where singles/doubles/triples cost CY£14/22/34, a bit more for rooms with private bath.

Places to Eat

There's a *supermarket* on Plateia Solomu, about 200m north-west of Plateia Eleftherias.

A huge *meze* (a traditional meal comprised of numerous small dishes) is only CY£6 at *Zanettos Taverna* (Trikoupi 65). *Kantinas* (Chytron 11) is situated in the new town, about 2km from the hostel. Open day and night, it serves excellent food with several vegetarian choices. *Ledra Café*, in the observatory, has a wide range of hot and cold snacks and meals.

Getting There & Away

Private bus companies in Lefkosia offer frequent services daily except Sunday, when schedules are greatly reduced.

Intercity, off Leonidou St at Omirou 3, has buses to Lemesos (CY£1.50, five daily), Paphos (CY£3, daily) and Platres (CY£2, daily at 12.15 pm). Kallenos operates from Plateia Solomou and has five buses a day to Larnaka (CY£1.50). From the same square there's a direct bus to Polis at noon daily (CY£4). From the Constanza car park, Klarios goes to Troödos at 11.30 am daily (CY£1.50) and more frequently to Kakopetria (CY£1.20).

Travel Express (✆ 771444) operates taxis to Larnaka (CY£2.10) and Lemesos (CY£3). Call the office to arrange a pick-up point.

LARNAKA
✆ 04

Larnaka is a coastal resort built over the ancient city of **Kition**. The actual ruins of Kition, 1.5km from town (signposted), are not that thrilling, though the Cyclopean city walls are impressive (open 7 am to 2.30 pm weekdays).

In Larnaka proper are a beach, a new waterfront promenade, an old Turkish area and a fort. North of the fort, touristy cafes line the seafront.

The CTO tourist office (✆ 654322) is on Plateia Vasileos Pavlou, two blocks west of the Sun Hall Hotel.

Places to Stay

The nearest camping ground is *Forest Beach Camping* (✆ 644514), 8km along the beach road towards Agia Napa, but it's a bit run down. To get there take the tourist bus from the north side of the Sun Hall Hotel.

The HI *hostel* (✆ 621188, N Rossou 27), just east of St Lazaros church, charges CY£4 a night; it's basic, but friendly with dorm beds only.

CYPRUS

About 500m west of the fort, the friendly two-star *Onisillos Hotel* (☎ 651100, fax 654468, Onisillos 17) has rooms with bathroom for CY£18/25, including breakfast.

Getting There & Away

The bus stop for Lefkosia (CY£1.50) and Lemesos (CY£1.70) is on the waterfront, almost opposite the Dolphin Café Restaurant.

For service taxis to Lemesos (CY£2.60) and Lefkosia (CY£2.10) call Travel Express (☎ 661010) to arrange a pick-up point.

LEMESOS
☎ 05

Lemesos (Limassol) is Cyprus' second-largest city and its main passenger and cargo port. Bland apartments and public gardens line the waterfront; behind these and to the west is the more attractive old town with a mosque, old-fashioned artisans' shops and the well-restored **castle** where Richard the Lionheart married Berengaria of Navarre in 1191. Inside is the **Medieval Museum**.

Close-by, near the mosque, is a newly restored **hammam** (Turkish bath) where a steam and sauna or a massage costs CY£5. It's open 2 to 10 pm daily and all sessions are mixed.

The CTO office (☎ 362756) is at Spyros Araouzou 15, on the waterfront near the old harbour.

Places to Stay & Eat

The cheapest hotels are clustered in the old town, on the eastern side of the castle. A good one to try is the *Luxor Guest House* (☎ 362265, Agiou Andreou 101). Its large, clean rooms cost CY£5 per person. Otherwise the two-star *Continental Hotel* (☎ 362530, fax 373030, Spyrou Araouzou 137), overlooking the waterfront, has pleasant rooms with private bath for CY£15/25, including breakfast.

A good place for lunch or a snack is the *Richard & Berengaria* cafe, by the castle. For an evening meal of traditional Cypriot dishes try the cosy *Rizitiko's Tavern* tucked away discreetly just to the right of the castle.

Getting There & Away

Intercity buses run daily to Lefkosia (CY£1.50) and Paphos (CY£1.50) from the station on the corner of Enoseos and Eirinis

Sts, north of the castle. From the same spot there are weekday buses (at noon) to Agros (CY£1) in the Troödos Mountains.

Ferries in summer run to Rhodes (CY£49) and less frequently to Crete and Piraeus (near Athens). Buy ferry tickets from any travel agency or direct from Salamis Tours Ltd (☎ 355555) or Poseidon Lines (☎ 745666). The port is 5km southwest of town; take bus No 1 from the station on A Themistokleous St.

TROÖDOS MASSIF
☎ 05

The mountains of the Troödos region are beautiful with their secluded Byzantine monasteries, 15th-century frescoed churches, small wine-making villages, pine forests, and numerous walking trails.

Platres is easy to reach by bus and is a good base for the Troödos area. The region's CTO office (☎ 421316) is on Platres' main square (closed Sunday).

The only reason to stay in **Troödos** itself, more a touristy hill station than a village, is for the nearby walks; maps are available at CTO in Platres.

In **Pedhoulas** village there is the small World Heritage-listed **Church of Archangelos**, with frescoes dating from 1474. The key to the church is at a nearby house (signposted).

The **Kykkos Monastery**, 20km west of Pedhoulas, is the best-known but also the most touristy monastery. It dates from the 12th century but has been completely renovated – all the mosaics, frescoes and stonework are new.

Omodos village is in a wine-growing region, and home-made wine is available for sale and tastings. The village is also home to the intimate Stavros Monastery.

Places to Stay

There are hotels or private rooms in most of the villages. In July and August it's wise to book ahead.

In a pine forest 2km north of Troödos is a *camping ground* (☎ 420124), open from May to October. Troödos' HI *hostel* (☎ 420200) is usually open from May to October and charges CY£5 for the first night and CY£4 thereafter. Rather more luxurious is the three-star *Troödos Hotel* (☎ 420135, fax 420160), with rooms for CY£27/38, including breakfast.

Platres' *Minerva Hotel* (☎ *421731, fax 421075*) is situated on the top road and charges CY£16/30 for a pleasant room with bathroom and breakfast. The Swiss-styled *Petit Palais* (☎ *421723, fax 421065*), priced in high season at CY£20/32, also includes breakfast. There are signposts to these and other hotels in Platres.

Getting There & Away
From Troödos village buses run to Lefkosia via Kakopetria (CY£0.60) daily at 1.30 pm. From Kakopetria there are about 12 buses at day to Lefkosia (CY£1.10). At 7 am there is a service taxi from Platres to Limassol (CY£2). At 6 am there is a bus from Pedoulas to Lefkosia (CY£2) but it no longer stops in Platres.

PAPHOS
☎ 06
Paphos, once the capital of Cyprus, is divided into Kato Paphos (Lower Paphos) on the coast, and plain old Paphos 1km inland. Kato Paphos has most of the sights but is full of huge hotels and expensive bars and eateries that spoil the old harbour area. Paphos itself is more pleasant and authentic. The CTO office (☎ 232841) is at Gladstonos 3, just down from Paphos' main square.

The **Tombs of the Kings**, a fascinating network of underground tombs dating from the 3rd century BC, are on the coastal road to Polis, about 2km north of Kato Paphos.

Places to Stay
The nearest camping ground is *Zenon Gardens* (☎ *242277*), 5km south of Kato Paphos and close to the beach.

The unkempt HI *hostel* (☎ *232588, Leoforos Eleftheriou Venizelou 37*) is quite a walk from Paphos centre (go up Leoforos Evagora Pallikaridi; the hostel is off to the right). Beds are CY£5 for the first and then CY£4.

The *Trianon Hotel* (☎ *232193, Makarios Avenue 99*) charges CY£5/12 and includes shared bathroom and kitchen facilities.

Getting There & Away
The Amaroza bus company has buses to Lemesos (CY£2) and Lefkosia (CY£3). Their office is at 79 Leoforos Evagora Pallikaridi, north of Paphos' main square.

For service taxis call Travel Express (☎ 233181) to arrange a pick-up point.

Turkish Republic of Northern Cyprus (TRNC)

NORTH NICOSIA (LEFKOŞA)
North Nicosia, the capital of the TRNC, is a quiet city with good examples of Gothic and Ottoman architecture – though it sometimes seems populated exclusively by Turkish soldiers.

Orientation & Information
The old city's Atatürk Square is the heart of North Nicosia. Girne Caddesi is the main thoroughfare and runs north from Atatürk Square to the well-preserved Girne Gate. To the east of the square is the Selimiye quarter, where you'll find most places of interest.

The tourist office inside Girne Gate has maps for most towns in North Cyprus (closed Sunday). The main post office is on Sarayönü Sokak, just west of Atatürk Square. The telephone office, in the new town on Kizilay Sokak, is open 8 am to midnight daily. You can check email at the Super Computer Internet Café (☞ megabir@ cypronet.net), Gultekin Sengor Sokak, opposite the football grounds.

Things to See & Do
The **Turkish Museum** at the northern end of Girne Caddesi is housed in a 17th-century Islamic monastery used by dervishes (Muslim ascetics) in the 19th century. It now displays dervish memorabilia. The museum is open 8 am to 2 pm weekdays.

The Selimiye quarter, east of Atatürk Square, is dominated by the **Selimiye Mosque**, which was originally a cathedral built between 1209 and 1326.

The **Büyük Hammam**, by the Antalya Pansiyon (ask directions), is a world-famous Turkish bath used by locals and tourists of both sexes. A steam bath and a massage (all masseurs are male) costs UK£10.

Places to Stay & Eat
Most of the budget accommodation in the city is intended for local workers rather than tourists and is definitely unsuitable for lone female travellers.

Passable is the *Altin Pansiyon* (☎ *22-85049, Girne Caddesi 63*), where a room costs UK£5/6. The old town's best hotel is the three-star *Saray* (☎ *22-83115, fax 22-84808)*, on Atatürk Square. Rooms here cost UK£26/40, including breakfast. It's more advisable (cheaper and safer) to move on from the capital and stay overnight in one of the outlying towns.

There are two friendly restaurants on Girne Caddesi – *Saricizmeli* and *Öz Amasyali*. A substantial meal at either is about UK£3. There's also a restaurant at the *Saray* hotel.

Getting There & Away
For information on travel from the Republic of Cyprus, see the Getting There & Away section at the beginning of this chapter.

The long-distance bus station is in the new town on the corner of Atatürk Caddesi and Kemal Aşik Caddesi. However, it is easier to catch the frequent minibuses to Kyrenia (UK£0.60) and Famagusta (UK£0.90) from the Itimat bus station just east of Girne Gate.

FAMAGUSTA (GAZIMAĞUSA)
The old part of Famagusta is enclosed by an impressive Venetian wall. Famagusta's St Nicholas Cathedral, now the Mustafa Pasha Mosque, is the finest example of Gothic architecture in Cyprus. Othello's Castle, part of the city walls and battlements, was built by the Lusignans in the 13th century. According to legend it was here that Christophore Moro (governor of Cyprus from 1506 to 1508) killed his wife, Desdemona, in a fit of jealous rage. There are good views from the ramparts.

The tourist office (☎ 36-62864) is on Fevzi Cakmak Caddesi, outside the city wall about 300m east of the Victory Monument.

Places to Stay & Eat
Inside the city walls is the pleasant *Altun Tabaya Hotel* (☎ *36-65563, Kizilkule Yolu 7);* follow signs from the gate east of the Victory Monument. Rooms with private bath and breakfast are UK£8/12.

Not far from the tourist office, but in a run-down section of the new town, the friendly *Panorama Hotel* (☎ *36-65880, fax 36-65990)*, on Ilker Karter Caddesi, has comfortable rooms (no breakfast) for UK£7/11.

In the old town opposite St Nicholas Cathedral, *Viyana Restaurant* serves good

filling meals (from UK£6) and has a pleasant outside eating area.

Getting There & Away
Minibuses to North Nicosia (UK£0.90) go frequently from the Itimat bus station on the Victory Monument roundabout, and from the small bus terminal on Lefkoşa Yolu, west of the monument. From the latter, minibuses leave every 30 minutes for Kyrenia (UK£1).

Ferries to Mersin in Turkey leave on Tuesday, Thursday and Sunday from the port behind Canbulat Yolu. The eight-hour trip costs UK£10. Buy tickets from 3 Bulent Ecevit Bulvari (☎ 36-65995).

ANCIENT SALAMIS
Salamis, 9km north of Famagusta, contains the ruins of Cyprus' most important pre-Christian city. Allow a few hours to explore the restored Roman amphitheatre and the gymnasium and adjacent baths. In summer the site is open 7 am to 7.30 pm daily.

There is a *bar/restaurant* in the car park by the ticket office, and a long sandy beach and a *camping ground* near the site. Taxis from Famagusta (there are no buses) charge UK£6 return.

KYRENIA (GIRNE)
Kyrenia is an attractive town built around a horseshoe-shaped harbour, dominated on one side by an impressive Byzantine castle. The castle's star attraction is the Shipwreck Museum, which houses the world's oldest shipwreck (circa 3000 BC) and its cargo. Both the castle and museum are open 9 am to 7 pm daily.

Behind the harbour, Hürriyet Caddesi runs west from the town hall roundabout all the way to the tourist office (☎ 81-52145).

Places to Stay
Most budget hotels are along Ecevit Caddessi and between Hürriyet Caddesi and the harbour. The central *Bingöl Guest House* (☎ *81-52749)*, on the roundabout, charges UK£6 per person. The utterly pleasant *New Bristol Hotel* (☎ *81-56570, fax 81-57365, Hürriyet Caddesi 42)* charges UK£8/12. For sea views and old-fashioned charm try the *Girne Harbour Lodge Motel* (☎ *81-57392, fax 81-53744)* at the west end of the harbour. It has good-value rooms with bath and breakfast for UK£10/18.

Getting There & Away

Minibuses to Famagusta (UK£0.90) and North Nicosia (UK£0.60), as well as shared taxis to North Nicosia (UK£0.75), depart from the roundabout in front of the town hall.

Ferries to Taşucu, in Turkey, leave at 9.30 am (UK£21, three hours) and 11.30 am (UK£17.00, seven hours) daily. Buy tickets at the port or from the Fergün Shipping Co Ltd (☎ 8152344) at the town hall roundabout.

Czech Republic

The Czech Republic, a nation squeezed between the Germanic and Slavic worlds, is full of medieval castles, fairy-tale chateaux and boisterous pubs pouring glasses of frothy Czech beer. The Czech Republic is doubly inviting for its mostly helpful, cultured people and its excellent transportation networks.

More than 90% of English-speaking visitors limit themselves only to Prague. The clever few who escape the capital will encounter some of Europe's finest architecture, minus the year-round crowds and high prices.

AT A GLANCE

Capital:	Prague
Population:	10.28 million
Official Language:	Czech
Currency:	1 koruna (Kč)
	= 100 haléřů

Facts about the Czech Republic

HISTORY

In antiquity the Bohemian basin was inhabited by the Celtic Boii tribe. Germanic tribes conquered the Celts in the 4th century AD, and between the 5th and 10th centuries the West Slavs settled here. From 830 to 907, the Slavic tribes united in the Great Moravian Empire.

In 995, the Czech lands were united under the native Přemysl dynasty. The Czech state became a kingdom in the 12th century and reached its peak under Přemysl Otakar II from 1253 to 1278.

In 1310 John of Luxembourg gained the Bohemian throne. His son, Charles IV, became king in 1346 and Holy Roman Emperor in 1355.

In 1415, the religious reformer Jan Hus, rector of Charles University, was burnt at the stake in Constance. His ideas inspired the religious and nationalistic Hussite movement that swept Bohemia from 1419 to 1434.

The Thirty Years' War, which devastated Central Europe from 1618 to 1648, began in Prague, and the defeat of the uprising of the Czech Estates at the 1620 Battle of White Mountain marked the beginning of a long period of forced Catholicisation, Germanisation and oppression. The Czechs began rediscovering their linguistic and cultural roots in the early 19th century during the so-called National Revival.

Following WWI, Czech and Slovak nationalists strived for a common state, leading to the formation of the Czechoslovak Republic on 28 October 1918.

After annexing Austria in the Anschluss of March 1938, Hitler turned his attention to Czechoslovakia. By the infamous Munich Pact of September 1938, Britain and France surrendered the border regions of Bohemia and Moravia to Nazi Germany, and in 1939 the Germans occupied the rest of the country.

At the end of WWII West Bohemia was liberated by US troops, while the rest of the country was liberated by the Soviet army. Unlike Germany and Poland, which were devastated during WWII, Czechoslovakia was largely undamaged.

A power struggle soon developed in Prague between communists and democrats. In early 1948, the communists staged the 'February coup d'etat' with the backing of the Soviet Union. In July, Communist Party chairman Klement Gottwald became president.

The 1950s were years of harsh repression and thousands of non-communists fled the country. In April 1968, the new first secretary of the Communist Party, Alexander Dubček, introduced liberalising reforms – the so-called Prague Spring – to create 'socialism with a human face'. Dubček refused requests from Moscow to withdraw his reforms and on the night of 20 August 1968 more than 200,000 Soviet and Warsaw Pact soldiers invaded Czechoslovakia.

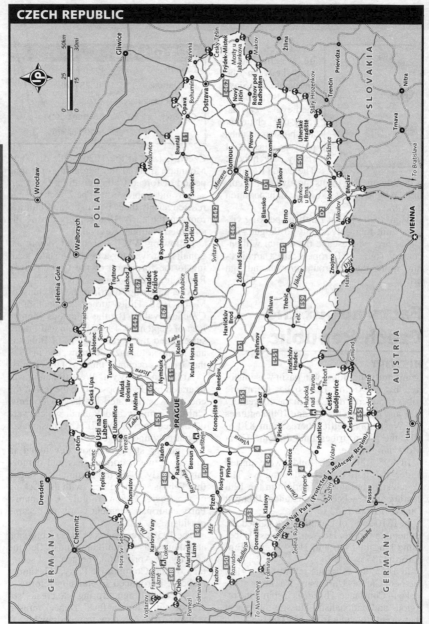

By 1989, Mikhail Gorbachev's *perestroika* was sending shock waves through the region. After the fall of the Berlin Wall on 9 November, an officially sanctioned student march on Prague's Národní třída was ruthlessly broken up by police on 17 November. The following Monday 250,000 protesters gathered in Václavské náměstí. The protests widened, culminating in the resignation of the Communist Party's Politburo. The mostly peaceful 'Velvet Revolution' was over.

With the strong central authority provided by the communists gone, old antagonisms between Slovakia and Prague re-emerged. The June 1992 elections sealed the fate of Czechoslovakia. The incompatibility of Václav Klaus (the prime minister) and Vladimír Mečiar (a left-leaning Slovak nationalist) soon became apparent, with the former pushing for economic reform while the latter wanted state intervention to save key industries in Slovakia.

Calls from president Václav Havel – the country's most famous dissident-playwright – for a referendum on national unity were rejected by politicians on both sides. In August 1992, Klaus and Mečiar agreed that the Czechoslovak federation would cease to exist at midnight on 31 December 1992. The peaceful 'velvet divorce' was over.

Since becoming an independent country, the Czech Republic has suffered from economic mismanagement. In late 1997 Klaus was forced to resign and a new government, headed by the former central bank boss, Josef Tošovský, was formed to govern until the June 1998 elections. The following month President Havel named the new minority government of the Social Democrats (ČSSD) headed by their leader and new prime minister, Miloš Zeman.

GEOGRAPHY
The Czech Republic (78,864 sq km) is comprised of two regions – Bohemia and Moravia. Bohemia nestles between the Šumava Mountains along the German border. The Czech Republic's highest peak, Mt Sněžka (1602m), is in the Giant Mountains. In between these ranges are rolling plains mixed with forests and farmland.

CLIMATE
The Czech climate is temperate, with cool, humid winters and warm summers. Prague has average daily temperatures above 14°C from May to September, above 8°C in April and October, and below freezing in December and January.

POPULATION & PEOPLE
The Czech Republic is fairly homogeneous: of its population of 10.28 million people, 95% are Czech, 3% are Slovak and the majority are Catholic.

SOCIETY & CONDUCT
It is customary to say *dobrý den* (good day) when entering a shop, cafe or quiet bar, and *na shledanou* (goodbye) when leaving. If you are invited to a Czech home bring fresh flowers. When entering someone's home remember to remove your shoes, unless you're told not to bother.

LANGUAGE
Czech and Slovak are closely related and mutually comprehensible West Slavic languages. German is predominantly understood by the older generation. Under the communists everybody learned Russian at school, but this has now been replaced by English.

Some useful Czech words that are frequently used in this chapter are: *most* (bridge), *náměstí* (square), *nádraží* (station), *třída* (avenue) and *ulice* (street). Toilets might be marked *záchody* or *WC*, while men's may be marked *páni* or *muži* and women's *dámy* or *ženy*. See the Language chapter at the back of this book for pronunciation guidelines and useful words and phrases.

Facts for the Visitor

HIGHLIGHTS
Some of the most picturesque 'historical' towns are Prague, Litoměřice, Český Krumlov, Kutná Hora, Tábor and Telč. The 14th-century Karlštejn Castle looks like something out of Disneyland. Konopiště and Český Krumlov castles have the same effect. The Prague Jewish Museum in the former Prague ghetto is easily the largest and most authentic of its kind in Central Europe.

SUGGESTED ITINERARIES
Three days
Spend two days in Prague and make a day trip to Kutná Hora.

One week
  Visit Prague, Kutná Hora, Litoměřice and
  Český Krumlov.
Two weeks
  As above, plus Telč, Brno and either Mariánské Lázně or Karlovy Vary.

PLANNING
When to Go

Crowds are a year-round problem in Prague, especially from June to August, but crowds are rarely a problem outside of the capital. The best times to visit the Czech Republic are mid-April to May and September. Many sights are closed from November to March.

Maps

Some of the best Czech country maps are GeoClub by SHOCart. Good maps of the Czech Republic available outside the country are those by Austrian publishers Freytag & Berndt.

TOURIST OFFICES

Throughout the country there is a network of *městské informační centrum/středisko* (municipal information centres). Čedok, the former government tourism monopoly, has offices around the country that change money and arrange accommodation and travel tickets.

VISAS & DOCUMENTS

Citizens of the USA can stay 30 days without a visa; most citizens of EU countries and New Zealand are allowed three months, while for citizens of the UK, Ireland and Canada (visas might be introduced for Canadians from January 2001) the limit is six months. Australians need a visa that costs the equivalent of 1000 Kč (about A$48) from embassies and consulates and is valid for up to three months.

Visas are not available at any border crossings.

EMBASSIES & CONSULATES
Czech Embassies Abroad

Czech Republic embassies and consulates abroad include:

Australia (☎ 02-9371 8878) 169 Military Rd, Dover Heights, NSW 2030
Canada (☎ 613-562 3875) 541 Sussex Drive, Ottawa, KIN 6Z6
New Zealand (☎ 04-564 6001) 48 Hair St, PO Box 43035, Wainuiomata, Wellington

UK (☎ 020-7243 7943) 26 Kensington Palace Gardens, London, W8 4QY
USA (☎ 202-274 9100) 3900 Spring of Freedom St NW, Washington, DC 20008

Foreign Embassies in the Czech Republic

Countries with embassies in Prague (area code ☎ 02) include:

Canada (☎ 72 10 18 00) Mickiewiczova 6, Hradčany, Praha 6
Slovakia (☎ 33 32 14 42) Pod hradbami 1, Střešovice, Praha 6
UK (☎ 57 53 02 78) Thunovská 14, Malá Strana, Praha 1
USA (☎ 57 53 06 63) Tržiště 15, Malá Strana, Praha 1

There is an Australian honorary consul in Prague (☎ 24 31 07 43) at Na Ořechovce 38, Střešovice, Praha 6. For nonemergency services contact the Australian embassy in Vienna, Austria. New Zealand citizens can contact the honorary consul (☎ 57 53 02 78) in Prague or the New Zealand embassy in Bonn, Germany.

MONEY

The Czech crown (Koruna česká; Kč) was made fully convertible in 1996. Banknotes come in denominations of 20, 50, 100, 200, 500, 1000, 2000 and 5000 Kč; coins are of 10, 20 and 50 *haléřů* (hellers) and one, two, five, 10, 20 and 50 Kč.

The Komerční, ČS, ČSOB or Živnostenská banks are usually efficient about changing travellers cheques for a standard 2% commission. There is a large network of *bankomaty* (Automatic Teller Machines; ATMs) throughout the country. Most accept Visa, Visa Plus, Visa electron, Maestro and MasterCard, Cirrus, Euro and EC cards. Many hotels, restaurants and shops accept major credit cards.

There is no longer a black market; anyone who approaches you offering such a deal is a thief.

Exchange Rates

Exchange rates are as follows:

country	unit		koruna
Australia	A$1	=	21.14 Kč
Canada	C$1	=	24.57 Kč
euro	€1	=	35.06 Kč

France	10FF	=	53.83 Kč
Germany	DM1	=	18.43 Kč
New Zealand	NZ$1	=	17.62 Kč
UK	UK£1	=	56.17 Kč
USA	US$1	=	36.75 Kč

COSTS

Food, transportation and admission fees are cheap; it's accommodation that is costly, particularly as foreigners pay up to double the local price for some hotel rooms. You could get away with spending US$15 a day in summer by camping or staying in cheap hostels. In a private home or a better hostel, count on US$25 to US$30. Costs drop dramatically outside Prague.

Refunds

It is possible to claim VAT refunds for purchases of more than 1000 Kč when made from one store on the same day, when leaving the country, if exported within 30 days of the purchase. This is only available from shops displaying a Tax Free Shopping sticker, who have to give you the export declaration form. This must be presented to the customs with the receipt and purchased item on departure and stamped, and presented to the seller within three months for the refund.

POST & COMMUNICATIONS
Post

Postcards cost 7 Kč to European countries and 8 Kč elsewhere. Letters cost 9 Kč and 13 Kč, respectively. Don't bother sending a parcel containing antiques or anything valuable: it is quite likely that it will not make it, as some postal staff tend to be light-fingered.

Telephone, Fax & Email

The Czech Republic's country code is ☎ 420. Czech Telecom is still replacing the antiquated telephone system, so changing telephone numbers will be a problem for a few years to come.

You can make international telephone calls at main post offices or directly from telephone booths. Three-minute operator-assisted international telephone calls cost 58 Kč to the USA. Local calls cost 4 Kč from public booths. Many phones accept phonecards (320 Kč), which are sold at newsstands and post offices.

Emergency telephone numbers in the Czech Republic are ☎ 158 (police), ☎ 155 (ambulance), ☎ 150 (fire) and ☎ 1230 or 1240 (automobile emergencies).

Faxes can only be sent from certain major post offices. Many large cities have cybercafes that charge 1 Kč or 2 Kč for one minute of Internet access.

INTERNET RESOURCES

The following are just a few of the huge number of useful Web sites for travellers to the Czech Republic.

Czech Ministry of Foreign Affairs English-language Web site packed with Czech Republic information and lots of links.
www.czech.cz
Czech Press Agency (ČTK) For info on the latest Czech Republic news.
www.ctknews.com
Czech Tourist Authority A good site with travel and local information.
www.visitczech.cz
Prague Information Service An excellent Web site that's packed with country and travel information, and lots of links.
www.prague-info.cz

BOOKS

Lonely Planet's *Czech & Slovak Republics* gives extensive information on the nuts and bolts of travelling in the Czech Republic.

An English-Czech phrasebook will prove invaluable, so consider Lonely Planet's *Central* or *Eastern Europe phrasebook*.

TIME

The Czech Republic is GMT/UTC plus one hour. Clocks are turned ahead one hour at the end of March and back again at the end of October.

WOMEN TRAVELLERS

Sexual violence has been on the rise in the Czech Republic but is still much lower than in the West. Nevertheless, solo female travellers should avoid deserted and unlit areas, especially at night.

GAY & LESBIAN TRAVELLERS

The SOHO Union of Homosexual Organisations (☎ 02-24 22 38 11, ✉ soho.v.cr@ atlas.cz) in Prague can provide information on activities and places to visit. The crisis line for gays and lesbians is ☎ 035-243 31 (10 am to 4 pm weekdays). A useful Web site for gay and lesbian travellers is at www.gay.cz/soho.

DISABLED TRAVELLERS

The Prague Wheelchair Users Organization
(☎ 24 82 72 10, ✆ pov@server1gts.cz) at
Benediktská 6, Josefov, has plenty of information about the Czech Republic.

DANGERS & ANNOYANCES

Crime is low compared with levels in Western Europe and only a real problem in
Prague's touristy areas. Robberies on international trains passing through the country
are a growing problem; the victims are
sometimes gassed to sleep in their compartments and then relieved of their valuables.

BUSINESS HOURS

On weekdays, shops open at around 8.30
am and close at 5 or 6 pm. Many small
shops, particularly in country areas, close
for lunch between noon and 2 pm. Almost
everything closes between 11 am and 1 pm
on Saturday and all day Sunday, except for
some department stores and chain supermarkets in major cities.

PUBLIC HOLIDAYS & SPECIAL EVENTS

Public holidays include January 1 (New
Year's Day), Easter Monday, 1 May
(Labour Day), 8 May (Liberation Day), 5
July (Cyril and Methodius Day), 6 July (Jan
Hus Day), 28 September (Czech Statehood
Day), 28 October (Republic Day), 17 No-
vember (Struggle for Freedom and Democ-
racy Day) and 24 to 26 December.

Since 1946 the Prague Spring International Music Festival has been held in the
second half of May (most performances are
sold out well in advance). Karlovy Vary
hosts the International Film Festival in July
and Dvořák Autumn Music Festival in September. In Brno there's the Easter Festival
of Spiritual Music and the International
Moravian Music Festival in September.

ACCOMMODATION

There are several hundred camping
grounds in the Czech Republic, which are
usually open from May to September. Most
have a small snack bar, and many have
small cabins for rent. Camping on public
land is prohibited.

Most hostels in the Czech Republic are affiliated with Hostelling International (HI). In
July and August many student dormitories
become temporary hostels and in recent
years a number of such dormitories in Prague
have been converted into year-round hostels.
A HI membership card is not usually required, though it usually gets you a reduced
rate. *Turistické ubytovny* (tourist hostels)
provide very basic dormitory accommodation and are not connected with HI. Watch
for the letters 'TU' on accommodation lists.

Private rooms are widely available – look
for 'privát' or 'Zimmer frei' signs. Many
tourist offices and travel agencies can book
them.

Hotels are usually rated from one to five
stars; three-star hotels charge about
1200/1300 Kč for singles/doubles, two-star
hotels about 400/600 Kč or 600/1000 Kč
with private bath (about 50% higher in
Prague). Some hotels will not rent rooms
until 2 pm during the high season.

FOOD & DRINKS

The cheapest places to eat at are *jídelna*
(buffet) and *samoobsluha* (self-service
restaurants). As a general rule a restaurant
calling itself *restaurace* is usually
cheaper than a 'restaurant'. You can be
sure of getting a good feed at a *vinárna*
(wine restaurant).

Always insist on seeing a *Jídelní lístek*
(menu) before ordering – if staff refuse to
show you a written menu, walk out. The
main menu categories are *předkrmy* (hors
d'oeuvres), *polévky* (soups), *studené jídlo*
(cold dishes), *teplé jídlo* (warm dishes),
masitá jídla (meat dishes), *ryby* (fish), *zelenina* (vegetables), *saláty* (salads), *ovoce*
(fruit), *zákusky* (desserts) and *nápoje*
(drinks).

Czechs love meat dishes with sauerkraut
and *knedlíky* – flat circular dumplings made
from *bramborové* (potato) or *houskové*
(bread). Vegetarian dishes include *smažený
sýr* (fried cheese) or *knedlíky s vejci* (scrambled eggs with dumplings).

Tipping is optional, but it's common to
round the bill up to the next 10 Kč or 20 Kč
as you're paying. Never leave coins worth
less than 1 Kč (it's insulting).

One of the first words of Czech you'll
learn is *pivo* (beer); the most famous Czech
brands are Budvar and Plzeňský Prazdroj.
South Moravia produces good *bílé víno*
(white wine), but *červené víno* (red wine) is
just average.

Getting There & Away

The national carrier, Czech Airlines (ČSA), flies to Prague from several cities around the world.

Bus services to/from Western Europe are still much cheaper than train services, even though some heavily discounted airfares can be cheaper than the train. There's a bus several times a day from Vienna's Mitte Busbahnhof to Brno (250 Kč, three hours), plus Eurolines buses to Prague from Paris (1900 Kč, 16½ hours), Amsterdam (2150 Kč, 15 hours) and most major European cities.

Still, the easiest access is by train. Sample 2nd-class international train fares from Prague are about 250 Kč to Bratislava (five hours, 396km), 500 Kč to Budapest (nine hours, 616km), 700 Kč to Vienna (six hours, 354km), 600 Kč to Warsaw (12 hours, 740km), 2120 Kč to Frankfurt (eight hours, 609km), 1350 Kč to Berlin (5½ hours, 377km) and 8000 Kč to London (about 14 hours, 1,285km). In the Czech Republic purchase international train tickets in advance from Czech Railways (České dráhy or ČD) or a travel agent. Most major trains require seat reservations.

Getting Around

BUS

The express buses of Česká automobilová doprava (ČSAD) are often faster and more convenient than trains operated by ČD. By European standards both buses and trains are cheap. Count on spending around 65 Kč for every 100km of travel.

Because of numerous footnotes, posted bus timetables are difficult to read. Two crossed hammers as a footnote means the bus only operates on weekdays (many bus services don't operate on weekends). The clerks at information counters seldom speak English (not even in major stations), so to get a departure time, try writing down your destination and the date you wish to travel, then point to your watch and pray. If the bus isn't *vyprodáno* (sold out) the ticket will indicate the *stání* (platform) and *sed* (seat). The letter 'R' inside a box or circle means that reservations are mandatory, while an R alone means that reservations are recommended but not compulsory.

TRAIN

Inter-Rail (Eurail pass-holders need to buy a separate extension route pass) passes are valid in the Czech Republic. When buying train tickets you must tell the ticket seller which type of train you want. Categories include: SC (SuperCity), which has an 85 Kč surcharge; EC/IC (EuroCity/InterCity), which have a 60 Kč surcharge; Ex (express); R and Sp (fast trains); and Os (local slow trains). Note that some Czech train conductors try to intimidate foreigners by pretending that there's something wrong with their ticket, so always make sure that you have a ticket and don't pay a 'fine' unless you first get a *doklad* (receipt).

CAR & MOTORCYCLE

You can drive in the Czech Republic using your normal driving licence if it has a photo (ie, an International Driving Permit is not required). Speed limits are 40km/h or 50km/h in built-up areas, 90km/h on open roads and 130km/h on motorways; motorcycles are limited to 80km/h. Most of the major freeways now have a 800 Kč annual toll charge, payable at most border crossings. If you are caught on a freeway without the toll sticker displayed on the windscreen of your vehicle, the fine will be up to 5000 Kč.

Prague

☎ 02

Prague (Praha; population 1.19 million) has an almost magical feel about it and is like a history lesson come to life, with an unsurpassed splendour that stems largely from two architectural golden ages: a Gothic period under Holy Roman Emperor Charles IV and a baroque period during the Habsburg Counter-Reformation. Unlike Warsaw, Budapest and Berlin, Prague and its stunning skyline escaped WWII almost unscathed.

Prague, almost exactly midway between Berlin and Vienna, is the seat of government and a leading European intellectual and cultural centre. How you feel about Prague's current tourist glut may depend on where you're coming from. Arriving from London, Paris or Rome it may all seem

CZECH REPUBLIC

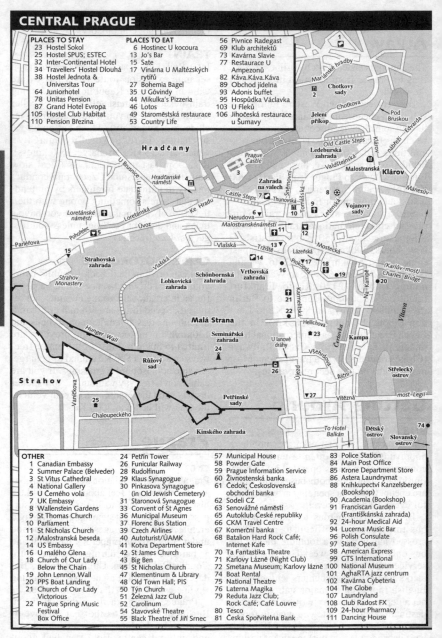

CENTRAL PRAGUE

PLACES TO STAY
23 Hostel Sokol
25 Hostel SPUS; ESTEC
32 Inter-Continental Hotel
34 Travellers' Hostel Dlouhá
38 Hostel Jednota &
 Universitas Tour
64 Juniorhotel
78 Unitas Pension
87 Grand Hotel Evropa
105 Hostel Club Habitat
110 Pension Březina

PLACES TO EAT
6 Hostinec U kocoura
13 Jo's Bar
15 Sate
17 Vinárna U Maltézských
 rytířů
27 Bohemia Bagel
35 U Góvindy
44 Mikulka's Pizzeria
46 Lotos
49 Staroměstská restaurace
53 Country Life

56 Pivnice Radegast
69 Klub architektů
73 Kavárna Slavie
77 Restaurace U
 Ampezonů
82 Káva.Káva.Káva
89 Obchod jídelna
93 Adonis buffet
95 Hospůdka Václavka
103 U Fleků
106 Jihočeská restaurace
 u Šumavy

OTHER
1 Canadian Embassy
2 Summer Palace (Belveder)
3 St Vitus Cathedral
4 National Gallery
5 U Černého vola
7 UK Embassy
8 Wallenstein Gardens
9 St Thomas Church
10 Parliament
11 St Nicholas Church
12 Malostranská beseda
14 US Embassy
16 U malého Glena
18 Church of Our Lady
 Below the Chain
19 John Lennon Wall
20 PPS Boat Landing
21 Church of Our Lady
 Victorious
22 Prague Spring Music
 Festival
 Box Office

24 Petřín Tower
26 Funicular Railway
28 Rudolfinum
29 Klaus Synagogue
30 Pinkasova Synagogue
 (in Old Jewish Cemetery)
31 Staronová Synagogue
33 Convent of St Agnes
36 Municipal Museum
37 Florenc Bus Station
39 Czech Airlines
40 Autoturist/ÚAMK
41 Kotva Department Store
42 St James Church
43 Big Ben
45 St Nicholas Church
47 Klementinum & Library
48 Old Town Hall; PIS
50 Týn Church
51 Železná Jazz Club
52 Carolinum
54 Stavoské Theatre
55 Black Theatre of Jiří Srnec

57 Municipal House
58 Powder Gate
59 Prague Information Service
60 Živnostenská banka
61 Čedok; Československá
 obchodní banka
62 Sodeli CZ
63 Senovážné náměstí
65 Autoklub České republiky
66 CKM Travel Centre
67 Komerční banka
68 Batalion Hard Rock Café;
 Internet Kafe
70 Ta Fantastika Theatre
71 Karlovy Lázně (Night Club)
72 Smetana Museum; Karlovy lázně
74 Boat Rental
75 National Theatre
76 Laterna Magika
79 Reduta Jazz Club;
 Rock Café; Café Louvre
80 Tesco
81 Česká Spořvitelna Bank

83 Police Station
84 Main Post Office
85 Krone Department Store
86 Astera Laundrymat
88 Knihkupectví Kanzelsberger
 (Bookshop)
90 Academia (Bookshop)
91 Franciscan Garden
 (Františkánská zahrada)
92 24-hour Medical Aid
94 Lucerna Music Bar
96 Polish Consulate
97 State Opera
98 American Express
99 GTS International
100 National Museum
101 AghaRTA jazz centrum
102 Kavárna Cybeteria
104 The Globe
107 Laundryland
108 Club Radost FX
109 24-hour Pharmacy
111 Dancing House

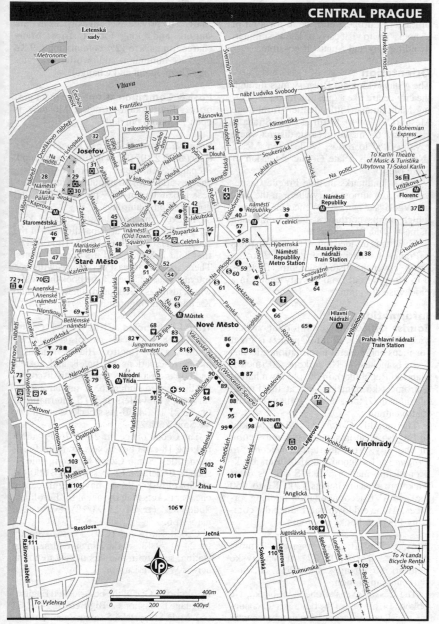

CENTRAL PRAGUE

CZECH REPUBLIC

quite normal, but if you've been elsewhere in Eastern Europe, you'll be in for a bit of a shock. Try to visit early or late in summer, avoiding July and August if possible.

Orientation

The Vltava (Moldau) River swings through the city centre like a question mark, separating Malá Strana (Little Quarter) from Staré Město (Old Town). North of Malá Strana is Hradčany, the medieval castle district where royalty used to reside, while Nové Město (New Town) is a late Gothic extension of Staré Město.

Major landmarks include Prague Castle, visible from almost everywhere in the city, and Václavské náměstí (Wenceslas Square), which points north-west to Staroměstské náměstí (Old Town Square).

The city is divided into 10 postal districts – Prague 1, and parts of Prague 2 to the south, cover the historical centre. Districts 3 to 10 spiral out from the city centre in a clockwise direction.

Information

Tourist Offices Prague Information Service (PIS; ☎ 187, ✆ info@pis.cz) is great for maps and general information. PIS has three branches: at Na příkopě 20 (metro: Náměstí Republiky); in the old town hall at Staroměstské náměstí; and at the Praha-hlavní nádraží train station, right next to the metro entrance.

The monthly *Culture in Prague* booklet in English is an invaluable guide to action in the city. The quarterly *Welcome to Prague* isn't as good but also offers background information. All PIS offices offer Ticketpro concert tickets (200 Kč to 950 Kč) and AVE accommodation-booking services. At the old town hall branch the company Pragotur books city tours.

Money The efficient American Express office (☎ 22 80 02 37) at Václavské náměstí 56 changes travellers cheques without commission.

The Československá obchodní banka, Na příkopě 14, has one of the best rates for changing travellers cheques at 1% commission with a 50 Kč minimum. As does Česká spořitelna, Václavské náměstí 16, which only charges 1% commission at its automatic-exchange machine that changes foreign banknotes.

Beware the exorbitant commission charged by private exchange offices in train stations and along tourist strips. Many charge from 4% to 12% commission (39 Kč to 95 Kč minimum) and/or offer low rates (eg, Chequepoint and Change).

Post & Communications The main post office, Jindřišská 14 (metro: Můstek), is open 7 am to 8 pm daily.

Email & Internet Access Kavárna Cyberteria (☎ 22 23 07 07, ✆ info@cyberteria.cz), Štěpánská 18, near Václavské náměstí, charges 50 Kč for 30 minutes of Internet access (open 10 am to 8 pm weekdays and noon to 6 pm Saturday).

An even cheaper place is Internet kafe (☎ 20 10 81 47, ✆ art@batalion.cz) in the Batalion Hard Rock Café, 28. října 3. The first hour is 80 Kč, and it's open 24 hours. There are also at least two places with free Internet access: The Globe bookshop/cafe, which also has free laptop connections, and Karlovy lázně nightclub.

Travel Agencies CKM Travel Centre (☎ 26 85 32, ✆ ckmprg@login.cz), Jindřišská 28 (metro: Hlavní Nádraží), makes reservations for hotels and hostels and books air and bus tickets with discounts for those aged under 26. A similar agency for young travellers is GTS international (☎ 22 21 15 04, ✆ gts.smecky@gtsint.cz), Ve Smečkách 27.

The Čedok office (☎ 24 19 76 99) at Na příkopě 18 sells bus tickets to major European cities. Some Czech bus companies – such as Bohemian Express (☎ 24 81 00 13) at Sokolovská 93 – have significantly cheaper tickets than the agent for Eurolines, Sodeli CZ (☎ 24 23 93 18), Senovážné náměstí 6.

Czech Railways (ČD) Travel Agency (☎ 24 21 79 48), at the Hlavní nádraží train station, sells train and bus tickets to points across Western Europe.

Bookshops One of the best-stocked English-language bookshops is Big Ben (☎ 24 82 65 65), Malá Štupartská 5 (metro: náměstí Republiky). Knihkupectví Kanzelsberger, Václavské náměstí 42, and Academia at No 34 have a good selection of maps and guidebooks.

There are two cafes with an excellent selection of English-language books: U knihomola (☎ 627 77 67) at Mánesova 79 (metro: Náměstí Míru) and The Globe (☎ 24 91 72 29) at Pštrossova 6 (metro: Národní Třída).

Laundry Laundry Kings, Dejvická 16 (metro: Hradčanská), is a popular US-style laundrette. It costs about 125 Kč to wash and dry a 6kg load of clothes. Other self-service laundrettes are Laundryland at Londýnská 71 (metro: Náměstí Míru), Astera in the passage at Jindřišská 5 (metro: Můstek) and Prague Laundromat at Korunní 14 (metro: Jiřího z Poděbrad).

Medical & Emergency Services Emergency medical aid for foreigners is available at Hospital Na Homolce (☎ 57 27 21 46), 5th floor, Roentgenova 2 (the sixth stop on bus No 167 from Anděl metro station), which has some of the best facilities in the country.

The 24-hour Canadian Medical Centre Prague (☎ 35 36 01 33 from 8.30 am to 5 pm weekdays, ☎ 0603 212 320 at other times), Veleslavínská 30/1 (seventh stop on tram No 20 or 26 from Dejvicá metro station), has English-speaking doctors.

There are several 24-hour *lékárna* (pharmacies) in the centre: in Prague 1 at Palackého 5 (also a 24-hour clinic) and in Prague 2 at Belgická 37 (metro: Náměstí Míru).

Dangers & Annoyances The crime rate is low but pickpocketing is rife. Some taxis in touristy areas grossly overcharge their customers (even Czechs). Try not to take a taxi from Václavské náměstí or Národní.

Hradčany

Prague's finest churches and museums are found in Hradčany, the photogenic castle district stretching along a hilltop west of the river. Early morning is a good time to visit and evening is even better (although all the museums will be closed). The easiest way to reach this area is by metro to Malostranská, then tram No 22 up the hill around to the back of Hradčany as far as the fourth stop (Památník Písemnictví). From here Pohořelec and Loretánská streets slope down to the castle gate.

The nearby **Loreta Convent** shelters a fabulous treasure of diamonds, pearls and gold

and is worth visiting despite the crowds (closed Monday; 80 Kč). Loretánská soon opens onto Hradčanské náměstí, with the main gate to Prague Castle at its eastern end. On the square at No 15 is the 18th-century Šternberský Palace, which contains the main branch of the **National Gallery**, with the country's best collection of 14th- to 18th-century European paintings, including whole rooms of Cranachs and Goyas (closed Monday; 90 Kč).

Prague Castle Prague Castle was founded in the 9th century, then rebuilt and extended many times. Always the centre of political power, it's still the official residence of the president. The castle is open daily. The three-day ticket (120 Kč) allows entry only to the Old Royal Palace, Basilica of St George, Powder Gate (Mihulka) and all the attractions of St Vitus Cathedral.

You enter the castle through Matthias Gate. Directly beyond is the **Chapel of the Holy Cross**, which contains the ticket and information office. On the northern side of the courtyard is the **Prague Castle Gallery** (100 Kč), with a good collection of baroque paintings.

The third courtyard is dominated by **St Vitus Cathedral**, a glorious French Gothic structure begun in 1344. You can climb the 287 steps of the cathedral's tower.

On the southern side of the cathedral is the entrance to the **Old Royal Palace**, where, on 23 May 1618, two Catholic councillors were thrown from the window of an adjacent chamber by irate Protestant nobles, an act that sparked the Thirty Years' War (1618-48).

As you leave the palace, the **Basilica of St George** (1142), a remarkable Romanesque church, is directly in front of you. In the Benedictine convent next to the church is a branch of the **National Gallery** with Czech art from the 16th to the 18th century (closed Monday; 90 Kč).

Behind this gallery, follow the crowd into **Golden Lane** (Zlatá ulička), a 16th-century quarter of tiny houses built into the castle walls. The novelist Franz Kafka, born in Prague in 1883, lived and wrote in the house at No 22.

Malá Strana

Malá Strana, below the protective walls of Prague Castle, was built in the 17th and 18th centuries. From Malostranská metro station, follow Valdštejnská around to Valdštejnské náměstí, past many impressive palaces.

Continue south on Tomášská and around the corner to Letenská to reach **St Thomas Church**, a splendid baroque edifice built in 1731. Behind Malostranské náměstí is the formerly Jesuit **St Nicholas Church** (1755), one of the finest baroque buildings in Prague (45 Kč).

After a wander around the square, follow the tram tracks south along Karmelitská and take narrow Prokopská towards the river. You'll soon reach a beautiful square surrounded by baroque palaces. Continue on the left on Lázeňská towards the massive stone towers of the **Church of Our Lady Below the Chain**.

To the left of the church, Lázeňská leads out to Mostecká with **Karlův most** (Charles Bridge) to the right. This enchanting bridge, built in 1357 and graced by 30 statues dating from the 18th century, was the only bridge in Prague until 1841. Climb the **tower** on the Malá Strana side for a bird's-eye view. Throughout the day, so many tourists and hawkers squeeze onto the bridge that you can hardly move; it's quieter at sunrise and after midnight.

Staré Město

To the right as you come off the bridge and around at the end of Novotného lávka is the **Smetana Museum**, dedicated to the Czech composer (closed Tuesday; 40 Kč). The view from the terrace in front of the museum is one of the best in Prague.

The heart of Staré Město is **Staroměstské náměstí** (Old Town Square). The square's most notable features are the **old town hall** (30 Kč) and its **clocktower** (30 Kč), which you can climb for a sweeping view. Below the clock tower is a 15th-century **astronomical clock** that entertains throngs of tourists every hour on the hour with mechanical apostles, a mock Christ, a skeleton and a cock.

At the centre of Staroměstské náměstí is a **monument** to the religious reformer Jan Hus, erected in 1915 on the 500th anniversary of his death (he was burned at the stake on a trumped-up charge of heresy against the Catholic Church). Facing the square is the Gothic **Týn Church** (1365) with its twin steeples; the tomb of the

16th-century Danish astronomer Tycho Brahe is in front of the main altar.

From Staroměstské náměstí follow Železná south-east to the **Carolinum** at Železná 9. It's the oldest remaining part of Prague University, founded by Charles IV in 1348. Next to this at Železná 11 is the neoclassical **Stavovské Theatre** (1783), where the premiere of Mozart's *Don Giovanni* took place on 29 October 1787, with the composer himself conducting.

Nearby **Václavské náměstí** is Prague's fashionable shopping boulevard, lined with majestic Art Nouveau facades. At the upper end of Václavské náměstí stands an **equestrian statue** of the 10th-century king Václav I (aka St Wenceslas), patron saint of Bohemia. In the 20th century, this vast square has often been the scene of public protests – just below the statue is a simple memorial to those who resisted the dictatorship.

Looming above the south-eastern end of Václavské náměstí is the **National Museum** with ho-hum collections covering prehistory, 19th- and early-20th-century history and mineralogy (70 Kč). The museum's neoclassical interior is the saving grace.

Jewish Quarter

The Jewish Quarter is behind Staroměstské náměstí, bordered by the streets Kaprova, Dlouhá and Kozí (metro: Staroměstská). The quarter includes a fascinating variety of monuments, all of which are now part of the **Prague Jewish Museum** (closed Saturday; 480 Kč). The collections have a remarkable origin – in 1942 the Nazis brought most of the pieces on display from 153 Jewish communities in Bohemia and Moravia for a planned 'museum of an extinct people'. The interior of the **Pinkas Synagogue** at Široká 3 bears the names of 77,297 Czech Jews and the names of the concentration camps where they perished (on the list are the three sisters of Franz Kafka).

Note that only men must cover their head to enter the following synagogues (staff sell paper yarmulkes).

The early Gothic **Staronová Synagogue**, one of the oldest in Europe, was built in 1270. If you don't buy the 480 Kč joint ticket, separate 200 Kč synagogue tickets are sold here.

Opposite the synagogue is the pink Jewish **town hall** with its picturesque 16th-century clock tower.

Follow the crowd down U starého hřbitova to the **Klaus Synagogue** (1694), which houses another section of the Prague Jewish Museum.

Behind the Klaus Synagogue (but entered from the Pinkas Synagogue) is the evocative **Old Jewish Cemetery**. There are more than 12,000 tombstones, the oldest dating from 1439. By the time the cemetery was closed in 1787, burials were layered up to 12 deep due to the extreme crowding of the graves.

Vyšehrad

Vyšehrad, easily accessible by metro, is home to the plain, modern **Congress Centre** (1981), which hosts musicals and exhibitions. From here the twin towers of the neo-Gothic **SS Peter & Paul Church** are visible to the west.

Walk towards them along Na Bučance, through the gates of the 17th-century **Vyšehrad Citadel** and past the Romanesque **Rotunda of St Martin**. Right behind SS Peter & Paul Church is **Slavín Cemetery**, the final resting place of many distinguished Czechs, including the composers Smetana and Dvořák.

Other Museums

Mozart Museum If you're into music make the trek up to Villa Bertrámka at Mozartova 169 – take the metro to Anděl, walk three blocks west on Plzeňská and turn left on Mozartova. The villa is where Mozart finished composing *Don Giovanni* in 1787. It's open daily and entry is 90 Kč.

Municipal Museum On your last afternoon in Prague, set aside a little time for this white neo-Renaissance building above the Florenc metro station (closed Monday; 30 Kč). On display are maps and photos of Prague's numerous monuments, plus a huge scale model of Prague created in 1834. The museum also sells a vast selection of postcards made from old photos of Prague.

Organised Tours

Pragotur, in the PIS office at the old town hall, arranges personal guides for two-hour city walking tours (up to 500 Kč per person).

Private companies operating from kiosks along Na příkopě offer city bus tours at similar prices. These are OK if your time is short, but at the crowded castle and at other major sights it's difficult to even hear your guide.

Čedok uses the services of Prague Sightseeing Tours, which has a wide range of walking tours and arranges 1½-hour Vltava cruises (380 Kč), as well as bus excursions to Karlštejn/Konopiště (750 Kč), Kutná Hora (790 Kč) and Karlovy Vary (1390 Kč). Most departures, but not all, are only during the high season (May to October).

Prague Walks (☎/fax 61 21 46 03) organises interesting tours such as a Ghost Tour or Velvet Revolution Walk.

Boat Excursions The Prague Passenger Shipping (PPS) riverboat terminal is on the right bank of the Vltava between Jiráskův most and Palackého most (metro: Karlovo Náměstí). From May to early October there are day-long cruises upriver to Štěchovice (220 Kč return) at 9 am from Friday to Sunday and holidays.

Shorter trips downriver to Troja Zoo (50 Kč, 1¼ hours each way) depart at 8.30, 9.30, 12.30 am and 1.30 pm, May to August.

From the Kampa landing next to Karlův most, there are 50-minute cruises (200 Kč) daily, March to December.

Places to Stay

No matter where you stay, advance bookings are *strongly* advised from May to August and at Easter and Christmas.

Camping *Universitní sportovní klub Caravan Camp* (☎ 57 21 01 40, *Plzeňská 279, Motol*) is Prague's most convenient camping ground. It's next to tram line Nos 4 and 9 (stop: Hotel Golf). The rates are 155 Kč per person and 110 Kč per tent.

The year-round and cheaper *Autokemp Džbán* (☎ 36 85 51, fax 36 90 06, *Nad lávkou 3, Vokovice*) is part of the Aritma sports complex (some 200m on from the sports ground). Facilities include huts and bungalows. From Dejvická metro station, take tram No 20 or 26 seven stops to the Nádraží Veleslavín stop.

Hostels The *Hostel Sokol* (☎ 57 00 73 97, *Hellichova 1*) is basic but convenient. Enter from Všehrdova 42. Take the metro to Malostranská and then tram No 12 or 22 two stops south. Dorm beds are 270 Kč.

There are five traveller's hostels spread around Prague, open from mid-June to August. Only the Staré Město branch of the

Traveller's Hostel Dlouhá (Roxy; ☎ *24 82 66 62,* ✆ *hostel@travellersroxy.cz, Dlouhá 33)* is open all year. Basic and not so clean dorms/doubles are 350/490 Kč per person.

Hostel Club Habitat (☎ *24 92 17 06,* ✆ *hostel@iol.cz, Na Zderaze 10, Nové Město)* is near Karlovo náměstí (metro: Karlovo Náměstí). It has beds in renovated rooms at 400 Kč.

Juniorhotel (☎ *24 23 17 54, fax 24 22 15 70,* ✆ *euroagentur@telecom.cz, Senovážné náměstí 21)* has dorm beds for 150 Kč. There are discounts for student and youth card-holders but not for HI members (metro: Náměstí Republiky).

In the heart of Žižkov, the popular *Clown & Bard Hostel (*☎ *22 71 64 53, Bořivojova 102)* charges 350 Kč for dorm beds or from 450 Kč per bed in doubles with small kitchens (metro: Jiřího z Poděbrad).

Penzion Máchova (☎ *22 51 01 07, fax 22 51 17 77,* ✆ *jana.dyrsmidova@telecom.cz, Máchova 11)* has dorm beds for up to 500 Kč, including breakfast (metro: Náměstí Míru).

Hotel Standart (☎ *87 52 58, fax 80 67 52,* ✆ *jsc@jsc.cz, Přístavní 1)* is a large hotel north of the centre. Dorm beds are good value at 350 Kč with HI card; rooms with shared bath are 620/800 Kč for singles/doubles. From Nádraží Holešovice metro station/Praha-Holešovice train station, take tram No 1, 3, 14 or 25 and get off at the second stop. If the Standart is full, *Pension Vltava (*☎ *80 97 95, Dělnická 35),* just around the corner, has rooms for 520/835 Kč.

Opposite is a new and great *Sir Toby's Hostel (*☎ *83 87 06 35, Dělnická 24).* Here dorm beds are 325 Kč and singles/doubles start at 650/900 Kč, including private shower and toilet.

If it's getting late and you don't have a bed, consider spending the night at the *Turistická ubytovna TJ Sokol Karlín (*☎ *24 81 74 74, Malého 1),* a five-minute walk from the Florenc bus station (metro: Florenc). To get there, walk east along Křižíkova past the Karlín Theatre and turn right on Pluku (just after the railway bridge). The hostel is before the next railway bridge. Dorm beds start at 180 Kč, but the doors don't open until 6 pm.

Student Dorms The following student dorms are open year-round. *Hostel Jednota (*☎ *22 21 17 73, fax 24 21 22 90, Opletalova*

38, Nové Město), near the Hlavní nádraží train station, has beds starting at 310 Kč, including breakfast. A *pension* at the same address has beds from 390 Kč per person.

One of the easiest places to arrange hostel accommodation on the spot is at the *Strahov* dorm complex opposite Spartakiádní stadión, west of the centre – bus Nos 143, 149 and 217 run directly there from the Dejvická metro station. The complex comprises 11 blocks of flats that operate as independent hostels in July and August; at other times of the year only five are open, however the standard is not great. Arrange your own room in person, or pre-book at a private-room agency (see Private Rooms following). At Block 4, *Hostel SPUS (*☎ *57 21 07 64,* ✆ *spus@praha.czcom.cz)* has rooms with one or two beds from 285/220 Kč per person. Noisy discos operate until late at Block Nos 1, 7 and 11.

Hostel Orlík (☎ *24 31 12 40, Terronská 6)* has beds in singles/doubles/triples for 530/420/400 Kč. It's a three-minute walk from the Dejvice metro station – walk northeast up Verdunská from the roundabout and take the second left. If it's full, walk five minutes farther up Terronská to the *Berhanu CK Hostel (*☎ *24 31 11 05, 28 Terronská),* which has dorm beds for 220 Kč.

Private Rooms AVE Limited (☎ 24 22 32 26, reservations ☎ 51 55 10 11, ✆ ave@ avetravel.cz), at the Hlavní nádraží and Holešovice train stations and at Ruzyně airport, rents a variety of *private rooms* at around 500 Kč per person, with discounts for longer stays. AVE can also arrange *hostel accommodation* starting at 200 Kč per person, as well as book hotels. The Hlavní nádraží branch is open 6 am to 10 pm daily.

Other room-finding agencies include ESTEC (☎ 57 21 04 10, fax 57 21 52 63, ✆ estec@jrc.cz), Vaníčkova 1, Block 2; and Stop City Accommodation (☎ 24 22 24 97), Vinohradská 24, about six blocks from the Hlavní nádraží train station.

Touts at train and bus stations may also offer private rooms from 300 Kč to 800 Kč per person, depending on the location. Bargain if you think the price is too high and check the location on a good map before accepting.

Pensions The old town's *Unitas Pension (*☎ *24 21 10 20, fax 24 21 08 00,* ✆ *unitas@*

cloister-inn.cz, Bartolomějská 9) has 40 dull rooms that were once prison cells – President Havel spent a night locked up in one of them. Singles/doubles with shared bath and breakfast are 1020/1200 Kč.

Just south of the IP Pavlova metro station is *Pension Březina (☎ 96 18 88 88, fax 24 26 67 77, ✉ brezina@netforce.cz, Legerova 41),* where basic rooms are 900/1100 Kč without shower and start at 1300/1500 Kč with shower.

North of the centre, one of the strangest (and best) choices is *Pension V sudech (☎ 688 04 28, Zenklova 217, Libeň).* Beds in beer-keg shaped bungalows are 200 Kč; the kegs are 'uncorked' from April to October only. Pension accommodation is from 400 Kč per person. From the Nádraží Holešovice metro station, take tram No 5, 14 or 17 to the 'Ke Stírce' stop and walk through the restaurant (reception is in the backyard).

North-west of the centre in Prague 6, the family-run *Pension Bob (☎ 20 92 07 18, fax 20 92 31 53, ✉ pensionbob@iol.cz, Kovárenská 2, Lysolaje)* has bright and clean rooms with bathroom for 1020/1540 Kč, including breakfast. The staff will also pick up and drop off guests at the airport and the stations. From the Dejvická metro station take bus No 160 or 355 to the Žákovská stop.

Hotels – City Centre *Hotel Balkán (☎ 57 32 71 80, třída Svornosti 28),* two blocks from the Anděl metro station, has doubles in an attractive four-storey building for 1500 Kč with bath or shower.

North of the centre, *Hotel Apollo Garni (☎ 688 06 28, fax 688 45 70, Kubišova 23, Libeň)* is a modern four-storey hotel that has rooms with bath or shower at 1360/1760 Kč, breakfast included.

Places to Eat
Tourism has had a heavy impact on Prague's restaurant scene and cheaper restaurants have almost disappeared from the historical centre. If you're on a low budget it might be worth walking a few streets away from the tourist centre or taking the metro to an outlying station and eating there. The suburbs of Žižkov and Smíchov have plenty of inexpensive places.

Bílá Labut, Tesco, Kotva and Krone department stores all have **supermarkets** in their basements.

Václavské náměstí & Around Tucked in a courtyard is *Hospůdka Václavka (Václavské náměstí 48),* which has hearty Czech pub food at around 60 Kč. *Obchod jídelna (Václavské náměstí 36)* is a cheap stand-up buffet at the rear of a butcher's shop. It has good stodge but it's best before 1 pm.

A bit farther from the square is *Jihočeská restaurace u Šumavy (Štěpánská 3),* serving inexpensive South Bohemian food, but check your bill.

Radost FX Café (Bělehradská 120, Vinohrady) has plenty of vegetarian dishes and good salads.

Staroměstské náměstí & Around *Staroměstská restaurace (Staroměstské náměstí 19)* has good Czech food and beer, but prices are inflated by as much as 50% on its outside terrace.

The *Pivnice Radegast (Templová 2),* off Celetná, has good local food – try the *guláš* (goulash) – but mediocre service.

Mikulka's Pizzeria (Dlouhá 8) has tasty pizzas with unusual toppings, including one with apple and cinnamon.

South of the square in a passage off Melantrichova 15, *Country Life* is the healthiest place to eat in Prague. There are inexpensive salad sandwiches, pizzas, goulash and vegetarian food.

Lotos (Platnéřská 13), just north of Klementinum, has an all-vegetarian menu with many dishes modelled on Bohemian cuisine, for under 150 Kč.

The subterranean *Klub architektů (Betlémské náměstí 5)* offers inventive Czech/international dishes, including vegetarian ones, for 80 Kč to 130 Kč.

Národní třída & Around *Café Louvre (Národní 22)* is best for breakfast; prices at lunch and dinner are a bit higher but the food is good.

West of Václavské náměstí, fans of Middle Eastern snacks can find felafels, kebabs or gyros at *Adonis buffet (Jungmannova 30).*

Back in the Old Town is *Restaurace U Ampezonů (Konviktská 11),* serving inexpensive, solid Bohemian food in pleasant surroundings.

U Fleků (Křemencova 11), is a German-style beer hall that verges on being a 'tourist trap'. Waiters circulate with mugs of excellent (but overpriced) dark ale that is brewed in-house. The food prices are shamelessly high.

CZECH REPUBLIC

In northern Nové Město, the vegetarian *U Góvindy (Soukenická 27)* is run by Hare Krishnas but nobody's preaching. Donations of at least 70 Kč get you a full lunch Monday to Saturday.

Malá Strana One of Prague's most popular expat hangouts is *Jo's Bar (Malostranské náměstí 7)*. The Mexican food isn't half bad and there's a cheap happy hour. Not far away, on the corner of Nerudova and Zámecká, *Hostinec U kocoura* serves inexpensive Bohemian beer and pub grub and is one of President Havel's favourites.

A good splurge is the *Vinárna U Maltézských rytířů (Prokopská 10)* with professional service and top-notch food, from a small menu of vegetarian and other dishes costing under 500 Kč.

In the southern part of Malá Strana, *Bohemia Bagel (Újezd 18)* has bagels with various toppings and is open 7 am to midnight daily.

Hradčany One of the few cheap options in this high-price area is *U Černého vola (Loretánské náměstí 1)*, just up from the Loreta Convent. Big mugs of beer and pub snacks cost less than 50 Kč.

Farther west, the excellent *Sate (Pohořelec 3)* serves tasty Indonesian dishes for around 100 Kč.

Cafes The classy *Kavárna Slavie (Národní 1)* is fairly upmarket. More relaxed is *Káva.Káva.Káva (Národní 37)*, where you can enjoy top-notch Arabian coffee along with carrot cake and other American-style goodies. *U knihomola* and *The Globe* (see under Bookshops in the earlier Information section) are two popular cafes-cum-bookshops.

Entertainment

For the most up-to-date information check the *Prague Post,* the best English-language newspaper in town; *Culture in Prague* guide; and the free *Do města – Downtown* guide.

For classical music, opera, theatre and some rock concerts, uncollected or extra tickets go on sale at box offices about 30 minutes before show time. In addition, agencies around Prague sell tickets for a commission – try Ticketpro (☎ 1051), Salvatorská 10, with branches around

Prague; Best Tour (☎ 87 89 47) at Václavské náměstí 27; or Čedok (see under Travel Agencies in the earlier Information section).

Bars & Clubs The *Rock Café, Národní 20,* adjacent to the Reduta Jazz Club, is in the same building as a punk-metal music shop that hosts mainly live hard-rock bands 8 pm to 3 am nightly; the cover is about 60 Kč. *Batalion Hard Rock Café,* downstairs at 28. října 3, has anything from rock, folk to jazz bands or DJs spinning discs.

The grungy *Klub Újezd (Újezd 18)* has several bars and a mixed clientele, nightly from 8 pm. Soak up the real Prague feel at *Lucerna Music Bar, Vodičkova 36,* inside a passage, has mainly Czech bands most evenings – anything from folk to jazz to rock or DJs.

Prague's prime dance venue is *Club Radost FX (Bělehradská 120),* with famous European and local DJs spinning discs (metro: IP Pavlova). The new *Karlovy lázně (Novotného lávka, Staré Město)* has a nightclub playing anything from the 1960s to latest techno on each of its three floors, while the basement has live bands. *Mecca (U Průhonu 3)* is another popular dance venue (metro: Nádraží Holešovice).

The alternative *Palác Akropolis (Kubelíkova 27, Žižkov)* features everything from local bands to plays and films.

The quaint *Malostranská beseda (Malostranské náměstí 21)* is popular with students and serves up jazz, folk, country, rock and rock opera nightly from 8.30 pm (metro: Malostranská).

At Block 7 in the student dorm complex in Strahov (see under Student Dorms in the earlier Places to Stay section), *Klub 007 Strahov* has grunge/alternative bands or DJs starting at 8 pm Monday to Saturday.

Jazz The excellent *Železná Jazz Club* (☎ 24 23 96 97, *Železná 16, Staré Město)* is in a renovated stone cellar that has plenty of atmosphere. It has nightly live jazz 9 pm to midnight. There's also nightly live jazz at the unpretentious *AghaRTA jazz centrum (Krakovská 5),* which is near the Muzeum metro stop. The cosy *U malého Glena (Karmelitská 23)* has jazz bands in its basement most nights starting at 9 pm (metro: Malostranská).

Classical Music Prague's main concert venue is the neo-Renaissance *Rudolfinum* (*náměstí Jana Palacha*), metro: Staroměstská. In late May it's one of the venues that hosts the Prague Spring Music Festival.

Organ concerts and recitals are performed almost daily in summer at various venues; look for fliers and posters around town. Seat prices start at around 350 Kč.

Theatre & Opera Opera, ballet and plays (in Czech) are performed at the charming neo-Renaissance *National Theatre (Národní 2); near the Národní Třída metro stop. Next door is the modern *Laterna Magika*, which offers a widely imitated combination of theatre, dance and film – tickets are often sold out two months in advance.

Opera and ballet are also presented at the neo-Renaissance *State Opera* on Wilsonova (metro: Muzeum). *Stavovské Theatre (Ovocný trh 1)* presents opera; it's near the Můstek metro stop. For musicals and operettas try the *Karlín Theatre of Music (Křižíkova 10)*, near the Florenc bus station (metro: Florenc).

Several theatres stage 'black theatre' or 'magic theatre' performances combining mime, film, dance, music etc – try *Black Theatre of Jiří Srnec (Celetná 17, Staré Město)* or *Ta Fantastika (Karlova 8, Staré Město)*.

Getting There & Away

Bus Buses to Karlovy Vary, Brno (140 Kč, 2½ hours) and other towns in the Czech Republic, as well as to Bratislava (240 Kč, 4½ hours), depart from the Florenc bus station at Křižíkova 4 (metro: Florenc). Some international buses to Western Europe also use the Florenc bus station – though Bohemian Express buses depart from the Holešovice train station and most Eurolines buses from Želivského bus stand next to Želivského metro station. Advance reservations are recommended on all services.

Train Prague has four main train stations. International trains between Berlin and Budapest often stop at the Holešovice station (metro: Nádraží Holešovice) on the northern side of the city. Other important trains terminate at Hlavní nádraží (metro: Hlavní nádraží) and Masarykovo nádraží (metro: náměstí Republiky). Some local trains to the south-west depart from the Smíchov station (metro: Smíchovské nádraží).

Hlavní nádraží handles trains to Benešov (32 Kč, one hour), České Budějovice (108 Kč, 2½ hours), Cheb via Plzeň (128 Kč, four hours), Karlovy Vary via Chomutov (120 Kč, four hours), Košice (350 Kč, 10 hours), Mariánské Lázně (120 Kč, three hours), Plzeň (74 Kč, two hours) and Tábor (68 Kč, 1½ hours). Trains to Kutná Hora (50 Kč, 1½ hours), Brno (150 Kč, 3½ hours) and Bratislava (250 Kč, 5½ hours) leave from either Hlavní nádraží, Holešovice or Masarykovo nádraží.

For information on international trains see the Getting There & Away section earlier in this chapter.

Getting Around

Public Transport The 12 Kč tickets – valid on trams, city buses, the metro and some local 2nd-class trains – are sold at newsstands, yellow machines at the entrance to all metro stations and at some tram and bus stops. Tram and bus drivers sell the same ticket for 15 Kč – no change given. Validate the ticket as you enter the bus/tram or metro. For a large piece of luggage or a bicycle, validate an extra half-price ticket. Once validated, tickets are good for one hour 5 am to 8 pm weekdays; and for 1½ hours 8 pm to 5 am weekdays, and the whole day on weekends. With a valid ticket you can change from buses to trams to the metro for free.

Jízdenka síťová (season tickets) are sold for periods of one (70 Kč), three (200 Kč), seven (250 Kč) or 15 (280 Kč) days.

Bicycle Rental A Landa (☎ 24 25 61 21), Šumavská 33, Vinohrady (metro: Náměstí Míru), rents bikes starting at 250 Kč a day.

Taxi Taxis are reasonable (30 Kč flag fall plus 22 Kč per kilometre), but only if the meter is turned on. If the driver won't turn on the meter, find another taxi or clearly establish the price before setting out. If you feel you're being overcharged ask for a *účet* (bill), which the driver is obliged to provide.

AROUND PRAGUE
Karlštejn Castle
Erected by Emperor Charles IV in the mid-14th century, this towering castle is a rewarding and easy day trip from Prague.

Highlights include the **Church of Our Lady** (1357), with its medieval frescoes, and the magnificent **Chapel of the Holy Rood** and its 128-painted panels by the 14th-century artist Master Theodoric.

Karlštejn Castle is open 9 am to noon and 1 to 6 pm Tuesday to Sunday in May, June and September (to 7 pm in July and August, 5 pm in April and October and 4 pm from November to March). There are 45-minute guided tours in English on Route I (200 Kč), and on Route II of the chapel (600 Kč). These can only be pre-booked on ☎ 02-74 00 81 11.

Getting There & Away Trains leave about once an hour from Prague's Smíchov train station for Karlštejn (23 Kč, 35 minutes). The castle, which crowns a ridge above the village, is a 20-minute walk from the train station.

Konopiště

The dramatic 14th-century **Konopiště Chateau** is halfway between Prague and Tábor, about 2km west of Benešov's train station. Archduke Franz Ferdinand d'Este, heir to the Austro-Hungarian throne, had Konopiště renovated in 1894 and added a large English park and rose garden. Ferdinand's huge collection of hunting trophies and weapons will shock animal lovers.

The chateau is open 9 am to 12.30 pm and 1 to 5 pm May to August; to 4 pm in September; to 3 pm in April and October; and to 3 pm weekends in November. It's closed Monday. Various tours (in English) cover the castle – Tours I and II last 45 minutes each and cost 120 Kč, while the hour-long Tour III costs 250 Kč.

Getting There & Away Twelve fast trains run daily from Prague's Hlavní nádraží station to Benešov (one hour). Most trains to/from Tábor (one hour) and České Budějovice (two hours) also stop here. There are occasional buses from Benešov's train station to the castle.

Kutná Hora
☎ 0327

In the 14th century, Kutná Hora, 66km east of Prague, was the second-largest town in Bohemia after Prague. Kutná Hora's wealth came from the rich veins of silver below the

town; the city's silver groschen coin was Central Europe's preferred currency at the time.

In the 16th century, Kutná Hora's boom ended and mining ceased in 1726. The town has changed little since then, which explains why it was added to Unesco's World Heritage List in 1996.

Besides the town itself, day-trippers from Prague are drawn by the macabre ossuary in Sedlec, on the outskirts of Kutná Hora.

Orientation & Information The main train station, Kutná Hora hlavní nádraží, is 3km east of the centre but only a 10-minute walk from the ossuary. The bus station is on the north-eastern edge of Kutná Hora's old town.

The helpful Information Centre (☎ 51 23 78, ☻ kv.info.kh@pha.pvtnet.cz), Palackého náměstí, sells local maps and books accommodation, and offers Internet access for 3 Kč per minute.

Things to See From the main train station, walk towards town and turn right at the huge Church of the Ascension of the Virgin – less than 1km ahead is the suburb of Sedlec and its ghastly **ossuary** (*kostnice*), decorated with the bones of some 40,000 people, arranged in the forms of bells, a chandelier and even the Schwarzenberg coat-of-arms. Entry is 30 Kč.

Continue 2km south-west along Masarykova and enter Kutná Hora's old town at Na námĕti – look for the Gothic **Church of Our Lady** on the left. Keep straight, turn right on Tylova, and go straight to Palackého náměstí. From this square's upper end, Jakubská (a lane to the left) leads to the tall tilting tower of **St James Church** (1330). Just beyond is the **former Royal Mint** (Vlašský dvůr) and its small but interesting mint museum (50 Kč).

From the front entrance to St James a series of cobbled, signposted streets slope up to the **Hrádek Mining Museum**. The main attraction is the 45-minute guided tour (minimum of three people) through 500m of **medieval mine shafts**. The museum is open daily except Monday, May to October. Entry is 100 Kč and includes the tour.

Places to Stay *Camping Santa Barbara* (☎ *51 29 51*) is north-west of town off

Česká, near the cemetery (*hřbitov*). The *private rooms* around town cost from 300 Kč to 500 Kč per person.

A friendly, welcoming place to stay is the hostel *U rytířů* (☎ *51 22 56, Rejskovo náměstí 123*), just off Husova. The 20 rooms vary in price and start at 200 Kč per person. In a pinch try the basic *TJ Turista* (☎ *51 49 61, náměstí Národního odboje 56*), where dorm beds are 160 Kč (140 Kč with youth cards). Reception is open 8 to 9 am and 5 to 6 pm.

The pleasant five-room *Hotel U hrnčíře* (☎ *51 21 13, Barborská 24*) charges 500 Kč per person. *Alkr Pension* (☎ *51 24 69, Lorecká 7*), right near the bus station, has comfortable rooms with bath and small kitchenettes for 350 Kč per person.

Getting There & Away Seven fast trains from Prague's Hlavní nádraží station and one fast train from Masarykovo nádraží stop at Kutná Hora hlavní nádraží (55 minutes) in the suburb of Sedlec, which is 3km from the city centre. Local trains from Prague's Masarykovo nádraží station also stop here (1½ hours). From the Sedlec station there are 15 daily local trains to Kutná Hora město station just on the outskirts of the town centre, and also local buses.

Litoměřice & Terezín
☎ 0416

Litoměřice, north-west of Prague and only 75 minutes away by bus, has a picturesque historical centre. Dominating the central square are the **All Saints Church** and the lavishly decorated **House of Ottavio Broggio**, an 18th-century architect who was born here and who designed many of Litoměřice's finest facades. West of the square at Michalská 7 is the excellent **North Bohemia Fine Arts Gallery** (closed Monday).

Litoměřice is only 3km north of Terezín, an 18th-century fortress used during WWII as a jail, Jewish ghetto and Nazi-run concentration camp. An hourly bus from Litoměřice stops at the main square, náměstí Československé armády, where the **Museum of the Ghetto** documents life in the ghetto. At the Lesser Fortress, a 10-minute walk east, you can tour the camp's prison barracks, morgues and former mass graves. Both are open daily and joint entry is 150 Kč.

Orientation & Information From Litoměřice's adjacent train and bus stations, walk down Dlouhá to the central square, Mírové náměstí. On the square are the tourist office (☎ 73 24 40) and a Komerční banka with an ATM.

Places to Stay *Autocamp Slavoj* (☎ *73 44 81*) is on Střelecký ostrov just south of the stations. It's open May to September. The best bargain in Litoměřice is *Penzion U pavouka* (☎ *73 16 37, fax 73 44 09, Pekařská 7*), where small doubles are 550 Kč, including breakfast. *Lovochemie Hotel* (☎ *73 54 36, fax 73 54 43, Vrchlického 10*), a 15-minute walk north-east of the main square, has singles/doubles with bath and breakfast for 560/900 Kč.

Bohemia

KARLOVY VARY
☎ 017

Karlovy Vary (population 60,000) is the largest and oldest of the Czech Republic's many spas. From the 19th century onwards, famous people such as Beethoven, Bismarck, Brahms, Chopin, Franz Josef I, Goethe, Liszt, Metternich, Tolstoy, Karl Marx and Yuri Gagarin came here to enjoy the waters at the town's 12 spas.

Karlovy Vary still has a definite Victorian air. The elegant colonnades and boulevards complement the many peaceful walks in the surrounding parks. The spa offers all the facilities of a medium-sized town without the bother.

Karlovy Vary's numerous sanatoriums are reserved for patients undergoing treatment. The only place open to the public is the **open-air thermal pool** (*bazén*) on the hill above the Thermal Sanatorium (open 8 am to 8.30 pm weekdays; 30 Kč per hour). The bazén also has a sauna and a fitness club.

Orientation & Information

TG Masaryka, the town's main pedestrian mall, runs east to the Teplá River. Upstream is the heart of the spa area.

Express trains from Prague use Karlovy Vary horní nádraží, north of town across the Ohře River. From the station, bus No 11 runs to the Vřídelní Colonnade.

Trains to/from Mariánské Lázně stop at Karlovy Vary dolní nádraží opposite the main ČSAD bus station.

Kur-Info (☎ 322 40 97), on the Vřídelní Colonnade, has maps and brochures.

Places to Stay

Rolava camp site (☎ *452 24*) is on a little lake of the same name, about 3km northwest of town. Take bus No 12 from Tržnice bus station five stops to the Třeboňská stop.

Private rooms cost 350 Kč per person and can be arranged at Čedok (☎ 322 33 35), Bechera 21, and at the W-privat Accommodation Agency (☎/fax 322 77 68), náměstí Republiky 5.

The fading *Adria Hotel* (☎/fax 322 37 65, Západní 1), opposite the ČSAD bus station, charges 830/1410 Kč with bathroom. There are cheaper pensions along Zahradní, such as *Hotel/Pension Kosmos* (☎/fax 322 31 68, 39 Zahradní). Rooms are 450/720 Kč or 750/1340 Kč with bathroom.

Getting There & Away

There are direct trains to/from Prague, but it's faster and easier to take one of the five daily buses. The only way to go directly to Plzeň (54 Kč, 1½ hours) and České Budějovice (126 Kč, four hours) is by bus. Book tickets in advance at the ČSAD station.

The train is best to/from Mariánské Lázně (38 Kč, 1½ hours, eight daily).

MARIÁNSKÉ LÁZNĚ
☎ 0165

Small, provincial Mariánské Lázně (population 15,500) is the Czech Republic's most famous spa, but in some ways it ranks second to the larger Karlovy Vary. Even so, the town's grand hotels, stately mansions, casinos, colonnades and gardens will delight romantics with a nostalgia for the 19th century.

Mariánské Lázně boasts 140 mineral springs, all of which are closed to the public. Thirty-nine spas are used for treating diseases of the kidneys and of the urinary and respiratory tracts. The town's elevation gives the spa a brisk climate that makes the Bohemian hills to the north all the more inviting.

Orientation & Information

The adjacent bus and train stations are 3km south of the town centre – head north up Hlavní třída or take trolleybus No 5 (5 Kč; pay with coins only).

The curt municipal Infocentrum (☎ 62 24 74), Hlavní třída 47, sells theatre tickets, maps and guidebooks. The Spa Information Service (☎ 62 55 50, ✉ spa@marienbad.cz), Mírové náměstí 5, has information on spa medical treatments.

Places to Stay

The City Service booth (☎ 62 42 18) on Hlavní třída, at the city bus stand, arranges *private rooms* starting at 350 Kč per person and can book hotels.

Just south of Motel Start on Plzeňská is *TJ Lokomotiva* (☎ *62 39 17*), a sports centre with inexpensive dorm beds. Reception is open 5 to 9 pm.

Holiday Pension (☎ *62 31 95, Plzeňská 98)* has doubles with breakfast for 1080 Kč.

Hotels line Hlavní třída – *Hotel Haná* (☎ *62 27 53, fax 62 27 53, 259 Hlavní třída)* charges 1500 Kč per double. Rooms are much cheaper – 490/880 Kč or 590/1080 Kč with bathroom – at the *Hotel Kossuth* (☎ *62 28 61, fax 62 28 62, Ruská 77)*, on a sidestreet above Hlavní třída.

Places to Eat

Restaurace Jalta, upstairs at Hlavní třída 43, serves good, simple food. The stand-up *Bistro* *(Hlavní třída 145)* has good salads. *Restaurace Classic* *(Hlavní třída 50),* next to the Excelsior Hotel, is a bit pricier but has some vegetarian dishes and salads. On the same street in a lane behind Hotel Cristal Palace, at No 61, is the *Čínská restaurace,* with mains starting at 100 Kč.

On some nights, jazz bands play at *New York Restaurant* *(Hlavní třída 233).* In a courtyard behind Hlavní 96, signs point the way to the cosy *Irish Pub*.

Getting There & Away

There are direct buses between Mariánské Lázně, Plzeň and Prague, as well as frequent trains to Plzeň (50 Kč, 1¼ hours) and Karlovy Vary (38 Kč, 1½ hours). Most international express trains between Nuremberg and Prague stop at Mariánské Lázně.

PLZEŇ
☎ 019

The city of Plzeň (Pilsen; population 173,000), halfway between Prague and

Nuremberg, is the capital of West Bohemia. Beer has been brewed at Plzeň for 700 years and the town is famous as the original home of Pilsner. Plzeň has sights enough to keep you busy for a day and devoted beer drinkers will not regret the pilgrimage.

Orientation
The main train station, Plzeň hlavní nádraží, is on the east side of town. The central bus station is west of the centre on Husova, opposite the Škoda factory. Between these is the old town, which is centred around náměstí Republiky. Tram No 2 travels from the train station to the centre of town and on to the bus station.

Information
The Information Centre (☎ 203 27 50, ℮ infocenter@mmp.plzen-city.cz), náměstí Republiky 41, has information about museums, accommodation and also has three Internet computers for the public. CKM (☎ 723 63 93), Dominikánská 1, can help with accommodation.

There's an ATM at the Československá obchodní banka on Americká, opposite the Tesco department store.

Things to See
The Gothic **St Bartholomew Church** in the middle of náměstí Republiky has the highest tower (102m) in Bohemia; you can climb it daily for 20 Kč.

Plzeň's most interesting sight by far is the **Brewery Museum** at Veleslavínova 6, northeast of náměstí Republiky. The museum (in an authentic medieval malt house) displays a fascinating collection of brewing-related artefacts; entry is 40 Kč. If all that reading makes you thirsty, visit the Pivnice Na Parkánu behind the museum.

Just around the corner at Perlová 4 is an entrance to Plzeň's fascinating medieval **underground corridors** (Plzeňské historické podzemí), which stretch for 9km below the town. They were originally built as refuges during sieges. Tours (minimum five people) are offered Tuesday to Sunday.

The famous **Pilsner Urquell Brewery** is a 10-minute walk from the underground corridors, just north of Plzeň's main train station. A one-hour tour (from 30 Kč) of the brewing room and fermentation cellar is held at 12.30 pm weekdays.

Places to Stay
Camping The camping ground *Oestende* (☎ 52 01 94, Malý Bolevec 41) in Bílá Hora is 5km north of the city (take bus No 20). It also has bungalows and is open May to mid-September.

Hostels *Sou H (☎ 738 20 12, Vejprnická 56)* is a year-round *ubytovna* (hostel) about 3km west of town but easily accessible on tram No 2 (direction: Skvrňany) from the train or bus station. Beds are 240 Kč per person.

Pensions & Hotels A fine old hotel is *Hotel Slovan (☎ 722 72 56, fax 22 70 12, ℮ hotelslovan@iol.cz, Smetanovy sady 1)*, which has singles/doubles for 600/1000 Kč, or 1400/2000 Kč with bath and breakfast included.

The impressive *Hotel Continental (☎ 723 64 79, fax 722 17 46, Zbrojnická 8)* has rooms starting at 860/1460 Kč with shower but no toilet, or 1492/2150 Kč with both, buffet breakfast included.

Pension Bárová (☎ 723 66 52, Solní 8), in a town house just off náměstí Republiky, has three attractive rooms with bath for 695/1020 Kč.

Places to Eat
There is a *supermarket* in the Tesco department store on Americká. *Fénix Bistro (náměstí Republiky 18)* is an inexpensive self-service lunch spot. Plzeň's institution for good-quality food and fine beer is *Pivnice U Salzmannů (Pražská 8)*, not far from the square. Decent inexpensive pizzas are served daily at *Pizzerie (Solní 9)*. *Zach's Pub (Palackého náměstí 2)* serves Guinness and English beers until 1 am, or you can dance to rock bands (to 11.30 pm) or pop tunes (to 5 am) at *Rock bar Elektra (Americká 24)*.

Getting There & Away
All international trains from Munich (1350 Kč, 5½ hours) and Nuremberg (1100 Kč, four hours) stop at Plzeň.

There are fast trains to České Budějovice (86 Kč, two hours) and Prague (74 Kč, two hours). Train services to Mariánské Lázně (50 Kč, 1½ hours) are also good. It's best to take a bus to Karlovy Vary (54 Kč, two hours).

CZECH REPUBLIC

ČESKÉ BUDĚJOVICE
☎ 038
České Budějovice (population 98,800), famous as the home of Budvar (Budweiser) beer, is a charming medieval city halfway between Plzeň and Vienna.

The town's main drawbacks are the lack of cheap accommodation and heavy summertime crowds – if you're pressed for time, consider skipping České Budějovice and head instead to the smaller, more scenic Český Krumlov.

Orientation & Information
From the adjacent bus and train stations, it's a 10-minute walk west down Lannova třída to the town's main square, náměstí Přemysla Otakara II.

The Tourist Information & Map Centre (☎/fax 635 25 89, @ mapcentrum@mbox .vol.cz), náměstí Přemysla Otakara II 28, sells maps, theatre tickets and guidebooks, and arranges accommodation for no commission.

The friendly municipal information centre (☎ 635 94 80), in the town hall at náměstí Přemysla Otakara II 2, sells maps and can also arrange accommodation.

Things to See
Náměstí Přemysla Otakara II, a great square surrounded by 18th-century arches, is one of the largest of its kind in Europe. Looming 72m above the square is the **Black Tower** (1553), with great views from the gallery (open 10 am to 6 pm, April to October; closed Monday).

West, near the river, is the former **Dominican monastery** (1265), with another tall tower and a splendid pulpit.

Beside the church is a medieval warehouse where salt was kept until it could be sent down the Vltava to Prague. The **Museum of South Bohemia** is on Dukelská, a few blocks south-east of the main square (closed Monday; 20 Kč).

The **Budvar Brewery** (☎ 770 53 41) is on Pražská, at the corner of K Světlé; it's open 10 am to 10 pm daily in summer (shorter hours in winter).

The one-hour tour costs from 70 Kč per person; individual travellers should book the 2 pm tour through the brewery or tourist offices; there are group tours at other times.

Places to Stay
Motel Dlouhá Louka – Autocamp (☎ 721 06 01, fax 721 05 95, Stromovka 8) is a 20-minute walk south-west of town – or take bus No 6 from the Dům kultury (two blocks south-east of the South Bohemia Museum). Tent spaces are available May to September and motel rooms – 580/980 Kč with breakfast – year-round.

Book *private rooms* (from 300 Kč per person) at either tourist office or at CTS (☎ 635 39 68), náměstí Přemysla Otakara II 38.

Pension Centrum (☎ 635 20 30, Mlýnská stoka 6), just off Kanovnická as you enter the old town, is a popular place. Clean doubles with bath are 850 Kč, including breakfast. A similar place is *AT Pension* (☎ 731 25 29, Dukelská 15), with rooms starting at 650/980 Kč. *Hotel Grand* (☎ 635 65 03, fax 635 65 62, Nádražní 27), opposite the train station, charges 650/940 Kč.

Places to Eat
The atmospheric *Masné krámy* is a popular, touristy (and semi-expensive) beer hall on the corner of Hroznová and 5. května. *Na dvorku (Kněžská 11)* is a quieter, friendlier beer hall.

Víno z Panské (Panská 14) serves wine straight from barrels and has both meat and vegetarian dishes (closed weekends). *Cukrárna U kláštera (Piaristická 13)*, just off the main square, is great for coffee and cakes (closed Sunday). The Prior department store on Lannova has a large *supermarket*.

Entertainment
Rock bands play often at *Černej velbloud (U tří lvů 4)*. At night the Restaurant Heaven, on the 3rd floor at náměstí Přemysla Otakara II 38, becomes the rock bar *Club Zeppelin*. Another popular club is *Hudební klub 2 (Sokolovský ostrov 2)*, near the football stadium.

Getting There & Away
There are fast trains to Plzeň (86 Kč, two hours), Tábor (44 Kč, one hour) and Prague (110 Kč, 2½ hours), and two daily trains to Linz in Austria (400 Kč, three hours).

For shorter distances you're better off travelling by bus, ie, to Český Krumlov (21 Kč, one hour). From České Budějovice's bus station, a bus to Vienna's Mitte Bahnhof departs on Friday (345 Kč, 3¼ hours), and to Linz (320 Kč, two hours; via Český Krumlov) on Wednesday, Friday and Saturday. Pay the driver.

ČESKÝ KRUMLOV
☎ 0337

Český Krumlov (population 15,000), 25km south of České Budějovice, is one of Europe's most picturesque medieval towns – in 1992 it was added to Unesco's World Heritage List.

In recent years Český Krumlov has become a haven for backpackers, thanks to its laid-back pace, its small and easily navigated historical centre and its many hostels. The only problem is the heavy summertime crowds.

Orientation & Information

The town is built on an S-shaped bend of the Vltava River, its 13th-century chateau occupying a ridge along the left bank. The main bus station is on Tavírna; the train station is 2km north of town, at the top of a steep hill.

Infocentrum (☎ 71 11 83, ✉ infocentrum@ckrf.ckrumlov.cz), náměstí Svornosti 1, sells maps and concert tickets, and books accommodation. The IPB, náměstí Svornosti, changes travellers cheques and has an ATM. The telephone centre is in the post office, Latrán 81.

Things to See

Get off the bus from České Budějovice at Český Krumlov Špičák, the first stop in town.

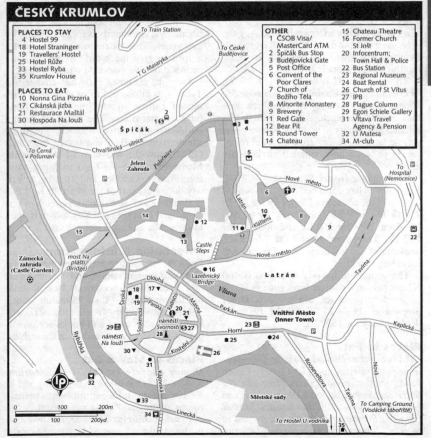

ČESKÝ KRUMLOV

PLACES TO STAY
4 Hostel 99
18 Hotel Straninger
19 Travellers' Hostel
25 Hotel Růže
33 Hostel Ryba
35 Krumlov House

PLACES TO EAT
10 Nonna Gina Pizzeria
17 Cikánská jizba
21 Restaurace Maštál
30 Hospoda Na louži

OTHER
1 ČSOB Visa/MasterCard ATM
2 Špičák Bus Stop
3 Budějovická Gate
5 Post Office
6 Convent of the Poor Clares
7 Church of Božího Těla
8 Minorite Monastery
9 Brewery
11 Red Gate
12 Bear Pit
13 Round Tower
14 Chateau
15 Chateau Theatre
16 Former Church St Jošt
20 Infocentrum; Town Hall & Police
22 Bus Station
23 Regional Museum
24 Boat Rental
26 Church of St Vítus
27 IPB
28 Plague Column
29 Egon Schiele Gallery
31 Vltava Travel Agency & Pension
32 U Matesa
34 M-club

Just above is **Budějovická Gate** (1598), which leads directly into the old town.

On the right, two blocks south, is the **chateau** entrance. The oldest part of the chateau is the lower section with its distinctive **round tower** (30 Kč); the massive upper chateau contains the palace halls that are open to visitors. The ticket office in the chateau's second courtyard sells tickets for three different chateau tours (130 Kč to 150 Kč).

Across the river on náměstí Svornosti are the Gothic **town hall** and a baroque **plague column** (1716). Below the square is **Egon Schiele Gallery**, Široká 70, with 50 of Schiele's watercolours and drawings (100 Kč). Nearby is the **Regional Museum**, with a surprisingly good collection housed in the old Jesuit seminary (closed Monday; 20 Kč).

Places to Stay

The *camping ground*, open June to August, is on the east bank of the Vltava River about 2km south of town. The facilities are basic but the management is friendly.

The excellent *U vodníka* (☎ *71 19 35,* ✉ *krumlovhostels@sendme.cz, Po vodě 55)* is next to the Vltava River. The three doubles are 600 Kč each. Facilities include a kitchen and library. The owners also operate the larger *Krumlov House* hostel (*Rooseveltova 68),* nearby, where dorm beds are 250 Kč.

The popular *Hostel Ryba* (☎ *71 18 01, Rybářská 5)* has dorm beds for 250 Kč. At the top of the old town, *Hostel 99* (☎ *71 28 12,* ✉ *hostel99@hotmail.com, Věžní 99)* has dorm beds for 250 Kč and doubles for 600 Kč. *Travellers' Hostel* (☎ *71 13 45, Soukenická 43)* has dorm beds for 250 Kč, including breakfast.

The going rate for private rooms is 400 Kč per person – contact Infocentrum.

Good value in the old town is *Hotel Straninger* (☎ *71 25 73, Široká 49),* with doubles only for 1500 Kč.

Places to Eat

Cikánská jizba (*Dlouhá 31)* is an unpretentious spot for cheap beer and hearty Czech food. Another good spot is *Hospoda Na louži,* on náměstí Na louži. Vegetarians can find good dishes at the *Restaurace Maštál* (*náměstí Svornosti 2).* If it's pizza you're after, try *Nonna Gina Pizzeria* on Klášterní.

Entertainment

On the corner of Rybářská and Plešivecké schody in a courtyard is *M-club*, which plays traditional rock music and has a pool table. For a drink, try the popular *U Matesa* (*Rybařská 24),* about 100m past Hostel Ryba.

Getting There & Away

The best way to reach Český Krumlov is by bus and the service from České Budějovice is frequent and fast (one hour). Trains are more frequent but slower.

TÁBOR
☎ 0361

God's warriors, the Hussites, founded Tábor in 1420 as a bastion against Catholic Europe. The town (population 37,000) was organised according to the biblical precept that 'nothing is mine and nothing is yours, because the community is owned equally by everyone'. This extreme nonconformism helped to give the word 'Bohemian' the connotations we associate with it today.

Over the centuries little has changed in Tábor – its hilltop old town remains a warren of narrow streets lined with ornate burgher mansions. The most imposing building on Žižkovo náměstí, the main square, is the early Renaissance town hall (1521), now the **Museum of the Hussite Movement** (open 8.30 am to 5 pm daily from April to October, and Tuesday to Friday during the rest of the year; 40 Kč); this is also the entrance to a 650m stretch of **underground passages** (40 Kč), which is open to the public and well worth a visit.

Orientation & Information

From the train station walk west through the park, past the bus station, and continue west on 9. května (which becomes Palackého třída) to Žižkovo náměstí – it's a 15-minute walk.

Infocentrum (☎ 48 62 30), Žižkovo náměstí 2, sells maps and books accommodation, and stocks bus and train timetables.

Places to Stay & Eat

Domov mládeže (☎ *25 28 37, Martina Koláře 2118)* has dorm beds starting at 110 Kč per person. Infocentrum books *private rooms* starting at 300 Kč per person.

Pension Dáša (☎ *25 62 53, Bílkova 735)* is close to the station and has deluxe rooms for 700/990 Kč. Friendly *Pension Alfa* (☎ 25 61 65, Klokotská 107), right in the centre of town, has doubles for 650 Kč.

Typical Bohemian cuisine is available in the modern *Atrium restaurace* at the corner of 9. května and Kollárova for under 100 Kč. A great alternative bar is *Café bar Sedm* (*Žižkovo náměstí 7*).

Getting There & Away
Tábor is on the main railway line between Prague and Vienna. The line from České Budějovice to Prague also passes through here. To Plzeň (84 Kč, 2½ hours) or Brno (107 Kč, 2½ hours) it's easier to take a bus.

Moravia

TELČ
☎ 066

Telč – perhaps the most photogenic town in the Czech Republic – was founded in the 14th century, but after a fire in 1530 the governor of Moravia, Lord Zachariáš, ordered the town and castle rebuilt in the Renaissance style. After the death of Zachariáš in 1589, building activity ceased and the town you see today is largely as it was then. In 1992, Telč was added to Unesco's World Heritage List.

Besides its stunning main square, náměstí Zachariáše z Hradce, Telč's greatest monument is the splendid Renaissance **Water Chateau** (1568), at the square's western end (closed Monday and from November to March). Each of the two tours in English are 120 Kč.

Orientation & Information
The bus and train stations are a few hundred metres apart on the eastern side of town, a 10-minute walk along Masarykova towards náměstí Zachariáše z Hradce. The Information Office (☎ 724 31 45) is in the town hall on the main square. The Komerční banka on the main square has an ATM and changes travellers cheques.

Places to Stay & Eat
The Information Office books *private rooms* starting at 300 Kč per person. There are 'Zimmer frei' (private room) signs on náměstí Zachariáše z Hradce at Nos 11, 12, 32, 36, 45 and 58. The friendly *Hotel Pod*

kaštany (☎ 721 30 42, Štěpnická 409), just outside the old town, charges 300/660 Kč for rooms without bathrooms and 550/850 Kč with bathrooms. The *restaurant* here is good. If Pod kaštany is full try *Pension Relax* (☎ 721 31 26, Na posvátné 29), which is farther east along Štěpnická. Rooms with bath and TV are 450/900 Kč, including breakfast. The prices are similar at *Pension Vacek* (☎ 721 30 99) on Furchova.

The restaurant most preferred by locals is *Restaurace U Zachariáše* on the square. It has local specialties for around 100 Kč. The restaurace in the *Hotel Černý orel* is more expensive but apparently not as good.

Getting There & Away
The railway line through Telč is fairly useless. Instead take a bus to/from České Budějovice (54 Kč, two hours), Brno (54 Kč, two hours) or Prague (128 Kč, 2½ hours). Tickets are sold by the drivers.

BRNO
☎ 05

Brno (population 388,000), midway between Budapest and Prague, has been the capital of Moravia since 1641. Brno has a rich cultural life and its compact centre (half of which is a pedestrian zone) holds a half-dozen notable sights. The town hasn't been overwhelmed by tourism the way Prague has. If you enjoy the diversions of a city (bars, restaurants, museums etc) you'll like Brno for a few days.

Orientation
Brno's Hlavní nádraží train station is at the old town's southern edge. Walk or take a tram up Masarykova, a busy thoroughfare opposite the station, to the triangular náměstí Svobody, Brno's main square. The bus station is 800m south of the train station, beyond Tesco (go through the pedestrian tunnel and follow the elevated walkway). There are two left-luggage offices at the train station and one at the bus station.

Information
The helpful Infocentrum (☎ 42 21 10 90) is in the old town hall at Radnická 8, and books rooms and sells maps. Look out for the free *Do města – Downtown* leaflet that

lists what's on in cinemas, theatres, galleries, nightclubs etc.

There are dozens of banks around town, most with ATMs. American Express is represented by BVV Fair Travel (☎ 42 21 77 45), Starobrněnská 20. The telephone centre is at Český telecom, Šilingrovo náměstí 3/4. The 24-hour post office is at the western end of the train station. You can surf the Internet at the @Internet café, Lidická 17, just south of Hotel Slovan (closed on Sunday).

GTS international (☎ 42 21 19 96), Skrytá 2, sells international bus and train tickets, as does Čedok (☎ 42 32 12 67), Nádražní 10-12.

Things to See

As you enter the city on Masarykova, turn left into Kapučínské náměstí to reach the 17th-century **Capucine monastery** (40 Kč). In the crypt below the church are the intact mummies of monks and local aristocrats deposited here before 1784.

At the western end of Kapučínské náměstí, the Dietrichstein Palace (1760) houses the **Regional Moravian Museum**.

On Radnická, off the northern side of Zelný trh, is Brno's 13th-century **old town hall** (20 Kč), which has a **tower** (10 Kč) that is worth climbing for the view. The town hall itself is worth a visit.

Špilberk Castle, in a park above the town centre, was founded in the 13th century and converted into a citadel and prison in the 17th century. Today it houses the superb **Municipal Brno Museum** (40 Kč), including a gallery. The casemates, which contain an exhibit of prison life, are also open to the public (20 Kč). Both are closed on Monday.

Other museums worth seeing are the **Moravian Gallery** at Pražákův Palace, Husova 18, with a 20th-century Czech art exhibit; and the **City Art Gallery** at Malinovského náměstí 2. Both are closed on Monday.

Places to Stay

Camping *Obora Camping* (☎ 79 11 05), open from May to September, is at the Brněnská přehrada (Brno dam). From the train station, take tram No 1 to the zoo and change to bus No 103; the camping ground is at the seventh stop.

Hostels The HI-affiliated *Hotel Interservis* (☎ 45 23 43 35), south of the centre

on Lomená, charges from 150 Kč for beds in two-person rooms. Take tram No 9 or 12 south to the end of the line, walk through the underpass, follow Luzná three blocks east, and turn right on Lomená. The hostel is the tall, modern building about two blocks down on your right.

Hotel Přehrada (☎ 46 21 01 67, *Kníničky 225, Brno Přehrada*) has rooms with shared facilities starting at 580 Kč and doubles with bathroom at 780 Kč, including breakfast. Student- and youth-card-holders pay 180 Kč per person for a bed. It's open March to November. Take tram No 1 from the main train station to the zoo, cross the road west to náměstí 28. dubna and take bus No 54 to the end.

The year-round *koleje Palacký vrch* (☎ 41 64 11 11, *Block K-1, Kolejní 2*), on the northern side of the city, has rooms starting at 760/960 Kč. Take tram No 13 north to the end of the line, then take trolleybus No 53 to the hostel.

Private Rooms A room far from the centre that's (usually) accessible by trolleybus or tram is about 350 Kč to 540 Kč per person. Contact Čedok, Infocentrum or Taxatour (☎ 42 21 33 48), at the train station.

Hotels The modern *Hotel Avion* (☎ 42 21 50 16, fax 42 21 40 55, ✉ avion@iq-net.cz, *Česká 20*) is reasonable; rooms with shower but no toilet are 845/1000 Kč; with shower and toilet, 1150/1560 Kč.

Hotel Pegas (☎ 42 21 01 04, fax 42 21 12 32, *Jakubská 4*) is on a quiet street right in the centre of town. Bright and clean rooms with bath and breakfast are 1200/1700 Kč. Not far is another place, *Hotel Slavia* (☎ 42 32 12 49, fax 42 21 08 43, ✉ hotel.slavia@iol.cz, *Solniční 15*) with polished rooms starting at 1450/1850 Kč.

Places to Eat

There's a good *supermarket* in the basement of Tesco, behind the train station.

Haribol (*Lužanecká 4*) is a small vegetarian restaurant open 10.30 am to 5 pm weekdays. The touristy *Pivnice Pegas* (*Jakubská 4*) has so-so food but brews its own dark and light beers on the premises.

Restaurace Špalíček (*Zelný trh 12*) is a good bet for Moravian food, as is the wine-restaurant *Vinárna U zlatého meče*

(Mečová 3). Good local food is served at **Restaurace Pod radničním kole** *(Mečová 5)*, which is in a cellar with plenty of charming atmosphere.

The popular **U Lucerny** (☎ 75 20 42, *Slováková 2*) is an excellent Italian restaurant also serving seafood at 90 Kč to 230 Kč for main courses. **Café Blau** *(Běhounská 18)* is a small and intimate modern place.

Entertainment

A popular cellar bar is **Charlie's hat** *(Kobližná 12)* and it even has a small dance floor where DJs spin anything from heavier rock to dance music (open until 4 am). North of the city centre is **Stará pekárna** *(Štefánikova 8)*, which has live bands playing anything from jazz to funk and rock on most nights (from 5 pm to 1 am daily).

Alterna *(Block B, Kounicova 48)* is an alternative *klub* with rock, punk, jazz and more, open from 7 pm nightly. From Česká take trolleybus No 134 or 136 three stops north.

Don't miss the **Radost Puppet Theatre** *(Bratislavská 32)*. It's kids' stuff but great fun if you haven't enjoyed puppets for a while.

Getting There & Away

The bus to Vienna's Mitte Bahnhof (250 Kč, 1½ hours) departs from platform No 20 at the bus station twice a day. For shorter trips, buses are faster and more efficient than the trains, ie, to Telč (54 Kč, two hours) České Budějovice (116 Kč, four hours) and Český Krumlov (136 Kč, five hours).

All trains between Budapest and Berlin stop at Brno. If you're going to/from Vienna, change trains at Břeclav. Direct trains to/from Bratislava (148 Kč, two hours) and Prague (150 Kč, three hours) are frequent.

Denmark

The smallest and southernmost of the Scandinavian countries, Denmark (Danmark in Danish) is a mix of lively cities and pastoral farmland.

The countryside abounds with ancient medieval churches, Renaissance castles and tidy 18th-century fishing villages. Denmark has some wonderful white sand beaches, the warmest waters in Scandinavia and scores of unspoilt islands to explore. Copenhagen is Scandinavia's largest and most cosmopolitan capital, with renowned museums and a spirited music scene.

Facts about Denmark

HISTORY

Although there were agricultural villages in the region in the Stone and Bronze Ages, present-day Denmark traces its linguistic and cultural roots to the arrival of the Danes, a tribe thought to have migrated south from Sweden around AD 500.

In the late 9th century, warriors led by the Viking chieftain Hardegon conquered the Jutland peninsula. The Danish monarchy, Europe's oldest, dates back to Hardegon's son, Gorm the Old, who established his reign in the early 10th century. Succeeding Danish kings went on to invade England and conquer most of the Baltic region.

In 1397 the Danish queen Margrethe I established a political union between Denmark, Norway and Sweden to counter the influence of the powerful Hanseatic League that had come to dominate the region's trade. Sweden withdrew from the union in 1523; Norway remained under Danish rule until 1814.

In the 16th century the Reformation swept through the country amid church burnings and civil warfare. The fighting

ended in 1536 with the ousting of the powerful Catholic church and the establishment of a Danish Lutheran church headed by the monarchy.

Denmark's golden age was under Christian IV (1588-1648), with Renaissance cities, castles and fortresses flourishing throughout his kingdom. In 1625 Christian IV, hoping to neutralise Swedish expansion, entered a protracted struggle known as the Thirty Years' War. The Swedes triumphed and in 1658 Denmark lost Skåne and its other territories on the Swedish mainland.

Literature, the arts, philosophy and populist ideas flourished in the 1830s, and Europe's 'Year of Revolutions' in 1848 helped inspire a democratic movement in Denmark that led to the adoption of a constitution on 5 June 1849. As a result, King Frederik VII was forced to relinquish most of his political power to an elected parliament and thus became Denmark's first constitutional monarch.

Denmark remained neutral in WWI and also declared its neutrality at the outbreak of WWII. Nevertheless, on 9 April 1940 an unfortified Denmark faced either a quick surrender or a full-scale invasion by German troops massed along its border. The Danish government settled for the former in exchange for some rights over internal affairs; in August 1943 the Germans took outright control. The Danish Resistance movement mushroomed and 7000 Jewish Danes were quickly smuggled into neutral Sweden.

Although the island of Bornholm was heavily bombarded by Soviet forces, the rest of Denmark emerged from WWII relatively unscathed. Denmark joined NATO in 1949 and the European Community (now the European Union or EU) in 1973. Support for the EU is tepid, however, as many

DENMARK

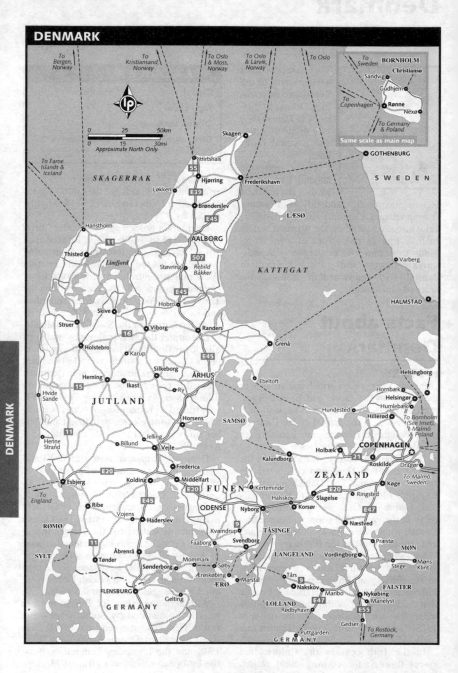

Danes fear the loss of local control to a European bureaucracy dominated by stronger nations. Denmark has one of the world's highest per capita GNPs and a high standard of living.

GEOGRAPHY
The majority of Denmark's 42,930 sq km is on the peninsula of Jutland, but there are also 406 islands, 90 of which are inhabited. Copenhagen is on Zealand, the largest island. Most of Denmark is a lowland of farms, marshland, rolling hills and heather-covered moors. The highest elevation is a mere 173m.

CLIMATE
Considering its northern latitude, Denmark has a fairly mild climate. May and June can be superb months to visit: the weather is generally warm and comfortable, and you'll beat the rush of summer tourists. While autumn can also be pleasant, it's not as scenic.

POPULATION & PEOPLE
Denmark's population is about 5.3 million. Foreign nationals account for 5% of the total, and 8% of Copenhagen's population. The four largest cities are Copenhagen (population 1.5 million), Århus (265,000), Odense (184,000) and Aalborg (155,000).

SOCIETY & CONDUCT
Danes pride themselves on being thoroughly modern, and the wearing of folk costumes, the celebration of traditional festivals and the clinging to old-fashioned customs is less prevalent than elsewhere in Scandinavia. Danes are tolerant of different lifestyles; in 1989 Denmark became the first European nation to legalise same-sex marriages.

Perhaps nothing captures the Danish perspective more than the concept of *hygge*, which, roughly translated, means 'cosy and snug'. It implies shutting out the turmoil and troubles of the outside world and striving instead for a warm, intimate mood.

LANGUAGE
Written Danish bears a strong resemblance to Swedish, Norwegian, Icelandic and Faroese. Spoken Danish, on the other hand, has evolved in a different direction, introducing sounds and pronunciation not found elsewhere.

Most Danes speak English. However, an effort to at least learn the basics will be appreciated. See the Language guide at the back of this book for pronunciation guidelines and useful words and phrases.

Facts for the Visitor

HIGHLIGHTS
Half-timbered houses and ancient churches are thick on the ground in Denmark, but a few places are unique. Ribe, the oldest town in Denmark, has an exquisite historic centre encircling a 12th-century cathedral. The tiny fortress island of Christiansø, off Bornholm, retains its ramparts and 17th-century buildings, with almost no trace of the 20th century. Ærøskøbing on Ærø has a town centre of 18th-century houses that's arguably the most picturesque in Denmark.

The Danish countryside holds a number of Viking sites, including a Viking ring fortress at Trelleborg in southern Zealand. The impressive Lindholm Høje, outside Aalborg, contains the largest plot of Viking and Iron-Age graves in Scandinavia.

Denmark has castles aplenty – the most strikingly set is Egeskov Castle in Funen.

Despite gentle hills here and there, Denmark is quite flat, which, combined with an extensive network of cycle routes, makes it a great place to explore by bike.

SUGGESTED ITINERARIES
Three days
  Spend two days in Copenhagen and one day exploring north Zealand.
One week
  Visit Copenhagen, north Zealand's castles and beaches, Odense, Århus and Ribe.
Two weeks
  As above plus Ærø, Skagen and other Jutland sights of interest (or Bornholm).

TOURIST OFFICES
Virtually every good-sized town in Denmark has a local tourist office, most often found in the *rådhus* (town hall) or elsewhere on *torvet* (the central square).

Danish Tourist Offices Abroad
UK (☎ 020-7259 5959, ✉ dtb.london@dt.dk), 55 Sloane St, London SW1X 9SY
USA (☎ 212-885 9700, ✉ info@goscandinavia .com), PO Box 4649, Grand Central Station, New York, NY 10163

DENMARK

EMBASSIES & CONSULATES
Danish Embassies Abroad
Australia (☎ 02-6273 2195) 15 Hunter St, Yarralumla, ACT 2600
Canada (☎ 613-562 1811) 47 Clarence St, Suite 450, Ottawa, Ontario K1N 9K1
Sweden (☎ 8-406 75 00) Jakobs Torg 1, 11186 Stockholm
UK (☎ 020-7333 0200) 55 Sloane St, London SW1X 9SR
USA (☎ 202-234 4300) 3200 Whitehaven St NW, Washington DC 20008

Foreign Embassies in Denmark
The following embassies are in Copenhagen:

Australia *Consulate*: (☎ 39 29 20 77) Strandboulevarden 122
Canada (☎ 33 48 32 00) Kristen Bernikows Gade 1
UK (☎ 35 44 52 00) Kastelsvej 40
USA (☎ 35 55 31 44) Dag Hammarskjölds Allé 24

MONEY
The Danish krone is most often written as DKK in international money markets, Dkr in northern Europe and kr within Denmark. The krone is divided into 100 øre. Coin denominations are 25 and 50 øre and 1, 2, 5, 10 and 20kr. Notes come in denominations of 50, 100, 200, 500 and 1000kr.

Most travellers cheques are accepted in Denmark, though it's wise to bring large-denomination cheques, as there's a hefty fee of 20kr per cheque (40kr minimum) at most banks. If you're exchanging cash, there's a 25kr fee for any size transaction. Post offices also exchange foreign currency at comparable rates. Major banks have ATMs that accept Visa, MasterCard and Cirrus/Plus cards.

Exchange Rates
The following currencies convert at these approximate rates:

country	unit		krone
Australia	A$1	=	4.85 kr
Canada	C$1	=	5.79 kr
euro	€1	=	7.46 kr
France	1FF	=	1.14 kr
Germany	DM1	=	3.82 kr
New Zealand	NZ$1	=	3.78 kr
Norway	1 Nkr	=	0.93 kr
Sweden	1 Skr	=	0.89 kr
UK	UK£1	=	12.33 kr
USA	US$1	=	8.60 kr

Costs
Costs in Denmark are not exorbitant by Scandinavian standards. Yet nothing is cheap either _ partly due to the 25% value-added tax (VAT), called *moms* in Danish, included in every price.

If you camp or stay in hostels and prepare your own meals you might get by on US$30 per day. Staying in modest hotels and eating at inexpensive restaurants, expect to spend about US$65 a day (US$85 if you're travelling alone). To this you need to add local transport, museum admission fees, entertainment and incidentals.

Tipping
Restaurant bills and taxi fares include service charges in the quoted prices, and further tipping is unnecessary.

POST & COMMUNICATIONS
Most post offices are open 9 or 10 am to 5 or 5.30 pm weekdays, to noon Saturday. It costs 4.50kr to mail a postcard or letter (up to 20g) to Western Europe, 5.50kr to other countries.

Denmark's international country code is ☎ 45. There are no area codes within Denmark; you must dial all eight digits. It costs 2kr minimum to make a local call at coin phones. You get about twice as much calling time for your money on domestic calls made from 7.30 pm to 8 am daily, all day Sunday. Card phones are typically found side by side with coin phones. Phonecards (30kr to 100kr) are sold at post offices and newspaper kiosks.

The direct-dial international access code for Denmark is ☎ 00.

The largest cities have Internet cafes that charge about 30kr an hour to go online. Public libraries also have Internet-capable computers, but as computer time often requires advance sign up, you may have to wait for a free slot.

INTERNET RESOURCES
The Danish foreign ministry site at www.denmark.org has a wealth of information, including updated weather and exchange rates, and links to many sites, such as the Danish Tourist Board.

TIME
Time in Denmark is GMT/UTC plus one hour. Clocks are moved forward one hour

on the last Sunday in March and back again on the last Sunday in October.

WOMEN TRAVELLERS

KVINFO, the Danish Centre for Information on Women and Gender (☎ 33 13 50 88), Christians Brygge 3, Copenhagen, can provide information on feminist issues. Also in Copenhagen, Kvindehuset (☎ 33 14 28 04), at Gothersgade 37, is a help centre and meeting place for women.

GAY & LESBIAN TRAVELLERS

Denmark is a popular destination for gay and lesbian travellers. Copenhagen in particular has an active, open gay community and lots of nightlife options.

Landsforeningen for Bøsser og Lesbiske (LBL; ☎ 33 13 19 48, ✉ lbl@lbl.dk), the national organisation for gay men and lesbians, is at Teglgårdstræde 13 in Copenhagen. A good English-language Web site with links to LBL and other gay organisations is www.copenhagen-gay-life.dk.

DISABLED TRAVELLERS

Overall, Denmark is user-friendly for the disabled. The Danish Tourist Board publishes *Access in Denmark – a Travel Guide for the Disabled*, an English-language booklet with information on options for accommodation, transportation and sightseeing for disabled travellers.

DANGERS & ANNOYANCES

Travelling in Denmark presents no unusual dangers. Nevertheless, be careful with your belongings, particularly in busy places such as Copenhagen's Central Station. In cities, you'll need to quickly become accustomed to the busy cycle lanes between vehicle roads and the pedestrian pavement.

Dial ☎ 112 for police or an ambulance.

BUSINESS HOURS

Office hours are generally 9 am to 4 pm weekdays. Most banks are open 9.30 am to 4 pm weekdays (to 6 pm Thursday). Stores are generally open to 5.30 pm weekdays and to 2 pm Saturday.

PUBLIC HOLIDAYS & SPECIAL EVENTS

Many Danes go on holiday during the first three weeks of July. Public holidays observed in Denmark are: New Year's Day, Maundy Thursday (Thursday before Easter), Good Friday, Easter, Common Prayer Day (4th Friday after Easter), Ascension Day, Whit Sunday, Whit Monday, 5 June (Constitution Day), 24 to 26 December.

The acclaimed 10-day Copenhagen Jazz Festival is held in early July, with outdoor concerts and numerous performances in clubs around the city. Roskilde has a grand Woodstock-style rock festival on the last weekend of June. There are folk festivals in Skagen near the end of June and in Tønder in late August. The 10-day Århus Festival in early September features an array of music and multicultural events. For information contact Dansk Musik Informations Center (☎ 33 11 20 66), Gråbrødre Torv 16, 1154 Copenhagen K. Web site: www.mic.dk

ACCOMMODATION
Camping & Cabins

Denmark's 516 camping grounds typically charge 40kr to 60kr per person to pitch a tent. A camping pass is required (45kr for the season) and can be picked up at any camping ground. Many sites rent simple cabins that sleep two to six people and cost 200kr to 450kr a day. Cabins often have cooking facilities, but you'll need a sleeping bag. Tourist offices have free booklets that list camping grounds throughout Denmark.

Hostels

Most of Denmark's 100 Hostelling International (HI) hostels, called *vandrerhjem* in Danish, have both dorm beds (70kr to 100kr) and private rooms (singles/doubles average 225/275kr). Travellers without a HI card can buy one in Denmark for 160kr or pay an extra 30kr a night. In summer, hostels can book out in advance; it's always wise to call ahead. Outside Copenhagen, check-in is generally between 4 and 8 or 9 pm; reception is usually closed, and the phone not answered, between noon and 4 pm. Most Danish hostels close in winter for a few weeks to several months.

All Danish hostels offer an all-you-can-eat breakfast (40kr or less) and many also provide dinner (65kr maximum). Nearly all hostels have guest kitchens. The national HI affiliate is Danhostel (☎ 31 31 36 12), Vesterbrogade 39, 1620 Copenhagen V. Web site: www.danhostel.dk

DENMARK

Private Rooms

Many tourist offices book rooms in private homes for a small fee, or provide a free list of rooms available. Rates vary but average about 200/275kr for singles/doubles. Dansk Bed & Breakfast (☎ 39 61 04 05,), Postbox 53, 2900 Hellerup, is a nationwide booking service. Web site: www.bbdk.dk.

If you're cycling or driving around Denmark, you'll come across farmhouses displaying *værelse* ('room') signs.

Hotels

Although the cheapest hotels – which typically cost around 450/600kr for singles/doubles – tend to be spartan, they're rarely seedy or unsafe. *Kro*, a name that implies country inn but is more commonly the Danish version of a motel, are generally cheaper than hotels. Both hotels and kros usually include an all-you-can-eat breakfast.

Rates listed in this chapter include all taxes and, unless otherwise noted, are for rooms with shared bath. The Danish Tourist Board's free *Hotels in Denmark* booklet, published annually, lists hotels and kros around the country.

FOOD & DRINKS

The cheapest restaurant food is generally pizza and pasta; you can eat your fill for about 40kr at lunch, 60kr at dinner. Danish food, which relies heavily on fish, meat and potatoes, generally costs double that. *Dagens ret*, which means daily special, is usually the best deal on the menu.

Nothing epitomises Danish food more than *smørrebrød* (literally 'buttered bread'), an open-faced sandwich that ranges from basic to very elaborate. Typically it's a slice of rye bread topped with roast beef, tiny shrimps or fish fillet and finished off with a variety of garnishes. The rich pastry known worldwide as 'Danish' is called *wienerbrød*, and nearly every second street corner has a bakery with mouthwatering varieties.

Other typical Danish dishes include *frikadeller* (ground-pork meatballs), *kogt torsk* (poached cod in mustard sauce), *flæskesteg* (roast pork with crackling), *hvid labskovs* (beef and potato stew), and *hakkebøf* (ground-beef burger with fried onions).

Denmark's Carlsberg and Tuborg breweries both produce excellent beers. The most popular spirit in Denmark is caraway-spiced Aalborg aquavit; it's drunk straight down as a shot, followed by a chaser of beer. *Øl* (beer), *vin* (wine) and spirits are sold at grocery stores, and prices are cheap compared to those in other Scandinavian countries.

Getting There & Away

AIR

Scandinavian Airlines (SAS) is the largest carrier serving Denmark. Other airlines flying into Copenhagen include Air France, Alitalia, Austrian Airlines, British Airways, British Midland, El Al, Finnair, Iberia, Icelandair, KLM, Lithuanian Airlines, LOT, Lufthansa, Maersk Air, Olympic Airways, Sabena, Swissair and Virgin Express.

BUS & TRAIN
Germany

Three railway lines go to/from Germany; 2nd-class fares from Copenhagen to Frankfurt costs 1105k. Eurolines operates buses from Copenhagen to Berlin (230kr) and Frankfurt (635kr) several times a week.

Norway

Trains operate daily between Copenhagen and Oslo via Sweden (400kr). Eurolines offers a daily bus service between Oslo and Copenhagen (445kr) via Gothenburg.

Sweden

Trains run many times a day between Copenhagen and Malmö, Sweden (60kr), via the new Øresund Fixed Link, the longest bridge-tunnel of its type in the world. The rail fare from Copenhagen is 200kr to Gothenburg, 370kr to Stockholm.

There are numerous buses between Copenhagen and Sweden, including Eurolines buses to Gothenburg (255kr) and Stockholm (420kr).

SEA
Germany

The frequent Rødbyhavn-Puttgarden ferry takes 45 minutes and is included in rail tickets for those travelling by train; otherwise, the cost for a car with passengers is 310kr.

Other ferries run from Rømø to Sylt (31kr, one hour), Rønne to Sassnitz-Mukran

(50kr to 100 kr, 3½ hours) and Gedser to Rostock (32kr, two hours).

Iceland & the Faroe Islands
Smyril Line (☎ 33 16 40 04) runs weekly ferries from Hanstholm to Tórshavn (Faroe Islands) and Seyðisfjörður (Iceland) from mid-May to early September. The boat leaves Hanstholm at 8 pm Saturday, arriving in Tórshavn at 6 am Monday. There's a two-day layover in the Faroe Islands, departing from Tórshavn at 6 pm Wednesday and arriving in Seyðisfjörður at 9 am Thursday.

The cheapest fares are for couchettes – 1410kr to Tórshavn and 2200kr to Seyðisfjörður (less 25% for students under 26). Bicycles cost 80kr more.

Norway
A daily overnight ferry operates between Copenhagen and Oslo. Ferries also run from Hirtshals to Oslo, Kristiansand and Moss; from Hanstholm to Bergen; and from Frederikshavn to Oslo and Larvik. For further details see the relevant Getting There & Away sections.

Poland
Polferries (☎ 33 11 46 45) operates ferries to Swinoujscie from both Copenhagen (340kr, 10 hours) and Rønne (160kr, 5½ hours).

Sweden
The cheapest and most frequent ferry to Sweden is the shuttle between Helsingør and Helsingborg (16kr, 20 minutes). Other ferries go from Frederikshavn to Gothenburg (90kr to 140kr, three hours), Rønne to Ystad (150kr, 1½ hours) and Grenå to Varberg (80kr to 140kr, four hours). There are also hydrofoils from Copenhagen to Malmö (89kr, 45 minutes).

UK
DFDS Seaways sails from Esbjerg (☎ 79 17 79 17) to Harwich at least three times a week (448/1098kr in winter/summer, 19 hours).

Getting Around

AIR
Denmark's domestic air routes are operated by Maersk Air (☎ 70 10 74 74). The regular one-way fare from Copenhagen is 715kr to

Bornholm and 815kr to Billund but if you buy your ticket a week in advance and stay over the weekend, you can get a return ticket for 575kr to Bornholm and 625kr to Billund.

BUS
All large cities and towns have a local bus system and most places are also served by regional buses, many of which connect with trains. There are also a few long-distance bus routes, including from Copenhagen to Aalborg or Århus. Domestic travel by bus on long-distance routes is about 20% cheaper than travel by train.

TRAIN
Scanrail, Eurail, Inter-Rail and other rail passes are valid on Danish State Railways (DSB) ferries and trains, but not on the few private lines.

There are two types of long-distance trains. The sleek InterCity (IC) trains have ultra-modern comforts and generally require reservations (15kr). Inter-regional (IR) trains are older and a bit slower, make more stops and don't require reservations. Both trains charge the same fares, as long as you avoid the InterCityLyn, an express aimed at businesspeople. Rail passes don't cover reservation fees or surcharges.

Fares work out to about 1kr per kilometre.

CAR & MOTORCYCLE
Denmark's roads are in good condition and well signposted.

In Denmark you drive on the right, seat belt use is mandatory and all drivers are required to carry a warning triangle. Speed limits range from 50km/h in towns to 110km/h on motorways. Cars and motorcycles must have dipped headlights on at all times. The blood alcohol limit is 0.05%. Unleaded petrol is relatively expensive. *Parkering forbudt* means 'no parking'.

Denmark's main motoring organisation, Forenede Danske Motorejere (FDM; ☎ 45 93 08 00), is based at Firskovvej 32, 2800 Lyngby.

BOAT
An extensive network of ferries carrying both passengers and vehicles links Denmark's main islands as well as most of the smaller populated ones. Generally where there's no bridge, there's a ferry.

DENMARK

Copenhagen

Copenhagen (Danish: København) is Scandinavia's largest and liveliest city, with a population of 1.5 million. Founded in 1167, it became the capital of Denmark in the early 15th century. Copenhagen is largely a low-rise city, with block after block of historic six-storey buildings. The city has an active nightlife that rolls into the early hours of the morning, and for sightseers there's a treasure trove of museums, castles and old churches to explore.

Orientation

Central Station (Hovedbanegården or København H), the main train station, is flanked on the west by the main hotel zone and on the east by Tivoli amusement park. At the northern corner of Tivoli is Rådhuspladsen, a central city square and the main bus transit point.

The Strøget pedestrian mall runs through the centre between Rådhuspladsen and Kongens Nytorv, at the head of the Nyhavn canal. Strøget is made up of five continuous streets: Frederiksberggade, Nygade, Vimmelskaftet, Amagertorv and Østergade. Other pedestrian streets run north from Strøget in a triangular pattern to the Latin Quarter, a popular student haunt.

Information

Tourist Offices The tourist office (☎ 70 22 24 42), Bernstorffsgade 1, just north of Central Station, distributes the informative *Copenhagen This Week*, free city maps and brochures for all Denmark. In summer it's open 9 am to 9 pm daily; at other times to 4.30 pm weekdays, to 2 pm Saturday.

Use It (☎ 33 73 06 20), Rådhusstræde 13, is an alternative information centre catering to young budget travellers but open to all. Staff here book rooms, store luggage, hold mail and put out a useful general guide called *Playtime* – all free of charge. In summer it's open 9 am to 7 pm daily; at other times 11 am to 4 pm weekdays (to 2 pm Friday). Web site: www.useit.dk

Copenhagen Card The Copenhagen Card allows unlimited travel on the buses and trains around Copenhagen and North Zealand and free admission to most museums and attractions. It costs 155/255/320kr for one/two/three days and is sold at Central Station, the tourist office and some hotels.

Money Banks, all of which charge transaction fees, are found on nearly every second corner in the city centre, but the Forex exchange booth at Central Station generally has the best rates.

Post & Communications The main post office is at Tietgensgade 37 (closed Sunday). The post office in Central Station is open daily.

You can make international phone calls from any public phone.

Email & Internet Access Babel (☎ 33 33 93 38), Frederiksborggade 33, and Netpoint (☎ 33 42 60 00) in the SAS Royal Hotel on Vestergade have Internet access for 30kr an hour. If you just want to check your email, Use It, Rådhusstræde 13, offers free Internet access, or drop by the Royal Library at the south side of Slotsholmen, where more than 100 online computers fill the hallways.

Travel Agencies Kilroy Travels (☎ 33 11 00 44), Skindergade 28, and Wasteels (☎ 33 14 46 33), Skoubogade 6, specialise in student and budget travel.

Medical & Emergency Services Frederiksberg Hospital (☎ 38 16 38 16), Nordre Fasanvej 57, has a 24-hour emergency ward. Private doctor visits (☎ 33 93 63 00 for referrals) usually cost around 350kr. Steno Apotek, a 24-hour pharmacy, is at Vesterbro-gade 6 opposite Central Station.

Things to See & Do

No trip to Copenhagen is complete without a visit to Tivoli and a stroll down Strøget. The most outstanding museums are Ny Carlsberg Glyptotek and Nationalmuseet.

City Centre From the Rådhus (town hall) walk down Strøget, which after a couple of blocks cuts between two squares, Gammel Torv and Nytorv. The former is one of Copenhagen's most popular hang-outs.

At the eastern end of Strøget is Kongens Nytorv, a square surrounded by gracious old buildings including the **Royal Theatre**, home of the Royal Danish Ballet, and

Charlottenborg, a 17th-century Dutch baroque palace housing the Royal Academy of Arts. The academy's rear building has changing exhibits of contemporary art (20kr).

Amalienborg Palace, home of the royal family since 1794, comprises four almost identical rococo mansions surrounding a central square that's the scene of a ceremonial noontime **changing of the guard**. You can visit the north-west mansion, featuring royal memorabilia and the study rooms of three kings (40kr).

Continue north along Amaliegade to Churchillparken, where you'll find **Frihedsmuseet**, which depicts the history of Danish Resistance against Nazi occupation (closed Monday; free).

It's a 10-minute walk past the immense **Gefion Fountain** and through the park to the statue of the famed **Little Mermaid** (Den Lille Havfrue), a diminutive bronze with an industrial harbour backdrop that tends to disappoint all but the most steadfast Hans Christian Andersen fans.

Latin Quarter Ascend the stairs of the **University Library** (enter from Fiolstræde) to see one quirky remnant of the 1807 British bombardment of Copenhagen: a cannonball and the target it hit, a book titled *Defensor Pacis* (Defender of Peace).

Opposite the university is **Vor Frue Kirke**, Copenhagen's neoclassical cathedral, housing the most acclaimed works of Bertel Thorvaldsen, his statues of Christ and the 12 apostles.

At the north side of the Latin Quarter is **Kultorvet**, a lively square with beer gardens, flower stalls and produce stands. The nearby **Rundetårn** (Round Tower) is the best vantage point for viewing the old city's red-tiled rooftops and church spires (closed Sunday morning; 15kr).

To the north, **Rosenborg Slot** is a 17th-century castle built by Christian IV in Dutch Renaissance style. The dazzling collection of crown jewels is the main attraction of the castle (50kr).

Slotsholmen On an island separated from the city centre by a moat-like canal, Slotsholmen is the site of **Christiansborg Palace** and the seat of Denmark's national government. Of the numerous sites to explore, grandest is the **Royal Reception Chambers**, the ornate Renaissance hall where the queen entertains other heads of state. Tours in English (40kr) are at 11 am and 1 and 3 pm daily. Other sights include **Thorvaldsens Museum**, with sculptures by Bertel Thorvaldsen; the partially excavated **Ruins of Absalon's Fortress**; and the **Museum of Royal Coaches**.

Christianshavn In 1971 an abandoned military camp on the east side of Christianshavn was taken over by squatters who proclaimed it the 'free state' of Christiania. About 1000 people settled into Christiania, starting their own collective businesses and schools. Visitors are welcome to stroll through car-free Christiania. Photography is frowned upon, and outright forbidden on Pusherstreet where hashish is openly (though not legally) smoked and sold. Guided tours (meet inside the entrance on Prinsessegade; 25kr) are given at noon and 3 pm daily in summer.

To reach Christianshavn, walk over the bridge from the north-east side of Slotsholmen or take bus No 8 from Rådhuspladsen.

Tivoli Right in the heart of the city, Tivoli is Copenhagen's century-old amusement park and a mishmash of gardens, food pavilions, amusement rides and stage shows. Fireworks light up the skies at 11.45 pm on Wednesday and Saturday. Tivoli is open 11 am to midnight daily from mid-April to late September. Entry is 49kr.

Museums The **Nationalmuseet** (National Museum), Ny Vestergade 10, holds the world's most extensive collection of Danish artefacts from the Palaeolithic period to the 19th century (closed Monday; 40kr, free Wednesday).

Statens Museum for Kunst, Denmark's substantial national gallery at Sølvgade 48, contains work by 19th-century Danish masters and European artists including Matisse, Picasso and Munch (closed Monday; 40kr, free Wednesday).

The superb **Ny Carlsberg Glyptotek** on HC Andersens Boulevard near Tivoli has an exceptional collection of Greek, Egyptian, Etruscan and Roman sculpture; a wing of paintings by Gauguin, Monet and Van Gogh and a complete set of Degas bronzes (closed Monday; 30kr, free Wednesday and Sunday).

COPENHAGEN (KØBENHAVN)

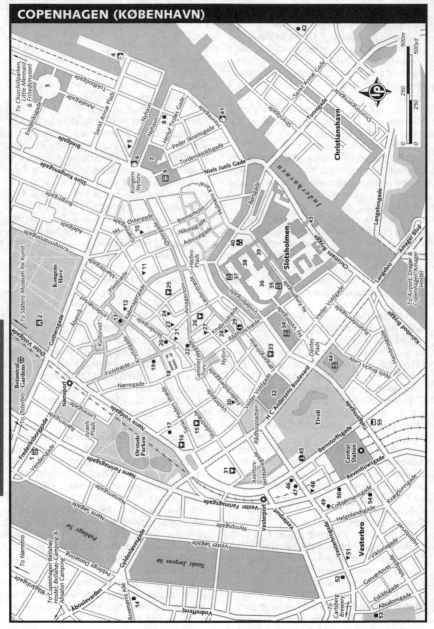

COPENHAGEN (KØBENHAVN)

PLACES TO STAY		OTHER		31	Pumphuset
8	Sømandshjemmet Bethel	1	Babel Internet Cafe	32	Rådhus
14	Cab-Inn Scandinavia	2	Rosenborg Slot	33	Mojo
52	Løven	3	Amalienborg Palace	34	Nationalmuseet
53	City Public Hostel	4	Boats to Oslo & Bornholm	35	Museum of Royal Coaches
54	Saga Hotel	6	Canal Boats	36	Christiansborg Palace
		7	Charlottenborg	37	Thorvaldsens Museum
PLACES TO EAT			(Royal Academy of Arts)	38	Royal Reception
5	Nyhavns Færgekro	9	Royal Theatre		Chambers
10	Netto Supermarket	13	Rundetårn	39	Folketing (Parliament)
11	Café Sommersko	15	Cosy Bar	40	Ruins of Absalon's Fortress
12	Studenterhusets	16	Never Mind	41	Boats to Malmö
21	Samos	17	LBL (Gay & Lesbian	42	Christiana
23	Jensen's Bøfhus		Organisation)	43	Royal Library
24	Pasta Basta	18	Vor Frue Kirke	44	Ny Carlsberg Glyptotek
27	Café Sorgenfri	19	University Library	45	Tourist Office
28	RizRaz	20	Kilroy Travels	46	Netpoint
30	Shawarma Grill	22	Wasteels	47	Steno Apotek (Pharmacy)
	House	25	Copenhagen Jazz House	49	Danwheel
48	Astor Pizza	26	Sebastian	50	Eurolines Office
51	Ankara	29	Use It	55	Main Post Office

Carlsberg Brewery At the brewery's visitor centre, Ny Carlsbergvej 140 (take bus No 6 westbound from Rådhuspladsen), free self-guided tours provide the lowdown on the history of Danish beer, capped off with a sampling of brew (closed weekends).

Organised Tours

Canal Tours Hour-long narrated boat tours wind through Copenhagen's canals from April to mid-October. The biggest company, DFDS Canal Tours, charges 50kr, but the best deal (20kr) is with Netto-Bådene; both leave from Nyhavn.

Special Events

Copenhagen Jazz Festival is the biggest event of the year, with 10 days of music in early July. For information, contact the festival office (☎ 33 93 20 13). Web site: www.cjf.dk

Places to Stay

Two places book *private rooms*: the tourist office (from 200/300kr plus a 50kr fee) and Use It (no fee and slightly lower rates). For contact details, see Information earlier.

Camping Bellahøj-Camping (☎ 38 10 11 50, *Hvidkildevej 66*), about 5km west of the centre, is open June to August; take bus No 11 from Rådhuspladsen. The year-round **Absalon Camping** (☎ 31 41 06 00, *Korsdalsvej 132*) is 9km west of the centre near Brøndbyøster station on the S-train's line B.

HI Hostels *Copenhagen Bellahøj* (☎ 38 28 97 15, fax 38 89 02 10, ✉ bellahoej@danhostel.dk, Herbergvejen 8), in a suburban area north-west of the centre, has 250 dorm beds (90kr) and 24-hour reception. From Rådhuspladsen you can take bus No 2-Brønshøj and get off at Fuglsangs Allé. It's closed from mid-January to 1 March.

Copenhagen Amager (☎ 32 52 29 08, fax 32 52 27 08, ✉ copenhagen-amager@danhostel.dk, Vejlands Allé 200), in Amager just off the E20, has 528 beds (90kr). Take the S-train to Sjælør station, then change to bus No 100S, which stops in front of the hostel. It's closed December to mid-January.

Both HI hostels are about 5km from the city centre.

City Hostels The *City Public Hostel* (☎ 33 31 20 70, fax 33 23 51 75, Absalonsgade 8) charges 120kr and is open early May to mid-August. Reception is 24 hours.

The 286-bed *Sleep-In* (☎ 35 26 50 59, fax 35 43 50 58, ✉ copenhagen@sleep-in.dk, Blegdamsvej 132A) is in Østerbro, a few kilometres north of the centre. Beds (80kr) are in a sports hall that's curtained off into two- to six-bed 'rooms'. It's open late June to 31 August. Take bus No 1 or 6 to Trianglen from Rådhuspladsen, then walk 300m south on Bledgdamsvej.

Sleep-In Green (☎ 35 37 77 77, Ravnsborggade 18), in the Nørrebro area close to cafes and nightlife, is open from late May to

DENMARK

late September. Beds cost 85kr. Take bus No 5 or 16, or walk north-west on Frederiksborggade over the canal.

The smallest operation, *YMCA Interpoint* (☎ *33 31 15 74, Valdemarsgade 15)* is open from the end of June to early August. There are only 28 beds (80kr), so call ahead for reservations. It's a 15-minute walk from Central Station (go along Vesterbrogade west until you reach Valdemarsgade), or take bus No 6 or 16.

The privately run *Sleep-In Heaven* (☎ *35 35 46 48,* ✆ *morefun@sleepinheaven.com, Struenseegade 7)*, in the Nørrebro area and open year-round, charges 100kr for a bed in a basement dorm. Take bus No 8 to the Kapelvej stop.

Hotels Løven (☎ *21 80 67 20, fax 33 15 86 46, Vesterbrogade 30)* has singles/doubles for 350/450kr and spacious flats from 550kr.

Saga Hotel (☎ *33 24 49 44, fax 33 24 60 33,* ✆ *booking@sagahotel.dk, Colbjørnsensgade 18)*, near Central Station, has rooms for 420/580kr.

Sømandshjemmet Bethel (☎ *33 13 03 70, fax 33 15 85 70, Nyhavn 22)* is top value, with unbeatable views of Nyhavn harbour and rooms for 395/495kr, or 495/595kr with private bath.

The quite modern *Cab-Inn Scandinavia* (☎ *35 36 11 11, fax 35 36 11 14,* ✆ *cab-inn@ cab-inn.dk, Vodroffsvej 57)* has compact rooms with private bath for 475/585kr.

Places to Eat

Central Station has a good *bakery*, a small, reasonably priced *food court* and a *supermarket* that's open to midnight daily. The *Netto* supermarket, near the east end of Strøget, has cheap prices.

Astor Pizza (*Vesterbrogade 7)*, just north of Central Station, has an all-you-can-eat pizza and salad bar for 39kr from 11 am to 5 pm, 49kr after 5 pm.

Ankara (*Vesterbrogade 35)* has a good-value buffet of Middle Eastern dishes for 39kr from noon to 4 pm, 59kr from 4 pm to midnight.

Shawarma Grill House at the west end of Strøget has good inexpensive felafels and kebabs. *Samos* (*Skindergade 29)*, just north of Strøget, has a top-notch buffet of Greek hot dishes and salads for 39kr from noon to 5 pm, 79kr after 5 pm.

At *RizRaz* (*Kompagnistræde 20)*, just south of Strøget, you can feast on a Mediterranean-style vegetarian buffet for 49kr (11.30 am to 5 pm) or 59kr (5 to 11 pm). The corner pub *Café Sorgenfri* (*Brolæggerstræde 8)* has reasonably priced Danish food.

For night owls, *Pasta Basta* (*Valkendorfsgade 22)* is open to at least 3 am and has a self-service table of cold pasta dishes and salads for 69kr. *Jensen's Bøfhus*, fronting Gråbrødre Torv, has steak or chicken lunch deals for 45kr until 4 pm.

Studenterhusets (*Købmagergade 52)* is a student hang-out with drinks, light eats and sandwiches. *Café Sommersko* (*Kronprinsensgade 6)* also draws a university crowd and has 50 different beers and a menu of moderately priced salads, sandwiches and hot dishes.

For a thoroughly Danish experience try *Nyhavns Færgekro* (*Nyhavn 5)*, right on the canal, which serves an all-you-can-eat buffet featuring 10 different herring dishes for 89kr (11.30 am to 5 pm).

Entertainment

The free publications *Nat & Dag* and *Musik Kalenderen* list concerts and entertainment schedules in detail. For free entertainment by street performers, stroll along Strøget, especially between Nytorv and Højbro Plads.

The westside Nørrebro area has a number of good bars and clubs, including *Rust* (*Guldbergsgade 8)*, a dance venue that attracts a college-age crowd, and *Stengade 30* (*Stengade 18)*, a lively alternative scene.

Closer to the centre is *Pumphuset* (*Studiestræde 52)*, with rock and blues groups. *Copenhagen Jazz House* (*Niels Hemmingsensgade 10)* is the city's leading jazz spot. *Mojo* (*Løngangstræde 21)* is big for blues. *Loppen* in Christiania has live music on Friday and Saturday, often rock or reggae.

Gay & Lesbian Venues Popular meeting places for both men and women are *Never Mind* (*Nørre Voldgade 2)* and also the cafe *Sebastian* (*Hyskenstræde 10)*. *Cosy Bar* (*Studiestræde 24)* is a late-night place for gay men.

Getting There & Away

Copenhagen's international airport is in Kastrup, 10km south-east of the centre. Most airline offices are north of Central

Station near the intersection of Vester Farimagsgade and Vesterbrogade.

Long-distance trains arrive and depart from Central Station. Most international buses also leave from Central Station; reservations on most routes can be made at Eurolines (☎ 33 88 70 00), Reventlowsgade 8.

DFDS Seaways' (☎ 33 42 30 00) ferry to Oslo departs daily at 5 pm and the Bornholmstrafikken (☎ 33 13 18 66) ferry to Bornholm departs nightly at 11.30 pm. Both leave from Kvæsthusbroen, north of Nyhavn. Boats to Malmö (☎ 33 32 12 60) leave frequently from Havnegade, south of Nyhavn.

Getting Around

To/From the Airport Trains run between the airport terminal and Central Station three times an hour (18kr, 12 minutes).

Public Transport Copenhagen has an extensive public transit system consisting of a metro rail network called S-train, whose 10 lines pass through Central Station (København H), and a vast bus system, whose main terminus is nearby at Rådhuspladsen.

The basic fare of 12kr for up to two zones covers most city runs and allows transfers between buses and trains for up to an hour. Third and subsequent zones cost 6kr more (maximum 42kr for travel throughout North Zealand). *Klippekort* (clip cards) good for 10 rides in two zones cost 80kr (three zones 110kr), or get a 24-hour pass allowing unlimited travel in all zones for 70kr.

On buses, fares are paid to the driver when you board, while on S-trains tickets are punched in the yellow time clock on the platform. For information on trains call ☎ 33 14 17 01, for buses call ☎ 36 13 14 15.

Taxi Taxis with *'fri'* signs can be flagged down; the cost is 22kr at flag fall plus about 10kr per kilometre (13kr at night and on weekends).

Bicycle Københavns Cykler, at Central Station, rents bicycles for 50kr a day. to find cheaper prices (35kr a day) walk a few blocks north-west to Danwheel at Colbjørnsensgade 3.

If you just want to ride in the city centre, look for a City Bike, a free-use bicycle that has solid spokeless wheels painted with sponsor logos. Deposit a 20kr coin in the stand to release the bike and return it to any rack to retrieve your coin.

Except during weekday rush hours, you can carry bikes on S-trains for 12kr.

AROUND COPENHAGEN

The **Louisiana Museum of Modern Art**, Denmark's foremost modern-art museum, is on a seaside knoll in a strikingly modernistic building – a fascinating place to visit even if you're not passionate about modern art. The museum is a 10-minute walk north on Strandvej from Humlebæk station, a 35-minute train ride from Copenhagen. It's open 10 am to 5 pm daily (to 10 pm Wednesday). Entry is 60kr.

Frilandsmuseet is a sprawling open-air museum of old countryside dwellings, workshops and barns in the town of Lyngby, a 10-minute walk from Sorgenfri station, which is 25 minutes from Central Station on the S-train's line B (closed Monday and from November to mid-April; 40kr).

Around Zealand

NORTH ZEALAND

Considering its proximity to Copenhagen, the northern part of Zealand (Danish: Sjælland) is surprisingly rural, with small farms and beech woodlands. One of the most popular day trips from Copenhagen is a loop tour taking in Frederiksborg Castle in Hillerød and Kronborg Castle in Helsingør, possibly with a stop at Fredensborg Palace in between.

Frederiksborg Castle

Hillerød, 30km north of Copenhagen, is the site of Frederiksborg Slot, an impressive Dutch Renaissance castle spread across three islands. The oldest part of the castle dates from Frederik II's time, though most of the present structure was built by his son Christian IV in the early 1600s.

The sprawling castle has a magnificent interior with wall-sized tapestries, gilded ceilings, royal paintings and antiques. It's open 10 am to 5 pm daily (to 3 pm from November to March); entry is 45kr.

Getting There & Away The S-train (A and E lines) runs every 10 minutes from Copenhagen to Hillerød (42kr, 40 minutes).

DENMARK

From Hillerød station follow the signs to Torvet and then continue along Slotsgade to the castle, a 15-minute walk in all.

Fredensborg Palace

Fredensborg, the royal family's summer residence, is an 18th-century Italianate mansion in the midst of formal gardens. Although the palace is not a must-see, the palace grounds, which border Denmark's second largest lake, make for pleasant walking. The palace interior can only be visited during July, from 1 to 5 pm (30kr).

Getting There & Away Fredensborg is midway along the rail line between Hillerød and Helsingør. Go left out of Fredensborg station and turn right onto the main road that runs through town to the palace, 1km away.

Helsingør

Helsingør (Elsinor) is a busy port town, with ferries shuttling across the Øresund strait to and from Sweden 24 hours a day. The tourist office (☎ 49 21 13 33), Havnepladsen 3, is opposite the train station.

Helsingør's top sight is **Kronborg Castle**, made famous as the Elsinore Castle in Shakespeare's *Hamlet* (closed Monday in winter). You can cross the moat and walk around the courtyard for free; tour the chapel, dungeons and royal quarters for 30kr; or get a combined ticket that includes the Danish Maritime Museum for 45kr.

The castle is on the north side of the harbour; the best way to get there is to walk past the tourist office up Brostræde and along historic Sankt Anna Gade.

Places to Stay *Helsingør Hostel* (☎ 49 21 16 40, fax 49 21 13 99, ❷ helsingor@ danhostel.dk, Nordre Strandvej 24), 2km north-west of the centre, has dorm beds/ doubles for 90/225kr. Beachside *Helsingør Camping* (☎ 49 21 58 56) is just east of the hostel. The tourist office books private *rooms* for 200/350kr, plus a 25kr fee.

Getting There & Away Trains from Hillerød (36kr, 30 minutes) run at least hourly. Trains from Copenhagen run a few times hourly (42kr, 55 minutes). For information on ferries to Helsingborg (16kr, 20 minutes), see Getting There & Away earlier in this chapter.

ROSKILDE

Roskilde, Denmark's original capital, was a thriving trade centre throughout the Middle Ages. It was also the site of Zealand's first Christian church, which was built by Viking king Harald Bluetooth in AD 980. Today it's a likeable, low-profile town worthy of a day trip from Copenhagen, from where there are frequent trains (42kr, 25 minutes).

Northern Europe's largest music festival rocks Roskilde each summer during the last weekend in June. The Roskilde tourist office (☎ 46 35 27 00) is at Gullandsstræde 15.

Things to See

Roskilde Domkirke Although most of Roskilde's medieval buildings vanished in fires over the centuries, the imposing cathedral still dominates the city centre. The cathedral has tall spires, a splendid interior and the crypts of 37 Danish monarchs. Take note of the 16th-century clock above the entrance, where a tiny St George on horseback marks the hour by slaying a yelping dragon. Entry is 12kr. The cathedral sometimes closes for weddings and funerals; check in advance by calling the tourist office.

Other City Sights From the north side of the cathedral, walk across a field where wildflowers blanket the unexcavated remains of Roskilde's original medieval town, continuing through a green belt all the way down to the **Viking Ship Museum**. This well-presented museum (52kr) contains five reconstructed Viking ships (circa AD 1000) excavated from the bottom of Roskilde Fjord in 1962; the harbourside grounds have workshops replicating Viking ships.

A short walk west along the harbour leads to the **Sankt Jørgensbjerg quarter**, where the cobbled walkway Kirkegade goes through a neighbourhood of old straw-roofed houses and into the courtyard of the 11th-century church, **Sankt Jørgensbjerg Kirke**.

Places to Stay & Eat

The tourist office books *private rooms* (150/300kr) for a 25kr reservation fee. *Roskilde Hostel* (☎ 46 35 21 84, fax 46 32 66 90, ❷ danhostel.roskilde@post.tele.dk, Vindeboder 7), adjacent to the Viking Ship Museum, has 100kr dorm beds.

On Skomagergade, *Strandberg Supermarket* has a cafeteria and *Jensen's Bøfhus* has inexpensive steak lunches. For a treat, the atmospheric Raadhus-Kælderen in the old town hall has a nice fish lunch for 68kr until 5 pm.

TRELLEBORG

Trelleborg, in the countryside of southern Zealand, is the best preserved of Denmark's four Viking ring fortresses. The earthen-walled fortress, which dates to AD 980, has two compounds, the inner of which is cut with gates at the four points of the compass. You can walk up onto the grassy circular rampart and readily grasp the fortress' precise geometric design. Cement blocks have been placed to show the outlines of the house foundations and interpretive plaques point out burial mounds and other features.

At Trelleborg's entrance there are a few replicated Viking buildings, including a Viking longhouse. Entry to the site is 35kr.

Getting There & Away

From Roskilde take a train to Slagelse (52kr, 33 minutes) and then either catch the infrequent bus No 312 to Trelleborg (12kr, 12 minutes), grab a taxi, or rent a bicycle from the shop near the Slagelse tourist office.

Bornholm

Bornholm, 200km east of Copenhagen, is a slow-paced island that makes for a delightful getaway. The centre of the island is a mix of wheat fields and forests, the coast is dotted with small fishing villages, and there's a scattering of 12th-century round churches.

The main transport hub, Rønne, has little to offer; catch the first bus to Gudhjem. In summer, bus No 7 leaves from the Rønne ferry terminal every two hours (from 8 am to 4 pm) and goes anticlockwise around the island, stopping at all major coastal villages.

Getting There & Away

Bornholmstrafikken (☎ 33 13 18 66) operates a ferry between Copenhagen and Rønne that leaves daily at 11.30 pm (189kr, seven hours). Add 62kr for a bunk, 52kr to take a bicycle. In midsummer there's also a daily ferry (except Wednesday) that leaves at 8.30 am and returns from Rønne at 3.30 pm.

The same company also operates several ferries a day to Rønne from Ystad, Sweden

(150kr one-way or same-day return, 1½ hours) and near-daily in the summer months from Sassnitz-Mukran, Germany (50/100kr weekdays/weekends, 3½ hours).

Another option is the train-ferry combination from Copenhagen to Rønne via Ystad, Sweden. This trip goes a few times a day (239kr, three hours).

GUDHJEM

Gudhjem is a pretty seaside village with half-timbered houses and sloping streets. The harbour was one of the settings for Bornholm novelist Martin Andersen Nexø's Oscar-winning film *Pelle the Conqueror*. The tourist office (☎ 56 48 52 10), Åbogade 7, is a block inland from the harbour.

Things to See & Do

At the dockside **Glasrøgeri** you can watch glass being hand blown. Stroll the footpath running south-east from the harbour for a pleasant coastal view. Gudhjem's shoreline is rocky, though sunbathers will find a small sandy beach at **Melsted**, 1km east. A bike path leads 4km south (inland) from Gudhjem to **Østerlars Rundkirke**, the most impressive of the island's round churches; bus Nos 3 and 9 also go by the church.

Places to Stay & Eat

Sletten Camping (☎ 56 48 50 71) is a 15-minute walk south of the village. Year-round *Gudhjem Hostel* (☎ 56 48 50 35, fax 56 48 56 35), at the harbourside bus stop, has 95kr dorm beds and books single/double *rooms* in private homes for 250/325kr.

Gudhjem Røgeri, a waterfront smoke-house, sells fish and salads deli-style, as well as pizza. It doubles as a nightspot with live folk music.

SANDVIG

Sandvig, a quiet village of attractive older houses, has a nice sandy beach right in town. Three kilometres south is Bornholm's best known sight, **Hammershus Slot**. These impressive castle ruins, dramatically perched on top of a sea cliff, date from the 13th century and are the largest in Scandinavia. There's an hourly bus to the ruins, but the best way to get there from Sandvig is via footpaths through the heather-covered hills of Hammeren – a wonderful hour-long hike. The trail begins down by the camping ground.

Places to Stay & Eat

Sandvig Familie Camping (☎ *56 48 04 47*) is near the beach on the north side of town. *Sandvig Hostel* (☎ *56 48 03 62, fax 56 48 18 62*), open 1 June to 1 October, is midway between Hammershus Slot and Sandvig; dorm beds cost 100kr, doubles 325kr. There are also moderately priced *pensions* in the village. There's a *snack bar* by the beach and a number of restaurants in the village centre.

CHRISTIANSØ

Tiny Christiansø is a charming 17th-century fortress island an hour's sail north-east of Bornholm. A seasonal fishing hamlet since the Middle Ages, Christiansø fell briefly into Swedish hands in 1658, after which Christian V decided to turn the island into an invincible naval fortress. By the 1850s the island was no longer needed as a forward base against Sweden and the navy withdrew. Soldiers who wanted to stay on as fishermen were allowed to live as free tenants in the old cottages. Their offspring, and a few latter-day fisherfolk and artists, currently constitute Christiansø's 100 residents. The entire island is an unspoiled reserve – there are no cats or dogs, no cars, and no modern buildings.

Christiansø is connected to a smaller island, Frederiksø, by a footbridge.

There's a **local history museum** in Frederiksø's tower and a great 360° view from Christiansø **lighthouse**. Otherwise the main activity is walking the footpaths along the fortified walls and batteries that skirt the island.

Places to Stay & Eat

Christiansø Gæstgiveriet (☎ *56 46 20 15*) has a few rooms with shared bath for 460kr including breakfast. In summer, *camping* (☎ *30 34 96 05*) is allowed in a small field at the Duchess Battery. There's a restaurant at the inn, a small food store and a snack shop.

Getting There & Away

Boats sail to Christiansø daily from Gudhjem and Monday to Saturday from Allinge between mid-May and mid-September. The mailboat from Svaneke makes the trip on weekdays all year round. All boats charge 145kr return on a day trip, 225kr for an open return.

Funen

Funen (Danish: Fyn) is Denmark's garden island. It's largely rural and green, with rolling woodlands, pastures, wheat fields and lots of old farmhouses. During May, the landscape is ablaze with solid patches of yellow rapeseed flowers.

The main railway line from Copenhagen runs straight through Odense, Funen's main city, and westward to Jutland. Svendborg and Faaborg are the main jumping-off points to Ærø, a scenic southern island.

Store Bælt (Great Belt), the channel that separates Zealand and Funen, was until a few years ago crossed only by boat. It's now spanned by Europe's longest combined road and rail bridge – the Storebæltsforbindelsen (Great Belt Fixed Link). If you're taking a train, the crossing is included in your rail fare; if you're driving there's a 225kr bridge toll.

ODENSE

Denmark's third largest city makes much ado about being the birthplace of Hans Christian Andersen. Of course, it plays down the fact that, after a fairly unhappy childhood, Hans got out of Odense as fast as he could.

Odense is an affable university city with lots of bike lanes and pedestrian streets, as well as an interesting cathedral and a number of worthy museums.

Orientation & Information

The tourist office (☎ 66 12 75 20) in the Rådhus is a 15-minute walk from the train station (closed Saturday afternoon and Sunday in the off season).

The cathedral is on Klosterbakken, two minutes from the tourist office; most other city sights are within walking distance. Net Café (☎ 65 91 02 78), Vindegade 43, offers Internet access from noon to midnight.

Things to See & Do

City Centre The east side of the city centre has some of Odense's oldest buildings; make a pleasant loop by strolling down Nedergade, a cobblestone street with leaning half-timbered houses and antique shops, and returning via Overgade. En route you pass **Vor Frue Kirke**, a 13th-century church.

Around the corner, **Møntergården**, a city museum at Overgade 48, has displays of Odense's history and a few 16th and 17th-century half-timbered houses that you can enter (closed Monday; 15kr).

At Hans Jensens Stræde 39, **HC Andersens Hus**, depicts Andersen's life story through his memorabilia and books (30kr). **HC Andersens Barndomshjem**, Munkemøllestræde 3, has a few rooms of exhibits in the house where Hans grew up (10kr).

Sankt Knuds Kirke, Odense's 13th-century Gothic cathedral, has an ornate gilded altar dating from 1520, but the cathedral's real intrigue lies in the basement, which holds the remains of a prior church and a glass case containing the skeleton of King Knud II, who in 1086 was killed in a tax revolt after unsuccessfully seeking sanctuary in the church.

The **Fyns Kunstmuseum**, in a stately Graeco-Roman building at Jernbanegade 13, contains a quality collection of Danish art, from paintings of the old masters to abstract contemporary works (closed Monday; 35kr).

Den Fynske Landsby This delightful open-air museum has period buildings authentically laid out like a small country village (55kr). The museum is in a green zone 4km south of the centre. You can take bus No 42 or, in summer, a boat (30kr) from Munke Mose down the river to Erik Bøglıs Sti, from where it's a 15-minute riverside walk to the museum.

Places to Stay
Odense Camping (☎ *66 11 47 02, Odensevej 102*) is 3.5km south of the city centre (take bus No 21 or 22). The tourist office books *rooms* in private homes for 175/300kr, plus a 25kr booking fee.

Odense City Hostel (☎ *63 11 04 25, fax 63 11 35 20)* is right at the train station, while *Odense Kragsbjerggaard Hostel* (☎ *66 13 04 25, fax 65 91 28 63, Kragsbjergvej 121)* occupies a former manor house 2km southeast of the centre via bus No 61 or 62; both have dorms for 100kr and pricier private rooms.

The pension-like *Det Lille Hotel* (☎/*fax 66 12 28 21, Dronningensgade 5)*, a 10-minute walk west of the train station, has straightforward rooms for 250/380kr. *Ydes*

Hotel (☎ *66 12 14 27, fax 66 12 14 31, Hans Tausensgade 11)* has pleasant rooms with bath for 330/450kr.

Places to Eat
The train station has a *bakery*, a *DSB Café*, a *Jensen's Bøfhus* with cheap lunches, and a *grocery store* that's open until midnight.

China Barbecue (Kongensgade 66) has a 49kr lunch buffet until 3 pm. *Café Biografen* at Brandts Klædefabrik is a student haunt with pastries, coffees, light meals and beer at reasonable prices. Another popular spot is *Birdy's Café (Nørregade 21)*, which has Mexican dishes for around 75kr.

Kærnehuset (Nedergade 6), a vegetarian collective, offers a 40kr meal at 6 pm Tuesday to Friday. *Naturkost (Gravene 8)* is a central health-food store.

Entertainment
Popular venues are *Ryan's*, a friendly Irish pub on Nørregade near Rådhus, and *Boogies (Nørregade 21)*, a dance spot that attracts students. The outdoor amphitheatre at *Brandts Klædefabrik* is a venue for free summer weekend concerts.

Getting There & Away
Odense is on the main railway line between Copenhagen (178kr, 1½ hours) and Århus (156kr, 1¾ hours). Buses leave from the rear of the train station.

Getting Around
In Odense you board city buses at the back and pay the driver (11kr) when you get off. The train station and tourist office sell an 'adventure pass' allowing free bus travel and museum entry (85/125kr for one/two days).

Bicycles can be rented for 45kr a day at City Cykler (☎ 66 13 97 83), Vesterbro 27, west of the city centre.

EGESKOV CASTLE
Egeskov is a gem of a Renaissance castle, complete with moat and drawbridge. Egeskov (literally 'oak forest') was built in 1554 in the middle of a small lake on top of a foundation of thousands of upright oak trunks. The expansive grounds include century-old privet hedges, English gardens and the 'a-maze-ing' bamboo grass labyrinth.

The castle is open 10 am to 5 pm daily (to 7 pm in July); the grounds usually stay open

DENMARK

an hour later. Entry to the grounds and an antique car museum is 60kr. To tour the castle interior is 50kr extra but it's most impressive from the outside.

Getting There & Away
Egeskov Castle is 2km west of Kvændrup on route 8. From Odense take bus No 801 to Kvændrup Bibliotek (36kr), where you can switch to bus No 920, which stops near the castle.

FAABORG
In the 17th century, Faaborg was a bustling harbour town with one of Denmark's largest fleets. Home to only 6000 people today, Faaborg retains many vestiges of that earlier era and its picturesque cobblestone streets and leaning half-timbered houses make for some pleasant ambling. Pick up a walking-tour map at the tourist office (☎ 62 61 07 07), adjacent to the bus station at Banegårdspladsen 2A.

Faaborg also has two fine museums. **Den Gamle Gaard**, at Holkegade 1, is an old merchant's house fitted out with period furnishings (25kr); and **Faaborg Museum** is a former winery at Grønnegade 75 that contains the best collection of Funen art in Denmark (30kr).

Places to Stay & Eat
Holms Camping (☎ 62 61 03 99) is 1km north of the town centre on route 43. The *Faaborg Hostel* (☎ 62 61 12 03, fax 62 61 35 08, Grønnegade 71), in a half-timbered building opposite the Faaborg Museum, has 90kr beds. *Christiansminde* (☎ 62 61 90 18, Assensvej 66), a guesthouse 1.5km west of the centre, has pleasant rooms for 210/320kr for singles/doubles.

Harlem Pizza on Torvet has long hours and good pizza, sandwiches and chicken. A fine upmarket option is the nearby *Ved Brønden*, which specialises in fish dishes.

Getting There & Away
Faaborg has no rail service. Bus Nos 961 and 962 from Odense, cost 48kr take an hour and run at least hourly to 11 pm.

There are numerous daily ferries to the nearby islands of Avernakø and Lyø (70kr return, bicycle 20kr) and a passenger boat to Bjørnø. For information on ferries to Ærø, see the Ærø section.

SVENDBORG
South Funen's largest municipality and a transit point for travel between Odense and Ærø, Svendborg itself is a rather ordinary town and there's not much reason to linger. The train and bus stations are two blocks north-west of the dock.

More appealing is the island of **Tåsinge**, just over the bridge from Svendborg, with its charming harbourside village of Troense and the nearby 17th-century castle **Valdemars Slot**, where the grounds and whitesand beach are open for free. Visitors can tour the castle's lavish interior for 55kr. In addition to the public bus, the MS *Helge* ferry carries passengers from Svendborg to Troense and Valdemars Slot every few hours in summer.

Places to Stay
Svendborg Hostel (☎ 62 21 66 99, fax 62 20 29 39, Vestergade 45), in the town centre, has 100kr beds. *Hotel Ærø* (☎ 62 21 07 60), opposite the Ærø ferry dock, has 13 straightforward rooms at 250/400kr for singles/doubles. The nearest camping facilities are on Tåsinge.

Getting There & Away
Trains depart from Odense hourly for Svendborg (52kr, one hour). Ferries to Ærøskøbing depart five times a day, the last at 10.30 pm in summer.

ÆRØ
Well off the beaten track, Ærø is an idyllic island with small fishing villages, rolling hills and patchwork farms. It's a great place to tour by bicycle _ the country roads are laced with thatched houses and old windmills, and the island has ancient passage graves and dolmens to explore.

Ærø has three main towns: Ærøskobing, Marstal and Søby. The Ærøskøbing tourist office (☎ 62 52 13 00) is near the waterfront at Vestergade 1. The Marstal tourist office (☎ 62 53 19 60) is at Havnegade 5, a few minutes walk south of the harbour.

Things to See & Do
Ærøskøbing A prosperous merchants' town in the late 17th century, Ærøskøbing has been preserved in its entirety and is one of the most handsome towns in Denmark. Its narrow cobblestone streets are tightly

lined with 17th- and 18th-century houses, many of them gently listing half-timbered affairs with hand-blown glass windows and decorative doorways.

The main attraction of Ærøskøbing is **Flaskeskibssamlingen**, at Smedegade 22, where Bottle Peter's lifetime work of 1700 ships-in-a-bottle and other local folk art are displayed in the former poorhouse (25kr).

Søby This town has a sizable fishing fleet and a popular yacht harbour. Five kilometres beyond Søby, at Ærø's northern tip, there's a pebble beach with clear water and a stone **lighthouse** with a view.

Marstal On the south-eastern end of the island, Marstal is Ærø's most modern town, though it too has a nautical character, with a **maritime museum** (30kr), shipyard and yacht harbour, plus a reasonably good beach on the south side of town.

Store Rise This village is the site of **Tingstedet**, a Neolithic Age passage grave in a field behind an attractive 12th-century church. A few kilometres to the south is **Risemark Strand**, the best of Ærø's few sandy beaches.

Places to Stay
There are camping grounds at Ærøskøbing, Søby and Marstal. The tourist offices have information on *B&Bs* around the island that average 340kr a double.

There's a *hostel* (☎ 62 52 10 44) in Ærøskøbing, 1km from town on the road to Marstal, open from 1 April to 31 October, and another in Marstal centre (☎ 62 53 10 64, *Færgestræde 29*), open from 1 May to 1 September.

In Ærøskøbing, the historic Hotel Ærøhus (☎ 62 52 10 03, *Vestergade 38*) has atmospheric rooms from 280/460kr. In Marstal, *Hotel Marstal* (☎ 62 53 13 52, *Dronningestræde 1A*), near the harbour, has 10 rooms for 270/395kr.

Places to Eat
All three towns have bakeries and restaurants. In Ærøskøbing on Vestergade, just west of the ferry dock, there's a small grocery store, a *rogeri* with inexpensive smoked fish and moderately priced restaurants.

At Marstal's harbour, there's a small food store and a simple *grill* with sandwiches. If you are looking for something more substantial, *Hotel Marstal* has a two-course daily special for 95kr.

Getting There & Away
There are year-round car ferries to Søby from Faaborg, to Ærøskøbing from Svendborg and to Marstal from Rudkøbing. All run about five times a day, take about an hour and charge 70kr a person, 20kr for a bike, 155kr for a car. If you have a car it's a good idea to make reservations (☎ 62 52 40 00).

There's also a ferry (☎ 62 58 17 17) between Søby and Mommark that runs a few times daily from spring to autumn at comparable fares.

Getting Around
Bus No 990 travels from Søby to Marstal via Ærøskøbing hourly on weekdays, half as frequently on weekends. A pass for unlimited one-day travel costs 52kr.

You can rent bikes for around 40kr a day at the hostel and camping ground in Ærøskøbing, Nørremark Cykelforretning at Møllevejen 77 in Marstal, and Søby Cykelforretning at Langebro 4 in Søby. The tourist office sells a 20kr cycling map.

Jutland

Thc Jutland (Danish: Jylland) peninsula, the only part of Denmark connected to the European mainland, was originally settled by the Jutes, a Germanic tribe whose forays included invading England in the 5th century. Jutland's southern boundary has been a fluid one, last drawn in 1920 when Germany relinquished its holdings in Sønderjylland.

Jutland's west coast has endless stretches of windswept sandy beaches, often a good kilometre wide and packed down hard enough to drive cars on. Most of the main cities, including Århus and Aalborg, are along the more sheltered east coast.

ÅRHUS
In the middle of Jutland's east coast, Århus has been an important trading centre and seaport since Viking times. Today it is Denmark's second largest city (population 265,000), a lively university city with more than 40,000 students. It has one of Denmark's best music and entertainment scenes,

DENMARK

a well-preserved historic quarter and plenty
to see and do.

The 10-day Århus Festival in early September turns the city into a stage for nonstop jazz, rock, classical music, theatre and
dance.

Orientation & Information

The train station is on the south side of the
city centre. The pedestrian shopping streets of
Søndergade and Sankt Clements Torv lead to
the cathedral in the heart of the old city.

The tourist office (☎ 89 40 67 00), in
Rådhus on Park Allé, is open 9.30 am to 6
pm weekdays, to 5 pm Saturday, to 1 pm
Sunday. Winter hours are shorter.

The main post office, next to the train
station, is open 9.30 am to 6 pm weekdays,
10 am to 1 pm Saturday.

Net-City (☎ 86 76 11 99), Frederiksgade
45, offers Internet access from noon to
midnight.

Kilroy Travels (☎ 86 20 11 44), Fredensgade 40, specialises in discount and
student travel.

Things to See & Do

Den Gamle By The Old Town is a fine
open-air museum of 75 half-timbered
houses brought here from around Denmark
and reconstructed as a provincial town,
complete with a functioning bakery, silversmith, bookbinder etc. It's on Viborgvej, a
20-minute walk west of the centre, and open
daily year-round. Entry is 55kr, though at
night you can walk the streets for free.

Århus Domkirke This impressive cathedral is Denmark's longest, with interesting
frescoes and a lofty nave that spans nearly
100m. The original Romanesque chapel at
the east end dates back to the 12th century,
while most of the rest of the church is 15th-
century Gothic.

Vor Frue Kirke This church off Vestergade
has a carved wooden altarpiece dating from
the 1530s, but far more interesting is what's
in its basement – the crypt of the city's original cathedral, dating from around 1060.
Enter via the stairway beneath the altar.

Vikinge-Museet Pop into the basement of
Unibank, Sankt Clements Torv 6, for a free
look at artefacts from a Viking village that

was excavated at this site in 1964 (closed
weekends).

Moesgård The Moesgård woods, 5km
south of the city centre, make for an absorbing half-day outing. The focal point is the
Moesgård Prehistoric Museum with quality
displays from the Stone Age to the Viking
Age (closed Monday in winter; 35kr). The
most unique exhibit is the 2000-year-old
Grauballe man, found preserved in a nearby
bog in 1952. The dehydrated, leathery body
is amazingly intact, right down to its red
hair and fingernails.

An enjoyable walking trail, dubbed the
prehistoric trackway, leads from behind the
museum through fields of grazing sheep to
Århus' best sandy **beach**. The marked trail
passes reconstructed historic sights including a dolmen, burial cists and an Iron Age
house. You can walk one way and catch a
bus back to town, or do the trail both ways
as a 5km loop. Bus No 6 from Århus train
station terminates at the museum, and bus
No 19 (summer only) at Moesgård beach;
both run about twice an hour.

Organised Tours

There are tours of the **Ceres Brewery** on
Tuesday, Wednesday and Thursday in summer. Passes (5kr) are distributed at the tourist office but tours often book out days ahead.

A guided 2½-hour bus tour leaves from
the tourist office (☎ 89 40 67 00 for bookings) at 10 am daily from mid-June to early
September. The 45kr tour is a good deal as it
includes entry into Den Gamle By and also
leaves you with a 24-hour public bus pass.

Places to Stay

The tourist office books *private rooms* for
175/275kr, plus a 25kr fee.

Camping *Blommehaven* (☎ 86 27 02 07)
has a seaside setting in the Marselisborg
woods, 6km south of Århus on bus No 19
or 6. It's open mid-April to mid-September.

Hostels The *Århus Hostel* (☎ 86 16 72 98,
fax 86 10 55 60, @ danhostel.aarhus@
get2net.dk, Marienlundsvej 10), at the edge
of the Risskov woods, 4km north of the city
centre, is reached by bus No 6 or 9. It's
closed mid-December to late January and
charges 90kr a bed.

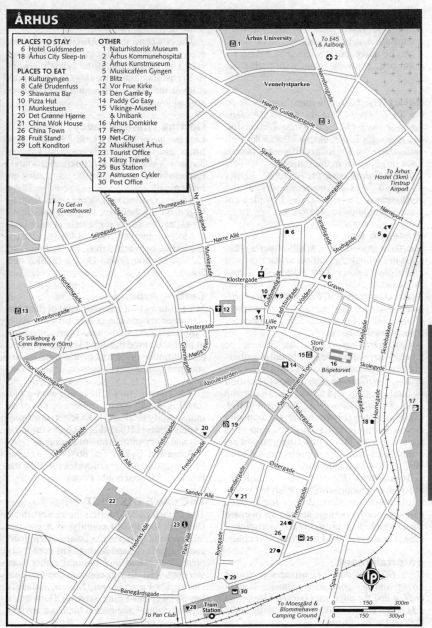

ÅRHUS

PLACES TO STAY
6 Hotel Guldsmeden
18 Århus City Sleep-In

PLACES TO EAT
4 Kulturgyngen
8 Café Drudenfuss
9 Shawarma Bar
10 Pizza Hut
11 Munkestuen
20 Det Grønne Hjørne
21 China Wok House
26 China Town
28 Fruit Stand
29 Loft Konditori

OTHER
1 Naturhistorisk Museum
2 Århus Kommunehospital
3 Århus Kunstmuseum
5 Musikcaféen Gyngen
7 Blitz
12 Vor Frue Kirke
13 Den Gamle By
14 Paddy Go Easy
15 Vikinge-Museet
   & Unibank
16 Århus Domkirke
17 Ferry
19 Net-City
22 Musikhuset Århus
23 Tourist Office
24 Kilroy Travels
25 Bus Station
27 Asmussen Cykler
30 Post Office

Århus University

To E45
& Aalborg

Vennelystparken

Nørrebrogade

Høegh Guldbergsgade

Sjællandsgade

To Århus
Hostel (3km)
Tirstrup
Airport

Nørregade

Nørreport

To Get-in
(Guesthouse)

Lollandsgade

Thunøgade

Ny Munkegade

Nørre Allé

Sejrøgade

Paradisgade

Studsgade

Hjortensgade

Munkegade

Klostergade

Guldsmedgade

Badstuegade

Volden

Graven

Vesterbrogade

To Silkeborg &
Ceres Brewery (50m)

Vestergade

Lille
Torv

Grønnegade

Møllestien

Mejlgade

Skolebakken

Thorvaldsensgade

Åboulevarden

Store
Torv

Bispetorvet

Skolegyde

Sankt Clements Torv

Fiskergade

Havnegade

Skolegade

Marstrandsgade

Christiansgade

Frederiksgade

Østergade

Fredensgade

Vester Allé

Sønder Allé

Sandergade

Fredriks Allé

Park Allé

Ryesgade

Spanien

Banegårdsgade

Train
Station

To Pan Club

To Moesgård &
Blommehaven
Camping Ground

0   150   300m
0   150   300yd

DENMARK

Århus City Sleep-In (☎ 86 19 20 55, fax 86 19 18 11, Havnegade 53), run by a youth organisation, is in a former mariners' hotel. It can be noisy, but it's cheap at 85kr for a dorm bed. A private room with bath costs 280kr.

Hotels The 62-room guesthouse *Get-in* (☎ 86 10 86 14, fax 86 10 86 24, Jens Baggesensvej 43), near Århus University, has rooms for 250/300kr, or 300/350kr with bath. There's a TV room and guest kitchen. Take bus No 7 from the station.

Hotel Guldsmeden (☎ 86 13 45 50, fax 86 13 76 76, Guldsmedgade 40), at the north side of the city centre, is a pleasant place with rooms for 445/645kr.

Places to Eat

The train station has a small *supermarket* open to midnight, a fruit stand out the front and a good bakery, *Loft Konditori*, across the street.

The countercultural *Kulturgyngen (Mejlgade 53)* serves one vegetarian and one meat dinner nightly for around 55kr, lunches for 35kr (closed Sunday).

Café Drudenfuss, on the corner of Graven and Studsgade, is a popular gathering place with inexpensive sandwiches and drinks. *Det Grønne Hjørne*, on the corner of Frederiksgade and Østergade, is a health food-oriented cafe with a 59kr lunch buffet. *China Town (Fredensgade 46)*, opposite the bus station, has 10 daily lunch specials for under 50kr. Or for just 20kr you can get a box lunch from the unpretentious *China Wok House* on Søndergade.

Munkestuen (Klostertorv 5) is a hole-in-the-wall restaurant with home-style Danish food (lunch for 55kr, dinner for 120kr). Cheaper nearby options are the *Shawarma Bar*, which has pitta bread sandwiches (25kr), and a branch of the *Pizza Hut* chain.

Entertainment

Blitz (Klostergade 34) attracts a young crowd and has good dance music. *Musikcaféen* and the adjacent *Gyngen (Mejlgade 53)* offer an alternative scene with rock, jazz and world music.

The Irish pub *Paddy Go Easy (Åboulevarden 60)* has football on big-screen TV and live music on weekends. The main gay and lesbian hang-out is the *Pan Club*

(Jægergårdsgade 42), a cafe and disco south of the train station.

The city concert hall, *Musikhuset Århus*, presents concerts by international performers. The free publication *What's On in Århus* lists current happenings in detail, pick it up at the tourist office and other venues around town.

Getting There & Away

Express buses (☎ 70 21 08 88) run a few times daily between Århus and Copenhagen's Valby station (200kr, 3½ hours). Express buses leave from the bus station on Fredensgade.

Trains to Århus, via Odense, leave Copenhagen on the hour to 10 pm (156kr, 3¼ hours) and there's a night train at midnight.

Mols-Linien (☎ 70 10 14 18) operates car ferries between Århus and Kalundborg (225kr, 2¾ hours) and Odden (375kr, one hour).

Getting Around

Most in-town buses stop in front of the train station or around the corner on Park Allé. City bus tickets are bought from a machine in the back of the bus for 13kr and are good for unlimited rides within the time period stamped on the ticket, which is about two hours.

You can also buy a 24-hour pass for bus travel in Århus county (90kr) or in Århus municipality alone (45kr). Or get a two-day 'Århus Pass' (110kr) that includes both the bus and entry into Århus museums.

Asmussen Cykler (☎ 86 19 57 00), at Fredensgade 54, rents bicycles for 50kr the first day, 35kr each additional day.

THE LAKE DISTRICT

The Danish Lake District, the closest thing Denmark has to hill country, is a popular 'active holiday' spot for Danes, with good canoeing, biking and hiking. The scenery is pretty, but placid and pastoral rather than stunning. The district contains the Gudenå, Denmark's longest river; Mossø, Jutland's largest lake; and Yding Skovhøj, Denmark's highest point – none of which are terribly long, large or high.

Silkeborg

Silkeborg, the Lake District's biggest town, has a rather bland and modern centre though it's bordered by green areas and waterways. The tourist office (☎ 86 82 19 11) is near the harbour at Åhavevej 2A.

Main attraction at the **Silkeborg Museum**, a cultural history museum on Hovedgårdsvej, is the Tollund Man, who was executed in 200 BC and whose leather-like body, complete with the rope still around his neck, was discovered in a nearby bog in 1950 (open daily in summer, less frequently in winter; 20kr).

To reach **Nordskoven**, a beech forest with hiking and bike trails, simply walk over the old railway bridge down by the hostel. You can rent bicycles at Schaufuss Cykeludlejning (☎ 86 81 39 38), Nørreskov Bakke 93, and canoes from Slusekiosken (☎ 86 80 08 93) at the harbour.

Places to Stay *Indelukkets Camping* (☎ 86 82 22 01, Vejlsøvej 7) is 2km south of town. *Silkeborg Hostel* (☎ 86 82 36 42, Åhavevej 55), a 10-minute walk east of the train station, has a scenic riverbank location; it's open March to November and charges 80kr. The tourist office has a list of *private rooms* priced around 175/300kr.

Getting There & Away Hourly trains connect Silkeborg with Skanderborg (37kr, 30 minutes) and Århus (59kr, 45 minutes), running via Ry.

Ry

A smaller town in a more rural setting than Silkeborg, Ry is a good place from which to explore the Lake District. The helpful tourist office (☎ 86 89 34 22), in the train station at Klostervej 3, is open until 5 pm weekdays, to 1.30 pm Saturday.

Things to See & Do The Lake District's most visited spot is the whimsically named **Himmelbjerget** (Sky Mountain) which, at just 147m, is one of Denmark's highest hills. It can be reached on a pleasant 6km hike from Ry, or by bus or boat. From the hill-top **tower** (5kr) there's a fine 360-degree view of the lakes and countryside.

Another good half-day outing is to cycle from Ry to **Boes**, a tiny hamlet with picturesque thatched houses and bounteous flower gardens. From there continue across the Danish countryside to **Øm Kloster**, the ruins of a medieval monastery (closed Monday;

30kr). The complete trip from Ry and back is about 18km.

Ry Cykel (☎ 86 89 14 91), Skanderborgvej 19, rents bikes for 50kr a day. If you want to explore the lakes in the district, Ry Kanofart (☎ 86 89 11 67), Kyhnsvej 20, rents canoes for 60kr an hour.

Places to Stay The lakeside *Sønder Ege Camping* (☎ 86 89 13 75, Søkildevej 65) is 1km north of town. *Ry Hostel* (☎ 86 89 14 07, ✉ mail@danhostel-ry.dk, Randersvej 88) is on the same lake. To get there from the train station cross the tracks, turn left and go 2.5km; or take the infrequent bus No 311. Dorm beds cost 100kr, double rooms from 225kr. The tourist office books *private rooms* from 175/250kr.

Getting There & Away Hourly trains connect Ry with Silkeborg (24kr, 20 minutes) and Århus (35kr, 30 minutes).

AALBORG

Jutland's second largest city, Aalborg is an industrial and trade centre, well known to bar hoppers as the leading producer of aquavit. Linked by bridge and tunnel, Aalborg spreads across both sides of the Limfjord, the long body of water that cuts Jutland in two.

Although it's often skipped over by travellers, Aalborg has a few worthwhile sites – the paramount attraction is Lindholm Høje, where you'll find Denmark's largest Viking burial ground.

Orientation & Information

The town centre is a 10-minute walk from the train and bus stations, north down Boulevarden. The tourist office (☎ 98 12 60 22), Østerågade 8, is open 9 am to 6 pm weekdays, to 5 pm Saturday; off-season hours are slightly shorter.

Things to See

Old Town The whitewashed **Buldolfi Domkirke** marks the centre of the old town, and has colourful frescoes in the foyer. On the cathedral's east side is the **Aalborg Historiske Museum** with interesting excavated artefacts (closed Monday; 20kr).

The alley between the museum and church leads to the rambling **Monastery of the Holy Ghost**, which dates to 1431. North-east of the cathedral on Østerågade are three noteworthy historic buildings: the **old town hall** (circa 1762), the five-storey **Jens Bangs Stenhus** (circa 1624) and **Jørgen Olufsens House** (circa 1616).

Nordjyllands Kunstmuseum This regional art museum at Kong Christian Allé 50, in a building designed by Finnish architect Alvar Aalto, has a fine collection of Danish modern art (closed Monday in the off season; 30kr). To get there, take the tunnel beneath the train station, cross Vesterbro and continue through the woods, a 10-minute walk in all.

Lindholm Høje On a hill-top pasture overlooking the city, Lindholm Høje is the site of 682 graves from the Iron and Viking Ages. Many of the **Viking graves** are marked by stones placed in an oval ship shape, with two larger end stones as stem and stern. It's an intriguing place to walk, as there's something almost spiritual about the site, which is open free from dawn to dusk. It's 15 minutes from Aalborg on bus No 6; cross the fence 50m beyond the bus stop and you're in the burial field.

A **museum** (20kr) depicting the site's history is at the opposite side of the field.

Places to Stay
Aalborg Hostel (☎ 98 11 60 44, fax 98 12 47 11, ✉ danhostel.aalborg@post5.tele.dk, Skydebanevej 50), at the marina 4km west of the centre, has dorm beds for 100kr and an adjacent *camping ground* with cabins; it's reached by bus No 8.

The tourist office books *rooms* in private homes for 200/300kr plus a 25kr fee. *Aalborg Sømandshjem* (☎ 98 12 19 00, fax 98 11 76 97, ✉ hansen@hotel-aalborg .com, Østerbro 27), about 1km east of the centre, has rooms for 475/625kr.

Places to Eat
Jomfru Ane Gade is a boisterous pedestrian street lined with restaurants and cafes. Popular eating spots include *Fellini*, an Italian restaurant with a 39kr lunch buffet, and *Frytøjet* with Danish and Mexican fare for around 50kr.

The pleasant *Café Luna*, a few minutes north of the train station on Boulevarden, has reasonably priced lasagne, sandwiches and salads. *Salling*, a department store on

Nytorv, has a basement supermarket with a good deli.

Algade, a pedestrian shopping street a block south of the tourist office, offers inexpensive options, including *Skibsted's Fish Market* at No 23 and *Café Underground* at No 21.

Cap off the night with a glass of wine at the smoulderingly romantic Duus Vinkjælder, a candle-lit, 300-year-old wine cellar in the Jens Bangs Stenhus.

Getting There & Away
Trains run at least hourly to Århus (127kr, 1½ hours) and every two hours to Frederikshavn (66kr, one hour). Express buses (☎ 70 10 00 30) run daily to Copenhagen (220kr, five hours).

Getting Around
City buses leave from Østerågade and Nytorv, near Burger King. The bus fare is 12kr to anywhere in greater Aalborg.

FREDERIKSHAVN
Frederikshavn is a major ferry town with a busy industrial port. There are a couple of local museums, but overall the town has no particular appeal and most travellers just pass through. If you're waiting for a train, you might want to climb the nearby whitewashed **gun tower** (15kr), a remnant of the 17th-century citadel that once protected the port.

An overhead walkway leads from the ferry terminal to the tourist office (☎ 98 42 32 66) at Skandiatorv 1. The train station and adjacent bus terminal are a 10-minute walk to the north.

Getting There & Away
Bus & Train Frederikshavn is the northern terminus of the DSB rail line. Trains run about hourly south to Aalborg (66kr) and on to Copenhagen (290kr). Nordjyllands Trafikselskab (NT) has both a train (40 minutes) and bus service (one hour) north to Skagen (36kr). NT sells a *klippekort* (clip ticket) for 74kr that's good for 120kr worth of travel.

Boat Stena Line (☎ 96 20 02 00) runs ferries from Frederikshavn to Gothenburg, Sweden (90kr to 140kr, two to 3¼ hours, six to 10 times daily); and to Oslo, Norway (140kr to 500kr; 10 hours; daily in summer, almost daily in winter).

Color Line (☎ 99 56 20 00) has ferries to Larvik, Norway (152kr to 372kr, 6¼ hours, daily).

Silja Line (☎ 96 20 32 00) operates a SeaCat catamaran to Gothenburg (100kr, two hours) daily in summer, almost daily in winter.

SKAGEN

A fishing port for centuries, Skagen's luminous heath and dune landscape was discovered in the mid-1800s by artists and in more recent times by summering urbanites.

The town's older neighbourhoods are filled with distinctive yellow-washed houses, each roofed with red tiles edged with white lines. Skagen is half-arty, half-touristy, with a mix of galleries, souvenir shops and ice-cream parlours.

Orientation & Information

Sankt Laurentii Vej, Skagen's main street, runs almost the entire length of this long, thin town, never more than five minutes from the waterfront. The tourist office (☎ 98 44 13 77) is in the train/bus station at Sankt Laurentii Vej 22.

Things to See & Do

Grenen Denmark's northernmost point is the long curving sweep of sand at Grenen, 3km north-east of Skagen. From the end of route 40 it's a 30-minute walk out along this vast beach to its narrow tip where the waters of the Kattegat and Skagerrak meet.

Skagens Museum This notable museum, Brøndumsvej 4, displays the paintings of PS Krøyer, Michael and Anna Ancher and other artists who flocked to Skagen between 1830 and 1930 to 'paint the light' (50kr).

Skagen By-og Egnsmuseum Evocatively presented, this open-air museum depicts Skagen's maritime history with the homes of fisherfolk and a picturesque old windmill (closed December to February and weekends in spring and autumn; 30kr). It's a 15-minute walk from the train station, west down Sankt Laurentii Vej, then south on Vesterled.

Tilsandede Kirke This whitewashed medieval church tower (closed September to May; 8kr) still rises up above the sand dunes

that buried the church and surrounding farms in the late 1700s. The tower, in a nature reserve, is 5km south of Skagen. By bike, take Gammel Landevej from Skagen and follow route 40.

Places to Stay & Eat

Grenen Camping (☎ 98 44 25 46), 1.5km north-east of Skagen centre, has a fine seaside location.

Skagen Hostel (☎ 98 44 22 00, fax 98 44 22 55, ✉ danhostel.skagen@adr.dk, Rolighedsvej 2), 1km west of the centre, has dorm beds for 100kr, singles/doubles from 250/300kr. The tourist office books *private rooms* for around 200/350kr, plus a 50kr fee.

Marienlund Badepension (☎ 98 44 13 20, ✉ badepension@marienlund.dk, Fabriciusvej 8), near the open-air museum, charges 280/530kr.

There are *pizzerias*, a *kebab shop*, a *burger joint* and an *ice-cream shop* on Havnevej. *Super Brugsen*, a grocery store on Sankt Laurentii Vej just west of the tourist office, has a bakery.

Getting There & Away

Either a bus or a train leaves Skagen station for Frederikshavn (36kr) about once an hour. The seasonal Skagerakkeren bus (No 99) runs between Hirtshals and Skagen (30kr, 1½ hours, six daily) from mid-June to mid-August.

HIRTSHALS

Hirtshals' character comes from its commercial fishing harbour and ferry terminal. The main street is lined with supermarkets catering to Norwegian shoppers who pile off the ferries to load up with relatively cheap Danish meats and groceries. The tourist office (☎ 98 94 22 20) is at Nørregade 40.

Hirtshals' main sight for nonshoppers is **Nordsømuseet**, an impressive aquarium that recreates a slice of the North Sea in a huge four-storey tank, Europe's largest (90kr).

Hirtshals Hostel (☎ 98 94 12 48, Kystvejen 53), 1km west of the train station, has 95kr dorm beds.

Getting There & Away

Train Hirtshals' main train station is 500m south of the ferry harbour. A private-line railway connects Hirtshals with Hjørring (18kr, 20 minutes). From Hjørring you can

DENMARK

take a DSB train to Aalborg (52kr) or to Frederikshavn (37kr).

Boat Color Line (☎ 99 56 20 00) runs year-round ferries to the Norwegian ports of Oslo (8¾ hours), Moss (nine hours) and Kristiansand (2½ to five hours). Fares on all three routes are from 152kr (midweek) to 372kr (summer weekends).

ESBJERG

Esbjerg was established as a port in 1868 following the loss of the Schleswig and Holstein regions to Germany. It's now Denmark's fifth-largest city, the centre of its North Sea oil activities and the country's largest fishing harbour. Although it has its fair share of early 20th-century buildings, Esbjerg lacks the intrigue found in the medieval quarters of other Danish cities and isn't on the itinerary of most travellers unless they're heading to or from the UK.

Torvet, the city square, is bordered by cafes, a bank, the post office and the tourist office (☎ 75 12 55 99). The train and bus stations are about 300m east of Torvet; the ferry terminal is 1km south.

Places to Stay

Three kilometres north-west of the city centre (bus No 4 or 12), *Esbjerg Hostel* (☎ 75 12 42 58, ☺ esbjerg@danhostel.dk, Gammel Vardevej 80) has dorm beds for 100kr, doubles for 290kr. The tourist office books *private rooms* at 175/300kr.

Getting There & Away

Trains between Esbjerg and Copenhagen (256kr, 3¼ hours) run about hourly until 10 pm.

For ferry service to the UK, see the Getting There & Away section earlier in this chapter.

LEGOLAND

At Legoland (☎ 75 33 13 33), the popular theme park in the town of **Billund**, 45 million plastic blocks have been arranged into a world of miniature cities, Lego pirates, safari animals and amusement rides. Though it's a mecca for kids who have grown up with Lego blocks, most adults will find Legoland less riveting.

The park is open 10 am to 8 pm daily (to 9 pm in midsummer) from April to late October. Admission is 145kr (but free after

the rides stop, two hours before closing). There are frequent buses from Vejle to Legoland (41kr, 25 minutes), as well as bus tour packages from many cities.

RIBE

Ribe, the oldest town in Scandinavia, dates back to AD 869 and was an important medieval trading centre. With its crooked cobblestone streets and half-timbered 16th-century houses, it's like stepping into a living history museum. The entire old town is a preservation zone, with more than 100 buildings in the National Trust.

Almost everything, including the hostel and train station, is within a 10-minute walk of Torvet, the town square which is dominated by a huge Romanesque cathedral. The tourist office (☎ 75 42 15 00), also at Torvet, is open to 5.30 pm daily in summer (to 2 pm Sunday).

Things to See & Do

You can climb the **cathedral steeple** for a towering view of the countryside (10kr). **Ribes Vikinger**, a substantial museum opposite the train station, has archaeological displays of Ribe's Viking history (45kr), while **Ribe Vikingecenter**, Lustrupvej 4, 3km south of the centre, is a recreated Viking village with costumed interpreters (50kr). **Ribe Kunstmuseum**, Skt Nicolajgade 10, has a good collection of 19th-century Danish art (30kr).

Places to Stay & Eat

The friendly *Ribe Hostel* (☎ 75 42 06 20, fax 75 42 42 88, ☺ ribedanh@post5.tele.dk, Skt Pedersgade 16) has dorm beds for 100kr, doubles for 295kr. The tourist office maintains a list of *rooms* in private homes from 175/275kr.

A few in-town taverns rent upstairs rooms for around 275/500kr with breakfast, including *Backhaus* (☎ 75 42 11 01, fax 75 42 52 87, Grydergade 12) and *Weis Stue* (☎ 75 42 07 00, Torvet).

On Nederdammen, between the hostel and Torvet, there's *Pizza Expressen*, with pizza by the slice, and *Peking House*, with Chinese lunch specials from 25kr.

Getting There & Away

Trains from Esbjerg to Ribe take 40 minutes and cost 37kr.

TØNDER

Tønder is another historic southern town that retains a few curving cobblestone streets with half-timbered houses. Its high point is during the last weekend of August when the Tønder Festival (☎ 74 72 46 10), one of Denmark's largest, brings a multitude of international and Danish folk musicians to town. The tourist office (☎ 74 72 12 20) is at Torvet 1.

Things to See & Do

Tønder Museum This museum at Kongevej 51, a 10 minute walk east of the train station, has regional history exhibits, including Tønder lace, once considered among the world's finest, and a wing with Danish surrealist and modern art (closed Monday in winter; 30kr).

Møgeltønder Slotsgade, the main street of this fetching village, is cobblestoned and lined with period houses sporting thatched roofs and colourful wooden doors. At one end of Slotsgade is the private castle of Prince Joachim and a small public park, while at the other end is a 12th-century church with one of the most lavish interiors in Denmark. Buses run from Tønder (4km west via route 419) hourly on weekdays, less frequently on weekends; or rent a bicycle at the cycle shop near the train station.

Places to Stay & Eat

Tønder Hostel (☎ 74 72 35 00, fax 74 72 27 97, @ danhostel@tonder-net.dk, Sønderport 4), on the east side of the centre, a 15-minute walk from the train station, has dorm beds for 100kr, doubles for 300kr. *Tønder Camping (☎ 74 72 18 49, Holmevej 2)* is just beyond the hostel.

The tourist office maintains a list of *private rooms* for around 175/250kr.

There's a *market* selling fruit and cheese at Torvet on Tuesday and Friday mornings. A short walk east of Torvet is *Spisehuset Asian (Østergade 37)*, which has inexpensive Chinese and grilled items; *Pizzeria Italiano (Østergade 40)*, with pizza and pasta; and an adjacent *bakery*.

Getting There & Away

Tønder is on route 11, 4km north of the German border. Trains run hourly on weekdays and slightly less frequently on the weekends from Ribe (52kr, 50 minutes) and Esbjerg (74kr, 1½ hours).

Estonia

Estonia (Eesti) is just 80km across the Gulf of Finland from Helsinki, and both socially and economically it's creeping closer week by week. Only fully independent since August 1991, Estonia's transition from Soviet socialist republic to western-style economy has been little short of miraculous. There are still certain problems with some of what the West would take for granted (hot water is sometimes not available) but things are far less problematic than just a few years ago.

Estonia is more Scandinavian in look and feel than Latvia or Lithuania. However, Estonia's German past lingers and is particularly evident in Tallinn's medieval Old Town, the best preserved Old Town in Eastern Europe. Tallinn is the hub of Estonian life, but Tartu (the second largest city), the coastal town of Pärnu, and the islands of Saaremaa and Hiiumaa are also appealing destinations.

Facts about Estonia

HISTORY

Estonia's pagan clans encountered Scandinavians (pushing east) and Slavs (pushing west) in the 8th to 12th centuries. However, they were little influenced from outside until the 12th century, when German traders and missionaries were followed by knights unleashed by Pope Celestinus III's 1193 call for a crusade against the northern heathens. Within about 25 years, what is now Latvia and the southern half of Estonia had been subjugated. Northern Estonia fell to Denmark.

In 1346 Denmark sold northern Estonia to German knights, sealing Estonia's servitude to German nobility until the early 20th century. Sweden, a rising power, took northern Estonia between 1559 and 1564 and southern Estonia in the 1620s, consolidating Estonian Protestantism. Under Peter the Great, Russia smashed Swedish power in the Great Northern War (1700-21), and Estonia became part of the Russian empire.

Russia's Soviet government, eager to get out of WWI, abandoned the Baltic region to Germany with the 1918 Treaty of Brest-Litovsk. The Bolsheviks then tried to win Estonia, Latvia and Lithuania back but were beaten by local opposition and outside military intervention – in Estonia's case, a British fleet and volunteer forces from Scandinavia. Damaged by the war and hampered by the disruption of trade with Russia and the world slump, independent Estonia suffered dire economic problems.

The Molotov-Ribbentrop Pact signed on 23 August 1939, which Nazi Germany and the USSR agreed on mutual nonaggression, secretly divided Eastern Europe into German and Soviet spheres of influence. The Baltics ended up in the Soviet sphere and by August 1940 they were under occupation, Communists had won 'elections', and the states had been 'accepted' into the USSR. When Hitler invaded the USSR in 1941, many in the Baltics saw the Germans as liberators, but during the German occupation an estimated 5500 people died in concentration camps.

There were demonstrations by Estonian students against 'Sovietisation' as early as 1980. By 1988 a reformist popular front had been formed in each republic to press for democratic change. Like Latvia and Lithuania, Estonia paid lip service to *perestroika* while dismantling its Soviet institutions. On 23 August 1989, the 50th anniversary of the Molotov-Ribbentrop Pact, an estimated two million people formed a human chain across all three republics, many of them calling for secession from the USSR. In November, Moscow granted the republics economic autonomy.

ESTONIA

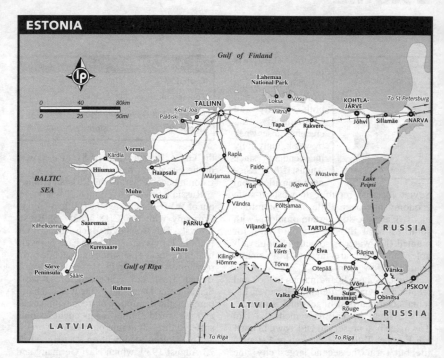

ESTONIA

In the spring of 1990 the Estonian Supreme Soviet – now called the Supreme Council or parliament – reinstated the pre-WWII constitution, but allowed a 'transition period' for independence to be negotiated. Estonia announced full independence on 20 August 1991.

Immediately following independence, ethnic tensions between Estonians and Russians arose. The several thousand Russian troops who remained on Estonian territory following the demise of the Soviet empire added further fuel to the fire. Under international pressure, the last Russian military personnel departed from Estonian soil on 31 August 1994.

Although Estonia's government plans to be ready for accession to the EU by 2003, it is unlikely to achieve full membership before 2005.

GEOGRAPHY
Estonia (45,277 sq km) is the smallest of the Baltic countries, slightly bigger than Denmark. Suur Munamägi (318m) in the southeast is the highest point in Estonia (and the Baltic countries). Nearly 50% of the land is forested. Offshore there are over 1500 islands, the biggest being Saaremaa to the west.

CLIMATE
From May to September daytime maximum temperatures are usually between 14°C and 22°C. July and August, the warmest months, are also the wettest. May, June and September are more comfortable. Mid-June is also favoured by 'white nights', when the skies darken for only a few hours each night.

April and October deliver cold, sharp, wintry days, as well as mild spring-like or autumnal ones. There's usually snow on the ground from December to late March.

POPULATION & PEOPLE
Estonia's population is 1.44 million, 65% of which is Estonian, 28% Russian, 2.5% Ukrainian and 1.5% Belorussian.

LANGUAGE
Like Finnish, Estonian is a Finno-Ugric language, part of the Ural-Altaic language family. English is on its way to becoming the lingua franca of the Baltic countries and many Estonians speak some. With older

people, German is often of more use. Russian can also be handy.

See the Language Guide at the back of this book for pronunciation guidelines and useful words and phrases.

Facts for the Visitor

HIGHLIGHTS
Tallinn's Old Town with its cobbled streets and gingerbread-like facades is a definite highlight. The city's numerous bars and inexpensive clubs, open virtually round the clock (especially in summer), make for many memorable evenings. The locals rave about the island of Saaremaa, which represents for them everything that is best about Estonia – solitude and nature.

SUGGESTED ITINERARIES
Three days
  Divide your time between Tallinn (with an evening walk along the Pirita waterfront) and Tartu.
One week
  Spend two days in Tallinn (don't miss Pirita and Keila-Joa), a day in Lahemaa National Park, one or two days on Saaremaa (don't miss Kuressaare and the Sõrve Peninsula), and a day or two in Tartu.

TOURIST OFFICES
There are tourist information centres all over Estonia. The Estonian Tourist Board (☎ 641 1420, 📧 info@tourism.ee), Mündi tänav 2, Tallinn, is also helpful.

Estonian embassies and consulates are often happy to answer questions relating to tourism and travel.

EMBASSIES & CONSULATES
Estonian Embassies Abroad
Estonian embassies abroad include:

Australia (☎ 02-9810 7468,
  📧 eestikon@ozc.com.au) 86 Louisa Road, Birchgrove, NSW 2041
Finland (☎ 9-622 0260, 📧 sekretar@estemb.fi) Itäinen Puistotie 10, 00140 Helsinki, Suomi
Latvia (☎ 7820 460,
  📧 sekretar@riia.vm.lv) Skolas 13, Rīga
Lithuania (☎ 2-220 486,
  📧 sekretar@estemb.lt) Mickeviciaus 4a, Vilnius
UK (☎ 020-7589 3428, 📧 loa@estonia.gov.uk) 16 Hyde Park Gate, London SW7 5DG
USA (☎ 202-588 0101,
  📧 info@estemb.org) 2131 Massachusetts Avenue, NW, Washington DC 20008
  Consulate: 660 3rd Avenue, 26th floor, New York, NY (☎ 212-883 0636)

Foreign Embassies in Estonia
The following are in Tallinn (area code ☎ 2):

Australia (☎ 650 9308, fax 667 8444)
  Kopli tänav 25
Canada (☎ 627 3310) Toomkooli tänav 13
Latvia (☎ 646 1313, fax 631 1366)
  Tõnismägi tänav 10
Lithuania (☎ 631 4030, 641 2014 for visas, fax 641 2013) Uus tänav 15
UK (☎ 667 4700, fax 667 4724) Wismari tänav 6
USA (☎ 631 2021, fax 631 2025)
  Kentmanni tänav 20

MONEY
Estonia introduced its own currency, the kroon (EEK), in June 1992. The kroon comes in one, two, five, 10, 25, 50, 100 and 500EEK denomination notes. One kroon is divided into 100 sents, and there are coins of five, 10, 20 and 50 sents as well as one and five EEK.

The best currencies to bring into the Baltics are US dollars or German marks, though most western currencies are perfectly acceptable. It is easy to change one Baltic currency into another, although rates are not always favourable.

A limited amount of travellers cheques may be useful, though commissions are often high. Credit cards are widely accepted, especially at the upper end of the market. A Visa card is particularly useful as there are now a fair number of Visa ATMs in Estonia.

Exchange Rates

country	unit		kroon
Australia	A$1	=	10.02EEK
Canada	C$1	=	11.92EEK
euro	€1	=	15.67EEK
France	1FF	=	2.39EEK
Germany	DM1	=	8.01EEK
Ireland	IR£1	=	19.89EEK
Netherlands	f1	=	7.11EEK
UK	UK£1	=	25.59EEK
USA	US$1	=	117.59EEK

Tipping
Tipping is not traditional in Estonia, but nobody is going to complain if you leave 10% or so on top of the bill.

ESTONIA

POST & COMMUNICATIONS

Mail service in and out of Estonia isn't too bad. Air-mail rates for letters/postcards (up to 20g) are 5.50/5.20EEK to European countries, 7/6.70EEK to the USA, Canada and Australia. Stamps can only be bought at post offices, tourist information offices and hotels.

Estonia's country code is ☎ 372. When calling from abroad, drop the initial 0 from Estonian area codes. If you want to make an international call from within Estonia dial ☎ 00 followed by the country code and telephone number. A three-minute call to the USA costs about US$4.40.

To call other cities within Estonia, dial ☎ 0 followed by the area code and phone number. Public telephones accept phonecards (30, 50 or 100EEK), which are available at post offices, hotels and street-side kiosks.

INTERNET RESOURCES

The Estonia-Wide Web (www.ee) is an informative Web site, and the *Tallinn In Your Pocket* guide also has a useful homepage (www.inyourpocket.com).

TIME

Estonian time is GMT/UTC plus two hours.

WOMEN TRAVELLERS

Unaccompanied women may want to avoid the sleazier bars and beer cellars. In some tourist hotels prostitution is a fact of life – if you are a woman sitting alone in a lobby, corridor or cafe, you may be propositioned.

GAY & LESBIAN TRAVELLERS

The overall attitude is more of curiosity than antagonism; the media have run many gay-positive articles since the topic opened up in the early 1990s. For information, contact the Estonian Gay League (☎ 056 607 654, ✆ eluell@saturn.zzz.ee), PO Box 142, Tallinn EEOO90.

DANGERS & ANNOYANCES

Theft from hotel rooms is a danger in all the Baltics, especially at lower-end hotels. Street crime has also become an unfortunate fact of contemporary life, and it is wise to avoid walking alone along darkened routes.

Most of the surly, rude, obstructive goblins employed in service industries during the Soviet era have miraculously become more pleasant, but there are still a few hangovers from the bad old days.

BUSINESS HOURS

Most shops in Estonia are open 9 or 10 am to 6 pm weekdays and to 4 or 5 pm Saturday, with many open on Sunday. Restaurants usually open from 11 am to around midnight.

Museum opening hours vary, but they are nearly always open 11 am to 4 pm and are usually closed Monday and/or Tuesday.

PUBLIC HOLIDAYS & SPECIAL EVENTS

Estonian national holidays are 1 January, 24 February (1918 Independence Day), Good Friday, 1 May (May Day), 23 June (Victory Day), 24 June (Jaanipäev), 21 August (New Independence Day), 26 December (Boxing Day).

The biggest occasion of the year is the night of 23 June – Jaanipäev (St John's Eve) – which, despite its Christian tag, is a celebration of pagan Midsummer's Night. The Baltika International Folk Festival (usually mid-July) – a week of music, dance and parades – is held in each Baltic capital in turn, taking place in Tallinn in 2001. The All-Estonian Song Festival, which climaxes with a choir of up to 30,000 people on a vast open-air stage performing to an audience of 100,000, is held every four years; it is next in Tallinn in 2003. Smaller annual festivals include the Tallinn Old Town Days and Tartu's popular Jazz Festival (both in June).

ACCOMMODATION

Though you can pitch a tent at most *kämpingud* (camping grounds), it's more common to stay in wooden cabins or brick bungalows. Camping grounds are usually open mid-May to early September.

The Estonian Youth Hostel Association (☎ 646 1457, ✆ eyha@online.ee, Tatari tänav 39-310), open 9 am to 7 pm weekdays, has some 15 hostels throughout Estonia. Advance bookings are recommended. Accommodation is mainly in small, two to four-bed rooms with prices between 100EEK and 200EEK a person, with a 10% discount for HI cardholders. See their Web site for more information: www.eyha.jg.ee.

Many tourist offices book private rooms (averaging 295/495EEK for singles/doubles) and farmstays (from 150EEK per person).

There is a shortage of budget hotels in Estonia, and those that do exist are often fully booked in summer.

FOOD & DRINKS

There are dozens of decent restaurants and cafes in Estonia, from semi-expensive western-style places to cheap cafeterias and food stands. Increasingly restaurants include at least one *taimetoit* (vegetarian dish) on the menu. Estonian specialities tend to be drenched in mayonnaise and sour cream.

A few helpful menu items include: *leib/sai* (bread/white bread), *supp* (soup), *liha* (meat), *looma* (beef), *sea* (pork), *kana* (chicken), *kala* (fish), *forrell* (smoked trout), *köögiviljad* (vegetables), *puuvili* (fruit), *juust* (cheese) and, of course, *arve* (the bill/check).

Õlu (beer), the favourite alcoholic drink in Estonia, is sold for around 10EEK a bottle, 25EEK in restaurants and bars. *Viin* (vodka) and *konjak* (brandy) are also popular. Try the delicious national liquer, Vana Tallinn.

Getting There & Away

For travel to or through parts of the CIS (such as St Petersburg or Kaliningrad), look into the visa situation well in advance.

BUS

Buses are the cheapest but least comfortable way of reaching Estonia. Eurolines (☎ 601 0700), Lastekodu tänav 46, in Tallinn, runs direct buses to Tallinn from Oslo, Stockholm, Frankfurt, Berlin, Munich, Stuttgart and Bremen daily. Other buses run from Tallinn to Vilnius (300EEK, 10½ hours, twice a day) and Rīga (200EEK to 250EEK, six hours, 13 a day).

Eurolines has booking agents throughout Germany; its main office is Deutsche Touring (☎ 069 7903 240), Römerhof 17, Berlin.

Buses leave Tallinn for St Petersburg (180EEK, eight hours) four times daily. There is also one bus daily from Tallinn to Kaliningrad (262EEK).

TRAIN

There is no longer a direct train between Tallinn and Rīga, and the *Baltic Express* between Warsaw and Tallinn is no longer running.

Between St Petersburg and Tallinn there is one overnight train each way (256EEK, nine hours;180EEK for open, *platzkart* seating) for the pleasure of being hassled by border guards at 3 am. There's also a nightly train between Moscow (St Petersburg station) and Tallinn (608EEK, 17hours).

BOAT
Finland

There are about 25 ferries and hydrofoils crossing between Helsinki and Tallinn every day. The operating companies all offer slight student discounts and charge higher prices for weekend travel. Hydrofoils make the trip in just over an hour.

Tallink has both ferries (☎ 631 8312) and *Tallink Express* hydrofoils (☎ 631 8320) running throughout the day. Tickets on the hydrofoil range from 300-380EEK, and on the larger ferry, from 270-320EEK. Its downtown office (☎ 640 3641) is at Pärnu maantee 12. In Helsinki, the booking office (☎ 9-2282 139) is at Etelaranta 14.

Lindaline (☎ 641 2412), make six return hydrofoil crossings daily. A one-way trip costs from 260EEK (10% discount for ISIC holders). Eckerö Line (☎ 631 8606) operate a daily auto catamaran, with one-way tickets starting at 180EEK. Nordic Jet Line (☎ 613 7000, 📧 njl@njl.ee) has several auto catamarans, making the trip in just over an hour several times a day; tickets range from 445EEK to 525EEK, including your car.

Silja Line (☎ 631 8331 or 631 0400) operates an overnight cruise ship, costing from 270EEK to 1080EEK, depending on whether or not you want a cabin. The ship also makes another run in afternoons, costing from 270EEK to 430EEK, taking 3½ hours.

Sweden

The two Estline (☎ 644 8308, Aia tänav 5a) ferries, *Regina Baltica* and the smaller *Baltic Kristina*, sail between Tallinn and Stockholm daily in summer. The trip takes around 15 hours. A one-way ticket costs 480EEK, plus either 90EEK for a deck seat or up to 800EEK more for cabins of different categories. Tickets should be booked in advance through the Estline office in Tallinn or the Frihamnen (Free Harbour) in Stockholm (☎ 08-667 0001). Web site: www.estline.ee

Getting Around

Within Estonia, buses are generally cheaper, more frequent and definitely faster than trains, but make sure you get an *ekspress* or *kiir* (fast) bus. On Estonian bus tickets, *koht* is your seat number. The Sebe bus company, which operates most local bus routes within Estonia, offers a 25% discount to ISIC cardholders on domestic trips of distances greater than 80km. Make sure to ask about student discounts before buying your tickets.

Tallinn

Tallinn (population 411,600) fronts a bay on the Gulf of Finland and is dominated by Toompea Hill. The aura of the 14th and 15th centuries survives intact in central Tallinn's jumble of medieval walls, turrets, spires and winding cobbled streets; the area has been judiciously restored and it's fascinating to explore. Estonia's capital also has a university, excellent bars and cafes, and plenty of noteworthy sights. Tallinn is on a similar latitude to St Petersburg and shares that city's summer 'white nights' and short, dark winter days.

Orientation

The city centre (Old Town), just south of the bay, comprises two parts: Toompea (the upper town) and the lower town, which spreads around the eastern foot of Toompea. The lower town's centre is Raekoja plats (Town Hall Square). The train station (Balti jaam) is north-west of the Old Town.

Information

Tourist Offices The Estonian tourist information centre (☎ 645 7777, ✉ turismiinfo@tallinnlv.ee) is smack in the Old Town's centre at Raekoja plats 10, and has lists of hotels and camping grounds in Tallinn and throughout Estonia.

Infoliinia (☎ 626 1111) is a free phone information service (in English) offering advice on anything and everything, 24 hours a day.

The tourist office and most hotels sell the Tallinn Card, which gives free admission to all museums and the zoo, free public transport, a free sightseeing tour and more. The card is valid for 24/48/72 hours and costs 195/270/325EEK.

Money There are exchange counters just about everywhere you turn: at the airport, the sea passenger terminal, the train station, the main post office and at all banks and major hotels. The local American Express agent is Estravel (☎ 626 6200, fax 626 6262), Suur-Karja tänav 15.

Post & Communications The main post office is at Narva maantee 1 on the north side of Viru väljak. You can make long-distance and international calls from Tallinn's ubiquitous card phones. Note that if you are calling Tallinn from elsewhere in Estonia, the area code is ☎ 2, or ☎ 22 with six-digit numbers.

You can surf the Web for 40EEK per hour at @5, on the fifth floor of the Kaubamaja department store, or on the second floor of the Central Post Office.

Travel Agencies A leading travel and tour company is Estravel, with a branch at Suur-Karja tänav 15 (☎ 626 6266, ✉ sales@estravel.ee) and a Web site at www.estravel.ee. Other good budget agencies are Estonian Holidays at Pärnu maantee 12 (☎ 631 4106, fax 631 4109, ✉ holidays@holidays.ee), and Baltic Tours at Pikk tänav 31 (☎ 630 0400, ✉ baltic.tours@bt.ee).

Bookshops Viruvärava Raamatukauplus, Viru 23, stocks maps and a limited choice of English-language books (but a wide array of Lonely Planet titles). The city's best selection of English-language books is at Allecto (☎ 660 6493) at Jukentali tänav 32-5.

Medical Services The Tallinn Central Hospital (☎ 620 7010) at Ravi tänav 18, just south of Liivalaia tänav and 300m west of the Hotel Olümpia, has a full range of services including a polyclinic and a 24-hour emergency room.

Things to See & Do

Raekoja Plats & Around Wide Raekoja plats (Town Hall Square) is dominated by the only surviving Gothic **town hall** (1371-1404) in northern Europe. Its spire is 17th century but Vana Toomas (Old Thomas), the warrior-and-flag weather vane at its top, has guarded Tallinn since 1530.

The **Raeapteek** (Town Council Pharmacy), on the north side of Raekoja plats, is another ancient Tallinn institution: there's been a pharmacy or apothecary's shop here since at least 1422. An arch beside it leads into short, narrow Saia käik (White Bread Passage), at the far end of which is the 14th-century **Holy Spirit Church** (Pühavaimu Kirik). Free music concerts are given here at 6 pm every Monday.

A medieval merchant's home at Vene 17, on the corner of Pühavaimu, houses Tallinn's most interesting museum, the **City Museum** (Linnamuuseum; closed Tuesday; 5/2.50EEK).

Toompea The best approach to Toompea is through the red-roofed 1380 **gate tower** at the west end of Pikk, and up Pikk jalg (Long Leg). The 19th-century Russian Orthodox **Alexandr Nevsky Cathedral** dominates Lossi plats at the top of Pikk jalg. Estonia's governing body meets in the pink, classical-style **Parliament building** at the western end of Lossi plats. The Parliament building is an 18th-century addition to **Toompea Castle**. Nothing remains of the original 1219 Danish castle except for three corner towers, the finest of which is the 14th-century **Pikk Hermann** (Tall Hermann).

The Lutheran **Toomkirik** (Dome Church), at the north end of Toom-Kooli, is Estonia's oldest church, dating from the 14th century. Inside are many fine carved tombs.

Across the street from the Dome Church, in an 18th-century noble's house at Kiriku plats 1, is the **Estonian Art Museum** (Kunstimuuseum; closed Tuesday).

A path leads down from Kiriku plats through a hole in the walls to an open space and lookout where, in summer, artists paint portraits. Nearby **Kiek-in-de-Kõk**, a tall tower built about 1475, is a museum with a number of floors of maps, weapons and models of old Tallinn (closed Monday; 7/3.50EEK).

Lower Town North Pikk, running north from Raekoja plats to the **Great Coast Gate** – the medieval exit to Tallinn port – is lined with the houses of medieval merchants and gentry. The **History Museum** (Ajaloomuuseum) at Pikk 17 features Estonian history up to the mid-19th century, with labelling in English (closed Wednesday;

5/1EEK). The 1911 **Drakon Gallery**, Pikk 18, has a fantastically sculpted facade of dragons and semi-nude maidens.

Farther north on Pikk, immediately beyond the four-storey beige block that used to house the KGB, the tower of **Oleviste Church** is a chief Tallinn landmark. The church's architect, Olav (Olaf), fell to his death from the 120m tower.

The Great Coast Gate is joined to **Fat Margaret** (Paks Margareeta), the rotund 16th-century bastion which protected this entrance to the Old Town. Its walls are more than 4m thick at the base. Inside is the **Sea Museum** (Meremuuseum), which has great views from the platform on the roof (closed Monday and Tuesday; 10/4EEK). In the grounds stands a **monument** erected in memory to the 852 people who died when the popular *Estonia* ferry sank in 1994 en route between Stockholm and Tallinn – now considered Europe's worst peacetime maritime tragedy.

Kadriorg To reach the pleasant, wooded **Kadriorg Park**, 2km east of the Old Town along Narva maantee, take tram No 1 or 3, or bus No 1 from Pärnu maantee. The park itself, and the 1718-36 **Kadriorg Palace** (Kadrioru Loss) in the park at Weizenbergi tee 37, were designed for the Russian tsar Peter the Great. Today, the palace is the residence of the president of Estonia. The **Estonian Foreign Art Museum** is located within, and it's worth a trip just to see the building's interiors. It's open 11 am to 6 pm daily, and adult/student admission will cost 25/15EEK.

Pirita Some 2.5km beyond Kadriorg, just before Pirita tee crosses the Pirita River, a side road leads down to the **Kalevi Yacht Club** and **Olympic Sailing Sports Centre** (☎ 639 8800). This was the base for the 1980 Olympic sailing events. In summer you can rent rowing boats and pedalboats beside the bridge where Pirita tee crosses the river. The long stretch of clean beaches on the other side of Pirita tee is packed in the summer months.

Particularly recommended is a late-evening walk along Pirita tee to watch the summer sun set across the bay. Bus Nos 1, 8 and 34 run between the city centre and Pirita.

ESTONIA

CENTRAL TALLINN

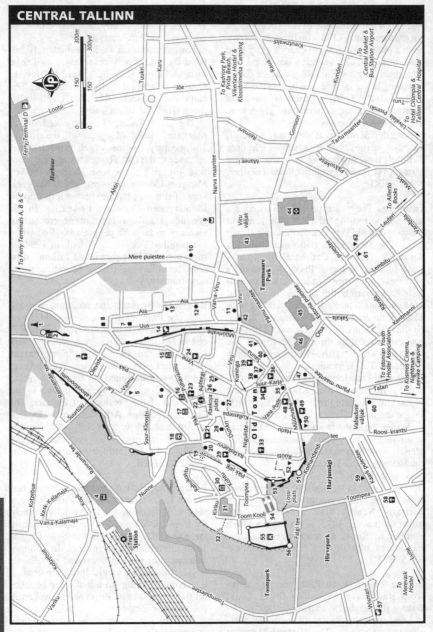

CENTRAL TALLINN

PLACES TO STAY		2	Fat Margaret Bastion; Sea	32	Lookout Point
7	Old House B&B		Museum; Great Coast Gate	33	Niguliste Church
8	Hostel	3	Oleviste Church	34	Nimeta Baar
28	Hotel Eeslitall;	4	Local Bus Station	35	Estravel
	Eeslitall Restaurant	6	Baltic Tours	36	Nimega Baar
38	The Barn	9	Main Post Office	39	X-Baar
		10	Rasastra	42	Viru Gate
PLACES TO EAT		11	Viruvärava Raamatukauplus		(Department Store)
5	Sammaria	12	Estline City Office	43	Hotel Viru
13	Kaubahall	14	Lithuanian Embassy	44	Kaubamaja; @5
25	Elevant	15	City Museum	45	Estonia Theatre;
26	Café Anglais	16	Drakon Gallery;		Concert Hall
37	Syrtaki Greek Kebabs	17	History Museum	46	Estonia Drama Theatre
40	Buon Giorno	18	Puppet Theatre	47	Estonian Holidays
41	Creperie Chez Mignon	19	Lookout Point	48	Hollywood Club;
50	Pizza Americana	20	Pikk Jalg Gate Tower		Sõprus Cinema
52	Mõõkala	21	Vinoteque	49	Gloria Wine Cellar
53	Neitsitorn	22	Tourist Information	51	Kiek-in-de-Kõk Tower
59	24-Hour Café		Centre	54	Alexandr Nevsky Cathedral
61	Imanta	23	Holy Spirit Church	55	Toompea Castle;
62	Eesti Maja	24	Kloostri Ait		Parliament
		27	Town Hall	56	Pikk Hermann
OTHER		29	Von Krahli Theatre Bar	57	British Embassy
1	Estonia Ferry Disaster	30	Estonian Art Museum	58	Kaarli Kirik Church
	Memorial	31	Toomkirik	60	Scandic Palace Hotel

Places to Stay

Rasastra (☎ 641 2291, @ rasatra@online.ee, Mere puiestee 4) can set up *B&B* in family homes and separate *apartments* throughout Estonia, Latvia and Lithuania from US$15 per person a night.

Camping *Kloostrimetsa* (☎ 239 191, *Kloostrimetsa tee 56A)*, near the TV tower in a nice stretch of forest, comes recommended. *Leevike* (☎ 493 294), 10km from the centre at Pärnu 600, has cabins for two/three/four persons for 200/350/500EEK with full facilities on site.

Hostels The *Vikerlase* (☎ 632 7781, *Vikerlase tänav 15-148)*, 6km east of the centre in the concrete suburb of Lasnamäe, has 15 basic two- to three-bed family rooms with shared showers and toilets. Take bus No 67 in front of Gonsiori tänav 4 to the last stop and keep walking some 100m. The *Merevaik* (☎ 529 604, *Sõpruse puiestee 182)*, southwest of the centre, is a similar establishment. Take trolleybus No 2 or 3 from diagonally opposite the Palace Hotel and get off at the Linnu tee stop. Both charge 100EEK per person, 90EEK for HI card holders.

Two places in the Old Town offer dream locations in clean surroundings. *Old House*

B&B (☎ 641 1464, *Uus tänav 22)* offers singles/doubles for 290/490EEK. A few doors down is *Hostel* (☎ 641 1281, *Uus tänav 26)* with singles/doubles that cost 240/400EEK (no breakfast though).

Hotels The *Barn* (☎ 631 3252) has an unbeatable location – 30 seconds' walk from Raekoja plats at Väike-Karja tänav 1. Follow signs for the erotic strip club, which is located above it. Shared dorm rooms are 195EEK per person; regular rooms start at 550EEK.

Dorell (☎ 626 1200, fax 423 387) at Karu tänav 39 (a 10-minute walk east of the Old Town along Narva maantee), offers 30 comfortable single/doubles with shared toilets for 420/460EEK, including breakfast. There's a bar and sauna on the premises. A good choice is *Hotel Eeslitall* (☎ 631 3755) in the Old Town a minute's walk from Raekoja plats, at Dunkri tänav 4. Below it is the popular Eeslitall restaurant. Singles/doubles cost 450/585EEK.

Places to Eat

A good source of basic foodstuffs and fresh fruit and vegetables is the *Kaubahall* (shopping hall) on Aia, near the Viru gates. Tallinn's always-bustling *Keskturg* (central market) is off Lastekodu tänav (take tram

No 2 or 4 to the Keskturg stop). It's open 7 am to 5 pm daily, and is worth a visit.

Restaurants The best place to sample Estonian food is *Eesti Maja (Lauteri 1)*, open 11 am to 11 pm daily. If you're not squeamish about pickled cabbage stew and black-pudding sausage, go for the 75EEK lunch buffet (noon to 4 pm weekdays).

Your best bet for a cheap, hearty meal (around 50EEK) is the cafeteria-style *Imanta*, which is inside the Foreign Ministry building at Rävala pst 9; it's open 10 am to 5 pm weekdays.

For good, simple Italian at reasonable prices, try *Buon Giorno (Müürivahe tänav 17)*, open 9 am to 10 pm daily. For delicious Indian food, step into *Elevant (Vene tänav 5)* and you may never want to leave. The food is first-rate (try their korma, 85EEK), and all meals come with a side salad. The *Creperie Chez Mignon (Müürivahe 23a)*, serves dinner and dessert crêpes in a cosy, candle-lit atmosphere.

Seafood fans will find their paradise at *Mõõkkala (Rüütli 16/18)*, one of the finest restaurants in Tallinn. A exquisite array of fish is served up for upwards of 90EEK.

The old favourite *Neitsitorn (Lühike jalg 9)* remains popular for its great views of the Old Town.

Cafes *Cafe Anglais (Raekoja plats 14)*, overlooking Town Hall Square, has some of the best homemade pastries in Tallinn and serves French-style sandwiches and hot salads. The only place to get decent kebabs and falafel in Tallinn is *Syrtaki Greek Kebabs (Sauna tänav 1)*, conveniently open until 2 am (4 am Friday and Saturday). Entirely vegetarian is *Sammaria (Vaimu tänav 3)*, a Christian-run cafe that serves soups and a small selection of light vegetarian fare for dirt cheap prices.

For pizza, *Pizza Americana (delivery ☎ 644 8837, Müürivahe tänav 2)* gets the job done.

Entertainment

The *Baltic Times* and *Tallinn In Your Pocket* have detailed entertainment listings.

Bars The top bars in town are *Nimeta Baar* ('bar with no name'), in the Old Town at Suur-Karja 4, and its sister *Nimega Baar* ('bar with a name') a few doors down. Another veteran on the scene is the relaxed *Kloostri Ait (Vene tänav 14)* which is a focal Tallinn meeting place. The *Von Krahli Theatre Bar (Rataskaevu 10)* has unique decor and great atmosphere.

For a sedate glass of wine in a candle-lit atmosphere head to *Vinoteque (Pikk 6)*. For an even cosier ambience try the lovely *Gloria Wine Cellar (Müürivahe 2)*.

After-hours hangouts include the 24-hour *Võiroos (Kaarli puiestee 4)* – it's nothing more than a shack, but is practically a Tallinn institution.

Clubs The hot club event in Tallinn is the once-monthly *Vibe* (check out their Web site for dates and locations at www.vibe.ee). *Hollywood* in the Sõprus cinema at Vana-Posti tänav 8 attracts the largest crowds.

The city's most popular (that is, the only) gay and lesbian club is *Nightman (Vineeri 4)*, a techno-happy disco that attracts a mixed crowd (closed Sunday to Tuesday). *X-Baar (Sauna 1)* is the only gay bar in town.

Theatre, Ballet & Opera The *Estonia Theatre (Estonia puiestee 4)* stages classical operas and ballets in repertory and the adjacent *Estonia Concert Hall* (Kontserti-saal) has concerts every night of the week. Tickets generally cost upwards of 25EEK. In summer there are numerous open-air concerts around town.

Of particular interest is the *Puppet Theatre (Nukuteater; Lai 1)*. Performances, while primarily aimed at children, are beautifully produced.

Getting There & Away

Bus Suburban buses (within 40km or so of Tallinn) depart from the bus station beside the train station. Most other services depart from the Autobussijaam (long-distance station), 2km from the centre along Tartu maantee (take tram No 2 south from Mere puiestee or tram No 4 east from Tammsaare Park). For information on international buses see the Getting There & Away section earlier in this chapter.

Domestic services from Tallinn's Autobussijaam include: Haapsalu (49EEK, 2½ hours), Kuressaare (110EEK, 4½ hours), Pärnu (60EEK, 2½ hours), Tartu (80EEK, three hours) and Narva (75EEK, four hours).

Train Tallinn's Baltic station (Balti jaam) is on the north-west edge of the Old Town at Toompuiestee 35, a short walk from Raekoja plats. For information about trains to places outside Estonia see the Getting There & Away section earlier in this chapter. Services within Estonia include Tartu (80EEK, three to four hours, four daily), Pärnu (40EEK, three to four hours, two daily), and Narva (77EEK, 3¼ to 4¼ hours, two daily).

Boat See the Getting There & Away section earlier in this chapter for information on the many ferries and cruises between Tallinn and Helsinki or Stockholm.

Tallinn's sea passenger terminals A, B and C are at the end of Sadama, about 1km north-east of the Old Town. Tram Nos 1 and 2 and bus Nos 3, 4 and 8 go to the Linnahall stop (by the Statoil petrol station), a five-minute walk from the terminal. Terminal D is best reached from Ahtri tänav. A shuttle bus costing 25EEK runs every 15 minutes between the terminal and the Viru, Scandic Palace and Olümpia hotels.

AROUND TALLINN
Keila-Joa
This small village near the coast, 30km west of Tallinn, boasts what is jokingly referred to as 'Estonia's Niagara Falls', a lovely small waterfall (6.1m) with a nearby 19th-century manor house. The large park and forest surrounding it are perfect for a day's picnicking or hiking (1.7km to the sea). Bus Nos 108, 110, 136 and 172 run from platform 1 on the east side of Tallinn's train station throughout the day. The *Joaveski Baar*, serving light meals and drinks right by the waterfall, offers accommodation in a small guest house.

Lahemaa National Park
☎ 32
Estonia's *rahvuspark* (national park), Lahemaa, is 70km east of Tallinn and makes an easy day trip. Several nature trails wind through it. The small coastal towns of **Võsu**, **Käsmu** and **Loksa** are popular seaside spots in summer, and there are many trails through the forests. Hiking, biking and boating opportunities are plentiful.

The showpiece of Lahemaa is **Palmse Manor**, about 8km north of Viitna. The existing building is a restored version of the 18th-century baroque house that belonged to the Baltic-German Von der Pahlen family. You can visit the house 10 am to 7 pm daily.

Information The Lahemaa National Park Visitors' Centre (☎ 34 196), open 9 am to 7 pm weekdays, is in a converted wagon-house and stable in Palmse. Anne Kurepalu, working out of the Park Hotel Palmse (see below) organises excellent, highly recommended guided tours of the park.

Places to Stay The visitors' centre can arrange accommodation to suit every budget; ask about the amazing *Park Hotel Palmse* (☎ 23 626, ✉ info@phpalmse.ee), where singles/doubles start at 550/790EEK. The *Viitna Holiday Centre* (☎ 93 651), among trees beside a clean lake has singles/doubles for 100/150EEK. There are two *hostels*. One is in a converted 1855 farmhouse 1.5km south-east of Palmse at Ojaäärse (☎ 34 108) and charges 105EEK per person; the other is on the grounds of Sagadi Manor (☎ 58 888) and its beauty redefines the notion of 'hostel'. Beds cost 180EEK.

Getting There & Away There are buses from Tallinn to Viitna, Käsmu, Võsu, Loksa, Leesi, Pärispea and elsewhere in the park.

Around Estonia

TARTU
☎ 07
Tartu (population 100,580), formerly known as Dorpat, is 190km south-east of Tallinn on the Emajõgi River, which flows into Lake Peipsi. Tartu was the cradle of the 19th-century Estonian nationalist revival and lays claim to being the spiritual capital of the country. It managed to escape Sovietisation to a greater degree than Tallinn and retains a sleepy pastoral air. The town is notable for its university, with over 7400 students, and its 18th-century architecture.

Orientation
Toomemägi Hill and the area of older buildings between it and the Emajõgi River are the focus of Tartu. At the heart of this older area are Raekoja plats (Town Hall Square) and the street Ülikooli, which runs across the west end of the square.

ESTONIA

Information

The tourist office (☎/fax 432 141, ℮ info@ tartu.tourism.ee) is at Raekoja plats 14. The main post office, Vanemuise 7, has an ATM that accepts Visa cards. The American Express agent is Estravel (☎ 447 979), at Reakoja plats 16.

Estonia's coolest, most welcoming Internet café is Café Virtual at Pikk tänav 40, open 11 am to 11 pm daily.

Travel agencies that can book hotels and sightseeing tours include Estravel (see above), and South Estonian Travel (☎ 474 553, ℮ lets.travel@kiirtee.ee) on the 2nd floor of the bus station.

Buy local maps, English-language books and the useful magazine *Tartu This Week* at the well-stocked Mattiesen bookshop,

Vallikraavi 4, or at the Raamatupood (university bookshop), Ülikooli 11.

Things to See

At the centre of town on Raekoja Plats is the beautifully proportioned **town hall** (1782-89), topped by a tower and weather vane. The wonderfully crooked building at No 18, formerly the home of Colonel Barclay de Tolly (1761-1818), now houses the **Kivisilla Art Gallery**.

The main **university** (☎ 375 100) building, with its six Corinthian columns, at Ülikooli tänav 18, dates from 1803-09. It contains the **Art Museum of Tartu University** and the **Student's Lock-Up** museum (where 19th-century students were held as punishment for their misdeeds). Farther north, the

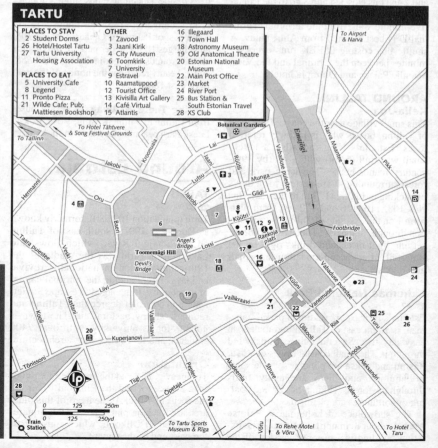

TARTU

PLACES TO STAY
2 Student Dorms
26 Hotel/Hostel Tartu
27 Tartu University
   Housing Association

PLACES TO EAT
5 University Cafe
8 Legend
11 Pronto Pizza
21 Wilde Cafe; Pub;
   Mattiesen Bookshop

OTHER
1 Zavood
3 Jaani Kirik
4 City Museum
6 Toomkirik
7 University
9 Estravel
10 Raamatupood
12 Tourist Office
13 Kivisilla Art Gallery
14 Café Virtual
15 Atlantis

16 Illegaard
17 Town Hall
18 Astronomy Museum
19 Old Anatomical Theatre
20 Estonian National
   Museum
22 Main Post Office
23 Market
24 River Port
25 Bus Station &
   South Estonian Travel
28 XS Club

Gothic brick **Jaani Kirik** (St John's Church), founded in 1330 but ruined in 1944, is being restored as a museum. It has rare **terracotta sculptures** around the main portal. The **Botanical Gardens**, founded in 1803 on the corner of Lai tänav and Vabaduse puiestee, are home to 6500 different species of plants. (open 9 am to 5 pm daily between May and September, but you're free to roam the lovely grounds until 9 pm).

Rising to the west of Raekoja plats is **Toomemägi Hill**, landscaped in the style of a 19th-century English park. The 13th-century Gothic **Toomkirik** (cathedral) at the top houses the **University History Museum** (closed Monday and Tuesday; 2EEK).

Also on the hill are the **Angel's Bridge** (Inglisild), with a good view of the city, the **Devil's Bridge** (Kuradisild), and an **astronomy museum** (closed Tuesday).

The **Estonian National Museum**, tracing the history, life and traditions of the Estonian people, is at Kuperjanovi tänav 9, just west of Toomemägi Hill (6EEK). There's a **City Museum** covering the history of Tartu up to the 19th century at Oru 2 (closed Tuesday), a superlative **sports museum** at Riia 27a, and a tiny **toy museum** at Lai 1. The latter two are closed Monday and Tuesday.

Places to Stay
The tourist office and some travel agencies can book *private rooms*. *Tartu University Student Village* (☎ *420 337*, @ *janikah@ ut.ee, Pepleri Tänav 14*), offers spotless singles/doubles for 250/400EEK in summer, and 180/350EEK from September to May. During summer months, no-frills rooms are sometimes available at another *student dorm*, *(Narva maantee 27)* for 70EEK a night. Inquire about these at the headquarters on Pepleri, but some travellers have reported no problems just showing up and asking for a room.

Hotels *Hotel Tähtvere* (☎ *421 708, Laulupeo 19*), not quite 1km north-west of the centre, has singles/doubles/quads with bath and TV for 150/250/600EEK. There's a sauna, tennis court, and sports complex on the premises.

The unexciting *Hotel Tartu* (☎ *432 091, Soola tänav 1),* across from the bus station, has passable rooms with shared facilities for 405/715EEK (660/990EEK with private

bath), but also offers 200EEK per person hostel accommodation to HI card-holders. Also good value is the *Rehe Motel* (☎ *412 234, fax 412 355)* 5km from the centre on the road to Võru. Singles/doubles cost 300/480EEK.

Places to Eat
For quick, cheap eating, you can't beat the atmospheric *University Cafe (Ülikooli 20).* On the first floor is a cafeteria where the meat and veggie meals won't cost you more than 20EEK, and on the second floor is a charming old-world cafe serving tasty pastries, coffee, and dainty omelettes (12EEK).

The *Cafe Wilde (Vallikraavi 4)* is a relaxing place to rest, read and savour some homemade delights. Its namesake is Peter Ernst Wilde, who ran a publishing house on the premises in the 18th century; another Wilde – Oscar – is celebrated upstairs at the popular *Wilde Irish Pub*, which serves great food.

Legend, a 24-hour bar and restaurant at Küütri 2, has a decor that defines 'eclectic'. Good pizza is served up 8 am to midnight daily in lively surroundings at *Pronto Pizza (Küütri tänav 3).*

Entertainment
In a class of its own stands *Illegaard* at Ülikooli tänav 5. Also an art gallery, this cellar bar-cum-cafe attracts an artsy crowd. *Zavood (Lai tänav 30)* is another popular spot for late-night carousing. *Atlantis (Narva maantee 2)*, and *XS (Vaksali tänav 21)*, which attracts a fun, mixed crowd, are the most popular dance clubs.

Getting There & Away
Over 30 buses a day run to/from Tallinn (80EEK, 2½ to 3½ hours). There are also four trains that run daily (80EEK, three to four hours).

OTEPÄÄ
☎ 76
The small hill-top town of Otepää, 44km south of Tartu, is the centre of a bucolic area much loved by the Estonians for its hills and lakes, and often referred to jokingly as the 'Estonian alps'. In winter Otepää is a popular skiing centre.

The best views are along the shores of the 3.5km-long **Pühajärv** (Holy Lake), on the south-west edge of town. The lake was blessed by the Dalai Lama when he visited Tartu in 1992 _ there's a monument to His Holiness on the east shore.

Orientation & Information

The centre of town is the triangular main 'square', Lipuväljak, with the bus station just off its eastern corner. The tourist office (☎ 55 364) is at Lipuväljak 13. The post office, bank and main food shop are beside the bus station.

Places to Stay

Smack in the town centre is *Kesklinna Hostel* (☎ 55 095, *Lipuväljak 11*) which has bare singles/doubles for 100/120EEK. The *Väike Munamäe Sports Centre* (☎/fax 61 711) at Väike Munamägi, 3km south-east of town, has a ski hill and passable rooms for 100EEK. The *Setanta Irish Pub and Motel* (☎ 68 200), 2km from the centre, has rooms from 650EEK.

Getting There & Away

There are 11 buses daily to and from Tartu which take just over an hour and cost 20EEK. There are two buses daily from Tallinn – one via Tartu, one via Viljandi – taking about 4½ hours. Other places served by bus to/from Otepää include Pärnu, Sangaste, Valga, Viljandi and Võru.

AROUND OTEPÄÄ

One of Estonia's prettiest sights, **Sangaste Castle** (Sangaste Loss; ☎ 27-91 343) is only 25km from Otepää. This fairy-tale brick castle, built in Tudor-cum-Gothic style between 1874 and 1881, is said to be modelled on Britain's Windsor Castle. Sangaste sits in parkland close by a river and it's possible to hire boats and bicycles. The castle is now a fancy hotel with doubles for 550EEK. There are buses between Otepää and Sangaste five times a day, and one that runs from Tartu.

VÕRU

☎ 78

Võru, 64km south of Tartu, is a small and ordinary town, but a good base for visiting Suur Munamägi (the highest point in the Baltics), the picturesque village of Rõuge and the castle at Vahtseliina (see Around Võru later in this section).

Orientation & Information

Võru lies on the eastern shore of Lake Tamula. The main streets, both running parallel to the shore, are Kreutzwaldi and Jüri. The central square is off Jüri; the bus station is 500m east along Tartu tänav.

The tourist office (☎/fax 21 881, Tartu maantee 31), can help with local and regional accommodation (closed Sunday). You can change money at the Hermes hotel (see Places to Stay & Eat).

Places to Stay & Eat

The central *Hermes Guesthouse* (☎ 21 326, *Jüri tänav 32a*) has singles/doubles from 200/300EEK.

The comfy cafe *Wõro* (*Jüri 11*) has great daily specials for 25EEK. The popular pub *Õlle nr 17* (*Jüri 17*) also has good grub.

Getting There & Away

There about 15 buses to/from Tartu (1½ hours, daily) seven from Tallinn (4½ hours, daily) plus two to/from Otepää and one to/from Pärnu (4½ hours).

AROUND VÕRU

The highest peak in the Baltic region at 318m, **Suur Munamägi** (literally 'Great Egg Hill'), is 17km south of Võru. It's topped by a 29m-high observation tower that commands views of up to 50km. The tower has odd opening hours but if you turn up between 10 am and 6 pm any day from May to September, you should be OK. To get there take a bus from Võru to Hanja or Ruusmäe.

Although all that's left of **Vahtseliina Castle** is a couple of towers, a length of wall, a ditch and some ramparts, their dramatic perch and remoteness make them evocative of a past age. The surrounding countryside with its sandstone cliffs and river valleys is enchanting. Vahtseliina Castle is on the eastern edge of the village of Vahtseliina, which is, rather confusingly, 5km east of the small town of Vastseliina, to which there are several buses daily from Võru.

PÄRNU

☎ 44

Pärnu (population 51,900), 127km south of Tallinn on the road to Rīga, is Estonia's leading seaside resort and magnet for party-loving Estonians and Finns. Out of season it's quiet and forlorn, but between June and

August it's buzzing. There are some good places to stay, wide leafy streets and white sandy beaches.

Orientation & Information

The main shopping street and heart of the old town is Rüütli, 100m south of the bus station, with the Hotel Pärnu at one end and Vallikäär park at the other. Running southward the streets become wider and greener before terminating (after about 1.5km) at Ranna puiestee and the beach.

The tourist office (☎ 73 000) is at Rüütli tänav 16. Ühispank, around the corner from the information centre on Nikolai tänav cashes travellers cheques and gives cash advances on credit cards. The main post office is at Akadeemia 7.

Things to See & Do

Parts of the 17th-century Swedish moat and ramparts survive in **Vallikäär park**, including the tunnel-like **Tallinn Gate** (Tallinna Värav) at the west end of Rüütli. A display of local history is included in the **Pärnu Museum** on the corner of Rüütli and Aia (closed Sunday).

The wide, white-sand **beach** just south of Ranna puiestee is surprisingly beautiful, as are the 1920s and 1930s buildings that front the beach (and now serve as cafes and restaurants). The eye-catching 1927 neoclassical structure at the sea end of Supeluse is the place to go for **mud baths** (☎ 42 461). A number of different 'cures' start at 95EEK.

The **Pärnu New Art Museum** (☎ 30 772) at Esplanaadi tänav 10, is among the cultural bright spots in all of Estonia. It's a large complex that's sometimes referred to by its old name, the Charlie Chaplin Centre, and it houses a cafe, an art bookshop and several galleries with rotating, daring, and almost always interesting exhibitions. It's open 9 am to 9 pm daily.

Places to Stay

Camping *Linnakämping Green* (☎ 43 776, Suure-Jõe 50b), 3km from the centre in a pleasant spot at the rowing centre on the river, offers boat and bike rentals and charges 100EEK per person.

Hostels The cheapest beds around are at the friendly and often crowded *Kajakas* (☎ 43 098, fax 42 181), just over 1km from

the bus station at Seedri tänav 2, a short walk to the beach. Singles/doubles/triples with shared bath are 180/290/390EEK. Breakfast is 30EEK extra.

Hotels The *Pärnu Mudaravilla* (☎ 25 520, Sääse tänav 7), offers singles/doubles for 300/470EEK, but for 460/480EEK the price includes daily mud treatments. Nearby at Pärna tänav 12, both the *Monaste* (☎ 41 472, 5th floor) and the *Leharu* (☎ 45 895, 4th floor) offer standard singles/doubles for 400/560EEK.

Places to Eat

The *Georg* (Rüütli 43), a block west from the bus station, is a smart and clean cafeteria with soups and salads for 8EEK and hot dishes for around 25EEK. For pizza, your best bet is *Steffani Pizzeria* (Nikolai tänav 24).

Väike Klaus (Superlase tänav 3) is a welcoming, supposedly German-styled pub that's a great place for a quick, spicy lunch (delicious goulash for 18EEK), a game of billiards upstairs, or a leisurely beer to counteract the healthy effects of those mud treatments.

Entertainment

Pärnu's night scene rocks, the highlight being the very flashy *Sunset Club* (Ranna 3). Other clubs like *Las Vegas* (Ranna 7) and *Mirage* (Rüütli 40), also pack them in. More subdued and with great food is *Alexandri Pub* (Väike Tööstuse 8).

Getting There & Away

There are more than 20 buses from Tallinn (67EEK, 2½ hours, daily).

SAAREMAA

☎ 45

Soviet industry and immigration barely touched the country's biggest island, Saaremaa, and it retains the appearance of agricultural, pre-WWII Estonia. In the Soviet era Saaremaa was closed to foreigners, and even mainland Estonians needed a permit to visit because of the presence of an early-warning radar system and rocket base.

To reach Saaremaa you must first cross to Muhu, the small island where the ferry from the mainland docks and which is connected to the eastern edge of Saaremaa by a 2.5km causeway. The capital of Saaremaa (and the best base for travellers) is Kuressaare (population 16,360), about 70km from Muhu.

Information

Kuressaare's tourist information office (☎ 33 120, ✉ info@oesel.tourism.ee) is at Tallinna maantee 2. You can change money at the bus station or at any of the several banks on the main square. The post office is at Torni 1.

Arensburg travel agency (☎ 33 360, ✉ abr@tt.ee), at Tallinna maantee 25, is extremely knowledgeable about the island and specialises in boat trips to remote islands and personalised biking and hiking tours.

Things to See

The island's most distinctive landmark is the restored 14th-century **Bishop's Castle** at the south end of Kuressaare. It now houses the **Saaremaa Regional Museum** (closed Monday and Tuesday).

At **Angla**, 40km from Kuressaare on the road to Leisi, is the island's biggest and most photogenic grouping of **windmills** – five of them lined up along the roadside. Two kilometres away, along the road opposite the windmills, is **Karja church**, a striking 13th to 14th-century German Gothic church.

At **Kaali**, 18km from Kuressaare on the road to the harbour, look for the 100m-wide, water-filled crater formed 2700 years ago by a meteor strike. In ancient Scandinavian mythology the site was known as 'the sun's grave', and as the sun had chosen to be buried there the Estonians were considered blessed folk.

Where Saaremaa's magic can really be felt, though, is along the **Sõrve Peninsula**, jutting out south and west of Kuressaare. This sparsely populated strip of land saw some of the heaviest fighting in WWII, and the marks are still there – by the lighthouse at the southern tip, **Sääre**, you can walk around the ruins of an old Soviet army base. A bike or car trip along the coastline provides some of the most spectacular sights on the island.

Places to Stay & Eat

Kuressaare The tourist information centre (see the preceding Information section) can fix you up with beds in *private flats* in town for around 150EEK per person.

Saaremaa School Hostel (☎ 52 042, Hariduse tänav 13) understands the back-packer, offering a place to crash on a gym floor for as low as 15EEK. For those who want a bed, a place in a double/triple/quad is 110/75/65EEK. The *Pärna Motel (☎/fax 57 521, Pärna tänav 3a)* is a very clean house transformed into a cosy motel, with kitchen and sauna. Doubles with private bath are 550EEK, without, 400EEK.

Pizza Primo (Turu tänav 4) is a reliable bet, and *Café Hansa*, inside an art gallery at Tallinna maantee 9, is small and cosy and serves unforgettable homemade pies. A fancier meal can be enjoyed at *Raekelder*, in the basement of the Town Hall – delicious meals start from 55EEK. *Lonkav Konn (Kauba tänav 6)* is Kuressaare's Irish pub, with pub grub and live music on weekends.

The *central market*, with a fine array of fresh produce and Estonian handicrafts, is just north of the main square. There's also a *grocery store* at Tallinna 1.

Out of Town *Kämping Mändjala (☎ 55 079, fax 54 035)* is the island's most pleasant camping ground, located in woods behind a sandy beach 10km along the coast road west of Kuressaare. Singles/doubles in two-person cabins cost 145/240EEK including breakfast. Buses from Kuressaare to Torgu or Sääre (three a day) go to the Mändjala bus stop, about half a kilometre beyond the site. *Motel and Kämping Tare (☎ 23 331)*, near the beach at Sutu, 13km east of Kuressaare, has sizeable doubles for 250EEK. Unheated wooden cabins cost 190EEK for a double, and pitching a tent is 20EEK. There's a field shower and kitchen facilities.

The *Süla Talu (☎ 46 927)*, in an isolated patch of woods in the village of Oja, 4km north-west of Kihelkonna on the west coast of the island, is a good place to experience rustic life – and explore remote coastlines and the island of Vilsandi. Places in wood cabins are 200EEK.

Getting There & Away

A vehicle ferry runs throughout the day from Virtsu on the mainland across the 7km strait to Muhu island, which is joined by a causeway to Saaremaa. At least eight buses travel each way between Tallinn and Kuressaare (110EEK, 4½ hours, daily). There are also three buses to/from Tartu daily and two a day to/from Pärnu.

Finland

For much of the 20th century, Finland (Suomi) was the least visible of the Scandinavian countries: Sweden had given the world ABBA, Norway had all those lovely fjords, but Finland stirred few notions in the average traveller's mind.

With the rise of mobile communications and the Internet, though, Finland has hit the world stage, with companies like Nokia exploring areas of communications once imagined only in science fiction. As the techno-wave breaks into the 21st century, Finland appears set to play an important role in the way the future is mapped out.

But in sharp contrast to its reputation for high-tech gadgetry, Finland is not a bleeping, pulsating place, but a land of quietness. With the exception of Helsinki – fast becoming an extremely popular travel destination – and perhaps Turku, this is not a locale to visit for wild frivolity and hedonism; it is a place for peace and tranquillity, where people respect silence and solemnity in a way seldom found elsewhere.

Facts about Finland

HISTORY

Human settlement in Finland dates back almost 10,000 years. The Finns' ancestors arrived on the north Baltic coast and established themselves in the forests, driving the nomadic Sami people to the north (where a small number still live today in Lapland).

By the end of the Viking era, Swedish traders had extended their interests to Ladoga and, in 1155 the Swedes made Finland a province. Swedish culture was swiftly imposed, but Sweden's heavy-handedness soon split the country along religious lines, and most Orthodox believers fled to Russia; famine then killed a third of the remaining Finnish population.

AT A GLANCE	
Capital:	Helsinki
Population:	5.2 million
Official Language:	Finnish, Swedish
Currency:	1 Finnish markka (mk) = 100 penniä

In 1809 Russia seized control of Finland and the capital was moved to Helsinki. The communist revolution in 1917 caused the downfall of the tsar and enabled the Finnish senate to declare independence.

Anti-communist violence broke out in the 1930s and relations with the Soviet Union remained uneasy; in November 1939 the Winter War between the two countries began. It was a harsh winter, with temperatures reaching -40°C, and soldiers from both sides died in their thousands. After 100 days, the massively outnumbered Finns were defeated, and Finland forced to cede part of its eastern lakelands. When no Western allies would help against the Soviet threat, Finland accepted assistance from Germany, and in return allowed transit of German troops on Finnish soil. With aid from Germany, Finland resumed hostilities with the Soviets in 1941 and won back large swathes of Karelia, at the cost of almost 100,000 Finnish lives.

By September 1944, growing Soviet strength forced another armistice, under the terms of which Finns turned and fought German forces entrenched in Lapland.

After WWII, Finland signed a new treaty with the USSR: Finland was to recognise Soviet security concerns and agree to Soviet aid in defending the frontier. This agreement helped craft an independent stance in East-West relations during the Cold War. With this new security came the opportunity for Finland to develop its economy and welfare system, and its Scandinavian links through the Nordic Council. The various Helsinki conferences and accords were significant in the gradual ending of the Cold War and the dismantling of the Soviet Union. Since then, Finland has overcome its worst post-war recession despite an endless

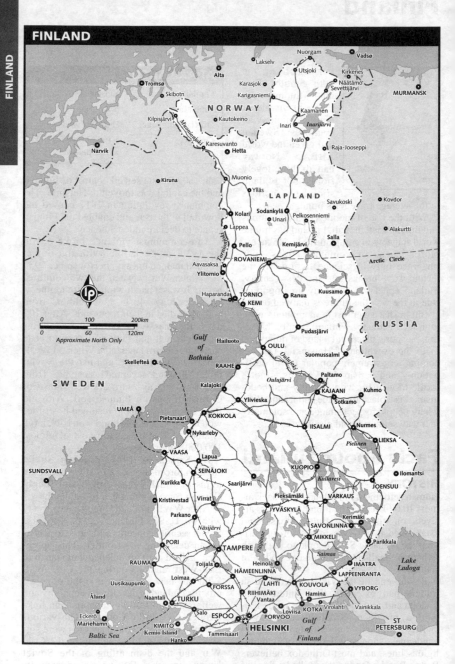

FINLAND

number of bankruptcies and economic reforms and over the past five years has gone from strength to strength economically.

In 1995 Finland joined the EU, giving this oft-forgotten country new opportunities. Signs of growing integration are common – many Finns now drink Guinness!

GEOGRAPHY

Finland is Europe's seventh-largest country, with one third of its area above the Arctic Circle. Helsinki is the northernmost European capital.

CLIMATE

The seasons differ enormously in Finland, ranging from constant darkness in Arctic winter to a two-month 'day' in northern Lapland's summer. In most parts of the country snow first falls in October and vanishes by the end of March, but in Lapland it lingers from September to late May. Helsinki – the world's fourth coldest capital city – can experience a freak snowstorm even in July.

POPULATION & PEOPLE

Finland has a population of 5.2 million, more than half of whom live in the south. Finland is one of Europe's most sparsely populated countries, with 17 people per square kilometre. There are around 300,000 Swedish-speaking Finns in the west, as well as in fishing communities along the coast and on the Åland islands; and a smaller number of Roma (Gypsies) in the south.

The Sami population of 6,500 in the deep north consists of three distinctive groups, each speaking its own dialect. The Scandinavian Sami region has its own flag, and many Samis look across the border at the more developed Sami community in Norway for a deeper cultural identity.

SOCIETY & CONDUCT

A capacity for silence and reflection are the traits that best sum up the Finnish character (however, get a Finn near a stack of duty-free liquor and see if this remains the case). The image of a log cabin with a sauna by a lake tells much about Finnish culture: independence, endurance (*sisu* or 'guts') and a love of open space and nature.

The Finns are a naturally reserved people, and at first meeting can be very polite and more formal than you may be used to.

This seemingly icy front never, ever lasts though, and almost every visitor leaves with a story of unexpected kindness from a Finn.

LANGUAGE

Finnish is spoken by just six million people, all but a few of whom live in Scandinavia and Russian Karelia.

Staff at hotels, hostels and tourist offices generally speak fluent English but bus drivers and restaurant and shop staff may not – but they'll always fetch a colleague or bystander who does.

Facts for the Visitor

HIGHLIGHTS

Finland is awash with museums and galleries and Kiasma, Helsinki's daring museum of contemporary art, is the best. In the north, Arktikum in Rovaniemi and Saamelaismuseo in Inari are top class.

Savonlinna is a beautiful town, and its Olavinlinna is the mightiest and best preserved of the northern medieval castles, set superbly between two lakes. Hikers should try a short walk in the lakes area, a romantic and very silent place (though be sure to take a mosquito head net).

SUGGESTED ITINERARIES

Two days
  Day one, Helsinki: visit Kiasma or the Mannerheim, then stroll over to the market square for lunch, then visit the Senaatintori. Day two, take a ferry to Suomenlinna.
One week
  After two days in Helsinki, explore the eastern cities of Savonlinna, Lappeenranta and Kuopio, or take an overnight train to Lapland.
Two weeks
  Spend a few days in Helsinki, then visit Turku and Tampere, then on to Savonlinna and the beautiful eastern lakeland. After this go up to Lapland, or back to Åland.

PLANNING
When to Go

May to September are the best months to visit Finland. The tourist season is in full swing from early June to late August, when all attractions, hostels and camping grounds are open, and there are festivals aplenty. During the rest of the year, Finland's tourist infrastructure hibernates.

Lapland's tourist season is different from the rest of the country: the mosquitoes are annoying in July but September is delightful with its *ruska* (autumn) colours.

Maps
Tourist offices supply good city and regional maps. Trekking, canoeing and road maps are available from Karttakeskus (☎ 0204-45 5911), Unioninkatu 32, 00100 Helsinki.

TOURIST OFFICES
Every Finnish town has a tourist office with English-language brochures and free maps. The main tourist information centre is run by the Finnish Tourist Board (☎ 09-4176 9300, ✉ mek@mek.fi) at Eteläesplanadi 4, Helsinki. The mailing address is PO Box 249, 00131 Helsinki.

Tourist Offices Abroad
Finland tourist offices abroad include:

Australia (☎ 02-9290 1950), Finnish Tourist Board, Level 4, 81 York Street, Sydney, NSW 2000
Denmark (☎ 3313 1362), Finlands Turistbureau, Nyhavn 43A, 1051 Copenhagen K
Estonia (☎ 2-699 7010), Soome Turismiarendamise, Uus 31, 10111 Tallinn
Norway (☎ 2310 0800), Finlands Turistkontor, Lille Grensen 7, 0159 Oslo 1
Sweden (☎ 08-5451 2430), Finska Turistbyrån Snickarbacken 2, 111 39 Stockholm
UK (☎ 020-7839 4048, ✉ mek.lon@mek.fi), Finnish Tourist Board 30-35 Pall Mall, 3rd Floor, London SW1Y 5LP
USA (☎ 212-885 9700), Finnish Tourist Board, 655 Third Avenue, New York, NY 10017

VISAS & DOCUMENTS
A valid passport is required to enter Finland. Citizens of EU countries (except Greece), Norway and Iceland can, however, come and go without one. Most Western nationals don't need a tourist visa for stays under three months.

Travel from Finland into Russia requires a visa.

EMBASSIES & CONSULATES
Finnish Embassies Abroad
Diplomatic missions abroad include:

Australia (☎ 02-6273 3800) 10 Darwin Avenue, Yarralumla, ACT 2600

Canada (☎ 613-236 2389) 55 Metcalfe Street, Suite 850, Ottawa K1P 6L5
France (☎ 01 44 18 19 20) 1 Place de Finlande, 57007 Paris
Germany (☎ 0228-382 980) Friesdorferstrasse 1, 53173 Bonn
Ireland (☎ 1-478 1344) Russell House, St Stephen's Green, Dublin 2
Netherlands (☎ 070-346 9754) Groot Hertoginnelaan 16, 2517 EG Den Haag
UK (☎ 020-7838 6200) 38 Chesham Place, London SW1X 8HW
USA (☎ 202-298 5800) 3301 Massachusetts Ave NW, Washington DC 20008

Foreign Embassies in Finland
The following diplomatic missions are all in Helsinki (area code ☎ 09):

Australia (☎ 447 233) Museokatu 25B
Canada (☎ 171 141) Pohjoisesplanadi 25B
France (☎ 171 521) Itäinen Puistotie 10
Germany (☎ 458 580) Krogiuksentie 4
Ireland (☎ 646 006) Erottajankatu 7
Netherlands (☎ 661 737) Raatimiekenkatu 2A
UK (☎ 2286 5100) Itäinen Puistotie 17
USA (☎ 171 931) Itäinen Puistotie 14A

MONEY
Currency
The *markka* is abbreviated as mk. Notes come in 20, 50, 100, 500 and 1000mk denominations and coins in one, five and 10mk, and 50 and 10 penniä.

Exchange Rates

country	unit		markka
Australia	A$1	=	3.87mk
Canada	C$1	=	4.61mk
euro	€1	=	5.95mk
France	1FF	=	0.91mk
Germany	DM1	=	3.04mk
Ireland	IR£1	=	7.55mk
New Zealand	NZ$1	=	2.79mk
UK	UK£1	=	9.83mk
USA	US$1	=	6.83mk

Exchanging Money
Finland has three national banks with similar rates and charges. In cities, independent exchangers such as Forex are a better alternative; they charge 10mk per cheque to exchange traveller's cheques. Banks are open 9.15 am to 4.15 pm weekdays. There is no American Express office that changes cheques in Finland.

Costs

Though it's a bargain compared to Sweden and Norway, Finland is still expensive. Your costs will depend on how you travel, and where; if you stick to the big cities like Helsinki and Tampere your costs will be much higher than in smaller towns and the countryside.

If you camp or stay in hostels and prepare your own meals you might get by on less than 180mk a day. If you stay in guesthouses (or private rooms in hostels) and eat at inexpensive restaurants, expect to pay about 300mk a day if travelling alone, or 250mk each with a partner.

Students with valid ID and seniors receive substantial discounts on museum admission prices quoted in this chapter, as well as on transportation (including ferries) – if you fit the bill, always ask.

Tipping & Bargaining

Tipping is not necessary and Finns generally don't do it. Bargaining is not common, except at flea markets.

POST & COMMUNICATIONS

Post offices are open 9 am to 5 pm weekdays, but stamps can be bought at bus or train stations and R-kiosks (newsstands). Postcards and letters weighing up to 20g cost 3.50mk within the EU, 2.70mk to other countries in Europe, and 3.40mk elsewhere.

The country code for calling Finland from abroad is ☎ 358. To make an international call from Finland first dial an international prefix (☎ 990, ☎ 994 or ☎ 999) and then the country code for the country you're calling.

International calls are expensive; calls placed weekdays between 10 pm and 8 am and all day Saturday and Sunday are cheapest. A three-minute call to the USA during peak time costs about 23mk. For national directory assistance dial ☎ 020 202, for international help ☎ 020 208.

Finland has 13 area codes, each starting with a zero. Include the zero when dialling within Finland, but omit it if you are calling from abroad.

Some public phones accept coins but most accept only plastic Telecards (30, 50 or 100mk). A short local call will cost at least 2mk. See the Telephones Appendix at the back of this book for more information.

All public libraries offer free Internet access, though in many cases you need to book hours or even days in advance. Internet cafes are not common.

INTERNET RESOURCES

Finland probably has more Web sites per capita than any other country – all tourist offices have a site, and so, it seems, does every other Finnish person, place and thing. A few good sites to start with are those of the Finnish Tourist Board (MEK; www.mek.fi), the Finnish Youth Hostel Association (SRM; www.srmnet.org) and the Helsinki city tourist office (www.hel.fi).

BOOKS

Lonely Planet's *Finland* is the most comprehensive guidebook available on this country. Guides to the architecture of Helsinki are available in that city's bookshops.

For a very readable history, see the paperback *A Short History of Finland* by Fred Singleton. *A Way to Measure Time* (Finnish Literature Society) contains contemporary Finnish literature by over 50 authors.

TIME

Finland is two hours ahead of GMT/UTC and summer time applies from early April to late October, when clocks go forward one hour.

WOMEN TRAVELLERS

The only likely annoyance is harassment by drunken men. Ignore them, and avoid neighbourhood pubs in the evening. Unioni Naisasialiitto Suomessa (☎ 643 158, Bulevardi 11A, Helsinki) is the national feminist organisation.

GAY & LESBIAN TRAVELLERS

Though you won't find the equivalent of Copenhagen's active gay community in Finland, it is as tolerant as other Nordic countries. Current information can be obtained from the Finnish organisation for gay and lesbian equality, SETA (Seksuaalinen tasavertaisus; ☎ 135 8302), Postios, PL55, 00531 Helsinki. Web site: www.seta.fi.

DISABLED TRAVELLERS

By law, most public and private institutions must provide ramps, lifts and special toilets for disabled persons, making Finland one of

FINLAND

the easiest countries to negotiate. Some national parks offer accessible trails.

DANGERS & ANNOYANCES

Violence mostly occurs in association with drunk males. Foreign males of dark complexion run the highest risk of street harassment, especially in smaller towns such as Joensuu. In Helsinki, it's best to avoid the main train station late at night.

Weather extremes in Lapland can cause unexpected danger at any time of the year. Exposure kills lone trekkers almost every winter, and cold rain can also be a problem in summer.

Wolves are not common, but are most likely seen in winter. Bears generally avoid people, though if they feel threatened females with cubs may attack.

BUSINESS HOURS

Shops are generally open 9 am to 5 pm weekdays, and to 1 pm on Saturday, though Helsinki shops often open longer hours. Public holidays are taken seriously – absolutely everything shuts at 6 pm on the eve of a holiday and reopens the morning after the holiday ends.

PUBLIC HOLIDAYS & SPECIAL EVENTS

Finland grinds to a halt twice a year: around Christmas (sometimes including the New Year) and during the Midsummer weekend. Plan ahead and avoid travelling during those times. The public holidays are: 1 January, 6 January (Epiphany), Good Friday to Easter Monday, 30 April and 1 May (May Day Eve and May Day), Ascension Day, Whit Sunday, Juhannus (Midsummer's Day) and Midsummer's Eve, 1 November (All Saints Day), 6 December (Independence Day), 24 December, 25 December and 26 December.

The foremost events are the Opera Festival in Savonlinna and the Jazz Festival in Pori, though every town and city in Finland puts on a barrage of festivals between mid-June and mid-August. The Lapp town of Sodankylä holds the annual Midnight Sun International Film Festival. A few smaller communities arrange some of the weirdest events imaginable (eg, the Wife-carrying World Championships in Iisalmi). Pick up the *Finland Festivals* booklet in any tourist office or contact Finland Festivals (☎ 09-621 4224), Uudemaankatu 36, 00120 Helsinki; or check out its Web site, www.festivals.fi.

Anyone who has been in Finland on *vappu* (May Day) will know it's a big day for Finns, and that more alcohol is consumed in the 48 hours surrounding 1 May than over a similar period at any other time of year.

ACTIVITIES

What would Finland be without the physically and mentally cleansing sauna? The traditional sauna is a wooden room with benches and a properly stoked wooden stove, though most Finnish saunas now have modern electrical heating. Temperatures from 80 to 100°C are the norm and bathing is done in the nude. A cold swim (fanatics roll in snow or jump in icy lakes during winter) afterwards completes the refreshment.

Canoes and kayaks can be hired in most towns near a lake – prices start at around 100mk a day or 500mk a week, but you will have to arrange the transport.

To fish you need a licence. In winter, ice-fishing is popular. Most fishing spots are owned privately or by local or national authorities, so you also need a local permit for the day or week; check local rules before you cast out.

Hiking or trekking is best from June to September. Wilderness huts line the northern trails (and must be shared). According to the law, a principle of common access to nature applies, so you are generally allowed to hike in any forested or wilderness area, and camp for a night anywhere outside inhabited, privately owned areas.

Nordic skiing is popular and there are cross-country trails (some lit) of varying difficulty. The season runs from October to April and, although daylight is limited before Christmas, you can ski in nocturnal twilight in Lapland from late October.

ACCOMMODATION

The Finnish Youth Hostel Association (SRM; ☎ 09-64 0377, ✉ info@srm.inet.fi), Yrjönkatu 38B, 00100 Helsinki, operates 133 hostels, with about half of them open year-round. Hostel prices quoted in this chapter are without the 15mk discount given to holders of a valid HI card. The invaluable free publication *Camping & Hostels*, published by the Finnish Tourist

Board, gives a full listing of camping and hostel accommodation.

Camp sites cost from 35mk to 80mk; if you don't have an International Camping Card buy a national Camping Card for 20mk (valid for one year).

Holiday cabins can be booked through regional tourist offices, generally for 1200mk a week or more for four people. For listings on the mainland and booking information, contact Lomarengas (☎ 09-3516 1321, ✉ sales@lomarengas.fi), Malminkaari 23, 00700 Helsinki.

FOOD

Restaurant meals are expensive, particularly at dinner. Fortunately, most restaurants offer special lunch menus for around 40mk, and these include salad, bread, milk, coffee and dessert, plus big helpings of hearty fare – sausage and potatoes or fish and potatoes are common.

Hostels and guesthouses often offer breakfast from about 25mk; it's cheaper to self-cater.

Most towns have a *kauppahalli* (covered market) where you can get sandwiches and snacks cheaply. The *grilli* is the venue for a takeaway meal of hamburgers or hot dogs for less than 25mk.

Genuine Finnish cuisine is not easy to find, but a 40mk to 60mk *seisova pöytä* (smorgasbord) with soups and fish is a grand experience.

DRINKS

Beer costs 20mk to 25mk a pint in cheaper bars, but as much as 33mk in ritzier joints. It costs as little as 5mk a bottle in supermarkets. Wines cost 30mk to 60mk a bottle.

Strong beers, wines and spirits are sold by the state network, aptly named Alko (open 10 am to 5 pm weekdays, and often only until 2 pm Saturday). Drinks containing more than 20 percent alcohol are not sold to those aged under 20; for beer and wine purchases the age limit is 18.

Local specialities include vodka, and cloudberry or cranberry liqueurs.

ENTERTAINMENT

Live music can vary from miserable to excellent; ask around, as most young Finns will love to let you in on the local music scene. In Helsinki, there are often large

dance parties; you'll see flyers in all the hipper Helsinki bars. Nightclubs charge from 20mk at the door, some up to an offensive 60mk (the usual age limit is 18 or 20 years, sometimes a whopping 24 years).

If possible, go to an ice hockey match – one of the few times you'll see Finns get animated. Football (soccer) matches are tame compared to other European countries, though the skill levels may surprise.

Getting There & Away

AIR

All major European carriers have flights to/from Helsinki. In addition to this, cheap London-Helsinki flights have been started by Buzz, KLM's budget carrier – go to its Web site at www.buzzaway.co.uk for the latest deals.

Holders of the GO25 or International Student Identity Card (ISIC) cards from student travel agents should also be able to pick up discount flights; in Finland, contact Kilroy Travels in Helsinki, Turku, Tampere and Oulu.

LAND
Bus

Buses run between Rovaniemi and the Norwegian border, and most buses continue on to the first Norwegian town. From Norway or southern Sweden there are buses (train passes are valid) to the Swedish town of Haparanda, from where you can easily walk (or take another bus) to the Finnish town of Tornio.

There are daily express buses from Turku and Helsinki to Vyborg and St Petersburg. These buses stop at other Finnish cities along the way, notably Porvoo and Hamina. Check current timetables and book tickets at the bus station or a travel agency.

Train

The *Tolstoi* sleeper departs Helsinki at 5.34 pm daily, arrives in Moscow at 8.38 am and costs 479mk one way, 2nd class. It departs Moscow at 10.17 pm daily.

The *Sibelius* and *Repin* offer daily service between Helsinki and St Petersburg (seven hours). The *Sibelius* departs Helsinki at 6.30 am (278mk 2nd class). The *Repin* departs at 3.35 pm and offers 2nd-class seats (278mk) or 1st-class sleeping berths (509mk). Return fares are double. From St Petersburg departures are at 4.35 pm *(Sibelius)* and 7.15 am *(Repin)*.

A Russian visa is required for all trains. Buy Russian rail tickets in Helsinki at the special ticket counter in the central station. Check timetables at www.vr.fi.

From Norway or southern Sweden there are trains to Boden.

SEA

Baltic ferries are some of the world's most impressive seagoing craft, and service between major cities is year-round. You should book when travelling in July, especially if you have a car.

Many ferries offer 50% discounts for holders of Eurail, Scanrail and Inter-Rail passes. Some services also offer discounts for seniors and for those with ISIC and GO25 cards.

Sweden

The Stockholm to Helsinki, Stockholm to Turku, and Kapellskär (Sweden) to Mariehamn (Åland) runs are covered by Silja Line and Viking Line, with daily departures year-round. Birka Cruises travels between Mariehamn and Stockholm.

Cabins are compulsory on Silja Line; they're optional on Viking. In summer, rates from Stockholm start at 79mk to Turku (11 to 12 hours) and 215mk to Helsinki (15 hours), plus around 200mk extra for a car.

Eckerö Linjen sails from Grisslehamn north of Stockholm to Eckerö in Åland – at three hours and 35mk (53mk in summer) it's the quickest and cheapest crossing from Sweden to Finland.

Silja Line also sails from Vaasa, Finland to Umeå, Sweden (150mk, 3½ hours) one to four times daily. In summer Silja sails from Pietarsaari (Jakobstad), Finland to Skellefteå, Sweden (200mk, 4½ hours) once daily and to Umeå once a week.

Estonia

The 80km trip from Helsinki to Tallinn is an easy and popular day trip. Car ferries cross in 3½ hours, catamarans and hydrofoils in about 1½ hours. In winter there are fewer departures, and the traffic is also slower due to the ice.

Ferries are cheapest, with return fares from 125mk in summer; Tallink, Silja Line and Eckerö Linjen all have daily departures. Catamarans and hydrofoils cost 157mk to 300mk return.

Germany

Silja Line and Finnlines have year-round service from Helsinki to Travemünde (32 to 36 hours) with bus service to Hamburg. Finnlines also operates year-round service from Helsinki to Lübeck (36 hours). Rates for Helsinki-Travemünde are from US$120 to US$600 one way.

Russia

At the time of writing there was no ferry service operating between Finland and Russia, though Kristina Cruises (☎ 05-218 1011) offers visa-free cruises from Helsinki to St Petersburg, and Karelia Lines (☎ 05-453 0380) offers visa-free cruises from Lappeenranta to Vyborg.

Getting Around

AIR

Finnair and SAS fly domestic – but not especially cheap – services between the big centres and to Lapland. Advance-purchase return tickets give up to 50% discounts, and summer deals are cheaper still. Seniors and children aged under 12 years receive a 70% discount. Those aged between 17 and 24 pay half-price and can fly stand-by to anywhere in Finland for 249mk one way.

BUS

Buses are the principal carriers outside the railway network – they travel 90% of Finland's roads. You may buy your ticket on board or book at a bus station or travel agency. Restricted services operate on Saturday and public holidays. Very few lines operate on Sunday.

Long-distance and express bus travel is handled by Oy Matkahuolto Ab (☎ 09-682 701) in Helsinki. Private lines operate local services but all share the same ticketing system. National timetables are available from bus stations, tourist offices (or on the Web site at www.expressbus.com).

Ticket prices depend on the length of journey. From Helsinki to Rovaniemi by express bus (13½ hours) costs around 500mk one way. A reserved seat (optional) carries a 12mk surcharge. Return tickets are about 10% cheaper than two one-way fares. Discounts are available for students and seniors, though usually only if the ticket is booked and the trip is more than 80km.

A Holiday Ticket is valid for two weeks and 1000km (390mk). There are no refunds. On some routes, buses accept train passes.

TRAIN

Finnish trains are efficient, fast and much cheaper than in Sweden and Norway. On longer routes there are two- and three-bed sleepers (costing from 60mk per bed) and special car-carriers. Rovaniemi is the main northern rail terminus.

VR Ltd Finnish Railways (☎ 09-707 3519) in Helsinki has its own travel bureau at main stations and can advise on all tickets. A one-way ticket from Helsinki to Rovaniemi (nine hours) is 339mk 2nd class. Single tickets are valid for eight days and return tickets valid for a month. Passengers under 17 years old pay half fare and children aged under six travel free (without a seat). There are also discounts for families and seniors.

International rail passes accepted in Finland include the Eurail pass, Eurail Flexipass, Scanrail Pass and Inter-Rail pass.

The Finnrail Pass is a one-month pass good for three/five/10 days of 2nd-class travel (there's no need for 1st class on trains this slick), and costs 620/830/1120mk. Tickets may be purchased before arrival in Finland (consult your local travel agent). Check at the train station on arrival for summer and regional special fares.

CAR & MOTORCYCLE

Finland's road network is good between centres, although in the forests you'll find many unsurfaced roads and dirt tracks. There are no road tolls. Petrol is expensive in southern Finland – around 7mk per litre – and even more in Lapland, costing up to 8mk.

Your headlights must be turned on at all times outside built-up areas. The speed limit is 50km/h in built-up areas and from 80km/h to 100km/h on highways. Traffic keeps to the right.

Small 10-year-old sedans and old vans can cost less than 10,000mk, but those that cost less than 5000mk should have been recently inspected (katsastettu).

Car rental companies such as Budget (☎ 686 6500), Hertz (☎ 0800-112 233) and Europcar (☎ 09-7515 5300) have offices in most cities. The smallest car costs from 180mk per day and 2mk per kilometre. Weekly rentals with unlimited mileage cost from 2000mk.

BICYCLE

Finland is bicycle-friendly, with miles of bike paths. Daily hire at about 50mk is common and a weekly rate should be around 250mk. SRM offers a cycling and hostel package that takes in the flat south and lakes. New bicycles range from 1000mk, but good second-hand models may cost less than 500mk.

BOAT

Lake and river ferries operate over the summer period. They're more than mere transport – a cruise is a bona fide Finnish experience. Many of the ferries that run between the islands along the coast are free, especially in Åland.

Helsinki

☎ 09

Helsinki, with its population of 540,000, is small and intimate compared to other Scandinavian capitals; its size makes it easy to walk around and its cafes, parks, markets and nearby islands are an absolute delight in summer.

The area has only been settled since 1550. While the Swedes (whose name for the city is Helsingfors) were here in the 1700s they built a mammoth fortress on nearby Suomenlinna Island. After falling to the tsar in 1808, Helsinki became the seat of the Russian Grand Duchy. The monumental buildings of Senaatintori (Senate Square) were designed by 19th-century architect Carl Ludwig Engel to give the new city an appropriate measure of oomph.

Orientation

Helsinki occupies a peninsula and is linked by bridge and ferry to nearby islands. Close towns include Espoo to the east and Vantaa, with the international airport, to the north.

The city centre surrounds the main harbour Eteläsatama and the *kauppatori* (market square); huge international ferry terminals lie either side.

Information

Tourist Offices The helpful and friendly Helsinki City Tourist Office (☎ 169 3757), Pohjoisesplanadi 19, is open daily from May to the end of September. The rest of the year it's closed Sunday.

The Finnish Tourist Board (☎ 4176 9300) has an office at Eteläesplanadi 4, across from the city tourist office. It's open daily from May to September, weekdays only the rest of the year.

The youth information centre Kompassi (☎ 3108 0080), in the Lasipalatsi Multimedia Centre at Mannerheimintie 22-24, has information on travelling for young people. It's closed Monday and Saturday.

Tikankontti (☎ 270 5221 or ☎ 0203-44 122), Eteläasplanadi 20, is the Helsinki office of Metsähallitus, the Finnish Forest and Park Service. It's open 10 am to 6 pm weekdays, and 10 am to 3 pm Saturday.

Helsinki Card This pass gives free urban travel, an 80% discount for entry fees to more than 50 attractions in and around Helsinki (including almost all of the sights in the following Things to See & Do section) and discounts on day tours to Porvoo and Tallinn. A card lasting one/two/three days costs 130/165/195mk, and 55/65/75 for children. If you buy one, make sure you take the free 1½-hour sightseeing tour.

Money Forex, at the train station, offers good rates and is open 8 am to 9 pm daily. The airport exchange counter is open 6.30 am to 11 pm daily, although a machine operates 24 hours. A counter at the Katajanokka ferry terminal is open 9 am to 6 pm weekdays. Western Union on the 7th floor of the Stockmann department store is open daily.

Post & Communications The main post office is at Mannerheiminaukio 1, opposite the train station; it's open 10 am to 7 pm weekdays, and 11 am to 4 pm weekends. The poste restante office (00100 Helsinki) is in the same building, and opens 8 am to 9 pm weekdays, 9 am to 6 pm Saturday and 11 am to 9 pm Sunday.

Email & Internet Access Web access at public libraries in Finland is free. The Rikhardinkadun Library, at Rikhardinkatu 3, has several terminals. The Kirjakaapeli library, upstairs in the Lasipalatsi Multimedia Centre at Mannerheimintie 22-24, has 23 terminals.

Below Kirjakaapeli next to the bus station is the chic Meteori Books (☎ 611 475), with around 10 terminals costing 15mk per 20 minutes.

Roberts Coffee, the cafe on the ground floor of Stockmann department store, has two free terminals, as does the cafe at Kiasma.

But the best place in town is the Helsinki University Library, Unioninkatu 36, with 20 free terminals at the rear of the 2nd floor. There are also free small lockers downstairs.

Travel Agencies Kilroy Travels (☎ 680 7811), Kaivokatu 10C, specialises in student and budget travel. Tour Expert, in the city tourist office, handles travel around Finland, to Tallinn and St Petersburg.

Bookshops Akateeminen Kirjakauppa, at Pohjoisesplanadi 39, has books, newspapers and periodicals in 40 languages. The Sokos and Stockmann department stores also have foreign newspapers.

Laundry A load of washing at Easywash, Runeberginkatu 47, costs 25mk; drying is 10mk extra; tram no 3 stops right outside. Café Tin Tin Tango, Töölöntorinkatu 7, has a washing machine (30mk).

Left Luggage Luggage can be left at the main train station. Lockers cost 10mk and the left-luggage counter charges 10mk per piece per day.

Medical Services Dial ☎ 112 for ambulance service, ☎ 10022 for police and ☎ 10023 for 24-hour medical advice. The police have stations at Helsinki's main train and bus stations.

English speakers should use the 24-hour clinic at Töölö Hospital (☎ 4711), Töölönkatu 40. There's a 24-hour pharmacy at Mannerheimintie 96.

Things to See & Do

An eccentric and superbly curvaceous building houses **Kiasma**, Mannerheiminaukio 2,

FINLAND

Finland's national museum of contemporary art. It's open 9 am to 5 pm Tuesday and 10am to 10pm Wednesday to Sunday (closed Monday); admission 25mk. Check out the Web site at www.kiasma.fng.fi.

The **Amos Anderson Art Museum**, Yrjönkatu 27, has great touring exhibitions of contemporary art, as well as a less interesting permanent collection. Entry is around 30mk; its Web site is at www.amosanderson.fi.

No visit to Helsinki is complete without a sauna at the sleek Art Deco **Yrjönkadun Uimahalli**, Yrjönkatu 21, with its two indoor swimming pools. There are separate hours for men and women, and bathing suits are not allowed. Entry is 25mk for a swim and sauna, and up to 60mk for a swim, steamroom and smoke sauna.

The monolithic **Parliament** building dominates the Mannerheimintie entrance to the centre of Helsinki; Alvar Aalto's angular **Finlandia Talo** (concert hall) is on the other side of the road.

The **Temppeliaukio Church** (Church in the Rock), which is hewn into rock on Temppelikatu, has a stunning 24m-diameter roof covered in 22km of copper stripping, and is worth a look.

The **Kansallimuseo** (National Museum), Mannerheimintie 34, was scheduled to reopen in late 2000 after major renovation. Just opposite it is the main branch of the **City Museum**.

North of the **Opera House**, on the corner of Mannerheimintie and Helsinginkatu, are the tiny, beautifully manicured **City Gardens**. Farther north is **Linnanmäki amusement park** (bus No 23 or tram No 3 or 8), open daily April to September. Day passes are 90mk (children 60mk); individual ride tickets 6mk.

Back in town, the Finnish national gallery **Ateneum**, Kaivokatu 2, covers Finnish and international art dating from the 18th century to the middle of the 20th century (closed Monday).

Senaatintori, Helsinki's majestic central square, is ringed with early-19th-century buildings. It was modelled after St Petersburg's and is occasionally used by B-list Hollywood film makers wanting a dramatic 'Russian' backdrop. CL Engel's stately **Tuomiokirkko** (Lutheran cathedral), finished in 1852, is the square's most prominent feature.

The Orthodox **Uspensky Cathedral** (opened 1868) above the harbour at Kanavakatu 1 is even more magnificent, inside and out. The red-brick exterior supports 13 gilded cupolas representing Christ and his disciples.

Stock up on fruit and vegetables at the main produce and craft market held daily in the **kauppatori** (market square), also known as the Fish Market.

The beautiful park bordered by Bulevardi, Lönnrotinkatu, Yrjönkatu and Annankatu houses the lovely **Old Church**. The **Hietalahti flea market** in Hietalahdentori (off Bulevardi) comes alive on summer evenings. The **Sinebrychoff Museum of Foreign Art**, nearby at Bulevardi 40, has Continental works and Orthodox icons (closed Tuesday).

Ferries and water taxis shuttle to **Suomenlinna** from the kauppatori (10mk one way, or use your Helsinki Card). You can ramble around the ruins of the mighty fortress, a World Heritage Site, or look around the museums, including the **Ehrensvärd Museum** which covers the history of the fortress and its many battles (open May to August).

Korkeasaari Island has the **zoo** and is best reached by ferry from the kauppatori (the 40mk return ticket includes zoo admission).

The massive **Cable Factory**, Nokia's main factory until the 1980s, has been converted into theatres, art galleries and dance studios, and there's a cafe and restaurant – definitely worth a visit.

The open-air centre on **Seurasaari Island** is Helsinki's folk museum. It's open 15 May to 15 September and entry is free except to the houses (20mk). Take bus No 24 from the central train station.

The most important sight in the town of **Espoo** is the pastiche castle **Tarvaspää**, Gallen-Kallelantie 27, the studio and now museum of Akseli Gallen-Kallela (35mk). Take tram No 4 to Munkkiniemi, then walk 2km or take bus No 33.

Organised Tours

A 1½-hour guided sightseeing tour by bus departs at 10 am daily from the Olympia Ferry Terminal; cost is 85mk.

Places to Stay

Bookings *at least* a week in advance are essential for hostels and hotels from May to

FINLAND

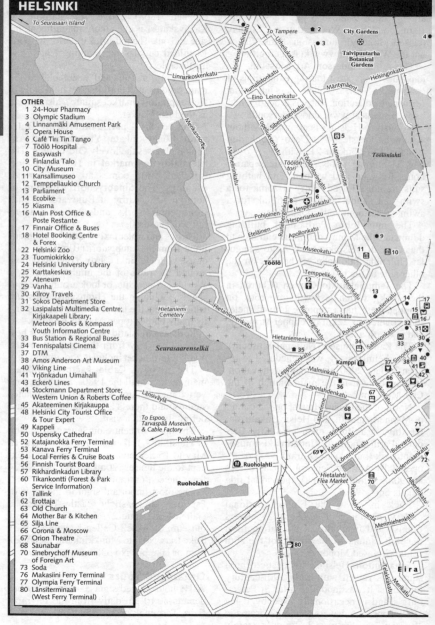

HELSINKI

To Seurasaari Island

To Tampere
City Gardens
Talvipuutarha
Botanical
Gardens

Linnankoskenkatu
Humalistonkatu
Eino Leinonkatu
Mäntymäent
Helsinginkatu

Töölönlahti

OTHER
1 24-Hour Pharmacy
3 Olympic Stadium
4 Linnanmäki Amusement Park
5 Opera House
6 Café Tiu Tin Tango
7 Töölö Hospital
8 Easywash
9 Finlandia Talo
10 City Museum
11 Kansallimuseo
12 Temppeliaukio Church
13 Parliament
14 Ecobike
15 Kiasma
16 Main Post Office &
    Poste Restante
17 Finnair Office & Buses
18 Hotel Booking Centre
    & Forex
22 Helsinki Zoo
23 Tuomiokirkko
24 Helsinki University Library
25 Karttakeskus
27 Ateneum
29 Vanha
30 Kilroy Travels
31 Sokos Department Store
32 Lasipalatsi Multimedia Centre;
    Kirjakaapeli Library;
    Meteori Books & Kompassi
    Youth Information Centre
33 Bus Station & Regional Buses
34 Tennispalatsi Cinema
37 DTM
38 Amos Anderson Art Museum
40 Viking Line
41 Yrjönkadun Uimahalli
43 Eckerö Lines
44 Stockmann Department Store;
    Western Union & Roberts Coffee
45 Akateeminen Kirjakauppa
48 Helsinki City Tourist Office
    & Tour Expert
49 Kappeli
50 Uspensky Cathedral
52 Katajanokka Ferry Terminal
53 Kanava Ferry Terminal
55 Local Ferries & Cruise Boats
56 Finnish Tourist Board
57 Rikhardinkadun Library
60 Tikankontti (Forest & Park
    Service Information)
61 Tallink
62 Erottaja
63 Old Church
64 Mother Bar & Kitchen
65 Silja Line
66 Corona & Moscow
67 Orion Theatre
68 Saunabar
70 Sinebrychoff Museum
    of Foreign Art
73 Soda
76 Makasiini Ferry Terminal
77 Olympia Ferry Terminal
80 Länsiterminaali
    (West Ferry Terminal)

Merikannonti
Mechelininkatu
Töölön
tori
Töölöntorinkatu
Mannerheimintie
Topeliuksenkatu
Sibeliuksenkatu
Nordenskiöldinkatu
Urhelukatu

Pohjoinen
Hesperiankatu
Eteläinen
Hesperiankatu
Apollonkatu
Museokatu
Runeberginkatu
Nervanderinkatu
Mannerheimintie

Töölö

Temppelikatu
Arkadiankatu
Pohjoinen
Rautatienkatu
Salomonkatu

Hietaniemi
Cemetery
Hietaniemenkatu
Hietaniemenkatu

Seurasaarenselkä

Leppäsuonkatu
Kamppi
Simonkatu
Malminkatu
Lapinlahdenkatu
Fredrikinkatu
Annankatu

Lapinlahti
Eerikinkatu
Kalevankatu
Lönnrotinkatu
Bulevardi
Uudenmaankatu
Albertinkatu

Länsiväylä
Lansiväylä

To Espoo,
Tarvaspää Museum
& Cable Factory
Porkkalankatu

Ruoholahti
Ruoholahti

Hietalahti
Flea Market
Ruoholahdenranta
Merimiehenkatu

Eira
Telakkakatu
Merikatu

Hietasaarenkuja

euro currency converter €1 = 5.95mk

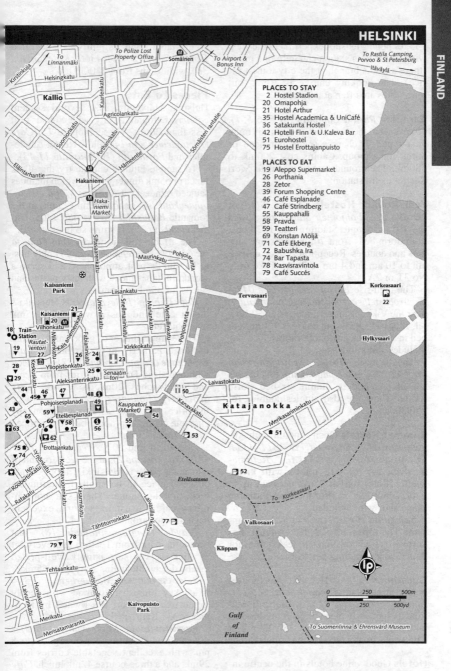

HELSINKI

FINLAND

PLACES TO STAY
2 Hostel Stadion
20 Omapohja
21 Hotel Arthur
35 Hostel Academica & UniCafé
36 Satakunta Hostel
42 Hotelli Finn & U.Kaleva Bar
51 Eurohostel
75 Hostel Erottajanpuisto

PLACES TO EAT
19 Aleppo Supermarket
26 Porthania
28 Zetor
39 Forum Shopping Centre
46 Café Esplanade
47 Café Strindberg
55 Kauppahalli
58 Pravda
59 Teatteri
69 Konstan Möljä
71 Café Ekberg
72 Babushka Ira
74 Bar Tapasta
78 Kasvisravintola
79 Café Succés

August. The Hotel Booking Centre (☎ 171 133, ❷ hotel@helsinkiexpert.fi) in the west wing of the train station can help in a pinch (there's also a branch at the city tourist office). The booking charge is 20mk, but room rates are often at a discount.

Camping *Rastila Camping (☎ 316 551),* 10km east of the centre in Vuosaari, is open year-round. It charges 60mk per head or 80mk for a group. Cabins cost 200mk to 580mk. The grounds are adjacent to Meri Rastila metro station.

Year-Round Hostels *Hostel Stadion (☎ 496 071, Pohjoinen Stadiontie 3B)* at the 1952 Olympic Stadium has 162 beds, with dorm beds from 70mk and some singles and doubles. Reception is open daily 8 am to 10 am and 4 pm to 2 am. Take tram No 3T or 7A.

The high-rise *Eurohostel (☎ 622 0470, ❷ eurohostel@eurohostel.fi, Linnankatu 9)* near the Viking Line terminal, is an HI hostel. It has 255 beds and charges 120mk per bed in simple, clean double rooms. The rate includes a morning sauna.

The central *Hostel Erottajanpuisto (☎ 642 169, Uudenmaankatu 9)* charges 140mk per bed in quaint six-bed dorm rooms. There are also singles/doubles for 250/300mk.

Summer Hostels Open June through August, *Hostel Academica (☎ 1311 4334, ❷ hostel.academica@hyy.fi, Hietaniemenkatu 14)* has 115 rooms with kitchenettes. Rates start at 95mk per bed, up to 230/320mk for singles/doubles; morning sauna and swim included.

Satakunta Hostel (☎ 6958 5231, Lapinrinne 1A), open June to late August, has dorm beds for 70mk and singles/doubles for 230/330mk including breakfast.

Guesthouses Most Helsinki guesthouses ooze sleaze, but not *Omapohja (☎ 666 211, Itäinen Teatterikuja 3)* near the train station. Its spotlessly clean, high-roofed rooms with huge windows go from 230/330mk. It fills weeks in advance so book ahead.

Hotels Good-value hotels in the centre include *Hotel Arthur (☎ 173 441, Vuorikatu 19),* with excellent rooms for 440/550mk

(380/480mk in summer), and the clean, comfortable and slightly dishevelled *Hotelli Finn (☎ 684 4360, Kalevankatu 3B),* with rooms from 230/330mk.

Places to Eat
Helsinki University has several student *cafeterias* around the city, where meals cost less than 20mk. These include *UniCafé (Hietaniemenkatu 14)* below Hostel Academica and *Porthania (Hallituskatu 11-13).*

To sample Finnish cuisine try the 40mk lunch or 65mk dinner buffet (which includes sauteed reindeer) at *Konstan Möljä (Hietalahdenkatu 14);* or try a blini (95mk) at the romantic *Babushka Ira (☎ 680 1405, Uudenmaankatu 28).* It's tiny so book ahead.

The affable folk at nearby *Bar Tapasta (☎ 640 724, Uudenmaankatu 13)* play host to Helsinki's best atmosphere and serve a wonderful tapas menu with tasty pastas and salads for 35mk to 45mk.

Café Ekberg (Bulevardi 9) is Helsinki's oldest cafe and has a wonderful 45mk lunch buffet.

There are a number of good cafes around Esplanadi park. If you're on a budget, *Café Esplanade (Pohjoisesplanadi 37)* is perfect, with oversized Danish pastries from 12mk and sandwiches 20mk to 25mk. *Café Strindberg (Pohjoisesplanadi 33)* is twice the price, but twice as classy; its snappy clientele chomp top-notch baguettes priced from 27mk to 35mk.

Opened in mid-2000, *Teatteri (☎ 6811 1310, Pohjoisespa 2),* at the western end of Esplanadi park, is Helsinki's hippest (and poshest) place to be spotted chatting on your mobile phone. There's a not-too-pricey cafe downstairs serving excellent baguettes for around 30mk.

Pravda (Pohjoisesplanadi 18), just across the park from Teatteri and every bit as slick, serves surprisingly well-priced meals; delectable mains start from 55mk.

Zetor (☎ 666 966, Mannerheimintie 3-5) is a jokey Finnish restaurant with deeply ironic tractor decor; it's owned by filmmaker Aki Kaurismäki.

Kasvisravintola (Korkeavuorenkatu 3) is a vegetarian restaurant open nightly to 8 pm, with excellent vegetable curries from 29mk, and a three-course 42mk lunch. *Café Succés (Korkeavuorenkatu 2)* over the road does great coffee and cakes.

For fast food, head to the *Forum shopping centre* basement *(Mannerheimintie 20)*. The *kauppahalli (Eteläranta 1)* is great for cheap sandwiches and snacks.

If you want to fend for yourself, *Aleppo*, a supermarket in the pedestrian tunnel by the train station, is open 8 am to 10 pm weekdays, 10 am to 8 pm weekends.

Entertainment

Bars *Vanha (Mannerheimintie 3)*, a music bar in this beautiful 19th-century students' house, is popular with city hipsters, as is the grungy little *U.Kaleva (Kalevankatu 3A)*, serving cheap beer and wine. Perfect for a quiet drink among Helsinki's folk in the know is *Erottaja (☎ 611 196, Erottajankatu 15-17)*.

The brewery pub in the cellar at *Kappeli (Eteläesplanadi 1)* is where worker ants come to wind down from a hard day's data entry. The outdoor tables on summer evenings can be great fun.

Soda (Uudenmaankatu 16-20) draws droves of shiny, happy people with its house and techno music. If Soda's not hip enough for you, try the ultra-chic club above *Teatteri (Pohjoisespa 2)*.

The stylish *Mother Bar & Kitchen (☎ 612 3990, Eerikinkatu 2)* has excellent DJs playing drum'n'bass and acid jazz music four nights a week, a wonderful vibe and a great tapas menu (21mk to 35mk). Nearby, *DTM (Annankatu 32)* is a popular gay bar that gets going after midnight. *Corona (Eerikinkatu 15)* and its neighbour *Moscow (Eerikinkatu 15)* are run by filmmakers Aki and Mika Kaurismäki; both attract a savvy, grungy crowd. The *Saunabar (Eerikinkatu 27)*, downstairs at the rear of the building, is popular with students and pool players.

Cinemas The *Tennispalatsi* multiplex *(Salomonkatu 15)* screens recent American movies (45mk). The nearby *Orion Theatre (Eerikinkatu 15)* is a cinema with a fondness for Woody Allen. Movies are always shown in their original language and have Finnish and Swedish subtitles.

Getting There & Away

Air There are flights to Helsinki from all major European cities. Vantaa airport is 19km north of the centre.

Bus Purchase long-distance and express bus tickets at the main bus station off Mannerheimintie (open 7 am to 7 pm weekdays, 7 am to 5 pm Saturday and 9 am to 6 pm Sunday), or on the bus itself. The express bus to St Petersburg costs 250mk one way and takes 8½ hours.

Train Express trains run daily to Turku, Tampere and Lappeenranta and there's a choice of day and overnight trains to Oulu, Rovaniemi and Joensuu.

Boat International ferries depart from four terminals and travel to Stockholm, Tallinn in Estonia, and Travemünde and Lübeck in Germany. See the Getting There & Away section earlier for more details.

Ferry tickets can be bought at the terminals, from the ferry companies' offices in the centre or (in some cases) from the city tourist office. Book tickets in advance for the June to August period.

Silja Lines' offices (☎ 9800-274 552) are at Mannerheimintie 2 and in the Olympia terminal. Viking Line (☎ 12 351) is at Mannerheimintie 14 and in the Katajanokka terminal. Eckerö Lines (☎ 228 8544) is at Mannerheimintie 10 and the Länsiterminaali (West Terminal). Tallink (☎ 2282 1211) is at Erottajankatu 19. A catamaran service to Tallinn departs from Kanava terminal.

Kanava and Katajanokka terminals are served by bus No 13 and tram Nos 2, 2V and 4; Olympia and Makasiini terminals by tram Nos 3B and 3T; and Länsiterminaali by bus No 15.

Getting Around

To/From the Airport Bus No 615 shuttles between Vantaa airport and platform No 10 at Rautatientori (Railway Square), next to the main train station; the trip takes 35 minutes (16mk, every 20 minutes on weekdays, every 30 minutes on weekends).

Finnair buses depart from the Finnair office at Asema-aukio, also next to the main train station, though on the other side of the building (27mk, every 20 minutes 5 am to midnight).

There are shared taxis (☎ 2200 2500) at 70mk per person; otherwise the fare is 120mk.

Public Transport A one-hour ticket for the bus, tram, metro, Suomenlinna ferry and

FINLAND

local trains within Helsinki's HKL network costs 10mk when purchased on board, 8mk when purchased in advance. The ticket allows unlimited transfers. A single tram ticket (no transfers) is 8mk on board, 6mk in advance.

Tourist tickets are available at 25/50/75mk for one/three/five days; 10-trip tickets cost 75mk.

HKL offices at the Rautatientori and Hakaniemi metro stations (open weekdays) sell tickets and passes, as do many of the city's R-kiosks (newsstands). Metro services run 6 am to 11.30 pm daily.

Bicycle Helsinki is ideal for cycling: the small inner city is flat, and there are well-marked and high-quality bicycle paths.

In July 2000 Helsinki installed 300 'City Bikes' at venues within a 2km radius of the kauppatori. Depositing a 10mk piece into the stand unlocks the bicycle; you can then return it at various stands around town and reclaim your 10mk. Ask at the Helsinki Tourist Office for more details.

Ecobike (☎ 4110 0800) at Mannerheimintie 13, in the small yellow hut across the road from parliament house, rents out bikes from 50mk a day during spring and summer.

AROUND HELSINKI
Porvoo
☎ 019

This picturesque medieval town is about 50km east of Helsinki – a perfect day trip. The historic **church** and several good museums are the main sights, but there are also cosy cafes on the cobblestone lanes of the old town and the squeaky clean *Porvoo Hostel (☎ 523 0012, Linnankoskenkatu 1-3)*. Beds cost from 90mk.

Frequent buses connect Porvoo with Helsinki, as do ferries in summer. The steamship *JL Runeberg* sails regularly to/from Helsinki in summer (150mk).

Southern Finland

Nowhere in Finland are there so many historical monuments as the southern coast between Turku and Hamina. This region, dotted with medieval churches, old manors and castles, is strongly influenced by early Swedish

settlers, and several Swedish dialects are still spoken in coastal communities.

TURKU
☎ 02

Though you might not know it due to its predominantly modern buildings, Turku (population 171,000) is the oldest city in Finland, founded in the 1200s, and also the former Swedish capital. It's now a large port and a major border crossing with Sweden, and Finland's fifth-largest city.

Information
The city tourist office (☎ 262 7444), Aurakatu 4, is open daily. The Forex office, Eerikinkatu 12, offers good rates and is open 8 am to 7 pm weekdays, 8 am to 5 pm Saturday. The main post office, Humalistonkatu 1, is open 9 am to 8 pm weekdays. A pharmacy open 8 am to 11 pm daily is at Aurakatu 10.

There are several Internet terminals at the public library, Linnankatu 2 (closed Sunday). There's also Surf City, Brahenkatu 2, charging 15mk per half-hour for Internet access (13mk for students).

Things to See & Do
The mammoth **Turku Castle** (Linnankatu) is open 10 am to 6 pm daily from May to September (2 pm to 7 pm Monday, 10 am to 3 pm Tuesday to Sunday the rest of the year). Admission costs 30mk. There's also a popular bar/cafe in the entrance quadrant. Take bus No 1 from the kauppatori.

Four **museum ships** (open summer only) dominate the river banks: the steam tug *Vetäjäv*, the minelayer *Keihässalmi* and the three-masted *Sigyn* each charge 10mk admission. The impressive *Suomen Joutsen* (Swan of Finland), a 1902 sailing ship, charges a steep 20mk.

Aboa Vetus and **Ars Nova**, at Itäinen Rantakatu 4-6, are, respectively, an archaeological museum and a modern art collection. Tickets are 50mk for both, or 35mk each.

Archipelago **cruises** are a popular activity in summer. There are day trips as well as evening dinner-and-dance cruises. Departures are from Martinsilta bridge and fares are from 45mk.

Places to Stay & Eat
Ruissalo Camping (☎ 258 9249), on an island 10km west of the centre (take bus No

8), is open from June to mid-August. Sites cost 70mk and there are also cabins.

Hostel Turku (☎ *262 7680, Linnankatu 39)* is open all year (reception closed 10 am to 3 pm daily). Dorm beds cost 60mk, and there are a couple of double rooms for 85mk per person.

The *Bridgettine Sisters Guesthouse* (☎ *250 1910, Ursininkatu 15A)* is run by the nuns of a Catholic convent. The clean, simple singles/doubles are a bargain at 210/320mk, including breakfast. Silence is expected around the corridors and reception areas after 10 pm. Book ahead.

There are cheap eateries everywhere around the market square, especially in the *kauppahalli* (closed Sundays). *Boat restaurants* (summer only) sound tacky, but are surprisingly nice; you'll find several near the Auransilta bridge.

Next to the bridge is the ultra-chic *Blanko (Aurakatu 1)*, where Turku's gorgeous young things shake their booty; there is an excellent tapas menu with meals from 35mk to 45mk. Footpath tables overlooking the main bridge are a great place to sip an afternoon beer in summer.

Verso (Linnankatu 3) is a vegetarian restaurant offering 40mk lunch specials 11 am to 2 pm weekdays. A few doors down is *Sergio's (Linnankatu 3)*, an Italian restaurant serving excellent pasta and the best coffee in town; the outside terrace overlooking the river is perfect for lunch if the sun's out.

Stop for a beer at the *riverside bar* across the river if the sun is shining, or if it's cloudy head up the hill to *Uusi Apteeki (Kaskenkatu 1)*, a wonderful bar in a converted old pharmacy, the antique shelving and desks filled with hundreds of old beer bottles.

Getting There & Away
Express trains run frequently to Helsinki, Rovaniemi, Tampere and Oulu.

Silja, Seawind and Viking ferries sail from Stockholm (9½ hours) and Mariehamn (six hours). Silja and Viking have offices at the harbour and in the Hansa shopping centre. Bus No 1 travels between the centre and the harbour.

NAANTALI
☎ 02
One of Finland's loveliest seaside towns, Naantali, 13km west of Turku, developed

after the founding of a convent in the 1440s. The harbour and old town with its church and quaint museums is good for strolling through. Nearby is beautiful **Kultaranta**, the summer residence of the president of Finland (guided tours are available). Scandinavian families come here for the *massively* popular **Moomin World** theme park (day pass 80mk, children 60mk), open June to August.

Tourist information is available at Naantalin Matkailu (☎ 435 0850), Kaivotori 2.

Places to Stay & Eat
Naantali Camping (☎ 435 0855), 800m north of the town centre, is open year-round and has cabins from 160mk and campsites for 80mk. *Hotel Anmarina (☎ 435 6066, Nunnakatu 5)*, right next to the harbour, is an excellent choice with single/double cabins from 300/400mk in summer and 100mk less at other times (cheaper for a full week's booking).

Naantali has excellent restaurants. *Merisali (Nunnakatu 1)* at the harbour offers an unbelievable 57mk lunch and dinner buffet. *Café Antonius (Mannerheiminkatu 9)* is a homy – and cheaper – option.

Getting There & Away
There are frequent buses from Turku, and in summer the steamship *Ukkopekka* cruises between Turku and Naantali several times each day.

RYMÄTTYLÄ
☎ 02
From Naantali, the road south leads to Rymättylä, a peaceful island village with a beautiful 14th-century vaulted **church**, which is open 9 am to 4 pm daily in summer.

The idyllic *Päiväkulma Hostel (☎ 252 1894, Kuristentie 225)*, open late May to late August, justifies a visit to Rymättylä. Beds in the old house cost from 75mk; there's a kitchen, seaside sauna and rowboat. Book well ahead.

KEMIÖ ISLAND
☎ 02
Kemiö Island offers excellent possibilities for bicycle tours. The 18th-century churches and the museums of **Sagalund** and **Dalsbruk** are worth a visit, and there is access to the **Archipelago National Park** via the park centre in Kasnäs.

Pensionat och Vandrarhotell (☎ 424 553, Kulla) in the village of Dragsfjärd is a delightful hostel (closed January and February) with dorm beds from 70mk. There are bicycles for rent.

All buses and trains between Helsinki and Turku stop at Salo, which has half a dozen daily bus connections to Kemiö Island.

Åland

☎ 018

The Åland islands are unique, autonomous islands with their own flag and culture. Several dialects of Swedish are spoken, and few Ålanders speak Finnish. Åland took its own flag in 1954 and has issued stamps (prized by collectors) since 1984.

The centre of Åland is Mariehamn, in the south of the main island group. You can take your wheels almost anywhere around the islands using the bridges or the network of car and bicycle ferries.

Information

The main tourist office is Ålands Turistinformation in Mariehamn (☎ 24000), at Storagatan 8. Web site: www.info.aland.fi.

Getting There & Away

Air There are weekday direct flights to/from Stockholm and daily flights to/from Helsinki via Turku. The airport is 4km north of Mariehamn and there's a bus service. Finnair has an office at Skarpansvägen 24 in Mariehamn.

Boat In Mariehamn, Eckerö Linjen is at Torggatan 2, Silja Line is at Norragatan 2, Birka Cruises is at Östra Esplanadsgatan 7 and Viking Line is at Storagatan 2. Viking and Silja Lines have daily ferries to Mariehamn from Turku as part of their links with Stockholm: you can stop-off 'between' countries. Viking also sails from Kapellskär in Sweden.

Birka Cruises sails between Stockholm and Mariehamn. Eckerö Linjen sails from Grisslehamn to Eckerö – this is the cheapest and quickest route from Sweden to Åland.

Getting Around

The five main buses depart from Mariehamn terminal on Torggatan near the library, and go to Eckerö, Geta, Saltvik, Vårdö (Hummelvik) and Lumparland (Långnäs) for fares ranging up to 33mk.

Ferries are constantly plying the shorter straits, and are always free. On longer routes, ferries take cars, bikes and pedestrians.

There are also three bicycle ferries in summer, for 30mk to 40mk per person with bicycle. For timetables ask the tourist office or Ålandstrafiken at Strandgatan 25, Mariehamn.

Bicycle is the best way to see these flat, rural islands. The most scenic roads have clearly marked separate bike lanes. Ro-No Rent has bicycles available at Mariehamn and Eckerö harbours with rates starting at 40mk per day, or 150mk per week.

MARIEHAMN

Mariehamn retains its village flavour despite the summer tourist rush. The main pedestrian street Torggatan is colourful, and there are some great museums.

Orientation & Information

Mariehamn lies on a peninsula and has two harbours, Västra Hamnen (West Harbour) and Östra Hamnen (East Harbour). Ferries from Sweden and mainland Finland dock at Västra Hamnen but just about everything else is at Östra Hamnen.

There's luggage storage in lockers (10mk) at the ferry terminal, or Ålandstrafiken will store backpacks for 5mk a day.

Things to See

The **Maritime Museum** at Västra Hamnen, a kitsch museum of fishing and maritime commerce, is devoted to the stalwart mariners of Åland (admission 20mk).

Trade and crafts displays are at the **Köpmannagar** (Merchant's House) in Parkgatan (open 1 to 3 pm weekdays in summer; free). Of more general interest is the fine **Ålands Museum** and **Åland Art Museum**, housed jointly at the east end of Storagatan (15mk).

Places to Stay & Eat

Gröna Uddens Camping (☎ 19041, Osternäsvägen), 1km south of town, charges 20mk per person per night. It's open mid-May to August.

The *Botel Alida* (☎ 13755) is a summer-only boat hostel (and year-round cafe) moored at the north end of Östra Hamnen.

It charges 90mk per bed in basic two-bunk cabins. *Gästhem Kronan (☎ 12617, Neptunigatan 52)* charges 215/330mk for clean singles/doubles in summer.

The best local cafe is *Bagarstugan (Ekonomiegatan 2)* – it does excellent soups. *Cha Shao Tropical (Torggatan 10)* does a good stir-fry. The boat restaurant *FP von Knorring (Östra Hamnen)* has a great beer terrace for sunny afternoons.

SUND

Åland's most striking attraction is the medieval **Kastelholm** castle, in Sund, 20km north-east of Mariehamn (take bus No 4). It's open daily in summer and you must join a guided tour (25mk) to explore inside.

Farther east, the ruins of the Russian fortress at **Bomarsund** are accessible year-round, as are the cemeteries on **Prästö Island**.

Near Bomarsund is *Puttes Camping (☎ 44016)*, open May to August, which charges 12mk per person and has cabins. *Prästö Stugor & Camping (☎ 44045)*, on Prästö Island, also has cabins in summer.

Café Uffe på Berget is popular for its splendid view over the islands, and its 30m observation tower is superb. It's on the main Mariehamn-Sund road near the town of Godby, just before the bridge to Sund.

ECKERÖ

Finland's westernmost municipality, Eckerö is linked by ferry to Sweden. The ferry terminal is at Storby village, and its historic **Post & Customs building** houses a cafe, post office and bank. Bus No 1 runs to Mariehamn.

East from Storby on the road to Mariehamn, the medieval **Eckerö Church** has beautiful interior paintings. There are other medieval churches along the road between Storby and Mariehamn – watch for signs.

Käringsund Camping (☎ 38309), at Storby, has cabins and 37mk campsites. *Ängstorps Gästhem (☎ 38665)*, at Storby, is one of the best places to stay in Åland. In summer, singles/doubles are 220/300mk.

Central Finland

TAMPERE
☎ 03
Set between the Näsijärvi and Pyhäjärvi lakes, Tampere is Finland's third-largest

city (population 189,500). Dozens of red-brick chimneys from former factories point skyward in this 19th-century textile manufacturing centre; most have now been transformed into cultural centres, bars or restaurants. There's plenty to see and do in Tampere, long known as the 'Manchester of Finland'.

Information
The city tourist office (☎ 212 6652, Verkatehtaankatu 2) is open weekdays in winter and daily in summer. Web site: www.tampere.fi. Vuoltsu, the international youth centre, provides information and free luggage storage; it's at Vuolteenkatu 13 and is open daily from June to September.

Vuoltsu houses an Internet cafe open noon to 6 pm Monday to Friday; terminals are 8mk per hour. There are also free Internet terminals at the public library, and the information centre has one terminal.

Things to See & Do
The city's most fascinating attraction, the **Lenin Museum**, Hämeenpuisto 28, is packed with relics of the Russian revolutionary (20mk).

Tampere's **cathedral**, built in National Romantic style, features the weird frescoes of Hugo Simberg and is open 9 am to 6 pm daily. The small but ornate **Orthodox church** is open 9.30 am to 3 pm weekdays from May to August.

Places to Stay & Eat
Camping Härmälä (☎ 265 1355 or in winter ☎ 09 6138 3210, Leirintäkatu 8) is 5km south of the city centre (take bus No 1). A site costs 85mk a night, or from 140mk for a three-person cabin. There are two lakeside saunas and rowing boats.

The clean *Hostel Tampere YWCA (☎ 254 4020, Tuomiokirkonkatu 12A)* is open June to August and charges 75mk in dorms, or 115mk per person in a double.

Hostel Uimahallin Maja (☎ 222 9460, Pirkankatu 10-12) is a HI hostel and, unfortunately for the winter visitor, Tampere's only year-round hostel. It's poorly kept by unhelpful staff, and often fully booked by school groups. Dorm beds are 105mk.

Hotel Iltatähti (☎ 315 161, Tuomiokirkonkatu 19) has clean, simple rooms for 220/270mk. Reception is open 9 am to 7 pm weekdays and midday to 6 pm weekends.

The main street, Hämeenkatu, abounds with cafes and pubs. The *Koskikeskus* on Hatanpään Valtatie and *Tullintori (Itsenäisyydenkatu 4)* shopping centres are good for fast food. Tampere University's student cafeteria in *Attila House (Yliopistonkatu 38)* has cheap meals; it's open 8.30 am to 5 pm weekdays and for lunch Saturday.

Getting There & Away
The main bus station is at Hatanpäänvaltatie 7. Express buses run to Helsinki and Turku.

Express trains run hourly to/from Helsinki. Intercity trains continue to Oulu and there are trains to Turku, Pori, Vaasa and Joensuu.

Getting Around
The bus service is extensive and a one-hour ticket costs 10mk. A 24-hour Traveller's Ticket is 25mk.

AROUND TAMPERE
Pori
☎ 02
If you're anywhere near Pori in July, try to get tickets to the **Pori Jazz Festival**, known worldwide among jazz and blues performers. Visitors and performers pour in from all over the world and hotels book out a year in advance. For tickets and information contact Pori Jazz (☎ 550 5550; Pohjoisranta 11, 28100 Pori); or check out their Web site at www.porijazz.fi.

The town itself, despite being one of Finland's oldest, isn't worth visiting when the festival isn't on.

During the festival, the tourist office (☎ 621 1273), Hallituskatu 9, offers cheap accommodation (around 100mk) on a first-come first served-basis. The *Tekunkorpi Summer Hostel (☎ 634 8400, Tekniikantie 4)* has beds from 95mk. *Liisanpuisto (Liisankatu 20)* is run by a catering college and offers a satisfying 42mk lunch. *Vanha Seppä (Liisankatu 16)* has pizza from 25mk and steaks from 55mk.

Frequent trains connect Pori with Tampere.

Hämeenlinna
☎ 03
Historical Hämeenlinna (population 47,500) and its medieval **Häme Castle** are at the southern tip of a lake network 100km northwest of Helsinki. Many visitors catch a ferry from Tampere. The tourist office (☎ 621 2388) is at Sibeliuksenkatu 5.

Hostel Hattelmala (☎ 616 6564, Visamäentie 35) has a kitchen, sauna and beds from 100mk to 150mk. Catch bus No 2, 13 or 17.

Trains and express buses from Tampere and Helsinki are frequent, and there's a Hämeenlinna-Tampere ferry (ask at the tourist office).

Pohjanmaa

The flat coastal area of Pohjanmaa (Österbotten) facing the Gulf of Bothnia is also known as the 'Swedish coast' for its preponderance of Swedish-speakers, or the 'tomato belt' for the dozens of glass hothouses that dot its fields. It has a lively capital, Oulu.

OULU
☎ 08
Oulu is a lively, fast-growing university town with a current population of 115,500. It was founded by King Karl IX of Sweden in 1605 and rebuilt after a fire in 1822; few old buildings remain. Its huge number of outdoor bars and terrific network of bike paths are best enjoyed in summer.

Information
The city tourist office (☎ 5584 1330), Torikatu 10, is open daily in summer. Across town, the public library (closed Sunday) has seven Internet terminals and a reading room packed with English-language magazines and newspapers.

Things to See & Do
Visiting **Tietomaa**, Scandinavia's largest science museum, could occupy a full day. It's open daily year-round, but expensive at 60mk. The nearby **Oulu City Art Museum** (closed Monday; 15mk) has intriguing temporary international and Finnish exhibitions.

The imposing 19th-century **cathedral** has Finland's oldest portrait (dating from 1611) in its vestry.

Places to Stay & Eat
Nallikari Camping (☎ 554 1541) is open all year. The seaside camping ground, 5km

north-east of town (take bus No 5), charges 35mk to 80mk per camp site and also rents out cabins.

Kesähostel Välkkylä (☎ *880 3311,* ✆ *unihostel@oyy.fi, Kajaanintie 36)*, east of the centre, is open summer only and charges 75mk to 100mk per bed; it has a kitchen, sauna, and laundry. *Kesähotelli Oppimestari* (☎ *884 8527, Nahkatehtaankatu 3)*, across from Tietomaa, is open June and July only. Beds in double rooms with kitchenettes cost 110mk each (singles 150mk).

There are local specialities in the indoor *kauppahalli* adjacent to the market square. *Da Mario's Pizzeria* (*Torikatu 24)* has tasty pizza.

The hip young things of Oulo sip their green tea in the dazzling Nordish elegance of *Café Kaldi (Isokatu 25)*; it's open until 8 pm weekdays and until 4 pm weekends and has great sweets as well.

Entertainment

Café Mibou (Asemakatu 21) packs in the students with its 20mk beer, way gone vibe and bookshelves packed with cartoons and comics.

45 Special (Saaristonkatu 12) is Oulu's best rock venue, with free entry most nights. *Oluthuone Leskinen (Saaristonkatu 15)*, across the road, is a friendly bar with a huge selection of Finnish and English beers.

Getting There & Away

Trains and buses connect Oulu with all main centres; the Helsinki direct train takes six hours (longer via Kajaani).

Eastern Finland

Eastern Finland (Karelia) is a romantic region of lakes, rivers, locks and canals. Karelia is the highlight of any trip to Finland, and if you've only got the time or money to visit one destination outside Helsinki, make this the place.

LAPPEENRANTA
☎ 05
Lappeenranta (population 57,000) was a frontier garrison town until the building of the Saimaa Canal in 1856 made it an important trading port, and despite the surrounding pulp factories it's one of the most

attractive stops on Lake Saimaa, Finland's largest lake.

The day cruise which goes along the Saimaa Canal to Vyborg, which was Finland's second-largest city until it was lost to Russia in World War II, is one of Lappeenranta's main attractions.

Information

The city tourist office (☎ 667 788) is above the bus station; in summer there's an additional information booth at the harbour. The main post office is at Pormestarinkatu 1. The public library, Valtakatu 47, has six Internet terminals; book ahead. The pharmacy at Valtakatu 37 is open until 10 pm daily.

Things to See & Do

The **fortress complex** above the harbour was started by the Swedes in the 18th century and finished by the Russians; today it houses museums and artists' workshops. The jewel-like **Orthodox church** is Finland's oldest.

There are daily cruises on **Lake Saimaa** in summer (60mk). Most interesting are the day cruises to Vyborg in Russia (from 120mk) aboard the **MS Karelia**. A Russian visa is not required. The Karelia Lines office (☎ 453 0380) at the harbour sells tickets.

Places to Stay & Eat

West of the centre, *Huhtiniemi Tourist Resort* (☎ *451 5555,* ✆ *huhtiniemi@lomaoksa .inet.fi, Kuusimäenkatu 18)* has dorm beds for 55mk from June to August, plus a lakeside camping ground (75mk to 90mk per site). *Finnhostel Lappeenranta* on the same site is open year-round and has beds from 80mk. Take bus No 5, 6 or 7. Just 300m west, *Karelia Park* (☎ *675 211, Korpraalinkuja 1)* is a summer hostel charging 90mk per person.

Gasthaus Turistilappee (☎ *415 0800, Kauppakatu 52)*, close to the train station, offers tidy rooms at 190/290mk a single/ double, breakfast and sauna included.

Pallon Pizzariina (Taipalsaarentie 39) and the charming *Drive-In Elvis (Kauppakatu 45)* are grillis with good options under 15mk. *Café Galleria (Koulukatu 15)* offers home-cooked lunches from 40mk.

Stalls at the *market square* sell *vety* (meat pie with ham, eggs and butter), a local favourite.

FINLAND

Kolme Lyhtä (Kauppakatu 21) is a typical eastern Finland bar, and next door is *Birra (Kauppakatu 19)*, where Lappeenranta's student population congregates to drink 18mk beer.

Getting There & Away
Trains and buses to and from Helsinki are frequent.

SAVONLINNA
☎ 015
Savonlinna is set between lakes near the stronghold of Olavinlinna castle in some of the prettiest of waterscapes. As a summer spot or opera venue it's unbeatable.

Hire bicycles in the summer from the tourist office (☎ 517 510) at Puistokatu 1. The library has a couple of Internet terminals but you'll need to book a day ahead. There's also a free terminal at Kirjakauppa Knut Posse (Olavinkatu 44); maximum time is 15 minutes.

Things to See & Do
The best-preserved medieval castle in the northern countries is **Olavinlinna**. It was used by both Swedish and Russian overlords but is today best known as the setting for the month-long Savonlinna Opera Festival.

Dozens of 1½ hour **scenic cruises** leave from the harbour at the kauppatori daily in summer (40mk).

Special Events
The **Savonlinna Opera Festival** in July is the most famous festival in Finland. Tickets average 400mk but can be picked up for as little as 100mk on some nights. Contact the Savonlinna Opera Festival (☎ 476 750, Olavinkatu 27, 57130) Savonlinna for more information, or see their Web site at www.operafestival.fi.

In August the castle hosts a **beer festival** and in September a **theatre festival**.

Places to Stay & Eat
Book accommodation well in advance if visiting during the Opera Festival; accommodation prices rise by as much as 100% during this time, and many festival-goers stay in nearby towns such as Mikkeli to avoid the grossly inflated prices.

Vuohimäki Camping (☎ 537 353, @ myyntipalvelu@lomaliitto.fi), 7km west of town, has sites for 75mk, cabins for 295mk to 370mk and singles/doubles for 210/290mk. The summer hostels *Vuorilinna* (☎ 739 5495), on Kasinosaari island, near the Casino Spa Hotel, and *Malakias* (☎ 33 283, Pihlajavedenkuja 6), 2km north-west of town, have shared rooms from 120mk to 170mk per person.

In summer the *SS Heinävesi* offers beds after the last cruise in the evening; two-person cabins on the upper deck cost 110mk per person and on the lower deck 100mk per person.

Pizzeria Capero (Olavinkatu 51) does excellent pizzas for 30mk to 40mk, and *Majakka (Satamakatu 11)*, opposite the harbour, is a good restaurant with a nautical theme and lunch specials from 35mk.

The lively market at the *kauppatori* (closed Sunday) is the place to find local pastries like *omena-lörtsy*, an apple turnover.

Getting There & Away
From Helsinki there are daily buses and trains via Parikkala. The main train station is a long walk from the centre; get off at the kauppatori platform instead. In summer there are ferries to Punkaharju and Kuopio.

AROUND SAVONLINNA
Between Savonlinna and Parikkala is **Punkaharju**, the famous pine-covered sand ridge that is one of the most overrated attractions in Finland; the surrounding forest and lakes, though, are beautiful – the perfect place to spend a couple of relaxing days. If you're just passing through, near the railway station is a **water tower** with a viewing platform you can climb for free; the view makes the dizzying 210-step ascent worth it (though it gets stinking hot up there in summer). It's opened 10 am to 8 pm daily from May to August.

Punkaharju can be reached from Savonlinna by train, bus or, in summer, a two-hour cruise (one-way/return 85/130mk). Ring the tourist centre (☎ 734 1233) for accommodation options or stay at the simple *Guesthouse Punkaharju* (☎ 441 371, Palomäentie 18); singles/doubles are 220/350mk. The lovely owners also run *Naaranlahti* (☎ 473 123, @ naaranlahti@kolumbus.fi), a gorgeous farm estate where you could easily spend a few days swimming in the lake, sweating in the sauna, cycling and fishing.

KUOPIO
☎ 017

Once away from the dreary train station and town square with its rowdy amusement park, you'll find Kuopio quite charming.

Information
The tourist office (☎ 182 585), Haapaniemenkatu 17, is open weekdays, and Saturdays from June to August.

Things to See & Do
The spectacular view from the 75-metre **Puijo Tower** on top of **Puijo Hill** is one of Kuopio's main attractions; take bus No 6. There are also mountain-biking and walking tracks and cross-county ski trails in the area.

Not to be missed is the world's largest **smoke sauna** at Jätkänkämpällä, adjacent to Rauhalahti Hostel. The 60-person sauna is fired up 2 to 8 pm Tuesday and Friday year-round, and costs 55mk. Bring a swimsuit for a dip in the lake – devoted sauna-goers do so even when the lake is covered with ice!

Places to Stay & Eat
Rauhalahti (☎ 473 473), on Kiviniementie, 5km south-west of the centre (take bus No 16, 19, 20 or 21), is a hotel-spa-hostel complex with doubles from 160mk. *Camping Rauhalahti* (☎ 361 2244), adjacent, is open mid-May to September and charges 65mk to 110mk for tent sites or 140mk to 420mk for cabins. *Puijo-Hovi* (☎ 261 4943, *Vuorikatu 35*), near the train station, is a clean guesthouse with singles/doubles for 190/240mk.

There are indoor and outdoor markets in the main square where you can try *kalakukko*, a local fish inside a rye loaf (eaten hot or cold). *Golden Rax Pizza & Pasta* (*Puijonkatu 45, 2nd floor*), serves a dreadful 42mk lunch and dinner buffet (who cares about taste at this price).

Wanha Satama at the harbour is a lively pub during the summer; at other times try *Henry's Pub* (*Käsityökatu 17*), where you can hear live rock Friday and Saturday nights. If drum'n'bass is more your thing, *Tahti* (*Kauppakatu 18*), round the corner from Henry's, is perfect, with happy hour between 3 and 10 pm every day.

Getting There & Away
Kuopio is easily reached by train or bus from Helsinki or Kajaani, or ferry from Savonlinna. The express bus station is north of the train station.

LIEKSA
☎ 013

The small centre of Lieksa, about 100km north of Joensuu on Lake Pielinen, is important if planning any outdoor activities in the region.

Information
Lieksan Matkailu Oy (☎ 520 2400), Pielisentie 7, the local tourist office, is open Monday to Saturday from June to August, Monday to Sunday in July, and weekdays only the rest of the year. It has information on accommodation, fishing, canoeing, smoke saunas and national parks as well as local hiking maps.

Places to Stay
You can get a cabin at the river mouth at *Timitraniemi Camping* (☎ 521 780, *Timitra*), open June to August. Cabins start from 180mk and sites are 25mk per person.

The small Vuonislahti train station south of Lieksa is the jumping-off point for the year-round lakeside hostel *Kestikievari Herranniemi* (☎ 542 110, ✉ tn@kestik .pp.fi, *Vuonislahdentie 185*) with 75mk dorm beds.

Getting There & Away
Trains run regularly to/from Joensuu and Nurmes, but the more scenic mode of transport is by ferry from Joensuu (via Koli, 160mk). The Koli car ferry runs twice a day from mid-May to mid-August.

TREKS AROUND KARELIA
Some of the best trekking routes in North Karelia were recently linked together to create **Karjalan Kierros**, an 800km loop of marked trails around Lake Pielinen.

For more information on these and other routes contact Metsähallitus (☎ 520 5711 or 0205 645 711), Urheilukatu 3A in Lieksa.

KOLI NATIONAL PARK
☎ 013

Finns regard the views from the heights of Koli overlooking Lake Pielinen as the best in the country. In summer, the national park has wonderful scenic hiking routes, and there's ferry service between Koli and

Lieksa (less than two hours) or Joensuu (seven hours) on select days from June to mid-August.

Places to Stay & Eat

At *Loma-Koli Camping* (☎ 673 212, Merilänrannantie 65), open June to August, camp sites are 35mk per person and there are four-bed cabins from 220mk.

The family-run *Koli Hostel* (☎ 673 131) on a gravel road 5km from the bus stop, has a kitchen, smoke sauna and beds from 55mk year-round.

Hotelli Koli (☎ 672 221, Ylä-Kolintie 39) at the top of Koli has a restaurant and singles/doubles from 520/620mk. Ask for keys at the hotel for the free four-bed *Ikolanaho* wilderness hut inside the park.

KAJAANI
☎ 08

Kajaani (population 40,000) is the centre of the Kainuu region. The **regional museum** near the train station has a good section on Lönnrot. The tourist office (☎ 615 5555) is at Pohjolankatu 16.

Places to Stay & Eat

Camping Onnela (☎ 622 703), on Onnelantie, has camp sites (80mk) and cabins (145mk to 270mk). The HI-affiliated *Huone ja Aamiainen* (☎ 622 254, Pohjolankatu 4), 200m from the train station, has spartan but clean singles/doubles for 150/215mk.

The main street, Kauppakatu, has many restaurants. *Pikantti*, at the corner of Urho Kekkonen katu, has excellent lunch buffets until 5 pm weekdays. When it's warm, the outside chairs at the *Brahe Public house* at the corner of Linnankatu on the cute town square, is Kajaani's best spot to sit with a beer or coffee and watch the passing parade.

Getting There & Away

Trains connect Kajaani with Kuopio, Nurmes and Oulu.

Lapland

☎ 016

Lapland is a place of extremes: continuous daylight in summer and continuous night in winter; and average daytime temperatures that range from -15°C in December to +15°C in June. If you care to brave the Arctic winter, October, February and March are ideal times to see the *aurora borealis* (Northern Lights).

Finnish Lapland is home to some 6500 Sami people and their living culture is best seen in the villages of Hetta, Inari or Utsjoki.

Getting Around

Because of hassle-free border crossings to Sweden and Norway, Lapland is at times the most international region in Finland. The popular route to Nordkapp goes either via road No 4 from Rovaniemi to Sodankylä to Inari, and farther to Karigasniemi, or along road No 21 near the Tornionjoki River valley to Kilpisjärvi.

Hitchhiking is a very natural means of transport in this large region with so few buses, but the waiting period can sometimes be lengthy.

TORNIO

The Swedish town of Haparanda across the Tornionjoki River is Tornio's twin, and they share tourist brochures, and even a famous **golf course** (☎ 431 711). If midnight golf is your thing, start from the Finnish side at, say, 12.30 am and hit the ball into yesterday (ie, Sweden).

Camping Tornio (☎ 445 945, ✉ sirkka.hyry@pp.inet.fi), on Matkailijantie, has sites for 90mk and cabins from 230mk.

Hostel Tornio (☎ 211 9244, Kivirannantie 13-15), 2.5km north of town, is open June to August and has dorm beds for 75mk.

From Kemi, take a bus from the train station. Road No 21 leads from Tornio up to the north.

KEMI

Kemi is an industrial town with huge pulp factories. It's not an attractive town, but it is home to one of Lapland's blockbuster attractions: the icebreaker *Sampo*.

A four-hour cruise on the *Sampo* (☎ 256 548) costs a whopping 850mk, but includes (for the very brave) ice swimming in special drysuits – a remarkable experience. Cruises are from mid-December through the end of April and bookings are advised.

The Kemi tourist office (☎ 259 467), Kauppakatu 19, is open daily in summer.

Kemi has no hostel, but in summer *Hotel Relletti* (☎ 233 541, Miilukatu 1), 1.5km south-east of the train station, has dorm beds for 125mk and doubles for 200mk.

There are trains from Helsinki and Rovaniemi. Buses to/from Tornio are free with a Finnrail pass.

ROVANIEMI
Rovaniemi (population 35,000) is the capital of and gateway to Lapland. The town itself is relatively uninteresting, built from a plan by Alvar Aalto (the main streets radiate out from Hallituskatu in the shape of reindeer antlers) after its complete destruction in World War II. And its proximity to the Arctic Circle means tour buses thunder through year-round.

Information
The helpful tourist office (☎ 346 270), Koskikatu 1, is open daily in summer (weekdays only other times).

The most convenient post office is at Koskikatu 9. The public library (closed Sunday), Hallituskatu 9, has several Internet terminals.

Things to See & Do
The huge **Arktikum**, Pohjoisranta 4, is one of Finland's best museums. Exhibits and interactive displays focus on arctic flora and fauna as well as the Sami and other people of arctic Europe, Asia and North America. Give yourself at least a couple of hours to get around it. Entry is 50mk (closed Mondays in winter).

The official **Arctic Circle marker** (Napapiiri) is 8km north of Rovaniemi (take bus No 8), as well as the 'official' **Santa Claus Village**. Its Santa Claus post office receives close to a million letters each year. Activities include an arctic circle initiation ceremony and computerised portraits with jolly ol' St Nick; those with a dry sense of humour should steer well clear.

Etiäinen at the Arctic Circle marker is the information centre for national parks and trekking, with information on hiking and fishing.

Places to Stay & Eat
Ounaskoski Camping (☎ 345 304, Jäämerentie 1) has 95mk sites.

The excellent hostel *Tervashonka* (☎ 344 644, Hallituskatu 16) has beds from 75mk and a well-equipped kitchen; there are also singles/doubles for 90/180mk. Reception is closed 10 am to 5 pm, and closes again at 10 pm (ring ahead if you're coming in on the night train).

Matka Borealis (☎ 342 0130, Asemieskatu 1), opposite the train station, is an excellent guesthouse with clean, simple singles/doubles from 190/260mk (10mk more in summer) including breakfast.

Café Sandwich (Koskikatu 11) is good for 20mk sandwiches. *Hai Long* (Valtakatu 35, upstairs) does decent Chinese; mains start from 35mk. You can pick up ingredients for a cheap meal at the **supermarket** on the market square.

The Irish Times pub (Valtakatu 35) below Hai Long Chinese has a great heated terrace in spring and summer and a pool tables downstairs.

Getting There & Away
The train from Helsinki travels via Oulu and terminates in Rovaniemi. There's one train connection daily to Kemijärvi, farther to the north.

Buses travel to Muonio, Enontekiö (Ounas-Pallas National Park) and Kilpisjärvi in the north-west, to Sodankylä, Inari, Karigasniemi and Utsjoki in the north-east, and into Norway.

AROUND ROVANIEMI
Ranua, 83km south of Rovaniemi on road No 78, is home to the excellent **Ranua Wildlife Park** (☎ 355 1921). This could be your only chance to see **hirvi** – the elusive Finnish moose. The park is open year-round; entry is 50mk.

INARI
The pleasant lakeside settlement of Inari is a great base for exploring northern Lapland. There are banks, a post office and the friendly Inari information office (☎ 661 666), open daily in summer (weekdays only other times).

Things to See & Do
Inari is probably northern Lapland's most interesting town, although one day is enough to see its attractions. The excellent **Saamelaismuseo** (closed Mondays in winter) is one of Finland's best open-air museums, and covers the crafts, reindeer-farming and fishing traditions of the Sami. Not far

FINLAND

away is a marked 7km walking track (starting from the Saamelaismuseo parking area) to the 18th-century **wilderness church**, with a hut and a sauna nearby.

In summer, boat trips leave for the prominent Ukko Island, an ancient cult site for the Inari Samis.

Places to Stay

There's a camping ground 3km towards Lemmenjoki. *Inarin Kultahovi* (☎ 671 221) is good, but *Hotel Inari* (☎ 671 026) is cheaper, with doubles from 180mk. There are also inexpensive cottages to the south of Inari; ask at the information office.

France

France's most salient characteristic is its exceptional diversity. The largest country in Western Europe, France extends all the way from the rolling hills of the north to the seemingly endless beaches of the south; from the wild coastline of Brittany to the icy crags of the Alps, with cliff-lined canyons, dense forest and vineyards in between.

Over the centuries, France has received more immigrants than any other country in Europe. From the ancient Celtic Gauls and Romans to the more recent arrivals from France's former colonies in Indochina and Africa, these peoples have introduced new elements of culture, cuisine and art, all of which have contributed to France's unique and diverse civilisation.

Once on the western edge of Europe, today's France stands firmly at the crossroads: between England and Italy, Belgium and Spain, North Africa and Scandinavia. Of course, this is exactly how the French have always regarded their country – at the very centre of things.

Facts about France

HISTORY
Ancient & Medieval History
Human presence in France is known to date from the middle Palaeolithic period, about 90,000 to 40,000 years ago. Around 25,000 BC the Stone Age Cro-Magnon people appeared and left their mark in the form of cave paintings and engravings.

The Celtic Gauls moved into what is now France between 1500 and 500 BC. By about 600 BC, they had established trading links with the Greeks, whose colonies on the Mediterranean coast included Massilia (Marseille). Julius Caesar's Roman legions took control of the territory around 52 BC. France remained under Roman rule until the 5th century, when the Franks (thus 'France') and other Germanic groups overran the country.

Two Frankish dynasties, the Merovingians and the Carolingians, ruled from the 5th to the 10th centuries. In AD 732, Charles Martel defeated the Moors at Poitiers, ensuring that France would not follow Spain and come under Muslim rule. Martel's grandson, Charlemagne, significantly extended the boundaries of the kingdom and was crowned Holy Roman Emperor in 800. During the 9th century, Scandinavian Vikings (the Normans) began raiding France's western coast and eventually founded the Duchy of Normandy.

Under William the Conqueror (the Duke of Normandy), Norman forces occupied England in 1066, making Normandy – and later, Plantagenet-ruled England – a formidable rival of the kingdom of France. A further third of France came under the control of the English Crown in 1154, when Eleanor of Aquitaine married Henry of Anjou (later Henry II of England).

In 1415, French forces were defeated at Agincourt; in 1420, the English took control of Paris, and two years later Henry IV of England became king of France. Just when it seemed that England had pulled off a dynastic union with France, a 17-year-old peasant girl known to history as Jeanne d'Arc (Joan of Arc) surfaced in 1429 and rallied the French troops at Orléans. She was captured, convicted of heresy and burned at the stake two years later, but her efforts helped to turn the war in favour of the French.

The Renaissance & the Reformation
The ideals and aesthetics of the Italian Renaissance were introduced in the 15th century, partly by the French aristocracy

returning from military campaigns in Italy. The influence was most evident during the reign of François I, and the chateaux of Fontainebleau, near Paris, and Chenonceau in the Loire are good examples of Renaissance architectural style.

By the 1530s the position of the Protestant Reformation sweeping Europe had been strengthened in France by the ideas of the Frenchman John Calvin, an exile in Geneva. The Wars of Religion (1562-98) involved three groups: the Huguenots (French Protestants); the Catholic League, led by the House of Guise; and the Catholic monarchy. The fighting brought the French state close to disintegration. Henry of Navarre, a Huguenot who had embraced Catholicism, eventually became King Henry IV. In 1598, he promulgated the Edict of Nantes, which guaranteed the Huguenots many civil and political rights.

The French Revolution

Louis XIV – also known as Le Roi Soleil (the Sun King) – ascended the throne in 1643 at the age of five and ruled until 1715. Throughout his long reign, he sought to extend the power of the French monarchy. He involved France in a long series of costly wars and poured enormous sums of money into the building of his extravagant palace at Versailles.

His successor, Louis XV (ruled 1715-74), was followed by the incompetent Louis XVI. By the late 1780s, Louis XVI and his queen, Marie-Antoinette, had managed to alienate virtually every segment of society. When the king tried to neutralise the power of the more reform-minded delegates at a meeting of the Estates General in 1789, the urban masses took to the streets and, on 14 July, a Parisian mob stormed the Bastille prison.

At first, the Revolution was in the hands of relative moderates. Yet it was not long before the moderate, republican Girondists (Girondins in French) lost power to the radical Jacobins, led by Robespierre, Danton and Marat, who established the First Republic in 1792. In January 1793, Louis was guillotined in what is now place de la Concorde in Paris. Two months later the Jacobins set up the notorious Committee of Public Safety. This body had virtually dictatorial control over the country during the Reign of Terror (September 1793 to July 1794).

Napoleon

In the resulting chaos, a dashing young general by the name of Napoleon Bonaparte chalked up a string of victories in the Italian campaign of the war against Austria, and his success soon turned him into an independent political force. In 1799, when it appeared that the Jacobins were again on the ascendancy in the legislature, Napoleon assumed power himself. Five years later he had himself crowned Emperor of the French by Pope Pius VII, and the scope and grand nature of Napoleon's ambitions became obvious to all.

In 1812, in an attempt to do away with his last major rival on the Continent, Tsar Alexander I, Napoleon invaded Russia. Although his Grande Armée (Grand Army) captured Moscow, it was wiped out shortly thereafter by the brutal Russian winter. Prussia and Napoleon's other enemies quickly recovered from their earlier defeats, and less than two years after the fiasco in Russia, the Allied armies entered Paris. Napoleon abdicated and was exiled to his tiny Mediterranean island-kingdom of Elba.

At the Congress of Vienna (1814-15), the Allies restored the House of Bourbon to the French throne. But in March 1815, Napoleon escaped from Elba, landed in southern France and gathered a large army as he marched northward towards Paris. His 'Hundred Days' back in power ended when his forces were defeated by the English at Waterloo in Belgium. Napoleon was then banished to the remote South Atlantic island of St Helena, where he died in 1821.

The 19th Century

The 19th century was a chaotic one for France. The second empire lasted from 1852 until 1870. During this period, France enjoyed significant economic growth. But as his uncle had done, Napoleon III embroiled France in a number of conflicts, including the disastrous Crimean War (1853-56). In 1870 the Prussian prime minister, Bismarck, goaded Napoleon III into declaring war on Prussia. Within months the thoroughly unprepared French army had been defeated and the emperor taken prisoner. When news of the debacle reached the French capital, the Parisian masses took to the streets and demanded that a republic be declared – the Third Republic.

WWI & WWII

Central to France's entry into WWI was the desire to regain Alsace and Lorraine, lost to Germany in 1871. This was eventually achieved but at immense human cost: of the eight million French men who were called to arms, 1.3 million were killed and almost one million crippled. The war was officially ended by the Treaty of Versailles in 1919.

During the 1930s the French, like the British, did their best to appease Hitler, but two days after the 1939 German invasion of Poland, the two countries reluctantly declared war on Germany. By June of the following year, France had capitulated. The British forces sent to help the French barely managed to avoid capture by retreating to Dunkirk and crossing the English Channel in small boats. The hugely expensive Maginot Line, a supposedly impregnable wall of fortifications along the Franco-German border, had proved useless: the German armoured divisions simply went through Belgium.

The Germans divided France into zones of direct occupation (in the north and along the west coast) and a puppet state based in the spa town of Vichy. Both the collaborationist government and French police forces in German-occupied areas were very helpful to the Nazis in rounding up French Jews and other targeted groups for deportation to concentration camps.

After the capitulation, General Charles de Gaulle, France's undersecretary of war, fled to London and established a French government-in-exile. He also established the Forces Françaises Libres (Free French Forces), a military force dedicated to continuing the fight against Germany. The liberation of France began with the US, British and Canadian landings in Normandy on D-Day (6 June 1944). Paris was liberated on 25 August.

Postwar France

The postwar Fourth Republic came to an end in 1958; de Gaulle was brought back to power to prevent a military coup and even civil war. He soon drafted a new constitution that gave considerable powers to the president at the expense of the National Assembly. This Fifth Republic continues to this day.

In 1969, de Gaulle was succeeded as president by the Gaullist leader Georges Pompidou, who in turn was followed by Valéry Giscard d'Estaing in 1974. François Mitterrand, a Socialist, was elected president in 1981 and re-elected for a second seven-year term in 1988. The closely contested presidential election of May 1995 resulted in Jacques Chirac winning the mandate with 52% of the vote. More surprising was the considerable success of the extreme-right Front National (FN) led by Jean-Marie Le Pen, which took 15% of votes in the first round.

In the 1997 election Chirac retained the presidency but his party lost support to a coalition of Socialists, Communists and Greens, led by Lionel Jospin, who became prime minister. The popular Jospin remains the favourite to succeed Chirac in the next presidential ballot, which has been scheduled for 2002.

France is one of the five permanent members of the United Nations (UN) Security Council, and a major force in the European Union (EU). France also belongs to NATO but withdrew from its joint military command in 1966.

GEOGRAPHY

France (551,000 sq km) is the largest country in Europe after Russia and Ukraine. It is shaped like a hexagon bordered by either mountains or water except for the relatively flat, north-east frontier that abuts Germany, Luxembourg and Belgium.

POPULATION & PEOPLE

France has a population of 60.2 million, more than 20% of whom live in the Paris metropolitan area. During the late 1950s and early 1960s, as the French colonial empire collapsed, more than one million French settlers returned to France from Algeria, Morocco, Tunisia and Indochina. In recent years, there has been a racist backlash against France's non-white immigrant communities, led by the FN party.

Some 80% of French people say they are Catholic, but although most have been baptised very few attend church. About 75,000 French Jews were killed during the Holocaust. The country's Jewish community now numbers some 650,000.

SOCIETY & CONDUCT

Some visitors to France conclude that it would be a lovely country if it weren't for the French. As in other countries, however, the more tourists a certain town or neighbourhood attracts, the less patient the locals tend to be. The following tips might prove useful when interacting with the French: never address a waiter or bartender as *garçon* (boy); *s'il vous plaît* is the way it's done nowadays. Avoid discussing money, keep off the manicured French lawns (watch for 'pelouse interdite' signs), and resist handling produce in markets. Always address people as *Monsieur* (Mr/sir), *Madame* (Mrs) and *Mademoiselle* (Miss); when in doubt use 'Madame'.

Finally, when you go out for the evening, it's a good idea to follow the local custom of dressing relatively well, particularly in a restaurant.

LANGUAGE

Around 122 million people worldwide speak French as their first language, and various forms of creole are used in Haiti, French Guiana and southern Louisiana. Thus the French tend to assume that all human beings should speak French; it was the international language of culture and diplomacy until WWI.

Your best bet is always to approach people politely in French, even if the only words you know are *'Pardon, Monsieur/ Madame/Mademoiselle, parlez-vous anglais?'* ('Excuse me sir/madam/miss, do you speak English?').

See the Language chapter at the back of this book for pronunciation guidelines and useful words and phrases.

Facts for the Visitor

HIGHLIGHTS
Every city and town in France has at least one museum, but a good number of the country's most exceptional ones are in Paris. In addition to the rather overwhelming Louvre, other Parisian museums not to be missed include the Musée d'Orsay (late-19th- and early 20th-century art), the Centre Pompidou (modern and contemporary art), the Musée Rodin, and the Musée National du Moyen Age (Museum of the Middle Ages) at the Hôtel de Cluny. Other cities known for their museums include Nice, Bordeaux, Strasbourg and Lyon.

The royal palace at Versailles is the largest and most grandiose of the hundreds of chateaux located all over the country. Many of the most impressive ones, including Chambord, Cheverny, Chenonceau and Azay-le-Rideau, are in the Loire Valley around Blois and Tours. The cathedrals at Chartres, Strasbourg and Rouen are among the most beautiful in France.

The Côte d'Azur – the French Riviera – has some of the best-known beaches in the world, but you'll also find lovely beaches farther west on the Mediterranean.

SUGGESTED ITINERARIES
Three days
  Visit Paris.
One week
  Paris plus a nearby area, such as the Loire Valley, Champagne, Alsace or Normandy.
Two weeks
  As above, plus one area in the west or south, such as Brittany, the Alps or Provence.

PLANNING
When to Go
Weather-wise, France is at its best in spring, though wintry relapses are not unknown in April and the beach resorts only begin to pick up in mid-May. Autumn is pleasant, too, though by late October it's a bit cool for sunbathing. Winter is great for snow sports in the Alps and Pyrenees, though prices rise considerably at Christmas, New Year and the February/March school holidays. Paris has all sorts of cultural activities during its rather wet winter.

In summer the weather is warm and even hot, especially in the south, and beaches, resorts and camping grounds are packed to the gills. In August, when millions of French people take their annual month-long holiday *(congé)*, beach-town hotel rooms are in extremely short supply, while in the half-deserted cities – only partly refilled by the zillions of foreign tourists – many shops, restaurants and even hotels simply shut down. If at all possible, avoid travelling in France in August.

Maps
For driving, the best road map is Michelin's *Motoring Atlas France* (1:200,000), which covers the whole country. Éditions Didier & Richard's series of 1:50,000 trail maps are adequate for most hiking and cycling excursions.

TOURIST OFFICES
Local Tourist Offices
Virtually every French city, town and one-chateau village has some sort of tourist office. See Information under each town or city for details.

Tourist Offices Abroad
The French government tourist offices provide brochures and tourist information.

Australia (☎ 02-9231 5244, fax 9221 8682, ✉ frencht@ozemail.com.au) 25 Bligh St, 22nd floor, Sydney, NSW 2000
Canada (☎ 514-288 4264, fax 845 4868, ✉ mfrance@mtl.net) 1981 McGill College Ave, Suite 490, Montreal, Que H3A 2W9
UK (☎ 020-7399 3500, fax 7493 6594, ✉ info@co.uk) 178 Piccadilly, London W1V 0AL
USA (☎ 212-838 7800, fax 838 7855, ✉ info@francetourism.com) 444 Madison Ave, New York, NY 10020

VISAS
Citizens of the USA, Canada, Australia, New Zealand, and most European countries can enter France for up to three months without a visa. South Africans, however, must have a visa (to avoid delays, apply before leaving home). The usual length of a tourist visa is three months.

FRANCE

EMBASSIES & CONSULATES
French Embassies Abroad
Australia (☎ 02-6216 0100, fax 6216 0127,
@ embassy@france.net.au) 6 Perth Ave,
Yarralumla, ACT 2600
Canada (☎ 613-789 1795, fax 562 3735,
@ res@amba-ottowa.fr) 42 Sussex Drive,
Ottawa, Ont K1M 2C9
New Zealand (☎ 04-384 2555, fax 384 2577,
@ consulfrance@actrix.gen.nz) Rural Bank
Building, 34-42 Manners St, Wellington
UK (☎ 020-7201 1000, fax 7201 1004,
@ press@ambafrance.org) 58 Knightsbridge,
London SW1X 7JT
Visa inquiries: ☎ 0891-887733
USA (☎ 202-944 6000, fax 944 6166,
@ visas-washington@amb-wash.fv) 4101
Reservoir Rd, NW Washington, DC 20007

Foreign Embassies in Paris
Australia (☎ 01 40 59 33 00, fax 01 40 59 33
10, metro Bir Hakeim) 4 rue Jean Rey, 15e
Canada (☎ 01 44 43 29 00, fax 01 44 43 29 99,
metro Franklin D Roosevelt) 35 ave
Montaigne, 8e
New Zealand (☎ 01 45 00 24 11, fax 01 45 01
43 44, metro Victor Hugo) 7ter rue Léonard
de Vinci, 16e
UK (☎ 01 44 51 31 00, fax 01 44 51 31 27,
@ ambassade@amb-grandebretagne.fr, metro
Concorde) 35 rue du Faubourg St Honoré, 8e
USA (☎ 01 43 12 22, fax 01 42 66 97 83,
@ ambassade@amb-usa.fr, metro Concorde),
2 ave Gabriel, 1er

MONEY
One French franc (FF) equals 100 centimes.
French coins come in denominations of
five, 10 and 20 centimes and half, one, two,
five, 10 and 20FF (the last two are two-
tone). Banknotes are issued in denominations of 20, 50, 100, 200 and 500FF. The
higher the denomination, the larger the bill.

Generally you'll get a better exchange
rate for travellers cheques than for cash.
Post offices usually offer the best exchange
rates for cash transactions and accept banknotes in a variety of currencies as well as
American Express travellers cheques – but
only if the cheques are in US dollars or
French francs. Banque de France, the central bank, offers the next-best exchange
rates and doesn't charge any commission.
Do not bring travellers cheques in Australian dollars as they are hard to change;
US$100 bills are also difficult to change.

Visa (Carte Bleue) is more widely accepted than MasterCard (Eurocard). Visa
card-holders with a PIN number can get cash
advances from banks and ATMs nationwide.
American Express cards are not very useful
except to get cash at American Express offices in big cities or to pay for things in upmarket shops and restaurants.

Exchange Rates

country	unit		franc
Australia	A$1	=	4.21FF
Canada	C$1	=	4.89FF
euro	€1	=	6.56FF
Germany	DM1	=	3.35FF
Japan	¥100	=	6.68FF
New Zealand	NZ$1	=	3.26FF
Spain	100 ptas	=	3.94FF
UK	UK£1	=	10.9FF
USA	US$1	=	7.26FF

Costs
If you stay in hostels or the cheapest hotels
and buy provisions from grocery stores
rather than eating at restaurants, it is possible to tour France on as little as US$30 a day
(US$35 in Paris). Eating out, lots of travel or
treating yourself to France's many little luxuries can increase this figure dramatically.
Always check to see if you qualify for the
tarif réduit (reduced rate for students, children, seniors and other groups).

Tipping
It is not necessary to leave a *pourboire* (tip)
in restaurants, hotels etc; under French law,
the bill must already include a 15% service
charge. Some people leave a few francs on
the table for the waiter, but this is not expected (especially for drinks). At truly posh
restaurants, however, a more generous gra-
tuity is expected. For a taxi ride, the usual
tip is 2FF to 5FF no matter what the fare.

POST & COMMUNICATIONS
Post
La Poste, the French postal service, is fast,
reliable and expensive. Postcards and letters
up to 20g cost 3FF within the EU, 4.40FF to
the USA, Canada and the Middle East, and
5.20FF to Australasia. Aerograms cost 5FF
to all destinations. All overseas packages are
now sent by air only, which is expensive.

Telephone
Public Telephones You can dial direct
from any public phone in France to almost

anywhere in the world. Almost all public phones now require *télécartes* (phonecards), which are sold at post offices, *tabacs* (tobacco shops), Paris metro ticket counters and supermarket check-out counters. Cards worth 50/120 units cost 48.60/96.70FF. Each unit is good for one three-minute local call. To make a call with a phonecard, pick up the receiver, insert the card and dial when the LCD screen reads 'Numérotez'.

Domestic Dialling France is divided into five telephone zones and all telephone numbers, no matter where you are calling from in France, comprise 10 digits. Paris and Île de France numbers begin with 01. The other codes are: ☎ 02 for the north-west; ☎ 03 for the north-east; ☎ 04 for the south-east (including Corsica); and ☎ 05 for the south-west. Numbers beginning with 0800 are free, but others in the series (eg, 0836) generally cost 2.23FF per minute.

International Dialling The international country code for France is ☎ 33. When dialling in from abroad, drop the initial '0' at the start of France's 10-digit phone numbers.

Direct-dial calls to almost anywhere in the world can be placed using a phonecard – dial ☎ 00, wait for the second tone, and then dial the country code, area code and local number. A three-minute call to the USA costs about 5/3FF peak/off-peak.

To make a reverse-charge call *(en PCV)* or person-to-person call *(avec préavis)* to other countries, dial ☎ 00 (the international operator), wait for the second tone and then dial ☎ 33 plus the country code of the place you're calling (for the USA and Canada, dial ☎ 11 instead of 1).

Minitel Minitel is a screen-based information service peculiar to France. Though useful, it can be expensive to use and the Internet is becoming a popular alternative. Minitel numbers consist of four digits (eg, 3611, 3614, 3615) and a string of letters. Most of the terminals in post offices are free for directory inquiries.

Fax
Virtually all post offices can send and receive domestic and international faxes (*télécopies* or *téléfaxes*). It costs around 12/60FF to send a one-page fax within France/USA.

Email
Email can be sent and received at cybercafes throughout France. La Poste has set up Internet centres at some 1000 post offices around France; a 50FF Cybercarte gives you an hour's access, and each 30FF 'recharge' is good for another hour. The commercial cybercafes that have sprung up around France charge about 20FF to 30FF for a half-hour's surfing.

INTERNET RESOURCES
Useful Web sites in English include:

The Paris Tourist Office (www.paris-touristoffice.com)
GuideWeb (www.guideweb.com), with information about selected regions in France

Many towns have their own Web sites, including:

Avignon (www.ot-avignon.fr)
Bordeaux (www.bordeaux-tourisme.com)
Chamonix (www.chamonix.com)
Dijon (www.ot-dijon.fr)
Marseille (www.marseilles.com)
Nice (www.nice-coteazur.com)
Strasbourg (www.strasbourg.com).

Gay and lesbian travellers should check out:

The Queer Resources Directory
(www.france.qrd.org)
The gay-and-lesbian guide to France
(www.gaipied.fr)

BOOKS
For a more comprehensive guide to the country and its capital, pick up a copy of Lonely Planet's *France* or *Paris*. Also useful are the *French phrasebook* and *World Food France*.

There are many excellent histories of France in English. Among the best is Fernand Braudel's two-volume *The Identity of France*, which out of print but still available in some bookshops. *France Today* by John Ardagh provides excellent insights into the way French society has evolved since WWII.

A Moveable Feast by Ernest Hemingway portrays Bohemian life in 1920s Paris. Henry Miller also wrote some pretty dramatic stuff set in the French capital of the 1930s, including *Tropic of Cancer* and *Tropic of Capricorn*.

FRANCE

Paul Rambali's *French Blues* is a series of uncompromising yet sympathetic snapshots of modern France. *A Year in Provence* by Peter Mayle is an irresistible account of country life in southern France. *Toujours Provence* is its witty sequel.

WOMEN TRAVELLERS

In general, women need not walk around in fear – women are rarely physically attacked on the street. However, the French seem to have given relatively little thought to sexual harassment, and many men tend to stare hard at passing women.

If you are subject to catcalls or are hassled in any way while walking down the street, the best strategy is usually to carry on and ignore the comment. Making a cutting retort is ineffective in English and risky in French if your slang isn't extremely proficient.

France's national rape crisis hotline, which is run by a women's organisation called Viols Femmes Informations, can be reached toll-free by dialling ☎ 0800 05 95 95 from 10 am to 6 pm weekdays.

GAY & LESBIAN TRAVELLERS

Most of France's major gay organisations are based in Paris. Centre Gai et Lesbien (CGL; ☎ 01 43 57 21 47, metro Ledru Rollin), 3 rue Keller, 11e, 500m east of place de la Bastille, is the headquarters for numerous organisations. Its bar, library and other facilities are open 2 to 8 pm Monday to Saturday. Paris' Gay Pride parade is held on the last weekend in June.

Gay publications include the monthlies *3 Keller*, *Action* and *Gay*. The weekly *e.m@le* has interviews, gossip and articles (in French) and good listings of gay clubs, bars and associations as well as personal classifieds. The monthly *Lesbia* gives a rundown of what's happening around the country. See also Internet Resources earlier for useful Web sites.

DISABLED TRAVELLERS

France is not particularly well equipped for *handicapés*: kerb ramps are few and far between, older public facilities and budget hotels often lack lifts, and the Paris metro, most of it built decades ago, is hopeless. Details of train travel for wheelchair users is available in SNCF's booklet *Guide du Voyageur à Mobilité Réduite*. You can also contact SNCF Accessibilité (the French rail company) toll-free at ☎ 0800 15 47 53.

Hostels in Paris that cater to disabled travellers include the Foyer International d'Accueil de Paris Jean Monnet and the Centre International de Séjour de Paris Kellermann (see Hostels & Foyers in the Paris section).

DANGERS & ANNOYANCES

The biggest crime problem for tourists in France is theft – especially of and from cars. Pickpockets are a problem, and women are a common target because of their handbags. Be especially careful at airports and on crowded public transport in cities.

France's laws regarding even small quantities of drugs are very strict, and the police have the right to search anyone at any time.

The rise in support for the FN in recent years reflects the growing racial intolerance in France. Especially in the south (eg, Provence and the Côte d'Azur), entertainment places such as bars and discos are, for all intents and purposes, segregated.

EMERGENCIES

Emergency telephone numbers in use all over France include:

ambulance	☎ 15
fire	☎ 18
police	☎ 17

BUSINESS HOURS

Tourist offices in larger towns generally open from 9 or 9.30 am to 5 or 6 pm Monday to Saturday, and Sunday mornings in winter; those in smaller towns tend to take a midday break of 1½ to two hours and close on Sunday. In summer, opening hours are often extended to 7 pm or later, and many offices open seven days a week.

Most museums are closed on either Monday or Tuesday and on public holidays, though in summer some open daily. Most small businesses open 9 or 10 am to 6.30 or 7 pm daily except Sunday and perhaps Monday, with a break between noon and 2 pm or 1 and 3 pm. In the south, midday closures are more like siestas and may continue until 3.30 or 4 pm.

Many food shops open daily except Sunday afternoon and Monday. As a result, Sunday morning may be your last chance to stock up on provisions until Tuesday. Most restaurants open only for lunch (noon to 2 or 3 pm) and dinner (6.30 to about 10 or 11 pm); outside Paris, very few serve meals throughout the day. In August, lots of establishments simply close so that their owners and employees alike can take their annual month-long holiday.

Banque de France branches throughout France are open Monday to Friday, but will change money and travellers cheques only in the morning. The opening hours of other banks vary.

PUBLIC HOLIDAYS & SPECIAL EVENTS

National *jours fériés* (public holidays) in France include: New Year's Day, Easter Sunday & Monday, 1 May (May Day), 8 May (1945 Victory Day), Ascension Thursday, Pentecost/Whit Sunday and Whit Monday, 14 July (Bastille Day), 15 August (Assumption Day), 1 November (All Saints' Day), 11 November (1918 Armistice Day) and Christmas Day.

Some of the biggest and best events in France include the Festival d'Avignon (early July to early August), with some 300 daily music, dance and drama events; Bastille Day celebrations, spread over 13 and 14 July; Francofolies, a six-day dance and music festival held in mid-July in La Rochelle, with performers from all over the French-speaking world, the Festival Interceltique, a 10-day Celtic festival in early August, held in the Breton town of Lorient; Lyon's Biennale de la Danse/d'Art Contemporain, a month-long festival (from mid-September) that's held in even-numbered years (in odd-numbered years the city holds a festival of contemporary art); and the Carnaval de Nice, held in Nice every spring around Mardi Gras (Shrove Tuesday).

ACCOMMODATION
Camping

France has thousands of seasonal and year-round camping grounds. Facilities and amenities, reflected in the number of stars the site has been awarded, determine the price. At the less fancy places, two people with a small tent pay 20FF to 55FF a night. Campers without a vehicle can usually get a spot, even late in the day, but not in July and August, when most are packed with families.

Refuges & Gîtes d'Étape

Refuges (mountain huts or shelters) are basic dorms operated by national park authorities, the Club Alpin Français and other private organisations. They are marked on hiking and climbing maps. Some are open year-round.

In general, refuges are equipped with mattresses and blankets but not sheets. Charges average 50FF to 70FF per night (more in popular areas). Meals, prepared by the *gardien* (attendant), are sometimes available. Most refuges are equipped with a telephone, so it's a good idea to call ahead and make a reservation.

Gîtes d'étape, which are usually better equipped and more comfortable than refuges, are found in less remote areas, often in villages. They also cost around 50FF to 70FF per person.

Hostels

In the provinces, *auberges de jeunesse* (hostels) generally charge 48FF to 73FF for a bunk in a single-sex dorm. In Paris, expect to pay 100FF to 140FF a night, including breakfast. In the cities, especially Paris, you will also find *foyers*, student dorms used by travellers in summer. Information on hostels and foyers is available from tourist offices. Most of France's hostels belong to one of three Paris-based organisations:

Fédération Unie des Auberges de Jeunesse (FUAJ; ☎ 01 44 89 87 27, fax 01 44 89 87 10) 27 rue Pajol, 18e, 75018 Paris (metro La Chapelle). Web site: www.fuaj.org

Ligue Française pour les Auberges de la Jeunesse (LFAJ; ☎ 01 44 16 78 78, fax 01 44 16 78 80) 67 rue Vergniaud, 13e, 75013 Paris (metro Glacière)

Union des Centres de Rencontres Internationales de France (UCRIF; ☎ 01 40 26 57 64, fax 01 40 26 58 20, ✆ ucrif@aol.com) 27 rue de Turbigo, 2e, 75002 Paris (metro Étienne Marcel)

Only FUAJ is affiliated with Hostelling International (HI).

Hotels

For two people sharing a room, budget hotels are often cheaper than hostels. Unless otherwise indicated, prices in this chapter refer to rooms in unrated or one-star hotels equipped with a washbasin. Most doubles, which generally cost the same or only marginally more than singles, have only one bed. Doubles with two beds usually cost a little more. A hall *douche* (shower) can be free or cost between 10FF and 25FF.

If you'll be arriving after noon (after 10 am at peak times), it's wise to book ahead. For advance reservations, most hotels require a deposit by post, though if you call on the day of your arrival, many will hold a room for you until a set hour (rarely later than 7 pm). Local tourist offices also make reservations, usually for a small fee.

FOOD & DRINKS

A fully fledged traditional French dinner – usually begun about 8.30 pm – has quite a few distinct courses: an apéritif or cocktail; an *entrée* (first course); the *plat principal* (main course); *salade* (salad); *fromage* (cheese); *dessert*; *fruit* (fruit; pronounced fwee); *café* (coffee); and a *digestif* liqueur.

Restaurants usually specialise in a particular cuisine while brasseries – which look very much like cafes – serve quicker meals of more standard fare (eg, steak and chips/French fries or omelettes). Restaurants tend to open only for lunch (noon to 2 or 3 pm) and dinner (6.30 to 10 or 11 pm); brasseries serve meals throughout the day.

Most restaurants offer at least one fixed-price, multicourse meal known in French as a *menu*. In general, *menus* cost much less than ordering each dish *à la carte* (separately). *Boissons* (drinks) cost extra unless the *menu* says *boisson comprise* (drink included).

Sitting in a cafe to read, write or talk with friends is an integral part of everyday life in France. A cafe on a busy boulevard will charge considerably more than a place that fronts a side street.

While *supermarchés* (supermarkets) and more expensive *épiceries* (grocery shops) are common, many people buy food from small neighbourhood shops, each with its own speciality – a *boulangerie* (bread bakery), *pâtisserie* (pastry bakery), *confiserie* (chocolate and sweets shop), *fromagerie* and *crémerie* (cheese shops), *boucherie* (general butcher) and *poissonnerie* (fish shop). A *charcuterie* is a delicatessen with pricey but delicious sliced meats, salads and ready-to-eat main dishes. Most towns hold *marchés découverts* (open-air markets) or *marchés couverts* and *halles* (covered markets) one or more times a week.

Nonalcoholic Drinks

Tap water in France is perfectly safe. Make sure you ask for *une carafe d'eau* (a jug of water) or *de l'eau du robinet* (tap water) or you may get costly *eau de source* (mineral water). A small cup of espresso is called *un café*, *un café noir* or *un express*; you can also ask for a *grand* (large) one. *Un café crème* is espresso with steamed cream. *Un café au lait* is espresso served in a large cup with lots of steamed milk. Decaffeinated coffee is *un café décaféiné* or simply *un déca*.

Other popular hot drinks include: *thé* (tea) – if you want milk you ask for '*un peu de lait frais*'; *tisane* (herbal tea); and *chocolat chaud* (hot chocolate).

Alcoholic Drinks

The French almost always take their meals with wine – *rouge* (red), *blanc* (white) or *rosé*. The least expensive wines cost less per litre than soft drinks. Wines that meet stringent regulations bear the abbreviation AOC (Appellation d'Origine Controlée). The cheapest wines have no AOC certification and are known as *vins ordinaires* or *vins de table* (table wines).

Alcoholic drinks other than wine include apéritifs, such as *kir* (dry white wine sweetened with *cassis* – blackcurrant liqueur), *kir royale* (champagne with cassis) and *pastis* (anise-flavoured alcohol drunk with ice and water); and digestifs such as brandy or Calvados (apple brandy). Beer is usually either from Alsace or imported. A *demi* (about 250ml) is cheaper *à la pression* (on draught) than from a bottle.

Getting There & Away

AIR

Air France and many of other airlines link Paris with the world. Other French cities with international air links (mainly within Europe) include Bordeaux, Lyon, Marseille, Nice, Strasbourg and Toulouse. For information on Paris' two international airports, Orly and Roissy-Charles de Gaulle, see Getting There & Away in the Paris section.

FRANCE

Flights between London and Paris can cost as little as UK£50 return; with the larger companies expect to pay at least UK£88. One-way discount fares to Paris start at L229,000 from Rome, 55,000 dr from Athens, I£55 from Dublin, 1200FF from İstanbul and 16,000 ptas from Madrid. Student travel agencies can supply details.

LAND
Britain
The highly civilised Eurostar (☎ 0870-518 6186 in the UK, ☎ 0836 35 35 39 in France) links London's Waterloo Station with Paris' Gare du Nord via the Channel Tunnel. The journey takes about three hours, not including the one-hour time change. Tickets for people aged 25 and under cost UK£45/75 one way/return; return fares booked 14/seven days ahead cost UK£69/80. Student travel agencies often have youth fares not available direct from Eurostar. Web site: www.eurostar.com.

Eurotunnel shuttle trains (☎ 0870-535 3535 in the UK, ☎ 03 21 00 61 00 in France) whisk buses and cars (and their passengers) from near Folkestone to Coquelles (just west of Calais) in 35 minutes. The regular one-way fare for a car and its passengers ranges from UK£109.50 (February and March) to UK£174.50 (July and August). To take advantage of promotional fares you must book at least one day ahead. Web site: www.eurotunnel.com.

Elsewhere in Europe
Bus Eurolines coach services (☎ 0836 69 52 52 in France) link France with other European countries. See the Getting There & Away chapter and Getting There & Away in the Paris section for information. Web site: www.eurolines.fr.

Train Paris, France's main rail hub, is linked with every part of Europe. Depending on where you're coming from, you sometimes have to change train stations in Paris to reach the provinces. For details on Paris' six train stations, see Getting There & Away in the Paris section.

BIJ (Billets International de Jeunesse, ie, International Youth Tickets), available to people under 26, save at least 20% on international 2nd-class rail travel; on some routes discounts (not available to Italy) are limited to night trains. BIJ tickets are not sold at train station ticket windows – you have to visit Voyages Wasteels or one of the student travel agencies. There's almost always at least one BIJ-issuer near major train stations.

People aged 12 to 25 get significant discounts on the superfast Thalys trains that link Paris with Brussels, Amsterdam and Cologne.

SEA
Ferry tickets are available from almost all travel agents.

Britain & the Channel Islands
Hoverspeed (☎ 0870-524 0241 in the UK, ☎ 0820 00 35 55 in France) runs giant catamarans (SeaCats) from Folkestone to Boulogne (55 minutes). Foot passengers pay UK£24 one way (or return if you come back within five days). Depending on the season, a car with up to nine passengers is charged UK£109 to UK£175 one way. Web site: www.hoverspeed.co.uk.

The Dover-Calais crossing is also handled by car ferries (1½ hours, 44 a day) run by SeaFrance (☎ 0870-571 1711 UK, ☎ 0804 04 40 45 France) and P&O Stena (☎ 0870-598 0980 in the UK, ☎ 0802 010 020 in France). Pedestrians pay UK£15/24 with SeaFrance/P&O Stena; cars are UK£122.50 to UK£170 one way. Web sites: www.seafrance.com and www.posl.com.

If you are travelling to Normandy, the Newhaven-Dieppe route is handled by Hoverspeed's SeaCats (2¼ hours, one to three a day). Poole is linked to Cherbourg by Brittany Ferries (☎ 0870-536 0360 in the UK, ☎ 02 98 29 28 00 in France), which has one or two 4¼-hour crossings a day; the company also runs ferries from Portsmouth to Caen (Ouistreham). On the Portsmouth-Cherbourg route, P&O Portsmouth (☎ 0870-598 0555 in the UK, ☎ 0803 013 013 in France) has three car ferries a day and, from mid-March to mid-October, two faster catamarans a day; the company also links Portsmouth with Le Havre. Web sites: www.brittany-ferries.com and www.poef.com.

If you're going to Brittany, Brittany Ferries links Plymouth with Roscoff (six hours, one to three a day) from mid-March to mid-November; the company also has services from Portsmouth to St Malo (8¾ hours).

FRANCE

For information on ferries from St Malo to the Channel Islands, Weymouth, Poole (via the Channel Islands) and Portsmouth, see Getting There & Away in the St Malo (Brittany) section.

Ireland

Irish Ferries (☎ 01-638 333 Ireland, ☎ 02 33 23 44 44 Cherbourg) has overnight runs from Rosslare to either Cherbourg (18 hours) or Roscoff (16 hours) every other day (three times a week from mid-September to October, with a break in service from November to February). Pedestrians pay I£40 to I£80 (I£32 to I£66 for students and seniors). Eurail pass-holders are charged 50% of the adult pedestrian fare. Web site: www.irish-ferries.com.

Morocco

Sète, 29km south-west of Montpellier, is linked with Tangier (36 hours, five to seven a month) by Compagnie Marocaine de Navigation (☎ 04 99 57 21 21 Sète, ☎ 09-94 23 50 Tangier). The cheapest one-way berth costs 970FF. Discounts are available if you're under 26 or in a group of four or more.

Getting Around

AIR

France's long-protected domestic airline industry is being opened up to competition, though Air France still handles the majority of domestic flights. For more details check out the Web site at www.airfrance.fr.

Full-fare flying within France is extremely expensive, but big discounts are available to people aged 12 to 24, couples, families and seniors. The most heavily discounted flights may be cheaper than long-distance rail travel. Further details on the complicated fare structures are available from travel agents.

BUS

Because the French train network is state-owned and the government prefers to operate a monopoly, the country has only very limited intercity bus service. However, buses (some run by the SNCF) are widely used for short distances, especially in rural areas with relatively few train lines (eg, Brittany and Normandy).

TRAIN

Eurail and Inter-Rail passes are valid in France.

France's excellent rail network, operated by the Société Nationale des Chemins de Fer Français (SNCF), reaches almost every part of the country. The most important train lines fan out from Paris like the spokes of a wheel. The SNCF's nationwide telephone number for inquiries and reservations (☎ 0836 35 35 39 in English) costs 2.23FF a minute. Web site: www.sncf.com.

The pride and joy of the SNCF is the high-speed TGV. There are now three TGV lines that go under a variety of names: the TGV Sud-Est & TGV Midi-Mediterranée link Paris' Gare de Lyon with the southeast, including Dijon, Lyon, the Alps, Avignon, Marseille, Nice and Montpellier; the TGV Atlantique Sud-Ouest & TGV Atlantique Ouest link Paris' Gare Montparnasse with western and south-western France, including Brittany, Tours, La Rochelle, Bordeaux, Biarritz and Toulouse; and the TGV Nord links Paris' Gare du Nord with Arras, Lille and Calais.

Reservations are optional unless you're travelling by TGV or want a couchette or special reclining seat. On popular trains (eg, on holiday weekends) you may have to reserve in advance to get a seat. Eurail pass-holders must pay all applicable reservation fees.

Before boarding the train, you must validate your ticket (and your reservation card, if it's separate) by time-stamping it in one of the *composteurs*, the bright orange posts that are located somewhere between the ticket windows and the tracks. Eurail and some other rail passes *must* be validated at a train station ticket window to initiate the period of validity.

Discounts

Passes for Nonresidents of Europe

The France Railpass allows unlimited rail travel within France for three to nine days over the course of a month. In 2nd class, the three-day version costs US$180 (US$145 each for two people travelling together); each additional day of travel costs US$30. The France Youthpass, available if you're 25 or under, costs US$164 for four days of travel over two months; additional days (up to a maximum of 10) cost US$20. In North

America, Rail Europe (☎ 1-800 456 7245) has details. Web site: www.raileurope.com.

Passes for Residents of Europe The Euro Domino France flexipass gives European residents who don't live in France three to eight days of midnight-to-midnight travel over a period of one month. The youth version (for people 25 and under) costs €120 for three days and €24 for each additional day; the adult version costs €150 for three days and €30 for each additional day.

Discounts for Everyone Discounts of 25% on one-way or return travel within France are available at all train station ticket windows to: people aged 12 to 25 (the Découverte 12/25 fare); one to four adults travelling with a child aged four to 11 (the Découverte Enfant Plus fare); people over 60 (the Découverte Senior fare); and – for return travel only – any two people who are travelling together (the Découverte À Deux fare).

No matter what age you are, the Découverte Séjour excursion fare gives you a 25% reduction for return travel within France if you meet two conditions: the total length of your trip is at least 200km; and you'll be spending a Saturday night at your destination.

The Découverte J30, which must be purchased 30 to 60 days before the date of travel, offers savings of 45% to 55%. The Découverte J8, which you must buy at least eight days ahead, gets you 20% to 30% off.

CAR & MOTORCYCLE

Driving in France is expensive: petrol is costly and tolls can reach hundreds of francs a day if you're going cross-country in a hurry. Three or four people travelling together, however, may find that renting a car is cheaper than taking the train.

In the centres of almost all French cities, parking is metered. Buy a time-stamped ticket from a kerbside *horodateur* (parking meter) and display it *inside* the car on the pavement side of the dashboard. There's often a two-hour maximum.

Unless otherwise posted, speed limits are 130km/h (110km/h in the rain) on *autoroutes* (dual carriageways/divided highways whose names begin with A); 110km/h (100km/h in the rain) on *routes nationales* (highways whose names begin with N) that have a divider down the middle; and 90km/h

(80km/h if it's raining) on nondivided routes nationales and *routes départementales* (rural highways whose names start with D). The moment you pass a sign with a place name on it you have entered the boundaries of a town or village, which means that the speed limit automatically drops to 50km/h; this limit applies until you pass an identical sign with a red bar across it.

The maximum permissible blood-alcohol level in France is 0.05%.

Big supermarkets on the outskirts of towns tend to offer the lowest petrol prices.

If you don't live in the EU and think you will need a car in France (or Europe) for 17 days (or a bit more) to six months, it is *much* cheaper to 'purchase' one from the manufacturer and then 'sell' it back than it is to rent one. The purchase-repurchase *(achat-rachat)* paperwork is not your responsibility (all you do is pay a remarkably cheap per-day rate). Both Renault's Eurodrive (☎ 1-800 221 1052 in the USA) and Peugeot's Vacation Plan/Sodexa (☎ 1-800 572 9655 or ☎ 1-800 223 1516 in the USA) offer great deals that – incredibly – include insurance with no deductible (excess). For further information check out the Web sites at www.eurodrive.renault.com and www.sodexa.com.

Paris

Paris (population 2.2 million – metropolitan area 10.5 million) has almost exhausted the superlatives that can reasonably be applied to a city. Notre Dame and the Eiffel Tower – at sunrise, at sunset, at night – have been described ad nauseam, as have the River Seine and the subtle (and not-so-subtle) differences between the Left and Right Banks. But what writers have been unable to capture is the grandness and even the magic of strolling along the city's broad avenues, which lead from impressive public buildings and exceptional museums to parks, gardens and esplanades. Paris is enchanting at any time, in every season. There are plenty of free and cheap ways to enjoy France's (very expensive) capital, but not if you attempt to cover the big-name attractions in a short period of time. Make sure you give yourself at least three or four days in Paris.

ORIENTATION

In central Paris (which the French call Intra-Muros – 'within the walls'), the Rive Droite (Right Bank) is north of the Seine, while the Rive Gauche (Left Bank) is south of the river. For administrative purposes, Paris is divided into 20 *arrondissements* (districts) that spiral out clockwise from the centre. Addresses in Paris always include the arrondissement number; we list them as part of the street address, using the usual French notation – 1er stands for the *premier* or 1st district, 4e for the *quartrième* or 4th district etc. When an address includes the full five-digit postal code, the last two digits indicate the arrondissement (ie, 75001 for the 1st, 75004 for the 4th).

The best map of Paris is Michelin's *Paris Plan* (1:10,000). It comes in booklet (No 11 or 14) and sheet form (No 10 or 12) and is available in bookshops and kiosks throughout the city.

INFORMATION
Tourist Offices

The best single source of information is Paris' main tourist office (☎ 0836 68 31 12, fax 01 49 52 53 00, metro George V) at 127 ave des Champs-Élysées, 8e. It's open 9 am to 8 pm (11 am to 7 pm on winter Sundays) every day of the year, except 1 May and Christmas Day. There are branch offices in the Gare de Lyon open 8 am to 8 pm Monday to Saturday and at the base of the Eiffel Tower open 11 am to 6 pm daily from May to September.

Money

All of Paris' six major train stations have bureaux de change that open to at least 7 pm daily, but the rates are not very good. The exchange offices at Orly (Orly-Sud terminal) and Roissy-Charles de Gaulle (both terminal complexes) open until 11 pm daily. By far the best rate in town is offered by Banque de France, whose headquarters (☎ 01 42 92 22 27, metro Palais Royal-Musée du Louvre) is three blocks north of the Louvre at 31 rue Croix des Petits Champs, 1er. The exchange service is open 9.30 am to 12.30 pm and 1.30 to 4 pm weekdays. There are other branches throughout the city. American Express (☎ 01 47 77 77 75, metro Auber or Opéra) is at 11 rue Scribe, 9e, facing the west side of Opéra Garnier. It's open 9.30 am to 6 pm weekdays (7 pm June to September), and 10 am to 5 pm at the weekend.

Post & Communications

Paris' 24-hour main post office (☎ 01 40 28 20 00, metro Sentier or Les Halles) is at 52 rue du Louvre, 1er. Foreign exchange is available 8 am to 7 pm weekdays, to noon Saturday.

Café Orbital (☎ 01 43 25 76 77, metro Odéon) at 13 rue de Médicis, 6e, opens 9 am to 10 pm daily, from noon on Sunday. Internet access costs 55FF per hour (discount for students). Web Bar (☎ 01 42 72 66 55, @ webbar@webbar.fr, metro Filles du Calvaire) is at 32 rue de Picardie, 3e, and charges 45/300FF for one/10 hours. It's open 11.30 am to 2 am daily.

Travel Agencies

Nouvelles Frontières (☎ 0825 00 08 25, Minitel 3615 NF, metro Luxembourg) specialises in discount air fares and has 14 outlets around the city including one at 66 blvd St Michel, 6e. Voyageurs du Monde (☎ 01 42 86 16 00, Minitel 3615 VOYAGEURS, metro Pyramides or Quatre Septembre), 55 rue Ste Anne, 2e, is open 9.30 am to 7 pm Monday to Saturday. There's also a good travel bookshop here and the agency has its own restaurant next door. Web site: www.nouvelles-frontieres.fr.

Bookshops

The famous English-language bookshop, Shakespeare & Company (☎ 01 43 26 96 50, metro St Michel), is at 37 rue de la Bûcherie, 5e, across the Seine from Notre Dame Cathedral. The largest English-language bookshop, WH Smith (☎ 01 44 77 88 99, metro Concorde) is at 248 rue de Rivoli, 1er, one block east of place de la Concorde. Abbey Bookshop (☎ 01 46 33 16 24, metro Cluny-La Sorbonne), 29 rue de la Parcheminerie, 5e, has free tea and coffee, a supply of Canadian newspapers and a good selection of fiction. Les Mots á la Bouche (☎ 01 42 78 88 30, metro Hôtel de Ville), 6 rue Ste Croix de la Bretonnerie, 4e, is Paris' premier gay bookshop.

Laundry

Near the BVJ hostels, the Laverie Libre Service (metro Louvre Rivoli), 7 rue Jean-

FRANCE

Jacques Rousseau, 1er, is open 7.30 am to 10 pm daily. The Laverie Libre Service (metro St Paul), 25 rue des Rosiers, 4e, is also open 7.30 am to 10 pm daily. Other laundrettes include: Lavomatique (metro Monge) at 63 rue Monge, 5e; Lav' Club (metro Gare de l'Est), 55 blvd de Magenta, 10e; and Montmartre's Laverie Libre Service (metro Blanche) at 4 rue Burq, 18e.

Medical Services

Paris has about 50 *assistance publique* (public health service) hospitals. An easy one to find is the Hôtel Dieu hospital (☎ 01 42 34 81 31, metro Cité), on the northern side of place du Parvis Notre Dame, 4e, the square in front of the cathedral. The *service des urgences* (emergency room) is open 24 hours.

Dangers & Annoyances

For its size, Paris is a safe city, but you should always use common sense; for instance, avoid the large Bois de Boulogne and Bois de Vincennes parks after nightfall. Although it's fine to use the metro until it stops running at about 12.30 am, some stations are best avoided late at night, especially if alone. These include Châtelet-Les Halles and its seemingly endless corridors; Château Rouge in Montmartre; Gare du Nord; Strasbourg-St Denis; Réaumur-Sébastopol; and Montparnasse-Bienvenüe.

Museum Hours & Discounts

The Carte Musées et Monuments pass gets you into some 75 museums and monuments without having to queue for a ticket. The card costs 80/160/240FF for one/three/five consecutive days and is on sale at the museums and monuments it covers, at some metro ticket windows and at the main tourist office.

THINGS TO SEE – LEFT BANK
Île de la Cité (1er & 4e)

Paris' most famous cathedral, **Notre Dame** (metro Cité or St Michel), is a magnificent example of Gothic architecture. It was begun in 1163 and completed around 1345. Exceptional features include the three spectacular rose windows, and the window on the north side of the transept. Notre Dame is open 8 am to 6.45 pm daily (free). The **North Tower**, from which you can view many of the cathedral's most ferocious-

looking gargoyles, can be climbed via long spiral steps (35/23FF).

One of the best views of Notre Dame is from the lovely park behind it, where you can see the church's mass of ornate flying buttresses. While there, have a look at the haunting **Mémorial des Martyrs de la Déportation**, in memory of the 200,000 people deported by the Nazis and French fascists during WWII.

The gem-like upper chapel of **Ste Chapelle**, illuminated by a veritable curtain of 13th-century stained glass, is inside the **Palais de Justice** (Law Courts; metro Cité) at 4 blvd du Palais. Ste Chapelle, built in only 33 months, was consecrated in 1248. This is one of Paris' finest small chapels. It's open 9.30 am to 6.30 pm daily from April to September and 10 am to 5pm the rest of the year. Entry is 35/23FF. A combined ticket with the nearby Conciergerie is 50/25FF. The **Conciergerie** was a luxurious royal palace when it was built in the 14th century – its **Salle des Gens d'Armes** (Cavalrymen's Room) is the oldest medieval hall in Europe – but was later transformed into a prison and continued as such until 1914. During the Reign of Terror (1793-94), among the almost 2600 people held here before being bundled off to the guillotine were Queen Marie-Antoinette and the Revolutionary radicals Danton and Robespierre. The Conciergerie has the same hours and entry fees as Ste Chapelle. The entrance is at 1 quai de l'Horloge.

Île St Louis (4e)

The smaller of Paris' two islands is just east of Île de la Cité. The 17th-century houses of grey stone and the small-town shops that line the streets and quays impart an almost provincial feel, making this a great place for a quiet stroll. On foot, the shortest route between Notre Dame and the Marais passes through Île St Louis.

Latin Quarter (5e & 6e)

This area is known as the Quartier Latin because, until the Revolution, all communication between students and their professors here took place in Latin. The 5e is increasingly touristy but still has a large population of students affiliated with the University of Paris and other institutions. Shop-lined **blvd St Michel**, known as the 'Boul Mich', runs

FRANCE

FRANCE

CENTRAL PARIS

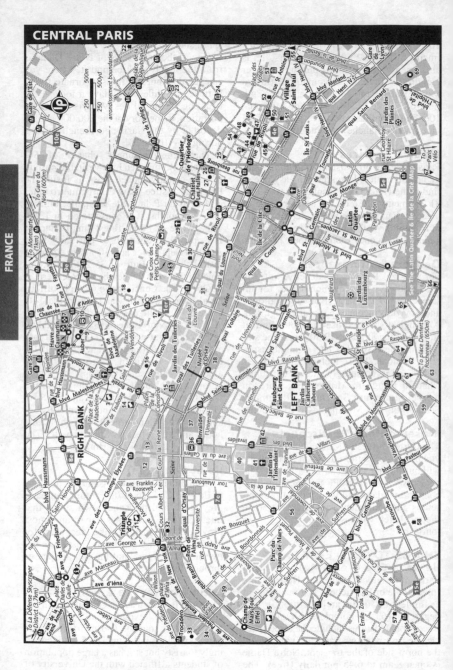

CENTRAL PARIS

PLACES TO STAY		OTHER		29	Église Saint Eustache
22	Auberge de Jeunesse	1	Arc de Triomphe	31	Louvre Museum
	Jules Ferry	2	Main Tourist Office	32	Bateaux Mouches
30	Centre International BVJ	3	UK Embassy		(Boat Tours)
	Paris-Louvre & Laundrette	4	La Madeleine Church	33	Palais de Chaillot
44	Hôtel Rivoli	5	Au Printemps	34	Jardins du Trocadéro
45	MIJE Maubisson		(Department Store)	35	Australian Embassy
46	Hôtel de Nice	6	Galeries Lafayette	36	Aérogare des Invalides
50	MIJE Fourcy		(Department Store)		(Buses to Orly)
51	MIJE Fauconnier	7	Galeries Lafayette	37	Palais Bourbon (National
52	Hôtel Moderne; Hôtel Pratic	8	Eurostar & Ferry Offices		Assembly Building)
57	Three Ducks Hostel	9	American Express	38	Musée d'Orsay
58	Aloha Hostel	10	Opéra Garnier	39	Eiffel Tower
		11	Canadian Embassy	40	Hôtel des Invalides
PLACES TO EAT		12	Grand Palais	41	Église du Dôme
17	Food Shops	13	Petit Palais	42	Musée Auguste Rodin
25	Aquarius	14	US Embassy	47	Stolly's Pub
43	Minh Chau	15	Musée de l'Orangerie	48	Laundrette
49	Restaurant Jo	16	WH Smith Bookshop	53	Maison de Victor Hugo
	Goldenburg	18	Voyageurs du Monde	54	Les Mots á la Bouche
61	Rue d'Odessa Crêperies	19	Banque de France	55	Colonne de Juillet
62	Mustang Café	20	Main Post Office	56	École Militaire
64	Le Caméléon	21	Rue Saint Denis Sex District	59	Gare Montparnasse
65	CROUS Restaurant	23	Web Bar	60	FNAC Store &
	Universitaire Assas	24	Musée Picasso		Ticket Outlet
66	CROUS Restaurant	26	Centre Pompidou	63	Cimetière du Montparnasse
	Universitaire Bullier	27	AJF Main Office	68	Paris Mosque & Hammam
67	Founti Agadir	28	Forum des Halles	69	Gare d'Austerlitz

FRANCE

along the border of the 5e and the 6e. The Latin Quarter landmark now known as the **Pánthéon** (metro Luxembourg or Cardinal Lemoine), at the eastern end of rue Soufflot, was commissioned as an abbey church in the mid-18th century. In 1791 it was converted into a mausoleum for the 'great men of the era of French liberty'; permanent residents include Victor Hugo, Émile Zola, Voltaire and Jean-Jacques Rousseau. Much of the Panthéon's ornate marble interior will be closed for some time during a massive renovation. Entry is 32/21FF. The **Sorbonne**, Paris' most famous university, was founded in 1253 as a college for 16 poor theology students. Today, the Sorbonne's main campus (bounded by rues Victor Cousin, St Jacques, des Écoles and Cujas) and other buildings nearby house several of the 13 autonomous universities created when the University of Paris was reorganised in 1968.

Jardin du Luxembourg (6e)
When the weather is warm, Parisians flock to the Luxembourg Gardens (metro Luxembourg) in their thousands to sit and read, write and sunbathe while their children sail little boats in the fountains. The gardens'

main entrance is across the street from 65 blvd St Michel. The **Palais du Luxembourg**, fronting rue de Vaugirard at the northern end of the gardens, was built for Maria de' Medici (Marie de Médicis in French), queen of France from 1600 to 1610. It now houses the Sénat, the upper house of the French parliament.

Musée National du Moyen Age (5e)
The Museum of the Middle Ages (metro Cluny-La Sorbonne) houses one of France's finest collections of medieval art. Its prized possession is a series of six 15th-century tapestries from the southern Netherlands known as *La Dame à la Licorne* (The Lady and The Unicorn). The museum's entrance is at 6 place Paul Painlevé. It's open 9.15 am to 5.45 pm daily (except Tuesday) and entry costs 38/28FF (28FF on Sunday).

Paris Mosque (5e)
Paris' central mosque (metro Monge) at place du Puits de l'Ermite was built between 1922 and 1926 in an ornate Moorish style. There are tours (15/10FF) from 9 am to noon and 2 to 6 pm, Saturday to Thursday. The mosque complex includes a small

souk (marketplace), a *salon de thé*, an excellent couscous restaurant and a hammam (Turkish bath; 85FF), open to men 2 to 9 pm on Tuesday and 10 am to 9 pm on Sunday only; on other days (open 10 am to 9 pm) it is reserved for women. The entrance is at 39 rue Geoffroy St Hilaire.

Catacombes (14e)

In 1785 it was decided that the hygiene problems posed by Paris' overflowing cemeteries could be solved by exhuming the bones and storing them in the tunnels of three disused quarries. One such ossuary is the Catacombes (☎ 01 43 22 47 63, metro Denfert Rochereau). During WWII these tunnels were used by the Resistance as headquarters. The route through the Catacombes begins from the small green building at 1 place Denfert Rochereau; it's a good idea to bring along a torch (flashlight). The site is open 2 to 4 pm Tuesday to Friday, 9 to 11 am and 2 to 4 pm at the weekend. Tickets cost 33/22FF.

Musée d'Orsay (7e)

This world-class museum (metro Musée d'Orsay), housed in a former train station along the Seine at 1 rue de Bellechasse, exhibits paintings, sculptures and works produced between 1848 and 1914. The museum opens 10 am (9 am Sunday) to 6 pm (9.45 pm Thursday) Tuesday to Sunday from late September to late June; in summer it opens at 9 am daily. Entry is 40/30FF (30FF Sunday).

Musée Auguste Rodin (7e)

This is one of the most pleasant museums in Paris (metro Varenne), housing Rodin's extraordinary bronze and marble sculptures – look for *The Kiss*, *Cathedral* and, of course, *The Thinker*. The museum is at 77 rue de Varenne and opens 9.30 am to 5.45 pm daily from April to September (to 4.45 pm the rest of the year). Entry is 28/18FF (18FF Sunday). Visiting just the garden (which closes at 5 pm) costs 5FF.

Invalides (7e)

The Hôtel des Invalides (metro Invalides for the Esplanade; Varenne or Latour Maubourg for the main building) was built in the 1670s by Louis XIV to provide housing for 4000 disabled veterans (*invalides*).

It also served as the headquarters of the military governor of Paris, and was used to store weapons and ammunition. On 14 July 1789 the Paris mob forced its way into the building and, after fierce fighting, took 28,000 firearms before heading for the Bastille prison. The Église du Dôme, built between 1677 and 1735, is considered one of the finest religious edifices erected under Louis XIV. The church, which houses the tomb of Napoleon, is open 10 am to 6 pm daily from April to September (to 5 pm the rest of the year); entry costs 38/28FF.

Eiffel Tower (7e)

The Tour Eiffel (metro Champ de Mars-Tour Eiffel) faced massive opposition from Paris' artistic and literary elite when it was built for the 1889 Exposition Universelle (World Fair). It was almost torn down in 1909 but, proving an ideal platform for new-fangled transmitting antennae, was spared. The tower is 320m high, including the television antenna at the tip. There are three levels open to the public. The lift (west and north pillars) costs 22FF for the 1st platform (57m), 44FF for the 2nd (115m) and 62FF for the 3rd (276m). The escalator (south pillar) to the 1st or 2nd platforms costs 18FF. The tower opens 9.30 am to 11 pm (9 am to midnight from mid-June to August) daily; the escalators run from 9.30 am to 6.30 pm (to 9 pm May and June, 11 pm July and August).

THINGS TO SEE – RIGHT BANK
Jardins du Trocadéro (16e)

The Trocadéro gardens (metro Trocadéro), whose fountain and nearby sculpture park are grandly illuminated at night, are across the Pont d'Iéna from the Eiffel Tower. The vast, colonnaded Palais de Chaillot, built in 1937, houses a couple of interesting museums: the Musée de l'Homme (Museum of Mankind; 30/20FF); and the Musée de la Marine (Maritime Museum; 38/28FF).

Louvre (1er)

The Louvre (☎ 01 40 20 51 51, metro Palais Royal-Musée du Louvre), built around 1200 as a fortress and rebuilt in the mid-16th century as a royal palace, became a public museum in 1793. The paintings, sculptures and artefacts on display have been assembled by French governments over the past five centuries and include works of art and artisanship from all over Europe as well as important collections of Assyrian, Egyptian, Etruscan, Greek, Roman and Islamic art. The Louvre's most famous work is Leonardo da Vinci's *Mona Lisa*. Since it takes several visits to get anything more than the briefest glimpse of the offerings, your best bet – after seeking out a few things you really want to see – is to choose a period or section of the museum and pretend the rest is across town. The Louvre's entrance is covered by a glass pyramid designed by American architect IM Pei. The Louvre opens daily except Tuesday and closes on some public holidays. Hours are 9 am to 6 pm (last admission 5.15 pm) Thursday to Sunday; 9 am to 9.45 pm (last admission 9.15 pm) Monday and Wednesday. Cassette tours in six languages can be rented (30FF) on the mezzanine level beneath the pyramid.

Musée de l'Orangerie (1er)
This museum (☎ 01 42 97 48 16, metro Concorde) in the south-west corner of the Jardin des Tuileries at place de la Concorde, is usually home to important impressionist works including a series of Monet's spectacular *Nymphéas* (Water Lilies), but is being renovated and will reopen at the end of 2001.

La Madeleine (8e)
The church of St Mary Magdalene (metro Madeleine) is 350m north of place de la Concorde along rue Royale. Built in the style of a Greek temple, it was consecrated in 1842 after almost a century of construction delays. The front porch affords a superb view of the square and, across the river, the 18th-century **Palais Bourbon** (now the home of the National Assembly).

Champs-Élysées (8e)
The 2km-long ave les Champs-Élysées links place de la Concorde with the Arc de Triomphe. Once popular with the aristocracy as a stage on which to parade their wealth, it has, in recent decades, been partly taken over by fast-food restaurants and overpriced cafes. The nicest bit is the park with the **Petit Palais** (with Renaissance clocks, tapestries and 19th-century French art) and the **Grand Palais** (temporary exhibitions). Both are on ave Winston Churchill.

Arc de Triomphe (8e)
Paris' second-most famous landmark (metro Charles de Gaulle-Étoile) is in the middle of place Charles de Gaulle. Also called place de l'Étoile, this is the world's largest traffic roundabout and the meeting point of 12 avenues. The Arc de Triomphe was commissioned in 1806 by Napoleon to commemorate his imperial victories; it was finally completed in the 1830s. An unknown soldier from WWI is buried under the arch, commemorated by a memorial flame that is lit with ceremony each evening at around 6.30 pm. The platform atop the arch (lift up, steps down) opens 9.30 am to 11 pm daily from April to September and 10 am to 10 pm the rest of the year. Entry is 40/25FF, and there's a small museum with a short videotape. The only sane way to reach the arch's base is via the underground passageways from its perimeter.

Centre Pompidou (4e)
This six-storey centre (metro Rambuteau or Châtelet-Les Halles), also known as the Centre Beaubourg, displays contemporary art. It has recently undergone a massive renovation and, thanks in part to its outstanding temporary exhibitions, is by far the most frequented sight in Paris. **Place Igor Stravinsky** and its crazy fountains attract street artists, mimes, musicians and the like.

Hôtel de Ville (4e)
Paris' city hall (metro Hôtel de Ville) at place de l'Hôtel de Ville was burned down during the Paris Commune of 1871 and rebuilt between 1874 and 1882. The small museum has imaginative exhibits on Paris. The visitors entrance is at 29 rue de Rivoli.

Marais Area (4e)
The Marais, east of the Centre Pompidou and north of Île St Louis, was a marsh *(marais)* until the 13th century, when it was converted to agricultural use. In the 17th century the nobility erected luxurious but discreet mansions known as *hôtels particuliers*. By the time renovation was begun in the 1960s, the Marais had become a poor but lively Jewish neighbourhood centred around **rue des Rosiers**. In the 1980s the area underwent serious gentrification and is today one of Paris' trendiest neighbourhoods. It is also something of a gay quarter.

In 1612 King Henry IV chose the Marais as the site for his Place Royale, known today as the **Place des Vosges** (metro Chemin Vert), an ensemble of 36 symmetrical houses with ground-floor arcades and large dormer windows north of rue St Antoine. Duels were once fought in the elegant park in the middle. The nearby **Maison de Victor Hugo** is where the author lived from 1832 to 1848 (closed Monday; 22/15FF).

Musée Picasso (3e)

The Picasso Museum (metro St Sébastien-Froissart), housed in the mid-17th-century Hôtel Salé, is just north-east of the Marais at 5 rue de Thorigny. Paintings, sculptures, ceramic works and drawings donated to the French government by the heirs of Pablo Picasso (1881-1973) to avoid huge inheritance taxes are on display, as is Picasso's personal art collection (Braque, Cézanne, Matisse, Rousseau etc). The museum's opening hours are 9.30 am to 5.30 pm daily except Tuesday. Admission costs 30/20FF (38/28FF when there are special exhibits).

Bastille (4e, 11e & 12e)

The Bastille is the most famous nonexistent monument in Paris; the notorious prison was demolished shortly after the mob stormed it on 14 July 1789 and freed all seven prisoners. Today, the site where it stood is known as place de la Bastille; the 52m-high **Colonne de Juillet** in the centre was erected in 1830. The new (and rather drab) **Opéra Bastille** is at 2-6 place de la Bastille.

Opéra Garnier (9e)

Paris' better-known opera house (metro Opéra) at place de l'Opéra was designed in 1860 by Charles Garnier. The ceiling of the auditorium was painted by Marc Chagall in 1964. The building also houses the excellent **Musée de l'Opéra** (30/20FF).

Montmartre (18e)

During the 19th century, Montmartre's Bohemian lifestyle attracted artists and writers, whose presence turned the area into Paris' most lively and vibrant artistic quarter. In English-speaking countries, Montmartre's mystique has been magnified by the notoriety of the **Moulin Rouge** (☎ 01 53 09 82 82, 82 blvd de Clichy, metro Blanche), a nightclub founded in 1889 and known for its twice-nightly revue of nearly naked chorus girls. Today it is an area of mimes, buskers, tacky souvenir shops and commercial artists. Perched at the very top of Montmartre is the **Basilique du Sacré Cœur** (Basilica of the Sacred Heart), built to fulfil a vow taken by Parisian Catholics after the disastrous Franco-Prussian War of 1870-71. On warm evenings, groups of young people gather on the steps below the church to contemplate the view, play guitars and sing. The basilica (metro Lamarck Caulaincourt) is open 7 am to 11 pm daily. The entrance to the dome and the crypt (15/8FF) is on the west side of the basilica. The recently rebuilt funicular up the hill's southern slope costs one metro/bus ticket each way.

Pigalle (9e & 18e)

Pigalle, only a few blocks south-west of the tranquil, residential areas of Montmartre, is one of Paris' major sex districts. Although the area along blvd de Clichy between the Pigalle and Blanche metro stops is lined with sex shops and striptease parlours, the area has plenty of legitimate nightspots and several all-night cafes. The new **Musée de l'Érotisme** (Museum of Eroticism; metro Blanche) at 72 blvd de Clichy tries to raise erotic art – both antique and modern – to a loftier plane (40/30FF).

Cimetière du Père Lachaise (20e)

Paris' most visited cemetery (metro Père Lachaise) is the final resting place of such notables as Chopin, Proust, Oscar Wilde, Édith Piaf, Sarah Bernhardt and, of course, Jim Morrison, lead singer for the Doors, who died in 1971. Maps indicating the locations of the graves are posted around the cemetery; Jim Morrison's grave is in Division 6. Admission to the cemetery is free and it's open to at least 5.30 pm daily. There are five entrances; the main one is opposite 23 blvd de Ménilmontant.

Bois de Boulogne (16e)

The 8.65-sq-km Bois de Boulogne, on the western edge of the city, is endowed with meandering trails, gardens, forested areas, cycling paths and *belle époque*-style cafes. Rowing boats can be rented at the **Lac Inférieur** (metro Ave Henri Martin), the largest of the park's lakes.

ORGANISED TOURS

Bus

From mid-April to late September RATP's Balabus follows a 50-minute route from the Gare de Lyon to the Grande Arche de la Défense and back, passing many of the city's most famous sights. It costs one metro/bus ticket; details are available at metro stations.

Bicycle

Paris à Vélo c'est Sympa! (☎ 01 48 87 60 01, ✆ info@parisvelosympa.com, metro Bastille), at 37 blvd Bourdon, 4e, runs well-reviewed bicycle tours of Paris and its major monuments (185/160FF). Book ahead.

Boat

In summer, the Batobus river shuttle (☎ 01 44 11 33 99) docks at seven stops along the Seine, including Notre Dame and the Musée d'Orsay. The boats come by every 25 minutes. A one-/two-day pass costs 60/80FF. The Bateaux Mouches company (☎ 01 42 25 96 10 or, for an English recording, ☎ 01 40 76 99 99, metro Alma Marceau), based on the north bank of the Seine just east of Pont de l'Alma, 8e, has a 1½-hour cruise with commentary for 40FF. Vedettes du Pont Neuf (☎ 01 46 33 98 38, metro Pont Neuf), whose home port is on the western tip of Île de la Cité near the Pont Neuf, operates one-hour boat circuits day and night for 50FF.

PLACES TO STAY

Accueil des Jeunes en France (AJF) makes same-day reservations at hostels, hotels and private homes for a 10FF fee; you pay at the office and take a voucher to the establishment. Prices start at 120FF per person. AJF's main office (☎ 01 42 77 87 80, metro Rambuteau) is at 119 rue St Martin, 4e, just west of the Centre Pompidou (closed Sunday). Paris' main tourist office (see Information earlier) also makes same-day bookings.

Camping

Camping du Bois de Boulogne (☎ 01 45 24 30 81, 2 allée du Bord de l'Eau) is along the Seine at the far western edge of the Bois de Boulogne, 16e. Two people with a tent pay 67FF to 88FF (105FF to 143FF with a vehicle). From the Porte Maillot metro stop, private shuttle buses (10FF) run to the site from April to October; at other times, take RATP bus No 244.

Hostels & Foyers

Some hostels impose a three-night maximum stay, especially in summer, though places that have age limits (eg, 30) tend *not* to enforce them. Only official hostels require HI cards. Curfews at Paris hostels tend to be 1 or 2 am though some are earlier. Few hostels accept reservations by telephone; those that do are noted in the text.

Louvre Area (1er) The *Centre International BVJ Paris-Louvre (☎ 01 53 00 90 90, 20 rue Jean-Jacques Rousseau, metro Louvre-Rivoli)* is only a few blocks northeast of the Louvre. Bunks in single-sex rooms cost 130FF, including breakfast.

Marais (4e) The organisation MIJE (☎ 01 42 74 23 45, fax 01 40 27 81 64) runs three hostels in renovated 17th- and 18th-century Marais residences. A bed in a single-sex dorm is 145FF, including breakfast. The nicest of the three, *MIJE Fourcy (6 rue de Fourcy, metro St Paul)*, is 100m south of rue de Rivoli. Two blocks away is *MIJE Fauconnier (11 rue du Fauconnier, metro Pont Marie)*; or *MIJE Maubisson (12 rue des Barres, metro Hôtel de Ville)*. Visit the MIJE Fourcy in person to make reservations (up to seven days in advance) for all three hostels. Individuals can make reservations for all three MIJE hostels by calling or faxing the central switchboard (see above).

Panthéon Area (5e) In a happening street with restaurants and pubs, the friendly 24-hour *Y&H Hostel (☎ 01 45 35 09 53, ✆ smile@youngandhappy.fr, 80 rue Mouffetard, metro Monge)* offers beds in cramped rooms for 117FF. Reservations require a deposit.

11e Arrondissement Though it's a bit institutional, *Auberge de Jeunesse Jules Ferry (☎ 01 43 57 55 60, fax 01 43 12 82 09, ✆ auberge@easynet.fr, 8 blvd Jules Ferry, metro République or Goncourt)* is relaxed and does not accept large groups (no screaming school kids!). Beds are 115FF and Internet access costs 5FF.

Auberge Internationale des Jeunes (☎ 01 47 00 62 00, fax 01 47 00 33 16,

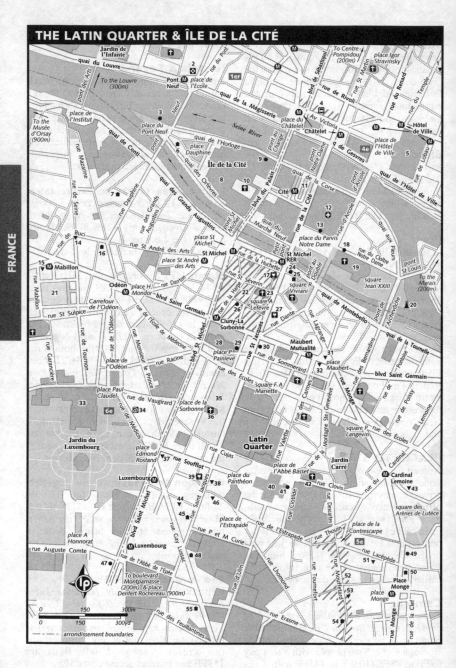

THE LATIN QUARTER & ÎLE DE LA CITÉ

THE LATIN QUARTER & ÎLE DE LA CITÉ

PLACES TO STAY
6 Hôtel Henri IV
7 Hôtel de Nesle
16 Hôtel Petit Trianon
25 Hôtel Esmeralda
45 Hôtel de Médicis
48 Hôtel Gay Lussac
50 Hôtel Saint Christophe
54 Y&H Hostel
55 Grand Hôtel du Progrès

PLACES TO EAT
1 Aquarius
14 CROUS Restaurant
    Universitaire Mabillon
15 Food Shops
21 Marché Saint Germain
22 Restaurants ('Bacteria Alley')
31 Food Shops
32 Fromagerie (Cheese Shop)
37 McDonald's
38 Perraudin
43 Le Petit Légume
44 Douce France Sandwich Bar

46 Tashi Delek Tibetan
    Restaurant
51 Ed l'Épicier Supermarket
52 Restaurants
53 Crêpe Stand

OTHER
2 Samaritaine
   (Department Store)
3 Vedettes du Pont Neuf
   (Boat Tours)
4 Noctambus (All-Night Bus)
   Stops
5 Hôtel de Ville (City Hall)
8 Palais de Justice &
   Conciergerie
9 Conciergerie Entrance
10 Sainte Chapelle
11 Flower Market
12 Hôtel Dieu (Hospital)
13 Hospital Entrance
17 Caveau de la Huchette
    Jazz Club
18 Notre Dame Tower Entrance

19 Notre Dame Cathedral
20 WWII Deportation Memorial
23 Église Saint Séverin
24 Shakespeare & Company
    Bookshop
26 Abbey Bookshop
27 Le Cloître Pub; Polly
    Maggoo Pub
28 Musée National du Moyen
    Age
29 Musée National du Moyen
    Age Entrance
30 Eurolines Bus Office
33 Palais du Luxembourg
    (French Senate Building)
34 Café Orbital
35 Sorbonne (University of Paris)
36 Église de la Sorbonne
39 Café Oz
40 Panthéon
41 Panthéon Entrance
42 Église Saint Étienne du Mont
47 Nouvelles Frontières
49 Lavomatique

FRANCE

aij@aijparis.com, 10 rue Trousseau, metro Ledru Rollin) is a clean, friendly hostel 700m east of place de la Bastille – walk along rue du Faubourg St Antoine until you come to rue Trousseau on your left. Dorm beds are 81FF to 91FF. Rooms are closed for cleaning between 10 am and 3 pm. Reservations are accepted (mandatory in summer).

Maison Internationale des Jeunes (☎ 01 43 71 99 21, e mij.cp@wanadoo.fr, 4 rue Titon, metro Faidherbe Chaligny) is about 1km east of place de la Bastille. A bed in a spartan dorm is 110FF. Same-day phone reservations are accepted.

12e Arrondissement Bookings are accepted up to two days in advance at *Centre International de Séjour de Paris (CISP) Ravel (☎ 01 44 75 60 06, fax 01 43 44 45 30, e 100616.2215@compuserve.com, 4-6 ave Maurice Ravel, metro Porte de Vincennes)*. Beds are 126FF, and private rooms are 206FF per person, including breakfast.

13e & 14e Arrondissements A bed costs 139/172/194FF in modern rooms for eight/four/two people at *Foyer International d'Accueil de Paris (FIAP) Jean Monnet (☎ 01 43 13 17 00, 30 rue Cabanis, 14e, metro Glacière)*, a few blocks south-east of place Denfert Rochereau.

Rooms outfitted for disabled people are available.

Centre International de Séjour de Paris (CISP) Kellermann (☎ 01 43 44 45 30, e 100616.2215@compuserve.com, 17 blvd Kellermann, 13e, metro Porte d'Italie) has dorm beds costing 126FF, and singles for 146FF. The centre also has facilities for disabled people on the 1st floor. Phone reservations are accepted up to two days in advance.

The institutional *Maison des Clubs UNESCO (☎ 01 43 36 00 63, e clubs.unesco.paris@wanadoo.fr, 43 rue de la Glacière, 13e, metro Glacière)* charges 130FF for a dorm bed; singles/doubles are 180/300FF.

15e Arrondissement A favourite with young backpackers is the friendly, helpful *Three Ducks Hostel (☎ 01 48 42 04 05, fax 01 48 42 99 99, e backpack@3ducks.fr, 6 place Étienne Pernet, metro Commerce)*. A bunk bed costs 97FF to 117FF, and phone reservations are accepted. *Aloha Hostel (☎ 01 42 73 03 03, e friends@aloha.fr, 1 rue Borromée, metro Volontaires)*, 1km west of Gare Montparnasse, is run by the same people and has the same prices.

Hotels
Marais (4e) One of the best deals in town is the friendly *Hôtel Rivoli (☎ 01 42 72 08*

41, 44 rue de Rivoli, metro Hôtel de Ville). Rooms range from 200FF (singles without shower) to 300FF (doubles with bath). The front door is locked at 2 am. *Hôtel Moderne* (☎ *01 48 87 97 05, 3 rue Caron, metro St Paul)* has singles/doubles starting at 160FF, doubles with shower from 260FF (300FF with shower and toilet). Triples cost 400FF (hall showers 15FF). Just around the corner, *Hôtel Pratic* (☎ *01 48 87 80 47, fax 01 48 87 40 04, 9 rue d'Ormesson)* has singles/ doubles for 250/305FF (370/390FF with shower). One of the nicest medium-priced hotels in the area is *Hôtel de Nice* (☎ *01 42 78 55 29, fax 01 42 78 36 07, 42bis rue de Rivoli, metro Hôtel de Ville).* Singles/ doubles/triples/quads go for 380/450/550/ 680FF; many of the rooms have balconies.

Notre Dame Area (5e) Because of its location directly across the Seine from Notre Dame, *Hôtel Esmeralda* (☎ *01 43 54 19 20, fax 01 40 51 00 68, 4 rue St Julien le Pauvre, metro St Michel)* is everybody's favourite. Its three simple singles (180FF) are booked months in advance. Doubles with bath start at 350FF.

Panthéon Area (5e) *Hôtel de Médicis* (☎ *01 43 54 14 66, 214 rue St Jacques, metro Luxembourg)* is exactly what a Latin Quarter dive for impoverished travellers should be like. Very basic singles/ doubles/triples start at 90/180/250FF. A better deal is *Grand Hôtel du Progrès* (☎ *01 43 54 19 20, fax 01 40 51 00 68, 50 rue Gay Lussac, metro Luxembourg).* Singles with washbasin start at 160FF and there are larger rooms with fine views of the Panthéon for 240FF. Hall showers are free. Large old-fashioned singles/doubles with bath are 310/330FF. The nearby *Hôtel Gay Lussac* (☎ *01 43 54 23 96, fax 01 40 51 79 49)* at No 29 is a cut above, with small singles averaging 220FF; doubles/quads with bath and toilet start at 360/450FF.

St Germain des Prés (6e) The wonderfully eccentric *Hôtel de Nesle* (☎ *01 43 54 62 41, 7 rue de Nesle, metro Odéon or Mabillon)* has frescoed rooms and a garden out the back. Singles/doubles with shower are 275/350FF; a double with shower/bath and toilet is 400/450FF. The only way to get a room is to book in person in the morning.

The nearby *Hôtel Petit Trianon* (☎ *01 43 54 94 64, 2 rue de l'Ancienne Comédie, metro Odéon)* also attracts lots of young travellers. Singles start at 180FF, doubles with shower at 380FF. The well-positioned *Hôtel Henri IV* (☎ *01 43 54 44 53, 25 place Dauphine, 1er, metro Pont Neuf)* is in a quiet square at the western end of Île de la Cité. Singles range from 125FF to 210FF, doubles 215FF to 245FF, and hall showers are 15FF; breakfast is included. Be sure to make your booking well ahead.

Montmartre (18e) The metro station Abbesses is convenient for all the following hotels. *Idéal Hôtel* (☎ *01 46 06 63 63, 3 rue des Trois Frères)* has simple but acceptable rooms starting at 125/180FF (hall shower 20FF). A cut above is the two-star *Hôtel des Arts* (☎ *01 46 06 30 52, fax 01 46 06 10 83, 5 rue Tholozé),* priced at 340/460FF with bath.

PLACES TO EAT

For standard restaurant opening times and other helpful tips, see Food & Drinks at the beginning of this chapter.

The *Monoprix* supermarket *(21 ave de l'Opéra)* opposite metro Pyramides is convenient for the Louvre district (closed Sunday). In the Latin Quarter try *Ed l'Épicier* *(37 rue Lacépède, metro Monge),* also closed Sunday. Otherwise fruits, vegetables and meats are on offer at Paris' neighbourhood *food markets,* most of which are closed Sunday afternoon and Monday. Paris' *open-air markets* – about 60 are scattered around town – set up two or three mornings a week in squares and streets like rue Mouffetard, 5e, and rue Daguerre, 14e. Get details from the tourist offices.

Other budget options are the 15 *restaurants universitaires* (student cafeterias) run by CROUS (☎ 01 40 51 36 00). Tickets (on sale at meal times) cost 14.50FF for ISIC card-holders and around 24FF for others. CROUS restaurants (usually called 'restos U') have variable opening times; check the schedule posted outside any of the following: *Bullier* (☎ *01 43 54 93 38, 2nd floor of Centre Jean Sarrailh, 39 ave Georges Bernanos, 5e, metro Port Royal); Assas* (☎ *01 46 33 61 25, 92 rue d'Assas, 6e, metro Port Royal);* and *Mabillon* (☎ *01 43 25 66 23, 3 rue Mabillon, 6e, metro Mabillon).*

Forum des Halles

The area between Forum des Halles and the Centre Pompidou is filled with scores of trendy restaurants, but few of them are particularly good or inexpensive. Streets lined with places to eat include rue des Lombards, the pedestrians-only rue Montorgueil, and the narrow streets north and east of Forum des Halles.

Marais (4e)

The heart of the old Jewish neighbourhood, rue des Rosiers (metro St Paul) has a few *kascher* (kosher) restaurants. *Hammam Café* at No 4 is bright and decorated with original Art Noveau mosaics; try the kosher pizzas (45FF to 98FF). Paris' best-known Jewish (but not kosher) restaurant, founded in 1920, is *Restaurant Jo Goldenberg* at No 7, with main dishes for around 80FF. *Minh Chau (10 rue de la Verrerie, metro Hôtel de Ville)* is a tiny but welcoming Vietnamese place with tasty main dishes (eg, grilled chicken with lemon grass, roast duck) for about 30FF. For vegetarian fare and a calming atmosphere head to *Aquarius (54 rue Ste Croix de la Bretonnerie, metro Rambuteau)*. A tasty two-course lunch costs 64FF; at dinner it's 95FF for three courses.

Bastille (4e, 11e & 12e)

Ethnic restaurants line rue de la Roquette and rue de Lappe, which intersects rue de la Roquette 200m north-east of place de la Bastille. At the Cuban-inspired *Havanita Café (11 rue de Lappe, metro Bastille)* cocktails are from 48FF, starters from 38FF to 78FF and excellent main courses from 69FF to 94FF. Happy hour is 5 to 8 pm.

Latin Quarter (4e, 5e & 6e)

There are plenty of good Greek, North African and Middle Eastern restaurants in the area bounded by rue St Jacques, blvd St Germain, blvd St Michel and the Seine. You should know that some people refer to rue de la Huchette and the nearby streets as 'Bacteria Alley' because of the high incidence of food poisoning at restaurants there. But the takeaway kebab and shwarma sandwiches (20FF) aren't bad.

The Moroccan *Founti Agadir (117 rue Monge, metro Censier Daubenton)* has some of the Left Bank's best couscous, grills and tajines for 75FF to 89FF. *Perraudin (157 rue St Jacques, metro Luxembourg)* is a reasonably priced, traditional French restaurant that hasn't changed much since the turn of the 19th century. Main courses cost 59FF, and there's a lunchtime *menu* for 65FF. A good place for a quick vegetarian lunch is *Le Petit Légume (36 rue des Boulangers, metro Cardinal Lemoine)*, with vegetarian *menus* at 50FF, 64FF and 75FF.

The area around rue Mouffetard is especially popular with students. Some of Paris' best discount crepes (11FF and upwards) are sold from a stall opposite 68 rue Mouffetard. For Tibetan food, a good choice is the friendly *Tashi Delek (4 rue des Fossés St Jacques, metro Luxembourg)*, with a lunch *menu* for 65FF and a dinner one at 105FF. There is a large cluster of *food shops* on rue de Seine and rue de Buci (metro Mabillon), and the covered *Marché St Germain* (metro Mabillon) on rue Lobineau has a huge array of produce and prepared foods. For sandwiches (13.50FF), try the popular hole-in-the-wall *Douce France (7 rue Royer Collard, 5e, metro Luxembourg)*. Place Maubert (metro Maubert Mutualité) is transformed into a lively *food market* from 7 am to 1.30 pm on Tuesday, Thursday and Saturday. *Food shops* are also found here, including a *fromagerie (47 ter blvd St Germain)*.

Montparnasse (6e & 14e)

Somewhat pricey but a real 'find' in this area is *Le Caméléon (☎ 01 43 20 63 43, 6 rue de Chevreuse, metro Vavin)*. The never-to-be-forgotten lobster ravioli is 92FF. Bookings are essential. *Mustang Café (☎ 01 43 35 36 12, 84 blvd du Montparnasse, metro Montparnasse Bienvenüe)* has passable Tex-Mex (platters and chilli from 47FF to 78FF) available to 5 am. There are *creperies* on rue d'Odessa and around the corner on rue du Montparnasse.

Montmartre (9e & 18e)

An old favourite is the dinner-only *Refuge des Fondus (☎ 01 42 55 22 65, 17 rue des Trois Frères, metro Abbesses or Anvers)*. The speciality is fondue – for 92FF you get an apéritif, hors d'œuvre, red wine and a good quantity of either cheese or meat fondue (minimum order for two people). Book ahead. *Le Mono (40 rue Véron, metro*

FRANCE

Abbesses) serves West African dishes (Togolese to be exact) from 25FF to 70FF. *Il Duca (26 rue Yvonne le Tac, metro Abbesses)* is an intimate Italian restaurant with good, straightforward food including a three-course *menu* for 89FF and homemade pasta dishes from 55FF to 76FF.

ENTERTAINMENT

The weekly *Pariscope* (3FF) has a six-page section in English that lists clubs, cultural events etc. *L'Officiel des Spectacles* (2FF) has similar listings but is in French only. Both are sold at newsstands.

Reservations and ticketing for all sorts of cultural events are handled by outlets in the FNAC stores at 136 rue de Rennes (☎ 01 49 54 30 00, metro St Placide) and on the 3rd underground level of the Forum des Halles department store at 1-7 rue Pierre Lesco (☎ 01 40 41 40 00, metro Châtelet-Les Halles). Also try the Virgin Megastores at 52-60 ave des Champs-Élysées (☎ 01 49 53 50 00) and 99 rue de Rivoli (☎ 01 49 53 52 90), both near the Franklin D Roosevelt metro station.

Bars & Pubs

Le Cloître (☎ 01 43 25 19 92, 19 rue St Jacques, 5e, metro St Michel) is an unpretentious, relaxed place with mellow background music. Informal, friendly *Polly Maggoo (☎ 01 46 33 33 64, 11 rue St Jacques)*, up the road, was founded in 1967 and still plays music from that era. *Café Oz (01 43 54 30 48, 18 rue St Jacques, 5e, metro Luxembourg)* is a casual, friendly Australian pub with Fosters on tap. In the Marais, *Stolly's (☎ 01 42 76 06 76, 16 rue de la Cloche Percée, 4e, metro Hôtel de Ville)*, just off rue de Rivoli, is an Anglophone bar that is always crowded, particularly during happy hour (4.30 to 8 pm).

Clubs

Many *discothèques* (ie, any place where there's music and dancing) are officially private, so the gorilla-like bouncers can refuse entry to whomever they don't like the look of. If you pass muster, expect to pay at least 50/10FF on weekdays/weekends.

Le Balajo (☎ 01 47 00 07 87, 9 rue de Lappe, 11e, metro Bastille) has been a mainstay of the Parisian dance-hall scene since 1936. There's accordion music (50FF entry) from 2.30 to 6.30 pm on Thursday and 3 to 7 pm on Sunday, and dancing (100FF, including one drink) on Thursday, Friday and Saturday from 11.30 pm to 5 am. *La Locomotive (☎ 01 53 41 88 88, 90 blvd de Clichy, 18e, metro Blanche)* is in Pigalle next to the Moulin Rouge nightclub. It occupies three floors, each offering a different ambience and style of music. It is open nightly from 11 pm (from midnight on Monday). Entry costs 70/55FF with/without a drink on weekdays, and women get in free before 12.30 am.

Jazz

Caveau de la Huchette (☎ 01 43 26 65 05, 5 rue de la Huchette, 5e, metro St Michel), with live jazz, is an old favourite. It's open from 9.30 pm to at least 2 am (3.30 am on Friday, 4 am on Saturday) nightly, with a cover charge of 60FF (55FF for students) during the week, 70FF (no discounts) at the weekend.

Opera

National de Paris now splits its performances between *Opéra Garnier (☎ 01 44 73 13 99, place de l'Opéra, 9e, metro Opéra)*, its old home, and *Opéra Bastille (☎ 01 44 73 13 99, 2-6 place de la Bastille, 11e, metro Bastille)*, which opened in 1989. Opera tickets cost 90FF to 670FF. Ballets cost 70FF to 420FF (45FF to 50FF for the cheapest seats). Concerts are 85FF to 255FF (45FF for the cheapest seats). Unsold tickets *(tarif spécial)* are offered 15 minutes prior to showtime to students and people aged under 25 or over 65 for about 100FF. Concerts held at *Notre Dame Cathedral (☎ 01 42 34 56 10)* don't keep to any particular schedule but are advertised on posters around town and usually cost 100/80FF for the full/reduced tariff.

GETTING THERE & AWAY

Air

Paris has two major international airports. Aéroport d'Orly (☎ 01 49 75 15 15) is 14km south of central Paris, while Aéroport Charles de Gaulle (☎ 01 48 62 22 80), also known as Roissy-Charles de Gaulle, is in the suburb of Roissy, 23km north-east of central Paris. See the later Getting Around section for information on getting to/from these airports.

FRANCE

Bus

Eurolines (www.eurolines.fr) runs buses from Paris to cities all over Europe. The company's terminal, Gare Routière Internationale (☎ 0836 69 52 52, metro Gallieni), is at Porte de Bagnolet on the eastern edge of Paris. It has an in-town ticket office (☎ 01 43 54 11 99, metro Cluny-La Sorbonne) at 55 rue St Jacques, open 9.30 am to 6.30 pm weekdays and 10 am to 5 pm Saturday.

Train

Paris has six major *gares* (train stations), each handling traffic to different parts of France and Europe. For information in English call ☎ 08 36 35 35 39; the switchboards are staffed from 7 am to 10 pm. All the stations have bureaux de change and easy access to the metro network, and there is a tourist office at each one except Gare St Lazare. Paris' major train stations are:

Gare d'Austerlitz (13e) – trains to the Loire Valley, Spain and Portugal and non-TGV trains to south-western France (Bordeaux, the Basque Country etc).

Gare de l'Est (10e) – trains east of Paris (Champagne, Alsace, Lorraine), Luxembourg, parts of Switzerland (Basel, Lucerne, Zürich), southern Germany (Frankfurt, Munich) and Austria.

Gare de Lyon (12e) – regular and TGV trains to points south-east of Paris, including Dijon, Lyon, Provence, Côte d'Azur, the Alps, parts of Switzerland, Italy and Greece.

Gare Montparnasse (15e) – trains to Brittany and places on the way (Chartres, Angers, Nantes); and the TGV Atlantique, which serves Tours, Bordeaux and other places in south-western France.

Gare du Nord (10e) – trains to northern France (Lille, Calais), the UK via the Channel Tunnel (TGV Nord), Belgium, Netherlands, northern Germany, Scandinavia, Moscow, etc.

Gare St Lazare (8e) – trains to Normandy and, via the Channel ports, ferries to England.

GETTING AROUND

RATP, Paris' public transit system, is one of the most efficient in the world. Free metro/RER (commuter rail/bus) maps are available at ticket windows and at tourist offices. For 24-hour information in English, call ☎ 0836 68 41 14.

To/From Orly Airport

Orly Rail is the quickest way to reach the Left Bank and the 16e. Take the shuttle bus to the Pont de Rungis-Aéroport d'Orly RER station (free), which is on the C2 line, and get on a train heading into the city. Another fast way into town is the Orlyval shuttle train (57FF); it stops near Orly-Sud's Porte F and links Orly with the Antony RER station, which is on line B4. Orlybus (35FF) takes you to the Denfert-Rochereau metro station, 14e. Air France buses (45FF) run to/from Gare Montparnasse, 15e (every 12 minutes), along Aérogare des Invalides in the 7e. RATP bus No 183 (8FF or one bus/metro ticket) goes to Porte de Choisy, 13e, but is very slow. Jetbus links both terminals with the Villejuif-Louis Aragon metro stop (20 minutes; 26.50FF). All services between Orly and Paris run every 15 minutes or so (less frequently late at night) from 5.30 or 6.30 am to 11 or 11.30 pm.

A taxi costs from 120FF to 175FF, plus 6FF per piece of luggage over 5kg.

To/From Charles de Gaulle Airport

The fastest way to get to/from the city is by Roissy Rail. Free shuttle buses take you from the airport terminals to the Roissy-Charles de Gaulle RER station. You can buy tickets to Charles de Gaulle (CDG) at RER stations for 49FF. If you get on at an ordinary metro station you can buy a ticket when you change to the RER. Air France bus No 2 goes to Porte Maillot, 16e and 17e, and the corner of ave Carnot near the Arc de Triomphe, 17e, for 60FF; bus No 4 goes to blvd de Vaugirard at the Gare Montparnasse, 15e, for 70FF. Roissybus goes to the American Express office near place de l'Opéra. RATP bus No 350 goes to Gare du Nord and Gare de l'Est, both in the 10e. Both RATP buses require six metro/bus tickets or 48FF. Most buses and trains from CDG to Paris run from 5 or 6.30 am to 11 or 11.30 pm.

Bus

Paris' extensive bus network tends to get overlooked by visitors, in part because the metro is so quick and easy to use. Bus routes are indicated on the free RATP maps No 1 (*Petit Plan de Paris*) and No 3 (*Grand Plan Île de France*). Short trips cost one bus/metro/RER ticket, while longer rides require two. Travellers without tickets can purchase them from the driver. Whatever kind of *coupon* (ticket) you have, you must

FRANCE

cancel it (oblitérer) it in the composteur (cancelling machine) next to the driver. If you have a Carte Orange, Formule 1 or Paris Visite pass (see Metro/RER/Bus Tickets later), just flash it at the driver – do not cancel your ticket. After the metro shuts down (between 12.25 and 12.45 am), the Noctambus network (look for the black owl silhouetted against a yellow moon) links the Châtelet-Hôtel de Ville area, 4e, with the Right Bank (lines A to H) and, to a lesser extent, the Left Bank (lines J and R). Noctambuses begin their runs from the even-numbered side of ave Victoria, 4e, which is between the Hôtel de Ville and place du Châtelet, every hour on the half-hour from 1.30 to 5.30 am. A ride requires three tickets (four tickets if your journey involves a transfer).

Metro & RER

Paris' underground network consists of two separate but linked systems: the Métropolitain, known as the *métro*, which now has 14 lines with the opening of the ultra-modern, driverless Météor linking the Madeleine stop with the Bibliothèque Nationale de France in the 13e and RER line C, and over 300 stations; and the RER, a network of suburban services that pass through the city centre. The term 'metro' is used in this chapter to refer to the Métropolitain as well as any station of the RER system within Paris proper. No point in Paris is more than 500m from a metro stop. Each metro train is known by the name of its terminus; trains on the same line have different names depending on which direction they are travelling. In the stations, white-on-blue *sortie* signs indicate exits and black-on-orange *correspondance* signs show how to get to connecting trains. The last metro train sets out on its final run between 12.25 and 12.45 am, and starts up again at 5.30 am. Metro travel is free after midnight.

Metro/RER/Bus Tickets

The same green 2nd-class tickets are valid on the metro, the bus and, for travel within the Paris city limits, the RER's 2nd-class carriages. They cost 8FF if bought separately and 55FF for a booklet (carnet) of 10. Children aged four to 11 pay half the fare. One ticket lets you travel between any two metro stations, including stations outside of the Paris city limits, no matter how many transfers are required. You can also use it on the RER commuter rail system for travel within Paris (within zone 1).

For travel on the RER to destinations outside the city, purchase a special ticket *before* you board the train or you won't be able to get out of the station and could be fined. Always keep your ticket until you reach your destination and exit the station; if you're caught without a ticket, or with an invalid one, you'll be fined.

The cheapest and easiest way to travel the metro is to get a Carte Orange, a bus/metro/RER pass whose accompanying magnetic coupon comes in weekly and monthly versions. You can get tickets for travel in up to eight urban and suburban zones; unless you'll be using the suburban commuter lines an awful lot though, the basic ticket – valid for zones 1 and 2 – is probably sufficient.

The weekly ticket costs 82FF for zones 1 and 2 and is valid from Monday to Sunday. Even if you'll be in Paris for only three or four days, it may very well work out cheaper than purchasing a carnet – you'll break even at 15 rides – and it will certainly cost less than buying a daily Mobilis or Paris Visite pass. The monthly Carte Orange ticket (279FF for zones 1 and 2) begins on the first day of each calendar month. Both are on sale in metro and RER stations from 6.30 am to 10 pm and at certain bus terminals.

To get a Carte Orange, bring a passport-sized photograph of yourself to any metro or RER ticket counter (four photos for about 25FF are available from automatic booths in train stations and certain metro stations). Request a Carte Orange (which is free) and the kind of coupon you'd like. To prevent tickets from being used by more than one person, you must write your surname (nom) and given name (prénom) on the Carte Orange, and the number of your Carte Orange on each weekly or monthly coupon you buy (next to the words Carte No).

The rather pricey Mobilis and Paris Visite passes, designed to facilitate bus, metro and RER travel for tourists, are on sale in many metro stations, the train stations and international airports. The Mobilis card (and its *coupon*) allows unlimited travel for one day in two to eight zones. The version valid for zones 1 and 2 costs 32FF. Paris

Visite passes, which allow the holder discounts on entries to certain museums and activities as well as transport, are valid for travel in either three, five or eight zones. The one- to three-zone version costs 55/90/120/175FF for one/two/three/five days. Children aged four to 11 pay half-price. They can be purchased at larger metro and RER stations, at SNCF bureaus in Paris and at the airports.

Taxi

Flag fall is 13FF; within the city it costs 3.53FF per kilometre from 7 am to 7 pm Monday to Saturday. At night and on Sunday it's 5.83FF per kilometre. Each piece of luggage over 5kg costs 6FF. The easiest way to find a taxi is to walk to the nearest *tête de station* (taxi rank); 500 are scattered around the city. Radio-dispatched taxis include Taxis Bleus (☎ 01 49 36 10 10) and G7 Taxis (☎ 01 47 39 47 39). If you order a taxi by phone, the meter is switched on as soon as the driver gets word of your call – wherever that may be (but usually not too far away). The usual tip is 2FF no matter what the fare.

AROUND PARIS
Disneyland Paris

It took US$4.4 billion to turn beet fields 32km east of Paris into the much heralded Disneyland Paris, which opened in 1992. Although it struggled financially for the first few years, what was then known as EuroDisney is now in the black, and the park has become the most popular tourist attraction in Europe, with 12.5 million visitors in 1998. Disneyland Paris is open 365 days a year. From early September to March the hours are 10 am to 6 pm (8 pm on Saturday, some Sundays and perhaps during school holiday periods); in spring and early summer, the park opens 9 am to 8 pm (to 11 pm at the weekend). From early July to early September it opens 9 am to 11 pm daily.

The one-day entry fee, which includes unlimited access to all rides and activities (except the shooting gallery and the video games arcade), costs 220FF (170FF for those aged three to 11) from April to early November. The rest of the year, except during the Christmas holidays, prices drop to 165/135FF. To get there, take RER line A4 to the terminus (Marne-la-Vallée Chessy) –

check destination boards to ensure your train goes all the way to the end. Otherwise there are trains (38FF, 35 minutes) every 15 minutes or so from the Nation stop on place de la Nation, 12e.

Versailles

The site of France's grandest and most famous chateau, Versailles served as the country's political capital and seat of the royal court from 1682 until 1789, when Revolutionary mobs dragged Louis XVI and Marie-Antoinette off to Paris, where they were later guillotined. In 1919 the Treaty of Versailles was signed in the chateau's Galerie des Glaces (Hall of Mirrors), officially ending WWI. Because Versailles is on most travellers' 'must-see' lists, the chateau can be jammed with tourists, especially on weekends, and most especially on Sundays. Try to arrive early in the morning. The tourist office (☎ 01 39 24 88 88, @ tourisme@ot-versailles.fr) is at 2bis ave de Paris, just north of the chateau.

Château de Versailles The enormous palace (☎ 01 30 83 78 00) was built in the mid-17th century during the reign of Louis XIV (the Sun King). Among the advantages of Versailles was its distance from the political intrigues of Paris. The plan worked brilliantly, all the more so because court life turned the nobles into sycophantic courtiers who expended most of their energy vying for royal favour. The chateau essentially consists of four parts: the main palace building, which is a classical structure with innumerable wings, sumptuous bedchambers and grand halls; the vast 17th-century gardens, laid out in the formal French style; and two out-palaces, the late-17th-century **Grand Trianon** (25/15FF) and the mid-18th-century **Petit Trianon** (15/10FF). The main building opens from 9 am to 5.30 pm (to 6.30 pm from May to September) daily, except Monday. The other attractions have slightly different hours. Entrance to the State Apartments, which include the Hall of Mirrors, costs 45FF (35FF after 3.30 pm, free for under 18s). Tickets are on sale at Entrée A (Entrance A), which is off to the right from the equestrian statue of Louis XIV as you approach the building. The gardens are open 7 am to nightfall daily. Entry is free except on Sunday from May to early

FRANCE

October when the baroque fountains 'perform' – this 'Grandes Eaux' show takes place from 3.30 to 5 pm and costs 30FF (students 20FF).

Several different guided tours are available in English. They last one hour, 1½ and two hours and cost 25FF, 37FF and 50FF respectively (17/26/34FF for those aged 10 to 17). To buy tickets and make advance reservations go to Entrée C or D. Cassette-guided tours lasting 80 minutes are available at Entrée A for 30FF.

Getting There & Away Bus No 171 (8FF or one metro/bus ticket, 35 minutes) takes you from Paris' Pont de Sèvres metro stop all the way to place d'Armes, right in front of the chateau. Versailles has three train stations: Versailles-Rive Gauche, Versailles-Chantiers and Versailles-Rive Droite. RER line C5 takes you from Paris' Gare d'Austerlitz and various other RER stations on the Left Bank to Versailles-Rive Gauche, which is 700m south-east of the chateau. SNCF trains go from Paris' Gare Montparnasse to Versailles-Chantiers, which is 1.3km south-east of the chateau, just off ave de Sceaux. SNCF trains also run from Paris' Gare St Lazare to Versailles-Rive Droite, 1.2km north-east of the chateau. Eurail passholders can travel free on SNCF (but not RER) trains.

Chartres

The indescribably beautiful 13th-century cathedral of Chartres rises abruptly from the corn fields 88km south-west of Paris. Crowned by two soaring spires – one Gothic, the other Romanesque – it dominates the attractive medieval town clustered around its base. During the Middle Ages, the city of Chartres grew and developed along the banks of the Eure River. Among the many buildings remaining from that period are private residences, stone bridges, tanneries, wash houses and a number of churches.

Orientation & Information The cathedral, visible from almost everywhere, is about 500m east of the train station, which is on place Pierre Sémard. The tourist office (☎ 02 37 18 26 26, ✆ chartres.tourism@wanadoo.fr) is across place de la Cathédrale from the cathedral's main entrance. Audioguide tours, in English, lasting 25 to 70

minutes (15FF to 30FF) can be hired from the cathedral bookshop.

Things to See Chartres' **Cathédrale Notre Dame** was built to replace an earlier structure devastated by fire in 1194. The construction of this early Gothic masterpiece took only 25 years, which is why the cathedral has a high degree of architectural unity. The 105m **Clocher Vieux** (old bell tower), the tallest Romanesque steeple still standing, is to the right as you face the Romanesque **Portail Royal** (the main entrance). The **Clocher Neuf** (new bell tower) has a Gothic spire dating from 1513 and can be visited daily (except Sunday morning) for 25FF. The 11th-century Romanesque **crypt**, the largest in France, can be visited on a half-hour guided tour (in French, with a written English translation) for 15FF (students 10FF). The cathedral itself is open from 7.30 am (8.30 am on Sunday) to 7.15 pm daily. Englishman Malcolm Miller gives fascinating tours (35FF, students 25FF) at noon and 2.45 pm daily except Sunday from Easter to November.

Places to Stay & Eat *Les Bords de l'Eure* camping ground (☎ 02 37 28 79 43), open May to early September, is about 2.5km south-east of the train station on rue de Launay. From the train station take bus No 8 to the Launay stop. The pleasant and calm *Auberge de Jeunesse* (☎ 02 37 34 27 64, 23 ave Neigre) is 1.5km east of the train station via the ring road (blvd Charles Péguy and blvd Jean Jaurès). To get there from the train station, take bus No 5 (direction Mare aux Moines) to the Rouliers stop. Beds are about 68FF, including breakfast (sheets 17FF).

Hôtel de l'Ouest (☎ 02 37 21 43 27, 3 place Pierre Sémard), opposite the train station, has somewhat dingy rooms with washbasin for 120FF, with shower and toilet for 190FF and with bath, toilet and TV from 210FF to 260FF. *Hôtel Au Départ* (☎ 02 37 36 80 43, 1 rue Nicole) has better singles/doubles/triples with washbasin for 120/190/300FF. Reception (at the Brasserie L'Ouest, 9 place Pierre Sémard) is closed Sunday.

For self-caterers, there are a number of *food shops* around the *covered market* (open Saturday until about 1 pm) on rue des

Changes, and there's a *Monoprix (12 rue Noël Ballay).*

Getting There & Away There are about three dozen trains a day to/from Paris' Gare Montparnasse (72FF, 55 to 70 minutes) that also stop at Versailles' Chantiers station (61FF, 45 minutes). The last train to Paris leaves Chartres just after 9 pm weekdays, 7.40 pm Saturday and 10 pm Sunday.

Alsace & Lorraine

The charming and beautiful region of Alsace, long a meeting place of Europe's Latin and Germanic cultures, lies in France's far north-eastern corner between the Vosges Mountains and the Rhine River. The Alsatian language is a Germanic dialect similar to that spoken in nearby parts of Germany and Switzerland. Since becoming part of France in the 17th century, the region (along with part of neighbouring Lorraine) was twice annexed by Germany: from the Franco-Prussian War (1871) until the end of WWI; and again between 1940 and 1944.

STRASBOURG

Strasbourg (population 423,000), just a few kilometres west of the Rhine, is Alsace's great metropolis and its intellectual and cultural capital. Towering above the restaurants and pubs of the lively old city is the cathedral, a medieval marvel in pink sandstone, near which you'll find one of the finest ensembles of museums in France.

When it was founded in 1949, the Council of Europe decided to base itself in Strasbourg as a symbol of Franco-German (and pan-European) cooperation. The city is also the seat of the European Parliament (the legislative branch of the EU), whose huge new home is used for one-week plenary sessions 12 times a year.

Orientation & Information
The train station is 400m west of the Grande Île (Large Island), the city centre, which is delimited by the Ill River to the south and the Fossé du Faux Rempart to the north. Place Kléber, the main public square, is 400m north-west of the cathedral.

The main tourist office (☎ 03 88 52 28 28, fax 03 88 52 28 29, @ otsr@strasbourg

.com), 17 place de la Cathédrale, is open daily. There's a branch office (☎ 03 88 32 51 49) in front of the train station, in the underground complex beneath place de la Gare. Both offices sell the three-day Strasbourg Pass (58FF), which gets you a variety of discounts. Web site: www.strasbourg.com.

The Best Coffee Shop, 10 quai des Pêcheurs, offers cheap email access from 10 am (2 pm on weekends) to 11.30 pm.

Cathédrale Notre Dame
Strasbourg's lacy Gothic cathedral was begun in 1176. The west facade was completed in 1284, but the spire (its southern companion was never built) was not in place until 1439. Many of the statues decorating the exterior are copies – the originals are in the Musée de l'Œuvre Notre-Dame (see Museums). The interior can be visited until 7 pm daily; the astronomical clock goes through it's paces at 12.30 pm (5FF). The 66m-high platform above the facade (from which the tower and its spire soar another 76m) can be visited daily – if you don't mind the 330 steps to the top (20/10FF).

Museums
Except for the Musée de l'Œuvre Notre-Dame and the Musée d'Art Moderne et Contemporain, which close on Monday, all of the city's museums open daily except Tuesday. Hours (except for the Musée d'Art Moderne) are 10 am to noon and 1.30 to 6 pm (10 am to 5 pm on Sunday). Most museums (except the 30FF Musée d'Art Moderne) charge 20/10FF.

The outstanding **Musée de l'Œuvre Notre Dame**, housed in a group of 14th- and 15th-century buildings at 3 place du Château, displays one of France's finest collections of Romanesque, Gothic and Renaissance sculpture, including many of the cathedral's original statues.

The **Château des Rohan**, 2 place du Château, was built between 1732 and 1742 as a residence for the city's princely bishops. It now houses three museums (combined ticket costs 40/20FF): the **Musée Archéologique** covers the period from prehistory to AD 800; the **Musée des Arts Décoratifs** gives you a sense of the lifestyle of the rich and powerful during the 18th century; and the **Musée des Beaux-Arts** has paintings from the 14th to 19th centuries.

FRANCE

STRASBOURG

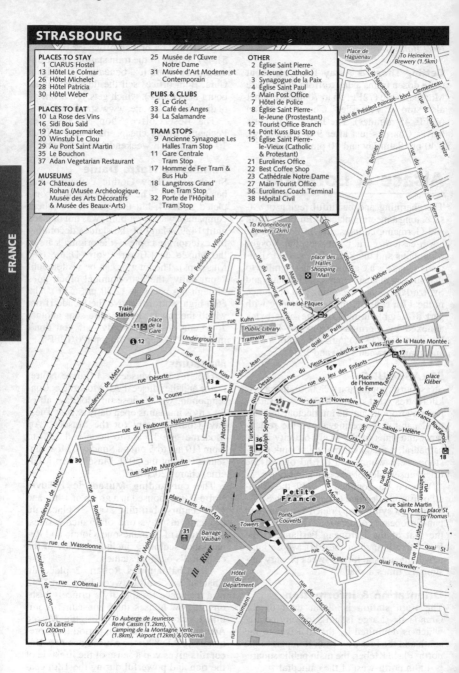

PLACES TO STAY
1 CIARUS Hostel
13 Hôtel Le Colmar
26 Hôtel Michelet
28 Hôtel Patricia
30 Hôtel Weber

PLACES TO EAT
10 La Rose des Vins
16 Sidi Bou Saïd
19 Atac Supermarket
20 Winstub Le Clou
29 Au Pont Saint Martin
35 Le Bouchon
37 Adan Vegetarian Restaurant

MUSEUMS
24 Château des
Rohan (Musée Archéologique,
Musée des Arts Décoratifs
& Musée des Beaux-Arts)

25 Musée de l'Œuvre
Notre Dame
31 Musée d'Art Moderne et
Contemporain

PUBS & CLUBS
6 Le Griot
33 Café des Anges
34 La Salamandre

TRAM STOPS
9 Ancienne Synagogue Les
Halles Tram Stop
11 Gare Centrale
Tram Stop
17 Homme de Fer Tram &
Bus Hub
18 Langstross Grand'
Rue Tram Stop
32 Porte de l'Hôpital
Tram Stop

OTHER
2 Église Saint Pierre-
le-Jeune (Catholic)
3 Synagogue de la Paix
4 Église Saint Paul
5 Main Post Office
7 Hôtel de Police
8 Église Saint Pierre-
le-Jeune (Prostestant)
12 Tourist Office Branch
14 Pont Kuss Bus Stop
15 Église Saint Pierre-
le-Vieux (Catholic
& Protestant)
21 Eurolines Office
22 Best Coffee Shop
23 Cathédrale Notre Dame
27 Main Tourist Office
36 Eurolines Coach Terminal
38 Hôpital Civil

FRANCE

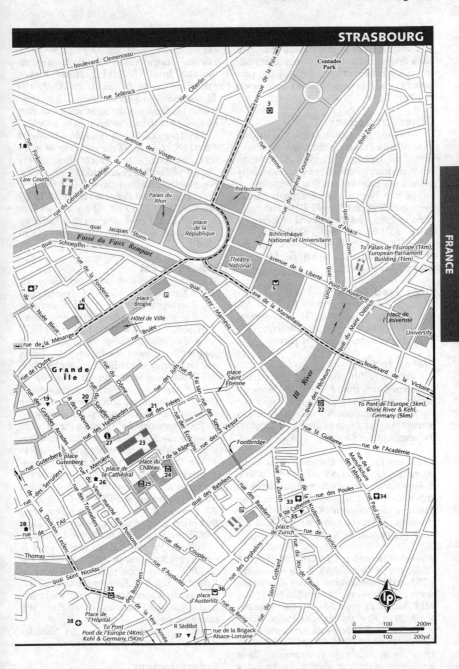

STRASBOURG

The new, superb **Musée d'Art Moderne et Contemporain** at place Hans Jean Arp has a diverse collection of works representing every major art movement of the past century or so. It opens 11 am to 7 pm (noon to 10 pm Thursday).

Other Attractions

Crisscrossed by narrow lanes, canals and locks, **Petite France**, in the south-west corner of the Grande Île, retains its old-time Alsatian atmosphere and charm, especially in the early morning and late afternoon.

The hugely expensive **European Parliament building** (☎ 03 88 17 20 07), inaugurated in 1999, and the Council of Europe's **Palais de l'Europe** (☎ 03 90 21 49 40), opened in 1977 – both about 2km north-east of the cathedral – can be visited. Phone in advance for reservations.

Organised Tours

Tours of Kronenbourg (☎ 03 88 27 41 59, tram stop Duc d'Alsace) and Heineken (☎ 03 88 19 59 53) breweries, both 2.5km from the city centre, can be reserved by phone.

Places to Stay

It's *extremely* difficult to find last-minute accommodation from Monday to Thursday during the one week each month when the European Parliament is in plenary session (except August; twice in October). Contact the tourist office for dates.

Camping The grassy *Camping de la Montagne Verte* (☎ 03 88 30 25 46, 2 rue Robert Forrer) is open from mid-March to October. It's a few hundred metres from *Auberge de Jeunesse René Cassin* (see Hostels), where you can pitch a tent for 42FF per person, including breakfast.

Hostels The modern *CIARUS* (☎ 03 88 15 27 88, fax 03 88 15 27 89, 7 rue Finkmatt), a 285-bed Protestant-run hostel about 1km north-east of the train station, has beds from 92FF, including breakfast. By bus, take No 4, 10, 20 or 72 to the place de Pierre stop.

The 286-bed *Auberge de Jeunesse René Cassin* (☎ 03 88 30 26 46, fax 03 88 30 35 16, 9 rue de l'Auberge de Jeunesse), 2km south-west of the train station, has beds for 73FF. To get there, take bus No 3 or 23 to the Auberge de Jeunesse stop.

Hotels The 15-room *Hôtel Le Colmar* (☎ 03 88 32 16 89, fax 03 88 21 97 17, 1 rue du Maire Kuss) has clean singles/doubles from 167/218FF. *Hôtel Weber* (☎ 03 88 32 36 47, fax 03 88 32 19 08, @ hotelpatricia@hotmail.com, 22 blvd de Nancy) is hardly in the most attractive part of town, but quiet doubles start at 140FF.

The 16-room, family-run *Hôtel Michelet* (☎ 03 88 32 47 38, 48 rue du Vieux Marché aux Poissons) – the street name means 'Street of the Old Fish Market' – has simple singles/doubles from 145/170FF. The dark, rustic *Hôtel Patricia* (☎ 03 88 32 14 60, fax 03 88 32 19 08, @ hotelpatricia@ hotmail.com, 1a rue du Puits) has ordinary but spacious doubles with great views from 180FF.

Places to Eat

A winstub serves both wine and hearty Alsatian fare such as *choucroute* (sauerkraut) and *baeckeoffe* (pork, beef and lamb marinated in wine and cooked with vegetables).

Winstub Le Clou (☎ 03 88 32 11 67, 3 rue du Chaudron) seats diners together at long tables (closed Wednesday for lunch and on Sunday and holidays); baeckeoffe is 97FF. *Au Pont St Martin* (☎ 03 88 32 45 13, 15 rue des Moulins) is a reasonably priced restaurant that specialises in Alsatian dishes but also has a few vegetarian options.

The dinner-only *Le Bouchon* (☎ 03 88 37 32 40, 6 rue Ste Catherine) offers excellent French cuisine at reasonable prices (69FF to 125FF for mains). The proprietor, a *chansonnière* of local repute, performs most nights at about 9 pm (closed Sunday and Monday). *La Rose des Vins* (☎ 03 88 32 74 40, 5 rue de Pâques) is a French restaurant that offers good value for money, including a 98FF *menu* (closed Saturday and Sunday).

Self-service vegetarian-organic food is on offer at *Adan* (☎ 03 88 35 70 84, 6 rue Sédillot), open noon to 2 pm Monday to Saturday. *Sidi Bou Saïd* (☎ 03 88 22 17 17, 22 rue du Vieux Marché aux Vins) has hearty Tunisian couscous for 60FF to 75FF (closed Monday).

Atac supermarket (47 rue des Grandes Arcades) is open Monday to Saturday.

Entertainment

La Salamandre (☎ 03 88 25 79 42, 3 rue Paul Janet), an informal dance club, is open

9 pm to 3 am Wednesday to Saturday. At the ever-popular, easy-going *Café des Anges* (☎ 03 88 37 12 67, *5 rue Ste Catherine*), you can dance from Tuesday to Saturday and on holiday eves from 9 pm to 4 am; things get going after 11 pm. The soul, funk, salsa and African music at the very informal *Le Griot* (☎ 03 88 52 00 52, *6 impasse de l'Écrevisse*) attracts a racially and ethnically mixed crowd; hours are 9 pm to 4 am (closed Sunday and Monday).

Strasbourg's happening live music venue is *La Laiterie* (☎ 03 88 23 72 37, *11-13 rue du Hohwald*), near the Laiterie tram stop.

Getting There & Away
Eurolines coaches arrive and depart from place d'Austerlitz; the office (☎ 03 88 22 73 74) is at 5 rue des Frères.

City bus No 21 links place Gutenberg with the Stadthalle in Kehl, across the Rhine in Germany.

Strasbourg's train station (☎ 08 36 35 35 39) is well connected with Paris' Gare de l'Est (215FF, four to five hours), Basel (Bâle; 103FF, 1½ hours) and Frankfurt (218FF, at least two hours). There are also daily trains to Nice (468FF), Amsterdam (413FF) and Prague (593FF). Certain trains to/from Paris charge a supplement.

Getting Around
Three tram lines form the centrepiece of Strasbourg's excellent public transport network. Single bus/tram tickets, sold by bus (but not tram) drivers and the ticket machines at tram stops, cost 7FF.

AROUND STRASBOURG
Colmar
Colmar (population 64,000), an easy day trip from Strasbourg by train (56FF, at least 30 minutes), is famous for the typically Alsatian architecture of its older neighbourhoods, and also for the stunning *Issenheim Altarpiece* in the **Musée d'Unterlinden** (closed on Tuesday from November to March; 35/25FF). The efficient tourist office (☎ 03 89 20 68 92) is opposite the museum at 4 rue d'Unterlinden.

Ave de la République stretches from the train station to the Musée d'Unterlinden (about 1km); the streets of the old city are to the south-east of the museum. **Petite Venise**, a neighbourhood of old, half-timbered buildings, runs along the Lauch River at the southern edge of the old city.

Colmar is a good base for exploring the quaint villages of the **Route du Vin d'Alsace** (Alsace Wine Route) and the forested – and, in winter, snow-covered – **Massif des Vosges** (Vosges Mountains). Quite a few destinations are accessible by bus – hours are available at the tourist office and posted at the bus station, which occupies a car park next to the train station.

The 110-bed *Auberge de Jeunesse Mittelhart* (☎ 03 89 80 57 39, fax 03 89 80 76 16, *2 rue Pasteur*), 2km north-west of the train station, has beds for 69FF, including breakfast. Reception is closed 10 am to 5 pm. By bus, take No 4 to the Pont Rouge stop.

NANCY
Delightful Nancy has an air of refinement that is found nowhere else in Lorraine, the region that borders Alsace to the northwest. This is largely thanks to the stunning, gilded **place Stanislas** (the central square), sumptuous cream-coloured buildings and shop windows filled with fine glassware, the former capital of the dukes of Lorraine seems as opulent today as it did during the 16th to 18th centuries, when much of the city centre was built.

Nancy thrives on a combination of innovation and sophistication. The **Musée de l'École de Nancy**, the city's premier museum, houses a superb collection of the sinuous, dream-like works of the Art Nouveau movement, which once flourished here (closed Tuesday; 30/20FF). It's about 2km south-west of the centre – by bus, take No 5 or 25 to the Nancy Thermal stop.

Other outstanding museums include the newly reopened **Musée des Beaux-Arts** (Fine Arts Muesum) at place Stanislas (30/15FF), and the **Musée Historique Lorrain** (Lorraine Historical Museum) at 64-66 Grande Rue (30FF). Both museums are closed Tuesday.

Orientation & Information
The heart of Nancy is the beautifully proportioned place Stanislas. The train station, at the bottom of busy rue Stanislas, is 800m south-west of place Stanislas.

The tourist office (☎ 03 83 35 22 41, fax 03 83 35 90 10, ✉ tourisme@ot-nancy.fr) is inside the Hôtel de Ville on place Stanislas.

FRANCE

FRANCE

Places to Stay & Eat

The 60-bed *Auberge de Jeunesse Remicourt* (☎ *03 83 27 73 67, fax 03 83 41 41 35, 149 rue de Vandœuvre in Villers-lès-Nancy)*, in an old chateau, is 4km south of the centre. A bed costs 80FF, including breakfast. By bus, take No 26 to the St Fiacre stop.

Two blocks south-west of place Stanislas, the welcoming and slightly off-beat, 29-room *Hôtel de l'Académie* (☎ *03 83 35 52 31, fax 03 83 32 55 78, 7bis rue des Michottes)* has singles/doubles with shower from 110/160FF.

Restaurant Le Gastrolâtre (☎ *03 83 35 51 94, 1 place Vaudémont)* has Lorraine and Provençal *menus* from 95FF to 195FF (closed on Monday at noon and Sunday). Around the corner and just a block from place Stanislas, rue des Maréchaux is lined with about a dozen restaurants of all sorts.

The *covered market (place Henri Mangin)* is open 7 am to 6 pm Tuesday to Saturday. On the other side of the square, inside the St Sébastien shopping centre, the *Casino* supermarket opens until 8.30 pm (closed Sunday).

Getting There & Away

From the train station on place Thiers there are direct services to Strasbourg (109FF, 70 to 95 minutes) and Paris' Gare de l'Est (206FF, three hours).

Normandy

Normandy (Normandie) derives its name from the Norsemen (Vikings) who took control of the area in the early 10th century. Modern Normandy is the land of the *bocage*, farmland subdivided by hedges and trees.

ROUEN

The city of Rouen (population 107,000), for centuries the lowest bridging point on the Seine, is known for its many spires, church towers and half-timbered houses, not to mention its Gothic cathedral and excellent museums. Rouen can be visited on a day or overnight trip from Paris.

Orientation & Information

The train station (Gare Rouen-Rive Droite) is at the northern end of rue Jeanne d'Arc, the major thoroughfare south to the Seine.

The tourist office (☎ 02 32 08 32 40, fax 02 32 08 32 44, @ otrouen@mcom.fr) is at 25 place de la Cathédrale. Guided city tours (35FF) depart from the office in summer at 10.30 am and 3 pm daily.

Things to See

Rouen's main street, rue du Gros Horloge, runs from the cathedral to **place du Vieux Marché**, where 19-year-old Joan of Arc was burned at the stake for heresy in 1431. You'll learn more about her life from the stained-glass windows at the adjacent Église Jeanne d'Arc than at the tacky **Musée Jeanne d'Arc** across the square at No 33.

Rouen's **Cathédrale Notre Dame**, the subject of a series of paintings by Claude Monet, is a masterpiece of French Gothic architecture. There are several guided visits (15/10FF) a day to the crypt, ambulatory (containing Richard the Lion-Heart's tomb) and Chapel of the Virgin.

The **Musée Le Secq des Tournelles** on rue Jacques Villon (opposite 27 rue Jean Lecanuet) is devoted to the blacksmith's craft and displays some 12,000 locks, keys and tongs made between the 3rd and 19th centuries (closed Tuesday; 15/10FF).

The **Musée des Beaux-Arts** facing the square at 26bis rue Jean Lecanuet features some major paintings from the 16th to 20th centuries, including some of Monet's cathedral series (closed Tuesday; 20/13FF).

La Tour Jeanne d'Arc on rue du Donjon, south of the train station, is the tower where Joan of Arc was imprisoned before her execution. There are two exhibition rooms (closed Tuesday; 10FF).

Places to Stay

The year-round *Camping Municipal* (☎ *02 35 74 07 59, rue Jules Ferry)*, in the suburb of Déville-lès-Rouen, is 5km north-west of town. From the Théâtre des Arts or the nearby bus station, take bus No 2 and get off at the *mairie* (town hall) of Déville-lès-Rouen. It's 59FF for two people and a tent.

The spotless and friendly *Hôtel Normandya* (☎ *02 35 71 46 15, 32 rue du Cordier)* is on a quiet street 300m southeast of the train station. Singles (some with shower) are 110FF to 140FF, doubles 10FF to 20FF more. The very French *Hostellerie du Vieux Logis* (☎ *02 35 71 55 30, 5 rue de Joyeuse)*, 1km east of the train station, has a pleasantly frayed atmosphere and a lovely garden out the back. Rooms start at 100FF. *Hôtel Le Palais* (☎ 02 35 71 41 40, *12 rue du Tambour*), between the Palais de Justice and the Gros Horloge, has doubles with shower for 140FF.

Places to Eat

A *covered market* is held daily (except Monday) from 6 am to 1.30 pm at place du Vieux Marché. The bistro-style *Les Maraîchers* at No 37 is the pick of the Vieux Marché's many restaurants, with its terrace and varied *menus* from 69FF (89FF in the evening).

Gourmand'grain (☎ 02 35 98 15 74, *3 rue du Petit Salut*), behind the tourist office, is a lunchtime vegetarian cafe with *menus* for 45FF and 69FF.

Getting There & Away

Buses to Dieppe (68FF, two hours) and Le Havre (84FF, three hours) are slower and more expensive than the train. The bus station (☎ 02 35 52 92 00) is at 25 rue des Charrettes near the Théâtre des Arts.

There are at least 20 trains a day to/from Paris' Gare St Lazare (124FF, 70 minutes). For train information, call ☎ 0836 35 35 39.

Getting Around

TCAR operates the local bus network and metro line. The metro links the train station with the Théâtre des Arts before crossing the Seine into the southern suburbs. Bus tickets cost 8FF, or 63FF for a magnetic card good for 10 rides.

BAYEUX

Bayeux (population 15,000) is celebrated for two trans-Channel invasions: the AD 1066 conquest of England by William the Conqueror (an event chronicled in the Bayeux Tapestry) and the Allied D-Day landings in WWII; Bayeux was the first town in France to be freed from the Nazis.

Bayeux is an attractive – though fairly touristy – town with several excellent museums. It's also a good base for the D-Day beaches.

Orientation & Information

The cathedral, Bayeux's central landmark, is 1km north-west of the train station.

The tourist office (☎ 02 31 51 28 28, fax 02 31 51 28 29) is at Pont St Jean just off the northern end of rue Larcher. It opens Monday to Saturday (also Sunday in July and August). A *billet jumelé* (multipass ticket) valid for most of Bayeux's museums (but not the Musée Mémorial) costs 38/22FF.

Things to See

The world-famous **Bayeux Tapestry** – a 70m-long strip of coarse linen decorated with woollen embroidery – was commissioned by Odo, bishop of Bayeux and half-brother to William the Conqueror, for the consecration of the cathedral in Bayeux in 1077. The tapestry recounts the story of the Norman invasion of 1066 – from the Norman perspective. Halley's Comet, which visited our solar system in 1066, also makes an appearance. The tapestry is housed in the **Musée de la Tapisserie de Bayeux** on rue de Nesmond, open 9 am to 7 pm daily (closed at lunch in the off season). Entry is 38/16FF.

Bayeux's **Cathédrale Notre Dame** is an exceptional example of Norman-Gothic architecture, dating from the 13th century.

The **Musée Mémorial 1944 Bataille de Normandie**, Bayeux's huge war museum on blvd Fabien Ware, displays a haphazard collection of photos, uniforms, weapons and lifelike scenes associated with D-Day and the Battle of Normandy. An excellent 30-minute film is screened in English. Admission is 33/16FF.

The **Bayeux War Cemetery**, a British cemetery on blvd Fabien Ware, a few hundred metres west of the museum, is the largest of the 18 Commonwealth military cemeteries in Normandy. Many of the headstones are inscribed with poignant epitaphs.

Places to Stay

Camping *Camping Municipal de Bayeux* (☎ 02 31 92 08 43) is 2km north of town, just south of blvd d'Eindhoven. It's open mid-March to mid-November, and charges 9.20/17.10FF per tent/person. Bus Nos 5 and 6 from the train station stop here.

Hostels The *Family Home* hostel and guesthouse (☎ 02 31 92 15 22, fax 02 31 92 55 72, *39 rue du Général de Dais*), in three old buildings, is an excellent place to meet other travellers. Beds in dorms are 100FF (95FF with HI card), single rooms 160FF. There's a kitchen, or you can have a multicourse French dinner (with wine) for 65FF.

FRANCE

The modern, if slightly sterile, *Centre d'Accueil Municipal* (☎ 02 31 92 08 19, 21 rue des Marettes) is 1km south-west of the cathedral. Singles are good value at 90FF.

Hotels The old but well-maintained *Hôtel de la Gare* (☎ 02 31 92 10 70, fax 02 31 51 95 99, 26 place de la Gare), opposite the train station, has rooms from 85/100FF. The central *Hôtel de l'Hôtel de Ville* (☎ 02 31 92 30 08, 31ter rue Larcher) has large and quiet rooms for 140/160FF; showers are free. Phone reservations are not accepted. A few hundred metres north, *Hôtel des Sports* (☎ 02 31 92 28 53, 19 rue St Martin) has decent rooms (most with shower) starting at 160/200FF.

Places to Eat
There are *food markets* on rue St Jean (Wednesday morning) and on place St Patrice (Saturday morning).

Le Petit Normand (☎ 02 31 22 88 66, 35 rue Larcher) specialises in traditional Norman food and has simple *menus* starting at 58FF (closed Sunday night and Wednesday, except in July and August). The *Hôtel Notre Dame* restaurant (☎ 02 31 92 87 24) offers Norman fare at its best; lunch *menus* cost 60FF, dinner *menus* 95FF (closed Sunday lunch and Monday from November to March). *Milano* (☎ 02 31 92 15 10, 18 rue St Martin) serves good pizza (closed Sunday from September to May).

Getting There & Away
The train station office (☎ 02 31 92 80 50) opens 7 am to 8.45 pm daily. Trains serve Paris' Gare St Lazare (171FF, via Caen), Cherbourg, Rennes and points beyond.

D-DAY BEACHES
The D-Day landings were the largest military operation in history. Early on the morning of 6 June 1944, swarms of landing craft – part of a flotilla of almost 7000 boats – ferried ashore 135,000 Allied troops along 80km of beaches north of Bayeux. The landings on D-Day were followed by the 76-day Battle of Normandy that began the liberation of Europe from Nazi occupation.

Arromanches
In order to unload the vast quantities of cargo necessary for the invasion, the Allies established two prefabricated ports. The remains of one of them, Port Winston, can be seen at Arromanches, a seaside town 10km north-east of Bayeux.

The **Musée du Débarquement** (Landing Museum; ☎ 02 31 22 34 31) explains the logistics and importance of Port Winston and makes a good first stop before visiting the beaches (closed Monday and in January; 35/20FF).

Omaha Beach
The most brutal combat of 6 June 1944 was fought 20km west of Arromanches at Omaha Beach. Today, little evidence of the war remains except the bunkers and munitions sites of a German fortified point to the west (look for the tall obelisk on the hill).

American Military Cemetery
The remains of the Americans who lost their lives during the Battle of Normandy were either sent back to the USA or buried in the American Military Cemetery at Colleville-sur-Mer. The cemetary contains the graves of 9386 American soldiers and a memorial to 1557 others whose bodies were never recovered.

Organised Tours
Tours of the D-Day beaches are offered by Bus Fly (☎ 02 31 22 00 08), based at the Family Home hostel in Bayeux (see Places to Stay in Bayeux). An afternoon tour to major D-Day sites costs 160/140FF, including museum entry fees.

Getting There & Away
Bus Verts (☎ 02 31 92 02 92), with an office opposite Bayeaux's train station (closed weekends and in July), sends bus No 70 west to the American cemetery at Colleville-sur-Mer and Omaha Beach. Bus No 74 serves Arromanches, and Gold and Juno Beaches. In July and August only, bus No 75 goes to Caen via Arromanches, Gold, Juno and Sword Beaches and then to the port of Ouistreham. There are timetables posted in the train station and at place G Despallières.

For three or more people, renting a car can actually be cheaper than a tour. Lefebvre Car Rental (☎ 02 31 92 05 96) on blvd d'Eindhoven in Bayeux charges 350FF per day with 200km free.

MONT ST MICHEL

It is difficult not to be impressed by Mont St Michel, with its massive abbey anchored at the summit of a rocky island. Around the base are the ancient ramparts and a jumble of buildings that house the small number of people who still live there.

At low tide, Mont St Michel looks out over bare sand stretching into the distance. At high tide – about six hours later – this huge expanse of sand is under water, though only the very highest tides cover the 900m causeway that connects the islet to the mainland. The French government is currently spending millions to restore Mont St Michel to its former glory, so parts of it may be scaffolded.

The Mont's major attraction is the **Abbaye du Mont St Michel** (☎ 02 33 89 80 00), at the top of the Grande Rue, up the stairway. It opens 9 am to 5.30 pm daily (9.30 am to 5 pm from October to April). It's worth taking the guided tour (in English) included in the ticket price (40/25FF). Even better are the evening tours (60/35FF) at 9 or 10 pm (except Sunday); visitors explore, at their own pace, the illuminated and music-filled rooms.

The nearest town, **Pontorson**, is 9km south and is the base for most travellers. Route D976 from Mont St Michel runs right into Pontorson's main thoroughfare, rue du Couësnon.

Information

The tourist office (☎ 02 33 60 14 30, fax 02 33 60 06 75, @ ot.mont.saint.michel@wanadoo.fr) is up the stairs to the left as you enter Mont St Michel at Porte de l'Avancée, and opens daily. There's another tourist office in Pontorson, open daily (closed Sunday in winter).

Places to Stay

Camping du Mont St Michel (☎ 02 33 60 09 33), open from mid-February to mid-November, is on the road to Pontorson (D976), 2km from the Mont. It charges 20/22FF per tent/person. Two-person bungalows with shower and toilet are 220FF.

Pontorson's *Centre Duguesclin* (☎ 02 33 60 18 65) operates as a 10-room hostel from Easter to mid-September. Beds are 48FF. The hostel is closed from 10 am to 6 pm, but there is no curfew. The hostel is 1km

west of the train station on rue du Général Patton, which runs parallel to the Couësnon River north of rue du Couësnon. The hostel is on the left side in a three-storey stone building opposite No 26.

Mont St Michel has about 15 hotels but most are expensive. *La Mère Poulard* (☎ 02 33 60 14 01, fax 02 33 48 52 31), the first hotel on the left as you walk up the Grande Rue, has doubles with shower from 300FF.

In Pontorson, across place de la Gare from the train station, there are a couple of cheap hotels. *Hôtel de l'Arrivée* (☎ 02 33 60 01 57, 14 rue du Docteur Tizon) has doubles for 95FF, or 165FF with shower.

Places to Eat

The tourist restaurants around the base of the Mont have lovely views but tend to be mediocre; *menus* start at about 80FF. A few places along the Grande Rue sell sandwiches, quiches and the like. The nearest *supermarket* to the Mont is next to Camping du Mont St Michel on the D976.

In Pontorson, *La Crêperie du Couësnon* (☎ 02 33 60 16 67, 21 rue du Couësnon) has crepes and savoury galettes (10FF to 30FF). *La Tour de Brette* (☎ 02 33 60 10 69, 8 rue du Couësnon), across from the river, has good *menus* from 60FF.

Getting There & Away

STN (☎ 02 33 58 03 07) sends bus No 15 from Pontorson's train station to Mont St Michel daily year-round; most of the buses connect with trains to/from Paris, Rennes and Caen.

There are trains to Pontorson from Caen (via Folligny) and Rennes (via Dol). From Paris, take the train to Caen (Gare St Lazare), Rennes (Gare Montparnasse) or to Pontorson via Folligny (Gare Montparnasse).

Getting Around

Bikes can be rented at Pontorson's train station (55FF per day plus 1000FF deposit) and from E Videloup (☎ 02 33 60 11 40), 1bis rue du Couësnon, which charges 50/80FF per day for one-speeds/mountain bikes.

Brittany

Brittany (Bretagne in French, Breizh in Breton), the westernmost region of France, is famous for its rugged countryside and wild coastline. Traditional costumes, including extraordinarily tall headdresses worn by the women, can still be seen at *pardons* (religious festivals) and other local festivals.

The indigenous language of Brittany is Breton, which, to the untrained ear, sounds like Gaelic with a French accent. It can sometimes still be heard in western Brittany and especially in Cornouaille, where perhaps a third of the population understands it.

QUIMPER

Situated at the confluence of two rivers, the Odet and the Steïr, Quimper (pronounced cam-pair) has managed to preserve its Breton architecture and atmosphere and is considered by many to be the cultural capital of Brittany. Some even refer to the city as the 'soul of Brittany'.

The Festival de Cornouaille, a showcase for traditional Breton music, costumes and culture, is held here every year between the third and fourth Sundays in July.

Orientation & Information

The old city, largely pedestrianised, is to the west and north-west of the cathedral. The train station is 1km east of the city centre on ave de la Gare; the bus station is to the right as you exit, in the modern-looking building.

You'll find the tourist office (☎ 02 98 53 04 05, fax 02 98 53 31 33, ✉ office.tour isme.quimper@ouest-mediacap.com) is on place de la Résistance (closed Sunday from mid-September to April).

Things to See

The old city is known for its centuries-old houses, which are especially in evidence on rue Kéréon and around place au Beurre.

The Cathédrale St Corentin, built between 1239 and 1515, incorporates many Breton elements, including – on the western facade between the spires – an equestrian statue of King Gradlon, the city's mythical 5th-century founder.

The Musée Départemental Breton, next to the cathedral in the former bishop's palace, houses exhibits on the history, costumes, crafts and archaeology of the area (25/15FF, closed Sunday morning and Monday). The Musée des Beaux-Arts, in the Hôtel de Ville at 40 place St Corentin, has a wide collection of European paintings from the 16th to early 20th centuries (25/15FF, closed Tuesday from September to June).

Faïenceries HB Henriot (☎ 02 98 90 09 36) has been turning out *faïence* (glazed earthenware) since 1690. Tours (20FF) of the factory, on rue Haute south-west of the cathedral, are held from 9 to 11.15 am and 1.30 to 4.15 pm weekdays (to 4.45 pm in July and August).

Places to Stay

It is extremely difficult to find accommodation during the Festival de Cornouaille in late July. The tourist office makes bookings in Quimper (2FF) and elsewhere in Brittany (5FF), and has a list of *private rooms*.

The year-round *Camping Municipal* (☎ *02 98 55 61 09*) charges 17.70FF per person, 3.90FF for a tent. It's on ave des Oiseaux just over 1km west of the old city. From the train station, take bus No 1 to the Chaptal stop.

The *Auberge de Jeunesse* (☎ *02 98 64 97 97, fax 02 98 55 38 37, 6 ave des Oiseaux)*, about 1km west of the old city, charges 67FF per dorm-room bed, including breakfast. Take bus No 1 or 8 to the Chaptal stop.

The spotless *Hôtel de l'Ouest* (☎ *02 98 90 28 35, 63 rue Le Déan)*, up rue Jean-Pierre Calloch from the train station, has large, pleasant singles/doubles from 100/150FF. Rooms with shower are 180/190FF. *Hôtel Pascal* (☎ *02 98 90 00 81, 17bis ave de la Gare)* has rooms with shower for 180/190FF. *Hôtel Le Celtic* (☎ *02 98 55 59 35, 13 rue Douarnenez)*, 100m north of Église St Mathieu, has doubles without/with shower for 125/165FF.

Places to Eat

There's a *Monoprix* supermarket (closed Sunday) on quai du Port au Vin, near the *covered market*.

Crepes, a Breton speciality, are your best bet for a cheap and filling meal. You'll find *creperies* everywhere, particularly along rue Ste Catherine across the river from the cathedral. Otherwise there are several decent restaurants on rue Le Déan not far from the train station, including the Chinese-Vietnamese *Le Lotus d'Or* (☎ *02 98 53 02 54)* at No 53 (closed Wednesday).

Le Jardin de l'Odet (☎ *02 98 95 76 76, 39 blvd Amiral de Kerguélen)* is a good splurge, with tasty Lyonnais cuisine and *menus* from 80FF (closed Sunday).

Getting There & Away
A half-dozen companies operate out of the bus station (☎ 02 98 90 88 89). Destinations include Brest, Pointe du Raz, Roscoff (for ferries to Plymouth, England), Concarneau and Quimperlé.

Inquire at the train station for SNCF buses to Douarnenez, Camaret-sur-Mer, Concarneau and Quiberon. A one-way ticket on the TGV train to Paris' Gare Montparnasse costs 384FF (four hours). You can also reach St Malo by train via Rennes. For rail information call ☎ 0836 35 35 35.

Getting Around
Torch VTT (☎ 02 98 53 84 41) at 58 rue de la Providence rents out mountain bikes for 65/90FF per half-day/day (cheaper in winter). It's closed Sunday, Monday and Thursday morning.

AROUND QUIMPER
Concarneau
Concarneau (Konk-Kerne in Breton), 24km south-east of Quimper, is France's third-most important trawler port. Concarneau is slightly scruffy and also a bit touristy, but it's refreshingly unpretentious and is near several decent beaches. The **Ville Close** (walled city), built on a small island measuring 350m by 100m and fortified between the 14th and 17th centuries, is reached via a footbridge from place Jean Jaurès.

Orientation & Information Concarneau curls around the busy fishing port (Port de Pêche), with the two main quays running north-south along the harbour. The tourist office (☎ 02 98 97 01 44, fax 02 98 50 88 81, @ otsi.concarneau@wanadoo.fr) is on quai d'Aiguillon, 200m north of the main (west) gate to the Ville Close (closed Sunday in the off season).

Places to Stay & Eat *Camping Moulin d'Aurore* (☎ 02 98 50 53 08, 49 rue de Trégunc), open April to September, is 600m south-east of the Ville Close. The *Auberge de Jeunesse* (☎ 02 98 97 03 47, fax 02 98 50 87 57) is on the water at quai de la Croix, next to the Marinarium. From the tourist office, walk south to the end of quai Peneroff

and turn right. Reception opens 9 am to noon and 6 to 8 pm; beds are 48FF. *Hôtel des Halles* (☎ 02 98 97 11 41, fax 02 98 50 58 54, place de l'Hôtel de Ville) charges 220FF for a double with shower and TV.

L'Escale (☎ 02 98 97 03 31, 19 quai Carnot) is popular with local Concarnois – a hearty lunch or dinner *menu* costs just 51FF (closed Saturday night and Sunday). For excellent home-style crepes, try the unpretentious *Crêperie du Grand Chemin* (17 ave de la Gare).

Getting There & Away The bus station is in the car park, to the north of the tourist office. Caoudal (☎ 02 98 56 96 72) runs up to four buses a day (three on Sunday) between Quimper and Quimperlé (via Concarneau and Pont Aven). The trip from Quimper to Concarneau costs 26FF and takes 30 minutes.

ST MALO
The Channel port of St Malo (population 52,300) is one of the most popular tourist destinations in Brittany – and with good reason. It has a famous walled city and good nearby beaches, and is an excellent base for day trips to Mont St Michel (see the earlier Normandy section).

Orientation & Information
St Malo consists of the resort towns of St Servan, St Malo, Paramé and Rothéneuf. The old city, signposted as Intra-Muros ('within the walls') and also known as the Ville Close, is connected to Paramé by the Sillon Isthmus. The train station is 1.2km east of the old city along ave Louis Martin.

The tourist office (☎ 02 99 56 64 48, fax 02 99 56 67 00, @ office.de.tourisme .saint-malo@wanadoo.fr) is just outside the old city on esplanade St Vincent (closed Sunday from October to March).

Cop Imprimu, 29 blvd des Talards, charges 30FF per half-hour of Web surfing and opens 9 am to 7 pm Monday to Friday, 9 am to noon on Saturday.

Old City
During the fighting of August 1944, which drove the Germans from St Malo, 80% of the old city was destroyed. After the war, the main historical monuments were lovingly reconstructed but the rest of the area was

FRANCE

rebuilt in the style of the 17th and 18th centuries. The **ramparts**, built over the course of many centuries, are largely original. They afford superb views in all directions.

The **Musée de la Ville**, in the Château de St Malo at Porte St Vincent, deals with the history of the city and the Pays Malouin, the area around St Malo (closed Monday in winter; 27/13.50FF).

The **Aquarium Intra-Muros** with over 100 tanks is built into the walls of the old city next to place Vauban (30/25FF). Europe's first circular aquarium, **Le Grand Aquarium St Malo**, is on ave Général Patton 1.5km south of the train station (56/44FF in summer, 44/30FF in the off season). Take bus No 5 from the train station and hop off at La Madelaine stop.

Île du Grand Bé
You can reach the Île du Grand Bé, where the 18th-century writer Chateaubriand is buried, on foot at low tide via the Porte des Bés. Be warned: when the tide comes rushing in, the causeway is impassable for about six hours.

St Servan
St Servan's fortress, **Fort de la Cité**, was built in the mid-18th century and served as a German base during WWII. The **Musée International du Long Cours Cap-Hornier**, housed in the 14th-century Tour de Solidor on esplanade Menguy, has interesting seafaring exhibits (closed Monday in the off season; 20/10FF). A combined ticket with the Musée de la Ville is 40/20FF.

Beaches
To the west, just outside the old city walls, is **Plage de Bon Secours**. The **Grande Plage**, which stretches north-eastward from the Sillon Isthmus, is spiked with tree trunks that act as breakers.

Places to Stay
Camping The year-round *Camping Municipal Cité d'Aleth* (☎ 02 99 81 60 91) is at the northern tip of St Servan next to Fort de la Cité. It charges 21/28FF per person/tent. In summer take bus No 1; at other times your best bet is bus No 6.

Hostel The *Auberge de Jeunesse* (☎ 02 99 40 29 80, fax 02 99 40 29 02, 37 ave du Père Umbricht)* is about 2km north-east of the train station (in Paramé). Dorm beds start at 72FF and doubles cost 170FF, breakfast included. From the train station, take bus No 5.

Hotels *Hôtel de l'Europe* (☎ 02 99 56 13 42, 44 blvd de la République)* is across the roundabout from the train station. Modern, nondescript doubles start at 180FF.

In the old city, *Hôtel Le Victoria* (☎ 02 99 56 34 01, fax 02 99 40 32 78, 4 rue des Orbettes)* charges 150FF for doubles (185FF with shower).

The friendly, family-run *Hôtel Aux Vieilles Pierres* (☎ 02 99 56 46 80, 4 rue des Lauriers)* is in a quiet part of the old city. Doubles start at 140FF (170FF with shower); hall showers are free.

Places to Eat
Tourist restaurants, creperies and pizzerias are chock-a-block in the area between Porte St Vincent, the cathedral and the Grande Porte, but if you're after better food, and better value, avoid this area completely.

As good as any for seafood is *La Morinière* (☎ 02 99 40 85 77, 9 rue Jacques Cartier)*, with *menus* at 70FF and 90FF (closed Wednesday). Or try the more intimate *Grain de Sable* (☎ 02 99 56 68 72) at No 2, which serves an excellent fish soup. In St Servan, *Crêperie du Val de Rance (11 rue Dauphine)* serves Breton-style crepes and galettes (8FF to 42FF).

Getting There & Away
Bus The bus station, served by several operators, is at esplanade St Vincent. Many of the buses departing from here also stop at the train station.

Courriers Bretons (☎ 02 99 19 70 70) has regular services to Cancale (21.50FF), Fougères (81FF, Monday to Saturday) and Mont St Michel (55FF, one hour). The first daily bus to Mont St Michel leaves at 9.50 am and the last one returns around 4.30 pm.

TIV (☎ 02 99 40 82 67) has buses to Cancale (21FF), Dinan (33FF) and Rennes (56.50FF). Buses to Dinard (20FF) run about once an hour until around 7 pm.

Train From the train station (☎ 0836 35 35 35) there is a direct service to Paris' Gare Montparnasse (315FF, 4¼ hours). Some go via Rennes (70FF). There are local services to Dinan (47FF) and Quimper (221FF).

Boat Ferries link St Malo with the Channel Islands, Weymouth and Portsmouth in England. There are two ferry terminals: hydrofoils, catamarans and the like depart from Gare Maritime de la Bourse; car ferries leave from the Gare Maritime du Naye. Both are south of the walled city.

From Gare Maritime de la Bourse, Condor (☎ 02 99 20 03 00) has catamaran and jetfoil services to Jersey (295FF one-day excursion) and Guernsey (295FF) from mid-March to mid-November. Condor's service to Weymouth (270FF, four hours) operates daily from late May to mid-October.

Émeraude Lines (☎ 02 23 18 01 80) has ferries to Jersey, Guernsey and Sark from Gare Maritime du Naye. Service is most regular between late March and mid-November.

Between mid-March and mid-December, Brittany Ferries (☎ 0803 82 88 28) has boats to Portsmouth (passengers 270FF; 850FF to 1620FF with a car) three times a day from the Gare Maritime du Naye. In winter, ferries sail four or five times a week.

The Bus de Mer ferry (run by Émeraude Lines) links St Malo with Dinard (20/30FF single/return, 10 minutes) from April to September. In St Malo, the dock is just outside the Porte de Dinan; the Dinard quay is at 27 ave George V.

From late May to mid-October, Condor Ferries (☎ 02 99 20 03 00) runs catamaran ferries between Poole and St Malo (280FF passengers, 1030FF to 2020FF with a car, 4¾ to 6½ hours, daily) from the Gare Maritime de la Bourse.

AROUND ST MALO
Dinard
St Malo's old city and beaches are geared towards middle-class families, and Dinard attracts a well-heeled clientele – especially from the UK. Indeed, Dinard has the feel of a turn-of-the-20th-century beach resort, with its candy-cane bathing tents and beachside carnival rides.

Beautiful seaside trails extend along the coast in both directions from Dinard. The famous **Promenade du Clair de Lune** (Moonlight Promenade) runs along the Baie du Prieuré. The town's most attractive walk is the one that links the Promenade du Clair de Lune with Plage de l'Écluse via the rocky coast of **Pointe du Moulinet**. Bikes are not allowed.

The tourist office (☎ 02 99 46 94 12, fax 02 99 88 21 07, ❷ dinard.office.de.tourime@wanadoo.fr) is in the round, colonnaded building at 2 blvd Féart (closed Sunday). Staying in Dinard can strain the budget, so consider making a day trip from St Malo (see that town's Getting There & Away section for details).

Loire Valley

From the 15th to 18th centuries, the fabled Loire Valley (Vallée de la Loire) was the playground of kings and nobles who expended vast fortunes to turn it into a neighbourhood of lavish chateaux. Today, the region is a favourite destination of tourists seeking the architectural glories of the Middle Ages and the Renaissance.

BLOIS
The medieval town of Blois (pronounced blwah) was a hub of court intrigue between the 15th and 17th centuries, and in the 16th century served as a second capital of France. The old city, seriously damaged by German attacks in 1940, retains its steep, twisting medieval streets. The town's highlight is outstanding Château de Blois.

Several of the Loire Valley's most rewarding chateaux, including Chambord and Cheverny, are a pleasant 20km bicycle ride from Blois.

Orientation & Information
In town, almost everything of interest is within walking distance of the train station, which is at the western end of ave Dr Jean Laigret. The old city is south and east of Château de Blois, which towers over place Victor Hugo.

The tourist office (☎ 02 54 90 41 41, fax 02 54 90 41 49, ❷ blois.tourism@wanadoo.fr), 3 ave Dr Jean Laigret, opens daily. The post office on rue Gallois has Internet access.

Things to See
Château de Blois (☎ 02 54 74 16 06) has a bloody history and an extraordinary mixture of architectural styles. Its four distinct

sections are early Gothic (13th century); Flamboyant Gothic (1498-1503); early Renaissance (1515-24), from the reign of François I; and classical (17th century). The chateau also houses an **archaeological museum** and the **Musée des Beaux-Arts** (Museum of Fine Arts), both open 9 am to noon and 2 to 5 pm mid-October to mid-March; and 9 am to 6.30 pm (8 pm in July and August) the rest of the year (35/25FF). The chateau's evening **sound-and-light show** (60/30FF) runs May to September. If you intend taking in a chateau visit and show, buy a money-saving combination ticket (75/55FF).

Opposite, the **Maison de la Magie** (House of Magic) has magic shows and displays objects invented by the 19th-century scientist/magician Robert Houdin, after whom the great Houdini named himself (48/42FF).

Large brown explanatory signs in English pinpoint tourist sights around the predominantly pedestrian-only old city. **Cathédrale St-Louis** is named after Louis XIV, who had it rebuilt after a hurricane in 1678. There's a great view of Blois and the River Loire from the lovely **Jardins de l'Évêché** (Gardens of the Bishop's Palace), behind the cathedral.

The 15th-century **Maison des Acrobates** (House of Acrobats), 3bis rue Pierre de Blois, is one of Blois' few medieval houses to survive the bombings of WWII. It is named after the cheeky characters carved in its timbers.

Places to Stay

Camping The two-star *Camping du Lac de Loire* (☎ *02 54 78 82 05*), open April to mid-October, is in Vineuil, which is 4km south of Blois. It costs 49FF for two people and a tent. There's no bus service from town except in July and August (phone the camp site or the tourist office for further details).

Hostel The *Auberge de Jeunesse* (☎/*fax 02 54 78 27 21, 18 rue de l'Hôtel Pasquier*), 4.5km south-west of Blois train station in Les Grouëts; is open from March to mid-November. Call first – it's often full. Dorm beds cost 68FF. The hostel closes from 10 am to 6 pm. From place de la République, take bus No 4.

Hotels Near the train station, your best bet is the one-star *Hôtel St-Jacques* (☎ *02 54 78 04 15, fax 02 54 78 33 05, 7 rue Ducoux*). Basic doubles cost upwards of 130FF. Opposite at No 6, the family-run *Hôtel Le Savoie* (☎ *02 54 74 32 21, fax 02 54 74 29 58*) has well-kept singles/doubles with shower, toilet and TV starting at 180/200FF.

North of the old city, the 12-room *Hôtel du Bellay* (☎ *02 54 78 23 62, fax 02 54 78 52 04, 12 rue des Minimes*) has doubles costing 135FF to 160FF (185FF with bath or shower). *Hôtel L'Étoile Tex* (☎ *02 54 78 46 93,* ✉ *etoiletex.cybercafe@caramail.com, 7 rue du Bourg Neuf*) has nine rooms costing 150FF to 180FF, and Internet access (1FF per minute).

Places to Eat

In the old city, *Le Rond de Serviette* (☎ *02 54 74 48 04, 18 rue Beauvoir*) claims to be Blois' most humorous and cheapest restaurant; its 49FF *menu* is unbeatable. Nearby, pasta and pizza are dished up at *La Scala* (☎ *02 54 74 88 19, 8 rue des Minimes*). Its leafy summer terrace gets full fast.

La Mesa (☎ *02 54 78 70 70, 11 rue Vauvert*) is a busy Franco-Italian joint, up an alleyway from 44 rue Foulerie. Its lovely courtyard is perfect for dining alfresco.

There's a *food market* on rue Anne de Bretagne on Tuesday, Thursday and Saturday until 1 pm, and an *Intermarché* supermarket near the station on ave Gambetta.

Getting There & Away

By train, there are four direct trains daily from Blois to Paris' Gare d'Austerlitz (123FF, 1½ to two hours), plus several more if you change train in Orléans. There are frequent trains to/from Tours (51FF, 40 minutes, 11 to 17 daily) and its TGV station, St-Pierre des Corps (49FF, 25 to 35 minutes, hourly). About three-quarters of the trains on the Blois-Tours line stop at Amboise (34FF, 20 minutes).

Getting Around

All buses (except No 4) within Blois – run by TUB – stop at the train station. Tickets cost 6FF (41FF for a carnet of 10).

Hire a bicycle from Cycles Leblond (☎ *02 54 74 30 13*), 44 Levée des Tuileries, which charges upwards of 30/180FF per day/week. To get there, walk eastward along Promenade du Mail.

BLOIS AREA CHATEAUX

Blois is surrounded by some of the Loire Valley's finest chateaux which languish in countryside perfect for cycling. Chambord, Cheverny and Chaumont are each about 20km from Blois.

Without your own wheels, the best way to see more than one chateau in a day is with an organised tour. From mid-May to 31 August, Blois-based TLC (☎ 02 54 58 55 55) organises two bus tours daily from Blois to Chambord and Cheverny (65/50FF); prices don't include entry fees.

Château de Chambord

Château de Chambord (☎ 02 54 50 50 02), begun in 1519 by François I (1515-47), is the largest and most-visited chateau in the Loire Valley. Its Renaissance architecture and decoration, grafted onto a feudal ground plan, may have been inspired by Leonardo da Vinci who, at the invitation of François I, lived in Amboise (45km south-west) from 1516 until his death three years later.

The chateau's famed **double-helix staircase**, attributed by some to Leonardo, consists of two spiral staircases that wind around the same central axis but never meet. Tickets to the 440-room chateau are sold from 9.30 am to 4.45 pm July and August; 9.30 am to 5.45 pm April to June and September; and 9.30 am to 4.45 pm October to March. Visitors already in the chateau can stay for 45 minutes after ticket sales end (40/25FF).

From mid-July to mid-October, Chambord hosts a **light show** every night. Tickets are sold from 10.30 pm until midnight in July, 10 to 11.30 pm in August, and 8.30 to 9.30 or 10 pm September to mid-October (80/50FF). Tickets covering show and chateau are available (100/55F).

Getting There & Around Chambord is 16km east of Blois and 20km north-east of Cheverny. During the school year, TLC bus No 2 averages three return trips (two/one on Saturday/Sunday) from Blois to Chambord (18.50FF, 45 minutes). In July and August, your only bus option is TLC's guided tour (see the Blois Area Chateaux introduction). In Chambord, you can rent a bicycle from the Echapée Belle kiosk, next to Pont

St-Michel in the castle grounds (25/70FF per hour/day).

Château de Cheverny

Privately owned Château de Cheverny (☎ 02 54 79 96 29), the most magnificently furnished of the Loire Valley chateaux, was completed in 1634. Visitors are treated to room after sumptuous room outfitted with the finest canopied beds, tapestries, paintings, painted ceilings and walls covered with embossed Córdoba leather. Three dozen panels illustrate the story of *Don Quixote* in the 1st-floor dining room. In the grounds, near the lake, is a **balloon pad** where you can take to the skies in a hot-air balloon from mid-March to mid-October (47/43FF).

Cheverny (☎ 02 54 79 96 29, ☺ chateau.cheverny@wanadoo.fr) opens 9.15 or 9.30 am to 6.15 pm (6.30 pm July and August) April to September; and 9.15 or 9.30 am to noon and 2.15 to 5.30 pm (5 pm November to February) the rest of the year (35/24FF).

Getting There & Away Cheverny is 16km south-east of Blois and 20km south-west of Chambord.

The TLC bus from Blois to Villefranche-sur-Cher stops at Cheverny (14.60FF). Buses leave at 6.50 am and 12.25 pm from Blois Monday to Saturday. Returning to Blois, the last bus leaves Cheverny at 6.58 pm. Times vary on Sunday and holidays; check schedules before setting off.

Château de Chaumont

Château de Chaumont (☎ 02 54 51 26 26), set on a bluff overlooking the River Loire, resembles a feudal castle. Its luxurious **stables** are its most famous feature; also note the **Salle du Conseil** (Council Chamber) on the 1st floor, with its majolica tile floor and tapestries, and **Catherine de' Medici's bedroom** overlooking the chapel. Tickets are sold 9.30 am to 6 pm mid-March to September; 10 am to 4.30 pm the rest of the year (33FF).

Getting There & Away Château de Chaumont is 17km south-west of Blois and 20km north-east of Amboise in the village of Chaumont-sur-Loire. The path leading up to the park and the chateau begins at the intersection of rue du Village Neuf and rue Maréchal Leclerc (D751). By rail, take a

FRANCE

local train from Blois to Onzain (36FF, 10 minutes, eight or more daily), a 2km walk across the river from the chateau.

TOURS
Lively Tours (population 270,000) has the cosmopolitan and bourgeois air of a miniature Paris, with wide 18th-century avenues and cafe-lined boulevards. The city was devastated by German bombardment in June 1940, but much of it has been rebuilt since. The French spoken in Tours is said to be the purest in France.

Orientation & Information
Tours' focal point is place Jean Jaurès, where the city's major thoroughfares – rue Nationale, blvd Heurteloup, ave de Grammont and blvd Béranger – join up. The train station is 300m east along blvd Heurteloup. The old city, centred around place Plumereau, is about 400m west of rue Nationale.

The tourist office (☎ 02 47 70 37 37, fax 02 47 61 14 22, @ info@ligeris.com), 78-82 rue Bernard Palissy, opens daily with a midday break at 12.30 pm.

Things to See
The **Musée de l'Hôtel Goüin** at 25 rue du Commerce is an archaeological museum, housed in a splendid Renaissance mansion built around 1510 (21/16FF). The **Musée du Compagnonnage** (Guild Museum) overlooking the courtyard of **Abbaye St-Julien**, 8 rue Nationale, is a celebration of the skill of the French artisan; exhibits include examples of woodcarving, metalwork and even cake-icing (25/15FF). The **Musée des Vins de Touraine** (Museum of Touraine Wines), a few metres away at No 16, is in the 13th-century wine cellars of Abbaye St-Julien (16/10FF).

The **Musée des Beaux-Arts**, at 18 place François Sicard, has a good collection of works from the 14th to 20th centuries (30/15FF). Most museums in Tours are closed on Tuesday.

Places to Stay
Camping The three-star *Camping Les Rives du Cher* (☎ 02 47 27 27 60, 63 rue de Rochpinard, St-Avertin) is 5km south of Tours and is open April to mid-October. It charges 14/14/8FF per tent/person/car. To get there, from place Jean Jaurès, take bus

No 5 straight to the St-Avertin bus terminal, then follow the signs.

Hostels *Le Foyer* (☎ 02 47 60 51 51, fax 02 47 20 75 20, @ fjt.tours@wanadoo.fr, 16 rue Bernard Palissy), about 500m north of the train station, is a workers dormitory. When there's space for travellers, singles/doubles cost 100/160FF. Reception closes Sunday.

Tours' *Auberge de Jeunesse* (☎ 02 47 25 14 45, ave d'Arsonval) is 5km south of the train station in Parc de Grand Mont. Beds cost 48FF. Until 8.30 or 8.45 pm, take bus No 1 or 6 from place Jean Jaurès; from 9.20 pm to about midnight, take Bleu de Nuit bus N1 (southbound).

Hotels *Hôtel Français* (☎ 02 47 05 59 12, 11 rue de Nantes) provides a cold welcome but is worth frequenting for penny-pinchers: singles/doubles/triples/quads with washbasin and bidet cost 120/140/150/170FF (140/160/170/180FF with shower or 155/190/220/250FF with shower and toilet). A hall shower/breakfast costs 10/28FF.

Mon Hôtel (☎ 02 47 05 67 53, 40 rue de la Préfecture), 500m north of the train station, touts singles/doubles costing upwards of 100/115FF (170/200FF with shower and toilet). Cheerful *Hôtel Vendôme* (☎ 02 47 64 33 54, @ hotelvendome.tours@wanadoo.fr, 24 rue Roger Salengro) is run by an exceptionally friendly couple. Simple but decent rooms start at 140/160FF (150/185FF with shower and toilet).

Places to Eat
In the old city, place Plumereau and rue du Grand Marché are loaded with places to eat, sit down or stand up. *Le Serpent Volant (54 rue du Grand Marché)* is a quintessential French cafe, while *Le Café (39 rue du Dr Bretonneau)* is a contemporary and funky favourite.

Budget travellers can try sweet-talking their way into *Les Tanneurs*, the university resto-cum-cafe near the main university building on rue des Tanneurs. To dine you need a student ticket.

Sandwich stalls selling filled baguettes and pastries line the Grand Passage shopping mall at 18 rue de Bordeaux. The *covered market (place Gaston Pailhou)* opens until 7 pm (1 pm Sunday).

Entertainment

Old-city cafe nightlife is centred around place Plumereau. *Les 3 Orfèvres* (☎ 02 47 64 02 73, 6 rue des Orfèvres) has live music starting at 11 pm most nights. Student nightlife comes to life down tiny rue de la Longue Echelle and the southern strip of adjoining rue Dr Bretonneau.

Live jazz venues include alternative cafe-theatre *Le Petit Faucheux* (☎ 02 47 38 67 62, 23 rue des Cerisiers) and brilliant *Bistro 64* (☎ 02 47 38 47 40, 64 rue du Grand Marché) which plays Latin, blues and *musique Française* in a 16th-century interior.

Getting There & Away

Eurolines (☎ 02 47 66 45 56) has a bus ticket office next to the tourist office at 76 rue Bernard Palissy (closed Sunday).

The train station is opposite the bus station on place du Général Leclerc. Trains run between Tours and Orléans (88FF, 1¼ hours, hourly), via St-Pierre des Corps (eight minutes), Amboise (28FF, 20 minutes) and Blois (51FF, 35 minutes). There are two trains daily to Loches (44FF, 45 minutes) and eight trains to Saumur (56FF, 40 minutes).

Paris' Gare Montparnasse is about 1¼ hours away by TGV (211FF to 277FF, 10 to 15 daily), often with a change of train at St-Pierre des Corps. Other services include to/from Paris' Gare d'Austerlitz (154FF, two to three hours), Bordeaux (224FF, 2¾ hours) and Nantes (135FF, 1½ to two hours).

Getting Around

From May to September, Amster' Cycles (☎ 02 47 61 22 23, fax 02 47 61 28 48), 5 rue du Rempart, rents road and mountain bikes for 80/330FF per day/week. Staff provide cyclists with a puncture repair kit and map.

TOURS AREA CHATEAUX

Several chateaux around Tours can be reached by train, SNCF bus or by bicycle. Several companies offer English-language tours of the chateaux – book ahead at the Tours tourist office or contact the company directly. Services Touristiques de Touraine (STT; ☎/fax 02 47 05 46 09, @ info@ stt-millet.fr) runs half-/full-day coach tours, April to mid-October, costing 190/300FF (including admission fees to three to four

chateaux). Full details are posted on STT's Web site: www.stt-millet.fr.

Château de Chenonceau

With its stylised moat, drawbridge, towers and turrets straddling the River Cher, the 16th-century Chenonceau is everything a fairy-tale castle should be, although its interior – crammed with period furniture, tourists, paintings, tourists, tapestries and tourists – is only of moderate interest.

Chenonceau (☎ 02 47 23 90 07, @ chateau.de.chenonceau@wanadoo.fr) opens 9 am until sometime between 4.30 pm (mid-November to January) and 7 pm (mid-March to mid-September). Admission costs 50/40FF.

Getting There & Away Château de Chenonceau, in the town of Chenonceaux (spelt with an 'x') is 34km east of Tours. Between Tours and Chenonceaux there are two or three trains daily (32FF, 30 minutes); alternatively, trains on the Tours-Vierzon line stop at Chisseaux (33FF, 24 minutes, six daily), 2km east of Chenonceaux. In summer, take CAT bus No 10 to/from Tours (13FF, one hour, one daily).

Château d'Azay-le-Rideau

Azay-le-Rideau, built on an island in the River Indre and surrounded by a quiet pool, is among the most elegant of the Loire's chateaux. Inside, seven rooms are open to the public, but their contents are disappointing (apart from a few 16th-century Flemish tapestries). Château d'Azay-le-Rideau is one of the few chateaux which allows visitors to picnic in its beautiful grounds.

The chateau (☎ 02 47 45 42 04) opens 9.30 am to 6 pm April to June and September; 9 am to 7 pm July and August; and 9.30 am to 12.30 pm and 2 to 5.30 pm October to March (35/23FF).

Getting There & Away Azay-le-Rideau, 26km south-west of Tours, is on SNCF's Tours-Chinon line (four or five daily Monday to Saturday, one on Sunday). From Tours, the 30-minute trip (50 minutes by SNCF bus) costs 27FF; the station is 2.5km from the chateau. The last train/bus to Tours leaves Azay at about 6.35 pm (8 pm on Sunday).

Amboise

The picturesque hillside town of Amboise, an easy day trip from Tours, is known for **Château d'Amboise** (☎ 02 47 57 00 98), perched on a rocky outcrop overlooking the town and affording panoramic views of Amboise and the Loire Valley from its ramparts. The remains of Leonardo da Vinci (1452-1519), who lived in Amboise for the last three years of his life, are supposedly under the chapel's northern transept.

Inside the chateau walls, opposite 42 place Michel Debré, is the innovative **Caveau des Vignerons d'Amboise**, a wine cellar where you can taste regional Touraine wines (free), Easter to October. The chateau entrance is at the end of Rampe du Château. From April to October, hours are 9 am to 6.30 pm (to 8 pm in July and August); the rest of the year, it's open 9 am to noon and 2 to 5 or 5.30 pm. Admission costs 40/33FF.

Da Vinci came to Amboise at the invitation of François I in 1516. Until his death at the age of 67 three years later, Leonardo lived and worked in **Le Clos Lucé** (☎ 02 47 57 62 88), 2 rue du Clos Lucé, a 15th-century brick manor house 500m south-east of the chateau along rue Victor Hugo. The building contains restored rooms and scale models of some 40 of Leonardo's inventions – fascinating stuff. Le Clos Lucé opens 9 am to 7 pm March to December (to 8 pm July and August); and 9 am to 6 pm (10 am to 5 pm in January) the rest of the year (39/32FF).

Information The tourist office (☎ 02 47 57 09 28, fax 02 47 57 14 35, @ tourisme .amboise@wanadoo.fr) is next to the river, opposite 7 quai du Général de Gaulle (closed Sunday November to Easter).

Getting There & Away Several daily trains run to Amboise from both Tours (28FF, 20 minutes) and Blois (34FF, 20 minutes). From Tours, you can also take CAT bus No 10 (19.60FF, 30 to 50 minutes).

South-Western France

LA ROCHELLE

La Rochelle (population 120,000), a lively port city midway down France's Atlantic coast, is popular with middle-class French families and students on holiday. The ever-expanding Université de La Rochelle, opened in 1993, adds to the city's vibrancy. The nearby Île de Ré is ringed by long, sandy beaches.

Orientation & Information

The old city is north of the Vieux Port (old port), which is linked to the train station – 500m south-east – by ave du Général de Gaulle.

The tourist office (☎ 05 46 41 14 68, fax 05 46 41 99 85) is in Le Gabut, the quarter on the south side of the Vieux Port.

Things to See

To protect the harbour at night and to defend it in times of war, a chain used to be stretched between the two 14th-century stone towers at the harbour entrance, the 36m **Tour St Nicolas** and **Tour de la Chaîne**; the latter houses displays on local history. West along the old city wall is **Tour de la Lanterne**, long used as a prison. All three towers are open daily; entry to each costs 25/15FF (45FF for combined ticket).

The **Musée Maritime Neptunea**, an excellent maritime museum at Bassin des Chalutiers, is the permanent home of Jacques Cousteau's research ship *Calypso* (not yet open to the public). The entry fee of 50/35FF includes tours of a *chalutier* (fishing trawler). Next door, a vast new **aquarium** is scheduled to open in early 2001.

The **Île de Ré**, a 30km-long, beach-fringed island that begins 9km west of La Rochelle, is reached by a 3km toll bridge. In July and August, and on Wednesday, weekends and holidays in June, city bus No 1 or 50 (known as No 21 between the train station and place de Verdun) goes to Sablanceaux (10FF, 25 minutes). Year-round, Rébus (☎ 05 46 09 20 15 in St Martin de Ré) links La Rochelle (the train station and place de Verdun) with St Martin de Ré and other island towns.

Places to Stay

Camping du Soleil (☎ 05 46 44 42 53, ave Marillac), about 1.5km south of the city centre, opens mid-May to mid-September and is often full. It is served by bus No 10.

Centre International de Séjour-Auberge de Jeunesse (☎ 05 46 44 43 11, fax 05 46

45 41 48, ave des Minimes) is 2km south-west of the train station. A dorm bed costs 72FF, including breakfast. To get there, take bus No 10.

The two-star, 63-room *Hôtel Le Commerce* (☎ 05 46 41 08 22, fax 05 46 41 74 85, 6-10 place de Verdun) has 11 doubles with washbasin for 135FF (165FF in season). In summer, breakfast (33FF) may be obligatory. In the pedestrianised old city, the friendly, 24-room *Hôtel Henri IV* (☎ 05 46 41 25 79, fax 05 46 41 78 64, place de la Caille) has spacious doubles from 170FF (220FF with shower and toilet).

A short block west of the Vieux Port, the 22-room *Hôtel de Bordeaux* (☎ 05 46 41 31 22, fax 05 46 41 24 43, ✆ hbordeaux@ free.fr, 43 rue St Nicolas) has quiet, pastel-coloured doubles from 175FF (285FF from June to September, including breakfast).

Places to Eat

French cuisine is available at the rustic *La Galathée* (45 rue St Jean du Perot), which has *menus* for 65FF (weekday lunch), 85FF and 130FF (closed Tuesday and Wednesday except in July and August). The stylish *Bistrot l'Entracte* (22 rue St Jean du Pérot) specialises in fish and seafood; the four-course *menu* costs 160FF (closed Sunday). There are dozens of other eateries between here and the quay along the northern side of the port.

The lively *covered market (place du Marché)* is open 7 am to 1 pm daily. The *Prisunic* supermarket, across from 55 rue du Palais, is open 8.15 am to 8 pm Monday to Saturday.

Getting There & Away

Eurolines ticketing is handled by Citram Littoral (☎ 05 46 50 53 57) at 30 cours des Dames (closed Saturday afternoon, Monday morning and Sunday).

By train from Paris, you can take a TGV from Gare Montparnasse (320FF to 380FF, three hours) or a non-TGV from Gare d'Austerlitz (264FF). Other destinations include Bordeaux (134FF, two hours) and Tours (160FF, two hours).

BORDEAUX

Bordeaux (population 650,000) is known for its neoclassical (if somewhat grimy) architecture, wide avenues and well-tended public parks. The city's cultural diversity (including 60,000 students), excellent museums and untouristy atmosphere make it much more than just a convenient stop between Paris and Spain. The marketing and export of Bordeaux wine are the city's most important economic activities.

Orientation & Information

Cours de la Marne stretches for about 2km from the train station north-westward to place de la Victoire, which is linked to the tourist office area (1.5km farther north) by the pedestrians-only rue Ste Catherine. The city centre lies between place Gambetta and the Garonne River.

The main tourist office (☎ 05 56 00 66 00, fax 05 56 00 66 01), 12 cours du 30 Juillet, opens daily year-round. There's a branch office at the train station (closed Sunday from October to April). Web site: www.bordeaux-tourisme.com.

For Internet access, Cyberstation (☎ 05 56 01 15 15), 23 cours Pasteur, opens 11 am to 2 am (2 pm to midnight on Sunday).

Things to See

The sights below are listed more-or-less from north to south. Entry to each museum costs 25/15FF (free for students and on the first Sunday of the month).

The excellent **Musée d'Art Contemporain** at 7 rue Ferrère hosts exhibits by contemporary artists (closed Monday). The **Jardin Public**, an 18th-century English-style park, is along cours de Verdun and includes Bordeaux's **botanical garden** and **Musée d'Histoire Naturelle** (Natural History Museum; closed Tuesday).

The most prominent feature of **esplanade des Quinconces**, a vast square laid out in 1820, is a towering fountain-monument to the Girondins, a group of moderate, bourgeois legislative deputies executed during the French Revolution.

The neoclassical **Grand Théâtre** at place de la Comédie was built in the 1770s. **Porte Dijeaux**, which dates from 1748, leads from **place Gambetta**, in whose centre there's a garden, to the pedestrianised commercial centre.

In 1137, the future King Louis VII married Eleanor of Aquitaine in **Cathédrale St André**. Just east of this cathedral, the 15th-century and 50m-high belfry, **Tour**

FRANCE

Pey-Berland, can be climbed for 25/15FF (closed Monday).

At 20 cours d'Albert, the **Musée des Beaux-Arts** occupies two wings of the 18th-century Hôtel de Ville and houses a large collection of paintings, including works by 17th-century Flemish, Dutch and Italian artists (closed Tuesday). The outstanding **Musée d'Aquitaine**, 20 cours Pasteur, illustrates the history and ethnography of the Bordeaux area (closed Monday).

The **Synagogue** (1882) on rue du Grand Rabbin Joseph Cohen (just west of rue Ste Catherine) is a mixture of Sephardic and Byzantine styles. During WWII the Nazis turned the complex into a prison. Visits are generally possible 9 am to noon and 2 to 4 pm Monday to Thursday – ring the bell marked *gardien* at 213 rue Ste Catherine.

Places to Stay

The 150-spot **Camping Les Gravières** (☎ 05 56 87 00 36, *place de Courréjean*), open all year, is 10km south-east of the city centre in Villenave d'Ornon. By bus, take line B from place de la Victoire towards Corréjean and get off at the terminus.

About 700m west of the train station, *Auberge de Jeunesse* (☎ 05 56 91 59 51, 22 cours Barbey) is being renovated and is scheduled to reopen in April 2001.

North of the centre near place de Tourny (from the station take bus No 7 or 8), *Hôtel Studio* (☎ 05 56 48 00 14, fax 05 56 81 25 71, 26 rue Huguerie) and three affiliated hotels offer charmless rooms with shower, toilet and (in most cases) cable TV starting at a minimum of 98/120FF. The hotel's mini-cybercafe charges guests 10FF an hour. Web site: www.hotel-bordeaux.com.

The 27-room *Hôtel de Famille* (☎ 05 56 52 11 28, fax 05 56 51 94 43, 76 cours Georges Clemenceau) has rather ordinary but homy doubles from 120FF.

A few blocks south-west of place Gambetta, the quiet, 16-room *Hôtel Boulan* (☎ 05 56 52 23 62, fax 05 56 44 91 65, 28 rue Boulan) has decent singles/doubles from 100/110FF (120/140FF with shower).

Places to Eat

The many inexpensive cafes and restaurants around place de la Victoire include the *Cassolette Café* (20 place de la Victoire), which serves family-style French food in small/large *cassolettes* (terracotta plates) that cost 11/33FF (open daily).

The popular *Chez Édouard (16 place du Parlement)* purveys French bistro-style meat and fish dishes; *menus* cost 59FF (lunch except on Sunday), 70FF and 99FF. There are numerous eateries to be found along nearby rue du Parlement, rue Ste Catherine, rue des Piliers de Tutelle and rue St Rémi.

Restaurant Baud et Millet (19 rue Huguerie) serves cheese-based cuisine (most dishes are vegetarian), including all-you-can-eat *raclette* for 110FF (closed Sunday).

The dinner-only *La Fournaise (23 rue de Lalande)* serves the delicious cuisine of Réunion; the *menus* cost 80FF to 140FF (closed Sunday and Monday).

The *Champion* supermarket (place des Grands Hommes), in the basement of the mirror-plated Marché des Grands Hommes, is open until 7.30 pm Monday to Saturday. Near *Marché des Capucins*, a covered food market just east of place de la Victoire (open 6 am to 1 pm, closed Monday), you'll find super-cheap *fruit and vegie stalls* along rue Élie Gintrec (open until 1 pm, closed Sunday).

Getting There & Away

Buses to places all over the Gironde (and nearby areas) leave from the Halte Routière (☎ 05 56 43 68 43), in the north-east corner of esplanade des Quinconces; schedules are posted.

Bordeaux's train station, Gare St Jean (☎ 08 36 35 35 39), is about 3km south-east of the city centre at the end of cours de la Marne. By TGV it takes only about three hours to/from Paris' Gare Montparnasse (352FF to 399FF). The trip to Bayonne (135FF) takes 1¾ hours.

BORDEAUX VINEYARDS

The Bordeaux wine-producing region, 1000 sq km in extent, is subdivided into 57 production areas called *appellations*, whose climate and soil impart distinctive characteristics to the wines grown there.

Over 5000 wine-producing chateaux (also known as *domaines*, *crus* and *clos*) produce the area's highly regarded wines, which are mainly reds. Many smaller chateaux accept walk-in visitors (some are closed during the October grape harvest); the larger and better-known ones usually require that you phone ahead.

Each winery has different rules about tasting – at some it's free (with the expectation that you'll seriously consider making a purchase), others charge entry fees, and others do not serve wine at all. Look for signs reading *dégustation* (wine tasting), *en vente directe* (direct sales), *vin à emporter* (wine to take away) and *gratuit* (free).

Opposite Bordeaux's main tourist office, the Maison du Vin de Bordeaux (☎/fax 05 56 00 22 66), open weekdays (and, in summer, on Saturday), has details on winery visits. It can also supply information on the many local *maisons du vin* (special wine-oriented tourist offices). See the Web site at www.vins-bordeaux.fr.

On Wednesday and Saturday (daily from May to October), the Bordeaux tourist office runs five-hour bus tours in French and English to the area's wine chateaux (160/140FF).

St Émilion
The medieval village of St Émilion, 39km east of Bordeaux, is surrounded by vineyards renowned for their full-bodied, deeply coloured red wines. The most interesting historical sites – including the **Église Monolithe**, carved out of solid limestone from the 9th to the 12th centuries – can be visited only on the 45-minute guided tours (33/20FF) offered by the tourist office (☎ 05 57 55 28 28), which is at place des Créneaux (open daily). The 50 or so wine shops include the cooperative Maison du Vin (☎ 05 57 55 50 55) at place Pierre Meyrat, around the corner from the tourist office, which is owned by the 250 chateaux whose wines it sells (open daily).

From Bordeaux, St Émilion is accessible by train (44FF, 35 minutes, two or three a day) and bus (at least once a day, except on Sundays and public holidays from October to April). The last train back usually departs at 6.27 pm.

BAYONNE
Bayonne (population 40,000) is the most important city in the French part of the Basque Country (Euskadi in Basque, Pays Basque in French), a region straddling the Franco-Spanish border.

Its most important festival is the annual Fêtes de Bayonne, beginning on the first Wednesday in August. The event includes a 'running of the bulls' like Pamplona's, except that here, the stars are cows.

Orientation & Information
The Adour and Nive Rivers split Bayonne into three: St Esprit, north of the Adour; Grand Bayonne, the oldest part of the city, on the west bank of the Nive; and the very Basque Petit Bayonne to its east.

The tourist office (☎ 05 59 46 01 46, fax 05 59 59 37 55, ✆ bayonne.tourisme@wanadoo.fr) is on place des Basques. Its brochure *Fêtes* is useful for cultural and sporting events while *Promenades and Discoveries*, in English, describes a self-guided walk around town.

You can log on at Cyber Net Café (☎ 05 59 55 78 98) on place de la République. Open 7 am to 2 am daily (from noon on Sunday), it charges 1FF per minute or 45FF an hour.

Things to See
Construction of the Gothic **Cathédrale Ste Marie**, place Monseigneur Vansteenberghe, began in the 13th century and was completed in 1451. The entrance to the beautiful 13th-century **cloister** is on place Louis Pasteur.

The **Musée Bonnat** (closed Tuesday; 20/10FF), 5 rue Jacques Laffitte in Petit Bayonne, has a diverse collection including a gallery of paintings by Rubens.

Places to Stay
Camping *Camping de Parme* (☎ 05 59 23 03 00, route de l'Aviation), 1.25km northeast of the Biarritz-La Négresse train station, charges 79FF for two people and tent. Open all year, it's usually booked up during July and August.

Hostel The lively *Auberge de Jeunesse d'Anglet* (☎ 05 59 58 70 00, fax 05 59 58 70 07, ✆ biarritz@fuaj.fr, 19 route des Vignes) in Anglet comes complete with a Scottish pub. Popular with surfers, it's open mid-February to mid-November; reservations are essential in summer. B&B costs 73FF and you can also pitch a tent here for 48FF per person, including breakfast.

From Bayonne, take bus No 7 and get off at Moulin Barbot, a 10-minute walk away. From Biarritz, town or station, take bus No 9.

FRANCE

Hotels You can tumble off the train into hyperfriendly *Hôtel Paris-Madrid* (☎ *05 59 55 13 98, fax 05 59 55 07 22)*, just beside the station. The cheapest singles are 95FF, and pleasant doubles without/with shower start at 130/160FF. Big rooms with bathroom and cable TV which can take up to four cost from 210FF.

Nearby, *Hôtel Monte Carlo* (☎ *05 59 55 02 68, 1 rue Ste Ursule)* has simple rooms from 90FF and larger ones with bathroom for two to four people from 170FF to 250FF.

In Petit Bayonne, *Hôtel des Basques* (☎ *05 59 59 08 02, place Paul Bert)* has large, pleasant rooms with washbasin and toilet for between 135FF and 180FF and rooms with full bathroom from 170FF. Showers cost 10FF.

The mid-range *Hôtel des Basses-Pyrénées* (☎ *05 59 59 00 29, fax 05 59 59 42 02, 12 rue Tour de Sault)* is built around a 17th-century tower. Doubles/triples/quads with bathroom start at 300/330/350FF. There are also a few rooms with washbasin for 150FF to 170FF and private parking (30FF). It's closed in January.

Places to Eat

Nowhere in town is more Basque than *Restaurant Euskalduna Ostatua* (*61 rue Pannecau)* near Hôtel des Basques, where main dishes are a bargain 35FF to 50FF. It's open for lunch, weekdays only. Over the Nive River and also open lunchtimes only is the family-run *Bar-Restaurant du Marché* (*39 rue des Basques)*. Here the cooking is homy and the owner's wife mothers everyone; the food will fill you to bursting for under 100FF.

A couple of blocks west, cheerful *Restaurant Dacquois* (*48 rue d'Espagne)* serves juicy sandwiches from 12FF and has a great-value 65FF *menu*.

The central market, *Les Halles* (*quai Amiral Jauréguiberry)* on the west side of the Nive River, is open every morning except Sunday.

Entertainment

The greatest concentration of pubs and bars is in Petit Bayonne, especially along rue Pannecau and quai Galuperie. *La Pompe* (☎ *05 59 25 48 12, 7 rue des Augustins)*, a lively disco, throbs from 10 pm to dawn, Thursday to Sunday.

Getting There & Away

Bus From place des Basques, ATCRB buses (☎ 05 59 26 06 99) run to St-Jean de Luz (22FF, 40 minutes, 10 daily) with connections for Hendaye (36FF, one hour). Two Transportes Pesa buses run to Irún and San Sebastián in Spain (38FF, 1¾ hours, daily except Sunday).

From the train station car park, RDTL (☎ 05 59 55 17 59) runs services northward into Les Landes. For beaches north of Bayonne, such as Mimizan Plage and Moliets Plage, get off at Vieux Boucau (39FF, 1¼ hours). TPR (☎ 05 59 27 45 98) has three buses daily to Pau (85FF, 2¼ hours).

Bayonne is one of three hubs in southwestern France for Eurolines, whose buses stop in place Charles de Gaulle, opposite the company office (☎ 05 59 59 19 33) at No 3.

Train The train station is just north of Pont St Esprit bridge. TGVs run to/from Paris' Gare Montparnasse (428FF, five hours). Two daily non-TGV trains go overnight to Paris' Gare d'Austerlitz (401FF or 471FF with couchette) in about eight hours.

There's a frequent service to Biarritz (13FF, 10 minutes), St-Jean de Luz (26FF, 25 minutes) and St-Jean Pied de Port (47FF, one hour), plus the Franco-Spanish border towns of Hendaye (37FF, 40 minutes) and Irún (38FF, 45 minutes).

Other destinations include Bordeaux (145FF, 2¼ hours, about 12 daily), Lourdes (126FF, 1¾ hours, six daily) and Pau (82FF, 1¼ hours, eight daily).

BIARRITZ

The classy coastal town of Biarritz (population 30,000), 8km west of Bayonne, has fine beaches and some of Europe's best surfing. Unfortunately, it can be a real budget-buster – consider making it a day trip from Bayonne, as lots of French holiday-makers do. Many surfers camp or stay at one of the two excellent youth hostels – in Anglet (see the Bayonne section) and in Biarritz.

Biarritz' Festival International de Folklore is held in early July.

Orientation & Information

Place Clemenceau, at the heart of Biarritz, is just south of Grande Plage, the main beach. The tourist office (☎ 05 59 22 37 10, fax 05 59 24 14 19, ✉ biarritz.tourisme@

biarritz.tm.fr) is one block east at 1 square d'Ixelles. It publishes *Biarritzcope*, a free monthly guide to what's on. In July and August, it has a branch at the train station.

Check your emails at Génius Informatique, 60 ave Édouard VII (1FF per minute, 50FF an hour).

Things to See & Do

The **Grande Plage**, lined in season with striped bathing tents, stretches from the Casino Bellevue to the stately Hôtel du Palais. North of the hotel is **Plage Miramar** and the 1834 **Phare de Biarritz**. Beyond this lighthouse the superb surfing beaches of **Anglet** extend for 4km (take bus No 9 from place Clemenceau).

The **Musée de la Mer**, Biarritz' sea museum, is on Pointe Atalaye overlooking **Rocher de la Vierge**, an islet, reached by a short footbridge, which offers sweeping coastal views. The museum (45/30FF) has a 24-tank aquarium plus seal and shark pools.

Places to Stay

Camping *Biarritz Camping* (☎ 05 59 23 00 12, 28 rue d'Harcet), open June to late September, is about 3km south-west of the town centre. Camping costs 105FF for two people and tent. Take bus No 9 to the Biarritz Camping stop.

Hostel For Biarritz' *Auberge de Jeunesse* (05 59 41 76 00, fax 05 59 41 76 07, ℮ aubergejeune.biarritz@wanadoo.fr, 8 rue Chiquito de Cambo), follow the railway westward from the train station for 800m. B&B is 85FF and half-board, 120FF.

The otherwise expensive *Hôtel Barnetche* (☎ 05 59 24 22 25, fax 05 59 24 98 71, 5 ave Charles Floquet) has dorm bunks for 100FF.

Hotels Nowhere is cheap in Biarritz, but prices drop by up to 25% in the low season. In the Vieux Port area, trim *Hôtel Palym* (☎ 05 59 24 16 56, 7 rue du Port Vieux) has singles/doubles with toilet at 170/220FF (290FF with bathroom). *Hôtel Atlantic* (☎ 05 59 24 34 08, 10 rue du Port Vieux) has singles/doubles with washbasin for 195/215FF and doubles/triples/quads with bathroom at 295/330/350FF.

The attractive *Hôtel Etche-Gorria* (☎ 05 59 24 00 74, 21 ave du Maréchal Foch) has doubles without/with bathroom for 180/290FF.

Places to Eat

Popular *Le Bistroye* (☎ 05 59 22 01 02, 6 rue Jean Bart) has delicious main dishes between 75FF and 95FF (closed Wednesday evening and all Sunday). Next door, *La Mamounia* (☎ 05 59 24 76 08) doles out couscous from 80FF and other Moroccan specialities from 95FF.

There are quite a few decent little restaurants around Les Halles. At *Bistrot des Halles* (☎ 05 59 24 21 22, 1 rue du Centre), for example, a three-course meal with wine from the chalkboard menu will set you back about 150FF.

The *covered market* off ave Victor Hugo opens 7 am to 1.30 pm daily.

Entertainment

Popular bar areas include the streets around rue du Port Vieux, the covered market area and around place Clemenceau. Two central discos are *Le Caveau* (4 rue Gambetta) and *Le Flamingo*, inside the Casino.

Getting There & Away

Most local STAB buses stop beside the town hall, from where Nos 1 and 2 go to Bayonne's town hall and station.

Biarritz-La Négresse train station is 3km south of the centre and served by bus Nos 2 and 9. SNCF has a town centre office (☎ 05 59 24 00 94) at 13 ave du Maréchal Foch.

AROUND BIARRITZ
St-Jean Pied de Port

The walled Pyrenean town of St-Jean Pied de Port, 53km south-east of Bayonne, was once the last stop in France for pilgrims heading for the Spanish pilgrimage city of Santiago de Compostela. Nowadays it's a popular departure point for latter-day hikers and bikers but can be hideously crowded in summer. The climb to the 17th-century **Citadelle** is worth it for the fine views.

The tourist office (☎ 05 59 37 03 57) is on place Charles de Gaulle. Riverside *Camping Municipal Plaza Berri* (☎ 05 59 37 11 19, ave du Fronton), open Easter to September, charges 42FF for two people and tent. Cheerful *Hôtel des Remparts* (☎ 05 59 37 13 79, 16 place Floquet) has rooms with bathroom from 210FF.

FRANCE

For lunch, *Chez Dédé* (☎ 05 59 37 16 40), just inside the Porte de France, has as many as seven good-value, tasty *menus*, ranging from the modest *menu du routard* at 50FF to the *suggestion du chef* at 135FF.

Half the reason for coming to St-Jean Pied de Port is the scenic train trip from Bayonne (47FF, one hour, up to four daily).

LOURDES

Lourdes (population 15,000) was just a sleepy market town in 1858 when Bernadette Soubirous, a 14-year-old peasant girl, saw the Virgin Mary within a small grotto in a series of 18 visions, later confirmed as bona fide apparitions by the Vatican. Bernadette, who lived out her short life as a nun, was canonised as Ste Bernadette in 1933.

Some five million pilgrims, including many seeking cures for their illnesses, converge on Lourdes annually from all over the world. In counterpoint to the fervent, almost medieval piety of the pilgrims is a tacky display of commercial exuberance.

Orientation & Information

Lourdes' two main east-west streets are rue de la Grotte and, 300m north, blvd de la Grotte. Both lead to the Sanctuaires Notre Dame de Lourdes. The principal north-south thoroughfare connects the train station with place Peyramale and the tourist office (☎ 05 62 42 77 40, fax 05 62 94 60 95, @ lourdes@sudfr.com). The office sells the *Visa Passeport Touristique* (169FF), allowing entry to five museums in Lourdes.

Things to See

The huge religious complex that has grown around the cave where Bernadette saw the Virgin is just west of the town centre. The main Pont St Michel entrance is open from 5 am to midnight.

Major sites include the **Grotte de Massabielle**, where Bernadette had her visions, its walls today worn smooth by the touch of millions of hands; the nearby **pools** in which 400,000 people immerse themselves each year; and the **Basilique du Rosaire** (Basilica of the Rosary). Dress modestly.

From the Sunday before Easter to mid-October, **torch-lit processions** leave at 8.45 pm nightly from Grotte de Massabielle, while the **Procession Eucaristique** (Blessed Sacrament Procession) takes place at 5 pm daily.

Places to Stay

Tiny *Camping de la Poste* (☎ 05 62 94 40 35, 26 rue de Langelle), a few blocks east of the tourist office, opens Easter to mid-October. Charging 15/21FF per person/tent, it also has a few excellent-value rooms with bathroom for 150FF.

Lourdes has plenty of budget hotels. Near the train station, the friendly *Hôtel d'Annecy* (☎ 05 62 94 13 75, 13 ave de la Gare) is open from Easter to October. Singles/doubles/triples/quads with washbasin are 95/152/176/198FF (140/195/215/223FF with bathroom).

In the town centre, *Hôtel St Sylve* (☎/fax 05 62 94 63 48, 9 rue de la Fontaine) has large rooms for 75/140FF (100/160FF with shower). The stylish *Hôtel de la Grotte* (☎ 05 62 94 58 87, fax 05 62 94 20 50, 66 rue de la Grotte) has fine balconies and a gorgeous garden. Its singles/doubles with all mod cons start at 390/420FF. Both these hotels are open April to October.

Places to Eat

Restaurants close early in this pious town; even *McDonald's* (7 place du Marcadal) is slammed shut at 10.30 pm. *Restaurant le Magret* (10 rue des Quatre Frères Soulas), opposite the tourist office, has excellent-value *menus* at 80FF and 150FF. Next door, *La Rose des Sables* specialises in couscous (from 78FF). Both are closed Mondays. The *covered market* is on place du Champ Commun, south of the tourist office.

Getting There & Away

The bus station, down rue Anselme Lacadé east of the covered market, serves regional towns including Pau (32FF, 1¼ hours, four to six daily). SNCF buses to the Pyrenean towns of Cauterets (39FF, one hour, five daily) and Luz-St-Sauveur (40FF, one hour, six daily) leave from the train station's car park.

The train station is 1km east of the sanctuaries. Trains connect Lourdes with many cities including Bayonne (106FF, 1¾ hours, three to four daily), Bordeaux (172FF, 2½ hours, six daily), Pau (39FF, 30 minutes, over 10 daily) and Toulouse (125FF, 2¼ hours, seven daily). There are five TGVs daily to Paris' Gare Montparnasse (478FF, six hours) and one overnight train to Gare d'Austerlitz (409FF, nine hours).

The Dordogne

The Dordogne (Périgord) was one of the cradles of human civilisation, and a number of local caves, including the world-famous Lascaux, are adorned with extraordinary prehistoric paintings. The region is also renowned for its cuisine, which makes ample use of those quintessentially French delicacies, *truffes du Périgord* (black truffles) and *foie gras*, the fatty liver of force-fed geese.

PÉRIGUEUX

Founded over 2000 years ago on a curve in the gentle Isle River, Périgueux (population 33,000) has one of France's best museums of prehistory, the **Musée du Périgord** at 22 cours Tourny (closed Tuesday and holidays). Admission costs 20/10FF.

The old city, known as **Puy St Front**, lies between blvd Michel Montaigne and the Isle River. Périgueux's tourist office (☎ 05 53 53 10 63, fax 05 53 09 02 50, ✉ tourisme .perigueux@perigord.tm.fr) is at 26 place Francheville, next to a fortified, medieval tower called **Tour Mataguerre**.

Places to Stay

The year-round *Barnabé Plage* camping ground (☎ 05 53 53 41 45) is about 2.5km east of the train station along the Isle River. Take bus No 8 to the rue des Bains stop.

About 600m south of the cathedral, *Foyer des Jeunes Travailleurs* (☎ 05 53 53 52 05, rue des Thermes Prolongée), just off blvd Lakanal, charges 73FF for a bed, including breakfast.

Near the train station, there are half-a-dozen inexpensive hotels along rue Denis Papin and rue des Mobiles de Coulm. The cheapest is the family-run, 16-room *Hôtel des Voyageurs* (☎ 05 53 53 17 44, 26 rue Denis Papin), where basic but clean doubles cost only 80FF (100FF with shower). Reception may be closed on weekend afternoons (hours posted). The two-star *Hôtel du Midi et Terminus* (☎ 05 53 53 41 06, fax 05 53 08 19 32, 18 rue Denis Papin) has doubles from 145FF.

Getting There & Away

The bus station (☎ 05 53 08 91 06) is on place Francheville and has buses to Sarlat (50.50FF, 1½ hours, one or two a day) via

the Vézère Valley town of Montignac (35FF, 55 minutes).

The train station (☎ 08 36 35 35 39), on rue Denis Papin (about 1km north-west of the tourist office), is served by local bus Nos 1, 4 and 5. Destinations include Bordeaux (99FF, 1¼ hours), Les Eyzies de Tayac (41FF, 30 minutes, two to four a day), Paris' Gare d'Austerlitz (268FF, four to five hours) and Sarlat (75FF).

SARLAT-LA-CANÉDA

This beautiful town, situated between the Dordogne and Vézère Rivers, is graced by numerous Renaissance-style, 16th- and 17th-century stone buildings. On Saturday mornings there's a colourful market on place de la Liberté and along rue de la République – edible (though seasonal) offerings include truffles, mushrooms, geese and parts thereof.

Sarlat stretches northward for 2km from the train station all the way to the Auberge de Jeunesse. The main drag is known as rue de la République where it passes through the heart-shaped old town. The tourist office (☎ 05 53 59 27 67, fax 05 53 59 19 44, ✉ ot24.sarlat@perigord.tm.fr) occupies the 15th- and 16th-century Hôtel de Maleville on place de la Liberté.

Places to Stay

The modest but friendly, 15-bed *Auberge de Jeunesse* (☎ 05 53 59 47 59, 05 53 30 21 27, 77 ave de Selves) is open from mid-March to mid-November. A bed costs 50FF; small tents can be pitched in the tiny back garden for 30FF a person (5FF more for the first night). Cooking facilities are available. Call ahead to see if there's space.

Doubles start at 250FF at the following two-star places: the seven-room *Hôtel de la Mairie* (☎ 05 53 59 05 71, 13 place de la Liberté), near the tourist office (open from March to December), and the 18-room *Hôtel Les Récollets* (☎ 05 53 31 36 00, fax 05 53 30 32 62, ✉ otelrecol@aol.com, 4 rue Jean-Jacques Rousseau), up an alley just west of rue de la République.

Getting There & Away

There are one or two buses a day (fewer in July and August) from place de la Petite Rigaudie to Périgueux (50.50FF, 1½ hours) via Montignac (35 minutes).

FRANCE

Sarlat's tiny train station (☎ 0836 35 35 39) is linked to Bordeaux (119FF, 2½ hours), Périgueux (75FF) and Les Eyzies de Tayac (47FF, 50 minutes, two a day).

VÉZÈRE VALLEY

Périgord's most important prehistoric sites are about 45km south-east of Périgueux and 20km north-west of Sarlat in the Vézère Valley, mainly between Les Eyzies de Tayac and Montignac. Worthwhile caves not mentioned below include the **Grotte du Grand Roc** and **La Roque St Christophe**. For details on public transport, see Getting There & Away under Périgueux and Sarlat.

Les Eyzies de Tayac

This dull, touristy village offers one of the region's best introductions to prehistory, the **Musée National de Préhistoire** (22/15FF), built into the cliff above the tourist office (closed Tuesday except in July and August). Also of interest is the **Abri Pataud** (28/14FF), an impressive Cro-Magnon rock shelter in the cliff face (closed Monday except in July and August).

The **Grotte de Font de Gaume**, a cave with 230 sophisticated polychrome figures of bison, reindeer and other creatures, and the **Grotte des Combarelles**, decorated with 600 often-superimposed engravings of animals, are 1km and 3km respectively north-east of Les Eyzies de Tayac on the D47. Home to some of the finest prehistoric art on public display, they are closed on Wednesday and charge 35/23FF for a tour – reserve in advance on ☎ 05 53 06 86 00.

Les Eyzies' tourist office (☎ 05 53 06 97 05, fax 05 53 06 90 79) is on the town's main street (closed on Sunday from October to February).

The 14-room *Hôtel des Falaises (☎ 05 53 06 97 35)*, almost across the street from the Abri Pataud, has unremarkable doubles with shower and toilet starting at 170FF.

Montignac

Montignac, 25km north-east of Les Eyzies, achieved sudden fame thanks to the **Lascaux Cave**, discovered in 1940 by four teenage boys who, it is said, were out searching for their dog. The cave's main room and a number of steep galleries are decorated with 15,000-year-old figures of wild oxen, deer, horses, reindeer and other creatures depicted in vivid reds, blacks, yellows and browns.

Lascaux has long been closed to the public to prevent deterioration, but **Lascaux II** is a meticulous replica of the original. Its main gallery opens 10 am to 12.30 pm and 1.30 to 6 pm daily (until 8 pm in July and August). There's no midday closure from April to October; and it's closed Monday from November to March and for three weeks in January. The last tour begins about an hour before closing time. Tickets, which from April to October are sold *only* in Montignac (next to the tourist office), cost 50FF, marginally more if you'd also like to visit **Le Thot** (☎ 05 53 50 70 44), a prehistoric theme park with a museum and mock-ups of Palaeolithic huts – it's all very *Flintstones* – that's about 5km south-west of town.

The 10-room *Hôtel de la Grotte (☎ 05 53 51 80 48, fax 05 53 51 05 96, place Tourny)* is 200m east of Montignac's tourist office and has very comfortable doubles/triples for 165/195FF.

Burgundy & the Rhône

DIJON

Dijon (population 230,000), the prosperous capital of the dukes of Burgundy for almost 500 years, is one of France's most appealing provincial cities. Graced by elegant medieval and Renaissance residences, it has a distinctly youthful air, in part because of the major university situated there.

Dijon is a good starting point for visits to the vineyards of the Côte d'Or, arguably the greatest wine-growing region in the world (don't mention this oenological opinion when you're in Bordeaux).

Orientation & Information

Dijon's main thoroughfare runs eastward from the train station to Église St Michel: ave Maréchal Foch links the train station with the tourist office; rue de la Liberté continues eastward past the Palais des Ducs. The social centre of Dijon is place François Rude, a popular hang-out in good weather.

The tourist office (☎ 03 80 44 11 44, fax 03 80 42 18 83) is 300m east of the train station at place Darcy (open daily). The annexe, at 34 rue des Forges, faces the north side of the Palais des Ducs (closed Sunday and, from mid-October to April, on Saturday). Web site: www.ot-dijon.fr.

The main post office, at place Grangier, has a Cyberposte.

Things to See

Dijon's major museums are open daily except Tuesday, with the exception of the Musée National Magnin, which is open daily except Monday. Except where noted, entry is free for under-18s and students and, on the first Sunday of the month, for everyone. La Clé de la Ville combination ticket (45FF), available at the tourist office, gives access to all of Dijon's museums and to one of the tourist office's tours.

The **Palais des Ducs et des États de Bourgogne** (Palace of the Dukes and States General of Burgundy), remodelled in the neoclassical style in the 17th and 18th centuries, was once the home of the powerful dukes of Burgundy. The front looks out onto the semicircular **place de la Libération**, a gracious, arcaded public square laid out in 1686. The east wing houses the **Musée des Beaux-Arts**, one of the richest and most renowned fine-arts museums in France. Hours are 10 am to 6 pm (22FF).

Some of Dijon's finest medieval and Renaissance town houses are just north of the Palais des Ducs along **rue Verrerie** and **rue des Forges**, Dijon's main street until the 18th century. The splendid Flamboyant Gothic **Hôtel Chambellan** (1490) at 34 rue des Forges now houses the tourist office annexe. There's some remarkable vaulting at the top of the spiral staircase.

Many of Burgundy's great historical figures are buried in the Burgundian-Gothic **Cathédrale St Bénigne**, built in the late 13th century. **Église St Michel**, begun in 1499, is a Flamboyant Gothic church with an impressive Renaissance facade added in 1661. The unusual **Église Notre Dame** was built in the Burgundian-Gothic style during the first half of the 13th century. The three tiers of the extraordinary facade are decorated with dozens of false gargoyles.

Next to the cathedral, at 5 rue du Docteur Maret, is the fascinating **Musée Archéologique**, which contains a number of rare Celtic and Gallo-Roman artefacts (14FF).

Just off place de la Libération, the **Musée National Magnin**, which is housed in a mid-17th-century residence at 4 rue des Bons Enfants, contains 2000 works of art assembled about a century ago (16/12FF).

Places to Stay

The two-star **Camping du Lac** (☎ 03 80 43 54 72, 3 blvd Chanoine Kir), open from April to mid-October, is 1.4km west of the train station behind the psychiatric hospital. By bus, take No 12 (towards Fontaine d'Ouche) to the Hôpital des Chartreux stop; services stop at around 8 pm.

The 260-bed **Centre de Rencontres Internationales et de Séjour de Dijon** (☎ 03 80 72 95 20, fax 03 80 70 00 61, 1 blvd Champollion) is 2.5km north-east of the centre. Dorm beds start at 72FF, including breakfast; a room for three is 140FF (no-breakfast). Take bus No 5 (towards Épirey) from place Grangier; at night take line A to the Épirey Centre Commercial stop.

Three blocks south of rue de la Liberté, the friendly, 24-room **Hôtel Monge** (☎ 03 80 30 55 41, fax 03 80 30 30 15, 20 rue Monge) has doubles/quads starting at 135/240FF. Hall showers are 15FF. **Hôtel Confort** (☎ 03 80 30 37 47, fax 03 80 30 03 43, 12 rue Jules Mercier), on a narrow street off rue de la Liberté, has plain doubles with shower from 180FF.

Just north of Église St Michel, the two-star **Hôtel Le Chambellan** (☎ 03 80 67 12 67, fax 03 80 38 00 39, 92 rue Vannerie) occupies a 17th-century building and has a rustic feel. Comfortable doubles start at 140FF. Three blocks to the north-east, **Hôtel du Lycée** (☎ 03 80 67 12 35, fax 03 80 63 84 69, 28 rue du Lycée) has ordinary doubles from 120FF.

Places to Eat

For a splurge, **La Toison d'Or** (☎ 03 80 30 73 52, 18 rue Ste Anne) serves up traditional Burgundian and French cuisine in a rustic medieval setting. Two-/three- course menus are 215/270FF (125/170FF for lunch); closed Sunday. **Chez Nous** (8 impasse Quentin), just down the alley from 6 rue Quentin and the Halles du Marché, serves a copious, Burgundian plat du jour (60FF) from noon to 2.15 pm.

Generous portions of excellent tajines and couscous (70FF to 115FF) are on offer

FRANCE

at *Restaurant Marrakech (20 rue Monge)*; closed Monday lunch. Breton crepes are the speciality of *Crêperie Kerine (36 rue Berbisey)*; there are Brazilian, Tunisian and Egyptian places on the same street at Nos 42, 44 and 116.

For cheap student eats, *Restaurant Universitaire Maret (3 rue du Docteur Maret)* opens on weekdays and one weekend a month from 11.40 am to 1.15 pm and 6.40 to 8 pm (closed during university holidays). Tickets (14.90FF for students) are sold on the ground floor at lunchtime (weekdays only) and during Monday dinner.

The cheapest place to buy picnic food is the *Halles du Marché*, a 19th-century covered market 150m north of rue de la Liberté that opens until 1 pm on Tuesday, Thursday, Friday and Saturday. The *Prisunic* supermarket *(11-13 rue Piron)* opens daily except Sunday.

Entertainment

Discos include the converted-factory-style *L'An-Fer (8 rue Marceau)*, open 11 pm to 5 am (closed on Monday and, from mid-July to mid-September, on Tuesday and Wednesday). Entry costs 50FF or 60FF from Friday to Sunday, 40FF the rest of the week (25FF without a drink). Things start to take off at around 1 am.

Coco-Loco (18 ave Garibaldi) is a friendly and hugely popular bar that attracts legions of students, especially late at night from Thursday to Saturday. Hours are 6 pm to 2 am (closed Sunday and Monday).

Getting There & Away

Buses link the bus station (attached to the train station) with some of the wine-making towns along the Côte d'Or (Beaune included).

The train station (Gare Dijon-Ville; ☎ 0836 35 35 39), has TGV services to/from Paris' Gare de Lyon (227FF to 275FF, 1¾ hours). There are non-TGV trains to Lyon (133FF to 153FF, 1½ to two hours) and Nice (380FF, eight hours).

Getting Around

Dijon's extensive urban bus network is run by STRD (☎ 03 80 30 60 90). Bus lines are known by their number and the name of the terminus station. In the city centre, seven different lines stop along rue de la Liberté, and five more have stops around place

Grangier. A Forfait Journée ticket, valid all day, costs 16FF and is available at the STRD's office at place Grangier (closed on Sunday).

AROUND DIJON

Burgundy's finest vintages come from the vine-covered Côte d'Or, the eastern slopes of the limestone escarpment running for about 60km south from Dijon. The northern section is known as the Côte de Nuits, the southern section as the Côte de Beaune. The tourist offices in Dijon and Beaune can provide details on *caves* (wine cellars) that offer tours and dégustation.

The Beaune tourist office handles ticketing for year-round, two-hour minibus tours of the Côte (190FF).

Beaune

The attractive town of Beaune (population 22,000), a major wine-making centre about 40km south of Dijon, makes an excellent day trip from Dijon. Its most famous historical site is the **Hôtel-Dieu**, France's most opulent medieval charity hospital (entry is 32/25FF). The tourist office (☎ 03 80 26 21 30, fax 03 80 26 21 39), 1km west of the train station, is opposite the entrance to the Hôtel-Dieu (open daily).

At the **Marché aux Vins**, on rue Nicolas Rolin 30m south of the tourist office, you can sample 18 wines for 50FF. The best reds are near the exit. **Patriarche Père et Fils** at 6 rue du Collège has one of the largest wine cellars in Burgundy; one-hour visits that include the sampling of 13 wines begin from 10.30 am (9.30 am in the warm months) to 11 am and 2 to 5 pm.

Places to Stay & Eat The best deal in town is the 12-room *Hôtel Rousseau (☎ 03 80 22 13 59, 11 place Madeleine)*. Run by a friendly older woman, it has large, old-fashioned singles/doubles from 140/185FF; a room for five is 380FF.

Caves Madeleine (8 rue du Faubourg Madeleine) is a cosy wine bar with family-style Burgundian *menus* for 69FF and 115FF (closed on Thursday and Sunday). *Restaurant Maxime (3 place Madeleine)* offers reasonably priced Burgundian cuisine in a rustic but elegant dining room; *menus* range from 76FF to 150FF (closed Sunday night, Monday and, except from

June to September, on Thursday night). There are a number of other restaurants nearby on rue du Faubourg Madeleine.

A good choice for a splurge is the refined **Restaurant Bernard & Martine Morillon** *(31 rue Maufoux)* which has traditional French *menus* for 180FF to 480FF (closed Tuesday at noon, Monday and in January).

Getting There & Away Beaune is linked to Dijon by both trains (38FF, 20 to 25 minutes) and Transco buses (40FF, one hour); the latter stop at a number of wine villages en route.

LYON

The grand city of Lyon (population 415,500) is part of a prosperous urban area of almost two million people, France's second-largest conurbation. Founded by the Romans over 2000 years ago, it has spent the last 500 years as a commercial, industrial and banking powerhouse. Lyon sports outstanding museums, a dynamic cultural life, an important university, lively pedestrian malls and such excellent cuisine that it's ranked among France's great gastronomic capitals – for people of all budgets.

Orientation & Information

The city centre is on the Presqu'île, a peninsula bounded by the Rhône and Saône Rivers. Place Bellecour is 1km south of place des Terreaux and 1km north of place Carnot, which is next to one of Lyon's train stations, Gare de Perrache. The other station, Gare de la Part-Dieu, is 2km east of the Presqu'île in a commercial district called La Part-Dieu. Vieux Lyon (old Lyon) sprawls the Saône's west bank.

The tourist office (☎ 04 72 77 69 69, fax 04 78 42 04 32, ✆ lyoncvb@lyon-france .com), place Bellecour, opens 10 am to 6 or 7 pm. Its Web site at www.lyon-france.com is worth a surf. The same building houses an SNCF reservations desk (closed Sunday). Thomas Cook exchange offices grace both train stations.

Check email at the Centre Régional Information Jeunesse (☎ 04 72 77 00 66), 9 quai des Célestins. It charges 10FF for the initial subscription, then 10FF for 30 minutes. The travel bookshop, Raconte-Moi La Terre (☎ 04 78 92 60 20, ✆ internet@ raconte-moi.com), at 38 rue Thomassin, has

a cybercafe where the rates are 60/130FF for one/three hours online.

Vieux Lyon

The old city, whose cobbled streets form a picturesque ensemble of restored **medieval and Renaissance houses**, lies at the base of Fourvière hill. Equally historic buildings line rue du Bœuf, rue Juiverie (spot the bugs on the window ledges), rue des Trois Maries and rue St Jean.

The mainly Romanesque **Cathédrale St Jean** has a Flamboyant Gothic facade and a 14th-century astronomical clock in the north transept.

The **Musée Gadagne** on place du Petit Collège is split into the Musée de la Marionnette, featuring puppets, and the Musée Historique, which paints the history of Lyon. Both are closed Tuesday (25/13FF).

Fourvière

Two thousand years ago, the Romans built the city of Lugdunum on Fourvière's slopes. Today the hill – topped by the Tour Métallique (1893), a sort of stunted Eiffel Tower – offers spectacular views of Lyon, its two rivers and – on clear days – Mont Blanc. The easiest way to the top is to ride the funicular railway (between 6 am and 10 pm) from place Édouard Commette in Vieux Lyon. Use a bus/metro ticket or buy a 12.50FF funicular return.

The excellent **Musée de la Civilisation Gallo-Romaine**, 17 rue Cléberg, is worth seeing even if you're not into Roman history (closed Monday and Tuesday; 20/10FF). The two neighbouring, rebuilt **Roman amphitheatres** host rock and classical music concerts during the Les Nuits de Fourvière festival, held mid-June to mid-September.

Presqu'île

The centrepiece of **place des Terreaux** is a monumental 19th-century fountain by Bartholdi, sculptor of New York's *Statue of Liberty*. Fronting the square is the **town hall**, built in 1655 but given its present facade in 1702. Its south side is dominated by Lyon's outstanding **Musée des Beaux-Arts** which showcases sculptures and paintings from every period of European art (closed Monday and Tuesday; 25/13FF).

The contemporary **statue of a giant on roller skates** on place Louis Pradel, north-east

FRANCE

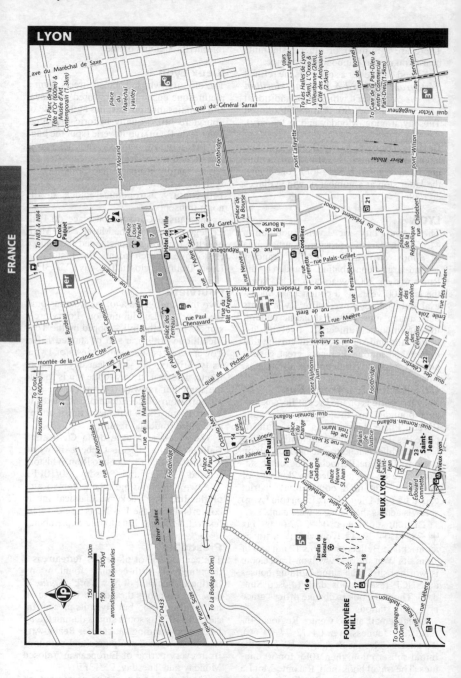

LYON

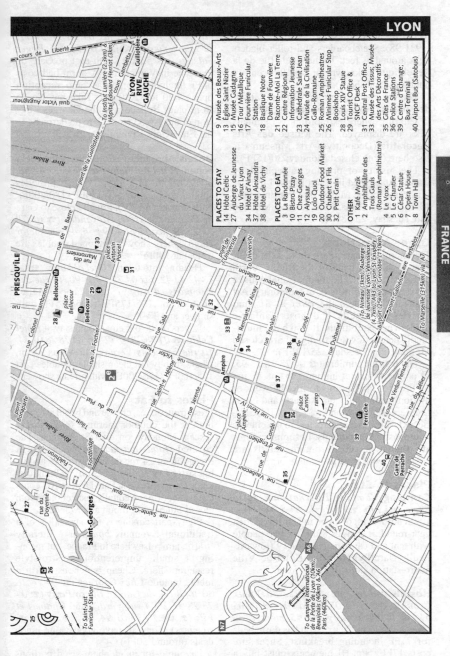

LYON

LYON RIVE GAUCHE

PRESQU'ÎLE

Saint-Georges

FRANCE

PLACES TO STAY
14 Hôtel Celtic
27 Auberge de Jeunesse du Vieux Lyon
34 Hôtel d'Ainay
37 Hôtel Alexandra
38 Hôtel de Vichy

PLACES TO EAT
3   La Randonnée
10 Bistro Pizay
11 Chez Georges
12 Alyssaar
19 Lolo Quoi
20 Outdoor Food Market
30 Chabert et Fils
32 Petit Grain

OTHER
1   Kafé Myzik
2   Amphithéâtre des Trois Gauls (Roman Amphitheatre)
4   Le Voxx
5   Le Chantier
6   César Statue
7   Opéra House
8   Town Hall
9   Musée des Beaux-Arts
13 Église Saint Nizier
15 Musée Gadagne
16 Tour Métallique
17 Fourvière Funicular Station
18 Basilique Notre Dame de Fourvière
21 Raconte-Moi La Terre
22 Centre Régional Information Jeunesse
23 Cathédrale Saint Jean
24 Musée de la Civilisation Gallo-Romaine
25 Roman Amphitheatres
26 Minimes Funicular Stop
28 Bookshop
29 Louis XIV Statue
31 Tourist Office & SNCF Desk
33 Central Post Office
35 Musée des Tissus; Musée des Arts Décoratifs
35 Gîtes de France
36 Police Stations
39 Centre d'Échange; Bus Terminal
40 Airport Bus (Satobus)

of the **opera house**, was sculpted from scrap metal by Marseilles-born sculptor César (1921-98). Skateboarders and roller bladers buzz around its feet. To the south, **rue de la République** is known for its 19th-century buildings (and shops).

The Lyonnais are proud of their **Musée des Tissus** (Textiles Museum) at 34 rue de la Charité, where extraordinary Lyonnais silks are displayed. The **Musée des Arts Décoratifs** (Decorative Arts Museum) is also here (both closed Monday; 30/15FF).

The history of printing, a technology firmly established in Lyon in the 1480s, is illustrated by the **Musée de l'Imprimerie** at 13 rue de la Poulaillerie (closed Monday and Tuesday; 25/13FF).

Other Attractions

The main city park, **Parc de la Tête d'Or**, sits on the east bank of the Rhône, north of La Part-Dieu. The inspirational **Musée d'Art Contemporain** (Contemporary Art Museum), borders the river at 81 quai Charles de Gaulle and hosts fantastic modern art exhibitions. It also has a multimedia centre devoted to digital art (closed Monday and Tuesday; 25/13FF).

The **Institut Lumière** (☎ 04 78 78 18 95, ✆ contact@institut-lumiere.org) at 25 rue du Premier-Film brings to life the work of motion-picture pioneers Auguste and Louis Lumière (closed Monday; 25/20FF). Classic and cult films are screened in the cinema in the institute's grounds. In summer, films are shown outside. Program details are posted at www.institut-lumiere.org.

Places to Stay

Camping *Camping International de la Porte de Lyon* (☎ 04 78 35 64 55) is some 10km north-west of Lyon in Dardilly. Open year-round, it charges 80FF for two people with tent and car. Bus No 3 or 19 (towards Ecully-Dardilly) from the Hôtel de Ville metro station stops right out front.

Hostels *Auberge de Jeunesse du Vieux Lyon* (☎ 04 78 15 05 50, fax 04 78 15 05 51, ✆ lyon@fuaj.org, 40-45 montée du Chemin Neuf) in Vieux Lyon has dorm beds for 71FF including breakfast. Sheet hire costs 17FF. Non-HI members must buy a welcome stamp for 19FF. Reception stays open 24 hours.

Auberge de Jeunesse Lyon-Vénissieux (☎ 04 78 76 39 23, fax 04 78 77 51 11, ✆ lyonvenissieux@fuaj.fr, 51 rue Roger Salengro) is 5.5km south-east of Gare de Perrache in Vénissieux. A dorm bed costs 68FF including breakfast and reception opens 7.30 to 12.30 am. Take bus No 35 from place Bellecour to the Georges Lévy stop or bus No 53 from Gare de Perrache to the États-Unis-Viviani stop.

Hotels Absolutely affordable is the rock-bottom *Hôtel de Vichy* (☎ 04 78 37 42 58, 60bis rue de la Charité) which provides singles/doubles for 140/150FF (180/200FF with shower and TV). Equally close to Gare de Perrache is *Hôtel Alexandra* (☎ 04 78 37 75 79, fax 04 72 40 94 34, 49 rue Victor Hugo) where shower-equipped doubles are a steal at 190FF.

Heading into town, *Hôtel d'Ainay* (☎ 04 78 42 43 42, fax 04 72 77 51 90, 14 rue des Remparts d'Ainay) has basic singles/doubles for 165/175FF (205/215FF with shower and TV).

Lovers of the old city should stay at *Hôtel Celtic* (☎ 04 78 28 01 12, fax 04 78 28 01 34, 10 rue François Vernay), in Vieux Lyon, where shabby but clean singles/doubles cost 135/160FF (170/200FF with private shower).

Places to Eat

Fresh fruit, olives, cheese and bread are piled high at the outdoor morning *food market* (except Monday) on quai St Antoine. The covered *food market* in the northern Presqu'île at 24 rue de la Martinière and its big sister *Les Halles de Lyon*, walking distance from Gare de la Part-Dieu at 102 cours Lafayette, offer an equally tasty choice (both closed Sunday afternoon and Monday).

Piggy-part cuisine is the speciality of a traditional Lyonnais *bouchon* – literally 'traffic jam' elsewhere in France, but meaning a small, unpretentious bistro-style restaurant here. Cheap bouchons worth a nibble include *Chez Georges* (☎ 04 78 28 30 46, 8 rue du Garet); *Bistro Pizay* (☎ 04 78 28 37 26, 4 rue Verdi); and *Chabert et Fils* (☎ 04 78 37 01 94, 11 rue des Marronniers). They all have good-value lunch deals (around 50FF).

Favoured for its elephant-sized portions is *La Randonnée* (☎ 04 78 27 86 81, 4 rue Terme) which has vegetarian platters

FRANCE

(50FF), lunchtime/evening formules (from 32/38FF) and *menus* (from 49/65FF).

Terraces, great for eating and lounging in the sun, include *Campagne* (☎ *04 78 36 73 85, 20 rue Cardinal Gerlier*) atop Fourvière hill and any one of the *cafes* on place des Terreaux. On touristy rue Mercière *Lolo Quoi* (☎ *04 72 77 60 90, 40-44 rue Mercière*) is a popular and chic spot, dressed in funky furnishings and not overly wallet-crunching if you stick to a tasty bowl of pasta (50FF).

Syrian *Alyssaar* (☎ *04 78 29 57 66, 29 rue du Bât d'Argent*) has spicy *menus* for 78FF, 87FF and 105FF, while Vietnamese *Petit Grain* (☎ *04 72 41 77 85, 19 rue de la Charité*) near the Textile Museum sports salads, meats and vegetarian platters from 43FF. Rue Ste-Marie des Terreaux and rue Ste-Catherine are lined with ethnic quick-eating joints.

Entertainment

Rue Ste-Catherine is cluttered with late-night bars.

At funky *Le Chantier* (☎ *04 78 39 05 56*) at No 20 clubbers slide down bum-first – courtesy of a metal slide – to the basement dance floor. On the Saône's left bank, *Le Voxx* (☎ *04 78 28 33 87, 1 rue d'Algérie*) lures live bands and a boisterous drinking crowd. On the right bank, *La Bodéga* (☎ *04 78 29 42 35, 35 quai Pierre Scize*) also rocks till late.

Local bands play at *Kafé Myzik* (☎ *04 72 07 04 26, 20 montée St-Sébastien*), a hole-in-the-wall club; at *Ninkasi* (☎ *04 72 76 89 09, 267 rue Marcel Mérieux*), a micro-brewery next to the football stadium which serves its own beer and runs a great-value food bar; and at *L'Oxxo* (☎ *04 78 93 62 03, 7 ave Albert Einstein*), a student bar in Villeurbanne which sports a decor of recycled aeroplanes and cable cars.

Getting There & Away

Bus Most intercity buses depart from the terminal under the Centre d'Échange, next to Gare de Perrache. Timetables are available from the TCL information office (☎ 04 78 71 70 00), on the middle level of the Centre d'Échange. Tickets are sold by the driver. Buses for destinations west of Lyon (☎ 04 78 43 40 74) leave from outside the Gorge de Loup metro station.

Train You can travel between Lyon's two stations – Gare de Perrache and Gare de la Part-Dieu – by metro (change at Charpennes) or by SNCF train.

Lyon has direct rail links to all parts of France and Europe. Trains to/from Paris (318FF to 398FF, two hours) use the capital's Gare de Lyon.

Getting Around

Lyon's metro system, run by TCL, has four lines (A to D), which run 5 am to midnight. Tickets (8FF) are valid for one-way travel on buses, trolleybuses, the funicular and the metro for one hour after time-stamping. A carnet of 10 tickets is 68FF. The Ticket Liberté (24FF, allows one day of unlimited travel) and the Ticket Liberté 2h (24FF, two hours of unlimited travel from 9 am to 4 pm) can be bought at metro ticket machines, or at the TCL information office (☎ 04 78 71 70 00) in the Centre d'Échange; at 43 rue de la République; or at Vieux Lyon metro station.

The French Alps

The French Alps, where craggy, snow-bound peaks soar above fertile, green valleys, is one of the most awe-inspiring mountain ranges in the world. In summer, visitors can take advantage of hundreds of kilometres of hiking trails and engage in all sorts of warm-weather sporting activities. In winter, the area's ski resorts attract enthusiasts from around the world.

CHAMONIX

The town of Chamonix sits in a valley surrounded by the most spectacular scenery in the French Alps. The area is almost Himalayan in its grandeur: deeply crevassed glaciers many kilometres long ooze down the valleys between the icy peaks and pinnacles around Mont Blanc (4807m), the highest mountain in the Alps.

There are some 330km of hiking trails in the Chamonix area. In winter, the valley offers superb skiing, with dozens of ski lifts.

Information

The tourist office (☎ 04 50 53 00 24, fax 04 50 53 58 90, ✉ info@chamonix.com) at place du Triangle de l'Amitié, opposite

FRANCE

place de l'Église, opens daily. Useful brochures on ski-lift hours and costs, refuges, camping grounds and parapente (paraskiing) schools are available. In winter it sells ski passes, valid for bus transport and all the ski lifts in the valley (except Lognan-Les Grands Montets).

The Maison de la Montagne, near the tourist office at 109 place de l'Église, houses the Office de Haute Montagne (2nd floor, ☎ 04 50 53 22 08), which has information and maps for walkers and mountaineers (closed Sunday).

You can log onto the Internet at the busy cyBar (☎ 04 50 53 64 80), 81 rue Whymper, or at the sometimes noisy Santa Fe Bar & Restaurant (☎ 04 50 53 99 14), 148 rue du Docteur Paccard. Both charge 1FF per minute.

Aiguille du Midi

The Aiguille du Midi (3842m) is a lone spire of rock 8km from the summit of Mont Blanc. The *téléphérique* from Chamonix to the Aiguille du Midi (200FF) is the highest and probably scariest cable car in the world – especially the final leg almost vertically up to the Aiguille; the views in all directions are truly awesome and should not be missed. In general, visibility is best early in the morning.

Between April and September, you can usually take a second cable car – depending on the winds – from the Aiguille du Midi across the glacier to **Pointe Helbronner** (3466m) and down to the Italian ski resort of **Courmayeur** (an extra 98FF return). A ride from Chamonix to the cable car's halfway point, **Plan de l'Aiguille** (2308m) – an excellent place to start hikes in summer – costs 66/85FF one way/return.

The téléphérique operates all year from 8 am to 3.45 pm (from 6 am to 4.45 pm in July and August). To avoid long queues, arrive before 9.30 am when the buses start to arrive. You can make advance reservations 24 hours a day by calling ☎ 04 50 53 40 00.

Le Brévent

Le Brévent (2525m), the highest peak on the west side of the valley, is known for its great views of Mont Blanc. It can be reached from Chamonix by a combination of *télécabine* (gondola) and téléphérique (☎ 04 50 53 13 18) for 57/84FF single/return.

Services run 8 am (9 am in winter) to 5 pm (an hour or so earlier in winter). Numerous hiking trails, including routes back to the valley, can be picked up at Le Brévent or at the cable car's midway station, **Planpraz** (1999m; 48/58FF one way/return).

Mer de Glace

The heavily crevassed Mer de Glace (Sea of Ice), the second-largest glacier in the Alps, is 14km long, 1950m across at its widest point and up to 400m deep. It has become a popular tourist destination thanks to a cogwheel railway, which has an upper terminus at an altitude of 1913m.

The train, which runs year-round (weather permitting), leaves from Gare du Montenvers (☎ 04 50 53 12 54) in Chamonix. Tickets cost 42/79FF single/return. A combined ticket valid for the train, the gondola to the ice cave (Grotte de la Mer de Glace; 15FF return) and entry to the cave (14FF) costs 116FF. The ride takes 20 minutes each way.

Activities

Hiking In late spring and summer (mid-June to October), the Chamonix area has some of the most spectacular hiking trails anywhere in the Alps. The combined map and guide, *Carte des Sentiers du Mont Blanc* (Mountain Trail Map; 75FF), is ideal for straightforward day hikes. The best map of the area is the 1:25,000 scale IGN map (No 3630OT) entitled *Chamonix-Massif du Mont Blanc* (58FF).

Skiing & Snowboarding The Chamonix area has 160km of marked ski runs, 42km of cross-country trails and 64 ski lifts of all sorts. Count on paying around 39/220FF a day/week for regular skis or boots. Ski Location Guy Perillat (☎ 04 50 53 54 76) at 138 rue des Moulins is open daily and also rents out snowboards (100/150FF a day without/with boots or 590/690FF a week). Cross-country skis are available from Le Grand Bi (☎ 04 50 53 14 16) at 240 ave du Bois du Bouchet.

Places to Stay

Camping There are some 13 camp sites in the Chamonix region. In general, camping costs 25FF per person and 12FF to 26FF for a tent site. *L'Île des Barrats* (☎ *04 50 53 51*

44), open May to September, is near the base of the Aiguille du Midi cable car. The three-star *Les Deux Glaciers (☎ 04 50 53 15 84, route des Tissières)* in Les Bossons, 3km south of Chamonix, is closed mid-November to mid-December. To get there, take the train to Les Bossons or Chamonix Bus to the Tremplin-le-Mont stop.

Refuges Most mountain refuges, which cost 90FF to 100FF a night, are accessible to hikers and are generally open mid-June to mid-September.

The easier-to-reach refuges include one at *Plan de l'Aiguille (☎ 04 50 53 55 60)* at 2308m, the intermediate stop on the Aiguille du Midi cable car, and another at *La Flégère (☎ 04 50 53 06 13)* at 1877m. It is advisable to call ahead to reserve a place, especially in July and August.

Hostels The *Chalet Ski Station (☎ 04 50 53 20 25, 6 route des Moussoux)* is a gîte d'étape next to the Planpraz/Le Brévent télécabine station. Beds cost 60FF a night. It's closed 10 May to 20 June and 20 September to 20 December.

The *Auberge de Jeunesse (☎ 04 50 53 14 52, fax 04 50 55 92 34, ✉ chamonix@ fuaj.org, 127 montée Jacques Balmat)* is a few kilometres south-west of Chamonix in Les Pélerins.

By bus, take the Chamonix-Les Houches line and get off at the Pélerins École stop. Beds are 74FF. The hostel is closed October to mid-December.

The *GîteVagabond (☎ 04 50 53 15 43, fax 04 53 68 21, 365 ave Ravanel le Rouge)* is a neat little hostelry with a guest kitchen, bar/restaurant with Internet access, barbecue area, climbing wall and parking. A bed in a four- or six-person dorm costs 70FF a night or 149FF for half-board.

Hotels The lively *Hôtel El Paso (☎ 04 50 53 64 20, fax 04 50 53 64 22, 37 impasse des Rhododendrons)* is great value. Doubles with shared bath in the low/high season cost 166/224FF, triples are 236/306FF. In summer a dorm bed costs 90FF.

The *Hôtel Valaisanne (☎ 04 50 53 17 98, 454 ave Ravanel le Rouge)* is a small, family-owned place 900m south-west of Chamonix town centre. It has doubles for 170/270FF in the low/high season.

Places to Eat

There are restaurants offering pizzas, pastas and fondue in the streets leading off from place Balmat. Handy *Poco Loco (47 rue du Docteur Paccard)* has pizzas from 33FF to 45FF and *menus* from 50FF. It also serves great hot sandwiches (from 23FF), sweet crepes (from 8FF), and burgers to eat in or take away.

Abuzz with hungry diners looking for salads, pizzas, vegetarian platters and Tex-Mex specialities is the sometimes crowded *Santa Fe (148 rue du Docteur Paccard)*, a popular eating as well as meeting place.

The *Super U* supermarket is at 117 rue Joseph Vallot.

Getting There & Away

Bus Chamonix's bus station is next to the train station. SAT Autocar (☎ 04 50 53 01 15) has buses to Annecy (95.30FF), Geneva (170FF, two hours) and Grenoble (161FF). There are no services to Italy since the closing of the Mont Blanc tunnel in March 1999.

Train The narrow-gauge train line from St Gervais-Le Fayet (20km west of Chamonix) to Martigny, Switzerland (42km north of Chamonix) stops at 11 towns in the Chamonix Valley. You have to change trains at Châtelard or Vallorcine on the Swiss border. From St Gervais there are trains to destinations all over France.

Chamonix-Mont Blanc train station (☎ 04 50 53 00 44) is on the east side of town. Major destinations include Paris' Gare de Lyon (469FF, six to seven hours), Lyon (186FF, 4½ hours) and Geneva (100FF, 2½ hours via St Gervais).

Getting Around

Bus transport in the valley is handled by Chamonix Bus (☎ 04 50 53 05 55), with an office at place de l'Église opposite the tourist office.

Between April and October, Le Grand Bi (☎ 04 50 53 14 16), 240 ave du Bois du Bouchet, rents three- and 10-speed bikes for 65FF a day, mountain bikes for 100FF (closed Sunday).

ANNECY

Annecy (population 50,350), situated at the northern tip of the incredibly blue Lac d'Annecy, is the perfect place to spend a relaxing

FRANCE

holiday. Walking around, taking in the lake, flowers and quaint buildings, is the essence of a visit to Annecy.

Orientation & Information

The train and bus stations are 500m north-west of the old city, which is centred around the canalised Thiou River. The modern town centre is between the main post office and the Centre Bonlieu complex. The lake town of Annecy-le-Vieux is just east of Annecy.

The tourist office (☎ 04 50 45 00 33, fax 04 50 51 87 20, ✆ ancytour@cybercable .tm.fr) is in the Centre Bonlieu north of place de la Libération.

The Emailerie (☎ 04 50 10 18 91, ✆ message@emailerie.com), on faubourg de Annonciades, opens 10 am to 10 pm (June to October) and 2 to 10 pm (closed Sunday) at other times of the year. Access costs 25/45FF per half- hour/hour.

Things to See & Do

The Vieille Ville, an area of narrow streets on either side of the Canal du Thiou, retains much of its 17th-century appearance despite recent gentrification. On the island in the middle, the Palais de l'Isle (a former prison) houses the Musée d'Histoire d'Annecy et de la Haute-Savoie (closed Tuesday; 20/5FF).

The Musée d'Annecy (☎ 04 50 33 87 30), housed in the 16th-century Château d'Annecy overlooking the town, puts on innovative temporary exhibitions and has a permanent collection of local craftwork (closed Tuesday; 30/10FF). The climb up to the chateau is worth it just for the view.

Just east of the old city, behind the Hôtel de Ville, are the flowery Jardins de l'Europe, shaded by giant California redwoods.

Places to Stay

Camping Municipal Le Belvédère (☎ 04 50 45 48 30, fax 04 50 45 55 56, Forêt du Crêt du Maure) is 2.5km south of the train station in a shaded forest. It costs about 47/67FF for one/two people to pitch a tent. From mid-June to early September you can take bus No 91 (Ligne des Vacances) from the train station.

The Auberge de Jeunesse (☎ 04 50 45 33 19, fax 04 50 52 77 52, 4 route du Semnoz) is 1km south of town in the Forêt du Semnoz. From mid-June to early September, bus No 91 goes there. Beds cost 72FF.

The small Hôtel Rive du Lac (☎ 04 50 51 32 85, fax 04 50 45 77 40, 6 rue des Marquisats), superbly located near the Vieille Ville and the lake, has one- or two-bed rooms with shower for 146FF.

One of the cheapest places close to the Vieille Ville is Central Hôtel (☎ 04 50 45 05 37, 6bis rue Royale) in a quiet courtyard. Doubles start at 160FF. Triples/quads cost 220/230FF.

Places to Eat

In the old city, there are a number of cheap, hole-in-the-wall sandwich shops along rue Perrière and rue de l'Isle, these include a couple of good creperies. In the new town centre, there are good pizzas (from 38FF), large salads (19FF to 43FF) and a children's menu (42FF) at Lous P'tious Onions (36 rue Sommeiller) in the Grand Passage. Menus start at 65FF. There are also a number of inexpensive places to eat along rue du Pâquier.

Les Oubliettes (10 quai de l'Isle), right next to the canal in the Vieille Ville, has pizzas from 40FF to 55FF and a wide choice of other main courses such as an expansive Menu Savoyard for 99FF. Just across the canal, Le Pichet (13 rue Perrière) has a big terrace and three-course menus for 66FF and 78FF.

Getting There & Away

Bus The bus station, Gare Routière Sud, is on rue de l'Industrie next to the train station. Voyages Crolard (☎ 04 50 45 08 12) has regular services to Roc de Chère on the eastern shore of Lac d'Annecy and Bout du Lac at the far southern tip, as well as to Albertville and Chamonix.

Autocars Frossard (☎ 04 50 45 73 90) sells tickets to Geneva, Grenoble, Nice and elsewhere. Autocars Francony (☎ 04 50 45 02 43) has buses to Chamonix.

Train The train station (☎ 0836 35 35 35) is a modernistic structure at place de la Gare. There are frequent trains to Paris' Gare de Lyon (451FF, 3¾ hours by TGV), Nice (404FF via Lyon, 352FF via Aix-les-Bains, eight to nine hours), Lyon (115FF, two hours), Chamonix (105FF, three hours) and Aix-les-Bains (39FF, 30 to 45 minutes).

GRENOBLE

Grenoble (population 153,300) is the intellectual and economic capital of the French Alps. Set in a broad valley surrounded by spectacular mountains, this spotlessly clean city has a Swiss feel to it.

Orientation & Information

The old city is centred around place Grenette, with its many cafes, and place Notre Dame. Both are about 1km east of the train and bus stations.

The Maison du Tourisme at 14 rue de la République houses the tourist office (☎ 04 76 42 41 41, fax 04 76 00 18 98, ✉ office-de-tourism-de-grenoble@wanadoo.fr), an SNCF information counter and an information desk for the local bus network (TAG).

At 8 rue Hache, Cybernet (☎ 04 76 51 73 18, ✉ services@neptune.fr) charges 30/47FF for 30/60 minutes online. It opens noon to 2 pm and 10 pm to 1 am.

Things to See

Built in the 16th century to control the approaches to the city (and expanded in the 19th century), **Fort de la Bastille** sits on the north side of the Isère River, 263m above the old city. The fort affords superb views of Grenoble and the surrounding mountain ranges. To reach the fort you can take the téléphérique (☎ 04 76 44 33 65) from quai Stéphane Jay (24/35FF single/return, 19/28FF for students). Several hiking trails lead up the hillside to the fort.

Housed in a 17th-century convent at 30 rue Maurice Gignoux (at the foot of the Fort de la Bastille hill), the **Musée Dauphinois** has displays on the history of the Dauphiné region (closed Tuesday; 20/10FF).

Grenoble's fine-arts museum, the **Musée de Grenoble**, 5 place de Lavalette, has a good collection of paintings and sculpture, including works by Matisse, Picasso and Chagall (closed Monday and Tuesday; 25/15FF).

The **Musée de la Résistance et de la Déportation de l'Isère**, 14 rue Hébert, examines the region's role in the Resistance, and the deportation of Jews from Grenoble to Nazi concentration camps (closed Tuesday; 20/10FF).

Activities

Skiing & Snowboarding There are a number of inexpensive, low-altitude ski stations near Grenoble, including Col de Porte and Le Sappey (north of the city) and St Nizier du Moucherotte, Lans-en-Vercors, Villard-de-Lans and Méaudre (west of the city). The tourist office has comprehensive information, including accommodation lists.

Hiking The place to go for hiking information is Info-Montagne (☎ 04 76 42 45 90), on the 1st floor of the Maison du Tourisme. It sells hiking maps and has detailed information on gîtes d'étape and refuges (closed Sunday).

Places to Stay

Camping The year-round *Camping Les Trois Pucelles* (☎ 04 76 96 45 73, 58 rue des Allobroges) is one block west of the Drac River in Grenoble's western suburb of Seyssins. From the train station, take the tram towards Fontaine and get off at the Maisonnat stop, then take bus No 51 to Mas des Îles and walk east on rue du Dauphiné.

Hostels In Échirolles, the *Auberge de Jeunesse* (☎ 04 76 09 33 52, fax 04 76 09 38 99, ✉ grenoble-echirolles@fuaj.org, 10 ave du Grésivaudan) is 5.5km south of the train station. To get there from cours Jean Jaurès take bus No 8 (direction Pont de Claix) and get off at the Quinzaine stop – look for the Casino supermarket. A bed for the night costs 68FF.

The friendly and central *Foyer de l'Étudiante* (☎ 04 76 42 00 84, 4 rue Ste Ursule) accepts travellers of both sexes from late June to late September. Singles/doubles cost 90/130FF a day and, for those who want to stay put, 450/700FF a week. It opens 7 to 12.30 am.

Hotels Near the train station, *Hôtel Alizé* (☎ 04 76 43 12 91, fax 04 76 47 62 79, 1 rue Amiral Courbet) has modern singles/doubles with washbasin for 138/202FF and with shower for 162/212FF.

There are lots of inexpensive hotels in the place Condorcet area, about 800m south-east of the train station. One of the best is *Hôtel Lakanal* (☎ 04 76 46 03 42, fax 04 76 17 21 24, 26 rue des Bergers). It attracts a young and friendly crowd and has simple singles/doubles with toilet for just 100/120FF. Rooms with shower and toilet cost 140/180FF. Breakfast is 20FF.

FRANCE

FRANCE

Places to Eat

Les Halles Ste Claire food market, near the tourist office, opens 6 am to 1 pm daily (except Monday). The *Restaurant Universitaire* (*5 rue d'Arsonval*) opens 11.20 am to 1.15 pm and 6.20 to 7.50 pm weekdays between mid-September and mid-June. Tickets (about 15/30FF for students/nonstudents) are sold at lunchtime only.

For good food at reasonable prices, try *Le Tonneau de Diogène* (*6 place Notre Dame*), which attracts a young, lively crowd. The *plat du jour* is 55FF, salads cost from 15FF to 38FF. It opens 8.30 am to 1 am.

La Panse (*7 rue de la Paix*) offers a 50FF and 76FF lunch *menu* and a 100FF day and evening *menu* that are especially good value. Hours are noon to 1.30 pm and 7.15 to 10 pm (closed Sunday).

Les Archers (*2 rue Docteur Bailly*) is a brasserie-style restaurant with great outside seating in summer. The *plat du jour* is 57FF, *huîtres* (oysters) are 106FF a dozen. It opens 10 am to 10 pm.

Getting There & Away

Bus The bus station (☎ 04 76 87 90 31) is next to the train station at place de la Gare. VFD (☎ 04 76 47 77 77) has services to Geneva (151FF, 2½ hours), Nice (311FF, five hours), Annecy (99FF, 1¾ hours), Chamonix (161FF, three hours) and to a number of ski resorts.

Intercars (☎ 04 76 46 19 77, fax 04 76 47 96 34) handles long-haul destinations such as Budapest (580FF), Madrid (540FF), Lisbon (830FF), London (550FF), Prague (520FF) and Venice (260FF).

Train The train station (☎ 0836 35 35 39) is served by both tram lines (get off at the Gare Europole stop). There is a regular fast service to Paris' Gare de Lyon (371FF, 3½ hours by TGV). There are three trains a day to Turin (246FF) and Milan (321FF) in Italy, two trains a day to Geneva (118FF), and regular services to Lyon, Nice and Monaco.

Getting Around

Buses and trams take the same tickets (7.50FF, or 56FF for a carnet of 10), which are sold by bus (but not tram) drivers and by ticket machines at tram stops.

Provence

Provence was settled by the Ligurians, the Celts and the Greeks, but it was after its conquest by Julius Caesar in the mid-1st century BC that the region really began to flourish. Many exceptionally well-preserved amphitheatres, aqueducts and other buildings from the Roman period can still be seen in Arles and Nîmes (see the Languedoc-Roussillon section later). During the 14th century, the Catholic church, then led by a series of French-born popes, moved its headquarters from feud-riven Rome to Avignon, thus beginning the most resplendent period in that city's history.

MARSEILLE

The cosmopolitan and much maligned port of Marseille (population 1.23 million), France's second-largest city and third-most populous urban area, is not in the least bit prettified for the benefit of tourists. Its urban geography and atmosphere are a function of the diversity of its inhabitants, the majority of whom are immigrants (or their descendants) from the Mediterranean basin, West Africa and Indochina. Although Marseille is notorious for organised crime and racial tensions, the city is worth exploring for a day or two.

Orientation & Information

The city's main street, La Canebière, stretches eastward from the Vieux Port. The train station is north of La Canebière at the top of blvd d'Athènes. The city centre is around rue Paradis, which becomes more fashionable as you move south.

The tourist office (☎ 04 91 13 89 00, fax 04 91 13 89 20, ✉ destination-marseille@wanadoo.fr) is next to the Vieux Port at 4 La Canebière. The annexe (☎ 04 91 50 59 18) at the train station opens weekdays only (Monday to Saturday in July and August).

The Le Rezo Cybercafé (☎ 04 91 42 70 02, ✉ lerezo@lerezo.com), 68 cours Julien, charges 30/50FF for 30 minutes/one hour access and is open 9.30 am to 8 pm Monday, 9.30 am to 10 pm Tuesday to Friday and 10 am to 11 pm Saturday.

Dangers & Annoyances Despite its fearsome reputation, Marseille is probably no more dangerous than other French cities.

As elsewhere, beware of bag-snatchers and pickpockets, especially at the train station. At night it's best to avoid the Belsunce area – the neighbourhood south-west of the train station bounded by La Canebière, cours Belsunce/rue d'Aix, rue Bernard du Bois and blvd d'Athènes.

Things to See & Do

Marseille grew up around the **Vieux Port**, where Greeks from Asia Minor established a settlement around 600 BC. The quarter north of quai du Port (around the Hôtel de Ville) was blown up by the Germans in 1943 and rebuilt after the war. The lively **place Thiars** pedestrian zone, with its many late-night restaurants and cafes, is south of the quai de Rive Neuve.

Corniche Président John F Kennedy runs along the coast from 200m west of the **Jardin du Pharo**, a park with good harbour views. Along its entire length, the corniche is served by bus No 83, which goes to the quai des Belges (the old port) and the Rond-Point du Prado metro stop.

If you like great panoramic views or over-wrought mid-19th-century architecture, consider a walk up to **Basilique Notre Dame de la Garde**, on a hill 1km south of the Vieux Port – the city's highest point. Bus No 60 will get you back to the Vieux Port.

Museums All the museums listed here charge 12FF to 18FF for admission; all admit students for half-price. The 'Passeport pour les musées' (50/25FF) is valid for 15 days and allows unlimited entry to all the city's museums.

The **Centre de la Vieille Charité** is home to Marseille's Museum of Mediterranean Archaeology and has superb permanent exhibits on ancient Egypt and Greece (closed weekends). It is in the mostly North African Panier quarter (north of the Vieux Port) at 2 rue de la Charité. The **Musée Cantini** off rue Paradis, at 19 rue Grignan, has changing exhibitions of modern and contemporary art (closed weekends).

Roman history buffs should visit the **Musée d'Histoire de Marseille** on the ground floor of the Centre Bourse shopping mall, just north of La Canebière (closed Tuesday). Its exhibits include the remains of a merchant ship that plied the waters of the Mediterranean in the late 2nd century AD.

Château d'If Château d'If (☎ 04 91 59 02 30), the 16th-century island fortress-turned-prison made infamous by Alexandre Dumas' *The Count of Monte Cristo*, can be visited 9 am until 7 pm daily (closed Monday from October to March). Admission costs 22FF. Boats (50FF return, 20 minutes each way) depart from quai des Belges in the Vieux Port and continue to the nearby **Îles du Frioul** (80FF return for chateau and islands).

Places to Stay

Camping & Hostels Tents can usually be pitched (26FF per person) on the grounds of *Auberge de Jeunesse de Bois Luzy* (☎ 04 91 49 06 18, fax 04 91 49 06 18, allées des Primevères), 4.5km east of the city centre in the Montolivet neighbourhood. Otherwise dorm beds (HI card required) are 44FF. Take bus No 6 from near the Canebière-Réformés metro stop or bus No 8 from La Canebière.

Auberge de Jeunesse de Bonneveine (☎ 04 91 73 21 81, fax 04 91 73 97 23, ✉ marseille@fuaj.org, 47 ave Joseph Vidal), 4.5km south of the Vieux Port, has beds for 72FF but is closed in January. Take bus No 44 from the Rond-Point du Prado metro stop and get off at place Louis Bonnefon.

Hotels – Train Station Area The two-star *Hôtel d'Athènes* (☎ 04 91 90 12 93, fax 04 91 90 72 03, 37-39 blvd d'Athènes) is at the foot of the grand staircase leading from the train station into town. Average but well-kept singles and doubles with shower and toilet cost 220FF to 300FF. Rooms in its adjoining one-star annexe called the *Hôtel Little Palace* cost between 120FF and 280FF for singles/doubles.

Hotels – Around La Canebière The *Hôtel Ozea* (☎ 04 91 47 91 84, 12 rue Barbaroux), across square Léon Blum from the eastern end of allées Léon Gambetta, has clean, old-fashioned doubles without/with shower for 120/150FF. There are no hall showers. Nearby *Hôtel Pied-à-Terre* (☎ 04 91 92 00 95, 18 rue Barbaroux) has rooms without/with shower for 120/150FF.

Places to Eat

Fresh fruits and vegies are sold at the *Marché des Capucins*, one block south of La Canebière on place des Capucins, and at

FRANCE

the *fruit and vegetable market* on cours Pierre Puget. Both are closed Sunday.

Restaurants along and near the pedestrianised cours Julien, a few blocks south of La Canebière, offer an incredible variety of cuisines: Antillean, Pakistani, Thai, Lebanese, Tunisian, Italian and more. An excellent-value Caribbean-themed eatery with 'student dishes' for 29FF is the *Mosaic (38 cours Julien).* Its *plat du jour* is only 19FF. *La Caucase (62 cours Julien),* specialising in Armenian dishes, is open nightly from about 6 pm, and has *menus* from 88FF. *Le Resto Provençal (54 cours Julien)* does regional French cuisine and has outdoor tables; mains are around 115FF, the *plat du jour* is 43FF and the lunch *menu* is 65FF (closed Sunday and Monday). The West Indian *Restaurant Antillais (10 cours Julien)* has starters from 20FF, main dishes from 40FF, and a 100FF *menu* that includes house wine.

Countless cafes and restaurants line the pedestrian streets around place Thiars, which is on the south side of the Vieux Port. Though many offer *bouillabaisse,* the rich fish stew for which Marseille is famous, it's difficult to find the real thing. Try *Le Mérou Bleu (32-36 rue St Saëns),* a popular seafood restaurant with a lovely terrace. Bouillabaisse is 89FF to 135FF, other seafood dishes 72FF to 125FF.

Entertainment

Listings appear in the monthly *Vox Mag* and weekly *Taktik* and *Sortir,* all free at the tourist office.

Marseille's Irish pub, *O'Malleys (rue de la Paix),* overlooks the Vieux Port on the corner with quai de Rive Neuve. Camperthan-camp and full of fun is the *Drag Queen Café (2 rue Sénac de Meilhan),* which hosts live bands. For rock, reggae, country and other live music, try *La Maison Hantée (10 rue Vian),* on a hip street between cours Julien and rue des Trois Rois.

Getting There & Away

Bus The bus station (☎ 04 91 08 16 40) at place Victor Hugo, 150m to the right as you exit the train station, offers services to Aix-en-Provence, Avignon, Cannes, Nice, Nice airport and Orange, among others.

Eurolines (☎ 04 91 50 57 55) has buses to Spain, Italy, Morocco, the UK and other

countries. Its counter in the bus station opens 8 am to noon and 2 to 6 pm (closed Sunday).

Train Marseille's passenger train station, Gare St Charles (☎ 08 36 35 35 39), is served by both metro lines. Trains from here go everywhere, including Paris' Gare de Lyon (379FF, 4¼ hours via the TGV), Avignon (92FF, one hour), Lyon (209FF, 3¼ hours), Nice (149FF, 1½ hours), Barcelona (342FF, 8½ hours) and Geneva (262FF, 6½ hours).

Ferry The Société Nationale Maritime Corse-Méditerranée (SNCM; ☎ 0836 67 95 00) runs ferries from the *gare maritime* (passenger ferry terminal) at the foot of blvd des Dames to Corsica (Corse). The SNCM office, 61 blvd des Dames (closed Sunday), also handles ticketing for the Moroccan ferry company, Compagnie Marocaine de Navigation (COMANAV).

Getting Around

Marseille has two easy-to-use metro lines, a tram line and an extensive bus network, which operate from 5 am to 9 pm. Night buses and tram No 68 run from 9 pm to 12.30 am. Tickets (9FF, 42FF for a carnet of six) are valid on all services for one hour (no return trips). Tram stops have modern blue ticket distributors that should be used to time-stamp your ticket before you board. For more information, visit the Espace Infos RTM (☎ 04 91 91 92 10), 6-8 rue des Fabres.

AROUND MARSEILLE
Aix-en-Provence

Aix-en-Provence is one of the most appealing cities in the whole of Provence, (population 134,200), it owes its atmosphere to the students who make up over 20% of the population. The city is renowned for its *calissons,* almond-paste confectionery made with candied melon, and for being the birthplace of the post-impressionist painter Cézanne. Aix hosts the Festival International d'Art Lyrique each July.

You'll find the main tourist office (☎ 04 42 16 11 61, fax 04 42 16 11 62, ✉ infos@ aixenprovencetourism.com) on place Général de Gaulle. Aix is an easy day trip from Marseille, and frequent trains (38FF) make the 35-minute journey.

The mostly pedestrianised **old city** is wonderful to explore, with its maze of tiny streets full of ethnic restaurants and specialist food shops, intermixed with elegant 17th- and 18th-century *hôtels particuliers* (private mansions).

Aix also has several interesting museums, the finest of which is the **Musée Granet** at place St Jean de Malte (closed Tuesday; 10FF). The collection includes Italian, Dutch and French paintings from the 16th to 19th centuries as well as some of Cézanne's lesser-known paintings. The **Musée des Tapisseries**, in the former bishop's palace at 28 place des Martyrs de la Résistance, is worth visiting for its tapestries and sumptuous costumes (closed Sunday; 15FF).

The **Atelier Paul Cézanne**, 9 ave Paul Cézanne, was the painter's last studio and has been left as it was when he died in 1906 (closed Tuesday; 16/10FF).

AVIGNON

Avignon (population 85,900) acquired its ramparts and its reputation as a city of art and culture during the 14th century, when Pope Clement V and his court, fleeing political turmoil in Rome, established themselves here. From 1309 to 1377 huge sums of money were invested in building and decorating the popes' palace. Even after the pontifical court returned to Rome amid bitter charges that Avignon had become a den of criminals and brothel-goers, the city remained an important cultural centre.

Today, Avignon maintains its tradition as a patron of the arts, most notably through its annual performing arts festival. The city's other attractions include a bustling (if slightly touristy) walled town and a number of interesting museums, including several across the Rhône in Villeneuve-lès-Avignon.

Orientation & Information

The main avenue in the Intra-Muros (walled city) runs northward from the train station to place de l'Horloge; it's called cours Jean Jaurès south of the tourist office and rue de la République north of it. The island that runs down the middle of the Rhône between Avignon and Villeneuve-lès-Avignon is known as Île de la Barthelasse.

The tourist office (☎ 04 32 74 32 74, fax 04 90 82 95 03, ✆ information@ot-avignon.fr), 41 cours Jean Jaurès, is 300m north

of the train station. It's open daily (10 am to noon on Sunday). During the Avignon Festival it opens 10 am to 8 pm daily (5 pm on Sunday). The main post office is on cours Président Kennedy, which is through Porte de la République from the train station. Cyberdrome (☎ 04 90 16 05 15, fax 04 90 16 05 14, ✆ cyberdrome@wanadoo.fr) on rue Guillaume Puy charges 25FF for 30 minutes online access (400FF for 10 hours) and opens 7 am to 1 am.

Palais des Papes & Around

Avignon's leading tourist attraction is the fortified Palace of the Popes, built during the 14th century. The seemingly endless halls, chapels, corridors and staircases were once sumptuously decorated, but these days they're nearly empty except for a few damaged frescoes. The palace opens 9 am to 7 pm (9 pm in July and 8 pm in August and September). Entry is 45/37FF, which includes a user-friendly audioguide in English.

At the far northern end of place du Palais, the **Musée du Petit Palais** houses an outstanding collection of 13th- to 16th-century Italian religious paintings (closed Tuesday; 30/15FF). Just up the hill is **Rocher des Doms**, a park with great views of the Rhône, Pont St Bénézet, Villeneuve-lès-Avignon and the Alpilles.

Pont St Bénézet

This impressive bridge was built in the 12th century to link Avignon with Villeneuve-lès-Avignon. Yes, this is the Pont d'Avignon mentioned in the French nursery rhyme. Originally 900m long, the bridge was repaired and rebuilt several times until all but four of its 22 spans were washed away in the 17th century. The bridge is closed Monday; entry is 17/9FF.

Museums

Housed in an 18th-century mansion, the **Musée Calvet**, 65 rue Joseph Vernet, has a collection of ancient Egyptian, Greek and Roman artefacts as well as paintings from the 16th to 20th centuries (30/15FF). Its annexe, the **Musée Lapidaire**, 27 rue de la République, houses sculpture and statuary from the Gallo-Roman, Romanesque and Gothic periods (closed Tuesday; 10FF).

At 17 rue Victor Hugo, the **Musée Louis Vouland** exhibits a fine collection of faïence

FRANCE

FRANCE

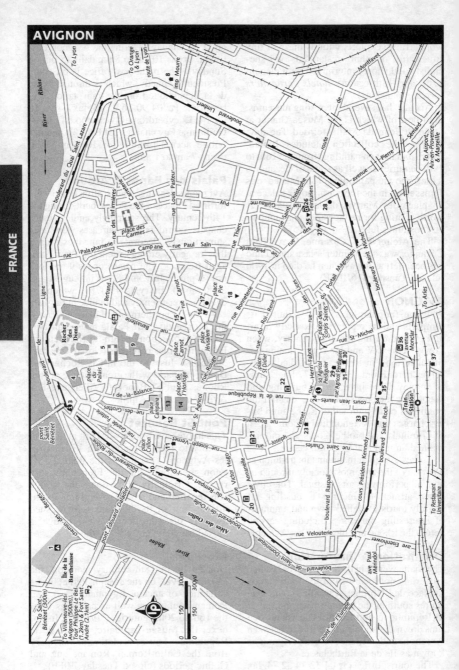

AVIGNON

AVIGNON

PLACES TO STAY		25	Sindabad		14	Hôtel de Ville
1	Camping Bagatelle;	27	Woolloomooloo		17	TCRA Bus Information
	Auberge Bagatelle					Office
8	Avignon Squash Club	**OTHER**			19	Porte Sainte Dominique
11	Hôtel Mignon	2	La Barthelasse Bus Stop		20	Musée Louis Voland
23	Hôtel Innova	3	Entrance to Pont Saint		21	Musée Calvet
29	Hôtel Le Parc		Bénézet; Tourist Office		22	Musée Lapidaire
30	Hôtel Colbert		Annexe		24	Tourist Office
31	Hôtel Splendid	4	Musée du Petit Palais		26	Cyberdrome Cybercafe
37	Hôtel Monclar	5	Cathédrale Notre		28	Cycles Peugeot
			Dame des Doms		32	Porte Saint Roch
PLACES TO EAT		6	Cinéma Utopia		33	Main Post Office
12	Natural Café; La Fourchette	7	Porte Saint Lazare		34	Porte de la République
15	Restaurant Song Long	9	Palais des Papes		35	TCRA Bus Information
16	Le Belgocargo	10	Porte de l'Oulle			Office
18	Les Halles Food Market	13	Opéra d'Avignon		36	Bus Station

and some magnificent 18th-century French furniture (closed Sunday and Monday; 20/10FF).

Villeneuve-lès-Avignon

Avignon's picturesque sister city also has a few interesting sights, all of which are included in a 45FF combined ticket sold at the major sights.

From Avignon, Villeneuve can be reached by foot or bus No 10 (from the main post office); buses marked 'Villeneuve puis Les Angles' are faster than those marked 'Les Angles puis Villeneuve'.

The **Chartreuse du Val de Bénédiction**, 60 rue de la République, was once the largest and most important Carthusian monastery in France (32/21FF).

The **Musée Pierre de Luxembourg** on rue de la République has a fine collection of religious paintings (closed Monday and February; 20/12FF).

The **Tour Philippe le Bel**, a defensive tower built in the 14th century at what was then the north-western end of Pont St Bénézet, has great views of Avignon's walled city, the river and the surrounding countryside. Entry is 10FF.

Another Provençal panorama can be enjoyed from the 14th-century **Fort St André** (25/15FF).

Special Events

The world-famous Festival d'Avignon, held every year during the last three weeks of July, attracts many hundreds of performers (actors, dancers, musicians etc) who put on some 300 performances each day.

Places to Stay

Camping The three-star *Camping Bagatelle* (☎ 04 90 86 30 39, *Île de la Barthelasse*), open year-round, is an attractive, shaded camping ground just north of Pont Édouard Daladier, 850m from the walled city. High-season charges are 23.80FF per adult, 11FF to pitch a tent and 7FF for parking. Reception opens 8 am to 9 pm, but you can arrive any time.

Hostels The 210-bed *Auberge Bagatelle* (☎ 04 90 85 78 45, fax 04 90 27 16 23) is part of a large, park-like area on Île de la Barthelasse that includes Camping Bagatelle. A bed costs 60FF.

From April to September a bunk in a converted squash court at the *Avignon Squash Club* (☎ 04 90 85 27 78, 32 blvd Limbert) costs 60FF. Reception opens 9 am to 10 pm (closed on Sunday from September to June), and 8 to 11 am and 5 to 11 pm in July and August. Take bus No 7 from the train station to the Université stop.

Hotels – Within the Walls Three hotels virtually rub shoulders on the same street – if one is full, try the next. *Hôtel Le Parc* (☎ 04 90 82 71 55, 18 rue Agricol Perdiguier) has singles/doubles without shower for 145/175FF and 195/215FF with shower.

The friendly, one-star *Hôtel Splendid* (☎ 04 90 86 14 46, fax 04 90 85 38 55, 17 rue Agricol Perdiguier) has singles/doubles with shower for 130/200FF and rooms with shower and toilet for 170/280FF.

The third in the trio, the two-star *Hôtel Colbert* (☎ 04 90 86 20 20, fax 04 90 85 97

FRANCE

00, 7 rue Agricol Perdiguier) has well-priced singles with shower for 160FF and doubles/triples with shower and toilet for 210/260FF.

The always-busy, one-star **Hôtel Innova** (☎ *04 90 82 54 10, fax 04 90 82 52 39, 100 rue Joseph Vernet)* has bright, comfortable and soundproofed rooms ranging in price from 140FF to 220FF. Breakfast is 25FF.

The one-star **Hôtel Mignon** (☎ *04 90 82 17 30, fax 04 90 85 78 46, 12 rue Joseph Vernet)* has spotless, well-kept and soundproofed singles with shower for 150FF and doubles with shower and toilet for 220FF.

Hotels – Outside the Walls The noisy, family-run **Hôtel Monclar** (☎ *04 90 86 20 14, fax 04 90 85 94 94, ✆ hmonclar84@ aol.com, 13 ave Monclar)* is in an 18th-century building just across the tracks from the train station. Eminently serviceable doubles start at 165FF with sink and bidet. The hotel has its own car park (20FF) and a pretty little back garden.

Places to Eat

The *Les Halles* food market on place Pie opens 7 am to 1 pm daily (except Monday). The **Restaurant Universitaire** *(ave du Blanchissage)*, south-west of the train station, opens 11.30 am to 1.30 pm and 6.30 to 7.30 pm October to June (closed Saturday dinner and Sunday, and during university holidays). People with student IDs can buy tickets (15FF to 30FF) at the CROUS office at 29 blvd Limbert, just east of the walled city, from 10.30 am to 12.30 pm daily (except Thursday and Sunday).

Restaurant Song Long *(1 rue Carnot)* offers a wide variety of excellent Vietnamese dishes, including 16 *plats végétariens* (vegetarian soups, salads, starters and main dishes from 28FF to 40FF). Lunch/dinner *menus* are 35FF, 40FF and 45FF. Song Long opens daily.

Le Belgocargo *(7 rue Armand de Pontmartin)*, a Belgian place tucked behind Église St Pierre, serves mussels 16 different ways for 49FF to 68FF and *waterzooi de volaille* (a creamy Belgian stew of chicken, leeks and herbs) for 58FF.

For hearty and healthy fodder in a rustic setting (tree trunks for benches), look no farther than the atmospheric **Natural Café** *(17 rue Racine)*. It's closed on Sunday and Monday. Adjoining it is the more conventional **La Fourchette** *(17 rue Racine)*, a Michelin-recommended place with *menus* for 150FF.

On the other side of town, a good choice is **Woolloomooloo** *(16bis rue des Teinturiers)*, a lively spot with vegetarian and Antillean dishes on offer (*menus* from 67FF to 89FF; closed Sunday and Monday). The small, bohemian **Sindabad** *(53 rue des Teinturiers)*, nearby, offers good Tunisian, oriental and Provençal home cooking and has a 50FF *plat du jour* (closed Sunday).

Entertainment

Cinéma Utopia *(4 rue des Escaliers Ste Anne)* is a student entertainment/cultural centre with a jazz club, cafe and four cinemas screening nondubbed films (follow the 'Promenade des Papes' signs east from place du Palais). From October to June, the **Opéra d'Avignon** (☎ *04 90 82 23 44, place de l'Horloge)* stages operas, plays, concerts and ballet. The box office opens 11 am to 6 pm (closed Sunday).

Getting There & Away

Bus The bus station (☎ 04 90 82 07 35) is down the ramp to the right as you exit the train station. Tickets are sold on the buses, which are run by about 20 different companies. Destinations include Aix-en-Provence (86FF, one hour), Arles (38FF, 1½ hours), Nice (165FF, 3½ hours), Nîmes (40FF, 1¼ hours) and Marseille (89FF, 35 minutes). Sunday services are less frequent.

Train The train station (☎ 0836 35 35 39) is across blvd St Roch from Porte de la République. There are frequent trains to Arles (36FF, 25 minutes), Nice (206FF, four hours), Nîmes (44FF, 30 minutes) and Paris (370FF, 3¼ hours via TGV).

Getting Around

TCRA municipal buses operate from 7 am to about 7.40 pm. Tickets cost 6.50FF if bought from the driver; a carnet of five tickets (good for 10 rides) costs 48FF from TCRA offices in the walled city at Porte de la République and at place Pie (closed Sunday).

Cycles Peugeot (☎ 04 90 86 32 49), 80 rue Guillaume Puy, has three- and 10-speeds for 60/130/240FF for one/three/seven days (plus 1000FF deposit).

FRANCE

AROUND AVIGNON
Arles

Arles (population 50,500) began its ascent to prosperity in 49 BC when Julius Caesar, to whom the city had given its support, sacked Marseille, which had backed the Roman general Pompey. It soon became a major trading centre, the sort of place that, by the late 1st century AD, needed a 20,000-seat amphitheatre and a 12,000-seat theatre. Now known as the **Arènes** and the **Théâtre Antique** respectively, the two structures are still used for bullfights and cultural events.

Arles is also known for its **Église St Trophime** and **Cloître St Trophime**; significant parts of both date from the 12th century and are in the Romanesque style. But the city is probably best known as the place where Van Gogh painted some of his most famous works, including *The Sunflowers*. The tourist office (☎ 04 90 18 41 20, fax 04 90 18 41 29, ✆ ot-arles@visitprovence.com) is on esplanade des Lices.

There are regular bus services to Marseille (87FF, 2½ hours), Aix-en-Provence (68FF, 1¾ hours) and Avignon (40FF, 1½ hours).

Languedoc-Roussillon

Languedoc-Roussillon stretches in an arc along the coast from Provence to the Pyrenees. From the plains of Bas Languedoc (Lower Languedoc) rise the region's towns and cities. Beaches are generally broad and sandy and the wine – Languedoc is France's largest wine-producing area – is red, robust and cheap. Inland are the rugged, sparsely populated mountains of Haut Languedoc (Upper Languedoc), a region of bare limestone plateaus rising above deep canyons.

Transport is frequent between cities on the plain, but buses in the interior are about as rare as camels. For train timetables and fares throughout the region, ring ☎ 0836 35 35 35.

MONTPELLIER

Montpellier (population 228,000) is one of France's fastest-growing cities. It's also one of the youngest, with students making up nearly a quarter of its population. The pedestrianised old city with its stone arches and fine hôtels particuliers is great to meander through – and the nearest beach is only 12km away.

Montpellier hosts a popular theatre festival in June and a two-week international dance festival in June/July.

Orientation & Information

The Centre Historique, surrounded by wide boulevards, has at its heart place de la Comédie, an enormous pedestrianised square. North-east of the square is esplanade Charles de Gaulle, a pleasant tree-lined promenade. To the east is Le Polygone, a modern shopping complex, and Antigone, a mammoth housing project. Westward sprawls the city's oldest quarter, a web of pedestrianised lanes between rue de la Loge and Grand Rue Jean Moulin. Bus and train stations are an easy walk south of the square.

Montpellier's main tourist office (☎ 04 67 60 60 60, fax 04 67 60 60 61, ✆ office.tourisme@mirt.fr) is at the south end of esplanade Charles de Gaulle. There's an annexe at the train station, open May to September.

To snack and surf, visit Dimension 4 Cybercafé, 11 rue des Balances. Open noon to midnight daily, it charges 1FF per minute or a bargain 35FF per hour.

Things to See

The **Musée Fabre**, 39 blvd Bonne Nouvelle, has one of France's richest collections of French, Italian, Flemish and Dutch works from the 16th century onwards (closed Monday). The **Musée Languedocien**, 7 rue Jacques Cœur, displays the region's archaeological finds (closed Sunday). Both charge 20/10FF.

As you wander the narrow streets of the old quarter, notice the fine **hôtels particuliers**, private mansions with large inner courtyards built by wealthy merchants during the 17th and 18th centuries.

Beaches The closest beach is at **Palavas-Flots**, 12km south of the city. Take bus No 17 or 28 from the bus station. About 20km south-east of Montpellier is **La Grande Motte**, famous for its futuristic, wacky architecture. Courriers du Midi runs hourly buses (24FF, 35 minutes).

FRANCE

Places to Stay

Camping The closest camp sites are around the suburb of Lattes, some 4km south of the city centre. *L'Oasis Palavasienne* (☎ 04 67 15 11 61, fax 04 67 15 10 62, route de Palavas), open April to September, charges 106FF for two people and tent. Take bus No 17 to the Oasis stop.

Hostel A bed at the *Auberge de Jeunesse* (☎ 04 67 60 32 22, fax 04 67 60 32 30, 2 impasse de la Petite Corraterie), ideally located in the old city, costs 48FF. Take the tram from the bus or train station.

Hotels At *Hôtel des Touristes* (☎ 04 67 58 42 37, fax 04 67 92 61 37, 10 rue Baudin), just off place de la Comédie, good-sized singles/doubles/triples with shower start at 150/180/260FF.

Friendly *Hôtel des Étuves* (☎ 04 67 60 78 19, 24 rue des Étuves) has singles/doubles with bathroom from 130/160FF. Close by, *Hôtel Majestic* (☎ 04 67 66 26 85, 4 rue du Cheval Blanc) has basic singles/doubles for 110/140FF and doubles/triples/quads with bathroom for 200/300/350FF.

Mid-range *Hôtel Le Guilhem* (☎ 04 67 52 90 90, fax 04 67 60 67 67, ✉ hotel-le -guilhem@mnet.fr, 18 rue Jean-Jacques Rousseau) occupies a 16th-century building. Spacious, tastefully furnished rooms start at 360FF.

Places to Eat

Tempting eating places abound in Montpellier's old quarter.

Barrel-vaulted *Tripti Kulai* (☎ 04 67 66 30 51, 20 rue Jacques Cœur) is a popular vegetarian place which does salads from 49FF and *menus* for 69FF and 85FF. It's open noon to 9.30 pm (closed Sunday).

La Tomate (☎ 04 67 60 49 38, 6 rue Four des Flammes), renowned primarily for its *cassoulet* and regional dishes, does salads the size of a kitchen garden plus dessert for 50FF and *menus* from 50FF upwards (closed Sunday and Monday).

For a midday takeaway sandwich, try one of the crunchy baguettes, brimming with salad and Alsacian goodies, at *Chez Fels* on rue de la Loge, just off place de la Comédie.

At vaulted *Le Menestrel* (☎ 04 67 60 62 51, impasse Périer), lunch/dinner *menus* start at 78/95FF; the *menu gastronomique* at

155FF is worth every centime (closed Sunday and Monday).

Largest of the covered markets is *Halles Laissac* occupying the ground floor of a multistorey car park. *Le Polygone* shopping complex is bursting with food shops.

Getting There & Away

Montpellier's bus station (☎ 04 67 92 01 43) is immediately south-west of the train station.

The two-storey train station at place Auguste Gibert is 500m south of place de la Comédie. Destinations include Paris' Gare de Lyon (379/452FF weekdays/weekends, four to five hours by TGV, about 10 a day), Carcassonne (113FF, 1¾ hours, at least 10 a day) and Nîmes (47FF, 30 minutes, at least 20 daily).

NÎMES

Nîmes (population 135,000) has some of Europe's best-preserved Roman structures. For a great overview, make the 15-minute uphill walk to the 30m-high **Tour Magne** (15FF), looking down over the Jardins de la Fontaine (Fountain Gardens) and crumbling **Temple de Diane**.

Orientation & Information

The hub of Nîmes is Les Arènes, the Roman amphitheatre. To its north, the fan-shaped, largely pedestrianised old city is bounded by blvd Victor Hugo, blvd Amiral Courbet and blvd Gambetta.

From esplanade Charles de Gaulle, ave Feuchères strikes south to the train and bus stations.

The main tourist office (☎ 04 66 67 29 11, fax 04 66 21 81 04, ✉ info@ot-nimes .fr) is at 6 rue Auguste. There's an annexe at the train station.

Nîmes' three *férias* (festivals) – the three-day Féria Primavera (Spring Festival) in February, the five-day Féria de Pentecôte (Whitsuntide Festival) in June, and the three-day Féria des Vendanges coinciding with the grape harvest on the third weekend in September – are celebrated with bullfights and concerts in Les Arènes and parades and music in the streets. In March, there's the week-long Printemps du Jazz festival while July and August are rich in dance, theatre, rock, pop and jazz events.

Things to See

Les Arènes, the amphitheatre (28/22FF) built around AD 100 to seat 24,000 spectators, is used to this day for theatre performances, music concerts and bullfights.

The rectangular **Maison Carrée**, a well-preserved Roman temple, was built around AD 5 to honour Augustus' two adopted sons and survived the centuries as a meeting hall, private residence, stable, church and archive.

Complementing it at the other side of the square is the striking glass and steel modern **Carrée d'Art** (Square of Art), which houses the **Musée d'Art Contemporain**.

Places to Stay

At year-round *Camping Domaine de la Bastide* (☎ 04 66 38 09 21), about 4km south of town on the D13, two people with tent pay about 55FF. Take bus D and get off at La Bastide, the terminus.

A dorm bed at the *Auberge de Jeunesse* (☎ 04 66 23 25 04, fax 04 66 23 84 27, ✉ nimes@fuaj.org) on chemin de la Cigale, 3.5km north-west of the train station, costs 52FF. From the train station, take bus No 2, direction Alès or Villeverte, and get off at the Stade stop.

In the old city, the friendly *Hôtel de la Maison Carrée* (☎ 04 66 67 32 89, 14 rue de la Maison Carrée) has basic singles for 145FF and singles/doubles/triples/quads with bathroom and TV for 180/220/330/350FF.

Hôtel Amphithéâtre (☎ 04 66 67 28 51, fax 04 66 67 07 79, 4 rue des Arènes) is one of the city's loveliest options with singles/doubles/triples starting at 185/240/305FF.

Places to Eat

Beneath the vaults of a restored 14th-century inn, *La Truye qui Filhe* (☎ 04 66 21 76 33, 9 rue Fresque) blends self-service format with a warm, homy atmosphere. Its *menu* is superb value at 52FF (open lunchtime only and closed in August). *Le Portofino (3 rue Corneille)*, near Maison Carrée, serves great home-made pasta dishes and has a lunchtime *menu* for 60FF.

The small *Restaurant Le Menestrel* (☎ 04 66 67 54 45, 6 rue École Vieille) is *the* place for rich local cuisine. Observe yourself in the giant overhead mirror as you tuck away one of its imaginative *menus* at 60FF, 85FF and 125FF.

Getting There & Away

Bus Nîmes' bus station is immediately south of the train station. Destinations include Pont du Gard (35FF, 45 minutes, five to six daily), Avignon (65FF, 30 minutes, at least 10 daily) and Arles (34FF, 30 to 45 minutes, four to eight daily).

Train The train station is at the south-eastern end of ave Feuchères. Destinations include Paris' Gare de Lyon (366FF to 431FF, four hours by TGV, seven daily), Arles (41FF, 30 minutes, 10 or more daily), Avignon (65FF, 30 minutes, at least 10 daily), Marseille (76FF, 1¼ hours, 12 daily) and Montpellier (66FF, 30 minutes, 15 or more daily).

AROUND NÎMES
Pont du Gard

The Roman general Agrippa slung the mighty Pont du Gard over the Gard River around 19 BC. You won't be alone here: this three-tier aqueduct, 275m long, 49m high and a Unesco world heritage site, attracts over two million visitors a year.

There's a tourist kiosk on each bank and a brand new information centre and display on the left bank, set back from the river.

Buses from Avignon (26km) and Nîmes (23km) stop 1km north of the bridge.

CARCASSONNE

From afar, Carcassonne (population 45,000) looks like a fairy-tale medieval city. Bathed in late-afternoon sun and high-lighted by dark clouds, the Cité (as the old walled town is known) is truly breathtaking.

Once inside the fortified walls, however, Carcassonne is less magical. Luring some 200,000 visitors in July and August alone, it can be a tourist hell in high summer. But even if purists sniff at Carcassonne's 'medieval' Cité – whose impressive fortifications were extensively renovated and rebuilt in the 19th century – what the heck; it *is* magic, one of France's greatest skylines.

The Ville Basse (lower town), a more modest stepsister to camp Cinderella up the hill and established in the 13th century, has cheaper eating places and accommodation and also merits a browse.

Orientation & Information

The Aude River separates the Ville Basse from the Cité on its hill. The main tourist

FRANCE

office (☎ 04 68 10 24 30, fax 04 68 10 24 38) is in the Ville Basse opposite square Gambetta. It has a small annexe in the Tour Narbonnaise within the Cité.

Alerte Rouge (Red Alert), 73 rue Verdun, is a cybercafe where you can plug in all day, every day, 10 am to 1 am, for a bargain 30FF an hour.

Things to See
The 1.7km-long double ramparts of **La Cité** (spectacularly floodlit at night) are spiked with 52 witches' hat towers. Within is a maze of narrow, medieval streets and the 12th-century **Château Comtal** (Count's Castle), visited by guided tour only (35/23FF). A 40-minute visit in English departs between two and five times a day, according to season.

Special Events
On 14 July at 10.30 pm, L'Embrasement de la Cité (Setting the Cité Ablaze) celebrates Bastille Day with a firework display rivalled only by Paris' pyrotechnics.

Throughout July, the Festival de la Cité brings the live arts to town. The concurrent Festival Off is an alternative, fringe celebration with street theatre and a host of events, both free and paying. In August, Carcassonne: Terre d'Histoire brings more music and theatre to the Cité while in October the Fête des Vendanges marks the grape harvest.

Places to Stay
Camping *Camping de la Cité* (☎ 04 68 25 11 77) is about 3.5km south of the main tourist office on route de St Hilaire. Open March to early October, it charges 75FF to 95FF for two people and tent. Take bus No 5 (hourly until 6.40 pm) from square Gambetta to the route de Cazilhac stop.

Hostels In the heart of the Cité on rue Vicomte Trencavel, the large, cheery *Auberge de Jeunesse* (☎ 04 68 25 23 16, fax 04 68 71 14 84, @ carcassonne@fuaj.org), closed mid-December to January, has dorm beds for 74FF, including breakfast.

B&B at the *Centre International de Séjour* (☎ 04 68 11 17 00, 91 rue Aimé Ramon) in the Ville Basse costs 68FF a night.

Hotels Handy for the train station is the recommended *Hôtel Astoria* (☎ 04 68 25 31 38,

fax 04 68 71 34 14, @ hotel-astoria@wana doo.fr, 18 rue Tourtel) and its equally agreeable annexe. Immaculate, basic singles/doubles cost 110/130FF (from 190FF with bathroom). A hall shower is 10FF.

Pricing policy at the friendly *Relais du Square* (☎ 04 68 72 31 72, fax 04 68 25 01 08, 51 rue du Pont Vieux) couldn't be simpler; large rooms, accommodating one to three people, cost 165FF, whatever their facilities, and quads are 235FF. So get there early in summer if you want your own bathroom.

At the welcoming, family-atmosphere *Hôtel Central* (☎ 04 68 25 03 84, fax 04 68 72 46 41, 27 blvd Jean Jaurès) freshly renovated doubles with shower are 140FF while doubles/triples/quads with bathroom and TV cost from 200/220/260FF.

Places to Eat
In the Ville Basse, *Le Gargantua*, the restaurant of Relais du Square (see Hotels earlier) has a weekday *menu du jour* at 69FF and others from 128FF. *L'Italia* (32 route Minervoise), handy for the station, is a pizza-plus joint that also does takeaways. Next door is the more stylish *Restaurant Gil* with Catalan-influenced *menus* from 100FF.

Getting There & Away
The train station is at the northern end of pedestrianised rue Georges Clemenceau. Carcassonne is on the main line linking Toulouse (74FF, 50 minutes, 10 or more daily) with Béziers (70FF, 50 minutes, five daily) and Montpellier (113FF, 1½ hours, at least 10 daily).

TOULOUSE
Toulouse (population 690,000), France's fourth-largest city, is renowned for its high-tech industries, especially aerospace; local factories have built the Caravelle, Concorde and Airbus passenger planes and also the Ariane rocket. Like Montpellier, it's a youthful place with over 110,000 students – more than any other French provincial city.

Most older buildings in the centre are in rose-red brick, earning the city its nickname *la ville rose* (the pink city).

Orientation & Information
The heart of Toulouse is bounded to the east by blvd de Strasbourg and its continuation,

blvd Lazare Carnot and, to the west, by the Garonne River. Its two main squares are place du Capitole and, 300m eastward, place Wilson. From place Wilson, the wide allées Jean Jaurès leads to the main bus station and Gare Matabiau, the train station, just across the Canal du Midi.

The busy tourist office (☎ 05 61 11 02 22, fax 05 61 22 03 63, ✉ ottoulouse@mip net.fr) is in the base of the Donjon du Capitole, a 16th-century tower on square Charles de Gaulle. It's open weekdays October to April and daily the rest of the year.

The OTU student travel agency (☎ 05 61 12 18 88) at 60 rue du Taur can help with cheap travel options.

Online time at Résomania cybercafe, 85 rue Pargaminières, is 40FF an hour. Also, France Telecom has several public access points around town, payable with a telecard.

Things to See & Do

Cité de l'Espace (Space City; ☎ 05 62 71 48 71) is a mindboggling interactive space museum and planetarium (69FF). Take bus No 15 from allées Jean Jaurès to the end of the line, then walk about 600m, aiming for the 55m-high rocket.

The **Galerie Municipale du Château d'Eau** is a world-class photographic gallery inside a 19th-century water tower at the western end of Pont Neuf, just across the Garonne River (15/10FF).

More traditional, the **Musée des Augustins**, 21 rue de Metz, has a superb collection of paintings and stone artefacts, many seized by the Revolutionary government or gathered from vandalised monuments (12FF, free for students). The gardens in the 14th-century **cloisters** of this former Augustinian monastery are gorgeous.

The nave of the magnificent Gothic **Église des Jacobins** seems to defy gravity as a single row of seven 22m-high columns runs smack down its middle, spreading their fan vaulting to support the roof. The remains of St Thomas Aquinas (1225-74), an early head of the Dominican order, are interred on the north side.

The **Basilique St Sernin** was once an important stop on the pilgrim route to Santiago de Compostela in Spain. With a length of 115m, it's France's largest and most complete Romanesque structure, topped by a magnificent eight-sided 13th-century **tower**

and spire, planted in the 15th century above the 11th-century chancel. The almost equally vast **Cathédrale de St Étienne**, just south of rue de Metz, also merits a visit.

Toulouse has about 50 handsome hôtels particuliers – grand, private, mostly 16th-century mansions. **Hôtel d'Assézat** on rue de Metz, one of the finest, nowadays houses the important Bemberg collection of paintings, bronzes and *objets d'art* (admission 30/18FF).

Several Toulouse operators do short **boat trips** on the Canal du Midi and Garonne River, leaving from quai de la Daurade or Ponts Jumeaux. Prices are around 50FF for a 1½-hour cruise and 125FF for a half-day outing.

Special Events

Toulouse is culturally vibrant. Major annual events include Festival Garonne with riverside music, dance and theatre (July), Musique d'Été with music of all definitions all around town on Tuesday and Thursday evenings (July and August) and Jazz sur Son 31, an international jazz festival (October).

Places to Stay

Many Toulouse hotels cater to businesspeople and so offer enticing discounts at weekends and during most of July and August. Then, many mid-range places offer much better value for money than budget alternatives.

Camping Year-round, the often packed *Camping de Rupé* (☎ 05 61 70 07 35, 21 chemin du Pont de Rupé*), 6km north-west of the train station, charges 72FF for two people and tent. Take bus No 59 (last departure 7.25 pm) from place Jeanne d'Arc to the Rupé stop.

Hotels Avoid the cheap hotels near the train station; most are fairly sordid.

The exceptionally friendly *Hôtel Beauséjour* (☎/fax 05 61 62 77 59, 4 rue Caffarelli), off allées Jean Jaurès, is great value. Simple rooms start at 110FF and doubles/triples with bathroom are 150/190FF. *Hôtel Splendid* (☎/fax 05 61 62 43 02) at No 13 has simple rooms from 90FF while singles/doubles/triples with bathroom are 130/150/210FF. Hall showers at both are 10FF.

FRANCE

Hôtel du Grand Balcon (☎ 05 61 21 48 08, fax 05 61 21 59 98, *8 rue Romiguières*), just off place du Capitole, is where French aviator-author Antoine de St-Exupéry put up in the 1920s; the lobby is a veritable shrine to him. Basic rooms are from 160FF to 210FF (230FF to 270FF with bathroom).

More upmarket, *Hôtel Albert 1er* (☎ 05 61 21 17 91, fax 05 61 21 09 64, ✉ *hotel.al bert.1er@wanadoo.fr, 8 rue Rivals*) has comfortable singles with bathroom and air con for between 230FF and 340FF (doubles 290FF to 410FF).

Places to Eat

Fill yourself at lunchtime, when there are some amazing deals. Look around: many places have lunch *menus* for 50FF to 60FF. Unmissable and an essential Toulouse experience are the small, spartan, lunchtime-only *restaurants* on the 1st-floor of *Les Halles Victor Hugo* covered market (great in itself for atmosphere and fresh produce). Fast, packed and no-nonsense, they serve up generous quantities of hearty fare for 55FF to 85FF.

Place St Georges is almost entirely taken over by cafe tables; at night it's one of the liveliest outdoor spots in town. Both blvd de Strasbourg and place du Capitole are lined with restaurants and cafes. *Restaurant Saveur Bio* (*22 rue Maurice Fonvieille*) serves tasty vegetarian food, including a 40FF lunchtime mixed plate, a great-value 60FF buffet and three 85FF *menus*.

Les Caves de la Maréchale (☎ 05 61 23 89 88, *3 rue Jules Chalande*) occupies the magnificently vaulted brick cellar of a pre-Revolution convent and specialises in regional cuisine. Lunch/dinner *menus* start at 85/135FF and there's a lunchtime 56FF *formule rapide*.

Bistrot Van Gogh (☎ 05 61 21 03 15, *21 place St Georges*), with its huge outdoor terrace, has lunch and dinner *menus* at 65/120FF. Alternatively, go a la carte and try its generous cassoulet (94FF) or *parillade* of eight different grilled fish (134FF).

Entertainment

For what's on where, pick up a copy of *Toulouse Hebdo* (3FF) or *Intramuros* (free from the tourist office). For life after dark, ask at the tourist office for their free listing *Toulouse By Night*.

Cafes around place St-Pierre beside the Garonne pull in a predominantly young crowd. Nearby, the *Why Not Café* (*5 rue Pargaminières*) has a beautiful terrace while *Café des Artistes* (*13 place de la Daurade*) is an art-student hang-out.

Toulouse has discos in double figures. Two hot spots near the centre are *La Strada* (*4 rue Gabriel Péri*), which may still be undergoing extensive renovation, and *L'Ubu* (*16 rue St-Rome*), closed Sunday.

Getting There & Away

Bus Toulouse's bus station (☎ 05 61 61 67 67), just north of the train station, serves mainly regional destinations, including Andorra (75FF, four hours, one to two daily). For longer-distance travel, both Intercars (☎ 05 61 58 14 53) and Eurolines (☎ 05 61 26 40 04) have offices here.

Train Toulouse's train station, Gare Matabiau, is on blvd Pierre Sémard, about 1km north-east of the city centre.

Destinations served by multiple daily direct trains include Bayonne (196FF, 3¾ hours), Bordeaux (165FF, 2½ hours) and Carcassonne (74FF, one hour).

The fare to Paris is 356FF by Corail (6½ hours, to Gare d'Austerlitz) and 447FF by TGV (5½ hours, to Gare Montparnasse via Bordeaux).

SNCF has an information and ticketing office at 5 rue Peyras.

Côte d'Azur

The Côte d'Azur, which includes the French Riviera, stretches along France's Mediterranean coast from Toulon to the Italian border. Many of the towns here – budget-busting St Tropez, Cannes, Antibes, Nice and Monaco – have become world-famous thanks to the recreational activities of the tanned and idle rich. The reality is rather less glamorous, but the Côte d'Azur still has a great deal to attract visitors: sunshine, 40km of beaches, all sorts of cultural activities and, sometimes, even a bit of glitter.

Unless you're camping or hostelling, your best bet is to stay in Nice, which has a generous supply of cheap hotels, and make day trips to other places. Note that theft from backpacks, pockets, cars and even laundrettes is a problem along the Côte d'Azur, especially at train and bus stations.

NICE

Known as the capital of the Riviera, the fashionable yet relaxed city of Nice (population 342,000) makes a great base from which to explore the entire Côte d'Azur. The city, which did not become part of France until 1860, has plenty of relatively cheap accommodation and is only a short train or bus ride away from the rest of the Riviera. Nice's pebbly beach may be nothing to write home about, but the city is blessed with a fine collection of museums.

Orientation & Information

Ave Jean Médecin runs from near the train station to place Masséna. Vieux Nice is the area delineated by the quai des États-Unis, blvd Jean Jaurès and the 92m hill known as Le Château. The neighbourhood of Cimiez, home to several very good museums, is north of the town centre.

The main tourist office (☎ 04 93 87 07 07, fax 04 93 16 85 16, 🖂 otc@nice.cote azur.org) at the train station opens daily; there's also an annexe at 5 promenade des Anglais (☎ 04 92 14 48 00).

American Express (☎ 04 93 16 53 53) is at 11 promenade des Anglais (closed Sunday). Opposite the train station, Le Change (☎ 04 93 88 56 80) at 17 ave Thiers (to the right as you exit the terminal building) offers decent rates and opens 7 am to midnight. The main post office is at 23 ave Thiers, one block from the train station.

Web Store (☎ 04 93 87 87 99, 🖂 info@ webstore.fr), 12 rue de Russie, charges 30/50FF for 30/60 minutes of Internet access and opens 10 am to noon and 2 to 7 pm Monday to Saturday.

Things to See

An excellent-value museum pass (140/ 70FF), available at tourist offices and participating museums, gives free admission to some 60 Côte d'Azur museums. Unless otherwise noted, the following museums are open daily except Tuesday from around 10 am to 5 or 6 pm (sometimes with a break for lunch in the off season), and entry is around 25/15FF.

The **Musée d'Art Moderne et d'Art Contemporain**, ave St Jean Baptiste, specialises in eye-popping French and American avant-garde works from the 1960s to the present. It is served by bus Nos 3, 5, 7, 16 and 17.

The main exhibit at the **Musée Chagall**, opposite 4 ave Docteur Ménard, is a series of incredibly vivid Marc Chagall paintings illustrating stories from the Old Testament.

The **Musée Matisse**, with its fine collection of works by Henri Matisse (1869-1954), is at 164 ave des Arènes de Cimiez in Cimiez, 2.5km north-east of the train station. Many buses pass by, but No 15 is most convenient; get off at the Arènes stop.

The **Musée Archéologique** and nearby **Gallo-Roman Ruins** (which include public baths and an amphitheatre) are next to the Musée Matisse at 160 ave des Arènes de Cimiez.

Nice's **Russian Orthodox Cathedral of St Nicholas**, crowned by six onion-shaped domes, was built between 1903 and 1912; step inside and you'll be transported to Imperial Russia (closed Sunday morning; 15/10FF). You'll need to dress appropriately: shorts or short skirts and sleeveless shirts are forbidden.

Activities

Nice's **beach** is covered with smooth pebbles, not sand. Between mid-April and mid-October, free public beaches alternate with private beaches (60FF to 70FF a day) that have all sorts of amenities (mattresses, showers, changing rooms, security etc). Along the beach you can hire paddle boats, sailboards and jet skis, and go parasailing (200FF for 15 minutes) and water-skiing (100FF to 130FF for 10 minutes). There are indoor showers (12FF) and toilets (2FF) open to the public opposite 50 promenade des Anglais.

Places to Stay

There are quite a few cheap hotels near the train station and lots of places in a slightly higher price bracket along rue d'Angleterre, rue d'Alsace-Lorraine, rue de Suisse, rue de Russie and ave Durante, also near the station. In summer the inexpensive places fill up by late morning – drop by or call by 10 am.

In summer, lots of backpackers sleep on the beach, however do *not* leave your bags unattended. Technically this is illegal, but the Nice police usually look the other way.

FRANCE

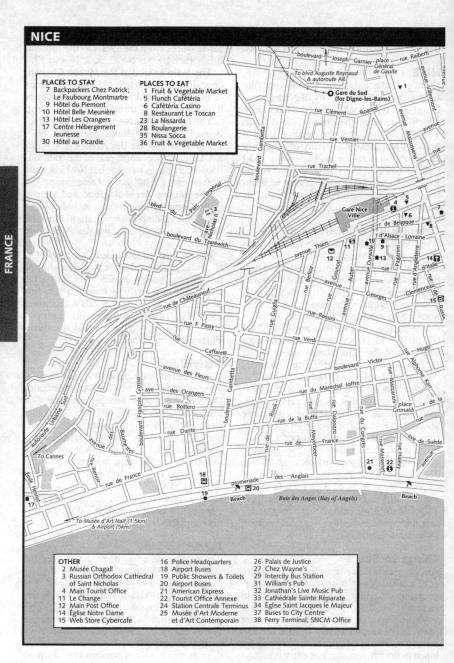

NICE

PLACES TO STAY
7 Backpackers Chez Patrick;
    Le Faubourg Montmartre
9 Hôtel du Piemont
10 Hôtel Belle Meunière
13 Hôtel Les Orangers
17 Centre Hébergement
    Jeunesse
30 Hôtel au Picardie

PLACES TO EAT
1 Fruit & Vegetable Market
5 Flunch Cafétéria
6 Cafétéria Casino
8 Restaurant Le Toscan
23 La Nissarda
28 Boulangerie
35 Nissa Socca
36 Fruit & Vegetable Market

OTHER
2 Musée Chagall
3 Russian Orthodox Cathedral
    of Saint Nicholas
4 Main Tourist Office
11 Le Change
12 Main Post Office
14 Église Notre Dame
15 Web Store Cybercafe
16 Police Headquarters
18 Airport Buses
19 Public Showers & Toilets
20 Airport Buses
21 American Express
22 Tourist Office Annexe
24 Station Centrale Terminus
25 Musée d'Art Moderne
    et d'Art Contemporain
26 Palais de Justice
27 Chez Wayne's
29 Intercity Bus Station
31 William's Pub
32 Jonathan's Live Music Pub
33 Cathédrale Sainte Réparate
34 Église Saint Jacques le majeur
37 Buses to City Centre
38 Ferry Terminal; SNCM Office

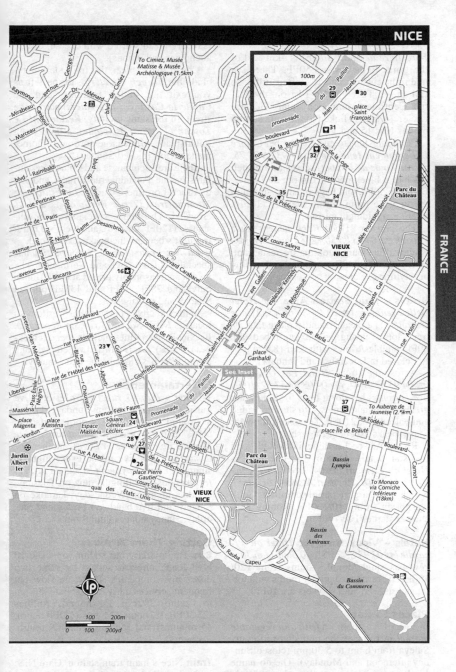

To Cimiez, Musée
Matisse & Musée
Archéologique (1.5km)

0   100m

FRANCE

VIEUX
NICE

Parc du
Château

See Inset

place
Garibaldi

place
Masséna

place
Magenta

de Verdun

Jardin
Albert
1er

place Pierre
Gautier

VIEUX
NICE

To Auberge de
Jeunesse (2.5km)

place Île de Beauté

Bassin
Lympia

To Monaco
via Corniche
Inférieure
(18km)

Bassin
des
Amiraux

Bassin
du Commerce

Parc du
Château

Hostels The *Auberge de Jeunesse (☎ 04 93 89 23 64, fax 04 92 04 03 10, route Forestière de Mont Alban)* is 4km east of the train. Beds cost 68.50FF. There's a midnight curfew, and it's often full – so call ahead. Take bus No 14 from the Station Centrale terminus on square Général Leclerc, which is linked to the train station by bus Nos 15 and 17.

From mid-June to mid-September *Centre Hébergement Jeunesse (☎ 04 93 86 28 75, 31 rue Louis de Coppet)* serves as a hostel. It's half a block north from rue de France. Beds are 50FF, and bags must be stored in the luggage room during the day (10FF). There is a midnight curfew.

The popular 21-bed *Backpackers Chez Patrick (☎ 04 93 80 30 72, 32 rue Pertinax)* is above Faubourg Montmartre restaurant. Dorm beds are 80FF, and there's no curfew or daytime closure.

Hotels – Train Station Area The *Hôtel Belle Meunière (☎ 04 93 88 66 15, 21 ave Durante)* is a clean, friendly place that attracts lots of young people. Dorm beds are 80FF, doubles/triples with bath 182/243FF. It's closed in December and January.

Across the street, *Hôtel Les Orangers (☎ 04 93 87 51 41, fax 04 93 82 57 82, 10bis ave Durante)* has dorm beds for 85FF, and great doubles and triples with shower, fridge and balcony for 210FF. The cheerful owner Marc speaks excellent English.

Rue d'Alsace-Lorraine is dotted with two-star hotels. One of the cheapest is *Hôtel du Piemont (☎ 04 93 88 25 15, fax 04 93 16 15 18, 19 rue d'Alsace-Lorraine)*, which has bargain singles/doubles with washbasin from 110/130FF. Rooms with shower start at 140/170FF.

Hotels – Vieux Nice The *Hôtel au Picardie (☎ 04 93 85 75 51, 10 blvd Jean Jaurès)* has single/double rooms from 120/150FF; there are also pricier rooms with toilet and shower. Hall showers are 10FF.

Places to Eat

In Vieux Nice, there's a *fruit and vegetable market* in front of the préfecture in cours Saleya from 6 am to 5.30 pm (closed Sunday afternoon and Monday). The no-name *boulangerie* at the south end of rue du Marché is the best place for cheap sandwiches, pizza slices and *michettes* (savoury bread stuffed with cheese, olives, anchovies and onions).

Cheap places near the train station include the *Flunch Cafétéria*, to the left as you exit the station building, and the *Cafétéria Casino (7 ave Thiers)* across the street. In the same vicinity, *Restaurant Le Toscan (1 rue de Belgique)*, a family-run Italian place, offers large portions of homemade ravioli (closed Sunday).

There are Vietnamese and Chinese restaurants on rue Paganini, rue d'Italie and rue d'Alsace-Lorraine. Nearby, *Le Faubourg Montmartre (32 rue Pertinax)* is always crowded. The house speciality is bouillabaisse (120FF for two), and there's a 68FF *menu*. It's beneath the backpackers hotel.

La Nissarda (17 rue Gubernatis) has specialities from Nice and Normandy. The *menus* are reasonably priced at 60FF (lunch only) and 78FF, 98FF and 138FF (closed Sunday and in August).

In the old city, a perennial favourite with locals is *Nissa Socca (5 rue Ste Reparate)*. Its Niçois specialities include *socca* (chickpea rissoles), *farcis* (stuffed vegetables) and *ratatouille*. It's closed June and January.

Entertainment

William's Pub (4 rue Centrale) has live music every night (except Sunday) starting at around 9 pm. There's pool, darts and chess in the basement. *Jonathan's Live Music Pub (1 rue de la Loge)*, another *bar à musique*, has live music every night in summer. *Chez Wayne's (15 rue de la Préfecture)* hosts a bilingual quiz on Tuesday, a ladies night on Wednesday, karaoke on Sunday and live bands on Friday and Saturday. Happy hour is until 9 pm.

Getting There & Away

Bus The intercity bus station, opposite 10 blvd Jean Jaurès, is served by some two dozen bus companies. There are slow but frequent services daily until about 7.30 pm to Cannes (32FF, 1½ hours), Antibes (25.50FF, 1¼ hours), Monaco (20FF return, 45 minutes) and Menton (28.50FF return, 1¼ hours).

Train Nice's main train station, Gare Nice Ville, is 1.2km north of the beach on ave Thiers. There is fast, frequent service (up to

40 daily trains) to points all along the coast, including Monaco (20FF, 20 minutes), Antibes (20FF, 25 minutes) and Cannes (32FF, 40 minutes). The two or three TGVs that link Nice with Paris' Gare de Lyon (455FF, seven hours) are infrequent; it can be more convenient to travel via Marseille.

Trains for Digne-les-Bains (109FF, 3¼ hours) make the scenic trip four times daily from Nice's Gare du Sud (☎ 04 93 82 10 17), 4bis rue Alfred Binet.

Getting Around
Local buses, run by Sunbus, cost 8/68FF for a single ticket/carnet of 10. Bus information and daily passes are available from the Sunbus information office (☎ 04 93 16 52 10) at Station Centrale on ave Félix Faure. To go from the train station to Vieux Nice and the bus station, take bus No 2, 5 or 17. Bus No 12 links the train station with the beach.

CANNES
The harbour, the bay, Le Suquet hill, the beachside promenade and the bronzed sunworshippers on the beach provide more than enough natural beauty to make Cannes (pop 67,300) worth at least a day trip. It's also fun watching the rich drop their money with such fashionable nonchalance.

Cannes is renowned for its many festivals and cultural activities, the most famous being the International Film Festival, which runs for two weeks in mid-May. People come to Cannes all year long, but the main season runs from May to October.

Orientation & Information
From the train station, follow rue Jean Jaurès west and turn left onto rue Vénizélos, which runs west into the heart of the Vieux Port. Place Bernard Cornut Gentille (formerly known as place de l'Hôtel de Ville), where the bus station is located, is on the north-western edge of the Vieux Port. Cannes' most famous promenade, the magnificent blvd de la Croisette, begins at the Palais des Festivals (four blocks south of the train station) and continues eastward around the Baie de Cannes to Pointe de la Croisette.

The main tourist office (☎ 04 93 39 24 53, fax 04 92 99 84 23, ☻ semoftou@ palais-festivals-cannes.fr) is on the ground floor of the Palais des Festivals (closed Sunday from September to June). There's

an annexe (☎ 04 93 99 19 77) at the train station (closed Sunday); turn left as you exit the station and walk up the stairs next to Frantour Tourisme.

The main post office is at 22 rue Bivouac Napoléon, two blocks inland from the Palais des Festivals. Asher Cyber Espace (☎ 04 92 99 03 01, ☻ asher@riviera.net), 44 blvd Carnot, is open 9.30 am to 7 pm (9 am to midnight Friday and Saturday; closed Sunday).

Vieux Port
Some of the largest yachts you'll ever see are likely to be sitting in the Vieux Port, a fishing port now given over to pleasure craft. The streets around the old port are particularly pleasant on a summer's evening, when the many cafes and restaurants light up the whole area with coloured neon.

The hill just west of the Vieux Port, **Le Suquet**, affords magnificent views of Cannes, especially in the late afternoon and on clear nights. The **Musée de la Castre**, housed in a chateau atop Le Suquet, has Mediterranean and Middle Eastern antiquities as well as objects of ethnographic interest from all over the world (closed Tuesday; 10FF, free for students).

Beaches
Each of the fancy hotels that line blvd de la Croisette has its own private section of the beach. Unfortunately, this arrangement leaves only a small strip of public sand near the Palais des Festivals. Other free public beaches – the **Plages du Midi** and **Plages de la Bocca** – stretch several kilometres westward from the old port along blvd Jean Hibert and blvd du Midi.

Îles de Lérins
The eucalyptus and pine-covered **Île Ste Marguerite**, where the Man in the Iron Mask (made famous in the novel by Alexandre Dumas) was held captive during the late 17th century, is just over 1km from the mainland. Many trails and paths crisscross the island. The smaller **Île St Honorat** is home to Cistercian monks who welcome visitors to their monastery and the seven small chapels dotted around the island.

Compagnie Maritime Cannoise (CMC; ☎ 04 93 38 66 33) runs ferries to Île St Honorat (50FF return, 20 minutes) and Île Ste

Marguerite (50FF return, 15 minutes). Both islands can be visited for 75FF. The ticket office is at the Vieux Port near the Palais des Festivals.

Places to Stay

Tariffs can be up to 50% higher in July and August – when you'll be lucky to find a room at any price – than in winter. During the film festival, all the hotels are booked up to a year in advance.

Hostels Cannes' *Centre International de Séjour de la Jeunesse* (*☎/fax 04 93 99 26 79, ❷ centre.sejour.youth.hostel.cannes@ wanadoo.fr, 35 ave de Vallauris)*, in a small villa about 400m north-east of the train station, has dorm beds for 80FF (HI card required; available for 70/100FF for those under/over 26). Reception is open 8 am to 12.30 pm and 2.30 to 10.30 pm (from 3 to 10 pm on weekends); curfew is at midnight (2 am on weekends).

The pleasant private hostel *Le Chalit* (*☎ 06 15 28 07 09, fax 04 93 99 22 11, ❷ le–chalit@libertysurf.fr, 27 ave du Maréchal Galliéni)* is a five-minute walk north-west of the station. Beds are 90FF. Le Chalit is open year-round and there is no curfew.

Hotels Heading towards the Auberge de Jeunesse, you pass the excellent-value but little-known *Hôtel Florella* (*☎/fax 04 93 38 48 11, 55 blvd de la République)*. Singles/doubles are 120/140FF, and doubles with shower and TV are 180FF.

The large *Hôtel Atlantis* (*☎ 04 93 39 18 72, fax 04 93 68 37 65, 4 rue du 24 Août)* may have a two-star rating, but its cheapest singles/doubles with TV and minibar cost only 155/195FF during the low season. The price rises to 195/220FF during festival time and in July and August.

Hôtel de Bourgogne (*☎ 04 93 38 36 73, fax 04 92 99 28 41, 11 rue du 24 Août)* has singles/doubles with washbasin for 143/ 186FF, and doubles with shower/shower and toilet for 223/286FF.

Places to Eat

A morning *food market* is held on place Gambetta, and at the *Marché Forville* north of place Bernard Cornut Gentille, both Tuesday to Sunday (daily in summer).

There are a few budget restaurants around the Marché Forville and many small (but not necessarily cheap) restaurants along rue St Antoine, which runs north-west from place Bernard Cornut Gentille.

Near the train station at *Au Bec Fin (12 rue du 24 Août)*, choose from two excellent *plats du jour* for 55FF to 69FF or a 105FF *menu* (closed Saturday evening and Sunday). Another good choice is the popular *Aux Bons Enfants (80 rue Meynadier)*, with regional dishes and a *plat du jour* for 94FF (closed Saturday dinner and Sunday).

One of the cheapest restaurants in Cannes is *Restaurant Le Croco (11 rue Louis Blanc)*, with pizzas, grilled meat and fish and shish kebabs. The *plat du jour* is 49FF and *menus* are 59FF (lunch) and 105FF (dinner).

Getting There & Away

Bus Buses to Nice (32FF, 1½ hours) and other destinations, the majority operated by Rapides Côte d'Azur, leave from place Bernard Cornut Gentille.

Train From the train station (*☎ 0836 35 35 39)* there is regular service to Antibes (13FF, 10 minutes), Nice (32FF, 40 minutes) and Marseille (133FF, two hours).

Getting Around

Bus Azur serves Cannes and destinations up to 7km from town. Its office (*☎ 04 93 39 18 71)* is at place Bernard Cornut Gentille, in the same building as Rapides Côte d'Azur. Tickets cost 7.70FF and a carnet of 10 is 51FF.

Alliance Location (*☎ 04 93 38 62 62)*, 19 rue des Frères, rents mountain bikes for 80FF a day.

ST TROPEZ

Since 1956 when the small fishing village of St Tropez found fame through the patronage of French actor Brigitte Bardot and her acolytes, things have never been the same. The once-isolated fishing village now draws in thousands of visitors a year seeking to share in a piece of the glamour that supposedly permeates this town. If you can, come by boat since the road traffic into and out of the town can be horrendous. If watching the rich dining on yachts is not your flute of Moët then there are the timeless backstreets where men still play pétanque and you might just glimpse a famous face or two.

Information

The tourist office (☎ 04 94 97 45 21, fax 04 94 97 82 66, ✆ tourisme@nova.fr), quai Jean Jaurès, opens 9.30 am to 1 pm and 3 to 10.30 pm in the high season. Hours vary slightly at other times of the year. It organises guided city tours in French and English (20/10FF for adults/children). Call in here for a good set of maps and brochures.

Things to See & Do

The **Musée de l'Annonciade** is a disused chapel on place Grammont in the Old Port which contains an impressive collection of modern art, including works by Matisse, Bonnard, Dufy, Derain and Rouault. Alternatively, the **Musée Naval** in the dungeon of the citadel at the end of Montée de la Citadelle has displays on the town's maritime history and on the Allied landings in 1944.

For a decent beach, you'll need to go 4km out of town to the excellent **Plage de Tahiti**. Naturists should get away from St Tropez to the beaches between the town and Le Lavandou to the west.

Places to Stay & Eat

Accommodation isn't cheap and even camping costs more than normal. St Tropez' cheapest hotel is the dingy *Hôtel La Méditerranée* (☎ 04 94 97 00 44, fax 04 94 97 47 83, 21 blvd Louis Blanc). Doubles start at 200FF. One rung up the price ladder is *Hôtel Les Chimères* (☎ 04 94 97 02 90, fax 04 94 97 63 57, Port du Pilon), at the south-western end of ave du Général Leclerc. Singles/doubles with shower and breakfast cost 328/358FF.

Move away from the waterfront to eat. Extremely tasteful and not too expensive is the informal *Café Sud* (12 rue Étienne Berny), tucked down a narrow street off places des Lices. It has a *menu* for 140FF and tables are outside in a star-topped courtyard. Close by, *Bistrot des Lices* (3 places des Lices) serves traditional Provençal cuisine, including wonderful ratatouille, with dishes from 120FF to 190FF.

Getting There & Away

St Tropez' bus station, ave Général de Gaulle, is on the south-western edge of

town on the one main road out of town. Frequent taxi boats run to Port Grimaud nearby and excursion boats run regularly to and from St Maxime and St Raphaël.

MENTON

Menton (population 28,800), reputed to be the warmest spot on the Côte d'Azur, is encircled by mountains. The town is renowned for lemons and holds a two-week Fête du Citron (Lemon Festival) each year between mid-February and early March. The helpful tourist office (☎ 04 93 57 57 00, fax 04 92 41 76 78, ✆ ot@villedementon.com) is in the Palais de l'Europe at 8 ave Boyer.

It's pleasant to wander around the narrow, winding streets of the Vieille Ville (old city) and up to the cypress-shaded **Cimetière du Vieux Château**, with the graves of English, Irish, North Americans, New Zealanders and others who died here during the 19th century. The view alone is worth the climb.

Église St Michel, the grandest baroque church in this part of France, sits perched in the centre of the Vieille Ville. The **beach** along the promenade du Soleil is public and, like Nice's, carpeted with smooth pebbles. Better private beaches lie east of the old city in the port area, the main one being **Plage des Sablettes**.

Camping St Michel (☎ 04 93 35 81 23, plateau St Michel), open April to mid-October, is 1km north-east of the train station. The adjacent *Auberge de Jeunesse* (☎ 04 93 35 93 14, fax 04 93 35 93 07, plateau St Michel) has beds for 68FF.

The bus station has services to Monaco (12.50FF return, 30 minutes) and Nice (28FF return, 1¼ hours). Take the train to get to Ventimiglia in Italy.

Monaco (Principauté de Monaco)

The Principality of Monaco (population 30,000), a sovereign state whose territory covers only 1.95 sq km, has been ruled by the Grimaldi family for most of the period since 1297. Prince Rainier III (born in 1923), whose sweeping constitutional powers make him far more than a figurehead, has reigned since 1949. The citizens of Monaco (Monégasques), of whom there are only 5000 out of a total population of 30,000, pay no taxes. The official language is French, although efforts are being made to revive the country's traditional dialect. There are no border formalities and Monaco makes a perfect day trip from Nice.

Orientation

Monaco consists of four principal areas: Monaco Ville, also known as the old city or the Rocher de Monaco, perched atop a 60m-high crag overlooking the Port de Monaco; Monte Carlo, famed for its casino and its Grand Prix motor race, north of the harbour; La Condamine, the flat area around the harbour; and Fontvieille, an industrial area south-west of Monaco Ville and the Port de Fontvieille.

Around 15 *ascenseurs publics* (public lifts) ease passage up and down Monaco's steep hills. Most of them operate 24 hours.

Information

Tourist Offices The Direction du Tourisme et des Congrès de la Principauté de Monaco (☎ 92 16 61 66, fax 92 16 60 00, ✉ dtc@monaco-congres.com), 2a blvd des Moulins, is across the public gardens from the casino. It's open daily (10 am to noon on Sunday). From mid-June to mid-September there are several tourist office kiosks open around the principality.

Money The currency of Monaco is the French franc. Both French and Monégasque coins are in circulation, but the latter are not widely accepted outside the principality.

In Monte Carlo, you'll find lots of banks in the vicinity of the casino. American Express (☎ 93 25 74 45), 35 blvd Princesse Charlotte, is near the main tourist office (closed Saturday and Sunday).

Post & Communications Monégasque stamps are valid only within Monaco, and postal rates are the same as in France. The main post office is at 1 ave Henri Dunant (inside the Palais de la Scala). Calls between Monaco and the rest of France are treated as international calls. Monaco's country code is ☎ 377. To call France from Monaco, dial 00 and France's country code (☎ 33).

Email & Internet Access Stars 'n' Bars (☎ 93 50 95 95, ✉ info@starsnbars.com), a bar and restaurant at 6 quai Antoine, 1er, charges 40FF for 30 minutes of Internet access and opens 11 am to midnight (closed Monday).

Palais du Prince

The changing of the guard takes place outside the Prince's Palace daily at 11.55 am. Daily from June to October about 15 state apartments are open to the public from 9.30 am to 6.20 pm. Admission costs 30/15FF. Guided tours (35 minutes) in English leave every 15 or 20 minutes. A combined ticket for entry to the **Musée des Souvenirs Napoléoniens** – a display of Napoleon's personal effects in the palace's south wing – is 40/20FF.

Musée Océanographique

If you're planning to visit just one aquarium, the world-famous Oceanographic Museum, with its 90 sea-water tanks, should be it. The museum, which is on ave St Martin in Monaco Ville, opens 9 am to 7 pm daily (to 8 pm in July and August). The entry fee – brace yourself – is 60/30FF.

Cathédrale de Monaco

The unspectacular 19th-century cathedral at 4 rue Colonel has one major draw: the grave of Grace Kelly (1929-82). The Hollywood star married Prince Rainier III in 1956, but was killed in a car crash. The remains of other members of the royal family, buried in the church crypt since 1885, rest behind Princess Grace's tomb.

Jardin Exotique

The steep slopes of the wonderful Jardin Exotique are home to some 7000 varieties of cacti and succulents from all over the world. The spectacular view is worth at least half the admission fee (40/19FF), which also gets you into the **Musée d'Anthropologie Préhistorique** and includes a half-hour guided visit to the **Grottes de l'Observatoire**, a system of caves 279 steps down the hillside. From the tourist office, take bus No 2 to the end of the line.

Places to Stay

Monaco's HI hostel, the *Centre de la Jeunesse Princesse Stéphanie* (☎ 93 50 83

20, fax 93 25 29 82, 24 ave Prince Pierre) is 120m uphill from the train station. You must be aged between 16 and 31 to stay here. Beds (70FF) are given out each morning on a first-come, first-served basis – numbered tickets are distributed from 8 am or so and registration begins at 11 am.

Hôtel Cosmopolite (☎ *93 30 16 95, fax 93 30 23 05,* ✉ *hotel-cosmopolite@monte-carlo.mc, 4 rue de la Turbie)*, the only one-star hotel in Monaco, has decent singles/doubles with shower for 282/314FF and doubles without shower for 228FF.

Places to Eat

There are a few cheap restaurants in La Condamine along rue de la Turbie. Lots of touristy restaurants of more or less the same quality can be found in the streets leading off from place du Palais. The flashy *Stars 'n' Bars (6 quai Antoine)* is a blues bar and restaurant with large portions of great salads (65FF to 75FF). It's open noon to 3 am daily (except Monday); the restaurant closes at midnight.

One of the few affordable restaurants specialising in Monégasque dishes is *U Cavagnetu (14 rue Comte Félix-Gastaldi)*, where a lunchtime *menu* is 85FF and in the evening jumps to between 115FF and 140FF.

Getting There & Away

There is no single bus station in Monaco – intercity buses leave from various points around the city.

The train station, which is part of the French SNCF network (☎ 0836 35 35 39), is on ave Prince Pierre. There are frequent trains to Menton (13FF, 10 minutes), Nice (42FF, 20 minutes) and Ventimiglia in Italy (21FF, 25 minutes).

FRANCE

Germany

Few countries in Western Europe have as fascinating and complicated a past as Germany. Despite the country's staid reputation for efficiency, it boasts a huge variety of museums, architecture from dozens of historical periods and a heavy emphasis on cultural and outdoor activities. Infrastructure is well organised, there is plenty of accommodation, and the frothy beer, heady wine and hearty food are superb.

In 1990 West and East Germany were reunified after 50 years of Cold War separation. Despite over a decade of integration, the social and economic differences of the formerly distinct countries will take many years to disappear altogether – another example of the intricate political and cultural layers that constitute modern Germany.

Facts about Germany

HISTORY

Germany, west of the Rhine and south of the Main rivers, was part of the Roman Empire. As the Empire crumbled, local tribes spread across Europe, establishing small kingdoms. The Frankish conqueror Charlemagne, from his court in Aachen, forged a huge empire that covered most of Christian Western Europe. The eastern branch of Charlemagne's empire developed in AD 962 into the Holy Roman Empire, organised under Otto I (Otto the Great).

The house of Habsburg, ruling from Vienna, took control of the empire in the 13th century. A semblance of unity in northern Germany was maintained by the Hanseatic League, a federation of German and Baltic city-states with Lübeck as its centre.

Things would never be the same in Europe after Martin Luther, a scholar from the monastery in Erfurt, nailed his '95 Theses'

AT A GLANCE	
Capital:	Berlin
Population:	82.5 million
Official Language:	German
Currency:	1 Deutschmark = 100 pfennig

to a church door in Wittenberg in 1517. Luther opposed the Catholic Church racket involving the selling of so-called 'indulgences', which absolved sinners from temporal punishment. Luther's efforts at reforming the Church gained widespread support, culminating in the Protestant movement and the Reformation.

Tensions between Protestant and Catholic states across Europe led to the catastrophic Thirty Years' War (1618-48). Germany became the battlefield for the great powers of Europe, losing more than one-third of its population and many of its towns and cities.

In the 18th century, the Kingdom of Prussia, with its capital in Berlin, became one of Europe's strongest powers. Thanks to the organisational talents of Friedrich Wilhelm I (the Soldier King) and his son Friedrich II (Frederick the Great) it expanded castwards at the expense of Poland, Lithuania and Russia.

After Napoleon's foray into Russia, Prussia led the war that put an end to his German aspirations in a battle at Leipzig in 1813. In 1815 the Congress of Vienna replaced the Holy Roman Empire with a German Confederation of 35 states; it had a parliament in Frankfurt and was led by the Austrian chancellor Klemens von Metternich.

The well-oiled Prussian civil and military machine eventually smashed this arrangement. In 1866, Otto von Bismarck (the Iron Chancellor) took Prussia to war against Austria and rapidly annexed northern Germany. Another successful war in 1870-71 saw Prussia defeat France and seize the provinces of Alsace and Lorraine. The Prussian king, Wilhelm I, became *Kaiser* (German emperor).

When WWI broke out in 1914 Germany's only ally was a weakened Austria-Hungary.

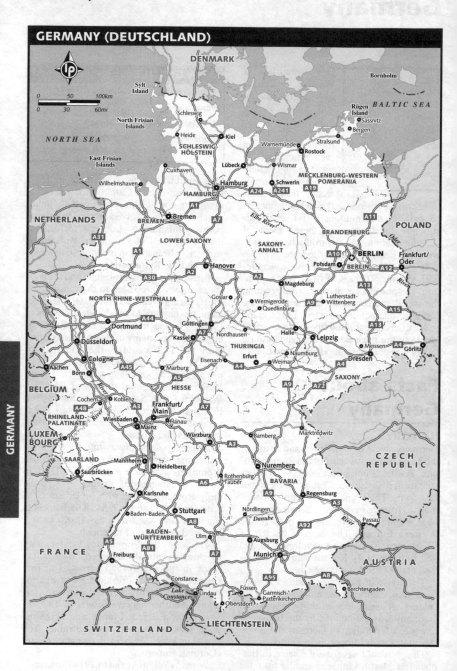

GERMANY (DEUTSCHLAND)

DENMARK

Bornholm

Sylt
Island

BALTIC SEA

Rügen
Island
Sassnitz
Bergen

Schleswig

North Frisian
Islands

Heide
Kiel

Warnemünde
Stralsund

NORTH SEA

SCHLESWIG-
HOLSTEIN

Rostock

East Frisian
Islands

Cuxhaven

Lübeck

Wismar

MECKLENBURG-WESTERN
POMERANIA

Wilhelmshaven

Hamburg
Schwerin

A24   A241   A19

A11

HAMBURG

A1

POLAND

NETHERLANDS

Bremen
A7

Elbe River

BREMEN

BRANDENBURG

Oder

A31

LOWER SAXONY

SAXONY-
ANHALT

A10   BERLIN

Frankfurt/
Oder

A1

Hanover

Potsdam
BERLIN

A12

A30

A2

Magdeburg

A13

NORTH RHINE-WESTPHALIA

Goslar

Wernigerode
Quedlinburg

Lutherstadt-
Wittenberg

A9

River

A15

Rhine

A44

Göttingen

Nordhausen

Halle

A13

Dortmund

Kassel
A7

Leipzig

Meissen
Görlitz

Düsseldorf

THURINGIA

Naumburg

A4

Aachen
Cologne

Marburg

Eisenach
Erfurt
Weimar

Dresden

Bonn

A45

A5

HESSE

A4

SAXONY

A9   A72

BELGIUM

Cochem
River
Koblenz

A48

Frankfurt/
Main

A7

RHINELAND-
PALATINATE

A3

Wiesbaden

Hanau

LUXEM-
BOURG

Mainz

CZECH
REPUBLIC

Trier

Moselle River

Würzburg

Bamberg

Marktredwitz

SAARLAND

Mannheim

A3

Saarbrücken

Heidelberg

Nuremberg

A6

Rothenburg/
Tauber

BAVARIA

Karlsruhe

A9

Regensburg

A3

Baden-Baden

Stuttgart

Nördlingen

Passau

A8

Danube

River

BADEN-
WÜRTTEMBERG

Ulm

A92

A5

A81

Augsburg

FRANCE

Freiburg

A7

Munich

AUSTRIA

A95

A8

Constance

Füssen

Berchtesgaden

Lake
Constance

Lindau

Garmisch-
Partenkirchen

Oberstdorf

SWITZERLAND

LIECHTENSTEIN

GERMANY

euro currency converter €1 = 1.95DM

Gruelling trench warfare on two fronts sapped the nation's resources and by late 1918 Germany was forced to sue for peace. The Kaiser abdicated and escaped to Holland and a new republic, known as the Weimar Republic, was proclaimed.

Following the war Germany was forced to pay massive reparations to its WWI foes. The subsequent hyperinflation and miserable economic conditions provided fertile ground for political extremists. One of these was Adolf Hitler, an Austrian drifter, German army veteran, and lousy watercolour painter. Hitler's National (or Nazi) Socialist German Workers' Party staged an abortive coup in Munich in 1923. This landed Hitler in prison for nine months, during which time he wrote his turgid *Mein Kampf*.

The Nazis increased their strength in general elections and in 1933 replaced the Social Democrats as the largest party in the Reichstag. Hitler was appointed chancellor and a year later assumed control as *Führer* (leader).

Hitler reoccupied the Rhineland in 1936 and in 1938 annexed Austria and parts of Czechoslovakia. Finally, in September 1939, after signing a pact that allowed both Stalin and himself a free hand in the east of Europe, Hitler attacked Poland, which led to war with Britain and France. Germany quickly invaded large parts of Europe, but after 1942 began to suffer increasingly heavy losses. Germany accepted unconditional surrender in May 1945, soon after Hitler's suicide. Chief among the horrors of WWII was the extermination of more than six million Jews, gypsies, communists and other 'undesirables' at Nazi extermination camps. The Holocaust was (and remains) a national shame.

At conferences in Yalta and Potsdam, the victorious Allies redrew the borders of Germany. In the Soviet zone, the communist Socialist Unity Party (SED) won the 1946 elections and began a rapid nationalisation of industry. In June 1948 the Soviet Union stopped all land traffic between Germany's western zones and Berlin. This forced the western allies to mount a military operation known as the Berlin Airlift, which brought food and other supplies to West Berlin by plane. In September 1949 the Federal Republic of Germany (FRG) was created out of the three western zones; in response the

German Democratic Republic (GDR) was founded in the Soviet zone the following month, with (East) Berlin as its capital.

As the west's bulwark against communism, the FRG received massive injections of US capital in the postwar years. A better life in the west increasingly attracted skilled workers that the GDR could ill afford to lose. So in 1961 it built a wall around West Berlin and sealed its border with the FRG.

After Mikhail Gorbachev came to power in the Soviet Union in March 1985, the East German communists gradually lost Soviet backing. But events in 1989 rapidly overtook the East German government, which refused to bite the bullet on economic and political reforms. Hungary relaxed its border controls in May 1989, and East Germans began flocking to the west. Then suddenly on 9 November 1989, a Politburo decision to allow direct travel to the west was mistakenly interpreted as the immediate opening of all GDR borders with West Germany. That same night thousands of people streamed into the west past stunned border guards. Millions more followed in the next few days and dismantling of the Berlin Wall began soon after.

Several months later the two Germanys and the wartime Allies signed the Two-Plus-Four Treaty, ending the postwar system of occupation zones. Germany recognised its eastern borders, officially accepting the loss of territories annexed by Poland and the Soviet Union after 1945. On 3 October 1990, based on a Unification Treaty, the German Democratic Republic was incorporated into the Federal Republic of Germany.

The economic and social costs of unifying Germany proved to be enormous. The government pumped massive sums of money into infrastructure, housing and environmental protection in eastern regions to bring standards up to those in the west.

In 1991 the German parliament, the Bundestag, voted to transfer Germany's capital from Bonn to Berlin, and the parliament and embassies are now located in Berlin.

GEOGRAPHY

Germany covers 356,866 sq km. The Central Uplands region divides northern Germany from the south. Extending from the deep schisms of the Rhineland massifs to the Black Forest, the Bavarian Forest, Ore

GERMANY

Mountains and the Harz Mountains, these low mountain ranges are Germany's heartland. The Rhine and Main rivers cut through the south-west of this region. Germany's alps lie entirely within Bavaria and stretch from Lake Constance in the west to Berchtesgaden in Germany's south-eastern corner. Many summits are well above 2000m; the highest is Zugspitze (2966m).

CLIMATE

The German climate can be variable – the most reliable weather is from May to October, which coincides with the standard tourist season (except for skiing). The mean annual temperature in Berlin is 11°C, the average range of temperatures varying from -1°C in January to 18°C in July. The average annual precipitation is 585mm and there is no special rainy season. The camping season is from May to September.

POPULATION & PEOPLE

There are 82.5 million people in Germany, about 15.5 million of whom live in eastern Germany. More than seven million foreigners live in Germany, mostly Turks, Italians, Greeks and people from the former Yugoslavia. In 1933 some 530,000 Jews lived in Germany; today the number is around 50,000.

SOCIETY & CONDUCT

Forget about the loud, beer-swilling 'Kraut lout' image; nor are Germans all that punctual or much into pop-eyed discipline these days. One feature of the country, though, is an enormous generation gap between older, traditional types and young Germans. That means you'll see Bavarian women in the *Dirndl* (skirt and blouse), some men in typical Bavarian *Lederhosen* (leather shorts), *Loden* (short jacket) and felt hat, but seemingly the rest of Germany skateboarding across historic town squares, on a very different sort of mission.

While Germans are generally not prudish or awkwardly polite, formal manners remain important. When making a phone call to anywhere in Germany, you'll find people more helpful if you first introduce yourself by name. Germans sometimes shake hands when greeting or leaving. Hugging and cheek-kissing is common between males and females who know one another.

LANGUAGE

German is spoken throughout Germany and Austria and in much of Switzerland. Although you will hear different regional dialects, the official language, *Hochdeutsch*, is universally understood. English is widely understood by young or educated Germans; away from large cities and in eastern Germany the situation is rather different.

Words that you'll often encounter on maps and throughout this chapter include: *Altstadt* (old city), *Bahnhof* (train station), *Brücke* (bridge), *Markt* (market, often the central square in old towns), *Platz* (square), *Rathaus* (town hall) and *Strasse* (street). German nouns are always written with a capital letter. See the Language Guide at the back of this book for pronunciation guidelines and useful words and phrases.

Facts for the Visitor

HIGHLIGHTS

Depending on how you see it, Munich's Oktoberfest will be a highlight or lowlight. Berlin, Hamburg and Munich are raunchy. To soak up Germany's fairy-tale charm, hit castles like Heidelberg, Neuschwanstein, Burg Rheinfels on the Rhine River, Burg Eltz on the Moselle, the medieval Königstein and Wartburg castles, Renaissance Wittenberg Castle and baroque Schloss Moritzburg. Towns which also impart this flavour are Wismar, Goslar and Regensburg, Meissen and Quedlinburg; Weimar has a special place in German culture, and Lübeck is one of Europe's true gems.

SUGGESTED ITINERARIES

Three days
  Visit Berlin or Munich.
One week
  Divide your time between Berlin and Munich, and throw in a visit to Dresden and/or Leipzig on the way.
Two weeks
  As for one week, but head over to Freiburg or Cologne and the Rhine or Moselle Valleys.

PLANNING
Maps

Most tourist offices have free city maps. Many Deutsche Bahn Service Point counters at main train stations have free city maps and local information.

GERMANY

TOURIST OFFICES

The German National Tourist Office's (DZT) headquarters is at Beethovenstrasse 69, 60325 Frankfurt/Main (☎ 069-97 46 40, fax 75 19 03, ❷ gnto–fra@com puserve.com). For local information, in virtually any city, the office to head for is the *Verkehrsamt* (tourist office) or *Kurverwaltung* (resort administration).

Tourist Offices Abroad

DZT representatives abroad include:

Australia
(☎ 02-9267 8148, fax 9267 9035) c/o German-Australian Chamber of Industry and Commerce, Box A 980, Sydney, NSW 1235

Canada
(☎ 416-968 1570, fax 968 19 86, ❷ germanto@idirect.com), 175 Bloor St East, North Tower, 6th floor, Toronto, Ont M4W 3R8

UK
(☎ 20-73 17 09 08, fax 495 61 29), PO Box 2695, London W1A 3TN

USA
German National Tourist Office (☎ 212-661-7200, fax 661 71 74, ❷ gntony@aol.com), 122 East 42nd St, 52nd floor, New York, NY 10168-0072
German National Tourist Office (☎ 310-234-02 50, fax 474 16 04, ❷ gntolax@aol.com), PO Box 641 009, Los Angeles, CA 90064

EMBASSIES & CONSULATES
German Embassies Abroad

Australia (☎ 02-6270 1911) 119 Empire Circuit, Yarralumla, ACT 2600
Canada (☎ 613-232 1101) 1 Waverley St, Ottawa, Ont K2P 0T8
New Zealand (☎ 04-473 6063) 90-92 Hobson St, Wellington
UK (☎ 0171-824 13 00) 23 Belgrave Square, London SW1X 8PZ
USA (☎ 202-298 8141) 4645 Reservoir Rd NW, Washington, DC 20007-1998

Foreign Embassies in Germany

The following embassies are in Berlin. Some of them will move in the next few years as construction on buildings moves along. The Web site www.bau.berlin.de/bauen/botschaften has useful information on this in English. The area code for Berlin is ☎ 030.

Australia (☎ 880 08 80) Friedrichstrasse 200, 10117
Canada (☎ 20 31 20) Friedrichstrasse 95, 10117

New Zealand (☎ 20 62 10) Friedrichstrasse 60, 10117
UK (☎ 20 18 40) Unter den Linden 32-34, 10117
USA (☎ 238 51 74) Neustädtische Kirchstrasse 4-5, 10117

MONEY

Until the euro is adopted in 2002, Germany will use the German Mark or Deutschmark (DM), which consists of 100 pfennig (Pf). Coins are one, two, five, 10 and 50 pfennigs. There are banknotes of DM5, DM10, DM20, DM50, DM100, DM200, DM500 and DM1000.

The easiest places to change cash in Germany are banks or foreign exchange counters at airports and train stations, particularly those of the Reisebank, which charge a flat DM5 to change cash.

Travellers cheques can be cashed at any bank. The Reisebank charges 1% or a minimum of DM10, or DM5 on amounts less than DM100.

There are ATMs in virtually all towns and cities; most accept Visa, MasterCard, American Express, Eurocard and bankcards linked to the Plus and Cirrus networks.

Exchange Rates

country	unit		Deutschmark
Australia	A$1	=	DM1.25
Canada	C$1	=	DM1.46
euro	€1	=	DM1.95
France	1FF	=	DM0.30
Japan	¥100	=	DM1.99
Netherlands	f1	=	DM0.89
New Zealand	NZ$1	=	DM0.97
UK	UK£1	=	DM3.25
USA	US$1	=	DM2.16

Costs

A tight budget can easily blow out in Germany. Camping, which costs around DM15 per person, and staying in hostels is the cheapest way to go, while private rooms can be had for around DM45 per person. If your budget allows it, you'll find decent accommodation in pensions and hotels for around DM60 in most places, and regardless of your budget, eating lunchtime restaurant specials (about DM12) and visiting museums on days when they are free is a great way to reduce costs. Unless stated otherwise, prices given for museums and sights are for adults/concession. Travelling on a

GERMANY

rail pass, you could get by on DM40 to DM45 a day. If you stay in hotels or pensions and eat evening meals a la carte, double that figure; then add the rail costs we give in the city sections if you're not travelling on a pass.

Tipping
Apart from in restaurants and taxis, tipping is not widespread in Germany. In restaurants, rather than leave money on the table, tip when you pay by stating a rounded-up figure or saying *es stimmt so* (that's the right amount). A tip of 10% is usually more than sufficient.

POST & COMMUNICATIONS
Post
Postcard rates are DM1 within Europe and DM2 to North America and Australasia. A 20g letter to anywhere in Europe costs DM1.10 and to North America and Australasia DM3.

Telephone, Fax & Email
Most pay phones in Germany accept only phonecards, available for DM12 and DM50 at post offices and some kiosks, tourist offices and banks. One call unit costs just over DM0.12 from a private telephone and DM0.20 from a public phone (DM0.19 using a DM50 phonecard). Calling from a private phone is most expensive between 9 am and 6 pm, when a unit lasts 90 seconds for a city call, 45 seconds for a regional call (up to 50km) and 30 seconds for a Deutschland call (over 50km) during the peak period. From telephone boxes city calls cost DM0.20 per minute. Calls to anywhere else in Germany from a phone box cost DM0.40 per minute.

To ring abroad from Germany, dial ☎ 00 followed by the country code, area code and number. Home direct services whereby you reach the operator direct for a reverse charge call from Germany are only possible for some countries. The prefix is ☎ 0130 followed by the home direct number – it's wise to check the number for your country before leaving home.

Main post offices have public fax-phones that operate with a phonecard for a DM2 service charge (plus the cost of the call).

Internet cafes exist in many large cities. Locations change frequently, so check at tourist offices. The price in an Internet cafe is anything from around DM6 to DM20 per hour.

INTERNET RESOURCES
For up-to-date information on Germany, visit the German Information Centre's Web site (www.germany-info.org). The Berlin tourist office also maintains a useful Web site (www.berlin.de).

BOOKS
Lonely Planet's *Germany* provides detailed information on the entire country; Lonely Planet also publishes *Berlin* and *Munich* city guides. Mark Twain's *A Tramp Abroad* is recommended for its comical observations of German life. For a more modern analysis of the German character and the issues facing Germany, pick up the Penguin paperback *Germany and the Germans* by John Ardagh.

WOMEN TRAVELLERS
Women should not encounter many difficulties while travelling in Germany. The Lübeck-based organisation Frauen gegen Gewalt (☎ 0451-70 46 40), Marlesgrube 9, can offer advice if you are a victim of harassment or violence. Frauenhaus München (☎ 089-354 83 11) in Munich can also counsel victims of assault.

Notice boards in student or alternative cafes and bookshops are good places to get information on local women's groups.

GAY & LESBIAN TRAVELLERS
Germans are generally tolerant of *Schwule* (gays) and *Lesben* (lesbians). Most progressive are the large cities, particularly Berlin and Frankfurt, where the sight of homosexual couples holding hands is not uncommon – though kissing in public is less common. Larger cities have many gay and lesbian bars and cafes.

Berlin Pride is held on the last weekend in June. Other 'Pride' festivals are held in mid-June in Bielefeld, Bochum, Hamburg and Wurzburg, in early July in Cologne and in late June in Mannheim.

DISABLED TRAVELLERS
Germany caters reasonably well to the needs of disabled travellers, with access ramps for wheelchairs and/or lifts where

necessary in public buildings, train stations, museums, theatres and cinemas. However, assistance is usually required when boarding any means of public transport in Germany. On Deutsche Bahn, you can arrange this when buying tickets.

DANGERS & ANNOYANCES

Theft and other crimes against travellers are relatively rare. In the event of problems, the police are helpful and efficient.

Africans, Asians and southern Europeans may encounter racial prejudice, especially in eastern Germany where they have been singled out as convenient scapegoats for economic hardship, though the animosity is directed towards immigrants, not tourists.

Most major hotels have doctors on call. In an emergency, look in the telephone book under *Ärztlicher Notdienst* (Emergency Doctor Service).

The emergency telephone number for police is ☎ 110 and the fire brigade/ambulance is ☎ 112.

BUSINESS HOURS

By law, shops in Germany may open from 6 am to 8 pm weekdays and to 4 pm on Saturday. Banking hours are generally on 8.30 am to 1 pm and 2.30 to 4 pm weekdays; many banks do not close for lunch and stay open on Thursday to 5.30 pm. Museums are generally closed on Monday.

PUBLIC HOLIDAYS & SPECIAL EVENTS

Germany has many holidays, some of which vary from state to state. Public holidays include New Year's Day, Good Friday to Easter Monday, 1 May (Labour Day), Whit Monday, Ascension Day, Pentecost, Corpus Christi (10 days after Pentecost), 3 October (Day of German Unity), 1 November (All Saints' Day), 18 November (Day of Prayer and Repentance); and usually Christmas Eve to the day after Christmas.

There are many festivals, fairs and cultural events throughout the year. Famous and worthwhile ones include: Berlin's International Film Festival in February; Frankfurt's Music Fair and Jazz Fair, both held in March; Dresden's Music Festival in late May/early June; Freiburg's International Theatre Festival in June; Munich's Opera Festival in June; Berlin Love Parade in July; Munich's Oktoberfest, held in September/October; and Christmas festivals in Munich, Nuremberg, Berlin and Heidelberg.

ACCOMMODATION

Accommodation in Germany is well organised, though some cities are short on budget hotels; private rooms – look for signs which read *Zimmer frei* (rooms available) or *Fremdenzimmer* (tourist rooms) – are one option in such situations. Budget hotel rooms can be hard to find in summer. Average budget prices are DM60 for a single and DM90 for a double (without bathroom).

If you're after a hotel or especially a private room, head straight for a local tourist office and use the *Zimmervermittlung* (room-finding service) for free or typically DM5.

Camping

Germany has 2000 organised camping grounds, but many sites are far from city centres and not always easy to reach on public transport. Most camping grounds are open from April to September. The best overall source of information is the Deutscher Camping Club (☎ 089-380 14 20, fax 33 47 37), Mandlstrasse 28, 80802 Munich.

Hostels

The Deutsches Jugendherbergswerk or DJH (☎ 05231-740 10, fax 05231-74 01 49, or write to: DJH Service GmbH, 32754 Detmold), coordinates all affiliated Hostelling International (HI) hostels in Germany. Germany's hostel network is possibly the most extensive in the world and most are open year-round.

You must have an HI card or join DJH when checking in (DM20/35 junior/senior). Dorm beds in DJH hostels cost around DM23 to DM45. Camping (where permitted) is usually half price. Most don't have communal kitchens though breakfast is always included in the overnight price. Lunch or an evening meal costs DM6 to DM9.

Theoretically, visitors aged under 27 get preference, but in practice prior booking or arrival determines who gets rooms. In Bavaria, though, the strict maximum age for anyone staying at a hostel is 26. Elsewhere, many hostels charge different prices for juniors (under 27) and seniors (everyone else).

FOOD & DRINKS

Germany is a meat-and-potatoes kind of country, although vegetarians will usually find suitable restaurants or fast-food places. Restaurants always display their menus outside with prices. Beware of early closing hours, and of the *Ruhetag* (rest day) at some establishments. Lunch is the main meal of the day, though getting a main meal in the evening is never a problem.

If you're on a low budget, look for cheap *Schnellimbiss* or *Imbiss* (stand-up food stalls).

Wurst (sausage), in its hundreds of forms, is by far the most popular main dish. Regional favourites include *Bratwurst* (spiced sausage), *Weisswurst* (veal sausage) and *Blutwurst* (blood sausage). Other popular choices include *Rippenspeer* (spare ribs), *Rotwurst* (black pudding), *gegrilltes Fleisch* or *Rostbrätl* (grilled meat) and *Schnitzel* (breaded pork or veal cutlet).

Potatoes feature prominently in German meals, either *Bratkartoffeln* (fried), *Kartoffelpüree* (mashed) or *Rösti* (grated and then fried), or as *Pommes Frites* (french fries). A Thuringian speciality is *Klösse*, a ball of mashed and raw potato that is cooked to produce something like a dumpling. A similar Bavarian version is the *Knödel*. In Baden-Württemberg, potatoes are often replaced by *Spätzle* – a local noodle variety.

Beer, the national beverage, is excellent and relatively cheap. *Vollbier* is 4% alcohol by volume, *Export* is 5% and *Bockbier* is 6%. *Helles Bier* is light, *dunkles Bier* is dark and *Pils* is more bitter. *Alt* is darker and more full-bodied. A speciality is *Weizenbier*, made with wheat instead of barley malt and served with a slice of lemon.

German wines are inexpensive and typically white, light and fruity. A *Weinschorle* or *Spritzer* is wine mixed with mineral water.

Getting There & Away

AIR

The main arrival/departure points in Germany are Berlin, Düsseldorf, Frankfurt and Munich. Flights are priced competitively among all major airlines, but the German national carrier, Lufthansa (☎ 01803-80 38 03), offers the most flexibility.

Flights to Frankfurt are usually cheaper than to other German cities. Ryanair and Buzz are cheap options, with some flights for under DM100 from/to London.

BUS

Within Europe it's generally cheapest (but slower) to get to/from Germany by bus. Eurolines operates routes throughout the continent. Some sample one-way fares and travel times are: London-Frankfurt (DM127, 14¼ hours), Amsterdam-Hamburg (DM75, 7½ hours), Amsterdam-Frankfurt (DM75, 5½ hours), Paris-Hamburg (DM108, 14 hours), Paris-Cologne (DM70, 6½ hours), Prague-Frankfurt (DM70, 8½ hours) and Barcelona-Frankfurt (DM172, 20½ hours). Eurolines' youth fares (aged under 26) are 10% less. For information (but not bookings), contact Deutsche-Touring GmbH (☎ 069-7 90 30, fax 790 32 19) at Am Römerhof 17, 60486 Frankfurt am Main. Web site: www.deutsche-touring.com

TRAIN

Trains are far quicker and more comfortable – and expensive – than buses to/from Germany. Major German cities with international train connections include: Berlin to/from Warsaw (DM57, six hours), Prague (DM96, five hours) and Budapest (DM184, 13 hours); Hamburg to/from Amsterdam (DM132, 4½ hours) and Paris (DM130, nine hours); Frankfurt to/from Paris (DM144, 10 hours), Vienna (DM166, 10 hours), Budapest (DM230, 13 hours), Zürich (DM161, four hours) and Milan (DM216, nine hours); and Munich to/from Paris (DM202, nine hours), Zürich (DM117, four hours), Milan (DM110, 7½ hours), Vienna (DM113, five hours), Zagreb (DM141, nine hours), Budapest (DM156, seven hours) and Prague (DM97, six hours).

Note that on overnight trains, getting a bunk only costs an extra DM26/38 in six/four-berth 2nd-class compartments.

BOAT

If you're heading to/from the UK or Scandinavia, the port options are Hamburg, Lübeck, Rostock and Kiel. The Hamburg-Harwich service runs at least three times a week (from DM106 to DM674 depending on the season, the day of the week and cabin comforts). The Puttgarden-Rødbyhavn ferry is popular with those heading to Copenhagen (see the Hamburg Getting There & Away section for details). In eastern Germany, there are five ferries in each direction daily all year between Trelleborg (Sweden) and Sassnitz near Stralsund (see the Rügen Island section) and another service to Klaipeda in Lithuania three times weekly.

There are daily services between Kiel and Gothenburg, Sweden (DM70 to DM160, 14 hours, daily) and Oslo (Non-cabin space is only available from mid-June to mid-August, otherwise, basic double cabins cost from DM120 to DM182, 19½ hours). A ferry between Travemünde (near Lübeck) and Trelleborg (Sweden) runs one to four times daily (DM50, 7½ hours). Ferries also run several times a week between the Danish island of Bornholm and Sassnitz (DM20 to DM30, three times a week). Car-ferry service is also good from Gedser (Denmark) to Rostock (DM6 to DM10, two hours, three per day). Silja runs fast ferries several times a week between Rostock-Tallin-Helsinki (DM150, up to 26 hours) from June to September. Finnlines has daily sailings from Lübeck to Helsinki (DM340, 36 hours).

Getting Around

BUS

Germany's domestic buses function in support of the train network, going places where trains don't. Bus stations or stops are usually near train stations, and schedule and route information is usually posted.

Eurolines (which was previously known as Europabus, a name you will still run into) operates within Germany as Deutsche-Touring GmbH, a subsidiary of the German Federal Railways (Deutsche Bahn – DB; ☎ 069-790 30, fax 7 90 32 19), Am Römerhof 17, 60486 Frankfurt am Main. It doesn't handle bookings. Also see the Frankfurt and Romantic Road sections for details.

TRAIN

Schedules on DB trains are integrated throughout the country, so that connections between trains are time-saving and tight, often only five minutes. Of course the obverse of this is that when a train is late – a not uncommon occurrence, especially during busy travel periods – connections are missed and you can find yourself stuck waiting for the next train.

German trains fall into specific classifications: InterCity Express (ICE) trains run between major cities and require a supplement of around 10% of the ticket price; InterCity (IC/EC) are the most common express trains, and you must pay DM7 *Zuschlag* (extra fare) before boarding; InterRegio (IR) are fast trains covering secondary routes, with a DM3 surcharge; Regional Express (RE) are local trains that make limited stops; RegionalBahn (RB) are the slowest trains, not missing a single cow town.

Standard DB ticket prices are distance-based at a rate of 27Pf per km. For distances of under 100km, you can often buy tickets at a machine rather than queue at a ticket window. For longer distances it is better to buy tickets at a ticket window. During peak travel periods, a seat reservation (DM5) on long-distance trains can mean the difference between squatting near the toilet or relaxing in your own seat. Seat reservations can be made right up to the last minute (an 'express reservation').

If you don't have an Inter-Rail or Eurail pass, there are numerous DB rail passes to choose from (all fares for 2nd class). The 'Guten Abend' ticket is valid for one day of unlimited travel between 7 pm and 2 am and costs DM59 (DM69 for ICE); eg, the 7.15 pm ICE from Hamburg to Munich, arriving at 1.26 am, costs DM69 instead of the usual DM256. Schönes Wochenende (Good Weekend) tickets are a bargain for budget travellers: they're valid for up to five people (or one or both parents and their children) on a Saturday or Sunday on RE/RB and SE (Stadt Express) trains and cost DM35. Theoretically, a group of five can travel from Cologne to Dresden for that price on a 12-hour trip through the wilds of Germany (pack the wine and Wurst!).

Travel agents outside Germany sell German Rail Passes valid for unlimited travel on all DB trains for a given number of days within a 30-day period. The following prices (in US$), good for 2nd-class travel, are for adults/two adults travelling together/those under 26: five days $196/294/156, 10 days $306/459/210 and 15 days $416/624/366. The passes include some buses (like those on the Romantic Road route) and some ships (such as those plying the Rhine and Moselle rivers). They do not include seat reservations. Eurail and Inter-Rail passes are also valid in Germany.

Almost all train stations have lockers (from DM2 depending on size). Larger stations have DB Service Points counters, which offer schedule information and are open long hours. Many have local maps that will help you find the tourist office.

CAR & MOTORCYCLE

The autobahn motorway system runs throughout Germany and can be hair-raising for those of us used to a more leisurely pace – don't underestimate the time it takes for a car in the rearview mirror to close in at 180km/h.

The usual speed limits are 50km/h in built-up areas and 100km/h on the open road. The blood-alcohol limit for drivers is 0.05%. Obey the road rules carefully: the German police are very efficient and issue heavy on-the-spot fines.

Parking in German cities is a hassle. Leaving your car in a central *Parkhaus* (car park) costs roughly DM20 per day or DM2.50 per hour.

BICYCLE

Simple three-speed bicycles can be hired from around DM15/60 per day/week, and more robust mountain bikes from DM18/90. A separate ticket must be purchased whenever you carry your bike on a train. These cost DM6/12 for distances under/over 100km. Most trains (but not ICEs) have a 2nd-class car with a bicycle compartment.

The central office of Germany's main cycling organisation is the Allgemeiner Deutscher Fahrrad Club (ADFC; ☎ 0421-34 62 90, fax 346 92 50, ✉ kontakt@adfc.de), Grünenstrasse 8-9, 28199 Bremen (Web site: www.adfc.de).

RIDE SHARING

Rides within (and beyond) Germany are arranged by *Mitfahrzentrale* agencies in many cities. You pay a reservation fee to the agency and a share of petrol and costs to the driver.

The local tourist office may be able to direct you to several such agencies. Check under 'Mitfahrzentrale' in the phone book, or call the area code and ☎ 194 40 in large cities in Germany.

Berlin

☎ 030

Berlin has more to offer than almost any city in Europe. It may be Germany's largest city, but there are more trees and parklands here than in Paris and more bridges than in Venice. With hundreds of construction cranes dotting the city, Berlin – once again the capital of the nation – is undergoing breathtaking changes, making it an exciting and dynamic destination.

The centre of 19th-century Prussian military and industrial might, this great city finally reached maturity in the 1920s, only to be bombed into rubble in WWII. After the war, the Potsdam Conference sealed Berlin's fate by allowing the victorious powers – the USA, Britain, France and the Soviet Union – to occupy separate zones.

In June 1948 the city was split in two when the three western Allies introduced a western German currency and established a separate administration in their sectors. The Soviets then blockaded West Berlin from June 1948 to May 1949, but an American-led airlift kept the city going. In October 1949 East Berlin became the capital of the GDR. The construction of the Berlin Wall in August 1961 prevented the drain of skilled labour (between 1945 and 1961 four million East Germans were lured westward by higher wages and political freedom).

On 9 November 1989 the Berlin Wall opened, releasing a flood of East German refugees. Yet after more than a decade of integration, the city's two halves are still adjusting – eastern neighbourhoods such as the Scheunenviertel are Berlin's new artistic and cultural centres, while outlying areas with their grim Communist-era apartment blocks are as bleak as ever.

Orientation

The ruins of Kaiser-Wilhelm-Gedächtnis-Kirche, a memorial church on Breitscheid-platz, a block away from Zoo train station, are a useful landmark in central Berlin. The tourist office and hundreds of shops are in the faded Europa-Center at the northern end of the square. The Kurfürstendamm runs 3.5km south-west from Breitscheidplatz. To the north-east, between Breitscheidplatz and Brandenburger Tor (Brandenburg Gate), is the vast Tiergarten city park.

Some of the city's finest museums are in Berlin-Mitte; the best landmark here is the monstrous Fernsehturm (TV Tower). Unter den Linden, a fashionable Mitte avenue, and its continuation, Karl-Liebknecht-Strasse, extend eastwards from Brandenburger Tor to Alexanderplatz, once the heart of East Berlin.

South of here, in areas once occupied by the Wall, the largest construction site in Europe continues hammering away on Potsdamer Platz. What used to be Checkpoint Charlie is now almost lost amid new construction.

Information
Tourist Offices The main office of Berlin Touristen-Information is at Budapester Strasse 45 in the Europa-Center and is open 8 am to 10 pm Monday to Saturday and 9 am to 9 pm Sunday. This office also handles hotel reservations. There is another branch in the southern wing of Brandenburger Tor (open 9.30 am to 6 pm daily). For telephone information and hotel reservations, call ☎ 25 00 25, fax 25 00 24 24 or email ✆ reservation@btm.de.

The tourist office sells the Berlin Welcome Card (DM32), which entitles you to unlimited transport for three days and discounted admission to major museums, shows, attractions, sightseeing tours and boat cruises in both Berlin and Potsdam.

EurAide's Zoo train station (Zoologischer Garten) office provides English-language city and train information and books rooms for DM7.50. The office is open 8 am to noon and 1 to 4 pm Monday to Saturday.

All foreign embassies can now be found in Berlin; see the Facts for the Visitor section earlier.

Money Reisebank has an exchange office at Hardenbergplatz 1 outside Zoo station, open 7.30 am to 10 pm daily. Show a EurAide newsletter for a reduction on commission charges.

Branches of the main German banks – all with ATMs – are plentiful around Breitscheidplatz and along the Ku'damm.

American Express has two offices: Friedrichstrasse 172 and Bayreuther Strasse 37.

Post & Communications The post office on the ground level of Zoo station is open to midnight daily. Make domestic and international calls at pay phones throughout the city – have plenty of coins ready or buy a phonecard for DM12 or DM50.

Email & Internet Access Close to Zoo station, Café Website, Joachimsthaler Strasse 41, has loads of computers hooked up for Internet access. You could also try Alpha Café, Dunckerstrasse 72 in Prenzlauer Berg (S8 or S10 to Prenzlauer Allee).

Travel Agencies Kilroy Travel (☎ 310 00 40) has especially good deals on air tickets, bus travel and car hire. There's a branch at Hardenbergstrasse 9 in Charlottenburg. Atlas Reisewelt is a big chain of travel agencies with several offices in Berlin. The most convenient branch is at Alexanderplatz 5 (☎ 242 73 70), inside the Kaufhof department store. STA Travel has offices at Gleimstrasse 28 (☎ 28 59 82 64) and at Goethestrasse 73 (☎ 311 09 50).

Bookshops The British Bookshop, Mauerstrasse 83-84 in Mitte, has a wide range of fiction and travel books (including Lonely Planet titles). Books in Berlin, Goethestrasse 69, has a good selection of English and American literature, as does Kiepert, Hardenbergstrasse 4-5. The Europa Presse Center, at ground level in Europa-Center, stocks international papers and magazines.

Laundry The Schnell und Sauber Waschcenter chain has laundrettes at Uhlandstrasse 53 and Leibnizstrasse 72 in Charlottenburg, and on Mehringdamm right outside the Mehringdamm U-Bahn station in Kreuzberg. It's around DM10 to wash and dry a load.

Medical Services For 24-hour medical aid call the Kassenärztliche Bereitschaftsdienst (Public Physicians' Emergency Service; ☎ 31 00 31). If you need a pharmacy after hours, dial ☎ 011 41.

The Zahnklinik Medeco, open 7 am to midnight daily, has English-speaking dentists. It's at Königin-Louise-Platz 1 (☎ 841 91 00) in Dahlem and at Klosterstrasse 17 (☎ 351 94 10) in Spandau.

Things to See & Do
State museums (denoted by SMB) have free admission on the first Sunday of every

GERMANY

month and are closed on Monday. Some require you to buy a day pass (DM8/4 adults/concession), valid for all SMB museums on that day. If you want to overindulge on museums, the Drei-Tages-Touristenkarte (DM15) gives unlimited access to SMB museums over three consecutive days. Cards can be purchased at the museums.

Around Alexanderplatz Alexanderplatz (or, affectionately, 'Alex'), the square named after Tsar Alexander I, was bombed in WWII and completely reconstructed in the 1960s. Nearby and soaring 368m above Berlin is the stupendously ugly **Fernsehturm** (TV Tower; 1969), open 10 am to 1 am daily. On a clear day it's worth paying DM9/4 to go up the tower or have a drink at the revolving Telecafé.

Museumsinsel Berlin's famed Museum Island is west of the Fernsehturm, on an island between two arms of the Spree River. East Germany's parliament, the Volkskammer, used to meet in the monstrous, asbestos-filled **Palace of the Republic** (1976) facing Marx-Engels-Platz.

North of Marx-Engels-Platz looms the great neo-Renaissance **Berliner Dom** (1904), the former court church of the Hohenzollern family. The imposing edifice beside it is Karl Friedrich Schinkel's 1829 neoclassical SMB **Altes Museum** and its famed rotunda; it has a permanent antiquities collection plus special exhibitions (DM8/4).

Three of the five museums on the Museumsinsel are undergoing badly needed facelifts – the **Neues Museum** (1855) will open in 2005, the **Alte Nationalgalerie** (Old National Gallery; 1876) opens from 2001 and the **Bodemuseum** (1904) is closed until mid-2004. Happily, the SMB **Pergamon Museum** and its feast of classical Greek, Babylonian, Roman, Islamic and Oriental antiquity is open (DM8/4). Highlights include the Ishtar Gate from Babylon (580 BC) and the reconstructed Pergamon Altar from Asia Minor (160 BC).

Nikolaiviertel The rebuilt 13th-century **Nikolaikirche** stands amid the forced charms of the Nikolaiviertel (Nikolai quarter), conceived and executed under the GDR's Berlin restoration program. Inside is a fascinating museum that exhibits relics of early Berlin

(DM3). Another medieval church, **Marienkirche**, is on Karl-Liebknecht-Strasse. It stands near the monumental **Rotes Rathaus** (Red Town Hall), which is a neo-Renaissance structure from 1860, which has been proudly restored and is once again the centre of Berlin's municipal government.

Unter den Linden The **Deutsches Historisches Museum**, tracing German history from AD 900 to the present, is closed until early 2002, before then you can catch some of its collection at the Kronprinzenpalais. Architect IM Pei has designed a glass roof for the museum – during construction, some sections may be closed.

Opposite the museum is the beautiful, colonnaded **Kronprinzenpalais** (Crown Prince's Palace), which has some Deutsches Historisches Museum exhibits (free). Next to the museum is Schinkel's **Neue Wache** (1818), a memorial to the victims of fascism and despotism that harbours Käthe Kollwitz's sculpture *Mother and Her Dead Son*. An equestrian **statue of Friedrich II**, usually at home in the middle of the avenue, is being restored. Across the street, beside the Alte Königliche Bibliothek (Old Royal Library; 1780), is Wenzeslaus von Knobelsdorff's **Staatsoper** (State Opera; 1743). The square in front is **Bebelplatz**, where a poignant below-ground memorial marks the spot where the Nazis had their first book-burning on 10 May 1933.

Just south is the Gendarmenmarkt, a quiet square with the **Deutscher Dom** at the southern end. The Dom houses a free museum featuring an excellent German history exhibit. For a great view climb the nearby **tower** (DM3/2).

Around Oranienburger Tor Known as the Scheunenviertel, this neighbourhood is one of the most vibrant in Berlin. The **Brecht-Weigel Gedenkstätte**, Chausseestrasse 125, is where the socialist playwright Bertolt Brecht and his wife Helene Weigel lived from 1948 until his death in 1956 (closed Monday; DM6/3).

Behind are two adjacent cemeteries – the one closest to the house is the **Dorotheen-städtischer Friedhof**, with tombs of the illustrious, such as Bertolt Brecht, philosopher Georg Friedrich Hegel and poet Johannes Becher.

Don't miss the **Neue Synagogue** on Oranienburger Strasse 28 (closed Saturday; DM5/3). Built in the Moorish-Byzantine style in 1866, it was desecrated by the Nazis, later destroyed by WWII bombing and now holds a permanent exhibit on Jewish life in Berlin.

Though 10,000 people are buried at the old **Jüdischer Friedhof** on Rosenthaler Strasse – including Moses Mendelssohn, the famous philosopher of the Enlightenment – few tombstones survived Nazi destruction in 1942.

If you travel westwards along Oranienburger Strasse you'll come across the rambling, crumbling **Tacheles** alternative art, culture and entertainment centre made famous by post-Wende squatters.

The nearby **Hackesche Höfe** (1907) is a cluster of Art Nouveau buildings with eight interconnected courtyards filled with galleries, shops and trendy cafes.

Tiergarten Unter den Linden ends at the 1791 **Brandenburger Tor** (Brandenburg Gate), a symbol of Berlin and once the boundary between east and west. It is crowned by the winged Goddess of Victory and a four-horse chariot.

Beside the Spree River, just north of Brandenburger Tor, is the **Reichstag** (1894), where at midnight on 2 October 1990 the reunification of Germany was enacted. The Reichstag is now Berlin's top attraction, thanks to a stunning reconstruction by Sir Norman Foster. The highlight is wending your way to the top of the gleaming metal and glass dome. Get there early (and that means 8 am) to avoid the hordes awaiting their ascent during the day (it's open until midnight, though last admission is at 10 pm; free). Tours of the Reichstag are free but you must reserve in writing to: Deutscher Bundestag, Besucherdienst, 11011 Berlin.

Just west of the Reichstag is the **Haus der Kulturen der Welt** (House of World Cultures), nicknamed the 'pregnant oyster' for its shape. The photo and art exhibits (often with Third World themes) are worth a look.

The huge city park, **Tiergarten**, stretches west from Brandenburger Tor towards Zoo station. Strasse des 17 Juni (named for the 1953 workers' uprising) leads westwards from Brandenburger Tor through the park. On the northern side of this street, the

Soviet War Memorial is flanked by the first Russian tanks to enter the city in 1945.

Farther to the west, the **Siegessäule** (Victory Column) commemorates 19th-century Prussian military adventures. It is crowned by a gilded statue of the Roman victory goddess, Victoria, which is visible from much of Tiergarten.

Potsdamer Platz One of the biggest attractions is the monumental construction site around Potsdamer Platz, the only area of Berlin which is neither east nor west. Sadly, the lipstick-red Infobox on stilts gazing over Leipziger Platz will have been moved by the time you read this, so you'll have to experience the action and mushrooming modern architecture – like the **Sony-Center** and **DaimlerCity** complex – from the ground. Nearby, on the corner of Wilhelmstrasse and Vossstrasse, is the site of **Hitler's bunker**, now covered by a grassy area.

Kulturforum Area The Kulturforum is a cluster of museums and concert halls – from the gold-plated **Berliner Philharmonie** to the adjacent **Musikinstrumenten-Museum** (Musical Instruments Museum; DM4/2) and its beautifully displayed collection. The SMB **Kunstgewerbemuseum** (Museum of Decorative Arts) shows arts and crafts from the 16th to the 20th century – don't miss Carlo Bugatti's crazy suite of furniture from the 1880s (DM4/2).

Across the plaza, the superb SMB **Neue Gemäldegalerie** (New Picture Gallery) focuses on European painting from the 13th to the 18th century, including stunning works from Rembrandt, Botticelli, Raphael, Goya and more (DM8/4 with a day pass).

To the south-east at Potsdamer Strasse 50 is the squat SMB **Neue Nationalgalerie** (New National Gallery), with 19th and 20th-century paintings and sculptures, including works by Picasso, Klee and German expressionists (DM8/4 with a day pass).

The **Bauhaus Archiv/Museum für Gestaltung** (Bauhaus Archive/Museum of Design), at Klingelhöferstrasse 14, is dedicated to the artists of the Bauhaus school (closed Tuesday; DM5/2.50). The building was designed by Bauhaus founder Walter Gropius.

Kreuzberg On Niederkirchnerstrasse, in the former SS/Gestapo headquarters, the

GERMANY

free **Topography of Terror** exhibition documents Nazi crimes and is open daily.

Almost nothing remains at the site of the famous **Checkpoint Charlie**, a major crossing between east and west during the Cold War. The history of the Berlin Wall is commemorated nearby in the **Haus am Checkpoint Charlie**, Friedrichstrasse 43-44, with tattered but fascinating escape memorabilia and photos (open daily; DM8/5).

The longest surviving stretch of the **Berlin Wall** is just west of the Warschauer Strasse terminus of the U1. This 300m section was turned over to artists who created the **East Side Gallery**, a permanent open-air art gallery. Note that this area is rife with violent punks, urban drifters and druggies.

The Daniel Libeskind-designed **Jüdisches Museum** (Jewish Museum) at Lindenstrasse 9-14 opens late in 2001; its provocative architecture has attracted tens of thousands of visitors. Twice-daily architectural tours in English cost DM8/5.

Kurfürstendamm Once the commercial heart of West Berlin, the Ku'damm can become a stultifying tourist ghetto in summer. The stark ruins of the **Kaiser-Wilhelm-Gedächtnis-Kirche** (1895) on Breitscheidplatz, engulfed in the roaring commercialism all round, are a world-famous landmark. A British bombing on 22 November 1943 left only the broken west tower standing.

Adjacent to Zoo station, on the corner of Kantstrasse and Joachimsthaler, the **Erotik-Museum** is a surprisingly artistic creation of Beate Uhse, the German porno and sex toy queen (DM10/8). It's open 9 am to midnight daily.

North-east of Europa-Center on Budapester Strasse is Germany's oldest **Zoo & Aquarium**, with more than 1400 species. The zoo (DM12) is open 9 am to 5 pm daily; the aquarium is open to 6 pm. A joint zoo-aquarium ticket is DM22.50/11 for adults/children.

Charlottenburg Built as a summer residence for Queen Sophie Charlotte, **Schloss Charlottenburg** (1699) is an exquisite baroque palace on Spandauer Damm northeast from Tiergarten. Make an effort to visit on a weekday, to avoid the heavy weekend crowds. The DM15/10 ticket is good for all tours and attractions. Take the U-Bahn to

Sophie-Charlotte-Platz, then walk for 15 minutes; or take bus No 145 from Zoo station right to the door.

Along the Spree River behind the palace are extensive French and English gardens (free). Across the street at the beginning of Schlossstrasse is the SMB **Ägyptisches Museum** (Egyptian Museum), with the main highlight being the 14th-century BC bust of Queen Nefertiti (DM8/4 with a day pass). The nearby **Sammlung Berggruen** is showing an incredible modern art collection entitled 'Picasso and His Time' until 2006 (DM8/4 with a day pass).

Organised Tours

Most city bus tours operate on the get-on, get-off as often as you wish principle, and take in 12 main sights, including Kurfürstendamm, the Brandenburg Gate, Schloss Charlottenburg, the Berliner Dom and Alexanderplatz. Tours usually run from 10 am to 6 pm and leave from near the Kaiser-Wilhelm-Gedächtnis-Kirche. The cost is DM30.

Highly recommended two- and three-hour walking tours with Berlin Walks (☎ 301 91 94) cost DM14/18 for those under/over 26. Walks – which leave outside Zoo station's main entrance – include Discover Berlin, Third Reich sites and Jewish Berlin.

Insider Tours (☎ 692 31 49) has three-hour walking tours (DM10/15) and four-hour bike tours (DM25/29). Both leave opposite the main entrance to Zoo station, next to McDonald's. Guide yourself for the price of a bus ticket (DM3.90) on bus No 100, which passes 18 major sights on its way from Zoo station to Michelangelostrasse in Prenzlauer Berg.

Cruises Reederei Bruno Winkler (☎ 349 95 95) runs a variety of tours on the Spree River. The most popular is a three-hour cruise (DM22) that leaves several times a day from mid-March to October from the Schlossbrücke, over the Spree just east of Schloss Charlottenburg.

Special Events

The International Film Festival Berlin (☎ 25 48 90), also known as Berlinale, is held in February; about 750 films are shown in a two-week span at various cinemas.

Berlin Pride – Germany's largest gay festival – is held on the last weekend in June. The Love Parade (☎ 390 66 60), in the middle of July, is the world's largest techno party – in recent years it has attracted more than one million people.

Places to Stay

Reservations – no less than two weeks in advance – are *strongly* recommended from May to September and on weekends. At other times of the year (excluding Christmas and New Year) finding a room is not difficult.

The city's tourist information office, Berlin Tourismus Marketing (BTM; ☎ 25 00 25, fax 25 00 24 24), handles hotel reservations at no charge to guests. Bed & Breakfast in Berlin (☎ 44 05 05 82, fax 44 05 05 83, @ bedbreakfa@aol.com), at Tietjenstrasse 36, in Tempelhof, can book singles, doubles and triples around the city.

Camping All camping grounds are far from the city centre and fill up quickly, so call ahead. Charges are DM9.50 per person plus DM7 for a small tent site.

Campingplatz Kohlhasenbrück (☎ 805 17 37, Neue Kreisstrasse 36) is in the suburb of Zehlendorf about 15km south-west of the city centre. It's open from April to September. Take the S7 to Griebnitzsee station – from here it's a 10-minute walk. Alternatively, get off at the previous stop, Wannsee, and take bus No 118 directly to the camping ground.

If it's full, *Campingplatz Dreilinden* (☎ 805 12 01) is 2km east along the Teltow Canal at Albrechts-Teerofen. Bus No 118 from Wannsee station stops there.

DJH Hostels All DJH hostels fill quickly, especially on weekends and between March and October. Phone reservations are not accepted – instead write a few weeks in advance (enclose an international postal reply coupon) to Deutsches Jugendherbergswerk, Zentralreservierung, Kluckstrasse 3, 10785 Berlin. None has cooking facilities, but breakfast is included in the price.

The only DJH hostel within walking distance of the centre is the impersonal 364-bed *Jugendgästehaus Berlin* (☎ 261 10 98, fax 265 03 83, Kluckstrasse 3), which charges DM24 for a dorm bed, DM34 per bed in a three-, four- or five-bed room or DM84 for a double room. It's in Schöneberg, near the Landwehrkanal (take the U1 to Kurfürstenstrasse).

Jugendgästehaus am Wannsee (☎ 803 20 35, fax 803 59 08, Badeweg 1) is on Grosser Wannsee, the lake south-west of the city. The hostel is a 10-minute walk from Nikolassee S-Bahn station (S1 and S7) – walk west over the footbridge and turn left at Kronprinzessinnenweg. Beds cost DM34/42 for juniors/seniors.

Jugendherberge Ernst Reuter (☎ 404 16 10, fax 404 59 72, Hermsdorfer Damm 48-50) is in the far north-west of Berlin. Take the U6 to Alt-Tegel, then bus No 125 to the door. Beds cost DM28/35 for juniors/seniors.

Independent Hostels There are some private hostels which give discounts to students with ID. None has a curfew.

In Charlottenburg, *Jugendgästehaus am Zoo* (☎ 312 94 10, fax 31 25 50 30, Hardenbergstrasse 9a) is three blocks from Zoo station. The rates are DM47/85/35 for singles/doubles/dorm (plus DM5 if you're over 27).

Nearby is the *Jugendhotel Berlin* (☎ 322 10 11, fax 322 10 12, Kaiserdamm 3). If you're under 26, you pay DM57/105 for singles/doubles (DM92/143 for over-26s) with bath and toilet. Take the U2 to Sophie-Charlotte-Platz.

Two moderately priced hotels near Mehringdamm station (U6 or U7) have dormitory accommodation. Friendly *Pension Kreuzberg* (☎ 251 13 62, fax 251 06 38, Grossbeerenstrasse 64) has dorm beds for DM43 and singles/doubles for DM75/98. *Hotel Transit* (☎ 789 04 70, fax 78 90 47 77, Hagelberger Strasse 53-54), in Kreuzberg, has multibed rooms with shower for DM33 per person and singles/doubles for DM90/105.

In Kreuzberg 36, you'll find *Die Fabrik* (☎ 611 71 16, fax 618 29 74, @ info@ diefabrik.com, Schlesische Strasse 18) in a huge converted factory (U15 to Schlesisches Tor). Dorm beds are DM30 and singles/ doubles/triples/quads spread out over five floors (no lift) are DM66/94/120/144; breakfast is an extra DM10.

Jugendgästehaus Schreberjugend (☎ 615 10 07, fax 614 63 39, Franz-Künstler-Strasse 10), in Kreuzberg, charges

GERMANY

CHARLOTTENBURG & WILMERSDORF

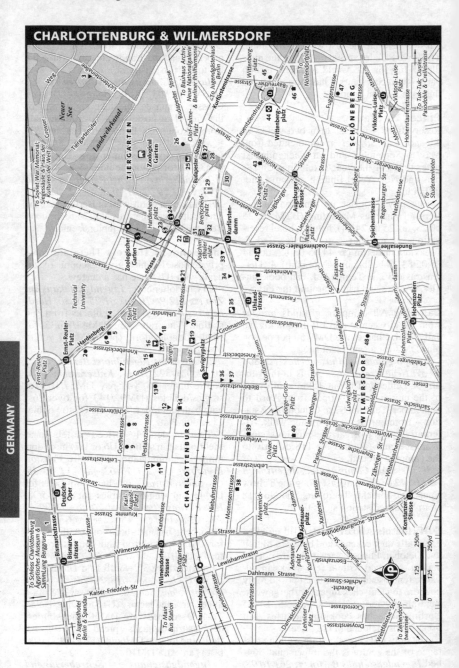

GERMANY

CHARLOTTENBURG & WILMERSDORF

PLACES TO STAY	18	Dicke Wirtin	21	Quasimodo
5 Jugendgästehaus am Zoo	20	Schwarzes Café	22	Erotik-Museum
14 Hotel-Pension Cortina	32	Pizzeria Amigo	23	Reisebank
15 Pension Knesebeck	33	Café Kranzler	24	BVG Information Kiosk
38 Hotel-Pension Majesty	34	Aschinger	25	Main Post Office
39 Hotel-Pension Alexandra	36	Zillemarkt	26	Aquarium
40 Hotel-Pension Modena	37	Ali Baba	27	Berlin Touristen-Information
41 Hotel-Pension Savoy			28	Europa-Center
43 Pension Fischer	**OTHER**		29	Kaiser-Wilhelm-Gedächtnis-
46 Hotel Auberge	1	Deutsche Oper Berlin		Kirche (Memorial Church)
	2	Kiepert Bookshop	30	Hugendubel Bookshop
PLACES TO EAT	6	Kilroy Travel	31	Café Website
3 Café am Neuen See	8	STA Travel	35	Australian Embassy
4 Technische Universität Mensa	9	Books in Berlin	42	City-Wache (Police Station)
(Student Cafeteria)	11	Aldi Supermarket; Schnell	44	KaDeWe Department Store
7 Satyam		und Sauber Laundrette	45	American Express
10 Il Pulcino	13	A-Trane Jazz Club	47	Connection Disco
12 Good Friend	16	Gainsbourg	48	Schnell und Sauber
17 Cour Careé	19	Hegel		Laundrette

DM37 per night in two- or three-bed rooms. Take the U6 or U15 to Hallesches Tor.

In Mitte, the excellent *Circus – The Hostel* (☎ 28 39 14 33, fax 28 39 14 84, @ circus@mind.de, Rosa-Luxemburg-Strasse 39-41), near Alexanderplatz, has comfortable singles/doubles/triples for DM50/80/105. Beds in larger rooms are DM25 to DM39 per person.

The Circus people jointly run *Clubhouse Hostel* (☎ 28 09 79 79, 28 09 79 77, @ mailto@clubhouse-berlin.de, Kalkscheune 2), just behind the Friedrichstadtpalast on Friedrichstrasse.

In the heart of Prenzlauer Berg's nightlife is *Lette 'm Sleep* (☎ 44 73 36 23, fax 44 73 36 25, @ info@backpackers.de, Lettestrasse 7). You'll pay DM25 to DM35 in three- to six-bed rooms or DM45 in doubles (with kitchenette).

Odyssee Globetrotter Hotel (☎ 29 00 00 81, Grünberger Strasse 23), in the second backyard of a Friedrichshain apartment building, has dorm beds for DM24 to DM32 and singles/doubles for DM50/72.

In Schöneberg, *Studentenhotel* (☎ 78 71 74 14, fax 78 71 74 12, @ info@studentenhotel.de, Meininger Strasse 10) offers bed and breakfast for DM44 per person in a double room, DM40 in a quad (U4 to Rathaus Schöneberg).

If you're on a really tight budget, head for the *Internationales Jugendcamp Fliesstal* (☎ 433 86 40, fax 434 50 63), open in July and August only. From the U6 Alt-Tegel

station take bus No 222 (direction 'Lübars') four stops. Space in communal tents is DM10 (blankets and foam mattresses provided); check-in is after 5 pm. No reservations are taken and officially this place is only for those aged 14 to 27, but usually no one gets turned away.

Hotels – Budget In Charlottenburg, *Hotel-Pension Majesty* (☎ 323 20 61, fax 323 20 63, Mommsenstrasse 55) charges from DM90/130 for simple singles/doubles.

Rock-bottom prices – DM50/80 without breakfast – are the draw at *Pension Fischer* (☎ 218 68 08, fax 213 42 25, 2nd floor, Nürnberger Strasse 24a).

Hotel-Pension Cortina (☎ 313 90 59, fax 312 73 96, Kantstrasse 140) has plenty of rooms from DM60/100.

Hotel-Pension Adler (☎ 282 93 52, Friedrichstrasse 124) is a bargain place in Mitte, with rooms with shared facilities costing DM69/89.

In the heart of the gay district around Nollendorfplatz, *Hotel Gunia* (☎ 218 59 40, fax 218 59 44, Eisenacher Strasse 10) charges DM100/140 for a single/double with bath (there's a single without bath for DM90).

In Charlottenburg, excellent *Pension Knesebeck* (☎ 312 72 55, fax 313 95 07, Knesebeckstrasse 86) has basic rooms for DM75/120 or DM85/140 with shower.

Hotels – Mid-Range The *Hotel-Pension Alexandra* (☎ 881 21 07, fax 88 57 78 18,

GERMANY

Wielandstrasse 32) has quiet, simple rooms for DM95/110 or DM120/125 with full facilities. At No 26, **Hotel-Pension Modena** (☎ 885 70 10, *fax 881 52 94)* charges from DM120/180 with own facilities (singles with shared shower go for DM80). **Hotel-Pension Savoy** (☎ *881 37 00, fax 888 37 46, Meinekestrasse 4)* is in a beautiful building with an antique lift. Singles are DM75 to DM125 and doubles start at DM175.

Mitte's **Artist Hotel-Pension Die Loge** (☎/fax *280 75 13, Friedrichstrasse 115)* caters to artists and actors. Its seven rooms cost DM90/120 each.

Hotel Auberge (☎ *235 00 20, fax 235 00 299,* ✉ *hotel-auberge@t-online.de, Bayreuther Strasse 10)*, in an interesting old building in Schöneberg, is a good place with large rooms from DM178/280.

In Kreuzberg, **Hotel am Anhalter Bahnhof** (☎ *251 03 42, fax 251 48 97,* ✉ *hotel-aab@t-online.de, Stresemannstrasse 36)* has simple, reasonably priced digs costing from DM120/170.

Places to Eat

Anyone, student or not, can eat lunch at the **Technische Universität Mensa** *(Hardenbergstrasse 34)*, three blocks from Zoo station. From 11 am to 2.30 pm, three-course lunches cost DM10. Ditto at the **Humboldt Universität Mensa** *(Unter den Linden 6)* in Mitte, entered via the main portal (take the first door on the left).

Berlin Cuisine In Charlottenburg, the old-fashioned **Zillemarkt** *(Bleibtreustrasse 48a)* serves hearty portions at fair prices. German soul food priced around DM20 is served up at the rustic **Grossbeerenkeller** *(Grossbeerenstrasse 90)* in Kreuzberg 61. **Bärenschänke** *(Friedrichstrasse 124)* in Mitte is a smoky neighbourhood pub serving local specialities. Right on Ku'damm at No 26 is **Aschinger**, a cosy cellar with dark beer and an all-you-can-eat salad bar (DM4.80). **Luisen-Bräu** *(Luisenplatz 1)* is a microbrewery near Schloss Charlottenburg, with a daily dish for DM9.80.

Berliner Kneipen (traditional Berlin pubs) have good food and plenty of beer. In Charlottenburg, **Dicke Wirtin** *(Carmerstrasse 9)* is an earthy place off Savignyplatz with daily stews for under DM6. The historic **Zur letzten Instanz** *(Waisenstrasse*

14) is in Mitte. **Alte Berliner Kneipe** *(Schlesische Strasse 6)* in Kreuzberg 36 is especially authentic – as is the nearby **Oberbaum-Eck** on the corner of Oberbaumstrasse and Bevernstrasse.

Asian *Tuk-Tuk (Grossgörschenstrasse 2)* in Schöneberg has Indonesian dishes from DM18 accompanied by soothing gamelan music. **Good Friend** *(Kantstrasse 30)*, near restaurant-packed Savignyplatz, is short on decor but big in the popularity stakes. Always busy is **Kamala** *(Oranienburger Strasse 69)* in Mitte, with curries and noodle dishes averaging DM17.

French *Cour Careé (Savignyplatz 5)* is a nice brasserie open daily to 2 am. In the Nikolaiviertel, the chic brasserie **Reinhard's** *(Poststrasse 28)* serves tasty Franco-German food; the *plat du jour* is around DM19.

Greek Highly recommended is **Ousies** *(Grunewaldstrasse 16)*, where the huge menu features treats like fried sardines stuffed with taramasalata (DM11.50).

International *Deininger (Friesenstrasse 23)* in Kreuzberg has an eclectic menu and all-you-can-eat dishes (DM12) every Monday and Tuesday night and a themed Sunday brunch. The chefs-in-training at **Kiezküche** *(Waldenser Strasse 2-4)* near the Tiergarten turn out refined dishes at absurdly low prices, eg, poached salmon for DM7.

Italian *Il Pulcino (Leibnizstrasse 74)* is a busy neighbourhood place in Charlottenburg; excellent pastas start at DM13. **Ali Baba** *(Bleibtreustrasse 45)* does good pizza (around DM12). **Pizzeria Amigo** *(Joachimsthaler Strasse 39)*, near Zoo station, serves a wicked spaghetti or pizza for less than DM10.

Spanish *Bar-Celona (Hannoversche Strasse 2)* is a friendly restaurant-bar near Brecht-Weigel Gedenkstätte. Tapas are under DM7. A fashionable crowd munches on tapas and bocadillos (from DM3) at **Pasodoble** *(Crellestrasse 39)* in Schöneberg.

Turkish The tastiest felafel we've ever eaten was from **Restaurant Rissani II** *(Mehringdamm 44)* in Kreuzberg. Mains average DM7.

Vegetarian *Satyam* *(Goethestrasse 5)* in Charlottenburg has a big Indian platter for DM9.50. Another good place is *Naturkost Vegetarisches Buffet, (Mehringdamm 48)* in Kreuzberg 61 (U6 or U7 to Mehringdamm). Specials cost less than DM10.

Cafes *Café Kranzler (Kurfürstendamm 18-19)*, near Zoo station, is one of Berlin's oldest coffee houses and a traditional *Konditorei* (cake shop). *Schwarzes Café (Kantstrasse 148)* in Charlottenburg is open around the clock.

Barcomi's (Bergmannstrasse 21) in Kreuzberg is a hole-in-the-wall place loved by locals for its great coffee and bagels. In S-Bahn arch No 192 on Georgenstrasse, near Museumsinsel, *Cafe Odéon* has snacks (DM6.50 to DM9) and a good old-timey atmosphere. On balmy summer nights head for *Café am Neuen See (Lichtensteinallee 1)*, right in Tiergarten park. From November to February it's only open on weekends.

Entertainment

Berlin's entertainment options are almost daunting. Areas to look out for include Kreuzberg 61 for an alternative but trendy scene; Kreuzberg 36 for a grungier, slightly edgy feel; Prenzlauer Berg for the most dynamic nightlife scene; and Friedrichshain for its emerging bar scene.

Pubs & Bars *Gainsbourg (Savignyplatz 5)* speaks to a 30-something artsy crowd. Nearby, cultured *Hegel (Savignyplatz 2)* is popular with expat Russians. In gentrifying Kreuzberg 36 is *Morgenland (Skalitzer Strasse 35)*. A longtime favourite is *Flammende Herzen (Flaming Hearts; Oranienstrasse 170)*; it's dark, romantic and, occasionally, gay. Dark and retro, *Astro (Simon-Dach-Strasse 40)* is a cool techno bar in Friedrichshain. *Obst und Gemüse (Oranienburger Strasse 48)* in Mitte is a pretty hip and popular bar. Plenty of cafe-pubs with outdoor tables are clustered around Käthe-Kollwitz-Platz in Prenzlauer Berg, including *Café Weitzmann (Husemannstrasse 2)*. Good pub-cafes on Crellestrasse in Schöneberg include *Café Mirell* at No 46 and the retro *Leuchturm* at No 17.

Beer Gardens A cult favourite is the open-air *Golgatha (Dudenstrasse 48-64)* in Viktoriapark in Kreuzberg 61. In the southwestern district of Zehlendorf is *Loretta am Wannsee (Kronprinzessinenweg 260)*, a huge garden; take the S1, S3 or S7 to Wannsee.

Nightclubs Nothing happens at most places until 11 pm at the earliest. Cover charges (when they apply) are DM5 to DM20 and usually don't include a drink.

Berlin *is* techno music and you'll be hard pressed to find a club that plays anything else. One of the oldest techno temples is *Tresor* (☎ *609 37 02, Leipziger Strasse 126a)* in Mitte. Upstairs is the affiliated *Globus*, which plays more hip-hop, funk and soul.

Popular and always packed is *Delicious Doughnuts* (☎ *28 09 92 74, Rosenthaler Strasse 9)*, an acid jazz club in Mitte. Kreuzberg's *SO 36* (☎ *61 40 13 07, Oranienstrasse 190)* is one of Berlin's longest-running techno nightclubs. *KitKat Club@Metropolis* (☎ *217 36 80, Nollendorf Platz 5)* in Schöneberg has Sex Trance Bizarre parties on Friday and Saturday nights (you only get in wearing erotic – or basically no – clothes).

A great club in Mitte is *Sophienklub* (☎ *282 45 52, Sophienstrasse 6)* off Rosenthaler Strasse, especially if you're tired of techno. Chances are you'll hear Britpop, 70s and 80s music, disco and Indie.

Gay & Lesbian Venues For listings and one-off parties check the free *Siegessäule* or the strictly gay *Sergej Szene Berlin*.

Hafen (Motzstrasse 19), near Nollendorfplatz, is full of gay yuppies. Next door is the legendary *Tom's Bar. Connection* (☎ *218 14 32, Fuggerstrasse 33)* is arguably the best gay disco in town.

Interesting places in Kreuzberg 36 include the *O-Bar (Oranienstrasse 168)* with a good mixed crowd and *Schoko-Café (Mariannenstrasse 6)*, a convival meeting place for lesbians. A good lesbian cafe is the smoke and alcohol-free *Café Seidenfaden (Dircksenstrasse 47)* in Mitte.

Jazz & Rock *A-Trane* (☎ *313 25 50, Bleibtreustrasse 1)* in Charlottenburg is *the* place in Berlin for jazz. *Quasimodo* (☎ *312 80 86, Kantstrasse 12a)* has nightly live jazz, blues or rock acts in the basement.

GERMANY

BERLIN-MITTE

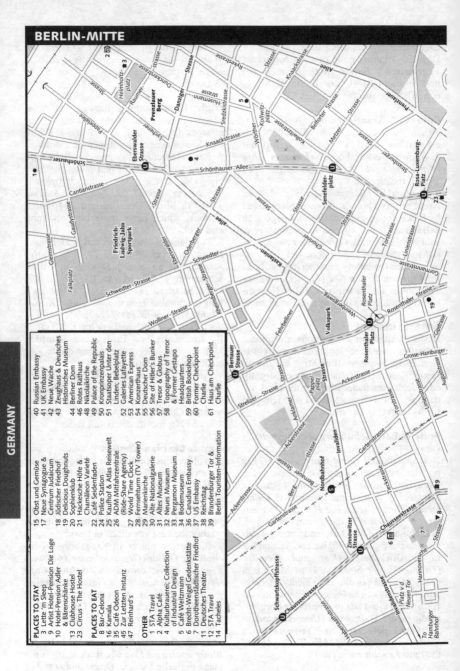

PLACES TO STAY
3 Lette 'm Sleep
9 Artist Hotel-Pension Die Loge
10 Hotel-Pension Adler
& Bärenschänke
13 Clubhouse Hostel
23 Circus – The Hostel

PLACES TO EAT
8 Bar-Celona
16 Kamala
35 Café Odeon
45 Zur Letzten Instanz
47 Reinhard's

OTHER
1 STA Travel
2 Alpha Café
4 Kulturbrauerei; Collection
of Industrial Design
5 Café Weltzrian
7 Brecht-Weigel Gedenkstätte
7 Dorotheenstädtischer Friedhof
11 Deutsches Theater
12 STA Travel
14 Tacheles
15 Obst und Gemüse
17 Neue Synagogue &
Centrum Judaicum
18 Jüdischer Friedhof
19 Delicious Doughnuts
20 Sophienklub
21 Hackesche Höfe &
Chamäleon Varieté
22 Café Seidenfaden
24 Police Station
25 Kaufhof & Atlas Reisewelt
26 ADM Mitfahrzentrale
(Ride-Share Agency)
27 World Time Clock
28 Fernsehturm (TV Tower)
29 Marienkirche
30 Alte Nationalgalerie
31 Altes Museum
32 Neues Museum
33 Pergamon Museum
34 Bodemuseum
36 Canadian Embassy
37 US Embassy
38 Reichstag
39 Brandenburger Tor &
Berlin Touristen-Information
40 Russian Embassy
41 UK Embassy
42 Neue Wache
43 Zeughaus & Deutsches
Historisches Museum
44 Berliner Dom
46 Rotes Rathaus
48 Nikolaikirche
49 Palace of the Republic
50 Kronprinzenpalais
51 Staatsoper Unter den
Linden; Bebelplatz
52 Galeries Lafayette
53 American Express
54 Konzerthaus
55 Deutscher Dom
56 Site of Hitler's Bunker
57 Tresor & Globus
58 Topography of Terror
& Former Gestapo
Headquarters
59 British Bookshop
60 Former Checkpoint
Charlie
61 Haus am Checkpoint
Charlie

GERMANY

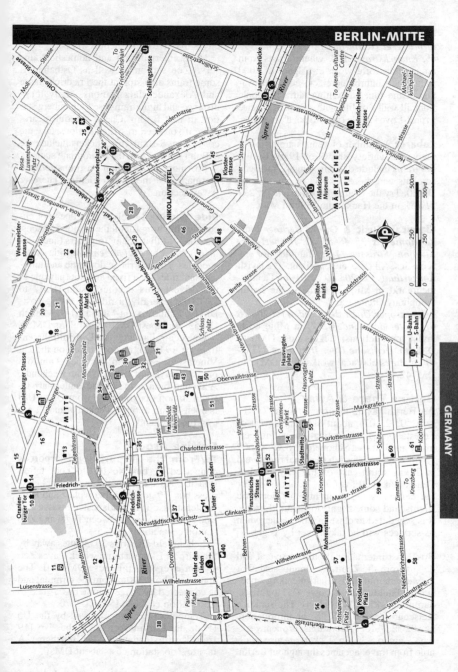

The hot spot in Prenzl'berg is the *Kulturbrauerei (Cultural Brewery; ☎ 441 92 69, Knaackstrasse 97)*, where artists from around the world work in a space of 8000 sq m. The Kulturbrauerei, closed for renovation at the time of writing, attracts people from all walks of life with events as diverse as post-Love Parade raves to poetry readings.

Cabaret A number of venues are trying to revive the variety shows of 1920s Berlin. Programs include dancers, singers, jugglers, acrobats and more. Expect to pay at least DM20. Try the *Chamäleon Varieté (☎ 282 71 18)*, in the Hackesche Höfe in Mitte.

Classical Music & Opera *Berliner Philharmonie (☎ 25 48 81 32, Herbert-von-Karajan Strasse 1)* is famous for its acoustics. All seats are excellent. The lavish *Konzerthaus (☎ 203 09 21 01)* on Gendarmenmarkt in Mitte is home to the Berlin Symphony Orchestra.

Staatsoper Unter den Linden (☎ 208 28 61, Unter den Linden 5-7) in Mitte hosts lavish productions; tickets cost DM6 to DM190. *Deutsche Oper Berlin (☎ 343 84 01)* features classical works from DM17 to DM142.

Getting There & Away

Air Berlin has three airports. Tegel (TXL; ☎ 41 01 23 07), about 8km north-west of Zoo station, serves destinations within Germany and Europe. Schönefeld (SXF; ☎ 609 10) mostly operates international flights and is 22km south-east of the city. Berlin-Tempelhof (THF; ☎ 695 11), 6km south of the centre, is the main hub for domestic flights, and some flights to Central Europe. It is scheduled to close by 2002, after when its services will be taken over by Tegel.

Bus Most international buses arrive at and depart from the Zentraler Omnibusbahnhof at Messedamm 8, in Charlottenburg opposite the Funkturm radio tower (U2 to Kaiserdamm or S45 to Witzleben). The station's Reisebüro (☎ 301 80 28 for information, ☎ 302 52 94 for reservations) is open weekdays 9 am to 5.30 pm. Tickets are also available from travel agencies throughout Berlin.

Train Until the opening of the new Lehrter Bahnhof in 2007, train services to/from

Berlin will remain confusing due to the city's massive construction works.

Many international and domestic trains serve Zoo station as well as Ostbahnhof; some trains also stop at the Friedrichstrasse and Alexanderplatz stations. Many long-distance and night trains use Lichtenberg station in east Berlin. Check schedules carefully; if you need to switch stations, take the convenient S-Bahn (train tickets include the S-Bahn ride to/from the appropriate station).

For more information on trains to/from Germany see the earlier Getting There & Away section.

Ride Sharing Lonely Planet does not encourage hitching for all the obvious reasons. Having said that, many travellers (and Germans) swear by *Mitfahrzentrale* (ride share) agencies. These arrange domestic and international rides for a fixed amount (payable to the driver) plus a commission (DM7 to DM20). Generally, a ride to Leipzig costs DM19, Frankfurt-am-Main DM49, Munich DM53, Budapest DM109 and Paris DM84.

One central agency is ADM Mitfahrzentrale (☎ 194 40), in Zoo station on the U2 Vinetastrasse platform. It's open 9 am to 8 pm weekdays and 10 am to 6 pm weekends. A second branch in the Alexanderplatz U-Bahn station (as you cross from U2 to U8) is open 10 am to 6 pm weekdays and 11 am to 4 pm weekends.

Getting Around

To/From the Airport Tegel airport is connected by bus No 109 to Zoo station (via the Ku'damm and Luisenplatz). Express bus X9 goes to Lützowplatz and Kurfürstenstrasse (via Budapester Strasse and Zoo station). A taxi between Tegel and Zoo station costs about DM35.

Schönefeld airport is 30 minutes away by the Airport Express train, which leaves Zoo station every 30 minutes (DM4.20). The station is about 300m from the terminal and is connected by a free shuttle bus. A taxi to Zoo station costs DM50 to DM70.

Tempelhof airport is served by the U6 (Platz der Luftbrücke) and by bus No 119 from Kurfürstendamm (via Kreuzberg). A taxi to Zoo station costs about DM30.

Public Transport Berliner Verkehrsbetriebe (BVG; ☎ 194 49) operates the

GERMANY

U-Bahn, buses, trams and ferries, while the Deutsche Bahn (DB; ☎ 01805-99 66 33) now runs the S-Bahn and regional RE, SE and RB trains (Eurail and Inter-Rail holders can use DB trains for free). The BVG kiosk on Hardenbergplatz in front of Zoo station has free route maps and general information.

Berlin's metropolitan area is divided into three tariff zones – A, B and C. Unless you're venturing to Potsdam, buy the AB ticket. Other tickets include: the Kurzstrecke (Short Trip) ticket (DM2.50), valid for three stops on the U-Bahn or S-Bahn, or six stops by bus or tram; the Langstrecke (Long Trip) ticket (DM3.90), valid for two hours of unlimited travel; and the Tageskarte (Day Pass), valid for unlimited travel until 3 am the following day for DM7.80 (zones AB or BC) or DM8.50 (zones ABC).

Bus drivers sell single and day tickets, but tickets for U/S-Bahn trains and other tickets must be purchased from the orange vending machines in U/S-Bahn stations. Tickets must be stamped (validated) in a red machine at the platform entrances to U/S-Bahn stations or at bus stops before boarding.

Bicycle Fahrradstation is the largest bike-rental agency with branches all over the city, including at the left-luggage office in Zoo station (☎ 29 74 93 19). Bikes cost from DM18 to DM23 a day.

AROUND BERLIN
Potsdam
☎ 0331

Potsdam, 24km from Berlin and easily accessible by S-Bahn, is an ideal day trip. In the mid-18th century Friedrich II (Frederick the Great) built many of the marvellous palaces in Potsdam's Sanssouci Park, to which visitors flock today. The Allies chose Schloss Cecilienhof for the Potsdam Conference of August 1945, which set the stage for the division of Berlin and Germany into occupation zones.

Orientation & Information The main train station and last stop for the S-Bahn is Potsdam-Stadt. From here, it is a 4km walk over the Lange Brücke and through the town centre to the gates of Sanssouci Park. Or take bus No 606 from the Lange Brücke

to Schloss Charlottenhof and the Neues Palais; tram No 98 also goes to the former.

The Potsdam-Information office (☎ 27 55 80, fax 27 55 99) is beside the Alter Markt at Friedrich-Ebert-Strasse 5. Sanssouci-Information (☎ 969 42 00), near the old windmill opposite Schloss Sanssouci, has details on the palaces in the park.

Things to See The vast **Sanssouci Park** is free and open from dawn to dusk. A day ticket to all the palaces within the park costs DM20/15. Otherwise, students get a 50% discount at each palace.

Georg Wenzeslaus von Knobelsdorff's **Schloss Sanssouci** (1747), a celebrated rococo palace with glorious interiors, is only accessible by guided tour – arrive early as the tickets often sell out by 2.30 pm. The palace is open 9 am to 5 pm Tuesday to Sunday from April to mid-October (to 4 pm November to April).

The late-baroque **Neues Palais** (1769), the summer residence of the royal family, is one of the most imposing buildings in the park and the one to see if time is limited. It's open the same hours as the Schloss Sanssouci but closes on Friday instead of Monday.

The **Bildergalerie** contains a rich collection of 17th-century paintings (closed Monday), and **Schloss Charlottenhof** can only be visited on a 30-minute German-language tour (closed Wednesday). Both of these sites close from November to April.

Sachsenhausen

In 1936 the Nazis opened a 'model' concentration camp at Sachsenhausen, 35km north of Berlin. By 1945 about 220,000 people from 22 countries had passed through the gates of Sachsenhausen – labelled, as at Auschwitz in south-western Poland, *Arbeit Macht Frei* (Work Sets You Free); about 100,000 died here. After the war, the Soviets and the leaders of the GDR used the camp for *their* undesirables.

Plan on spending at least two hours at Sachsenhausen. Among the many museums and monuments within the triangular-shaped, walled grounds are **Barracks 38 & 39**. Rebuilt after an arson attack by neo-Nazis in 1992, they contain excellent displays about the camp's history. An information office (☎ 03301-80 37 15) sells maps and helpful English-language guides.

GERMANY

The camp is open 8.30 am to 6 pm from April to September, closing at 4.30 pm the rest of the year (closed Monday; free). From Berlin take the S1 to Oranienburg (DM4.20, 40 minutes). The camp is 2km north-east of the station – an easy, signposted 20-minute walk.

Saxony

DRESDEN
☎ 0351

In the 18th century, Dresden, the capital of Saxony, was famous throughout Europe as the 'Florence of the north', largely due to the Italian artists and craftsmen who flocked to the Dresden court during the reigns of Augustus the Strong (ruled 1694-1733) and his son Augustus III (1733-63). In February 1945 much of Dresden was devastated by Allied fire-bombing raids – at least 35,000 people died. This horrific attack is the basis for *Slaughterhouse Five* by Kurt Vonnegut, who was a POW in Dresden at the time.

In the postwar years Dresden's great baroque buildings have been restored. In spite of some modern rebuilding in concrete and steel, Dresden is an impressive city – budget at least two days to cover all of its main sights.

Orientation & Information

Most trains stop at Dresden's two main stations: Dresden Hauptbahnhof, on the southern side of town, and Dresden-Neustadt north of the river. The ramshackle Hauptbahnhof is more convenient unless you're staying in Neustadt. To reach the Altstadt from the Hauptbahnhof, follow the pedestrian mall, Prager Strasse, north past some classic GDR monoliths.

Dresden-Information (☎ 49 19 20, fax 49 19 21 16), Prager Strasse 10, is open from 10 am to 6 pm weekdays and from 9.30 am to 5 pm Saturday. A second Neustadt branch is in the underpass below the Goldener Reiter statue; a third branch is in the Schinkelwache near the Semperoper.

All offices sell the Dresden Card (DM29), which is valid for 48 hours and gives free entry to 11 museums, discounts on city tours and free use of public transport. Internet access costs DM5 per half-hour at Cyberb@r

on the 3rd floor of Karstadt department store, Prager Strasse 12.

Things to See & Do

Cross the wide Wilsdruffer Strasse to the **Stadtmuseum** (closed Friday to Sunday; DM4/2). North-west up Landhausstrasse is Neumarkt and the site of the ruined **Frauenkirche** (Church of Our Lady) built in 1738. Until the fire-bombings in 1945 it was Germany's greatest Protestant church; it is now undergoing major renovations.

Walk north-west from Neumarkt to Augustusstrasse with the stunning 102m-long **Procession of Princes**, a porcelain mural on the outer wall of the old royal stables.

Augustusstrasse leads directly to Schlossplatz and the baroque Catholic **Hofkirche** (1755). Just south of the church is the Renaissance **Schloss**, which is being reconstructed as a museum – the tower and a palace exhibit are now open to the public (closed Monday; DM5/2).

On the western side of the Hofkirche is Theaterplatz, with Dresden's glorious opera house, the neo-Renaissance **Semperoper**. The baroque **Zwinger** (1728), one of Dresden's star attractions, occupies the southern side of Theaterplatz. Among its five museums, the most important is the **Historisches Museum**, which has a superb collection of ceremonial weapons (closed Monday; DM3).

East of the Augustusbrücke (bridge) is the **Brülsche Terrace**, an elevated riverside promenade that is saddled with the overwrought moniker of 'The Balcony of Europe'. At the eastern end is the **Albertinum** (1885), with the **Gemäldegalerie Alte Meister** (closed Monday), which boasts Raphael's *Sistine Madonna*; the **Gemäldegalerie Neue Meister** (closed Tuesday), with renowned 19th- and 20th-century paintings; and the **Grünes Gewölbe** (Green Vault; closed Tuesday), with a collection of jewel-studded precious objects. South-east of the Altstadt is the **Grosser Garten**, enchanting in summer and home to a fine zoo.

Elbe River Excursions From May to November Sächsische Dampfschifffahrts GmbH (☎ 86 60 90) has one-hour river tours (DM20). Boats also go to Meissen (DM27, two hours). Schedules vary, so check at the waterfront ticket office just east of Augustusbrücke.

Places to Stay

Dresden-Information arranges beds in *private rooms* for DM6.

Hostels The central *Jugendgästehaus Dresden* (☎ 49 26 20, fax 492 62 99, Maternistrasse 22) is a 15-minute walk north-west of the Hauptbahnhof; or take tram No 7, 9, 10 or 26 to the corner of Ammonstrasse and Freiberger Strasse. Beds cost DM33/38 for people under/over 26.

The non-DJH *Jugendherberge Rudi Arndt* (☎ 471 06 67, fax 472 89 59, Hübnerstrasse 11) is a 10-minute walk south of the Hauptbahnhof. Dorm beds are DM25/30.

In the heart of Neustadt nightlife, *Die Boofe* (☎ 801 33 61, fax 801 33 62, ☻ boofe@t-online.de, Louisenstrasse 20) charges DM27/49.50/79 for dorms/singles/doubles, while *Mondpalast* (☎/fax 8 04 60 61, ☻ mondpalast@t-online.de, Katherinenstrasse 11-13) charges DM25/40/64. For both, take tram No 7 or 8 to Louisenstrasse.

Hotels Five minutes from the Hauptbahnhof along Prager Strasse are the *Hotel Ibis Bastei* (☎ 48 56 66 61), the *Hotel Ibis Königstein* (☎ 48 56 66 62) and the *Hotel Ibis Lilienstein* (☎ 48 56 66 63). Their rates are as similar as their 1960s-style architecture, with rooms from DM110/130 a single/double.

In the Neustadt, *Pension Edith* (☎ 802 83 42, Priesnitzstrasse 63) has single/double rooms with shower for DM79/109.

Places to Eat

Restaurants and cafes in the Altstadt are hard on the budget. The only real find is the stylish and tasty *aha* (*Kreuzstrasse 7*), just off Altmarkt. It serves innovative organic fare daily to midnight.

In the Neustadt, not far from the Augustusbrücke, *Restaurant Kügelgenhaus* (*Hauptstrasse 13*) has a good range of local Saxon dishes; there's also a beer cellar below the restaurant. *Trattoria Vecchia Napoli* (*Alaunstrasse 33*) has oven-fresh pizza and good pasta dishes from DM9. *Café Scheune* (*Alaunstrasse 36*) has a tasty vegetarian Indian meal for two for DM28. *Raskolnikoff* (*Böhmische Strasse 34*) has cheap Russian dishes like *borscht* and *wareniki* (dough baked with potatoes and mushrooms).

Entertainment

Dresden is synonymous with opera and performances at the *Semperoper* are brilliant. Dresden's two other great theatres are the *Staatsschauspiel*, near the Zwinger and the *Staatsoperette* in Leuben in the far east of the city.

A variety of musical events are presented in the *Kulturpalast* (☎ 486 6250), which changes its programs daily. *Jazzclub Tonne* (☎ 802 60 17, Am Brauhaus 3) has live jazz five nights a week (cover DM12 to DM20).

There's a great variety of bars in the Neustadt, from the dark *Mondfisch* (*Louisenstrasse 37*) to the *Mona Lisa* (*Louisenstrasse 77*) cocktail bar.

Getting There & Away

Frequent IC trains link Dresden to Berlin (DM59, two hours), Leipzig (DM40, 1¼ hours), Hanover (DM110.60, 4½ hours) and Cologne (DM198, 7½ hours), where you can connect to major cities all over Germany. There are trains to Warsaw (DM135), Budapest (DM142), Vienna (DM123) and Prague (DM98).

AROUND DRESDEN
Meissen
☎ 03521

Meissen, just 27km north-west of Dresden, is a perfectly preserved old German town and the centre of a rich wine-growing region. Its medieval quarter, Albrechtsburg, crowns a ridge high above the Elbe River. Various steeply stepped lanes lead up to the Albrechtsburg, whose towering medieval **cathedral**, with its altarpiece by Lucas Cranach the Elder, is visible from afar (open daily; DM3.50/2.50).

Beside the cathedral is the remarkable 15th-century **palace** (open daily but closed early January; DM6/4); Europe's first porcelain factory was opened here in 1710. Today's **porcelain factory** is at Talstrasse 9, 1km south-west of town. There are often long queues for the workshop demonstrations (DM9/7), but you can view the porcelain collection in the museum at your leisure (a further DM5).

Meissen straddles the Elbe River, with the old town on the western bank and the train station on the eastern bank. The train/pedestrian bridge behind the station is the quickest way across. From the bridge,

GERMANY

continue up Obergasse then bear right through Hahnemannsplatz and Rossplatz to the Markt, Meissen's central square. The helpful Meissen-Information (☎ 419 49, fax 41 94 19) is at Markt 3.

Places to Stay & Eat The non-DJH *Jugendgästehaus* (*☎/fax 45 30 65, Wilsdruffer Strasse 28*), a 20-minute walk south of Markt, has dorm beds for DM18. *Pension Burkhardt* (*☎ 45 81 98, fax 45 81 97, Neugasse 29*) is halfway between Rossmarkt and the porcelain factory. Attractive rooms with bath are DM70/110 a single/double.

Kartoffelkäfer (*Marktgasse 1*) is all things spud to spud-lovers, with hearty meals from DM9.20. *Zollhof* (*Elbstrasse 7*) serves Saxon dishes (light meals under DM10 and mains for under DM20).

Getting There & Away From Dresden take the S-Bahn (DM8.70, 40 minutes) or a boat (see the earlier Elbe River Excursions section).

Görlitz
☎ 03581

Görlitz, 100km east of Dresden on the Neisse River, emerged from WWII with its beautiful old town undamaged. Of particular interest are the **town hall** (1537), the **Peterskirche** (1497) and the 16th-century **Dreifaltigkeitskirche** on Obermarkt. The tourist office (☎ 475 70, fax 47 57 27) is at Obermarkt 29.

Places to Stay & Eat The *DJH hostel* (*☎/fax 40 65 10, Goethestrasse 17*), south of the station, charges DM21. Central *Gästehaus Lisakowski* (*☎ 40 05 39, Landeskronstrasse 23*) offers simple singles/doubles for DM60/90. *Hotel Bon-Apart* (*☎ 480 80, Elisabethstrasse 41*) is a delightful place and charges from DM90 per person.

Zum alten Brauhaus (*Bruderstrasse 3*) serves local specialities from DM10 and has a beer garden.

Getting There & Away To/from Dresden there are RB trains every hour (DM29, two hours) and IR trains every two hours (DM29, 90 minutes). There are four IR trains a day to/from Berlin (DM58, 3½ hours). Görlitz is on the border with Poland; night trains to Warsaw (DM80) stop here

and there is one IR train a day to/from Wroclaw (DM27, 2½ hours).

LEIPZIG
☎ 0341

Leipzig, the second-largest city in eastern Germany, is a major business and transport centre. It has a strong cultural tradition and has much to offer book and music lovers (Bach's time here is celebrated by a museum and an active choir). Since reunification in 1990, Leipzig has experienced a restoration and construction boom that has brought new life to its many fine old buildings.

Orientation & Information
From Leipzig's train station (the largest in Europe), head through the underpass below Willy-Brandt-Platz and continue south for five minutes; the central Markt square is a few blocks south-west. The wide Augustusplatz, three blocks east of Markt, is fronted by the Universitt, Gewandhaus concert hall and the functional Opernhaus (opera house).

Leipzig-Information (☎ 710 42 65, fax 710 42 71), Richard-Wagner-Strasse 1, directly opposite the train station, is open 9 am to 7 pm daily (to 4 pm Saturday and 2 pm Sunday). Staff sell the one-day Leipzig Card (DM9.90), good for discounts at museums and free travel on public transport.

You can wash your dirty clothes at Maga Pon, a combination laundrette and cafe at Gottschedstrasse 3, and surf the Internet (DM5 for half an hour) at Cyberb@r on the top floor of Karstadt, Neumarkt 38.

Things to See
The Markt's Renaissance **Altes Rathaus** (1556) is one of Germany's most beautiful town halls. **Nikolaikirche** (1165), between Markt and Augustusplatz, has a truly remarkable interior. South-west of Markt is **St Thomas Church** (1212), with the tomb of composer Johann Sebastian Bach in front of the altar. Bach worked in Leipzig from 1723 until his death in 1750. The St Thomas Boys Choir, which he once led, is still going strong. Opposite the church, at Thomaskirchhof 16, is the **Bach Museum** (DM6/4).

North along Dittrichring, where it intersects with Goerdelerring, is the former East German Stasi (secret police) headquarters, which houses the free **Museum in der Runden Ecke**, with exhibits outlining Stasi methods of investigation – some appalling, some worthy of Inspector Clouseau (closed Monday).

The best of Leipzig's fine museums, **Museum der bildenden Künste** (Museum of Fine Arts), is in temporary quarters at Grimmaische Strasse 1-7 until 2002 (DM5/2.50).

South-east of the city centre is Leipzig's most impressive sight, the 91m-tall **Völkerschlachtdenkmal** (Battle of Nations Monument), built in 1913 to commemorate the 1813 defeat of Napoleon's armies by the Prussians, Austrians and Russians (DM5/2.50).

Places to Stay

Leipzig-Information runs a free room-finding service (☎ 710 42 55).

Campingplatz Am Auensee (☎ 465 16 00, Gustav-Esche-Strasse 5) is in the woods on the city's north-western outskirts; take tram No 10 or 28 to the end of the line at Wahren, then walk eight minutes. Camping costs DM12 per person plus DM5 for a car or tent site.

Leipzig's two youth hostels are both 5km east of the centre. The *Jugendpension (☎ 194 30, Rudolf-Breitscheid-Strasse 39)* is near the Battle of Nations Monument – take tram No 15 to Völkerschlachtdenkmal. Beds are DM22 to DM30. The larger *Jugendherberge (☎ 245 70 11, Volksgartenstrasse 24)* charges about the same. Take tram No 17, 27 or 37 (direction 'Schönefeld') to Löbauer Strasse and walk five minutes farther north.

North-west of the main train station is *Pension am Nordplatz (☎ 960 31 43, fax 564 98 71, Nordstrasse 58)*, with basic rooms from DM80/100 a single/double. Other reasonable options include the family-run *Weisses Ross (☎ 960 59 51, Rossstrasse 20)*, with rooms from DM70/95. Farther east of the city centre, *Pension Prima (☎ 688 34 81, Dresdner Strasse 82)* has simple rooms for DM50/70.

Places to Eat

Al Salam (Nikolaistrasse 33) has cheap Middle Eastern food: doners are DM3 while the vegetarian platter is DM7.50. *Paulaner Palais*, with locations at Klostergasse No 3

and No 5, has hearty meals for around DM15. Martin Luther's favourite pub was *Thüringer Hof (Burgstrasse 19)*, where great dishes cost from DM13. Founded in 1525, *Auerbachs Keller*, in the Mädler Passage, is one of Germany's classic restaurants – Goethe mentions it in his play *Faust*.

Entertainment

Moritz-Bastei (Universitätsstrasse 9), spread over three underground floors, has live music or disco most nights. *Spizz (Markt 9)* is a trendy cafe by day and slick place for drinking and dancing by night.

Getting There & Away

Leipzig is linked by fast trains to all major German cities, including Dresden (DM40, 1¼ hours), Berlin (DM58, two hours) and Munich (DM140, 5½ hours).

Thuringia

ERFURT
☎ 0361

This trading and university centre, founded as a bishop's residence by St Boniface in 742 AD, is the lively capital of Thuringia (Thüringen). Erfurt was only slightly damaged during WWII, and its astonishingly well-preserved medieval quarter with numerous burgher town houses, churches and monasteries is listed by Unesco as a World Heritage Site. If you visit only one city in Thuringia, make it Erfurt.

Orientation & Information

Bahnhofstrasse leads north from the train station to Anger, a large square in the heart of the city. Continue straight, following the tram tracks along Schlösserstrasse, to Fischmarkt. The efficient tourist office (☎ 664 00, fax 664 02 90, ❷ service@erfurt-tourist-info.de) at Fischmarkt 27 is open 10 am to 7 pm weekdays and to 4 pm Saturday (till 6pm from January to March). From here it's a short walk west along Marktstrasse to Domplatz, Erfurt's most impressive square.

Erfurt's Classic-Card (DM25) allows unlimited use of public transportation and entry to museums for 72 hours.

See the Web site at www.erfurt-tourist-info.de for more information.

GERMANY

Things to See & Do

The Fischmarkt, a handsome medieval square, is fronted by the neo-Gothic **Rathaus** (Town Hall; 1873), the **Haus Zum Breiten Herd** (1584) and the **Haus Zum Roten Ochsen** (1562).

A few blocks west of Fischmarkt, Erfurt's largest and finest square, Domplatz, is dominated by the 13th-century Gothic **Dom St Marien** and the **Severikirche**, which stand together on a hill. Both are worth a visit.

From Fischmarkt, the eastbound street beside the town hall leads to the medieval **Krämerbrücke** (1325), a stunning bridge lined on both sides with timber-framed shops. Farther north, on the same side of the River Gera, is **Augustinerkloster**, a late-medieval monastery that was home to Martin Luther early in the 16th century (open daily, only by arrangement from November to March; DM5.50/4).

Places to Stay

The tourist office books beds in private rooms for DM40/80, plus a DM5 booking fee. Erfurt's *Jugendherberge* (☎ 562 67 05, fax 562 67 06, @ jugendherberge-erfurt@ t-online.de, Hochheimer Strasse 12) is south-west of the centre and costs DM25/30 for juniors/seniors. Take tram No 5 from Erfurt train station southbound to the terminus.

Pension Schuster (☎ 373 50 52, Rubenstrasse 11) has clean, bright single/double rooms for DM65/70 (breakfast DM5 extra) with a bathroom. *Pension am Park* (☎ 345 34 71, fax 345 33 44, Löberwallgraben 22) has fairly good rooms with shared facilities for DM75/100 (check-in is after 2 pm). *Ibis* (☎ 664 10, fax 664 11 11, @ h1648@accorhotels.com, Barfüsserstrasse 9) is central and standard, but good value at DM120 for doubles without breakfast (singles cost the same).

Places to Eat

There's a convenient REWE *supermarket* in the InterCity Hotel on Willy-Brandt-Platz at the train station.

You should have no trouble finding good eats in Erfurt. *Suppen-Grün (Regierungsstrasse 70)* serves wholesome organic-vegetarian broths (from DM6.50) until 3 pm daily except Sunday. The microbrewery *Erfurter Brauhaus (Anger 21)* offers cheap, hearty fare to accompany its own brew –

pilsener and *Schwarzbier*. The best nightlife is in the Andreasviertel, a few paces northwest of Fischmarkt. *P33 (Pergamentergasse 33)* serves a Sunday brunch with music, and is a good spot for an evening beer.

Getting There & Away

Every two hours a direct IR train connects Frankfurt (DM72, 3½ hours) and Erfurt. The same train goes to/from Berlin (DM81, 3½ hours) and to/from Weimar (DM8, 14 minutes) and Eisenach (DM15, 40 minutes). Regional trains also run between Weimar and Eisenach. IC trains go to/from Leipzig (DM54, two hours, every two hours).

WEIMAR
☎ 03643

Weimar is well known as the place where the German republican constitution was drafted after WWI (hence, the 1919-33 Weimar Republic). Weimar is also associated with the nearby Buchenwald concentration camp.

Many famous people lived and worked here, including Lucas Cranach the Elder, Johann Sebastian Bach, Friedrich Schiller, Johann Wolfgang von Goethe, Franz Liszt, Friedrich Nietzsche, Walter Gropius, Vasili Kandinsky and Paul Klee. The Bauhaus movement, which laid the foundations of modern architecture, functioned in the city from 1919 to 1925.

Orientation & Information

The centre of town, just west of the Ilm River, is a 20-minute walk south of the train station. Buses run frequently between the station and Goetheplatz, from where it's a short walk east to Herderplatz or Markt.

Weimar-Information (☎ 240 00, fax 24 04 40, @ tourist-info@weimar.de), Markt 10, is open 9.30 am to 7 pm weekdays, till 5 pm Saturday, and till 4 pm Sunday. From November to March it keeps slightly shorter hours. A smaller tourist office (☎ 24 00 45, fax 24 00 46) inside Weimar Hauptbahnhof is open 10 am to 8 pm daily. The three-day Weimar Card (DM20) is valid for unlimited bus/tram travel and for entry to many museums. For more information, see the Web site at www.weimar.de.

Times Square, inside Weimar Hauptbahnhof, is a great if expensive Internet cafe where you can drink and surf (open daily; DM3 per 15 minutes).

Things to See

The 16th-century **Herderkirche** on Herder-platz has an altarpiece (1555) by Lucas Cranach the Elder; his son, Lucas Cranach the Younger, completed the work.

On Burgplatz, a block east of Herder-platz, is Weimar's main art museum, the **Schlossmuseum** (closed Monday; DM6/3). The large collection, with masterpieces by Cranach, Dürer and others, occupies three floors of this castle.

Platz der Demokratie, with a renowned music school founded by Franz Liszt in 1872, is just south of the castle. The square spills over into the Markt and its **Cranach-haus**, where Lucas Cranach the Elder spent his last two years and died (in 1553).

West of Markt (via some narrow lanes) is Theaterplatz, with statues of Goethe and Schiller, and the **German National Theatre**, where the constitution of the German Republic was drafted in 1919. Opposite the theatre is the **Bauhaus Museum** (closed Monday; DM5/3).

From Theaterplatz, Schillerstrasse curves around to the **Schillers Wohnhaus** at No 12 (closed Tuesday; DM5/3). The **Goethes Wohnhaus**, a block ahead and then to the right, is where the immortal work *Faust* was written (closed Monday; DM8/5). Both have interesting exhibits on Weimar's dynamic duo.

The **Liszthaus** is south on Marienstrasse by the edge of Park an der Ilm (closed Monday; DM4/3). The yellow complex across the road, erected by the famous architect Henry van de Velde between 1904 and 1911, houses the **Bauhaus University**.

Places to Stay

For a flat fee of DM5, Weimar-Information arranges *private rooms* from about DM40 per person.

Hostels Weimar has four DJH hostels. The *Jugendherberge Germania* (☎ 85 04 90, fax 85 04 91, Carl-August-Allee 13), in the street running south (downhill) from the station, charges DM25/30 for juniors/seniors. *Am Poseckschen Garten* (☎ 85 07 92, fax 85 07 93, Humboldtstrasse 17) is more central but least comfortable. Beds for juniors/seniors are DM25/30. The *Jugendgästehaus Maxim Gorki* (☎ 85 07 50, fax 85 07 49, Zum Wilden Graben 12), on the southern uphill

side of town (take bus No 8 from the station), charges DM26/31 for juniors/seniors. The *Jugendgästehaus Am Ettersberg* (☎ 42 11 11, fax 42 11 12) at Ettersberg-Siedling (bus No 6 from the main train station to Obelisk) charges the same.

Pensions *Savina II* (☎ 51 33 52, fax 86 69 11, @ pensionsavina@compuserve.com, Meyerstrasse 60) has bright rooms near the station (with attached kitchen) from DM78/138. Its sister, the tiny *Pension Savina I* (Rembrandtweg 13) charges DM59/104 (same contact details). *Pension am Theater* (☎ 889 40, fax 88 94 32, Erfurter Strasse 10) has nice rooms with all facilities for DM85/125.

Places to Eat

Zum Zwiebel (☎ 50 23 75, Teichgasse 6) serves cheap, hearty meals. *Brasserie Central* (☎ 85 27 74, Rollplatz 8a) is open till late and serves generous main dishes such as lamb goulash in wine sauce for DM18. The *Residenz* (Grüner Markt 4) gets a gourmandising and quaffing young crowd until late. *Felsenkeller* (Humboldtstrasse 37) is run by the local Felsenbräu brewery. The atmosphere is great, the beer is cheap, the food is good and fairly priced – no wonder it's often full.

Entertainment

The *German National Theatre* (☎ 755 334) on Theaterplatz is the main stage for Weimar's cultural activities. Buy tickets at the tourist office.

The *Kasseturm*, a beer cellar in the round tower on Goetheplatz, has live music, disco and cabaret. *ACC* (Burgplatz 2) is a nice cafe-bar that serves good food, has occasional music and has a gallery upstairs.

Getting There & Away

There are frequent direct IR trains to Berlin-Zoo (DM75, three hours) via Naumburg and Halle, and to Frankfurt/Main (DM78, three hours) via Erfurt and Eisenach. IC/EC trains go to Dresden (DM65, 2½ hours) and Leipzig (DM31, 1¼ hours).

AROUND WEIMAR
Buchenwald

A visit to Buchenwald, a notorious Nazi concentration camp, is a powerful experience.

GERMANY

On 11 April 1945, as American troops approached, Buchenwald's prisoners rebelled at 3.15 pm (the clock tower above the entrance still shows that time), overcame the SS guards and liberated themselves. After the war the Soviet victors turned the tables by establishing Special Camp No 2, in which thousands of (alleged) anti-Communists and former Nazis were worked to death.

The Buchenwald **museum** and memorial are on Ettersberg Hill, 7km north-west of Weimar. You first pass a memorial and the **mass graves** of 56,500 victims from 18 nations, including German antifascists, Jews and Soviet and Polish prisoners of war.

The camp and museum at Buchenwald are open 9.45 am to 6 pm Tuesday to Sunday (in winter 8.45 am to 5 pm). Last entry is 45 minutes before closing. Every 40 minutes bus No 6 runs via Goetheplatz and Weimar's train station to Buchenwald.

EISENACH
☎ 03691

Eisenach, birthplace of Johann Sebastian Bach, is a small and picturesque – if slightly dull – town on the edge of the Thuringian Forest. Martin Luther went into hiding at Eisenach's Wartburg castle after being excommunicated by the pope in 1521.

Orientation & Information

Markt, Eisenach's central square, is a 15-minute walk from the train station – follow Bahnhofstrasse west to Karlsplatz, and continue west along the pedestrianised Karlstrasse. Except for the Wartburg, which is 2km south-west of town, most sights are close to Markt.

The well-organised Eisenach-Information (☎ 194 33, fax 67 09 60, @ tourist-in fo@eisenach-tourist.de) is at Markt 2. Its three-day Classic-Card (DM24) provides free admission to the castle and most museums and free use of public transport.

Things to See

The superb **Wartburg** castle, on a hill overlooking Eisenach, is world famous. Martin Luther translated the New Testament from Greek into German while in hiding here (1521-22), thus making an enormous contribution to the development of the written German language. Castle tours (ask for the English-language leaflet) include a museum, Luther's study and the amazing Romanesque Great Hall. Tours run continuously from 8.30 am to 5 pm (9 am to 3.30 pm in winter) and cost DM11/6; arrive early to avoid the crowds.

To reach the Wartburg on foot from Markt, go one block west to Wydenbrugkstrasse and follow the steep, signposted Schlossberg lane 2km south-west to the castle. A shuttle bus to the castle (DM2.50 return) runs every hour from April to October from the terminal in front of the train station.

Places to Stay & Eat

Jugendherberge Artur Becker (☎ 74 32 59, fax 74 32 60, Mariental 24) is in the valley below Wartburg. The cost for juniors/seniors is DM25/30. Take bus No 3 from the station to Liliengrund.

Eisenach-Information charges no commission to book *private rooms* for around DM45 per person. Otherwise, *Gasthof Storchenturm* (☎/fax 21 52 50, Georgenstrasse 43) has small rooms for DM53/85 with shower and toilet.

The *Kartoffelkeller* (☎ 73 26 26, Sophienstrasse 44) serves quite good spud dishes for about DM10 to DM20.

Getting There & Away

Use the frequent regional or IR services to Erfurt (DM15, 40 minutes) and Weimar (DM19, 50 minutes) rather than the IC as they are far cheaper and take only a few minutes longer. IR services run direct to Frankfurt/Main and Berlin-Zoo.

Saxony-Anhalt

WERNIGERODE
☎ 03943

Wernigerode, flanked by the foothills of the Harz Mountains, has a romantic castle and some 1000 half-timbered houses in its old town. For backpackers the main draw is hiking in the nearby mountains and perhaps riding the scenic, steam-powered Harzquerbahn train to Nordhausen (DM19) and Brocken (DM30) which is the highest mountain in northern Germany (1142m).

Orientation & Information

From Bahnhofsplatz, Rudolf-Breitscheid-Strasse leads south-east to Breite Strasse, which in turn runs south-west to the old town's main square, the Markt. The tourist office (☎ 194 33, fax 63 20 40, ✉ wernigerod-tg@netco.de) is at Nicolaiplatz 1 near Markt.

Things to See & Do

First built in the 12th century, the neo-Gothic **castle** has been renovated and enlarged over the centuries and received its current fairy-tale facade from Count Otto of Stolberg-Wernigerode in the last century. The castle's **museum** is worth a look for the chapel and Great Hall (closed Monday from November to April; DM8/7).

There are plenty of short walks and day hikes nearby, foremost in the forest behind the castle. The tourist office offers trail suggestions; you'll need a good topographic map for some trails.

Wernigerode is the northern terminus for steam train services throughout the Harz Mountains and Hochharz National Park.

Places to Stay & Eat

The non-DJH *Jugendgästaehaus (☎/fax 63 20 61, Friedrichstrasse 53)* has dorm beds for DM27. Take bus No 1 or 4 to Kirchstrasse. The tourist office also arranges *private rooms* free of charge.

Hotel zur Tanne (☎ 63 25 54, fax 67 37 35, Breite Strasse 59) charges DM40/60 for simple singles/doubles. *Pension Schweizer Hof (☎/fax 63 20 98, Salzbergstrasse 13)* caters to hikers with route information and has rooms from DM65/100. *Hotel zur Post (☎ 690 40, fax 69 04 30, Marktstrasse 17)* has rooms with a bathroom for DM95/160.

Altwernigerode Kartoffelhaus (Marktstrasse 14) serves well-priced traditional and potato dishes. *Nonnenhof* at Am Markt adjoining Gothisches Haus has regional specialties for around DM15.

Getting There & Away

For details on bus services in the western Harz, see the Getting Around section under Western Harz Mountains in Lower Saxony. Harzer Schmalspurbahnen (☎ 55 81 43, fax 55 81 48), Marktstrasse 3, runs services to Brocken from Wernigerode which cost DM26/42 one way/return (1¾ hours one-way). There is a three-day steam-train pass for DM80 and a one-week pass for DM100 (Web site at www.hsb-wr.de).

There are frequent trains to Goslar (DM12, 30 minutes) which connect with services to Hanover (DM36, 2½ hours). Frequent direct trains go to Halle (DM31, two hours), and also to Halberstadt (DM8, 30 minutes) with connections to Magdeburg (DM22, 1½ hours), where you can change trains for Berlin (DM62, three hours).

QUEDLINBURG
☎ 03946

Quedlinburg, one of Germany's true gems, dates back over 1000 years. In the old town, street after cobbled street is lined with handsome half-timbered houses that are slowly being restored. Since 1992 Quedlinburg has been listed by Unesco as a World Heritage Site.

Orientation & Information

The old town is a 10-minute walk from the train station down Bahnhofstrasse. Quedlinburg-Information (☎ 90 56 24, fax 90 56 29, ✉ Q.T.M@t-online.de) is at Markt 2. From May to September it opens 9 am to 7 pm weekdays, 10 am to 4 pm weekends. It closes an hour earlier in March, April, October and December, and in November, January and February it's open till only 5 pm weekdays. See the Web site at www.quedlinburg.de for more tourist information.

Things to See

A prominent Markt landmark is the Renaissance **Rathaus** (1615). Quedlinburg's main focal point is the **Schlossberg**, the old castle district on a hill south-west of the Markt. The area features the Romanesque **Church of St Servatii** (1129), also called the Dom, with a 10th-century crypt, priceless reliquaries and early Bibles (closed Monday; DM6/4). Also try to visit the **Lyonel-Feininger-Galerie** (closed Monday; DM6/3) where you can view excellent works by this Bauhaus artist who fled the Nazis and settled in America.

Places to Stay & Eat

Quedlinburg-Information books *private rooms*. The central *Familie Klindt (☎ 70 29 11, Hohe Strasse 19)* has budget, basic rooms for DM30/50. *Hotel Zum Augustinern (☎ 77 16 11, fax 70 12 35, Reichenstrasse 35a)* has good rooms for DM70/110 with facilities.

GERMANY

Kartoffelhaus No 1 (Breite Strasse 37) serves filling meals for all budgets. *Brauhaus Lüdde (Blasiistrasse 14)* has hearty pub food from DM14 to DM22 and brews its own pilsener, *Altbier* and the sweetish low-alcohol *Pubarschknall*.

Getting There & Away

There are hourly trains to/from Halberstadt (DM6, 17 minutes) where you can connect to Wernigerode (DM12, one hour). Direct trains go to Magdeburg (DM19, 1¼ hours), where you can change for Berlin-Zoo (DM60, three hours). Going to/from Halle (DM24, two hours), you must change at the hamlet of Wegeleben.

LUTHERSTADT WITTENBERG

☎ 03491

Wittenberg is where Martin Luther did most of his work, including launching the Protestant Reformation in 1517. Ever quotable, Luther hurled vitriol at the corrupt church in Rome, even calling the Vatican a 'gigantic, bloodsucking worm'. Thousands make pilgrimages every year, and the town has done its best to profit from the monk's legacy – including adding 'Lutherstadt' to the name in 1938. Wittenberg can be seen in a day, but is worth a longer look.

Orientation & Information

Hauptbahnhof Lutherstadt Wittenberg, the stop for all fast trains, is a 15-minute walk from the city centre – go under the tracks and follow Collegienstrasse.

Wittenberg-Information (☎ 49 86 10, fax 49 86 11, ✉ wb_info@wittenberg.de), sells *The Historic Mile* (DM4.80), a good English-language guide to the city.

Things to See

The **Lutherhaus** is a Reformation museum inside Lutherhalle, a former monastery at Collegienstrasse 54 (open 9 am to 6 pm daily April to October, 10 am to 5 pm the rest of the year; DM7/3). It contains an original room furnished by Luther in 1535.

The large altarpiece at the **Stadtkirche St Marien** was created jointly by Renaissance painter Lucas Cranach the Elder and his son in 1547. It shows Luther, Melanchthon and other Reformation figures. In June 1525 Luther married ex-nun Katharina von Bora in this church, where he also preached. The

Luther-Eiche, the site where Luther burnt the papers threatening his excommunication, is on the corner of Lutherstrasse and Am Bahnhof.

Just off the Markt is the **Cranachhaus**, Schlosstrasse 1, which has a picturesque courtyard. **Wittenberg Castle**, at the west end of town, houses the church onto whose door Luther allegedly nailed his '95 Theses' on 31 October 1517. His tombstone lies below the pulpit. The castle is open 10 am to 5 pm Monday to Saturday from May to October, 11.30 am to 5 pm Sunday. The rest of the year it closes at 4 pm daily (free).

Places to Stay

Wittenberg-Information books *private rooms* from DM40 per person.

The often-mobbed *Jugendherberge* (☎ /fax 40 32 55) is housed upstairs in Wittenberg Castle (DM22/27 juniors/seniors, sheets DM6). *Gasthaus Central* (☎/fax 41 15 72, Mittelstrasse 20) has clean singles/doubles for DM58/92 with bathroom.

Getting There & Away

Wittenberg is on the main train line between Berlin (DM39, one hour), Leipzig (DM23, 45 minutes) and Halle (DM16, one hour). Every two hours IC trains run to/from Berlin-Ostbahnhof, stopping at Schönefeld airport (DM31, 50 minutes).

NAUMBURG

☎ 03445

Naumburg is one of those pretty medieval towns for which Germany is famous. It is strategically located between Halle, Leipzig and Weimar. The sights – mainly the streets of the old town and the art-filled cathedral, the **Dom St Peter & Paul** – can be seen in a two-hour break between trains.

Orientation & Information

Naumburg/Saale, the main train station, is 1.5km north-west of the old town – follow Markgrafenweg, turn left on Rossbacher Strasse and walk to Bauernweg, which heads uphill to the cathedral and, five minutes farther, to the central square, Markt. Alternatively, bus Nos 1 and 2 run frequently from the train station to Markt or nearby Theaterplatz.

Naumburg's helpful tourist office (☎ 20 16 14, fax 26 60 47, ✉ stadt.naumburg@

GERMANY

t-online.de) is at Markt 6 (closed Sunday). The tourist office can help with some great hikes and bike rides along the rivers. There is a souvenir store posing as a tourist office across from the cathedral.

Places to Stay

The tourist office books *private rooms* for DM30 per person. The large *Jugendherberge* (☎ /fax 70 34 22, *Am Tennisplatz 9*), 1.5km south of the town centre, has double rooms at DM28/34 juniors/seniors. Multibed rooms go for DM24/29.

Gasthaus St Othmar (☎/fax 20 12 13, *Othmarsplatz 7*) is a restored historic hotel with rooms from DM50/90 with shower and toilet. *St Wenzel* (☎ 717 90, *fax 717 93 01, Fr-Nietsche-Strasse 21a*), a 10 minute walk from Markt, has nice rooms for DM60/90 with facilities.

Getting There & Away

Frequent IR trains stop at Naumburg going to/from Berlin (DM64, 2½ hours), Weimar (DM12, 30 minutes) and Frankfurt (DM89, 3½ hours). Frequent IC trains go to/from Leipzig (DM22, 45 minutes).

Northern Germany

HAMBURG
☎ 040

Hamburg should be high on your list of German cities to visit. The nightlife is great, the museums are world class, and it has a bustling port. The Reeperbahn, originally a red-light district for sailors, is rather tame these days, whereas the Schanzenviertel has a lively alternative and anarchist student scene.

Hamburg's first settlement (around AD 800), though, was a far cry from anarchism: this was the site of a moated fortress known as Hammaburg. In the 13th century Hamburg became the Hanseatic League's trading gateway to the North Sea and was second in importance only to Lübeck. With the decline of the Hanseatic League in the 16th century, Hamburg thrived as Lübeck sank into (near) oblivion.

In WWII, more than half of Hamburg was flattened and 55,000 people died in Allied air raids that spawned horrific firestorms.

Orientation

The main train station, the Hauptbahnhof, is near Aussenalster lake and close to most sights. The port is west of the city centre, facing the Elbe.

Information

Tourist Offices The small office at the Hauptbahnhof's Kirchenallee exit (☎ 30 05 12 00, fax 300 51 333, ✪ info@hamburg-tourism.de) has a room-finding service and is open 7 am to 11 pm daily. A branch at St Pauli harbour, between piers four and five, is open from 10 am to 7 pm daily.

Both sell the Hamburg Card, valid for free or discounted admission to many museums, and free use of public transport. A one-day card is DM12.80 and a card valid on the day of purchase and following two days costs DM26.50.

The Hamburg Jugend Spass card (DM12.50), only available at youth hostels, gives even steeper discounts to anyone under 27.

For more information, see the Web site at www.hamburg-tourism.de.

Money The Reisebank above the Hauptbahnhof's Kirchenallee exit is open 7.30 am to 10 pm daily.

Post & Communications The main post office is on the corner of Dammtorstrasse and Stephansplatz. There's a smaller post office near the Hauptbahnhof's Kirchenallee exit.

Email & Internet Access Surf-In, in the Lust for Life store at Mönchebergstrasse 1, charges DM3 for 30 minutes online.

Laundry The Schnell & Sauber chain has a laundrette at Nobistor 34, near the Safeway store; an SB Wasch-Center is on the eastern side of Neuer Pferdemarkt (U-Bahn to Feldstrasse).

Things to See & Do

Altstadt The Altstadt is centred on Rathausmarkt. The 647-room **Rathaus** is one of the most interesting city halls in Germany, and the 40-minute English-language tour is worthwhile at DM2.

Nearby on Ost-West-Strasse, the lone remaining tower of the **St Nikolai Church**

GERMANY

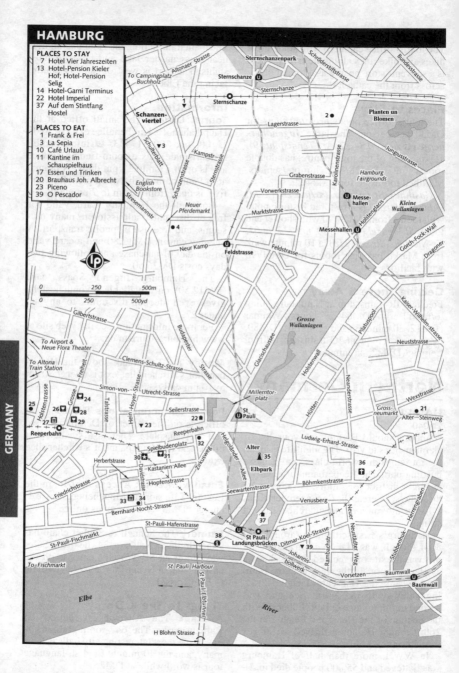

HAMBURG

PLACES TO STAY
7 Hotel Vier Jahreszeiten
13 Hotel-Pension Kieler
   Hof; Hotel-Pension
   Selig
14 Hotel-Garni Terminus
22 Hotel Imperial
37 Auf dem Stintfang
   Hostel

PLACES TO EAT
1 Frank & Frei
3 La Sepia
10 Café Urlaub
11 Kantine im
   Schauspielhaus
17 Essen und Trinken
20 Brauhaus Joh. Albrecht
23 Piceno
39 O Pescador

HAMBURG

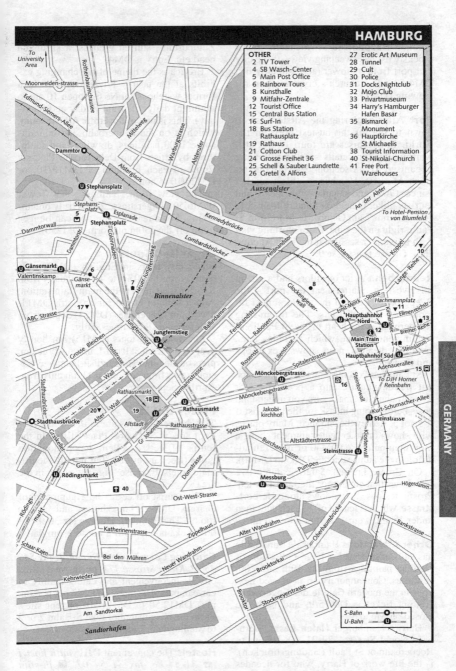

OTHER

2 TV Tower
4 SB Wasch-Center
5 Main Post Office
6 Rainbow Tours
8 Kunsthalle
9 Mitfahr-Zentrale
12 Tourist Office
15 Central Bus Station
16 Surf-In
18 Bus Station
   Rathausplatz
19 Rathaus
21 Cotton Club
24 Grosse Freiheit 36
25 Schell & Sauber Laundrette
26 Gretel & Alfons

27 Erotic Art Museum
28 Tunnel
29 Cult
30 Police
31 Docks Nightclub
32 Mojo Club
33 Privatmuseum
34 Harry's Hamburger
   Hafen Basar
35 Bismarck
   Monument
36 Hauptkirche
   St Michaelis
38 Tourist Information
40 St-Nikolai-Church
41 Free Port
   Warehouses

contains a moving anti-war memorial. The baroque **Hauptkirche St Michaelis** a few blocks west has sweeping views of the city and port from its **tower** (accessible by lift; DM4.50). The church's crypt is open for viewing (DM1).

Port After exploring the Altstadt, stroll down to one of the busiest ports in the world. Port cruises are touristy but still worthwhile; for details see the following Organised Tours section. The Fischmarkt (Fish Market), Hamburg's oldest market (since 1703) and popular with locals and tourists alike, is held on Sunday from 5 to 10 am (from 7 am October to March) in St Pauli, right on the Elbe. Cap a morning visit with a live jazz session at the Fish Auction Hall, Grosse Elbstrasse 9.

Reeperbahn A lot of sailors had a girl in this western quarter near the port – the Reeperbahn is one of the world's most famous red-light districts. The 600m-long Reeperbahn is the heart of the St Pauli entertainment district, which includes bars, cabarets, theatres, peep shows, sex shops and a casino.

St Pauli has become tamer in recent years, but if you venture into a peep show or Reeperbahn club, make sure you understand costs before going in; ask for the price list if it's not posted by the entrance. Many places with shows or other 'entertainment' have a minimum purchase (DM40 or more) in addition to the admission fee (DM5 to DM10).

On Grosse Freiheit, **Safari** features live sex shows that are not for the faint-hearted. Prostitutes pose in windows along **Herbertstrasse**, which is fenced off at each end; men under 18 and women are not allowed in.

Other Attractions Hamburg's **Kunsthalle** has old masters and a large collection of German paintings from the 19th and 20th centuries. Contemporary art is housed next door in the modern **Galerie der Gegenwart**. A joint ticket is DM15/9, and both are closed on Monday.

Harry's Hamburger Hafen Basar, Bernhard-Nocht-Strasse 89-91 (S-Bahn to Reeperbahn or St Pauli Landungsbrücken), is the life work of Harry, who for decades bought trinkets and souvenirs from sailors and assorted others. Now run by Harry's

daughter, it has a wealth of curiosities – Zulu drums, stuffed giraffes, a shrunken head etc. Entry is DM4.

Erotica is the theme of the changing exhibits at the nearby **Privartmuseum**, in a former warehouse at No 69 (open 10 am to midnight daily, till 1 am Friday and Saturday). This is part of the **Erotic Art Museum**, which is on the Reeperbahn and contains some 1800 paintings, drawings and sculptures by artists from Delacroix to Picasso. Entry to each museum is DM15/10, or DM20/10 to both.

The view from Hamburg's **TV Tower** (DM6.50), Lagerstrasse 2-8, is truly breathtaking. For a real scream, you can bungee jump off the 130m platform (DM250).

Organised Tours

Basic city tours in English (DM22, 1¾ hours) depart 9.30 am to 4.45 pm daily from Kirchenallee, next to the main train station. Add a harbour cruise for an extra DM11. Two-hour fleet cruises (DM23) depart from Jungfernstieg three times daily.

One-hour port tours (DM15) run hourly year-round from St Pauli-Landungsbrücken, piers one to nine. The English-language version leaves from pier one at 11 am only from April to September.

Places to Stay

The cheapest options are in the sleazy red-light area in St Georg. Places listed in the tourist office's excellent accommodation guide (free) are mostly (but not all!) legitimate hotels. Exercise 'big city' sense in the area.

The tourist office at the Hauptbahnhof charges DM6 to book hotels and private rooms. The Hamburg-Hotline (☎ 30 05 13 00) books hotels from 8 am to 8 pm daily.

Camping *Campingplatz Buchholz* (☎ *540 45 32, Kieler Strasse 374*) north-west of the city, is inconvenient and caters mainly to car-campers. The rates are DM7 per person, plus DM12.50 to DM14.50 for tent sites. From the Hauptbahnhof take S-Bahn 2 or 3 to Stellingen or Eidelstedt.

Hostels The convenient DJH *youth hostel* (☎ *31 34 88, fax 31 54 07,* ✉ *jh-stint fang@t-online.de, Albert-Wegener-Weg 5*) offers a view of the port. Beds are DM27/32 a junior/senior. Take the U or S-Bahn to St Pauli-Landungsbrücken.

The DJH *Horner Rennbahn* (☎ 651 16 71, fax 655 65 16, **❷** *jgh-hamburg@t-on line.de, Rennbahnstrasse 100*) is less convenient (DM30/35.50). Take U-Bahn 3 to Horner Rennbahn, then walk 10 minutes north past the racecourse and leisure centre.

The private hostel *Schanzenstern* (☎ 439 84 41, fax 439 34 13, Bartelsstrasse 12), in the lively Schanzenviertel, has beds in clean dorms for DM33 and singles/doubles/triples for DM60/90/115 excluding breakfast (it's just off Susannenstrasse).

Pensions & Hotels Most budget hotels are along Steindamm and a few blocks east of the main train station along Bremer Reihe. *Hotel-Pension Selig* (☎ 24 46 89, fax 24 98 45, Bremer Reihe 23) has reasonable, basic rooms for DM60/120. *Hotel-Pension Kieler Hof* (☎ 24 30 24, fax 24 60 18, Bremer Reihe 15) has rooms with shower cabins for DM60/100. (Both of these exclude breakfast.) *Hotel-Garni Terminus* (☎ 280 31 44, fax 24 15 80, Steindamm 5) offers basic rooms from DM75/100, or DM90/120 with a bathroom.

The highly recommended *Hotel-Pension von Blumfeld* (☎ 24 58 60, fax 24 32 82, Lange Reihe 54), north-east of the main train station, has nice rooms for DM60/90. In St Pauli, the family-run *Hotel Imperial* (☎ 31 17 20, fax 319 60 21, **❷** *Hotel-Impe rial@t-online.de, Millerntorplatz 3-5*) charges DM95/150 for singles/doubles during the week and from DM115/165 on weekends. *Hotel Vier Jahreszeiten* (☎ 349 40, fax 34 94 26 00, **❷** *vier-jahreszeiten@hvj.de, Neuer Jungfernstieg 9-14*) is *the* place in town to lighten your wallet, with rooms starting at DM400 for a single.

Places to Eat
Near the Hauptbahnhof *Kantine im Schauspielhaus*, downstairs in the Deutsches Schauspielhaus on Kirchenallee, is one of the best kept secrets in this part of town, with plain but filling lunches for DM10. The student *Café Urlaub* (Lange Reihe 63), which is open from breakfast until 2 am, is a good eating and drinking option.

Gänsemarkt Essen und Trinken (Gänsemarkt 21) is a food hall in an arcade where

you can choose from Asian, Mediterranean and German cuisine at budget prices. *Brauhaus Joh. Albrecht* (Adolfsbrücke 7) is an boutique brewery where most dishes cost less than DM20.

Schanzenviertel This bristling, bustling anarcho-ethnic neighbourhood is north of St Pauli – take the U or S-Bahn to Sternschanze. Lots of cafes and restaurants line Schanzenstrasse and Susannenstrasse, including the *Frank and Frei* student hangout on the corner of the two. *La Sepia* (Schulterblatt 36) serves terrific seafood, sometimes with live music.

St Pauli/Port Area There's a cluster of good Portuguese and Spanish restaurants along Ditmar-Koel-Strasse and Reimarus-Strasse near St Pauli Landungsbrücken. *O Pescador*, on the corner of the two, serves a variety of mid-priced meat and fish dishes. Just off the Reeperbahn, *Piceno* (Hein-Hoyer-Strasse 8) is good for Italian fare at reasonable prices in a cosy, relaxed atmosphere.

Entertainment
St Pauli is the place for nightclubs. *Tunnel* (☎ 317 24 30, Grosse Freiheit 10) usually serves up techno and house; *Cult* (Grosse Freiheit 2) is another favourite; *Docks* (☎ 31 78 83 11, Spielbudenplatz 19) sometimes has live bands; as does the hip *Grosse Freiheit 36* (Grosse Freiheit 36). At *Gretel & Alfons* across the street, you can have a drink where the Beatles once quaffed. The *Mojo Club* (☎ 43 52 32, Reeperbahn 1) should absolutely *not* be missed by fans of jazz or cutting-edge music (Web site: www.mojo.de). The *Cotton Club* (34 38 78, Alter Steinweg 10) has more traditional jazz flavours.

Getting There & Away
Bus The central bus station is south-east of the Hauptbahnhof on Adenauerallee. International destinations not served directly by train from Hamburg, such as Amsterdam (DM80, 6½ hours) and London (DM136, 17½ hours), are served by Eurolines buses. Rainbow Tours (☎ 32 09 33 09, fax 32 09 30 99), Gänsemarkt 45, has return tickets to London for DM69 – a bargain even if you don't use the return portion.

Train From the Hauptbahnhof there are frequent RE/RB trains to Lübeck (DM16, 45 minutes) and Kiel (DM30, 1¼ hours), various trains to Hanover (DM50, 1½ hours) and Bremen (DM33, 1¼), as well as IC trains to Berlin (DM88, 2½ hours) and ICE trains to Frankfurt (DM191, 3½ hours) via Hanover. There are overnight services to Munich, Vienna and Paris as well as Zurich via Basel.

Hamburg-Altona station has a monopoly on some services to the north – Kiel, and Westerland on Sylt (DM71, three hours).

Ride Share A convenient Mitfahr-Zentrale (☎ 194 40) is at Ernst-Merck-Strasse 8 near the main train station. Sample one-way prices are Cologne DM44, Frankfurt am Main DM49, Amsterdam DM47 and Berlin DM31.

Ferry Hamburg is 20 hours by car ferry from the English port of Harwich. DFDS Seaways (☎ 389 03 71, fax 38 90 31 41) runs services at least three times a week in either direction. The Fischereihafen terminal is at Van-der-Smissen-Strasse 4, about 1km west of the Fischmarkt – take S-Bahn 1 to Königstrasse, or bus No 383 to/from Altona station.

Scandlines (☎ 01805-72 26 35 46 37) runs a 24-hour ferry from Puttgarden to Rødbyhavn (DM5 to DM10, 45 minutes), a popular way to reach Copenhagen. If you're travelling by train, the cost of the ferry is included in the ticket.

MECKLENBURG-WESTERN POMERANIA
Schwerin
☎ 0385

Schwerin, almost completely surrounded by lakes, is one of the most picturesque towns in eastern Germany, and its popularity is rising. Taking in the sights of this easily walked town can occupy a day or more.

Orientation & Information Downhill to the east of the train station is Pfaffenteich lake; at its south end you'll find Schwerin's main street, Mecklenburgstrasse. The town's centre, the Markt, is one block east. Farther south, around Alter Garten on the Schweriner See, are the Marstall (former royal stables), the Schloss (castle), and museums, parks and tour boats.

Schwerin-Information (☎ 592 52 13, fax 55 50 94, ✉ Stadtmarketing-Schwerin@t-online.de), Am Markt 10, is open 10 am to 6 pm weekdays. On weekends it closes at 2 pm (closed May to September on Sunday).

Things to See & Do On the Markt, the 14th-century Gothic **Dom** is a superb example of red-and-black brick architecture. You can climb the church's 19th-century tower for DM2.

Schwerin's neo-Gothic **Schloss** is on an island connected to the Schlossgarten by a causeway. Admission to the superb interior is DM8/6.

On the city side of Alter Garten, the **Staatliches Museum** has an excellent collection of works by old Dutch masters (open 10 am to 8 pm Tuesday and 10 am to 6 pm Wednesday to Sunday, closing one hour earlier November to March; DM7/3.50). The dramatic cream-coloured building next to the art museum is the **Mecklenburgisches Staatstheater Schwerin** (state theatre).

From May to September, **Schweriner See tour boats** run every 30 minutes from the Weisse Flotte quay, next to the Staatliches Museum. Cruises lasting 1½ hours cost DM15.

Places to Stay & Eat The computerised list in front of the train station shows which hotels/pensions have rooms and where they are located. Schwerin-Information books *private rooms* from about DM30 per person. The *Jugendherberge Schwerin (☎ 326 00 06, fax 326 03 03, Waldschulweg 3)* is about 4km south of the city centre (take bus No 14 from Marienplatz; DM25/DM30 juniors/ seniors). *Pension Galinat (☎ 73 34 61, Steinstrasse 1)* has nice, basic rooms for DM50/75, or DM75/110 with a bathroom.

The *food hall* in the shopping centre on Wittenburger Strasse known as *Der Wurm* (The Worm) serves cheap Asian and German chow. *Unity Bar (Arsenalstrasse 36)* plays music spanning jazz to acid and is open late. They also have a decent snack menu.

Getting There & Away Various IR trains serve Rostock (DM22, 1¼ hours), Stralsund (DM44, 2¼ hours), Magdeburg (DM52, 2½ hours), Lübeck (DM20, 1¼ hours) and Hamburg (DM34, 1¼ hours) at least every two hours. Frequent trains go to/from Wismar (DM10, 30 minutes). Travel to/from Berlin (DM65, two hours) requires a change at Wittenberge.

Rostock
☎ 0381
Rostock, the largest city in lightly populated north-eastern Germany, is a major Baltic port and shipbuilder. The years since reunification have been difficult – unemployment has soared and neo-Nazi attacks on foreign workers have brought worldwide condemnation. Now, however, the city is working hard to improve conditions. The city centre along Kröpeliner Strasse and the former dock area on the Warnow have been redeveloped into pleasant pedestrian quarters. The sights can easily occupy a day and the beach resort of Warnemünde is only 12km north.

Information Rostock-Information (☎ 194 33 or 381 22 22, fax 381 26 01, ✉ tourist info@rostock.de) is in the old post office building at Neuer Markt 3-8, about 1.5km from the train station – to get there take tram No 11 or 12.

Places to Stay & Eat Rostock-Information books *private rooms* for DM30 per person, plus a DM5 counter fee.

The 85-berth *Jugendgästeschiff Traditionsschiff* (☎ *71 62 24, fax 71 40 14*) is in the converted freighter *Dresden* at Schmarl-Dorf, between Rostock and Warnemünde. Take the S-Bahn to Lütten Klein station, then bus No 35 (direction 'Schmarl-Fähre') to avoid the walk past the unwelcoming apartment blocks. It costs DM27.50/39 a junior/senior, and the setting is pleasant. The last bus runs at about 8 pm.

Burger King and *Jimmy's Hamburger* jostle for position on Kröpeliner Strasse and Briete Strasse. *Kölsch- und Altbierhaus* (*Wokrenter Strasse 36*), between Lange Strasse and the harbour, has a woodsy, pub atmosphere and cheap lunches.

Getting There & Away There are hourly trains from Wismar (DM15, 1¼ hours), and frequent IR trains to/from Berlin-Zoo (DM75, three hours), Stralsund (DM20, one hour), Schwerin (DM22, 1¼ hours) and Hamburg (DM54, 2¼ hours).

Several ferry companies run to Trelleborg (Sweden) and Gedser (Denmark) from Rostock's seaport (take tram No 19 or 21 to Seehafen Fähre). TT-Line (☎ 040- 360 14 42, fax 360 14 07, www.TTLine.de) departs Rostock for Trelleborg several times daily using fast and slow boats. The crossing takes three to six hours and costs from DM50 to DM100 one way, depending on the season. Bicycles are DM10 to DM20 extra. To Gedser, Scandlines charges DM6 to DM10 per person for trips that take up to two hours. Tickets and timetable information are available at the train station.

Warnemünde
Warnemünde, actually part of Rostock, is among eastern Germany's most popular beach resorts. Frequent S-Bahn trains connect Warnemünde to Rostock, so the town can easily be used as a base for day trips to Rostock, Stralsund and even Schwerin. This small fishing village with a broad beach is a great choice, but in summer finding accommodation is like winning a lottery. Warnemünde-Information (☎ 54 80 00, fax 548 00 30), Am Strom 59, is just across the bridge from the train station. It can help with accommodation, or ask at Rostock-Information in Rostock.

Stralsund
☎ 03831
Stralsund, an enjoyable city on the Baltic Sea north of Berlin, is almost completely surrounded by lakes and the sea. It is an attractive historic town with fine museums, pleasant walks and a restful, uncluttered waterfront. The island of Rügen is just across the Strelasund.

Orientation & Information From the Hauptbahnhof, walk east across the Tribseer Damm causeway to Neuer Markt. The Alter Markt, a few blocks north, is where you'll find Stralsund-Information (☎ 246 90, fax 24 69 49) at No 9.

Things to See The massive 14th-century **Marienkirche** on Neuer Markt is a red-brick edifice typical of north German Gothic architecture. Climb the tower's 350 or so steps for a sweeping view of Stralsund (DM2). There are two excellent museums on Mönchstrasse. The **Meeresmuseum** is

GERMANY

an oceanic museum and aquarium in a 13th-century convent church (DM7/3.50). The **Kulturhistorisches Museum** has a large collection housed in the cloister of an old convent (closed Monday; DM6/3).

Places to Stay & Eat Stralsund's excellent *Jugendherberge* (☎ *29 21 60, fax 29 76 76, Am Kütertor 1)* is in the 17th-century waterworks. (closed in December and January; DM25/30 juniors/seniors). Take bus No 4 or 5 from the main train station. Stralsund-Information handles reservations for private rooms, pensions and hotels (DM5). *Hotel-Pension Klabautermann* (☎ *29 36 28, fax 28 06 12, Am Querkanal 2)*, near the port, has a view of the city and charges DM70/120; take Langenstrasse east from Markt to the water.

Torschliesserhaus (☎ *29 30 32)* is next to the hostel and has dishes for under DM11. *Braugasthaus Zum Alten Fritz* (*Greifswalder Chausee 84-5)* has good beer and some interesting and well-priced dishes (open daily; take bus No 3 from the main train station).

Getting There & Away Frequent IR trains run to/from Rostock (DM20, one hour), Berlin (DM65, three hours), Schwerin (DM44, 2¼ hours) and Hamburg (DM73, 3¼ hours).

International trains between Berlin and Stockholm or Oslo use the car ferry connecting Fährhafen Sassnitz on Rügen Island with Trelleborg and Malmö (Sweden). If you're heading to Sweden, be sure to travel in a carriage labelled for Malmö, as the train may split up at Sassnitz. Two or three daily connections to Stockholm (changing at Malmö) are available. See also Rügen Island, and the Getting There & Away section at the beginning of this chapter.

Rügen Island

Germany's largest island is north-east of Stralsund and connected by a causeway. The **chalk cliffs** that tower above the sea are worth the trip out here. Much of Rügen and its surrounding waters are either national park or protected nature reserves.

The main resort area is around Binz, Sellin and Göhren, on a peninsula on Rügen's east side. A lovely hike from Binz to Sellin skirts the cliffs above the sea

through beech and pine forest and offers great coastal views.

Tourismus Verband Rügen (☎ 03838-807 70, fax 25 44 40) is at Am Markt 4 in Bergen and publishes a monstrous magazine listing all accommodation on the island along with other useful information. In Sassnitz, the tourist office (☎ 038392-51 60, fax 516 16, ☻ fvb-sassnitz@t-online.de), Seestrasse 1, handles inquiries and also books hotel and private rooms for an outrageous fee of DM15 by telephone, or DM8 over the counter. Binz Information (☎ 038393-27 82, fax 307 17, ☻ fremdenverkehrsverein -binz@t-online.de), Heinrich-Heine-Strasse 7, books rooms over the counter (free).

Places to Stay In Binz, the *Jugendherberge* (☎ *038393-325 97, fax 325 96, ☻ jugendher berge-binz@t-online.de, Strandpromenade 35)* is across from the beach (DM36/43.50 juniors/seniors). The *Jugendherberge Prora* (☎ *038393-328 44, fax 328 45, ☻ jh-pr ora@t-online.de, Strandstrasse 12)* is at Prora-Ost, five minutes from the Prora-Ost station (DM27/32 juniors/seniors).

Getting There & Away Local trains run almost hourly between 8 am and 9 pm between Stralsund and Sassnitz (DM15, one hour). Scandlines (☎ 038392-644 20 or 01805-72 26 35 46) runs five passenger-vehicle ferries daily from the vast Sassnitz ferry terminal, 5km south of town, to/from Trelleborg, Sweden (DM20 to DM30 one way). Scandlines also has at least three services weekly to/from Rønne on Bornholm, Denmark, for DM20 to DM30.

SCHLESWIG-HOLSTEIN
Lübeck
☎ 0451

Medieval Lübeck was the capital of the Hanseatic League, an association of towns that ruled trade on the Baltic Sea from the 12th to the 16th century. This beautiful city, with its red-stone buildings, is a highlight of the region and well worth taking the time to explore.

Orientation & Information Lübek's old town is on an island ringed by the canalised Trave River, a 15-minute walk east from the main train station. Take Konrad-Adenauer-Strasse across the Puppenbrücke (Doll

Bridge) to Holstentor gate, then follow Holstenstrasse east from An der Untertrave to Kohlmarkt, from where Breite Strasse leads north to Markt.

Lübeck-Information (☎/fax 1 22 54 19) is near the Rathaus at Breite Strasse 62. Ask about the Lübeck-Travemünde Card (DM9/18 for 24/72 hours) for discounts on museums, cruises and other attractions, as well as free public transport.

For tourist information on the town, see the Web site at www.Luebeck-info.de.

Things to See & Do The landmark **Holstentor**, a fortified gate with huge twin towers, serves as the city's symbol as well as its museum (closed Monday; DM5).

Buddenbrookhaus (DM8/5), the family house where Thomas Mann was born and which he made famous in his novel *Buddenbrooks*, is on Mengstrasse one block north of the Markt's massive **Rathaus** (DM4/2).

Lübeck's **Marionettentheater** (Puppet Theatre), on the corner of Am Kolk and Kleine Petersgrube, is an absolute must (closed Monday). Afternoon seats cost DM8 and evening seats are DM13 to DM22. It's best to book ahead; call ☎ 700 60, or go to the theatre itself.

Places to Stay & Eat The *Jugendgästehaus Lübeck* (☎ 702 03 99, fax 770 12, Mengstrasse 33) is clean, comfortable and well situated in the middle of the old town, 15 minutes' walk from the train station (DM28.50/37 for juniors/seniors in dorms). It also has single and twin-bed rooms for DM42 per person. The *Folke-Bernadotte-Heim* (☎ 334 33, fax 345 40, Am Gertrudenkirchhof 4) is a little outside the old town, in the suburb of St Gertrud, and is slightly cheaper. The YMCA's *Sleep-Inn* (☎ 719 20, fax 789 97, Grosse Petersgrube 11) charges DM15 per bed in dorms, DM40 per double, and there are apartments from DM30 per person. Breakfast is DM7 and sheets DM8 extra (closed mid-December to mid-January).

The best eating and drinking options are in the area directly east of the Rathaus. *Tipasa (Schlumacherstrasse 12-14)* serves specials on weekday afternoons for around DM10. It's also a great place to eat and drink in the evening. *Hieronymus (Fleischhauerstrasse 81)* is a relaxed, rambling restaurant spread over three floors of a 15th-century building. Most dishes on the creative menu cost DM10 to DM20 and are quite filling.

Getting There & Away There are frequent train services to Kiel (DM22, 1¼ hours) and Schwerin (DM20, 1¼ hours). Trains to/from Copenhagen also stop here.

Kiel
☎ 0431

Kiel, the capital of Schleswig-Holstein, doesn't have an awful lot of sights, but if you're a salty sea dog, it'll be your kind of place. Located at the end of a modest firth, it has long been one of Germany's most important Baltic Sea harbours.

Kiel's most famous attraction is **Kieler Woche** (Kiel Week) in the last full week of June. The festival of yachting regattas is attended by more than 4000 of the world's sailing elite and half a million spectators. Even if you're not into sailing, the atmosphere is electric – just make sure you book a room in advance.

To experience Kiel's love for the sea in less energetic fashion, take a one-hour ferry ride to the village of **Laboe** at the mouth of the firth. Ferries leave hourly from Bahnhofbrücke pier, behind the Hauptbahnhof.

Orientation & Information Kiel's main street, Holstenstrasse, runs north-south from St Nikolai church to Sophienhof, a large indoor shopping mall connected by an overpass to the main train station. The tourist office (☎ 67 91 00, fax 679 10 99, ✉ info@kiel-tourist.de) is at Andreas-Gayk-Strasse 31, a northern extension of Sophienblatt. Edit(ha's) Internet cafe at Alter Markt 13 is a good place to surf the web on the fjord.

Places to Stay & Eat The tourist office charges DM3.50 to book accommodation.

The *Jugendherberge (☎ 73 14 88, fax 73 57 23, Johannesstrasse 1)* is in the suburb of Gaarden (DM28/33 for junior/seniors). You can walk across the pretty drawbridge behind the train station, or take the Laboe ferry to Gaarden, from where it's a 10 minute walk; or take bus No 11 or 12 from the main train station to Kieler Strasse. *Hotel Runge (☎ 733 33 96, 73 19 92, Elisabethstrasse 16)* in Gaarden charges

GERMANY

DM60/100 for singles/doubles. The central *Hotel Schweriner Hof (☎ 614 16, fax 67 41 34, Königsweg 13)* has singles/doubles from DM70/110, rooms with shower and toilet for DM110/140.

The *Klosterbrauerei (☎ 90 62 90, Alter Markt 9)* is a private brewery with good beer and well-priced food.

Getting There & Away Regional buses run to/from Lübeck, Schleswig and Puttgarden from the bus station on Auguste-Viktoria-Strasse, just north of the Hauptbahnhof. Numerous RE trains run every day between Kiel and Hamburg-Altona or Hamburg Haupt-bahnhof (DM30, 1¼ hours).

The daily Kiel-Gothenburg ferry (DM70 to DM160, 14 hours) leaves from Schwe-denkai and is run by Stena Line (☎ 0180-533 36 00). Web site: www.stenaline.de. Color Line ferries (☎ 730 03 00) run direct to/from Oslo (DM120 to DM182, 19½ hours) from Norwegenkai, across the fjord in Gaarden. Web site: www.color-line.de.

North Frisian Islands
Sylt ☎ 04651   Amrum ☎ 04682
The Frisian Islands reward those who make the trek with sand dunes, sea, pure air and – every so often – sunshine. The most popular of the North Frisian Islands is **Sylt**, a famous resort known for its spa facilities, water sports and fancy restaurants. It can be very crowded in summer; the neighbouring island of **Amrum** is far more relaxed and less touristy.

Information The information office next to Westerland's train station on Sylt (☎ 99 88, fax 99 81 00) can help with finding accommodation. On Amrum, the friendly tourist office (☎ 940 30, fax 94 03 20) faces one of the harbour car parks.

Activities In Westerland, a visit to the indoor waterpark and health spa **Sylter Welle** (☎ 99 82 42) is great fun, especially when it's too cold for the beach. It includes saunas, solariums, a wave pool and a slide. It's open 10 am to either 9 pm or 10 pm daily (DM25/17). For a real thrill, though, visit one of Sylt's beach saunas – the tourist office can point you in the right direction.

The best way to explore the islands is by bicycle. In Westerland on Sylt, Fahrrad am

Bahnhof (☎ 58 03) is convenient, situated at the train station (DM9 per day). On Amrum, the tourist office keeps a list of rental places.

Getting There & Away Frequent regional trains go from Hamburg-Altona to Wester-land (DM64, 2¾ hours). For Amrum, take a Sylt-bound train from Hamburg-Altona (DM70, four hours) and change at Niebüll for Dagebüll Hafen (DM86, six hours), from where there are frequent ferries to Amrum (DM27 return, two hours).

Bremen & Lower Saxony

BREMEN
☎ 0421
Bremen is, after Hamburg, the most important harbour in Germany, even though the open sea lies 113km to the north. It has vibrant student cafes, and a congenial Alt-stadt area around Am Markt and Domsheide that makes it an enjoyable place to explore on foot.

Orientation & Information
The heart of the city is Am Markt (follow the tram route from the tourist office), but its soul is the port, which provides about 40% of local employment. The tourist office (☎ 30 80 00, fax 308 00 30, ✉ btz@brem en-tourism.de) is directly in front of the main train station; ask about the Bremen tourist card (from DM19.50 for two days), which provides unlimited public transport and substantial discounts on city sites. A smaller booth is at the New Town Hall.

See also the Web site at www.brem en-tourism.de.

Things to See & Do
Am Markt's landmarks include the ornate **Rathaus** and the **St Petri-Dom** cathedral with its museum (DM3/2) and tower (DM1).

Nearby **Böttcherstrasse** is a re-creation of a medieval alley, complete with brick houses, galleries, museums and restaurants. The **Paula-Becker-Modersohn-Haus** at No 8 has works by its namesake contemporary painter, while the main focus of **Roselius-Haus** at No 6 is on paintings and applied

GERMANY

arts from the 12th to the 19th century (closed Monday; DM8/4 for all three). Shop-keepers and cafe owners cast out their nets for tourists in the **Schnoorviertel**, an area featuring historic fisher cottages.

Beck's Brewery (☎ 50 94 5555), Am Deich 18/19, has tours in English from Tuesday to Saturday at 1.30 pm (DM5 including tasting).

Places to Stay & Eat

The closest camping ground is *Campingplatz Bremen* (☎ 21 20 02, Am Stadtwaldsee 1). Take tram No 5 from the train station to Kuhlenkampfallee, then bus No 28 to the Campingplatz stop.

Jugendgästehaus Bremen (☎ 17 13 69, fax 17 11 02, Kalkstrasse 6) is across from Beck's brewery (DM30/35 junior/seniors). Take tram No 1 or 8 from the train station to Am Brill.

The friendly *Hotel Garni Gästehaus Walter* (☎ 55 80 27, fax 55 80 29, Buntentorsteinweg 86-88) has pleasant single/double rooms from DM45/75, or from DM65/98 with shower and toilet. Take tram No 4 or 5 from the main train station. The Art Nouveau *Hotel Bölts am Park* (☎ 34 61 10, fax 34 12 27, Slevogtstrasse 23) has very nice rooms from DM95/155 with facilities.

Ostertorsteinweg (near Am Dobben) is a lively student area with well-priced eateries and bars. *Piano (Fehrfeld 64)*, just east of Am Dobben, serves tasty baked casseroles for around DM12 to DM16. *Beck's Bistro (Markt 9)* does good lunch specials.

Getting There & Away

Frequent regional and IC trains run to Hamburg (DM40, one hour). There are hourly IC trains to Cologne (DM100, three hours). A couple of ICE trains run direct to Frankfurt (DM172, 3½ hours) and Munich (DM241, six hours) daily. Change trains in Hanover for Berlin (DM135, 3½ hours). For Amsterdam (four hours), change in Osnabrück.

HANOVER
☎ 0511
If you've just arrived from Amsterdam, you'll find provincial Hanover, the capital of Lower Saxony, no great shakes. It's fairly low on sights, but has a very good park and a couple of worthwhile museums. Hanover has close links with the English-speaking world. In 1714, the eldest son of Electress Sophie of Hanover ascended the British throne as King George I. This Anglo-German union lasted until 1837.

Information

The tourist office (☎ 16 84 97 11, fax 16 84 97 08), Ernst-August-Platz 2, is next to the main post office near the Hauptbahnhof. It sells the HannoverCard (DM14/22 for one/three days) and the *Red Thread Guide* (DM4), an easy-to-follow city walking guide.

Things to See

Hanover's chief attractions are the glorious parks of **Herrenhäuser Gärten**, especially the baroque **Grosser Garten** and the **Berggarten** and their museums (take tram No 4 or 5). Notables include the **Fürstenhaus** (DM6/3.50), with treasures from the Guelph palaces, and the **Sprengel Museum** (closed Monday; DM8/6), which exhibits contemporary art, the highlights being Picasso and Max Beckmann.

Places to Stay & Eat

Hanover's swished-up *Jugendherberge* (☎ 131 76 74, fax 185 55, Ferdinand-Wilhelm-Fricke-Weg 1) is 3km from town; from the Hauptbahnhof take U-Bahn 3 or 7 to Fischerhof, then cross the river on the Lodemannbrücke bridge and turn right. Beds are DM27/32 a junior/senior.

Hotel Flora (☎ 38 39 10, fax 383 91 91, Heinrichstrasse 36) has good singles/doubles from DM70/120, or with a bathroom for DM90/140. *Hotel Gildehof* (☎ 36 36 80, fax 30 66 44, Joachimstrasse 6) charges DM85/125 for clean rooms, or DM112/147 with a bathroom.

The *Markthalle*, on the corner of Karmarschstrasse and Leinestrasse, is the place to snack or load up on picnic supplies before hitting the parks. *Brauhaus Ernst August* (☎ 36 59 50, Schmiedestrasse 13A) brews its own Hannöversch beer and serves tasty German dishes from around DM11 to DM31.

Getting There & Away

Hanover's train station is a major hub. ICE trains to/from Hamburg (DM67, 1½ hours), Munich (DM215, 4½ hours), Frankfurt (DM140, 2½ hours) and Cologne (DM104,

GERMANY

2¾ hours) leave hourly, and every two hours to Berlin-Zoo (DM101, 1¾).

FAIRY-TALE ROAD

The Fairy-Tale Road (Märchenstrasse), so called because of the number of legends and fairy tales that sprang from this region, is worth a day or two. The route begins at Hanau and runs to Kassel and Göttingen (passing near Hanover) and ends in Bremen. The stretch between Hanover and Göttingen is perhaps the most interesting – the towns here include **Hamelin** (Hameln) of Pied Piper fame; **Bodenwerder**, where the great adventurer Baron von Münchhausen made his home; and **Bad Karlshafen**, a whitewashed, meticulously planned baroque village that is too beautiful to miss.

Information

At Hamelin's Fremdenverkehrsverband Weserbergland-Mittelweser office (☎ 930 00, fax 93 00 33), Inselstrasse 3, there is a free regional room-finding service and plenty of brochures on the Fairy-Tale Road. The tourist office in Hamelin (☎ 20 26 18, fax 20 25 00) is at Deisterallee 1. In Bodenwerder, the tourist office (☎ 405 41, fax 61 52) is at Weserstrasse 3. In Bad Karlshafen it is in the Kurverwaltung (☎ 99 99 24, fax 99 99 25) by the 'harbour'.

Local telephone codes are ☎ 05151 for Hamelin, ☎ 05533 for Bodenwerder and ☎ 05672 for Bad Karlshafen.

Places to Stay

In Hamelin the camping ground *Fährhaus an der Weser* (☎ 611 67) is on Uferstrasse, across the Weser River from the old town and 10 minutes' walk north. There's also a *DJH hostel* (☎ 34 25, fax 423 16, Fischbeckerstrasse 33). In Bodenwerder, the *DJH hostel* (☎ 26 85, fax 62 03) is on Richard-Schirrmann-Weg; in Bad Karlshafen, there's the DJH hostel *Hermann Wenning* (☎ 338, fax 83 61, Winnefelderstrasse 7). Beds in these hostels are DM22/27 for juniors/seniors.

Getting There & Away

There are frequent regional trains between Hanover and Hamelin (DM15, 45 minutes). From Hamelin's train station, bus No 520 follows the Weser River to Holzminden via Bodenwerder. Bus No 221 from Holzminden

(board at 'Hafendamm') runs to Höxter bus station. From here bus No 220 goes to Bad Karlshafen, where trains connect to/from Göttingen.

GÖTTINGEN

☎ 0551

Göttingen is leafy in summer, teeming with strapping young German students, and makes an ideal stopover on the way north or south between Munich and Hamburg. Bismarck spent his wild years here, and the Brothers Grimm studied and worked here too. Around 40 Nobel Prize winners are linked in some way to Göttingen's hallowed halls.

Information

The main tourist office is in the old Rathaus on Markt 9 (☎ 49 98 00, fax 499 80 10, @ tourismus@goettingen.de). A smaller tourist office is in the round building in front of the train station (☎ 499 80 40).

Things to See

The **Great Hall** in the Rathaus on the Markt has colourful frescoes of notables, with some local bigwigs grafted onto scenes for good measure. Just outside, students mill about the **Gänseliesel** fountain, the town's symbol. The 15th-century **Junkernschänke** at Barfüsserstrasse 5, with its colourful carved facade, is the most stunning of the town's half-timbered buildings.

Places to Stay & Eat

The *Jugendherberge Göttingen* (☎ 576 22, fax 438 87, Habichtsweg 2) charges DM27/32 for juniors/seniors. From the train station's main entrance, cross Berliner Strasse, go right to Groner-Tor-Strasse and take bus No 6 or 9 from across the street.

The friendly *Hotel Garni Gräfin von Holtzenorff* (☎ 639 87, fax 63 29 85, Ernst-Ruhstrat-Strasse 4) charges DM49/85 for basic singles/doubles and DM75/120 with bathroom. Take bus No 13 to Florenz-Sartorius-Strasse. *Berliner Hof* (☎ 38 33 20, fax 383 32 32, @ BerlinerHof.Goettingen@t-online.de, Weender Landstrasse 43) charges DM75/100 for rooms with shower and toilet.

A filling lunchtime meal at the *Zentralmensa*, through the arch off Weender Landstrasse, costs DM6 or less. There's another Mensa on Wilhelmsplatz. *Salamanca*

(Gartenstrasse 21b) offers tasty, well-priced food in a student atmosphere until late.

Entertainment
The *Irish Pub (Mühlenstrasse 4)* offers free live music. *Der Nörgelbuff (Groner Strasse 23)* has live blues, rock and jazz; *Blue Note (Wilhelmsplatz 3)* is the place to get down and dance. *Die Oper (☎ 48 79 98, Nikolaistrasse 1b)* is for young boppers. A couple of bars downstairs cater to a mixed crowd.

Getting There & Away
Hourly ICE trains go to/from Hanover (DM51, 30 minutes), Berlin (DM122, 2¾ hours), Hamburg (DM103, 1¾ hours), Frankfurt (DM94, 1¾ hours) and Munich (DM180, four hours). Direct trains depart every two hours for Goslar in the Harz Mountains (DM23, 1¼ hours).

GOSLAR
☎ 05321
Goslar, a centre for Harz Mountains tourism, is a 1000-year-old city with beautifully preserved half-timbered buildings. The town (and the nearby Rammelsberg Mine) is listed as a World Heritage Site by Unesco.

Information
The tourist office (☎ 780 60, fax 78 06 44, ✆ goslarinfo@t-online.de), Markt 7, can help with accommodation. For information on the Harz Mountains, visit the Harzer Verkehrsverband (☎ 3 40 40, fax 34 04 66, ✆ harzerverkehrsverband@t-online.de) at Marktstrasse 45 (open weekdays).

Things to See & Do
Marktplatz has several photogenic houses. The **Kaiserpfalz** is a reconstructed 11th-century palace that's usually jammed with tour-bus visitors (DM8/4). Just below is the restored **Domvorhalle**, which displays the 11th-century Kaiserstuhl throne, used by German emperors.

At the **Rammelsberger Bergbaumuseum**, about 1km south of the town on Rammelsberger Strasse, you can delve into the area's mining history and descend into mine shafts on a variety of tours (DM10 to DM35).

Places to Stay & Eat
The *youth hostel (☎ 222 40, fax 413 76, Rammelsberger Strasse 25)* is behind the Kaiserpfalz. Take bus C to Theresienhof from the train station. Beds are DM22/27 a junior/senior.

Except on Thursday when it's closed, *Hotel und Campingplatz Sennhütte (☎ 225 02, Clausthaler Strasse 28)*, 3km south of town on Route B241, is a good choice for cheap singles/doubles (DM40/80) and tent sites (DM5.50 per person, DM4.50 per tent).

Many trails lead into the nearby mountains, including the one to Hahnenklee. From the train station take bus No 434 to the Sennhütte stop.

The tourist office arranges *private rooms*; otherwise *Haus Bielitza (☎ 207 44, Abzuchtstrasse 11)* has passable rooms for DM35/55 (hall shower DM3.50). *Gästehaus Schmitz (☎ 234 45, fax 30 60 39, Kornstrasse 1)* offers the best value, with bright rooms with bath for DM55/70.

The Kaiserpassage shopping arcade on Breite Strasse has a couple of eating options; while *Brauhaus Wolpertinger (Marstallstrasse 1)* is a restaurant with traditional German fare (DM15 to DM30). *Didgeridoo (Hoher Weg 13)* serves well-priced kangaroo burgers and barbecued meats and has Australian wines.

Getting There & Away
Goslar is regularly connected by train to Göttingen (DM23, 1¼ hours), Hanover DM23, 1½ hours) and Wernigerode (30 minutes). For information on getting to/from the Harz region, see Getting Around in the following section.

WESTERN HARZ MOUNTAINS
The Harz Mountains (Harzgebirge) don't have the dramatic peaks and valleys of the Alps, but they are a great four-seasons getaway without the Alpine tackiness and tourism.

Information
Make sure to pick up the booklet *Grüner Faden* (Green Thread; DM3), available at tourist offices in the Harz and at many hotels.

For weather reports (in English) contact Goslar's Harzer Verkehrsverband (see Information in the earlier Goslar section).

Alpenverein and Harzclub offices in many towns are good places to receive trail recommendations.

GERMANY

Places to Stay

Many of the 30 or so camping grounds in the Harz Mountains are open year-round; pick up the free *Campingführer* brochure from tourist offices. In the resorts a DM2.50 per day Kurtaxe (resort tax) is slapped on hotel accommodation (less at hostels and camp sites).

Hahnenklee *Campingplatz am Kreuzeck* (☎ 05325-25 70) is 2km north of Hahnenklee (bus No 434 from Goslar or Hahnenklee). The *Jugendherberge* (☎ 22 56, fax 35 24, Hahnenkleer Strasse 11) is near the Bockswiese bus stop (same bus) on the road from Goslar (DM22/27 for juniors/ seniors). The tourist office (☎ 05325-5 10 40), at Kurhausweg 7, can help find a cheap private room.

Bad Harzburg *Campingplatz Wolfenstein* (☎ 05322- 35 85) is about 3km east of town at Wolfstein on Ilsenburger Strasse (bus No 74 or 77 from the train station). The youth hostel *Braunschweiger Haus* (☎ 45 82, fax 18 67, Waldstrasse 5) has beds for DM23/27 juniors/seniors. Take bus No 73 from the train station.

Clausthal-Zellerfeld *Campingplatz Waldweben* (☎ 05323-817 12, Spiegeltaler Strasse 31) is around 1km west of Zellerfeld. The *Jugendherberge* (☎ 842 93, fax 838 27, Altenauer Strasse 55) charges DM22/27 for juniors/seniors (bus No 408). The hostel is usually closed on the first weekend of the month from mid-September to mid-May.

Getting Around

Frequent trains link Goslar with Wernigerode. Four direct trains depart daily for Göttingen via Bad Harzburg. Bus No 77 shuttles several times daily between Bad Harzburg and Wernigerode (DM6, one hour). Bus Nos 408 and 432 run between Goslar and Altenau, while bus Nos 408 and 434 go to Clausthal-Zellerfeld.

Central Germany

RHINELAND-PALATINATE

Rhineland-Palatinate (Rheinland-Pfalz), a region of wine and great natural beauty, is perfect if you want to get off the busy Rhine River tourist route.

Moselle Valley

Exploring the vineyards and wineries of the Moselle (Mosel) Valley is an ideal way to get a taste of German culture. Though the entire route is packed with visitors from June to October, getting off the beaten path is always easy. The most interesting section of the Moselle Valley runs 195km northeast from Trier to Koblenz.

Information Koblenz's tourist office (☎ 0261-30 38 80, fax 303 88 11, ✉ touris tik@koblenz.de) is at Bahnhofsplatz in front of the main train station.

Koblenz's telephone area code is ☎ 0261; in Cochem it's ☎ 02671.

Things to See & Do While not to be compared with Trier or Cochem, Koblenz is a nice enough place to spend half a day or so. Immediately across the Rhine is the impressive **Festung Ehrenbreitstein** fortress, which houses the DJH hostel.

Don't miss **Burg Eltz**, a towering medieval castle at the head of the Eltz Valley (closed from 2 November to March; DM9/6); take a train to Moselkern, from where it's a 50-minute walk up through the forest.

Cochem, though heavily geared to tourists, remains a pretty picture-postcard German town with narrow alleyways and gates. The famous **Reichsburg** castle is a 15-minute walk up the hill from town (daily tours from mid-March to mid-November; DM7). Cochem's HH Hieronimi (☎ 02671-221), just across the river at Stadionstrasse 1-3, is a family-run winery with DM9 tours. Weingut Rademacher (☎ 02671-41 64), diagonally behind the train station at Pinnerstrasse 10, has winery tours for DM9.50/13 with four/six wine tastings.

Places to Stay Tourist offices offer roomfinding services. In May, on summer weekends or during the local wine harvest (mid-September to mid-October), accommodation is hard to find.

In Koblenz, the camping ground *Rhein Mosel* (☎/fax 0261-80 24 89), open April to mid-October, is on Schartwiesenweg at the confluence of the Moselle and Rhine rivers opposite the Deutsches Eck. The daytime passenger ferry from town puts you within a five-minute walk. The excellent DJH *hostel* (☎ 0261-97 28 70, fax 972 87 30, ❷ *jh-koblenz@djh-info.de*) in the old Ehrenbreitstein fortress has beds for DM25.20 – book ahead in summer. From the Hauptbahnhof take bus No 7, 8 or 9.

In Cochem, the riverside *Campingplatz Am Freizeitszentrum* (☎ 44 09), open from Easter to late October, is in Stadionstrasse, downstream of the northern bridge. The *DJH hostel* (☎ 86 33, fax 85 68, ❷ *jh-cochem@djh-info.de, Klottener Strasse 9*) is also on the eastern bank, near the bridge. Beds are DM23.80.

Getting There & Away Buses between Trier and Bullay (DM13, three hours), about three-fifths of the way towards Koblenz, are run by Moselbahn (☎ 0651-210 76); buses leave from outside the train stations in Trier and Bullay.

Local and fast trains run every hour between Trier and Koblenz (DM30, 1½ hours), but the only scenic stretch of track is between Cochem and Koblenz.

From early May to mid-October, Köln-Düsseldorfer (KD) ferries (☎ 0221-208 83 18) sail daily between Koblenz and Cochem (DM37 one way, 4½ hours). From Cochem, the Gebrüder Kolb Line (☎ 02673-15 15) runs boats upriver to Trier and back (DM71/96 single/return) between May and mid-October. Eurail and DB passes are valid for all normal KD Line services, and travel on your birthday is free!

Trier
☎ 0651
Trier is touted as Germany's oldest town, with more Roman ruins than anywhere else north of the Alps. Thanks to its university, Trier can get fairly lively. The town's chief landmark is the **Porta Nigra**, the imposing 2nd-century city gate on the northern edge of the town centre (DM4/2). Trier's superb Romanesque **Dom** shares a 1600-year history with the nearby and equally impressive **Konstantin Basilika**.

Orientation & Information From the Hauptbahnhof, head west along Bahnhofstrasse and Theodor-Heuss-Allee to the Porta Nigra, where you'll find Trier's tourist office (☎ 97 80 80, fax 447 59, ❷ info@tit.de). It

has a free room-finding service, organises guided walking tours in English (DM10), and sells the three-day Trier-Card (DM17).

Places to Stay The year-round camping ground *Trier-City* (☎ 869 21, *Luxemburger Strasse 81*) is on the Moselle. The *DJH Jugendgästehaus* (☎ 14 66 20, fax 146 62 30, ❷ *jh-trier@djh-info.de, An der Jugendherberge 4*) is also down by the riverside. It has dorm beds for DM29.10, doubles for DM38.60 and singles for DM54.40.

Hotel Hochwald (☎ 758 03, fax 743 54, *Bahnhofplatz 5*) is opposite the train station and charges DM48 for plain singles. Single/double rooms with shower and toilet cost DM66/130.

Places to Eat The bustling *Bistro Krim* (☎ 739 43, *Glockenstrasse 7*) offers generous Mediterranean-inspired dishes at affordable prices. *Astarix* (☎ 722 39, *Karl-Marx-Strasse 11*) is a favourite student hang-out in an arcade that serves large salads and limited main dishes for under DM10 (open till late). *Cafeteria-Restaurant Haus Runne* (☎ 209 26 77, *Engelstrasse 25*) serves very good budget lunches.

Getting There & Away There are hourly local and fast trains to/from Saarbrücken (DM22, 1½ hours) and Koblenz (DM30, 1½ hours), as well as a service to Luxembourg and Metz (in France). For information on river ferries see Getting There & Away in the previous Moselle Valley section.

Rhine Valley – Koblenz to Mainz
A trip along the Rhine is on the itinerary of most travellers. The section between Mainz and Koblenz offers the best scenery, especially the narrow tract downriver from Rüdesheim. Spring and autumn are the best times to visit; summer is busy and in winter most towns become dormant.

Information Mainz's tourist office (☎ 06131-28 62 10, fax 286 21 55, ❷ tourist@info-mainz.de) is at Brückenturm am Rathaus (bus No 7, 13, 17, 19 or 27 to Rheingoldhalle). Mainz's C@fé Enterprise, Bilhildisstrasse 2 on Münsterplatz, has Internet facilities.

For information in Koblenz, see the Moselle Valley section earlier.

GERMANY

Things to See & Do One of the valley's most impressive castles is **Burg Rheinfels** in St Goar. Across the river, just south of St Goarshausen, is the Rhine's most famous sight – the **Loreley Cliff**. Worse things don't happen at sea: legend has it that Loreley, the nubile young maiden, lured sailors to their horny, horrible deaths here. It's worth the trek to the top of the Loreley for the view, but try to get up there early to beat the lemmings.

The town of **Rüdesheim**, tanked on tourism, is only for those studying mass tourism at its worst, or for travellers seeking out the bucolic paths in the hills above.

Mainz, 30 minutes south-west by train from Frankfurt, has an attractive old town. Of particular interest are the massive St Martin's cathedral and the Stephanskirche, with stained-glass windows by Marc Chagall. Mainz's Gutenberg Museum contains the first printed Bible. The Roman Ship Museum houses an ancient Rhine galley built by the Romans.

Oberwesel and **Bacharach**, respectively 40km and 45km south of Koblenz, are the best towns for a tipple-'n-nibble experience. For tastings in other towns, ask for recommendations at the tourist offices or just follow your nose.

Places to Stay *Camping* Good possibilities include: Oberwesel's *Schönburg* (☎ *06744-245*), open from May to October and right beside the river; Bacharach's *Sonnenstrand* (☎ *06743-17 52*), open from April to mid-November situated just 500m south of the centre; and St Goarshausen's *Auf der Loreley* (☎ *06771-430*), right on the legendary rock and open all year (call if it's unattended).

Hostels There are *DJH hostels* in Oberwesel (☎ *06744-933 30, fax 74 46, Auf dem Schönberg,* 🖂 *jh-oberwesel@djh-info.de*); *St Goar* (☎ *06741-388, fax 28 69,* 🖂 *jh-st-goar@djh-info.de, Bismarckweg 17*); *St Goarshausen* (☎ *06771-2619, fax 81 89*), *Auf der Loreley* (right on top of the Loreley); *Bacharach* (☎ *06743-12 66, fax 26 84,* 🖂 *jh-bacharach@djh-info-de*), a legendary facility housed in the Burg Stahleck castle; *Rüdesheim* (☎ *06722-27 11, fax 482 84,* 🖂 *ruedesheim@djh-hessen.de*), at Am Kreuzburg; and in Mainz, *Jugendgästehaus* (☎ *06131-853 32, fax*

824 22, 🖂 *jh-mainz@djh-info.de, Otto-Brunfels-Schneise 4*).

Getting There & Away You can travel non-stop on IC/EC trains or travel by regional RB or SE services (DM25, 1½ hours). Sit on the river bank for a magnificent view.

The Köln-Düsseldorfer (KD) Line (☎ 0221-20 88 318) has daily slow and fast boats between Koblenz and Mainz. The most scenic stretch is Koblenz-Rüdesheim (DM42.40); the journey takes about four hours downstream (Rüdesheim-Koblenz) and about 6½ hours upstream (Koblenz-Rüdesheim).

SAARLAND & SAARBRÜCKEN
☎ 0681

Though distinctly German since the early Middle Ages, the Saarland region was ruled by France for several periods during its turbulent history. Reoccupied by the French after WWII, it only joined the Federal Republic of Germany in 1957, after the population snubbed French efforts to turn it into an independent state. Since WWII, the steady economic decline of the coal and steel industries has made Saarland the poorest region in western Germany.

Saarbrücken, capital of Saarland, has an interesting mixed French and German feel. Though lacking major tourist sights, Saarbrücken is a friendly city which chugs along at a relaxed pace.

Orientation & Information
Saarbrücken's Hauptbahnhof is in the north-western corner of the old town, which stretches out on both sides of the Saar River. The tourist office (☎ 93 80 90, fax 938 09 39) is two minutes from the main train station at Reichstrasse 1 (closed Sunday).

Places to Stay & Eat
The excellent *Jugendherberge* (☎ *330 40, fax 37 49 11, Meerwiesertalweg 31*) is a half-hour walk north-east of the train station, or take bus No 49 or 69 to Prinzenweiher. Beds cost DM29 in four-person dorms, or DM36 in two-person rooms. *Hotel Schlosskrug* (☎ *354 48, fax 37 50 22, Schmollerstrasse 14*) on the edge of the lively area around Max-Ophüls-Platz has basic single/double rooms for DM50/95.

Gasthaus Zum Stiefel (*Am Stiefel 2*) is in a laneway off St Johanner Markt. It has an upmarket restaurant at the front and a cheaper pub out the back. *Café Kostbar* (*Nauwieserstrasse 19*) has well-priced set menus.

Getting There & Away

There are frequent trains to the connecting cities of Mannheim (DM76, 2¼ hours), Koblenz (DM55, 2½ hours), Mainz (DM46, two hours) and Frankfurt (DM60, 2½ hours), as well as services across the border to Metz.

FRANKFURT/MAIN

☎ 069

'Bankfurt', 'Krankfurt', and more obscene variants – call it what you will, Frankfurt/Main is the financial and trade-fair centre of western Germany. Unless you're in the market for a good story to tell about how you missed that important flight, don't confuse Frankfurt/Main with Frankfurt/Oder, which is on the Oder River in the 'Wild East'.

Frankfurt is Germany's most important transport hub, so you'll probably end up here at some point. Keep in mind that Frankfurt is not all that typical of Germany – that goes especially for the architecture. But if you look closely, you'll find a jovial southern Hessen folk whose main preoccupations seem to be eating and drinking, and who speak in a dialect that has dispensed with half the German alphabet.

Orientation

The airport is 11 minutes by train, southwest of the city centre. The safest route to the city centre through the sleazy Hauptbahnhof (main train station) area is along Kaiserstrasse.

Information

Tourist Offices Frankfurt's most convenient tourist office (☎ 21 23 88 49/51, fax 212 37 88) is in the main hall of the train station. It's open 8 am to 9 pm weekdays, and 9 am to 6 pm weekends and holidays. For its efficient room finding service there's a charge of DM5. Tourismus + Congress (☎ 21 23 03 96, fax 21 23 07 76), Kaiserstrasse 56, handles room reservations free of charge (closed weekends). Call ☎ 21 23 08 08 to reserve rooms by phone.

One- and two-day Frankfurt cards (DM12/19) give 50% reductions at most museums, the zoo and Palmengarten, as well as unlimited travel on public transport.

Money The Reisebank's Hauptbahnhof branch at platform No 1 is open 6.30 am to 10 pm daily. American Express and Thomas Cook are opposite each other on Kaiserstrasse at Nos 10 and 11 respectively.

Post & Communications The main post office is on the ground floor of the Hertie department store at Zeil 90. There's a smaller branch in the Hauptbahnhof.

Email & Internet Access Cyberyder (☎ 91 39 67 54), Töngesgasse 31, charges DM6.50 for half an hour online.

Medical Services The Uni-Klinik (☎ 630 11) at Theodor Stern Kai in Sachsenhausen is open 24 hours a day.

Things to See & Do

The **Römerberg**, Frankfurt's old central area, has restored 14th- and 15th-century buildings that show how the city looked prior to WWII.

East of Römerberg is the newly restored **Dom**, the coronation site of Holy Roman emperors from 1562 to 1792. It's dominated by the elegant 15th-century Gothic **tower** – one of the few structures left standing after bombings in 1944.

Anyone with an interest in German literature should visit the **Goethe Haus** museum and library, Grosser Hirschgraben 23-25, where Goethe was born in 1749 (open 9 am to 6 pm weekdays, till 4 pm from October to March, 10 am to 4 pm on weekends; DM7/3).

A bit farther afield, the botanical **Palmengarten** (DM7/3; U-Bahn to Bockenheimer Warte), the creative **Frankfurt Zoo** (DM11/5), and the southern bank of the river leading east are good places to unwind.

Museums Most museums are closed on Monday and offer free entry on Wednesday. The **Museum für Moderne Kunst** (Museum of Modern Art), Domstrasse 10, features work by Joseph Beuys, Claes Oldenburg and many others (DM10/5). Also on the north bank is the **Jüdisches Museum** (DM5/2.50, free Saturday).

GERMANY

CENTRAL FRANKFURT

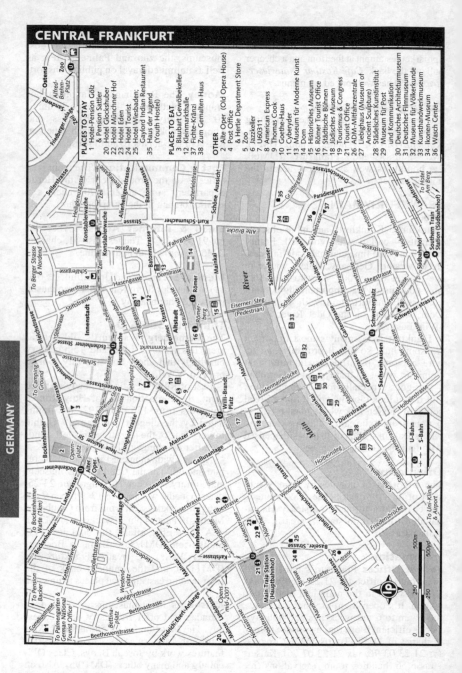

PLACES TO STAY
1 Hotel-Pension Gölz
    & Pension Sattler
20 Hotel Glockshuber
22 Hotel Münchner Hof
23 Hotel Eden
24 Hotel Tourist
25 Hotel Wiesbaden;
    Gaylord Indian Restaurant
35 Haus der Jugend
    (Youth Hostel)

PLACES TO EAT
3 Blaubart Gewölbekeller
12 Kleinmarkthalle
37 Fichte-Kränzi
38 Zum Gemalten Haus

OTHER
2 Alte Oper (Old Opera House)
4 Post Office
    & Hertie Department Store
5 Zoo
6 Jazzkeller
7 U60311
8 American Express
9 Thomas Cook
10 Goethe-Haus
11 Cyberyder
13 Museum für Moderne Kunst
14 Dom
15 Historisches Museum
16 Römer Tourist Office
17 Städtische Bühnen
18 Jüdisches Museum
19 Tourismus & Congress
21 Tourist Office
24 ADM-Mitfahrzentrale
27 Liebighaus (Museum of
    Ancient Sculpture)
28 Städelsches Kunstinstitut
29 Museum für Post
    und Kommunikation
30 Deutsches Architekturmuseum
31 Deutsches Filmmuseum
32 Museum für Völkerkunde
33 Kunsthandwerkmuseum
34 Ikonen-Museum
36 Wasch Center

Numerous museums line the south bank of the Main River along the so-called **Museumsufer** (Museum Embankment). Artistic pickings are plenty at the **Städelsches Kunstinstitut** at Schaumainkai 63, with a world-class collection by artists from the Renaissance to the 20th century, including Botticelli, Dürer, Van Eyck, Rubens, Rembrandt, Vermeer, Cézanne and Renoir (open 10 am to 5 pm Tuesday to Sunday, to 8 pm Wednesday; DM10/8).

Places to Stay

Camping *Campingplatz Heddernheim* (☎ 57 03 32, *An der Sandelmühle 35*) is in the Heddernheim district; take U-Bahn 1, 2 or 3 to the Heddernheim stop. It's open all year and costs DM9.50 per person plus DM5.50 for tent sites.

Hostels The big and often crowded *Haus der Jugend* (☎ 610 01 50, fax 61 00 15 99, *Deutschherrnufer 12*) is within walking distance of the city centre and Sachsenhausen's nightspots. Dorm beds are DM27/34 under/over age 20, and space in four-bed dorms is DM39.50. Breakfast is free and dinner is DM8.90. From the Hauptbahnhof take S-Bahn 2, 3, 4, 5 or 6 to Lokalbahnhof, then walk north for 10 minutes. Check-in begins at 2 pm and there's a midnight curfew.

Pensions & Hotels Most of Frankfurt's lower-budget accommodation is in the sleazy Bahnhofsviertel surrounding the main train station. *Hotel Eden* (☎ 25 19 14, fax 25 23 37, *Münchener Strasse 429*) has rooms for DM85/125 with toilet and shower. *Hotel Münchner Hof* (☎ 23 00 66, fax 23 44 28, *Münchener Strasse 46*) has reasonable, basic rooms for DM80/100, or DM100/140 with toilet and shower. *Hotel Tourist* (☎ 23 30 95/96/97, fax 23 69 86, *Baseler Strasse 23-25*) charges DM95/140 for small rooms with facilities. *Hotel Wiesbaden* (☎ 23 23 47, fax 25 28 45, *Baseler Strasse 52*) is one of the area's better establishments with rooms from DM115/150.

Hotel Glockshuber (☎ 74 26 28, fax 74 26 29, *Mainzer Landstrasse 120*), north of the main train station, is another pleasant option. Basic rooms here start at DM65/110. Sachsenhausen's *Hotel Am Berg* (☎ 61 20 21, fax 61 51 09, *Grethenweg 23*) to the

south, charges DM65/95, or DM125 for doubles with a bathroom.

In the pleasant Westend, *Pension Backer* (☎ 74 79 92, fax 74 79 00, *Mendelssohnstrasse 92*) has basic rooms for DM50/70. *Hotel-Pension Gölz* (☎ 74 67 35, fax 74 61 42, @ *Hotel Goelz@aol.com, Beethovenstrasse 44*) has basic rooms for DM69, and singles/doubles with a bathroom for DM85/130. *Pension Sattler* (☎ 74 60 91) at No 46 charges DM110/160 for quite good singles/doubles with a bathroom. In Bockenheim to the north-west, *Hotel West* (☎ 247 90 20, fax 707 53 09, *Gräfstrasse 81*) has fairly good rooms for DM90/150 with facilities.

Places to Eat

For Indian cuisine, *Gaylord (Baseler Strasse 54)* has curry lunch specials from DM15 and evening main dishes for around DM22.

Known to locals as Fressgass (Munch-Alley), the Kalbächer Gasse and Grosse Bockenheimer Strasse area, between Opernplatz and Börsenstrasse, has some medium-priced restaurants and fast-food places with outdoor tables in summer. *Blaubart Gewölbekeller (Kaiserhofstrasse 18)* serves well-priced hearty dishes in a beer cellar atmosphere. It's also a lively place to drink until late.

Apple-wine taverns are a Frankfurt tradition, serving *Ebbelwoi* (an alcoholic apple cider) along with hearty food. *Fichte-Kränzi (Wallstrasse 5)* has a friendly atmosphere and well-priced food. *Zum Gemalten Haus (Schweizer Strasse 67)* is a lively place full of paintings of old Frankfurt.

In hip Bornheim to the north, *Café Gegenwart (Berger Strasse 6)* is a large bar/restaurant serving large, hearty dishes from DM14; if the weather cooperates you can sit outside.

Fresh produce markets are held from 8 am to 6 pm Thursday and Friday at Bockenheimer Warte and Südbahnhof respectively. The *Kleinmarkthalle*, off Hasengasse, is a great produce market with loads of fruit, vegetables, meats and hot food.

Entertainment

Journal Frankfurt (DM3.30) has good listings in German of music clubs and what's on in town, and the English-language

GERMANY

MainCity series of guides is well worth browsing. Pick these up at any newsagent or newspaper kiosk.

Ballet, opera and theatre are strong points of Frankfurt's entertainment scene. For information and bookings, contact Städtische Bühnen (☎ 21 23 79 99) at Willy-Brandt-Platz.

Frankfurt's jazz scene is very good. *Blues & Beyond (Berger Strasse 159)* is a small venue which often has jazz; the *Jazzkeller (Kleine Bockenheimer Strasse 18a)* is also a cool place. *U60311*, on Rossmarkt, has techno and house music.

Getting There & Away
Air Germany's largest airport, Flughafen Frankfurt/Main (☎ 69 03 05 11) has two terminals linked by an elevated railway. Departure and arrival halls A, B and C are in Terminal 1, with Lufthansa flights handled in hall A; halls D and E are in the new Terminal 2. The airport train station has two sections: platforms below terminal 1 handle regional and S-Bahn connections, whereas IR, IC and ICE connections are in a separate long-distance train station. Signs point the way.

Bus Long-distance buses leave from the south side of Hauptbahnhof, where there's a Eurolines/Europabus office (☎ 23 07 35/6) that caters to major European destinations and handles reservations.

Train The Hauptbahnhof handles more departures and arrivals than any other station in Germany. Night trains depart for Copenhagen (DM246, 11½ hours), Milan (DM216, nine hours), Nice (DM203, 16 hours), Paris (DM144, eight hours), Prague (DM138, nine hours), Warsaw (DM268, 13 hours) and Vienna (DM149, 10 hours). For rail information, call ☎ 01805-99 66 33.

Ride Share The ADM-Mitfahrzentrale (☎ 194 40) is on Baselerplatz, a three-minute walk south of the train station. A sample of fares (including fees) is: Berlin DM54, Hamburg DM49, Cologne DM23, Dresden DM49 and Munich DM41.

Getting Around
To/From the Airport The S-Bahn's S8/S9 line runs every 15 minutes between the airport and Frankfurt Hauptbahnhof (DM5.90, 11 minutes), usually continuing via Hauptwache and Konstablerwache to Offenbach. Taking a taxi or the frequent airport bus (DM5.90 from the Südbahnhof) is slower.

Public Transport Frankfurt's excellent transport network (RMV) integrates all bus, tram, S-Bahn and U-Bahn lines. Single or day tickets can be purchased from automatic machines at most stops. Press *Einzelfahrt Frankfurt* for destinations in zone 50, which takes in most of Frankfurt; a plane symbol indicates the button for the airport. Tickets cost DM3.60 for peak times. A *Tageskarte* (24-hour ticket) costs DM8.20 and is also valid for the airport trip.

COLOGNE
☎ 0221
Cologne (Köln) has been an important city since Roman times, when it was known as Colonia Agrippinensis, the capital of the province of Germania. In later years it remained one of northern Europe's main cities (the largest in Germany until the 19th century). Though devastated in WWII, Cologne was quickly rebuilt and many of its old churches and monuments have been meticulously restored.

After Berlin, Munich and Hamburg, Cologne should be high on your list of cities to visit. Its Dom (cathedral) is famous, but it's also a buzzing, interesting place.

Orientation & Information
The pedestrianised Hohe Strasse runs north-south through the middle of the old town. The Hauptbahnhof is just north of the cathedral. The main bus station is behind the train station on Breslauer Platz.

The tourist office (☎ 22 12 33 45, fax 22 12 33 20, @ koelntourismus@koeln.org) is opposite the cathedral's main entrance, at Unter Fettenhennen 19. Staff book rooms for a DM5 fee (no telephone bookings). *Monatsvorschau*, the monthly what's-on booklet, is a good investment at DM2.

Moderne Zeiten (☎ 206 72 51), Richmodstrasse 13, is a very hip place where you can surf the Web and chew chow.

Things to See
The sheer size of Cologne's **Dom**, with spires rising to a height of 157m, is

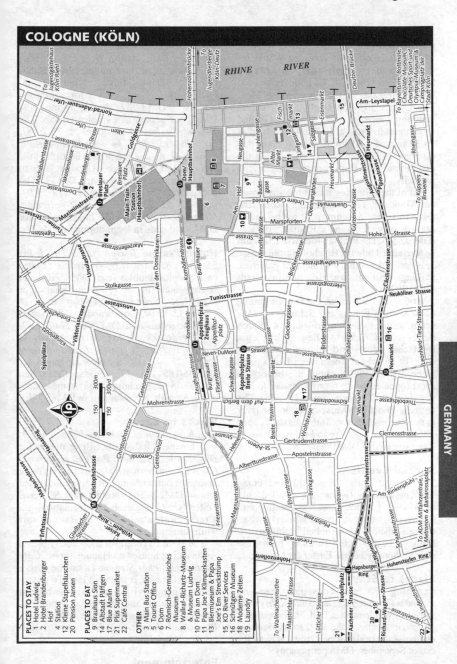

COLOGNE (KÖLN)

RHINE RIVER

GERMANY

PLACES TO STAY
1 Hotel Ludwig
2 Hotel Brandenburger Hof
4 Station
12 Kleine Stapelhäuschen
20 Pension Jansen

PLACES TO EAT
9 Brauhaus Sion
14 Altstadt Päffgen
17 Blue Marlin
21 Plus Supermarket
22 Café Central

OTHER
3 Main Bus Station
5 Tourist Office
6 Dom
7 Römisch-Germanisches Museum
8 Wallraf-Richartz-Museum & Museum Ludwig
10 Früh am Dom
11 Papa Joe's Klimperkasten
13 Biermuseum & Papa Joe's Em Streckstrump
15 KD River Services
16 Schnütgen Museum
18 Moderne Zeiten
19 Laundry

overwhelming. Building began in 1248, was stopped in 1560, and started again in 1842. Miraculously, it survived WWII intact. Behind the high altar, the **Magi's Shrine** (circa 1150-1210) is believed to contain the remains of the Three Wise Men. The Dom's 509-step **south tower** offers stunning views of town (DM3). Guided Dom tours in English (DM7/4) are held at 10.30 am and 2.30 pm Monday to Saturday (Sunday at 2.30 pm only); meet inside the main portal. The Dom is open 7 am to 7.30 pm daily.

All of the following museums are closed on Monday. The interesting **Römisch-Germanisches Museum**, next to the cathedral, displays Cologne's Roman artefacts (DM5/2.50). The **Wallraf-Richartz-Museum & Museum Ludwig**, Bischofsgartenstrasse 1, is one of the country's finest art galleries, making brilliant use of natural light (DM10/5).

At Cäcilienstrasse 29, the former church of St Cecilia houses the **Schnütgen Museum**, an overwhelming display of church riches (DM5/2.50). The multi-media **Deutsches Sport- und Olympia-Museum**, south of the city at Rheinaufen 1, is a great place to find out all about the history of sport (open 10 am to 6 pm Tuesday to Friday, 11 am to 7 pm weekends; DM8/4). The enticing **Chocolate Museum** is on the river in the Rheinauhafen, near the Altstadt (open 10 am to 6 pm Tuesday to Friday, 11 am to 7 pm weekends; DM10/5).

Special Events

Try to visit during the wild and crazy Cologne Carnival (Karneval), rivalled only by Munich's Oktoberfest. People dress in clown suits, as popular personalities or whatever else their alcohol-fuelled brains invent. Karneval begins on the Thursday before the seventh Sunday before Easter (got that?).

Places to Stay

Camping The most convenient camping ground is *Campingplatz der Stadt Köln* (☎ 83 19 66) on Weidenweg in Poll, 5km south-east of the city centre. Take U16 to Marienburg and cross the bridge (open from May to the end of September; DM8 per person).

Hostels The bustling *Jugendherberge Köln-Deutz* (☎ 81 47 11, fax 88 44 25,

JH-DEUTZ@t-online.de, Siegesstrasse 5a) in Deutz is a 15-minute walk east from the main train station over the Hohenzollernbrücke, or three minutes from Bahnhof Köln-Deutz (also called Messe-Osthallen). The cost for juniors/seniors is DM32/37; double rooms cost DM46 per person and singles DM53. The *Jugendgästehaus Köln-Riehl* (☎ 76 70 81, fax 76 15 55, *jgh-koeln-riehl@t-online.de, An der Schanz 14)* is north of the city in Riehl. Take the U15 or U16 to Boltensternstrasse. Beds are DM39. The backpackers' hostel *Station* (☎ 912 53 01, fax 912 53 03, *station@t-online.de, Marzellenstrasse 44-48)* has singles for DM40 and beds in large dorms for DM27.

Hotels *Pension Jansen* (☎ 25 18 75, fax 25 18 75, Richard-Wagner-Strasse 18) has basic singles/doubles from DM55/100 and is convenient to the restaurant quarter of town. *Hotel Brandenburger Hof* (☎ 12 28 89, fax 13 53 04, Brandenburger Strasse 2) has basic rooms from DM75/90. *Hotel Ludwig* (☎ 16 05 40, fax 16 05 44 44, *hotel@hotelludwig.com, Brandenburger Strasse 22-24)* has very pleasant rooms for DM145/185. *Das Kleine Stapelhäuschen* (☎ 2 57 78 62, Fischmarkt 1-3) in the middle of the Altstadt, has rooms from DM85/140.

Places to Eat

Brauhaus Sion (*Unter Taschenmacher 9)* is a big beer hall with filling meals for DM20 or less. *Altstadt Päffgen* (*Heumarkt 62)* at the northern or Salzgasse end is more upmarket but authentic. It serves meals for around DM22. The Internet cafe Moderne Zeiten (see Orientation & Information) has a *restaurant* attached where you can surf while slinging pasta.

You'll find a couple of moderately priced Asian eating houses on Händelstrasse. *Café Central* (*Jülicher Strasse 1)*, on the corner of Händelstrasse, is open till late. To put together a picnic, visit a *market*; the biggest is on Tuesday and Friday at Aposteln-Kloster near Neumarkt. The supermarket *Plus* (*Aachener Strasse 64)* is in the Belgisches Viertel.

Entertainment

Papa Joe's Klimperkasten (*Alter Markt 50)* is a lively jazz pub and has a wonderful pianola. *Papa Joe's Em Streckstrump (Buttermarkt 37)* is more intimate. *Metronom (Weyerstrasse 59)*, near the Kwartier Latäng (Latin Quarter) to the south-west, is Cologne's most respected evening bar for jazz enthusiasts, with live performances mainly on weekdays. *Wallmachenreuther (Brusseler Platz 9)* is an off-beat bar in the Belgisches Viertel which also serves food.

There are more than 20 local breweries, all producing a variety called *Kölsch*, relatively light and slightly bitter. *Früh am Dom (Am Hof 12-14)* is popular; the *Biermuseum (Buttermarkt 39)*, beside Papa Joe's, has 18 varieties on tap. *Küppers Brauerei (☎ 934 78 10, Alteburger Strasse 157)* is in Bayenthal south of the city (take the U16 to Bayenthalgürtel) and has a nice beer garden.

Getting There & Away
Deutsche Touring's Eurolines (☎ 13 52 52) has overnight trips to Paris (DM58, 6½ hours). The office is at the main train station at the Breslauer Platz exit.

There are frequent train services to nearby Bonn (DM9, 18 minutes) and Düsseldorf (DM12, 20 minutes) as well as to Aachen (DM20, one hour). Frequent direct IC/EC (DM93, 3¼ hours) and ICE (DM104, 2¾ hours) trains go to Hanover. There are IC/EC links with Frankfurt/Main (DM68, 2¼ hours) – a new ICE line is being built to Frankfurt's airport – and ICE trains to Berlin (DM190, 4½ hours). The Thaly high-speed train connects Paris and Cologne via Aachen and Brussels (DM108/128 weekdays/weekends, four hours, seven times daily; with only a small discount for rail pass holders).

KD River Cruises (☎ 208 83 18 for information), Frankenwerft 1, has services all along the Rhine.

The ADM Mitfahrzentrale (☎ 194 40) is at Triererstrasse 47 near Barbarossaplatz in the south-west.

BONN
☎ 0228
This small city on the Rhine became West Germany's temporary capital in 1949 and recently lost its parliament, which has moved to Berlin. The deck of public servants was reshuffled – some stayed, others went to Berlin with the politicians. Bonn,

though pleasant, is no great shakes these days, so you might like to make it a day trip from Cologne.

Information
The tourist office (☎ 77 50 00 or 194 33, fax 77 50 77, ✉ bonninformation@bonn.de) is behind the Karstadt department store in Windeckstrasse, a three-minute walk along Poststrasse from the Hauptbahnhof.

Ludwig van Beethoven was born in 1770 at the **Beethoven-Haus**, Bonngasse 20, which houses memorabilia concerning his life and music, including his last piano, specially made with an amplified sounding board to accommodate his deafness (open 10 am to 6 pm Monday to Saturday from April to October, 11 am to 4 pm Sunday; DM8/6).

The free **Haus der Geschichte der Bundesrepublik Deutschland**, Adenauerallee 250, covers the history of Germany from 1945 to the present (closed Monday). It's part of the **Museumsmeile**, a row of museums that includes the **Kunstmuseum** with its collection of 20th-century art, and changing exhibitions at the **Kunst- und Ausstellungshalle der Bundesrepublik Deutschland**.

The **Frauenmuseum**, Im Krausfeld 10, promotes and exhibits art created by women (closed Monday; DM8/5).

There are about 70 trains a day to/from Cologne (DM9, 18 minutes) in the north and Koblenz (DM22, 30 minutes) in the south.

DÜSSELDORF
☎ 0211
Though there are no 'must see' sights in Düsseldorf, it's quite nice to visit anyway, especially once you've wended your way to the Rhine River. Most of Düsseldorf was razed from the skies in WWII but it was reconstructed and is now one of the most elegant and wealthy cities in all of Germany. This capital of North Rhine-Westphalia is an important centre for fashion and commerce – and beer connoisseurs will find a couple of nice surprises here.

Information
The main tourist office (☎ 17 20 20, fax 16 10 71, ✉ vvd@t-online.de) is opposite the main exit of the train station towards the north end of Konrad-Adenauer-Platz. It levies DM5 for room bookings made over

the counter. There's an Internet cafe behind the Rathaus at Rathausufer 8.

Things to See

The **Kunstmuseum Düsseldorf** at Ehrenhof, north of the Oberkasseler Brücke, has a comprehensive European collection (closed Monday; DM5/2.50). The **Kunstsammlung Nordrhein-Westfalen**, Grabbeplatz 5, has a huge collection of modern art (closed Monday; DM12/8).

The **Goethe-Museum Düsseldorf** in Schloss Jägerhof, Jacobistrasse 2, pays tribute to the life and work of the great man of letters (closed Monday and Saturday morning; DM4/2).

German-literature buffs will also want to visit the **Heinrich-Heine-Institut**, Bilker Strasse 12-14. Heine was born here and lived in France when the political burner was turned up a notch, only returning to Germany when things cooled down (closed Monday and Saturday morning; DM4/2). Heine's house at Bolkerstrasse 53 is now a literary pub.

Places to Stay & Eat

Campingplatz Nord Unterbacher See (☎ 899 20 38), open from 4 April to late September, is at Kleiner Torfbruch in Düsseldorf-Unterbach – take S-Bahn 7 to Düsseldorf-Eller, then bus No 735 to Kleiner Torfbruch.

The *Jugendgästehaus* (☎ 55 73 10, fax 57 25 13, ✉ jgh-duesseldorf@t-online.de, *Düsseldorfer Strasse 1)* is in posh Oberkassel across the Rhine from the Altstadt. It charges DM38 in small dorms and has some singles (DM47) and doubles (DM43 per person). Take U-Bahn 70, 74, 75, 76 or 77 to Luegplatz, where it's a short walk.

Hotel Komet (☎ 17 87 90, fax 178 79 50, *Bismarckstrasse 93)* has reasonable rooms for DM69/98 with bathroom (breakfast from DM7). *Hotel Amsterdam* (☎ 840 58, fax 840 50, *Stresemannstrasse 20)* has rooms with private shower from DM80/145.

The *Brauerei zur Uer (Ratinger Strasse 16)* is a rustic place to eat your fill for under DM20. Ratinger Strasse is also home to a couple of other pub-style places where you can eat and drink.

Anadolou (Mertensgasse 10) serves delicious Anatolian sit-down and takeaway food including vegetarian dishes.

Entertainment

For bars try Bolkerstrasse, Kurze Strasse and Andreasstrasse in Düsseldorf's Altstadt, referred to as the 'longest bar in the world'. The beverage of choice is *Alt* beer, a dark and semisweet brew. Try Gatzweilers Alt at *Zum Schlüssel (Bolkerstrasse 43-7)*. *Zum Uerige* on Berger Strasse is the place to buy Uerige Alt beer.

Getting There & Away

There are ICE services to Hanover (DM95, 2¾ hours), and various services to Cologne (DM12, 30 minutes). IR trains go to Frankfurt/Main (DM82, 3½ hours) and most other major German cities.

AACHEN
☎ 0241

Aachen was known in Roman times for its thermal springs. The great Frankish conqueror Charlemagne was so chuffed by the waters that he settled here and made it the capital of his kingdom in AD 794. It is now an industrial and commercial centre and home to the country's largest technical university. It's possible to visit this pleasant town on a day trip from Cologne.

Orientation & Information

The Hauptbahnhof is south-east of the town centre, just beyond Alleenring, Aachen's outer ring road. The inner ring road, or Grabenring, has different names (most ending in 'graben') and encloses the old city.

The helpful tourist office (☎ 1 80 29 60/1, fax 1 80 29 30, ✉ mail@aachen-tourist.de) is at Atrium Elisenbrunnen, just inside the Grabenring east of the cathedral (closed Sunday). Vision Internet Café is at Neupforte 25.

For budget rooms, call the reservation service well in advance on ☎ 180 29 50/1.

Things to See & Do

Aachen's drawing card is its **cathedral** (Dom, Kaiserdom or Münster), open 7 am to 7 pm daily. The cathedral's subtle grandeur is topped by its historical significance – Charlemagne is buried here, and no fewer than 30 Holy Roman emperors were crowned here from 936 to 1531. Don't miss this cathedral – it's rightly on Unesco's World Heritage List.

The entrance to the **Domschatzkammer** (cathedral treasury), with one of the richest collections of religious art north of the Alps, is nearby on Klostergasse (DM5/4).

The **Ludwig Forum for International Art**, in a former umbrella factory on Jülicherstrasse 97-109, has works by Warhol, Lichtenstein, Baselitz and others (closed Monday; DM6/3). A visit to the city-owned **Carolus Thermen** baths (☎ 180 29 00) when they open in late 2000 will set you back DM14 for two hours (DM24 with sauna), or DM26 for up to five hours of splashy activity (DM40 with sauna). Take bus No 34 from the city centre.

Places to Stay & Eat

The *Jugendgästehaus* (☎ *71 10 10, fax 711 01 20, Maria-Theresia-Allee 280)* is 4km south-west of the train station on a hill overlooking the city. Take bus No 2 to Ronheide, or bus No 12 to the closer Colynshof at the foot of the hill. It charges DM38.50 in dorms, and has some singles/doubles for DM63.50/77. The central *Hotel Drei Könige* (☎ *483 93, fax 361 52, Büchel 5)* has a few simple rooms for DM65/105. *Hotel Marx* (☎ *375 41, fax 267 05,* @ *Hotel-Marx@gmx.de, Hubertusstrasse 33-35)* offers basic rooms for DM60/100.

Aachen is full of lively cafes, restaurants and pubs, especially along Pontstrasse, referred to by locals as 'Quartier Latin'. *Café Kittel (Pontstrasse 39)* is a popular student hang-out serving light meals, including vegetarian dishes. *Gaststätte Labyrinth (Pontstrasse 156-158)* is a rambling beer-hall-type place that lives up to its name. Good, filling meals range from DM10 to DM16.

Getting There & Away

There are fast trains almost every hour to Cologne (DM20, 45 minutes) and Liège (DM16, 40 minutes). The high-speed Thaly passes through seven times daily on its way to Brussels (DM40, two hours) and Paris (DM118, 3¼ hours).

Baden-Württemberg

STUTTGART
☎ 0711

Stuttgart is Baden-Württemberg's state capital and the hub of its industries. At the forefront of Germany's post-WWII economic recovery, Stuttgart started life less auspiciously in AD 950 as a stud farm. Lacking historical monuments, the city attracts visitors with its air of relaxed prosperity and its Mercedes-Benz and Porsche museums.

Orientation & Information

The main train station is immediately north of the central pedestrian shopping street, Königstrasse. The tourist office (☎ 222 82 40, fax 222 82 53), Königstrasse 1a, is opposite the main train station. The Königstrasse department stores Karstadt and Kaufhof have Internet terminals on their top floors – the former, at No 1, charges DM5 per half-hour and the latter, at No 6, asks for DM6.

Things to See & Do

Stretching south-west from the Neckar River to the city centre is the **Schlossgarten**, an extensive strip of parkland divided into three sections (Unterer, Mittlerer and Oberer), complete with ponds, swans, street entertainers and modern sculptures. At their northern edge the gardens take in the **Wilhelma zoo** and botanical gardens (open daily; DM14/7). At their southern end they encompass the sprawling baroque **Neues Schloss** and the Renaissance **Altes Schloss**. The **Staatsgalerie**, adjoining the park at Konrad-Adenauer-Strasse 30, houses an excellent collection from the Middle Ages to the present (closed Monday; DM9/5).

The Mittlerer Schlossgarten's excellent **Carl Zeiss Planetarium** is named for the company that invented the planetarium (open daily; DM9/5).

Motor Museums The motor car was first developed by Gottlieb Daimler and Carl Benz at the end of the 19th century. The free **Mercedes-Benz Museum** (closed Monday) in the suburb of Sindelfingen tells the story of the company's rise. Take S-Bahn No 1 to Neckarstadion.

For even faster cars, visit the free **Porsche Museum**, open 9 am to 4 pm daily (to 5 pm weekends). Take S-Bahn No 6 to Neuwirtshaus.

Better than either museum is a Mercedes-Benz **factory tour** of the Sindelfingen plant. You must book in advance for the free weekday tours (☎ 07031-90 24 93).

GERMANY

Places to Stay

You can camp at *Campingplatz Stuttgart* (☎ 55 66 96, fax 55 74 54, *Mercedesstrasse 40*), by the river and 500m from the Bad Cannstatt S-Bahn station. Adults pay DM9 each plus DM4 for the site. The DJH *youth hostel* (☎ 24 15 83, fax 236 10 41, *Haussmannstrasse 27*) is a signposted 15-minute walk east of the main train station. Beds cost DM24/29 for juniors/seniors and the curfew is midnight. The non-DJH *Jugendgästehaus* (☎ 24 11 32, *Richard-Wagner-Strasse 2*), south-east of the centre, charges DM40/70/90 for singles/doubles/triples. Take U-Bahn No 15 to Bubenbad. The cheapest deal for those aged 16 to 27 is *Tramper Point Stuttgart* (☎ 817 74 76, fax 237 28 10, *Wiener Strasse 317*), which has portable beds in a communal room for DM13. It's open from late June to early September and check-in is from 5 to 11 pm. Take U-Bahn 6 to Sportpark Feuerbach.

Hotel Espenlaub (☎ 21 09 10, fax 210 91 55, *Charlottenstrasse 27*) has pleasant singles/doubles starting at DM60/90 without bathroom. Rooms at the *Gasthof Alte Mira* (☎ 222 95 02, fax 222 95 03 29, *Büchsenstrasse 24*) start at DM60/100.

Places to Eat

Stock up on picnic supplies at the *Markthalle*, a superb Art Nouveau-style market on Dorotheenstrasse (closed Sunday). Lunch is only DM7 at the university mensa's ground-floor *cafeteria* (*Holzgartenstrasse 11*) and the small *Mensa Stüble* in the basement.

Otherwise try the healthy spreads at *iden* (*Eberhardtstrasse 1*), a spacious vegetarian restaurant. *Weinstube Stetter* (*Rosenstrasse 32*) in the Bohnenviertel (Bean Quarter) has local specialities like *Maultaschen* (a German form of ravioli) from DM8.20. The surrounding streets boast many more pubs and eateries. *Calwer Eck Bräu* (*Calwerstrasse 31*) brews its own excellent beer and serves a wide range of dishes from DM15.

Getting There & Away

ICE trains run to Frankfurt/Main (DM88, 80 minutes), Berlin (DM256, six hours), Munich (DM87, two hours) and most major German cities. Regional and long-distance buses leave from the station next to the main train station.

AROUND STUTTGART
Tübingen
☎ 07071

In this gentle, picturesque university town, just 35km south of Stuttgart, you can wander through winding alleys and enjoy views of half-timbered houses and old stone walls. On **Marktplatz**, the centre of town, is the 1435 **Rathaus** with its ornate baroque facade and astronomical clock. The nearby late-Gothic **Stiftkirche** houses tombs of the Württemberg dukes and has excellent medieval stained-glass windows. From the heights of the Renaissance **Schloss Hohentübingen** (now part of the university) there are fine views over the steep, red-tiled rooftops of the old town.

The tourist office (☎ 913 60, fax 350 70, ✉ mail@tuebingen-info.de) is by the main bridge, Neckarbrücke. Hourly trains to/from Stuttgart take one hour (DM16.40).

Places to Stay & Eat There is a *camping ground* (☎ 431 45, *Rappenberghalde 61*); follow the signs from the Alleenbrücke. The DJH *youth hostel* (☎ 230 02, fax 250 61, *Gartenstrasse 22/2*) charges DM26/31 for juniors/seniors. Central *Hotel Am Schloss* (☎ 929 40, fax 92 94 10, ✉ info@hotelam schloss.de, *Burgsteige 18*) has simple singles/doubles from DM72/130. Its restaurant's *Maultaschen* are a local institution. The Turkish food at *Restaurant Istanbul* (*Karlstrasse 1*) is fighting fresh (averaging DM6).

HEIDELBERG
☎ 06221

The French destroyed Heidelberg in 1693 – they may have been the last visitors to dislike this charming town on the Neckar River. Mark Twain began his European travels here and recounted his comical observations in *A Tramp Abroad*.

With a sizable student population, Heidelberg is surprisingly lively for a city of its size. But be warned: this place is chock-a-block with tourists in July and August.

Orientation & Information

From the main train station, walk east along Kurfürsten-Anlage to Bismarckplatz, where medieval Heidelberg begins to reveal itself. The pedestrianised Hauptstrasse leads east through the heart of the old city, from Bismarckplatz via Marktplatz to Karlstor.

Castellers, Vilafranca del Penedesi, Spain

Venice Carnival, Italy

Oktoberfest, Munich, Germany

Folk dancing, Portugal

Cliffs of Santorini, Greek Islands

The Island of Murano, home of Venetian glass, Italy

Sunset at the magnificent travertine terraces in Pamukkale, Turkey

The main tourist office (☎ 194 33, fax 14 22 22, ✉ cvb@heidelberg.de), outside the train station at Willy-Brandt-Platz 1, is open 9 am to 7 pm Monday to Saturday (10 am to 6 pm Sunday from mid-March to mid-November). There are smaller tourist offices at the funicular train station near the castle, and on Neckarmünzplatz.

The main post office is to the right as you leave the train station. You can exchange foreign currency at the Reisebank in the station or at several banks around Bismarckplatz. Café Gekco, Bergheimer Strasse 8, charges DM4 for 30 minutes on the Internet.

Things to See & Do

Heidelberg's large Gothic-Renaissance **Schloss** is the city's chief attraction. The building's half-ruined state actually adds to its romantic appeal. Entry is DM4/2, which covers the **Grosses Fass** (Great Vat), an enormous 18th-century keg capable of holding 221,726L, and **Deutsches Apotheken-museum** (German Pharmaceutical Museum). It costs nothing to wander the grounds and garden terraces.

To reach the castle either walk 10 minutes up from town, or take the **funicular railway** from lower Kornmarkt station (DM3 return). For DM8.50 return, the funicular continues up to the **Königstuhl**, where there's a TV and lookout tower.

Dominating Universitätsplatz are the 18th-century **Alte Universität** (Old University) and the **Neue Universität** (New University). The **Studentenkarzer** (students' jail) is on Augustinergasse (closed Sunday and Monday; DM1.50). From 1778 to 1914 this jail held uproarious students imprisoned for heinous crimes such as drinking, singing and womanising.

The **Kurpfälzisches Museum** (Palatinate Museum) on Hauptstrasse contains paintings, sculptures and the jawbone of the 600,000-year-old Heidelberg Man, one of the oldest humans ever found (closed Monday; DM5/3, DM3/2 on Sunday).

A stroll along the **Philosophenweg**, north of the Neckar River, gives a welcome respite from Heidelberg's tourist hordes. Leading through steep vineyards and orchards, the path offers the great views of the Altstadt and the castle that inspired German philosopher Hegel.

Places to Stay

Finding accommodation can be difficult in high season – arrive early in the day or book ahead.

Camping *Camping Haide* (☎ 06223-21 11) is on the river and charges DM8.50 per person and from DM6 per site. Take bus No 35 to Orthopädische Klinik.

Hostels In summer, fax reservations at least a week in advance for the DJH *youth hostel* (☎ 41 20 66, fax 40 25 59, Tiergartenstrasse 5). It's across the river from the train station – from the station or Bismarckplatz, take bus No 33 towards Ziegelhausen. Beds are DM24/29 for juniors/seniors.

The ideally situated *Jeske Hotel* (☎ 237 33, Mittelbadgasse 2) charges just DM24 for beds.

Hotels Tiny *Pension Astoria* (☎ 40 29 29, Rahmengasse 30) is in a quiet residential street north of the river just across Theodor-Heuss-Brücke, and has singles/doubles for DM70/115. Near the Alte Brücke (Karl-Theodor-Brücke) is the *Hotel Vier Jahreszeiten* (☎ 241 64, fax 16 31 10, Haspelgasse 2), with rooms from DM85/120.

Hotel Kohler (☎ 97 00 97, fax 97 00 96, Goethestrasse 2), east and within walking distance of the station, has high season singles/doubles from DM115/170 (much cheaper at other times). Also in the old town is *Hotel Am Kornmarkt* (☎ 243 25, fax 282 18, Kornmarkt 7), which charges from DM90/140.

Places to Eat

If you can bluff your way into the student *mensa* near the University Library, lunch is a mere DM5. For takeaways and picnics, seek out fast-food places and delicatessens along Hauptstrasse, though for cheaper sit-down food, Bergheimer Strasse, west of Bismarckplatz, has a few cheap sit-down restaurants and pubs with main courses priced around DM14.

Raja Rani (Mittelbadgasse 5) is an Indian cafe and takeaway place with simple, tasty (and often vegetarian) curries from DM5 a plate. They make their own sausage and beer at *Vetter Alt Heidelberg Brauhaus* (Steingasse 9), which is bustling year round. A large tavern, *Zum Güldenen*

GERMANY

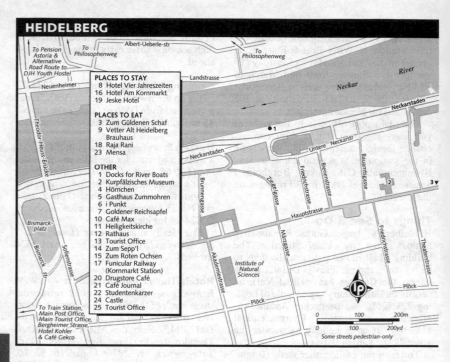

HEIDELBERG

To Pension Astoria & Alternative Road Route to DJH Youth Hostel

To Philosophenweg

Albert-Ueberle-str

To Philosophenweg

River

Neckar

Neuenheimer

Landstrasse

Neckarstaden

Theodor-Heuss-Brücke

Neckarstaden

Untere Neckarstr

Bauamtsgasse

Friedrichstrasse

Bienenstrasse

Ziegelgasse

Brunnengasse

Bismarck-platz

Bismarck-str

Sofienstrasse

Akademiestrasse

Institute of Natural Sciences

Hauptstrasse

Märzgasse

Friedrichstrasse

Theaterstrasse

Plöck

Plöck

Some streets pedestrian-only

0   100   200m
0   100   200yd

PLACES TO STAY
8 Hotel Vier Jahreszeiten
16 Hotel Am Kornmarkt
19 Jeske Hotel

PLACES TO EAT
3 Zum Güldenen Schaf
9 Vetter Alt Heidelberg Brauhaus
18 Raja Rani
23 Mensa

OTHER
1 Docks for River Boats
2 Kurpfälzisches Museum
4 Hörnchen
5 Gasthaus Zummohren
6 i Punkt
7 Goldener Reichsapfel
10 Café Max
11 Heiligkeitskirche
12 Rathaus
13 Tourist Office
14 Zum Sepp'l
15 Zum Roten Ochsen
17 Funicular Railway (Kornmarkt Station)
20 Drugstore Café
21 Café Journal
22 Studentenkarzer
24 Castle
25 Tourist Office

To Train Station, Main Post Office, Main Tourist Office, Bergheimer Strasse, Hotel Kohler & Café Gekco

Schaf (Hauptstrasse 115) has vegetarian fare from DM14 and local specialities from DM16. Many student pubs (see Entertainment) have main courses priced from around DM14.

Entertainment

Zum Roten Ochsen (Hauptstrasse 217) and the adjacent *Zum Sepp'l* are historic student pubs that are a bit too touristy nowadays. Better are *Gasthaus Zum Mohren (Untere Strasse 5-7)* and *Hörnchen*, with outdoor tables on Heumarkt. *Goldener Reichsapfel* on Untere Strasse is another good student pub, as is the modern *i Punkt*, diagonally opposite.

On the Markt's northern side, *Café Max* is a big favourite. At *Café Journal (Hauptstrasse 162)* you can linger for hours over coffee and English-language papers. Serious chess players gather at the small *Drugstore Café (Kettengasse 10)*.

Getting There & Away

From mid-May to late September, Deutsche-Touring has a daily Castle Road bus service between Heidelberg and Rothenburg ob der Tauber (DM47, five hours). Otherwise there are hourly ICE/IC trains to/from Frankfurt/Main (DM22.40, one hour), Stuttgart (DM38, 45 minutes) and Munich (DM104, three hours). Mannheim (12 minutes) has train connections to cities throughout Germany.

The local ride-share service, Citynetz Mitfahr-Service (☎ 194 44), is at Bergheimer Strasse 125.

Getting Around

Bismarckplatz is the main public transport hub. Single bus tickets are DM3.30 and a 24-hour pass is DM10.

BADEN-BADEN
☎ 07221

Baden-Baden's natural hot springs have attracted visitors since Roman times, but this small city only really became fashionable in the 19th century when the likes of Victor Hugo and the future King Edward VII of Britain came to bathe in and imbibe its therapeutic waters.

Today Baden-Baden is Germany's premier (and ritziest) health spa.

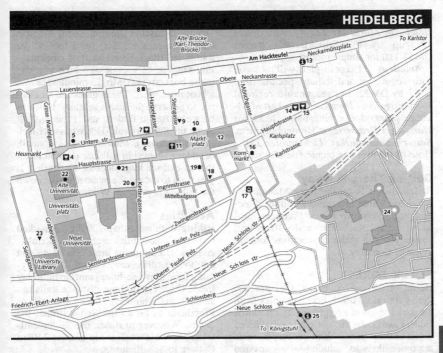

Orientation & Information

The train station is 7km north-west of town. Bus Nos 201, 205 and 216 run frequently to/from Leopoldsplatz, the heart of Baden-Baden. Almost everything is within walking distance of this square. Sophienstrasse leads east to the more historic part of town. North of Sophienstrasse are the baths, the Stiftskirche and the Neues Schloss.

The tourist office (☎ 27 52 00, fax 27 52 02) is in the Trinkhalle; collect some information and sample the local drop (see Things to See & Do). If you stay at a hotel, the DM5 spa *Kurtaxe* (visitors' tax) entitles you to a Kurkarte, which brings various discounts.

Things to See & Do

The ancient **Römische Badruinen** (Roman Bath Ruins) on Römerplatz are worth a quick look.

On either side of Römerplatz are the two places where you can take the waters. The 19th-century **Friedrichsbad** (☎ 27 59 20) is decadently Roman in style and offers a bathing program for DM36. An extra DM12 gets you a soap-and-brush massage. No clothing is allowed inside and several of the bathing sections are mixed, so leave your modesty at the reception desk. The **Caracalla-Therme** (☎ 27 59 40) is a vast complex of outdoor and indoor pools. It's DM19 for two hours of watery bliss, and bathing suits are required (bring your own towel).

At the ornate **Trinkhalle**, Kaiserallee 3, you can have a free drink of the spa water piped in hot from the ground. Next door is the **Kurhaus**, which houses the opulent casino where Dostoyevsky was inspired to write *The Gambler*. Guided tours run between 9.30 am and noon daily (DM6).

Places to Stay & Eat

Baden-Baden's *DJH hostel* (☎ *522 23, fax 600 12, Hardbergstrasse 34*) is 3km north-west of the centre and charges DM24/29 for juniors/seniors. Take bus No 201 to Jugendherberge stop.

The tourist office charges no commission to book private rooms starting at DM20 per person. Otherwise, *Gästehaus Löhr* (☎ *330 29, Adlerstrasse 2*), just off Augustaplatz, is a good deal by Baden-Baden's standards – rooms cost from DM60/110 a single/double (a single without bath is DM35). Reception is at the Café Löhr, Lichtentaler Strasse 19. *Hotel Am Markt* (☎ 227 47, *Marktplatz 17*), up by the Stiftskirche, charges DM54/110 for simple rooms.

Amadeus on Leopoldsplatz will rock you with vegetarian and Italian specials from DM7 to DM22. For reasonable regional specialities like *Flammkuchen* (a sort of Alsatian pizza) and a nice patio, head for *Warsteiner Brasserie* on Hindenburgplatz. *Kaiser's supermarket (Lichtentaler 15)* is close to the lush and picnic-friendly parks.

Getting There & Away

Baden-Baden is on the busy Mannheim-Basel train line; fast trains in either direction stop every two hours. Frequent local trains serve Karlsruhe and Offenburg, where you can make connections to/from much of Germany.

BLACK FOREST

Home of the cuckoo clock, the moniker 'Schwarzwald' (Black Forest) comes from the dark canopy of evergreens. The fictional Hansel and Gretel encountered their wicked witch in these parts – 20th-century hazards are more likely to include tour groups and their buses. However, a 20-minute walk from even the most crowded spots puts you in quiet countryside dotted with traditional farmhouses and amiable dairy cows.

Orientation & Information

The Black Forest lies east of the Rhine between Karlsruhe and Basel. It's roughly triangular in shape, about 160km long and 50km wide. Baden-Baden, Freudenstadt, Titisee and Freiburg act as convenient information posts for Black Forest excursions.

Freudenstadt's tourist office (☎ 07441-86 40, fax 851 76, ℮ touristinfo@freuden stadt.de) is on Am Marktplatz and has information on the northern part of the region (closed Sunday). Additional tourist offices are in Titisee (☎ 07651-98 04 0, fax 98 04 40, ℮ touristinfo@titisee.de), inside the Kurhaus at Strandbadstrasse 4, and Feldberg (☎ 07655-80 19, fax 801 43, ℮ tourist-info@feldberg-schwarz.de), at Kirchgasse 1.

Things to See

The area between Freudenstadt and Freiburg is cuckoo-clock country, a name that takes on new meaning when you see the prices

people are willing to pay. In Furtwangen, visit the **Deutsches Uhrenmuseum** (German Clock Museum; DM5/3) for a look at the traditional Black Forest skill of clockmaking. On Titisee's namesake lake you can take a **boat cruise** (DM6, 25 minutes) or rent a boat in summer. The engines are all electric to preserve the lake's serenity. Halfway between Baden-Baden and Freudenstadt along the Schwarzwald-Hochstrasse (Black Forest Highway), **Mummelsee** is a small, deep lake steeped in folklore (legend has it that an evil sea king inhabits the depths). If you want to escape the busloads, hike down the hill to the peaceful **Wildsee**.

Activities

Hiking With more than 7000km of marked trails, the possibilities are, almost literally, endless. Hiking maps are everywhere and any tourist office can set you off on anything from easy one-hour jaunts to multiday treks. Three classic long-distance trails run south from the northern Black Forest city of Pforzheim as far as the Swiss Rhine: the 280km Westweg to Basel, the 230km Mittelweg to Waldhut-Tiengen and the 240km Ostweg to Schaffhausen.

The southern Black Forest, especially the area around the 1493m Feldberg summit, offers some of the best hiking; small towns like Todtmoos or Bonndorf serve as useful bases for those wanting to get off the more heavily-trodden trails.

Skiing The Black Forest ski season runs from late December to March. While there is some good downhill skiing, the Black Forest is more suited to cross-country skiing. The Titisee area is the main centre for winter sports, with uncrowded downhill runs at Feldberg (day passes DM38) and numerous graded cross-country trails. In midwinter, ice-skating is also possible on the Titisee and the Schluchsee.

Places to Stay

Camping Facilities include *Campingplatz Wolfsgrund* (☎ 07656-573) on the Schluchsee and *Terrassencamping Sandbank* (☎ 07651-82 43), one of four camping grounds on the Titisee.

Hostels Some convenient hostels are in *Freudenstadt* (☎ 07441-77 20, fax 857 88,

Eugen-Nägele-Strasse 69); **Triberg** (☎ 07722-41 10, fax 66 62, Rohrbacher Strasse 3), a steep climb from town; **Feldberg** (☎ 07676-221, fax 12 32, Passhöhe 14); **Titisee** (☎ 07652-238, fax 756, Bruderhalde 27) – take bus No 7300; and **Neustadt** (☎ 07652-73 60, fax 42 99, Rudenberg 6) on the eastern edge of town. All charge between DM23 and DM24 for juniors and DM28 and DM29 for seniors.

Hotels & Pensions In Freudenstadt is **Gasthof Pension Traube** (☎/fax 07441-853 28, Markt 41), which charges DM50/100 for singles/doubles.

Triberg's **Hotel Central** (☎ 07722-43 60) is right on Markt and charges DM50/88 for singles/doubles with all the facilities (it's DM5 more per person if you stay just one night).

A few minutes away from the Titisee, **Gasthaus Rehwinkel** (☎ 07651-83 41, Neustädter Strasse 7) has rooms from DM39/78.

Near the Feldberg slopes, **Berggasthof Wasmer** (☎ 07676-230, fax 430, An der Wiesenquelle 1) is a good option with rooms from DM42/84.

Getting There & Away

The Mannheim-Basel train line has numerous branches that serve the Black Forest. Trains for Freudenstadt and the north leave from Karlsruhe. Triberg is on the busy line linking Offenburg and Constance. Titisee has frequent services from Freiburg, with some trains continuing to Feldberg and others continuing to Neustadt. To reach Feldberg, take one of the frequent buses from the train stations in Titisee or Bärental.

FREIBURG
☎ 0761

The gateway to the southern Black Forest, Freiburg (full name: Freiburg im Breisgau) is a fun place thanks to the city's large and thriving university community. The monumental 13th-century cathedral is the city's key landmark but the real attractions are the vibrant cafes, bars and street-life.

Orientation & Information

The city centre is an easy 10-minute walk from the train station – walk east along Eisenbahnstrasse to the tourist office, then continue through the bustling pedestrian zone to Münsterplatz, dominated by the red-stone cathedral.

The tourist office (☎ 3 88 18 80, fax 3 70 03, 📧 touristik@fwt-online.de) sells a helpful guide in English (DM6) and has piles of information on the Black Forest.

PingWing Internet Center, Niemensstrasse 3, offers half an hour's Internet access for DM5. Café Fleck Waschsalon, Predigerstrasse 3, has a laundrette (open until 1 am daily) and a cafe.

Things to See

The major sightseeing goal is the 700-year-old **Münster** cathedral, a classic example of both high and late-Gothic architecture looming over Münsterplatz. Climb the cathedral's stunning **spire** (DM2.50/1.50) for great views of Freiburg. South of the Münster stands the picturesque **Kaufhaus**, the 16th-century merchants' hall.

The **university quarter** is north-west of the Martinstor (one of the old city gates) and is usually bustling with people sporting tattoos and body piercings.

Freiburg's main museum, the **Augustinermuseum** on Augustinerplatz has a fine collection of medieval art (DM4/2). The **Museum für Ur- und Frühgeschichte** (Museum of Prehistory; free) is in Columbipark, on the corner of Eisenbahnstrasse and Rotteckring. Both are closed Monday.

The popular trip by cable car to the **Schauinsland** peak (1286m) is a quick way to reach the Black Forest highlands. From Freiburg take tram No 4 south to Günterstal and then bus No 21 to Talstation. The five-hour hike from Schauinsland to the Untermünstertal offers some of the best views with the fewest people; return to Freiburg via the train to Staufen and then take the bus. The cable car runs 9 am to 5 pm daily, slightly longer in summer, and costs DM13/20 one way/return.

Places to Stay

To reach the year-round **Camping Hirzberg** (☎ 350 54, fax 28 92 12, Karthäuserstrasse 99) take tram No 1 to Messeplatz (direction: Littenweiler) and then go under the road and across the stream.

Freiburg's DJH **youth hostel** (☎ 676 56, fax 603 67, Karthäuserstrasse 151), on the eastern edge of the city, is often full, so phone ahead. Take tram No 1 to Römerhof (direction: Littenweiler) and follow the signs down Fritz-Geiges-Strasse. Beds are DM26/31 for juniors/seniors. There is an 11.30 pm curfew, but you can ask for an extension to 1 am.

The least expensive place in central Freiburg is *Hotel Schemmer* (☎ 20 74 90, *Eschholzstrasse 63)*, behind the train station. Basic singles/doubles cost DM65/95. The historic *Hotel Zum Schützen* (☎ 72 02 10, *Schützenallee 12)*, on the way to the youth hostel, is also a reasonable compromise for location and value, with rooms from DM65/95. In the Altstadt, *Hotel Löwen* (☎ 331 61, *Herrenstrasse 47)* is near the Schwabentor and has simple rooms for DM65/90. Right on Münsterplatz, *Hotel Rappen* (☎ 313 53 54) has rooms for DM80/100 with glorious views of the Münster and an inspirational buffet breakfast.

Places to Eat
The university-subsidised *mensas (Rempartstrasse 18 and Hebelstrasse 9a)* have salad buffets and other filling fodder. You may be asked to show a student ID when buying meal tickets. *Papala Pub (Moltkestrasse 30)* is a retro cafe reverberating with classic rock. Fill up on starchy chow from DM7.80, or risk the *Volles Risiko* menu that includes several surprise courses for DM22.

The popular *UC Uni-Café*, on the corner of Universitätsstrasse and Niemanstrasse, has a cool patio where you will see and be seen. The nearby *Salatstuben (Löwenstrasse 1)* has a wide choice of wholesome salads for DM2.30 per 100g. *Caruso (Kaiser Joseph Strasse 258)* has a laidback Latino vibe and a fantastic international menu (lunch specials average DM13).

Entertainment
If the weather is at all nice, walk over the pedestrian bridge at the Schwabentor and head up the hill to *Greiffenberg-Schlössle*, a vast beer garden with stunning views. *Jazzhaus (Schnewlinstrasse 1)* has live jazz every night (from DM5). *Galerie (Milchstrasse 7)* has a cosy seating area warmed by a wood stove in winter, and a lilac-scented patio in summer. Everybody is happy at *Alter Simon (Konvikstrasse 43)*, where the merry scene spills onto the street until well past midnight.

Getting There & Away
Freiburg lies on the Mannheim-Basel train line and is served by numerous ICE and EC trains in both directions. The trains to Titisee depart every 30 minutes (DM16 return). The regional bus station is next to platform 1. Bus No 1076 runs to/from Colmar in France four times a day. For ridesharing information contact the Citynetz Mitfahr-Service (☎ 194 44) at Belfortstrasse 55.

DANUBE RIVER
The Danube (Donau), one of Europe's great rivers, rises in the Black Forest. In Austria, Hungary and Romania it is a mighty, almost intimidating, waterway, but in Germany it's narrower and more tranquil, making it ideal for hiking and biking tours.

Donaueschingen is the gateway to the Donauradwanderweg (Danube Bike Trail), a beautiful and level trail that stretches 583km east through Ulm and Regensburg to Passau on the Austrian border. From there you can continue on to Vienna and beyond. The booklet *Donauradwanderführer* (DM16.80) provides maps and descriptions of the German route and is available from bookshops and tourist offices. Tourist offices also have a free brochure in English called *Tips, Info and Facts for Carefree Travels along the German Danube*, which gives useful information about the river's towns, along with listings of camping facilities, hostels and bike-rental places.

In Donaueschingen, bikes can be rented from Rothweiler (☎ 0771-131 48), Max-Egan-Strasse 14, for DM20 per day.

ULM
☎ 0731
A city well worth a visit, Ulm is famous as the birthplace of Albert Einstein and for its huge **Münster** cathedral and its 161m-high **steeple** – the tallest in Europe. Although construction began in 1377, it took more than 500 years for the entire structure to be completed. Climbing to the top via the 768 spiralling steps yields great views and a dizzy head (DM4).

Schwörmontag (Oath Monday), held on the second to last Monday in July, has been going on since 1397. After the mayor makes an oath, the populace moves down to the river for a raucous procession of rafts and barges. Later, all-night parties take place on the town's streets and squares.

Greater Ulm is actually two cities. On the south side of the Danube, the Bavarian city of Neu Ulm is a bland, modern city. On the north side is Ulm, which contains all the main attractions.

Ulm's tourist office (☎ 161 28 30, fax 161 16 41, ✉ unt@tourismus.ulm.de) is on Münsterplatz. Internet access costs DM7 a half-hour and DM11 an hour at connect onlinecafe, Frauenstrasse 31.

Places to Stay & Eat

The DJH *youth hostel* (☎ *38 44 55, fax 38 45 11, Grimmelfinger Weg 45)* charges DM20/24 juniors/seniors. From the train station, take tram No 1 to Ehinger Tor, then bus No 4 to Schulzentrum – from here it's a five-minute walk. Across the river in Neu-Ulm, the *Rose* (☎ *778 03, Kasernstrasse 42a)* has singles/doubles from DM35/70. Central *Hotel-Restaurant Bäumle* (☎ *622 87, fax 602 26 04, Kohlgasse 6)* has good rooms from DM55/75. Its rustic restaurant downstairs has creative regional fare. Quaff the local dark beer at *Drei Kannen (Hafenbad 31)*, a historic restaurant and beer garden. *Lloyd*, a bar and cafe on the Dreiköniggasse, 200m north of the cathedral, is cheap and plays good rock.

Getting There & Away

Ulm is a hub for frequent fast trains to Lindau, Munich and Stuttgart and the north.

LAKE CONSTANCE

Lake Constance (Bodensee) is a perfect cure for travellers stranded in landlocked southern Germany. Often jokingly called the 'Swabian Ocean', this giant bulge in the sinewy course of the Rhine offers a choice of water sports, relaxation or cultural pursuits.

The lake's southern side belongs to Switzerland and Austria, whose snow-capped mountaintops provide a perfect backdrop when viewed from the northern (German) shore.

The German side of Lake Constance features three often-crowded tourist centres in Constance (Konstanz), Meersburg and the island of Lindau. It's essentially a summer area, too often foggy or at best hazy in winter.

Orientation & Information

The tourist office (☎ 07531-13 30 30, fax 13 30 60, ✉ info@touristinformation .stadt.konstanz.de) is at Bahnhofplatz 13, 150m from the train station's exit (closed Sunday).

Meersburg lies across the lake from Constance and is an ideal base for exploring the long northern shore. Its helpful tourist office (☎ 07532-43 11 11, fax 43 11 20, ✉ info@meersburg.de) is in the city museum building at Kirchstrasse 4. Nearby Friedrichshafen, the largest and most 'central' city on the lake's northern shore, has its tourist office (☎ 07541-300 10, fax 7 25 88) near the Stadtbahnhof train station at Bahnhofsplatz 2. Lindau's tourist office (☎ 08382-91 80, fax 91 82 90) is directly opposite the train station.

Activities

Water Sports In Constance, five public beaches are open from May to September, including the **Strandbad Horn** with shrub-enclosed nude bathing. Take bus No 5 or walk for 20 scenic minutes around the shore.

Meersburg is a good base for watery pursuits and is popular with windsurfers. Rudi Thum's (☎ 07532-55 11) at the yacht harbour rents equipment and offers sailing courses.

Lindau's water isn't quite as crowded as the land; Windsurf-Schule Kreitmeir (☎ 08382-233 30) at Strandbad Eichwald has a windsurfing school and equipment rental. For boat rental contact Grahneis (☎ 08382-55 14).

Cycling A 270km bike track circumnavigates Lake Constance through Germany, Austria and Switzerland, tracing the often steep shoreline beside vineyards and pebble beaches. The route is well signposted. The widely available tourist booklet *Rad Urlaub am Bodensee* lists routes, rental places and a wealth of other information for the region.

In Constance, Velotours (☎ 07531-982 80), Fritz-Arnold-Strasse 2b, rents out bikes (daily/weekly DM20/100) and organises cycling tours.

Places to Stay

Pitch at tent at *Campingplatz Litzelstetten-Mainau* (☎ *07531-94 30 30)* a 20-minute walk towards Mainau Island from Constance.

Park Camping Lindau am See (☎ 08382-722 36) is 3km south-east of Lindau.

There are DJH hostels in *Constance* (☎ 07531-322 60, fax 311 63, Zur All-mannshöhe 18) – catch bus No 4 from the station to the 'Jugendherberge' stop, rates are DM22/27 for juniors/seniors; *Lindau* (☎ 08382-967 10, fax 96 71 50, Her-bergsweg 11), which charges DM29 and ac-cepts juniors and families only; and in *Friedrichshafen* (☎ 07541-724 04, fax 749 86, Lindauer Strasse 3), 15 minutes from the harbour, DM26/31 for juniors/seniors.

Getting Around

Trains link Lindau, Friedrichshafen and Constance, and buses fill in the gaps. The most enjoyable albeit slowest way to get around is by boat (☎ 07531-28 13 98), which, from Easter to late October, calls several times a day at the larger towns along both sides of the lake; there are discounts for rail pass-holders. The seven-day Bodensee-Pass costs DM57 and gives one free day of travel on the boats plus six days at half price on all boats, buses, trains and mountain ca-bleways on and around Lake Constance (in-cluding its Austrian and Swiss shores).

Bavaria

MUNICH
☎ 089

Munich (München), the main attraction in Bavaria (Bayern), is a beer-quaffing, sausage-eating city that can be as cosmopoli-tan as anywhere in Europe. Depite what you may have heard, Munich is more than a vast open-air beer hall – give yourself at least two or three days to cover its museums and gar-dens, and to sample the local brews.

Munich has been the capital of Bavaria since 1503, but really achieved eminence under the guiding hand of Ludwig I in the 19th century. It has seen many turbulent times – WWI practically starved the city, the Nazis got their start here in the 1920s, and WWII brought bombing and more than 6000 deaths. Today Munich is the centre of Germany's burgeoning high-tech industries.

Orientation

The main train station is just west of the centre – walk east along Bayerstrasse, through Karlsplatz and then along Neuhauser Strasse and Kaufingerstrasse to Marienplatz, the hub of Munich.

North of Marienplatz are the Residenz (the former royal palace), Schwabing (the famous student section) and the parklands of the Englischer Garten. East of Marien-platz is the Platzl quarter with its beer houses and restaurants, as well as Maximil-ianstrasse, a fashionable street that's fun for strolling and window-shopping.

Information

Tourist Offices The busy main tourist of-fice (☎ 23 33 02 56, fax 23 33 02 57, @ tourismus@muenchen.btl.de) is at the main train station, to the right as you exit via the eastern entrance. It's open 9 am to 8 pm Monday to Saturday and 10 am to 6 pm Sunday. The room-finding service is free and you can book in person; call ☎ 23 33 03 00 or write to Fremdenverkehrsamt München, D-80313 München. A second branch is on Marienplatz.

EurAide (☎ 59 38 89, @ euraide@com puserve.com), near platform 11 at the train station, is an excellent source of informa-tion in English and books rooms for DM7. It's open 7.45 am to noon and 1 to 4.30 pm daily from May to mid-October (these hours on weekdays plus Saturday morning mid-October to April).

The Jugendinformationszentrum (Youth Information Centre; ☎ 51 41 06 60), on the corner of Landwehrstrasse and Paul-Heyse-Strasse, has youth-related city information and offers cheap Internet access (closed on weekends).

The excellent *Young People's Guide* (DM1) is available from all tourist offices. The English-language monthly *Munich Found* (DM4) is also useful.

Money Reisebank has two offices at the main train station; if you show a EurAide newsletter, you'll pay less commission. Otherwise there are branches of all major German banks on or near Marienplatz. American Express is at Promenadeplatz 6 and Thomas Cook at Petersplatz 10.

Post & Communications Munich's main post office at Bahnhofplatz 1 is open 8 am to 8 pm weekdays and until noon Saturday. The poste restante address is: Hauptpostlagernd

(Poste Restante), Bahnhofplatz 1, 80074 Munich.

Email & Internet Access Internet Café, Nymphenburger Strasse 145, offers an hour's free access if you order a dish of its so-so Italian food costing more than DM10; otherwise it's DM7 for 30 minutes at this popular traveller hang-out. Karstadt am Dom, Neuhauser Strasse 21, has Internet terminals on its 4th floor for DM3 a half-hour. The Jugendinformationszentrum (see Tourist Offices earlier in this section) also offers Internet access.

Travel Agencies ABR Reisebüro (☎ 120 40), in the main train station, is a full-service travel agency. Council Travel (☎ 39 50 22), near the university at Adalbertstrasse 32 to the north, is a good budget agency.

Bookshops The best travel bookshop in town is Geobuch, opposite Viktualienmarkt at Rosental 6. Hugendubel, on Marienplatz, has a good selection of Lonely Planet guides and tons of English-language offerings.

Laundry City SB-Waschcenter, Paul-Heyse-Strasse 21, is close to the main train station and is open 7 am to 10 pm daily. Loads cost DM6.

Medical & Emergency Services Medical help is available at the Kassenärztlicher Notfalldienst (☎ 55 14 71). There's a pharmacy with English-speaking staff in the main train station.

Things to See & Do

Except where noted, museums are closed on Monday.

Marienplatz & Around The neo-Gothic **Altes Rathaus** (old town hall) with its incessantly photographed **Glockenspiel** (carillon), which does its number at 11 am and noon (also at 5 pm from May to October), towers over the pivotal Marienplatz.

Two important churches on this square are the **Peterskirche** and, behind the Altes Rathaus, the **Heiliggeistkirche**. Head west along the shopping street Kaufingerstrasse to the late Gothic **Frauenkirche** (Church of Our Lady), the landmark church of Munich; the monotonous red brick is very Bavarian

in its simplicity. Continue west on Kaufingerstrasse to **Michaelskirche**, Germany's grandest Renaissance church.

Farther west is the **Richard Strauss Fountain** and then the medieval **Karlstor** (an old city gate). Double back towards Marienplatz and turn right onto Eisenmannstrasse, which becomes Kreuzstrasse, and Herzog-Wilhelm-Strasse. The two streets converge at the medieval gate of **Sendlinger Tor**.

Go down Sendlinger Strasse and turn right on Hermann-Sack-Strasse to reach the **Stadtmuseum** on St-Jakobs-Platz, where the outstanding exhibits cover beer brewing, fashion, musical instruments, photography and puppets (DM5/4).

Residenz This huge palace housed Bavarian rulers from 1385 to 1918, and features more than 500 years of architectural history. Apart from the palace itself, the **Residenz Museum** (open daily; DM8/6) has an extraordinary array of 100 rooms containing the Wittelsbach house's belongings, while the **Schatzkammer** (DM8/6) exhibits a ridiculous quantity of jewels, crowns and ornate gold.

Deutsches Museum If you combined Disneyland and the Smithsonian Institute you'd get something similar to this vast science and technology museum, which covers 13km of corridors on eight floors. It's definitely too large to see everything, so pursue specific interests. Entry is DM12/5 for adults/children and a visit to the planetarium is DM3 extra. Take the S-Bahn to Isartor or tram No 18 to the 'Deutsches Museum' stop.

Alte Pinakothek This is a veritable treasure house of European masters from the 4th to 18th centuries. Highlights include Dürer's Christ-like *Self Portrait* and his *Four Apostles*, Rogier van der Weyden's *Adoration of the Magi* and Botticelli's *Pietà*. Entry is DM7/4. Immediately north, at Barer Strasse 29, the **Neue Pinakothek** contains mainly 19th-century painting and sculpture. Entry is DM7/4 (free on Sunday). See both with a combined card (DM12/6).

The huge new **Pinakothek der Moderne**, a block east of the Alte Pinakothek, is planned to open in October 2001. It will bring together four collections of modern art, graphic art, applied art and architecture from galleries and museums around the city.

GERMANY

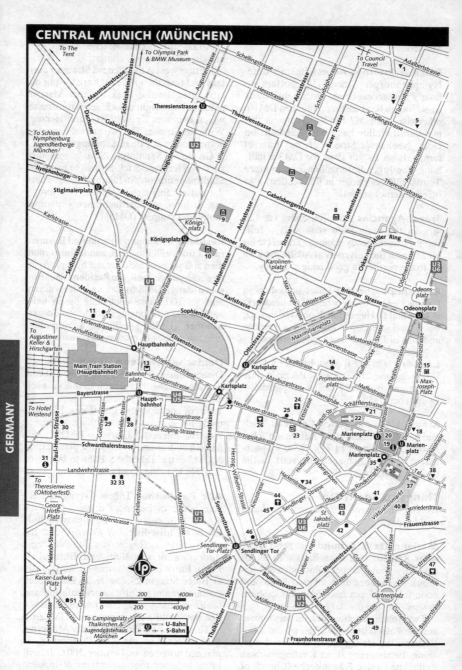

CENTRAL MUNICH (MÜNCHEN)

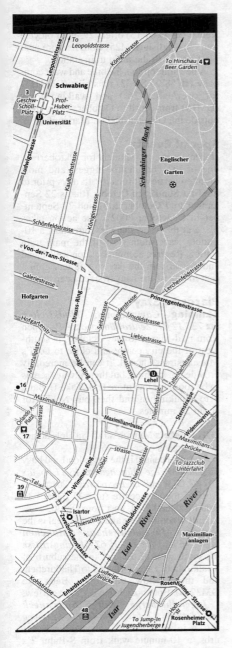

CENTRAL MUNICH (MÜNCHEN)

PLACES TO STAY
11 4 you münchen
28 Euro Youth Hotel
29 Jugendhotel Marienherberge
32 Pension Marie-Luise
33 Pension Alpina
40 Hotel-Pension am Markt
42 Hotel Blauer Bock
50 Gärtnerplatz-Theater
51 Pension Haydn

PLACES TO EAT
1   Vorstadt Café
2   Alter Simpl
5   Schall und Rauch
18 Alois Dallmayr
21 Münchner Suppenküche
34 Prinz Myschkin
38 Weisses Brauhaus
45 Cipriani

OTHER
3   Universität
4   Chinesischer Turm
6   Neue Pinakothek
7   Alte Pinakothek
8   Pinakothek der Modern
9   Glyptothek
10 Antikensammlungen
12 ADM-Mitfahrzentrale
13 Main Tourist Office
14 American Express
15 Residenz
16 Nationaltheater
17 Hofbräuhaus
19 Tourist Office
20 Altes Rathaus &
    Glockenspiel
22 Frauenkirche
23 Karstadt am Dom
24 Michaelskirche
25 Richard Strauss Fountain
26 Augustiner Bierhalle
27 Karlstor
30 City SB-Waschcenter
31 Jugendinformationszentrum
35 Hugendubel
36 Peterskirche
37 Heiliggeistkirche
39 Zentrum für Aussergewöhnliche
    Museen
41 Geobuch
43 Stadtmuseum & Stadtcafé
44 Asamkirche
46 Sendlinger Tor
47 Bei Carla
48 Deutsches Museum
49 Morizz

GERMANY

Other Museums On Königsplatz there are two museums worth a look. The **Glyptothek** and the **Antikensammlungen** feature one of Germany's best antiquities collections (mostly Greek and Roman). Entry is DM6 or DM10 for both (both free on Sunday).

Auto-fetishists can thrill to the **BMW Museum** at Peutelring 130 (open daily; DM5.50/4). Take U-Bahn 3 from Marienplatz to Olympiazentrum.

Its a mixed bag and that's the delight of the **Zentrum für Aussergewöhnliche Museen** (Centre for Unusual Museums), Westenriederstrasse 26. Displays range from chamber pots to the Easter Bunny to the Austrian Empress Elisabeth (open daily; DM8/5).

Englischer Garten One of the largest city parks in Europe, this is a great place for strolling, especially along the Schwabinger Bach. In balmy summer weather, nude sunbathing is the rule rather than the exception. Be wary of leaving your belongings unattended.

Dachau Dachau was the first Nazi concentration camp, built in March 1933. More than 200,000 Jews, political prisoners, homosexuals and others deemed 'undesirable' by the Third Reich were imprisoned in the camp; more than 30,000 died at Dachau and countless others died after being transferred to other death camps. A visit includes camp relics, a memorial and a very sobering museum. An English-language documentary is shown at 11.30 am and 3.30 pm. Entry is free and it's open 9 am to 5 pm Tuesday to Sunday. Take S-Bahn 2 to Dachau and then bus No 724 or 726 (Sunday and holidays) to the camp. A two-zone ticket (DM7.20) is needed for the trip.

Organised Tours

Munich Walks (☎ 235 90 20) runs excellent English-language tours from April to October (DM18/14 for over/under 26s). The Discover Munich tour covers the heart of the city; the Infamous Third Reich Sites tour covers exactly that. Both leave from in front of the EurAide office.

Mike's Bike Tours (☎ 25 54 39 87) runs 3½-hour guided city cycling tours in English (DM36) from the archway in front of the Old Town Hall on Marienplatz.

From April to early October, Radius Bike Rental (☎ 59 61 13) offers 2½-hour bicycle tours in English (DM25) from its store near platform 27 in the main train station.

A new tour option, the bike and walk company (☎ 58 95 89 33) runs bike (DM31/27 for over/under 26s) and walking tours (DM15) from April to October. Tours meet outside the Glockenspiel on Marienplatz.

Special Events

Hordes come to Munich for Oktoberfest, one of the continent's biggest and most drunken parties. It runs for 15 days prior to the first Sunday in October (that's 22 September to 7 October 2001 and 21 September to 6 October 2002). The action takes place at the Theresienwiese grounds, a 10-minute walk south-west of the main train station. Reserve accommodation well ahead and go early in the day so you can grab a seat in one of the hanger-sized beer 'tents'.

Places to Stay

Camping *Campingplatz Thalkirchen* (☎ 723 17 07, *Zentralländstrasse 49*), open from mid-March to late October, is south-west of the city centre and close to DJH's Miesingstrasse hostel. It can be incredibly crowded in summer, but there always seems to be room for one more tent. Take U-Bahn 3 to Thalkirchen and then bus No 57 for about 20 minutes.

DJH Hostels Munich's DJH hostels do not accept guests over age 26.

The most central is the large, loud and busy *Jugendherberge München* (☎ 13 11 56, *fax 167 87 45, Wendl-Dietrich-Strasse 20*), north-west of the city centre (take U-Bahn 1 to Rotkreuzplatz). Beds cost from DM30.

Still decently close and a better deal is the modern *Jugendgästehaus München* (☎ 723 65 50, *fax 724 25 67, Miesingstrasse 4*), south-west of the city in the suburb of Thalkirchen. Take U-Bahn 3 to Thalkirchen, and then follow the signs. Beds are DM32.50. Both hostels have a 1 am curfew.

Jugendherberge Burg Schwaneck (☎ 74 48 66 72, *fax 74 48 66 80, Burgweg 4-6*) is in an old castle in the southern suburbs, a 10-minute walk from S-Bahn 7's Pullach station. Dorm beds start at DM23.

Munich's summer favourite is *The Tent* (☎ 51 41 06 16), less famously known as

Jugendlager am Kapuziner Hölzl. This mass camp is open from late June to early September. A thermal mattress and blanket costs DM13 with a small breakfast. There's no curfew and priority is given to those under age 24. Take tram No 17 from the main train station to Botanischer Garten, then walk straight on to Franz-Schrank-Strasse to In den Kirschen.

Private Hostels People over age 26 often have to pay a surcharge at the following hostels.

Newcomer to the hostel scene, *Jump-In Jugendherberge* to the south-east (☎ 48 95 34 37, *Hochstrasse 51*) has beds from DM29. Catch the S-Bahn to Karlsplatz and then tram No 27 to Ostfriedhof. Call before arriving – you can only check in during certain hours.

Kolpinghaus St Theresia (☎ 12 60 50, *fax 12 60 52 12, Hanebergstrasse 8)* charges DM36/43/49 for singles/doubles/triples. Take U-Bahn 1 to Rotkreuzplatz, then walk 10 minutes north.

4 you münchen (☎ 552 16 60, *fax 55 21 66 66, Hirtenstrasse 18)* has an under-27 section with dorm beds for DM24 and nice singles/doubles for DM61.50/92; travellers 27 or older pay DM69/99 for singles/doubles in the adjoining hotel section.

Just near the main train station, *Euro Youth Hotel* (☎ 59908811, fax 59908877, ❻ info@euro-youth-hotel.de, *Senefelder Strasse 5)* has dorm beds for DM29, beds in three- to four-bed rooms for DM36 and doubles for DM42.

Women under 26 can try *Jugendhotel Marienherberge* (☎ 55 58 05, *Goethestrasse 9)*, where dorm beds start at DM30 and singles/doubles cost DM40/70.

Hotels There are plenty of fairly cheap, if scruffy, places near the station. The cramped *Pension Marie-Luise* (☎ 55 42 30, *Landwehrstrasse 35)* offers rooms from DM55/80. Nearby at No 49, *Pension Alpina* (☎/fax 538 07 22) has basic rooms from DM55/85. Neither place includes breakfast.

An ideal compromise of location, price and cleanliness is *Pension Haydn* (☎ 53 11 19, *Haydnstrasse 9)*, near the Goetheplatz U-Bahn station and within walking distance of the main train station. Rooms without bath start at DM75/110 a single/double.

The friendly *Hotel Westend* (☎ 508 09 00, fax 502 58 96, *Landsberger Strasse 20)* is a fabulous deal with nice rooms from DM70/100. It's a 10-minute walk west of the main train station or three stops on tram No 18 or 19.

The good-value *Hotel-Pension am Markt* (☎ 22 50 14, *Heiliggeiststrasse 6)* is just off the Viktualienmarkt. Rooms start at DM64/110. At *Hotel Blauer Bock* (☎ 23 17 80, fax 23 17 82 00, *Sebastiansplatz 9)* reasonably large singles/doubles/triples start at DM70/110/195 and include a buffet breakfast.

Places to Eat

At *Viktualienmarkt*, just south of Marienplatz, you can put together a picnic for DM10 or less, or you can grab a cheap meal and a beer to enjoy in the lively beer garden. More prosperous picnickers might prefer the legendary *Alois Dallmayr (Dienerstrasse 14)*, one of the world's greatest (and priciest) delicatessens.

Student-card holders can fill up for around DM4 in any of the university *mensas (Leopoldstrasse 13, Arcistrasse 17 and Helene-Mayer-Ring 9)*. *Münchner Suppenküche (Schäfflerstrasse 7)* has meaty and vegetarian soups averaging DM8.

Weisses Brauhaus (Tal 7) serves the classic Munich *Weisswürste* (sausage). At other times it offers typical beer-quaffers' dishes. In Schwabing, *Alter Simpl (Türkenstrasse 57)* is a busy student joint with good jazz and a reasonable menu.

Stylish *Prinz Myschkin (Hackenstrasse 2)* offers gourmet vegetarian cooking blending South-East Asian, Indian and Italian influences, with rotating daily menus and main courses for as little as DM16. *Cipriani (Sendlinger Strasse 28)* in the Asam-Hof, a small courtyard just off Sendlinger Strasse, is a good spot for Italian *panini*.

Cafes *Stadtcafé*, at the Stadtmuseum, is a popular haunt for Munich's intellectual types. *Vorstadt Café (Türkenstrasse 83)* and *Schall und Rauch (Schellingstrasse)* are examples of the many lively student hangouts in Schwabing.

Entertainment

Nationaltheater, on Max-Joseph-Platz, is the home of the Bavarian State Opera and

GERMANY

the site of many cultural events (particularly in July). Buy tickets at Maximilianstrasse 11 or call ☎ 21 85 19 20.

Munich has a good jazz scene – the landmark *Jazzclub Unterfahrt* (☎ 448 27 94, *Kirchenstrasse 96*), near the Ostbahnhof station, has live music from 9 pm (except Monday).

Much of Munich's gay and lesbian nightlife is centred just south of Sendlinger Tor. There's good food and cocktails at *Morizz (Klenzestrasse 43)*, popular with gay men of all ages. *Bei Carla (Buttermelcherstrasse 9)* is a friendly cafe popular with lesbians.

Beer Halls & Beer Gardens Germans drink an average 250L of beer each per year; Munich residents average 350L. Many places sell beer in a *Mass*, a hefty 1L mug.

Of the beer halls, most famous is the enormous and tourist-packed *Hofbräuhaus (Am Platzl 9)*. That there is a Planet Hollywood across the street tells you everything you need to know about the place. Far better is the *Augustiner Bierhalle (Neuhauser Strasse 27)*, an authentic old-style Munich beer hall with cheap chow.

On a summer day there's nothing better than the Englischer Garten's classic *Chinesischer Turm* beer garden, although the nearby *Hirschau* beer garden on the banks of the Kleinhesseloher See is less crowded. *Augustiner Keller (Arnulfstrasse 52)* has a large and leafy beer garden about five minutes west of the main train station.

Join thousands of locals at *Hirschgarten*, a beautiful beer garden set in the woods. Take the S-Bahn west to Laim, exit the station north, turn right on Winfried Strasse, enter the park and follow your ears.

Getting There & Away

Air Munich is second in importance only to Frankfurt-am-Main for international and national connections. Flights will take you to all major destinations worldwide. Main German cities are serviced by at least half a dozen flights daily.

Bus Deutsche Touring (☎ 545 87 00, fax 54 58 70 21), near platform 26 at the main train station, has services from Munich to major German and European cities and to Romantic Road towns (see Getting There &

Away in the later Romantic Road section). Buses stop at the northern side of the train station.

Train There are rapid connections at least every two hours to all major cities in Germany, as well as frequent EC trains to European cities such as Innsbruck (two hours), Vienna (five hours), Prague (six hours), Zürich (4¼ hours), Verona (5½ hours) and Paris (eight hours).

High-speed ICE services from Munich include Frankfurt/Main (DM147, 3½ hours), Hamburg (DM268, six hours) and Berlin (DM277, 6½ hours), via Hanover.

Ride-Sharing The ADM-Mitfahrzentrale (☎ 194 40) is near the main train station at Lämmerstrasse 4. Destinations and charges (including booking fees) include: Berlin DM52, Frankfurt/Main DM40 and Leipzig DM42.

Getting Around

To/From the Airport Munich's gleaming Flughafen Franz Josef Strauss is connected by S-Bahn No 8 to Marienplatz and the main train station (DM14.40). The service takes 40 minutes and runs every 20 minutes from 4 am until around 12.30 am.

Public Transport Munich's excellent public transport network (MVV) is zone-based, and most places of interest to tourists (except Dachau and the airport) are within the 'blue' *Innenraum* (inner zone). MVV tickets are valid for the S-Bahn, U-Bahn, trams and buses, but must be validated before use. The U-Bahn ends around 12.30 am on weekdays and 1.30 am on weekends, but there are some later buses and S-Bahns. Rail passes are valid only on the S-Bahn. Bicycle transport is free, but forbidden on weekdays during the morning and evening rush hour.

Kurzstrecke (short-ride tickets) cost DM1.80 and are good for rides no longer than four stops on buses and trams and two stops on the U and S-Bahns. Longer trips cost DM3.60. It's cheaper to buy a *Mehrfahrtenkarte* (10-ticket strip) for DM15, and stamp one strip per adult on short rides two strips for longer rides in the inner zone. *Tageskarte* (day passes) for the inner zone cost DM9.

Bicycle Radius Bike Rental (see the earlier Organised Tours section) rents out two-wheelers from DM25/75 per day/week.

AUGSBURG
☎ 0821

Originally established by the Romans, Augsburg later became a centre of Luther's Reformation. Today it's a lively provincial city criss-crossed by streams, with an ambience and vitality matched by few other places in Germany. For some it will be a day trip from Munich, for others an ideal base or a gateway to the Romantic Road.

Its tourist offices are at Bahnhofstrasse 7 (☎ 502 07 22; closed on weekends) and at Rathausplatz (☎ 502 07 24).

Things to See & Do
The onion-shaped towers of the modest **St Maria Stern Kloster** on Elias-Holl-Platz started a fashion that spread throughout southern Germany in the 16th century. More impressive towers are at the **Rathaus**, the adjacent **Perlachturm** and the **St Ulrich und Afra Basilika** on Ulrichsplatz, near the south edge of the old town. The **Bertolt-Brecht-Gedänkstätte**, Am Rain 7, is a museum dedicated to playwright Brecht (who once lived here) and the work of young artists (closed Monday and Tuesday; DM3.50/2).

Places to Stay & Eat
The worn but central DJH *youth hostel* (☎ 339 09, fax 15 11 49, Beim Pfaffenkeller 3), just east of St Mary's Cathedral, charges DM20 and imposes a strict age limit of 26. Perhaps the best value in Augsburg is *Hotel Von den Rappen* (☎ 21 76 40, Äussere Uferstrasse 3), where modern singles/doubles go for DM54/85; there's also a Bavarian restaurant downstairs.

Bauerntanz (Bauerntanz-Gässchen 1), just a heave past Barfusgasse, has been proudly serving cheap local food and beer since 1572. *3 Königinnen (Meister-Veits-Gässchen 32)*, south of the Fuggerei houses, has a cool beer garden on a quiet street.

Getting There & Away
Trains between Munich and Augsburg are frequent (DM16, 40 minutes). Frequent ICE/IC trains also serve Ulm (DM36, 40 minutes), Stuttgart (DM66, 1½ hours) and Nuremberg (DM45, one hour). Connections

to/from Regensburg take two hours via Ingolstadt. Deutsche Touring's Romantic Road bus stops at Augsburg's train station.

ROMANTIC ROAD
Originally conceived as a way of promoting tourism in western Bavaria, the Romantic Road (Romantische Strasse) links a series of picturesque Bavarian towns and cities from Würzburg south to Füssen in the Alps. The trip has become one of the most popular in Germany and you will have to decide if you want to fall for the sales pitch and join the throngs to see these admittedly pretty towns. The main places for information are the tourist offices in Würzburg and Augsburg. Private accommodation – look for 'Zimmer Frei' signs – costs DM25 to DM40 per person and is plentiful in most towns. You must be age 26 or less to stay at the DJH hostels.

Getting There & Away
From April to October, Deutsche Touring runs one coach daily in each direction between Frankfurt-am-Main and Munich (12 hours) and another between Dinkelsbühl and Füssen (4½ hours). The bus makes short stops in some towns, but it's silly to do the whole trip in one go (reserve a seat for the next day as you disembark). The full fare from Frankfurt-am-Main to Füssen is DM129. Eurail and German Rail passes are valid and Inter-Rail gets a 50% discount (plus a DM10 'registration' fee and DM3 for each piece of luggage).

For information and reservations contact Deutsche-Touring GmbH (☎ 089-59 38 89, fax 089-550 39 65) at Am Römerhof 17, 60486 Frankfurt-am-Main. (This office doesn't accept bookings, but does give info.)

In the north of the Romantic Road route, Würzburg is well-served by trains. To start at the southern end, take the hourly RE train from Munich to Füssen (DM35, two hours). Rothenburg is linked by train to Würzburg, Nuremberg and Munich via Steinach. To reach Dinkelsbühl, take a train to Ansbach and catch a bus from there. Nördlingen is on a train line with connections to Stuttgart, Augsburg and Munich.

Rothenburg ob der Tauber
☎ 09861
Rothenburg is the main attraction along the route and is absolutely mobbed in summer.

GERMANY

Granted the status of a 'free imperial city' in 1274, it's full of cobbled lanes and picturesque old houses and enclosed by towered walls, all of which are worth exploring. Note that its museums only open in the afternoon from November to March. The tourist office (☎ 404 92, fax 8 68 07, ⊙ info@rothenburg.de) is at Markt 1.

The **Rathaus** on Markt was commenced in Gothic style in the 14th century but completed in Renaissance style. The tower gives a majestic view over the town and the Tauber valley. The **Reichsstadt Museum** in the former convent (DM5/3) features the superb *Rothenburger Passion* in 12 panels by Martinus Schwarz (1494) and the Judaika room.

Camping options are about 1.5km north of the town walls at Detwang, west of the road on the river. There are signs to *Tauber-Romantik* (☎ 61 91), open from Easter to late October.

Rothenburg's jammed DJH *youth hostel* (☎ 941 60, fax 94 16 20, *Mühlacker 1*), housed in two enormous old buildings, has beds for DM22. Inside the old town, *Gasthof Butz* (☎ 22 01, ⊙ *gasthofbutz@rothen burg.com, Kapellenplatz 4*) has single/double rooms from DM60/120. *Pension Eberlein* (☎ 46 72, fax 34 99, *Winterbachstrasse 4*), behind the train station, has basic rooms from DM55/75.

Dinkelsbühl
☎ 09581
South of Rothenburg, Dinkelsbühl is another walled town of cobbled streets. The hour-long walk around the town's **walls** and its almost 30 towers is the scenic highlight. The tourist office (☎ 902 40, fax 902 79, ⊙ touristik.service@dinkelsbuehl.de) is at Marktplatz 1.

DCC-Campingplatz Romantische Strasse (☎/fax 78 17) is open all year. Dinkelsbühl's DJH *youth hostel* (☎ 95 09, fax 48 74, *Koppengasse 10*) charges DM18. *Fränkischer Hof* (☎ 579 00, fax 57 90 99, *Nördlinger Strasse 10*) has rooms from DM45/80.

Nördlingen
☎ 09081
The town of Nördlingen is encircled by original 14th-century walls – you can climb the tower of the **St Georg Kirche** for a

bird's-eye view. The town is within the basin of the **Ries**, a huge crater left by a meteor more than 15 million years ago. You'll find the tourist office (☎ 43 80, fax 841 13, ⊙ stadt.noerdlingen@t-online.de) at Marktplatz 2.

The DJH *youth hostel* (☎ 841 09, *Kaiserwiese 1*) charges DM19; follow the many signs. By the church is *Gasthof Walfisch* (☎ 31 07, *Hallgasse 15*), with singles/doubles for DM35/65.

Füssen
☎ 08362
Just short of the Austrian border, Füssen has a monastery, castle and splendid baroque architecture, but it is primarily visited for the two castles in nearby Schwangau associated with King Ludwig II. The castles provide a fascinating glimpse into the king's state of mind – or lack thereof. Füssen's tourist office (☎ 70 77, fax 391 81, ⊙ kurverwaltung@fussen.de) is at Kaiser-Maximilian-Platz 1.

Hohenschwangau is where Ludwig lived as a child, but more interesting is the adjacent **Neuschwanstein**, his own creation (albeit with the help of a theatrical designer). Although it was unfinished at the time of his death in 1886, there is plenty of evidence of Ludwig's twin obsessions: swans and Wagnerian operas. The sugary pastiche of architectural styles inspired Disney's Fantasyland castle. There's a great view of Neuschwanstein from the Marienbrücke (bridge) over a waterfall and gorge just above the castle, from where you can hike the Tegelberg for even better vistas.

Take the bus from Füssen train station (DM2.50), share a taxi (DM14) or walk the 5km. Both castles are open daily and entry is only by guided tour (DM12/9): Neuschwanstein 9 am to 5.30 pm (10 am to 4 pm October to March) and Hohenschwangau 8.30 am to 5.30 pm (9 am to 4.30 pm mid-October to mid-March). Go early to avoid the massive crowds.

The DJH *youth hostel* (☎ 77 54, fax 27 70, *Mariahilferstrasse 5*) is by the train tracks, 10 minutes west of the station. Dorm beds cost DM20, curfew is a draconian 10 pm and the hostel is closed from mid-November to Christmas. The tourist office has lists of private rooms from DM30 per person.

GERMANY

WÜRZBURG

☎ 0931

Surrounded by forests and vineyards, the charming city of Würzburg straddles the upper Main River. Rebuilt after bombings late in the war, Würzburg is a centre of art, wine and beautiful architecture.

Information

The tourist office (☎ 37 23 98, **@** touris mus@wuerzburg.de) is in the rococo masterpiece Haus zum Falken on Oberer Markt. In the same building, the Stadtbücherei (☎ 37 34 38) has Internet access for DM3 a half-hour (make sure you book).

Things to See & Do

The magnificent **Residenz**, spread along Balthasar-Neumann-Promenade, is a baroque masterpiece by Neumann (whose image appears on the DM50 note). It is well worth the DM8/6 admission. The **Dom St Kilian** interiors and the adjacent **Neumünster** in the old town continue the baroque themes of the Residenz.

Another Neumann effort is the fortified **Alter Kranen** (old crane), which serviced a dock on the river bank south of Friedensbrücke. Today it is known as the **Haus des Frankenweins**, where you can taste wines from nearby vineyards for around DM2 per glass.

The **Marienberg** fortress, across the river on the hill, is reached by crossing the 15th-century stone **Alte Mainbrücke**. Visit the fortress museums and wander the walls enjoying the panoramic views.

Würzburg's most important son is Wilhelm Conrad Röntgen, discoverer of the X-ray. The **Röntgen Gedächtnisstätte**, Röntgenring 8, is a tribute to his visionary work and is open on weekdays for free.

Places to Stay & Eat

The nearest camping ground is **Kanu-Club** (☎ 725 36, Mergentheimer Strasse 13b), on the western bank of the Main River (take tram No 3 or 5). The **Jugendgästehaus Würzburg** (☎ 425 90, fax 41 68 62, Burkarderstrasse 44), below the fortress, charges DM25 for beds; you must be aged 26 or younger to stay here. Take tram No 3 or 5 from the train station.

Two places with absolutely no frills but clean rooms are **Pension Siegel** (☎ 529 41,

fax 529 67, Reisgrubenstrasse 7), with singles/doubles from DM48/92; and **Pension Spehnkuch** (☎ 547 52, fax 547 60, Röntgenring 7), which charges DM50/94/135 for singles/doubles/triples.

Sternbäck on Sternplatz is a student hangout with a 1920s feel and 19 varieties of baked potato from DM5.90. One of Würzburg's most popular eating and drinking spots is **Bürgerspital** (Theaterstrasse 19), with a good selection of Franconian wines (including its own vintages) and excellent house specialities (from DM16).

Getting There & Away

IC/EC trains run to/from Frankfurt-am-Main (DM54, 80 minutes) and Nuremberg (DM42, one hour). Würzburg is a major stop on the Hamburg-Munich line. It is also on Deutsche Touring's Romantic Road bus route; to/from Rothenburg by bus is 2½ hours. The main bus station is next to the train station, off Röntgenring.

BAMBERG

☎ 0951

Bamberg is practically a byword for magnificence, an untouched monument to the Holy Roman Emperor Heinrich II (who conceived it). Its appeal rests in its sheer number of fine buildings (in a jumble of styles) and relaxed feel. Unesco has recognised this fun and beautiful town as a World Heritage Site.

The tourist office (☎ 87 11 61, fax 87 19 60, **@** info@bamberg.de) is at Geyerswörthstrasse 3 on the island in the River Regnitz A handy machine dispenses a wad of information (DM1) after business hours.

Things to See & Do

Most attractions are spread either side of the Regnitz River, but the colourful **Altes Rathaus** (old town hall) is actually on it, precariously perched on an islet.

The princely and ecclesiastical district is centred on Domplatz, where the Romanesque and Gothic **cathedral**, housing the statue of the chivalric king-knight, the *Bamberger Reiter*, is the biggest attraction.

Above Domplatz is the **Kirche St Michael**, the former Benedictine monastery of St Michael. This is a must-see for its baroque art and the herbal compendium painted on its ceiling. The garden terraces give a

GERMANY

marvellous overview of the city's splendour. There is also the **Fränkisches Brauereimuseum**, which shows how the monks brewed their robust *Benediktiner Dunkel* beer (closed Monday; DM3.50/2.50).

Places to Stay & Eat
Campingplatz Insel (☎ 563 20) is at Bug on the west bank of the Regnitz, a few kilometres south of the city (take bus No 18). *Jugendherberge Wolfsschlucht (☎ 560 02, fax 552 11, Oberer Leinritt 70)* is on the same bank but closer to town; turn south off Münchener Ring towards the clinic complex, go east at Bamberger Strasse, then walk north along the river. Beds (only for those aged 26 or under) are DM20.

Hotel Alt-Bamberg (☎ 98 61 50, fax 20 10 07, Habergasse 11), near the Rathaus, charges DM68/115 for singles/doubles with bath. *Gasthof Fässla (☎ 265 16, fax 20 19 89, Obere Königstrasse 19-21)* has rooms for DM63/98 upstairs and a brewery and earthy restaurant downstairs. The 17th-century *Wirtshaus zum Schlenkerla (Dominikanerstrasse 6)* offers Franconian specialities, along with its own house-brewed *Rauchbier*, a dark-red local speciality that has a startling smoky flavour.

Getting There & Away
There are hourly RE and RB trains to/from Würzburg (DM27) and Nuremberg (DM16.40), both taking one hour. Bamberg is also served by IC trains every two hours running between Munich (DM78, 2½ hours) and Berlin (DM25.60, five hours).

NUREMBERG
☎ 0911
Nuremberg (Nürnberg) is the largest city of northern Bavaria's Franconia region, with a population of 500,000. Though the flood of tourists to this historical town never seems to cease – especially during its world-famous Christmas market – it's still worth the trip. Nuremberg played a major role during the Nazi years and during the war crimes trials afterwards. The city was re-built after Allied bombs reduced it to rubble on the night of 2 January 1945.

Orientation & Information
From the train station, the mostly pedestrianised Königsstrasse leads through the old town and its main squares. There are tourist offices at the train station's main hall (☎ 233 61 32, fax 233 61 66) and on the Hauptmarkt (☎/fax 233 61 35). The main post office is at Bahnhofplatz 1 by the station. There's a laundrette at Fünferplatz 2. Maximum Internet cafe, Färberstrasse 11, offers one hour of surfing between noon and 3 pm for DM5; normally it's DM5 for 30 minutes.

Things to See & Do
The spectacular **Germanisches National Museum** at Kartäusergasse 1 is the most important general museum of German culture. It has works by German painters and sculptors, an archaeological collection, arms and armour (closed Monday; DM6/3).

Close by, the **Neues Museum**, Luitpoldstrasse 5, opened its modern art and design collection, contained in a sleek, streamlined building, in April 2000 (closed Monday; DM6/4).

The **Handwerkerhof**, a re-creation of Nuremberg's old crafts quarter, is walled in opposite the train station. It's thoroughly quaint (read: over-priced). The bustling Hauptmarkt is the site of Germany's most famous *Christkindlmarkt* (Christmas market), lasting from the Friday before Advent to Christmas Eve.

It's a not a bad climb up Burgstrasse to the **Kaiserburg** castle, which has good views of the city. You can visit the palace complex, chapel, well and tower on a DM10 ticket. The walls spread west to the tunnel-gate of **Tiergärtnertor**, where you can stroll behind the castle to the gardens.

Near Tiergärtnertor is the renovated **Albrecht-Dürer-Haus**, where Dürer, Germany's Renaissance draughtsman, lived from 1509 to 1528 (DM5).

The Nazis chose Nuremberg as their propaganda centre and a site for mass rallies, which were held at **Luitpoldhain**, a (never completed) sports complex of megalomaniac proportions. After the war, the Allies deliberately chose Nuremberg as the site for the trials of Nazi war criminals. A chilling documentary film, *Fascination and Force*, can be seen in the museum at the rear of the Zeppelin stand at Luitpoldhain (closed Monday and November to April; DM2/1). Take S-Bahn No 2 to Dutzendteich. A new museum called the **Dokumentationszen-**

trum covering the entire Nazi era is scheduled to open in 2002.

Places to Stay

Campingplatz im Volkspark Dutzendteich (☎ 81 11 22, Hans-Kalb-Strasse 56) is near the lakes in the Volkspark, south-east of the city centre (U1 to Messezentrum). It charges DM10 per site plus DM8 per person, and is open from May to September.

The excellent *Jugendgästehaus* (☎ 230 93 60, fax 23 09 36 11) is in the historical Kaiserstallung next to the castle. Dorm beds including sheets cost DM29 (under age 27 only). The cheapest option for those aged 27 and over is the remote *Jugend-Hotel Nürnberg* (☎ 521 60 92, Rathsbergstrasse 300), north of the city (take tram No 3 to Ziegelstein). Dorm beds start at DM27 and there are singles/doubles from DM37/58.

The most reasonable accommodation in the city centre is the *Pension Altstadt* (☎ 22 61 02, Hintere Ledergasse 4), with basic singles/doubles from DM55/90, and *Pension Sonne* (☎ 22 71 66, Königstrasse 45), with rooms from DM 57/75. Friendly *Pension Vater Jahn* (☎ 44 45 07, Jahnstrasse 13), south-west of the main train station, has rooms from DM50/80.

Places to Eat

A top draw is the *Bratwursthäusle* (Rathausplatz 1), where you can try Nuremberg's famous *Bratwurstl* (small grilled sausages; closed Sunday). Be sure to order at least a dozen with both *Meerrettich* (horse radish) and *Kartoffelsalat* (potato salad).

Kaiserburg (Ubere Krämersgasse 20) has an ancient wood interior and hot dishes from DM9.80. Just around the corner, *Créperie Mignonne (Untere Schmiedgasse 5)* has crepes from DM12.50. *Altstadthof Brewery (Bergstrasse 19)* is a rambling place with beer and hearty standards from DM9. Probably the loveliest place to sit on a sunny day is the *Café am Trödelmarkt*, on an island overlooking the covered bridge.

Getting There & Away

IC trains run frequently to/from Frankfurt-am-Main (DM73, 2½ hours), Munich (DM61, 1½ hours) and Berlin (DM144, 5½ hours). IR trains run every two hours to Stuttgart (DM54, two hours). Several EC trains travel daily to Vienna and Prague

(both six hours). Buses to regional destinations – including Rothenburg – leave from the station just east of the main train station.

REGENSBURG
☎ 0941

On the Danube River, Regensburg has relics of all periods yet lacks the packaged feel of some other German cities. It escaped the fate of carpet bombing, and here, as nowhere else in Germany, you enter the misty ages between the Roman and the Carolingian.

Orientation & Information

From the train station walk up Maximillianstrasse for 10 minutes to reach the centre. The tourist office (☎ 507 44 10, fax 507 44 19, @ tourismus@info.regensburg .baynet.de) is in the Altes Rathaus. C@fe Netzblick, Am Römling 9, is a bar-cum-Internet cafe offering half an hour's access for DM5.

Things to See

Dominating the skyline are the twin spires of the cathedral **Dom St Peter**, which was built during the 14th and 15th centuries from unusual green limestone. During the same period, merchants built Italian-style patrician houses with their characteristic defensive towers. Two of the best, **Goldener Turm** and **Baumburger Turm**, are near the Kohlenmarkt. The **Altes Rathaus** was progressively extended from medieval to baroque times and remained the seat of the Reichstag for almost 150 years. From May to September there are daily tours in English at 3.15 pm (not Sunday; DM5).

The **Roman wall**, with its Porta Praetoria arch, follows Unter den Schwibbögen onto Dr-Martin-Luther-Strasse.

The lavish castle **Schloss Thurn und Taxis**, near the train station, is divided into three separate sections: the castle proper (Schloss), the monastery (Kreuzgang) and the royal stables (Marstall). A combined ticket for all three is DM18/14. Nearby is **St Emmeram Basilika**, a baroque masterpiece containing untouched Carolingian and episcopal graves and relics.

Places to Stay & Eat

Bus No 6 from the train station goes to the entrance of *Azur-Camping* (☎ 27 00 25, Weinweg 40). The *youth hostel* (☎ 574 02,

GERMANY

fax 524 11, Wöhrdstrasse 60) charges DM27 (for juniors only) and is closed in December. Take bus No 3, 8 or 9 to the 'Eisstadion' stop. In the city centre *Diözesanzentrum Obermünster (☎ 597 02, fax 597 22 30, Obermünsterplatz 7)* charges DM50/90 for singles/doubles; ring ahead if you can't arrive before 5 pm.

Arty *Hinterhaus (Rote-Hahnen-Gasse 2)*, in a covered alley, serves fresh fare, with good vegetarian choices, from DM7. Just across the river is the *Alte Linde (Müllerstrasse 1)*, with a leafy beer garden and tasty German standards. One of the oldest eateries in the world, the *Historische Wurstküche* has been serving Bratwurstl for centuries from its spot at the southern end of the Steinerne Brücke.

Getting There & Away

Regensburg is on the train line between Nuremberg (DM34, one hour) and Austria. There are EC/IC trains in both directions every two hours, as well as IR trains to Munich (DM38, 1½ hours) and Passau (DM39, one hour).

BAVARIAN ALPS

While not quite as high as their sister summits farther south in Austria, the Bavarian Alps (Bayerische Alpen) rise so abruptly from the rolling hills of southern Bavaria that their appearance seems all the more dramatic. There are a myriad of hiking and winter sports possibilities.

Berchtesgaden

☎ 08652

Berchtesgaden is perhaps the most scenic place in the Bavarian Alps. To reach the centre cross the footbridge from the train station and walk up Bahnhofstrasse. The tourist office (☎ 96 70, fax 96 74 00, **☻** info@berchtesgaden.de) is just across the river from the train station at Königsseer Strasse 2.

Tours of the **Salzbergwerk** salt mine are offered daily (closed Sunday from mid-October to March; DM21/11 for adults/children, 1½ hours).

Nearby **Obersalzberg** was a second seat of government for the Third Reich. Hitler, Himmler, Goebbels and the rest of the Nazi hierarchy all maintained homes here. To reach the town take bus No 9538 (DM7.90 return) from the Nazi-built Berchtesgaden

train station. Just down the hill from the Obersalzberg stop, the new **Dokumentation Obersalzberg museum** records Hitler and his cronies' lives in the area, plus the horrors of their time in power. The DM5/3 entry also gets you into the eerie **Hitler's bunker**.

Kehlstein, a spectacular meeting house seldom used by Hitler despite its reputation as the 'Eagle's Nest', is a popular destination (closed from November to mid-May). The views are stunning and the history is compelling. Entrance (DM22) includes transport on special buses linking the summit with Hintereck/Obersalzberg as well as the 120m elevator ride through solid rock to the peak. Be sure to reserve a spot on a bus going down when you exit the one going up.

The wilds of **Berchtesgaden National Park** unquestionably offer some of the best hiking in Germany. A good introduction to the area is a 2km path up from St Bartholomä beside the Königssee to the Watzmann-Ostwand, a massive 2000m-high rock face – scores of mountaineers have died attempting to climb it. Another popular hike goes from the southern end of the Königssee to the Obersee.

Of the five camping grounds in the Berchtesgaden area, the nicest are up at Königssee: *Grafenlehen (☎ 41 40)* and *Mühleiten (☎ 45 84)*. Both charge DM10 per site plus DM8 per person. The *youth hostel (☎ 21 90, fax 663 28, Gebirgsjägerstrasse 52)* charges DM23 for a B&B (age 26 and under only). From the train station take bus No 9539 to Strub, then continue a few minutes on foot. The hostel closes in November and December.

Hotel Watzmann (☎ 20 55, fax 5174, Franziskanerplatz 2) is just opposite the chiming church in the old town. Simple singles/doubles cost from DM33/66. The hotel closes in November and December. *Hotel Floriani (☎ 660 11, fax 634 53, Königsseer Strasse 37)* is near the station and charges from DM65/110.

To Berchtesgaden, it's usually best to go by train to/from Munich (DM48, 2½ hours) or Salzburg (one hour), with a change at Freilassing.

Garmisch-Partenkirchen

☎ 08821

The year-round resort of Garmisch-Partenkirchen is Munich's favourite getaway spot. The huge **ski stadium** outside town hosted the 1936 Winter Olympics. From the pedestrian Am Kurpark, walk up Klammstrasse, cross the tracks and veer left on the first path to reach the stadium and enjoy the spectacular views. The tourist office (☎ 18 07 00, fax 18 07 55, ℮ tourist-info @garmisch-partenkirchen.de) is at Richard Strauss Platz 2.

An excursion to the **Zugspitze** (2963m), Germany's highest peak, is the most popular outing from Garmisch. There are various ways up, including a return trip by rack-railway (just west of the main train station) or summit cable car and Eibsee cable car for DM76. For information on guided hiking or mountaineering courses check with Bergsteigerschule Zugspitze (☎ 589 99), Dreitorspitz Strasse 13, Garmisch.

About 20km north of Garmisch lies the touristy town of **Oberammergau**, which becomes a focus of world attention every 10 years when a good portion of the local populace perform day-long Passion plays. The next series of performances – which date back to the 17th century – will be in 2010.

The camping ground nearest to Garmisch is *Zugspitze (☎ 31 80)*, along highway B24. Take the 'Weiss-Blaue' bus (outside and left across the street as you exit the train station) in the direction of the Eibsee. Sites cost DM5 plus DM9.50 per person.

The *youth hostel (☎ 29 80, fax 585 36, Jochstrasse 10)* is in the suburb of Burgrain. Beds cost DM21 (age 26 and under only) and it's closed from November to Christmas. From the train station take bus No 3, 4 or 5 to the Burgrain stop.

Five minute's walk from the station is the quiet *Hotel Schell (☎ 957 50, fax 95 75 40, Partnachauenstrasse 3)*, while in the town centre is *Gästehaus Becherer (☎ 547 57, Höllentalstrasse 4)*. Both charge from DM45/90 and don't mind you staying only one night (unlike many places in Garmisch).

Garmisch-Partenkirchen is serviced from Munich by hourly trains (DM27, 1½ hours) – a special return fare from Munich or Augsburg (DM68) includes the trip up the Zugspitze. RVO bus No 1084 from in front of the train station links Garmisch with Füssen (DM13, two hours) four times daily via Oberammergau.

GERMANY

Greece

The first travel guide to Greece was written 1800 years ago by the Greek geographer and historian Pausanias, so the tourism industry isn't exactly in its infancy.

The country's enduring attraction is its archaeological sites; those who travel through Greece journey not only through the landscape but also through time, witnessing the legacy of Europe's greatest ages – the Mycenaean, Minoan, classical, Hellenistic and Byzantine.

The magnetism of Greece is also due to less tangible attributes – the dazzling clarity of the light, the floral aromas that permeate the air. Then again, many visitors come to Greece simply to get away from it all and relax in one of Europe's friendliest and safest countries.

Facts about Greece

HISTORY

The Greek Islands were the birthplace of two of Europe's oldest civilisations, the Cycladic and the Minoan, which flourished between 3000 and 1500 BC. The focus then shifted to mainland-based Mycenaeans, who were eventually swept aside by the Dorians in the 12th century BC. The next 400 years are often referred to as the 'age of darkness', which is a bit unfair for a period that saw the arrival of the Iron Age and the emergence of geometric pottery.

By 800 BC, when Homer's *Odyssey* and *Iliad* were first written down, Greece was undergoing a cultural and military revival with the evolution of city-states, the most powerful of which were Athens and Sparta. Greater Greece (Magna Graecia) was created, with south Italy as an important component.

The period that followed was an unparalleled time of growth and prosperity, resulting in what is called the classical (or golden) age. In this period the Parthenon

AT A GLANCE	
Capital:	Athens
Population:	10.6 million
Official Language:	Greek
Currency:	1 drachma = 100 lepta

was commissioned by Pericles, Sophocles wrote *Oedipus the King,* and Socrates taught young Athenians to think.

The golden age ended with the Peloponnesian War (431-404 BC) in which the militaristic Spartans defeated the Athenians. So embroiled were they both in this war that they failed to notice the expansion of Macedonia to the north under King Philip II, who easily conquered the war-weary city-states. Philip's ambitions were surpassed by those of his son, Alexander the Great, who marched into Asia Minor, Egypt, Persia and what are now parts of Afghanistan and India. In 323 BC he met an untimely death at the age of 33.

Roman incursions into Greece began in 205 BC, and by 146 BC Greece and Macedonia had become Roman provinces. In AD 330 Emperor Constantine chose Byzantium as the new capital of the Roman Empire and renamed the city Constantinople. After the subdivision of the Roman Empire in AD 395, Greece became part of the Eastern Roman Empire, leading to the illustrious Byzantine age.

In 1453 Constantinople fell to the Turks, and most of Greece soon became part of the Ottoman Empire. By the 19th century the Ottoman Empire had become the 'sick man of Europe' and the Greeks, seeing nationalism sweep Europe, fought their War of Independence (1821-32).

In 1831 the first president of Greece, Ioannis Kapodistrias, was assassinated and in the ensuing anarchy the European powers stepped in again and declared that Greece should become a monarchy. In January 1833 Otho of Bavaria was installed as king. In 1862 he was peacefully ousted and the Greeks chose George I, a Danish prince, as king.

After WWI, Prime Minister Venizelos, underestimating the new-found power of

GREECE

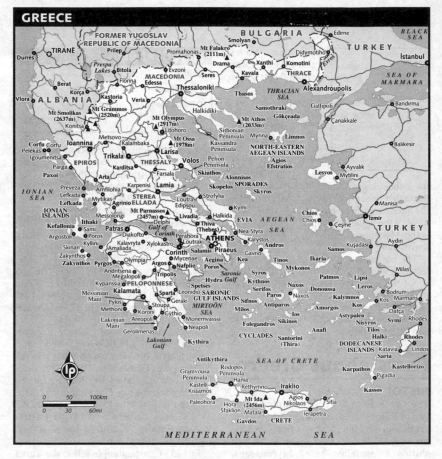

Turkey under the leadership of Atatürk, sent the army to occupy Smyrna (the present-day Turkish port of İzmir), which had a large Greek population. After early successes, the Greek army was humiliated. The outcome was the Treaty of Lausanne (1923), which ordered a massive population exchange between the countries to eliminate the grounds for future disputes. Almost 1.5 million Greeks left Turkey, while some 400,000 Turks left Greece.

The German occupation of Greece in 1941 was the start of eight years of increasingly bitter war. The resistance movements polarised into royalist and communist factions, leading to a brutal civil war that lasted until 1949 and left the country in complete chaos. The sense of despair became the trigger for a mass exodus. Almost a million Greeks headed off in search of a better life elsewhere, primarily to Australia, Canada and the USA.

Continuing political instability led to the so-called 'colonels' coup d'etat' in 1967. The Greek army's junta distinguished itself by inflicting appalling brutality, repression and political incompetence upon the people. In 1974 the army attempted to assassinate Cyprus' leader, Archbishop Makarios. Makarios escaped, and the junta replaced him with the extremist Nikos Samson, prompting mainland Turkey to occupy North Cyprus in support of the island's 20% Turkish minority. This continued occupation remains one of the most contentious issues in Greek politics.

Greece joined the European Community (now EU) in 1981. Later that year, it elected its first socialist government. The increasingly less left-wing PASOK party has dominated ever since, first under the charismatic Andreas Papandreou, and now under the reformist Costas Simitis. Simitis has presided over a remarkable economic turnaround since 1996, and the country was scheduled to be admitted to the single European currency in early 2001.

MYTHOLOGY
Greek mythology is based on the gods worshipped in ancient times. The main characters are the 12 principle deities, who lived on Mt Olympus, which the Greeks thought to be at the exact centre of the world.

The supreme deity was **Zeus**, who was also god of the heavens. He was the fortunate possessor of an astonishing libido and mythology is littered with his offspring. Zeus was married to his sister, **Hera**, who was the protector of women and the family. She was able to renew her virginity each year by bathing in a spring. She was the mother of **Ares**, the god of war, and **Hephaestus**, god of the forge.

Demeter was the goddess of earth and fertility, the goddess of love (and lust) was the beautiful **Aphrodite**. **Athena**, the powerful goddess of wisdom and guardian of Athens, is said to have been born (complete with helmet, armour and spear) from Zeus' head.

Poseidon, the brother of Zeus, was god of the sea and preferred his sumptuous palace in the depths of the Aegean to Mt Olympus. **Apollo**, god of the sun, was also worshipped as the god of music and song. His twin sister, **Artemis**, was the goddess of childbirth and the protector of suckling animals.

Hermes, messenger of the gods, completes the first XI – the gods whose position in the pantheon is agreed by everyone. The final berth is normally reserved for **Hestia**, goddess of the hearth. She was too virtuous for some, who promoted the fun-loving **Dionysos**, god of wine, in her place.

Other gods included **Hades**, god of the underworld; **Pan**, god of the shepherds; **Asclepius**, the god of healing; and **Eros**, the god of love.

Greek heroes such as **Heracles** and **Theseus** were elevated almost to the ranks of the gods.

Xena, sadly, does not feature anywhere. The strapping warrior princess of TV fame is a script writer's invention – not a myth!

GEOGRAPHY
Greece consists of the southern tip of the Balkan peninsula and about 2000 islands, only 166 of which are inhabited. Most of the country is mountainous. The Pindos Mountains in Epiros continue down through central Greece and the Peloponnese, and re-emerge in the mountains of Crete.

Looking at the harsh, rocky landscapes of the 20th century, it's hard to believe that in ancient times Greece was a fertile land with extensive forests – much of the land was cleared to make way for olive tree cultivation.

CLIMATE
The Greek climate is typically Mediterranean with mild, wet winters followed by hot, dry summers.

POPULATION & PEOPLE
The population of Greece (1997 census) is 10.62 million, 97% of whom nominally belong to the Greek Orthodox Church. By far the largest city is Athens, with more than 3.7 million in the greater Athens area.

SOCIETY & CONDUCT
Greece is steeped in traditional customs. Name days (celebrated instead of birthdays), weddings and funerals all have great significance. Weddings are highly festive, with dancing, feasting and drinking sometimes continuing for days.

If you want to bare all, other than on a designated nudist beach, remember that Greece is a conservative country and it may be offensive to locals.

LANGUAGE
English is almost a second language, especially with younger people. Even in remote villages there are invariably one or two people who can speak English.

See the Language chapter at the back of this book for pronunciation guidelines and useful Greek words and phrases. Transliteration from the Greek alphabet into Roman characters is a knotty problem – there are six ways of rendering the vowel sound 'ee' in Greek, and two ways of rendering the 'o' and 'e' sounds. This book has merely attempted to be

GREECE

consistent within itself, not to solve this long-standing difficulty. Please bear with us if signs in Greek don't agree with our spelling.

Odos means street, *plateia* means square and *leoforos* means avenue. These words are often omitted on maps and other references, so we have generally done the same throughout this chapter.

Facts for the Visitor

HIGHLIGHTS

Many islands are overrun with tourists in summer. For tranquillity, try lesser-known islands such as Anafi (near Santorini); Koufonisi, Donoussa, Shinoussa and Iraklia (near Naxos); and Symi (near Rhodes) – see the sections on the Cyclades and the Dodecanese islands for more information. If you enjoy mountain walks, then Naxos, Crete, Samothraki and Samos are all rewarding. If you prefer the beach, try Paros. The top 'party' islands are Mykonos, Ios and Santorini.

Greece has more ancient sites than any country in Europe. The most famous (and crowded) are the Acropolis, Delphi, Knossos and Olympia. The Sanctuary of the Great Gods on Samothraki is one of Greece's most evocative sites, and it's off the package-tourist circuit.

Two of Greece's most spectacular Byzantine, medieval cities are in the Peloponnese – the ghostly city of Mystras, west of Sparta, and Monemvassia. Rhodes is the finest surviving example of a fortified medieval town, while Naxos' *hora* (main village) is a maze of whitewashed Venetian houses.

SUGGESTED ITINERARIES

Depending on the length of your stay, you might want to visit the following places:

Three days
  Visit Athens and perhaps Delphi. Visiting the islands would be almost impossible unless you fly.
One week
  Spend two days in Athens and four days in either the Peloponnese (Olympia, Nafplio/Mycenae and Sparta/Mystras), the Cycladic Islands (Santorini, Paros and/or Ios) or Crete.
Two weeks
  Spend two days in Athens, three days in the Peloponnese, three or four days on the Cycladic Islands, and a few days either on the Dodecanese Islands or on Crete, allowing at least three days travelling time.

PLANNING

When to Go

Many places go into hibernation between late November and early April, particularly on the islands; hotels and restaurants close, and ferries operate on drastically reduced schedules. The cobwebs are dusted off in time for Easter, and conditions are perfect until the end of June. From July until mid-September, northern Europe heads for Greece en masse. The pace slows down again by mid-September, and conditions are ideal once more until the end of October.

Maps

The best maps – for both motoring and trekking – are produced by local company Road Editions.

TOURIST OFFICES

The Greek National Tourist Organisation (GNTO) is known as EOT in Greece. There is either an EOT office or a local tourist office in almost every town of consequence. Most of these offices do no more than give out brochures and maps. Popular tourist destinations have tourist police who often have ferry schedules and can help in finding accommodation.

Tourist Offices Abroad

Greek overseas tourist offices include:

Australia (☎ 02-9241 1663) 51 Pitt St, Sydney, NSW 2000
Canada (☎ 416-968 2220) 1300 Bay St, Toronto, Ontario M5R 3K8
  (☎ 514-871 1535) Suite 101, 1233 Rue de la Montagne, Montreal, Quebec H3G 1Z2
UK (☎ 020-7734 5997) 4 Conduit St, London W1R 0DJ
USA (☎ 312-782 1084) Suite 160, 168 North Michigan Ave, Chicago, Illinois 60601
  (☎ 213-626 6696) Suite 2198, 611 West 6th St, Los Angeles, California 92668
  (☎ 212-421 5777) Olympic Tower, 645 5th Ave, New York, NY 10022

VISAS & DOCUMENTS

Nationals of Australia, Canada, EU countries, Israel, New Zealand and the USA can stay in Greece for up to three months without a visa. In the past, Greece has refused entry to those with North Cyprus (Turkish-occupied) passport stamps, though there are reports that this is less of a problem now. To be on the safe side, ask the North Cyprus immigration officials to stamp a piece of paper rather than your passport.

EMBASSIES & CONSULATES
Greek Embassies Abroad
The following are a selection of Greek embassies abroad:

Australia (☎ 02-6273 3011) 9 Turrana St, Yarralumla, Canberra, ACT 2600
Canada (☎ 613-238 6271) 76-80 Maclaren St, Ottawa, Ontario K2P 0K6
New Zealand (☎ 04-473 7775) 5-7 Willeston St, Wellington
UK (☎ 020-7229 3850) 1A Holland Park, London W11 3TP
USA (☎ 202-939 5818) 2221 Massachusetts Ave NW, Washington, DC, 20008

Foreign Embassies in Greece
The following embassies are in Athens:

Australia (☎ 645 0404) Dimitriou Soutsou 37
Canada (☎ 727 3400) Genadiou 4
New Zealand (☎ 771 0112) Xenias 24
UK (☎ 723 6211) Ploutarhou 1
USA (☎ 721 2951) Leoforos Vasilissis Sofias 91

MONEY
The Greek unit of currency is the drachma (dr). Coins come in denominations of five, 10, 20, 50 and 100 dr. Banknotes come in 50, 100, 500, 1000, 5000 and 10,000 dr denominations. At the time of writing, Greece was expected to adopt the single European currency, the Euro, in 2000. Travellers can expect to find prices quoted in both drachma and Euros in preparation for the changeover.

Greek banks exchange all major currencies, in either cash or travellers cheques and also Eurocheques. All post offices have exchange facilities and charge less commission than banks. All major credit cards are accepted, but only in larger establishments. If you run out of money, you can get a cash advance on Visa at the Greek Commercial Bank and on Access, MasterCard and Eurocard at the National Bank.

Exchange Rates
Exchange rates are as follows:

country	unit		drachma
Australia	A$1	=	215.08 dr
Canada	C$1	=	252.30 dr
euro	€1	=	337.55 dr
France	10FF	=	514.59 dr
Germany	DM1	=	172.60 dr
Japan	¥100	=	350.22 dr
New Zealand	NZ$1	=	163.39 dr
UK	UK£1	=	550.75 dr
USA	US$1	=	374.35 dr

Costs
Greece is a cheap country by European standards. You can get by on US$25 per day by staying in hostels, eating at cheap restaurants and seldom taking buses or ferries. Allow at least US$50 per day to stay at nicer hotels, travel around and eat out regularly.

Tipping & Bargaining
In restaurants where the service charge is included on the bill, but it is the custom to leave a small tip. Accommodation is nearly always negotiable outside high season, especially if you are staying more than one night. Souvenir shops are another place where substantial savings can be made during the low season. Prices in other shops are normally clearly marked and non-negotiable.

POST & COMMUNICATIONS
Postal rates for cards and small air-mail letters (up to 20g) are 170 dr to EU destinations, and 200 dr elsewhere. The service is slow but reliable. Post offices are usually open 7.30 am to 2 pm weekdays. In major cities they stay open until 8 pm and are also open on Saturday.

The phone system is modern and efficient. All public phone boxes use phonecards, sold at OTE telephone offices and *periptera* (kiosks). Four cards are available: 100 units (1000 dr), 200 units (1800 dr), 500 units (4200 dr) and 1000 units (8200 dr). Direct-dial long-distance and international calls can also be made from public phones. The international access code is ☎ 00. A three-minute call to the USA costs 708 dr.

Greece's country code is ☎ 30.

Main post offices have fax facilities. Internet cafes are springing up everywhere, including the islands; most places charge about 1500 dr per hour.

INTERNET RESOURCES
The following are just a few of the huge number of useful Web sites for travellers to Greece.

GREECE

Corfu Online: Links to Greece & Corfu A good place to start with hundreds of links to a huge range of sites covering everything from accommodation to Zeus.
www.viking1.com/corfu/link.htm.

A Travel Guide to Greece This is the front door for an assortment of interesting sites by Matt Barrett.
www.greektravel.com

Vacation in Greece This site has travel information, links to online reservation services, and ferry schedules.
www.odysseas.com

BOOKS

For more detailed information see Lonely Planet's *Greece* and *Greek Islands* guides. *Zorba the Greek* by Nikos Kazantzakis may seem an obvious choice, but read it and you'll understand why it's the most popular of all Greek novels translated into English.

TIME

Greece is GMT/UTC plus two hours. Clocks are turned one hour ahead on the last Sunday in March and back again on the last Sunday in September.

TOILETS

You'll find public toilets at all major bus and train stations, but they are seldom pleasant. You will need to supply your own paper.

Greek plumbing cannot handle toilet paper. Always put it in the bin provided.

WOMEN TRAVELLERS

Many foreign women travel alone in Greece. Hassles occur, but they tend to be a nuisance rather than threatening. Violent offences are rare. In rural areas it's a good idea to dress conservatively. It is perfectly OK to wear shorts, short skirts, etc in touristy places.

GAY & LESBIAN TRAVELLERS

Greece is a popular destination for gay travellers. Athens has a busy gay scene, but most people head for the islands – Mykonos and Lesvos in particular. Paros, Rhodes, Santorini and Skiathos also have their share of gay hang-outs.

There is no legislation against homosexual activity, but it is wise to be discreet and to avoid open displays of togetherness. The main gay rights organisation, Elladas Omofilofilon Kommunitas, can be contacted by email on ✆ eok@nyx.gr.

DISABLED TRAVELLERS

If mobility is a problem, the hard fact is that most hotels, museums and ancient sites are not wheelchair accessible.

DANGERS & ANNOYANCES

Greece has the lowest crime rate in Europe. Athens is developing a bad reputation for petty theft and scams, but elsewhere crimes are most likely to be committed by other travellers. Drug laws are strict. There's a minimum seven-year sentence for possession of even a small quantity of dope.

BUSINESS HOURS

Banks are open 8.30 am to 2.30 pm weekdays (to 2 pm Friday). Some city banks also open 3.30 to 6.30 pm and on Saturday morning. Shops are open 8 am to 1.30 pm and 5.30 to 8.30 pm on Tuesday, Thursday and Friday, and 8 am to 2.30 pm on Monday, Wednesday and Saturday, but these times are not always followed.

PUBLIC HOLIDAYS & SPECIAL EVENTS

Public holidays are as follows: 1 January (New Year's Day), 6 January (Epiphany), First Sunday of Lent, Good Friday, Orthodox Easter Sunday, 1 May (Labour Day), 15 August (Feast of the Assumption), 28 October (Okhi Day), and 25 to 26 December (Christmas).

Easter is Greece's most important festival, with candle-lit processions, feasting and firework displays. Orthodox Easter is 50 days after the first Sunday in Lent.

ACCOMMODATION

Prices throughout Greece are subject to strict controls set by the tourist police. By law, prices must be displayed in every room – if you think you have been ripped off, contact the tourist police. Many places – especially in rural areas and on the islands – are closed from late October to mid-April.

Camping

Rates at Greece's 350 camping grounds average around 1400 dr per person. Most are open only from April to October. Greece has 55 mountain refuges, which are listed in the booklet *Greece Mountain Refuges & Ski Centres,* available for free at EOT and EOS offices.

GREECE

Hostels

There are youth hostels in most major towns and on half a dozen islands. The only place affiliated with Hostelling International (HI) is the excellent Athens International Youth Hostel. Most are run by the Greek Youth Hostel Organisation (☎ 01-751 9530, fax 751 0616, ✉ y-hostels@otenet.gr), Damareos 75, 116 33 Athens. There are affiliated hostels in Athens, Olympia, Patras and Thessaloniki on the mainland, and on the islands of Crete and Santorini. Rates vary from 1600 dr to 2000 dr and you don't have to be a member to stay in any of them.

There is a XEN (YWCA) hostel for women in Athens.

Domatia

Domatia are the Greek equivalent of a British B&B, minus the breakfast. Many domatia are purpose-built appendages to family homes. Rates start at 4000/6000 dr for singles/doubles, rising to 9000/12,000 dr.

Hotels

Hotels are classified as deluxe, A, B, C, D or E class. Expect to pay 6000/9000 dr for singles/doubles in D and E class, and about 10,000/15,000 dr in a decent C-class hotel. You can bargain if you're staying more than one night. Prices are about 40% cheaper between October and May.

FOOD & DRINKS

There are many varieties of restaurants. An *estiatoria* is a straightforward restaurant with a printed menu. A *taverna* is cheaper and more traditional. A *psistaria* specialises in charcoal-grilled dishes. *Ouzeria* (ouzo bars) often have such a good range of *mezedes* (appetisers) that they can be seen as eating places.

Typical snacks include *gyros* (meat sliced from a rotating skewer) and *souvlaki* (individual meat skewers), both wrapped in pita bread with salad and lashings of *tzatziki* (a yoghurt, cucumber and garlic dip). Other snacks are *spanakopitta* (spinach and cheese pie) and *tyropitta* (cheese pie).

Greece is famous for its appetisers – standards include tzatziki, *melitzanosalata* (aubergine dip), *taramasalata* (fish-roe dip), *dolmades* (stuffed vine leaves), *fasolia* (beans) and *oktapodi* (octopus).

Moussaka (layers of aubergine and mince meat, topped with bechamel sauce

and baked) is on every menu, alongside a number of other taverna staples: *moschari* (oven-baked veal and potatoes), *keftedes* (meatballs), *stifado* (meat stew), *pastitsio* (macaroni with mince meat and bechamel sauce, baked) and *yemista* (either tomatoes or green peppers stuffed with mince meat and rice). The most popular fish are *barbouni* (red mullet), *ksifias* (swordfish) and *kalamaria* (fried squid).

Fortunately for vegetarians, salad is a mainstay of the Greek diet. The most popular is *horiatiki salata* (cucumbers, peppers, onions, olives, tomatoes and feta cheese), normally listed on English-language menus as Greek or country salad.

Greece is traditionally a wine-drinking society. A speciality is *retsina* (resinated white wine). Mythos and Alpha are two local brews for beer drinkers to seek out. The most popular aperitif is the aniseed-flavoured ouzo.

Greek coffee comes three main ways: *glyko* (thick and sweet), *metrio* (less sweet) and *sketo* (no sugar). Instant coffee is called *Nescafé*. *Nescafé me ghala* is coffee with milk. Real (ground) coffee is available at smarter cafes.

Getting There & Away

AIR

There are no less than 16 international airports, but most of these only handle summer charter flights to the islands. Athens handles the vast majority of international flights; Thessaloniki is also well served. The Greek national carrier is Olympic Airways.

From London, Olympic Airways, British Airways and Virgin Atlantic offer 30-day return tickets to Athens for about UK£240 in high season; Olympic and British Airways have returns to Thessaloniki for about UK£225. At the time of writing, the cheapest fares were being offered by EasyJet (☎ 0870 6 000 000).

Charter flights from London and major European cities to Athens are readily available for UK£99/189 one way/return in high season, dropping to UK£79/129 in low season. Fares are about UK£109/209 to most island destinations in high season.

Departure Tax

The international airport departure tax of 6800 dr is included in the price of all tickets.

LAND

Overland travel to Greece is virtually a thing of the past. Buses and trains can't compete with cheap air fares, and the turmoil in former Yugoslavia has cut the shortest overland route. All bus and train services now go via Italy and take ferries over to Greece.

Bus

The Hellenic Railways Organisation (OSE) has buses from Athens to İstanbul (23,000 dr, 22 hours) at 11 pm daily, and to Tirana (12,600 dr, 21 hours), leaving at 8.30 pm daily except Sunday.

Train

Unless you have a Eurail pass, travelling to Greece by train is prohibitively expensive. There are daily trains between Athens and İstanbul (20,000 dr, 23 hours), leaving Athens at 11.15 pm.

SEA

Greece is part of the Eurail network, and passes are valid on ferries operated by Adriatica di Navigazione and Hellenic Mediterranean Lines from Brindisi to Corfu, Igoumenitsa and Patras. Eurailers still need to make a reservation. Everyone must pay port taxes – 1800 dr to Italy and 3000 dr to Turkey and Cyprus.

Italy

The most popular crossing is from Brindisi to Patras (18 hours), via Corfu (nine hours) and Igoumenitsa (10 hours). There are numerous services. One-way deck fares start at about 7600 dr in low season and 12,000 dr in high season.

There are ferries to Patras from Ancona, Bari, Trieste and Venice, stopping at either Corfu or Igoumenitsa. In the summer months there are also ferries from Bari and Brindisi to Kefallonia.

Turkey

There are five regular ferries between the Greek Islands and Turkey: Lesvos-Ayvalık, Chios-Çeşme, Samos-Kuşadası, Kos-Bodrum and Rhodes-Marmaris. All are daily services

in summer, dropping to weekly in winter. Tickets must be bought a day in advance and you will be asked to hand over your passport. It will be returned on the boat.

Cyprus & Israel

Both Salamis Lines and Poseidon Lines operate ferries from Piraeus to the Israeli port of Haifa, travelling via Rhodes and Lemessos on Cyprus. Deck-class fares from Piraeus are 19,000 dr to Lemessos and 28,000 dr to Haifa.

Getting Around

AIR

Most domestic flights are operated by Olympic Airways and its offshoot, Olympic Aviation. It offers a busy schedule in summer with flights from Athens to 25 islands and a range of mainland cities. Sample fares include Athens-Iraklio for 21,400 dr, Athens-Rhodes for 23,400 dr and Athens-Santorini for 22,200 dr. It is advisable to book at least two weeks in advance, especially in summer. Aegean Air, Air Greece and Cronus Airlines provide competition on a few major routes.

The above fares include the 3400-dr tax on domestic flights, paid when you buy your ticket.

BUS

Buses are comfortable, they run on time and there are frequent services on all major routes. Almost every town on the mainland (except in Thrace) has at least one bus a day to Athens. Reckon on paying about 1200 dr per hour of journey time. Tickets should be bought at least an hour in advance in summer to ensure a seat.

TRAIN

Inter-Rail and Eurail passes are valid in Greece, but you still need to make a reservation. In summer, make reservations at least two days in advance.

Trains are a poor alternative to bus travel. There are only two main lines (Thessaloniki and Alexandroupolis in the north and to the Peloponnese) plus a few branch lines (including the spectacular Diakofto-Kalavryta mountain railway). Beware that there are two distinct levels of service: the painfully slow, dilapidated trains that stop at all stations and the faster, modern express trains.

You'll find information about schedules at www.ose.gr.

CAR & MOTORCYCLE

Car hire is expensive, but it's a great way to explore off the beaten track. You'll find the best deals at smaller local companies, especially outside high season.

Mopeds are cheap (about 3000 dr per day) and available everywhere, but be warned: Lonely Planet receives many letters complaining about companies hiring out poorly maintained mopeds, and most insurance policies won't pay out for injuries caused by defective machines.

The Greek automobile club, ELPA, offers reciprocal services to members of other national motoring associations. If your vehicle breaks down, dial ☎ 104.

Road Rules

No casual observer would guess that it was compulsory to wear seat belts in the front seats of vehicles, or that it was compulsory to wear a helmet on motorcycles of more than 50cc – always insist on a helmet when renting a motorcycle.

The speed limit for cars is 120km/h on toll roads, 90km/h outside built-up areas and 50km/h in built-up areas. For motorcycles, the speed limit outside built-up areas is 70km/h. Drink-driving laws are strict – a blood alcohol content of 0.05% incurs a penalty and over 0.08% is a criminal offence.

GREECE - MAIN FERRY ROUTES

BOAT

Every island has a ferry service of some sort. The hub of Greece's ferry network is Piraeus, the main port of Athens. Patras is the hub for ferries to the Ionian islands, while Volos and Agios Konstantinos are the hubs for the Sporades.

Some of the smaller islands are virtually inaccessible in winter, when schedules are cut back to a minimum. Services start to pick up in April and are running at full steam from June to September. The local port police always know the latest schedules.

Fares are fixed by the government. The small differences in price you may find between ticket agencies are the result of some agencies sacrificing part of their designated commission to qualify as a 'discount service'. Unless you specify otherwise, you will automatically be sold deck class, which is the cheapest fare.

Hydrofoils and high-speed catamarans operate competing services on some of the most popular routes. They cost about twice as much as the ferries, but get you there in half the time.

Athens Αθήνα

☎ 01

Ancient Athens ranks alongside Rome and Jerusalem for its influence on Western civilisation, but the modern city (population 3.7 million) is a place few people fall in love with. However inspiring the Acropolis might be, most visitors have trouble coming to terms with the surrounding urban sprawl, the appalling traffic congestion and the pollution.

Greece's capital is not, however, without redeeming features. The Acropolis is but one of many important ancient sites, and the National Archaeological Museum has the world's finest collection of Greek antiquities. Culturally, Athens is a fascinating blend of east and west. King Otho and the middle class that emerged after independence may have been intent on making Athens a European city, but the influence of Asia Minor is everywhere.

Orientation

Although Athens is a huge, sprawling city, nearly everything of interest to travellers is within a small area bounded by Plateia Omonias (Omonia Square) to the north, Plateia Monastirakiou (Monastiraki Square) to the west, Plateia Syntagmatos (Syntagma Square) to the east and the Plaka district to the south.

Most people opt to stay in Plaka, the delightful old Turkish quarter. Its labyrinthine streets are nestled on the north-eastern slope of the Acropolis.

Information

Tourist Offices Close to Syntagma, the main EOT tourist office (☎ 331 0561, fax 325 2895, ✉ gntoeexi.gr), at Amerikis 2, has ferry, bus and train information and a helpful city map that shows trolleybus routes. The office is open 9 am to 7 pm weekdays and 9.30 am to 2 pm Saturday.

The tourist police (☎ 924 2700) are open 24 hours at Dimitrakopoulou 77, Koukaki. Take trolleybus No 1, 5 or 9 from Syntagma. They also have a 24-hour information service (☎ 171).

Money The National Bank of Greece in Syntagma has 24-hour automatic exchange machines. In Plaka, Acropole Foreign Exchange, Kydathineon 23, is open 9 am to midnight daily.

American Express (☎ 324 4975), Ermou 2, on Syntagma, is open 8.30 am to 4 pm weekdays and to 1.30 pm Saturday. Thomas Cook travellers cheques are handled by Eurochange (☎ 322 0155), nearby at Karageorgi Servias 4.

Post & Communications The main post office is at Eolou 100 in Omonia. If you're staying in Plaka, get your mail sent to the Syntagma post office. The OTE telephone office at 28 Oktovriou-Patission 85 is open 24 hours. The office at Stadiou 15, Syntagma, is open to 11.30 pm daily.

Email & Internet Access Internet cafes include: Skynet Internet Centre, corner of Voulis and Apollonos, Plaka; Sofokleus.com Internet Café, Stadiou 5, Syntagma; and Museum Internet Café, Oktovriou-Patission 46.

Travel Agencies The bulk of the city's travel agencies are around Syntagma square, particularly in the area just south of the square on Filellinon, Nikis and Voulis.

Sun-seekers at Es Canar, Ibiza, Spain

Amalfi Coast, Italy

Whitewashed Fira, Santorini, Greek Islands

The Modernist La Pedrera aparment block, designed by Gaudí, Barcelona, Spain

CHRISTOPHER GROENHOUT

Campo Maior, Alto Alentejo, Portugal

CARLOS COSTA

Santorini, Greek Islands

CHRIS CHRISTO

Hassan II Mosque, Casablanca, Morocco

ADAM McCROW

Reputable agencies include STA Travel (☎ 321 1188, 321 1194, ❷ robissa@spark .net.gr), at Voulis 43, and ETOS Travel (☎ 324 1884, fax 322 8447, ❷ usit@ usitetos.gr), at Filellinon 1. Both these places also issue International Student Identity Cards (ISIC).

Bookshops Athens has three good bookshops with English-language titles. The biggest is Eleftheroudakis, which has branches at Panepistimiou 17 and Nikis 4. The others are Pantelides Books, Amerikis 11, and Compendium Books, Nikis 28. Compendium has a second-hand section.

Laundry Plaka has a convenient laundrette at Angelou Geronta 10, just off Kydathineon.

Medical Services For emergency medical treatment, ring the tourist police (☎ 171) and they'll tell you where to find the nearest hospital. Don't wait for an ambulance – get a taxi. Hospitals give free emergency treatment to tourists.

Dangers & Annoyances Pickpockets have become a major problem in Athens. Their favourite hunting grounds are the metro system and the crowded streets around Omonia, particularly Athinas, and the Sunday market on Ermou.

Also be wary of taxi drivers working in league with some hotels around Omonia. The scam involves taxi drivers picking up late-night arrivals and persuading them that the hotel they want to go to is full – even if they have a booking. Also note that when taxi drivers do go to the correct hotel, they sometimes attempt to claim commissions from hotel owners.

Lonely Planet receives a steady flow of letters warning about bar scams, particularly around Syntagma. The most popular version goes like this: friendly Greek approaches solo male traveller and discovers that the traveller knows little about Athens; friendly Greek then reveals that he, too, is from out of town. Why don't they go to this great little bar and have a beer? The crunch comes at the end of the evening when the traveller is presented with an exorbitant bill and the smiles disappear. The conmen who play the role of the friendly Greek can be

very convincing; some people have been conned more than once.

Things to See

Acropolis Most of the buildings now gracing the Acropolis were commissioned by Pericles in the 5th century BC. The entrance to the Acropolis is through the **Beule Gate**, a Roman arch added in the 3rd century AD. Beyond this is the **Propylaia**, the monumental gate that was the entrance in ancient times. To the south of the Propylaia is the small, graceful **Temple of Athena Nike**, which is not accessible to visitors.

Standing supreme over the Acropolis is the monument that more than any other epitomises the glory of ancient Greece: the **Parthenon**, completed in 438 BC and unsurpassed in grace and harmony. The base curves upwards slightly towards the ends, and the columns become slightly narrower towards the top, with the overall effect of making them both look straight. Above the columns are the remains of a Doric frieze. The best surviving pieces are the famous Elgin Marbles, carted off by Lord Elgin in 1801 and now in London's British Museum.

To the north is the **Erechtheion** with its much-photographed Caryatids (six maidens who support the southern portico). These are plaster casts – the originals (except for the one taken by Lord Elgin) are in the **Acropolis Museum**. The site and museum are open 8 am to 8 pm daily (entry 2000 dr).

Theatre of Dionysos The importance of theatre in the life of the Athenian city-state can be gauged from the dimensions of the enormous Theatre of Dionysos, just south of the Acropolis. Built between 342 and 326 BC on the site of an earlier theatre, it could hold 17,000 people spread over 64 tiers of seats, of which about 20 survive. It's open 8.30 am to 2.30 pm daily. Entry is 500 dr.

Ancient Agora The Agora was the marketplace of ancient Athens. Socrates spent much time here expounding his philosophy. The main monuments are the well-preserved **Temple of Hephaestus**, the 11th-century **Church of the Holy Apostles** and the reconstructed **Stoa of Attalos**, which houses the site's museum. The agora is open 8 am to 8 pm Tuesday to Sunday (to 5 pm in winter). Entry is 1200 dr.

GREECE

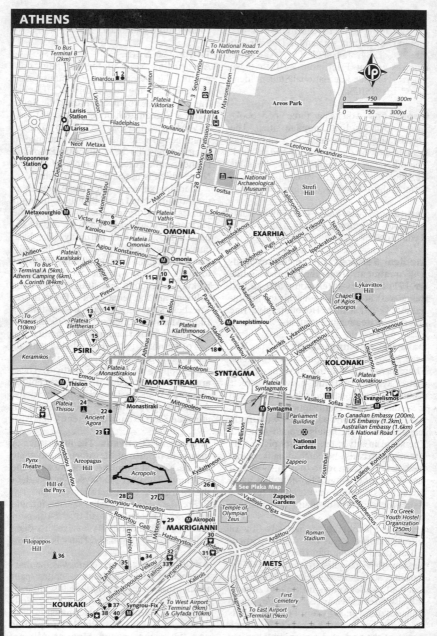

ATHENS

To Bus
Terminal B
(2km)

Einardou 1 2

To National Road 1
& Northern Greece

Larisis
Station
Larissa

Filadelphias

Peloponnese
Station

Neof Metaxa

Metaxourghio
Victor Hugo 6
Karolou

To Bus
Terminal A (5km),
Athens Camping (6km),
& Corinth (84km)

To
Piraeus
(10km)

Keramikos

Ermou
Thision

Plateia
Thisiou
Ancient
Agora

Pynx
Theatre

Hill
of the Pnyx

Filopappos
Hill

36

KOUKAKI

Aharnon
3 Septemvriou

Plateia
Viktorias
Viktorias

3
4

Mavromateon

Areos Park

0   150   300m
0   150   300yd

Leoforos Alexandras

Strefi
Hill

National
Archaeological
Museum

Tositsa

28 Oktovriou (Patission)

Mami

Plateia
Vathis

Solomou

EXARHIA

Lykavittos
Hill

Chapel
of Agios
Georgios

Kleomenous

Veranzerou
Plateia
Omonias
Omonia

Plateia
Karaïskaki

Agiou Konstantinou

OMONIA

Themistokleous

Emmanual Benaki

Zoodohou Pigis

Akadimias

Solonos

Voukourestiou

Panepistimiou

Panepistimiou

Amerikis

Plateia
Klafthmonos

Stadiou

Lykavittou

KOLONAKI

Plateia
Kolonakiou

12

11 10
9

8

13
14
16
17

15

18

Athinas

Eolou

Plateia
Eleftherias

PSIRI

Plateia
Monastirakiou

MONASTIRAKI
Monastiraki

24
22
23

25

26

Kolokotroni

Ermou
Mitropoleos

Kanaris

SYNTAGMA

Plateia
Syntagmatos
Syntagma

Vasilisis Sofias

19
20
21

Evangelismos

To Canadian Embassy (200m),
US Embassy (1.2km),
Australian Embassy (1.6km)
& National Road 1

Nikis

Filellinon

Amalias

Parliament
Building

National
Gardens

PLAKA

Kydathineon

Zappeio

See Plaka Map

28 27

Acropolis

Dionysiou Areopagitou

Areopagus
Hill

Rovertou Galli
Erethiou

Mitseon

29
30

Akropoli

MAKRIGIANNI

Hatzihrystou

Zappeio
Gardens

Temple of
Olympian
Zeus

Vasilissis Olgas

Vasileos Konstantinou

Eratosthenous

To Greek
Youth Hostel
Organization
(250m)

35

34

32
33

31

Lembesi

Roman
Stadium

METS

Ardittou

Zabrtes
Veikou

Dimitrakopoulou
Falirou
Syngrou

Kallirois

First
Cemetery

37
38 40
39

Syngrou-Fix

To West Airport
Terminal (9km)
& Glyfada (10km)

To East Airport
Terminal (9km)

GREECE

ATHENS

PLACES TO STAY	OTHER		21	UK Embassy
1 Hostel Aphrodite	2	Atlantik Supermarket	22	Stoa of Attalaos
6 Athens International	3	OTE	23	Church of the
Youth Hostel	4	Mavromateon Bus Terminal		Holy Apostles
26 Hotel Dioskouros	5	Museum Internet Café	24	Temple of Hephaestus
35 Art Gallery Pension	7	AN Club; Rembetika Boemissa	25	Stavlos
37 Marble House Pension	8	Main Post Office	27	Theatre of Dionysos
	9	Bus 091 to Airport	28	Theatre of Herodes
PLACES TO EAT	10	Marinopoulos Supermarket		Atticus
13 Bengal Garden	11	Bus 049 to Piraeus	30	Lamda Club
14 Pak Bangla Indian	12	Bus 051 to Bus Terminal A	31	Granazi Bar
Restaurant	16	Fruit & Vegetable Market	32	Porta Bar
15 Embros	17	Rembetika Stoa Athanaton	34	Hellaspar Supermarket
29 Socrates Prison	18	Vasilopoulou Delicatessen	36	Monument of Filopappos
Taverna	19	Benaki Museum	39	Tourist Police
33 To 24 Hours	20	Goulandris Museum of	40	Olympic Airways
38 Gardenia Restaurant		Cycladic & Ancient Greek Art		Head Office

Roman Agora The Romans built their agora just west of its ancient counterpart. Its principle monument is the wonderful **Tower of the Winds**, built in the 1st century BC by a Syrian astronomer named Andronicus. Each side represents a point of the compass, and has a relief carving depicting the associated wind. The site is open 8.30 am to 2.30 pm Tuesday to Sunday. Entry is 500 dr.

Temple of Olympian Zeus Begun in the 6th century BC and finally completed by the Emperor Hadrian in AD 131, this was the largest temple in Greece. Fifteen of the original 104 massive Corinthian columns (17m high with a base diameter of 1.7m) remain standing. The site is open 8.30 am to 2.30 pm Tuesday to Sunday. Entry is 500 dr.

Roman Stadium The stadium, just east of the temple, hosted the first Olympic Games of modern times in 1896. It was originally built in the 4th century BC as a venue for the Panathenaic athletic contests. The seats were rebuilt in Pentelic marble by Herodes Atticus in the 2nd century AD, and faithfully restored in 1895.

Changing of the Guard Every Sunday at 11 am traditionally costumed *evzones* (guards) marches down Vasilissis Sofias to the Tomb of the Unknown Soldier in front of the parliament building on Syntagma.

National Archaeological Museum This is the most important museum in the country, with finds from all major sites. The crowd-pullers are the magnificent, exquis-

itely detailed gold artefacts from Mycenae and the spectacular **Minoan frescoes** from Santorini (Thira), which are here until a suitable museum is built on the island. The museum is at 28 Oktovriou-Patission 44 and is open 8.30 am to 8 pm daily (from noon Monday). Entry is 2000 dr.

Benaki Museum This museum, on the corner of Vasilissis Sofias and Koumbari, houses the collection of Antoine Benaki, the son of an Alexandrian cotton magnate. The collection includes ancient sculpture, Persian, Byzantine and Coptic objects, icons, two El Greco paintings and a superb collection of traditional costumes.

Goulandris Museum of Cycladic & Ancient Greek Art This private museum at Neofytou Douka 4 was custom-built to display a fabulous collection of Cycladic art, with an emphasis on the Early Bronze Age. Particularly impressive are the beautiful marble figurines (closed Tuesday and Sunday; 1000 dr).

Lykavittos Hill Pine-covered Lykavittos is the highest of the eight hills dotted around Athens. From the summit you can enjoy all-embracing views of the city – pollution permitting. The main path to the summit starts at the top of Loukianou, or you can take the funicular railway (500 dr) from the top of Ploutarhou.

Organised Tours
The main operators – Key Tours (☎ 923 3166) at Kallirois 4, CHAT Tours (☎ 322

GREECE

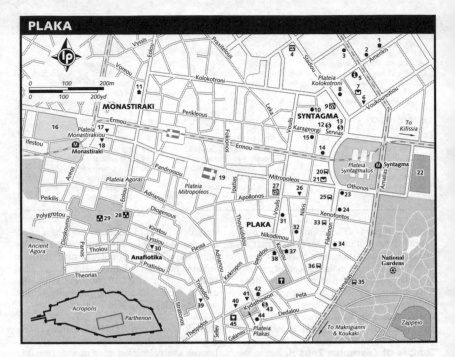

3137) at Stadiou 4, and GO Tours (☎ 322 5951), Voulis 31-33 – offer identical tours and prices, including a half-day bus tour (10,000 dr) of the major sights.

Special Events
The Athens Festival (mid-June to late September) is the city's most important cultural event, with plays, ballet and classical-music concerts. Performances are held at 9 pm in the Theatre of Herodes Atticus. For tickets contact the Athens Festival Box Office (☎ 322 1459) at Stadiou 4.

Places to Stay
Rooms fill up quickly in July and August; book ahead if possible. Plaka, the most popular area in which to stay, has good accommodation right across the price spectrum.

Camping   The closest site is *Athens Camping* (☎ 581 4114, Athinon 198), 7km west of the centre on the road to Corinth.

Hostels   There are only a few youth hostels worth knowing about. They include the excellent HI-affiliated *Athens International*

Youth Hostel (☎ 523 4170, Victor Hugo 16). Location is the only drawback; otherwise the place is almost too good to be true. Beds are 1720 dr for HI members. It costs 4200 dr to join HI or 700 dr for a daily stamp.

The women-only *XEN (YWCA;* ☎ 362 4291, fax 362 2400, Amerikis 11) has singles/doubles for 10,000/12,000 dr with private bath.

Hotels – Plaka *Student & Travellers' Inn* (☎ 324 4808, fax 321 0065, @ students-inn@ath.forthnet.gr, Kydathineon 16) is a well-run place in the heart of Plaka with spotless rooms. It has beds in large dorms for 4000 dr, four-person dorms for 4500 dr and three-person dorms for 5000 dr. There are also singles/doubles for 8000/11,000 dr. All rooms share communal bathrooms.

Hotel Dioskouros (☎ 324 8165, Pittakou 6) is a quiet place with large doubles with shared bathroom for 9000 dr.

Acropolis House Pension (☎ 322 2344, fax 322 6241, Kodrou 6-8) is a beautiful 19th-century house with rooms for 12,700/14,600 dr or 14,300/17,150 dr with private bath.

PLAKA

PLACES TO STAY	OTHER		22	Parliament Building
1 XEN	2	Pantilides Books	23	ETOS Travel
11 Hotel Tempi	3	Eleftheroudakis	24	Olympic Airways
37 Hotel Adonis	4	OTE	25	Bus 040 to Piraeus
38 Acropolis House Pension	5	EOT Tourist Office	27	Skynet Internet Centre
42 Student & Travellers' Inn	7	Parcel Post Office	28	Tower of the Winds
	8	Athens Festival Box Office	29	Roman Agora
PLACES TO EAT	9	Sofokleos.com Internet Café	31	STA Travel
6 Brazil Coffee Shop	10	Pan Express Travel	32	Compendium Books
17 Savas	12	Eurochange	33	Buses to Cape Sounion
18 Thanasis	13	National Bank of Greece	34	OSE Office
26 Furin Kazan Japanese	14	American Express		(Train Tickets)
Restaurant	15	Eleftheroudakis	35	Bus 024 to Bus Terminal B
30 Eden Vegetarian Restaurant	16	Flea Market	36	Trolley Stop for Plaka
39 Ouzeri Kouklis	19	Athens Cathedral	43	Acropole Foreign Exchange
40 Plaka Psistaria	20	Buses to Airport	44	Laundrette
41 Byzantino	21	Syntagma Post Office	45	Brettos

Hotel Adonis (☎ *324 9737, fax 323 1602, Kodrou 3)*, opposite, is a comfortable modern hotel with air-con rooms starting at 12,000/17,000 dr. It has good views of the Acropolis from the 4th-floor rooms and from the rooftop bar.

Hotels – Monastiraki The friendly, family-run *Hotel Tempi* (☎ *321 3175, fax 325 4179,* @ *tempihotel@travelling.gr, Eolou 29)* occupies a quiet pedestrian mall near Monastiraki square. The rooms at the front have balconies overlooking a square. Rates are 6000/10,000 dr with shared bath, or 11,500 dr for doubles with private bath.

Hotels – Koukaki This pleasant residential area is just south of the Acropolis.

Marble House Pension (☎ *923 4058, Zini 35A)* is a quiet place with rooms for 5500/9500 dr or 7000/11,000 dr with bath. All rooms come with bar fridge and safety box.

The comfortable *Art Gallery Hotel* (☎ *923 8376, fax 923 3025,* @ *ecotec@ otenet.gr, Erehthiou 5)* is a family-run place with rooms for 14,000/16,500 dr including balcony and bath.

From Syntagma take trolleybus No 1, 5, 9 or 18 (they travel along Veïkou) and get off at the 'Drakou' stop for Art Gallery Pension, at 'Zini' for Marble House.

Hotels – Omonia & Around There are dozens of hotels in Omonia, but most are either bordellos masquerading as cheap hotels or overpriced C-class hotels. An exception is the excellent *Hostel Aphrodite* (☎ *881*

0589, fax 881 6574, @ *hostel-aphrodite@ ath.forthnet.gr, Einardou 12)*, 10 minutes from the train stations. Dorm beds are priced from 3500 dr. There are also singles/doubles for 6000/10,000 dr with shared bath, and doubles with private bathroom for 11,000 dr. Aphrodite also offers Internet access.

Places to Eat
Plaka It's hard to beat dining out beneath the floodlit Acropolis. You do, however, pay for the privilege – particularly at the outdoor restaurants around the square on Kydathineon. The best of this bunch is *Byzantino* *(Kydathineon 20)*. One of the best deals in Plaka is the nearby *Plaka Psistaria* *(Kydathineon 28)* with a range of gyros and souvlakia.

Ouzeri Kouklis *(Tripodon 14)* is an old-style ouzeri with an oak-beamed ceiling and marble tables. It serves only mezedes (appetisers), which are brought on a large tray for you to take your pick. The whole selection, enough for four hungry people, costs 9600 dr.

One of Athens' few vegetarian spots is the long-running *Eden Vegetarian Restaurant (Lyssiou 12)*. Soya is substituted for meat in tasty vegie versions of moussaka (1500 dr) and other Greek favourites.

Monastiraki *Thanasis* and *Savas*, opposite each other at the bottom end of Mitropoleos, are great for cheap gyros and souvlaki.

Syntagma Fast food is the order of the day around busy Syntagma with an assortment of Greek and international offerings.

GREECE

Anyone suffering from a surfeit of Greek salad and souvlakis should head for the **Furin Kazan Japanese Restaurant** *(Apollonos 2)*. Noodle dishes start at 1800 dr and rice dishes at 1600 dr. It's open 11.30 am to 5.30 pm Monday to Saturday. Follow your nose to the **Brazil Coffee Shop** *(Voukourestiou 2)* for the best coffee in town.

South of the Acropolis   **To 24 Hours** *(Syngrou 44)* is a great favourite with Athenian night owls. As the name suggests, it's open 24 hours. It calls itself a *patsadakia,* which means that it specialises in *patsas* (tripe soup), but it also has a wide selection of taverna dishes.

Socrates Prison *(Mitseon 20)* is not named after the philosopher, but after the owner (also called Socrates) who reckons the restaurant is his prison. It's a stylish place with an imaginative range of mezedes starting at 850 dr and main dishes at 1500 dr.

Gardenia Restaurant *(Zini 31)* at the junction with Dimitrakopoulou, claims to be the cheapest taverna in Athens; it has moussaka for 800 dr, large beers for 400 dr and draught retsina for 650 dr. On top of this, the food is of a high standard and the service is friendly.

Psiri   The narrow streets of Psiri, just northwest of Monastiraki, are dotted with numerous trendy ouzeris, tavernas and music bars, particularly the central area between Plateia Agion Anargyron and Plateia Iroön.

Embros *(Plateia Agion Anargyron 4)* is a popular spot with seating in the square. You can choose from about 20 mezedes, including delicious cheese croquettes (1150 dr) and chicken livers wrapped in bacon (1600 dr).

The streets north of Psiri, around Plateia Eletherias, have recently been adopted by the city's Bangladeshi community and it's the area to head for a good curry and a cold beer. Try the **Bengal Garden** *(Korinis 12)* or the smarter **Pak Bangla Indian Restaurant** *(Menandrou 13)*.

Entertainment

Discos & Bars   Discos operate in central Athens only between October and April. In summer, the action moves to the coastal suburbs of Glyfada and Ellinikon.

Most bars around Plaka and Syntagma are places to avoid, especially if there are guys outside touting for customers. One place that's recommended is **Brettos** *(Kydathineon 41),* a delightful old family-run place right in the heart of Plaka. Huge old barrels line one wall, and the shelved are stocked with an eye-catching collection of coloured bottles.

Most bars in Athens have music as a main feature. Thisio is a good place to look, particularly on Iraklidon. **Stavlos** *(Iraklidon 10)* occupies an amazing old rabbit warren of a building.

Gay & Lesbian Venues   Check the streets off Syngrou, south of the Temple of Olympian Zeus. Popular spots include the long-running **Granazi Bar** *(Lembesi 20)* and the more risque **Lamda Club**, *(Lembesi 15)*. Lesbians can try the nearby **Porta Bar** *(Falirou 10)*.

Folk Dancing   **Dora Stratou Dance Company** performs at its theatre on Filopappos Hill, nightly at 10.15 pm from mid-May to October, with additional performances at 8.15 pm Wednesday. Tickets are 1500 dr. Filopappos Hill is west of the Acropolis, off Dionysiou Areopagitou – take bus No 230 from Syntagma.

Sound-and-Light Show   From early April to late October there are nightly shows in English (1500 dr) at 9 pm at the theatre on the Hill of the Pnyx (☎ 322 1459), opposite Filopappos Hill. The show is timed so that you can cross to the folk dancing.

Rembetika Clubs   Rembetika is the music of the working classes. Songs are accompanied by bouzouki, guitar, violin and accordion. **Rembetika Stoa Athanaton**, in the meat market at Sofokleous 19, is the best venue. It's open 3 to 7.30 pm and midnight to 6 am daily except Sunday, late September to mid-May. The year-round **Rembetika Boemissa** *(Solomou 19, Exarhia)* operates from 11 pm to 4 am daily (closed Monday). Neither place charges admission, but drinks are expensive.

Getting There & Away

Air   Athens' dilapidated airport, Ellinikon, is 9km south of the city. There are two main terminals: West for all Olympic Airways flights and East for other flights. An old military terminal is dusted off for charter flights in summer. A new international airport at Spata (21km east of Athens) is due to open in 2002.

The Olympic Airways head office (☎ 926 7251) is at Syngrou 96. The office at Filellinon 13, near Syntagma, is more convenient.

Bus Athens has two main intercity bus stations. The EOT has comprehensive schedules for both. Terminal A is north-west of Omonia at Kifissou 100 and has departures to the Peloponnese, the Ionian islands and western Greece. Take bus No 051 from the junction of Zinonos and Menandrou, near Omonia.

Terminal B is north of Omonia off Liossion and has departures to central and northern Greece as well as to Evia. Take bus No 024 from outside the main gate of the National Gardens on Amalias. Get off at Liossion 260 and turn right onto Gousiou – you'll see the terminal at the end of the road.

Buses for Attica leave from the Mavromateon terminal at the junction of Alexandras and 28 Oktovriou-Patission.

Train Athens has two train stations, located about 200m apart on Deligianni, 1km north-west of Omonia. Trains to the Peloponnese leave from the Peloponnese station, while international trains and trains to northern Greece leave from Larisis station.

The Larissa stop on metro Line 2 is right outside Larisis station. The Peloponnese station is across the footbridge at the southern end of Larisis station.

Buy tickets at the stations or at the OSE office at Filellinon 17, Sina 6 or Karolou 1.

Ferry See the Piraeus section for information on ferries to/from the islands.

Getting Around

To/From the Airport A 24-hour express-bus service runs between central Athens and both the East and West terminals, also calling at the charter terminal when in use.

Service No E91 leaves Stadiou, near Omonia, every 20 minutes from 6 am to 9 pm, every 40 minutes from 9 pm until 12.20 am, and then hourly through the night. It stops at Syntagma (outside the post office) five minutes later. The trip takes from 30 minutes to an hour. The return service is No E92. The fare is 250 dr (500 dr from midnight to 6 am); pay the driver. There are also express buses between the airport and Plateia Karaïskaki in Piraeus.

A taxi from the airport to Syntagma should cost 1500 dr to 2500 dr.

Bus & Trolleybus You probably won't need to use the normal blue-and-white suburban buses. Route numbers and destinations, but not the actual routes, are listed on the free EOT map. The map does, however, mark the routes of the yellow trolleybuses, making them easy to use. They run from 5 am to midnight and cost 120 dr.

There are two 24-hour bus services to Piraeus – bus No 040 leaves from the corner of Syntagma and Filellinon, and No 049 leaves from the Omonia end of Athinas. They run every 20 minutes from 6 am to midnight, and then hourly.

Tickets can be bought at kiosks and periptera. Once on a bus, validate your ticket by putting it into a machine.

Metro Although sections of the long-awaited new Metro system finally came on line in late 1999, much work remains to be done before the system becomes fully operational – supposedly before the Olympics in 2004.

Line 1 runs from Piraeus to the northern suburb of Kifissia, with useful stops at Monastiraki, Omonia (city centre) and Plateia Viktorias (National Archaeological Museum).

Line 2 has useful stops at Larissa (for the train stations), Omonia, Panepistimiou and Syntagma (city centre). Line 3 will eventually run north-east from Monastiraki to a Stavros, where it will connect with trains to the international airport at Spata.

Ticket prices are 150 dr for most journeys, including Monastiraki-Piraeus. There are ticket machines and ticket booths at all stations, and validating machines at platform entrances. The penalty for travelling without a validated ticket is 4800 dr.

Trains operate between 5 am and midnight.

Taxi Athenian taxis are yellow. Flagfall is 200 dr, with a 160 dr surcharge from ports, and train and bus stations, and 300 dr from the airport. After that it's 66 dr per km (called tariff 1), 122 dr from midnight to 5 am. There's a minimum fare of 500 dr, which should be sufficient cover most rides around the city.

Athenian taxi drivers are notorious for pulling every scam in the book. If a taxi driver refuses to use the meter, try another – and make sure it's set on the right tariff.

To hail taxis, shout your destination as they pass. They will stop if they are going your way even if the cab is already occupied. Take note of the meter when you get in, and pay the difference when you get out – plus 200 dr flagfall.

AROUND ATHENS
Piraeus Πειραιάς
☎ 01

Piraeus has been the port of Athens since classical times. These days the streets are every bit as traffic-clogged as Athens, and behind the veneer of banks and shipping offices most of Piraeus is pretty seedy. The only reason to come is to catch a ferry or hydrofoil.

Note that all train services to the Peloponnese from Athens actually start and terminate at Piraeus, although some schedules don't mention it.

Orientation & Information Piraeus consists of a peninsula surrounded by harbours. The most important of them is the Great Harbour. All ferries leave from here, as well as hydrofoil and catamaran services to Aegina and the Cyclades. There are dozens of shipping agents around the harbour, as well as banks and a post office.

Zea Marina, on the other side of the peninsula, is the main port for hydrofoils to the Saronic Gulf Islands (except Aegina). There's also an EOT office (☎ 452 2586) at Zea Marina.

Getting There & Away The metro is the fastest link between the Great Harbour and Athens. The station is close to the ferries, at the northern end of Akti Kalimassioti. There are trains every 10 minutes from 5 am to midnight.

Otherwise there are two 24-hour bus services between central Athens and Piraeus. Bus No 049 runs from Omonia to the Great Harbour, and bus No 040 runs from Syntagma to the tip of the Piraeus Peninsula.

This is the service to catch for Zea Marina – get off the bus at the Hotel Savoy on Iroön Politehniou.

Ferry If you want a cabin or to take your car on a ferry, buy an advance ticket in Athens. Otherwise, wait until you get to Piraeus; agents selling ferry tickets are thick on the ground around Plateia Karaïskaki.

The following information is a guide to ferry departures between June and mid-September. Schedules are similar in April, May and October, but are radically reduced in winter – especially to small islands. The Athens EOT has a reliable schedule, updated weekly.

Cyclades
There are daily ferries to Amorgos, Folegandros, Ios, Kimolos, Kythnos, Milos, Mykonos, Naxos, Paros, Santorini, Serifos, Sifnos, Sikinos, Syros and Tinos; two or three ferries a week to Iraklia, Shinoussa, Koufonisi, Donoussa, and Anafi; none to Andros or Kea.
Dodecanese
There are daily ferries to Kalymnos, Kos, Leros, Patmos and Rhodes; three a week to Karpathos and Kassos; and weekly services to the other islands.
North-Eastern Aegean
There are daily ferries to Chios, Lesvos (Mytilini), Ikaria and Samos; and two a week to Limnos.
Saronic Gulf Islands
There are daily ferries to Aegina, Poros, Hydra and Spetses all year.
Crete
There are two boats a day to Iraklio; daily services to Hania and Rethymno; and three a week to Agios Nikolaos and Sitia.

The various departure points are shown on the map of Piraeus. Note that there are two departure points for Crete – ask when you buy a ticket. All ferries display a clock face showing their departure time and have their ports of call written in English above their bows.

Hydrofoil & Catamaran Minoan Lines operate Flying Dolphins (hydrofoils) and high-speed catamarans to the Cyclades from early April to the end of October, and year-round services to the Saronic Gulf.

All services to the Cyclades and Aegina leave from Great Harbour, near Plateia Themistokleous. Some services to Poros,

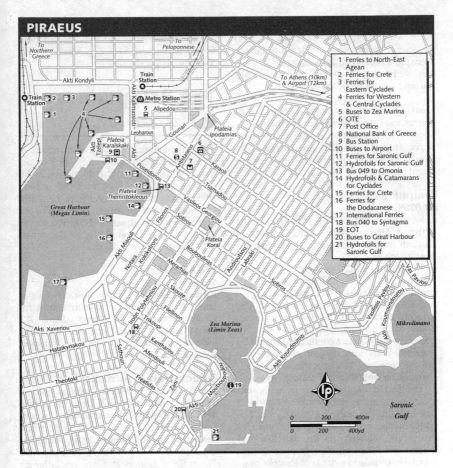

PIRAEUS

To Northern Greece
Akti Kondyli
Train Station
Akti Kalimassioti
To Peloponnese
To Athens (10km) & Airport (12km)

Train Station
Metro Station
Alipedou
Leoharous
Gounari
Plateia Ipodamias

Akti Tzelepi
Plateia Karaïskaki
Akti
Poseidonos
Antistaseos
Karaoli
Tsamadou

Plateia Themistokleous
Vasileos Georgiou
Filonos
Sotiros
Plateia Korai
Bouboulinas
Andronikou
Labraki
Sotiros

Great Harbour (Megas Limin)

Akti Miaouli
Notara
Kolokotroni
Merarhias
Skouze
Iroön Polytehniou
Filellinon
Trikoupi
Kantharou
Afendouli
Freatidas
Zani
Akti Koundourioti

Zea Marina (Limin Zeas)

Akti Xaveriou
Hatzikyriakou
Theotoki

Vas Pavlou
Vasilios Pavlou
Koumoundourou
Mikrolimano

Saronic Gulf

0   200   400m
0   200   400yd

1 Ferries to North-East Agean
2 Ferries for Crete
3 Ferries for Eastern Cyclades
4 Ferries for Western & Central Cyclades
5 Buses to Zea Marina
6 OTE
7 Post Office
8 National Bank of Greece
9 Bus Station
10 Buses to Airport
11 Ferries for Saronic Gulf
12 Hydrofoils for Saronic Gulf
13 Bus 049 to Omonia
14 Hydrofoils & Catamarans for Cyclades
15 Ferries for Crete
16 Ferries for the Dodacanese
17 International Ferries
18 Bus 040 to Syntagma
19 EOT
20 Buses to Great Harbour
21 Hydrofoils for Saronic Gulf

Hydra and Spetses also leave from here, but most leave from Zea Marina. For the latest departure information, pick up a timetable from Pan Express Travel (☎ 324 8704), in the arcade at Voulis 7, Syntagma in Athens. There are also offices quayside at Great Harbour and at Zea Marina.

Saronic Gulf Islands
Νησιά του Σαρωνικού
The Saronic Gulf islands are the closest island group to Athens. Accommodation can be hard to find between mid-June and September, and on weekends year-round.

Aegina (Αίγινα) is the closest island to Athens and is popular with day-trippers. Many make for the lovely **Temple of Aphaia**, a well-preserved Doric temple 12km east of Aegina town. Buses to the small resort of Agia Marina can drop you at the site.

Poros (Πόρος) has some reasonable beaches, but not much else to get excited about. It's popular with Brits, but it's hard to work out why.

Hydra (Ύδρα) is the island with the most style; it has a fine natural harbour surrounded by gracious stone mansions stacked up around rocky hillsides. The main attraction is peace and quiet – there are no motorised vehicles on the island. Accommodation is expensive, but of a high standard. *Hotel Dina* (☎ 52 248) has singles/doubles overlooking the harbour for 10,000/12,000 dr, less on weekdays.

Pine-covered **Spetses** (Σπέτσες) is perhaps the most beautiful island in the group.

GREECE

It also has the best beaches, so it's packed with package tourists in summer. The old harbour in Spetses town is a delightful place to explore. *Orloff Apartments* (☎ 72 246) has well-equipped studios behind the old harbour for 6000/10,000 dr.

Getting There & Away Ferries to all four islands leave from Great Harbour in Piraeus. All hydrofoil services to Aegina leave from Great Harbour. Services to Poros, Hydra and Spetses are split between Great Harbour and Zea Marina.

Delphi Δελφοί
☎ 0265
Like so many of Greece's ancient sites, the setting at Delphi – overlooking the Gulf of Corinth from the slopes of Mt Parnassos – is stunning.

In 6th century BC, Delphi had become the Sanctuary of Apollo and thousands of pilgrims came to consult the oracle (always a peasant woman of 50 years or more). The pilgrim, after sacrificing a sheep or goat, would ask a question, and the priestess' incoherent mumblings were then translated by a priest. Wars were fought, voyages embarked upon, and business transactions undertaken on the strength of these prophecies.

The **Sacred Way** leads up from the entrance of the site to the **Temple of Apollo**. It was here that the oracle supposedly sat. The path continues to the theatre and stadium. Opposite this sanctuary is the **Sanctuary of Athena** and the much photographed **tholos**, which is a columned rotunda of Pentelic marble. It was built in the 4th century BC and is the most striking of Delphi's monuments.

The site, 1.5km east of modern Delphi, is open 7.30 am to 7.15 pm weekdays and 8.30 am to 2.45 pm weekends. Entry is 1200 dr. There are five buses a day to Delphi from Athens (2900 dr, three hours).

Orientation & Information The bus station, phone office, a bank and the tourist office are all on modern Delphi's main street, Vasileon Pavlou. The tourist office (☎ 82 900), at No 44, is open 7.30 am to 2.30 pm weekdays.

Places to Stay & Eat *Apollon Camping* (☎ 82 750) is 1.5km west of modern Delphi. *Hotel Tholos* (☎/fax 82 268, Apollonos

31) has rooms for 5000/9000 dr and is open March to November and on Friday and Saturday in winter. The adjacent *Taverna Vakhos* has good-value meals.

The Peloponnese
Η Πελοπόννησος

The Peloponnese, the southern extremity of the rugged Balkan peninsula, is rich in history. The principal site is Olympia, birthplace of the Olympic Games. Other ancient sites – Epidaurus and Mycenae in the northeast – are all within striking distance of the pretty Venetian town of Nafplio. In the south are the magical old Byzantine towns of Monemvassia and Mystras.

PATRAS Πάτρα
☎ 061
Patras is Greece's third-largest city (population 153,300) and the principal port for ferries to Italy and the Ionian islands. It's not particularly exciting and most travellers hang around only long enough for transport connections.

Orientation & Information
The city is easy to negotiate and is laid out on a grid stretching uphill from the port to the *kastro* (castle). Most services – including ferry offices – are along the waterfront, known as Othonos Amalias in the middle of town and Iroön Politehniou to the north. The train station is in town on Othonos Amalias, and the bus station is close by.

Customs and the EOT office (☎ 361 653) are clustered together inside the port fence off Iroön Politehniou. The 24-hour tourist police office (☎ 220 902) is opposite EOT.

For Internet access, head inland to the Rocky Racoon Music Bar, Gerokostopoulou 56. It's open 9 am to 3 am daily.

Places to Stay & Eat
Most travellers head for *Pension Nicos* (☎ 623 757), up from the waterfront on the corner of Patreos and Agiou Andreou 121. It has doubles with shared facilities for 6500 dr and singles/doubles with bathroom for 4000/7000 dr.

The C-class *Hotel Rannia* (☎ 220 114, fax 220 537, Riga Fereou 53), facing

Plateia Olgas, has comfortable air-con rooms with TV for 10,000/15,000 dr – 8000/12,000 dr outside high season.

Europa Centre (Othonos Amalias 10) is a convenient cafeteria-style place close to the international ferry dock. It has a range of taverna dishes as well as spaghetti (starting at 900 dr) and a choice of vegetarian meals (900 dr).

Getting There & Away

The best way to travel to Athens is by train. The buses may be faster, but they drop you a long way from the city centre at Terminal A on Kifissou. This can be a real hassle if you're arriving in Athens after midnight – when there are no connecting buses. The trains take you close to the city centre, five minutes from Syntagma on the metro.

Bus There are buses to Athens (3650 dr, three hours) every 30 minutes. There are also 10 buses a day to Pyrgos (for Olympia).

Train There are nine trains a day to Athens. Four are slow trains (1580 dr, five hours) and five are express intercity trains (2580 dr, 3½ hours). The last intercity train leaves at 6 pm. Trains also run south to Pyrgos.

Ferry There are daily ferries to Kefallonia (3450 dr, four hours), Ithaki (3500 dr, six hours) and Corfu (6000 dr, 10 hours). Services to Italy are covered in the Getting There & Away section at the start of this chapter. Ticket agents line the waterfront.

DIAKOFTO-KALAVRYTA RAILWAY

This spectacular rack-and-pinion line climbs up the deep gorge of the Vouraikos River from the small coastal town of Diakofto to the mountain resort of **Kalavryta**, 22km away. It is a thrilling journey, with dramatic scenery all the way. There are four trains a day in each direction.

Diakofto is 45 minutes east of Patras by train.

NAFPLIO Ναύπλιο
☎ 0752

Nafplio ranks as one of Greece's prettiest towns. The narrow streets of the old quarter are filled with elegant Venetian houses and neoclassical mansions.

There are terrific views of the old town and the surrounding coast from the hill-top **Palamidi Fortress**. The climb is strenuous – there are almost 1000 steps. The fortress is open 8 am to 6.45 pm daily. Entry is 800 dr.

Orientation & Information

The municipal tourist office (☎ 24 444) is at 25 Martiou, opposite the OTE office. The bus station is on Syngrou, the street that separates the old town from the new. For Internet access, head to the Diplo Internet Cafe, Bouboulinas 43.

Places to Stay & Eat

The cheapest beds are at *Hotel Economou* (☎ 23 955, Argonafton 22), which has two rooms set up as dorms for backpackers. It charges 2000 dr per person. Argonafton runs off Argous, the road to Argos.

Most people prefer to stay in the old part of town, where there are numerous signs for domatia. Singles/doubles start at 4000/6000 dr. The stylish *Hotel Byron (☎ 22 351, fax 26 338, @ byronhotel@otenet.gr, Platanos 2)* has beautifully furnished singles for 13,000 dr, and doubles range from 16,000 dr to 22,000 dr.

Taverna Ellas, on the old town's main square, Plateia Syntagmatos, has tasty staples priced from 1200 dr. For a good night out, try *Taverna Paleo Arhontiko (☎ 22 449, corner Ypsilandou & Sofroni)*. Reservations are essential on Friday and Saturday nights. Reckon on 6000 dr for two, plus wine.

Getting There & Away

There are hourly buses to Athens (2650 dr, 2½ hours) via Corinth, as well as services to Argos (for Peloponnese connections), Mycenae and Epidaurus.

EPIDAURUS Επίδαυρος

The huge well-preserved **Theatre of Epidaurus** is the crowd-puller at this site, but don't miss the more peaceful **Sanctuary of Asclepius** nearby. Epidaurus was regarded as the birthplace of Asclepius, the god of healing. The setting alone would have been enough to cure many ailments. The site is open 8 am to 4.30 pm daily (from noon Monday). Entry is 1500 dr. You can enjoy the theatre's astounding acoustics first hand during the Epidaurus Festival from mid-June to mid-August.

GREECE

There are two buses a day from Athens (2250 dr, 2½ hours), three a day from Nafplio (600 dr, 40 minutes). Extra buses run during the festival.

MYCENAE Μυκήνες

Mycenae was the most powerful influence in Greece for three centuries until about 1200 BC. The rise and fall of Mycenae is shrouded in myth, but the site was settled as early as the 6th millennium BC. Described by Homer as 'rich in gold', Mycenae's entrance, the **Lion Gate**, is Europe's oldest monumental sculpture.

Excavations have uncovered the palace complex and a number of tombs. The so-called **Mask of Agamemnon**, discovered by Heinrich Schliemann in 1873, now holds pride of place at the National Archaeological Museum in Athens along with other finds from the site.

The site is open 8 am to 7 pm daily; admission is 1500 dr. There are three buses a day from Nafplio (600 dr, one hour).

SPARTA Σπάρτη
☎ 0731

The bellicose Spartans sacrificed all the finer things in life to military expertise and left no monuments of any real consequence. Ancient Sparta's forlorn ruins lie amid olive groves at the northern end of town. Modern Sparta is a neat and rather unspectacular town, but a convenient base from which to visit Mystras.

Orientation & Information

Sparta is laid out on a grid system. The main streets are Paleologou, which runs north-south through the town, and Lykourgou, which runs east-west. The municipal tourist office (☎ 24 852) is in the town hall on the main square, Plateia Kentriki. For Internet access, try the Cosmos Club Internet Cafe, Palaeolgou 34.

Places to Stay & Eat

Camping Mystras (☎ 22 724), on the Sparta-Mystras road, is open year-round.

Back in town, the family-run *Hotel Cecil* (☎ 24 980, fax 81 318, Palaeologou 125) has singles/doubles with bathroom and TV for 8000/10,000 dr.

Restaurant Elysse (Palaeologou 113) offers Lakonian specialities like *chicken bar-*

douniotiko (1300 dr), which is chicken cooked with onions and fetta cheese.

Getting There & Away

The bus terminal is at the eastern end of Lykourgou. There are 10 buses a day to Athens (3900 dr, 3¼ hours), three to Monemvassia (1900 dr, 2½ hours) and two to Kalamata (1200 dr, 2½ hours). There are also frequent buses to Mystras (250 dr, 30 minutes).

MYSTRAS Μυστράς

The ruins at Mystras, 7km from Sparta, spill from a spur of Mt Taygetos, crowned by a mighty fortress built by the Franks in 1249. The streets of Mystras are lined with palaces, monasteries and churches, most of them dating from 1271 to 1460, when the town was the effective capital of the Byzantine Empire. The buildings are among the finest examples of Byzantine architecture in the whole of Greece and contain many superb frescoes.

The site is open 8 am to 7 pm daily. Entry is 1200 dr, which includes the museum (closed Monday). Take a taxi or hitch a ride to the upper Fortress Gate and work your way down. Take some water.

MONEMVASSIA Μονεμβασία
☎ 0732

Monemvassia is no longer an undiscovered paradise, but mass tourism hasn't lessened the impact of this extraordinary old town. Monemvassia occupies an outcrop of rock that rises dramatically from the sea. It was separated from the mainland by an earthquake in AD 375 and access is by a causeway from the village of Gefyra.

From the causeway, a road curves around the base of the rock for about 1km until it comes to a narrow L-shaped tunnel. You emerge, blinking, in the Byzantine town. The cobbled main street is flanked by stairways leading to a network of stone houses. Steps (signposted) lead to the ruins of a 16th-century **fortress**. The views are great, and there is the added bonus of being able to explore the Byzantine **Church of Agia Sophia**, perched precariously on the edge of the cliff.

There's no EOT office but the staff at Malvasia Travel (☎ 61 752), near the bus station, are helpful.

Places to Stay & Eat

Camping Paradise (☎ 61 123) is 3.5km to the north.

There is no budget accommodation in Monemvassia, but there are *domatia* in Gefyra as well as cheap hotels. The basic *Hotel Akrogiali (☎ 61 360),* opposite the National Bank of Greece, has rooms with shower for 6000/9000 dr. If your budget permits, treat yourself to a night in one of the traditional settlements in Monemvassia. The pick of them is *Malvasia Guest Houses (☎ 61 113, fax 61 722).* Doubles are priced from 12,000 dr including breakfast.

Taverna Nikolas is the best place to go for a hearty meal in Gefyra. *Matoula* in Monemvassia has a great setting overlooking the sea.

Getting There & Away

There are four buses a day to Athens (5800 dr, 5½ hours).

In July and August there are hydrofoils to Piraeus via the Saronic Gulf islands.

GYTHIO Γύθειο
☎ 0731

Gythio, once the port of ancient Sparta, is an attractive fishing town at the head of the Lakonian Gulf. It is the gateway to the rugged Mani peninsula to the south.

The main attraction at Gythio is the picturesque islet of **Marathonisi**, linked to the mainland by a causeway. According to mythology it is ancient Cranae, where Paris (a prince of Troy) and Helen (the wife of Menelaus of Sparta) consummated the love affair that sparked the Trojan War. An 18th-century tower on the islet has been turned into a **museum** of Mani history.

Places to Stay & Eat

Gythio's *camping grounds* are dotted along the coast south of town and can be reached on any bus heading to Areopoli. There are numerous *domatia* on the waterfront near the main square. They include *Xenia Rooms to Rent (☎ 22 719),* opposite the causeway to Marathonisi. It has singles/doubles with bathroom for 4000/6000 dr.

The waterfront is lined with countless fish tavernas with very similar menus. For a real treat, head inland to the tiny *General Store & Wine Bar (☎ 24 113, Vasileos Georgiou 67).* You'll find an unusually imaginative

menu featuring dishes like orange and pumpkin soup (600 dr) and fillet of pork with black pepper and ouzo (2800 dr).

Getting There & Away

There are five buses a day to Athens (4350 dr, 4¼ hours) via Sparta (750 dr, one hour). Services to the Inner Mani include five buses to Areopoli (500 dr, 30 minutes), two to Gerolimenas (1150 dr, two hours) and one to the Diros caves (700 dr, one hour).

There are daily ferries to Kythira (1600 dr, two hours) in summer, continuing twice a week to Kastelli-Kissamos on Crete (5100 dr, seven hours). Tickets are sold at Golden Ferries (☎ 22 996, fax 22 410), opposite the tourist office on Vasileos Pavlou.

THE MANI

The Mani is divided into two regions, the Lakonian (inner) Mani in the south and Messinian (outer) Mani in the north-west below Kalamata.

The Lakonian Mani is wild and remote, its landscape dotted with the dramatic stone tower-houses that are a trademark of the region. They were built as refuges from the clan wars of the 19th century. The best time to visit is in spring, when wildflowers briefly enliven the barren countryside.

The region's principal village, **Areopoli**, is about 30km south-west of Gythio. Just south of here are the magnificent **Diros Caves**, where a subterranean river flows (3500 dr). **Gerolimenas**, 20km farther south, is a tiny fishing village built around a sheltered bay. **Vathia**, a village of towers built on a rocky peak, is 11km south-east of Gerolimenas.

The Messinian Mani runs north along the coast from Itilo to Kalamata. The beaches here are some of the best in Greece, set against the dramatic backdrop of the Taygetos mountains. **Itilo** is split by a ravine that is the traditional dividing line between inner and outer Mani. The picturesque coastal village of **Kardamyli**, 37km south of Kalamata, is the starting point for walks up the **Taygetos Gorge**. It takes about 2½ hours to walk to the deserted Monastery of the Saviour. Strong footwear is essential and take plenty of water.

Places to Stay & Eat

The cheapest accommodation in Areopoli can be found at *Perros Bathrellos Rooms*

GREECE

(☎ 0733-51 205) on Kapetan Matapan, the main street of the old town, above *Taverna Barbar Petros*. Rooms are 4000/6000 dr.

In Gerolimenas, *Hotel Akrotenaritis* *(☎ 0773-54 205)* has air-cond singles/doubles with bathroom for 5000/10,000 dr, while *Hotel Akrogiali (☎ 0773-54 204)* has an excellent restaurant overlooking the pebble beach.

Kardamyli has lots of domatia. *Olivia Koumounakou (☎ 0721-73 326),* opposite the post office, has doubles with bath for 7000 dr. There's also a communal kitchen.

Getting There & Around

Areopoli is the focal point of the Inner Mani's bus network. There are two buses a day to the Diros Caves and Gerolimenas, and occasional buses to Vathia. There are also five buses a day to Gythio.

Getting to Kalamata involves changing buses at Itilo, 11km north of Areopoli. There are also three buses a day to Itilo, and two buses a day from Itilo to Kalamata via Kardamyli.

OLYMPIA Ολυμπία
☎ 0624

The site of ancient Olympia lies 500m beyond the modern town, surrounded by the green foothills of Mt Kronion. In ancient times, Olympia was a sacred place of temples, priests' dwellings and public buildings, as well as being the venue for the quadrennial Olympic Games. The first Olympics were staged in 776 BC, reaching the peak of their prestige in the 6th century BC. The city-states were bound by a sacred truce to stop fighting for three months and compete.

The Olympia site, one of the highlights of the Peloponnese, is dominated by the immense, ruined **Temple of Zeus**, to whom the games were dedicated. The site is open 8 am to 7 pm weekdays and 8.30 am to 3 pm weekends. Entry is 1200 dr. The museum (1200 dr), north of the archaeological site, keeps similar hours. Allow a whole day to see both.

The efficient tourist office on Olympia's main street is open daily year-round and also changes money.

Places to Stay & Eat

Camping Diana (☎ 22 314), 250m west of town, has good facilities and a pool. The

youth hostel (☎ 22 580, Praxitelous Kondyli 18) has dorm beds for 1700 dr, including hot showers. *Pension Achilleys (☎ 22 562, Stefanopoulou 4)* has rooms with shared bath for 4000/7000 dr.

Getting There & Away

There are four buses a day from Athens (5900 dr, 5½ hours). There are also regular buses and trains to Olympia from Pyrgos, 24km away on the coast.

Northern Greece

IGOUMENITSA Ηγουμενίτσα
☎ 0665

Igoumenitsa, opposite Corfu, is the main port of north-western Greece. Few people stay any longer than it takes to buy a ticket out. The bus station is on Kyprou. To get there from the ferries, follow the waterfront (Ethnikis Antistasis) north for 500m and turn up El Venizelou. Kyprou is two blocks inland and the bus station is on the left.

Places to Stay & Eat

If you get stuck, there are *domatia* around the port. The central *Hotel Egnatias (☎ 23 648, Eleftherias 1)* has comfortable rooms with bath for 8500/11,500 dr.

Bilis (Agion Apostolon 15), opposite the Corfu ferry quay, is handy for a quick meal.

Getting There & Away

Bus services include nine a day to Ioannina (1900 dr, two hours) and four to Athens (8850 dr, 8½ hours).

Ferries run every hour to Corfu (1400 dr, 1½ hours). In summer there are daily ferries to the Italian ports of Brindisi and Bari. Ticket agents are opposite the port.

IOANNINA Ιωάννινα
☎ 0651

Ioannina is the largest town in Epiros, sitting on the western shore of Lake Pamvotis. The **old town** juts out into the lake on a small peninsula. Inside the impressive fortifications lies a maze of winding streets flanked by traditional Turkish houses. The **nisi** (island) is a serene spot in the middle of the lake, with four monasteries set among the trees. Ferries (200 dr, 10 minutes) leave from just north of the old town.

Orientation & Information

The town centre is around Plateia Dimokratias. Averof runs north-east from here towards the old town, while Dodonis runs south and becomes the road to Athens. The main bus terminal is 300m north of Plateia Dimokratias along Markou Botsari.

The helpful EOT office (☎ 25 086) is 100m along Dodonis, set back on a small square at Napoleon Zerva 2. Robinson Travel (☎ 29 402), 8th Merarhias Gramou 10, specialises in treks in the Zagoria region.

For Internet access, try the Giannena Club, 100m from the tourist office at Stoa Saka 30-32.

Places to Stay

Camping Limnopoula (☎ 25 265) is on the lakeside 2km north of town. The cheapest hotel is *Agapi Inn* (☎ 20 541, Tsirigoti 6), near the bus station. Basic rooms cost 5000/7000 dr. Next door is the co-owned *Hotel Paris* with more comfortable rooms for 6000/9000 dr.

Getting There & Away

There are 12 buses a day to Athens (7700 dr, seven hours), nine to Igoumenitsa (1950 dr, 2½ hours), five to Thessaloniki (6500 dr, seven hours) and three to Trikala via Kalambaka (3050 dr, 3½ hours). The road from Ioannina to Kalambaka across the Pindos mountains is one of Greece's most spectacular drives.

ZAGORIA & VIKOS GORGE
☎ 0653

The Zagoria region covers a large expanse of the Pindos mountains north of Ioannina. It's a wilderness of raging rivers, crashing waterfalls and deep gorges. The remote villages that dot the hillsides are famous for their impressive grey-slate architecture.

The fairytale village of **Monodendri** is the starting point for treks through the dramatic Vikos Gorge, with its awesome sheer limestone walls. It's a strenuous 7½-hour walk from Monodendri to the twin villages of **Megalo Papingo** and **Mikro Papingo**. The trek is popular and the path is clearly marked. Ioannina's EOT office has information.

Places to Stay

There are some wonderful places to stay, but none of them come cheap.

The options in Monodendri include the lovely, traditional *Monodendri Pension & Restaurant* (☎ 71 300), with doubles for 9000 dr. The immaculate *Pension Gouris (mobile/cellphone ☎ 094-789 909)* in Tsepelovohas has doubles for 12,000 dr. *Xenonas tou Kouli (☎/fax 41 115)* is one of several options in Megalo Papingo. Rates start at 12,000 dr for doubles. The owners are official EOS guides. The only rooms in Mikro Papingo are at *Xenonas Dias* (☎ 41 257), a beautifully restored mansion with doubles for 11,000 dr.

Getting There & Away

Buses to the Zagoria leave from the main bus station in Ioannina. There are buses to Monodendri at 6 am and 4.15 pm weekdays; to Tsepelovo at 6 am and 3 pm Monday, Wednesday and Friday; and to the Papingo villages at 6 am and 2.30 pm Monday, Wednesday and Friday.

METEORA Μετέωρα
☎ 0432

Meteora, just north of the town of Kalambaka, is an extraordinary place. The massive, sheer columns of rock that dot the landscape were created by wave action millions of years ago. Perched precariously atop these seemingly inaccessible outcrops are monasteries that date back to the late 14th century.

There were once monasteries on each of the 24 pinnacles, but only five are still occupied. They are **Megalou Meteorou** (closed Tuesday and Wednesday), **Varlaam** (closed Friday), **Agiou Stefanou**, **Agias Triados**, **Agiou Nikolaou** and **Agias Varvaras Rousanou** (closed Wednesday). Most are open 9 am to 1 pm and 3 to 6 pm. Entry to each is 400 dr.

Meteora is best explored on foot, following the old paths where they exist. Allow a whole day to visit all of the monasteries and take food and water. Dress modestly; women must wear skirts or trousers that reach below their knees, men must wear long trousers, and arms must be covered.

Places to Stay & Eat

Kastraki, 2km from Kalambaka, is the best base for visiting Meteora. *Vrachos Camping* (☎ 22 293), on the edge of the village, is an excellent site. There are dozens of *domatia* in Kastraki, prices range from

4000/6000 dr. *Hotel Sydney* (☎/*fax 23 079*), on the road into town from Kalambaka, has comfortable doubles with bath for 9000 dr.

In Kalambaka, *Koka Roka Rooms* (☎ *24 554*), at the beginning of the path to Agia Triada, is a popular travellers place. Doubles with bath are 8000 dr; the *taverna* downstairs is good value. Telephone for a lift from the bus or train station.

Getting There & Away
There are daily buses to Kalambaka from Trikala and Ioannina. Local buses shuttle constantly between Kalambaka and Kastraki; five a day continue to Megalou Meteorou.

There were no trains between Kalambaka and Volos at the time of writing because of upgrading work on the line. Normally, these trains would provide useful connections with trains from Athens and Thessaloniki at Paleofarsalos.

THESSALONIKI Θεσσαλονίκη
☎ 031
Thessaloniki (population 750,000), also known as Salonica, is Greece's second-largest city and a sophisticated place with good restaurants and a busy nightlife. It was once the second city of Byzantium, and there are some magnificent Byzantine churches, as well as a scattering of Roman ruins.

Orientation & Information
Plateias Eleftherias and Aristotelous, both on Nikis, are the main squares. The city's most famous landmark is the White Tower at the eastern end of Nikis. The train station is on Monastiriou, the westerly continuation of Egnatia, beyond Plateia Dimokratias.

The EOT office (☎ 271 888), Plateia Aristotelous 8, is open 8 am to 8 pm weekdays and to 2 pm Saturday. The tourist police (☎ 554 871) are at Dodekanisiou 4 on the 5th floor, open 7.30 am to 11 pm daily.

The main post office is at Aristotelous 6 and the OTE telephone office is at Karolou Dil 27. You can check email at the Globus Internet Café, Amynta. It's closed from mid-July to mid-August.

Things to See
The **archaeological museum**, at the eastern end of Tsimiski, houses a superb collection of treasures from the royal tombs of Philip II (1500 dr). The **White Tower** (no longer white) now houses a **Byzantine Museum**, with splendid frescoes and icons. It's open Tuesday to Sunday 8 am to 2.30 pm; admission is free.

Places to Stay
The *youth hostel* (☎ 225 946, Alex Svolou 44) has dorm beds for 2000 dr (10% less for HI members). The dorms are locked from 11 am to 6 pm, and there's a midnight curfew. Take bus No 10 from outside the train station to the 'Kamara' stop.

The best budget hotel is the family-run *Hotel Acropol* (☎ 536 170, Tantalidou 4), off Egnatia. Clean rooms with shared bath are 6000/9000 dr, though most of the time it charges a bargain 5000 dr per room. *Hotel Atlas* (☎ 537 046, Egnatia 40) charges 6000/9000 dr and has good doubles with bath for 12,000 dr. Just around the corner is the quiet *Hotel Averof* (☎ 538 498, Leontos Sofou 24) with pleasant rooms for 5000/8000 dr.

Places to Eat
Ta Nea Ilysia, opposite the Hotel Averof on Leontos Sofou, is a popular place with main dishes priced from 1050 dr. The colourful *O Loutros Fish Taverna* occupies an old Turkish bathhouse near the flower market on Komninon. Most dishes here cost 2000 dr to 3000 dr.

Entertainment
Young people frequent the many bars along the waterfront before hitting the clubs. A good area to check out is Ta Ladadika, near the ferry quay. There's live bouzouki and folk music at 11 pm every night at *Show Avantaz*, opposite the Turkish consulate at Agiou Dimitriou 156.

Getting There & Away
Bus Buses to Athens (8700 dr, 7½ hours), Igoumenitsa (8200 dr, eight hours) and Trikala (4000 dr, 5½ hours) leave from Monastiriou 65 and 67; buses to Alexandroupolis leave from Koloniari 17, behind the train station. Buses to Litihoro (for Mt Olympus) leave from Promitheos 10. These cost 1850 dr and take 1½ hours.

The OSE has two buses a day to Athens from the train station, as well as international services to İstanbul, Sofia and Korça (Albania).

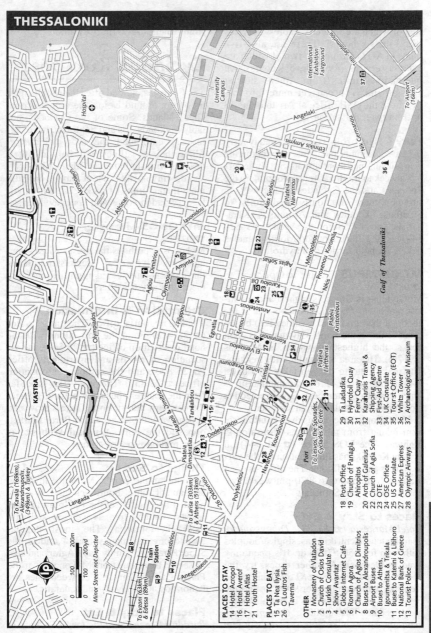

THESSALONIKI

KASTRA

Hospital

University Campus

International Exhibition Fairground

To Airport (16km)

To Kavala (169km), Alexandroupolis (349km) & Turkey

To Evzoni (63km) & Edessa (89km)

To Larisa (303km) & Athens (513km)

Train Station

Langada

Gulf of Thessaloniki

Port

To Lesvos, the Sporades, Cyclades & Crete

Minor Streets not Depicted

0   100   200m
0   100   200yd

PLACES TO STAY
14 Hotel Acropol
16 Hotel Averof
17 Hotel Atlas
21 Youth Hostel

PLACES TO EAT
15 Ta Nea Ilysia
26 O Loutros Fish Taverna

OTHER
1   Monastery of Vlatadon
2   Church of Osios David
3   Turkish Consulate
4   Show Avantaz
5   Globus Internet Café
6   Roman Agora
7   Church of Agios Dimitrios
8   Buses to Alexandroupolis
9   Airport Buses
10 Buses to Athens, Igoumenitsa & Trikala
11 Buses to Katerini & Litihoro
12 National Bank of Greece
13 Tourist Police
18 Post Office
19 Church of Panagia Ahiropitos
20 Arch of Galerius
22 Church of Agia Sofia
23 OTE
24 OSE Office
25 US Consulate
27 American Express
28 Olympic Airways
29 Ta Ladadika
30 Hydrofoil Quay
31 Ferry Quay
32 Karaharisis Travel & Shipping Agency
33 First-Aid Centre
34 UK Consulate
35 Tourist Office (EOT)
36 White Tower
37 Archaeological Museum

GREECE

Train There are nine trains a day to Athens, five of which are intercity express services (8250 dr, six hours). There are also five trains to Alexandroupolis, two of which are express services (4990 dr, 5½ hours). All international trains from Athens stop at Thessaloniki. You can get more information from the OSE office at Aristotelous 18 or from the train station.

Ferry & Hydrofoil There's a Sunday ferry to Lesvos, Limnos and Chios throughout the year. In summer there are at least three ferries a week to Iraklio (Crete), stopping in the Sporades and the Cyclades on the way. In summer there are daily hydrofoils to Skiathos, Skopelos and Alonnisos. Karaharisis Travel & Shipping Agency (☎ 524 544, fax 532 289), Koundourioti 8, handles tickets for both ferries and hydrofoils.

MT OLYMPUS Ολυμπος Ορος
☎ 0352
Mt Olympus is Greece's highest and mightiest mountain. The ancients chose it as the abode of their gods and assumed it to be the exact centre of the Earth. Olympus has eight peaks, the highest of which is Mytikas (2917m). The area is popular with trekkers. The main route to the top takes two days, overnighting at one of four mountain refuges (open May to September). Good protective clothing is essential, even in summer.

Most people base themselves at **Litohoro**, 5km inland from the Athens-Thessaloniki highway. The EOS office (☎ 81 944) on Plateia Kentriki has information on the various treks and conditions. The office is open 9 am to 1 pm and 6 to 8.30 pm weekdays, and 9 am to 1 pm Saturday.

Places to Stay & Eat
Hotel Markesia (☎ 81 831, Dionyssou 5), near Plateia Kentriki, has singles/doubles with bath for 6500/7500 dr. It's open only June to October. At other times, try the cheery *Hotel Enipeas* (☎ 81 328) on Plateia Kentriki, with doubles for 9000 dr and the best views of Mt Olympus in town. Rooms are priced at 8000/10,000 dr. *Olympus Taverna*, on Agiou Nikolaou, serves tasty fare at reasonable prices.

Getting There & Away
There are 10 buses a day to Litihoro from

Thessaloniki (1800 dr, 1½ hours) and three from Athens (7500 dr, 5½ hours).

Cyclades Κυκλάδες

The Cyclades, named after the rough circle they form around Delos, are quintessential Greek islands. Some of the Cyclades, notably Mykonos, Ios and Santorini, have vigorously embraced the tourist industry, filling their coastlines with bars and their beaches with sunlounges. Others, like Anafi and the tiny islands east of Naxos, are little more than clumps of rock, each with a village, secluded coves and very few tourists.

MYKONOS Μύκονος
☎ 0289
Mykonos is perhaps the most visited – and most expensive – of all Greek islands. It has the most sophisticated nightlife and is a mecca for gay travellers.

Orientation & Information
There is no tourist office. The tourist police (☎ 22 482) are at the port, along with the hotel reservation office (☎ 24 540), the association of rooms and apartments office (☎ 26 860), and the camping information office (☎ 22 852). The post office is not far from the southern bus station, the OTE near the northern bus station. There's slow and expensive Internet access at Porto Market, opposite the port. A useful Web site is www.mykonosgreece.com.

Things to See
The capital and port is Mykonos town – a tableau of chic boutiques and brightly painted houses. Here, the **folklore museum** (closed Sunday; free) is well stocked with local memorabilia. The most popular beaches are the mainly nude **Paradise**, the **Super Paradise** (mainly gay), **Agrari** and **Elia**, all served by caïque from Mykonos town and Platys Gialos. The less crowded ones are **Panormos**, **Kato Livadi** and **Kalafatis**.

Places to Stay & Eat
Paradise Beach Camping (☎ 22 852, fax 24 350, ✉ paradise@paradise.myk.forthnet.gr) charges 1500 dr per person and 1100 dr per tent. Two-person beach cabins are 10,000 dr; four-person cabins are 22,000 dr (with

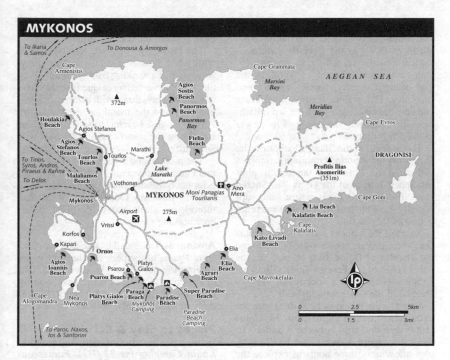

MYKONOS

To Ikaria & Samos
To Donousa & Amorgos
Cape Armenistis
Cape Grammata
AEGEAN SEA
Agios Sostis Beach
Mersini Bay
372m
Panormos Beach
Panormos Bay
Meridias Bay
Cape Evros
Houlakia Beach
Agios Stefanos
Ftelia Beach
Marathi
DRAGONISI
Agios Stefanos Beach
Tourlos Beach
Tourlos
Lake Marathi
Profitis Ilias Anomeritis (351m)
To Tinos, Syros, Andros, Piraeus & Rafina
To Delos
Malaliamos Beach
Vothonas
MYKONOS
Moni Panagias Tourlianis
Ano Mera
Cape Goni
Mykonos
Lia Beach
Kalafatis Beach
Airport
275m
Cape Kalafatis
Vrissi
Korfos
Kato Livadi Beach
Kapari
Ornos
Elia
Agios Ioannis Beach
Psarou
Platys Gialos
Elia Beach
Psarou Beach
Agrari Beach
Cape Mavrokefalas
Cape Alogomandra
Nea Mykonos
Platys Gialos Beach
Paraga Beach
Mykonos Camping
Paradise Beach
Super Paradise Beach
Paradise Beach Camping
To Paros, Naxos, Ios & Santorini
0   2.5   5km
0   1.5   3mi

bath). **Mykonos Camping** (☎ 24 578), near Platys Gialos Beach, charges 2000/ 1100 dr per person/tent. Minibuses for these sites usually meet the ferries.

Rooms fill up quickly in summer, so it's wise to succumb to the first domatia owner who accosts you. Outside of July and August you can negotiate some excellent bargains. Kalogera is a good street to seek out lodgings – there are a number of mid-range hotels here, including **Hotel Philippi** (☎ 22 294, fax 24 680), offering simple doubles/triples with bath for 17,000/22,000 dr. Nearby, **Rooms Chez Maria** (☎ 22 480) has attractive singles/doubles for 15,000/20,000 dr.

Busy **Niko's Taverna**, near the Delos quay, offers good seafood. **Sesame Kitchen**, next to the maritime museum on Matogianni, serves vegetarian dishes. **Antonini's Taverna**, on Taxi Square, is popular with locals for its good-value traditional fare.

Entertainment

Troubador (formerly the Down Under Bar) and the nearby **Skandinavian Bar & Disco** are popular, and **Rhapsody** in Little Venice plays jazz and blues. **Club Paradiso**, 300m above Paradise Beach, has all-night raves starting at 3 am. Entry is 5000 dr. **Porta**, **Kastro Bar**, **Icaros** and **Manto** are popular gay haunts. **Pierro's** is the place for late-night dancing.

Getting There & Away

There are flights from Mykonos to Athens (19,100 dr), Santorini (15,400 dr) and in summer to Rhodes and Thessaloniki. The Olympic Airways office (☎ 22 490) is on Plateia Louka, by the southern bus station.

There are ferries daily to Mykonos from Piraeus (4800 dr, six hours). From Mykonos there are daily ferries to most Cycladic Islands, and weekly services to Crete, the North-Eastern Aegean and the Dodecanese. For ferry schedules contact the port police (☎ 22 218).

Getting Around

The northern bus station is near the port, behind the OTE office. It serves Agios Stefanos, Elia, Kalafatis and Ano Mera. The southern bus station, south-east of the windmills, serves Agios Yiannis, Psarou, Platys Gialos, Ornos and Paradise Beach.

GREECE

DELOS Δήλος

Just south-east of Mykonos, the uninhabited island of Delos is the Cyclades' archaeological jewel. According to mythology, Delos was the birthplace of Apollo – the god of light, poetry, music, healing and prophecy. Delos flourished as a religious and commercial centre from the 3rd millennium BC, reaching the height of its power in the 5th century BC.

To the north of the island's harbour is the **Sanctuary of Apollo**, containing temples dedicated to him, and the much photographed **Terrace of the Lions**. The **Sacred Lake** (dry since 1926) is where Leto supposedly gave birth to Apollo. The **museum** is east of this section.

South of the harbour is the **Theatre Quarter**, where private houses were built around the **Theatre of Delos**. East of here are the **Sanctuaries of the Foreign Gods**. Climb Mt Kynthos (113m) for a spectacular view of Delos and the surrounding islands.

Entry to the island is 1200 dr. There are excursion boats to Delos from Mykonos (1900 dr round trip) between 9 and 10.15 am daily except Monday, but boat schedules allow only three hours to explore the site. There's a cafeteria on the island.

PAROS Πάρος
☎ 0284

Paros is an attractive island and has some of the finest beaches in the Cyclades.

Orientation & Information

Paros' main town and port is Parikia, on the west coast. Agora, also known as Market St, is Parikia's main commercial thoroughfare running south-west from the main square, Plateia Mavrogenous (opposite the ferry terminal). The OTE is on the south-west waterfront; turn right from the ferry pier. The post office is also on the waterfront, but to the north of the pier. Wired Cafe is on Market St; Memphis.net is just north of the quay. A good Web site is www.parosweb.com.

Things to See

One of the most notable churches in Greece is Parikia's **Panagia Ekatontapyliani**, which features a beautiful, highly ornate interior (no shorts allowed).

Petaloudes, 8km from Parikia, is better known as the Valley of the Butterflies. In summer, huge swarms of the creatures almost conceal the copious foliage.

The charming village of **Naoussa**, filled with white houses and labyrinthine alleyways, is still a working fishing village. Popular beaches served by caïque from Naoussa include **Kolimvythres**, with bizarre rock formations, and the mainly nude **Monastiri**. Paros' longest beach, **Hrysi Akti** (Golden Beach) on the south coast, is popular with windsurfers.

The picturesque villages of **Lefkes**, **Marmara** and **Marpissa** are all worth a visit and offer good walking opportunities. The Moni Agiou Antoniou (Monastery of St Anthony), on a hill above Marpissa, offers breathtaking views.

Antiparos This small island, less than 2km from Paros, has superb beaches but is becoming too popular for its own good. One of the chief attractions is the **cave**, considered one of Europe's most beautiful (open daily in summer only; 600 dr).

Places to Stay & Eat

Paros has a number of camping grounds: *Koula Camping* (☎ 22 081), *Parasporas* (☎ 22 268) and *Krios Camping* (☎ 21 705) are near Parikia. *Antiparos Camping* (☎ 61 221) is on Agios Giannis Theologos Beach, just north of Antiparos village. Alternatively, head for Naoussa, which has *Naoussa Camping* (☎ 51 595) and *Surfing Beach* (☎ 51 013). There's an information office at Naoussa's bus terminal that can help with finding rooms.

In Parikia, *Rooms Mike* (☎ 22 856) is popular with backpackers. Doubles/triples cost 12,000/15,000 dr, with use of a small kitchen. Walk 50m left from the pier and it's next to Memphis.net cybercafe. The very friendly owners of *Rooms Rena* (☎/fax 21 427) offer spotless doubles/triples with bath, balcony and fridge for 13,000/16,000 dr; turn left from the pier then right at the ancient cemetery.

There are countless tavernas and cafes lining the waterfront and surrounding the main square. If you're after a cheap, quick fix, *Zorba's* on the main square does a tasty gyros. Just off Market St is the oddly named *Happy Green Cow*, dishing up good vegetarian fare. For something more upmarket, try *I Trata* or *Porphyra*, on opposite sides of the ancient cemetery, north of the pier. Both offer excellent seafood at reasonable prices.

There are a few good bars tucked away in the old town, and the far southern end of Parikia's waterfront has numerous clubs.

Getting There & Away
Flights to/from Athens cost 18,900 dr. From Paros there are daily ferries to Piraeus (4900 dr, five hours), frequent ferries to/from Naxos, Ios, Santorini and Mykonos, and less frequent ones to Amorgos and Astypalea, then across to the Dodecanese and the North-Eastern Aegean. For the port police call ☎ 21 240.

Getting Around
The bus station is 100m north of the ferry quay. There are frequent buses to Aliki, Pounta, Naoussa, Lefkes, Piso Livadi and Hrysi Akti. For Petaloudes take the Aliki bus. In summer there are hourly excursion boats to Antiparos from Parikia, or you can catch a bus to Pounta and a ferry across.

NAXOS Νάξος
☎ 0285
Naxos, the biggest, greenest and perhaps most beautiful island of the archipelago, is popular but large enough to allow you to escape the hordes.

Orientation & Information
Naxos town (Chora), on the west coast, is the island's capital and port. There is no EOT, but the privately owned Naxos Tourist Information Centre (NTIC; ☎ 25 201, fax 25 200), opposite the quay, makes up for this, offering numerous services including room-finding and luggage storage.

The OTE is on the waterfront, 150m past the National Bank of Greece. The post office is three blocks farther on. Internet access is available at Rental Centre on Plateia Protodikiou, which is also known as Central Square.

Things to See
The winding alleyways of **Naxos town**, lined with immaculate whitewashed houses, clamber up to the crumbling 13th-century kastro (castle) walls. The well-stocked archaeological museum is here (closed Monday; 600 dr).

After the town beach of Agios Georgios, south beyond the harbour-front, sandy **beaches** continue southwards as far as Pyrgaki Beach and become progressively less crowded.

On the north coast, **Apollonas** has a rocky beach and a pleasant sheltered bay. If you're curious about the *kouros* statues, you can see the largest one, 10.5m long and dating from the 7th century BC, just outside of Apollonas, lying abandoned and unfinished in an ancient marble quarry.

The gorgeous **Tragaea region** is a vast Arcadian olive grove with Byzantine churches and tranquil villages. **Filoti**, the largest settlement, perches on the slopes of **Mt Zeus** (1004m). It takes three hours to climb the trail to the summit.

Places to Stay & Eat
Naxos' three camping grounds are *Camping Naxos* (☎ 23 500), 1km south of Agios Georgios Beach; *Camping Maragas* (☎ 24 552), Agia Anna Beach; and *Camping Apollon* (☎ 24 117), 700m from Agios Prokopios Beach.

Dionyssos Youth Hostel (☎ 22 331) is the best budget choice, with dorm beds for 2000 dr, doubles/triples with private bath for 4000/5000 dr and cooking facilities for guests. It's signposted from Agiou Nikodemou, also known as Market St. Book through NTIC. *Pension Irene* (☎ 23 169), south-east of the town centre, has doubles for around 14,000 dr.

Popi's Grill, on the waterfront, serves good-value souvlaki for 1700 dr. *Taverna Galini*, out by Pension Irene, is a favourite with locals and serves up delicious seafood. In the winding alleys around the kastro, you'll find *Manolis Garden* serving excellent Greek fare. If you're hankering for curry in this part of the world, follow the signs for *Dolfini*.

Nightlife is centred around the southern end of the waterfront.

Getting There & Away
Naxos has daily flights to Athens (20,000 dr), daily ferries to Piraeus (4900 dr, six hours) and good ferry connections with most islands in the Cyclades. At least once a week there are boats to Crete, Thessaloniki, Rhodes and Samos. For the port police, call ☎ 22 300.

GREECE

Getting Around

Buses run to most villages and the beaches as far as Pyrgaki. The bus terminal is in front of the quay. There are four buses daily to Apollonas (1200 dr) and five a day to Filoti (450 dr).

IOS Ιος
☎ 0286

Ios epitomises the Greece of sun, sand and sex; in high season it's the *enfant terrible* of the islands. Come here if you want to bake on a beach all day and drink all night. Yet it's not only young hedonists who holiday on Ios – the island is also popular with the older set (anyone over 25), but the two groups tend to be polarised. The young stay in 'the village' and others at the port. Non-ravers should avoid the village from June to September.

Ios has a tenuous claim to being Homer's burial place. His tomb is supposedly in the island's north, although no-one seems to know exactly where.

Gialos Beach, at the port, is OK. **Koumbara Beach**, a 20-minute walk west of Gialos, is less crowded and mainly nudist. **Milopotas**, 1km east, is a superb long beach. Vying with Milopotas for best beach is **Manganari**, on the south coast, reached by bus or, in summer, by excursion boats from the port.

Orientation & Information

The capital, Ios town ('the village', also known as the Hora), is 2km inland from the port of Ormos. The bus terminal in Ormos is straight ahead from the ferry quay on Plateia Emirou. To walk from Ormos to Ios town, turn left from Plateia Emirou, then immediately right and you'll see the stepped path leading up to the right after 100m. The walk takes about 20 minutes.

There is no EOT tourist office, but information is available at the port from travel agencies, most of which offer free luggage storage and use of safes to reduce thefts. An increasing number of venues – from hotels (Francesco's, Far Out) and bars (Fun Pub) to travel agents – offer Internet access.

Places to Stay & Eat

Far Out Camping (☎ 91 468, fax 92 303, ✉ farout@otenet.gr), on Milopotas Beach, is a seriously slick operation, attracting up to

2000 people a night in summer. Camping costs 1600 dr per person; tents can be hired for 400 dr. Bungalows cost from 2500 dr to 4000 dr per person. There are loads of features – pools, bar, restaurants, mini market, travel agency, safe boxes and sports facilities. If you prefer a quieter campsite, try *Camping Stars* (☎ 91 302), also in Milopotas, or *Camping Ios* (☎ 91 050) in Ormos.

There is a wonderful view of the bay from *Francesco's* (☎/fax 91 223, ✉ fragesco@otenet.gr) in the village. Dorm beds cost 2500 dr; doubles/triples with private bath are 10,000/12,000 dr. It's a lively meeting place with a bar and terrace.

In the village, *Taverna Lord Byron*, *Pithari Taverna* and *Fun Pub* are the most popular eateries. For a seafood treat, head to *Filippos* on the road between the port and Koumbara Beach.

Entertainment

The party crowd reckons the port is dull, while the older set thinks the village is crazy, so take your pick. At night the tiny central square has so many party-goers that it can take 30 minutes to get from one side to the other. Surprisingly, bars in the square charge competitive prices.

Scorpions, *Dubliners* and *Sweet Irish Dreams* are perennial favourites; *Blue Note* and *Red Bull* are also popular.

Getting There & Around
Ios has daily connections with Piraeus (5300 dr, seven hours), and there are frequent ferries to the major Cycladic islands. For schedules contact the port police (☎ 91 264).

There are regular buses between the port, the village and Milopotas Beach.

SANTORINI (THIRA)
Σαντορίνη (Θήρα)
☎ 0286
Around 1450 BC, the volcanic heart of Santorini exploded and sank, leaving an extraordinary landscape – a malevolently steaming core almost encircled by sheer cliffs. It's possible that the catastrophe destroyed the Minoan civilisation, but neither this theory nor the claim that the island was part of the lost continent of Atlantis have been proven.

Santorini is one of the most popular islands in the Cyclades, with a good mix of beaches, archaeological sites and chaotic bars. The main drawback is a lack of budget accommodation.

Orientation & Information
The capital, Fira, perches on top of the caldera (submerged crater) on the west coast. The port of Athinios is 12km away. There is no EOT or tourist police, but the helpful Dakoutros Travel Agency (☎ 22 958, 24 286, fax 22 686) sells boat and plane tickets and can arrange accommodation and excursions. It's in the southern part of the main square (Plateia Theotokopoulou), opposite the taxi station. The post office is a block south of the taxi station; Lava Internet Cafe is just north of the square and the OTE is 200m farther on.

Things to See & Do
Fira The commercialism of Fira has not quite reduced its all-pervasive dramatic aura. The best of the town's museums is the exceptional new **Museum of Prehistoric Thera** (closed Monday; 1200 dr), with wonderful displays of well-labelled artefacts predominantly from ancient Akrotiri. To get there, walk south from the main square, past the bus station and take the next street on the right. The **Megaron Gyzi Museum**, behind the Catholic monastery, houses local memorabilia, including fascinating photographs of Fira before and immediately after the 1956 earthquake.

Around the Island Excavations in 1967 uncovered the remarkably well preserved Minoan settlement of **Akrotiri** (closed Monday; 1200 dr). Less impressive than Akrotiri, the site of **Ancient Thira** is still worth a visit for the stunning views. **Moni Profiti Ilia**, a monastery (with folk museum) built on the island's highest point, can be reached along a path from Ancient Thira; the walk takes about one hour.

Santorini's **beaches** are of black volcanic sand that becomes very hot, making a beach mat essential. Kamari and Perissa get crowded – those near Oia and Monolithos are quieter.

From Imerovigli, just north of Fira, a 12km coastal path leads to the picturesque village of **Oia** (pronounced **ee**-ah), famed for postcard-perfect sunsets. On a clear day there are breathtaking views of neighbouring islands.

Of the surrounding islets, only **Thirasia** is inhabited. At Palia Kameni you can bathe in hot springs, and on Nea Kameni you can clamber around on volcanic lava.

Places to Stay & Eat
Beware of the aggressive accommodation owners who meet boats and buses and claim that their rooms are in Fira when in fact they're in Karterados. Ask to see a map to check their location.

Camping Santorini (☎ 22 944), 1km east of the main square, has many facilities including a restaurant and swimming pool. The cost is 1000 dr per person and 1000 dr per tent. *Thira Hostel* (☎ 23 864), 200m north of the square, sleeps as many as 145. It has dorms with up to 10 beds for 3000 dr per person, roof beds for 2000 dr, plus doubles/triples with private bath for 10,000/12,000 dr. It also has a cheap *restaurant*.

There are plenty of rooms to rent near the main square and on the road running east towards Camping Santorini, including *Pension Petros* (☎ 22 573), offering basic but pleasant doubles for 17,000 dr. The location

GREECE

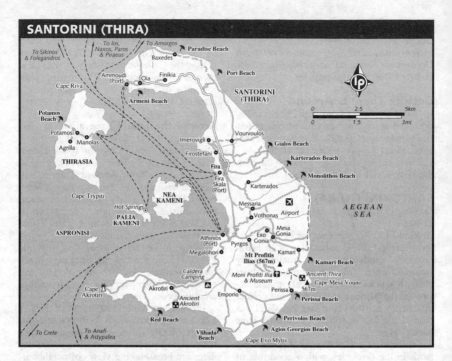

SANTORINI (THIRA)

can be a bit noisy, however. A short walk north-east of the centre of town will take you to a quiet rural area with plenty of domatia. *Pension Stella* has doubles/triples for 16,000/19,000 dr; *Pension Horizon* charges 17,000/20,000. To book, ring Dakoutros Travel (see Orientation & Information earlier in this section).

Toast Club, on the square, is a fast-food operation (pizza and pasta) popular with budget travellers. *Restaurant Stamna*, just east of the square, has good-value daily specials. *Naoussa*, not far from the cable-car station, is excellent. The food served by other restaurants in this area does not always represent good value for money, but you may not mind given the million-dollar view.

Bars and clubs are clustered along one street, Erythrou Stavrou. From the main square, facing north, turn left at George's Snack Corner then take the first right.

Getting There & Away
Flights cost 22,200 dr to Athens, 22,900 dr to Rhodes, 15,400 dr to both Mykonos and Iraklio (Crete). The Olympic Airways office (☎ 22 493) is 200m south of the hospital.

Daily ferries to Piraeus cost 5900 dr and take around nine hours. There are frequent connections with Crete, Ios, Paros and Naxos. Ferries travel less frequently to/from Anafi, Sikinos, Folegandros, Sifnos, Serifos, Kimolos, Milos, Karpathos and Rhodes. For schedules contact the port police (☎ 22 239).

Getting Around
There are daily boats from Athinios and Fira Skala to Thirasia and Oia. Palia Kameni and Nea Kameni can only be visited on excursions from Fira.

Large ferries use Athinios port, where they are met by buses. Small boats use Fira Skala, which is served by donkey or cable car (1000 dr each); otherwise it's a clamber up 600 steps.

The bus station is just south of Fira's main square. Frequent buses go to Oia, Kamari, Perissa, Akrotiri and Monolithos.

Crete Κρήτη

All of Crete's large towns are on the north coast, and it's here that the package tourist industry thrives – Crete has the dubious distinction of playing host to a quarter of all visitors to Greece.

The island was the birthplace of Minoan culture, Europe's first advanced civilisation, which flourished from 2800 to 1450 BC. Later, Crete passed from the warlike Dorians to the Romans, and then to the Genoese, who in turn sold it to the Venetians. Under the Venetians, Crete became a refuge for artists, writers and philosophers; the young Cretan painter Domenikos Theotokopoulos moved to Spain and won immortality as El Greco.

Getting There & Away

The international airport is at Iraklio, Crete's capital. Hania and Sitia have domestic airports. There are several flights a day from Athens to Iraklio (21,000 dr) and Hania (21,300 dr), and weekly flights to Sitia (23,000 dr). In summer there are three flights a week to Rhodes from Iraklio and two to Santorini.

Kastelli-Kissamos, Rethymno, Hania, Iraklio, Agios Nikolaos and Sitia have ferry ports. Ferries travel most days to Piraeus from Hania (5900 dr), Rethymno and Iraklio (7000 dr); less frequently from Agios Nikolaos and Sitia (7600 dr, 4½ hours). There are at least two boats a week from Iraklio to Santorini and on to other Cycladic Islands. In summer there's at least one ferry a week from Iraklio to Rhodes (6200 dr, 11 hours) via Kassos and Karpathos and at least three a week from Agios Nikolaos to Rhodes via Sitia, Kassos and Karpathos. In summer, a twice-weekly boat sails from Iraklio to Cyprus via Rhodes and then on to Israel.

Getting Around

Frequent buses run between towns on the north coast, and less frequently to the south coast and mountain villages. See the long-distance bus Web site www.ktel.org for information. Parts of the south coast are without roads, so boats are used to connect villages.

IRAKLIO Ηράκλειο
☎ 081

Iraklio, Crete's capital, lacks the charm of Rethymno or Hania; its old buildings are virtually swamped by modern apartment blocks. Don't leave town without visiting the excellent **archaeological museum** (1500 dr), opposite the EOT.

Orientation & Information

Iraklio's two main squares are Plateia Venizelou and Plateia Eleftherias; Dikeosynis and Dedalou run between them. The main thoroughfare is 25 Avgoustou, leading from the waterfront to Plateia Venizelou. The EOT (☎ 228 225) and Olympic Airways (☎ 229 191) are on Plateia Eleftherias. The tourist police (☎ 283 190) are at Dikeosynis 10.

Most of the city's banks are on 25 Avgoustou. The central post office is on Plateia Daskalogiani, the OTE is just north of El Greco Park. You can access the Internet at Netcafe, on 1878, or Istos Cyber Cafe, Malikouti 2. There is a laundrette and left-luggage storage area at Washsalon, Handakos 18.

Places to Stay & Eat

Beware of taxi drivers who tell you that the pension of your choice is dirty, closed or has a bad reputation. They're paid commissions by the big hotels.

There are few domatia in Iraklio and not many budget accommodation options. **Rent Rooms Hellas** (☎ 288 851, Handakos 24) is a hostel popular with backpackers despite the number of draconian rules posted in the rooftop reception and bar. Singles/doubles/triples are 4500/6000/75000 dr; dorm beds are 2000 dr. As a last resort there's the **youth hostel** (☎ 286 281, Vyronos 5) off 25 Avgoustou, where beds in small, crowded dorms cost 1800 dr.

Hotel Lena (☎ 223 280, Lahana 10) is one of the nicer budget hotels. Singles/doubles with shared facilities cost 6500/9000 dr; with private bath 8500/11,000 dr.

Plateia Venizelou has countless fast-food outlets and cafe-bars, while Theosadaki, the little street between 1866 and Evans, is lined with tavernas. One of the best is **Giakoumis Taverna** (Theosadaki 5). **Ippokampos Ouzeri**, on the waterfront just west of 25 Avgoustou, offers a huge range of good-value mezedes and is always packed. Arrive early to get a table. **Pagopeion**, by Agios Titos church, has good food with imaginative titles, and the toilets alone are worth a visit. There's a bustling, colourful **market** on 1866.

GREECE

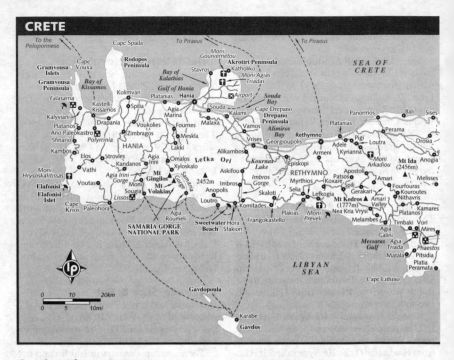

CRETE

Getting There & Away

For air and ferry information, see Getting There & Away at the start of the Crete section. For the port police, call ☎ 244 912.

Bus station A, just inland from the new harbour, serves eastern Crete (Agios Nikolaos, Ierapetra, Sitia, Malia and the Lassithi Plateau). Bus station B, 50m beyond the Hania Gate, serves the south (Phaestos, Matala, Anogia). The Hania/Rethymno terminal is opposite bus station A.

KNOSSOS Κνωσσός

Knossos, 8km south-east of Iraklio, is the most famous of Crete's Minoan sites and is the inspiration for the myth of the Minotaur. According to legend, King Minos of Knossos was given a bull to sacrifice to Poseidon, but instead decided to keep it. This enraged Poseidon, who punished the king by causing his wife Pasiphae to fall in love with the beast. The result of this bizarre union was the Minotaur (half-man, half-bull) who lived in a labyrinth beneath the king's palace, feeding on youths and maidens.

In 1900 the ruins of Knossos were uncovered by Arthur Evans. Archaeologists tend to disparage Evans' reconstruction, however, the buildings – courtyards, private apartments, baths and more – give a good idea of what a Minoan palace may have looked like.

A whole day is needed to see the site, which is open 8 am to 7 pm daily, April to October; entry is 1500 dr. Arrive early to avoid the crowds. Iraklio's local bus No 2 goes to Knossos every 10 minutes from bus station A (260 dr) and also stops on 25 Avgoustou.

HANIA Χανιά
☎ 0821

Lovely Hania, the old capital of Crete, has a harbour with crumbling, softly hued Venetian buildings. It oozes charm; unfortunately it also oozes package tourists. The **archaeological museum**, at Halidon 21, is housed in the former Venetian Church of San Francesco; the Turks have since converted it into a mosque (closed Monday, 500 dr). The **fortress** separates the old harbour from the new.

Orientation & Information

Hania's bus station is on Kydonias, a block south-west of Plateia 1866, the town's main

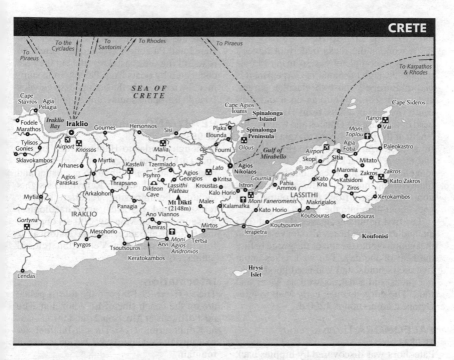

CRETE

square. Halidon runs from here to the old harbour. Hania's port is at Souda, 10km from town. The airport is on the Akrotiri Peninsula, 14km from Hania.

The EOT office (☎ 92 943) is at Kriari 40, 20m from Plateia 1866. The central post office is at Tzanakaki 3 and the OTE is next door. Internet access is available at Vranas Studios on Ag Deka, or from e-Kafe.com, Theotokopoulou 53.

Places to Stay & Eat

The nearest camping ground is *Camping Hania* (☎ 31 138), 3km west of town, right on the beach. Take a Kalamaka bus from Plateia 1866. The budget choice is *Pension Fidias* (☎ 52 494, Sarpaki 6), behind the Orthodox cathedral, which offers beds in three-bed dorms for 2500 dr. Doubles, some with bath, start at 5500 dr. *Hotel Meltemi* (☎ 92 802, Agelou 2), next to the fortress, is run down but has character and a fantastic location. Doubles start at 7000 dr. *Rooms for Rent George* (☎ 88 715, Zambeliou 30), one block from the waterfront, has singles/doubles/triples for 4000/7000/9000 dr.

The lively central *food market* houses a few inexpensive tavernas. For al fresco dining, try *Tsikoydadiko* (*Zambeliou 31*) or the classy *Tholos Restaurant* (*Agion Deka 36*). Both serve good Greek cuisine at reasonable prices. Another good choice is the excellent *Tamam* (*Zambeliou 51*).

The authentic *Cafe Crete* (*Kalergon 22*) has live Cretan music every evening, and there are numerous cafes and bars around the harbour, particularly near the fortress.

Getting There & Away

For air and ferry information, see Getting There & Away at the start of the Crete section. Olympic Airways (☎ 40 268) is at Tzanakaki 88. For the port police at Souda, call ☎ 89 240.

There are frequent buses to Iraklio, Rethymno and Kastelli-Kissamos, and less frequent ones to Paleohora, Omalos, Hora Sfakion, Lakki and Elafonisi leaving from the bus station on Kydonias. Buses for Souda (the port) leave frequently from outside the food market, and for beaches just west of Hania from the south-eastern corner of Plateia 1866.

GREECE

SAMARIA GORGE
Φαράγγι της Σαμαριάς
It's a wonder the rocks underfoot haven't worn away completely as so many people trample through the Samaria Gorge. But it is one of Europe's most spectacular gorges, and worth seeing. You can do it independently by taking a bus from Hania to the head of the gorge at Omalos and walking the length of the gorge (16km) to Agia Roumeli, from where you take a boat to Hora Sfakion and then a bus back to Hania. Or you can join one of the daily excursions from Hania (many companies also offer an 'easy' option, which starts from Agia Roumeli and goes about 4km into the gorge).

The first public bus leaves Hania at 6.15 am and excursion buses also leave early so that people get to the top of the gorge before the heat of the day. The walk takes about five or six hours, and you need good walking shoes and a hat, as well as water and food. The gorge is open early May to mid-October; admission is 1200 dr.

PALEOHORA Παλαιοχώρα
☎ 0823
Paleohora was discovered by hippies back in the 1960s and from then on its days as a tranquil fishing village were numbered. It remains a relaxing, if overrated, resort favoured by backpackers. There's a helpful tourist office three blocks south of the bus stop.

Farther east, along Crete's south-west coast, are the resorts of Sougia, Agia Roumeli, Loutro and Hora Sfakion; of these, Loutro is the most appealing and the least developed.

Places to Stay & Eat
Camping Paleohora (☎ 41 120) is 1.5km north-east of town, near the pebble beach. *Homestay Anonymous (☎ 41 509)* is a great place for backpackers. It has clean rooms set around a small courtyard; singles/doubles here go for 4000/5500 dr and there is a communal kitchen. *Oriental Bay Rooms (☎ 41 076)*, at the northern end of the pebble beach (on the road to the camping ground), has comfortable doubles/triples with bath for 7000/8000 dr.

There's a very good vegetarian restaurant, *The Third Eye*, close to the sandy beach.

Getting There & Away
There are at least three buses a day between Hania and Paleohora (1600 dr). There's no road linking the coastal resorts, but they are connected by boats from Paleohora in summer. Twice weekly the boat goes to Gavdos Island (Europe's southernmost point).

RETHYMNO Ρέθυμνο
☎ 0831
Although similar to Hania in its Venetian and Turkish buildings (not to mention its package tourists), Rethymno is smaller and has a distinct character. Rethymno's sights include the imposing **Venetian fortress** (closed Monday; 900 dr), an **archaeological museum** (closed Monday; 500 dr) opposite the fortress entrance, and an **historical & folk art museum** on Vernardou (closed Sunday; 600 dr).

Information
The EOT (☎ 29 148) and the tourist police are on the beach side of El Venizelou. The post office is at Moatsou 21 and the OTE is at Kountouriotou 28. There's Internet access upstairs at Galero cafe, beside Rimondi fountain.

Places to Stay & Eat
Elisabeth Camping (☎ 28 694) is on Myssiria Beach, 3km east of town. The *youth hostel (☎ 22 848, Tombazi 45)* is a friendly place; beds are 1800 dr in dorms or on the roof. *Olga's Pension (☎ 53 206, Souliou 57)*, in the heart of town, is colourful and eclectically decorated, with rooms spread off a network of terraces bursting with greenery. Doubles/triples with private bath are 9000/12,000 dr.

Stella's Kitchen, beneath Olga's Pension, offers hearty breakfasts and cheap snacks. *Taverna Kyria Maria (Diog Mesologiou 20)*, tucked behind the Rimondi fountain, is a cosy family-run taverna. *Gounakis Restaurant & Bar (Koroneou 6)* has live Cretan music every evening and reasonably priced food. The area east of Rimondi fountain is a good place to investigate. The *Punch Bowl* is here, on Arabatzoglou.

Getting There & Away
For ferries, see Getting There & Away at the start of the Crete section. For the port police, call ☎ 22 276.

GREECE

Frequent buses run to Iraklio (1800 dr) and Hania (1600 dr), and less frequent ones to Agia Galini, Arkadi Monastery and Plakias.

SITIA Σητεία
☎ 0843
Skirting a commanding hotel-lined bay with a long sandy beach, Sitia is an attractive town with considerably less tourists.

Orientation & Information
The municipal tourist office is on the waterfront just before the town beach. The post office is on Dimokratou, off El Venizelou, and the OTE is on Kapetan Sifis, which runs inland from Plateia El Venizelou, the main square. The ferry port is a bit of a hike; it's signposted from the main square.

Places to Stay & Eat
It's possible to camp in the grounds of the *youth hostel (☎ 22 693, Therissou 4)*, on the road to Iraklio, for 1200 dr. Dorm beds here cost 1500 dr; doubles/triples with shared facilities are 3500/5000 dr. The immaculate *Hotel Arhontiko (☎ 28 172, Kondylaki 16)* has doubles/triples for 5000/6500 dr. To find it, walk towards the ferry dock along El Venizelou, turn left up Filellinon and then right into Kondylaki.

The waterfront is buzzing with tavernas and bars; inland you'll find *Kali Kardia Taverna (Foundalidhou 20)* and *O Mixos (Kournarou 15)*. Both are excellent value and popular with locals.

Getting There & Away
For air and ferry information, see Getting There & Away at the start of the Crete section. To contact the port police, call ☎ 22 310.

There are at least three buses daily to Ierapetra and five to Iraklio via Agios Nikolaos. In summer there are two or three buses daily to Vaï (for its lovely palm-tree-fringed beach) and Zakros.

Dodecanese
Δωδεκάνησα

More verdant and mountainous than the Cyclades and with comparable beaches, the islands of the Dodecanese offer more than natural beauty – here more than anywhere

else you get a sense of Greece's proximity to Asia. There are 16 inhabited islands in the group; the most visited are Rhodes, Kos, Patmos and Symi.

RHODES Ρόδος
☎ 0241
According to mythology, the sun god Helios chose Rhodes as his bride and bestowed light, warmth and vegetation upon her. The blessing seems to have paid off, for Rhodes produces flowers in profusion and enjoys more sunny days than most Greek Islands.

Medieval **Rhodes City**, the island's capital and port, is the 'must see' of the Dodecanese. Almost everything of interest lies within its 12m-thick town walls, considered one of the finest surviving examples of medieval fortifications.

The main port is east of Rhodes City's old town, and north of here is Mandraki Harbour, supposed site of the Colossus of Rhodes, a giant bronze statue of Apollo (built 292-280 BC) that was one of the Seven Wonders of the World. The statue stood for a mere 65 years before being toppled by an earthquake.

Information
The EOT office (☎ 23 255, @ eot-rodos@ otenet.gr) is on the corner of Makariou and Papagou; the tourist police (☎ 27 423) are next door. In summer there is also a municipal tourist office on Plateia Rimini, open longer hours than the EOT. The main post office is on Mandraki and the OTE is at Amerikis 91. Rock Style cybercafe is at Dimokratias 7, just south of the old town, and Minoan Internet Cafe is at Iroon Politechnou 13 (new town).

Things to See & Do
Rhodes City In the old town, the 15th-century Knights' Hospital houses an impressive **archaeological museum** (closed Monday; 800 dr). Particularly noteworthy is the exquisite *Aphrodite of Rhodes* statue.

Odos Ippoton – the Avenue of the Knights – is lined with magnificent medieval buildings. The most imposing is the **Palace of the Grand Masters**, which was restored as a holiday home for Mussolini, but was never used (closed Monday; 1200 dr).

The 18th-century **Turkish bath** on Plateia Arionos offers a rare opportunity to bathe

GREECE

Turkish-style in Greece (closed Sunday and Monday; 500 dr).

The massive **city walls** are closed to the public except on guided walks (1200 dr) that leave at 2.45 pm on Tuesday and Saturday, starting from the courtyard at the Palace of the Grand Masters.

Acropolis of Lindos The imposing acropolis, about 35km south of Rhodes City, is the island's most important ancient city (closed Monday, 1200 dr). It shares a rocky outcrop with a **crusader castle**. Down below it there are labyrinths of winding streets with whitewashed houses. Take a bus from Rhodes City's east-side station.

Places to Stay
Faliraki Camping (☎ 85 358), 2km north of Faliraki Beach, has a restaurant, bar, minimarket and pool, and charges 800/1500 dr per tent/person. Take a bus from the east-side bus station.

The popular *Rodos Youth Hostel (☎ 30 491, Ergiou 12)* has a lovely garden and a kitchen. Roof beds are 1000 dr, dorm beds are 1500 dr, and doubles without/with bath are 3500/6000 dr. *Pension Sunlight (☎ 21 435, Ipodamou 32)*, above Stavro's Bar, has doubles/triples with bath for 10,000/12,000 dr. The friendly *Pension Andreas (☎ 34 156, fax 74 285, Omirou 28D)* has a terrace bar with terrific views. Clean, pleasant doubles with shared bathroom cost 10,000 dr, doubles/triples/quads with private bath are 12,500/15,500/18,000 dr.

Other good choices include *Pink Elephant (☎ 22 469, Irodotou 42)* and *Hotel Spot (☎ 34 737, Perikleous 21)*. Both have clean, bright doubles with private bath for 12,000 dr.

Places to Eat
For the best Greek coffee in town and a game of backgammon or chess, try *Kafekopteion (Sokratous 76)*. Head to *Kringlan Swedish Bakery (1 Dragioumi 14)*, in the new town, for exceptional sandwiches and pastries. One of the best-value places to eat in the old town is *Fisherman's Ouzeria* on Sofokleous. *Taverna Kostas (Pythagora 62)* and *Yiannis Taverna*, on Platanos, are highly popular and also good value. Indian food fans should visit *India Restaurant (Konstantopedos 16)*, opposite

the Swedish bakery. *Kasbah (Platonos 4)* serves huge Moroccan-influenced meals.

The funky *Kafe Besara (Sofokleous 11)* and *Marco Polo Cafe (Agios Fanouriou 40)* are popular for day-time snacks and evening drinks. A popular place for big-time bar-hopping is Orfanidou in the city's north-west, lined with bars representing almost every nationality.

Getting There & Away
There are daily flights from Rhodes to Athens (23,400 dr), and regular summer services to Iraklio, Mykonos and Santorini. The Olympic Airways office (☎ 24 571) is at Ierou Lohou 9.

Most daily ferries from Rhodes to Piraeus (9000 dr, 14½ hours) sail via the Dodecanese north of Rhodes, but at least once a week there is service via Karpathos, Kassos, Crete and the Cyclades. The EOT has schedules, or contact the port police (☎ 27 695). There are daily excursion boats to Symi (5000 dr return), but the regular ferry is cheaper (1600 dr one way).

Between April and October there are regular boats from Rhodes to Marmaris (Turkey); one-way tickets cost 11,000 dr (13,500 dr return), plus US$10 Turkish port tax. During summer there are also ferries to Israel (from 28,000 dr) via Cyprus (17,000 dr), plus port taxes.

Getting Around
There are frequent buses to/from the airport (450 dr) from the west-side bus station.

Rhodes City's west-side bus station, next to the New Market, serves the west coast, Embona and Koskinou; the east-side station, nearby on Plateia Rimini, serves the east coast, including Lindos, and inland southern villages. The EOT has a schedule.

SYMI Σύμη
☎ 0241
Symi town is outstandingly attractive and easily accessible by boat from Rhodes, but you'll have more fun if you stay over when the day-trippers have gone. Budget accommodation is scarce, however. *Catherinettes Rooms to Let (☎ 72 698)*, *Hotel Glafkos (☎ 71 358)* and *Rooms to Let Helena (☎ 71 931)*, all scattered around the harbour, are some worthwhile options. *O Meraklis* and

Taverna Neraida are cheap and cheerful eateries; at night, *Sunflower* sandwich and salad bar turns into an excellent vegetarian restaurant. Aside from the excursion boats, a number of ferries and hydrofoils between Rhodes and Kos also call at Symi. The port police are on ☎ 71 205.

KOS Κως
☎ 0242
Kos is renowned as the birthplace of Hippocrates, father of medicine. Kos town manifests the more ghastly aspects of mass tourism, and the beaches are horrendous, with wall-to-wall sunlounges. The island is crowded but there a few areas where you can try to escape the masses.

Orientation & Information
Kos town, on the north-east coast, is the main town and port. The municipal tourist office (☎ 24 460, @ dotkos@hol.gr), Vasileos Georgiou 1, is near the hydrofoil pier. The post office is on Vasileos Pavlou; the OTE is on the corner of Vironos and Xanthou. Internet access is available at Cafe Del Mare, Megalou Alexandrou 4.

Things to See
Before you beat a hasty retreat from Kos town, check out the 13th-century **fortress** and the **archaeological museum**. On a pine-clad hill 4km from Kos town stand the extensive ruins of the renowned healing centre of **Asclepion** (closed Monday; 800 dr). The villages in the **Asfendion** region of the Dikeos Mountains are tranquil. There is a long stretch of coast along Kefalos Bay. **Paradise** is the most appealing of these beaches, but don't expect to have it to yourself.

Places to Stay & Eat
Kos Camping (☎ 23 910) is 3km along the eastern waterfront; take any bus from the harbourfront heading to Agios Fokas. Otherwise, head straight for the convivial *Pension Alexis (☎ 28 798, 25 594, Irodotou 9)*, close to the harbour (the entrance is in Omirou). Singles/doubles/triples with shared bath cost 5000/7500/9000 dr. Friendly English-speaking Alexis is also the owner of *Hotel Afendoulis (☎ 25 321, Evripilou 1)*, where comfortable, well-kept singles/doubles/triples with private bath cost 7500/11,000/13,0000 dr.

Olympiada, behind the Olympic Airways office, and *Filoxenia Taverna*, on the corner of Pindou and Alikarnassou, are popular with locals. *Creta Corner*, on the corner of Artemisias and Korai, serves excellent, well-priced food, and there's often live Greek music.

Kos town is well known for its nightlife. The streets of Diakon and Nafklirou are lined with bars that are jam-packed in high season.

Getting There & Away
Apart from European charter flights, there are daily flights from Kos to Athens (21,400 dr). The Olympic Airways office (☎ 28 330) is at the southern end of Vasileos Pavlou.

There are frequent ferries from Rhodes that continue on to Piraeus (7700 dr, 11½ hours) via Kalymnos, Leros and Patmos. There are less frequent connections to Nisyros, Tilos, Symi, Samos and Crete. Daily excursion boats go to Nisyros, Kalymnos and Rhodes. Ferries travel daily in summer to Bodrum in Turkey costing 9,000 dr one way (10,000 dr return). For the port police, call ☎ 26 594.

Getting Around
Buses for Asclepion, Agios Fokas (for the camping ground) and Lampi leave from opposite the town hall on the harbourfront; all other buses leave from the station behind the Olympic Airways office.

PATMOS Πάτμος
☎ 0247
Starkly scenic Patmos gets crowded in summer, but manages to remain reasonably tranquil. Orthodox and Western Christians have long made pilgrimages to this holy island.

Orientation & Information
The tourist office (☎ 31 666), post office and police station are all in the white Italianate building at the island's port and capital of Skala. There's a cybercafe, Millennium, a few blocks inland from the port, just up from the OTE.

Things to See
The **Monastery of the Apocalypse**, on the site where St John wrote the Revelations, is between the port and the hora. The attraction

here is the cave where the saint lived and dictated his revelations. The hora's white-washed houses huddle around the fortified **Monastery of St John the Theologian**, which houses a vast collection of monastic treasures, including embroidered robes, or-nate crosses and early manuscripts and icons. Opening hours for both monasteries are 8 am to 1 pm daily and 4 to 6 pm Tues-day, Wednesday and Sunday. Entrance to the monasteries is free; entry to the treasury costs 1200 dr.

Places to Stay & Eat

Stefanos Camping (☎ *31 821*) is on Meloi Beach, 2km north-east of Skala. There are a few budget pensions along the hora road, including *Pension Maria Paskeledi* (☎ *32 152*), where singles/doubles/triples with shared bathroom cost 4000/7000/9000 dr.

There is a cluster of mid-range hotels about 500m to the right of the port as you disem-bark. *Hotel Australis* (☎ *31 576*) and *Villa Knossos* (☎ *32 189*), next to each other, offer pleasant singles/doubles for 10,000/15,000 dr and both have wonderful gardens.

O Pantelis Taverna, one block back from the waterfront, and *Grigoris Taverna*, opposite the passenger-transit port building, are popular eateries. *Restaurant Pisofani* serves up good fresh fish.

Getting There & Away

Frequent ferries travel between Patmos and Piraeus (7200 dr, 9½ hours), and to Rhodes (4400 dr) via Leros, Kalymnos and Kos. There are also frequent boats to Samos. For the port police, call ☎ 34 131.

Getting Around

Skala, Hora, Grikos and Kambos are con-nected by buses that depart from the port. In summer there are frequent excursion boats to the various beaches and to the islets of Arki and Marathi.

North-Eastern Aegean Islands

SAMOS Σάμος
☎ 0273

Samos was an important centre of Hellenic culture and is reputedly the birthplace of the philosopher and mathematician Pythagoras. Lush and humid, its mountains are skirted by pine, sycamore and oak-forested hills.

Pythagorio, where you'll disembark if you've come from Patmos, is touristy and expensive; Vathy (20 minutes by bus) is cheaper.

Orientation & Information

Samos has three ports: Vathy (Samos town) and Karlovasi on the north coast, and Pythagorio on the south-east coast. Vathy's unhelpful EOT office (☎ 28 530) is in a side street one block north of Plateia Pythagora. A better bet is ITSA Travel (☎ 23 605/6, @ itsa@otenet.gr), directly opposite the port. Friendly staff here can help with ferries, excursions and accommo-dation, plus there's free luggage storage.

The post office is on Smyrnis, four blocks from the waterfront. The OTE is on Plateia Iroön, behind the municipal gardens. There is a cybercafe on the waterfront, 250m from Plateia Pygathora and next to the police station.

Things to See

Very little is left of the **ancient city** of Samos, on which the town of Pythagorio now stands. The Sacred Way, once flanked by 2000 statues, has been transformed into the airport's runway. The extraordinary **Evpalinos Tunnel** is the site's most impres-sive surviving relic. The 1km tunnel was dug by prisoners in the 6th century BC and was used as an aqueduct to bring water from the springs of Mt Ampelos. Part of it can still be explored. It's 2km north of Pythagorio (closed Monday; 800 dr).

Vathy's **archaeological museum** is out-standing, with an impressive collection of statues, votives and pottery (closed Mon-day; 800 dr).

Places to Stay & Eat

In Vathy, *Pythagoras Hotel* (☎ *28 422, fax 28 893,* @ *smicha@otenet.gr*) is a good budget option. Doubles/triples in high sea-son go for 9000/11,000 dr, but considerably less at other times. There's also a good value *restaurant* here. The hotel is 800m to the left of the quay.

The friendly *Pension Vasso* (☎ *23 258*) is open year-round and has singles/doubles/triples for 5000/9000/12,000 dr with balcony and bath. To get there from the quay, turn right onto the waterfront, left into Stamatiadou and walk up the steps. Nearby, *Hotel Ionia* (☎ *28 782*) is cheap, with singles/doubles with shared bathroom for 4000/6000 dr.

The popular *Taverna Gregoris*, near the post office, serves good food at reasonable prices. *O Kipos* (The Garden), one block back from the waterfront on Kalomiri, offers good traditional fare in a lovely outdoor setting.

Getting There & Away
There are daily flights to/from Athens (17,400 dr). There are daily ferries to Piraeus (6700 dr, 13 hours), some via Paros and Naxos, others via Mykonos, and two ferries a week to Chios (3000 dr, four hours). There are ferries to Patmos (3100 dr one way, 2½ hours) or excursion boats for daytrippers (8000 dr return).

There are daily boats to Kuşadası (for Ephesus) in Turkey, costing 13,000/14,000 dr one way/return, plus US$10 Turkish port tax. For the port police in Vathy call ☎ 27 318.

Getting Around
To get to Vathy's bus station, follow the waterfront and turn left onto Lekadi, 250m south of Plateia Pythagora (just before the police station). Buses run to all the island's villages.

LESVOS (MYTILINI)
Λέσβος (Μυτιλήνη)
☎ 0251
Lesvos is the third largest Greek island. It has always been a centre of artistic and philosophical achievement and creativity, and it remains a spawning ground for innovative ideas in the arts and politics.

Orientation & Information
Mytilini, the capital and port of Lesvos, is a large town built around two harbours. All passenger ferries dock at the southern harbour. The tourist police (☎ 22 776) are at the entrance to the quay; the EOT (☎ 42 511) is 50m up the road at Aristarhou 6. The post office is on Vournazon, west of the southern harbour, and the OTE is in the same street. Internet access is available at Net Club, 200m south of the southern harbour on Eliti.

Things to See
Mytilini's imposing **castle** was built in early Byzantine times and renovated in the 14th century. The new **archaeological museum** is signposted north of the quay. Don't miss the **Theophilos Museum**, which houses the works of the prolific primitive painter Theophilos. It's 4km from Mytilini in the village of Varia (take a local bus). Entry to each of these attractions is 500 dr; all are closed Monday.

Places to Stay & Eat
Most of Mytilini's domatia are in little side streets off Ermou, near the northern harbour. *Salina's Garden Rooms* (☎ *42 073, Fokeas 7*) has doubles starting at 6500 dr with shared facilities; nearby *Thalia Rooms* (☎ *24 640, Kinikiou 1*) has doubles starting at 7500 dr with private bath. Nearest to the quay is *Iren* (☎ *22 787, Komninaki 41*), where clean but simple doubles/triples cost 9000/11,000 dr.

The ramshackle but atmospheric *Ermis Ouzeri* has yet to be discovered by the tourist crowd. It's at the northern end of Ermou on the corner with Kornarou. There are popular tavernas spilling over the pavement south of the harbour; *Stratos Psarotaverna* offers good fish dishes.

Around the Island
Northern Lesvos is best known for its exquisitely preserved traditional town of **Mithymna** (also known as Molyvos), which is a good place to spend a few days. The neighbouring beach resort of **Petra**, 6km south, is also popular. Western Lesvos is a popular destination for lesbians who come on a kind of pilgrimage in honour of Sappho, one of the greatest poets of ancient Greece. The beach resort of **Skala Eresou** is built over ancient Eresos, where she was born in 628 BC. Southern Lesvos is dominated by **Mt Olympus** (968m), with pine forests decorating its flanks.

Getting There & Away
There are daily flights from Lesvos to Athens (19,900 dr), and less frequent services to Thessaloniki (20,900 dr), Limnos (13,400 dr) and Chios (10,900 dr). The Olympic Airways office (☎ 28 659) is at Kavetsou 44.

In summer there are daily boats to Piraeus (7200 dr, 12 hours), some via Chios.

There are three a week to Kavala (6500 dr, 11 hours) via Limnos and two a week to Thessaloniki (8400 dr, 13 hours). Ferries to Ayvalik in Turkey cost 16,000 dr one way (21,000 dr return). The port police (☎ 28 827) are on Pavlou Kountouriotou.

Getting Around
There are two bus stations in Mytilini. The one for long-distance buses is just beyond the south-western end of Pavlou Kountouriotou. For local buses go to the harbour's northernmost section.

SAMOTHRAKI Σαμοθράκη
☎ 0551
This wild, alluring island has only recently been discovered by holiday-makers and is deservedly popular with walkers. Experienced trekkers can climb Mt Fengari (1611m), the highest mountain in the Aegean.

Samothraki's big attraction is the Sanctuary of the Great Gods, an ancient site at Paleopolis shrouded in mystery. No-one knows quite what went on here, only that it was a place of initiation into the cult of the Kabeiroi, the gods of fertility. The site's winding pathways lead through lush shrubbery to extensive ruins. The site's most celebrated relic, the *Winged Victory of Samothrace*, which now has pride of place in Paris' Louvre, was discovered here in 1863. Admission to the site and its small museum is 500 dr each; closed Monday.

Samothraki's port is Kamariotissa on the north-west coast. The island's capital, the hora (also called Samothraki), is 5km inland. Most people stick to the resorts of Kamariotissa, Loutra (Therma) and Pahia Ammos, leaving the rest of the island untouched.

There are two camping grounds at Loutra and a number of domatia in the port and hora. Ferries link Samothraki with Limnos, and Kavala and Alexandroupolis on the mainland.

Ionian Islands
Τα Επτάνησα

CORFU Κέρκυρα
☎ 0661
Corfu (population 105,000) is the most important island in the group. The old town of Corfu, wedged between two fortresses, occupies a peninsula on the island's east coast. The narrow alleyways of high shuttered tenements in mellow ochres and pinks are an immediate reminder of the town's long association with Venice.

The town's old fortress, Palaio Frourio, stands on an eastern promontory, separated from the town by an area of parks and gardens known as the Spianada. The Neo Frourio (new fortress) lies to the north-west.

Orientation & Information
Ferries dock at the new port, west of the new fortress. The long-distance bus station is on Avrami, just inland from the port.

The EOT office (☎ 37 520) is on Rizospaston Vouleflon, between the OTE and the post office. The tourist police (☎ 30 265) are at Samartzi 4.

Things to See
Corfu Town's archaeological museum, Vraili 5, houses a collection of finds from Mycenaean to classical times. The star attraction is the pediment from the Temple of Artemis, decorated with gorgons (closed Monday; 800 dr).

The Church of Agios Spiridon, Corfu's most famous church, has an elaborately decorated interior. Pride of place is given to the remains of St Spiridon, displayed in a silver casket; four times a year they are paraded around town.

Around the Island The main resort on the west coast is Paleokastritsa, which is built round a series of pretty bays. Farther south, there are good beaches around the small village of Agios Gordios.

Places to Stay & Eat
Corfu Town There are no decent budget places in town. A lot of people wind up at *Hotel Europa* (☎ *39 304*), but only because it's close to the port (signposted off Xenofondos Stratigou). It charges 5500/6000 dr for singles/doubles. A bit nicer is *Hotel Ionian* (☎ *30 268, Xenofondos Stratigou 46*), also near the port. It charges 8500/ 11,000 dr for rooms with bath.

There are several cheap restaurants near the new port. The tiny *O Thessalonikios*, on Xenofondos Stratigou, serves succulent spit-roast chicken (1200 dr).

GREECE

Agios Gordios Most backpackers jump off the ferry and head straight for the ***Pink Palace*** (*☎ 53 103, fax 53 025, ℮ pink-palace@ker.forthnet.gr*), a huge complex of restaurants, bars and budget rooms that tumbles down a hillside outside Agios Gordios. It charges 6500 dr per day for bed, breakfast and dinner, or 7500 dr in the smart new wing. The palace is open April to November, and staff are there to meet the boats. Facilities include public telephones and Internet access.

Getting There & Away

There are daily buses to Athens (8650 dr, 11 hours) and Thessaloniki (8500 dr, 11 hours) from the Avrami terminal in Corfu town. The fare to Athens includes the ferry to Igoumenitsa.

There are hourly ferries to Igoumenitsa (1400 dr, 1½ hours) and a daily ferry to Paxoi (3300 dr, 1½ hours). In summer there are daily services to Patras (5800 dr, 10 hours) on the international ferries that call at Corfu on the way from Italy.

Hungary

A short hop from Vienna, Hungary is just the place to kick off an Eastern European trip. The allure of Budapest, once a great imperial city, is obvious at first sight, but other cities like Pécs, the warm heart of the south, and Eger, the wine capital of the north, have much to offer travellers. Throughout Hungary you'll find much of the glamour and excitement of Western Europe at less than half the cost.

AT A GLANCE

Capital:	Budapest
Population:	10.4 million
Official Language:	Hungarian
Currency:	1 forint (Ft) = 100 filler

Facts about Hungary

HISTORY

Until the early 5th century, all of Hungary west of the Danube (Transdanubia), was included in the Roman province of Pannonia. The Romans were forced to abandon Pannonia in 451, when the Huns, led by Attila, established a short-lived empire.

Seven Magyar tribes under the leadership of Árpád – the *gyula* (chief military commander) – swept in from beyond the Volga River in 896 and occupied the Danube Basin. Hungary's first king and patron saint, Stephen I (István), was crowned on Christmas Day in 1000, marking the foundation of the Hungarian state.

In 1456 at Nándorfehérvár (now Belgrade) Hungarians under János Hunyadi stopped the Ottoman Turkish advance into Hungary. Under Hunyadi's son, Matthias Corvinus (ruled 1458-90), Hungary experienced a brief flowering of Renaissance culture.

In 1526 the Turks defeated the Hungarian army at Mohács. When the Turks were expelled in 1686 by the Austrian, Hungarian and Polish armies, Hungary was subjected to Habsburg domination. From 1703 to 1711 Ferenc Rákóczi II, Prince of Transylvania, led an unsuccessful war of independence against the Austrians.

After WWI and the collapse of the Habsburg empire, Hungary became independent, but the 1920 Trianon Treaty stripped the country of 68% of its territory and 58% of its population. Many of the problems Trianon created remain today and still colour Hungary's relations with some of its neighbours.

In 1941 Hungary's desire to recover its lost territories drew it into war alongside the Nazis. During WWII Hungary deported hundreds of thousands of Jews to Auschwitz and other labour camps. In December 1944 a provisional government was established at Debrecen, and by early April 1945 all of Hungary was liberated by the Soviet army.

After the war the communists divided large estates among the peasantry and nationalised industry. On 23 October 1956 student demonstrators demanding the withdrawal of Soviet troops were fired upon; the next day Imre Nagy, a reform-minded communist, was made prime minister. On 1 November Nagy announced that Hungary would leave the Warsaw Pact and become neutral. The Soviet forces began to redeploy and on 4 November Soviet tanks moved into Budapest, crushing the uprising. The fighting continued until 11 November – 3000 Hungarians died and 200,000 fled to Austria. Nagy was arrested and deported to Romania, where he was executed two years later.

In June 1987 Károly Grósz took over as premier and in May 1988 became party secretary general. Under Grósz, Hungary began moving towards full democracy. At a party congress in October 1989 the communists agreed to give up their monopoly on power, paving the way for free elections in March 1990. A new program advocating social democracy and a free-market economy was adopted. As Gorbachev looked on, Hungary changed political systems with scarcely a murmur and the last Soviet troops left in 1991.

HUNGARY

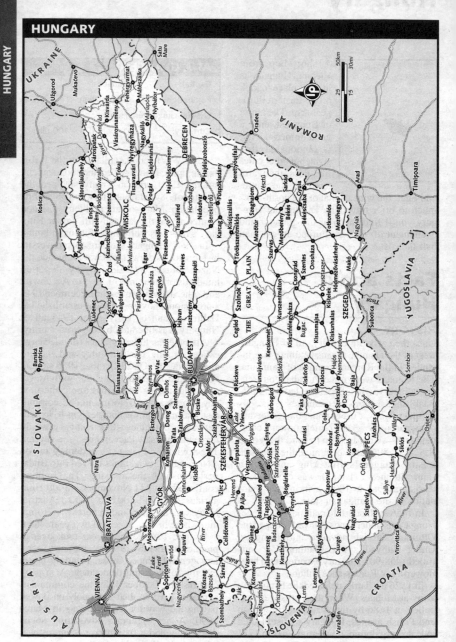

After a decade of economic transition and hardship, Hungary has emerged as the strongest economy in Eastern and Central Europe. Hungary became a fully fledged member of NATO in March 1999, and is eagerly awaiting accession to the EU, which should be granted around 2003.

GEOGRAPHY

Hungary occupies the Carpathian Basin in the very centre of Eastern Europe. It shares borders with seven countries: Austria, Slovakia, Ukraine, Romania, Yugoslavia, Croatia and Slovenia.

Hungary has an area of 93,030 sq km. The Danube divides the country into the Great Plain (Nagyalföld) in the east and Transdanubia (Dunántúl) in the west. The Tisza crosses the Great Plain about 100km east of the Danube. Hungary's 'mountains' are actually hills that seldom exceed 1000m.

POPULATION & PEOPLE

Some 10.4 million Hungarians live within the national borders, and another five million abroad. Minorities within Hungary include Germans, Slovaks, Romanians, Croatians and Serbs. The number of Roma ('Gypsy') is estimated at 150,000 to 250,000.

SOCIETY & CONDUCT

In general Hungarians are not uninhibited like the Romanians or the sentimental Slavs, who will laugh or cry at the drop of a hat (or a drink). They are a somewhat reserved, formal people. Forget about the impassioned, devil-may-care Roma stereotype – it doesn't exist.

Hungarians put surnames before given names: John Smith is always Smith John in Hungarian. In this chapter, people's names are written in the western manner, but addresses are always written in Hungarian.

LANGUAGE

Hungarians speak Magyar, a member of the Finno-Ugric language group that is related very, very distantly to Finnish and Estonian. Many older Hungarians understand German, particularly in the north-west, but it's unusual to meet someone on the street who understands English outside of Budapest.

See the Language Guide at the back of the book for pronunciation guidelines and useful words and phrases.

Facts for the Visitor

SUGGESTED ITINERARIES

Three days
    Visit Budapest, and possibly Szentendre
One week
    Visit Budapest, the Danube Bend and one or two of the following places: Sopron, Kőszeg, Pécs, Győr, Szeged or Eger
Two weeks
    Visit Budapest, Győr, Sopron, the north shore of Lake Balaton, Pécs and Eger

PLANNING
When to Go

Though it can get pretty wet in May and early June, spring is beautiful. Summer is warm, sunny and unusually long, but the resorts are crowded. If you avoid Lake Balaton, you'll do OK. Like Paris, Budapest comes to a grinding halt in August. Winters are cold, cloudy and damp or windy.

Maps

In this small country you can get by with the *Road Map Hungary*, available free from the Hungarian National Tourist Office (HNTO). Otherwise, you can pick up Cartographia's excellent road atlas.

TOURIST OFFICES
Local Tourist Offices

The Hungarian National Tourist Office (HNTO) has a chain of almost 100 tourist information bureaus called Tourinform across the country. The main Tourinform office (☎ 1-317 9800, fax 317 9656, @ hungary@tourinform.hu) is in Budapest at V Sütő utca 2. Web site: www.hungarytourism.hu

If your query is about private accommodation, international train transport or changing money, visit a commercial travel agency such as Ibusz.

Tourist Offices Abroad

Austria (☎ 1-513 9122, fax 513 1201) Opernring 5/2, A-1010 Vienna
Czech Republic (☎ 02-2109 0135, fax 2109 0139) Rumunská 22, 22537 Prague 2
France (☎ 01 53 70 67 17, fax 47 04 83 57) 140 Avenue Victor Hugo, 75116 Paris
Germany (☎ 030-243 1460, fax 243 14613) Karl Liebknecht Strasse 34, D-10178 Berlin
Netherlands (☎ 070-320 9092, fax 327 2833) Postbus 93076, 2593 AB The Hague
Romania (☎ 064-555 433, fax 414 520) CP 352, 3400 Cluj-Napoca

HUNGARY

UK (☎ 020-7823 1032, fax 7823 1459)
46 Eaton Place, London SW1X 8AL
USA (☎ 212-355 0240, fax 207 4103) 150 East
58th St, 33rd floor, New York NY 10155-3398

VISAS & DOCUMENTS

Citizens of the USA, Canada, most European countries and New Zealand do not require visas to visit Hungary for up to 90 days. Nationals of South Africa can stay visa-free up to 30 days, while UK citizens have six months. Australians (among others) still require visas, which are issued at Hungarian consulates or missions, most international highway border crossings, Ferihegy airport and the International Ferry Pier in Budapest. Visas are never issued on trains, and rarely on buses. Single-entry visas valid for 90 days cost US$40 and require three photos. A double-entry tourist visa costs US$75 and you must have five photos.

EMBASSIES & CONSULATES
Hungarian Embassies & Consulates

Australia
  Embassy: (☎ 02-6282 2555) 17 Beale Crescent, Deakin, ACT 2600
  Consulate: (☎ 02-9328 7859) Suite 405, Edgecliff Centre 203-233, New South Head Road, Edgecliff, NSW 2027
Austria (☎ 1-533 2631) 1 Bankgasse 4-6, 1010 Vienna
Canada
  Embassy: (☎ 613-230 9614) 299 Waverley St, Ottawa, Ont K2P 0V9
  Consulate: (☎ 416-923 8981) Suite 1115, 121 Bloor St East, Toronto, Ont M4W 3M5
Croatia (☎ 01-483 4900) Krlezin Gvozd 11a, 10000 Zagreb
France (☎ 01 43 54 66 96) 92 Rue de Bonaparte, 75006 Paris
Germany
  Embassy: (☎ 030-2031 0100) Markgraffen-strasse 36, Berlin
  Consulate: (☎ 089-911 032) Vollmannstrasse 2, 81927 Munich
Ireland (☎ 01-661 2902) 2 Fitzwilliam Place, Dublin 2
Netherlands (☎ 070-350 0404) Hogeweg 14, 2585 JD The Hague
Romania (☎ 01-311 0062) Strada Calderon 63-65, Bucharest 70202
Slovakia (☎ 07-544 30541) Sedlárska ul 3, 81425 Bratislava
Slovenia (☎ 061-152 1882) Ulica Konrada Babnika 5, 61210 Ljubljana-Semtvid
UK (☎ 020-7235 5218) 35 Eaton Place, London SW1X 8BY

Ukraine (☎ 044-212 4134) Ul Rejterszkaja 33, Kyiv 252901
USA
  Embassy: (☎ 202-362 6730) 3910 Shoemaker St NW, Washington DC 20008
  Consulate: (☎ 212-752 0669) 223 East 52nd St, New York, NY 10022
  Consulate: (☎ 310-473 9344) 11766 Wilshire Blvd, Suite 410, Los Angeles, CA 90025
Yugoslavia (☎ 011-444 0472) Ul Ivana Milutinovica 74, Belgrade 11000

Embassies & Consulates in Hungary

The following places are all in Budapest (area code ☎ 1).

Australia (☎ 201 8899) XII Királyhágó tér 8-9
Austria (☎ 351 6700) VI Benczúr utca 16
Canada (☎ 275 1200) XII Budakeszi út 32
Croatia (☎ 355 1522) XII Nógrádi utca 28b
France (☎ 332 4980) VI Lendvay utca 27
Germany (☎ 467 3500) XIV Stefánia út 101-103
Ireland (☎ 302 9600) V Szabadság tér 7
Netherlands (☎ 326 5301) II Füge utca 5-7
Romania (☎ 268 0271) XIV Thököly út 72
Slovakia (☎ 251 1700) XIV Stefánia út 22-24
Slovenia (☎ 325 9202) II Cseppkő utca 68
UK (☎ 266 2888) V Harmincad utca 6
Ukraine (☎ 355 2443) XII Nógrádi utca 8
USA (☎ 475 4400) V Szabadság tér 12
Yugoslavia (☎ 342 0566) VI Dózsa György út 92b

MONEY
Currency

The unit of currency is the Hungarian Forint (Ft). Coins come in denominations of one, two, five, 10, 20, 50 and 100Ft, and notes come in 200, 500, 1000, 2000, 5000 and 10,000Ft.

Exchange Rates

country	unit		forint
Australia	A$1	=	168Ft
Canada	C$1	=	204Ft
euro	€1	=	261Ft
France	10FF	=	398Ft
Germany	DM1	=	134Ft
Japan	¥100	=	282Ft
NZ	NZ$1	=	128Ft
UK	UK£1	=	427Ft
USA	US$1	=	302Ft

Exchanging Money

There are ATMs that accept any number of credit cards and some bank cards throughout the country. It's always useful to carry a little foreign cash, preferably US dollars or German Deutschmarks. You can exchange cash, travellers cheques and Eurocheques at banks – Országos Takarékpenztár (OTP) charges no commission on travellers cheques – and travel offices, which take a commission of 1% to 3%. K&H banks everywhere give cash advances on most credit cards. Credit cards are widely accepted, especially Visa and MasterCard.

You are allowed to change leftover forints back into hard currency, but you need to have the official exchange receipts with the date and your passport number clearly legible; the limit is about half the total on each of your transactions.

Because of the rapidly changing value of the forint, many hotels quote their rates in Deutschmarks. In such cases, we have done the same.

Costs

Hungary is a bargain compared to most Western European countries. If you stay in private rooms, eat at medium-priced restaurants and travel on public transport, you should easily survive on US$25 a day. Those camping or staying in dorms and doing some self-catering could do it for US$15. Prices listed in this chapter are high season costs.

Tipping

Hungarians routinely tip waiters, taxi drivers and even petrol-station attendants about 10%. In restaurants, do this immediately on payment of the bill – don't leave money on the table.

POST & COMMUNICATIONS

Surface mail costs 32Ft to neighbouring countries and 130Ft to the rest of Europe. Foreign air mail costs 140Ft for a letter or postcard to countries outside Europe.

Hungary's international phone code is ☎ 36. You can make domestic and international calls from most public telephones, both coin and card phones. Phonecards are sold at post offices in 50/120 units for 800/1800Ft.

To make a local call, pick up the receiver and listen for the continuous dial tone. For domestic long-distance calls dial ☎ 06 and wait for the second, more musical, tone. For direct-dial international calls dial ☎ 00 and

wait for the second tone. To reach an international operator dial ☎ 199. A three-minute call to the USA costs about 550Ft.

You can send faxes from most main post offices. Budapest has several Internet cafes and most year-round hostels offer email services.

INTERNET RESOURCES

Tourinform has two informative Web sites: www.tourinform.hu and www.hungarytou rism.hu. The site at www.hungary.com offers a broad range of topics, from links to government offices to hotels (go to the 'Exhibition Hall' link).

TIME

Hungary is on GMT/UTC plus one hour. Clocks are turned one hour ahead at the end of March and back again at the end of September. In Hungary, 'half eight' means 7.30 and not 8.30.

WOMEN TRAVELLERS

Hungarian men can be very sexist in their thinking, however women do not suffer any particular form of harassment. Most men – even drunks – are effusively polite with women. Nevertheless the usual care should be taken. Two useful organisations are Women United Against Violence (helpline ☎ 1-267 4900), PO Box 660, Budapest 1462, and the Feminist Network at PO Box 701, Budapest 1399.

GAY & LESBIAN TRAVELLERS

There are magazines for both gay men (Mások) and lesbians (Labrisz), which are published sporadically. There's also a gay Web site at www.gayguide.net/Europe /Hungary/Budapest. For help call the Háttér Gay & Lesbian Association (helpline ☎ 329 3380, 6 to 11 pm) or Gay Switchboard (helpline mobile/cellphone ☎ 06-309 323 334, 4 to 8 pm weekdays).

DISABLED TRAVELLERS

Wheelchair ramps, toilets fitted for the disabled and so on are virtually nonexistent though audible traffic signals for the blind are becoming increasingly commonplace.

For more information contact the Hungarian Disabled Association (MEOSZ; ☎ 1-388 2387, fax 1-388 2339) at San Marco utca 76, Budapest 1035.

DANGERS & ANNOYANCES

Hungary is hardly a violent or dangerous society, but crime increased dramatically in the 1990s (from a communist-era base of virtually nil). Violence is seldom directed towards travellers, though racially motivated attacks against Roma, Africans and Arabs are not unknown. As a traveller you are most vulnerable to pickpockets and taxi louts.

The following emergency numbers are valid throughout Hungary: police ☎ 107, fire brigade ☎ 105 and ambulance ☎ 104.

BUSINESS HOURS

Grocery stores and supermarkets open from about 7 am to 7 pm weekdays and department stores 10 am to 6 pm. Most shops stay open until 8 pm on Thursday but close at 1 or 2 pm on Saturday. Post offices open on 8 am to 6 pm weekdays, 8 am to 1 pm Saturday. Banks usually close no later than 4 pm Monday to Thursday and as early as 1 pm on Friday.

PUBLIC HOLIDAYS & SPECIAL EVENTS

Hungary's public holidays are: New Year's Day, 1848 Revolution Day (15 March), Easter Monday, International Labour Day (1 May), Whit Monday (May/June), St Stephen's Day (20 August), 1956 Remembrance Day (23 October), Christmas Day and Boxing Day.

The most outstanding annual events include: the Budapest Spring Festival (March), Sopron Festival Weeks (mid-June to mid-July), Győr Summer Cultural Festival (mid-June to mid-July), Kőszeg Street Theatre Festival (late July), Pannonia Festival in Pécs (July and August), Szeged Open-Air Festival (mid-July to August), Festival of Music on Óbuda Island in Budapest (August), wine harvest festivals nationwide (September) and Budapest Autumn Festival (mid-October to early November).

ACCOMMODATION

Hungary has more than 400 camping grounds. Small, private camping grounds are usually preferable to the large and noisy 'official' camping grounds. Prices vary from 500Ft to 2000Ft for two adults plus tent. Most camping grounds open from May to September and also rent small bungalows (from 3000Ft).

Generally the only year-round hostels are in Budapest; they charge around 2000Ft a night. From 1 July to 20 August, the cheapest beds (from 800Ft) are in vacant student dorms.

Private rooms – look for *szoba Kiadó* or *Zimmer frei* signs – are assigned by travel agencies who give you a voucher bearing an address or sometimes even the key to the flat. There's often a 30% supplement on the first night if you stay for less than three or four nights.

Panzió (pensions) are really just small hotels charging from 4000Ft in the provinces to twice that in Budapest for a double. Hotels, called *szálló* or *szálloda*, run the gamut from luxurious five-star palaces to run-down old communist era hovels.

FOOD

For many Hungarians, lunch is the main meal of the day – *étterem* and *vendéglő* (restaurants) usually offer a cheap set-lunch *menü* on weekdays. A *csárda* is an old-style inn or tavern offering traditional fare and wine. *Borozó* denotes a wine bar, *pince* is a beer or wine cellar and a *söröző* is a pub offering beer and sometimes meals. A *bisztró* is an inexpensive restaurant that is often self-service.

The main menu categories are *előételek* (appetisers), *levesek* (soups), *saláták* (salads), *készételek* (ready-to-serve meals that are heated up), *frissensült* (freshly prepared meals), *halételek* or *halak* (fish dishes), *szárnyasok* (poultry dishes), *tészták* (desserts) and *sajtok* (cheeses).

Hungarian *gulyás* (goulash) is a thick beef soup cooked with onions and potatoes. Cabbage is an important vegetable, either as *töltött káposzta* (stuffed) or made into *káposzta leves* (a thick soup). Other delicacies include *libamaj* (goose liver) and *sült libacomb* (roast goose leg). *Csirke paprikás* (chicken paprika) served with *galuska* (tiny dumplings) is a crowd pleaser. *Halászlé* (fisherman's soup) is a rich mixture of several kinds of poached fish, tomatoes, green peppers and paprika.

Vegetarians dishes include *rántott sajt* (fried cheese), *gombafejek rántva* (fried mushroom caps), *gomba leves* (mushroom soup), *gyümölcs leves* (fruit soup), *sajtos kenyer* (sliced bread with soft cheese) and *túrós csusza* (pasta with cheese). *Palacsinta* (pancakes/crepes) may be made with *sajt* (cheese), *gomba* (mushrooms), *dió* (nuts) or *mák* (poppy seeds).

DRINKS

Wine has been produced in Hungary for thousands of years and you'll find it available by the glass or bottle everywhere. *Pálinka* is a strong brandy distilled from a variety of fruits but most commonly apricots or plums. Ask for a *pohár* (glass) or *korsó* (half-litre mug) of beer by name and don't just say *sör* (beer), or you may get an expensive imported brand rather than a cheaper Hungarian brew such as Dreher and Kőbanyai.

Getting There & Away

AIR

Malév Hungarian Airlines flies direct to Budapest's Ferihegy airport from North America, the Middle East, Asia and more than three dozen European cities. The airline has ticketing desks at Terminal 2A (☎ 1-296 7179) and 2B (☎ 1-296 7544).

Malév doesn't offer student discounts on flights originating in Hungary, but youth fares are available to people aged under 26 (summer only). These might not always be cheaper than discounted tickets to other cities in the former Soviet bloc. Return prices (you must stay away at least one Saturday night) include: Moscow 63,300Ft; Warsaw 42,500Ft; and Prague 42,500Ft.

LAND
Bus

Most international buses are run by Eurolines or its Hungarian associate, Volánbusz. There are two international bus stations in Budapest with services to/from: Berlin (17,900Ft, 15 hours) with connections to Hamburg (20,900Ft, 18½ hours), London (28,900Ft, 25 hours), Paris (24,900Ft, 22 hours), Rome (20,900Ft, 20 hours) via Florence (16,900Ft, 16½ hours) and Vienna (5790Ft, 3¼ hours).

Other useful international buses include those to Bratislava/Pozsony (2500Ft, four hours), Prague (6990Ft, 8¾ hours), Zakopane in Poland (4600Ft, 8¼ hours) and the Romanian towns of Timişoara/Temesvár (4100Ft, eight hours) and Cluj-Napoca/Kolozsvár (4900Ft, 9½ hours).

Train

In Budapest, most international trains arrive and depart from Keleti (Eastern) station; trains to some destinations in Romania leave from Nyugati (Western) station, while Déli (Southern) station handles trains to/from Zagreb and Rijeka in Croatia. For 24 hour information on international train services call ☎ 1-461 5500.

There are big discounts on return fares from Hungary to former communist countries: 30% to Bulgaria, Slovenia and Poland, 40% to Czech Republic, Latvia and Lithuania; 50% to Belarus, Croatia, Russia and Ukraine; and 55% to Romania (70% if you buy your ticket in Romania). Under 26s qualify for up to 30% BIJ (Billet International de Jeunesse) discount to Western Europe.

In Hungary it's easiest to buy tickets at Magyar Államvasutak (MÁV) ticket offices. Note that you must pay a supplement (700Ft one-way) on many Eurocity (EC) express trains. On other international trains, reservations (650Ft) are recommended in summer.

RIVER

A hydrofoil service on the Danube between Budapest and Vienna (5½ hours, 282km) via Bratislava operates daily from April to the end of October, twice daily from late July to early September. Fares are AS780/1100 one-way/return, but ISIC student-card holders pay AS600/900 and Eurail Pass holders get a 50% discount, with some restrictions. Taking a bicycle along will cost AS200 each way. Contact Mahart Tours in Budapest (☎ 1-318 1704) or in Vienna (☎ 0222-729 2161).

Getting Around

BUS

Volán buses are a good alternative to the trains and fares are only slightly more expensive than comparable 2nd-class train fares. For short trips on the Danube Bend or Lake Balaton areas, buses are recommended. Tickets are usually available from the driver, but ask at the station to be sure. Timetables are posted at stations and stops.

Important footnotes include *naponta* (daily), *hétköznap* (weekdays), *munkanapokon* (workdays), *munkaszüneti napok kivételével naponta* (daily except holidays), *szabadnap kivételével naponta* (daily except Saturday), *szabad és munkaszüneti napokon* (Saturday and holidays) and *szabadnap* (on Saturday).

TRAIN

Eurail and Inter-Rail passes are valid in Hungary.

MÁV operates reasonably reliable, comfortable and not overcrowded train services. Second-class train fares are 286Ft for 50km, 694Ft for 100km, 1392Ft for 200km and 2536Ft for 500km. First class is 50% more. If you buy your ticket on the train rather than in the station, there's a 500Ft surcharge (1500Ft on Intercity trains). Seat reservations may be compulsory (indicated on the timetable by an 'R' in a box), mandatory on trains departing from Budapest (an 'R' in a circle) or simply available (just plain 'R').

There are several types of train. Express (Ex on the timetable) trains often require a seat reservation (120Ft). The two dozen or so Intercity (IC) trains levy a 320Ft supplement and you must book a seat. IC trains stop at main centres only and are the fastest and most comfortable trains.

The other types of train are *gyorsvonat* (fast trains) and *személyvonat* (slow passenger trains). In all stations a yellow board indicates *indul* (departures) and a white board *érkezik* (arrivals).

CAR & MOTORCYCLE

You must drive on the right. Wearing a seat belt when you're sitting in the front of the car is compulsory and motorcyclists must wear helmets. There is virtually a ban on drink-driving and this rule is *very* strictly enforced. Speed limits are also strictly enforced: 50km/h in built-up areas, 80km/h on secondary and tertiary roads, 100km/h on highways and 120km/h on motorways.

The 24-hour breakdown number is ☎ 188 (nationwide) or ☎ 1-212 2938 in Budapest.

Budapest

☎ 1

The capital of Hungary straddles a curve of the Danube River where Transdanubia

meets the Great Plain. More romantic than Warsaw, more cosmopolitan than Prague, Budapest is home to one-fifth of Hungary's population.

Strictly speaking, the story of Budapest only begins in 1873 when hilly, residential Buda merged with flat, industrial Pest to form what was at first called Pest-Buda. But Budapest is much older than that: the Romans built the town of Aquincum here, and layer upon layer of history blankets Buda's Castle District.

Orientation

Most visitors arrive at one of the three main train stations: Keleti and Nyugati stations are in Pest, and Déli is on the Buda side. All are on metro lines which converge at Deák tér in the centre of town.

Pest is very much the bustling heart of the city, while Buda, on the west bank, is where you'll find the historic Castle District and quiet Buda Hills.

Budapest is divided into 22 kerület (or districts), each with a Roman numeral, and which often precedes the street name in written addresses.

Information

Tourist Offices Your best source of information is Tourinform (☎ 317 9800, fax 356 1964, ✉ hungary@tourinform.hu). Its main office is at V Sütő utca 2 (metro: Deák tér) and it's open 8 am to 8 pm daily. There's also a 24-hour pre-recorded infoline on ☎ 06 8066 0044.

See Travel Agencies later in this section for details of commercial travel agencies, which book accommodation, arrange transport and change money.

Discount Cards The Budapest Card is sold at many outlets in the capital. It gives free admission to most museums and galleries, discounts on tours, thermal baths, shops and restaurants and also acts as a public transport pass. A two-day card costs 2800Ft, a three-day card 3400Ft.

Also worth considering is the Hungary Card, valid for a year.

Money OTP banks change cash and travellers cheques without commission, and there are ATMs and quite a few foreign-currency exchange machines around the town. The closest OTP branch to Deák tér for foreign exchange is at Nádor utca 6, open 7.45 am to 5 pm Monday, and until 4 pm Tuesday to Friday (metro: Bajscy-Zsilinszky út).

Tribus Hotel Service (see Travel Agencies later in this section) is handy for changing travellers cheques if you arrive late at night.

Post & Communications The main post office, V Petőfi Sándor utca 13, is near Deák tér. Make the cheapest international phone calls from a phone box using a phonecard.

Most hostels have Internet access but it can be more expensive than cafes. Matáv Pont, V Petőfi Sándor utca 17, has Internet access for 300/500Ft for 30/60 minutes. A little dearer, but open until midnight, AMI Internet Cafe is at Váci utca 40.

Travel Agencies An excellent one-stop shop is Vista, on the corner of VI Andrássy út and Paulay Ede utca. Its Visitor Center (☎ 268 0888) books rooms, has a telephone call centre and is open non-stop.

Another useful place for room bookings is the 24-hour Tribus Hotel Service (☎ 318 4848 or 318 5776), V Apáczai Csere János utca 1. It also changes travellers cheques.

The main Ibusz office (☎ 317 1806), at V Ferenciek tere 10, changes money, books rooms and accepts credit card payments. Its branch at VII Dob utca 1 (metro: Astoria or Deák tér) books train tickets. Web site: www.ibusz.hu

The main Express office (☎ 317 8600) is at V Semmelweis utca 4 (metro: Astoria). Its branch at Szabadság tér 16 (☎ 312 3849) books hostels and colleges, while the branch around the corner at V Zoltán utca 10 (☎ 311 6418) books international and domestic trains, Eurolines buses and takes phone (credit card) bookings. All Express offices sell IYHF and ISIC cards (900Ft).

Bookshops Bestsellers, at V Október 6 utca 11 (metro: Arany János), is one of the best English-language bookshops with novels, travel guides, magazines and newspapers.

Laundry One central laundromat is at Városház utca 5 (metro: Ferenciek tere).

Medical Services International Medical Services (☎ 329 9349), XIII Váci út 202 (metro: Gyöngyösi utca) is a private clinic

where consultations start at 6700Ft. It is open 7.30 am to 8 pm.

Emergency The emergency police help number is ☎ 107 – or go straight to the police station of the district (kerület) you're in. Tourinform or your hotel may also be able to help. Police headquarters (☎ 443 5259) is at XIII Teve utca 6.

Things to See & Do
Pest The most attractive boulevard in Budapest is leafy Andrássy út, which stretches north-east from Bajscy-Zsilinsky út out to City Park. The neo-Renaissance **State Opera House** at No 22 has tours at 3 and 4 pm daily which are worth taking if you can't catch a performance (1000Ft, students 450Ft).

The 96m-high neo-Renaissance dome of **St Stephen's Basilica** (1906) west of here looms over Bajscy-Zsilinsky út. The mummified right hand – the so-called Holy Right or Holy Dexter – of St Stephen is kept in the chapel at the rear of the church.

Heading north, stately Szabadság tér is a large square lined with impressive buildings, including the Art Nouveau **National Bank** building (1900) and the **Hungarian Television Building** (1906), formerly the Budapest Stock Exchange.

The incredible neo-Gothic **Parliament** (1904) nearby on Kossuth Lajos tér runs tours in English but only when Parliament isn't sitting.

The twin-towered **Great Synagogue** (1859) at VII Dohány utca 2-8, the largest functioning synagogue in Europe, contains the **Jewish Museum** (open 10 am to 5 pm Monday to Thursday, to 3 pm Friday and to 2 pm Sunday; 600/300Ft).

The **National Museum**, VIII Múzeum körút 14-16, houses Hungary's main collection of historical relics in a neoclassical building (1847). It's open 10 am to 6 pm (5 pm in winter) Tuesday to Sunday; admission is 400/150Ft.

One of Budapest's most famous monuments is the dramatic **Heroes' Square** (Hősök tere). To get there, take the yellow metro line (M1) north-east to Hősök tere. The metro line, the oldest underground railway in Europe, was completed the same year as the square. On the south-east side of the square is the **Műcsarnok**, an exhibition hall built in 1896 and now used for cutting

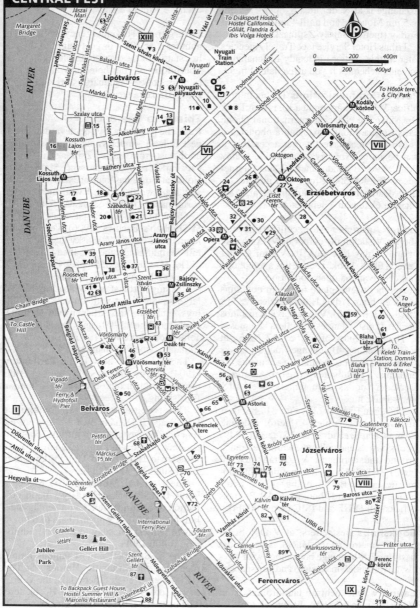

CENTRAL PEST

CENTRAL PEST

PLACES TO STAY

2	Hotel Metro
8	Best Youth Hostel
10	Yellow Submarine
12	Hostel Bánki (summer only)
26	Medosz Hotel
27	Caterina Hostel
62	Hostel Marco Polo
81	Hotel Ibis Centrum
85	Citadella Hotel
91	Hotel Corvin; Hotel Sissi

PLACES TO EAT

3	Okay Italia
4	Okay Italia
14	Semiramis
29	Felafel Faloda
31	Művész
32	Cafe Eckermann; Goethe Institute
38	Central European University & Cafeteria
39	Self-Service Cafeteria
40	Gandhi
47	Café Gerbeaud
58	Hannah
60	New York Café
69	Cabar
71	Govinda
72	Fatál
73	Alföldi
79	Darshan Café; Biopont
80	Stex Ház
82	Marie Kristensen Sandwich Bar

83	Nagycsarnok (Great Market)
89	Iran Persia Sandwich Club

OTHER

1	OTP Bank
5	OTP Bank
6	Bahnhof
7	Post Office
9	Bábszínház (Puppet Theatre)
11	Kaiser's Supermarket
13	Beckett's Irish Bar
15	Ethnography Museum
16	Parliament
17	Express (Transport Tickets)
18	Express (Room Bookings)
19	Soviet Army Memorial
20	Hungarian Television Building
21	National Bank Building
22	US Embassy
23	Mystery Bar
24	Piaf
25	Budapest Operetta Theatre
28	Liszt Academy of Music
30	MÁV Ticket Office
33	State Opera House
34	Tütü Tangó
35	Vista Travel Agency
36	St Stephen's Basilica
37	Bestsellers Bookshop
41	Duna Palota Restaurant & Booking Office
42	OTP Bank
43	Erzsébet tér Bus Station
44	Centrum Bus Stop (to Airport)

45	Corvinus Kempinski Hotel
46	American Express
48	Malév Office
49	Pesti Vigadó (Concert Hall)
50	Tribus Hotel Service
51	Main Post Office
52	Matáv Pont Internet Centre
53	Tourinform
54	Merlin Club
55	Ibusz (Train Tickets)
56	K&H Bank
57	Great Synagogue & Jewish Museum
59	Old Man's Music Pub
61	Julius Meinl Supermarket
63	Portside
64	OTP Bank
65	Express (Main Office)
66	Laundromat
67	Ibusz Main Office & Jégbüfé
68	Inner Town Parish Church
70	AMI Internet Cafe
74	Action Bar
75	Irish Cat Pub
76	National Museum
77	Kenguru (Car Pooling)
78	Nothin' But the Blues
84	Rudas Baths
86	Independence Monument
87	Cliff Chapel
88	Gellért Hotel & Baths
90	Museum of Applied Arts

edge art exhibits. On the other side is the **Museum of Fine Arts** (1906), housing Hungary's richest collection of foreign art. **City Park** extends to the west of the square.

Buda Most of what remains of medieval Budapest is on **Castle Hill** (Várhegy), perched above the Danube. The easiest way to get there from Pest is to stroll across Chain Bridge (Széchenyi lánchíd) and take the *sikló*, a funicular railway, from Clark Ádám tér up to Szent György tér, near the Royal Palace. The sikló is pricey – 350Ft uphill and 300Ft going down – and it's easy to walk up, taking the path to the left of the sikló entrance.

Another option is to take the metro to Moszkva tér, cross the bridge above the square and walk straight up Várfok utca to the **Vienna Gate** (Bécsi kapu). A minibus marked 'Várbusz' follows this same route from the start of Várfok utca.

From the Vienna Gate, take a sharp right on Petermann bíró utca to the **Magdalene Tower**, all that's left of a Gothic church destroyed here in WWII. Walk south-east along Tóth Árpád sétány, the ramparts promenade, until you glimpse the neo-Gothic tower of **Matthias Church** on Szentháromság utca. The church houses the **Museum of Ecclesiastical Art** (200Ft), which you enter through the crypt. The church is closed from mid-January to mid-February.

Behind the church is the **Fishermen's Bastion**, a late-19th-century structure offering great views of Pest, the Parliament building and the Danube.

From the **Holy Trinity Statue** in the centre of Szentháromság tér, Tárnok utca runs south-east to the gate of the **Royal Palace**, which contains two important museums. The **National Gallery** (closed Monday) has a huge collection of Hungarian works of art ranging from Gothic to contemporary. The

Budapest History Museum (closed Tuesday in the off-season) in Wing E traces the city's 2000 years of history.

Beneath Castle Hill is an extensive system of caves, tunnels and cellars, part of which has been transformed into **The Labyrinth**. It costs 900Ft but it's well worth a visit. Enter at Úri utca 9.

South of Castle Hill is Gellért Hill, home to the **Citadella**, a commanding fortress built by the Habsburgs after the 1848-49 Revolution. At night, with the city lit up, the panorama is spectacular. The **Independence Monument**, the lovely lady with the palm proclaiming freedom, was erected in tribute to the Soviet soldiers who died liberating Hungary in 1945.

To walk up there take the stairs on the Buda side of Erzsébet Bridge which lead up behind the 'waterfall'. Or climb up through the park opposite the Gellért Baths. If you don't feel like exerting yourself, bus No 27 runs almost to the top of the hill from Móricz Zsigmond körtér, south-west of the Gellért Hotel (and accessible on trams No 18, 19, 47 and 49).

Thermal Baths Some bathhouses require you to wear a bathing suit while others do not; take one just in case. Most of the public baths hire out bathing suits and towels if you don't have your own. Some baths become gay venues on male-only days – especially the Király and Rác. Not much actually goes on except for some intensive cruising.

Enter the famous **Gellért Baths** through the side entrance of the stately Gellért Hotel on XI Kelehegyi út. The temperature of the pools here is a constant 44°C and a large outdoor pool is open in summer. Entry costs 1500Ft, or 750Ft after 5 pm on weekdays and after 2 pm on weekends.

The **Széchenyi Baths**, XIV Állatkerti út 11, just outside the Széchenyi Fürdő metro station in City Park, are less touristy than the Gellért, with separate sections for men and women. Entry is 400Ft.

The Turkish-built **Rudas Baths** (1566) at I Döbrentei tér 9, are for men only (closed Saturday afternoon and Sunday). **Rác Baths** nearby on Hadnagy utca 8-10 admit women on Monday, Wednesday and Friday, men on Tuesday, Thursday and Saturday. Admission is 550Ft at both. The **Király Baths**, II Fő utca 84 (metro: Batthyány tér), genuine

Turkish baths erected in 1570, admit men and women on opposite days to the Rác.

Organised Tours

Ibusz has a three-hour city bus tour with stops for 5500Ft and Budatours (☎ 353 0558) has a two-hour tour without stops for 4800Ft, departing from Roosevelt tér.

IA Tours (mobile/cellphone ☎ 06 30 211 8861) has a popular 3½ hour walking tour which departs at 10 am and 2 pm daily from mid-May to the end of September from the steps of Műcsarnok in Heroes' Square, and at 10 am only the rest of the year (2500Ft).

From May to early September there are 1½-hour Mahart cruises daily (900/450Ft) on the Danube. Buy your ticket and board the boat at a small ticket office by the river at Vigadó tér (metro: Vörösmarty tér).

Places to Stay

Camping *Római Camping* (☎ 368 6260, III Szentendrei út 189) is in a shady park north of the city. To get there take the HÉV suburban railway from the Batthyány tér metro station to the Római Fürdő station, which is within sight of the grounds. A tent site for two people costs 3000Ft. Cabins are available, but only from mid-April to mid-October. Use of the adjacent swimming pool is included.

Zugligeti Niche Camping (☎ 200 8346, XII Zugligeti út 101) is at the bottom station of the Buda Hills chair lift (take bus No 158 from Moszkva tér to the terminus). Camping costs 500Ft per tent plus 850Ft per person.

Year-Round Hostels In Pest, the *Museum Guest House* (☎ 318 9508, ❷ museumgh@ reemail.hu, Mikszáth Kálmán tér 4, 1st floor) is a central, pokey but creatively decorated place charging 1800Ft each for its 20 dorm beds. The nearest metro station is Kálvin tér.

At the intersection of Teréz körút and Podmaniczky utca, right near Nyugati station, is *Yellow Submarine* (☎ 331 9896, Teréz Körút 56, 3rd floor), an IYHF place with dorm beds from 1800Ft. Diagonally opposite, *Best Youth Hostel* (☎ 332 4934, ❷ bestyh@mail.datanet.hu, VI Podmaniczky utca 27) is a touch dearer but the rooms are bigger and facilities marginally better.

Caterina Hostel (☎ 291 9538, VI Andrássy út 47, 3rd floor) is well situated near

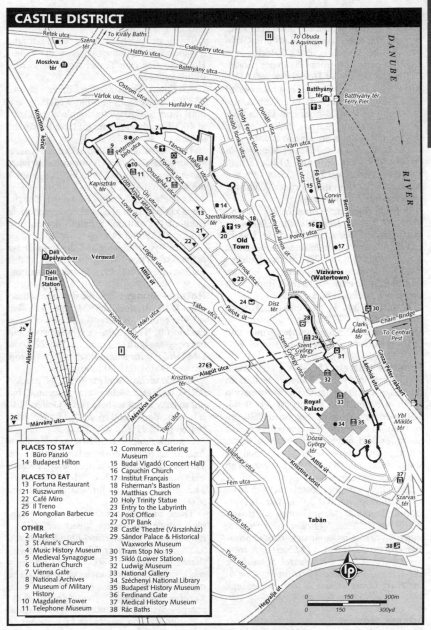

CASTLE DISTRICT

Retek utca
Széna tér
To Király Baths
Csalogány utca
To Óbuda & Aquincum
DANUBE
Moszkva tér
Hattyú utca
Batthyány utca
Ostrom utca
Várfok utca
Hunfalvy utca
Batthyány tér
Batthyány tér Ferry Pier
Krisztina körút
Vám utca
Szabó Ilonka utca
Toldy Ferenc utca
Donáti utca
Iskola utca
Fő utca
RIVER
Vienna Gate
Petermann bíró utca
Táncsics Mihály utca
Fortuna utca
Országház utca
Úri utca
Tóth Árpád sétány
Kapisztrán tér
Corvin tér
Lovas út
Szentháromság tér
Old Town
Hunyadi János út
Ponty utca
Bem rakpart
Déli pályaudvar
Vérmező
Logodi utca
Attila út
Tárnok utca
Viziváros (Watertown)
Déli Train Station
Krisztina körút
Mikó utca
Tábor utca
Palota út
Dísz tér
Clark Ádám tér
Chain Bridge
To Central Pest
Alagút utca
Krisztina tér
Szent György utca
Szent György tér
Lánchíd utca
Groza Péter rakpart
Alkotás utca
Tigris utca
Mészáros utca
Royal Palace
Ybl Miklós tér
Márvány utca
Dózsa György tér
Attila út
Naphegy utca
Fém utca
Tabán
Dezső utca
Tigris utca
Szarvas tér
Hegyalja út

PLACES TO STAY
1 Büro Panzió
14 Budapest Hilton

PLACES TO EAT
13 Fortuna Restaurant
21 Ruszwurm
22 Café Miro
25 Il Treno
26 Mongolian Barbecue

OTHER
2 Market
3 St Anne's Church
4 Music History Museum
5 Medieval Synagogue
6 Lutheran Church
7 Vienna Gate
8 National Archives
9 Museum of Military History
10 Magdalene Tower
11 Telephone Museum
12 Commerce & Catering Museum
15 Budai Vigadó (Concert Hall)
16 Capuchin Church
17 Institut Français
18 Fisherman's Bastion
19 Matthias Church
20 Holy Trinity Statue
23 Entry to the Labyrinth
24 Post Office
27 OTP Bank
28 Castle Theatre (Várszínház)
29 Sándor Palace & Historical Waxworks Museum
30 Tram Stop No 19
31 Sikló (Lower Station)
32 Ludwig Museum
33 National Gallery
34 Széchenyi National Library
35 Budapest History Museum
36 Ferdinand Gate
37 Medical History Museum
38 Rác Baths

0   150   300m
0   150   300yd

lively Liszt Ferenc tér. Dorm beds cost US$8 and singles/doubles are US$10 per person. The nearest metro station is Oktogon. If the hostel is full, Caterina can arrange apartments from US$15 per person.

The big *Diáksport Hostel* (☎ 340 8585, XIII Dózsa György út 152) is a bit isolated (metro: Dózsa György út), but compensates by having its own 24-hour bar. Dorm beds in crowded rooms start at 2250Ft; teensy singles and doubles are also available.

The newly renovated *Hostel Marco Polo* (☎ 342 9587, VII Nyár utca 6) is excellent but pricey. Beds cost DM27/35 in 12/6 bed dorms, DM39/46 in quads/triples. Web site: www.hostelmarcopolo.com

In Buda *Backpack Guest House* (☎ 385 8946, XI Takács Menyhért utca 33) has a pretty garden. Dorm beds cost from 1600Ft and there's one small double (2400Ft). Get there on bus No 7 or 7A (green numbers) from Keleti train station, tram No 49 from central Pest, or tram No 19 from Buda. Web site: www.backpackbudapest.hu

Also in Buda is the chaotic *Martos Hostel* (☎ 463 3777, XI Sztoczek utca 5-7). Singles are 2000Ft and doubles, triples and quads cost from 1600Ft per person.

Summer Hostels The Travellers' Youth Hostels company runs summer hostels in student accommodation. The information booth at Keleti train station (☎ 343 0748, ✉ travellers@matavnet.hu; open 7.30 am to 9 pm, to 11 pm in summer daily) makes bookings and might transport you there. All the Travellers' hostels are open 24 hours a day and there's no curfew. Web site: www.travellers-hostels.com

Travellers' summer hostels include: *Hostel California* (☎ 340 8585, XIII Angyalföldi út 2, metro: Dózsa György út), *Hostel Bánki* (☎ 312 5268, VI Podmaniczky utca 8, metro: Nyugati pályaudvar), *Hostel Summer Hill* (☎ 329 8644, XI Ménesi út 5, tram No 18, 19, 47 or 49), *Hostel Schönherz* (XI Irinyi József utca 42, tram No 4 or 6) and *Hostel Universitas* (XI Irinyi József utca 9-11, tram No 4 or 6).

Private Rooms Rooms generally cost 3000/5000Ft for a single/double, with a 30% supplement if you stay less than four nights. The following agencies arrange rooms; if you're approached at the train sta-

tions, agree on a price beforehand and check the location.

If you arrive late or on a weekend, try the 24-hour Vista Visitor Center or the Tribus Hotel Service (see Travel Agencies earlier in this section).

At Keleti Train Station, Ibusz (☎ 342 9572) is open 8 am to 6 pm weekdays and until 4 pm Saturday. Its double rooms start at 4000Ft and singles might have to pay the same.

The tourist information office at Nyugati station (☎ 302 8580) arranges *private rooms* for about 5000/6500Ft. It's open 7 am to 8 pm daily.

At Déli station, try Budapest Tourist (☎ 355 7167), in the sunken forecourt in front of the station. Singles/doubles cost around 4000/5000Ft.

Vista Visitor Center and the main Ibusz office (see Travel Agencies earlier in this section) are close to Erzsébet tér bus station.

Hotels – Budget The most central cheap hotel is the *Medosz* (☎ 374 3000, VI Jókai tér 9), near the restaurants and bars of Liszt Ferenc tér. The rooms are well-worn but have private bath and satellite TV; they cost DM45/65/80 for single/double/triple in low season, DM61/85/100 in high.

The *Citadella Hotel* (☎ 466 5794, fax 386 0505), on XI Citadella sétány, is central, but not so easy to get to, being atop Gellért Hill. It has big, dark wood rooms for 8400Ft with shared bath; 9200Ft with shower.

Domnik Panzió (☎ 343 7655, XIV Cházár András utca 3), beside a large church on Thököly út, is two stops north-east of Keleti train station on bus No 7 (black number). The plain rooms with shared bath are 5200/6500/8400Ft.

There are two institutional, but cheap, places out in the dreary streets near Rákosrendező HÉV station. *Hotel Flandria* (☎ 350 3181, XIII Szegedi út 27) has rooms with shared bath for 5700/8000/9800/10,900Ft a single/double/triple/quad (less in winter). The mammoth *Hotel Góliát* (☎ 270 1456, XIII Kerekes utca 12-20), two blocks away, charges 5200/6200/6700/7700Ft. Access to both hotels is on bus No 4 or tram No 14 along Lehel/Béke utca.

Hotels – Mid-Range Very close to Nyugati train station is *Hotel Metro* (☎ 329 3830,

Kádár utca 7), with faded singles/doubles/ triples with bath for 9800/12,400/ 15,000Ft. You'd do much better in the spotless **Hostel Marco Polo** (see the Year-Round Hostels section earlier).

The central, three-star **Hotel Corvin** (☎ *218 6566, Angyal utca 31)* has singles/doubles with all the mod cons for DM149/169, while *Hotel Sissi* (☎ *215 0082, Angyal utca 33)*, next door, has slightly nicer rooms for DM165/180. You should be able to get big discounts most of the year.

The Ibis chain has a couple of good midrange places. **Hotel Ibis Centrum** (☎ *215 8585, Ráday utca 6)*, right near Kálvin tér, has light, airy singles/doubles for 19,800/ 22,200Ft, and a nice garden. A couple of kilometres north of the centre, **Hotel Ibis Volga** (☎ *329 0200, Dózsa György út 65)* has older-style rooms for DM122/145, and new rooms with air-con for DM150/170. It's right outside Dózsa György út metro station.

Near Castle Hill, on the Buda side, **Büro Panzió** (☎ *212 2929, II Dékán utca 3)* looks basic from the outside but the rooms (DM80/100/130) are comfortable.

Places to Eat

Pest The *Nagycsarnok (Great Market)*, on Fővám tér, might be a bit of a tourist trap but the food stalls on the upper level are good for a cheap snack and self-caterers can buy bread, cheese, fruit and sliced meats.

American fast food joints abound, but you can also experience fast food Communist-style at the *self-service cafeteria (V Arany János utca 5)*, which is open 11.15 am to 3 pm weekdays. The **Central European University cafeteria** *(V Nádor utca 9)* has set meals for around 600Ft from 11.30 am to 4 pm weekdays.

Felafel Faloda (VI Paulay Ede utca 53) has felafel, salads, juices and smoothies and opens 10 am to 8 pm weekdays. More cheap Middle Eastern food can be found at *Semiramis (V Alkotmány utca 20)*, **Cabar** *(V Iranyi utca 25)* and the **Iran Persia Sandwich Club** *(IX Ráday utca 17)*.

Marie Kristensen Sandwich Bar (Ráday utca 7) has a large selection of sandwiches (around 250Ft) and does a cheap cooked breakfast until 10 am. *Okay Italia (XIII Szent István körút 20* and *V Nyugati tér 6)* has pizzas from 750Ft, pastas for 950Ft and a good range of antipasto.

Darshan Cafe (VIII Krúdy Gyula utca 8) is an Aztec-inspired hang out, good for a drink and meal, while *Stex Ház (József körút 55-57)*, close by, does soups, sandwiches, pasta, fish and meat dishes (most 500Ft to 800Ft). It's open virtually 24 hours and transforms into a lively bar late at night.

For a splurge, try *Fatál (V Váci utca 67)*, which serves massive Hungarian meals in an atmospheric old cellar. Main courses are around 1000Ft. Typical Hungarian meals are also served at *Alföldi (V Kecskeméti utca 4)*, where mains cost 400Ft to 800Ft.

Vegetarians could try *Gandhi, (V ker Vigyázó Ferenc utca 4)*, with a daily set menu (from 860Ft); *Biopont, (Krúdy Gyula utca 7)*, with a 660Ft set menu; or *Govinda (V Belgrád rakpart 18)*, an Indian eatery. For a kosher lunch, you could head for *Hannah (VII Dob utca 35)*, in a courtyard behind the Orthodox Synagogue (open 11.30 am to 4 pm weekdays).

Like Vienna, Budapest is famous for its elegant coffee and cake shops. The **Café Gerbeaud** *(Vörösmarty tér 7)* has been a fashionable meeting place for the city's elite since 1870, but it's pricey. *Művész (VI Andrássy út 29)*, near the State Opera House, has a better selection of cakes at lower prices. The sumptuous 1895 *New York Café (VII Erzsébet körút 9-11)*, near Blaha Lujza tér metro, is incredibly ornate and formal.

Budapest has a growing number of hip modern cafes which often serve light meals – you'll find lots on Liszt Ferenc tér (metro: Oktogon) or Ráday utca (metro: Kálvin tér). *Cafe Eckermann (VI Andrássy út 24)*, below the Goethe Institute, has exotic teas, juices, toasted sandwiches and 'big coffees' served in bowls.

Buda In the Castle District, *Fortuna Önkiszolgáló (I Hess András utca 4)*, above the Fortuna restaurant, is a cheap self-service place open 11.30 am to 2.30 pm weekdays. *Café Miro (Úri utca 30)* is a bright, modern place, good for a coffee or a meal such as sandwiches (250Ft), ham and eggs (490Ft) or steak (1200Ft). Crowded *Ruszwurm (I Szentháromság utca 7)*, near Matthias Church, is *the* spot for coffee and cake.

Near Déli train station, *Il Treno (XII Alkotás utca 15)* has pasta (800Ft), pizzas (from 700Ft) and a salad bar. Nearby, *Mongolian Barbecue (XII Márvány utca 19a)* offers all the food you can eat and all the beer you can drink for 1900Ft before 5 pm, 2990Ft after.

The simple but excellent Italian fare at **Marcello** *(XI Bartók Béla út 40)* attracts students from the nearby university.

Entertainment
Pubs & Clubs The crowded *Old Man's Music Pub (VII Akácfa utca 13)* has a lively bar area, a bluesy music venue (from 9 pm nightly) and a pizzeria (3 pm to 3 am). A bar with a small dance floor and a nautical theme, *Portside (VII Dohány utca 7)* attracts the pretty young things and stays open until 4 am on Friday and Saturday.

The *Merlin Club (V Gerlóczy utca 4)*, near Deák tér, has live jazz most nights, as does the eclectically hip *Tütü Tangó (VI Hajós utca 2)*, open until midnight.

For your dose of Guinness, head to the *Irish Cat Pub (V Múzeum körút 41)*, with music some nights, or *Beckett's Irish Bar (V Bajcsy-Zsilinzky út 72)*, where the food is also good and expats abound. *Nothin' But the Blues (VIII Krúdy Gyula utca 6)* is cheap and popular with backpackers, and has music every night.

A nice spot to chill out along the banks of the Danube is *Zöld Párdon*, an outdoor dancing and drinking venue on the Buda side of Petöfi Bridge. You can while away the afternoon here, then fire up for dancing after 10 pm.

For a big throbbing disco, head to *Bahnhof (VI Teréz körút 55)*, in a southern wing of the Nyugati train station building – enter via the lane next to McDonald's. When everything else is dying down, part the velvet curtains at *Piaf (VI Nagymező utca 25)* and let the night continue.

Gay & Lesbian Venues Lesbians frequent *Angel (VII Szövetség utca 33)*, a gay venue that is becoming increasingly mixed. *Mystery Bar (V Nagysándor József utca 3)* is a quiet gay bar, while the name of the *Action Bar (V Magyar utca 42)* says it all.

Opera & Operetta You should pay at least one visit to the ornate *State Opera House (☎ 332 7914, VI Andrássy út 22)*. Budapest's second opera house, the modern (and ugly) *Erkel Theatre (III Köztársaság tér 30)*, is near Keleti train station. Operettas

are presented at the *Budapest Operetta Theatre (VI Nagymező utca 17)*, which often has special summer programs.

Classical Music Budapest's main concert hall is the *Pesti Vigadó (V Vigadó tér 2)*. Other concerts are held at the stunning *Liszt Academy of Music (VI Liszt Ferenc tér 8)*.

Folk & Traditional Shows *Hungária Koncert (☎ 317 2754)* organises folk and Gypsy concerts featuring the Hungarian State Folk Ensemble and two other groups at the *Duna Palota* restaurant *(Zrínyi utca 5)*, *Bábszínház (Andrássy út 69)* and *Budai Vigadó (Corvin tér 8)*. Tickets cost 4400Ft, 3900Ft for students.

Folklór Centrum (☎ 203 3868, XI Fehérvári út 47-51) also presents a program of Hungarian dancing accompanied by live Gypsy music at 8.30 pm every Monday and Friday between May and mid-October. The performance here is one of the best of its kind in Budapest.

Getting There & Away
Air The main ticket office for Malév Hungarian Airlines is at V Dorottya utca 2 near Vörösmarty tér. For information and phone bookings call ☎ 235 3804 or free-call outside Budapest on ☎ 06-4021 2121.

Bus Most buses to Western and Central Europe, some neighbouring countries and destinations in Hungary south and west of Budapest leave from V Erzsébet tér (☎ 317 2562 for international services, ☎ 317 2345 for domestic services, metro: Deák tér). The international ticket office is upstairs.

In general, buses to/from Eastern Europe, as well as Greece and Turkey and destinations north and east of the capital, leave from the station at Népstadion (☎ 252 1896 for international services, ☎ 252 4496 for national services; XIV Hungária körút 48-52; metro: Népstadion).

Most buses to the Danube Bend leave from the bus station next to Árpád híd metro station.

Train Budapest-Keleti (Eastern) station (☎ 314 5010 or 313 6835) handles almost all international trains, plus domestic trains to/from the north and north-east. For some Romanian destinations as well as domestic ones to/from the Great Plain and the

Danube Bend head for Budapest-Nyugati (Western) station (☎ 349 0115). For trains bound for Transdanubia and Lake Balaton, go to Budapest-Déli (Southern) train station (☎ 375 6293 or 355 8657).

The MÁV ticket office (☎ 322 8405) at VI Andrássy út 35 (metro: Opera) sells international train tickets and can make advance seat reservations for domestic express trains at the same price you'd pay at the station. Ibusz at VII Dob utca 1 (metro: Astoria or Deák tér), also sells train tickets and can make seat reservations.

Car & Motorcycle One of the cheapest car rental agencies is Americana Rent-a-Car (☎ 320 8287), attached to the Hotel Ibis Volga at Dózsa György út 65. Web site: www.americana.matav.hu

Kenguru (☎ 266 5857), VIII Kőfaragó út 15 (metro: Blaha Lujza tér), matches up drivers and riders for a fee, mostly to points abroad. The cost is around 8.7Ft per kilometre. Approximate one-way fares include: Amsterdam 11,800Ft, London 13,650Ft, Munich 6150Ft, Paris 12,350Ft, Prague 4600Ft and Vienna 2300Ft. Web site: www.kenguru.hu

Boat Hydrofoils to Vienna, via Bratislava on request, depart from the International Ferry Pier on Belgrád rakpart, mid-way between the Szabadság and Erzsébet bridges on the Pest side. For fares, see the Hungary Getting There & Away section.

Mahart ferries link Budapest with the towns of the Danube Bend – see each town's section for fares and schedules. Boats leave from below Vigadó tér on the Pest side and the first stop is at Batthyány tér in Buda.

Getting Around
To/From the Airport The Centrum Bus, which costs 600Ft, runs every half-hour between 5.30 am and 9.30 pm from Erzsébet tér, immediately outside the Corvinus Kempinsky Hotel (metro: Deák tér). Coming from the airport, buses operate between 6 am and 10 pm.

The Airport Minibus Service (☎ 296 8555) ferries passengers in eight-seater vans from the airport directly to their hotel, hostel or private home. The fare is 1500Ft and tickets are available in the airport arrival

halls. If you're going *to* the airport, you need to book 24 hours ahead.

A rail line connecting Ferihegy with Nyugati train station is under construction.

Public Transport Three underground metro lines meet at Deák tér: the yellow M1, the red M2 and the blue M3. The HÉV (pronounced 'heave') suburban railway, which runs north from Batthyány tér, is almost like a fourth metro line. The metro operates from 4.30 am until just after 11 pm.

On trams, trolleybuses, regular buses and the HÉV (as far as the city limits) the fare is a flat 95Ft. On the metro the fare is 65Ft (three stops within 30 minutes) or 150Ft (one hour of travel with one transfer). Ticket inspectors are out in force on the metro – and they *will* fine you, no matter what your excuse.

The Danube Bend

Between Vienna and Budapest, the Danube breaks through the Pilis and Börzsöny hills in a sharp bend. This scenic area's historic monuments, easy access, good facilities and forest trails combine to put it at the top of any visitor's list.

SZENTENDRE
☎ 26
Early in the 19th century Szentendre, 19km north of Budapest, became a favourite of painters and sculptors; it has been known for its art and artists ever since and galleries abound. You can easily see Szentendre on a day trip from Budapest, but the town makes a good – if hugely crowded and touristy – base for the Danube Bend.

Orientation & Information
From Szentendre's HÉV and bus station, it's a short walk under the subway and up Kossuth Lajos utca to Fő tér, the centre of the old town. The Mahart riverboat terminal is at the end of Czóbel Béla sétány, 2km farther north.

Tourinform (☎ 317 965) is at Dumtsa Jenő utca 22.

Things to See
All of the museums are closed on Monday; the ecclesiastical collection shuts on Tuesday as well.

In an alley off the eastern side of Fő tér is the **Margit Kovács Museum**, devoted to the ceramicist Margit Kovács (1902-77) who combined Hungarian folk, religious and modern themes. The **Ferenczy Museum**, Fő tér 6, displays the artwork of the Ferenczy clan, pioneers of Szentendre's artist colony.

Narrow stepped lanes lead up from Fő tér to Castle Hill and the **Parish Church of St John**, from where you'll get splendid views of the town. Just north is the tall red tower of **Belgrade Church** (1764), the finest example of Szentendre's Serbian churches. Beside the church is the **Serbian Ecclesiastical Art Collection** (100Ft).

The large **Hungarian Open-Air Ethnographic Museum** includes reassembled houses and buildings from around the country. It's 3km north-west of Szentendre on Sztaravodai út – buses from stand No 8 at the bus station run to the museum about 10 times a day. It's open 9 am to 5 pm Tuesday to Sunday, mid-March to October only. Entry is 300/150Ft.

Places to Stay

Ibusz on Bogdányi utca organises *private rooms* from around 3500Ft.

Two kilometres north of Szentendre on Pap Island is *Pap Sziget Camping (☎ 310 697)*, open from May to October. Camping is 1000Ft to 1200Ft for two people with a tent, and bungalows with bath cost 7000Ft a double. The motel rooms with shared bath are 3000Ft per person. To get there, take bus No 1, 2 or 3.

The most central pension is *Bükkös (☎ 312 021, Bükkös 16)*, halfway between the stations and Fő tér. Good singles/doubles with bath are DM60/70.

Getting There & Away

Buses from Budapest's Árpád híd bus station, on the blue metro line, run to Szentendre frequently. Onward services to Visegrád (45 minutes) and Esztergom (1½ hours) are frequent.

Take the HÉV from Budapest's Batthyány tér metro station to the end of the line (40 minutes); the last train leaves from Szentendre for Budapest at 11.30 pm.

Mahart ferries run between Budapest and Szentendre (650/975Ft one-way/return, 1½ hours, daily), with connections to Visegrád and Esztergom.

VISEGRÁD
☎ 26

In the 14th century a royal palace was built at the foot of Visegrád's hills and for nearly two centuries Hungarian kings and queens alternated between Visegrád and Buda. The destruction of Visegrád came with the Turks and later in 1702 when the Habsburgs blew up the citadel.

Today tiny Visegrád, superbly situated on an abrupt loop of the Danube River, is a low-key and less crowded alternative to Szentendre and Esztergom.

Orientation & Information

The small town stretches along the highway south of the ferry pier. Visegrád Tours, by the entrance of the big Sirály Restaurant, has information and can book accommodation.

Things to See

All trace of the royal palace was lost until 1934 when archaeologists, following descriptions in literary sources, uncovered the **palace ruins** at Fő utca 29 (closed Monday; 120Ft). Original palace bits and pieces are in the museum at **Solomon's Tower**, a few hundred metres north of the ruins (closed Monday and November to April; 200/100Ft).

Visegrád Citadel is on a high hill directly above – you can hike up there from Solomon's Tower, via a trail marked 'Fellegvár' that turns south-east at a fork. From the town centre another, less steep, trail leads to the citadel from behind the Catholic church on Fő tér. Entry to the citadel is 260Ft.

Places to Stay

Up on Mogyoróhegy (Hazelnut Hill), about 2km north-east of the citadel, *Jurta Camping (☎ 398 217)* has bungalows and camp sites. Buses run there only between June and August.

Visegrád Tours can organise *private rooms* for around 1500Ft per person. Many houses along Fő utca and Széchenyi utca have signs advertising 'Zimmer frei'.

A friendly pension, *Haus Honti (☎ 398 120, fax 397 274, Fő utca 66)* has doubles with shower for 5500Ft, including breakfast.

Getting There & Away

Buses run frequently between Budapest's Árpád híd station, the Szentendre HÉV station and Eztergom.

Mahart ferries link Visegrád with Esztergom and Budapest (700/1050Ft one-way/return).

ESZTERGOM
☎ 33

Esztergom, at the western entrance to the Danube Bend, is one of Hungary's most historically important cities. Stephen I, founder of the Hungarian state, was born and crowned at Esztergom, the royal seat from the late 10th to the mid-13th centuries.

While the cathedral area and the banks of the Danube and Little Danube are peaceful and pretty, Esztergom's small town centre is a mixture of drab architecture and relatively heavy traffic.

Orientation & Information
The train station is at the southern edge of town – walk north on Baross Gábor út, then along Ady Endre utca to Simor János utca. The bus station is a 10-minute walk south of the train station. The ferry terminal is on Primas Island.

Three travel agencies that will be able to help with information are: Komturist (☎ 312 082), Lörincz utca 6; Gran Tours (☎ 417 052), Széchenyi tér 25; and Cathedralis Tours (☎ 415 260), on the corner of Bajcsy-Zsilinsky and Batthány Lajos utca.

Things to See
You can't miss Esztergom Cathedral, built on a hill liigh above the Danube. It's the largest church in Hungary. The treasury behind the altar is worth a look (200Ft). Sometimes the staircases to the top of the cathedral are open to visitors.

Beside the cathedral, at the southern end of the hill, is the Castle Museum (closed Monday; 200Ft). The views from this hill are great.

In the fairytale Watertown district is the Christian Museum (closed Monday; 200Ft), at Berényi Zsigmond utca 2. It houses the best collection of medieval religious art in the country.

The outdoor thermal baths, halfway between the cathedral and Széchenyi tér, are open 9 am to 6 pm May to September. Entry is 270/130Ft.

Places to Stay
Open May to late September, Gran Camping (☎/fax 489 563, Nagy-Duna sétány 3) is by the Danube. A camp site for two people costs DM20, a dorm bed is DM10.

Gran Tours books private rooms from 1900Ft. The large Platán Panzió (☎ 411 355, Kis-Duna sétány 11) charges 3300Ft for doubles with shared bath.

Friendly Alabárdos (☎ 312 640, Bajcsy-Zsilinszky utca 49), right near the cathedral, has singles/doubles for 4500/5500Ft. The nearby Ria Panzió (☎ 313 115, Batthyány Lajos utca 11) is more expensive.

Places to Eat
For pizza, pasta and salads, head for the small Kaktusz Pizzeria (Bajcsy-Zsilinsky utca 25-27), or much cheaper McAllenney Pizzeria (Kossuth Lajos utca 11). Csülök Csárda (Batthyány utca 9) has good home cooking and huge main courses from 800Ft.

Getting There & Away
Buses from Budapest's Árpád híd station to Esztergom may travel via Dorog (1¼ hours) or via Visegrád and Szentendre (two hours). Trains to Esztergom depart from Budapest's Nyugati train station (1½ hours).

A ferry (120Ft per person one-way) crosses the Danube to Štúrovo in Slovakia 10 times a day between 7.20 am and 4.20 pm.

Mahart riverboats travel to/from Budapest (740/1110Ft one-way/return, five hours) once a day from late May to mid-June, and twice a day from mid-June to late September.

Western Transdanubia

Conquered by the Romans but never fully occupied by the Turks, this enchanting corner of Hungary contains picturesque small towns and cities with a decidedly European air.

Bland Komárom is the gateway to Hungary for visitors arriving from Komárno in Slovakia. There's a good camping ground (next to the public thermal baths) within walking distance of the train station and border crossing, and a couple of inexpensive hotels.

GYŐR
☎ 96

Győr (pronounced 'jyeur') is a historic city midway between Budapest and Vienna.

HUNGARY

Győr is Hungary's third-largest industrial centre, but you'd never know it when you're standing in the charming old centre. Most travellers give it a miss, but it's less touristy than Esztergom, Sopron or Eger and well worth a visit.

Orientation & Information

The large City Hall rises up across from the train station. The bus station is just south, through the tunnel under the train tracks. Baross Gábor utca, which leads to the old town, lies diagonally across from City Hall.

There's a Tourinform office (☎ 311 771) in the pedestrian mall on the corner of Árpad út and Baross Gábor utca.

Things to See

Széchenyi tér is the heart of Győr and features **St Ignatius Church** (1641), with its superb pulpit, pews and ceiling frescoes. At Széchenyi tér 4, the **Imre Patkó Collection** of paintings and Asian and African art is one of Hungary's finest small collections.

A short walk north-west of Széchenyi tér is **Káptalandomb** (Chapter Hill), the oldest part of Győr. The large baroque **cathedral** on the hill was originally Romanesque; the Gothic **Héderváry Chapel** on the cathedral's southern side contains a glittering 15th-century bust of King (and St) Ladislas.

The streets behind the cathedral are full of old palaces; at the bottom of the hill on Jedlik Ányos utca is the outstanding **Ark of the Covenant**, a large baroque statue dating from 1731.

Győr's well-maintained **thermal baths** are west of the Rába River – cross Rába kettős híd (Rába Double Bridge) over the little island and walk north to Ország út 4. The covered pool is open all year and the pools and grassy strand from May to September.

Places to Stay

Kiskút-liget Camping (☎ 411 042), near the stadium 3km north-east of town, has a year-round motel (3600/4300/4620/5720Ft a single/double/triples/quad) and camp sites for about 400Ft. Take bus No 8 from beside City Hall.

Ibusz (☎ 311 700), Kazinczy utca 3, books *private rooms* from 2500Ft a double.

The pension *Kuckó* (☎ 316 260, Arany János utca 33) charges 5400/6700Ft for rooms with bath. The pick of the crop is

Teátrum (☎ 310 640, fax 328 827, Schweidel utca 7) with rooms for 5300/6500Ft.

Places to Eat

Rábaparti (Zechmeister utca 15) serves tasty, reasonably priced Hungarian fare. *Halászcsárda* (Apáca utca 4), near the market, is a typical inn with fish dishes where the lunch *menü* can cost as little as 350Ft. *Komédias Restaurant* (Czuczor Gergely utca 30) is also worth trying, with most mains around 700Ft. For a cheap self-service lunch, try **Márka** (Bajcsy-Zsilinszky út 30).

Getting There & Away

There are buses to Budapest (hourly), Pécs (two daily), Esztergom (two daily), Balatonfüred (eight daily), Vienna (four daily) and beyond. To reach Fertőd, take the Sopron bus to Kapuvár and change there.

Express trains connect Győr to Budapest's Déli and Keleti train stations (1½ hours) and to Sopron (one hour). To travel to/from Vienna's Westbahnhof (126km) you may have to change trains at Hegyeshalom.

SOPRON
☎ 99

Sopron (Ödenburg in German) sits right on the Austrian border, 217km west of Budapest and only 69km south of Vienna. In 1921 the town voted to remain part of Hungary, while the rest of Bürgenland (the region to which Sopron used to belong) went to Austria. In the small, horseshoe-shaped old town, still partly enclosed by medieval walls, almost every building is historically important – this is Sopron's principal charm.

Orientation & Information

From the main train station, walk north on Mátyás király utca, which becomes Várkerület after a few blocks. Várkerület and Ógabona tér form a loop around the old town. The bus station is on Lackner Kristóf utca, off Ógabona tér.

Tourinform (☎ 338 892) is at Előkapu 11, right near the Fire Tower. Ciklámen Tourist (☎ 312 040), a travel agency, is at Ógabona tér 8 on the corner of Lackner Kristóf utca.

Things to See

The 60m-high **Fire Tower** above the old town's northern gate is a true architectural hybrid: the square base dates from the 12th century, the arcaded balcony from the 16th and the baroque spire from 1680. Climb to the top for a good view (closed Monday).

There are several excellent museums on Fő tér. **Fabricius House** at No 6 is a comprehensive historical museum. **Storno House** at No 8 is a famous Renaissance palace (1560) that is now a museum of Romanesque and Gothic art.

A unique museum of Jewish life is housed in the 14th-century **Old Synagogue** at Új utca 22 (closed Tuesday and October to February). Jews were an important part of the community until their expulsion in 1526.

Places to Stay

Lővér Camping (☎ *311 715, Kőszegi út*) on Pócsi-domb about 5km south of the city centre, is open from mid-April to mid-October. Doubles with shared bath are 2200Ft and camping costs from 580Ft. Bus No 12 from both the bus and train stations stops directly in front of the camp site.

The *Brennbergi Hostel* (☎/fax *313 116*), on Brennbergi út, is pretty far to the west of the city centre, but a bed is under 1000Ft a night and there's also a pension charging 1300Ft per person. It's open from mid-April to mid-October.

Ciklámen Tourist has *private rooms* for about 3000/4000Ft. The pension *Bástya* (☎ *325 325, Patak utca 40*) charges 6000/8000Ft for singles/doubles. The more central *Jégverem* (☎ *312 004, Jégverem utca 1*), with five rooms in an 18th-century ice cellar in the Ikva district, charges 3000Ft per person.

Places to Eat

The best place for an inexpensive lunch or light meal is *Cézár Pince* (*Hátsókapu 2*), in a medieval cellar off Orsolya tér (open until 9.30 pm). Around the corner, the 1950s-inspired *City Diner* (*Várkerület 104*) has burgers done several ways (220Ft) and Mexican dishes.

Forum Pizzeria (*Szent György utca 3*) has decent pizza (around 650Ft), pasta (500Ft) and a salad bar. To sample Sopron's wines go to *Gyógygődőr*, a deep cellar at Fő tér 4.

The ice cream and cakes at *Dömötöri* (*Széchenyi tér 13*) are worth trying, as are the reliable meals at *John Bull pub* next door.

Getting There & Away

There are frequent buses to major Hungarian towns as well as Vienna on weekdays.

Express trains en route to Vienna's Südbahnhof pass through Sopron at least three times a day, however local services to Wiener Neustadt (where you can change for Vienna) are not as frequent. There are four express trains a day to Budapest-Keleti via Győr and Komárom, and around eight local trains to Szombothely.

KŐSZEG
☎ 94

Kőszeg (Güns in German) is a small town at the foot of the Kőszeg Hills, just 3km from the Austrian border. It has played pivotal roles in the nation's defence on several occasions througout history. **Mt Írottkő** (882m), which is south-west of town and straddling the border, is the highest point in Transdanubia.

At its centre is the old town, a colourful well-preserved **medieval precinct**, which includes **Jurisics Castle** (1263), now a historical museum (closed Monday). Jurisics tér, Kőszeg's pleasant main square, hasn't changed much since the 18th century.

Orientation & Information

The train station is a 15-minute walk to the south-east of the old town on Alsó körút; buses stop just a block from Várkör on Liszt Ferenc utca.

For information try Savaria Tourist (☎ 360 238) at Várkör 69 or Ibusz (☎ 360 376) at Várkör 35-37.

Places to Stay

Savaria Tourist can arrange *private rooms* from 3000Ft per double. *Jurisics Castle Hostel* (☎ *360 227, Rajnis József utca 9*), in a small building near the entrance to the castle, is well-worn, but the location makes it attractive. Doubles cost 2700Ft.

Getting There & Away

Kőszeg is at the end of a 18km railway spur from Szombathely, to which there are 15 departures a day. To travel to/from anywhere else, you must take a bus. At least six buses a day run to/from Sopron, and there are two a day to Keszthely. Two buses a week head for Oberpullendorf and Vienna in Austria.

Lake Balaton

Lake Balaton, 77km long, is the largest freshwater lake in Europe outside Scandinavia. The south-eastern shore is shallow and in summer the warm, sandy beaches are a favourite family holiday spot. Better scenery, more historic sites and deeper water are found on the northern shore – Keszthely and Balatonfüred are good bases. Balaton's very popularity is its main drawback, particularly in July and August.

Orientation & Information

The phone code for Balatonfüred and Badacsony is ☎ 87; Keszthely's code is ☎ 83. Balatonfüred's adjacent bus and train stations are on Dobó István utca, 1km north-west of the spa centre and lake. Tourinform (☎ 342 237) is at Petőfi Sándor utca 2 and Balatontourist (☎ 343 471) is near the ferry pier. Ibusz (☎ 342 028), at Zsigmond utca 1, is also helpful.

Keszthely's adjacent bus and train stations are close to the lake ferry terminal. From the stations follow Mártírok útja up the hill, then turn right onto Kossuth Lajos utca into the town. Tourinform (☎ 314 144) is at Kossuth Lajos utca 28 and Ibusz (☎ 314 320) is at Erzsébet királyné utca 2.

Things to See & Do

Balatonfüred This spa town has an easygoing grace and has been the lake's most fashionable bathing resort since the late 18th century. Some parts of town still bear an aristocratic air, while in other parts there are topless bars. Balatonfüred has three public beaches (entry about 200Ft); the best is **Aranyhíd** to the east of Tagore sétány.

Badacsony This small town lies between Balatonfüred and Keszthely in a picturesque region of basalt peaks that can claim some of the best hikes in Hungary. From October to April and as late as mid-May many travel agencies, pensions and restaurants are closed.

From May to September, open-top jeeps marked 'Badacsonyhegyi járat' depart from opposite the post office whenever at least six passengers climb aboard (500Ft per person). They drop you at the Kisfaludy House restaurant, where a map of the trails is posted.

Keszthely Pronounced 'kest-hay', this is a fairly large town with good facilities and boat services on the lake from June to early September. Since it's not totally dependent on tourism, Keszthely is one of the lake's few year-round towns.

Keszthely's most important sight is the **Festetics Palace**, the one-time residence of the wealthy Festetics family. It's closed on Monday; entry is an exorbitant 1300Ft, students 650Ft.

Europe's largest thermal lake, **Gyógytó** lies 7km north-west of Keszthely, in the small town of Hévíz. The thermal lake is an astonishing sight: a milky-blue surface of almost five hectares, covered most of the year with water lilies. The lake is open for swimming until 4.30 or 5.30 pm year-round. Entry is 490/990Ft per half/full day.

Places to Stay

Balatonfüred *Füred Camping* (☎ 343 823, Széchenyi utca 24) is beside the lakeside Hotel Marina, 3km from the train station. It's open April to mid-October. *Lajos Lóczy Gymnasium* (☎ 343 428, Bartók Beutca 4), near the station, charges around 1300Ft for a bed in summer. Friendly *Ring Pension* (☎ 342 884, Petőfi Sándor utca 6a) has neat, clean singles/doubles with shared bath from 3500Ft.

Badacsony *Badacsony Camping* (☎ 431 091), open May to early September, is at the water's edge and about 1.5km west of the ferry pier. There are several small *pensions* on the road above the railway line, a 10-minute walk from the station. Most close from October to April or mid-May.

Keszthely *Zalatour Camping* (☎ 312 782), on Ernszt Géza sétány, has large bungalows for four people from DM50 to DM70 and smaller holiday houses for DM18 to DM24. The site has access to Helikon Beach. To get there, head south across the train tracks. In July and August you can stay at *Ferenc Pethe College* (☎ 311 290, Festetics György út 5) for about 2000Ft per person.

Getting There & Away

From Budapest's Déli station there are frequent express trains to Balatonfüred (two hours) via Badacsony. Change at Tapolca for Keszthely.

Buses from Budapest leave for towns around Lake Balaton from the bus station at Erzsébet tér. Hévíz doesn't have a train station, but a bus goes to/from Keszthely almost every half-hour from stand No 3 (30 minutes).

Getting Around

Train services on both the northern and southern sides of the lake are fairly frequent. A better way to see Lake Balaton up close is on a Mahart passenger ferry. From April to October, ferries operate between Siófok, Balatonfüred and Tihany, as well as Fonyód and Badacsony. During the main summer season, June to early September, ferries ply the entire length of the lake from Balatonkenese to Keszthely (five hours) with frequent stops on both shores. One-way trips on the lake cost 360Ft to 700Ft, depending on the kilometres travelled. Return trips are slightly cheaper than double the one-way fare.

Southern Transdanubia

PÉCS
☎ 72

Pécs (pronounced 'pairch') is a large, historical city between the Danube and Drava rivers. City walls were erected after the Mongol invasion of 1241, but 1543 marked the start of almost 150 years of Turkish domination. The Turks left their greatest monuments at Pécs and these – together with imposing churches, a lovely synagogue and a lively student atmosphere – make it a good stop on the way to/from Croatia.

Orientation & Information

The bus and train stations are south of the centre, three blocks apart – find your way north to Széchenyi tér, the centre of the old town.

Tourinform (☎ 213 315) is at Széchenyi tér 9. The Corvina Art Bookshop at Széchenyi tér 7-8 has an excellent selection of English-language books.

Things to See

All of Pécs' museums, except the synagogue, are closed on Monday.

Széchenyi tér is the bustling heart of Pécs, dominated to the north by the Inner Town Parish Church, or **Mosque Church**, as it was originally the Gazi Kassim Pasha Mosque. It's the largest Turkish building in Hungary. Behind at Széchenyi tér 12 is the **Archaeological Museum**. From here go west along Janus Pannonius utca for a block to the **Csontváry Museum** at No 11, which displays the work of surrealist painter Tivadar Csontváry (1853-1919).

Káptalan utca, which climbs north-east from here, is lined with museums. The **Vasarely Museum** at No 3 houses Victor Vasarely's op art. Across the street at No 2 is the **Zsolnay Porcelain Museum**.

Walk westward to Dóm tér and the enormous four-towered **Basilica of St Peter**. In summer there are organ concerts on Friday evening. West of the **Bishop's Palace** (1770), which stands in front of the cathedral, is a 15th-century **barbican**, the only stone bastion to survive from the old city walls.

To the south of Dóm tér is leafy Szent István tér. Here you'll see a stairway down to an excavated 4th-century **Christian chapel** with striking frescoes. There's a **Roman mausoleum** a little farther south at Apáca utca 14.

The **synagogue** (1869) on Kossuth tér, an oblong square south of Széchenyi tér, is open to visitors every day except Saturday from May to October.

Places to Stay

In July and August, the *Négy Kollégium* at Janus Pannonius University (☎ *251 203, Szántó Kovács János utca 1/c*) will accommodate travellers in dormitory rooms for 800Ft to 1400Ft. Ask Tourinform about other college dorms.

Ibusz (☎ 212 176), at Apáca utca 1, arranges *private rooms* from 2200/3200Ft for singles/doubles.

The small but very central *Főnix Hotel* (☎ *311 680, Hunyadi János út 2*) charges from 4290/5690Ft for singles/doubles with shared bath, more with attached bath.

Places to Eat

Kiraly utca is lined with eateries, including *Planet Pécs (Király utca 2)*, a groovy place for a pizza and *Dóm Snack (Király utca 3)*, which does pizza and pasta for around 600Ft. *Alibaba (Perczel Mór utca 23)* is a small takeaway place serving gyros and felafel. *Az Elefánthoz (Jókai tér 6)* is a bustling Italian restaurant, with excellent pizza, pasta and meal-sized salads.

Getting There & Away
There are regular buses to Szeged, two daily to Kecskemét, Hévíz and one a day to Sopron. To/from Croatia, there are three buses a day between Pécs and Osijek, and three more between Barcs on the border and Zagreb.

Some 10 trains a day connect Pécs with Budapest-Déli or Budapest-Keleti. A daily train runs from Pécs to Osijek.

The Great Plain

The Great Plain (Nagyalföld) of southeastern Hungary is a wide expanse of level *puszta* (prairie) drained by the Tisza River. Visitors to the region are introduced to the lore of the Hungarian shepherds and their unique animals: Nonius horses, long-horned grey cattle and *racka* sheep.

KECSKEMÉT
☎ 76
Lying near the geographical centre of Hungary, Kecskemét is a clean, leafy city famous for its apricots, *barack pálinka* (apricot brandy) and level puszta. Central Kecskemét has more than its share of impressive public and religious architecture and there is a vibrant student atmosphere.

Orientation & Information
The bus and main train stations are opposite one another in József Katona Park. A 10-minute walk south-west along Nagykőrösi utca leads to the first of Kecskemét's many squares, Szabadság tér.

You'll find Tourinform (☎ 481 065) on the western side of the town hall at Kossuth Lajos tér 1.

Things to See
Dominating Kossuth Lajos tér is the massive Art Nouveau **town hall** (1897) with a carillon that plays on the hour. Flanking the town hall are the neoclassical **Great Church** (1806) and the earlier **Church of St Nicholas**. Facing Szabadság tér, the **Ornamental Palace** (1902) is covered in multicoloured majolica tiles – check out the **Decorative Hall** with its stucco peacock, bizarre windows and tiles.

Of the many museums and art galleries, the most interesting is the **Museum of Naive Artists** in the Stork House (1730) on Gáspár András utca, just off Petőfi Sándor utca. The rewarding **Photography Museum** is housed in a former Orthodox synagogue at Katona József tér 12 (closed Monday and Tuesday).

Places to Stay
Autós Camping (☎ 329 398, Csabay Géza körút 5) is on the south-western side of town and is open from mid-April to mid-October. Catch bus Nos 1 or 11 from the train station. In summer, the *Teachers' College* (☎ 486 186, Piaristák tere 4) in the centre of town has beds for 1200Ft in triple rooms. Tourinform can make college bookings.

Color Panzió (☎ 483 246, Jókai utca 26) charges 5000Ft a double or triple. Nicer rooms can be found at *Caissa Panzió* (☎ 481 685, Gyenes tér 18) around the corner. Singles/doubles with shared bathroom start at 2600/3200Ft, or 4400/5400Ft with bath and TV.

Hotel Pálma (☎ 321 045, Arany János utca 3) is central and good value. Rooms in the 'tourist' section cost 2850/5100Ft with shared bathroom. In the hotel section you'll pay 4300/5900Ft with bath, phone and TV. It has another 80 dorm beds in a nearby building.

Places to Eat
Jalta (Batthyány utca 2), opposite the Hotel Három Gúnár, is a homy wine cellar with a menu that's in both English and German. Modern *Taverna Hellasz*, behind the shopping centre on the corner of Lechner and Kisfaludy utcas, has excellent Greek meals such as superb lamb gyros for 750Ft. A comfortable spot for coffee, snacks and stiff drinks is the bar on the ground floor of the *House of Technology* (a former synagogue) on Jókai utca.

Entertainment
Kecskemét is a city of music and theatre; you'd be crazy not to attend at least one performance here. The *Ferenc Erdei Cultural Centre (Deák Ferenc tér 1)* is a good source of information.

Getting There & Away

There are almost hourly buses to Budapest, and every few hours to Szeged and at least two a day to Pécs. Buses also run to Arad in Romania twice a week and to Subotica in Yugoslavia a couple of times daily.

Kecskemét is on the train line linking Budapest-Nyugati with Szeged.

KISKUNSÁG NATIONAL PARK

Many of the park's alkaline ponds, dunes and grassy 'deserts' are off-limits to casual visitors. But you can get a close look at this environmentally fragile area – and see the famous horseherds go through their paces – at **Bugac**, 30km south-west of Kecskemét.

The best way to get there on your own is by bus from Kecskemét. The 11 am bus from the main terminal gets you to the park entrance around midday, giving you time to walk (3km) or take a horse and carriage (1000Ft) to the puszta for the horse show, which begins at 1.15 pm. Entry to the park is 1000Ft.

It is easier – but pricier – to get there with Bugac Tours in Kecskemét (☎ 482 500); its office is at Szabadság tér 5 and it has another one at the park entrance. Tours cost from US$17 to US$30 per person, depending on whether you join the tour in Kecskemét or make your own way to the park entrance. The tours include a horse and carriage ride to the puszta, the horse show and lunch at the touristy csárda.

The **horse show** usually runs from April to the end of September. The horseherds perform tricks such as whip cracking and bareback riding.

The **Bugaci Karikás Csárda**, with its folk-music ensemble and its gulyás, is a lot more fun than it appears. It has a *camping ground* for 60 people.

SZEGED

☎ 62

Szeged (Segedin in German), the most important city on the southern Great Plain, straddles the Tisza River just before it enters Yugoslavia. The Maros River from Romania enters the Tisza just east of the city centre.

Szeged is more architecturally homogenous than many other Hungarian cities, with few modern buildings intruding on the stately city centre and the main square, Széchenyi tér. Don't miss the **Reök Palace**,

a mind-blowing Art Nouveau structure on Kölcsey utca. Szeged's **Great Synagogue** (1903), Gutenberg utca 13, is the most beautiful Jewish house of worship in Hungary and is still in use. The symbol of Szeged is the rather ugly **Votive Church**, though its cavernous interior is impressive.

Besides architecture, Szeged is known for its large student population, its midsummer Open-Air Festival, its paprika and Pick salami, the finest in Hungary.

Orientation & Information

The main train station is south of the city centre on Indóház tér; tram No 1 connects the train station to the city centre. The bus station, to the west of the centre on Mars tér, is within easy walking distance via pedestrianised Mikszáth Kálmán utca.

Tourinform (☎ 420 509) is at Victor Hugo utca 1. Other agencies include Szeged Tourist (☎ 321 800) on Klauzál tér, just off Victor Hugo utca, and Ibusz (☎ 471 177), Oroszlán utca 3.

Places to Stay

Partfürdő Camping (☎ 430 843, *Középkikötő sor*) is in Újszeged (New Szeged), along the river opposite the city centre, and *Napfény Camping* (☎ 421 800, *Dorozsmai út 4*) is across a large bridge near the western terminus of tram No 1.

Plenty of student accommodation is open to travellers in July and August, including *István Apáthy College* (☎ 420 488, *Eötvös utca 4*), next to the Votive Church. Private rooms with bath cost around 1500Ft per person and dorms cost 800Ft. *Loránd Eötvös College* (☎ 310 641, *Tisza Lajos körút 103*) charges similar prices. Go directly to the hostels or ask Proko Travel (☎ 484 225, ✉ proko@mail.tiszanet.hu), Kígyó utca 3, to organise it.

Ibusz and Szeged Tourist have *private rooms* (2000Ft to 2500Ft per person). If you arrive by bus you'll be within walking distance of *Pölös Panzió* (☎ 498 208, *Pacsirta utca 17a*), which charges 4000/4800Ft.

Places to Eat

Hági (*Kelemen utca 3*), an old Szeged stand-by in the centre, serves reliable and reasonably priced Hungarian and South Slav dishes. *Lesö Harcsa Halászcsárda* (*Roosevelt tér 14*) is a Szeged institution and serves up *halászlé* by the cauldron. *Jumbo Grill (Mikszáth Kálmán utca 4)* has salads and excellent grilled chicken. *Festival*, on Oskola utca, a self-service place opposite the Votive Church, offers cheap Chinese dishes.

Entertainment

The *National Theatre* (☎ 479 279, *Deák Ferenc utca 12-14*) has always been the centre of cultural life in Szeged and usually stages opera and ballet. The Szeged Open-Air Festival (mid-July to August) unfolds on Dóm tér – the outdoor theatre here seats some 6000 people. Tickets and information are available from the festival ticket office at Deák Ferenc utca 30.

Szeged isn't all highbrow: there's a vast array of bars and clubs around Dugonics tér. The *JATE Club (Toldy utca 1)* is the best place to meet students on their own turf.

Getting There & Away

There are seven daily buses to Budapest, two to Debrecen, two to Eger, 10 to Kecskemét and six to Pécs. To Romania, buses run to Arad at 8.45 am daily and to Timişoara on Tuesday, Wednesday, Friday and Saturday. Buses run to Senta (Hungarian: Zenta) in Yugoslavia twice daily and to Subotica several times a day.

Szeged is on a main train line to Budapest-Nyugati. Another line connects the city with Hódmezővásárhely and Békéscsaba, where you can change trains for Romania. South-bound local trains leave for Subotica in Yugoslavia twice daily.

Northern Hungary

EGER

☎ 36

Eger (Erlau in German) is a lovely baroque city with Hungary's finest examples of Copf (Hungarian: Zopf) architecture, a transitional style between late baroque and neoclassicism found only in Central Europe. It was at Eger Castle in 1552 that 2000 Hungarian defenders temporarily stopped the Turkish advance into Europe and helped to preserve Hungary's identity.

Today Eger is famous for its potent Bull's Blood (Egri Bikavér) red wine. Dozens of wine cellars are open for tastings in

Szépasszonyvölgy (Valley of the Beautiful Women), just a 20-minute walk west of the city centre.

Orientation & Information

The train station is a 15-minute walk south of the city centre via Vasút utca, just west of Deák Ferenc utca. The bus station is above Széchenyi István utca, Eger's main drag. Tourinform (☎ 321 807) is at Dobó István tér 2.

Things to See & Do

The first thing you see as you come into town centre from the bus or train station is the neoclassical **Eger Cathedral** (1836) on Eszterházy tér.

Directly opposite the cathedral is the Copf-style **Lyceum** (200Ft, students 100Ft) with a frescoed library on the 1st floor, and an observation deck with a great view of the city and a camera obscura which projects 'live' images of Eger into a darkened room. The Lyceum is open to 9.30 am to 3 pm daily in summer (until 12.30 pm in the off season).

At the eastern end of Kossuth utca, across Dózsa György tér, a cobblestone lane leads up to **Eger Castle**, built in the 13th century after the Mongol invasion. The castle's **István Dobó Museum**, in the former Bishop's Palace (1470), is named after the national hero who led the resistance to the Turks in 1552. Below the castle are underground casemates hewn from solid rock, which you can tour with a guide (300Ft for museum and casemates).

The **Minorite church** (1773) on Dobó István tér is one of the most beautiful baroque buildings in Hungary. After so much history, unwind in the **Archbishop's Garden** (Érsek kert). It has open-air and covered swimming pools as well as thermal baths.

The choice of **wine cellars** at Szépasszonyvölgy can be a bit daunting. If you're interested in good wine, visit cellars 5, 13, 18, 23, 31 and 32.

Places to Stay

Tulipán Camping (☎ 410 580, *Szépasszonyvölgy utca 71*) charges 500Ft to 600Ft for tent sites and the same per person. Bungalows are also available. The valley's wine cellars are within easy stumbling distance.

A number of colleges can offer accommodation in July and August, including the

300-bed *Attila József College* (☎ *410 571/2, Mátyás király út 62)* near the train station. Express can tell you about others. Rates at most are around 1000Ft.

Egertourist (☎ 411 724) can organise *private rooms* from 2500Ft per person and flats from 4500Ft for two people. Villa Tours (☎ 410 215) also has private rooms at similar prices.

The cheapest place is the somewhat institutional *Tourist Motel* (☎ *429 014, Mekcsey István utca 2)* with singles/doubles with shared bath from 1800/2800Ft in the old wing, 2400/4000Ft in the new wing, and doubles with private bath for 4900Ft.

Places to Eat

Express (Pyrker tér 4), just below the north-east side of the bus station, is a self-service restaurant with meals as low as 250Ft.

HBH Bajor (Bajcsy-Zsilinszky utca 19) serves good reliable Hungarian/Germanic food. *Kondi* salad bar *(Széchenyi utca 2)* and *Gyros (Széchenyi utca 10)*, a local bar/restaurant with Greek salads (330Ft) and souvlaki (620Ft), are also good. For pizza, try the *Pizza Club (Fazolka Henrik utca 1)*.

Entertainment

Tourinform, the *County Cultural Centre (Knézich Károly utca 8)*, or the city's *ticket office* (☎ *312 660, Széchenyi utca 3)* can tell you what concerts and plays are on. Venues are the Géza Gárdonyi Theatre, the Lyceum and Eger Cathedral. There are organ concerts from mid-May to mid-October at Eger Cathedral (11.30 am Monday to Saturday, 12.45 pm Sunday; 300/100Ft).

Getting There & Away

There are regular buses to Budapest, Kecskemét, Szilvásvárad and Szeged.

Eger is on a minor rail line linking Putnok and Füzesabony; for Budapest you usually have to change at Füzesabony. There are up to four direct trains a day to/from Budapest-Keleti. Trains to Szilvásvárad leave around six times a day.

SZILVÁSVÁRAD
☎ 36

To the north of Eger are the Bükk range of hills, most of which fall within the 388 sq km **Bükk National Park**. A good place to begin a visit is the village of Szilvásvárad, 27km from Eger – an easy day trip. It's an ideal base for hiking in the Szalajka Valley and is also the centre of horse breeding in Hungary, with some 250 prize Lipizzaners at the **Lipizzaner Stud Farm** at the top of Fenyves utca.

Szilvásvárad is also the place to ride on a scenic narrow-gauge train for about 5km to **Szalajka-Fátyolvízesés** (April to October). Stay on the train for the return trip or walk back along well-trodden, shady paths. From Szalajka-Fátyolvízesés, you can walk for 15 minutes to the **Istállóskő Cave**, where Palaeolithic pottery shards were discovered, or climb 958m **Mt Istállóskő**, the highest peak in the Bükk.

Orientation & Information

The bus from Eger stops in the centre of town. From the Szilvásvárad-Szalajkavölgy train station follow Egri út east for about 10 minutes to the centre of town. There's no local tourist office, but Tourinform in Eger has information and sells Cartographia's *A Bükk* (400Ft), the best map of the Bükk region.

Places to Stay

Hegyi Camping (☎ *355 207, Egri út 36a)* has small holiday houses for two for 3400Ft. Camping costs around 500Ft per tent and per person. *Hegyi Panzió* (☎ *355 545)*, at the camping ground entrance, has doubles with bath for 5800Ft.

Hotel Lipicai (☎ *355 100, Egri út 12)* is a bit on the dark and dingy side, though the rooms are reasonable. Singles/doubles are 3150/6300Ft.

Getting There & Away

Buses to/from Eger are very frequent and they're faster than the train.

Iceland

Nowhere are the forces of nature more evident than in rugged Iceland (Ísland), with snow-capped peaks, glaciers, hot springs, geysers, active volcanoes, waterfalls, icecaps, tundra, lava deserts, and craters. For 'stopover' visitors on the way to/from mainland Europe, there's plenty to see in and around Reykjavík, Iceland's capital and main transport hub.

AT A GLANCE

Capital:	Reykjavík
Population:	279,000
Official Language:	Icelandic
Currency:	1 Icelandic króna (Ikr) = 100 aurar

Facts about Iceland

HISTORY

Irish monks were the first people to arrive on Iceland, around 700 AD. Although they regarded Iceland as a hermitage until the early 9th century, the Age of Settlement is traditionally defined as the period between 874 and 930 when political strife on the Scandinavian mainland caused many Nordic people to flee westward.

The human history of Iceland was chronicled almost from the beginning. The *Íslendingabók* was written by the 12th-century scholar Ari Torgilsson (Ari the Learned) about 250 years after the fact. He also compiled the more detailed *Landnámabók*, a comprehensive chronicle of that era. The *Íslendingabók* credits the first permanent settlement to Norwegian Ingólfur Arnarson who set up in 874 at a place he called Reykjavík (Smoky Bay) because of the steam from thermal springs there.

In the early 13th century, violent feuds and raids by private armies ravaged the countryside and the chaos eventually led to the cession of control to Norway in 1281. In 1397, the Kalmar Union (of Norway, Sweden and Denmark) brought Iceland under Danish rule.

By the early 1800s, a growing sense of Icelandic nationalism was perceived in Copenhagen. Free trade was restored in 1855 thanks to lobbying by Icelandic scholar Jón Sigurdsson and, by 1874, Iceland had drafted a constitution. The Republic of Iceland was established on 17 June 1944.

After the Nazi occupation of Denmark in WWII, Iceland's vulnerability became a matter of concern, and so British troops occupied the island. When the British withdrew in 1941, the government allowed US troops to move in and take over Keflavík, now the site of Reykjavík's international airport. Despite protests by the government and people, the US military presence continues.

GEOGRAPHY

Iceland (103,000 sq km) is the second-largest island in Europe. The south-eastern coast is 798km from Scotland, the eastern end is 970km from Norway, and the Westfjords lie 287km east of Greenland. Only 21% of the land is arable. Over 50% of the country lies above 400m and its highest point, Hvannadalshnúkur, rises 2119m from beneath the glacier Öræfajökull.

CLIMATE

In January, Reykjavík enjoys an average of three sunny days and in July, only one. Fierce, wind-driven rains alternate with drizzle, gales and fog to create a miserable climate. Basically, it's a matter of 'if you don't like the weather now, wait five minutes – it will probably get worse'. May, June and July are the 'driest' months of the year.

POPULATION & PEOPLE

Most Icelanders are descended from the early Scandinavian and Celtic settlers. The population of 279,000 is increasing by only about 1% annually and 62% (172,000) of these people live in Reykjavík and environs.

Icelanders are noted for being self-reliant, stoic and reserved, which gregarious

ICELAND

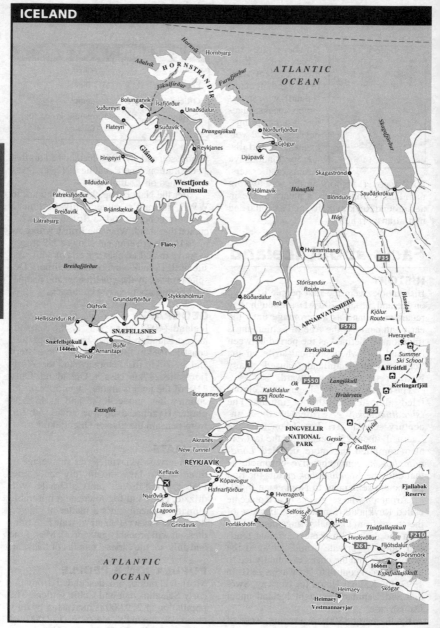

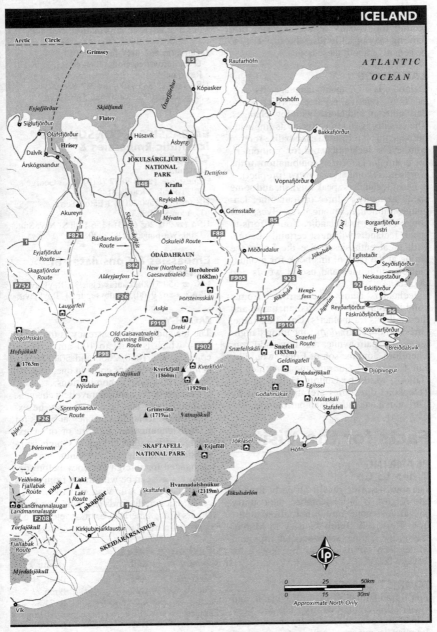

ICELAND

visitors may find a little disconcerting. Objecting too vocally to whaling and bird hunting may upset locals, who are likely to be sensitive about these issues.

LANGUAGE

Icelandic is a Germanic language. Its closest 'living relative' is Faroese, which is also derived from Old Norse, with few changes. The country is so protective of its linguistic heritage that it refuses to cannibalise foreign words. The Icelandic word for 'computer', for example, is *tölva*, a combination of the words *tala* (number) and *völva* (prophet).

Most Icelanders speak English, and some speak as many as three or four other languages, although, among themselves, they converse only in Icelandic. Your efforts to speak Icelandic will most certainly be met with great enthusiasm. See the Language Guide at the back of this book for pronunciation guidelines and useful words and phrases.

Icelanders' names are constructed from a combination of their Christian name and their father's (or mother's) Christian name. Girls add the suffix *dóttir*, meaning daughter, to the patronymic, and boys add *son*. Therefore, Jón, the son of Einar, would be Jón Einarsson. Gudrun, the daughter of Halldór, would be Gudrun Halldórsdóttir. Telephone directories are alphabetised by Christian name rather than patronymic.

Facts for the Visitor

PLANNING
When to Go

The tourist season runs from early June to late August. By 30 September, the country has almost gone into hibernation, apart from Reykjavík. From January to March, skiing, ice-fishing, snow-scooter trips and winter jeep safaris can be arranged from Reykjavík.

TOURIST OFFICES

You'll find tourist offices in Reykjavík and towns all over the country. They're very helpful and employees usually speak Scandinavian languages, English, German and French. In addition to providing information, the staff will book tours, sell bus passes and make hotel and transport reservations.

Ask for the free *Around Iceland* and *Iceland*. For advance information, contact:

Iceland (☎ 562 3045, fax 562 3057,
    @ tourinfo@tourinfo.is) Bankastræti 2, IS-101 Reykjavík
USA (☎ 212-885 9700, fax 212-885 9710,
    @ goiceland@aol.com) 655 Third Ave, New York, NY 10017

EMBASSIES & CONSULATES
Icelandic Embassies & Consulates
Australia
    Consulate: (☎ 03-9827 7819) 44 St George's Rd, Toorak, Victoria 3142
UK (☎ 020-7590 1100) 1 Eaton Terrace, London SW1 8EY
USA (☎ 202-265 6653) 1156 15th St NW, Suite 1200, Washington, DC 20005

Embassies & Consulates in Iceland
UK (☎ 550 5100), Laufásvegur 31, Reykjavík
USA (☎ 562 9100), Laufásvegur 21, Reykjavík

MONEY

The Icelandic unit of currency is the króna (Ikr), which is equal to 100 aurar. Notes come in 500, 1000, 2000 and 5000 krónur denominations. Coins come in one, five, 10, 50 and 100 krónur denominations.

Foreign-denomination travellers cheques, postal cheques and banknotes may be exchanged for Icelandic currency at banks for a small commission. Beware of other exchange offices that charge sky-high commissions. Any leftover krónur may be exchanged for foreign currency before departure. Cash can be withdrawn from banks using a MasterCard, Visa or Cirrus ATM card. Major credit cards (MasterCard, Visa, Diners Club, American Express, etc) are accepted at most places.

Exchange Rates

country	unit		krónur
Australia	A$1	=	Ikr46.71
Canada	C$1	=	Ikr55.73
euro	€1	=	Ikr71.88
France	1FF	=	Ikr10.96
Germany	DM1	=	Ikr36.75
Ireland	IR£1	=	Ikr91.26
New Zealand	NZ$1	=	Ikr34.14
UK	UK£1	=	Ikr118.78
USA	US$1	=	Ikr85.52

Costs

If you stay in hostels and eat at snack bars you can keep expenses to about US$45 a day. Student-card holders get substantial discounts on flights, museum admissions and bus fares (in winter). Discounts aren't always advertised, so you're advised to ask.

Tipping

Tipping isn't required in Iceland; restaurants automatically add service charges to the bill.

POST & COMMUNICATIONS

To mail letters with the efficient Icelandic postal system costs Ikr50 to Europe, Ikr75 to most other destinations.

Iceland's country code is ☎ 354, and there are no area codes. When dialling in from abroad, simply dial ☎ 354 plus the seven-digit phone number.

Within Iceland, direct dialling is available via satellite to Europe, North America and elsewhere. The international access code is ☎ 00. For operator assistance (collect calls), call ☎ 533 5010. A three-minute phone call to the USA costs Ikr180 at all times.

INTERNET RESOURCES

The Icelandic Tourist Board has detailed country information, as well as tips on organised tours, accommodation and festivals. Web sites: www.icetourist.is and www.goiceland.org. The Website www.nat.is also has comprehensive information.

TIME

Iceland doesn't have daylight-saving time, so it keeps to GMT/UTC all year; from late October to late March, Iceland is on the same time as London (GMT/UTC) but it's one hour behind London in summer.

DANGERS & ANNOYANCES

Iceland has a low crime rate, so there are few dangers or annoyances for travellers. Police don't carry guns, and prisoners go home on public holidays.

When visiting geothermal areas avoid thin crusts of lighter coloured soil around fumaroles (vents for hot gases) and mudpots, snowfields that may overlie hidden fissures, loose sharp lava chunks, and slippery slopes of scoria (volcanic slag).

BUSINESS HOURS

Weekday shopping hours are 9 am to 6 pm, although some shops open at 8 am and close at 4 pm or later. Shops usually open at 9 or 10 am and close between 1 and 5 pm on Saturday. Some shops in Reykjavík are now open on Sunday.

PUBLIC HOLIDAYS & SPECIAL EVENTS

The following public holidays are observed in Iceland: 1 January, Maundy Thursday, Good Friday, Easter Day, Easter Monday, 3rd Thursday in April (First Day of Summer), 1 May (Labour Day), Ascension Day, Whit Sunday, Whit Monday, 17 June (Independence Day), 1st Monday in August (Shop & Office Workers' Holiday), 24 to 26 December.

The first day of summer, or *Sumardagurinn fyrsti*, is celebrated in carnival style, with the biggest bash staged in Reykjavík. The first day of winter, *Fyrsti vetrardagur*, occurs on the third Saturday of October, but it's not an occasion that inspires much merriment. Midsummer is celebrated around 24 June in Iceland but with less fervour than on the Scandinavian mainland.

Reykjavík hosts a biennial arts festival that includes a large range of events, including paintings, song and dance. Ask the tourist office for details. *Þjódhátíð Vestmannaeyjar* takes place in early August in Vestmannaeyjar, commemorating the day in 1874 when foul weather prevented the populace from celebrating the establishment of Iceland's constitution.

ACCOMMODATION

Camping provides the most effective relief from high accommodation prices. Bring an easily assembled, stable, seam-sealed and well-constructed tent (storm-force winds and deluges aren't uncommon in summer). A porch for storing wet gear, cooking implements and boots is vital. You'll also need a good sleeping bag. Organised camping grounds are known as *tjaldsvæði*. Amenities and charges vary, but usually you'll pay about Ikr400 to Ikr700 per person.

In Iceland, Hostelling International (HI) hostels are called *farfuglaheimili*, which translates into something like 'little home for migrating birds'. HI members pay Ikr1250 and others pay Ikr1500. For information on

ICELAND

hostels, contact Bandalag Íslenskra Farfugla (Icelandic Hostel Association; ☎ 553 8110, fax 588 9201, ✉ info@hostel.is), Sundlaugavegur 34, IS-105 Reykjavík.

Most Edda hotels, operated by Icelandair Hotels, are school dormitories that are used as hotels during summer holidays (early June to late August). Some offer sleeping-bag accommodation (a bed on which you roll out your sleeping bag) or dorm facilities as well as conventional lodging. Single/double rooms cost Ikr4300/5400. Sleeping-bag and dorm accommodation range from Ikr950 to Ikr1500 per person.

There are several types of *gistiheimilið* (guesthouses), from private homes that let out rooms in order to bring in extra cash, to others that are quite elaborate. Hostel-style sleeping-bag accommodation may be available. In some cases, a continental breakfast is included. Sleeping-bag accommodation costs about Ikr1500; double rooms range from Ikr3000 to Ikr9000; and self-contained units, between Ikr4000 and Ikr9000. Rooms are always cheaper if booked through a travel agent abroad.

FOOD & DRINKS
Although traditional Icelandic delicacies may remind foreigners of the nightmare feast in *Indiana Jones and the Temple of Doom*, they aren't always as bad as they sound. The glaring exception is *hákarl*, putrefied shark meat that has been buried in sand and gravel for three to six months to ensure sufficient decomposition.

Moving towards the less bizarre, Icelanders make a staple of *harðfiskur*, haddock that's cleaned and dried in the open air until it has become dehydrated and brittle. It's torn into strips and eaten with butter as a snack. Icelanders also eat broiled *lundi*, or puffin, which looks and tastes like calves' liver. Whale blubber, whale steaks and seal meat are also available, but you might resist for various reasons. A unique Icelandic treat, *skyr*, is a delicious yoghurt-like concoction made of pasteurised skimmed milk and bacteria culture.

Reykjavík has several intimate pub-style cafes where you can drink beer, eat a meal or chat over coffee for hours without attracting comment. These places are great value, with light meals for about Ikr800. The word 'restaurant' usually denotes an upmarket establishment, often associated with expensive hotels.

Coffee is a national institution in Iceland. Alcohol is another matter: high taxes are levied in the hope that they will discourage excessive consumption (in fact, beer didn't become legal until 1989). Nowadays beer, wine and spirits are available to people over 20 years from licensed bars, restaurants and *ÁTVR*, or State Monopoly stores. Drinking in restaurants and pubs is definitely for the wealthy – a glass of house wine costs about Ikr500, and the price for beer is up to Ikr800 for 500ml. The traditional Icelandic alcoholic brew is *brennivín* (burnt wine), a sort of schnapps made from potatoes and caraway.

Getting There & Away

AIR
Icelandair, Iceland's national carrier, serves Keflavík directly from many European airports including Amsterdam, Copenhagen, Frankfurt, Glasgow, Hamburg, London, Oslo, Paris and Stockholm. Flights from London to Iceland cost from UK£167 return.

During the high season (20 May to 29 September), there are daily Icelandair flights from Keflavík to New York JFK and Baltimore/Washington. For the latest information, call ☎ 800-223 5500 within the USA.

The budget airline Go (☎ 0845 605 4321 in the UK) flies London (Stanstead) to Keflavík four days a week from May to September; fares start at UK£59 one-way. Atlantic Airways (☎ 570 3030) flies to Iceland (Reykjavík) from the Faroes three to five times a week from April to September, with possible connections from Aberdeen and Glasgow. The discounted return Faroes-Iceland Apex fare is Dkr2300.

Other airlines serve Iceland, mainly in summer, including LTU from Germany. Combined air/ferry tickets to Iceland are now available from the UK and Scandinavia. Contact your travel agent for full details.

SEA
Ferry
You can travel from the European mainland by ferry. Although this takes longer

than flying and isn't much cheaper, it allows you the option of taking a vehicle.

Smyril Line's *Norröna* operates from late May to early September out of Hanstholm in Denmark. The *Norröna* sails from Hanstholm on Saturday, arriving in Tórshavn in the Faroe Islands on Monday morning. All Iceland-bound passengers must disembark while the ship continues to Lerwick (Shetland) and Bergen (Norway). It returns to Tórshavn on Wednesday, gathers up Iceland passengers, and sails overnight to Seyðisfjörður. Note that Iceland passengers cannot remain aboard while the ship sails to Norway; they must spend two nights in the Faroes en route. To stay longer in the Faroes, you'll have to break your journey there and pay for two sectors. The high-season deck fare between Hanstholm and Seyðisfjörður (which includes a couchette or sleeper) is Dkr2200 each way. Hanstholm to Tórshavn is Dkr1410 and Tórshavn to Seyðisfjörður is Dkr1320. Discounts of 25% are available to holders of student cards.

Cargo Ship

The Icelandic cargo-shipper Eimskip can take passengers on its vessel *Brúarfoss*. The ship sails every second Thursday from Reykjavík to the Faroe Islands and Hamburg, returning via Denmark, Sweden, Norway and the Faroes. The trip to Hamburg takes four days and costs Ikr28,800 per person, one way in a double cabin (full board). Contact the sales agent in Iceland: Úrval-Útsýn Travel (☎ 585 4000, fax 585 4065), Lágmúli 4, IS-108 Reykjavík.

The Samskip Line (☎ 01482-322399, fax 01482-229529) has its UK base at Silvester House, The Maltings, Silvester St, Hull, England. It is cheaper but facilities are considerably more basic.

Getting Around

BUS

Although Iceland is small and has a well-established public transport system, there are no railways and the highway system is Europe's least developed.

Bifreiðastöð Íslands (BSÍ; ☎ 552 2300 or ☎ 562 3320), a collective organisation of Iceland's long-distance bus operators, covers the country with feasible connections.

Many routes are straightforward but on some minor routes connections may take up to two days. Many buses stop running in September and don't resume until June. Interior routes rarely open before July and most close by early to mid-September.

BSÍ offers two bus passes, the Hringmiði ('Ring Pass' or Full-Circle Pass) and the Tímamiði ('Time Pass' or Omnibuspass). The former allows a circuit of the Ring Road in either direction (without reversing your route), stopping anywhere you like. It costs Ikr16,100 (Ikr23,800 with the Westfjords extension) – not much less than the normal fare – but you're entitled to 5% discount on ferries (if tickets are bought from BSÍ) and 10% discount at a few camping grounds and other accommodation. There's also 5% discount on some organised tours if bought from BSÍ.

Ask for a free copy of the *Leiðabók* (bus timetable).

Reykjavík

Iceland's capital Reykjavík, home to 172,000 of the country's 279,000 people, is the world's most northerly capital city and one of its smallest. Though Reykjavík is historically and architecturally unexciting by European standards, it dominates Iceland politically, socially, culturally, economically and psychologically. In essence, everything that happens in the country happens in Reykjavík.

Reykjavík (Smoky Bay) was the first place in Iceland to be intentionally settled. The original settler, Ingólfur Arnarson, tossed his high-seat pillars (a bit of pagan paraphernalia) overboard in 874 AD, and built his farm near where they washed ashore. Ingólfur claimed the entire southwest corner of the island, then set about planting his hayfields at Austurvöllur, the present town square.

Orientation

Reykjavík's heart is between Tjörnin and the harbour, and many old buildings remain. Nearly everything in the city lies within walking distance of the old settlement, and most meeting and lounging activity takes place around Lækjartorg and the adjacent pedestrian shopping street, Austurstræti. The shopping district extends east along

ICELAND

REYKJAVÍK

Laugavegur from Lækjargata to the Hlem-mur bus terminal.

Information

Tourist Offices The main tourist office, Upplýsingamiðstöð Ferðamála (☎ 562 3045), is at Bankastræti 2, near Lækjargata. From 15 May to 15 September it's open 8.30 am to 7 pm daily, with shorter hours (and closed Sunday) the rest of the year.

There are other branches at the new city hall (☎ 563 2005) and at the BSÍ long-distance bus terminal. Pick up a copy of *Reykjavík This Month*, published monthly in summer.

The Reykjavík Tourist Card, available at the tourist offices, gives you free entry to museums, swimming pools, etc, and includes a bus pass. It costs Ikr900/1200/1500 for one/two/three days.

Money Banks can be found on Austurstræti and Bankastræti. After-hours banking is available at the Change Group, with branches at Keflavík international airport and in town at Bankastræti 2, but it charges 8.75% commission.

Post & Communications The main post office on Pósthússtræti is open from 10 am to 4.30 pm weekdays. The substation in the Kringlan shopping centre closes at 6.30 pm (7.30 on Friday) and is also open from 10 am to 6 pm Saturday.

Public phones at the Lækjartorg bus terminal, on the corner of Hafnarstræti and

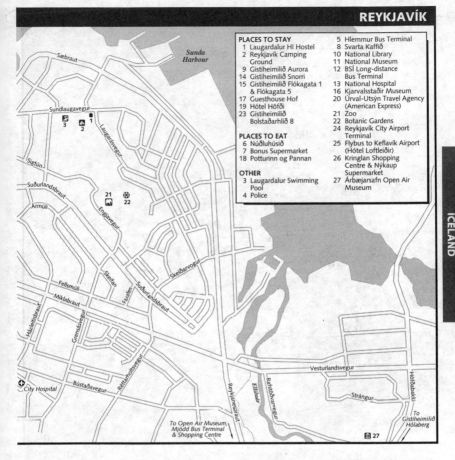

REYKJAVÍK

PLACES TO STAY
1 Laugardalur HI Hostel
2 Reykjavík Camping
   Ground
9 Gistiheimilið Aurora
14 Gistiheimilið Snorri
15 Gistiheimilið Flókagata 1
   & Flókagata 5
17 Guesthouse Hof
19 Hótel Höfði
23 Gistiheimilið
   Bolstaðarhlíð 8

PLACES TO EAT
6 Núðluhúsið
7 Bonus Supermarket
18 Potturinn og Pannan

OTHER
3 Laugardalur Swimming
   Pool
4 Police

5 Hlemmur Bus Terminal
8 Svarta Kaffið
10 National Library
11 National Museum
12 BSÍ Long-distance
   Bus Terminal
13 National Hospital
16 Kjarvalsstaðir Museum
20 Úrval-Utsýn Travel Agency
   (American Express)
21 Zoo
22 Botanic Gardens
24 Reykjavík City Airport
   Terminal
25 Flybus to Keflavík Airport
   (Hótel Loftleiðir)
26 Kringlan Shopping
   Centre & Nýkaup
   Supermarket
27 Árbæjarsafn Open Air
   Museum

ICELAND

Lækjargata, can be used from 7 am (8 am Saturday, 9 am Sunday) to 11.30 pm. The tourist office on Bankastræti also has phone and fax facilities.

The NMT-450 mobile-phone network covers the whole country; for details, call Iceland Telecom (24 hours) on ☎ 550 6000 or ☎ 800 7000 (toll free). For GSM services in southwest Iceland, ring Tal-Talk on ☎ 1414 (24 hours, toll free).

Internet access is free at the National Library (☎ 525 5600), at Arngrímsgata 3, but it's wise to book in advance.

Medical & Emergency Services There is a 24-hour emergency ward at the city hospital (☎ 525 1700) on Fossvogur near Áland. Less urgent cases should consult the Health Centre (☎ 585 2600), at Vesturgata 7; open 8 am to 7 pm weekdays.

Call ☎ 112 for police, ambulance or fire.

Things to See

The **old town** includes the area bordered by Tjörnin, Lækjargata, the harbour and the suburb of Seltjarnarnes, including the east bank of Tjörnin and both sides of Lækjargata. The Lækjartorg area is the socialising centre of town.

The houses on the southern side of **Hafnarstræti** were used by Danish traders during the trade monopoly between 1602 and 1855. Today, tourist shops here sell woollens, pottery and souvenirs.

Old Reykjavík grew up around **Tjörnin**, the pleasant lake in the centre of town. The

CENTRAL REYKJAVÍK

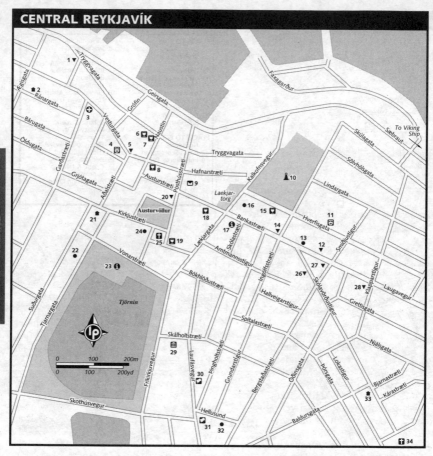

park at Tjörnin has jogging and bike trails, a fountain and colourful flower gardens. Reykjavík's new **Raðhus** (city hall), on the northern bank of Tjörnin, could be described as a sort of postmodern floating palace. The **National Gallery**, behind the church Fríkirkjan near Tjörnin, is worth visiting for exhibitions by Icelandic artists (closed Monday; Ikr400). **Stjórnarráðið**, the white building opposite Lækjartorg, contains government offices. It's one of the city's oldest buildings, originally an 18th-century jail. On nearby **Árnarhóll** (Eagle Hill) there's a statue of the first settler, Ingólfur Arnarson.

The grey basalt building south of Austurvöllur (Ingólfur's hayfields and the old town square), built in 1881, houses the **Alþing**. The government has now outgrown the present building and an extension is currently being constructed.

Reykjavík's most imposing structure, the immense church **Hallgrímskirkja**, at the top of Skólavörðustígur, was unashamedly designed to resemble a mountain of basaltic lava. The stark, light-filled interior is enhanced by the worthwhile view from its 75m tower. The tower's open 10 am to 6 pm daily in summer (Ikr200).

The excellent **Volcano Show**, Hellusund 6a, was filmed by locals Vilhjálmur and Ósvaldur Knudsen, and offers an insight into the volcanic spectre under which Icelanders live. The daily two-hour shows (in English) begin at 10 am and 3 and 8 pm in summer. Admission is Ikr850 (Ikr650 for the one-hour option).

CENTRAL REYKJAVÍK

PLACES TO STAY	OTHER	
2 Guesthouse Vikingur	3 Health Centre	17 Tourist Information Centre & Reykjavík Excursions
21 Salvation Army Guest House	4 Kaffileikhúsið í	18 Astro
33 Gistiheimilið Svala	Hlaðvarpanum	19 Skuggabarinn
	6 Glaumbar Pub	22 Tjarnarbíó - 'Light Nights'
PLACES TO EAT	7 Gaukur á Stöng	Production
1 Amigo's	8 Dubliner	23 Ráðhús & Tourist Information
5 Café Victor	9 Central Post Office	24 Alþing
12 Ítalía	10 Árnarhóll & Ingólfur	25 Domkirkja
14 Café Sólon Íslandus	Arnarson Statue	29 National Gallery
20 Café Paris	11 National Theatre & Archives	30 USA Embassy
26 Grænn Kostur	13 Icelandair	31 UK Embassy
27 Asia	15 Spotlight Club	32 Volcano Show
28 Á næstu grösum	16 Stjórnarráðið	34 Hallgrímskirkja

Renovation of the **National Museum**, Suðurgata 41, should be completed by January 2003. A visit is obligatory for anyone interested in Norse culture and Icelandic history. It will be open 11 am to 5 pm, daily except Monday, mid-May to mid-September, with shorter hours the rest of the year (Ikr300).

Jóhannes Kjarval, born in 1885, was Iceland's most popular artist. The surrealism that characterises his work was derived from the ethereal nature of the distinctive Icelandic landscape. **Kjarvalsstaðir**, the Kjarval Museum, is in Miklatún park on Flókagata (Ikr400).

The **zoo** (open daily; Ikr400) and **botanic gardens** (open daily; free) are in the huge park south of the Reykjavik HI hostel.

Also known as the Open-Air Museum, **Árbæjarsafn** is a 12.5-hectare historic farm set up as a museum in 1957 (Ikr400). It includes a collection of old homes and buildings moved from various places to illustrate life in early Iceland. Take the museum bus, No 10 or 110, from the city centre.

Places to Stay

It's wise to book ahead in summer – even at the camping ground.

Camping The *Reykjavík Camping Ground* (☎ 568 6944), with cooking and laundry facilities, is 15 minutes on bus No 5 from Lækjartorg (from mid-June to August there's a free shuttle bus from the BSÍ terminal at 7.15 am). It's open from mid-May to mid-September and costs Ikr350 per person/tent.

Hostels Beside the camping ground, there's the clean *Laugardalur HI Hostel* (☎ 553 8110, fax 588 9201, Sundlaugavegur 34). Until the extension is completed in May 2001, the hostel will get crowded and noisy – book well ahead. Beds are Ikr1500 (Ikr1250 for HI members). Breakfast is Ikr600.

Guesthouses & Hotels The cheapest option is the *Salvation Army Guest House* (☎ 561 3203, fax 561 3315, Kirkjustræti 2), with singles/doubles for Ikr3300/4300, and sleeping-bag accommodation from Ikr1600 to Ikr2000. Breakfast is Ikr700.

In summer, *Guesthouse Vikingur* (☎ 562 1290, fax 562 1293, Ránargata 12) has rooms for Ikr4900/6500. *Gistiheimilið Svala* (☎ 562 3544, fax 562 3650, Skólavörðustígur 30) is an old house on a quiet central street. Rooms cost Ikr4000/6000 (including breakfast).

More basic is *Gistiheimilið Bólstaðarhlíð 8* (☎ 552 2822, Bólstaðarhlíð 8), a 10-minute walk from the BSÍ terminal. Sleeping-bag accommodation is Ikr1500 and rooms start at Ikr3200/4300.

Gistiheimilið Snorri (☎ 552 0598, fax 551 8945, Snorrabraut 61) charges Ikr1500 for sleeping-bag accommodation and singles/doubles cost from Ikr3800/4800, including breakfast. Nearby is *Guesthouse Hof* (☎/fax 551 6239, Brautarholt 4), which offers bed and breakfast for Ikr4200/6200 and extra beds for Ikr1500. Also nearby, *Gistiheimilið Flókagata 1* (☎ 552 1155, fax 562 0355) charges Ikr5500/7900 for rooms or Ikr2100 for sleeping-bag accommodation (all including breakfast).

ICELAND

Gistiheimilið Aurora (☎ 552 5515, fax 551 4894, Freyjugata 24) charges Ikr4500/6300 for bed and breakfast and sleeping-bag accommodation is Ikr1800.

The only budget-priced hotel is *Hótel Höfði* (☎ 552 6477, fax 562 3986, Skipholt 27), with rooms starting at Ikr5400/7300.

Places to Eat

Some upmarket restaurants offer a *Tilboðs-réttir*, a scaled-down menu for the budget conscious. However, many less pretentious places serve better food for similar prices. For a quick bite on the run, nothing beats the **snack kiosks** on Lækjartorg, Haf-narstræti and the Austurstræti mall. There's a *Nýkaup* supermarket in the Kringlan Centre, but the cheaper *Bonus* is on Lau-gavegur near Snorrabraut.

Friendly *Potturinn og Pannan (Brautarholt 22)* has an all-day soup and salad buffet (Ikr890) and, in the evening, fish, lamb and beef dishes for about Ikr1600. *Ítalía (Laugavegur 11)* has pasta dishes for Ikr1200 to Ikr1450 and pizzas for about Ikr1300. Nearby *Grænn Kostur (Skölavörðustígur 8)* does a great vegetarian daily special for Ikr640.

The excellent vegetarian restaurant, *Á næstu grösum*, on the corner of Laugave-gur and Klapparstígur, serves macrobiotic and standard vegetarian meals for Ikr750 (closed Sunday lunch).

For Chinese and Japanese dishes, *Asía (Laugavegur 10)* has buffet lunches for Ikr950. For delicious Thai food, try *Nud-luhusid (Vitastígur 10)*; filling meals go for Ikr680 to Ikr850. The popular *Amigo's (Tryggvagata 8)* does good Mexican food; enchiladas cost around Ikr1300.

There are several pub-style cafes serving inexpensive food. *Café Victor,* on Ingólfs-torg, offers light meals for around Ikr700 to Ikr900. The popular but stuffy *Café Paris (Austurstræti 14)* has light lunches for Ikr400 to Ikr650. Iceland's only bohemian cafe (complete with art gallery) is *Café Sólon Íslandus (Bankastræti 7)*.

Entertainment

Pubs & Clubs Some of the best pubs in-clude the enduring *Gaukur á Stöng (Tryg-gvagata 22)*, the sportsbar *Glaumbar (Tryggvagata 20)* and the Irish-style *Dubliner (Hafnarstræti 4)*, where you'll

also get bar meals. The pub/cafe *Svarta kaffið (Laugavegur 54)* serves relatively cheap beer between 6 and 9 pm daily (Ikr400 for 500ml).

For an unforgettable cultural experience, try a Friday night crawl with the beautiful youth through Reykjavík's 'in' bars and clubs. Cover charges range from Ikr500 to Ikr1000 and there are queues on weekend evenings. *Skuggabarinn*, next to Hótel Borg, is popular with people in their 20s; you'll get dance music and chart sounds here. Other popular spots include *Astro (Austurstræti 22)*, with techno and dance music and the wild gay bar/club *Spotlight (Hverfisgata 8-10)*.

Theatre Reykjavík has several theatre groups, an opera, a symphony orchestra and a dance company. Important venues are the *National Theatre* (☎ 551 1200, Hverfisgata 19) and *Kaffileikhúsið í Hlaðvarpanum* (☎ 551 9055, Vesturgata 3). For other venues, check the papers or contact the tourist offices. In summer, the Viking-theme tourist show *Tjarnarbíó (Light Nights; Tjarnargata 12)* plays from 9 pm Thursday to Saturday.

Getting There & Away

Air Reykjavík city airport serves all do-mestic routes, flights to the Faroe Islands and Greenland. All other flights operate through Keflavík international airport. Ice-landair (☎ 505 0710, fax 505 0482) has an office at Laugavegur 7 in central Reykjavík.

Bus Long-distance buses use the BSÍ termi-nal (☎ 552 2300) at Vatnsmýrarvegur 10.

Getting Around

To/From the Airport The Flybus to Ke-flavík international airport leaves Hótel Loftleidir two hours prior to international departures. The 50-minute journey costs Ikr700. From 15 June to 31 August, the bus leaves from the Laugardalur Youth Hostel at 5 am daily, 5.30 am for Glasgow and London flights, and at other times throughout the day, then picks up at all main hotels. Buses from Keflavík airport into town leave about 35 minutes after the arrival of an international flight.

Bus Reykjavík's excellent city bus system (☎ 551 2700) runs from 7 am to midnight, with night buses at weekends. The two central terminals are at Hlemmur near the corner of Laugavegur and Raudarárstígur, and on Lækjargata near Lækjartorg. The fare is Ikr150 (no change given), and *skiptimiði* (transfer tickets) are available. The Reykjavík Tourist Card includes a bus pass. The museum bus visits most museums, operating four times daily (except Monday) from mid-June to late August (Ikr300).

Bicycle Bicycles may be hired from the BSÍ bus terminal, the youth hostel and camping ground, all for Ikr1500 per day. Gistiheimilið Hólaberg (☎ 567 0980), Hólaberg 80, does mountain-bike hire for only Ikr750 per day.

Around Reykjavík

BLUE LAGOON
The Blue Lagoon (Bláa Lónið) isn't a lagoon, but rather a pale blue 20°C pool of effluent (silica mud and dead algae) from the Svartsengi power plant, 70km southwest of Reykjavík. A swim can be an ethereal experience with clouds of vapour rising and parting at times to reveal the stacks of the power plant and moss-covered lava in the background. Bring enough shampoo for several rinses or your hair will become a brick-like mass afterwards.

In summer the bath house is open from 9 am to 10 pm daily (shorter hours in winter). Entry is Ikr700 (for three hours). From the BSÍ terminal in Reykjavík, take one of three daily Grindavík buses (Ikr600).

THE GOLDEN TRIANGLE
The term 'Golden Triangle' refers to Gullfoss, Geysir and Þingvellir, the 'Big Three' destinations for Icelandair's stopover visitors.

If Iceland has a star attraction, it's **Gullfoss**, where the river Hvitá drops 32m in two falls. About 10km down the road is **Geysir**, after which all the world's spouting hot springs are named. The Great Geysir died in the early 20th century, plugged by debris tossed in to encourage it to perform. Fortunately, the faithful stand-in **Strokkur** (Butter Churn) spouts approximately every eight minutes. Þingvellir is Iceland's most significant historical site, since the Alþing was established here in 930 AD. In 1928, its history and wealth of natural attractions led to the creation of Iceland's first national park. Most of the historical buildings are concentrated in a small area of the park and the remainder is left to nature. A maze of hiking trails crisscrosses the plain. Of particular interest are: **Almannagjá**, a large tectonic rift; **Lögberg** (Law Rock), which served as the podium for the Alting from 930 to 1271; **Þingvallavatn**, Iceland's largest lake; and the clear blue wishing spring, **Peningagjá**.

Places to Stay & Eat
Þingvellir has *Keyhotel Valhöll* (☎ 482 2622, fax 483 4775) near the church, with three dining rooms and fairly elegant rooms for Ikr9800/11,500. Nearby at Leirur is the main *camping ground* (☎ 482 2660), costing Ikr350 per person. There's also a petrol station selling basic snacks. *Hótel Geysir* (☎ 486 8915, fax 486 8715) has sleeping-bag accommodation for Ikr1500 and rooms starting at Ikr3300/4600. The souvenir shop/cafe sells burgers, chips, etc.

Getting There & Away
The popular Reykjavík Excursions and Allrahandra Golden Circle day tours cost Ikr5300 and Ikr4900 per person respectively, without lunch. They leave Reykjavík at 8.40 am and 8.30 am daily in summer, respectively, running via the Eden souvenir shop in Hveragerði, the Kerið crater, the southern bishopric at Skálholt, Gullfoss, Geysir and Þingvellir.

BSÍ tours run between Reykjavík, Gullfoss and Geysir, departing at 8.30 am and 12.30 pm daily from the BSÍ terminal (tour price Ikr3180). Public buses between Reykjavík and Þingvellir depart BSÍ at 1.30 pm daily (Ikr1200 one-way).

ÞÓRSMÖRK
Þórsmörk (the Woods of Thor), about 130km south-east of Reykjavík, is one of the most beautiful places in Iceland, a glacial valley with scrub birch, flowers, braided rivers and clear streams surrounded by snowy peaks and glaciers. There's great hiking but it gets busy and noisy on summer weekends. Þórsmörk is a terminus for two of Iceland's most popular hikes, Landmannalaugar to Þórsmörk and Þórsmörk to Skógar.

ICELAND

Places to Stay

The three Þórsmörk area huts – Þórsmörk (Ferðafélag Íslands; ☎ 568 2533, fax 568 2535, @ fi@fi.is), Básar (Útivist; ☎ 561 4330, fax 561 4606) and Húsadalur (Austurleið; ☎ 545 1717, fax 545 1718) – are often crowded in summer.

Camp sites at any of the three centres cost Ikr500 per person.

Getting There & Away

In summer, buses leave BSÍ in Reykjavík at 8.30 am daily and at 5 pm Monday to Thursday, arriving at Húsadalur (over the hill from Þórsmörk) at around noon and 9 pm, respectively. Buses depart Húsadalur for Reykjavík at 7.30 am on weekdays (three hours) and at 3.30 pm daily (3½ hours).

Ireland

Ireland's long history is easy to trace through its Stone Age passage tombs and ring forts, medieval monasteries and castles, its elegant Georgian architecture and staunch literary figures. The island's tragic side is almost as easy to spot; the reminders of Ireland's long and difficult relationship with Britain are ubiquitous.

The north-eastern corner of Ireland is part of the UK and its official name is Northern Ireland. It is also referred to as 'the North', or Ulster, a reference to the historical province of Ulster that, following the partition of Ireland in 1921, was ceded to Britain. The rest of Ireland is known as the Republic of Ireland, although you may hear it referred to as Éire, the Irish Republic, the Republic, Southern Ireland or 'the South'.

Facts about Ireland

HISTORY

Celtic warriors probably reached Ireland from mainland Europe around 300 BC and were well ensconced by 100 BC. Christian monks including St Patrick arrived around the 5th century AD, and as the Dark Ages enveloped the continent, Ireland became a lonely outpost of European civilisation.

In the 1500s, the Protestant Henry VIII moved to enforce English control over Ireland. Under his daughter and successor, Elizabeth I, Ireland's colonisation by Protestant settlers got seriously under way, sowing the seeds for the divided Ireland that exists today.

In 1690 the Protestant William of Orange landed at Carrickfergus, just north of Belfast, with an army of 36,000 men to fight the Catholic James II (recently deposed from the English throne for his religious views). The ensuing Battle of the Boyne took place on 12 July; William's victory was a turning point, and is commemorated to this day by northern Protestants as a pivotal triumph over 'popes and popery'.

By early in the 18th century, the dispirited Catholics in Ireland held less than 15% of the land. The War of American Independence (1775-83) and the French Revolution (1789-99) stirred Irish hopes, both Protestant and Catholic, for a fairer deal from Britain. What they got instead was the Act of Union in 1800, joining Ireland politically with Britain.

In 1828 Daniel O'Connell (1775-1847) stood for a seat representing Ireland in the British parliament, even though, being a Catholic, he could not legally take the seat. O'Connell won easily, and rather than risk a Catholic rebellion the British parliament passed the 1829 Act of Catholic Emancipation. O'Connell unfortunately died just as Ireland was suffering its greatest tragedy – the potato famine.

Introduced from South America, the easily grown potato was the staple food of a rapidly growing but desperately poor Irish people. From 1800 to 1840 the population had rocketed from four to eight million, but successive failures of the potato crop between 1845 and 1851, the so-called Great Famine, resulted in mass emigration and the starvation of more than 1.1 million people.

In the late 19th and early 20th centuries, the British parliament finally began to contemplate Irish home rule, until the bungled uprising in 1916. Though it is now celebrated as a glorious bid for Irish freedom, the Easter Rising was, in fact, heavy with rhetoric, light on planning and decidedly lacking in public support.

In the 1918 general election, Irish republicans (mostly Catholics) stood under the

IRELAND

Counties

1 Derry	9 Sligo	17 Meath	25 Tipperary
2 Antrim	10 Mayo	18 Louth	26 Ladis
3 Tyrone	11 Roscommon	19 Offaly	27 Kilkenny
4 Fermanagh	12 Galway	20 Kildare	28 Carlow
5 Armagh	13 Longford	21 Dublin	29 Wicklow
6 Down	14 Cavan	22 Clare	30 Cork
7 Donegal	15 Monaghan	23 Kerry	31 Waterford
8 Leitrim	16 Westmeath	24 Limerick	32 Wexford

banner of Sinn Féin (We Ourselves or Ourselves Alone) and won a majority of the Irish seats. The Anglo-Irish War, which lasted from 1919 to 1921, pitted Sinn Féin and its military wing, the Irish Republican Army (IRA), against the British. After months of negotiations in London, an Irish delegation led by Michael Collins signed the Anglo-Irish Treaty on 6 December 1921.

The treaty gave 26 counties of Ireland independence and allowed six largely Protestant counties in Ulster the choice of opting out (a foregone conclusion). In the north, the Protestant majority made sure their rule was absolute by systematically excluding Catholics from power.

In January 1969 a civil-rights march from Belfast to Derry (Londonderry) was attacked by a Protestant mob; in August 1969 British troops were sent into Derry and Belfast to maintain law and order. The peaceful civil-rights movement lost ground and the IRA, which had been hibernating, found itself with new recruits for an armed independence struggle. Passions reached fever pitch in 1972 when 13 unarmed Catholics were shot dead by British troops in Derry on 'Bloody Sunday' (30 January).

'The Troubles' rolled back and forth throughout the 1970s and into the 1980s. In August 1994 the announcement of a 'permanent cessation of violence' on behalf of the IRA by Sinn Féin's leader, Gerry Adams, offered the almost unimagined prospect of peace in Ulster. When Protestant paramilitary forces responded with their own cease-fire in October 1994, most British troops were withdrawn from Northern Ireland.

Peace negotiations were shattered in February 1996 by an IRA bomb in London. In June 1997 Britain's Northern Ireland Secretary, Dr Mo Mowlam, promised to admit Sinn Féin to all-party talks following any new cease-fire. Encouraged by this, the IRA declared another cease-fire on 20 July 1997.

To worldwide acclaim these talks produced the Good Friday agreement on 10 April 1998. This complex agreement allows the people of Northern Ireland to decide their political future by majority vote, and it commits its signatories to 'democratic and peaceful means of resolving differences on political issues'. It further established a new Northern Irish parliament and high-level political links between the Republic and Northern Ireland. In May 1998 the Good Friday agreement was approved by 71% of voters in referendums held simultaneously on both sides of the Irish border. Though this historic vote is not a guarantee of peace, it is the best hope in a generation even despite the continuing violence of splinter groups such as the so-called 'Real IRA'. This particular group, comprising former IRA members who are vehemently opposed to the Good Friday agreement, was responsible for Ireland's single most lethal act of terrorism – the August 1998 bombing in Omagh, Northern Ireland, which killed 28 people and wounded at least 330 others.

Since the Good Friday Agreement the peace process has stopped and started, the new parliament being suspended then reinstated. In Derry there is an official inquiry into the events surrounding Bloody Sunday, which some say is a token gesture. And although at times it seems that the Troubles have been reduced to political banter between the parties, one thing is for sure: Ireland, the island, has an optimistic future and most agree that the 'war' is over.

GEOGRAPHY

Ireland is divided into 32 counties: 26 in the Republic and six in Northern Ireland. The island measures 84,421 sq km (about 83% is the Republic) and stretches 486km north to south and 275km east to west. The jagged coastline extends for 5631km. The midlands of Ireland are flat, generally rich farmland with huge swaths of brown peat (which is rapidly being depleted for fuel).

CLIMATE

Ireland has a relatively mild climate with a mean annual temperature of 10°C. June, July and August are the sunniest months; December and January the gloomiest. Annual rainfall is about 1000mm, and it often rains every day for weeks on end.

POPULATION & PEOPLE

The total population of Ireland is around 5.2 million. The Republic's population is 3.6 million and Northern Ireland has about 1.6 million people. The Irish are an easy-going, loquacious, fun-loving people. They are used to tourists and there are few social taboos. In Northern Ireland people have been wary of discussing the Troubles – but

IRELAND

this is changing. Do not take humorous Irish scepticism or sarcasm too seriously.

RELIGION
Almost everybody is either Catholic or Protestant, with the Republic 95% Catholic and Northern Ireland about 60% Protestant. The Jewish community in Ireland is tiny but long-established.

Facts for the Visitor

HIGHLIGHTS
Some of the best scenery in the Republic includes the Ring of Kerry, the Dingle Peninsula, the barren stretches of the Burren, the rocky Aran Islands and the Cliffs of Moher. In Northern Ireland the Causeway Coast and the Glens of Antrim are a must.

Ireland is littered with castles, forts and religious sites in various stages of ruin. Prime examples can be found at Glendalough, Cashel, Kilkenny, Blarney, and, in Northern Ireland, Carrickfergus and Dunluce.

SUGGESTED ITINERARIES
Depending on the length of your stay, you might want to see and do the following things in Ireland:

Three days
  Visit Dublin and Glendalough.
One week
  Visit Dublin, Glendalough, Kilkenny, the Burren and Galway.
Two weeks
  As above, plus the Ring of Kerry (Iveragh Peninsula), Killarney and Cork.

PLANNING
When to Go
The tourist season begins the weekend before St Patrick's Day (17 March) and is in full swing from Easter onward. In July and August the crowds are biggest and the prices are highest. Many tourist facilities close or have shorter opening hours in the quieter winter months.

Maps
There are many good-quality maps of Ireland. For cycling and driving the four-part Ordnance Survey Holiday Map series (1:250,000) is recommended.

TOURIST OFFICES
The Irish tourist board, Bord Fáilte and the Northern Ireland Tourist Board (NITB) operate separate offices.

Every town big enough to have half-a-dozen pubs will have a tourist office. Many of the smaller offices are closed in winter.

Tourist Offices Abroad
Overseas offices of Bord Fáilte include:

Australia (☎ 02-9299 6177) 5th floor, 36 Carrington St, Sydney, NSW 2000
Canada (☎ 416-929 2777) Suite 1150, 160 Bloor St East, Toronto, ON M4W 1B9
New Zealand (☎ 09-379 3708) Dingwall Bldg, 87 Queen St, Auckland 1
UK (☎ 020-7493 3201) Ireland House, 150 New Bond St, London W1Y 0AQ
USA (☎ 212-418 0800) 345 Park Ave, New York, NY 10154

Overseas offices of the NITB include:

Australia (☎ 02-9299 6177) All Ireland Desk, c/o Irish Tourist Board, 36 Carrington St, Sydney, NSW, 2000
Canada (☎ 416-925 6368) Suite 1501, 2 Bloor St West, Toronto, ON M5R 3J8
New Zealand (☎ 09-379 3708) Dingwall Bldg, 87 Queen St, Auckland 1
UK (☎ 020-7766 9920) British Travel Centre, 24 Haymarket, London SW1Y 4DG
USA (☎ 212-922 0101) Suite 701, 551 5th Ave, New York, NY 10176

EMBASSIES
Irish Embassies Abroad
Irish embassies abroad include the following:

Australia (☎ 02-6273 3022) 20 Arkana St, Yarralumla, ACT 2600
Canada (☎ 613-233 6281) 130 Albert St, Ottawa, ON K1A 0L6
UK (☎ 020-235 2171) 17 Grosvenor Place, London SW1X 7HR
USA (☎ 202-462 3939) 2234 Massachusetts Ave NW, Washington DC 20008

Foreign Embassies in Ireland
Foreign embassies in Ireland include the following:

Australia (☎ 01-676 1517) 6th floor, Fitzwilton House, Wilton Terrace, Dublin 2
Canada (☎ 01-478 1988) 65-68 St Stephen's Green, Dublin 2
UK (☎ 01-205 3742) 29 Merrion Rd, Dublin 4
USA (☎ 01-668 9946) 42 Elgin Rd, Dublin 4

In Northern Ireland, nationals of most countries should contact their embassy in London. The USA has an embassy (☎ 028-9032 8239) at Queens House, 14 Queen St, Belfast.

MONEY

The Irish pound or punt (IR£), like the British pound sterling (£), is divided into 100 pence (p). Pounds sterling (see the Britain chapter) are used in Northern Ireland, though several banks also issue their own Northern Irish pound notes, which are equivalent to sterling but not readily accepted in Britain.

Most major currencies and types of travellers cheques are readily accepted in Ireland. Eurocheques can also be cashed here. Major credit cards, particularly Visa and MasterCard (often called Access), are widely accepted. You can obtain cash advances on your card from banks and from automatic teller machines (ATMs).

Exchange Rates

Exchange rates are as follows:

country	unit		Irish pound
Australia	A$1	=	IR£0.51
Canada	C$1	=	IR£0.59
euro	€1	=	IR£0.78
France	1FF	=	IR£0.12
Germany	DM1	=	IR£0.40
Japan	¥100	=	IR£0.80
New Zealand	NZ$1	=	IR£0.39
UK	UK£1	=	IR£1.32
USA	US$1	=	IR£0.87

Costs

For the budget traveller IR£40 per day should cover hostel accommodation, getting around, a meal in a restaurant and possibly something for the folks at home – leaving just enough for a pint at the end of the day.

Tipping

Even though Ireland's not really a tipping culture, staff in cafes and restaurants are often paid as though it is. Keep this in mind when settling your bill. Fancy hotels and restaurants usually add a 10% or 15% service charge onto the bill. Pub staff are not tipped, but taxi drivers can be – 10% if you feel like it.

POST & COMMUNICATIONS

Post

Post offices (An Post) in the Republic are open 9 am to 5.30 pm Monday, Thursday and Friday, 9.30 am to 5.30 pm Tuesday and Wednesday and 9 am to 1 pm Saturday; smaller offices close for lunch. Postcards cost 28p to EU countries and 38p outside Europe, while aerograms cost 32p to EU countries, 52p outside Europe. Post office hours and postal rates in Northern Ireland are the same as in Britain (see Post & Communications in the Britain chapter for details).

Telephone, Fax & Email

See the Telephones appendix in the back of this book for information about dialling international calls to or from the Republic or Northern Ireland (ie, the UK). The important difference is that to call Northern Ireland from the Republic, you do not use ☎ 0044 as for the rest of the UK. Instead you dial ☎ 028 and then the local number. International calls can be dialled directly from pay phones.

Dial ☎ 1190 for directory assistance throughout the island.

Faxes can be sent from post offices or other specialist offices. To send international telegrams, phone ☎ 196 in the Republic or ☎ 0800 190 190 in Northern Ireland. Internet cafes are slowly springing up all over the country (IR£5 per hour).

INTERNET RESOURCES

The following are just a few of the huge number of useful Web sites for travellers to Ireland.

Bord Fáilte Official site of the Irish tourist board.
www.ireland.travel.ie
Dublin Tourism Centre An overview of travelling and tourism in Ireland.
www.visit.ie/dublin
Northern Irish Tourism Board Official site of the NITB.
www.ni-tourism.com
The *Irish Times* An award-winning site with Irish news, arts features and its much-loved crossword puzzles.
www.irish-times.ie

BOOKS

Lonely Planet's *Ireland* and *Dublin* guides offer comprehensive coverage of the island

and its most visited city. For food-lovers, Lonely Planet's *World Food Guide: Ireland* is a must.

One of the better books about Irish history is *The Oxford Companion to Irish History* (1998) edited by SJ Connolly.

WOMEN TRAVELLERS

Women travellers will find Ireland a blissfully relaxing experience, with little risk of hassle on the street or anywhere else. Nonetheless, walking alone at night, especially in certain parts of Dublin, is unwise. There's little need to worry about what you wear in Ireland. Nor is finding contraception the problem it once was, although anyone on the pill should bring adequate supplies with them.

GAY & LESBIAN TRAVELLERS

Only Dublin, and to a certain extent Belfast and Cork, have open gay communities. The *Gay Community News* is available at bars and cafes or by subscription to GCN (☎ 01-671 0939/9076, ✉ gcn@tinet.ie) at 6 South William St, Dublin 2. Information is also available from the following organisations:

OUThouse Community Centre (☎ 01-670 6377) 6 South William St, Dublin 2
Web site: indigo.ie/~outhouse
Northern Ireland Gay Rights Association (NIGRA; ☎ 028-9066 4111) Cathedral Bldgs, Lower Donegall St, Belfast

DISABLED TRAVELLERS

Bord Fáilte's various accommodation guides indicate which places are wheelchair accessible, and the NITB publishes *Accessible Accommodation in Northern Ireland*. The National Rehabilitation Board (☎ 01-874 7503) and Dtour have a Web site at www.ireland.iol.ie/infograf/dtour with information applicable to both the Republic and Northern Ireland. Disability Action (☎ 028-9049 1011), in Belfast, can also provide useful information.

DANGERS & ANNOYANCES

Ireland is probably safer than most countries in Europe, but the usual precautions should be observed. Drug-related crime is on the increase, and Dublin has its fair share of pickpockets. Be careful with your belongings when you visit pubs and cafes.

If you're travelling by car note that Dublin is notorious for car break-ins and petty theft. Car theft is also a problem in Belfast.

EMERGENCIES

The emergency number in both the Republic and Northern Ireland is ☎ 999.

BUSINESS HOURS

Offices are open 9 am to 5 pm weekdays, shops a little later. On Thursday and/or Friday, shops stay open later. Many are also open on Saturday.

PUBLIC HOLIDAYS & SPECIAL EVENTS

Public holidays in both the Republic and Northern Ireland are: New Year's Day, 17 March (St Patrick's Day), Good Friday, Easter Monday, 25 and 26 December. Both countries also have one 'bank holiday' Monday in May, June, August and/or October when most shops and businesses are closed. Protestants in Northern Ireland celebrate Orangeman's Day on 12 July.

The All-Ireland hurling and football finals both take place in Dublin in September. There are some great regional cultural events around the island, like the Galway Arts Festival in late July. In Dublin, Leopold Bloom's Joycean journey around the city is marked by various events on Bloomsday (16 June). The Dublin International Film Festival, in April, is also a highlight. In Northern Ireland, July is marching month and every Orangeman in the country hits the streets on the 'glorious 12th'. Other events include the Belfast Festival at Queen's in November.

ACCOMMODATION

Bord Fáilte offices book local accommodation for a fee of IR£1 (or IR£2 to book in another town). This can be handy when it may take numerous phone calls to find a free room. The NITB provides a similar booking service.

All accommodation prices in this chapter are high-season rates (generally June to August); at other times of year, subtract 15% to 25% from the listed prices.

There are hordes of hostels in Ireland, but in summer they can be heavily booked. An Óige (☎ 01-830 4555, ✉ anoige@iol.ie), which means 'youth', is the Irish branch of Hostelling International (HI), as is the Youth Hostel Association of Northern Ireland (YHANI; ☎ 028-9031 5435). These hostels are open to members of HI, An Óige and YHANI (annual membership IR£10), or to any overseas visitor for an additional nightly charge of IR£1. If you pay the extra charge 10 times, you become a member.

Two alternative associations with reliable accommodation include Independent Holiday Hostels (IHH; ☎ 01-836 4700, ✉ ihh@iol.ie) and the 'back-to-basics' Independent Hostels Owners association (IHO; ☎ 073-30130).

FOOD

Traditional meals (like Irish Stew, often found in pubs) are hearty and cheap. A bowl of the day's soup and some fantastic soda or brown bread can be a cheap lunch. Seafood is excellent in the west, and there are good vegetarian restaurants all over the island.

In Ireland a drink means a beer, either lager or stout. Stout is usually Guinness, the famous black beer of Dublin, although in Cork it can mean a Murphy's or a Beamish. Simply asking for a Guinness will get you a pint (570ml, IR£2 to IR£2.25 in a pub). If you want a half-pint (285ml, IR£1 to IR£1.20), ask for a 'glass' or a 'half'.

In the Republic, pub hours are 10.30 am to 11.30 pm Monday to Wednesday, 10.30 am to 12.30 am Thursday to Saturday and 12.30 pm to 11.30 pm on Sunday. In Northern Ireland, pub hours are 11.30 am to 11 pm Monday to Saturday, and 12.30 to 2 pm and 7 to 10 pm Sunday.

Getting There & Away

AIR

Aer Lingus (☎ 886 8888) is the Irish national airline with international connections to other countries in Europe and to the USA.

Dublin, Shannon and Cork are linked by a variety of airlines to many cities in Britain. The standard return economy fare from London to Dublin is around £155, but advance-purchase fares can see tickets as low as £60. Ryanair has some of the best deals, sometimes as low as £20 one-way.

LAND

As the flights are so cheap, getting to Ireland by land (including ferry) is not very popular. For details in London, contact Eurolines (☎ 0870-514 3219) or National Express (☎ 0870-580 8080). London to Dublin by bus takes about 12 hours and costs from £20/38 to £30/55 one-way/ return. To Belfast it's 13 hours and slightly more expensive.

SEA

There's a great variety of ferry services from Britain and France to Ireland. Prices vary drastically, depending on season, time of day, day of the week and length of stay. One-way fares for an adult foot passenger can be as little as IR£20, but nudge close to IR£50 in summer. For a car plus driver and up to four adult passengers, prices can range from IR£170 to IR£300. There are often special deals, discounted return fares and other money savers worth investigating.

Britain

Following is a list of shipping lines.

Irish Ferries (☎ 0870-517 1717) For services from Holyhead to Dublin (3¼ hours by ferry) and Pembroke to Rosslare Harbour (four hours by ferry).

Isle of Man Steam Packet Company and SeaCat Services (☎ 0870-552 3523) For catamaran services from Douglas (Isle of Man) to Belfast (2¾ hours, May to September) and Dublin (2¾ hours, May to September), Liverpool to Dublin (four hours), and Heysham (four hours), and Stranraer (1½ hours) and Troon (2½ hours) to Belfast.

Norse Irish Ferries (☎ 028-9077 9090) For services from Liverpool to Belfast (8½ hours).

P&O European Ferries (☎ 0870-242 4777) For services from Cairnryan to Larne (one hour by fast ferry, 2½ by ferry); Fleetwood to Larne (eight hours); and Liverpool to Dublin (eight hours).

Stena Line (☎ 0870-570 7070) For services from Holyhead to Dublin (3¾ hours) and Dun Laoghaire (1¾ hours by fast ferry); Fishguard to Rosslare Harbour (3½ hours by ferry, 1¾ hours by catamaran); and Stranraer to Belfast (3¼ hours by ferry, 1¾ hours by catamaran).

Swansea Cork Ferries (☎ 01792-456 116) For services from Swansea to Cork (10 hours, mid-May to mid-September).

France

Eurail passes are valid for crossings between Ireland and France on Irish Ferries; InterRail passes give reductions. You must book in advance to receive the discount.

IRELAND

Irish Ferries run from Roscoff and Cherbourg to Rosslare Harbour, April to January, taking 14 hours and 18½ hours respectively.

For Roscoff to Cork, Brittany Ferries (☎ 021-277801 in Cork) sails once weekly from April to early October (leaving Friday from Roscoff, Saturday from Cork). The trip takes 14 hours.

Getting Around

PASSES & DISCOUNTS

Eurail passes are valid for train travel in the Republic of Ireland, but not in Northern Ireland, and entitle you to a reduction on Bus Éireann's three-day Irish Rambler tickets (see the Bus section following). They are also valid on some ferries between France and the Republic. InterRail passes offer a 50% reduction on train travel within Ireland and discounts on some ferries to/from France and Britain.

For IR£7, students can have a Fairstamp affixed to their ISIC card by any USIT agency. This gives a 50% discount on Iarnród Éireann (Irish Rail) services.

Irish Rambler tickets are available from Bus Éireann for bus-only travel within the Republic. They cost IR£30 (for travel on three out of eight consecutive days), IR£70 (eight out of 15 days) or IR£100 (15 out of 30 days).

For train-only travel within the Republic, the Irish Explorer ticket (IR£90) is good for five travel days out of 15. In Northern Ireland the Freedom of Northern Ireland pass allows unlimited travel on Ulsterbus and Northern Irish Railways for one day (IR£10) or seven consecutive days (IR£35). The Irish Rover ticket combines services with Bus Éireann and Ulsterbus for three days (IR£40), eight days (IR£90) or 15 days (IR£140).

BUS

Bus Éireann is the Republic's national bus line, with services all over the Republic and into Northern Ireland. Fares are much cheaper than regular rail fares. Return fares are usually only a little more expensive than one-way fares, and special deals (eg, same-day returns) are often available. Most intercity buses in Northern Ireland are operated by Ulsterbus.

TRAIN

Iarnród Éireann, the Republic of Ireland's railway system, operates trains on routes that fan out from Dublin. Distances are short in Ireland and fares are often twice as expensive as the bus, but travel times can be dramatically reduced. As with buses, special fares are often available, and a mid-week return ticket is often not much more than the single fare.

Northern Ireland Railways has four routes from Belfast, one of which links up with the Republic's rail system.

CAR & MOTORCYCLE
Road Rules

As in Britain, driving is on the left and you should only overtake (pass) to the right of the vehicle ahead of you. The driver and front-seat passengers must wear safety belts; in Northern Ireland passengers in the rear must also wear them. Motorcyclists and their passengers must wear helmets.

Speed limits in both Northern Ireland and the Republic appear in kilometres, miles or both and are generally the same as in Britain: 112km/h (70 mph) on motorways, 96km/h (60 mph) on other roads and 48km/h (30 mph) or as signposted in towns. On quiet, narrow, winding rural roads it's simply foolish to speed. Ireland's blood-alcohol limit is .08% and strictly enforced.

The Automobile Association (AA) breakdown number in the Republic is ☎ 1800-667788; in Northern Ireland it's ☎ 0800-887766. Also in Northern Ireland, the Royal Automobile Club (RAC) breakdown number is ☎ 0800-828282.

BICYCLE

You can either bring your bike with you on the ferry or plane, or rent one in Ireland. Typical rental costs are IR£7 to IR£10 a day or IR£30 to IR£40 a week. Raleigh Rent-a-Bike (☎ 01-626 1333), Raleigh House, Kylemore Rd, Dublin 10, has dozens of outlets around the country.

Dublin

☎ 01

Dublin (Baile Átha Cliath) is Ireland's capital and largest, most cosmopolitan city (population 952,700). Dublin is growing at a furious pace; the city centre is an intricate mass of shops, restaurants, pubs and people. Cybercafes and world-class restaurants now sit happily next to smoky pubs and chophouses. And in spite of rapid changes, Dublin remains a city of character and characters.

Orientation

North of the river, O'Connell St is the major shopping thoroughfare. Immediately south of the river is the often-raucous Temple Bar district, Dame St, Trinity College and St Stephen's Green. For shopping, the pedestrianised Grafton St and its surrounding streets and lanes are always busy.

Information

Tourist Offices The Dublin Tourism Centre is in the de-sanctified St Andrew's Church on St Andrew St, west of Trinity College. Services include accommodation bookings, car rentals, maps, concert tickets and more. In July and August (when it can be a madhouse), the centre is open 9 am to 7 pm Monday to Saturday and until 3.30 pm Sunday. At other times of year it's open until 5.30 pm Monday to Saturday.

There is a 24-hour information line (☎ 1850 230 330, ✉ information@dublintourism.ie), but Dublin Tourism is so-so about answering email queries. Try its Web site at www.visitdublin.com.

The Northern Ireland Tourist Board (☎ 679 1977), 16 Nassau St, is open 9 am to 5.30 pm weekdays and 10 am to 5 pm Saturday.

Post & Communications Dublin's famous General Post Office (GPO) is on O'Connell St, north of the river. South of the river there are post offices on Anne St South and St Andrew St.

Email & Internet Access Planet Cyber Cafe (☎ 679 0583), 13 St Andrews St, is open until at least 10 pm daily, and charges IR£5 per hour. Does Not Compute (☎ 670 4464), opposite Dublin's Viking Adventure, and Global Internet Café, just north of the O'Connell Bridge, are other alternatives.

Travel Agencies The USIT travel office (☎ 679 8833), 19 Aston Quay, near O'Connell Bridge, opens 9 am to 6 pm weekdays (8 pm Thursday) and 10 am to 5.30 pm Saturday.

Trinity College & Book of Kells

Ireland's premier university was founded by Elizabeth I in 1592. In summer, walking tours depart regularly from the main gate on College Green; 9.30 am to 4.30 pm Monday to Saturday and noon to 4 pm Sunday. The tour costs IR£5.50, which includes the fee to see the Book of Kells, an illuminated manuscript dating from around AD 800, and one of Dublin's prime attractions. It's on display in the East Pavilion of the Colonnades (IR£4.50).

Museums & Galleries

The highlight of the exhibits at the **National Museum**, on Kildare St, is the Treasury, with its superb collection of Bronze Age, Iron Age and medieval gold objects. Other exhibits focus on the 1916 Easter Rising and the struggle for Irish independence (closed Monday; free).

The small **Dublin Civic Museum**, 58 William St South, focuses on Dublin's long and tumultuous history (closed Monday; free).

Dublin Writers Museum, 18-19 Parnell Square, celebrates the city's long and continuing role as a literary centre, with displays on Joyce, Swift, Yeats, Wilde, Beckett and others (IR£3.10).

Almost next-door, **Hugh Lane Municipal Gallery** has works by contemporary Irish artists, as well as retrospectives and a large Impressionist collection (closed Monday; free).

The **National Gallery**, Merrion Square West, has an excellent collection with strong Irish content. It is open daily, and there are guided tours on Saturday (3 pm) and Sunday (2.15, 3 and 4 pm). Entry is free.

The **Irish Museum of Modern Art** (IMMA) at the old Royal Hospital Kilmainham, is renowned for its conceptual installations and temporary exhibits (closed Monday; free).

In Temple Bar, around Meeting House Square, are the **National Photographic Archive** and the **Gallery of Photography**. In fact, in and around Meeting House square is a cauldron of cultural activities, including the **Irish Film Archive**, the multimedia centre **Arthouse**, contemporary galleries and studios. For information call the Temple Bar Culture Line (☎ 671 5717).

IRELAND

DUBLIN

PLACES TO STAY
1 Dublin International Youth Hostel
2 Waverley House
3 MEC Budget Accommodation Centre
7 Park House B&B; Gardiner Lodge
8 Backpackers Ireland: Eurohostel; Abraham House
9 Jacobs Inn
11 Isaac's Hostel
12 Backpackers Citi Hostel
13 Globetrotters Tourist Hostel & Townhouse
14 Cardijn House
26 Abbey Hostel
31 Ashfield House
41 Kinlay House; Dublin Bike Tours
50 Barnacles Temple Bar House
54 Oliver St John Gogarty Hostel
59 Brewery Hostel
95 Avalon House

PLACES TO EAT
15 101 Talbot
18 Bewley's Oriental Café
23 Winding Stair Bookshop & Café
25 The Epicurean Food Hall
33 Bewley's Oriental Café
35 Elephant & Castle
36 La Paloma
37 The Chameleon
39 The Brazen Head
44 Poco Loco
51 Cafe Irie; Juste Pasta
56 La Mezza Luna
57 Mermaid Café
58 Leo Burdock's
61 Yamamori
63 Stag's Head
64 Boulevard Café
66 QV2
68 O'Neill's
71 Trocadero; Café Rouge
73 Cornucopia
75 Alpha Café
76 Good World Restaurant
81 Rajdoot Tandoori
83 Bewley's Oriental Café
84 Café Java
91 Pasta Fresca

OTHER
4 Dublin Writers Museum
5 Hugh Lane Municipal Gallery
6 Gate Theatre
10 Busáras (Bus Station)
16 Dublin Bus (Bus Átha Cliath)
17 General Post Office
19 Slatterys
20 Old Jameson Distillery
21 Ceol-The Irish Traditional Music Centre
22 Handel's
24 Pravda
27 Global Internet Café
28 Iarnród Éireann (Irish Rail) Travel Centre
29 Abbey Theatre; Peacock Theatre
30 John Mulligan's
32 USIT Travel Office
34 Palace Bar
38 Clarence
40 Christ Church Cathedral
42 Does Not Compute
43 Dublin's Viking Adventure
45 Front Lounge
46 Irish Film Archive; Gallery of Photography; National Photographic Archive
47 Irish Film Centre (IFC)
48 Norseman
49 Temple Bar
52 Auld Dubliner
53 Oliver St John Gogarty Bar
55 Arthouse
60 Guinness Hopstore
62 The Globe
65 Planet Cyber Cafe
67 Post Office
69 Trinity College Old Library & Book of Kells
70 Dublin Tourism Centre
72 International Bar
74 Northern Ireland Tourist Board
77 The Long Hall
78 Hogan's
79 Grogan's Castle Lounge
80 Dublin Civic Museum
82 McDaid's
85 John Kehoe's
86 Davy Byrne's
87 National Gallery
88 National Museum
89 Post Office
90 Gaiety Theatre
92 Jute
93 St Patrick's Cathedral
94 Marsh's Library
96 Royal College of Surgeons
97 O'Donoghue's
98 Irish Ferries

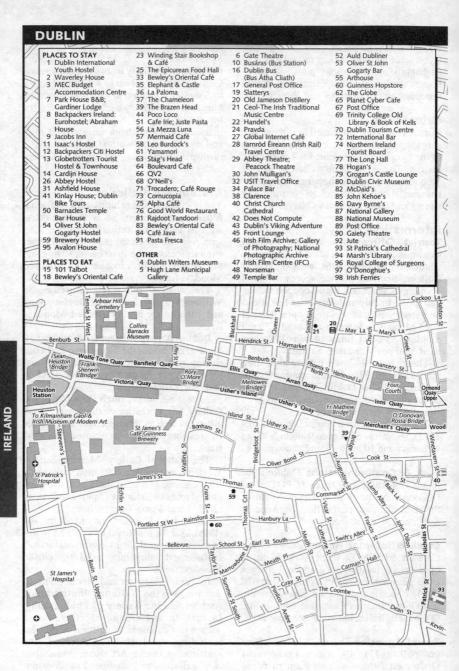

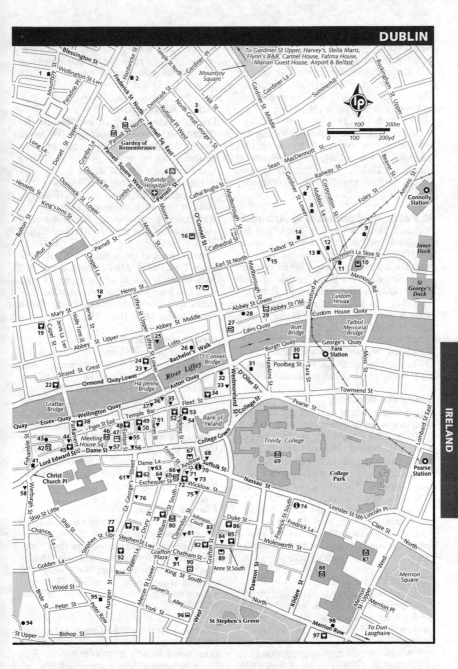

Christ Church Cathedral & Around

In the south aisle, Christ Church Cathedral (1169) has a monument to the 12th-century Norman warrior Strongbow. Note the church's precariously leaning north wall (it's been that way since 1562). Open 10 am to 5 pm daily (IR£2).

On Essex St West is **Dublin's Viking Adventure** where costumed 'Norse' guides lead visitors through life-size mock-ups of Viking-era Dublin. The adventure is open 10 am to 4.30 pm Tuesday to Saturday (IR£4.95).

St Patrick's Cathedral & Around

A church stood on the site of St Patrick's Cathedral, on Patrick's Close, as early as the 5th century, but the present building dates from 1191. It's noted for its connections with Jonathan Swift, author of *Gulliver's Travels* and dean of St Patrick's from 1713 to 1745 (he's interred there). Open 9 am to 6 pm daily (closed during times of worship; IR£2.30).

Just south of the cathedral is the not-to-be-missed **Marsh's Library** dating from 1701, boasting some 25,000 volumes lovingly stacked in dark oak bookcases (IR£1).

Guinness Brewery

Rather than a tour of the brewery, the main attraction is the **Guinness Hopstore** (☎ 408 4800) on Crane St, south-east of the city centre. Historical displays and a lame audiovisual program (although an upgrade was planned late 2000) preface a free half-pint Guinness. Guinness stout was first brewed by Arthur Guinness in 1759.

It's open 9.30 am to 5 pm Monday to Saturday and 10.30 am to 4.30 pm Sunday April to September. The rest of the year it opens 9.30 am to 4 pm Monday to Saturday and noon to 4 pm Sunday (IR£5).

Kilmainham Gaol

The grey, sombre Kilmainham Gaol (☎ 453 5984) played a key role in Ireland's struggle for independence and was the site of mass executions following the 1916 Easter Rising. The tour includes an excellent audiovisual introduction to the prison from its opening in 1796 to its closure in 1924. The gaol is on Inchicore Rd near the IMMA, west of Christ Church Cathedral;

take bus No 51 or 79 from Aston Quay. It's open 9.30 am to 4.45 pm daily April to September; the rest of the year it opens 9.30 am to 4 pm weekdays and 10 am to 4.45 pm Sunday (IR£3.50).

Other Attractions

Dublin's finest **Georgian architecture**, including its famed doorways, is found around **St Stephen's Green** and **Merrion Square**, both of which are prime picnic spots whenever the sun shines.

The **Old Jameson Distillery** (☎ 807 2355) on Bow St, north of the Liffey, is a defunct brewery with displays on the whiskey-making process. The audiovisual show is a dud, but the free whiskey-tasting is a big hit. Tours are held daily (IR£3.95).

At the back of the distillery is Ceol – **The Irish Traditional Music Centre** (☎ 817 3820), which is a must for lovers of jigs, reels and lonely ballads. The centre is full of interactive displays tracing the roots of Irish music (open daily; IR£4.95).

Organised Tours

A hop-on hop-off service that does a 75-minute city circuit with commentary runs daily from mid-April to late September. The IR£5 ticket lets you travel all day.

Theme tours include The Dublin Literary Pub Crawl (☎ 670 5602) on which you are accompanied by actors performing pieces from Irish literature, and the Musical Pub Crawl (☎ 478 0193). Each lasts about two hours and costs around IR£6. Bookings can be made via Dublin Tourism, through hostels or by calling direct.

Places to Stay

At unexpected times Dublin can be bedless for a radius of up to 60km. So we recommend advance reservations any time, even for hostels. For B&Bs and hotels, Dublin Tourism will do the work for a small fee. Contact it in person, by email (@ reservations@dublintourism.ie) or phone ☎ 1800 668 668.

Hostels – North of the Liffey

Jacobs Inn (☎ 855 5660, 21-28 Talbot Place) and the often noisy *Isaac's Hostel* (☎ 836 3877, 2-5 Frenchman's Lane) are sister hostels. Dorm beds at Jacobs are IR£9.25 to IR£11.25; doubles cost up to IR£43. Isaac's charges IR£7.50 to IR£9.95 for dorms and up to IR£19.95/42 for singles/doubles.

IHH **Cardijn House** (☎ 878 8484, 15 Talbot St), aka 'Goin' My Way', is an older hostel, east of O'Connell St. The nightly cost is IR£9.

Gardiner St Lower is a goldmine of hostels. The welcoming IHH **Globetrotters Tourist Hostel** (☎ 873 5893, 47 Gardiner St Lower) is a modern place with good security, dorm beds from IR£12, and a full Irish breakfast. The simple IHO **Backpackers Ireland: Eurohostel** (☎ 836 4900, 80 Gardiner St Lower) has dorm beds for IR£8/10 midweek/weekend. Adjacent is IHH **Abraham House** (☎ 855 0600, 82 Gardiner St Lower). It's well-run and clean, with beds in small/large dorms for IR£9/13 (add IR£2 for peak times) and singles/doubles for IR£22/30. The IHO's pleasant **Backpackers Citi Hostel** (☎ 855 0035, 61-62 Gardiner St Lower) charges IR£8 to IR£11 for dorm beds and IR£35 to IR£50 for private doubles.

If you don't mind street noise, the central **Abbey Hostel** (☎ 878 0700, 29 Bachelor's Walk) overlooks the River Liffey, has new facilities and a friendly vibe. Dorms cost from IR£11 to IR£16.

IHH **MEC Budget Accommodation Centre** (☎ 878 0071, 42 North Great George's St) is a sprawling 100-bed hostel in an old Georgian townhouse. Dorm beds cost from IR£8.50 to IR£13.50.

Although An Óige's 363-bed **Dublin International Youth Hostel** (☎ 830 1766, 61 Mountjoy St) is very safe, it suffers from its rough-and-tumble surroundings. From Dublin airport, bus No 41A stops on Dorset St Upper, a short walk away. Beds are IR£10 to IR£11 including continental breakfast.

Hostels – South of the Liffey The big IHH **Kinlay House** (☎ 679 6644, 2-12 Lord Edward St), beside Christ Church Cathedral, is central, but some rooms can be noisy. Rates are IR£10 per person in four-bed dorms, and IR£16/24 a single/double.

IHH's **Avalon House** (☎ 475 0001, 55 Aungier St) is in a renovated Georgian building just west of St Stephen's Green. Beds in its standard dorms are IR£8 to IR£12.

Just north of Trinity College, **Ashfield House** (☎ 679 7734, 19-20 D'Olier St) has all the amenities of a semi-deluxe hotel but fills up quickly. Dorm beds are IR£11 to IR£14, singles/doubles IR£35/46.

In Temple Bar a good choice is the IHH **Barnacles Temple Bar House** (☎ 671 6277, 19 Temple Lane), with dorm beds for IR£9 to IR£11 and doubles starting at IR£50. **Oliver St John Gogarty Hostel** (☎ 671 1822, 18-21 Anglesea St) adjoins a boisterous pub but is surprisingly quiet. Dorm beds cost IR£12 to IR£17, doubles IR£38.

The IHH **Brewery Hostel** (☎ 453 8600, 22-23 Thomas St) is close to the Guinness Hopstore and has great facilities, including a secure carpark. Unfortunately the neighbourhood is scruffy and it's a longish walk to the centre. Dorm beds start at IR£8.50, doubles IR£38, including breakfast.

B&Bs If you want something close to the city centre and cheap (relatively), Gardiner Sts Upper and Lower are the places to look.

North of the city, friendly **Harvey's** (☎ 874 5140, 11 Gardiner St Upper) has singles/doubles for IR£25/35. Similarly priced B&Bs nearby include: **Stella Maris** (☎ 874 0835, 13 Gardiner St Upper), **Flynn's B&B** (☎ 874 1702, 15 Gardiner St Upper), **Carmel House** (☎ 874 1639, 16 Gardiner St Upper), **Fatima House** (☎ 874 5410, 17 Gardiner St Upper) and **Marian Guest House** (☎ 874 4129).

Nicer B&Bs along Gardiner St Lower include **Gardiner Lodge** (☎ 836 522, 87 Gardiner St Lower), **Park House B&B** (☎ 855 0034, 90 Gardiner St Lower) and the highly recommended **Townhouse** (☎ 878 8808, 47-48 Gardiner St Lower), joined to Globetrotters hostel. All three charge IR£35 to IR£37.50 per person.

Hardwicke St, only a short walk from Gardiner St Upper, has a few B&Bs including **Waverley House** (☎ 874 6132, 4 Hardwicke St). Singles cost IR£30 and doubles from IR£46 to IR£70.

Places to Eat
Restaurants – Around Temple Bar Although at times a mecca for tourists and rowdy rugby rogues, the Temple Bar district is convenient and caters to all tastes and budgets. **La Mezza Luna** (☎ 671 2840), on Dame St near the corner of Temple Lane, is enormously popular; book or be prepared to wait. It has vegetarian dishes starting at

IRELAND

IR£4.95. *Mermaid Café (70 Dame St)* is renowned for creative seafood dishes and decadent desserts; mains start at IR£12.95, the majority around the mid to high teens.

Omelettes (from IR£6.50) are a speciality at the popular and bustling, but somewhat overpriced *Elephant & Castle (18 Temple Bar)*. It stays open until midnight on Friday and Saturday, until 11.30 pm on other days. *The Chameleon (1 Fownes St)* specialises in Indonesian dishes such as *rijstaffel* and *gado gado* for around IR£6; it's open in the evening. *Cafe Irie,* upstairs at 12 Fownes St, has fried tofu for IR£3.20 and a huge selection of sandwiches. Next door, the cute *Juste Pasta* serves pasta starting at IR£5.95 and 'not pasta' at IR£6.50. *La Paloma*, on Asdill's Row, has a wide range of Spanish tapas and mains for around IR£12.

Poco Loco (32 Parliament St) offers straightforward Tex-Mex, and its combination plates are great value at IR£6.95.

Although it's not in Temple Bar proper, *Leo Burdock's (2 Werburgh St)* doles out Dublin's best fish and chips.

Restaurants – Around Grafton St

Popular *Café Java (5 Anne St South)* serves excellent brunches (bagels and scrambled eggs) at around IR£4.95. *Cornucopia (19 Wicklow St)* is a popular wholefood cafe, catering for special diets with all sorts of creative concoctions for less than IR£7 (closed Sunday). *Alpha Café*, upstairs on the corner of Wicklow and Clarendon Sts, is cheap and has fried everything (grills from IR£3). The fashionable *Boulevard Café (27 Exchequer St)* serves grilled meats, gourmet pizzas and pastas (IR£5.50 to IR£12) to midnight daily.

Straightforward preparation, large helpings and late opening hours are the selling points at *Trocadero (3 St Andrew's St),* where mains cost around IR£10. The adjacent *Café Rouge,* part of a French-theme chain, serves great coffees and pastries and has good-value lunches (IR£5.95) and dinner specials (IR£7.95). Across the road, *QV2 (14-15 St Andrew's St)* is an elegant Dublin institution that looks more expensive than it is. There are lunch and earlybird specials for IR£7.50.

Pasta Fresca (3-4 Chatham St), just off Grafton St's southern end, has authentic pasta dishes from IR£5.95 to IR£8.95 and

antipasta starting at IR£2.50. *Rajdoot Tandoori (26-28 Clarendon St),* in the Westbury Centre behind the Westbury Hotel, has superb tandoori dishes starting at IR£8.60.

On South Great George's St, *Yamamori,* No 71-72, serves sushi and delicious Japanese noodle soups from IR£5, and Dublin's finest Chinese dishes are cooked up at the *Good World Restaurant* at No 18; a full meal will set you back at least IR£12.

Restaurants – North of the Liffey

This area is a bit barren when it comes to full-service restaurants. Try *101 Talbot,* oddly enough at 101 Talbot St, which serves adventurous pastas starting at IR£5.50 and interesting mains from IR£8.50 to IR£12.50 (closed Sunday and Monday).

Pubs

Pub meals are offered 11.30 am to 2 pm or so weekdays, and the going rate is IR£5 to IR£7 for a major feast of meat, veggies and potatoes. The wonderfully old-looking *Stag's Head,* on the corner of Dame Lane and Dame Court, turns out simple, well-prepared meals. The lunch buffet at *O'Neill's,* opposite the Dublin Tourism Centre, is highly recommended. *The Brazen Head* on Bridge St, always packed at lunchtime, offers everything from sandwiches to a carvery buffet.

Cafes

There are three branches of *Bewley's Oriental Café* around the centre. Bewley's, something of a Dublin institution, has above-average cafeteria-style breakfasts (IR£3), sandwiches (to IR£3) and full meals (to IR£5). The people-watching is first rate, and you can sit all day reading the paper without feeling guilty. The 78 Grafton St branch is the flagship, open 7.30 am to 1 am daily (to 7 pm Sunday). The branch at 11-12 Westmoreland St is open 7.30 am to 9 pm daily. There is a smaller branch north of the Liffey at 40 Mary St.

Winding Stair Bookshop & Café, on Ormond Quay Lower, north of the Liffey opposite Ha'penny Bridge, is a rambling bookshop with teas, pastries and sandwiches.

The Epicurean Food Hall, with entrances on Lower Liffey and Middle Abbey Sts, has several cafes, but the highlights here are the delis, celebrating world food from Japanese to Eastern European. It's open until 7 pm daily.

Entertainment

For events, reviews and particularly for club listings, get a free copy of the fortnightly *Event Guide,* available from music venues, cafes, hostels etc. Its Web site is at www.eventguide.ie.

Pubs The Temple Bar district is choc-a-block with pubs that feature live music. Notables here include the *Temple Bar* on Temple Lane, the *Norseman* on the corner of Temple Bar and Eustace St, the restored *Oliver St John Gogarty Bar (57-58 Fleet St),* and the *Auld Dubliner (24-25 Temple Bar).*

Other atmospheric spots for a pint include *The Long Hall* on South Great George's St, the *Palace Bar* on Fleet St, *John Kehoe's* on Anne St South, *John Mulligan's (8 Poolbeg St);* and *Grogan's Castle Lounge* on the corner of William and Castle Sts.

Davy Byrne's (21 Duke St), off Grafton St, has been famous ever since Leopold Bloom dropped in for a sandwich. It's now an anaemic yuppie bar.

Pubs with live music from blues to rock to traditional Irish include the *International Bar (23 Wicklow St), McDaid's (3 Harry St),* and touristy *O'Donoghue's (15 Merrion Row),* one of the most renowned music pubs in Ireland.

North of the river on Capel St, both *Slatterys* and *Handel's* are busy music pubs.

Dublin's very 'hip' pubs attract fashion-conscious crowds worthy of London and New York. Hipster spots include *Front Lounge* on Parliament St; *The Globe* and *Hogan's* on South Great George's St; *Jute (2 Aungier St); Clarence (6-8 Wellington Quay),* inside the U2-owned Clarence Hotel; and the northside's Russianesque *Pravda* on Liffey St.

Cinema & Theatre The *Irish Film Centre (IFC; ☎ 679 5744, 6 Eustace St)* has two screens in the Temple Bar showing off-beat and art films. The complex also has a bar, cafe and bookshop.

The *Abbey Theatre (☎ 878 7222)* and the smaller *Peacock Theatre* are on Abbey St Lower near the river. The *Gate Theatre (☎ 874 4045)* is on Parnell Square East. The *Gaiety Theatre (☎ 677 1717)* is on King St South.

Getting There & Away

Bus Busáras (☎ 836 6111), Bus Éireann's central bus station, is just north of the Liffey on Store St. Standard one-way fares from Dublin include: Cork (IR£13, 3½ hours), Galway (IR£9, 3¾ hours) and Rosslare Harbour (IR£10, three hours). There are seven buses a day (only three on Sunday) to Belfast (IR£11.50, three hours).

Train Connolly station (☎ 836 3333), just north of the Liffey, is the station for Belfast, Derry, Sligo, other points north and Wexford. Heuston station (☎ 836 5421), south of the Liffey and well west of the centre, is the station for Cork, Galway, Killarney, Limerick, Waterford and most other points to the west, south and south-west. For travel information and tickets, the Iarnród Éireann Travel Centre (☎ 836 6222) is at 35 Abbey St Lower.

Regular one-way services from Dublin include: Belfast (IR£19, 2¼ hours), Cork (IR£33.50, 3¼ hours), Galway (IR£22, three hours) and Limerick (IR£26.50, 2¼ hours).

Boat There are two direct services from Holyhead on the north-western tip of Wales, one to Dublin Port, and the other to Dun Laoghaire at the southern end of Dublin Bay. Stena Lines (☎ 204 7777), in Dun Laoghaire, and Irish Ferries (☎ 661 0715), 2-4 Merrion Row, are the main carriers. See the Getting There & Away section earlier in this chapter for details.

Getting Around

To/From the Airport Dublin airport (☎ 844 4900) is 10km north of the centre. There's an Airlink Express service to/from Busáras for IR£3 and to/from Heuston train station for IR£3 (both 30 minutes).

To/From the Ferry Terminals Buses go to Busáras from the Dublin Ferryport terminal (☎ 855 2222), Alexandra Rd, after all ferry arrivals. Buses also run from Busáras to meet ferry departures. To travel between Dun Laoghaire's ferry terminal (☎ 880 1905) and Dublin, take the Dublin Area Rapid Transport (DART).

Local Transport Dublin Bus (Bus Átha Cliath; ☎ 873 4222) has an office at 59 O'Connell St. Buses cost IR£1.20 for one to

IRELAND

three stages, up to a maximum of IR£2.60. These tickets give you two trips valid for a month, and single fares can be bought on the bus. One-day passes cost IR£3.50.

DART provides quick rail access to the coast as far north as Howth (IR£1.10) and south to Bray (IR£1.30). Pearse station is handy for central Dublin.

Bicycle Dublin Bike Tours (☎ 679 0899), Lord Edward St, has bike rental for IR£10 per day and tours year round. Other rental places open during high season; contact Dublin Tourism for details.

AROUND DUBLIN
Dun Laoghaire
☎ 01

Dun Laoghaire (pronounced 'dun leary'), only 13km south of central Dublin, is both a popular resort and a busy harbour with ferry connections to Britain.

On the southern side of the harbour is the **Martello Tower**, where James Joyce's epic novel *Ulysses* opens. It now houses the **James Joyce Museum** (☎ 280 9265). *Ulysses* follows its characters around Dublin during a single day (16 June 1904).

The tower is open 10 am to 5 pm Monday to Saturday and 2 to 6 pm Sunday, April to October (IR£2.70). Phone in advance at other times of the year.

Bus No 7, 7A, 8 or 46A, or the DART rail service (IR£1.10, 20 minutes), will take you from Dublin to Dun Laoghaire.

Places to Stay The small *Marina House* (☎ 284 1524), on Old Dunleary Rd, (turn left at the DART station at Salt Hill & Monkstown) has dorm beds for IR£12.

Glendalough
☎ 0404

Glendalough (Gleann dá Loch; pronounced 'glen-da-lock'), was founded in the late 6th century by St Kevin, an early Christian bishop who established a monastery on the Upper Lake's south shore. During the Middle Ages, when Ireland was known as 'the island of saints and scholars', Glendalough became a monastic city catering to thousands of students and teachers.

The Glendalough Visitor Centre (☎ 45325), opposite the Lower Lake car park, overlooks a round tower, a ruined cathedral, and the tiny Church of St Kevin. It has historical displays, an audio-visual program, and is open 9.30 am to 5 pm daily (IR£2). From here a trail leads 1km west to the panoramic Upper Lake, with a car park (IR£1.50) and more ruins nearby.

Places to Stay An Óige's *Glendalough Hostel* (☎ 45342) is 600m west of the visitor centre. Dorms cost up to IR£10.50. At the village of Laragh, 3km east of the monastic site, the basic *Wicklow Way Hostel* (☎ 45345), beside The Laragh Inn, charges IR£7 for a dorm bed and IR£25 per person for a private room.

Getting There & Away St Kevin's Bus Service (☎ 01-281 8119) runs daily to Glendalough from outside Dublin's College of Surgeons, across from St Stephen's Green. Buses leave at 11.30 am and 6 pm daily, returning to Dublin at 4.15 pm. It's recommended to stay the night and return on the 7.20 am or 9.45 am service (9.45 am only on weekends). The one-way/return fare is IR£6/10.

The South-East

WEXFORD
☎ 053

Little remains of Wexford's Viking past – apart from its narrow streets and name, Waesfjord, or 'Ford of Mud Flats'. Cromwell was in one of his most destructive moods when he included Wexford on his 1649-50 Irish tour, destroying the churches and 'putting to the sword' three-quarters of the town's 2000 inhabitants.

Wexford is a convenient stopover for those travelling to France or Wales via the Rosslare Harbour ferry port, 21km south-east of Wexford.

Orientation & Information
The train and bus stations are at the northern end of town, on Redmond Place. The tourist office (☎ 23111), on The Cresent, overlooking the River Slaney, is open Monday to Saturday. The curiously tight North Main and South Main Sts are a block inland and parallel to the quays.

Things to See & Do
About 5km north-west of Wexford, beside the Dublin-Rosslare (N11) road at Ferry-carrig, the **Irish National Heritage Park** (☎ 20733) is an outdoor theme-park condensing Irish history from the Stone Age to the early Norman period. The 14 reconstructed sights are animated by a not-to-be-missed free guided tour. Entry is IR£5, and the park opens 9.30 am to 6.30 pm (last admission at 5.30 pm) daily, March to November.

Places to Stay
Ferrybank Camping & Caravan Park (☎ 44387) is open Easter to late September and charges from IR£5 to IR£10 for a tent site. From the quays, cross the River Slaney via the Wexford Bridge (R741) and walk straight for five minutes.

The IHH *Kirwan House* (☎ 21208) on Mary St is a small and friendly hostel. It has Internet access, dorm beds for IR£8 and private rooms for IR£12 per person. From the tourist office, turn right at Henrietta St, then right at South Main St, take a quick left at Allen St, right at High St and left at Mary St.

Westgate House (☎ 22167), 150m south of the train station, has rates starting at IR£25 per person. Other B&Bs can be found along Redmond Rd, right from the train station.

Places to Eat
North and South Main Sts have something for most tastes, including sandwiches and picnic supplies at *Greenacres Food Hall* *(54 North Main St)*, Chinese at *Chan's Restaurant* *(90 North Main St)*, and pub grub at *Tim's Tavern* *(51 South Main St)*. For traditional fish and chips try *Premier* *(104 South Main St)*.

Getting There & Away
Wexford's O'Hanrahan train station (☎ 33114 or 33162) is on the Dublin (IR£11) to Rosslare Harbour (IR£4, 25 minutes) line. Bus Éireann runs from the train station to Rosslare Harbour (IR£2.50, 20 minutes), or Dublin (IR£7.50, three hours) and beyond.

ROSSLARE HARBOUR
☎ 053
Rosslare Harbour has frequent ferry services to France and Wales (see the Getting There

& Away section at the beginning of this chapter). There is absolutely no reason to linger at Rosslare Harbour, so catch the first bus or train (outside the ferry terminal) to Wexford or elsewhere. If you do stay, An Óige's *Rosslare Harbour Hostel* (☎ 33399) is on Goulding St, across the park at the back of Hotel Rosslare, just uphill from the ferry terminal. Beds in dorms range from IR£8 to IR£10.50.

WATERFORD
☎ 051
Although Waterford (Port Láirge) is a busy port and modern commercial centre, it also retains vestiges of its Viking and Norman past. Strongbow took the city in 1170, and in later centuries it was the most powerful political centre in Ireland.

Today Waterford is famed for its crystal, but it's also a college town, and during the academic year the crowded pubs are plenty of fun.

Orientation & Information
The main shopping street runs directly back from the River Suir, beginning as Barronstrand St and changing names as it runs south to intersect with Parnell St, which runs north-east back up to the river, becoming The Mall on the way.

The tourist office (☎ 87 5823), in The Granary, is near the river at 41 Merchant's Quay. It's open 9 am to 5 pm Monday to Saturday year-round (Sunday in July and August). Hidden away in Parnell Court, off Parnell St, Voy@ger Internet Cafe (☎ 84 3900) is open from 10 am to 10 pm daily.

Waterford Crystal Factory
The first Waterford glass factory was established in 1783 but closed in 1851 as a result of punitive taxes imposed by the British government. The business wasn't revived until 1947.

The visitor centre (☎ 33 2500) is 2km south-west out on the road to Cork (N25). A guided tour (IR£3.50) takes you through the factory, where you can see big-cheeked glass blowers and fragile exhibits. Public transport runs from the top of the mall at Broad St to the factory every 10 minutes (IR£1.50 return). The factory is open 8.30 am to 4 pm daily (shorter hours in the low season).

Other Attractions

On Merchants Quay, **The Granary** (☎ 30 4500), a gutted old grain store sleekly redesigned, houses the **Waterford Treasures**. The exhibition is tastefully designed and documents 1000 years of the city's history with close-to-fascinating artefacts, art, and interactive and audiovisual presentations (open 9.30 am to 9 pm June to August and 10 am to 5 pm the rest of the year; IR£4).

Places to Stay & Eat

The only Waterford hostel we can recommend is the IHH *Barnacles Viking House* (☎ 853827), on Coffee House Lane, off Parade Quay. Dorm beds cost IR£7.50 to IR£9, including breakfast and a personal security locker. Doubles are IR£14.50 to IR£16.50. It's wise to book ahead.

The Mall and Parnell St have several cheap B&Bs. *Derrynane House* (☎ 875179, 19 The Mall) has singles/doubles for IR£16/32. Attractively positioned near the Christ Church Cathedral, *Beechwood* (☎ 876677, 7 Cathedral Square) has rooms for IR£18/32.

Haricot's Wholefood (11 O'Connell St) has vegetarian and meaty dishes for IR£5 to IR£7. It's relaxed and boasts 'Nu-tron friendly food'. On John St, *Cafe Luna* has thick coffee and is popular after pub closing time.

Entertainment

The venerable *T & H Doolan* (32 George's St) is packed on weekends, and has the best traditional music in town. On John St is the popular *Geoff's,* and at the junction with Manor Rd, *Peig's Bar* has music sessions and is the pick of the four or so pubs that are there.

Getting There & Away

The train station (☎ 873401) is across the river from the town centre. There are regular rail connections to Dublin (IR£13, 2½ hours), Rosslare Harbour (IR£6, 80 minutes), Kilkenny and Wexford. Bus Éireann (☎ 879000) has a sparkly new depot opposite the tourist office and sends buses to Dublin (IR£7), Wexford (IR£7.30), Rosslare Harbour (IR£8.80) and Cork (IR£9).

KILKENNY

☎ 056

Despite the occasional heavy brewery-waft through its main streets, Kilkenny (Cill Chainnigh) is perhaps the most attractive large town in the country. Even though it was ransacked by Cromwell during his 1650 campaign, Kilkenny retains some of its medieval ground-plan, particularly the narrow streets.

Orientation & Information

Most places of interest can be found on or close to Parliament St and its continuation, High St, which runs parallel to the River Nore; or along Rose Inn St, which changes its name to John St, and leads away from the river to the north-east. The tourist office (☎ 51500), open Monday to Saturday, is in Shee Alms House on Rose Inn St. Access the Internet at Compustore in the Market Cross Shopping Centre on James St. It's open 10 am to 6 pm daily.

Things to See & Do

Overlooking a sweeping bend in the River Nore, stronghold of the powerful Butler family, **Kilkenny Castle** (☎ 21450) has a history dating back to 1172, though the present castle is a more recent structure. The **Long Gallery**, with its vividly painted ceiling, is quite remarkable. Guided tours are compulsory and cost IR£3.50. The castle is open 10 am to 7 pm daily in summer; hours are slightly shorter at other times.

The approach on foot to **St Canice's Cathedral** from Parliament St leads over Irishtown Bridge and up **St Canice's Steps**, which date from 1614; the wall at the top contains fragmentary medieval carvings. Around the cathedral is a **round tower** (which you can climb for IR£1).

On Parliament St, **Rothe House** is a restored Tudor merchant's house dating from 1594 (IR£2). **Smithwicks Brewery**, also on Parliament St, shows a video and has tastings on weekdays at 3 pm from June to September. Free tickets are available at the tourist office.

Places to Stay

The small *Tree Grove Caravan & Camping Park* (☎ 70302) is 1.5km south of Kilkenny on the New Ross Rd (R700). A tent for two costs IR£6; IR£7 if you have a car.

Open year-round, IHH *Kilkenny Tourist Hostel* (☎ 63541, 35 Parliament St) is central and has helpful staff who can guide you to the best things to do around town.

Dorm beds cost up to IR£9 and private rooms to IR£12 per person.

There are plenty of B&Bs, especially south of the city along Patrick St and north of the city on Castlecomer Rd. The central *Bregagh Guesthouse (☎ 22315),* Dean St, near St Canice's Cathedral, has rooms for IR£25 per head. A few doors down, *Kilkenny B&B (☎ 64040)* has a variety of rooms starting at IR£16 a head.

Places to Eat
Italian Connection (38 Parliament St) has good-value pizzas starting at IR£4.75 and pasta at IR£7. *Edward Langton's (69 John St)* is a stylish, award-winning pub with affordable lunches but pricey set dinners. For simpler pub grub try *Caisleán Uí Cuain,* opposite the castle. *Kytelers,* home of Kilkenny's most famous witch, Dame Alice Kyteler, has a good restaurant and bar meals.

Entertainment
The best pub in town for traditional Irish music is *Maggie's* on St Keiran St. Others include *Ryan's* on Friary St, *John Cleere's* and *The Pumphouse,* popular for all types of music, on Parliament St.

Getting There & Away
McDonagh train station (☎ 22024), Dublin Rd, east of the town centre via John St, has trains to Dublin's Heuston Station (IR£12) and Waterford (IR£5).

Bus Éireann (☎ 051-87 9000) operates out of the train station. Buses head to Dublin (IR£7), Cork (IR£5.30), Galway, Wexford, Waterford and Rosslare Harbour.

CASHEL
☎ 062
The **Rock of Cashel** (☎ 61437) is one of Ireland's most spectacular archaeological sites. On the outskirts of town rises a huge lump of limestone bristling with ancient fortifications. Mighty stone walls encircle a complete round-tower, a roofless abbey and the country's finest 12th-century **Romanesque chapel**. The complex is open 9 am to 4.30 pm (to 7.30 pm in summer) daily, and admission is IR£3.50.

The tourist office (☎ 61333), open from 9.30 am to 5.30 pm daily April to September (weekdays only at other times), is in the town hall on Cashel's main street.

The IHH *Cashel Holiday Hostel (☎ 62330, 6 John St)* has dorm beds for IR£8.50 and doubles starting at IR£12 per person. Buses on line 8 (Dublin to Cork) pass through Cashel.

The South-West

CORK
☎ 021
Cork (Corcaigh), the Irish Republic's second-largest city, is home to a major university and prides itself on its heady mix of pubs, cafes and restaurants, and its love of the arts. The Cork International Jazz Festival and the International Film Festival both take place in October.

The Black and Tans (demobilised British soldiers reunited to fight the IRA) were at their most brutal in Cork and much of the town was burnt down during the Anglo-Irish War. Cork was also a centre for the civil war that followed independence (Irish leader Michael Collins was ambushed and killed nearby).

Orientation & Information
The city centre is an island between two channels of the River Lee. Oliver Plunkett St and the curve of St Patrick's St are the main areas to shop, eat and drink. The train station and several hostels are north of the river; MacCurtain St and Glanmire Rd Lower are the main thoroughfares there.

The less-than-helpful tourist office (☎ 427 3251) is on Grand Parade. It's open 9.15 am to 5.30 pm (closed 1 to 2.15 pm) Monday to Saturday; daily in July and August.

Internet access is available at i dot Café (☎ 427 3544) in the Gate Multiplex centre on North Main St. There is a laundrette at 14 MacCurtain St (across from Isaac's Hostel).

Things to See
North of the river there's a fine view from the tower of the 18th-century **St Anne's Church, Shandon** (☎ 4505 906). The quirky salmon-shaped weathervane was apparently chosen because the local monks reserved for themselves the right to fish for salmon in the river. The church is open 10 am to 5 pm Monday to Saturday. It costs IR£3.50 to climb the tower, ring the Shandon Bells and watch an audiovisual presentation about the area.

IRELAND

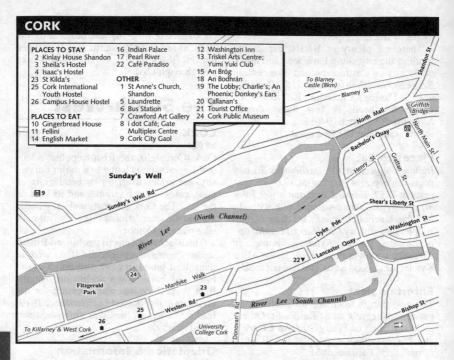

CORK

PLACES TO STAY
2 Kinlay House Shandon
3 Sheila's Hostel
4 Isaac's Hostel
23 St Kilda's
25 Cork International
     Youth Hostel
26 Campus House Hostel

PLACES TO EAT
10 Gingerbread House
11 Fellini
14 English Market

16 Indian Palace
17 Pearl River
22 Café Paradiso

OTHER
1 St Anne's Church,
    Shandon
5 Laundrette
6 Bus Station
7 Crawford Art Gallery
8 i dot Café; Gate
    Multiplex Centre
9 Cork City Gaol

12 Washington Inn
13 Triskel Arts Centre;
     Yumi Yuki Club
15 An Bróg
18 An Bodhrán
19 The Lobby; Charlie's; An
     Phoenix; Donkey's Ears
20 Callanan's
21 Tourist Office
24 Cork Public Museum

The ground floor of the small **Cork Public Museum** is mostly devoted to Cork's role in the fight for Irish independence, while the 1st floor has archaeological displays. Entry is free on weekdays and 75p Sunday afternoons.

Cork City Gaol (☎ 430 5022) received its first prisoners in 1824 and its last in 1923. The taped tour around the restored cells and the audiovisual show on the prison's history are quite moving. The complex is off Sunday's Well Rd and is open 9.30 am to 6 pm daily, March to October (reduced hours at other times). Entry is IR£3.50.

Crawford Art Gallery (☎ 427 3377) is an impressive example of cutting-edge architecture melding into an existing 18th-century building. The permanent collection has works by Irish artists like Jack Yeats and Seán Keating as well as works of the British Newlyn and St Ives' schools (closed Sunday; free).

Places to Stay

Camping Opposite the entrance to the airport, on the N27, is *Bienvenue Ferry Caravan & Camping* (☎ 431 2711). Tent sites are IR£8 for two people and the airport bus, 500m away, will take you to Cork for IR£2.50.

Hostels Across the river from the bus station, IHH *Isaac's Hostel* (☎ 450 0011, 48 MacCurtain St) has beds in large/small dorms for IR£7.95/9.25. It's a modern place, but can be a tad impersonal.

Back from MacCurtain St, off Wellington Rd, is the clean and friendly *Sheila's Hostel* (☎ 450 5562, 4 Belgrave Place). The facilities are superb. Dorm beds start at IR£7.50, doubles at IR£22.

Behind St Anne's Church is the modern *Kinlay House Shandon* (☎ 450 8966), Bob & Joan's Walk. Dorm beds cost IR£8, doubles IR£25.

South of the river, *Kelly's Hostel* (☎ 431 5612, 25 Summerhill South) has beds starting at IR£6.50 and boasts the best showers in Cork.

Out by the university, to the west of the centre, the An Óige *Cork International Youth Hostel* (☎ 454 3289, 1-2 Western Rd) is excellent value at IR£9 for dorm beds. The much smaller *Campus House Hostel*

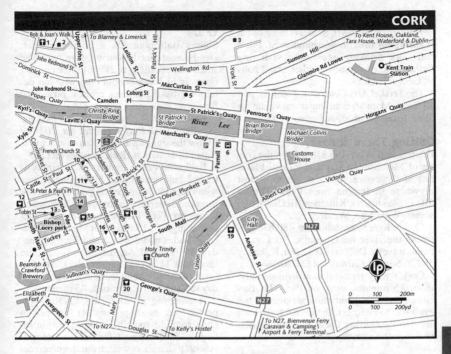

CORK

Bob & Joan's Walk
To Blarney & Limerick
To Kent House, Oakland,
Tara House, Waterford & Dublin

Upper John St
Leitrim St
St Patrick's Hill

John Redmond St
Dominick St
Wellington Rd
York St
Summer Hill
Glanmire Rd Lower
Kent Train Station

John Redmond St
Popes Quay
Camden
Coburg St
MacCurtain St

Kyrl's Quay
Christy Ring Bridge
Lavitt's Quay
Camden Pl
St Patrick's Bridge
St Patrick's Quay
Penrose's Quay
Horgans Quay

Kyle St
Cornmarket St
French Church St
Emmet Pl
Merchant's Quay
River Lee
Brian Boru Bridge
Michael Collins Bridge
Customs House

Castle St
St Paul St
Academy St
St Patrick's St
Robert St
Oliver Plunkett St
Albert Quay
Victoria Quay

St Peter & Paul's St
Tobin St
Grand Pde
Princes St
Marlborough St
Cook St
Morgan St
South Mall
City Hall
N27

Bishop Lucey park
Tuckey St
Holy Trinity Church
Union Quay
Anglesea St

Beamish & Crawford Brewery
Sullivan's Quay

Elizabeth Fort
Evergreen St
Mary St
George's Quay
N27

To N27
Douglas St
To Kelly's Hostel
To N27, Bienvenue Ferry
Caravan & Camping
Airport & Ferry Terminal

0   100   200m
0   100   200yd

Places to Eat (continued)

(☎ 434 3531, 3 Woodland View, Western Rd), just a few doors down, has beds for IR£8. Bus No 8 from the bus station stops outside the An Óige hostel.

B&Bs Glanmire Rd Lower, a short distance east of the train station, is lined with economical B&Bs. *Kent House* (☎ 450 4260, 47 Glanmire Rd Lower)* has singles/doubles starting at IR£23.50/38; *Oakland* (☎ 450 0578, 51 Glanmire Rd Lower)* charges IR£25/40; and rates at *Tara House* (☎ 450 0294, 52 Glanmire Rd Lower)* start at IR£21/35.

On the opposite side of town, Western Rd also has plenty of more-exclusive (and therefore expensive) B&Bs, including *St Kilda's* (☎ 427 3095)*, a big blue house with its own car park. It charges IR£70 for a double.

Places to Eat

For self-catering, head straight for the well-stocked food stalls inside the *English Market,* off the western end of St Patrick's St.

Between St Patrick's St and the pedestrianised area of Paul St are several narrow lanes packed with restaurants. For coffees and light meals, try the popular *Gingerbread House,* or *Fellini,* with its French film paraphernalia. Both are on Carey's Lane.

Yumi Yuki Club, on Tobin St, is attached to the Triskel Arts Centre and has Japanese food and performances.

Princess St is a haven of ethnic cuisine. There's authentic Chinese at mid-range *Pearl River,* and delicious (if expensive) Indian at the adjacent *Indian Palace.*

For vegetarians, *Café Paradiso,* opposite Jury's Hotel on Western Rd, has friendly staff, good coffee and inventive dishes (closed Sunday and Monday).

Entertainment

In Cork, Murphy's is the stout of choice, not Guinness. Don't be bullied; drink what you want. *Cork's List,* a free fortnightly entertainment publication, is available from pubs, cafes and the like.

On Union Quay *The Lobby, Charlie's, An Phoenix* and *Donkey's Ears* are all side by side, and at least one of them has live music (from rock to traditional) most nights. *An Bodhrán (42 Oliver Plunkett St)*

IRELAND

regularly features music, as does *An Bróg* (*78 Oliver Plunkett St*). Students hang out at *Washington Inn,* on Washington St. For a real Cork drinking experience visit tiny *Callanan's,* or any of the other small pubs on George's Quay.

The *Triskel Arts Centre* on Tobin St, just off South Main St, is an important venue for films, theatre, music, and other arts.

Getting There & Away

The bus station (☎ 450 8188) is on the corner of Merchant's Quay and Parnell Place, east of the centre. You can get to almost anywhere in Ireland from Cork: Dublin (IR£13, 4½ hours), Killarney (IR£9.40, two hours), Waterford, Wexford etc.

Cork's Kent train station (☎ 450 6766) is across the river on Glanmire Rd Lower. Trains travel to Dublin (IR£33.50), Kilkenny (IR£26.50) and Galway (IR£31.50).

Cork's ferry terminal is at Ringaskiddy, about 15 minutes away on the N28. Bus Éireann runs frequent daily services to the terminal (45 minutes). Details for ferries are listed in the Getting There & Away section earlier in this chapter.

AROUND CORK
Blarney
☎ 021

Just north-west of Cork, Blarney (An Bhlarna) is a village with one overwhelming drawcard – the 15th-century **Blarney Castle** (☎ 438 5252). Even the most jaded visitor will feel compelled to kiss the **Blarney Stone** and get the 'gift of the gab'. It was Queen Elizabeth I, exasperated with Lord Blarney's ability to talk endlessly without ever actually agreeing to her demands, who invented the phrase. Bending over backwards to kiss the sacred rock requires a head for heights, though you're unlikely to fall since there's someone there to hold you in position.

The castle's opening hours are 9 am to 6.30 or 7 pm Monday to Saturday, or to sundown in winter, and 9.30 am to 5.30 pm Sunday (IR£3.50).

There are many B&Bs surrounding the castle, plus an unaffiliated *Blarney Tourist Hostel* (☎ 438 5580). It is a few kilometres west of Blarney on the road to Killarney. Dorm beds are IR£7, doubles IR£17.

Buses run regularly from the Cork bus station (IR£2.50 return, 30 minutes).

BALTIMORE & CLEAR ISLAND
☎ 028

Sleepy Baltimore has a population that swells enormously during summer. The small tourist office (☎ 21766) at the harbour opens in high season, but otherwise has details for fishing, sailing cruises, buses and ferries on the door.

Baltimore has plenty of B&Bs, plus the excellent IHH *Rolf's Hostel* (☎ 20289); follow the signs up a hill 700m east of town. Dorm beds start at IR£8, doubles IR£23.

Baltimore's main draw is its proximity to Clear Island, which is an Irish-speaking area with about 150 Irish-speaking inhabitants, one shop and three pubs. From June to September, ferries (☎ 39135) leave Baltimore (weather permitting) at 2.15 and 7 pm Monday to Saturday and at noon, 2.15, 5 and 7 pm on Sunday. In July and August there is an extra service at 11 am (12 pm Sunday). At other times of the year boats leave at 2.15 pm Monday to Saturday (IR£8 return, 45 minutes).

A *camping ground* (☎ 39119), signposted from the shop, costs IR£3 per person (June to mid-September). Dorm beds in An Óige's basic *Cape Clear Island Hostel* (☎ 39198), a short walk from the pier, cost IR£7.50 (March to the end of November).

BANTRY & THE BEARA PENINSULA
☎ 027

Bantry is famed for its mussels from Bantry Bay. Its major attraction is the colourful old **Bantry House** (☎ 50047), superbly situated overlooking the bay. The gardens are beautifully kept, and the house is noted for its French and Flemish tapestries. Entry to the gardens is IR£2, to the house an extra IR£4.

Bantry's tourist office (☎ 50229), on the east end of Wolfe Tone Square, is open April to October. Frequent buses to Cork, Killarney, Glengarriff and beyond stop just off the main square at Barry Murphy's pub.

The IHH *Bantry Independent Hostel* (☎ 51050) is on Bishop Lucey Place just off Glengarriff Rd, about 600m north-east of the town centre. Doubles/dorm beds cost IR£20/8 in the high season. The *Small Independent Hostel* (☎ 51140), right beside the harbour on the north bank, has dorm beds for IR£6.50.

From Bantry the N71 follows the coast north-west to Glengarriff from where the

IRELAND

R572 runs south-west to the Beara Peninsula, a harsh, rocky landscape ideal for walking and cycling. It's possible to drive the 137km 'Ring of Beara' in one day, but that would be missing the point.

Coming from Glengarriff, the first village on the peninsula is **Adrigole**, a quiet place with lots of rocks, and *Hungry Hill Lodge* (☎ 60228), whose new facilities include camping for IR£4 per person, dorms beds starting at IR£8, doubles at IR£20.

Other peninsula hostels include *Beara Hostel* (☎ 70184), 3km west of Castletownbere, with dorm beds for IR£7 and camping for IR£4. *Garranes Hostel* (☎ 73147), between Castletownbere and Allihies, has a superb location overlooking Bantry Bay and charges IR£7.50 for a dorm bed.

In the village of **Allihies**, the IHH *Village Hostel* (☎ 73107) charges IR£8.50 for dorm beds, IR£4 for tent sites (April to the end of October). In among the surrounding copper mines is An Óige's *Allihies Hostel* (☎ 73014), with beds for IR£7 (June to the end of September). *Glanmore Lake Lodge* (☎ 064-83181) is in an old schoolhouse 5km from Lauragh, with dorm beds for IR£7 (Easter to the end of September).

The West Coast

KILLARNEY
☎ 064

By the time you reach Killarney (Cill Airne) you will have seen plenty of touristy Irish towns, but nothing will prepare you for a Killarney summer weekend chock-a-block with tour coaches. Still, with a national park and three lakes right on its doorstep, there are easy escapes for walkers and cyclists. Killarney is also a convenient base for touring the Ring of Kerry (see Ring of Kerry section later).

Killarney's busy tourist office (☎ 31633), open Monday to Saturday (closed 1 to 2.15 pm) year-round and on Sunday from June to August, is on Beech Rd. The main post office is on New St. Web Talk on High St and Café Internet on New St provide Internet access daily.

Killarney National Park

Killarney's 10,236-hectare national park has a pedestrian entrance immediately opposite St Mary's Cathedral, and a drivers' entrance off the N71. Within the park are beautiful Lough Leane, Muckross Lake and the Upper Lake.

The restored 14th-century **Ross Castle** is a 2.5km walk from St Mary's Cathedral. Entry to the castle is IR£2.50. Hour-long **cruises of Lough Leane** leave the castle daily in summer; make bookings at the tourist office. From late September to May boats depart on weekends only.

The core of Killarney National Park is **Muckross Estate**, donated to the government in 1932 by Arthur Bourn Vincent. The estate is 5km from Killarney and you can walk around the estate's rooms, with their faded 19th-century fittings, daily for IR£4.

Gap of Dunloe

In summer the Gap, a heather-clad valley at the foot of Purple Mountain (832m), is Killarney tourism at its worst. Rather than paying over IR£30 for a one-hour horse-and-trap ride through the Gap, consider hiring a bike and cycling to Ross Castle. From here take a boat across to Lord Brandon's Cottage and cycle down through the Gap and back into town via the N72 and a path through the golf course. Including bike hire, this should cost you about IR£14. The 90-minute boat trip alone justifies the trip.

Places to Stay

Camping *Fleming's White Bridge Caravan & Camping Park* (☎ 31590) is 1.6km east out along the Cork road (N22), and *Flesk Muckross Caravan Park* (☎ 31704) is 1.5km south out on the Kenmare road (N71). Tent sites at both are IR£5 per person (mid-March to October).

Hostels Just off Park Rd and closest to the bus and train station, the modern, well-equipped *Killarney Railway Hostel* (☎ 35299) has dorm beds for IR£8.50, private rooms for IR£15 and doubles for IR£25.

Off New St, in the town centre, Bishop's Lane leads to the much-recommended *Neptune's Hostel* (☎ 35255). Dorm beds start at IR£7.50, and singles/doubles are IR£19/24.

The small *Súgán* (☎ 33104), on Lewis Rd, has a cosy dining room with a rack of strumable guitars and bikes for hire. Ask for

IRELAND

a map of the town and Killarney will come alive. Dorms are IR£9.

An Óige's large *Killarney International Hostel* (☎ 31240) is 2km west of town; a hostel bus meets trains from Dublin and Cork. Dorm beds range from IR£7.50 to IR£8.50. But for the real out-of-town experience, the IHH *Peacock Farm Hostel* (☎ 33557), a quiet rural oasis, is 7km away in Gortdromakiery; call to arrange a free pick-up. Dorm beds are IR£7 (April to the end of September).

B&Bs In high season finding a room can be tricky, so it's worth paying the IR£1 booking-fee and letting the tourist office do the hunting. Both *West End House* (☎ 32271), along New St beside the Shell petrol station, and *Killarney Townhouse,* a bit farther down New St, have singles/doubles for IR£30/45. Otherwise, the road to Muckross is a good place to look.

Places to Eat
For good coffee try *Coffee House,* on High St. On New St, *Country Kitchen* has breakfast and lunch-time sandwiches and salads. *Allegro,* on High St, serves basic pizza, pasta and burgers, and has traditional meals for IR£4.95. The inviting *Bricín,* above a craft shop on High St, serves lunchtime specials including vegetarian meals for IR£4.50. For a cheap meal, *Teo's* on New St has a half-pizza and chips for IR£2.

Entertainment
The musical part of the tourist-oriented *The Laurels* is behind the main pub and reached by a side alley off Main St. Pubs with more authentic music include *Danny Mann Inn* on New St, and *Courtney's* on High St. But the most popular is the *Killarney Grand* on Main St, which has nights of poetry readings, and interesting takes on traditional Irish music.

Getting There & Away
Bus Éireann (☎ 34777) operates from outside the train station (☎ 31067), with services to Cork (IR£10), Galway (via Limerick; IR£13.50), Dublin (IR£15) and Rosslare Harbour (IR£16). Travelling by train to Cork (IR£10) usually involves changing at Mallow, but there is a direct route to Dublin (IR£34) via Limerick Junction.

Getting Around
In the same lane as Neptune's Hostel is O'Sullivan's (☎ 31282), which rents bikes for IR£6 per day.

THE RING OF KERRY
☎ 066
The Ring of Kerry, a 179km circuit around the Iveragh Peninsula, with its dramatic coastal scenery, is one of Ireland's premier tourist attractions.

Most travellers tackle the Ring by bus on a guided day-trip from Killarney. By car or on bike, dealing with big buses on the narrow roads can be frustrating; getting off the main highway can provide some relief. The **Ballaghbeama Pass** cuts across the peninsula's central highlands and has spectacular views and remarkably little traffic. The shorter **Ring of Skellig**, at the end of the peninsula, has fine views of the Skellig Rocks and is also less touristy. You can forgo roads completely by walking the **Kerry Way**, which winds through the Macgillycuddy's Reeks mountains past **Carrantuohil** (1038m), the highest mountain in Ireland.

Places to Stay
It's wise to book your next night as you make your way around the Ring. Hostels typically charge IR£8 to IR£9 for dorm beds.

Cycling hostel-to-hostel around the Ring, there's the IHH *Laune Valley Farm* (☎ 976 1488) 2km east of Killorglin, the IHO *Caitin Baiters Hostel* (☎ 9477614) in Kells, the IHH *Sive Hostel* (☎ 9472717) in Cahirciveen, the IHO *Ring Lyne Hostel* (☎ 9476103) in Chapeltown and An Óige's *Valentia Island* (☎ 9476154) in Knightstown on Valentia Island, the An Óige *Baile an Sceilg* (☎ 9479229), and the IHH *Fáilte Hostel* (☎ 064-42333) in Kenmare.

An Óige's *Black Valley Hostel* (☎ 064-34712) in the Macgillycuddy's Reeks mountains is a good starting point for walking the Kerry Way. It's open March to late November.

Getting Around
Bus Éireann (☎ 064-34777) operates a Ring of Kerry bus service daily from May to September. Buses stop at Killorglin, Glenbeigh, Kells, Cahirciveen, Waterville, Caherdaniel and Sneem before returning to Killarney. (Some services terminate at Waterville.)

IRELAND

THE DINGLE PENINSULA
☎ 066

The Dingle Peninsula is just as beautiful as, and far less crowded than the Ring of Kerry, with narrow roads that discourage heavy bus-traffic.

The region's main hub, Dingle Town (An Daingean), is a fishing village with a dozen good pubs. The western tip of the peninsula, noted for its extraordinary number of ring forts and high crosses, is predominantly Irish-speaking.

Dingle Town
In the winter of 1984 fisherfolk noticed a solitary bottlenose dolphin that followed their boats. Tours (☎ 915 2626) leave Dingle's pier for a one-hour trip to find **Fungie the dolphin**. The cost is IR£6 (free if Fungie doesn't show, but he usually does). You can swim with him for IR£10; wetsuit hire is extra.

Open daily, **Dingle Oceanworld** (☎ 915 2111), opposite the harbour, has a walk-through tunnel and touch pool for IR£4.50.

East of Dingle Town
From Tralee the N86 heads west along the coast. The 'quick' route to Dingle Town is south-west from Camp via Anascaul and the N86. The scenic route follows the R560 north-west and crosses the wildly scenic **Connor Pass** (456m).

West of Dingle Town
From Dingle follow signs for the 'Slea Head Drive', a scenic coastal stretch of the R559. First stop is the village of **Ventry** and its excellent post-office-cum-delicatessen-cum-wineshop. A few kilometres south-west, **Slea Head** offers some of the peninsula's best views.

Ferries run to the bleak **Blasket Islands** (IR£10 return, 20 minutes), off the tip of the peninsula, from Dunquin. Dunquin's **Blasket Centre** (☎ 56444), open 10 am to 6 pm daily Easter to September (to 7 pm daily July and August), focuses on the hearty islanders who lived on Great Blasket until 1953 (IR£2.50).

Places to Stay
The going rate for a dorm bed in and around Dingle is IR£7 to IR£9.50.

In Dingle Town, the inviting **Grapevine Hostel** (☎ 915 1434) on Dykegate St has beds in dorms and four-bed rooms. For a more rural setting try the popular **Rainbow Hostel** (☎ 915 1044), 1km west of town (call for free pick-up from the bus stop); camping is also available. East along the Tralee road, the IHH **Ballintaggart Hostel** (☎ 915 1454), in a 19th-century house, has a free shuttle service to/from town, plus bike hire. The clean, friendly-but-basic **Marina Hostel** (☎ 915 1065) is near the pier.

Hostels east of Dingle include the IHH **Fuchsia Lodge** (☎ 915 7150), in Anascaul, and the IHH **Connor Pass Hostel** (☎ 713 9179) in Stradbally, near Castlegregory (mid-March to November).

West of Dingle, look for An Óige's year-round **Dunquin Hostel** (☎ 915 6121) near the Blasket ferry and the IHO **Black Cat Hostel** (☎ 915 6286) in Ballyferriter (May to October).

Getting There & Away
Buses stop outside the car park at the back of the Super Valu store. Buses for Dingle Town leave from Tralee. Two buses daily depart from Killarney for Dingle in the summer. Note that there are few services on Sunday.

THE BURREN
County Clare's greatest attraction is the Burren, a harsh and inhospitable stretch of country battered by the cranky Atlantic Ocean. *Boireann* is Irish for 'Rocky Country', and the name is no exaggeration.

The Burren is an area of major interest, with many ancient dolmens, ring forts, round towers and high crosses. There's also some stunning scenery, a good collection of hostels and some of Ireland's best music pubs.

Doolin
☎ 065

Tiny Doolin, famed for its music pubs, is a convenient base for exploring the Burren and the awesome Cliffs of Moher.

Doolin's popularity among backpackers has skyrocketed over the past few years, and at night the three or so pubs are packed with a cosmopolitan crowd. In summer it can be difficult to get a bed, so book ahead. Some of the hostels rent bikes for around IR£8 a day plus deposit.

Places to Stay Down by the harbour, *O'Connors Riverside Camping & Caravan*

Park (☎ *707 4314*) charges IR£4 to IR£6 for a tent plus IR£1.50 per person (April to September). Both the Aille River and Rainbow hostels allow camping for around IR£4 per person.

Doolin's hostels charge around IR£8 for dorm beds. *Paddy Moloney's Doolin Hostel* (☎ *707 4006),* a large and modern IHH hostel in the lower village, has two doubles for IR£20 apiece. The upper village has three IHH hostels: 16-bed *Rainbow Hostel* (☎ *707 4415),* 30-bed *Aille River Hostel* (☎ *707 4260),* and 24-bed *Flanagan's Village Hostel* (☎ *707 4564).* Aille River, in a converted farmhouse, is the nicest of the bunch.

Getting There & Away There are direct buses to Doolin from Limerick, Ennis, Galway and even Dublin; the main Bus Éireann stop is across from Paddy Moloney's Doolin Hostel. See the Aran Islands section for information on ferries to and from Inishmór.

Cliffs of Moher
Eight kilometres south of Doolin are the towering Cliffs of Moher (203m), one of Ireland's most famous natural features. In summer the cliffs are overrun by day-trippers, so consider staying in Doolin and hiking along the Burren's quiet country lanes where the views are just as good and crowds are never a problem. Either way, be careful walking along these sheer cliffs, especially in wet or windy weather.

Near the Cliffs of Moher visitor centre (☎ 065-708 1171) is O'Brien's Tower. Apparently, local landlord Cornelius O'Brien (1801-57) raised it to impress 'lady visitors'. Today's visitors pay IR£1 to climb the tower.

The Cliffs of Moher are free and never close. The visitor centre is open daily, there is an adjacent shop/cafe and it costs IR£1 to use the car park.

GALWAY
☎ 091
The city of Galway (Gaillimh) is delightful, with its narrow streets, fast-flowing river, old stone and wooden shop-fronts, and good restaurants and pubs. On weekends people come from as far as Dublin for the nightlife, and during the city's festivals the streets are bursting. Galway is one of Europe's fastest-growing cities, and Ireland's

fourth-largest, and is also a departure point for the rugged Aran Islands.

Orientation & Information
Galway's tightly packed town-centre is spread evenly on both sides of the River Corrib.

The tourist office (☎ 563081) on Victoria Place, just off Eyre Square, is open 9 am to 5.45 pm weekdays and 9 am to 12.45 pm Saturday; from Easter to September its hours are extended and it opens daily.

The main post office is on Eglington St. Bubbles laundrette is on Mary St. Celtel e-centre, near the entrance to Kinlay House, has Internet access.

Things to See
Galway is a great place to wander around, and a copy of the *Tourist Guide of Old Galway,* available from the tourist office, points out many curiosities.

Eyre Square is the uninspired focal point of the eastern part of the city centre. In the centre of the square is **Kennedy Park**, honouring a visit by John F Kennedy in 1963. To the north of the square is a controversial statue to the Galway-born writer and hell-raiser Pádraic O'Conaire (1883-1928). South-west of the square, on Shop St, **St Nicholas Collegiate Church** dates from 1320 and has several interesting tombs.

Across the road, in the Bowling Green area, is the **Nora Barnacle House Museum** (☎ 564743), the former home of the wife and life-long muse of James Joyce. The small museum, dedicated to the couple, opens mid-May to mid-September (closed Sunday; IR£1).

Little remains of Galway's old city walls apart from the **Spanish Arch**, right by the river mouth. Next to the arch is the small and unimpressive **Galway City Museum**, open 10 am to 1 pm and 2 to 5 pm Monday to Saturday (IR£1).

Special Events
The Galway Arts Festival in July is huge. For information on the festival's music, arts, and street spectaculars check out its Web site at www.galwayartsfestival.com.

Places to Stay
Camping The *Silver Strand Caravan & Camping Park* (☎ *592040)* is on the coast

just beyond Salthill. Large/small tents are IR£7/6 plus 50p per adult (Easter to September). Take bus No 1 from Eyre Square to Salthill.

Hostels It's wise to book your hostel during summer, festivals and on weekends. Prices range from IR£8 in winter to IR£12 in peak times.

The modern and well-maintained IHH *Great Western House* (☎ *561139 or free call* ☎ *1800 425929*), Frenchville Lane, is opposite the bus and train station.

On the same street but closer to Eyre square is the happiest hostel in Galway: the 50-bed *Galway Hostel* (☎ *566959*).

Despite the four flights of stairs, the IHH *Kinlay House* (☎ *565244*), opposite the

tourist office, is a good central choice. Around the corner on Queen St, is the scruffy IHO *Celtic Tourist Hostel* (☎ *566606*).

Barnacle's Quay Street House (☎ *568644, 10 Quay St*) is a justly popular IHH property with 98 beds, and is surrounded by good pubs and cafes.

Near the Salmon Weir Bridge, *Corrib Villa* (☎ *562892, 4 Waterside St*) is in a three-storey townhouse with good kitchen facilities.

On the other side of the river, at the junction of Upper and Lower Dominick Sts, is the possibly too-laid-back *Arch View Hostel* (☎ *586661*). At IR£6 to IR£7, this hostel is the cheapest in Galway.

Continue north-west from Upper Dominick St along Henry and St Helen Sts,

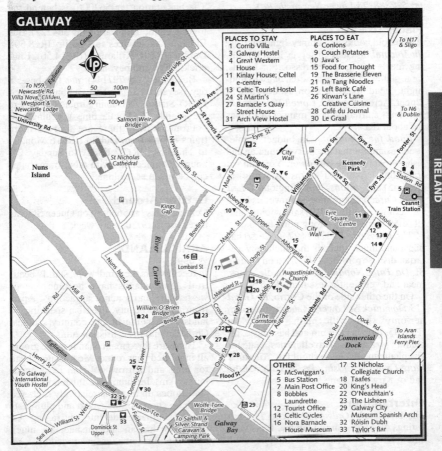

GALWAY

PLACES TO STAY	PLACES TO EAT
1 Corrib Villa	6 Conlons
3 Galway Hostel	9 Couch Potatoes
4 Great Western House	10 Java's
11 Kinlay House; Celtel e-centre	15 Food for Thought
	19 The Brasserie Eleven
13 Celtic Tourist Hostel	21 Da Tang Noodles
24 St Martin's	25 Left Bank Café
27 Barnacle's Quay Street House	26 Kirwan's Lane Creative Cuisine
31 Arch View Hostel	28 Café du Journal
	30 Le Graal

OTHER		
2 McSwiggan's	17 St Nicholas Collegiate Church
5 Bus Station	18 Taafes
7 Main Post Office	20 King's Head
8 Bobbles Laundrette	22 O'Neachtain's
12 Tourist Office	23 The Lisheen
14 Celtic Cycles	29 Galway City Museum Spanish Arch
16 Nora Barnacle House Museum	32 Róisín Dubh
	33 Taylor's Bar

IRELAND

then turn left onto St Mary's Rd to reach An Óige's 200-bed **Galway International Youth Hostel (☎ 527411)**, open June to August. It's on the St Mary's College campus, but ring before you make the journey out there. From Eyre Square you can take bus No 1 straight to the college.

B&Bs Expect to pay IR£20 to IR£25 per person for B&B accommodation in Galway. There are not many around the city centre, but it's worth trying **St Martin's (☎ 568286, 2 Nuns Island St)**, which is situated right on the Corrib. Otherwise, walk 10 minutes from the centre on Newcastle Rd (it becomes the N59 to Clifden). Among the many choices here are **Villa Nova (☎ 524849, 40 Lower Newcastle Rd)** and **Newcastle Lodge (☎ 527888, 28 Lower Newcastle Rd)**.

Places to Eat

Among old books and library-lighting, **Café du Journal** on Quay St serves light but filling meals and good espresso. For bagels, large sandwiches and desserts, daily to midnight, head to **Java's** on Abbeygate St Upper. Across the road, **Couch Potatoes** has big spuds stuffed with all manner of fillings for about IR£4.

Food for Thought is a budget wholefood-restaurant that also serves chicken and fish, on Abbeygate St Lower. You can get traditional fish and chips (starting at IR£4.45) at **Conlons,** on Eglinton St. **Left Bank Café**, on Dominick St Lower, is basic but complements hefty sandwiches and IR£4.50 mains with strong coffees.

The Brasserie Eleven (19 Middle St) has pizza and lunch specials that include vegetarian dishes from IR£4.95. Also on Middle St, **Da Tang Noodles** serves noodle soups, meat and veggie, for less than IR£5.50.

On the other side of the Corrib, **Le Graal (13 Dominick St Lower)** is a charming dinner-only spot with mains starting at IR£6.95. It opens at 6 pm and has music, including jazz nights. Travellers desperate for an epicurean adventure should try **Kirwan's Lane Creative Cuisine (☎ 568266),** at the end of Kirwan's Lane.

Entertainment

The fortnightly **Galway & Mayo List** has listings of what's on in Galway. It is available free from hostels, cafes and pubs.

Galway has dozens of good pubs, among them 100-year-old **O'Neachtain's (17 Cross St Upper)**. **King's Head,** farther north on High St, has a carnivalesque execution scene in the front window and music most nights in summer. Almost next door, there is the much-recommended **Taafes**, a music and sports bar. **McSwiggan's,** on Daly's Place, is big, always busy, and has good meals for IR£6.95. **The Lisheen** (5 Bridge St) is one of the better traditional-music venues in Galway.

Across the river the choice spot for traditional music is **Monroe's Tavern,** on the corner of Dominick St Upper and Fairhill St. The nearby **Róisín Dubh** is good for alternative music and often has international acts.

Getting There & Away

The bus station (☎ 562000) is behind the Great Southern Hotel, off Eyre Square, next to the Ceannt train station (☎ 564222). Bus Éireann has services to Doolin (IR£8.50), Dublin (IR£9), Killarney (IR£14.50), Limerick, Sligo and beyond.

Bus Nestor (☎ 797144) runs five buses a day (seven on Friday) to Dublin's Tara St DART Station via Dublin Airport. Often there are specials (IR£5 at the time of writing).

From Galway there are four or more trains to and from Dublin (IR£16 Monday to Thursday, IR£22 Friday to Sunday; 2¾ hours). Connections with other train routes can be made at Athlone.

Getting Around

Celtic Cycles (☎ 566606) on Queen St rents bikes for IR£7/30 a day/week.

ARAN ISLANDS
☎ 099

In recent years the windswept, starkly beautiful Aran Islands have become one of western Ireland's major attractions. Apart from natural beauty, the Irish-speaking islands have some of the country's oldest Christian and pre-Christian ruins.

There are three main islands in the group, all inhabited year round. Most visitors head for long and narrow (14.5km by a maximum 4km) Inishmór (or Inishmore). The land slopes up from the relatively sheltered northern shores of the island and plummets on the southern side into the raging Atlantic. Inishmaan and Inisheer are much smaller and receive far fewer visitors.

Orientation & Information

A tourist office (☎ 61263) operates on the waterfront at Kilronan (April to mid-September), the arrival point and major village of Inishmór. You can change money here at some of the local shops.

Things to See

Inishmór, the 'Big Island', has four impressive stone forts of uncertain age, though 2000 years is a good guess. Halfway down the island, about 8km west of Kilronan, semi-circular **Dún Aengus**, perched terrifyingly on the edge of the sheer southern cliffs, is the best-known of the four.

About 1.5km north is **Dún Eoghanachta**, while halfway back to Kilronan is **Dún Eochla**; both are smaller but perfectly circular ring-forts. Directly south of Kilronan and dramatically perched on a promontory is another fort, **Dún Dúchathair**.

Ionad Árann (☎ 61355), just off the main road leading out of Kilronan, introduces the landscape and traditions of the islands. It opens 10 am to 5 pm daily, April to October (IR£2.50).

Places to Stay

Inishmór hostels typically charge IR£7 to IR£10 for dorm beds. Although most are open year-round, it's a good idea to ring ahead in the off season.

In Kilronan, the modern, justly popular *Kilronan Hostel* (☎ 61255), also known as Tí Joe Mac's Hostel, is a short walk from the pier.

St Kevin's Hostel, between Tí Joe Mac's and the Spar supermarket, is a bit rundown and opens only in summer; inquire at the *Dormer House B&B* (☎ 61125) opposite. Small and basic, *Aharla Hostel* (☎ 61305) is just off the road to Kilmurvey.

A few kilometres north-west of Kilronan, the IHO *Mainistir House Hostel* (☎ 61169 or 61322) has breakfast included and transport that meets the ferry. Also with a pick-up facility, the IHO *Dún Aengus Hostel* (☎ 61318) is near the beach on the west side of Kilmurvey Bay, 7km from Kilronan (April to October).

The numerous B&Bs in and around Kilronan include the large *Dormer House* (☎ 61125), behind Tí Joe Mac's. Open year-round, it has rooms starting at IR£18 per person.

Getting There & Away

Air You can fly to the islands and back with Aer Árann (☎ 091-593034) for IR£35. The mainland departure point is Connemara regional airport at Minna, near Inverin, 38km west of Galway. A connecting bus from outside the Galway tourist office costs IR£2.50 each way. Flights take less than 10 minutes.

Boat Island Ferries (☎ 091-568903 in Galway) serves Inishmór year-round (IR£15 return, 40 minutes). Unfortunately the boat leaves from Rossaveal, 37km west of Galway, which means it's an extra IR£4 to catch an Island Ferries bus from outside the tourist office in Galway. Buses leave 1½ hours before departure time and are scheduled to meet arriving ferries. If you have a car you can go straight to Rossaveal.

Another option is to leave from Doolin in County Clare (see earlier). Doolin Ferries (☎ 065-74455 in Doolin) run to Inishmór mid-May to August (IR£20 return, 55 minutes).

Getting Around

On Inishmór, bikes are definitely the way to go. Aran Cycle Hire (☎ 61132), just up from Kilronan's pier, charges IR£5 per day.

Plenty of small operators offer speedy bus tours to some of the island's principal sights for around IR£5; they'll find you as you get off the ferry.

CONNEMARA & WESTPORT

The north-west corner of County Galway is the wild and barren region known as Connemara. It's a stunning patchwork of bogs, lonely valleys, pale-grey mountains and small lakes. Connemara's isolation has allowed the Irish language to thrive and it's widely spoken here.

By car or bicycle the most scenic routes through Connemara are Oughterard-Recess (via the N59), Recess-Kylemore Abbey (via the R344) and Leenane-Louisburgh (via the R335).

From Galway, Lally Coaches (☎ 091-562905) and O'Neachtain Tours (☎ 091-553188) arrange day-long tours of Connemara for around IR£10.

Things to See

Just west of Recess (Straith Salach) on the N59, turning north at the R334, you'll pass

IRELAND

through the stunning Lough Inagh Valley. From Kylemore you can take the N59 east to Leenane (An Líonán), then detour north on the R335 to Louisburgh and onwards to **Westport**.

Westport (Cathair na Mairt) is a popular stop on the way to/from Sligo and Donegal. It has a pleasant main street and a handful of good pubs. The tourist office (☎ 098-25711) is north over the River Carrowbeg. Westport's major attraction, **Croagh Patrick**, about 7km west of the town, is the hill from which St Patrick performed his snake-expulsion act (Ireland has been serpent-free ever since). Climbing the 765m peak is a ritual for thousands of pilgrims on the last Sunday of July.

Places to Stay

Oughterard has numerous B&Bs and a good hostel. *Canrawer House Hostel* (☎ 095-552388) is at the Clifden end of town, just over 1km down a signposted turning. It has dorm beds starting at IR£8, and bike hire.

An Óige's excellent *Ben Lettery Hostel* (☎ 095-51136) is on the N59, halfway between Recess and Clifden (Easter to September).

In Westport there is *Old Mill Hostel* (☎ 098-27045) in a courtyard off James St; and the almost-luxurious *Club Atlantic Holiday Hostel* (☎ 098-26644) on Alta-mount St near the train station. Both charge IR£7 to IR£8 for dorm beds. The IHO *Granary Hostel* (☎ 098-25903), on The Quay, has beds for IR£6 (March to October).

Getting There & Away

From Westport there are bus connections to Belfast, Cork, Galway, Limerick, Shannon, Sligo and Waterford. Buses depart from the Octagon at the end of James St. The train station (☎ 25253) is on Altamount St, south-east of the town centre. There are three daily rail connections to Dublin via Athlone.

Buses link Galway with Oughterard and Leenane.

The North-West

SLIGO
☎ 071

William Butler Yeats (1865-1939) was ed-ucated in Dublin and London, but his poetry

is muddied with the county of his mother's family. He returned to Sligo (Sligeach) many times, and there are plentiful re-minders of his presence in this sleepy, lar-gish town.

The tourist office (☎ 61201), open week-days year-round and on weekends in July and August, is on Temple St, just south of the centre. Cygo Internet Café is at 19 O'Connell St.

Things to See

Sligo's two major attractions are outside town. **Carrowmore**, 5km to the south-west, is the site of a megalithic cemetery (☎ 61534) with over 60 stone rings, passage tombs and other Stone Age remains. It's the largest Stone Age necropolis in Europe. The visitor centre here is open 9.30 am to 6.30 pm daily May to October (IR£1.50).

A few kilometres north-west of Carrow-more is the hilltop cairn-grave known as **Knocknarea**. About 1000 years younger than Carrowmore, the huge cairn is said to be the grave of the legendary Maeve, Queen of Con-naught in the 1st century AD. Several trails lead to the top of the 328m-high grassy hill.

Places to Stay & Eat

From the town centre, the IHH's *Eden Hill Holiday Hostel* (☎ 43204) on Pearse Rd is a 10-minute walk via the Dublin road. It costs IR£7.80 for a dorm bed. North, on Markievicz Rd, the IHH *White House Hos-tel* (☎ 45160) costs IR£7. The smaller and more basic IHO *Yeats County Hostel* (☎ 46876) is opposite the bus and train sta-tion at 12 Lord Edward St, and costs IR£6.50.

Sligo's less expensive B&Bs are on the various approaches to town. *Renate House* (☎ 62014), in the centre on Upper John St, is a small B&B with singles/doubles start-ing at IR£23.50/34.

Bar Bazzar: Coffee Culture, on Market St near the monument, has coffee, snacks and secondhand books. *Bistro Bianconi (44 O'Connell St)* serves decent Italian dishes for around IR£11, salads and pizzas starting at IR£8.

Getting There & Around

Bus Éireann (☎ 60066) has services to Dublin (IR£10, four hours). There's also a Galway-Sligo-Donegal-Derry service. Buses operate from below the train station

(☎ 69888), which is just west of the centre along Lord Edward St. Trains leave three times a day for Dublin via Boyle, Carrick-on-Shannon and Mullingar.

DONEGAL & AROUND
☎ 073

Donegal Town (Dún na nGall) is not the major centre in County Donegal, but it's a pleasant and laid-back place and well worth a visit.

The triangular Diamond is the centre of Donegal; a few steps south along the River Eske is the tourist office (☎ 21148), open 9 am to 5 pm weekdays June to September.

The cliffs at **Slieve League**, dropping some 300m straight into the Atlantic Ocean, are a recommended, two- or three-day side trip from Donegal. To drive to the cliff edge, take the Killybegs-Glencolumbcille road (R263) and, at Carrick, take the turn-off signposted **Bunglas**. Continue beyond the narrow track signposted for Slieve League (this trail is good for hikers) to the one signposted for Bunglas. Starting from Teelin, experienced walkers can spend a day walking via Bunglas and the somewhat-terrifying One Man's Path to Malinbeg, near Glencolumbcille.

Places to Stay
The comfortable IHH/IHO *Donegal Town Independent Hostel* (☎ 22805) is 1km north-west of town on the Killybegs road (N56). Dorm beds are IR£7 and private rooms are IR£8.50 per person. Camping in the grounds is IR£4 per person.

An Óige's *Ball Hill Hostel* (☎ 21174) has an absolutely stunning setting at the end of a quiet road, right on the shores of Donegal Bay. To get here, take the Killybegs road south-west, and 5km along, look out for the signs. Beds are IR£7.50 (Easter to September). The location is pretty remote, so stock up on food before arriving.

If you're walking around the Slieve League area, a convenient base is the IHH's year-round *Derrylahan Hostel* (☎ 38079), 2km south-east of Carrick and 3km north-west of Kilcar. Beds are IR£7, and there's a small food shop. Call for free pick-up from Kilcar.

Getting There & Away
From Donegal, Bus Éireann (☎ 21101) has connections to Derry, Enniskillen and

Belfast to the north; Sligo and Galway to the west; and Limerick and Cork to the south. The bus stop is on the Diamond, outside the Abbey Hotel. McGeehan's Coaches (☎ 075-46150) does a Donegal-Dublin trip (stopping at Carrick and Kilcar), departing from the police station opposite the tourist office. Otherwise there are daily Bus Éireann coaches from Donegal to Killybegs, with onward buses to Kilcar and Carrick.

Northern Ireland

☎ 028

More than a quarter-century of internal strife has seriously affected tourism in Northern Ireland. Though this was understandable in the dark days of the late 1960s and early 1970s, wanton violence was never a serious threat to visitors. In 1995, following the declaration of the first IRA ceasefire, the numbers of visitors from abroad jumped dramatically. Although the numbers fell in 1996 after hostilities resumed, ratification in 1998 of the Good Friday Agreement provided a dose of positive international press, and tourism figures are once again rising.

Northern Ireland has plenty going for it: the Causeway Coast road, the Glens of Antrim, the old walls of Derry, cosmopolitan Belfast. But even with the coming of peace and the end of military roadblocks, the signs of the Troubles can't be ignored: the street murals in Belfast and Derry, shuttered shopfronts, deserted fortified police-stations, and the occasional armoured car and circling helicopter are still as much a part of Northern Ireland as green fields and smoke-filled pubs.

BELFAST
Had the Troubles never happened, the capital of Northern Ireland would simply be a big, rather ugly industrial city, pleasantly situated and with some impressive Victorian architecture. As it is, Belfast (Béal Feirste) has been deformed by violence for nearly 30 years, and until recently its residents were forced to incorporate bomb threats and army checkpoints into their daily routines.

Yet if your only view of the city has been through the media's lens, you may be surprised to find that Belfast is actually busy and

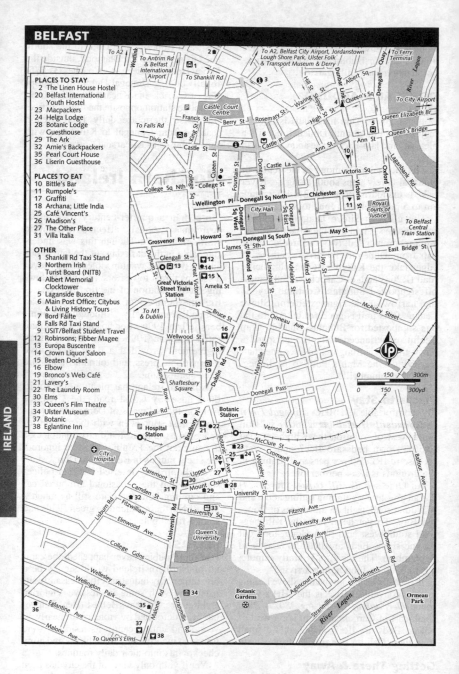

BELFAST

PLACES TO STAY
2 The Linen House Hostel
20 Belfast International Youth Hostel
23 Macpackers
24 Helga Lodge
28 Botanic Lodge Guesthouse
29 The Ark
32 Arnie's Backpackers
35 Pearl Court House
36 Liserin Guesthouse

PLACES TO EAT
10 Bittle's Bar
17 Rumpole's
17 Graffiti
18 Archana; Little India
25 Café Vincent's
26 Madison's
27 The Other Place
31 Villa Italia

OTHER
1 Shankill Rd Taxi Stand
3 Northern Irish Turist Board (NITB)
4 Albert Memorial Clocktower
5 Laganside Buscentre
6 Main Post Office; Citybus & Living History Tours
7 Bord Fáilte
8 Falls Rd Taxi Stand
9 USIT/Belfast Student Travel
12 Robinsons; Fibber Magee
13 Europa Buscentre
14 Crown Liquor Saloon
15 Beaten Docket
16 Elbow
19 Bronco's Web Café
21 Lavery's
22 The Laundry Room
30 Elms
33 Queen's Film Theatre
34 Ulster Museum
37 Botanic
38 Eglantine Inn

IRELAND

bustling, livelier and far more cheerful than its grim reputation leads visitors to expect.

Orientation & Information

The city centre is a compact area with the imposing City Hall as the central landmark. Belfast's principal shopping district is north of the square. To the south lies the Golden Mile, a restaurant- and pub-filled stretch of Dublin Rd, Shaftesbury Square, Bradbury Place and Botanic Ave.

The helpful Northern Ireland Tourist Board (NITB; ☎ 9024 6609), 59 North St (a new location is planned, but undecided at the time of writing), is open 9 am to 5.15 pm (in summer until 7 pm) Monday to Saturday, and noon to 4 pm Sunday in July and August. Bord Fáilte (☎ 9032 7888), 53 Castle St, has information on the Irish Republic.

The main post office is on Castle Place, and there's a smaller branch on Shaftesbury Square. The USIT/Belfast Student Travel office (☎ 9032 4073) is at 13B Fountain Centre, College St. The Laundry Room is at 37 Botanic Ave; and Bronco's Web Cafe is at 122 Great Victoria St.

Around the City

At the north-eastern corner of City Hall (1906) is a statue of Sir Edward Harland, the Yorkshire-born engineer who founded Belfast's Harland & Wolff shipyards. The yard's most famous construction was the ill-fated *Titanic*, the 'unsinkable' boat that sank in 1912. A memorial to the disaster and its victims stands on the east side of City Hall.

Across from the Europa Hotel on Great Victoria St, the famed Crown Liquor Saloon (1885) displays Victorian architecture at its most extravagant.

The Ulster Museum (☎ 9038 3000) is in the Botanic Gardens (which open at 8 am and close at sunset), near the university. It has excellent exhibits on Irish art, wildlife, dinosaurs, steam and industrial machines, and more. Entry is free (except for some major exhibitions) and the museum is open 10 am to 5 pm weekdays, 1 to 5 pm Saturday, and 2 to 5 pm Sunday.

Falls & Shankill Roads

The Catholic Falls Rd and the Protestant Shankill Rd have been battlefronts since the 1970s. Even so, these areas are quite safe and worth venturing into, if only to see the large **murals** expressing local political and religious passions.

If you don't fancy a tour (see Organised Tours later), the ideologically sound way to visit the sectarian zones of the Falls and Shankill Rds is by what is known locally as the 'people taxi'. Shankill Rd taxis go from North St; Falls Rd taxis from Castle St. The Falls Rd taxis occupy the first line at the Castle St taxi park, with signs up in Gaelic. They're used to doing tourist circuits of the Falls and typically charge £10 to £12 (the cabs hold up to five people) for a one-hour tour that takes in the main points of interest.

Ulster Folk & Transport Museum

Belfast's biggest tourist attraction (☎ 9042 8428) is 11km north-east of the centre beside the Bangor road (A2) near Holywood. The 30 buildings on this 60-hectare site range from city terrace-homes to thatched farm-cottages. A bridge crosses the A2 to the Transport Museum, where you can see various Ulster-related vehicles including a prototype of the Vertical Take-Off and Landing (VTOL) aircraft.

The museums are open daily, but times vary throughout the year. You'll be sure to find them open 10.30 am to 5 pm except Sunday, when they open at noon. Joint entry is £4. From Belfast take Ulsterbus No 1 or any Bangor-bound train that stops at Cultra station.

Organised Tours

A Citybus tour (☎ 9045 8484) covers all the main sights at 1 pm every Wednesday and Saturday (3½ hours). The popular Living History tour takes in Belfast's Troubles-related sights Thursday and Sunday at 1 pm. Tickets cost £8.50. Both tours leave Castle Place, outside the main post office, year-round (off-season they're subject to demand).

Special Events

For two weeks in late October and early November the people of Belfast get excited about the arts at the Festival at Queen's (☎ 9066 7687).

Places to Stay

Hostels *Arnie's Backpackers (☎ 9024 2867, 63 Fitzwilliam St)* has dorm beds from £7 to £8.50. With only 22 beds, demand for space far exceeds supply.

IRELAND

The YHANI *Belfast International Youth Hostel* (☎ *9031 5435, 22-32 Donegall Rd*) is large (112 beds), modern and very clean. There's a laundry and small cafe, but no kitchen facilities. Dorm beds cost £9, private/twin rooms £16/22.

The Ark (☎ *9032 9626, 18 University St*) has 31 beds. Dorms cost £6.50 to £7.50 and twins are £12 per person. *Macpackers* (☎ *9022 0845, 1 Cameron St)*, linked to Steve's Backpackers in Derry, has beds for £7.50 per night. At the other end of the central city is *The Linen House Hostel* (☎ *9058 6400, 18-20 Kent St)*, with dorm beds for £6.50 to £8.50 and singles/doubles for £10/24.

B&Bs The tourist office makes B&B reservations for a minimal fee; credit-card bookings can be made over the phone (☎ *0800-317153*). Many B&Bs are in the university area, which is close to the centre, safe and well-stocked with restaurants and pubs.

The large and comfortable *Helga Lodge* (☎ *9032 4820, 7 Cromwell Rd*) has singles/doubles starting at £22/40. Nearby is the handsome *Botanic Lodge Guesthouse* (☎ *9032 7682, 87 Botanic Ave)*, which costs £25/40.

The basic *Pearl Court House* (☎ *9066 6145, 11 Malone Rd*) charges £23.50 per person. *Liserin Guesthouse* (☎ *9066 0769, 17 Eglantine Ave*) charges £20/40 for a room with a shower and TV.

Places to Eat

Restaurants There are numerous budget restaurants along the Golden Mile from Dublin Rd south to University Rd and Botanic Ave.

Graffiti (*50 Dublin Rd*) serves excellent, filling pasta-dishes for under £6.75. There are often queues for tables at *Villa Italia* (*37-41 University Rd)*, a vibrant Italian restaurant and pizzeria.

Archana prides itself as the only Balti House in Belfast. It's upstairs at 53 Dublin Rd, and serves Balti curries from £5.50. Downstairs the superb *Little India* dishes up Belfast's best fauna-free curries from £5.50. There's also a £2.50 lunch special of two veggie dishes and rice.

Botanic Ave has lots of cafes. Try *The Other Place* (*79 Botanic Ave)*, which is lively and good for coffee. More on the ritzy side is *Madison's* (*59-63 Botanic Ave)*. Across the road you'll find a range of ethnic cuisines from Thai to Mexican and French at *Café Vincent's*. Main dishes cost £6 to £10.

Pubs At the *Crown Liquor Saloon*, on Great Victoria St, you can get oysters and Irish stews, and at the same time take in the magnificent decor.

Keeping a low profile, *Rumpole's* (*81 Chichester St*) is good for steak-and-spud lunches. A block farther north, *Bittle's Bar* is a small pub entered from 70 Upper Church Lane. It specialises in traditional dishes.

Entertainment

Belfast's guide to what's on is the *Big List*, available at cafes and pubs.

Worthy of more than one visit is *Robinsons* on Great Victoria St, with its many bars, historic paraphernalia (including personal-hygiene products) and a walk-through to *Fibber Magee* on Blackstaff Square. Across the road the often rowdy *Beaten Docket*, on Great Victoria St, is also busy at night.

A major landmark along the Golden Mile at Bradbury Place, *Lavery's* is intensely popular with students, bikers and hardened drinkers. More comfortable is the student-filled *Elms* (*36 University Rd)*. Farther south and facing each other across Malone Rd are *Eglantine Inn* and *Botanic*, two student-bars known as the 'Egg and Bott'. If you crave a quiet pint try the *Elbow*, on Dublin Rd.

Queen's Film Theatre (*free call* ☎ *0800 3 28 28 11)*, on University Square Mews, has independent, classic, cult and arthouse films.

Getting There & Away

For security reasons there are no left-luggage facilities at Belfast train or bus station. For all Ulsterbus, Northern Ireland Railways (NIR) and local bus information call ☎ 9089 9411 or ☎ 9033 3000.

Bus Belfast has two separate bus stations. The Laganside Buscentre, in Oxford St near the river, has bus connections to counties Antrim, Down and Derry. Buses to everywhere else in Northern Ireland, the Republic, the international airport and the Larne ferries, leave from the Europa Buscentre in Glengall St.

Belfast-Dublin buses take about three hours and start at £10.50 one way. For connections to Derry and Donegal contact the Lough Swilly Bus Company (☎ 7126 2017) in Derry.

Train Belfast has two main train stations – Great Victoria St, next to the Europa Buscentre, and Belfast Central, east of the city centre on East Bridge St.

Destinations served from Belfast Central include Derry and Dublin. Dublin-Belfast trains take two hours at £19/29 one way/return. From Belfast Central a free (with your bus or train ticket) Linkline bus to Donegall Square in the city centre leaves every 10 minutes. A local train also connects with Great Victoria St. Great Victoria St station has services to Derry and Larne Harbour.

Boat From Belfast there are three main ferry routes connecting Belfast to Stranraer, Liverpool and the Isle of Man. See the Getting There & Away section at the beginning of this chapter for more details.

Norse Irish ferries to Liverpool leave from Victoria terminal, 5km north of central Belfast; take a bus from Europa Buscentre.

THE BELFAST-DERRY COASTAL ROAD

Ireland isn't short of fine stretches of coast, but the Causeway Coast from Portstewart in County Derry to Ballycastle in County Antrim, and the Antrim Coast from Ballycastle to Belfast, are magnificent.

From late May to late September, Ulsterbus's Antrim Coaster bus No 252 operates between Belfast and Coleraine (four hours), stopping at all the main tourist sights. Also, its open-topped Bushmills Bus (No 177) is a double-decker that runs from the Giant's Causeway to Coleraine in July and August. The trip takes just over an hour. Bus No 162 runs year-round along the Antrim coast between Larne and Cushendun.

Glens of Antrim

Between Larne and Ballycastle, the nine Glens of Antrim are extremely picturesque stretches of woodland where streams cascade into the sea. The picture-perfect port of **Cushendall** has been dubbed the 'Capital of the Glens', while **Glenariff**, a few kilometres

to the south, lays claim to the title 'Queen of the Glens'. Between Cushenden and Ballycastle, eschew the main A2 road for the narrower and more picturesque B92, and take the turn-off down to sweeping Murlough Bay.

The YHANI *Cushendall Youth Hostel* (☎ 2177 1344) is 1km north of the village. Dorm beds cost £8.25 (March to mid-December).

Ballycastle

Ballycastle, where the Atlantic Ocean meets the Irish Sea, is a quiet harbour town and a natural base for exploring the coasts to the west or south.

The welcoming IHH/IHO *Castle Hostel* (☎ 2076 2337, 62 Quay Rd), just past the Marine Hotel, charges £7 a night. The IHO *Ballycastle Backpackers* (☎ 2076 3612, 4 North St), near the waterfront and main bus stop, charges £6.

Carrick-a-Rede Island

Open from May to mid-September, but closed any time the wind is too strong, the 20m rope bridge connecting Carrick-a-Rede Island to the mainland is a heart-stopper, swaying some 25m above the furious sea. The island is the site of a salmon fishery and a nesting ground for gulls and fulmars. You can cross the bridge free, but the National Trust car park costs £2; it's a 1.25km walk from there to the bridge.

Giant's Causeway

Chances are you've seen pictures of the Giant's Causeway (Clochán an Aifir), Northern Ireland's number-one tourist attraction. The hexagonal basalt columns are impressive and do look as if a giant might have accidentally tipped out all 37,000 of them. According to legend, giant Finn Mc-Cool fancied a female of his race on the Scottish island of Staffa and built some stepping stones to the island where, indeed, similar rock formations are found.

The more prosaic explanation is that lava erupted from an underground fissure and crystallised some 60 million years ago. The phenomenon is very clearly explained in the **Causeway Visitors' Centre** (☎ 2073 1855) by a new exhibition and audiovisual show (£1.50). Skip the tourist banality and head straight for the natural wonder.

It costs nothing to make the pleasant 1.5km pilgrimage to the actual site, starting from outside the visitors' centre. About four buses a day (fewer on Sunday) between Portrush and Ballycastle pass the Giant's Causeway.

A recommended walk is from the Giant's Causeway 16km east along the coast (not the highway), past Dunseverick Castle to the beach at Whitepark Bay, where you'll find the year-round YHANI *Whitepark Bay Hostel* (☎ 2073 1745), with beds starting at £10.50.

Bushmills

Bushmills, 4km south-west of the Giant's Causeway, is a small town off the A2. The town itself is grimy and grey; the real attraction, 500m south of the main square, is the **Old Bushmills Distillery** (☎ 2073 3272), the only place in the world where Bushmills whiskey is distilled. Whiskey was first officially bottled here in 1608, but records indicate that the activity was going on for hundreds of years before that. After a noisy tour of the industrial process (it's quieter on weekends, when production is halted), you're rewarded with a whiskey-tasting session.

From April to October, distillery tours leave every 20 minutes, 9.30 am to 4 pm Monday to Saturday and noon to 4 pm Sunday. In the off season, tours leave at 10.30 and 11.30 am and 1.30, 2.30 and 3.30 pm weekdays (£3.50).

Dunluce Castle

Abandoned back in 1641, the ruins of 14th-century Dunluce Castle (☎ 2073 1938), dramatically placed overlooking the sea between Bushmills and Portrush, still bear a hint of the castle's former eminence. The south wall, facing the mainland, has two openings cut into it to hold cannons salvaged from the wreck of the *Girona*, a Spanish Armada vessel that foundered nearby in 1588. Perched 30m above the sea, the castle was of obvious military value, and there are extensive remains inside the walls, giving a good idea of life here.

Entry to the castle is £1.50 and guided tours are available. It opens 10 am to 6 pm weekdays and 2 to 6 pm Sunday (closed Tuesday) April to September; the rest of the year it closes at 4 pm.

DERRY

Derry or Londonderry; even choosing what you call Northern Ireland's second-largest city can be a political statement. In practice it's better known as Derry whatever your politics.

Doire, the original Irish name, means 'oak grove', and the 'London' prefix was added as a reward for the town's central role in the struggle between Protestant King William III and Catholic King James II.

In the 1960s, resentment at the long-running domination and gerrymandering of the city council by Protestants boiled over in the (Catholic dominated) civil rights marches of 1968. Simultaneously, attacks by Protestants on the Catholic Bogside district began, leading to a veritable siege. The British government decided that open warfare could only be prevented by military intervention, and on 14 August 1968 British troops entered Derry. In January 1972, 'Bloody Sunday' saw the deaths of 14 unarmed Catholic civil rights marchers in Derry at the hands of the British army, an event that marked the beginning of the Troubles in earnest.

Today Derry is as safe to visit as anywhere else in Northern Ireland. The arts are alive, and festivals, such as the Banks of the Foyle Halloween Carnival and the Foyal Film Festival, draw crowds from everywhere.

Orientation & Information

The old centre of Derry is the small, walled city on the west bank of the River Foyle. The heart of the walled city is The Diamond, intersected by four main roads: Shipquay St, Ferryquay St, Bishop St Within and Butcher St. The Catholic Bogside area is below the walls to the northwest. To the south is a Protestant estate known as the Fountain.

Derry's NITB (☎ 7126 7284) and Bord Fáilte (☎ 7136 9501) share an office just outside the walled city at the Tourist Information Centre, 44 Foyle St.

The main post office is on Custom House St, just north of the Tower Museum. Access the Internet for free until 1 pm, or £2.50 per hour after, at the Central Library (☎ 7127 2300), 35 Foyle St.

Things to See

Until the mid-1990s, the presence of the army and protective iron gates made Derry's magnificent **city walls** hard to appreciate. The gates are still there, but now they're open and it's possible to walk all around the walls, which were built between 1613 and 1618. They're about 8m high, 9m thick, and go around the old city for a length of 1.5km. A major highlight for the traveller, the gates give an excellent overview of Bogside and its defiant **murals** – one notably proclaiming 'You Are Now Entering Free Derry'. From the city walls between Butcher's Gate and the army barracks, you can see many of the in-your-face building-side murals.

Just inside Coward's Bastion to the north, O'Doherty's Tower houses the excellent **Tower Museum** (☎ 7137 7633), which traces the story of Derry from the days of St Columbcille to the present. The museum is open 10 am to 5 pm Tuesday to Saturday; 10 am to 5 pm Monday to Saturday and 2 to 5 pm Sunday in July and August (£3.50).

Places to Stay

There are only two hostels in Derry, so consider booking ahead. The largest of the two is the YHANI *Derry City Hostel* (☎ 7128 4100, 6 Magazine St) in the walled city near Butcher's Gate, just 150m from the bus station. The cheapest dorm beds without breakfast are £6.50 and the most expensive £8; doubles cost £30.

Not so formal is *Steve's Backpackers* (☎ 7137 7989, 4 Asylum Rd), a small, friendly, year-round hostel north of the walled city. From Butchers Gate follow Waterloo St until it turns into Strand Rd, continue for another 500m and turn left into Asylum Rd. Beds are £7.50.

Within walking distance of the bus station, the friendly *Acorn House* (☎ 7127 1156, 17 Aberfoyle Terrace, Strand Rd) has singles/doubles starting at £20/32. *Clarence House* (☎ 7126 5342, 15 Northland Rd) charges £19/50; the double comes with an ensuite.

Places to Eat

Just outside the Ferryquay Gate, south-east of the walled city, modern *Fitzroy's* has entrances at 3 Carlisle Rd and 2-4 Bridge St, and moves from cool cafe to sophisticated mains at night. *The Sandwich Company*, on The Diamond, and *The Bailey*, a few doors along on Bishop St, are handy for a simple lunch.

On Shipquay St, *Townsman* serves above-average pub food. *The Strand Bar*, on Strand Rd about 200m from the northern corner of the walled city, has meals upstairs starting at £8.95, along with a pub, night-club and live music.

Entertainment

Derry's liveliest pubs are those along Waterloo St: *The Gweedore Bar, Dungloe, Tracy's,* and *Peadar O'Donnell's,* which is good for traditional music. *Metro Bar* (3-4 Bank Place), just inside the walls, is Derry's most trendy (and crowded) pub.

The Oscar-nominated *The Nerve Centre* (☎ 7126 0562, 7-8 Magazine St) is a multi-media venue with music, art-house cinema, a cafe and bar.

Getting There & Away

The Ulsterbus station (☎ 7126 2261) is just outside the city walls on Foyle St, near the Guildhall.

Of the many services to Belfast, bus No 212, the Maiden City Flyer, is the fastest (£7.10, one hour 40 minutes).

Each day at 9 am a bus leaves for Cork, arriving at 7.15 pm. Bus Éireann operates a Derry-Galway service, via Donegal and Sligo.

Derry's Waterside train station (☎ 7134 2228) is across the River Foyle from the centre, but is connected to it by a free Linkline bus. To Belfast, there are seven trains Monday to Saturday and three on Sunday (three hours).

Italy

Italy is vibrant, seductive, even extraordinary. It has style, fine food and delicious wine, and more museums and churches than you could ever hope to explore in a lifetime. Beneath it all there remains, happily, a chaotic Mediterranean flair.

Of course, not everything is wonderful. The 'economic miracle' of the past decades has transformed the country, leading to expanded industry, poor urban planning and unchecked resort construction.

Do some research before arriving in Italy and strike a fair balance between the cities and the countryside – from Roman ruins and tiny medieval hill towns to the grandeur of the Alps and Dolomites, there is much more to the country than just Rome, Venice and Florence.

Facts about Italy

HISTORY

The traditional date for the founding of Rome by the mythical figure Romulus is 753 BC, but the country had already been inhabited for thousands of years. Palaeolithic Neanderthals lived in Italy during the last Ice Age more than 20,000 years ago, and by the start of the Bronze Age, around 2000 BC, the peninsula had been settled by several Italic tribes.

From about 900 BC the Etruscan civilisation developed until these mysterious people, whose origins are still controversial, dominated the area between the Arno and Tiber Valleys. By the end of the 3rd century BC, however, the Romans had overwhelmed the last Etruscan city.

The new Roman republic, after recovering from the invasion of the Gauls in 390 BC, began its expansion into southern Italy. Rome claimed Sicily following the First Punic War against Hannibal in 241 BC, after his legendary crossing of the Alps.

AT A GLANCE	
Capital:	Rome
Population:	57.8 million
Official Language:	Italian
Currency:	1 Italian lira (L) = 100 centesimi

Rome defeated Carthage in 202 BC and within a few years claimed Spain and Greece as colonies.

In the 1st century BC, under Julius Caesar, Rome conquered Gaul and moved into Egypt. After Caesar's assassination by his nephew, Brutus, on the Ides of March in 44 BC, a power struggle began between Mark Antony and Octavius, leading to the deaths of Antony and Cleopatra in Egypt in 31 BC and the establishment of the Roman Empire in 27 BC. Octavius, who had been adopted by Julius Caesar as his son and heir, took the title of Augustus Caesar and became the first emperor. Augustus ruled for 45 years, a period of great advancement in engineering, architecture, administration and literature.

By the end of the 3rd century, the empire had grown to such an extent that Emperor Diocletian divided it between east and west for administrative purposes. His successor, Constantine, declared religious freedom for Christians and moved the seat of power to the eastern capital, Byzantium, which he renamed Constantinople. During the 4th century, Christianity was declared the official state religion and grew in power and influence.

By the early 5th century, German tribes had entered Rome, and in 476 the Western Roman Empire ended when the German warrior, Odoacer, deposed the emperor and declared himself ruler of Italy. The south and Sicily were dominated by Muslim Arabs until the Normans invaded in 1036.

The Middle Ages in Italy were marked by the development of powerful city-states in the north. This was the time of Dante, Petrarch and Boccaccio, Giotto, Cimabue and Pisano.

In the 15th century the Renaissance, which began in Florence, spread throughout

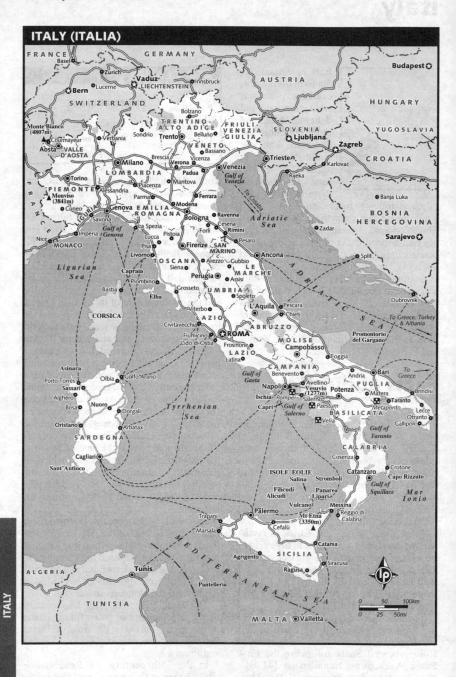

ITALY (ITALIA)

the country, fostering genius in the likes of Brunelleschi, Donatello, Bramante, Botticelli, Da Vinci, Masaccio, Lippi, Raphael and, of course, Michelangelo.

By the early 16th century much of the country was under Spanish rule. This lasted until 1713 when, following the War of Spanish Succession, control of Italy passed to the Austrians. It was not until after the invasion by Napoleon in 1796 that a degree of unity was introduced into Italy, for the first time since the fall of the Roman Empire.

In the 1860s Italy's unification movement, known as the Risorgimento, gained momentum, and in 1861 the Kingdom of Italy was declared under the rule of King Vittorio Emanuele. Venice was wrested from Austria in 1866 and Rome from the papacy in 1870.

Mussolini & WWII

In the years after WWI, Italy was in turmoil. In 1921 the Fascist Party, formed by Benito Mussolini in 1919, won 35 of the 135 seats in parliament. In October 1921, after a period of considerable unrest and strikes, the king asked Mussolini to form a government, and he became prime minister with only 7% representation in parliament.

Mussolini formed the Rome-Berlin axis with Hitler in 1936 and Italy entered WWII as an ally of Germany in June 1941. After a series of military disasters and an invasion by the Allies in 1943, the king led a coup against Mussolini and had him arrested. After being rescued by the Germans, Mussolini tried to govern in the north, but was fiercely opposed by Italian partisans, who finally shot him in April 1945.

The Italian Republic

In 1946, following a referendum, the constitutional monarchy was abolished and the republic established. Italy was a founding member of the European Economic Community (EEC) in 1957. The country was seriously disrupted by terrorism in the 1970s following the appearance of the Red Brigades, who kidnapped and assassinated the Christian Democrat prime minister, Aldo Moro, in 1978.

In the decades that followed WWII, Italy's national government was dominated by the centre-right Christian Democrats, usually in coalition with other parties (excluding the communists). Italy enjoyed significant economic growth in the 1980s, but the 1990s heralded a new period of crisis for the country, both economically and politically.

The 1990s

Against the backdrop of a severe economic crisis, the very foundations of Italian politics were shaken by a national bribery scandal known as *tangentopoli* (bribesville). Investigations eventually implicated thousands of politicians, public officials and business people, and left the main parties in tatters, effectively demolishing the centre of the Italian political spectrum.

After a period of right-wing government, new elections in 1996 brought a centre-left coalition known as the Olive Tree to power. Led by economist Romano Prodi, it included the communists for the first time in Italian history. A program of fiscal austerity was ushered in to guarantee Italy's entry into Europe's economic and monetary union (EMU), which occurred in 1998. Although the prime minister has been replaced three times (the government is currently led by socialist Giuliano Amato, who inherited the position from Prodi's successor Massimo d'Alema in March 2000), the Olive Tree coalition is holding on.

The 1990s have also seen Italy moving more decisively against the Sicilian Mafia, prompted by the 1992 assassinations of two prominent anti-Mafia judges. A major offensive in Sicily, plus the testimonies of several *pentiti* (informers or supergrasses), led to several important arrests – most notably of the Sicilian godfather, Salvatore 'Toto' Riina, who is now serving a life sentence. The man believed to have taken power after Riina's arrest, Giovanni Brusca, was arrested in May 1996 and implicated in the murders of anti-Mafia judges, Giovanni Falcone and Paolo Borsellino. A number of subsequent high profile arrests have undoubtedly dented the Mafia's confidence, but the battle is far from won.

GEOGRAPHY

Italy's boot shape makes it one of the most recognisable countries in the world. The country, incorporating the islands of Sicily and Sardinia, is bound by the Adriatic, Ligurian, Tyrrhenian and Ionian Seas, which all form part of the Mediterranean Sea.

ITALY

About 75% of the Italian peninsula is mountainous, with the Alps dividing the country from France, Switzerland and Austria, and the Apennines forming a backbone which extends from the Alps into Sicily. There are four active volcanoes: Stromboli and Vulcano (in the Aeolian Islands), Vesuvius (near Naples) and Etna (Sicily).

CLIMATE

Summers are uniformly hot, but are often extremely hot and dry in the south. Winters can be severely cold in the north – particularly in the Alps, but also in the Po Valley – whereas they are generally mild in the south and in Sicily and Sardinia.

GOVERNMENT & POLITICS

For administrative purposes Italy is divided into 20 regions, each of which have some degree of autonomy. The regions are then subdivided into provinces and municipalities.

The country is a parliamentary republic, headed by a president who appoints the prime minister. The parliament consists of a senate and chamber of deputies, both of which have equal legislative power. The seat of national government is in Rome. Until reforms were introduced in 1994, members of parliament were elected by what was probably the purest system of proportional representation in the world.

Two-thirds of both houses are now elected on the basis of who receives the most votes in their district, basically the same as the first-past-the-post system in the UK. The old system generally produced unstable coalition governments – Italy had 53 governments in the 48 years between the declaration of the republic and the introduction of electoral reforms.

POPULATION & PEOPLE

The population of Italy is 57.8 million. The country has the lowest birth rate in Europe – a surprising fact considering the Italians' preoccupation with children and family. Foreigners may like to think of Italy as a land of passionate, animated people who gesticulate wildly when speaking, love to eat, drive like maniacs and don't like to work. However, it will take more than a holiday in Italy to understand its vigorous and remarkably diverse inhabitants. Overall the people remain fiercely protective of their regional customs, including their dialects and cuisine.

ARTS
Architecture, Painting & Sculpture

In the south of Italy and in Sicily, where Greek colonisation preceded Roman domination, there are important Greek archaeological sites such as the temples at Paestum, south of Salerno, and at Agrigento in Sicily. Pompeii and Herculaneum give an idea of how ancient Romans actually lived.

Byzantine mosaics adorn churches throughout Italy, most notably at Ravenna, in the Basilica of San Marco in Venice, and in Monreale cathedral near Palermo. There are also some interesting mosaics in churches in Rome. In Apulia, you can tour the magnificent Romanesque churches, a legacy of the Normans (the region's medieval rulers) and their successors, the Swabians.

The 15th and early 16th centuries in Italy saw one of the most remarkable explosions of artistic and literary achievement in recorded history – the Renaissance. Patronised mainly by the Medici family in Florence and the popes in Rome, painters, sculptors, architects and writers flourished and many artists of genius emerged. The High Renaissance (about 1490-1520) was dominated by three men – Leonardo da Vinci (1452-1519), Michelangelo Buonarrotti (1475-1564) and Raphael (1483-1520).

The baroque period (17th century) was characterised by sumptuous, often fantastic architecture and richly decorative painting and sculpture. In Rome there are innumerable works by the great baroque sculptor and architect Gianlorenzo Bernini (1598-1680).

Literature

Before Dante (1265-1321) wrote his *Divina Commedia* (Divine Comedy) and confirmed vernacular Italian as a serious medium for poetic expression, Latin was the language of writers. Among the greatest writers of ancient Rome were Cicero, Virgil, Ovid and Petronius.

A contemporary of Dante was Petrarch (1304-74). Giovanni Boccaccio (1313-75), author of *Decameron*, is considered the first Italian novelist.

Machiavelli's *The Prince*, although a purely political work, has proved the most lasting of the Renaissance works.

Italy's richest contribution to modern literature has been in the novel and short story. Authors Cesare Pavese (1908-50) and Carlo Levi (1902-75) both endured internal exile in southern Italy during Fascism. Levi based *Christ Stopped at Eboli* on his experiences in exile in Basilicata. Umberto Eco (born 1932) shot to fame with his first and best-known work, *The Name of the Rose*.

Cinema

From 1945 to 1947, Roberto Rossellini produced three neorealist masterpieces, including *Rome Open City* starring Anna Magnani. Vittorio de Sica produced another classic in 1948, *The Bicycle Thief*. Schooled with the masters of neorealism, Federico Fellini in many senses took the creative baton from them and carried it into the following decades, with films such as *La Dolce Vita*. The career of Michelangelo Antonioni reached a climax with *Blow-up* in 1967. Bernardo Bertolucci had his first international hit with *Last Tango in Paris*. He made the blockbuster *The Last Emperor* in 1987. Franco Zeffirelli's most recent film was *Jane Eyre*. Other notable directors include the Taviani brothers, Giuseppe Tornatore, Nanni Moretti and Roberto Benigni, director of the Oscar-winning *Life is Beautiful* (1998).

Theatre

At a time when French playwrights ruled the stage, the Venetian Carlo Goldoni (1707-1793) attempted to bring Italian theatre back into the limelight with the *commedia dell' arte*, the tradition of improvisational theatre. Luigi Pirandello (1867-1936), author of *Six Characters in Search of an Author*, won the Nobel Prize in 1934. Modern Italian theatre's most enduring representative is actor/director Dario Fo, who won the Nobel Prize for literature in 1997.

SOCIETY & CONDUCT

It is difficult to make blanket assertions about Italian culture, if only because Italians have lived together as a nation for little over 100 years. Prior to unification, the peninsula was long subject to a varied mix of masters and cultures. This lack of unity contributed to the survival of local dialects and customs. Even today many Italians tend to identify more strongly with their region or home town than with the nation. An Italian is first and foremost a Tuscan or Sicilian, or even a Roman or Neapolitan.

In some parts of Italy, especially in the south, women might be harassed if they wear skimpy or see-through clothing. Modest dress is expected in all churches, and even churches that are major tourist attractions, such as St Peter's in Rome, strictly enforce dress codes (no shorts, bare arms or shoulders).

LANGUAGE

English is most widely understood in the north, particularly in major centres such as Milan, Florence and Venice. Staff at most hotels and restaurants usually speak a little English, but you will be better received if you attempt to communicate in Italian.

Italian, a Romance language, is related to French, Spanish, Portuguese and Romanian. Modern literary Italian developed in the 13th and 14th centuries, predominantly through the works of Dante, Petrarch and Boccaccio, who wrote chiefly in the Florentine dialect. Although many dialects are spoken in everyday conversation, so-called standard Italian is the national language of schools, media and literature, and is understood throughout the country.

Many older Italians still expect to be addressed by the third person formal (ie, *Lei* instead of *Tu*). It is not polite to use the greeting *ciao* when addressing strangers, unless they use it first; use *buongiorno* and *arrivederci*.

See the Language chapter at the back of this book for pronunciation guidelines and useful words and phrases.

Facts for the Visitor

HIGHLIGHTS

Whittling down a short list of highlights for Italy is almost an impossible task. Bearing that in mind, you could try the following: Florence, Siena, Italian food, the ancient ruins at Pompeii and Herculaneum, Venice and the rugged Aeolian Islands.

SUGGESTED ITINERARIES

Three days
   Visit Rome to see the Forum, the Colosseum, St Peter's Basilica and the Vatican museums.

ITALY

One week
  Visit Rome and Florence, with detours in Tuscany to Siena and San Gimignano. Or visit Rome and Naples, with detours to Pompeii, Vesuvius and the Amalfi Coast.
Two weeks
  As above, plus Bologna, Verona, Ravenna and at least three days in Venice.

PLANNING
When to Go
The best time to visit Italy is in the off season, particularly from April to June and September to October, when the weather is good, prices are lower and there are fewer tourists. During July and August (the high season) it is very hot, prices are inflated, the country swarms with tourists, and hotels by the sea and in the mountains are usually booked out. Note that many hotels and restaurants in seaside areas close down for the winter months.

Maps
For maps of cities, you will generally find those provided by the tourist office adequate. Excellent road and city maps are published by the Istituto Geografico de Agostini and are available in all major bookshops.

TOURIST OFFICES
Local Tourist Offices
There are three main categories of tourist office in Italy: regional, provincial and local. Their names vary throughout the country. Provincial offices are sometimes known as the Ente Provinciale per il Turismo (EPT) or, more commonly, the Azienda di Promozione Turistica (APT). The Azienda Autonoma di Soggiorno e Turismo (AAST) and Informazioni e Assistenza ai Turisti (IAT) offices usually have information only on the town itself. In some of the very small towns and villages the local tourist office is called a Pro Loco, and is often little more than a room with a desk.

The quality of service offered varies dramatically throughout the country; don't be surprised if you encounter lethargic, disinterested staff. You should, however, be able to get a map, an *elenco degli alberghi* (a list of hotels), a *pianta della città* (map of the town) and information on the major sights. Staff speak English in larger towns, but in the more out-of-the-way places you may

have to either speak Italian or rely on sign language. Tourist offices are generally open from 8.30 am to 12.30 or 1 pm and 3 to 7 pm Monday to Friday and on Saturday morning. Hours are usually extended in summer.

The Centro Turistico Studentesco e Giovanile (CTS) has offices all over Italy and specialises in discounts for students and young people, but is also useful for travellers of any age looking for cheap flights and sightseeing discounts. It is linked with the International Student Travel Confederation. You can get a student card here if you have documents proving that you are a student.

Tourist Offices Abroad
Information about Italy can be obtained at Italian State Tourist Offices (Web site www.enit.it) throughout the world, including:

Australia (☎ 02-9262 1666, fax 9262 5745) c/o Italian Chamber of Commerce, Level 26, 44 Market St, Sydney, NSW 2000
Canada (☎ 514-866 7668, ✉ initaly@ican.net) Suite 1914, 1 Place Ville Marie, Montreal, Quebec H3B 2C3
UK (☎ 020-7408 1254, ✉ enitlond@globalnet .co.uk) 1 Princes St, London W1R 8AY
USA (☎ 212-245 4822, ✉ enitny@bway.net) Suite 1565, 630 Fifth Ave, New York, NY 10111
  (☎ 310-820 1819) Suite 550, 12400 Wilshire Blvd, Los Angeles, CA 90025
  (☎ 312-644 0996, ✉ enitch@italiantourism .com) 500 North Michigan Ave, Chicago, IL 60611

Sestante CIT (Compagnia Italiana di Turismo), Italy's national travel agency, also has offices throughout the world (known as CIT outside Italy). It can provide extensive information on Italy, as well as book tours and accommodation. It can also make train bookings. Offices include:

Australia (☎ 03-9650 5510) Level 4, 227 Collins St, Melbourne, Vic 3000
  (☎ 02-9267 1255), 263 Clarence St, Sydney, NSW 2000
Canada (☎ 514-845 4310, 800 361 7799) Suite 750, 1450 City Councillors St, Montreal, Quebec H3A 2E6
  (☎ 905-415 1060, 800 387 0711) Suite 401, 80 Tiverton Court, Markham, Toronto, Ontario L3R 0G4
UK (☎ 020-8686 0677, 8686 5533, ✉ ciao@citalia.co.uk) Marco Polo House, 3/5 Lansdown Rd, Croydon CR9 1LL

ITALY

USA (☎ 212-730 2121, @ citnewyork@msn
.com) 10th floor, 15 West 44th Street, New
York, NY 10036
(☎ 310-338 8615, @ citlax@email.msm.com)
6033 West Century Blvd, Suite 980,
Los Angeles, CA 90045

EMBASSIES & CONSULATES
Italian Embassies & Consulates
Australia
Embassy: (☎ 02-6273 3333, fax 6273 4223,
@ ambital2@dynamite.com.au) 12 Grey St,
Deakin, Canberra, ACT 2600
Consulate: (☎ 03-9867 5744, fax 9866 3932,
@ itconmel@netlink.com.au) 509 St Kilda Rd,
Melbourne, Vic 3004
Consulate: (☎ 02-9392 7900, fax 9252 4830,
@ itconsyd@armadillo.com.au) Level 43, The
Gateway, 1 Macquarie Place, Sydney, NSW 2000
Canada
Embassy: (☎ 613-232 2401, fax 233 1484,
@ italcomm@trytel.com) 21st floor, 275
Slater St, Ottawa, Ontario K1P 5H9
Consulate: (☎ 514-849 8351, fax 499 9471,
@ consitmtl@cyberglobe.net) 3489
Drummond St, Montreal, Quebec H3G 1X6
Consulate: (☎ 416-977 1566,
@ consolato.it@toronto.italconsulate.org)
136 Beverley St, Toronto, Ontario M5T 1Y5
France
Embassy: (☎ 01 49 54 03 00, fax 01 45 49 35 81,
@ stampa@dial.oleane.com) 7 rue de
Varenne, Paris 75007
Consulate: (☎ 01 44 30 47 00, fax 01 45 66
41 78) 5 blvd Augier, Paris 75116
New Zealand
Embassy: (☎ 04-473 53 39, fax 472 72 55,
@ amhwell@xtra.co.nz) 34 Grant Rd,
Thorndon, Wellington
UK
Embassy: (☎ 020-7312 2209, fax 7312 2230,
@ emblondon@embitaly.org.uk) 14 Three
Kings Yard, London W1Y 2EH
Consulate: (☎ 020-7235 9371, fax 7823 1609)
38 Eaton Place, London SW1X 8AN
USA
Embassy: (☎ 202-328 5500, fax 328 5593,
@ itapress@ix.netcom.com) 1601 Fuller St,
NW Washington, DC 20009
Consulate: (☎ 213-820 0622, fax 820 0727,
@ cglos@aol.com) Suite 300, 12400 Wilshire
Blvd, West Los Angeles, CA 90025
Consulate: (☎ 212-737 9100, fax 249 4945,
@ italconsny@aol.com) 690 Park Ave,
New York, NY 10021-5044
Consulate: (☎ 415-931 4924, fax 931 7205)
2590 Webster St, San Francisco, CA 94115

Embassies & Consulates in Italy
The headquarters of most foreign embassies
are in Rome, although there are generally

British and US consulates in other major
cities. The following addresses and phone
numbers are for Rome (area code ☎ 46):

Australia (☎ 85 27 21) Via Alessandria 215
Austria (☎ 844 01 41) Via Pergolesi 3
  Consulate: (☎ 855 29 66) Viale Liegi 32
Canada (☎ 44 59 81) Via G B de Rossi 27
  Consulate: (☎ 44 59 81) Via Zara 30
France (☎ 68 60 11) Piazza Farnese 67
  Consulate: (☎ 68 80 21 52) Via Giulia 251
Germany (☎ 88 47 41) Via Po 25c
  Consulate: (☎ 88 47 41) Via Francesco Siacci 2c
New Zealand (☎ 440 29 28) Via Zara 28
Spain (☎ 687 81 72) Largo Fontanella
Borghese 19
  Consulate: (☎ 687 14 01) Via Campo Marzio 34
Switzerland (☎ 808 36 41) Via Barnarba
Oriani 61
  Consulate: (☎ 808 83 61) Largo Elvezia 15
UK (☎ 482 54 41) Via XX Settembre 80a
USA (☎ 467 41) Via Vittorio Veneto 119a-121

MONEY
Until the euro notes and coins are in circu-
lation, Italy's currency will remain the lira
(plural: lire). The smallest note is L1000.
Other denominations in notes are L2000,
L5000, L10,000, L50,000, L100,000 and
L500,000. Coin denominations are L50,
L100 (two types of silver coin), L200, L500
and L1000.

Like other continental Europeans, Italians indicate decimals with commas and
thousands with points.

Major credit cards – including Visa,
MasterCard and American Express – are
widely accepted throughout Italy. They can
be used for purchases and in hotels and
restaurants (although smaller *trattorie* and
pensioni might not accept them). They can
also be used to get money from *bancomats*
(ATMs) or, if you don't have a PIN, over
the counter in major banks.

Exchange Rates

country	unit		lire
Australia	A$1	=	L1241.85
Canada	C$1	=	L1444.84
euro	€1	=	L1936.27
France	1FF	=	L295.182
Germany	DM1	=	L989.999
Ireland	£IR1	=	L2458.56
Japan	¥100	=	L1972.57
New Zealand	NZ$1	=	L964.079
UK	UK£1	=	L3222.28
USA	US$1	=	L2143.12

ITALY

Costs

A *very* prudent traveller could get by on L80,000 per day, but only by staying in youth hostels, eating one meal a day (at the hostel), buying a sandwich or pizza by the slice for lunch and minimising the number of galleries and museums visited, since the entrance fee to most major museums is cripplingly expensive at around L12,000.

Italy's railways offer a few cut-price options for students. Museums and galleries also usually give discounts to students, but you will need a valid student card.

A basic breakdown of costs during an average day could be: accommodation L25,000 (youth hostel) to L60,000; breakfast (coffee and croissant) L3000; lunch (sandwich and mineral water) L6000; public transport (bus or underground railway in a major town) L6000; entry fee for one museum L12,000; a sit-down dinner L14,000 to L30,000.

Tipping & Bargaining

You are not expected to leave a tip on top of restaurant service charges, but it is common practice among Italians to leave a small amount, say around 10%. In bars they will leave any small change as a tip, often only L100 or L200. You can tip taxi drivers if you wish but it's not obligatory.

Bargaining is common throughout Italy in the various flea markets, but not normally in shops. You can try bargaining for the price of a room in a *pensione*, particularly if you plan to stay for more than a few days or out of season.

POST & COMMUNICATIONS
Post

Stamps *(francobolli)* are available at post offices and authorised tobacconists (look for the official *tabacchi* sign: a big 'T', often white on black). Since letters often need to be weighed, what you get at the tobacconist's for international airmail will occasionally be an approximation of the proper rate. Main post offices in the bigger cities are generally open 8 am to 6 pm weekdays. Many are open on Saturday morning too.

Postcards and letters up to 20g sent airmail cost L1400 to Australia and New Zealand, L1300 to the USA and L800 to EU countries (L900 to the rest of Europe). Aerograms are a cheap alternative, costing only L900 to send anywhere. They can be purchased at post offices only.

A new service, *posta prioritaria* (priority post – a little like the UK's 1st class post), began in 1999. For L1200, postcards and letters up to 20g posted to destinations within Italy, the EU, Switzerland and Norway are supposed to arrive the following day. Sending letters express *(espresso)* costs a standard extra L3600, but may help speed a letter on its way.

Telephone, Fax & Email

Italy's country code is ☎ 39. Area codes are an integral part of the telephone number, even if you're dialling a local number. Not content to make the area code part of the phone number, as of December 2000 the initial 0 in Rome's telephone numbers has been changed to a 4. Thus any number in Rome begins with 46.

Local and long distance calls can be made from any public phone, or from a Telecom office in larger towns. Italy's rates, particularly for long-distance calls, are among the highest in Europe. Local calls cost a minimum of L200. Most public phones accept only phonecards, sold in denominations of L5000, L10,000 and L15,000 at tobacconists and newsstands, or from vending machines at Telecom offices.

To make a reverse-charge (collect) call from a public telephone, dial ☎ 170. All operators speak English.

International faxes can cost L8000 for the first page and L5000 per page thereafter. You can send faxes from specialist fax/photocopy shops, post offices and from some tabacchi shops. Some Telecom public phones can also send faxes.

Italy has a growing number of Internet cafes, where you can send and receive email and surf the Net for around L10,000 to L15,000 an hour.

INTERNET RESOURCES

There is an Italy page at Lonely Planet's Web site (www.lonelyplanet.com) and you can visit the Thorn tree to share tips with fellow travellers. The following are just a few of the huge number of useful Web sites for travellers to Italy: Alfanet (www.alfanet .it) has a Welcome Italy page, with a link to information about a number of cities; CTS (www.cts.it) has useful information from

Italy's leading student travel organisation; Rome (www.informaroma.it) has information on the city's monuments and museums, virtual tours and links to other pertinent sites; and the Vatican (www.christusrex.org) has information about Vatican City, including virtual tours of the main monuments and the Musei Vaticani.

BOOKS

Lonely Planet has a series of comprehensive guides to Italy. The *Italy* guide covers the whole country, while the new *Tuscany & Umbria* and *Sicily* guides concentrate on those specific regions. If you're a hiking enthusiast, a good companion is Lonely Planet's *Walking in Italy*.

A History of Contemporary Italy: Society and Politics 1943-1988 by Paul Ginsborg is well written and absorbing. Luigi Barzini's classic *The Italians* is a great introduction to Italian people and culture, while *Excellent Cadavers: The Mafia and the Death of the First Italian Republic* by Alexander Stille is a shocking and fascinating account of the Mafia in Sicily. Interesting introductions to travelling in Italy include *A Traveller in Italy* by HV Morton, who also wrote similar guides to Rome and southern Italy.

WOMEN TRAVELLERS

Italy is not a dangerous country for women, but women travelling alone will often find themselves plagued by unwanted attention from men. Most of the attention falls into the nuisance/harassment category and it is best to simply ignore the catcalls, hisses and whistles. However, women touring alone should use common sense. Avoid walking alone in dark and deserted streets and look for centrally located hotels that are within easy walking distance of restaurants. In the south, including Sicily and Sardinia, the unwelcome attention paid to women travelling alone can border on the highly intrusive, particularly in the bigger cities. Women should also avoid hitchhiking alone.

GAY & LESBIAN TRAVELLERS

Homosexuality is legal in Italy and generally well tolerated in major cities, though overt displays of affection might get a negative response in smaller towns and villages, particularly in the south. The national organisation for gays (men and women) is AGAL (☎ 051 644 70 54, fax 051 644 67 22) in Bologna.

DISABLED TRAVELLERS

The Italian travel agency CIT (see Tourist Offices earlier) can advise on hotels which have special facilities. The UK-based Royal Association for Disability and Rehabilitation, or RADAR (☎ 020-7250 3222), publishes a useful guide called *Holidays & Travel Abroad: A Guide for Disabled People*.

DANGERS & ANNOYANCES

Theft is the main problem for travellers in Italy, mostly in the form of petty thievery and pickpocketing, especially in the bigger cities. Always carry your cash in a money belt and avoid flashing your dough in public. Motorcycle bandits are a minor problem in Rome, Naples, Palermo and Syracuse. If you are using a shoulder bag, make sure that you wear the strap across your body and have the bag on the side away from the road.

Never leave valuables in a parked car. It is a good idea to park your car in a supervised car park if you are leaving it for any amount of time. Car theft is a major problem in Rome and Naples. Throughout Italy you can call the police (☎ 113) or *carabinieri* (☎ 112) in an emergency.

BUSINESS HOURS

Business hours can vary from city to city, but generally shops and businesses are open 8.30 am to 1 pm and 5 to 7.30 pm Monday to Saturday, and some are also open on Sunday morning. Banks are generally open 8.30 am to 1.30 pm and from 2.30 to 4.30 pm Monday to Friday, but hours vary between banks and cities. Large post offices are open 8 am to 6 or 7 pm Monday to Saturday. Most museums close on Monday, and restaurants and bars are required to close for one day each week.

All of this has become more flexible since opening times were liberalised under new trading hour laws that came into effect in April 1999. At the time of writing it was difficult to determine what effect this has had on day to day practicalities, as Italians tend to value their time off and are not necessarily rushing to keep their shops open throughout the week.

ITALY

PUBLIC HOLIDAYS & SPECIAL EVENTS

National public holidays include: 6 January (Epiphany); Easter Monday; 25 April (Liberation Day); 1 May (Labour Day); 15 August (Ferragosto or Feast of the Assumption); 1 November (All Saints' Day); 8 December (Feast of the Immaculate Conception); 25 December (Christmas Day); and 26 December (Feast of St Stephen).

Individual towns also have public holidays to celebrate the feasts of their patron saints. Some of these are the Feast of St Mark in Venice on 25 April; the Feast of St John the Baptist on 24 June in Florence, Genoa and Turin; the Feast of St Peter and St Paul in Rome on 29 June; the Feast of St Januarius in Naples on 19 September; and the Feast of St Ambrose in Milan on 7 December.

Annual events in Italy worth keeping in mind include:

Carnevale During the 10 days before Ash Wednesday, many towns stage carnivals. The one held in Venice is the best known, but there are also others, including ones at Viareggio in Liguria and Ivrea near Turin.

Holy Week There are important festivals during this week everywhere in Italy, in particular the colourful and sombre traditional festivals of Sicily. In Assisi the rituals of Holy Week attract thousands of pilgrims.

Scoppio del Carro Literally 'Explosion of the Cart', this colourful event held in Florence in Piazza del Duomo on Easter Sunday features the explosion of a cart full of fireworks and dates back to the Crusades. If all goes well, it is seen as a good omen for the city.

Corso dei Ceri One of the strangest festivals in Italy, this is held in Gubbio (Umbria) on 15 May, and features a race run by men carrying enormous wooden constructions called *ceri*, in honour of the town's patron saint, Sant'Ubaldo.

Il Palio On 2 July and 16 August, Siena stages this extraordinary horse race in the town's main piazza.

ACCOMMODATION
Camping

Camping facilities throughout Italy are usually reasonable and vary from major complexes with swimming pools, tennis courts and restaurants, to simple camping grounds. Average prices are around L8000 per person and L11,000 or more for a site. Lists of camping grounds in and around major cities are usually available at tourist information offices.

Hostels

Hostels in Italy are called *ostelli per la gioventú* and are run by the Associazione Italiana Alberghi per la Gioventú (AIG), which is affiliated with Hostelling International (HI). An HI membership card is not always required, but it is recommended that you have one. Pick up a list of all hostels in Italy, with details of prices and locations, from the AIG office (☎ 46 487 11 52) in Rome, at Via Cavour 44.

Many Italian hostels are located in castles and old villas, most have bars and the cost per night often includes breakfast. Many also provide dinner, usually for around L16,000. Prices, including breakfast, range from L16,000 to L24,000. Closing times vary, but are usually from 9 am to 3 or 5 pm and curfews are around midnight. Men and women are often segregated, although some hostels have family accommodation.

Pensioni & Hotels

There is often no difference between an establishment that calls itself a *pensione* (pension) and one that calls itself an *albergo* (hotel); in fact, some use both titles. *Locande* (similar to pensioni) and *alloggi*, sometimes also known as *affittacamere* (room rentals), are generally cheaper, but not always. Tourist offices have booklets listing all pensioni and hotels, including prices, and lists of locande and affittacamere.

FOOD & DRINKS

Eating is one of life's great pleasures for Italians. Cooking styles vary notably from region to region and significantly between the north and south. In the north the food is rich and often creamy; in central Italy the locals use a lot of olive oil and herbs and regional specialities are noted for their simplicity, fine flavour and the use of fresh produce. As you go farther south the food becomes hotter and spicier and the *dolci* (cakes and pastries) sweeter and richer.

Vegetarians will have no problems eating in Italy. Most eating establishments serve a selection of *contorni* (vegetables prepared in a variety of ways).

If you have access to cooking facilities, buy fruit and vegetables at open-air markets

ITALY

and salami, cheese and wine at *alimentari* or *salumerie* (a cross between a grocery store and a delicatessen). Fresh bread is available at a *forno* or *panetteria*.

Restaurants in Italy can be divided into several categories. A *tavola calda* (literally 'hot table') usually offers inexpensive, pre-prepared meat, pasta and vegetable dishes in a self-service style. The *rosticceria* usually serves up cooked meats, but often has a larger selection of takeaway food. A pizzeria will of course serve pizza, but usually also offers a full menu. An *osteria* is likely to be either a wine bar offering a small selection of dishes, or a small *trattoria*. Many of the establishments that are in fact restaurants *(ristoranti)* call themselves trattoria and vice versa for reasons best known to themselves.

Most eating establishments charge a *coperto* (cover charge) of around L2000 to L3000, and a *servizio* (service charge) of 10% to 15%. Restaurants are usually open for lunch from 12.30 to 3 pm, but will rarely take orders after 2 pm. In the evening, opening hours vary from north to south. In the north they eat dinner earlier, usually from 7.30 pm, but in Sicily you will be hard-pressed to find a restaurant open before 8.30 pm. Very few restaurants stay open after 11.30 pm.

A full meal will consist of an antipasto, which can vary from *bruschetta*, a type of garlic bread with various toppings, to fried vegetables, or *prosciutto e melone* (ham wrapped around melon). Next comes the *primo piatto*, a pasta dish or risotto, followed by the *secondo piatto* of meat or fish. Italians often then eat an *insalata* (salad) or contorni and round off the meal with *dolci* and *caffé*, often at a bar on the way home or back to work.

Wine made in Italy is justifiably world-famous. Fortunately, wine is reasonably priced, so you will rarely have to pay more than L12,000 for a bottle of drinkable wine and as little as L6000 will still buy something of reasonable quality. You should make sure you try the famous chianti and *brunello* in Tuscany, but also the *vernaccia* of San Gimignano, the *barolo* in Piedmont, the *lacrima christi* or *falanghina* in Naples and the *cannonau* in Sardinia. Beer is known as *birra* and the cheapest local variety is Peroni.

Getting There & Away

AIR

There are frequent flights to Rome, Milan, Naples and other major Italian cities on a variety of international carriers. Although it is expensive to pay full fare for plane travel in Europe, examples of cheap one-way fares at the time of writing were: Rome-Paris L220,000 (L360,000 return); Rome-London L210,000 (L258,000 return); and Rome-Amsterdam L329,000 return. Italy Sky Shuttle (☎ 020-8748 1333), part of the Air Travel Group, 227 Shepherd's Bush Rd, London W6 7AS, specialises in cheaper charter flights.

Within Italy, information on discount fares is available from CTS and Sestante CIT offices (see the earlier Tourist Offices section).

LAND
Bus

Eurolines is the main international carrier in Europe. Its representative in Italy is Lazzi, with offices in Florence (☎ 055 35 71 10) at Piazza Adua; and in Rome (☎ 46 884 08 40) at Via Tagliamento 27b. Buses leave from Rome, Florence, Milan, Turin, Venice and Naples, as well as numerous other Italian towns, for major cities throughout Europe including London, Paris, Barcelona, Madrid, Amsterdam, Budapest, Prague, Athens and İstanbul. Ticket prices are: Rome-Paris L187,000 (L297,000 return); Rome-London L260,000 (L398,000 return); and Rome-Barcelona L211,000 (L376,000 return).

Train

Eurostar (ES) and Eurocity (EC) trains run from major destinations throughout Europe direct to major Italian cities. On overnight hauls you can book a *cuccetta* (known outside Italy as a couchette or sleeping berth).

If you're under 26 you can take advantage of Billet International de Jeunesse tickets (BIJ, also known in Italy as BIGE), which can cut fares by around 50%. They are sold at Transalpino offices at most train stations and at CTS and Sestante CIT offices in Italy, Europe and overseas. Examples of one-way 2nd-class fares are: Rome-Amsterdam L218,900, Rome-Paris L170,000 and

ITALY

Rome-London L284,300. Throughout Europe and in Italy it is worth paying extra for a couchette on night trains. A couchette from Rome to Paris is an extra L48,000.

You can book tickets at train stations or at CTS, Sestante CIT and most travel agencies. Eurostar and Eurocity trains carry a supplement (see Train in the Getting Around section).

Hitching

Hitching is never safe in any country and we don't recommend it. Your best bet is to inquire at hostels throughout Europe, where you can often arrange a lift. The International Lift Centre in Florence (☎ 055 28 06 26) and Enjoy Rome (☎ 46 445 18 43) might be able to help organise lifts. It is illegal to hitch on the *autostrade* (freeway).

SEA

Ferries connect Italy to Spain, Croatia, Greece, Turkey, Tunisia and Malta. There are also services to Corsica (from Livorno) and Albania (from Bari and Ancona). See Getting There & Away under Brindisi (for ferries to/from Greece), Ancona (to/from Greece, Albania and Croatia), Venice (to/from Greece) and Sicily (to/from Malta and Tunisia).

Getting Around

AIR

Travelling by plane is expensive within Italy and it makes much better sense to use the efficient and considerably cheaper rail and bus services. The domestic airlines are Alitalia, Meridiana and Air One. The main airports are in Rome, Pisa, Milan, Bologna, Genoa, Torino, Naples, Catania, Palermo and Cagliari, but there are other, smaller airports throughout Italy. Domestic flights can be booked directly with the airlines or through Sestante CIT, CTS and other travel agencies.

Alitalia offers a range of discounts for students, young people and families, and for weekend travel.

BUS

Numerous bus companies operate within Italy. It is usually necessary to make reservations only for long trips, such as Rome-Palermo or Rome-Brindisi. Otherwise, just arrive early enough to claim a seat.

Buses can be a cheaper and faster way to get around if your destination is not on major rail lines, for instance from Umbria to Rome or Florence, and in the interior areas of Sicily and Sardinia.

TRAIN

Travelling by train in Italy is simple, relatively cheap and generally efficient. The Ferrovie dello Stato (FS) is the partially privatised state train system and there are several private railway services throughout the country.

There are several types of trains: Regionale (R), which usually stop at all stations and can be very slow; interRegionale (iR), which run between the regions; Intercity (IC) or Eurocity (EC), which service only the major cities; and Eurostar Italia (ES), which serves major Italian and European cities.

To travel on the Intercity, Eurocity and Eurostar Italia trains, you have to pay a *supplemento*, an additional charge determined by the distance you are travelling and the type of train.

All tickets must be validated in the yellow machines at the entrance to all train platforms.

It is not worth buying a Eurail or Inter-Rail pass if you are going to travel only in Italy. The FS offers its own discount passes for travel within the country. These include the Cartaverde for those aged 26 years and under. It costs L40,000, is valid for one year, and entitles you to a 20% discount on all train travel. You can also buy a *biglietto chilometrico* (kilometric ticket), which is valid for two months and allows you to cover 3000km, with a maximum of 20 trips. It costs L214,000 (2nd class) and you must pay the supplement if you catch an Intercity or Eurostar train. Its main attraction is that it can be used by up to five people, either singly or together.

CAR & MOTORCYCLE

Travelling with your own vehicle certainly gives you more flexibility. The drawbacks in Italy are that cars can be inconvenient in larger cities where you'll have to deal with heavy traffic, parking problems, the risk of car theft, the exorbitant price of petrol and toll charges on the autostrade.

Roads are generally good throughout the country and there is an excellent system of autostrade. The main north-south link is the Autostrada del Sole, which extends from Milan to Reggio di Calabria (called the A1 from Milan to Naples and the A3 from Naples to Reggio).

Petrol prices are high in Italy. Petrol is called *benzina*, unleaded petrol is *benzina senza piombo* and diesel is *gasolio*.

Call the Automobile Club d'Italia (ACI) on ☎ 116 for roadside assistance.

Road Rules

In Italy people drive on the right-hand side of the road and pass on the left. Unless otherwise indicated, you must give way to cars coming from the right. It is compulsory to wear seat belts if they are fitted to the car (front seat belts on all cars and back seat belts on cars produced after 26 April 1990). If you are caught not wearing your seat belt, you will be required to pay a L62,500 on-the-spot fine.

Helmets are compulsory for all motorcycle and moped riders and passengers.

Some Italian cities, including Rome, Bologna, Florence, Milan and Turin, have introduced restricted access for both private and rental cars in their historical centres. These restrictions, however, do not apply to vehicles with foreign registrations. *Motorini* (mopeds) and scooters (such as Vespas) are able to enter the zones without any problems.

Speed limits, unless otherwise indicated by local signs, are: on autostrade 130km/h for cars of 1100cc or more, 110km/h for smaller cars and motorcycles under 350cc; on main, nonurban highways 100km/h; on secondary nonurban highways 90km/h; and in built-up areas 50km/h.

The blood-alcohol limit is 0.08% and random breath tests have now been introduced.

Rental

If you want to rent a car or motorcycle, you will need a valid EU driving licence, an International Driving Permit, or your driving permit from your own country. If you're driving your own car, you'll need an international insurance certificate, known as a Carta Verde (Green Card), which can be obtained from your insurer.

BOAT

Navi (large ferries) service the islands of Sicily and Sardinia, and *traghetti* (smaller ferries) and *aliscafi* (hydrofoils) service areas such as Elba, the Aeolian Islands, Capri and Ischia. The main embarkation points for Sicily and Sardinia are Genoa, La Spezia, Livorno, Civitavecchia, Fiumicino and Naples.

Tirrenia Navigazione is the major company servicing the Mediterranean and it has offices throughout Italy. Most long-distance services travel overnight and all ferries carry vehicles (you can usually take a bicycle free of charge).

Rome

☎ 46

Rome (Roma), a phenomenal mix of history, legend and monuments, is at the heart of the Western world's two great historical powers: the Catholic Church and the Roman Empire. Deservedly, it is on most travellers' 'must-see' list, so brace yourself for the summertime crush. Realistically, you need at least a week to explore Rome – one of the great pleasures of being in the city is wandering through the many beautiful *piazzas* (squares), stopping frequently for a *caffé* and *paste* (pastries).

Whatever time you devote to Italy's capital, put on your walking shoes, buy a good map and plan your time carefully – the city will eventually seem less chaotic and overwhelming than it first appears.

Rome's origins lie in a group of Etruscan, Latin and Sabine settlements on the surrounding hills. It is, however, the legend of Romulus and Remus that has captured the popular imagination. They were the twin sons of Rhea Silvia and the Roman war god Mars, and were raised by a she-wolf after being abandoned on the banks of the Tiber (Tevere). The myth says Romulus killed his brother during a battle over who should govern, and then established the city on Palatine Hill.

ORIENTATION

Rome is a vast city, but the historical centre is relatively small. Most of the major sights are west – and within walking distance – of the central train station, Stazione

ITALY

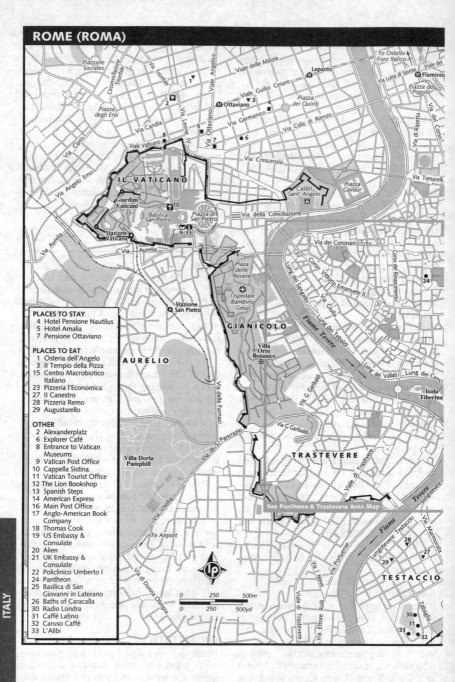

ROME (ROMA)

PLACES TO STAY
4 Hotel Pensione Nautilus
5 Hotel Amalia
7 Pensione Ottaviano

PLACES TO EAT
1 Osteria dell'Angelo
3 Il Tempio della Pizza
15 Centro Macrobiotico Italiano
23 Pizzeria l'Economica
27 Il Canestro
28 Pizzeria Remo
29 Augustarello

OTHER
2 Alexanderplatz
6 Explorer Café
8 Entrance to Vatican Museums
9 Vatican Post Office
10 Cappella Sistina
11 Vatican Tourist Office
12 The Lion Bookshop
13 Spanish Steps
14 American Express
16 Main Post Office
17 Anglo-American Book Company
18 Thomas Cook
19 US Embassy & Consulate
20 Alien
21 UK Embassy & Consulate
22 Policlinico Umberto I
24 Pantheon
25 Basilica di San Giovanni in Laterano
26 Baths of Caracalla
30 Radio Londra
31 Caffé Latino
32 Caruso Caffé
33 L'Alibi

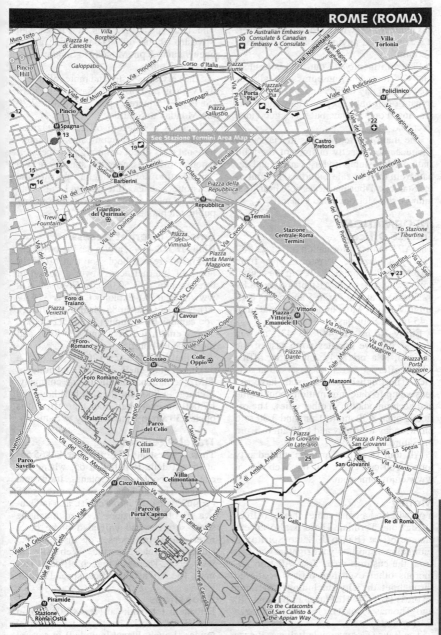

ROME (ROMA)

ITALY

Termini. Invest L6000 in the street map and bus guide *Roma*, with a red-and-blue cover; it's available at any newsstand in Stazione Termini.

Plan an itinerary if your time is limited. Many of the major museums and galleries are open all day until 5 or 7 pm, and some remain open until 10 pm. Many museums are closed on Monday, but it is a good idea to check.

The main bus terminus is in Piazza dei Cinquecento, directly in front of the train station. Many intercity buses arrive and depart from the Piazzale Tiburtina, in front of the Stazione Tiburtina, accessible from Termini on the Metropolitana Linea B.

INFORMATION
Tourist Offices
The APT tourist information office (☎ 487 12 70) at Stazione Termini is open from 8.15 am to 7.15 pm daily. It's in the central courseway. The main APT office (☎ 48 89 92 53/55) is at Via Parigi 5 and opens 8.15 am to 7.15 pm Monday to Friday and until 1.45 pm on Saturday.

Enjoy Rome (☎ 445 18 43), at Via Varese 39 (five minutes north-east of the station), is a privately run tourist office which offers a free hotel-reservation service. The English-speaking staff have extensive up-to-date information about Rome and accommodation in other cities. The office is open 8.30 am to 1 pm and 3.30 to 6 pm Monday to Friday and 8.30 am to 1 pm on Saturday.

All tourist offices arrange guided city tours. You can check out the Web site at www.enjoyrome.com.

Money
You will find a bank and exchange offices at Stazione Termini. There is also an exchange office (Banco di Santo Spirito) at Fiumicino airport, to your right as you exit from the customs area. You will find numerous other exchange offices scattered throughout the city, including American Express (☎ 6 76 41, Piazza di Spagna 38) and Thomas Cook (☎ 482 81 82, Piazza Barberini 21).

The Banca Commerciale Italiana, Piazza Venezia, is reliable for receiving money transfers and will give cash advances on both Visa and MasterCard.

Post & Communications
The main post office is at Piazza San Silvestro 19, just off Via del Tritone, and is open 9 am to 6 pm Monday to Sunday (Saturday to 2 pm).

The service is faster and more reliable at the Vatican post office in Piazza San Pietro (St Peter's Square), open 8.30 am to 7.30 pm Monday to Saturday.

There is a Telecom office at Stazione Termini, from where you can make international calls direct or through an operator. Another office is near the station, in Via San Martino della Battaglia opposite the Pensione Lachea. International calls can easily be made with a phonecard from any public telephone.

Email & Internet Access
Bibli (☎ 588 40 97, at Via dei Fienaroli 28) in Trastevere is a bookshop that offers 10 hours of Internet access over a period of three months for L50,000. Its Web site is at www.bibli.it. At Explorer Café (☎ 324 17 57), Via dei Gracchi 85 (near the Vatican), you can pay by the hour (about L12,000) to access email, the Web and CD-Rom and multi-media libraries.

Nolitel Italia (☎ 42 00 70 01, Via Sicilia 54), near Via Veneto, is an official outlet of TIM, the national mobile phone company. It charges L8000 for the first half hour and L7,000 for every half hour thereafter. It is open 9.30 am to 7 pm Monday to Saturday.

Travel Agencies
There is a Sestante CIT office (☎ 474 65 55) at Piazza della Repubblica 65, where you can make bookings for planes, trains and ferries. The student tourist centre, CTS (☎ 462 04 31, ✉ info@cts.it), at Via Genova 16, off Via Nazionale, offers much the same services and will also make hotel reservations, but focuses on discount and student travel. See the Web site at www.cts.it. There is a branch office at Termini. The staff at both offices speak English.

Bookshops
Feltrinelli International (☎ 487 01 71), at Via VE Orlando 78, has literature and travel guides (Lonely Planet included) in several languages, including Japanese. The Anglo-American Book Company (☎ 679 52 22), at Via della Vite 27, off Piazza di Spagna, also

has an excellent selection of literature, travel guides and reference books. The Lion Bookshop (☎ 32 65 04 37), at Via dei Greci 33-36, also has a good range, as does the Economy Book & Video Center (☎ 474 68 77), at Via Torino 136, off Via Nazionale, which also has second-hand books.

Laundry
There is an Onda Blu coin laundrette at Via Lamarmora 10, near the train station. It is open 8 am to 10 pm daily.

Medical & Emergency Services
Emergency medical treatment is available in the casualty sections of public hospitals, including Policlinico Umberto I (☎ 06 4 99 71), Viale del Policlinico 155, near Stazione Termini.

There is a pharmacy in Stazione Termini, open 7 am to 11 pm daily (closed in August). Otherwise, closed pharmacies usually post a list in their windows of others open nearby.

The questura (police headquarters; ☎ 4 68 61) is at Via San Vitale 15. It's open 24 hours a day and thefts can be reported here. Its Foreigners' Bureau (Ufficio Stranieri; ☎ 46 86 29 77) is around the corner at Via Genova 2.

Dangers & Annoyances
Thieves are active in and around Stazione Termini, at major sights such as the Colosseum and Roman Forum, and in the city's most expensive shopping streets, such as Via Condotti. Pickpockets like to work on crowded buses, particularly the No 64 from St Peter's to Stazione Termini.

THINGS TO SEE & DO
Piazza del Campidoglio
This piazza, designed by Michelangelo in 1538, is on the **Capitolino** (Capitoline Hill), the most important of Rome's seven hills. Capitolino was the seat of the ancient Roman government and is now the seat of Rome's municipal government.

The two palaces flanking the piazza make up the **Musei Capitolini**, well worth visiting for their collections of ancient Roman sculpture, including the famous *Capitoline Wolf*, an Etruscan statue dating from the 6th century BC. They are open 10 am to 9 pm Tuesday to Sunday. Admission is L12,000.

The **Chiesa di Santa Maria d'Aracoeli** is between the Campidoglio and the Monumento Vittorio Emanuele II at the highest point of the Capitoline Hill. The church is built on the site where legend says the Tiburtine Sybil told the Emperor Augustus of the coming birth of Christ.

Piazza Venezia
This piazza is overshadowed by the neoclassical monument dedicated to Vittorio Emanuele II, which is often referred to by Italians as the *macchina da scrivere* (typewriter) because it resembles one. Built to commemorate Italian unification, the piazza incorporates the **Altare della Patria** and the tomb of the unknown soldier, as well as the **Museo del Risorgimento**. Also in the piazza is the 15th-century **Palazzo Venezia**, which was Mussolini's official residence and now houses a museum.

Roman Forum & Palatine Hill
The commercial, political and religious centre of ancient Rome, the Forum stands in a valley between the Capitoline and Palatine (Palatino) Hills. You can enter the Forum from Via dei Fori Imperiali, which leads from Piazza Venezia to the Colosseum. Entrance to the Forum is free, but it costs L12,000 to head up to the Palatine. The Forum and Palatine Hill are open 9 am to 7 pm Monday to Saturday in summer (to 4 pm in winter), and 9 am to 1 pm on Sunday year-round.

As you enter the Forum, to your left is the **Tempio di Antonino e Faustina**, erected by the senate in AD 141 and transformed into a church in the 8th century. To your right are the remains of the **Basilica Aemilia**, built in 179 BC and demolished during the Renaissance when it was plundered for its precious marble. The Via Sacra, which traverses the Forum from north-west to south-east, runs in front of the basilica. Towards the Campidoglio is the **Curia**, once the meeting place of the Roman senate and converted into a Christian church in the Middle Ages. In front of the Curia is the **Lapis Niger**, a large piece of black marble which legend says covered the grave of Romulus. Under the Lapis Niger is the oldest known Latin inscription, dating from the 6th century BC.

The **Arco di Settimo Severo** was erected in AD 203 in honour of emperor Septimus

ITALY

Severus and his sons, and is considered one of Italy's major triumphal arches. A circular base stone beside the arch marks the *umbilicus urbis*, the symbolic centre of ancient Rome. To the south is the **Rostrum**, used in ancient times by public speakers and once decorated by the rams of captured ships.

South along the Via Sacra is the **Tempio di Saturno**, one of the most important temples in ancient Rome. Eight granite columns remain. The **Basilica Julia**, in front of the temple, was the seat of justice, and nearby is the **Tempio di Giulio Cesare** (Temple of Julius Caesar), which was erected by Augustus in 29 BC on the site where Caesar's body was burned and Mark Antony read his famous speech. Back towards the Palatine Hill is the **Tempio dei Castori**, built in 489 BC in honour of the Heavenly Twins, or Dioscuri. It is easily recognisable by its three remaining columns.

Back on the Via Sacra is the **Case delle Vestali**, home of the virgins who tended the sacred flame in the adjoining **Tempio di Vesta**. If the flame went out, it was seen as a bad omen. The next major monument is the vast **Basilica di Costantino**. Its impressive design inspired Renaissance architects. The **Arco di Tito**, at the Colosseum end of the Forum, was built in AD 81 in honour of the victories of the emperors Titus and Vespasian against Jerusalem.

From here climb the **Palatino**, where wealthy Romans built their homes and where legend says Romulus founded the city.

Worth a look is the impressive **Domus Augustana**, which was the private residence of the emperors, and the **Domus Flavia**, the residence of Domitian; the **Tempio della Magna Mater**, built in 204 BC to house a black stone connected with the Asiatic goddess, Cybele; and the **Casa di Livia**, thought to have been the house of the wife of Emperor Augustus, and decorated with frescoes.

Colosseum

Originally known as the Flavian Amphitheatre, Rome's most famous monument was begun by Emperor Vespasian in AD 72 in the grounds of Nero's Golden House, and completed by his son Titus. The massive structure could seat 80,000 and featured bloody gladiatorial combat and wild beast shows that resulted in thousands of human and animal deaths.

In the Middle Ages the Colosseum became a fortress and was later used as a quarry for travertine and marble for the Palazzo Venezia and other buildings. Restoration works have been underway since 1992. Opening hours are 9 am to 7 pm daily in summer (to one hour before sunset in winter). Entry is L10,000.

Arch of Constantine

On the north-west side of the Colosseum is the triumphal arch built to honour Constantine following his victory over his rival Maxentius at the battle of Milvian Bridge (near the present-day Zona Olimpica, north-west of the Villa Borghese) in AD 312. Its decorative reliefs were taken from earlier structures.

Baths of Caracalla

This huge complex, covering 10 hectares, could hold 1600 people and included shops, gardens, libraries and entertainment. Begun by Antonius Caracalla and inaugurated in AD 217, the baths were used until the 6th century. Summer opening hours are 9 am to 7 pm Monday to Saturday and 9 am to 2 pm on Sunday (until 3 pm in winter). Entry is L8000.

Baths of Diocletian

Started by Emperor Diocletian, these baths were completed in the 4th century. The complex of baths, libraries, concert halls and gardens covered about 13 hectares and could house up to 3000 people. After the aqueduct which fed the baths was destroyed by invaders in AD 536, the complex fell into decay. Parts of the ruins are now incorporated into the Michelangelo-designed **Basilica di Santa Maria degli Angeli**.

The church incorporates what was the great central hall and *tepidarium* (lukewarm room) of the original baths. During the following centuries Michelangelo's work was drastically changed and little evidence of his design, apart from the great vaulted ceiling of the church, remains. The church is open 7.30 am to 12.30 pm and 4 to 6.30 pm. Through the sacristy is an entrance to a stairway leading to the upper terraces of the ruins.

Piazza di Spagna & Spanish Steps

This piazza, church and famous staircase (Scalinata della Trinitá dei Monti) have long provided a major gathering place for foreigners. Built with a legacy from the French in 1725, but named after the Spanish Embassy to the Holy See, the steps lead to the church of Trinitá dei Monti, which was built by the French.

In the 18th century the most beautiful men and women of Italy gathered here, waiting to be chosen as artists' models. To the right as you face the steps is the house where Keats spent the last three months of his life, and where he died in 1821. In the piazza is the boat-shaped fountain of the **Barcaccia**, believed to be by Pietro Bernini, father of the famous Gian Lorenzo. One of Rome's most elegant shopping streets, **Via Condotti**, runs off the piazza towards Via del Corso.

Villa Borghese

This beautiful park was once the estate of Cardinal Scipione Borghese. His 17th-century villa houses the **Museo e Galleria Borghese**, a collection of important paintings and sculptures gathered by the Borghese family. It is possible to visit only with a reservation (☎ 32 81 01), so call well in advance. It's open 9 am to 10 pm Tuesday to Saturday, and to 8 pm on Sunday. Entry is L10,000, plus a L2000 booking fee. Just outside the park is the **Galleria Nazionale d'Arte Moderna**, Viale delle Belle Arti 131. It's open 9 am to 10 pm Tuesday to Saturday, and to 8 pm on Sunday. Entry is L8000. The important Etruscan museum, **Museo Nazionale di Villa Giulia**, is along the same street in Piazzale di Villa Giulia. It opens 9 am to 7 pm Tuesday to Saturday, and to 11 am on Sunday; entry is L10,000. Due to the large number of visitors, admittance is every two hours only.

Pantheon

This is the best-preserved ancient Roman building. The original temple was built in 27 BC by Marcus Agrippa, son-in-law of Emperor Augustus. Although the temple was rebuilt by Emperor Hadrian around AD 120, Agrippa's name remains inscribed over the entrance. The Pantheon's extraordinary dome is considered the most important achievement of ancient Roman architecture. The Italian kings, Vittorio Emanuele II and Umberto I, and the painter Raphael, are buried inside.

The Pantheon is in Piazza della Rotonda and is open 9 am to 6.30 pm Monday to Saturday and 9 am to 1 pm on Sunday. Admission is free.

Trastevere

You can wander through the narrow medieval streets of this area; it is especially beautiful at night and is one of the more interesting areas for bar-hopping or a meal. Of particular note here is the **Basilica di Santa Maria in Trastevere**, in the lovely piazza of the same name. It is believed to be the oldest place of worship dedicated to the Virgin in Rome.

Museo Nazionale Romano

This museum, located in three separate buildings, houses an important collection of ancient art, including Greek and Roman sculpture. The museum is largely located in the restored Palazzo Altemps, Piazza Sant' Apollinare 44, near Piazza Navona. It contains numerous important pieces from the Ludovisi collection, including the *Ludovisi Throne*. Entry is L10,000. Another part of the same museum is located in the Palazzo Massimo alle Terme, in Piazza dei Cinquecento. It contains a collection of frescoes and mosaics from the Villa of Livia, excavated at Prima Porta. Entry is L12,000. Both sections open 9 am to 6.45 pm Tuesday to Saturday (to 7.45 pm on Sunday).

Squares & Fountains

Trevi Fountain The high-baroque Fontana di Trevi, north-east of the Pantheon, was designed by Nicola Salvi in 1732. The famous custom is to throw a coin into the fountain (over your shoulder while facing away) to ensure your return to Rome. If you throw a second coin you can make a wish.

Piazza Navona This vast and beautiful square, lined with baroque palaces, was laid out on the ruins of Domitian's stadium. It features three fountains, including Bernini's masterpiece, the **Fontana dei Fiumi** (Fountain of the Rivers).

Campo de' Fiori A flower and vegetable market is held every morning except Sunday on this bar- and trattoria-lined piazza. The **Palazzo Farnese** (Farnese Palace), in the piazza of the same name, is just off

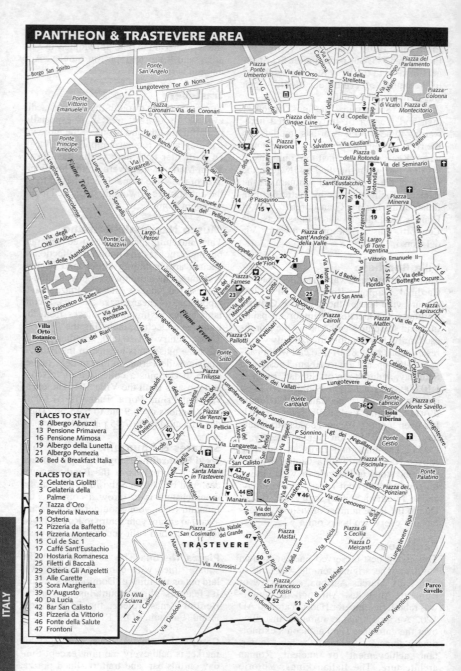

PANTHEON & TRASTEVERE AREA

PLACES TO STAY
8 Albergo Abruzzi
13 Pensione Primavera
16 Pensione Mimosa
19 Albergo della Lunetta
21 Albergo Pomezia
26 Bed & Breakfast Italia

PLACES TO EAT
2 Gelateria Giolitti
3 Gelateria della Palme
7 Tazza d'Oro
9 Bevitoria Navona
11 Osteria
12 Pizzeria da Baffetto
14 Pizzeria Montecarlo
15 Cul de Sac 1
17 Caffé Sant'Eustachio
25 Hostaria Romanesca
25 Filetti di Baccalà
29 Osteria Gli Angeletti
31 Alle Carette
35 Sora Margherita
39 D'Augusto
40 Da Lucia
42 Bar San Calisto
43 Pizzeria da Vittorio
46 Fonte della Salute
47 Frontoni

ITALY

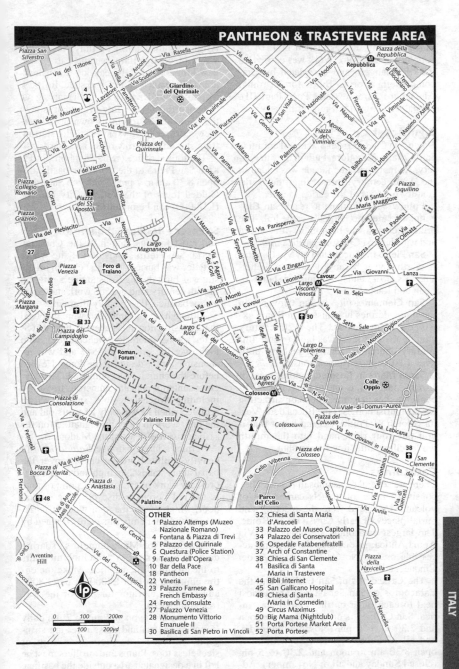

PANTHEON & TRASTEVERE AREA

Piazza San Silvestro

Via Rasella

Via del Tritone

Via delle Quattro Fontane

Piazza della Repubblica

Repubblica

Via delle Terme di Diocleziano

Via Modena

Via del Lavatore

Via della Panetteria

Via Arcione

Via Scuderie

Giardino del Quirinale

Via Nazionale

Via Firenze

Via Torino

Via Viminale

Via Massimo D'Azeglio

Via delle Muratte

Via dei Lucchesi

Via della Dataria

Via del Quirinale

Via Piacenza

Via Cenova

Via San Vitale

Via Napoli

Via di Umiltà

Piazza del Quirinale

Via della Consulta

Via Milano

Via Parma

Piazza del Viminale

Via Agostino De Pretis

Via Cesare Balbo

Via Urbana

Piazza Collegio Romano

Via del Corso

Piazza dei SS Apostoli

Via di Pilotta

Via della Consulta

Via Milano

Piazza Esquilino

V di Santa Maria Maggiore

Piazza Graziolo

Via del Plebiscito

Via IV Novembre

Largo Magnanapoli

Via Panisperna

Via Cavour

Via del Quattro Cantoni

Via Paolina

Via dell'Olmata

27

Piazza Venezia

Foro di Traiano

Via Alessandrina

Via d Zingari

Via Sforza

Via Giovanni

Lanza

Aracoeli

28

Via dei Fori Imperiali

Via M dei Monti

Largo Leonina

Largo Visconti Venosta

Via in Selci

Piazza Margana

Via del Teatro di Marcello

32

33

Largo C Ricci

Via Cavour

Via degli Annibaldi

30

Via delle Sette Sale

Piazza del Campidoglio

34

Roman Forum

Largo D Polveriera

Viale del Monte Oppio

Piazza di Consolazione

Largo G Agnesi

Colle Oppio

Palatine Hill

Colosseo M

Viale di Domus Aurea

Via dei Fienili

Palatine Hill

37

Colosseum

Piazza del Colosseo

Via Labicana

38

San Clemente

Piazza di Bocca D Verita

Piazza di S Anastasia

Piazza del Colosseo

Via San Giovanni in Laterano

48

Palatino

Parco del Celio

Via Celio Vibenna

Piazza della Navicella

Aventine Hill

Via del Circo Massimo

49

0   100   200m
0   100   200yd

OTHER
1 Palazzo Altemps (Muzeo Nazionale Romano)
4 Fontana & Piazza di Trevi
5 Palazzo del Quirinale
6 Questura (Police Station)
9 Teatro dell'Opera
10 Bar della Pace
18 Pantheon
22 Vineria
23 Palazzo Farnese & French Embassy
24 French Consulate
27 Palazzo Venezia
28 Monumento Vittorio Emanuele II
30 Basilica di San Pietro in Vincoli

32 Chiesa di Santa Maria d'Aracoeli
33 Palazzo del Museo Capitolino
34 Palazzo dei Conservatori
36 Ospedale Fatebenefratelli
37 Arch of Constantine
38 Chiesa di San Clemente
41 Basilica di Santa Maria in Trastevere
44 Bibli Internet
45 San Gallicano Hospital
48 Chiesa di Santa Maria in Cosmedin
49 Circus Maximus
50 Big Mama (Nightclub)
51 Porta Portese Market Area
52 Porta Portese

ITALY

Campo de' Fiori. A magnificent Renaissance building, it was started in 1514 by Antonio da Sangallo. Work was carried on by Michelangelo and completed by Giacomo della Porta. Built for Cardinal Alessandro Farnese (later Pope Paul III), the palace is now the French Embassy.

Significant Churches

Down Via Cavour from Stazione Termini is **Santa Maria Maggiore**, built in the 5th century. Its main baroque facade was added in the 18th century, preserving the 13th-century mosaics of the earlier facade.

Follow Via Merulana to reach **San Giovanni in Laterano**, Rome's cathedral. The original church was built in the 4th century and was the first Christian basilica in Rome.

San Pietro in Vincoli, just off Via Cavour, is worth a visit because it houses Michelangelo's *Moses* and his unfinished statues of Leah and Rachel.

San Clemente, on Via San Giovanni in Laterano, defines how history in Rome exists on many levels. The 12th-century church at street level was built over a 4th-century church which was, in turn, built over a 1st-century Roman house.

Santa Maria in Cosmedin, north-west of Circus Maximus, is one of the finest medieval churches in Rome. The main attraction for the tourist hordes is the Bocca della Verità (Mouth of Truth). Legend has it that if you put your right hand into the mouth while telling a lie, it will snap shut.

Catacombs

There are several catacombs in Rome. They consist of miles of tunnels carved out of volcanic rock, and were the meeting and burial places of early Christians in Rome. The largest catacombs are along the Via Appia Antica, just outside the city and accessible on bus No 660 (from Piazza dei Cinquecento).

The **Catacombs of San Callisto** and the **Catacombs of San Sebastiano** are almost next to each other on the Via Appia Antica. San Callisto is open 8.30 am to noon and 2.30 to 5.30 pm (closed Wednesday and all of February). San Sebastiano is open 8.30 am to noon and 2.30 to 5 pm (closed Sunday and all of November). Admission to each costs L8000 and is with a guide only.

Vatican City

After the unification of Italy, the papal states of central Italy became part of the new kingdom of Italy, causing a considerable rift between church and state. In 1929, Mussolini, under the Lateran Treaty, gave the pope full sovereignty over what is now the Vatican City, with its own postal service, currency, newspaper, radio station, train station and army of Swiss Guards.

The tourist office (☎ 69 88 44 66), in Piazza San Pietro to the left of the basilica, is open 8.30 am to 7 pm Monday to Saturday. Guided tours of the Vatican City gardens (L18,000) can be organised here.

St Peter's Basilica & Square The largest and most famous church in the Christian world, **San Pietro** stands on the site where St Peter was buried. The first church on the site was built during Constantine's reign in the 4th century, and in 1506 work started on a new basilica, designed by Bramante.

Although several architects were involved in its construction, it is generally held that St Peter's owes more to Michelangelo, who took over the project in 1547 and was responsible for the design of the dome. He died before the church was completed. The cavernous interior contains numerous treasures, including Michelangelo's superb *Pietá*, sculpted when he was only 24 years old and the only work to carry his signature (on the sash across the breast of the Madonna).

Bernini's huge, baroque *Baldacchino* (a heavily sculpted bronze canopy over the papal altar) stands 29m high and is an extraordinary work of art. Another point of note is the red porphyry disc near the central door, which marks the spot where Charlemagne and later emperors were crowned by the pope.

Entrance to Michelangelo's soaring dome is to the right as you climb the stairs to the atrium of the basilica. Make the entire climb on foot for L7000, or pay L8000 and take the elevator for part of the way (recommended).

The basilica is open 7 am to 7 pm daily (6 pm in winter) and dress rules are stringently enforced – no shorts, miniskirts or sleeveless tops. Prams and strollers must be left in a designated area outside the basilica.

Bernini's **Piazza San Pietro** (St Peter's Square) is considered a masterpiece. Laid

ITALY

out in the 17th century as a place for Christians of the world to gather, the immense piazza is bound by two semicircular colonnades, each of which is made up of four rows of Doric columns. In the centre of the piazza is an obelisk that was brought to Rome by Caligula from Heliopolis (in ancient Egypt). When you stand on the dark paving stones between the obelisk and either of the fountains, the colonnades appear to have only one row of columns.

The Pope usually gives a public audience at 10 or 11 am every Wednesday in the Papal Audience Hall. You must make a booking, either in person or by fax to the Prefettura della Casa Pontifica (☎ 69 88 30 17, fax 69 88 58 63), between 9 am and 1 pm on the Monday or Thursday before the audience. Go through the bronze doors under the colonnade to the right as you face the basilica.

Vatican Museums From St Peter's follow the wall of the Vatican City (to the right as you face the basilica) to the museums, or catch the regular shuttle bus (L2500) from the piazza in front of the tourist office. The museums are open 8.45 am to 3.45 pm Monday to Friday (to 12.45 on Saturday). Admission is L15,000. The museums are closed on Sunday and public holidays, but open on the last Sunday of every month from 9 am to 1 pm (free admission, but queues are always very long). Guided visits to the Vatican gardens cost L18,000 and can be booked by calling ☎ 69 88 44 66.

The Vatican museums contain an incredible collection of art and treasures collected by the popes, and you will need several hours to see the most important areas and museums.

The **Museo Pio-Clementino**, containing Greek and Roman antiquities, is on the ground floor near the entrance. Through the tapestry and map galleries are the **Stanze di Rafaello**, once the private apartment of Pope Julius II, decorated with frescoes by Raphael. Of particular interest is the magnificent **Stanza della Segnatura**, which features Raphael's masterpieces *The School of Athens* and *Disputation on the Sacrament*.

From Raphael's rooms, go down the stairs to the sumptuous **Appartamento Borgia**, which is decorated with frescoes by Pinturicchio. Then go down another flight of stairs to the **Sistine Chapel**, the private

papal chapel built in 1473 for Pope Sixtus IV. Michelangelo's wonderful frescoes of the *Creation* on the barrel-vaulted ceiling and *Last Judgment* on the end wall have both been restored to their original brilliance. It took Michelangelo four years, at the height of the Renaissance, to paint the ceiling; 24 years later he painted the extraordinary *Last Judgment*. The other walls of the chapel were painted by artists including Botticelli, Ghirlandaio, Pinturicchio and Signorelli. To best enjoy the ceiling frescoes, a pocket mirror is recommended so that you don't have to strain your neck.

PLACES TO STAY
Camping
About 15 minutes from the centre by public transport is *Village Camping Flaminio* (☎ 333 26 04, Via Flaminia Nuova 821). It costs L16,000 per person and L22,000 for a site. Tents and bungalows are available for rent. From Stazione Termini catch bus No 910 to Piazza Mancini, then bus No 200 to the camping ground. At night, catch bus No 24N from Piazzale Flaminio (just north of Piazza del Popolo).

Hostel
The HI *Ostello del Foro Italico* (☎ 323 62 67, Viale delle Olimpiadi 61) costs L25,000 a night, breakfast and showers included. Take Metro Linea A to Ottaviano, then bus No 32 to Foro Italico.

B&B
This type of accommodation in private houses is a recent addition to Rome's budget accommodation options. Bed & Breakfast Italia (☎ 687 86 18, fax 46 687 86 19, @ md4095@mclink.it), at Corso Vittorio Emanuele II 282, is one of several B&B networks. Central singles/doubles with shared bathroom cost L50,000/95,000, or L70,000/130,000 with private bath. Also worth checking out is Rome Sweet Home (☎/fax 69 92 48 33, @ romesweethome@tiscalinet.it), at Via della Vite 32. Prices are generally more expensive (L70,000/100,000) but the B&Bs are stunning. You can check out the Web site at www.romesweethome.it.

Hotels & Pensioni
North-East of Stazione Termini To reach the pensioni in this area, head to the

ITALY

right as you leave the train platforms onto Via Castro Pretorio. The excellent *Fawlty Towers* (☎ 445 48 02, *Via Magenta 39*) offers hostel-style accommodation at L40,000 per person, or L45,000 with a shower. Run by the people at Enjoy Rome, it offers lots of information about Rome and added bonuses are the sunny terrace and satellite TV.

Nearby in Via Palestro there are several reasonably priced pensioni. *Pensione Restivo* (☎ 446 21 72, ✉ info@enjoyrome.com, *Via Palestro 55*) has reasonable singles/doubles at L70,000/110,000, including the cost of showers. There's a midnight curfew. *Pensione Katty* (☎ 444 12 16, *Via Palestro 35*) has basic rooms from L55,000/90,000. Nearby is *Pensione Ester* (☎ 495 71 23, *Viale Castro Pretorio 25*) with comfortable doubles/triples for L70,000/100,000. *Hotel Positano* (☎ 49 03 60, *Via Palestro 49*) is a more expensive option. Very pleasant rooms with bathroom, TV and other comforts cost L120,000/160,000.

Two good pensioni share the same building at Via San Martino della Battaglia 11. *Pensione Lachea* (☎ 495 72 56) has large doubles/triples for L70,000/90,000. *Hotel Pensione Dolomiti* (☎ 49 10 58) has singles/doubles for L65,000/95,000.

Papa Germano (☎ 48 69 19, ✉ info@hotelpapagermano.it, *Via Calatafimi 14a*) is one of the more popular budget places in the area. It has singles/doubles for L55,000/80,000 or a double with private bathroom for L100,000.

Across Via XX Settembre, about 1km from the station, *Pensione Ercoli* (☎ 474 54 54, *Via Collina 48*) has singles/doubles for L90,000/140,000.

West of Stazione Termini This area is seedier, but prices remain the same. Via F Turati and the parallel Via Principe Amedeo, harbour a concentration of budget pensioni, so you shouldn't have any trouble finding a room. The area improves as you get closer to the Colosseum and Roman Forum.

On Via Cavour, the main street running south-west from the piazza in front of Termini, is *Everest Pensione* (☎ 488 16 29, *Via Cavour 47*), with clean and simple singles/doubles for L60,000/90,000. *Hotel Sandy* (☎ 445 26 12, *Via Cavour 136*) has dormitory beds for L35,000 a night.

Better quality hotels in the area include *Hotel Oceania* (☎ 482 46 96, *Via Firenze 50*), which can accommodate up to five people in a room. It has doubles for up to L260,000. *Hotel Kennedy* (☎ 446 53 73, *Via F Turati 62*) has good quality singles/doubles with bath for up to L149,000/249,000.

City Centre The *Pensione Primavera* (☎ 68 80 31 09, *Piazza San Pantaleo 3*), on a square just off Via Vittorio Emanuele II, has immaculate doubles with bathroom for up to L180,000. The *Albergo Abruzzi* (☎ 679 20 21, *Piazza della Rotonda 69*) overlooks the Pantheon – which excuses, to an extent, its very basic, noisy rooms. You couldn't find a better location, but it's expensive at L105,000/150,000 for singles/doubles. Bookings are essential throughout the year at this popular hotel.

The strictly no-smoking *Pensione Mimosa* (☎ 68 80 17 53, *fax 683 35 57, Via Santa Chiara 61*), off Piazza della Minerva, has very pleasant rooms for L90,000/110,000.

Another good choice is *Albergo della Lunetta* (☎ 686 10 80, *fax 689 20 28, Piazza del Paradiso 68*), which charges L90,000/140,000, or L110,000/190,000 with private shower. Reservations are essential.

Albergo Pomezia (☎/*fax 686 13 71, Via dei Chiavari 12*) has rooms for L120,000/170,000, breakfast included. Use of the communal shower is free.

Near St Peter's & the Vatican Bargains do not abound in this area, but it is comparatively quiet and still reasonably close to the main sights. Bookings are an absolute necessity because rooms are often filled with people attending conferences and so on at the Vatican. The simplest way to reach the area is on the Metropolitana Linea A to Ottaviano. Bus No 64 from Termini stops at St Peter's.

Pensione Ottaviano (☎ 39 73 72 53, ✉ gi.costantini@agora.stm.it, *Via Ottaviano 6*), near Piazza Risorgimento, is the best bargain in the area. It has beds in dormitories for L35,000 per person. At *Hotel Pensione Nautilus* (☎ 324 21 18, *Via Germanico 198*) you will pay L90,000/110,000 for basic singles/doubles or L130,000/160,000 with private bathroom. *Hotel Amalia* (☎ 39 72 33 56, *fax 39 72 33 65, hotelamalia@iol.it, Via Germanico 66)* has a beautiful courtyard entrance and clean, sunny rooms for L105,000/140,000, including breakfast and use of the communal shower. Triples cost L182,000.

PLACES TO EAT

Rome bursts at the seams with trattorias, pizzerias and restaurants – and not all of them overrun by tourists. Eating times are generally from 12.30 to 3 pm and from 8 to 11 pm. Most Romans head out for dinner around 9 pm, so it's better to arrive earlier to claim a table.

The antipasto dishes in Rome are particularly good, and many restaurants will allow you to make your own mixed selection. Some typical pasta dishes are: *bucatini all'*

Amatriciana (large, hollow spaghetti with a salty sauce of tomato and bacon); *penne all'arrabbiata* (penne with a hot sauce of tomatoes, peppers and chilli); and *spaghetti carbonara* (pancetta, eggs and cheese). Romans eat many dishes prepared with offal. Try the *paiata* if you can stomach it – it's pasta with veal intestines. *Saltimbocca alla Romana* (slices of veal and ham) is a classic meat dish, as is *straccetti con la rucola*, fine slices of beef tossed in garlic and oil and topped with fresh rocket. In winter you can't go past *carciofi alla Romana* (artichokes stuffed with garlic and mint or parsley).

Good options for cheap, quick meals are the hundreds of bars, where *panini* (sandwiches) cost L2500 to L5000 if taken *al banco* (at the bar). There's also takeaway

STAZIONE TERMINI AREA

PLACES TO STAY & EAT		OTHER	15 Telecom Office	26 Museo Nazionale Romano
1 Pensione Katty	31 Everest Pensione	2 Telecom Office	16 Urban Bus Station	27 Teatro dell'Opera
3 Pensione Lachea;	33 Hotel Kennedy	4 Hospital (Policlinico Umberto I)	17 Baths of Diocletian	28 Questura (Police Station)
Hotel Pensione Dolomiti	35 Hotel Sandy	9 ENIT Tourist Office	18 APT Tourist Office	29 Foreigners' Bureau
5 Pensione Ester		11 Enjoy Rome Tourist Office	19 Feltrinelli International	30 CTS Travel Agency
6 Pensione Restivo		13 CTS Travel Agency	21 Sestante CIT Travel Agency	32 Italian Youth Hostels
7 Hotel Positano		14 APT Branch Tourist Office	22 Basilica di Santa	Association Office
8 Papa Germano			Maria degli Angeli	34 Basilica di Santa
10 Trattoria Da Bruno			23 Eurojet Travel Agency	Maria Maggiore
12 Fawlty Towers			24 SAIS Bus Office	36 The Druid's Den
20 Hotel Oceania			25 Economy Book & Video Center	37 Circolo degli Artisti

pizzerias, usually called pizza a taglio, where a slice of freshly cooked pizza, sold by weight, can cost as little as L2000. Bakeries are numerous and are another good choice for a cheap snack. Try a huge piece of pizza bianca, a flat bread resembling focaccia, for around L2000 a slice (sold by weight).

There are numerous outdoor *markets*, notably the lively daily market in Campo de' Fiori. Other, cheaper food markets are held in Piazza Vittorio Emanuele, near the station, and in Via Andrea Doria, near Largo Trionfale, north of the Vatican.

Restaurants, Trattorias & Pizzerias

The restaurants near Stazione Termini are generally to be avoided. The side streets around Piazza Navona and Campo de' Fiori harbour many budget trattorias and pizzerias, and the areas of San Lorenzo (to the east of Termini, near the university) and Testaccio (across the Tiber near Piramide) are popular local eating districts. Trastevere offers an excellent selection of rustic eating places hidden in tiny piazzas, and pizzerias where it doesn't cost the earth to sit at a table on the street.

City Centre The *Pizzeria Montecarlo (Vicolo Savelli 12)* is a very traditional place, with paper sheets for tablecloths. A pizza with wine or beer will cost as little as L17,000. *Pizzeria da Baffetto (Via del Governo Vecchio 11)* is a Roman institution. The pizzas are huge and delicious. Expect to join a queue if you arrive after 9 pm and don't be surprised if you end up sharing a table. Pizzas cost around L10,000 to L15,000, a litre of wine costs L9000 and the cover charge (*coperto*) is only L2000. Farther along the street at No 18 is a tiny, nameless *osteria* where you can eat an excellent, simple meal for around L25,000. There's no written menu, but don't be nervous – the owner/waiter will explain slowly (in Italian). Back along the street towards Piazza Navona is *Cul de Sac 1 (Piazza Pasquino 73)*, a wine bar which also has light meals at reasonable prices.

Centro Macrobiotico Italiano (Via della Vite 14) is a vegetarian restaurant, which also serves fresh fish in the evenings. It charges an annual membership fee (which reduces as the year goes by), but tourists can usually eat there and pay only a small surcharge.

There are several small restaurants in the Campo de' Fiori. *Hostaria Romanesca* is tiny, so arrive early in winter. In summer there are numerous tables outside. A dish of pasta will cost around L12,000, and a full meal around L40,000.

Just off Campo de' Fiori is *Filetti di Baccalá (Largo dei Librari)*, which serves only deep-fried cod fillets for L6500 and wine for L9000 a litre. Across Via Arenula, in the Jewish quarter, is *Sora Margherita (Piazza delle Cinque Scole 30)*. Open only at lunchtime, it serves traditional Roman and Jewish food, and a full meal will cost around L38,000.

West of the Tiber On the west bank of the Tiber, good-value restaurants are concentrated in Trastevere and the Testaccio district, past Piramide. Many of the establishments around St Peter's and the Vatican are geared for tourists and can be very expensive. There are, however, some good options. Try *Il Tempio della Pizza (Viale Giulio Cesare 91)* or the highly recommended *Osteria dell'Angelo (Via G Bettolo 24)*, along Via Leone IV from the Vatican City, although this place can be difficult to get into if you get there after 8 pm.

In Trastevere, try *Frontoni*, on Viale di Trastevere, opposite Piazza Mastai, for fantastic panini made with pizza bianca. *D'Augusto,* on Piazza dei Renzi, just around the corner from the Basilica Santa Maria in Trastevere (turn right as you face the church and walk to Via della Pelliccia), is a very popular cheap eating spot. The food might be average, but the atmosphere is as traditionally Roman as you can get, especially in summer with tables outside in the piazza. A meal with wine will cost around L29,000. *Da Lucia (Vicolo del Mattinato 2)* is more expensive at around L50,000 a full meal, but the food is good and the owners are delightful. In summer you'll sit beneath the neighbours washing.

For a Neapolitan-style pizza, try *Pizzeria da Vittorio (Via San Cosimato 14)*. You'll have to wait for an outside table if you arrive after 8.30 pm, but the atmosphere is great. A bruschetta, pizza and wine will cost around L30,000.

You won't find a cheaper, noisier, more chaotic pizzeria in Rome than *Pizzeria Remo (Piazza Santa Maria Liberatrice 44)* in Test-

ITALY

accio. Nearby is *Il Canestro*, on Via Maestro Giorgio, which specialises in vegetarian food and is relatively expensive. You won't get much change out of L60,000. *Augustarello (Via G Branca 98)*, off the piazza, specialises in the very traditional Roman fare of offal dishes. The food is reasonable and a meal will cost around L25,000.

Between Termini & the Forum You will find typical local fare and good pizzas at prices students can afford at *Pizzeria l' Economica (Via Tiburtina 44)*.

If you have no option but to eat near Stazione Termini, try to avoid the tourist traps with overpriced full menus. *Trattoria da Bruno (Via Varese 29)* has good food at reasonable prices – around L8500 for pasta and up to L17,000 for a second course. Home-made gnocchi is served on Thursday. A decent pizzeria is *Alle Carrette (Vicolo delle Carrette 14)*, off Via Cavour near the Roman Forum. Pizza and wine will cost around L16,000. Just off Via Cavour is *Osteria Gli Angeletti*, on Via dell'Angeletto, an excellent little restaurant with prices at the higher end of the budget range. You'll pay L10,000 to L14,000 for a pasta and around L16,000 for a second course.

Gelati
Gelateria Giolitti (Via degli Uffici del Vicario 40), near the Pantheon, and *Gelateria della Palme (Via della Maddalena 20)*, just around the corner, both have a huge selection of flavours. In Trastevere, *Fonte della Salute (Via Cardinale Marmaggi 2-6)* also has excellent gelati.

ENTERTAINMENT
Rome's best entertainment guide is the weekly *romac'é* (L2000), which has an English-language section; it's available at all newsstands. Another good entertainment guide is *Trovaroma*, a weekly supplement in the Thursday edition of the newspaper *La Repubblica*. It provides a comprehensive listing of what's happening in the city, but in Italian only, and also publishes a daily listing of cinema, theatre and concerts.

Metropolitan is a fortnightly magazine for Rome's English-speaking community (L1500). It has good entertainment listings and is available at outlets including the Economy Book & Video Center, at Via

Torino 136, and newsstands in the city centre, including at Largo Argentina.

Nightclubs
Among the more interesting and popular Roman live music clubs is *Radio Londra (Via di Monte Testaccio 67)* in the Testaccio area. In the same street are the more sedate music clubs *Caruso Caffé* at No 36 and *Caffé Latino* at No 96, both generally offering jazz or blues. More jazz and blues can be heard at *Alexanderplatz (Via Ostia 9)* and *Big Mama (Via San Francesco a Ripa 18)* in Trastevere. *Circolo degli Artisti (Via Lamarmora 28)*, near Piazza Vittorio Emanuele, is a lively club, popular among Rome's hip set.

Roman discos are outrageously expensive. Expect to pay up to L30,000 to get in, which may or may not include one drink. Perennials include *Alien (Via Velletri 13)*, *Piper '90 (Via Tagliamento 9)* and *Gilda-Swing (Via Mario de' Fiori 97)*. The best gay disco is *L'Alibi (Via di Monte Testaccio 44)*.

Cafes & Bars
Remember that prices skyrocket in bars as soon as you sit down, particularly near the Spanish Steps, in the Piazza della Rotonda and in Piazza Navona, where a *cappuccino a tavola* (at a table) can cost L5000 or more. The same cappuccino taken at the bar will cost around L1800 – but passing an hour or so watching the world go by over a cappuccino, beer or wine in any of the above locations can be hard to beat!

For the best coffee in Rome head for *Tazza d'Oro*, on Via degli Orfani, just off Piazza della Rotonda, and *Caffé Sant' Eustachio (Piazza Sant'Eustachio 82)*. Try the granita di caffé at either one.

Vineria in Campo de' Fiori, also known as *Giorgio's*, has a wide selection of wine and beers. In summer it has tables outside, but prices are steep – it's better to stand at the bar. *Bar della Pace (Via della Pace 3-7)* is big with the trendy crew, but being hip has a price. *Bevitoria Navona (Piazza Navona 72)* has wine by the glass. In Trastevere, the alternative set seem to prefer *Bar San Calisto (Piazza San Calisto)*, where you don't have to pay extra to sit at the outside tables. Near Piazza Santa Maria Maggiore, *The Druid's Den (Via San Martino ai Monti 28)* is a popular Irish pub,

ITALY

which means you can get Guinness and Kilkenny on tap.

GETTING THERE & AWAY
Air
The main airline offices are in the area around Via Veneto and Via Barberini, north of Stazione Termini. Qantas, British Airways, Alitalia, Air New Zealand, Lufthansa and Singapore Airlines are all in Via Bissolati. The main airport is Leonardo da Vinci, at Fiumicino (see Getting Around later in this section).

Bus
The main terminal for intercity buses is in Piazzale Tiburtina, in front of the Stazione Tiburtina. Catch the Metropolitana Linea B from Termini to Tiburtina. For information about which companies operate services to which destinations and from where, go to the APT office, or Enjoy Rome (see Tourist Offices). At Eurojet (☎ 481 74 55, fax 474 45 21, ✆ eurojet@adv.it), Piazza della Repubblica 54, you can buy tickets for and get information about several bus services. Otherwise, there are ticket offices for all of the companies inside the Tiburtina station. COTRAL buses, which service Lazio, depart from numerous points throughout the city, depending on their destinations.

Train
Almost all trains arrive at and depart from Stazione Termini. There are regular connections to all major cities in Italy and throughout Europe. Some journey times and costs for Eurostar trains from Rome (which require booking and a special supplement) are as follows: Florence (L48,000, 1¾ hours); Milan (L79,500, 4½ hours) and Naples (L37,500, two hours). For train timetable information phone ☎ 147-88 80 88 (from 7 am to 9 pm), or go to the information office at the station (English is spoken). Timetables can be bought at most newsstands in and around Termini and are particularly useful if you are travelling mostly by train. Services at Termini include telephones, money exchange (see the earlier Information section) and luggage storage (☎ 47 30 62 75, beside track 22) which charges L5000 per piece every six hours. Some trains depart from the stations Ostiense and at Tiburtina.

GETTING AROUND
To/From the Airport
The main airport is Leonardo da Vinci (☎ 65 95 36 40 for flights only) at Fiumicino. Access to the city is via the airport-Stazione Termini direct train (follow the signs to the station from the airport arrivals hall), which costs L16,000 and takes 35 minutes. Another train makes stops along the way, including Trastevere and Ostiense, and terminates at Stazione Tiburtina (L8000). The trip takes about 50 minutes. A night bus runs from Stazione Tirburtina to the airport from 12.30 to 3.45 am, stopping at Termini at the corner of Via Giolitti about 10 minutes later.

Bus
The city bus company is ATAC (☎ 167-43 17 84 for information in English). Details on which buses head where are available at the ATAC information booth in the centre of Piazza dei Cinquecento. Another central point for main bus routes in the centre is Largo Argentina, on Corso Vittorio Emanuele south of the Pantheon. Buses run from 5.30 am to midnight, with limited services throughout the night on some routes. A fast tram service, the No 8, connects Largo Argentina with Trastevere, Porta Portese and the suburb of Monte Verde.

Rome has an integrated public transport system, so you can use the same ticket for the bus, subway and suburban railway. Tickets cost L1500 and are valid for 75 minutes. They must be purchased *before* you get on the bus and validated in the orange machine as you enter. The fine for travelling without a ticket is L100,000, to be paid on the spot, and there is no sympathy for 'dumb tourists'. Tickets can be purchased at any tobacconist, newsstand, or at the main bus terminals. Daily tickets cost L6000 and weekly tickets cost L24,000.

Metropolitana
The Metropolitana (Metro) has two lines, A and B. Both pass through Stazione Termini. Take Linea A for Piazza di Spagna, the Vatican (Ottaviano) and Villa Borghese (Flaminio), and Linea B for the Colosseum, Circus Maximus and Piramide (for Testaccio and Stazione Ostiense). Tickets are the same as for city buses (see Bus earlier in this section). Trains run approximately

ITALY

every five minutes between 5.30 am and 11.30 pm (12.30 am on Saturday).

Taxi

Taxis are on radio call 24 hours a day in Rome. Cooperativa Radio Taxi Romana (☎ 46 35 70) and La Capitale (☎ 46 49 94) are two of the many operators. Major taxi ranks are at the airports, Stazione Termini and Largo Argentina in the historical centre. There are surcharges for luggage (L2000 per item), night service (L5000), Sunday and public holidays (L2000) and travel to/from Fiumicino airport (L14,000). Flag fall is L4500 (for the first 3km), then L1200 for every kilometre.

Car & Motorcycle

Most of the historic centre is closed to normal traffic, although tourists are permitted to drive to their hotels. *Vigili* (traffic police) control the entrances to the centre and will let you through once you mention the name of your hotel.

A major parking area close to the centre is at the Villa Borghese. Entrance is from Piazzale Brasile at the top of Via Veneto. There is a supervised car park at Stazione Termini.

AROUND ROME
Ostia Antica

The Romans founded this port city at the mouth of the Tiber in the 4th century BC and it became a strategically important centre of defence and trade. It was populated by merchants, sailors and slaves, and the ruins of the city provide a fascinating contrast to a place such as Pompeii. It was abandoned after barbarian invasions and the appearance of malaria, but Pope Gregory IV re-established the city in the 9th century.

Of particular note in the excavated city are the mosaics of the **Terme di Nettuno** (Baths of Neptune); a **Roman theatre** built by Augustus; the **forum** and **temple**, dedicated to Jupiter, Juno and Minerva; and the **Piazzale delle Corporazioni**, where you can see the offices of Roman merchants, distinguished by mosaics depicting their trades. The site is open 9 am to 7 pm (last admission 6 pm) Tuesday to Sunday and entry is L8000. To get there take the Metropolitana Linea B to Magliana and then the Ostia Lido train (getting off at Ostia Antica).

Tivoli
☎ 0774
Set on a hill by the Anio River, Tivoli was a resort town of the ancient Romans and became popular as a summer playground for the rich during the Renaissance. It is famous today for the terraced gardens and fountains of the Villa d'Este and the ruins of the spectacular Villa Adriana, built by the Roman emperor Hadrian.

The local tourist office (☎ 33 45 22) is in Largo Garibaldi near the COTRAL bus stop.

Things to See Hadrian built his summer house, **Villa Adriana**, in the 2nd century AD. Its construction was influenced by the architecture of the famous classical buildings of the day. It was successively plundered by barbarians and Romans for building materials and many of its original decorations were used to embellish the Villa d'Este. However, enough remains to give an idea of the incredible size and magnificence of the villa. You will need about four hours to wander through the vast ruins.

The villa is open 9 am to about one hour before sunset daily (around 7.30 pm; last entry at 6.30 pm) between April and September. Entry is L8000.

The Renaissance **Villa d'Este** was built in the 16th century for Cardinal Ippolito d'Este on the site of a Franciscan monastery. The villa's beautiful gardens are decorated with numerous fountains, which are its main attraction. Opening hours are the same as for Villa Adriana and entry is L8000. Both villas are closed on Monday.

Getting There & Away Tivoli is about 40km east of Rome and is accessible by COTRAL bus. Take Metro Linea B from Stazione Termini to Ponte Mammolo; the bus leaves from outside the station every 20 minutes. The bus also stops near the Villa Adriana, about 1km from Tivoli. Otherwise, catch local bus No 4 from Tivoli's Piazza Garibaldi to Villa Adriana.

Tarquinia
☎ 0766
Believed to have been founded in the 12th century BC and to have been the home of the Tarquin kings who ruled Rome before the creation of the republic, Tarquinia was an important economic and political centre

ITALY

of the Etruscan League. The major attractions here are the painted tombs of its *necropoli* (burial grounds). The IAT tourist information office (☎ 85 63 84) is at Piazza Cavour 1.

Things to See & Do The 15th-century Palazzo Vitelleschi houses the **Museo Nazionale Tarquiniense** and an excellent collection of Etruscan treasures, including frescoes removed from the tombs. There are also numerous sarcophagi that were found in the tombs. The museum is open 9 am to 7 pm Tuesday to Sunday. Entry is L8000 and the same ticket covers entry to the **necropolis**, a 15- to 20-minute walk away (or catch one of four daily buses). The necropolis has the same opening hours as the museum. Ask at the tourist office for directions.

Getting There & Away Buses leave approximately every hour for Tarquinia from Via Lepanto in Rome, near the Metropolitana Linea A Lepanto stop, arriving at Tarquinia a few steps away from the tourist office.

Northern Italy

GENOA
☎ 010

Travellers who write off Genoa (Genova) as just another dirty port town do the city a disservice. This once-powerful maritime republic, birthplace of Christopher Columbus (1451-1506) and now capital of the region of Liguria, can still carry the title La Superba (The Proud). It is a city of contrasts, where tiny backstreets lead onto grand thoroughfares and piazzas lined with marble and stucco palaces.

Orientation & Information
Most trains stop at Genoa's two main stations, Principe and Brignole. The area around Brignole is closer to the city centre and has better accommodation choices. Principe is closer to the port, an area which should be avoided by women travelling alone.

From Brignole walk straight along Via Fiume to reach Via XX Settembre and the historical centre.

The main IAT tourist office (☎ 24 87 11, ✉ aptgenova@apt.genova.it) is on the waterfront at Via del Porto Antico, in the Palazzina Santa Maria. It's open 9 am to 6.30 pm daily. There are branches at Stazione Principe and the airport.

The main post office is in Via Dante, just off Piazza de Ferrari. Telecom Italia is on Piazza Verdi, open 8 am to 9 pm daily.

Things to See & Do
The labyrinthine port area, Genoa's oldest quarter, features the 12th-century **Cattedrale di San Lorenzo** and the **Palazzo Ducale** in Piazza Matteotti. The palaces of the Doria family, one of the most important local families in the 14th and 15th centuries, surround tiny **Piazza San Matteo**.

Take a walk along **Via Garibaldi**, which is lined with palaces. Some are open to the public and contain art galleries, including the 16th-century **Palazzo Bianco** and the 17th-century **Palazzo Rosso**, where the Flemish painter Van Dyck lived. Italian and Flemish Renaissance works are displayed in the **Galleria Nazionale di Palazzo Spinola**, Piazza Superiore di Pellicceria 1.

The **aquarium**, Europe's biggest and well worth a visit, is on the waterfront at Ponte Spinola. Admission is L19,000.

Places to Stay
The HI *Ostello Genova* (☎ 242 24 57, ✉ hostelge@iol.it, Via Costanzi 120) is just outside Genoa in Righi. B&B is L23,000, and an evening meal of pasta is L5000. Catch bus No 40 from Stazione Brignole.

On the 3rd floor of a lovely old palazzo near Stazione Brignole, the friendly *Carola* (☎ 839 13 40, Via Gropallo 4) has pleasant singles/doubles/triples for L45,000/75,000/100,000. To get there, turn right as you leave the station, walk up Via de Amicis to Piazza Brignole and turn right into Via Gropallo. *Albergo Rita* (☎ 87 02 07), a few doors up at No 8, has singles/doubles for L50,000/75,000.

Places to Eat
Don't leave town without trying the local *pesto genovese* (pasta with a sauce of basil, garlic and pine nuts), *pansotti* (ravioli in walnut sauce) and, of course, several focaccia.

Plenty of shops sell sandwiches and pizza by the slice in the Brignole and port areas. *Da Maria (Vico Testa d'Oro 14)* is a good deal, with full meals for L13,000, including wine. The tourist menu at *La Locanda del Borgo* (*Via Borgo Incrociati 45*), north of Stazione Brignole (use the unsavoury pedestrian tunnel), costs around L15,000.

Getting There & Away

Buses for Rome, Florence, Milan and Perugia leave from Piazza della Vittoria. Eurolines buses leave from the same piazza for Barcelona, Madrid and Paris. Book at Geotravels (☎ 58 71 81) in the piazza.

Genoa is connected by train to the major Italian and European cities. For train information call ☎ 147 88 80 88.

The city's busy port is a major embarkation point for ferries to Sicily, Sardinia and Corsica. Major companies are:

Corsica Ferries (☎ 019 21 55 11 in Savona)
Moby Lines (☎ 25 27 55 for Corsica), Ponte Asserato
Tirrenia (☎ 254 30 58 for Sicily and Sardinia), at the Stazione Marittima, Ponte Colombo
Grandi Navi Veloci and Grandi Traghetti (☎ 58 93 31 for Sardinia, Sicily, Malta and Tunisia), Via Fieschi 17

RIVIERA DI LEVANTE
☎ 0185

The Ligurian coastal region from Genoa to La Spezia (on the border with Tuscany) rivals the Amalfi Coast in its spectacular beauty. It also has several resorts which, despite attracting thousands of summer tourists, have managed to remain unspoiled. Both spring and autumn can bring suitable beach weather.

There are tourist offices in most towns, including Santa Margherita (☎ 28 74 86), at Via XXV Aprile 4, and La Spezia (☎ 0187 77 09 00), near the waterfront at Via Mazzini 45. Staff can help with accommodation.

Things to See & Do

Santa Margherita Ligure, a pretty resort town, is a good base from which to explore the nearby resorts of **Portofino**, a haunt of the rich and famous, and **Camogli**, a fishing village turned resort. The medieval Benedictine monastery of **San Fruttuoso** is a hilly 2½-hour walk from Camogli or Portofino, and you can catch the ferry back.

The five tiny coastal villages of the **Cinque Terre** – Riomaggiore, Manorola, Corniglia, Vernazza and Monterosso – are easily reached by train from La Spezia.

These mountainside fishing and wine-growing villages are linked by unforgettably scenic walking and hiking tracks.

Places to Stay

In Santa Margherita, the *Nuova Riviera* (☎ 28 74 03, 📧 gisabin@tin.it, Via Belvedere 10) is a clean, nonsmoking hotel 15 minutes or so from the station (follow Via Roma to Piazza Mazzini). Singles/doubles/triples/quads start at L75,000/95,000/130,000/160,000 with breakfast. Nearby, *Albergo Annabella* (☎ 28 65 31, Via Costasecca 10) has large singles/doubles for L60,000/80,000. Right by the station there's *Albergo Azalea* (☎ 28 81 60, Via Roma 60), with rooms from L65,000/95,000.

The orderly *Ostello 5 Terre* (☎ 0187 92 02 15, 📧 ostello@cdh.it, Via B Riccobaldi 21) in Manorola has B&B from L25,000, and an evening meal for around L12,000; book well ahead. In La Spezia, try *Albergo Parma* (☎ 0187 74 30 10, Via Fiume 143) opposite the station, with rooms from L45,000/75,000.

Getting There & Away

The entire coast is served by train and all points are accessible from Genoa. Buses leave from Santa Margherita's Piazza Martiri della Libertà for Portofino.

Boats leave from near the bus stop in Santa Margherita for Portofino (L10,000 return), San Fruttuoso (L20,000 return) and the Cinque Terre (L35,000 return). From La Spezia to the Cinque Terre by boat it's L33,000 return.

TURIN
☎ 010

Turin (Torino) is the capital of the Piedmont region. The House of Savoy, which ruled this region for hundreds of years (and Italy until 1945), built a gracious baroque city of boulevards and arcaded buildings. Italy's industrial expansion began here with companies such as Fiat and Olivetti.

Orientation & Information

The Porta Nuova train station is the point of arrival for most travellers. To reach the city centre, cross Corso Vittorio Emanuele II and walk through the grand Carlo Felice and San Carlo piazzas until you come to Piazza Castello.

ITALY

The tourist office is at Piazza Castello 161 (☎ 53 51 81), and there's also a branch at the Porta Nuova train station (☎ 53 13 27).

Things to See

Turin's historical centre is Piazza Castello, which features the sumptuous **Palazzo Madama**, home to the Museo Civico d'Arte Antica. The gardens of the adjacent 17th-century **Palazzo Reale** (Royal Palace) were designed by Louis le Nôtre, who also designed the gardens at Versailles.

The **Cattedrale di San Giovanni**, west of the Palazzo Reale, houses the **Shroud of Turin**, the linen cloth believed to have been used to wrap the crucified Christ. Scientists claim that the shroud dates back to the 12th century. The shroud is displayed for only a few days each year, but a reasonable copy is displayed in the cathedral.

Turin's **Museo Egizio**, in Via Accademia delle Scienze 6, is considered one of the best museums of ancient Egyptian art after those in London and Cairo. It opens 9 am to 7 pm Tuesday to Saturday and to 2 pm on Sunday (L12,000).

Places to Stay

Campeggio Villa Rey (☎ 819 01 17, Strada Superiore Val San Martino 27) opens from March to October. The *Ostello Torino* (☎ 660 29 39, Via Alby 1) is in the hills east of the Po River. Catch bus No 52 from the Porta Nuova station (No 64 on Sunday). B&B is L19,000 and a meal is L14,000.

The *Canelli* (☎ 54 60 78, Via San Dalmazzo 5b), off Via Garibaldi, has bare singles/doubles/triples for L40,000/55,000/ 66,000. The two-star *Albergo Magenta* (☎ 54 26 49, Corso Vittorio Emanuele II 67) charges L50,000/75,000.

Getting There & Away

Intercity Sadem buses terminate at the main bus station at Corso Inghilterra 1, near the Porta Susa train station, with services to Italy's major cities. Frequent trains connect with Milan, Venice, Genoa and Rome.

MILAN

☎ 02

Milan (Milano) is Italy's capital of fashion and finance. The city has Celtic origins, and became an important trading and transport centre following the arrival of the Romans

in 222 BC. From the 13th century the city flourished under the rule of two powerful families: the Visconti and, later, the Sforza.

You should note that Milan closes down almost completely in August, when most of the city's inhabitants are taking their annual holidays.

Orientation

From Stazione Centrale, the main train station, take the efficient underground (known as the MM, or Metropolitana Milanese) into town. The MM3 goes to the Duomo and the city centre. The city of Milan is huge – use the Duomo and the Castello Sforzesco, at the other end of Via Dante, as points of reference. The main shopping areas and sights are around and between the two.

Information

Tourist Offices The main APT office (☎ 72 52 43 01), at Via Marconi 1, in Piazza del Duomo, stocks the useful city guide *Milan is Milano*. The office is open until at least 5 pm daily. A second APT office is at Stazione Centrale.

Milan city council operates an information office in Galleria V Emanuele II, just off Piazza del Duomo.

Money Exchange offices at Piazza Duomo include Banca Ponti at No 19 and there are also somewhat expensive offices in Stazione Centrale, open daily. The American Express office (☎ 87 66 74), at Via Brera 3, is open 9 am to 5 pm Monday to Friday.

Post & Communications The main post office is at Via Cordusio 4, off Via Dante. The Telecom Italia office at Stazione Centrale is open 8 am to 8 pm daily.

Email & Internet Access Milan's first and best cybercafe is the Hard Disk Cafe (www.hdc.it), Corso Sempione 44. For basic service close to the station, try Boomerang on the corner of Via Gasparotto and F Filzi. It charges L3000 for 10 minutes and L8000 for half an hour. The Telecom office in the Galleria also has Internet access (L200 per minute).

Bookshops The American Bookstore, at Via Campiero 16, has a good selection of English-language books.

Medical Services The public hospital, Ospedale Maggiore Policlinico (☎ 550 31), is at Via Francesco Sforza 35, close to the centre. There is an all-night pharmacy in Stazione Centrale (☎ 669 09 35).

Dangers & Annoyances Milan's main shopping areas are popular haunts for groups of thieves. Be particularly careful in the square in front of Stazione Centrale.

Things to See
Start with the extraordinary **Duomo**, commissioned by Gian Galeazzo Visconti in 1386. With its marble facade shaped into spiky pinnacles, statues and pillars, this tumultuous structure is certainly memorable – as is the view from the roof (stairs L6000, lift L9000).

Join the throngs and take a *passeggiata* through the Galleria Vittorio Emanuele II to **La Scala**, Milan's famous opera house. Entry to the theatre's **museum** is L6000.

At the end of Via Dante is the huge **Castello Sforzesco**, a Visconti fortress which was entirely rebuilt by Francesco Sforza in the 15th century. Its museums hold an interesting collection of furniture, artefacts and sculpture, including Michelangelo's unfinished *Pietà Rondanini*. The castle is open 9.30 am to 5.30 pm Tuesday to Sunday (free).

Nearby in Via Brera is the 17th-century Palazzo di Brera, which houses the **Pinacoteca di Brera** gallery and a vast collection of paintings, including Mantegna's masterpiece, the *Dead Christ*. The gallery is open 9 am to 5.45 pm Tuesday to Saturday and to 8 pm on Sunday (L12,000).

Leonardo da Vinci's *Last Supper* can be viewed by prior appointment in the **Cenacolo Vinciano**, Piazza Santa Maria delle Grazie 2; phone ☎ 199 199 100 to make a booking. The famous fresco was restored in 1995, but centuries of damage from floods, bombing and decay have left their mark. The building is open 9 am to 7 pm Tuesday to Saturday, to 8 pm on Sunday (L12,000).

Special Events
St Ambrose's Day (7 December) is Milan's major festival, with celebrations at the Fiera di Milano (MM1 Amendola Fiera).

Places to Stay
Milan's hotels are among the most expensive and heavily booked in Italy – it's strongly recommended to reserve ahead. The tourist office makes bookings (which hotels will hold for one hour).

Hostels The HI *Ostello Piero Rotta* (☎ 39 26 70 95, Viale Salmoiraghi 1) is northwest of the city centre; take the MM1 to the QT8 stop. B&B is L26,000, and the hostel is closed from 9 am to 3.30 pm, with lights out at 12.30 am.

Protezione della Giovane (☎ 29 00 01 64, Corso Garibaldi 123) is run by nuns for single women aged 16 to 25. Beds are L37,000 a night, and bookings are required.

Hotels – Around Stazione Centrale
One of Milan's nicest one-star hotels is *Due Giardini* (☎ 29 52 10 93, Via B Marcello 47), with rooms overlooking a tranquil back garden; simple but comfortable doubles are L150,000 with bathroom and TV. To get there turn right off Via D Scarlatti, which is to the left as you leave the station.

Budget options nearby in busy Via Vitruvio, off Piazza Duca d'Aosta, include *Albergo Salerno* (☎ 204 68 70) at No 18, with clean singles/doubles for L65,000/90,000, and the *Italia* (☎ 669 38 26) at No 44, with rooms for L55,000/85,000.

The no-frills *Nettuno* (☎ 29 40 44 81, Via Tadino 27) has rooms for L60,000/90,000. Near Piazza della Repubblica, *Verona* (☎ 66 98 30 91, Via Carlo Tenca 12) has rooms for L80,000/150,000 with shower, TV and telephone.

The friendly *Hotel San Tomaso* (☎ 29 51 47 47, @ hotelsantomaso@tin.it) has simple singles/doubles/triples for L60,000/100,000/135,000, all with shower and TV. It's on the 3rd floor at Viale Tunisia 6, just off Corso Buenos Aires. On the 6th floor in the same building, the *Hotel Kennedy* (☎ 29 40 09 34) has reasonable singles/doubles for L60,000/90,000. A double or triple with bathroom is L120,000.

Closer to the centre, the *Euro Hotel* (☎ 20 40 40 10, @ eurohotel.viasirtori@tin.it, Via Sirtori 26), off Piazza G Oberdan, is a good bet, with modern singles/doubles/triples with shower, TV and breakfast for L110,000/140,000/180,000.

Hotels – City Centre The *Albergo Commercio* (☎ 86 46 38 80, Via Mercato 1) has basic singles/doubles with shower for

ITALY

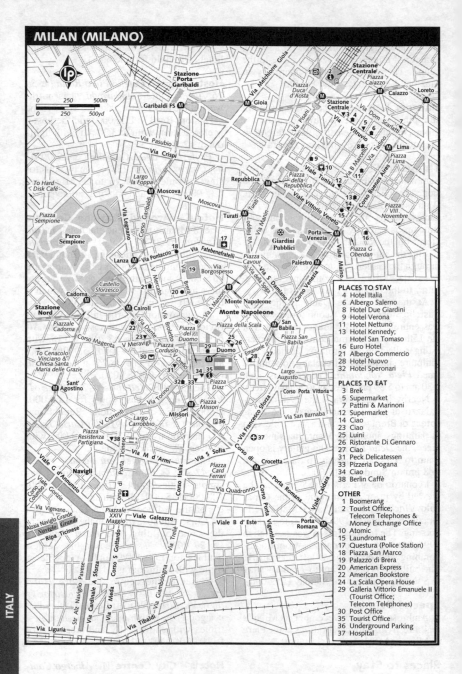

MILAN (MILANO)

0 250 500m
0 250 500yd

Stazione Porta Garibaldi

Stazione Centrale

Piazza Caiazzo

Caiazzo

Loreto

Garibaldi FS

Gioia

Piazza Duca d'Aosta

Stazione Centrale

Via Dom Scarlatti

Vitruvio

Via Pasubio

Via Crispi

Largo la Foppa

Moscova

Lima

Piazza Lima

To Hard Disk Café

Via Tunisia

Piazza della Repubblica

Repubblica

Corso Buenos Aires

Piazza VIII Novembre

Piazza Sempione

Via Moscova

Turati

Viale Vittorio Veneto

Parco Sempione

Porta Venezia

Piazza G Oberdan

Lanza

Via Fatebenefratelli

Piazza Cavour

Palestro

Castello Sforzesco

Giardini Pubblici

Via Borgospesso

Cadorna

Stazione Nord

Cairoli

Monte Napoleone

Piazzale Cadorna

Monte Napoleone

San Babila

Piazza della Scala

Piazza San Babila

Corso Magenta

To Cenacolo Vinciano & Chiesa Santa Maria delle Grazie

Piazza del Duomo

Duomo

Largo Augusto

Sant' Agostino

Piazza Cordusio

Corso Porta Vittoria

Piazza Diaz

Piazza Missori

Missori

Via San Barnaba

Largo Carrobbio

Piazza Resistenza Partigiana

Via M d'Armi

Piazza Card Ferrari

Crocetta

Porta Romana

Navigli

Via S Sofia

Via Quadronno

Corso di Porta Romana

Viale G d'Annunzio

Piazzale XXIV Maggio

Viale Galeazzo

Viale B d'Este

Porta Romana

Ripa Ticinese

Via Tibaldi

Via Liguria

PLACES TO STAY
4 Hotel Italia
6 Albergo Salerno
8 Hotel Due Giardini
9 Hotel Verona
11 Hotel Nettuno
13 Hotel Kennedy;
   Hotel San Tomaso
16 Euro Hotel
21 Albergo Commercio
28 Hotel Nuovo
32 Hotel Speronari

PLACES TO EAT
3 Brek
5 Supermarket
7 Pattini & Marinoni
12 Supermarket
14 Ciao
23 Ciao
25 Luini
26 Ristorante Di Gennaro
27 Ciao
31 Peck Delicatessen
33 Pizzeria Dogana
34 Ciao
38 Berlin Caffè

OTHER
1 Boomerang
2 Tourist Office;
   Telecom Telephones &
   Money Exchange Office
10 Atomic
15 Laundromat
17 Questura (Police Station)
18 Piazza San Marco
19 Palazzo di Brera
20 American Express
22 American Bookstore
24 La Scala Opera House
29 Galleria Vittorio Emanuele II
   (Tourist Office;
   Telecom Telephones)
30 Post Office
35 Tourist Office
36 Underground Parking
37 Hospital

ITALY

L60,000/90,000; the entrance is around the corner on Via delle Erbe. In a great location near Piazza del Duomo, *Hotel Speronari* (☎ *86 46 11 25, Via Speronari 4*) has comfortable rooms for L75,000/110,000. *Hotel Nuovo* (☎ *86 46 05 42, Piazza Beccaria 6*) is also in the thick of things, just off Corso Vittorio Emanuele II and the Duomo. Rooms are L60,000/80,000.

Places to Eat

Around Stazione Centrale There's a reasonable *supermarket* inside the station, as well as those close by at Via D Vitruvio 32 and on the corner of Via Lecco and F Casati.

Ciao (Corso Buenos Aires 7) is part of a chain (there are others on Corso Europa and at Via Dante 5), but the food is pretty good and relatively cheap. Pizza and pasta cost from L5000 and salads start at L4500. The *Brek* chain is similar.

Pattini & Marinoni (Corso Buenos Aires 55) sells breads, sandwiches and pizza by the slice; there's another outlet at Via Solferino 5.

City Centre *Ristorante Di Gennaro (Via S Radegonda 14)* serves up excellent pizza and focaccia. *Pizzeria Dogana*, on the corner of Via Capellari and Via Dogana, has outside tables and serves pastas and pizzas from L10,000.

One of Milan's oldest fast-food outlets is *Luini (Via S Radegonda 16)*, just off Piazza del Duomo. It sells *panzerotti* (a savoury turnover made with pizza dough) stuffed with tomatoes, garlic and mozzarella for around L4000. The best gourmet takeaway is the *Peck* delicatessen. Its *rosticceria* is at Via Cesare Cantù 3, where you can buy cooked meats and vegetables. Another outlet is at Via Spadari 7-9 (near the Duomo).

Berlin Caffè (Via G Mora 7) is a good choice for a coffee or wine, and has a small wholefood menu.

Piazza San Marco is *the* place to be, especially in summer.

Entertainment

Music, theatre and cinema dominate Milan's entertainment calendar. The opera season at *La Scala* opens on 7 December. For tickets go to the box office (☎ *72 00 37 44*) in the portico in Via Filodrammatici, open noon to 6 pm daily.

Milan has a reasonable selection of bars, from the disco-pubs and wine bars surrounding Piazza San Marco to pricey bars such as *Atomic (Via Casati 24)*.

For football fans a visit to Stadio Olympico Meazza (San Siro) is a must, with AC Milan and Inter Milan drawing crowds of up to 85,000. Ticket prices start at around L25,000, and can be bought at branches of Cariplo (AC Milan) and Banca Popolare di Milano (Inter) banks.

Getting There & Away

Bus stations are scattered throughout the city, though some companies use Piazza Castello as a terminal. Check with the APT for routes and fares.

From Stazione Centrale there are frequent trains to Venice, Florence, Bologna, Genoa, Turin and Rome, as well as to major cities throughout Europe. Call ☎ 147 88 80 88 for timetable information or visit the busy office in Stazione Centrale. Regional trains stop at Stazione Porta Garibaldi and Stazione Nord, on the MM2 line.

Getting Around

Milan's public transport system is extremely efficient, with underground (MM), tram and bus services. Tickets are L1500, valid for one underground ride or 75 minutes on buses and trams.

Taxis won't stop if you hail them in the street – head for the taxi ranks or call Radiotaxidata (☎ 53 53) or Autoradiotaxi (☎ 85 85).

MANTUA
☎ 0376

Legend, perpetuated by Virgil (who was born in a nearby village in AD 70) and Dante, claims that Mantua (Mantova) was founded by the soothsayer Manto, daughter of Tiresias. From the 14th to the 18th century the city was ruled by the Gonzaga family, who embellished the town with palaces decorated by artists such as Mantegna and Pisanello. You can easily visit the city on a day trip from Milan, Verona or Bologna.

Information

The APT office (☎ 32 82 53), Piazza Andrea Mantegna 6, is a 10-minute walk from the train station along Corso Vittorio Emanuele. It's open 8.30 am to 12.30 pm

ITALY

and 3 to 6 pm Monday to Saturday, and 9.30 am to 12.30 pm on Sunday.

Things to See
Piazza Sordello is surrounded by some impressive buildings, including the cattedrale, an eclectic structure which combines a Romanesque tower, baroque facade and Renaissance interior. The piazza itself is dominated by the massive Palazzo Ducale, former seat of the Gonzaga family. There is much to see in the palace, in particular the Gonzaga apartments and art collection, and the famous Camera degli Sposi (Bridal Chamber) with frescoes by Andrea Mantegna. The palace is open 9 am to 6 pm Tuesday to Sunday (L12,000).

Don't miss Palazzo Tè, the Gonzaga's lavishly decorated summer palace. It is open 9 am to 5.30 pm Tuesday to Sunday (L12,000).

Places to Stay
There are camp sites 2km from Mantua at Corte Chiara (☎ 39 08 04) and 7km from town at Sacchini (☎ 44 87 63), priced at around L20,000 per person. In Mantua, Albergo ABC (☎ 32 33 47, Piazza Don Leoni 25) has singles/doubles with bathroom and breakfast for L100,000/140,000.

Getting There & Away
Mantua is accessible by train and bus from Verona (40 minutes), and by train from Milan and Bologna (with a change at Modena).

VERONA
☎ 045
Forever associated with Romeo and Juliet, Verona has much more to offer than the relics of a tragic love story. Verona's golden era was during the 13th and 14th centuries, under the rule of the della Scala (also referred to as the Scaligeri) family. The period was noted for the savage family feuding on which Shakespeare based his play.

Orientation & Information
Buses leave for the historical centre from outside the train station; otherwise it's a 20-minute walk, heading right from the bus station, crossing the river and walking along Corso Porta Nuova to Piazza Brà. From there take Via Mazzini and turn left at Via Cappello to reach Piazza delle Erbe.

The main tourist office (☎ 806 86 80), at Via degli Alpina 9, facing Piazza Brà ☎, is open 9 am to 6 pm Monday to Saturday (to 8 pm in summer). There's a branch at the train station. The main post office is on Piazza Viviani.

Things to See & Do
Piazza Brà's Roman amphitheatre, known as the Arena, was built in the 1st century and is now Verona's opera house.

Walk along Via Mazzini to Via Cappello and Juliet's House (Casa di Giulietta), its entrance smothered with lovers' graffiti. Farther along the street to the right is Porta Leoni, one of the gates to the old Roman Verona; Porta Borsari, the other city gate, is north of the Arena at Corso Porta Borsari.

Piazza delle Erbe, the city's lively centre, is lined with Verona's characteristic pink marble palaces and filled with market stalls. Just off the square is the elegant Piazza dei Signori, flanked by the medieval town hall, the Renaissance Loggia del Consiglio and the della Scala (Scaligeri) residence, partly decorated by Giotto and nowadays known as the Governor's Palace. Take a look at the Duomo, on Via Duomo, for its Romanesque main doors and Titian's glorious Assumption.

Places to Stay
The HI Ostello Villa Francescatti (☎ 59 03 60, Salita Fontana del Ferro 15) has B&B for L22,000 (including sheets) and dinner for L14,000. An HI or student card is necessary. The hostel runs the adjacent camping ground, where it costs L10,000 per person. Take bus No 73 from the station to Piazza Isolo and follow the signs.

Casa della Giovane (☎ 59 68 80, Via Pigna 7), just off Via Garibaldi, is for women only and costs L23,000 a night for a bed in a small dormitory. Doubles are L26,000. Catch bus No 73.

Albergo Castello (☎ 800 44 03, Corso Cavour 43) has singles/doubles for L75,000/110,000. Albergo Ciopeta (☎ 800 68 43, Vicolo Teatro Filarmonico 2), near Piazza Brà, charges L80,000/130,000.

Places to Eat
Boiled meats are a local speciality, as is the crisp Soave white wine.

Both the Castello and Ciopeta Hotels have well-priced restaurants. Pizzeria Liston (Via

Pietro Liston 19) has good pizzas from L11,000. *Brek* in Piazza Brà has a view of the Arena and the usual cheap dishes from L8000.

Entertainment
Opera is performed from July to September at the *Arena*, with tickets starting at L40,000. There is a lyric-symphonic season in winter at the 18th-century *Teatro Filarmonico* (☎ *800 28 80, Via dei Mutilati 4)*, just off Piazza Brà. Information is available from the Fondazione Arena di Verona (☎ 805 18 11), Piazza Brà 28.

Getting There & Away
The main APT bus terminal is in front of the train station, an area known as Porta Nuova. Buses leave for surrounding areas, including Mantua, Ferrara and Brescia.

Verona is on the Brenner Pass railway line to Austria and Germany, and is directly linked by train to Milan, Venice, Florence and Rome.

PADUA
☎ 049
Although famous as the city of St Anthony and for its university, which is one of the oldest in Europe, Padua (Padova) is often seen as a convenient and cheap place to stay while visiting Venice. In fact the city offers a rich collection of art treasures, and its many piazzas and porticoed streets are a stress-free pleasure to explore.

Orientation & Information
From the train station it's a 15-minute walk to the centre of town; or take bus No 3 or 8 along Corso del Popolo.

The tourist office at the train station is open 9.15 am to 6.30 pm Monday to Saturday (to noon on Sunday). The post office is at Corso Garibaldi 33, and there's a telephone office next door.

Things to See
Thousands of pilgrims come to Padua every year to visit the **Basilica del Santo**, in the hope that St Anthony, patron saint of Padua and of lost things, will help them find what they're looking for. The church houses the saint's tomb along with important artworks, including 14th-century frescoes and bronze sculptures by Donatello. A bronze equestrian

statue, known as the *Gattamelata* (Honeyed Cat), also by Donatello, is outside.

The **Musei Civici agli Eremitani** and adjoining **Cappella degli Scrovegni** are at Piazza Eremitani 8. The chapel's emotionally charged frescoes depicting the life of Christ were painted by Giotto between 1303 and 1305. The transcendent 38 panels are considered one of the world's greatest works of figurative art. The museum and chapel are open 9 am to 7 pm (to 6 pm in winter) Tuesday to Sunday. It's advisable to book in summer.

A combined L15,000 ticket (L10,000 for students) allows entry to the city's monuments and can be bought at any of the main sights.

Places to Stay
The non-HI *Ostello della Città di Padova* (☎ *875 22 19, Via A Aleardi 30)* has B&B for L23,000. Take bus No 3, 8 or 12 from the train station to Prato della Valle (a piazza about five minutes away) and then ask for directions.

Verdi (☎ *875 57 44, Via Dondi dell' Orologio 7)*, in the university district off Via Verdi, has basic clean singles/doubles for L40,000/64,000. The two-star *Sant'Antonio* (☎ *875 13 93, Via Santo Fermo 118)*, near the river and the northern end of Via Dante, has comfortable rooms for L60,000/90,000.

Places to Eat
Grab a sandwich at *Dalla Zita (Via Gorizia 16)*, off Piazza Pedrocchi. *Birroteca da Mario (Via Breda 3)*, off Piazza della Frutta, is a good choice for panini and pizza. *Trattoria al Pero (Via Santa Lucia 72)*, near Piazza dei Signori, serves regional dishes for around L15,000. Daily food *markets* are held in Piazza delle Erbe and Piazza della Frutta.

Getting There & Away
Padua is linked by train to Milan, Venice and Bologna, and is easily accessible from most major Italian cities. Regular buses serve Venice, Milan, Trieste and surrounding towns. The terminal is in Piazzale Boschetti, off Via Trieste, near the train station.

VENICE
☎ 041
Perhaps no other city in the world has inspired the superlatives heaped upon Venice

(Venezia) through the centuries. It was, and remains, a phenomenon – La Serenissima (the Most Serene Republic). The secret to discovering its romance and beauty is to *walk*. Parts of Dorsoduro and Castello see few tourists even in the high season (July to September), and it's easy to lose yourself for hours in the narrow winding streets between the Accademia and the train station.

The islands of the lagoon were first settled during the barbarian invasions of the 5th and 6th centuries AD, when the people of the Veneto sought refuge in the marshy region, gradually building the unique city on a raft of wooden posts driven into the subsoil. The waters that today threaten the city's existence once protected it from its enemies. Following years of Byzantine rule, Venice evolved into a republic ruled by a succession of *doges* (chief magistrates). This period of independence lasted 1000 years, the city eventually growing in power to dominate half the Mediterranean, the Adriatic and the trade routes to the Levant. It was from here that Marco Polo set out on his voyage to China.

Today Venice is increasingly being left to the tourists, as regular floods (caused by high tides) and soaring property values make it impractical as a place of residence. Most of the 'locals' live in industrial Mestre, which is linked to the city by a 4km-long bridge.

Orientation

Venice is built on 117 small islands and has some 150 canals and 400 bridges. Only three bridges cross the Grand Canal: the Rialto, the Accademia and, at the train station, the Scalzi.

The city is divided into six *sestieri* (sections): Cannaregio, Castello, San Marco, Dorsoduro, San Polo and Santa Croce. Streets are called *calle*, *ruga* or *salizzada*; side streets can be called *caletta* or *ramo*. A street beside a canal is a *fondamenta*, a canal is a *rio* and a quay a *riva*. The only square in Venice called a piazza is San Marco – all the others are called *campo*.

There are no cars in the city and all public transport is via the canals on *vaporetti* (passenger boats). To cross the Grand Canal between the bridges, use the cheaper *traghetto* (public gondolas).

It's worth buying the street-referenced *Venezia* map published by FMB, as the free

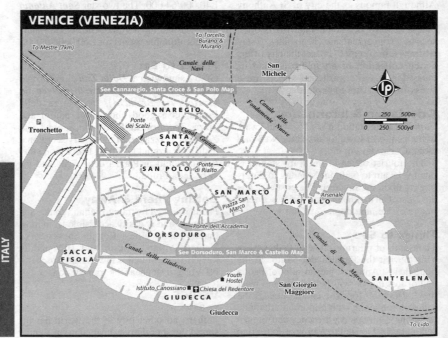

tourist office map provides only a vague guide to the complicated network of streets.

Information

Tourist Offices Venice has three APT tourist office branches: at the train station (☎ 529 87 27), open 8 am to 7 pm daily; at Piazza San Marco 71F (☎ 520 89 64), open 9.30 am to 3.30 pm daily; and the Venice Pavilion (☎ 522 63 56), on the waterfront next to the Giardini Ex Reali (turn right from San Marco), open 10 am to 6 pm daily. Hours can vary a little seasonally.

People aged between 14 and 29 can buy a Rolling Venice card (L5000), which offers significant discounts on food, accommodation and museum fees. It's available July to September from tourist offices; at other times private offices distribute the cards.

Money Most of the main banks have branches around the Rialto and San Marco. American Express on Salizzada San Moisé changes money without charging commission. It's open 9 am to 5.30 pm weekdays and to 12.30 pm at weekends. Thomas Cook, on Piazza San Marco, is open 9.10 am to 7.45 pm Monday to Saturday (to 5 pm on Sunday).

Post & Communications The main post office is on Salizzada del Fontego dei Tedeschi, near the Ponte di Rialto (Rialto Bridge). Buy stamps at window No 9 or 10 in the central courtyard. There are several Telecom Italia offices in the city, including those at the post office, near the Rialto and on Strada Nova.

Email & Internet Access Nethouse (☎ 277 11 90), at Campo Santo Stefano 2967-2958, is open from 9 am to 2 am daily, with 60 screens, printing, fax and helpful staff. Rates are L4500 for 15 minutes and L18,000 per hour. The smaller and less frenetic Puntonet, at Campo Santa Margherita 3002, charges L10,000 per hour, and L3000 for 15 minutes.

Bookshops There is a good selection of English-language guidebooks and general books on Venice in the bookshop just over the bridge at Calle de la Cortesia 3717d, and at Studium, behind the basilica on the corner of Calle de la Canonica, on the way from San Marco to Castello.

Things to See & Do

For an overview, catch the No 1 vaporetto along the Grand Canal and then go for a long walk. Start at **San Marco** and either delve into the tiny lanes of tranquil **Castello** or head for the Accademia Bridge to reach the narrow streets and squares of **Dorsoduro** and **San Polo**.

Remember that most museums are closed on Monday.

Piazza & Basilica di San Marco One of the most famous squares in the world, Piazza San Marco is enclosed by the basilica and the arcades of the Procuratie Vecchie, Procuratie Nuove and Libreria Sansoviniana (home to the Museo Correr, Biblioteca Marciana and Museo Archeologico). The piazza hosts flocks of pigeons and tourists, both competing for space in the high season. Stand and wait for the famous bronze *mori* (Moors) to strike the bell of the Law Courts' 15th-century **Torre dell'Orologio** (clock tower).

The basilica, with its elaborately decorated facade, was built to house the body of St Mark, which had been stolen from its burial place in Egypt by two Venetian merchants. The saint has been reburied several times in the basilica (at least twice the burial place was forgotten) and his body now lies under the high altar. The present basilica was built in the Byzantine style in the 11th century and richly decorated with magnificent mosaics over the next five centuries. The famous bronze horses (part of Venice's booty from the Sack of Constantinople in 1204) prancing above the entrance are replicas of the originals displayed in the basilica's **museum** (L3000). Don't miss the flashy **Pala d'Oro** (L3000), a gold altarpiece decorated with silver, enamel and precious stones; it's behind the basilica's altar.

The basilica's 99m freestanding **bell tower** was built in the 10th century, but suddenly collapsed on 14 July 1902 and was later rebuilt. It costs L8000 to get to the top.

Palazzo Ducale The official residence of the doges and seat of the republic's government was built in the 9th century, and later expanded and remodelled. The palace's **Sala del Maggior Consiglio** has paintings by Tintoretto and Veronese. The palace is open 9 am to 7 pm daily (last entry at 5.30

ITALY

pm). Admission is L18,000 and the same ticket covers entry to the nearby Museo Correr, Biblioteca Marciana and Museo Archeologico, as well as the Palazzo Mocenigo (San Stae area), and Burano and Murano Museums.

The **Bridge of Sighs** (Ponte dei Sospiri) connects the Palazzo Ducale to Venice's old prisons. The bridge evokes romantic images, probably because of its association with Casanova, a native of Venice who was incarcerated in the prisons. It was, however, the thoroughfare for prisoners being led to the dungeons.

Galleria dell'Accademia The Academy of Fine Arts contains Italy's most important collection of Venetian art, including works by Tintoretto, Titian and Veronese. It is open 9 am to 7 pm Tuesday to Saturday, to 8 pm on Sunday and to 2 pm Monday (L12,000).

For a change of pace visit the nearby **Collezione Peggy Guggenheim**, a modern art collection displayed in the former home of the American heiress. The palazzo is set in a sculpture garden where Miss Guggenheim and her many pet dogs are buried. It is open 10 am to 6 pm Wednesday to Monday (L12,000).

Churches The **Chiesa del Redentore** (Church of the Redeemer) on Giudecca Island was built in the 16th century by the architect Palladio, and is the scene of the annual Festa del Redentore (see the Special Events section). The **Chiesa di Santa Maria della Salute** was built at the entrance to the Grand Canal and dedicated to the Madonna after a plague in the 17th century. It contains works by Tintoretto and Titian. Also be sure to visit the Gothic churches **SS Giovanni e Paolo** and the **Frari**.

Entry to each church is L3000, or buy the Chorus Pass (L15,000) which gains entry to 13 churches.

The Lido Easily accessible by vaporetto Nos 1, 6, 14 and 61, this thin strip of land east of the centre separates Venice from the Adriatic. Once a fashionable beach resort, it is still very popular and thoroughly crowded in summer.

Islands The island of **Murano** is the home of Venetian glass. Visit the Glassworks

Museum to see the evolution of the famous glassware. Despite the constant influx of tourists, **Burano** is a relatively sleepy fishing village, renowned for its lace. Visit tiny **Torcello** to see the Byzantine mosaics in its cathedral, notably the exquisite mosaic of the Madonna in the apse.

Excursion boats leave for the three islands from San Marco (L30,000 return). If you want to go it alone, vaporetto No 12 goes to all three from Fondamenta Nuove (L6000 one way).

Gondola Rides These might represent the quintessential romantic Venice, but at around L120,000 (L150,000 after 8 pm) for a 50-minute ride they are expensive. It is possible to squeeze up to six people into one gondola and still pay the same price.

Special Events

Venice's major event is Carnevale, held during the 10 days before Ash Wednesday, when Venetians don spectacular masks and costumes for what is literally a 10-day street party.

The Venice Biennale, a major exhibition of international visual arts, is held every odd-numbered year, and the Venice International Film Festival is held every September at the Palazzo del Cinema, on the Lido.

Festa del Redentore (Festival of the Redeemer), on the third weekend in July, features a spectacular fireworks display. The Regatta Storica, a gondola race on the Grand Canal, is held on the first Sunday in September.

Places to Stay

There's no denying that Venice is expensive. The average cost of a basic single/double (without bath) in a one-star hotel is L90,000/120,000. Hotel proprietors may charge extra for a compulsory breakfast. Prices skyrocket in peak periods (Christmas, Carnevale, Easter), but can drop dramatically at other times of the year. Prices quoted here are high season.

Book ahead whenever possible and, since street numbers in Venice are confusing, ring when you arrive to ask for specific directions.

Camping There are numerous camping grounds, many with bungalows, at Litorale del Cavallino, north-east of the city. The tourist office has a full list, or try *Marina di Venezia (☎ 530 09 55, ✆ camping@marinave.it, Via Montello 6 at Punta Sabbioni)*, open from April to September.

Hostels The HI *Ostello Venezia (☎ 523 82 11, fax 523 56 89, Fondamenta delle Zitelle 86)* is on the island of Giudecca. It is open to HI members only, though you can buy a card there. B&B is L27,000 and meals are L14,000. From the train station take vaporetto No 82 (L6000 one way) and get off at Zitelle. Curfew is 11.30 pm. *Istituto Canossiano (☎/fax 522 21 57, Ponte Piccolo 428)* is nearby, and has dorm beds for women only at L23,000 per night. Take vaporetto No 82 and get off at Palanca.

Foresteria Valdese (☎/fax 528 67 97, Castello 5170) has dorm beds for L30,000 and doubles from L85,000 per night. Follow Calle Lunga from Campo Santa Maria Formosa. *Ostello Santa Fosca (☎ 71 57 75, ✆ cpu@iuav.unive.it, Cannaregio 2372)*, less than 15 minutes from the station through Campo Santa Fosca, has dorm beds for L30,000; check-in is 4 to 7 pm.

Hotels – Cannaregio The two-star *Edelweiss Stella Alpina (☎ 71 51 79, Calle Priuli detta dei Cavalletti 99d)*, near the station in the first street on the left after the Scalzi church, has decent singles/doubles for L110,000/160,000.

In the next street on the left, *Hotel Santa Lucia (☎ 71 51 80, Calle della Misericordia 358)* has singles for L80,000 and doubles with shower and breakfast for L170,000. In the same street, the friendly *Hotel Villa Rosa (☎ 71 89 76, Calle della Misericordia 389)* has pleasant, well-furnished singles/doubles/triples/quads with bathroom, breakfast and TV for L130,000/190,000/240,000/280,000.

Albergo Adua (☎ 71 61 84, Lista di Spagna 233a) has clean singles/doubles with shower for L130,000/200,000. The adjacent *Hotel Minerva (☎ 71 59 68, Lista di Spagna 230)* has modest rooms for L70,000/95,000.

Hotel Rossi (☎ 71 51 64) is just off Lista di Spagna (via a Gothic archway) at the end of tiny Calle de le Procuratie. Singles/doubles/triples/quads with bathroom and bare essentials are L100,000/160,000/195,000/230,000. In the same street, the two-star

Hotel Guerrini (☎ 71 53 33) has comfortable singles/doubles without bathroom for L80,000/160,000.

Around the corner *Casa Gerotto (☎ 71 53 61, Campo San Geremia 283)* and the neighbouring *Alloggi Calderan* together offer singles/doubles in a hostel atmosphere for around L110,000/140,000. *Al Gobbo (☎ 71 50 01, Campo San Geremia 312)* has sparkling-clean rooms with bathroom and breakfast for L120,000/150,000.

Hotels – San Marco The *Hotel Noemi (☎ 523 81 44, Calle dei Fabbri 909)* is only a few steps from Piazza San Marco and has basic rooms for L90,000/130,000. *Locanda Casa Petrarca (☎ 520 04 30, San Marco 4394)* is one of the area's nicest cheap hotels, with rooms for L75,000/140,000.

Hotel ai Do Mori (☎ 520 48 17, Calle Larga San Marco 658) is just off Piazza San Marco. It has pleasant rooms, some with views of the basilica, for L120,000/150,000.

Hotels – Castello *Locanda Silva (☎ 522 76 43, Fondamenta del Rimedio 4423)*, off Campo Santa Maria Formosa, has basic rooms for L70,000/110,000. Next door, *Locanda Canal (☎ 523 45 38)* has better doubles with bathroom for L160,000. *Hotel Doni (☎ 522 42 67, Fondamenta del Vin 4656)*, off Salizzada San Provolo, has clean, quiet rooms for L75,000/95,000.

Hotels – Dorsoduro, San Polo & Santa Croce This is the most authentic area of Venice, in which you can still find the atmosphere of a living city.

Hotel Al Gallo (☎ 523 67 61, Corte dei Amai 197g), off Fondamenta Tolentini, has excellent doubles with shower for L115,000. *Albergo Casa Peron (☎ 71 00 21, Salizzada San Pantalon 84)* has clean rooms with shower for L100,000/150,000, including breakfast. To get there from the station, cross Ponte dei Scalzi and follow the signs to San Marco and Rialto until you reach Rio delle Muneghette, then cross the wooden bridge.

Hotel Dalla Mora (☎ 71 07 03) is on a lovely small canal just off Salizzada San Pantalon, near the Casa Peron. It has airy singles/doubles/triples/quads with bathroom for L95,000/150,000/190,000/230,000. Bookings are a must.

ITALY

CANNAREGIO, SANTA CROCE & SAN POLO

Albergo Antico Capon (☎ *528 52 92, Campo Santa Margherita 3004b),* is on one of the nicest squares in Venice, and has rooms with bathroom for L120,000/150,000.

Elegant *Hotel Galleria* (☎ *523 24 89,* ℮ *galleria@tin.it, Dorsoduro 878a)* has rooms in a 17th-century palace facing the Grand Canal at Ponte dell'Accademia. This must be the last affordable hotel on the Grand Canal, though you'll have to put up with some canal traffic noise. Rooms are L100,00/150,000.

Hotels – Mestre Only 15 minutes from Venice by bus or train, Mestre makes a cheap if somewhat drab alternative to staying in Venice. The two-star *Albergo Roberta* (☎ *92 93 55, Via Sernaglia 21)* has

large, clean rooms for L90,000/130,000. The one-star *Albergo Giovannina* (☎ *92 63 96, Via Dante 113)* has decent singles for L50,000 and doubles with bathroom for L90,000.

Places to Eat

Many bars serve a wide range of Venetian panini and *tramezzini* (sandwiches) for L2500 to L5000 if you eat them while standing at the bar. The staples of the Veneto region's cuisine are rice and beans. Try the *risi e bisi* (risotto with peas), followed by a glass of *fragolino*, the Veneto's fragrant strawberry wine.

For fruit and vegetables, as well as delicatessens, head for the *market* in the streets on the San Polo side of the Rialto Bridge.

CANNAREGIO, SANTA CROCE & SAN POLO

PLACES TO STAY
4 Hotel Edelweiss
    Stella Alpina
5 Hotel Villa Rosa
6 Hotel Santa Lucia
7 Albergo Adua
8 Hotel Minerva
9 Hotel Rossi
11 Hotel Guerrini
12 Casa Gerotto &
    Alloggi Calderan
13 Hotel Al Gobbo
16 Ostello Santa Fosca

PLACES TO EAT
14 Trattoria
    alla Palazzina
15 Pizzeria all'Anfora
17 Paradiso Perduto
19 Standa Supermarket
20 Cantina do Mori
21 Osteria del Bomba

OTHER
1 Intercity Bus Station
2 Tourist Office
3 Ponte dei Scalzi
10 Park & Playground
18 Iguana
22 Ospedale Civile

There's a **Standa** supermarket on Strada Nova and a **Mega 1** supermarket just off Campo Santa Margherita.

The best gelati in Venice is said to be sold at **Gelati Nico** (*Fondamenta Zattere 922*). **Il Doge**, on Campo Santa Margherita, also has excellent ice cream.

Cannaregio *Trattoria alla Palazzina* (*Cannaregio 1509*) is near the station, just over the first bridge after Campo San Geremia, with a garden at the rear and tasty if pricey pizzas (L13,000 to L20,000). *Osteria del Bomba* (*Calle de l'Oca 4297*), near Campo dei Santi Apostoli, has pasta from L8000 and excellent bar snacks. Popular *Paradiso Perduto* (*Fondamenta della Misericordia 2539a*) is a lively restaurant-bar.

San Marco & Castello For cheap panini try *Al Vecio Penasa* (*Calle delle Rasse 4587*). *Cip Ciap*, just over the Ponte del Mondo Novo, serves filling pizza by the slice (L3000 to L5000). In Campo Santa Margherita student favourite *Bar DuChamp*, has panini for around L6000 and you can sit outside at no extra charge. *Vino Vino* (*San Marco 2007*) is a popular bar-osteria at Ponte Veste, near Teatro La Fenice. The menu changes daily, with mains usually around L15,000. *Antica Carbonera*, in Calle Bembo (a continuation of Calle dei Fabbri), is an authentic old trattoria with pasta from L13,000 and a full meal for around L60,000.

Dorsoduro, San Polo & Santa Croce A good-value pizzeria/trattoria is *Da Silvio*

ITALY

DORSODURO, SAN MARCO & CASTELLO

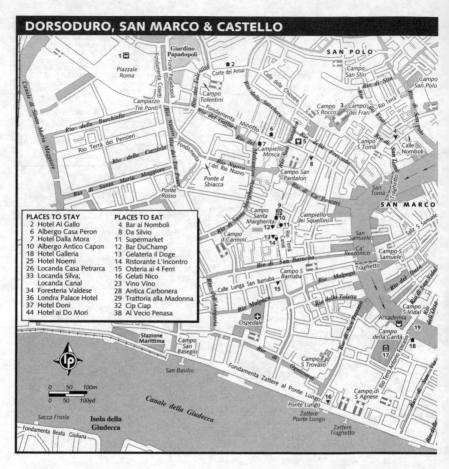

PLACES TO STAY
2 Hotel Al Gallo
6 Albergo Casa Peron
7 Hotel Dalla Mora
10 Albergo Antico Capon
18 Hotel Galleria
25 Hotel Noemi
26 Locanda Casa Petrarca
33 Locanda Silva;
    Locanda Canal
34 Foresteria Valdese
36 Londra Palace Hotel
37 Hotel Doni
44 Hotel ai Do Mori

PLACES TO EAT
4 Bar ai Nomboli
8 Da Silvio
11 Supermarket
12 Bar DuChamp
13 Gelateria il Doge
14 Ristorante L'Incontro
15 Osteria ai 4 Ferri
16 Gelati Nico
23 Vino Vino
28 Antica Carbonera
29 Trattoria alla Madonna
32 Cip Ciap
38 Al Vecio Penasa

(Crosera San Pantalon 3817) with a garden and outside tables. ***Bar ai Nomboli***, on the corner of Calle dei Nomboli and Rio Terrà dei Nomboli, has a great selection of gourmet sandwiches.

Pizzeria all'Anfora (Lista dei Bari 1223), across the Scalzi Bridge from the train station, has pizzas for L7500 to L14,000. ***L'Incontro** (Rio Terrà Canal 3062a)* serves excellent food, with full meals around L45,000.

Cantina do Mori, on Sottoportego dei do Mori, off Ruga Rialto, is a small, popular wine bar that also serves sandwiches. ***Trattoria alla Madonna***, Calle della Madonna, two streets west of the Rialto, is an excellent trattoria specialising in seafood. A full meal could cost up to L60,000, but it would be worth the splurge.

For authentic Venetian *ombra* and *cichetti* (a glass of wine served with bar snacks) try ***Osteria ai 4 Ferri***, in Calle Lunga San Barnaba off Campo San Barnaba.

Entertainment

The free weekly booklet *Un Ospite di Venezia*, available at hotels and tourist offices, has entertainment listings. Venice lost its opera house, the magnificent Teatro La Fenice, to a fire in January 1996. Reconstruction is slowly under way, and in the interim performances are held at PalaFelice (☎ 521 01 61), a tentlike structure on the car-park island of Tronchetto.

In Cannaregio, ***Paradiso Perduto*** (see Places to Eat) has live music and outdoor tables. A few doors up, ***Iguana** (Fonda-*

DORSODURO, SAN MARCO & CASTELLO

OTHER

1 Intercity Bus Station
3 Frari
5 Cafe Blue
9 Puntonet
17 Galleria dell'Accademia
19 Ponte dell'Accademia
20 Nethouse
21 Collezione Peggy Guggenheim
22 Chiesa di Santa Maria della Salute
24 American Express
27 Bookshop
30 Ponte di Rialto
31 Main Post Office & Telecom Telephones
35 Questura (Police Station)
39 Bridge of Sighs
40 Palazzo Ducale
41 Basilica di San Marco
42 Studium Bookshop
43 Torre dell'Orologio (Clock Tower)
45 Thomas Cook Exchange Office
46 Procuratie Vecchie
47 Tourist Office
48 Procuratie Nuove
49 Bell Tower
50 Libreria Sansoviniana
51 Tourist Office

menta della Misericordia 2515) pumps out live and loud Latino music, and serves Mexican food. In Dorsoduro, there's *Café Blue (Salizzada San Pantalon 3778)*, a pub-like drinking den near trendy Campo Santa Margherita.

Getting There & Away
Bus ACTV buses (☎ 528 78 86) leave from Piazzale Roma for surrounding areas, including Mestre, Chioggia, Padua and beyond. Tickets and information are available at the office in the piazza.

Train The Stazione Santa Lucia (☎ 147 88 80 88), known in Venice as the *ferrovia*, has services to Padua, Verona, Trieste, Milan and Bologna, and is easily accessible from

Florence and Rome. You can also leave from Venice for major points in Germany, Austria and the former Yugoslavia.

Boat Minoan Lines (☎ 271 23 45), at Porto Venezia, Zona Santa Marta, runs ferries to Greece year-round.

Getting Around
From Piazzale Roma, vaporetto No 1 zigzags its way along the Grand Canal to San Marco and then to the Lido. There is the faster No 82 if you're in a hurry. The No 12 vaporetto leaves from Fondamenta Nuove for the islands of Murano, Burano and Torcello. A full timetable is available at the tourist office. Vaporetto tickets cost L6000 (plus L6000 for luggage). A 24-hour

ticket is L18,000, and a 72-hour ticket L35,000.

Water taxis are exorbitant, with a set charge of L27,000 for a maximum of seven minutes, then L500 per 15 seconds.

FERRARA
☎ 0532

Ferrara was the seat of the Este dukes from the 13th century to the end of the 16th century. The city still retains much of the austere splendour of its heyday – its streets are lined with graceful palaces and in its centre is the Castello Estense, surrounded by a moat.

Information
The tourist office (☎ 20 93 70, @ infotur .comfe@fe.nettuno.it) inside the Castello Estense is open 9 am to 1 pm and 2 to 6 pm daily.

Things to See
The historical centre is small, encompassing medieval Ferrara to the south of the **Castello Estense**, and the area to the north. The castle houses government offices, but certain areas are open to the public.

The beautiful Romanesque-Gothic **Duomo** has an unusual triple facade of pink and white marble, and houses important works of art in its museum. The Renaissance Palazzo dei Diamanti, along Corso Ercole I d'Este, is home to the **Pinacoteca Nazionale** gallery (L8000; closed Monday).

The 14th-century **Palazzo Schifanoia**, at Via Scandiana 23, another of the Este palaces, houses a civic museum and features the city's finest Renaissance frescoes. It's open 9 am to 7 pm daily (L8000).

Places to Stay
Albergo Centro Storico (☎ 20 33 74, *Via Vegri 15*) is central but basic, with singles/ doubles for L40,000/60,000. South of the cathedral, *Pensione Artisti* (☎ 76 10 38, *Via Vittoria 66*) has singles for L30,000 and doubles without/with bathroom for L60,000/85,000. Better singles/doubles are available at the two-star *Albergo Nazionale* (☎ 20 96 04, *Corso Porta Reno 32*) for L80,000/120,000 with bathroom.

Getting There & Away
Ferrara is on the Bologna-Venice train line, with frequent services to both cities. It's 40 minutes to Bologna and 1½ hours to Venice. Trains also run directly to Ravenna.

Buses run from the train station to Modena.

BOLOGNA
☎ 051

Elegant, intellectual and wealthy, Bologna stands out among Italy's many beautiful cities. The regional capital of Emilia-Romagna, it is famous for its porticoes (arcaded streets), its harmonious architecture, its university (the oldest in Europe) and, above all, its gastronomic tradition, having given the world tortellini, lasagne, mortadella and the eponymous spaghetti bolognese.

Information
The IAT office (☎ 23 96 60) at Piazza Maggiore 6, under the portico of the castle, is open 9 am to 7 pm Monday to Saturday and to 2 pm on Sunday. There are branch offices at the train station and the airport. Pick up a map and the useful English-language booklet *A Guest in Bologna*.

The main post office is in Piazza Minghetti. Telecom phones are at Piazza VIII Agosto 24 and the train station.

Things to See
Bologna's beautiful centre is formed by Piazza Maggiore, the adjoining Piazza del Nettuno with its Fontana di Nettuno (Neptune's Fountain), and Piazza Porta Ravegnana, with its two leaning towers to rival that of Pisa.

The **Basilica di San Petronio** in Piazza Maggiore is dedicated to the city's patron saint, and is noted for its artworks and red-and-white marble facade (the colours of Bologna). It was here that Charles V was crowned emperor by the pope in 1530.

The adjacent **Palazzo Comunale** (town hall) is a huge building combining several architectural styles in remarkable harmony. It features a bronze statue of Pope Gregory XIII (a native of Bologna), an impressive winding staircase and Bologna's collection of art treasures.

The **Basilica di Santo Stefano** is a group of four churches (originally there were seven), including the 11th-century Chiesa del Crocefisso which houses the bones of San Petronio. The **Basilica di San Domenico**, erected in the early 16th century, houses the sarcophagus of the founder of

ITALY

the Dominican order and a shrine featuring figures carved by a young Michelangelo.

Places to Stay

Budget hotels in Bologna are virtually nonexistent, and the city's busy trade-fair calendar means that hotels are often heavily booked. The best options are the two HI hostels: *Ostello San Sisto (☎ 51 92 02, Via Viadagola 14)* charges L18,000 with breakfast, while *Ostello Due Torri (☎ 50 18 10, Via Viadagola 5)* charges L21,000. Take bus No 93 or 20b from Via Irnerio, off Via dell'Indipendenza near the station. Ask the driver where to get off and then follow the signs.

Albergo Garisenda (☎ 22 43 69, Galleria del Leone 1) is under the two towers and has decent singles/doubles for L70,000/100,000. *Apollo (☎ 22 39 55, Via Drapperie 5)*, off Via Rizzoli, has singles/doubles for L60,000/95,000 and doubles/triples with bathroom for L130,000/165,000. *Albergo Marconi (☎ 26 28 32, Via G Marconi 22)* has cheap singles/doubles for L55,000/70,000.

Places to Eat

Mercato Ugo Bassi (Via Ugo Bassi 27) is a covered market offering all the local fare. There is also a *market* in the streets southeast of Piazza Maggiore.

Pizzeria Bella Napoli (Via San Felice 40) serves good pizzas at reasonable prices. *Pizzeria Altero (Via Ugo Bassi 10)* has good pizza by the slice for only L1500. The self-service *Due Torri (Via dei Giudei 4)*, under the towers, is excellent value, but is open for lunch only.

Getting There & Around

Bologna's train station on Piazza delle Medaglie d'Oro is a major transport junction for northern Italy. Buses to major cities depart from the terminal on Piazza XX Settembre, around the corner from the train station.

Bus No 25 goes from the train station to the historical centre.

RAVENNA
☎ 0544

Ravenna is best known for its exquisite mosaics, relics of the time it was capital of the Western Roman Empire, stronghold of Theodoric the Great (king of the Ostrogoths) and western seat of the Byzantines.

The town is easily accessible from Bologna and is worth a day trip, at the very least.

The IAT tourist office (☎ 354 04), at Via Salara 8, is open 8.30 am to 6 pm Monday to Saturday and 10 am to 4 pm on Sunday.

Things to See

The pick of Ravenna's mosaics are found in the **Basilica di Sant'Apollinare Nuovo**, the **Basilica di San Vitale**, the **Mausoleo di Galla Placidia** (these are the oldest) and the **Battistero Neoniano**. These buildings are all in the town centre and an admission ticket to the four, as well as to the **Museo Arcivescovile**, costs L10,000. The mosaics in the **Basilica di Sant'Apollinare in Classe**, 5km away, are also notable.

Special Events

Ravenna's music festival, held from late June to early August, features international artists performing in churches and at the open-air Rocca di Brancaleone. An annual theatre and literature festival is held each September in honour of Dante, who spent his last 10 years in Ravenna. In winter, opera and dance are staged at the *Teatro Alighieri*.

Places to Stay & Eat

The HI *Ostello Dante (☎ 42 11 64, Via Aurelio Nicolodi 12)* opens from March to November. Take bus No 1 from Viale Pallavacini (left of the station). B&B is L23,000.

Al Giaciglio (☎ 394 03, Via Rocca Brancaleone 42), the city's sole one-star, has singles/doubles for L45,000/65,000. From the station walk straight ahead on Viale Farini and turn right into Via Rocca Brancaleone. The two-star *Ravenna (☎ 21 22 04, Via Maroncelli 12)*, near the train station, has rooms for L70,000/90,000.

The best bet for a quick meal is the *Bizantino* self-service restaurant in the city's fresh-produce market in Piazza Andrea Costa.

Getting There & Around

Ravenna is accessible by train from Bologna (1½ hours), sometimes with a change at Castel Bolognese.

COOP San Vitale, on Piazza Farini in front of the train station, rents out bikes for L2000/15,000 per hour/day.

ITALY

SAN MARINO
☎ 0549

A few kilometres from Rimini is the ancient Republic of San Marino, an unashamed tourist trap perched on top of Monte Titano (600m). The world's oldest surviving republic, San Marino was formed in AD 300 by a stonemason said to have been escaping religious persecution. The tiny state (only 61 sq km) strikes its own coins and has its own postage stamps and army.

Wander along the city walls and drop in at the two fortresses. San Marino's main attraction is the splendid view of the mountains and coast.

The Ufficio di Stato per il Turismo (☎ 88 29 98) is in the Palazzo del Turismo at Contrada Omagnano 20. San Marino is accessible from Rimini by bus.

The Dolomites

This spectacular limestone mountain range in the Alps stretches across Trentino-Alto Adige into the Veneto. The Dolomites are the Italians' favoured area for skiing, and there are excellent hiking trails.

Information

Information about Trentino-Alto Adige can be obtained in Trent from the APT del Trentino (☎ 0461 83 90 00, ☺ apt@ provincia.tn.it), at Via Romagnosi 3; in Rome (☎ 46 36 09 58 42, fax 46 320 24 13), at Via del Babuino 20; and in Milan (☎ 02 86 46 12 51, fax 02 72 00 21 88), at Piazza Diaz 5. Bolzano's tourist office (☎ 0471 30 70 00, ☺ bolzano@sudtirol.com), Piazza Walther 8, also has information on the region, and there's a telephone information service on ☎ 0471 41 38 08.

The APT Dolomiti at Cortina (☎ 0436 27 11) can provide information on trekking and skiing in the Veneto.

Skiing

The Dolomites' numerous ski resorts range from expensive and fashionable Cortina d'Ampezzo in the Veneto, to family-oriented resorts such as those in the Val Gardena in Trentino-Alto Adige. All the resorts have helpful tourist offices with loads of information on facilities, accommodation and transport.

The high season is from around Christmas to early January, and early February to April, when prices rise considerably. A good way to save money is to buy a *settimana bianca* (literally 'white week' – a package-deal ski holiday) through travel agencies in Italy.

If you want to go it alone, but plan to do a lot of skiing, invest in a ski pass, valid for unlimited use of lifts at several resorts. The cost in the 2000-2001 high season for a six-day pass was around L270,000. The Superski Dolomiti pass (☎ 0471 79 53 97), which allows access to 460 lifts and 1200km of ski runs, costs L300,000. The average cost of ski and boot hire per day is around L25,000 for downhill and L20,000 for cross-country skiing.

Hiking

Without doubt, the Dolomites provide the most breathtaking opportunities for walking in the Italian Alps – from a half-day stroll to multiday hikes. The walking season is roughly from July to late September. Alpine refuges usually close around 20 September.

Buy a map of the hiking trails that also shows the locations of Alpine refuges. The best maps are the Tabacco 1:25,000 series, sold at newsagents and bookshops in the area where you plan to hike. Lonely Planet's *Walking in Italy* guide outlines several treks in detail.

Hiking trails are generally well-marked, usually with numbers on red-and-white bands painted on trees and rocks along the trails.

Recommended areas to walk in the Dolomites include:

Alpe di Siusi A vast plateau above the Val Gardena, at the foot of the spectacular Sciliar.
Cortina area Featuring the magnificent Parco Naturale di Fanes-Sennes-Braies and, to the south-west, the Marmolada Group, Mt Pelmo and Mt Civetta.
Sesto Dolomites North of Cortina towards Austria.
Pale di San Martino Accessible from San Martino di Castrozza.

Warning Remember that even in summer the weather is extremely changeable in the Alps. Though it might be sweltering when you set off, be prepared for cold and wet weather on even the shortest walks.

Getting There & Away

Trentino-Alto Adige has an excellent public transport network. The region's two main bus companies are SAD (in Alto Adige and the Veneto) and Atesina (in Trentino). Larger towns and many ski resorts are also accessible from cities throughout Italy – including Rome, Florence, Bologna, Milan and Genoa – by a network of long-distance buses operated by companies including Lazzi, SITA, Sena and STAT.

Information about these services is available from tourist offices, bus stations throughout Trentino-Alto Adige, or from the following offices: Lazzi Express in Rome (☎ 46 884 08 40) at Via Tagliamento 27b, and in Florence (☎ 055 28 71 18) at Piazza della Stazione 47r; and SITA at Florence's bus station (☎ 055 21 47 21).

Getting Around

In summer the areas around the major resorts are well serviced by local buses; tourist offices have schedules and prices. In winter most resorts have 'ski bus' shuttle services from the towns to the main ski facilities.

CORTINA D'AMPEZZO
☎ 0436

Italy's most famous, fashionable and expensive ski resort, Cortina is also one of the best equipped and certainly the most picturesque. The area is very popular for trekking and climbing, with well-marked trails and numerous refuges.

The main APT tourist office (☎ 27 11) has information on Cortina's (expensive!) accommodation. *International Camping Olympia* (☎ 50 57) is north of Cortina at Fiames and is open year-round. *Casa Tua* (☎ 22 78, @ casatua@tin.it, Zuel 100) in Cortina charges L50,000 to L90,000 per person, depending on the season. SAD buses connect Cortina with Bolzano, via Dobbiaco, and long-distance services are operated by ATVO, Zani, Lazzi and SITA.

CANAZEI
☎ 0462

The resort of Canazei in the Fassa Dolomites has more than 100km of trails and is linked to the challenging network of runs known as the Sella Ronda. Canazei also offers cross-country and summer skiing on Marmolada – at 3342m, the highest peak in the Dolomites.

The Marmolada *camping ground* (☎ 60 16 60) is open all year, and there is also a choice of hotels, furnished rooms and apartments. Contact the AAST tourist office (☎ 60 11 13, fax 60 25 02) for full details. The resort is accessible by Atesina bus from Trent and SAD bus from Bolzano.

VAL GARDENA
☎ 0471

This is one of the most popular skiing areas in the Alps, due to its reasonable prices and first-class facilities for downhill, cross-country and Alpine skiing. There are superb walking trails in the Sella Group and the Alpi di Siusi. The Vallunga, behind Selva, is great for family walks and cross-country skiing.

The valley's main towns are Ortisei, Santa Cristina and Selva, all offering plenty of accommodation and easy access to runs. The tourist offices at Santa Cristina (☎ 79 30 46, fax 79 31 98) and Selva (☎ 79 51 22, fax 79 42 45) have extensive information on accommodation and facilities. Staff speak English and will send details on request. The Val Gardena is accessible from Bolzano by SAD bus, and is connected to major Italian cities by coach services (Lazzi, SITA and STAT).

SAN MARTINO DI CASTROZZA
☎ 0439

Located in a sheltered position beneath the Pale di San Martino, this resort is popular among Italians and offers good facilities and ski runs, as well as cross-country skiing and a toboggan run. The APT office (☎ 76 88 67, fax 76 88 14) will provide a full list of accommodation, or try *Garni Suisse* (☎ 680 87, Via Dolomiti 1), where singles/doubles with breakfast cost L43,000/86,000. Buses travel regularly from Trent, Milan, Venice, Padua and Bologna.

Central Italy

The landscape in central Italy is a patchwork of textures bathed in a beautiful soft light – golden pink in Tuscany, and greenish gold in Umbria and the Marches. The people remain close to the land, but in each of the regions there is also a strong artistic and cultural tradition. Even the smallest medieval hill town can harbour extraordinary works of art.

FLORENCE

☎ 055

Cradle of the Renaissance, home of Dante, Machiavelli, Michelangelo and the Medici, Florence (Firenze) is overwhelming in its wealth of art, culture and history. Even in summer – the season of huge crowds, hot weather and severe air pollution – it is one of the most enticing cities in Italy.

Florence was founded as a colony of the Etruscan city of Fiesole in about 200 BC and later became the strategic Roman garrison settlement of Florentia. In the Middle Ages the city flourished as a banking and commerce centre, which sparked a period of building and growth previously unequalled in Italy. Under Medici rule in the 15th century, Florence reached the zenith of its artistic, cultural and political development and gave birth to the Italian Renaissance.

The Grand Duchy of the Medici was succeeded in the 18th century by the House of Lorraine (related to the Austrian Habsburgs). Following Italy's unification movement (the Risorgimento), Florence became capital of the new Kingdom of Italy from 1865 to 1871. During WWII, parts of the city, including all of the bridges except the Ponte Vecchio, were destroyed by bombing. After a devastating flood in 1966 destroyed or severely damaged many important works of art, a worldwide fundraising effort helped Florence with its massive restoration works.

Orientation

The central train station, Santa Maria Novella, is a good reference point. Budget hotels and pensions are concentrated east of the station around Via Nazionale and south of the station near Piazza Santa Maria Novella. From the station it's a 10-minute walk (along Via de' Panzani and then Via de' Cerretani) to Piazza del Duomo and the historical centre.

A good map of the city, on sale at newsstands, is *Firenze: Pianta della Città*, with a white, red and black cover.

Information

Tourist Offices The Florence City Council (Comune di Firenze) operates a tourist information office (☎ 21 22 45) opposite the main train station at Piazza della Stazione 4, next to the Chiesa di Santa Maria Novella; there's another office at Borgo Santa Croce 29r (☎ 234 04 44). Opening hours are 8.30 am to 5.30 pm Monday to Saturday (to 1.30 pm on Sunday). The main APT office (☎ 29 08 32/3) is just north of the Duomo at Via Cavour 1r, open 8.15 am to 7.15 pm Monday to Saturday and to 1.30 pm Sunday. At all offices you can pick up a map of the city, a list of hotels and other useful information.

Consorzio ITA, inside the train station on the main concourse, makes hotel bookings for a small fee.

Post & Communications The main post office is on Via Pellicceria, off Piazza della Repubblica. It's open 8.15 am to 7 pm Monday to Saturday. The Telecom phone centre at Via Cavour 21r is open 7 am to 11 pm daily, and there's another in the train station.

Email & Internet Access Internet Train has 10 branches in Florence, including offices not far from the station at Via Guelfa 24r (☎ 21 47 94) and in Santa Croce at Via dei Benci 36 (☎ 263 85 55). It charges L6000/12,000 per half-hour/hour and also offers postal and money-transfer services. Lively Caffè Mambo at Via G Verdi 49 has a separate Internet area and charges L2500 for 15 minutes.

Bookshops For new and second-hand books in English try the Paperback Exchange at Via Fiesolana 31r; Internazionale Seeber at Via de' Tornabuoni 70r; or Feltrinelli International at Via Cavour 12-20r.

Laundry Onda Blu, east of the Duomo at Via degli Alfani 24bR and at Via Guelfa 22aR, is self-service and charges L5500 to wash and L5500 to dry.

Medical Services The main public hospital is Ospedale Careggi (☎ 427 71 11), Viale Morgagni 85, north of the city centre. Tourist Medical Service (☎ 47 54 11), at Via Lorenzo il Magnifico 59, can be phoned 24 hours a day and the doctors speak English, French and German.

All-night pharmacies include the Farmacia Comunale (☎ 28 94 35) inside the train station, and the central Molteni (☎ 28 94 90) at Via dei Calzaiuoli 7r.

FLORENCE (FIRENZE)

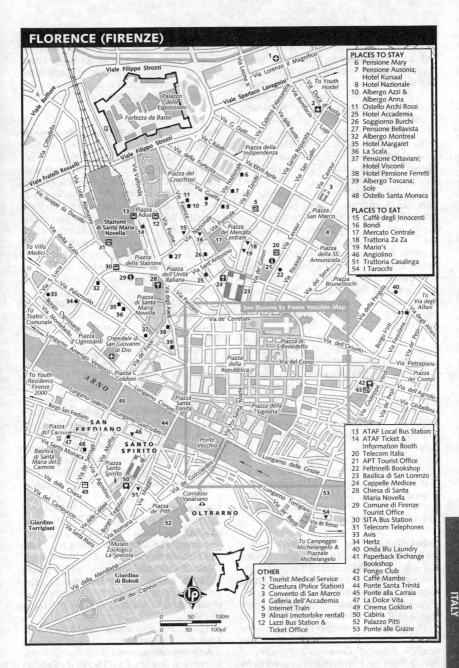

PLACES TO STAY
6 Pensione Mary
7 Pensione Ausonia;
   Hotel Kursaal
8 Hotel Nazionale
10 Albergo Azzi &
   Albergo Anna
11 Ostello Archi Rossi
25 Hotel Accademia
26 Soggiorno Burchi
27 Pensione Bellavista
32 Albergo Montreal
35 Hotel Margaret
36 La Scala
37 Pensione Ottaviani;
   Hotel Visconti
38 Hotel Pensione Ferretti
39 Albergo Toscana;
   Sole
48 Ostello Santa Monaca

PLACES TO EAT
15 Caffè degli Innocenti
16 Bondi
17 Mercato Centrale
18 Trattoria Za Za
19 Mario's
46 Angiolino
51 Trattoria Casalinga
54 I Tarocchi

13 ATAF Local Bus Station
14 ATAF Ticket &
   Information Booth
20 Telecom Italia
21 APT Tourist Office
22 Feltrinelli Bookshop
23 Basilica di San Lorenzo
24 Cappelle Medicee
28 Chiesa di Santa
   Maria Novella
29 Comune di Firenze
   Tourist Office
30 SITA Bus Station
31 Telecom Telephones
33 Avis
34 Hertz
40 Onda Blu Laundry
41 Paperback Exchange
   Bookshop
42 Pongo Club
43 Caffè Mambo
44 Ponte Santa Trinità
45 Ponte alla Carraia
47 La Dolce Vita
49 Cinema Goldoni
50 Cabiria
52 Palazzo Pitti
53 Ponte alle Grazie

OTHER
1 Tourist Medical Service
2 Questura (Police Station)
3 Convento di San Marco
4 Galleria dell'Accademia
5 Internet Train
9 Alinari (motorbike rental)
12 Lazzi Bus Station &
   Ticket Office

ITALY

Things to See & Do

Duomo With its elaborate nougat facade and skyline-dominating dome, the Duomo is one of Italy's most famous monuments, and the world's fourth-largest cathedral. Named the Cattedrale di Santa Maria del Fiore, it was begun in 1294 by the Sienese architect Arnolfo di Cambio but took almost 150 years to complete.

The Renaissance architect Brunelleschi won a public competition to design the enormous **dome**, which is decorated with frescoes by Vasari and Zuccari, and stained-glass windows by Donatello, Andrea del Castagno, Paolo Uccello and Lorenzo Ghiberti. Climb to the top for an unparalleled view of Florence (open 8.30 am to 7.30 pm Monday to Friday and on Saturday to 5 pm; entry L10,000).

Giotto designed and began building the **bell tower** next to the cathedral in 1334, but died before it was finished. This unusual and graceful structure is 82m high. You can climb to the top daily from 9 am to 7.30 pm (L10,000).

The Romanesque **baptistry**, believed to have been built between the 5th and 11th centuries on the site of a Roman temple, is the oldest building in Florence. Dante was baptised here. The building is famous for its gilded bronze doors, particularly the celebrated east doors facing the Duomo, entitled the *Gates of Paradise*, by Lorenzo Ghiberti. The south door, by Andrea Pisano, dates from 1336 and is the oldest. Most of the doors are copies – the original panels are being removed for restoration and are placed in the Museo dell'Opera del Duomo as work is completed. The baptistry is open noon to 6.30 pm Monday to Saturday, and 8.30 am to 1.30 pm on Sunday (L5000).

Uffizi Gallery The Palazzo degli Uffizi, built by Vasari in the 16th century, contains some of the world's most famous Renaissance paintings. The vast collection, dating from the 13th to 18th centuries, is Italy's most important, and represents the huge legacy of the Medici family.

The gallery's masterpieces include 14th-century gems by Giotto and Cimabue; Botticelli's *Birth of Venus* and *Allegory of Spring* from the 15th century; and works by Filippo Lippi, Fra Angelico and Paolo Uccello. *The Annunciation* by Leonardo da Vinci is also here, along with Michelangelo's *Holy Family*, Titian's *Venus of Urbino* and renowned works by Raphael, Andrea del Sarto, Tintoretto, Caravaggio and Tiepolo. The gallery is open 8.30 am to 10 pm daily except Monday (Sunday to 8 pm). Entry is L12,000.

Palazzo Vecchio & Piazza della Signoria
Designed by Arnolfo di Cambio and built between 1298 and 1340, the Palazzo Vecchio is the traditional seat of the Florentine government. In the 16th century it became the ducal palace of the Medici family before they moved to the Palazzo Pitti. Visit the beautiful **Michelozzo** courtyard just inside the entrance, and the lavishly decorated **apartments** upstairs. The palazzo is open 9 am to 7 pm daily (Thursday and Sunday to 2 pm). Admission is L11,000.

The palace's turrets, battlements and 94m-high bell tower form an imposing backdrop to Piazza della Signoria, scene of many important political events in the history of Florence, including the execution of the religious and political reformer Savonarola; a bronze plaque marks the spot where he was burned at the stake in 1498. The **Loggia della Signoria**, at a right angle to the Palazzo Vecchio, contains important sculptures.

Ponte Vecchio This famous 14th-century bridge, lined with gold and silversmith shops, was the only one to survive Nazi bombing in WWII. Originally, the shops housed butchers. A corridor along the 1st floor was built by the Medici family to link the Palazzo Pitti with the Palazzo Vecchio.

Palazzo Pitti This immense and imposing palazzo was built for the Pitti family, great rivals of the Medici, who moved in a century later. The **Galleria Palatina** has 16th- and 17th-century works by Raphael, Filippo Lippi, Tintoretto, Veronese and Rubens, hung in lavishly decorated rooms. The gallery is open 8.30 am to 10 pm Tuesday to Saturday (to 8 pm on Sunday). Entry is L12,000.

The palace also houses the **Museo degli Argenti** (Silver Museum) and **Galleria d'Arte Moderna**, open 8.30 am to 2 pm Tuesday to Sunday. Don't leave the Palazzo Pitti without visiting the beautiful Renaissance **Giardino di Boboli** (L4000).

ITALY

DUOMO TO PONTE VECCHIO

PLACES TO STAY
9 Albergo Firenze
10 Pensione Maria
    Luisa de' Medici
11 Brunori
18 Aily Home

PLACES TO EAT
4 Hosteria Il Caminetto
8 Gelateria Perché No?
12 Gelateria Vivoli
19 Trattoria da Benvenuto
20 Angie's Pub
21 Fiaschetteria

OTHER
1 Baptistry
2 Bell Tower
3 Duomo
5 Internazionale Seeber
   Bookshop
6 Cinema Odeon
7 Main Post Office
13 Museo del Bargello
14 Farmacia Molteni
    (chemist)
15 Palazzo Vecchio
16 Loggia della Signoria
17 Uffizi Gallery
22 Comune di Firenze
    Tourist Office
23 Internet Train
24 Chiesa di Santa Croce

Museo del Bargello A medieval palace, the Bargello (also known as the Palazzo del Podestà) was the seat of the local ruler and, later, of the chief of police. The palace now houses a rich collection of sculpture, notably works by Michelangelo and Benvenuto Cellini, as well as Donatello's bronze *David*, the first sculpture since antiquity to depict a fully naked man. It's open 8.30 am to 2 pm Tuesday to Sunday (L8000).

Galleria dell'Accademia Michelangelo's *David* is housed in this gallery, as are four of the artist's unfinished *Slaves* (or *Prisoners*). Early Florentine works are on show in the gallery upstairs. The Accademia is at Via Ricasoli 60, and opens 8.30 am to 10

pm Tuesday to Saturday, and to 8 pm on Sunday (L12,000).

Basilica di San Lorenzo & Cappelle Medicee The basilica, rebuilt by Brunelleschi in the early 15th century, contains his **Sagrestia Vecchia** (Old Sacristy), which was decorated by Donatello. It's also worth visiting the **Biblioteca Laurenziana**, a huge library designed by Michelangelo to house the Medici collection of some 10,000 manuscripts.

Around the corner, in Piazza Madonna degli Aldobrandini, are the Cappelle Medicee (Medici Chapels). The **Cappella dei Principi**, sumptuously decorated with precious marble and semi-precious stones, was the principal burial place of the Medici grand dukes. The graceful and simple **Sagrestia Nuova** was designed by Michelangelo and contains his beautiful sculptures *Night & Day*, *Dawn & Dusk* and the *Madonna with Child*. The chapels are open 8.30 am to 5 pm Tuesday to Sunday (L11,000).

Other Attractions The Dominican church of **Santa Maria Novella** was built during the 13th and 14th centuries, and its white-and-green marble facade was designed by Alberti in the 15th century. The church is decorated with frescoes by Ghirlandaio and Masaccio. The **Cappella di Filippo Strozzi** contains frescoes by Filippo Lippi.

The **Convento di San Marco** (Monastery of St Mark) pays homage to the work of Fra Angelico, who lived here from 1438 to 1455 and covered the monastery's walls and many of the monks' cells with dazzling frescoes. Also worth seeing are the peaceful cloisters and the cell of the monk Savonarola. The monastery is open 8.30 am to 2 pm Tuesday to Sunday (L8000).

Head up to **Piazzale Michelangelo** for a magnificent view of Florence. To reach the piazzale cross the Ponte Vecchio, turn left and walk along the river, then turn right at Piazza Giuseppe Poggi (or take bus No 13 from the station).

Organised Tours

I Bike Italy (☎ 234 23 71) offers single- and two-day guided bike rides (and walking tours) in the countryside around Florence, with stops at vineyards. It supplies 24-speed bikes, helmets and English-speaking guides. The Fiesole ride costs US$65, Chianti US$80 and Siena (two days) US$235. Check out the Web site at www.ibikeitaly.com.

Special Events

Florence's major festivals include the Festa del Patrono (Feast of St John the Baptist) and the Calcio Storico (Historical Football), featuring football matches played in 16th-century costume, both held on 24 June; and the Scoppio del Carro (Explosion of the Cart), held in front of the Duomo on Easter Sunday.

Italy's oldest music festival, Maggio Musicale Fiorentino, is usually held in June. For information contact the Teatro Comunale (☎ 21 11 58).

Places to Stay

There are more than 150 budget hotels in Florence so it's fairly easy to find a room, even in peak season. However, it is wise to book ahead.

Always ask the full price of a room before putting your bags down – Florence's hotels and pensions are notorious for billpadding, particularly in summer. Many charge L10,000 for breakfast (even if you don't want it) and showers are L3000 or more. Prices listed here are high season.

Camping Near Piazzale Michelangelo is *Campeggio Michelangelo* (☎ 681 19 77, *Viale Michelangelo 80*). Take bus No 13 from the train station. *Villa Camerata* (☎ 60 03 15, *Viale Augusto Righi 2-4*) is next to the HI hostel, north-east of the centre. *Campeggio Panoramico* (☎ 59 90 69, *Via Peramonda 1*), in Fiesole 8km north-east of Florence, also rents out bungalows.

Hostels The HI *Ostello Villa Camerata* (☎ 60 14 51, *Viale Augusto Righi 2-4*) charges L26,000 for B&B and L14,000 for dinner. There is also a bar. It is open to HI members only and reservations (essential in summer) can be made by mail. Take bus No 17 or 17b from the right of the train station as you leave the platforms. The trip takes 30 minutes. Note that the hostel is closed 9 am to 2 pm daily.

The private *Ostello Archi Rossi* (☎ 29 08 04, *Via Faenza 94r*) is a good option for a bed in a dorm room for L30,000, as is *Ostello Santa Monaca* (☎ 26 83 38, *Via Santa Monaca 6*).

Farther west, *Youth Residence Firenze 2000* (☎ 233 55 58, ✉ scatizzi@dada.it, *Via le Raffaello Sanzio 16*) has shared rooms with en-suite for L55,000 per person.

Hotels – Around the Station The *Pensione Bellavista* (☎ 28 45 28, *Largo Alinari 15*), at the start of Via Nazionale, has basic singles/doubles for L90,000/130,000; two of the doubles have views of the Duomo.

Albergo Azzi (☎ 21 38 06, *Via Faenza 56*) has helpful management and rooms for L70,000/110,000, including breakfast. The same management runs the *Albergo Anna* upstairs.

Across Via Nazionale there is *Hotel Accademia* (☎ 29 34 51, *Via Faenza 7*) which partially occupies an 18th-century palace, complete with magnificent stained-glass doors and carved wooden ceilings. Pleasant singles cost L140,000 and a double with bathroom is L230,000, breakfast and TV included.

On the same street at No 20, **Soggiorno Burchi** (☎ *41 44 54*) has singles/doubles with bathroom for L90,000/110,000.

Hotel Nazionale (☎ *238 22 03, Via Nazionale 22*) has rooms for L90,000/130,000 including breakfast. At No 24, **Pensione Ausonia** (☎ *49 65 47*) is run by a young couple who go out of their way to help travellers. They offer a range of accommodation, starting with standard singles/doubles/triples with breakfast for L90,000/145,000/190,000, and also operate the more expensive **Hotel Kursaal** (☎ *49 63 24*) downstairs.

Pensione Mary (☎ *49 63 10, Piazza dell' Indipendenza 5*) charges L100,000/130,000.

Hotels – Around Piazza Santa Maria Novella
Via della Scala, which runs north-west off the piazza, is lined with pensions. **La Scala** (☎ *21 26 29*) at No 21 is small and has doubles/triples for L85,000/150,000. **Hotel Margaret** (☎ *21 01 38*) at No 25 is pleasantly furnished and has singles/doubles for L80,000/100,000. **Albergo Montreal** (☎ *238 23 31*) at No 43 has singles for L85,000 and doubles/triples/quads with bathroom for L100,000/150,000/185,000.

The **Sole** (☎ *239 60 94, Via del Sole 8*) charges L70,000/100,000 or L120,000 for a double with bath. In the same building, **Albergo Toscana** (☎ *21 31 56*) has singles/doubles with bathroom for L90,000/150,000. Slightly north, the family-run **Hotel Pensione Ferretti** (☎ *238 13 28, Via delle Belle Donne 17*) has comfortable singles for L70,000; rooms with bathroom are L90,000/140,000, and breakfast is included.

Ottaviani (☎ *239 62 23, Piazza Ottaviani 1*), just off Piazza Santa Maria Novella, charges L70,000/90,000, breakfast included. In the same building is **Visconti** (☎ *21 38 77*), with a pleasant breakfast terrace and rooms for L65,000/90,000.

Hotels – From the Duomo to the Arno
This central and historical area is a 15-minute walk from the station. One of the better deals is the small **Aily Home** (☎ *239 65 05, Piazza Santo Stefano 1*), overlooking the Ponte Vecchio. Singles cost L40,000 and doubles (three of which overlook the bridge) cost L70,000.

Albergo Firenze (☎ *21 42 03, Piazza dei Donati 4*), south of the Duomo, has singles/doubles with bathroom and breakfast for L100,000/140,000. **Brunori** (☎ *28 96 48, Via del Proconsolo 5*) has doubles for L96,000. **Pensione Maria Luisa de' Medici** (☎ *28 00 48, Via del Corso 1*) is in a 17th-century palace. Doubles cost from L80,000, including breakfast.

Places to Eat
Avoid the mediocre self-service restaurants that line the streets between the Duomo and the Arno River. Be adventurous and seek out the small trattorias in the district of Oltrarno (south of the Arno) and near the Mercato Centrale (covered market) in San Lorenzo. The **market**, open 7 am to 2 pm Monday to Friday, offers fresh produce, cheeses and meat at reasonable prices.

Simplicity and quality are the hallmarks of food in Tuscany. Start your meal with *fettunta* (known elsewhere in Italy as bruschetta), a thick slice of toasted bread, rubbed with garlic and soaked in olive oil. *Ribollita* is a filling soup of vegetables and white beans, reboiled with chunks of bread and garnished with olive oil. Another traditional dish is *bistecca Fiorentina* (beef-steak Florentine) – big enough for two.

Among the best outlets for gelati are **Gelateria Vivoli** in Via dell'Isola delle Stinche, off Via dei Calzaiuoli, and **Perché No?** (*Via dei Tavolini 19r*), off Via dei Calzaiuoli.

City Centre The **Trattoria da Benvenuto** (*Via Mosca 16r*) offers a quick meal of pasta, bread and wine for L16,000. **Angie's Pub** (*Via dei Neri 35r*) has sandwiches and foccaccia (L4500 to L6500), as well as hamburgers, hot dogs and beer on tap. At **Fiaschetteria** (*Via dei Neri 17r*), sample the range of panini from L2500 and value-for-money pastas for around L8000. **Hosteria Il Caminetto** (*Via dello Studio 34*), just south of Piazza del Duomo, has a small vine-covered terrace. Pasta dishes are around L14,000.

Around San Lorenzo The ever-popular **Mario's** (*Via Rosina 2r*) is open only at lunchtime. This small bar and trattoria serves pasta dishes for around L7000. A few doors down, *Trattoria Za Za (Piazza del Mercato Centrale 20)* is another local favourite, with prices similar to Mario's. *Bondi (Via dell'Ariento 85)* specialises in focaccia and pizza (from L3000). *Caffè degli Innocenti (Via Nazionale 57)* has a selection of pre-prepared panini and good cakes for around L2500 to L4500.

Oltrarno Bustling, popular *Trattoria Casalinga (Via dei Michelozzi 9r)* serves great food at fair prices – a full meal is L15,000 to L20,000. *I Tarocchi (Via de' Renai 16)* serves excellent pizza (L7500 to L10,000), traditional pastas (L9000 to L11,000) and plenty of salads and vegetable dishes (L8000). *Angiolino (Via Santo Spirito 36r)* is an excellent trattoria where a full meal costs around L40,000.

Entertainment
Hotels and tourist offices have copies of the various free publications listing the theatrical and musical events, and newsstands sell the English-language entertainment guide *Vista*.

Concerts, opera and dance are performed year-round at the *Teatro Comunale (☎ 277 92 36, Corso Italia 16)*. The main seasons are September to December and January to April.

Nightclubs include *La Dolce Vita*, spilling onto Piazza del Carmine, south of the Arno, and *Pongo (Via G Verdi 59r)*, with an assortment of live music. The tiny but noisy *Cabiria* bar in Piazza Santo Spirito is popular, especially in summer.

English films are screened at a number of cinemas: the *Astro* in Piazza San Simone, near Santa Croce (every night except Monday); the *Odeon* on Piazza Strozzi (Monday and Wednesday); and the *Goldoni*, Via de' Serragli (Wednesday).

Shopping
The main shopping area is between the Duomo and the Arno, with boutiques concentrated along Via Roma, Via dei Calzaiuoli and Via Por Santa Maria, leading to the goldsmiths lining the Ponte Vecchio.

The open-air market (closed Sunday), in the streets of San Lorenzo near the Mercato Centrale, offers leather goods, clothing and jewellery at low prices, but quality can

vary. The flea market (closed Sunday) at Piazza dei Ciompi, off Borgo Allegri near the Church of Santa Croce, is not as extensive but there are great bargains.

Getting There & Away
The SITA bus terminal (☎ 21 47 21), at Via Santa Caterina da Siena 17, is just south of the train station. Buses leave for Siena, San Gimignano and Volterra. Lazzi (☎ 28 71 18) is at Piazza della Stazione 47r.

Florence is on the main Rome-Milan rail line, and most trains are the fast Eurostars, for which you have to book and pay a supplement. Regular trains also go to/from Venice (three hours). For information, call ☎ 147 88 80 88.

Getting Around
ATAF buses service the city centre and Fiesole. The terminal for the most useful buses is in a small piazza to the left as you exit the train station. Bus No 7 leaves from here for Fiesole and also stops at the Duomo. Tickets must be bought before boarding at tobacconists and newsstands or from automatic vending machines at major bus stops (L1500 for one hour, L2500 for three hours, L6000 for 24 hours).

To rent a car try Hertz (☎ 28 22 60), at Via M Finiguerra 17r, or Avis (☎ 21 36 29), Borgo Ognissanti 128r. For motorcycles and bicycles try Alinari (☎ 28 05 00), at Via Guelfa 85r. Ask at the station for information about the city council's free bicycles for use between 8 am and 7.30 pm.

PISA
☎ 050
Once a maritime power to rival Genoa and Venice, Pisa now makes the most of its one remaining claim to fame: its leaning tower. The busy port city was the site of an important university and the home of Galileo Galilei (1564-1642). Pisa was devastated by the Genoese in the 13th century, and its history eventually merged with that of Florence. Today Pisa is a relaxing town, its charm intact despite the many day-trippers.

Orientation & Information
Pisa's main square is the Campo dei Miracoli. There are APT tourist offices at the train station and west of Campo dei Miracoli at Via Carlo Cammeo 2.

ITALY

Things to See

The Pisans can justly claim that their central square, **Campo dei Miracoli** (Field of Miracles), is one of the most beautiful in the world. Set in its sprawling lawns are the cathedral, the baptistry and the leaning tower.

The Romanesque **cathedral**, begun in 1064, has a beautiful facade of tiered arches. The bronze doors of the transept, facing the leaning tower, are by Bonanno Pisano. The marble **baptistry**, started in 1153, contains a beautiful pulpit by Nicola Pisano.

Pisa's famous leaning **bell tower** was in trouble from the start – its architect, Bonanno Pisano, managed to complete only three tiers before the structure started to lean. The problem is shifting soil, which adds about 1mm each year to the tower's lean. Today it leans 5m off the perpendicular. The tower has been closed for over a decade, and is braced by strengthening cables, weighted with more than 1000 tons of lead and is undergoing a ground-levelling process – all in all, it resembles a construction site. It's hoped that the weights and steel cables will eventually be removed, leaving the tower still leaning but without the risk of collapse.

It costs L3000 to see the cathedral, and from L10,000 to L18,000 for all or just a few of the sights.

Places to Stay

The non-HI *Ostello per la Gioventù* (☎ 89 06 22, *Via Pietrasantina 15*) has dorm beds for L24,000; the doors are closed from 9 am to 6 pm. Take bus No 3 from the station.

Albergo Gronchi (☎ 56 18 23, *Piazza Arcivescovado 1*), near the Campo dei Miracoli, has modern singles/doubles for L35,000/58,000. *Hotel di Stefano* (☎ 55 35 59, *Via Sant'Apollonia 35*) has good-quality rooms for L65,000/85,000. Near the train station, *Albergo Milano* (☎ 231 62, *Via Mascagni 14*) has a friendly owner and pleasant rooms for L60,000/80,000.

Places to Eat

Pizzeria da Matteo (*Via l'Arancio 46*) is a good choice for quick, cheap meals. Head to *La Bottega del Gelato* in Piazza Garibaldi for gelati, or grab a cocktail and bar snack at *Krott* (*Lungarno Pacinotti 2*). There's an open-air food *market* in Piazza delle Vettovaglie, off Borgo Stretto.

Getting There & Away

Lazzi (☎ 46 288) buses run to Florence via Lucca and Prato. CPT (☎ 50 55 11) operates buses to Livorno (via Tirrenia).

The city is linked by direct trains to Florence, Rome and Genoa. Local trains head for Lucca and Livorno.

SIENA
☎ 0577

Surrounded by its ancient ramparts, Siena is Italy's best-preserved medieval town. The historical centre is jam-packed with majestic Gothic buildings in various shades of the colour known as 'burnt sienna'.

According to legend, Siena was founded by the sons of Remus (one of the founders of Rome). In the Middle Ages the city became a free republic, but its success and power led to serious rivalry with Florence, both politically and culturally. Painters of the Sienese School produced significant works of art, and the city was home to St Catherine and St Benedict.

Siena is divided into 17 *contrade* (districts), and each year 10 are chosen to compete in the Palio, an extraordinary horse race held on 2 July and 16 August in the shell-shaped Piazza del Campo.

Orientation & Information

Leaving the train station, cross the concourse to the bus stop opposite and catch bus No 9 or 10 to Piazza Gramsci, then walk into the centre along Via dei Termini (it takes about five minutes to reach Piazza del Campo). From the intercity bus station in Piazza San Domenico, it's a five-minute walk along Via della Sapienza and then turn right into Via delle Terme.

The APT office (☎ 28 05 51) is at Piazza del Campo 56. It opens 8.30 am to 7.30 pm Monday to Saturday (from 11 November to 21 March it opens 8.30 am to 1 pm and 3 to 7 pm Monday to Friday, and to 1 pm on Saturday).

The main post office is at Piazza Matteotti 1. The Telecom office is at Via dei Termini 40.

Things to See & Do

Siena's uniquely shell-shaped **Piazza del Campo** (known simply as Il Campo) has been the city's focus since the 14th century. The piazza's sloping base is formed by the

ITALY

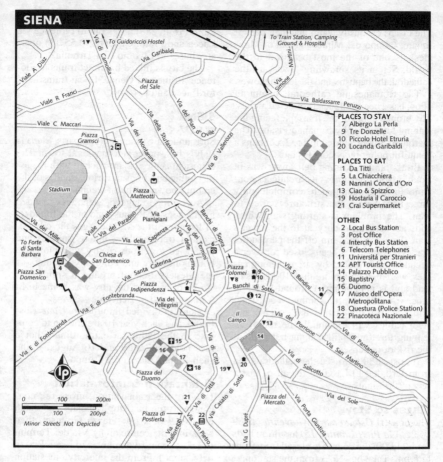

SIENA

PLACES TO STAY
7 Albergo La Perla
9 Tre Donzelle
10 Piccolo Hotel Etruria
20 Locanda Garibaldi

PLACES TO EAT
1 Da Titti
5 La Chiacchiera
8 Nannini Conca d'Oro
13 Ciao & Spizzico
19 Hostaria il Caroccio
21 Crai Supermarket

OTHER
2 Local Bus Station
3 Post Office
4 Intercity Bus Station
6 Telecom Telephones
11 Università per Stranieri
12 APT Tourist Office
14 Palazzo Pubblico
15 Baptistry
16 Duomo
17 Museo dell'Opera
Metropolitana
18 Questura (Police Station)
22 Pinacoteca Nazionale

imposing **Palazzo Pubblico** (town hall), considered one of Italy's most graceful Gothic buildings. Its Sienese art treasures include Simone Martini's *Maestà* and Ambrogio Lorenzetti's *Allegories of Good & Bad Government*. There is also a chapel with frescoes by Taddeo di Bartolo. The town hall is open from 10 am to 7 pm daily (to 11 pm in July and August), and entry is L10,000 (L5000 for students).

The spectacular **Duomo** is another Gothic masterpiece, and one of the most enchanting cathedrals in Italy. Its black-and-white striped marble facade has a Romanesque lower section, with carvings by Giovanni Pisano. The upper section is 14th-century Gothic with 19th-century mosaics. The inlaid-marble floor (largely covered) fea-

tures various works depicting biblical stories, and the marble and porphyry **pulpit** was carved by Nicola Pisano, father of Giovanni. Other artworks include a bronze statue of St John the Baptist by Donatello and statues of St Jerome and Mary Magdalene by Bernini.

Through a door from the north aisle is the **Libreria Piccolomini**, which Pope Pius III (pope during 1503) built to house the illustrated books of his uncle, Pope Pius II. It features frescoes by Pinturicchio and a Roman statue of the Three Graces. Entry is L2000.

The **Museo dell'Opera Metropolitana** (Duomo Museum), on Piazza del Duomo, houses works of art which formerly adorned the cathedral, including the famous *Maestà* by Duccio di Buoninsegna and Giovanni Pisano's 12 marble statues. Entry is L6000.

ITALY

The **baptistry**, behind the cathedral, has a Gothic facade and is decorated with 15th-century frescoes and a font by Jacopo della Quercia. It is open 9 am to 7.30 pm daily (L3000).

The 15th-century Palazzo Buonsignori houses the **Pinacoteca Nazionale** (National Picture Gallery), with innumerable master-pieces by Sienese artists, including the *Madonna dei Francescani* by Duccio di Buoninsegna, *Madonna col Bambino* by Simone Martini and a series of Madonnas by Ambrogio Lorenzetti. The gallery is open 9 am to 7 pm Tuesday to Saturday, to 1.30 pm on Monday and from 8 am to 1 pm on Sunday (L8000).

Places to Stay

Book ahead, particularly in August and during the Palio, when accommodation is nearly impossible to find.

The *Colleverde* camping ground (☎ 28 00 44, Strada di Scacciapensieri 47) is outside the historical centre – take bus No 8 from Piazza del Sale, near Piazza Gramsci. It's open 21 March to 10 November and costs L15,000 per person, L15,000 per tent.

The *Guidoriccio* hostel (☎ 52 212, Via Fiorentina) is 3km from town in Stellino. Take bus No 15 from Piazza Gramsci. B&B is L29,000 and an evening meal is L16,000.

In the heart of the old town, *Tre Donzelle* (☎ 28 03 58, Via delle Donzelle 5) has singles/doubles for L50,000/80,000. Nearby, the two-star *Piccolo Hotel Etruria* (☎ 28 80 88, Via delle Donzelle 1) has renovated rooms with bathroom for L75,000/120,000. *Locanda Garibaldi* (☎ 28 42 04, Via Giovanni Dupré 18) has basic rooms for L45,000/85,000 and a small, reasonably priced trattoria.

Albergo La Perla (☎ 47 144, Via delle Terme 25, 2nd floor) is a short walk from the Campo. Small but clean rooms with shower are L80,000/110,000.

Places to Eat

There are several supermarkets in the town centre, including *Crai (Via di Città 152-156)* and *Consorzio Agrario*, on Via Piani Giani. *Nannini Conca d'Oro (Banchi di Sopra 22)* is one of the city's finest cafes.

The ubiquitous self-service *Ciao* and ready-to-go *Spizzico* are right on the Campo at No 77. For a traditional hostaria, try *Il Caroccio (Via Casato di Sotto 32)*, off the Campo, where bistecca alla Fiorentina is L40,000 a kilo.

For local specialities, try *La Chiacchiera (Costa di Sant'Antonio 4)*, off Via Santa Caterinaserves. Pasta dishes cost from L7000 and a bottle of house wine is L5000. There are several trattorias farther north, in a less frenetic neighbourhood. *Da Titti (Via di Camollia 193)* is a no-frills establishment with big wooden bench tables where a full meal with wine costs around L28,000.

Getting There & Away

Regular Tra-In buses run from Florence to Siena, arriving at Piazza San Domenico. Buses also go to San Gimignano and other points in Tuscany, and there's a daily bus to Rome. For timetable information about buses to Perugia ask at the Balzana travel agency (☎ 28 50 13); these buses leave from the train station.

Siena is not on a main train line, so from Rome it is necessary to change at Chiusi and from Florence at Empoli, making buses a better alternative.

SAN GIMIGNANO
☎ 0577

Few places in Italy rival the beauty of San Gimignano, a town that has barely changed since medieval times. Famous for its towers (13 of the original 72 remain), it was built as a demonstration of power by its prominent families in the Middle Ages.

Try to visit during the week, as this hill-top town is packed with tourists at weekends. The Pro Loco tourist office (☎ 94 00 08, ✉ prolocosg@tin.it) is at Piazza del Duomo 1.

Things to See & Do

Climb San Gimignano's tallest tower, **Torre Grossa** (also known as the town hall tower), off Piazza del Duomo, for a memorable view of the Tuscan hills. The tower is reached from within the **Palazzo del Popolo** which houses the **Museo Civico**, whose star attraction is Lippo Memmi's 14th-century *Maestà*. The **Duomo** has a Romanesque interior, frescoes by Ghirlandaio in the Cappella di Santa Fina and a particularly gruesome *Last Judgment* by Taddeo di Bartolo. The city's most impressive square is **Piazza della Cisterna**, named for the 13th-century well at its centre.

ITALY

Places to Stay

Hotels in town are expensive, but there are numerous rooms for rent in private homes – contact the tourist office (see earlier).

The nearest camping ground is *Il Boschetto di Piemma* (☎ 94 03 52), about 3km from town in Santa Lucia. It is open from April to mid-October and there is a bus service to the site. The rates are L9000 per person, and L12,000 per tent.

The non-HI *hostel* (☎ 94 19 91, *Via delle Fonti 1*) is open from March to October and charges L29,000 for B&B, and L16,000 for a meal.

Places to Eat

Friendly *Trattoria Chiribiri (Piazzetta della Madonna 1)*, off Via San Giovanni, has hearty minestrone for L8000 and ravioli for L10,000. A fresh-produce *market* is held on Thursday morning in Piazza del Duomo.

Getting There & Away

Regular buses connect San Gimignano with Florence and Siena. Buses arrive at Porta San Giovanni, a short walk from Piazza del Duomo.

PERUGIA

☎ 075

Perugia, capital of the Umbria region, is one of Italy's better-preserved medieval hill towns. It is noted for the feuding between its families, the Baglioni and the Oddi, and for the violent wars against its neighbours during the Middle Ages.

Perugia also has a strong artistic and cultural tradition. It was the home of the painter Perugino, and one of his students, Raphael, also worked here. Perugia's University for Foreigners, established in 1925, attracts thousands of students from around the world. Perugia's noted jazz festival, Umbria Jazz, is held in July.

Orientation & Information

The centre of all activity in Perugia is Corso Vannucci. The main train station is a few kilometres downhill from the historical centre; catch any bus heading for Piazza Italia. Tickets cost L1200 and must be bought before boarding.

The IAT tourist office (☎ 572 33 27) is at Piazza IV Novembre 3, opposite the cathe-

dral at one end of the Corso. It opens 8.30 am to 1.30 pm and 3.30 to 6.30 pm Monday to Saturday, and 9 am to 1 pm Sunday. The main post office is on Piazza Matteotti.

The monthly magazine *Perugia What, Where, When*, sold at newsstands for L1000, has events listings and other useful information.

Things to See

Perugia's austere **Duomo** has an unfinished facade in the characteristic Perugian red-and-white marble. Inside are frescoes, decorations and furniture by artists from the 15th to 18th centuries. The **Palazzo dei Priori**, just down from the Duomo on Corso Vannucci, is a rambling 13th-century palace housing the impressively frescoed **Sala dei Notari** and the **Galleria Nazionale dell'Umbria**, with works by Perugino and Fra Angelico. Between the two buildings, in Piazza IV Novembre, is the 13th-century **Fontana Maggiore**, designed by Fra Bevignate in 1278 and carved by Nicola and Giovanni Pisano.

At the other end of Corso Vannucci is the **Rocca Paolina** (Paolina Fortress), the ruins of a massive 16th-century fortress built upon the foundations of the palaces and homes of the powerful families of the day, notably the Baglioni. The fortress itself was destroyed by the Perugians after the declaration of the kingdom of Italy in 1860.

Raphael's magnificent fresco *Trinity with Saints* can be seen in the church of **San Severo**, on Piazza San Severo. One of the last works by the painter in Perugia, it was completed by Perugino after Raphael's death in 1520.

Etruscan remains in Perugia include the **Arco Etrusco** (Etruscan Arch), near the university, and the **Pozzo Etrusco** (Etruscan Well), near the Duomo.

Places to Stay

Book ahead in July and August. The non-HI hostel *Centro Internazionale per la Gioventù* (☎ 572 28 80, *@ ostello@edisons.it, Via Bontempi 13*) charges L18,000 a night. Sheets are an extra L2000. The hostel's terrace has one of the best views in Perugia. Daytime closing is from 9.30 am to 4 pm and the hostel closes from mid-December to mid-January.

Pensione Anna (☎ 573 63 04, *Via dei Priori 48*), off Corso Vannucci, has singles/

doubles for L50,000/80,000. Nearby, the *Hotel Morlacchi* (☎ 572 03 19, Via Tiberi 2) has attractively presented singles/doubles/triples with bathroom for L70,000/100,000/130,000. *Pensione Paola* (☎ 572 38 16, Via della Canapina 5) is five minutes from the centre, down the escalator from Via dei Priori. Cheap but pleasant rooms are L43,000/65,000. Just off Corso Vannucci, *Piccolo Hotel* (☎ 572 29 87, Via Bonazzi 25) has small doubles with bathroom for L75,000.

Places to Eat

Good places for pizza are *L'Era Nuova*, just behind the trendy Medio Evo bar on Corso Vannucci, *Il Segreto di Pulcinella* (Via Larga 8) and *Tit-Bit* (Via dei Priori 105). All charge L9000 and up for a pizza. There's a tiny but popular *takeaway pizza place* (Via dei Priori 3). The *Tavola Calda* (Piazza Danti 16) has good, cheap food.

Getting There & Away

There are some direct trains from Rome and Florence, but most require a change at Foligno (from Rome) or Terontola (from Florence). Local trains leave from the St Anna station.

Intercity buses leave from Piazza Partigiani, at the bottom of the Rocca Paolina escalators. Destinations include Rome, Florence, Siena, Assisi, Gubbio and nearby Lake Trasimeno. Bus and train timetables are available at the tourist office.

ASSISI

☎ 075

Despite the millions of tourists and pilgrims it attracts every year, Assisi, home of St Francis, is beautiful and even tranquil (as long as you keep away from the main tourist drags). From Roman times its inhabitants have been aware of the visual impact of their city: perched halfway up Mt Subasio, its pink-and-white marble buildings literally shimmer in the sunlight. In September 1997, a strong earthquake rocked the town, causing part of the vault of the upper church of the Basilica di San Francesco to collapse. While the upper basilica has since reopened, the painstaking task of restoration continues.

The APT tourist office (☎ 81 25 34, ✉ aptas@krenet.it) is on Piazza del Comune.

Things to See

Most people come to Assisi to visit its religious monuments. Dress rules are applied rigidly – absolutely no shorts, miniskirts or low-cut dresses/tops are allowed.

St Francis' Basilica is composed of two churches, one built on top of the other. The lower church is decorated with frescoes by Simone Martini, Cimabue and a pupil of Giotto, and it contains the crypt where St Francis is buried. The upper church has a classic vaulted ceiling, and was decorated by the great painters of the 13th and 14th centuries, in particular Giotto and Cimabue. The frescoes in the apse and entrance received the most damage in the 1997 earthquake.

The impressively frescoed 13th-century **Basilica di Santa Chiara** contains the remains of St Clare, friend of St Francis and founder of the Order of Poor Clares.

The massive 14th-century **Rocca Maggiore** fortress offers spectacular views of the valley below, including the **Basilica di Santa Maria degli Angeli**, a huge church built around the first Franciscan monastery. St Francis died in its **Cappella del Transito**, in 1226.

Places to Stay

Peak periods, when you need to book well in advance, are Easter, August and September, and the Feast of St Francis (3 and 4 October). The tourist office can help with private rooms and pensions.

The small HI *Ostello della Pace* (☎ 81 67 67, Via Valecchi 177) is open all year; B&B is L25,000. The hostel is on the bus line between Santa Maria degli Angeli and Assisi. The non-HI hostel *Fontemaggio* and camping ground (☎ 81 36 36) has B&B for L25,000 and singles/doubles for L50,000/100,000. From Piazza Matteotti, at the far end of town from the basilica, it's a 30-minute uphill walk along Via Eremo delle Carceri to No 8.

Albergo Italia (☎ 81 26 25), on Vicolo della Fortezza, just off Pizza del Comune, has rooms with shower for L45,000/69,000.

Places to Eat

For a snack of pizza by the slice for around L2000, head for *Pizza Vincenzo* (Via San Rufina 1a), just off Piazza del Comune. A good self-service in the same area is *Il Foro Romano* (Via Portico 23). *Il Pozzo Romano*

ITALY

(Via Santa Agnese 10), off Piazza Santa Chiara, has pizzas for around L9000 and a tourist menu for L22,000. Dine under ancient architraves at **Dal Carro** *(Vicolo dei Nepis 2)*, off Corso Mazzini, with superior pasta dishes from L7000.

Getting There & Away

Buses connect Assisi with Perugia, Foligno and other local towns, leaving from Piazza Matteotti. Buses for Rome and Florence leave from Piazzale dell'Unità d'Italia. Assisi's train station is in the valley, in the suburb of Santa Maria degli Angeli. It's on the same line as Perugia and a shuttle bus runs between the town and the station.

ANCONA
☎ 071

The main reason to visit Ancona, a largely unattractive and industrial port city in the Marches, is to catch a ferry to Croatia, Greece or Albania. The easiest way to get from the train station to the port is by bus No 1.

Ancona is on the Bologna-Lecce train line and is easily accessible from major Italian towns, including Rome (via Foligno). All ferry operators have information booths at the ferry terminal, off Piazza Kennedy. Prices listed here are for one-way deck class in the 2000 high season. Companies include the following: Superfast (☎ 207 02 40) to Patras in Greece (L136,000); Minoan Lines (☎ 20 17 08) to Igoumenitsa and Patras (L124,000); Adriatica (☎ 20 49 15) to Durrës in Albania (L155,000) and to Split in Croatia (L80,000).

If you're stuck here waiting for a ferry, there are a couple of options for dining and accommodation. Many backpackers choose to bunk down at the ferry terminal, although the city has many cheap hotels. The relatively new **Ostello della Gioventú** *(☎/fax 4 22 57, Via Lamaticci)* has B&B for L24,000. **Albergo Fiore** *(☎ 433 90, Piazza Rosselli 24)* has singles/doubles for L42,000/72,000 and is just across from the train station.

URBINO
☎ 0722

This town in the Marches can be difficult to reach, but it is worth the effort to see the birthplace of Raphael and Bramante, which has changed little since the Middle Ages

and remains a centre of art, culture and learning.

The IAT tourist information office (☎ 27 88, ✉ iat@comune.urbino.ps.it) is at Piazza Duca Federico 35 and is open 9 am to 1 pm Monday to Saturday.

Things to See & Do

Urbino's main sight is the huge **Palazzo Ducale**, designed by Laurana and completed in 1482. Enter the palace from Piazza Duca Federico and visit the **Galleria Nazionale delle Marches**, featuring works by Raphael, Paolo Uccello and Verrocchio. The palace is open 9 am to 7 pm Tuesday to Saturday, 9 am to 9 pm on Sunday and 9 am to 2 pm Monday. Entry is L8000.

Also visit the **Casa di Rafaello**, at Via Raffaello 57, where the artist Raphael was born, and the **Oratorio di San Giovanni Battista**, with 15th-century frescoes by the Salimbeni brothers.

Places to Stay & Eat

Urbino is a major university town and most cheap beds are taken by students during the school year. The tourist office has a full list of *affittacamere* (room rentals). **Pensione Fosca** *(☎ 32 96 22, Via Raffaello 61)* has singles/doubles for L42,000/60,000.

There are numerous bars around Piazza della Repubblica in the town centre and near the Palazzo Ducale which sell good panini. Try **Pizzeria Galli** *(Via Vittorio Veneto 19)* for takeaway pizza by the slice. **Ristorante Da Franco**, just off Piazza del Rinascimento, next to the university, has a self-service section where you can eat a full meal for around L22,000.

Getting There & Away

There is no train service to Urbino. There is a bus link to the train station at the town of Fossato di Vico, on the Rome-Ancona line. There are also buses to Rome twice a day. All buses arrive at Borgo Mercatale, down Via Mazzini from Piazza della Repubblica. The tourist office has timetables for all bus services.

Southern Italy

The land of the *mezzogiorno* (midday sun) will surprise even the most world-weary

ITALY

traveller. Rich in history and cultural traditions, the southern regions are poorer than those of the north, and certainly the wheels of bureaucracy grind more slowly as you travel closer to the tip of the boot. The attractions here are simpler and more stark, the people more vibrant and excitable, and myths and legends are inseparable from official history. Campania, Apulia and Basilicata cry out to be explored and absolutely nothing can prepare you for Naples.

NAPLES
☎ 081

Crazy and confusing, but also seductive and fascinating, Naples (Napoli), capital of the Campania region, has an energy that is palpable. Beautifully positioned on the Bay of Naples and overshadowed by Mt Vesuvius, it is one of the most densely populated cities in Europe.

Naples has its own secret society of criminals, the Camorra, which traditionally concentrated its activities on the import and sale of contraband cigarettes, but has now diversified into drugs, construction, finance and tourist developments.

Orientation

Both the Stazione Centrale (central train station) and the main bus terminal are just off the vast Piazza Garibaldi. Naples is divided into *quartieri* (districts). The main shopping thoroughfare into the historical centre, Spaccanapoli, is Corso Umberto I, which heads south-west from Piazza Garibaldi to Piazza Bovio. West on the bay are Santa Lucia and Mergellina, both fashionable and picturesque and a far cry from the chaotic, noisy historical centre. South-west of Mergellina is Posillipo, where the ultra-wealthy live, and in the hills overlooking the bay is the residential Vomero district, a natural balcony across the city and bay to Vesuvius.

Information

Tourist Offices The EPT office at the station (☎ 26 87 79) will make hotel bookings, but make sure you give specific details on where you want to stay and how much you want to pay. Some staff speak English. Ask for *Qui Napoli* (Here Naples), published monthly in English and Italian, which lists events in the city, as well as information about transport and other services. The office is open 8.30 am to 8 pm Monday to Saturday, and 9 am to 2 pm on Sunday.

There's an AAST office in Piazza del Gesú Nuovo (☎ 552 33 28), near Piazza Dante, open 8.30 am to 7.30 pm Monday to Saturday and until 3.30 pm on Sunday.

Money There is a branch of the Banca Nazionale del Lavoro at Via Firenze 39; otherwise there are plenty of exchange booths throughout the city which often offer lower rates than the banks.

Post & Communications The main post office is in Piazza G Matteotti, off Via Armando Diaz. It's open 8.15 am to 7.30 pm Monday to Friday, and to 1 pm on Saturday. There is a Telecom office at Via A Depretis 40, open 9 am to 10 pm daily. Internetbar, Piazza Bellini 74, provides Internet access. The postcode for central Naples is 80100.

Medical & Emergency Services The Ospedale Loreto-Mare (☎ 20 10 33) is near the station on Via A Vespucci. The pharmacy in the central station is open 8 am to 8 pm daily. The questura (police station; ☎ 794 11 11) is at Via Medina 75, just off Via A Diaz, and has an office for foreigners where you can report thefts etc. To report a stolen car call ☎ 794 14 35.

Dangers & Annoyances The petty crime rate in Naples is extremely high. Carry your money and documents in a money belt and never carry a bag, purse or wear your jewellery if you can help it. The city council has started to crack down on bag-snatching thieves on motorcycles, but you should still stay alert. Car theft is also a major problem, so think twice before bringing a vehicle to the city.

Women should be careful at night near the station and around Piazza Dante. The area west of Via Toledo and as far north as Piazza Caritá can be particularly threatening.

Things to See & Do

Start by walking around Spaccanapoli, the historic centre of Naples. From the station and Corso Umberto I turn right into Via Mezzocannone, which will take you to Via Benedetto Croce, the main street of the quarter. To the left is Piazza del Gesú

ITALY

NAPLES (NAPOLI)

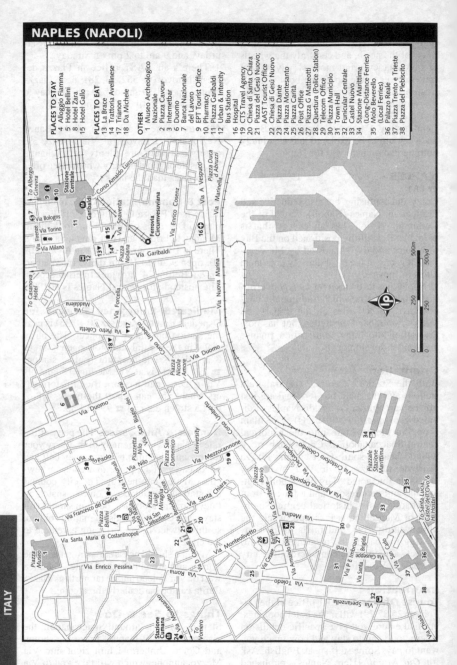

PLACES TO STAY
4 Alloggio Fiamma
5 Hotel Bellini
8 Hotel Zara
15 Hotel Gallo

PLACES TO EAT
13 La Brace
14 Trattoria Avellinese
17 Trianon
18 Da Michele

OTHER
1 Museo Archeologico Nazionale
2 Piazza Cavour
3 Internetbar
6 Duomo
7 Banca Nazionale del Lavoro
9 EPT Tourist Office
10 Pharmacy
11 Piazza Garibaldi
12 Urban & Intercity Bus Station
16 Hospital
19 CTS Travel Agency
20 Chiesa di Santa Chiara
21 Piazza del Gesù Nuovo; AAST Tourist Office
22 Chiesa di Gesù Nuovo
23 Piazza Dante
24 Piazza Montesanto
25 Piazza Cantà
26 Post Office
27 Piazza G Matteotti
28 Questura (Police Station)
29 Telecom Office
30 Piazza Municipio
31 Town Hall
32 Funicular Centrale
33 Castel Nuovo
34 Stazione Marittima (Long-Distance Ferries)
35 Molo Beverello (Local Ferries)
36 Palazzo Reale
37 Piazza Trento e Trieste
38 Piazza del Plebiscito

Nuovo, with the Neapolitan baroque **Chiesa di Gesú Nuovo** and the 14th-century **Chiesa di Santa Chiara**, restored to its original Gothic-Provençal style after it was severely damaged by bombing during WWII. The beautiful **Chiostro delle Clarisse** (Nuns' Cloisters) should not be missed.

The **Duomo**, on Via Duomo, has a 19th-century facade but was built by the Angevin kings at the end of the 13th century, on the site of an earlier basilica. Inside is the **Cappella di San Gennaro**, which contains the head of St Januarius (the city's patron saint) and two vials of his congealed blood. The saint is said to have saved the city from plague, volcanic eruptions and other disasters. Every year the faithful gather to pray for a miracle, namely that the blood will liquefy and save the city from further disaster (see Special Events later in this section).

Turn off Via Duomo into **Via Tribunali**, one of the more characteristic streets of the area, and head for Piazza Dante, through the 17th-century **Port'Alba**, one of the gates to the city. Via Roma, the most fashionable street in old Naples, heads to the left (becoming Via Toledo) and ends at Piazza Trento e Trieste and the **Piazza del Plebiscito**.

In the piazza is the **Palazzo Reale**, the former official residence of the Bourbon and Savoy kings, now a museum. It is open 9 am to 1.30 pm Tuesday to Sunday and also from 4 to 7.30 pm on weekends. Admission is L8000. Just off the piazza is the **Teatro San Carlo**, one of the most famous opera houses in the world thanks to its perfect acoustics and beautiful interior.

The 13th-century **Castel Nuovo** overlooks Naples' ferry port. The early-Renaissance triumphal arch commemorates the entry of Alfonso I of Aragon into Naples in 1443. It is possible to visit the **Museo Civico** in the castle. South-west along the waterfront at Santa Lucia is the **Castel dell'Ovo**, originally a Norman castle, which is surrounded by a tiny fishing village, the **Borgo Marinaro**.

You will find the **Museo Archeologico Nazionale** in Piazza Museo, north of Piazza Dante. The museum contains one of the most important collections of Graeco-Roman artefacts in the world, mainly the rich collection of the Farnese family, and the art treasures that were discovered at Pompeii and Herculaneum. It opens 9 am to

10 pm Tuesday to Saturday, and to 8 pm Sunday (L12,000).

To escape the noisy city centre, catch the Funicolare Centrale (funicular), in Via Toledo, to the suburb of **Vomero** and visit the Certosa di San Martino, a 14th-century Carthusian monastery, rebuilt in the 17th century in Neapolitan-baroque style. It houses the **Museo Nazionale di San Martino**. The monastery's church is well worth a visit, as are its terraced gardens, which afford spectacular views of Naples and the bay. The monastery is open 9 am to 2 pm Tuesday to Sunday (L8000).

Special Events
Religious festivals are lively occasions in Naples, especially the celebration of St Januarius, the patron saint of the city, held three times a year (the first Sunday in May, 19 September and 16 December) in the Duomo.

Places to Stay
Hostel The HI *Ostello Mergellina Napoli* (☎ *761 23 46, Salita della Grotta 23)*, in Mergellina, is modern and safe. B&B is L26,000. It's open all year and imposes a maximum three-night stay in summer. Take the Metropolitana to Mergellina, and signs will direct you to the hostel from the waterfront.

Hotels – Around Stazione Centrale
The following hotels are safe and offer a reasonable standard of accommodation. *Hotel Zara* (☎ *28 71 25,* ✉ *hotelzar@tin.it, Via Firenze 81)* is clean with singles/doubles for L35,000/60,000. Via Firenze is off Corso Novara, to the right as you leave the train station. *Albergo Ginevra* (☎ *28 32 10, Via Genova 116)* is another reliable and well-kept place with rooms for L42,000/67,000. *Casanova Hotel* (☎ *26 82 87, Corso Garibaldi 333)* is quiet and safe, with rooms for L35,000/70,000; triples with shower are L95,000. *Hotel Gallo* (☎ *20 05 12, fax 28 18 49, Via Spaventa 11)*, left out of the train station, has rooms of different standards (ask to see them first) for L110,000/160,000.

Hotels – Around Spaccanapoli The best option in this area is the popular *Hotel Bellini* (☎ *45 69 96, Via San Paolo 44)*, which has

ITALY

singles/doubles for L70,000/120,000. *Alloggio Fiamma (☎ 45 91 87, Via Francesco del Giudice 13)* has pretty basic doubles/triples for L80,000/110,000.

Places to Eat

Naples is the home of pasta and pizza. In fact, once you have eaten a good Neapolitan pizza, topped with fresh tomatoes, oregano, basil and garlic, no other pizza will taste the same. Try a *calzone*, a filled version of a pizza, or *mozzarella in carozza* (mozzarella deep-fried in bread), which is sold at tiny street stalls. Also sold at street stalls is *misto di frittura* (deep-fried vegetables). Don't leave town without trying the *sfogliatelle* (light, flaky pastry filled with ricotta).

Restaurants According to the locals the best pizza in Naples (and Italy) is served at *Da Michele (Via Cesare Sersale 1)*. The place is always crowded and you'll need to queue with a numbered ticket. Another excellent option is the nearby *Trianon (Via Pietro Colletta 46)* near Via Tribunali. There's a wide selection from L5000. *La Brace (Via Spaventa 14)* is also recommended; you can eat well for around L25,000. Down the same street is *Trattoria Avellinese (Via Silvio Spaventa 31-35)*, just off Piazza Garibaldi, which specialises in cheap seafood.

The area around Piazza Sannazzaro, south-west of the centre, also has good offerings. *Pizzeria da Pasqualino (Piazza Sannazzaro 79)* has outdoor tables and serves good pizzas and seafood. A meal will cost around L20,000 with wine. *Daniele (Via A Scarlatti 104)*, is a bar with a restaurant upstairs. *Cibo Cibo (Via Cimarosa 150)*, is another good budget spot. In Vomero, *Trattoria da Sica (Via Bernini 17)* has excellent local dishes – try the *spaghetti alle vongole e pomodorini* (spaghetti with clams and cherry tomatoes).

Shopping

The narrow streets of Naples are full of markets, notably in the area off Via Mancinio (off Piazza Garibaldi), near Piazza Caritá (which separates Via Roma and Via Toledo) and around Piazza Montesanto.

Getting There & Away

Buses leave from Piazza Garibaldi, just outside the train station, for Salerno, Benevento, Caserta and Bari, Lecce and Brindisi in Apulia.

Naples is a major rail-transport centre for the south, and regular trains for most major Italian cities arrive and depart from the Stazione Centrale. There are up to 30 trains a day for Rome.

Traghetti (small ferries), *aliscafi* (hydrofoils) and *navi veloce* (fast ships) leave for Capri, Sorrento, Ischia and Procida from the Molo Beverello, in front of the Castel Nuovo. Some hydrofoils leave for the bay islands from Mergellina, and ferries for Ischia and Procida also leave from Pozzuoli. All operators have offices at the various ports from which they leave. Hydrofoils cost twice as much as ferries, but the trip takes half the time.

Ferries to Palermo and Cagliari (Tirrenia ☎ 147 89 90 00) and to the Aeolian Islands (Siremar ☎ 091 761 36 88; SNAV ☎ 761 23 48) leave from the Stazione Marittima on Molo Angioino, next to Molo Beverello (see the Getting There & Away sections under Sicily and Sardinia).

Getting Around

You can make your way around Naples by bus, tram, Metropolitana (underground) and funicular. City buses leave from Piazza Garibaldi in front of Stazione Centrale bound for the centre of Naples, as well as for Mergellina. Tickets, called GiraNapoli, cost L1500 for 90 minutes and are valid for all forms of transport. Day tickets cost L4500.

Tram No 1 leaves from east of Stazione Centrale for the city centre. To reach Molo Beverello and the ferry terminal from Stazione Centrale, take bus No R2 152 (known as 'La Sepsa') or the M1 subway line.

Metropolitana trains head west to Mergellina, stopping at Piazza Cavour, Piazza Amedeo and the funicular to Vomero. Another line, now under construction, will eventually connect Piazza Garibaldi and Piazza Medaglie d'Oro.

AROUND NAPLES
Pompeii, Herculaneum & Mt Vesuvius
☎ 081

Famously buried under a layer of lapilli (burning fragments of pumice stone) during the devastating eruption of Mt Vesuvius in AD 79, **Pompeii** provides a fascinating insight into how the ancient Romans lived. It was a resort town for wealthy Romans, and among the vast ruins are impressive temples, a forum, one of the largest known Roman amphitheatres, and streets lined with shops and luxurious houses. Many of the site's mosaics and frescoes have been moved to Naples' Museo Archeologico Nazionale. The exception is the Villa dei Misteri, where the frescoes remain *in situ*.

Legend has it that **Herculaneum** (Ercolano) was founded by Hercules. First Greek, then Roman, it was also destroyed by the AD 79 eruption, buried under mud and lava. Most inhabitants of Herculaneum had enough warning and managed to escape. The ruins here are smaller and the buildings, particularly the private houses, are remarkably well preserved. Here you can see better examples of the frescoes, mosaics and furniture that used to decorate Roman houses.

The ruins at Pompeii and Herculaneum are open daily from 9 am to one hour before sunset. Entry is L12,000.

If you want to have a look into the huge crater of **Mt Vesuvius**, catch the Trasporti Vesuviani bus (see the following Getting There & Away section). You'll then need to walk about 1.5km to the summit, where you must pay L9000 to be accompanied by a guide to the crater. See Lonely Planet's *Walking in Italy* guide for detailed information on walking circuits on Vesuvius.

Information There are tourist offices (AACST) at Via Sacra 1 (☎ 850 72 55) in the new town, and just outside the excavations at Piazza Porta Marina Inferiore 12 (☎ 167 01 33 50 toll-free). Both offer information for visitors, notes on guided tours and simple site maps.

Getting There & Away Both sites are accessible from Naples via the Circumvesuviana train. For Pompeii, get off at the Pompeii-Villa dei Misteri stop; the Porta Marina entrance is close by. For Herculaneum, get off at the Ercolano stop.

Trasporti Vesuviani buses (☎ 739 28 33) do a loop from Pompeii (Piazza Anfiteatro) to Herculaneum (train station) to Mt Vesuvius (Quota 1000 car park). Return tickets to Mt Vesuvius are L7000 return Herculaneum and L12,000 from Pompeii.

SORRENTO
☎ 081
This major resort town is in a particularly beautiful area, but is heavily overcrowded in summer with package tourists and traffic. However, it is handy to the Amalfi Coast and Capri.

The centre of town is Piazza Tasso, a short walk from the train station along Corso Italia. The AAST tourist office (☎ 807 40 33), at Via Luigi de Maio 35, is inside the Circolo dei Forestieri complex. It is open 8.45 am to 2.30 pm and 4 to 6.45 pm Monday to Saturday.

Places to Stay
There are several camping grounds, including *Nube d'Argento* (☎ 878 13 44, Via del Capo 21), which costs L12,000 per person and up to L15,000 for a tent site.

The HI *Ostello La Caffeteria* (☎ 807 29 25, Via degli Aranci 160), near the train station, offers B&B for L26,000.

Getting There & Away
Sorrento is easily accessible from Naples on the Circumvesuviana train line. SITA buses leave from outside the train station for the Amalfi Coast. Hydrofoils and ferries leave from the port, along Via de Maio and down the steps from the tourist office, for Capri and Napoli all year round and Ischia in summer only.

CAPRI
☎ 081
This beautiful island is only an hour by ferry from Naples. The island is famous for its grottoes and for 12 villas built by successive Roman emperors, including Augustus and Tiberius. A short bus ride will take you to Anacapri, the town uphill from Capri – a good alternative if rooms are full in Capri.

Boat tours of the grottoes, including the famous **Grotta Azzurra** (Blue Grotto), leave from the Marina Grande and a round trip will cost L26,500 (which includes the cost of a motorboat to the grotto, rowing boat into the grotto and entrance fee). It is cheaper to catch a bus from Anacapri (although the rowboat and entrance fee still total around L16,000).

For information on ferries to the island, see the Getting There & Away section under Naples.

ITALY

Orientation & Information

There are tourist offices at Marina Grande (☎ 837 06 34), where all the ferries arrive, in Piazza Umberto I (☎ 837 06 86, fax 837 09 18, ✉ touristoffice@capri.it) in the centre of town, and at Piazza Vittoria 4 in Anacapri (☎ 837 15 24). Online information can be found at www.capri.it.

Places to Stay

Stella Maris (☎ 837 04 52, Via Roma 27), just off Piazza Umberto I, is right in the noisy heart of town. Doubles range from L100,000 to 160,000. *Villa Luisa* (☎ 837 01 28, Via D Birago 1) is a private house with a couple of doubles for rent at L95,000; the views are terrific.

In Anacapri near the town centre, the *Loreley* (☎ 837 14 40, ✉ loreley@ caprinet.it, Via G Orlandi 16) has singles/ doubles with bathroom starting at L80,000/135,000. *Caesar Augustus* (☎ 837 14 21, Via G Orlandi 4) is a beautiful hotel which becomes a knockout bargain in the off season and when there are empty rooms. In season, rooms start at L150,000/200,000. It opens from 1 May to the end of October.

AMALFI COAST
☎ 089

The Amalfi Coast swarms with rich tourists in summer and prices are correspondingly high. However, it remains a place of rare and spectacular beauty and if you can manage to get there in spring or autumn, you will be surprised by the reasonably priced accommodation and peaceful atmosphere.

There are tourist information offices in the individual towns, including Positano (☎ 87 50 67) at Via Saracino 2, and Amalfi (☎ 87 11 07), on the waterfront at Corso Roma 19.

Positano

This is the most beautiful town on the coast, but for exactly this reason it has also become the most fashionable. It is, however, still possible to stay here cheaply. The hills behind Positano offer some great walks if you tire of lazing on the beach.

On the way from Positano to Amalfi is the town of **Praiano**, which is not as scenic but has more budget lodging options, including the only camping ground on the Amalfi Coast.

Places to Stay In Positano, *Villa Maria Luisa* (☎ 87 50 23, Via Fornillo 40) is the pick of the budget options, with double rooms with terraces for L100,000 in the low season and L130,000, breakfast included, in August. *Villa delle Palme* (☎ 87 51 62), around the corner in Via Pasitea, is run by the same management and charges L125,000 for a double in the low season, and L140,000 at the height of summer.

In Praiano, *La Tranquillitá* (☎ 87 40 84, ✉ contraq@contraqpraiano.com) has a pensione, bungalows and a small camping ground. It costs L25,000 per head to camp there if you have your own tent. For a double room or bungalow it is L100,000 (with breakfast) and in summer there is compulsory half-pension at L105,000 per head including room, private bathroom, breakfast and dinner. The SITA bus stops outside the pensione. The entire establishment closes down in winter, reopening at Easter.

Amalfi

One of the four powerful maritime republics of medieval Italy, Amalfi today is a popular tourist resort. It has an impressive **Duomo**, and nearby is the **Grotta dello Smeraldo**, which rivals Capri's Blue Grotto.

In the hills behind Amalfi is **Ravello**, accessible by bus and worth a visit if only to see the magnificent 11th-century **Villa Rufolo**, once the home of popes and, later, of the German composer Wagner. The 20th-century **Villa Cimbrone**, is set in beautiful gardens, which end at a terrace offering a spectacular view of the Gulf of Salerno. There are numerous walking paths in the hills between Amalfi and Ravello. Pick up *Walks from Amalfi – The Guide to a Web of Ancient Italian Pathways* (L12,000) in Amalfi.

Places to Stay The HI *Ostello Beato Solitudo* (☎ 081 802 50 48, Piazza G Avitabile) is in Agerola San Lazzaro, a village just 16km west of Amalfi. It charges L17,500 for a bed only. A bus leaves every 45 minutes from Amalfi, the last at 8.50 pm.

In Amalfi, *Albergo Proto* (☎ 87 10 03, Salita dei Curiali 4) has doubles/triples from L125,000/175,000, breakfast included. *Hotel Lidomare* (☎ 87 13 32, Via Piccolomini 9) has homy singles/doubles for L80,000/135,000 – just follow the signs from Piazza del Duomo and go left up a flight of stairs.

Getting There & Away

The coast is accessible by regular SITA buses, which run between Salerno (a 40-minute train trip from Naples) and Sorrento (accessible from Naples on the Circumvesuviana train line). Buses stop in Amalfi at Piazza Flavio Gioia, from where you can also catch a bus to Ravello.

Hydrofoils and ferries also service the coast, leaving from Salerno and stopping at Amalfi and Positano. From Positano in summer you can catch a boat to Capri.

PAESTUM

☎ 0828

The evocative image of three Greek temples standing in fields of poppies is not easily forgotten and makes the trek to this archaeological site well worth the effort. The three temples, just south of Salerno, are among the world's best preserved monuments of the ancient Greek world. There is a tourist office (☎ 81 10 16) open 9 am to 2 pm daily and an interesting museum (L8000) at the site, open 9 am to 7 pm (to 10 pm in summer) daily (except the first and third Mondays of the month). The ruins are open daily from 9 am to two hours before sunset and entry is L8000.

Paestum is accessible from Salerno by ATACS bus or by train.

MATERA

☎ 0835

This ancient city in the region of Basilicata evokes powerful images of a peasant culture which existed until just over 30 years ago. Its famous *sassi* (the stone houses built in the two ravines which slice through the city) were home to more than half of Matera's population (about 20,000 people) until the 1950s, when the local government built a new residential area just out of Matera and relocated the entire population.

The two sassi wards, which are known as **Barisano** and **Caveoso**, had no electricity, running water or sewerage until well into last century. The oldest sassi are at the top of the ravines, and the dwellings which appear to be the oldest were established in the 20th century. As space ran out in the 1920s, the population started moving into hand-hewn or natural caves, an extraordinary example of civilisation in reverse. The sassi zones are accessible from Piazza Vittorio Veneto and Piazza del Duomo in the centre of Matera.

There is a tourist office (☎ 33 19 83) at Via de Viti De Marco 9, off the main Via Roma. Itinera (☎ 26 32 59, ✉ arttur@tin.it) organises guided tours in English of the sassi wards for around L50,000 an hour (maximum five people). You can find information about Matera on the Web at www.materanet.com.

Places to Stay & Eat

There are few options for budget accommodation here and it is best to book in advance. The fairly bare *Albergo Roma (☎ 33 39 12, Via Roma 62)* has singles/doubles for L45,000/65,000.

The local fare is simple and the focus is on vegetables. *Da Aulo (Via Padre Minozzo 21)* is economical and serves typical dishes of Basilicata. There is a fruit and vegetable market near Piazza V Veneto, between Via Lucana and Via A Persio.

Getting There & Away

SITA buses connect Matera with Potenza, Taranto and Metaponto. The town is on the private Ferrovie Apulo-Lucane train line, which connects with Bari, Altamura and Potenza. There are also three Marozzi buses a day from Rome to Matera. Buses arrive in Piazza Matteotti, a short walk down Via Roma from the town centre.

BRINDISI

☎ 0831

As the major embarkation point for ferries from Italy to Greece, Brindisi swarms with travellers in transit. There is not much to do here, other than wait, so most backpackers gather at the train station or at the port in the Stazione Marittima. The two are connected by Corso Umberto I – which becomes Corso Garibaldi – and are a 10-minute walk from each other; otherwise, you can take bus No 3 or 9.

The EPT tourist information office (☎ 56 21 26) is at Lungomare Regina Margherita 12. Another information office is inside the ferry terminal. Be careful of bag snatchers and pickpockets in the area around the train station and the port.

Places to Stay & Eat

The non-HI *Ostello per la Gioventú* (☎ 56 80 24, *Via N Brandi 4, Casale)* is about 2km out of town. B&B costs L20,000. Take bus No 3 from Via Cristoforo Colombo near the train station. *Hotel Venezia* (☎ 52 75 11, *Via Pisanelli 4)* has singles/doubles for L27,000/ 50,000. Turn left off Corso Umberto I onto Via S Lorenzo da Brindisi to get there.

There are numerous takeaway outlets along the main route between the train and boat stations, but if you want a meal, head for the side streets. *Vecchio Vicolo* (*Vicolo D'Orimini 13),* between the station and the port, has good-value meals for around L20,000.

Getting There & Away

Marozzi runs several buses a day to/from Rome (Stazione Tiburtina), leaving from Viale Regina Margherita in Brindisi. Appia Travel (☎ 52 16 84), Viale Regina Margherita 8-9, sells tickets (L65,000, nine hours). Brindisi is directly connected by train to the major cities of northern Italy, as well as Rome, Ancona and Naples.

Boat Ferries leave Brindisi for Greek destinations including Corfu, Igoumenitsa, Patras and Cefalonia. Adriatica (☎ 52 38 25), at Corso Garibaldi 85-87, is open from 9 am to 1 pm and 4 to 7 pm; you can check in here until 7 pm (after 8 pm check-in is in front of the ship). Other major ferry companies are Hellenic Mediterranean Lines (☎ 52 85 31), at Corso Garibaldi 8; and Italian Ferries (☎ 59 03 21), at Corso Garibaldi 96-98.

Adriatica and Hellenic are the most expensive, but also the most reliable. They are also the only lines that can officially accept Eurail and Inter-Rail passes, which means you pay only L20,500 to travel deck class. For a *poltrona* (airline-type chair) you'll pay L32,000, and for a second-class cabin L48,000. If you want to use your Eurail or Inter-Rail pass, it is important to reserve some weeks in advance in summer. Even with a booking in summer, you must still go to the Adriatic or Hellenic embarkation office in the Stazione Marittima to have your ticket checked.

Discounts are available for travellers under 26 years of age and holders of some Italian rail passes. Note that in July and August fares increase by 40% and ferry services are also increased. Average prices in the 2000 high season for deck class were: Adriatica and Hellenic to Corfu, Igoumenitsa, Cefalonia or Patras cost L120,000 (L100,000 return); Med Link to Patras cost L70,000 on deck. Prices go up by an average L25,000 for a poltrona, and for the cheapest cabin accommodation prices jump by L40,000 to L65,000. Bicycles can be taken on board free, but the average high-season fare for a motorcycle is L60,000 and for a car around L130,000.

The port tax is L12,000, payable when you buy your ticket. It is essential to check in at least two hours prior to departure.

AROUND BRINDISI
Lecce
☎ 0832

Baroque can be grotesque, but never in Lecce. The style here is so refined and particular to the city that the Italians call it Barocco Leccese (Lecce baroque). The most famous example of the style is the **Basilica di Santa Croce**. Artists worked for 150 years to decorate the building, creating an extraordinarily ornate facade.

Lecce's numerous bars and restaurants are a pleasant surprise in such a small city. There is an APT information office (☎ 24 80 92) at Via Vittorio Emanuele 24 near Piazza Duomo. Take bus No 2 from the station to the town centre.

Places to Stay The *Torre Rinalda* (☎ 38 21 62) is a camp site near the sea that is accessible by STP bus from the terminal in Lecce's Via Adua. It costs L12,000/16,000 per person/site. In Lecce try *Hotel Cappello* (☎ 30 88 81, *Via Montegrappa 4)* near the station. Singles/doubles are L57,000/90,000 with bathroom.

Getting There & Away STP buses connect Lecce with towns throughout the Salentine peninsula, leaving from Via Adua. Lecce is directly linked by train to Brindisi, Bari, Rome, Naples and Bologna. The Ferrovie del Sud Est runs trains to all major points in Apulia.

REGGIO DI CALABRIA
☎ 0965

The port city of Reggio di Calabria, on the Strait of Messina, was founded in approximately 720 BC by Greek colonists. In 1908 the city was destroyed by an earthquake (which also razed Messina) and has since been totally rebuilt.

Reggio's only really impressive sight is the **Museo Nazionale** (National Museum), which houses a remarkable collection documenting Greek civilisation in Calabria. Of particular interest are the *Bronzi di Riace* (Bronze Warriors of Riace), two Greek statues found off the coast of Riace in 1972. Reggio's **lungomare**, the promenade along the port, overlooks Sicily – in certain atmospheric conditions, such as at dawn, it is possible to see the fabled 'mirage of Morgana' (the reflection of Messina in the sea).

There is an information booth at the Stazione Centrale train station (☎ 271 20) and at Corso Garibaldi 329 (☎ 89 20 12) where you can pick up a map and a list of hotels. The main tourist office is at Via Roma 3 (☎ 211 71).

Getting There & Away
From Reggio there are regular trains to Naples and Rome, and to Metaponto, Taranto and Bari. Reggio has two stations: Stazione Lido (at the port) and Stazione Centrale (in the town centre at Piazza Garibaldi).

SNAV (☎ 2 95 68) runs up to 20 daily hydrofoils from the port, just north of Stazione Lido, to Messina. Some continue onwards to the Isole Eolie (Aeolian Islands). It is easier, particularly if you arrive from the north by train, to catch a ferry to Messina from Villa San Giovanni, 15 minutes north of Reggio by train.

Sicily

Sicily, the largest island in the Mediterranean, is a land of Greek temples, Norman churches and castles, Arab and Byzantine domes and splendid baroque churches and palaces. Its landscape, dominated by the volcano Mt Etna (3330m) on the east coast, ranges from fertile coast to mountains in the north to a vast, dry plateau at its centre.

Sicily, with a population of about five million, has a mild climate in winter. Summer can be relentlessly hot, when the beaches swarm with holidaying Italians and other Europeans. The best times to visit are in spring and autumn, when it is hot enough for the beach, but not too hot for sightseeing.

Most ferries from Italy arrive at Sicily's capital, Palermo, which is a convenient jumping-off point. If you're short on time, spend a day in Palermo and then perhaps head for Taormina and Agrigento. Syracuse is another highlight.

The Mafia remains a powerful force in Sicily, despite taking a hammering from the authorities throughout the 1990s. But the 'men of honour' are little interested in the affairs of tourists, so there is no need to fear you will be caught in the crossfire of a gang war while in Sicily.

Getting There & Away
Bus services from Rome to Sicily are operated by Segesta (☎ 46 481 96 76 in Rome), which has two departures daily from Rome's Piazza Tiburtina. The buses service Messina (L55,000, nine hours), Palermo (L66,000, 12 hours) and Syracuse (L66,000, 12 hours). SAIS Trasporti (☎ 091 617 11 41 in Palermo) also has a daily service to Catania and Palermo (L75,000).

One of the cheapest ways to reach Sicily is to catch a train to Messina. The cost of the ticket covers the 3km ferry crossing from Villa San Giovanni (Calabria) to Messina.

Sicily is accessible by ferry from Genoa, Livorno, Naples, Reggio di Calabria and Cagliari, and also from Malta and Tunisia. The main companies servicing the Mediterranean are Tirrenia (☎ 091 33 33 00 in Palermo; ☎ 46 474 20 41 in Rome) and Grimaldi (☎ 091 58 74 04 in Palermo; ☎ 46 42 81 83 88 in Rome) which runs Grandi Traghetti and Grandi Navi Veloci. Prices are determined by the season and jump considerably in the summer period (July to September).

At the time of writing, high-season fares for a poltrona were: Genoa-Palermo with Grimaldi Grandi Navi Veloci (L150,000, 20 hours); Naples-Palermo with Tirrenia (L88,000, 10 hours); and Cagliari-Palermo with Tirrenia, (L70,000; 10 hours). A bed in a shared cabin with four beds costs an additional L25,000 to L35,000. Cars cost upwards of L130,000.

PALERMO
☎ 091
An Arab emirate and later the seat of a Norman kingdom, Palermo was once regarded as the grandest and most beautiful city in

Europe. Today it is in a remarkable state of decay, due to neglect and heavy bombing during WWII, yet enough evidence remains of its golden days to make Palermo one of the most fascinating cities in Italy.

Palermo is a large but easily manageable city. The main streets of the historical centre are Via Roma and Via Maqueda, which extend from the central station to Piazza Castelnuovo, a vast square in the modern part of town.

Information

Tourist Offices The main APT tourist office (☎ 58 61 22) is at Piazza Castelnuovo 35. It's open 8.30 am to 2 pm and 2.30 to 6 pm Monday to Friday (to 2 pm on Saturday). There are branch offices at the Stazione Centrale (☎ 616 59 14) and airport (☎ 59 16 98) with the same opening hours as the main office.

Money The exchange office at the Stazione Centrale is open 8 am to 8 pm daily. American Express is represented by Ruggieri & Figli (☎ 58 71 44), at Via Emerico Amari 40, near the Stazione Marittima.

Post & Communications The main post office is at Via Roma 322 and the main Telecom telephone office is opposite the station in Piazza G Cesare, open 8.30 am to 9.30 pm daily. The postcode for Palermo is 90100.

Medical & Emergency Services For an ambulance call ☎ 30 66 44. The public hospital, Ospedale Civico (☎ 666 22 07), is at Via Carmelo Lazzaro. The all-night pharmacy, Lo Cascio (☎ 616 21 17), is near the train station at Via Roma 1. The questura (police station; ☎ 21 01 11) is at Piazza della Vittoria and is open 24 hours a day.

Dangers & Annoyances Contrary to popular opinion, Palermo is not a hotbed of thievery, but you will have to watch your valuables, which may attract pickpockets and bag snatchers. The historical centre can be a little dodgy at night, especially for women walking alone. Travellers should also avoid walking alone in the area northeast of the station, between Via Roma and the port (though there is safety in numbers).

Things to See

The intersection of Via Vittorio Emanuele and Via Maqueda marks the **Quattro Canti** (four corners of historical Palermo). The four 17th-century Spanish baroque facades are each decorated with a statue. Nearby is **Piazza Pretoria**, with a beautiful fountain (**Fontana Pretoria**), created by Florentine sculptors in the 16th century. Locals used to call it the Fountain of Shame because of its nude figures. Also in the piazza are the baroque **Chiesa di Santa Caterina** and the **Palazzo del Municipio** (town hall). Nearby is Piazza Bellini and Palermo's most famous church, **La Martorana**, with a beautiful Arab-Norman bell tower and its interior decorated with Byzantine mosaics. Next to it is the Norman **Chiesa di San Cataldo**, which also mixes Arab and Norman styles and is easily recognisable by its red domes.

The huge Norman **cattedrale** is along Via Vittorio Emanuele, on the corner of Via Bonello. Although modified many times over the centuries, it remains an impressive example of Norman architecture. Opposite Piazza della Vittoria and the gardens is **Palazzo Reale**, also known as Palazzo dei Normanni, now the seat of the government. Enter from Piazza Indipendenza to see the **Cappella Palatina**, a magnificent example of Arab-Norman architecture, built during the reign of Roger II and decorated with Byzantine mosaics. Upstairs, the **Sala di Ruggero** (King Roger's former bedroom) is decorated with 12th-century mosaics and can only be visited with a guide (free of charge).

Take bus No 8/9 from under the trees across the piazza from the train station to the nearby town of **Monreale** to see the magnificent mosaics in the famous 12th-century cathedral of **Santa Maria la Nuova**.

Places to Stay

The best camping ground is *Trinacria* (☎ 53 05 90, *Via Barcarello 25*), at Sferracavallo by the sea. It costs L9000/L9500/L500 per person/tent/car. Catch bus No 616 from Piazzale Alcide de Gasperi, which can be reached by bus No 101 or 107 from the station.

There is a new hostel called *Casa Marconi* (☎ 657 06 11, *Via Monfenera 140*) which has cheap, good quality singles/doubles for L35,000/60,000. To get there, take bus No 246 from the station and get off at Piazza Montegrappa; the hostel is 300m away.

Near the train station try *Albergo Orientale* (☎ *616 57 27, Via Maqueda 26*), in an old and somewhat decayed palace. Singles/doubles are L35,000/55,000. Just around the corner is *Albergo Rosalia Conca d'Oro* (☎ *616 45 43, Via Santa Rosalia 7*) with very basic singles/doubles/triples at L40,000/60,000/90,000 without bath.

Hotel Sicilia (☎ *616 84 60, Via Divisi 99*), on the corner of Via Maqueda, has rooms of a higher standard at L50,000/75,000 with bath. An excellent and popular choice is *Hotel Joli* (☎ *611 17 65, Via Michele Amari 11*) which has clean and comfortable rooms for L60,000/90,000; book early.

Places to Eat
The Palermitani are late eaters and restaurants rarely open for dinner before 8 pm. At *Osteria Lo Bianco* (*Via E Amari 104*), at the Castelnuovo end of town, a full meal will cost around L30,000. *Trattoria Stella* (*Via Alloro 104*) is in the courtyard of the old Hotel Patria. A full meal will come to around L40,000. One of the city's best-loved restaurants is *Hostaria da Ciccio* (*Via Firenze 6*), just off Via Roma. A meal will cost around L30,000.

The *vucciria*, Palermo's open-air markets, are held daily (except Sunday) in the narrow streets between Via Roma, Piazza San Domenico and Via Vittorio Emanuele. Here you can buy fresh fruit and vegetables, meat, cheese and virtually anything else you want. There are even stalls which sell steaming-hot boiled octopus.

Getting There & Away
The main (Intercity) terminal for destinations throughout Sicily and the mainland is in the area around Via Paolo Balsamo, to the right (east) as you leave the station. Offices for the various companies are all in this area, including SAIS Traporti (☎ 616 60 28), at Via Balsamo 16, and Segesta (☎ 616 79 19), at Via Balsamo 26.

Regular trains leave from the Stazione Centrale for Milazzo, Messina, Catania and Syracuse, as well as for nearby towns such as Cefalú. Direct trains go to Reggio di Calabria, Naples and Rome. For a one-way ticket to Rome you pay L73,200 in 2nd class plus a L26,000 Intercity supplement.

Boats leave from the port (Molo Vittorio Veneto) for Sardinia and the mainland (see the Getting There & Away section under Sicily). The Tirrenia office (☎ 33 33 00) is at the port.

Getting Around
Palermo's buses are efficient and most stop outside the train station. Useful routes include the No 7 along Via Roma from the train station to near Piazza Castelnuovo, and the No 39 from the station to the port. Buy tickets (L1500; valid for one hour) before boarding.

TAORMINA
☎ 0942
Spectacularly located on a hill overlooking the sea and Mt Etna, Taormina was long ago discovered by the European jet set, which has made it one of the more expensive and touristy towns in Sicily. But its magnificent setting, its Greek theatre and the nearby beaches remain as seductive now as they were when Goethe and DH Lawrence visited here.

The AAST tourist office (☎ 2 32 43) in Palazzo Corvaja, just off Corso Umberto near Largo Santa Caterina, has extensive information on the town.

Things to See & Do
The Greek theatre (cntry L4000) was built in the 3rd century BC and later greatly expanded and remodelled by the Romans. Concerts and theatre are staged there in summer and it affords a wonderful view of Mt Etna. From the beautiful Trevelyan Gardens there is a panoramic view of the sea. Along Corso Umberto is the Duomo, with a Gothic facade.

The local beach is Isola Bella, a short bus ride from Via Pirandello or by the *funivia* (cable car) which costs L5000 return.

Places to Stay & Eat
You can camp near the beach at *Campeggio San Leo* (☎ *2 46 58, Via Nazionale*) at Capo Taormina. The cost is L10,000 per person per night, and L14,000 for a tent site.

There are numerous *affittacamere* (room rentals) in Taormina and the tourist office has a full list. *Il Leone* (☎ *2 38 78, Via Bagnoli Croce 127*), near the Trevelyan Gardens, charges L45,000 per person with

ITALY

breakfast. *Pensione Svizzera* (☎ *237 90,* @ *svizzera@tau.it, Via Pirandello 26),* on the way from the bus stop to the town centre, has very pleasant rooms for L80,000/120,000 with private bathroom.

Ristorante La Piazzetta (Via Paladini 5) has excellent full meals for around L30,000. *Da Rita (Via Calapitrulli 3)* serves pizza, bruschetta and lots of big salads. To drink a good Sicilian wine or sangria go to *Arco Rosso (Via Naumachie 7).* Eat a typical Sicilian summer breakfast at *Bam Bar (Via Di Giovanni 45).* Order a granita of crushed ice with fresh fruit or almonds.

Getting There & Away
Bus is the easiest way to get to Taormina. SAIS buses leave from Messina, Catania and also from the airport at Catania. Taormina is on the main train line between Messina and Catania, but the station is on the coast and regular buses will take you to Via Pirandello, near the centre; bus services are heavily reduced on Sunday.

MT ETNA
☎ 095
Dominating the landscape in eastern Sicily between Taormina and Catania, Mt Etna (3323m) is Europe's largest live volcano. It has four live craters at its summit and its slopes are littered with crevices and extinct cones. Eruptions of slow lava flows can occur locally, but are not really dangerous. Etna's most recent eruption was in 1999. You can climb to the summit (it's a seven-hour hike), but the handiest way is to take the cable car (SITAS ☎ 91 41 41) from **Rifugio Sapienza** on the Nicolosi side of the mountain. The all-inclusive price for the cable car, a 4WD vehicle to near the tip of the crater and a guide is L65,000. From the north side, there is a 4WD minibus (Le Betulle/STAR, ☎ 64 34 30) from Piano Provenzana. A three-hour guided tour costs L60,000.

Mt Etna is best approached from Catania by AST bus (☎ 53 17 56; L7000 return), which departs from Via L Sturzo (in front of the train station) at 8.15 am, returning from Rifugio Sapienza at 4.30 pm. A private Circumetnea train line (☎ 37 48 42) circles Mt Etna from Giarre-Riposto to Catania. It starts from Catania at Stazione Borgo, Corso delle Province 13 (take bus No 29 or 36 from Cata-

nia's main train station). From Taormina, you can take an FS train to Giarre, where you can catch the Circumetnea.

In nearby Catania, Natura e Turismo (NeT; ☎ 33 35 43, fax 53 79 10, @ natur@ tin.it), Via Quartararo 11, organises guided walks and excursions on Mt Etna and in surrounding areas.

SYRACUSE
☎ 0931
Once a powerful Greek city to rival Athens, Syracuse (Siracusa) is one of the highlights of a visit to Sicily. Founded in 743 BC by colonists from Corinth, it became a dominant sea power in the Mediterranean, prompting Athens to attack the city in 413 BC. Syracuse was the birthplace of the Greek mathematician and physicist Archimedes, and Plato attended the court of the tyrant Dionysius, who ruled from 405 to 367 BC.

The main sights of Syracuse are in two areas: on the island of Ortygia and at the archaeological park 2km across town. There are two tourist information offices. The AAT (☎ 46 42 55), at Via Maestranza 33, on Ortygia, opens 9 am to 1 pm and 4.30 to 8.30 pm weekdays (mornings only on Saturday). The APT (☎ 6 77 10), at Via San Sebastiano 45, opens 8.30 am to 1.30 pm Monday to Saturday. There is a branch office of the APT, with the same opening hours, at the archaeological park.

Things to See
On the island of **Ortygia** the buildings are predominantly medieval, with some baroque palaces and churches. The main archaeological zone is the **Neapolis-Parco Archeologico**, with a 5th-century BC Greek theatre, its seating area carved out of solid rock. The park is open 9 am to one hour before sunset daily. Admission is L4000.

The **Museo Archeologico Paolo Orsi** (☎ 46 40 22), about 500m east of the archaeological zone, off Viale Teocrito, contains the best-organised and most interesting archaeological collection in Sicily. The museum is open 9 am to 1 pm and 3.30 to 6.30 pm Tuesday to Sunday. Admission is L8000.

Places to Stay
Camping facilities are at *Agriturist Rinaura* (☎ *72 12 24),* about 4km from the city near

the sea. Camping costs L8000 per person and L19,000 for a site. Catch bus No 21, 22 or 24 from Corso Umberto. *Hotel Gran Bretagna* (☎ 6 87 65, *Via Savoia 21*), just off Largo XXV Luglio on Ortygia, has very pleasant singles/doubles for L63,000/99,000 with bath or L53,000/87,000 without. *Hotel Aretusa* (☎ 2 42 11, *Via Francesco Crispi 75*), close to the train station, has comfortable and clean rooms for L45,000/70,000.

Places to Eat
On Ortygia, *Ristorante Osteria da Mariano* (*Vicolo Zuccalá 9*) serves typical Sicilian food. *Pizzeria Trattoria Zsa Zsa* (*Via Roma 73*) serves 65 different kinds of pizza, antipasti and pasta. At both places a full meal will cost under L25,000. A good pizzeria is *Il Cenacolo* (*Via del Consiglio Reginale 10*).

Getting There & Away
SAIS buses leave from Riva della Posta on Ortygia, for Catania, Palermo and Rome. AST buses also service Palermo from Piazza della Posta. Syracuse is easy to reach by train from Messina and Catania.

AGRIGENTO
☎ 0922
Founded in approximately 582 BC as the Greek Akragas, Agrigento is today a pleasant medieval town, but the Greek temples in the valley below are the real reason to visit. The Italian novelist and dramatist Luigi Pirandello (1867-1936) was born here, as was the Greek philosopher and scientist Empedocles (circa 490-430 BC).

The AAST tourist office (☎ 2 04 54), at Via Cesare Battisti 15, opens 8.30 am to 1.30 pm and 4.30 to 7 pm Monday to Friday (to 1 pm Saturday).

Things to See
Agrigento's **Valley of the Temples** is one of the major Greek archaeological sights in the world. Its five main Doric temples were constructed in the 5th century BC and are in various states of ruin because of earthquakes and vandalism by early Christians. The only temple to survive relatively intact is the **Tempio della Concordia**, which was transformed into a Christian church. The **Tempio di Giunone**, a five-minute walk uphill to the east, has an impressive sacrificial altar. The **Tempio di Ercole** is the oldest of the structures.

Across the main road which divides the valley is the massive **Tempio di Giove**, one of the most imposing buildings of ancient Greece. Although now completely in ruins, it used to cover an area measuring 112m by 56m, with columns 18m high. **Telamoni**, colossal statues of men, were also used in the structure. The remains of one of them are in the **Museo Archeologico**, just north of the temples on Via dei Templi (a copy lies at the archaeological site). Close by is the **Tempio di Castore e Polluce**, which was partly reconstructed in the 19th century. The temples are lit up at night and are open until one hour before sunset. To get to the temples from the town, catch bus No 1, 2 or 3 from the train station.

Places to Stay & Eat
Bella Napoli (☎ 2 04 35, *Piazza Lena 6*), off Via Bac Bac at the end of Via Atenea, has clean and comfortable singles/doubles for L25,000/55,000 (L44,000/75,000 with private bathroom). For a decent, cheap meal try the excellent *La Forchetta* (*Piazza San Francesco 9*).

Getting There & Away
Intercity buses leave from Piazza Rosselli, just off Piazza Vittorio Emanuele, for Palermo, Catania and surrounding small towns.

AEOLIAN ISLANDS
☎ 090
Also known as the Lipari Islands, the seven Aeolian Islands (Isole Eolie) are so named because the ancient Greeks believed they were the home of Aeolus, the god of wind. Homer wrote of them in the *Odyssey*.

The islands of most interest to travellers are Lipari, Vulcano and Stromboli – all accessible by ferry from Palermo and Messina. Ferries also run between the seven islands.

Information
The main AAST tourist information office (☎ 988 00 95) for the islands is on Lipari at Corso Vittorio Emanuele 202. Other offices are open on Vulcano, Salina and Stromboli during summer.

Things to See
On **Lipari** visit the castello with its archaeological park and museum. You can also go

ITALY

on excellent walks on the island. Catch a local bus from the town of Lipari to the hilltop village of Quattrocchi for a great view of the island.

Vulcano, with the smell of sulphur always in the air, is a short boat trip from Lipari's port. The main volcano, Vulcano Fossa, is still active. Make the one-hour hike to the crater, or take a bath in therapeutic hot mud.

Stromboli is the most spectacular of the islands. Climb its volcanic cone (924m) at night to see the Sciara del Fuoco (Trail of Fire), a stream of lava that's the main reason for coming. People make the trip (four to five hours) without a guide during the day, but at night you should go with a guided group – contact AGAI/GAE (☎/fax 98 62 54, ✉ stromboli@iol.it).

Places to Stay
Lipari The camping ground *Baia Unci* (☎ 981 19 09) is at Canneto, about 3km out of Lipari town. It costs L18,000 a night per person. The HI *Ostello per la Gioventú Lipari* (☎ 981 15 40, Via Castello 17) is inside the walls of the citadel. A bed costs L18,500 a night. It's open March to October.

Lo Nardo Maria (☎ 988 0431, fax 981 31 63, Vicolo Ulisse) is a private home with four comfortable double rooms costing L50,000 between October and April but double that amount during summer. There is a terrace with views.

Stromboli The popular *Casa del Sole* (☎ 98 60 17, Via Soldato Cincotta), on the road to the volcano, has singles/doubles for L35,000/40,000. If you want to splurge try the hotel *La Sirena* (☎ 988 99 97, Via Pecorini Mare) which charges L70,000/120,000 with bath.

Vulcano On Vulcano, if you can cope with the sulphurous fumes, try *Pensione Agostino* (☎ 985 23 42, Via Favaloro 1). Close to the mud bath, it has doubles with bathroom from L50,000 to L100,000 depending on the season. *Hotel Arcipelago* (☎ 985 20 02) is beautifully positioned on Vulcano's northern coast and costs L185,000 for half-board.

Getting There & Away
Ferries and hydrofoils leave for the islands from Milazzo (which is easy to reach by train from Palermo and Messina) and all ticket offices are along Via Rizzo at the port. SNAV runs hydrofoils (L19,500 one way). Siremar also runs hydrofoils, but its ferries are half the price. Both companies have offices at the port. If arriving at Milazzo by train, you will need to catch a bus to the port. If arriving by bus, simply make the five-minute walk back along Via Crispi to the port area. SNAV also runs hydrofoils from Palermo twice a day in summer and three times a week in the off season.

Sardinia

The second-largest island in the Mediterranean, Sardinia (Sardegna) was colonised by the Phoenicians and Romans, followed by the Pisans, Genoese and finally the Spaniards. But it is often said that the Sardinians, known on the island as *Sardi*, were never really conquered – they simply retreated into the hills.

The landscape of the island ranges from the 'savage, dark-bushed, sky-exposed land' described by DH Lawrence, to the beautiful gorges and valleys near Dorgali and the unspoiled coastline between Bosa and Alghero. Try to avoid the island in August, when the weather is hot and the beaches are overcrowded.

Getting There & Away
Sardinia is accessible by ferry from Genoa, Livorno, Fiumicino (the port of Rome), Civitavecchia, Naples, Palermo, Trapani, Bonifacio (Corsica) and Tunis. The main company is Tirrenia, which runs a Genoa-Cagliari service (L102,000, 20 hours); Genoa-Porto Torres or Olbia (L83,000, 13 hours); Civitavecchia-Cagliari (L77,000, 13½ hours); Civitavecchia-Olbia (L40,400, seven hours); Naples-Cagliari (L78,000, 16 hours); and Palermo-Cagliari (L73,000, 14 hours). For online information including departures, timetables and fares, check out Tirrenia's Web site at www.tirrenia.com.

CAGLIARI
☎ 070
This attractive city offers an interesting medieval section, the beautiful beach of Poetto, and salt lakes with a population of pink flamingoes.

ITALY

Buses, trains and boats arrive at the port area. The main street along the port is Via Roma, and the old city stretches up the hill to the castle. The AAST information booth (☎ 66 92 55), at Piazza Matteotti 9, is open 8 am to 8 pm daily in July and August and 8 am to 2 pm in other months. There are also information offices at the airport and in the Stazione Marittima.

The Ente Sardo Industrie Turistiche office (ESIT; ☎ 167 01 31 53 or 6 02 31, fax 66 46 36), at Via Goffredo Mameli 97, is open 8 am to 8 pm daily during summer (reduced hours the rest of the year). It has information on the whole island.

Places to Stay & Eat

There arc numerous budget pensioni near the station. Try the *Locanda Firenze (☎ 66 85 05, Corso Vittorio Emanuele 149)* which has comfortable singles/doubles for L43,000/58,000. *Locanda Miramare (☎ 66 40 21, Via Roma 59)* has rooms for L56,000/75,000. Nearby is *Albergo La Perla (☎ 66 94 46, Via Sardegna 18)* with rooms for L46,000/58,000.

Several reasonably priced trattorias can be found in the area behind Via Roma, particularly around Via Sardegna and Via Cavour. *Trattoria da Serafino (Via Lepanto 6)*, on the corner of Via Sardegna, has excellent food at reasonable prices. *Trattoria Gennar-gentu (Via Sardegna 60)* has good pasta and seafood and a full meal costs around L33,000. *Trattoria Ci Pensa Cannas*, down the street at No 37, is another good choice, with meals for around L26,000.

Getting There & Away

ARST buses (☎ 409 83 24) leave from Piazza Matteotti for nearby towns. PANI buses (☎ 65 23 26) leave from farther along Via Roma at Piazza Darsena.

The main train station is also in Piazza Matteotti. Ask at ESIT for information about the private Trenino Verde (green train) that runs along a scenic route between Cagliari and Arbatax.

AROUND SARDINIA

Cala Gonone, a fast-developing seaside resort, is an excellent base from which to explore the coves along the eastern coastline. From the port catch a boat to the **Grotta del Bue Marino**, where a guide will take you on a 1km walk to see vast caves with stalagmites, stalactites and lakes.

Alghero, one of the most popular tourist resorts in Sardinia, is on the island's west coast and is a good base from which to explore the magnificent coastline which links it to **Bosa** in the south. From Alghero you can visit the famous **Grotte di Nettuno** (Neptune's Caves) on the Capocaccia to the north.

ITALY

Latvia

Latvia (Latvija) is perhaps the most geographically disadvantaged country in the Baltic region, lacking Estonia's proximity to a Western country (Finland) or Lithuania's close ties with Poland and Germany. Latvia has been 'stuck in the middle' in some ways, but has worked hard in recent years to promote tourism as a way to increase international recognition and point the way to its natural splendours.

The vibrant capital Rīga remains Latvia's chief tourist magnet as it is the largest and most cosmopolitan city in the Baltic region. Partially because it has more preserved Art Nouveau buildings than any other city in the world, it is a city of striking beauty. Several attractive destinations lie within day-trip distance of it, among them the coastal resort of Jūrmala and Sigulda Castle overlooking the scenic Gauja River valley.

AT A GLANCE	
Capital:	Rīga
Population:	2.43 million
Official Language:	Latvian
Currency:	1 lat = 100 santīmi

Facts about Latvia

HISTORY

Peoples arriving in the south-eastern Baltic region from the south introduced settled agriculture to Latvia by about 2000 BC and eventually grouped into what are called the 'Baltic' tribes. These tribes were dragged into recorded history in the 12th century by the German *Drang nach Osten* (push to the east) of traders, missionaries and crusading knights.

The Knights of the Sword, also known as the Livonian Order, were founded in Rīga in 1202. By 1290 they controlled the seaboard from modern Poland to Estonia, plus inland Latvia. The existing inhabitants became serfs to a German nobility, which dominated until the early 20th century.

In 1561 Latvia came under Polish control after the Livonian Order appealed for protection against Russia's Ivan the Terrible. During the 1620s Sweden took most of Latvia. Russia's Peter the Great destroyed Swedish power in the Great Northern War (1700-21), and most of Latvia became part of the Russian empire.

After WWI, fighting broke out between Latvian nationalists (who had declared independence in November 1918), Bolsheviks trying to incorporate Latvia into Soviet Russia, and lingering German occupation forces. In 1921 Moscow signed a peace treaty with the independent Latvian parliamentary republic. From 1934 authoritarian leader, Kārlis Ulmanis, headed a nonparliamentary government of unity.

Latvia was occupied partly or wholly by Nazi Germany from 1941 to 1945. Some Latvians collaborated in the murders of as many as 90,000 Jews at the Salaspils concentration camp near Rīga and Latvia's Jewish population was virtually wiped out.

Latvia's subsequent conquest by the Red Army was followed by farm collectivisation and nationalisation. There was some armed resistance until 1952, and an estimated 175,000 Latvians were killed or deported as a result of Soviet occupation. With postwar industrialisation, Latvia received an influx of migrant workers from all over the Soviet Union, which increased local resentment towards Soviet rule.

On 23 August 1989 about two million Latvians, Lithuanians and Estonians formed a 650km human chain that stretched from Vilnius, through Rīga, to Tallinn, in protest at the 50th anniversary of the Molotov-Ribbentrop Pact (a secret Nazi-Soviet pact that put the Baltics under the Soviet yoke). A reformist, pro-independence Latvian Popular Front was formed, and its supporters won a big majority in the March 1990 elections to Latvia's Supreme Soviet (now parliament). A transition period that was envisaged for independence to be negotiated

faded as hardliners regained the ascendancy in Moscow in the winter of 1990-91. On 20 January 1991 Soviet troops, in an attempt to destabilise the Baltics, stormed the Interior Ministry building in Rīga, killing four people.

The August 1991 coup attempt in Moscow turned the tables and Latvia declared full independence on 21 August. It was recognised first by the West, then by the USSR on 6 September. Latvia's first democratic elections were held in June 1993.

Only citizens of the pre-1940 Latvian Republic and their descendants automatically became citizens of modern Latvia, leaving roughly 30% of the population (mainly Russians) noncitizens without the right to vote – even in local elections.

With the government encouraging foreign investment and credit, the private sector has grown rapidly. Denmark, the USA, Russia and Germany are Latvia's largest foreign investors. Germany, Russia, Sweden, the UK and Finland are its biggest trading partners. In early 2000, inflation in Latvia was under 3.5%, and the average monthly gross wage was $243. Official unemployment was a high 14.3%.

GEOGRAPHY

Green and rolling Latvia covers an area of 64,600 sq km. Over half of this area is less than 100m above sea level. The Daugava, flowing from Belarus through Rīga to the sea at the Gulf of Rīga, is the most voluminous of Latvia's rivers. The Gauja, flowing down from the north-east, is the longest at 452km. Woodland (half of it pine) covers 46% of Latvia.

CLIMATE

Latvia has a damp climate, with over 600mm of precipitation a year. July is the warmest month (temperatures can reach 28°C) and also the wettest. The east is usually 1°C warmer than the coast in summer and 4°C colder in winter.

POPULATION & PEOPLE

Latvia's population is 2.43 million. Only 55.5% is ethnic Latvian (Russians account for 32.4% of the population, Belarussians, Ukranians and Polish make up the rest), and Latvians are a minority in all the country's major cities, including the capital, where 47% are Russian and only 44% Latvian.

LANGUAGE

Even more than Estonians, Latvians regard their language (Latvian) as an endangered species. English is widely spoken in Rīga, and Russian is useful throughout the country. See the Language Guide at the back of this book for pronunciation guidelines and useful words and phrases.

Facts for the Visitor

HIGHLIGHTS

Apart from the obvious destination of Rīga, the other highly recommended spot in Latvia is the Gauja valley. For the adventurous, the ideal way to experience the scenery is to canoe down the Gauja River from Valmiera, but for those pressed for time a day's hiking from Sigulda is a pleasant alternative.

SUGGESTED ITINERARIES

Three days
Spend one or two days in Rīga, the remainder in Sigulda.
One week
Visit Rīga, Jūrmala, Sigulda, Līgatne, Cēsis and either Kurzeme (Kuldiga) or Latgale.

TOURIST OFFICES

Latvia has no tourist information offices abroad but its embassies and consulates may have information. There are other agents who specialise in the Baltic region who could also help.

VISAS & DOCUMENTS

It is recommended to check Latvia's ever-changing visa regime before your trip at its Foreign Ministry Web site: www.mfa.gov.lv.

A valid passport is the only requirement for citizens of 30 countries including Belgium, the Czech Republic, Denmark, Estonia, Finland, France, Germany, Ireland, Italy, Japan, Lithuania, the Netherlands, Norway, Spain, the UK, and the USA.

Citizens of some 20 additional countries including Australia, Canada, Israel, New Zealand, and South Africa, need to have an invitation to get a Latvian visa, and can get a 10-day on-the-spot visa at Rīga's International Airport. A single entry tourist visa should cost around US$15.

EMBASSIES & CONSULATES
Latvian Embassies
Australia
    Consulate-General: (☎ 03-9499 6920) 38 Longstaff St, Ivanhoe East, Victoria 3073
Canada (☎ 613-238 6014) 280 Albert Street, Suite 300, Ottawa, Ontario K1P 5G8
Finland (☎ 09-4764 7244) Armfeltintie 10, 00150 Helsinki
UK (☎ 0171-312 0040) 45 Nottingham Place, London W1M 3FE

USA (☎ 202-726 8213, fax 726 6785) 4325 17th Street NW, Washington DC 20011

Embassies in Latvia
The following embassies are in Rīga:

Canada (☎ 722 63 15) Doma laukums 4
Estonia (☎ 781 20 20) Skolas iela 13
Lithuania (☎ 732 15 19, fax 732 15 89) Elizabetes iela 2
UK (☎ 733 81 26) Alunāna iela 5
USA (☎ 721 00 05) Raiņa bulvāris 7

MONEY

The Latvian lats (plural: lati) is the country's only legal tender and comes in 5Ls, 10Ls, 20Ls, 50Ls, 100Ls and 500Ls denomination notes. One lats is divided into 100 santīmi, and there are one, two, five, 10, 20 and 50 santīmi coins and also one and two lati coins.

Most banks change travellers cheques, and credit cards are widely accepted at hotels and upper-end restaurants. There are many ATMs in Latvia, many of which accept Visa/Plus, MasterCard/Cirrus and Eurocard. Most major banks give cash advances on Visa, MasterCard and Eurocard.

Exchange Rates

country	unit		lati
Australia	A$1	=	0.32Ls
Canada	C$1	=	0.41Ls
euro	€1	=	0.54Ls
France	1FF	=	0.83Ls
Germany	DM1	=	0.27Ls
Ireland	IR£1	=	0.69Ls
Netherlands	f1	=	0.25Ls
UK	UK£1	=	0.89Ls
USA	US$1	=	0.61Ls

POST & COMMUNICATIONS

Letters/postcards (up to 20g) cost 0.30/0.20Ls to Europe and 0.40/0.30Ls elsewhere. Stamps can only be bought from post offices or hotels.

Telephone

Latvia's international country code is ☎ 371.

Public phones are scattered all over the country that accept chip cards worth 2Ls, 3Ls, 5Ls or 10Ls which can be bought from kiosks, shops and post offices. Phones that accept coins greater than 5 santīmi, can be found at train and bus stations. To call other

LATVIA

cities in Latvia, simply dial the area code followed by the telephone number.

All international calls require the access code ☎ 00, the country and city codes, then the subscriber number. Charges are 0.23Ls per minute to Estonia and Lithuania and from 0.41Ls to 0.59Ls per minute to all other countries. A three minute call to the US will cost US$8.85.

Analogue Phones Analogue numbers have only six digits. To call a digital number within Latvia from an analogue phone dial ☎ 1, wait for the tone, then dial the number. To dial an analogue number from a digital phone, add a 2 before the six-digit number.

INTERNET RESOURCES
Rīga In Your Pocket's Web site, at www .inyourpocket.com, has country information and hotel listings.

GAY & LESBIAN TRAVELLERS
Rīga is the most gay-friendly of the Baltic regon capitals but open displays of same-sex affection are rarely seen. The active Homosexuality Information Centre (☎ 722 70 52, ✉ info@gay.lv.) at Puškina iela 1a can offer advice, and runs a 24-hour hotline (☎ 951 95 51).

DANGERS & ANNOYANCES
Theft from hotel rooms is a danger in the region, especially at lower-end hotels. Though street crime is a growing problem, Latvia is still safer than most western countries.

Drinking unboiled tap water is generally safe in Rīga, though we would still recommend boiling it. Though plenty of Latvians swim, pollution makes swimming anywhere on the coast risky. Between May and September there's a risk of tick-borne encephalitis in parks in Rīga and in Jūrmala's wooded areas backing on to the beach. Consider immunisation with a vaccine or specific tick-borne encephalitis immunoglobulin, readily available in Europe or the Baltics.

PUBLIC HOLIDAYS & SPECIAL EVENTS
Latvian national holidays are 1 January, Good Friday, 23 June (Ligo – Midsummer Festival), 24 June (Jāni – St John's Day), 18 November (1918 Latvian Republic Day), 26 and 31 December.

Latvia shares some major cultural events with Estonia and Lithuania, the most important being the Baltika International Folk Festival. The All-Latvian Song and Dance Festivals, held every five years, will again take place in 2003. The Folk Song Festival will take place in Riga during the summer of 2001. For more information about folk-related events, contact the Melndailis National Folk Art Centre (☎ 722 89 85) in Rīga.

ACCOMMODATION
Latvia has some decent *kempings* (camping grounds) but only a small network of youth hostels. In summer, colleges in Rīga sometimes accept travellers. Tourist offices can help with private rooms, though Latvia has plenty of budget hotels. It's sometimes cheaper to book hotel rooms through travel agencies such as Latvia Tours (see Travel Agencies, Rīga); they may find you a room even when the hotel claims to be full. In summer it's a good idea to book in advance, especially at bottom-end hotels.

FOOD & DRINKS
The Latvian diet leans heavily on dairy products, grains and *zivs* (fish), though meat is common. *Šprotes* (sprats) crop up as a starter in many places. You may also find *siļe* (herring), *līdaka* (pike) and *lasis* (salmon). *Zupa* (soup) and *desa* (sausage) are popular. In summer and autumn good use is made of the many types of berry. Throughout Latvia you will find a mouth-watering choice of freshly baked cakes, breads and pastries for as little as 0.15Ls a piece.

A few food words in Latvian are *maize* (bread), *salāti* (salad), *kartupeli* (potatoes), *vista* (chicken), *saknes* (vegetables), *augļi* (fruit), *siers* (cheese) and the *rēķinu* (bill/cheque).

The best *alus* (beer) is produced by the Aldaris brewery. A 330ml bottle of Aldaris Zelta costs 0.35Ls. A wide range of cheaper, cloudy beers is available from other breweries, all named after Latvian regions or towns (Baltija, Rīga etc). A Latvian speciality for the brave is *Rīgas Melnais Balzāms* (Riga Black Balsam), a thick, dark, vaguely noxious liquid with supposedly medicinal properties. It's better to drink it 50/50 with vodka or mixed in with coffee or coke.

Getting There & Away

For any travel through Russia, Belarus or Kaliningrad, look into the visa situation well ahead of departure.

Within Latvia, buses are generally cheaper and definitely faster than the trains.

AIR

Rīga has scheduled flights to/from Helsinki with Finnair, London with British Airways, Frankfurt with Lufthansa, Prague with ČSA, Warsaw with LOT, and Vienna with Austrian Airlines.

Air Baltic, the Latvian state airline, together with SAS which supports it, flies to Vilnius, Copenhagen, Stockholm, Kiev, Frankfurt, Helsinki, Tallinn, Budapest, Warsaw and London.

BUS

Eurolines (☎ 721 40 80), inside the central bus station in Rīga, runs several daily buses to Tallinn (6Ls, six hours), Vilnius (4Ls, six hours), St Petersburg (8Ls, 10½ hours) and Berlin, and buses several times weekly to Moscow (12Ls, 16½ hours), Prague (38Ls, 28 hours), Munster (DM165, 33 hours), Hanover, Cologne, Stuttgart, Munich, Nuremberg and Bremen. Buses to Brussels, Paris and Kyiv are handled by Norma-A, which also has an office inside the bus station (☎ 721 45 12 or 728 13 18).

TRAIN

The Baltic Express is no longer running from Rīga and the only way to get to Tallinn is to change in Valga, though the bus is much more convenient. There is also one overnight train between Rīga and Vilnius via Kaunas (eight hours), and one overnight train to St Petersburg (13 hours).

BOAT

Ferry Rīga's ferry terminal (☎ 732 98 82) is at Eksporta iela 1, on the river about 1.5km downstream (north) of the Akmens Bridge. Tickets for the Travemünde (Germany) ferry (DM275 for a one-way ticket in a four-person cabin, 34 hours), which runs every four days, are sold here by Hanza Maritime Agency (☎ 732 37 30, @ hanza@hanza.lv), Eksporta iela 10.

Rīga

☎ 2

Rīga has always been the Baltic region's major metropolis, and with 790,000 people (100,000 less than it had in 1990) it has a big-city feel. During the 1930s the city was the west's major post for observing 'the Russian bear' to the east, and the city was a thrumming mix of diplomats, traders and intrigues – earning it the accolade of 'the Paris of the east'.

Today, like its neighbouring Baltic capitals, Rīga has a well-preserved, historic old quarter, which isn't as postcard-pretty as Tallinn's or Vilnius', but it boasts what these cities cannot: magnificent architecture throughout its entire extended city centre. Rīga is also a fascinating mix of Latvian, Russian and German influences.

Orientation

Rīga straddles the Daugava River; the east bank holds all the places of interest, including Old Rīga (Vecrīga). Rīga's axial street, running north-east from Akmens Bridge (Akmens tilts), is called Kaļķu iela as it passes through the old city, then Brīvības bulvāris as far as the towering Hotel Latvija, about 2km from the river.

The train and bus stations are five minutes' walk apart on the south-east edge of Old Rīga. The ferry terminal is 500m north of Old Rīga.

Information

Tourist Offices The Rīga Tourist Information Bureau (☎ 704 43 77, @ tourinfo@ lgs.lv) is behind the Occupation Museum at Rātslaukums 7. Open daily, it organises walking, hiking, biking and yachting tours, sells maps and guidebooks and provides visitors with a wealth of information.

Rīga In Your Pocket is a helpful guide to the city, available at bookshops and kiosks. Information on just about anything can be found through two helpful telephone information services (☎ 722 22 22 and 777 07 77).

Money Rīga's 24-hour exchanges include Ahāts on the edge of Old Rīga at Basteja bulvāris 12, and Marika at Basteja bulvāris 14. Twenty-four hour ATMs accepting MasterCard, Visa, Cirrus and Plus are everywhere in Rīga.

LATVIA

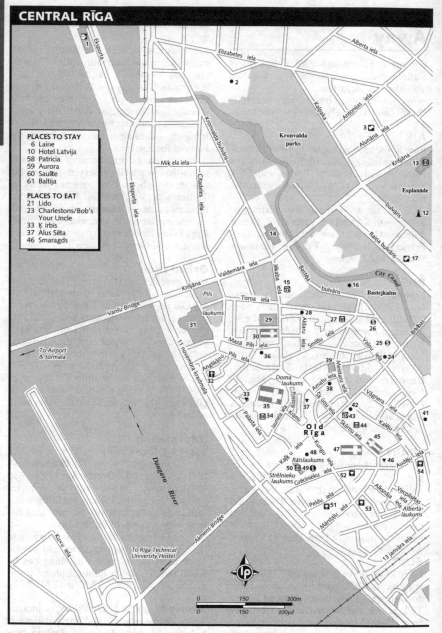

CENTRAL RĪGA

PLACES TO STAY
6 Laine
10 Hotel Latvija
58 Patricia
59 Aurora
60 Saulīte
61 Baltija

PLACES TO EAT
21 Lido
23 Charlestons/Bob's Your Uncle
33 Ķirbis
37 Alus Sēta
46 Smaragds

Eksporta
Elizabetes iela
Alberta iela
Kronvalda bulvāris
Kronvalda parks
Ķelpaka
Antonijas iela
Alunāna iela
Krišjāna
Esplanāde
bulvāris
Miķ ela iela
Citadeles iela
Eksporta iela
Valdemāra iela
Raiņa bulvāris
Krišjāna
Pils
laukums
Vanšu Bridge
Torņa iela
Jēkaba iela
Bastela bulvāris
City Canal
Bastejkalns
Brīvkas
11 novembra krastmala
Maza Pils iela
Aldaru iela
Smiltu iela
Valņu iela
To Airport & Jūrmala
Angļikāņu
Pils iela
Rožena
Amatu iela
Meistaru iela
Vāgnera iela
Doma laukums
Šķūnu iela
Kaļēju iela
Jauniela
Krāmu
Palasta iela
Old Rīga
Kungu iela
Skārņu iela
Vecpilsētas iela
Daugava River
Rātslaukums
Kaļķu iela
Strēlnieku laukums
Grēcinieku iela
Peldu iela
Alksnāja iela
Alberta laukums
Kuxu iela
Mārstaļu iela
Akmens Bridge
To Rīga Technical University Hostel
13 janvāra iela

0   150   300m
0   150   300yd

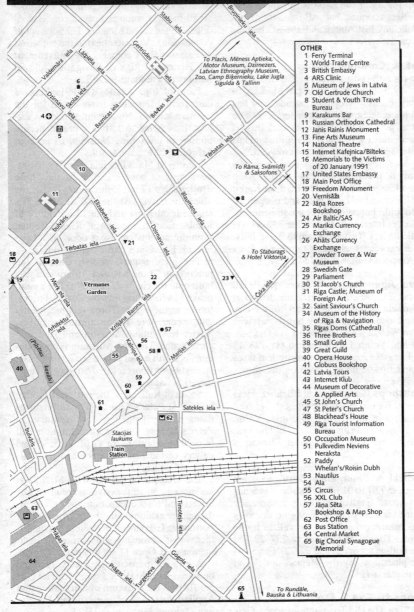

CENTRAL RĪGA

OTHER

1 Ferry Terminal
2 World Trade Centre
3 British Embassy
4 ARS Clinic
5 Museum of Jews in Latvia
7 Old Gertrude Church
8 Student & Youth Travel
  Bureau
9 Karakums Bar
11 Russian Orthodox Cathedral
12 Janis Rainis Monument
13 Fine Arts Museum
14 National Theatre
15 Internet Kafejnica/Bilteks
16 Memorials to the Victims
  of 20 January 1991
17 United States Embassy
18 Main Post Office
19 Freedom Monument
20 Vernisāža
22 Jāņa Rozes
  Bookshop
24 Air Baltic/SAS
25 Marika Currency
  Exchange
26 Ahāts Currency
  Exchange
27 Powder Tower & War
  Museum
28 Swedish Gate
29 Parliament
30 St Jacob's Church
31 Riga Castle; Museum of
  Foreign Art
32 Saint Saviour's Church
34 Museum of the History
  of Rīga & Navigation
35 Rīgas Doms (Cathedral)
36 Three Brothers
38 Small Guild
39 Great Guild
40 Opera House
41 Globuss Bookshop
42 Latvia Tours
43 Internet Klub
44 Museum of Decorative
  & Applied Arts
45 St John's Church
47 St Peter's Church
48 Blackhead's House
49 Rīga Tourist Information
  Bureau
50 Occupation Museum
51 Pulkvedim Neviens
  Neraksta
52 Paddy
  Whelan's/Roisin Dubh
53 Nautilus
54 Ala
55 Circus
56 XXL Club
57 Jāņa Sēta
  Bookshop & Map Shop
62 Post Office
63 Bus Station
64 Central Market
65 Big Choral Synagogue
  Memorial

Latvia Tours (see Travel Agencies) is the agent for American Express. It cannot cash travellers cheques, but will issue them and replace any lost American Express cheques and cards.

Post & Communications Rīga's most user-friendly post office, at Brīvības bulvāris 19, is open 7 am to 11 pm Monday to Friday, 8 am to 10 pm weekends, and has telephone, telegraph, and fax services. The central post office, at Stacijas laukums, is immediately east of the train station and has similar services but is always crowded.

Email & Internet Access Internet Klub (☎ 750 35 95), in the Old Town on Kaļķu iela 10, charges 2Ls an hour and is open 10 am to midnight daily. Other possibilities include the Internet Kafejnica (☎ 732 33 61) at Jēkaba iela 20, open 10 am to 9 pm daily. The local access telephone number in Rīga for America Online is ☎ 724 24 57.

Travel Agencies Latvia Tours (☎ 708 50 05, fax 782 00 20, ✉ lt@latviatours.lv) at Kaļķu iela 8 arranges short tours of the city as well as day trips. Check out its services on the Web at www.latviatours.lv. The Student and Youth Travel Bureau (☎ 728 48 18), Lāčplēša 29, can help find student fares and has tips on doing Latvia on the cheap.

Bookshops Jāņa Rozes – at Elizabetes iela 85a and Barona 5 – is the biggest and best bookshop in the Baltics. Globuss, Valņu iela 26, stocks Penguin Classics. The best place for maps is Jāņa Sēta at Elizabetes iela 83/85.

Medical & Emergency Services ARS Clinic (☎ 720 10 01/07) at Skolas iela 5 has a 24-hour, English-speaking emergency service (☎ 720 10 03/05), on-site doctor's visits from 8 am to 8 pm, as well as home service. The AIDS Centre (☎ 737 22 75) has a hotline service (☎ 52 22 22). For a 24-hour pharmacy, try the Mēness aptieka at Brīvības iela 121.

Things to See & Do

Old Rīga The Old Town retains many German buildings that have stood since the 17th century or earlier. Kaļķu iela neatly divides the old city in half. Just north of

Kaļķu iela, the brick **Rīgas Doms** (cathedral), which was founded in 1211, is now an all-in-one church and organ concert hall (closed Sunday and Monday; 1/0.50Ls adult/ concession). A cloister next to the cathedral at Palasta iela 4 contains the **Museum of the History of Rīga & Navigation** (closed Sunday to Tuesday; 1/0.40Ls).

Parts of **Rīga Castle** at Pils laukums 3 date from 1330 when it was built for the German knights. Now, painted canary yellow, it is home to Latvia's president and houses an unexciting **Museum of Foreign Art** (closed Monday; 0.50Ls).

Nearby at Mazā Pils iela there's a photogenic row of houses known as the **Three Brothers**. No 17 is a 15th-century house, the oldest in Latvia. At the end of Mazā Pils iela is Jēkaba iela and the 13th-century **St Jacob's Church**, the seat of Rīga's Roman Catholic archbishop. Next door, at Jēkaba iela 11, is Latvia's **parliament** building.

The picturesque **Swedish Gate** at the junction of Torņa iela and Aldaru iela was built onto the city walls in 1698. The round, peaked 14th-century **Powder Tower** (Pulvertornis) at the end of Torņa iela has been a gunpowder store, prison, torture chamber, Soviet Revolution Museum and students' party venue. The **War Museum** it now contains is worth a visit just to see its immense, wrought-iron doors (closed Sunday to Tuesday; 0.50Ls).

South of Kaļķu iela, the red-brick Gothic bulk of **St Peter's Church** (Pētera Baznīca) dates mainly from the 15th century. St Peter's is now used as an exhibition hall (closed Monday). There's a lift to the second gallery of the 72m **spire** for a marvellous view of Old Rīga (1Ls).

The **Occupation Museum** on Strēlnieku laukums is an impressive account of the Soviet and Nazi occupations of Latvia, although the exhibition has been criticised for portraying Latvians as blameless lambs. Either way it's probably Rīga's most interesting museum. Open 11 am to 5 pm daily; free.

A row of particularly pretty restored buildings faces St Peter's on Skārņu iela. At No 10/16 is the **Museum of Decorative and Applied Arts**, full of outstanding Latvian work (closed Monday; 0.05Ls).

East of Old Rīga, the **City Canal** (Pilsētas kanāls) snakes through parks laid between wide 19th-century boulevards. On Brīvības bulvāris near the junction with Raiņa bulvāris stands the central landmark of the park ring, the **Freedom Monument** (Brīvības piemineklis), a hub of the Latvian independence movement in the 1980s and early 1990s.

In Bastejkalns, west of the monument, five red stone slabs lie as **Memorials to the Victims of 20 January 1991**, killed here when Soviet troops stormed the nearby Interior Ministry. The **Fine Arts Museum** at Krišjāna Valdemāra iela 10A, on the northern corner of the Esplanāde park, houses what is probably the best art collection in the Baltics (closed Tuesday; 1.40Ls).

New Rīga The commercial soul of the city lies beyond the ring of Elizabetes iela in a grid of broad, six-storey streets. It is in this part of town that Rīga really starts to feel like a major city. Along the boulevards are many impressive and flamboyant 19th and early 20th-century buildings in Rīga's characteristic Jugendstil style. One of the best examples, designed by Mikhail Eisenstein, father of the renowned film maker Sergei, is at Elizabetes iela 10b. Other impressive buildings line Alberta iela.

The **Museum of Jews in Latvia**, Skolas 6, 3rd floor, has a captivating exhibit on the extermination of the Jews in Latvia during WWII. Ask to see the 10-minute introductory video containing some chilling footage shot by an amateur German soldier. It's open 10 am to 5 pm weekdays. The **Big Choral Synagogue Monument** down Gogoļa iela marks the place where hundreds of Jews were burned to death on 4 July 1941 inside a synagogue that once stood on the premises.

Suburbs Rīga's **Motor Museum** (Motormuzejs) is a long way out at Eizenšteina iela 6, 8km east of the old city, but it's worth the trip to see the cars that once belonged to Stalin and Brezhnev (closed Monday; 1Ls). Bus No 21 from the Russian Orthodox cathedral goes to the Pansionāts stop on Šmerļa iela, 500m from the museum.

Beside Lake Jugla on the eastern edge of the city, the open-air **Latvian Ethnography Museum** is a collection of over 900 buildings from rural Latvia, mostly wooden and dating from the 18th and 19th centuries. It's open 10 am to 5 pm daily mid-May to mid-

October (closed last day of every month; 0.50Ls). Take bus No 1 from opposite the Russian Orthodox cathedral.

Places to Stay

Camping *Dzirnezers* (☎ 951 415), 15km north of Rīga on the road to Tallinn, offers magnificent views of Lake Dzirnezers from the small cabins it rents out, but there's no hot water. Tents cost only 1.50Ls to pitch, and beds in cabins start at 4Ls. Bike and boat rental is available. All buses to Tallinn, Limbaži and Ainaži can stop at the Siguli stop near the camping ground.

Hostels The Hostel Association runs the hostel *Placis* (☎ 755 12 71, @ amans@ parks.lv, Laimodotas iela 2a) where singles are 5Ls (with a 20% discount for IYH cardcarriers). To get there, take trolleybus No 4 from the Circus stop on Merķeļa iela to the Teika stop. The *Rīga Technical University Hostel* (☎ 708 92 61, Āzenes iela 22a) on the other side of the river has decent beds for 3Ls a night. Take trolleybus No 7 from the centre and get off one stop after Akmens Bridge.

Private Rooms Patricia (☎ 728 48 68, fax 728 66 50, @ tourism@parks.lv), at Elizabetes iela 22-6, offers *rooms* in private flats all over Latvia from 9Ls and up. They also assist in renting and buying flats, as well as travel throughout the Baltics and discount car rental. Check out its Web site at www.rigalatvia.net.

Hotels There are a handful of cheap options right by the train station. The best of the worst is *Aurora* (☎ 722 44 79, Marijas iela 5), though rooms do tend to be noisy. Singles/doubles cost 4.30/6.80Ls. *Saulīte* (☎ 722 45 46), just round the corner at Merķeļa iela 12, has rooms without private toilet from 7Ls, from 16Ls with. *Baltija* (☎ 722 74 61, Raiņa bulvāris 33) is only for the absolutely desperate; smelly rooms cost from 4.50/5.50Ls.

Viktorija (☎ 701 41 11, Čaka iela 55), 1km north-east from the station, is in a mild 'red light district' but is the fanciest, cleanest budget hotel you'll find in Rīga. Excellent value rooms with shared toilets and showers are 8/12Ls, while nicely renovated ones are 26/38Ls. *Laine* (☎ 728 98 23, Skolas iela 11), on the 3rd and 4th floors of a run-down, central building, has rooms with shared, clean communal bathrooms from 15/25Ls (better rooms are available for double the price).

Places to Eat

Dining out in Rīga will be one of your best Baltic memories. Though more expensive than Vilnius or Tallinn, the selection is much wider and there is excellent food in all budget categories.

Rīga's colourful *central market* is behind the bus station and open 7 am to 4 pm daily.

No trip to Rīga would be complete without a visit to *Staburags* (*Čaka 55*) to the city's east, which serves authentic and enormous portions of fatty but delicious Latvian cooking (ask for a doggie bag – the staff are used to it). You will never forget the roast pig leg, much less be able to finish it. Another must is the culinary double-whammy *Charlestons* and *Bob's Your Uncle* (*Blaumaņa iela 38/40*). The former is a relaxed dining room serving a superb array of dishes and fronted by a first-rate cappuccino bar with takeaway salads and cakes. In the pleasant courtyard, *Bob's Your Uncle* is a sandwich and pancake haven with the most sumptuous omelettes imaginable (open for breakfast from 8 am daily) and fill-up lunches for under 2.50Ls.

The restaurant-cafe that blows the rest away is the exquisite *Smaragds* on a quiet Old Town corner at Jāņa 18, where the dreamy, deep velvet decor whisks you back into the 19th century.

The Latvian beer bar *Alus Sēta* (*Tirgoņu iela 6*), dishes out mammoth portions of ribs and other hunks of meat for around 5Ls a head.

Cafes Some of the most delicious food in town is also the cheapest at the two Hare Krishna cafes *Rāma* and *Svāmīdži*, both at Barona iela 56, where they serve blessed food 9 am to 9 pm daily, 11 am to 6 pm Sunday. At Rama, a healthy, gut-busting vegetarian meal can be had for 1.50Ls (wash it down with homemade ginger tea for 0.15Ls), and downstairs at Svāmīdži, set meals cost only 0.50Ls – less a 10% discount for ISIC card-holders!

The other vegetarian paradise is *Ķirbis* (*Doma laukums 1*), open 9 am to 11 pm daily. Delicious warm meals (and fresh

juices) displayed cafeteria-style are enjoyed in a spacious, half-outdoors setting for under 3Ls. This, together with *Lido*, on the corner of Elizabetes and Tērbatas iela, should redefine your notion of fast food. Also buffet style, Lido's mouth-watering array of all kinds of foods, salads and desserts, are prepared in front of you. It's open 8 am to 11 pm daily, but a second location, at Getrūdes 54, is open around the clock.

Entertainment

Bars & Clubs Rīga's hot spot is the Irish pub *Paddy Whelan's* at Grēcinieku iela 4. Upstairs is the more expensive *Roisin Dubh* bar, run by the same management. Just round the corner at Peldu iela 26/28, *Pulkvedim Neviens Neraksta* is an off-beat dance bar popular with a grunge-hip crowd.

For live rock, pop and jazz try *Ala* (☎ 722 39 57, Audēju iela 11) where local bands often play at weekends (open 10 am to 4 am daily). There are plenty of billiard tables too. Other alternative cellar bars where wild dancing is freely permitted include *Karakums* (*Lāčplēša iela 18*) and the more bohemian *Saksofons* (☎ 731 28 54, Stabu iela 43), where you can listen to great jazz and grunge bands in a smoke-filled cellar.

If clubland's your space, try *Vernisāža* (*Tērbatas iela 2*), Rīga's largest, most popular club which features a dance floor which rises a few meters every so often, causing a few spilled drinks. *Nautilus* (*Kungu iela 8*) has a submarine theme going and is a good place to disco or chill out. The biggest gay club is *XXL* (*A Kalniņa 4*).

Circus Rīga has the only permanent circus in the Baltics, at Merķeļa iela 4. It's worth a visit for the bizarre nature of some of the acts (performing pigs and stubborn, non-performing domestic cats). The circus goes on holiday from June to September. Admission ranges from 1Ls to 3Ls.

Classical Music, Opera & Cinema The *Rīgas Doms* has spectacular acoustics, and its frequent organ recitals and other concerts are well worth attending. The ticket office is opposite the west door and schedules are listed there. The highly regarded Latvia Philharmonia performs at the *Great Guild* (☎ 721 3798, Amatu iela 6).

A night at Rīga's 1860 *Opera House* (*Aspazijas bulvāris 3*), is a must. Buy tickets at the box office inside or at Teātra iela 10/12, 100m away, just past the Hotel Rīga. Tickets range from 1Ls to 10Ls.

Getting There & Away

Air Lidosta Rīga (Rīga airport) is at Skulte, 8km west of the city centre. For airport information, call ☎ 720 70 09 or 720 71 36. International connections to/ from Rīga are covered in the Getting There & Away section earlier in this chapter. One of the major carriers is Air Baltic (☎ 722 91 66), with an office at Kaļķu iela 15. SAS (☎ 721 61 39) is also at Kaļķu iela 15.

Bus National and international buses use Rīga's *autoosta* (main bus station; ☎ 900 00 09) at Prāgas iela 1, behind the railway embankment. Timetables are posted in the main hall. Services include: Cēsis (1.10Ls, two hours), Bauska (1.10Ls, 1½ hours), Daugavpils (2.55Ls to 3Ls, four hours), Jelgava (0.60Ls, one hour), Liepāja (2.55Ls, four hours), Sigulda (0.70Ls, one hour), Valmiera (2.30Ls, 2½ hours) and Ventspils (four hours).

Train Rīga's *centrālā stacija* (train station; ☎ 583 21 34), on Stacijas laukums, is split into two parts: one for long-distance trains (the bigger block, on the left as you face the station) and one for slow 'suburban' trains, which travel to destinations up to 150km away from Rīga. A huge wall chart shows the stations on each suburban line.

The timetable for *atiešanas laiks* (departures) is on the right as you enter the main hall; *pienakšanas laiks* (arrivals) are posted up on the opposite side. To buy a ticket 24 hours or more before departure go to the *iepriekšpārdošanas kases* (advance booking hall), reached via the 'suburban' hall.

Getting Around

To/From the Airport Bus No 22 runs to the airport every 20 minutes from the 13th janvāra stop opposite the bus station. Expect to pay at least 7Ls for a taxi to/from the centre.

Public Transport All the routes of buses, trolleybuses and trams are clearly marked on the *Rīga City Map*. Tickets (0.20Ls) are sold inside by a controller. City transport runs 5.30 am to 12.30 am daily.

AROUND RĪGA
Salaspils

Between 1941 and 1944 an estimated 45,000 Jews from Rīga and about 55,000 Jews and prisoners of war from other Nazi-occupied countries were murdered in the concentration camp at Salaspils, 15km south-east of Rīga. Giant, gaunt sculptures stand on the site as a memorial, and there's also a **museum**. The inscription on the huge concrete barrier at the entrance translates as 'Behind this gate the earth groans'. Both the grounds and the museum are free.

From Rīga take a suburban train (10 daily) on the Ogre-Krustpils line to Dārziņi (not Salaspils) station. A path leads from the station to the *piemineklis* (memorial) – about a 15-minute walk.

Jūrmala
☎ 7

Jūrmala is the combined name for a string of small towns and resorts stretching for 30km west along the coast from Rīga. Jūrmala's long sandy beaches are backed by dunes and pine woods, and its shady streets are lined with low-rise wooden houses. In Soviet times 300,000 visitors a year from all over the USSR flooded the region's holiday homes and sanatoriums. Today it still swarms with fun-in-the-sun lovers.

The main reason to visit Jūrmala is to walk along the beach, over the dunes, and through the woods (be wary of forest ticks). The main Jūrmala townships are between Bulduri and Dubulti, centred on Majori and Dzintari.

The main street in **Majori** is the 1km pedestrian-only Jomas iela, across the road from Majori's train station, then to the right. Majori's tourist office (☎ 64 276) is at Jomas 42 (closed weekends).

Places to Stay Camping is available at *Jaunķemeri* (☎ 773 65 75, *Kolkas 6*), in Jaunķemeri. *Zinātnes nams* (☎ 775 12 05, *Vikingu 3*), five minutes' walk from the Lielupe station, offers singles/doubles for 9/12Ls including breakfast.

Places to Eat Every second building on Jomas iela offers some eating option. More

LATVIA

refined places include the cosy *Barbara (Jomas 66/3)*, a candle-lit bistro which claims to be Spanish. The menu touts paella and tortilla for around 3.50Ls. The Middle-Eastern *Orients*, which has an outlet at both ends of Majori at Jomas iela 86 and 33, has some of the most scrumptious dishes in town and is worth the wait for a table. *Café de la presse (Jomais iela 57)* is one of the hottest spots to hang 24 hours long.

Getting There & Away About three trains an hour go from Rīga to Jūrmala (0.40Ls, 40 minutes) along the Ķemeri-Tukums line. All trains stop at Majori.

Sigulda
☎ 2

One of the best trips from Rīga is to Sigulda, 53km east on the southern lip of the picturesque Gauja valley. It's close enough to visit in a day but there's plenty to justify a longer stay, including long walks and canoeing. In mid-May Sigulda hosts the annual International Hot Air Balloon Contest.

Sigulda is also the main gateway to the 920-sq-km Gauja National Park, which stretches north-east as far as Valmiera. The park is down the hill from town and across the river.

Information The friendly Tourist Information Centre (☎ 971 335) in the kiosk at Pils iela 4a, open 10 am to 7 pm daily, can help find accommodation. The national park office (☎ 971 345) is at Raiņa iela 15. The Makars Tourism Agency (see Places to Stay) organises a full range of trips along the Gauja river at reasonable prices.

Unibanka (open 9 am to 4 pm weekdays) at Rīgas iela 1 has a currency exchange and a cash machine.

Things to See & Do Little remains of Krimulda Castle, built between 1207 and 1226, but its *pilsdrups* (ruins) are perhaps all the more evocative for this. On the way to the ruins from the town you pass the 1225 **Sigulda Church**, rebuilt in the 18th century, and the 19th-century **New Sigulda Castle**.

To the west of Raiņa iela is a **cable car** (0.50Ls) that runs every hour or so between 7.25 am and 6.25 pm across to 13th-century

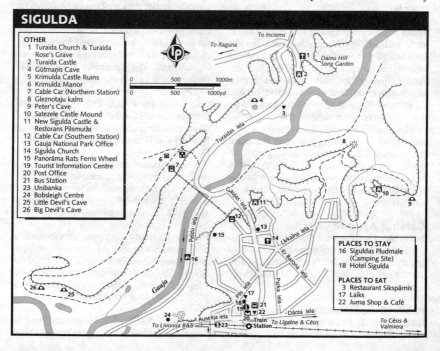

SIGULDA

OTHER
1 Turaida Church & Turaida Rose's Grave
2 Turaida Castle
4 Gūtmaņis Cave
5 Krimulda Castle Ruins
6 Krimulda Manor
7 Cable Car (Northern Station)
8 Gleznotāju kalns
9 Peter's Cave
10 Satezele Castle Mound
11 New Sigulda Castle & Restorans Pilsmuiža
12 Cable Car (Southern Station)
13 Gauja National Park Office
14 Sigulda Church
15 Panorāma Rats Ferris Wheel
19 Tourist Information Centre
20 Post Office
21 Bus Station
23 Unibanka
24 Bobsleigh Centre
25 Little Devil's Cave
26 Big Devil's Cave

PLACES TO STAY
16 Siguldas Pludmale (Camping Site)
18 Hotel Sigulda

PLACES TO EAT
3 Restaurant Sikspārnis
17 Laiks
22 Juma Shop & Café

LATVIA

Krimulda Castle, which is also in ruins. Follow the path past the ruins to the viewing tower, in front of which are some steep wooden steps. Walk down all 358 steps to the bottom and follow the wooden riverside path north-east leading to **Gūtmaņis Cave** (Gūtmaņa ala), adorned with graffiti going back as far as 1667.

The red-brick **Turaida Castle**, founded in 1214 on the site of a Liv stronghold, was mostly destroyed in a fire in 1776. The restored structure is better viewed from afar. The **museum** (open 10 am to 5 pm daily; 0.50Ls) inside provides a detailed account of the Livonian state from 1319 to 1561. The neighbouring **tower** (42m) offers breathtaking views of the entire valley (0.80Ls).

Activities On weekdays year round, it costs only 3Ls to ride the 1km, 121m-high **bobsleigh** run at the Bobsleigh Centre (☎ 973 813).

The Bungee Jumping Club of Latvia (☎ 921 27 31) organises jumps on Saturday and Sunday from 6.30 pm, from the 43m high cable car which crosses the Gauja valley for 13Ls. They can also arrange jumps out of hot air balloons, available for hire at 70Ls for 5-6 hour 'flights' over the region (☎ 732 61 55).

Places to Stay At *Siguldas Pludmale* (☎ 973 724, 924 49 48, Peldu iela 1), also the headquarters of the Makars Tourism Agency, you can pitch a tent for 1Ls a night plus a further 1Ls per person. They can also arrange B&B in private homes around Sigulda from 7Ls per person.

The top place in town is *Hotel Sigulda* (☎ 972 263, Pils 6), with singles/doubles for 20/24Ls.

Places to Eat *Juma* (Raiņa 1), is an excellent shop that sells ready-made salads and foods. *Laiks* (Pils iela 8) serves tasty meals 8 am to 2 am daily in a trendy, smoky bar replete with pool table, darts, and one-armed bandits. *Juma Café* (Raiņa 1) serves even tastier, cheaper cafe fare 7 am to 11 pm daily.

Getting There & Away Trains from Rīga, running every half hour on the Rīga-Cēsis-Valmiera line, take 1¼ hours and cost 0.78Ls. There are 14 buses a day between Rīga and Sigulda, but only two stop in the town centre (0.70Ls, two hours) – taking the train is a better idea.

Rundāle

The 18th-century **Rundāle Palace** (Rundāles Pils) is the architectural highlight of provincial Latvia. It was designed by Bartolomeo Rastrelli, the baroque genius from Italy who created many of St Petersburg's finest buildings. If you have visited any other Rastrelli creations, the poor upkeep of this one may come as a disappointment, although the Gilded Hall is a sight worth beholding. The 138-room palace and pitifully overgrown park open 11 am to 6 pm Wednesday to Sunday (1.20/0.80Ls adults/students).

Getting There & Away Unless you have your own transport, the best way to reach Rundāle, 77km south of Rīga, is to go to Bauska (see below) and take a bus heading to Rundāles Pils (not Rundāle).

Bauska

☎ 39

Bauska, 65km south of Rīga on the main Rīga-Vilnius road, is worth a stop in its own right if only to see the imposing **Bauska Castle** (Bauskas Pilsdrupas). Built between 1443 and 1456 for the Livonian Knights, it was blown up during the Great Northern War in 1706, but was recently rebuilt.

The castle is located 1km west of the town centre on a hillock between the Mēmele and Mūsa Rivers. From the bus station, walk towards the centre along Zalē iela then branch left along Uzvaras iela beside the park at the top of Kalna iela.

Getting There & Away Only buses go to Bauska. Rīga-Bauska buses run 30 times daily, starting at 5.30 am, and take a tedious 1½ hours (1.10Ls). Several express buses run during the week.

Liechtenstein

Blink and you might miss Liechtenstein; the country measures just 25km from north to south, and an average of 6km from west to east. In some ways you could be forgiven for mistaking it for a part of Switzerland. The Swiss franc is the legal currency, all travel documents valid for Switzerland are also valid for Liechtenstein, and the only border regulations are on the Austrian side. Switzerland also represents Liechtenstein abroad, subject to consultation.

But a closer look reveals that Liechtenstein is quite distinct from its neighbour. The ties with Switzerland began only in 1923 with the signing of a customs and monetary union. Before that, it had a similar agreement with Austria-Hungary. Although Liechtenstein shares the Swiss postal system, it issues its own postage stamps.

Unlike Switzerland, Liechtenstein joined the United Nations (1990) and, in 1995, the European Economic Area (EEA). Despite going separate ways over the EEA issue, the border between Liechtenstein and Switzerland will remain unregulated. Liechtenstein has no plans to seek full EU membership.

Liechtenstein is a very prosperous country. In 1998 it suffered from an unusually high level of unemployment: 2% (482 people!).

AT A GLANCE	
Capital:	Vaduz
Population:	31,320
Official Language:	German
Currency:	1 Swiss franc (Sfr) = 100 centimes

must approve every act before it becomes law. Prince Franz Josef II was the first ruler to live in the castle above the capital city of Vaduz. He died in 1989 after a reign of 51 years, and was succeeded by his son, Prince Hans-Adam II. Prince Hans-Adam is currently agitating for constitutional reforms that will actually limit his own powers in some respects.

Liechtenstein has no military service, its minuscule army (80 men!) was disbanded in 1868. It is a country known for its wines, postage stamps, dentures (an important export) and its status as a tax haven. In 2000, Liechtenstein's financial and political institutions were rocked by allegations that money laundering is rife in the country.

Despite its small size, Liechtenstein has two political regions (upper and lower) and three distinct geographical areas: the Rhine valley in the west, the edge of the Tirolean Alps in the south-east, and the northern lowlands. The current population is 31,320, with a third of that total made up of foreign residents.

Facts about Liechtenstein

Liechtenstein was created by the merger of the domain of Schellenberg and the county of Vaduz in 1712 by the powerful Liechtenstein family. It was a principality under the Holy Roman Empire from 1719 to 1806 and, after a spell in the German Confederation, it achieved full sovereign independence in 1866. A modern constitution was drawn up in 1921 but even today, the prince retains the power to dissolve parliament and

Facts for the Visitor

Sightseeing highlights are few. Many tourists come to Liechtenstein only for the stamps – a stamp in the passport and stamps on a postcard for the folks back home. But it's worth lingering to appreciate the art collection, and to enjoy the scenery.

The information on entry regulations and currency etc, that appears in the Switzerland chapter, applies to Liechtenstein too. The same emergency numbers apply as in Switzerland: dial ☎ 117 for the police, ☎ 144 for an ambulance or ☎ 118 in the event of a fire.

LIECHTENSTEIN

To St Gallen (50km) & Lake Constance

To Lake Constance & Bregenz

Feldkirch

Sennwald

Ruggell

Schellenberg

To Vienna (630km)

Mauren

Tisis

Eschen

Schaanwald

Haag

Bendern

Nendeln

N13

Rhine

16

Planken

AUSTRIA

Buchs

Schaan

SYHA Hostel

VADUZ

Gaflei

Silum

Sevelen

Triesenberg

Steg

SWITZERLAND

Triesen

Malbun

Trübbach

Balzers

To Zürich (95km)

N3

Sargans

0   2.5   5km
0   1.5   3mi

Liechtenstein's telephone country code is ☎ 423. There are no regional telephone codes in this tiny country.

Getting There & Away

Liechtenstein has no airport (the nearest is in Zürich), and there are only a few trains that stop within its borders, in the town of Schaan. Getting there by postbus is easiest. There are usually three buses each hour from the Swiss border towns of Buchs (Sfr2.40) and Sargans (Sfr3.60) which stop in Vaduz. Buses run every 30 minutes from the Austrian border town of Feldkirch; sometimes you have to change at Schaan to reach Vaduz (the Sfr3.60 ticket is valid for both buses).

By road, route 16 from Switzerland passes through Liechtenstein via Schaan and terminates at Feldkirch. The N13 follows the Rhine along the Swiss/Liechtenstein border; minor roads cross into Liechtenstein at each motorway exit.

Getting Around

Postbus travel within Liechtenstein is cheap and reliable; all fares cost Sfr2.40 or Sfr3.60, and a weekly/monthly pass is only Sfr10/20 (half-price for students and senior citizens).

The only drawback is that some services finish early; the last of the hourly buses from Vaduz to Malbun, for example, leaves at 6.20 pm (takes 35 minutes). Get a timetable from the Vaduz tourist office.

Vaduz

Although it's the capital of Liechtenstein, Vaduz is little more than a village, with a population of 5100.

Orientation & Information

Two adjoining streets, Äulestrasse and the pedestrian-only Städtle, enclose the town centre. Everything important is within this small area, including the postbus station.

The Vaduz tourist office (☎ 232 14 43, fax 392 16 18, ☺ touristinfo@lie-net.li), Städtle 37, has a free room-finding service and information on the whole country. It is open 8 am to noon and 1.30 to 5.30 pm Monday to Friday. From May to October it's also open till 4 pm on Saturday. Staff members are kept busy putting surprisingly dull souvenir entry stamps in visitors' passports (Sfr2). Pick up the excellent *Tourist Guide*, which tells you everything you might want to know about the country.

The main post office (postcode FL-9490), Äulestrasse 38, is open 8 am to 6 pm Monday to Friday, and 8 to 11 am Saturday. Postal rates are the same as in Switzerland. The post office has an adjoining philatelic section, open 8.30 am to noon and 1.30 to 4.30 pm weekdays only. The Telecom FL shop, Austrasse 77, 1km south of Vaduz, provides free Internet access.

The hospital, Krankenhaus Vaduz (☎ 235 44 11), is at Heiligkreuz 25.

Bikes can be rented from Melliger AG (☎ 232 16 06), Kirchstrasse 10, for Sfr20 per day; they can be picked up the evening before rental begins.

Things to See & Do

Although the **castle** is not open to the public, it is worth climbing the hill for a closer

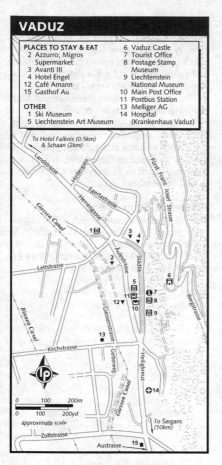

VADUZ

PLACES TO STAY & EAT
2 Azzurro; Migros
    Supermarket
3 Avanti III
4 Hotel Engel
12 Café Amann
15 Gasthof Au

OTHER
1 Ski Museum
5 Liechtenstein Art Museum

6 Vaduz Castle
7 Tourist Office
8 Postage Stamp
    Museum
9 Liechtenstein
    National Museum
10 Main Post Office
11 Postbus Station
13 Melliger AG
14 Hospital
    (Krankenhaus Vaduz)

To Hotel Falknis (0.5km)
& Schaan (2km)

Landstrasse
Hintergass
Egertastrasse
Herrengasse
Giessen Canal
Lettstrasse
Aulestrasse
Städtle
Fürst Franz Josef Strasse
Giessenstrasse
Bergstrasse
Bianna Canal
Kirchstrasse
Gerberweg
Giessen Canal
Heiligkreuz
Zoltstrasse
Austrasse
To Sargans (10km)

0   100   200m
0   100   200yd
approximate scale

LIECHTENSTEIN

Places to Stay

Hotel Falknis (☎ 232 63 77, Landstrasse 92) is a 15-minute walk (or take the postbus) from the centre of Vaduz towards Schaan. Reasonable singles/doubles are Sfr50/100 with a shower on each floor. *Gasthof Au (☎ 232 11 17, fax 232 11 68, Austrasse 2)* is the only other budget option in Vaduz. Rooms are Sfr80/120 with private shower, or Sfr60/95 without; triples are Sfr145. Eating is pleasant and fairly inexpensive in the garden restaurant here.

Places to Eat

Most restaurants are pricey in Vaduz, so look out for lunchtime specials. *Hotel Engel (Städtle 13)* has good meals from Sfr17, with some vegetarian choices. *Avanti III (Städtle 5)* provides cheap but basic fodder. On Äulestrasse, try *Café Amann* (closes 7 pm weekdays, noon Saturday, and all day Sunday), or *Azzurro*, next to the *Migros supermarket*. Azzurro is a stand-up place with pizzas from Sfr10, open till 7 or 8 pm (5 pm Sunday).

AROUND VADUZ

Northern Liechtenstein is dotted with small communities. There's little to do except enjoy the quiet pace of life and view the village churches. Pottery-making is demonstrated on weekdays at Schaedler Keramik (☎ 373 14 14) in **Nendeln** (admission free). The Rofenberg in **Eschen-Nendeln** was formerly a place of public execution and is now the site of the Holy Cross Chapel. **Schellenberg** has a Russian monument, commemorating the night in 1945 when a band of 500 heavily armed Russian soldiers crossed the border. They had been fighting for the German army, but they came to defect, not attack.

Triesenberg, on a terrace above Vaduz, commands an excellent view over the Rhine valley and has a pretty onion-domed church. There's also a museum (closed Sunday except in summer, and Monday; admission Sfr2, students Sfr1) devoted to the Walser community, which journeyed from Valais (Switzerland) to settle here in the 13th century. The Walser dialect is still spoken here.

Balzers, in the extreme south of the country, is dominated by the soaring sides of Gutenberg Castle. The castle is closed to the public.

look. There's a good view of Vaduz and the mountains, and a network of marked **walking trails** along the ridge.

Liechtenstein Art Museum, or Kunstmuseum, is opposite the tourist office in a new building. It comprises a range of works, including parts of the prince's art collection, and is open 10 am to 5 pm (8 pm Thursday), closed Monday; entry is Sfr8 (students Sfr5). The **Postage Stamp Museum**, next to the tourist office, contains 300 frames of national stamps issued since 1912 (open daily; free). A **Ski Museum** awaits at Bangarten 10, open weekday afternoons (Sfr5). The **National Museum**, Städtle 43, will be closed until about 2003.

Look out for processions and fireworks on 15 August, Liechtenstein's national holiday.

Places to Stay

Check the Vaduz tourist office hotel list for private rooms or cheaper accommodation outside Vaduz that is within a short bus ride of the capital. Schaan, for example, has *Hotel Post* (☎ 232 17 18, fax 233 35 44), by the bus station, providing singles/doubles from Sfr45/90 with shower, and small singles for Sfr38 without.

Triesenberg has a *camp site* (☎ 392 26 86), with dorm beds for Sfr12.

The *SYHA hostel* (☎ 232 50 22, fax 232 58 56, Untere Rütigasse 6), 10 minutes' walk from Schaan towards Vaduz, is open from March to November. Beds cost Sfr28.30 including breakfast. From 9.30 am to 5 pm reception is closed and the doors are locked.

MALBUN

Liechtenstein's ski resort, Malbun, lies at 1600m amid the mountains in the south-

east. It has some good runs for novices (and two ski schools) as well as more difficult runs. A one-day pass for all ski lifts costs Sfr35 (students/seniors Sfr29). Skis, shoes and poles cost Sfr43 for a day, and can be hired from the sports shop (☎ 263 37 55).

The road from Vaduz terminates at Malbun. The tourist office (☎ 263 65 77, fax 263 73 44, ✆ malbuninfo@lie-net.li) is by the first bus stop (there are only two) and is open 9 am to noon and 1.30 to 5 pm weekdays (1 to 4 pm on Saturday). It's closed from mid-April to 31 May and 1 November to mid-December.

Places to Stay & Eat

The village has six hotels, each with a restaurant. Singles/doubles start at Sfr45/90 at *Alpenhotel Malbun* (☎ 263 11 81, fax 263 96 46), or Sfr70/110 at *Turna* (☎ 232 34 21, fax 263 51 73, ✆ lampert1@bluewin).

Lithuania

Lithuania, south of Latvia and Estonia, is in many ways the most vibrant of the trio, as it showed the world by its daring and emotional drive for independence. Lithuania (Lietuva) owes much to the rich cultural currents of Central Europe – with neighbouring Pol-and it once shared an empire stretching to the Black Sea.

Vilnius, the historic, lively capital, is the obvious base for visitors. But Lithuania has other sizable cities such as Kaunas, briefly its capital this century, and the seaport of Klaipėda, formerly the German town Memel.

Facts about Lithuania

HISTORY

By the 10th century AD the south-eastern Baltic was occupied by three related groups of tribes: the Livs in present-day Latvia, the Prussians in the present Kaliningrad region of Russia and modern north-east Poland, and the Lithuanians in between.

Gediminas, leader of a united Lithuania from 1316 to 1341, profited from the decline of the early Russian state based in Kiev. He pushed Lithuania's borders south and east, but found his own willingness to accept Christianity opposed by pagan kin. After his death his son Algirdas, based in Vilnius, pushed the borders past Kiev.

In 1386 Algirdas' son and successor Jogaila married Jadwiga, Queen of Poland, becoming Wladyslaw II of Poland and a Christian, forging an alliance against the knights and initiating a 400-year bond between the two states. Together they won control of a huge swathe of land from the Baltic to the Black Sea. But Lithuania ended up the junior partner, its gentry adopting Polish culture and language.

Polish and Lithuanian forces briefly took Moscow in 1610, but in 1654 Russia invaded and took significant territory. In the 18th century, divisions in the Polish-Lithuanian state weakened until it finally vanished from the map when Russia, Austria and Prussia carved it up in the Partitions of Poland (1772, 1793 and 1795-96).

With the collapse of the old order in Eastern Europe in 1917-18, Lithuanian nationalists declared independence on 16 February 1918 and managed to fend off an attempted Soviet takeover. Independent Lithuania's capital was Kaunas.

In 1940, following the signing of the Molotov-Ribbentrop Pact, Lithuania found itself part of the USSR. Within a year around 40,000 Lithuanians were killed or deported. Up to 300,000 people, mostly Jews, died in concentration camps and ghettos during the 1941-44 Nazi occupation.

Between 1945 and 1952, with Soviet control re-established, an estimated further 200,000-plus people were killed or deported. The Lithuanian forests were the centre of armed resistance to Soviet rule, which may have involved tens of thousands of people.

In the late 1980s Lithuania came to lead the Baltic push for independence after candidates supporting its popular front, Sajūdis, won 30 seats in the March 1989 elections for the USSR Congress of People's Deputies. In December 1989 Lithuania became the first Soviet republic to legalise noncommunist parties. In February 1990 Sajūdis was elected to form a majority in Lithuania's new Supreme Soviet, which on 11 March declared Lithuania independent.

The independence momentum flagged as the Baltic republics' economic reliance on the USSR became clear. Then in January 1991 Soviet troops and paramilitary police stormed key buildings in Vilnius, apparently

LITHUANIA

789

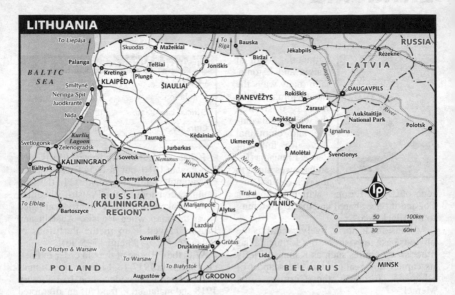

to pave the way for a communist coup and Soviet crackdown. Fourteen people were killed and many more injured in the storming of the Vilnius TV tower. Lithuanians barricaded their parliament, the violence drew heavy condemnation from the west, and the threat subsided.

Lithuania and the other Baltic republics were finally brought real independence by the failed coup in Moscow in August 1991, which resulted in western and then, on 6 September, Soviet recognition of Lithuanian independence. The country became the first of the Baltic ex-republics to be free of any Soviet presence when the last troops based on Lithuanian soil departed for Russia on 31 August 1993.

In January 1998, Lithuanian politics took a surprising turn when Valdas Adamkus, who had lived most of his life in the US, won the presidential elections by a slim majority. In May 1999 Adamkus appointed Rolandas Paksas, popular Vilnius mayor and champion stunt pilot, as his new prime minister, but after resigning, he's back to being Vilnius' mayor. The government's policies are directed towards integration with the EU and NATO.

GEOGRAPHY
Lithuania (65,300 sq km) is bigger than Latvia or Estonia. Half Lithuania's short coastline is on Neringa, a spit with high dunes and pine forests stretching 97km north from near Kaliningrad. Inland Lithuania is dotted with over 4000 mostly shallow lakes.

CLIMATE
Lithuania's climate is similar to Latvia's with the warmest period, late June to mid August (average temperature 20°C), also being the wettest. Temperatures may not rise above freezing from mid-November to mid-March.

Winter is foggy and lasts about six weeks longer in the inland east of the country than the coastal west.

POPULATION & PEOPLE
Lithuania's population is 3.7 million. The main minority groups are Russians (8.5%) and Poles (7%). Like the Poles, Lithuanians are predominantly Roman Catholic, and much more enthusiastic about their creed than the Lutherans to the north.

LANGUAGE
Lithuanian is one of only two surviving languages of the Baltic branch of the Indo-European language family (the other is Latvian). Despite the small Russian minority, most Lithuanians, both young and old, speak decent Russian, and you're likely to get further with it than with English. See the Language Guide at the back of this book for

pronunciation guidelines and useful words and phrases.

Facts for the Visitor

HIGHLIGHTS

Vilnius' Old Town is the definite highlight. No less enchanting are the castles of Trakai and the coastal region of Neringa, a magnificent silent world of windswept sand dunes and pine trees. Klaipėda's Sea Museum & Aquarium is also worth a look.

TOURIST OFFICES

Tourist information sources include Lithuanian embassies, and Tourist Information Bureaus located in every main centre in Lithuania.

EMBASSIES & CONSULATES
Lithuanian Embassies & Consulates Abroad

Australia
  Consulate: (☎ 02-9498 2571) 40B Fiddens Wharf Rd, Killara, NSW 2071
Canada (☎ 613-567 5458) 130 Albert Street, Suite 204, Ottawa, Ontario K1P 564
UK (☎ 0171-486 6401) 84 Gloucester Place, London W1HN
USA (☎ 202-234 5860) 2622 16th St NW, Washington, DC 20009

Embassies in Lithuania

The following are in Vilnius (area code ☎ 22):

Australia (☎/fax 223 369) Gaono gatvė 6
Canada (☎ 220 898) Gedimino 64
Estonia (☎ 757 970) Mickevičiaus 4a
Finland (☎ 221 621) Klaipėdos gatvė 6
Latvia (☎ 231 260) Čiurlionio gatvė 76
Poland (☎ 709 001) Smėlio gatvė 20a
UK (☎ 222 070) Antakalnio gatvė 2
USA (☎ 223 031) Akmenų gatvė 6

MONEY

Lithuania introduced its national currency, the litas (plural litau; abbreviated Lt), on 25 June 1993, replacing the transitional 'talonas'. The litas is a fully convertible currency that has been pegged to the US dollar at a rate of 4 to 1. There are plans to peg it instead to the euro.

The litas comes in one, two, five, 10, 20, 50, 100 and 200 Lt notes. One litas equals 100 centų (ct), and there are one, two, five, 10, 20 and 50 centų coins.

The best currencies to bring into Lithuania are US dollars and/or German marks.

Credit cards are widely accepted, especially at upper-end hotels and restaurants. Travellers cheques and Eurocheques can be cashed at banks and major post offices. Vilniaus Bankas ATMs accept Visa cards, while Taupomasis Bank ATMs accept MasterCard.

Costs

Costs are relatively low in Lithuania. In general, good and services are priced even lower than in neighbouring Latvia and Estonia. There is also a good network of youth hostels in the country to keep accommodation costs down. Transport remains affordable. Backpackers can get by on as low as US$13 a day.

Exchange Rates

country	unit		litas
Australia	A$1	=	2.30Lt
Canada	C$1	=	2.71Lt
euro	€1	=	3.59Lt
France	1FF	=	0.54Lt
Germany	DM1	=	1.82Lt
Ireland	IR£1	=	4.52Lt
Netherlands	f1	=	1.62Lt
UK	UK£1	=	5.82Lt
USA	US$1	=	4.00Lt

POST & COMMUNICATIONS

Letters/postcards weighing under 20g cost 1.70 Lt/1.20 Lt air mail or 1.30/1 Lt surface mail. Stamps can be bought at post offices or hotels.

Lithuania's international country code is ☎ 370. To call other cities within Lithuania, simply dial ☎ 8, wait for the tone, then dial the area code and phone number. Lithuania has two kinds of card phones – both the magnetic and the chip cards cost 3.54 Lt to 28.32 Lt and are available from news kiosks and post offices.

To make an international call dial ☎ 8-tone-10 followed by the country code and phone number. A three-minute call to the US costs about $4.45.

INTERNET RESOURCES

Online versions of the handy *In Your Pocket* city guides to Vilnius, Klaipėda and Kaunas (www.inyourpocket.com) have up-to-date information. There are lots of links and strong background information at both neris.mii.lt and www.ciesin.ee/Lithuania.

LITHUANIA

GAY & LESBIAN TRAVELLERS

Lithuania is the least tolerant of the Baltics. The Lithuanian Gay League (☎ 633 031, ✆ forter@ektaco.ee) in Vilnius arranges accommodation for gay and lesbian travellers. There is only one gay club in Lithuania (see Entertainment in the Vilnius section). Check out www.gay.lt on the Web.

DISABLED TRAVELLERS

The Association of Invalids (☎ 757 716, Saltoniškiu 29/3) can help direct you to local services.

PUBLIC HOLIDAYS & SPECIAL EVENTS

Lithuania's national holidays are 1 January, 16 February (1918 Independence Day), 11 March (Restoration of Independence), Good Friday, Easter Monday, 1 May (Labour Day), 6 July, 1 November (All Saint's Day), 25 and 26 December.

The next Lithuanian Song Festival will take place in 2002. The Baltika International Folk Festival is due in Vilnius in mid-July 2002. Other annual festivals include the Kaunas International Jazz Festival during April, the week-long Life Theatre Festival in Vilnius in May, and the pagan-flavoured Vilnius City Masks Festival celebrating the Autumn equinox at the end of September. For more information contact the Lithuanian Folk Culture Centre at B Radvilaitės 8 in Vilnius (☎ 612 594). Web site: neris.mii .lt/heritage/lfcc

ACCOMMODATION

Accommodation in the cities and smaller towns can be heavily booked, especially in summer, so it's worth booking ahead.

There are camping grounds at holiday towns such as Palanga, Trakai and Druskininkai. Your best bet is to contact the local tourist centre for information. Most camping grounds also have small unheated cabins for hire.

It is possible find fairly cheap hostels or student rooms in Vilnius and throughout Lithuania. A number of agents offer accommodation in private flats in Vilnius.

Hotels in Lithuania are fairly user-friendly. In recent years most older hotels have undergone extensive renovation, often resulting in a range of room prices based on the degree of renovation in the rooms.

FOOD & DRINKS

Traditional Lithuanian meals are based on potato, and one that must be tried – even if only once – is *cepelinai*, a fist-sized parcel of potato dough stuffed with cheese, meat or mushrooms. Other staples include *bulvinai blynai* (pancakes made of grated potato) and *koldūninė* (ravioli-style dumplings stuffed with cheese, mushrooms or meat). Dairy products such as *varškė* (cottage cheese) and *rūgusis pienas* (sour milk) are also dietary mainstays.

A few basic menu items include: *duona* (bread), *salatos/mišrainė* (salad), *sriuba* (soup), *karbonadas* (fried pork), *kepsnys* (fried meat), *vištiena* (chicken), *zuvis* (fish), *daržovės* (vegetables), *vaisiai* (fruit) and the *sąskaita* (the bill/check).

The best Lithuanian *alus* (beer) is made by local breweries such as Utenos and Kalnapalis. 'Utenos porteris' is a good, hard-hitting dark ale. Lithuanians also drink *midus* (mead) and *gira* (made from fermented grains or fruit). There are also any number of potent liqueurs, like *Krupnikas*, a honey liqueur, and *Starkas*, made from apple and pear tree leaves, which is great mixed with Coca-Cola or apple juice.

Getting There & Away

Lithuania has quite cheap air, bus and rail links with Warsaw, which in turn has flights, trains and cheap buses to/from many Western European cities. In Polish, Vilnius is Wilno; in Lithuanian Warsaw is Varšuva. You can also easily reach Lithuania overland through Latvia, by air or sea from Germany and Sweden, or by air from many points in Europe.

Be sure to obtain a Russian or Belarus visa if you plan to travel onto, or through, Belarus or Kaliningrad.

AIR

Lithuanian Airlines (Lietuvos Avialinijos; LAL) and other major carriers have flights to/from Vilnius and Amsterdam, Berlin, Copenhagen, Frankfurt, London, Paris, Stockholm, Warsaw and Moscow. There are also flights from Helsinki (Finnair) and Vienna (Austrian Airlines). The Latvian state airline, Air Baltic, flies from Vilnius to Rīga twice a day. Estonian Air flies to Tallinn daily.

LAND
Four buses daily run between Vilnius and Warsaw (10 hours, 80 Lt), departing from Vilnius bus station.

Daily buses also run between Vilnius and Białystok (45 Lt) and Gdańsk (overnight, 83 Lt). The Varita bus company (☎ 730 219), at Ukmergės gatvė 12a in Vilnius, runs a bus every Sunday from Vilnius to Saarbrücken for 325 Lt one-way; a 20% student discount is available, and there are discounts for children.

Varita also sell tickets to Paris on buses operated by Kautra (☎ 27 201 963). Buses leave Vilnius twice a week, stopping in Kaunas, Strasbourg, Nice, Metz, and Reims en route to Paris. A return ticket costs 790 Lt. A 10% student discount is available.

Every second day (on even-numbered dates) there is an overnight train between Vilnius and Warsaw. There is a daily express train between Vilnius and Berlin.

Trains from Vilnius to Kaliningrad (seven hours) run three times a day; St Petersburg (15-17 hours) once or twice a day; Moscow (18 hours) two or three times a day; and Lviv, Kharkiv and Chernivtsi several times a week.

SEA
Ferries sail from Klaipėda to/from Kiel in Germany daily (26-29 hours), to/from Mukran in Germany three times a week (19 hours), to/from Stockholm twice each week (18 hours), to/from Kiel four times weekly (26 hours). For tickets contact Krantas Travel (☎ 26-227 084) at Pylimo gatvė 4, or Passenger Service (☎ 26-395 050) at Perkėlos 10 in Klaipėda. Cargo ferries offering limited cabin space for passengers also sail between Klaipėda and Copenhagen and Fredericia in Denmark twice a week (22-34 hours). Tickets can be booked through DFDS Baltic Line (☎ 26 496 400) at Minijos gatvė 180 in Klaipėda.

Getting Around

Within Lithuania, as in all the Baltic republics, buses are generally cheaper, more frequent and definitely faster than trains. Trains are a good option for destinations within 20 or 30km of Vilnius.

Vilnius

☎ 22

The greenest and prettiest of the Baltic capitals, Vilnius (population 578,400) lies 250km inland on the Neris River. The winding streets of Old Vilnius – a wonderland of three-storey baroque and classical buildings – are a pleasure to explore. Evidence of the Polish connection can be seen in the many Catholic churches and the array of central European architectural styles from past centuries. It's also a relaxed and friendly city, one of the only places in the Baltic region where people seem to actually smile on the street.

In the 17th and early 18th centuries Vilnius suffered fires, war, famine and plague, but in the 19th century it grew again as industry developed, and the town became a refuge for dispossessed Polish-Lithuanian gentry. It was devastated, however, in WWI when the Germans occupied it for 3½ years. When the shooting died down, Vilnius found itself in Poland, where it remained until 1939. By then its population was one-third Jewish and it developed into one of the world's three major centres of Yiddish culture (the others being Warsaw and New York). The Germans occupied Vilnius for another three years during WWII; nearly all of Vilnius' Jews were killed in its ghetto or at the Paneriai death camp.

Orientation
The heart of central Vilnius is Katedros aikštė, the cathedral square with Gediminas Hill rising behind it. South of Katedros aikštė are the streets of the Old Town; to the west Gedimino prospektas is the axis of the newer part of the centre. The train and bus stations are just beyond the south edge of the old city, 1.5km from Katedros aikštė.

Information
Tourist Offices Vilnius Tourist Information Centre (☎ 629 660, ✉ turizm.info@ vilnius.sav.lt, Vilniaus gatvė 22) is open 9 am to 6 pm weekdays only. Its smaller branch (☎ 626 470, Pilies gatvė 42) is open

CENTRAL VILNIUS

PLACES TO STAY
34 Teacher's University Hostel
38 Litinterp
51 AAA Mano Liza Guesthouse
56 Lithuanian Youth Hostels & Old Town Youth Hostel
57 Elektros Tinklai
58 Hotel Gintaras
59 Mikotel

PLACES TO EAT
2 Ritos Slėptuvė
18 Prie Parlamento & Ministerija Nightclub
20 Namai Presto
21 Čili
22 Kuba
23 McDonald's
37 Gabi
42 Užupio Café
46 The PUB
48 Savas Kampas
60 McDonald's

OTHER
1 National Gallery
3 Lithuanian Airlines
4 Varita Bus Company
5 Lithuanian Tours
6 The Farmer's Market
7 Decorative & Applied Arts Museum
8 Gedimino Tower
9 Vilnius Cathedral
10 National Museum
11 Men's Factory
12 Lithuanian Opera & Ballet Theatre
13 National Library
14 Parliament
15 Church of the Saint Virgin's Apparition
16 Angaras Nightclub
17 Taupomasis Bank
19 Museum of the Genocide of the Lithuanian People
24 City Hall
25 Central Post Office
26 Vilnius Bankas
27 Academic Drama Theatre & Interneto Kavinė
28 Tourism Information Centre
29 Telecommunications Centre
30 Frank Zappa Memorial
31 State Jewish Museum
32 US Embassy
33 Student and Youth Travel
35 Vilnius University
36 St John's Church
39 Mickiewicz Museum
40 St Anne's Church
41 St Michael's Church
43 Church of the Holy Mother of God
44 Tourism Information Centre
45 Gero Viskio Baras
47 VOO2 Internet Café
49 Lithuanian Art Museum
50 St Kazimieras Church
52 Philharmonic Concert Hall
53 Holy Spirit Church
54 St Teresa's Church
55 Gates of Dawn
61 Bus Station
62 24-hour Currency Exchange & Express Mail Service (EMS)

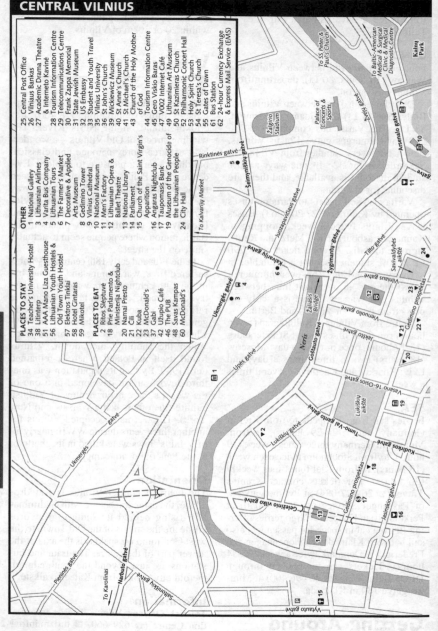

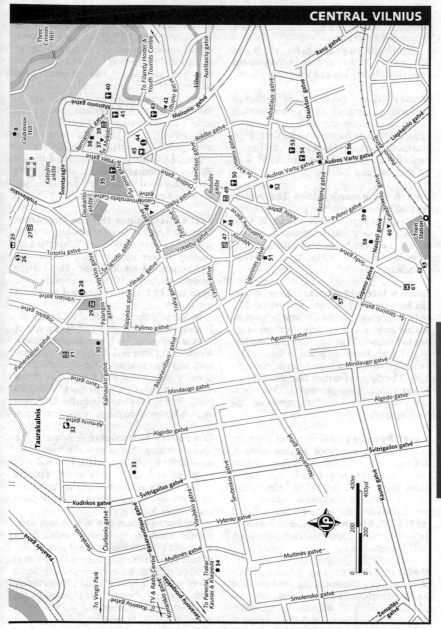

CENTRAL VILNIUS

LITHUANIA

9 am to 7 pm weekdays, and 10 am to 4 pm Saturday. Web site: www.vilnius.lt/tourism/organiz/infocentr.htm

English-speaking hotlines include ☎ 231 414 and ☎ 726 006, and can help you out with virtually any kind of information.

Money Vilnius' best 24-hour exchange (and with good rates to boot) is on your left as you exit the train station at Geležinkelio gatvė 6. Vilniaus Bankas and its Visa ATM is at Gedimino prospektas 12, while Taupomasis Bank and its MasterCard ATM is on the same street at No 56.

Post & Communications The central post office at Gedimino prospektas 7 is open 7 am to 7 pm weekdays, 9 am to 4 pm Saturday. It also has telephone facilities. Express mail can be sent with the state Express Mail Service (EMS; ☎ 236 232) at Geležinkelio gatvė 6.

Email & Internet Access Internet access can be found at Interneto Kavinė (☎ 221 481), inside the Drama Theatre at Gedimino prospektas 4, open 8 am to 8 pm Monday to Friday, 10 am Saturday and Sunday. VOO2 is another cool place to surf, at Ašmenos gatvė 8, open from 8 am to midnight daily. The cheapest surfing is at the National Library, Gedimino prospektas 51, which will ask you for a 5 Lt membership and nothing more.

Travel Agencies Several travel agencies in Vilnius can help book accommodation, tickets, visas and other services within Lithuania and the rest of the Baltics. Lithuanian Tours (☎ 724 176) at Šeimyniškių gatvė 12 offers a worldwide booking system; Lithuanian Student and Youth Travel (☎ 313 737, ✆ info@lsyt.lt), Basanavičiaus gatvė 30, room 13, offers cheap fares for ISIC holders.

Medical Services Two private clinics offer an English-speaking service: the Baltic-American Medical and Surgical Clinic (☎ 342 020) inside Vilnius University Antakalnio hospital at Antakalnio gatvė 124, and the cheaper Medical Diagnostic Centre (☎ 709 120), Grybo gatvė 32, which is open weekdays 8 am to 8 pm, Saturday 9 am to 2 pm.

Things to See

Katedros Aikštė & Around On top of the 48m **Gediminas Hill** (Gedimino kalnas), behind the cathedral, the **Gedimino Tower** is a good starting point. Walk up the path from Katedros aikštė. The red-brick tower was part of the upper castle. Inside the tower is a museum (open Wednesday to Sunday) featuring old Vilnius, and on top there's an observation platform.

Katedros aikštė, scene of most of the mass gatherings during Lithuania's independence campaign, is dominated by the **Vilnius Cathedral**, reconsecrated in 1989 after being used as a picture gallery during the Soviet era.

East of Gediminas Hill The white **Three Crosses** (Trys Kryžiai) overlooking the city are said to have stood there since the 17th century, in memory of three monks who were crucified on the spot. The current crosses, erected in 1989, are replicas of the three knocked down and buried by Soviet authorities.

Inside **St Peter & St Paul's Church** (Šv Petro ir Povilo Bažnyčias), at the far end of Kosciuškos gatvė, is a sea of white stucco sculptures of real and mythical people, animals and plants. Most of the decoration was done by Italian sculptors between 1675 and 1704. If you don't want to walk, trolleybus No 2, 3 or 4 goes there from the Gedimino stop on Vrublevskio gatvė, near the cathedral.

Old Town – Pilies Gatvė & Around The area stretching 1km or so south from Katedros aikštė was built up in the 15th and 16th centuries and the area is worth repeated visits. The focal streets are Pilies gatvė and its southward continuations, Didžioji gatvė and Aušros Vartų gatvė.

The central buildings of **Vilnius University** occupy most of the block between Pilies gatvė and Universiteto gatvė. The university, founded in 1579, was one of the greatest centres of Polish learning and produced many notable scholars in the 17th and early 19th centuries, before being closed by the Russians in 1832. Reopened in 1919, today it has over 14,000 students.

The 12 linked courtyards can be entered by several passages and gates: the southern gate on Šv Jono gatvė brings you into the Didysis or Skarga Courtyard, with three sides of galleries in the early 17th century Mannerist style, and Šv Jono Bažnyčia (St John's Church), which has an outstanding 18th century Baroque main façade.

East of Pilies gatvė, the old rooms of the Polish Romantic poet Adam Mickiewicz (1798-1855) at Bernardinų gatvė 11 are now the **Mickiewicz museum**, open 10 to 5 pm Tuesday to Friday, 10 am to 2 pm weekends, closed Monday.

Across Maironio gatvė is the fine 1581 brick façade of **St Anne's Church** (Šv Onos Bažnyčia), a high point of Lithuanian Gothic architecture with its sweeping curves and delicate pinnacles.

Farther down Maironio at No 12 stands the lovely Russian Orthodox Church of the Holy Mother of God (1346), damaged in the late 17th century and reconstructed from 1865-68, behind which lies the Užupio bridge (1895) stretching over the thin Vilna rivulet into one of Vilnius' most interesting neighbourhoods, **Užupis**. Once an area for derelicts and criminals, it has been taken over by several groups of artists who squat in its many crumbling buildings and hold impromptu art shows.

Old Town – Didžioji Gatvė & Around

Southern Didžioji gatvė widens into a plaza that was long one of the centres of Vilnius life. The large **St Kazimieras' Church** (Šv Kazimiero Bažnyčios) at Didžioji gatvė 43 is Vilnius' oldest baroque church, built by the Jesuits between 1604 and 1615. Under Soviet rule it spent two decades as a museum of atheism.

Pretty Aušros Vartų gatvė was once the start of the Moscow road. On the east side of the street, just above a 16th-century house, is the big, pink, domed, 17th-century **Holy Spirit Church**, Lithuania's chief Russian Orthodox church. The amazingly preserved bodies of three 14th-century martyrs lie in a chamber in front of the altar.

At the southern end of Aušros vartų gatvė are the **Gates of Dawn** (Aušros Vartai) – in fact just a single gate tower, the only one of the original nine in the town wall that's still intact. Just before the gate, a door on the left opens on to a staircase leading to an 18th-century chapel directly over the gate arch. This houses a supposedly miracle-working **icon of the Virgin**, one of Eastern Europe's leading pilgrimage destinations.

New Town The main street of modern Vilnius, laid out in 1852, is **Gedimino prospektas**, dotted with shops, banks, restaurants and offices. Lukiškių aikštė, which is the square at roughly the mid-point on Gedimino prospektas, used to be Lenin Square. The large building facing the square, at Gedimino prospektas 4 (enter around the corner at Auku 2a), used to be the Vilnius KGB headquarters and prison and is now a **Museum of the Genocide of the Lithuanian People** (closed Monday). The museum guides are all former inmates.

Close by at Pamėnkalnio gatvė 12 is the excellent **Lithuanian State Jewish Museum**, with a second branch nearby on Pylimo 4, both open 9 am to 5 pm Monday to Thursday, to 4 pm Friday.

At Kalinuasko gatvė 1 stands a 4.2m-high memorial to the American rock 'n' roll legend **Frank Zappa**, erected by the Lithuanian Frank Zappa fan club in 1995 after a long dispute with local authorities who found the idea preposterous.

Just over 1km south-west of parliament, at the western end of Čiurlionio gatvė, is Vilnius' biggest city park, the pleasant **Vingis parkas**, whose huge stage is the usual setting for the Lithuanian Song Festival.

The 326m **TV tower** (where Soviet tanks and troops killed 14 people and injured many more as they fought through the crowd encircling it on 13 January 1991) is in the suburb of Karoliniškes, across the river from Vingis parkas. Trolleybus No 7 from the train station to Justiniškės stops within a few minutes' walk of the tower.

Places to Stay

It's wise to book ahead in summer. Litinterp (☎ 223 850, @ vilnius@litinterp.lt, Bernardinų gatvė 7-2) can arrange B&B accommodation in the Old Town from 70/120 Lt a single/double. It also handles bookings in Klaipėda, Nida, Palanga and Kaunas, rents cars and organises English-speaking city guides. Bookings can be made via the Internet at www2.omnitel.net/litinterp.

Hostels Lithuanian Youth Hostel Association (Lietuvos Jaunimo Nakvynės Namai; ☎ 625 357, @ livijus@pub.osf.lt), runs the *Filaretų Hostel* (☎ 254 627, Filaretų gatvė 17) in the Užupis area. Beds cost from 24 Lt to 32 Lt with breakfast. A second location, the *Old Town Youth Hostel (Aušros vartų 20-15a)* is the place to head to. This is exactly what hostels are meant to be – clean, homy and loads of fun. It's also in a prime location; follow the many signs for it east of the train station – it's only 500m away.

Second best is definitely the *Youth Tourists' Centre (☎ 613 576, Polocko gatvė 7),* also in charming Užupis, with sparse doubles and triples overlooking a bend in the river for only 20 Lt per person.

The *Teacher's University Hostel (☎ 230 704, fax 262 291),* in a drab slab of a building at Vivulskio gatvė 36, always has places available in large singles/doubles/triples for 65/66/99 Lt (students pay only 27 Lt for a bed in a shared room).

Hotels The best option is *Elektros Tinklai (☎ 260 254, Šv Stepono 11),* about 500m from the train station, in a lively though run-down area. Their comfortable doubles/triples are only 20 Lt per person and accordingly they fill up fast – advance reservations are a must!

Your best mid-range bet is the cheerful, quiet *Mikotel (☎ 609 626, Pylimo gatvė 63),* just a few minutes walk from the train station. These are the nicest rooms you're likely to find for 180/240 Lt (152/192 Lt on weekends) – ask for one on the top floor, with a skylight.

If desperate, *Hotel Gintaras (☎ 738 003, Sodų gatvė 14)* in front of the train station, will do. The black market types hanging around and the drab Soviet atmosphere are notable features. Singles/doubles start at 64/95 Lt and rise to 140/199 Lt for the renovated ones.

Places to Eat

Fresh milk straight from the cow's udder, home-made honey and smoked eels are just some of the culinary delights at the *farmers' market* at Kalvarijų gatvė 6, open 7 am to noon daily (except Monday). *Kuba*, a cafeteria/cafe/take-out counter at Gedimino prospektas 24 has salads and sandwiches to go.

For a cheap and cheerful meal in the company of well-fed ex-pats and locals, there are two British-run options. *The PUB (Dominikonų gatvė 9),* in the Old Town, dishes up shepherd's pie, lasagne, shaslik, and a whole host of other mammoth-sized meals for around 13 Lt. Even better is *Prie Parlamento (Gedimino prospektas 46)* whose specialities include delicious vegetarian meals, a great breakfast menu, and sinful chocolate brownies and crumbles.

Užupio Café (Užupio gatvė 2), open daily from 11 am until the last client leaves, has the best patio in the city – tree-shaded and overlooking the river – plus a cosy interior dining room in a building whose foundations date from the 13th century. A variety of tasty meals are around 13 Lt.

Savas Kampas (Vokiečių gatvė 4) has something to keep everyone happy, including a jovial atmosphere. It has a pub feel in the evenings, and is open 9 am to midnight daily.

Ritos Slėptuvė (Goštauto gatvė 8) is as eclectic as they come and serves great, if mostly Yank-styled food. The retro-US-meets-USSR decor is worth a visit, as is the bakery in the entrance (real cupcakes, mmm). It stays open until 4 am weekends.

Cafes The *Namai Presto (Gedimino prospektas 32a)* serves the closest thing to a decent latte in town (but is that 35% cream they use for the froth?) and has a huge selection of teas, and a few cakes too. It's open at 7.30 am daily (11 am Sunday). Equally popular is the no-smoking *Gabi (Šv Mykolo gatvė 6),* which is packed most lunchtimes. Filling meals can be enjoyed for under 13 Lt.

If all this good food has given you a craving for junk, head to *McDonald's* on the corner of Gedimino prospektas and Vilniaus gatvė – there's also a drive-through opposite the train station at Seinų gatvė 3 with a children's playground out front. For good pizza, head to *Čili* – one of its outlets is on Gedimino prospektas 23.

Entertainment

See *Vilnius In Your Pocket,* the weekly *Baltic Times* or the local daily *Lietuvos Rytas* for events listings.

Bars & Clubs Aside from the previously mentioned The PUB and Prie Parlamento, try *Ministerija* in the latter's basement – there are often energetic live bands, and when there's not, you'll find good dancing. At *Bix (Etmonų gatvė 6),* you can play pool, hang out with alternative and grunge kids, relax with a brew, or enjoy good food – it's one of the best places to meet interesting people. *Gero Viskio Baras (Pilies gatvė 34)* is another extremely popular bar with downstairs disco.

The spacious *Angaras (Jasinkio gatvė 14)* is one of the most happening discos, with pool tables and a large lounge area. The country's first and only gay club, the *Men's Factory (Žigimantų gatvė 2)* is hidden away in a courtyard and has an Eastern European charm to it.

Classical Music, Opera & Ballet The State Symphony and Lithuania Chamber Orchestras have good reputations, as does the Lithuanian Philharmonia. Concert halls include the *Philharmonic* at Didžioji gatvė 45. The *Lithuanian Opera & Ballet Theatre* is a modern building with poor acoustics at Vienuolio gatvė 1.

Getting There & Away

Air Vilnius' *aerouostas* (airport) is 5km south of the city at Rodūnės kelias 2, in the suburb of Kirtimai. Local travel agents (see Information earlier) generally have the best air fare deals. Otherwise contact the airlines directly. Air Baltic has an office at the airport (☎ 306 666), Lithuanian Airlines (LAL) at Ukmergės gatvė 12 (☎ 752 588).

Bus The *Auto-busų stotis* (long-distance bus station; ☎ 262 482) is just south of the Old Town at Sodų gatvė 22. The ticket hall on the right is for destinations within Lithuania. Eurolines (☎ 251 377) have their office there as well. Domestic departures from Vilnius include: Druskininkai (2½ hours), Kaunas (two hours), Klaipėda (five to 6½ hours), Palanga (seven hours), Šiauliai (4½ hours) and Trakai (45 minutes).

Train The *geležinkelio stotis* (train station; ☎ 330 088) is slightly to the left behind the bus station at Geležinkelio 16. Timetables are displayed in English. A handful of daily trains go to Kaunas (two to three hours), Klaipėda (five hours), Šiauliai (four hours) and Trakai (1½ hours).

Getting Around

To/From the Airport Take bus No 2 from Lukiškių square or Hotel Lietuva, or bus No 1 from the train station. A taxi from the airport to the city centre should cost no more than 20 Lt.

Public Transport Bus and trolleybus tickets are distinct and cost 0.60 Lt (0.30 Lt for students) at most kiosks. Buying a ticket directly from the driver costs 0.75 Lt. Tickets must be punched inside the carriage.

Around Vilnius

PANERIAI

Between July 1941 and July 1944, about 100,000 people were killed in the Nazi concentration camp at Paneriai, which is 10km south-west of central Vilnius. The entrance to the wooded site is marked by a memorial, the **Panerių Memorialas**, which now states that 70,000 of the victims here were Jewish – in the past the victims were referred to simply as 'Soviet citizens'. A path leads to the small **Paneriai Museum** (closed Sunday and Tuesday). From here paths lead to a number of grassed-over pits where the Nazis burnt the exhumed bodies of their victims in order to hide the evidence of their crimes.

Getting There & Away

Take bus No 8 from Vilnius' train station and get off near the footbridge over the Paneriai marshalling yards. Cross the bridge and turn right along the street at the far side of the tracks, Agrastų gatvė, which leads 900m straight to the site.

TRAKAI
☎ 238

Gediminas reputedly made Trakai, 27km west of Vilnius, his capital in 1321. Its two lakeside castles were built within the next 100 years to fend off the German knights. Today it's a small, quiet town on a north-pointing peninsula between two vast lakes. From the train station in Trakai, follow Vytauto gatvė north to the central square, where you'll find the bus station, then continue north to Karaimų gatvė and the main points of interest.

The tourist information office (☎/fax 51 934, ✉ tic@is.lt), at Vytauto gatvė 69, is open 9 am to 6 pm weekdays, and 10 am to 3 pm Saturday.

Things to See

Among the wooden cottages along Karaimų gatvė, at No 30, is an early 19th-century **Kenessa** (prayer house) of the Karaites, or

LITHUANIA

Karaimai, a Judaist sect originating in Baghdad and adhering only to the Law of Moses. About 100 Karaites still live in Trakai. There is also a beautiful 15th-century **cemetery** 200m south of Karaimų, along Žalioji gatvė, which begins 300m north-west of the castle area.

The remains of Trakai's **Peninsula Castle** are towards the north end of town, in a park close to the shore of Lake Luka. The castle is thought to have been built between 1362 and 1382. The painstakingly restored, Gothic red-brick **Island Castle** probably dates from around 1400. The moated main tower has a cavernous central court and a range of galleries, halls and rooms, some housing the **Trakai History Museum** (5/2.50 Lt).

Places to Stay
Kempingas Slėnyje (☎ 51 387) is a top camping ground 6km north of Trakai on the road to Vievis. It costs 12 Lt a night to pitch a tent. Double/triple rooms in the hostel cost 60/80 Lt. In Trakai, the comfy **Galvė Hotel** (☎ 51 345, Karaimų gatvė 41) has singles/doubles for 25/50 Lt.

Getting There & Away
More than 30 buses run daily from Vilnius' bus station to Trakai (3 Lt; 40 minutes). Seven daily trains also go from Vilnius to Trakai (40 minutes).

DRUSKININKAI
☎ 33
At 130km south-west of Vilnius, this stretches the definition of a day trip, but in the nearby village of Grūtas is what has recently become the second most-visited tourist attraction in Lithuania, after the Hill of Crosses. The **Soviet Sculpture Park** (Grūto Parkas; ☎ 55 511), inaugurated in June 2000, contains several dozen Soviet-era statues and monuments (of Stalin, Lenin and local leaders) spread out over a forested area. It's open 9 am to 6 pm daily.

There are five daily buses to Druskininkai from Vilnius, and several slow trains (which go through a slice of Belarus on the way – this is the only way to see Belarus without a visa, albeit from the inside of a train!). From Druskininkai, the village of Grūtas is 7km east (on the road to Vilnius). It's best to take a taxi from the centre. If you're bussing from Vilnius, ask to be let off at the Gruto stop,

cross the road and it's a 1.5km walk. There is a tourist information centre (☎ 41 777) on the 2nd floor of Druskininkai's bus station.

Central Lithuania

KAUNAS
☎ 27
Kaunas (population 412,200), 100km west of Vilnius, is about 90% ethnic Lithuanian, which means that it's generally considered more 'Lithuanian' than the capital. Kaunas was Lithuania's capital between WWI and WWII, when Vilnius was taken over by Poland. Though Kaunas can seem listless after Vilnius, it is a cultural bastion with a big student population and some fine architecture, museums and galleries.

Orientation & Information
The most attractive part of Kaunas is its historic heart, Rotušės aikštė (City Hall Square), on a point of land between two rivers at the western end of the city centre. To the east, the new town is centred on the pedestrianised Laisvės alėja, dotted with shops, hotels, restaurants, galleries and museums.

The bus and train stations are around 1km south of Laisvės alėja's eastern end, down Vytauto prospektas. Kaunas is big, and it takes the best part of an hour to walk from the train station to Rotušės aikštė.

There is a tourist information centre (☎ 323 436, ✉ turizma@takas.lt) at Mickevičiaus 36/40. It's recommended you contact the centre as it can get hotel discounts and find available space when the hotels will say they're booked. The central post and telephone office is at Laisvės alėja 102. For Web access, go to Kavinė Internetas at Daukšos 12, open 10 am to 10 pm daily.

Things to See
Kaunas' museums are all closed on Monday.

Rotušės Aikštė Many of the 15th- and 16th-century German **merchants' houses** around this pretty square have been restored, some now contain cafes or shops. In the square's south-west corner is a **statue of Maironis**, or Jonas Maculevičiaus, the Kaunas priest and writer whose works were banned by Stalin but who is now Lithuania's national poet. The **Lithuanian Liter-**

ary **Museum** is in the house behind, where Maironis lived from 1910 to 1932. Not far off, at Muziejaus 7, is the worthwhile **Lithuanian Sports Museum** with a focus on Lithuania's basketball talents.

A reconstructed tower and sections of wall are all that remain of the 11th-century **Kaunas Castle**, just a short walk north of Rotušės aikštė.

New Town The blue, neo-Byzantine **St Michael the Archangel Church** (1893) on Nepriklausomybės aikštė (Independence Square), dominates the east end of Laisvės alėja.

Directly to the right as you face the cathedral, in front of the **Mykolas Žilinskas Art Museum** at Nepriklausomybės aikštė 12, stands **Man**, a glorious statue of a man revealing his manhood. It has been the centre of controversy since its erection in 1991.

Straddling Donelaičio gatvė, a block north of Laisvės alėja, is Vienybės aikštė (Unity Square), which is fronted by the 14,000-student Kaunas Technical University and the smaller Vytautas Magnus University. Not far away at Donelaičio gatvė 64 is the **Military Museum of Vytautas the Great**, which isn't a military museum at all but a museum of the history of Lithuania. Of particular interest is the wreck of the aircraft in which two of Lithuania's greatest modern heroes, Darius and Girėnas (pictured on the 10 Lt note), attempted to fly nonstop from New York to Kaunas in 1933.

Next door is the **M-K Čiurlionis Museum**, at Putvinskio gatvė 55, which has an extensive collection of paintings by Čiurlionis (1875-1911), Lithuania's greatest artist and composer. Across the street at Putvinskio gatvė 64 is the fascinating **Devil Museum** (Velnių Muziejus), with a bizarre collection of more than 1700 devil-shaped or inspired statuettes, ashtrays and pipes.

Places to Stay

The Lithuanian Hostels Association has three-bed rooms for 40 Lt per person at the **Respublika Guesthouse** (Svečių Namai; ☎ 748 972, Prancūzų gatvė 59), about a 1.25km walk east of the train station. Call before you go to make sure it's still operating.

To obtain reliable information about B&B possibilities, contact Litinterp (☎ 228 718, 📧 litinterp@kaunas.omnitel.net) agency at

Kumelių gatvė 15-4 (its prices start at about 60 Lt). The **Hotel Lietuva** (☎ 205 992, Daukanto gatvė 21) has drab but decent singles/doubles for 90/140 Lt. A somewhat fancier option is **Neris** (☎ 204 224, Donelaičio gatvė 27), offering neat singles/doubles in a friendly atmosphere from 180/220 Lt.

Places to Eat

Kuba (Laisvės alėja 51) is a good bet. The upstairs cafeteria has a large selection you can peruse before ordering, and downstairs is a trendy cocktail bar. **Miesto Sodas** (Laisvės alėja 93) is a favourite during the summer, with a huge, usually packed terrace and an array of sandwiches, burgers and salads for under 12 Lt. Local carnivores titter at the grain 'kotlets' on the menu, but **Arbatinė** (Laisvės alėja 100) is vegan heaven – no meat, no dairy, just plain healthy vegetarian fare.

Cool hang-outs include **Fortas** (Donelaičo gatvė 65), an Irish bar open to the wee hours, and **B&O** (Muitinės gatvė 9) the rock/alternative bar.

Getting There & Away

Bus Bus Kaunas long-distance bus station (☎ 201 955) is at Vytauto prospketas 24. International buses run by the Kautra bus company (Eurolines affiliates; ☎ 322 222 or 746 613) go to Paris, Minsk, Kaliningrad, St Petersburg, Rīga, Pärnu, Tallinn, Berlin and several other destinations in Germany. Other buses travel to Vienna, Warsaw, Prague and Amsterdam. There are many daily domestic connections to Vilnius, Klaipėda and Palanga.

Train Kaunas train station (☎ 221 093) is at Čiurlionio gatvė 16, at the southern end of Vytauto prospektas. There are many daily trains to/from Vilnius and others to/from Klaipėda, Rīga, Šiauliai and Šeštokai.

Boat Between June and August the *Raketa* speed boat sails daily except Monday from Kaunas pier (prieplauka) on the east edge of the city at Raudondvario plentas 107 (☎ 261 348) to Nida (four hours). Check with the tourist information centre (see Information) to confirm it is still running when you visit; in summer 2000, they were only accepting group reservations.

AROUND KAUNAS

Built in the late 19th century, **Ninth Fort**, 7km from central Kaunas, was used by the Nazis in WWII as a death camp. An estimated 80,000 people, including most of Kaunas' Jewish population, were murdered here. One of the prison buildings remains, and the site of the mass grave is marked by stark, monumental sculptures. The museum is open from 10 am to 6 pm daily (except Tuesday).

Buses to Ninth Fort leave regularly from Kaunas' main bus station.

ŠIAULIAI

☎ 21

Šiauliai (population 146,800), 140km north of Kaunas, is Lithuania's fourth-largest city. The city's real magnet is the strange Hill of Crosses. If you're using public transport you may have to spend a night in Šiauliai, unless you're going to/from Rīga.

Orientation & Information

The main north-south street is Tilžės gatvė, with the bus station towards its south end and the tall St Peter & Paul's Church towards its north end, almost 1km away. To the south, Tilžės gatvė becomes the road to Kaliningrad, to the north the road to Rīga. The main east-west axis is Vilniaus gatvė, which crosses Tilžės gatvė 300m south of the church.

The tourist information centre (☎ 422 644, @ tourism.info@siauliai.lt) is at Vilniaus gatvė 213. Web site: www.siauliai.lt

Hill of Crosses

About 10km north of Šiauliai, 2km east off the road to Joniškis and Rīga, the Hill of Crosses (Kryžių kalnas) is a place of national pilgrimage. It's a two-hump hillock covered by thousands upon thousands of crosses. Some are devotional, others are memorials (many for people deported to Siberia). At least three times in the Soviet era the crosses were bulldozed, only to spring up again.

Buses leave from platform No 2 at the main bus station and stop at the beginning of the 2km tree-lined road to the hill (look for the sign Kryžiu kalnas 2). Taxis will take you there for about 20 Lt.

Places to Stay

Šiauliai's tourist office arranges *private rooms* for about 60 Lt per person, including breakfast. The Lithuanian Hostels Association operates a *hostel* (☎ 427 845, Rygos gatvė 36), offering a bed in a shared room for 16 Lt a night.

Getting There & Away

Bus There are buses to/from Kaunas (three hours; 20 daily), Vilnius (four hours; 13 daily), Klaipėda (2½ hours; six daily), Rīga (three hours; seven daily) and Tallinn (8½ hours, one daily).

Train The station is at Dubijos gatvė 44, about 700m east of the bus station. Two or three trains a day go to/from Rīga (two to 2½ hours), one daily to Vilnius (four hours), and two daily to Klaipėda.

Western Lithuania

KLAIPĖDA

☎ 26

The port of Klaipėda (population 202,300), Lithuania's third-largest city, is 315km west of Vilnius, at the mouth of the Kuršių Lagoon. Before WWI Klaipėda was the German town of Memel. Lithuania seized it in 1923, Hitler annexed it in 1939, and the Red Army took over at the end of WWII. Today, it is a lovely, laid-back city with plenty to offer, not the least of which is its proximity to the Curonian Spit (Neringa).

Orientation & Information

Klaipėda's main street, running roughly north-south, is H. Manto gatvė, which becomes Tiltų gatvė south of the Danės River. The old town is centred on Tiltų gatvė. The central post office is at Liepų gatvė 16.

The tourist information bureau (☎ 213 977) at Tomo gatvė 2 is open 9am to 5 pm daily, closed Sunday.

Things to See

An important landmark on Teatro aikštė (Theatre Square), off Turgaus gatvė south of the river, is the 1820 **Klaipėda Theatre**. Hitler stood on its balcony in 1939 to proclaim the re-connection of Memel to Germany. North of the river is a thin **riverside park** immediately east of the H Manto gatvė bridge. Klaipėda's **art gallery** and adjacent sculpture park are at Liepų gatvė 33 (closed Monday). The **Clock & Watch Museum**,

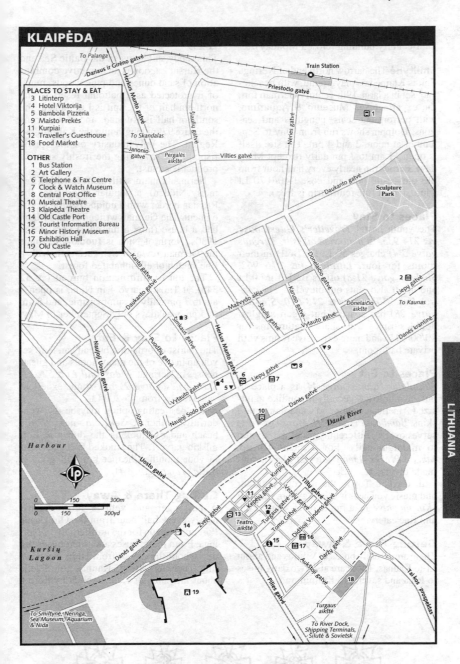

KLAIPĖDA

To Palanga

Dariaus ir Girėno gatvė

Train Station

Priestočio gatvė

PLACES TO STAY & EAT
3 Litinterp
4 Hotel Viktorija
5 Bambola Pizzeria
9 Maisto Prekės
11 Kurpiai
12 Traveller's Guesthouse
18 Food Market

OTHER
1 Bus Station
2 Art Gallery
6 Telephone & Fax Centre
7 Clock & Watch Museum
8 Central Post Office
10 Musical Theatre
13 Klaipėda Theatre
14 Old Castle Port
15 Tourist Information Bureau
16 Minor History Museum
17 Exhibition Hall
19 Old Castle

To Skandalas

Janonio gatvė

Pergalės aikštė

Vilties gatvė

Šiaulių gatvė

Nėries gatvė

Daukanto gatvė

Sculpture Park

Kanto gatvė

Daukanto gatvė

Mažvydo alėja

Šiaulių gatvė

Karuso gatvė

Donelaičio gatvė

Liepų gatvė

Donelaičio aikštė

To Kaunas

2

Vytauto gatvė

Danės krantinė

Sinkaus gatvė

3

Herkus Manto gatvė

Danės River

Puodžių gatvė

Naujoji Uosto gatvė

Vytauto gatvė

Naujojo Sodo gatvė

Jūros gatvė

9

Liepų gatvė

6

5

4

8

7

10

Danės gatvė

Harbour

LP

0   150   300m
0   150   300yd

Uosto gatvė

Kuršių gatvė

Tiltų gatvė

11

Kepėjų gatvė

Vežėjų gatvė

12

Turgaus gatvė

Tomo gatvė

Didžioji Vandens gatvė

13

Teatro aikštė

Kuršių Lagoon

Danės gatvė

14

15

16

17

Daržų gatvė

Aukštoji gatvė

18

Pilies gatvė

Taikos prospektas

19

Turgaus aikštė

To Smiltynė, Neringa, Sea Museum, Aquarium & Nida

To River Dock, Shipping Terminals, Šilutė & Sovietsk

LITHUANIA

Liepų gatvė 12, is housed in a sumptuous 18th-century building (closed Monday).

Smiltynė The narrow north end of Neringa Spit is Klaipėda's playground, with beaches and, set in a large 19th-century German fort, the excellent **Sea Museum & Aquarium**, with performing seals, penguins and sea-lions. Dolphin shows run from May to September at noon, 2 and 4 pm. The site itself is open 11 am to 7 pm daily (except Monday). Ferries run nearly every half hour from the old castle port and cost 1.40/0.70 Lt adult/student (the return trip is free).

Places to Stay
The youth hostel *Traveller's Guesthouse* (☎ 214 935, ✉ oldtown@takes.lt, Turgaus gatvė 3-4) charges 50 Lt for B&B in their rooms for four. *Litinterp* (☎ 216 962, Šimkaus gatvė 21-8) offers B&B for 60 Lt and up. It also rents out bicycles. The central *Hotel Viktorija* (☎ 213 670, Šimkaus gatvė 28) has spartan but clean singles/doubles/triples with shared bathrooms for 40/60/80 Lt and more expensive rooms with private bathroom.

Places to Eat
Skandalas (Kanto gatvė 44) is a place to put on your list, especially if you like giant-sized American steaks and Canadian potato skins. *Bambola Pizzeria* (H. Manto gatvė 1) serves over 40 different types of pizza 9 am to midnight daily. For a cheap fill-up, *Maisto Prekės* (Liepų gatvė 20) has home-made blyniys for 4 Lt.

In the Old Town, the raucous laughter and music you hear is coming from *Kurpiai* (Kurpių gatvė 1), a fun two-floor jazz club and fine eatery.

Getting There & Away
There are 10 daily buses to Vilnius and about 11 to Kaunas. There are also two daily buses to Rīga and several to Kaliningrad.

NERINGA
☎ 259
This sandy spit between the Baltic Sea and the Kuršių Lagoon is an attractive combination of sand dunes and pine woods, much of it protected as a national reserve. The northern half of the spit is Lithuanian, the southern half is Russian, and a road runs the entire 97km length into the Kaliningrad Region. The only industry on the spit is fishing, and savouring the freshly smoked product is a must.

Neringa's main settlement is **Nida** (formerly Nidden), a popular resort near the Russian border with a unique natural environment. The German writer Thomas Mann had a house (now a museum) here in the 1930s. North of Nida is **Juodkrantė** (once the German town of Schwarz-ort), with a fine stretch of elk-inhabited forest.

The tourist information bureau (☎ 52 345), at Taikos gatvė 4 in Nida, is open 9 am to 7 pm daily in summertime, and 8 am to 5 pm weekdays only September to May.

Places to Stay & Eat
The tourist information bureau can help set you up in one of the many hotels and guest-houses in Neringa. *Nidos Smiltė* (☎ 52 221, Skruzdynés gatvė 2) has some excellent value rooms from 45-200 Lt.

The best eating option may be the wonderfully authentic *Seklyčia*, next to the beach and overlooking the dunes at Lot-miškio gatvė 1. The smoked fish just melts in your mouth. Cheaper but still good is *Agila* (Taikos gatvė 4).

Getting There & Away
A passenger and vehicle ferry departs nearly every half hour from the Old Castle Port in Klaipėda for the northern tip of Neringa. From there, buses and microbuses run throughout the day to/from Nida. See Getting There & Away, Kaunas for details about the summer Kaunas-Nida hydrofoil.

Luxembourg

The Grand Duchy of Luxembourg (Luxemburg, Letzeburg) has long been a land of transit. For centuries its ownership has passed from one European superpower to another; and for decades, travellers wrote it off as merely an expensive stepping stone to other European destinations.

Tiny Luxembourg may be more of a tax shelter than a budget haven for travellers, but many people miss the best by rushing through. Its countryside is beautiful, dotted with feudal castles, deep river valleys and quaint wine-making towns. The capital, Luxembourg City, is often described as the most dramatically situated in Europe.

Facts about Luxembourg

HISTORY

Luxembourg's history reads a little like a fairy tale. More than 1000 years ago, in 963, a count called Sigefroi (or Siegfried, count of Ardennes) built a castle high on a promontory, laying the foundation stone of the present-day capital and the beginning of a dynasty which spawned rulers throughout Europe.

By the end of the Middle Ages, the strategically placed, fortified city was much sought after – the Burgundians, Spanish, French, Austrians and Prussians all waging bloody battles to conquer and secure it. Rebuilt more than 20 times in 400 years, it became the strongest fortress in Europe after Gibraltar, hence its nickname, 'Gibraltar of the north'.

Listed as a French 'forestry department' during Napoleon's reign, it was included in the newly formed United Kingdom of the Netherlands, along with Belgium, in 1814. It was cut in half 16 years later when Belgium severed itself from the Netherlands

and Luxembourg was split between them. This division sparked the Grand Duchy's desire for independence, and in 1839 the Dutch portion became present-day Luxembourg. Later, after the country declared itself neutral, much of the fortifications were dismantled.

Luxembourg entered the 20th century riding high on the wealth of its iron-ore deposits. When this industry slumped in the mid-1970s, the Grand Duchy not only survived but continued to prosper by introducing favourable banking and taxation laws, which made it a world centre of international finance.

GEOGRAPHY

At only 82km long and 57km wide, Luxembourg (2586 sq km) occupies a tiny spot between Belgium, Germany and France. Riddled with rivers, it is divided between the forested Ardennes highlands to the north, and farming and mining country to the south.

CLIMATE

Luxembourg has a temperate climate with warm summers and cold winters – it's especially cold in the Ardennes, which sometimes get snow. The sunniest and warmest months are May to August, although April and September can be very pleasant as well. Precipitation is spread evenly throughout the year.

POPULATION & PEOPLE

Luxembourg's 420,000 inhabitants maintain an independent character. Christianity was established early, and today more than 95% of the population are Roman Catholic.

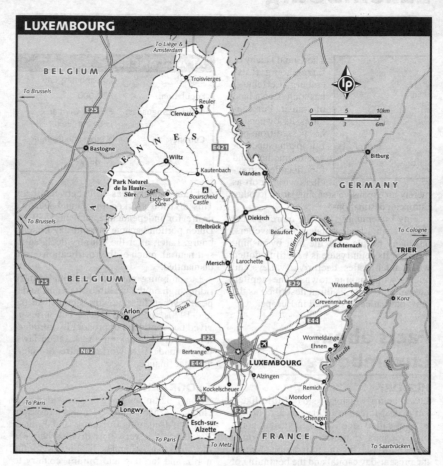

LUXEMBOURG

LANGUAGE
There are three official languages in Luxembourg: French, German and Letzeburgesch. The latter is most closely related to German and was proclaimed as the national tongue in 1984. English is widely spoken in the capital and by younger people around the countryside.

Luxembourgers speak Letzeburgesch to each other but generally switch to French when talking to foreigners. Common words are *moien* (good morning/hello) and *äddi* (goodbye). Like French speakers, Luxembourgers say *merci* for 'thank you'. In the business world, French or German are used. For a rundown on these two languages and some useful words and phrases, see the Language chapter at the back of this book.

Facts for the Visitor

HIGHLIGHTS
Luxembourg's highlights include strolling along the capital's Chemin de la Corniche, spending a lazy afternoon visiting wineries along the Moselle Valley, hiking almost anywhere in the north; and taking in the expansive view from Bourscheid Castle.

SUGGESTED ITINERARIES
Three days
  Spend them in Luxembourg City and in either Echternach or Vianden.
One week
  Spend two days in Luxembourg City, two days exploring the centre and north (Vianden, Clervaux or Diekirch), two days in the Müllerthal region (Echternach and Beaufort) and a day along the Moselle Valley.

PLANNING
Passes & Discounts

Those keen on exploring should consider one of two passes (both available from tourist offices in Luxembourg City). The Luxembourg Card (valid from Easter to 31 October) gives free admission to many attractions throughout the country plus unlimited use of public transport. It costs f350/600/850 for an adult for one/two/three days. The Stater Museeskaart is a two-day card allowing admission to Luxembourg City's major museums and costs f250/400 for an adult/family.

TOURIST OFFICES

The Office National du Tourisme headquarters (☎ 42 82 82 10, fax 42 82 82 38, ✉ tourism@ont.smtp.etat.lu), PO Box 1001, L-1010, Luxembourg City, will send you information, but is not open to the public. Its Web site is at www.etat.lu/tourism.

Tourist Offices Abroad

UK (☎ 020-7434 2800, fax 7734 1205, ✉ tourism@luxembourg.co.uk) 122 Regent St, London W1R 5FE

USA (☎ 212-935 88 88, fax 935 58 96, ✉ luxnto@aol.com) 17 Beekman Place, New York, NY 10022

EMBASSIES & CONSULATES
Luxembourg Embassies Abroad

In countries where there is no representative, contact the Belgian or Dutch diplomatic missions.

UK (☎ 020-7235 6961) 27 Wilton Crescent, London SW1X 8SD

USA (☎ 202-265 41 71) 2200 Massachusetts Ave, NW Washington, DC 20008

Foreign Embassies in Luxembourg

The nearest Australian, Canadian and New Zealand embassies are in Belgium. The following embassies are in Luxembourg City:

Belgium (☎ 44 27 46 1) 4 Rue des Girondins, L-1626

France (☎ 45 72 71 1) 8 Blvd Joseph II, L-1840

Germany (☎ 45 34 45 1) 20-22 Ave Émile Reuter, L-2420

UK (☎ 22 98 64) 14 Blvd Roosevelt, L-2450

USA (☎ 46 01 23) 22 Blvd Emmanuel Servais, L-2535

MONEY

The unit of currency is the Luxembourg franc – written as 'f' or 'flux' – which is issued in f1, f5, f20 and f50 coins, and notes of f100, f1000 and f5000.

The Luxembourg franc is equal to the Belgian franc (for exchange rates, see the Belgium chapter), but while Belgian currency is commonly used in Luxembourg, the reverse does not apply.

Banks are the main exchange bureau and charge about f200 commission per transaction. All major credit cards are commonly accepted; ATMs are located at the airport and around Luxembourg City. Tipping is not obligatory and bargaining is impossible.

POST & COMMUNICATIONS

Post offices (except in Luxembourg City) are open 9 am to 5.30 pm weekdays. It costs f21 to send a letter (under 20g) within Europe and f30 outside.

Luxembourg's international country code is ☎ 352. International phone calls can be made using f125, f250 or f550 phonecards. The cost of a three-minute phone call, in peak time, to the USA is f111.

There are no telephone area codes in Luxembourg. Local telephone calls are time-based and cost a minimum of f10. Numbers prefixed with 0800 are toll-free numbers.

Send faxes from post offices. They cost f180/280/350 to the UK/USA/Australia, plus f30/130/200 per page respectively. It costs f80 to receive a fax.

Internet access facilities are very limited and only in Luxembourg City will you find cybercafes.

TIME

Luxembourg is one hour ahead of GMT/UTC. Clocks are moved forward one hour on the last Sunday in March, and back again on the last Sunday in October.

WOMEN TRAVELLERS

Women should face few problems travelling around Luxembourg. However, in the event of attack, contact the women's crisis organisation Waisse Rank (☎ 40 20 40), 84 Rue Adolphe Fischer, Luxembourg City.

GAY & LESBIAN TRAVELLERS

Luxembourg's national homosexual and lesbian organisation is Rosa Lëtzebuerg

LUXEMBOURG

(mobile/cellphone ☎ 091-31 10 37), 94 Blvd Patton, L-2316 Luxembourg. Attitudes to homosexuality are relaxed and in Luxembourg City you'll find a few of gay bars. The age of consent is 16. Luxembourg Pride is a small festival held in mid-June. A Web site looking at gay Luxembourg is www.ogayane.com (only in French).

DISABLED TRAVELLERS

Disabled travellers will find little joy in getting around in Luxembourg – lifts are not commonplace, ramps are few, and pavements are uneven. For information contact Info-Handicap (☎ 36 64 66), 20 Rue de Contern, L-5955 Itzig.

DANGERS & ANNOYANCES

Luxembourg is a safe country to travel around. In the event of an emergency, call ☎ 113 for the police or ☎ 112 for medical assistance.

BUSINESS HOURS

Trading hours are 9 am to 5.30 pm weekdays (except Monday when some shops open about noon), and a half or full day on Saturday. Many shops close for lunch between noon and 2 pm. Banks have shorter hours: 8.30 am to 4.30 pm weekdays and, in the capital, on Saturday mornings.

PUBLIC HOLIDAYS & SPECIAL EVENTS

Public holidays include New Year's Day, Easter Monday, May Day (1 May), Ascension Day, Whit Monday, National Day (23 June), Assumption Day (15 August), All Saints' Day (1 November) and Christmas Day (25 December).

For a small country, Luxembourg is big on festivals. Pick up the tourist office's *Calendar of Events* brochure for local listings. The biggest national events are carnival, held six weeks before Easter, and Bonfire Day (Bürgsonndeg) one week later.

ACCOMMODATION

In summer it's wise to book all accommodation in advance. The national tourist office has free hotel and camping brochures, and charges f20 to book a hotel room. For accommodation in B&Bs or *gîtes ruraux* (rural houses), contact the Association for Rural Tourism (☎ 95 71 84, fax 95 71 85,

@ tourural@pt.lu), Château de Wiltz, L-9516 Wiltz. It publishes a free brochure (in English) listing many options.

Camping grounds are abundant in the central and northern regions. Rates are f50 to f65 per adult at 'Category 3' grounds, from f100 and f280 in the more plentiful (and better equipped) 'Category 1' grounds. Children are charged half the adult rate, and a tent site is equivalent to an adult rate.

There are 11 hostels – most close irregularly throughout the year, so ring ahead. The nightly dorm rate, including breakfast, varies from f375 to f575 for members under 26 years, and f455 to f670 for older members. Sheets cost f125, and nonmembers must pay an extra f110 a night. For more details contact Hostelling International (HI; ☎ 22 55 88, fax 46 39 87, @ information@youthhostels.lu), 2 Rue du Fort Olisy, L-2261 Luxembourg City.

B&Bs, mainly in rural areas, usually go for between f1200 to f1600 for two people, while the cheapest hotels charge f1000/1400 for a basic single/double room with breakfast.

FOOD & DRINKS

Luxembourg's cuisine is similar to that of Belgium's Wallonia region – plenty of pork, freshwater fish and game meat – but with a German influence in local specialities like liver dumplings with sauerkraut. The national dish is *judd mat gaardebounen* (smoked pork with beans). Strict vegetarians will find little joy. A *plat du jour* (dish of the day) in the cheapest cafe costs about f260. Beer, both local (Mousel) and Belgian, is plentiful, and the Moselle Valley white wines are highly drinkable.

Getting There & Away

The international airport, Findel, is 6km east of the capital. The national carrier, Luxair, flies to a number of European destinations, including London, Paris and Frankfurt. Its main office (☎ 4798 42 87) is at the airport.

Eurolines buses do not pass through Luxembourg; Busabout buses from the UK do (see Getting Around at the start of this book for details).

There are hourly trains to Brussels (f890 for a one-way 2nd-class ticket, 2¾ hours) and Amsterdam (f1634, 5½ hours). Other destinations include Paris (f1550, four hours, six trains per day) and Trier in Germany (f306, 40 minutes, 11 per day).

By car or motorcycle, the E411 is the major route to Brussels; the A4 leads to Paris and the E25 to Metz; the main route to Germany is the E44 via Trier.

It's possible to take a cruise boat from points along the Moselle to destinations in Germany. For example, from Remich to Konz (three hours) it costs f490/590 one-way/return. For more details, see the Moselle Valley section.

Getting Around

The Benelux Tourrail pass (see the Belgium Getting Around section) costs f4400 for a 2nd-class ticket for people above 26 years and f3300 for those under 26. It's also valid for travelling on national buses.

Unlike its Benelux partners, Luxembourg does not have an extensive rail system, so getting around, once you leave the main north-south rail line, can take time. The bus network (operated by CFL) is comprehensive and the fare system for both train and bus is simple: f40 for a 'short' (about 10km or less) trip, or f160 for a 2nd-class unlimited day ticket (known as a *Billet Reseau*), which is also good for travelling on inner-city buses. It's valid from the time of purchase until 8 am the next day.

Luxembourgers drive on the right-hand side, and the blood-alcohol limit for drivers is 0.08%. The speed limit on motorways is 120km. Fuel prices are among the cheapest in Western Europe: lead-free/diesel costs f33/26 per litre. For motoring information, contact Club Automobile de Luxembourg (☎ 45 00 45 1), 54 Route de Longwy, L-8007 Bertrange.

Bikes can be hired for about f400 per day in Luxembourg City. It costs f40 to take your bike on a train.

Luxembourg City

Strikingly situated high on a promontory overlooking the Pétrusse and Alzette valleys, the Grand Duchy's 1000-year-old capital is a composed blend of old and new. One of Europe's financial leaders, it's a wealthy city with an uncommonly tranquil air and unusually clean streets. The historical value of the city's fortifications and older quarters were acknowledged in 1994 when they were added to Unesco's list of World Heritage sites.

Orientation

The city centre's main squares are Place d'Armes and Place Guillaume II. To the south – across Pont Adolphe and Pont Passerelle, two impressive bridges that span the Pétrusse Valley – is the train station quarter. The station itself is 1.25km from Place d'Armes.

The Grund, or lower town, is a picturesque, cobblestoned quarter below the fortifications, and home these days to some brisk nightlife. Across the Alzette Valley rise the modern towers of the European Centre (Centre Européen) on the Kirchberg Plateau.

Information

Tourist Offices The Luxembourg City tourist office (☎ 22 28 09, fax 46 70 70, @ touristinfo@luxembourg-city.lu), Place d'Armes, is open 9 am to 6 or 7 pm daily. It hands out free city maps, a comprehensive walking tour pamphlet and the handy *Luxembourg Weekly* events guide.

The national tourist office (☎ 42 82 82 20, fax 42 82 82 30, @ tourism@ont.smtp .etat.lu) is inside the train station. It's open 9 am to 6 or 7 pm daily.

Money The Kredietbank Luxembourg, Place de la Gare next to the station, is a convenient bank. The exchange office at the train station has poorer rates but is open 8.30 am to 9 pm daily.

Post & Communications The main post office, 25 Rue Aldringen, is open from 7 am to 7 pm weekdays, and until 5 pm Saturday. There's a branch office at 38 Place de la Gare, near the train station. Faxes can be sent from either.

For Internet access try Café Chiggeri (☎ 22 82 36), 15 Rue du Nord, a stylish cafe with just one computer terminal, or CDROMWorld (☎ 26 48 03 12, @ info@ cdromworld.lu) at 41 Ave de la Gare in the Galerie Mercure (f100 for 30 minutes).

LUXEMBOURG

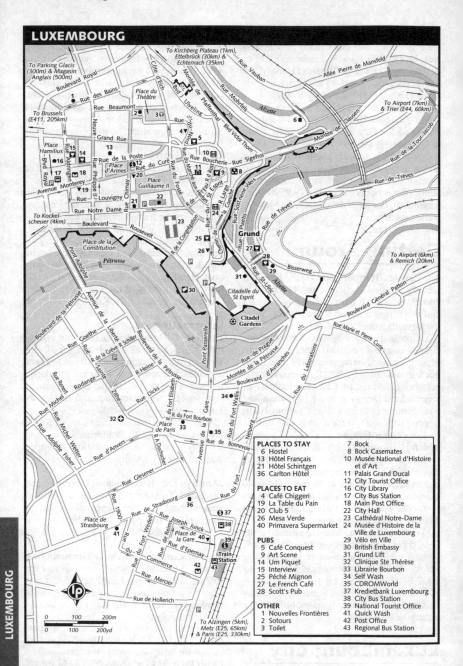

LUXEMBOURG

To Kirchberg Plateau (1km),
Ettelbrück (30km) &
Echternach (35km)

To Parking Glacis
(300m) & Magasin
Anglais (500m)

To Brussels
(E411, 205km)

To Kockel-
scheuer (4km)

Grund

Place de la
Constitution

Citadelle du
St Esprit

Citadel
Gardens

To Airport (7km)
& Trier (E44, 60km)

To Airport (6km)
& Remich (20km)

To Alzingen (5km),
Metz (E25, 65km)
& Paris (E25, 330km)

PLACES TO STAY	7 Bock
6 Hostel	8 Bock Casemates
13 Hôtel Français	10 Musée National d'Histoire
21 Hôtel Schintgen	et d'Art
36 Carlton Hôtel	11 Palais Grand Ducal
	12 City Tourist Office
PLACES TO EAT	16 City Library
4 Café Chiggeri	17 City Bus Station
19 La Table du Pain	18 Main Post Office
20 Club 5	22 City Hall
26 Mesa Verde	23 Cathédral Notre-Dame
40 Primavera Supermarket	24 Musée d'Histoire de la
	Ville de Luxembourg
PUBS	29 Vélo en Ville
5 Café Conquest	30 British Embassy
9 Art Scene	31 Grund Lift
14 Um Piquet	32 Clinique Ste Thérèse
15 Interview	33 Librairie Bourbon
25 Péché Mignon	34 Self Wash
27 Le French Café	35 CDROMWorld
28 Scott's Pub	37 Kredietbank Luxembourg
	38 City Bus Station
OTHER	39 National Tourist Office
1 Nouvelles Frontières	41 Quick Wash
2 Sotours	42 Post Office
3 Toilet	43 Regional Bus Station

Travel Agencies Sotours (☎ 46 15 14 1), 15 Place du Théâtre, specialises in student and youth fares. Nouvelles Frontières (☎ 46 41 40), Rue des Bains, has occasional discount air fares.

Bookshops Librairie Bourbon (☎ 49 22 06), 11 Rue du Fort Bourbon, has books relating to Luxembourg, English-language novels, travel guides and maps. Magasin Anglais (☎ 22 49 25), 19 Allée Scheffer, has a wall of English-language books. It's a 15-minute walk north-west of Place d'Armes.

Laundry There's a Quick Wash on Place de Strasbourg and a Self Wash at 2 Rue du Fort Wallis. Both are open Monday to Saturday.

Medical Services In the case of a medical emergency or if you need a pharmacy outside normal working hours call ☎ 112. For a hospital, head to Clinique Ste Thérèse (☎ 49 77 61) on Rue Ste Zithe.

Things to See & Do

From Place d'Armes, head south down Rue Chimay to **Place de la Constitution**, where there are excellent views over the Pétrusse Valley and of the spectacular bridges that span it. East along Blvd Roosevelt, the gardens which surround the 17th-century **Citadelle du St Esprit** offer superb panoramas up both valleys and over the Grund.

Follow the natural curve north to the **Chemin de la Corniche** – a pedestrian promenade hailed as 'Europe's most beautiful balcony' – which winds along to the **Bock**, the cliff on which Count Sigefroi built his mighty fort.

The castle and much of the fortifications were dismantled between 1867 and 1883 following the Treaty of London. There's little left – the main attractions are the view and the nearby entrance to the **Bock Casemates**, a 23km network of underground passages. Long ago, they housed bakeries, slaughterhouses and thousands of soldiers; during WWI and WWII they were used as a bomb shelter for 35,000 people. They are open 10 am to 5 pm daily from March to October; entry costs f70.

The **Grund** district lies in the valley directly below, accessible from the other side of the Bock or by a free **lift** dug in the cliff near the citadel at Place du St Esprit.

From the Bock, it's a short walk to Rue du Marché-aux-Herbes where you'll find the **Palais Grand Ducal**. Originally a town hall, the palace was built in the 1570s during Spanish rule and later expanded; the royal family took up residence here at the end of the 19th century. It has been extensively restored in recent years and is open to visitors from mid-July to 31 August. The nearby **Place Guillaume II** is lined with formal government edifices.

The **Musée National d'Histoire et d'Art**, Place Marché-aux-Poissons, contains Roman and medieval relics, but most of it is closed for renovations until late 2001. The **Musée d'Histoire de la Ville de Luxembourg**, Rue du St Esprit 14, is a state-of-the-art complex covering the history of Luxembourg City (closed Monday; f200).

Places to Stay

Camping About 4km south of the city is *Kockelscheuer* (☎ 47 18 15, 22 Route de Bettembourg) in Kockelscheuer (take bus No 2 from the train station). It's open from Easter to 31 October.

Hostel The HI *hostel* (☎ 22 68 89, fax 22 33 60, ☻ luxembourg@youthhostels.lu, 2 Rue du Fort Olizy) is located in a valley below the old city. Bus No 9 from the airport or train station stops nearby, otherwise it's a 30-minute walk from the station. It's open all year, and charges f650/1140 for a single/double for members aged under 26 and f750/1340 for members over 26. Dorms start at f435/520. Nonmembers pay an extra f110 a night.

Hotels The big, old *Carlton Hôtel* (☎ 29 96 60, fax 29 96 64, ☻ carlton@pt.lu, 9 Rue de Strasbourg) has clean singles from f750 to f2500, and doubles between f1400 and f3000; breakfast is f150 extra.

Hôtel Schintgen (☎ 22 28 44, fax 46 57 19, 6 Rue Notre Dame) is well located and has decent single/double/triple rooms starting at f2600/3200/3500.

The most delightful mid-range option is *Hôtel Français* (☎ 47 45 34, fax 46 42 74, 14 Place d'Armes). It's small, modern, superbly sited and dotted with *objets d'art* – all in all a winning combination. Prices begin at f3400/4400. Its Web site is at www.hotelfrancais.lu.

LUXEMBOURG

Places to Eat

On Wednesday and Saturday mornings there's a *food market* on Place Guillaume II. The *Primavera* supermarket is in the Galerie Kons.

Club 5 (☎ *46 17 63, 5 Rue Chimay*) is a trendy brasserie with a good-value *plat du jour* (f350).

A convivial cafe-cum-bakery with no-smoking surroundings is *La Table du Pain* (☎ *24 16 08, 19 Ave Monterey*). It covers two floors and serves salads (f250) and open sandwiches (f160 to f200) from 7 am to 7 pm daily.

Café Chiggeri (☎ *22 82 36, 15 Rue du Nord*) draws a hip crowd with its range of international meals, including vegetarian fare (f320).

The only purely vegetarian option is *Mesa Verde* (☎ *46 41 26, 11 Rue du St Esprit*), an exotically colourful restaurant that's often full.

Entertainment

Le French Café (*Rue de Trèves*) has a moody ambience and a great line-up of international beers. *Scott's Pub*, on Bisserweg, is popular with lovers of loud blues and rock (weekend); it's calmer on weekdays.

In the old centre, *Art Scene* (*6 Rue Sigefroi*) has live jazz or blues from 10 pm every Friday and Saturday night. There's no cover charge, but drink prices are hiked up on these nights. *Pêché Mignon* (*17 Rue du St Esprit*) is a trendy cafe with musical and literary evenings. The raw *Interview* (*19 Rue Aldringen*) is popular with young people while the nearby *Um Piquet* (*30 Rue de la Poste*) has a cosier feel. The city's gay scene revolves around *Café Conquest* (☎ *22 21 41, 7 Rue du Palais de Justice*).

Getting There & Away

For information on international flights and train services, see the Getting There & Away section at the beginning of this chapter. For national destinations, see the Getting There & Away section for each place. Turn left as you leave the train station to find CFL buses heading to towns within Luxembourg.

Getting Around

Bus No 9 (three services hourly) connects Findel airport with the hostel, Place Hamilius and the train station (f40, plus f50 for luggage). Alternatively the Luxair bus (f150) picks up at the station and Place Hamilius. A taxi to Findel costs f800.

Vélo en Ville (☎ 47 96 23 83), 8 Bisserweg, rents bikes for f250 a half-day, f400 a day or f2000 a week (20% off for those aged under 26).

Around Luxembourg

MOSELLE VALLEY

Less than half an hour's drive east of the capital, the Luxembourg section of the Moselle Valley is one of Europe's smallest wine regions. More than a dozen towns line the **Route du Vin** (Wine Road), which follows the Moselle from Wasserbillig to the small, southern border town of Schengen.

Wine tasting is the obvious attraction and there are several *caves* (cellars) where you can sample the fruity, white vintages. Try the **Caves Bernard-Massard** in Grevenmacher or **St Martin** in Remich. Both run tours (f100) daily from April to October.

Places to Stay

Next to the butterfly garden in Grevenmacher, there's *Camping de la Route du Vin* (☎ *75 02 34, Route du Vin*), open from April to September. In Remich, *Camping Europe* (☎ *69 80 18, Rue du Camping*) is 100m from the bus station. It's open from Easter to mid-September.

Remich has several riverfront hotels, the cheapest being *Beau Séjour* (☎ *69 81 26, fax 66 94 82, 30 Quai de la Moselle*) which has rooms (shared toilet) from f1100/1900. In Wormeldange, *Relais du Postillon* (☎ *76 84 85, fax 76 81 86, 113 Rue Principale*) has pleasant rooms from f1700/2100.

Getting There & Away

The region is difficult to explore without your own transport. Trains stop at Wasserbillig only; buses from Luxembourg City go to Grevenmacher (twice daily) from where there are connections to other towns.

From Easter to October, it's possible to cruise the Moselle on board either the new *MS Princesse Marie-Astrid* or the *Musel*. They call in at Remich, Wormeldange, Grevenmacher and Wasserbillig, before continuing to Konz and Saarburg in Germany. A sample fare is f390/490 one-way/return between Remich and Grevenmacher (two hours).

CENTRAL LUXEMBOURG

While there's not much to keep you in central Luxembourg, the area can make a good exploration base. The town of **Ettelbrück** is the nation's central rail junction; more pleasant is the nearby town of **Diekirch** which is home to the **Musée National d'Histoire Militaire**, the country's excellent wartime museum.

Hourly trains from Luxembourg City to Ettelbrück take 30 minutes; to Diekirch, it takes 40 minutes. The tourist office in Diekirch (☎ 80 30 23), at 1 Esplanade, is a 10-minute walk from the station.

Places to Stay

Camping de la Sûre (☎ *80 94 25, Route de Gilsdorf 34*) is by the river in Diekirch and open from 1 April to 30 September. The Ettelbrück *hostel* (☎ *81 22 69, fax 81 69 35, Rue G D Joséphine-Charlotte*) is a 20-minute walk from the station; closed December and January. *B&B Weber-Posing* (☎ *80 32 54, 74 Rue Principale*) in Gilsdorf, about 2km west of central Diekirch, has large, old-fashioned rooms for f700 per person. *Hiertz* (☎ *80 35 62, fax 80 88 69, 1 Rue Clairefontaine*), in the heart of Diekirch, has one of the region's best restaurants and decent rooms for f2300/2900.

MÜLLERTHAL

The Müllerthal region lies north-east of the capital, based around the old, Christian town of **Echternach**. The area is also called *Petite Suisse* (Little Switzerland), due to its woodlands and fascinating sandstone plateaus. Outdoor enthusiasts love this area – it's great for hiking, cycling and rock climbing. From Echternach walking paths wind through rocky chasms and past waterfalls to **Berdorf**, situated on the tableland 6km away, and on to the hidden castle of **Beaufort** (open April to 25 October) another 6km (approximately).

There are only buses from the capital city to Echternach (40 minutes). From Echternach, buses connect to other towns. There's an information office in Echternach (☎ 72 02 30), Porte St Willibrord, and smaller offices in Beaufort (☎ 83 60 81), 9 Rue de l'Église, and Berdorf (☎ 79 06 43), 7 Rue Laach.

Places to Stay

Camping Officiel (☎ *72 02 72, 5 Route de Diekirch*) is about 200m from the bus station in Echternach. In Beaufort, the big *Camping Plage* (☎ *83 60 99, Grand Rue*) is open all year.

There are two *hostels* – one in Echternach (☎ *72 01 58, fax 72 87 35,* @ *echternach@ youthhostels.lu, 9 Rue André Duchscher*) and the other at Beaufort (☎ *83 60 75, fax 86 94 67, 6 Rue de l'Auberge*).

Hotels are plentiful in Echternach: try *Aigle Noir* (☎ *72 03 83, fax 72 05 44, 54 Rue de la Gare*), about 40 steps from the bus station, which has basic rooms for f1250/1500, or *Hôtel Le Pavillon* (☎ *72 98 09, fax 72 86 23,* @ *diedling@pt.lu, 2 Rue de la Gare*), it has 10 well-equipped rooms for f1800/2400 (f2100/2700 from May to September).

THE ARDENNES

The Grand Duchy's northern region is known as the Luxembourg Ardennes. It's spectacular country – winding valleys with fast-flowing rivers cut deep through green plateaus crowned by castles.

Of the three main towns, **Clervaux**, in the far north, is the most accessible; **Vianden**, in the east, is more appealing but also more touristy. To the west, the town of **Wiltz** holds no special appeal, though the tiny hamlet of **Esch-sur-Sûre** nearby attracts a staggering number of tourists simply because of its picturesque location.

Clervaux's tourist office (☎ 92 00 72) is ensconced in its castle. Vianden's new office (☎ 83 42 57) is at 1 Rue du Vieux Marché. The tourist office at Wiltz (☎ 95 74 44) is also in the castle.

There are trains every two hours to Clervaux (one hour) from Luxembourg City. To reach Vianden, take the Luxembourg City-Ettelbrück train and then take a connecting bus. To get to Wiltz (1½ hours) take the Luxembourg City-Clervaux train to Kautenbach, and another train from there.

Clervaux

The town has two main sights: its feudal **castle**, in the town centre, and the turreted **Benedictine abbey**, high in the forest above.

The castle houses Edward Steichen's famous photography collection, *Family of Man*, which is open 10 am to 6 pm from Tuesday to Sunday (closed January and February; f150).

The closest camping ground is *Camping Officiel* (☎ 92 00 42, *33 Klatzewé*), open April to mid-November. *Hôtel du Parc* (☎ 92 06 50, fax 92 10 68, *2 Rue du Parc*) occupies a lovely, old mansion and has just seven rooms from f1650/2600.

Vianden

Vianden's top attraction is its impeccably restored **chateau**, open 10 am to 4 pm daily (to 6 pm in summer). Admission is f180. The chateau's striking position can be photographed from the **télésiège** (chair lift) which climbs the nearby hill daily from Easter to mid-October.

Vianden was home to author Victor Hugo during his exile from France in 1870-71. There are plans to turn the house where he lived (across the river from the tourist office and denoted with a plaque) into a museum.

Campers can head to *Op dem Deich* (☎ 83 43 75), on the river to the south of town and about 200m from the bus station. It's open from Easter to 31 September. Vianden's **hostel** (☎ 83 41 77, fax 84 94 27, ✉ *vianden@youthhostels.lu*, *3 Montée du Château*) sits in the shadow of the chateau. The friendly *Auberge de l'Our* (☎ 83 46 75, fax 84 91 94, *35 Rue de la Gare*) has

bright rooms starting at f950/1600 (bathroom facilities are communal).

Wiltz

Built on the side of a small plateau, Wiltz is more spacious, but less picturesque, than Clervaux or Vianden. The rather sterile **chateau** sits on the edge of the Ville Haute and is home to an exhibition on the 1944 Battle of the Bulge. It's open daily from June to mid-September.

Camping Kaul (☎ 95 00 79, *Rue Jos Simon*), about 800m from the train station, is open from May to October. The **hostel** (☎ 95 80 39, fax 95 94 40, ✉ *wiltz@youthhostels.lu*, *6 Rue de la Montagne*) is a 1km climb from the train station.

Auberge La Ballade (☎ 95 73 24, fax 95 92 27, *144 Rue du X Septembre*) is a rustic inn with four modern rooms, located 1km from the train station. Rooms start at f800/1200.

Esch-sur-Sûre

The tiny village of Esch-sur-Sûre is off the Wiltz-Ettelbrück road. It's built on a rocky peninsula skirted by the Sûre River and is lorded over by steep cliffs and a ruined castle. It's all very picturesque and, in summer, tourists come here in vast numbers.

A worthwhile detour is to the **Maison du Parc Naturel** (☎ 89 93 31 1), 15 Rte de Lultzhausen. It's 500m from the village and contains a working collection of old textile-making machines.

Macedonia (Македонија)

The Former Yugoslav Republic of Macedonia (FYROM) is at the south end of what was once the Yugoslav Federation. Its position in the centre of the Balkan Peninsula between Albania, Bulgaria, Serbia and Greece has often made it a pol-itical powder keg, though in 1992 Macedonia became fully independent – the only republic to emerge peacefully from the breakup of ex-Yugoslavia.

In this book, Lonely Planet uses the name Macedonia rather than the Former Yugoslav Republic of Macedonia. This is to reflect what its inhabitants prefer to call their country and is not intended to prejudice any political claims.

For travellers Macedonia is a land of contrasts, ranging from Skopje with its time-worn Turkish bazaar and lively cafes, to the many medieval monasteries around Ohrid. Macedonia's fascinating blend of Orthodox mystery and the exotic Orient, together with Lake Ohrid's world-class beauty, afford a variety of opportunities for relaxation and exploration.

Facts about Macedonia

HISTORY

Historical Macedonia (from where Alexander the Great set out to conquer the ancient world in the 4th century BC) is today contained mostly in present-day Greece, a point Greeks are always quick to make when discussing contemporary Macedonia's use of that name. The Romans subjugated the Greeks of ancient Macedonia and the territory to the north in the mid-2nd century BC, and when the empire was divided in the 4th century AD this region became part of the Eastern Roman Empire ruled from Constantinople. Slav tribes settled here in the

AT A GLANCE	
Capital:	Skopje
Population:	2 million
Official Language:	Macedonian
Currency:	1 Macedonian denar (MKD) = 100 deni

7th century, changing the ethnic character of the area.

In the 9th century the region was conquered by Bulgaria and later became the centre of a powerful Bulgarian state. After the crushing defeat of Serbia by the Turks in 1389, the Balkans became part of the Ottoman Empire.

In 1878 Russia defeated Turkey, and Macedonia was ceded to Bulgaria by the Treaty of San Stefano. The Western powers, fearing the creation of a powerful Russian satellite in the heart of the Balkans, forced Bulgaria to give Macedonia back to Turkey.

In 1893 Macedonian nationalists formed the Internal Macedonian Revolutionary Organisation (IMRO) to fight for independence from Turkey, culminating in the Ilinden uprising of August 1903 that was brutally suppressed by October that year. Although nationalist leader Goce Delčev died before the revolt he has become the symbol of Macedonian nationalism.

The First Balkan War in 1912 brought Greece, Serbia, Bulgaria and Montenegro together against Turkey. In the Second Balkan War in 1913 Greece and Serbia ousted the Bulgarians and split Macedonia between themselves.

On 8 September 1991 a referendum on independence was held in Macedonia and 74% voted in favour. In January 1992 the country declared its full independence from former Yugoslavia. For once Belgrade cooperated by ordering all federal troops present to withdraw.

Greece delayed diplomatic recognition of Macedonia by demanding that the country find another name, alleging that the term Macedonia implied territorial claims on northern Greece. Thus Macedonia was forced to use the absurd 'temporary' title

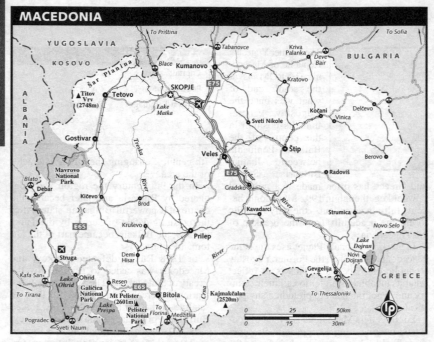

FYROM (Former Yugoslav Republic of Macedonia) in order to be admitted to the UN in April 1993. When the US (following six EU countries' lead) recognised FYROM in February 1994, Greece declared an economic embargo against Macedonia and closed the port of Thessaloniki to the country's trade. The embargo was lifted in November 1995 after Macedonia changed its flag and agreed to discuss its name with Greece. To date, this tricky issue remains unresolved.

GEOGRAPHY

Much of Macedonia (25,333 sq km) is a plateau between 600m and 900m high. The Vardar River cuts across the middle of the country, passing the capital, Skopje, on its way to the Aegean Sea near Thessaloniki. Ohrid and Prespa lakes in the south-west drain into the Adriatic via Albania; at 294m, Lake Ohrid is the deepest lake on the Balkan peninsula. Titov Vrv (2748m) in the northwest is Macedonia's highest peak. The country's three national parks are Pelister (west of Bitola), Galičica (between lakes Ohrid and Prespa) and Mavrovo (between

Ohrid and Tetovo). A fourth national park may be established in the Šara region west of Tetovo.

CLIMATE

Macedonia's summers are hot and dry. Winter brings warm Aegean winds but Macedonia still receives a lot of snow.

POPULATION & PEOPLE

Macedonia's population of two million is comprised of 66% Macedonian Slavs who bear no relation whatsoever to the Greek-speaking Macedonians of antiquity. The largest minority groups are ethnic Albanians (23%), Turks (4%), Roma (3%), Serbs (2%), and others (2%). Tensions between ethnic Albanians and Macedonians derive partly from the high birth rate of the former (three times the national average). In spring 1999, 250,000 Albanian refugees from Kosovo flooded into the country but almost all have returned.

SOCIETY & CONDUCT

Before the Rain, Milcho Manchevski's visually stunning vision of how inter-ethnic war in Macedonia might begin, was filmed mainly in Ohrid.

Macedonians welcome visitors. Show respect to your hosts by learning a few words of Macedonian. Be aware that churches and mosques are not built for tourists, but are working places of worship. Dress and behave accordingly.

Most of the Albanians and Turks are Muslim, while most Slavs are Orthodox.

LANGUAGE

Macedonian is closely related to Bulgarian.

The Cyrillic alphabet is used predominantly in Macedonia. Street names are printed in Cyrillic script only. Road signs use both Cyrillic and Latin scripts.

For a quick introduction to Macedonian and some useful words and phrases, see the Language chapter at the end of this book.

Facts for the Visitor

HIGHLIGHTS

The Byzantine monasteries of Ohrid are worth a visit, as is Sveti Naum 30km from Ohrid. Lake Ohrid itself is simply beautiful. The Čaršija (old Turkish bazaar) in Skopje is very colourful.

PLANNING
Maps

The tourist office in Skopje has maps of Macedonia.

What to Bring

You can find most things in Macedonia, but bring along a converter and adapter if you plan to use electrical appliances.

TOURIST OFFICES

Only Skopje has an official tourist office but people in other travel agencies and shops are friendly and will help you out.

VISAS & EMBASSIES
Visas

Citizens of EU countries and New Zealanders do not need visas to enter Macedonia. For Americans and Australians a 30-day visa is issued free of charge at your port of entry. Canadians and South Africans must buy visas for £7, or the equivalent, obtainable either before you go or at the border.

Macedonia Embassies Abroad

Macedonian embassies are found in the following countries. There are no embassies as yet in Australia or New Zealand.

Canada (☎ 613-234 3882, fax 233 1852) 130 Albert St Suite 1006, Ottowa ON, KIP 5G4
Turkey (☎ 012-446 9204) Filistin sokak 30-2/3, Gaziosman Pasha, Ankara
UK (☎ 0207-499 5152, fax 499 2864) 19a Cavendish Square, London, W1M 9AD
USA (☎ 202-337 3063, fax 337 3093) 3050 K Street NW, Washington DC, 20007

Foreign Embassies in Macedonia

The following embassies are in Skopje:

Albania (☎ 614 636, fax 614 200) ul H T Karpoš 94a
Bulgaria (☎ 116 320, fax 116 139) ul Zlatko Šnajder 3
Canada (☎ 125 228, fax 122 681) 12-ta Udama Brigada 2a
Greece (☎ 130 198, fax 115 718) ul Borka Talevski 6
Turkey (☎ 113 270, fax 117 024) ul Slavey Planina-B 8
UK (☎ 116 772, fax 117 005) ul Veljko Vlahović 26
USA (☎ 116 180, fax 117 103) Bulevar Ilindenska
Yugoslavia (☎ 129 298, fax 129 427) Pitu Guli 8

MONEY
Currency

Colourful Macedonian denar (MKD) banknotes come in denominations of 10 MKD, 50 MKD, 100 MKD, 500 MKD, 1000 MKD and 5000 MKD and there are coins of one, two and five denari. Prices may be quoted and payment accepted in Deutschmarks and (occasionally) US dollars, particularly at larger establishments, but denars are preferred for smaller, everyday transactions.

Small private exchange offices exchange money (cash only) for a good rate, as do the banks, which change travellers cheques as well. A handful of ATMs can be found in central Skopje.

Exchange Rates

country	unit		denar
Australia	A$1	=	35.58 MKD
Canada	C$1	=	40.56 MKD
euro	€1	=	54.32 MKD
France	10FF	=	82.81 MKD
Germany	DM1	=	27.77 MKD

MACEDONIA

Japan	¥100	=	55.20 MKD
New Zealand	NZ$1	=	27.15 MKD
UK	UK£1	=	89.72 MKD
US	US$1	=	59.85 MKD

Costs

Except for accommodation in Skopje, Macedonia is not an expensive country. In Skopje, if you stay in a private room, you might keep costs to 1800 MKD to 2100 MKD a day (outside Skopje, budget 1200 MKD to 1500 MKD per day).

POST & COMMUNICATIONS

Mail addressed c/o Poste Restante, 1000 Skopje 2, Macedonia, can be claimed at the post office next to Skopje train station. Mail addressed c/o Poste Restante, 6000 Ohrid, Macedonia, can be picked up at Ohrid's main post office near the bus station.

Macedonia's country code is ☎ 389. Long-distance phone calls cost less at main post offices than in hotels. Drop the initial zero in the city codes when calling Macedonia from abroad. The international access code in Macedonia is ☎ 99. Phonecards (available at post offices) work in public phones.

Skopje and Ohrid both have numerous cheap Internet cafes.

INTERNET RESOURCES

The Virtual Macedonia site has useful background and practical information (www.vmacedonia.com/index2.html).

BOOKS

Good background books include *Who Are the Macedonians?* by Hugh Poulton, *Black Lamb and Grey Falcon* by Rebecca West, and Robert Kaplan's *Balkan Ghosts*.

TOILETS

Public toilets are of the grotty 'squattie' type. Bring your own paper, but try to use hotel and restaurant toilets.

WOMEN TRAVELLERS

Women travellers should feel no particular concern about travelling in Macedonia.

GAY & LESBIAN TRAVELLERS

Homosexuality in Macedonia is technically legal. However, it's not considered mainstream so be discreet.

DANGERS & ANNOYANCES

Macedonia is a safe country in general. Travellers should be on the lookout for pickpockets in bus and train stations and exercise common sense in looking after belongings.

BUSINESS HOURS

Businesses hours are usually in the range of 8 am to 8 pm weekdays and 8 am to 2 pm on Saturday.

PUBLIC HOLIDAYS & SPECIAL EVENTS

Public holidays in Macedonia are New Year (1 and 2 January), Orthodox Christmas (7 January), Easter Monday and Tuesday (March/April), May Day (1 May), Ilinden or Day of the 1903 Rebellion (2 August), Republic Day (8 September) and 1941 Partisan Day (11 October).

ACTIVITIES

Macedonia's top ski resort is Popova šapka (1845m) on the southern slopes of Šar Planina west of Tetovo. Hiking in any of the three national parks (Mavrovo, Galičica and Pelister) is a good way to get to know the countryside. Spelunking is also a popular sport; try at Lake Matka near Skopje.

ACCOMMODATION

Skopje's hotels are very expensive but its convenient HI hostel is open throughout the year. Ohrid has cheap *private rooms* and its hostel opens in summer.

FOOD & DRINKS

Turkish-style grilled mincemeat is available almost everywhere in Macedonia and there are self-service cafeterias in most towns for the less adventurous. Balkan *burek* (cheese or meat pie) and yoghurt makes for a cheap breakfast. Watch for Macedonian *tavče gravče* (beans in a skillet) and Ohrid trout, that is priced according to weight.

Other dishes to try are *teleška čorba* (veal soup), *riblja čorba* (fish soup), *čevapčinja* (kebabs), *mešena salata* (mixed salad) and *šopska salata* (mixed salad with grated white cheese).

The strong and cheap *Skopsko Pivo* is the local beer. It's strong and reasonably cheap. The national firewater is *rakija,* a strong distilled spirit made from grapes. *Mastika,* an ouzo-like spirit, is also popular.

Getting There & Away

AIR

Yugoslavian Airlines (JAT), Macedonian Airlines (MAT), Adria Airlines, Croatia Airlines, Avioimpex, Olympic Airways, Malev Airlines, Turkish Airlines, and British Airways offer flights from Skopje to a number of European destinations. Sample one-way prices (not including airport taxes) are: Amsterdam (US$235); Athens (US$195); Belgrade (US$100); London (US$395); Rome (US$183); Zagreb (US$200); and Zurich (300 SFr). Return prices are usually a much better deal. There's an ATM at the Skopje airport.

It may be cheaper to fly into Thessaloniki in northern Greece though only one train a day runs to Skopje. Travel agents abound in Ohrid and Skopje.

LAND
Bus

The international bus station in Skopje is next to the City Museum. Buses make the trip to Sofia (620 MKD, 6 hours, three times daily), İstanbul (1280 MKD, 14 hours, three to four daily) and Belgrade (850 MKD, 6 hours, three times daily). Buses through Yugoslavia travel to Munich, Zagreb, Budapest, Vienna, and Sarajevo. A Yugoslavia transit visa will be difficult to obtain.

Buses from Skopje to Prishtina run five to six times a day from the domestic bus station in Skopje.

Train

Trains run twice a day between Skopje and Belgrade via Niš (1200 MKD, 8-9 hours). Sleepers are available. One train runs daily between Skopje and Thessaloniki (700 MKD, 6 hours).

Buy international tickets from Feroturist Travel Agency (☎ 163 248) in the Skopje train station, open Monday to Friday 7 am to 8 pm, Saturday from 7 am to 2 pm, Sunday from 7 am to 9 pm.

Getting Around

Bus travel is well developed in Macedonia with fairly frequent services from Skopje to Ohrid (280 MKD, three hours) and Bitola.

Don't bother with the train – the local train from Skopje to Bitola takes four hours to cover 229km.

A quick way of getting around the country if the buses are not convenient is by taxi, especially if there are two or more of you to share the cost. A half-hour trip, from Skopje to Lake Matka for example, should cost 350 MKD. Taxis are a possibility for getting to Kosovo: 640 MKD will get you to the Macedonia-Kosovo border, where taxis are waiting on the other side to whisk you to Prishtina (DM30-70).

Many car rental places are available in Skopje (and some in Ohrid).

Skopje (Скопје)

☎ 091

Macedonia's capital, Skopje (population 600,000), is strategically set on the Vardar River at a crossroads of Balkan routes almost exactly midway between Tirana and Sofia, capitals of neighbouring Albania and Bulgaria. After the Romans, conquerors included the Slavs, Byzantines, Bulgarians, Normans and Serbs, until the Turks arrived in 1392 and managed to hold onto Uskub (Skopje) until 1912.

A devastating earthquake in July 1963 killed 1066 people and virtually demolished the town. The rebuilding wasn't exactly ideal; the post office building and telecommunications complex next to it are particularly hideous examples of this architectural overkill. Fortunately, much of the old town survived, along with the fortress atop the hill, preserving Skopje's historic beauty.

Orientation

Most of central Skopje is a pedestrian zone, with the 15th-century Turkish stone bridge (Kamen Most) over the Vardar River linking the old and new towns. South of the bridge is Ploštad Makedonija (the former Ploštad Maršal Tito). The train station is a 15-minute walk south-east of the stone bridge. The domestic bus station is just over the stone bridge on the northern side.

Information

The helpful, English-speaking tourist information office (☎ 116 854) is opposite the Daud Pasha Baths on the viaduct between

MACEDONIA

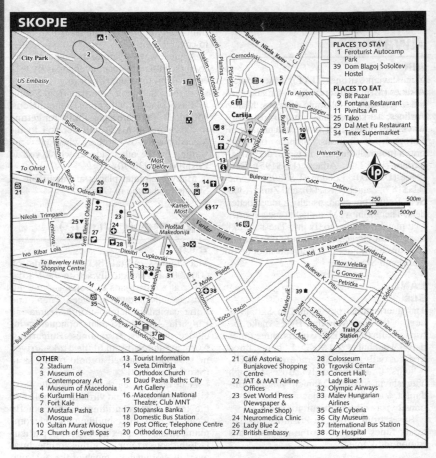

SKOPJE

PLACES TO STAY
1 Feroturist Autocamp Park
39 Dom Blagoj Šošolčev Hostel

PLACES TO EAT
5 Bit Pazar
9 Fontana Restaurant
11 Pivnitsa An
25 Tako
29 Dal Met Fu Restaurant
34 Tinex Supermarket

OTHER
2 Stadium
3 Museum of Contemporary Art
4 Museum of Macedonia
6 Kuršumli Han
7 Fort Kale
8 Mustafa Pasha Mosque
10 Sultan Murat Mosque
12 Church of Sveti Spas
13 Tourist Information
14 Sveta Dimitrija Orthodox Church
15 Daud Pasha Baths; City Art Gallery
16 Macedonian National Theatre; Club MNT
17 Stopanska Banka
18 Domestic Bus Station
19 Post Office; Telephone Centre
20 Orthodox Church
21 Café Astoria; Bunjakoveć Shopping Centre
22 JAT & MAT Airline Offices
23 Svet World Press (Newspaper & Magazine Shop)
24 Neuromedica Clinic
26 Lady Blue 2
27 British Embassy
28 Colosseum
30 Trgovski Centar
31 Concert Hall; Lady Blue 1
32 Olympic Airways
33 Malev Hungarian Airlines
35 Café Cyberia
36 City Museum
37 International Bus Station
38 City Hospital

the Turkish bridge and Čaršija. Opening hours are 9 am to 7 pm Monday to Friday, 9 am to 4 pm Saturday (they close an hour earlier on weekdays from mid-November to March). Detailed maps of Skopje are sold here for 250 MKD.

There are many private exchange offices scattered throughout the old and new towns where you can change your cash at a good rate. Banks also abound.

Skopje has a number of ATMs. There are two in the Bunjakoveć Shopping Centre, one in Trgovski Centar off Ploštad Makedonija.

There is a 24-hour telephone centre inside the post office.

The Café Astoria in the Bunjakoveć Shopping Centre at Bul Partizanska Ohredi 27a charges 100 MKD per hour for online time. Café Cyberia, on Bulevar Makedonija near its intersection with Sveti Kliment Ohridski, charges 70 MKD per hour.

A recommended travel agency is Kompas Holidays (☎/fax 222 441 or 110 089, ✉ komphol@mt.net.mk), inside the Trgovski Centar.

Left luggage at the train station is open 24 hours.

Things to See & Do

The 1466 **Daud Pasha Baths**, north-east of Kamen Most, were once the largest Turkish baths in the Balkans. The **City Art Gallery** (closed on Monday) now occupies its six domed rooms. Farther north and well worth exploring is **Čaršija**, the old market area. Steps up on the left lead to the tiny **Church** of Sveti Spas with a finely carved iconostasis done in 1824. It's half buried because when it was constructed in the 17th century no church was allowed to be higher than a mosque.

Beyond the church is the **Mustafa Pasha Mosque** (1492), with an earthquake-cracked dome; you can pay to climb the 124 steps of the minaret. The park across the street are the ruins of **Fort Kale**, with an 11th-century Cyclopean wall and good views of Skopje.

The lane on the north side of Mustafa Pasha Mosque leads back down into Čaršija and the **Museum of Macedonia**, which covers the history of the region fairly well, but with Cyrillic explanations.

Skopje's old Oriental bazaar district is among the largest and most colourful of its kind left in Europe.

Places to Stay

Camping From April to mid-October you can pitch a tent at the *Feroturist Autocamp Park* (☎ *228 246, fax 162 677*); prices are 192 MKD per person and tent. The camping ground is situated between the river and the stadium, just a 15-minute walk upstream from Kamen Most along the right (south) bank.

Hostel HI's *Dom Blagoj Šošolčev Hostel* (☎ *114 849, fax 235 029, Prolet 25*), near the train station, is a good bet. It's open all year with 24-hour reception and has clean rooms. Singles go for 1210/1520 MKD for HI members/non-members, doubles for 1210/865 MKD – though in the off-season you may be able to get a double for a single price. Add 60 MKD for breakfast.

Private Rooms & Pansions The tourist information office (☎ *116 854*), on the viaduct two blocks north of the Turkish stone bridge, can arrange singles/doubles in private homes beginning at 1120 MKD per person. Insist on something near the centre or you may find yourself beyond the train station.

For a bit more, the tidy *Pansion Brateks* (☎ *176 606, mobile/cellphone* ☎ *070 24 3232, ul Atso Karomanov 3*) is a possibility if you don't mind the half-hour walk to the centre. Make sure to book well in advance. Singles/doubles are 1920/3200 MKD. German is spoken but not English.

Places to Eat

The *Bit Pazar* next to the Čaršija stocks salad items. A good supermarket is *Tinex* on ul Dame Gruev, near the intersection with ul Makedonija.

There is a cheap *restaurant* in the basement of the Hostel (see Places to Stay).

The *Dal Met Fu Restaurant*, across Ploštad Makedonija at the beginning of ul Makedonija, is good for pizza and pasta. *Tako* (☎ *114 808, Sveti Kliment Ohridski*), is a small, smoke-free spot for fast-food burritos, fajitas, and the like.

Colourful, small restaurants in Čaršija serve *evap inja* and *burek*. For a sit-down meal try the *Fontana* restaurant, on a little square with a fountain in the Čaršija, or the atmospheric *Pivnitsa An* opposite.

Entertainment

Check the *Concert Hall* on ul Makedonija 12, for performances. The kingpin of the disco scene is *Colosseum*, on Dimitri Čupkovski. Another snappy nightspot is *ZZ Top*, a bit south-east of centre in the Beverley Hills shopping centre. *Club MNT*, downstairs below the Macedonian National Theatre, cranks up around 10 pm. Live jazz, blues and rock music can be heard at the *Lady Blue 1* and *Lady Blue 2* clubs, the latter on the corner of Ivo Ribar Lola and Sveti Kliment Ohridski and the former in the Concert Hall complex.

Getting There & Away

There are two bus routes from Skopje to Lake Ohrid; opt for the one through Tetovo which is shorter and more scenic (167km). Book a seat to Ohrid the day before if you're travelling in high season.

For information on international trains and buses, see the Getting There & Away section earlier in this chapter.

Getting Around

Arrange transport from the airport in advance, otherwise you'll be charged 1280 MKD to 2240 MKD for a taxi ride into town (25km). Do not get into a taxi without an official taxi sign.

Skopje's taxi system is excellent, once you get beyond the unofficial taxis at the airport. All taxis have metres. The first few kilometres is a flat 50 MKD, and then it's 15 MKD per kilometre.

AROUND SKOPJE
Lake Matka
A half-hour's drive southwest of Skopje is beautiful Lake Matka, great for hiking or spelunking. Take bus No 60 (30 MKD) to the last stop, Matka (about 40 minutes away) and walk about 300m along the path above the dam. The path will take you to *Pioneerski Dom* (☎ 352 655), right on the lake. Basic accommodation costs 320 MKD a night. Food is available, as is heat, but the lodge is closed in January and February and when it snows.

Ohrid (Охрид)

☎ 096

Lake Ohrid, a natural tectonic lake in the south-west corner of Macedonia, is the deepest lake in the Balkans (294m) and one of the world's oldest. One third of its 450-sq-km surface area belongs to Albania.

The town of Ohrid is *the* Macedonian tourist mecca with a medieval citadel and plenty of churches to explore.

Orientation & Information
Ohrid's bus station is next to the post office in the centre of town. The tourist office (☎ 266 494), at ul Partizanska 3 in front of the bus station, arranges bus tickets and private rooms. Ohridska Banka, on the Sveti Kliment Ohridski mall changes travellers cheques and cash and does Visa advances without commission. There are plenty of exchange bureaus for cash.

There are several Internet access points around town. The 24-hour Cybercity, on the third storey of the Ohrid mall across from the post office has slow Internet access costing 60 MKD per hour. Other Internet cafes have bounced up; ask around.

There's a left luggage office at the bus station.

Things to See & Do
Most churches and museums at Ohrid are open daily, except Monday, from 9 am to 3 pm; some have a morning break from 10.30 to 11 am. Most charge 100/50 MKD or 100/30 MKD admission prices for adult foreigners/foreign students.

Ohrid's picturesque old town rises from Sveti Kliment Ohridski, the main pedestrian mall, up towards the Church of Sveti Kliment and the citadel. A medieval town wall still isolates this hill from the surrounding valley. Penetrate the old town on Car Samuil as far as the **Archaeological Museum** in the four-storey dwelling of the Robevi family (1827) at No 62. Farther east, along Car Samuil is 11th-century **Sveti Sofija**, also worth the 100/30 MKD adult/student price. Aside from the frescoes there's an unusual Turkish *mimbar* (pulpit) remaining from the days when this was a mosque, and an upstairs portico with a photo display of the extensive restoration work.

From near here ul Ilindenska climbs up towards the North Gate, to the right is the 13th-century **Church of Sveti Kliment**, almost covered inside with vividly restored frescoes of biblical scenes.

In the park just below the citadel are the ruins of an Early Christian **basilica** with 5th-century mosaics covered by protective sand, and nearby is the shell of **Sveti Pantelejmon**, Ohrid's oldest church, which is being refurbished.

The tiny 13th-century **Sveti Jovan Bogoslov Kaneo** church is on a point overlooking the lake. There's a rocky beach at the foot of the cliffs and in summer young men perform death-defying leaps into the water from the clifftop above the lake.

It's worthwhile to make the journey (70 MKD, six buses daily) to Sveti Naum, 28km south of Ohrid and home to the impressive 17th-century **Church of Sveti Naum** rising on a hill above the lake. The original church was built here in 900, and St Naum was buried here in 910. The gorgeous frescoes inside the church are mostly 19th century, though fragments of 16th- and 17th-century work remain. You can probably find an English speaker on hand to act as a guide. The monastery offers a view of the Albanian town of Pogradec across the lake. The monastery around the church now houses a nice but pricey hotel.

Special Events
The five-day Balkan Festival of Folk Dances & Songs, held at Ohrid in early July, draws folkloric groups from around the Balkans. The Ohrid Summer Festival, held from mid-July to mid-August, features classical concerts and performances in the Church of Sveti Sofija as well.

Places to Stay

Camping The *Autocamp Gradište* (☎ *22 578)*, open from May to mid-September, is halfway to Sveti Naum and is popular with young people. It's accessible on the Sveti Naum bus; ask the driver to let you off at your site.

Private Rooms *Private rooms* from the tourist office near the bus station (☎ 266 494), ul Partizanska 3, cost from 320 MKD to 800 MKD per person per night, plus another 20 MKD per person per night tax. *'Mimi' Apostolov Rooms* (☎/*fax 31 549, ul Strašo Pinđura 2)* has eight comfortable, heated rooms with phone and satellite TV for 800 MKD including breakfast. *Stefan Kanevče* (☎ *34 813)* has nice, rustic *sobi* (rooms) in Kaneo on the lake. A room goes for 320 MKD plus an extra 160 MKD for a hearty breakfast, if you want it.

Hostels & Hotels The HI *Mladost Hostel* (☎ *21 626)* is located on the lakeside a little over 2km west of Ohrid, towards Struga and is open in summer only. Get there on the Struga bus (15 MKD) and ask for Mladost.

Expect to pay around 1560/2400 MKD per night, including breakfast, for a decent single/double room at the fairly central *Hotel Palace* (☎ *260 440, fax 35 460)*, on ul Partizanska, close to the bus station.

Places to Eat

Stock up on fresh vegetables at the busy *Popular Market* just north of the old plane tree.

Any number of fast-food and pizza joints speckle the old town area. Try *Cosa Nostra*, not far from the Archaeological Museum – it's popular for pizza. Across the way, restaurant *Dolga* has a glorious sea view from its outdoor patio and does good trout but is a bit more expensive (approximately 500 MKD for a good-sized portion of two trout).

The *Star Chinar* (Old Plane Tree), a neat, modern restaurant near the old plane tree cooks up some tasty local specialities. About 100m west of the old plane tree is the Turkish-style *Restoran Neim* on the south side of Goce Delčev. It dishes up some excellent *musaka* or *polneti piperki* (stuffed peppers).

Entertainment

The mellow *Jazz In*, just towards the water from Sveti Sophia, dominates the after-hours scene. Ohrid's movie theatre is *Dom Na Kultura* at Grigor Prličev, facing the lakeside park. Various cultural events are also held here.

Getting There & Away

Avioimpex flies once a week from Ohrid to Zürich (250 Sfr plus a 20 Sfr airport tax); MAT flies regularly from Skopje to Ohrid and once a week from Dusseldorf to Ohrid (US$180 plus airport tax). Adria Airlines flies three times a week from Ljubljana to Ohrid(US$120).

Ten buses a day run between Ohrid and Skopje (280 MKD, three hours, 167km), via Kičevo. Another three go via Bitola and another two via Mavrovo. The first route is a much shorter, faster, more scenic and cheaper one, so try to take it. During the summer rush, it pays to book a seat the day before.

There are six buses a day to Bitola (140 MKD, 1¼ hours) and three overnight buses to Belgrade (1530 MKD, 14 hours).

To go to Albania catch a bus or boat to Sveti Naum monastery, that is near the border crossing. In summer there are six buses a day from Ohrid to Sveti Naum (80 MKD, 29km), in winter three daily. The bus continues on to the border post. From Albanian customs it's 6km to Pogradec; taxis are waiting and should charge only US$6 to US$10 for the ride.

Malta

Malta, Gozo and Comino don't take up much space on the map, but their strategic position in the Mediterranean has for centuries made them irresistible to both navigators and invaders.

Today Malta is an economical and cheerful destination for a beach holiday. The weather is excellent, food and accommodation are good value and the water is sparkling clean.

Facts about Malta

HISTORY

Malta's well-preserved megalithic temples, built between 3600 and 2500 BC, are the oldest surviving free-standing structures in the world.

From 800 to 218 BC, Malta was colonised by the Phoenicians and, for the last 250 years of this period, by Phoenicia's principal North African colony, Carthage. After the Punic Wars between Rome and Carthage, Malta became part of the Roman Empire.

Arabs from North Africa arrived in 870 but were expelled in 1090 by a Norman king, Roger of Sicily. For the next 400 years Malta's history was linked to Sicily, and its rulers were a succession of Normans and Angevins (French), Aragonese and Castilians (Spanish). In 1530 the islands were given to the Knights of the Order of St John of Jerusalem by Charles V, Emperor of Spain; the rent was two Maltese falcons a year, one to be sent to the emperor and the other to the Viceroy of Sicily.

In 1798 Napoleon arrived, seeking to counter the British influence in the Mediterranean. The Maltese defeated the French in 1800 with the assistance of the British, and in 1814 Malta officially became part of the British Empire. During WWII the British developed Malta into a major naval base.

In 1947 the island was given a measure of self-government. Dr George Borg

Olivier led the country to independence in 1964, while Dominic Mintoff, as prime minister, established the republic in 1974.

GEOGRAPHY

The Maltese archipelago consists of three inhabited islands: Malta (246 sq km), Gozo (67 sq km) and Comino (2.7 sq km), which lie 93km south of Sicily. The soil is generally thin and rocky. There are few trees and, for most of the year, little greenery to soften the stony, sun-bleached landscape.

CLIMATE

Malta has an excellent climate, although it can get very warm (around 30°C) during midsummer. Winter temperatures average around 14°C. The rainfall is low, at around 580mm a year, and it falls mainly between November and February.

POPULATION & PEOPLE

Malta's population is around 378,000, with most people living in Valletta and its satellite towns. Gozo has 29,000 inhabitants. Comino has a mere handful of farmers, six or seven in winter.

SOCIETY & CONDUCT

Mediterranean culture is dominant, but many signs of British influence exist. The Catholic Church is the custodian of national traditions and its huge churches dominate the villages. Divorce and abortion are illegal.

LANGUAGE

The Maltese language (Malti) is Semitic in origin and is believed to be based on Phoenician. Nearly all Maltese in built-up areas speak English, and an increasing number speak Italian. French and German are also understood.

MALTA

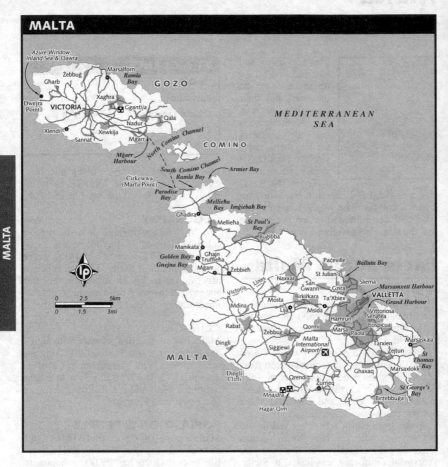

See the Language chapter at the back of the book for pronunciation guidelines and useful words and phrases.

Facts for the Visitor

HIGHLIGHTS

The evocative prehistoric temples of Hagar Qim and Mnajdra are superb; the 16th-century city of Valletta and the hill-top town of Mdina are also magnificent . To get away from it all, head to the quiet island of Gozo.

PLANNING
When to Go

Outside the high season (mid-June to late September) accommodation prices drop by about 40%. The season of *festas* (or more correctly *festi*) begins in earnest at the beginning of June and lasts until the end of September.

TOURIST OFFICES

The Malta Tourist Authority has its main overseas office in London (☎ 020-7292 4900) at Malta House, 36-38 Piccadilly, London, W1V OPP. Other offices are in Paris, Milan, Amsterdam and New York. Embassies and offices of Air Malta also provide tourist information.

NSTS, a student travel agency and Hostelling International (HI) representative, has offices in Valletta (☎ 244983, @ nsts@ nsts.org), 220 St Paul St, and on Gozo (☎ 553977), 45 St Francis Square, Victoria.

EMBASSIES & CONSULATES
Maltese Embassies

Australia (☎ 02-6295 1586) 261 La Perouse St, Red Hill, Canberra, ACT 2603

Canada (☎ 416-207 0922) The Mutual Group Centre, 3300 Bloor St West, Suite 730, West Tower Etobicoke, Ontario

UK (☎ 020-7292 4800) 36-38 Piccadilly, London, W1V OPQ

USA (☎ 202-462 3611) 2017 Connecticut Ave, NW Washington, DC, 20008

Foreign Embassies in Malta

Australia (☎ 338201) Ta'Xbiex Terrace, Ta'Xbiex MSD 11

Canada (☎ 233122) 103 Archbishop St, Valletta

UK (☎ 233134/37) 7 St Anne St, Floriana

USA (☎ 235960/65) Development House, 3rd floor, St Anne St, Floriana

MONEY

The Maltese lira (Lm; a £ symbol is also sometimes used) is divided into 100 cents. There are one, two, five, 10, 25, 50c and Lm1 coins; and Lm2, Lm5, Lm10 and Lm20 notes. The currency is often referred to as the pound.

There is a 24-hour exchange bureau at the airport, but no currency exchange at the ferry terminal.

Exchange Rates

country	unit		lira
Australia	A$1	=	Lm0.26
Canada	C$1	=	Lm0.29
euro	€1	=	Lm0.41
Germany	DM1	=	Lm0.21
Italy	L1000	=	Lm0.21
New Zealand	NZ$1	=	Lm0.20
UK	UK£1	=	Lm0.66
US	US$1	=	Lm0.43

Costs

Malta is cheap by Western European standards. For around Lm10 per day, you'll get pleasant hostel accommodation, a simple restaurant meal and decent street-side snacks.

Tipping & Bargaining

Restaurants and taxis expect a 10% tip. Bargaining for handicrafts at stalls or markets is essential, but most shops have fixed prices. You won't get far bargaining for taxis, but make sure you establish the fare in advance.

POST & COMMUNICATIONS
Post

Post office branches are found in most towns and villages. Local postage costs 6c; postcards or letters sent airmail to Europe cost 16c, to the USA 22c, and to Australia 27c.

Telephone, Fax & Email

The country code for Malta is ☎ 356. There are no area codes in Malta.

Public telephones are widely available and take either coins or phonecards, which are sold at Maltacom offices, post offices and stationery shops for Lm2, Lm3 or Lm5. Local calls cost 10c.

For local telephone inquiries phone ☎ 190; for overseas inquiries phone ☎ 194. The international direct dialling code is ☎ 00. International calls are heavily discounted between 6 pm and 8 am and all day on weekends. A three-minute call to the USA costs about Lm1.50. You can send faxes from larger Maltacom offices.

See the Valletta, Sliema and St Julian's section for email and Internet cafes.

INTERNET RESOURCES

There's a wealth of information on the Malta Tourist Authority's Web site (www.tourism.org.mt) and on the Search-Malta site (www.searchmalta.com).

WOMEN TRAVELLERS

Malta remains a conservative society by western standards. Young males have adopted the Mediterranean macho style, but they are not usually aggressive. Walking alone at night in Gzira is not recommended, as this is a centre for prostitution.

Dress conservatively, particularly if you intend to visit churches (shorts are out). Topless bathing is not acceptable.

DISABLED TRAVELLERS

The Association for the Physically Handicapped (☎ 693863) is a good contact for disabled people wanting to travel to Malta. It is at the Rehabilitation Fund Rehabilitation Centre, Corradino Hill, Paola PLA 07.

PUBLIC HOLIDAYS & SPECIAL EVENTS

Fourteen national public holidays are observed in Malta: 1 January (New Year's Day), 10 February (St Paul's Shipwreck),

19 March (St Joseph's Day), Good Friday, 31 March (Freedom Day), 1 May (Labour Day), 7 June (commemoration of 1919 independence riots), 29 June (Feast of Sts Peter and Paul, and Harvest Festival), 15 August (Feast of the Assumption), 8 September (Feast of Our Lady of Victories), 21 September (Independence Day), 8 December (Feast of the Immaculate Conception), 13 December (Republic Day), and 25 December (Christmas Day).

Every village has a *festa* (usually in summer), often to celebrate the feast day of its patron saint. Tourist offices can provide details.

ACCOMMODATION

The Malta Tourist Authority produces a listing of all types of accommodation on Malta, Gozo and Comino, from luxury five-star hotels to small and affordable guesthouses. It's worth noting that off-season prices can be considerably lower than those in the high season.

Camping is not permitted, but the NSTS (see Tourist Offices earlier in this section) runs several hostels on Malta and Gozo. An HI card is required and can be obtained from NSTS or from Valletta's Hibernia House hostel (☎ 333859, fax 230330).

NSTS offers a special hostelling package that includes airport transfers, seven overnight stays (with breakfast), including at least one night at Hibernia House, a week's bus pass and entry to Valletta's Aquacentre Beach Club. The package costs Lm62 for accommodation in eight-bed dorms. NSTS must be notified seven days in advance of arrival.

FOOD & DRINKS

The most obvious culinary influence in Malta is Sicilian, and most of the cheaper restaurants serve pasta and pizza. English standards (eg, grilled chops, sausages and mash) are available in tourist areas. Maltese specialities include *pastizzi* (savoury flaky pasties filled with either ricotta cheese or mushy peas); *timpana* (a rich macaroni, cheese and egg pie); and *bragioli* (spicy beef rolls).

The local beers are very good – Hop Leaf (40c for a small bottle) is highly recommended. Most table wines are also very drinkable.

Getting There & Away

AIR

Malta is well connected to Europe and North Africa by Air Malta, Alitalia, KLM, Lufthansa and Swissair – though flights aren't particularly cheap. Charter flights from England or Scotland offer outstanding value, particularly in winter. Contact a travel agent or NSTS (see Tourist Offices earlier in this section).

SEA

Malta has regular sea links in summer with Sicily (Palermo, Pozzallo, Licata and Catania) and with northern Italy (Genoa and Livorno). Cars can be brought over by ferry and may be imported for up to three months at a time.

The Italy-Malta ferry services are always changing so it is best to confirm with a travel agent such as SMS (☎ 232211), 311 Republic St, Valletta. Ferry companies include Virtu Ferries (☎ 318854 in Malta, and ☎ 095-376933 in Catania) and MA.RE.SI Shipping (☎ 320620), both of which have services to Pozzallo and Reggio Calabria. The Grimaldi Group Grandi Traghetti (☎ 244373) serves Genoa and Tunis. The car-ferry journey to Catania takes around 12 hours and costs Lm20 (plus Lm35 for cars). Virtù Ferries operates a fast catamaran service to Catania, Pozzallo and Licata (Lm34 open return; three hours).

Note that the ferries do not have money-changing facilities, nor are there any at Malta's port. There is no public transport from the port up to the city of Valletta – you will need to catch a taxi or make the steep 15-minute walk.

Getting Around

BUS

Malta and Gozo are served by a network of buses run by the Malta Public Transport Authority (ATP). Most buses on Malta originate from the main City Gate bus terminus, just outside Valletta's city gates (☎ 250007/08/09 for information). A free bus map is available from ATP kiosks and tourist information offices.

CAR & MOTORCYCLE

Like the British, the Maltese drive on the left side of the road. If the speed limits (70km/h on highways and 35km/h in urban areas) don't slow you down, the many potholes in the roads will.

All the car hire companies have representatives at the airport. In early 2000 Hertz was offering a weekly summer rate of Lm75 for a small car (Lm53 a week in the low season). Its head office (☎ 314636) is at 66 Gzira Road, Gzira. Local garages such as Ada (☎ 691007) charge slightly less. La Ronde (☎ 322962), Belvedere Street, Gzira, hires out motorcycles from Lm3 per day (insurance and delivery included). One litre of petrol costs 30 cents. Call ☎ 242222 for 24-hour breakdown assistance and towing.

BOAT

Regular ferries operated by the Gozo Channel Co (☎ 243964) link Malta and Gozo, and buses connect with all ferry services. Ferries depart from Cirkewwa in Malta and from Mgarr, Gozo. Services are more or less hourly from 6 am to 11 pm. The crossing takes 30 minutes and costs Lm1.75 return. There is also a ferry service (☎ 335689) between Valletta and Sliema (at the end of the Strand) approximately every half-hour from 8 am to 6 pm.

TAXI

Taxis are expensive. A fare from the airport to Sliema is around Lm8; from Valletta to St Julian's, around Lm6. Make sure you establish a price in advance. Wembley Motors (☎ 374141), in St Andrews, offers a 24-hour service.

Valletta, Sliema & St Julian's

Valletta, city of the Knights of the Order of St John, is architecturally superb and seemingly unchanged since the 16th-century. The city is the seat of Malta's government, and overlooks the magnificent Grand Harbour to the south-east and Marsamxett Harbour to the north-west. The Maltese think of the suburbs surrounding Valletta as separate towns, but they effectively create one large city with a population of around 250,000.

Orientation

On the northern side of Marsamxett Harbour lies Sliema, a fashionable residential area. Farther north-west are the tourist haunts of St Julian's and Paceville.

The ferries from Italy dock in the Grand Harbour below Valletta, and from there it's a steep 15-minute climb up the hill to the main City Gate bus terminus.

Information

The local tourist office (☎ 237747) is at 1 City Arcade, Valletta. NSTS (☎ 244983), 220 St Paul St, Valletta, is a student travel agency and a representative for Hostelling International (HI).

There are several banks on Valletta's main street, Republic St, including branches of the HSBC Bank at No 15. There is another HSBC Bank at 32 Merchants St. You can also change money at Thomas Cook (☎ 235948) at 20 Republic St, Valletta.

At the time of writing, the main post office had moved from its usual home in the Auberge d'Italie, in Merchants Street, to a building under St James Cavalier on Castile Square. It's open 8 am to 6 pm Monday to Saturday.

Check email at the YMCA (☎ 240680), 178 Merchants St, Valletta, where Internet access costs 75c per half hour (closed Sunday). At the Ghall Kafé (☎ 319686), 118 St George's Road in Paceville, you'll pay Lm1 for 40 minutes.

Things to See

Among the city's more impressive buildings is the **Auberge de Castile** on Castile Square, designed by the Maltese architect Girolamo Cassar (who was one of the two architects who designed Valletta). It was once the palace for the Spanish and Portuguese knights of the Order of St John of Jerusalem. It is now the office of the prime minister and is not open to the public. The nearby **Upper Barrakka Gardens**, originally the private gardens of the Italian knights, offer a magnificent view of the Grand Harbour.

The Auberge de Provence, designed by Cassar for the knights from Provence, now houses the **National Museum of Archaeology**, worth visiting for its collection of relics from the island's Copper Age temples (Lm1).

St John's Co-Cathedral & Museum is the church of the Order of St John of Jerusalem.

MALTA

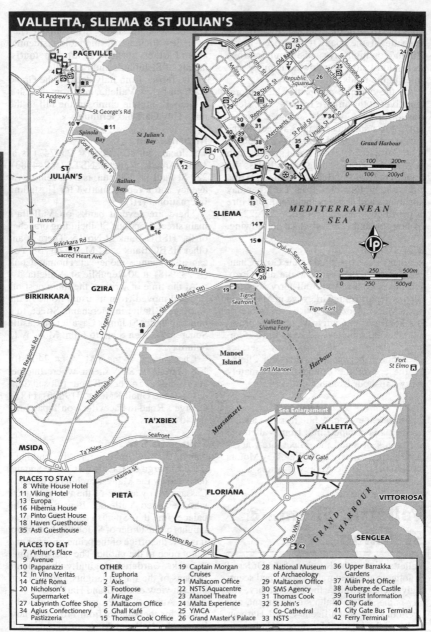

VALLETTA, SLIEMA & ST JULIAN'S

PACEVILLE

St Andrew's Rd

St George's Rd

Spinola Bay

St Julian's Bay

ST JULIAN'S

Balluta Bay

Tunnel

Birkirkara Rd

Sacred Heart Ave

BIRKIRKARA

GZIRA

Gorg Borg Olivier St

Dingli St

SLIEMA

Tower Rd

Qui-si-Sana Place

MEDITERRANEAN SEA

Manoel Dimech Rd

The Strand (Marina Stt)

D'Argens Rd

Testaferrata St

Tigne Seafront

Tigne Fort

Valletta-Sliema Ferry

Manoel Island

Fort Manoel

Harbour

Fort St Elmo

TA'XBIEX

Seafront

Ta'Xbiex Seafront

Marsamxett

See Enlargement

VALLETTA

MSIDA

Marina St

PIETÀ

FLORIANA

City Gate

GRAND HARBOUR

VITTORIOSA

Wenzu Rd

Pinto Wharf

SENGLEA

Grand Harbour

National Museum of Archaeology (28)

Republic Square

St John St · Old Bakery St

Malta St · St John St · Strait St

South St · Republic St

Merchants St · St Paul St · St Ursula St

St Christopher St · Archbishop St

Old Theatre St

PLACES TO STAY
8 White House Hotel
11 Viking Hotel
13 Europa
16 Hibernia House
17 Pinto Guest House
18 Haven Guesthouse
35 Asti Guesthouse

PLACES TO EAT
7 Arthur's Place
9 Avenue
10 Papparazzi
12 In Vino Veritas
14 Caffé Roma
20 Nicholson's Supermarket
27 Labyrinth Coffee Shop
34 Agius Confectionery Pastizzeria

OTHER
1 Euphoria
2 Axis
3 Footloose
4 Mirage
5 Maltacom Office
6 Ghall Kafé
15 Thomas Cook Office

19 Captain Morgan Cruises
21 Maltacom Office
22 NSTS Aquacentre
23 Manoel Theatre
24 Malta Experience
25 YMCA
26 Grand Master's Palace

28 National Museum of Archaeology
29 Maltacom Office
30 SMS Agency
31 Thomas Cook
32 St John's Co-Cathedral
33 NSTS

36 Upper Barrakka Gardens
37 Main Post Office
38 Auberge de Castile
39 Tourist Information
40 City Gate
41 City Gate Bus Terminal
42 Ferry Terminal

It's on St John St, and has an austere facade and a baroque interior. The museum houses a collection of precious tapestries.

The **Grand Master's Palace**, Republic St, is the seat of the Maltese parliament. It contains an armoury and a fresco depicting the Great Siege. The **Manoel Theatre** (1731), one of the oldest in Europe, is appropriately located on Old Theatre St. Apart from performances (generally in winter), entry is by guided tour (Lm1.65) at 10.45 and 11.15 am weekdays and 11.30 am Saturday.

Valletta's **Malta Experience** (☎ 243776) provides a short and interesting audio-visual introduction to Maltese history (enter from St Lazarus Bastion). It costs Lm2.50 and starts every hour on the hour from 11 am to 4 pm weekdays, 11 am to 1 pm weekends.

The **Hypogeum**, an important series of underground prehistoric temples at Paola, was closed at the time of writing.

Activities
The NSTS Aquacentre Beach Club (☎ 338568), Qui-si-Sana Place, Tigne, offers a range of reasonably priced activities, including the hire of flippers and masks (Lm1.50 per hour, Lm1 for students), sailboards (Lm4/2.75 an hour) and sailing boats (Lm4/3 an hour). You can also scuba dive (Lm15/13 per dive including equipment).

Organised Tours
Captain Morgan Cruises (☎ 343373) operates short harbour cruises (Lm6.25) and a variety of half and full-day cruises around the islands (from Lm13.95). Boats leave from the Strand in Sliema. Buy tickets at any of the travel agencies on the waterfront.

Places to Stay
Hostel NSTS runs the *Hibernia House* hostel (☎ 333859, fax 230330), Depiro St, in Sliema. An HI card is required and can be obtained from NSTS or at the hostel itself. Beds cost Lm2.85. Take bus No 62 or 67 to Balluta Bay, walk up the hill along Manoel Dimech Rd, then turn left into Depiro St; the hostel is 100m along on the right.

For information on NSTS hostelling packages see the Accommodation section earlier in this chapter.

Guesthouses & Hotels In general, guesthouses tend to be family operated and are cheaper than hotels. Guesthouses can be found in and around Paceville and St Julian's. All prices below include breakfast.

In Valletta, the *Asti Guest House* (☎ 239506, 18 St Ursula St), in a former convent, has cheap, basic rooms with share bathrooms (Lm5.50 per person).

The *Pinto Guest House* (☎ 313897), Sacred Heart Ave, St Julian's, is a steep walk up from Balluta Bay, but it's worth the hike for the spacious rooms and excellent views. A twin room costs Lm6 per person. The *Viking Hotel* (☎ 316702 or 340930), Spinola Rd, St Julian's, charges Lm10.

Right in the centre of Paceville is the *White House Hotel* (☎ 378016), Paceville Ave. Comfortable rooms with bath or shower cost Lm10 per person (Lm7 low season).

Europa (☎ 330080, 138 Tower Rd, Sliema), is well located and has pleasant rooms with bath and TV for Lm17 per person (Lm13 off season).

In Gzira, *Haven Guest House* (☎ 335862, 193 The Strand), is spotlessly clean and charges Lm7.70 per person.

Places to Eat
Nicholson's supermarket is on the top level of the Plaza shopping centre, St Anna Square, Sliema. There are cheap restaurants, bars and cafes on the Strand in Sliema, in Paceville and around St Julian's Bay.

For lunch in Valletta try the *Labyrinth coffee shop* (44 Strait St), which has generous salads (from Lm1.60), delicious pies (60c to 70c) and great coffee (35c). There's a more extensive menu in the basement supper club, which is open until midnight. The cheapest lunch is a couple of delicious pastizzi (15c each) from *Agius Confectionery Pastizzeria* (273 St Paul St).

Arthur's Place, Ball St, Paceville, has an interesting range of Maltese and vegetarian dishes. Main courses are Lm2 to Lm3.50. The terrace at *Papparazzi*, overlooking St Julian's Bay, is a prime people-watching spot. The bistro serves good pastas, pizzas, steaks and burgers prices (Lm2 to Lm5). Pizza costs around Lm2 at the *Avenue*, in Gort St, Paceville.

Some good options are on Tower Rd in Sliema. *Caffè Roma*, on the corner of Ghar Il-Lembi St, has homemade pastas (Lm1.30 to Lm2.50) and pizzas (Lm2). Vegetarians could try *In Vino Veritas* (59 Dingli St), on

MALTA

the corner of Tower Rd. The lasagne (Lm1.65), vegetarian rice (Lm1.65) and homemade cakes are excellent.

Entertainment
Paceville, Malta's nightlife centre, is quiet Monday to Thursday but jumping on Friday, Saturday and Sunday. *Mirage*, a disco for the young crowd, is opposite *Footloose*, a loud rock-music pub on St George's Rd. *Euphoria* and *Axis* are other places to party till late. Nightclubs cost around Lm2.50 to enter and drinks are expensive.

Getting Around
Bus No 8 leaves from outside the departures hall at Malta international airport terminal about every half hour and goes to Valletta City Gate bus terminus. The journey costs 15c (pay the driver). Most arrivals are transferred by courtesy car or coach to their hotels. Taxis operate on official rates; to Sliema or St Julian's it's Lm8.

Around Malta

NORTH COAST
Although the north coast is fairly exposed, it's a good place for walking as it's relatively uninhabited. The sandy beach at **Mellieha Bay**, west of St Paul's Bay, is the best on Malta, although it does get crowded. Catch bus No 44 or 48 from Valletta.

Bugibba, the traditional name for the town on St Paul's Bay, is the bay's main tourist centre and it's ghastly. There's no reason to stay here, though the nightlife hots up in summer, and there are numerous cheap hotels and restaurants. Catch bus No 43, 44, 45 or 49 from Valletta.

Cirkewwa is the port where the Gozo ferry docks. **Paradise Bay**, one of Malta's better sandy beaches, is a short walk to the south of the town.

MDINA
Until the knights arrived and settled around the Grand Harbour, the political centre of Malta was Mdina. Set inland on an easily defendable rocky outcrop, it has been a fortified city for more than 3000 years. You could spend hours wandering through Mdina's narrow, quiet streets. Also check out the beautiful main piazza and the **Mdina**

Dungeons, below the Vilhena Palace. They have been restored to all their dubious glory and have tableaux depicting former inmates. Open 9.30 am to 5 pm daily (Lm1.40).

Catch bus Nos 80 or 81 from Valletta to reach Mdina and Rabat.

SOUTH COAST
The most interesting temples on Malta are **Hagar Qim** and **Mnajdra**, built between 3600 and 2500 BC near the village of Qrendi. The temples are open 7.45 am to 2 pm daily in summer and 8.15 am to 5 pm (4.15 pm on Sunday) the rest of the year (Lm1). These Copper Age megalithic temples are reminiscent of Stonehenge, and a visit is a must.

Gozo

Gozo is much smaller than Malta and has a distinctive character; the countryside is more attractive, the pace is slower and there are fewer tourists. The capital is Victoria (also known as Rabat), but most travellers stay at the small resort of Marsalforn. You can cram the sights into one day, but the real charm of Gozo is to experience it slowly.

Victoria has a decent range of shops and banks but no hotels. There's a wonderful view over the island from the 17th-century citadel. The tourist office (☎ 558106), in Independence Square, has a useful map.

Marsalforn is the main resort town and can be crowded on weekends. There's one large hotel, a scattering of smaller places to stay and a dozen restaurants, all built around an attractive bay. Follow the coast road west from the harbour for a fabulous walk past eroded cliffs. By foot Marsalforn is 4km from Victoria, or catch bus No 21 from Victoria's Main Gate St.

The **Ggantija** temple complex near Xaghra village is spectacular. There's a dramatic stretch of coastline around Dwejra Point, including the imposing **Azure Window**, a gigantic rock arch in the cliff, only a few hundred metres from the Inland Sea.

St Joseph Hostel (☎ 556439) in Ghanjsielem, a 15-minute walk uphill from Mgarr Harbour, has beds in summer – book-through NSTS (see Valletta section).

For information on Malta-Gozo ferry services see Getting Around earlier in this chapter.

Morocco

Known to the Arabs as *al-Maghreb al-Aqsa* (farthest land of the setting sun), Morocco stands at the western extremity of the Arab and Muslim world. For many, Morocco's greatest charm lies in the labyrinths of its imperial cities – Fès, Marrakesh, Meknès and Rabat. Nothing in Europe can prepare you for the visual feast of the great mosques and *medersas* (Koranic schools) that bejewel Morocco's major cities.

The countryside exerts its own fascination. The snowcapped High Atlas mountains, the great river valleys of the south with their magnificent red-earth kasbahs (citadels) and the vast expanse of the desert all offer a taste of the exotic.

Facts about Morocco

HISTORY

Morocco is largely populated by descendants of Berbers who settled the area thousands of years ago. Later the Romans gained a tenuous hold in this corner of North Africa, only to fade slowly away before the arrival of Islam in the 7th century when Arab armies swept across the North African coast and into Spain.

In the 11th century the Almoravids took control of Morocco and Muslim Spain and founded Marrakesh. They were supplanted by the Almohads, who raised Marrakesh, Fès and Rabat to heights of splendour, before crumbling as Christian armies regained Spain. The Alawites took over in the 17th century and, during the rule of Sultan Moulay Ismail (1672-1727), built the Imperial City at Meknès.

As colonialism swept across Africa, the 1912 Treaty of Fès ceded large swathes of Morocco to France and a smaller zone in the north to Spain. The colonialists, under

the enlightened French resident-general, Marshal Lyautey, built *villes nouvelles* (new cities) so preserving the medinas (ancient quarters) in many larger cities.

After WWII Moroccan opposition to the French took a violent turn, and in 1953 the French exiled Sultan Mohammed V, stoking even greater discontent. In 1955 Mohammed V was allowed to return and independence was granted the following year. The Spanish withdrew from much of the country at the same time but have retained the coastal enclaves of Ceuta and Melilla.

Following independence Sultan Mohammed V was crowned king, followed by his son King Hassan II who, despite moves towards democracy and several attempted coup, retained all effective power until his death in July 1999. His son, Mohammed VI, has already adopted a more populist and reforming agenda vowing to tackle the huge developmental problems Morocco faces, particularly high unemployment, poverty and illiteracy.

The Moroccan government hopes that the free-trade agreement with the EU, that came into effect in March 2000 will accelerate economic development. The payoff for Europe should be a tighter clamp on the flow of drugs (a multi-billion dollar trade) and access to new markets.

It was hoped that with the new King the dispute in the western Sahara would be resolved. Since the 'Green March' in 1975 Morocco has occupied the former Spanish colony. The Algerian-backed Polisario Front resists Moroccan rule, though a UN-brokered cease-fire has been in place since 1991. A referendum on the territory's future has been planned since then, but stalling tactics mean that a vote is unlikely to take place until 2002.

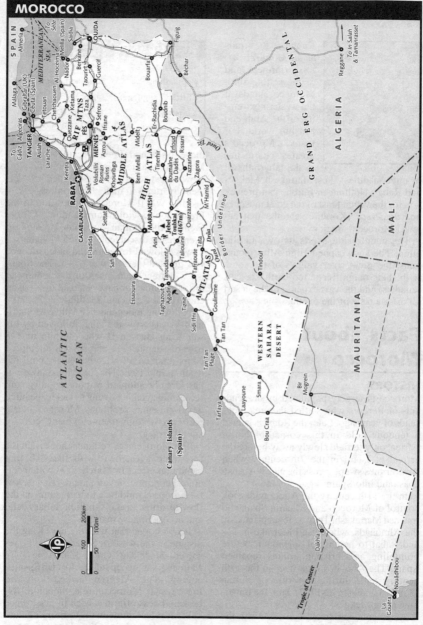

GEOGRAPHY

Morocco, one of Africa's most geographically diverse countries, is traversed by four mountain ranges. From north to south they are the Rif, the Middle Atlas, the High Atlas and the Anti-Atlas. In the extreme south, at the edge of the Anti-Atlas Mountains, eroded gorges gradually peter out in the endless sand and stone wastes of the Sahara Desert.

POPULATION & PEOPLE

Morocco's population is around 30 million and growing at around 1.8% per year. The largest city is Casablanca at about five million. The bulk of the population is made up of Arab and Berber peoples. Morocco once hosted a large population of Jews, but most left after the founding of Israel in 1948. Trade with trans-Saharan Africa brought a population of black Africans into Morocco.

SOCIETY & CONDUCT

Despite western influences, Morocco is largely a conservative Sunni Muslim society. Though Islam is far from strictly orthodox in Morocco, a high degree of modesty is demanded of both sexes in dress as well as behaviour. Women, in particular, are well advised to keep their shoulders and upper arms covered and to opt for long skirts or trousers (beach resorts are an exception).

If invited into a Moroccan home, it is customary to remove your shoes before stepping onto the carpet. Food is served in common dishes and eaten with the right hand (the left hand is used for personal hygiene after visiting the toilet and should not be used to touch any common source of food or water, or to hand over money).

All mosques and active religious buildings (and some cemeteries) are off limits to non-Muslims.

You should always ask permission before taking photographs – urban Moroccans usually have no problem with this. As a rule, women especially do *not* want to be photographed. Respect their right to privacy and don't take photos.

LANGUAGE

Arabic is the official language, but Berber and French are widely spoken. Spanish is spoken in former Spanish-held territory (particularly the north) and some English in the main tourist centres. Don't expect much beyond Moroccan Arabic (*darija*) and French outside the main tourist spots.

Pick up your own copy of Lonely Planet's *Moroccan Arabic phrasebook*, or see the Language Guide at the back of this book for pronunciation guidelines and useful words and phrases.

Facts for the Visitor

HIGHLIGHTS

The four great cities of Morocco's imperial past are Fès, Marrakesh, Meknès and Rabat. Here you will discover Morocco's greatest monuments – mosques and medersas surrounded by the colour of the medina and its *souqs* (markets).

In just a few days you can sample the breathtaking heights of the Atlas mountains, sprinkled with Berber villages, and then head south to take in the atmosphere of the oases and *kasbahs* (citadels) of the Drâa Valley and enjoy the Dadès and Todra gorges to the south-east of Marrakesh.

The Atlantic coast is dotted with tranquil towns – notably Essaouira – bearing the marks of European occupation.

SUGGESTED ITINERARIES

Four days
    Head straight for Fès or Chefchaouen in the Rif mountains.
One week
    Take your pick of the imperial cities (Fès, Meknès, Marrakesh and Rabat).
Two weeks
    Take in an imperial city, do some trekking or see the southern oases and gorges and visit Essaouira or Chefchaouen.

PLANNING
When to Go

The most pleasant times of the year to explore Morocco are during spring (April to May) and autumn (September to October).

Midsummer can be very enjoyable on the coast but viciously hot in the interior where the *chergui*, a hot wind from the desert, can push temperatures above 40°C.

Winter can be idyllic in Marrakesh and farther south during the daytime, but bone-chillingly cold at night – bring a sleeping bag. Snow blocks the passes in the High Atlas and other mountain ranges during winter.

MOROCCO

Maps

The best map to buy is the Michelin No 959 *Morocco* (scale 1:1,000,000). The Cartography Division of the Conservation & Topography Department (☎ 29 50 34, fax 29 55 49) on Ave Hassan II, Rabat stocks maps of Morocco.

TOURIST OFFICES

The national tourist body, ONMT, has offices (usually called Délégation Régionale du Tourisme) in the main cities. Head office (☎ 73 05 62) is in Rabat on Rue al-Abtal. Several cities also have local offices known as *syndicats d'initiative*. Some are much better than others, though all have brochures and simple maps to dispense.

The ONMT maintains offices in Australia (Sydney), Belgium (Brussels), Canada (Montreal), France (Paris), Germany (Düsseldorf), Italy (Milan), Japan (Tokyo), Spain (Madrid), the UK (London) and the USA (New York and Orlando).

EMBASSIES & CONSULATES
Moroccan Embassies Abroad

Australia (☎ 02-9922 4999) Suite 2, 11 West St, North Sydney, NSW 2060
Canada (☎ 416-236 7391) 38 Range Rd, Ottawa KIN 8J4
France (☎ 01-45 20 69 35) 5 Rue Le Tasse, Paris 75016
Germany (☎ 228 35 50 44) Gotenstrasse, 7-9-5300, Bonn 2
Japan (☎ 03-478 3271) Silva Kingdom 3, 16-3, Sendagaya, Shibuya-ku, Tokyo 151
Spain (☎ 91-563 1090) Calle Serrano 179, 28002 Madrid
UK (☎ 0171-581 5001) 49 Queen's Gate Gardens, London SW7 5NE
USA (☎ 202-462 7979) 1601 21st St NW, Washington DC 20009

Foreign Embassies in Morocco

Embassies in Rabat (area code ☎ 07) include:

Canada (☎ 67 28 80) 13 Rue Jaafar as-Sadiq, Agdal
France
Embassy: (☎ 77 78 22) 3 Rue Sahnoun, Agdal
Service de Visas: (☎ 70 24 04) Rue Ibn al-Khatib
Germany (☎ 70 96 62) 7 Zankat Madnine
Japan (☎ 63 17 82) 39 Ave Ahmed Balafrej Souissi
Spain
Embassy: (☎ 76 89 89) 3-5 Zankat Madnine
Consulate: (☎ 70 41 47) 57 Rue du Chellah
UK (☎ 72 96 96) 17 Blvd de la Tour Hassan
USA (☎ 76 22 65) 2 Ave de Marrakesh

MONEY

The unit of currency is the dirham (Dr), made up of 100 centimes. There's not much of a black market and little reason to use it. In the Spanish enclaves of Ceuta and Melilla the currency is the Spanish peseta (pta).

Banking services are generally quick and efficient. Branches of BMCE (Banque Marocaine du Commerce Extérieur) often have separate currency exchange desks. Almost all banks charge commission on travellers cheques. Automatic teller machines (*guichets automatiques*) are a common sight in major towns and many accept Visa, MasterCard, Electron, Cirrus, Maestro and InterBank.

Major credit cards are widely accepted in the main tourist centres although their use often attracts a surcharge. American Express, represented by the travel agency Voyages Schwartz, has offices in Casablanca, Marrakesh, Rabat and Tangier. Commission on travellers cheques is usually Dr10 per cheque.

Exchange Rates

Australian, Canadian and New Zealand dollars are not quoted in banks and are generally not accepted.

country	unit		dirham
Australia	A$1	=	Dr6.14
Canada	C$1	=	Dr7.47
euro	€1	=	Dr9.57
France	1FF	=	Dr1.46
Germany	DM1	=	Dr4.89
Japan	¥100	=	Dr10.41
New Zealand	NZ$1	=	Dr4.62
UK	UK£1	=	Dr15.61
USA	US$1	=	Dr11.03

Costs

You can get by on US$20 to US$25 a day by staying in cheap hotels and eating at cheap restaurants. For life's basic luxuries, such as hot showers, the occasional splurge at a good restaurant and the odd taxi, plan on US$30 to US$35 a day.

If you are under 26, don't forget that an international student card can get you big reductions on internal flights (and some international flights) and international rail fares departing from Morocco.

Tipping & Bargaining

The judicious distribution of a few dirham for services willingly rendered can make your

MOROCCO

life a lot easier, but don't be railroaded. Between 5% and 10% of a restaurant bill is fine.

Bargaining is an integral part of the street life in Morocco. When souvenir-hunting, decide beforehand how much you are prepared to spend on an item (get an idea of upper-end prices at government-run Ensemble Artisanals in major cities). Vendors often start with hugely inflated prices so wait until the price has reduced significantly before making your first (low) offer. Approach your limit slowly.

POST & COMMUNICATIONS
Post
The Moroccan post is fairly reliable. Outgoing parcels must be inspected by customs (at the post office) before you seal them and pay for postage. Some post offices offer a private packing service.

Telephone & Fax
Morocco's country code is ☎ 212. Drop the initial zero on city area codes when dialling in from overseas.

Morocco's telephone system is good. Private sector *téléboutiques* are widespread though fractionally more expensive than the official phone offices, which are being phased out. Attendants sell phonecards (*télécartes*) and provide change. Phonecards for public phones are available from post offices.

Reverse charge (collect) calls to most countries are possible; ask to *téléphoner en PCV* (pronounced 'peh-seh-veh'). The Moroccan phone book (*Annuaire des Abonnés au Téléphone*) lists toll-free numbers that connect you to an operator in the country you wish to call.

When calling overseas from Morocco, dial ☎ 00, your country code and then the city code and number.

Calls are expensive: a three-minute call to the USA will cost about US$3 and a three-minute call to Europe at least US$2. For international calls, there is a 20% reduction between 8 pm and 8 am weekdays and throughout the weekend.

Many téléboutiques have fax machines. Prices per page are about Dr50 to Europe and Dr70 to North America and Australia.

INTERNET RESOURCES
Email and Internet access (not many places offer coffee and cake) has sprung up all over Morocco. One-hour access costs Dr10 to Dr25. The Net is quicker in the morning.

There are numerous Internet sites about Morocco – www.maghreb.net, www.mincom.gov.ma, www.morocco.com and www.i-cias.com/mor.htm will get you started.

BOOKS
See Lonely Planet's *Morocco* for more detailed information on the country.

The Moors: Islam in the West by Michael Brett & Werner Forman details Moorish civilisation at its height, with superb colour photographs. *Histoire du Maroc* by Bernard Lugan is a potted history of the country. *The Conquest of Morocco* by Douglas Porch examines the takeover of Morocco by Paris.

Doing Daily Battle by Fatima Mernissi, translated by Mary Jo Lakeland, is a collection of fascinating interviews with Moroccan women. It's also worth seeking out the fiction of Peter Bowles, who lived and worked in Tangier for many years.

WOMEN TRAVELLERS
Though a certain level of sexual harassment is almost the norm, it is generally of the leering, verbal variety. In bigger cities, female travellers will receive hopeful greetings from every male over the age of 13! Ignore them.

Women will avoid a great deal of grief by dressing modestly – shoulders and upper arms covered, long skirts and trousers and avoiding anything skintight. It's wise not to walk around alone at night – after dark all 'good' Moroccan women are at home.

More often than not, Moroccan cafes are all-male preserves and female travellers may prefer to have coffee or tea at *pâtisseries* (pastry shops).

GAY & LESBIAN TRAVELLERS
Homosexual acts are officially illegal in Morocco – in theory you can be jailed, fined or both. However, while not openly admitted or shown, male homosexuality is relatively common. Be discreet as aggression towards gay male travellers is not unheard of. Gay women shouldn't encounter any particular problems, though it's commonly believed that there are no Moroccan lesbians.

DANGERS & ANNOYANCES
Morocco's era as a hippy paradise, riding the Marrakesh Express and all that, is long past.

Drug busts are common and this is not a good place to investigate local prison conditions.

Those disembarking (and embarking) the ferry in Tangier should expect some hassle from touts and hustlers trying to pull you one way or the other (usually to a hotel/ferry ticket office where they can expect a commission). Ceuta and Melilla are far more pleasant ports of entry.

On some of the more popular tourist routes – in particular the road between Marrakesh and Ouarzazate – you may come across professional hitchhikers and people pretending that their cars have broken down. Once you stop to assist them various scams unfold.

Morocco has its share of pickpockets and thieves but they're not a major problem.

The police can be reached on ☎ 19 and the highway emergency service on ☎ 177.

Guides

A few years ago special *Brigade Touristique* (tourist police) were set up in the main tourist centres to clamp down on Morocco's notorious *faux guides* (false guides) and hustlers. Any person suspected of trying to operate as an unofficial guide could face jail and/or a huge fine.

This has reduced, but not eliminated, the problem of the faux guide. Plenty still hang around the entrances to city medinas and outside bus and train stations. They can be persistent and sometimes unpleasant. If you don't want their services, ignore their offers and try not to get your feathers ruffled.

If you end up with one of these people remember their main interest is the commission gained from certain hotels or on articles sold to you in the souqs.

Official guides can be engaged through tourist offices at the fixed price of Dr120 per half day (plus tip). It's well worth taking a guide when exploring the intricate and confusing medinas of Fès and Marrakesh. Their local knowledge is extensive and they'll save you from being hassled by other would-be guides. If you don't want a shopping expedition included in your tour, make this clear beforehand.

BUSINESS HOURS

Banking hours are 8.30 to 11.30 am and 2.30 to 4.30 pm weekdays with Friday lunch lasting from 11.15 am to 3 pm and 9 am to 3 pm during Ramadan. These times can vary a little. In some of the main tourist cities currency exchange offices keep longer hours and open over the weekend. Post offices generally keep similar hours, but don't close until around 6 pm. Téléboutiques and cybercafes are open until around 10 pm. Many museums and some monuments are closed on Tuesday.

PUBLIC HOLIDAYS & SPECIAL EVENTS

All banks, post offices and most shops are shut on the main public holidays: New Year's Day, 11 January (Independence Manifesto), 1 May (Labour Day), 23 May (National Day), 9 July (Young People's Day), 13 July (Feast of the Throne), 14 August (Allegiance of Wadi-Eddahab), 20 August (Anniversary of the King's and People's Revolution), 6 November (Anniversary of the Green March), 18 November (Independence Day).

Morocco also celebrates many Islamic holidays and festivals, all tied to the lunar calendar. The most important is Aïd al-Fitr, held at the end of the holy fasting month of Ramadan (usually during December or January). The festivities generally last four or five days, during which just about everything grinds to a halt.

Aïd al-Adha, which marks the end of the Islamic year (usually in March), celebrates Abraham's submission to God through the offer of his son Isaac for sacrifice. Again, most things shut down for four or five days. Mawlid an-Nabi (or Mouloud), celebrates the Prophet Mohammed's birthday and is usually in June.

Local festivals, mostly in honour of *marabouts* (saints) and known as *moussems* or *amouggars*, are common among the Berbers and usually held in summer.

ACCOMMODATION

Morocco has many official camping grounds, where you'll pay around Dr10 per person plus Dr10 to pitch a tent. There are extra charges for vehicles, electricity and hot water.

There are *auberges de jeunesse* (hostels) at Asni, Azrou, Casablanca, Chefchaouen, Fès, Marrakesh, Meknès, Rabat and Tangier. They cost Dr20 to Dr30 a night.

Cheap, unclassified hotels are clustered around certain parts of medinas of the bigger cities. They charge from Dr30/50 for singles/doubles. Showers are often cold, but there are always *hammams* (public bathhouses) nearby. Some are bright and spotless, others haven't seen a mop for years.

Slightly more expensive are unclassified or one-star hotels outside the medinas, where singles/doubles with shower start at Dr60/120. Rooms in two-star hotels start at Dr150/200.

The three-star category (from Dr200/250) gets you a TV and a telephone. Five-star hotels (from Dr1000 for a double) range from rather sterile modern places to former palaces.

FOOD & DRINKS

Moroccan cuisine features a sublime use of spices and the freshest local produce. Restaurant food, particularly in touristy areas, can be variable. Head for the places full of locals and you won't go far wrong.

If you're on a very tight budget, you can eat for as little as Dr50 per day. A three-course meal in a medium-priced restaurant will cost around Dr80, in a traditional Moroccan palace restaurant or a smart French place, expect to pay around Dr150.

Typical dishes include *tajine*, a meat and vegetable stew. *Couscous*, steamed semolina served with meat and vegetables, is traditionally eaten on Friday. *Harira* is a substantial soup made from lamb stock, chickpeas, onions and tomatoes, usually eaten as a first course in the evening. Brochettes (skewered meat barbecued over hot coals) and roast chicken served with crispy *frites* (fried potatoes) are other staples.

Pastilla, a speciality of Fès, is a delicious dish of pigeon meat and lemon-flavoured eggs, plus almonds, cinnamon, saffron and sugar, encased in fine pastry dough.

For vegetarians, fresh fruit and vegetables are widely available. When ordering couscous or tajine, be sure to specify *sans viande* (without meat). The traditional *salade marocaine* is made from finely diced green peppers, tomatoes and red onions.

Food markets (*souqs*), vegetable stalls and bakeries are found all over the country. Quality is usually high and prices low (in season stawberries can cost Dr5 per kilo!).

Morocco is bursting at the seams with cafes where sipping mint tea or coffee is a serious (male) occupation. English-style tea is usually served black and invariably known as *thé Lipton*. Coffee is served in the French style: short black or large milky white.

Beer is reasonably easy to find in the villes nouvelles. A bottle of local Stork or Flag beer typically costs from Dr12 to Dr15 in bars.

Getting There & Away

AIR

The main entry point is the Mohammed V airport 30km south-east of Casablanca. Inter-national flights also land at Tangier, Agadir, Marrakesh, Fès and Ouarzazate. Air France and Royal Air Maroc (RAM) are the major carriers, but other airlines operating to Morocco include Alitalia, British Airways, Iberia, KLM, Lufthansa, Swissair and Gulf Air.

Charter flights to Morocco from cities such as Paris, Amsterdam, Brussels and Düsseldorf cost around UK£200 or less.

In the high season, scheduled flights between London and Casablanca can cost as much as UK£350. It's cheaper to fly to Málaga (from as little as UK£69 one way) in southern Spain and catch a ferry.

LAND

Eurolines and the Moroccan national bus line, CTM (Compagnie des Transports Marocains), run buses between Morocco and many European cities. One-way/return tickets from London to Marrakesh cost UK£116/192. For a one-way ticket from Morocco the cost starts at Dr615 for Malaga and rises to Dr1200 for Paris.

Trains give you the option of couchettes and breaking your trip along the way. From London, Rail Europe sells tickets as far as Algeciras. One-way/return tickets valid for two months are UK£123/208. The one-way fare from Casablanca to London is Dr2220, less with a student card (including the Tangier-Algerciras ferry).

The Moroccan rail system is part of the Inter-Rail network. An Inter-Rail ticket (around UK£290) entitles you to a month of free unlimited 2nd-class travel on trains in up to 28 countries in Europe, including Morocco.

MOROCCO

SEA
Spain

Ferries are operated by Trasmediterranea, Islena de Navigación SA, Comarit, Limadet, Buquebus and Euroferrys. The most popular route is Algeciras-Tangier; others are Algeciras-Ceuta, Ceuta-Málaga, Almeria-Melilla, Málaga-Melilla, Gibralter-Tangier and Cadiz-Tangier.

Algeciras-Tangier There's a ferry roughly every hour, or 1½ hours, between 7 am and 9.30 pm. One way trips (2½ hours) cost 3200ptas (Dr210).

Cadiz-Tangier IMTC operate this twice daily, 3 hour, service for 3900ptas (Dr250) one-way.

Algeciras & Málaga-Ceuta There are up to 22 hydrofoil (35 minutes) and six ferry crossings (90 minutes) per day between Algeciras and Ceuta. The one-way fares are 2945ptas and 1800ptas respectively.

Buquebus operate the twice daily Ceuta-Malaga hydrofoil (4995 ptas, 90 minutes).

Almeria & Málaga-Melilla There are six Trasmediterranea overnight services a week from Almeria to Melilla, and Malaga to Melilla and vice versa. The crossing takes 6½ to eight and 7½ to 10 hours respectively. The cheapest one-way fare is 4020ptas on either service.

Gibraltar-Tangier

Bland Shipping runs this thrice-weekly, service. The voyage (which takes about two hours) costs Dr260/510 (UK£18/35) one way/return.

France

The Sète-Tangier and Nador ferry service is operated by the Compagnie Marocaine de Navigation and the crossing is usually made every four to five days, takes 38 hours and costs roughly between 1500FF and 3630FF.

Getting Around

AIR

If time is limited, consider the occasional internal flight with Royal Air Maroc (RAM). If you're under 22 or a student under 31, you are entitled to at least 25% (and often up to 60%) off all fares. The standard/student one-way fare between Casablanca and Tangier is Dr688/263 (about US$70/28); between Casablanca and Agadir it's Dr908/323 (about US$90/32).

BUS

CTM (Compagnie des Transports Marocains) is really the only national company, although other companies (with smaller networks), such as SATAS, are just as good. On major inter-city routes CTM runs 1st and 2nd-class services. There are more of the former than the latter, so you'll often be paying the 25% higher fare. Advance booking is advisable, especially in smaller towns with few services. In many places, CTM has its own terminal. Sample 1st-class CTM fares are Casablanca-Fès Dr80 and Marrakesh-Fès Dr128.

There's an official baggage charge on CTM buses (Dr5 per pack). On other lines baggage handlers may demand a little cash – Dr3 is OK.

TRAIN

Travel by train when you can. You have a choice of 1st and 2nd class on *ordinaire* and *rapide* trains. The latter are a little faster, have air-con and are more comfortable. The former are cheaper, but restricted to the odd evening service. Fares in 2nd class are roughly comparable with bus fares (there is no need to go 1st class). Couchettes are available on night trains between Marrakesh and Tangier.

Supratours runs luxury buses in conjunction with trains to some destinations not on the rail network, including Tetouan, Agadir and Essaouira. You can buy a bus-rail ticket to any place on the combined network.

CAR & MOTORCYCLE

You drive on the right-hand side of the road in Morocco; if you're already on a roundabout, give way to traffic entering from the right. It's compulsory for drivers and passengers to wear seatbelts. An International Driving Permit is officially required, but most national licences are sufficient.

Main roads are in decent condition, but many secondary roads are not so hot. The expanding motorway network now stretches from Casablana to just short of Tangier and from Rabat to Fès. Tolls are payable and the speed limit on the motorway is 120km/h – elsewhere it's 100km/h or 40km/h to 60km/h in built-up areas. Mountain roads can be blocked by snow in winter, and desert roads are sometimes awash with sand drifts. The accident rate in Morocco is high; night driving is particularly hazardous.

There are frequent police and customs roadblocks. Always stop; often you'll be waved through, but have your licence and passport handy.

Most towns have paid parking areas which cost a few dirham for a few hours or Dr10 overnight.

It's worth renting a car to explore the southern oases and kasbah routes. Major companies have reps in main cities. The cheapest rentals (three days with unlimited kilometres) start at Dr1400, plus 20% tax. Renters must be at least 21. Shop around and haggle!

LOCAL TRANSPORT

The big cities have useful local bus networks. A ride costs about Dr2.50.

Petits taxis (city taxis) are equally useful and cheap – provided the driver uses the meter and you have some idea of the fare. Fares around town shouldn't be more than Dr10. Fares rise by about 50% after 8 pm.

Grands taxis work a little like buses. Usually ageing Mercedes, they take six passengers to a fixed destination for a standard fare and leave when full. They often leave more frequently than buses, are quicker and up to 50% more expensive.

You can hire grands taxis privately. Always agree on a price with the driver, and discuss any stops you might want to make before leaving.

Mediterranean Coast & the Rif

TANGIER
☎ 09

Tangier (Tanja to locals), a major port of entry for travellers, was once home to hordes of the world's best hustlers. First time arrivals can still find it hard going, though things have settled down a *bit* these days, but give the place time and you'll find it a likeable city buzzing with energy.

Tangier has been coveted for millennia as a strategic site commanding the Strait of Gibraltar. In 1923, as a compromise between the European powers, the city and surrounding areas were declared an 'international zone' controlled by France, Spain, Britain, Portugal, Sweden, the Netherlands, Belgium, Italy and the USA.

During the Inter(national) Zone years, which ended with independence in 1956, Tangier became a fashionable Mediterranean resort renowned for its high-profile gay scene and popular with freebooters, artists, writers, exiles and bankers. However, it was also an infamous haven for paedophiles.

Information

The Délégation Régionale du Tourisme (☎ 94 80 50, 29 Blvd Pasteur) can arrange official guides and offers a limited range of brochures.

There are banks along Blvd Pasteur and Blvd Mohammed V – the BMCE on Blvd Pasteur has ATMs and an exchange booth that is open until 8 pm daily. Crédit du Maroc is further south on Blvd Mohammed V.

The main post office (for poste restante; c/o Tangier Prinicple 90000) is on Blvd Mohammed V.

Internet access (Dr10 per hour) is available at Cyber Café Mam Net (53 Rue du Prince du Moulay Abdallah), Maghreb Net on Rue al-Antaki, and Cyber Café Adam on Rue Ibn Rochd.

Librairie des Colonnes (☎ 93 69 55, 54 Blvd Pasteur), has a good selection of Francophone literature while Librairie Dar Baroud, at the Hôtel Continental, stocks a good range of books in English.

Things to See & Do

In the heart of the medina the **Petit Socco**, with its cafes and restaurants, is the focus of activity. In the days of the international zone this was the sin and sleaze centre – and it retains something of its seedy air.

North of the Petit Socco, the Rue des Almohades takes you to the **kasbah**, built on the highest point of the city. Enter from Bab el-Assa at the end of Rue Ben Raissouli in the medina. The gate opens onto a large open courtyard that leads into the 17th-century **Dar el-Makhzen**, the former sultan's palace and now a museum (closed Tuesday; Dr10).

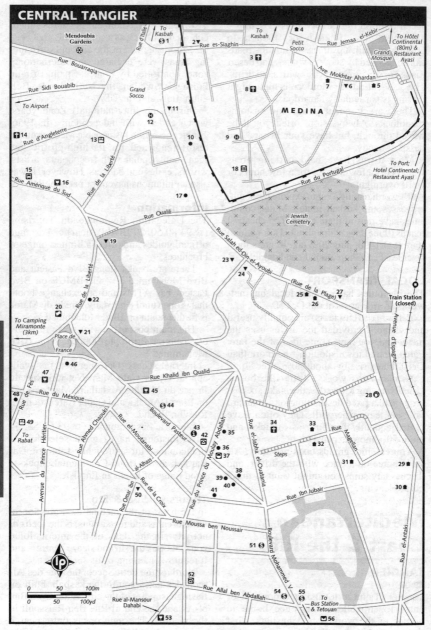

CENTRAL TANGIER

CENTRAL TANGIER

PLACES TO STAY	OTHER	39 Librairie des Colonnes
4 Pensión Mauritania	1 BMCE Bank (ATMs)	40 Avis
5 Hôtel Olid	3 Church of the Immaculate	41 Casa Pepé
7 Pension Palace	Conception	(Liquor Store)
25 Pensión Miami	8 Spanish Church	42 Telephone & Fax Office;
26 Pension le Détroit	9 Hammam	Cyber Espace Pasteur
29 Hôtel Marco Polo	10 Covered Market	43 Délégation Régionale
30 Youth Hostel	12 Hammam	du Tourisme
31 Hôtel Magellan	13 Cinéma Rif	44 BMCE (Late Bank
32 Ibn Batouta	14 St Andrew's Church	& ATMs)
33 El Muniria; Tangier Inn	15 Local Bus Terminal	45 Paname
	16 Dean's Bar	46 Royal Air Maroc
PLACES TO EAT	17 Covered Market	47 Hole-in-the-Wall
2 Restaurant Mamounia Palace	18 American Legation Museum	48 Depôt de Nuit
6 Restaurant Ahlan	20 French Consulate	(Night Pharmacy)
11 Restaurant Economique	22 British Airways office	49 Cinéma Le Paris
19 Restaurant Populaire	28 Petrol Station	51 Crédit du Maroc
21 Café de Paris	34 Church	52 Cyber Café
23 Sandwich Genève	35 Budget	Mam Net
24 Sandwich Cervantes	36 Limadet Boat Ticket Office	53 London Pub
27 Hassi Baida;	37 Trasmediterranea;	54 Banque Populaire
Restaurant Africa	Limadet Office	55 Wafabank
50 Pizzeria Piazza Capri	38 Iberia Airlines	56 Main Post Office

The **American Legation Museum** is a fine old building housing a fascinating collection of 17th to 20th-century paintings and prints, mostly focusing on Morocco. Knock on the door, it's open weekdays. Entrance is free.

Places to Stay

Camping and Hostels *Camping Miramonte* (☎ 94 75 04) is in a pleasant location above Jew's Bay about 3km west of the centre. It costs Dr15 per adult, plus Dr10 to pitch a tent and Dr10 for a car. Turn left off Ave Hassan II on to Rue des USA then first right down a narrow street to the grey gates (it's a Dr10 petits taxi ride).

Beds cost Dr27 at the *Youth Hostel* (☎ 94 61 27, 8 Rue al-Antaki). Hot showers are Dr5.

Hotels – Medina There are numerous cheap hotels around the Petit Socco and along Ave Mokhtar Ahardan, which connects the Petit Socco and the port area, though many are occupied with refugees from West Africa. Most are basic, some have hot showers and singles/doubles cost around Dr40/80.

Two of the best are *Pension Palace* (☎ 93 61 28, 2 Ave Mokhtar Ahardan), and the *Hôtel Olid* (☎ 93 13 10) across the road. Basic rooms cost Dr40/80. The Palace's

rooms are small but spotless, and some surround a quiet courtyard. The Olid's rooms have cold showers.

A good choice on the Petit Socco is *Pensión Mauritania* (☎ 93 46 77). Clean rooms with washbasin cost Dr35 to Dr45 per person.

The wonderful and full-of-character *Hôtel Continental* (☎ 93 10 24, fax 93 11 43, 36 Dar Baroud) is perched above the port northeast of the centre. Singles/doubles go for Dr186/240 including breakfast.

Hotels – Ville Nouvelle Good value, and straight down the line, is *Pension Le Détroit* (☎ 93 48 38), whilst *Pensión Miami* (☎ 93 29 00) remains popular. Both charge Dr50/80 for singles/doubles in summer and both are on Rue Salah ed-Din el-Ayoubi.

There's a better selection of hotels up the steep and winding Rue Magellan. *Hôtel Magellan* (☎ 37 23 19) has reasonable rooms for Dr40/80, whilst farther up on the same street, are hotels *El Muniria* (☎ 93 53 37) and *Ibn Batouta* (☎ 93 93 11). The latter has recently been renovated and has immaculate *en suite* rooms (Dr120/200) and a roof cafe. William Burroughs wrote *Naked Lunch* while staying at the Muniria, which has characterful rooms, with shower, for Dr110/130.

The German-run *Hôtel Marco Polo* (☎ 94 11 24), Rue el-Antaki, has impeccable

MOROCCO

single/double rooms (Dr189/217) plus a restaurant and lively bar.

Places to Eat
Medina Down hill from the Hôtel Continental, *Restaurant Ayasi (7 Rue Dar el-Baroud),* unsigned, serves xcellent *bessara* (pea soup) in the morning for Dr5 and fish, chicken and tajines (Dr20) after 11 am. On the east side of the Grand Socco, the tiny stall-like *Restaurant Economique* serves harira, bessara and brochettes all day. *Restaurant Ahlan,* on Ave Mokhtar Ahardan, is popular for lunch and light evening meals.

North of the Petit Socco, *Restaurant Andalus (7 Rue Commerce)* is a pleasant hole-in-the-wall serving great, cheap meals including liver (Dr35) and swordfish (Dr45). *Restaurant Mamounia Palace (☎ 93 50 99)* on Rue es-Siaghin offers full 'Moroccan feasts', tour-group style (Dr100 a throw).

Ville Nouvelle For really cheap food and self-catering head to the covered *market* and food stalls close to the Grand Socco. The *Sandwich Cervantes* and *Sandwich Genève*, opposite each other on Rue Salah ed-Din el-Ayoubi, offer rolls filled with meat or fish and salad for Dr10.

Down the hill, *Restaurant Africa* and the adjacent *Hassi Baida* have set meals for Dr50 and main courses from Dr30. The Africa serves alcohol.

Restaurant Populaire, down the steps from Rue de la Liberté, is a local favourite serving excellent Moroccan food (especially fish dishes) at reasonable prices (Dr40). Don't miss it.

If you're desperate for western-style fast food, *Excel Food,* on Blvd Pasteur, isn't bad. *Pizzeria Piazza Capri (☎ 93 72 21, 2 Rue de la Croix)* makes a decent pizza for around Dr30.

A coffee at the ageing *Café de Paris,* on the Place de France, is a must.

Entertainment
Bars The famous *Dean's Bar*, Rue Amérique du Sud, has beer and tapas from Dr13. The *Tangier Inn*, on Rue Magellan, is full of Interzone history, while other colourful bars include the *Hole in the Wall* on Ave du Prince Héritier and the *Paname* (*15 Blvd Pasteur*).

London Pub, on Rue al-Mansour Dahabi, has live music every night and is a very civilised place. The much-reduced European gay population still frequents the beach bars south of town – the *Macumba*, *Miami Beach* and *Coco Beach*.

Getting There & Away
Most CTM buses leave from an office near the port entrance. Others leave from the bus station on Place Jamia el-Arabia, south of the centre (a Dr8 taxi ride away). Most non-CTM buses leave from here to hundreds of destinations. Regular CTM departures include Casablanca (Dr110, seven hours), Rabat (Dr83, 5½ hours), Tetouan (Dr13.50, one hour) and Fès (Dr85, six hours).

The only train station in operation in Tangier – Tangier Morora – is about 5km south-east of town. Trains from Tangier split at Sidi Kacem to Rabat (five hours), Casablanca (six hours) and Marrakesh (10½ hours), or to Meknès (five hours), Fès (six hours) and Oujda (12 hours). The only cheap *ordinaire* service south leaves at 10.30 pm. Four trains depart daily from Tanger Morora. The 7.15 am and 4.30 pm services go as far as Casa Voyageurs, the 10.30 am only goes as far as Sidi Kacem (where you can get connections as far as Marrakesh or west to Oujda via Fès and Meknès), whereas the 10.30 pm *ordinaire* service (with couchettes) goes as far as Marrakesh. Some second class fares include Rabat (Dr87, five hours), Casablanca (Dr74, Casa-Voyageurs, six hours), Meknès (Dr77, four hours), Fès (Dr93, five hours), Taza (Dr128, seven hours) and Oujda (Dr 197, 11 hours). The *ordinaire* service to Marrakesh takes about 10 hours and costs (Dr193/274) with a couchette, (Dr143/214) without (1st and 2nd-class fares shown).

Grands taxis leave from the bus station to Tetouan (Dr20), Asilah (Dr20) and Fnideq (Ceuta Frontier; Dr25).

If you're heading to Spain or Gibraltar by boat, buy tickets from virtually any travel agency or at the port. The Limadet and Trasmediterranea offices are on Rue du Prince du Moulay Abdallah.

TETOUAN
☎ 09
Tetouan's flavour is unmistakably Spanish-Moroccan – a result of its settlement by

Arab-Berber and Jewish refugees from Muslim Andalucía in the 16th century and subsequent occupation by the Spanish during the protectorate years. The cheerfully whitewashed and tiled houses of the medina are dramatically set against the brooding Rif Mountains.

Although it's well worth spending time here and the hustlers and touts have calmed down in recent years, be prepared for a little initial hassle.

Information

The tourist office (☎ 96 19 16) is at 30 Blvd Mohammed V. A branch of BMCE on Place Moulay el-Mehdi has an ATM. The Spanish Consulate (☎ 70 35 34) is beside the post office on Place Moulay el-Mehdi.

Good Internet access (Dr10 per hour) is offered at Cyber Primo, on Place Moulay el-Mehdi, and Cyber World (8 Salah Eddine Al Ayoubi).

Things to See

Place Hassan II, the town's showpiece, links the old and new parts of the city. Some fine 19th-century houses can be found in the area towards Bab el-Okla, the eastern gate. Just inside Bab el-Okla, the excellent **Musée Marocain** (closed Tuesday; Dr10) has some well-presented exhibits of Moroccan and Andalucían life.

Just outside Bab el-Okla is the **Artisanat School**, where children learn traditional crafts (open weekdays; Dr10).

Also worthy of a visit is the **Archaeology Museum**, a small collection housed just off Place al-Jala. In the entrance porch you're greeted by a striking mosaic of the three Graces from the Roman ruins of Lixus, where most of the exhibits originate (open weekdays; Dr10).

Places to Stay

The nearest camping ground is *Camping Alboustane* (☎ 68 88 22) on the beach at Martil, 8km away.

Pension Iberia (☎ 96 36 79), above the BMCE bank on Place Moulay el-Mehdi, has single/double rooms for Dr40/70. Hot showers are Dr5.

The *Hôtel Cosmopolita* (☎ 96 48 21, 3 Rue du Prince Sidi Mohammed), is good value, clean and tidy. Rooms are Dr35/70 (hot showers cost Dr7).

Places to Eat

El Yesfi Snack, on Rue ben Tachfine does great baguettes with various meats, chips and salad which cost Dr16.

Restaurant Saigon on Rue Mohammed ben Larbi Torres, is good value though there's nothing Vietnamese about it – tajine etc, Dr30. Also popular is the licensed *Restaurant Restinga*, off Blvd Mohammed V.

Getting There & Away

The long-distance bus station is at the junction of Rue Sidi Mandri and Rue Moulay Abbas. There are CTM buses to Casablanca (Dr105, seven hours), Chefchaouen (Dr16.50, 11½ hours, five daily), Fès (Dr68, five hours), Rabat (Dr80, 5½ hours) and Tangier (Dr13, one hour, twice daily). Many other companies have buses to these and other destinations, including Marrakesh (Dr130).

A local bus to Martil (Dr2.50) leaves from Rue Moulay Abbas, close by.

Grands taxis to Chefchaouen (Dr25) and Tangier (Dr20) leave from Rue al-Jazeer. Taxis for Ceuta (Dr15) leave from the corner of Rue Mourakah Anual and Rue Sidi Mandri. The border is open 24 hours, but transport dries up after 7 pm.

CHEFCHAOUEN

Formally called Chaouen (or Xauen by the Spanish), this is a delightful town in the Rif Mountains and a favourite with travellers. The air is cool and clear, and the atmosphere friendly and relaxed.

Founded by Moulay Ali ben Rachid in 1471, the town prospered with the arrival of Muslim refugees from Spain. They gave the town its unique Hispanic look of whitewashed houses, though the blue that the town is so famous for only dates back to the 1930s – before then doors and window frames were a traditional Muslim green.

Information

The post office and two banks (no ATMs) are on the main street, Ave Hassan II.

Groupe Chaouni Info offer the cheapest Internet access (D10 to Dr20 per hour). Internet Cafe Sefiani Network on Ave Tarik Tetouan costs Dr30 per hour.

Things to See & Do

The old **medina** is easy to navigate – all painted streets are dead-ends. Many of the weaving looms, once so common, are now gone, although you may see a few crammed into tiny ground-floor rooms at the north end of town.

Numerous cafes surround the shady and cobbled **Plaza Uta el-Hammam** which is dominated by the 15th century **kasbah** (entry to the museum and gardens is Dr10) and **Great Mosque**.

The lively **market** in the new town is held on Monday and Thursday.

The mountains surrounding the town provide some excellent trekking. Contact the president of the Association Randonnée et Culture at Casa Hassan (☎ 98 81 96) for further information.

Places to Stay

On the side of the hill, north of the Hôtel Asma are the *camping ground* (very pleasant) and *hostel* (poor). They're a steep 30-minute walk (follow the signs to the hotel) from town. Call ☎ 98 69 79 for both places. Sleeping out under the stars in the camp site costs Dr 10.

The cheap hotels are in the medina. The best of the bunch is probably *Pensión La Castellana* (☎ 98 62 95, 4 Sidi Ahmed el-Bouhali), just off the western end of Plaza Uta el-Hammam. Singles/doubles cost Dr30/60, including hot showers. *Pension Mauritania* (☎ 98 61 84, 15 Zankat Qadi Alami) remains popular and *Pension Znika* (☎ 98 66 24, 4 Rue Znika) is clean, light and airy. Both charge Dr30 per person.

North-east of Plaza de Makhzen is the *Hostel Gernika* (☎ 98 74 34), run by two Spanish women. It has nine beautifully furnished doubles (with showers) for Dr120.

Places to Eat

At the small restaurants and cafes on Plaza Uta el-Hammam, a full meal costs Dr20 to Dr30.

On the north side of Plaza de Makhzen, a hole-in-the-wall *restaurant* serves excellent bessara for Dr5. There are often stalls selling soup (Dr3) or snails (Dr2 for a bowl of the slippery suckers) in Plaza Uta el-Hammam or just outside Bab al-'Ain (the main gate). The *Restaurant Assada*, just inside Bab al-'Ain to the north, is another tiny local spot offering good-value standards (about Dr18). Outside the medina, and up from the

Bab al-'Ain, are the popular and reasonable *Restaurant Moulay Ali ben Rachid* and *Restaurant Zouar*.

For a splurge (Dr50 for three courses!) try *Salon Aladin* or *Restaurant Tissemlal*. Both are up a side street off Plaza Uta el-Hammam.

Getting There & Away

The bus station is a 20-minute walk southwest of the old town centre. Many buses (especially to Fès) are through services that are often full. Give yourself a fighting chance and book a seat in advance.

If you can't get a bus to Fès (Dr52, 4½ hours), try the Ouezzane bus (Dr15, 1½ hours), then catch an ongoing bus or a grand taxi on to Fès. There are also buses that go to Tetouan, Ceuta, Tangier, Rabat and Casablanca.

Grands taxis to Tetouan (Dr25) leave from just off Plaza Mohammed V. Taxis heading to Ouezzane (Dr25) and points south and east leave from Ave Abdallah.

Spanish Morocco

Ceuta and Melilla came under Spanish control during the 16th and 15th centuries respectively. Today about 70% of their inhabitants are Spanish. Morocco occasionally tries half-heartedly to reclaim the cities, but Rabat is not keen to rock the boat as Spain and the EU are increasingly important trading partners.

Travellers come here mainly for ferry services to and from Spain but they are also tranquil places for the travel weary. Visa requirements are the same as for Spain. Don't forget that these enclaves keep Spanish, not Moroccan time and have cheap, tax-free goods (including petrol). For details on exchange rates for the Spanish peseta, see the Spain chapter.

CEUTA

☎ 956

Known as Sebta in Morocco, Ceuta offers a couple of day's distraction (the **Museo de la Legión**, on Paseo de Colón, is worth a look) but it's expensive. If you're heading for Morocco, you could catch an early fast-ferry from Algeciras and continue through to Tetouan or Chefchaouen.

Information

The tourist office (☎ 50 14 01) is near the end of Avenida Muelle Cañonero Dato, beside the dock. It can also provide brochures, good maps and an accommodation list (closed Sunday).

Plenty of banks, with ATMs, line the main street, Paseo de Revellín, and its continuation, Calle Camoens. You can buy dirham at the border if you have cash.

Places to Stay

Finding somewhere to stay in Ceuta can be a nightmare, so try and book in advance. Places are marked by a blue-and-white F (for *fondas* or inn) or CH (for *casas de huéspedes* or boarding house) signs. Prices are subject to 3% tax.

The best value is the small *Pensión Charito* (☎ 51 39 82, 5 Calle Arrabal), a 15-minute walk along the waterfront from the ferry terminal. Basic singles/doubles are 1500/2000 ptas (cold showers only).

Or try *Pensión Revellín* (☎ 51 67 62, 2 Paseo de Revellín) where rooms cost 1200/2200 ptas. *Pensión La Bohemia* (☎ 51 06 15, 16 Paseo de Revellín) charges 2000/3000 ptas for fresh, clean rooms. Both have hot showers.

Getting There & Away

The No 7 bus runs between Plaza de la Constitución and the *frontera* (frontier; 75 ptas, 20 minutes). If you want to head for the border after coming straight off the ferry, there's a No 7 stop just up from the tourist office on Calle Edrisis, opposite the ramparts.

Once through the border, there are plenty of grands taxis to Tetouan (Dr15 a seat, two hours).

The ferry terminal is 800m west of the town centre. There are frequent fast-ferry (hydrofoil), and cheaper ferry departures to Algeciras. Two hydrofoil services per day head to Malaga.

MELILLA
☎ 952

Smaller but more run down than Ceuta, Melilla retains a lingering fascination because of its medieval fortress – impressive renovations were taking place at the time of writing. Until the end of the 19th century, almost all of Melilla was contained within these massive walls.

Information

There's a well-stocked tourist desk (☎ 67 54 44) in the Palicio de Congresos y Exposiciones, on Calle Fortuny. Most of the banks (with ATMs) are on Avenida de Juan Carlos I Rey, and you can buy and sell dirham.

There's a Banque Populaire branch on the Moroccan side of the border – cash only.

Places to Stay

Be warned, accommodation in Melilla is expensive. Cheapest, if a little rough and ready, is *Pensión del Puerto,* off Avenida General Macías. A bed should cost 1500 ptas. *Hostal Residencia Rioja* (☎ 68 27 09, 10 Calle Ejército Español) has bright, basic singles/doubles for 3500/4500 ptas. Both have hot showers.

Getting There & Away

No 2 bus runs from Plaza de España to the border (75 ptas) every 30 minutes from 7.30 am to 10 pm. On the Moroccan side there are frequent buses (Dr2.20) and grands taxis to Nador (Dr4) until about 8 pm.

Trasmediterranea runs daily ferries to Malaga and Almería. Buy your tickets at their office on Plaza de España or in the ferry terminal. Spanish rail and coach tickets can be booked at travel agents in town. Also check out flights to Malaga.

The Middle Atlas

MEKNÈS
☎ 05

Although a town of considerable size even in the 13th century, Meknès didn't reach its peak until Moulay Ismail, the second Alawite sultan, made it his capital in 1672 and built an enormous palace complex. An earthquake in 1755 severely damaged Meknès and the city was allowed to decay until recently, when its tourism potential was recognised and major restoration begun. If you have time, Meknès is worth a day or so on the way to/from Fès.

Information

The tourist office (☎ 52 44 26) is near the main post office facing Place de France.

Banks with ATMs are concentrated in the ville nouvelle. BMCE operates a bureau de change on Ave des Forces Armées Royales

(FAR; opposite the Hôtel Volubilis), 10 am to 2 pm and 4 to 8 pm daily.

Club Internet, next door to the Hotel Continental, and Winword Internet next to Pizza Fongue charge Dr10 per hour.

Things to See

Unless otherwise noted, these sights are open 9 am to noon and 3 to 6 pm daily.

The focus of the old city is the massive, highly decorated **Bab el-Mansour**, the main entrance to Moulay Ismail's 17th-century **Imperial City**. The gate faces Place el-Hedim, where storytellers and musicians gather in the evening. On the north side of the square is the **Dar Jamaï Museum** (Wednesday to Monday; Dr10), housed in a beautiful 19th-century palace with traditional ceramics, jewellery and textiles.

The easiest access to the **medina** is through the arch immediately to the left of the museum. The covered main street leads to the **Grand Mosque** and the 14th-century **Medersa Bou Inania**, an Arabic theology college.

For the Imperial City, follow the road through the gate, round from Bab el-Mansour, through the *mechouar* (a parade ground where Moulay Ismail reviewed his famed black regiments), to the small, white **Koubbat as-Sufara'**, where foreign ambassadors were once received. Beside it is the entrance to a huge underground granary.

Opposite and a little to the left, through another restored gate, is the **Mausoleum of Moulay Ismail**, one of the few functioning Islamic monuments open to non-Muslims (free entry).

From the tomb, the road leads into a long, walled corridor flanking the **Dar el-Makhen**, now the King's residence (closed to visitors). Follow the road around and, beyond the camp site, look for the spectacular **Heries-Souani**, built as a granary. The storerooms are impressive in size, and wells for drawing water can still be seen. Above is a pleasant rooftop cafe.

Places to Stay

Camping There's a good, shady camp site, *Camping Agdal* (☎ 55 18 28), near the Heri es-Souani, priced at Dr17 per person, Dr10 for a tent and Dr7 for hot showers. It's a long walk from the transport hubs so take a taxi (about Dr12).

Hostel The *hostel* (☎ 52 46 98) is close to the Hôtel Transatlantique in the ville nouvelle. It's open 8 to 10 am, noon to 3pm, and 6 to 10 pm Monday to Saturday; 10 am to 6 pm on Sunday. A dorm bed costs Dr27. Family rooms are Dr30 per person.

Hotels In the medina, *Hôtel Maroc* (☎ 53 00 75), on Rue Rouamzine, has quiet, clean rooms around a flowered courtyard for Dr60/120. *Hôtel Regina* (☎ 53 02 80), Rue Dar Smen, is a biggish place with rooms around a central, covered courtyard from Dr60 to Dr150.

One of the best in the ville nouvelle is *Hotel Toubkal*. Rooms with balcony are clean, bright and a reasonable Dr50/90.

Across the road, *Hotel Continental* (☎ 52 54 71, 92 Ave des FAR) has bright rooms, some with shower for Dr110/140; or Dr140/160 with full bathroom.

Places to Eat

In the old town a number of simple restaurants along Rue Dar Smen serve cheap standard fare. The aptly named *Restaurant Économique* at No 123 is good, as is *Snack Bounana* in a square near the medersa.

There are a few cheap eats and rotisseries along Ave Mohammed V and on the roads leading to the train station. Try *Marhaba Restaurant*, a tiled place on Ave Mohammed V, and *Boveda* next to the Excelsior; both of these have tajine for Dr30. If you're after pizza (Dr20) head for *Pizza Fongue* on Zankat Accra.

More upmarket, *Pizzeria Le Four,* on Rue Atlas, off Mohammed V, is a licensed and popular Italian restaurant. Pizza costs from Dr40 (plus 14% tax). Opposite, the *Montana* has a bar.

There is a *market* in the ville nouvelle and a shop selling alcohol.

Getting There & Away

The CTM bus station is on Ave des FAR near the junction with Ave Mohammed V. The main bus station (where CTM buses also stop) is just outside Bab el-Khemis, west of medina. Destinations include Agadir, Casablanca (four hours), Chefchaouen (five hours), Fès (one hour), Marrakesh, Rabat, Tangier (six hours) and Tetouan. Grands taxis to the same destinations and Moulay Idriss (Dr7) also leave from here.

The main train station is on Ave du Sénégal. El-Amir Abdelkader station, parallel to Ave Mohammed V, is more convenient. All trains to Fès (one hour), Oujda (6½ hours), Casablanca (4½ hours), Rabat (2¼ hours) and Marrakesh (seven hours) stop here.

AROUND MEKNÈS

Volubilis (Oualili in Arabic) Volubilis, 33km from Meknès, has the best-preserved Roman ruins in Morocco, dating from the 2nd and 3rd centuries AD. The site is noted for its mosaic floors, many of which have been left *in situ*.

Volubilis is open from sunrise to sunset daily (Dr20). To get there, take a grand taxi (Dr7) or bus (Dr6) from Place de la Foire in Meknès and hop out at the turn-off to Moulay Idriss. From there it's a pleasant half-hour walk along the main road. Going back, you can hitch or walk to Moulay Idriss and wait for a bus or taxi.

FÈS

☎ 05

Fès is the oldest of Morocco's imperial cities and has been the capital of Morocco on several occasions. Fassis, the people of Fès, justifiably look on their city as the cultural and spiritual capital of Morocco.

The medina of Fès el-Bali (Old Fès) is one of the largest surviving medieval cities in the world. Its narrow, winding alleys and covered bazaars are crammed with craft workshops, restaurants, mosques, medersas, markets and extensive dye pits and tanneries. The exotic smells, the hammering of metal workers, the call of the muezzin and the jostling crowds all make for an unforgettable experience.

Orientation & Information

Fès consists of three distinct parts. The original walled city of Fès el-Bali lies to the east. South-west is the French-built ville nouvelle with most of the restaurants and hotels. Between the two is the Merenid walled city of Fès el-Jdid.

The ONMT office (☎ 62 34 60) is on Place de la Résistance in the ville nouvelle.

Official guides (including nine women), at Dr120/150 for a half/full day are available from here or through hotels. Plenty of unofficial guides hang around and will guide you for a lot less.

The main post office is in the ville nouvelle, as are most banks with ATMs. Fès has dozens of Internet cafes charging Dr10 per hour. Try Club Internet, east of the post office, on Rue des Mérinides.

Things to See

Fès el-Bali The most convenient entry point to the walled medina is Bab Bou Jeloud, the main western gate. Unfortunately, many of the religious sites and monuments are closed to non-Muslims, for those that aren't entry costs Dr10.

Just in from the bab is the **Medersa Bou Inania**, built by the Merenid sultan Bou Inan between 1350 and 1357. It's open to non-Muslims from 8 am to 5 pm daily, except at prayer times.

In the guts of the city is the **Kairaouine Mosque**, one of the largest mosques in Morocco. Founded between 859 and 862 for refugees from Tunisia, it has one of the finest libraries in the Muslim world.

Nearby, the **Medersa el-Attarine**, built by Abu Said in 1325, displays some particularly beautiful Merenid craftsmanship. Open daily.

On the boundary between Fès el-Bali and Fès el-Jdid, is the interesting **Dar Batha** (Musée du Batha) on Place de l'Istiqlal. Built as a palace over 100 years ago, it houses historical and artistic artefacts from ruined or decaying medersas, as well as Fassi embroidery, tribal carpets and ceramics. Open everyday except Tuesday.

Fès el-Jdid The other walled city, built by the Merenids in the 13th century, has an old Jewish quarter (mellah) and a couple of mosques and synagogues (one with a **museum**), but is less interesting than Fès el-Bali.

The grounds of the **Dar el-Makhzen** (Royal Palace) comprise 80 hectares of pavilions, medersas, mosques and pleasure gardens closed to the public.

At the northern end of the main street, Sharia Moulay Suleiman, is the enormous **Bab Dekkaken**, formerly the main entrance to the royal palace. Between it and Bab Bou Jeloud are the **Bou Jeloud Gardens**, through which flows Oued Fès, the city's main water source.

Borj Nord & Merenid Tombs For a spectacular view of Fès, walk or taxi up to the

MOROCCO

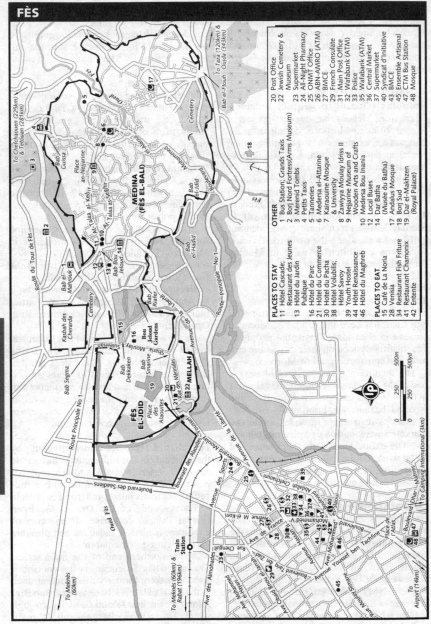

FÈS

MEDINA
(FÈS EL-BALI)

FÈS
EL-JDID

22 MELLAH

PLACES TO STAY
11 Hôtel Cascade;
   Restaurant des Jeunes
13 Hôtel du Jardin
   Publique
16 Hôtel du Parc
21 Hôtel du Commerce
30 Hôtel du Pacha
38 Hôtel Volubilis;
   Hôtel Savoy
39 Youth Hostel
44 Hôtel Renaissance
46 Hôtel du Maghreb

PLACES TO EAT
15 Café de La Noria
28 Venisia
34 Restaurant Fish Friture
41 Restaurant Chamonix
42 Entente

OTHER
1 Bus Station; Grands Taxis
2 Borj Nord Fortress(Arms Museum)
3 Merenid Tombs
4 Petits Taxis
5 Tanneries
6 Medersa el-Attarine
7 Kairaouine Mosque
  & University
8 Zawiyya Moulay Idriss II
9 Nejjarine Museum of
  Wooden Arts and Crafts
10 Medersa Bou Inania
12 Local Buses
14 Dar Batha
   (Musée du Batha)
17 Andalus Mosque
18 Borj Sud
19 Dar el-Makhzen
   (Royal Palace)
20 Post Office
22 Jewish Cemetery &
   Museum
23 Supermarket
24 All-Night Pharmacy
25 ONMT Office
26 ABN-AMRO (ATM)
27 BMCE
29 French Consulate
31 Main Post Office
32 Wafabank (ATM)
33 Police
35 Wafabank (ATM)
36 Central Market
37 Supermarket
40 Syndicat d'Initiative
43 BMCE
45 Ensemble Artisanal
47 CTM Bus Station
48 Mosque

Borj Nord fortress and Merenid Tombs. The whole of Fès lies at your feet. The 16th-century borj, built by Saadian sultan Ahmed al-Mansour, houses the **Arms Museum**. The tombs are mostly ruins but dramatic against the city backdrop. Don't come here alone too early or late, there have been some reports of attacks on solo sightseers. Open daily except Tuesday.

Places to Stay

Camping The well-maintained *Camping International* (☎ 73 14 39) is about 3km from town on the Sefrou and has great facilities including a pool and bar. It costs Dr40 adult, plus Dr30 per tent and Dr30 per car. Bus No 38 from Place Atlas passes here.

Hostel The *Youth Hostel* (☎ 62 40 85, 18 Rue Abdeslam Serghini) is a small, clean place with TV and hot showers. It costs Dr45/55 (non-members Dr50/60) in dormitory/two-bed accommodation with breakfast. Open 8 to 10 am, noon to 3 pm and 6 to 10 pm daily.

Hotels – Medina The most colourful hotels are around Bab Bou Jeloud at the entrance to Fès el-Bali. They are basic and not all have showers (cold), but there are hammams all over.

Hôtel du Jardin Publique (☎ 63 30 86) outside the gate, down an alley, has clean, large singles/doubles (a couple with balconies) for Dr40/60.

Inside the gate, *Hôtel Cascade* (☎ 63 84 42) has simple rooms for Dr40/60. There are two roof terraces and usually a trickle of hot water.

Staying in Fès el-Jdid doesn't offer the full-on medina buzz, but it's central. Closest to Bab Bou Jeloud is *Hôtel du Parc* with rooms at Dr30/50. The best place is *Hôtel du Commerce,* on Place des Alaouites. Simple, spotless rooms, some with balconies, cost Dr40/60.

Hotels – Ville Nouvelle The central *Hôtel Renaissance* (☎ 62 21 93, 29 Rue Abdel el-Khattabi) is an old, dark, cavernous place but remains popular. Clean rooms, some with balcony, cost Dr50/80. There's a cold shower and a terrace.

Brighter and cleaner, *Hôtel du Maghreb* (☎ 62 15 67, 25 Ave Mohammed es-Slaoui)

has rooms with brass bed and balcony for Dr50/80 and hot shower for Dr10.

Closer to the student area is *Hôtel Savoy* (☎ 62 06 08) on Blvd Abdallah Chefchaouni. Reasonably clean, airy rooms with wash basins cost from Dr50 to Dr120. The showers are usually hot (Dr10).

Around the corner, *Hôtel Volubilis* has brightly decorated rooms from Dr30 per person. Those on the terrace and with balconies for Dr70 are better.

Places to Eat

There are *supermarkets* near the train station and opposite the central market.

There are plenty of snack stands in the popular Bab Bou Jeloud area, where you can get a filling roll for about Dr10. The *Restaurant des Jeunes*, near the Hotel Cascade, has simple meals for around Dr50.

In the ville nouvelle there are a few cheap eats around Blvd Mohammed V and the central market. On Ave de France, the popular *Venisia* is one of the best snack bars in town.

For a more substantial meal, *Restaurant Chamonix*, a block south of the market, offers the usual (set menu Dr50) plus pizzas. Nearby, on Blvd Mohammed V, the pleasant *Restaurant Fish Friture* serves cheap, good seafood and pizzas from Dr40.

For a splurge (Dr100 to Dr200 per head), try one of the traditional restaurants set in centuries-old buildings in the medina.

For a peaceful cup of coffee or tea, the *Café de la Noria* in the Bou Jeloud Gardens is unbeatable.

In the ville nouvelle, there are heaps of cafes and patisseries – take your pick. *Entente* (85 Blvd Mohammed V) is a good place.

Getting There & Away

Bus CTM buses (☎ 73 23 84) originate at the bus station at Place Baghdadi, near Bab Bou Jeloud, and call in at the CTM station on Blvd Dhar Mahres, near the mosque in the ville nouvelle, half an hour later.

There are daily departures to Agadir, Casablanca (five hours) via Rabat (3½ hours) and Meknés (one hour), Ouarzazate via Erfoud and Rissani, Marrakesh (nine hours), Oujda (six hours), Tangier (six hours), and Tetouan (five hours).

Train The train station is in the ville nouvelle, 10 minutes' walk from the town centre.

MOROCCO

There are daily departures to Casablanca (5½ hours), via Rabat (3½hours) and Meknès (one hour), Oujda (six hours), Marrakesh (eight hours), and Tangier (five hours).

Taxi Grands taxis to Casablanca (Dr100), Meknès (Dr15) and Rabat (Dr60) leave from the bus station.

Getting Around
Bus Fès has good local bus services (around Dr2) although they are like sardine cans at times. Useful routes include:

No 9 Place de l'Atlas-Ave Hassan II-Dar Batha
No 12 Bab Bou Jeloud-Bab Guissa-Bab el-Ftouh
No 16 Train Station-Airport
No 47 Train Station-Bab Bou Jeloud

Taxi You can expect to pay about Dr10 for a (red) petits taxi from the train station to Bab Bou Jeloud. Only grands taxis go out to the airport (Dr80).

TAZA
☎ 05
Taza overlooks the Taza Gap – the only feasible pass between the Rif Mountains and the Middle Atlas. If you have your own transport, then a drive around **Mt Tazzeka**, with a visit to the incredible caverns of the **Gouffre du Friouato**, is recommended. In Taza itself, the medina is relaxed and worth a wander.

Places to Stay & Eat
In the medina, the basic but cheerful *Hôtel de l'Étoile* (☎ 27 01 79), on Moulay el-Hassan, has showerless rooms with fireplaces and brass beds for Dr35.

In the centre of the new town (about 3km from the medina), the *Hôtel Guillaume Tell* (☎ 67 23 47) offers big rooms for Dr40/60. Showers are cold.

The *Hôtel du Dauphiné* (☎ 67 35 67), Place de l'Indépendance, is an attractive colonial-style place with a restaurant and lively bar. En suite rooms cost Dr130/165.

The best of Taza's few eateries is *Restaurant Majestic* on Ave Mohammed V, near the hotels. You can eat well for around Dr30.

Getting There & Away
Buses and grands taxis leave for Fès, Tangier, Nador and Oujda several times a day from a lot near the station on the Fès-Oujda road. The CTM terminal is on Place de l'Indépendance, more convenient for the hotels. There are daily trains to Casablanca via Fès, Meknès and Rabat, as well as to Marrakesh and Tangier.

The Atlantic Coast

RABAT
☎ 07
Rabat's role as Morocco's capital dates from the days of the French protectorate. Today few of Rabat's people are involved in the tourist trade, it's a relaxed, sophisticated place and worth visiting for a few days.

Information
The ONMT office (☎ 73 05 62) is inconveniently located on Rue al-Abtal in Agdal, west of the city (take bus No 3 from Blvd Hassan II). Banks are concentrated along Ave Mohammed V (many with ATMs and exchange kiosks).

The post office is on Ave Mohammed V, and téléboutiques are found all over town. Wave Cyber Cafe (53 Allal Ben Abdellah) and INT Plus on Ave Mohammed V, charge around Dr10 per hour.

Things to See
Follow Rue Souika then north up Rue des Consuls (where there's an informal morning carpet souk on Tuesday and Thursday) to reach the **Kasbah des Oudaias**, built out on the bluff overlooking the Atlantic Ocean. It houses the **Museum of Moroccan Arts** (open daily, Dr10). The main entrance is via the impressive **Almohad Bab Oudaia** gate, built in 1195.

Rabat's most famous landmark is the **Tour Hassan**, the incomplete minaret (ruined in a 1755 earthquake) of the great mosque begun by Yacoub al-Mansour. On the same site is the **Mausoleum of Mohammed V**, dedicated to the present King's grandfather.

Beyond the city walls, at the end of Ave Yacoub el-Mansour, are the remains of the ancient Roman city of Sala, which subsequently became the independent Berber city of **Chellah** and then later still the Merenids' royal burial ground. Entry is Dr10.

If you're after something completely different, learn to surf at **Oudayas Surf Club**

(☎ 26 06 83). The stylish club house is perched above the Atlantic west of the kasbah.

Places to Stay

At Salé beach, and well signposted, is *Camping de la Plage (☎ 84 45 66)*, Dr15 per person, Dr18 for a two-person tent and Dr12 per car. It's Dr10 for power and water.

The *youth hostel (☎ 72 57 69, 43 Rue Marassa)*, opposite the walls of the medina, is pleasant and costs Dr32 per night. There are cold showers, but no cooking facilities.

Hôtel d'Alger (☎ 72 48 29, 34 Rue Souk Semara) is about the cheapest, reasonable deal in the medina (singles/doubles Dr35/70). However, *Hôtel Al Maghrib Al Jadid (☎ 73 22 07, 2 Rue Sebbahi)* is more geared towards travellers – clean, bright rooms cost Dr50/80. Hot showers are Dr5.

Numerous cheapies are found near the Central Market, but in a league of its own is *Hôtel Dorhmi (☎ 72 38 98, 313 Ave Mohammed V)*. Comfortable rooms will cost Dr80/100; hot showers Dr7.

In the ville nouvelle, *Hôtel Mamounia (☎ 72 44 79, 10 Rue de la Mamounia)* has simple rooms for Dr50/90, some with balconies; hot showers cost Dr5. Don't be put off by the entrance.

Places to Eat

There's a group of small restaurants under a common roofed area just off Blvd Hassan II, west of the Central Market. At the popular *Café de la Jeunesse*, you can get a full meal of kebabs, chips, salad and bread for Dr25. However, the tajines across the street at *Café Restaurant Afrique du Nord* have the edge (Dr25) and the harira is good and cheap (Dr3.50).

Just along the road, *Restaurant de la Libération* does meat or fish, with chips and veg (or couscous on Fridays) for Dr29.

Getting There & Away

Bus The bus station is inconveniently situated 5km from the centre of town so take a local bus (No 30) or Petits taxi (Dr15).

CTM and cheaper non-CTM buses leave for most destinations including Casablanca, Chefchaouen, Fès, Tangier, Tetouan and Marrakesh.

Train Rabat Ville train station is centrally located on Ave Mohammed V. Don't get off at Rabat Agdal station. There are 23 trains to Casablanca (Dr27, 50 minutes) and daily departures to Tangier (5½ hours), Meknès and Fès (four hours) and Marrakesh (4½ hours).

Taxi Grands taxis for Casablanca (Dr27) leave from outside the main bus station. Taxis for Fès (Dr55), Meknès (Dr40) and Salé (Dr3) leave from near the Hôtel Bou Regreg on Blvd Hassan II.

AROUND RABAT

In **Salé** you can experience the sights, smells and sounds of the Morocco of yesteryear without the tourist hordes. The main sight inside the walls is the classic Merenid **medersa** built in 1333 next to the grand mosque (Dr10).

Grands taxis to Rabat (Dr3) leave from Bab Mrisa. Bus No 16 also links the two, or catch the small boats across the river below Bab Bou Haja.

CASABLANCA
☎ 02

Morocco's largest city has a long history. It was colonised by the Portuguese in the 16th century (who stayed until 1755), but its renaissance came when the resident-general of the French protectorate, Lyautey, developed Casablanca giving it the wide boulevards, public parks and imposing Mauresque civic buildings (a blend of French colonial and traditional Moroccan styles).

Casablanca is cosmopolitan and an excellent barometer of liberal Islam, although central Casablanca can be seedy.

Information

Helpful ONMT (☎ 27 11 77, 55 Rue Omar Slaoui) is open weekdays. There's a Syndicat d'Initiative, at 98 Blvd Mohammed V.

BMCE branches with ATMs are on Ave Lalla Yacout and Ave des FAR. Crédit du Maroc, on Ave Mohammed V, will change travellers cheques and is open Saturday mornings. There are banks with ATMs at Mohammed V international airport.

American Express is represented by Voyages Schwartz (☎ 22 29 47), 112 Rue Prince Moulay Abdallah, and the main post office is on Place Mohammed V.

Internet access (about Dr20 per hour) is available at First Cyber (62 Rue Allah Ben Abdellah) and Euro Net (51 Rue Tata).

MOROCCO

Things to See

Don't miss the beautiful **Hassan II Mosque**, which overlooks the Atlantic Ocean just beyond the northern tip of the medina. Completed in 1993, it is the third biggest religious monument in the world and open to non-Muslims. Multi-language guided tours cost Dr100 per person (Dr50 for students) every day except Friday.

Casablanca's so-so **beaches** are west of town along Blvd de la Corniche in the suburb of 'Ain Diab. It's a trendy area and very crowded in summer. Bus No 9 goes to 'Ain Diab from Place Oued al-Makhazine, just to the west of Place des Nations Unies.

Places to Stay

About 5km south-west of town, on the main road to El-Jadida, is *Camping de l'Oasis* (☎ 23 42 57), which charges Dr10 per person, per tent and per car. Bus No 31 runs past it.

There's a *youth hostel* (☎ 22 05 51, fax 22 76 77, 6 Place de l'Amiral Philibert) in the medina, just off Blvd des Almohades. It's large, comfortable and clean and costs Dr45 per person including breakfast; double/triple rooms cost Dr120/180.

The hotels in the medina are unclassified, cheap and not up to much – there are better deals in the ville nouvelle.

Hôtel du Palais (☎ 27 61 21, 68 Rue Farhat Hachad) is good, clean and cheap. Spacious singles/doubles go for Dr62/76. Showers are cold.

Around the central market and near Rue Allal ben Abdallah, is a cluster of cheapies. *Hôtel Touring* (☎ 31 02 16, 87 Rue Allal ben Abdallah) has big, old rooms for Dr62/78 (Dr7 for a hot shower).

A good choice is friendly *Hôtel Colbert* (☎ 31 42 41, 38 Rue Chaoui), opposite the market. Simple rooms with washbasin go for Dr68/83 (hot showers cost Dr10). En suite rooms cost Dr84/100.

A little more upmarket is the welcoming *Hôtel Rialto* (☎ 27 51 22, 9 Rue Salah Ben Bouchaib). Spotless rooms with shower cost Dr84/120.

Places to Eat

There are a few cheap restaurants around the clock tower entrance to the medina, but of the numerous budget restaurants along Rue Chaoui *Restaurant Amine* stands out, with large portions of fresh seafood and good *pastilla* from Dr25.

In the market, on Blvd Mohammed V, are hosts of good *food stalls* (some even sell ham!).

La Bodéga (☎ 54 18 42, 129 Rue Allal Ben Abdallah) is a Spanish style tapas bar and restaurant. It's expensive but good fun with live music, and it's very woman friendly.

Getting There & Away

Bus The flash CTM bus station is on Rue Léon L'Africain with daily departures going all over the country. CTM also operates international services from here.

Aulad Ziane is the new bus station for almost all non-CTM services. It's bright and almost tranquil! However, it's about a Dr10 petit taxi ride away (or catch bus No 10 from Blvd Mohammed V).

Train Most long distance departures for destinations across the country leave from Casa-Voyageurs station, 4km east of the city centre (bus No 30 runs past it from Blvd Mohammed V; a petits taxi costs Dr10).

Rapide shuttle trains to Mohammed V Airport (Dr30, 38 minutes) and north to Rabat (Dr27, 50 minutes) leave from the central Casa-Port station, via Casa-Voyageurs.

Taxi Grands taxis to Rabat (Dr27) leave from Blvd Hassan Seghir, near the CTM bus station. A grand taxi to Mohammed V airport costs Dr150 (Dr200 after 8 pm).

Getting Around

You'll find plenty of petits taxis in Casablanca – just make sure the meter is on. Expect to pay Dr10 for a ride in or around the city centre.

SAFI

☎ 04

Safi (Asfi) is a modern Atlantic fishing port and industrial centre in a steep crevasse formed by the Oued Chabah. It has a lively walled medina and souq, with battlements dating from the brief Portuguese era – the **Qasr al-Bahr** (Castle on the Sea) is worth visiting.

The town is also well known for its pottery and the **National Ceramics Museum** can be found here. The museum is housed in the kechla, a massive defensive structure dominating the east end of the medina.

MOROCCO

Places to Stay

About 2km north of town, just off the coast road to El-Jadida, is *Camping International*. It's a shady site with a small swimming pool and costs Dr12 per person, Dr9 per car, Dr9 per tent and Dr10 for a hot shower.

There are some basic cheapies (from Dr30 per person) clustered around the port end of Rue du Souq and along Rue de R'bat.

Hôtel Majestic (☎ *46 40 11*), next to the medina wall at the junction of Ave Moulay Youssef and Place de l'Indépendance, is the best value. Rooms that are well-maintained and pleasant, with washbasin and bidet, start from Dr40. A hot shower is Dr5.

The two-star *Hôtel Anis* (☎ *46 30 78*), just off Rue de R'bat to the south of the medina, has comfortable singles/doubles with shower and toilet for Dr135/159.

Places to Eat

The hole-in-the-wall seafood restaurants in the alleys off Rue du Souq in the medina offer cheap, excellent food for about Dr20 a head. The *Restaurant de Safi*, on Rue de la Marine, offers reasonably priced brochettes and other Moroccan dishes. Almost next door, the *Restaurant Gegene* serves fish and Italian dishes.

The more expensive *Restaurant Le Refuge* (☎ *46 43 54*), a few kilometres north of Safi on the coast road to Sidi Bouzid, has a good reputation for seafood.

Getting There & Away

CTM and other companies share a terminal south-east of the town centre. There are regular departures to Casablanca and several to Marrakesh, Essaouira and Agadir. A couple of buses head north to El-Jadida. Some are through services from elsewhere, but you shouldn't have too much trouble on main runs.

ESSAOUIRA
☎ 04

Essaouira (pronounced esa-wee-ra) is one of Morocco's most popular coastal towns among independent travellers. Along with a magnificent beach (much appreciated by windsurfers), it has a pleasant laid-back atmosphere.

Essaouira's fortifications and brawny town walls are an interesting mix of Portuguese, French and Berber military architecture. Inside are tranquil squares, friendly cafes and small *thuya* woodcarving workshops.

Information

The Syndicat d'Initiative (☎ 47 50 80) is on Rue de Caire, just inside Bab as-Sebaa.

The post office is a 10-minute walk southeast from Place Prince Moulay Hassan; Cyberdrive on the same street charges Dr20 per hour for Internet access.

Crédit du Maroc, also on Place Prince Moulay Hassan, and Wafabank on Ave de l'stiqlal have ATMs.

Things to See & Do

You can walk along most of the **ramparts** on the seaward part of town and visit the two main *skalas* (forts) during daylight hours (Dr10).

The small **museum** (Dr10) on Darb Laalouj al-Attarin has displays of jewellery, costumes, weapons, musical instruments and carpets. Opening hours are 8.30 am to 6 pm Wednesday to Monday.

The **beach** stretches some 10km down the coast to the sand dunes of Cap Sim. It's possible to hire **windsurfing** gear in Essaouira – beware, the currents are strong.

There have been reports of tourists being attacked on remote sections of the beach, so take care.

Places to Stay

The best sea views are from the terraces of *Hôtel Civilisation des Remparts* (☎ *47 51 10, 18 Rue Ibn Rochd*) and *Hôtel Smara* (☎ *47 56 55, 26 Rue de la Skala*). Both have basic rooms around covered courtyards for Dr60/80, with a shared shower (Dr5).

Along Rue Ibn Rochd, *Hotel Majestic* (☎ *47 49 09*) charges Dr50/100 for bright, airy rooms with a shared shower (Dr5). It also has one of the highest panoramas in Essaouira from its terrace.

Residence Shahrazed (☎ *47 29 77, fax 47 64 36, 1 Rue Youssef El Fassi*), next door to the tourist office, charges Dr120/200 for rooms with bathroom, or a double is Dr100 without a bath.

Places to Eat

For snacks there are a few simple places along Rue Mohammed ben Abdallah, Rue Zerktouni and just inside Bab Doukkala.

MOROCCO

In the port area *Chez Sam* and *Le Coquillage* have set menus starting at Dr70. En route to the port you can eat an al fresco lunch at the cheap *fish grills* set up outdoors.

Getting There & Away
The bus terminal is 1km north-east of the town centre. CTM has regular buses to Agadir (three hours), Casablanca (6½ hours) and Marrakesh (2½ hours). Grands taxis to Agadir leave from a nearby lot.

Supratours (☎ 47 23 17) runs buses from near Bab Marrakesh to the Marrakesh train station and Agadir.

AGADIR
☎ 08
Agadir is a modern city, completely rebuilt after a devastating earthquake in 1960. Though one of the more expensive and least appealing resorts in Morocco (but it's popular with European package tourists), Agadir offers an escape from the restraints of everyday Moroccan life.

It's also a good take-off point for the coast and, to the east, the Atlas mountains. Bird-watchers will find a rewarding estuarine area just a few kilometres south of town.

Information
You'll find the ONMT tourist office (☎ 84 63 78) in the market just off Ave Prince Sidi Mohammed. There's also a Syndicat d'Initiative (☎ 84 03 07) on Blvd Mohammed V.

The main post and phone office is on Ave du Prince Moulay Abdallah, and there's another in Talborjt. Internet cafes, including AgadirNet, opposite the tennis club on Ave Hassan II, charge Dr10 to Dr15 per hour. There are numerous banks with ATMs.

Places to Stay & Eat
Campervans dominate at Agadir's *camp site* (☎ 84 66 83) on the port side of town. It charges Dr10/15 per adult/tent.

On noisy Rue Yacoub el-Mansour, *Hôtel Amenou* (☎ 84 15 56) has rooms for Dr65/80. *Hotel Tamri* (☎ 82 18 80, *1 Ave du Président Kennedy*) has a bright plant-filled courtyard and rooms with bathroom for Dr80/100.

There are snack stands on Rue Yacoub el-Mansour. On the roads leading up here are *restaurants* all offering good three-course menus for around Dr35.

Getting There & Away
CTM buses leave from Rue Yakoub el-Mansour daily for Casablanca, Essaouira, Marrakesh, Rabat, Tafraoute and Tangier.

The main bus terminal is actually located in Inezgane, 13km south of Agadir. If you arrive here jump in a grand taxi (Dr3) or local bus No 5/6 to Agadir.

TAROUDANNT
☎ 08
Taroudannt, with its magnificent red-mud walls, has played an important part in Morocco's history, and briefly was the capital under the Saadians in the 16th century.

Today, it's a pleasant place, with some nice accommodation options, to while away a few days. It also makes a base from which to explore the western High Atlas.

Things to See
You can explore the **ramparts** of Taroudannt by foot, bicycle (Dr5 per hour) or horse-drawn carriage (Dr35).

High-quality items abound in the Berber and Arab **souqs**, especially traditional jewellery, and there are large **markets** held outside the ramparts on Thursday and Sunday. Some modest **tanneries** lie just beyond Bab Taghount, north-west of the centre, Place Assarag.

North of Place Talmoklate, there are banks with ATMs, post offices and Internet access (try Infonet which charges Dr10 per hour).

Places to Stay & Eat
There are plenty of cheapies, around or close to Place Assarag. On the square, *Hotel Roudani* has rooms on a terrace for Dr40 including hot showers.

Hotel Mantaga (☎ 85 27 63) has a good terrace overlooking Place la Victoire, cold showers and rooms for Dr30/50.

The best deal is *Hotel Taroudannt* (☎ 85 24 16). Rooms gathered around a tranquil, leafy courtyard full of character and terraces cost Dr70/90 without bathroom or Dr100/120 with.

Small *restaurants* and *snack stands* line the street between Place Assarag and Place Talmoklate; try *Barcelone* on Place Assarag.

Getting There & Away
The SATAS and CTM offices are on Place Assarag, other companies and grands taxis

are based just outside Bab Zorgan, the southern gate. CTM has a morning bus to Casablanca via Agadir and an evening bus to Ouarzazate. SATAS buses go to Tata and Ourzazate. Local buses leave for Marrakesh via the spectacular Tizi n'Test pass.

The High Atlas

MARRAKESH
☎ 04

Marrakesh is one of Morocco's most important artistic and cultural centres. It was founded in 1062 by the Almoravid sultan Youssef bin Tachfin, but experienced its heyday under his son, Ali, who built the extensive *khettara* (underground irrigation canals) that still supply the city's gardens with water. Although Fès later gained in prominence, Marrakesh remained the southern capital until 1269.

The Saadians made Marrakesh the capital again in the 16th century and built the *mellah* (Jewish quarter), Mouassine mosque and the mosque of Ali ben Youssef. In the 17th century, Moulay Ismail moved the capital to Meknès, although Marrakesh remained an important base of power. The town was revitalised by the French and tourism has ensured its relative prosperity since then.

Orientation & Information
As in other major Moroccan towns, the ville nouvelle and the medina are separate entities.

The tourist office (☎ 44 88 89) is in the ville nouvelle on the Place Abdel Moumen ben Ali. Other offices can be found at 170 Ave Mohammed V and near La Mamounia.

There are plenty of ATMs and money-exchanges, some (ie, Bank Populaire near Djemaa el-Fna) open on Saturday mornings.

The main post office is on Place du 16 Novembre, in the ville nouvelle. There is a branch office (and a phone centre) on the Djemaa el-Fna. Internet places charge between Dr15 and Dr20 an hour.

Things to See
The focal point of Marrakesh is the **Djemaa el-Fna**, a huge square in the medina. Although lively at any time of day, it comes into its own in the late afternoon and evening, when rows of open-air food stalls

are set up and mouthwatering aromas fill the air. Musicians, snake charmers, magicians, acrobats and benign lunatics take over the rest of the space, along with hustlers, ageing water sellers and bewildered tourists.

The **souqs** of Marrakesh are some of the best in Morocco, producing a wide variety of high-quality crafts, and a fair amount of rubbish. High-pressure sales tactics are common and you should never believe a word you are told about the quality of most goods.

Koutoubia Mosque is the most famous landmark in Marrakesh (not open to non-Muslims). Built by the Almohads in the late 12th century, it's the best-preserved and oldest of the Almohads' three famous minarets, the other two being the Tour Hassan in Rabat and the Giralda in Seville (Spain).

The **Ali ben Youssef Medersa**, next to the mosque of the same name, was built by the Saadians in 1565 and contains some beautiful examples of stucco decoration. The largest theological college in the Maghreb, it once housed up to 900 students and teachers in small, bare dormitories (Dr10).

The **Palais de la Bahia** was built in the late 19th century as the residence of Bou Ahmed, the Grand Vizier of Sultan Moulay al-Hassan I. It's a rambling structure with fountains, gardens and shady courtyards. The palace is open daily and entry is free, but you must take (and pay) a guide.

Built about the same time and definitely worth a visit is the nearby Dar Si Said, now the **Museum of Moroccan Arts**. It served as a palace for Bou Ahmed's brother, Sidi Said, and houses collections of Berber jewellery, carpets, Safi pottery and leather work (closed Tuesday; Dr10).

Next door to the Kasbah Mosque are the **Saadian Tombs**. Sixty-six Saadians, including Al-Mansour, his successors and their closest family members, lie buried under the two main structures. The tombs are open daily (except Friday morning) for Dr10.

Special Events
The Festival of Folklore held in June attracts some of the best troupes in Morocco. In July the famous Fantasia features charging Berber horsemen outside the ramparts.

Places to Stay
Hostel The *Youth Hostel* (☎ 44 77 13), not far from the train station, costs Dr14

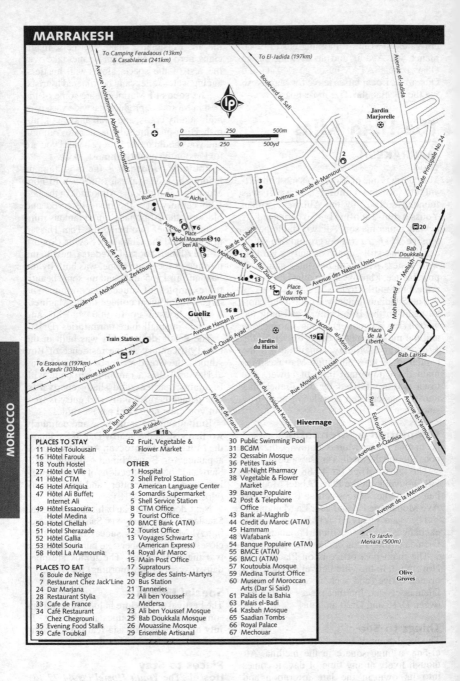

MARRAKESH

To Camping Feradaous (13km) & Casablanca (241km)

To El-Jadida (197km)

Jardin Marjorelle

Avenue Mohammed Abdelkrim el-Khattabi

Avenue el-Jadida

Route Principale No 24...

Boulevard de Safi

Avenue Yacoub el-Mansour

Rue Ibn Aicha

Avenue de France

Avenue Abdel Moumen ben Ali

Rue de la Liberté

Rue Tariq Ibn Zaid

Mohammed V

Bab Doukkala

Rue Mohammed el-Mellakh

Boulevard Mohammed Zerktouni

Avenue des Nations Unies

Avenue Moulay Rachid

Gueliz

Avenue Hassan II

Place du 16 Novembre

Train Station

Rue el-Quadi Ayad

Rue Ibn el-Quadi

Rue el-Jahed

Ave Yacoub al-Mini

Place de la Liberté

Jardin du Hartsi

Bab Larissa

To Essaouira (197km) & Agadir (303km)

Avenue Hassan II

Rue Echouhada

Avenue el-Yarmouk

Avenue du President Kennedy

Rue Moulay el-Hassan

Hivernage

Rue

Avenue de France

Avenue el-Qadissa

Avenue de la Ménara

To Jardin Menara (500m)

Olive Groves

PLACES TO STAY		OTHER	
11 Hotel Toulousain	62 Fruit, Vegetable & Flower Market	1 Hospital	30 Public Swimming Pool
16 Hôtel Farouk		2 Shell Petrol Station	31 BCdM
18 Youth Hostel		3 American Language Center	32 Qessabin Mosque
27 Hôtel de Ville	**OTHER**	4 Somardis Supermarket	36 Petites Taxis
41 Hôtel CTM		5 Shell Service Station	38 Vegetable & Flower Market
46 Hotel Afriquia		8 CTM Office	38 Vegetable & Flower Market
47 Hôtel Ali Buffet; Internet Ali		9 Tourist Office	39 Banque Populaire
49 Hôtel Essaouira; Hotel Medina		10 BMCE Bank (ATM)	42 Post & Telephone Office
50 Hotel Chellah		12 Tourist Office	43 Bank al-Maghrib
51 Hotel Sherazade		13 Voyages Schwartz (American Express)	44 Credit du Maroc (ATM)
52 Hôtel Gallia		14 Royal Air Maroc	45 Hammam
53 Hôtel Souria		15 Main Post Office	48 Wafabank
58 Hotel La Mamounia		17 Supratours	54 Banque Populaire (ATM)
		19 Eglise des Saints-Martyrs	55 BMCE (ATM)
PLACES TO EAT		20 Bus Station	56 BMCI (ATM)
6 Boule de Neige		21 Tanneries	57 Koutoubia Mosque
7 Restaurant Chez Jack'Line		22 Ali ben Youssef Medersa	59 Medina Tourist Office
24 Dar Marjana		23 Ali ben Youssef Mosque	60 Museum of Moroccan Arts (Dar Si Said)
28 Restaurant Stylia		25 Bab Doukkala Mosque	61 Palais de la Bahia
33 Cafe de France		26 Mouassine Mosque	62 Palais el-Badi
34 Café Restaurant Chez Chegrouni		29 Ensemble Artisanal	64 Kasbah Mosque
35 Evening Food Stalls			65 Saadian Tombs
39 Cafe Toubkal			66 Royal Palace
			67 Mechouar

MOROCCO

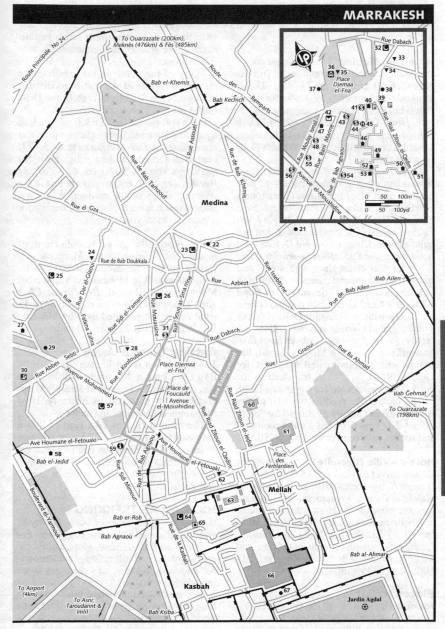

(membership compulsory). Open 8 to 9 am and noon to 11 pm, it's just a bit far from the action.

Hotels – Medina There are plenty of small hotels in the area south of the Djemaa el-Fna. *Hotel Afriquia* (☎ 44 24 03, 45 Sidi Bouloukat) charges from Dr40 for basic rooms but has a fantastic courtyard and terrace. *Hotel Chellah* (☎ 44 29 77, 14 Derb Sekaya) has large, clean singles/doubles, around a courtyard, for Dr40/80 plus Dr10 for a hot shower.

Hôtel Essaouira (☎/fax 44 38 05, 3 Sidi Bouloukate) has a terrace cafe – a good place to meet other travellers. Clean rooms cost Dr35/70, and a hot shower is Dr5. Next door, the *Hôtel Medina* (☎ 44 29 97, 1 Sidi Bouloukat) is of a similar design but not quite as nice. Clean rooms are Dr40/80 and hot showers are Dr5. *Hôtel Souria* (☎ 42 67 57) is another clean place with a cool and tranquil courtyard and rooms for Dr60/100.

With good views of Djemaa el-Fna, *Hôtel CTM* (☎ 44 23 25), on Place Djemaa el-Fna, has rooms with breakfast for Dr70/100/160. Totally geared towards travellers, *Hôtel Ali* (☎ 44 49 79, fax 44 05 22, ✆ hotelali@ hotmail.com), on Rue Moulay Ismail, has rooms with bathroom and breakfast for Dr85/120/170. You can also sleep in the dorm or on the roof terrace for around Dr40.

The pick of the medina two-star places is *Hôtel Gallia* (☎ 44 59 13, 30 Rue de la Recette). It's spotless, has a quiet courtyard and rooms with shower for Dr210/270.

Hotels – Ville Nouvelle Handy to the train station, *Hôtel Farouk* (☎ 43 19 89, 66 Ave Hassan II) has rooms with showers at Dr70/ 100/130. There's a restaurant and it organises excursions to the High Atlas and desert.

Another good choice is *Hotel Toulousain* (☎ 43 00 33, 44 Rue Tariq Ibn Ziad), a calm and cool place with courtyard and parking. Rooms without shower are Dr80/ 100; Dr105/135 with.

Places to Eat

Medina In the evening, the Djemaa el-Fna fills with all sorts of *food stalls*. Snacks are a few dirham; a full meal less than Dr30. At other times you can sit on the one of the many terraces (including the ground-level *Café Restaurant Chez Chegrouni*) enjoying the spectacle and a meal, coffee or ice cream (consumption is always obligatory). Otherwise there are several other small *restaurants* along Rue Bani Marine and Rue de Bab Agnaou.

Many of the hotels in the medina have restaurants – *Hôtel Ali* has a good-value buffet 6.30 to 10.30 pm nightly for Dr60 (Dr50 for hotel guests).

For a splurge (at least Dr300 per head) in a palace restaurant, one of the best for sheer atmosphere is *Dar Marjana* (☎ 44 57 73) near Bab Doukkala. Just eclipsing it for quality of food is *Stylia* (☎ 44 35 87, 34 Rue Ksour). Both restaurants are lost in the winding alleys of the medina. When you make a reservation (obligatory), arrange for a guide to meet you.

Ville Nouvelle A good collection of restaurants, offering French, Moroccan and Italian cuisine for around Dr60, can be found around Ave Mohammed V and Blvd Mohammed Zerktouni. *Restaurant Chez Jack'Line* (☎ 44 75 47) is a quirky French-style restaurant presided over by Madame Jack'Line and her 23-year-old parrot.

Getting There & Away

The bus station is outside the city walls by Bab Doukkala, a 20-minute walk or Dr12 taxi ride from the Djemaa el-Fna. CTM operates out of here and its office on Blvd Mohammed Zerktouni in Gueliz.

The train station on Ave Hassan II is a long way from Djemaa el-Fna, so take a taxi or bus No 8 ride into the centre There are regular trains to Casablanca (three hours), Fès (eight hours), Meknès (seven hours) and Rabat (four hours).

HIGH ATLAS TREKKING

If you have good shoes or boots, plenty of warm clothes and a sleeping bag, the ascent of **Jebel Toubkal** (4167m), Morocco's highest mountain, is worth making. It's a beautiful area and on clear days there are some incredible views.

You don't need mountaineering skills, as long as you don't go in winter and take the normal route from Imlil and stay at the Toubkal refuge for the night. You can do this trek in two days up to the Toubkal refuge the first day, and up to the summit and back down again the second.

The usual starting point for the trek is the village of Imlil, 17km south of Asni on the Tizi n'Test road from Marrakesh to Agadir. Other possible starting points are the villages of Setti Fatma and Oukaïmeden in the Ourika Valley, but these involve longer treks.

Guides

You don't need a guide for the normal two-day trek, but longer treks will almost certainly require a guide and mule. You can arrange this in Imlil at the CAF Refuge or Bureau des Guides. In Marrakesh, the Hôtel Ali (☎ 44 49 79, fax 44 05 22, ✉ kotelali@hotmail.com) and the Hôtel de Foucauld (☎ 44 54 99, fax 44 13 44), near the Dje-maa el-Fna, are good places to track down experienced mountain guides.

Official guides carry ID cards and the official prices for guides, mules and muleteers are published annually in *The Great Trek through the Moroccan Atlas*, a very useful tourist office booklet generally available only in Marrakesh (and in French). At the time of writing guides charged Dr250 and mules were Dr85 per day.

Imlil

Most trekkers stay in Imlil for the first night. Stock up here for the trek, as there's nothing available farther up the mountain.

Places to Stay & Eat The cheapest place to stay in Imlil is the *Club Alpin Français (CAF) Refuge* in the village square. It offers dormitory-style accommodation for Dr24 (CAF members), Dr39 (HI members) and Dr52 (nonmembers), plus there's a common room with an open fireplace, cooking facilities (Dr5 for use of gas), cutlery and crockery. You can camp here for Dr12 per tent, Dr6 per person. Bookings for *refuges* (huts) farther up cannot be made from here.

Good deals in Imlil include the *Hôtel L'Aine* (☎ 48 56 25), which charges Dr40 per person in comfortable and bright rooms, and the *Café Soleil* (☎ 48 56 22) which charges Dr40 per person for very basic rooms; hot showers included.

The beautifully restored *Kasbah du Toubkal* (☎ 48 56 11, fax 48 56 36, ✉ kasbah@discover.ltd.uk), on the hill above Imlil, has good Moroccan-style salons and luxury double rooms. Prices are between Dr300 and Dr 600 per person, full board.

All the hotels have restaurants offering standard Moroccan meals from around Dr30. *Café Imouzar,* just off the square, has cheaper but excellent eats.

The Two-Day Trek

The first day takes you from Imlil to the Toubkal refuge (3207m) via the villages of Aroumd and Sidi Chamharouch. This takes about five hours. Bottled drinks are usually available at both these villages. The trail then climbs steeply and clearly to the refuge.

The Toubkal refuge (3207m) was totally rebuilt in 1999 and now has dorm beds for over 70 people, hot showers (Dr10), a kitchen (Dr7 per hour for gas) and a generator. Bring your own bedding. Officially bookings must be made through Caf (☎ 02-27 00 90, fax 29 72 92, BP 6178), in Casablanca. Web site: www.clubalpin.com. However, you can usually find out if space is available down in Imlil (it's often crammed in July and August), the warden now has two, rather unreliable, mobile/cellphones (☎ 01-65 51 33 or 62 49 81). Beds cost Dr64 per person for non-CAF members and Dr48 for HI members.

The ascent from the hut to the summit should take you about four hours and the descent about two. Carry water with you; any water from the streams on the mountainside should be boiled or treated. There's a fair chance you'll pick up giardia. Remember it can be bitterly cold at the top, even in summer.

Other Treks

The five-hour trek north-east from Imlil over the Tizi n'Tamatert pass (2279m) to Tacheddirt is an enjoyable walk. In the village there's a small *CAF refuge* (priced the same as the one in Imlil). It's a great launching point for many of other treks, including a one or two-day walk to the village of Setti Fatma at the head of the Ourika Valley and the climb up to Oukaïmeden. There are cheap hotels here and transport to Marrakesh from both villages.

Getting There & Away

There are frequent buses (Dr10) and grands taxis (Dr13) to Asni from Bab er-Rob in Marrakesh. From Asni, trucks operate fairly frequently to Imlil and will take passengers for around Dr15. Grands taxis cost DR15.

MOROCCO

Southern Morocco

OURZAZATE
☎ 04

The best thing about Ouarzazate (pronounced war-za-zat) is the journey to/from Marrakesh over the dramatic Tizi n'Tichka pass. Ouarzazate has little to recommend it, though you may pass through on the way to Zagora and the Dadès and Todra gorges.

Places to Stay
There's a *camping ground* (signposted) 3km from the bus station off the road towards Tinerhir (Dr10 per person and tent).

A good cheapie is *Hôtel Royal* (☎ *88 22 58, 24 Ave Mohammed V*) with singles starting at Dr30. Across the road, the *Hôtel Es-Salam* (☎ *88 25 12*) has large and bright rooms, without shower, starting at Dr40.

Getting There & Away
CTM has a bus station on Blvd Mohammed V. Buses go to M'Hamid, Zagora, Marrakesh (four hours), Agadir (seven hours), Taroudannt, Casablanca, Boumalne du Dadès and Tinerhir. Other buses and grands taxis leave from the bus station 1km north-west of town.

Since the Drâa Valley makes such a spectacular journey, consider renting a car. However, you'll save money by doing it in Marrakesh rather than the international agencies in Ouarzazate.

AÏT BENHADDOU
In Aït Benhaddou (which is 32km northwest off the road to Marrakesh and has a fantastic kasbah) is the *Auberge La Baraka* (☎ *89 03 05, fax 88 62 73*), where clean doubles with shower are Dr60. Farther along the road leading to Telouet, *Auberge Etoile Filante D'or* (☎ *89 03 22, fax 88 61 13*) has sparkly bedsheets and a terrace where you can sleep for Dr20. Both have restaurants.

Local buses travel to Aït Benhaddou from Ouarzazate, but it's a lot easier to get there by taxi (Dr7).

DRÂA VALLEY & ZAGORA
For the 100km before Zagora, the Drâa flows through a sea of *palmeraies* (oasis-like areas) and imposing craggy desert cliffs and past dozens of imposing, earth-red kasbahs. It's a magical drive, especially in the soft mauve light of the early evening.

Zagora's attractions are limited to a sign saying 'Tombouctou 52 jours' (by camel) and its large Wednesday and Sunday souks.

Hotels can arrange desert camel treks, but if you've the time it's better to head to Merzouga (see the Merzouga & The Dunes entry later in this chapter).

Places to Stay & Eat
Zagora *Camping Sindbad*, off Ave Hassan II, is the only camp site in town; *Camping d'Amezrou* and *Camping de la Montagne* are off the M'Hamid road. They all charge around Dr10 per person/tent.

Hôtel Vallée du Drâa (☎ *84 72 10*), on Blvd Mohammed V, has rooms for Dr45/70. Next door, *Hôtel des Amis* (☎ *84 79 24*), on Blvd Mohammed V, offers basic rooms with shower for Dr35/60/75.

One of Zagora's most relaxing places is the *Hôtel La Fibule* (☎ *84 73 18*) on the southern side of the Oued Drâa. Doubles without/with shower cost Dr180/360 including breakfast, and there's an excellent *restaurant*, bar and swimming pool.

Getting There & Away
There's a CTM bus from M'Hamid that goes to Zagora (two hours), Ouarzazate (seven hours) and Marrakesh (12 hours). Other daily buses leave Zagora for Casablanca, Erfoud, Marrakesh, Meknès, Ouarzazate, Rabat and Rissani.

BOUMALNE DU DADÈS & THE DADÈS GORGE
☎ 04

Towering ochre-coloured cliffs and fabulous rock formations of the Dadès Gorge, just over 100km east of Ouarzazate along the road to Er-Rachidia, are one of Morocco's most magnificent natural sights. Along the road are magnificent *ksour* (fortified strongholds), both ruined and lived-in.

From Boumalne du Dadès, a good bitumen road wiggles past 63km of palmeraies, Berber villages and some beautiful ruined kasbahs to Msemrir, before continuing as *piste* (dirt track) to Imilchil, in the heart of the High Atlas.

Places to Stay & Eat
In the Gorge There are half a dozen simple hotels lining the road, all have restaurants and

will let you sleep on their terrace or camp by the river from around Dr10/5 per person.

Close to the narrowest part of the gorge, and right on the river, is **Hotel Atlas Berbere** (☎ 83 17 42). Built in earthen kasbah style, it has rooms for Dr50/80. Back towards Boumalne, **Chez Pierre** (☎ 83 02 67) is a tasteful auberge with a sumptuous menu and half board for Dr360 per person.

Boumalne du Dadès Hotel Bougafer, across from the bus station, has simple rooms for Dr50/70. Up on the hill, **Kasbah Tizzarouine** (☎/fax 83 02 56) has comfortable cave rooms with bathroom for Dr250 per person half board.

Getting There & Around
The CTM office is in the centre of town. It has daily buses to Marrakesh and Tinerhir. Other buses leave for Agadir, Casablanca, Erfoud, Fés, Marrakesh, Rabat and Zagora.

Occasional grands taxis (and Berber camionettes on market days) run to Aït Oudinar (Dr10) in the gorge.

TINERHIR & THE TODRA GORGE
☎ 04
The spectacular pink canyons of the Todra Gorge, 15km from Tinerhir, rise up at the end of a lush valley of mud-brick villages and palmeraies. It's best visited in the morning, when the sun penetrates to the bottom, turning the rock from rose pink to a deep ochre.

Places to Stay & Eat
Todra Gorge There are three good camp sites along the road to the gorge, about 9km from Tinerhir. You'll pay around Dr10 per person and Dr15 per tent. There's a small grocery shop across from the first site.

Just before the gorge, **Hôtel le Mansour** (☎ 83 42 13) has a Berber tented cafe and basic rooms for Dr50. Next door, **Hôtel Étoile des Gorges** (☎ 83 51 58) has basic rooms for Dr60 and a cheap tented restaurant.

Inside the gorge, **Hôtel Restaurant Les Roches** (☎ 83 48 14, fax 83 36 11) offers doubles without/with shower for Dr100/150. Next door, **Hôtel Restaurant Yasmina** (☎ 83 42 07) has rooms for Dr110/200. In summer you can sleep on the roof (Dr20).

Tinerhir There's a handful of budget hotels virtually in a row along Ave Hassan II. The **Hôtel Salam** (☎ 83 50 20), next to the CTM office, has basic rooms for Dr30/60. Back behind Ave Hassan II, near the central market, is **Hôtel de l'Avenir** (☎/fax 83 45 99) with pleasant rooms for Dr60/100/130, including breakfast. Trekking can be organised here and the restaurant does paella.

Hôtel Tombouctou (☎ 83 46 04, fax 83 35 05, Ave Bir Anzarane) is a beautiful old kasbah; single/double/triple rooms with bathroom will cost you Dr250/300/350; Dr90/160/200 without.

Getting There & Away
CTM has a bus to Marrakesh, otherwise there are several private buses also running to Agadir, Casablanca, Fés, Meknés, Tangier and Zagora.

Some grands taxis head up to the Todra Gorge (Dr7) and, on market days, you can find camionettes heading to more remote High Atlas villages.

MERZOUGA & THE DUNES
About 50km south of Erfoud are the tiny villages of Hassi Labied and Merzouga and the famous **Erg Chebbi**, Morocco's only genuine Saharan dune.

It's a magical landscape with the dunes changing colour from pink to gold to red at different times of the day. Sometimes in spring, shallow lakes appear, attracting flocks of pink flamingos and other water birds.

Merzouga itself is tiny but it does have téléboutiques, general stores, a mechanic and, of course, a couple of carpet shops.

Places to Stay & Eat
Kasbah style auberges flank the western side of Erg Chebbi to the north and south of the villages. Basic but comfortable rooms cost about Dr30/60 and you can usually sleep on the roof or in the salon or Berber tent for about Dr25. All have views of the dunes and offer food (including the local *kalia* – minced mutton with tomato, onion and 44 spices), Berber music, sand toys (snowboards, skis, etc) and camel treks (around Dr100 for two hours; Dr200 to Dr300 per night).

South of Merzouga, **Auberge la Palmeraie** is a super chilled out place with pink rooms, not facing the dunes; prices start at Dr50.

Nearby, **Kasbah Le Touareg** (☎/fax 57 72 15) is slightly more upmarket with

MOROCCO

colourful rooms for Dr100. The more basic rooftop turret rooms have excellent views for Dr60.

Ksar Sania (☎ *57 74 14, fax 57 72 30*) offers the area's most comfortable doubles from Dr70 to Dr180 and its restaurant has a French menu for Dr90.

Getting There & Away

A camionette to Merzouga leaves Rissani and returns daily (1½ hours), there are also 4WD taxis between the two on Sunday, Tuesday and Thursday. If you're driving you may want to engage a local guide (Dr100).

Another daily bus runs between Erfoud and Merzouga (one hour). Apart from the 'sunrise tours', the only other option is to charter a 4WD taxi (about Dr300), or hitch a ride with tourists.

There are daily buses to and from Fès (eight hours) and Meknès (eight hours) from Rissani and Erfoud.

The Netherlands

A small country with a big reputation for liberalism, the Netherlands (Nederland, or Holland as it's commonly, but incorrectly, known) swims in a sea of familiar images. A land of bikes, dikes, fields of blazing flowers, windmills and few hills – these quintessential images of the Netherlands do exist outside the major cities and the once-radical, still exuberant, capital of Amsterdam.

The countryside's endlessly flat landscape, broken only by slender church steeples in scenes which inspired the nation's early artists, is a cyclist's nirvana. And while you may be pressed to find untouched spaces and solitude, you'll discover a hard-fought-for land, with proud people and farmers who, yes, still wear traditional clogs.

Facts about the Netherlands

HISTORY

The Netherlands' early history is linked with Belgium and Luxembourg: the three were known as the Low Countries until the 16th century, when the region's northern provinces united to fight the Spanish (see the Belgium History section). The most powerful of these provinces was Holland, with its main city of Amsterdam. To the outside world, Holland thus became synonymous with the independent country that was to emerge in this corner of Europe (a bit like saying England when you mean Britain).

Led by Prince William of Orange, the Revolt of the Netherlands lasted 80 years, ending in 1648 with a treaty that recognised the 'United Provinces' as an independent republic. As part of the deal, the Schelde River was closed to all non-Dutch ships. This destroyed the trade of the largest port in that time, Antwerp, but ensured the prosperity of its rival, Amsterdam.

Amsterdam stormed onto the European scene in what was the province of Holland's most glorified period: the Golden Age from about 1580 to about 1740, after which the British began dominating the world seas. The era's wealth was generated by the Dutch East India Company, which sent ships to the Far East in search of spices and other exotic goods, while colonising the Cape of Good Hope and Indonesia and establishing trading posts throughout Asia. Later the West Indies Company sailed to West Africa and the Americas, creating colonies in Surinam, the Antilles and New Amsterdam (today's New York).

It didn't last. In 1795 the French invaded and Napoleon made his younger brother Louis king. When the largely unpopular French occupation came to an end, the United Kingdom of the Netherlands – incorporating Belgium and Luxembourg – was born. The first king, William I of Orange, was crowned in 1814, and the House of Orange still rules (Queen Beatrix took over from her mother, Juliana, in 1980).

In 1830 the Belgians rebelled and became independent; Luxembourg followed soon after.

The Netherlands stayed neutral in WWI, but was unable to do so in WWII when the Germans invaded on 10 May 1940. A Dutch resistance movement formed, but only a small minority of the country's Jews survived the war.

In 1949, despite military attempts to hold on to Indonesia, the colony won independence. Surinam followed much later gaining a peaceful handover of sovereignty in 1975. The Antilles still have close ties with the Netherlands but are self-ruled.

The social consciousness of the 1960s found fertile ground in the Netherlands, especially in Amsterdam, which became the

THE NETHERLANDS (NEDERLAND)

radical heart of Europe. The riotous squatters' movement stopped the demolition of much cheap inner-city housing, the lack of which is a problem that has continued into the 21st century.

GEOGRAPHY

The Netherlands (33,920 sq km) is largely artificial, its lands reclaimed from the sea over many centuries and the drained polders protected by dikes. More than half of the country is below sea level. Only in the southeast Limburg province will you find hills.

CLIMATE

The Netherlands has a temperate maritime climate with cool winters and mild summers. The wettest months are July and August, though precipitation is spread pretty evenly throughout the year. The sunniest months are May to August, and the warmest are June to September. Because it's such a flat country, wind has free reign – something you'll soon notice if you take to cycling.

POPULATION & PEOPLE

The population of the Netherlands is 15.65 million, making it the most densely populated country in Western Europe. This concentration is intensified in the Randstad, the western hoop of cities which includes Amsterdam, The Hague and Rotterdam. Catholics are the largest religious grouping, accounting for 19% of the population. The Dutch Reformed Church, to which half the population belonged 100 years ago, attracts about 15% today, though it's still the official church of the royal family.

SOCIETY & CONDUCT

The Dutch are well known for their tolerance which perhaps has stemmed largely from *verzuiling* (pillarisation), the custom of dividing society into compartments or pillars which, although separate from each other, support society as a whole. In this way any group which demands a place in society can have it and the balance is kept by an overall attitude of 'agreeing to disagree'.

It's customary to greet shopkeepers and bar/cafe owners when entering their premises.

LANGUAGE

Most English speakers use the term 'Dutch' to describe the language spoken in the Netherlands, and 'Flemish' for that spoken in the northern half of Belgium and a tiny north-western corner of France. Both are in fact the same language, the correct term for which is Netherlandic, or *Nederlands*. The differences between Dutch and Flemish (*Vlaams*), in their spoken as well as written forms, are similar to those between UK and North American English. The people of the northern Fryslân (Friesland) province speak their own language.

Netherlandic has a formal and informal version of the English 'you'. The formal version is *U* (written with a capital letter and pronounced *ü*), the informal version is *je* (pronounced *yer*). As a general rule, people who are older than you should still be addressed with *U*. For pronunciation guidelines and some useful words and phrases, see the Language Chapter at the back of this book.

Facts for the Visitor

HIGHLIGHTS

Amsterdam has three not-to-be-missed museums: the Rijksmuseum, the Van Gogh Museum and the Anne Frankhuis (Anne Frank's house). The Keukenhof gardens (see The Randstad section) are a must, especially for flower aficionados. Anyone into a bit of dirt should investigate *wadlopen* – mud-flat-walking (see The North section). Museum and cycling buffs will be in their glory throughout – a visit to the Kröller-Müller Museum (see the Hoge Veluwe section) can superbly combine the two.

SUGGESTED ITINERARIES

Three days
 Spend two days in Amsterdam, and one day at the Keukenhof gardens or The Hague.
One week
 Spend two days in Amsterdam, one day each in The Hague, Leiden, the Keukenhof gardens, and the Hoge Veluwe national park, and the remaining day visiting Rotterdam (Kinderdijk windmills) or Waterland Neeltje Jans (see the Delta Region section).
Two weeks
 Spend three days in Amsterdam, two days in The Hague, one day each in Maastricht, Leiden, the Keukenhof gardens, Delft, Rotterdam (Kinderdijk), a day in the Delta Region (Waterland Neeltje Jans and Middelburg) and another in the Hoge Veluwe national park, and if you have any time left over, head to Schiermonnikoog, Den Bosch or Alkmaar.

NETHERLANDS

PLANNING
When to Go

Spring is the ideal time to visit as there's less chance of rain and the bulbs are in bloom – daffodils from about early to late April, and tulips from about late April to mid-May. For details on climate considerations, see the Climate section earlier in this chapter.

Maps

Lonely Planet's *Amsterdam City Map* is plastic-coated against rain and has a handy street index. Good road maps of the Netherlands include those produced by Michelin (1:400,000) and the Dutch motoring organisation ANWB (1:300,000). ANWB also has provincial maps detailing cycling paths and picturesque road routes (1:100,000).

Passes & Discounts

Avid museum goers should buy the Museumjaarkaart (Museum Year Card), which gives free entry into 440 museums and art galleries. It costs f55 for adults (f25 for those aged under 24) and is issued at museums or tourist information (VVV) offices (you'll need a passport photo). Unless stated otherwise, all the museums and art galleries mentioned in this chapter are free with the Museumjaarkaart.

TOURIST OFFICES

The ubiquitous VVV – the national tourist organisation – sells brochures on everything and maps, and will book accommodation for a fee of f4.50 to f6 per person. Some VVV offices have telephone numbers prefixed by ☎ 0900. These numbers cost f1 a minute, and are answered by recorded messages in Dutch – wait for the message to end to be answered personally.

The Netherlands Board of Tourism (NBT; ✆ info@nbt.nl), Vlietweg 15, Postbus 458, 2260 MG Leidschendam, takes postal and email inquiries only.

Tourist Offices Abroad

NBT's overseas offices include:

Canada (☎ 416-363 1577) 25 Adelaide St East, suite 710, Toronto, Ont M5C 1Y2
UK (☎ 020-7802 8108, ✆ information@nbt.org .uk) PO Box 523, London, SW1E 6NT
USA (☎ 212-370 7360, ✆ info@goholland .com) 355 Lexington Ave, New York, NY 10017

EMBASSIES & CONSULATES
Netherlands Embassies Abroad

Diplomatic missions abroad include:

Australia (☎ 02-6273 3111) 120 Empire Circuit, Yarralumla, Canberra, ACT 2600
Canada (☎ 613-237 5030) Suite 2020, 350 Albert St, Ottawa, Ont K1R 1A4
New Zealand (☎ 04-471 6390) 10th floor, Investment House, corner Ballance & Featherston Sts, Wellington
UK (☎ 020-7590 3200) 38 Hyde Park Gate, London SW7 5DP
USA (☎ 202-244 5300) 4200 Linnean Ave, NW Washington, DC 20008

Foreign Embassies & Consulates in the Netherlands

Countries with diplomatic representation in the Netherlands include:

Australia (☎ 070-310 82 00) Carnegielaan 4, 2517 KH The Hague
Canada (☎ 070-311 16 00) Sophialaan 7, 2514 JP The Hague
New Zealand (☎ 070-346 93 24) Carnegielaan 10, 2517 KH The Hague
UK
 Embassy: (☎ 070-427 04 27) Lange Voorhout 10, 2514 ED The Hague
 Consulate: (☎ 070-676 43 43) Koningslaan 44, 1075 AE Amsterdam
USA
 Embassy: (☎ 070-310 92 09) Lange Voorhout 102, 2514 EJ The Hague
 Consulate: (☎ 020-575 53 09) Museumplein 19, 1071 DJ Amsterdam

MONEY

The currency is the guilder, divided into 100 cents and symbolised as 'Dfl' or 'f' (originally 'florin'). There are 5c, 10c, 25c, f1, f2.50 and f5 coins, and f10, f25, f50, f100, f250 and f1000 notes.

Banks stick to official exchange rates and charge 2.50% to 2.75% (with a minimum of f7.50) for exchanging cash, and f10 commission for travellers cheques. De Grenswisselkantoren (GWK), the national exchange organisation, has similar rates but the commissions are slightly cheaper. There are GWK branches at all major border posts and train stations. With a student card there's 25% less commission on cash.

In larger cities there are many private exchange bureaus that close late but generally ask high commissions or offer lousy rates. Many post offices will exchange cash and travellers cheques. Although all major credit cards are recognised, the Netherlands is still very much a cash-based society. ATMs are located at Schiphol airport and at Centraal Station in Amsterdam, as well as countless other locations around the country.

Exchange Rates

country	unit		guilder
Australia	A$1	=	f1.41
Canada	C$1	=	f1.64
euro	€1	=	f2.20
France	1FF	=	f0.34
Germany	DM1	=	f1.13
Japan	¥100	=	f2.24
New Zealand	NZ$1	=	f1.10
UK	UK£1	=	f3.67
USA	US$1	=	f2.44

Costs

Travelling costs relatively little due to the country's size. You can survive on about f60 a day by staying in hostels and eating in cafes. Tipping is not compulsory, but 'rounding up' the bill is always appreciated in taxis, restaurants and pubs with table or pavement service.

POST & COMMUNICATIONS
Post

Letters cost f0.80 within the Netherlands, f1.80 for up to 20g within Europe, f2.80 outside. In general, post offices are open 9 am to 5 or 6 pm Monday to Friday, and until noon or 1 pm Saturday.

Telephone & Fax

The Netherlands country code is ☎ 31.

Local telephone calls are time-based – the minimum charge from a Telecom phone is f0.25, then roughly f0.20 per minute. Telephone numbers prefixed with ☎ 0900 are more expensive (between f0.50 and f1 a minute).

Telephones take f10 and f25 phonecards and, in some cases, credit cards. Coin-operated telephones are rare. International calls can be made from public phones and post offices, using phonecards designed specifically for international calls.

International faxes can be sent (but not received) from post offices but they are very expensive – f25 for the first page plus f3/5 to countries within/outside Europe for each additional page. Much cheaper is

Kinko's (☎ 020-589 09 10, fax 589 09 20) at Overtoom 62 in Amsterdam.

Email & Internet Access

Cybercafes are plentiful. In major towns they're open until about 11 pm, and charge f2.50 to f3.50 for 20 minutes. The local *bibliotheek* (library) in most towns is also good for Internet access.

INTERNET RESOURCES

The best place to start a virtual visit to the Netherlands is DDS (De Digitale Stad – The Digital City at www.dds.nl. Also good is the Amsterdam city site (www.amsterdam.nl).

BOOKS

Lonely Planet publishes a detailed *Amsterdam* city guide, *Amsterdam Condensed* for short-term visitors and *The Netherlands* country guide. For a humorous look at Dutch ways, pick up *The UnDutchables* by the non-Dutch Colin White & Laurie Boucke or, more seriously, *Culture Shock! Netherlands* by Hunt Janin.

WOMEN TRAVELLERS

The women's movement has some strength and women travellers will find *vrouwen* (women's) cafes, bookshops and help centres in many cities. Het Vrouwenhuis (Women's House; ☎ 020-625 20 66, ✉ info@vrouwenhuis.nl), Nieuwe Herengracht 95, 1011 RX Amsterdam, is well known.

Unwanted attention from men is not a big problem in the Netherlands. However, in the event of rape or attack, De Eerste Lijn (☎ 020-613 02 45) is an Amsterdam-based help line, open 10.30 am to 11 pm weekdays and 4 to 11 pm on weekends.

GAY & LESBIAN TRAVELLERS

The Netherlands is one of the most liberal countries in Europe where attitudes to homosexuality are concerned. The age of consent is 16, discrimination on the basis of homosexual orientation is illegal, and gay and lesbian couples can legally marry.

Most provincial capitals have at least one gay and lesbian bar or cafe, as well as a branch of COC, a gay and lesbian information service. In Amsterdam, COC (☎ 020-626 30 87) is at Rozenstraat 14.

The Gay & Lesbian Switchboard (☎ 020-623 65 65) is an information and

NETHERLANDS

help line based in Amsterdam. *Gay News Amsterdam* and *Gay & Night* are free monthly publications listing gay-friendly hotels, bars, etc. The Amsterdam Pride parade is in the first week of August. For gay-related Web sites within the Netherlands check out www.dds.nl/plein/homo.

DISABLED TRAVELLERS

Many government buildings, museums, hotels and restaurants have lifts and/or ramps. Many trains and some taxis have wheelchair access, and most train stations have a toilet for the handicapped. For the visually impaired, train timetables are published in Braille and Dutch bank notes have raised symbols on the corners for identification.

For more information contact the Nederlands Instituut voor Zorg & Welzijn (☎ 030-230 66 03, fax 231 96 41), Postbus 19152, 3501 DD Utrecht. It's at www.nizw.nl on the Web.

DANGERS & ANNOYANCES

Petty crime is fairly common in Amsterdam – pickpockets often use distraction as their key tool, so keep your hands on your valuables, especially at Centraal Station in Amsterdam, the post office, and other tourist strongholds. Bike thefts are also common. Locals use two chains to lock up their bikes, and even that's no guarantee.

Despite popular belief to the contrary, drugs are illegal. Possession of more than 5g of marijuana or hash can, strictly speaking, get you a large fine and/or land you in jail – hard drugs can definitely land you in jail. Small amounts of 'soft' drugs for personal use are generally, though not officially, tolerated, but could complicate matters if you're already in trouble with the police over something else. Don't buy drugs from street dealers – you'll end up getting ripped off or mugged.

In the event of an emergency, the national telephone number for police, ambulance and fire brigade is ☎ 112.

BUSINESS HOURS

The working week starts leisurely at around lunchtime on Monday. For the rest of the week most shops open at 8.30 or 9 am and close at 5.30 or 6 pm, except Thursday or Friday when many close at 9 pm, and on Saturday at 4 pm. In Amsterdam and tourist centres, you will find many shops open on Sunday. Banks are generally open 9 am to 4 or 5 pm Monday to Friday. Many museums are closed on Monday.

PUBLIC HOLIDAYS & SPECIAL EVENTS

Public holidays fall on New Year's Day, Good Friday (but most shops stay open), Easter Sunday and Monday, Queen's Day (30 April), Ascension Day, Whit Sunday and Monday, Christmas Day and Boxing Day.

The Holland Festival brings many of the top names in music, opera, dance and theatre to Amsterdam for performances throughout June. Another big event in Amsterdam is Koninginnedag (Queen's Day), the 30 April national holiday held on the former Queen Juliana's birthday.

Religious celebrations like carnival are confined to the southeastern provinces of North Brabant and Limburg.

Floriade is a huge horticultural exhibition staged every 10 years – the next will run from mid-April to mid-October in 2002.

ACCOMMODATION

Rarely cheap and often full, accommodation is best booked ahead especially in Amsterdam or if you're going to be in the Randstad during the Keukenhof season.

You can book hotel accommodation ahead (no deposit required) through the Netherlands Reservation Centre which has a Web site at www.hotelres.nl, or via the Amsterdam Reservation Center (☎/fax 777 000 888, ✉ reservations@amsterdamtourist.nl).

Camping grounds are copious but prices vary – on average f7/8/4.50 per adult/tent/car. The NBT has a selective list of sites or there's the ANWB's annual camping guide (f19.95), both available from some VVVs or bookshops.

The country's official hostel organisation is the Nederlandse Jeugdherberg Centrale (NJHC; ☎ 020-551 31 55, fax 639 01 99, ✉ info@njhc.org), Prof Tulpstraat 2, 1018 HA Amsterdam. The Web site is at www.njhc.org. The NJHC has four categories of hostels, with nightly rates in a dorm varying from f22.50 to f28 for members (in July and August f25.50 to f31.50) including breakfast. Category four hostels charge f34.25 to f38.75. At all hostels, a nonmember pays f5 extra. Some hostels have rooms – expect to

NETHERLANDS

pay between f75 to f90 for a single, and f100 to f135 for a double. Private hostels in large cities have similar prices.

B&Bs start at f35 per person a night. Local VVVs have lists or you can book through Bed & Breakfast Holland (☎ 020-615 75 27, fax 669 15 73, ✉ bbrholland@ hetnet.nl), Theophile de Bockstraat 3, 1058 TV Amsterdam.

Hotels start at f75/100 for basic singles/ doubles with breakfast. In the mid-range, prices start from f120/200. Prices will sometimes rise during the high season (roughly 15 March to 15 November); prices quoted throughout this chapter are for the high season.

FOOD

What traditional Dutch cuisine lacks in taste sensation, it certainly makes up for in quantity. And thanks to the sizeable Indonesian, Surinamese and Turkish communities – and to the culinary revolution that has taken over Amsterdam in recent years – there are plenty of spicy or interesting options. Vegetarians will find at least one meat-free dish at *eetcafés* (eating pubs).

The national fast-food habit is *frites* – chips or french fries – usually sold from a *frituur* (chip shop). *Broodjes* (open-face sandwiches) are everywhere. Dinner traditionally comprises thick soups and meat, fish or chicken dishes fortified with potatoes. Most restaurants have a *dagschotel* (dish of the day) for between f15 and f20, while eetcafés serve meals or cheap snacks. Otherwise, the Indonesian *rijsttafel* ('rice table') of boiled rice with oodles of side dishes is pricey but worth a try, as are Zeeland mussels (best eaten during months with an 'r' in their name according to local tradition).

As for sweets, *appelgebak* (apple pie) ranks up there with frites, while *poffertjes* (miniature pancakes sprinkled with icing sugar) are sure-fire tourist food, as are *pannekoeken* (pancakes) and *stroopwafels* (hot wafers glued together with syrup).

DRINKS

Dutch beer is served cool and topped by a two-finger-thick head of froth – a sight that can horrify Anglo-Saxon drinkers. Many Belgian beers – such as Duvel and Westmalle Triple – have become immensely popular in the Netherlands, and are reasonably priced.

Dutch *genever* (gin) is made from juniper berries; a common combination, known as a *kopstoot* ('head butt'), is a glass of genever with a beer chaser – two or three of those is all most people can handle.

Getting There & Away

AIR

The Netherlands' international airport is Schiphol, 18km south-west of central Amsterdam. It's one of western Europe's major international hubs, and services flights from airlines worldwide as well as the national carrier, KLM Royal Dutch Airlines.

LAND

Bus

Eurolines is the main international bus company servicing the Netherlands. It has regular buses from Amsterdam to a crop of European destinations as well as North Africa. Depending on the service, there are stops in Breda, Rotterdam, The Hague and Utrecht. Eurolines buses cross the Channel either on ferries departing from Calais in France or via the Eurotunnel. Members of Hostelling International (HI) get a 10% discount on Eurolines tickets. For more detailed information, see the Amsterdam (or other relevant city) Getting There & Away section.

Train

Nederlandse Spoorwegen (NS; Netherlands Railways) operates regular and efficient train services to all its neighbouring countries. For international train information and reservations, call ☎ 0900-92 96.

The main line south from Amsterdam passes through The Hague and Rotterdam and on to Antwerp (f52.50, two hours, hourly trains) and Brussels (f62.50, 2¾ hours, hourly trains). The line south-east runs to Cologne (f91, 2¾ hours, every two hours) and farther into Germany. The line east goes to Berlin, with a branch north to Hamburg. All these fares are one way in 2nd class; people aged under 26 get a 25% discount (bring your passport). The *Weekendretour* (weekend return) ticket gives a 40% discount on return fares to Belgium or Germany when travelling between Friday and Monday.

NETHERLANDS

The high-speed Thalys train runs five times daily between Amsterdam and Paris-Nord (f161/132 on weekdays/weekends, 4¼ hours). Those under 26 get a 45% discount. Thalys is at www.thalys.com on the Web.

To/from the UK, the only train-ferry route is via Hook of Holland (Hoek van Holland) to Harwich in England and on to London's Liverpool St station (f137/55 adults/children, six hours). Alternatively, go by train to Brussels and connect with a Eurostar train direct (via the Channel Tunnel) to London's Waterloo station (f250 to f280, six hours). Those under 25 years pay f110.

SEA

Stena Line's high-speed *Stena HSS* sails from Hook of Holland to Harwich in 3¾ hours. Fares for a car with driver range from f520 to f830. There are also special five-day return tickets for between f370 to f690. A one-way passenger ticket costs f140/100 for an adult/child.

P&O/North Sea Ferries operates an overnight boat (14½ hours) between Europoort (near Rotterdam) and Hull. Basic rates for cars start at f200/250 in the low/high season. Adult tickets are f125/160 and child fares go for f37/48.

DFDS Seaways sails daily from Ijmuiden (near Amsterdam) to Newcastle. Rates for cars are f110/135/215 in the low/mid/high season; passenger fares start at f85/110/160. The journey takes 15 hours.

Getting Around

For all national train/bus/tram information, call ☎ 0900-92 92 (f0.75 per minute).

BUS

Buses are used for regional transport rather than for longer trips, which are better travelled by train. They provide a vital service, especially in parts of the north and east, where trains are less frequent or nonexistent.

TRAIN

NS trains are fast and efficient, with at least one InterCity train every 15 minutes between major cities, and half-hourly trains on branch lines.

If you're returning on the same day, it's cheaper to buy a *dagretour* (day return)

rather than two single tickets. A One-Day Ticket gives unlimited 2nd/1st-class travel and costs f75/117. With this ticket you can also buy a Public Transport Day Card for f9 which gives unlimited use of city buses, trams and metros.

CAR & MOTORCYCLE

Foreign drivers need a Green Card as proof of insurance. Road rules are basically stick to the right and give way to the right (except at major crossroads and roads with right of way). Watch out for cyclists – they're abundant. Speed limits are 50km/h in built-up areas, 80km/h in the country, 100km/h on major through roads and 120km/h on motorways. Fuel prices per litre are f2.53 to f2.59 for *loodvrij* (lead-free), f2.65 for leaded and f1.75 for diesel. The maximum permissible blood-alcohol concentration is 0.05%. For other motoring information, contact the Royal Dutch Touring Association (ANWB, ☎ 020-673 08 44), Museumplein 5, 1071 DJ Amsterdam.

BICYCLE

With 10,000km of cycling paths, a *fiets* (bicycle) is *the* way to go. The ANWB publishes cycling maps for each province. Major roads have separate bike lanes, and, except for motorways, there's virtually nowhere bicycles can't go. That said, in places such as the Delta region and along the coast you'll need muscles to combat the North Sea headwinds. To take a bicycle on a train (not allowed in peak hours) costs f10 for up to 80km, f15 for greater distances, or f25 for a *dagkaart* (day card). Private bike rental outlets charge about f15/50 per day/week; hire shops at train stations charge f9.50/38 a day/week. You must return the bike to the same station.

LOCAL TRANSPORT

Buses and/or trams operate in most cities, and Amsterdam and Rotterdam also have metros.

Fares operate nationally. Buy a *strippenkaart* (strip card), valid throughout the country, and stamp off a number of strips depending on how many zones you cross. The ticket is then valid on all buses, trams, metro systems and city trains for an hour, or longer depending on the number of strips you've stamped. Around central Amsterdam for example, you'll use two strips – one for the journey plus one for the zone. A zone farther will cost three strips, and so on. When riding on trams it is up to you to stamp your card (fare dodgers will face a f64.50 on-the-spot fine). The buses are more conventional, with drivers stamping the strips as you get on. Bus and tram drivers sell two/three-strip cards for f3/4.50. More economical are 15/45-strip cards for f12/35.25, which you must purchase in advance at train or bus stations, post offices or some VVV offices. If all this sounds too complicated, simply invest in a *dagkaart* (day card), available in some large cities.

Amsterdam

☎ 020

Personal freedom, liberal drug laws, the gay centre of Europe – these images have been synonymous with the Dutch capital since the heady 1960s and 1970s, when Amsterdam was one of Europe's most radical cities. Though Amsterdam foundered somewhat in the 1980s and continues to face a chronic housing shortage and growing numbers of homeless, it is still exuberant and famously tolerant.

More obvious, however, are the rich historical and lively contemporary airs that meld here, as you'll experience when exploring the myriad art galleries and museums, relaxing in the canalside cafes or enjoying the open-air entertainment that beats through the heart of summer.

Orientation

Amsterdam's major sights, accommodation and nightlife are scattered around a web of concentric *grachten* (canals) known as the canal belt.

The centre, easily covered on foot, has two main parts: the medieval core and the 'newer', 17th-century canal-lined quarters which surround it. Corked to the north by Centraal Station, the old city centre is encased by the Kloveniersburgwal and Singel canals. The city's central point is Dam Square, five minutes' walk straight down Damrak from Centraal Station.

Information

Tourist Offices The two busiest VVV offices are at Centraal Station: one of them is on platform two (open 8 am to 8 pm Monday to Saturday and 9 am to 5 pm Sunday) and the other is outside at Stationsplein 10 (open 9 am to 5 pm daily). A third tourist office at Leidseplein operates every day from 9 am to 5 pm. Other VVV offices are at Stadionplein and at Schiphol airport. For telephone information, call ☎ 0900-400 40 40 (f1.05 per minute) from 9 am to 5 pm weekdays, or you can send an email to @ info@amsterdamtourist.nl.

The VVV offices sell a f39.50 Amsterdam Culture & Leisure Pass which gives free entry to several museums and discounts on canal boats, some restaurants, etc.

Money There are 24-hour GWK offices at Centraal Station and Schiphol airport. Private exchange bureaus along Damrak and Leidsestraat stay open late but often have lousy rates. The main post office also handles foreign exchange. There are ATMs at the ABN-AMRO bank on Dam Square and on Leidseplein.

American Express is at Damrak 66 (☎ 504 80 00 to report lost or stolen cards, ☎ 06-022 01 00 for travellers cheques). Thomas Cook has offices at Damrak 1-5 (☎ 620 32 36) and at Leidseplein 31a (☎ 626 70 00).

Post The main post office is at Singel 250, and is open 9 am to 6 pm weekdays (until 8 pm Thursday), and from 10 am to 1.30 pm Saturday.

Email & Internet Access For those on a tight budget, In de Waag (☎ 422 77 72) on Nieuwmarkt is a pleasant cafe with a couple of computers and free Internet access (you must buy a drink). Alternatively, book a free half-hour session at the Openbare Bibliotheek (Public Library) at Prinsengracht 587.

The Internet Café (☎ 627 10 52, @ info@internet.nl), Martelaarsgracht 11, has 34 terminals, a trendy clientele, and charges f2.50 for 20 minutes.

Travel Agencies Amsterdam is a major European centre for cheap fares to anywhere in the world. A few of the better known budget agencies are: Budget Air (☎ 627 12 51) at Rokin 34; Eurolines Amsterdam (☎ 560 87 88) at Rokin 10; and NBBS Reizen (☎ 624 09 89) at Rokin 66 which is a nationwide 'student' travel agency.

NETHERLANDS

CENTRAL AMSTERDAM

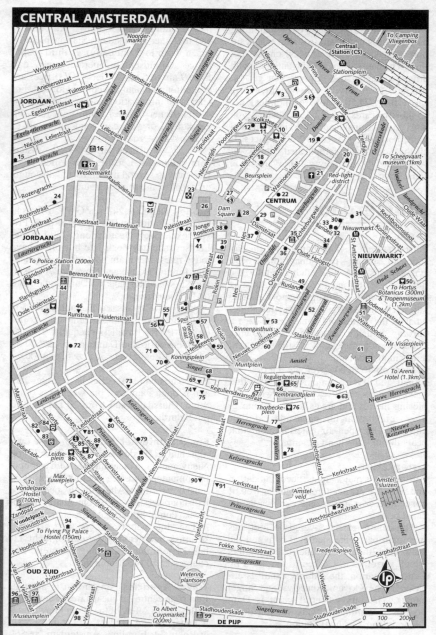

NETHERLANDS

CENTRAL AMSTERDAM

PLACES TO STAY		OTHER			47	Amsterdams Historisch
13	Canal House Hotel	4	The Internet Cafe			Museum
15	Hotel van Onna	5	Thomas Cook		48	Schuttersgalerij
19	Kabul Hostel	6	Tourist Office		49	The Book Exchange
20	The Crown	7	Rijwielshop		50	Bimhuis
29	Grand Hotel	8	In den Olofspoort		51	Rembrandthuis
	Krasnapolsky	9	Sexmuseum De Venustempel		54	Begijnhof
33	The Shelter	10	De Kuil		56	Hoppe
34	Zosa	11	In de Wildeman		57	W H Smith Bookshop
52	Stadsdoelen Hostel	12	Yellow Bike		59	American Book Centre
78	Seven Bridges	14	Café 't Smalle		61	City Hall/Muziektheater
89	Hans Brinker Hostel	16	Anne Frankhuis		62	Joods Historisch Museum
92	Hotel Prinsenhof	17	Westerkerk		63	iT
94	Smit Hotel	18	American Express		64	Sinners in Heaven
		21	Oude Kerk		65	De Kroon
PLACES TO EAT		22	Condomerie Het		66	Escape
1	Bolhoed		Gulden Vlies		67	Tuschinskitheater
2	De Keuken van 1870	23	Magna Plaza		68	Bloemenmarkt
3	Dorrius	24	COC Café		71	The Odeon
30	Albert Heijn Supermarket	25	Main Post Office		72	Public Library & Café
41	Supper Club	26	Koninklijk Paleis		76	Schiller
46	Miramare	27	ATM		77	Bridge of 15 Bridges
53	Atrium	28	Nationaal Monument		79	Conscious Dreams
55	Kantijl en de Tijger	31	Cybercafé In de Waag		80	Clean Brothers Laundry
58	Vlaams Frites Huis	32	Webers Holland		82	Melkweg
60	Café De Jaren	35	Hash Marihuana Hemp		83	Stadsschouwburg
69	Gary's Muffins		Museum		84	Boom Chicago
70	Albert Heijn Supermarket	36	Laundry		85	Tourist Office
73	Metz & Co	37	Damstraat Rent-a-Bike		86	The Bulldog
74	Le Pêcheur	38	Eurolines Amsterdam		87	Jazz Café Alto
75	Rose's Cantina	39	Budget Air		93	Paradiso
81	Shoarma/falafel places	40	NBBS Reizen		95	Rijksmuseum
88	Bojo	42	Vrolijk Bookshop		96	Stedelijk Museum
90	Hollandse Glorie	43	Saarein		97	Van Gogh Museum
91	Albert Heijn	44	Woonbootmuseum		98	ANWB
	Supermarket	45	La Tertulia		99	Heineken Museum

Bookshops Waterstones (☎ 638 38 21), Kalverstraat 152, is strong on guides, maps and novels, and stocks translated Dutch literature.

The American Book Centre (☎ 625 55 37), Kalverstraat 185, gives 10% discounts to students. The Book Exchange (☎ 626 62 66), Kloveniersburgwal 58, is a rabbit warren of second-hand books. Vrolijk (☎ 623 51 42), Paleisstraat 135, is a lesbian and gay bookshop.

Laundry The Clean Brothers have a laundrette at Kerkstraat 56 near Leidseplein, open 7 am to 9 pm daily. There's also a big laundrette at Oude Doelenstraat 12.

Medical & Emergency Services The Central Doctors Service (☎ 0900-503 20 42) handles 24-hour medical, dental and pharmaceutical emergencies and inquiries.

The closest hospital to the centre is Onze Lieve Vrouwe Gasthuis (☎ 599 91 11), at 1e Oosterparkstraat 279, near the Tropenmuseum. The main police station (☎ 559 91 11) is at Elandsgracht 117.

Things to See & Do

Walking Tour The best place to start is **Dam Square** (the 'Dam'), where the Amstel River was dammed in the 13th century, giving the city its name. Today it's the crossroads for the crowds surging along the pedestrianised Kalverstraat and Nieuwendijk shopping streets. The **Koninklijk Paleis** (Royal Palace) on Dam Square is occasionally open to the public – check with the VVV.

Heading west from Dam Square along Raadhuisstraat, you cross the main canals to the **Westerkerk** whose 85m-high tower is the highest in the city. In the church's

NETHERLANDS

shadow stands a **statue of Anne Frank**, the young Jewish diarist. Across Prinsengracht from here spreads the **Jordaan**, Amsterdam's trendiest quarter, with renovated gabled houses and canal-front cafes.

South from the Dam along NZ Voorburgwal, the quaint **Spui** square acts as a facade to hide one of the inner city's most tranquil spots, the **Begijnhof**. Such *hofjes*, or groupings of almshouses, were built throughout the Low Countries in the Middle Ages to house Catholic women, the elderly and poor. From the Begijnhof you can walk though the **Schuttersgalerij** (Civic Guard Gallery), a glass-covered passageway adorned with enormous group portraits of dignitaries from the 16th to 18th centuries, to the **Amsterdams Historisch Museum**.

Continuing south-west, Leidsestraat ends where the city's nightlife takes off at **Leidseplein**. From there it's just a few minutes' walk south-east past **Vondelpark** – a summer-long entertainment venue – to the everinundated **Museumplein** where you'll find the Rijksmuseum, Van Gogh Museum and Stedelijk Museum (see the following section).

Back across the canals, the **Muntplein tower** denotes the colourful **Bloemenmarkt** (flower market), a floating flower market established in 1862 (closed Sunday). Close by is **Rembrandtplein**, a nightlife hub, and the **Bridge of 15 Bridges**, so called because from here you can see 15 bridges (they're best viewed at night when lit up). Farther north, the sleaze of the **red-light district** extends along the parallel OZ Voorburgwal and OZ Achterburgwal canals, past **Oude Kerk**, the city's oldest church.

Museums & Galleries Amsterdam's museums are expensive and if you intend visiting more than a few, it's worth buying the Museumjaarkaart (see the Planning section at the beginning of this chapter).

The excellent **Rijksmuseum**, Stadhouderskade 42, is the Netherlands' largest art collection, concentrating on Dutch artists from the 15th to 19th centuries and housing Rembrandt's famous *Night Watch*. It occupies a palatial 19th-century building and is the best introduction you'll get to Dutch art. Opening hours are 10 am to 5 pm daily (f15). Visit the museum's Web site at www.rijksmuseum.nl.

The must-see **Van Gogh Museum**, Paulus Potterstraat 7, boasts the largest collection of Vincent's works in the world, including hundreds of drawings and some 200 paintings. Highlights include the dour *Potato Eaters*, the famous *Sunflowers* and the ominous *Wheatfield with Crows*, one of his last paintings. It's open 10 am to 5 pm daily (f12.50). The museum is at www.vangoghmuseum.nl on the Web. Next door, the **Stedelijk Museum** has the country's best collection of modern and contemporary Dutch art. The Stedelijk is open 11 am to 5 pm daily; tickets cost f9.

The **Anne Frankhuis**, at Prinsengracht 263, is arguably the city's most famous canal house; come early to avoid the queues. Anne wrote her famous diary here, and excerpts from it are used to describe the persecution of the Jews during WWII. It's open 9 am to 9 pm daily from April to August, and until 5 pm from September through March. Entry is f10 (the Museumjaarkaart is not accepted).

For a wider picture, the **Joods Historisch Museum**, Jonas Daniël Meijerplein 2, details Jewish society and the Holocaust. It's open 11 am to 5 pm daily (f8). Take tram No 9 from the Centraal Station or the metro to Waterlooplein.

The **Rembrandthuis**, Jodenbreestraat 4-6, displays sketches by the master housed in his former home (open 10 am to 5 pm, closed Sunday morning; f12.50). Take the metro to Waterlooplein.

The **Amsterdams Historisch Museum**, Kalverstraat 92, explores the city's rich history via an impressive collection of paintings, models and archaeological finds. Opening hours are 10 am to 5 pm weekdays; from 11 am on weekends (f12).

The excellent **Scheepvaartmuseum** (Maritime Museum), Kattenburgerplein 1, is lorded over by the *Amsterdam*, a replica of the 18th-century East India Company rig. The museum is open 10 am to 5 pm Tuesday to Saturday (also Monday from June to September) and from noon Sunday (f14.50). It's about 15 minutes' walk east of Centraal Station, or take bus No 22.

The **Tropenmuseum** (Museum of the Tropics), Linnaeusstraat 2, realistically depicts African, Asian and Latin American lifestyles (10 am to 5 pm weekdays, from noon weekends; f12.50). Take tram No 9 or bus No 22 from Centraal Station.

For a peek at life on a houseboat, head to the **Woonbootmuseum's** *Hendrika Maria* on Prinsengracht opposite No 296 (10 am to 5 pm, closed Sunday and Monday; f3.75).

Beer production stopped in 1988 but the **Heineken Museum**, in the 130-year-old former brewery building at Stadhouderskade 78, still coerces beer buffs to its weekday tours at 9.30 and 11 am (also 2.30 pm from 1 June to 15 September). In July and August, there are extra tours on Saturday at 11 am and 2.30 pm (f2).

As is to be expected, Amsterdam has a handful of museums that you'd probably find nowhere else in the world. The name says it all at the **Hash Marihuana Hemp Museum** at OZ Achterburgwal 148. It's open 11 am to 10 pm daily (f8). The **Sexmuseum De Venustempel**, Damrak 18, is the first museum most people encounter upon arriving in the city by train. All things pornographic are extolled here – what a start to Amsterdam! Entry is f4.50.

Organised Tours

Yellow Bike (☎ 620 69 40), Nieuwezijds Kolk 29 (just off NZ Voorburgwal), organises bicycle tours of the city (f32, three hours) or a countryside tour taking in a windmill and clog factory (f42.50, six hours, bring your own lunch). Tours run April to November only.

Places to Stay

Amsterdam is popular all year but in peak times it's overrun – bookings are essential. Most of the private hostels and youth hotels don't take advance reservations, so turn up early. Unless noted otherwise, hotel prices include breakfast.

Camping The closest ground is *Vliegenbos* (☎ 636 88 55, Meeuwenlaan 138) across the harbour from Centraal Station. Open April to September, it charges f14.75 for one person with a tent plus f7.75/15.50 for a motorbike/car. Take bus No 32 or 36 from Centraal Station, or use the free ferry from behind Centraal Station and then walk 20 minutes.

Hostels & Youth Hotels Hostels & Youth Hotels can be found in the following areas.

Old City Centre Accurately advertised as the 'cheapest B&B in town', *The Shelter* (☎ 625 32 30, Barndesteeg 21) is a Christ-

ian hostel in the red-light district. It has single-sex dorms, midnight curfews, and charges f23 per night (maximum age 35).

Five minutes' walk south is *Stadsdoelen* (☎ 624 68 32, fax 639 10 35, Kloveniersburgwal 97), one of the city's two official NJHC hostels. It charges f31.25 (nonmembers f5 more); the closest metro is Nieuwmarkt.

In the heart of the red-light district is the lively *Kabul* (☎ 623 71 58, fax 620 08 69, Warmoesstraat 38). Singles/doubles/triples go for f90/125/150 (or f110/175/225 on weekends) and dorm beds cost between f35 and f55 (weekends f40 to f60).

Beyond the Old City Centre The main NJHC hostel, *Vondelpark* (☎ 589 89 99, fax 589 89 55, ☻ fit.vondelpark@njhc.org, Zandpad 5) is one of Europe's largest hostels. It's newly renovated, well-run and is open all year. Dorm rates range from f35.50 to f40 depending on the season (nonmembers pay f5 extra), and there are singles from f75 to f90, and doubles from f100 to f135. Get tram No 1, 2 or 5 to Leidseplein from where it's a five-minute walk.

Nearby is the *Flying Pig Palace* (☎ 400 41 87, fax 421 08 02, Vossiusstraat 46), a popular backpacker's abode. A bed in a three/four/12-bed dorm costs f50/48/34, and there are double rooms for f110. There's a small kitchen for guests to use. Check out the Web site at www.flyingpig.nl.

The huge, modern *Hans Brinker* (☎ 622 06 87, fax 638 20 60, Kerkstraat 136) is popular with visiting well-off students and has singles/twins/triples from f115/125/195. It's at www.hans-brinker.com on the Web.

Hotels Hotels can be found in the following areas.

Old City Centre Situated on one of the main red-light canals is *The Crown* (☎ 626 96 64, fax 420 64 73, OZ Voorburgwal 21). It has a lively bar, and rooms start at f80/130.

Zosa (☎ 330 62 41, fax 330 62 42, ☻ info@zosa-online.com, Kloveniersburgwal 20) is an innovative little hotel with just six ultra-modern rooms for f200/250.

The *Grand Hotel Krasnapolsky* (☎ 554 91 11, fax 622 86 07, ☻ info@krasnapolsky.nl, Dam 9), right on Dam Square, is one of the city's historic showpieces. Rooms start at f550/628; breakfast costs f38.

NETHERLANDS

Beyond the Old City Centre A sage choice on a quiet canal is *Seven Bridges* (☎ 623 13 29, *Reguliersgracht 31*). Every room is furnished differently and they start at f120/230. It has already been discovered so book well ahead.

Another good option to try out is *Hotel Prinsenhof* (☎ 623 17 72, *fax 638 33 68*, *@ prinshof@xs4all.nl, Prinsengracht 810*). Rooms with beamed ceilings start at f85/125, or f160/165 with private shower. Triples go for f175.

The large *Smit Hotel* (☎ 671 47 85, *fax 662 91 61, @ hotel.smit@wxs.nl, PC Hooft-straat 24*) has decent rooms for f155/210. It's close to the major museums. Tram No 2 or 5 stops nearby.

In the Jordaan, the efficient *Hotel van Onna* (☎ 626 58 01, *fax 623 68 62, Bloem-gracht 104*) has small, sparsely-decorated modern rooms for f80/160; book ahead.

Hotel Arena (☎ 694 74 44, *fax 663 26 49*, *@ info@hotelarena.nl, 's-Gravesandestraat 51*) has metamorphosed many times over the years. It's now a big hotel with pristine white rooms, all with private facilities. Doubles go from f150 to f210, and a triple/quad is f200/250. Breakfast is f15 extra. Take the metro to Weesperplein then follow the signs for about 600m.

The *Canal House Hotel* (☎ 622 51 82, *fax 624 13 17, @ canalhousehotel@ compuserve.com, Keizersgracht 148*) has 26 rooms, all individually furnished in ornate, 17th-century style. Prices range from f285 to f365. The hotel's Web site is at www.canalhouse.nl.

Places to Eat
Restaurants abound: try the neon-lit streets off Leidseplein for a veritable diner's market, the Jordaan for discreet eetcafés or the city centre for fast-food factories, student cafeterias and vegetarian hideaways.

Restaurants The following areas have a good selection of eateries.

Old City Centre The *De Keuken van 1870* (☎ 624 89 65, *Spuistraat 4*) is an unpretentious Dutch diner that began last century as a soup kitchen. Open until 9 pm, it offers a basic three-course meal for f12.

For much classier Dutch, try *Dorrius* (☎ 420 22 24, *Nieuwezijds Voorburgwal*

5). Traditional main courses range from f30 to f45.

Kantijl en de Tijger (☎ 620 09 94, *Spuis-traat 291*) is an Indonesian restaurant with modern, minimalist decor. Mains hover around f25; the bami goreng is delicious.

Reservations are essential at the *Supper Club* (☎ 638 05 13, *Jonge Roelensteeg 21*). This ultra-trendy restaurant occupies one big, stark, white room where you dine on mattresses – novel to say the least. The four-course set meal costs f95.

Beyond the Old City Centre Greek and Italian cuisine competes fiercely with steak houses and Dutch fare in the streets off Lei-dseplein. Here you'll find *Bojo* (☎ 622 74 34, *Lange Leidsedwarstraat 51*), a cheap Indonesian eatery open until the early hours of the morning.

The *Hollandse Glorie* (☎ 624 47 64, *Kerkstraat 222*) is laced and intimate, with Dutch mains from f28. *Rose's Cantina* (☎ 625 97 97, *Reguliersdwarsstraat 38*) is a big ever-popular Mexican restaurant with huge pitchers of sangria. Main courses range from f26 to f44.

In the Jordaan, *Miramare* (☎ 625 88 95, *Runstraat 6*) has tasty pizzas from f11.50.

Bolhoed (☎ 626 18 03, *Prinsengracht 60*) is a colourful vegetarian haunt serving excellent organic and vegan food – mains from f24 to f35 and a three-course meal for f35. You'll need to reserve for dinner.

Le Pêcheur (☎ 624 31 21, *Reguliersd-warsstraat 32*) is a stylish seafood restaurant with a pleasant terrace garden. Mains hover around f40. It's closed on Sunday.

Cafes & Eetcafés Huge *Café De Jaren* (☎ 625 57 71, *Nieuwe Doelenstraat 20*) has a sun deck and English newspapers. Reservations are necessary for the 1st-floor section with its all-you-can-eat salad bar (f18).

For late-night munchies try *Gary's Muffins* (☎ 420 24 06, *Reguliersdwarsstraat 53*), open until 1 am (3 am on weekends).

The university's (smokefree) student cafeteria, *Atrium* (*OZ Achterburgwal 237*), attracts a wide assortment of diners (not just students), and does cheap, self-service meals for f10. It's open noon to 2 pm and 5 to 7 pm, weekdays only.

Metz & Co (☎ 520 70 48, *Leidsestraat 34*) is a chic department store with a 6th-floor

NETHERLANDS

cafe open until 5 or 6 pm daily (9 pm on Thursday). Breakfast, soup, salad and sandwiches are the go, and the view is superb.

There are inexpensive, authentic *Chinese* and *Thai eateries* at Nieuwmarkt, and *Surinamese cafes* near Albert Cuypmarkt.

Fast Food Amsterdam's favourite frituur, the *Vlaams Frites Huis (Voetboogstraat 33)* is open until 6 pm daily.

There's a clutch of little *shwarma/felafel eateries* on Leidsestraat. Most are open until about 4 am and do excellent, all-you-can-eat felafels for f6.

Self-Catering The *Albert Heijn Food Plaza (NZ Voorburgwal)* is open 8 am to 10 pm Monday to Saturday and from 11 am to 7 pm Sunday. Other *Albert Heijn* supermarkets are located at Vijzelstraat 119, on Nieuwmarkt, and on the corner of Singel and Leidsestraat.

Entertainment

Pick up the monthly, *What's On* guide (f4) from the VVV or from the Amsterdam Uit Buro (AUB; ☎ 0900-01 91) ticket shop at Leidseplein 26.

Classical music, theatre and ballet are high priorities in Amsterdam, as are African and world music.

Gay nightlife is centred on Reguliersdwarsstraat and Kerkstraat and the streets off Rembrandtplein; the COC (see the Gay & Lesbian Travellers section earlier in this chapter) has venue lists.

Pubs The intimate *Hoppe (Spui 18)* has been enticing drinkers behind its thick curtain for more than 300 years (the entrance is to the right of the pub-with-terrace of the same name). *In de Wildeman (Kolksteeg 3)* attracts connoisseurs with its sizeable beer menu. *In den Olofspoort (Nieuwebrugsteeg 13)* is a typical genever-tasting house.

In the Jordaan, *Café 't Smalle (Egelantiersgracht 12)* has the quaintest floating terrace you're ever likely to see. The trendy *De Kroon (Rembrandtplein 17)* and the smooth *Schiller (Rembrandtplein 26)* are both recommended.

There's a throng of gay bars and cafes, although not nearly as many options for lesbians. *Saarein (Elandsstraat 119)* is the most popular women's bar, open until about

1 am (closed Monday). *COC Café (Rozenstraat 14)* is a gay and lesbian cafe open evenings only.

Live Music The *Jazz Café Alto* (☎ 626 32 49, *Korte Leidsedwarsstraat 115)* has nightly jazz sessions from 9.30 pm. A larger jazz venue is the *Bimhuis* (☎ 623 13 61, *Oude Schans 73)*.

The legendary *Melkweg (Milky Way;* ☎ 531 81 81, *Lijnbaansgracht 234a)* moves from late until early with live rock, reggae and African rhythm. The equally hallowed *Paradiso* (☎ 626 45 21, *Weteringschans 6)* has everything from dance parties to world music or classical.

'Smoking' Coffee Shops You'll have little difficulty pinpointing the 350-odd coffee shops whose trade is marijuana and hash rather than tea and cake. One of the most famous and expensive is *The Bulldog (Leidseplein 13-17)*. *La Tertulia (corner Prinsengracht and Oude Looiersstraat)* is candid and colourful; *De Kuil, (Oudebrugsteeg 27)* is popular and central.

Nightclubs One of the oldest clubs in town is *The Odeon (Singel 460)*, a big student haunt open nightly. *Escape (Rembrandtplein 11)* is capable of drawing 2000 people on a Saturday night. *iT (Amstelstraat 24)* is the largest gay/mixed nightclub – it's open Thursday to Sunday and there's usually a queue. *The* place to be seen is *Sinners in Heaven (Wagenstraat 3)*, open Thursday to Sunday. The club at *The Arena* (see the previous Places to Stay section) has '60s to '90s dance music on Friday and Saturday nights.

Cinema The 80-year-old, Art Deco *Tuschinskitheater* (☎ 0900-93 63, *Reguliersbreestraat 26)* is the city's cinematic showpiece. For foreign and art films try *Desmet* (☎ 627 34 34, *Plantage Middenlaan 4a)* behind the Hortus Botanicus.

Theatre & Dance The premier performing arts venues are the *Stadsschouwburg* (☎ 624 23 11, *Leidseplein 26)* and the *Muziektheater* (☎ 625 54 44, *Waterlooplein 22)*. The comedy club *Boom Chicago* (☎ 530 73 00, *Leidseplein 12)* has an English-language program.

NETHERLANDS

Shopping

The free brochure, *Mike's Guide*, gives a snapshot of the city's most zany shops. *Art & Antiques in Amsterdam* (also free) pinpoints enticing shops in the so-called Spiegelkwartier (Nieuwe Spiegelstraat and nearby sidestreets).

Some interesting shops include: Condomerie Het Gulden Vlies (☎ 627 41 74), Warmoesstraat 141, which is well situated for its trade; Webers Holland (☎ 638 17 77), Kloveniersburgwal 26, with avant-garde fashion; Conscious Dreams (☎ 626 69 07), Kerkstraat 17, which trades in magic mushrooms and aphrodisiacs; and Magna Plaza, a grandiose shopping complex on Nieuwezijds Voorburgwal.

Getting There & Away

Air Amsterdam has long been known for its cheap air tickets (see Travel Agencies in the Amsterdam Information section). Airline offices in Amsterdam include: KLM (☎ 474 77 47 for 24-hour reservations and information), Postbus 7700, 1117 ZL Schiphol; Malaysia Airlines (☎ 626 24 20), Weteringschans 24a, 1017 SG Amsterdam; and Qantas (☎ 683 80 81), Stadhouderskade 6, 1054 ES Amsterdam.

Bus Eurolines operates from Amstel Station, which is connected to Centraal Station by metro. Tickets can be bought from the Eurolines office (☎ 560 87 88) at Rokin 10. High season prices apply between 1 July and 31 August.

To London (f90/100 in the low/high season, 10-11 hours) there are three or four services per day, with buses stopping at Utrecht, The Hague, Rotterdam and Breda.

Other Eurolines services include Antwerp (f35, 3½ hours), Brussels (f35, five hours), Cologne (f55/65, 4½ hours), Copenhagen (f145/155, 13 hours) and Paris (f75/95, 8½ hours).

Train The international information and reservations office at Centraal Station is open 6.30 am to 10 pm daily; for all international information call ☎ 0900-92 96. For national information, ask at the ticket windows or call ☎ 0900-92 92.

For fares and journey times to other destinations in the Netherlands, check the Getting There & Away sections for those places. For information on trains to neighbouring countries, including train/ferry services to London, see the Getting There & Away section earlier in this chapter.

Getting Around

To/From the Airport There are trains every 10 minutes between Schiphol and Amsterdam Centraal Station (f6.50, 20 minutes). Taxis cost about f60.

Bus, Tram & Metro Amsterdam's comprehensive public transport network is operated by the Gemeentevervoerbedrijf (GVB), which has an information office next to the VVV on Stationsplein, open 7 am to 9 pm weekdays and from 8 am weekends. Pick up the free transport map.

Buses, trams and the metro use strip cards (see Local Transport in the Getting Around section earlier in this chapter), or you can buy one/two/three-day daycards for f11/17/22 (f5 per day extra up to nine days) from the GVB (one to eight-day tickets are sold from some VVV offices also). All services run from about 5 or 6 am until midnight when the more limited night buses takes over.

The Circle Tram 20 is designed to meet the needs of tourists. It operates from 9 am to 6 pm daily and departs every 12 minutes from Centraal Station. One/two/three-day tickets cost f10/15/19, or f6/10/12.50 for children.

For all information, the national public transport number is ☎ 0900-92 92.

Car & Motorcycle A 17th-century city enmeshed by waterways is hardly the place for motorised transport. Anti-car feelings are strong and the city council has done much to restrict access and parking. The *Amsterdam by Car* leaflet, free from the VVV, pinpoints parking areas and warns of dire penalties – a wheel clamp and a f130 fine – for nonconformists. If you do bring your car, the best place to park is the 'Transferium' parking garage at Amsterdam Arena stadium which charges f12.50 per day and includes two return metro tickets to the city centre (20 minutes).

Motorcycles can usually be parked on pavements providing they don't obstruct pedestrians, but security is a big problem with any parked vehicle, irrespective of the

NETHERLANDS

time of day. For any queries, contact the Parking Control Department (☎ 555 03 33).

Moped The Moped Rental Service (☎ 422 02 66), Marnixstraat 208, charges f15 for the first hour plus f12.50 for each extra hour, f50 for six hours or f80 per day. No driving licence is required but there's a hefty f1000 deposit.

Bicycle Tram tracks and the other 400,000 bikes are the only real obstacle to cycling; local cyclists can get very impatient when pedestrians block cycle paths. It's advisable to book rental bikes ahead in summer. Try Damstraat Rent-a-Bike (☎ 625 50 29), Damstraat 20, which charges f15/68 per day/week plus a f50 deposit or credit card imprint. The Rijwiel Shop (☎ 624 83 91), to the left out of Centraal Station, charges f9.50/38 per day/week with a f200 deposit or credit card imprint.

Canal Boat, Bus & Bike Canal cruises (f12 an hour) leave from in front of Centraal Station, along Damrak and Rokin and near the Rijksmuseum. They're a very touristy thing to do ... but they're also a great way to see the city from a different perspective. Night cruises are especially enchanting, as many of the bridges are illuminated and the whole scene takes on something of an unreal quality.

The Canal Bus (☎ 623 98 86) stops at the tourist enclaves between Centraal Station and the Rijksmuseum and has a day ticket for f25. Better value is the Amsterdam Transport Pass (f31.50) which gives one days' travel on the Canal Bus plus discounts at selected museums and restaurants. The Museumboot (☎ 530 10 90) offers a f25 day ticket (f20 if bought after 1 pm) good for unlimited travel. In summer, canal 'bikes' can be hired from kiosks at Centraal Station and Leidseplein, with two/four-seaters costing f12.50/22.50 per hour (plus a f50 deposit).

AROUND AMSTERDAM

Bus tours to nearby sights can be booked through the VVV, and include trips to Aalsmeer, Alkmaar (f45), The Hague, Delft and Fryslân. For information on the Keukenhof, see the following Randstad section.

The world's biggest flower auction is held Monday to Friday at **Aalsmeer**, south of

Amsterdam; take bus No 172 from Centraal Station. Bidding starts early, so arrive between 7.30 and 9 am. Admission costs f7.50.

To get to the once typical, but unfortunately now tourist-filled, fishing village of **Volendam**, take bus No 110 from Centraal Station (35 minutes). To the similar village and former island of **Marken**, now connected to the mainland by a dike, get bus No 111 (45 minutes) or go to Volendam and take the ferry (summer only).

The **Alkmaar cheese market**, which is staged at 10 am every Friday in summer in the town's main market square, attracts droves. Arrive early if you want to get more than a fleeting glimpse of the famous round cheeses being weighed and whisked away. There are two trains per hour from Centraal Station (f11.50, 30 minutes) and it's a 10-minute walk at the other end.

The Randstad

The Netherlands' most densely populated region, the Randstad (literally, 'Urban Agglomeration') spreads in a circle from Amsterdam, incorporating The Hague, Rotterdam and Utrecht, and smaller towns like Haarlem, Leiden, Delft and Gouda. A compact area, its many sights are highlighted by the bulb fields which explode into intoxicating colours between March and May.

HAARLEM
☎ 023
Less than 15 minutes by train from Amsterdam (f6.50, every 15 minutes), Haarlem is a small but vibrant town, close to the wealthy seaside resort of Zandvoort. The Haarlem VVV (☎ 0900-616 16 00) is at Stationsplein 1 next to the train station.

The **Frans Hals Museum**, Groot Heiligland 62, features portraits by Frans Hals, the town's favourite 17th-century artist. The **Teyler Museum**, Spaarne 16, is the country's oldest museum, with a curious collection including drawings by Raphael and Michelangelo. Worth a look is the **St Bavokerk** church on Grote Markt – it houses the Müller organ which Mozart played as a youngster.

KEUKENHOF
Near the town of Lisse between Haarlem and Leiden, the Keukenhof, the world's

NETHERLANDS

largest garden, attracts a staggering 800,000 people in a mere eight weeks every year. Its beauty is something of an enigma, combining nature's talents with artificial precision to create a garden where millions of bulbs – tulips, daffodils and hyacinths – bloom beautifully every year, perfectly in place and exactly on time. It's open from late March to late May but the exact dates vary each year, so you should check with the VVV at Leiden or the Keukenhof (☎ 0252-46 55 55, ✉ info@keukenhof). Admission costs f19 (concession f9.50). It's at www.keukenhof.nl on the Web.

From Amsterdam, the Keukenhof can be reached either by a bus tour (f47/75 for a half/full day and booked at the VVV) or by train to Leiden (f13.75 return, or ask about the discounted Rail Idee fare). Once in Leiden, pick up bus No 54 (25 minutes, two per hour), which runs directly there, and departs from the bus station (in front of the train station).

LEIDEN
☎ 071

Home to the country's oldest university, Leiden is an effervescent town with an intellectual aura generated by the 15,000 students who make up a seventh of the population. The university was a present to the town from William the Silent for withstanding a long Spanish siege in 1574. A third of the townsfolk starved before the Spaniards retreated on 3 October, now the date of Leiden's biggest festival.

Orientation & Information
Most of the sights lie within a network of central canals, about a 10-minute walk from the train station.

The VVV (☎ 0900-222 23 33, fax 516 12 27), Stationsweg 2D, is open 10 am to 6.30 pm weekdays and 10 am to 4.30 pm Saturday (also 11 am to 3 pm Sunday from April to 15 September). The main post office, Schipholweg 130, is about 300m north-east of the station, or there's a central branch at Breestraat 46. For Internet access head to the Centrale Biblioteek (☎ 514 99 43), Nieuwstraat 4.

Things to See & Do
In summer canal cruises leave from near the bridge at Beestenmarkt. To tour the town's many hofjes (almshouses), pick up the walking tour booklet from the VVV.

The Rijksmuseum van Oudheden (National Museum of Antiquities), Rapenburg 28, tops Leiden's list of museums. Its striking entrance hall contains the Temple of Taffeh, a gift from Egypt for the Netherlands' help in saving ancient monuments from inundation when the Aswan High Dam was built. It's open 10 am to 5 pm Tuesday to Friday, from noon on weekends (f7).

The 17th-century Museum De Lakenhal (Cloth Hall), Oude Singel 28, houses works by old masters and period rooms (f8).

Leiden's landmark windmill, De Valk (Falcon), Binnenvestgracht 1, is a museum that will blow away notions that windmills were a Dutch invention (closed Monday and Sunday morning; f5).

The Hortus Botanicus, Rapenburg 73, Europe's oldest botanical garden, dates back 400 years (closed Saturday in winter; f5).

Places to Stay
The *Camping De Wasbeek* (☎ 301 13 80, *Wasbeeklaan 5b*) is at Warmond, a few kilometres north of Leiden, and is open all year.

The nearest NJHC hostel, *De Duinark* (☎ 0252-37 29 20, fax 37 70 61, *Langevelderlaan 45*), is in Noordwijkerhout, 45 minutes away near Noordwijk an Zee – take bus No 60 (two per hour) to Sancta Maria hospital and walk 10 minutes.

The canal-front *Pension Witte Singel* (☎ 512 45 92, fax 514 28 90, *Witte Singel 80*), south of the town centre, has rooms for f60/92, or f85/120 with private bath facilities. It's 20 minutes' walk from the station.

The *Rose Hotel* (☎ 514 66 30, fax 521 70 96, *Beestenmarkt 14*) is central, popular with young travellers, but a bit scruffy. Rooms cost f90/135. Alternatively, the stately *Hotel De Doelen* (☎ 512 05 27, fax 512 84 53, ✉ info@dedoelen.com, *Rapenburg 2*) has pleasant rooms from f100/150 (breakfast costs f12.50).

Places to Eat
The *Oudt Leyden Pannekoekenhuysje* (☎ 513 31 44, *Steenstraat 51*) does enormous pancakes for f8 to f18. The predominantly vegetarian *Splinter Eethuis* (☎ 514 95 19, *Noordeinde 30*) has organic two-course meals for f18.50 (closed Monday to Wednesday).

NETHERLANDS

De Waterlijn (☎ 512 12 79, Prinsessekade 5) is a floating cafe that's popular with locals craving a coffee or cake. Self-caterers will find a *De Boer* supermarket opposite the train station.

Entertainment

Evenings revolve around the town's lively cafes. Check the notice boards at either *De Burcht (Nieuwstraat)*, a literary bar next to the remains of a 12th-century citadel, or the ever-popular *Bacchus (Breestraat 49)*. The *Kijkhuis* cinema (☎ 566 15 85, *Vrouwenkerksteeg 10*) has an alternative film circuit.

Getting There & Away

There are trains that run every 15 minutes to Amsterdam (f13.25, 35 minutes), Haarlem (f9.50, 30 minutes), The Hague (f5.50, 15 minutes) and Schiphol (f9.50, 17 minutes). For information on buses from Leiden to the Keukenhof gardens, see the previous Keukenhof section.

THE HAGUE
☎ 070

Officially known as 's-Gravenhage ('the Count's Domain') because a count built a castle here in the 13th century, The Hague – Den Haag in Dutch – is the country's seat of government and residence of the royal family, though the capital city is Amsterdam. It has a refined air, created by the many stately mansions and palatial embassies that line its green boulevards. The city is known for its prestigious art galleries, a huge jazz festival held annually near the seaside suburb of Scheveningen, and the miniature town of Madurodam.

Orientation

Trains stop at Station Hollands Spoor (HS), a 20-minute walk south of the city, or Centraal Station, five minutes from the centre. The area between Spui and Centraal Station has recently experienced a massive facelift in order to create The Hague's New Centre – a prestigious commercial and residential area.

Information

The VVV (☎ 0900-340 35 05, fax 346 24 12, @ reservations@denhaag.com for hotel reservations), Koningin Julianaplein 30, is open 9 am to 5.30 pm Monday to Saturday, and 10 am to 2 pm on Sunday in July and August.

There's a GWK money exchange bureau in Centraal Station and the main post office is on Kerkplein. There's a laundry to the east behind Centraal Station at Theresiastraat 250.

Internet users should head to either Café Tweeduizendvijf (☎ 364 40 94), Denneweg 7f, or to the bank of terminals at the Centrale Bibliotheek (☎ 353 44 55), Spui 68.

Things to See

Those interested in the city's eclectic **architecture** can take a two-hour guided tour (Saturday only from May to August) organised by the VVV. The cost is f30 for an adult plus child.

Museums The showpiece is the **Mauritshuis**, Korte Vijverberg 8, an exquisite 17th-century mansion housing a superb collection of Dutch and Flemish masterpieces and a touch of the contemporary. It's open 10 am to 5 pm Tuesday to Saturday, Sunday from 11 am (f12.50). The museum's Web site is at www.mauritshuis.nl.

Admirers of De Stijl, and in particular of Piet Mondriaan, won't want to miss out on the **Gemeentemuseum** (Municipal Museum), Stadhouderslaan 41. It's open 11 am to 5 pm Tuesday to Sunday (f10).

Binnenhof The parliamentary buildings, or Binnenhof (Inner Court), have long been the heart of Dutch politics although nowadays the parliament meets in a building outside the Binnenhof. Tours take in the 13th-century **Ridderzaal** (Knight's Hall) and must be booked in advance at the VVV. They are run daily (except Sunday) from 10 am to 4 pm; f6.50 (concession f5).

Koninklijk Paleis There are three royal palaces but the only one accessible to the public is the **Lange Voorhout Paleis Museum** which stages temporary art exhibitions. You can pass the palaces on a two-hour 'Royal Tour' (f30) which leaves from the VVV at 1 pm (Tuesday to Saturday May through August).

Peace Palace Home of the International Court of Justice, the Peace Palace *(Vredepaleis)* on Carnegieplein can be visited by

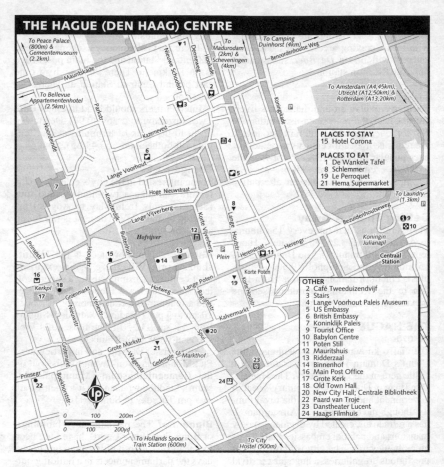

THE HAGUE (DEN HAAG) CENTRE

PLACES TO STAY
15 Hotel Corona

PLACES TO EAT
1 De Wankele Tafel
8 Schlemmer
19 Le Perroquet
21 Hema Supermarket

OTHER
2 Café Tweeduizendvijf
3 Stairs
4 Lange Voorhout Paleis Museum
5 US Embassy
6 British Embassy
7 Koninklijk Paleis
9 Tourist Office
10 Babylon Centre
11 Poten Still
12 Mauritshuis
13 Ridderzaal
14 Binnenhof
16 Main Post Office
17 Grote Kerk
18 Old Town Hall
20 New City Hall; Centrale Bibliotheek
22 Paard van Troje
23 Danstheater Lucent
24 Haags Filmhuis

guided tours (f5) – inquire at the VVV. To get there, take tram No 7 or bus No 4 from Centraal Station.

Madurodam Everything that's quintessential Netherlands is in this tiny 'town' that's big with tourists. It's at George Maduroplein 1 and is open from 9 am to 6 pm daily (until 8 pm from March to June, and until 11 pm July to August). Admission is f21. Take tram Nos 1 and 9 or bus No 22 from the Centraal Station. It's at www.madurodam.nl on the Web.

Places to Stay

The **Camping Duinhorst** (☎ 324 22 70, Buurtweg 135) is to the east of Scheveningen and is open April to September.

The modern NJHC **City Hostel** (☎ 315 78 88, fax 315 78 77, @ denhaag@ njhc.org, Scheepmakerstraat 27), is the only bright spot on the budget scene. Singles range from f80 to f85, doubles from f90 to f109, and dorms from f35.50 to f40. It's a five-minute walk from Station HS, or take tram Nos 1, 9 or 12 from Centraal Station to the stop Rijswijkseplein.

The pleasant **Bellevue Appartementenhotel** (☎ 360 55 52, fax 345 35 08, Beeklaan 417) has self-contained singles/doubles from f65/120 (f12.50 extra for breakfast), and street parking. Take tram No 3 (direction: Kijkduin) and get off at Valkenbosplein from where it's a 300m walk. For a diplomat-style splurge there's **Hotel Corona** (☎ 363 79 30, fax 361 57 85,

@ corona@greenpark.nl, Buitenhof 39). It
has charming rooms from f285/330; on
weekends, these prices drop to f185/220.
Breakfast costs f30.

Places to Eat
The cobbled streets off Denneweg are one
of the livelier areas. Here you'll find *De
Wankele Tafel (☎ 364 32 67, Mauritskade
79)*, a budget-friendly vegetarian haunt with
three-course meals from f12.50 to f21
(closed Sunday).

The ever-popular *Le Perroquet (☎ 363
97 86, Lange Poten 12)*, serves satay specials for f19. It's also good for the ubiquitous *koffie met appelgebak* (coffee with
apple pie). *Schlemmer (☎ 360 90 00, Lange
Houtstraat 17)* is a tastefully-decorated
brasserie with a limited international menu
(mains from f20 to f30).

Self-caterers should head to *Hema*, on
Grote Marktstraat.

Entertainment
During the second week of July, the North
Sea Jazz Festival considerably invigorates
the music scene. If you're into ballet, be sure
to catch a performance by the renowned
Nederlands Danstheater in the *Danstheater
Lucent (☎ 360 49 30, Spui)*. Casual dress
will do; no performances in July and August.

Poten Still (Herenstraat 15) is a small,
popular Irish pub on a grungy nightlife
street. *Stairs (Nieuwe Schoolstraat 21)* is a
gay bar/disco.

The *Haags Filmhuis (☎ 365 99 00, Spui
191)* screens foreign and art movies. The
*Paard van Troje (☎ 360 16 18, Prinseg-
racht 12)* is The Hague's answer to Amsterdam's Melkweg and Paradiso 'cultural
activity centres'. It reopens in mid-2001
after extensive renovations.

Getting There & Away
Eurolines buses stop at the bus station
above Centraal Station. Tickets can be
bought at Broere Reizen (☎ 382 40 51)
travel agent inside the Babylon Centre.
London services originate in Amsterdam,
arriving in The Hague about one hour later.
For more details, see the Amsterdam Getting There & Away section.

From Centraal Station, there are trains to
Amsterdam (f17.25, 45 minutes), Gouda
(f8.50, 20 minutes), Leiden (f5.50, 15

minutes), Rotterdam (f7.50, 20 minutes)
and Schiphol airport (f13.25, 40 minutes).
Just 9km away, Delft can be reached by
tram No 1 (30 minutes) which departs from
next to Centraal Station.

Getting Around
There's a public transport information kiosk
inside Centraal Station. Buses and some
trams leave from above Centraal Station,
while other trams take off from the side.
Tram No 8 goes to Scheveningen via the
Peace Palace, while tram Nos 1 and 9 follow Nieuwe Parklaan past Madurodam to
the coast. Tram No 9 links Centraal Station
and HS.

DELFT
☎ 015
In the 17th century, potters in Delft began
duplicating Chinese porcelain so successfully that it became known as delftware.
Today, tourists flock to Delft mainly to buy
pottery. If you're here in summer you'll
probably wish you weren't; in winter Delft's
old-world charm and narrow, canal-lined
streets make it a pleasant overnight stay.

Orientation & Information
The train and neighbouring bus station are
a 10-minute stroll south of the central
Markt. The VVV (☎ 212 61 00, fax 215 86
95) is at Markt 85. Delft's post office is on
Hippolytusbuurt. Internet users should head
to the Centrale Bibliotheek (☎ 212 34 50),
Kruisstraat 71.

Things to See & Do
The 14th-century **Nieuwe Kerk** houses the
crypt of the Dutch royal family as well as
the mausoleum of William the Silent. The
church is open from Monday to Saturday
(f4). The Gothic **Oude Kerk**, with 140 years'
seniority and a 2m tilt in its tower, is at
Heilige Geestkerkhof.

The **Prinsenhof**, St Agathaplein 1, is
where William the Silent held court until
assassinated here in 1584. It now displays
historical and contemporary art (closed
Monday and Sunday morning; f5).

In summer, **canal boats** leave from
Koornmarkt.

Delftware The most central and modest outlet is **Atelier de Candelaer**, Kerkstraat 14, a

small painting studio and shop. The town's two main delftware factories are outside the centre. **De Delftse Pauw**, Delftweg 133, is the smaller, employing painters who work mainly from their homes; take tram No 1 to Pasgeld, walk up Broekmolenweg to the canal and turn left. It has free, daily tours. **De Porceleyne Fles**, Rotterdamseweg 196 to the south, is the only original factory, operating since 1653. It charges f5 for tours; bus No 63 from the train station stops nearby, or it's a 25-minute walk from the town centre.

Places to Stay

The closest camping ground is **Delftse Hout** (☎ 213 00 40, Korftlaan 5) just to the northeast of town. It's open all year; get bus No 64 from the station. **Pension De Vos** (☎ 212 32 58, Breestraat 5), is homy and has doubles (no singles) for f70. **Herberg De Emauspoort** (☎ 219 02 19, fax 214 82 51, @ emauspoort@emauspoort.nl, Vrouwenreght 11) is excellent value, with lovely rooms from f85/135, plus two gorgeous, gypsy-style caravans for f135/150.

Places to Eat

The **Eetcafé De Ruif** (☎ 214 22 06, Kerkstraat 23) is a rustic eatery with generous meals and a floating terrace – the dagschotel (f15.50) is good value. Vegetarians need look no further than **De Zaag en de Fries** (☎ 213 70 15, Vrouw Jutteland 17), an earthy restaurant serving organic meals. For Dutch fare try **Spijshuis De Dis** (☎ 213 17 82, Beestenmarkt 36). The house speciality, De Bokkepot (f29), is a hearty stew of rabbit, chicken and beef. The **Albert Heijn** supermarket (Brabantseturfmarkt 41) services self-caterers.

Entertainment

The multi-faceted **Speakers** (Burgwal 45) is the town's most lively nightspot. For a slightly quieter haunt head round the corner to **Kobus Kuch** (Beestenmarkt 1). Beer connoisseurs should aim for the cosy **Trappistenlokaal** (Vlamingstraat 4). The **Filmhuis Lumen** (☎ 214 02 26, Doelenplein 5), to the north of the centre, has an alternative film circuit and a good cafe.

Getting There & Away

It's 10 minutes by train to Rotterdam (f5.50), less to The Hague (f4.25). Tram No 1 leaves for The Hague (30 minutes) every 10 minutes from in front of the train station.

ROTTERDAM
☎ 010

Rotterdam is not your quintessential Dutch city. Bombed to oblivion on 14 May 1940, its centre is ultra-modern, with mirrored skyscrapers and some extraordinarily innovative buildings. The city prides itself on this experimental architecture, as well as having the world's largest port.

Orientation & Information

The heart of the city is formed by the pedestrianised shopping streets based around Lijnbaan. The VVV (☎ 414 00 00, fax 412 17 63), Coolsingel 67, is open 9.30 am to 5 or 6 pm Monday to Saturday (until 9 pm Friday), and from noon to 5 pm Sunday from 1 April to 30 September.

The main post office is at Coolsingel 42, opposite the VVV. Internet users should head to Time2surf, Stadhuisplein 32, near the VVV.

Things to See & Do

Rotterdam's sights lie within a region bordered by the old town of **Delfshaven** (accessible by metro), the Maas River (Maas in Dutch) and the Blaak district. Those interested in architecture should buy the guidebook *Two Architecture Walks* (f9.95) from the VVV.

The most famed sight in Delfshaven is the **Oude Kerk**, Aelbrechtskolk 20, where the Pilgrim Fathers set sail to the New World.

The city's many museums are headed up by the **Boijmans van Beuningen**, Museumpark 18, a rich gallery of 14th-century to contemporary art (closed Monday; f7.50).

The **Schielandshuis** museum on Korte Hoogstraat 31, the only central 17th-century building to survive the German bombing blitz, gives insight into that tragic day (closed Monday; f6).

Spido runs daily 75-minute harbour cruises (f16) and day trips (f42) to the harbour's heart at Europoort.

The **Euromast**, a 185m-high tower, pricks the skyline at Parkhaven 20 (f15.50). A combination ticket for a Spido harbour cruise and the Euromast costs f27.

With an Escher-like design, the **Kijk-Kubus** (Cube Houses), Overblaak 70, offer

NETHERLANDS

a new angle on modern living. The display house (f3.50) is open from 11 am to 5 pm daily; take the metro to Blaak.

Places to Stay
The *Stadscamping* (☎ *415 34 40, Kanaalweg 84*) is 40 minutes' walk north-west of the station, or you can take bus No 33.

The NJHC *hostel* (☎ *436 57 63, fax 436 55 69,* ✆ *rotterdam@njhc.org, Rochussenstraat 107*) is 20 minutes' walk from the station, or get the metro to Dijkzigt.

The best budget hotel is *Hotel Bienvenue* (☎ *466 93 94, fax 467 74 75, Spoorsingel 24*) which has pleasant rooms, all with TV, from f81/100. It is two blocks straight up the canal from the rear entrance of Centraal Station.

The name says it all at *Hotel Bazar* (☎ *206 51 51, fax 206 51 59, Witte de Withstraat 16*) in the heart of town. It's an original hotel/restaurant with lantern-lit rooms from f115/135.

Places to Eat
The *Westerpaviljoen* (☎ *436 26 45, Mathenesserlaan 155*) is a large cafe popular with all types – basic meals cost between f12 and f17. *Dudok* (☎ *433 3102, Meent 88*) is a pricier but more central version of the same. Named after a well-known Dutch architect, this brasserie is said to have Rotterdam's best appelgebak. *Blaeu* (☎ *433 07 75, Wijnstraat 20*) has a view of the Kijk-Kubus and reasonably-priced Dutch specialities. *De Pijp* (☎ *436 68 96, Gaffelstraat 90*) is over a century old (and looks every bit of it) and is still going strong. Mains range from f27 to f34, and reservations are essential. Self-caterers will find an *Albert Heijn* supermarket on Lijnbaan, the main shopping street.

Entertainment
The many terrace cafes on Stadhuisplein and at Oude Haven near the Kijk-Kubus are popular with a young crowd. Rotterdam is home to one of the country's biggest music venues, the *Ahoy'* (☎ *293 33 00*) – check the monthly *R'uit* guide (free from the VVV) for listings.

Getting There & Away
Eurolines buses stop at Conradstraat (to the right as you leave the train station) where Eurolines also has an office (☎ 412 44 44)

at No 20. Eurolines services to London leave from Amsterdam (see Amsterdam Getting There & Away section), arriving in Rotterdam 1¼ hours later.

Trains run every 15 minutes to Amsterdam (f23.25, one hour), Delft (f5.50, 10 minutes), The Hague (f7.50, 20 minutes) and Utrecht (f15.25, 40 minutes). Half-hourly services run to Middelburg (f33, 1½ hours) and Hook of Holland (f8.50, 30 minutes).

For information on the ferries from Hook of Holland and Europoort to England, see the Getting There & Away section at the beginning of this chapter. P&O/North Sea Ferries' bus (f12.50) leaves daily at 4 pm from Conradstraat (next to Centraal Station) to connect with the ferry at Europoort.

Around Rotterdam
The **Kinderdijk**, the Netherlands' picture-postcard string of 19 working windmills, sits between Rotterdam and Dordrecht near Alblasserdam. On Saturday afternoons in July and August the mills' sails are set in motion. One windmill is open daily from 1 April to 30 September – get the metro to Zuidplein then bus No 154 (1¼ hours).

GOUDA
☎ 0182
Think Dutch cheese, and most people will say Gouda. This pretty little town, 25km north-east of Rotterdam, is best known for its cheese market, held at 10 am every Thursday morning from July through August. Enormous rounds of cheese – some weighing up to 25kg – are brought to the Markt where they're weighed and sold. Surprisingly, the Markt is the largest in the country, as Gouda was a major player in the cloth trade in the Middle Ages. For more information, the VVV (☎ 0182-51 36 66) is at Markt 27.

Regular trains connect Gouda with Rotterdam (f7.50, 18 minutes) and Amsterdam (f17.25, one hour).

UTRECHT
☎ 030
Lorded over by the Dom, the country's tallest church tower, Utrecht is an antique frame surrounding an increasingly modern interior. Its 14th-century sunken canals, once-bustling wharfs and cellars now brim with chic restaurants and cafes.

Orientation & Information

The most appealing quarter lies between Oudegracht and Nieuwegracht and the streets around the Dom.

The VVV (☎ 0900-414 14 14, fax 233 14 17), Vredenburg 90, is five minutes from the train station; it's open 9 am to 6 pm weekdays and until 5 pm Saturday.

Things to See & Do

The 112m-high **Dom Tower** has 465 steps leading up to excellent views. From 1 April to 31 October, the tower is open 10 am to 5 pm weekdays and noon to 5 pm weekends. The rest of the year it's open weekends only (f7.50).

The **Museum Van Speelklok tot Pierement**, Buurkerkhof 10, has a colourful collection of musical clocks and street organs (closed Monday and Sunday morning; f12).

For religious and medieval art buffs, **Het Catharijneconvent Museum**, Nieuwegracht 63, winds through a 15th-century convent and has the country's largest collection of medieval Dutch art (closed Monday; f10).

Places to Stay

The year-round *Camping De Berekuil* (☎ *271 38 70, Ariënslaan 5)* is easily reached by bus No 57 from the station.

The *Strowis Hostel (☎/fax 238 02 80, ✆ strowis@xs4all.nl, Boothstraat 8)* is a colourful budget option in the heart of town. Double rooms cost f80 and dorms (four to 14 beds) are f20 to f25. There's a kitchen for guests to use. It's a 15-minute walk from Centraal Station or take bus No 54 to Janskerkhof then walk 200m.

The *Park Hotel (☎ 251 67 12, fax 254 04 01, Tolsteegsingel 34)* has homy rooms with private shower and toilet for f125, and parking. It's about 25 minutes' walk from the station, or take bus No 2.

Places to Eat

The Oudegracht is lined with outdoor restaurants and cafes. *De Winkel van Sinkel (☎ 230 30 30, Oudegracht 158)* is a huge cafe occupying an old warehouse. Pasta dishes start at f18.50 and there are various vegetarian options.

De Baas (☎ 231 51 85, Lijnmarkt 8) is a cheap, colourful eatery, open Tuesday to Saturday (evenings only). *Moby Dick (☎ 670 03 00, Kromme Nieuwegracht 16)* does meat, fish and vegetarian dishes for between f24 and f36.

Shoarma (pitta-bread) eateries are plentiful along Voorstraat. *Eettafel Veritas (Kromme Nieuwe Gracht 54)* is a student mensa open 5 pm to 8 pm weeknights.

For self-caterers, there's an *Albert Heijn* supermarket in Hoog Catharijne (the huge shopping centre next to the train station), and another at Voorstraat 38.

Getting There & Away

Eurolines buses stop at Jaarbeursplein out the back of the train station; tickets can be bought from Wasteels (☎ 293 08 70) a travel agent at Jaarbeurstraverse 6 (on the covered walkway which joins the station to Jaarbeursplein). Buses arrive in Utrecht 45 minutes after leaving Amsterdam – for more details, see the Amsterdam Getting There & Away section.

As Utrecht is the national rail hub, there are frequent trains to Amsterdam (f11.50, 30 minutes), Arnhem (f17.25, 40 minutes), Den Bosch (f13.25, 30 minutes), Gouda (f9.50, 22 minutes), Maastricht (f42, two hours), Rotterdam (f15.25, 40 minutes) and The Hague (f17.25, 45 minutes).

Arnhem & the Hoge Veluwe

☎ 026

About an hour's drive east of Amsterdam, the Hoge Veluwe is the Netherlands' best-known national park and home of the prestigious Kröller-Müller Museum. To the south, the town of Arnhem was the site of fierce fighting between the Germans and allied British and Polish airborne troops during the failed Operation Market Garden in WWII. Today it's a peaceful town, the closest base to the nearby war museum and the national park.

Orientation & Information

The town's pedestrianised centre, based around the well-hidden Korenmarkt, is five minutes' walk from the train station. The VVV (☎ 0900-202 40 75, fax 442 26 44), Willemsplein 8, is one block to the left out of the station. Buses leave from the right as you exit the station.

Things to See

In Arnhem, the main attraction is the **Museum voor Moderne Kunst** (Modern Art Museum), Utrechtsestraat 87, occupying a neoclassical building overlooking the Rhine. It's a 10-minute walk from the station. Out of town, Oosterbeek's wartime **Airborne Museum**, Utrechtseweg 232, is open 11 am to 5 pm weekdays and from noon on Sunday – get there on bus No 1.

Hoge Veluwe Stretching for nearly 5500 hectares, the Hoge Veluwe is a mix of forests and woods, shifting sands and heathery moors. It's home to red deer, wild boar, mouflon (a Mediterranean goat), and the **Kröller-Müller Museum** with its vast collection of Van Gogh paintings. The museum is open 10 am to 5 pm, Tuesday to Sunday.

The park is best seen on foot or bicycle – the latter are available free of charge at the park entrances or from the visitors' centre inside the park.

To get to the park, take the special bus (No 12) which leaves from Stationsplein in Arnhem at least four times daily from April to 30 October. A return ticket costs f9 (concession f5.50).

The park is open 8 am to sunset daily and costs f8 (f8.50 for a car). A combination ticket for the park and the museum costs f16. The yearly Museumjaarkaart is not valid.

Places to Stay & Eat

The *Alteveer Hostel* (☎ 442 01 14, *Diepenbrocklaan 27*) is to the north of town, 10 minutes on bus No 3. *Pension Parkzicht* (☎ 442 06 98, *fax 443 62 02, Apeldoornsestraat 16*) is 10 minutes' walk downhill from the station and has rooms for f52.50/95. Almost opposite the train station is *Hotel Haarhuis* (☎ 442 74 41, *fax 442 74 49, Stationsplein 1*), a chain hotel with comfortable rooms for f175/240.

Terrace cafes rim the Korenmarkt – *Wampie* is the oldest and most trendy. *Mozaïk* (☎ 351 55 65, *Ruiterstraat 43*) is a popular Turkish restaurant, and also does vegetarian meals (f30).

Getting There & Away

Trains to Amsterdam (f25, 65 minutes) and Rotterdam (f30.50, 75 minutes) go via Utrecht (f17.25, 40 minutes), while the line south passes Den Bosch (f17.25, 45 minutes) and continues to Maastricht (f36, two hours).

The Delta Region

The Netherlands' aptly named province of Zeeland ('Sea Land') makes up most of the Delta region. Spread over the south-west corner of the country, it was until recent decades a solitary place, with isolated islands battered by howling winds and white-capped seas, and small medieval towns seemingly lost in time. But after a devastating flood in 1953 came the decision to defend Zeeland from the sea – and thus the Delta Project (see the later Around Middelburg section) became a reality.

The region's main town, Middelburg, makes a good base for exploration or, for something more quaint, head to Willemstad.

MIDDELBURG
☎ 0118

Middelburg is the long-time capital of Zeeland. It makes for a pleasant overnight stop and has a handful of worthy sights. The VVV (☎ 65 99 44) is centrally located at Nieuwe Burg 40.

Things to See & Do

Near the VVV is the Gothic **Stadhuis** (Town Hall) which, like much of the central district, was destroyed during the 1940 German blitz which flattened Rotterdam. Dating back to the mid-15th century, it was convincingly restored. A few streets away is **Lange Jan**, the town's other distinctive tower, rising from the former 12th-century **Abdij** (Abbey) complex. The tower can be climbed from mid-April to 31 October. For insight into the province's history, visit the **Zeeuws Museum** (Zeeland Museum) inside the Abbey.

Places to Stay & Eat

The nearest NJHC hostel, *Kasteel Westhove* (☎ 58 12 54), is in a medieval castle about 15km west between the villages of Domburg and Oostkapelle. It's open mid-March to mid-October – from Middelburg station, take the hourly ZWN bus No 53. In town, *B&B De Kaepstander* (☎ 64 28 48, *Koorkerkhof 10*) is a quaint place with rooms for f50/90. *Hotel Roelant* (☎ 62 76 59, *fax 62 89 73, Koepoortstraat 10*) has functional

NETHERLANDS

rooms starting at f57/115. A nice spot for a light meal is **Sint Jan** (☎ *62 89 95, St Janstraat 40)*, a cosy cafe next to the 16th-century fish market.

Getting There & Away
Trains run regularly to Amsterdam (f48, 2½ hours) and Rotterdam (f33, 1½ hours).

AROUND MIDDELBURG
The disastrous 1953 flood was the impetus for the Delta in which the south-west river deltas were blocked using a network of dams, dikes and a remarkable 3.2km storm-surge barrier which is lowered only in rough conditions. Finished in 1986, the project is explained at **Waterland Neeltje Jans** (☎ 0111-65 27 02), a theme park next to the storm-surge barrier's command centre. The f20 admission to Neeltje Jans includes entry to the Delta Expo and to a dolphin rehabilitation centre, and allows a walk on the storm-surge barriers. It's open 10 am to 5.30 pm daily (closed Monday and Tuesday from 1 November to 31 March). To get there from Middelburg, take the ZWN bus No 104 (30 minutes, twice hourly).

WILLEMSTAD
☎ 0168
Sitting on the edge of the Delta region but officially part of Brabant province, Willemstad is a picturesque fortified village. Built in the mid-16th century, the village was given to the nation's saviour, William the Silent, in 1582 as compensation for his expenses in leading the Revolt of the Netherlands.

The VVV (☎ 47 60 55, fax 476 054) is at Hofstraat 1. Overnighters will find two mid-range hotels: **Willemstad** (☎ *47 22 50, Voorstraat 42)* and **Het Wapen van Willemstad** (☎ *47 34 50, Benedenkade 12)*.

Public transport to Willemstad is limited to an hourly bus from Roosendaal or Breda, or buses from Rotterdam (45 minutes).

The North

The Netherlands' northern region is made up of several provinces, including Fryslân and Groningen, and capped by the Frisian Islands. Even to the Dutch, the lake-land province of Fryslân is a bit 'different' from the rest of the Netherlands. Here the people

have their own flag, anthem and language – Frysk (Frisian). In 1996, the province's name was officially changed from Friesland to Fryslân (as it is spelt in Frysk).

LEEUWARDEN
☎ 058
As the economic and cultural capital of Fryslân, Leeuwarden radiates an air of proud independence. The city developed from three *terp* (artificial dwelling mound) settlements which merged in the 15th century, though it's better remembered as the birth place of Mata Hari, the dancer executed by the French in 1917 on suspicion of spying for the Germans.

The VVV (☎ 0900-202 40 60, fax 215 35 93), Stationsplein 1, has city and provincial information. More can be gained from the **Frisian Museum**, Turfmarkt 11, as well as the **Frisian Literair Museum**, Grote Kerkstraat 21, a literary museum occupying Mata Hari's former house.

For a cheap hotel head to **De Pauw** (☎ *212 36 51, fax 216 07 93, Stationsweg 10)*, conveniently located near the train and bus stations. More central and comfortable is **Hotel 't Anker** (☎ *212 52 16, fax 212 82 93, Eewal 69)* with rooms for f85/120.

From Amsterdam there are hourly trains to Leeuwarden (f48, two hours) or you can take bus No 350 from Alkmaar across the Afsluitdijk.

GRONINGEN
☎ 050
This lively provincial capital has been an important trading centre since the 13th century. Its prosperity increased with the building in 1614 of the country's second oldest university and, later, the discovery of natural gas. The VVV (☎ 313 97 74, fax 313 63 58), Gedempte Kattendiep 6, is half-way between the train station and the city centre.

The city's colourful **Groninger Museum**, Museumeiland 1, is opposite the train station. It's open 10 am to 5 pm Tuesday to Sunday.

Groningen is the best place to arrange **wadlopen**, a serious pastime – strenuous and at times dangerous – involving kilometres-long, low-tide walks in mud that can come up to your thighs. To get into the thick of it contact Dijkstra Wad Walking Tours (☎ 0595-528 300) at Pieterburen to the north of town.

For overnighters, there's the clean *Simplon* (☎ *313 52 21, Boterdiep 73*). This youth centre has large dorms for f21.50 per person (take bus No 1 from the train station). More centrally, *Hotel Friesland* (☎ *312 13 07, Kleine Pelsterstraat 4*) has doubles for f77.

Hourly trains depart from Amsterdam to Groningen (f51, 2¼ hours) and from Groningen to Leeuwarden (f15.25, 50 minutes).

FRISIAN ISLANDS

The Netherlands is capped by the Frisian or Wadden Islands, a group of five islands including Ameland, Schiermonnikoog and Texel. They are important bird-breeding grounds as well as being an escape for stressed southerners. Ferries connect the islands to the mainland, and bikes can be hired for getting around.

Texel
☎ 0222

The largest and most populated island, Texel's 30km of beach can seem overrun all summer but even more so in June when the world's largest catamaran race is staged here. The biggest village is Den Burg where you'll find the VVV (☎ 31 47 41, fax 31 00 54), Emmalaan 66.

Campers can head to *De Krim Vakantiecentrum* (☎ *39 01 11, fax 39 01 21, Roggeslootweg 6*) in Cocksdorp which is open all year. The main NJHC hostel (open summer only) is the pleasant *Panorama* (☎ *31 54 41, Schansweg 7*). *Hotel 't Koogerend* (☎ *31 33 01, fax 31 59 02, Kogerstraat 94*) in Den Burg is moderately priced.

Trains from Amsterdam to Den Helder (f23.25, 1½ hours) are met by a bus that whisks you to the awaiting hourly car ferry. The voyage takes 20 minutes, and costs f10 (concession f5); cars/bicycles are charged f48.50/6.

Ameland
☎ 0519

Ameland is noted for its birds and four quaint villages. The main one, Nes, is home to the VVV (☎ 54 65 46, fax 54 29 32), Rixt van Doniastraat 2.

The *Camping Duinoord* (☎ *54 20 70, fax 54 21 46*), Jan van Eijckweg 4, is in Nes. The *NJHC hostel* (☎ *55 53 53, Oranjeweg 59*) is near the lighthouse at Hollum – get

bus No 130 from Nes. *Hotel Nobel* (☎ *55 41 57, fax 55 45 15,* @ *nobel@xs4all.nl, Kosterweg 16*), in the quiet village of Ballum, has rooms for f75/110.

From Leeuwarden, take bus No 60 to the port at Holwerd. On weekdays there are six boats a day; weekends four (hourly services from 1 June to 31 August). Returns cost f20.50 (concession f10.80) and f9.70 for bikes, and cars start at f140. The journey takes 45 minutes.

Schiermonnikoog
☎ 0519

With one of the nation's most tongue-tying names, Schiermonnikoog is the smallest island of the group and off-limits to cars. In the only village, about 3km from the ferry terminus, you'll find the VVV (☎ 53 12 33), Reeweg 5.

Two accommodation options are *Camping Seedune* (☎ *53 13 98, Seeduneweg 1*) and *Hotel Tjattel* (☎ *53 11 33, Langestreek 94*), which has rooms for f120/240.

There are four ferries (three on Sunday) from the village of Lauwersoog, between Leeuwarden and Groningen. To get there from Leeuwarden take bus No 50; from Groningen, bus No 63. The voyage takes 45 minutes each way and return tickets cost f21.70 (concession f12) and f10 for a bike.

The South-East

Sprinkled with woods, heather and the odd incline, the Netherlands' south-eastern corner is made up of the North Brabant and Limburg provinces.

DEN BOSCH
☎ 073

Den Bosch (officially known as 's-Hertogenbosch, 'The Count's Forest') is the capital of North Brabant. The town's pedestrianised centre is based around the Markt, a 10-minute walk east of the train station. The VVV (☎ 0900-112 23 34), Markt 77, is housed in the town's oldest building.

Things to See

The **Noordbrabants Museum**, Verwersstraat 41, features exhibits about Brabant life and art from earlier times (closed Monday). The other main attraction is **St Janskathedraal**,

NETHERLANDS

one of the most ornate churches in the Netherlands. It's a few minutes' walk from the Markt at the end of Kerkstraat, the main shopping thoroughfare.

Places to Stay & Eat
For accommodation there's **Hotel All Inn** (☎/fax 613 40 57, Gasselstraat 1), one block east of the Markt, with basic rooms for f45 per person (breakfast is f10 extra). Considerably more upmarket is **Hotel Central** (☎ 692 69 26, fax 614 56 99, ✉ info@hotel-central.nl, Burg Leoffplein 98). This place overlooks the Markt (though the entrance is at the rear) and has modern rooms for f210/260 (breakfast f25).

Van Puffelen (☎ 689 04 14, Molenstraat 4) is a spacious eetcafé (closed Monday) with eclectic cuisine (including vegetarian dishes). For a sweet local snack try a *Bossche Bol*, a big chocolate-coated blob bought from bakeries.

Getting There & Away
Trains run regularly to Amsterdam (f23.25, one hour) via Utrecht (f13.25, 30 minutes), Arnhem (f17.25, 45 minutes) and Maastricht (f33, 1½ hours).

MAASTRICHT
☎ 043
The Netherlands' oldest city, Maastricht sits at the bottom end of the thin finger of land which juts down between Belgium and Germany – and is influenced by them both. Capital of the largely Catholic Limburg province, its history stretches back to 50 BC when the Romans set up camp on a bank of the Maas River. Today, spanning both banks, this lively city has a reputation even in its own country as being something a little 'foreign'.

Orientation & Information
The west bank of the Maas is the city's main hub, with the old, now largely pedestrianised, centre and its trendy Stokstraat quarter. On the east bank there's the Wyck, an area of 17th-century houses, intimate cafes and bars and, further south, Céramique, the new showpiece quarter.

The VVV (☎ 325 21 21) is housed in Het Dinghuis ('The Thing House'), which is on the corner of Kleine Staat and Jodenstraat. It's open 9 am to 5 or 6 pm Monday

to Saturday (from May to October it also opens 11 am to 3 pm Sunday).

There's a GWK money exchange office at the train station. The main post office is at Grote Staat 5. For Internet access go to the Stadsbibliotheek (☎ 350 56 00) in the Centre Céramique, Ave Céramique 50.

Things to See & Do
The premier museum, **Bonnefanten**, Ave Céramique 250 in Céramique, features art and architecture from the Limburg area (closed Monday; f10). Visit its Web site at www.bonnefantenmuseum.nl.

The main basilica is the 10th-century **Sint Servaasbasiliek** on Vrijthof (entrance on Keizer Karelplein). It's large and somewhat stark, but has a rich treasure house (f4). Farther south, on the Onze Lieve Vrouweplein, is **Onze Lieve Vrouwebasiliek**, a smaller Gothic structure.

Stiphout Cruises, Maaspromenade 27, operates 50-minute boat trips along the Maas River for f11.

Places to Stay
The closest camping ground is the four-star *De Dousberg* (☎ 343 21 71, Dousbergweg 102). It's 700m from *Dousberg Parc Hostel* (☎ 346 67 66, fax 346 67 55, Dousbergweg 4), which is 5km west of the train station. It charges f34 for dorm bed, or f93/108 for rooms. Bus No 11 runs to the hostel's front door twice hourly. At night time, a Call-Bus will get you there.

Hotel Le Guide (☎ 321 61 76, fax 325 99 13, Stationsstraat 17) has cheerful rooms (some of them with private bathroom facilities) for f98/117. The lovely *Hotel Botticelli* (☎ 352 63 00, fax 352 63 36, ✉ reception@botticellihotel.nl, Papenstraat 11) was an 18th-century mansion of a wine merchant. The rooms range from f130 to f275, and breakfast costs f22.

The VVV has a list of *B&Bs* ranging from f55 to f80 per person.

Places to Eat
In the centre, Platielstraat is lined with restaurants and cafes. Nearby, there's *De Bóbbel* (☎ 321 74 13, Wolfstraat 32), a charming brown cafe with decent snacks for about f12. A range of regional specialities (mains from f31) is offered by the *De Gulden Clock* (☎ 325 27 09), Wycker Brugstraat 54.

For fabulous food and informal dining (reservations not taken) head to *Café Sjiek* (☎ *321 01 58, St Pieterstraat 13)*, pronounced 'chic', an atmospheric little eet-café that has been around for years. For good French food at reasonable prices try the *Petit Bonheur (☎ 321 51 09, Achter de Molens 2)*.

Picnic supplies can be bought from *Super de Boer* supermarket on Kleine Staat.

Entertainment

If the weather is good, Vrijthof and the more intimate Onze Lieve Vrouweplein are taken over by people-watching terrace cafes. *De Kadans (☎ 326 17 00, Kesselkade 62)*, a big bistro-cum-disco, is *the* most happening spot in town. Alternatively, you could cross the river to the Wyck where there are plenty of rustic cafes including *Take One (Rechtstraat 28)*, a beer specialist's haven. *Cinema Lumière (☎ 321 40 80, Bogaardenstraat 40)* screens non-mainstream films.

Getting There & Away

Within the Netherlands, major train lines include those to Amsterdam (f51, 2½ hours) and Den Bosch (f33, 1½ hours). Major international connections include those to Liège in Belgium (f14.50, 30 minutes, hourly), Cologne in Germany (f38, 1½ hours, hourly), and Luxembourg City (f59, three hours, hourly).

Getting Around

Stadsbus buses run local routes as do Call-Buses – evening minibuses which must be booked by telephone. For information or bookings for either, call ☎ 350 57 07. The main bus station is next to the train station. Bikes can be hired at Aan de Stasie (☎ 321 11 00), Stadtionsplein, a bike shop to the left as you exit the train station.

Norway

Norway (Norge) is a ruggedly beautiful country of high mountains, deep fjords and icy blue glaciers. It stretches 2000km from beach towns in the south to treeless Arctic tundra in the north. Norway offers incredible wilderness hiking, year-round skiing and some of the most scenic ferry, bus and train rides imaginable. Summer days are long – in the northernmost part of the country the sun doesn't set for weeks on end.

AT A GLANCE

Capital:	Oslo
Population:	4.5 million
Official Language:	Norwegian
Currency:	1 Norwegian krone = 100 øre

Facts about Norway

HISTORY

The first settlers of Norway arrived more than 10,000 years ago with the end of the Ice Age. As the glaciers retreated north, these early hunters and gatherers followed, pursuing migrating reindeer herds.

Norway's greatest impact on history was during the Viking Age, a period usually dated from the plundering of England's Lindisfarne monastery by Nordic pirates in 793. Over the next century, the Vikings made raids throughout Europe and established settlements in the Shetland, Orkney and Hebrides islands, the Dublin area, and in Normandy. Viking leader Harald Fairhair unified Norway around 900 and King Olaf, adopting the religion of the lands he had conquered, converted Norway's people to Christianity a century later.

The Viking Age ended in 1066 with the defeat of the Norwegian king Harald Hardrada at the Battle of Stamford Bridge in England. In 1380 Norway was absorbed into a union with Denmark that lasted over 400 years.

Denmark's ill-fated alliance with France in the Napoleonic Wars resulted in its ceding of Norway to Sweden in January 1814 under the Treaty of Kiel. Tired of forced unions, on 17 May 1814 Norway adopted its own constitution, though its struggle for independence was quickly quelled by a Swedish invasion.

In 1884 a parliamentary government was introduced in Norway and a growing nationalist movement eventually led to a peaceful secession from Sweden in 1905. By referendum Norwegians voted in favour of a monarchy over a republic. Having no royalty of their own, Norway's parliament selected Prince Carl of Denmark to be king. Upon acceptance, he took the title Håkon VII and named his infant son Olav, both prominent names from Norway's Viking past.

Norway stayed neutral during WWI. Despite restating its neutrality at the start of WWII, the country was attacked by the Nazis on 9 April 1940 and, after a two-month struggle, fell to the Germans. In one of the most renowned sabotage efforts of WWII, Norwegian Resistance fighters destroyed the German heavy-water plant at Rjukan in southern Norway, shattering Germany's efforts to develop an atomic bomb. During their retreat at the end of the war, the Nazis torched and levelled nearly every town and village in northern Norway.

The royal family returned to Norway in June 1945. King Håkon died in 1957 and was succeeded by his son, Olav V, a popular king who reigned until his death in January 1991. The current monarch is Harald V, Olav's son.

Norway joined the European Free Trade Association (EFTA) in 1960 but has been reluctant to forge closer bonds with other European nations. In 1972 Norwegians voted against joining the European Community (EC). In 1994 a second national referendum was held, this time on joining the EC's successor, the European Union (EU), and voters rejected that as well. North Sea oil fields, discovered on the Norwegian

NORWAY

NORWAY

NORWEGIAN

SEA

Nordkapp Honningsvåg
Hammerfest
Vardø
Kirkenes
Storskog
Alta
Finnmark
Karasjok
Tromsø
Kautokeino
Andenes
Vesterålen
Troms
E6
Lofoten
Narvik
Svolvær
Stamsund Skutvik
Vestfjord
FINLAND
BODØ Fauske
Arctic Circle
Nordland
Mo i Rana
ATLANTIC
Mosjøen
OCEAN
E6
Nord
Trøndelag
SWEDEN
Steinkjer
TRONDHEIM E14
Hell
Sør
Trøndelag
ÅLESUND Åndalsnes
Røros
Måløy
Nordfjord Geiranger Dombås
E136
Mt Galdhøpiggen ▲ Rondane
(2469m)
Balestrand Jotunheimen
Sognefjord E6
Flåm Lillehammer
Voss Finse E16
Geilo
BERGEN
Hardangervidda
E134 Rjukan
Haugesund Kongsberg OSLO
Telemark E18
Tau SKIEN Moss
STAVANGER FREDRIKSTAD
Kragerø Larvik Halden
E39 Risør
Arendal *Skagerrak*
Mandal KRISTIANSAND
Bottenhavet
HELSINKI
TALLINN
ESTONIA
STOCKHOLM *BALTIC*
SEA

0   100   200km
0   50   100mi
Approximate North Only

Selimiye Camii of Edirne, Turkey

Fountain in front of Ayuntamiento, Valencia, Spain

Astronomical clock, Prague, Czech Republic

Detail on Dracula's house in Sighişoara, Romania

The Island Church, Lake Bled, Slovenia

Prizren in Kosovo, once the capital of 'Old Serbia', Yugoslavia

continental shelf in the 1960s, have brought prosperity to Norway, which has one of the world's highest per capita incomes.

GEOGRAPHY
Norway (323,878 sq km) is long and narrow, with a coastline deeply cut by fjords – long, narrow inlets of the sea bordered by high, steep cliffs. Mountains, some capped with Europe's largest glaciers, cover more than half of the country's land mass. Nearly a third of Norway lies north of the Arctic Circle – the point at which there is at least one full day when the sun never sets and one day when it never rises.

CLIMATE
Due to the warming effects of the Gulf Stream, Norway's coastal areas have a surprisingly temperate climate. In Bergen the average temperature in winter never drops below 0°C and in Vardø (in the far north) the average winter temperature is only -4°C. The mountainous inland areas have a more extreme range of temperatures with colder winter weather.

POPULATION & PEOPLE
Norway has 4.5 million people and the lowest population density in Europe. The largest cities are Oslo (population 500,000), Bergen (227,000), Trondheim (147,000) and Stavanger (108,000).

Most Norwegians are of Nordic, Alpine and Baltic origin. In addition, there are about 30,000 Lapps (called Sami in Norway), many of whom still live a traditional nomadic life herding reindeer in the far north.

SOCIETY & CONDUCT
Norwegians tend to be an independent and outdoor-oriented people. On summer weekends hiking, fishing and boating are popular; in winter Norwegians head for the ski runs. 'No trespassing' signs are virtually unknown and public access to wilderness areas is guaranteed.

The wearing of elaborate regional folk costumes is still commonplace at weddings and other festive events. Traditional folk dancing and singing is enjoying a resurgence in popularity and visitors can enjoy these activities at festivals around the country. Storytelling is another centuries-old tradition.

One simple rule of etiquette: as a guest in a Norwegian home, you shouldn't touch your drink before your host makes the toast '*skål*', which you should answer in return.

LANGUAGE
Norway has two official languages. They are quite alike, and every Norwegian learns both at school. Bokmål, literally 'book language', referred to in the Language Guide at the back of this book as BM (or indicated within brackets), is the urban-Norwegian variety of Danish, the language of the former rulers. BM, also called Dano-Norwegian, is used by more than 80% of the population.

The other language is Nynorsk or 'New Norwegian' (NN) – as opposed to Old Norwegian, the language in Norway before 1500. Nynorsk has a rural base and is the predominant language in the western fjord area and the central mountain districts.

In speech the distinction between BM and NN is no problem, since Norwegians understand both of them. English is also widely spoken in Norway, especially in the urban areas and in most tourist destinations.

Facts for the Visitor

HIGHLIGHTS
The 470km trip on the Oslo-Bergen railway is Norway's finest. Don't miss the side trip on the Flåm line, which winds sharply down the Flåm Valley, stopping at a thundering waterfall mid-route. Another special train trip is the Rauma line from Dombås to Åndalsnes.

Nothing typifies Norway more than its glacier-carved fjords, and ferrying along these inland waterways is Norway's top sightseeing activity. The cruise down the Geirangerfjord is Norway's most stunning and shouldn't be missed.

SUGGESTED ITINERARIES
Three days
  Spend one day each in Oslo and Bergen, and take a cruise on the scenic Nærøyfjord via Flåm.
One week
  Spend two days each in Oslo and Bergen, and take a three-day jaunt through the fjords of central Norway.
Two weeks
  As above, but continue north through Åndalsnes, Trondheim and the Lofoten Islands.

PLANNING
When to Go
Norway is at its best and brightest from May to September. Late spring is particularly pleasant. Unless you're heavily into winter skiing or searching for the Aurora Borealis, Norway's cold, dark winters are not the prime time to visit.

Maps
For drivers, the best road maps are the Cappelens series, available in Norwegian bookshops. Most local tourist offices have free, simple town maps. Topographical hiking maps can be purchased from the Norwegian Mountain Touring Association (DNT), which has offices throughout Norway.

TOURIST OFFICES
There are tourist offices in nearly every town of any size in Norway, usually near the train station, dock or town centre. In smaller towns they may be open only during peak summer months, while in cities they're open year-round.

Tourist Offices Abroad
Norwegian tourist office abroad include:

UK (☎ 0207-839 6255) Charles House,
   5 Lower Regent St, London SW1Y 4LR
USA (☎ 212-885 9700) PO Box 4649,
   Grand Central Station, New York, NY 10163

EMBASSIES & CONSULATES
Norwegian Embassies Abroad
Norwegian embassies abroad include:

Australia (☎ 02-6273 3444) 17 Hunter St,
   Yarralumla, ACT 2600
Canada (☎ 613-238 6570) Royal Bank Centre, 90
   Sparks St, Suite 532, Ottawa, Ontario K1P 5B4
UK (☎ 020-7591 5500) 25 Belgrave Square,
   London SW1X 8QD
USA (☎ 202-333 6000) 2720 34th St NW,
   Washington DC 20008

Foreign Embassies in Norway
The following embassies are in Oslo:

Australia (☎ 22 41 44 33) Jernbanetorget 2
Canada (☎ 22 99 53 00) Wergelandveien 7
New Zealand (☎ 66 84 95 30) Billingstadsletta
   19B, Asker
Russia (☎ 22 55 32 78) Drammensveien 74
UK (☎ 22 13 27 00) Thomas Heftyes gate 8
USA (☎ 22 44 85 50) Drammensveien 18

MONEY
The Norwegian krone is most often written NOK in international money markets, Nkr in Northern Europe and kr within Norway. One Norwegian krone equals 100 øre. There are 50 øre and one, five, 10 and 20 kroner coins, while bills are in 50, 100, 200, 500 and 1000-kroner denominations.

Post offices and banks exchange major foreign currencies and accept all travellers cheques. Cashing fees are calculated per cheque, so you'll save money by bringing travellers cheques in large denominations. There are ATMs throughout Norway; most accept major credit cards and Cirrus/Plus bank cards. Visa, Eurocard, MasterCard, American Express and Diners Club cards are widely accepted throughout Norway.

Exchange Rates
The following currencies convert at these approximate rates:

country	unit		kroner
Australia	A$1	=	Nkr5.21
Canada	C$1	=	Nkr6.22
euro	€1	=	Nkr8.03
France	1FF	=	Nkr1.22
Germany	DM1	=	Nkr4.10
Ireland	IR£1	=	Nkr10.19
New Zealand	NZ$1	=	Nkr3.77
UK	UK£1	=	Nkr13.26
USA	US$1	=	Nkr9.21

Costs
Norway can be very expensive, though if you sleep at camping grounds and prepare your own meals you might squeak by on US$25 to US$30 a day. If you stay at hostels and eat at inexpensive restaurants budget US$40 per day. This is still bare-bones – entertainment, alcohol and transport all cost extra. Trying to cover the whole country can be quite expensive – not because the per-km rate is particularly high, but because the distances are great.

Tipping
Service charges and tips are included in restaurant bills and taxi fares, and no additional tip is expected.

POST & COMMUNICATIONS
Norway has an efficient postal service. Postcards and letters (up to 20g) cost 5kr to

Nordic countries, 6kr to the rest of Europe and 7kr elsewhere.

Norway's country code is ☎ 47. Norway has no telephone area codes – all eight digits must be dialled. A three-minute call to the USA costs 30kr.

Most pay phones accept one, five and 10kr coins. Domestic calls cost a minimum of 2kr. The lowest rates apply from 5 pm to 8 am, and on weekends. Cardphones are generally found side by side with coin phones. *Telekort* (phonecards) are sold in 40, 90 and 140kr denominations and work out a bit cheaper than using coins. Phonecards are sold at post offices and the ubiquitous Narvesen newspaper kiosks.

Faxes can be sent from many post offices and hotels. Many public libraries have computers with Internet access, but access to nonresidents is often restricted. The larger cities have cybercafes and throughout the country many hotels, including the nationwide Rainbow chain, have Internet computers in their lobbies that work with credit cards.

INTERNET RESOURCES

General and tourism-related information about Norway can be accessed on the Internet at www.visitnorway.com. The Fjord Norway Travel Guide has information specific to fjord areas throughout Norway. Web site: www.fjordnorway.com/.

TIME

Time in Norway is GMT/UTC plus one hour. Clocks are turned one hour ahead on the last Sunday in March and back again on the last Sunday in October.

WOMEN TRAVELLERS

The main Norwegian feminist organisation is Kvinnefronten (☎ 22 37 60 54), Holsts gate 1, 0473 Oslo. Norway is generally a safe place to travel in, but in cases of attack or abuse women can call the Krisesenter (☎ 22 37 47 00) in Oslo or ☎ 112 nationwide.

GAY & LESBIAN TRAVELLERS

Norwegians are generally tolerant of different lifestyles, but public displays of affection (regardless of sexual preference) are not common. Gay and lesbian travellers can find gay entertainment spots in the larger cities. The largest gay event of the year is the week-

long Oslo Pride (mid to late June). For gay issues and activities, contact Landsforeningen for Lesbisk og Homofil Frigjøring (LLH; ☎ 22 36 19 48), St Olavs plass 2, 0165 Oslo.

DISABLED TRAVELLERS

Norway can be a challenging destination for disabled travellers, and those with special needs should plan ahead. The Norwegian Tourist Board's main accommodation brochure and the hostel association's handbook both list nationwide accommodation that is wheelchair accessible. Some, but not all, trains have coaches designed for wheelchair users. Norges Handikapforbund publishes a brochure in English with information for disabled travellers that can be picked up at tourist offices.

BUSINESS HOURS

Business hours are generally 9 am to 4 pm weekdays, though stores often stay open to 7 pm Thursday and to 2 pm Saturday.

Be aware that many museums have short hours (11 am to 3 pm is quite common). On Sunday most stores are closed, including bakeries, grocers and many restaurants.

PUBLIC HOLIDAYS & SPECIAL EVENTS

Public holidays are: 1 January, Maundy Thursday, Good Friday, Easter Monday, 1 May (Labour Day), 17 May (Constitution Day), Ascension Day, Whit Monday, 25 and 26 December.

Constitution Day (17 May) is Norway's biggest holiday, with many Norwegians taking to the streets in traditional folk costumes; the biggest celebration is in Oslo. Midsummer's Eve, which is celebrated with bonfires on the beach, is generally observed on 23 June, Saint Hans Day. The Sami people (Lapps) hold their most colourful celebrations at Easter in Karasjok and Kautokeino, with reindeer races, *joik* (traditional chanting) and other festivities.

ACCOMMODATION
Camping

Norway has nearly 1000 camping grounds. Sites cost 80kr to 125kr, and many places rent simple cabins (often with cooking facilities) from about 250kr a day. The Norwegian Tourist Board publishes a free annual camping guide that lists most camping grounds.

You can also pitch a tent anywhere in the wilderness for two nights, as long as you camp at least 150m from the nearest house and leave no trace of your stay. From 15 April to 15 September lighting a fire in the proximity of woodlands is strictly forbidden.

The Norwegian Mountain Touring Association (DNT) maintains a network of mountain huts a day's hike apart. Keys for unstaffed huts must be picked up in advance at DNT offices in nearby towns, while at staffed huts hikers simply show up – no one is ever turned away. Nightly fees average about 200kr. Contact the DNT head office, Den Norske Turistforening (☎ 22 82 28 00), Postboks 7 Sentrum, 0101 Oslo; check their Web site at www.dntoa.no.

Hostels

There are 88 Hostelling International (HI) *vandrerhjem* (hostels) in Norway. Some are lodge-style facilities open year-round, while others occupy school dorms in summer only. Beds are 80kr to 200kr per person (25kr extra without an HI card), breakfast is sometimes included. Some offer dinner for about 85kr and nearly all hostels have kitchens. In summer it's best to call ahead and make reservations – you can also book ahead on the Web site: www.vandrerhjem.no.

The free, annually updated, list of all hostels is available at tourist offices and hostels. Note that the word *lukket* next to a hostel listing refers to the hours when the reception office is closed and the phone is not answered – usually 11 am to 4 pm.

Norway's hostelling organisation is Norske Vandrerhjem (☎ 23 13 93 00, fax 23 13 93 50), Dronningens gate 26, 0154 Oslo.

Private Rooms & Hotels

Next to camping and hostelling, the cheapest option is a private room – look for '*husrom*' and '*sjøhus*' – booked through tourist offices. The average rate is 200/300kr for a single/double.

Although normal hotel prices are high, nationwide chains such as Rainbow and Rica offer good summer and weekend deals. With Rainbow, you'll get the lowest rates with a Scan Hotel Pass (sold at hotels for 90kr), which usually pays for itself on the first night. One important consideration in this land of sky-high food prices is that hotels usually include an all-you-can-eat buffet breakfast, while most pensions do not.

FOOD & DRINKS

Food prices can be a shock. To keep within a budget, expect to frequent grocery stores and bakeries. Common throughout Norway is the *konditori*, a bakery with a few tables where you can sit and eat pastries and inexpensive sandwiches. Other relatively cheap eats are found at *gatekjøkken* (food wagons and streetside kiosks). Only marginally more expensive, but with more nutritionally balanced food, are *kafeterias*, which have simple meals from about 50kr. Meals at moderately priced restaurants cost 90kr to 120kr, though many places feature a *dagens rett* (daily special) for about 75kr.

Norwegian specialities include grilled or smoked *laks* (salmon), *reker* (boiled shrimp), *torsk* (cod) and other seafood. Expect to see *geitost* (sweet goat cheese) and *sild* (pickled herring) at the breakfast buffet.

The legal drinking age is 18 years for beer and wine, 20 years for spirits. Supermarkets sell beer, while government-run *vinmonopolet* stores sell wine and spirits. These shops are generally open to 5 pm weekdays, to 1 pm Saturday. Wine is the most reasonably priced alcoholic beverage, costing from 75kr a bottle.

Getting There & Away

AIR

SAS, British Airways, KLM, Air France, Lufthansa, Sabena, Swissair, Finnair and Icelandair link Oslo with major European and North American cities. Bergen, Stavanger and Trondheim also have direct international flights.

LAND
Denmark

Trains run a few times daily (including an 11 pm night train) from Oslo to Copenhagen (nine hours) via Sweden. The trip costs 490kr.

Finland

The E8 highway runs from Tornio, Finland, to Tromsø and there are secondary higways connecting Finland with the northern Sami towns of Karasjok and Kautokeino. All three routes have bus services.

Russia
Russia has a short Arctic border with northern Norway and there's a bus between Kirkenes and Murmansk, Russia; see the Kirkenes section for details.

Sweden
Bus Nor-Way Bussekspress runs express buses at least three times daily from Oslo to Gothenburg (310kr, five hours) and Stockholm (345kr, eight hours).

Train There are daily trains from Oslo to Stockholm (502kr, seven hours), Gothenburg (414kr, four hours) and Helsingborg (490kr, 7½ hours). Ask about 'Nordic' fares – when available they can cut about 100kr from these prices.

SEA
Denmark
DFDS Seaways (☎ 22 94 44 00) runs overnight ferries from Oslo to Copenhagen daily; the cheapest cabin fare is 550/930kr in winter/summer (less 25% with a student ID). In summer you can also opt for a reclining chair (640kr). Cars cost 300kr. The departure in either direction is at 5 pm, arriving at 9 am.

Color Line (☎ 22 94 44 00) runs daily ferries between Kristiansand and Hirtshals, the shortest connection (four hours) and most frequent service (three to five sailings a day in summer) between Norway and Denmark. Color Line also operates ferries several days a week between Oslo and Hirtshals and between Moss (via Larvik) and the Danish ports of Hirtshals and Frederikshavn. Fares on all the routes are the same, ranging from 160kr on winter weekdays to 390kr on summer weekends for a passenger, from 200kr to 555kr for a car.

Fjord Line (☎ 55 54 88 00) sails from Bergen to Hanstholm on Monday, Wednesday and Friday at 4.30 pm, stopping en route in Egersund. The fare ranges from 300kr on winter weekdays to 750kr on summer weekends. Cars cost from 370kr to 680kr.

Stena Line (☎ 23 17 91 00) operates ferries from Oslo to Frederikshavn daily in summer, less frequently the rest of the year.

Boats leave Oslo at 8 pm, take 11 hours and cost 550kr in summer, as low as 150kr in winter.

Germany
Color Line has a ferry between Oslo and Kiel (19 hours, daily). Departures in both directions are at 2 pm. The cheapest cabin costs from 600kr to 820kr.

Iceland & the Faroe Islands
Smyril Line (☎ 55 32 09 70) runs weekly in summer between Bergen and Seyðisfjörður (Iceland), via the Faroe Islands. One-way fares from Bergen are 610kr to 840kr to Tórshavn (Faroe Islands) and 1290kr to 1840kr to Iceland. These fares are for a couchette. The boat leaves Bergen at 3 pm on Tuesday.

Sweden
DFDS Seaways runs daily overnight ferries between Oslo and Helsingborg (640kr in summer). The boats leave Oslo at 5 pm southbound and Helsingborg at 7 pm northbound. DFDS Seaways also provides service between Kristiansand and Gothenburg (110kr to 300kr, six hours) three times a week.

UK
Fjord Line sails from Bergen to Newcastle, via Stavanger, twice weekly in winter and thrice weekly in summer. Summer sailings are on Sunday, Tuesday and Friday from Bergen and on Monday, Wednesday and Saturday from Newcastle. The cheapest summer fare is 1010kr for a reclining chair; winter fares begin at 440kr per person in a four-berth cabin.

DFDS Seaways sails between Kristiansand and Newcastle, with departures from Kristiansand at 6.15 pm on Sunday and Thursday and from Newcastle at 3 pm on Monday and Friday. Cheapest cabin fares are 580kr in the winter and 1170kr in the summer.

Getting Around

The handy *NSB Togruter*, available free at train stations, has rail schedules and information on linking buses. Boat and bus departures vary with the season and the day (services on Saturday are particularly sketchy), so pick up the latest *ruteplan* (timetable) from regional tourist offices.

AIR

Norway has nearly 50 airports with scheduled commercial flights. Because of the great distances, air travel in Norway may be worthy of consideration even by budget travellers.

Norway's main domestic airlines are SAS, Braathens and Widerøe. Typical fares from Oslo (one way) are 1295kr to Trondheim and 2400kr to Tromsø, but a variety of discounts are available. Widerøe has a 500kr summer ticket (valid June to August) for flights within any one of four sectors, which are divided at Trondheim, Bodø and Tromsø.

Braathens's Visit Norway Pass, valid May to September, divides Norway into northern and southern sectors at Trondheim. Flights between any two points in one sector cost the equivalent of US$85.

BUS

Norway has an extensive bus network and long-distance buses are quite comfortable. Fares are based on distance and average about 1.15kr per km. Many bus companies have student and family discounts of 25% to 50% – always ask.

The main company, Nor-Way Busseks-press (☎ 22 33 01 90), operates a far-reaching network of express buses, with routes connecting every main city in the country. It offers a good-value pass that's valid for seven/14 consecutive days of unlimited bus travel for 1375/2200kr.

TRAIN

Eurail, Inter-Rail and Scanrail passes are valid in Norway.

All railway lines are operated by the Norwegian State Railways (NSB). From Oslo, the main lines go to Stavanger, Bergen, Åndalsnes, Bodø and Sweden. Second-class travel, particularly on long-distance trains, is generally comfortable; 1st-class travel, which costs 30% more, is not worth the extra money.

The Norway Rail Pass, which allows unlimited train travel within the country, can be purchased either before or after you arrive in Norway. For 2nd-class travel on any three/five days within a 30 day period the cost is US$139/194 abroad or 1124/1540kr in Norway.

If you're not travelling with a rail pass, there's a discounted 'minipris' ticket available for travel on long-distance trains but you must buy the ticket at least five days in advance. The minipris covers many, but not all, departures; those that are eligible are marked by green dots in the *NSB Togruter* schedule. On regular train tickets you can make unlimited en route stops, but no stops are allowed on minipris tickets.

To be assured of a seat you can always make reservations for an additional 25kr; on many long-distance trains, including all those between Oslo and Bergen, reservations are mandatory. Second-class sleepers offer a good way to get a cheap sleep: a bed in a three-berth cabin costs 115kr.

CAR & MOTORCYCLE

In Norway, you drive on the right side of the road. All vehicles, including motorcycles, must have dipped headlights on at all times. The wearing of seat belts is obligatory. On motorways and other main roads the maximum speed is generally 90km/h, while the limit in built-up areas is 50km/h unless otherwise posted. The maximum permissible blood alcohol concentration is 0.05%.

Main highways, such as the E16 (Oslo-Bergen) and the E6 (Oslo-Kirkenes) are kept open year-round; smaller roads, especially mountain passes, are often closed until May or June. In snow-covered areas you need studded tyres or tyre chains. The Road User Information Centre (☎ 22 65 40 40) has up-to-date road conditions throughout the country.

If you plan to travel along Norway's west coast, keep in mind that there are numerous ferry crossings, which can be time consuming and costly. For a complete list of ferry schedules, fares and reservation phone numbers, consider investing in the latest copy of *Rutebok for Norge* (210kr), available in larger bookshops and Narvesen kiosks.

The main office of the national automobile club, Norges Automobilforbund (NAF; ☎ 22 34 14 00), is at Storgata 2, 0155 Oslo.

Oslo

Oslo, the oldest of Scandinavia's capitals, was founded in 1050 by Harald Hardrada. After being levelled by fire in 1624, the city was rebuilt in brick and stone by King Christian IV, who renamed it Christiania, a name that stuck until 1925 when Oslo took back its original name.

Despite being Norway's largest city, Oslo (population 500,000) is remarkably low-key, casual and manageable. The city centre is a pleasant jumble of old and new architecture. Oslo has good museums, plenty of parks and an abundance of statues.

Orientation

From Oslo's central train station (Oslo Sentralstasjon, also Oslo S), Karl Johans gate, the main street, leads through the heart of the city to the Royal Palace. Most central city sights, including the harbour district and Akershus Fortress, are within a 15-minute walk of Karl Johans gate, as are the majority of Oslo's hotels and pensions.

Information

Tourist Offices The main tourist office (☎ 22 11 78 80), west of Rådhus near the harbour, is open 9 am to 7 pm daily in summer, 9 am to 4 pm weekdays in winter. There's a branch office at Oslo S, open until 11 pm daily.

At Use It (☎ 22 41 51 32), the youth information office at Møllergata 3, you can get advice on everything from cheap accommodation to hitching. It is open until 5 pm weekdays.

Oslo Card The Oslo Card provides free entry to most museums and free travel on all Oslo public transport. It costs 180/290/410kr for one/two/three days and is sold at the tourist office, post offices and some hotels. Students, who get half-price entry at many sights, may do better buying a public transport pass and paying separate museum admissions.

Money There are banks and ATMs throughout the city, in Oslo S and at the airport. If you're exchanging a small amount you usually get the best deal at American Express, north of Rådhus at Fridtjof Nansens plass 6.

Post & Communications The main post office is at Dronningens gate 15. There are convenient branch post offices at Oslo S and on Karl Johans gate opposite Stortinget.

Check your email for free at Use It (access only until 11.30 am on weekdays) or for 25kr at Studenten Nett-Café, Karl Johans gate 45, or Akers Mic, a CD shop at Akersgata 39.

Travel Agencies Kilroy Travels (☎ 23 10 23 10), Nedre Slottsgate 23, specialises in student and youth travel.

Bookshops Tanum Libris at Karl Johans gate 43 and the nearby Norli on Universitetsgata both have a good selection of English-language books, maps and travel guides.

Medical & Emergency Services Jernbanetorvets Apotek, opposite Oslo S, is a 24-hour pharmacy. Oslo Kommunale Legevakt (☎ 22 11 80 80), Storgata 40, is a medical clinic with 24-hour emergency services.

Things to See & Do

Oslo's highlights include the Bygdøy Peninsula with its folk museum and Viking ships; Vigeland Park, which features the sculptures of Gustav Vigeland; and Akershus Fortress with its castle and harbour views.

Karl Johans gate Along Oslo's main pedestrian street, Karl Johans gate, you'll find **Stortinget**, the nation's parliament building; **Eldsvollsplass**, a city square filled with fountains and statues; the century-old **National Theatre**; and the **Royal Palace**, which is surrounded by a large public park.

Rådhus Oslo's twin-towered, red-brick city hall, opposite the harbour, has showy wall murals decorating the interior. You can view the main hall from the front corridor or, for 25kr, walk through it all.

National Gallery The free Nasjonalgalleriet, Universitetsgata 13, has the nation's largest collection of Norwegian art. Some of Munch's best known works are on display, including the iconic *Scream*. There are also works by Gauguin, Monet and Picasso (closed Tuesday).

Historic Museum The free Historisk Museum at Frederiks gate 2 comprises three museums under a single roof. Most interesting is the ground floor **antiquities collection**

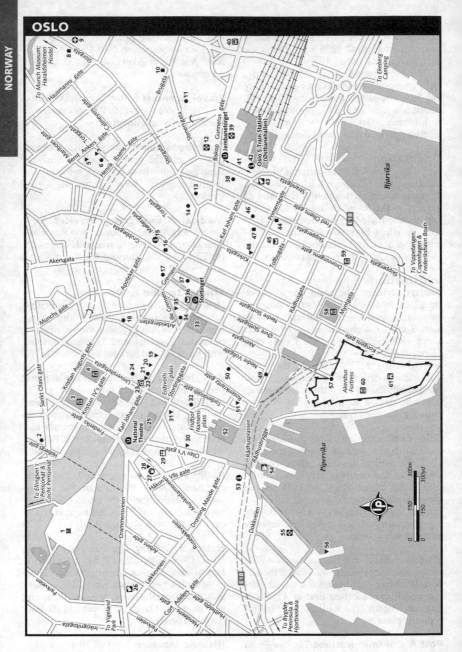

OSLO

NORWAY

OSLO

PLACES TO STAY		OTHER		34	Akers Mic
8	Albertine Hostel	1	Royal Palace	36	Post Office
10	Hotel Spectrum	2	Hertz Car Rental	37	Kilroy Travels
16	KFUM Sleep In	3	Historic Museum	38	Jernbanetorgets Apotek
44	City Hotel	4	National Gallery		(Pharmacy)
47	Fønix Hotel	6	Rockefeller Music Hall	40	Galleri Oslo (Bus Station)
		9	Oslo Kommunale Legevakt	41	Jernbanetorget
PLACES TO EAT			(Medical Clinic)	42	Turist Office
5	Saigon Lille Café	11	Oslo Spektrum	43	Australian Consulate
7	Lille Amir	13	NAF (Norges Automobilforbund)	45	Main Post Office
12	Oslo City Shopping Centre	14	DNT Office	46	Norske Vandrerhjem Office
19	Oluf Lorentzen	15	Use It	49	Skansen
	Grocery Store	17	So What	50	Potpurriet
20	Paleet Complex	18	London	52	Rådhus
22	Brassiere 45	21	Tanum Libris Bookshop	53	Main Tourist Office
28	Vegeta Vertshus	23	Studenten Nett-Café	54	Ferry to Bygdøy
30	Baker Brun	24	Norli Bookshop	55	Aker Brygge
31	Baker Hansen	25	National Theatre	57	Fortress Entrance
35	7-eleven	26	US Embassy	58	National Museum of
39	Byporten (Shopping Centre)	27	Petrol Station		Contemporary Art
48	Kiwi Grocery Store	29	Saga Cinema	59	Astrup Fearnley Museet
51	Baker Hansen	32	American Express	60	Norway's Resistance Museum
56	Fiske Røkeriet	33	Stortinget (Parliament)	61	Akershus Castle

with its exceptional displays of Viking-era coins, jewellery and ornaments. The 2nd-floor has a **numismatic collection** of coins dating from 995, while the top floor holds the **ethnographical collection** with displays on non-European cultures (closed Monday).

Akershus Fortress This medieval fortress and castle was built by King Håkon V around 1300. The park-like grounds, which offer excellent views of the city and Oslofjord, are the venue for a host of concerts in summer. Entry into the fortress (free) is either through a gate at the end of Akersgata or over a drawbridge at the southern end of Kirkegata. The fortress grounds are open 6 am to 9 pm; after 6 pm use the Kirkegata entrance.

In the 17th century, Christian IV renovated **Akershus Castle** (20kr) into a Renaissance palace, though the front is still decidedly medieval. Its chapel is still used for royal events, and the crypts of kings Håkon VII and Olav V lie beneath it. Tours in English at 11 am, 1 and 3 pm, led by university students in period costume, provide a good anecdotal history, or you can wander through on your own.

During WWII the Nazis used Akershus as a prison and execution grounds; today it is the site of **Norway's Resistance Museum** (25kr).

National Museum of Contemporary Art This museum at Bankplassen 4 features Scandinavian modern art (closed Monday; 40kr, free Thursday). A block to the east is the **Astrup Fearnley Museet**, which has quality, changing exhibits of Norwegian and foreign modern art (closed Monday; 40kr).

Munch Museum Dedicated to the life and work of Norway's most renowned artist, Edvard Munch (1863-1944), this museum at Tøyengata 53 is the repository for some 5000 drawings and paintings that Munch bequeathed to the city of Oslo (50kr). Take the T-bane (metro) to Tøyen, from where it's a five-minute, signposted walk.

Vigeland Park Frognerparken, or Vigeland Park, is a wonderful city park with expansive green spaces, duck ponds and rows of shady trees. Its central walkway is lined with life-sized statues by Gustav Vigeland. The most impressive piece is the monolith of writhing bodies, said to be the world's largest granite sculpture. The park is free and always open. To get there take tram No 12 or 15 from Jernbanetorget or the National Theatre.

For a more in-depth look at Gustav Vigeland and his work, head across the park to the **Vigeland Museum** at Nobels gate 32 (closed Monday; 30kr).

Holmenkollen The Holmenkollen **ski jump**, perched on a hillside above Oslo, draws the world's top jumpers in a ski festival each March and doubles as a concert site in summer. From the top of the ski jump there's a bird's-eye view of Oslo city and fjord – a lift goes part of the way, and then you climb 114 steps. The 60kr entry fee includes a **ski museum** with a collection of skis and sleds dating back as far as 600.

From Oslo, take T-bane line 1 for the 25-minute ride to Holmenkollen station, from where it's a 15-minute walk up to the jump.

Bygdøy Bygdøy Peninsula holds some of Oslo's top attractions. Give yourself at least half a day, more if possible. Ferries operate from late April to late September, making the 10-minute run to Bygdøy (20kr) every 40 minutes, starting at 7.45 am (9.05 am on weekends). The ferries leave from Rådhusbrygge 3 (opposite Rådhus) and stop first at Dronningen, from where it's a 10-minute walk up to the folk museum. The ferry continues to Bygdøynes, where you'll find the *Kon-Tiki* and *Fram* ships, and the maritime museum. From the folk museum it's a five-minute walk to the Viking ships and 15 minutes more to Bygdøynes. The route is signposted. All five museums are open daily year-round.

Norwegian Folk Museum More than 150 buildings, mostly from the 17th and 18th centuries, have been gathered from around the country and are clustered according to region in Norway's largest open-air museum (70kr). Dirt paths wind past old barns, rough-timbered farmhouses with sod roofs, and a rare stave church. There's also a worthwhile cultural exhibition hall just inside the main entrance. Sunday is a good day to visit, as there's usually folk music and dancing.

Viking Ship Museum This captivating museum houses three Viking ships that were excavated from the Oslofjord region. The ships had been drawn ashore and used as tombs for nobility, who were buried with all they expected to need in the hereafter: jewels, furniture, food and servants (30kr).

Kon-Tiki Museum This museum displays the *Kon-Tiki* balsa raft that Norwegian explorer Thor Heyerdahl sailed from Peru to Polynesia in 1947 to prove that Polynesia's first settlers could have come from South America. Also on display is the papyrus reed boat *Ra II* in which Heyerdahl crossed the Atlantic in 1970 (30kr).

Polarship Fram This museum holds Fridtjof Nansen's 39m rigged schooner *Fram*, which was launched in 1892 and used for polar expeditions, including the 1911 discovery of the South Pole by Roald Amundsen (25kr).

Norwegian Maritime Museum This rather mundane museum has small fishing boats, displays of dried cod and an abundance of model ships. The balcony on the top floor of the larger wing has a good view of the Oslofjord Islands (30kr).

Activities

Hiking A network of trails leads off into the Nordmarka from Frognerseteren, at the end of T-bane line 1. One good hardy walk is from Frognerseteren over to Lake Sognsvann, where you can take T-bane line 5 back to the city.

Skiing Oslo's ski season is roughly December to March. There are over 1000km of ski trails in the Nordmarka area north of Oslo, many of them floodlit. Easy-access tracks begin right at the end of T-bane lines 1 and 5. Tomm Murstad Skiservice (☎ 22 13 95 00) at the Voksenkollen station, one T-bane stop before Frognerseteren, has skis for hire.

Places to Stay

Camping Oslo has two large camping grounds with full facilities. Both charge 120kr for two people and a tent. ***Ekeberg Camping*** (☎ 22 19 85 68, *Ekebergveien 65*), on a knoll south-east of the city, is open June to August. Take bus No 34 from Oslo S to the Ekeberg stop, a 10-minute ride.

The lakeside ***Bogstad Camping*** (☎ 22 51 08 00, *Ankerveien 117*) in Holmenkollen is open year-round. Take bus No 32 from Oslo S to the Bogstad Camping stop, a 30-minute ride.

Private Rooms Use It (see Information) help travellers book rooms in *private homes* for 125kr a person – there's no minimum stay and no booking fee. The Oslo S tourist office books private rooms (from 170/300kr singles/doubles) and hotel rooms; it charges a 20kr booking fee, and there's a two-night minimum stay at most places.

HI Hostels Oslo has four HI-affiliated hostels; all include breakfast in their price.

Haraldsheim Hostel (☎ 22 22 29 65, fax 22 22 10 25, ✉ post@haraldsheim.oslo.no, Haraldsheimveien 4) is open year round. Rates without/with bath are 160/180kr in a dorm, 280/350kr for a single room, and 380/460kr for a double. The hostel is 4km from the centre; take tram No 13 or 17.

IMI (☎ 69 88 19 00, Staffeldtsgata 4), in a boarding school just north of the Royal Palace, is open from mid-June to mid-August. It costs 170kr for a dorm bed and 300/440kr for singles/doubles. Trams 10 and 17 stop nearby.

Open mid-May to mid-August, the *Holtekilen Hostel* (☎ 67 51 80 40, fax 67 59 12 30, ✉ holtekil@alfanet.no, Michelets vei 55, Stabekk) is 9km south-west of Oslo and charges 165kr for dorm beds and 270/430kr for singles/doubles. Take bus No 151 or 161.

LBM-Ekeberg Hostel (☎ 22 74 18 90, fax 22 74 75 05, Kongeveien 82), 7km south-east of Oslo, is open June to mid-August. Dorm beds are 175kr, singles/doubles 280/440kr. Take tram 18 or 19 to Holtet.

Private Hostels From mid-June to mid-August, a convenient non-HI option is *Albertine Hostel* (☎ 22 99 72 00, fax 22 99 72 20, Storgata 55), at the rear of the Anker Hotel. Beds in four/six-person dorms are 145/120kr. A private double room costs 360kr.

The convenient *KFUM Sleep In* (☎ 22 20 83 97), a YMCA hostel at Møllergata 1 (enter from Grubbegata), has beds at 130kr and is open from early July to mid-August.

Pensions & Hotels *Ellingsen's Pensjonat* (☎ 22 60 03 59, fax 22 60 99 21, Holtegata 25), five blocks north of the Royal Palace, has small but adequate singles/doubles for 290/470kr. Closer to the centre is *Cochs Pensjonat* (☎ 23 33 24 00, fax 23 33 24 10, Parkveien 25), just north of the Royal Palace. Rooms are 340/480kr with shared

bath, 430/580kr with bath and cooking facilities.

Fønix Hotel (☎ 22 42 59 57, fax 22 33 12 10, Dronningens gate 19), just a few blocks from Oslo S, has the city's lowest hotel rates: 395/550kr for singles/doubles with shared bath; request a renovated room. Also relatively cheap is *City Hotel* (☎ 22 41 36 10, fax 22 42 24 29, Skippergata 19), which has simple but adequate rooms for 440/640kr, or 565/770kr with private bath.

The Rainbow chain's *Hotel Spectrum* (☎ 23 36 27 00, fax 22 83 22 23, Brugata 7), east of Oslo S, has pleasant rooms and weekday rates of 680/780kr, weekend rates of 470/590kr.

Places to Eat

One way to save money is to frequent bakeries, many of which have reasonably priced sandwiches as well as pastries and wholegrain breads. *Baker Hansen* and *Baker Brun* are two good chains with numerous shops around Oslo. Among grocery stores, you'll find some of the best prices at *Kiwi*, which has branches throughout Oslo.

Oslo S & Around There are relatively cheap cafes, bakeries, fast-food stands and grocery stores inside Oslo S. *Oslo City* and *Byporten*, shopping complexes at the north side of Oslo S, also have numerous eateries.

Aker Brygge Aker Brygge, the shopping complex along the west side of the harbour, has a small food court with a *bakery*, *ice-cream shop*, *burger stand* and *pizzeria*.

Lining the harbour are ice-cream and hot-dog vendors as well as docked boats that have been converted into pricey beer halls and restaurants. The best deal is at *Fiske Røkeriet*, a waterside stall selling smoked mackerel for 20kr a half fish – buy a loaf of bread, grab a harbourside bench and make yourself a tasty sandwich.

Elsewhere in Oslo The grocery store *Oluf Lorentzen* (Karl Johans gate 33) has whole roasted chickens for 45kr. The 24-hour *7-Eleven* on Lille Grensen sells cheap coffee and hot dogs.

The shopping complex *Paleet* (Karl Johans gate 37) offers some of the better food deals in the city centre, including *Ma'raja* with an Indian lunch buffet for 59kr; *Mr*

Hong, with Chinese meals for around 60kr; and *Egon*, with a pizza and salad buffet for 79kr until 6 pm daily. The nearby *Brassiere 45 (Karl Johans gate 45)* has good fish and pasta dishes for around 80kr.

Vegeta Vertshus (Munkedamsveien 3) features a single-serving vegetarian buffet that includes casseroles and salads for 80kr for a small plate, 90kr for a normal-size plate.

Grønland, a neighbourhood of Asian and Middle Eastern immigrants, a few minutes' walk north-east of the bus station, has good, affordable eateries. *Punjab Sweet House (Grønland 24)* is recommended; it serves up plates of curry, rice and naan bread for around 50kr.

Also tasty is *Saigon Lille Café (Bernt Ankers gate 7)*, which has a full menu of Vietnamese meals for 58kr, and *Lille Amir*, on Torggata opposite the Rockefeller Music Hall, which has felafels and shwarmas.

Entertainment

The tourist office's monthly brochure *What's on in Oslo* lists current concerts, theatre and special events, while the free *Natt & Dag* entertainment newspaper covers the club scene. The city's largest concert halls – *Oslo Spektrum*, near Oslo S, and *Rockefeller Music Hall (Torggata 16)* – host big-name international musicians. *Saga cinema* on Olav V's gate shows first-run movies in their original language.

Skansen (Rådhusgata 25), in a former public toilet, is one of the city's hottest dance clubs. Just a stone's throw from Sleep In is *So What (Grensen 9)* a club with alternative music. The main hang-out for gay men is *London (CJ Hambros plass 5)*, while lesbians favour *Potpurriet (Øvre Vollgate 13)*.

Getting There & Away

Air All flights land at Oslo's international airport in Gardermoen, 50km north of the city. SAS (☎ 81 00 33 00) and Braathens (☎ 81 52 00 00) airlines have ticket offices in Oslo S near the airport train platform.

Bus Long-distance buses arrive and depart from Galleri Oslo, a 10-minute walk east of Oslo S.

Train All trains arrive and depart from Oslo S in the city centre. The reservation windows are open 6.30 am to 11 pm daily. There's also an information desk where you can get details on travel schedules throughout Norway.

Boat Boats to/from Copenhagen and Frederikshavn (Denmark) use the docks off Skippergata, near Vippetangen. Bus No 60 brings you close to the terminal.

Boats from Hirtshals (Denmark) and Kiel (Germany) dock at Hjortneskaia, west of the central harbour, from where there are connecting buses to Oslo S.

Getting Around

To/From the Airport High-speed trains run every 20 minutes between Oslo S and Oslo International airport in Gardermoen, cost 120kr and take 20 minutes. Or, you can take a local train or an express airport bus – these options take twice as long but only cost 80kr and operate frequently.

Public Transport Oslo has an extensive network of buses, trams, subways (the T-bane) and ferries. A one-way ticket on any of these services costs 20kr and includes a free transfer within an hour of purchase. A *dagskort* (day ticket) good for unlimited 24-hour travel (45kr) and one-week cards (150kr) are sold at Narvesen kiosks, staffed underground stations, and Trafikanten (below the tower at the front entrance of Oslo S). The latter also has a free public transport map, *Sporveiskart Oslo*.

Taxi Taxi charges average 34kr (44kr at night and on weekends) at flag fall and 13kr per km. There are taxi stands at the train station, shopping centres and city squares. Taxis with lit signs can be flagged down.

Southern Norway

Sørlandet, the curving south coast, is magnetic for Norwegians when the weather turns warm. The coast is largely rocky with a heavy scattering of low, stone islands.

STAVANGER

Stavanger, Norway's fourth-largest city, was once a bustling fishing centre and in its heyday had more than 50 sardine canneries. The city now holds the title 'Oil Capital of

Norway' – perhaps no greater tourist draw than pickled herring, but it has brought prosperity and a cosmopolitan community that includes nearly 3000 British and US oil people.

Most visitors to Stavanger arrive on the ferry from England and make a beeline for Bergen or Oslo. If your time is limited, that's not a bad idea.

Orientation & Information

The adjacent bus and train stations are a 10-minute walk from the harbour. The Kulturhus, a town centre of sorts, holds the public library, a cinema and an art gallery.

The tourist office (☎ 51 85 92 00), opposite the inner harbour, is open 9 am to 8 pm daily in summer.

Things to See & Do

A fun quarter to stroll through is **Gamle Stavanger**, on the west side of the harbour, where cobblestone walkways lead past early 18th-century whitewashed houses – said to be northern Europe's best preserved wooden-house settlement.

Stavanger Domkirke, on the southern end of Kirkegata, is an impressive medieval stone cathedral dating from the 12th century. You can get a good view of the city and the harbour oil rigs from **Valbergtårnet**, a 150-year-old tower at the end of Valberggata.

The **Maritime Museum**, in a seaside warehouse at Nedre Strandgate 17, gives a good glimpse into Stavanger's maritime history. The **Canning Museum**, in an old sardine cannery at Øvre Strandgate 88A, speaks for itself. A 40kr one-day ticket includes entry to all local museums.

Pulpit Rock The area's most popular outing is the two-hour hike to the top of the awesomely sheer Pulpit Rock (Preikestolen), 25km east of Stavanger. You can inch up to the edge of its flat top and peer 600m straight down to the Lysefjord. From Stavanger take the 8.20 or 9.15 am ferry to Tau (29kr, 40 minutes) from where there's a connecting bus (45kr) to the trailhead; allow a full day. The bus operates from late June to early September.

If you'd rather look up at Pulpit Rock from the bottom, the **Clipper** sightseeing boat (☎ 51 89 52 70) leaves Stavanger daily to cruise the steep-walled Lysefjord. Tickets (215kr) can be purchased at the tourist office.

Places to Stay & Eat

The lakeside *Mosvangen Hostel* (☎ 51 87 29 00, Henrik Ibsens gate 21), 3km from the city centre (bus No 97), charges 135kr for a dorm bed, 270kr for a double. There's a *camping ground* (☎ 51 53 29 71) next door. *Preikestolen* (☎ 97 16 55 51), a sod-roofed summer hostel, is within walking distance of Pulpit Rock.

The tourist office books *private rooms* from 250/350kr singles/doubles plus a 30kr booking fee. *Commandør Hotel* (☎ 51 89 53 00, ✉ comhot@online.no, Valberggata 9) has pleasant rooms with private baths for 500/650kr in summer.

The central pub *Dickens* (Skagenkaien 6) has generous daily specials for around 75kr. The nearby *Mai Thai* (Skagen 27) has good Asian food and reasonable lunch deals.

Getting There & Away

An express bus to Oslo (500kr, 10½ hours) leaves Stavanger daily at 8.30 am.

Stavanger's only train line runs to Oslo (650kr, eight hours), via Kristiansand. On weekdays there's also an overnight train, which leaves Stavanger at 10.40 pm. All trains require a reservation.

For information on ferries to/from England, see the Getting There & Away section at the start of this chapter.

Flaggruten's (☎ 51 86 87 80) express passenger catamaran to Bergen costs 530kr and takes four hours. Ask about discounts, including 50% off for rail pass holders. There are four sailings each way on weekdays, two on weekends.

KRISTIANSAND

Kristiansand, the closest port to Denmark, is the first glimpse of Norway for many travellers. The capital of Sørlandet, Kristiansand has a grid pattern of wide streets laid out by King Christian IV, who founded the city in 1641. It's a busy seaside holiday resort for Norwegians but of less interest to foreign visitors, who generally pile off the ferries and onto the next train.

For a quick look around, walk south-east along Vestre Strand gate to its end and then along Strandepromenaden to **Christiansholm Fortress** (circa 1674), where there's a coastal view from the cannon-ringed wall. From there walk inland along the tree-lined Festningsgata and turn left onto Gyldenløves gate, passing the **town square** and **cathedral** on the way back to the transport terminals.

Orientation & Information

The train, bus and ferry terminals are together on the west side of the city centre. Markens gate, a pedestrian street a block inland, is the central shopping and restaurant area.

The tourist office (☎ 38 12 13 14) is at Vestre Strandgate 32, opposite the bus station.

Places to Stay & Eat

Roligheden Camping (☎ *38 09 67 22*), at a popular beach 3km east of town, can be reached by bus No 15. The modern *Kristiansand Hostel* (☎ *38 02 83 10, Skansen 8*), about a 10-minute walk east of the fortress, is open year-round and charges 170kr for dorm beds, 320/370kr for singles/doubles.

The 10-room *Sjøgløtt Hotel* (☎ *38 02 21 20, Østre Strandgate 25*) has rooms with shared bath for 350/590kr.

There are good *bakeries* on Rådhus gate near the post office and opposite the *McDonald's* on Markens gate. *Mega* grocery store, opposite the train station, has a cheap cafeteria. *Peppe's Pizza* (*Gyldenløves gate 7*) offers a pizza and salad lunch buffet.

Getting There & Away

Express buses head north at 9 am daily to Voss (490kr, 11 hours) and Bergen (560kr, 12 hours) via Odda. There are daily trains to Oslo (430kr, five hours) and Stavanger (310kr, 3¼ hours), as well as express buses.

For information on ferries to Denmark see the Getting There & Away section at the start of this chapter.

TELEMARK

Most of the Telemark region is sparsely populated and rural, with steep mountains, deep valleys, high plateaus and a myriad of lakes. Unfortunately, travel around Telemark is geared primarily to the automobile. Train lines run only through the south-eastern part of Telemark and buses are infrequent.

Telemark Canal

The Telemark canal system, 105km of waterways with 18 locks, runs from the industrialised city of Skien to the small town of **Dalen**. From mid-May to early September century-old sightseeing boats (☎ 35 90 00 20) make the unhurried, 10-hour journey (290kr one way). At the height of summer, the boats operate in both directions daily.

Buøy Camping Dalen (☎ *35 07 75 87*), 1km from the Dalen dock, has hostel-style rooms for 200kr, doubles for 300kr and cabins for 425kr. Skien has a year-round *hostel* (☎ *35 50 48 70, Moflatvien 65*) and a hotel nearby, *Nye Hotell Herkules* (☎ *35 59 63 11, Moflatvien 59*), with singles/doubles for 445/610kr.

Rjukan

The long, narrow industrial town of Rjukan is squeezed into the deep Vestfjord valley at the base of **Mt Gausta** (1883m), Telemark's highest peak. A trail to the mountaintop starts at Lake Hedder, 16km south-east of town. The **Industrial Workers Museum**, 7km west of Rjukan, has an exhibit of the Norwegian Resistance's daring sabotage of the heavy-water plant that was built here by the Nazis during WWII.

There's a year-round *hostel* (☎ *35 09 05 27*) in Rjukan. Daily express buses connect Rjukan to Oslo (240kr, 3½ hours) via Kongsberg.

Kongsberg

The settlement of Kongsberg was founded in 1624 following the discovery of one of the world's purest silver deposits in the nearby Numedal Valley. The national mint is still located in town, but the last mine, no longer able to turn a profit, closed in 1957. The tourist office (☎ 32 73 50 00), Storgata 35, is opposite the train station.

Things to See & Do The **Norwegian Mining Museum**, Hyttegata 3, just over the bridge in an 1844 smelting building, has exhibits of mining, minting and skiing (50kr). The **Lågdal folk museum**, which has a collection of period farmhouses and an indoor museum with recreated 19th-century workshops, is 10-minutes south of the train station: turn left on Bekkedokk, take the walkway parallel to the tracks and follow the signs (25kr).

In summer there are daily tours of the old **silver mines** at Saggrenda, 8km from Kongsberg, which include a train ride through cool subterranean shafts (55kr). Weekday buses to the mines (get off at Søvverket) leave from Kongsberg on the hour.

Places to Stay & Eat The *Kongsberg Hostel* (☎ 32 73 20 24) is 2km from the train station; walk south on Storgata, cross the bridge and take the pedestrian walkway over route 40. Dorm beds cost 185kr, doubles 440kr.

Of Kongsberg's two central hotels, the *Gyldenløve Hotel* (☎ 32 73 17 44), a member of the Best Western chain, usually has the cheapest summer and weekend rates.

Gamle Kongsberg Kro, on the south side of the river, has good food, a varied menu and moderate prices. There's a bakery at the *Rimi* grocery store west of the train station.

Getting There & Away There are daily trains to/from Oslo (125kr, 1½ hours). Daily express buses connect Kongsberg with Rjukan (152kr, two hours) and Oslo (120kr, 1½ hours).

Central Norway

The central part of Norway stretches west from Oslo to the historic city of Bergen and north to the mountain town of Åndalsnes, taking in Norway's highest mountains, largest glacier and most spectacular fjords.

OSLO TO BERGEN

The Oslo-Bergen railway line is Norway's most scenic, a seven-hour journey past forests, alpine villages and the starkly beautiful Hardangervidda Plateau.

Midway between Oslo and Bergen is **Geilo**, a ski centre where you can practically walk off the train and onto a lift. Geilo has a *hostel* (☎ 32 09 03 00) near the train station, and there is good summer hiking in the mountains above town.

From Geilo the train climbs 600m through a tundra-like landscape of high lakes and snow-capped mountains to the tiny village of **Finse**, near the glacier Hardangerjøkulen. Finse has year-round skiing and is in the middle of a network of summer hiking trails.

Myrdal, the next train stop, is the connecting point for the spectacularly steep Flåm railway, which twists its way down 20 splendid kilometres to Flåm village on the Aurlandsfjord, an arm of the Sognefjord.

Many people go down to Flåm, have lunch and take the train back up to Myrdal where they catch the next Oslo-Bergen train.

A better option is to take the ferry from Flåm up the waterfall-laden Nærøyfjord to Gudvangen where there's a connecting bus that climbs a steep valley on the dramatically scenic ride to Voss. From Voss, trains to Bergen run nearly hourly. To include a cruise of the Nærøyfjord in a day trip from Oslo to Bergen, you'll need to take the 8.11 am train from Oslo, which connects with the afternoon ferry from Flåm. For details on Flåm see the Sognefjord section.

BERGEN

Set on a peninsula surrounded by seven mountains, Bergen's history is closely tied to the sea. It became one of the central ports of the Hanseatic League, which dominated trade in northern Europe during the late Middle Ages. The Hanseatic influence is still visible in the sharply gabled row of houses that line Bergen's picturesque harbour.

Even though it's Norway's second-largest city, Bergen (population 227,000) has a pleasant, slow pace, not to mention a university, good museums and a noted philharmonic orchestra. Odds are that you'll see rain, as it falls 275 days a year. Still, that's not as dismal as it sounds – the low skyline of red-tiled roofs manages to look cheery even on drizzly days.

Bergen is the main jumping-off point for journeys into the western fjords; numerous buses, trains, passenger ferries and express boats set off daily. The railway sells a packaged 'Norway in a Nutshell' ticket (560kr) combining a morning train from Bergen to Flåm, a ferry up the spectacular Nærøyfjord to Gudvangen, a bus to Voss and a train back to Bergen in time for a late dinner. It makes for a very scenic day trip.

Orientation

The bus and train stations are a block apart on Strømgaten, a 10-minute walk from the city centre. Much of the city is built up around the waterfront and many of the sights, restaurants and hotels are within a few blocks of Vågen, the inner harbour.

Information

The tourist office (☎ 55 32 14 80), opposite the inner harbour at Vågsallmenningen 1, stocks the handy *Bergen Guide*. Hours are 8.30 am to 10 pm daily (to 4 pm in winter, closed Sunday in the off season).

BERGEN

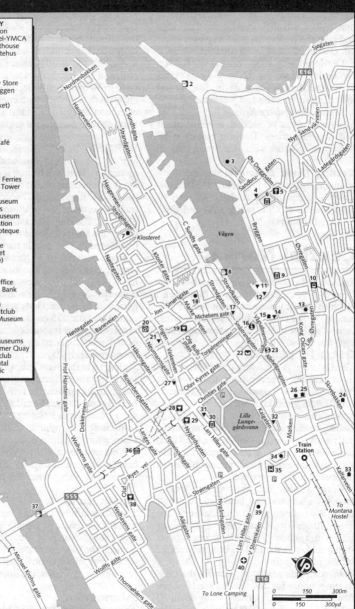

PLACES TO STAY
7 Kloster Pension
15 Bergen Hostel-YMCA
24 Olsnes Guesthouse
25 Marken Gjestehus
33 Intermission

PLACES TO EAT
4 Spar Grocery Store
11 Zachariasbryggen Complex
12 Torget (Market)
14 Godt Brød
17 Burger King
21 Café Opera
27 Godt Brød
31 Stenersens Café
32 Ma-Ma Thai

OTHER
1 Aquarium
2 International Ferries
3 Rosenkrantz Tower
5 Mariakirken
6 Bryggens Museum
8 Express Boats
9 Hanseatic Museum
10 Funicular Station
13 Jarlens Vaskoteque (Laundrette)
16 Tourist Office
18 Vinmonopolet (Liquor Store)
19 Rick's
20 Netropolis
22 Main Post Office
23 Kreditkassen Bank
26 DNT Office
28 Kafé Fincken
29 Garage Nightclub
30 Bergen Art Museum
34 Library
35 Bus Station
36 University Museums
37 Coastal Steamer Quay
38 Hulen Nightclub
39 Avis Car Rental
40 Medical Clinic

For information on wilderness hiking and hut rentals, contact DNT (☎ 55 32 22 30) at Tverrgaten 4.

The tourist office and local hotels sell the Bergen Card (150/230kr for 24/48 hours), which allows free transport on local buses, free funicular rides and admission to museums (the Hanseatic Museum is not covered).

The main post office, on Småstrandgaten, is open to 6 pm weekdays, to 3 pm on Saturday.

You can check email for a fee at the Internet cafe Netropolis (☎ 55 55 85 44), 20 Teatergaten; or for free (but with a lengthy queue) at the library next to the train station.

Things to See & Do

Bryggen Bryggen, the site of the old medieval quarter, is a compact area that's easily explored on foot. The street side of Bryggen's long timber buildings hold museums, restaurants and shops, while the alleys that run along their less-restored sides offer an intriguing look at the rough-plank construction of centuries past.

The worthwhile **Hanseatic Museum**, in a timber building dating from the 16th century, retains its period character and furnishings and offers a glimpse of the austere working and living conditions of Hanseatic merchants (open daily; 35kr).

The **Bryggens Museum** occupies the site of Bergen's earliest settlement; exhibits include excavated medieval tools, pottery and skeletons (open daily; 30kr).

The Romanesque church **Mariakirken** dates from the 12th century and is Bergen's oldest building. It has 15th-century frescoes and a splendid baroque pulpit and is open on weekdays (10kr).

Opposite the harbour is the **Rosenkrantz Tower**, built in the 1560s by Bergen's governor as a residence and defence post. You can climb up spiral staircases to the lookout on top (20kr). It's open daily from mid-May to August, otherwise on Sunday only.

Other City Sights The university, at the end of Christies gate, has a **Maritime Museum** with models of Viking ships (20kr) and a **Cultural History Museum** with Viking weaponry, medieval altars and folk art (closed Monday; 30kr).

The three-part **Bergen Art Museum**, housed in two buildings on Rasmus Meyers Allé, opposite the lake fountain, exhibits a superb collection of Norwegian art from the 18th and 19th centuries, including many works by Munch and JC Dahl, as well as contemporary works by Picasso, Klee and others. It's open from 11 am to 5 pm daily (closed on Mondays in winter; 35kr).

The **Bergen Aquarium** has an outdoor tank with seals and penguins as well as indoor fish tanks. It's near the northern tip of the peninsula, a 15-minute walk from the centre (or take bus No 11). Entry is 75kr.

Activities

For an unbeatable city view, you can take the **funicular** to the top of 320m Mt Fløyen. If you also want to do some hiking, well-marked trails lead into the forest from the hill-top station. Trails 1 and 3 are the longest, each making 5km loops through hilly woodlands. For a good 40-minute walk back to the city, take trail 4 and connect with trail 6. The funicular runs 7.30 am to 11 pm (midnight in summer) on the hour and half-hour and costs 20kr one way.

The **Ulriksbanen cable car** to the top of 642m Mt Ulriken offers a panoramic view of the city and surrounding fjord and mountains. The tourist office sells a 90kr ticket that includes the cable car and a return bus from Bergen. It's also possible to take the cable car one way and walk across to the funicular station at Mt Fløyen along a well-beaten trail that takes about three hours.

Special Events

The Bergen International Festival held for 11 days at the end of May, is the big cultural event of the year with dance, music and folklore events throughout the city.

Places to Stay

Camping *Lone Camping (☎ 55 39 29 60, Hardangerveien 697, Haukeland)* is 30 minutes east of Bergen by bus No 900.

Private Rooms The tourist office books private singles/doubles from 200/300kr, plus a 25kr booking fee.

Hostels The 175-bed *Bergen Hostel-YMCA (☎ 55 60 60 50, fax 55 60 60 51, ⓔ ymca@online.no, Nedre Korskirkeal-menning 4)* is a central place to crash but can be noisy. It's open from 1 June to mid-September and costs 100kr to 125kr for a dorm bed. Breakfast is an extra 40kr.

A cosier in-town option is **Intermission** (☎ 55 31 32 75, *Kalfarveien 8*), in a period home near the train station, open mid-June to mid-August. A dorm bed with breakfast costs 120kr.

The 276-bed **Montana Hostel** (☎ 55 20 80 70, *fax 55 20 80 75*, ❸ *montvh@ online.no, Johan Blyttsvei 30*), 5km from the city centre by bus No 31, is open from 1 April to 20 December. Dorm beds cost 140kr and doubles 500kr, breakfast included.

Guesthouses The inviting **Marken Gjestehus** (☎ 55 31 44 04, *fax 55 31 60 22*, ❸ *markengjestehus@smisi.no, Kong Oscargate 45*) has dorm beds for 160kr in a four-bed room and private rooms at 310/410kr for singles/doubles. There's a guest kitchen, coin laundry, TV room and lockers.

Olsnes Guesthouse (☎ 55 31 20 44, *Skivebakken 24*) is a five-minute walk from the train station (turn uphill opposite the Leprosy Museum). Open from mid-May to October, it has nine adequate rooms and a shared kitchen. Singles/doubles cost 185/295kr with shared bath, 205/345kr with private bath.

Kloster Pension (☎ 55 90 21 58, *fax 55 23 30 22, Strangehagen 2*) has 18 clean, simple rooms for 340/500kr with shared bath and a few doubles with private bath for 650kr; rates include breakfast.

Places to Eat

The *fish market* at Torget is the place to buy fruit and seafood, including tasty open-faced salmon rolls (10kr). It's open 7 am to 4 pm Monday to Saturday. The **Spar** grocery store, opposite Bryggens Museum, has 25kr grilled chickens.

The bus station is a mecca of cheap eats with inexpensive fast food, a *fruit stand*, a *bakery* and two *grocery stores*. A great place for a snack is the bustling **Godt Brød** on Vaskerelven; it has a cafe with sandwiches and cakes and bakery with organic whole-grain breads. There's also a branch of **Godt Brød** (*Nedre Korskirkealmenning 17*) near the Bergen Hostel-YMCA.

Ma-Ma Thai (*Kaigaten 20*), a cosy Asian restaurant, attracts university students with discounted specials, including 55kr lunches served daily from 2 to 5 pm.

Another student haunt, **Café Opera** (*Engen 24*), serves pastas, salads and Mexican dishes for around 75kr. **Stenersens Café**, on the ground floor of the Bergen Art Museum, has baguette sandwiches and light meals at reasonable prices.

The waterfront Zachariasbryggen complex, at the inner harbour, houses several pubs and eateries including the **Baker Brun** konditori with good pastries and sandwiches, a **Peppe's Pizza** and an *ice-cream shop*.

Entertainment

The popular **Rick's**, at the head of Ole Bulls plass, has live music, a disco and pub. **Garage** (*Christies gate 14*) attracts a student crowd, as does the cave-like **Hulen** (*Olaf Ryes vei 47*) behind the student centre. **Kafé Fincken** (*Nygårdsgaten 2A*) is the main gay and lesbian venue in town.

Getting There & Away

Air The airport is in Flesland, 19km southeast of central Bergen. The SAS Flybussen (45kr) runs a couple of times an hour between the airport and the Bergen bus station, stopping en route on Olav Kyrres gate near Hotel Norge.

Bus Daily express buses run to Odda in Hardanger (200kr, 3½ hours) and to the western fjord region. From Bergen it costs 349kr (seven hours) to Stryn, 503kr (10½ hours) to Ålesund and 694kr (14½ hours) to Trondheim. There's a bus from Bergen to Stavanger (360kr, 5¾ hours) at least twice daily.

Train Trains to Oslo (550kr, seven hours) depart several times a day; seat reservations are required. In addition, local trains run regularly between Bergen and Voss (125kr, 1¼ hours). Lockers at the train station cost 10kr.

Boat There are daily Sognefjord express boats to Balestrand and Flåm, northbound express boats to Måløy and southbound express boats to Stavanger. All leave from the west side of Vågen.

The coastal steamer, *Hurtigruten*, heads for northern ports daily, departing from the quay south of the university at 8 pm in summer and 10.30 pm in winter.

Ferries to Newcastle, Iceland and Denmark dock north of Rosenkrantz tower; for details see this chapter's introductory Getting There & Away section.

Getting Around
The bus fare within the city boundaries is 18kr per ride. A free bus runs between the post office and the bus station.

SOGNEFJORD
The Sognefjord is Norway's longest (200km) and deepest (1300m) fjord – a wide slash across the map of western Norway. In some places the sheer, lofty walls rise more than 1000m straight up out of the water. The Sognefjord's broad main waterway is impressive, but it's only by cruising into the fjord's narrower arms that you get closest to the steep rock faces and the cascading waterfalls. The loveliest branch is the deeply cut Nærøyfjord, Norway's narrowest fjord.

Fylkesbaatane operates a year-round express boat between Bergen and Sogndal, stopping at a dozen towns en route, and a second summer-only boat that terminates in Flåm instead of Sogndal. The summer boat leaves Bergen at 8 am daily and arrives in Flåm at 1.25 pm. The return boat leaves Flåm at 3.30 pm, arriving in Bergen at 8.40 pm. From Bergen it costs 320kr to Balestrand, 435kr to Flåm.

Flåm
Flåm, a tiny village at the head of the Aurlandsfjord, is a transit point for travellers taking the Gudvangen ferry or the Sognefjord express boat. It's also the only place on the Sognefjord with rail connections. The tourist office (☎ 57 63 21 06) at the train station rents bikes and the Heimly Pensjonat rents boats. The docks are just beyond the train station.

Places to Stay & Eat The pleasant *Flåm Camping & Hostel* (☎ 57 63 21 21), minutes from the station, has just 20 beds (book early) and charges 105/300kr for a dorm bed/double. *Heimly Pensjonat* (☎ 57 63 23 00) has a great fjord view and straightforward rooms from 450/600kr for singles/doubles.

The *Heimly Cafeteria* has reasonably priced sandwiches, and the *Furukroa Cafeteria*, at the ferry dock, has fast food as well as Norwegian meals.

Getting There & Away The Flåm railway runs between Myrdal and Flåm (115kr) numerous times a day in sync with the Oslo-Bergen service. At Flåm, buses and boats head out to towns around the Sognefjord.

The most scenic boat ride from Flåm is the ferry up the Nærøyfjord to Gudvangen, leaving at 3 pm daily all year and at 9 am, 11.15 am and 1.15 pm from June to early September. The ferry from Flåm to Gudvangen costs 155kr. At Gudvangen a connecting bus (65kr) takes you on to Voss. Tickets are sold at the Flåm tourist office.

Balestrand
Considering that it's the main resort destination on the Sognefjord, the village of Balestrand is remarkably low-key and there are some good, inexpensive places to stay. The tourist office (☎ 57 69 12 55) at the dock rents bikes for 50kr a half-day.

Places to Stay At *Sjøtun Camping* (☎ 57 69 12 23), a 15-minute walk south along the fjord, you can pitch a tent amid apple trees or rent a rustic four-bunk cabin for 200kr.

The lodge-like *Balestrand Hostel* (☎ 57 69 13 03, fax 57 69 16 70) has dorm beds/doubles for 165/400kr, breakfast included; it's open late June to mid-August. The Victorian-style *Bøyum Pensjonat* (☎ 57 69 11 14), open in summer only, has singles/doubles for 200/300kr. Both places are minutes from the dock.

Getting There & Away In addition to the Sognefjord express boat, local boats run daily to Flåm, Hella and Fjærland. Buses go to Sogndal (72kr) and Bergen (230kr).

Fjærland
Fjærland is a farming village at the head of scenic Fjærlandsfjord and near two arms of the massive glacier Jostedalsbreen, an inviting location for day-trippers.

The Balestrand tourist office sells a packaged ticket (331kr) that includes the morning ferry to Fjærland, a connecting sightseeing bus and the afternoon return ferry. The tour includes the Norwegian Glacier Museum, which has extensive displays on Jostedalsbreen, and visits two arms of the glacier: the Supphellebreen, where you can walk up to the glacier's edge and touch the ice, and the creaking blue-iced

Bøyabreen, where it's not uncommon to witness ice breaks dropping into the meltwater. Alternatively, a taxi from the Fjærland dock to the glacier costs about 300kr return.

Getting There & Away Ferries run twice a day in summer between Fjærland and Balestrand (110kr, 1½ hours), stopping in Hella en route. Buses connect Fjærland with Sogndal (44kr, 30 minutes) and Stryn (130kr, two hours).

Sogndal

Sogndal is a modern regional centre of little note but it's a starting point for day trips in the surrounding area. Of most interest is the glacier **Nigardsbreen** 70km to the north. The tourist office (☎ 57 67 30 83) is at Kulturhus on Gravensteinsgata, about 500m east of the bus station.

The tourist office books *private rooms* for 200/350kr a single/double. The summer *hostel* (☎ *57 67 20 33*) 15-minutes east of the bus station charges 95kr for a dorm bed, 160/220kr for singles/doubles.

Getting There & Away Buses run from Sogndal to Kaupanger (20kr) and Hella (50kr). Daily summer buses go north-east to Lom (160kr, 3½ hours) and on to Otta (240kr, 4½ hours), a hiking centre between the Jotunheimen and Rondane mountains on the Dovre railway line.

Nigardsbreen

Nigardsbreen, the most attractive arm of the Jostedalsbreen glacier, is a popular summer destination, with guided hikes across the glacier's rippled blue ice. Outings include easy 1½-hour walks (100kr), hardy four hour blue-ice treks (300kr) that require hiking boots and warm clothing, and a couple of day-long options. More information is available from Jostedal Breheimsenteret (☎ 57 68 32 50), the Web site at www.jostedal.com, or at nearby tourist offices.

A bus leaves Sogndal at 8.25 am for the glacier, and a return bus leaves Nigardsbreen at 5 pm. The fare is 90kr each way. Although this gives you time to do a short hike, if you're doing a longer hike you might want to stay at the nearby *Nigardsbreen Camping* (☎ *57 68 31 35*), which has huts as well as tent sites.

ÅNDALSNES

Åndalsnes, at the edge of the Romsdalsfjord, is the northern gateway to the western fjords. Most visitors arrive on the train from Dombås, a scenic route that descends through a deeply cut valley with dramatic waterfalls. Just before reaching Åndalsnes the train passes **Trollveggen**, whose jagged and often cloud-shrouded summit is considered the ultimate challenge among Norwegian mountain climbers.

The town of Åndalsnes is rather nondescript, but the scenery is top notch. Camping grounds are plentiful and it has one of the finest hostels in Norway. The tourist office (☎ 71 22 16 22) is at the train station.

Places to Stay

Åndalsnes Camping (☎ *71 22 16 29*), 3km from the centre on the south-east side of the Rauma River, has simple cabins for 160kr. It rents bicycles/canoes for 100/170kr a day and cars for 550kr a day.

The best option is the sod-roofed *Setnes Hostel* (☎ *71 22 13 82*), 2km from the train station on route 9. Open from mid-May to mid-September, it has pleasant singles/doubles for 275/420kr and dorm beds for 175kr, all including breakfast. If you don't want to walk, catch the Ålesund bus, which meets the train and goes past the hostel.

If the hostel is full, the nearby *Romsdal Gjestegård* (☎ *71 22 13 83*) has rooms for 350/580kr with breakfast and pleasant two-bedroom cabins with kitchens for 550kr.

Getting There & Away

The train from Dombås runs at least three times daily (155kr, 1½ hours), in sync with Oslo-Trondheim trains. Buses to Ålesund (148kr, 2½ hours) meet the trains. Buses to Geiranger (122kr, three hours) via the Trollstigen highway operate from 15 June to 31 August, leaving Åndalsnes at 8.45 am and 5.45 pm. If you're driving, the mountain pass is reopened by at least 1 June every year.

FROM ÅNDALSNES TO GEIRANGER

The **Trollstigen** (Troll's Path) winding south from Åndalsnes is a thriller of a road with hairpin bends and a 1:12 gradient. The bus makes photo stops at the thundering 180m **Stigfossen waterfall** on its way up the precipitous mountain pass.

You could break your journey in **Valldal** – there are camping grounds, cabins and a hostel – though most travellers continue on, taking the short ferry across to **Eidsdal**. From there a waiting bus continues along the Ørneveien (Eagle's Highway), ending with a magnificent bird's-eye view of the Geirangerfjord before descending into Geiranger village.

GEIRANGERFJORD

The 16km Geirangerfjord is narrow and winding with towering rock faces, a scattering of abandoned farms clinging to the cliffsides, and breathtakingly high waterfalls. The villages of Geiranger and Hellesylt, at either end of the fjord, are connected by ferry. The cruise down the Geirangerfjord is magnificent and shouldn't be missed.

Geiranger

Geiranger, at the head of the Geirangerfjord, is surrounded by high mountains with cascading waterfalls. Although the village has only 300 residents, it's one of Norway's most visited spots. Nevertheless, it's reasonably serene in the evening when the cruise ships and tour buses have gone.

There's great hiking all around Geiranger to abandoned farmsteads, waterfalls and some beautiful vista points. One special walk is to **Storseter waterfall**, a 45-minute hike that actually takes you between the rock face and the cascading falls. The tourist office (☎ 70 26 30 99), at the pier next to the post office, has a photo album detailing trails.

You can get a splendid cliff-top view of Geiranger valley and fjord from the Dalsnibba lookout (1476m); there's a bus (37kr) from Geiranger at 9.40 am in summer.

Places to Stay Hotels in Geiranger are quickly booked out by package tourists, but cabins and camping spots are plentiful. A dozen camping grounds skirt the fjord and hillsides, including *Geiranger Camping* (☎ 70 26 31 20), in town at the head of the fjord.

'Husrom' signs around the village advertise *private rooms* for around 200kr to 350kr – the tourist office maintains a list of such places and can help you book one.

Vinjebakken (☎ 70 26 32 05), a hostel-style chalet about a 15-minute uphill walk from the dock, has a beautiful fjord view

and friendly management. Open mid-June to mid-August, there are male and female dorms, each with 10 beds (125kr).

The *Grande Fjord Hotell* (☎ 70 26 30 90), on the fjord 2km north-east of the village, has cabins, tent space and moderately priced motel rooms.

Getting There & Away In summer there are daily buses to Åndalsnes (122kr) leaving Geiranger at 1 and 6.35 pm. The Geiranger-Hellesylt ferry cruises the fjord four to 10 times a day from May to September (passengers 34kr, cars 105kr; 70 minutes).

Hellesylt

Although this end of the fjord is not as spectacular as Geiranger, the village of Hellesylt has a fine summer *hostel* (☎ 70 26 51 28) perched just above town with 100kr dorms and a row of cabins (250kr) with fjord views. The tourist office (☎ 70 26 50 52) is near the dock. Buses heading south to Stryn leave from the pier where the ferry pulls in (66kr, one hour).

LILLEHAMMER

Lillehammer (population 24,500) has long been a popular ski resort for Norwegians, and since hosting the 1994 Winter Olympics it has attracted foreign visitors as well.

Orientation & Information

Lillehammer centre is small and easy to explore. Storgata, the main pedestrian walkway, is two short blocks east of the adjacent bus and train stations. The tourist office (☎ 61 25 92 99), Elvegata 19, is open daily in summer.

Things to See & Do

It's possible to tour the former Winter Olympic sites, including Håkons Hall (the hockey venue), which houses the **Norwegian Olympic Museum** (50kr). If you prefer a more interactive experience, there's a downhill **ski and bobsleigh simulator** (40kr) beneath the ski jump.

The Olympics aside, Lillehammer's main attraction is the exceptional **Maihaugen folk museum**, a collection of 175 historic buildings in a traditional village setting. It's open from 9 am to 6 pm daily June to mid-August and at least 11 am to 4 pm Tuesday to Sunday at other times; admission is 70kr. Maihaugen is a 20-minute walk from the train station; go up Jernbanegata, turn right onto Anders Sandvigs gate, and then left up Maihaugvegen.

Places to Stay & Eat
Lillehammer Camping (☎ 61 25 33 33), on Lake Mjøsa 700m south of the Skibladner dock, has modern cabins.

The *Lillehammer Hostel (☎ 61 26 25 66)*, upstairs at the bus station, has 26 rooms each with four beds, shower and toilet. Beds cost 170kr, singles/doubles 350/460kr, breakfast included.

A good budget option is *Gjeste Bu (☎ 61 25 43 21, Gamleveien 10)*, a guesthouse with dorm beds for 80kr and singles/doubles from 175/250kr. There's a shared kitchen.

Storgata is lined with shops, bakeries and restaurants; you can get a reasonably priced meal at several places, including *Peppe's Pizza (Storgata 69)* and *Vertshuset Solveig (Storgata 84)*.

Getting There & Away
Lillehammer is on the Dovre railway line between Oslo (275kr, 2½ hours) and Trondheim (450kr, five hours).

Northern Norway

The counties of Sør Trøndelag, Nord Trøndelag, Nordland, Troms and Finnmark comprise a vast area – over 1500km – mostly north of the Arctic Circle. Trains run as far north as Bodø and from there it's all buses and boats. Because distances are long, bus travel costs can pile up, though Inter-Rail and Scanrail holders get a 50% discount on most long-distance bus routes. An interesting alternative to land travel is the *Hurtigruten* coastal steamer, which pulls into every sizeable port between Bergen and Kirkenes, passing some of Scandinavia's finest coastal scenery along the way.

RØROS
Røros is an old copper-mining town with a well-preserved historic district that's on Unesco's World Heritage List. The first mine opened in 1644 and the last one closed in 1986. The town is good for strolling and

everything's within close proximity. The tourist office (☎ 72 41 11 65) is on Peder Hiortsgata 2, a two-minute walk north-east of the train station.

Things to See & Do
Røros' main attractions are the turf-roofed **miners' cottages** and other centuries-old timber buildings, a 1784 **church** with a baroque interior, **slag heaps**, and the old smelting works, which is now a **mining museum** with intricate scale models of life in the mines (50kr).

You can also visit the defunct **Olav copper mine**, 12km north-east of town (45kr). In summer, subterranean tours into the mine (5°C – dress warmly) are given six times daily between 10.30 am and 6 pm. In July and early August a special bus to the mine departs from the train station (60kr return) at 1 pm (11.30 am on Saturday).

Places to Stay
Idrettsparken Hostel (☎ 72 41 10 89, Øra 25), at the edge of a sports stadium 1km from the train station, has camping, dorm beds (180kr) and private rooms (280/380kr for singles/doubles). Walk east from the train station, cross the tracks opposite Bergstadens Hotel and follow the signs.

The central *Vertshuset Røros (☎ 72 41 24 11, Kjerkgata 34)* has pleasant rooms and flats from 715/890kr for singles/doubles.

Getting There & Away
Røros is 46km west of the Swedish border, via route 31. It's also a stop on the eastern railway line between Oslo (490kr, six hours) and Trondheim (225kr, 2½ hours).

TRONDHEIM
Trondheim, Norway's third-largest city (population 147,000) and its first capital, is a lively university town with a rich medieval history. It was founded at the estuary of the winding Nidelva River in 997 by the Viking king Olaf Tryggvason. After a fire razed most of the city in 1681, Trondheim was redesigned by General Caspar de Cicignon with wide streets and a Renaissance flair.

Orientation & Information
The central part of town is on a triangular peninsula that's easy to explore on foot. The train station and coastal steamer quay

are across the canal, a few minutes north of the centre.

Torvet, the central square, has the tourist office (☎ 73 80 76 60; closed weekends off-season), a fruit market and a head-on view of the cathedral.

Things to See & Do

The grand **Nidaros Domkirke** cathedral is the city's most prominent landmark and Scandinavia's largest medieval building. From spring to autumn it's open 9 am to at least 3 pm weekdays (to 2 pm Saturday) and 1 to 4 pm Sunday. The 25kr admission includes entrance to the adjacent 12th-century **Archbishop's Palace**, the oldest secular building in Norway. The cathedral, which is the site of Norwegian coronations, displays the crown jewels in summer every day except Friday.

The **Museum of Applied Art**, Munkegata 5, has a fine collection of contemporary arts and crafts (closed Saturday; 40kr). The **Trondhjems Kunstforening**, an art museum at Bispegata 7, has Munch lithographs and other Scandinavian works (30kr).

The excavated ruins of early medieval churches can be viewed free in the basement of the SpareBank 1 Midt-Norge at Søndre gate 4 and inside the entrance of the public library nearby. Also not to be missed are the old waterfront warehouses, best viewed from **Gamle Bybro** (the Old Town Bridge). There's a good city view from the top of the 17th-century **Kristiansten Fort**, a 10-minute uphill walk from Gamle Bybro.

The **Ringve Museum**, Lade Allé 60, 4km north-east of the city centre (bus No 4), is a fascinating music history museum in a period estate. Tours in English are given at 11.30 am, 12.30 and 3.30 pm daily in July and August (less frequently the rest of the year). Entry is 60kr.

Places to Stay

The tourist office books *private rooms* averaging 275/350kr for singles/doubles, plus a 20kr booking fee.

From late June to mid-August, university students operate an informal crash pad called **Trondheim InterRail Centre** (☎ 73 89 95 38, ✆ tirc@stud.ntnu.no, Elgeseter-gate 1), a five-minute walk south of the cathedral. A bed costs 105kr, breakfast included. This friendly operation has 40kr

dinners, inexpensive beer and free Internet access.

The **Trondheim Hostel** (☎ 73 87 44 50, ✆ tr-vanas@online.no, Weidemannsvei 41), 2km south-east of the train station (bus No 63), is open from 3 January to 18 December and has dorm beds for 170kr, singles/doubles for 370/480kr, breakfast included.

Pensjonat Jarlen (☎ 73 51 32 18, fax 73 52 80 80, Kongens gate 40) has straightforward rooms with TV, shower and kitchenette at 350/450kr for singles/doubles.

Places to Eat

Kafé Gjest Baardsen in the library on Kongens gate has inexpensive cakes, salads and sandwiches. On Brattørgata, on the north side of the city, you'll find *Café Dali* and *Café 3-B*, which serve simple eats, have alternative music and are popular with students.

Pizzakjelleren (Fjordgata 7) offers a simple 59kr pizza buffet from noon to around midnight, while *Peppe's Pizza (Kjøpmannsgata 25)* is a bit pricier but right on the water.

The *Det Lille Franske* bakery opposite the tourist office has good takeaway sandwiches. There's a small health-food store, *Hardangerfrukt*, at Fjordgata 62. Or you can munch out on inexpensive fish cakes at the *Ravnkloa fish market*.

Getting There & Away

Air The airport is in Værnes, 32km east of Trondheim. Airport buses (50kr) leave from the SAS Royal Garden Hotel in conjunction with SAS and Braathens flights.

Train There are six trains to Oslo daily (640kr) and two to Bodø (720kr). If you're in a hurry to get north, consider taking the overnight train from Oslo, tossing your gear into a locker at the station and spending the day exploring Trondheim before continuing on an overnight train to Bodø.

There are also trains from Trondheim to Storlien in Sweden (145kr, two hours) at 11 am and 4.36 pm daily, with onward connections to Stockholm.

Boat On its northbound journey, the coastal steamer arrives in Trondheim at 8 am (6 am in winter) and departs at noon; southbound, it arrives at 6.30 am and departs at 10 am.

BODØ

Besides being the terminus for the northern railway line, Bodø is Nordland's biggest town (population 40,500) and a jumping-off point for the Lofoten islands. As the town was levelled during WWII and completely rebuilt in the 1950s, Bodø itself is rather ordinary in appearance, though it does have a lovely mountain backdrop.

The tourist office (☎ 75 52 60 00), Sjøgata 21, and an adjacent Kreditkassen bank are near the waterfront in the city centre. From the tourist office, the bus station is a five-minute walk west.

Places to Stay & Eat

Bodøsjøen Camping (☎ 75 56 36 80) is 3km from town via bus No 12. The 58-bed *Bodø Hostel* (☎ 75 52 11 22) is conveniently located on the top floor of the train station and open year round; dorm beds cost 140kr, doubles 280kr.

Glasshuset, an indoor shopping centre midway between the tourist office and bus station, has a grocery store, cafeteria, pizzeria, bakery and Burger King.

Getting There & Away

Trondheim trains arrive in Bodø at 9.55 am and 6.40 pm. If you're continuing north by bus, be sure to get off one stop before Bodø at Fauske, where the two daily express buses to Narvik (272kr, 4¾ hours) connect with the train. Southbound trains leave Bodø at 11.30 am and 8.55 pm daily.

The northbound coastal steamer arrives in Bodø at 12.30 pm and departs at 3 pm; southbound, it's in port from 1 to 4 am. The coastal steamer and Lofoten car ferry docks are a five-minute walk north of the train station, while express catamaran boats dock beside the bus station.

LOFOTEN ISLANDS

The spectacular Lofoten Islands are peaks of glacier-carved mountains that shoot straight up out of the sea. From a distance they appear as an unbroken line, known as the Lofoten Wall, and are separated from the mainland by the Vestfjord.

Although fish stocks have dwindled in recent years, fishing continues to be the Lofoten Islands' largest industry and the cod is still hung outside on wooden racks to dry through early summer. Fishermen's *rorbu*

(winter shanties) and *sjøhus* (dorm-style beach houses) double as summer tourist lodges.

The main islands – Austvågøy, Vestvågøy, Flakstadøy and Moskenesøy – are linked by bridge or tunnel, with buses running the entire length of the Lofoten road (E10) from Fiskebøl in the north to Å at road's end in the south-west. Lofoten Trafikklag (☎ 76 06 40 40) offers various discounts. There are 50% reductions with Inter-Rail passes; with a Scanrail pass you get half-price fares only if the journey includes a rail connection.

Svolvær

By Lofoten standards the main port town of Svolvær on the island of Austvågøy is busy and modern. On the square facing the harbour you'll find a couple of banks, a taxi stand and the regional tourist office, Destination Lofoten (☎ 76 07 30 00).

A fun excursion is the cruise into the spectacularly steep and narrow **Trollfjord**. The M/S *Trollfjord* (☎ 76 07 17 90) departs from Svolvær harbour to the fjord (300kr) at 11 am daily, weather permitting.

Places to Stay The *Svolvær Sjøhus* (☎ 76 07 03 36), a rustic dockside beach house, has rooms from 350kr for either singles or doubles; turn right on the first road past the library, a five-minute walk east of the harbour. *Havna Hotel* (☎ 76 07 10 55), near the tourist office, has comfortable rooms with private bath from 550/750kr for singles/doubles.

Getting There & Away Buses to Leknes leave Svolvær (80kr, two hours) every couple of hours on weekdays, less frequently on weekends.

A car ferry runs between Svolvær and the mainland town of Skutvik a few times a day (55kr for a passenger, 188kr for a car; two hours). The coastal steamer leaves Bodø at 3 pm daily, arriving in Svolvær at 9 pm (328kr). Express boats leave Bodø for Svolvær at 5.15 pm weekdays, 8.30 pm on Sunday (229kr, 3½ hours).

Borg

Norway's largest Viking building, an 83m chieftain's house, has been excavated in Borg, near the centre of Vestvågøy island.

The site's rewarding **Lofotr Vikingmuseum** (80kr) has a full-scale reconstruction of the building and a replicated Viking ship. The museum is a stop on the Svolvær-Leknes bus route.

Stamsund

This traditional fishing village makes a fine destination largely because of its dockside hostel, a magnet for travellers who sometimes stay for weeks on end. A grocery store, post office and bus stop are a couple of minutes uphill from the hostel.

Places to Stay At *Justad Hostel/Rorbuer* (☎ *76 08 93 34, fax 76 08 97 39)*, bunks in the old beach house cost 80kr, double rooms 200kr and pleasant four-person cabins 400kr. Manager Roar Justad lends rowing boats for free (catch and cook your own dinner!) and rents bicycles for 80kr. The hostel is open from 15 December to 15 October.

Getting There & Away The coastal steamer stops en route (7.30 pm northbound, 9.15 pm southbound) between Bodø (306kr) and Svolvær (109kr). In summer, buses from Leknes to Stamsund run seven times a day, less on weekends (27kr).

Reine

The delightful village of Reine, on the island of Moskenesøy, is on a calm bay backed by lofty mountains and has an almost fairy-tale setting. In summer ferries run from Reine to **Vindstad** through the scenic Reinefjord (23kr; 40 minutes). From Vindstad you can make a one-hour hike over a ridge to the abandoned beachside settlement of **Bunes** on the other side of the island. On most weekdays you can take a morning ferry from Riene and then catch an afternoon ferry back.

All buses from Leknes to Å stop in Reine; the bus stop is near the post office.

Places to Stay *Reine Rorbuer* (☎ *76 09 22 22)* has seaside rorbu that can sleep eight for 1150kr. There are *'sjøhus'* signs along the road advertising cheaper private rooms.

Å

Å is a special place – a preserved fishing village with a shoreline of red rorbu, cod drying on racks everywhere and picture-postcard scenes at almost every turn. Many of Å's 19th-century buildings have been set aside as the **Norwegian Fishing Village Museum**, complete with old boats, boathouses, a bakery, etc. A second period museum, the **Lofoten Stockfish Museum**, details the history of cod fishing; a combined ticket to both museums is 55kr.

The camping ground at the end of the village has a hillside view of Værøy Island, which lies on the other side of the **Moskenesstraumen**, the swirling maelstrom that inspired the fictional tales of Jules Verne and Edgar Allen Poe.

Places to Stay & Eat *Moskenesstraumen Camping* (☎ *76 09 11 48)* has simple cabins for 300kr. *Å Hostel* (☎ *76 09 11 21, fax 76 09 12 82)*, open year round, offers accommodation in some of the museum's historic seaside buildings for 125kr a person. The inviting *Å-Hamna Rorbuer* (☎ *76 09 12 11, fax 76 09 11 14)*, also at the museum, has pleasant rooms in a restored 1860s home for just 200kr a double and cosy four-bedded rorbu from 400kr.

Food choices are limited – the best bet is to use the kitchen where you're staying. You can buy fresh fish from local fishermen and pick up other supplies at the small *food shop* behind the hostel office.

Getting There & Away There's a daily bus at 8 pm from Leknes to Å (78kr, two hours) and at 4 pm from Å to Leknes; on most days there are also a couple of earlier buses.

Ofotens og Vesteraalens Dampskibsselskab (OVD; ☎ 76 11 82 34) runs car ferries from Bodø to Moskenes, 5km north of Å. The trip takes four hours, costs 122kr for a passenger, 441kr for a car, and in summer operates about five times daily.

TROMSØ

Tromsø (population 57,500), the capital of Troms county, is the world's northernmost university town. In contrast to some of the more sober communities that dot Norway's north coast, Tromsø is a spirited place with street music, cultural happenings and more pubs per capita than any other city in Norway. Many polar expeditions have departed from Tromsø, earning the city the nickname 'Gateway to the Arctic'.

NORWAY

Orientation & Information
Tromsø's city centre and airport are on the island of Tromsøya, which is linked by a bridge to the mainland. The tourist office (☎ 77 61 00 00) is at Storgata 61 (closed weekends off-season).

Things to See & Do
The city centre has many period buildings, including the 1861 cathedral, **Tromsø Domkirke**, one of Norway's largest wooden churches. Tromsø's most striking church, however, is the **Arctic Cathedral**, on the mainland just over the bridge (15kr). This modernist building bears a resemblance to Australia's Sydney Opera House.

The **Tromsø University Museum**, at the southern end of Tromsøya, has well-presented displays on Arctic birds, Sami culture and regional history (20kr). Take bus No 28 from Storgata, opposite the bank.

The harbourside **Polar Museum** has Arctic frontier exhibits, some interesting and others, such as the display on clubbing baby seals, of more questionable taste (30kr).

The **Polaria**, at the south side of the city, has extensive polar displays, a 180-degree cinema showing polar films and an aquarium with arctic fish and seals (70kr).

The **cable car** 420m up Mt Storsteinen (60kr return) runs April to September, from 10 am to 5 pm daily, and until 1 am on clear nights from 20 May to 20 August. Take bus No 26 from Stortorget harbour.

Places to Stay
Tromsdalen Camping (☎ 77 63 80 37) on the mainland, 2km east of the Arctic Cathedral, has tent space and cabins; take bus No 24 from Stortorget harbour.

Tromsø Hostel (☎/fax 77 68 53 19, Gitta Jønsonsvei 4, Elverhøy), 2km west of the city centre, is reached via bus No 30. It's open from 20 June to 18 August and costs 125kr for dorms, 200/250kr for singles/doubles.

The tourist office books *rooms* in private homes, starting from 200/350kr plus a 25kr booking fee.

Two guesthouses on the hillside a few minutes' walk from the centre are *Ami Hotel* (☎ 77 68 22 08, fax 77 68 80 44, Skolegata 24) and *Hotell Nord* (☎ 77 68 31 59, fax 77 61 35 05, Parkgata 4). Rates with breakfast and shared bath are 420/550kr at Ami Hotel and 475/620kr at Hotell Nord.

Places to Eat
Buy fresh boiled shrimp from *fishing boats* at Stortorget harbour and a loaf of bread at the nearby *bakery* and you've got yourself a meal. The harbourside *Domus* grocery store has a cheap 2nd-floor cafeteria. Good central places are *Paletten Kafé*, which has inexpensive sandwiches; *Meieriet (Grønnegata 37)*, with snacks and affordable meals; and *Amtmannens Datter (Grønnegata 81)*, with reasonably priced pub fare and free Internet access.

Getting There & Away
Tromsø is the main airport hub for the northern region, with direct flights to Oslo, Bergen, Bodø, Trondheim, Honningsvåg and Kirkenes.

There are a few daily express buses between Tromsø and Narvik (296kr, 4½ hours), including one at 10.30 am. Buses to Alta (334kr, 6½ hours) leave Tromsø daily in the afternoon year round as well as at 8.15 am in summer.

The coastal steamer arrives at 2.45 pm and departs at 6.30 pm northbound and arrives at 11.45 pm and departs at 1.30 am southbound. The fare is 946kr to Bodø, 650kr to Hammerfest.

HAMMERFEST
Hammerfest has a population of 10,000 and an economy based on fishing.

Most visitors arrive on the coastal steamer and have two hours to look around. The tourist office (☎ 78 41 21 85) at Kirkegata 21 is a few minutes' walk from the dock. At the same site is the **Museum of Reconstruction** (40kr), which details the rebuilding of Hammerfest after WWII. Nearby in the town hall the free **Royal & Ancient Polar Bear Society** has arctic hunting displays.

Places to Stay & Eat
Storvannet Camping NAF (☎ 78 41 10 10), 2km east of the town centre, has reasonably priced cabins. The central *Rica Hotel* (☎ 78 41 13 33, Sørøygata 15) has summer rates of 710/840kr for singles/doubles. The *Domus* supermarket on Strandgata, east of the town hall, has an inexpensive cafeteria.

Getting There & Away
The coastal steamer stops at 5.30 am northbound and 11.45 am southbound daily.

FFR (☎ 78 40 70 00) runs a daily boat to Honningsvåg from mid-June to mid-August (310kr, 2¼ hours). The boat leaves Hammerfest at 7 pm; the return boat leaves Honningsvåg at 1.30 am. You can also get a return ticket for 835kr (spouses 670kr) that includes a bus and entry fee to Nordkapp to see the midnight sun.

HONNINGSVÅG

Honningsvåg, the only sizable settlement on the island of Magerøy, has a little museum and a 19th-century church, but the centre of attention is at Nordkapp, 34km away.

The tourist office (☎ 78 47 25 99), midway between the bus station and quay, covers the Nordkapp area and in winter can arrange snowscooter expeditions to Nordkapp.

Places to Stay & Eat

Nordkapp Camping (☎ 78 47 33 77), open from mid-May to 30 September, is 8km north of Honningsvåg on the road to Nordkapp (18kr by bus). Hostel-style dorm beds cost 135kr, small cabins 440kr and double rooms with private bath 500kr.

Honningsvåg's hotels are expensive; the cheapest, *SIFI Sommer Hotell (☎ 78 47 28 17)*, 3km north of the centre, charges 550/700kr for singles/doubles.

There's a *grocery store* on Storgata up from the coastal steamer quay. The reasonably priced *Kafé Corner* is behind the tourist office.

Getting There & Away

During summer a bus leaves Alta every day except Saturday at 3.55 pm, stopping in Honningsvåg at 8.15 pm and arriving at Nordkapp at 9.45 pm. From Alta the fare is 300kr to Honningsvåg and 360kr to Nordkapp.

The coastal steamer departs from Honningsvåg northbound at 5 pm in summer and 2.45 pm in winter, and southbound at 6.45 am year round.

NORDKAPP

Nordkapp (North Cape), a high rugged coastal plateau at 71°10'21'', is Europe's northernmost point and the main destination for travellers to the far north. The sun never drops below the horizon from mid-May to late July. Long before other Europeans took an interest in the area, Nordkapp was considered a power centre by the Sami people.

Nowadays there's a 175kr entrance fee and a touristy complex with exhibits, eateries, souvenir shops and a post office. The 180-degree theatre runs a good short movie but to really appreciate Nordkapp take a walk out along the cliffs.

Getting There & Away

An asphalt road winds across a rocky plateau and past herds of grazing reindeer up to Nordkapp. Depending on the snowfall, it's usually open from May to mid-October; the National Road User Information Center (☎ 22 65 40 40) gives opening dates.

In summer, buses run from Honningsvåg to Nordkapp (60kr, 45 minutes) at 12.15 and 9 pm. The buses return from Nordkapp at 2.50 pm and 12.30 am.

Poland

Travellers to Poland will delight in its heroic past, urban vitality and natural beauty. Poland's history begins with tales of medieval kings and armour-clad crusaders, lauds the astronomic advances of the great Copernicus and the romantic inspirations of Chopin, lays bare the savageries of WWII, and triumphs in the Solidarity-led revolution against communism. The enduring character of Poland's cities is displayed in the old-world splendour of regal Kraków, the modern clamour of ambitious Warsaw, and the resilient spirit of maritime Gdańsk. Outside enthusiasts will be impressed by the undeveloped coastline and intricate waterways in the north, as well as the rugged mountain ranges in the south.

Gone are the days of ill-mannered communism and questionable *kielbasa*. Poland now provides an accommodative tourist infrastructure and a flourishing consumer culture. One welcome remnant of the past remains: prices are significantly lower than in Western Europe. Often overlooked as a tourist destination, Poland represents one of Europe's last bargains.

AT A GLANCE

Capital:	Warsaw
Population:	38.5 million
Official Language:	Polish
Currency:	1 złoty (zł) = 100 groszy

Facts about Poland

HISTORY

Poland is situated midway along the northern European plain that stretches from the Atlantic to the Urals. This location has drawn the region's people into the ebb and flow of great power politics, as reflected in the dramatic fluctuations of Poland's territorial demarcation.

In the early middle ages, Western Slavs moved into the flatlands between the Vistula and Oder Rivers, from whence they were called Polanians, or people of the plains. In 966, Mieszko I adopted Christianity in exchange for official recognition from Rome of his status as regional overlord. He thus founded the Piast dynasty, which ruled Poland for over 400 years. His son, Bolesláv the Brave, was crowned Poland's first king in 1025.

Poland's early success as a regional power proved short-lived. German encroachment prompted the relocation of the royal capital from Poznań to Kraków in 1038. In 1226 the Prince of Mazovia invited a band of Germanic crusaders to help convert the pagan tribes still living in the north. Accepting the job, the Teutonic Knights quickly slashed their way to a sizable swath of the Baltic coast, whereupon pagans and Poles alike were harshly dispatched. The south had its own problems to contend with as marauding Tatars overran Kraków twice in the mid-13th century.

The kingdom was finally reconstituted under Kazimierz III the Great, who reigned from 1333-1370. The nuptials between the Polish Princess Jadwiga and the Grand Duke of Lithuania Jagiełło in 1386 set the stage for Poland's golden age. The joining of Poland and Lithuania created a continental great power, which stretched from the Baltic to the Black Seas. It assembled a fearsome army, which dealt the Teutonic Knights bloody defeat at the Battle of Grunwald in 1410. In the 16th century, the enlightened King Zygmunt I ushered in the Renaissance, lavishly patronising the arts and sciences. At this time, Copernicus was busy reordering the cosmos. While the rest of Europe was torn by religious strife, Poland displayed tolerance, becoming a haven for the persecuted, especially Jews. In 1569, Poland and Lithuania formally merged into a single state.

When the Jagiellonian dynasty expired in 1572, Poland's imported Swedish king moved the capital to Warsaw. At this point, the nobility reasserted its dominance over

the throne by making the king an elected official of the parliament (Sejm). The noble-dominated Sejm operated on the principle of the *liberum veto*, meaning that a disgruntled viscount could obstruct legislation. In effect, the nobles orchestrated a political arrangement that preserved their privileges.

Poland entered a period of irreversible decline. Through the 17th century, regional rivals Sweden and Russia marched back and forth across Polish territory. A last gasp of glory occurred under King Jan III Sobieski, who in 1683 smashed the Otto-man siege of Vienna and drove the Turks out of Europe. Unfairly, so it seems, the Austrians then allied against the Poles. In the late 18th century, the 'enlightened' despots of Russia, Prussia and Austria greedily conspired to

carve up the Polish state. Over a series of three partitions, Poland was systematically removed from the map of Europe.

In the 19th century, Poland, now subject to three empires, experienced a nationalist revival. The romantic movement in the arts preserved folk traditions and lamented independence lost. National revolutionaries plotted insurrections and died martyrs' deaths. In reaction, Russia and Germany enacted policies of forced assimilation in their Polish holdings.

In the early 20th century, the empires of Eastern Europe were finally dismembered, and the Versailles Treaty in 1919 declared Poland again to be a recognised sovereign state. In 1926, the military hero Marshal Jozef Piłsudski deposed Poland's fledgling parliamentary democracy in favour of presidential authoritarianism.

On 1 September 1939, WWII began when a Nazi blitzkrieg poured down on Gdańsk. The Polish army's determined stand proved no match for the German war machine. Refusing to collaborate with their Nazi occupiers, Polish resistance continued in underground partisan groups and in several ultimately tragic uprisings.

WWII fundamentally reshaped society. Six million Polish inhabitants, roughly 20% of the prewar population, died during the war. Nazi Germany used Poland as the main site for its policies of racial purification, whereby Slavic Poles were relegated to the role of slave labourers, and Jews were brutally annihilated in death camps. At the war's end, Poland's borders were redrawn yet again. The Soviet Union claimed the eastern territories for itself and extended the western boundary at the expense of Germany. The border changes were accompanied by the forced resettlement of more than one million Poles, Germans and Ukrainians. As a result, Poland became an ethnically homogenous state.

Stalin once said that imposing the communist system on Poland would be like trying to fit a saddle onto a cow. He tried anyway, and proved himself right. The cycle of anticommunist protests – met alternatively by coercion and concessions – culminated in the paralysing strikes of 1980-81, led by the Solidarity trade union. This time the regime survived only by declaring martial law.

In 1989, the communists, Solidarity and the Catholic Church sat down to round-table negotiations to address the political stalemate. Discussions resulted in parliamentary elections wherein a fixed number of seats would be openly contested. The communists failed to win even one seat in open competition, thus exposing the widespread contempt for their rule. Solidarity showed itself to be more than a trade union. Openly supported by the Church and the Polish pope, John Paul II, it had become the political embodiment of Polish nationalism, waging battle against yet another foreign oppressor.

The Polish elections of June 1989 triggered a succession of events that by the end of the year saw the collapse of communism across Eastern Europe. The exaltations over communism's demise, however, were soon tempered by the uncertainties of the road ahead. The post-communist transition brought radical changes, which induced new social hardships and political crises. By century's end, Poland appears to have successfully consolidated a democratic polity, built the foundations for a market economy, and reoriented its foreign relations toward the West.

GEOGRAPHY
Bordered by seven states and one sea, Poland covers an area of 312,677 sq km, just smaller than Germany. The northern edge of Poland meets the Baltic Sea at a broad, sandy, 524km coastline. The southern border is defined by the Sudenten and Carpathian mountain ranges. The area in between is a vast plain, sectioned by wide north-flowing rivers.

CLIMATE
Poland has a moderate continental climate with considerable maritime influence along the Baltic coast. Spring and fall can be rainy. Expect snow between December and March, lingering until April or even May in the mountains.

POPULATION & PEOPLE
The population in Poland in 1998 was about 38.5 million. Warsaw (1.7 million) is by far the largest city and is followed by Łódź (825,000) and Kraków (720,000). Upper Silesia is the most densely inhabited area while the north-eastern border regions remain the least populated.

SOCIETY & CONDUCT
Poles are friendly and polite, but not overly formal. The way of life in large urban centres increasingly mimics Western styles and manners. In the countryside, however, a more conservative culture predominates, evidenced by traditional gender roles and strong family ties. In both urban and rural settings, Poles are devoutly religious.

LANGUAGE
Most Poles do not speak any language other than Polish. Most tourist offices and upmarket hotels staff at least one English speaker, but visitors will do well to learn a few key phrases in Polish. See the Language Guide at the back of the book for pronunciation and basic vocabulary.

POLAND

Facts for the Visitor

HIGHLIGHTS

Poland's rich history is recounted by imposing medieval castles, charming old town squares and disquieting wreckage of WWII. Visitors can witness medieval knight life at Malbork Castle, the impressive fortress of the Teutonic Knights. The royal grandeur of Poland's past is preserved in Krakow's Old Town. Auschwitz is the most vivid reminder of the atrocities of WWII. For nature buffs, Zakopane is the base for hiking and skiing in the Tatras, Poland's most magnificent mountain range.

SUGGESTED ITINERARIES

Depending on the length of your stay, you might want to visit the following places:

Two days
   Visit Kraków with a day trip to Oświęcim.
One week
   Spend two days in Warsaw; two days in Kraków, plus a day trip to Oświęcim; two days in Zakopane, perhaps including a rafting trip down the Dunajec Gorge.
Two weeks
   All of the above, with an extra day in both Warsaw and Kraków. Then travel north, stopping at Malbork for one day. Spend two days in Gdańsk and two days at the beach on the Hel Peninsula.

PLANNING
When to go

The tourist season runs from May to September, peaking in July and August. To escape the crowds, the best time to visit is either May to June or September to October. July and August are the months when the Polish take their holidays. Many camp sites and hostels are closed December to March.

TOURIST OFFICES

Most larger cities have municipal tourist offices that sell maps and tourist publications. Orbis is the largest travel agency in Poland whose offices often have helpful English-speaking staff. The Polish Tourists Association (PTTK) offices also sell maps and arrange guides, though English is seldom spoken. Almatur is the Student Travel & Tourism Bureau and has offices in major provincial capitals.

Tourist Offices Abroad

Polish overseas tourist offices include:

UK (☎ 020-7580 8811, fax 7580 8866)
   1st floor, Remo House, 310-312 Regent St, London W1R 5AJ
USA
   Chicago: (☎ 312-236 9013, ☎ 236 9123, fax 236 1125) Suite 224, 33 North Michigan Ave, Chicago, IL 60601
   New York: (☎ 212-338 9412, fax 338 9283) Suite 1711, 275 Madison Ave, New York, NY 10016

EMBASSIES & CONSULATES
Embassies & Consulates Abroad

Polish embassies and consulates include:

Australia
   Embassy: (☎ 02-6273 1208) 7 Turrana St, Yarralumla, ACT 2600 (Canberra)
   Consulate: (☎ 02-9363 9816) 10 Trelawney St, Woollahra, NSW 2025 (Sydney)
Canada
   Embassy: (☎ 613-789 0468) 443 Daly Ave, Ottawa 2, Ontario K1N 6H3
   Consulate: (☎ 514-937 9481) 1500 Ave des Pins Ouest, Montreal, Quebec H3G 1B4
   Consulate: (☎ 416-252 5471) 2603 Lakeshore Blvd West, Toronto, Ontario M8V 1G5
   Consulate: (☎ 604-688 3530) Suite 1600, 1177 West Hastings St, Vancouver, BC V6E 2K3
UK
   Embassy: (☎ 020-7580 0475) 73 New Cavendish St, London W1N 7RB
   Consulate: (☎ 0131-552 0301) 2 Kinnear Rd, Edinburgh EH3 5PE
USA
   Embassy: (☎ 202-234 3800) 2640 16th St NW, Washington, DC 20009
   Consulate: (☎ 212-889 8360) 233 Madison Ave, New York, NY 10016
   Consulate: (☎ 312-337 8166) 1530 North Lake Shore Drive, Chicago, IL 60610
   Consulate: (☎ 310-442 8500) Suite 555, 12400 Wilshire Blvd, Los Angeles, CA 90025

Embassies & Consulates in Poland

Diplomatic representations (in Warsaw unless otherwise stated) include:

Australia (☎ 022-521 34 44, fax 627 35 10) ul Nowogrodzka 11
Canada (☎ 022-629 80 51, 629 64 57) ul Matejki 1/5
UK (☎ 022-628 10 01, fax 621 71 61) Al Róż 1
USA (☎ 022-628 30 41) Al Ujazdowskie 29/31
   Consulate in Kraków: (☎ 012-429 66 55) ul Stolarska 9
   Consulate in Poznań: (☎ 061-851 85 16, fax 851 89 66) ul Paderewskiego 8

POLAND

The tower of St Euphemia Cathedral overlooks the active fishing port of Rovinj, Croatia.

Busker, Prague, Czech Republic

Performer, Lublin Upland, Poland

Fiacre driver, Vienna, Austria

Bran Castle, Transylvania, Romania – associated with that legendary blood-sucker, Count Dracula

GUY MOBERLY

Fat Mo's, Budapest, Hungary

MARK HONAN

International hot-air balloon festival, Vaud Alps, Switzerland

RICHARD NEBESKÝ

Mustek Metro Station, Prague, Czech Republic

DAVID GREEDY

Szechenyi Bath, Budapest, Hungary

KRZYSZTOF DYDYŃSKI

Old Town Square, Warsaw

MONEY

For exchanging cash, private currency exchange offices *(kantors)* are ubiquitous in cities and common in small towns. Foreign bank notes should be in perfect condition or kantors may refuse to accept them.

Travellers cheques are obviously more secure than cash; however, not all banks handle these transactions, rates are generally lower, and most banks also charge a commission. American Express offices (in Warsaw and Kraków only) are the best places to change travellers cheques.

With the recent institution of automatic teller machines (ATMs; *bankomaty*), credit cards are becoming the most convenient option of getting local currency in the cities. Credit cards are increasingly useful for buying goods and services, though their use is still limited to upmarket establishments.

Exchange Rates

Exchange rates are as follows:

country	unit		złoty
Australia	A$1	=	2.51 zł
Canada	C$1	=	2.95 zł
euro	€1	=	3.95 zł
France	10FF	=	6.02 zł
Germany	DM1	=	2.02 zł
Japan	¥100	=	4.08 zł
NZ	NZ$1	=	1.90 zł
UK	UK£1	=	6.45 zł
USA	US$1	=	4.37 zł

Costs

Seeing Poland in relative comfort should cost about US$35 per day. This includes accommodation in budget hotels, food in medium-price restaurants and travelling by train or bus. Food and accommodation both average about US$12 per person per day. If you camp or stay in hostels and eat primarily at self-service cafeterias, you should be able to reduce this average to US$20 per day.

Reduced rates (usually 50%) for many tourist attractions and means of transportation are available to students and seniors. Museum admission fees are usually around US$1 to US$2, and most museums have one free-entry day during the week.

Tipping

The service charge at restaurants is included in the price. In low-price restaurants guests rarely leave an additional tip. In upmarket establishments it is customary to tip 10% of the bill.

POST & COMMUNICATIONS

Post services are operated by the Poczta Polska, while communications facilities are provided by the Telekomunikacja Polska. Both companies usually share one office, called the post office *(poczta)*. In any town, the Poczta Główna (main post office) will usually have the widest range of facilities.

Old public telephones operate on tokens *(żetony)*, which can be bought from the post office. More common, newly installed telephones operate on magnetic phonecards, which you can buy at post offices, kiosks and convenience stores. Cards come in 25/50/100 units for US$1.75/3.50/7. One unit represents one three-minute local call. Cards can be used for domestic and international calls.

Poland's international country code is ☎ 48. When dialling in from abroad, drop the initial '0' from all city codes. International direct-dialling is possible from card phones (the international access code is ☎ 00). You can also make operator-assisted international calls from post offices, for a slightly higher fee.

Many cities have cybercafes that charge about US$2 for an hour of Internet access.

INTERNET RESOURCES

The following are just a few of the huge number of useful Web sites for travellers to Poland.

Poland This is the official Web site of Poland. It's maintained by the Ministry of Foreign Affairs, and it provides tourist information, news and useful links.
www.poland.pl
The Warsaw Voice This is an insightful English-language weekly newspaper.
www.warsawvoice.com.pl

TIME

All of Poland lies within the same time zone, GMT/UTCg1. Poland puts the clocks forward an hour in late March and back again in late September.

TOILETS

The use of a public toilet costs from US$0.10 to US$0.50. *Dla Panów* or *Méski* for men, *Dla Pań* or *Damski* for women.

POLAND

WOMEN TRAVELLERS

Travel for women in Poland is mostly hassle-free except for occasional encounters with the local drunks. Harassment of this kind is almost never dangerous. Steer clear of drunks and cheap drink bars.

GAY & LESBIAN TRAVELLERS

The Polish gay and lesbian movement is still very much underground. Warsaw's best source of information is the Rainbow/Lambda centre (☎ 628 52 22), ul Czerniakowska 178 m 16. It's open 6 to 9 pm Tuesday, Wednesday and Friday, and English is spoken.

DANGERS & ANNOYANCES

Poland is a relatively safe country, even though crime has increased steadily since the fall of communism. In Warsaw, beware of pickpockets, especially near the train station and on crowded buses. International trains to/from Poland are also notorious for theft, particularly the Berlin-Warsaw and Prague-Warsaw overnight trains.

Heavy drinking is unfortunately a way of life in Poland and drunks may at times be disturbing. Poles also smoke a lot. Avoid drinking tap water; bottled water is easily available.

BUSINESS HOURS

Most shops are open 7 or 8 am to 6 or 7 pm weekdays and half a day on Saturday. The overwhelming majority of museums are closed Monday and close one or two hours ealier in the off season.

PUBLIC HOLIDAYS & SPECIAL EVENTS

Official public holidays include: 1 January (New Years' Day), Easter Monday, 1 May (Labour Day), 3 May (Constitution Day), Corpus Christi, 15 August (Assumption Day), 1 November (All Saints' Day), 11 November (Independence Day), and 25 and 26 December (Christmas).

Among the classical music highlights are Warsaw's Mozart Festival (June/July) and Wrocław's Wratislavia Cantans (September). The best of contemporary music is presented at the Warsaw Autumn International Festival in September. Jazz fans will enjoy Warsaw's Summer Jazz Days in June and the Jazz Jamboree in late October.

ACCOMMODATION

Camping

Poland has hundreds of camping grounds, many offering good-value cabins. Theoretically, most camping grounds are open May to September, but they tend to close early if things are slow.

Hostels

Polish *schroniska młodzieżowe* (hostels) are operated by Polskie Towarzystwo Schronisk Młodzieżowych (PTSM). PTSM is a member of the Hostelling International (HI) network, which currently operates about 130 year-round hostels and 440 seasonal ones (open July and August only). Hostels are open to all, but offer a 25% discount for HI members. Curfew is 10 pm, but some hostels may be flexible. Most hostels are closed between 10 am and 5 pm. Beds cost from US$4 to US$8.

PTTK (see Tourist Offices) runs an array of hostels, called Dom Turysty or Dom Wycieczkowy. Beds cost US$4 to US$7. Some PTTK hostels, especially in large cities, are now under private management and are more expensive.

Private Rooms

In major cities, accommodation agencies – the Biuro Zakwaterowania or Biuro Kwater Prywatnych – arrange rooms in private homes for around US$16/24 a single/double. In popular holiday resorts look for *pokoje* (rooms) and *noclegi* (lodging) signs.

Hotels

Various state-run lodging networks, previously accessible to few, have now opened to all. This category includes sports hotels (to provide facilities for local and visiting teams) and workers' hotels (to provide lodging facilities for workers), both of which fall into the bottom price bracket.

FOOD & DRINKS

The cheapest place to eat in Poland is a *bar mleczny* (milk bar), a no-frills self-service cafeteria that serves mostly vegetarian dishes. Restaurants *(restauracja)* range from unpretentious cheap eateries to luxurious establishments.

Poles start off their day with breakfast *(śniadanie)* which is roughly similar to its Western counterpart. The most important

POLAND

and substantial meal of the day, the *obiad*, is normally eaten between 2 and 5 pm. Obiad usually includes a hearty soup as well as a main course. The third meal is supper *(kolacja)*, which is often similar to breakfast.

Wódka (vodka), the national drink, is drunk neat, not diluted or mixed, and comes in various colours and flavours. Poles also appreciate the value of a cold beer *(zimne piwo)*; Polish beer is cheap and good.

Getting There & Away

AIR
The national carrier, LOT Polish Airlines, links Warsaw with major cities around the world. Most major European and some American carriers also fly to Warsaw. At the time of writing, the cheapest return fares available were US$550 from New York, US$300 from London, and US$1200 from Sydney.

TRAIN
Domestic train fares in Poland are far cheaper than international ones. Accordingly, you will save money by buying a ticket to the first city you arrive at inside Poland, then taking a local train.

Plenty of Western European cities are linked by train (direct or indirect) with major Polish cities. The Warsaw-Berlin route (via Frankfurt/Oder and Poznań) is serviced by several trains a day, including three EuroCity express trains (6½ hours). Direct trains also travel between Berlin and Gdańsk (via Szczecin, nine hours), and Berlin and Kraków (via Wrocław, 11 hours).

Trains between Prague and Warsaw (three a day) travel via either Wrocław (12 hours) or Katowice (10 hours). Two trains per day travel between Vienna and Warsaw (11 hours) via Katowice. Two trains run daily between Budapest and Warsaw (12 hours) via Bratislava and Katowice. All of these destinations south of Poland are also accessible by daily trains direct from Kraków. One train from Warsaw goes all the way to Bucharest via Kraków.

Direct trains from Warsaw head east to Vilnius in Lithuania (12 hours), Minsk (10 hours) and Hrodna (seven hours) in Belarus,

Kyiv (20 hours) and Lviv (12 hours) in Ukraine, and Moscow (20 hours) and St Petersburg (27 hours) in Russia. These trains only have sleeping cars.

Remember that you need transit visas for the countries you will be passing through en route. For example, the Warsaw-Vilnius-St Petersburg train travels via Hrodna, Belarus, and the Warsaw-Bratislava-Budapest rail line passes through the Czech Republic.

BUS
The cheapest way to travel to Poland from the UK, France, Holland and other Western European countries is by bus. Fregata – with an office (☎ 020-7734 5101) in London at 100 Dean St – sends buses from London's Victoria coach station to Warsaw and Kraków. Budget Bus/Eurolines (☎ 020-560 87 87), Amstel Coach Station, Julianaplein 5, Amsterdam, runs buses from Amsterdam to Kraków, Warsaw and Gdańsk.

A few buses a week travel between Budapest and Kraków (US$20, 10 hours). The Polish PKS bus company runs daily buses from Warsaw to Lviv (US$17), Minsk (US$21) and Vilnius (US$19).

BOAT
Poland has a regular ferry service to/from Denmark and Sweden operated by the Unity Line, Stena Line and Polferries. The Unity Line covers the Świnoujście-Ystad route (720Skr, nine hours, daily). The Stena Line runs between Gdynia and Karlskrona (11 hours, six days a week). Polferries services the Świnoujście-Copenhagen route (540Skr, 10 hours, five times a week), the Świnoujście-Malmö route (820Skr, nine hours, daily), and the Gdańsk-Nynäshamn route (820Skr, 18 hours, every day during summer, three times a week low season). Polferries now operates a new route between Świnoujście and Ronne (320 SEK, once a week). All routes operate year-round.

Getting Around

AIR
LOT Polish Airlines operates domestic flights daily to/from most major Polish cities. The regular one-way fare on domestic flights to/from Warsaw is around US$140 (less 10% with ISIC card). People

POLAND

under age 20 and students under age 26 may qualify for cheaper stand-by fares. Buy tickets at any LOT or Orbis office, or from travel agencies.

TRAIN

Inter-Rail passes are valid in Poland. A Polrail Pass, valid for unlimited rail travel throughout the country, can be bought abroad or in Poland. Passes cost US$65/75/85 for 2nd-class travel over 8/15/21 days. Persons under 26 can buy a 'Junior' pass for about 25% less.

The PKP Polish Railways operates *pociągi ekspresowe* (express trains), which often require seat reservations (indicated by an 'R' in a square on train timetables); *pociągi pospieszne* (fast trains), which do not usually require reservations; and *pociągi osobowe* which (ordinary trains) are OK for short trips and never require reservations. Speedy InterCity trains have been introduced on some major routes; they require seat reservations.

Almost all trains carry two classes: *druga klasa* (2nd class) and *pierwsza klasa* (1st class), which is 50% more expensive.

In any city, the main train station is identified by the name *Główny*. Train *odjazdy* (departures) are usually listed on a yellow board while *przyjazdy* (arrivals) are on a white board. Timetables also indicate which *peron* (platform) the train departs from.

If you get on a train without a *bilety* (ticket), you can buy one directly from the conductor for a small supplement, but you should find him/her right away. *Kuszetki* (couchettes) and *miejsca sypialne* (sleepers) can be booked in advance at larger stations. These tickets, as well as advance tickets for journeys over 100km, can also be bought at Orbis offices.

BUS

Buses in Poland are often a good option for short distances or for travelling in the mountains. Most buses are operated by the state bus company PKS, which runs ordinary buses (marked in black on timetable boards) that make numerous stops, and fast buses (marked in red or in bold) that travel longer distances and ignore minor stops. The ordinary/fast bus fares are rough US$3/4 per 100km.

The biggest private bus company is Polski Express, which operates on several major long-distance routes out of Warsaw. It's faster, more comfortable and cheaper than PKS.

PKS tickets must be purchased at the terminal itself. Tickets for Polski Express buses can be bought at terminals and from major Orbis offices.

CAR & MOTORCYCLE

The speed limit in Poland is 110km/h on highways and motorways, 90km/h on open roads and 60km/h in urban areas. Radar-equipped police are active, especially in villages, and speeding fines are levied frequently. Seat belts are compulsory in the front seat. The blood alcohol limit is 0.02%, so it's best not to drink at all before driving. Service stations are easy to find and sell several grades of petrol, most for about US$0.75 per litre.

Avis, Budget, Hertz and some other international agencies are now well-represented in Poland, as well as plenty of local operators. Car rental is not cheap; the prices are comparable to, or even higher than, full-price rental in Western Europe, and there are seldom any promotional discounts. Rental agencies will require you to produce your passport, a driver's licence held for at least one year, and a credit card. You need to be at least 21 or 23 years of age to rent a car.

Warsaw

☎ 022

The capital of Poland, Warsaw (Warszawa; population 1.7 million), is the heart of the nation's political and economic life. It is Poland's most cosmopolitan, progressive urban centre.

The city suffered extensively during WWII, when 700,000 residents perished and 85% of Warsaw's buildings were destroyed. Very few of the 350,000 Jews who were living in Warsaw in 1939 survived. Parts of the historic city, most notably the Old Town (Stare Miasto), have been meticulously rebuilt to their previous condition. Most of the urban landscape, however, is modern, including grey Stalinist edifices and shiny new skyscrapers.

Orientation

The main part of the city sits on the western bank of the Vistula, including the Old

Town. To the south stretches the new city centre, overlooked by the Palace of Culture & Science. The central train station is in this area. A few kilometres to the south-east is Łazienki Park, linked to the Old Town by the 4km Royal Way (Szlak Królewski).

Information
Tourist Offices The city tourist office (☎ 94 31, ✆ info@warsawtour.pl) has offices at the airport, at Warszawa Zachodnia train station, in the PKO Bank Rotunda on the corner of ul Marszałkowska and Al Jerozolimskie, and in the Historical Museum of Warsaw at the Old Town Square.

Another city tourist office (☎/fax 524 51 84, ✆ msitur@msiwarszawa.com.pl) is at the Warszawa Centralna. The private tourist office (☎ 635 18 81, fax 831 04 64) is at Plac Zamkowy 1/13, opposite the Royal Castle.

Two free monthly magazines are *Warszawa: What, Where, When* and *Welcome to Warsaw*. The best publication is the comprehensive *Warsaw Insider* monthly (US$1.50).

Money Kantors and ATMs are easy to find around the centre. The best place to change all travellers cheques is the American Express office (☎ 551 51 52), ul Krakowskie Przedmieście 11 (open weekdays). The Marriott also has an American Express outlet (☎ 630 69 52), which is open daily.

Post & Communications The main post office, ul Świętokrzyska 31/33, is open 8 am to 8 pm for mail and round the clock for telephones.

Cybercafes are springing up all around Warsaw. The most atmospheric places are Casablanca, ul Krakowski Przedmieście 4/6, and Piękna Internet Café (☎ 622 33 77), ul Piękna 68a. Planeta 808, ul Królewska 2, is also convenient. Near the central train station, the British Council, al Jerozolimskie 59, provides free Internet access, but it is closed Sunday.

Travel Agency Almatur (☎ 826 35 12, 826 26 39), ul Kopernika 23, handles student travel and discounts.

Bookshops The American Bookstore (☎ 660 56 37), ul Koszykowa 55, is the best place for English-language publications,

including Lonely Planet titles. Smaller outlets are at ul Nowy Świat 41 and 61.

Medical & Emergency Services The Medical Centre (☎ 621 06 46, 630 51 15), in the Hotel Marriott building (3rd floor), has specialist doctors, carries out laboratory tests and attends house calls. Ring your embassy for other recommendations. Do not drink Warsaw's poor-quality tap water. Bottled water is available from shops and supermarkets.

Things to See
Old Town The main gateway to the Old Town is the Castle Square (Plac Zamkowy). In 1945, the massive **Royal Castle** was a heap of rubble, but it was rebuilt from 1971 to 1984 and is now a museum (open daily). Entry is by guided tour. Purchase separate tickets for the various exhibits at the Zamek Królewski-Kasy Biletowe, ul Świętojańska 2 (US$4/2, free on Sunday). In summer, arrive early and be prepared to wait.

Enter the Old Town along ul Świętojańska and follow it to the 14th-century Gothic **St John's Cathedral**, and the **Old Town Square** (Rynek Starego Miasta). Try to catch the 15-minute film shown at noon at the **Historical Museum of Warsaw** (closed Monday), Rynek Starego Miasta 42, which graphically depicts the wartime destruction of the city.

Continue north on ul Nowomiejska to the **Barbican**, part of the medieval walled circuit around Warsaw, and further to the **New Town Square** (Rynek Nowego Miasta).

The Royal Way (Szlak Królewski) This 4km route from the Royal Castle to Łazienki Palace, the royal summer residence, follows ul Krakowskie Przedmieście, ul Nowy Świat and Al Ujazdowskie.

Just south of the Royal Castle is **St Anne's Church**, one of the most ornate churches in the city. A few hundred metres farther south is the **Carmelite Church**, and beside it, the powerful **Radziwiłł Palace**, the Polish White House. The Saxon Gardens hold the **Tomb of the Unknown Soldier** in a fragment of an 18th-century royal palace. The ceremonial changing of the guard takes place on Sunday at noon. South of the tomb is the **Zachęta Gallery of Contemporary Art** (closed Monday) featuring modern painting, sculpture and photography.

POLAND

POLAND

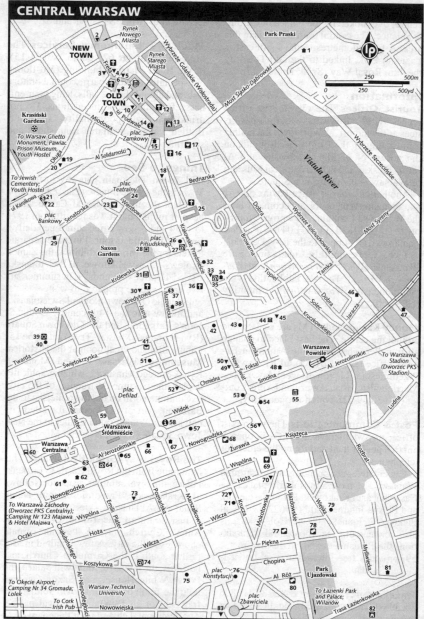

CENTRAL WARSAW

CENTRAL WARSAW

PLACES TO STAY		45	Salad Bar Tukan	40	Our Roots	
1	Hotel Praski	49	Café Blikle	41	Main Post Office	
9	Bursa Szkolnistwa	50	Bar Mleczny Familijny	42	American Bookstore	
	Artystyczna	52	Bar Krokiecik	43	Almatur	
15	Dom Literatury	56	Bar Mleczny Szwajcarski	44	Chopin Museum; Morgan's	
19	Pokoje Gościnne Federacja	70	Restauracja Adler	51	Filharmonia Narodowa	
	Metalowcy	72	Bar Mleczny Bambino	53	EMPiK	
29	Hotel Saski	73	Warsaw Tortilla Factory;	54	Former Communist Party	
34	Hotel Harenda; Pub Harenda		Ground Zero		Headquarters;	
38	Hotel Mazowiecki	83	Salad Bar Tukan		Warsaw Stock Exchange	
46	Hotel Belfer			55	National Museum	
47	Hotel Na Wodzie	**OTHER**		57	Kasy Teatralne ZASP	
48	Youth Hostel	6	Barbican	58	City Tourist Office;	
62	Hotel Marriott	7	Historical Museum of		PKO Bank Rotunda	
66	Hotel Polonia		Warsaw	59	Palace of Culture & Science	
67	Hotel Forum;	12	St John's Cathedral	60	Polski Express Bus Stop	
	Mazurkas Travel	13	Royal Castle	61	LOT Office	
81	Youth Hostel Agrikola	14	Private Tourist Office	63	Bus Travel Centre	
		16	St Anne's Church	64	British Council	
PLACES TO EAT		17	Pub pod Barylką	65	Fotoplastikon	
2	Restauracja Ekologiczna	21	Bank Pekao	68	Australian Embassy	
	Nowe Miasto	23	Rabarbar; Barbados	69	Szpilka	
3	Restauracja pod Samsonem	24	Teatr Wielki	71	Biuro Kwater Prywatnych	
4	Sklep z Kawą Pożegnanie z	25	Radziwiłł Palace		Syrena Univel	
	Afryką	26	American Express Office		(Private Rooms)	
5	Bar Mleczny pod	27	Planeta 808	74	Piękna Internet Café	
	Barbakanem	28	Tomb of the Unknown	75	American Bookstore	
8	Restauracja Maharaja		Soldier	76	Orbis	
10	Kmicic	31	Zachęta Gallery of	77	US Embassy	
11	Karczma Gessler		Contemporary Art	78	Canadian Embassy	
18	Pizzeria Giovani	32	Warsaw University	79	Parliament House	
20	Restauracja Tay-Ho	35	Casablanca	80	UK Embassy	
22	Salad Bar Tukan	36	Church of the Holy Cross	82	Ujazdów Castle; Centre of	
30	Salad Bar Tukan	37	Bank Pekao		Contemporary Art;	
33	Bar Mleczny Uniwersytecki	39	Nożyk Synagogue		Qchnia Artystyczna	

Back on the Royal Way is the 17th-century **Church of the Holy Cross**, where the heart of Chopin is preserved in the second pillar on the left-hand side of the main nave. Towards the river is the **Chopin Museum**, ul Tamka 41, with such memorabilia as Chopin's last piano and a collection of his manuscripts.

Returning to the Royal Way, head south along ul Nowy Świat (New World St), crossing Al Jerozolimskie (Jerusalem Ave), where the former Communist Party Headquarters sits on the corner and now houses the Warsaw Stock Exchange.

A few paces towards the river is the large **National Museum** (closed Monday), which has a magnificent collection of Polish sculpture and painting, from the medieval period to the present. Further south, the cutting-edge **Centre of Contemporary Art** (closed Monday) is accommodated in Ujazdów Castle, which dates from the 1620s.

Łazienki This park and palace complex is best known for its 18th-century **Palace upon the Water**, which was the summer residence of Stanisław August Poniatowski, the last king of Poland (open 9.30 am to 3.30 pm daily, closed Monday). On Sunday in summer, piano recitals are held at the **Chopin Monument** just off Al Ujazdowskie.

Wilanów Another park and palace complex is about 6km south-east of Łazienki (take bus No 116 from Al Ujazdowskie). The centrepiece is the mighty **Wilanów Palace**, a former summer residence of King Jan III Sobieski, who defeated the Turks at Vienna in 1683. Entry is by guided tour (open 9.30 am to 2.30 pm, closed Tuesday; US$3/2). Individual tourists should visit on a weekend or holiday. In the park behind the palace is the **Orangery**, which houses an art gallery. The **Poster Museum** (Muzeum Plakatu), in the former royal stables, has exhibits of Poland's world renowned poster art (closed Monday).

Other Attractions The 1950s **Palace of Culture & Science** was a 'gift of friendship' from the Soviet Union. It remains Poland's tallest building (234m). The observation terrace on the 30th floor provides a panoramic view. The **Fotoplastikon**, Al Jerozolimskie 51, just south of the palace, is reputedly the last working example in Europe of a once-popular 3D apparatus. A 20-minute session (US$1) consists of 48 stereoscopic slides from the turn of the 20th century.

A five-minute walk north-west, the neo-Romanesque **Nożyk Synagogue** (1902) is the only synagogue in Warsaw that survived WWII, albeit in a sorry state. It was restored and today is open for religious services (Thursday only for tourists). The vast Mirów and Muranów districts stretching to the north-west beyond the synagogue were once inhabited predominantly by Jews. During WWII the Nazis established a ghetto here. After crushing the Ghetto Uprising they razed the quarter to the ground. Today the **Warsaw Ghetto Monument,** at the corner of ul Anielewicza and ul Zamenhofa, commemorates the victims. The nearby **Pawiak Prison Museum**, ul Dzielna 24/26, occupies the building that was Warsaw's main Gestapo prison during the Nazi occupation. Possibly the most moving remnant of the Jewish legacy is the vast **Jewish Cemetery** (closed Friday and Saturday), ul Okopowa 49/51.

Organised Tours

Mazurkas Travel (☎/fax 629 18 78) in the lobby of the Hotel Forum, ul Nowogrodzka 24/26, is Warsaw's major tour operator. Our Roots (☎ 620 05 56), ul Twarda 6, next to the Nożyk Synagogue, is the Jewish tourist bureau.

Places to Stay

Warsaw's hotels are expensive and the choice is limited. Book ahead when possible, or make a beeline for the tourist offices when you arrive.

Camping Warsaw has several camping grounds. The largest, most central and most popular is *Camping Nr 34 Gromada* (☎ 825 43 91, ul Żwirki i Wigury 32) in the

Ochota suburb. Open May to September, it has budget cabins and hotel-style rooms. It is accessible from the airport on bus Nos 175 and 188, and from the central train station on bus Nos 136 and 175.

In the same suburb, close to the central bus terminal, is the smaller *Camping Nr 123 Majawa* (☎ 823 37 48, ul Bitwy Warszawskiej 1920r 15/17), which has all-year heated cabins (US$31 a double with bath), and the all-year *Hotel Majawa* (US$25 a double without bath).

Youth Hostels The tourist offices will know which *student dorms* are open as hostels in summer. Otherwise, Warsaw now has four all-year youth hostels.

The 110-bed *youth hostel* (☎/fax 827 89 52, ul Smolna 30), close to the National Museum, is the most central, accessible by any eastbound tram from the train station.

Another central option is the new *youth hostel Agrikola* (☎ 622 91 10, ul Myśliwiecka 9), close to the Trasa Łazienkowska (the main west-east city motorway).

A *youth hostel* (☎ 632 88 29, ul Karolkowa 53a) is 2km west of the train station in the Wola suburb and is accessible by tram No 12 or No 24. A smaller *youth hostel* (☎ 831 17 66, ul Międzyparkowa 4/6) is on the northern outskirts of the New Town. Take bus No 174 from the train station or No 175 from the airport.

Private Rooms The Biuro Podroży Syrena (☎/fax 629 49 78, ✉ syrena-pl@yahoo.co.uk), ul Krucza 17, arranges accommodation in private homes. The rooms are in the central districts and cost US$17/25 a single/double.

Hotels A few budget options are close to the Old Town. The cheapest is *Bursa Szkolnistwa Artystycznego* (☎ 635 79 05, 635 41 74, ul Miodowa 24a) in an art school dorm. It charges only US$9/13 for a bed in a double without/with bath, but it has vacancies only in the summer and on weekends. Another cheap option is *Pokoje Gościnne Federacja Metalowcy* (☎ 831 40 21, fax 635 31 38, ul Długa 29). It costs US$14/22/39 a single/double/quad without bath – good value for its location.

Also central, *Hotel Mazowiecki* (☎ 682 20 69, fax 827 23 65, ul Mazowiecka 10) is a former army dorm. A single/double/triple costs US$32/42/52 without bath, US$50/62/72 with bath.

Just across the river in the Praga district, the new *Hotel Praski* (*☎/fax 818 49 89, ul Solidarności 61*) charges US$30/41/50 for a single/double/triple without bath, and US$61/72 for a double/triple with bath. Breakfast is included.

Hotel Belfer (*☎ 622 55 62, ☎/fax 625 51 85, Wybrzeże Kościuszkowskie 31/33*) is a large former teachers' hotel on the Vistula bank and has singles/doubles without bath at US$30/39 and singles/doubles/triples with bath and breakfast at US$41/52/64.

The nearby *Hotel Na Wodzie* (*☎/fax 628 58 83*) is in the *Aldona*, a boat anchored to the river shore between the railway and Poniatowski bridges. It operates April to November and offers adequate single/double cabins without bath for US$16/22.

The ideally located *Dom Literatury* (*☎/fax 828 39 20, ul Krakowskie Przedmieście 87/89*) rents out rooms without/with bath for about US$38/50 per person. Near the central train station, the old-fashioned *Hotel Polonia* (*☎ 628 72 41, fax 628 66 22, Al Jerozolimskie 45*) costs US$40/58 a single/double without bath, US$60/98 with bath.

Places to Eat

Old & New Town *Bar Mleczny pod Barbakanem* (*ul Mostowa 27/29*), next to the Barbican, is a popular milk bar that serves cheap, unpretentious food. Nearby the popular, yet inexpensive *Restauracja pod Samsonem* (*ul Freta 3/5*) serves a tasty mix of Polish and Jewish cuisine. *Restauracja Ekologiczna Nowe Miasto* (*Rynek Nowego Miasta 13/15*) offers a variety of vegetarian dishes and salads, reputedly prepared from organically grown vegetables.

The Old Town boasts some of Warsaw's best restaurants specialising in traditional Polish cuisine. The most popular is *Karczma Gessler* (*Rynek Starego Miasta 21*) in a romantic cellar. A more affordable but less atmospheric option is *Kmicic* (*ul Piwna 27*).

The Old Town also shelters some fine Asian eateries, including *Restauracja Tay-Ho* (*ul Długa 29*) for Vietnamese and *Restauracja Maharaja* (*ul Szeroki Dunaj 13*) for Thai.

Arguably the best coffee in town is served in *Sklep z Kawą Pożegnanie z Afryką* (*ul Freta 4/6*).

New Centre & Around This section of the city covers the large area to the south of the Old Town, including the Royal Way.

Three milk bars have survived along the Royal Way: *Bar Mleczny Uniwersytecki* (*ul Krakowskie Przedmieście 20*), *Bar Mleczny Familijny* (*ul Nowy Świat 39*) and *Bar Mleczny Szwajcarski* (*ul Nowy Świat 5*). All are very cheap. *Bar Mleczny Bambino* (*ul Krucza 21*) is a few blocks to the west. The self-service *Bar Krokiecik* (*ul Zgoda 1*) is also deservedly popular thanks to its good inexpensive food.

For pizza and other affordable Italian food, try *Pizzeria Giovani* (*ul Krakowski Przedmieście 37*). *Restauracja Adler* (*ul Mokotowska 69*) is popular for its generous portions, cosy atmosphere and hearty Bavarian dishes. The cheapest and most authentic Mexican food in Warsaw is near the central train station at *Warsaw Tortilla Factory* (*ul Wspólna 62*).

A chain called *Salad Bar Tukan* has opened at several locations, including Plac Bankowy 2, ul Kredytowa 2, ul Tamka 37, and ul Nowowiejska 5, and offers just about the widest choice of salads in town.

Qchnia Artystyczna, in the Ujazdów Castle, has interesting food – mostly vegetarian – in artistic, postmodern surroundings.

Serving sweets and light meals, *Café Blikle* (*ul Nowy Świat 33*) is one of the most popular cafes along the Royal Way.

Entertainment

Check Friday's *Gazeta Wyborcza* for events. The *Warsaw Insider* (see Information earlier) has a thorough review of dining and drinking out options. The Kasy Teatralne ZASP, Al Jerozolimskie 25, sells tickets for most of the city theatres and musical events.

Jazz & Blues *Pub Harenda*, in the hotel of the same name, hosts jazz jam sessions on Tuesday and Wednesday. *EMPiK* offers free live blues every day but Sunday at the megastore on ul Nowy Świat. *Rabarbar* (*ul Wierzbowa 9/11*) is a fondue restaurant but also has live jazz on weekends. In July and August, open-air jazz concerts are staged at the Old Town Square, on Saturday at 7 pm.

Bars, Pubs & Discos Popular discos include *Ground Zero* (*ul Wspólna 62*) and the trendy *Barbados* (*ul Wierzbowa 9*).

Warsaw is flooded with bars and pubs these days. Warsaw has two authentic Irish pubs, which are both great places to meet expats and enjoy a Guinness. *Morgan's* is in the basement of the Chopin museum on ul Tamka. The out-of-the-way *Cork Irish Pub (al Niepodległóści 19)* is worth the trip for its beautiful stained glass windows.

If you prefer something more local, go to *Pub pod Barylką (ul Garbarska 5/7)* on the Mariensztat Square. It is a Polish pub offering 20-plus kinds of Polish beer.

Szpilka (plac Trzech Krzyży 18) is one of the hippest places in town for food, drinks and music. *Lolek*, in Park Mokotowskie, is a large pub with a prehistoric theme.

Classical Music, Opera & Ballet The main venue is *Teatr Wielki* (Grand Theatre), near the Saxon Gardens. *Opera Kameralna (Chamber Opera; Al Solidarnóści 76b)* performs operas in a more intimate setting. *Filharmonia Narodowa (National Philharmonic; ul Jasna 5)* has a concert hall (enter from ul Sienkiewicza 10) and a chamber hall (enter from ul Moniuszki 5).

Getting There & Away

Air Okęcie airport, 10km south-west of the city centre, handles all domestic and international flights. LOT and foreign carriers link Warsaw with Europe and beyond. The main LOT office is in the Marriott Hotel building at Al Jerozolimskie 65/79.

Train The Warszawa Centralna handles all international and most domestic trains. Be alert on platforms and while boarding trains – pickpocketing is on the increase here.

From Warsaw Central InterCity trains go to Gdańsk (3½ hours, 333km), Katowice (three hours, 303km), Kraków (2½ hours, 292km), Lublin (two hours, 175km), Poznań (three hours, 311km) and Szczecin (six hours, 525km). International destinations include Berlin (6½ hours), Bratislava (nine hours), Bucharest, Budapest (11 hours), Cologne (10½ hours), Dresden (nine hours), Frankfurt/Main (11 hours), Hrodna (seven hours), Kyiv (20 hours), Leipzig, Minsk, Moscow (20 hours), Prague, St Petersburg (27 hours), Vienna (8½ hours) and Vilnius (12 hours).

Domestic and international train tickets are available directly from the counters at the station (allow an hour for possible queuing) or from Orbis offices. International train tickets can also be bought from Almatur and other travel agencies.

Other major train stations include Warszawa Zachodnia (West Warsaw), next to the central bus terminal, and Warszawa Wschodnia (East Warsaw) in the Praga suburb. Warszawa Śródmieście station, a few hundred metres east of Warsaw Central, handles local trains.

Bus Warsaw has two PKS bus terminals. Dworzec Centralny PKS (central bus terminal) handles all domestic buses heading south and west. The terminal adjoins the Warszawa Zachodnia train station. Dworzec PKS Stadion (Stadium bus terminal), behind the main city stadium, adjoining the Warszawa Stadion train station, handles domestic buses to the north, east and south-east. Both terminals are accessible by commuter train from Warszawa Śródmieście.

The Polski Express company runs coaches from Okęcie airport and from the bus stop on Al Jana Pawła II, next to the central train station. Tickets for Polski Express are available from its offices and from selected Orbis outlets.

A wide range of options for travel to Western Europe are offered by Anna Travel (☎ 825 53 89) at Warsaw central train station, and from the Bus Travel Center (☎ 628 62 53) at Al Jerozolimskie 63. Tickets are also available from select Orbis outlets or from Almatur.

Getting Around

To/From the Airport The cheapest way to/from the airport is bus No 175, which goes into the centre and up to the Old Town, passing en route the Warsaw Central train station and the hostel at ul Smolna. Watch your bags and pockets closely. Buy tickets for you and your luggage at the airport's newsstand, and punch them aboard the bus.

The special AirportCity bus goes from the airport to the Bristol and Europejski hotels, calling at Warsaw Central train station (US$2/1). The bus runs from 6 am to 11 pm.

Taxi fare from the airport is about US$6. Make sure you take one of the taxis with rates and a phone number posted on the window. Other 'mafia' taxis will charge astronomical rates.

Bus, Tram & Metro Warsaw has about 30 tram routes and over 100 bus routes. Public transport operates from about 5 am to about 11 pm. The fare is a flat US$0.50 (50% less for students under age 26 with an ISIC card). Buy tickets beforehand from Ruch kiosks and punch them on board. Daily and weekly passes are available from the Dział Sprzedaży Biletów office, ul Senatorska 37.

Warsaw's 12.5km-long metro runs from the southern Ursynów suburb to the city centre (Centrum station), with an extension to the northern Młociny suburb scheduled for 2004. The metro takes tram/bus tickets, but punch them on the silver metal strip.

Taxi The official taxi rate is about US$0.40 per km with an initial charge of US$0.90. Rates increase by 50% after 10 pm and on weekends. Taxis can be flagged down on the street, but they are easier to find at a taxi stand. You can also order a taxi by phone for no extra charge. Taxis that do not have a phone number and rates posted on their window will likely charge outrageous prices.

Małopolska

KRAKÓW
☎ 012
Kraków (population 720,000) is Poland's third largest city and one of its oldest, dating from the 7th century. Kraków was the capital of the Polish kingdom from 1038 to 1596. Particularly good times came with the reign of King Kazimierz the Great, a generous patron of art and scholarship. In 1364 he founded the Kraków Academy (later renamed the Jagiellonian University).

Kraków is the only large city in Poland whose architecture survived WWII intact. Unfortunately, the town has instead suffered from tens of thousands of tonnes of pollution emitted annually by the huge steelworks at nearby Nova Huta. Now the city's historical monuments are being gradually restored.

No other city better captures Poland's intriguing history: the Old Town harbours towering Gothic churches and the splendid Wawel Castle; Kazimierz, the now silent Jewish quarter, recounts a more tragic story. In 1978 Unesco included the historic centre of Kraków on its first World Cultural Heritage list.

Orientation
Kraków's Old Town is centred around the Main Market Square (Rynek Główny). On the southern tip of the Old Town sits the Wawel castle, and farther south stretches the district of Kazimierz. The bus and train stations are next to each other on the north-eastern rim of the Old Town.

Information
Tourist Offices KART city tourist office (☎ 422 04 71, 422 60 91), ul Pawia 8, opposite the train station, is open Monday to Saturday (weekdays only during the low season).

Two private travel agencies have opened their own offices: the Jordan tourist office (☎ 421 21 25, fax 422 82 26, ✉ hotel@jordan.krkow.pl), ul Długa 9 (open daily); and the Dexter tourist office (☎ 634 08 08, fax 633 63 13, ✉ lepka@dexter.com.pl) in the Cloth Hall (open Monday to Saturday).

Tourist offices stock two free monthly magazines, *Welcome to Cracow* and *Kraków: What, Where, When*. The useful *Krakow Insider* magazine covers museums, restaurants, cafes, pubs etc.

As well as offering activity-based tours, Almatur (☎ 422 46 68), ul Grodzka 2, issues ISIC student cards.

Money Kantors and ATMs are scattered throughout the Old Town. Change your travellers cheques at the American Express counter in the Orbis office at Rynek Główny 41 (closed Sunday).

Post & Communications The main post office is at ul Westerplatte 20. There are telephone centres at the main post office (open 24 hours), at Rynek Główny 19 (open to 10 pm daily) and at ul Lubicz 4, opposite the central train station (24 hours).

The oldest cybercafe in town is the Cyber Café u Luisa, set in a spectacular vaulted cellar at Rynek Główny 13. The Centrum Internetowa, Rynek Główny 9, and the Looz Internet Café, ul Mikołajska 11, are also convenient.

Bookshops For English-language literature check the English Book Centre, Plac Matejki 5. The widest choice of publications related to Jewish issues is at the Jarden Jewish Bookshop, ul Szeroka 2, in Kazimierz.

POLAND

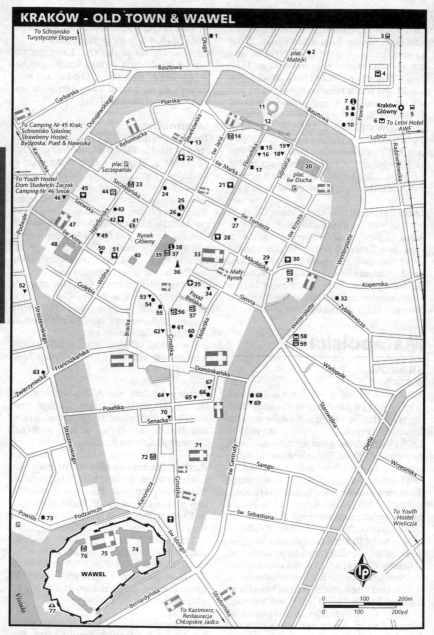

KRAKÓW - OLD TOWN & WAWEL

KRAKÓW - OLD TOWN & WAWEL

PLACES TO STAY
1 Pokoje Gościnne Jordan;
   Jordan Tourist Office
9 Hotel Warszawski
10 Hotel Polonia
15 Dom Gościnny UJ
17 Hotel Pokoje Gościnne SARP
24 Hotel Saski
32 Dom Turysty PTTK; Jan-Pol
55 Dom Polonii; Intercrac
66 Hotel Wawel Tourist
68 Hotel Monopol
73 Pensjonat Rycerska

PLACES TO EAT
13 Kuchnia Staropolska u
   Babci Maliny
16 Jama Michalika
18 Różowy Słoń
19 Jadłodajnia Sąsiedzi
27 Sklep z Kawą Pożegnanie
   z Afryką
29 Jadłodajnia u Pani Stasi;
   Pizzeria Cyklop
34 Różowy Słoń
46 Kawiarnia u Zalipianek
49 Jadłodajnia Kuchcik
50 Salad Bar Chimera
52 Różowy Słoń
53 Taco Mexicano
62 Akropolis Grill

64 Restauracja pod Aniołami
65 Taco Mexicano
67 Restauracja Korsykańska
   Paese
69 Bar Wegetariański Vega
70 Restauracja pod Temidą

OTHER
2 English Book Centre
3 Bus No 208 to Airport &
   Minibuses to Wieliczka
4 Central Bus Terminal
5 Buses to Oświćcim;
   Telephone Station
6 Post Office
7 KART City Tourist Office
8 Biuro Turystyki i
   Zakwaterowania Waweltur
11 Barbican
12 Florian Gate
14 Czartoryski Museum
20 Teatr im Słowackiego
21 Pub pod Jemiołą
22 Equinox
23 Szołajski Museum
25 Cultural Information Centre
26 Orbis; American Express
28 Jazz Club U Muniaka
30 Black Gallery
31 Looz Internet Café
33 St Mary's Church

35 Profimed
36 Statue of Adam Mickiewicz
37 Gallery of 19th-Century
   Polish Painting
38 Dexter Tourist Office
39 Cloth Hall
40 Town Hall Tower
41 Bank Pekao
42 Klub Pasja
43 Sklep Podróżnika
44 Teatr Stary
45 Klub Kulturny
47 St Anne's Church
48 Collegium Maius
51 Piwnica pod Baranami
54 Telephone Station
56 Cyber Café U Luisa;
   Klub U Luisa
57 Centrum Internetowy
58 Main Post Office
59 Main Telephone Centre
60 US Consulate
61 Almatur
63 Filharmonia
71 Church of SS Peter & Paul
72 Wyspiański Museum
74 Wawel Castle
75 Wawel Cathedral
76 Wawel Cathedral
   Museum
77 Dragon's Cave

Medical Services Profimed (☎ 421 79
97), Rynek Główny 6, is a private medical
clinic. The US consulate (☎ 422 12 94) has
a list of English-speaking doctors.

Things to See

Rynek Główny, Kraków's wonderful market
square, is the largest medieval town square
in Europe. The 16th-century Renaissance
Cloth Hall *(Sukiennice)* dominates the centre of the square and houses a large craft
market on the ground floor. Upstairs is the
Gallery of 19th-Century Polish Painting (a
branch of the National Museum), with several famous historical works by Matejko.

The 14th-century **St Mary's Church** fills
the north-east corner of the square. The huge
main altarpiece (1489) by Wit Stwosz (Veit
Stoss) of Nuremberg is the finest Gothic
sculpture in Poland. The altar's wings are
opened daily at noon. A trumpet call *(hejnał)*
occurs hourly from the church's highest
tower. It recalls a 13th-century trumpeter
who was cut down by a Tatar arrow in the
middle of sounding a warning of invasion.

On the opposite side of the Cloth Hall is
the 15th-century **Town Hall Tower**, which
you can climb to the top.

Around the Old Town Take ul
Floriańska north to the **Florian Gate** (1307),
the only remaining of seven original gates.
Behind it is the **Barbican**, a defensive bastion
built in 1498. The **Czartoryski Museum**, ul
Św Jana 19, features a collection of European art, including Leonardo da Vinci's
Lady with an Ermine. **Szołajski Museum**,
Plac Szczepańska 9, has an extensive collection of Gothic and Renaissance religious
artwork. It was closed for renovation at the
time of writing.

At ul Jagiellońska 15, is the 15th-century
Collegium Maius (☎ 422 05 49), the oldest
surviving building of the Kraków Academy, where Nicolaus Copernicus studied.
The guided tour is obligatory (English-
speaking guides available).

South on ul Grodzka is the early 17th-
century Jesuit **Church of SS Peter & Paul**,
the first baroque church built in Poland. The

POLAND

parallel ul Kanonicza (arguably Kraków's most picturesque street) boasts the **Wyspiański Museum**, dedicated to this renowned poet, painter, playwright and stained-glass designer.

Wawel Hill Just south of the Old Town is Wawel, a hill topped with a castle and cathedral that are the very symbols of Poland. **Wawel Cathedral** (1364) was for four centuries the coronation and burial place of Polish royalty, and 100 kings and queens are interred in the crypt. The tower houses Poland's largest bell (11 tonnes). The cathedral and accompanying **museum** are open daily except Sunday morning. The ticket office is diagonally opposite its entrance.

The 16th-century **Wawel Castle** (closed Monday) is behind the cathedral. The exhibits (housed in the buildings surrounding the splendid Italian Renaissance courtyard) require separate tickets, which can be purchased at the gate (about US$2 each). Reserve at least three hours for the castle and the cathedral. Arrive early, especially during the summer.

Behind the complex, outside the castle wall, you can visit the notorious **Dragon's Cave** (May to September), home of the earliest ruler of this land. As the story goes, the legendary Prince Krak had to outwit the resident dragon before he could found the city of Kraków in its prime location overlooking the Vistula.

Kazimierz This suburb, a short walk southeast of Wawel, was until the 1820s an independent town. In the 15th century, the Jews were expelled from Kraków and they resettled in a small prescribed area in Kazimierz, separated by a wall from the larger Christian quarter. The Jewish quarter became home to Jews fleeing persecution from all corners of Europe. At the outbreak of WWII 70,000 Jews lived in this section of Kraków.

During the war the Nazis relocated Jews to a walled ghetto in Podgórze. They were exterminated in the nearby Płaszów death camp, as portrayed in Stephen Spielberg's film *Schindler's List*. The current Jewish population in Kraków is estimated at 100.

The Jewish quarter is punctuated with synagogues, which miraculously survived the war. Of these, the most important is the late 15th-century Old Synagogue (the oldest Jewish religious building in Poland), today housing the **Jewish Museum** (closed Saturday and Sunday). A short walk north is the small 16th-century **Remu'h Synagogue** (open weekdays). Behind it, the **Remu'h Cemetery** boasts extraordinary Renaissance gravestones. The recently restored **Izaak's Synagogue** (closed Saturday) shows documentary films on life in the Jewish ghetto.

Wieliczka Wieliczka, 15km south-east of Kraków's centre, is famous for its **salt mine**, which is on the Unesco World Cultural Heritage list. Visitors see three upper levels of the mine, ranging from 64m to 135m below the ground. This eerie world of pits and chambers was hewn out by hand from solid salt. The highlight is the richly ornamented Chapel of the Blessed Kinga.

The mine is open 7.30 am to 6.30 pm daily, 16 April to 15 October, and 8 am to 4 pm the rest of the year. The obligatory guided tour takes three hours and is a 3km walk through the mine. It's only 14°C in the mine!

Some English tours (US$8) are scheduled in summer. Otherwise, English-language brochures are available (US$2). Minibuses to Wieliczka depart every 10 minutes from just north of the bus terminal. Request the driver to let you off at the mine.

Organised Tours

A joint program of tours is operated by Orbis (☎ 422 40 35), Rynek Główny 41; Jan-Pol (☎ 421 42 06), in the Dom Turysty PTTK, ul Westerplatte 15/16; and Intercrac (☎ 422 63 41) in the Dom Polonii, Rynek Główny 14.

The Jarden Jewish Bookshop (☎ 421 71 66), ul Szeroka 2, in Kazimierz's Jewish quarter, is the best known agency offering a choice of tours discovering Jewish heritage, including Retracing Schindler's List (two hours, US$14). Alternatively, buy the brochure (US$2) in the bookshop, and set off on your own.

Special Events

Kraków's major events include the Organ Music Days (April), the Polish and International Festivals of Short Films (May/June), the Jewish Culture Festival (June), the International Festival of Street Theatre (July), Music in Old Kraków (August) and the All Saints' Day Jazz Festival (October/November).

Places to Stay

Kraków is Poland's premier tourist destination, so finding a bed in summer can be tricky. Try to book in advance or inquire at a tourist office immediately upon arrival.

Camping The pleasant *Camping Nr 46 Smok* (☎ 429 72 66, *ul Kamedulska 18*), 4km west of the centre, is Kraków's only camping ground operating year-round. From Kraków Główny train station, take tram No 2 to the end of the line in Zwierzyniec and change for any westbound bus except No 100.

Camping Nr 45 Krak (☎ 637 21 22, *ul Radzikowskiego 99*) is next to Motel Krak, on the Katowice road about 5km north-west of the centre. It is the city's largest and best equipped camping ground and is open May to September. The traffic noise can be considerable. Bus No 238 from Kraków Główny train station goes there.

Hostels Kraków has several year-round hostels. The closest to the city is the *youth hostel* (☎ 633 88 22, *☎/fax 633 89 20, ul Oleandry 4*) 2km west of the train station (take tram No 15 and get off just past Hotel Cracovia). It is often full and can also be disturbingly noisy.

The all-year *Schronisko Turystyczne Ekspres* (☎ 633 88 62, *ul Wrocławska 91*), 2km north-west of the centre, does not close during the day and has no curfew. Take bus No 130 from the train station to the fifth stop.

The new *youth hostel* (☎ 653 24 32, *ul Grochowa 21*), on the 3rd floor of a student dormitory, is located in a quiet suburb 6km from the centre. Take bus No 115 from the train station and ask the driver to let you off at the Węglarska stop.

Several summer-only hostels are fair options during those months. *Strawberry Hostel* (☎ 636 14 09, *ul Racławicka 9*) provides minibus transportation from the train station. The large July-August *Schronisko Szkolne* (☎ 637 24 41, *ul Szablowskiego 1*) is 4km north-west of the Old Town. Tram No 4 from the station lets you off nearby.

Student Hostels Several student hostels operate each summer, but they change from year to year. The tourist offices will have current information. Options will probably include: the closest to the centre, *Dom Studencki Żaczek* (☎ 633 54 77, *Al 3 Maja 5*);

Letni Hotel AWF (☎ 648 20 09, *Al Jana Pawła II 82*), on the road to Nowa Huta; and *Bydgoska* (☎ 637 44 33, *ul Bydgoska 19*), *Piast* (☎ 637 49 33, *ul Piastowska 47*) and *Nawojka* (☎ 633 52 05, *ul Reymonta 11*), all close to each other about 3km west of the station. Each will cost around US$15/20 a single/double and each has its own cafeteria.

Private Rooms The Biuro Turystyki i Zakwaterowania Waweltur (☎ 422 16 40, ☎/fax 422 19 21), ul Pawia 8, next door to the municipal tourist office, will arrange for accommodation in *private rooms* at US$21/32 for a single/double in the Old Town, and slightly less farther out. Check the location carefully before deciding.

Hotels The vast *Dom Turysty PTTK* (☎ 422 95 66, ☎/fax 422 57 19, ✉ hotel@janpol.com.pl, ul Westerplatte 15/16) no longer has dorm rooms, thus unfortunately eliminating the cheapest central option. Now, it offers only singles/doubles for US$65/80 with bath and US$32/45 without. Prices include breakfast and are still among the cheapest for a room near the Old Town.

Several other affordable options are just outside the Old Town. The most appealing is *Pokoje Gościnne Jordan* (☎ 421 21 25, fax 422 82 26, ✉ hotel@jordan.krkow.pl, ul Długa 9), which is one block north of the Old Town. The reception is in the tourist office next door. Modern rooms with bath and breakfast are US$38/44. Another affordable option is the drab *Hotel Monopol* (☎ 422 70 15, ul Św Gertrudy 6). Rooms are US$38/50 with a sketchy bath, or US$25 for a single without bath.

Hotel Saski (☎ 421 42 22, fax 421 48 30, ul Sławkowska 3) is ideally located in a historic townhouse just off Rynek Główny and costs US$35/45/55 for singles/doubles/triples without bath, US$60/82/92 with bath.

Hotel Pokoje Gościnne SARP (☎ 292 02 66, ☎/fax 429 17 78, ul Floriańska 39) is a homy guest house on the top floor of a former architects' dormitory. It has only six rooms for US$39/52, so it's often full.

Several affordable hotels are near the train station. *Hotel Warszawski* (☎ 422 06 22, ul Pawia 6) costs US$36/50 for rooms without bath or US$62/75 for a newly renovated room with bath. Just around the corner,

Hotel Polonia (☎ *422 12 33, fax 422 16 21,* @ *polonia@bci.krakow.pl, ul Basztowa 25*) has small rooms bath at similar prices.

Places to Eat

Old Town & Around The Old Town is tightly packed with restaurants, ranging all the way from rock bottom to top notch. One of the best budget places is the self-service *Kuchnia Staropolska u Babci Maliny* (*ul Sławkowska 17*), in the basement of the Polska Akademia Umiejętności.

Other inexpensive eateries include the legendary *Jadłodajnia u Pani Stasi* (*ul Mikołajska 16*), just off Mały Rynek; *Jadłodajnia Kuchcik* (*ul Jagiellońska 12*); *Restauracja pod Temidą* on ul Grodzka; and *Jadłodajnia Sąsiedzi* (*ul Szpitalna 40*). Most of these places are open until 6 pm Monday to Saturday.

Salad Bar Chimera (*ul Św Anny 3*) is a cosy place with an array of salads. *Bar Bistro Różowy Słoń* (*ul Straszewskiego 24*) has opened several other outlets, including ul Sienna 1 and ul Szpitalna 38. A step up for Polish fare is *Kawiarnia u Zalipianek* (*ul Szewska 24*). In summer you can eat on its open terrace facing the Planty.

Bar Wegetariański Vega (*ul Św Gertrudy 7*) is a cheap veggie place. For pizza try the *Pizzeria Cyklop* (*ul Mikołajska 16*). *Taco Mexicano* (*ul Poselska 20*) now has an additional restaurant with outdoor seating at Rynek Główny 19. The Greek *Akropolis Grill* (*ul Grodzka 9*) has affordable prices. *Restauracja Korsykańska Paese* (*ul Poselska 24*) offers Corsican and mainland French cuisine in a bright atmosphere.

For the best coffee in town, go to *Sklep z Kawą Pożegnanie z Afryką* (*Coffee Shop Farewell to Africa; ul Św Tomasza 21*). It is a sophisticated shop and cafe, which sells about 70 kinds of coffee. This chain is now serving coffee in non-smoking venues all over Poland.

Wawel & Kazimierz The highly recommended *Restauracja Chłopskie Jadło* (*ul Agnieszki 1*), a short walk south of Wawel, looks like an old country inn and serves traditional Polish food at good prices. A few steps away is the tiny *Bar Orientalny Hoang Hai* (*ul Stradomska 13*), which does good hearty Chinese-Vietnamese food at low prices.

For Jewish food, go to the adjacent restaurants of the same name; *Café Ariel* (*ul Szeroka 17 and 18*), in Kazimierz. The two restaurants share not only their name, but also their menu. They offer live evening performances of Jewish, Gypsy and Russian folk songs (US$5).

The expensive *Restauracja pod Aniołami* (*ul Grodzka 35*) serves excellent Polish food in a beautiful old building.

Entertainment

The Cultural Information Centre (☎ 421 77 87), ul Św Jana 2, provides detailed information about events, publishes the monthly guide *Karnet*, and also sells tickets to some of the events.

Jazz The main jazz outlets include *Jazz Club u Muniaka* (*ul Floriańska 3*), open Thursday to Saturday, and *Klub u Luisa* (*Rynek Główny 13*), open weekends.

Discos, Bars & Pubs Popular haunts include *Equinox* (*ul Sławkowska 13/15*) and *Klub Pasja* (*ul Szewska 5*). Most student clubs run discos on Friday and Saturday nights. Try *Klub Rotunda* (*ul Oleandry 1*) if you are staying at the youth hostel nearby.

More than 50 pubs are in the Old Town alone, many housed in ancient vaulted cellars. All are smoking venues, so sometimes breathing is a problem.

Klub Kulturny (*ul Szewska 25*) has a lively crowd and dungeon-like interior. *Pub pod Jemiołą* (*ul Floriańska 20*), in the alley behind the music store, is also popular. *Black Gallery* (*ul Mikołajska 24*) is a crowded, underground pub that stays open late.

If you are in Kazimierz, check out the artsy *Ptaszyl* (*ul Szeroka 10*).

Classical Music, Opera & Theatre The best known venue is the *Teatr Stary* (*Old Theatre; ul Jagiellońska 1*), which attracts the cream of the city's acting crop. The spectacular *Teatr im Słowackiego* (*Słowacki Theatre; plac Św Ducha 1*) hosts theatre, opera and ballet performances. *Filharmonia* (*ul Zwierzyniecka 1*) is home to one of the best orchestras in the country.

Getting There & Away

Train The central train station, Kraków Główny, handles all international and most domestic rail traffic. Tickets and couchettes can be booked at Kraków Główny station or from the Orbis office at Rynek Główny 41.

Frequent InterCity express trains go to Warsaw in 2½ hours, and cheaper regular trains take three hours. Frequent trains leave for Częstochowa (2½ hours, 132km) and Wrocław (4½ hours, 268km). Fast trains travel daily to Poznań (seven hours, 398km) and Lublin (four hours, 269km). Trains to Zakopane are slower than the buses (three hours). The early morning and mid-afternoon service to Oświęcim (1½ hours, 65km) is also not as convenient as the bus.

Internationally, one or two direct trains go daily to Berlin (11 hours), Bratislava (eight hours), Bucharest, Budapest (8½ hours), Dresden (9½ hours), Frankfurt/Main (15 hours), Leipzig (11 hours), Prague and Vienna.

Bus Central bus terminal is next to Kraków Główny train station. Two buses leave each morning for Częstochowa (119km).

PKS buses run frequently to Zakopane and are considerably faster than the trains. A private company also runs to Zakopane, for which you can buy tickets from Biuro Turystyki i Zakwaterowania Waweltur (see the Private Rooms section earlier). Nine buses a day go to Oświęcim (two hours, 64km), which is also more convenient than the train. Most of these are privately run and depart from behind the train station, where a schedule is posted. You can purchase your ticket on the bus.

Agencies near the station can book buses to Amsterdam, Budapest, London, Paris, Vienna and a variety of destinations in Germany.

OŚWIĘCIM
☎ 033

Oświęcim is a medium-sized industrial town about 60km west of Kraków. The Polish name may be unfamiliar to outsiders, but the German name is not: Auschwitz, the largest Nazi concentration camp, was the scene of the most extensive experiment in genocide in the history of humankind.

Auschwitz camp was established in April 1940 in the prewar Polish army barracks on the outskirts of Oświęcim. Originally intended to hold Polish political prisoners, the camp eventually developed into the largest centre for the extermination of European Jews. Towards this end, two additional camps were set up in subsequent years: Birkenau (Brzezinka) and Monowitz (Monowice). This death factory eliminated 1½ to two million people of 27 nationalities, 85% to 90% of whom were Jews.

Auschwitz

Auschwitz was only partially destroyed by the fleeing Nazis, and many of the original buildings stand to this day as a bleak document of the camp's history. A dozen of the 30 surviving prison blocks today house the museum, including some general exhibitions and others dedicated to victims from particular countries.

From the visitors centre, enter the barbed-wire encampment through the gate with the ironic inscription 'Arbeit Macht Frei' (Work Makes Free). You can visit the exhibitions in the prison blocks and complete the tour with a look at the chilling gas chamber and crematorium. The experience is vivid and disturbing.

Every half-hour the cinema in the visitor's centre shows a 15-minute documentary about the liberation of the camp by Soviet troops on 27 January 1945. Check the schedule for the English-language viewing.

The museum opens 8 am to 7 pm daily in June, July and August; closes at 6 pm in May and September; at 5 pm in April and October; at 4 pm in March and November; and at 3 pm in December, January and February. Admission is free; the cinema is US$0.50. Get a copy of the small *Auschwitz Birkenau Guide Book*, which is quite enough to get you round the grounds. Otherwise, three-hour tours in English and German are organised daily at 11.30 am (US$4 per person). From 15 April to late October, a special bus shuttles visitors between Auschwitz and Birkenau. It departs hourly 10.30 am to 4.30 pm from just outside the entrance to the visitors' centre, opposite the cafeteria *Bar Smak*.

Birkenau

It was actually Birkenau, not Auschwitz, where the extermination of huge numbers of Jews took place. Vast (175 hectares), purpose-built and efficient, the camp had over 300 prison barracks and four huge gas chambers complete with crematoria. Each

POLAND

gas chamber accommodated 2000 people and electric lifts raised the bodies to the ovens. The camp could hold 200,000 inmates at a time.

Birkenau can be visited in the same opening hours as Auschwitz and entry is free. Make sure to leave enough time (at least an hour) to walk around the camp – it is really vast. Return to Auschwitz by shuttle bus or to the train station by taxi.

Getting There & Away

For most tourists, the jumping-off point for Oświęcim is Kraków, from where many tours to the camp are organised.

A few early morning and mid-afternoon trains travel from Kraków Główny station. More convenient, 10 buses per day travel from Kraków to Oświęcim (two hours, 64km), departing from behind the train station. Ask the driver to let you off at Auschwitz.

To get back to Kraków, you may be able to take one of the hourly buses that stop just outside the Auschwitz entrance. Otherwise, check the schedules at the Oświęcim train station and at the bus stop across the street.

CZĘSTOCHOWA

☎ 034

Częstochowa, north of Katowice, is the spiritual heart of Poland. It owes its fame to the miraculous icon of the Black Madonna, kept in Jasna Góra (Bright Mountain) Monastery, which has attracted pilgrims from all corners of the globe since its founding in 1382.

In 1430, the holy icon was stolen by the Hussites, who slashed the face of the Madonna. As the story goes, the wounds began to bleed, thus frightening the thieves who abandoned the icon and ran off. The monks who found the panel wanted to clean it, and a spring miraculously bubbled from the ground. The spring exists to this day, and St Barbara's Church was founded on the site. The picture was restored and repainted, but the scars on the face of the Virgin Mary were left as a reminder of the miracle.

Orientation & Information

The main thoroughfare in the city centre is Al Najświętszej Marii Panny (referred to in addresses as Al NMP), a wide, tree-lined avenue with Jasna Góra Monastery at its

western end and Plac Daszyńskiego at the eastern end. Both the train and bus stations are just south of Al NMP at the eastern end of town. Most of the places to stay and eat are clustered around the monastery or along Al NMP.

The Centrum Informacji Turystycznej (☎ 368 22 50, ☎/fax 368 22 60), Al NMP 65, is open daily (closed Sunday in the low season). The Centrum Internetowe, a cybercafe, is on the top floor of the Dom Handlowy Seka, Al NMP 12d (open till 10 pm daily).

Things to See & Do

Jasna Góra Monastery retains the appearance of a fortress. The compound houses a church, a chapel and the monastery. The large baroque church is beautifully decorated, but the image of the Black Madonna is on the high altar of the adjacent chapel. Upstairs in the monastery is the Knights' Hall (Sala Rycerska) where a copy of the icon is on display for close examination.

Three museums are housed within the defensive walls (all open daily): the Arsenal with a variety of old weapons; the 600th Anniversary Museum (Muzeum Sześćsetlecia) containing Lech Wałęsa's 1983 Nobel Peace Prize; and the Treasury (Skarbiec) featuring votive offerings presented by the faithful. At 106m, the monastery tower is the tallest church tower in Poland. It is normally open daily April to November, but it was closed for renovations at the time of writing.

Special Events

The major Marian feasts at Jasna Góra are 3 May, 16 July, 15 August, 26 August, 8 and 12 September, and 8 December. The most widely celebrated is the Assumption (15 August), when up to half a million of the faithful flock to Jasna Góra.

Places to Stay & Eat

The all-year *Camping Nr 76 Oleńka* (*☎/fax 324 74 95, ul Oleńki 10/30)*, west of the monastery, has rudimentary chalets and camping facilities. Rooms are US$18/25/32 for three/four/five people. An inexpensive *snack bar* is on the grounds.

The *youth hostel* (*☎ 324 31 21, ul Jasnogórska 84/90)* is two blocks north of Al NMP. It is open only in July and August and has modest facilities. Otherwise, try the Church-run **Hale Noclegowe** (☎ 365 66 88 ext 224, ul Klasztorna 1), just next to the monastery. You pay US$3.50 per head in a four- to nine-bed dorm with shared facilities and cold water only.

The Church's bigger and better lodging facility is **Dom Pielgrzyma** (Pilgrim's Home; ☎ 324 70 11, fax 365 18 70, ✉ dp@ jasnagora.pl), right behind the monastery. This large hostel has singles/doubles/triples with bath for US$12/18/25. It has a cheap *cafeteria* on the premises.

Hotel Polonia (☎ 324 68 32, fax 365 11 05, ul Piłsudskiego 9) is opposite the train station and offers rooms for US$25/30/35 with bath and breakfast.

Getting There & Away

The new, purpose-built train station on ul Piłsudskiego handles half a dozen fast trains to Warsaw (2½ hours, 235km) and Kraków (2½ hours, 132km). A few trains go to Łodz (1½ hours, four hours) and Wrocław (four hours) and Zakopane (eight hours). Trains run every hour or so to Katowice (1½ hours, 86km), from where there are connections to other cities.

The bus terminal is close to the central train station. Buses departing from here include three daily to Kraków (114km), three to Wrocław (176km) and one each day to Zakopane (222km).

ZAKOPANE & THE TATRAS
☎ 018

The Tatras, 100km south of Kraków, are the highest range of the Carpathian Mountains, with towering peaks and steep rocky sides dropping hundreds of metres to lakes. The whole range, roughly 60km long and 15km wide, stretches across the Polish-Slovakian border. The Polish Tatras include twenty peaks exceeding 2000m, the highest of which is Mt Rysy (2499m).

Set at the northern foot of the Tatras, Zakopane (population 30,000) is the most famous mountain resort in Poland. Though Zakopane is essentially a base for either skiing or hiking in the Tatras, the town itself has an enjoyable laid-back atmosphere.

Orientation & Information

Zakopane is nestled below Mt Giewont. Its bus and train stations are adjacent in the north-eastern part of town, from which it's a 10-minute walk down ul Kościuszki to the pedestrian mall of ul Krupówki. The funicular to Mt Gubałówka is just off the northern end of ul Krupówki. The cable car to Mt Kasprowy Wierch is at Kuźnice, 3km south.

The helpful Centrum Informacji Turystycznej (☎ 201 22 11), ul Kościuszki 17, is open daily and is staffed with knowledgeable English-speakers.

Orbis (☎ 201 50 51), ul Krupówki 22, sells domestic and international train tickets, arranges accommodation in private houses and selected holiday homes, and organises tours.

Other useful travel agencies include Tatry (☎ 201 43 43), ul Chramcówki 35, just off the train station (private rooms, tours); and Kozica (☎ 201 22 12), ul Jagiellońska 1, right behind the Bar FIS (private rooms, tickets).

The best choice of maps and guidebooks on the Tatras is in Księgarnia Górska, the bookshop on the 1st floor of Dom Turysty PTTK. GraNet Internet Café, ul Krupówki 2, is open daily.

Funicular to Mt Gubałówka
elevation 1120m

Mt Gubałówka offers an excellent view over the Tatras and is a favourite destination for people who do not feel like hiking. The funicular covers the 1388m-long route in less than five minutes (US$2.50 return).

Cable Car to Mt Kasprowy Wierch
elevation 1985m

Operating since 1935, the cable-car trip from Kuźnice travels to the summit of Mt Kasprowy Wierch. The one-way journey takes 20 minutes (US$4/6 single/return). In the summer, many people return to Zakopane on foot down the Gąsienicowa Valley.

The cable car normally shuts down for a few weeks in May and June, and again between October and December (dates are variable). In midsummer, it runs from 7.30 am to 8 pm; in winter, from 7.30 am to 4 pm.

If you buy a return ticket, your trip back is automatically reserved two hours after departure time. Buy tickets at the Kuźnice cableway station (expect queues) or from some travel agencies, who will charge a fee. PKS buses leave for Kuźnice frequently from the bus terminal, as do the private

POLAND

minibuses that park in front of the Bar FIS across the street.

Hiking & Cycling in the Tatras

The *Tatrzański Park Narodowy* map, available from the PTTK office, shows all the walking trails in the area. Late spring and early autumn are the best times to visit, as trails are overrun by tourists in July and August. The Tatras can be dangerous, particularly during the snowy period (roughly November to May). Bring good footwear, warm clothing and rain gear.

Several picturesque small valleys are south of Zakopane, including the Dolina Strążyska. You can continue from the Strążyska by the red trail up to Mt Giewont (1909m; 3½ hours from Zakopane) and then walk down on the blue trail to Kuźnice in two hours.

Two long and beautiful forested valleys, the Dolina Chochołowska and the Dolina Kościeliska, are in the western part of the park, known as Tatry Zachodnie (West Tatras). Both valleys are served by PKS buses and private minibuses from Zakopane. These valleys offer some of the best trails for cycling. Bicycles are available for rental from Cykle SC, ul Krupówki 52 (US$2 per hour).

Though camping is not allowed in the park, eight year-round PTTK mountain refuges (beds US$5 to US$8, doubles US$40 to US$50) provide cheap accommodation. No one is ever turned away, though you may have to crash on the bare floor (bring a sleeping bag). All refuges serve simple hot meals, but kitchens close early (around 7 pm). Before you set off, check the current conditions at the PTTK office in Zakopane.

Skiing in the Tatras

Zakopane is known as Poland's winter sports capital and was a prime contender for the 2006 winter Olympics. Mt Kasprowy Wierch and Mt Gubałówka offer the best conditions and the most challenging slopes in the area. Take the funicular or cable car as described earlier, and purchase your lift tickets on the mountain (US$1 per ride). Ski equipment rental is available at Mt Gubałówka.

Places to Stay

Zakopane has heaps of places to stay. Accommodation prices fluctuate considerably.

Peak seasons are December to February and July to August. The prices listed here are for the high season.

Camping The all-year *Camping Nr 97 Pod Krokwią* (☎ 201 22 56, ul Żeromskiego 34) has heated bungalows, which cost about US$10 per person. From the bus/train stations, take any bus to Kuźnice or Jaszczurówka and get off at the Rondo.

Other summer camping grounds in the Tatras include *Camping za Strugiem* (☎ 201 45 66, ul Za Strugiem 38), which has cabins, and *Auto Camping Nr 252 Comfort* (☎ 201 49 42, ul Kaszelewskiego 7a) on the Kościelisko road.

Hostels The year-round *Youth Hostel Szarotka* (☎ 206 62 03, ul Nowotarska 45) is a 10-minute walk from the centre. Beds are US$8 to US$12 depending on the size of the room. The all-year *Schronisko Młodzieżowe Żak* (☎ 201 57 06, ul Marusarzówny 15) is cheaper and smaller.

The central *Dom Turysty PTTK* (☎ 206 32 07, fax 206 32 84, ✉ informacja@ domturysty.zakopane.pl, ul Zaruskiego 5) has heaps of rooms – singles/doubles/ triples with bath cost US$25/40/45, those without are cheaper. You can stay in a dorm for US$6 to US$10.

Private Rooms The business of *private rooms* for hire is flourishing in Zakopane. Most travel agencies make these arrangements. In the peak seasons, they may not want to arrange accommodation for a period shorter than three nights. Expect a bed in a double room to cost US$6 to US$10 in the high season. Locals may also approach you in the bus or train station to offer rooms in their homes. In either case, check the location before committing.

You may also look for signs saying *pokoje, noclegi* or *zimmer frei* posted outside of private homes. The places that call themselves *pensjonat* may offer better facilities, but are usually more expensive.

In the low season, finding a private room for hire is much more difficult.

Holiday Homes These days, most holiday homes are open to the general public, offering rooms without/with bath for US$10/18. The major agent is FWP (☎ 201 27 63, fax

206 69 74), which has its office in the DW Podhale, ul Kościuszki 19.

Places to Eat

Among the cheapest eateries are *Zboecka (ul Krupówki 28), Bar Rzepka (ul Krupówki 43)* and *Pizzeria Joker (ul Krupówki 51)*. Another inexpensive option is *Restauracja Świarna (ul Kościuszki 4)*.

The folksy *Stek Chałupa (ul Krupówki 33)* serves tasty Polish dishes cafeteria-style. Opposite, *Restauracja Kolorowa* is popular for its pleasant atmosphere.

Getting There & Away

Several trains travel to Kraków (3½ hours, 147km) but buses are faster and also more frequent. Trains also go daily to Warsaw (10 hours, 439km), but it is faster to take the bus to Kraków, from where you can catch an IC or express train.

PKS fast buses run hourly to Kraków (US$4, 2½ hours); however, a private company has faster, cheaper buses to Kraków, departing from ul Kościuszki 19. A few buses per week go to Budapest (US$16, nine hours), and a daily morning bus travels to Poprad in Slovakia (US$3), from where you can catch the express train to Prague.

ZAMOŚĆ
☎ 084

Zamość was founded in 1580 by Jan Zamoyski, chancellor and commander in chief of Renaissance Poland, who intended to create an ideal urban settlement and impregnable barrier against raids from the east. In 1992 Zamość was added to Unesco's World Cultural Heritage list.

Information

The helpful tourist office (☎ 639 22 92) is in the town hall on Rynek Wielki (closed weekends low season).

Cybercafé NetSystem SC (☎ 639 34 75), ul Peowiaków 9, is a 10-minute walk from the Rynek and is open weekdays only. Head north on al Piłsudskiego and take the first right on ul Peowiaków.

Things to See

Begin your exploring on **Rynek Wielki**, an impressive Renaissance square surrounded by Italian-style burghers' houses and dominated by the 16th-century **town hall**. The **regional museum** is in one of the loveliest houses on the square (closed Monday), with a wide array of exhibits.

The nearby **Zamoyski Palace** lost much of its character when it was converted into a military hospital in the 1830s. A few paces to the north-east is the former **Academy**, Poland's third institution of higher education, founded in 1594. On the eastern edge of the Old Town is the best surviving **bastion** of the seven bastions the town originally had.

Before WWII, Jews accounted for about 45% of Zamość's population of 12,000, inhabiting the area to the east of the Academy. The most significant Jewish architectural relic is the Renaissance **synagogue** from the 1610s, on the corner of ul Zamenhofa and ul Bazyliańska. It is now a public library.

A 10-minute walk south of the Old Town is the **Rotunda**, a ring-shaped fort built in the 1820s. During WWII the Nazis executed 8000 local residents here. Today it is a memorial to the victims.

Places to Stay

Camping Duet (☎ 639 24 99, ul Królowej Jadwigi 14), 1km west of the Old Town, offers year-round chalets (US$16/19/24/29 a single/double/triple/quad with bath), tennis courts, and an indoor swimming pool with sauna and jacuzzi.

Just down the road from the camping ground, *Hotel Sportowy (☎ 638 60 11, ul Królowej Jadwigi 8),* in the sports centre, is a 10-minute walk from the Rynek. Rooms with bath cost US$20/25/29/34. A bed in a dorm without bath is US$8.

The July-August *youth hostel (☎ 627 91 25, ul Zamoyskiego 4)* is in a school, about 1.5km east of the Old Town, not far from the bus terminal.

Only a few places to stay are in the Old Town. The musty but adequate *Dom Turysty Marta (☎ 639 26 39, ul Zamenhofa 11)* costs US$5 per person in a dorm or US$11/15 for a single/double. All rooms have shared facilities. More comfortable is the *Hotel Renesans (☎ 639 20 01, ul Grecka 6),* which offers modern rooms with private bath for US$28/42. The spiffy *Hotel Arkadia (☎ 638 65 07, Rynek Wielki 9)* has just four rooms: three doubles (US$38 each) and one suite (US$63).

Places to Eat

For a simple cheap meal, go to *Bar Mleczny Asia (ul Staszica 10)*. The *Restauracja-Kawiarnia Ratuszowa*, in the town hall, also has reasonable food at low prices. For a more gratifying lunch or dinner, try the *Restauracja-Kawiarnia Muzealna* in a cellar next to the regional museum.

Entertainment

Two 'artistic' bars are located in the old fortifications: *Oberża Kazamat (ul Bazyliańska 36)* or *Kawiarnia Artystyczna Brama* in the Old Lublin Gate. Both host various live music events.

Getting There & Away

The bus terminal is 2km east of the centre. Buses to Lublin (2½ hours, 89km) run every half-hour. Cheaper and faster are the private minibuses that leave regularly from behind the bus terminal. Two fast buses go directly to Kraków (six hours, 318km), and four go to Warsaw (247km).

To get to Warsaw, take a special PKP bus, which travels to Lublin train station and meets the express train to Warsaw. A convenient morning fast train takes six hours to Kraków. Orbis, ul Grodzka 18, books and sells train tickets.

LUBLIN
☎ 081

In 1569 the political union of Poland and Lithuania was signed in Lublin, creating the largest European state of the time. Lublin's Old Town has retained much of its historic architectural fabric. However, the quarter looks dilapidated. Note that the Old Town gets deserted after 9 pm and can be dangerous.

Orientation & Information

The bus station is in the city centre, while the train station is located, less conveniently, 2km south of the town's heart. The centre consists of the Old Town, as well as the New Town that stretches to the west along its main thoroughfare, ul Krakowskie Przedmieście.

The tourist office (☎ 532 44 12), ul Narutomiza 54, is in the New Town, a few blocks south of ul Krakowskie Przedmieśscie (closed Sunday).

Email and Internet access can be found at Educom (☎ 532 79 91), Rynek 8, in the Old Town; and Not Kawiarnia Internetowa (☎ 532 25 85), ul Sklodowskiej 3, near the university.

Things to See

Built atop a hill just north-east of the Old Town, the original 14th-century castle was largely destroyed. The building that stands today actually functioned as a prison until 1944. During the Nazi occupation, over 100,000 people passed through this building, later deported to death camps. The building now houses the extensive **Lublin Museum** (closed Monday and Tuesday), which contains the 14th-century **Chapel of the Holy Trinity**.

Majdanek, 4km south-east of Lublin's centre, was one of the largest death camps in Europe. About 240,000 people, representing 51 nationalities from 26 countries (including over 100,000 Jews), were exterminated here. Barracks, guard towers and long lines of formerly electrified double barbed wire remain as they were. Even more chilling are the crematorium and gas chambers, which can be toured. The museum is open 8 am to 5 pm daily except Monday (to 3 pm October to April). Entrance is free. Trolleybus No 156 from ul Królewska will take you to Majdanek.

Places to Stay

The all-year, 80-bed *youth hostel (☎ 533 06 28, ul Długosza 6)*, 2km west of the Old Town, is in the heart of the university district (take trolleybus No 150 from the train station, bus No 5 from the bus terminal).

South of the youth hostel is *Dom Nauczyciela (☎ 533 82 85, ul Akademicka 4)*, a clean teachers' hostel, costing US$16/20 for a single/double without bath. Some of the rooms were recently renovated and go for US$33/42 for a double/triple with bath.

Two budget places in the Old Town provide excellent value and convenient location. The 28-bed *Wojewódzki Ośrodek Metodyczny (☎ 743 61 33, ul Dominikańska 5)* is US$8 per person with shared bath. Next to the castle, the church-run *Archidiecezjalny Dom Rekolekcyjny (☎ 532 41 38, ul Podwale 15)* has dorms (some with bath, others without) for the same price.

The basic *Hotel Piast (☎ 532 16 46, ul Pocztowa 2)* is next door to the train station, which is not a very pleasant part of town.

Singles/doubles with shared facilities will cost US$11/14.

Places to Eat & Drink

Lublin still has a few milk bars, such as *Bar Staromiejski (ul Jezuicka 1)*, at the foot of the Kraków Gate, and *Bar Uniwersalny Ludowy (ul Krakowskie Przedmieście 60)*. A more modern place for a budget lunch is fast-food *Bar Pod Basztą (ul Królewska 6)*.

A slew of eating establishments have appeared in the Old Town, which is gradually coming back to life. *Pueblo Desperados (Rynek 5)* makes a valid attempt at Mexican food, especially considering the low prices. Vegetarians will appreciate the tiny *Gopal Bar Wegetarianski (ul Jezuicka 14)*, serving Indian dishes during the day. *Piwnica u Biesów (Rynek 18)*, in the cellar, has a good ambience for a few drinks.

Getting There & Away

The main train station, Lublin Główny, is linked to the Old Town by trolleybus No 160 and bus Nos 13 and 17. Fast trains run daily to Warsaw (2½ hours, 175km) and Kraków (two hours, 345km).

The central bus terminal, Dworzec Główny PKS, is at the foot of the castle near the Old Town. Daily buses run to Kozłówka (one hour, 38km), Kazimierz Dolny (one hour, 44km), Zamość (two hours, 89km), Kraków (five hours, 269km) and Warsaw (three hours).

AROUND LUBLIN
Kozłowka

The hamlet of Kozłówka, 38km north of Lublin, is famous for its sumptuous late-baroque palace, which until WWII was the residence of the wealthy Zamoyski family. Today it is a museum displaying much of the original decoration. Its most striking feature is an extensive collection of socialist realist artwork from the communist era. The palace is open March to November (closed Monday), and is an easy day trip from Lublin.

Silesia

WROCŁAW
☎ 071

Silesia has spent much of its history under Austrian and Prussian rule. As a result of

Polish nationalist uprisings after WWI, most of the Upper Silesia was incorporated into Poland. The remainder of the Silesian region joined Poland only in the aftermath of WWII German residents were then deported, and the area was resettled with Poles from Poland's prewar eastern territories, which had been claimed by the Soviet Union.

Wrocław returned to Poland in 1945 in a sorry state. During the final phase of WWII, the Nazis held out for 81 days, surrendering only after Berlin fell on 2 May 1945. In the course of this siege 70% of the city was destroyed.

Today, Wrocław offers a beautifully restored old market square, a picturesque cluster of churches by the river, and a lively cultural scene.

Orientation & Information

The train and bus stations are near to each other, 1km south of the Old Town.

Get a copy of the practical and free magazine, *Welcome to Wrocław*, from the municipal tourist office (☎ 344 11 11, fax 344 29 62), Rynek 14, which is open Monday to Saturday.

The Orbis office (☎ 343 26 65) is at Rynek 29. PTTK (☎ 343 03 44), Rynek-Ratusz 11/12, can arrange foreign-language guides with advance notice. Almatur (☎ 344 47 28), ul Kościuszki 34, sells ISIC cards.

Internet Café Web is in the courtyard at ul Ruska 46. The Kawiarna pod Kalamburem, ul Kuźnicza 29, also has a cybercafe in its back courtyard, which you enter from ul Nożownicza.

Things to See

At 173m by 208m, this is Poland's second-largest old market square (after Kraków's). The **town hall** (1327-1504) on the southern side of the central block is certainly one of the most beautiful in Poland. Inside, the **Historical Museum** (closed Monday and Tuesday) shows off its splendid interiors.

In the north-western corner of the Rynek are two small houses called **Jaś i Małgosia**, or Hansel and Gretel, linked by a baroque gate. Just behind them looms the monumental 14th-century **St Elizabeth's Church** with its 83m-high tower.

One block east of the Rynek is the Gothic **St Mary Magdalene's Church** with

POLAND

a Romanesque portal from around 1280 incorporated into its southern external wall. Farther east along ul Wita Stwosza is the 15th-century Bernardine church and monastery, now home to the **Museum of Architecture** (closed Monday and Tuesday).

In the park behind the museum is the **Panorama Racławicka** (closed Monday), a huge 360-degree painting of the 1794 Battle of Racławice. In this famous battle, the Polish peasant army led by Tadeusz Kościuszko defeated the Russian forces intent on partitioning Poland. Headphones providing an English explanation of the painting are included in the ticket price (US$5/3). Arrive early to beat the crowds.

Just to the east is the **National Museum** (closed Monday). Highlights include Silesian medieval art and modern Polish painting.

Cross the Most Pokoju, the bridge over the Odra River. Turn left when the tram tracks bend right and walk west into Ostrów Tumski, the cradle of the city, which has been inhabited since about the 8th century. Its focal point is the mighty twin-towered Gothic **cathedral**.

Special Events

Wrocław's major annual events include the Musica Polonica Nova contemporary music festival (February), Jazz on the Oder (May) and the Wratislavia Cantans oratorio and Cantata Festival (September).

Places to Stay

The all-year *Camping Nr 267 Ślęża* (☎ 343 44 42, ul Na Grobli 16/18) is on the bank of the Oder, 2km east of the Old Town. Take tram No 4 to Plac Wróblewskiego from the train station and walk 1km eastward.

Hostels Wrocław has two all-year *youth hostels*. One is near the train station (☎ 343 88 56, ul Kołłątaja 20). The other, larger hostel (☎ 345 73 96, ul Kiełczowska 43) is in the distant suburb of Psie Pole, about 10km north-east of the train station. Bus N can take you there from ul Sucha between the train station and bus terminal.

Bursa Nauczycielska (☎ 344 37 81, ul Kotlarska 42) is ideally located just a block north-east of the Rynek. This teachers' hostel costs US$14/24 for a single/double or US$8/7 for a bed in a triple/quad. Rooms do not have private bath, but are clean.

Another teachers' hostel, *Dom Nauczyciela* (☎ 322 92 68, ul Nauczycielska 2) is 1.5km east of the Old Town. It has singles/doubles with shared facilities for US$14/21, or you can pay US$7 for a bed in a five-person room.

The tourist office may know about *student dorms* that are open as hostels in summer.

Private Rooms Oder Tourist, in the Hotel Piast, across from the train station at ul Piłsudskiego 98, arranges *private rooms* for about US$12/18 a single/double. Check the location before committing.

Hotels *Hotel Savoy* (☎ 344 30 71, fax 372 53 79, Plac Kościuszki 19) has singles/doubles/triples with bath for US$27/32/42. It offers an excellent location midway between the station and the old town, and is good value.

There are a few affordable hotels are in the immediate vicinity of the Old Town; *Hotel Mirles* (☎ 344 43 84, ul Kazimierza Wielkiego 45) is among the cheapest. It has just three doubles (US$25) and two triples (US$42) with shared bath.

Places to Eat

The best and most central milk bar is *Bar Wegetariański Vega*, next to the town hall. *Bar Rybny Karpik* on the corner of ul Grodzka and ul Odrzańska serves cheap fish. For simple Greek fare, try *Bar Zorba*, in the middle of the block in the centre of the Rynek.

The cosy *Pizzeria Rancho* (ul Szewska 59) is a reasonable place for pizza. A bit upmarket, *Karczma Lwowska*, upstairs at Rynek 4, offers Ukrainian cuisine.

Entertainment

Wrocław is an important cultural centre with theatre, opera and classical music as well as discos, pubs and jazz. For information on the lively cultural scene, pick up the free monthly, *Co Jest Grane*.

Irish Pub (Plac Solny 5) is rather expensive, but has live music on some nights. One of the cheapest watering holes is the open-air *Kalogródek* on the corner of ul Uniwersytecka and ul Kuźnicza. Wrocław's most original drinking spot is *Restauracja & Bar Spiż*, a subterranean microbrewery beside the town hall.

Getting There & Away

The bus terminal is south of the main train station, but trains are better for most destinations. Buses go to Prague and plenty of cities in Western Europe. Tickets are available from Virgo (at the terminal itself), Orbis and Almatur.

From the main train station (Wrocław Główny), fast trains travel to Katowice (2½ hours, 190km), some of which continue to Kraków (4½ hours, 268km). Trains also go to Warsaw (5½ hours, 385km) and Poznań (two hours, 165km). International destinations include Berlin (six hours), Budapest (12 hours), Dresden (4½ hours), Frankfurt/Main (10½ hours) and Prague (6½ hours).

Wielkopolska

POZNAŃ
☎ 061

Poznań (population 590,000), midway between Berlin and Warsaw, is the focal point of early Polish history. In the 9th century, the Polanian tribes fortified the island of Ostrów Tumski; from 968 to 1038, Poznań was the de facto capital of Poland. The settlement soon expanded beyond the island, and in 1253 the new town centre was established on the left bank of the Warta River.

By the 15th century, Poznań was already a trading centre famous for its fairs. This commercial tradition was reinstituted in 1925, and today the fairs – held for a few days each month – dominate the economic and cultural life of the city, attracting hordes of visitors and business people. July and August are fair-free, relatively quiet months, and perhaps better for tourists to visit.

Orientation & Information

The Old Town is about 2km north-east of the main train station, with the new city centre between them.

The municipal tourist office (☎ 852 61 56), Stary Rynek 59, is open Monday to Saturday. The city tourist office (☎ 851 96 45, @ cim@man.poznan.pl), ul Ratajczaka 44, also open Monday to Saturday, stays open later in the evening. Glob-Tour (☎ 866 06 67), in the main hall of the main train station, is open round the clock. All three offices provide useful information.

Poznań has a comprehensive what's-on monthly, *iks* (US$1), containing a useful city map.

The Internet Club (☎ 853 78 18), at ul Garncarska 10 m 1, is convenient and also friendly (closed Sunday). Alternatively, Internet Cafe (☎ 852 79 33), Plac Wolności 8, is closer to the Old Town and has super fast computers.

Things to See

Old Town Square The Stary Rynek has been restored to its historic shape and looks beautiful, except for two large postwar concrete buildings. The focal point is the decorative facade of the Renaissance **town hall** (1550-60). High above the clock, two metal goats butt their horns together daily at noon, striking each other 12 times. Near the entrance is the **whipping post**, once the site of public floggings. The **Historical Museum of Poznań** reveals the city's past via splendid period interiors (closed Saturday).

Around the Old Town The 17th-century **Franciscan Church**, one block west of the square, has an ornate baroque interior adorned with wall paintings and rich stucco work. The hill opposite the church is the site of the former castle, now the **Museum of Decorative Arts** (closed Monday and Thursday), with exhibits from the 13th century to the present.

The nearby **National Museum** (closed Monday) holds the typical collection of art, including medieval church woodcarving, Polish paintings and other European paintings.

Two blocks south of the Stary Rynek is a large pink baroque **parish church** with a spacious three-naved interior fitted out with monumental altars. The **Ethnographic Museum**, which is nearby, boasts an interesting collection of folk woodcarving and traditional costumes of the region (closed Monday and Thursday).

Other Attractions The island of **Ostrów Tumski**, 1km east of the Old Town (take any eastbound tram from Plac Wielkopolski), is dominated by the monumental, double-towered, 14th-century **cathedral**. Relics of the original pre-Romanesque church from 968 can be seen in the crypt. The Byzantine-style Golden Chapel (1841), mausoleum of Mieszko I and Boleslaus the Brave, is behind the high altar.

East of Ostrów Tumski is **Lake Malta**, a 70-hectare artificial lake that is a favourite weekend destination for Poles. The lake holds sailing regattas, outdoor concerts and other events. The carnival atmosphere is enhanced by games, concessions and a thrilling toboggan run. Take tram No 1, 4 or 8 from Plac Wielkopolski.

About 1km north of the Old Town is the 19th-century Prussian **citadel**, where 20,000 German troops held out for a month in February 1945. The fortress was destroyed by artillery fire but a park was laid out on the site, which incorporates two war museums and the Commonwealth war cemetery.

Special Events
Poznań's pride is the trade fairs, the largest of which take place in January, June, September and October. Culturally, major events include the Poznań Musical Spring (contemporary music) in April and the 'Malta' International Theatre Festival in late June.

Places to Stay
The all-year *Camping Nr 155 Malta* (☎ 876 62 03, ul Krańcowa 98) is on the north-eastern shore of Lake Malta, 3km east of the Old Town. Bungalows for two/three/ five people, all with bath and kitchenette, cost US$40/70/100.

The *youth hostel* (☎ 866 40 40, ul Berwińskiego 2/3) is a 10-minute walk south-west of the train station along ul Głogowska. It is small and fills up fast. The newer and more comfortable *youth hostel* (☎ 848 58 36, ul Drzymały 3) is 3km north of the train station (take tram No 11) and 3km from the Old Town (tram No 9).

The tourist offices should know which *student dorms* open in summer as student hostels. They will also know about several inexpensive *workers' hostels*, but most are in the outer suburbs.

Private rooms are let by Biuro Zakwaterowania Przemysław (☎ 866 35 60, ul Głogowska 16), opposite the train station (open Monday to Saturday). Rooms normally cost US$10/15 a single/double but prices increase at fair times. Glob-Tour arranges private rooms for marginally more.

Dom Turysty (☎ 852 88 93, Stary Rynek 91), set in the 1798 former palace (enter from ul Wroniecka), has singles/doubles/triples

without bath for US$26/40/45, and singles/doubles with bath for US$38/60. It also has dorms with shared facilities for US$12 a bed. Breakfast is included in the price. Midway between the train station and the Old Town, *Hotel Lech* (☎ 853 01 51, ul Św Marcin 74) has rooms with bath and breakfast for US$30/40.

Places to Eat
The modernised *Bar Mleczny Apetyt* (Plac Wolności 1) is popular and cheap. Other central milk bars include *Bar Mleczny Przysmak* (ul Roosevelta 22) and the basic *Bar Mleczny pod Kuchcikiem* (ul Św Marcin 75).

Uni-Pozmeat Bar (Plac Wolności 14) is the outlet restaurant for a local meat factory. Vegetarians can try the simple *Bar Wegetariański* (ul Wrocławska 21).

The very cheap and popular *Bistro Avanti* (Stary Rynek 76) serves heaping plates of spaghetti for less than US$1. It has another branch at the train station. Comparably cheap and filling Italian fare is served at *Spaghetti Bar Piccolo* (ul Rynkowa 1 or ul Ratajczaka 37) and *Spaghetteria Al Dente* (ul 3 Maja).

Restauracja Turystyczna, downstairs from the Dom Turysty hotel (enter from ul Wroniecka), has inexpensive Polish food. *Restauracja pod Psem* (ul Garbary 54) is tastier but pricier.

Getting There & Away
Poznań is a busy railway hub. About 10 trains per day travel to Warsaw (three hours, 311km), including EuroCity and InterCity trains that take three hours. Equally frequent is transport to Wrocław (two hours, 165km) and Szczecin (three hours, 214km). Five fast trains go direct to Kraków (seven hours, 398km). Gdańsk (3½ hours, 313km) is serviced by four express and two fast trains, and Toruń (two hours, 142km) by three-fast and four-ordinary trains. All pass via Gniezno (one hour, 51km).

Six trains run daily to Berlin (261km), including three EuroCity trains, which take three hours. Direct trains also go to Budapest (14 hours), Cologne (10½ hours) and Moscow (23 hours).

The PKS bus terminal is a 10-minute walk east of the train station, but the train is a better bet for most destinations.

Pomerania

TORUŃ
☎ 056

Toruń (population 210,000) is a historic city, characterised by its narrow streets, burghers' mansions, and mighty Gothic churches. The town is most famous as the birthplace of Nicolaus Copernicus, who spent his youth here and for whom the local university is named. Toruń is perhaps the best preserved Gothic town in the country, and the historic quarter was included on the Unesco World Heritage List in 1997.

Orientation & Information
Set on the northern bank of the Vistula, Toruń's historic quarter includes the Old Town (Stare Miasto) to the west, and the New Town (Nowe Miasto) to the east. The bus station is a five-minute walk north of the historic quarter, while the main train station is south across the river.

The friendly and knowledgeable municipal tourist office (☎ 621 09 31) is now at Rynek Staromiejski 1 in the Town Hall and is open daily (closed Sunday in off season).

A cybercafe, Klub Internetowy Jeremi (☎ 663 51 00), is at Rynek Staromiejski 33 above the Irish Pub. Another cybercafe with more of a pub atmosphere is Hacker (☎ 663 53 99), ul Podmurna 28.

Things to See
The Old Town Square (Rynek Staromiejski) is the focal point of the Old Town. The massive 14th-century brick old town hall now shelters the Regional Museum (closed Monday).

Just off the north-western corner of the square is the late 13th-century St Mary's Church. Behind the church you'll find the Planetarium, whose antiquated presentations include some in English and German during the summer. Strangely, the castle-like building opposite the church on ul Piekary is the town's prison.

Copernicus was born in 1473 in the brick Gothic house, ul Kopernika 15, which now houses the disappointing Museum of Copernicus.

One block east of the museum stands the Cathedral of SS John the Baptist & John the Evangelist, constructed between the 13th and 15th centuries. Its massive tower

houses Poland's second-largest bell (after Wawel Cathedral in Kraków), the Tuba Dei, cast in 1500, which is rung before mass. Farther east are the ruins of the Castle of the Teutonic Knights, destroyed in 1454 by angry townsfolk protesting the order's oppressive regime.

Places to Stay
Camping Nr 33 Tramp (☎ 654 71 87, ul Kujawska 14) is near the south end of the bridge, a five-minute walk from the main train station. It operates from May to September and has simple cabins (US$14/16/18 a double/triple/quad) and a building with hotel-style rooms (US$12/14 a double/triple). Facilities are shared.

The all-year youth hostel (☎ 654 45 80, ul Św Józefa 22/24) is 2km north-west of the centre. Bus No 11 links the hostel with the train station and the Old Town.

Bursa Szkolna (☎ 622 67 37, ul Słowackiego 47/49), 1km west of the Old Town, charges US$4 per bed in dorms of four to eight beds.

Dom Wycieczkowy PTTK (☎ 622 38 55, ul Legionów 24) is a 10-minute walk north from the Old Town. Singles/doubles with shared facilities are US$15/18, or you can share a quad for US$7 per person.

The cheapest central hotel is Hotel Polonia (☎ 622 30 28, Plac Teatralny 5), one block north of the square. It is rather run-down, but it has singles/doubles/triples with shared facilities for only US$17/20/24. The old Hotel Trzy Korony (☎ 622 60 31, Rynek Staromiejski 21) costs US$20/23/28 for a room without bath or US$48/58 for a double/triple with a new, private bath. Renovations are ongoing, so the cheaper rooms may not be available for much longer.

Places to Eat
Two central milk bars are the basic Bar Mleczny Małgośka (ul Szczytna 10/12) and the better Bar Mleczny pod Arkadami (ul Różana 1), just off the Rynek Staromiejski.

Grill Bar Landa (ul Ślusarska 5), off Rynek Nowomiejski, has a choice of salads. Alladyn (ul Żeglarska 27) serves inexpensive Middle Eastern food. On the Rynek, Sphinx is popular for Mediterranean cuisine.

The Restauracja Palomino (ul Wielkie Garbary 18), on the 1st floor (on the corner of ul Królowej Jadwigi), specialises in grilled foods. *Zajazd Staropolski*, in the hotel of the same name, offers good-value Polish food.

Toruń is famous for its *pierniki* (gingerbread) – try it at *Sklep Firmowy Katarzynka* (*ul Żeglarska 25*).

Entertainment

The *Toruńskie Vademecum Kultury* is a useful cultural monthly distributed free by the tourist office.

Piwnica, which is set in a splendid, spacious cellar in the town hall, is one of the most popular local drinking haunts that often has live music. *Barani Łeb* (*ul Podmurna 28*) is in the basement of the cybercafe. Just outside the Monastery Gate near the river, *Tratwa* has a congenial atmosphere and an outdoor beer garden.

Getting There & Away

The Toruń Główny train station is about 2km south of the Old Town, on the opposite side of the Vistula, linked by bus Nos 22 and 27. A few trains depart daily to Malbork (2½ hours, 138km), Gdańsk (three hours, 211km) and Poznań (2½ hours, 142km). Three trains go to Warsaw (three hours, 237km).

Polski Express has a dozen departures a day to Warsaw (US$7, 3½ hours, 209km).

MALBORK
☎ 055

Malbork (population 40,000), about 50km south-east of Gdańsk, boasts a monumental medieval fortress. The Teutonic Knights commenced construction of Malbork Castle in 1276, and moved their order's capital from Venice in 1309. Constant territorial disputes with Poland and Lithuania finally culminated in the Battle of Grunwald in 1410. The order was defeated but continued to hold the castle until 1457.

Malbork Castle was placed on the Unesco World Heritage List in 1997. It is open 9 am to 5 pm Tuesday to Sunday (to 2.30 pm October to April). The compulsory 2½-hour guided tour (in Polish) costs US$4.50/3 for adults/concession, but it is easy to lose the guide and wander freely. Allow three hours to visit the castle.

Given the number of train connections, Malbork is an easy day trip from Gdańsk or stopover between destinations (Gdańsk-Toruń or Gdańsk-Warsaw).

Information & Orientation

The train and bus stations are at the eastern end of town, 1km from the castle. As you leave the train station turn right and cut across the busy highway, then head straight down ul Kościuszki to the castle. A cybercafe, Inet Cafe, is located on the first floor of the train station building at ul Dworcowa 17.

Places to Stay & Eat

The cheapest place to stay is the all-year *youth hostel* (☎ 272 24 08, *ul Żeromskiego 45*) in the local school. Another cheap but dodgy place is the *Hotel Szarotka* (☎ 270 14 44, *ul Dworcowa 1*), near the train station. *Hotel Zbyszko* (☎ 272 26 40, fax 272 33 95, *ul Kościuszki 43*), between the station and the castle, costs US$26/35/42 with bath, including breakfast. Located 1.2km north of the castle, *Hotel Parkowy* (☎ 272 24 13, *ul Portowa 3*) has slightly cheaper rooms and also operates *Camping Nr 197* on its grounds. Both hotels have *restaurants*.

GDAŃSK
☎ 058

Gdańsk (population 470,000) is an important port and shipbuilding centre on the Baltic Sea. It is the biggest, oldest and most interesting component of the Tri-City, a conurbation comprising Gdańsk, Sopot and Gdynia, which stretches 30km along the Gulf of Gdańsk.

The importance of this strategic port was emphasised in 1939 when the Nazis bombarded Westerplatte and thus commenced WWII. The war devastated the town almost completely, but it is hardly evident today. The historic quarters have been completely restored and the town looks lovely.

Demographically predominantly German and architecturally reminiscent of Flanders, Gdańsk was effectively an independent city-state for most of its history. Today the town is most famous as the birthplace of Solidarity, which is perhaps symbolic of its free spirit.

Orientation

The Gdańsk Główny train station is a 10-minute walk from the heart of the historic quarter. The bus terminal is next to the train station. The city centre consists of three historic districts: the Old Town to the north, the Main Town in the middle, and the Old Suburb to the south. The centre is linked to other areas of the city (as well as Sopot and Gdynia) by commuter train.

Information

Tourist Offices The useful private Agencja Informacji Turystycznej (☎ 301 93 27), ul Długa 45, opposite the main town hall, is open daily. The municipal tourist office (☎ 301 43 55, ☎ /fax 301 66 37), ul Heweliusza 27, on the northern edge of the Old Town, is open weekdays only.

Post & Communications The main post office is at ul Długa 22. The most convenient cybercafe is Rudy Kot (☎ 301 39 86), ul Garncarska 18/20. A more out of the way place is Comptrade (☎ 341 47 14) in Gdańsk Wrzeszcz, Room 34, 2nd floor, Al Grunwaldzka 102 (weekdays only).

Travel Agencies Almatur (☎ 301 24 24), Długi Targ 11, provides its usual services, including ISIC student cards. PTTK (☎ 301 60 96) is in the Upland Gate. Orbis (☎ 301 45 44), Podwale Staromiejskie 96/97, sells transportation tickets and organises tours.

Things to See

Main Town This historic quarter boasts the richest architecture and the most thorough restoration. Ul Długa (Long Street) and Długi Targ (Long Market) form its main thoroughfare, known as the **Royal Way**, along which Polish kings traditionally paraded. They entered the Main Town through the **Upland Gate** (1574), passed through the **Golden Gate** (1614), and proceeded east to the Renaissance **Green Gate** (1568).

The towering Gothic main town hall on the west end of Długi Targ contains the **Historical Museum of Gdańsk** (closed Monday). Behind **Neptune's Fountain** (1613) stands the **Artus Court** where local merchants used to congregate. The nearby **Golden House** (1618) has perhaps the richest facade in town.

Two blocks north along the waterfront is St Mary's Gate, housing the **Archaeological Museum** (closed Monday). Follow the picturesque **ul Mariacka** (St Mary's St) to the gigantic **St Mary's Church** (1343-1502). Inside, note the unique 14m-high astronomical clock. The fabulous panorama from the

78m-high tower is well worth the 405-step climb. Farther north on the waterfront is the 15th-century **Gdańsk Crane**, capable of hoisting loads up to 2 tonnes. It is now home to the **Maritime Museum** (closed Monday).

Old Town & Old Suburb Destroyed almost totally in 1945, the Old Town was not rebuilt to its previous shape, apart from a handful of churches. The largest and most remarkable of these is **St Catherine's Church**, Gdańsk's oldest, begun in the 1220s. Opposite is the **Great Mill**, built by the Teutonic Knights around 1350. In 1945 it was producing 200 tonnes of flour per day.

Right behind St Catherine's is **St Bridget's Church**. Formerly Lech Wałęsa's place of worship, the priest often spoke on social and political issues in his sermons. The church remains a record of the Solidarity period.

On the northern outskirts of town, at the entrance to the shipyards (where Solidarity was born in August 1980), is the **Monument to the Shipyard Workers**, erected in late 1980 in memory of 44 workers killed in the riots of December 1970. This striking set of three 40m-tall steel crosses was the first monument in a communist regime to commemorate its victims.

The Old Suburb was also reduced to rubble in 1945, and little of the former urban fabric has been reconstructed, except for the Franciscan monastery, which today shelters the **National Museum** (closed Monday).

Westerplatte Set at the entrance to the harbour from the sea, Westerplatte is where WWII broke out at 4.45 am on 1 September 1939, when the German battleship *Schleswig-Holstein* began shelling the Polish naval post. The 182-man garrison held out against ferocious attacks for seven days before surrendering. The site, 7km north of the city centre, is now a memorial, including some ruins, a small museum and a massive monument to the defenders.

Bus No 106 goes to Westerplatte from the main train station. A more attractive way to get there is by excursion boat (April to October), which departs from the landing next to the Green Gate (US$8/5 return).

Places to Stay

Both tourist offices provide information about accommodation options. The private

POLAND

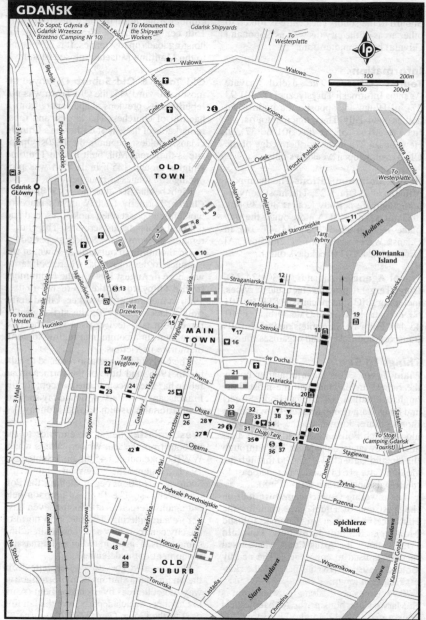

GDAŃSK

To Sopot; Gdynia &
Gdańsk Wrzeszcz
Brzeźno (Camping Nr 10)

Jana z Kolna

To Monument to
the Shipyard
Workers

Gdańsk Shipyards

To
Westerplatte

Błędnik

3 Maja

Podwale Grodzkie

Wały

Jagiellońskie

Podwale Grodzkie

1 ▪ Wałowa

Łagiewniki

Gnilna

Rajska

Hewilliusza

Gdańsk
Główny

Gdańsk
Główny

3 ▪

4 ●

6 ▮

5 ▼

Garncarska

Targ
Drzewny

13 ⑤

14 ▣

To Youth
Hostel

Hucisko

Wałowa

Krosna

2 ● ⓘ

OLD
TOWN

Osiek

Pocłty Polskie)

Olejarna

Stolarska

7 ●

8

9 ●

10 ●

Podwale Staromiejskie

Targ
Rybny

11 ▼

Motława

To
Westerplatte

Ołowianka
Island

Ołowianka

Straganiarska

Świętojańska

Szeroka

12 ▮

19 ▮

18 ▮

Panská

MAIN
TOWN

15 ▼

Węglarska

Kozia

17 ▼

16 ▮

Św Ducha

22 ▮

Targ
Węglowy

23 ▮

24 ▮

Tkacka

Piwna

21

25 ▮

Mariacka

20 ▮

Długa

30 ▮

32

38 34

33 ●

Chlebnicka

39

26 ▮

28 ▼

29 ▮

27 ▪

31

35 ●

Długi Targ

36 ● 37

40 ●

41

42 ▪

Ogarna

Zbytki

Podwale Przedmiejskie

Rzeźnicka

Garbary

Pocztowa

Okopowa

Okopowa

3 Maja

Na Stoku

Radunia Canal

Kocurki

Żabi Kruk

43

44 ▮

OLD
SUBURB

Toruńska

Lastadia

Stara Motława

Spichlerze
Island

Stągiewna

Żytnia

Pszenna

To Stog
(Camping Gdańsk
Tourist)

Chmielna

Wspornikowa

Nowa Motława

Kamienna Grobla

Chmielna

Stara Stocznia

0   100   200m
0   100   200yd

POLAND

To Stog
(Camping Gdańsk
Tourist)

GDAŃSK

PLACES TO STAY		
1 Youth Hostel	4 Gdańsk-Tourist	24 Golden Gate
12 Dom Aktora	6 Old Town Hall;	25 Celtic Pub
27 Hotel Zaułek	Irish Pub	26 Main Post Office
37 Hotel Jantar	7 Great Mill	29 Agencja Informacji
42 Dom Harcerza	8 St Catherine's	Turystycznej
	Church	30 Main Town Hall;
	9 St Bridget's Church	Historical Museum
PLACES TO EAT	10 Orbis	of Gdańsk
5 Green Way	13 Bank Pekao	31 Neptune's Fountain
11 Restauracja Kubicki	14 Rudy Kot	32 Artus Court
15 Bar Mleczny Turystyczny	16 Cotton Club	33 Golden House
17 La Pasta	18 Gdańsk Crane;	34 Jazz Club
28 Bar Mleczny Neptun	Maritime Museum	35 Almatur
38 Pub u Szkota	19 Maritime Museum	36 Bank Gdański
39 Jadłodajnia u Plastyków	20 Archaeological Museum;	40 Excursion Boats
	St Mary's Gate	41 Green Gate
OTHER	21 St Mary's Church	43 Church of the
2 Municipal Tourist Office	22 Latający Holender	Holy Trinity
3 Bus Terminal	23 Upland Gate; PTTK	44 National Museum

tourist office can also find and book a room for a small service charge.

Camping The camping grounds in Gdańsk are open only in the summer. The nearest to the city centre (about 5.5km to the northeast) is *Camping Gdańsk-Tourist (☎ 307 39 15, ul Wydmy 1)* in the seaside holiday centre in the suburb of Stogi (near Gdańsk's best beach). Take tram No 8 to Plaża Stogi from the main train station.

Camping Nr 10 (☎ 343 55 31, ul Hallera 234), in the suburb of Brzeżno, is accessible by tram No 13 from the main train station. It is the closest camping ground to the ferry terminal, a short ride by tram No 15.

Hostels The most convenient *youth hostel (☎ 301 23 13, ul Wałowa 21)* is a five-minute walk north-east of the main train station. The next closest is the *youth hostel (☎ 302 60 44, ul Kartuska 245b)*, 3.5km west of the main train station. Take bus No 161 or 167 from ul 3 Maja at the back of the station.

From July to September, the Politechnika Gdańska opens 10 *hostels* in its dorms, all of which are in Gdańsk Wrzeszcz. A bed in a double or triple will cost US$5 to US$15, depending on the facilities and standards. The hostels' central office (☎ 347 25 47, 347 25 89) is at ul Wyspiańskiego 7a.

Two budget places are conveniently sited in the Main Town. *Dom Harcerza (☎ 301 36 21, fax 301 24 72, ul Za Murami 2/10)* has decent doubles/triples without bath for

US$24/27. *Hotel Zaułek (☎ 301 41 69, ul Ogarna 107/108)* is a former workers' dorm with cell-like singles/doubles/triples for US$13/17/22. Facilities are shared, unisex and mildly offensive. Both places potentially offer dorm beds, but may refuse in summer.

Private Rooms Gdańsk-Tourist (☎ 301 26 34, fax 301 63 01), Podwale Grodzkie 8, opposite the train station (open daily in summer), is the main agency that handles *private rooms*. Singles/doubles in the central area are US$15/24, while rooms farther from the centre cost US$12/20. When making your choice, work out the distance to the commuter train line. Agencja Informacji Turystycznej, a private tourist office, may also have some central private rooms for about US$15 per person.

Hotels The old *Hotel Jantar (☎ 301 27 16, fax 301 35 29, Długi Targ 19)* has singles/doubles without bath for US$26/39 and doubles/triples with bath for US$50/56. It's a bit run-down, but good value for the central lcoation.

Another central option is the small *Dom Aktora (☎/fax 301 59 01, ul Straganiarska 55/56)*. It has three apartments with kitchens, as well as a single/double, which share a bath for US$38/50.

Places to Eat
Ultra-budget dining is provided by two central milk bars: *Bar Mleczny Neptun*

(ul Długa 33/34) and the more basic **Bar Mleczny Turystyczny** (ul Węglarska 1/4). Another good place for a tasty, cheap lunch is the **Jadłodajnia u Plastyków** (ul Chlebnicka 13/16).

Green Way (ul Garncarska 4/6) has tasty vegetarian fare, including sandwiches, crepes and hearty entrees. **La Pasta** (ul Szeroka 32) has pretty decent pizzas and cheap Italian food.

Restauracja Kubicki (ul Wartka 5), on the waterfront, has served tasty Polish food at reasonable prices since 1918.

Pub u Szkota (ul Chlebnicka 10) is a cosy double-level restaurant and bar. Food is affordably priced, and the Scottish decor is pleasant.

Entertainment

The main jazz venues are **Jazz Club** (Długi Targ 39/40) and **Cotton Club** (ul Złotników 25/29).

Latający Holender (Wały Jagiellońskie 2/4), in the basement of the LOT building, provides a laid-back atmosphere for beers. **Celtic Pub** (ul Lektykarska 3) and **Irish Pub**, in the fabulous vaulted cellar of the old town hall, both have live music at times and discos on weekends.

Getting There & Away

Train The main train station, Gdańsk Główny, is on the western outskirts of the Old Town. A dozen trains a day travel to Warsaw (3½ hours, 329km). Six fast trains go daily to Olsztyn (2½ hours, 179km), all

via Malbork (one hour, 51km). Two express and three fast trains go to Wrocław (seven hours, 478km), all via Poznań (3½ hours, 313km). Six fast trains go to Toruń (three hours, 211km). Four fast trains depart for Szczecin (five hours, 374km); one of these continues to Berlin (nine hours).

A commuter train, known as SKM (Fast City Train), runs constantly between Gdańsk Główny and Gdynia Główna (30 minutes, 21km) from 5 am till midnight, stopping at a dozen intermediate stations, including Sopot. You buy tickets in the stations and validate them in the machines at the platform entrance (not on the train itself).

Bus The bus terminal is behind the central train station, connected by an underground passageway. Plenty of buses link Gdańsk to Western European cities; travel agencies (including Almatur and Orbis) have information and sell tickets.

Ferry Car ferries to Nynäshamn in Sweden depart from Gdańsk, while those to Karlskrona in Sweden start from Gdynia. See Getting There & Away at the beginning of this chapter for details. The Orbis office can sell tickets.

From mid-May to late September excursion boats travel from Gdańsk's wharf near the Green Gate to Sopot (US$8/11 one-way/return ticket, 45 minutes), Gdynia (US$10/15) and across the Gulf of Gdańsk to the Hel Peninsula (US$11/16, two hours). Students pay about two-thirds normal fare.

Portugal

The 'far side' of Europe offers more than beaches and port wine. As Portugal moves into the economic mainstream of the European Union (EU), the country still seems to gaze nostalgically over its shoulder and out to sea, pondering the remains of a far-flung colonialist realm.

Beyond the crowded Algarve, Portugal has wide appeal: a simple but hearty cuisine based on seafood and lingering conversation, an enticing architectural blend that wanders from Moorish to Manueline to surrealist styles, and a changing landscape that occasionally lapses into Impressionism. Like the *emigrantes* – economically inspired Portuguese who eventually find their way back to their roots – *estrangeiros* (foreigners) who have had a taste of the real Portugal can only be expected to return.

Facts about Portugal

HISTORY

The early history of Portugal goes back to the Celts, who settled the Iberian Peninsula around 700 BC. A subsequent pattern of invasion and re-invasion was established by the Phoenicians, Greeks, Romans and Visigoths.

In the 8th century the Moors crossed the Strait of Gibraltar and commenced a long occupation which introduced Islamic culture, architecture and agricultural techniques to Portugal. The Moors were ejected in the 12th century by powerful Christian forces in the north of the country who mobilised attacks against them with the help of European Crusaders.

In the 15th century Portugal entered a phase of conquest and discovery inspired by Prince Henry the Navigator. Explorers such as Vasco da Gama, Ferdinand Magellan and Bartolomeu Diaz discovered new trade

AT A GLANCE

Capital:	Lisbon
Population:	10 million
Official Language:	Portuguese
Currency:	1 Portuguese escudo = 100 centavos

routes and helped create an empire that, at its peak, extended to Africa, Brazil, India and the Far East. This period of immense power and wealth ended in 1580 when Spain occupied the Portuguese throne. The Portuguese regained it within 90 years, but their imperial momentum had been lost.

At the close of the 18th century Napoleon mounted several invasions of Portugal, but was trounced by troops of the Anglo-Portuguese alliance. A period of civil war and political mayhem in the 19th century culminated in the abolition of the monarchy in 1910 and the founding of a democratic republic.

A military coup in 1926 set the stage for the dictatorship of António de Oliveira Salazar, who clung to power until his death in 1968. General dissatisfaction with his regime and a ruinous colonial war in Africa led to the so-called Revolution of the Carnations, a peaceful military coup on 25 April 1974.

The granting of independence to Portugal's African colonies in 1974-75 produced a flood of nearly a million refugees into the country. The 1970s and early 1980s saw extreme swings between political right and left, and strikes over state versus private ownership.

Portugal's entry into the EU in 1986 and its acceptance as a member of the European Monetary System in 1992 launched a new era of stability. Despite continuing backwardness in agriculture and education, the country has tamed inflation and is now enjoying steady economic growth. In 1999 the Socialist Party was re-elected for a second four-year term.

Expo '98, which triggered some vast infrastructure projects and attracted eight million visitors, brought Portugal back into world focus. In 2001 Porto is European Capital of Culture and in 2004 Portugal hosts the European Football Championships.

PORTUGAL

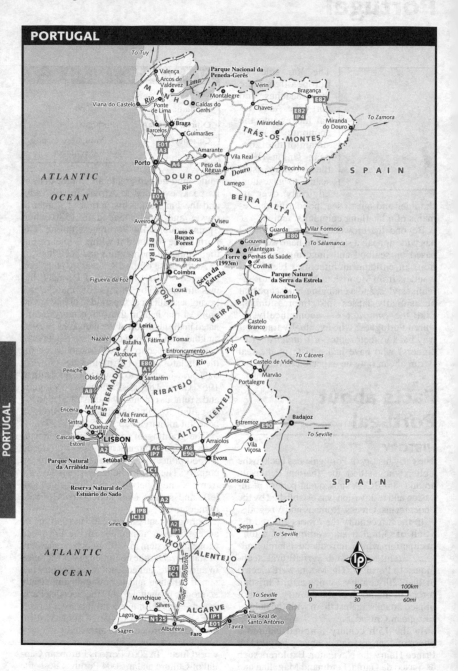

PORTUGAL

PORTUGAL

GEOGRAPHY

Portugal is about twice the size of Switzerland, 560km from north to south and 220km from east to west.

The northern and central coastal regions are densely populated. The northern interior is characterised by lush vegetation and mountains; the highest range, the Serra da Estrela, peaks at Torre (1993m). The country's south is less populated and, apart from the mountainous backdrop of the Algarve, flatter and drier.

POPULATION & PEOPLE

Portugal's population of 10 million does not include an estimated three million Portuguese living abroad as migrant workers. The country is 99% Roman Catholic, with fewer than 120,000 Protestants and about 5000 Jews.

SOCIETY & CONDUCT

Despite prosperity and foreign influence, the Portuguese have kept a firm grip on their culture. Folk dancing remains the pride of villages everywhere, and local festivals are celebrated with gusto.

Televised soccer matches, a modern element of male Portuguese life, ensure the continuation of the traditional long lunch break. Bullfighting is popular, despite pressure from international animal-rights activists; the season runs from late April to October.

The Portuguese tend to be very friendly but socially conservative: win their hearts by dressing modestly outside of the beach resorts, and by greeting and thanking them in Portuguese. Shorts and hats are considered offensive inside churches.

LANGUAGE

Portuguese is a Romance language, derived from Latin. It's spoken by 10 million people in Portugal and 130 million in Brazil, and is the official language of five African nations.

Nearly all tourist office staff speak English. In Lisbon, Porto and the Algarve it's easy to find English-speakers, but this isn't the case in the countryside, and among older folk.

See the Language guide at the back of this book for pronunciation guidelines and useful words and phrases.

Facts for the Visitor

HIGHLIGHTS

Tops for scenery are the mountain landscapes of the Serra da Estrela and Peneda-Gerês National Park. Architecture buffs should visit the monasteries at Belém and Batalha, and the palaces of Sintra. Combining the best of both worlds are Portugal's old walled towns such as Évora and Marvão. In Lisbon don't miss the Gulbenkian museum, and Europe's largest Oceanarium.

SUGGESTED ITINERARIES

Two days
  Spend them in Lisbon.
One week
  Devote four or five days to Lisbon and Sintra, the rest to Óbidos and Nazaré.
Two weeks
  As for one week, plus two days in Évora and the rest in the Algarve (including one or two days each in Tavira, Lagos and Sagres).

PLANNING
When to Go

Peak tourist season is June to early September. Going earlier (late March or April) or later (late September to early October) gives you fewer crowds, milder temperatures, spectacular foliage, and seasonal discounts including up to 50% for accommodation (prices in this chapter are for peak season). The Algarve tourist season lasts from late February to November.

Midsummer heat is searing in the Algarve and Alentejo, and in the upper Douro valley, but tolerable elsewhere. The north is rainy and chilly in winter. Snowfall is common in the Serra da Estrela, which has basic ski facilities.

Maps

Michelin's No 940 *Portugal; Madeira* map is accurate and useful even if you're not driving. Topographic maps are published (and sold) by two mapping agencies in Lisbon: the civilian Instituto Português de Cartográfia e Cadastro (☎ 213 819 600, fax 213 819 697, @ ipcc@ipcc.pt), Rua Artilharia Um 107, and the military Instituto Geográfico do Exército (☎ 218 520 063, fax 218 532 119, @ igeoe@igeoe.pt), Avenida Dr Alfredo Bensaúde. A Porto bookshop stocking the (better) military versions is Porto Editora, Praça Dona Filipa de Lencastre 42.

PORTUGAL

TOURIST OFFICES
Local Tourist Offices
Called *postos de turismo* or just *turismos,* local tourist offices are found throughout Portugal and offer information, maps and varying degrees of assistance.

Portuguese tourist offices abroad operate under the administrative umbrella of ICEP (Investimentos Comércio e Turismo de Portugal).

Tourist Offices Abroad
Canada (☎ 416-921 7376, fax 921 1353, ✉ iceptor@idirect.com) 60 Bloor St West, Suite 1005, Toronto, Ontario M4W 3B8
UK (☎ 020-7494 1441, fax 7494 1868, ✉ iceplondt@aol.com) 22-25a Sackville St, London W1X 1DE
USA (☎ 212-354 4403, fax 764 6137, ✉ tourism@portugal.org) 590 Fifth Ave, 4th floor, New York, NY 10036-4785

VISAS & DOCUMENTS
Visas
No visa is required for any length of stay by nationals of EU countries. Those from Canada, Israel, New Zealand and the USA can stay up to 60 days in any half-year without a visa. Others, including nationals of Australia and South Africa, need visas (and should try to get them in advance) unless they're spouses or children of EU citizens.

Outside Portugal, visa information is supplied by Portuguese consulates. In Portugal, contact the Foreigners Registration Service (Serviço de Estrangeiros e Fronteiras; ☎ 213 585 545), Rua São Sebastião da Pedreira 15, Lisbon, for information. It's open 9 am to noon and 2 to 4 pm weekdays.

EMBASSIES & CONSULATES
Portuguese Embassies Abroad
Australia (☎ 02-6290 1733) 23 Culgoa Circuit, O'Malley, ACT 2606
Canada (☎ 613-729 0883) 645 Island Park Drive, Ottawa, Ont K1Y 0B8
UK (☎ 020-7235 5331) 11 Belgrave Square, London SW1X 8PP
USA (☎ 202-328 8610) 2125 Kalorama Rd NW, Washington, DC 20008

Foreign Embassies in Portugal
The following embassies are in Lisbon. There are no embassies for Australia (call the Canadian embassy in emergencies) or New Zealand (call its honorary consul on ☎ 213 509 690 on weekday mornings).

Canada (☎ 213 164 600) Avenida da Liberdade 196
UK (☎ 213 924 000) Rua de São Bernardo 33
USA (☎ 217 273 300) Avenida das Forças Armadas

MONEY
Currency
The unit of Portuguese currency is the escudo, further divided into 100 centavos. Prices are written with a $ sign between escudos and centavos; eg, 25 escudos 50 centavos is 25$50. There are 200$00, 100$00, 50$00, 20$00, 10$00, 5$00, 2$50 and 1$00 coins. Notes currently in circulation are 10,000$00, 5000$00, 2000$00, 1000$00 and 500$00. Portugal will withdraw the escudo in 2002 and adopt the EU currency, the euro.

Exchange Rates

country	unit		escudos
Australia	A$1	=	128$58
Canada	C$1	=	149$60
euro	€1	=	200$48
France	1FF	=	30$56
Germany	DM1	=	102$51
Japan	¥100	=	204$24
New Zealand	NZ$1	=	99$82
Spain	100 ptas	=	120$49
UK	UK£1	=	333$64
USA	US$1	=	221$90

Changing Money
Portuguese banks can change most foreign cash and travellers cheques but charge a commission of around 2500$00. Better deals for travellers cheques are at private exchange bureaus in Lisbon, Porto and tourist resorts.

Better value (and handier) are 24-hour Multibanco ATMs at most banks. Exchange rates are reasonable, and normally the only charge is a handling fee of about 1.5% to your home bank. Major credit cards are widely accepted – especially Visa and MasterCard.

Costs
Portugal remains one of the cheapest places to travel in Europe. On a rock-bottom budget – using hostels or camping grounds, and mostly self-catering – you can get by on US$20 to US$25 a day. With bottom-end accommodation and cheap restaurant meals, figure around US$30. Outside major tourist areas, prices dip appreciably.

Tipping

A reasonable restaurant tip is 10%. For a snack, a bit of loose change is sufficient. Taxi drivers appreciate 10% of the fare, and petrol station attendants 50$00 to 100$00.

POST & COMMUNICATIONS
Post

Postcards and letters up to 20g cost 100$00 to European countries (90$00 to Spain), 140$00 to non-European countries. For parcels, 'economy air' (or surface airlift; SAL) costs about a third less than air mail and usually arrives a week or so later.

Addresses in Portugal are written with the street name first, followed by the building address and often a floor number with a ° symbol, eg, 15-3°. An alphabetical tag on the address, eg, 2-A, indicates an adjoining entrance or building. R/C (*rés do chão*) means ground floor.

Telephone

In 1999 Portugal completely revised its telephone numbering system. Aside from a few assistance numbers, all domestic numbers now have nine digits. All digits must be dialled from any location, effectively rendering area codes obsolete.

Portugal's country code is ☎ 351. To call abroad from Portugal, dial ☎ 00 and then the number. For operator help or to make a reverse-charge (collect) call, dial ☎ 172. For domestic inquiries, dial ☎ 118; for numbers abroad, dial ☎ 177. Multilingual operators are available.

Local calls from public coin telephones start at 30$00. The largest acceptable coin is 50$00, making these impractical for long-distance and international calls. Handier (and cheaper) are Credifones, which accept cards available from newsagents, tobacconists and telephone offices in 650$00, 1300$00 or 1900$00 denominations. International charges drop by 10% to 25% after 9 pm and 20% to 50% at the weekend; a three-minute direct-dial call from Portugal to the USA, using a Credifone during the evening/weekend, costs 200/90$00.

Fax

Post offices operate Corfax, costing 820$00 for the first page to Europe and 1250$00 to North America or Australia. Some private shops offer much cheaper services.

Email & Internet Access

Many towns have a branch of the Instituto Português da Juventude or IPJ, a state-funded youth-centre network. Most of these offer free Internet access during certain hours. Some municipal libraries also have free access. Some newer youth hostels have access for around 500$00 per hour. Cyber-cafes in bigger towns charge 100$00 to 600$00 (or more) per hour.

INTERNET RESOURCES

Three useful Web sites on Portugal are:

A Collection of Home Pages about Portugal
  www.well.com/user/ideamen/portugal.html
Portugal Info
  www.portugal-info.net
Excite City.Net
  www.city.net/countries/portugal

BOOKS

For a more comprehensive guide to the country and its capital city, pick up a copy of Lonely Planet's *Portugal* or *Lisbon. The Portuguese: The Land and Its People* by Marion Kaplan is an excellent overview of Portugal and its place in the modern world. The *Landscapes of Portugal* series by Brian & Aileen Anderson should be considered by walkers, with coverage of both car tours and walks in various regions.

WOMEN TRAVELLERS

Outside Lisbon and Porto, an unaccompanied foreign woman is an oddity, and older people may fuss over you as if you were in need of protection. Women travelling on their own or in small groups report few hassles, but in Lisbon and Porto, women should be cautious about where they go alone after dark. Hitching is not recommended for solo women anywhere in Portugal.

GAY & LESBIAN TRAVELLERS

In much of Portugal there is little understanding or acceptance of homosexuality. But Lisbon has a flourishing gay scene, with an annual Gay Pride Festival (around June 28) and a gay and lesbian community centre, the Centro Comunitário Gay e Lésbico de Lisboa (☎ 218 873 918), Rua de São Lazaro 88. For information on gay-friendly bars, restaurants, discos and clubs, check out the Web sites www.ilga-portugal.org and www.portugalgay.pt.

PORTUGAL

DISABLED TRAVELLERS

Turintegra, part of Cooperativa Nacional Apoio Deficientes (CNAD; ☎/fax 218 595 332), Praça Dr Fernando Amado, Lote 566-E, 1900 Lisbon, arranges holidays for disabled travellers.

DANGERS & ANNOYANCES

Crime against foreigners usually involves pickpocketing, theft from cars or pilfering from camping grounds (though armed robberies are on the increase), mostly in the Algarve, Estoril Coast, parts of Lisbon and a few other cities.

Avoid swimming on beaches which are not marked as safe: Atlantic currents are notoriously dangerous (and badly polluted near major cities).

The national emergency number (for police, fire etc) is ☎ 112.

BUSINESS HOURS

Most banks are open 8.30 am to 3 pm weekdays. Most museums and other tourist attractions are open 10 am to 5 pm weekdays but are often closed at lunchtime and all day Monday. Shopping hours are generally 9 am to 7 pm weekdays, and 9 am to 1 pm Saturday. Lunch is given serious and lingering attention between noon and 3 pm.

PUBLIC HOLIDAYS & SPECIAL EVENTS

Public holidays in Portugal include New Year's Day, Carnival (Shrove Tuesday; February/March), Good Friday and the following Saturday, Liberty Day (25 April), May Day, Corpus Christi (May/June), National Day (10 June), Feast of the Assumption (15 August), Republic Day (5 October), All Saints' Day (1 November), Independence Day (1 December), Feast of the Immaculate Conception (8 December) and Christmas Day. Amongst Portugal's most interesting cultural events are:

Holy Week Festival Easter week in Braga features colourful processions.
Festas das Cruzes Held in Barcelos in May, the Festival of the Crosses is known for processions, folk music and regional handicrafts.
Feira Nacional da Agricultura In June, Santarém hosts the National Agricultural Fair, with bullfighting, folk singing and dancing.
Festa do Santo António The Festival of St Anthony fills the streets of Lisbon on 13 June.

Festas de São João Porto's big street bash is the St John's Festival, from 16 to 24 June.
Festas da Nossa Senhora da Agonia Viana do Castelo's Our Lady of Suffering Festival, for three days nearest to 20 August, is famed for folk arts, parades and fireworks.

ACCOMMODATION

Most tourist offices have lists of accommodation to suit a range of budgets, and can help you find and book lodgings. Although the government uses stars to grade some types of accommodation, criteria seem erratic.

Camping

Camping is popular, and the cheapest option. *Roteiro Campista* (900$00), sold in larger bookshops, contains details of nearly all Portugal's camping grounds. Depending on facilities and season, prices are 300$00 to 600$00 per adult plus 300$00 to 500$00 for a small tent. Many camping grounds close in the low season.

Hostels

Portugal has 38 *pousadas da juventude* (youth hostels), all part of the Hostelling International (HI) system. Low rates are offset by segregated dorms, midnight curfews and partial daytime exclusion at most (but not all) of them.

In high season, dorm beds cost 1700$00 to 2900$00, and most hostels also offer basic doubles for 3800$00 to 4600$00 (without bath) or 4100$00 to 6500$00 (with). Bed linen and breakfast are included. Many hostels have kitchens where you can do your own cooking, plus TV rooms and social areas.

Advance reservations are essential in summer. Most hostels will call ahead to your next stop at no charge, or you can pay 300$00 per set of bookings through the country's central HI reservations office, Movijovem (☎ 213 524 072, fax 213 528 621, ✉ movijovem@mail.telepac.pt), Avenida Duque d'Ávila 137, Lisbon.

Private Rooms

A *quarto* or *quarto particular* is a room with shared facilities in a private house. Tourist offices sometimes have lists, or watch for 'quartos' signs. Rooms are typically 4500-6000$00 for a double. At a *dormida* or rooming house, doubles are about 4500$00.

PORTUGAL

Hotels & Guesthouses

The Portuguese equivalent of B&Bs are the *residencial* and *pensão* (plural *pensões*). Both are graded from one to three stars. High-season pensão rates for a double start around 5000$00; a residencial, where breakfast is normally included, is a bit more.

The government grades hotels with one to five stars. For a high-season double figure 15,000$00 to as much as 50,000$00. *Estalagem* and *albergaria* refer to upmarket inns. Breakfast is usually included.

FOOD & DRINKS

Bars and cafes offer snacks or even a small menu. For full meals try a *casa do pasto* (a simple, cheap eatery), *restaurante*, *cervejaria* (a bar-restaurant) or *marisqueira* (seafood restaurant). Lunchtime typically lasts from noon to 3 pm, evening meals from 7 to 10.30 pm.

The *prato do dia* (dish of the day) is often a bargain at around 800$00. A full portion or *dose* is ample for two decent appetites; a *meia dose* (half-portion) is a quarter to a third cheaper. The titbits at the start of a meal, including bread, cheese, butter and olives, cost extra.

Common snacks are *pastéis de bacalhau* (codfish cakes), *prego em pão* (meat and egg in a roll) and *tosta mista* (toasted cheese and ham sandwich). Prices start around 300$00. Seafood offers exceptional value, especially *linguado grelhado* (grilled sole), *bife de atum* (tuna steak) and the omnipresent *bacalhau* (dried cod) cooked in dozens of ways. Meat is hit-or-miss, but worth sampling are local *presunto* (ham), *borrego* (roast lamb) and *cabrito* (kid).

A small black espresso coffee is a *bica*. Half-and-half coffee and milk is a *café com leite*. Coffee with lots of milk at breakfast is a *galão*. Tea *(chá)* comes with lemon *(com limão)* or with milk *(com leite)*. Yummy pastries are sold in the ubiquitous *pastelarias* (cake shops).

Local beers (*cerveja*) include Sagres in the south and Super Bock in the north. A 20cL draught is called *um imperial*; *uma garrafa* is a bottle.

Portuguese *vinho* (wine) offers great value in all varieties: *tinto* (red), *branco* (white) and *vinho verde* (semi-sparkling). Restaurants often have *vinho da casa* (house wine) for as little as 350$00 for 350ml. Port,

synonymous with Portugal, is produced in the Douro Valley near Porto and drunk in three forms: ruby, tawny and white.

Getting There & Away

AIR

British Airways (BA), TAP Air Portugal and the no-frills carrier Go have daily direct flights from London to Lisbon; BA and TAP also go to Porto and Faro, and Go goes to Faro. High-season return fares for a direct London-Lisbon flight start at about UK£160 with Go.

Within Portugal, ask Top Tours (Lisbon ☎ 213 155 885, Porto ☎ 222 074 020) or youth travel agencies Usit Tagus (Lisbon ☎ 213 525 986, Porto ☎ 226 094 146) and Wasteels (Lisbon ☎ 218 869 793, Porto ☎ 225 370 539).

LAND
Bus

Portugal's main Eurolines agents are Internorte (Porto ☎ 226 093 220), Intercentro (Lisbon ☎ 213 571 745) and Intersul (Faro ☎ 289 899 770), serving north, central and southern Portugal, respectively. UK-based Busabout (☎ 020-7950 1661) is a Europewide hop-on-hop-off coach network with Portugal stops in Porto, Lisbon and Lagos.

Spain Eurolines connections include Madrid-Lisbon (5700 ptas/6860$00), Madrid-Porto (4560 ptas/5490$00) and Seville-Lisbon (4870 ptas/5870$00), all at least three times weekly; and Seville-Lagos (2630 ptas/ 3170$00) four to six times weekly.

UK & France Eurolines services from London (Victoria coach station), with a 7½-hour layover and change of coach in Paris, include at least four weekly to Porto (UK£105/770FF one way from London/Paris, 40/25 hours), five to Lisbon (UK£108/735FF) and two to Faro/Lagos (UK£113/785FF). Eurolines in the UK is at ☎ 0870-514 3219.

The independent line IASA (Paris ☎ 01 43 53 90 82, Porto ☎ 222 084 338, Lisbon ☎ 213 143 979) runs five coaches weekly on four routes: Paris-Viana do Castelo;

Paris-Braga; Paris-Porto; and Paris-Coimbra-Lisbon. One-way/return fares range from 640/990FF to 695/995FF

Train

The main rail route from Spain is Madrid-Lisbon via Valência de Alcântara; the journey (with an express departure daily) takes 10½ hours.

The *Sud Express* runs from Paris via Irún (where you change trains), from where there are two standard routes: the *Sud-Expresso* across Spain to Coimbra in Portugal, where you can continue to Lisbon or change for Porto; and an express service to Madrid.

Getting Around

BUS

A host of regional companies operate a network of comfortable, direct intercity *expressos*, fast regional *rápidas*, and *carreiras* which stop at every crossroad. Local weekend services can thin out to nothing, especially up north and when school is out.

TRAIN

Caminhos de Ferro Portugueses (CP), the state rail company, operates three main services: *rápido* or *intercidade* (IC on timetables), *interregional* (IR) and *regional* (R). IC and IR tickets cost at least twice the price of regional services, with reservations either mandatory or recommended. A special fast IC service called Alfa links Lisbon, Coimbra and Porto. Frequent train travellers may want to buy the *Guia Horário Oficial* (350$00), containing all domestic and international timetables. Inter-Rail and Eurail passes are valid in Portugal.

CAR & MOTORCYCLE

Automóvel Clube de Portugal (ACP), Portugal's motoring club, provides car breakdown assistance for members and affiliates, but anyone can get road information and maps from its head office (☎ 213 180 100, fax 213 180 227), Rua Rosa Araújo 24, Lisbon.

Portuguese drivers are among Europe's most reckless and accident-prone. Although city driving (and parking) is hectic, rural roads have surprisingly little traffic. EU subsidies have funded major road upgrades, and there are now long stretches of motorway,

some of them toll roads. Driving is on the right. Speed limits for cars and motorcycles are 50km/h in cities and public centres, 90km/h on normal roads and 120km/h on motorways (but 50, 70 and 100km/h for motorcycles with sidecars). Front passengers in cars must wear seat belts. Motorcyclists and passengers must wear helmets, and motorcycles must have headlights on day and night. Drink-driving laws are strict, with a maximum legal blood-alcohol level of 0.05%.

Lisbon

Despite the crowds, noise and traffic of a capital city, Lisbon's low skyline and breezy position beside the Rio Tejo (River Tagus) lend it a small, manageable feel. Its unpretentious atmosphere and pleasant blend of architectural styles make it a favourite with travellers. Lisbon (Lisboa to the Portuguese) is also one of Europe's most economical destinations.

Orientation

Activity centres on the Baixa district, focused at Praça Dom Pedro IV, known by all as the Rossio. Several kilometres west is Belém with its cluster of attractions. Parque das Nações, the former Expo '98 site with its grand Oceanarium, lies on the revamped north-eastern waterfront.

Information

Tourist Offices Turismo de Lisboa (☎ 213 433 672, fax 213 610 359) has a new information centre, CRIA (Centro de Representação, Informação e Animação de Lisboa), in Praça do Comércio, dealing specifically with Lisbon inquiries.

A tourist office (☎ 213 463 314, fax 213 468 772) run by ICEP, the national tourist organisation, in the Palácio Foz on Praça dos Restauradores, deals only with national enquiries. Both offices are open 9 am to 8 pm daily. Turismo de Lisboa also has several kiosks around town. All have free maps and the bi-monthly *Follow me Lisboa*, listing sights and current events. All sell the Lisboa Card, good for unlimited travel on nearly all city transport and free or discounted admission to many museums and monuments; a 24/48/72-hour card costs 2100/3500/4500$00.

Money Banks with 24-hour cash-exchange machines are at the airport, Santa Apolónia train station and Rua Augusta 24. A better deal is the exchange bureau Cota Câmbios, Rossio 41, open 9 am to 9 pm daily. American Express is represented by Top Tours (☎ 213 155 885, fax 213 155 873), Avenida Duque de Loulé 108 (closed weekends).

Post & Communications The central post office is on Praça do Comércio. A telephone office at Rossio 68 is open until 11 pm daily. A more convenient post and telephone office on Praça dos Restauradores is open until 10 pm weekdays and to 6 pm at weekends.

Email & Internet Access Portugal Telecom's Net Center (☎ 213 522 292), Avenida Fontes Pereira de Melo 38, offers Internet access at 200$00 per half-hour, from 9 am to 5 pm weekdays.

Access costs 100$00 per quarter-hour at Espaço Ágora (☎ 213 940 170), Rua Cintura, Armazém 1 (behind Santos train station), open 2 pm to 1 am daily; and 175$00 per quarter-hour at a bar called the Web Café (☎ 213 421 181), Rua do Diário de Notícias 126, from 4 pm to 2 am daily.

Travel Agencies Trusty youth-travel agencies are Usit Tagus (☎ 213 525 986, fax 213 532 715), Rua Camilo Castelo Branco 20, and Wasteels (☎ 218 869 793, fax 218 869 797), Rua dos Caminhos do Ferro 90.

Bookshops The city's biggest bookseller is Livraria Bertrand, whose biggest shop is at Rua Garrett 73. Diário de Notícias, Rossio 11, has a modest range of guides and maps.

Laundry Self-service Lave Neve, Rua da Alegria 37, is open until 7 pm weekdays and noon Saturday.

Medical Services The British Hospital (☎ 213 955 067 or ☎ 213 976 329), Rua Saraiva de Carvalho 49, has English-speaking staff.

Dangers & Annoyances Take normal precautions against theft, particularly on rush-hour transport. At night avoid wandering alone in the Alfama and Cais do Sodré districts.

A tourist-oriented, multilingual police office (☎ 213 421 634) is in the Palácio Foz building beside the ICEP tourist office in Praça dos Restauradores.

Things to See & Do

Baixa The Baixa district, with its imposing squares and straight streets, is ideal for strolling. From the Rossio, ascend at a stately pace by funicular (*elevador*) or lift into the surrounding hilly districts.

Castelo de São Jorge The castle, dating from Visigothic times, has been tarted up but still commands superb views. Take bus No 37 from Rossio or tram No 28, which clanks up steep gradients and the incredibly narrow streets from Largo Martim Moniz.

Alfama Though increasingly gentrified and full of tourist restaurants, this ancient district below the castle is a fascinating maze of alleys.

The terrace at **Largo das Portas do Sol** provides a great viewpoint. The **Casa do Fado**, at Largo do Chafariz de Dentro 1, offers an excellent audio-visual look at the history of *fado* (traditional, melancholy Portuguese style of singing). It's open 10 am to 6 pm daily except Tuesday; admission costs 450$00 (students 225$00).

Belém This quarter is 6km west of Rossio. **Mosteiro dos Jerónimos** (Jerónimos Monastery, 1496), the city's finest sight, is a soaring extravaganza of Manueline architecture (closed Monday; cloisters 500$00, free Sunday morning).

Sitting obligingly in the river a 10-minute walk away is the Manueline-style tower, **Torre de Belém**, *the* tourist icon of Portugal (closed Monday; 500$00, free Sunday morning).

To reach Belém take the train or bus No 43 from Cais do Sodré or tram No 15 from Praça da Figueira.

Museums The following museums are open 10 am to 6 pm (from 2 pm Tuesday; closed Monday).

The **Museu Calouste Gulbenkian** is considered Portugal's finest museum. Allow several hours to view its paintings, sculptures, jewellery and more.

The adjacent **Centro de Arte Moderna**

PORTUGAL

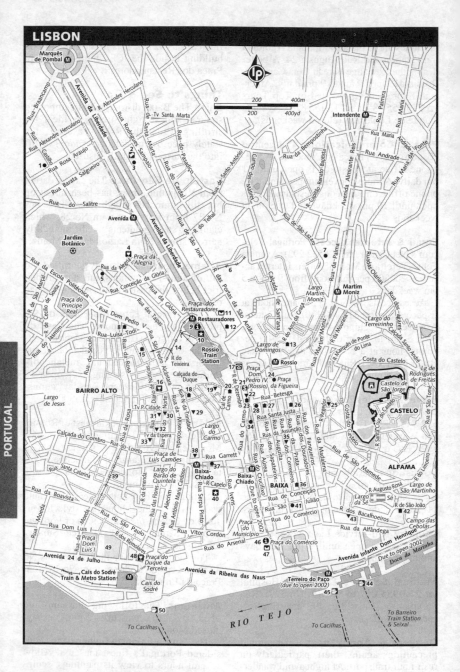

LISBON

LISBON

PLACES TO STAY		32	Restaurant A Primavera	14	Elevador da Glória
8	Pensão Londres	33	Adega do Ribatejo	16	Web Café
12	Pensão Imperial		(Casa de Fado)	17	Telephone Office
13	Pensão Residencial Gerês	35	Restaurant Adega Regional	21	Cota Câmbios
15	Pensão Globo		da Beira	24	Carris Kiosk
18	Pensão Duque	38	Café A Brasileira	28	Diário de Notícias
20	Hospedaria Bons Dias	43	Hua Ta Li	34	Elevador de Santa Justa
23	Pensão Santo Tirso			37	Livraria Bertrand
26	Pensão Norte	**OTHER**		39	Elevador da Bica
27	Pensão Arco da Bandeira	1	Automóvel Clube de Portugal	40	Police Sation
36	Pensão Prata		(ACP)	41	24-hour Exchange Machine
42	Pensão São João da Praça	2	Canadian Embassy	44	Terreiro do Paço Ferry
	& Sé Guest House	3	Instituto Português da		Terminal
			Juventude (IPJ)	45	Cais de Alfândega Ferry
PLACES TO EAT		4	Hot Clube de Portugal		Terminal
19	Restaurante O Sol	5	Lave Neve	46	Turismo de Lisboa Tourist
22	Nicola	6	Elevador de Lavra		Office (CRIA)
25	Restaurant São Cristóvão	7	Gay & Lesbian Community	47	Central Post Office
29	Cervejaria da Trindade		Centre	48	Ó Gilíns Irish Pub
30	Restaurant Sinal Vermelho	9	ICEP National Tourist Office	49	Mercado da Ribeira
31	Adega Machado	10	Tourist Police Office	50	Cais do Sodré Car Ferry
	(Casa de Fado)	11	Post & Telephone Office		Terminal

exhibits modern Portuguese art. Entry to each costs 500$00 (free to students, children and seniors, and to all on Sunday). The handiest metro station is São Sebastião.

One of Lisbon's most attractive museums is the **Museu Nacional do Azulejo** (400$00), north-east of Santa Apolónia station. Take bus No 104 from Praça do Comércio (weekdays) or No 59 from Rossio (weekends).

The **Museu Nacional de Arte Antiga** (Antique Art Museum), Rua das Janelas Verdes, houses the national collection of works by Portuguese painters (500$00). From Praça da Figueira take bus No 40 or 60 or tram No 15.

The centrepiece of Parque das Nações, the vast **Oceanarium** – Europe's largest – hosts 25,000 fish, birds and mammals in a giant two-floor aquarium. It's open 10 am to 6 pm daily; entry costs 1700$00 (900$00 for seniors and those under 16). Take the metro to Oriente station, an equally impressive Expo project.

Organised Tours

Carris (☎ 213 613 000) offers tours by open-top bus (2000$00) and tram (2800$00).

Transtejo (☎ 218 820 348) runs cruises on the Tejo for 3000$00 from the Terreiro do Paço ferry terminal.

Places to Stay

Camping *Lisboa Camping – Parque Municipal* (☎ 217 623 100, *Parque Florestal de Monsanto*) is 6km north-west of Rossio. Take bus No 43 from Cais do Sodré.

Hostels A 24-hour *pousada da juventude* (☎ 213 532 696, fax 213 537 541, *Rua Andrade Corvo 46*) is close to Picoas metro station, or take bus No 46 from Santa Apolónia station or Rossio. The newer *casa da juventude* (☎ 218 920 890, fax 218 920 891, *Via de Moscavide*) is 1km north of Gare do Oriente. Take bus No 44 from Praça dos Restauradores or Oriente to the Avenida da Boa Esperança roundabout; the hostel is 250m down the road.

The beachside *pousada da juventude de Catalazete* (☎ 214 430 638, fax 214 419 267) is on Estrada Marginal in Oeiras, 12km west of Lisbon; take the train from Cais do Sodré station to Oeiras.

Hotels & Guesthouses *Baixa & Restauradores* The cheapies are invariably on upper floors of old buildings. Adequate doubles with shared bath start around 4000$00 at homy *Pensão Santo Tirso* (☎ 213 470 428, *Rossio 18*), and 5000$00 at *Pensão Prata* (☎ 213 468 908, *Rua da Prata 71*) and *Pensão Arco da Bandeira* (☎ 213 423 478, *Rua dos Sapateiros 226*). Slightly pricier are *Pensão Duque* (☎ 213 463 444,

PORTUGAL

Calçada do Duque 53) and **Pensão Norte** (☎ *218 878 941, Rua dos Douradores 159)*.

More salubrious, with doubles around 7000$00, are **Pensão Imperial** (☎ *213 420 166, Praça dos Restauradores 78)* and friendly **Hospedaria Bons Dias** (☎ *213 471 918, Calçada do Carmo 25)*. Security-conscious **Pensão Residencial Gerês** (☎ *218 810 497, fax 218 882 006, Calçada do Garcia 6)* charges 9000$00.

Bairro Alto & Rato Near the Elevador da Glória, pleasant **Pensão Globo** (☎ *213 462 279, Rua do Teixeira 37)* has doubles without bath from 4500$00. **Pensão Londres** (☎ *213 462 203, fax 213 465 682, Rua Dom Pedro V 53)* has spacious rooms, the upper ones with great views; doubles start at 7200$00. **Casa de São Mamede** (☎ *213 963 166, fax 213 951 896, Rua Escola Politécnica 159)* has doubles in an elegant old house for 15,000$00.

Alfama Behind the cathedral, both at Rua São João da Praça 97, **Pensão São João da Praça** (☎/*fax 218 862 591, 2nd floor)* and **Sé Guest House** (☎ *218 864 400, 1st floor)* offer doubles from 6000$00 to 12,000$00 (all with breakfast).

Places to Eat

There are dozens of restaurants and cafes in the Baixa (best for lunchtime bargains) and Bairro Alto (pricier evening venues). A trendy restaurant and bar zone is riverside Doca de Santo Amaro, near Alcântara-Mar station.

Baixa & Alfama *Restaurante Adega Regional da Beira (Rua dos Correeiros 132)* is one of many reasonably priced places along this street. Vegetarian **Restaurante O Sol** *(Calçada do Duque 23)* offers set meals for under 1000$00. **Restaurante São Cristóvão** *(Rua de São Cristóvão 30)* is famous for its Cape Verdean dishes. A bargain Chinese restaurant is **Hua Ta Li** *(Rua dos Bacalhoeiros 109)*.

For a coffee or a meal, two old, atmospheric cafes are **Nicola** *(Rossio 24)* and **Café A Brasileira** *(Rua Garrett 120)*.

Bairro Alto & Saldanha Tiny **Restaurante A Primavera** *(Travessa da Espera 34)* has a family ambience complemented by honest cooking. The smarter **Restaurante Sinal Vermelho** *(Rua das Gáveas 89)* has especially good desserts.

Cervejaria da Trindade *(Rua Nova da Trindade 20-C)* is a converted convent decorated with *azulejos* (hand-painted tiles). Main dishes start at around 1400$00.

Bright **Bella Italia III** *(Avenida Duque d'Ávila 40-C)* is a pastelaria-cum-restaurant with pizzas and half-portions of Portuguese fare for under 1000$00.

Belém An attractive row of restaurants in Belém with outdoor seating includes **A Floresta** *(Rua Vieira Portuense 2)*.

Entertainment

Many Lisbon *casas de fado* (which are also restaurants) produce pale tourist imitations of fado, at high prices. All have a minimum charge of 2000$00 to 4500$00. In the Bairro Alto, try **Adega Machado** *(Rua do Norte 91)* or the simpler **Adega do Ribatejo** *(Rua Diário de Notícias 23)*.

Hot Clube de Portugal *(Praça da Alegria 39)* is at the centre of a thriving jazz scene, with live music three or four nights weekly after 10 pm (closed Sunday and Monday).

Ó Gilíns Irish Pub *(Rua dos Remolares 8-10)* is open 11 am to 2 am daily, with live Irish tunes most Saturday nights and jazz with Sunday brunch.

Lisbon's disco-clubs include the good **Lux Fragil** *(Avendida Infante Dom Henrique, Cais da Pedra à Santa Apolónia)* and, for some African music beats, **Luanda** *(Travessa de Teixeira Júnior 6)*. Other bar-discos are by the river: **Rock City**, on Rua Cintura do Porto de Lisboa, has live rock nightly except Monday. **Dock's Club** *(Rua da Cintura do Porto de Lisboa 226)* carries on until 4 am nightly except Sunday.

Getting There & Away

Bus A dozen different companies, including Renex (☎ 218 874 871), operate from Gare do Oriente. The Arco do Cego terminal (☎ 213 545 439), Avenida João Crisóstomo (metro: Saldanha), is the base for Rede Expressos (☎ 213 103 111) and EVA (☎ 213 147 710), whose network covers the whole country.

Train Santa Apolónia station (☎ 218 884 025) is the terminus for northern and central

Portugal and all international services (trains also stop en route at the better connected Gare do Oriente). Cais do Sodré station is for Belém, Cascais and Estoril. Rossio station serves Sintra.

Barreiro station, across the river, is the terminus for southern Portugal; connecting ferries leave frequently from the pier at Terreiro do Paço. The North-South railway line, over the Ponte de 25 Abril, goes to suburban areas and will eventually carry on to southern Portugal.

Ferry Cais da Alfândega is the terminal for several ferries including to Cacilhas (110$00), a transfer point for some buses to Setúbal. A car ferry (for bikes too) runs from Cais do Sodré terminal.

Getting Around

Bus & Tram Individual bus and tram tickets are 80$00 from Carris kiosks; tickets bought on board cost 160$00. A four/seven-day Passe Turístico, valid for all trams and buses and the metro, costs 1720/2430$00.

Buses and trams run from 6 am to 1 am, with some night services. The Aero-Bus runs between Cais do Sodré and the airport via Praça dos Restauradores every 20 minutes from 7 am to 9 pm (460$00).

The clattering, old-fashioned trams (*eléctricos*) are an endearing component of Lisbon; try No 28 to the old quarter from Largo Martim Moniz.

Metro The metro is useful for hops across town and to Parque das Nações (metro: Oriente). Individual tickets cost 100$00; a *caderneta* of 10 tickets is 850$00. A *bilhete diário* (day ticket) is 270$00. The metro operates from 6.30 am to 1 am.

AROUND LISBON
Sintra

If you take only one trip from Lisbon, make it Sintra. Beloved by Portuguese royalty and English nobility, its thick forests and startling architecture provide a complete change from Lisbon. The tourist office (☎ 219 231 157, fax 219 235 176), Praça da República 23, in the historic centre, has a good map and accommodation information. During weekends and the annual July music festival, expect droves of visitors. In high season it's wise to pre-book accommodation.

Things to See The Palácio Nacional de Sintra – Manueline and Gothic, with Moorish origins – dominates the centre with its twin chimneys (closed Wednesday; 600$00).

One of Sintra's best museums is the **Museu do Brinquedo** on Rua Visconde de Monserrate, with 20,000 toys from around the world (closed Monday; 500$00).

A 3km climb from the centre leads to the ruined **Castelo dos Mouros** with a fine view over town and surroundings. It's open 9 am to 7 pm daily (to 5 pm in winter). Twenty minutes farther on is the architecturally bizarre **Palácio da Pena**, built in 1839 (closed Monday; 600$00). Cars are prohibited; Stagecoach bus No 434 runs regularly from the bus station via the tourist office, for 600$00.

Rambling, romantic **Monserrate Gardens**, 4km from town, are open 10 am to 5 pm (admission free). En route is the extraordinary, mystical **Quinta da Regaleira**, open 10 am to 6 pm daily (to 4 pm in winter) for 2000/1000$00.

Places to Stay A *pousada da juventude* (☎ 219 241 210) is at Santa Eufémia, 4km from the centre; reservations are essential. *Casa de Hóspedes Adelaide* (☎ 219 230 873, Rua Guilherme Gomes Fernandes 11), a 10-minute walk from the station, has reasonable doubles from 4000$00. Better-value private rooms are around 4500$00 (the tourist office has a list). Across the tracks, *Piela's* (☎ 219 241 691, Rua João de Deus 70 – moving in 2001 to Avenida Desiderio Cambournac 1-3) has doubles without bath from around 6000$00.

Places to Eat Close to the tourist office is the recommended *Tulhas (Rua Gil Vicente 4-6)*. Simple *A Tasca do Manel (Largo Dr Vergilio Horta 5)* serves dishes from around 900$00. *Restaurante Parririnha (Rua João de Deus 41)* serves great grilled fish. *Bistro-bar Ópera Prima (Rua Consiglieri Pedroso 2-A)* has live jazz, soul and blues several nights weekly.

Getting There & Away The Lisbon-Sintra railway terminates in Estefânia, 1.5km north-east of the historic centre. Sintra's bus station, and another train station, are a further 1km east in the new-town district of Portela de Sintra. Frequent shuttle buses run to the historic centre from the bus terminal.

PORTUGAL

Trains run every 15 minutes all day from Lisbon's Rossio station. Buses run regularly from Sintra to Estoril and Cascais.

Cascais

Cascais, the 'in' beach resort on the coast west of Lisbon, is packed with tourists in summer. The sea roars into the coast at **Boca do Inferno** ('hell's mouth'), 2km west of Cascais. Spectacular, windy **Cabo da Roca**, Europe's westernmost point, is 16km from Cascais and Sintra (served by buses from both towns). Long, wild **Guincho** beach, 3km from Cascais, is a popular surfing venue.

The Cascais tourist office (☎ 214 868 204, fax 214 672 280), Rua Visconde de Luz 14, has accommodation lists and bus timetables. Smartprint (☎ 214 866 776), Rua Frederico de Arouca 45, has Internet access for 155$00 per five minutes. Transrent (☎ 214 864 566), at Centro Commercial Cisne, Avenida Marginal (near the post office), rents bicycles and motorcycles.

Places to Stay & Eat *Camping Orbitur do Guincho* (☎ *214 871 014, fax 214 872 167*) is 7km from Cascais near Guincho beach. *Residencial Avenida* (☎ *214 864 417, Rua da Palmeira 14*) has doubles without bath for 6000$00. The tourist office can recommend private rooms from around 5000$00.

A Económica (*Rua Sebastião J C Melo, 11*) serves standard fare at low prices. Try delicious fish kebabs at *A Tasca* (*Rua Afonso Sanches 61*).

Getting There & Away Trains run frequently all day to Estoril and Cascais from Cais do Sodré station in Lisbon.

The Algarve

Boisterous and full of foreigners, the Algarve is about as far from traditional Portugal as one can get. The largest town is Faro but the beach, golf and nightclub scenes are focused on central Algarve, particularly Albufeira and Lagos. West of Lagos, the shore grows increasingly steep and rocky.

Dangers & Annoyances

Theft is a significant problem in the Algarve. Don't leave anything valuable unattended in your vehicle, tent or on the beach.

Swimmers should beware of dangerous currents, especially on the west coast. Beaches are marked by coloured flags: red means no bathing, yellow means yes to wading but no to swimming, green means anything goes.

FARO

Low-key Faro is the main transport hub and commercial centre. The waterfront around Praça de Dom Francisco Gomes has pleasant gardens and cafes. Faro's beach, **Praia de Faro**, is 6km south-west of the city on Ilha de Faro; take bus No 16 from opposite the bus station or, from May to September, a ferry from Arco da Porta Nova, close to Faro's port. The tourist office (☎ 289 803 604, fax 289 800 453), Rua da Misericórdia, has leaflets on just about every Algarve community.

Places to Stay & Eat

A big, cheap *municipal camping ground* (☎ *289 817 876*) is on Praia de Faro. The *pousada da juventude* (☎ *289 826 521, Rua da Polícia de Segurança Pública 1*) has double rooms as well as dorm beds; it's open from 8 am to midday and 6pm to midnight.

Friendly *Residencial Adelaide* (☎ *289 802 383, fax 289 826 870, Rua Cruz dos Mestres 7*) has doubles from 6000$00 and rooftop space when they're full.

A Garrafeira do Vilaça (*Rua São Pedro 33*) is popular for budget fare. Lively *Sol e Jardim* (*Praça Ferreira de Almeida 22*) serves good seafood.

Getting There & Away

From the bus station, just west of the centre, there are at least a dozen daily express coaches to Lisbon (about four hours) and frequent buses to other coastal towns. Bus Nos 14 and 16 run from the airport into town (and to Praia de Faro).

The train station is a few minutes' walk west of the bus station. Two IR and three IC trains run daily to Lisbon (Barreiro), and seven to Lagos.

TAVIRA

Tavira is one of the Algarve's oldest and most beautiful towns, with a hilltop **castle** and dozens of old churches. **Ilha da Tavira**, 2km from Tavira, is an island beach connected to the mainland by ferry. Walk 2km

PORTUGAL

beside the river to the ferry terminal at Quatro Águas or take the (summer-only) bus from the bus station.

Information

The tourist office (☎ 289 322 511) is at Rua da Galeria 9. Internet access is available at PostNet, Rua Dr Silvestre Falcão, costing 200$00 per 15 minutes. Rent bicycles and motorcycles from Lorisrent, next door to the tourist office. Exploratio (mobile ☎ 919 338 226) runs walking and biking tours.

Places to Stay & Eat

Ilha da Tavira has a *camping ground*, but the ferry stops running at 11 pm (1 am from July to September).

Popular *Pensão Residencial Lagoas* (☎ 289 322 252, Rua Almirante Cândido dos Reis 24) has doubles from 5000$00 without bath. Central *Residencial Imperial* (☎ 289 322 234, Rua José Pires Padinha 24) charges 8000$00 (with bath and breakfast). Riverside *Pensão Residencial Princesa do Gilão* (☎ 289 325 171, Rua Borda d'Água de Aguiar 10) is slightly pricier.

Cantinho do Emigrante (Praça Dr Padinha 27), on the north side of the river, serves bargain fare. Or try *Casa de Pasto A Barquinha (Rua Dr José Pires Padinha 142)* on the other side.

Getting There & Away

Some 15 trains and at least four express buses run daily between Faro and Tavira (30 to 50 minutes).

LAGOS

This tourist resort has some of the Algarve's finest beaches. The beach scene includes **Meia Praia**, a vast strip to the east; and to the west **Praia da Luz** and the more secluded **Praia do Pinhão**.

Espadarte do Sul (☎ 289 761 820) operates **boat trips** from Docapesca harbour, including snorkelling and game fishing. On the seaside promenade, local fishermen offer motorboat jaunts to the nearby **grottoes**.

Information

The tourist office (☎ 289 763 031) is 1km north-east of the centre, at Situo São João roundabout (closed weekends during winter). Rent bicycles and mopeds from Motoride (☎ 289 761 720), Rua José Afonso 23.

Places to Stay & Eat

Two nearby camping grounds are *Trindade* (☎ 289 763 893), 200m south of the town walls, and *Imulagos* (☎ 289 760 031), with a shuttle bus from the waterfront road.

The excellent *pousada da juventude* (☎ 289 761 970) is at Rua Lançarote de Freitas 50 and has Internet access (300$00 per half-hour).

Residencial Marazul (☎ 289 769 749, Rua 25 de Abril 13) has smart doubles from around 11,000$00. *Private rooms* are plentiful, for around 5500$00.

For Algarve specialities, try *O Cantinho Algarvio (Rua Afonso d'Almeida 17)*. A local favourite is *Restaurante Bar Barros (Rua Portas de Portugal 83)*. Several bars around Rua 25 de Abril serve snacks. *Mullens (Rua Cândido dos Reis 86)* is a wood-panelled pub with good food.

Getting There & Away

Bus and train services depart frequently for other Algarve towns and around a dozen times daily to Lisbon; by train, change at Tunes for Lisbon.

SILVES

Silves was the capital of Moorish Algarve, rivalling Lisbon for influence. Times are quieter now, but the huge **castle** is well worth a visit.

The tourist office (☎ 289 442 255), Rua 25 de Abril, is open weekdays and Saturday morning.

Places to Stay & Eat

Residencial Sousa (☎ 289 442 502, Rua Samoura Barros 17) has doubles without bath for around 5000$00.

Residencial Ponte Romana (☎ 289 443 275), beside the old bridge, offers doubles with bath from 6000$00.

Restaurante Rui (Rua C Vilarinho 27) is Silves' best (and priciest) fish restaurant. For cheaper meals, try riverfront restaurants opposite the old bridge.

Getting There & Away

Silves train station is 2km from town; trains from Lagos (35 minutes) stop six times daily (from Faro, change at Tunes), to be met by local buses. Six buses run daily to Silves from Albufeira (40 minutes).

PORTUGAL

SAGRES

Sagres is a small fishing port perched on dramatic cliffs in Portugal's south-western corner. In its **fort**, on a wide windy promontory, Henry the Navigator trained the explorers who later founded the Portuguese empire. Among nearby beaches, a good choice is at the small village of **Salema**, 17km east.

No Sagres visit would be complete without a trip to **Cabo de São Vicente** (Cape St Vincent), 6km to the west. A solitary lighthouse stands on this barren cape, Europe's south-westernmost point.

Information

The tourist office (☎ 289 624 873), just beyond the central Praça da República on Rua Comandante Matoso, is open weekdays and Saturday morning. Turinfo (☎ 289 620 003), open daily on Praça da República, rents cars and bikes, books hotels and arranges jeep and fishing trips.

Places to Stay & Eat

The *Parque de Campismo Sagres* (☎ *289 624 351*) is 2km from town, off the Vila do Bispo road. Many Sagres folk rent *rooms* for around 5000$00 a double. Cheap, filling meals can be had at *Restaurante A Sagres* at the roundabout as you enter the village.

Getting There & Away

About 15 buses run daily to Sagres from Lagos (45-65 minutes), fewer on Sunday. Three continue out to Cabo de São Vicente on weekdays.

Central Portugal

ÉVORA

One of Portugal's architectural gems and a Unesco World Heritage Site, the walled town of Évora is the capital of Alentejo province, a vast landscape of olive groves, vineyards and wheat fields. The town's charm lies in the narrow streets of the well preserved inner town.

Orientation & Information

The focal point is Praça do Giraldo, from where you can wander through backstreets until you meet the city walls. An annotated map is available from the tourist office (☎ 266 702 671) Praça do Giraldo 73.

Outside the tourist office is an automatic cash-exchange machine. Oficin@ bar at Rua da Moeda 27 has Internet access for 100$00 per 10 minutes.

Things to See & Do

On Largo do Marquês de Marialva is the **Sé**, Évora's cathedral, with cloisters and a museum of ecclesiastical treasures, both closed Monday (450$00 for both museum and cloisters).

The **Museu de Évora** features some fantastic 16th-century Portuguese and Flemish painting (350$00). Opposite is the Romanera **Temple of Diana**, subject of Évora's top-selling postcard.

The **Igreja de São Francisco**, south of Praça do Giraldo, includes the ghoulish **Capela dos Ossos** (Chapel of Bones), constructed with the bones and skulls of several thousand people (100$00).

Évora's big bash, and one of Alentejo's biggest country fairs, is the Feira de São João, held from approximately 22 June to 2 July.

Places to Stay

Accommodation gets tight in Évora in summer; booking ahead is essential.

An *Orbitur camping ground* (☎ *266 705 190*) is about 2km south of town (buses to Alcaçovas stop there). There is a *pousada da juventude* (☎ *266 744 848, Rua Miguel Bombarda 40*) in town.

Recommended *private rooms* are those at Rua Romão Ramalho 27 (☎ *266 702 453*); doubles cost 5000$00. *Residencial O Alentejo* (☎ *266 702 903, Rua Serpa Pinto 74*) has doubles with bath for 6000$00. At handsome *Pensão Policarpo* (☎/fax *266 702 424, Rua da Freiria de Baixo 16*), doubles start at 9500$00. *Residencial Solar Monfalim* (☎ *266 750 000, fax 266 742 367, Largo da Misericórdia 1*) is a minipalace with doubles from 14,500$00.

Places to Eat

O Portão (*Rua do Cano 27*) is a popular budget choice. Pricier *Café Restaurant O Cruz* (*Praça 1 de Maio 20*) offers good traditional fare.

Jovial *Taberna Tipica Quarta-Feira* (*Rua do Inverno 16*) packs in locals for its speciality creamed spinach and pork dishes. *Pane & Vino* (*Páteo do Salema 22*) has

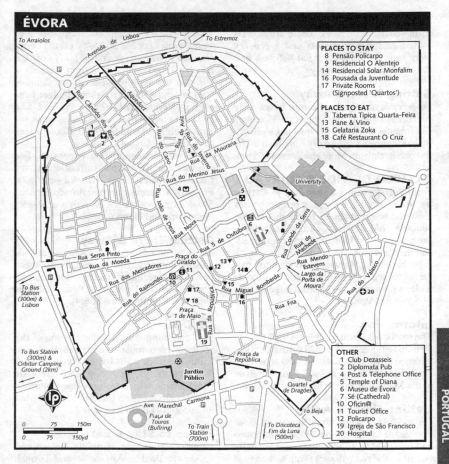

ÉVORA

PLACES TO STAY
8 Pensão Policarpo
9 Residencial O Alentejo
14 Residencial Solar Monfalim
16 Pousada da Juventude
17 Private Rooms
   (Signposted 'Quartos')

PLACES TO EAT
3 Taberna Tipica Quarta-Feira
13 Pane & Vino
15 Gelataria Zoka
18 Café Restaurant O Cruz

OTHER
1 Club Dezasseis
2 Diplomata Pub
4 Post & Telephone Office
5 Temple of Diana
6 Museu de Évora
7 Sé (Cathedral)
10 Oficin@
11 Tourist Office
12 Policarpo
19 Igreja de São Francisco
20 Hospital

---

great pizzas. Ice-cream fans will appreciate *Gelataria Zoka (Largo de São Vicente 14)*.

Entertainment

Popular student bars north-west of the centre include *Club Dezasseis (Rua do Escrivão da Cámara 16)* and *Diplomata Pub (Rua do Apóstolo 4)*, with frequent live music. *Discoteca Fim da Luna (Avenida Combatentes da Grande Guerra 56)* is near the train station.

Getting There & Away

Évora has six weekday express coach connections to Lisbon (1¼ hours) and two to Faro (four to five hours), departing from the terminal off Avenida Túlio Espanca (700m south-west of the centre). Three daily fast train runs from Lisbon (2½ hours).

Getting Around

Call Bike Lab (☎ 266 735 500) to rent a bike. Policarpo (☎ 266 746 970), Alcárcova de Baixo 43, organises tours of the city and surrounds.

MONSARAZ

This small, walled village high above the plain is well worth the trip, for its medieval atmosphere, clear light and magnificent views. Of architectural interest is the **Museu de Arte Sacra**, probably a former tribunal, with a rare 15th-century fresco. The **castle's** parapets have the best views.

Places to Stay & Eat

Several places along the main Rua Direita have *double rooms* for around 5000$00.

PORTUGAL

The tourist office (☎ 266 557 136) on the main square has details. There are several tourist-geared *restaurants* and a *grocery store* near the main gate. Eat before 8 pm: the town goes to bed early.

Getting There & Away
On weekdays only, two to four buses daily run 17km to/from Reguengos de Monsaraz (35 minutes), which is connected to Évora by half a dozen buses daily (one hour). The last one back from Monsaraz leaves at 5 pm.

CASTELO DE VIDE & MARVÃO
From Portalegre it's a short hop to **Castelo de Vide**, noted for its picturesque houses clustered below a castle. Highlights are the **Judiaria** (old Jewish quarter) in a well-preserved network of medieval backstreets, and the view from the castle. Try to spend a night here or in **Marvão**, a mountaintop medieval walled village 12km from Castelo de Vide, with grand views across large chunks of Spain and Portugal.

Information
The tourist offices at Castelo de Vide (☎ 245 901 361, fax 245 901 827), Rua de Bartolomeu Álvares da Santa 81, and at Marvão (☎ 245 993 886, fax 245 993 526), Largo de Santa Maria, can help with accommodation.

Getting There & Away
On weekdays only, three buses run from Portalegre to Castelo de Vide (20 minutes) and two to Marvão (45 minutes). One daily bus links the two villages (with a change at Portagem, a junction 5km from Marvão).

NAZARÉ
This once-peaceful 17th-century fishing village was 'discovered' by tourism in the 1970s. Fishing skills and distinctive local dress have gone overboard and in high season it's a tourist circus, but the beautiful coastline and fine seafood still make it worthwhile.

Lower Nazaré's beachfront retains a core of narrow streets now catering to tourists. The upper section, O Sítio, on the cliffs, is reached by a vintage funicular railway. The beaches attract huge summer crowds. Beware of dangerous currents.

The tourist office (☎ 262 561 194), at the end of Avenida da República by the funicular is open 10 am to 10 pm daily in high season.

Places to Stay & Eat
Two good, well-equipped camp sites are: *Vale Paraíso* (☎ 262 561 546), off the Leiria road, and *Orbitur* (☎ 262 561 111) off the Alcobaça road, both 2.5km from Nazaré.

Many townspeople rent *rooms*; doubles start around 4500$00. Among budget pensões is *Residencial Marina* (☎ 262 551 541, Rua Mouzinho de Albuquerque 6), with doubles around 6000$00. Room prices skyrocket in August.

Seafront restaurants are expensive. For cheaper fare in simple surroundings, try *Casa Marques (Rua Gil Vicente 37)*. Friendly *A Tasquinha (Rua Adrião Batalha 54)* does a good *carne de porco á Alentejana* (pork and clams).

Getting There & Away
The nearest train station, 6km away at Valado, is connected to Nazaré by frequent buses. Nazaré has numerous bus connections to Lisbon (1½ hours), Óbidos (40 minutes) and Coimbra (two hours).

ÓBIDOS
This charming walled village is one of the prettiest (and most touristy) in Portugal. Climb the town walls for the views, wander the back alleys, then pop into **Igreja de Santa Maria**, which features fine azulejos.

The tourist office (☎ 262 959 231, fax 262 959 014) is on Rua Direita.

Places to Stay & Eat
Private rooms are available for around 4500$00 a double. Among several Turihab properties is romantic *Casa do Poço (☎ 262 959 358, Travessa da Mouraria)* where doubles cost around 11,500$00. *Residencial Martim de Freitas (☎ 262 959 185, Estrada Nacional 8)*, outside the walls, has doubles from 6000$00.

Cheap cafes outside the walls include *Café Snack Bar O Aqueduto*. Inside, *Café-Restaurante 1 de Dezembro*, next to the Igreja de São Pedro, has pleasant outdoor seating. There's a small grocery store just inside the town gate.

Getting There & Away
There are regular bus connections from Lisbon, directly (two hours) or via Caldas da Rainha, 10 minutes away. From the train station, outside the walls at the foot of the

hill, five services daily go to Lisbon (four with a change at Cacém).

COIMBRA

Coimbra is famed for its 13th-century university, and for its traditional role as a centre of culture and art, complemented in recent times by industrial development. Lower Coimbra's main attraction is the **Mosteiro de Santa Cruz** with its ornate pulpit and medieval royal tombs. In the upper town, visit the **old university** with its baroque library and Manueline chapel, and the **Machado de Castro Museum**, with a fine collection of sculpture and painting.

At **Conimbriga**, 16km south of Coimbra, are the well-preserved ruins of a Roman town, plus a good museum (site open daily, museum closed Monday; 350$00). Direct buses depart at 9.05 or 9.35 am (only 9.35 am at weekends) from the terminal at Rua João de Ruão 18, returning at 1 and 6 pm (only 6 pm at weekends).

Coimbra's annual highlight is Queima das Fitas, a boozy week of fado and revelry beginning on the first Thursday in May, when students celebrate the end of the academic year.

Information

The regional tourist office (☎ 239 855 930, fax 239 825 576), Largo da Portagem, has pamphlets and cultural-events information, but a municipal tourist office (☎ 239 832 591) on Praça Dom Dinis, and another (☎ 239 833 202) on Praça da República, are more useful. All have good city maps.

The Centro de Juventude (☎ 239 790 600) at Rua Pedro Monteiro 73 offers free Internet access 9 am to 5 pm weekdays, with a half-hour maximum.

Places to Stay & Eat

For Coimbra's *pousada da juventude* (☎ 239 822 955, Rua António Henriques Seco 12-14), take northbound bus No 46 from Coimbra A train station.

Near Coimbra A train station, doubles with bath are 5000$00 at **Pensão Lorvanense** (☎ 239 823 481, Rua da Sota 27) and 6500$00 at central **Pensão Residencial Larbelo** (☎ 239 829 092, Largo da Portagem 33). **Pensão Flôr de Coimbra** (☎ 239 823 865, Rua do Poço 5) has doubles from 5000$00, and its dining room

offers a small daily (except Sunday) vegetarian menu.

Near the university, **Casa Pombal Guesthouse** (☎ 239 835 175, Rua das Flores 18) has everything from 7000$00 bathless doubles to bird's-eye views at 8200$00 with bath, and a huge breakfast.

The lanes west of Praça do Comércio, especially Rua das Azeiteiras, feature a concentration of plain, good-value restaurants. *Restaurante Democrática (Travessa da Rua Nova)* has Portuguese standards, with some half-portions under 900$00.

East of the university, *Bar-Restaurante ACM (Rua Alexandre Herculano 21A)* has plain fare from 700$00 per dish. Behind the *Centro de Juventude (Rua Pedro Monteiro 73)* is a canteen with main dishes under 800$00, and at three *university canteens*, a student card will get you a meal for about 400$00.

Getting There & Away

At least a dozen buses and as many trains run daily from Lisbon and Porto, plus frequent express buses from Faro and Évora. The main long-distance train stations are Coimbra B, 2km north-west of the centre, and central Coimbra A (on timetables called just 'Coimbra'). Most long-distance trains call at both.

SERRA DA ESTRELA

The forested Serra da Estrela is Portugal's highest mainland mountain range (topping out at 1993m Torre), and the core of a designated *parque natural*. With its outlying ranges it stretches nearly across Portugal, and offers some of the country's best hiking.

Orientation & Information

The best place for information on the Parque Natural de Serra de Estrela is the main park office in Manteigas (☎ 275 980 060, fax 275 980 069). Other good sources for regional information are the tourist offices at Guarda (☎ 271 212 115) and Covilhã (☎ 275 319 560). Park offices and some tourist offices sell an English edition of *Á Descoberta da Estrela*, a walking guide (850$00).

Places to Stay

The *pousada da juventude* (☎ 275 335 375) at Penhas da Saúde, 10km above Covilhã, offers meals (or you can cook your own), dorms and a few functional doubles.

Buses come from Covilhã twice daily in August only, and hitching is fairly safe and easy; the only other options are your feet or bike, or a taxi (about 1600$00). This makes a good base for excursions.

Guarda also has a *pousada da juventude* (☎ *271 224 482*), and Seia, Gouveia, Guarda and Covilhã have some modestly priced guesthouses.

Getting There & Away
Several buses run each day from Coimbra, along the park's perimeter to Seia, Gouveia, Guarda or Covilhã, plus others from Porto and Lisbon to Guarda and Covilhã. Twice-daily intercidade trains link Lisbon and Coimbra to Guarda, and two daily intercidade trains run from Lisbon to Covilhã on the Lisbon-Paris line.

The North

PORTO
Porto is Portugal's second-largest city, and the focus of the port-wine trade. Its reputation as an industrial centre belies considerable charm; indeed its old centre has been declared a Unesco World Heritage Site, and the city has, with Rotterdam, been named European City of Culture for 2001.

The city clings to the north bank of the Rio Douro, spanned here by five bridges. On the far bank is Vila Nova de Gaia and its port-wine lodges, a major attraction.

Orientation
Central Porto's axis is Avenida dos Aliados. At its southern end are Praça da Liberdade and São Bento train station, which are also major local bus hubs. Another is Jardim da Cordoaria, about 400m westward. The picturesque Ribeira district lies along the waterfront, below São Bento and in the shadow of the great Ponte de Dom Luís I bridge.

Information
Tourist Offices The main municipal tourist office (☎ 222 052 740, fax 223 323 303), Rua Clube dos Fenianos 25, is open 9 am to 5.30 pm weekdays. A smaller office (☎ 222 009 770) at Rua Infante Dom Henriques 63 is open during these hours and from 9.30 am to 4.30 pm weekends. Longer hours apply from July to September. There's a national tourist office (☎ 222 057 514, fax 222 053 212) at Praça Dom João I 43.

Money Banks with ATMs and exchange desks are everywhere. Better rates for travellers cheques are at the exchange bureaus Portocambios, Rua Rodrigues Sampaio 193, and Intercontinental, Rua de Ramalho Ortigão 8.

Top Tours (☎ 222 074 020), Rua Alferes Malheiro 96, is Porto's American Express representative.

Post & Communications The main post office (the place for poste-restante mail) is on Praça General Humberto Delgado. A telephone office at Praça da Liberdade 62 is open 10 am to 10 pm daily.

Email & Internet Access The Instituto Português da Juventude (☎ 226 003 173), Rua Rodrigues Lobo 98, offers free Internet access on weekdays. At Portweb (☎ 222 005 922), Praça General Humberto Delgado 291, access costs 100$00 per hour from 9 am to 4 pm daily, and 240$00 from 4 pm to 2 am.

Travel Agencies Two youth-oriented agencies, selling discounted plane and train tickets, rail passes and international youth/student cards, are Usit Tagus (☎ 226 094 146), Rua Campo Alegre 261, and Wasteels (☎ 225 370 539), Rua Pinto Bessa 27/29 near Campanhã station.

Laundry Lavandaria Olimpica, Rua Miguel Bombarda, and Lavandaria 5 á Sec in the Central Shopping centre have laundry and dry-cleaning services. A cheaper service, Lavandaria São Nicolau, is on Rua Infante Dom Henrique. All are closed Sunday.

Medical Services Santo António Hospital (☎ 222 077 500) is at Rua Vicente José Carvalho.

Emergency Requests for police help should go to the 'tourism police' office (☎ 222 081 833) at Rua Clube dos Fenianos 11, open 8 am to 2 am daily.

Things to See & Do
The riverfront **Ribeira** district is the city's beating heart, with narrow lanes, grimy bars, good restaurants and river cruises.

The 225 steps of the **Torre dos Clérigos** on Rua dos Clérigos lead to the best panorama of the city (10 am to noon and 2 to 5 pm daily; 200$00).

The **Sé**, the cathedral dominating central Porto, is worth a visit for its mixture of architectural styles and ornate interior (closed Sunday morning; 250$00).

The **Soares dos Reis National Museum**, Rua Dom Manuel II 44, offers masterpieces of 19th and 20th-century Portuguese painting and sculpture (10 am to 12.30 pm and 2 to 6 pm, closed all day Monday and Tuesday morning; 350$00).

Porto's finest new museum is the **Serralves Museum of Contemporary Art**, Rua de Serralves 947/999 (10 am to 7 pm, except to 10 pm Thursday, closed Monday; 800$00).

At the **Bolhão market**, east of Avenida dos Aliados, you can get anything from seafood to herbs and honey. It's open until 5 pm weekdays and to 1 pm Saturday.

Across the river in Vila Nova de Gaia, some two dozen **port-wine lodges** are open for tours and tastings on weekdays and Saturday, and a few on Sunday. The tourist office by the waterfront has details.

Porto's one remaining tram, the No 1E, trundles daily from the Ribeira to the coast at Foz do Douro and back to Boavista every half-hour all day. The **Museu dos Carros Eléctricos** (Tram Museum), Cais do Bicalho, has dozens of restored trams (closed Monday; 350$00).

Special Events

Porto's big festival is the Festa de São João (St John's Festival) in June. Also worth catching are several music festivals, including Celtic music in April-May, rock in August, and fado in October.

Places to Stay

Camping *Camping da Prelada (☎ 228 312 616, Rua Monte dos Burgos)* is 4km north-west of the centre (take bus No 6 from Praça de Liberdade or bus No 50 from Jardim da Cordoaria).

Three camping grounds near the sea in Vila Nova de Gaia are *Campismo Salgueiros (☎ 227 810 500, Praia de Salgueiros)*, *Campismo Marisol (☎ 227 135 942, Praia de Canide)* and *Campismo Madalena (☎ 227 122 520, Praia da Madalena)*. Bus No 57 runs to all of them from São Bento station.

Note that the sea at all these places is too polluted for swimming.

Hostel The fine *pousada da juventude (☎ 226 177 257, Rua Paulo da Gama 551)*, 4km west of the centre, is open 24 hours. Doubles and dorm-style quads are available, and reservations are essential. Take bus No 35 from Largo dos Lóios (a block west of Praça da Liberdade), or No 1 from São Bento station.

Guesthouses Porto's cheapest guesthouses are around Praça da Batalha. Two reliable ones where doubles with bath start at 4000$00 are *Residencial Afonso (☎ 222 059 469, Rua Duque de Loulé 233)* and *Residencial Santo André (☎ 222 055 869, Rua Santo Ildefonso 112)*. *Pensão Astória (☎ 222 008 175, Rua Arnaldo Gama 56)* has elegant doubles, some with river views, for 5000$00 with bath and breakfast.

Near the centre, plain doubles with shower at *Residencial União (☎ 222 003 078, Rua Conde de Vizela 62)* and *Pensão Porto Rico (☎ 223 394 690, Rua do Almada 237)* start at 5000$00. *Pensão Chique (☎ 223 322 963, Avenida dos Aliados 206)* has small doubles for 6500$00 with breakfast. Those at *Residencial Vera Cruz (☎ 223 323 396, fax 223 323 421, Rua Ramalho Ortigão 14)* are 8000$00. *Pensão Pão de Açucar (☎ 222 002 425, Rua do Almada 262)* has handsome doubles with shower from 9500$00; bookings are essential.

Near the university, *Pensão Estoríl (☎ 222 002 751, Rua de Cedofeita 193)* and the better-value *Pensão São Marino (☎ 223 325 499, Praça Carlos Alberto 59)* offer doubles with shower from 6500$00, with breakfast.

Places to Eat

Excellent value in the centre is the self-service mezzanine at *Café Embaixador (Rua Sampaio Bruno 5)*, with grills, salads and vegetables; it's open until 10 pm daily except Sunday. Near the university, *Restaurante A Tasquinha (Rua do Carmo 23)* has good regional dishes for 1000$00 to 2000$00. Cheerful *Restaurante Romão (Praça Carlos Alberto 100)* has northern specialities for around 900$00 per dish. A lively student haunt is *Café Ancôra Douro (Praça de Parada Leitão 49)*.

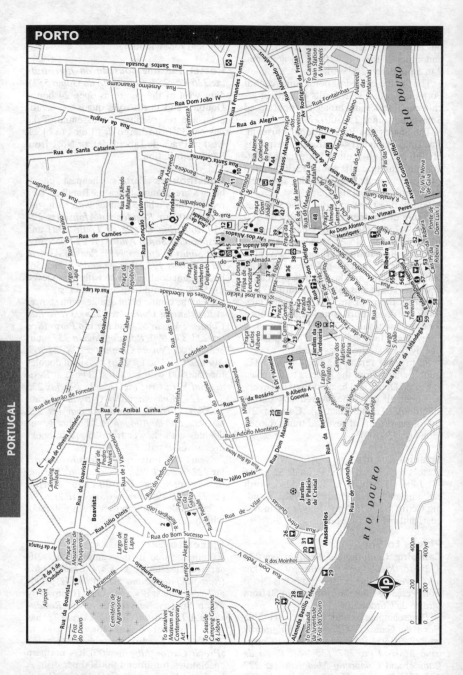

PORTO

PLACES TO STAY	OTHER	27	Voice
6	Pensão Estoríl	1	STCP Kiosk	28	Tram Museum
17	Residencial Vera Cruz	2	Instituto Português da	29	Maré Alta
18	Pensão Pão de Açucar		Juventude (IPJ)	30	Club Mau-Mau
19	Pensão Porto Rico	3	Usit Tagus	31	Mexcal
20	Pensão São Marino	4	Internorte Tickets and Buses	32	Cordoaria Bus Stand
36	Residencial União	5	Lavandaria Olimpica	33	Casa Oriental
40	Pensão Chique	7	Top Tours & American	34	Torre dos Clérigos
45	Residencial Santo		Express	35	Renex Tickets & Buses
	André	8	REDM; AV Minho; Carlos	37	Porto Editora Bookshop
46	Residencial Afonso		Soares Tickets & Buses	38	Telephone Office
51	Pensão Astória	9	Shopping Centre	41	Portocambios Exchange
		10	STCP Kiosk	42	National Tourist Office
PLACES TO EAT		11	Bolhão Market	43	Rodonorte Bus Station
21	Restaurante Romão	12	Main Post Office	47	Rede Expressos Bus Station
22	Café Ancôra Douro	13	Town Hall	48	São Bento Train Station
23	Restaurante A	14	Municipal Tourist Office;	49	STCP Kiosk
	Tasquinha		Tourism Police	50	Sé (cathedral)
39	Café Embaixador	15	Portweb	54	Mcia-Cave
44	Café Majestic	16	Intercontinental Exchange	55	Academia
52	Casa Filha da	24	Santo António Hospital	56	Ryan's Irish Pub
	Mãe Preta	25	Soares dos Reis National	57	Municipal Tourist Office
53	Pub-Petisqueira		Museum	58	Lavandaria São Nicolau
	O Muro	26	Solar do Vinho do Porto	59	Tram Terminus

An exception to the Ribeira's overpriced, touristy eateries is *Pub-Petisqueira O Muro (Muro dos Bacalhoeiros 88)*, with eclectic decor and good *feijoado de marisco* (a rich bean and seafood stew); it's open noon to 2 am daily. *Casa Filha da Mãe Preta (Cais da Ribeira 39)* has Douro views, and main dishes mostly under 2000$00. *Café Majestic (Rua Santa Catarina 112)* is an extravagant Art Nouveau relic with expensive coffees and afternoon teas.

Entertainment
Solar do Vinho do Porto (Rua de Entre Quintas 220) has a huge port-wine list and a terrace with views of the city. It's open to 11.45 pm weekdays, to 10.45 pm Saturday.

Lively pubs in the Ribeira include *Academia (Rua São Jão 80)*, *Ryan's Irish Pub (Rua Infante Dom Henrique 18)* and *Meia-Cave (Praça da Ribeira 6)*.

A newer generation of clubs in the riverfront area called Massarelos, 2km west of the Ribeira, includes *Mexcal* and *Club Mau-Mau* on Rua da Restauração, *Maré Alta* on Rua do Ouro, and *Voice* at Rua do Capitão Eduardo Romero 1.

Getting There & Away
Bus Renex (☎ 222 003 395), with a 24-hour ticket office at Rua das Carmelitas 32,

is the choice for Lisbon and the Algarve. From a terminal at Rua Alexandre Herculano 370, Rede Expressos (☎ 222 006 954) goes all over Portugal. From or near Praceto Régulo Magauanha, off Rua Dr Alfredo Magalhães, REDM (☎ 222 003 152) goes to Braga, AV Minho (☎ 222 006 121) to Viana do Castelo, and Carlos Soares (☎ 222 051 383) to Guimarães. Rodonorte (☎ 222 005 637) departs from its terminal at Rua Ateneu Comércial do Porto 19, mainly to Vila Real and Bragança.

Northern Portugal's main international carrier is Internorte (see the Getting There & Away section of this chapter), whose coaches depart from the booking office (☎ 226 052 420) at Praça da Galiza 96.

Train Most international trains, and all intercidade links, start at Campanhã station, east of the centre. Interregional and regional services depart from either Campanhã or the central São Bento station (bus Nos 34 and 35 run frequently between these two). At São Bento you can book tickets for services from any Porto station; for information call ☎ 225 364 141 between 8 am and 11 pm daily.

Getting Around
Central hubs of Porto's extensive bus system include Jardim da Cordoaria, Praça da

PORTUGAL

Liberdade and São Bento station (Praça Almeida Garrett). Tickets are cheapest from STCP kiosks (eg, opposite São Bento station, and beside Bolhão market) and many newsagents and tobacconists: 90$00 for a short hop, 125$00 to outlying areas or 320$00 for an airport return trip. Tickets bought on the bus are always 180$00. Also available is a 400$00 day pass.

It costs about 600$00 to cross town by taxi.

Work has begun on Porto's own Metro (underground railway), planned to reach Campanhã station, Vila Nova de Gaia and several coastal resorts to the north.

ALONG THE RIO DOURO

The Douro Valley is one of Portugal's scenic highlights, with 200km of expansive panoramas from Porto to the Spanish border. In the upper reaches, port-wine vineyards wrap round every hillside.

The river, tamed by eight dams and locks since the late 1980s, is navigable right across Portugal. Highly recommended is the train journey from Porto to Peso da Régua (2½ hours, about a dozen trains daily), the last 50km clinging to the river's edge; four trains continue daily to Pocinho (4½ hours). Douro Azul (☎ 223 393 950) and other companies run one and two-day river cruises, mostly from March to October. Cyclists and drivers can choose river-hugging roads along either bank, though they're crowded at weekends.

The elegant, detailed colour map *Rio Douro* (600$00) is available from Porto bookshops.

VIANA DO CASTELO

This attractive port at the mouth of the Rio Lima is renowned for its historic old town and its promotion of folk traditions. The town's focal point is **Praça da República**, with its delicate fountain and elegant buildings. Atop **Santa Luzia hill**, the Templo do Sagrado Coração de Jesus offers a grand panorama across the river. A funicular railway climbs the hill 9 am to 6 pm (hourly in the morning, every 30 minutes in the afternoon) from behind the train station.

The Festas de Nossa Senhora da Agonia, held for three days nearest to 20 August, is a large religious and folk festival, with processions, parades, fireworks and more.

The tourist office (☎ 258 822 620) on Rua Hospital Velho has information on festivals and the region in general.

Places to Stay

The tourist office has listings of *private rooms*. A *pousada da juventude* (☎ 258 800 260, Rua da Argaçosa) is about 1km east of the town centre.

Pensão Vianense (☎ 258 823 118, Avenida Conde da Carreira 79) and *Casa de Hóspedes Guerreiro* (☎ 258 822 099, Rua Grande 14) have plain doubles with shared facilities from 5000$00. Doubles with bath (breakfast included) are about 6000$00 at central *Pensão Dolce Vita* (☎ 258 824 860, Rua do Poço 44) and 7500$00 at *Pensão-Restaurant Alambique* (☎ 258 821 364, Rua Manuel Espregueira 86).

Places to Eat

Most pensões have good-value restaurants, open to non-guests too. *A Gruta Snack Bar* (Rua Grande 87) has lunchtime salads for under 500$00.

Adega do Padrinho (Rua Gago Coutinho 162) offers traditional dishes for under 1100$00 per half-portion. Seafood is pricey, but try the cervejaria half of *Os Três Arcos* (Largo João Tomás da Costa 25), with half-portions from 1000$00. *Viana's Restaurante* (Rua Frei Bartolomeu dos Mártires 179), near the fish market, specialises in bacalhau.

Getting There & Away

Half a dozen express coaches go to Braga and to Porto every day (fewer at weekends), with daily express services on to Coimbra and Lisbon. Daily train services run north to Spain and south to Porto and Lisbon.

BRAGA

Crammed with churches, Braga is considered Portugal's religious capital. In the centre is the **Sé**, an elegant cathedral complex. Admission to its treasury museum and several tomb chapels is 300$00.

At Bom Jesus do Monte, a hill-top pilgrimage site 5km from Braga, is the extraordinary **Escadaria do Bom Jesus** stairway, with allegorical fountains, chapels and a superb view. Buses run frequently from Braga to the site, where you can climb the steps or ascend by funicular railway.

During Easter week, huge crowds attend Braga's Holy Week Festival. The tourist office (☎ 253 262 550) on Praça da República can help with accommodation and maps.

Places to Stay

The *pousada da juventude* (☎ 253 616 163, *Rua de Santa Margarida 6*) is a 10-minute walk from the city centre. A bargain in the centre is the *Hotel Francfort* (☎ 253 262 648, *Avenida Central 7*), where well-kept old doubles start at 3500$00. *Casa Santa Zita* (☎ 253 618 331, *Rua São João 20*) is a hostel for pilgrims (and others) with doubles from 4500$00. *Grande Residência Avenida* (☎ 253 609 020, *Avenida da Liberdade 738*) is good value with doubles from 6000$00.

Places to Eat

Lareira do Conde (☎ 253 611 340, *Praça Conde de Agrolongo 56*) specialises in inexpensive grills. Around the corner from the bus station, *Retiro da Primavera* (☎ 253 272 482, *Rua Gabriel Pereira de Castro 100*) has good half-portions for under 900$00. *Casa Grulha* (☎ 253 262 883, *Rua dos Biscaínhos 95*) serves good-value *cabrito assudo* (roast kid, a local speciality). *Taberna do Felix* (☎ 253 617 701, *Praça Velha 17*) has simple, imaginative dishes from 1000$00.

For people-watching over coffee or beer, settle down at *Café Vianna* on Praça da República.

Getting There & Away

Intercidade trains arrive twice daily from Lisbon, Coimbra and Porto, and there are daily connections north to Viana do Castelo and Spain. Daily bus services link Braga to Porto and Lisbon.

PENEDA-GERÊS NATIONAL PARK

This wilderness park along the Spanish border has spectacular scenery and a wide variety of fauna and flora. Portuguese day-trippers and holiday-makers tend to stick to the main villages and camping areas, leaving the rest of the park to hikers.

The park's main centre is **Vila do Gerês** (or Caldas do Gerês, or just Gerês), a sleepy, hot-spring village.

Orientation & Information

Caldas do Gerês' tourist office (☎ 253 391 133) is in the colonnade at the upper end of the village. For park information go round the corner to the park office (☎ 253 390 110).

Other park offices are at Arcos de Valdevez, Montalegre and the head office (☎ 253 203 480) on Avenida António Macedo in Braga. All have a map of the park (530$00) with some roads and tracks (but not trails), and a free English-language booklet on the park's human and natural features.

Activities

Hiking A long-distance footpath is being developed, mostly following traditional roads or tracks between villages where you can stop for the night. Park offices sell map-brochures (300$00) for two sections so far.

Day hikes around Gerês are popular; at weekends and all summer the Miradouro walk from the **Parque do Merendas** (picnic area), above the village, is crowded. A more strenuous option is the old Roman road from Mata do Albergaria (10km up-valley from Gerês by taxi or hitching), past the **Vilarinho das Furnas** reservoir to Campo do Gerês. More distant destinations include **Ermida** and **Cabril**, both with simple accommodation and cafes.

Guided walks are organised by PlanAlto (☎ 253 351 005) at Cerdeira camping ground in Campo do Gerês, and Trote-Gerês (☎ 253 659 860) at Cabril.

Cycling Mountain bikes can be hired from Água Montanha Lazer (☎ 253 391 779) in Rio Caldo, Pensao Carvalho Araújo (☎ 253 391 185) in Gerês, or PlanAlto (see Hiking above).

Horse Riding The national park operates facilities (☎ 253 391 181) from beside its Vidoeiro camping ground, near Gerês. Trote-Gerês (see Hiking earlier) also has horses for rent.

Water Sports Rio Caldo, 8km south of Gerês, is the base for water sports on the Caniçada reservoir. Água Montanha Lazer rents canoes and other boats. For paddling the Salamonde reservoir, Trote-Gerês (see Hiking earlier) rents canoes from its camping ground at Cabril.

Organised Tours

Agência no Gerês (☎ 253 391 141), at the Hotel Universal in Gerês, runs two to 5½-hour minibus trips around the park in summer, for 1000$00 to 2000$00 per person.

PORTUGAL

Places to Stay & Eat

The *pousada da juventude* (☎ 253 351 339) and *Cerdeira Camping Ground* (☎ 253 351 005) at Campo do Gerês make good hiking bases.

Trote-Gerês runs its own *Parque de Campismo Outeiro Alto* (☎ 253 659 860) at Cabril. The park runs a *camping ground* (☎ 253 391 289) 1km north of Gerês at Vidoeiro, and others at Lamas de Mouro and Entre-Ambos-os-Rios.

Gerês has plenty of pensões, though many are block-booked by spa patients in summer.

Try *Pensão da Ponte* (☎ 253 391 121) beside the river, with doubles from 6000/7500$00 without/with bath. At the top of the hill, *Pensão Adelaide* (☎ 253 390 020) has doubles with bath from 7000$00.

Trote-Gerês runs the comfortable *Pousadinha de Paradela* (☎ 276 566 165) in Paradela, with doubles from 5000$00.

Most Gerês pensões serve hearty meals to guests and non-guests. There are several restaurants, plus shops in the main street for picnic provisions.

The Cerdeira Camping Ground at Campo do Gerês has a good-value *restaurant*.

Getting There & Away

From Braga, 10 coaches daily run to Rio Caldo and Gerês, and seven to Campo do Gerês (fewer at weekends). Coming from Lisbon or Porto, change at Braga.

Romania

A country where mass tourism means you, a horse and cart and a handful of farmers, Romania *is* the Wild West of Eastern Europe. With its medieval castles, frescoed monasteries and quaint farming villages, this country really is an unexpected delight. Much of its charm comes from being a developing nation, struggling to catch up with the West since communism's collapse, yet retaining many ancient customs. This results in certain inconveniences and inefficiencies; yet most of our readers' letters declare Romania to be the most exciting, best-value destination in Eastern Europe.

AT A GLANCE

Capital:	Bucharest
Population:	22.4 million
Official Language:	Romanian
Currency:	1 leu = 100 bani

Facts about Romania

HISTORY

Ancient Romania was inhabited by Thracian tribes, more commonly known as the Dacians. In the 1st century BC, a Dacian state was established to counter the advance of Roman legions north of the Danube. The last Dacian king, Decebalus, consolidated this state but was unable to prevent the Roman conquest in AD 105-6.

Faced with Goth attacks in AD 271, Emperor Aurelian withdraw the Roman legions south of the Danube, but the Romanised Vlach peasants remained in Dacia. From the 10th century the Magyars swept into Transylvania; by the 13th century it was under the Hungarian crown.

In the 14th and 15th centuries the Romanian-speaking principalities of Wallachia and Moldavia offered strong resistance to the Ottomans' northern expansion. Vlad Ţepeş (the Impaler) and Ştefan cel Mare (the Great) became legendary figures in this struggle, the former being legendary not only for the Turks he impaled on wooden stakes but for providing the inspiration for Bram Stoker's Count Dracula. Vlad, who ruled as prince of Wallachia in 1456-62 and 1476-77, was not a vampire but simply named Dracula (meaning 'son of the dragon') after his father, Vlad Dracul.

When the Turks conquered Hungary in the 16th century, Transylvania became a vassal of the Ottoman Empire. In 1600 the three Romanian states – Transylvania, Wallachia and Moldavia – were briefly united under Michael Viteazul (the Brave). In 1687 Transylvania fell under Habsburg rule; Turkish suzerainty persisted in Wallachia and Moldavia well into the 19th century.

After the Russian defeat in the Crimean War (1853-56), Romanian nationalism grew and in 1859 Alexandru Ioan Cuza was elected to the thrones of Moldavia and Wallachia, creating a national state, which took the name Romania in 1862.

In 1916 Romania entered WWI on the side of the Triple Entente (Britain, France and Russia) with the objective of taking Transylvania – where 60% of the population was Romanian – from Austria-Hungary. The latter was defeated in 1918 and the unification of Romania was at last achieved.

In June 1941 the country's fascist dictator, General Ion Antonescu, joined Hitler's anti-Soviet war. The results were gruesome: 400,000 Romanian Jews and 36,000 Roma (Gypsies) were murdered at Auschwitz and other camps. (After the war Antonescu was executed as a war criminal.) On 23 August 1944 Romania suddenly changed sides, captured 53,159 German soldiers, and declared war on Nazi Germany. By this act, Romania salvaged its independence and shortened WWII.

After the war, the Soviet-engineered return of Transylvania enhanced the prestige of local communist parties: in 1947 the

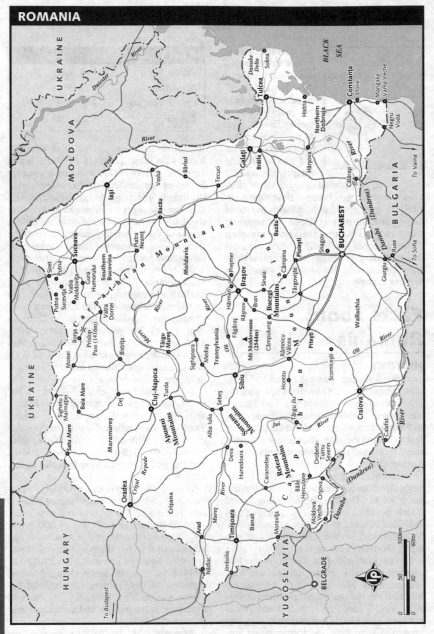

ROMANIA

monarchy was abolished and the Romanian People's Republic proclaimed. Soviet troops withdrew in 1958 and after 1960 Romania adopted an independent foreign policy under Gheorghe Gheorghiu-Dej (ruled 1952-65) and Nicolae Ceauşescu (1965-89).

Ceauşescu's domestic policy was chaotic and megalomaniacal. In November 1987 workers rioted in Braşov and in winter 1988-89 the country suffered its worst food shortages in decades. On 17 December 1989 a huge crowd on Timişoara's Blvd 30 Decembrie (now Piaţa Victoriei) was confronted by the Securitate (secret police) and army troops. Similar clashes in Bucharest prompted Ceauşescu and his wife (and partner-in-crime) Elena to flee by helicopter on 22 December. The couple were consequently arrested and, on Christmas Day, executed by a firing squad.

In 1990 a new constitution was ratified and elections in September were won by the left-wing National Salvation Front (FSN). Romania's first president, Ion Iliescu, was ousted by Emil Constantinescu of the reform-minded Democratic Convention of Romania (CDR) in 1996 presidential elections. Internal party bickering hampered promised reforms, leading to anti-government demonstrations and the forced resignation of Prime Minister Victor Ciorba in early 1998. During Radul Vasile's nine months in office as prime minister, harsh – yet effective – free-market reforms were made, including the controversial closure of some of Romania's loss-making coal mines in the Jiu Valley. Following Vasile's dismissal in December 1999, Constantinescu appointed Mugur Isărescu prime minister of the ruling coalition. Parliamentary and presidential elections were due to be held in November 2000.

Romania joined the Council of Europe in 1993, started accession talks with the European Union (EU) in March 2000 (of which it hopes to become a full member by 2007-10), and is slated to join NATO in 2002.

GEOGRAPHY

Covering 237,500 sq km, oval-shaped Romania is larger than Hungary and Bulgaria combined. The Danube River drains the whole country. Mt Moldoveanu (2544m), of the Făgăraş range in the U-shaped Carpathian Mountains, is the highest point.

CLIMATE

The average annual temperature is 11°C in the south and on the coast, but only 2°C in the mountains. Romanian winters are famously harsh, cold and snowy from mid-December to mid-April.

POPULATION & PEOPLE

Romania has a population of 22.4 million; 87% are Romanian Orthodox. Bucharest is the largest city, followed by Constanţa, Iaşi, Timişoara, Galaţi, Braşov, Cluj-Napoca and Craiova.

The government estimates that 400,000 Roma live in Romania, but a more accurate figure would be two million, making it the world's largest Roma community. The Roma have their own member of parliament but anti-Roma sentiment remains strong. For decades the situation of the 1.6 million Hungarians in Romania has soured relations with Hungary.

LANGUAGE

Romanian is closer to classical Latin than other Romance languages – speakers of Italian, Spanish and French should be able to understand some Romanian. This is one Eastern European country where Russian won't get you very far. Lots of younger people in Bucharest and larger cities speak English; countrywide some older people speak French. Beyond that, in Romania's rural heart, scarcely any English is spoken.

See the Language Guide at the back of this book for useful words and pronunciation guidelines.

Facts for the Visitor

HIGHLIGHTS

Bran Castle near Braşov is on everyone's 'must-see' list, but don't ignore neigbouring Râşnov Castle, Bucharest's Palace of Parliament or the Village Museum, also in the capital. Peleş Castle in Sinaia is among Eastern Europe's finest royal pads. Romania's best-preserved medieval towns – notably Braşov and Sighişoara – are in Transylvania.

SUGGESTED ITINERARIES

Two days
  Visit Braşov, Bran and Sinaia.

ROMANIA

One week

as above, plus Sighişoara and perhaps Cluj-Napoca. Southbound travellers should add a day in Bucharest.

Two weeks

Visit Bucharest, Braşov, Sinaia, Bran/Râşnov, Sighişoara and Bucovina's painted monasteries.

PLANNING
Maps

For maps, contact a Romanian National Tourist Office abroad. In Romania, there is at least one bookshop in every large town that stocks quality city and country maps published by Bucharest map-makers, Amco Press, or Budapest's Dimap. Street names in Romania are prone to change.

TOURIST OFFICES
Local Tourist Offices

Romania has no national tourist office network. In Bucharest, some travel agencies double as tourist offices. Elsewhere there are efficient, independently run tourist information centres, including in Predeal, Poiana Braşov and Arad.

Tourist Offices Abroad

Romania's National Authority for Tourism (☎ 1-410 12 62, ☻ turism@kappa.ro) runs a string of tourist offices abroad (Web site: www.turism.ro).

UK (☎ 20-7224 3692, fax 7935 6435, ☻ uktourff@romania.freeserve.co.uk) 22 New Cavendish Street, London W1M 7LH

USA (☎ 212-545 84 84, fax 251 04 29, ☻ ronto@erols.com) 14 East 38th St, 12th Floor, New York, NY 10016

VISAS & DOCUMENTS

American citizens may travel visa-free for 30 days. All other Western visitors require a visa. Single-entry visas (US$35 to US$50) are valid for 30 days; EU and Canadian citizens can buy one at the border for US$33 (payable in any currency). Single-entry (US$35 to US$38) and double-entry (US$35 to US$50) transit visas are only available from Romania embassies abroad. Australians and New Zealanders are advised to buy visas prior to departure from their home country.

Upon entering the country, fill in an entry form *(talon de intrare)* and retain the bottom half *(talon de ieisire)* to show when you exit the country.

EMBASSIES & CONSULATES
Romanian Embassies & Consulates Abroad

Australia (☎ 02-6286 2343, fax 6286 2433, ☻ roembcbr@cyberone.com.au) 4 Dalman Crescent, O'Malley, ACT 2606 Canberra

Canada (☎ 613-789 5345, fax 613-789 4365, ☻ romania@cyberus.ca) 655 Rideau St, Ottawa, Ontario K1N 6A3

UK (☎ 020-7937 9666, fax 7937 8069, ☎/fax 7937 4675, ☻ romania@roemb.demon.co.uk) 4 Palace Green, London W8 4QD

USA (☎ 202-387 6902, 332 4846, fax 232 4748, ☻ consular@roembus.org) 1607 23rd Street NW, Washington DC 20008; (☎ 212-682 9120, fax 972 8463, ☻ mail@romconsny.org) *consulate:* 200 East 38th Street, New York, NY 10016; (☎ 310-444 0043, fax 445 0043, ☻ consulat@romanian.org) *consulate:* 11766 Wilshire Blvd, 1230, Los Angeles, CA 90025

Embassies & Consulates in Romania

The following embassies and consulates are all in Bucharest (area code ☎ 01).

Australia (☎ 320 98 02) Blvd Unirii 74
Canada (☎ 222 98 45) Str Nicolae Iorga 36
UK
   Embassy: (☎ 312 03 03/04/05, ☻ britemb@dnt.ro) Str Jules Michelet 24
   Consulate: (☎ 210 46 57, 210 49 90)
USA
   Embassy: (☎ 210 40 42) Str Tudor Arghezi 7-9
   Consulate: (☎ 210 40 42) Str Nicolae Filipescu 26

MONEY

The unit of currency is the Romanian leu (plural: lei). There are coins of 50, 100 and 500 lei and banknotes of 1000, 5000, 10,000, 50,000 and 100,000 lei. Because of high inflation, prices in this chapter are listed in US$ (rounded to the nearest dollar). In Romania, you must pay for everything in lei.

Currency exchanges are plentiful in towns and cities, and a rarity in the countryside. You can change travellers cheques (into dollars or lei) and get Visa and MasterCard cash advances (in lei only) for a 1.5% to 3% commission at most branches of Banca Comercială Română and Banca Ion Ţiriac. ATM machines giving 24-hour advances (Cirrus,

Plus, Visa, MasterCard, Eurocard) are abundant in the capital and major cities; in Bucharest, there is an ATM at Otopeni airport and Gara de Nord train station.

Exchange receipts are required to change excess lei back into hard currency. Changing money on the street is illegal, risky and the quickest way to end up being ripped off. Don't do it.

Exchange Rates

country	unit		leu
Australia	A$1	=	12,989 lei
Canada	C$1	=	15,279 lei
euro	€1	=	20,383 lei
France	10FF	=	31,074 lei
Germany	DM1	=	10,422 lei
Japan	¥100	=	21,238 lei
NZ	NZ$1	=	9755 lei
UK	UK£1	=	33,675 lei
USA	US$1	=	22,727 lei

POST & COMMUNICATIONS

The Romanian postal service is improving, but still slow and unreliable. Stamps *(timbre)* are sold at post offices. Post-restante mail can be collected at Bucharest's main post office at Str Matei Millo 10.

Romania's country code is ☎ 40. When dialling in from abroad, drop the initial zero from city area codes. To use one of the orange-coloured RomTelecom cardphones for local, regional or international calls, buy a magnetic phonecard *(cartela telefonică)* at any telex-fax or post office. Only cards worth 50,000 lei (about $2.50) are available. To exchange a spent card mid-way through a call, press the button labelled 'K', then insert a new card.

Cybercafes are abundant in Bucharest where you can access the Internet 24 hours a day for $1.50 to $2 per hour. Elsewhere, there's at least one Internet cafe in every town.

INTERNET RESOURCES

Breaking news, views and local press digests feature on the Central European Web site, found at www.centraleurope.com /romaniatoday. Locally-published city guide *Bucharest In Your Pocket* posts its entire contents for free at www.inyourpocket.com.

The most interactive site around is RomaniaBYNET at www.romaniaBYNET .com – it has chat rooms, e-cards, hyperlinks to radio stations in Romania with

Internet relay, the best of Romanian pop music, etc.

BOOKS

Lonely Planet's guide to *Romania & Moldova* provides in-depth coverage. *A History of Romania,* edited by Kurt Treptow, is a comprehensive history; also available on CD-ROM. *Athene Palace* by RG Waldeck is a memoir of Bucharest's grand hotel and the political intrigues which filled its lobby prior to WWII. Dracula fiends should indulge in Kurt Treptow's *Vlad III Dracula: The Life and Times of the Historical Dracula.*

WOMEN TRAVELLERS

Romania is generally a safe place for women, although the usual rules apply: do not wander alone late at night; avoid sitting in empty compartments on long-distance and overnight trains, etc. If you should encounter offensive behaviour, a few strong words – such as shouting *poliţia!* – is usually sufficient to ward off trouble.

GAY & LESBIAN TRAVELLERS

In June 2000, article 200 of Romania's penal code was amended to decriminalise homosexual relations conducted in private. Showing affection in public, however, remains a criminal offence for gays and lesbians in Romania, who can still be thrown in jail for five years for holding hands, kissing or indulging in any other public act which demonstrates a homosexual relationship. The Orthodox Church considers homosexuality a sin, and a surprising number of young Romanians feel that gay and lesbian relationships are 'unnatural'. Hotel managers might turn away openly gay couples, so be discreet if you're travelling with a same-sex partner.

Bucharest is the only city in Romania to have an active gay and lesbian community, represented by ACCEPT (☎ 01-252 16 37, fax 252 56 20, ✆ accept@fx.ro), CP 34-56, Bucharest. Web site: accept.ong.ro.

DANGERS & ANNOYANCES

Bucharest has a serious stray dog problem – a bizarre legacy of systemisation in the 1980s when scores of city-centre homes were demolished, forcing dog-owners to let their pets loose on the streets. Most dogs roaming the city centre are harmless if left alone; bitches with puppies can be snappy.

Street scams are rife. Beware of anyone stopping you on the street and asking if you want to change money. Say no, walk away and keep calm if a second man suddenly appears, arrests the first, and demands to see your passport and/or wallet. Under no circumstances hand over either. If he flashes ID and refuses to leave you alone, insist on being accompanied to the nearest police station – on foot (taking a taxi with a thief is not a good idea). This usually sends them scampering.

Never accept a ride with anyone at Bucharest's Gara de Nord train station who claims to be from the Villa Helga; hostel staff do not meet guests at the station.

BUSINESS HOURS

Banking hours are 9 am to 2 or 3 pm weekdays. Most shops and markets close on Sunday. Many museums close on Monday. Shops are open 9 am to midday and 2 pm to 5 or 6 pm.

PUBLIC HOLIDAYS & SPECIAL EVENTS

Public holidays are New Year (1 and 2 January), Easter Monday (March/April), National Unity Day (1 December) and Christmas (25 and 26 December).

Many festivals take place in summer, including the three-day Bucharest carnival in June and the Golden Stag international pop music festival in Braşov in July. In September there's Sibiu's Cibinium music festival and, in October, Cluj-Napoca's Musical Autumn.

ACCOMMODATION

Camp sites with bungalows are called *popas turisticas*. Many sites are unkempt and lack toilets and/or showers. Most open from around May to September.

In mountainous areas there's a network of cabins *(cabana)* with restaurants and dormitories. Reservations are not required, but arrive early to bag a bed. Many open year-round and cater for skiers in winter.

Romania has several accredited HI hostels – including in Bucharest. The hostels in Cluj-Napoca and Sighişoara are student dorms and only open in summer. Outside the capital, private rooms costing $10 to $20 per person are widely available; landladies often meet you at train stations.

Romanian hotels are rated on a star system. One-star hotels, while generally clean, often have shared baths and toilet, and charge $10 to $25 per person. Two-star hotels charge around $30 per person; rooms have TV and private bath. Some hotels include breakfast *(mic dejun)* in the price.

FOOD & DRINKS

Romanian restaurants are affordable; outside Bucharest, it is hard to spend more than $15 per day on food. Always have a look at the menu, even a menu in Romanian, to check how prices are listed; dishes priced per 100g should be treated with caution.

Romanian favourites include *ciorbă de perişoare* (a spicy soup made with meatballs and vegetables), *ciorbă de burtă* (tripe soup), *ghiveci* (vegetable stew), *tocană* (onion and meat stew) and *ciorbă de legumă* (vegetable soup often cooked with meat stock). Restaurants and beer gardens often offer *mititei* or *mici* (pronounced 'meech'; grilled meatballs). Other common dishes are *muşchi de vacă/porc/miel* (cutlet of beef/pork/lamb), *ficat* (liver), *piept de pui* (chicken breast) and *cabanos prăjit* (fried sausages). Vegetarians should plump for a non-meaty *caşcaval pane* (breaded fried cheese) or *castraveţi* (tomato and cucumber salad). Cooking styles include grilled *(la grătar)*, fried *(prăjit)*, boiled *(fiert)* and roasted on a spit *(la frigare)*. Almost every dish comes with *cartofi* (potatoes) or *orez* (rice).

Folk dishes are harder to find but delicious, especially *ardei umpluţi* (stuffed peppers) and *sarmale* (cabbage or vine leaves stuffed with spiced meat and rice). *Mămăligă* is a cornmeal polenta that goes well with everything. Typical desserts include *plăcintă* (turnovers), *paturi cu brinză* (cheese pastries), *clătite* (pancakes) and *papănaşi* (a curd tartlet).

Local Romanian beer is notable for its low price (about $0.75 for a half-litre). Red wines are called *negru* and *roşu*, while white wine is *vin alb*. A bottle of decent Romanian wine shouldn't cost more than $4 ($10 in Bucharest). *Must* is a fresh unfermented wine available during the wine harvest. *Ţuică* (plum brandy) is a strong liqueur drunk at the start of a meal. A couple of toasts are *poftă bună* (bon appétit) and *noroc!* (cheers!).

Beware of *Ness*, an instant coffee made from vegetable extracts, served super sweet and tepid. Proper cafes serve *cafea filtru* (filtered coffee) and espresso (but don't get your hopes up). Unless you specifically ask, coffee and *ceai* (tea) are almost never served *cu lapte* (with milk). *Apă minerală* (mineral water) is cheap and widely available.

Getting There & Away

AIR
Romania's state-owned carrier TAROM operates weekly flights between Bucharest's Otopeni airport and most European capitals – including Amsterdam, Berlin, Budapest, Prague, Warsaw and Zagreb – and to/from Düsseldorf, Frankfurt, Milan, Chicago, New York and Tel Aviv.

TAROM offers special youth fares to people aged up to 25 on its European and transatlantic flights, and aged up to 24 on its weekly flights to/from Tel Aviv. Youth tickets are valid for one year and subject to no restrictions. Students aged 24 to 31 years are eligible for youth fares too.

For information, contact TAROM in Britain (☎ 020-7935 3600, fax 7487 2913), 27 New Cavendish Street, London, W1M 7RL; or in the USA (☎ 212-687 6014, fax 661 6056), 342 Madison Ave, Suite 168, New York 10173. The Web site is at tarom.digiro.net.

BUS
Although many private bus companies operate daily buses between Western Europe and Romania, it is more comfortable and faster to travel by train. The exception is travel between Bucharest and Istanbul, where the bus is substantially faster (11 to 14 hours), although it is only slighter cheaper ($20/40 single/return) than the train. There are four to eight buses every day to/from İstanbul.

Numerous private bus companies operate daily buses between Germany (from where there are connections to the rest of Western Europe) and Romania. Tickets are sold from ticketing agencies in Romania's larger cities; these are listed in the relevant Getting There & Away sections.

TRAIN
International train tickets are sold at CFR offices – look for the 'Agenţie de Voiaj CFR' signs – and at larger train stations like Bucharest's central station, Gara de Nord. Even if you are travelling on a rail pass you still need a seat reservation ($2 to $4), included in tickets purchased in Romania.

Major trains to/from Romania include the *Pannonia Expres* from Munich, Vienna, Prague, Bratislava and Budapest; the *Carpaţi* from Warsaw via Kraków, Sibiu and Braşov; and the *Dacia Expres* from Vienna and Budapest. The trip between Budapest and Bucharest takes 12 hours.

The *Bucureşti Expres* shuttles every day between Bucharest-Gara de Nord and Belgrade-Dunav (13 hours), via Timişoara. The *România Expres* runs to/from Moscow, via Chişinău and Kyiv (28 hours). There are two trains a day between Bucharest and Sofia; while the overnight Bucureşti-Istanbul express (called *Bosor*) crosses eastern Bulgaria.

Sample 2nd-class single fares to/from Bucharest, including a bed in a six-bunk couchette, include Budapest ($30), Belgrade ($23) and Sofia ($38).

CAR & MOTORCYCLE
Drivers need vehicle registration papers, liability insurance and a driving licence. Make sure your car is in good condition and carry a petrol can, oil and basic spares. Car rental is expensive. Expect long queues at Romanian border checkpoints, particularly on weekends. Beware of unauthorised people charging dubious 'ecology', 'disinfectant' or other dodgy taxes at the border; ask for a receipt.

BOAT
There are passenger and car ferries year-round into Bulgaria from Calafat and Giurgiu in Romania.

Getting Around

BUS
Romania's buses are less reliable and more crowded than its trains, and on rural routes only one or two buses may run daily. Schedules posted in bus stations are often incomplete and out of date, so always check

at the ticket window. Purchase your ticket at a bus station *(autogară)* before boarding.

TRAIN

Inter-Rail (not Eurail) passes are valid in Romania. Căile Ferate Române (CFR; Romanian State Railways) posts its train timetable on its Web site: www.cfr.ro.

There are four types of trains: slow locals *(personal)* and three expresses *(accelerat, rapid* and *inter-city* or *IC)*. On express trains you pay a supplement of $0.50 to $3 for the required seat reservation.

First-class express is approximately double the price of 2nd class. At major stations there are separate ticket halls or windows for 1st and 2nd class; queues are shorter in 1st-class. Irrespective of class, fares are low: it costs about $0.85 to travel 100km in 1st class on a local train and $2.95 to travel the equivalent in 2nd class on an express.

If possible, buy tickets a day in advance at a CFR office. Note that CFR offices do not sell tickets for express trains leaving the same day; in this case you must buy a ticket at the station *no more than one hour* before departure. Tickets list the code number of your train along with your assigned *vagon* (carriage) and *locul* (seat).

CAR & MOTORCYCLE

Romania has two short stretches of *autostradă* (motorway), linking Bucharest-Ploieşti (114km) and Cernavodă-Piteşti (15km); the latter is a toll road. Some major roads *(drum naţional)* have been resurfaced but most are pot-holed and irregularly signposted. Many have no markings and are unlit at night – as are many vehicles.

The speed limit for cars is 60km/h in built-up areas or 80km/h on the open road. Motorbikes are limited to 60km/h in built-up areas and 70km/h on the open road. Drink driving is severely punished in Romania; the blood alcohol limit is 0.01%.

Western-grade petrol *(benzină)* and diesel *(motorină)* are the norm, including unleaded 95-octane *(fără plumb* or *benzină verde)*, premium and super (96-98 octane). Members of major automobile clubs (such as AA and AAA) are covered by Romania's Automobil Clubul Român (ACR) which has a Web site at www.acr.ro. In the event of a breakdown, call ACR's 24-hour emergency service number (☎ 927).

Bucharest

☎ 01

Tree-lined boulevards, park-girdled lakes and pompous public monuments give Bucharest (Bucureşti, pop 2.2 million) a smooth Parisian flavour. During the 1980s Romania's capital was transformed by President Nicolae Ceauşescu, with his House of the People as its centrepiece. The revolution of December 1989 put an end to its Stalinist makeover, yet reminders of the Ceauşescu era remain – from ugly Soviet-style apartments to half-built buildings and stray dogs.

Yet, on a fast-track to recovery since the mid-1990s, Bucharest's greatest and grandest old edifices have been restored and fashionable new shops, restaurants and night spots are mushrooming. The city is at its best in spring, when relaxed crowds fill its beer gardens and parks.

Orientation

Bucharest's main train station, Gara de Nord, is a few kilometres north-west of the centre, conveniently connected by metro to the central stations of Piaţa Victoriei and Piaţa Unirii. The main boulevard (and the north-south metro line) runs between Piaţa Victoria, Piaţa Romană, Piaţa Universităţii and Piaţa Unirii and changes its name three times.

Information

Tourist Offices Bucharest has no tourist office. Try a privately run travel agency such as Contact Tour (☎ 211 09 79, @ contour@fx.ro), Blvd Dacia 45 or Nova Tours (☎ 315 13 57, @ Nova.Tour@snmail.softnet.ro), Blvd Nicolae Bălcescu 21.

Money Currency exchanges dot the length of Blvd Nicolae Bălcescu. Capitol Exchange at No 34 and Alliance Exchange at No 30 are open 24 hours. There are many ATMs around town which accept Visa and MasterCard, including at Otopeni airport; next to IDM Exchange at Gara de Nord; and outside the CFR office at Str Domniţa Anastasia 10-14.

Banca Comercială Română, opposite the university at Blvd Regina Elisabeta 5, cashes travellers cheques and gives cash advances on credit cards. It has two ATMs outside, as does its branch office at Calea Victoriei 155.

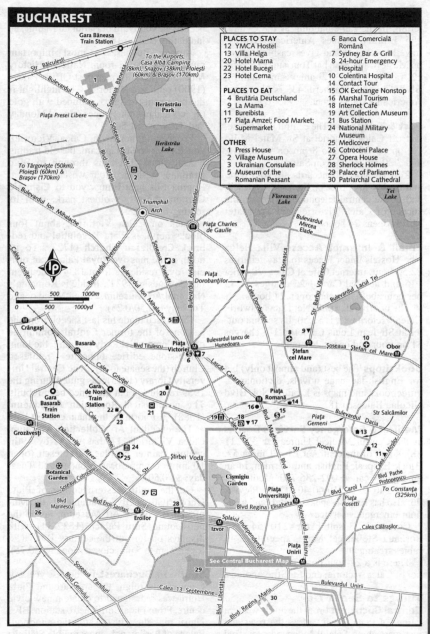

BUCHAREST

PLACES TO STAY
12 YMCA Hostel
13 Villa Helga
20 Hotel Marna
22 Hotel Bucegi
23 Hotel Cerna

PLACES TO EAT
4 Brutăria Deutschland
9 La Mama
11 Bureibista
17 Piaţa Amzei; Food Market; Supermarket

OTHER
1 Press House
2 Village Museum
3 Ukrainian Consulate
5 Museum of the Romanian Peasant

6 Banca Comercială Română
7 Sydney Bar & Grill
8 24-hour Emergency Hospital
10 Colentina Hospital
14 Contact Tour
15 OK Exchange Nonstop
16 Marshal Tourism
18 Internet Café
19 Art Collection Museum
21 Bus Station
24 National Military Museum
25 Medicover
26 Cotroceni Palace
27 Opera House
28 Sherlock Holmes
29 Palace of Parliament
30 Patriarchal Cathedral

Bank Austria Creditanstalt, Calea Victoriei 88, in the same building as the Central Uni Library, cashes American Express travellers cheque and gives cash advances on MasterCard. Marshal Tourism (☎ 659 68 12, fax 223 12 03, ✆ amex@marshal.ro), Blvd General Magheru 43, is the local American Express agent.

Post & Telephone The central post office, just off Calea Victoriei at Str Matei Millo 10, opens 7.30 am to 8 pm on weekdays, and 7.30 am to 2 pm on Saturday.

RomTelecom phonecards are sold here, at the telex-fax office on Str Tache Ionescu, and at the central telephone office, on the corner of Calea Victoriei and Str Matei Millo (opens 24 hours).

Email & Internet Access Villa Helga (see Hostels under Places to Stay) charges $2.50/hour. Internet Café at Calea Victoriei 136 and at Blvd Carol I 25 charges $1.85 per hour; both branches open 24 hours.

The hourly rate at PC-Net Data Network, Calea Victoriei 25, is $1.50. Its second outlet at Str Jean Louis Calderon 1-5 charges $1 an hour and opens 24 hours.

Bookshops The best (and almost only) bet for English-language novels, dictionaries, guidebooks and maps is Librăria Noi, Blvd Nicolae Bălcescu 18.

Medical & Emergency Services Doctors at the Centrul Medical Unirea (☎ 327 11 88), south of the centre at Blvd Unirea 57, Block E, speak English and German; in an emergency call ☎ 092-286 770. Medicover (☎ 310 40 66 or 310 40 40), Calea Plevnei 96, also has English-speaking staff and a 24-hour emergency service.

Colentina Hospital (☎ 210 54 85), Şoseaua Ştefan cel Mare, specialises in rabies treatments.

There is a 24-hour pharmacy on the corner of Calea Victoriei and Str Stravopoleos.

Things to See & Do

Central Bucharest From the north-western corner of Piaţa Unirii, across the river and just west along Splaiul Independenţei, find narrow Str Şelari. Enter the old city on this street and view the ruins of Vlad Ţepeş' **Old Court** and Bucharest's oldest church (1546)

on Str Franceză. Cross the street and drink a beer in the courtyard of **Hanul lui Manuc**, an inn dating back to 1808.

Among Bucharest's most important museums is the 41-room **National History Museum**, in the former Post Office Palace (1900) on Calea Victoriei. The highlight is the basement treasury, crammed with gold objects and precious stones (closed Monday and Tuesday; $1.50).

Proceeding north on Calea Victoriei, you'll come to **Str Lipscani**, the old trading bazaar street that runs through to Blvd Brătianu. A short detour west along Blvd Regina Elisabeta brings you to **Cişmigiu Garden**, the city's oldest park, with its rowing-boat lake.

Back on Calea Victoriei, about four blocks north, is **Piaţa Revoluţiei** and red-brick **Creţulescu Church** (1722). To its north is the massive **Royal Palace**, an official royal residence from 1834 (its current facade dates to 1937). Inside is Romania's **National Art Museum**, closed Monday and Tuesday ($0.50/0.25).

Ceauşescu made his last speech from the balcony of the former **Central Committee of the Communist Party** building, the long, white-stone edifice opposite Creţulescu Church (the senate today). The **Central University Library** (1895) was gutted during the 1989 revolution but has since been rebuilt. The neoclassical **Romanian Athenaeum** (1888), just north, is the main concert hall.

The excellent **Art Collection Museum**, Calea Victoriei 111, has works by 19th-century painter Nicolae Grigorescu (open 10 am to 6 pm, closed Monday and Tuesday; $1/0.50).

On the south-western corner of Piaţa Universităţii at Blvd Brătianu 2 is the **Municipal History & Art Museum**, inside the neo-Gothic Şuţu Palace (1832-34), with displays on turn-of-the-century Bucharest (open 9 am to 5 pm, closed Monday; $0.75).

Southern Bucharest In the last years of Ceauşescu's reign, the area around **Piaţa Unirii** was redesigned to create a new civic centre. From Piaţa Unirii metro station, Blvd Unirii runs directly towards the enormous **Palace of Parliament**, an incredible Stalinist structure that was still unfinished when Ceauşescu was overthrown in 1989. Three shifts of 20,000 workers toiled for over five years to build what is the second-largest building in the world (after the US Pentagon). Today it houses Romania's parliament. Seven of its 3100 furnished rooms can be visited as part of a 45-minute guided tour in English (☎ 311 36 11, @ cic@cic.camera.ro), every 10 minutes between 10 am and 4 pm ($1.50). The entrance is on the southern side along Calea 12 Septembrie.

Northern Bucharest Walk, or take the metro, to Piaţa Victoriei to view Romania's largest collection of folklore treasures in the **Museum of the Romanian Peasant**, Şoseaua Kiseleff 3 (open 10 am to 6 pm, closed Monday; $1/0.25). From here, walk along tree-lined **Şoseaua Kiseleff** or take the metro north-west to Piaţa Charles de Gaulle, then walk 500m west to the **Triumphal Arch** (1936), a deliberate replica of Paris' Arc de Triomphe.

A short walk north is one of Bucharest's best sights, the **Village Museum**, with full-scale displays of nearly 300 churches, wooden houses and farm buildings, first assembled here in 1936 in a rich mixture of styles (closed Monday in winter; $1.50). It is surrounded by **Herăstrău Park**, with lush gardens and a lake.

Places to Stay

Camping In Băneasa, *Casa Albă* (☎ 230 52 03, ☎/fax 230 62 55, Aleea Privighetorilor 1-3) is a restaurant with adjoining camp site, open from mid-April to October. A two-bed wooden hut costs $15; or negotiate a fee to pitch your tent. Take bus No 301 from Piaţa Romană to Şoseaua Bucureşti-Ploieşti; get off at the stop after Băneasa airport and head east along Aleea Privighetorilor. Bus No 783 to/from Otopeni airport also stops here.

Hostels Clean and friendly, 32-bed *Villa Helga* (☎/fax 610 22 14, @ helga@rotravel.com, Str Salcâmilor 2) provides a dorm bed, breakfast, kitchen facilities, free laundry and locally produced Carpaţi cigarettes for $12/72 a night/week. It's in the centre, east of Piaţa Romană. Take bus No 79 or 133 from Gara de Nord for six stops to Piaţa Gemini or bus No 783 from Otopeni airport to Piaţa Română, then walk or take bus No 79, 86, 133 or 126 two stops east along Blvd Dacia to Piaţa Gemini. The hostel is open 24 hours.

Around the corner, the *YMCA* (☎/fax 210 09 09, Str Silvestru 33) also has a hostel with shared rooms and kitchen access for $12 a night. From Gara de Nord take bus No 133 or 123, or trolleybus No 26 to Moşilor station. Reception hours are 2 pm to 6 pm, but it's best to call first.

Hotels – Around Gara de Nord Exit the station and walk 30m right to the noisy, but surprisingly clean, *Hotel Bucegi* (☎ 637 52 25, fax 637 51 15, Str Witing 2). Singles with shared bath cost $10, doubles without/with bath cost $13/20, and triples/quads with bathroom are a steal at $15/20.

Across the street, renovated *Hotel Cerna* (☎ 637 40 87, Blvd Golescu 29) charges $12/16 for a single/double ($20/32 with bath).

Cheerful *Hotel Marna* (☎ 650 68 20, fax 312 94 55, Str Buzeşti 3) is perhaps the best of this bunch, with a welcoming reception. Basic singles/doubles cost $14/19, including breakfast.

Hotels – City Centre *Hotel Carpaţi* (☎ 315 01 40, fax 312 18 57, Str Matei Millo 16) is Bucharest's most aesthetically pleasing budget option. Renovated singles with shared bath cost $11 and doubles with private shower *or* toilet cost $27; some have a balcony.

Hotel Muntenia (☎ 314 60 10, 314 17 84, fax 314 17 82, Str Academiei 19-21) is noisy but has a great location near the university. It costs $14.50/24 for a single/double ($32 for doubles with shower) and $40/43 for a triple/quad.

Downtrodden but quiet *Hotel Dâmboviţa* (☎ 315 62 44, Blvd Schitu Măgureanu 6) touts singles/doubles for $10/16 ($16 for singles with shower).

Places to Eat

Open-air markets with fruit and veg include Piaţa Amzei, between Calea Victoriei and Blvd General Magheru; and Piaţa Gemeni, spitting distance from Villa Helga. *Unic* and *Vox Maris* supermarkets are both on Piaţa Amzei. The German-style bakery *Brutăria Deutschland (Piaţa Dorobanţi and Str Edgar Quinet 5)* bakes the best bread in town. *Stalls* selling *covrigi* (rings of hard bread speckled with salt crystals) and other munch-while-you-walk snacks are easy to find in central Bucharest.

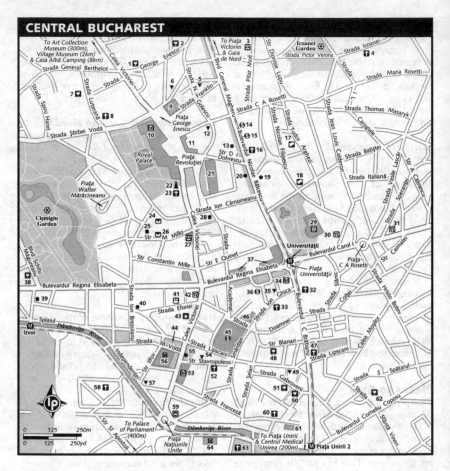

CENTRAL BUCHAREST

Hefty portions of munch-worthy Romanian cuisine are dished up for delicious prices at *Tipsy* (see Entertainment, later in this chapter); and at *La Mama* (☎ 212 40 86, Str Barbu Văcărescu 3), a contemporary spot north of the centre. Salads/main dishes cost $1/2.50, making advance reservations essential.

Cheap and cheerful spots within walking distance of the hostels are *Bureibista* (☎ 210 9704, Calea Moșilor 26) and *Nicorești* (☎ 211 24 80, Str Maria Rosetti 40). Dine at either for $2.

In the centre, *Bistro Atheneu* (☎ 313 49 00, Str Episcopiei 3) is an old favourite. Its high-quality food, French-inspired atmosphere and serenading musicians draw large crowds. Salads/mains average $2.50/5.

Jars of pickled gherkins and vibrant Transylvanian fabrics lend *Boema* (☎ 315 72 98, Str Rosetti 10) a rustic feel. Nearby, *Menuet* (☎ 312 0143, Str Nicolae Golescu 14) dishes up excellent Romanian cuisine, including the crispiest, gooiest and tastiest cașcaval pane around.

Hidden in the basement of a concrete block off Piața Universități is *Café de la Joie* (☎ 315 09 37, Str Bibliotecii 4), a candlelit bistro that oozes soul. French classics spin on the turntable. Count on paying around $6 a head, including wine. *Mes Amis* is an intimate spot tucked down Str Zarafi (off Str Lipscani), where you can also dine by candlelight.

Nearby, *Caru cu Bere* (☎ 313 75 60, Str Stavropoleos 3) is a beer hall dating to 1875

CENTRAL BUCHAREST

PLACES TO STAY
25   Hotel Carpaţi
28   Hotel Muntenia
39   Hotel Dâmboviţa

PLACES TO EAT
5   Menuet
6   Bistro Atheneu
12   Boema
35   Café de la Joie
49   Mes Amis
54   Caru cu Bere
57   Count Dracula Club

OTHER
1   Terminus
2   Planter's Club
3   Telex-Fax Office
4   Church of the Icon
7   Salsa, You & Me II
8   German Lutheran Church
9   Romanian Athenaeum
10   Royal Palace; National
        Art Museum
11   Central University Library;
        Bank Austria Creditanstalt

13   Nic Supermarket
14   Capitol Exchange
15   Alliance Exchange
16   Italian Church
17   US Embassy
18   US Consulate
19   Librăria Noi
20   Nova Tours
21   Senate (Central Committee
        of the Communist Party)
22   Memorial Bust of
        Corneliu Coposu
23   Creţulescu Church
24   Branch Post Office
26   Central Post Office
27   Central Telephone Office
29   Ion Luca Caragiale National
        Theatre & Lăptăria lui Enache
30   PC-Net Data Network
31   Internet Café
32   Colţea Church
33   Student Church
34   Municipal History
        & Art Museum
36   Bancă Comercială Română
37   University

38   Tipsy
40   CFR Train Ticket Office
41   Cinemateca Romănă
42   PC-Net Data Network
43   Police Station
44   Bucharest Financial Plaza
45   National Bank of
        Romania
46   Romanian National Library
47   New St George's Church
48   Club A
50   Swing House
51   Backstage
52   Stavropoleos Church
53   National History Museum
55   24-hour Pharmacy
56   Economic Consortium
        Palace
58   Prince Mihai Monastery
59   Double T (Buses to
        Western Europe)
60   Old Princely Court
61   Choral Temple
62   Hanul lui Manuc
63   Princess Bălaşa Church
64   Justice Palace

and worth a visit for its Gothic-style decor. Traditional Romanian dishes appear dirt-cheap – until you realise prices are listed per 100g. Count on paying around $3.50 in total.

Another interior worth a peek is the ghoulish **Count Dracula Club** (☎ 312 13 53, ✉ romantic@fx.ro, Splaiul Independenţei 8a) where human skulls and pickled bats enliven the dining experience. Eat in the coffin-clad chapel for the full house-of-horror experience.

Entertainment

Planter's Club (Str Mendeleev 35) and **Terminus** (Str George Enescu 5) are Bucharest's mainstream drinking holes, packed with English-speaking crowds until 5 am most nights. Near Cişmigiu Garden, **Tipsy** is a simple but soulful bar which claims to be Romania's only plub (pub-cum-club). **Sydney Bar & Grill** (Calea Victoriei 224), an Australian-inspired bar overlooking Piaţa Victoriei, opens 24 hours.

Top joints for jigging to live-band beats include **Backstage** (Str Gabroveni 14), **Swing House** (Str Gabroveni 20) and **Lăptăria lui Enache** (Blvd Nicolae Bălcescu 2), which is hidden on the 4th floor of the National Theatre. **Club A** (Str Blanari

4), just off Blvd Brătianu, is run by university students from the architecture faculty. Bongos, steel drums and body-beat dancing fills **Salsa, You & Me II**, a large nightclub behind Hotel Bucureşti on Str Luterană.

Sherlock Holmes (Blvd Mihail Kogălniceanu 49), near the Opera House, is a simple cellar bar that plays host to the city's gay and lesbian populace. It opens 24 hours.

Getting There & Away

Bus Bucharest's central bus stop is on Calea Griviţei. Services are poor, timetables are stuck on lamp posts, and drivers sell tickets.

Private bus companies operating buses to Turkey, such as Ortadoğu Tur (☎ 312 24 23 or 637 67 78, Piaţa Gara de Nord 1), are clustered around Piaţa Gara de Nord.

Tickets for daily buses to Western Europe are sold by Double T (☎ 313 36 42, ✉ doublet@fx.ro), Calea Victoriei 2 and Touring (☎ 230 36 61, ✉ touring.rez@ eurolines.ro), Str Sofia 26.

Train Almost all express trains and many local trains use Gara de Nord (☎ 223 08 80), Bucharest's central train station at Blvd Gării de Nord 2. To enter the station, flash your valid train ticket or buy a platform ticket

ROMANIA

($0.10) at the entrance. Avoid waiting in long queues by buying your ticket in advance from the CFR office at Str Domniţa Anastasia 10-14, open 7.30 am to 7.30 pm on weekdays and from 8 am to noon on Saturday. For more information see Getting There & Away at the beginning of this chapter.

Getting Around
For buses, trams and trolleybuses, buy tickets ($0.15) at streetside kiosks marked *casă de bilete* or *bilete* and validate them on board. Public transport runs 5 am to midnight (reduced service on Sunday).

The metro has three lines, handy for getting around the centre. Trains run every five to seven minutes. Buy a magnetic-striped card for two/10 rides ($0.30/1.50) at a subterranean kiosk at the station.

Wallachia

Wallachia is a flat, tranquil region of farms and small-scale industrial complexes. Most travellers quickly pass through on arriving or departing Bulgaria by ferry, car or foot.

The small town of **Calafat**, on the Danube opposite Vidin, Bulgaria, makes a convenient entry or exit point. Car and passenger ferries cross the river hourly year-round ($12.50 per car plus $2 extra per person, in hard currency only; 30 minutes) and there are frequent local trains to/from Craiova (2½ hours), from where you can catch an express train to Bucharest or Timişoara. The ferry landing is right in the centre of Calafat, about four blocks from the train station.

Drobeta-Turnu Severin is on the Danube opposite Yugoslavia, with one local bus crossing the border daily.

Transylvania

BRAŞOV
☎ 068
Braşov (Brassó in Hungarian) is one of Romania's most visited cities – and for good reason. Piaţa Sfatului, the central square, is the finest in the country, lined with baroque facades and pleasant outdoor cafes. Within easy reach is the ski resort of Sinaia, the castles of Bran and Râşnov and trails that lead into the dramatic Bucegi Mountains.

Orientation
The train station is far from the city centre; take bus No 4 to Parcul Central or Str Mureşenilor. Bus station (*autogară*) 1 is next to the train station (international buses arrive/depart from here). Bus station 2, Str Avram Iancu 114, is west of the train station near the 'Stadion Tineretului' local bus stop (bus Nos 12 and 22 go to/from the city centre).

Information
There's a tourist desk in the lobby of the Hotel Aro Palace, Blvd Eroilor 25, but it's not of much use. Banca Comercială Română, Piaţa Sfatului 14, changes travellers cheques, gives cash advances on Visa/MasterCard and has an ATM. There are also ATMs outside the Hotel Aro Palace restaurant on Blvd Eroilor and opposite McDonald's on Str Ferdinand.

The main post office is opposite the Heroes Cemetery. Braşov's telephone centres are at Str Ferdinand 12 (closed for renovation at time of writing); on Blvd Eroilor (open 7 am to 7 pm daily); and one block west of Str Ferdinand off Blvd Eroilor (open 7 am to 1 pm, and 2 pm to 7 pm weekdays).

Hercules, Piaţa Sfatului 7, in Discul de Aur's, charges $0.75 per hour for Internet access; open 24-hours.

Things to See
The Council House (1420), in the middle of Piaţa Sfatului, is now the **Braşov Historical Museum**. The museum was closed for renovation at the time of writing. The 58m Trumpeter's Tower above the building dates from 1582. The Gothic **Black Church** (1384-1477), still used by German Lutherans, looms just south of the square (closed Sunday; $0.40/0.20 adults/concession). During July and August recitals are given on the 1839 organ (6 pm Tuesday, Thursday and Saturday; $2).

The black-spired Orthodox **Church of St Nicolae din Scheii** (1595) is on Piaţa Unirii. The adjacent **First Romanian School Museum** houses icons, paintings on glass and old manuscripts (closed Monday; $0.25).

The art gallery inside the **Muzeul de Etnografie** (Ethnographic Museum), Blvd Eroilor 21, next to the Hotel Capitol, has a good Romanian collection upstairs (closed Monday; $0.40).

ROMANIA

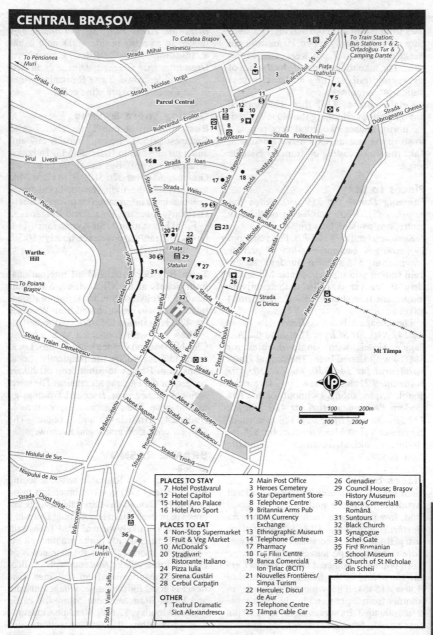

CENTRAL BRAŞOV

PLACES TO STAY
7 Hotel Postăvarul
12 Hotel Capitol
15 Hotel Aro Palace
16 Hotel Aro Sport

PLACES TO EAT
4 Non-Stop Supermarket
5 Fruit & Veg Market
10 McDonald's
20 Stradivari;
   Ristorante Italiano
24 Pizza Iulia
27 Sirena Gustári
28 Cerbul Carpatin

OTHER
1 Teatrul Dramatic
   Sică Alexandrescu

2 Main Post Office
3 Heroes Cemetery
6 Star Department Store
8 Telephone Centre
9 Britannia Arms Pub
11 IDM Currency
   Exchange
13 Ethnographic Museum
14 Telephone Centre
17 Pharmacy
18 Fuji Film Centre
19 Banca Comercială
   Ion Ţiriac (BCIT)
21 Nouvelles Frontières/
   Simpa Turism
22 Hercules; Discul
   de Aur
23 Telephone Centre
25 Tâmpa Cable Car

26 Grenadier
29 Council House; Braşov
   History Museum
30 Banca Comercială
   Română
31 Suntours
32 Black Church
33 Synagogue
34 Schei Gate
35 First Romanian
   School Museum
36 Church of St Nicholae
   din Scheii

ROMANIA

The **Mt Tâmpa cable car** (telecabina) rises from 640m to 960m and offers a stunning view of Braşov (open 10 am to 6 pm weekdays, and to 7 pm weekends; $1 return). The hike to the top follows a series of zigzagging trails starting at the telecabina station (45 minutes).

Cetatea Braşov (1580), a whitewashed fort on a hill overlooking the old town from the north, houses two good beer patios, a so-so disco and an expensive restaurant. Take the steps leading up from Str Nicolae Iorga.

Places to Stay

Camping Darste (☎ *259 080, Calea Bucureşti 285)*, 10km south-east of the city centre, has wooden huts for $6.

Suntours (☎/fax 474 179), Piaţa Sfatului 19, arranges accommodation in *private rooms* from $15 (closed Sunday). At the train station you may encounter Maria and Grig Bolea (☎ 311 962); their private rooms are fine, but ignore their alarmist travel advice.

The cheapest hotel is *Hotel Aro Sport* (☎ *142 840, Str Sf Ioan 3)*, behind the Aro Palace Hotel, with singles/doubles for $11/14 with shared bath. The central *Hotel Postăvarul* (☎ *144 330, fax 141 505, Str Politehnicii 2)* charges $14/21/32 for single/double/triple rooms without bath. The modern *Pensionea Muri* (☎ *418 740, fax 422 564, Str de Mijloc 62)*, 1.5km north of the center, offers clean doubles for $38 including breakfast. A single in a double room is $28.

Places to Eat

Pizza Iulia (Str Nicolai Bălcescu 1), a local favourite for pizza and pasta, has good food, low prices and friendly staff. *Sirena Gustări (Piaţa Sfatului 14)*, is a good place to try Romanian specialities such as *sarmale* (stuffed grape leaves) and *mămăligă* (corn polenta). Adjacent is the famous *Cerbul Carpatin*, in the Saxon-built Hirscher House (1545). The wine cellar opens in summer from 7 pm to midnight and a large restaurant upstairs serves meals until 10 pm year-round. *Stradivari (Piaţa Sfatului 1)* serves excellent pizzas in a cellar downstairs from Ristorante Italiano.

Braşov's *fruit and vegetable market* is at the northern end of Str Nicolae Bălcescu.

Entertainment

Britannia Arms Pub (Str Ferdinand 57), tucked in an alley beside McDonald's, has a traditional smoke-filled atmosphere. *Grenadier (Str Grigoraş Dinicu 2)* attracts a more elite crowd. Taste Romanian wines at the *Cetatea Braşov* wine cellar.

Getting There & Away

Bus From bus station 1, there's a bus to Budapest ($15, 17 hours, Thursday at 7 am) and a private bus to Istanbul ($33, 16 hours, Thursday at 8 am). Buy tickets for these from Ortadoğuu Tur (☎ 326 319), Blvd Gării 24A, not far from the train station. Local travel agencies have information on private buses to Germany, Hungary, Poland and Bulgaria.

From bus station 2, Str Avram Iancu 114, buses to Bran/Râşnov leave hourly ($0.30; pay the driver).

Train Buy domestic and all international train tickets at the CFR office, Str Ferdinand 53 (closed Sunday). International tickets can also be purchased from Wasteels (☎ 424 313) inside the train station hall.

Braşov is well connected to Sighişoara, Cluj-Napoca and Oradea by fast trains. Local trains to/from Sinaia run frequently. Local trains from Braşov to Sibiu drop off hikers headed for the Făgăraş Mountains. The international trains *Dacia*, *Ister* and *Traianus* go to Budapest. The *Pannonia Expres* runs to Budapest, Bratislava and Prague. The *Carpaţi* goes to Warsaw and Kraków.

BRAN & RÂŞNOV
☎ 068

It's hard to visit Romania without seeing **Bran Castle** (1378) in travel brochures or on postcards. Though this fairy-tale castle is impressive in itself, Bran is not Count Dracula's castle – it's unlikely the real Vlad Ţepeş ever set foot here. Still, it's fun to run through the castle's 57 rooms. Beside the entrance is an **Ethnographic Village Museum** with a collection of Transylvanian farm buildings. One ticket is good for the castle, village museum and **Vama Bran Museum** below the castle (closed Monday; $2.60/1.80 adults/students).

Râşnov offers the dual attractions of a convenient camping ground and the ruins of 13th-century **Râşnov Castle** (closed Monday; $0.50) which is more dramatic and a lot less touristy than the castle at Bran.

Places to Stay & Eat

In Râşnov, *Camping Valea Cetatii* and *Hotel Cetate* (☎ 230 266), ajoin each other directly below the castle on the road to Poiana Braşov. The camp site, open from June to August, has cabins for $5 per person; tents $2.50. The hotel, open year round, offers doubles/triples with private bath for $15/19.

ANTREC (☎/fax 236 884, Str Lucian Bologa 10, Bran) arranges inexpensive *private rooms* and is open daily year-round.

Cabana Bran Castel (☎ 236 404) is a rustic chalet on the hillside about 600m behind the castle, with dorm beds for $4 (in summer it's often full).

The one-star *Han Bran* (☎ 236 556), two blocks from the castle, charges $10/15 for doubles/triples (meals extra); hot water flows from 7.30 pm to 11 pm. The front terrace is a good place for a meal. *Vila Bran* (☎ 236 866, Str Principala 238), positioned in a picturesque orchard, has singles/doubles for $15/24, including breakfast. The *Bran Benzin* petrol station (☎ 238 088), at the northern end of Bran, has doubles without/with bath for $13.50/16.

Getting There & Away

Buses to Bran and Râşnov ($0.50) leave hourly from Braşov's bus station 2. It's best to visit Bran first and then stop at Râşnov on the way back. Return buses leave Bran every hour between 5.30 am and 7.30 pm.

From the bus stop in Bran, the castle is easy to spot. From the stop in Râşnov, walk 100m east towards the mountains, turn right at Piaţa Unirii and watch for the hillside stairs in the courtyard of the unmarked Casă de Cultură (on your left). The castle is a 15-minute walk uphill.

SINAIA
☎ 044

This popular winter ski resort at the foot of the Bucegi Mountains is a convenient day trip from Bucharest or Braşov. Peleş Castle alone is worth the trip to Sinaia.

Orientation & Information

From the train station, directly below the centre of town, climb the stairway across the street to busy Blvd Carol I. The Hotel Montana and cable car are toward the left, the monastery and palace are uphill to the right.

Palace Agenţie de Turism, Str Octavian Goga 11 opposite Villa Parc, sells hiking maps of the Bucegi Mountains. Surmont Sport, at the base of the cable car station on Str Cuza Vodă, sells hiking maps, skis, tents and imported outdoor gear. Banca Comercială Română, on Blvd Carol I just past the Hotel Montana, changes money and has an ATM.

Things to See & Do

Sinaia Monastery, named after Mt Sinai, has a large Orthodox church dating from 1846 and an older frescoed church built in 1695.

Just past the monastery is the road to Peleş Castle (1883), one of Romania's best sights (closed Monday and Tuesday; $3). The 160-room palace was built for the Prussian prince Carol I, first king of Romania (ruled 1866-1914). The queue can be long on weekends. Tours are held in various languages.

Sinaia is a great base for hiking in the Bucegi Mountains and even non-hikers should take the cable car from Hotel Montana to Cota 1400 (a station near Hotel Alpin) and continue on the cable car or ski lift up to Cota 2000 (near Cabana Mioriţa). The complete trip costs under $6 and can be done from 8 am to 3.45 pm Tuesday to Sunday.

Places to Stay

Hang around at the train station for a few minutes and you'll probably be offered a *private room*. The going rate is $8 to $10 per person.

Cabana *Hotel Alpin* (☎ 312 351) is at Cota 1400 by the cable-car station. Just below, at 1300m, is the year-round *Cabana Brădet* (☎ 311 551), with dorm beds for $6. Rates are similar at *Cabana Valea cu Brazi* (☎ 313 635), above the cable car at 1500m; a path leads up from Hotel Alpin.

The cheapest hotel option is *Pensiuna Parc* (☎ 314 821, Blvd Carol I) with doubles with shared bath for $10. Farther down is the attractive *Hotel Păltiniş* (☎ 314 651, Blv Carol I 65) priced at $20/27 with bath.

Villa Parc (☎ 313 856, Str Octavian Goga 2) has doubles without/with bath for $12/15.

Getting There & Away

Sinaia is on the Bucharest-Braşov rail line – 126km from the former and 45km from the latter. All express trains stop here and local trains to Buşteni (8km), Predeal (19km) and Braşov are quite frequent.

BUCEGI MOUNTAINS

The Bucegi Mountains are Romania's best-kept secret, rivalling Slovakia's Tatra Mountains and even the Alps when it comes to trekking. Getting lost is difficult thanks to a network of marked trails, while most cabanas are open year-round to shelter and feed hikers and cross-country skiers. The only danger is the weather: winter is severe, waist-deep snow lingers as late as May and summer thunderstorms are common. If you sleep in cabanas, it's a good idea to bring extra food.

Day Hikes

Catch a morning train from Braşov or Sinaia to Buşteni, then take the Buşteni cable car (closed Tuesday; $2) up to Cabana Babele (2206m). From Babele you hike south to Cabana Piatra Arsă (1950m), where you pick up a blue trail that descends to Sinaia via Poiana Stânii (a five-hour walk in total). The beginning of the blue trail is poorly marked at Piatra Arsă, so study the large map on the cabana's wall. This trip across alpine pastures and through the forest is varied and downhill all the way.

A variation on the above involves taking the Sinaia cable car up to Cabana Miorița (1957m), near the crest. You can then walk north to Cabana Piatra Arsă (1½ hours) and on to Cabana Babele (another hour), where you can catch the Buşteni cable car down the mountain. This hike is uphill (350m gain) and you must take two cable cars.

Longer Hikes

A more ambitious expedition involves taking one of the two cable cars mentioned previously and hiking north-west across the mountains to Bran Castle, where there are buses to Braşov. You can do this in one strenuous day if you get an early start from Babele, but it's preferable to take two days and camp free-lance or spend a night at Cabana Omul.

As you look north from Babele, you'll see a red-and-white TV transmitter on a hill. To the left is a yellow-marked trail that leads to **Cabana Omul** (two hours) on the summit (2505m). North of Babele the scenery gets dramatic. To go from Omul to

Bran Castle takes another six hours, following the yellow-triangle trail. Eventually you come out on a logging road beside a river, which you follow for 2½ hours to Bran Castle.

SIGHIŞOARA

☎ 065

Sighişoara (Schässburg in German, Segesvár in Hungarian), birthplace of Vlad Ţepeş, is a perfectly preserved medieval town in beautiful hilly countryside. Eleven towers stand along Sighişoara's intact city walls. Inside the walls are sloping cobblestone streets lined with 16th-century burgher houses. All trains between Bucharest and Budapest (via Oradea) pass through here, as do several trains a day from Braşov. Many readers have written to us saying Sighişoara was their favourite town in Romania.

Orientation

Follow Str Gării south from the train station to the Soviet war memorial, where you turn left towards the large Orthodox church. Cross the Târnava Mare River on the footbridge here and take Str Morii to the left, then keep going all the way up to Piaţa Hermann Oberth and the old town. Many of the facilities you'll want to use are along a short stretch of Str 1 Decembrie. Piaţa Cetăţii, surrounded by fine old houses, is the heart of old Sighişoara.

Information

Steaua Agenţie de Turism (☎ 771 072), Str 1 Decembrie 10, has information on weekly buses to Hungary and Germany (closed Sunday).

Change travellers cheques and get Visa/MasterCard cash advances at Banca Comercială Română, Str 1 Mai 12. The telephone centre in the main post office on Piaţa Hermann Oberth is open 7 am to 9 pm weekdays, and to 8 pm Saturday.

Kolping Internet Café, Str Ilarie Chendi 3, charges $0.50 per hour for Internet access (closed Sunday).

Things to See

The first tower you reach above Piaţa Hermann Oberth is the massive **clock tower** on Piaţa Muzeului (the 1648 clock still keeps time). The 14th-century tower houses a small but good **museum**. Under the tower on the left as you enter the citadel is the **Torture Room Museum** (opens end of 2000).

On the western side of the clock tower, in a small house, is a **museum** containing antique firearms and a small Dracula exhibition. All three museums are open 9 am to 5.30 pm Tuesday to Sunday, and 10 am to 5.30 pm Monday; entry is $1.25.

Across Piața Muzeului is the house where Vlad Țepeș, second son of Vlad Dracul, was born in 1431; it's now the Restaurantul Cetatea. Also known as 'The Impaler' or 'Draculea' (Son of Dracula), Țepeș became a Wallachian prince who led Romanian resistance against Ottoman expansion in the 15th century.

Places to Stay
The best camping ground is at *Hula Daneş* (☎ 771 052), 4km out of town on the road to Mediaş. There are 3 buses a day marked 'Cris' from the bus station (beside the train station).

The Steaua Agenție de Turism (see Information) arranges *private rooms* at $7.50 per person. Kolping Bildungswerk (☎ 774 909, Str Manastiri 10) provides accommodation, in the heart of the citadel, at $5 per person in two-, four- and six-bed rooms (meals extra).

Bobby's Hostel (☎ 772 232, Str Tache Ionescu 18), is open from 20 June to mid September. Dorm beds are $5, doubles are $6 per person. Bobby can arrange for backpackers to be met at the train station, which is a 25-minute walk away.

The best hotel deal is the small, clean *Hotel Chic* (☎ 775 901, Str Libertății 44), directly opposite the train station – look out for the 'Non-Stop Hotel Restaurant' sign. Doubles are $10. The dreary two-star *Hotel Steaua* (☎ 771 594, fax 771 932, Str 1 Decembrie 12), has musty single/doubles priced at $10/14 or $14/18 with bath (breakfast included).

Places to Eat
Dracula freaks can dine at *Restaurantul Cetatea*, in Vlad Țepeș's former house in the citadel. There's a good restaurant upstairs and a *berarie* (pub) downstairs. Popular *Ristorante Pizzeria 4 Amici* has two outlets: one at Str Morii 7 and the other at Str Octavian Goga 12. *Pizzeria Perla* on Piața Hermann Oberth has a good selection of pizzas, pastas, soups and cutlets. The daily *market*, off Str Tîrnavei, has a good selection of fruit, vegetables and cheeses.

Getting There & Away
The Agenție de Voiaj CFR on Str 1 Decembrie 2 sells domestic and international train tickets, from 7.30 am to 7.30 pm weekdays. All trains between Bucharest (via Braşov) and Cluj-Napoca stop at Sighişoara.

Buses leave from the bus station adjacent to the train station. The Steaua Agenție de Turism (see Information) can book weekly buses to Hungary and Germany.

CLUJ-NAPOCA
☎ 064
Cluj-Napoca is as much Hungarian as it is Romanian. Known as Klausenburg to the Germans and Kolozsvár to the Hungarians, it added the old Roman name of Napoca to its official title to emphasise its Daco-Roman origin, but it is simply referred to as Cluj. Because Cluj is a major university town it has a relaxed, inviting atmosphere, fine architecture and several good museums. It's well worth a day or two.

Orientation
The train station is 1.5km north of the city centre. To get to the centre, walk left out of the station, buy a ticket at the red L&M kiosk across the street and catch tram No 101 or a trolleybus south down Str Horea. Get off the trolley bus immediately after crossing the river; on tram No 101, go two stops, then walk south and cross the river.

All major bus services arrive/depart from bus station (*autogară*) 2, over the bridge from the train station, north of town. Bus station 1, Str Aurel Vlaicu on the eastern side of town, no longer operates.

Information
The Transylvanian Ecological Club (☎/fax 431 626) at Str Sindicatelor, arranges tours and activities in rural areas of Transylvania; open 11 am to 5 pm weekdays.

Youth Hostels România (☎ 198 067, fax 186 616) has an office at Piața Ştefan cel Mare 5 and is open 9 am to 4 pm weekdays.

Banca Comercială Română, Str George Barțiu 10-12, changes travellers cheques, gives cash advances on Visa/MasterCard and also has an ATM. The telephone centre is just behind the main post office at Str Ferdinand 33.

Supernet, Str Iuliu 1, charges $0.80 per hour for Internet access; open 24 hours.

Places to Stay

ANTREC (☎ 198 135, 424 536, Piaţa Avram Iancu 15), arranges *rooms* in private houses from $5 per person (meals extra).

In July and August, *Hostel Do-Re-Mi* (☎/fax 186 616, Str Braşov 2-4), has dorm beds for $7. From the train station take trolleybus No 3 three stops to Piaţa Cipariu, walk south along Str Andrei Mureşanu, then take the first right along Str Zrínyi Miklóos. At the end of the street turn left onto Str Braşov and go 50m to the right.

The five-storey *Hotel Delta* (☎ 132 507), at bus station No 2 across the bridge from the train station, is convenient and cheap at $5 for a bed in a shared room. Opposite the train station, *Hotel Pax* (☎ 136 101, Piaţa Gării 2) is noisy but clean. Singles/ doubles/triples with shared bath are $12/17/23. Some 150m east of the train station, *Hotel Junior* (☎ 432 028), on Str Câii Ferate, has simple rooms for $15 per person including breakfast. The centrally located *Hotel Continental* (Str Napoca 1) offers hostel-style doubles with shared bath for $9 per person including breakfast. Bookings must be made through Continental Tours (☎ 191 441, fax 193 977).

Places to Eat

Pizza Y (Piaţa Unirii 1) serves 34 types of pizza as well as fresh salads and pasta. *Restaurant Privighetoarea*, (Str Ferdinand 16), near Hotel Vlădeasu, serves hearty portions of meat, soups, spicy meatballs and breaded cheese. If you want game or quail (seasonal), head for *Hubertus* (Blvd 21 Decembrie 1989).

Getting There & Away

Buy domestic and international train tickets at the CFR office, Piaţa Mihai Viteazul 20; open 7 am to 7 pm weekdays. There are express trains from Cluj to Oradea (2½ hours), Sighişoara (three hours), Braşov (five hours), Timişoara (six hours) and Bucharest (eight hours).

A bus to Budapest leaves from the bus station twice a week ($6.50). Tickets are sold at the bus station.

Crişana & Banat

ORADEA
☎ 059

Of all the cities of the old Austro-Hungarian empire, Oradea (Grosswardein in German, Nagyvárad in Hungarian) is probably the one that has best retained its 19th-century elegance. When Oradea was ceded to Romania in 1920, this example of Habsburg majesty became the backwater it remains today, a time capsule for romantics in search of a simpler world. Oradea's most impressive architectural monuments are on the two city-centre squares, Piaţa Unirii and Piaţa Ferdinand.

Orientation & Information

The train station is a few kilometres north of town; tram Nos 1 and 4 run south from Piaţa Bucureşti (across from the station) to Piaţa Unirii.

The Cibela Agenţie de Turism (☎ 130 737), at Str Vulcan 1, is open 8 am to 6 pm weekdays, 9 am to 1 pm Saturday. Banca Comercială Română, at the southern end of Piaţa Independenţei, cashes travellers cheques, gives Visa and MaterCard cash advances and has an ATM.

Access the Internet at Liberty Internet Café, Str Ferdinand 35; open 24 hours.

Places to Stay & Eat

The Art-Nouveau *Hotel Vulturul Negru* (☎ 135 417, Str Independenţei 1) is musty and worn but otherwise OK. It charges $7/14 for a single/double without bath, and $17 for a double with bath. *Hotel Parc* (☎ 411 699, Str Ferdinand 5) is friendly, clean and charges $8/13 without bath and $18 for a double with bath. Breakfast is $2.

Restaurant Oradea & Grădină de Vară (Piaţa Ferdinand 5-7) has a lovely terrace, good grilled meats and occasional live music in summer. *Pinacoteca Fausto's* (Str Ferdinand 3) is a popular hang-out serving beer and a selection of Romanian dishes. *Restaurant Olivery* (Str Moscovei 12) is an unpretentious cellar restaurant with quality food at reasonable prices.

Getting There & Away

International train tickets are sold only at the Agenţie de Voiaj CFR, Str Ferdinand 2, 7 am to 7 pm weekdays. Express trains run south to Arad and east to Cluj-Napoca. Four trains run daily from Oradea to Budapest-Nyugati station ($16): the *Claudiopolis* and *Corona* express trains and two local trains, the *Varadinium* and *Partium*.

Most of the travel agencies can arrange buses to Budapest, Kraków and cities throughout Austria and Germany.

TIMIŞOARA
☎ 056

Timişoara (Temeschburg in German, Temesvár in Hungarian) is Romania's fourth-largest city, with outdoor cafes and regal Habsburg-era buildings fronting its three main squares. Opera and drama thrive here, thanks in part to its 8000 university students. It was also the centre of protests in December 1989, igniting the countrywide protests that eventually toppled Ceauşescu.

Orientation & Information
Timişoara-Nord train station is just west of the city centre. Walk east on Blvd Ferdinand to the Opera House and Piaţa Victoriei. A block north is the verdant Piaţa Libertăţii. Piaţa Unirii, the old town square, is two blocks farther north.

Timişoara's bus station is right beside the Idsefin Market, three blocks from the train station. Take Str General Dragalina south, cross the canal and follow it west to the next bridge.

The friendly Agenţie de Turism Banatul (☎ 198 862), Str 1 Mai 2, on the eastern side of Hotel Timişoara, sells town maps.

Cash travellers cheques and get Visa/MasterCard cash advances at Banca Comercială Română at Str 9 Mai just off Piaţa Libertăţii, or at BCIT on Piaţa Unirii.

The telephone office on Blvd Mihai Eminescu, just off Piaţa Victoriei, is open 7 am to 9 pm daily.

Access the Internet at Internet Java, Str Pacha 6, inside the Java Coffee House; open 24 hours.

Things to See
The centre of town is Piaţa Victoriei, a beautifully landscaped pedestrian mall lined with shops, cinemas and cafes, with the Opera House at its head. Just east of the piaţa is the 15th-century Huniades Palace, which houses the Banat History Museum (closed Monday; $1.50).

Towering over the mall's south-western end is the exotic Romanian Orthodox Metropolitan Cathedral (1946), in front of which are memorials to the people who died in the fighting here in December 1989.

Heading north from the Opera House, pedestrianised Str Alba Iulia leads to the gardens of Piaţa Libertăţii and the old town hall (1734). Two blocks north, Piaţa Unirii is Timişoara's most picturesque square. Walk east down Str Palanca to the Ethnographic Museum, Str Popa Şapcă 8, with Banat folk costumes and crafts (closed Monday; $0.50).

Places to Stay
The well maintained *Camping International* (☎ 225 596), open year-round, is in the Green Forest. From the station catch trolleybus No 11 to the end of the line. The bus stop is less than 50m from the campsite. The site has two/four-bed bungalows for $15/30; tent camping is $2 for two people. There's a small restaurant on the premises.

Timişoara's cheapest hotel is *Casă Tineretului* (☎ 162 419, Str Arieş 19), a large, modern building about 2km south of the city centre. Rooms with shared bath are $10 per person. From the train station take tram No 8 to Calea Martirilor.

In the centre is the reasonably priced *Hotel Banatul* (☎ 191 903, Blvd Ferdinand 5). Renovated single/doubles are $12/17 and unrenovated doubles are $10.

Places to Eat
Restaurant N&Z (Str Alba Iulia 1), just off Piaţa Libertăţii, serves typical Romanian dishes. Its menu is displayed in pictures outside. The *Crama Bastion (Str Popa Şapcâ)*, a wine cellar in a section of the city's 18th-century fortifications, has a small menu of meat and rice dishes. Nearby, the Italian-inspired *Horse Pizzeria (Str Popa Şapcâ)* serves 19 types of pizzas and delicious salads.

Getting There & Away
Bus Twice-weekly buses on Tuesday and Friday connect Timişoara to Békéscsaba (138km) and Szeged (257km) in Hungary. To Budapest ($8, eight hours) the service is weekly. The international ticket window is open 9 am to 5 pm weekdays; otherwise you can usually pay the driver.

Train The service to Bucharest (eight hours) is fairly frequent via Băile Herculane, Drobeta-Turnu Severin and Craiova; sleepers are available to/from Bucharest. Direct express trains link Timişoara to Iaşi via Cluj-Napoca and Suceava.

Two daily express trains connect Timişoara with Belgrade (3¾ hours). The *Bucureşti* leaves Timişoara Nord at 7.58 am, the *Banat* leaves at 4.10 pm. Advance reservations are required for both. All international tickets must be purchased at the CFR office, Blvd Ferdinand 1, open 8 am to 8 pm weekdays.

Southern Bucovina

The painted churches of Bucovina are among the greatest artistic monuments of Europe – in 1993 they were collectively designated a world heritage site by Unesco. The exteriors of many churches are completely covered with magnificent 16th-century frescoes and, remarkably, most of the intense colours have been preserved despite five centuries of rain and wind.

Bucovina's monasteries are generally open from 9 am to 5 or 6 pm daily. Admission to each is less than $1.

SUCEAVA
☎ 030
Suceava was the capital of Moldavia from 1388 to 1565 and a thriving commercial centre on the Lviv-Istanbul trading route. Today it's the seat of Suceava County and gateway to the painted churches of Bucovina. Its historic fortress and old churches are easily seen in a day.

Orientation & Information
Piaţa 22 Decembrie marks the centre of town. Suceava has two train stations – Gara Suceava and Gara Suceava Nord. From Gara Suceava cross the street, buy a ticket at a kiosk and take trolleybus No 2 or 3 to the town centre (it's about six stops from the station). From Gara Suceava Nord take trolleybus No 5.

Bucovina Estur (☎/fax 522 694), Str Ştefan cel Mare 24, arranges private rooms, organises monastery tours and rents cars; open 9 am to 6 pm weekdays, and 9 am to 1 pm Saturday.

Banca Comercială Română, Str Ştefan cel Mare 31, cashes travellers cheques and has an ATM. The telephone centre, on the corner of Str Nicolae Bălcescu and Str Firmu, is open 7 am to 9 pm weekdays, and 8 am to 4 pm Saturday.

Assist Internet Café and Computer Shop, Str Ana Ipatescu 7, opposite McDonald's, charges $0.75 per hour for Internet access; open 9 am to 1 am daily.

Places to Stay & Eat
Bucovina Estur (see Information) arranges *private rooms* for $15 per person. The five-storey *Hotel Socim (☎/fax 522 662, Str Jean Bart 24)*, 200m from Gara Suceava, has beds in a double or triple with shared bath for $3.50 per person. Hot water is available 6 to 9 am and 4 to 9 pm. Better value is *Motel West (☎ 512 199, Str Humorului 11)*, 4km from the city centre on the road to Humor Monastery. A bed in a double room is $7.50 per person. Central *Hotel Gloria (☎ 521 209, fax 520 005, Str Mihai Vasile Bumbac 4)* has singles/doubles for $20/25 including breakfast.

Eating options in Suceava are limited. *Restaurant Suceava (Str Bălcescu 2)* has a tasty chicken *kievskaia* for $2. Local favourite *Country Pizza (Str George Enescu 27)*, just west of the centre, serves a small selection of pizza slices with a variety of generous toppings for $1.20. There is a *supermarket* opposite Restaurant Suceava which is open to 11 pm.

Getting There & Away
Bus The bus station is in the centre of town at Str Armenească. Tickets for international destinations are sold at window No 4. Nine buses a day run to Gura Humorului (47km); five to Rădăuţi ($1.20, 62km) and seven to Botoşani ($1.20, 42km).

Train Express trains to Bucharest (seven hours) and Cluj-Napoca (6½ hours) are fairly regular. Local trains go to Gura Humorului, Putna, Câmpulung Moldovenesc and Vatra Dornei. The CFR office, Str Bălcescu 8, is open 7 am to 8 pm weekdays.

GURA HUMORULUI
☎ 030
This small logging town, 36km west of Suceava on the train line to Cluj-Napoca, is

an ideal base for visiting the Voroneţ and Humor monasteries. Most trains stop here; the adjacent train and bus stations are a seven-minute walk from the town centre.

The post office is on the corner of Str Bucovinei and Str 9 Mai. The CFR office, Str Ferdinand 10, is opposite the old cinema.

Places to Stay & Eat

You can *camp* freely by the Moldavian river, 1km south of town at the foot of the wooden hills. Otherwise try the unappealing *Hotel Carpaţi* (☎ 231 103, Str 9 Mai 3), beside the post office. Singles/doubles with communal showers (no hot water) are $5/8 per person.

In town, *Restaurant Select* at Str Bucovinei 1 has a menu in English. The adjacent *Mini Market* sells basic supplies.

Getting There & Away

Gura Humorului is on the main railway line between Suceava and Cluj-Napoca.

Buses from Gura Humorului's station at Str Ştefan cel Mare 37 include seven daily to Suceava and Humor; three to Voroneţ and two to Rădăuţi and Piatra Neamţ.

If you have limited time, you can bargain with taxi drivers here for tours to the monasteries. You can also walk the 4km south to Voroneţ through beautiful countryside. It's a 6km hike north to Humor monastery from the town centre.

AROUND GURA HUMORULUI

The *Last Judgment*, which fills the entire western wall at **Voroneţ Monastery** (9 am to 6 pm; $0.55), is perhaps the most marvellous Bucovine fresco. Inside, facing the iconostasis, is the famous portrait of Ştefan the Great offering Voroneţ to Christ. The vibrant blue pigment used in the frescoes here is known worldwide as 'Voroneţ blue'.

Humor Monastery (open 9 am to 6 pm; entry $0.55), run by kindly nuns, has the most impressive interior frescoes of all the monasteries. The predominant colour here is deep red. On the church's southern exterior wall the 1453 siege of Constantinople is depicted. On the porch is the *Last Judgment* and, in the first chamber inside the church, scenes of martyrdom.

MOLDOVIŢA

Moldoviţa monastery (1532) is in the middle of a quaint Romanian farming village

with a life of its own. It's open 10 am to 6 pm and admission costs $0.55. Moldoviţa consists of a strong, fortified enclosure with towers and brawny gates, with a magnificent painted church at its centre. The monastery has undergone careful restoration in recent years.

Places to Stay & Eat

Mărul de Aur (☎ 336 180), between the train station and the monastery, has tired doubles or triples for $7.50. Downstairs the smoke-filled *restaurant* serves basic meals and beer 24 hours.

Getting There & Away

Moldoviţa is right above Vatra Moldoviţei's train station (be sure to get off at Vatra Moldoviţei, not Moldoviţa). From Suceava there are eight daily trains to Vama (1½ hours), and from Vama three daily trains for Vatra Moldoviţei (50 minutes) at 7.27 am, 2.58 pm and 11.09 pm, returning to Vama at 4.29 am, 12.10 pm and 5.57 pm.

SUCEVIŢA

Suceviţa monastery is the largest and finest of Bucovina's monasteries. The church inside the fortified quadrangular enclosure (built between 1582 and 1601) is almost completely covered in frescoes. Green and red dominate here. It's open 8 am to 8 pm; entry $0.55.

Places to Stay & Eat

Freelance *camping* is possible in the field across the stream from the monastery. Otherwise the renovated *Hanul Suceviţa*, about 1km north-east towards Rădăuţi, offers double rooms with bath for $20. The *restaurant* is open year-round.

Popasul Bucovinean (☎/fax 565 389), 5km south of Suceviţa on the road to Vatra Moldoviţei, has two villas and an excellent Moldavian restaurant. Singles/doubles are $20/28; wooden huts $8.

Getting There & Away

Suceviţa is the most difficult monastery to reach on public transport. There are two buses from Rădăuţi (17km) at 6.30 am and 3 pm. At the time of writing the bus service between Suceviţa and Moldoviţa (36km) had ceased. The road connecting the monasteries winds over a high mountain pass (1100m).

ROMANIA

St Petersburg

If Moscow is Europe's most Asiatic capital, then St Petersburg, with a population of almost five million, is Russia's most European city. Created by Peter the Great as his 'window on the west', it was built with 18th and 19th-century European pomp and orderliness by mainly European architects. The result is a city that remains one of Europe's most beautiful; where Moscow intimidates, St Petersburg enchants.

Though St Petersburg is Russia's biggest port and a huge industrial centre, it's also a cosmopolitan place with thriving arts and entertainment scenes. For travellers on the way to/from Finland, Estonia, Latvia and Lithuania, St Petersburg is definitely worth a few days' exploration.

Facts about St Petersburg

HISTORY

In the Great Northern War (1700-21) Peter the Great captured the Swedish outposts on the Neva River, and in 1703 founded the Peter & Paul Fortress on the Neva. In 1709 he named the city Sankt Pieter Burkh and three years later made it his capital. By the time of Peter's death in 1725, Sankt Pieter Burkh had a population of 40,000. Between 1741 and 1825 under Elizabeth, Catherine the Great and Alexander I, it became a cosmopolitan city with a royal court.

St Petersburg was the hub of the 1905 revolution, started on 'Bloody Sunday' (9 January 1905) when strikers marching to petition the tsar in the Winter Palace were fired on by troops. In a wave of patriotism at the start of WWI, the city's name was changed to Petrograd. The city was again the cradle of revolution in 1917 when, following workers' protests leading to the end of the monarchy in March, Lenin returned

AT A GLANCE

Population:	4.2 million
Official Language:	Russian
Currency:	1 Russian rouble (R) = 100 kopecks

from exile to lead his Bolshevik Party to power on 25 October. The Union of Soviet Socialist Republics (USSR) was established in 1922 and in 1924, following Lenin's death, Petrograd was renamed Leningrad.

During the 1930s the city was a hub of Stalin's industrialisation program. When the Germans attacked in June 1941 it took Hitler's troops just 10 weeks to reach Leningrad. During the '900 Days' siege (actually 872), between 500,000 and a million people died before the Wehrmacht withdrew. After the war, Leningrad was extensively rebuilt.

During the 1991 putsch that led to the overthrow of Mikhail Gorbachev and the rise of Boris Yeltsin, the army, in true Leningrad style, refused to aid Moscow's coup leaders. As hundreds of thousands of Leningraders filled Palace Square, Anatoly Sobchak, the city's mayor, appeared on local TV denouncing the coup.

Almost as soon as Dzerzhinsky's statue hit the asphalt in Moscow, the Leningrad city council was proposing to change the city's name back to St Petersburg. The 1990s has seen the city re-blossom after decades of neglect (its population now stands at 4.7 million), and it has reassumed its regal position as one of the world's most beautiful cities.

LANGUAGE

To get by in St Petersburg, it is essential that you can at least decipher Cyrillic script. Otherwise you can't make sense of street names, bus destination placards or railway timetables.

People involved in the tourist industry may speak English or German, but a rudimentary knowledge of Russian is invaluable. See the Language guide at the back of this book for the pronunciation guidelines and useful words and phrases.

Facts for the Visitor

WHEN TO GO

St Petersburg's latitude – level with Seward, Alaska and Cape Farewell, Greenland – gives it nearly 24-hour daylight in midsummer but long, grey winters. From June to August temperatures reach 20°C. Winter usually sees the Neva River freeze over, with January temperatures averaging -8°C; it can get very slushy so bring along good waterproof boots or rubbers.

Hotels and tourist attractions are less crowded between October and February. In summer, the city is packed.

VISAS & DOCUMENTS

You need a visa to enter any part of Russia. A Russian visa is a separate document, not a stamp in your passport or an attached piece of paper. Numerous travel agencies in the Baltic region can help with a visa, or get one from a Russian embassy. Most visas cannot be obtained at the Russian border, though tourist visas are issued at St Petersburg's airport.

To apply yourself, you need your passport (valid for at least a month beyond your return), three passport photos, a completed application form (available at the embassy) including entry/exit dates, the relevant invitation or proof of accommodation depending on the type of visa you are applying for (this is when it's easier to arrange a visa through a travel agency), and a handling fee (around US$30). Most embassies offer a 'quick visa', issued within two or three days, which costs double, sometimes more.

Visas

There are six types of Russian visas available to foreign visitors, but only two are useful for the average traveller. A **tourist visa** (single or multiple entry) requires written confirmation of hotel reservations, usually done through travel agencies. A **transit visa**, valid for 48 hours, is for 'passing through' and does not require proof of accommodation.

Registration The company or organisation that invited you to Russia is responsible for your registration. When you check in to a hotel, you will have to surrender your passport and visa for a few hours so the hotel can register you. If you are travelling independently, you must remember that *all* Russian visas must be registered with OVIR (the Department of Visas and Registration) within three working days of your arrival in Russia. St Petersburg's main OVIR office (☎ 278 2481) is at Kirochnaya ulitsa 4, open 9.30 am to 5.30 pm weekdays.

EMBASSIES & CONSULATES
Russian Embassies Abroad

Australia (☎ 02-6295 9033) 78 Canberra Ave, Griffith, ACT 2603
Canada (☎ 613-235 4341) 285 Charlotte Street, Ottawa, Ontario K1N 8L5
Estonia (☎ 646-4166) Pikk tänav 19, 10133 Tallinn
Finland (☎ 09-66 14 49) Tehtaankatu 1b, 00140 Helsinki
Latvia (☎ 2-7332 151) Atonijas iela 2, Riga
Lithuania (☎ 2-721 763) Latviu 53/54, Vilnius
UK (☎ 020-7229 8027) 5 Kensington Palace Gardens, London W8 4QS
USA (☎ 202-939 8907) 1825 Phelps Place NW, Washington, DC 20008

Foreign Consulates in St Petersburg

Canada (☎ 325 8448) Malodetskoselsky prospekt 32
UK (☎ 325 6036) ploshchad Proletarskoy Diktatury 5
USA (☎ 275 1701) ulitsa Furshtatskaya 15

MONEY

The Russian rouble (R) is the only legal currency. Transactions in other currencies are technically forbidden, even though some travel agencies, museums, and merchants will happily accept Deutschmarks or US dollars. Confusingly, some prices listed in US dollars (the most accepted foreign currency) require payment in roubles (at current exchange rates). Because the rouble is not stable, prices in this chapter are given in US dollars. At the time of writing, US$1 was worth about 28 roubles. All prices listed in this chapter are in US dollars.

American Express (☎ 329 6060) has a full-service office at the Grand Hotel Europe, Mikhailovsky ulitsa 1/7. Promstroy Bank and St Petersburg Savings Bank are two prominent banks; both have a head office located at Nevsky prospekt 38 (entrance across from the Grand Hotel Europe). Most major hotels can handle all your banking needs. ATM machines are located inside every metro station, in department stores, main post offices and along major streets.

POST & COMMUNICATIONS
Post
If you're travelling on to Scandinavia, consider saving mail to send from there. From St Petersburg, letters or cards take about two weeks to Europe and three weeks to the US and Australia. Postcards have more chance of arriving if you put them in an envelope.

St Petersburg's *glavpochtamt* (central post office) is at Pochtamtskaya ulitsa 9. For quicker service try Westpost (☎ 275 0784, **ℰ** westpost@westpost.ru), Nevsky prospekt 86, which mails letters/postcards via Finland for a substantial fee.

Telephone & Fax
Russia's international country code is ☎ 7.

To make an international call dial ☎ 8, wait for the tone, then dial ☎ 10 followed by the country code, area code and phone number. To make a long-distance call within Russia and the CIS dial ☎ 8 (wait for tone) followed by the area code and phone number.

The state-run long-distance telephone office is at ulitsa Bolshaya Morskaya 3/5, where you can pre-pay the operator to connect long-distance and international calls; you can also dial direct from the international card phones inside. Similar card phones are found throughout the city; phonecards are sold at metro stations, hostels and hotels. A three-minute peak-time call to the US costs around $6.

To make a local call from the older, token-operated pay phones, put a metro token in the slot on top, dial the number and wait for the token to drop before speaking. When your party answers, press the black button on the front of the phone. Coin-operated phones (accepting rouble coins) are found inside every metro station.

Faxes can be sent and received from the state telephone offices and from the Business Centres in major hotels.

Email & Internet Access
The most pleasant and least expensive place to surf or email is at the central telephone office (see Telephone). Cityline (☎ 279 1164),

Nevsky prospekt 88, also has terminals for hire. Both places charge up to $2.80 an hour.

INTERNET RESOURCES
There is a wealth of information about St Petersburg on the web; the best starting point is www.spb.ru. The city's English-language newspaper, the *St Petersburg Times*, is at www.sptimes.ru. For an excellent introduction to the world of Russian art, check out www.museum.ru – with links to many of the country's best museums, including the Hermitage.

TIME
St Petersburg time is GMT/UTC plus three hours. Clocks are turned one hour ahead on the last Sunday in March, and back again on the last Sunday in September.

DANGERS & ANNOYANCES
Pick-pocketing, purse-snatching and petty theft is as rife in St Petersburg as in any other major city. Don't drink St Petersburg's tap water – it harbours *Giardia lamblia*, an intestinal parasite that can cause diarrhoea and nausea. Stick to bottled water, which is readily available at supermarkets and hotels; avoid ice and be careful with unpeeled raw fruit and vegetables.

Dive-bombing mosquitoes are rife in summer and it is advisable to bring mosquito repellent, coils or a net.

Getting There & Away

AIR
St Petersburg has direct air links with most major European capitals and airlines, many offering several connections each week (eg, Lufthansa offers six flights a week to/from Frankfurt).

You can also fly to just about anywhere within Russia, but only a few times a week in some cases. Tickets can be purchased at the Central Airline Ticket Office, Nevsky prospekt 7, and from travel agencies such as Ost-West Contaktservice.

BUS
St Petersburg's bus station, Avtovokzal No 2 (☎ 166 5777) – there is no number one –

at naberezhnaya Obvodnogo kanala 36, 1km from Ligovsky Prospekt metro, serves Tampere, Vyborg, Pskov, Novgorod, Moscow, Novaya Ladoga, Petrozavodsk and many other smaller destinations. For buses to and from Central and Eastern Europe, Eurolines (☎ 168 2740) operates several comfortable daily buses, leaving from in front of Baltisky Vokzal (Baltic Station). Eurolines' office is at ulitsa Shkapina 10, 50m west of Baltisky Vokzal. For service to/from Finland, Finnord (☎ 314 8951) and Sovavto (☎ 123 5125) have daily buses. A one-way ticket to Helsinki costs about $40.

TRAIN

St Petersburg has four major long-distance train stations: Finlandsky Vokzal (Finland Station) on ploshchad Lenina, Vyborg Side, serves trains on the Helsinki railway line; Moskovsky Vokzal (Moscow Station), at ploshchad Vosstaniya on Nevsky prospekt, handles trains to/from Moscow, the far north, Crimea, the Caucasus, Georgia and Central Asia; Vitebsky Vokzal (Vitebsk Station), at Zagorodny prospekt 52, deals with Smolensk, Belarus, Kiev, Odessa and Moldova; and Varshavsky Vokzal (Warsaw Station), naberezhnaya Obvodnogo kanala 118, covers the Baltic countries and Eastern Europe. Baltiysky Vokzal (Baltic Station), just along the road from the Warsaw Station, is mainly for suburban trains.

Domestic and international train information and tickets are available from counter No 13 at the Central Train Ticket Centre, naberezhnaya kanala Griboedova 24. Sindbad Travel issues tickets to Moscow and Helsinki on the spot, and has a ticket-buying service for other destinations, adding $5 to the ticket price. Foreigners have to pay up to six times more than Russians for tickets.

Two trains to Helsinki depart daily from St Petersburg ($50, six hours). There are overnight services to both Tallinn and Riga. There are also daily trains to Vilnius, Warsaw and Berlin.

Getting Around

TO/FROM THE AIRPORT

St Petersburg's airport is at Pulkovo, 17km south of the city centre. From Moskovskaya metro, bus No 39 runs to Pulkovo-1, the domestic terminal, and No 13 to Pulkovo-2, the international terminal. Taxis from the airport can cost up to $40, but from the centre, a private cabbie will get you there for $5 to $10.

PUBLIC TRANSPORT

Handy, free metro maps are available at most stations. Tokens (zhetony) cost $0.12, and a variety of magnetic-strip cards for multiple-entry are also available from the booths in the stations, which open around 5.30 am and close just after midnight every day. Tickets for buses, trolleybuses and tramways are bought inside from controllers.

TAXI

There are now official, metered taxis in St Petersburg as well as unofficial taxis (private cars). The average price for a ride across town in either is about $2.

The City

☎ 812
Orientation

The heart of St Petersburg spreads south and east from the Winter Palace and the Admiralty on the Neva's south bank, its skyline dominated by the golden dome of St Isaac's Cathedral. Nevsky prospekt, stretching south-east from the Admiralty, is the main street, containing many of the city's sights, shops and restaurants.

The north side of the city has three main areas. The westernmost is Vasilevsky Island, at whose eastern end – the Strelka – many of the city's fine early buildings still stand.

The middle area is Petrograd Side, a cluster of delta islands whose south end is marked by the tall golden spire of the SS Peter & Paul Cathedral. The third (eastern) area is Vyborg Side, divided from Petrograd Side by the Bolshaya Nevka channel.

Information

Tourist Offices The city is still without an official, state tourist office, but the HI St Petersburg Hostel (☎ 329 8018) at 3-ya Sovetskaya ulitsa 28 is very helpful. At the same address is the budget travel agency Sindbad Travel (see Travel Agencies).

The twice-weekly St Petersburg Times is packed with practical information and listings of clubs, pubs, restaurants, museums, theatres, etc.

Post & Communications For information on where to telephone, send mail or access the Internet, see the information under Facts for the Visitor earlier in the chapter.

Travel Agencies Sindbad Travel (☎ 327 8384, ☺ sindbad@sindbad.ru) at the HI St Petersburg Hostel is a student and discount air-ticket office, specialising in one-way and short or no-advance purchase tickets. Its second location (☎ 324 0880) is at Universitetskaya naberezhnaya 11. Web site: www.sindbad.ru

Ost-West Contaktservice (☎ 327 3416, ☺ info@ostwest.com), ulitsa Mayakovskogo 7, is another friendly, helpful agency that can help with any travel need. Web site: www.ostwest.com

Bookshops Anglia (☎ 279 8284), naberezhnaya Fontanki 40, is the city's English-language book haven, and stocks many Lonely Planet titles.

Medical & Emergency Services You can get Western-quality treatment (at stellar prices) at the 24-hour American Medical Center (AMC; ☎ 326 1730), Serpukhovskaya ulitsa 10. Apteka Petrofarm at the corner of Nevsky prospekt and Bolshaya Konyushennaya ulitsa is an all-night pharmacy.

Things to See & Do
Museum hours change like quicksilver, as do their weekly days off. Most are open 11 am to 6 pm (exceptions are noted) and close on Monday or Tuesday, but it's best to check the hours in the *St Petersburg Times*.

The Historic Heart From Gostiny Dvor or Nevsky Prospekt metro, a 15-minute walk along Nevsky prospekt brings you to **Dvortsovaya ploshchad** (Palace Square), where the stunning green, white and gold **Winter Palace** (Zimny dvorets) appears like a mirage. The baroque/rococo palace, commissioned from Rastrelli in 1754 by Empress Elizabeth and boasting 1057 rooms and 117 staircases, houses part of the **Hermitage** (☎ 110 9079), one of the world's great art museums.

The remainder of the Hermitage is housed in four linked buildings – the Little Hermitage, the Old and New Hermitages and the Hermitage Theatre – running west to east from the palace. The main ticket hall is inside the main entrance on the river side of the Winter Palace. The Hermitage is open 10.30 am to 6 pm daily except Monday. Entry for non-Russians is $10 (free for ISIC card-holders).

The **Alexander Column** (47.5m) in Dvortsovaya ploshchad commemorates the 1812 victory over Napoleon. Across the road from Dvortsovaya ploshchad is the gilded spire of the old **Admiralty**, the former headquarters of the Russian navy. West of the Admiralty is **ploshchad Dekabristov** (Decembrists' Square), at the river end of which stands the most famous statue of Peter the Great, the **Bronze Horseman**.

The golden dome of **St Isaac's Cathedral**, built between 1818 and 1858, looms just south of ploshchad Dekabristov. About 600m west of ploshchad Dekabristov is the **St Petersburg History Museum**, naberezhnaya Krasnogo Flota 44, which has good information on the 1941-44 siege (closed Wednesday; $0.75).

Nevsky Prospekt Russia's most famous street runs 4km from the Admiralty to the Alexandr Nevsky Monastery, from which it takes its name. The inner 2.5km to Moscow Station is St Petersburg's main shopping centre.

Across the Moyka River, Rastrelli's **Stroganov Palace** (1752-54) has kept most of its original appearance. A block beyond are the great colonnaded arms of the **Kazan Cathedral**. Inside is the **Museum of the History of Religion**, which includes the grave of Field Marshal Kutuzov, the Russian commander against Napoleon in 1812.

Nevsky prospekt crosses the Fontanka on the **Anichkov Bridge**, with the famous 1840s statues of rearing horses at its four corners. From here, the red **Beloselsky-Belozersky Palace** (1840s) provides a photogenic baroque backdrop. At the end of Nevsky prospekt is the **Alexandr Nevsky Monastery**, founded by Peter the Great in 1713 and still operating. The **Tikhvin Cemetery** within is where some of Russia's most famous artistic figures, including Tchaikovsky, are buried ($2/1).

CENTRAL ST PETERSBURG

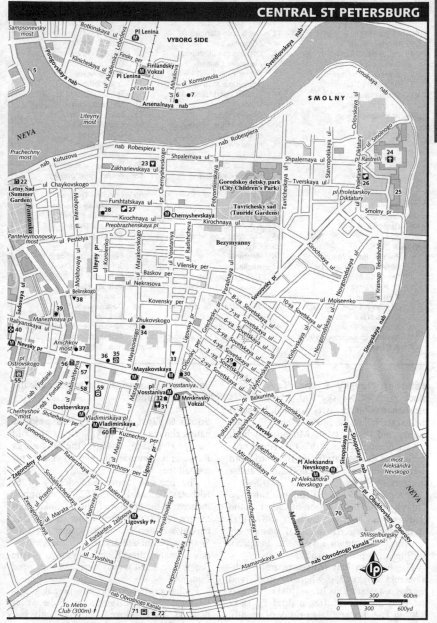

CENTRAL ST PETERSBURG

CENTRAL ST PETERSBURG

PLACES TO STAY
- 6   Holiday Hostel
- 29   HI St Petersburg Hostel;
  Sindbad Travel
- 30   Hotel Oktyabrskaya
- 32   Oktyabrsky Filial
- 45   Grand Hotel Europe;
  American Express
- 72   Hotel Kievskaya

PLACES TO EAT
- 1   Troitsky Most
- 2   Troitsky Most
- 12   Tinye
- 33   Cheburechnaya
- 38   Kafe Lagindze
- 46   Laima
- 57   Gushe
- 58   Green Crest
- 65   Café Idiot

OTHER
- 3   Political History Museum
  (Ksheshinskaya Palace)
- 4   Peter's Cabin
- 5   Cruiser Aurora
- 7   Kresty Prison
- 8   SS Peter & Paul Cathedral
- 9   Central Naval Museum
- 10   Museum of Zoology
- 11   Museum of Anthropology
  & Ethnography

- 13   The Bronze Horseman
- 14   Admirality
- 15   Dvortsovaya ploshchad;
  Alexander Column
- 16   Winter Palace
  (Hermitage Museum)
- 17   Pushkin Flat-Museum
- 18   Sindbad
- 19   Marble Palace
- 20   Church of the Resurrection
  of Christ
- 21   Russian Museum
- 22   Summer Palace
- 23   JFC Jazz Club
- 24   Smolny Cathedral
- 25   Smolny Institute
- 26   UK Consulate
- 27   US Consulate
- 28   Main OVIR
- 31   Fish Fabrique
- 34   Ost-West Contaktservice
- 35   Cityline
- 36   Westpost
- 37   Anglia
- 39   St Petersburg State
  Circus
- 40   Passazh Department Store
- 41   Theatralnaya Kassa Theatre
  (Ticket Office)
- 42   Promstroy Bank;
  St Petersburg Savings Bank
- 43   Philharmonia Large Hall

- 44   Philharmonia Small Hall
- 47   Apteka Petrofarm
  (24-Hour Pharmacy)
- 48   Telephone Office
- 49   Central Airline
  Ticket Office
- 50   St Isaac's Cathedral
- 51   Stroganov Palace
- 52   Kazan Cathedral
- 53   Central Train
  Ticket Centre
- 54   Gostiny Dvor
  Department Store
- 55   Pushkin Theatre
- 56   Beloselsky-Belozersky
  Palace
- 59   Lensoviet Theatre
- 60   Dostoevsky Museum
- 61   Tovstonov Bolshoy
  Dramatic Theatre
- 62   City Club; Money
  Honey Saloon
- 63   Central Post Office
- 64   St Petersburg History
  Museum
- 66   Yusupov Palace
- 67   Mariinsky Theatre
- 68   Dostoevsky Flat
- 69   69 Club
- 70   Alexandr Nevsky Monastery
- 71   Avtovokzal No 2
  (Bus Station)

Between Nevsky & the Neva Just a block north of Nevsky Prospekt metro is **ploshchad Iskusstv** (Arts Square), home to the **Large Hall** of the St Petersburg Philharmonia and the **Russian Museum**, which houses one of the country's two finest collections of Russian art (open 10 am to 5 pm daily, closed Tuesday; $5.60/2.80 adults/students).

The stunningly beautiful, multidomed **Church of the Resurrection of Christ** on the Griboedova Canal was built in 1887-1907 on the spot where Alexander II, despite his reforms, was blown up by the People's Will terrorist group in 1881.

The **Pushkin Flat-Museum**, naberezhnaya reki Moyki 12, is where the poet lived for the last year of his life – Russia's greatest poet died here after a duel in 1837 (closed Tuesday and last Friday of month; $2/1).

Between Mars Field and the Fontanka River is the lovely **Summer Garden**, laid out for Peter the Great with fountains, pavilions and a geometrical plan to resemble the park at Versailles.

South & West of Nevsky Prospekt At naberezhnaya reki Moyki 94 is the old **Yusupov Palace**, where the notorious Rasputin was murdered (open to visitors for a small fee).

The baroque spires and domes of **St Nicholas' Cathedral** (1753-62), rising among the trees at the bottom of ulitsa Glinki, shelter many 18th-century icons and a fine carved wooden iconostasis. Just west of Sennaya ploshchad and across the Griboedova Canal at ulitsa Kaznacheyskaya 7 is the flat where Dostoevsky wrote *Crime and Punishment*.

Farther east at Kuznechny pereulok 5 is the **Dostoevsky Museum**, where the writer died in 1881 (closed Monday and last Wednesday of month; $1.20/0.60).

Vasilevsky Island The **Strelka** (Tongue of Land) has one of the best views of the city.

The **Central Naval Museum** is full of maps, excellent model-ships and the *Botik*, a 19th-century submarine (closed Monday, Tuesday and last Thursday of month; $2/1). Just south is the **Museum of Zoology**, said to be one of the biggest and best in the world (closed Friday; $0.60/0.30).

Peter the Great's own personal collection of 'curiosities' (bugs, snakes and a truly ghoulish collection of preserved freaks, foetuses and body parts) is housed in the blue sand white building with the steeple, the **Museum of Anthropology & Ethnography** (closed Thursday; $1.50).

Petrograd Side Petrograd Side is a cluster of delta islands between the Malaya Neva and Bolshaya Nevka channels. Founded in 1703, the **Peter & Paul Fortress** is the oldest building in St Petersburg. Its main use up to 1917 was as a political prison; famous inmates included Dostoevsky, Gorky and Trotsky. The fort is closed Wednesday and the last Tuesday of the month; entry is free.

Most spectacular of all is the **SS Peter & Paul Cathedral**, with its landmark needle-thin spire and magnificent baroque interior. It houses the tombs of Peter the Great, Catherine the Great and the family of Nicholas II (reburied here in 1998).

East of Kamennoostrovsky prospekt at ulitsa Kuybysheva 4 is the Ksheshinskaya Palace, which houses the **Museum of Political History in Russia** (closed Thursday; $2.40/1.20).

East of the fortress at Petrovskaya naberezhnaya 6 is St Petersburg's first residence, **Peter's Cabin**, where Peter lived in 1703 while supervising the construction of the fortress and city.

Just east of that, moored at the eastern end of the island, is the **Cruiser Aurora**, which fired the (blank) shot that signalled the start of the 1917 revolution (closed Tuesday; free).

Organised Tours

Practically every travel agency and hotel organises tours; Peter's Tours which leave from the HI St Petersburg Hostel are unbeatable (book through the hostel or email in advance at @ pkozyrev@hotmail.com – see Places to Stay for contact details).

Eighty-minute 'City on the Neva' cruises – up the river and back from the Hermitage

No 2 landing or from the Fontanka bridge (at Nevsky prospekt) – leave every 40 minutes and cost around $5.

Special Events

The last 10 days of June are a massive celebration that includes the White Nights Dance Festival. The Russian Winter (25 December to 5 January) and Goodbye Russian Winter (late February to early March) festivities are centred outside the city. The St Petersburg Music Spring, an international classical-music festival, is held in April or May. The mid-November International Jazz Festival, *Osenie Ritmy* (Autumn Rhythms), is spread around St Petersburg's jazz clubs.

Places to Stay

Hostels The *HI St Petersburg Hostel* (☎ 329 8018, fax 329 8019, ryh@ryh.spb, 3-ya Sovetskaya ulitsa 28) could not have a better location – it's a five-minute walk north-east of Moskovsky vokzal (Moscow Station) and ploshchad Vosstaniya. A place in rooms with three to six beds costs $19; in a double room, $24.

The *Holiday Hostel* (☎/fax 542 7364, ulitsa Mikhailova 1, Vyborg Side) is just south of Finlandsky Vokzal (Finland Station) and next door to the Kresty Prison. A bed in a double room costs $15 with breakfast ($12 in a room with three to six beds).

While not close to the centre, the *Petrovskogo College Student Hostel* (☎ 252 7563, fax 252 4019, ulitsa Baltiyskaya 26, metro Narvsakya) has excellent deals: a place in a double/triple is $4/6.

Hotels The best hotel deals in the city, hands down, belong to *Hotel Oktyabrskaya* (☎ 277 6330, fax 315 75 01, Ligovsky prospekt 10) and its *Oktyabrsky Filial* (☎ 277 7281, Ligovsky prospekt 43/45), both opposite Moskovsky vokzal.

Both offer a wide range of rooms. The Filial is the more run-down option, with singles/doubles from $7/10 – no room is more than $30 a night. The Oktyabrskaya has singles/doubles/ triples starting at $30/38/45.

South of the centre is the dumpy but cheerful *Hotel Kievskaya (ulitsa Dnepropetrovskaya 49)*, and its superior *Kievsky*

Filial (Kurskaya ulitsa 40), a block away. Bookings for both can be made on ☎ 166 5811, fax 166 5398. Both have singles/doubles with shared facilities for $6/10, or $14/22 with toilet and breakfast.

Places to Eat

Some of the best Georgian food can be had at *Cheburechnaya (ulitsa Vosstaniya 13)*. It's no-frills dining, but the meals are first-rate – fill up on succulent *dolma* (stuffed fig leaves) for $1.30, or *seljanka* soup so thick you need a fork to eat it. It's open 10 am to midnight daily.

Kafe Lagindze (Belinskogo 1) is another excellent choice for Georgian food.

Chinese can be sampled at the heavenly *Red Rose (Kamennoostrovsky prospekt 44/46)* or *Tinye (1-ya linia 18)*, on Vasilevsky Island, which has huge soups (under $2) and main meals for under $6.

If you fancy Indian food, your head will swivel in ecstasy at *Swagat (☎ 217 2111, Bolshoy prospekt 91)*, also on Vasilevsky Island. Swagat also delivers.

One of the coolest places is *Café Idiot (☎ 315 1675 naberezhnaya reki Moyki 82)*, open noon to 11 pm daily. All the food is vegetarian (most meals cost under $5), there's a non-smoking room (the only one in Russia?) and the atmosphere is relaxed.

Vegetarians will also like *Troitsky Most*, with branches at Malaya Posadskaya 2 and Kronversky prospekt 9/2). They serve vegie burgers, lots of salads, dry soya meals, and are open 24 hours.

The very pleasant *Green Crest (Vladimirsky prospekt 7)* has 10 different kinds of salads (takeaways available), vegie stew and some fish and meat dishes. A few doors up at the corner of Nevsky prospekt, the *Gushe* bakery has some of the most addictive pastries in the city as well as light, healthy meals.

The undisputed champion of Russian fast food is *Laima*, found at naberezhnaya kanala Griboedova 14 and Bolshoy prospekt 88 (Petrograd Side). The huge menu includes about 20 salads, delicious soups, stuffed peppers, chicken and fish fillets, kebabs, freshly squeezed juices and milkshakes – with no meal more than $3. Ask for the English menu. Laima is open around the clock.

Entertainment

Bars, Clubs & Discos *City Club (Apraksin Dvor 14)* is an excellent, lively place. Upstairs there's a dance floor and pool tables, and downstairs there's the *Money Honey Saloon*, which has great live rock and country bands.

The excellent *JFC Jazz Club (☎ 272 98 50, Shpalernaya ulitsa 33)* has some of the city's best jazz and blues in a cosy, New York-style space.

Fish Fabrique (ulitsa Pushkinskaya 10) attracts the alternative artsy set – there's never a dull moment.

To boogie, the cavernous *Metro Club (☎ 166 0204, Ligovsky prospekt 174)* is hugely popular, has three dance halls, theme nights, and is a lot of fun.

69 Club (2-ya Krasnoarmeyskaya ulitsa 6) is St Petersburg's premiere gay nightclub, but so popular everyone seems to go there (except women, who pay double to get in).

Circus The *St Petersburg State Circus (☎ 210 4649, naberezhnaya reki Fontanki 3)*, 500m south of the Summer Garden, has shows at 7 pm nightly (except Monday and Thursday), plus afternoon and lunch-time performances at weekends. Tickets bought here cost from $0.40, but foreigners can be charged $10.

Ballet, Opera, Theatre & Classical Music September to early summer is the main season for the arts in St Petersburg. Most theatres and concert halls are closed on Monday.

The Kirov Ballet and Opera are at the *Mariinsky Theatre (Teatralnaya ploshchad 1)*. You can buy tickets (around $4) at the *teatralnaya kassa* (theatre ticket office; ☎ 314 9385) at Nevsky prospekt 42.

The St Petersburg Philharmonic performs at the *Bolshoy Zal (Large Hall; ☎ 311 7333, ploshchad Iskusstv)* and at the nearby *Maly Zal imeni MI Glinki (Small Hall; Nevsky prospekt 30)*.

The premier drama theatre is the *Pushkin (ploshchad Ostrovskogo 2)*. Other top theatres include the *Lensoviet Theatre (Vladimirsky prospekt 12)* and the *Tovstonov Bolshoy Dramatic Theatre (naberezhnaya reki Fontanki 65)*.

Around St Petersburg

PETRODVORETS

Petrodvorets (also known as Petergof), 29km west of St Petersburg, is an estate built by Peter the Great. Though heavily damaged by the Germans in WWII (and now largely a reconstruction), Petrodvorets is Russia's most popular attraction, receiving up to six million visitors a year.

The centrepiece of the grounds is the **Grand Cascade & Water Avenue**, a symphony of over 140 fountains and canals. Between the cascade and the formal **Upper Garden** is the **Grand Palace** (closed Monday and the last Tuesday of the month). The finest room in this vast museum of lavish rooms and galleries is Peter's study, apparently the only room to survive the Germans.

The estate also features other buildings of interest – **Monplaisir** (Peter's villa), the **Hermitage**, and **Marly** – and other parks and pavilions. To the east an old Orangery houses the **Historical Museum of Wax Figures**, containing 49 figures of big-wigged Russians from the 18th and 19th centuries.

The grounds are open 9 am to 10 pm daily. The museums are open 11 am to 8 pm daily from late May to late September.

Getting There & Away

The easiest way to get there on your own is to take comfy double-decker bus No 849 or 851 from outside the Baltisky Vokzal ($0.30, 40 minutes), which leaves regularly throughout the day and lets you off at Petrodvoret's main entrance on Sankt Peterburgsky prospekt.

From May to September, an alternative is the *Meteor* hydrofoil from the jetty in front of St Petersburg's Hermitage museum, which goes every 20 to 30 minutes from 9.30 am to at least 7 pm. The trip takes half an hour and will cost you a whopping $15 each way.

Slovakia

Slovakia, one of Europe's youngest countries, split from Czechoslovakia in 1993 after 74 years of junior partnership. The few budget travellers who pass through generally go no farther than Slovakia's capital, Bratislava, missing out on the rugged High Tatra mountains along the Polish border and the gentler natural beauty of the Malá Fatra mountains in Central Slovakia – both of which offer some of the best terrain in Europe for outdoor activities.

Slovakia is also rich in architecture, arts and folk culture. In East Slovakia, a string of unspoiled 13th-century medieval towns founded by Saxon Germans shelter Gothic artworks of the first order. There are about 180 castles and castle ruins in Slovakia, the largest and most photogenic being Spišský hrad, east of Levoča.

AT A GLANCE

Capital:	Bratislava
Population:	5.4 million
Official Language:	Slovak
Currency:	1 koruna (Sk) = 100 halier

Facts about Slovakia

HISTORY

Slavic tribes occupied what is now Slovakia in the 5th century AD, and in 833 the region became part of the Great Moravian Empire. By 1018 the whole of Slovakia was annexed to Hungary and it remained so for 900 years – Bratislava served as the Hungarian capital from 1526 to 1784.

The independent state of Czechoslovakia emerged after WWI, but power was concentrated in Prague and in 1938 Slovakia declared its autonomy. A fascist puppet state headed by Jozef Tiso was set up, and Slovakia became a German ally. In August 1944, Slovak partisans began the Slovak National Uprising (SNP) against the Tiso regime, an event that is now a source of national pride.

The second Czechoslovakia, established after WWII, was again centralised in Prague. Although the 1960 constitution granted Czechs and Slovaks equal rights,

only the 1968 'Prague Spring' reforms, which were introduced by Alexander Dubček (a rehabilitated Slovak communist), implemented this concept. In August 1968, after Soviet troops invaded Czechoslovakia, democratic reform was quashed and political power remained in Prague.

The fall of communism in Czechoslovakia in 1989 led to a resurgence of Slovak nationalism. In February 1992 the Slovak parliament rejected a treaty that would have perpetuated a federal Czechoslovakia.

The rift deepened with the June 1992 elections, which, in Slovakia, brought to power the nationalist Movement for a Democratic Slovakia (HZDS) headed by the autocratic Vladimír Mečiar. In July the Slovak parliament voted to declare sovereignty; the peaceful split with the Czech Republic was formalised on 1 January 1993.

Ex-boxer Mečiar dominated Slovak politics for the next five years. His authoritarian rule, the passing of anti-democratic laws and the mistreatment of Slovakia's Hungarian and Roma minorities brought criticism from human rights organisations, the EU and the US government.

Mečiar's controversial reign came to end when Mikuláš Džurinda, leader of the right-leaning Slovak Democratic Coalition (SDK), was elected prime minister in 1998. But Slovak society remains deeply polarised, and there is still support for Mečiar – he took 43% of the vote in the 1999 presidential election, narrowly losing to former communist Rudolf Schuster. The next parliamentary elections are scheduled for 2002.

GEOGRAPHY

Slovakia (49,035 sq km) forms a clear physical barrier between the plains of Poland and Hungary. Slovakia, south of

SLOVAKIA

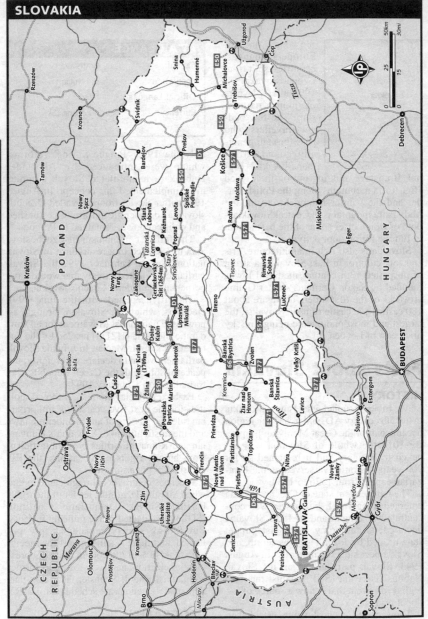

Nitra, is a fertile lowland stretching down to the Danube (Dunaj in Slovak), which forms the border with Hungary.

At 2654m Gerlachovský štít is the highest peak in the spectacular Vysoké Tatry (High Tatra) range, which Slovakia shares with Poland. Forests, mainly beech and spruce, cover 40% of the country despite centuries of deforestation.

CLIMATE

Slovakia experiences hot summers and cold winters. The warmest, driest and sunniest area in the country is the Danube lowland east of Bratislava. Because of the altitude spring and autumn are much shorter in the High Tatra mountains, which experience the highest rainfall.

POPULATION & PEOPLE

Slovakia has a population of 5.38 million, of which 85.6% are Slovaks, 10.7% Hungarians and 1% Czechs. The 600,000 ethnic Hungarians live mostly in southern and eastern Slovakia. Official figures say 1.5% of the Slovak population are Gypsies (Roma), but the figure may be as high as 400,000. As elsewhere in Eastern Europe, there is much prejudice against the Roma.

SOCIETY & CONDUCT

The rural Slovaks still adhere to their peasant traditions, evident in the folk costumes you'll see in remote Slovak villages on Sundays.

Slovaks are very polite people and it is customary to say *dobrý den* (good day) when entering a shop, hotel or restaurant, and *do videnia* (goodbye) when leaving. Despite the general surliness that Slovaks sometimes show to each other, they are friendly and hospitable to foreigners. If you are invited to someone's home remember to bring flowers for your hosts. If your hosts remove their shoes, do the same.

LANGUAGE

Although many people working in tourism have a good knowledge of English or German, in rural areas people speak Slovak only.

Slovak and Czech are similar but not identical. You won't be taken to task if you mix Czech with Slovak. Any effort to communicate in the local language will be appreciated.

See the Language Guide at the back of this book for details on Slovak pronunciation and some useful words and phrases.

Facts for the Visitor

HIGHLIGHTS

Bratislava's old town and castle are worth exploring, as are the historic town of Levoča and the castle of Spišský hrad.

The rocky peaks of the Vysoké Tatry offer excellent hiking and mountaineering, while the Malá Fatra has good hiking and skiing.

SUGGESTED ITINERARIES

Three days
    Visit Bratislava and Trenčín.
One week
    Visit Bratislava, the Vysoké Tatry and Košice.
Two weeks
    Visit most of the places in this chapter.

PLANNING
Maps

The Austrian publisher Freytag & Berndt has a good 1:500,000 map of Slovakia – *Slovenská republika*. Excellent hiking and skiing maps (1:25,000 and 1:50,000) are published by Vojenský kartografický ústav (VKÚ).

TOURIST OFFICES

Slovakia has an extensive network of Mestské informačné centrum (municipal information centres) that are in the Association of Information Centres of Slovakia (AiCES). They have exchange facilities, organise sightseeing tours and guides, and assist with accommodation. The staff speak English.

Commercial agencies include Satur, Tatratour and Slovakoturist.

VISAS

Nationals of most European countries, Australia and New Zealand do not need a visa for tourist visits of up to 90 days (UK and Irish citizens up to 180 days; US, Canadian, Italian and South African citizens up to 30 days).

EMBASSIES & CONSULATES
Slovakian Embassies Abroad

Australia (☎ 02-6290 1516) 47 Culgoa Circuit, O'Malley, Canberra, ACT 2606

SLOVAKIA

Austria (☎ 01-37 13 09) Armbrustergasse 24, 1-1190 Wien
Canada (☎ 613-749 4442) 50 Rideau Terrace, Ottawa, Ontario KIM 2A1
UK (☎ 020-7243 0803) 25 Kensington Palace Gardens, London W8 4QY
USA (☎ 202-965 5160) 2201 Wisconsin Ave NW, Suite 250, Washington, DC 20007

Foreign Embassies in Slovakia
The following are in Bratislava (area code ☎ 07):

Canada (☎ 52 44 21 75) Mišíkova 28D
Czech Republic (☎ 52 93 12 02) 29.augusta 5
UK (☎ 54 41 96 32) Panská 16
USA (☎ 54 43 33 38) Hviezdoslavovo nám 4

MONEY
The Slovak crown (Slovenská koruna; Sk) is divided into 100 hellers (halier). There are coins of 10, 20 and 50 hellers, and one, two, five and 10 Sk. Notes come in denominations of 20, 50, 100, 200, 500, 1000 and 5000 Sk.

The Slovak crown is not fully convertible – change your excess crowns before leaving Slovakia. Banks that change travellers cheques (1% commission) include the Všeobecná úverová banka (VÚB), Slovenská sporiteľňa and the Investičná banka. Satur travel agencies and post office exchange windows deduct 2%.

Credit cards can be used in most major hotels and many restaurants and shops. Larger branches of the major banks give cash advances from credit cards. ATMs (*bankomat*) are common, and most are linked to the Visa, MasterCard, Eurocard, Plus and Cirrus networks.

Exchange Rates

country	unit		koruna
Australia	A$1	=	27.09 Sk
Canada	C$1	=	31.86 Sk
euro	€1	=	42.51 Sk
France	10FF	=	64.80 Sk
Germany	DM1	=	21.73 Sk
Japan	¥100	=	44.29 Sk
New Zealand	NZ$1	=	20.34 Sk
UK	UK£1	=	70.22 Sk
USA	US$1	=	47.39 Sk

Costs
You'll find food, admissions and transport cheap and accommodation manageable, except in Bratislava. If you camp or stay in hostels, eat in local pubs and take local transport expect to spend about US$15 to US$20 a day.

POST & COMMUNICATIONS
Post
Mail is fairly reliable. Express Mail Services (for letters and parcels under 2kg) are available from most post offices. A postcard/letter to Europe is 7/12 Sk; overseas it's 10/16 Sk (airmail). Most post offices are open 7 or 8 am to 5 or 8 pm weekdays and 8 am to noon Saturday; in large towns such as Bratislava and Košice they open on Sunday.

Telephone, Fax & Email
Slovakia's country code is ☎ 421. Drop the initial zero from the area code when dialling in from abroad.

Calls are most easily placed from main post offices or telephone centres, and from cardphones on the street. Coin phones (5 Sk for local calls) often do not work. A three-minute direct-dial call from Slovakia costs about 68 Sk to the UK, 85 Sk to the USA or Australia. The international access code is ☎ 00. Phonecards are sold at post offices and shops in denominations of 150, 210, 270 or 520 Sk.

Faxes can be sent from a handful of major post offices. Internet access is available at an increasing number of places (see Email & Internet Access in the Bratislava and Košice sections).

INTERNET RESOURCES
EU Net's Slovakia Web site (slovakia.eunet .sk) has regional information and travel tips. Slovakia.org (www.slovakia.org) has information on Bratislava and other Slovak cities.

BOOKS
For a readable history, try Stanislav J Kirschbaum's *A History of Slovakia – The Struggle for Survival*. William Shawcross' *Dubček & Czechoslovakia* is a biography of the late leader and an account of the 1968 Prague Spring. Lonely Planet's *Czech & Slovak Republics* gives extensive information on Slovakia.

WOMEN TRAVELLERS
Sexual violence is low in comparison to Western countries and assaults on solo female travellers are rare.

GAY & LESBIAN TRAVELLERS

Homosexuality has been legal since the 1960s and the age of consent is 16. The local gay organisation is Ganymedes, PO Box 4, 830 00 Bratislava. It has a Trust Line (Linka dôvery; ☎ 0905-61 82 91), available on Tuesday and Thursday between 6 and 8 pm. The Lesbian organisation is Museion, PO Box 121, 814 99 Bratislava.

DISABLED TRAVELLERS

There are very few facilities for disabled people. Transport is a major problem as buses and trams have no wheelchair access. The Slovak Union for the Disabled (Slovenský zväz telesne postihnutých; ☎ 07-52 44 24 20) is at Pražská 11, Bratislava.

DANGERS & ANNOYANCES

Though crime is low in Slovakia, an increasing number of robberies take place on international trains passing through the country. The victims are usually sleeping passengers (occasionally passengers are gassed to sleep in their compartments and then relieved of their valuables). Minor annoyances include waiters and Bratislava taxi drivers who overcharge foreigners.

Ring the police (☎ 158) or ambulance (☎ 155) from anywhere in Slovakia.

BUSINESS HOURS

Shops open from 8 or 9 am and close at 5 or 6 pm on weekdays. Only major department stores such as Tesco are open on weekends. Many small shops, particularly in rural areas, close for lunch between noon and 2 pm.

Most museums are closed on Monday and the day following a public holiday. Many gardens, castles and historic sites in Slovakia are closed from November to March and open on weekends only in April and October.

PUBLIC HOLIDAYS & SPECIAL EVENTS

Public holidays are 1 January, 6 January (Three Kings Day), Easter Friday and Easter Monday, 1 May (Labour Day), 5 July (Cyril and Methodius Day), 29 August (SNP Day), 1 September (Constitution Day), 15 September (Our Lady of Sorrows Day), 1 November (All Saints' Day) and 24 to 26 December.

During late June or early July folk dancers from all over Slovakia meet at the Východná Folklore Festival, 32km west of Poprad. There are folk festivals in June in Červený Kláštor and Kežmarok, and in many other towns from June to August. The two-week Bratislava Music Festival is held in late September-early October, and the Bratislava Jazz Days weekend is in late October.

ACCOMMODATION

There are hundreds of camping grounds, usually open from May to September. Most lack hot water but have a small snack bar, and many also rent small cabins. Camping on public land is prohibited.

Though tourist hostels (Turistické ubytovňy) are not connected to the Hostelling International (HI) network, they do provide cheap, but very basic, dormitory accommodation. Slovakia has a few hostels and Juniorhotels where HI cards may get you a discount. In July and August many student dorms become temporary hostels – AiCES and Satur offices should have details. Hostel beds generally cost from US$4 to US$7.

Private rooms – look for *'privát'* or *'Zimmer frei'* signs – are available in tourist areas, and AiCES and Satur offices can book them.

Hotels in Bratislava are considerably more expensive than in the rest of the country. There are five categories from one star (budget) to five star (luxury). Two-star hotel rooms are typically US$15/20, three-star around US$25/40 (but up to US$60 in Bratislava).

FOOD & DRINKS

A *jedáleň* or *bistro* (self-service restaurant) is good for a cheap breakfast or lunch; sometimes these places have really tasty dishes such as barbecued chicken or hot German-style sausages. Also try Slovakia's beer halls – if the place is crowded with locals, is noisy and looks chaotic, chances are it will have great lunch specials at low prices. In Slovakia dinner is eaten early (between 6 and 7 pm) and latecomers may have little to choose from.

Check the prices on the *Jedálny lístok* (menu) before ordering, and send back anything you didn't ask for and don't want. The main categories are *predjedlá* (starters), *polievky* (soups), *hotová jedlá* (ready-to-serve dishes), *mäsité jedlá* (meat dishes), *ryby* (fish), *zelenina* (vegetables), *šaláty* (salads), *ovoce* (fruit), *zákusok* (dessert) and *nápoje* (drinks).

Tipping is optional but it's common to round up the bill to the next 5 Sk (10 Sk if the bill is over 100 Sk).

Slovak wine is good and cheap. Well-known brands are Kláštorné (a red) and Venušíno čáro (a white). Slovak *pivo* (beer) is good – try Zlatý Bažant from Hurbanovo or Martiner from Martin. Spirits include *Demänovka* (sweetened with honey) and *slivovice* (plum brandy).

Local Specialities

Soups include *hovädzia polievka* (beef broth), *zemiaková polievka* (potato soup) and *cesnaková polievka* (garlic soup).

Slovakia's traditional dish is *bryndžové halušky* (small dumplings topped with cheese and bacon). *Segedín* (a beef goulash with sauerkraut in cream sauce) usually comes with *knedle* (bread dumplings). *Kapor* (carp) and *pstruh* (trout) can be crumbed and fried or baked. Vegetarian dishes include *vysmážaný syr* (fried cheese).

Ovocné knedle (fruit dumplings) come with cottage cheese or crushed poppy seeds. A common dessert is *palačinky so zavareninou* (jam pancakes).

Getting There & Away

Czech Airlines (ČSA) flies between Bratislava and Prague (5777 Kč return) several times a day with connections to major European cities, New York, Montreal and Toronto. Return flights from New York to Bratislava (via Prague) can cost as little as US$575, and London to Bratislava (via Prague) from UK£175.

Seven buses each day link Bratislava to Vienna Airport (Schwechat) and to central Vienna (Mitte Busbahnhof; 285 Sk one way, 1½ hours). For more information on international buses see Getting There & Away in the Bratislava section.

There are trains going from Bratislava to Vienna (Südbahnhof) three times a day (260 Sk, 1½ hours). From Vienna there are rail connections to most Western European cities. Bratislava is linked to Budapest (three hours) by several daily express trains.

There are daily sleeper services from Bratislava to Kiev, changing at Košice (30 hours, 1443km), and to Moscow, changing at Warsaw (33 hours, 1991km).

Hydrofoils ply the Danube between Bratislava and Vienna once every day, Wednesday to Sunday for 745 Sk one way (1¾ hours), 1150 Sk return (May to mid-October). Buy tickets at the hydrofoil terminal, Fajnorovo nábrežie 2. There is also a once-daily (twice daily in August) hydrofoil service between Bratislava and Budapest from mid-April to October. The trip downstream to Budapest costs 2170 Sk one way, 3130 Sk return and takes four hours.

Getting Around

BUS

Plan on doing most of your travel by train, with side trips by bus. Bus tickets in Slovakia cost 84 Sk per 100km.

When trying to decipher posted bus schedules beware of departure times bearing footnotes you don't completely understand, as these buses often don't show up. Check the time at the information window whenever possible. It is helpful to know that *premáva* means 'it operates' and *nepremáva* means 'it doesn't operate'.

TRAIN

Slovak Republic Railways (ŽSR) provides efficient service at low rates. Most of the places covered in this chapter are on or near the main railway line between Bratislava and Košice. From Košice, there are daily express trains to Kraków and Budapest. Most train stations in Slovakia have an *úschovňa* (left-luggage office; 10 Sk to 20 Sk) and/or lockers (5 Sk).

CAR & MOTORCYCLE

You can drive in Slovakia using your home driving licence. Speed limits are 40km/h to 60km/h in built-up areas, 90km/h on open roads and 130km/h on motorways; motorbikes are limited to 90km/h. Beware of speed traps; on-the-spot fines are up to 2000 Sk.

Tolls for unlimited use of the country's highways are 60 Sk for 15 days or 200 Sk for a year, for vehicles up to 1.5 tonnes. You can be fined 5000 Sk if you do not have a sticker (available from most petrol stations). Unleaded petrol costs about 35 Sk per litre.

For roadside assistance call ☎ 154.

Bratislava

☎ 07

Bratislava (population 452,000), only 16km from the Hungarian border, is Slovakia's capital and largest city. Many beautiful monuments in the old town, as well as numerous museums and art galleries, hint at the city's rich past under Hungarian rule.

Bratislava is fairly cosmopolitan and definitely worth a day or two – if you can find cheap accommodation. Unlike Prague and Budapest, Bratislava is rarely swamped by tourists, except on summer weekends when the Austrians invade.

Orientation

Bratislava's main train station, Hlavná stanica, is several kilometres north of town. Tram No 1 runs from the stop downhill from the station to nám L. Štúra, near the centre. A few trains use the Bratislava-Nové Mesto station, on the north-eastern side of the city.

The Autobusová stanica (main bus station) is on Mlynské nivy, 1km east of Štúrova.

Information

Tourist Offices The Bratislava Information Service (BIS; ☎ 54 43 37 15, @ bis@bratislava.sk), Klobučnícka 2, sells an indexed city map and the event guide *Kam v Bratislave* (*Where in Bratislava*; 15 Sk, in Slovak only). It's open 8 am to 7 pm weekdays (to 4.30 pm October to May), 8.30 am to 1 pm Saturday. There is a smaller BIS office at Hlavná stanica.

The Slovak Spectator, an English-language paper sold at newsstands and bookshops, also has events listings.

Money The VÚB bank at Hlavná stanica, near the BIS desk, has an ATM and is open 7.30 am to 6 pm daily. Another branch is in the centre of town on the corner of Poštová and Obchodná. Many other banks around town have ATMs and exchange offices.

Bratislava's American Express representative is Tatratour (☎ 52 92 78 88), at Mickiewiczova 2.

Post & Telephone The main post office, nám SNP 34, is open 7 am to 8 pm weekdays, to 6 pm Saturday. There are phone centres at Kolárska 12 (open 7 am to 9 pm weekdays, 8 am to 8 pm weekends) and the main train station (24 hours).

Email & Internet Access There's an Internet Klub at the Múzeum Café (☎ 52 96 56 81) on Múzejná, at the rear of the Slovak National Museum – the entrance is in the cafe, to the right of the bar. It's open 9 am to 9 pm weekdays and from noon weekends. One minute costs 2 Sk (minimum 15 minutes). The same rates apply at the Bulgarian Cultural Centre's Internet Club (☎ 0903-96 71 21) at Jesenského 7, open 9 am to 6.30 pm Monday to Saturday, and the Österreich Institut's Cafe Internet (☎ 54 43 49 17) at Baštová 9, open 9 am to 9 pm weekdays. Netcafe, along a passage at Obchodná 53, is open noon till midnight daily, and charges only 60 Sk an hour.

Travel Agencies Satur (☎ 55 41 01 28), Jesenského 9, arranges international and domestic air, train and bus tickets, as well as local accommodation.

Bookshops Eurobooks, Jesenského 5, stocks books in English, including Lonely Planet guides. Interpress Slovakia, on the corner of Michalská and Sedlárska, sells foreign newspapers and magazines.

Buy maps of almost anywhere in Slovakia at Knihy Slovenský spisovate, on the corner of Rybárska brána and Laurinská.

Medical & Emergency Services For medical emergencies call ☎ 155. The main outpatient clinic is at Mýtna 5 and has a pharmacy. The 24-hour pharmacy (*lekáreň*) is at nám SNP 20. The main police station (*polícia*) is at Sasinkova 23.

Things to See & Do

Unless otherwise noted, all of Bratislava's galleries and museums are closed on Monday and admission is typically around 20 Sk to 40 Sk.

The **Slovak National Museum**, opposite the hydrofoil terminal, features anthropology, archaeology, natural history and geology exhibits. Further up the riverfront is the ultramodern **Slovak National Gallery**,

SLOVAKIA

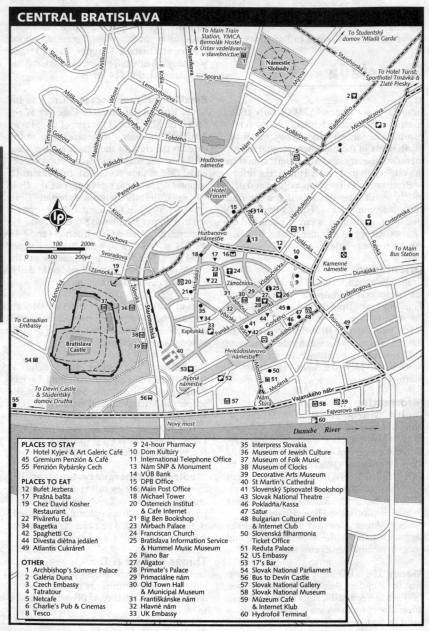

CENTRAL BRATISLAVA

SLOVAKIA

To Main Train
Station, YMCA,
Bernolák Hostel
& Ústav vzdelávania
v stavebníctve

To Študentský
domov 'Mladá Garda'

To Hotel Turist;
Sporthotel Trnávka &
Zlaté Piesky

Námestie
Slobody

To Hotel Forum

Hodžovo
námestie

Hurbanovo
námestie

Kamenné
námestie

To Main
Bus Station

To Canadian
Embassy

Bratislava
Castle

To Devín Castle
& Študentský
domov Družba

Hviezdoslavovo
námestie

Rybné
námestie

Nový most

Danube River

PLACES TO STAY	9 24-hour Pharmacy	35 Interpress Slovakia
7 Hotel Kyjev & Art Galeric Café	10 Dom Kultúry	36 Museum of Jewish Culture
45 Gremium Penzión & Café	11 International Telephone Office	37 Museum of Folk Music
55 Penzión Rybársky Cech	13 Nám SNP & Monument	38 Museum of Clocks
	14 VÚB Bank	39 Decorative Arts Museum
PLACES TO EAT	15 DPB Office	40 St Martin's Cathedral
12 Bufet Jezbera	16 Main Post Office	41 Slovenský Spisovateľ Bookshop
17 Prašná bašta	17 Michael Tower	43 Slovak National Theatre
19 Chez David Kosher	20 Österreich Institut	46 Pokladňa/Kassa
Restaurant	& Cafe Internet	47 Satur
22 Piváreňu Eda	21 Big Ben Bookshop	48 Bulgarian Cultural Centre
34 Bagetka	23 Mirbach Palace	& Internet Club
42 Spaghetti Co	24 Franciscan Church	50 Slovenská filharmónia
44 Divesta diétna jedáleň	25 Bratislava Information Service	Ticket Office
49 Atlantis Cukráreň	& Hummel Music Museum	51 Reduta Palace
	26 Piano Bar	52 US Embassy
OTHER	27 Aligator	53 17's Bar
1 Archbishop's Summer Palace	28 Primate's Palace	54 Slovak National Parliament
2 Galéria Duna	29 Primaciálne nám	56 Bus to Devín Castle
3 Czech Embassy	30 Old Town Hall	57 Slovak National Gallery
4 Tatratour	& Municipal Museum	58 Slovak National Museum
5 Netcafe	31 Františkánske nám	59 Múzeum Café
6 Charlie's Pub & Cinemas	32 Hlavné nám	& Internet Klub
8 Tesco	33 UK Embassy	60 Hydrofoil Terminal

holding Bratislava's major art collection, with a good Gothic section. The gallery's annexe is close by at nám L. Štúra 4.

Crowded, narrow Rybárska brána penetrates the old town to Hlavné nám, at the centre of which is **Roland's Fountain** (1572). To one side is the old town hall (1421), now the **Municipal Museum**, with torture chambers and an extensive historical collection.

Leave the courtyard through the east gate and you'll be on a square in front of the **Primate's Palace** (1781). Enter to see the Hall of Mirrors where Napoleon and the Austrian emperor Franz I signed a peace treaty in 1805. On Saturday the palace is crowded with couples being married, but it's still open to visitors.

On Františkánske nám, **Mirbach Palace** (1770) is a beautiful rococo building that houses a good art collection.

From the palace, narrow Zámočnícka leads to the **Michael Tower** (closed Tuesday), with a collection of antique arms. There's a great view from the top.

On the way to Bratislava Castle you can visit the **Decorative Arts Museum** and the **Museum of Clocks** (both closed Tuesday). Farther north is the **Museum of Jewish Culture** (closed Saturday).

From the 1st to the 5th centuries, **Bratislava Castle** was a frontier post of the Roman Empire. It later served as the seat of Hungarian royalty until it burnt down in 1811. Reconstructed between 1953 and 1962, the castle now houses a large **Historical Museum** in the main building, and an interesting **Museum of Folk Music** in a northern wing. The Slovak National Parliament meets in the modern complex that overlooks the river, just beyond the castle.

For a good view (even from the toilets) head to **Nový most** (New Bridge) and its expensive cafe, perched 80m above the river.

Places to Stay

Satur and BIS book private rooms (from 400 Sk per person), summer-only hostels (from 200 Sk per person) and hotels. Reservations are recommended year-round.

Hostels The shabby but friendly *YMCA* (☎/fax 52 49 51 56), on the corner of Šancová and Karpatská, rents out doubles and triples for 200 Sk or 250 Sk per bed, but it's often full. In July and August the 12-storey *Bernolák Hostel* (☎ 52 49 71 69, fax 52 49 77 24, Bernolákova 1), about five blocks east of the main train station, rents doubles with shower at 260 Sk per person. There's a swimming pool and disco (audible throughout the building).

Študentský domov 'Mladá Garda' (☎ 44 25 31 36, fax 44 45 96 90, Račianska 103), north-east of town (tram No 3, 5, 7 or 11), has accommodation from July to mid-September, at around 200 Sk per person.

Študentský domov Družba (☎ 65 42 00 65, Botanická 25) is 20 minutes west of the city centre near the Danube (take tram No 1 from the main train station, No 4 or 12 from nám L. Štúra). Available in summer only, it has double rooms with bathroom and TV for 850 Sk.

The hostel of the *Ústav vzdelávania v stavebníctve (Institute for Adult Education in the Building Industry;* ☎ 54 77 20 60, Bardošová 33), on a hill 1.5km north-west of the main train station, is 390 Sk per person, and the accommodation is good. This place is often full, so ask someone to help you call ahead before going there (take trolleybus No 212 from Hodžovo nám to ulica Stromová and hike up the hill).

Hotels & Pensions The best deal near the centre of town is *Penzión Rybársky Cech* (☎ 54 11 83 34, fax 54 41 83 33, Žižkova 1a), beneath the castle, with singles/doubles for 500/1000 Sk and a river-view apartment at 1700 Sk.

A good place in the heart of town is *Gremium Penzión* (☎ 54 13 10 26, fax 54 13 10 37, Gorkého 11), at 890/1600 Sk for singles/doubles, including breakfast. You will need to book ahead to get one of the few rooms.

The group-oriented *Hotel Kyjev* (☎ 52 96 10 82, fax 52 92 68 20, ✉ rezervacia@kyjev-hotel.sk) is a graceless tower block overlooking Tesco on Špitálska, but the location is central and rooms with bathroom and TV are reasonable value at 2200/2400 Sk, including breakfast.

The two-storey *Športhotel Trnávka* (☎/fax 43 42 34 97, Nerudova 8), next to a small stadium north-east of town, is seedy and rooms are small, but at 400/540/775 Sk with shared bath for singles/doubles/triples, it's good value. Take trolleybus No 205 from Cintorínska near Hotel Kyjev, or No 204 eastbound from Šancová down the hill from the main train station. On Friday and Saturday nights ask for a room away from the disco.

Hotel Turist (☎ *55 57 27 89, fax 55 57 31 80, Ondavská 5*) has pleasant rooms with bathroom and balcony for 950/1250/1450 Sk, not including breakfast. Take bus No 204 from Šancová (downhill from the train station) to the Zimný štadión stop; Ondavská is the third street on the right after the stop.

Zlaté Piesky Zlaté piesky (Golden Sands) is a lake resort 7km north-east of Bratislava, with bungalows, a motel, a hotel and two camping grounds. Tram Nos 2 (from the main train station) and 4 (from the city centre) terminate here.

Across the bridge from the tram stop is the **Hotel Flora** (☎ *25 79 88, fax 25 79 45*), with doubles from 590 Sk with shower and toilet. Next to the Flora is the lakeside **Inter-camp Zlaté piesky** (☎/*fax 44 25 73 73*) with three-bed bungalows with private bath for 900 Sk. Tent camping is possible and the site is open from mid-April to mid-October.

Places to Eat

There is a good **supermarket** in the basement of Tesco department store. One of the few places to get an early breakfast is **Bufet Jezbera** (*nám SNP 11*). It's open 6.30 am to 3.15 pm on weekdays only. **Bagetka**, in a passage at Zelená 8, sells cheap (less than 80 Sk), freshly made sandwiches.

Spaghetti & Co on the corner of Hviezdoslavovo nám and Rybárska brána has excellent pastas (60 Sk to 185 Sk) and pizzas (80 Sk to 150 Sk) and is open to 1 am daily.

The **Divesta dietná jedáleň** (*Laurinská 8*) is great for a quick meat or vegetarian meal. It's open 10 am to 3 pm weekdays.

Two good, inexpensive pubs with typical Slovak food are **Prašná bašta** (*Zámočnícka 11*) and **Piváreň u Eda**, on Biela.

Chez David Kosher Restaurant (*Zámocká 13*), directly below the castle, is upmarket but not intolerably so. Carp served in the Jewish style is a speciality.

Atlantis (*Štúrova 13*) serves the best ice cream in Bratislava. The **Gremium Art Galerie Café** (*Gorkého 11*) has a good atmosphere and pool tables upstairs.

Entertainment

World-class opera and ballet are presented at the **Slovak National Theatre** on Hviezdoslavovo nám, except on Sunday and in August. Tickets are sold at the 'Pokladňa/Kasse' office on the corner of Jesenského and Komenského.

The **Slovenská filharmonia** is based in the Reduta Palace. There's often something happening at the **Dom kultúry** (*House of Culture; nám SNP 12*).

Charlie's Pub (*Špitálska 4; enter from Rajská*) has loud pop music, TVs all around and people dancing among the tables. There is a small cover charge on weekends. Cinemas in the same complex often show films in English.

Two bars that have live jazz bands several times a week are **17's Bar** (*Hviezdoslavovo nám 17*) and **Aligator** (*Laurinská 7*). A pleasant and quiet place for a drink is the **Piano Bar** (*Laurinská 11*). The **Galéria Duna** (*Radlinského 11*) is a student-oriented club that has rock bands, dance music or whatever the alternative scene has to offer – check the program on its Web site at www.duna.sk.

Getting There & Away

Bus Bratislava's Autobusová stanica (main bus station; ☎ 55 42 27 73) is on Mlynské nivy, 1km east of the city centre. Buy domestic tickets from the driver if the bus is not full. Advance tickets for buses marked 'R' on timetables may be purchased inside at the AMS counter.

There are seven buses a day to Komárno (92 Sk, 2½ hours), nine to Košice (348 Sk, 7½ hours), and one to Starý Smokovec and Tatranská Lomnica (316 Sk).

Seven buses a day connect Bratislava with Vienna (Mitte Busbahnhof; 285 Sk, 1½ hours). In Bratislava buy your ticket for this bus at the ticket window inside the bus station. Ten express buses a day run to Prague (290 Sk, 4¾ hours).

Eurolines has buses between major European cities and Bratislava, including five a week from Brussels (2930 Bf one way, 16 hours) via Vienna, four a week from Zürich (59 Sfr, 13 hours), and three a week (five in summer) from London (UK£84, 24 hours). A 10% reduction is available to those aged under 26 or over 59. The Zürich bus continues to Košice twice a week (94 Sfr, 21 hours).

Other international buses from Bratislava go to Belgrade (9½ hours, twice a week), Budapest (four hours, daily), Frankfurt (12 hours, four weekly), Kraków (eight hours, weekly), Munich (8¼ hours, four times a week), Paris (20 hours, twice a week), Thessaloniki (21 hours, twice weekly) and Warsaw (12½ hours, weekly).

Buy tickets for international buses in crowns at either the international ticket window in the station or at the adjacent Eurolines office, depending on the destination.

Train For information on international express trains, see the Getting There & Away section at the beginning of this chapter.

From Hlavná stanica there are domestic services to major Slovak towns, including Košice (350 Sk, five hours) via Trenčín, Žilina and Poprad. Couchettes are available on the night train.

Getting Around
Buy tram and trolleybus tickets (6/12/18 Sk for 10/30/60 minutes with unlimited transfers) at the orange 'automat' machines at major stops or at Dopravný podnik Bratislava (DPB) offices at the train and bus stations and on Obchodná. If you are carrying luggage (even a large backpack) buy a separate half-fare ticket for it, otherwise inspectors mercilessly hand out 700 Sk fines. *Turistické cestovné lístky* (tourist tickets) valid for one/two/three/seven days (70/130/160/240 Sk) are also available.

Sightseeing boats (80 Sk) and ferries to Devín Castle (95 Sk return, 1¾ hours) leave from the hydrofoil terminal at Fajnorovo nábrežie. Boats to Devín run twice daily (except Monday) from May to early October.

AROUND BRATISLAVA
Devín Castle, across the river from Austria, was a frontier post of the Roman Empire from the 1st to the 5th centuries. In the 9th century it was a major stronghold of the Great Moravian Empire. The castle withstood the Turks but was blown up in 1809 by the French. Today the Gothic ruins are photogenic and make a good day trip. The castle is open Tuesday to Sunday, May to October.

To reach Devín, take a ferry (see Getting Around under Bratislava) or catch bus No 29 (every 30 minutes) from the terminal near

Nový most. Stay on the bus to the end of the line and walk back to the castle.

West Slovakia

TRENČÍN
☎ 0831
For centuries Trenčín has guarded the southwest gateway to Slovakia. Laugaricio, a Roman military post, was established here in the 2nd century AD – a rock inscription in Trenčín dated AD 179 mentions the Romans' victory over the Germanic Kvad tribes.

The mighty castle that now towers above the town was first mentioned in 1069. In the 13th century the castle's master, Matúš Čák, held sway over much of Slovakia. Though the castle and town were destroyed by fire in 1790, much has been restored.

Orientation & Information
From the adjacent bus and train stations walk west through the park and take the passage under the highway to Mierové nám, the main square.

The AiCES office (☎ 743 35 05), Štúrovo nám 10, can help with accommodation. The VÚB bank, at Mierové nám 48, changes travellers cheques, and another VÚB branch across the square at No 37 has an ATM.

Things to See
At the south-western end of Mierové nám are the baroque **Piarist Church** and the 16th-century **town gate** that plays old-fashioned tunes on the hour. The **art gallery** (closed Monday) next to the church features works by local artists.

A covered stairway from the corner of the main square leads up to **Trenčín Castle**, open daily year-round. A one-hour tour is 80 Sk. The castle's great central tower provides a sweeping view of the area. At night the castle is illuminated with green and purple lights. A two-hour show called Medieval Days, which includes sword fighting, is held from 9 pm every second Friday or Saturday from May to September.

Places to Stay & Eat
The camping ground *Vodácky klub na ostrove* (☎ 753 40 13) is on Ostrov Island, just opposite the large sports stadium near the city centre. Camping is 50 Sk per person

and 65 Sk per tent. Two- and four-bed cabins are 120 Sk per person. The site is open May to mid-September.

In the centre of town the only cheap accommodation is at *Penzión Svorad* (*☎/fax 743 03 22, Palackého 4*). Rooms with shared facilities cost 500/750 Sk.

There's a *supermarket* in the Prior department store on Vajanského.

Plzeňská pivnica, in a damp basement in pasáž Zlatá Fatima, serves hearty and inexpensive Slovak meals. A step up in quality, and in price, is *Restaurant Lanius* (*Mierové nám 22*).

Getting There & Away
All express trains on the Bratislava-Košice rail line stop here. There are six buses a day to Bratislava, Žilina and Košice. A few buses go to Brno in the Czech Republic.

Central Slovakia

ŽILINA
☎ 089

Žilina (population 86,700), midway between Bratislava and Košice, is the gateway to the Malá Fatra mountains. Though the sixth-largest city in Slovakia, it's still a pleasant, untouristy town with an attractive main square.

Orientation & Information
The adjacent bus and train stations are near the Váh River on the north-east side of town, a five-minute walk from Mariánské nám, Žilina's old town square. Another five minutes south from Mariánské nám is Štúrovo nám.

CK Selinan (☎ 562 14 78), Burianova medzierka 4, in a lane off the western side of Mariánské nám, has information about Žilina and the Malá Fatra.

The VÚB bank, Na bráne 1, changes travellers cheques and has an ATM. Tatratour, Mariánské nám 21, is the American Express representative.

The telephone centre is in the post office next to the train station.

Places to Stay
Pension GMK Centrum (*☎ 62 21 36, Mariánské nám 3*) has smallish rooms from 750/1200 Sk, including shower. Nicer is

Penzión Majovey (*☎ 62 41 52, fax 62 52 39, Jána Milica 3*), where rooms are 700/900 Sk.

The comfortable *Hotel Polom* (*☎ 562 11 51, Hviezdoslavova 22*), opposite the train station, has rooms for 820/1050 Sk with shower, TV and breakfast.

Places to Eat
Gastro (*Jána Milica 1*), on the corner of Národní, serves generous sandwiches and inexpensive buffet food. The trendy *Radničná vináreň* (*Mariánské nám 28*) is a cellar restaurant serving good, inexpensive meat dishes. *Campari Pizza* (*Zaymusova 4*), on the north side of Štúrovo nám, has a nice terrace where you can dine on pizza and cheap red wine.

Getting There & Away
Žilina is on the main Bratislava-Košice rail line. Express trains from Žilina take six hours to Prague, 1½ hours to Trenčín, three hours to Bratislava, two hours to Poprad and three hours to Košice.

There are several buses a day to Brno and Prague.

THE MALÁ FATRA
☎ 089

The Malá Fatra (Little Fatra) mountains stretch 50km across north-western Slovakia; Veľký Kriváň (1709m) is the highest peak. Much of this scenic range is included in Malá Fatra National Park.

At the heart of the park is Stará dolina, a beautiful mountain valley. Hiking possibilities here range from easy treks through the forest to scenic ridge walks. There are plenty of places you can stay and eat, though in midsummer and winter accommodation is tight. The valley is an easy day trip from Žilina.

Information
The Horská služba (Mountain Rescue Service; ☎ 569 52 32), on the access road to Hotel Boboty, has detailed park information.

If you plan to hike you should get the VKÚ's 1:50,000 *Malá Fatra Vrátna turistická mapa*.

It is also important to familiarise yourself with the trail markers, as some foreign hikers have confused them with logging markers and become lost.

Things to See & Do

To explore this area, take the bus from Žilina to **Chata Vrátna** (750m). From here, a two-seater chair lift climbs 770m to the Snilovské sedlo (1520m), a saddle midway between Chleb (1647m) and Veľký Kriváň. Take along a sweater or jacket as it's a lot cooler on top.

From Snilovské sedlo you can follow the red trail south-east along the mountain ridges past Hromové (1636m), then northeast to Poludňový grúň (1460m) and Stoh (1608m) to the **sedlo Medziholie** (1185m), a saddle below the rocky summit of **Veľký Rozsutec** (1610m). An orange trail skirting the side of Stoh avoids a 200m climb.

From Medziholie it's easy to descend another green trail to **Štefanová**, a picturesque village of log houses with private rooms available (ask around). You can do the hike from Snilovské sedlo to Štefanová (where you can get buses back to Žilina) via Medziholie in about four hours. Other possible hikes from Snilovské sedlo are the blue trail to Starý Dvor via Baraniarky (three hours) and the red trail west to Strečno train station via the Starý hrad ruins (6½ hours).

Skiing There is good downhill skiing and snowboarding for all levels, with 20 or so inexpensive lifts operating in the valley. Reasonable skis, boots and snowboards are available for hire. The best time is from late December to March.

Places to Stay & Eat

No camping is allowed in the Vrátna valley. The nearest *camping grounds* are at Nižné Kamence, 3km west of Terchová, and at Varín, both on the way to/from Žilina. There's a *grocery store* beside the Vrátna road junction in Terchová.

Accommodation in some chalets can be booked through Slovakotour Terchová (☎ 569 52 22). *Chata Vrátna* (☎ 69 57 39, fax 69 57 31), an 88-bed wooden chalet at 750m, is usually full with hikers in summer and skiers in winter. Regular hotel double/triple/quad rooms are 520/720/870 Sk, while the dormitory is 230 Sk per person. *Restaurant Koliba* faces the bus stop below the hotel.

Štefanová The *Chata pod Skalným mestom* (☎ 69 53 63), a few minutes up the green trail in Štefanová village, costs 300 Sk per person. A few hundred metres beyond is the similar *Chata pod Lampášom* (☎ 69 53 92), which charges 700 Sk per person for bed, breakfast and dinner. It's open year-round.

Reštaurácia Štefanová (☎ 69 53 25) rents cabins in the forest year-round, except in November. There are also several *privaty* around the village – look for the 'zimmer frei' signs.

The comfortable *Hotel Boboty* (☎ 569 52 28, fax 569 57 37), a five-minute walk up from the bus stop, near Štefanová, costs from 400/800 Sk for singles/doubles with shower, rising to 800/1000 Sk during holidays – breakfast is extra. The hotel has a sauna, a swimming pool and a restaurant.

Getting There & Away

Buses from Žilina to Chata Vrátna (one hour, nine daily) leave from platform No 10. Buses leave throughout the day from Štefanová to Žilina. The bus station at Žilina has an information counter – if you're on a day trip it's wise to confirm the times of afternoon buses returning to Žilina before setting out.

East Slovakia

THE VYSOKÉ TATRY
☎ 0969

The Vysoké Tatry (High Tatra) are the only truly alpine mountains in Central Europe. This granite massif is only 27km long and covers just 260 sq km, forming the northernmost portion of the 1200km-long Carpathian range. At 2654m, Gerlachovský štít (Mt Gerlach) is the highest peak in the Carpathians.

Enhancing the natural beauty packed into this relatively small area are 30 valleys and almost 100 little mountain lakes. The lower slopes are covered by dense coniferous forest. From 1500m to 1800m, there's a belt of shrubs and dwarf pines, and above this are alpine flora and bare rock.

Since 1949, most of the Slovak portion of this jagged range has been included in the Tatra National Park (TANAP), which complements a similar park in Poland. A 600km network of hiking trails reaches all the alpine valleys and many peaks. The red-marked

SLOVAKIA

Tatranská magistrála trail contours the southern slopes of the Vysoké Tatry for 65km
through a variety of striking landscapes.
Other routes are also colour-coded and easy
to follow. Park regulations require you to
keep to the marked trails.

When to Go
There's snow by November (on some of the
highest passes as early as September) and
from November to June the higher trails are
closed. July and August are the warmest
(and most crowded) months; August and
September are the best for high-altitude hiking. At 750m, the camping grounds will be
too cold for a tent from October to mid-
May. Hotel prices are at their lowest from
April to mid-June.

Orientation
The best centre for visitors is Starý
Smokovec, a turn-of-the-20th-century resort that is well connected to the rest of the
country by road and rail.

Tram-style electric trains run frequently
between the three main tourist centres: Štrbské Pleso (1320m), Starý Smokovec (990m)
and Tatranská Lomnica (850m). At Poprad
these trains link up with the national rail
system. Buses also run frequently between
the resorts. Cable cars, chair lifts and a funicular railway carry you up the slopes to
hiking trails that soon lead you away from
the throng.

Information
The main AiCES Tatry information centre
(☎ 442 34 40) in Dom služieb shopping centre, north-west of the Starý Smokovec train
station, has plenty of information and can
help with accommodation. Another office
(☎ 449 23 91) is opposite the Štrbské Pleso
train station. During the summer/winter seasons they are open 8.30 am to 6 pm daily, and
during the off season they open 8.30 am to 4
pm weekdays and 8 am to 1 pm Saturday.

The helpful Satur office (☎ 442 24 97,
✉ smokovec@satur.sk), just above the train
station at Starý Smokovec, provides a guiding service, accommodation and tours. The
TANAP Mountain Rescue Service office,
next to Satur, provides short-term weather
reports.

The Tatra National Park has a Web site
at www.tanap.sk which has information on

mountain guides, equipment rental and trail
conditions.

Things to See
Above Starý Smokovec From Starý
Smokovec a funicular railway (60 Sk;
closed April and November) carries you up
to Hrebienok (1280m), a ski resort with a
view of the Veľká Studená Valley. If it's not
running it takes less than an hour to walk up
to Hrebienok (via the green trail). From
Hrebienok the red Magistrála trail leads to
several waterfalls while the green trail continues to the Malá Studená Valley.

You can hike to the summit of Slav-
kovský štít (2452m) via the blue trail from
Starý Smokovec (seven to eight hours,
round trip). Check the weather first, and
take along warm clothes, waterproofs, and
a map and compass.

Štrbské Pleso From Starý Smokovec take
a morning train to the ski resort of Štrbské
Pleso and its glacial lake (at 1346m). Then
take the Magistrála trail (it runs along the
south shore of the lake) up to Popradské
pleso, another idyllic lake at 1494m (just over
one hour). From here the Magistrála zigzags
up the mountain towards Sliezsky dom and
Hrebienok (four hours). For a shorter hike, go
up the blue trail from Popradské pleso to the
Hincovo lakes (1½ hours).

Tatranská Lomnica In 1937 a 30-person
cable car (*lanová dráha*) began operating
from Tatranská Lomnica up to the mountain
lake of Skalnaté pleso (1751m, 120 Sk one
way). The cable car (closed Tuesday) is very
popular with tourists, so during the peak season get to the ticket office early.

A modern gondola with four-seat cabins
(closed every first Monday of each summer
month, 120 Sk one way) also runs to Skalnaté
pleso via Štart from above the Horec Hotel in
Tatranská Lomnica – it is faster and has
shorter queues than the cable car.

While waiting to depart, visit the **Tatra
National Park Museum**, a few hundred metres from the bus station (open 8 am to noon
and 1 to 4.30 pm weekdays, 8 am to noon
weekends). The exhibition on the natural
and human histories of this area is excellent.

There's an observatory at Skalnaté pleso
and a smaller cable car (15 persons; 300 Sk
one way) to the summit of **Lomnický štít**

(2632m), where you get a sweeping view of the entire High Tatra range. You're only allowed 30 minutes there and if you miss your car down you'll have to wait until another car has room for you. From Skalnaté pleso it's only two hours walk down the Magistrála trail to Hrebienok and the funicular railway down to Starý Smokovec.

Activities

Satur arranges rafting on the Dunajec River from June to September (750 Sk). In summer you can bungee jump from a 50m tower from Friday to Sunday in Štrbské Pleso, at Areál Snow, near the lift stations; cost is 750 Sk.

In winter Štrbské Pleso, Starý Smokovec and Tatranská Lomnica have fairly average downhill skiing and snowboarding, as well as some good cross-country skiing trails. Ski/snowboard hire costs from 220/390 Sk a day.

Places to Stay

Hotel prices almost double in the high seasons (mid-December to February and mid-June to September). Prices quoted here are for the high seasons.

Camping *Eurocamp FICC (☎ 446 77 41, fax 446 73 46)*, a five-minute walk from Tatranská Lomnica-Eurocamp train station on the line to Studený potok, has luxury bungalows (1800 Sk for four people) and camp sites (90 Sk per tent plus 120 SK per person), as well as restaurants, bars, a supermarket, a swimming pool and more. This place is open all year.

A short walk south is the less expensive *Športcamp (☎ 446 72 88)*, and a short walk north (towards Tatranská Lomnica) is *Hotel & Intercamp Tatranec (☎ 446 77 03)*, with hotel rooms (600 Sk per person), four-person bungalows (1600 Sk) and camping (80 Sk plus 80 Sk per person).

Chaty Up on the hiking trails there are nine moutain huts *(chaty)*, but given their limited capacity they are often full in midsummer. Food is available at these chalets, but you should take along some supplies. Prices range from 300 Sk to 500 Sk per person.

Satur in Starý Smokovec can reserve beds at most chalets.

Hotels – Around Starý Smokovec The cheapest place to stay – if you have a HI or ISIC card – is the year-round *Hotel Junior (☎ 442 26 61, fax 442 24 93)*, just below the Horný Smokovec train station. Basic rooms, ranging from singles to six-bed rooms, go for 230/360/490/560/600 Sk. Breakfast is 90 Sk extra.

One of the best deals is *Pension Vesna (☎ 442 27 74, fax 442 31 09, ✉ vesna@sinet.sk)*, a white two-storey building behind the large sanatorium, opposite the Nový Smokovec train station. Spacious three-bed apartments with private bath are 700 Sk per person, and the owner speaks English.

Also inexpensive is the four-storey *Hotel Šport (☎ 42 23 61/3, fax 42 27 19)*, a five-minute walk east from Starý Smokovec's train station. Rooms are 390/680 Sk with shared bath.

Hotels – Tatranská Lomnica The best value in town is the bright, new *Penzión Encian (☎ 446 75 20)*, on the main road just a few minutes' walk west of the train station, with rooms for 300 Sk per person.

Hotels – Štrbské Pleso The 11-storey *Hotel Panoráma (☎ 49 21 11, fax 49 28 10)* is the pyramidal eyesore just near the Obchodný dom Toliar department store, above the Štrbské Pleso train station. Singles/doubles there cost 1015/1830 Sk with bath, breakfast extra.

There are cheaper options down the hill in Tatranská Štrba. *Hotel Junior Rysy (☎ 448 48 45, fax 448 42 96, ✉ hotel.rysy@ke.telecom.sk)* is only a few minutes' walk from the Tatranská Lieskovec stop on the rack railway between Tatranská Štrba and Štrbské Pleso, and offers comfortable en suite rooms for 600/900 Sk excluding breakfast.

Getting There & Away

Bus There are regular express buses from Bratislava to Tatranská Lomnica via Nitra, Banská Bystrica and Starý Smokovec.

From Starý Smokovec there are eight buses a day to Lysa Polana (one hour); six to Levoča (one hour); four to Žilina; three to Trenčín; three to Bratislava; and one to Brno in the Czech Republic.

The Hungarian Volánbusz bus to/from Budapest and Tatranská Lomnica (seven hours) runs twice a week.

Train From Poprad – which is served by express trains from Prague, Bratislava and Košice – there are electric trains every half-hour to Starý Smokovec (14 Sk) and Štrbské Pleso (26 Sk). At the stations in Starý Smokovec and Tatranská Lomnica you can reserve sleepers and couchettes from Poprad to Bratislava, Prague, Karlovy Vary and Brno.

POPRAD
☎ 092

Poprad is a modern industrial city with little to interest visitors. However, it is an important transport hub and you'll pass through at least once on the way to the High Tatra mountains. The AiCES office (☎ 772 17 00), nám Sv Egídia 2950/114, covers the whole Tatra region.

Places to Stay & Eat

If you arrive late, you could stay at the run-down *Hotel Európa* (☎ 772 18 83), just outside the Poprad train station, for 400/600 Sk with shared bath.

There's a *supermarket* above the Prior department store at the west end of the town square. Ulica 1.mája, north of the main square, has several good eateries including *Bagetéria Astoria* and a cheap *pizzeria*.

Getting There & Away

There are buses to most towns in Slovakia from the large bus station next to the train station. Banská Bystrica (124km), Levoča (26km), Spišské Podhradie (41km) and Bardejov (125km) are most easily reached by bus.

Poprad is a major junction on the rail line from Bratislava to Košice. Express trains run from there to Žilina (two hours) and Košice (1½ hours) every few hours. Electric trains climb 13km to Starý Smokovec, the main High Tatra resort, every hour or so.

LEVOČA
☎ 0966

Levoča, 26km east of Poprad, is one of Slovakia's finest walled towns, with a square full of beautiful Renaissance buildings. The town is an easy stop on the way from Poprad to Košice.

Orientation & Information

The train station is 1km south of town, down the road beside the Hotel Faix. AiCES

(☎ 451 37 63) is on the main square at nám Majstra Pavla 58. The VÚB, nám Majstra Pavla 28, changes travellers cheques; there's an ATM next to the information office.

Things to See

Fifteenth-century walls and bastions greet the traveller arriving by bus at nám Štefana Kluberta, just outside the **Košice Gate**. The street beyond the gate leads to nám Majstra Pavla, Levoča's central square, which is full of things to see. The 15th-century **St James' Church** (40 Sk; closed Sunday mornings) contains a gigantic Gothic high altar (1517) by Master Pavol, one of the largest and finest altars of its kind in Europe. The Madonna on this altar appears on the 100 Sk banknote.

Next to St James' is the Gothic town hall, enlivened by Renaissance arcades. It houses the **Museum of the Spiš Region** (closed Monday). Beside the town hall is a 16th-century cage where prisoners were once exhibited.

There's a good **craft museum** in the 15th-century house at No 40 (closed Monday). At No 20 is the **Master Pavol Museum** (closed Monday).

Places to Stay & Eat

The hostel-style *Hotel Texon* (☎ 451 44 93, 0905-34 93 60, J Francisciho 45) has basic double rooms for 200 Sk per person. It's often locked, so phone ahead or ask at the information centre. The 25-room *Hotel Faix* (☎ 451 23 35, Probstnerova cesta 22), between the train station and the old town, has basic doubles with shower for 700 Sk. The hotel restaurant is good. Best value is the modern *Hotel Arkáda* (☎ 451 23 73, fax 451 22 55, nám Majstra Pavla 26). Large, bright rooms with TV and bath cost 1140/1700 Sk.

A good place for an inexpensive meal is *Reštaurácia Slovenská* at nám Majstra Pavla 62. The popular *Vegetarián* (Uholná 137) off the north-west corner of the main square, is open 10 am to 8 pm daily, except Sunday.

Getting There & Away

Frequent buses run to Poprad (30 minutes), Spišské Podhradie (20 minutes) and Košice (two hours). All buses stop at nám Štefana Kluberta, while some local buses stop at the train station at the southern end of town. Frequent local trains connect with Spišská Nová Ves, which is 13km south on the main line from Bratislava to Košice.

SPIŠSKÉ PODHRADIE
☎ 0966
Spišské Podhradie, 15km east of Levoča, is just an ordinary country town, but nearby Spišský hrad (castle) and Spišská Kapitula are major sights.

Things to See & Do
If arriving by bus from Levoča, ask the driver to stop at **Spišská Kapitula**, on a ridge, 1km west of Spišské Podhradie. This 13th-century ecclesiastical settlement is completely encircled by a 16th-century wall, and the single street running between the two medieval gates is lined with picturesque Gothic houses. At the upper end is the magnificent **St Martin's Cathedral** (1273), with twin Romanesque towers and a Gothic sanctuary.

Crowning a long ridge on the far side of Spišské Podhradie is the 180m-long **Spišský hrad**, the largest castle in Slovakia. In 1993 it was added to Unesco's World Heritage List. The castle is directly above the train station, 1km south of Spišské Podhradie's bus stop. Cross over the train tracks near the station and follow the yellow markers. The first gate is always locked, so carry on to the second one higher up. Although the castle burnt down in 1780, the ruins and the site are spectacular. The castle is closed on Monday and from October to April. Entry is 50 Sk.

Places to Stay
The only place there is to stay is *Penzión Podzámok* (☎ *81 17 55, fax 81 12 48, Podzámková 28)*, with beds at around 400 Sk per person. To get there, turn left after the bridge just south of Mariánské nám.

Getting There & Away
Buses to/from Levoča (15km), Spišská Nová Ves (25km) and Poprad (41km) are frequent.

A secondary rail line connects Spišské Podhradie to Spišské Vlachy (9km), a station on the main line from Poprad to Košice. Departures are scheduled to connect with the Košice trains.

KOŠICE
☎ 095
Slovakia's second-largest city, Košice (population 241,900) has museums, churches, a good state theatre and a vast main square lined with smart baroque buildings. Daily trains between Kraków and Budapest stop here, making Košice the perfect arrival or departure point for a visit to Slovakia.

Orientation & Information
The adjacent bus and train stations are just east of the old town. From here, a five-minute walk along Mlynská will bring you into Hlavná (Main Street), which broadens to accommodate the squares of Hlavné nám and nám Slobody.

AiCES (☎ 622 88 88), Hlavná 8, sells maps and guidebooks, books concert tickets and has accommodation listings. It also provides Internet access at 40 Sk for one hour.

The VÚB bank, Hlavná 112, changes travellers cheques and has an ATM. The main post office is at Poštová 2, 300m west of Hlavná. The telephone centre is on Bencúrova, about 300m north of the train station.

Satur (☎ 622 31 22), Hlavná 1 (in Hotel Slovan), reserves sleepers and couchettes and sells international train and bus tickets.

Things to See
Košice's top sight is the **Cathedral of St Elizabeth** (1345-1508), a magnificent late-Gothic edifice on the main square. Beside the cathedral is the 14th-century **St Michael's Chapel** and the **Košice Program House**, nám Slobody 27. The latter building dates from 1779 and now houses the **East Slovak Art Gallery** (Východoslovenská galéria; 5 Sk).

In the centre of the square is the ornate **State Theatre** (1899). Beside it is the rococo former **town hall** (1780), now offices.

The **East Slovak Museum** is on nám Maratónu mieru at the northern end of Hlavná (20 Sk). Don't miss the Košice Gold Treasure in the basement, a hoard of almost 3000 gold coins dating from the 15th to the 18th centuries and discovered by chance in 1935.

The **Mikluš Prison**, Pri Miklušovej Väznici 10, is a connected pair of 16th-century houses once equipped with medieval torture chambers and cells. Buy tickets behind the nearby gate at Hrnčiarska 7. This is also the ticket office for the **Ferenc Rákóczi House Museum** and the **Weapons Museum**, both of which are in the same courtyard as the ticket office. All are closed Monday and can only been seen on a one-hour tour (20 Sk), with a minimum group of 10 required.

Places to Stay
South of the city is *Autocamping Salaš Barca* (☎ 623 33 97). Take tram No 3 south along Južná trieda from the train station to the Juh SAD stop (about 200m before an overpass), then head right (west) on Alejová (the Rožňava Highway) for about 500m till you see the entrance to the camp site on the left. It is open 15 April to 30 September and there are cabins (360/540 Sk for a double/triple) and tent space (50 Sk per person, 40 Sk per tent). The cabins are available year-round and there's a restaurant.

Domov mládeže (☎ 642 90 52, Medická 2) is a hostel on the western side of town which charges 150 Sk per person in two- and three-bed rooms.

TJ Metropol turistická ubytovňa (☎ 625 59 48, fax 76 31 10, Štúrova 32) is an attractive sports complex where cheerful rooms with shared bath are 300 Sk per person plus 70 Sk for breakfast. It's an easy walk from town but is often full with groups. You get a lot of tram noise in the very early morning.

The basic *Hotel Európa* (☎ 622 38 97), a grand three-storey building just across the park from the train station, costs 570/740 Sk with shower/toilet.

The 12-storey prefabricated *Hotel Hutník* (☎ 633 75 11, fax 633 77 80, Tyršovo nábrežie 1), with rooms from 600/800 Sk with bath, is a last resort.

Places to Eat
The *Gastrodom supermarket* is on Mlynská next to the Hotel Európa. Great baguette sandwiches are made at *Bagetèria (Hlavná 74)*. The two-storey *Reštaurácia Ajvega (Orlia 10)* is an inexpensive, friendly restaurant with a partly vegetarian menu.

A popular place to eat or have a drink is the inexpensive *Bakchus (Hlavná 8)*. Through the passageway is an open courtyard with tables on sunny days. A better restaurant for more leisurely dining is upstairs at *Zlatý ducat (Hlavná 16)*.

Entertainment
The renovated *State Theatre* on nám Slobody holds regular performances. The *Bomba klub (Hlavná 5)* is a popular bar, down in a cellar from the passageway. The *Jazz Klub (Kováčská 39)* has live jazz twice a week. Club fans can try the *Hacienda Disco Club (Hlavná 65)*.

Getting There & Away
Buses are best for Levoča (four daily) and Spišské Podhradie (four daily).

Slovenia

Prosperous, orderly and maybe just a tad complacent, Slovenia (Slovenija) is the little Switzerland of the Balkans. Formerly the most affluent part of Yugoslavia, Slovenia went right on making money even as the rest of Yugoslavia erupted into a spasm of bloodletting. Although on the fast track to join the European Union, this independent republic costs less to visit than other European countries and offers a wealth of relatively untouristed attractions.

The capital city, Ljubljana, is graced with a tree-lined promenade at its centre and Piran makes a good base to explore the Slovenian coastline. The lush Soča Valley and the mountainous interior dotted with Lakes Bled and Bohinj offer further reminders of Switzerland. An added bonus is that Slovenia is a nation of polyglots, and communicating with these friendly people is never difficult.

Facts about Slovenia

HISTORY

The early Slovenes settled in the Danube Basin and eastern Alps in the 6th century. The Austro-German monarchy took over in the early 14th century and continued to rule (as the Habsburg Empire from 1804) right up until 1918.

After WWI and the dissolution of the Austro-Hungarian Empire, Slovenia was included in the Kingdom of Serbs, Croats and Slovenes. During WWII much of Slovenia was annexed by Germany, with Italy and Hungary taking smaller bits of territory. In 1945 Slovenia joined the Socialist Federal Republic of Yugoslavia.

The rise to power of Slobodan Milošović on a wave of Serbian nationalism in the late 1980s was a big concern to Slovenes. When Belgrade abruptly ended the autonomy of Kosovo in late 1988, Slovenes feared the

same could happen to them. As a result, in December of 1990, Slovenia became the first Yugoslav republic to hold free elections and 88% of the electorate voted in favour of independence.

The Slovenian government pulled the republic out of the Yugoslav Federation on 25 June 1991. To dramatise their bid for independence, the Slovenian leaders deliberately provoked a 10 day battle with the Yugoslav federal army. But resistance from the Slovenian militia was determined and, as no territorial claims or minority issues were involved, the Yugoslav government agreed to a truce brokered by the European Community (EC).

Slovenia got a new constitution in late December; on 15 January 1992 the EC formally recognised the country. Slovenia was admitted to the United Nations in May 1992 and has since been invited to join the European Union (EU). In November 1997 the Slovene president, Milan Kučan, was returned for his second term after winning nearly 56% of the popular vote.

GEOGRAPHY

Slovenia is wedged between Austria and Croatia and shares much shorter borders with Italy and Hungary. Measuring just 20,256 sq km, Slovenia is the smallest country in Eastern Europe, about the size of Wales or Israel. Much of Slovenia is mountainous, culminating in the north-west with the Julian Alps and the nation's highest peak, Mt Triglav (2864m). From this jagged knot, the main Alpine chain continues east along the Austrian border, while the Dinaric range runs south-east along the coast into Croatia. Beneath the limestone plateau of the Karst region is Europe's most extensive network of karst caverns.

SLOVENIA (SLOVENIJA)

CLIMATE

Slovenia gets most of its rain in March, April, October and November. January is the coldest month with an average temperature of -2°C, and July is the warmest (21°C). Snow can linger in the mountains as late as June. The coast and western Slovenia as far north as the Soča Valley has a Mediterranean climate with mild, sunny weather much of the year.

POPULATION & PEOPLE

Slovenia was the most homogeneous of all the Yugoslav republics; about 87% of the population (estimated at 1.97 million in 1999) are Slovenes, 72% of whom identify themselves as Roman Catholic. The most populous cities are Ljubljana (280,000), Maribor (134,000), Celje (41,000) and Kranj (36,700).

LANGUAGE

Slovene, a South Slavic language written in the Roman alphabet, is closely related to Croatian and Serbian. Slovene is grammatically complex and has something rare in linguistics: the singular, dual and plural forms. It's one *miza* (table) and three or more *mize* (tables) but two *mizi*. See the Language Guide at the back of this book for pronunciation guidelines and useful words and phrases.

Virtually everyone in Slovenia speaks at least one other language – Croatian, Serbian, German, English and/or Italian. English is definitely the preferred second language of the young.

Facts for the Visitor

HIGHLIGHTS

Ljubljana, Piran and Koper all have outstanding architecture; the hilltop castles at Bled and Ljubljana are impressive and the Soča Valley is indescribably beautiful during spring.

SUGGESTED ITINERARIES

Three days
  Visit Ljubljana
One week
  Visit Ljubljana, Bled, Bohinj, and Piran
Two weeks
  Visit all the places covered in this chapter

PLANNING
When to Go
In July and August hotel rates are increased and there are lots of tourists, especially on the coast. September is an excellent month to visit, as the days are long and the weather is still warm.

Books & Maps
Lonely Planet's *Slovenia* is the only complete, independent guide to the country in English. *Discover Slovenia*, published annually by Cankarjeva Založba (3300 SIT), is a good country introduction.

The Geodesic Institute of Slovenia (Geodetski Zavod Slovenije; GZS) is the country's principal cartographic agency, producing national (1:300,000) and regional (1:50,000) topographical maps as well as city plans. The Alpine Association of Slovenia (Planinska Zveza Slovenije; PZS) has 30 different hiking maps.

TOURIST OFFICES
The Slovenian Tourist Board (Center za Promocijo Turizma Slovenije; CPTS; ☎ 01 589 1840, fax 589 1841, ✉ cpts@cpts.tradepoint.si) in Ljubljana's World Trade Centre is the umbrella organisation for tourist offices in Slovenia.

The best office for face-to-face information in Slovenia is the Ljubljana Tourist Information Centre (see the Ljubljana section later in this chapter).

Most places in this chapter have some form of tourist office; if not seek assistance at a travel agency (eg, Kompas) or from hotel or museum staff.

Tourist & Travel Offices Abroad
CPTS offices abroad include:

UK (☎ 020-7287 7133, fax 7287 5476), 49 Conduit St, London W1R 9FB
USA (☎ 212-358 9686, fax 358 9025), 345 East 12th St, New York, NY 10003

Kompas has offices in:

Australia (☎ 07-3831 4400), 323 Boundary St, Spring Hill, 4000 Queensland
Canada (☎ 514 938 4041), 4060 Ste Catherine St West, Suite 535, Montreal, Que H3Z 2Z3
USA (☎ 954 771 9200), 2826 East Commercial Blvd, Fr Lauderdale, FL 33306

EMBASSIES & CONSULATES
Slovenian Embassies & Consulates
Diplomatic missions abroad include:

Australia (☎ 02 6243 4830), Advance Bank Centre, Level 6, 60 Marcus Clark St, Canberra, ACT 2601
Canada (☎ 613 565 5781), 150 Metcalfe St, Suite 2101, Ottawa, Ont K2P 1P1
UK (☎ 0171-495 7775), Cavendish Court, Suite One, 11-15 Wigmore St, London W1H 9LA
USA (☎ 202-667 5363), 1525 New Hampshire Ave NW, Washington, DC 20036

Embassies & Consulates in Slovenia
All embassies and consulates are in Ljubljana, area code ☎ 01.

Australia (☎ 425 4252), Trg Republike 3/XII
Canada (☎ 430 3570), Miklošičeva cesta 19
UK (☎ 200 3910), Trg Republike 3/IV
USA (☎ 200 5500), Prešernova 30

MONEY
Currency
Slovenia's currency, the tolar, is abbreviated SIT and divided into 100 stotin. There are coins of 50 stotin and one, two and five tolars and banknotes of 10, 20, 50, 100, 200, 500, 1000, 5000 and 10,000 tolars.

Most prices in Slovenia are in tolars, but a few hotels, guesthouses and even camping grounds quote prices in Deutschmarks (DM) – though you are never required to pay in the German currency.

It is simple to change cash and travellers cheques at banks, travel agencies and *menjalnica* (private exchange offices). Visa, MasterCard/Eurocard and American Express are widely accepted at upmarket restaurants, hotels and some travel agencies.

ATMs linked to Cirrus or Plus are available in Ljubljana and some coastal towns; their locations are noted in the Information sections of the individual towns. Clients of Visa can get cash advances in tolars from any A Banka branch, MasterCard and Eurocard holders from any branch of Nova Ljubljanska Banka.

Exchange Rates
country	unit		tolar
Australia	A$1	=	123 SIT
Canada	C$1	=	139 SIT

SLOVENIA

euro	€1	=	202 SIT
France	FF1	=	30 SIT
Germany	DM1	=	104 SIT
Japan	¥100	=	193 SIT
UK	UK£1	=	327 SIT
US	US$1	=	208 SIT

Costs

Slovenia is cheaper than neighbouring Italy and Austria, but about 50% more expensive than Hungary. If you stay in private rooms or at guesthouses, eat at mid-range restaurants and travel 2nd class by train or bus, you can get by on US$40 a day. Staying at hostels or college dormitories and eating at self-service restaurants will cut costs considerably.

POST & COMMUNICATIONS
Post

Domestic mail costs 19 SIT. For international mail, the base rate is 90 SIT and 70 SIT to 90 SIT for a postcard. Then you have to add on the airmail charge for every 10g: 20 SIT for Europe, 25 SIT for North America and 30 SIT for Australasia.

Telephone, Fax & Email

The country code for Slovenia is ☎ 386. Drop the initial zero from city area codes when dialling in from overseas.

Public telephones on the street never accept coins; they require a telephone card (*telefonska kartica*) which is available at post offices and some newsstands. The cheapest phone card is 700 SIT for 25 impulses; a local one-minute call absorbs one impulse. A three-minute call from Slovenia costs about 277 SIT to neighbouring countries, 214 SIT to Western Europe (including the UK) and the USA, and 434 SIT to Australia. Rates are 20% cheaper from 7 pm to 7 am.

Cybercafes are a rarity in Slovenia. Currently the only public access to the internet is at Klub K4 in Ljubljana.

INTERNET RESOURCES

CPTS has an excellent Web site with information on all of Slovenia (www.slovenia-tourism.si). Also check out the City of Ljubljana site (www.ljubljana.si). The Alpine Association of Slovenia (www.pzs.si) can provide information on hiking and mountaineering.

TIME

Slovenia is one hour ahead of GMT/UTC.

WOMEN TRAVELLERS

The Društvo Mesto Žensk (City of Women Association), part of the Government Office for Women's Affairs (☎ 01-438 1580), is at Kersnikova ul 4 in Ljubljana. In the event of an assault ring ☎ 080 124 or any of the following six numbers: ☎ 9780 to ☎ 9785.

GAY & LESBIAN TRAVELLERS

The gay association Roza Klub (☎ 01-430 4740), Kersnikova ul 4, organises a disco every Sunday night at the Klub K4 in Ljubljana. Lesbians should contact the organisation LL (☎ 01-430 4740) at Metelkova ul 6 in Ljubljana. GALfon (☎ 01-432 4089) is a hotline and source of general information for gays and lesbians. It operates from 7 to 10 pm daily.

DISABLED TRAVELLERS

Physically challenged travellers should contact the Zveza Paraplegikov Republike Slovenije (ZPRS; ☎ 01-432 7138) at Štihova ul 14 in Ljubljana.

DANGERS & ANNOYANCES

Slovenia is hardly a violent or dangerous place. In an emergency dial the police (☎ 113) or fire/first aid (☎ 112).

BUSINESS HOURS

Shops, groceries and department stores are open 7.30 or 8 am to 7 pm weekdays and to 1 pm Saturday. Bank hours are generally 8 am to 4.30 or 5 pm on weekdays (often with a lunchtime break) and to noon on Saturday. Many post offices are open 7 am to 8 pm weekdays, to 1 pm Saturday.

PUBLIC HOLIDAYS & SPECIAL EVENTS

Public holidays in Slovenia include 1 and 2 January, 8 February (Prešeren Day), Easter Sunday and Monday, 27 April (Insurrection Day), 1 and 2 May, 25 June (National Day), 15 August (Assumption Day), 31 October (Reformation Day), 1 November (All Saints' Day), Christmas Day and 26 December (Independence Day).

The highlights of Slovenia's summer festival season (July and August) are the

International Summer Festival in Ljubljana; the Piran Musical Evenings; the Primorska Summer Festival at Piran, Koper, Izola and Portorož; and Summer in the Old Town in Ljubljana, with three or four cultural events a week.

ACCOMMODATION

In summer, camping is the cheapest way to go and there are good camping grounds all over the country. It is forbidden to camp 'rough' in Slovenia.

Slovenia has only a handful of official hostels – two in Ljubljana and one each in Bled and Koper, but not all are open year-round. Some college dormitories accept travellers in summer.

Private rooms arranged by tourist offices and travel agencies can be inexpensive, though a surcharge of up to 50% is typically levied on stays of less than three nights. Beat the surcharge by going directly to any house with a sign reading '*Sobe*' (rooms).

Guesthouses (*penzion* or *gostišče*) can be good value, though in July and August the rates are higher and you may have to take at least one meal. Hotel rates vary according to the season. Many resort hotels, particularly on the coast, close in winter.

FOOD & DRINKS

Slovenian cuisine is heavily influenced by the food of its neighbours. From Austria, it's *klobasa* (sausage), *zavitek* (strudel) and *Dunajski zrezek* (Wiener schnitzel). *Njoki* (potato dumplings), *rižota* (risotto) and the ravioli-like *žlikrofi* are obviously Italian, and Hungary has contributed *golaž* (goulash), *paprikaš* (chicken or beef 'stew') and *palačinke* (thin pancakes filled with jam or nuts and topped with chocolate).

No Slovenian meal is complete without soup, be it the simple *goveja juha z rezanci* (beef broth with little egg noodles), *zelenjavna juha* (vegetable soup) or *gobova kremna juha* (creamed mushroom soup). There are many types of Slovenian dumplings; the cheese ones called *štruklji* are the most popular.

A popular Slovenian drink is *žganje*, a strong brandy distilled from a variety of fruits but most commonly plums. Beer is also popular – Union, brewed in Ljubljana, is lighter-tasting and sweeter than Zlatorog, the excellent and ubiquitous beer made by Laško.

Getting There & Away

AIR

There are daily direct flights from Ljubljana's airport with Adria Airways (Slovenia's national airline), British Airways, Lufthansa and Swissair.

LAND
Bus

Buses from Ljubljana serve several international destinations including Belgrade, Frankfurt, Munich, Rijeka, Split, Varaždin and Zagreb (2570 SIT, three a day).

Nova Gorica is the easiest exit/entry point between Slovenia and Italy. You can catch up to five buses a day to/from the Italian city of Gorizia or simply walk across the border at Rožna Dolina. Koper also has good connections with Italy: some 17 buses a day on weekdays go to/from Trieste, 21km to the north-east. There's also a daily bus (except Sunday) from Trieste to Ljubljana (1810 SIT)

There is no direct bus from Ljubljana to Budapest. Take one of five daily buses to Lendava; the Hungarian border is 5km to the north. The first Hungarian train station, Rédics, is only 2km beyond the border.

Train

The main train routes into Slovenia from Austria are Vienna to Maribor and Salzburg to Jesenice. Tickets cost 6763 SIT from Ljubljana to Salzburg (4½ hours) and 10,103 SIT to Vienna (six hours).

There are three trains a day between Munich and Ljubljana (seven hours, 11,266 SIT) including one overnight train.

Four trains a day run from Trieste to Ljubljana (3791 SIT, three hours). From Croatia it's Zagreb to Ljubljana (2260 SIT, 2½ hours), or Rijeka to Ljubljana (2099 SIT, 2½ hours) via Pivka. There are two daily trains from Ljubljana to Budapest (8833 SIT, 7½ hours). There is no direct train to Belgrade, but three trains daily to Zagreb connect with Belgrade trains (6650 SIT).

SEA

Between early April and October on Friday, Saturday and Sunday the *Prince of Venice*, a 39m Australian-made catamaran seating some 330 passengers, sails between Izola and Venice (8750/12,500 SIT one-way/return, 2½ hours) with an additional sailing on Tuesday from late June to early September. The price includes a sightseeing tour in Venice. From Izola there are frequent buses to Portorož, Piran and Koper.

Another catamaran, the *Marconi*, links Trieste with Piran (15,000/30,000 SIT return, two hours) on Wednesday, Friday and Sunday from mid-May to September.

Getting Around

BUS
Except for long journeys, buses are preferable to (the much slower) trains in Slovenia. In Ljubljana you can buy a ticket with seat reservation (200 SIT) the day before, but many people simply pay the driver on boarding. The one time you really might need a reservation is Friday afternoon. There is a 220 SIT charge for each bag placed underneath the bus.

Footnotes you might see on Slovenian bus schedules include: *vozi vsak dan* (runs daily); *vozi ob delavnikih* (runs on working days – Monday to Friday); *vozi ob sobotah* (runs on Saturday); and *vozi ob nedeljah in praznikih* (runs on Sunday and holidays).

TRAIN
Slovenske Železnice (SŽ; Slovenian Railways) operates on just over 1200km of track.

On posted timetables in Slovenia, *odhod* or *odhodi vlakov* means 'departures' and *prihod* (or *prihodi vlakov*) is 'arrivals'. If you don't have time to buy a ticket, conductors sell them for an extra charge of 200 SIT.

CAR & MOTORCYCLE
The use of seat belts in the front seat of cars is compulsory, and a new law requires all vehicles to show their headlights throughout the day outside built-up areas. Speed limits for cars are 50km/h in built-up areas, 90km/h on secondary roads, 100km/h on main highways and 130km/h on motorways. Several motorways charge inexpensive tolls. Slovenia's automobile club is the Avto Moto Zveza Slovenije (AMZS); for breakdown service ring ☎ 987.

The permitted blood-alcohol level for motorists is *very* low, and the law is strictly enforced.

Ljubljana

☎ 01

Ljubljana (Laibach in German), by far Slovenia's largest city with a population of 280,000, is a pleasant, self-contented town. Its most beautiful parts are the Old Town below the castle and the embankments along the narrow Ljubljanica River.

Ljubljana began as the Roman town of Emona. The Habsburgs took control in the 14th century and later built many of the pale-coloured churches and mansions that earned the city the nickname 'White Ljubljana'.

Despite the patina of imperial Austria, contemporary Ljubljana has a vibrant Slavic air and is refreshingly youthful – more than 25,000 students attend Ljubljana University's 14 faculties and three art academies. In summer Ljubljana is like a mini-Prague without the hordes of tourists.

Orientation
The tiny bus station and renovated train station are opposite one another on Trg Osvobodilne Fronte (known as Trg OF) at the northern end of the centre (called Center). The 24-hour left-luggage office *(garderoba)* at the train station is on platform No 1 (200 SIT per piece).

Information
Tourist Offices The Tourist Information Centre (TIC; ☎ 306 1215, fax 306 1204, ✉ pcl.tic-lj@ljubljana.si) is at Stritarjeva ul 2. It's open 8 am to 7 pm weekdays and 10 am to 6 pm Saturday. The branch office (☎ 433 9475) at the train station is open daily. The free brochure *Ljubljana Where?* is a goldmine of useful information.

The Cultural Information Centre (☎ 221 3025), next to Trg Francoske Revolucije 7, has a free booklet listing all the city's museums and galleries.

The main office of the Alpine Association of Slovenia (☎ 434 3022) is at Dvoržakova ul 9.

Money The currency exchange office inside the train station is open 6 am to 10 pm daily. It accepts travellers cheques and charges no commission for cash exchanges but does not offer a good rate. Most branches of A Banka have ATMs that accept Visa and Plus; there's one near the train station at Trg Osvobodilne Fronte 2 and another next to the Tourist Information Centre at Stritarjeva ul 2. There are three ATMs that accept Mastercard, Maestro and Cirrus as well: Banka Koper, at Cigaletova ul 4; outside the Globtour agency in the Maximarket passageway connecting Trg Republike with Plečnikov trg; and inside Nova Ljubljanska Banka, Trg Republike 2 (open 8 am to 5 pm weekdays, 9 am until noon Saturday). Next to the SKB Banka on Trg Ajdovščina is a currency exchange machine that changes the banknotes of 18 countries into tolar at a good rate. The Hida exchange bureau in the Seminary building near the open-air market at Pogarčarjev trg 1 is open 7 am to 7 pm weekdays and to 2 pm Saturday.

Post & Communications Poste restante is held for 30 days in the post office at Slovenska cesta 32 (postal code 1101). Make international telephone calls or send faxes from here or from the main post office at Pražakova ul 3.

There's only one cybercafe with public-access to the Internet in Ljubljana: the Klub K4 Café (☎ 431 7010) at Kersnikova ul 4.

Travel Agencies Erazem (☎ 433 1076), Trubarjeva cesta 7, is a budget travel agency geared to backpackers and students. It can provide information and make bookings, and has a useful message board. It also sells ISIC cards (900 SIT) and, for those under 26 but not studying, FIYTO cards (700 SIT). Mladi Turist (☎ 425 9131), Salendrova ul 4, sells hostel cards for those who have resided in the country for six months. Slovenijaturist (☎ 431 5055), Slovenska cesta 58, sells BIJ international train tickets (one-third cheaper than regular fares) to those under 26 years of age.

Bookshops Ljubljana's largest bookshop is Mladinska Knjiga at Slovenska cesta 29. It has an extensive collection of novels in English as well as guidebooks, maps and English-language newspapers.

Medical Services You can see a doctor at the medical centre (klini ni center; ☎ 433 6236 or 431 3123), Zaloška cesta 7, in Tabor east of the Park Hotel. The emergency unit (urgenca) is open 24 hours a day.

Things to See & Do

Opposite the TIC in the Kresija building is the celebrated **Triple Bridge**. In 1931, Jože Plečnik added the side bridges to the original central span dating from 1842. On the northern side of the bridge is Prešernov trg with its pink **Franciscan church** (1660) and a **statue** (1905) of poet France Prešeren and some lovely Art Nouveau buildings.

On the south side of the bridge in Mestni trg, the baroque **Robba Fountain**, designed by Italian sculptor Francesco Robba in 1751, stands before the 18th-century **town hall**.

To the south of Mestni trg is **Stari trg**, atmospheric by day or night. North-east are the twin towers of the **Cathedral of St Nicholas** (1708), which contains impressive frescoes. Behind the cathedral is Ljubljana's colourful open-air **produce market** (closed Sunday).

Študentovska ul, opposite the Vodnik statue in the market square, leads up to **Ljubljana Castle**. The castle has been under renovation for decades, but you can climb the 19th-century **Castle Tower** 10 am to dusk daily (200 SIT) and view the exhibits in a Gothic chapel and the **Pentagonal Tower** (closed Saturday and Monday).

From the Museum of Modern Art (see below) an underpass leads to Ljubljana's green lung, **Tivoli Park**. The park's Recreation Centre, Celovška cesta 25, has tennis courts, an indoor swimming pool and a roller-skating rink. There's also a popular sauna called Zlati Klub, with a small outside pool where you can sunbathe in the nude (mixed sexes). Entry is 1500 SIT on weekdays and until 1 pm and 1800 SIT at the weekend.

Museums The excellent **National Museum**, Muzejska ul 1, erected in 1885, has prehistory, natural history and ethnography collections. The highlight is a 6th century BC Celtic situla, a kind of pail sporting a fascinating relief. The museum is open 10 am to 6 pm Tuesday to Sunday. Entry is 500/300 SIT.

The **National Gallery**, Cankarjeva ul 20, offers Slovenian portraits and landscapes from the 17th to 19th centuries, as well as copies of medieval frescoes; the gallery's new wing at Puharjeva ul 9 (separate entrance) has a permanent collection of European paintings from the Middle Ages to the

LJUBLJANA

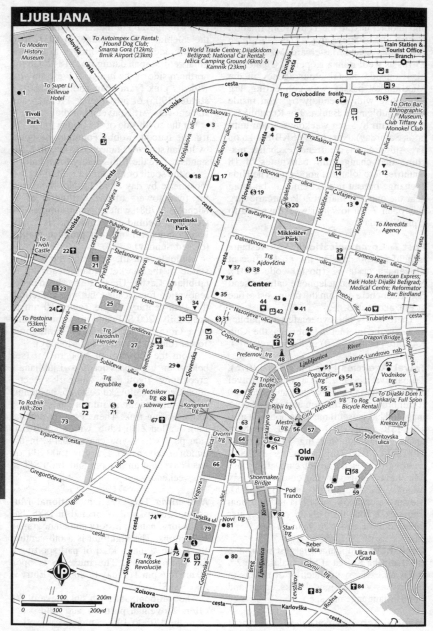

To Modern History Museum

To Avtoimpex Car Rental; Hound Dog Club; Šmarna Gora (12km); Brnik Airport (23km)

To World Trade Centre; Dijaškidom Bežigrad; National Car Rental; Ježica Camping Ground (6km) & Kamnik (23km)

Train Station & Tourist Office Branch

To Super Li Bellevue Hotel

Tivoli Park

Celovška cesta

cesta

Trg Osvobodilne fronte

To Orto Bar; Ethnographic Museum; Club Tiffany & Monokel Club

Tivolska

Dvoržakova ulica

Gosposvetska

Vodnikova ulica

Kersnikova ulica

Trdinova

Slovenska

Cigaletova

Prežakova

ulica

ulica

Čufarjeva

ulica

Kolodvorska

To Meredita Agency

Argentinski Park

Tavčarjeva

Dalmatinova

Trg Ajdovščina

Miklošičev Park

Komenskega ulica

Štefanova

Prešihova

Cankarjeva

Župančičeva

cesta

Tomšičeva

Center

Miklošičeva

Pražakova

To American Express; Park Hotel; Dijaški Bežigrad; Medical Centre; Reformator Bar; Birdland

Puharjeva ul.

Tivolska

Slovenska

Prešernov

Prečna ulica

Trubarjeva

cesta

Nazorjeva ulica

Čopova

Prešernov trg

Ljubljanica River

Dragon Bridge

Kopitarjeva ul.

Resljeva cesta

To Tivoli Castle

To Postojna (53km); Coast

Prešernova

Subičeva ulica

Beethovnova

Slovenska

Trg Narodnih Herojev

Trg Republike

Plečnikov trg subway

Kongresni trg

Dvorni trg

Adamič-Lundrovo nab

Vodnikov trg

To Dijaški Dom I. Cankarja; Full Spon Bicycle Rental

Ljubljanica

Ciril-Metodov trg

Mestni trg

To Rog Bicycle Rental

Old Town

Krekov trg

Študentovska ulica

To Rožnik Hill; Zoo

Erjavčeva cesta

Gregorčičeva

Igriška

ulica

Rimska

cesta

Vegova ulica

Shoemaker Bridge

Pod Trančo

Turjaška ul.

Novi trg

Stari trg

Reber ulica

Ulica na Grad

Trg Francoske Revolucije

Krakovo

Zoisova cesta

Karlovška

Breg

Ljubljanica

River

Gornji trg

Levstikov trg

Rožna ul.

cesta

| 0 | 100 | 200m |
| 0 | 100 | 200yd |

LJUBLJANA

PLACES TO EAT		21	National Gallery	55	Bishop's Palace
12	Burek Stand	22	Serbian Orthodox Church	56	Robba Fountain
33	Joe Pena's Cantina y Bar	23	Museum of Modern Art	57	Town Hall
34	Daj-Dam	24	US Embassy	58	Ljubljana Castle
36	Šestica	25	Opera House	59	Pentagonal Tower
37	Super 5 Food Stand	26	National Museum	60	Castle Tower
51	Ribca Seafood Bar	27	Parliament Building	61	Café Boheme
74	Foculus Pizzeria	28	Gajo Jazz Club	62	Maček
82	Pizzeria Romeo	29	Mladinska Knjiga Bookshop	63	Delikatesa
		30	Post Office (Poste Restante)	64	Filharmonija
OTHER		31	Hida Exchange Bureau	65	Burja Delicatessen
1	Tivoli Recreation Centre; Zlati	32	Komuna Cinema	66	Ljubljana University
	Klub Sauna; Klub Manhattan	35	Kompas Travel Agency;	67	Ursuline Church
2	Ilirija Swimming Pool	38	SKB Banka	68	Brewery Pub
3	Alpine Association of	39	Klub Central Disco;	69	Maximarket Shopping
	Slovenia		Hotel Turist		Arcade; Maxim Self-Service
4	Slovenijaturist Travel Agency;	40	TrueBar		Restaurant
	Burek Stand	41	Art Nouveau Bank	70	Globtour Travel Agency
5	Main Post Office		Buildings	71	Nova Ljubljanska Banka
6	Canadian Embassy	42	Union Cinema	72	UK & Australian Embassy
7	Post Office (Customs)	43	Grand Hotel Union	73	Cankarjev Dom
8	City Airport Buses	44	Eldorado		(Cultural Centre)
9	Bus Station	45	Franciscan Church	75	Ilirija Column
10	A Banka with ATM	46	Erazem Travel Agency	76	Križanke Ticket Office
11	Kompas Cinema	47	Centromerkur Department	77	Križanke/Summer
13	Avis Car Rental		Store		Festival Theatre
14	Kinoteka Cinema	48	Prešeren Monument	78	Cultural Information Centre
15	Kompas Hertz Car Rental	49	Alba Laundry	79	National & University
16	City Bus Ticket Kiosks	50	Tourist Information		Library
17	Klub K4; University		Centre (TIC)	80	Mladi Turist
	Student Centre	52	Produce Market	81	Academy of Arts
18	Adria Airways Office	53	Cathedral of Saint Nicholas		& Sciences
19	A Banka	54	Seminary/Hida Exchange	83	Church of St James
20	Banka Koper with ATM		Bureau	84	Church of St Florian

20th century and is used for temporary exhibits (closed Monday, 500/300 SIT and free on Saturday).

The **Museum of Modern Art**, diagonally opposite the National Gallery, hosts the International Biennial of Graphic Arts in the summer of every odd-numbered year (closed Monday, 500/300 SIT and free on Sunday).

The new **Slovenian Ethnographic Museum**, Metlikova ul 2, is definitely worth a visit (closed Monday, 500/300 SIT).

Organised Tours

From June to September, a two-hour tour in English (700 SIT) departs from the town hall at 5 pm daily (other times of year at 11 am on Sunday).

Places to Stay

The TIC lists about 40 private rooms, but only a few are in the centre. Single/double prices start at 2500/4000 SIT.

Camping On the Sava some 6km north of Center is the year-round *Camping Ježica* (☎ 568 3913, @ acjezica@siol.net, Dunajska cesta 270); catch bus No 6 or 8. The rates are 1200 SIT per person with a caravan or tent.

Hostels & Student Dorms Four student dormitories (*dijaški dom*) open their doors to foreign travellers in July and August. The most central by far is *Dijaški Dom Tabor* (☎ 232 1067, Vidovdanska ul 7), opposite the Park Hotel and affiliated with Hostelling International (HI). It charges 3100 SIT for a single room and 2300 SIT for a bed in a double or triple, including breakfast.

Dijaški Dom Bežigrad (☎ 534 2867, Kardeljeva ploščad 28), another HI member, is in the Bežigrad district 2km north of the train and bus stations. It has doubles/triples with shower and toilet for 2900/2400 SIT per person and rooms with one to three beds with shared facilities for 2000 SIT per

SLOVENIA

person. An HI card gets you about 10% off. The Bežigrad has 50 rooms available from late June to late August but only about 20 the rest of the year which are available weekends only. *Dijaška Dom Ivana Cankarja* (☎ *174 8600, Poljanska cesta 26*) is just out of the town centre and has singles/doubles/triples for 3460/2800/2600 SIT per person including breakfast (10% less for students) for rooms with shared facilities.

Hotels One of the cheapest deals in town is the 15-room *Super Li Bellevue Hotel* (☎ *433 4049, Pod Gozdom 12*) on the northern edge of Tivoli Park. There are no rooms with private bath, but bright and airy singles with basins are 5300 SIT, doubles 7300 SIT.

The 122-room *Park Hotel* (☎ *433 1306, fax 433 0546, Tabor 9*) is where most people end up, as it's the city's only large budget hotel close to the centre and the Old Town. It's pretty basic, but the price is right: 5800/7200 SIT for singles/doubles with breakfast and shared shower and 6954/8880 SIT with private shower. Students with cards get a 20% discount. The staff are very helpful and friendly.

A reasonable alternative in the town centre is the three-star *Hotel Turist* (☎ *432 2343, fax 231 9291, Dalmatinova 15*), which has singles/doubles for 10,000/14,600 SIT (2000 SIT less off-season).

Places to Eat

The *supermarket* in the basement of the Maximarket mall on Trg Republike has the largest selection in town (closed Sunday). For picnic supplies try the *Delikatesa (Kongresni trg 9)* or *Burja* at No 11.

There are *burek stands* (about 250 SIT) at several locations in Ljubljana and among the best are the one on Pražakova ul next to Slovenijaturist, and the one at Kolodvorska ul 20 which is open 24 hours. If you want something more substantial, head for the outdoor *Super 5*, which faces Slovenska cesta from the shopping mall in Trg Ajdovščina.

Among the two cheapest places for lunch are the *Maxim* self-service restaurant in the basement of the Maximarket shopping arcade on Trg Republike, and *Daj-Dam (Cankarjeva cesta 4)*, which has a vegetarian menu (950 SIT). For a quick and very

tasty lunch, try the fried squid (670 SIT to 900 SIT) or whitebait (300 SIT to 470 SIT) at *Ribca*, a basement seafood bar below the Plečnik Colonnade in Pogarčarjev trg.

A more upmarket alternative for Slovenian specialities is *Šestica (Slovenska cesta 40)*, a 200-year-old standby with a pleasant courtyard. The lunch menus for 1000 SIT and 1200 SIT are excellent value.

For Italian try *Foculus (Gregorčičeva ul 3)* or *Pizzeria Romeo (Stari trg 6)*. The friendly and spacious *Joe Pena's Cantina y Bar (Cankarjeva cesta 6)* serves up hearty portions of Mexican food (main courses 1500 SIT to 1900 SIT) and vegetarians will find a lot on the menu of *Full Spon (Zarnikova ul 3)*, a student hangout.

Entertainment

Pubs & Bars Some pleasant and congenial places for a *pivo* or glass of *vino* are *True-Bar* and *Reformator Bar (Trubarjeva cesta 18)*. In good weather, locals and visitors alike head to the adjoining *Maček* and *Café Boheme (Cankarjevo nabrežje 19 and 21)* for an outdoor drink along the river.

Clubs The most popular clubs are *Eldorado (Nazorjeva ul 4)* and *Klub Central (Dalmatinova ul 15)* next to the Hotel Turist. The student *Klub K4 (Kersnikova ul 4)* has a disco on some nights. Other popular venues are *Hound Dog (Trg Prekomorskih Brigad 4)* in the Hotel M and *Klub Manhattan* in the Tivoli Recreation Centre.

Gay & Lesbian Venues A popular spot for gays and lesbians alike on Sunday night is the *Roza Klub* at the Klub K4. At the Metelkova squat, Ljubljana's version of Christiania in Copenhagen, between Metelkova ul and Maistrova ul, there's a cafe-pub for gays called *Club Tiffany*. *Monokel Club* is a popular spot for lesbians in the same building.

Rock & Jazz Ljubljana has a number of excellent rock clubs with canned or live music including *Orto Bar (Grablovi eva ul 1)* and the *Brewery Pub (Plečnikov trg 1)*. For jazz, you can't beat the *Gajo Jazz Club (Beethovnova ul 8)* near the Parliament building. *Birdland (Trubarjeva cesta 50)* has a jam session on Wednesday night and occasional jazz concerts on the weekend.

Classical Music, Opera & Dance Ljubljana is home to two orchestras. Concerts are held in various locations all over town, but the main venue is *Cankarjev Dom* on Trg Republike. The ticket office (☎ 252 2815) is in the basement of the nearby Maximarket mall. Also check for concerts at the *Filharmonija*, Kongresni trg 10, and the *Opera House*, Župančičeva ul 1.

Buy tickets to the Ljubljana Summer Festival and anything else staged at the *Križanke* from the office (☎ 426 4340) behind the Ilirija Column at Trg Francoske Revolucije 1-2.

Getting There & Away

For information on international buses and trains to/from Ljubljana, see the Getting There & Away section earlier in this chapter.

Bus If you're heading for Bled or Lake Bohinj, take a bus rather than a train.

The timetable in the shed-like bus station (☎ 434 3838) on Trg OF lists all routes and times. Here are some sample one-way fares: Bled (980 SIT), Bohinj (1480 SIT), Koper (1900 SIT), Novo Mesto (1170 SIT), Piran (2120 SIT) and Postojna (900 SIT).

Train All domestic and international trains arrive at the station (☎ 231 6768) at Trg OF 6. Local trains leave Ljubljana regularly for Bled (760 SIT), Jesenice (64km, 690 SIT), Koper (1380 SIT) and Novo Mesto (760 SIT). A 200 SIT surcharge is required on fast domestic InterCity trains.

Getting Around

Ljubljana's bus system, run by LPP (☎ 519 4114), is user-friendly. Pay on board (140 SIT) or use tiny yellow plastic tokens (100 SIT) available at newsstands, tobacco shops and post offices. Full-day bus passes (*dnevna vozovnica*) cost 300 SIT.

You can rent bicycles at Rog (☎ 231 5868), next to Rozmanova ul 1, for 1500 SIT per day (closed Sunday). Kos Damjan (☎ 505 3606), Tugomerjeva ul 35, charges 1000 SIT per day.

Julian Alps

Lakes Bled and Bohinj make ideal starting points – Bled with its comfortable facilities,

Bohinj right beneath the rocky crags. Most of the region falls within the boundaries of Triglav National Park, established in 1924.

BLED
☎ 04

Bled (population 11,113) is a fashionable resort set on an idyllic, 2km-long lake with a small island and church in the centre and a dramatic castle towering overhead. To the north-east, the highest peaks of the Karavanke Range form a natural boundary with Austria. Bled is a favourite destination for travellers and it can get crowded – and expensive – in summer.

Orientation & Information

Bled village is at the north-eastern end of the lake below the castle. The bus station and tourist office (☎ 574 1122) are about 500m apart on Cesta Svobode (the main Lesce-Bled train station is about 4km south-east). Kompas (☎ 574 1515), Ljubljanska cesta 4, in the Triglav shopping centre, sells hiking maps and arranges private rooms. The Triglav National Park information centre (☎ 574 1188), Kidričeva cesta 2, is on the lake's northern shore (closed weekends).

Kompas and the tourist office change money but there is no ATM in town.

Things to See & Do

There are several trails up to **Bled Castle**, set atop a steep cliff 100m above the lake. The easiest heads south from behind the hostel at Grajska cesta 17. The castle is open daily and entry is 500/250 SIT.

Bled's other striking feature is tiny **Bled Island** at the western end of the lake. Most people reach the island on a *pletna* (gondola). The price (1500 SIT per person) includes a half-hour visit to the island, church and belfry, or you can hire a four-person rowing boat (4000 SIT) from various spots on the shore. **Vintgar Gorge**, 4.5km northwest, is an excellent half-day hike from Bled. Walk north-west on Prešernova cesta then north on Partizanska cesta to Cesta v Vintgar. This will take you to Podhom, where signs point the way to the gorge entrance (open daily May to October, 400/200 SIT).

Places to Stay

Many houses around the lake sport *Sobe* and *Zimmer frei* signs. Kompas books singles/

doubles with shared bath from around DM21/30.

Camping ground *Zaka* (☎ *574 1117*), open April to October, is at the western end of the lake, 2.5km from the bus station. Facilities include a restaurant and supermarket. Call ahead, as Zaka fills up quickly in summer. Rates are DM9 to DM12.50 per person.

The *Bledec* hostel (☎ *574 5250, Grajska cesta 17*), a few hundred metres north-west of the bus station, has a total of 56 beds and costs DM20 per person (DM26 with breakfast). It's open from December to late October.

The cheapest hotel is the 212-bed *Hotel Krim* (☎ *574 1662, fax 574 3729, Ljubljanska cesta 7*) in the town centre which has singles/doubles at the height of the season for DM75/110. On the waterfront, the attractive *Pension Mlino* (☎ *574 1404, fax 574 1506, Cesta Svobode 45*) has singles/doubles for DM60/90.

Places to Eat

Bled's best choice for an affordable meal is *Gostilna Pri Planincu* (*Grajska cesta 8*), a stone's throw from the bus station. There's a fruit and vegetable *market* near the bus station and a *supermarket* in the Triglav shopping centre.

Getting There & Around

Buses run at least hourly to Bohinj (as far as the Zlatorog hotel), Kranj, Ljubljana and Podhom-Zasip. One bus daily goes to Bovec via Kranjska Gora and the heart-stopping Vršič Pass from July to mid-September.

Lesce-Bled train station gets up to 15 trains a day from Ljubljana (55 minutes) via Škofja Loka, Kranj and Radovljica. They continue on to Jesenice (15 minutes), where about eight cross the Austrian border, continuing on to Germany.

Kompas rents out mountain bikes for 1100/1600 SIT per half-day/day.

BOHINJ
☎ 04

Bohinj is a larger, less developed glacial lake 26km south-west of Bled. It is exceedingly beautiful, with high mountains rising directly from the basin-shaped valley.

There is no town called Bohinj; the name refers to the entire valley, its settlements

and the lake. The region's largest town is Bohinjska Bistrica, 6km east of the lake. The main settlement right on the lake is Ribčev Laz. About 1km north, across the Bohinjka River, sits the town of Stara Fužina. Ukanc is a lakefront village 5km west of Ribčev Laz.

Orientation & Information

In Ribčev Laz, all in a row just up from the bus stop, are the tourist office (☎ 572 3370, open daily), a supermarket and the Alpinum travel agency, which organises any number of activities in Bohinj.

Things to See & Do

The **Church of St John the Baptist**, across the stone bridge at the northern end of Ribčev Laz, has exquisite 15th-century frescoes and is probably the most beautiful church in Slovenia.

Alpinsport (☎ 572 3486), to the right just before Ribčev Laz's stone bridge, rents out canoes and kayaks from DM25 per day and organises kayaking trips on the Sava (3400 SIT).

The **Vogel cable car**, above the Zlatorog camping ground in Ukanc, travels 1km up into the mountains every half-hour year-round (except November) for 1000/700 SIT return. From the upper station (1540m) you can scale **Mt Vogel** (1922m) in a few hours for a sweeping view of the region.

Places to Stay & Eat

The large and beautifully situated *Zlatorog* camping ground (☎ *572 3441*), open from May to September, costs 1000 SIT to 1600 SIT per person. It's near the lake in Ukanc, 5km west of Ribčev Laz.

The tourist office can arrange singles/doubles with shower in Ribčev Laz, Stara Fužina and neighbouring villages for 1920/3200 SIT (up to 2400/4000 SIT in July and August). There's a 30% surcharge for stays of less than three days.

In Ukanc, the nine-room pension *Stare* (☎ *572 3403, fax 572 3254*) has doubles with shower and breakfast for 7600 SIT to 8400 SIT.

In Ribčev Laz there's a *Mercator* supermarket (closed Sunday) and, next to the Alpinum travel agency, the *MK* restaurant and pizzeria. If you've got wheels of any sort head for *Gostišče Rupa*, at house No 87 in Srednja Vas, about 5km north-east of Ribčev Laz. It has some of the best home-cooking in Slovenia.

Getting There & Around

There are hourly buses between Ribčev Laz and Ljubljana via Bled, Kranj and Bohinjska Bistrica. All buses stop in Ribčev Laz before carrying on to the Zlatorog Hotel in Ukanc. The closest train station is at Bohinjska Bistrica on the Jesenice-Nova Gorica line.

Alpinsport rents mountain bikes for 2900 SIT per day.

TREKKING MT TRIGLAV

Starting from Ukanc or Stara Fužina, trails lead deep into the Julian Alps via a network of mountain huts (*planinska koča* or *planinski dom*) spaced about five hours apart. The huts in the higher regions are open July to September, in the lower regions from June to October. Beds cost about 2000 SIT per person, and meals are available. Warm clothes, sturdy boots and strong legs are indispensable.

The best time to hike is August to October. Keep to the trails that are well marked with a red circle and a white centre. Before setting out buy a copy of the 1:20,000 *Triglav* map or the 1:50,000 *Julijske Alpe – Vzhodni Del* (Julian Alps – Eastern Part), available at bookshops and tourist offices.

Soča Valley

BOVEC & KOBARID
☎ 05

The Soča Valley, defined by the bluer-than-blue Soča River, stretches from Triglav National Park to Nova Gorica and is one of the most beautiful spots in Slo venia. Of course it wasn't always that way: in WWI this was the site of the infamous Soča (or Isonzo) Front, which claimed the lives of an estimated one million people and was immortalised by Ernest Hemingway in his novel *A Farewell to Arms*.

Today visitors flock to the town of **Kobarid** which commemorates these events at the award-winning **Kobarid Museum** (500 SIT).

Many also head to **Bovec**, 21km north, for some of the best white-water rafting in Europe. The season lasts from April to October. In Bovec contact Soča Rafting (☎ 389 6200 or mobile/cellphone ☎ 041 724 472) or Bovec Rafting Team (☎ 388 6128). Rafting trips last from 1½ to 2½ hours and cost 4790/5980 SIT on weekdays/weekends (including neoprene long johns, wind breaker, life jacket, helmet and paddle). Kayaks cost 3230 SIT for four hours including equipment.

Places to Stay

The tourist office (☎ 389 0000) in the Kobarid Museum and, in Bovec, the Avrigo Tours agency (☎ 388 6123) book private doubles for 4820 SIT (there are few singles available). There are four camping grounds in Bovec and one in Kobarid.

Getting There & Away

There are up to six buses a day between Kobarid and Bovec. Other destinations include Ljubljana (two to five daily), Nova Gorica (four to six daily) and Cerkno (up to five daily). In July and August a daily bus to Ljubljana goes via the Vršič Pass and Kranjska Gora. From Bled there are three trains a day to Most na Soči (55 minutes) from which there are regular buses to Kobarid and Bovec (45 minutes).

Karst Region

POSTOJNA CAVE
☎ 05

Postojna Cave, vying with Bled as Slovenia's top tourist spot, can be like visiting Disneyland on a busy weekend. Visitors get to see about 5.7km of the cave's 27km on a 1½-hour tour in their own language; about 4km are covered by an electric train shuttling through colourfully lit karst formations. The tour ends with a viewing tank full of *Proteus anguinus*, the salamander-like beasties inhabiting Slovenia's karst caves. Dress warmly as the cave is a constant 8°C.

From May to September, tours leave on the hour between 9 am and 6 pm daily. In March and April and again in October there are tours at 10 am, noon, 2 and 4 pm with an extra daily tour at 5 pm in April and additional tours at the weekend in October. From November to February tours leave at 10 am and 2 pm daily, and at noon and 4 pm at the weekends. Entry is 2100/1050 SIT.

Orientation & Information

The cave is 2km north-west of Postojna's bus station. The train station is 1km south-east of the centre. The unhelpful tourist office (☎ 720 1610), Tržaška cesta 4, is open 8 am to 6 pm weekdays and to noon on Saturday. Kompas (☎ 726 4281), Titov trg 2a, has private rooms from 2400 SIT per person.

Getting There & Away

Almost all buses between Ljubljana and the coast stop here. There are direct trains and buses to Postojna from Ljubljana (one hour) and Koper (1½ hours) but the bus station is closer to the caves.

The Coast

KOPER
☎ 05

Only 21km south of Trieste, Koper (population 24,595) is the largest and least touristy of several coastal towns along the north side of the Istrian Peninsula. The town's Italian name, Capodistria, recalls its former status as capital of Istria under the Venetian Republic in the 15th and 16th centuries which is evident in the Venetian-flavoured architecture of the Old Town. As Slovenia's only shipping port, Koper is a lively business and industrial centre.

Orientation & Information

The adjacent bus and train stations are in the same modern building 1km south-east of the Old Town, at the end of Kolodvorska cesta. The tourist office (☎ 627 3791), opposite the marina at Ukmarjev trg 7, is open daily in summer but closed Sunday off-season.

Things to See

From the stations you enter Prešernov trg through the Muda Gate (1516). Walk past the bridge-shaped Da Ponte Fountain (1666) and into Čevljarska ul (Shoemaker's St), a narrow pedestrian way that opens onto Titov trg, the medieval central square. Most of the things to see in Koper are clustered here.

The 36m City Tower (1480), which you can climb, stands next to the mostly 18th-century Cathedral of St Nazarius. To the north is the sublime Loggia (1463), now a cafe and gallery, and to the south is the Praetorian Palace (1452); both are good examples of Venetian Gothic style.

The Koper Regional Museum, in the Belgramoni-Tacco Palace at Kidričeva ul 19, contains 16th- to 18th-century Italianate sculptures and paintings (closed Sunday).

Places to Stay & Eat

The tourist office and Kompas (☎ 627 2346), Pristaniška ul 17, have *private rooms* for 2000 SIT to 2500 SIT per person, mostly in the new town beyond the train station. Both levy a 30% surcharge for stays less than three nights.

In July and August the HI-affiliated *Dijaški Dom Koper* hostel (☎ 627 3252, Cankarjeva ul 5), in the Old Town east of Trg Brolo, rents 380 beds in triple rooms for 2300 SIT per person. Show an HI card for 10% discounts. The rest of the year only about 10 beds are available.

The only hotel in the Old Town, the recently renovated *Hotel Koper* (☎ 610 0500, fax 610 0594, Pristaniška ul 3), has comfortable singles/doubles for 9200/14,800 SIT off-season and 11,100/17,800 SIT in July and August.

There's an outdoor *market* on Pristaniška ul and a *Coop* supermarket in the department store on Piranska cesta. The pizzeria *Atrij (Triglavska ul 2)* is open most days to 10 pm. An atmospheric spot for a meal is *Istrska Klet (Župančičeva ul 39)* in an old palace. Main courses are priced from 700 SIT to 1000 SIT.

Getting There & Away

There are buses almost every 20 minutes on weekdays to Piran (17km) and Portorož via Izola, and every 40 minutes at the weekend. Buses also leave every hour or 90 minutes for Ljubljana (1920 SIT, 2¼ hours) via Divača and Postojna. You can also take the train to Ljubljana (1180 SIT, 2¼ hours).

PIRAN
☎ 05

Picturesque Piran (Pirano in Italian), sitting at the tip of a narrow peninsula, is everyone's favourite town on the Slovenian coast – brace yourself for heavy crowds in summer. Piran is a gem of Venetian Gothic architecture with a history dating back to the ancient Greeks and is now protected as a cultural monument. The trail east to the beaches (also crowded in summer) offers stunning views of the coast as it passes beneath the bluffs.

Orientation & Information

Buses stop just south of Piran Harbour and next to the library on Tartinijev trg which is the heart of Piran's Old Town.

The tourist office (☎ 673 2507) on Stjenkova ul rents rooms but keeps very brief hours. Head instead for the Maona travel agency (☎ 673 1291), Cankarjevo nabrežje 7, which arranges private rooms and organises boat cruises.

Banka Koper, Tartinijev trg 12, changes travellers cheques and cash on weekdays and Saturday morning. Outside the bank is an ATM.

Things to See

The **Maritime Museum**, in a 17th-century palace at Cankarjevo nabrežje 3 has exhibits on the sea, sailing and salt-making. Piran's small **aquarium**, Tomažičeva ul 4, packs a tremendous variety of sea life into 25 tanks (open daily, 350 SIT).

The **town hall** and **court house** stand on Tartinijev trg, in the centre of which is a **statue** of the local violinist and composer Giuseppe Tartini (1692-1770).

Piran is dominated by the **Church of St George**, a Renaissance and baroque structure north of Tartinijev trg. The free-standing **bell tower** (1609) was modelled on the campanile of San Marco in Venice; the octagonal **baptistry** next to it has altars, paintings and a Roman sarcophagus from the 2nd century.

PIRAN

PLACES TO STAY & EAT
3   Val Hostel
5   Tri Vdove
6   Pavel Restaurant
7   Delfin Restaurant
31 Neptun Restaurant
32 Jestvina Supermarket
33 Surf Bar Restaurant

OTHER
1   Punta Lighthouse
2   Church of St Clement
4   Cistern
8   Church of St Stephen
9   Dolphin Gate
10 Market
11 Church of St George
12 Bell Tower
13 Baptistry
14 Church of St Francis & Monastery
15 Our Lady of the Snows Church
16 Venetian House
17 Town Hall
18 Tartini Memorial
19 Church of St Peter
20 Banka Koper
21 Old Flag Poles
22 Bus Stop
23 Court House
24 Tourist Office (Rooms)
25 Piran Hotel
26 Aquarium
27 Giuseppe Tartini Hotel
28 Maritime Museum
29 Post Office
30 Maona Travel Agency
34 Customs Office
35 Bus Stop

GULF OF TRIESTE

Trail to Beaches; Fiesa Hotel; Camping Ground (700m)

PIRAN BAY

Piran Harbour

Marina

Customs Wharf

Town Walls

To Car Park (200m); Portorož (5km)

SLOVENIA

To the east of the church is a 200m stretch of the 15th-century **town walls**, which can be climbed for superb views of Piran and the Adriatic.

Cruises

From May to October Maona and other travel agencies can book you on any number of cruises – from a loop that takes in the towns along the coast (1200 SIT) to day-long excursions to Venice, Trieste (4000 SIT) or Croatia's Brioni National Park (8500 SIT return).

Places to Stay

The tourist office and the Maona travel agency arrange *private rooms* throughout the year. Singles are 2300 SIT to 3600 SIT, doubles 3300 SIT to 5500 SIT, plus a 50% surcharge for stays less than three nights.

The closest camping site is *Camping Jezero Fiesa* (☎ 673 3150) at Fiesa, 4km by road from Piran (but less than 1km via the coastal trail east of the Church of St George). It's open June to September and can get very crowded – call ahead.

The convenient hostel *Val* (☎ 674 2555, fax 674 2556, Gregorčičeva ul 38a), charges 2700 SIT to 3300 SIT per person, including breakfast. It's open from late April to October.

Though not in Piran proper, the 22-room hotel *Fiesa* (☎ 746 897, fax 746 896), overlooking the sea near Camping Jezero Fiesa, is one of the nicest places to stay on the coast. Singles/doubles are 4000/8000 SIT, rising to 5200/10,400 SIT in July and August.

Places to Eat

The *Jestvina* supermarket is opposite Trg Bratsva 8 (closed Sunday).

Piran has a heap of seafood restaurants along Prešernovo nabrežje, including *Pavel*, *Pavel 2* and *Tri Vdove*. Most are fairly expensive – about 2500 SIT for dinner with drinks. Cheaper fish spots include the *Delfin* (*Kosovelova ul 4*), and the semi-upmarket *Neptun* (*Župančičeva ul 7*) behind the Maona travel agency.

The *Surf Bar* (*Grudnova ul 1*), on a small street north-east of the bus station, is a mellow place for a meal or drink.

Getting There & Away

The I&I bus company (☎ 41 750 in Koper) links Piran with Portorož and Lucija (bus No 1); Portorož and Fiesa (bus No 2; mid-April to August only); Strunjan and Portorož (bus No 3); and Portorož, Sečovlje and Padna (bus No 4).

Buses from Piran also serve Ljubljana via Divača and Postojna (up to 10 daily) and Nova Gorica (two daily). Six buses head for Trieste on weekdays, and there's a daily departure for Zagreb and another for Croatian Istria.

PORTOROŽ

☎ 05

Every coastal country has a honky-tonk beach resort, and Portorož is Slovenia's very own Blackpool, Bondi or Atlantic City. The 'Port of Roses' is essentially a solid strip of high-rise hotels, restaurants, bars, travel agencies, discos and beaches that charge admission (around 400 SIT). Though it's not to everyone's taste, Portorož can be a fun place to watch Slovenes, Italians, Austrians and others at play.

The bus station is opposite the main beach on Postajališka pot. The tourist office (☎ 674 0231) at Obala 16, a short distance west of the bus station, books *private rooms* and *apartments* – as do Atlas Express (☎ 674 5077), Obala 55, and Kompas (☎ 674 7032), Obala 41. The going rate for doubles is 3300 SIT to 5000 SIT. Getting a room for less than three nights (for which there's a 50% surcharge) is difficult.

Spain

Spaniards approach life with such exuberance that most visitors have to stop and stare. In almost every town in the country, the nightlife will outlast the foreigners. Then just when foreigners think they are coming to terms with the pace, they are surrounded by the beating drums of a fiesta, with day and night disappearing into a blur of dancing, eating and drinking.

Spain also has a wealth of history and architecture, from Roman aqueducts and Moorish palaces to medieval castles and modern Art Nouveau churches. Then, of course, you have the weather – from April to October the sun shines with uncanny predictability on the Mediterranean coast and the Balearic Islands.

Facts about Spain

HISTORY

From around 8000 to 3000 BC, people from North Africa known as Iberians crossed the Strait of Gibraltar and settled the peninsula. Around 1000 BC Celtic tribes entered northern Spain, while Phoenician merchants were establishing trading settlements along the Mediterranean coast. They were followed by Greeks and Carthaginians who arrived from around 600 to 500 BC.

The Romans arrived in the 3rd century BC. Christianity came to Spain during the 1st century AD. In AD 409 Roman Hispania was invaded by Germanic tribes and by 419 the Christian Visigoths, another Germanic people, had established a kingdom. This lasted until 711, when the Moors – Muslim Berbers and Arabs from North Africa – crossed the Strait of Gibraltar and defeated Roderic, the last Visigoth king.

By 714 Muslim armies had occupied the entire peninsula. Islamic Spain – known as al-Andalus – was to last almost 800 years in parts of the country. In 722 a small army

AT A GLANCE	
Capital:	Madrid
Population:	39.8 million
Official Language:	Spanish (Castilian)
Currency:	1 peseta (pta) = 100 centimos

under the Visigothic leader, Pelayo, inflicted the first defeat on the Muslims – this marked the beginning of the Reconquista, the spluttering reconquest of Spain by the Christians. In 1085, Alfonso VI, king of León and Castile, took Toledo. This prompted the Muslim leaders to request help from North Africa, which arrived in the form of the Almoravids. They recaptured much territory and ruled it until the 1140s. The Almoravids were followed by the Almohads, another North African dynasty.

During the Reconquista, the kingdoms of Castile and Aragón emerged as Christian Spain's two main powers, and in 1469 they were united by the marriage of Isabel, princess of Castile, and Fernando, heir to the throne of Aragón. They united Spain and laid the foundations for the Spanish golden age. They also revived the notorious Inquisition, which expelled and executed thousands of Jews and other non-Christians. In 1492 the last Muslim ruler of Granada surrendered to them, marking the completion of the Reconquista.

Also in 1492, while searching for an alternative passage to India, Columbus stumbled on the Bahamas and claimed the Americas for Spain. This sparked a period of exploration and exploitation that was to yield Spain enormous wealth while destroying ancient American empires. For three centuries, gold and silver from the New World were used to finance the rapid expansion of the Spanish empire and to prop it up during its slow decline.

The disastrous Spanish-American War of 1898 marked the end of the Spanish empire. The early 20th century was characterised by military disasters in Morocco and growing instability as radical forces struggled to overthrow the established order. In 1923, with

SPAIN

SPAIN

Spain on the brink of civil war, Miguel Primo de Rivera made himself military dictator, ruling until 1930. The 1936 elections told of a country split in two between the Republican government (an uneasy alliance of leftist parties known as the Popular Front) and the right-wing Nationalists (an alliance of the army, Church and the fascist Falange Party).

Nationalist plotters in the army rose against the government in July 1936. During the subsequent Spanish Civil War (1936-39), the Nationalists, led by General Francisco Franco, received heavy military support from Nazi Germany and fascist Italy. By 1939 Franco had won and an estimated 350,000 Spaniards had died. After the war, thousands of Republicans were executed, jailed or forced into exile.

Franco's 35-year dictatorship began with Spain isolated internationally and crippled by recession. It wasn't until the 1950s and 1960s, when the rise in tourism and a treaty with the USA combined to provide much needed funds, that the country began to recover. By the 1970s Spain had the fastest-growing economy in Europe.

Franco died in 1975, naming Juan Carlos his successor. King Juan Carlos is widely credited with having overseen Spain's transition from dictatorship to democracy. The first elections after the civil war were held in 1977, a new constitution was drafted in 1978, and a failed military coup in 1981 was seen as a futile attempt to turn back the clock. Spain joined the European Community (EC) in 1986, and celebrated its return to the world stage in style in 1992, with Expo '92 in Seville and the Olympic Games in Barcelona. In 1997 it became fully integrated into the North Atlantic Treaty Organisation (NATO), and in 1999, with the fastest growing economy on the continent, it met the criteria for launching the new European currency, the euro.

GEOGRAPHY

Spain (505,000 sq km) is probably Europe's most geographically diverse country, with landscapes ranging from the near-deserts of Almería to the lush, green countryside and deep coastal inlets of Galicia, and from the sunbaked plains of Castilla-La Mancha to the rugged mountains of the Pyrenees.

CLIMATE

In July and August temperatures reach as high as 45°C in parts of Andalucía – even Madrid is unbearably hot and almost deserted. In winter the rains never seem to stop in the north, except when they turn to snow. Madrid regularly freezes in December, January and February. At these times Andalucía is the place to be, with temperatures reaching the mid-teens in most places and good skiing in the Sierra Nevada.

POPULATION & PEOPLE

Spain has a population of 39.8 million. The biggest cities are Madrid (three million), Barcelona (1.5 million), Valencia (750,000) and Seville (715,000). Each region proudly preserves its own unique culture, and some – Catalonia and the País Vasco in particular – display a fiercely independent spirit. Only about 20% of Spaniards are regular churchgoers, but Catholicism is deeply ingrained in the culture. As the writer Unamuno said, 'Here in Spain we are all Catholics, even the atheists'.

SOCIETY & CONDUCT

Spaniards are gregarious people, on the whole very tolerant and easy-going towards foreigners. It's difficult to cause offence, though disrespectful behaviour in churches – including excessively casual dress – won't go down well.

Bullfighting is enjoying a resurgence despite continued pressure from international animal-rights activists. It's a complex activity that's regarded as much as an art form as a sport by aficionados. If you decide to see a *corrida de toros*, the season runs from March to October. Madrid, Seville and Pamplona are among the best places to see one.

LANGUAGE

Spanish, or Castilian *(castellano)* as it is more precisely called, is spoken by just about all Spaniards. Catalan is spoken by about two-thirds of people in Catalonia and the Balearic Islands and half of those in the Valencia region. Galician (which sounds like a cross between Spanish and Portuguese) is spoken by many in the north-west. Basque (of obscure, non-Latin origin) is spoken by a minority in the País Vasco and Navarra.

English isn't as widely spoken as many travellers seem to expect, but you should be able to find English-speakers in the main cities and tourist areas.

See the Spanish Language Guide at the back of this book for pronunciation guidelines and useful words and phrases.

Facts for the Visitor

HIGHLIGHTS

Spain is home to some of the finest art galleries in the world. The Prado in Madrid has few rivals, and there are outstanding art museums in Bilbao, Seville, Barcelona, Valencia and Córdoba. Fascinating smaller galleries include the Dalí museum in Figueres and the abstract art museum in Cuenca.

Try not to miss the Muslim-era gems of Andalucía – the Alhambra in Granada, the alcázar in Seville and the mezquita in Córdoba – as well as Barcelona's extraordinary La Sagrada Família church by Antoni Gaudí.

There's outstanding mountain scenery – often coupled with extremely picturesque villages – in the Pyrenees, Picos de Europa, and in parts of Andalucía (such as the Alpujarras). On the coasts, the rugged inlets of Galicia and stark, hilly Cabo de Gata in Andalucía stand out.

SUGGESTED ITINERARIES

Three days
   Visit Seville and Granada, or Barcelona and San Sebastián.
One week
   Spend two days each in Barcelona, Madrid and Seville, allowing one day for travel.

SPAIN

Two weeks
As above, plus San Sebastián, Toledo, Salamanca and/or Cuenca, Córdoba and/or Granada,
and maybe Cáceres and/or Trujillo.

PLANNING
When to Go
The ideal months to visit are May, June and
September (plus April and October in the
south). In July and August prepare yourself
for the crush of Spanish and foreign tourists,
and for the extreme heat.

Books & Maps
If you're planning in-depth travels in Spain,
get hold of Lonely Planet's *Spain*.

The New Spaniards, by John Hooper, is a
fascinating summary of modern Spanish society and culture. Classic accounts of life and
travel in Spain include Gerald Brenan's
South from Granada (1920s), Laurie Lee's
As I Walked Out One Midsummer Morning
(1930s), George Orwell's *Homage to Catalonia* (about the civil war), and *Iberia* by
James Michener (1960s). Of foreign literature set in Spain, Ernest Hemingway's civil
war novel *For Whom the Bell Tolls* is a must.

Some of the best maps for travellers are
published by Michelin, which produces a
1:1 million *Spain Portugal* map and six
1:400,000 regional maps.

TOURIST OFFICES
Local Tourist Offices
Most towns (and many villages) have an
oficina de turismo (tourist office) that will
supply maps and basic information on local
sights, attractions, accommodation etc. Staff
are helpful and often speak some English.

The travel agency TIVE, with offices in
major cities throughout Spain, specialises
in discounted tickets and travel arrangements for students and young people. Its
head office is in Madrid (☎ 91 543 74 12,
fax 91 544 00 62) at Calle de Fernando El
Católico 88.

Tourist Offices Abroad
Spanish tourist offices abroad include:

Canada (☎ 416-961-3131, ✆ toronto@
tourspain.es) 2 Bloor St W, 34th floor,
Toronto M4W 3E2
UK (☎ 020-7486 8077,
✆ londres@tourspain.es) 22-23 Manchester
Square, London W1M 5AP

USA (☎ 212-265-8822, ✆ oetny@tourspain.es)
666 Fifth Ave, 35th floor, New York,
NY 10103

VISAS
Citizens of the USA, Canada, Australia and
New Zealand can stay up to 90 days without
a visa. South Africans must obtain a visa in
advance; the 90-day, multiple-entry visa is
useful if you plan to leave Spain – say to
visit Gibraltar or Morocco – then re-enter.

EMBASSIES & CONSULATES
Spanish Embassies Abroad
Diplomatic missions abroad include:

Australia (☎ 02-6273 3555,
✆ embespau@mail.mae.es) 15 Arkana St,
Yarralumla, Canberra, ACT 2600
Canada (☎ 613-747-2252,
✆ spain@DocuWeb.ca) 74 Stanley Ave,
Ottawa, Ontario K1M 1P4
UK (☎ 020-7235 5555, ✆ espemblon@
espemblon.freeserve.co.uk, 39 Chesham Place,
London SW1X 8SB
USA (☎ 202-452 0100) 2375 Pennsylvania Ave
NW, Washington, DC 20037

Embassies in Spain
Some 70 countries have embassies in
Madrid, including:

Australia (☎ 91 441 93 00) Plaza del Descubri-
dor Diego de Ordás 3-2, Edificio Santa
Engrácia 120
Canada (☎ 91 431 45 56) Calle de Núñez
de Balboa 35
New Zealand (☎ 91 523 02 26) Plaza de la
Lealtad 2
UK (☎ 91 308 06 18) Calle de Fernando el
Santo 16
USA (☎ 91 577 40 00) Calle de Serrano 75

MONEY
Currency
Spain's unit of currency for everyday transactions until early in 2002 is the peseta
(pta). Coin denominations include one, five
(known as a *duro*), 10, 25, 50, 100, 200 and
500 ptas. There are notes of 1000, 2000,
5000 and 10,000 ptas.

Exchange Rates

country	unit		pesetas
Australia	A$1	=	106.71 ptas
Canada	C$1	=	124.16 ptas
euro	€1	=	166.38 ptas

euro currency converter €1 = 166 ptas

France	1FF	=	25.36 ptas
Germany	DM1	=	85.07 ptas
Japan	¥100	=	169.5 ptas
New Zealand	NZ$1	=	82.84 ptas
UK	UK£1	=	276.89 ptas
USA	US$1	=	184.16 ptas

Exchanging Money

Banks – open 8.30 am to 2 pm weekdays and to 1 pm Saturday – generally give better exchange rates than currency-exchange offices, and travellers cheques attract a slightly better rate than cash. ATMs accepting a wide variety of cards are common throughout Spain.

Costs

Spain is one of Western Europe's more affordable countries. It's possible to scrape by on US$20 to US$25 a day by staying in the cheapest possible accommodation, avoiding eating in restaurants or going to museums or bars, and not moving around too much. Places like Madrid, Barcelona, Seville and San Sebastián will place a greater strain on your money belt. A more reasonable budget would be US$35 to US$40 a day.

Tipping

In restaurants, menu prices include a service charge, and tipping is a matter of personal choice – most people leave small change (5% is plenty). It's also common to leave small change in bars and cafes.

POST & COMMUNICATIONS
Post

Main post offices in provincial capitals are usually open 8.30 am to 8.30 pm weekdays and about 9 am to 1.30 pm Saturday. Stamps are also sold at *estancos* – tobacconist shops with the 'Tabacos' sign in yellow letters on a maroon background. A standard, airmail letter or card costs 70 ptas within Europe, 115 ptas to the USA or Canada, and 185 ptas to Australia or New Zealand. Aerograms cost 85 ptas regardless of destination.

Common abbreviations used in Spanish addresses are 1, 2, 3 etc, which mean 1st, 2nd, 3rd floor, and s/n *(sin número)*, which means the building has no number.

Telephone, Fax & Email

Spain's country code is ☎ 34. Area codes in Spain are an integral part of the phone number: all numbers are nine digits long, without area codes.

Public pay phones are blue, common and easy to use. They accept coins and *tarjetas telefónicas* (phonecards), which come in 1000 and 2000-pta denominations and are available at main post offices and estancos. A three-minute call from a pay phone costs 25 ptas within a local area, 65 ptas to other places in the same province, 110 ptas to other provinces, or 230 ptas to another EU country. Provincial and inter-provincial calls except those to mobile/cellphones are around 50% cheaper between 8 pm and 8 am and all day Saturday and Sunday; local and international calls are around 10% cheaper between 6 pm and 8 am and all day Saturday and Sunday.

A three-minute call to the USA during peak rate costs 280 ptas, to Australia it's 820 ptas.

Most main post offices have a fax service, but you'll often find cheaper rates at shops or offices with 'Fax Público' signs. Cybercafes are springing up in major Spanish cities. An hour online can cost anywhere from 200 ptas to 900 ptas.

INTERNET RESOURCES

The Spanish Tourist Office (Turespaña) Web site is at www.tourspain.es. An Internet search under 'Spain, Travel' will reveal dozens of sites.

TIME

Spain is GMT/UTC plus one hour in winter, or two hours in summer (from the last Sunday in March to the last Sunday in September).

WOMEN TRAVELLERS

Spain has one of the lowest incidences of reported rape in the developed world, and physical harassment is much less frequent than you might expect. Still, women should be prepared to ignore stares and catcalls.

The Asociación de Asistencia a Mujeres Violadas in Madrid (☎ 91 574 01 10), open 10 am to 2 pm and 4 to 7 pm weekdays, offers advice and help to rape victims, and can provide details of similar centres in other cities, though only limited English is spoken.

GAY & LESBIAN TRAVELLERS

Attitudes are fairly tolerant, especially in the cities. Madrid, Barcelona, Sitges, Ibiza and Cádiz all have active gay and lesbian scenes. A good source of information on gay venues and organisations throughout Spain is the Barcelona-based Coordinadora Gai-Lesbiana (☎ 93 298 00 29, fax 93 298 06 18), Carrer de Finlandia 45; find its Web site at www.pangea.org/org/cgl. In Madrid, the equivalent is Cogam (☎/fax 91 532 45 17), Calle del Fuencarral 37.

DISABLED TRAVELLERS

You'll find some wheelchair-accessible accommodation in main centres, but it may not be in the budget category – although 25 Spanish youth hostels are classed as suitable for wheelchair users.

Spanish tourist offices abroad provide a basic information sheet with some useful addresses. INSERSO (☎ 91 347 88 88), Calle de Ginzo de Limea 58, 28029 Madrid, is the government department responsible for the disabled, with branches in all of Spain's 50 provinces.

DANGERS & ANNOYANCES

Don't leave belongings unattended in youth hostels – there is a high incidence of theft. Beware of pickpockets in cities and tourist resorts (Barcelona and Seville have bad reputations). There is also a relatively high incidence of muggings in such places, so keep your wits about you.

In 1992 Spain's liberal drug laws were severely tightened. No matter what anyone tells you, it is not legal to smoke dope in public bars, hotel rooms or guesthouses.

Emergency numbers for police throughout Spain are ☎ 091 (national police) and ☎ 092 (local police).

BUSINESS HOURS

Generally, people work weekdays from 9 am to 2 pm and then from 4.30 or 5 to 8 pm. Shops and travel agencies are usually open on Saturday, though some may skip the evening session. Museums all have their own unique opening hours.

PUBLIC HOLIDAYS & SPECIAL EVENTS

The following holidays are observed virtually everywhere: 1 January (New Year's Day), 6 January (Epiphany or Three Kings' Day), Good Friday, 1 May (Labour Day), 15 August (Feast of the Assumption), 12 October (National Day), 1 November (All Saints' Day), 8 December (Feast of the Immaculate Conception) and 25 December (Christmas Day).

When a holiday falls close to a weekend, Spaniards like to make a *puente* (bridge) – meaning they also take the intervening day off.

There are innumerable local *ferias* (fairs); a major one is La Tamborada in San Sebastián on 20 January. *Carnaval* is a time of fancy-dress parades around the country about seven weeks before Easter (wildest in Cádiz and Sitges). Valencia's week-long mid-March party, Las Fallas, has first-class fireworks and processions. The wildest Semana Santa festival (the week leading up to Easter Sunday) is held in Seville; Seville also hosts the Feria de Abril, a week-long party in late April. Sanfermines, with the running of the bulls, is held in Pamplona in July. Barcelona's week-long party, the Festes de la Mercè, happens around 24 September.

ACCOMMODATION

Spain has more than 800 camping grounds, officially rated from 1st to 3rd class. Most charge around 500 ptas per tent and per person, though facilities and settings vary enormously. Many sites are open all year, though quite a few close from October to Easter.

Spain's *albergues juveniles* (youth hostels) are often the cheapest option for lone travellers, but two people can usually get a double elsewhere for a similar price. Many hostels have curfews, are closed during the day and lack cooking facilities. Most are members of the country's Hostelling International (HI) organisation, Red Española de Albergues Juveniles (REAJ), whose head office (☎ 91 347 77 00) is at Calle de José Ortega y Gasset 71, 28006 Madrid. Prices often depend on the season and whether you're under age 26; typically beds cost from 900 ptas to 1700 ptas. You can buy HI cards for 1800 ptas at virtually all hostels.

There are officially three categories of hotels – *hoteles* (from one to five stars), *hostales* (one to three stars) and *pensiones*. In practice, there are all sorts of overlapping categories, especially at the budget end of the market. In broad terms, the cheapest are usually *fondas* and *casas de huéspedes*, followed by pensiones. All charge about 2500 ptas to 4000 ptas for doubles with shared bath. Some hostales and *hostal-residencias* come in the same price range, but others have rooms with private bath that cost up to around 8000 ptas. Hoteles are usually beyond the means of budget travellers. Room rates in this chapter are generally high-season prices, which in most resorts and other busy tourist places means July and August, Semana Santa and occasionally Christmas and New Year.

FOOD & DRINKS

It's a good idea to reset your stomach's clock in Spain, unless you want to eat alone or with other tourists. Most Spaniards start the day with *desayuno* (a light breakfast), followed by the main meal of the day, *almuerzo* or *comida* (lunch), between 1.30 and 4 pm. The *cena* (evening meal) is usually lighter and may be eaten as late as 10 or 11 pm.

Most cafes and bars serve *tapas* – saucer-sized mini-snacks that are part of the Spanish way of life. Tapas come in infinite varieties, from calamari rings to spinach with chickpeas. A typical tapa costs 100 ptas to 250 ptas. A *ración* is a meal-sized serving of these snacks; a *media ración* is a half-ración. *Bocadillos* (sandwiches) are also common.

Spain's restaurants serve good, simple food at affordable prices. Many restaurants offer a *menú del día* (menu of the day) – the budget traveller's best friend. For between 850 ptas and 1500 ptas, you typically get a starter, a main course, dessert, bread and wine. The *plato combinado* (combined plate) is a near relative of the *menú* – maybe a steak and egg with chips and salad, or fried squid with potato salad. You'll pay more for your meals if you order à la carte, but the food will be better.

One of Spain's most characteristic dishes is *paella* – rice, seafood and often chicken or meat, all simmered up with saffron. *Gazpacho*, a soup made from tomatoes, breadcrumbs, cucumber and/or green peppers, is eaten cold. *Tortillas* (omelettes) are an inexpensive stand-by and come in many varieties. *Jamón serrano* (cured ham) is a treat for meat-eaters but can be expensive.

Finding vegetarian fare can be a headache – it's not uncommon for 'meatless' food to be flavoured with meat stock. Common vegetarian snacks are *bocadillo de tortilla de patata* (roll filled with potato omelette) and *bocadillo vegetal*, which has a filling of salad and, often, a fried egg (*sin huevo* means 'without egg').

Coffee addicts should specify how they want their fix: *café con leche* is about 50% coffee, 50% hot milk; *café solo* is a short black; *café cortado* is a short black with a little milk. The most common way to order a *cerveza* (beer) is to ask for a *caña*, which is a small draught beer. *Corto* and, in the País Vasco, *zurrito*, are other names for this. A larger beer (about 300ml) is often called a *tubo*, or in Catalonia a *jarra*. All these words apply to *cerveza de barril* (draught beer) – if you just ask for a cerveza you're likely to get bottled beer.

Vino (wine) comes *blanco* (white), *tinto* (red) or *rosado* (rosé). *Tinto de verano*, a kind of wine shandy, is good in summer. *Sangría*, a sweet punch made with red wine, fruit and spirits, is very refreshing.

To specify tap water (safe to drink almost everywhere), ask for *agua del grifo*.

Getting There & Away

AIR

Spain's many international airports include Madrid, Barcelona, Bilbao, Santiago de Compostela, Seville, Málaga, Almería, Alicante, Valencia, Palma de Mallorca, Ibiza and Maó (Menorca). In general, the cheapest destinations by air are Málaga, the Balearic Islands, Barcelona and Madrid.

The youth and student travel agency TIVE, and the general travel agency Halcón Viajes, both with branches in most main cities, have some good fares: generally you're looking at around 13,000 ptas to 15,500 ptas one way to London, Paris or Amsterdam. It's at least 30,000 ptas to the USA.

BUS

There are regular bus services to Spain from all major centres in Europe, including Lisbon, London and Paris. In London, Eurolines (☎ 0990-143 219) has services at least three times a week to Barcelona (UK£84, 23 to 25 hours), Madrid (UK£77, 27 hours) and Málaga (UK£79, 34 hours). Tickets are sold by major travel agencies, and people under 26 qualify for a 10% discount. In

SPAIN

Spain, services to the major European cities are operated by Eurolines affiliates such as Linebús and Julià Via. There are also bus services to Morocco from some Spanish cities.

TRAIN

Reaching Spain by train is more expensive than bus unless you have a rail pass, though fares for those under 26 come close to the bus price. Normal one-way fares from London (using the ferry) to Madrid (via Paris) are UK£104. For more details, contact the Rail Europe Travel Centre (☎ 0990-848 848) in London or a travel agent.

SEA

There are two direct ferry services from the UK. Brittany Ferries (UK ☎ 0870 536 0360) runs Plymouth-Santander ferries (24 hours) twice weekly from mid-March to mid-November and a weekly Portsmouth-Santander service (30 hours). P&O European Ferries (UK ☎ 08702 424 999) runs Portsmouth-Bilbao ferries (35 hours) twice weekly most of the year. Prices on all services are similar: one-way passenger fares range from about UK£50 in winter to UK£85 in summer (cabins extra).

Ferry services between Spain and Morocco include Algeciras-Tangier, Algeciras-Ceuta, Gibraltar-Tangier, Málaga-Melilla, Almería-Melilla and Almería-Nador. Those to/from Algeciras are the fastest, cheapest and most frequent, with up to 20 ferries/hydrofoils a day to Ceuta (90/40 minutes) and 14 to Tangier (two hours/one hour). One-way passenger fares on the ferry/hydrofoil are 1801/2945 ptas (Ceuta) and 2960/3440 ptas (Tangier).

Don't buy Moroccan currency until you reach Morocco, as you will get ripped off in Algeciras.

Getting Around

AIR

Spain has four main domestic airlines – Iberia and its subsidiary Binter Mediterráneo (☎ 902 40 05 00 for both), Air Europa (☎ 902 40 15 01) and Spanair (☎ 902 13 14 15). They compete, along with a couple of smaller airlines, to produce some fares that can make flying worthwhile if you're in a hurry, especially for longer or return trips.

Among travel agencies, TIVE and Halcón Viajes often have cheap fares, especially if you're under age 26.

BUS

Spain's bus network is operated by dozens of independent companies and is more extensive than the train system, serving remote towns and villages as well as the major routes. Buses to/from Madrid are often cheaper than (or barely different from) cross-country routes: for instance Seville to Madrid costs 2745 ptas while the shorter Seville-Granada trip is 2700 ptas.

Many towns and cities have one main bus station where most buses arrive and depart, and these usually have an information desk. Tourist offices can also help with bus schedules but they don't sell tickets.

TRAIN

Eurail and Inter-Rail passes are valid in Spain, but Inter-Rail users have to pay supplements on Talgo and InterCity services and on the high-speed AVE service between Madrid and Seville. All pass-holders making reservations for long-distance trains pay a fee of 500 ptas to 1500 ptas.

RENFE, the national railway company, runs numerous types of train, and travel times on the same route can greatly vary. So can fares, which may depend not just on the type of train, but also the day of the week and time of day. RENFE's trains are mostly modern and comfortable, and late arrivals are now the exception rather than the rule.

Regionales are all-stops trains – cheap and slow. *Cercanías* provide regular services from major cities to the surrounding suburbs and hinterland, sometimes even crossing regional boundaries (they are also, by the way, run by RENFE). Among *largo recorrido* (long-distance) trains the standard daytime train is the *diurno* (its nighttime equivalent is the *estrella*). Quicker is the InterCity (IC), mainly because it makes fewer stops. The *Talgo* is the quickest and dearest. Best of all is the AVE high-speed service that links Madrid and Seville in just 2½ hours. The Talgo 200 uses part of this line to speed down to Málaga from Madrid.

There's a bewildering range of accommodation types, especially on overnight trains. Fortunately ticket clerks understand the problem and are usually happy to go through a few options with you. The cheapest sleeper option is usually a *litera*, a bunk in a six-berth 2nd-class compartment.

You can buy tickets and make reservations at stations, RENFE offices in many city centres, and travel agencies that display the RENFE logo. RENFE's Tarjeta Turística is a rail pass for non-Europeans valid for three to 10 days travel in a two-month period: in 2nd class, four days costs US$155, while 10 days is US$365. Students and under-26s may want to inquire about the ExploreRail card, valid for seven, 15 or 30 days of unlimited travel at 19,000/23,000/30,000 ptas.

CAR & MOTORCYCLE

Spain's roads vary enormously but are generally quite good. Fastest are the *autopistas*, multilane freeways between major cities. On some, mainly in the north, you have to pay hefty tolls (eg, 1580 ptas from the French border to Barcelona). Minor routes can be slow going but are usually more scenic. Petrol is relatively expensive at around 114 ptas for a litre of unleaded.

Speed limits are 120km/h on autopistas, 90 or 100km/h on other country roads and 50km/h in built-up areas. The maximum allowable blood-alcohol level is 0.05% and seat belts must be worn at all times. Motorcyclists must wear a helmet and keep their headlights on day and night.

The head office of the Spanish automobile club Real Automovil Club de España (RACE; ☎ 900-20 00 93) is at Calle de José Abascal 10, 28003 Madrid. You can dial RACE's 24-hour, nationwide emergency service toll-free ☎ 900-11 22 22.

Madrid

Spain's capital may lack the glamour and beauty of Barcelona and the historical richness of so many other Spanish cities (it was insignificant until Felipe II made it his capital in 1561), but it more than makes up for this with a remarkable collection of museums and galleries, some lovely parks and gardens, and a wild nightlife. Give it a few days, and Madrid is sure to grow on you.

Orientation

The area of most interest to visitors lies between Parque del Buen Retiro in the east and Campo del Moro in the west. These two parks are more or less connected by Calle del Alcalá and Calle Mayor, which meet in the middle at Puerta del Sol. Calle Mayor passes the main square, Plaza Mayor.

The main north-south thoroughfare is Paseo de la Castellana, which runs (changing names to Paseo de los Recoletos and finally Paseo del Prado) all the way from Chamartín train station in the north to Madrid's other big station, Atocha.

Information

Tourist Offices The main Oficina de Turismo (☎ 91 429 49 51), at Calle del Duque de Medinaceli 2, is open 9 am to 7 pm weekdays, to 1 pm Saturday. There are branch offices at Barajas airport (☎ 91 305 86 56) and Chamartín train station (☎ 91 315 99 76) open 8 am to 8 pm Monday to Friday and 8 am to 1 pm Saturday. There's another office (☎ 91 364 18 76) at Ronda de Toledo 1, in the Centro Comercial de la Puerta de Toledo; and one in Plaza Mayor.

Money Banks with ATMs are ubiquitous in central Madrid. American Express (☎ 91 527 03 03, lost travellers cheques ☎ 900-99 44 26), Plaza de las Cortes 2, is open 9 am to 5.30 pm weekdays, to noon Saturday.

If you're desperate there are plenty of bureaux de change around Puerta del Sol and Plaza Mayor that offer appalling rates, but often stay open until midnight.

Post & Communications The main post office is in the gigantic Palacio de Comunicaciones on Plaza de la Cibeles. Telefónica's *locutorio* (phone centre), at Gran Vía 30, is open 9.30 am to midnight daily. Private phone companies around town can undercut Telefónica by 50%.

Email & Internet Access Dozens of cafes and shops offer Internet connections, including Aroba52 on Calle de los Reyes (metro: Plaza de España; 300 ptas an hour) and La Casa de Internet, Calle de Luchana 20 (metro: Bilbao; 900 ptas per hour).

Travel Agencies For cheap tickets try Viajes Zeppelin (☎ 91 542 51 54), Plaza de Santo Domingo 2. Another good bet is TIVE, the student and youth travel organisation, at Calle de Fernando el Católico 88

SPAIN

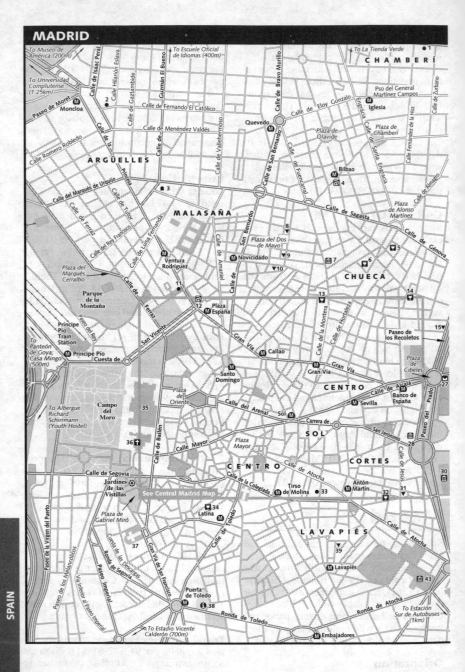

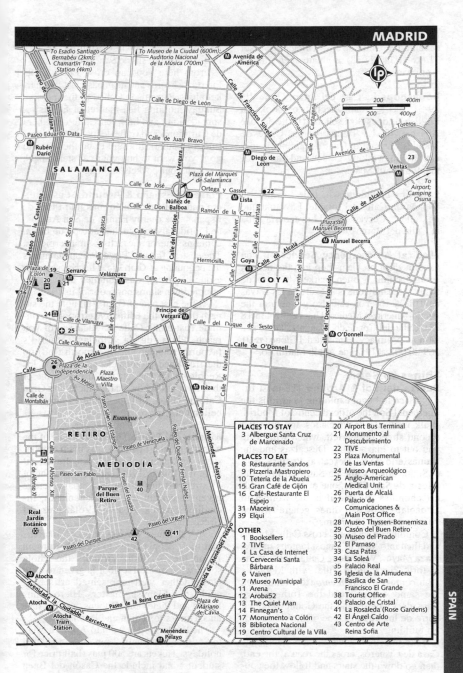

MADRID

0   200   400m
0   200   400yd

To Esadio Santiago
Bernabéu (2km);
Chamartín Train
Station (4km)

To Museo de la Ciudad (600m);
Auditorio Nacional
de la Música (700m)

Avenida de
América

Calle de Diego de León

Calle de Francisco Silvela

Calle de Ardemans

Calle de Cartagena

Paseo Eduardo Data

Rubén
Darío

Calle de Serrano

Paseo de Serrano

Calle de Juan Bravo

Calle de Vergara

Diego de
León

Avenida de

los Toreros

23

Ventas

SALAMANCA

Paseo de la Castellana

Plaza del Marqués
de Salamanca

Calle de José

Ortega y Gasset

22

Lista

To
Airport;
Camping
Osuna

Núñez de
Balboa

Calle de Don
Balboa

Ramón de la Cruz

Calle de Alcalá

Calle de Serrano

Calle de Lagasca

Calle del Príncipe

Calle de

Ayala

Calle de Alcántara

Calle Conde de Peñalver

Plaza de
Manuel Becerra

Manuel Becerra

Calle de

Calle de

Hermosilla

Goya

Calle de Alcalá

GOYA

Plaza de
Colón

19

17

20

21

Serrano

Velázquez

Calle de Goya

Calle de Velázquez

16

18

Calle de Fuente del Berro

Calle del Doctor Esquerdo

24

Calle de Vilanueva

25

Príncipe de
Vergara

Calle del Duque de Sesto

Calle de O'Donnell

O'Donnell

Calle Columela

Retiro

Calle de Alcalá

Avenida de

Calle de O'Donnell

26

Plaza de la
Independencia

Plaza
Maestro
Villa

Calle de
Montalbán

Calle

Av Mejico

Estanque

Ibiza

Calle de Narváez

RETIRO

Paseo Salón del Estanque

Paseo de Venezuela

MEDIODÍA

Calle de Alfonso XII

29

Paseo San Pablo

Paseo del Duque de Fernán Núñez

Paseo del Ecuador

40

Menéndez Pelayo

Parque
del Buen
Retiro

Real
Jardín
Botánico

Paseo del Uruguay

Paseo del Durque

42

41

Atocha

Avenida de la Ciudad de Barcelona

Paseo de la Reina Cristina

Plaza de
Mariano
de Cavia

Atocha

Atocha
Train
Station

Avenida de Menéndez Pelayo

Menéndez
Pelayo

PLACES TO STAY
3 Albergue Santa Cruz
   de Marcenado

PLACES TO EAT
8 Restaurante Sandos
9 Pizzeria Mastropiero
10 Tetería de la Abuela
15 Gran Café de Gijón
16 Café-Restaurante El
   Espejo
31 Maceira
39 Elqui

OTHER
1 Booksellers
2 TIVE
4 La Casa de Internet
5 Cervecería Santa
   Bárbara
6 Vaiven
7 Museo Municipal
11 Arena
12 Aroba52
13 The Quiet Man
14 Finnegan's
17 Monumento a Colón
18 Biblioteca Nacional
19 Centro Cultural de la Villa

20 Airport Bus Terminal
21 Monumento al
   Descubrimiento
22 TIVE
23 Plaza Monumental
   de las Ventas
24 Museo Arqueológico
25 Anglo-American
   Medical Unit
26 Puerta de Alcalá
27 Palacio de
   Comunicaciones &
   Main Post Office
28 Museo Thyssen-Bornemisza
29 Casón del Buen Retiro
30 Museo del Prado
32 El Parnaso
33 Casa Patas
34 La Soleá
35 Palacio Real
36 Iglesia de la Almudena
37 Basílica de San
   Francisco El Grande
38 Tourist Office
40 Palacio de Cristal
41 La Rosaleda (Rose Gardens)
42 El Ángel Caído
43 Centro de Arte
   Reina Sofia

SPAIN

(☎ 91 543 74 12) and in the Instituto de la Juventud at Calle de José Ortega y Gasset 71 (☎ 91 347 77 78). Both are open 9 am to 1 pm weekdays.

Bookshops La Casa del Libro, Gran Vía 29-31, has a broad selection of books in English, as does Booksellers at Calle de José Abascal 48. La Tienda Verde, Calle de Maudes 38 (metro: Cuatro Caminos), specialises in walking guides and maps for many parts of Spain.

Laundry Laundrettes include Lavandería España on Calle del Infante, Lavomatique on Calle de Cervantes, and Lavandería Alba at Calle del Barco 26.

Medical & Emergency Services If you have medical problems pop into the nearest Insalud clinic – often marked 'Centro de Salud'. A handy one is at Calle de las Navas de Tolosa 10. You can also get help at the Anglo-American Medical Unit (☎ 91 435 18 23), Calle del Conde de Aranda 1. There is a 24-hour pharmacy, Farmacia del Globo (☎ 91 369 20 00), at Plaza de Antón Martín 46.

Things to See
Puerta del Sol & Around The most fitting place to begin exploring Madrid is the Puerta del Sol, the official centre of Madrid. Walk up Calle de Preciados and take the second street on the left, which will bring you out to Plaza de las Descalzas and the **Monasterio de las Descalzas Reales**.

South down Calle de San Martín is the **Iglesia de San Ginés**, one of Madrid's oldest churches. Behind it is the wonderful **Chocolatería de San Ginés**, generally open 7 to 10 am and 1 to 7 pm.

Continue down to and cross Calle Mayor, and then into Madrid's most famous square, **Plaza Mayor**. West along Calle Mayor is the historic **Plaza de la Villa**, with Madrid's 17th-century *ayuntamiento* (**town hall**). On the same square stand the 16th-century **Casa de Cisneros** and the Gothic-Mudéjar **Torre de los Lujanes**, one of the city's oldest buildings.

Take the street down the left side of the Casa de Cisneros, cross the road at the end, then go down the stairs and follow the cobbled Calle del Cordón out onto Calle de Segovia. Almost directly in front of you is

the Mudéjar tower of the **Iglesia de San Pedro**. Farther down Costanilla de San Pedro is the **Iglesia de San Andrés**.

From here you can cross Plaza de la Puerta de Moros and head east past the market along Plaza de la Cebad to the massive Sunday morning flea market of **El Rastro**, spread along and between Calle de Ribera de Curtidores and Calle de los Embajadores (metro: Latina). It's said to be the place to go if you want to buy your car stereo back – watch your pockets and bags.

Plaza de España & Around At its northern end, Calle de Bailén runs into Plaza de España. The nearby Ermita de San Antonio de Florida, also called the **Panteón de Goya**, contains one of the artist's masterpieces. The eastern flank of Plaza de España marks the beginning of **Gran Vía**. This Haussmann-esque boulevard was slammed through the tumbledown slums north of Sol in 1911.

At the east end of Gran Vía, note the superb dome of the **Edificio Metropolis**. Continue east along Calle de Alcalá until you reach **Plaza de la Cibeles**, Madrid's favourite roundabout. Head north (left) up the tree-lined promenade of Paseo de los Recoletos. On the left you'll pass some of the city's best-known cafes, including Gran Café de Gijón, El Espejo and El Gran Pabellón del Espejo.

Museo del Prado The Prado is one of the world's great art galleries. Its main emphasis is on Spanish, Flemish and Italian art from the 15th to 19th centuries, and one of its strengths lies in the generous coverage given to certain individual geniuses, including Spain's greats – Velázquez, El Greco and Goya.

Of Velázquez's works, it's *Las Meninas* that most people come to see; it's in room 12 on the 1st floor. Virtually the whole south wing of the 1st floor is given over to Goya. Other well-represented artists include the Flemish masters Hieronymus Bosch and Pieter Paul Rubens, and the Italians Tintoretto, Titian and Raphael.

The Prado is open 9 am to 7 pm Tuesday to Saturday, and until 2 pm on Sunday and holidays. Tickets are 500 ptas (half price for students) and include the Casón del Buen Retiro, a subsidiary gallery a short walk east that contains the collection's 19th-century works. Entry is free on Sunday and Saturday afternoon (2.30 to 7 pm), as well as on selected national holidays.

Centro de Arte Reina Sofia At Calle de Santa Isabel 52, opposite Atocha station, the Reina Sofia museum houses a superb collection of predominantly Spanish modern art. The exhibition focuses on the period 1900-1940, and includes, in room 7, Picasso's famous *Guernica* – his protest at the German bombing of the Basque town of Guernica during the civil war in 1937. Room 9 is devoted to Salvador Dalí's surrealist work and room 13 contains a collection of Joan Miró's late works.

The gallery is open 10 am to 9 pm Wednesday to Monday, to 2.30 pm Sunday. Entry costs 500/250 ptas.

Museo Thyssen-Bornemisza Purchased by Spain in 1993 for something over US$300 million, this extraordinary collection of 800 paintings was formerly the private collection of a German-Hungarian family, the Thyssen-Bornemiszas. Starting with medieval religious art, it moves on through Titian, El Greco and Rubens to Cézanne, Monet and Van Gogh, then from Miró, Picasso and Gris to Pollock, Dalí and Lichtenstein. The museum is at Paseo del Prado 8, almost opposite the Prado, and opens 10 am to 7 pm Tuesday to Sunday. Entry is 700/400 ptas.

Palacio Real This over-the-top 18th-century palace hasn't been used as a royal residence for some time and today is only used for official receptions and, of course, tourism. Tours cover some elaborately decorated rooms, a good selection of Goyas, 215 absurdly ornate clocks and five Stradivarius violins still used for concerts and balls. All palace chandeliers are original and no two are the same.

The palace is open 9.30 am to 6 pm Monday to Saturday, 9 am to 2.30 pm Sunday and holidays (it closes an hour earlier from October to April). Entry is 900/400 ptas but is free on Wednesday for EU citizens (bring your passport). The nearest metro station is Opera.

Monasterio de las Descalzas Reales The Convent of the Barefoot Royals, on Plaza de las Descalzas, was founded in 1559 by Juana of Austria, daughter of the Spanish king Carlos I and became one of Spain's richest religious houses thanks to gifts from noblewomen. On the obligatory guided tour you'll be confronted by a number of tapestries based on works by Rubens, and a wonderful painting entitled *The Voyage of the 11,000 Virgins*.

The convent is open 10.30 am to 12.45 pm and from 4 to 5.30 pm Tuesday to Saturday (but closed Friday afternoon); and 11 am to 1.45 pm Sunday and holidays. Entry is 700/400 ptas; free on Wednesday for EU citizens.

Panteón de Goya The Ermita de San Antonio de la Florida contains not only Goya's tomb, directly in front of the altar, but also one of his greatest works – the entire ceiling and dome, beautifully painted with religious scenes.

The panteón is the first of two small churches 700m north-west along Paseo de la Florida from Príncipe Pío metro station. The chapel is open 10 am to 2 pm and 4 to 8 pm Tuesday to Friday (mornings only in July and August), and 10 am to 2 pm weekends. Entry is 300 ptas (free on Wednesday and Sunday).

Museo Arqueológico This museum on Calle de Serrano traces the history of the peninsula from the earliest prehistoric cave paintings to the Iberian, Roman, Carthaginian, Greek, Visigothic, Moorish and Christian eras. It's open 9.30 am to 8.30 pm Tuesday to Saturday and to 2 pm Sunday. Entry is 500/250 ptas (free Sunday and from 2.30 pm on Saturday).

Real Jardín Botánico This beautiful botanic garden next to the Prado is the perfect answer to an overdose of art and history. It's open 10 am to dark daily (250 ptas).

Parque del Buen Retiro This is another great place to escape hustle and bustle. On a warm spring day walk between the flowerbeds and hedges or just sprawl out on one of the lawns. Stroll along **Paseo de las Estatuas**, a path lined with statues originally from the Palacio Real. Perhaps the most important, and certainly the most controversial, of the park's other monuments is the 19th-century **El Ángel Caído** (The Fallen

SPAIN

CENTRAL MADRID

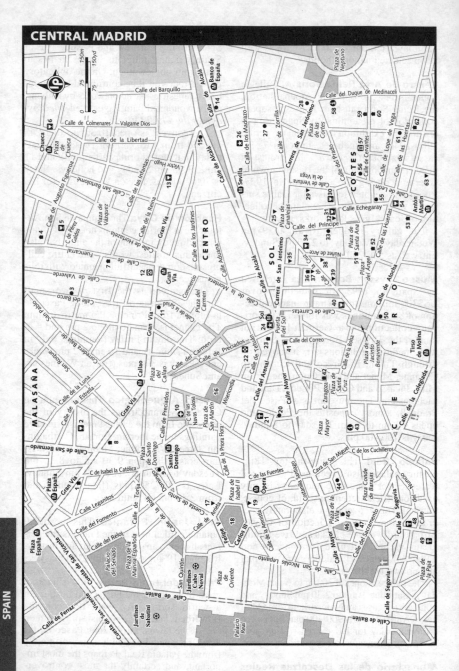

CENTRAL MADRID

	PLACES TO STAY				
1	Hostal Alcázar Regis	38	La Trucha	26	Police Station
4	Hostal Medieval	39	Las Bravas	27	Teatro de la Zarzuela
7	Hostal Ginebra	63	Restaurante La Sanabresa	28	American Express
8	Hostal Lamalonga			30	Carbones Bar
23	Hostal Cosmopolitan		**OTHER**	31	Viva Madrid
36	Hostal Tineo	2	Morocco Disco	33	Teatro de la Comedia
41	Hostal Riesco	3	Lavandería Alba (Laundrette)	34	Suristán
42	Hostal Santa Cruz	5	Cruising Bar	40	Torero Disco
51	Hostal Delvi	6	Rimmel Bar	43	Tourist Office
52	Hostal Vetusta	9	Viajes Zeppelin	44	Mercado de San Miguel
53	Hostal Matute	10	Centro de Salud	45	Torre de los Lujanes
59	Hostal Dulcinea	11	La Casa del Libro	46	Ayuntamiento (Town Hall)
60	Hostal Gonzalo	12	Telefónica Phone Centre	47	Casa de Cisneros
62	Hostal López	13	Cock Bar	48	Iglesia de San Pedro
		14	Renfe Train Booking Office	49	Iglesia de San Andrés
	PLACES TO EAT	15	Edificio Metropolis	50	Teatro Calderón
17	Restaurante La Paella Real	16	Monasterio de las Descalzas	54	Café Populart
19	Café del Real		Reales	55	Lavandería España
25	La Finca de Susana	18	Teatro Real		(Laundrette)
29	Restaurante Integral Artemisa	20	Chocolatería de San Ginés	56	Lavomatique (Laundrette)
32	La Trucha	21	Iglesia de San Ginés	57	Casa de Lope de Vega
35	Museo del Jamón	22	El Corte Inglés Department	58	Main Tourist Office
37	La Casa del Abuelo		Store	61	Convento de
		24	Police Station		las Trinitarias

Angel), said to be the first statue in the world dedicated to the devil.

Places to Stay

Finding a cheap place to stay is never a real problem in Madrid. In summer the city is drained of people, thanks to the horrific heat, so if you are mad enough to be here then, you may be able to bargain with hotel and pension owners.

Camping *Camping Osuna* (☎ 91 741 05 10), on Avenida de Logroño near the airport, charges 660 ptas per person and per tent. Take metro No 5 to Canillejas (the end of the line), from where it's about 500m.

Hostels There are two HI hostels in Madrid. *Albergue Richard Schirrman* (☎ 91 463 56 99) is in the Casa de Campo park (metro: El Lago; bus No 33 from Plaza Ópera). It's 1200 ptas for a bed and breakfast (1700 ptas for travellers over age 26).
Albergue Santa Cruz de Marcenado (☎ 91 547 45 32, Calle de Santa Cruz de Marcenado 28) has the same rates (metro: Argüelles; bus Nos 1, 61 and Circular).

Hostales & Pensiones Hostales and pensiones can be found in the following three main areas.

Plaza de Santa Ana Santa Ana is one of Madrid's 'in' districts. It's close to Sol, it's within walking distance of the Prado and Atocha train station, and it has countless bars, cafes and restaurants.

On the square itself at No 15, *Hostal Delvi* (☎ 91 522 59 98, 3rd floor) is friendly enough with OK rooms, including tiny singles. You will pay from 2000/2500 ptas for singles/doubles without bath or 4000 ptas for en-suite doubles. *Hostal Gonzalo* (☎ 91 429 27 14, Calle de Cervantes 34) is in sparkling nick. Singles/doubles with private shower and TV are 5000/6200 ptas. The staff will take a few hundred pesetas off the bill if you stay at least three days. Across the road at No 19, *Hostal Dulcinea* (☎ 91 429 93 09) has well-maintained if simply furnished rooms and is often full. Rooms cost 5500/6000 ptas.

The excellent *Hostal Matute* (☎ 91 429 55 85, Plaza de Matute 1) has spacious, somewhat musty singles/doubles for 3500/5000 ptas without own bath and 4500/6000 ptas with. *Hostal Vetusta* (☎ 91 429 64 04, Calle de las Huertas 3) has admittedly small, but cute, rooms with shower starting at 4000/4500 ptas; try for one looking onto the street.

Roughly halfway between Atocha train station and Santa Ana, *Hostal López*

SPAIN

(☎ 91 429 43 49, Calle de las Huertas 54) is a good choice. Singles/doubles start at 3600/4500 ptas; 4200/5200 ptas with bath.

Puerta del Sol You can't get more central than Plaza de la Puerta del Sol. Generally you'll pay for this privilege, but there are still some good deals in the surrounding streets. The pick of the bunch is *Hostal Riesco* *(☎ 91 522 26 92, Calle de Correo 2, 3rd floor)*. Singles/doubles with full bath cost 4000/5800 ptas. *Hostal Tineo (☎ 91 521 49 43, Calle de la Victoria 6)* charges a standard 3500/5500 ptas for singles/doubles with washbasin only. They range up to 5000/6500 ptas for rooms with private bathroom.

Hostal Santa Cruz (☎ 91 522 24 41, Plaza de Santa Cruz 6) is in a prime location. Rooms here start from about 3600/5200 ptas. If you don't mind the traffic, *Hostal Cosmopolitan (☎ 91 522 66 51, Puerta del Sol 9, 3rd floor)* has basic singles/doubles with washbasin for just 1800/3300 ptas.

Gran Vía Gran Vía itself is laden with accommodation. *Hostal Lamalonga (☎ 91 547 26 31, Gran Vía 56)* is reliable. Rooms with private bath start at 4500/6500 ptas. *Hostal Alcázar Regis (☎ 91 547 93 17, fax 91 559 07 85)*, No 61, is not a bad choice either, with singles/doubles costing 4000/6000 ptas.

Calle de Fuencarral is similarly choked with hostales and pensiones, especially at the Gran Vía end. *Hostal Ginebra (☎ 91 532 10 35, Calle de Fuencarral 17)* is decent. Singles with washbasin only start at 3200 ptas, while singles/doubles with full bathroom cost 4200/5000 ptas. All rooms have TV and phone. *Hostal Medieval (☎ 91 522 25 49, Calle de Fuencarral 46)* has spacious and bright singles/doubles with shower for 3000/4500 ptas. Doubles with full private bathroom cost 5500 ptas.

Places to Eat

Around Santa Ana There are tons of Gallego seafood restaurants in this area, but the best is the newly opened *Maceira*, away from the main tourist hubbub, at Calle de Jesús 7. At *La Casa del Abuelo (Calle de la Victoria 14)*, on a backstreet south-east of Puerta del Sol, you can sip a *chato* (small glass) of the heavy El Abuelo red wine while munching on heavenly king prawns, grilled or with garlic. Next, duck around the corner to *Las Bravas*, on Callejón de Álvarez Gato, for a caña and the best patatas bravas in town.

La Trucha (Calle de Núñez de Arce 6) is one of Madrid's great bars for tapas. It's just off Plaza de Santa Ana, and there's another branch nearby at Calle de Manuel Fernández y González 3.

Something of an institution is the *Museo del Jamón* – visit one of these places and you'll understand the name. There's one at Carrera de San Jerónimo 6.

If it's just plain cheap you want, *Restaurante La Sanabresa (Calle del Amor de Dios 12)* has very good *menú del día* for just 900 ptas.

La Finca de Susana (Calle de Arlabán 4) is a great new spot, with vegetarian and meat dishes in a soothing atmosphere. Vegetarians could also try *Elqui (Calle de Buenavista 18)*, a self-service, buffet-style place open daily except Monday for lunch (until 4 pm), and Friday and Saturday evening for dinner (à la carte). *Restaurante Integral Artemisa (Calle de Ventura de la Vega 4)* is excellent; a full meal will set you back 2000 ptas.

Around Plaza Mayor It's very touristy, but when the sun is shining (or rising) there's not a finer place to be than at one of the plaza's outdoor cafes. Calle de la Cava San Miguel and Calle de Cuchilleros are packed with mesones that aren't bad for a little tapas bar hopping.

Other Areas At *Casa Mingo (Paseo de la Florida 34)*, near the Panteón de Goya, a full roast bird, salad and large bottle of cider comes to less than 2000 ptas.

If you're after paella at all costs, head for *Restaurante La Paella Real (Calle de Arrieta 2)* near Plaza de Oriente, which does a whole range of rice-based dishes from 1800 ptas.

In the Malasaña area around Plaza del Dos de Mayo, *Restaurante Sandos (Plaza del Dos de Mayo 8)* can do you a cheap, outdoor pizza and beer, or a set menu from 850 ptas. Better still is the crowded *Pizzeria Mastropiero (Calle de San Vicente Ferrer 34)*, on the corner of Calle del Dos de Mayo, a popular Argentine-run joint where you can get pizza by the slice.

SPAIN

In the Plaza de España area the long-established *Restaurante Veracruz (Calle de San Leonardo de Dios 5)* has a set *menú* (including a bottle of wine) for 950 ptas. It's closed Sunday.

Cafes Madrid has hundreds of fine places for a coffee and light meal. Our favourites include the historic and elegant *Café-Restaurante El Espejo (Paseo de Recoletos 31)*; the equally graceful *Gran Café de Gijón* just down the road; and *Café del Real (Plaza de Isabel II)*, an atmospheric place with a touch of faded elegance. A teahouse with a hint of the 1960s is the *Tetería de la Abuela (Calle del Espíritu Santo 19)*. Along with the great range of teas you can indulge in scrummy crepes.

Entertainment

The weekly *Guía del Ocio* (125 ptas), available at newsstands, gives a good rundown of what's on in Madrid. It's handy even if you can't read Spanish.

Bars The epicentres of Madrid's nightlife are the Santa Ana-Calle de las Huertas area, and the Malasaña-Chueca zone north of Gran Vía. The latter has a decidedly lowlife element.

Any of the bars on Plaza de Santa Ana makes for a pleasant stop. Though it gets crowded at weekends, look into *Viva Madrid (Calle de Manuel Fernández y González 7)*. On the same street, *Carbones* is a busy place open till about 4 am with good mainstream music on the jukebox. *La Venencia (Calle de Echegaray 7)* is an ill-lit, woody place that serves six varieties of sherry. *Café Popullart (Calle de las Huertas 22)* often has music, generally jazz or Celtic. Just beyond the hubbub of Calle de las Huertas is *El Parnaso (Calle de Moratín 25)*, a quirky but engaging bar.

In Malasaña, *Cervecería Santa Bárbara (Plaza de Santa Bárbara 8)* is a classic Madrid drinking house.

Irish pubs are popular in Madrid: two good ones are *The Quiet Man (Calle de Valverde 44)* and *Finnegan's (Plaza de las Salesas 9)*.

Calle de Pelayo Campoamor is lined with an assortment of bars, graduating from noisy rock bars at the north end to gay bars at the south end – in the Chueca area, the heart of Madrid's gay nightlife. *Rimmel (Calle de Luis de Góngora 4)* and *Cruising (Calle de Pérez Galdós 5)* are among the more popular gay haunts.

The quaintly named *Cock Bar (Calle de la Reina 16)* once served as a discreet salon for high-class prostitution. These days it's merely a good bar with plenty of atmosphere.

Live Music & Discos A good place for Latin rhythms is *Vaiven (Travesía de San Mateo 1)* in Malasaña. Entry is free and a beer is about 600 ptas. *Morocco (Calle del Marqués de Leganés 7)*, also in Malasaña, is popular on the Madrid disco circuit. It gets going about 1 am.

Near Plaza de Santa Ana, Calle de la Cruz has a couple of good dance spaces. *Torero*, No 26, has Spanish music upstairs and international fare downstairs. *Suristán*, No 7, pulls in a wide variety of bands, from Cuban to African. Things usually start at 11.30 pm, sometimes with a cover charge of up to 1000 ptas. Near Plaza de España, *Arena (Calle de la Princesa 1)* offers music for all tastes – funky, house, techno and acid jazz – until 6.30 am from Wednesday to Sunday.

La Soleá (Calle de la Cava Baja 27) is regarded by some as the last real flamenco bar in Madrid. *Casa Patas (Calle de Cañizares 10)* hosts recognised masters of flamenco song, guitar and dance.

Opera & Classical Music The city's grandest stage, the recently reopened *Teatro Real*, is the scene for opera. The *Teatro Calderón (Calle de Atocha 18)* plays second fiddle. The *Centro Cultural de la Villa*, under the waterfall at Plaza de Colón, stages everything from classical concerts to opera to flamenco. Also important for classical music is the *Auditorio Nacional de Música (Avenida del Príncipe de Vergara 146, metro: Cruz del Rayo)*.

Spectator Sports

Tickets for football (soccer) games can be bought on the day of the match, starting from around 2500 ptas. Real Madrid's home is the huge Estadio Santiago Bernabéu (metro: Santiago Bernabéu). Atlético Madrid play at Estadio Vicente Calderón (metro: Pirámides).

Bullfights take place most Sundays between March and October. Madrid has

Spain's largest bullring, the Plaza Monumental de las Ventas (metro: Ventas), and a second bullring by metro Vista Alegre. Tickets (2000 ptas or less) are best bought in advance either from agencies or at the rings.

Getting There & Away

Air Scheduled and charter flights from all over the world arrive at Madrid's Barajas airport, 13km north-east of the city. The main Iberia office (☎ 91 587 75 36; reservations ☎ 902 40 05 00) is at Calle de Velázquez 130.

Bus There are eight bus stations dotted around Madrid. Most buses to the south (and some international services) use the Estación Sur de Autobuses (Calle de Méndez Álvaro; metro: Méndez Álvaro). Tourist offices can tell you which station you need for your destination.

Train Atocha station, south of the city centre, is used by most trains to/from southern Spain (some use Chamartín) and many destinations around Madrid. Trains from the north terminate at Chamartín (metro: Chamartín), although some pass through and terminate at Atocha instead.

The main RENFE booking office (☎ 91 328 90 20), at Calle del Alcalá 44, is open 9.30 am to 8 pm weekdays.

Getting Around

To/From the Airport The metro runs right into town from the airport, at the upper level of the T2 terminal. Alternatively, an airport bus service runs to/from an underground terminal in Plaza de Colón every 12 to 15 minutes. The trip takes 30 minutes in average traffic and costs 385 ptas. A taxi between the airport and city centre should cost around 2000 ptas.

Bus Generally, the underground (metro) is faster and easier than buses for getting around the city. Bus route maps are available from tourist offices. A single ride is 135 ptas. A 10-ride *Metrobus* ticket (705 ptas) can be used on buses and metro. Some 20 night-owl buses run from Puerta del Sol and Plaza de la Cibeles between midnight and 6 am.

Metro Madrid has a very efficient, safe and simple underground system. Trains run

from 6.30 am to 1.30 am daily. Fares are the same as on buses.

Taxi Madrid's taxis are inexpensive by European standards. Flag fall is 190 ptas, after which it's 90 ptas per km (120 ptas between 10 pm and 6 am).

AROUND MADRID
El Escorial

The extraordinary, 16th-century, monastery-palace complex of San Lorenzo de El Escorial lies one hour north-west of Madrid, just outside the town of the same name.

El Escorial was built by Felipe II, king of Spain, Naples, Sicily, Milan, the Netherlands and large parts of the Americas, to commemorate his victory over the French in the battle of St Quentin (1557) and as a mausoleum for his father Carlos I, the first of Spain's Habsburg monarchs. El Escorial's austere style, loved by some and hated by others, is a quintessential monument of Spain's golden age. It's open 10 am to 6 pm Tuesday to Sunday (to 5 pm October to March). Entry is 900/400 ptas, including a guided tour.

Getting There & Away Almost all visitors to El Escorial visit on a day trip from Madrid. The Herranz bus company runs up to 30 services a day from the Intercambiador de Autobuses at Madrid's Moncloa metro station to San Lorenzo de El Escorial (405 ptas). Only about 10 run on Sunday and holidays.

Castilla y León

SEGOVIA

Segovia is justly famous for its magnificent Roman aqueduct, but it also has a splendid, ridge-top, old city worthy of more than a fleeting visit. Originally a Celtic settlement, Segovia was conquered by the Romans around 80 BC. The Visigoths and Moors also left their mark before the city ended up in Castilian hands in the 11th century.

The main tourist office (☎ 921 46 03 34) is on Plaza Mayor, with another branch (☎ 921 46 29 06) beside the aqueduct.

Things to See

You can't help but see the 1st century AD **aqueduct**, stretching away from the east end of the old city. It's over 800m long, up to 29m high, has 163 arches – and not a drop of mortar was used in its construction.

At the heart of the old city is the 16th-century, Gothic **catedral** on the pretty Plaza Mayor. The austere interior is anchored by an imposing choir and enlivened by 20-odd chapels.

Perched on a cliff top at the west end of the old city, Segovia's **alcázar**, with its turrets, towers and spires, is a 15th-century fairy-tale castle. It was virtually destroyed by fire in 1862, but has been completely rebuilt and converted into a museum (400 ptas).

Places to Stay
About 2km along the road to La Granja is **Camping Acueducto** (☎ *921 42 50 00*), open April to September.

Fonda Aragón (☎ *921 46 09 14*) and **Fonda Cubo** (☎ *921 46 09 17*), both at Plaza Mayor 4, are shabby but the cheapest places in town. Both have singles only, costing 1600 ptas at the Aragón and 1300 ptas at the Cubo.

More pleasant is **Hostal Plaza** (☎ *921 46 03 03, Calle del Cronista Lecea 11*), where singles/doubles start at 3100/4500 ptas.

Also central and good is **Hostal Juan Bravo** (☎ *921 46 34 13, Calle de Juan Bravo 12*), which charges 3800 ptas for rooms without bath, or 4800 ptas for those with.

Places to Eat
The simple **Bar Ratos** (*Calle de los Escuderos*) makes generously stuffed sandwiches from 350 ptas. Atmospheric **Cueva de San Esteban** (*Calle de Valdeláguila 15*) has delicious set lunches for 1000 ptas. Segovia's speciality is *cochinillo asado* (roast suckling pig); a good place to sample this is at **Mesón José María** (*Calle del Cronista Lecea 11*), a favourite among Segovians.

Getting There & Away
Up to 30 daily buses run to Madrid (825 ptas, 1½ hours), and others serve Ávila and Salamanca. The bus station is 500m south of the aqueduct, just off Paseo Ezequiel González. Trains to Madrid leave every two hours (790 ptas, 1¾ hours).

ÁVILA
Ávila's 11th- and 12th-century *muralla* (city wall), with its eight monumental gates

and 88 towers, is one of the best preserved medieval defensive perimeters in the world.

Ávila is also distinguished by being the highest city in Spain (1130m) and – less proudly – the place where Tomás de Torquemada orchestrated the most brutal phase of the Spanish Inquisition, sending off 2000 people to be burnt at the stake in the late 15th century. St Teresa of Ávila, the 16th-century mystic and reformer of the Carmelite order, was born in what is now the **Convento de Santa Teresa**.

Ávila's tourist office (☎ 920 21 13 87) is at Plaza de la Catedral 4.

Places to Stay & Eat
Hostal Jardín (☎ *920 21 10 74, Calle de San Segundo 38*) has scruffy but adequate singles/doubles from 3000/4000 ptas. Better is **Hostal El Rastro** (☎ *920 21 12 18, Plaza del Rastro 1*), which is full of character and also has a good *restaurant*. Rooms start at 3880/5560 ptas.

Restaurante Los Leales (*Plaza de Italia 4*) has a solid *menú* for 1000 ptas.

Getting There & Away
There are up to 30 trains a day to Madrid (865 ptas, 1½ hours); trains to Salamanca cost the same. Buses are slower and pricier.

The bus and train stations are, respectively, 700m and 1.5km east of the old town. The old town is linked with the train station by bus No 1.

SALAMANCA
If any major Castilian city can be said to jump with action, it's Salamanca. Year round, its countless bars, cafes and restaurants are jam-packed with students and young visitors from around the world. This is one of Spain's most inspiring cities, both in terms of the beauty of its architecture and its modern, laid-back lifestyle.

Information
The Oficina Municipal de Turismo (municipal tourist office; ☎ 923 21 83 42), on Plaza Mayor, open daily, concentrates on city information. A second branch (☎ 923 26 85 71), in the Casa de las Conchas, focuses on the wider region (closed Saturday afternoon and Sunday).

The post office is at Gran Vía 25. For Internet access try Campus Cibermático at

SPAIN

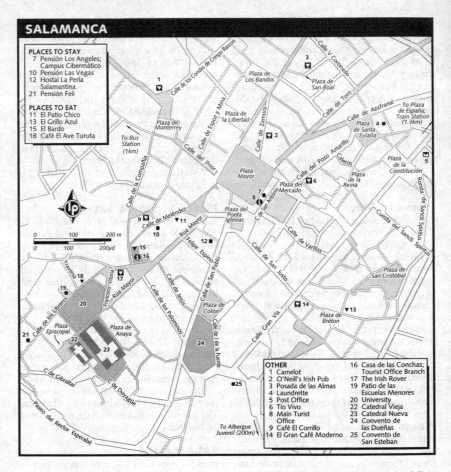

SALAMANCA

PLACES TO STAY
7 Pensión Los Angeles;
   Campus Cibermático
10 Pensión Las Vegas
12 Hostal La Perla
   Salamantina
21 Pensión Feli

PLACES TO EAT
11 El Patio Chico
13 El Grillo Azul
15 El Bardo
18 Café El Ave Turuta

OTHER
1 Camelot
2 O'Neill's Irish Pub
3 Posada de las Almas
4 Laundrette
5 Post Office
6 Tío Vivo
7 Main Turist
   Office
9 Café El Corrillo
14 El Gran Café Moderno
16 Casa de las Conchas;
   Tourist Office Branch
17 The Irish Rover
19 Patio de las
   Escuelas Menores
20 University
22 Catedral Vieja
23 Catedral Nueva
24 Convento de
   las Dueñas
25 Convento de
   San Esteban

Plaza Mayor 10 (below the Pensión Los Angeles). There's a coin-operated laundrette at Pasaje Azafranal 18.

Things to See

Salamanca's harmonious **Plaza Mayor** (1755), designed by José Churriguera, is ringed by medallions of sundry famous figures; until the 19th century, bullfights took place here.

The most stunning features of the late-Gothic **Catedral Nueva** (New Cathedral; 1733) are its doorways which are decorated with dizzying detail. From inside, you can enter the adjacent **Catedral Vieja** (Old Cathedral) for 300 ptas. Begun as early as 1120, this church is a bit of a hybrid, incorporating some Gothic and Byzantine elements into the original Romanesque structure.

Salamanca's **University** was founded in 1218. Its main facade, on Calle de los Libreros, is a tapestry in sandstone, bursting with images of mythical and historical figures ... and the famously elusive frog. Join the throngs trying to find the little creature.

Other major sights include the **Convento de San Esteban** and the **Convento de las Dueñas**. The 15th-century **Casa de las Conchas**, named for the scallop shells clinging to its facade, is a symbol of Salamanca.

Places to Stay

Salamanca is always in season, so book ahead when possible. The central HI *Albergue Juvenil* (☎ *923 26 91 41*, 🖂 *esterra@*

mmteam.disbumad.es, Calle Escoto 13-15) charges 1750 ptas per bunk, including bed linen and breakfast. Bus No 16 connects the hostel with the centre.

Pensión Los Angeles (☎ 923 21 81 66, Plaza Mayor 10) has low-frills singles/doubles with washbasin for 1900/2900 ptas. A favourite of young travellers is the tiny *Pensión Las Vegas (☎ 923 21 87 49, Calle de Meléndez 13)*, where clean rooms cost 2000/3500 ptas. *Hostal La Perla Salamantina (☎/fax 923 21 76 56, Calle de Sánchez Barbero 7)* has bright rooms with washbasin for 2100/3500 ptas. Cheerful rooms at *Pensión Feli (☎ 923 21 60 10, Calle de los Libreros 58)*, near the university, go for 2400/3400 ptas.

Places to Eat

El Patio Chico (Calle de Meléndez 13) is a lively place for beers and filling tapas (400 ptas each), plus a set menu for 1500 ptas. At *Café El Ave Turuta (Calle de los Libreros 24)* full meals can be had from 700 ptas. For more atmosphere, go to bustling *El Bardo (Calle de la Compañia 8)* nearby, which does decent paella for 1100 ptas. *El Grillo Azul (☎ 923 21 92 33, Calle Grillo 1)* has budget-priced vegetarian fare.

Entertainment

Salamanca, with its myriad bars, is the perfect, after-dark playground. A drink at *Tío Vivo (Calle de Clavel 3)* is a must, if only to experience the whimsical decor. *El Gran Café Moderno (Gran Vía 75)*, a Salamanca classic, is made to look like an early 20th-century Parisian street. *Café El Corrillo (Calle de Meléndez 8)* is great for a beer and live jazz. *O'Neill's (Calle de Zamora 14)* and *The Irish Rover*, by the Casa de las Conchas, are Salamanca's popular Irish pubs.

Great discos include *Camelot*, inside an actual convent on Calle de la Compañía, and *Posada de las Almas*, on Plaza de San Boal, a fantasy world inhabited by life-sized, papier-mache figures and doll houses.

Getting There & Away

Salamanca's bus station is about 1km northwest of Plaza Mayor. AutoRes has a frequent express service to Madrid (2250 ptas, 2½ hours), as well as a few nonexpress buses (1750 ptas, 3¾ hours). Other destinations served regularly include Santiago de Compostela, Cáceres, Ávila, Segovia, León and Valladolid.

Four trains leave daily for Madrid (2130 ptas, 2½ hours) via Ávila (865 ptas, 1¾ hours). A train for Lisbon leaves at 4.41 am.

Getting Around

Bus No 4 runs past the bus station and round the old town perimeter to Gran Vía. From the train station, bus No 1 is the best bet, heading down Calle de Azafranal. Going the other way, it can be picked up along Gran Vía.

LEÓN

León is far too often left off travellers' itineraries. For those who get here, a fresh and pleasant city awaits, with long boulevards, open squares, excellent nightlife and one of Spain's greatest cathedrals.

The tourist office (☎ 987 23 70 82) is opposite the cathedral main entrance. For Internet access go to Calle de la Rúa 8.

Things to See

León's breathtaking 13th-century **catedral** is a wonder of Gothic architecture. Its most outstanding feature is its stained-glass windows: 128 of them, with a surface of 1800 sq metres in all.

About 500m north-west of here is a great monument from the earlier Romanesque period: the **Real Basílica de San Isidoro**. It contains the **Panteón Real** where Leonese royalty lie buried beneath a canopy of some of the finest frescoes in all of Spain. It can only be seen on a guided tour (400 ptas).

The last in León's trio of major sights is the *Hostal de San Marcos*, at the end of the Gran Vía de San Marcos. This former pilgrim's hospital, with its golden-hued, 100m-long facade (1513), now houses a luxury hotel and the Museo de León.

Places to Stay

Pensión Berta (☎ 987 25 70 39, Plaza Mayor 8) has rickety but clean doubles for 3000 ptas. The decidedly no-frills *Fonda Roma (☎ 987 22 46 63, Avenida de Roma 4)* is in an attractive old building and has rooms for 900/1500 ptas. *Hospedaje Suárez (☎ 987 25 42 88, Calle de Ancha 7)* offers the same standard and prices. For more comfort, try the friendly *Hostal Londres (☎ 987 22 22 74, Avenida de Roma 1)*

SPAIN

where charming doubles with bath start at 4500 ptas.

Places to Eat

Restaurante Honoré (Calle de los Serradores 4) has a good *menú* for 950 ptas. *Casa Palomo*, on tiny Calle de la Escalerilla, is a quality establishment with a lunch *menú* for 1300 ptas. Next door is the popular *Restaurante & Sidrería Vivaldi*, where you can wash down your meal with a cider from Asturias. A bustling hang-out is *Pizzeria La Competencia*, wedged into tight Calle Mulhacín, where the cheap and delicious pizza perfectly complements the house wine (400 ptas/bottle).

Alimerika is a well-stocked supermarket at Avenida Roma 2.

Entertainment

León's nocturnal activity flows thickest in the aptly named *Barrio Húmedo* (Wet Quarter), the crowded tangle of lanes leading south off Calle de Ancha. Its epicentre is Plaza de San Martín, a particularly pleasant and car-free square. Outside of the Barrio, *El Gran Café*, on Calle de Cervantes, is a classy and popular spot, but there are plenty of other possibilities along this street as well as on Calle de Fernando Regueral and Calle del Sacramento.

Getting There & Away

Alsa has up to 12 buses daily to Madrid (2665 ptas, 3½ hours). Other destinations include Bilbao and San Sebástian.

Up to 10 trains a day leave for Madrid (3600 ptas, 4¼ hours) and three go to Barcelona (5700 ptas, 11 hours).

Castilla-La Mancha

Best known as the home of Don Quixote, Castilla-La Mancha conjures up images of endless empty plains and lonely windmills. This Spanish heartland is home to two fascinating cities, Toledo and Cuenca.

TOLEDO

The narrow, winding streets of Toledo, perched on a small hill above the Río Tajo, are crammed with museums, churches and other monumental reminders of a splendid and turbulent past.

Toledo is quite expensive and packed with tourists and souvenir shops. Try to stay at least one night – the street and cafe life is far more enjoyable once the tour buses head back to Madrid in the evening.

As the main city of Muslim central Spain, Toledo was the peninsula's leading centre of learning and the arts in the 11th century. Its unique architectural combinations, with Arabic influences everywhere, are a strong reminder of Spain's mixed heritage. Until Muslim Spain was conquered in 1492, Christians, Jews and Muslims co-existed peaceably here, for which Toledo still bears the label 'Ciudad de las Tres Culturas' (City of the Three Cultures).

Information

The tourist office (☎ 925 22 08 43) is just outside Toledo's main gate, the Puerta Nueva de Bisagra, at the northern end of town. A smaller, more helpful office is in the *ayuntamiento* (town hall) across from the cathedral. Discad Multimedia provides Internet access at Miguel de Cervantes 17, east of Plaza de Zocodover towards the river.

Things to See

Most of Toledo's attractions open from about 10 am to 1.30 pm and 3.30 pm to 6 pm (7 pm in summer). Many – including the alcázar, Sinagoga del Tránsito and Casa y Museo de El Greco (but not the cathedral) – are closed Sunday afternoon and/or all day Monday.

The **catedral**, in the heart of the old city, is stunning. You could easily spend an afternoon admiring the glorious stone architecture, stained-glass windows, tombs of kings in the Capilla Mayor, and art by the likes of El Greco, Velázquez and Goya. Entry to the cathedral is free, but you have to buy a ticket (700 ptas) to enter four areas – the Coro, Sacristía, Capilla de la Torre and the Sala Capitular, which contain some of the finest art and artisanry.

The **alcázar**, Toledo's main landmark, was fought over repeatedly from the Middle Ages to the civil war, when it was besieged by Republican troops. Today it's a fascinating museum with displays relating to the 1936 siege. Entry is 200 ptas.

Museo de Santa Cruz, on Calle de Cervantes, displays furniture, fading tapestries

SPAIN

TOLEDO

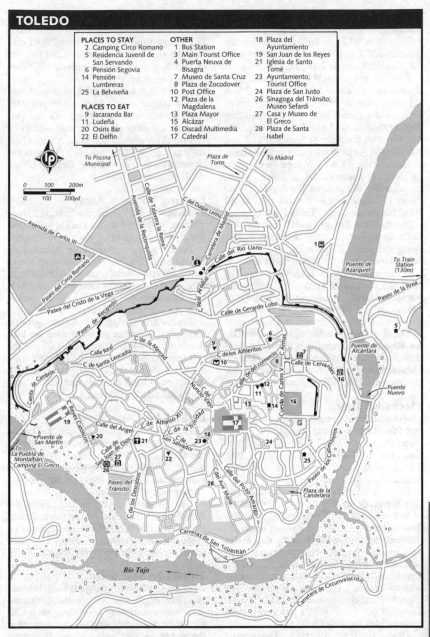

PLACES TO STAY
2 Camping Circo Romano
5 Residencia Juvenil de San Servando
6 Pensión Segovia
14 Pensión Lumbreras
25 La Belviseña

PLACES TO EAT
9 Jacaranda Bar
11 Ludeña
20 Osiris Bar
22 El Delfín

OTHER
1 Bus Station
3 Main Tourist Office
4 Puerta Neuva de Bisagra
7 Museo de Santa Cruz
8 Plaza de Zocodover
10 Post Office
12 Plaza de la Magdalena
13 Plaza Mayor
15 Alcázar
16 Discad Multimedia
17 Catedral
18 Plaza del Ayuntamiento
19 San Juan de los Reyes
21 Iglesia de Santo Tomé
23 Ayuntamiento; Tourist Office
24 Plaza de San Justo
26 Sinagoga del Tránsito; Museo Sefardi
27 Casa y Museo de El Greco
28 Plaza de Santa Isabel

and paintings. Upstairs is an impressive collection of works by El Greco (who lived in Toledo from 1577 to 1614), including the masterpiece *La Asunción* (Assumption of the Virgin). Entry is 200 ptas.

The queues outside an unremarkable church, the **Iglesia de Santo Tomé**, on Plaza del Conde, are for El Greco's masterpiece *El Entierro del Conde de Orgaz*. The painting depicts the burial of the Count of Orgaz in 1322 by San Esteban (St Stephen) and San Agustín (St Augustine). Entry is 200 ptas.

The so-called **Casa y Museo de El Greco** on Calle de Samuel Leví, in Toledo's former Jewish quarter, contains the artist's famous *Vista y Plano de Toledo*, plus about 20 of his minor works. Entry is 200 ptas.

Nearby, the **Sinagoga del Tránsito**, on Calle de los Reyes Católicos, is one of two synagogues left in Toledo. Built in 1355 and handed over to the Catholic church in 1492, when most of Spain's Jews were expelled from the country, it houses the interesting **Museo Sefardí**, examining the history of Jewish culture in Spain. Entry is 400 ptas (free on Saturday afternoon and Sunday).

The city's most visible sight, **San Juan de los Reyes**, is a Franciscan monastery and church founded by Fernando and Isabel. Outside hang the chains of Christian prisoners freed after the fall of Granada in 1492.

Places to Stay

The most central camping ground is *Camping Circo Romano* (☎ 925 22 04 42) at Avenida de Carlos III 19. A better choice is *Camping El Greco* (☎ 925 22 00 90), 2.5km south-west of town and well signposted. Both are open year-round.

Toledo's HI hostel, *Residencia Juvenil de San Servando* (☎ 925 22 45 54), is well set in the Castillo de San Servando east of the Río Tajo. B&B costs 1200 ptas if you're under 26.

Cheap accommodation in the city is not easy to come by, especially from Easter to September. *La Belviseña* (☎ 925 22 00 67, Cuesta del Can 5) is basic but good value, with rooms from 1500 ptas per person. The friendly *Pensión Segovia* (☎ 925 21 11 24, Calle de los Recoletos 2) has simple singles/doubles for 2200/3000 ptas.

The excellent *Pensión Lumbreras* (☎ 925 22 15 71, Calle de Juan Labrador 9) has reasonable rooms round a pleasant courtyard for 1700/3200/4500 ptas.

Places to Eat

El Delfin, Calle del Taller del Moro, has a lunch menu for 950 ptas. For outdoor dining, the *Osiris Bar*, on the shady Plaza del Barrio Nuevo, is a decent choice, with set lunches from 1300 ptas.

If you just want to pick at a paté and cheese platter over a beer, try the chilled-out *Jacaranda Bar* (*Callejón de los Dos Codos 1*). You could eat the equivalent of a full meal for about 1200 ptas. An excellent little place for a full meal (1500-pta *menú*) or simply a beer and tapas is *Ludeña* (*Plaza de la Magdalena 13*).

Getting There & Away

To reach most major destinations from Toledo, you need to backtrack to Madrid (or at least Aranjuez).

Toledo's bus station is on Avenida de Castilla-La Mancha. There are buses every half-hour from about 6 am to 10 pm to/from Madrid's Estación Sur (585 ptas). The Asia line sends buses from Toledo to Cuenca at 5.30 pm Monday to Friday.

Trains from Madrid's Atocha station (660 ptas) are more pleasant than the bus; the first from Madrid departs at 7.05 am, the last from Toledo at 8.56 pm. Toledo's train station is 400m east of Puente de Azarquiel.

Bus No 5 links the train and bus stations with Plaza de Zocodover.

CUENCA

Cuenca's setting is hard to believe. The old town is cut off from the rest of the city by the Júcar and Huécar rivers, sitting at the top of a deep gorge. Most of its famous monuments appear to teeter on the edge – a photographer's delight.

The Infotur office (☎ 969 23 21 19), Calle de Alfonso VIII 2, just before the arches of Plaza Mayor, is very helpful. La Repro, close to the train and bus stations, doubles as an Internet cafe and photocopying shop.

Things to See & Do

Cuenca's **Casas Colgadas** (Hanging Houses), originally built in the 15th century, are precariously positioned on a cliff top, their balconies literally hanging over the gorge. A footbridge across the gorge provides some spectacular views. Inside one of the Casas Colgadas is the **Museo de Arte Abstracto Español**, containing works by Fernando Zobel, Sempere, Millares and Chillida, members of the 1950s Generación Abstracta school of art (500 ptas).

Nearby on Calle del Obispo Valero is the **Museo Diocesano** (200 ptas). Of the religious art and artefacts inside, the 14th-century, Byzantine diptych is the jewel in the crown.

South of Plaza Mayor in a former convent is the **Museo de Las Ciencias** (science museum). Displays range from a time machine to the study of the resources of Castilla-La Mancha (free).

Cuenca's strange **catedral** is on Plaza Mayor. The lines of the unfinished facade are Norman-Gothic and reminiscent of French cathedrals, but the stained-glass windows look like they'd be more at home in the abstract art museum.

Places to Stay & Eat
Up at the top of the old town is the clean and simple *Pensión La Tabanqueta (☎ 969 21 12 90, Calle de Trabuco 13)*, priced at 2000 ptas per person.

There are several places down in the new town on Calle de Ramón y Cajal, which runs from near the train station towards the old town. The friendly *Pensión Marín (☎ 969 22 19 78, Calle de Ramón y Cajal 53)* is a short walk from the train station and has rooms for 1300/2400 ptas. At the foot of the old town *Pensión Tintes (☎ 969 21 23 98, Calle de los Tintes 7)* has basic rooms for about 1500 ptas a head in summer.

Most of the restaurants and cafes around Plaza Mayor are better for drinking and people-watching than for good-value eating.

Getting There & Away
There are up to nine buses a day to/from Madrid (1325 ptas to 1650 ptas, 2½ hours), and daily buses to Barcelona, Teruel and Valencia. There are five trains a day direct to Madrid Atocha (1405 ptas, 2½ hours) and four trains a day to Valencia.

Bus No 1 or 2 from near the bus and train stations will take you up to Plaza Mayor in the old town.

Catalunya

BARCELONA
After hosting the Olympic Games in 1992, Barcelona finally took its place on the list of the world's great cities. If you only visit one city in Spain, it should probably be Barcelona.

Catalonia's modernist architecture of the late 19th and early 20th centuries – a unique melting pot of Art Nouveau, Gothic, Moorish and other styles – climaxes here in the inspiring creations of Antoni Gaudí, among them La Sagrada Família church and Parc Güell. Barcelona also has world-class museums including two devoted to Picasso and Miró, a fine old quarter (the Barri Gòtic) and unbeatable nightlife.

Orientation
Plaça de Catalunya is the main square in Barcelona. Most travellers base themselves in Barcelona's old city (Ciutat Vella), the area bordered by the Port Vell harbour (to the south), Plaça de Catalunya (north), Ronda de Sant Pau (west) and Parc de la Ciutadella (east).

La Rambla, Barcelona's best known boulevard, runs through the heart of the old city from Plaça de Catalunya down to the harbour. On the east side of La Rambla is the medieval quarter (Barri Gòtic), and on the west the seedy Barri Xinès. North of the old city is the gracious suburb l'Eixample, where you'll find the best of Barcelona's modernist architecture.

Information
Tourist Offices The helpful Centre d' Informació Turisme de Barcelona (☎ 906-30 12 82), underground at Plaça de Catalunya 17-S, is open 9 am to 9 pm daily. Other offices are at Estació Sants (the main train station) and the EU passenger arrivals hall at the airport.

Money There are dozens of banks with ATMs around the city. The American Express office, at Passeig de Gràcia 101, is open 9.30 am to 6 pm weekdays, 10 am to noon Saturday. There's another branch on La Rambla dels Capuxtins 74.

Post & Communications The main post office, on Plaça d'Antoni López, is open 8 am to 9.30 pm Monday to Saturday.

Email & Internet Access Among dozens of options, El Café de Internet (☎ 93 302 11 54), upstairs at Gran Via de les Corts

SPAIN

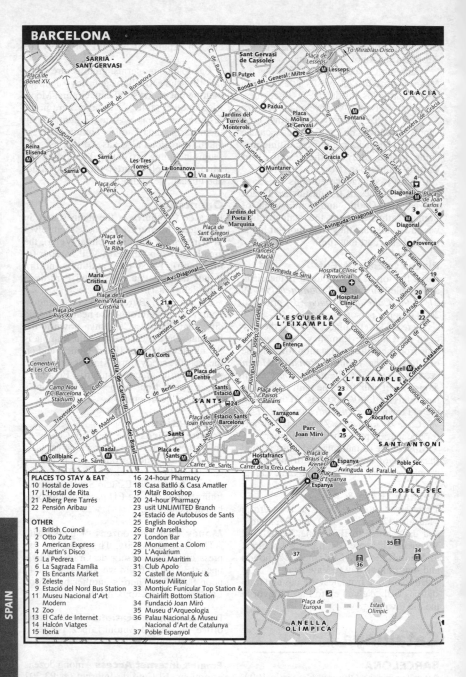

BARCELONA

PLACES TO STAY & EAT
10 Hostal de Joves
17 L'Hostal de Rita
21 Alberg Pere Tarrés
22 Pensión Aribau

OTHER
1 British Council
2 Otto Zutz
3 American Express
4 Martin's Disco
5 La Pedrera
6 La Sagrada Família
7 Els Encants Market
8 Zeleste
9 Estació del Nord Bus Station
11 Museu Nacional d'Art
  Modern
12 Zoo
13 El Café de Internet
14 Halcón Viatges
15 Iberia

16 24-hour Pharmacy
18 Casa Batlló & Casa Amatller
19 Altaïr Bookshop
20 24-hour Pharmacy
23 usit UNLIMITED Branch
24 Estació de Autobusos de Sants
25 English Bookshop
26 Bar Marsella
27 London Bar
28 Monument a Colom
29 L'Aquàrium
30 Museu Marítim
31 Club Apolo
32 Castell de Montjuïc &
  Museu Militar
33 Montjuïc Funicular Top Station &
  Chairlift Bottom Station
34 Fundació Joan Miró
35 Museu d'Arqueologia
36 Palau Nacional & Museu
  Nacional d'Art de Catalunya
37 Poble Espanyol

SPAIN

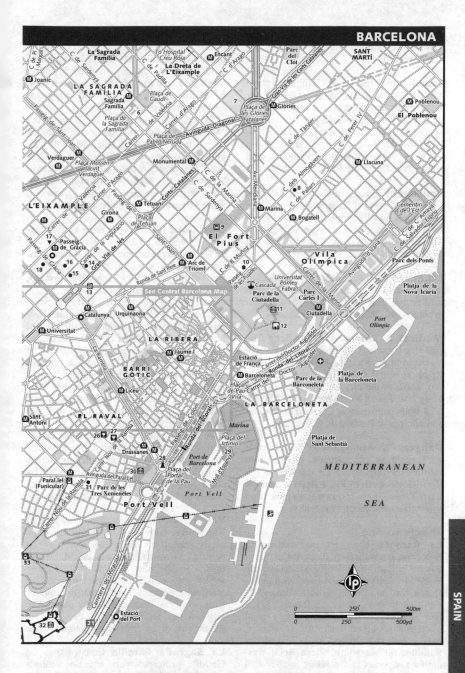

BARCELONA

La Sagrada Família

To Hospital
Creu Roja

La Dreta de
L'Eixample

Encant

Parc
del
Clot

SANT
MARTÍ

Ⓜ Joanic

C. de Sardenya

C. de Pi
i Margall

C. de Padilla

C. d'Aragó

Gran Via de les Corts Catalanes

LA SAGRADA
FAMÍLIA

Plaça de
Gaudí

Sagrada
Família

Plaça de
les Glòries
Catalanes

Glòries

Ⓜ Poblenou

El Poblenou

C. de Pere IV

6

7

Carrer de València

Carrer d'Aragó

Avinguda-Diagonal

Passeig de Sant-Joan

Plaça de
la Sagrada
Família

Plaça de
Pablo-Neruda

C. de Tànger

Verdaguer

Monumental

Ⓜ Llacuna

Plaça Mossèn
Jacint
Verdaguer

C. de la Marina

C. dels Almogàvers

Carrer d'Aragó

Passeig de

Marina

C. de Pallars

8

L'EIXAMPLE

Ⓜ Tetuan

Girona

Plaça de
Tetuan

Ⓜ Marina

Bogatell

Cementiri
de l'Est

C. de C. Arnau
Espriu

C. de Salvador Espriu

València

Carrer de

Carrer de la Diputació

Gran Via de les

El Fort
Pius

9

17
Passeig
de Gràcia

Vila
Olímpica

Parc dels Ponts

Passeig de Gràcia

16
14
15

Arc de
Triomf

C. de B. Muñoz

10

Avinguda d'Icària

18

Ronda de Sant Pere

Passeig de
les Pujades

Universitat
Pompeu
Fabra

Parc
Carles I

Platja de la
Nova Icària

13

See Central Barcelona Map

Cascada

Parc de la
Ciutadella

Catalunya

Urquinaona

11

Parc
Olímpic

Ⓜ Universitat

LA RIBERA

Ⓜ Jaume I

12

Ciutadella

Port
Olímpic

La Rambla

BARRI
GÒTIC

Estació
de França

Carrer del Doctor Aiguader

Ronda del Litoral

Ⓜ Liceu

Ⓜ Barceloneta

Doctor

Carrer del

Ronda del Litoral

Platja de
la Barceloneta

Ⓜ Sant
Antoni

EL RAVAL

Plaça de
Pau
Vila

Carrer del

Parc de la
Barceloneta

LA BARCELONETA

Marina

26
27

Plaça del
Ictinio

Platja de
Sant Sebastià

MEDITERRANEAN

Drassanes

28

Passeig de Colom

Ronda del Litoral

Port de
Barcelona

29

30

Plaça del
Portal
de la Pau

SEA

Paral·lel
(Funicular)

Avinguda del Paral·lel

31
Parc de les
Tres Xemeneies

Carrer Nou de la Rambla

Port Vell

Port Vell

Moll d'Espanya

5

5

5

Carretera de Miramar

3
3

3

UP

0   250'   500m
0   250   500yd

32

21

Estació
del Port

SPAIN

Catalanes 656, charges 600 ptas for 30 minutes of Internet access (800 ptas per hour for students).

Travel Agencies USIT Unlimited (☎ 93 412 01 04), at Ronda de l'Universitat 16, sells youth and student air, train and bus tickets. It has a branch in the Turisme Juvenil de Catalunya office at Carrer de Rocafort 116-122. Halcón Viatges (☎ 902-30 06 00) is a reliable chain of travel agents with a branch at Carrer de Pau Claris 108.

Bookshops Quera, in the Barri Gòtic at Carrer de Petritxol 2, specialises in maps and guides. In l'Eixample, Altaïr is a superb travel bookshop at Carrer de Balmes 71. The English Bookshop, Carrer d'Entença 63, has a good range of literature.

Laundry Lavomatic, at Carrer del Consolat de Mar 43-45, is a rare self-service laundromat. A 7kg load costs 575 ptas and drying costs 105 ptas for five minutes.

Medical & Emergency Services The Guàrdia Urbana (City Police; ☎ 092) have a station at La Rambla 43, opposite Plaça Reial. Hospital Creu Roja (☎ 93 300 20 20), north of the city at Carrer del Dos de Maig 301, has an emergency room. There's a 24-hour pharmacy at Carrer d'Aribau 62 and another at Passeig de Gràcia 26.

Dangers & Annoyances Watch your pockets, bags and cameras on the train to/from the airport, on La Rambla, in the Barri Gòtic south of Plaça Reial and in the Barri Xinès. These last two areas have been somewhat cleaned up in recent years.

Things to See

La Rambla The best introduction to Barcelona is a walk from Plaça de Catalunya down La Rambla, a long pedestrian strip shaded by leafy trees and lined with newsstands, bird and flower stalls, and cafes.

About halfway down La Rambla is the fragrant Mercat de la Boqueria, a good place to stock up on fresh fruit, vegetables, nuts, bread, pastries and more. Just off La Rambla, farther south, Plaça Reial was, until a few years ago, a seedy square of ill repute; now it's quite pleasant with numerous cafes, bars and a couple of music clubs.

Just off the other side of La Rambla, at Carrer Nou de la Rambla 3-5, is Gaudí's moody **Palau Güell** (10 am to 1.30 pm and 4 to 6.30 pm Monday to Saturday, 400 ptas). Pick up a *Ruta del Modernisme* ticket, which allows you to see other Gaudí goodies around the city.

Down at the end of La Rambla stands the **Monument a Colom**, a statue of Columbus atop a tall pedestal. A small lift will take you to the top of the monument for 250 ptas. Just west in the 14th-century Royal Shipyards, the **Museu Marítim** has an impressive array of boats, models, maps and more (10 am to 7 pm daily, 800 ptas).

Barri Gòtic Barcelona's serene Gothic **cathedral** is open 8.30 am to 1.30 pm and 4 to 7.30 pm daily – be sure to visit the cloister. Each Sunday at noon, crowds gather in front of the cathedral to dance the *sardana*, the Catalan national dance.

Just east of the cathedral is the fascinating **Museu d'Història de la Ciutat** (City History Museum) composed of several buildings around **Plaça del Rei**, the palace courtyard of the medieval monarchs of Aragón. The museum includes a remarkable subterranean walk through excavated portions of Roman and Visigothic Barcelona. It's open 10 am to 2 pm and 4 to 8 pm Tuesday to Saturday, 10 am to 2 pm Sunday. Entry is 500 ptas.

A few minutes' walk west of the cathedral, **Plaça de Sant Josep Oriol** is something of a hang-out for bohemian musicians and buskers. The plaza is surrounded by cafes and towards the end of the week becomes an outdoor art and craft market.

Waterfront For a look at the new face of Barcelona, take a stroll along the once seedy waterfront. From the bottom of La Rambla cross the Rambla de Mar footbridge to the Moll d'Espanya, a former wharf in the middle of the old harbour, Port Vell, where you'll find **L'Aquàrium**, one of Europe's best aquariums (1550 ptas). The city **beaches** start north-east of Port Vell, on the far side of the drab La Barceloneta area.

La Sagrada Família Construction on Gaudí's principal work and Barcelona's most famous building began in 1882 and is taking a *long* time. The church is not yet half built; many feel it should be left as a monument to the master, whose career was cut short when he was hit by a tram in 1926.

Today there are eight towers, all over 100m high, with 10 more to come – the total of 18 representing the 12 Apostles, the four Evangelists and the mother of God, with the tallest tower (170m) standing for her son. You can climb high inside some of the towers by spiral staircases, or you can take a lift some of the way up.

La Sagrada Família – which is on Carrer de Sardenya, on the corner of Carrer de Mallorca (metro: Sagrada Família) – is open 9 am to 6 pm daily (to 7 or 8 pm in summer). Entry is 800 ptas.

More Modernism Many of the best modernist buildings are in l'Eixample. These include Gaudí's beautifully coloured **Casa Batlló**, at Passeig de Gràcia 43, and also **La Pedrera** (at No 92), an apartment block with a grey-stone facade that ripples round the corner of Carrer de Provença. Next door to Casa Batlló (No 41) is **Casa Amatller**, by another leading modernist architect, Josep Puig i Cadafalch.

Another modernist high point is the **Palau de la Música Catalana** concert hall, at Carrer de Sant Pere més alt 11, in the La Ribera area east of the Barri Gòtic.

Museu Picasso & Around The Museu Picasso, in a medieval mansion at Carrer de Montcada 15-19 in La Ribera, houses the most important collection of Picasso's work in Spain – more than 3000 pieces. It concentrates on Picasso's Barcelona periods (1895-1900 and 1901-04). There are also two rooms devoted to Picasso's 1950s series of interpretations of Velázquez's *Las Meninas*. The museum is open 10 am to 8 pm Tuesday to Saturday, to 3 pm Sunday. Entry is 725 ptas (free on the first Sunday of the month).

The **Museu Textil i d'Indumentària** (Textile & Costume Museum), opposite the Museu Picasso, has a good collection of tapestries, clothing and other textiles from centuries past and present (closed Monday). Entry is 400 ptas, or 700 ptas if combined with the adjacent **Museu Barbier-Mueller d'Art Precolombí**, which holds a world-class collection of pre-Colombian art (closed Monday, 500 ptas).

Parc de la Ciutadella As well as being a great place for a picnic or a stroll, this large park east of the Ciutat Vella has some more specific attractions. Top of the list is the monumental **cascada** (waterfall), created in the 1870s with the young Gaudí lending a hand. The **Museu Nacional d'Art Modern de Catalunya** has a good collection of 19th- and early 20th-century Catalan art (closed Monday, 500 ptas). Barcelona's **zoo**, at the southern end of the park, is famed for its albino gorilla (1550 ptas).

Parc Güell This park, in the north of the city, is where Gaudí turned his hand to landscape gardening. It's a strange, enchanting place where Gaudí's passion for natural forms really took flight – to the point where the artificial almost seems more natural than the natural. The house in which Gaudí lived most of his last 20 years has been converted into a **museum** (closed Saturday from October to March, 300 ptas).

To reach Parc Güell, take the metro to Lesseps then walk 10 to 15 minutes, following the signs north-east along Travessera de Dalt, then left up Carrer de Larrard.

Montjuïc This hill, overlooking the city centre from the south-west, is home to some of Barcelona's best museums and attractions, some fine parks, and the main 1992 Olympic sites – well worth some of your time.

On the north side of the hill, the impressive Palau Nacional houses the **Museu Nacional d'Art de Catalunya**, with a first-rate collection of Romanesque frescoes, woodcarvings and sculpture from medieval Catalonia (closed Monday, 900 ptas).

Nearby is the **Poble Espanyol** (Spanish Village), by day it's a tour group's paradise with craft and souvenir shops; after dark it becomes a nightlife jungle, with bars and restaurants galore. It's open to 2 or 4 am most nights (until 8 pm Monday). Entry is 975 ptas (free Sunday to Thursday after 9 pm).

Above the Palau Nacional is the **Estadi Olímpic**, the former Olympic stadium. The **Fundació Joan Miró**, a short distance downhill east of the Estadi Olímpic, is one of the best modern art museums in Spain, with many works by Miró (closed Monday, 800 ptas).

At the top of Montjuïc is the **Castell de Montjuïc**, complete with a military museum and great views.

SPAIN

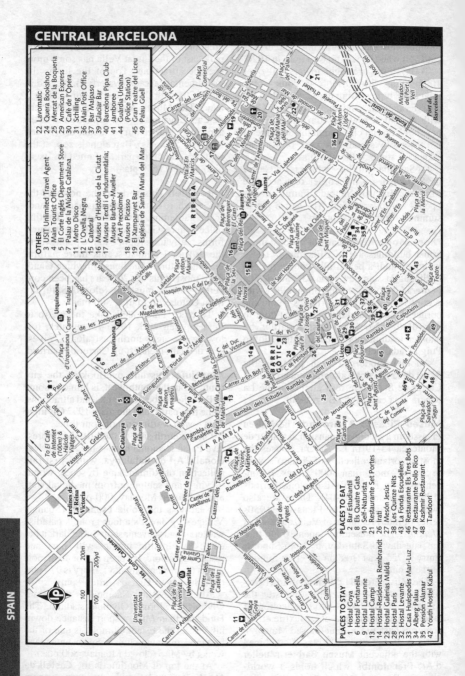

CENTRAL BARCELONA

OTHER
3 UST Unlimited Travel Agent
4 Main Tourist Office
5 El Corte Inglés Department Store
7 Palau de la Música Catalana
11 Metro Disco
12 L'Ovella Negra
15 Catedral
16 Museu d'Història de la Ciutat
17 Museu Textil i d'Indumentària;
  Museu Barbier-Mueller
  d'Art Precolombí
18 Museu Picasso
19 El Xampanyet Bar
20 Església de Santa Maria del Mar
22 Lavomatic
24 Quera Bookshop
25 Mercat de la Boqueria
29 American Express
30 Café de l'Opera
31 Schilling
36 Main Post Office
37 Bar Malpaso
39 Glaciar Bar
40 Barcelona Pipa Club
41 Jamboree
44 Guàrdia Urbana
  (Police Station)
45 Gran Teatre del Liceu
49 Palau Güell

PLACES TO STAY
1 Hostal Goya
6 Hostal Fontanella
9 Hostal Lausanne
13 Hostal Campi
14 Hostal-Residencia Rembrandt
23 Hostal Galerías Maldá
28 Hostal Paris
32 Hostal Levante
33 Casa Huéspedes Mari-Luz
34 Alberg Palau
35 Pension Alamar
42 Youth Hostel Kabul

PLACES TO EAT
2 Bar Estudiantil
8 Els Quatre Gats
10 Self-Naturista
21 Restaurante Set Portes
26 Irati
27 Mesón Jesús
38 Les Quinze Nits
43 La Fonda Escudellers
46 Restaurante Els Tres Bots
47 Restaurante Pollo Rico
48 Kashmir Restaurant
  Tandoori

SPAIN

To reach Montjuïc either walk or take bus No 61 from Plaça d'Espanya (metro: Espanya); the bus links most of the main sights and stops at the foot of a chair lift (475 ptas) up to the castle. A funicular railway (250 ptas) from Paral.lel metro station also runs to the chair lift. The chair lift and funicular are both closed weekdays from November to mid-June.

Organised Tours

The Bus Turístic service covers two circuits (24 stops) linking virtually all the major sights. Tourist offices and many hotels have leaflets explaining the system. Tickets, available on the bus, are 2000 ptas for one day, or 2500 ptas for two consecutive days of unlimited rides. Tickets entitle you to discounts of up to 300 ptas on entry fees and to more than 20 sights en route.

Special Events

Barcelona's biggest festival is the Festes de la Mercè, several days of merrymaking held around 24 September. There are many other festivals – tourist offices can clue you in.

Places to Stay

Camping *Camping Cala Gogó* (☎ 93 379 46 00), 9km south-west of Barcelona, can be reached by bus No 65 from Plaça d' Espanya. In Viladecans, on Carretera C-246, *El Toro Bravo* (☎ 93 637 34 62) and *La Ballena Alegre* (☎ 93 658 05 04) are more pleasant; take bus No L95 from the corner of Ronda de la Universitat and Rambla de Catalunya. All charge upwards of 3400 ptas.

Hostels Barcelona's hostels are not great value for two people, though they're certainly likely places to meet other travellers.

Youth Hostel Kabul (☎ 93 318 51 90, Plaça Reial 17) is a rough-and-ready place but it has no curfew and is OK if you're looking for a party atmosphere. Beds cost 2000 ptas. Security is slack but there are safes available for valuables. Bookings are not taken.

Alberg Palau (☎ 93 412 50 80, Carrer del Palau 6) is smaller and more pleasant, and has a kitchen. Beds are 1600 ptas including breakfast. It's open 7 am to midnight.

Hostal de Joves (☎ 93 300 31 04, Passeig de Pujades 29), near metro Arc de Triomf, is small and rather grim. Beds are 1500 ptas, including breakfast. The curfew is 1 or 2 am and hostel cards are required in July and August.

Alberg Mare de Déu de Montserrat (☎ 93 210 51 51, Passeig Mare de Déu del Coll 41-51) is the biggest and most comfortable hostel, but is 4km north of the city centre. Beds are 1900 ptas if you have an ISIC card or are under age 25; otherwise they're 2500 ptas. A hostel card is required and it's closed during the day and after 3 am. The hostel is a 10-minute walk from Vallcarca metro or a 20-minute ride from Plaça de Catalunya on bus No 28.

Alberg Pere Tarrés (☎ 93 410 23 09, Carrer de Numància 149) is a five-minute walk from Les Corts metro and charges 1500 ptas to 2000 ptas for bed and breakfast. The hostel is closed during the day and after 2 am.

Pensiones & Hostales Generally, the areas closer to the port and on the west side of La Rambla are seedier and cheaper; as you move north towards Plaça de Catalunya, standards (and prices) rise.

Hostal Galerias Maldà (☎ 93 317 30 02, Carrer del Pi 5), upstairs in an arcade, is about as cheap as you'll find. It's a rambling, family-run establishment with basic singles/doubles for 1500/3000 ptas. *Hostal Paris* (☎/fax 93 301 37 85, Carrer del Cardenal Casañas 4) caters to backpackers, with 42 mostly large rooms from 3000 ptas a single to 7000 ptas a double with bath.

Casa Huéspedes Mari-Luz (☎ 93 317 34 63, Carrer del Palau 4) is bright and sociable, with dorms for 2000 ptas a bed and doubles for 5500 ptas to 5800 ptas. *Pensión Alamar* (☎ 93 302 50 12, Carrer de la Comtessa de Sobradiel 1) has 12 singles for 2500 ptas, and one double room for 5000 ptas. *Hostal Levante* (☎ 93 317 95 65, Baixada de Sant Miquel 2) is a good, family-run place with singles for 3500 ptas, or doubles for 5500/6500 ptas with/without private bath.

Hostal Fontanella (☎/fax 93 317 59 43, Via Laietana 71) is a friendly, immaculate place, with 10 (in some cases smallish) rooms costing 3000/5000 ptas or 4000/6900 ptas with bathroom. The friendly *Hostal Campi* (☎ 93 301 35 45, fax 93 301 41 33, Carrer de la Canuda 4). is an excellent deal: singles/doubles without private bath

SPAIN

cost 2700/5000 ptas, or roomy doubles with shower and toilet cost 6000 ptas.

Up near Plaça de Catalunya is the excellent **Hostal Lausanne** (☎ *93 302 11 39, Avinguda Portal de l'Àngel 24, 1st floor*), with good security and rooms (mostly doubles) from 5500 ptas. **Hostal-Residencia Rembrandt** (☎ *93 318 10 11, Carrer Porta-ferrissa 23*) charges 3000/5000 ptas, or 4000/7000 ptas with shower or bath, but is often fully booked.

A few cheapies are spread strategically across the upmarket L'Eixample area, north of Plaça de Catalunya. **Hostal Goya** (☎ *93 302 25 65, fax 93 412 04 35, Carrer de Pau Claris 74*), has 12 nice, good-sized rooms starting at 3100/4500 ptas, or 5600 ptas with shower. **Pensión Aribau** (☎ *93 453 11 06, Carrer d'Aribau 37*) offers reasonable singles/doubles for 3500/6500 ptas. The singles only have a basin but do come with a TV, while the doubles have shower, toilet, TV and even a fridge.

Places to Eat

There are plenty of budget restaurants within walking distance of La Rambla. On Carrer de Sant Pau, west off La Rambla, **Kashmir Restaurant Tandoori**, at No 39, does tasty curries and biryanis from around 800 ptas. **Restaurante Pollo Rico**, at No 31, has a somewhat seedy downstairs bar where you can have a quarter chicken or an omelette with chips, bread and wine for 500 ptas; the restaurant upstairs is more salubrious and only slightly more expensive. **Restaurante Els Tres Bots**, at No 42, is grungy but cheap, with a set menu for 875 ptas.

In the Barri Gòtic, **Self-Naturista** (*Carrer de Santa Anna 13*) is a self-service vegetarian restaurant with a good lunch *menú* (965 ptas). **Mesón Jesús** (*Carrer dels Cecs de la Boqueria 4*) is a cosy, down-home place with lunch *menús* for 1400 ptas. A Basque favourite is **Irati** (*Carrer del Cardenal Cassanyes 17*). The set menu is 1500 ptas, or try the excellent tapas.

Les Quinze Nits (*Plaça Reial 6*) and **La Fonda Escudellers**, on Carrer dels Escudellers, are two stylish bistro-like restaurants (under the same management) with a wide range of tasty Catalan and Spanish dishes; three courses with wine and coffee go for 2500 ptas. Expect to queue. Carrer dels Escudellers also has a couple of good night-

time takeaway felafel joints; around 300 ptas a serve.

Restaurante Set Portes (☎ *93 319 30 33, Passeig d'Isabel II 14*) is a classic dating from 1836 and specialising in paella (1475 ptas to 2225 ptas). It's essential to book. Another famous institution is **Els Quatre Gats** (*Carrer Montsió 3*), Picasso's former hang-out, and now a bit pricey.

L'Eixample has a few good restaurants to offer as well. **Bar Estudiantil**, on Plaça de la Universitat, does economical plats combinats, eg, chicken, chips and *berenjena* (aubergine) or *botifarra* (beans and red pepper), each for around 600 ptas. This is a genuine student hang-out, open late. **L'Hostal de Rita** (*Carrer d'Aragó 279*), a block east of Passeig de Gràcia, is an excellent mid-range restaurant with a four-course lunch *menú* for 995 ptas, and à la carte mains for 700 ptas to 1000 ptas.

Entertainment

Barcelona's entertainment bible is the weekly *Guía del Ocio* (125 ptas) – helpful even if you don't speak Spanish.

Bars Barcelona's huge variety of bars are at their busiest from about 11 pm to 2 or 3 am, especially from Thursday to Saturday.

The liveliest place on La Rambla is **Cafè de l'Òpera** (*La Rambla 74*), opposite the Liceu opera house. It gets packed with all and sundry at night. **Glaciar** (*Plaça Reial 3*) is popular with a young crowd of foreigners and locals. Tiny **Bar Malpaso** (*Carrer d'En Rauric 20*), just off Plaça Reial, plays great Latin and African music. Another hip low-lit place with a more varied (including gay) clientele is **Schilling** (*Carrer de Ferran 23*).

El Xampanyet (*Carrer de Montcada 22*), near the Museu Picasso, is another small place, specialising in *cava* (Catalan champagne; around 500 ptas a bottle), with good tapas too.

West of La Rambla, **L'Ovella Negra** (*Carrer de les Sitges 5*) is a noisy, barn-like tavern with a young crowd. **Bar Marsella** (*Carrer de Sant Pau 65*) specialises in absinthe (*absenta* in Catalan). If by 2.30 am you still need a drink and you don't want a disco, your best bet (except on Sunday) is the **London Bar** (*Carrer Nou de la Rambla 36*), open until about 5 am, with occasional live music.

SPAIN

Live Music & Discos Many music places don't get started until midnight and don't hit their stride until 3 am or so. Women – and maybe male companions – may get in free at some discos if the bouncers like your looks. Count on 300 ptas to 800 ptas for a beer in any of these places. Cover charges can be anything from zero to 3000 ptas, which may include a drink.

Barcelona Pipa Club (Plaça Reial 3) has jazz Thursday to Saturday starting around midnight (ring the bell to get in). Entry is around 1000 ptas. *Jamboree (Plaça Reial 17)* has jazz, funk, and a disco later, from about 1.30 am. *Club Apolo (Carrer Nou de la Rambla 113)* has live world music several nights a week, followed by live salsa or a varied disco. Expect entry of around 2000 ptas for both of these. *Otto Zutz (Carrer de Lincoln 15)* is for beautiful people dressed in black. The crowd's cool and the atmosphere is great.

Zeleste (Carrer dels Almogàvers 122), in Poble Nou, is a cavernous warehouse-type club, regularly hosting visiting bands. *Mirablau*, at the foot of the Tibidabo funicular, is a bar with great views and a small disco floor; it's open till 5 am.

The two top gay discos are *Metro (Carrer de Sepúlveda 185)* and *Martin's (Passeig de Gràcia 130)*. Metro attracts some lesbians and heteros as well as gay men; Martin's is for gay men only.

Opera & Classical Music The *Gran Teatre del Liceu* opera house on La Rambla, gutted by fire in 1994, reopened in 1999 to much fanfare. It and the lovely *Palau de la Música Catalana (Carrer de Sant Pere més alt 11)* are the chief venues for opera, dance and orchestral music.

Getting There & Away

Air Barcelona's airport, 14km south-west of the city at El Prat de Llobregat, has international and domestic flights. Iberia (☎ 902 40 05 00) is at Passeig de Gràcia 30; Spanair (☎ 902 13 14 15) and Air Europa (☎ 902 40 15 01) are at the airport.

Bus The terminal for virtually all domestic and international buses is the Estació del Nord at Carrer d'Alí Bei 80 (metro: Arc de Triomf). The information desk there (☎ 93 265 65 08) is open 7 am to 9 pm daily. A few international buses go from Estació d'Autobuses de Sants, beside the Estació Sants train station.

Several buses a day go to most main Spanish cities including Madrid (3400 ptas, seven or eight hours), Zaragoza (1655 ptas, 4½ hours), Valencia (2900 ptas, 4½ hours) and Granada (7915 ptas, 13 to 15 hours). Buses run several times a week to London (14,075 ptas), Paris (11,975 ptas) and other European cities.

Train Virtually all trains travelling to/from destinations within Spain stop at Estació Sants (metro: Sants-Estació); most international trains use Estació de França (metro: Barceloneta).

For some international destinations you have to change trains at Montpellier or the French border. There are direct trains daily to Paris, Zürich and Milan.

Daily trains run to most major cities in Spain. There are seven trains a day to Madrid (5100 ptas, 6½ to 9½ hours), two to San Sebastián (4600 ptas, eight to 10 hours) and 10 to Valencia (4600 ptas, as little as three hours on high-speed Euromed train). Trains also go to Granada (6400 ptas, eight hours).

Tickets and information are available at the stations or from the RENFE office in Passeig de Gràcia metro/train station on Passeig de Gràcia, open 7 am to 10 pm daily (to 9 pm Sunday).

Getting Around

To/From the Airport Trains link the airport to Estació Sants and Catalunya station on Plaça de Catalunya every half-hour. The trip takes 15 to 20 minutes and a ticket costs 355 ptas. A taxi from the airport to Plaça de Catalunya will cost around 2500 ptas.

Bus, Metro & Train Most places of interest are within a 10-minute walk of a metro station. Buses and suburban trains are only needed for a few destinations. A single metro, bus or suburban train ride costs 150 ptas. A T-1 ticket (825 ptas) is valid for 10 rides, while a T-DIA ticket (625 ptas) gives unlimited travel for one day.

AROUND BARCELONA
Monestir de Montserrat

Unless you are on a pilgrimage, the prime attraction of Montserrat, 50km north-west of Barcelona, is its setting. Montserrat's information centre (☎ 93 877 77 77), to the left along the road from the top cable-car station, is open 10 am to 6 pm daily.

The **Benedictine Monastery of Montserrat** sits high on the side of a mountain (1236m) of truly weird rocky peaks, and is best reached by cable car. The monastery was founded in 1025 to commemorate an apparition of the Virgin Mary on this site. Pilgrims still come from all over Christendom to pay homage to its Black Virgin (La Moreneta), a 12th-century wooden sculpture of Mary, regarded as Catalonia's patroness.

The Black Virgin is high above the main altar of the 16th-century **basilica**, the only part of the monastery open to the public. The Montserrat Escolania (boys' choir) sings in the basilica Monday to Saturday at 1 and 7 pm (1 pm only on Sunday), except in July.

The two-part **Museu de Montserrat**, on the plaza in front of the basilica, has an excellent collection ranging from an Egyptian mummy to art by El Greco, Monet and Picasso (600/400 ptas).

Places to Stay There are several accommodation options at the monastery (all ☎ 93 877 77 77). Cheapest are the blocks of simple two-person apartments (up to 5990 ptas) at the *Cel.les de Montserrat*. Overlooking Plaça de Santa Maria is the comfortable *Hotel Abat Cisneros*, with rooms for 6725/11,650 ptas.

Getting There & Away Trains run often from Plaça d'Espanya station in Barcelona to Aeri de Montserrat (1½ hours). Return tickets (1905 ptas) include the cable car between Aeri de Montserrat and the monastery.

COSTA BRAVA

The Costa Brava (Rugged Coast) ranks among Europe's most popular holiday spots, along with Spain's Costa Blanca and Costa del Sol. However the Costa Brava stands alone in its spectacular scenery and proximity to Northern Europe, both of which have sent prices skyrocketing.

The main jumping-off points for the Costa Brava are the inland towns of Girona (Gerona in Castilian) and Figueres (Figueras). Along the coast the most appealing resorts are, from north to south,

Cadaqués, L'Escala (La Escala), Tamariu, Llafranc, Calella de Palafrugell and Tossa de Mar.

Tourist offices along the coast can help with accommodation, transport schedules and more; they include Girona (☎ 972 22 65 75), Figueres (☎ 972 50 31 55), Palafrugell (☎ 972 30 02 28) and Cadaqués (☎ 972 25 83 15).

Coastal Resorts

The Costa Brava is all about picturesque inlets and coves. Some longer beaches at places like L'Estartit and Empúries are worth visiting out of season, but there has been a tendency to build tall buildings wherever engineers think it can be done. Fortunately, in many places it just can't.

Cadaqués, about one hour's drive east of Figueres at the end of an agonising series of hairpin bends, is perhaps the most picturesque of all Spanish resorts, and is haunted by the memory of the artist Salvador Dalí, who lived here. It's short on beaches, so people spend a lot of time sitting at waterfront cafes or wandering along the beautiful coast.

About 10km north-east of Cadaqués is **Cap de Creus**, a rocky peninsula with a single restaurant at the top of a craggy cliff.

Farther down the coast, past L'Escala and L'Estartit, you eventually come to Palafrugell, itself a few kilometres inland with little to offer, but near three beach towns that have to be seen to be believed. The most northerly of these, and also the smallest, least crowded and most exclusive, is **Tamariu**. **Llafranc** is the biggest and busiest, and has the longest beach. **Calella de Palafrugell**, with its picture-postcard setting, is never overcrowded and always relaxed.

Other Attractions

When you have had enough beach for a while, make sure you put Figueres' **Teatre-Museu Dalí**, on Plaça Gala i Salvador Dalí, at the top of your list of things to do. This 19th-century theatre was converted by Dalí himself and houses a huge collection of his strange creations. It's open 9 am to 7.15 pm daily July to September; 10.30 am to 5.15 pm Tuesday to Sunday October to June. Entry is 1000 ptas (800 ptas October to May).

Historical interest is provided by **Girona**, with a lovely medieval quarter centred on a

SPAIN

Gothic cathedral, and the ruins of the Greek and Roman town of **Empúries**, 2km from L'Escala.

Among the most exciting attractions on the Costa Brava are the **Illes Medes**, off the coast from the package resort of L'Estartit. These seven islets and their surrounding coral reefs have been declared a natural park to protect their diverse flora and fauna. You can arrange glass-bottom boat trips and diving from L'Estartit.

Places to Stay

Figueres Figueres' HI hostel, *Alberg Tramuntana (☎ 972 50 12 13, Carrer Anicet Pagès 2)* is two blocks from the tourist office. It charges 1700 ptas if you're under 26 or have an ISIC or IYTC card, 2275 ptas otherwise (breakfast included). Alternatively, *Pensión Isabel II (☎ 972 50 47 35, Carrer de Isabel II 16)* has reasonable rooms with bath for 2800 ptas. Don't sleep in Figueres' Parc Municipal – people have been attacked here at night.

Girona *Pensión Viladomat (☎ 972 20 31 76, Carrer dels Ciutadans 5)* has comfortable singles/doubles starting at 2000/4000 ptas.

Cadaqués *Camping Cadaqués (☎ 972 25 81 26)* is at the top of the town as you head towards Cabo de Creus. Two adults with a tent and a car pay 2880 ptas plus IVA. At these prices, a room in town in probably a better bet. *Hostal Marina (☎ 972 25 81 99, Carrer de Frederico Rahola 2)* has doubles at up to 5500 ptas plus IVA, or 8000 ptas with private bath.

Near Palafrugell There are camping grounds at all three of Palafrugell's satellites, all charging similar hefty rates. In Calella de Palafrugell try *Camping Moby Dick (☎ 972 61 43 07)*; in Llafranc, *Camping Kim's (☎ 972 30 11 56)*; and in Tamariu, *Camping Tamariu (☎ 972 62 04 22)*.

Hotel and pensión rooms are relatively thin on the ground here, as many people come on package deals and stay in apartments. In Calella de Palafrugell, the friendly *Hostería del Plancton (☎ 972 61 50 81)* is one of the best deals on the Costa Brava, with rooms at 2200 ptas per person, but it's only open from June to September. *Residencia Montaña (☎ 972 30 04 04,*

Carrer de Cesàrea 2), in Llafranc, is not a bad deal at 6300 ptas plus IVA. In Tamariu, *Hotel Sol d'Or (☎ 972 30 04 24, Carrer de Riera 18)*, near the beach, has doubles with bathroom for 6550 ptas.

Getting There & Away

A few buses run each day from Barcelona to Tossa del Mar, L'Estartit and Cadaqués. To reach the small resorts near Palafrugell you first need to get to Girona. Both Girona and Figueres are on the railway line connecting Barcelona to Portbou on the French border. The fare from Barcelona to Girona is 790 ptas to 910 ptas, to Figueres it's 1125 ptas to 1290 ptas.

Getting Around

There are two or three buses a day from Figueres to Cadaqués and three or four to L'Escala. Figueres bus station (☎ 972 67 42 98) is across the road from the train station.

Several daily buses run to Palafrugell from Girona's bus station (behind the train station), and there are buses from Palafrugell to Calella de Palafrugell, Llafranc and Tamariu. Most other coastal towns (south of Cadaqués) can be reached by bus from Girona.

TARRAGONA

Tarragona is a modern city with a large student population and a lively beach scene – the perfect antidote to hectic Barcelona. Founded in 218 BC, Tarragona was for a long time the capital of much of Roman Spain, and Roman structures figure among its most important attractions. Tarragona's other main attraction, Port Aventura (Spain's answer to EuroDisney), is just a few kilometres south-west.

Orientation & Information

Tarragona's main street is Rambla Nova, which runs approximately north-west from a cliff top overlooking the Mediterranean. A few blocks east and parallel to Rambla Nova is Rambla Vella, which marks the beginning of the old town. The train station is south-west, on the coast.

Tarragona's main tourist office (☎ 977 24 50 64) is at Carrer Major 39.

Things to See

The **Museu d'Història de Tarragona** comprises four separate Roman sites around the

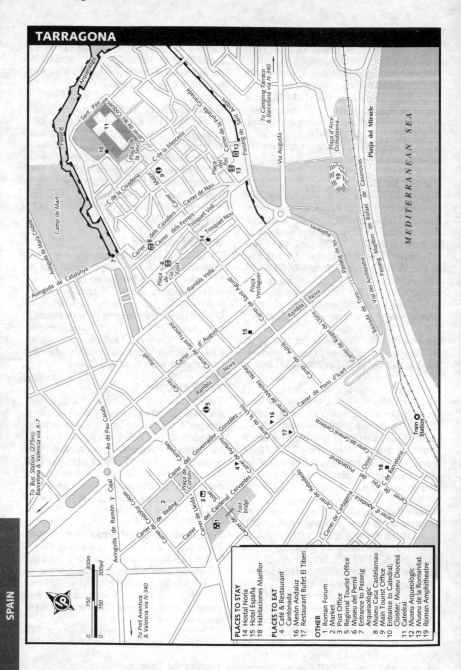

TARARAGONA

MEDITERRANEAN SEA

Platja del Miracle

SPAIN

PLACES TO STAY
14 Hostal Noria
15 Hotel España
18 Habitaciones Mariflor

PLACES TO EAT
4 Café & Restaurant
  Cantonada
16 Mesón Andaluz
17 Restaurant Bufet El Tiberi

OTHER
1 Roman Forum
2 Market
3 Post Office
5 Regional Tourist Office
6 Museu del Pernil
7 Entrance to Passeig
  Arqueològic
8 Museu Casa Castellarnau
9 Main Tourist Office
10 Entrance to Catedral;
   Cloister; Museu Diocesá
11 Catedral
12 Museu Arqueològic
13 Museu de la Romanitat
19 Roman Amphitheatre

city, plus the 14th-century noble mansion now serving as the **Museu Casa Castelarnau**, Carrer dels Cavallers 14. Most of these places close on Monday. Admission to each is 300 ptas.

A good site to start with is the **Museu de la Romanitat**, on Plaça del Rei, which includes part of the vaults of the Roman circus, where chariot races were held. Nearby, close to the beach, is the well-preserved Roman **amphitheatre**. On Carrer de Lleida, a few blocks west of Rambla Nova, are the substantial remains of a **Roman forum**. The **Passeig Arqueològic** is a peaceful walkway along a stretch of the old city walls.

The **Museu Arqueològic**, on Plaça del Rei, has a good collection of frescoes, mosaics, sculpture and pottery dating back to the 2nd century BC (closed Monday, 400 ptas).

The **catedral** sits grandly at the highest point of Tarragona, overlooking the old town. Some parts of the building date back to the 12th century AD (closed weekends). Entrance is through the beautiful cloister with the excellent **Museu Diocesà**.

Places to Stay
Camping Tàrraco (☎ 977 23 99 89) is near Platja Arrabassada beach, off the N-340 road, 2km north-east of the centre.

Rooms fill up quickly in summer – book ahead if possible. *Hostal Noria* (☎ 977 23 87 17, Plaça de la Font 53) is decent value at 2700/4600 ptas but is often full. *Habitaciones Mariflor* (☎ 977 23 82 31, Carrer del General Contreras 29) occupies a drab building near the station, but has clean rooms for 2100/4000 ptas. *Hotel España* (☎ 977 23 27 12, Rambla Nova 49) is a well-positioned, but unexciting, one-star hotel where rooms with bath cost 3300/6000 ptas plus IVA.

Places to Eat
For Catalan food, head to the stylish *Restaurant Bufet El Tiberi (Carrer de Martí d'Ardenya 5)*, which offers an all-you-can-eat buffet for 1450 ptas. Nearby *Mesón Andaluz (Carrer de Pons d'Icart 3, upstairs)* is a backstreet local favourite, with a good three-course *menú* for 1500 ptas. *Café Cantonada (Carrer de Fortuny 23)* is a popular place for tapas; next door, *Restaurant Cantonada* has pizzas and pasta from around 850 ptas.

Getting There & Away
There are frequent trains to/from Barcelona (660 ptas, one to 1½ hours) and Valencia (2095 ptas, 3½ hours). Trains to Madrid (from 4900 ptas) go via Valencia (seven hours total) or Zaragoza (six hours total).

AROUND TARRAGONA
Port Aventura
Port Aventura (☎ 902 20 22 20), Spain's biggest and best amusement park, lies 7km south-west of Tarragona, near Salou. If you have 4600 ptas to spare (3400 ptas for kids), it makes a fun day out. There are hair-raising rides like a virtual submarine and the Dragon Khan, claimed to be Europe's biggest roller coaster. There is a noticeable American influence. It is open 10 am to 8 pm daily from Semana Santa to October (to midnight mid-June through mid-September). Night tickets, valid from 7 pm, are 3400 ptas.

Trains run to Port Aventura's station, about 1km from the park, several times daily from Tarragona and Barcelona (1305 ptas return).

Balearic Islands

Floating out in the Mediterranean waters off the east coast of Spain, the Balearic Islands (Islas Baleares) are invaded each summer by a hedonistic and multinational force. Not surprising really, when you consider the ingredients on offer – fine beaches, relentless sunshine and a wild nightlife.

Beyond the crowded bars and beaches, there are Stone Age ruins, small fishing villages, some spectacular bushwalks and endless olive groves and orange orchards. Most place names and addresses are given in Catalan, the main language spoken in the islands. The prices quoted here are for high season – out of season, you will often find things are much cheaper.

Getting There & Away
Air Scheduled flights from major Spanish cities are operated by several airlines, including Iberia, Air Europa and Spanair. The cheapest and most frequent flights run between Palma de Mallorca and Barcelona (about 10,000 ptas return) and Valencia.

While it's possible to find cheap charter flights to the mainland from the islands, inter-island flights are expensive.

SPAIN

Boat Trasmediterránea (☎ 902 45 46 45) is the major ferry company with offices in (and services between) Barcelona (☎ 93 295 90 00), Valencia (☎ 96 367 65 12), Palma de Mallorca (☎ 971 40 50 14), Maó (☎ 971 36 60 50) and Ibiza city (☎ 971 31 51 00). You can check out the Web site at www.trasmediterranea.com.

High-season fares from the mainland to any island are 6920 ptas for a 'Butaca Turista' (standard seat) or 11,410 ptas for a bunk in a four-bed cabin. Taking a car will cost 19,315 ptas. Routes include Barcelona-Palma (eight hours), Barcelona-Maó (nine hours), Barcelona-Ibiza city (9½ hours; 14½ hours via Palma), Valencia-Palma (8½ hours), Valencia-Ibiza city (seven hours), Palma-Ibiza city (4½ hours) and Palma-Maó (6½ hours).

Inter-island services (Palma-Ibiza city and Palma-Maó) cost 3540 ptas for a Butaca Turista. In summer Trasmediterránea also operates the following 'Fast Ferry' services: Barcelona-Palma (8990 ptas, 4¼ hours), Valencia-Palma (6920 ptas, 6¼ hours), Valencia-Ibiza city (6920 ptas, 3¼ hours) and Palma-Ibiza city (5750 ptas, 2¼ hours).

Another company, Balearia (☎ 902 16 01 80) operates two or three daily ferries from Denia (on the coast between Valencia and Alicante) to Sant Antoni de Portmany and one to Ibiza city (6295 ptas one way, four hours). Another service links Ibiza to Palma (3245 ptas, three hours).

Iscomar (☎ 902 11 91 28) has from one to four daily car ferries (depending on the season) between Ciutadella on Menorca and Port d'Alcúdia on Mallorca (4400 ptas one way). Cape Balear (☎ 902 10 04 44) operates up to three daily fast ferries (75 minutes) to Ciutadella from Cala Ratjada (Mallorca) in summer for around 8000 ptas return.

MALLORCA

Most of the five million annual visitors to Mallorca, the largest of the Balearic Islands, come for the three 's' words: sun, sand and sea. There are other reasons for visiting – Palma de Mallorca (Palma), the capital, is on a bay famous for its brilliant sunsets, while the Serra de Tramuntana mountain range is a trekker's heaven. Mallorca's best beaches are along the north-east and east coasts – as are most of the main tourist resorts.

Information

All major resorts have at least one tourist office. Palma has four – Plaça d'Espanya (☎ 971 75 43 29), Carrer de Sant Domingo 11 (☎ 971 72 40 90), Plaça de la Reina and the airport. The *Hiking Excursions* brochure covers 20 of the island's better walks.

Things to See & Do

Palma The enormous **catedral**, on Plaça Almoina, is visible from the ferry as you approach the island. It houses an excellent museum (500 ptas). In front of the cathedral is the dull **Palau de l'Almudaina**, the one-time residence of the Mallorcan monarchs (450 ptas). Far better is the rich and varied **Museu de Mallorca** (300 ptas).

The **Banys Árabs** (Arab baths) near the cathedral are the only remaining monument to the island's former Muslim rulers. The **Fundació Joan Miró**, with a collection housed in the artist's Palma studio, is 2km west of the centre at Carrer de Joan de Saridakis 29.

Around the Island Mallorca's north-west coast, dominated by the Serra de Tramuntana mountains, is a beautiful region of olive groves, pine forests and small villages; it also has a rugged and rocky coastline. There are a few highlights for drivers: the hair-raising road to the small port of **Sa Calobra** and the amazing trip along the peninsula leading to the island's northern tip, **Cap Formentor**.

If you don't have your own wheels, take the Palma-Sóller train, one of the most spectacular excursions on the island. **Sóller** is a good base for trekkers – the easy three-hour return walk to the beautiful village of **Deià** is a fine introduction to Mallorca.

There are long stretches of sandy, undeveloped beach south of **Port d'Alcúdia** on the north-east coast. The lovely **Cala Mondragó**, on the south-east coast, is backed by a solitary hostal. Farther south the attractive port town of **Cala Figuera** has escaped many of the ravages of mass tourism.

Places to Stay & Eat

Palma The *Pensión Costa Brava* (☎ 971 71 17 29, Carrer de Ca'n Martí Feliu 16) is a backstreet cheapie with reasonable rooms from 2000/3300 ptas. The cluttered 19th-century charm of *Hostal Pons* (☎ 971 72 26

58, Carrer del Vi 8) overcomes its limitations (spongy beds, only one bathroom); the rates here are 2500 ptas per person. *Hostal Apuntadores (☎ 971 71 34 91, Carrer dels Apuntadores 8)* has smart rooms for 2700/3200 ptas, doubles with bath at 4800 ptas, and hostel beds for 1800 ptas. Next door, *Hostal Ritzi (☎ 971 71 46 10)* has kitchen facilities and comfortable rooms with shower for 3500/5000 ptas, or doubles with bath for 5500 ptas to 7500 ptas.

For Palma's best range of eateries, wander the streets between Plaça de la Reina and the port; Carrer dels Apuntadors is lined with restaurants. For a simple, cheap meal with the locals head for *Bar Martín (Carrer de la Santa Creu 2)*. The rustic *Restaurant Celler Sa Premsa (Plaça del Bisbe Berenguer de Palou 8)* is an almost obligatory stop for its hearty meals. For vegetarian food try *Bon Lloc (Carrer de Sant Feliu 7)*.

Other Areas Ask the tourist office for a list of old *monasteries* around the island, several of which offer cheap beds.

In Deiá, the excellent *Fonda Villa Verde (☎ 971 63 90 37)* charges 6000/8300 ptas. Beside the train station in Sóller, the popular *Hotel El Guía (☎ 971 63 02 27)* has rooms for 5405/8415 ptas. Nearby (go past Hotel El Guía and turn right), *Casa de Huéspedes Margarita (☎ 971 63 42 14)* has singles/doubles/triples for 2800/3800/4500 ptas.

Getting Around

Bus No 17 runs every half-hour from the airport to Plaça Espanya in central Palma (300 ptas, 30 minutes). Taxis cost around 2000 ptas.

Island buses depart from or near Palma's bus station at Plaça Espanya – tourist offices have details. Mallorca's two train lines also start from Plaça Espanya. One goes to the inland town of Inca and the other to Sóller (380 ptas to 735 ptas).

It's worth renting a car solely for the drive along the north-west coast. There are about 30 rental agencies in Palma along Passeig Marítim.

IBIZA

Ibiza (Eivissa in Catalan) is one of the world's most bizarre melting pots, each year attracting more than a million hippies, gays, fashion victims, nudists, party animals and plain ol' beachgoers. Besides the weather, Ibiza's main drawcards are the notorious nightlife and the many picturesque beaches.

The capital, Ibiza city, is on the island's south-eastern side. This is where most travellers arrive and also makes the best base. The next-largest towns are Santa Eulária des Riu, on the east coast, and Sant Antoni de Portmany on the west coast. Other big resorts are scattered around the island.

Information

Ibiza city's tourist office (☎ 971 30 19 00) is on Passeig des Moll opposite the Estación Marítima. The post office is at Carrer de Madrid s/n, or you can go online for 900 ptas an hour at Ibiform (☎ 971 31 58 69), Avinguda de Ignacio Wallis 8 (1st floor).

Things to See & Do

Ibiza City Shopping is a major pastime in Ibiza – the port area of **Sa Penya** is crammed with funky clothes boutiques and market stalls. From here you can wander up into **D'Alt Vila**, the old walled town, with its upmarket restaurants, galleries and the **Museu d'Art Contemporani**. There are fine views from the walls and from the top of the **catedral**. The **Museu Arqueològic** next door is also worth a visit.

Around the Island There are good beaches south of Ibiza city at **Ses Salines**, accessible by bus (125 ptas, 30 minutes). **Cala de Boix**, on the north-east coast, is the only black-sand beach in the islands. Farther north are the lovely beaches of **S'Aigua Blanca**. On the north coast near Portinatx, **Cala Xarraca** is in a picturesque, semi-protected bay. On the south-west coast, **Cala d'Hort** has a spectacular setting overlooking two rugged rock-islets, Es Verda and Es Verdranell.

Places to Stay & Eat

Ibiza City There are hostales in the streets around the port, although in mid-summer cheap beds are scarce. *Hostal-Residencia Ripoll (☎ 971 31 42 75, Carrer de Vicent Cuervo 14)* has singles/doubles costing 3800/5800 ptas. You get clean rooms and friendly hosts nearby at *Hostal Sol y Brisa (☎ 971 31 08 18, Avinguda de Bartomeu Vicent Ramón 15)*. Singles/doubles with

SPAIN

shared bathrooms cost from 3500/6000 ptas. On the waterfront, *Hostal-Restaurante La Marina* (☎ *971 31 01 72*) has good doubles with views for 5000 ptas to 7000 ptas. One of the best choices is *Casa de Huéspedes La Peña* (☎ *971 19 02 40, Carrer de la Virgen 76*) at the far end of Sa Penya. Doubles with shared bath range up to 4000 ptas.

Bland, overpriced eateries abound in the port area. The no-frills *Comidas Bar San Juan* (*Carrer Montgri 8*) offers outstanding value with main courses from 500 ptas to 850 ptas. *Ca'n Costa* (*Carrer de la Cruz 19*) is another family-run eating house with a *menú* for 900 ptas to 1100 ptas. If you want an intimate and romantic night, head for the candle-lit *La Scala* (*Carrer de sa Carrossa 6*), up in D'Alt Vila.

Other Areas One of the best of Ibiza's half-dozen camping grounds is *Camping Cala Nova* (☎ *971 33 17 74*), 500m north of the resort town of Cala Nova.

Near the Ses Salines bus stop, *Hostal Mar y Sal* (☎ *971 39 65 84*) has doubles at 5500 ptas. Near the S'Aigua Blanca beaches, *Pensión Sa Plana* (☎ *971 33 50 73*) has a pool and rooms with bath from 5000/6500 ptas including breakfast. Or you could stay by the black-sand beach, Cala Boix, at *Hostal Cala Boix* (☎ *971 33 52 24*), where B&B costs 2500 ptas per person.

Entertainment
Ibiza's raucous club scene draws legions willing to pay up to 7000 ptas cover (!). Some of the big names are *Pacha*, *El Divino* and *Privilege*.

Getting Around
Hourly buses run between the airport and Ibiza city (125 ptas); otherwise, a taxi costs around 1700 ptas. Buses to other parts of the island leave from the series of bus stops along Avenida d'Isidoro Macabich – the tourist office has timetables.

FORMENTERA
An easy day trip from Ibiza, Formentera is the smallest and least developed of the four main Balearic Islands. It has fine beaches and some excellent walking and cycling trails. It can get crowded in midsummer, but most of the time it is possible to find a strip of sand out of earshot of other tourists.

Ferries arrive at La Savina on the northwest coast; the tourist office (☎ 971 32 20 57) is behind the rental agencies at the harbour. The island's pretty capital, Sant Francesc Xavier, is 3km south. At the eastern end of the island is the Sa Mola lighthouse. Es Pujols is the main tourist resort (and the only place with any nightlife to speak of).

Getting There & Away
There are 20 to 25 ferries daily between Ibiza city and Formentera. The trip costs 2085 ptas one-way by fast ferry (25 minutes) or 2300 ptas return by regular ferry (one hour).

MENORCA
Menorca is perhaps the least overrun of the Balearic islands. In 1993 it was declared a Biosphere Reserve by Unesco, with the aim of preserving important environmental areas such as the Albufera d'es Grau wetlands.

The capital, Maó (Mahón in Spanish), is at the island's eastern end. Its busy port is the arrival point for most ferries. The main road runs down the middle of the island to Ciutadella, Menorca's second-largest town, with a smaller harbour and many historic buildings. Secondary roads lead north and south to the resorts and beaches.

Information
The main tourist office (☎ 971 36 37 90) is in Maó at Plaça de S'Esplanada 40. Offices open during summer at the airport and in Ciutadella on Plaça des Born.

Places to Stay & Eat
Menorca has two summer-only *camping grounds*: one near the resorts of Santa Galdana, about 8km south of Ferreries; and one near Son Bou, south of Alaior.

In Maó, *Hostal Orsi* (☎ *971 36 47 51, Carrer de la Infanta 19*), run by a Glaswegian and an American, is bright, clean and well located. Rooms are 2600/4400 ptas. *Hostal La Isla* (☎ *971 36 64 92, Carrer de Santa Catalina 4*) has excellent rooms with bath for 2300/4100 ptas.

In Ciutadella, *Hostal Oasis* (☎ *971 38 21 97, Carrer de Sant Isidre 33*) is set around a spacious courtyard and has its own *Italian restaurant*. Doubles with bath and breakfast cost 5500 ptas.

SPAIN

Getting Around

A taxi from the airport to Maó costs around 1200 ptas – there are no buses.

TMSA (☎ 971 36 03 61) runs six buses a day between Maó and Ciutadella (560 ptas), with connections to the major resorts on the south coast.

Valencia

VALENCIA CITY

Valencia, birthplace of paella and Spain's vibrant third city, is blessed with great weather and hosts the country's wildest party – Las Fallas (12 to 19 March), an exuberant blend of fireworks, music, all-night partying and over 350 *fallas*, giant sculptures which all go up in flames on the final night.

Orientation & Information

The action part of the city is oval, bounded by the old course of the Turia River and the sickle-shaped inner ring road of Calles Colón, Játiva and Guillem de Castro. These trace the walls of the old city, demolished in 1865 as a job-creation project.

Within are three major squares: Plazas del Ayuntamiento, de la Reina (also known as Plaza de Zaragoza) and de la Virgen.

The main tourist office is at Calle Paz 48 (☎ 96 398 64 22). Three smaller ones are at the train station, town hall and Teatro Principal. All have reams of information in English.

The imposing neobaroque main post office is on Plaza del Ayuntamiento. Poste restante is on the 1st floor.

Among several Cybercafes in town is the noisy, 48-terminal Www.confederacion.com (yes, that's the name) at Calle Ribera 8. Just off Plaza del Ayuntamiento, it charges 500 ptas per hour.

Things to See

The tree Museo de Bellas Artes ranks among Spain's best, with works by El Greco, Goya, Velázquez, Ribera, Ribalta and Valencian impressionists such as Sorolla and Pinazo.

The Instituto Valenciano de Arte Moderno (IVAM, pronounced 'eebam'; 350 ptas, free Sunday), beside Puente de las Artes, houses an impressive permanent collection of 20th-century Spanish art and hosts excellent quality temporary exhibitions.

Roam around Valencia's **catedral** with its three magnificent portals – one Romanesque, one Gothic and one baroque. Climb the Miguelete bell tower (200 ptas) for a sweeping view of the old town.

The aesthetically stunning, ultramodern **Ciudad de las Artes y de las Ciencias** promises to become Valencia's premier attraction. Already open is the **Hemisfèric** (☎ 96 399 55 77), at once planetarium, IMAX cinema and laser show (admission to each, 1100 ptas). An interactive science museum, the **Museo de las Ciencias Príncipe Felipe** (☎ 902 100 031), opens as of 2001 (1000 ptas).

Playa de la Malvarrosa, bordered by a string of restaurants, is Valencia city's beach. Take bus No 19 from Plaza del Ayuntamiento, No 1 or 2 from the bus station or the high-speed tram.

Playa El Salér, 10km south of town, is backed by shady pine wood. Autocares Herca (☎ 96 349 12 50) buses (150 ptas, 30 minutes) run hourly (every half hour in summer) from the junction of Gran Vía de las Germanias and Calle Sueca.

Places to Stay

Camping The nearest camping ground, *Devesa Gardens* (☎/fax 96 161 11 36), open year round, is 13km south of Valencia near El Saler beach.

Hostels *Alberge Las Arenas* (☎/fax 96 356 42 88, Calle Eugenia Viñes 24), open year round, is a pebble's throw from Malvarrosa beach and within earshot of its wild summer nightlife. Take bus No 32 from Plaza del Ayuntamiento.

Hotels Central and near the covered market, *Hospedería del Pilar* (☎ 96 391 66 00, Plaza del Mercado 19) has clean and basic singles/doubles/triples at 1600/2995/3900 ptas (2140/3850/4815 ptas with shower). Nearby, most rooms at the vast *Hostal El Rincón* (☎ 96 391 79 98, Calle de la Carda 11) are small but nicely priced at 1500/2800 ptas. It also has eight spacious renovated rooms with bathroom and aircon – excellent value at 2000/3600 ptas.

Near Plaza del Ayuntamiento, *Pensión París* (☎/fax 96 352 67 66, Calle Salvá 12) has spotless singles/doubles/triples at 2500/3600/5400 ptas (doubles/triples with shower, 4200/6000 ptas). At the recently renovated and welcoming **Hostal Moratín** (☎/fax 96 352 12 20, Calle Moratín 15), singles/doubles with shower are 2900/4500 ptas (3500/5500 ptas with bathroom).

Places to Eat

Plaza del Ayuntamiento has the usual range of burger bars. Just off it, you can eat local and well at unpretentious **La Utielana**, tucked away just off Calle Prócida, for around 1500 ptas. **Cervecería-Restaurante Pema** (Calle Mosén Femades 3) lets you choose anything from a simple tapa to a full-blown meal. Its weekday lunch *menú* at 1100 ptas, including a drink and coffee, must be central Valencia's best deal.

Just off Plaza de la Virgen, **Restaurante El Generalife** (Calle Caballeros 5) has an excellent-value *menú* for 1200 ptas. Also in the Barrio del Carmen, tiny **La Lluna** (Calle San Ramón 23), with a *menú* at 900 ptas, has simple, good-value vegetarian food.

Everyone, not only self-caterers, can have lots of fun browsing around the bustling **Mercado Central**, Valencia's *modernista* covered market (1928).

Entertainment

Valencia has four main nightlife zones, each bursting with bars: Barrio del Carmen; the old quarter in-vogue Mercado de Subastos on the west side of town; Plaza de Canovas for young up-and-comers; and Plaza de Xuquer, a student haunt.

Finnegan's, an Irish pub on Plaza de la Reina, draws English-speakers. If it's just a cheap drink you're after, no-frills **Oasis Cafe**, just off Plaza del Carmen, is about the cheapest in the barrio. Watch out for the drug dealers in the square; they'll have your wallet before you can say 'sell me a spliff'.

Getting There & Away

Bus The bus station (☎ 96 349 72 22) is beside the old riverbed on Avenida de Menéndez Pidal. Bus No 8 connects it to Plaza del Ayuntamiento.

Major destinations include Madrid (2875 ptas to 3175 ptas, up to 12 daily), Barcelona (2900 ptas, up to 12 daily) and Alicante (1980 ptas, 2¼ hours)

Train Express trains run from Estación del Norte (☎ 96 352 02 02 or 902-24 02 02)

to/from Madrid (5700 ptas, 3½ hours, up to 10 daily), Barcelona (mostly 4500 ptas, three to five hours, 12 daily) and Alicante (1400 to 3200 ptas, 1½ to two hours, up to eight daily).

ALICANTE (ALACANT)

Alicante is a dynamic town with an interesting old quarter, good beach and frenetic nightlife. It becomes even wilder for the Fiesta de Sant Joan, 24 June, when Alicante stages its own version of Las Fallas (see the Valencia city section).

Of its five tourist offices, the main, regional one (☎ 965 20 00 00) is at Rambla de Méndez Núñez 23.

Things to See & Do

The **Castillo de Santa Bárbara** (free), a 16th-century fortress, overlooks the city. Take the lift (400 ptas return), reached by a footbridge opposite Playa del Postiguet, or walk via Avenida Jaime II or the new Parque de la Ereta.

The **Museo de la Asegurada** (closed Sunday afternoon and Monday, free), on Plaza Santa María, houses an excellent collection of modern art, including a handful of works by Dalí, Miró and Picasso.

Playa del Postiguet is Alicante's city beach. Larger and less crowded beaches are at **Playa de San Juan**, easily reached by bus Nos 21 and 22.

Most days, Kontiki (☎ 96 521 63 96) runs boat trips (1800 ptas return) to the popular **Isla de Tabarca**, an island where there's good snorkelling and scuba diving from quiet beaches.

Be sure to fit in a stroll along Explanada de España, rich in cafes and running parallel to the harbour.

Places to Stay

About 10km north of Alicante, **Camping Costa Blanca**, outside Campello and 200m from the beach, has a good pool. Alicante's youth hostel, **La Florida** (☎ 96 511 30 44, Avenida de Orihuela 59), is 2km west of the centre and open to all – but only between July and September.

At the outstanding **Pensión Les Monges Palace** (☎ 96 521 50 46, Calle de Monges 2) rooms cost 3900/4200/5000 ptas with washbasin/shower/full bathroom and have satellite TV and aircon (700 ptas supplement).

SPAIN

Pensión La Milagrosa (☎ *96 521 69 18, Calle de Villavieja 8*) has clean, basic rooms for 1500 ptas to 2000 ptas per person (according to season) and a small guest kitchen. *Hostal Mayor* (☎ *96 520 13 83, Calle Mayor 5*) has pleasant singles/doubles/triples with full bathroom at 3000/6000/9000 ptas (cheaper out of season).

Places to Eat

Restaurante El Canario (*Calle de Maldonado 25*) is a no-frills eatery with a hearty menú for 950 ptas. Nearby, *Restaurante Mixto Vegetariano* (*Plaza de Santa María 2*) is a simple place with vegetarian and meat menús from 1000 ptas. *Restaurante Don Camillo* (*Plaza del Abad Penalva 2*) has above-average pasta dishes for up to 975 ptas.

Entertainment

Alicante's nightlife zone clusters around the cathedral – look out for *Celestial Copas*, *La Naya*, *Nazca* and *Fitty*. In summer the disco scene at Playa de San Juan is thumping. There are also dozens of discos in the coastal resorts between Alicante and Denia; FGV 'night trains' ferry partygoers along this notorious stretch.

Getting There & Away

There are daily services from the bus station on Calle de Portugal to Almería (2570 ptas, 4½ hours), Valencia (1980 ptas, 2¼ hours), Barcelona (4650 ptas, eight hours), Madrid (3345 ptas, five hours) and towns along the Costa Blanca.

From the train station on Avenida de Salamanca there are frequent services to Madrid (4700 ptas, four hours), Valencia (1400 ptas to 3200 ptas, two hours) and Barcelona (6500 ptas, around five hours).

COSTA BLANCA

The Costa Blanca (the White Coast), one of Europe's most popular tourist regions, has its share of concrete jungles. But if you're looking for a full-blown social scene, good beaches and a suntan, it's unrivalled. Unless you're packing a tent, accommodation is almost impossible to find in July and August, when rates skyrocket.

Xábia

In contrast to the very Spanish resort of Denia, 10km north-west, over two thirds of the annual visitors to Xábia (Jávea) are foreigners. This laid-back resort is in three parts: the old town (3km inland), the port, and the beach zone of El Arenal, lined with pleasant bar-restaurants.

Camping El Naranjal (☎ *96 579 10 70*) is a 10-minute walk from El Arenal. The port area is pleasant and has some reasonably priced pensiones. In the old town, *Hostal Levante* (☎ *96 579 15 91, Calle Maestro Alonso 5*) rents out basic singles/doubles for 2700/4500 ptas (5500 ptas with shower, 6500 ptas with bathroom).

Calpe (Calp)

Calpe, 22km north-east of Benidorm, is dominated by the Gibraltaresque **Peñon de Ilfach** (332m), a giant molar protruding from the sea. The climb towards the summit is popular – while you're up there, enjoy the seascape and decide which of Calpe's two long sandy beaches you want to laze on.

Camping Ifach and *Camping Levante*, both on Avenida de la Marina, are a short walk from Playa Levante. *Pensión Centrica* (☎ *96 583 55 28*), on Plaza de Ilfach, just off Avenida Gabriel Miró, has pleasant, simple rooms for 1500 ptas per person.

Benidorm

It's dead easy to be a snob about Benidorm, which long ago sold its birthright to cheap package tourism (nearly five million visitors annually), and indeed many of the horror tales are true. But beneath the jungle of concrete high-rises are 5km of white beaches and after dark there's a club scene to rival Ibiza's.

Almost everyone here is on a package deal and major hotels can be reasonable value out of high season, but there's no truly budget accommodation. *Hotel Nou Calpí* (☎/fax *96 681 29 96, Plaza Constitución 5*) has singles/doubles with full bathroom for 2700/5000 ptas (3000/6500 ptas July to October), including breakfast.

Andalucía

The stronghold of the Muslims for nearly eight centuries and the pride of the Christians for centuries thereafter, Andalucía is perhaps Spain's most exotic and colourful region. The home of flamenco, bullfighting

SPAIN

and some of the country's most brilliant fiestas, it's also peppered with reminders of the Muslim past – from treasured monuments like the Alhambra in Granada and the mezquita in Córdoba to the white villages clinging to its hillsides.

SEVILLE

Seville (Sevilla) is one of the most exciting cities in Spain, with an atmosphere both relaxed and festive, a rich history, some great monuments, beautiful parks and gardens, and a large student population. Seville is an expensive place, so it's worth planning your visit carefully. In high summer, the city is stiflingly hot. Seville is best during its spring festivals, though rooms then are expensive.

Sitting on the Río Guadalquivir, which is navigable to the Atlantic Ocean, Seville was once Spain's leading Muslim city. It reached its greatest heights later, during the 16th and 17th centuries, when it held a monopoly on Spanish trade with the Americas.

Information

The main tourist office (☎ 95 422 14 04) at Avenida de la Constitución 21 is open 9 am to 7 pm Monday to Friday, 10 am to 7 pm Saturday, 10 am to 2 pm Sunday. It's often extremely busy, so you might try the other tourist offices: Paseo de las Delicias 9 (☎ 95 423 44 65), open 8.30 am to 2.45 pm Monday to Friday; and Calle de Arjona 28 (☎ 95 450 56 00), open 8 am to 8.45 pm Monday to Friday, 8.30 am to 2.30 pm weekends.

Seville's many Internet and email services typically charge around 300 ptas an hour. One good-value place is Cibercafé Torredoro.net (☎ 95 450 28 09), Calle Núñez de Balboa 3A.

Librería Beta, Avenida de la Constitución 9 and 27, has guidebooks and novels in English. Tintorería Roma, Calle del Castelar 2C, will do a load of laundry for 1000 ptas.

Things to See & Do

Cathedral & Giralda Seville's immense cathedral, one of the biggest in the world, was built on the site of Muslim Seville's main mosque between 1401 and 1507. The adjoining tower, La Giralda, was the mosque's minaret and dates from the 12th century; climb up for great views. One

highlight of the cathedral's lavish interior is Christopher Columbus' supposed tomb inside the south door (no one's 100% sure that his remains didn't get mislaid somewhere in the Caribbean). The entrance to the cathedral and Giralda for non-group visitors at our last check was the Puerta del Perdón on Calle Alemanes. Opening hours are 11 am to 5 pm Monday to Saturday (700/200 ptas full/student) and 2 to 7 pm Sunday (free).

Alcázar Seville's alcázar, the residence of Muslim and Christian royalty for many centuries, was begun in AD 913 as a Muslim fortress. The highlights are the **Palacio de Don Pedro**, exquisitely decorated by Muslim artisans for a Castilian king, Pedro the Cruel, in the 1360s; and the large, immaculately tended **gardens**.

The alcázar is open 9.30 am to 7 pm Tuesday to Saturday (to 5 pm from October to March), 9.30 am to 5 pm Sunday and holidays. Entry is 700 ptas (free for students).

Museums & Bullring The **Archivo de Indias**, beside the cathedral, houses more than 40 million documents dating from 1492 through to the decolonisation of the Americas. There are changing displays of fascinating maps and documents. Opening hours are 10 am to 1 pm Monday to Friday (free).

The **Museo de Bellas Artes**, on Plaza del Museo, has an outstanding collection of Spanish art, focusing on Seville artists like Murillo and Zurbarán (250 ptas, free for EU citizens; closed Monday).

Seville's **Plaza de Toros** (Bullring), on Paseo de Cristóbal Colón, is one of the oldest and most famous in Spain, dating from 1758. Interesting 300-ptas tours are given in English and in Spanish, about every 20 minutes from 9.30 am to 2 pm and 3 to 6 or 7 pm daily (bullfight days: 10 am to 3 pm).

Walks & Parks If you're not staying in the **Barrio de Santa Cruz**, the old Jewish quarter immediately east of the cathedral and alcázar, make sure you take a stroll among its quaint streets and plant-filled plazas. South of the city centre, the large **Parque de María Luisa** is a pleasant place to get lost in, with its maze of paths, tall trees, fountains and shaded lawns. Another enjoyable walk is along the **riverbank**.

SPAIN

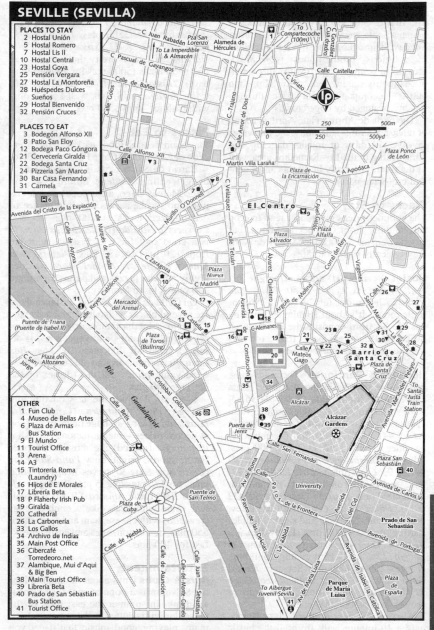

SEVILLE (SEVILLA)

PLACES TO STAY
2 Hostal Unión
5 Hostal Romero
7 Hostal Lis II
10 Hostal Central
23 Hostal Goya
25 Pensión Vergara
27 Hostal La Montoreña
28 Huéspedes Dulces Sueños
29 Hostal Bienvenido
32 Pensión Cruces

PLACES TO EAT
3 Bodegón Alfonso XII
8 Patio San Eloy
12 Bodega Paco Góngora
21 Cervecería Giralda
22 Bodega Santa Cruz
24 Pizzeria San Marco
30 Bar Casa Fernando
31 Carmela

OTHER
1 Fun Club
4 Museo de Bellas Artes
6 Plaza de Armas Bus Station
9 El Mundo
11 Tourist Office
13 Arena
14 A3
15 Tintorería Roma (Laundry)
16 Hijos de E Morales
17 Librería Beta
18 P Flaherty Irish Pub
19 Giralda
20 Cathedral
26 La Carbonería
33 Los Gallos
34 Archivo de Indias
35 Main Post Office
36 Cibercafé Torredeoro.net
37 Alambique, Mui d'Aqui & Big Ben
38 Main Tourist Office
39 Librería Beta
40 Prado de San Sebastián Bus Station
41 Tourist Office

Special Events

The first of Seville's two great festivals is Semana Santa, the week leading up to Easter Sunday. Throughout the week processions of religious brotherhoods (*cofradías*), dressed in penitents' garb with tall pointed hoods (eerily reminiscent of Ku Klux Klan outfits), accompany sacred images through the city, watched by huge crowds.

The Feria de Abril, in late April, is a kind of release after this solemnity: the festivities involve six days of music, dancing and horse riding in the Los Remedios area west of the river, plus daily bullfights and a general city-wide party.

Places to Stay

The summer prices given here tend to drop substantially from October to March, but around Semana Santa and the Feria de Abril they typically rise about 50%.

Hostel Seville's HI hostel, *Albergue Juvenil Sevilla* (☎ 95 461 31 50, *Calle Isaac Peral 2*) has room for 277 all in twin or triple rooms. It's about 10 minutes south by bus No 34 from opposite the main tourist office. Bed and breakfast is 1605/2140 ptas for under/over 26s most of the year.

Hostales & Pensiones There are some good-value options in the Barrio de Santa Cruz. *Hostal Bienvenido* (☎ 95 441 36 55, *Calle Archeros 14*) has singles/doubles from 1900/3700 ptas. *Hostal La Montoreña* (☎ 95 441 24 07, *Calle San Clemente 12*) provides clean rooms at 2000/3000 ptas. Friendly *Huéspedes Dulces Sueños* (☎ 95 441 93 93, *Calle Santa María La Blanca 21*) has nice, air-conditioned rooms for 2000/4000 ptas. *Pensión Cruces* (☎ 95 422 60 41, *Plaza de las Cruces 10*) has a few dorm beds at 1500 ptas and singles/doubles starting at 2000/4000 ptas. Pretty *Pensión Vergara* (☎ 95 421 56 68, *Calle Ximénez de Enciso 11*), in a 15th-century building, charges 2000/4000 ptas. Sociable *Hostal Goya* (☎ 95 421 11 70, *Calle Mateos Gago 31*) has nice clean rooms with bath or shower from 4300/6000 ptas.

Also try the area north of Plaza Nueva, only a 10-minute walk from all the hustle and bustle. Friendly *Hostal Unión* (☎ 95 422 92 94, *Calle Tarifa 4*) has clean rooms at 2000/3500 ptas (3000/4500 ptas with bath). Little *Hostal Romero* (☎ 95 421 13 53, *Calle Gravina 21*) offers clean, bare rooms for 2000/3500 ptas. *Hostal Lis II* (☎ 95 456 02 28, ✉ lisII@sol.com, *Calle Olavide 5*), in a pretty house, charges 2300/4500 ptas (5000 ptas for doubles with bath). *Hostal Central* (☎ 95 421 76 60, *Calle Zaragoza 18*) has well-kept rooms with bath for 4500/6500 ptas.

Places to Eat

The main central food market is the *Mercado del Arenal* on Calle Pastor y Landero.

Barrio de Santa Cruz is a good area for budget eating. *Bodega Santa Cruz*, on Calle Mateos Gago, a bar popular with visitors and locals, serves up a big choice of decent-sized tapas at 200 ptas or less. *Cervecería Giralda* (*Calle Mateos Gago 1*) is a good spot for breakfast; tostadas are from 120 ptas to 480 ptas. *Pizzeria San Marco* (*Calle Mesón del Moro 6*) does highly popular pizzas and pastas for around 850 ptas (closed Monday).

On Calle de Santa María La Blanca there are several places with outdoor tables: at the *Carmela* a media-ración of *tortilla Alta-Mira* (with potatoes and vegetables) is almost a meal for 700 ptas. The busy *Bar Casa Fernando*, around the corner, does good-value *platos del día* (dishes of the day) for 500 ptas.

West of Avenida de la Constitución, *Bodega Paco Góngora* (*Calle Padre Marchena 1*) serves a huge range of seafood at decent prices – media-raciones of fish *a la plancha* (grilled) are mostly 675 ptas. Farther north, bright, busy *Patio San Eloy* (*Calle San Eloy 9*) serves heaps of good tapas for 175 ptas to 215 ptas. *Bodegón Alfonso XII* (*Calle Alfonso XII 33*) is excellent value with deals like scrambled eggs (*revuelto*) with cheese, ham and spinach for 550 ptas, or a bacon, eggs and coffee breakfast for 400 ptas.

Entertainment

Bars & Clubs Until about midnight, Plaza del Salvador is a popular spot for an open-air drink. In summer the east bank of the Guadalquivir is dotted with temporary bars, many playing good music that'll get you dancing, and busy deep into the night.

There are some hugely popular bars just north of the cathedral, such as *P Flaherty*

Irish Pub, on Calle Alemanes (600 ptas for a pint of Guinness), and more around crowded Calle Adriano, west of Avenida de la Constitución. Busy music bars actually on Adriano include *A3* and *Arena*. There are quieter bodegas (traditional wine bars), most with tapas, on nearby Calle García de Vinuesa and Calle Dos de Mayo. A good one is *Hijos de E Morales (Calle García de Vinuesa 11)*. Plaza de la Alfalfa is another good area: there are at least five throbbing music bars north on Calle Pérez Galdós.

The *Fun Club (Alameda de Hércules 86)* is a small, busy dance warehouse, open Thursday to Sunday with live bands some nights. Several good pub-like bars line the same street farther north.

Across the river, *Alambique*, *Mui d'Aqui* and *Big Ben*, side by side on Calle de Betis, all play good music and attract an interesting mix of students and travellers.

Flamenco Seville is Spain's flamenco capital and you're most likely to catch spontaneous atmosphere (if unpredictable quality) in one of the bars staging regular flamenco nights with no entry charge. These include *La Carbonería (Calle Levíes 18)*, thronged nearly every night from about 11 pm, and *El Mundo (Calle Siete Revueltas 5)*, with flamenco at 11 pm Tuesday. Of the tourist-oriented venues, *Los Gallos (Plaza de Santa Cruz 11)* is a cut above the average, with two shows nightly (3500 ptas).

Spectator Sports

Seville's bullfights are among the best in the country. The season runs from Easter to October, with fights most Sundays about 6.30 pm, and every day during the Feria de Abril and the preceding week. The bullring is on Paseo de Cristóbal Colón. Tickets start around 1500 ptas or 3000 ptas depending who's fighting.

Getting There & Away

Air Seville airport (☎ 95 444 90 00) has a range of domestic and international flights. Air Europa fares to Barcelona start at 16,500 ptas.

Bus Buses going to Extremadura, Madrid, Portugal and Andalucía west of Seville leave from the Plaza de Armas bus station. Buses to eastern Spain and other parts of

Andalucía use the Prado de San Sebastián bus station.

Daily services include around 10 buses each to Córdoba (1225 ptas, 1¾ hours), Granada (2400 ptas, three hours), Málaga (1900 ptas, 2½ hours) and Madrid (2745 ptas, six hours).

For Portugal, there are five weekly direct buses to Lisbon (4800 ptas, eight hours), and daily buses to/from places on the Algarve such as Faro, Albufeira and Lagos.

Train Seville's Santa Justa train station is about 1.5km north-east of the city centre on Avenida de Kansas City. To/from Madrid there are 14 super-fast AVE trains each day (8400 ptas to 9900 ptas, 2½ hours); the few other trains cost 6600 ptas to 8300 ptas and take 3¼ to 3¾ hours. There are no overnight AVE trains.

Other daily trains include about 20 to Córdoba (1090 ptas to 2800 ptas, 45 minutes to 1¼ hours) and three or more each to Granada (2415 ptas to 2665 ptas, three hours), Málaga (2130 ptas, 2½ hours) and Barcelona (6300 ptas to 10,700 ptas, 11 to 13 hours). At least one Barcelona train is overnight. For Lisbon (7000 ptas, 16 hours) you must change at Cáceres.

Getting Around

The airport is about 7km from the city centre, off the N-IV Córdoba road. Airport buses (750 ptas) run up to 12 times daily – tourist offices have details.

Bus Nos C1 and C2, across the road from the Santa Justa train station, follow a circular route via Avenida de Carlos V, close to Prado de San Sebastián bus station and the city centre, and Plaza de Armas bus station. Bus No C4, south on Calle de Arjona from Plaza de Armas bus station, goes straight to the city centre.

CÓRDOBA

In Roman times Córdoba was the capital of Baetica province, covering most of Andalucía. Following the Muslim invasion in AD 711 it soon became the effective Muslim capital on the peninsula, a position it held until the Córdoban Caliphate broke up in the 11th century. Muslim Córdoba at its peak was the most splendid city in Europe, and its Mezquita (Mosque) is one of the most magnificent of all Islamic buildings.

From the 11th century Córdoba was over-shadowed by Seville and then, in the 13th century, both cities fell to the Christians in the Reconquista.

The legacies of these great civilisations make laid-back Córdoba one of the most interesting historical centres in Spain. It's at its best from mid-April to mid-June, when the weather's just right and Córdoba stages most of its annual festivals.

Orientation & Information

The old city, immediately north of the Río Guadalquivir, is a warren of narrow streets focused on the mezquita. Córdoba's main square is Plaza de las Tendillas, 500m north of the Mezquita.

The regional tourist office (☎ 957 47 12 35) faces the Mezquita at Calle de Torrijos 10. It's open from 10 am to 6, 7 or 8 pm (according to season) Monday to Saturday, 10 am to 2 pm Sunday and holidays. The municipal tourist office (☎ 957 20 05 22) is on Plaza de Judá Levi, a block west of the Mezquita.

Most banks and ATMs are around Plaza de las Tendillas. One ATM handier to the old city is on the corner of Calle San Fernando and Lucano.

Things to See

The inside of the famous **mezquita**, begun by Abd ar-Rahman I, emir of Córdoba, in AD 785, and enlarged by subsequent generations, is a mesmerising sequence of two-tier arches in stripes of red brick and white stone. From 1236 the mosque was used as a church and in the 16th century a cathedral was built right in its centre. Opening hours are 10 am to 7.30 pm Monday to Saturday (to 5.30 pm October to March), 3.30 to 7.30 pm Sunday and holidays (2 to 5.30 pm October to March). Entry is 800 ptas.

The Judería, medieval Córdoba's Jewish quarter, north-west of the Mezquita, is an intriguing maze of narrow streets and small plazas. Don't miss the beautiful little **Sinagoga** on Calle Judíos (open daily except Monday).

South-west of the Mezquita stands the **Alcázar de los Reyes Cristianos** (Castle of the Christian Monarchs), with large and lovely gardens. Entry is 300 ptas (free on Friday).

The **Museo Arqueólogico**, Plaza de Jerónimo Páez 7, is also worth a visit (250

ptas, free for EU citizens). South of the river, across the **Puente Romano**, is the **Torre de la Calahorra**, housing a museum on the intellectual achievements of Islamic Córdoba, with excellent models of the mezquita and Granada's Alhambra (open daily, 500 ptas).

Places to Stay

Córdoba's excellent youth hostel, *Albergue Juvenil Córdoba* (☎ 957 29 01 66), is perfectly positioned on Plaza de Judá Leví. Most of the year, bed and breakfast is 1605/2140 ptas for under/over 26s.

Huéspedes Martínez Rücker (☎ 957 47 25 62, ✉ hmrucker@alcavia.net, Calle Martínez Rücker 14), a stone's throw from the mezquita, is clean and friendly, with singles/doubles for 2000/3500 ptas. *Hostal Rey Heredia* (☎ 957 47 41 82, Calle Rey Heredia 26) has rooms around a plant-filled patio from 1500/3000 ptas. Just north of the Mezquita, the charming *Hostal Séneca* (☎/fax 957 47 32 34, Calle Conde y Luque 7) has rooms for 2550/4700 ptas, or with attached bath for 4750/5900 ptas, including breakfast. It's advisable to phone ahead.

There are some good hostales to the east, further from the tourist masses. *Hostal La Fuente* (☎ 957 48 78 27, Calle San Fernando 51) provides compact singles at 3500 ptas and doubles at 6000 ptas, all with bath and air-con, and serves a decent breakfast. *Hostal Los Arcos* (☎ 957 48 56 43, Calle Romero Barros 14) has singles/doubles around a pretty patio for 2500/4000 ptas, and doubles with bath for 5000 ptas. *Hostal Maestre* (☎ 957 47 24 10), next door, has spacious rooms with bath at 3000/5000 ptas. Old-fashioned *Hostal El Portillo* (☎ 957 47 20 91, Calle Cabezas 2) has seven rooms at 1500/3000 ptas.

Places to Eat

A *food market* on Plaza de la Corredera opens Monday to Saturday.

Tiny *Bar Santos* (Calle Magistral González Francés 3) is a good stop opposite the mezquita for *bocadillos* (200 ptas to 300 ptas) and *raciones* (500 ptas). *Café Bar Judá Levi*, on Plaza Judá Levi, serves *platos combinados* from 700 ptas.

To the east, *Taberna Salinas* (Calle Tundidores 3) is a lively tavern serving good, inexpensive Córdoban fare. Raciones cost

SPAIN

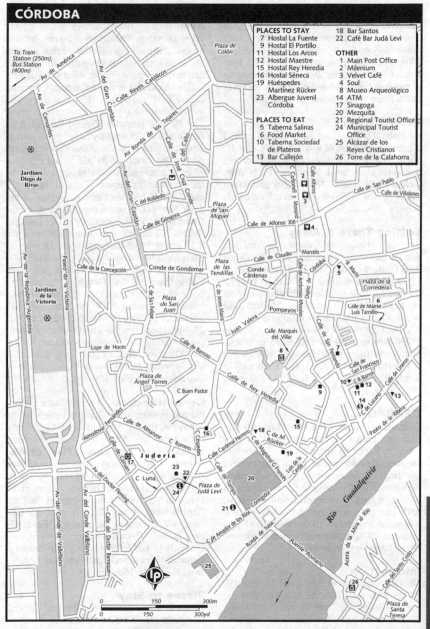

CÓRDOBA

PLACES TO STAY
7 Hostal La Fuente
9 Hostal El Portillo
11 Hostal Los Arcos
12 Hostal Maestre
15 Hostal Rey Heredia
16 Hostal Séneca
19 Huéspedes
    Martínez Rücker
23 Albergue Juvenil
    Córdoba

PLACES TO EAT
5 Taberna Salinas
6 Food Market
10 Taberna Sociedad
    de Plateros
13 Bar Callejón

18 Bar Santos
22 Café Bar Judá Levi

OTHER
1 Main Post Office
2 Milenium
3 Velvet Café
4 Soul
8 Museo Arqueológico
14 ATM
17 Sinagoga
20 Mezquita
21 Regional Tourist Office
24 Municipal Tourist
    Office
25 Alcázar de los
    Reyes Cristianos
26 Torre de la Calahorra

euro currency converter 100 ptas = €0.60

SPAIN

around 700 ptas to 800 ptas (closed Sunday). *Taberna Sociedad de Plateros (Calle San Francisco 6)* is another popular tavern with reasonably priced tapas and raciones (closed Monday). On pedestrian Calle Enrique Romero de Torres, *Bar Callejón* serves platos combinados for 500 ptas to 900 ptas and a three-course *menú* for 1200 ptas.

Entertainment
Córdoba's livelier bars are scattered around the north and west of town. *Soul (Calle Alfonso XIII 3)* attracts a studenty/arty crowd and stays open until 3 am nightly. Nearby *Velvet Café (Calle Alfaros 29)* and *Milenium (Calle Alfaros 33)* have live bands some nights.

Getting There & Away
The train station, on Avenida de América, and the bus station, behind it on Plaza de las Tres Culturas, are about 1km north-west of Plaza de las Tendillas. At least 10 buses a day run to/from Seville (1225 ptas) and five or more to/from Granada, Madrid and Málaga (all 1500 ptas to 1600 ptas).

About 20 trains a day run to/from Seville (1050 ptas to 2700 ptas, 45 to 75 minutes). Options to/from Madrid range from several AVEs (6100 ptas to 7200 ptas, 1¾ hours) to a middle-of-the-night Estrella (3700 ptas, 6¼ hours).

GRANADA
Granada, capital of the last Muslim kingdom in Spain from the 13th to 15th centuries, is home to Spain's greatest Muslim monument, one of the most magnificent buildings on the continent – the Alhambra. South-east of the city, the Sierra Nevada mountain range (mainland Spain's highest, with Europe's most southerly ski slopes) and the Alpujarras valleys, with their picturesque villages, are well worth exploring if you have time to spare.

Information
Granada's provincial tourist office (☎ 958 22 66 88), on Plaza de Mariana Pineda, opens 9.30 am to 7 pm Monday to Friday, 10 am to 2 pm Saturday. The regional tourist office, on Calle de Mariana Pineda, opens the same hours but is busier.

Net, Calle Santa Escolástica 13, has Internet access for 200 ptas an hour; open daily.

Things to See
Alhambra The Alhambra is one of the greatest accomplishments of Islamic art and architecture. None of the reams written about its fortress, palace, patios and gardens can really prepare you for what you will see.

The **Alcazaba** is the Alhambra's fortress, dating from the 11th to 13th centuries. The views from the tops of its towers are great. The **Palacio Nazaries** (Nasrid Palace), built for Granada's Nasrid dynasty in the 13th to 15th centuries, is the Alhambra's centrepiece. The beauty of its patios and intricacy of its stucco and woodwork, epitomised by the Patio de los Leones (Patio of the Lions) and Sala de las Dos Hermanas (Hall of the Two Sisters), is stunning. Don't miss the **Generalife**, the soul-soothing palace gardens.

The Alhambra and Generalife are open 8.30 am to 8 pm daily (to 6 pm October to March); admission is 1000 ptas. The 8000 tickets for each day can sell out fast, especially from May to October, but you can book ahead, for an extra 125 ptas, at any branch of Banco BBV (in many Spanish cities), or by Visa or MasterCard on ☎ 902-22 44 60 between 9 am and 6 pm. Any tickets available for same-day visits are sold at the Alhambra ticket office and, 9 am to 2 pm Monday to Friday, at Banco BBV on Plaza Isabel la Católica.

Other Attractions It's a pleasure to ramble around the steep, narrow streets of the **Albayzín**, the old Muslim district across the river from the Alhambra (not too late at night), or the area around **Plaza de Bib-Rambla**. On your way, stop by the **Museo Arqueológico** (Archaeological Museum) and **El Bañuelo** (Arab Baths), on Carrera del Darro at the foot of the Albayzín, and the **Capilla Real** (Royal Chapel), on Calle Oficios, which houses the tombs of Fernando and Isabel, the Christian conquerors of Granada in 1492. Next door to the chapel is Granada's **catedral**, part of which dates from the early 16th century.

Places to Stay
Granada's youth hostel, *Albergue Juvenil Granada (☎ 958 27 26 38, Calle Ramón y Cajal 2)* is 1.7km west of the centre and a 600m walk south-west of the train station. Most of the year, bed and breakfast is 1605/2140 ptas for under/over 26s.

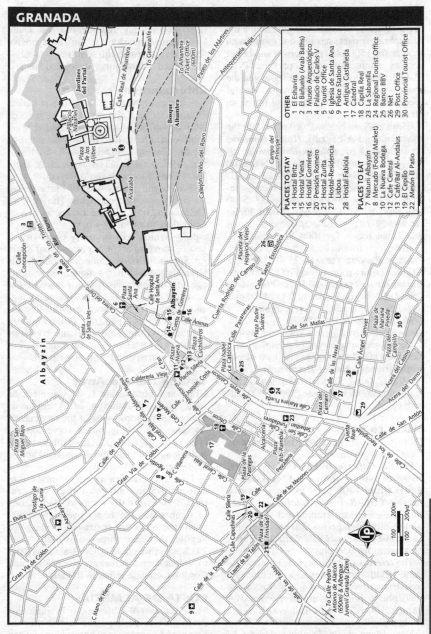

GRANADA

OTHER
1 El Eshavira
2 El Bañuelo (Arab Baths)
3 Museo Arqueológico
4 Palacio de Carlos V
5 Tourist Office
6 Iglesia de Santa Ana
9 Police Station
11 Antigua Castañeda
17 Catedral
18 Capilla Real
23 La Sabanilla
24 Regional Tourist Office
25 Banco BBV
26 Net
29 Post Office
30 Provincial Tourist Office

PLACES TO STAY
14 Hostal Britz
15 Hostal Viena
16 Hostal Gomérez
20 Pensión Romero
21 Hostal Zurita
27 Hostal-Residencia Lisboa
28 Hostal Fabiola

PLACES TO EAT
7 Naturli Albayzín
8 Mercado (Food Market)
10 La Nueva Bodega
12 Cafe Central
13 Café/Bar Al-Andalus
19 El Cepillo
22 Mesón El Patio

Posada Doña Lupe (☎ 958 22 14 73, Avenida del Generalife s/n), just above the Alhambra car park, has interior rooms with shower for 1500 ptas per person and better doubles ranging up to 7500 ptas plus IVA. Management does not like to show you the rooms first, but in our experience they're adequately clean. The Alhambra bus from Plaza Nueva stops nearby.

Close to Plaza Nueva (well placed for the Alhambra and Albayzín), *Hostal Gomérez (☎ 958 22 44 37, Cuesta de Gomérez 10)* has well-kept singles/doubles at 1600/2700 ptas. *Hostal Britz (☎/fax 958 22 36 52, Cuesta de Gomérez 1)* provides clean, adequate rooms for 2340/3900 ptas (4000/5400 ptas with bath). Close by, *Hostal Viena (☎ 958 22 18 59, Calle Hospital de Santa Ana 2)* has rooms for 3000/4000 ptas.

Also try around Plaza de la Trinidad. *Pensión Romero (☎ 958 26 60 79, Calle Sillería 1)* has rooms for 1700/2900 ptas. *Hostal Zurita (☎ 958 27 50 20, Plaza de la Trinidad 7)* is good value at 2000/4000 ptas (5000 ptas for doubles with bathroom).

Hostal Fabiola (☎ 958 22 35 72, Calle de Ángel Ganivet 5) is a good, family-run place where singles/doubles/triples with bath are 1800/4000/5000 ptas. Two blocks north, friendly *Hostal-Residencia Lisboa (☎ 958 22 14 13, Plaza del Carmen 27)* has rooms for 2600/3900 ptas (3900/5600 ptas with bath).

Places to Eat

There's a large, covered *food market* on Calle San Agustín.

Popular *Cafe Central*, on Calle de Elvira, offers everything from good breakfasts to *menús* (from 1100 ptas) to fancy coffees. Nearby *Café/Bar Al-Andalus* on Plaza Nueva does cheap Arabic food – tasty felafel in pitta bread costs 300 ptas. Reliable *La Nueva Bodega (Calle Cetti Meriém 3)* has a *menú* for 950 ptas.

The *teterías* (Arabic-style tea houses) on Calle Calderería Nueva, a picturesque pedestrian street west of Plaza Nueva, are atmospheric but they are also expensive. *Naturii Albayzín (Calle Calderería Nueva 10)* is a good vegetarian restaurant.

Near Plaza de la Trinidad, *Mesón El Patio (Calle de los Mesones 50)* has a pleasant patio and serves breakfast of coffee, juice, bread, eggs and bacon for 500 ptas

(from 10 am) plus mid-priced Spanish food later in the day. *El Cepillo*, on Calle Pescadería, nearby, is an inexpensive seafood restaurant with *menús* at 800 ptas – it's packed at lunchtime, and closed Sunday.

Entertainment

The highest concentration of music bars is on and around Calle de Pedro Antonio de Alarcón – from Plaza de la Trinidad, walk south on Calle de las Tablas. Also interesting are Carrera del Darro and its continuation, Paseo de los Tristes, leading from Plaza Nueva towards the Albayzín.

Bars in the streets west of Plaza Nueva are lively on weekend nights. The *Antigua Castañeda*, on Calle de Elvira, is one of Granada's most famous bars, serving great tapas – which will probably come free if you're standing at the bar after about 8 pm. *La Sabanilla (Calle San Sebastían 14)* is Granada's oldest bar – though showing its age, it's worth a visit. Don't miss *El Eshavira (Postigo de la Cuna 2)*, a roomy jazz and flamenco club down a dark alley off Calle Azacayas (open from 10 pm nightly).

In the evening there are flamenco shows in the 'gypsy caves' at Sacromonte, but they are touristy and a bit of a rip-off.

Getting There & Away

Granada's bus station is on Carretera de Jáen, the continuation of Avenida de Madrid, 3km north-west of the city centre. At least nine daily buses serve Madrid (1950 ptas, five to six hours); others run to Barcelona, Valencia and destinations across Andalucía.

The train station is on Avenida Andaluces, 1.5km south-west of the city centre. Of the two daily trains to Madrid, one of them takes 9½ hours overnight (3600 ptas), the other six hours (3800 ptas). To Seville, there are three trains daily (from 2415 ptas, three hours). One train runs daily to Valencia and Barcelona. For Málaga and Córdoba, change trains in Bobadilla.

COSTA DE ALMERÍA

The coast east of Almería city in south-east Andalucía is perhaps the last section of Spain's Mediterranean shore where you can have a beach to yourself (not in high summer, admittedly). This is Spain's sunniest region, so even in late March it can be warm

SPAIN

enough to take in some rays and try out your new swimsuit.

The most useful tourist offices are in Almería (☎ 950 62 11 17), San José (☎ 950 38 02 99) and Mojácar (☎ 950 47 51 62).

Things to See & Do
The **Alcazaba**, an enormous, 10th-century Muslim fortress, is well worth a visit in Almería city.

The best thing about the region is the wonderful coastline and semidesert scenery of the **Cabo de Gata** promontory. All along the 50km coast from El Cabo de Gata village to Agua Amarga, some of the most beautiful and empty beaches on the Mediterranean alternate with precipitous cliffs and scattered villages. The main village is laid-back **San José**, from where you can walk or drive to some excellent beaches – try **Playa de los Genoveses** or **Playa de Mónsul**, both within 7km south-west.

Mojácar, 30km north of Agua Amarga, is a white town of Muslim origin perched on a hill 2km from the coast, with a resort strip below. The old town is a pretty place and it's not hard to spend some time here.

Places to Stay
In the centre of Almería *Hostal Universal* (☎ *950 23 55 57, Puerta de Purchena 3*) has simple but sizable singles/doubles for 2000/4000 ptas. Near the bus and train stations, *Hostal Americano* (☎ *950 28 10 15, Avenida de la Estación 6*) is a bit better, with well-kept rooms from 2850/5540 ptas to 3915/6410 ptas.

San José's friendly non-HI *Albergue Juvenil* (☎ *950 38 03 53, Calle Montemar s/n*) opens from April to September, with bunks for 1300 ptas. On Calle Correo in San José's centre, *Hostal Bahía* (☎ *950 38 03 07*) has attractive singles/doubles with bathroom for 5000/7500 ptas.

In Mojácar the cheaper places are mostly up in the old town. *Pensión Casa Justa* (☎ *950 47 83 72, Calle Morote 7*) is reasonable, with rooms starting at 2500/5000 ptas. *Hostal La Esquinica* (☎ *950 47 50 09, Calle Cano 1*) charges 2500/4500 ptas.

Getting There & Away
Almería is accessible by bus and train from Madrid, Granada and Seville, and by bus only from Málaga, Valencia and Barcelona.

Buses also run from Almería to San José daily except non-summer Sundays. Mojácar can be reached by bus from Almeriá, Granada, Málaga and Madrid and, with a change at Vera, 16km north of Mojácar, from Alicante, Valencia and Barcelona.

MÁLAGA
The large port city of Málaga has a bustling street life, a thumping nightlife in the narrow streets behind Plaza de la Constitución, a 16th-century **catedral**, and a Muslim palace/fortress, the **Alcazaba**, from which the walls of the Muslim Castillo de Gibralfaro climb to the top of the hill dominating the city. A major new museum devoted to the work of Málaga-born artist Pablo Picasso is due to open in Málaga in 2002. The helpful regional tourist office (☎ 95 221 34 45), in the centre at Pasaje Chinitas 4, opens daily.

The Costa del Sol, a string of tightly packed resorts running south-west from Málaga towards Gibraltar, is of little attraction unless you're more interested in foreign package tourists than in Spain.

Places to Stay & Eat
Málaga's friendly, central *Pensión Córdoba* (☎ *95 221 44 69, Calle Bolsa 9*) has singles/doubles at 1500/3000 ptas. *Hostal Derby* (☎ *95 222 13 01, Calle San Juan de Dios 1*) has spacious rooms with bath for 4500/6000 ptas.

Café Central, on Plaza de la Constitución, is a noisy local favourite: food prices are reasonable, with plenty of choice. A short walk north-east, *La Posada (Calle Granada 33)* is great for tapas and raciones of *carnes a la brasa* (grilled meats) – 1600 ptas for lamb chops.

Getting There & Away
Málaga airport has a good range of domestic as well as international flights. Trains and buses run every half-hour from the airport to the city centre. The city is also linked by train and bus to all major Spanish centres. The bus and train stations are round the corner from each other, 1km west of the city centre.

RONDA
Ronda, one of the prettiest towns in Andalucía, is a world apart from the nearby Costa del Sol. Straddling the savagely deep

El Tajo gorge, the town stands at the heart of attractive hill country that's dotted with whitewashed villages. Ronda is a pleasure to wander around, but during the day it's packed with day-trippers up from the coast.

The regional tourist office (☎ 95 287 12 72) is at Plaza de España 1.

Things to See & Do

The 18th-century **Puente Nuevo** (New Bridge), an amazing feat of engineering, crosses the gorge to the originally Muslim old town (La Ciudad). At the Casa del Rey Moro, Calle Santo Domingo 17, you can climb down **La Mina**, a Muslim-era stairway cut inside the rock right to the bottom of the gorge (open daily, 600 ptas). Also in La Ciudad, don't miss: **Iglesia de Santa María la Mayor**, a church whose tower was once the minaret of a mosque; the **Museo del Bandolero**, dedicated to the banditry for which Andalucía was once renowned; or the beautiful **Baños Arabes** (Arab Baths), open Wednesday to Sunday.

Ronda's **Plaza de Toros** (1785), in the newer part of town north of the gorge, is considered the home of bullfighting; inside is the small but fascinating **Museo Taurino** (400 ptas).

Places to Stay & Eat

These necessities are found in the newer part of town on the north side of the gorge. *Pensión La Purísima* (☎ 95 287 10 50, Calle Sevilla 10) has nine reasonable rooms at 2000/3000 ptas. *Hotel Morales* (☎/fax 95 287 15 38, Calle Sevilla 51) has pleasant rooms with bath for 3500/6000 ptas and is full of information on exploring the area.

El Molino, on Plaza del Socorro, is popular for pizzas, pasta and platos combinados from 550 ptas to 775 ptas. *Restaurante Hermanos Macías (Calle Pedro Romero 3)*, nearby, is a reliable eatery with main dishes from 800 ptas to 1600 ptas.

Getting There & Away

There are several daily buses to/from Seville (1285 ptas, 2½ hours) and Málaga (1075 ptas, two hours). The bus station is on Plaza de Concepción García Redondo.

A few direct trains go to/from Granada (1775 ptas, 2¼ hours), Málaga (1175 ptas, two hours), Algeciras, Córdoba and Madrid. Going to/from Seville, change at

Bobadilla or Antequera. The station is on Avenida de Andalucía.

ALGECIRAS

This unattractive town west of Gibraltar is the major port linking Spain with Morocco. Keep your wits about you and ignore offers from the legions of money-changers, drug-pushers and ticket-hawkers. The tourist office (☎ 956 57 26 36), which is on Calle Juan de la Cierva near the ferry port, opens 9 am to 2 pm Monday to Friday.

There's loads of budget accommodation in the streets behind the waterfront. *Hostal España (☎ 956 66 82 62, Calle José Santacana 4)* has large, clean rooms at 1200 ptas per person but it's right by the market which gets noisy early.

Getting There & Away

Bus The Comes line, on Calle San Bernardo, 400m inland from the port, runs to/from La Línea (for Gibraltar), Seville and Madrid. Portillo, Avenida Virgen del Carmen 15 (200m north of the port) has buses that go to/from Málaga and Granada. Bacoma, inside the port, runs to/from Valencia, Barcelona and France.

Train Direct trains run to/from Ronda, Granada and Madrid. Change at Bobadilla for Seville, Córdoba and Málaga.

Boat Trasmediterránea (☎ 902-45 46 45), EuroFerrys (☎ 956 65 11 78) and other companies operate at least 20 daily ferries to/from Tangier in Morocco and 40 or more to/from Ceuta, the Spanish enclave on the Moroccan coast. Buy your ticket in the port or at agencies on Avenida de la Marina – prices are the same. To Tangier, adults pay 3500 ptas one-way by ferry (2½ hours), or 4440 ptas by hydrofoil (one hour). To Ceuta, it's 1945 ptas by ferry (90 minutes) or 3095 ptas by 'fast ferry' (40 minutes). Buquebus ferry service (☎ 902-41 42 42) crosses to Ceuta in 30 to 35 minutes for 2945 ptas.

TARIFA

The town of Tarifa perches at continental Europe's most southerly point, 21km southwest of Algeciras. The strong winds here make Tarifa one of Europe's top windsurfing spots, with an international scene, and it's a nice place to hang out for a couple of days.

SPAIN

Enjoy exploring the winding old streets and visit the castle, **Castillo de Guzmán**, dating from the 10th century. A 10km Atlantic beach beloved of windsurfers, **Playa de los Lances**, stretches north-west from the town.

Pensión Correo (☎ 956 68 02 06, *Calle Coronel Moscardó 9*) has attractive rooms from 2000 ptas per person. *Pensión África* (☎ 956 68 02 20, *Calle María Antonia Toledo 12*) provides bright, comfy rooms for 2500/4000 ptas (3500/5000 ptas with private bath). There are plenty of eating options on and near the central Calle Sancho IV El Bravo.

The Comes bus line links Tarifa with Algeciras, La Línea, Seville and Málaga.

Gibraltar

The British colony of Gibraltar occupies a huge lump of limestone – 5km long and 1km wide – near the mouth of the Mediterranean Sea. It's an interesting port of call if you're in the region.

Gibraltar is internally self-governing and an overwhelming majority of Gibraltarians – many of whom are of Genoese or Jewish ancestry – want to retain British sovereignty. Spain has offered Gibraltar autonomous-region status within Spain, but Britain and Gibraltar reject any compromise over sovereignty.

Information

Citizens of EU countries, the USA, Canada, Australia and New Zealand do not require visas to enter Gibraltar; however, anyone who needs a visa for Spain should have at least a double-entry Spanish visa if they intend to return to Spain from Gibraltar.

Gibraltar has a helpful tourist office at the border; the main office (☎ 45000) is in Duke of Kent House, Cathedral Square (open Monday to Friday). There's another branch (☎ 74982) at The Piazza on Main St, open daily.

The currency is the Gibraltar pound or pound sterling. You can use pesetas but conversion rates aren't in your favour. Exchange rates for buying pesetas are, however, a bit better than in Spain. Change any unspent Gibraltar pounds before you leave.

Gibraltar's country code is ☎ 350, but the code from Spain is ☎ 9567. To phone

Spain from Gibraltar, simply dial the nine-digit Spanish number.

Gibraltar has lots of British shops, including a Safeway supermarket in the Europort area.

Things to See & Do

Central Gibraltar is nothing special, but the **Gibraltar Museum**, on Bomb House Lane, has an interesting historical, architectural and military collection and includes an old Muslim bathhouse (Monday to Saturday, £2).

The **Upper Rock Nature Reserve**, covering most of the upper rock, has spectacular views and several interesting spots to visit. Entry is £5 and includes all the sights. Cable-car tickets (see Getting Around) include entry to the reserve, the Apes' Den and St Michael's Cave.

The rock's most famous inhabitants are its colony of **Barbary macaques**, the only wild primates in Europe. Some of these hang around the **Apes' Den** near the middle cable-car station, others can often be seen at the top station or Great Siege Tunnels.

From the top cable-car station, you can see Morocco in decent weather. **St Michael's Cave**, a 20-minute downhill walk south, is a big natural grotto renowned for its stalagmites and stalactites.

The **Great Siege Tunnels**, a 30-minute walk north (mostly downhill), were hewn from the rock by the British during a long Spanish siege from 1779 to 1783 to provide gun emplacements.

Places to Stay

The *Emile Youth Hostel* (☎ 51106, *Montagu Bastion, Line Wall Rd*) has dorm places for £12 including continental breakfast. The ramshackle *Toc H Hostel* (☎ 73431), tucked into the city walls at the south end of Line Wall Rd, has beds at £6 a night and cold showers.

The *Queen's Hotel* (☎ 74000, 1 Boyd St) has singles/doubles at £20/30 (£36/40 with private bath or shower). Reduced rates of £14/20 and £16/24 are offered for students and young travellers. All prices include English breakfast.

Places to Eat

Most of the many pubs do British pub meals. The *Cannon Bar* (27 Cannon Lane) has some of the best fish and chips in town,

SPAIN

with big portions for £4.75. *Three Roses Bar (60 Governor's St)* does a big all-day breakfast for £3.50.

For a restaurant meal, the chic *House of Sacarello (57 Irish Town)* has excellent daily specials for around £6.

Getting There & Away

There are no regular buses to Gibraltar, but the bus station in La Línea, Spain, is only a five-minute walk from the border.

The passenger catamaran *Mons Calpe II* sails daily except Monday and Saturday to/from Tangier (1¼ hours) for £18/33 one-way/return. There are normally two weekly vehicle ferries too. You can buy tickets for the catamaran at Bland Travel (☎ 77012), 81 Irish Town, and for the ferry at Tourafrica (☎ 77666), ICC Building, Main St.

Getting Around

Bus Nos 3 and 9 run direct from the border into town. On Sunday there are no buses – but the 1.5km walk is interesting, as it crosses the airport runway.

Weather permitting, Gibraltar's cable car leaves its lower station on Red Sands Rd every few minutes from 9.30 am to 5.15 pm, Monday to Saturday. One-way/return fares are £3.65/4.90. For the Apes' Den, disembark at the middle station.

Extremadura

Extremadura, a sparsely populated tableland bordering Portugal, is far enough off the beaten tourist trails to give you a genuine sense of exploration. Trujillo, Cáceres and Mérida are the three not-to-be-missed old towns here. Try to avoid coming from June to August, when Extremadura is uncomfortably hot.

TRUJILLO

Trujillo is blessed with the broad and fine Plaza Mayor, from which its remarkably well-preserved old town, packed with aged buildings, rises. If you approach from Plasencia you might imagine that you've fallen through a time warp into the 16th century.

With just 9000 people, Trujillo can't be much bigger now than in 1529, when its most famous son, Francisco Pizarro, set off with his three brothers for an expedition that culminated in the bloody conquest of the Inca empire.

The tourist office (☎ 927 32 26 77) is on Plaza Mayor.

Things to See

On Plaza Mayor's south side, the **Palacio de la Conquista** (closed to visitors) sports the carved images of Francisco Pizarro and his Inca princess bride Inés Yupanqui. Their daughter Francisca lived in this house with her husband Hernando, the only Pizarro brother to return alive to Spain. Two noble mansions that you *can* visit are the 16th-century **Palacio de los Duques de San Carlos**, also on the Plaza Mayor (100 ptas), and the **Palacio de Orellana-Pizarro**, which is through the alley on the plaza's southwest corner (free).

Up the hill, the **Iglesia de Santa María la Mayor** is an interesting hotchpotch of 13th- to 16th-century styles, with some fine paintings by Fernando Gallego of the Flemish school. Higher up, the **Casa-Museo de Pizarro** has informative displays (in Spanish) on the lives and adventures of the Pizarro family. At the top of the hill, Trujillo's **castillo** is an impressive though empty structure, primarily of Moorish origin (200 ptas for each).

Places to Stay & Eat

Camas Boni (☎ 927 32 16 04, Calle Domingo de Ramos 7) is small with well-kept rooms from 2000/3000 ptas, and doubles with bath for 4500 ptas. *Casa Roque (☎ 927 32 23 13, Calle Domingo de Ramos 30)* has singles at 3000 ptas and doubles with bath at 3500 ptas.

Don't miss *Restaurante La Troya*, on Plaza Mayor, if you're a meat-eater. The *menú* costs 1990 ptas, but it will save you from eating much else for the next few days. La Troya also serves good tapas. *Cafetería Nuria*, on Plaza Mayor, has various dishes from 550 ptas upwards.

Getting There & Away

The bus station is 500m south of Plaza Mayor, on Carretera de Mérida. At least six daily buses run to/from Cáceres (390 ptas, 45 minutes) and Madrid (2350 ptas, 2½ to four hours), and four or more go to/from Mérida (1020 ptas, 1¼ hours).

SPAIN

CÁCERES

Cáceres is larger than Trujillo with an even bigger old town, built in the 15th and 16th centuries, so perfectly preserved that it can seem lifeless at times. The old town is worth two visits –one by day to look around and one by night to soak up the atmosphere of accumulated ages.

The tourist office (☎ 927 24 63 47) is on Plaza Mayor. Ciberjust, on Calle Diego Maria Crehuet 7, is the best Internet cafe in town.

Things to See

The **old town** is surrounded by walls and towers built by the Almohads in the 12th century. Cáceres' 15th-century cathedral, the **Iglesia de Santa María**, is just off Plaza Mayor. Many of the old town's churches and imposing medieval mansions can only be admired from outside, but you *can* enter the interesting **Museo de Cáceres** on Plaza de Veletas (closed Monday, 200 ptas). It's housed in a 16th-century mansion built over a 12th-century Moorish *aljibe* (cistern), the museum's prize exhibit. Also worth a look is the **Casa-Museo Árabe Yussuf Al-Borch**, Cuesta del Marqués 4, a private house decked out with Islamic trappings to capture the feel of Moorish times (200 ptas).

Places to Stay

Pensión Márquez (☎ 927 24 49 60, Calle de Gabriel y Galán 2), off the bottom end of Plaza Mayor, is a family-run place with clean rooms for 1500/3000 ptas. *Hostal Castilla (☎ 927 24 44 04, Calle Ríos Verdes 3)*, one block from the plaza, has good rooms for 2000/4000 ptas.

Places to Eat

Cafetería El Puchero (Plaza Mayor 33) is a popular hang-out with a huge variety of food options, from bocadillos (400 ptas) and raciones to solid platos combinados (675 ptas to 900 ptas). *Cafetería El Pato*, a block down the arcade, has excellent coffee and an upstairs restaurant with three-course *menús*, including wine, for 1200 ptas to 2000 ptas.

Getting There & Away

Daily services to Trujillo (450 ptas), Madrid (2420 ptas, 3½ hours), Mérida (675 ptas, 1¼ hours), Salamanca (1705 ptas, three to four hours), Zafra and Sevilla (2090 ptas, four hours) and Badajoz leave from the bus station.

Three to five trains a day run to/from Madrid (from 2385 ptas, 3½ to five hours) and Mérida (one hour). Another two or three run to/from Plasencia (1¼ hours), Badajoz (two hours) and Barcelona. The sole daily train to Lisbon (4475 ptas, six hours) leaves in the middle of the night.

MÉRIDA

Once the biggest city in Roman Spain, Mérida is home to more Roman ruins than anywhere else in the country. A joint ticket (800/400 ptas full/concession) gives entry to the **Teatro Romano**, **Anfiteatro**, the **Casa del Anfiteatro**, the **Casa Romana del Mithraeo** the **Alcazaba**, the **Iglesia de Santa Eulalia** and the **Arqueologica de Moreria**. Entry to the Teatro Romano and Anfiteatro alone is 600 ptas. The theatre was built in 15 BC and the gladiators' ring, or Anfiteatro, followed seven years later. Combined they could hold some 20,000 spectators.

The tourist office (☎ 924 31 53 53) is at Avenida de José Álvarez Saenz de Buruaga, by the gates to the Roman theatre. Ware Nostrum is a funky Internet cafe on Calle del Baños.

Places to Stay & Eat

Pensión El Arco (☎ 924 31 83 21, Calle de Miguel de Cervantes 16) is great value and deservedly popular with backpackers. Spotless rooms with shared bath cost 1800/3500 ptas. *Hostal Bueno (☎ 924 30 29 77, Calle Calvario 9)* is also good, with rooms priced at 2500/4500 ptas.

Casa Benito, on Calle de San Francisco, is an old-style wood-panelled bar and restaurant, with local fare at reasonable prices. Two good eateries can be found on Calle de Felix Valverde Lillo: *Restaurante El Briz*, at No 5, which does a great *montado de lomo* (pork loin sandwich) for 350 ptas, and *Restaurante Antillano* at No 15.

Getting There & Away

Seven daily buses run to Badajoz (680 ptas), Sevilla (1550 ptas to 1590 ptas) and Madrid (from 2755 ptas), and at least four run to Cáceres (675 ptas) and Trujillo (820 ptas).

At least four trains a day run to Badajoz, and two or more go to Cáceres, Ciudad Real and Madrid (2945 ptas, five to six hours).

SPAIN

Galicia, Asturias & Cantabria

Galicia has been spared the mass tourism that has reached many other parts of Spain. Its often wild coast is indented with a series of majestic inlets – the Rías Altas and Rías Bajas – which hide some of Spain's prettiest and least known beaches. Inland are rolling green hills dotted with picturesque farmhouses. In winter, Galicia can be freezing, but in summer it has one of the most agreeable climates in Europe – though you must expect some rain.

Asturias and Cantabria, east of Galicia, are equally green and beautiful, especially around the Picos de Europa mountains.

SANTIAGO DE COMPOSTELA

This beautiful small city marks the end of the Camino de Santiago, a name given to several major medieval pilgrim routes from as far away as France, still followed by plenty of the faithful and/or energetic today. Thanks to its university, Santiago is a lively city almost any time, but is most festive around 25 July during the Feast of Santiago (St James).

Santiago's regional tourist office (☎ 981 58 40 81), at Rúa do Vilar 43, opens daily.

Things to See & Do

The goal of the Camino de Santiago is the **catedral** on magnificent **Praza do Obradoiro**. Under the main altar lies the supposed tomb of Santiago Apóstol (St James the Apostle). It's believed the saint's remains were buried here in the 1st century AD and rediscovered in 813, after which he grew into the patron saint of the Christian Reconquista. The cathedral is a magnificent Romanesque creation of the 11th to 13th centuries; its masterpiece is the Pórtico de la Gloria inside the west facade.

Santiago's compact old town is a work of art, and a walk around the cathedral leads through inviting squares. It's also good to stroll in the beautifully landscaped park, **Carballeira de Santa Susana**, south-west of the cathedral.

Places to Stay & Eat

Santiago is just crawling with accommodation. A quiet and cheap place is **Hospedaje Forest** (☎ 981 57 08 11, Callejón de Don Abril Ares 7), where decent singles/doubles start at 1600/2900 ptas. **Hostal Paz de Agra** (☎ 981 58 90 45, Rúa da Caldererería 37) is a spotless old house with rooms for 2500/4000 ptas (3500/5000 ptas with private bath). Little **Hostal Suso** (☎ 981 58 66 11, Rúa do Vilar 65) has comfortable modern doubles with bath for 5350 ptas.

For a solid meal including wine and dessert for less than 1000 ptas, try **Restaurante Cuatro Vientos** (Rúa de Santa Cristina 19). Popular with readers of travel guides, **Casa Manolo** (Rúa Travesa 27) has a good-value set meal for 750 ptas.

Entertainment

For traditional, occasionally live, Celtic music, head for **Café das Crechas** (Via Sacra 3). **Paraíso Perdido**, on the tiny square of Entrealtares, is one of Santiago's oldest bars. The local drinking and dancing scene is centred in the new town, especially around Praza Roxa. **Black** (Avenida de Rosalía de Castro s/n) is a popular disco.

Getting There & Away

Santiago's bus station is just over 1km northeast of the cathedral, on Rúa de Rodríguez Viguri (city bus No 10 runs to Praza de Galicia, on the south edge of the old town). As well several buses a day to/from other Galician cities such as La Coruña, Pontevedra and Vigo, daily services head to/from Madrid (5135 ptas, nine hours), Barcelona (8½ hours), Salamanca and Seville.

The train station is 600m south of the old town at the end of Rúa do Horreo (city bus Nos 6 and 9 from nearby go to Praza de Galicia). Up to four trains a day run to Madrid (5900 ptas, eight to 11 hours), and frequent trains head to La Coruña (515 ptas, one hour), Pontevedra (515 ptas, one hour) and Vigo.

RÍAS BAJAS

The grandest of Galicia's inlets are the four Rías Bajas, on the west-facing coast. From north to south these are the Ría de Muros, Ría de Arousa, Ría de Pontevedra and Ría de Vigo. All are dotted with low-key resorts, fishing villages and good beaches.

Tourist offices in the region include one at Calle del General Mola 3, Pontevedra (☎ 986 85 08 14) and one by the Estación Marítima (port) in Vigo (☎ 986 43 05 77).

SPAIN

Things to See & Do

There's a string of beaches along the south shore of the Ría de Muros, the nearest to Santiago. The village of **Porto do Son** makes a relaxed stop here.

The small city of **Pontevedra** has managed to preserve its medieval centre and is ideal for wandering around. Out at the end of the north side of the Ría de Pontevedra is the good **La Lanzada** beach, about 7km long and often good for windsurfing, though not exactly deserted or remote. There are some good, tranquil beaches around the villages of **Aldán** and **Hio**, near the south-west end of the Ría de Pontevedra. Buses run to Hio from Cangas, which you can reach by bus from Vigo.

Vigo, Galicia's biggest city, is a disappointment given its wonderful setting, although its small, tangled old town is worth a wander.

The best beaches in the Rías Bajas are on the **Islas Cíes** off the end of the Ría de Vigo. One of these three islands is off limits for conservation reasons. The other two, Isla del Faro and Isla de Monte Agudo, are linked by a white sandy crescent – together forming a 9km breakwater in the Atlantic. You can only visit the islands from Easter to mid-September, and numbers are strictly limited. Boats from Vigo cost 2000 ptas return; from mid-June they go every day, before that, only at weekends.

Places to Stay

In Porto do Son, *Hostal O Chinto*, on Avenida de Galicia, by the port, has doubles with shared bathrooms for 4000 ptas, and good seafood in the bar below. There's a string of *camping grounds* and several *hostales* along La Lanzada beach.

In Pontevedra, *Casa Alicia* (☎ *986 85 70 79, Avenida de Santa María 5*) and *Casa Maruja* (☎ *986 85 49 01, Praza de Santa María 12*), round the corner, are good. The former has homey doubles around 3000 ptas; the latter charges 3000/4000 ptas.

Hostal Stop (☎ *986 32 94 75*), in Hio, south of Pontevedra, has rooms for 3000/5000 ptas in summer.

In Vigo, *Hotel Pantón* (☎ *986 22 42 70, Rúa de Lepanto 18*) has rooms with bath and TV for 4700/5900 ptas plus IVA in high summer, but 3800/4600 ptas or less from October to June.

Camping is the only option if you want to stay on the Islas Cíes – book *camp sites* (575 ptas plus IVA per person and per tent) in the port in Vigo. You can then organise a return boat ticket for the days you require.

Getting There & Away

Pontevedra and Vigo are the area's transport hubs, with a reasonable network of local buses fanning out from them. Both are well served by buses and trains from Santiago de Compostela, and Vigo has services from more distant places like Madrid and Barcelona. Two trains a day run from Vigo to Porto in Portugal (3½ hours).

PICOS DE EUROPA

This small mountainous region straddling Asturias, Cantabria and Castilla y León is some of the finest walking country in Spain. The spectacular scenery ensures a continual flow of visitors from all over Europe and beyond.

The Picos begin only 20km from the coast, and cover an area around 40km long and 25km wide, comprising three limestone massifs. The Picos are a national park, with its main information office (☎ 985 84 86 14) at Casa Dago, Cangas de Onís. Plenty of information on walks is available here and at other offices around the Picos. Good maps, available locally, are published by Adrados Ediciones, including *Picos de Europa* (1:80,000). Serious trekkers will find Lonely Planet's *Walking in Spain* useful.

Places to Stay & Eat

The main access towns Cangas de Onís, Arenas de Cabrales and Potes all have a wide range of hostales.

A few hundred metres from Lago de Enol, a good starting point for walks, *Refugio Vega de Enol* (☎ 985 84 85 76) has bunks for 500 ptas and meals. You can camp free nearby. In Sotres, another good launch, *Pensión La Perdiz* (☎ 985 94 50 11) charges 3100/4000 ptas for singles/doubles with bath (less without), and the good, clean *Albergue Peña Castil* (☎ 985 94 50 70) offers bunks for 1100 ptas to 1300 ptas and has a restaurant.

In Espinama (for a southern approach), the attractive *Hostal Puente Deva* (☎ 942 73 66 58) has rooms for 3400/5000 ptas, and a restaurant.

SPAIN

Getting There & Away

From the roads encircling the Picos, three main routes lead into the heart of the mountains: from Cangas de Onís to Covadonga and Lago de Enol, from Arenas de Cabrales to Sotres, and from Potes to Fuente Dé.

A few buses from Santander, León and Oviedo serve the three main access towns. Others buses run from Cangas de Onís to Covadonga, Covadonga to Lago de Enol (July and August only), and Potes to Espinama and Fuente Dé (late June to mid-September).

SANTANDER

Santander, capital of Cantabria, is a cosmopolitan city with wide waterfront boulevards, leafy parks and crowded beaches. Semana Grande, celebrated during late July, is a wild party, but accommodation all along the north coast in the second half of July and August needs to be booked ahead.

Santander's main attractions are its beaches and its bars. The main beach, El Sardinero, sees surfers out in force by mid-March, despite the cold.

The city tourist office (☎ 942 21 61 20) is in the harbour-side Jardines de Pereda. The regional one (☎ 942 31 07 08) is nearby at Plaza Porticada 5.

Places to Stay & Eat

The following room rates come down substantially from October to May/June.

Pensión La Porticada (☎ *942 22 78 17, Calle Méndez Núñez 6*), near the train, bus and ferry terminals, has reasonable rooms for 4000/5000 ptas. *Hospedaje Botín* (☎ *942 21 00 94, Calle de Isabel II 1*) has spacious, impeccably clean rooms for 3500/5900 ptas.

The older part of town has lots of atmospheric old wine bars serving food. *Mesón Goya* (*Calle Daóiz y Velarde 25*) is one of the more economical, with salmon or a beef fillet *a la plancha* for 800 ptas to 1000 ptas.

Entertainment

In the old town, Calle Río de la Pila and the Plaza de Cañadío area teem with all kinds of *bars*. In summer there's quite a good scene along the main drag behind El Sardinero.

Getting There & Away

Santander is one of the major entry points to Spain, thanks to its ferry link with Plymouth, England.

The ferry terminal and train and bus stations are all in the centre of Santander, within 300m of each other. Six buses a day go to Madrid (3300 ptas) via Burgos. Several head east to Bilbao, San Sebastián (1790 ptas, 2½ hours) and Irún, and west to Oviedo. Others run to Pamplona, Barcelona, Salamanca and elsewhere.

Trains to Bilbao (925 ptas, 2½ hours, three daily) and Oviedo are run by FEVE, a private line that does not accept rail passes. Trains to Madrid and Castilla y León are run by RENFE, so rail passes are valid. To Madrid there are three trains most days (from 4300 ptas, 5½ to 8¾ hours), via Ávila.

SANTILLANA DEL MAR

This marvellously preserved village, with cobbled streets lined by lovely medieval stone buildings, lies 30km west of Santander. It would be well worth a visit even if the **Cuevas de Altamira**, with their world-famous, 14,000-year-old animal paintings, weren't just 2km to the south-west. A maximum of 20 people a day are allowed into the caves and the waiting list is three years long. For those of us who can't wait, a new museum at the caves, complete with full-scale replica of the caves, will open from 2001.

Places to Stay & Eat

Santillana has heaps of accommodation, but little in the real budget range. *Hospedaje Octavio* (☎ *942 81 81 99, Plaza Las Arenas 6*) has charming rooms with timber-beam ceilings and private bath for 3500/5500 ptas. *Casa Cossío* serves a good range of fare, with a *menú* for 1150 ptas.

Getting There & Away

Several daily buses call in at Santillana en route between Santander and San Vicente de la Barquera, farther west.

País Vasco, Navarra & Aragón

The Basque people have lived in Spain's País Vasco (Basque Country, or Euskadi in the Basque language), Navarra and the adjoining Pays Basque in the south-west of France for thousands of years. They have their own ancient language called Euskara, a distinct physical appearance, a rich culture and a proud history.

Along with this strong sense of identity has come, among a significant minority of Basques in Spain, a desire for independence. During the Franco years the Basque people were brutally repressed and Euskadi ta Askatasuna (ETA), a separatist movement, began its terrorist activities. With Spain's changeover to democracy in the late 1970s, the País Vasco was granted a large degree of autonomy, but ETA has pursued its violent campaign.

ETA terrorism may be a deterrent to tourism but it hasn't affected the beauty of the País Vasco region. Although the Bilbao area is heavily industrialised, the region has a spectacular coastline. The main draws are elegant San Sebastián, Bilbao's Guggenheim Museum and the Basque cuisine, considered the best in Spain.

South-east of the País Vasco, the Navarra and Aragón regions reach down from the Pyrenees into drier, more southern lands. The Aragonese Pyrenees offer the best walking and skiing on the Spanish side of this mountain range. Walkers should head for the Parque Nacional de Ordesa y Monte Perdido, whose main access point is the village of Torla. Weatherwise the best months up there are late June to mid-September.

SAN SEBASTIÁN

San Sebastián (Donostia in Basque) is a stunning city. Famed as a ritzy resort for wealthy Spaniards, it has also been a stronghold of Basque nationalist feeling since well before Franco. The surprisingly relaxed town of 180,000 people curves round the beautiful Bahía de la Concha. Those who live here consider themselves the luckiest people in Spain, and after spending a few days on the perfect crescent-shaped beach in preparation for the wild evenings, you may begin to understand why.

Information

The municipal tourist office (☎ 943 48 11 66) is at Boulevard Reina Regente 8 (closed Sunday afternoon). The regional tourist office (☎ 943 02 31 50), open daily, is at Paseo de los Fueros 1. The main post office is on Calle de Urdaneta, behind the cathedral. Donosti-Net, Calle de Embeltrán 2 in the old town (Parte Vieja), is a good Internet cafe.

Things to See & Do

The Playa de la Concha and Playa de Ondarreta are among the most beautiful city beaches in Spain. You can reach Isla de Santa Clara, in the middle of the bay, by boat from the harbour. In summer, you can also swim out to rafts anchored in the bay.

San Sebástian's revamped Aquarium has 10 large tanks teeming with tropical fish, morays, sharks and other finned creatures. There are also exhibits on pirates, Basque explorers and related themes (1100 ptas).

The free Museo de San Telmo, in a 16th-century monastery on Plaza de Zuloaga, has a varied collection with a heavy emphasis on Basque paintings (closed Sunday afternoon and Monday).

Overlooking Bahía de la Concha from the east is Monte Urgull, topped with a statue of Christ that enjoys sweeping views. It only takes 30 minutes to walk up – a stairway starts from Plaza de Zuloaga in the old town.

Places to Stay

Rooms are hard to find in July and August, so arrive early or book ahead, and be aware of huge, seasonal price differences. Prices below are for peak periods.

Camping Igueldo (☎ 943 21 45 02) is out beyond Monte Igueldo, but is connected to the centre by bus No 16. It's open year round. The HI hostel, *Albergue La Sirena* (☎ 943 31 02 68, ✉ udala-youthhostel@donostia.org, Paseo de Igueldo 25), offers bed and breakfast for 2000/2255 ptas for juniors/seniors.

In the lively Parte Vieja, the best bet is *Pensión San Lorenzo* (☎ 943 42 55 16, Calle de San Lorenzo 2), where nicely decorated doubles with bath cost 3500 ptas. Other assets include metered Internet access and off-season kitchen use. Also good is *Pensión Loinaz* (☎ 943 42 67 14, Calle de San Lorenzo 17), which charges 4000/5500 ptas.

The area near the cathedral is more peaceful than the Parte Vieja. *Pensión La Perla* (☎ 943 42 81 23, Calle de Loyola 10) has excellent singles/doubles with shower and toilet for 3500/5500 ptas; some overlook the cathedral. Also recommended is the friendly *Pensión Añorga* (☎ 943 46 79 45, Calle de Easo 12) with rooms for 4000/5000 ptas.

SPAIN

Places to Eat

It's almost a shame to sit down in a restaurant when the bars have such good tapas, or as they are known here, *pinchos*. Many of them cluster in the Parte Vieja, where *Bar Txepetxa (Calle Pescadería 5)* and *Borda Berri (Calle Fermín Calbetrón 12)* are recommended. Also here is *Juantxo Taberna (☎ 943 42 74 05, Calle de Embeltrán 6)*, famous for its cheap, super-sized sandwiches. The tiny *Koskol (Calle de Iñigo 5)* has a delicious, generous lunch *menú* for 1000 ptas, while *Restaurante La OKA (Calle de San Martín 43)* is a fun vegetarian spot (lunch daily, plus Saturday dinner).

Entertainment

The Spanish habit of bar-hopping has been perfected in San Sebastián's Parte Vieja – one street alone has 28 bars. Typical drinks are a *zurrito* (beer in a small glass) and *txacolí* (a tart Basque wine). If you'd like to have a swig of Basque *sidra* (cider) head for *Sagardotegia Itxaropena (Calle de Embeltran 16)*.

Once the Parte Vieja quietens down, usually at around 1 or 2 am, the crowd heads to Calle de los Reyes Católicos behind the cathedral.

Getting There & Away

Bus The bus station is a 20-minute walk south of the Parte Vieja on Plaza de Pío XII; ticket offices are along the streets north of the station. Buses leave from here for destinations all over Spain. PESA runs a half-hourly express service to Bilbao (1120 ptas, one hour), while La Roncalesa buses go to Pamplona up to 10 times daily (790 ptas, two hours). Buses to Madrid (3800 ptas) run nine times each day.

Train The Renfe train station is across the river on Paseo de Francia. There are daily trains to Madrid (6400 ptas, eight hours) and to Barcelona (5000 ptas, 8¼ hours). There is one daily direct train to Paris and several others that require a change at Hendaye (France). Other destinations include Salamanca and Lisbon.

Eusko Tren, a private company (international passes not valid) has trains to Hendaye (115 ptas) and Bilbao (900 ptas, 2¾ hours) departing from Amara station on Calle de Easo.

COSTA VASCA

Spain's ruggedly beautiful Costa Vasca (Basque Coast) is one of its least touristy coastal regions. A combination of rainy weather, chilly seas and terrorism tends to put some people off.

The coastal stretch between San Sebastián and Bilbao to the west is considered to be some of the finest surfing territory in Europe. **Zarautz** hosts a World Surfing Championship each September. At the picturesque village of **Getaria** the main attraction is wandering the narrow streets by the fishing harbour, while nearby **Zumaia** has better beaches.

Mundaka, 12km north of Gernika, is a surfing town and home to legendary 'left-handers'. The Mundaka Surf Shop rents gear and gives surfing lessons. *Camping Portuondo (☎/fax 94 687 77 01)*, about 1km south of town, has lovely terraced grounds and also rents bungalows.

Getting Around

If you don't have your own transport, there are buses from San Sebastián to Zarautz and Getaria, and from Bilbao to Gernika. From Gernika you can take a bus to Bermeo, which will drop you in Mundaka. Eusko Tren from Bilbao and San Sebástian also serves many coastal towns.

BILBAO

Once the industrial heart of the north, Bilbao has now spruced itself up and, in 1997, created for itself a tourist gold mine – the US$100 million **Museo Guggenheim de Arte Contemporáneo**. Designed by US architect Frank Gehry, this fantastical, swirling structure was inspired in part by the anatomy of a fish and the hull of a boat – both allusions to Bilbao's past and present economy. The interior makes wonderful use of space, with light pouring in through a central glass atrium of cathedral proportions. The permanent exhibit of modern and contemporary art is still small but choice with artists like Picasso, Mondrian and Kandinsky among those represented. All the other galleries are used for high-calibre temporary exhibits.

Museum hours are 10 am to 8 pm (Mondays in July and August only); admission is 1200/600 ptas. Arrive early and ask about free guided English-language tours.

Some 300m up the street, the excellent **Museo de Bellas Artes** has works by El Greco, Velázquez, Goya as well as 20th-century masters like Gauguin. Basque artists are shown as well (closed Monday, 600/300 ptas).

The main tourist office (☎ 94 479 57 60) is on Paseo Arenal 1 and there's also an information kiosk by the Guggenheim (closed Monday). For Internet access, go to El Señor de la Red, Calle Rodríguez Arias 69.

Places to Stay & Eat
Albergue Bilbao Aterpetxea (☎ *94 427 00 54,* ✉ *aterpe@albergue.bilbao.net, Carretera Basurto-Kastrexana Errep 70*) is a 10-minute, direct bus ride (No 58) away from the centre and charges from 1900 ptas to 2500 ptas, including breakfast.

Pensión Méndez (☎ *94 416 03 64, Calle de Santa María 13*) is central but can be a bit noisy. Singles/doubles cost 3000/4000 ptas.

Hostal La Estrella (☎ *94 416 40 66, Calle de María Múñoz 6*) is a charming place where rooms with washbasin cost 2700/4800 ptas and those with bath are 4000/6500 ptas.

Las Siete Calles (Seven Streets), the nucleus of Bilbao's old town, brims with tapas bars and restaurants. *Rio-Oja (Calle de Perro 6)* is among the many places for cheap food and drink. *Cafe Boulevard (Calle de Arenal 3)*, Bilbao's oldest coffeehouse (1871), has breakfasts, full meals and tapas at wallet-friendly prices.

Getting There & Away
Bus Buses to Madrid (3400 ptas) and Barcelona (4850 ptas) depart from Calle de la Autonomía 17. Most other destinations are served from the huge Termibus station in the south-west corner of town (metro: San Mamés).

Train Four daily trains go to Madrid (5800 ptas, 6¼ hours) and two go to Barcelona (4900 ptas, nine hours), leaving from the central Abando train station. The Eusko Tren station with regional services is about 1km south of the centre.

PAMPLONA
The madcap festivities of Pamplona's Sanfermines festival run from 6 to 14 July and are characterised by nonstop partying and, of course, the running of the bulls. The safest place to watch the *encierro* (running) is on TV. If that's too tame, see if you can sweet-talk your way on to a balcony overlooking one of the streets where the bulls run. The bulls are let out at 8 am, but you should show up at 6 am for a decent vantage point.

If you visit at any other time of year, Pamplona (Iruñea in Basque) is a pleasant, modern city with lovely parks and gardens and a compact old town with a lively bar and restaurant scene.

The tourist office (☎ 948 22 07 41) is on Plaza San Francisco and is open weekdays only (plus Saturday morning in July and August).

Places to Stay & Eat
The nearest camping ground is *Camping Ezcaba* (☎ *948 33 03 15)*, 7km north of the city. It fills up a few days before Sanfermines. A bus service (direction Arre/Oricain) runs four times daily from Calle de Teovaldos (near the bullring).

For Sanfermines you need to book well in advance (and pay as much as triple the regular rates). During the festival, beds are also available in *casas particulares* (private houses) – check with the tourist office or haggle with the locals at the bus and train stations. Otherwise, join the many who sleep in one of the parks, plazas or shopping malls. There's a left-luggage office *(consigna)* at the bus station.

Pamplona's old centre is filled with cheap pensiones renting out basic singles/doubles for around 2000/3500 ptas. Contenders on Calle San Nicolás include *Fonda Aragonesa* (☎ *948 22 34 28)*, at No 32, *Habitaciones San Nicolás* (☎ *948 22 13 19)*, at No 13, and *Habitaciones Otano* (☎ *948 22 50 95)* at No 5. Near the tourist office, *Camas Escaray Lozano* (☎ *948 22 78 25, Calle Nueva 24)* has probably the nicest rooms in this range. Right by the indoor market and next to the bull running route is *Habitaciones Redin* (☎ *948 22 21 82, Calle de Mercado 5)*.

Calle de San Nicolás is packed with tapas bars, with *Baserri*, at No 32 offering the best quality. Almost as good is *Otano* (☎ *948 22 26 38)* across the street.

Getting There & Away
The bus station is on Avenida de Yangüas y Miranda, a five-minute walk south of the old

SPAIN

town. There are 10 buses daily to San Sebastián (790 ptas) and eight to Bilbao (1580 ptas). Four daily head for Madrid (3220 ptas) and two to Barcelona (2190 ptas).

Pamplona is on the San Sebastián-Zaragoza railway line, but the station is awkwardly situated north of town. If you arrive this way, catch bus No 9 to the centre.

ZARAGOZA

Zaragoza, capital of the region of Aragón and home to half its 1.2 million people, is often said to be the most Spanish city of all. Once an important Roman settlement (under the name Caesaraugusta) and later a Muslim centre, it is today primarily an industrial and commercial city, but a lively one – and with a handsome and interesting old heart on the south side of the Río Ebro.

The city tourist office (☎ 976 20 12 00), in a surreal-looking glass cube on Plaza del Pilar, opens 10 am to 8 pm daily.

Things to See

Zaragoza's focus is the vast 500m-long main square, **Plaza de Nuestra Señora del Pilar** (Plaza del Pilar for short). Dominating the north side is the **Basílica de Nuestra Señora del Pilar**, a 17th-century church of epic proportions. People flock into the church to kiss a piece of marble pillar believed to have been left by the Virgin Mary when she appeared to Santiago (St James) in a vision here in AD 40.

At the south-east end of the plaza is **La Seo**, Zaragoza's brooding 12th- to 16th-century cathedral. Its north-west facade is a Mudéjar masterpiece. The inside, reopened in 1998 after 18 years of restoration, features a 15th-century main altarpiece in coloured alabaster.

The odd trapezoid structure in front of La Seo is the outside of a remarkable edifice housing ancient Caesaraugusta's **Roman forum**. Well below ground level are the remains of shops, porticos and a sewerage system, all brought to life by an imaginative audiovisual show (closed Sunday afternoon and Monday, 300/200 ptas full/students).

A little over 1km west of the plaza, the **Palacio de la Aljafería**, housing Aragón's *cortes* (parliament), is Spain's greatest Muslim building outside Andalucía. It was built as the palace of Zaragoza's Muslim rulers, who held the city from 714 to 1118

(open daily except Thursday, Friday afternoon and winter Sunday afternoons; free).

Places to Stay

Zaragoza's HI hostel, *Albergue Juvenil Baltasar Gracián* (☎ 976 55 13 87, Calle Franco y López 4) is open all year, except August.

The cheapest rooms elsewhere are in El Tubo, the maze of lanes and alleys south of Plaza del Pilar. A good choice is *Pensión La Peña* (☎ 976 29 90 89, Calle Cinegio 3), with singles/doubles for 1500/3000 ptas. Another good cheapie is *Fonda Manifestación* (☎ 976 29 58 21, Calle Manifestación 36), at 2500/3500 ptas. *Hostal Plaza* (☎ 976 29 48 30, Plaza del Pilar 14), perfectly located, has comfy rooms with shower for 4300/4900 ptas plus IVA.

Places to Eat & Drink

Cafetería Piccolo, on Calle Prudencio, a block south of the basilica, serves decent platos combinados from 800 ptas and stays open until 1 or 2 am. The bright *La Milagrosa (Calle Don Jaime I 43)* provides inexpensive breakfasts, and raciones for 300 ptas to 700 ptas.

The small plazas and narrow streets south-west of La Seo harbour contain some brilliant *tapas bars*: check out Plaza Santa Marta, Plaza de San Pedro Nolasco and Plaza Santa Cruz.

Entertainment

El Tubo has a plentiful quota of bars but much of the action takes place about 1km further south-west, on and around Calle Doctor Cerrada A good place to start is *Morrissey (Gran Vía 33)*, which often has live bands Thursday to Saturday.

Getting There & Away

Bus stations are scattered all over town: the tourist office can tell you what goes where from where. The Agreda company runs to most major Spanish cities from Paseo de María Agustín 7. The trip to Madrid costs 1750 ptas and to Barcelona 1655 ptas.

Up to 15 trains daily run from El Portillo station to both Madrid (3100 ptas to 4000 ptas, three to 4½ hours) and Barcelona (2900 ptas to 4100 ptas, 3½ to 5 hours). Some Barcelona trains go via Tarragona. Trains also run to Valencia via Teruel, and to San Sebastián via Pamplona.

TERUEL

A good stop on the way to the coast from Zaragoza, or from Cuenca in Castilla-La Mancha, is Teruel, which has a distinct flavour thanks to four centuries of Muslim domination in the middle ages and some remarkable Mudéjar architecture dating from after its capture by Christians in 1171.

The tourist office (☎ 978 60 22 79) is at Calle de Tomás Nogués 1.

Things to See

Teruel has four magnificent Mudéjar towers, on the cathedral of **Santa María** and the churches of **San Salvador**, **San Martín** and **San Pedro**. These, and the painted ceiling inside Santa María, are among Spain's best examples of Mudéjar architecture and artisanry.

The **Museo Provincial de Teruel**, on Plaza del Padre Polanco, is worth a visit, mainly for its well-presented archaeological collection dating back to *Homo erectus*.

Places to Stay & Eat

Fonda del Tozal (☎ 978 60 10 22, Calle del Rincón 5) is a rickety old house run by a friendly family. Most of the rooms (1500/3000 ptas for singles/doubles) have cast-iron beds, enamel chamber pots and exposed ceiling beams. In winter you might prefer *Hostal Aragón* (☎ 978 60 13 87, Calle de Santa María 4), which has mod cons such as heating. Rooms are 2150/3200 ptas, or 3200/4860 ptas with private bath, plus IVA. Both places are just a couple of minutes' walk from the cathedral.

Teruel is famed for its ham – if you can't fit a whole leg of it in your backpack, at least sample a *bocadillo con jamón* (long bread roll with ham, tomato and olive oil). One of the best places for hamming it up is *La Taberna de Rokelin* (Calle de Tozal 33), a narrow bar with a beautiful rack of smoked pig hocks.

Getting There & Away

The bus station is on Ronda de Ambeles. Daily buses head to Barcelona (6½ hours), Cuenca (2¾ hours), Valencia (two hours) and Madrid (2415 ptas, 4½ hours).

By rail, Teruel is about midway between Valencia and Zaragoza, with three trains a day to both places.

SPAIN

Sweden

Sweden has everything: thousands of lakes, rocky islands, excellent hostels, an efficient transport network, Samis and reindeer in the north and Danish castles in the south. The statistics are astounding; there are more than 25,000 Iron Age graveyards or burial mounds, 1140 prehistoric fortresses, 2500 open-air rune stones, 3000 churches and more than 10,000km of trekking and bicycle paths.

Only one thing is missing – the tourists, especially backpackers. For that you can blame Sweden's high prices.

Facts about Sweden

HISTORY

In the 9th century the missionary St Ansgar visited Birka near modern Stockholm, just as the Viking Age was getting under way. In the 11th century the groundwork was laid for a Swedish state by the Christian king Olof Skötkonung. At the time southern Sweden belonged to Denmark and was (and still is) strongly influenced by it. The Union of Kalmar in 1397 brought together the kingdoms of Denmark, Norway and Sweden, and for a while Danish monarchs held the Swedish throne.

In 1471 the Swedish regent, Sten Sture, fought the Danes in Stockholm and gained a small degree of autonomy for the Swedes. When the Danish king Christian II executed Sture's son in 1520, the Swedes rebelled under the leadership of a young nobleman, Gustav Vasa. In 1523 he was crowned King Gustav I and set about creating a powerful, centralised Swedish nation-state.

A period of expansion began under Gustav II Adolf. By the time he died in battle in 1632, Sweden controlled the Baltic countries and much of Finland.

AT A GLANCE	
Capital:	Stockholm
Population:	8.9 million
Official Language:	Swedish
Currency:	1 Swedish krona (Skr) = 100 öre

The megalomania of Karl XII, who ruled the Swedish empire from 1697 to 1718, was crushed by Peter the Great at Poltava in 1709 and Sweden lost its Baltic territories. Over the next 50 years the crown lost much of its power to the Swedish Riksdag (parliament). Gustav III led a coup that interrupted this development, until he was murdered by a conspiracy of aristocrats in 1792. Unrestricted power vested in the monarch was ended by an aristocratic revolt in 1809 – the same year that Sweden lost Finland to Russia.

Sweden declared itself neutral at the outbreak of WWI and WWII. During WWII Sweden sold weapons to both the Allied and Axis powers. Following the war, Swedes had a change of heart and decided to save themselves from the evils of war, want and capitalism. This institutionalised niceness saved oppressed refugees in the Third World, built the most comprehensive welfare state in the world, established equality among Swedish workers (90% are union members), liberated women and made life easier for the old and disabled.

The economic pressures prevailing in the 1970s began to cloud Sweden's social goals, and it was under Olof Palme that support for social democracy first wavered. Even the social democrats (who built the system) admit that the era of *folkhemmet* (the Swedish welfare state) is over. Even so, the idea of cradle-to-grave welfare is deeply entrenched in the Swedish psyche.

Serious current account problems in the early 1990s provoked frenzied speculation against the Swedish krona, forcing a massive devaluation of the currency. With both their economy and national confidence severely shaken, Swedes voted in favour of joining the EU, effective from 1 January

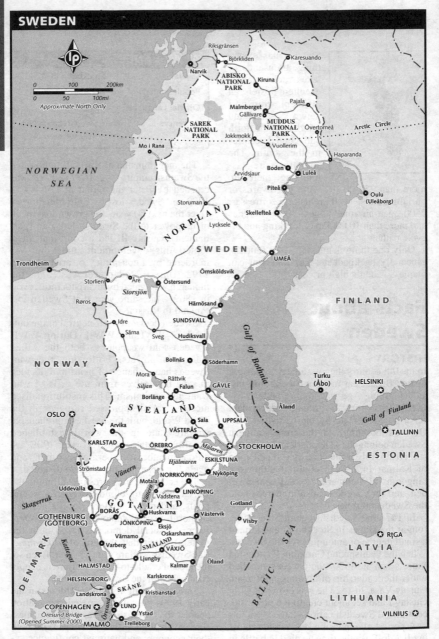

SWEDEN

0   100   200km
0   50   100mi
Approximate North Only

Riksgränsen
Björkliden
Karesuando
Narvik
ABISKO NATIONAL PARK
Kiruna
Malmberget
Gällivare
Pajala
SAREK NATIONAL PARK
Jokkmokk
MUDDUS NATIONAL PARK
Övertorneå
Arctic Circle
Mo i Rana
Vuollerim
Haparanda
Boden
Arvidsjaur
Luleå
Piteå
NORWEGIAN SEA
Oulu (Uleåborg)
Storuman
Skellefteå
Lycksele
NORRLAND
SWEDEN
UMEÅ
Trondheim
Örnsköldsvik
Storlien
Åre
Östersund
Storsjön
FINLAND
Røros
Härnösand
Idre
SUNDSVALL
Särna
Sveg
Hudiksvall
NORWAY
Bollnäs
Söderhamn
Mora
Rättvik
Siljan
Falun
Turku (Åbo)
HELSINKI
Borlänge
GÄVLE
Gulf of Bothnia
OSLO
SVEALAND
Arvika
Sala
UPPSALA
Åland
Gulf of Finland
VÄSTERÅS
KARLSTAD
ÖREBRO
Mälaren
STOCKHOLM
TALLINN
Strömstad
Hjälmaren
ESKILSTUNA
ESTONIA
Vänern
NORRKÖPING
Nyköping
Uddevalla
Motala
Vättern
Vadstena
LINKÖPING
Skagerrak
GÖTALAND
Gotland
GOTHENBURG (GÖTEBORG)
BORÅS
Huskvarna
Västervik
Visby
JÖNKÖPING
Eksjö
RĪGA
Värnamo
Oskarshamn
DENMARK
Varberg
SMÅLAND
VÄXJÖ
LATVIA
Kattegat
HALMSTAD
Ljungby
Kalmar
Öland
HELSINGBORG
Karlskrona
BALTIC SEA
SKÅNE
Landskrona
Kristianstad
LITHUANIA
COPENHAGEN
LUND
Øresund Bridge (Opened Summer 2000)
Ystad
MALMÖ
Trelleborg
VILNIUS

1995. Since then Sweden's welfare state 'model' has undergone major reforms and the economy has improved considerably. Sweden remains one of the strongest industrial nations in Europe – demonstrated by names such as Volvo, Ericsson, SAAB and ABB – and is also one of the world's wealthiest countries.

GEOGRAPHY

There are approximately 100,000 lakes in Sweden. The rocky south-west coast is most notable for its fjords and rocky skerries. Anything north of Svealand is called Norrland, which comprises a nearly uniform expanse of forest and rivers. The trees thin out in Jämtland and Lappland and the mountains assert themselves, providing a natural frontier with Norway in the north-west.

CLIMATE

Summer in Sweden can be hot, sunny and beautiful. In July the average temperature in the northern mountains is about 11°C (there may be occasional freezing temperatures and snowfalls), and in Stockholm and Malmö about 18°C. However, August can be wet. Snow in Lappland lies on the ground for anything between 150 and 200 days a year.

Malmö gets 17½ hours of daylight around Midsummer. Stockholm has an average of nine hours of sunshine daily from May to July.

POPULATION & PEOPLE

Some 8.9 million people live in Sweden. More than 500,000 are foreign nationals, including over 100,000 Asians, and 18% of the population is either foreign-born or has at least one non-Swedish parent. Sweden has two native minorities, both concentrated in the north-east: 17,000 Sami (formerly called Lapps), and about 30,000 Finns.

SOCIETY & CONDUCT

Swedes are decent and serious people, proud of their country's historical pre-eminence. The 17th-century expansionist kings and the Vikings – who are remembered in boisterous drinking sessions – are seen as good role models. Elk (moose), the stubborn wild animal, is another symbol of Sweden. So is *snus*, ground snuff-like tobacco that males (and a few females) keep under their stiff upper lips.

Other Scandinavians resent Sweden's quietly assumed superiority – if Sweden meets, say Italy in a sports event, Norwegians and Finns will applaud when Italy scores.

LANGUAGE

Swedish is a Germanic language, and is spoken throughout Sweden and in parts of Finland. Swedes, Danes and Norwegians can, however, make themselves mutually understood since their languages are similar. Most Swedes speak English as a second language. See the Language chapter at the back of this book for pronunciation guidelines and useful words and phrases.

Facts for the Visitor

HIGHLIGHTS

Castles in Sweden can be palaces with gardens such as Drottningholm near Stockholm, lakeside residences such as Vadstena Slott in Vadstena, formidable fortresses such as Kalmar and Örebro castles and impressive ruins such as those at Borgholm on Öland.

Lund is the oldest remaining town in Sweden, and Visby is the only walled medieval town. Also noteworthy are Gothenburg and Birka (a Viking town site on an island near Stockholm).

SUGGESTED ITINERARIES

Three days
    Visit Stockholm, with a day trip to Birka.
One week
    Visit Stockholm and Gothenburg, and stop briefly at some other towns, including Uppsala.
Two weeks
    Visit Stockholm, Gothenburg and Uppsala, and tour the Skåne region or visit Gotland.

PLANNING
When to Go

If you want sunshine, visit between late May and late July, bearing in mind that August can be wet. Many hostels, camping grounds and attractions open only in summer, from late June to mid-August. However, big cities are in full swing year-round.

TOURIST OFFICES

Sweden has about 350 local tourist offices. Most are open long hours in summer and short hours (or not at all) in winter; some exhibit nomadic tendencies. The following offices and organisations abroad can assist with promotional material and inquiries:

Australia (☎ 02-6270 2700, @ sweden@ netinfo.com.au) Embassy of Sweden, 5 Turrana St, Yarralumla, ACT 2600
UK (☎ 020-7870 5600, @ info@swetourism .org.uk) Swedish Travel & Tourism Council, 11 Montagu Place, London, W1H 2AL
USA (☎ 212-885 9700, @ info@gosweden.org) Danish & Swedish Tourist Board, PO Box 4649, Grand Central Station, New York, NY 10163

VISAS & DOCUMENTS
Citizens of most countries can enter Sweden with a passport for stays of up to three months, but citizens of South Africa and many other African, Asian and some Eastern European countries require 90-day tourist visas (Skr250; contact the nearest Swedish embassy).

Bring an HI membership card, and you'll pay Skr75 to Skr180 per night in each of the 300 STF hostels. Students with an ISIC card (and often seniors) are eligible for concessions in museums, theatres and cinemas.

EMBASSIES & CONSULATES
Swedish Embassies Abroad
Australia (☎ 02-6270 2700) 5 Turrana St, Yarralumla, ACT 2600
Canada (☎ 613-241 8553) 377 Dalhousie St, Ottawa K1N 9N8
UK (☎ 020-7917 6400) 11 Montagu Place, London W1H 2AL
USA (☎ 212-467 2600) 1501 M Street, NW, Suite 900, Washington DC 20005-1702

Foreign Embassies in Sweden
These are in Stockholm (area code ☎ 08):

Australia (☎ 613 2900) Block 5, Sergels Torg 12
Canada (☎ 453 3000) 7th floor, Tegelbacken 4
New Zealand (☎ 611 2625) Sture Plan 2
UK (☎ 671 9000) Skarpögatan 6-8
USA (☎ 783 5300) Dag Hammarskjölds väg 31

MONEY
The Swedish krona (plural kronor), often called the 'crown' by Swedes speaking English, is abbreviated to SEK or Skr but usually just kr within Sweden. There are

four coins: the 50 öre and Skr1, Skr5 and Skr10 pieces. One Swedish krona equals 100 öre. Prices are rounded off to the nearest 50 öre. There are notes of Skr20, Skr50, Skr100, Skr500 and Skr1000.

Forex, found in the largest cities and at some ferry terminals, is one of the cheapest and easiest places to exchange money and charges Skr15 per travellers cheque. Banks charge up to Skr60 per cheque; post offices charge Skr50 per transaction but have slightly better rates than Forex. The X-Change centres also offer good deals.

There are numerous ATMs in Sweden. The national Minuten and Bankomat ATM networks accept Visa, Plus, EC, Eurocard, Cirrus and MasterCard.

Exchange Rates

country	unit		kronor
Australia	A$1	=	Skr5.46
Canada	C$1	=	Skr6.51
euro	€1	=	Skr8.39
France	1FF	=	Skr1.28
Germany	DM1	=	Skr4.29
New Zealand	NZ$1	=	Skr3.97
Japan	¥100	=	Skr9.23
UK	UK£1	=	Skr13.87
USA	US$1	=	Skr9.64

Costs
Sweden can be expensive. The absolute minimum daily cost – sleeping at hostels, buying food at markets, avoiding alcohol and always asking for discounted bus/train tickets – is about US$40.

Otherwise, it's a question of cutting corners. Bring a tent and you can sleep for free in forests. Brew your own coffee at hostels (each cup saves you at least US$2). Stuff yourself at breakfast buffets for about US$5 (included in the price of most hotels), look for special lunch deals at restaurants (from around US$6) instead of dining a la carte in the evening. Takeaway pizzas are another inexpensive option. Intoxicate yourself in merry Central Europe, and in Sweden opt instead for the cheap *lättöl* (light beer).

Tipping
Tipping isn't necessary in restaurants, though adding a few kronor for good service is no problem. In taxis, round up the meter if you can manage it, particularly if there's luggage.

POST & COMMUNICATIONS
Post
Letters (up to 20g) to other parts of Sweden cost Skr5, Skr6 to Nordic and Baltic countries, Skr7 to Europe and Skr8 beyond. Main city post offices are generally open 9 am to 6 pm weekdays and until 1 pm Saturday. Stamps can be bought at post offices and at Pressbyrån newsagents.

Telephone, Fax & Email
Sweden's international country code is ☎ 46. Almost all public telephones in the country now take Telia phonecards, which cost Skr35/60/100 for 30/60/120 credits; Telia Travel Cards are much cheaper for inter-national calls. Many Telia booths also accept credit cards. Numbers with '020' or '0200' prefixes can be dialled toll-free from anywhere in Sweden.

To make an overseas call dial ☎ 00 followed by the country code and phone number. A three-minute call to the USA costs Skr16 with a 100-unit Telia Travel Card.

To send a fax from a post office (though many don't offer a fax service) costs a flat fee of Skr25 plus Skr25 per page to the UK, or Skr50 per page to Australia or the USA.

Most public libraries offer free Internet access (with a half-hour or one-hour time limit), but computers normally have to be booked several hours – sometimes days – in advance. Cybercafes can be found in large cities and typically charge around Skr1/50 per minute/hour.

INTERNET RESOURCES
The Global Visitor's Guide to Sweden (www.visit-sweden.com), maintained by the Swedish Tourist Board, with good general information about the country. Most towns in Sweden have their own Web sites, including Stockholm (www.stockholmtown .com), Gothenburg (www.gbg-co.se), Malmö (www.tourism.malmo.com) and Uppsala (www.uppsala.se).

Gay and lesbian travellers should check out the Swedish Federation of Gays and Lesbians site (www.rfsl.se).

WOMEN TRAVELLERS
Equality of the sexes is strongly emphasised in Sweden. Kvinnojouren (☎ 08-544 60016) is the national organisation that deals with violence against women and Kvinnohusgruppen (☎ 08-643 2200), Blekingegatan 67B Stockholm, is the women's shelter organisation.

Ask for a women-only compartment if you don't want male company in a 2nd-class rail sleeping section. Some Stockholm taxi firms offer discounts for women at night.

GAY & LESBIAN TRAVELLERS
Liberal Sweden allows same-sex 'registered partnerships', granting most marriage rights. The organisation concerned with equality for lesbians and gays is Riksförbundet för Sexuellt Likaberättigande (RFSL; ☎ 08-736 0212, @ forbund@rfsl.se), Gay-Hus, Sveavägen 59, Stockholm. RFSL produces *KOM UT!*, a free Swedish-language monthly.

DANGERS & ANNOYANCES
Sweden is relatively safe but crimes perpetrated against travellers are on the increase; take care in museums and transport terminals in Stockholm, where gangs operate at all hours. Crime associated with illegal drugs and the few trouble spots of big cities are the main concerns.

Mosquitoes are a major headache in early summer; bring a trusted repellent. Winter travellers should note that there are long, cold stretches. If you're out of doors in the far north or during winter, exposure is a threat best avoided by common sense.

Sweden's toll-free general emergency number is ☎ 112.

BUSINESS HOURS
Normal shopping hours are 9 am to 6 pm weekdays, to between 1 and 4 pm Saturday. Department stores are open longer and sometimes also on Sunday. Banks usually open at 9.30 am and close at 3 pm, but some city branches open from 9 am to 5 or 6 pm.

Most museums have short opening hours, many tourist offices are closed at weekends from mid-August to mid-June and some hotels are closed from Christmas to New Year.

PUBLIC HOLIDAYS & SPECIAL EVENTS
Public holidays include: 1 January, 6 January (Epiphany), Good Friday, Easter Monday, 1 May (Labour Day), Ascension Day, Whit Monday, the first Friday afternoon and Saturday after 21 June (Midsummer's Eve & Day), All Saints' Day, 25 and 26 December.

Midsummer is the year's major festival, with celebrations throughout the country. The Lucia festival on 13 December is also very popular – choirs sing, and everyone drinks *glögg*, a hot alcoholic fruit punch.

ACCOMMODATION
Camping

Sweden has over 700 camping grounds and a free English-language guide with maps is available. You must have the free Svenskt Campingkort to stay at Swedish camping grounds; apply at least one month before your journey to Sveriges Campingvärdars Riksförbund (fax 0522-642430, @ adm@ scr.se), Box 255, SE-45117 Uddevalla. If this isn't possible, you'll be given a temporary card on arrival.

Some camping grounds are open during winter, but the main season is May to August. Prices vary with facilities, from Skr50 to Skr190. Most camping grounds have kitchens and laundry facilities and many have self-catering cabins or rooms (from around Skr200).

By law, you're allowed to camp (for free) anywhere outside private property, and fires may be set where safe (not on bare rocks) with fallen wood.

Hostels

Sweden has well over 400 *vandrarhem* (hostels). Of these, 318 are 'official' hostels affiliated with Svenska Turistföreningen (STF; ☎ 08-463 2100, @ info@stfturist.se), which is part of the Hostelling International (HI) network. Dorm beds cost Skr115 to Skr220 per night, though you get a Skr40 discount with an HI card; nonmembers can join STF and HI at affiliated hostels or at most tourist offices (Skr250/75 adult/child). For more information write to Box 25, SE-10120 Stockholm, or visit the STF Web site at www.meravsverige.nu.

Around 120 hostels belong to the 'rival' Sveriges Vandrarhem i Förening (SVIF). No membership is required and rates range from Skr60 to Skr160. A handful of hostels aren't affiliated with either STF or SVIF.

Most Swedish hostels are hard to enter outside reception opening hours; most of the day (and much of the winter) the doors are firmly locked. The secret is to phone and make a reservation during reception hours (generally between 5 and 7 pm); write down the four-digit door code and ask where the room key will be when you arrive.

Hotels

There are few cheap hotels in Sweden. Budget travellers may find weekend and summer (mid-June to mid-August) rates reasonable, often below Skr700 for a double. Stockholm, Gothenburg and Malmö offer cut-price 'packages' that include a hotel room, free entry to the main city attractions and free local transport – plus an optional discounted return train ticket. Tourist offices and travel agents can usually give details.

FOOD & DRINKS

Budget travellers should stuff themselves at breakfast buffets and visit discount food stores for supplies. Restaurants are often expensive (dinner and drinks around Skr200), but many offer good lunch deals – look for the *dagens rätt* (today's special), which generally costs Skr50 to Skr65. Note that lunch is only served from around 11.30 am to 2 pm.

Chinese restaurants are less likely to be a cheap option in Sweden, but Middle Eastern fare such as takeaway kebabs or felafel and pizzas are budget alternatives. In cafes, getting a coffee of any size for less than Skr15 is rare, although often there's *påtår* (free refill).

Light supermarket beer – *lättöl* – is good value, but definitely drink it chilled. Strong beer, wines and spirits are expensive and sold only by the state-owned monopoly Systembolaget.

Getting There & Away

AIR

There aren't many cheap direct flights to/from Stockholm originating outside of Europe. Within Europe there are some good deals to Sweden – the Irish carrier Ryanair flies between London (Stansted) and Kristianstad or Nyköping from just UK£45 return (plus taxes). Also note that it's often easier to find a cheap flight to Copenhagen (Denmark), just 23 minutes away from Sweden by train.

LAND

Direct access to Sweden by land is possible from Norway, Finland and Denmark. However, trains and buses from numerous European cities travel directly to Sweden by ferry (usually included in the ticket price). The new Öresund toll bridge linking Copenhagen with Malmö was opened in summer 2000, creating a major direct rail/road link with Denmark.

Denmark

Bus Eurolines runs buses five days per week from Stockholm/Gothenburg to Copenhagen (Skr390/210, nine/4½ hours). Much cheaper Säfflebussen buses between Gothenburg and Copenhagen run four times daily (Skr150, four hours).

Kystlinien (☎ 0200 218218) bus No 109 runs regularly from Malmö/Lund across the bridge to Copenhagen Kastrup airport (Skr115). They also run daily buses from Halmstad to Kastrup (Skr160, 3¾ hours) via the Helsingborg-Helsingør ferry.

Train Trains run every 20 minutes from Copenhagen to Malmö (Skr65, 38 minutes). Around seven daily X2000 trains run from Copenhagen to Stockholm, Halmstad and Gothenburg (rail passes valid).

Finland

Bus Bus services from Luleå to Haparanda, Övertorneå and Pajala in Sweden are operated by Länstrafik i Norrbotten and Tapanis Buss runs express coaches from Stockholm to Tornio three or four days each week (Skr400, 15 hours).

Train Train passengers can reach Boden or Luleå in Sweden and Kemi in Finland (free bus connections for rail pass holders); in summer, trains run from Boden to Tornio (Finland).

Norway

Bus There are many direct services, including daily Säfflebussen runs from Gothenburg/Stockholm to Oslo (Skr150/280).

Train The main rail links run from Stockholm to Oslo (Skr273), from Gothenburg to Oslo (Skr246), from Stockholm to Östersund and Storlien (Norwegian trains continue to Trondheim), and from Luleå to Kiruna and Narvik.

Europe

Bus Eurolines' services run from several European cities, including London to Stockholm (Skr2060 return, 30 to 35 hours, four runs per week) via Amsterdam and Hamburg. Gothenburg-Berlin costs Skr440 to Skr510 (12½ hours, five per week), while Stockholm-Berlin costs Skr795 (17 hours, once weekly). Eurolines is represented in Stockholm by Busstop (☎ 08-440 8570) at Cityterminalen, and tickets can be bought from Swebus Express at Nils Ericsson Terminalen in Gothenburg. Call ☎ 020-987377 or hit www.eurolines.se for information and timetables.

Train Direct trains from Berlin run twice daily to Malmö (nine hours), via Sassnitz and Trelleborg.

SEA
Denmark

There are numerous ferries between Denmark and Sweden. The quickest and most frequent services are between Helsingør and Helsingborg (Skr17 to Skr20). Flygbåtarna passenger-only sailings between Copenhagen (Havnegade) and Landskrona runs up to seven times daily (Skr70).

There are also services between Jutland and Sweden. Stena Line cruises between Gothenburg and Frederikshavn up to 11 times daily (from Skr90, three hours) but SeaCat takes only two hours.

Finland

There are daily year-round services from Stockholm to Turku (from around Skr130) and Helsinki (from around Skr210); rail passes give 50% discount. There are inexpensive connections to Åland from Kapellskär (from around Skr100) and Grisslehamn (from Skr50), both accessible via Norrtälje, north of Stockholm. Farther north, there's a connection from Umeå to Vasa.

Baltic States & Russia

From Stockholm, Estline (☎ 08-667 0001) sails daily to Tallinn in Estonia (from Skr300, 15 hours) and Lisco Line (☎ 08-667 5235) sails three days weekly to Klaipėda in Lithuania (from Skr550, 17 hours). There are currently no boat links to Latvia or Russia, but check with the tourist office in Stockholm.

Germany

Trelleborg is the main gateway with more than a dozen ferries arriving daily from Travemünde (Skr250), Rostock (Skr85 to Skr250) and Sassnitz (Skr60 to Skr75). Stena Line cruises daily between Gothenburg and Kiel (Skr350/750 low/high season, 10 hours).

Poland

There are daily services (less frequent in winter) from Świnoujście to Ystad and Malmö, from Gdynia to Karlskrona, and from Gdańsk to Nynäshamn.

UK

DFDS Seaways (☎ 031-650650) have two crossings per week from Gothenburg to Newcastle via Kristiansand (Norway). These take 25 hours and single fares start at UK£54/114 in low/high season.

Getting Around

Sweden's efficient public transport relies on 23 different regional traffic networks (länstrafik). The general confusion is partly solved by the Tågplus system, where one ticket is valid on trains and on any länstrafik bus. Tågplus is only warranted if you're not using any other discount scheme.

AIR

Sweden has 10 domestic airlines, most of them using Stockholm Arlanda as a hub. SAS (Scandinavian Airlines) daily domestic flights serve the country from Malmö in the south to Kiruna in the north. Skyways runs an even larger network. Flying in Sweden is expensive, but substantial discounts are available. People under age 25 can buy one-way SAS stand-by tickets (Skr130) to/from Stockholm and any other major Swedish city, which is great value for Lappland destinations. Braathens Malmö Aviation stand-by tickets are available to all travellers for Skr200 or Skr300.

BUS

You can travel by bus in Sweden either on national long-distance routes, or using any of the 23 regional länstrafik networks.

Länstrafik is usually complemented by regional trains, and one ticket is valid on all

services. Rules vary but transfers are usually free within one to four hours. Most counties are divided into zones. Travel within one zone costs from Skr13 to Skr17. Every time you enter a new zone, the price is increased. There are thick timetables for each county, or dozens of thin local timetables – they're free or almost free. Study them carefully, and check out the various discount schemes.

Long-distance buses are either extended regional services (prices vary) or more extensive 'national' networks. The largest is Swebus Express (reservations not required), but there's also Svenska Buss (☎ 020 676767), cheaper Säfflebussen (☎ 0533-16006), and Ybuss in Norrland (☎ 0200 334444), which all require advance seat reservations.

Passengers under 25 (under 20 with Ybuss) and over 60 years get 30% discount.

TRAIN

Sweden has an extensive railway network, and trains are certainly the fastest way to explore the country. There are several train operators in Sweden, although the national network, Sveriges Järnväg (SJ), covers most main lines. Full price 2nd-class tickets are expensive, but there are discounts (see Passes & Discounts later in this section). All tickets include a seat reservation when required, and night trains provide the option of a sleeper (supplement from Skr90) or a seat.

In summer, almost 25 different tourist trains offer special rail experiences. The most notable is the scenic Inlandsbanan – 1067km from Mora to Gällivare costs Skr525, but a special Skr750 card allows two weeks' unlimited travel. Service on this line is slow – six hours from Mora to Östersund and 15 hours from Östersund to Gällivare.

You can bring a bicycle on many länstrafik trains without prior arrangement, unlike on SJ trains.

For information on train tickets and timetables call ☎ 020 757575 from anywhere in Sweden, or hit the Internet at www.sj.se, www.inlandsbanan.se, or www.tagkom.com.

Passes & Discounts

Eurail, Inter-Rail and ScanRail passes are valid on SJ trains and buses and on all regional trains, but not on Inlandsbanan or the local SL (Storstockholms Lokaltrafik) *pendeltåg* trains around Stockholm. Rail pass-holders are required to pay a supplement of Skr50 (including the obligatory seat reservation) on X2000 trains. Reservation supplements for non-X2000 trains (Skr30) aren't obligatory, and there are no supplements for regional länstrafik trains.

Discount rail tickets in Sweden are confusing and often have strings attached. Just remember that people under age 26 always get a 30% discount. Other options include SJ's Reslust Card and, for people under age 25, the Reslust Max 25 Card. These cost Skr150, are valid for one calendar year and give up to 80% discount on tickets. The catch is that with either card you must book and pay at least seven days in advance. From outside Sweden, purchase cards and tickets from Sweden Booking (☎ 0498-203380) for a Skr100 fee.

CAR & MOTORCYCLE

An international driver's licence is unnecessary; your home-country's licence is sufficient to drive in Sweden.

In Sweden you drive on the right and give way to the right. Headlights must be on at all times. Seat belts must be worn in all seats. The blood-alcohol limit is stringent at 0.02%. The normal maximum speed on motorways and remote highways is 110km/h. Speeds on other roads are 50km/h in built-up areas and 90km/h on highways. Especially in forested areas at dawn and dusk, drivers should be alert to wild animals crossing roads – colliding with a 400kg elk may cause more than one fatality. Sandboxes on many roads may be helpful in mud or snow.

The national motoring association affiliated to AIT is Motormännens Riksförbund (☎ 08-690 3800), Sveavägen 159, SE-10435 Stockholm.

Cars can be hired from petrol stations at reasonable rates, but must be returned to the hiring point. Statoil (☎ 020 252525) charges from Skr190 per day plus Skr1.40 per km, including insurance, and can accept drivers as young as 18.

Stockholm

☎ 08

Stockholm is without a doubt one of the world's most beautiful national capitals. The 24,000 islands and islets of the *skärgård* (archipelago) protect Stockholm's urbanised islands from the open seas.

Around 1.8 million people live in Greater Stockholm, and over 15% are foreigners who give the city a spirited, international feel. The city's 10 royal residences include the largest palace in the world still in use, and the World Heritage-listed Drottningholm. Stockholm has the best selection of budget accommodation in Scandinavia, and although it isn't really cheap, it's mostly clean and comfortable.

Orientation

Stockholm is built on islands, except for the modern centre (Norrmalm), focused on the ugly Sergels Torg square. This business and shopping hub is linked to Centralstationen (the central train station) by a network of subways and the gardens of Kungsträdgården lie to the east. The subways connect with the metro (*tunnelbana*, or T) stations.

The triangular island Stadsholmen and its neighbours accommodate the old town (Gamla Stan), connected to Norrmalm by several bridges.

Information

Tourist Offices The helpful Stockholm Information Service (☎ 789 2490, @ info@ stoinfo.se) is in Sweden House at Hamngatan 27, by Kungsträdgården. The office is open 8 am to 7 pm weekdays from June to August, 9 am to 5 pm weekends (otherwise 9 am to 5 pm, 3 pm at weekends).

Conviently located at Centralstationen, Hotellcentralen (☎ 789 2425) has city information and maps, and books hotels and hostels. It's open until 6 pm daily (until 9 pm from May to September).

Stockholm Card The Stockholm Card is available from tourist offices and larger museums at Skr199/398/498 for 24/48/72 hours. It gives free entry to most attractions (including museums) and free travel on public transport (including the Katarinahissen lift, but excluding local ferries and airport buses).

Money At Centralstationen, Forex (open 8 am to 9 pm daily) charges Skr15 per travellers cheque. The post office in the station's main hall charges a flat fee of Skr50

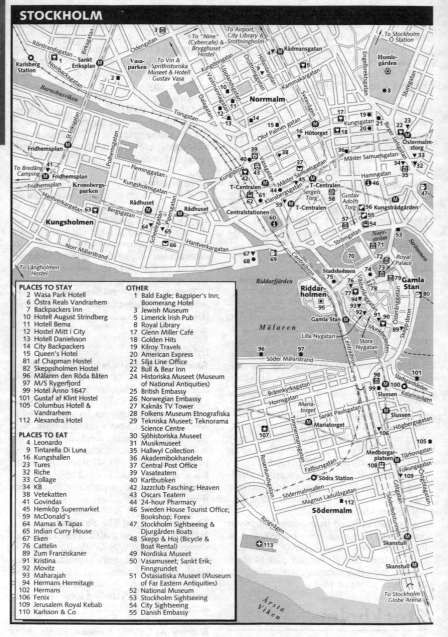

STOCKHOLM

SWEDEN

PLACES TO STAY
2   Wasa Park Hotell
6   Östra Reals Vandrarhem
7   Backpackers Inn
10   Hotell August Strindberg
11   Hotell Bema
12   Hostel Mitt i City
13   Hotell Danielsson
14   City Backpackers
15   Queen's Hotel
81   af Chapman Hostel
82   Skeppsholmen Hostel
96   Mälaren den Röda Båten
97   M/S Rygerfjord
99   Hotel Anno 1647
101   Gustaf af Klint Hostel
105   Columbus Hotell &
      Vandrarhem
112   Alexandra Hotel

PLACES TO EAT
4   Leonardo
9   Tintarella Di Luna
16   Kungshallen
23   Tures
32   Riche
33   Collage
34   KB
38   Vetekatten
41   Govindas
46   Hemköp Supermarket
59   McDonald's
64   Mamas & Tapas
65   Indian Curry House
67   Eken
76   Cattelin
89   Zum Franziskaner
91   Kristina
92   Movitz
93   Maharajah
94   Hermans Hermitage
102   Hermans
106   Fenix
109   Jerusalem Royal Kebab
110   Karlsson & Co

OTHER
1   Bald Eagle; Bagpiper's Inn;
    Boomerang Hotel
3   Jewish Museum
5   Limerick Irish Pub
6   Royal Library
17   Glenn Miller Café
18   Golden Hits
19   Kilroy Travels
20   American Express
21   Silja Line Office
22   Bull & Bear Inn
24   Historiska Museet (Museum
    of National Antiquities)
25   British Embassy
26   Norwegian Embassy
27   Kaknäs TV Tower
28   Folkens Museum Etnografiska
29   Tekniska Museet; Teknorama
    Science Centre
30   Sjöhistoriska Museet
31   Musikmuseet
35   Hallwyl Collection
36   Akademibokhandeln
37   Central Post Office
39   Vasateatern
40   Kartbutiken
42   Jazzclub Fasching; Heaven
43   Oscars Teatern
44   24-hour Pharmacy
46   Sweden House Tourist Office;
    Bookshop; Forex
47   Stockholm Sightseeing &
    Djurgården Boats
48   Skepp & Hoj (Bicycle &
    Boat Rental)
49   Nordiska Museet
50   Vasamuseet; Sankt Erik;
    Finngrundet
51   Östasiatiska Museet (Museum
    of Far Eastern Antiquities)
52   National Museum
53   Stockholm Sightseeing
54   City Sightseeing
55   Danish Embassy

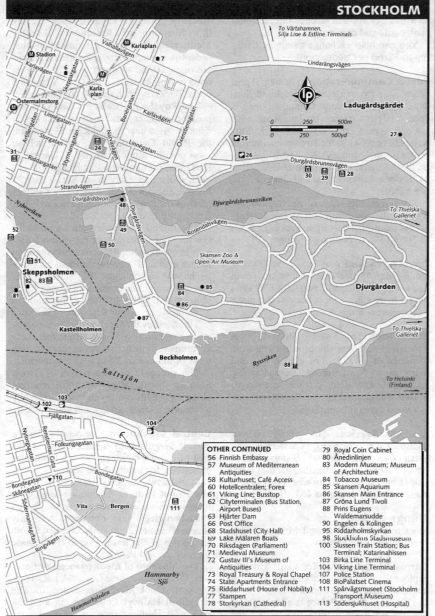

STOCKHOLM

To Värtahamnen,
Silja Line & Estline Terminals

Valhallavägen · Karlaplan

Stadion

Karlavägen

Skeppargatan

Karla-plan

Östermalmstorg

Linnégatan

Artillerigatan

Storgatan

Styrmansgatan

Banérgatan

Karlavägen

Narvavägen

Oxenstiernsgatan

Linnégatan

Riddargatan

Strandvägen

Nybroviken

Djurgårdsbron

Djurgårdsvägen

Djurgårdsbrunnsviken

Rosendalsvägen

Lindarängsvägen

Ladugårdsgärdet

0   250   500m
0   250   500yd

Djurgårdsbrunnsvägen

Skeppsholmen

Skansen Zoo &
Open-Air Museum

Djurgården

To Thielska
Galleriet

To Thielska
Galleriet

Kastellholmen

Beckholmen

Ryssviken

Saltsjön

To Helsinki
(Finland)

Fjällgatan

Nytorgsgatan

Renstiernas Gata

Folkungagatan

Bondegatan

Bondegatan

Skånegatan

Södermannagatan

Ringvägen

Vita   Bergen

Hammarby
Sjö

Hammarbyleden

OTHER CONTINUED

56	Finnish Embassy	
57	Museum of Mediterranean Antiquities	
58	Kulturhuset; Café Access	
60	Hotellcentralen; Forex	
61	Viking Line; Busstop	
62	Cityterminalen (Bus Station, Airport Buses)	
63	Hjärter Dam	
66	Post Office	
68	Stadshuset (City Hall)	
69	Lake Mälaren Boats	
70	Riksdagen (Parliament)	
71	Medieval Museum	
72	Gustav III's Museum of Antiquities	
73	Royal Treasury & Royal Chapel	
74	State Apartments Entrance	
75	Riddarhuset (House of Nobility)	
77	Stampen	
78	Storkyrkan (Cathedral)	

79	Royal Coin Cabinet
80	Ånedinlinjen
83	Modern Museum; Museum of Architecture
84	Tobacco Museum
85	Skansen Aquarium
86	Skansen Main Entrance
87	Gröna Lund Tivoli
88	Prins Eugens Waldemarsudde
90	Engelen & Kolingen
95	Riddarholmskyrkan
98	Stockholms Stadsmuseum
100	Slussen Train Station; Bus Terminal; Katarinahissen
103	Birka Line Terminal
104	Viking Line Terminal
107	Police Station
108	BioPalatset Cinema
111	Spårvägsmuseet (Stockholm Transport Museum)
113	Södersjukhuset (Hospital)

and has slightly better rates. The station also has ATMs that accept international bank cards and credit cards.

You can also exchange money at banks (up to Skr60 per transaction).

Post & Communications The central post office is at Drottninggatan 53 (closed Sunday). The post office at Centralstationen is open to 10 pm weekdays (to 7 pm weekends).

Café Access (☎ 5083 1488) in Kulturhuset charges Skr30 for 30 minutes Internet access (closed Monday). Nine (☎ 612 9009), on the northern side of town at Odengatan 44, is open daily to 1 am and charges Skr1 per minute.

The large city library on Sveavägen, north of the city centre, offers free Internet access from 11 am to 5 pm weekdays – call ☎ 5083 1130 to book a computer.

Travel Agencies Kilroy Travels (☎ 234515), Kungsgatan 4, specialises in discount youth and student flights. STF (☎ 020 292929) no longer has a sales office, but you can make telephone bookings for its tour packages.

Bookshops The Sweden Bookshop, in Sweden House, has the broadest selection of books in English. For guidebooks and maps, go to Kartbutiken, Kungsgatan 74. Akademibokhandeln on the corner of Mäster Samuelsgatan and Regeringsgatan is a good general bookshop.

Medical Services The central 24-hour pharmacy (☎ 454 8130) is at Klarabergsgatan 64. The hospital Södersjukhuset (☎ 616 1000), in Södermalm, handles casualties from the central city area. You can also contact the duty doctor (☎ 463 9100) at night.

Things to See

Most museums are closed Monday – exceptions are noted below.

Gamla Stan Allow at least half a day to explore Gamla Stan; it's the oldest and most attractive part of Stockholm.

The 'new' **Royal Palace** is a highlight of the old town. With 608 rooms, it's the largest royal palace in the world still in use. The **State Apartments** are the most interesting section of the palace, with two floors of royal pomp and portraits of the pale

princes. Crowns are displayed at the **Royal Treasury**, near the **Royal Chapel**. **Gustav III's Museum of Antiquities** displays Mediterranean treasures acquired by that eccentric monarch. Royal Palace attractions are open 10 am to 4 pm daily in summer, noon to 3 pm the rest of the year. Admission costs Skr50 for each (Skr80 combined).

The **Royal Coin Cabinet** (Skr45) is opposite the palace, next to the small Finnish Church. Also near the palace is **Storkyrkan**, the Royal Cathedral of Sweden, whose most notable attraction is the St George & the Dragon sculpture dating from 1494. It's open daily and entry costs Skr10 (Stockholm Card not valid). Inquire if summer tours of the tower are still held in English at 2 pm daily (Skr20).

The island of Riddarholmen, west of Gamla Stan, has some of the oldest buildings in Stockholm. **Riddarholmskyrkan**, no longer a church but now the royal necropolis, has the sarcophagus of Gustav II Adolf, Sweden's mightiest monarch; it's open 10 am to 4 pm daily May to August, and noon to 3 pm on weekends in September (Skr20).

The **Medieval Museum** on Strömparterren is a relatively recent addition (open daily in summer; Skr40). In summer there are free tours of the nearby **Riksdagen** (parliament).

The streets of the eastern half of Gamla Stan are medieval enough, still winding along their 14th-century lines and linked by a fantasy of lanes, arches and stairways.

Central Stockholm Few people like the central **Sergels Torg** square, a few blocks east of Centralstationen, but it's the centre of activity for much of the year.

Stadshuset, the City Hall, looks like a church but features the mosaic-lined Gyllene salen, and the hall where the Nobel Prize banquet is held. Entry is by tour only (open 10 am to 2 pm daily; Skr40). Climb to the top of the tower (Skr40) for a good view of the old town.

The **Museum of Mediterranean Antiquities**, Fredsgatan 2, near Gustav Adolfs Torg, is worth a look (Skr50/free under 20). The delightful **Hallwyl Collection**, in an 1898 palace at Hamngatan 4, is shown hourly (Skr60), once daily in English (1 pm).

The **National Museum** on Södra Blasieholmskajen has the main national collection of painting and sculpture, and hosts other temporary exhibitions (Skr60). The museum is open daily except Monday.

There are three worthwhile museums across the bridge on Skeppsholmen: **Östasiatiska Museet** (Museum of Far Eastern Antiquities; open daily except Monday; Skr40), the **Modern Museum** (Skr60) and the adjoining **Museum of Architecture** (Skr45). A combined ticket for the latter two costs Skr80.

In Vasastaden, north of the centre and near the T-Odenplan metro station, **Vin & Sprithistoriska Museet** (Wine & Liquor Museum), Dalagatan 100, details the weird story behind *brännvin* (snaps) and the birth of the conservative Swedish alcohol policy (closed Monday and Thursday; Skr40). The small **Jewish Museum** at Hälsingegatan 2 is open noon to 4 pm Sunday to Friday (Skr30, Stockholm Card not valid).

ABBA fans can check out band paraphernalia at the small **Musikmuseet**, at Sibyllegatan 2 (Skr30). The main national historical collection is housed at **Historiska Museet**, Narvavägen 13 (T-Karlaplan). Don't miss the incredible Gold Room (Skr60).

Djurgården To reach Djurgården, take bus No 47 from Centralstationen or, in summer, a ferry from Nybroplan or Slussen.

Skansen, the world's first open-air museum, today has over 150 traditional houses and other exhibits from all over Sweden occupying its attractive hill top. You could spend all day here, wandering between the **zoo**, the handicraft precinct, the quirky **Tobacco Museum**, the excellent **aquarium**, and the open-air stages. Skansen is open daily in summer (Skr60/30) with shorter hours at other times (from Skr30/10). The aquarium is open daily and costs Skr50 extra.

Skansen is surrounded by other museums. **Nordiska museet** was founded by Artur Hazelius (who also started Skansen), and the enormous Renaissance-style castle houses notable temporary exhibitions (Skr60). The interesting **Vasamuseet**, on the western shore of Djurgården, houses a resurrected warship and looks at the lives of the 17th-century sailors (open daily; Skr60). Moored behind the museum are the icebreaker *Sankt Erik* and the lightship *Finngrundet*, both open daily in summer (Skr25).

The **Gröna Lund Tivoli** fun park is open daily in summer and is always crowded.

The Åkbandet day pass (Skr195) allows unlimited rides. General park admission is an extra Skr45 (free with Stockholm Card).

Prins Eugens Waldemarsudde was a private palace of a painter-prince who preferred art to royal pleasures; the buildings, art galleries and the old windmill are surrounded by picturesque gardens (open Tuesday to Sunday; Skr60).

Ladugårdsgärdet Just north of Djurgården are several interesting attractions. **Sjöhistoriska Museet** exhibits maritime memorabilia (open daily; Skr40), **Tekniska Museet & Teknorama Science Centre** has exhaustive exhibits on Swedish inventions and includes the **Telecommunications Museum** (open daily; Skr50), and **Folkens Museum Etnografiska** which brings the entire world under one roof (Skr40). Nearby is the 155m **Kaknäs TV Tower**, the tallest building in town (lift to the top, Skr25). Take bus No 69 from Centralstationen to Ladugårdsgärdet.

Södermalm Mostly residential, Södermalm is a suburb with more character than other parts of Stockholm. Head to the northern cliffs for good views and old houses. Still better are the views from **Katarinahissen**, an old lift that takes you to the heights from Slussen (Skr5).

Stockholms Stadsmuseum displays the streets and houses of Stockholm, and it is worthwhile once you have developed some romantic attachment to Stockholm (Skr40). **Spårvägsmuseet** (Stockholm Transport Museum), in the Söderhallen transport depot at Tegelviksgatan 22, has a large collection of vintage trams and buses (open daily; Skr20, free with the SL Tourist Card).

Organised Tours

The city is best seen from the water, so consider a cruise (Skr90/140 for one/two hours) with Stockholm Sightseeing (☎ 587 14020); they run early April to mid-December from Strömkajen (near the Grand Hotel), Nybroplan and Klara Mälarstrand (near Stadshuset). City Sightseeing (☎ 587 14030) runs daily three-hour coach tours of the city from Skr130 to Skr240.

Special Events

The biggest annual event is the Stockholm Water Festival, which runs for 10 days in early August and involves all manner of concerts and cultural events as well as regattas and fireworks. A special pass (Skr99) is required for most concerts and events, but some require up to Skr150 more.

Places to Stay

Reservations are a good idea in summer. Otherwise the tourist office and Hotellcentralen (see Information, earlier in this section) make bookings for a small fee (Skr20/50 for hostels/hotels). A number of agencies book *private rooms* in and around Stockholm from around Skr200 per person – try Bed & Breakfast Service Stockholm (☎ 700 6272, ☺ info@bedbreakfast.a.se) at Kungsbron 1.

Note that most hotels in Stockholm offer discount rates on weekends and in summer (mid-June to early August).

Camping *Bredäng Camping (☎ 977071, Stora Sällskapets väg 51)* is in Bredäng, 10km south-west of Stockholm (T-Bredäng). Sites start at Skr75, and it's open between April and October.

Hostels Most travellers head first to Skeppsholmen (walk or take bus No 65 from Centralstationen). The popular, gently rolling STF boat hostel *af Chapman (☎ 463 2266, ☺ info@chapman.stfturist.se)* has bunks for Skr130; breakfast is Skr45. On dry land beside the boat hostel, and with the same reception and prices, is the larger *Skeppsholmen Hostel*.

Nearer to Centralstationen is *City Backpackers (☎ 206920, ☺ city.backpackers@swipnet.se, Upplandsgatan 2A)*, one of the best-equipped hostels (sauna, kitchen, laundry etc) in Stockhom. Dorm beds will cost you Skr150.

A bit farther north, *Hostel Mitt i City (☎ 217630, Västmannagatan 13, 5th floor)*, has beds from Skr175 (including breakfast). It's open 24 hours, year-round. *Brygghuset (☎ 312424, Norrtullsgatan 12N)*, near T-Odenplan, is open late May to early September. Dorm beds cost Skr130.

Open only from 26 June to 12 August, *Backpackers Inn (☎ 660 7515, Banérgatan 56)*, near (T-Karlaplan), has 300 beds in a school building and charges Skr100 (more for non-HI members). Nearby, *Östra Reals Vandrarhem (☎ 664 1114, Karlavägen 79)*,

also in an old school, is open from 16 June to 12 August. Beds cost Skr125 (there are no kitchen facilities).

There are many hostels in and around Södermalm. The boat hostel *Gustaf af Klint (☎ 640 4077, Stadsgårdskajen 153)* has dorm beds (Skr120) and beds in four/two-berth cabins (Skr140/160).

Mälaren den Röda Båten (☎ 644 4385, Söder Malärstrand, Kajplats 6) is easily the cosiest of Stockholm's floating hostels and has a fine restaurant. Dorm beds are Skr150 and cabin bunks Skr195. A bit farther west, M/S *Rygerfjord (☎ 840830, ☺ hotell@rygerfjord.se, Söder Malärstrand, Kajplats 14)* has a few bunks from Skr145, and hotel rooms from Skr275 per person (including breakfast).

Columbus Hotell & Vandrarhem (☎ 644 1717, ☺ columbus@columbus.se, Tjärhovsgatan 11) is in a quiet location in Södermalm (T-Medborgarplatsen). There are 100 beds (from Skr165), a kitchen and a restaurant. Hotel rooms cost from Skr495/695 a single/double.

The former prison on the small island of Långholmen now houses a small museum and the STF *Långholmen* hostel (☎ 668 0510, ☺ vandrarhem@langholmen.com). Dorm beds start at Skr160 (bookings essential) and hotel rooms are Skr595/895 on weekends and in summer.

Hotels Just north of the centre, *Hotell Bema (☎ 232675, Upplandsgatan 13)* has good singles/doubles discounted in summer and on weekends to Skr450/550 – excellent value. Not far away, *Hotell August Strindberg (☎ 325006, Tegnérgatan 38)* is a quiet spot with simple rooms for Skr575/690 and *Hotell Danielsson (☎ 411 1065, Västmannagatan 5)* has rooms in summer for Skr350/500.

A bit farther north is *Hotell Gustav Vasa (☎ 343801, Västmannagatan 61)*, with rooms from Skr475/625 in summer.

The pleasant, central *Queen's Hotel (☎ 249460, Drottninggatan 71A)* has basic singles/doubles discounted to Skr475/575 in summer.

Wasa Park Hotell (☎ 340285, Sankt Eriksplan 1), is just north-west of the business district (T-Sankt Eriksplan) and has rooms year-round from Skr425/550.

In Södermalm, *Alexandra Hotel (☎ 840320, Magnus Ladulåsgatan 42)*, has summer and weekend deals from Skr375/735. The simplest rooms at *Hotel Anno 1647 (☎ 442 1680, Mariagränd 3)*, just off Slussen, are reasonable value in summer at Skr530/630.

Places to Eat

The cheapest snacks are found at the numerous *gatukök* outlets, which serve chips, burgers and sausages. There are also several 24-hour 7-Eleven shops, which serve coffee and sandwiches.

Gamla Stan On Stora Nygatan look for *Maharajah* at No 20, with cheap Indian fare, and the vegetarian *Hermans Hermitage* at No 11 (dinner Skr70). *Kristina*, on Västerlånggatan, serves pizza from Skr39 and *Cattelin*, on Storkyrkobrinken, has inexpensive Swedish dishes (from Skr89). Locals prefer Gamla Stan's traditional restaurants, including *Movitz (Tyska Brinken 34)*, in an arched cellar. *Zum Franziskaner (Skeppsbron 44)* serves German sausages and is the oldest restaurant in town; the lunch special is Skr55.

Norrmalm *Kungshallen*, on Hötorget, is a food court where you can eat anything from Tex-Mex to Indian at budget prices. The traditional cafe *Vetekatten (Klara Norra Kyrkogatan 26)* is nearby. There's a 24-hour *McDonald's* on Vasagatan, outside Centralstationen. *Collage (Smålandsgatan 2)* offers main courses from Skr89. Surprisingly reasonable lunches for Skr60 are available at *Eken*, within the City Hall.

Birger Jarlsgatan has many good places, and *Riche*, at No 4, should be seen for its decor alone (main courses from Skr80). Nearby *KB (Smålandsgatan 7)* is a traditional restaurant with Swedish cuisine from Skr65. Farther north the highly recommended *Tures (Sturegallerian 10)* serves excellent Swedish grub from Skr75 to Skr182.

At *Leonardo (Sveavägen 55)*, pizzas are baked in a stone oven (from Skr73 to Skr95).

Tintarella Di Luna (Drottninggatan 102) is a pleasant Italian cafe which serves things like panini (Skr35) and focaccia (Skr40).

The handiest central supermarket is *Hemköp (Klarabergsgatan 50)*.

Södermalm *Jerusalem Royal Kebab (Götgatan 60)* is open 24 hours and has kebabs and felafels from just Skr15. For budget vegetarian food, go to *Hermans (Fjällgatan 23A)*. *Fenix (Götgatan 44)* is a local pub with a variety of evening meals. Another popular restaurant worth a visit is *Karlsson & Co (Bondegatan 54)*.

Kungsholmen Popular lower-budget restaurants around Scheelegatan include the *Indian Curry House (Scheelegatan 6)* and *Mamas & Tapas (Scheelegatan 3)*. The Hare Krishna-run *Govindas (Fridhemsgatan 22)*, near T-Fredhemsplan, offers an imaginative vegetarian buffet for Skr65.

Entertainment

Stockholm This Week, available free at tourist offices, has entertainment listings. The free English-language paper *D&N* concentrates on the contemporary music and entertainment scenes.

Pubs & Clubs *Kvarterskrog* (pubs), also known as krog, are generally open 5 pm to 1 am. In Södermalm there are krog on Götgatan and in the Skånegatan area. In the Kungsholmen area, try Scheelegatan.

The *Glenn Miller Café (Brunnsgatan 21)*, near Stureplan, plays jazz CDs, while *Golden Hits (Kungsgatan 29)* does the same with 1950s tunes. Stockholm's main live jazz venue is *Jazzclub Fasching (Kungsgatan 63)*. Next door *Heaven* also has regular live music on Friday and appeals to the 18 to 25 year-old group (Skr60 admission).

In Gamla Stan, *Stampen (Stora Nygatan 5)* has live jazz nightly, while *Engelen & Kolingen (Kornhamnstorg 59)* hosts local bands most nights (entry Skr40 to Skr60).

Kungsholmen's *Hjärter Dam (Polhemsgatan 23)* is a gay-and-straight bar/restaurant.

North of the city centre, the lively *Limerick Irish Pub*, on the corner of Döbelnsgatan and Tegnérgatan, has typical pub food with the inevitable Guinness on tap. Around Rörstandsgatan there are many pubs, including the *Bald Eagle* (American), *Bagpiper's Inn* (Scottish) and *Boomerang Hotel* (Australian). The English-style *Bull & Bear Inn (Birger Jarlsgatan 16)* serves pub grub for under Skr100.

Cinema & Theatre *BioPalatset (☎ 234700, Medborgarplatsen)* has 10 screens and shows Hollywood films daily.

Stockholm has outstanding dance, opera and music performances – for an overview, pick up the free *Teater Guide* from tourist offices. Tickets aren't cheap and are often sold out, especially for Saturday shows. The classic *Oscars Teatern* at the corner of Vasagatan and Kungsgatan runs Broadway-style musicals. The small *Vasateatern*, directly opposite, sometimes stages plays in English.

Getting There & Away

Air International air services to Copenhagen, Oslo, Bergen, Helsinki, Reykjavík and St Petersburg are run by SAS (☎ 020 727555). Finnair (☎ 020 781100) fly to Turku, Vasa and Tampere and there are around 15 flights per day to Helsinki. Skyways (☎ 797 7130) has the most comprehensive network of domestic flights. For more information see the main Getting There & Away section earlier in this chapter.

Bus Cityterminalen, opposite Centralstationen, is Stockholm's long-distance bus station. The station's Busstop ticket office represents the big concerns such as Swebus Express, Eurolines, Svenska Buss and Säfflebussen, along with many of the direct buses to the north.

Train From Centralstationen (Stockholm C) there are direct trains to/from Copenhagen, Oslo, Storlien (for Trondheim) and Narvik. SL pendeltåg commuter services also run to/from Nynäshamn, Södertälje and Märsta.

Boat For more information on ferries to/from Stockholm, see the main Getting There & Away section earlier in this chapter.

Silja Line ferries (☎ 222140) depart for Helsinki and Turku (in Finland) from Värtahamnen – walk from T-Gärdet or take bus No 76 from T-Ropsten. The company has an office on Kungsgatan in Stockholm.

Viking Line ferries (☎ 452 4000) sail to Turku and Helsinki from the terminal at Tegelvikshamn – walk 1.5km from T-Slussen, or take a bus from Viking Line's Cityterminalen office (Skr30).

Birka Cruises (☎ 714 5520) ferries to Mariehamn (in Finland) depart from Stadsgårdsterminalen (T-Slussen), while Ånedinlinjen (☎ 456 2200) boats to Mariehamn leave from the quay at Tullhus 1 on Skeppsbron in Gamla Stan.

Getting Around

To/From the Airport Every five or 10 minutes, Flygbuss buses run between Arlanda airport and Cityterminalen (Skr60, 40 minutes). The Flygbuss desk is in the international arrivals terminal. A taxi to/from the city centre costs Skr320 to Skr440 (agree on the fare before you get in).

If you're using the Bromma airport for domestic flights, the bus from Cityterminalen costs Skr40.

Public Transport Storstockholms Lokaltrafik (SL) runs Stockholm's *tunnelbana* (T) metro trains, local trains and buses. There are SL information centres at T-Centralen, in the basement level of the station hall and at the Sergels Torg entrance (☎ 686 1185).

The Stockholm Card (see Information earlier in this section) covers travel on all SL trains and buses in greater Stockholm. The SL Tourist Card (Skr60/120 for 24/72 hours) is identical except that it only gives free entry to a few attractions. Rail passes aren't valid on SL trains.

Public transport tickets cost Skr14 (two 'coupons') for one zone, then Skr7 extra for each additional zone, up to five coupons for four or five zones. You can buy a 20-coupon discount ticket for Skr95. Tickets are valid for one hour and must be stamped at the start of the journey.

Bicycle Skepp & Hoj (☎ 660 5757) on Djurgården (by the bridge) rents bicycles for Skr150/500 per day/week. Bicycles can be carried free on SL local trains, except on weekdays between 6 and 9 am and 3 and 6 pm, but are prohibited in Centralstationen and on the metro.

Boat City ferry services connect Gröna Lund Tivoli on Djurgården with Nybroplan and Slussen. The ferries run as frequently as every 10 minutes in summer; a single trip costs Skr20 (free with SL Tourist and Stockholm cards).

AROUND STOCKHOLM
Ekerö
☎ 08

Surprisingly rural, Ekerö consists of several large islands on Lake Mälaren (to the west of central Stockholm), three Unesco

World Heritage-listed sites and a dozen medieval churches. If you're too hassled to cycle, take the metro to T-Brommaplan and change to bus Nos 311 or 312.

Drottningholm The royal residence and parks of Drottningholm aren't among Greater Stockholm's finest attractions, despite the hype. The Renaissance-inspired palace, with geometric baroque gardens, was built about the same time as Versailles in the late 17th century. The highlights inside are the **Karl X Gustav Gallery** and the painted ceilings of the **State Bedchamber**. The palace is open daily from May to August, and entry costs Skr50.

Slottsteater, the court theatre, has a museum but the original 18th-century building itself is unique (hourly tours Skr50/free). At the far end of the gardens is the 18th-century **Kina slott**, a lavishly decorated 'Chinese palace' (Skr50).

Adelsö The World Heritage Site on Adelsö comprises the **medieval church** and **burial mounds** that are associated with nearby Birka.

SL bus No 311 runs to Adelsö church from T-Brommaplan metro station. The STF hostel *Adelsögården* (☎ *560 51400*), just south of the ferry pier, is open mid-June to August and beds cost Skr110. A walking trail from the hostel leads via some prehistoric sites to the church.

Birka Birka, a Unesco World Heritage Site, is the site of a trading centre dating from the Viking Age, on Björkö in Lake Mälaren. From early May to late September the ferry *Victoria* sails to Birka from Stockholm's Stadshusbron pier. The return fare is Skr200.

Archaeologists have excavated Birka's cemetery, harbour and fortress. A visit to the small **museum** and a guided tour of the settlement's burial mounds and fortifications (in English) are included in the ferry price.

In summer boats run seven times daily to/from Adelsö and Birka (Skr105, including museum admission).

Sigtuna
☎ 08

Sigtuna, about 40km north-west and the most pleasant town around Stockholm, is also one the oldest in Sweden; **Stora gatan**

is probably Sweden's oldest main street and ruins of the churches of St Per, St Olof and St Lars remain. **Mariakyrkan** has restored medieval paintings. Among the museums, visit **Lundströmska gården** and the extensive **Sigtuna Museum**.

The tourist office (☎ 592 50020) is at Drakegården house, Stora gatan 33. The STF hostel *Ansgarsliden* (☎ *592 58478, Manfred Björkquists allé 12*) has beds in summer only from Skr90. *Sigtuna Grillen*, opposite the bus station, serves reasonable pizzas from Skr37.

Getting to Sigtuna from Stockholm is easy: take a train to Märsta and, just outside the station, change to bus No 570 or 575. In summer there are cruises from Stockholm and Uppsala.

Skåne

MALMÖ
☎ 040

Malmö is a lively and friendly city, perhaps due to the influence of Copenhagen across Öresund. The new 16km Öresund bridge and tunnel link, which includes Europe's longest bridge (7.8km), has brought the two cities even closer.

Orientation & Information

Stortorget square is the focus of the city. Centralstationen (the central train station) is near the ferry port, just outside the city centre's encircling canals.

The Malmö tourist office (☎ 300150, ✉ touristinfo@tourism.malmo.com), inside Centralstationen, is open daily in summer. The discount card Malmökortet allows free entry to several museums, free bus transport and discounts on sightseeing tours. It costs Skr150/275/400 for one/two/three days.

There's a Forex exchange counter (open from 8 am) opposite the tourist office within the train station. The central post office is at Skeppsbron 1. The Cyberspace C@fé, Engelbrektsgatan 13, charges Skr22 for 30 minutes of Internet access.

The best bookshop is Lundgrens at Södergatan 3.

Things to See

The main museums of Malmö are based at the moated **Malmöhus castle**. Sights include

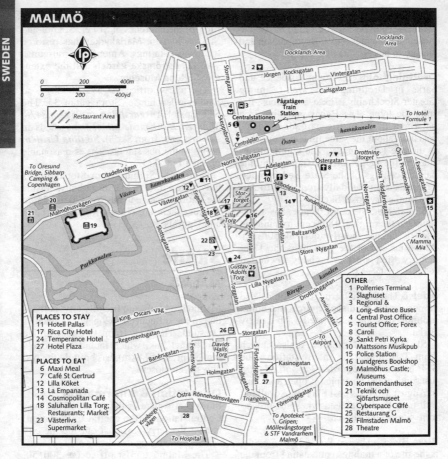

the royal apartments, with their ornate interiors and portrait collections, and the exhibitions on display at both the Stadsmuseum and Konstmuseum. Especially interesting are the aquarium and the Naturmuseum. The ticket includes the **Kommendanthuset** arsenal, opposite the castle, and also **Teknik och Sjöfartsmuseet** just to the west. The latter is a technology and maritime museum. The museums are all open daily during the summer months and a combined entry ticket costs Skr40.

Sankt Petri kyrka, on Göran Olsgatan, is characteristic of 14th-century Gothic style from the Baltic region, although it has been mostly rebuilt. The restored parts of the late-medieval town at **Lilla Torg** are now occupied by various restaurants, galleries and boutiques. It's worth wandering around Drottningtorget and down Adelgatan for more examples of old Malmö.

Places to Stay

Camping The year-round *Sibbarp Camping* (☎ *155165, Strandgatan 101*), by the Öresund bridge, has sites from Skr115 to Skr170. Take bus No 12B or 12G from Gustav Adolfs Torg.

Hostels The large, well-equipped *STF Vandrarhem Malmö* (☎ *82220, Backavägen 18*), 3km south of the city centre, is open from 10 January to 18 December and offers beds for Skr130 and breakfast for Skr40 (take bus No 21 from Centralplan in front of Centralstationen).

SWEDEN

Private Rooms Rooms or apartments from Skr200 per person are available through City Room (☎ 79594). The agency has no office address but is staffed on weekdays during office hours. Otherwise, contact the tourist office.

Hotels Of the cheapish hotels near Centralstationen only *Hotel Pallas (☎ 611 5077, Norra Vallgatan 74)* is recommended; singles/doubles are Skr280/380. *Hotel Formule 1 (☎ 930580, Lundavägen 28)*, 1.5km east of Stortorget, has rooms for Skr250 (up to three people).

On weekends and in summer the pleasant *Temperance Hotel (☎ 71020, Engelbrektsgatan 16)* charges Skr390/550, while *Hotel Plaza (☎ 77100, Kasinogatan 6)* has discounted rooms from Skr490/660 on weekends and in summer. The *Rica City Hotel (☎ 660 9550)* has a prime location on Stortorget and charges from Skr540/690.

Places to Eat

Ethnic *food stalls* at Möllevångstorget offer the cheapest snacks (felafel from Skr12). The hot dog stall *Maxi Meal* outside Centralstationen is reasonable (from Skr15) and *Mamma Mia (Föreningsgatan 67)* does excellent pizza and a drink from Skr40.

For excellent ciabatta sandwiches and broccoli soup, visit *Cosmopolitan Café (Djäknegatan 7)*. *Lilla Köket (Norra Vallgatan 88)* serves daily specials from 11 am to 8 pm (from Skr47). In the old St Gertrud courtyard, *Café St Gertrud (Östergatan 7)* has weekday lunch specials for Skr48. The cheap but highly recommended Mexican restaurant *La Empanada (Själbodgatan 10)* serves burritos from Skr30.

Saluhallen Lilla Torg has an indoor market and several restaurants. The *Västerlivs* supermarket is opposite the Temperance Hotel on Engelbrektsgatan.

Entertainment

Mattssons Musikpub (Göran Olsgatan 1) has jazz bands three nights a week except in July and August. The best club in town is the huge *Slaghuset (Jörgen Kocksgatan 7A)*. Admission costs Skr60. *Restaurang G*, in the middle of Gustav Adolfs torg, has a gay bar.

Cinema tickets at the *Filmstaden Malmö (☎ 600 8150, Storgatan 22)* cost Skr75.

Getting There & Away

The new integrated Öresundregionen transport system is now operational, with trains from Helsingborg via Malmö and Copenhagen to Helsingør. Malmö-Copenhagen (Skr65) takes 38 minutes.

Air Sturup airport is 31km south-east of the city (see Getting Around later in this section) and SAS flies nonstop to Stockholm up to 16 times daily. Trains run directly to Copenhagen airport, which has a much better flight selection.

Bus Regional and long-distance buses depart from Stormgatan. Swebus Express runs daily to Stockholm and Gothenburg. Säfflebussen (☎ 0533-16006) runs daily to Trelleborg and Helsingborg. Länstrafik buses to Helsingborg cost Skr70. Trains are best for trips to Lund or across the Öresund bridge.

Train Pågatågen local trains run to Helsingborg (Skr70), Lund (Skr30), Ystad (Skr60) and other destinations in Skåne.

SJ trains run regularly to/from Helsingborg (Skr90) and Gothenburg (Skr190) via Lund. Direct trains run between Stockholm and Malmö (Skr305), including regular X2000 services (Skr50 supplement for rail pass holders).

Boat Malmö can be reached from Poland – the ferry terminal is near the train station.

Getting Around

The Flygbuss runs from Centralstationen to Sturup airport (Skr60).

Bicycles can be rented for Skr60/300 per day/week from Cykelkliniken on Carlsgatan, near Centralstationen.

LUND

☎ 046

Lund, the second oldest town in Sweden, has a well preserved medieval quarter, a university founded in 1666, and some top-class museums. Modern Lund retains its quiet, airy campus feel and consequently has a youthful population.

Information

The tourist office (☎ 355040) is opposite the cathedral at Kyrkogatan 11. The main post office is at Knut den Stores torg 2. You can access the Internet at the Cyberspace Café, Bantorget 6, or for free at the public library (there's a 30-minute limit, and email is barred), St Petri kyrkogatan 6.

Things to See

Lund's Romanesque **cathedral** off Stortorget is magnificent, especially if you visit at noon or 3 pm (1 and 3 pm on Sunday) when the astronomical clock strikes up.

As far as Swedish museums go, you can't find many that are better than **Kulturen**, a few blocks north-east of the cathedral (enter from Tegnérsplatsen). The collection fills two city blocks. It's open daily in summer and entry costs Skr40. There are guided tours in English on Sunday.

Also worth a visit are **Historiska museet**, just behind the cathedral, and the adjoining cathedral museum **Domkyrkomuseet** (closed Monday; combined entry Skr10).

Drottens kyrkoruin is at Kattesund 6. The 11th-century church ruins can be viewed from the street, but the underground museum, focusing on medieval Lund, is the main draw (closed Monday; Skr10/free).

Hökeriet (☎ 350404), on the corner of St Annegatan and Tomegapsgatan, is a rather interesting old-fashioned general store, open daily in summer (free). The tiny **Antikmuseet**, Sölvegatan 2, is in a university department and can be seen free of charge during office hours.

Places to Stay

The tourist office books *private rooms* from Skr175 per person, plus a Skr50 booking fee.

STF's central *Tåget Hostel* (☎ 142820), 300m north-west of the train station, occupies old sleeping carriages – quiet yet cramped and perhaps too familiar to weary train travellers. Beds cost Skr110, breakfast is Skr45. The SVIF hostel *Lundabygdens Vandrarhem* (☎ 323251, Brunnshögsvägen 3), 4km north-east of the centre, charges Skr130/200 for singles/doubles and it's Skr50 for breakfast. Take bus No 4.

Hotell Ahlström (☎ 211 01 74, Skomakaregatan 3), has singles/doubles for Skr425/595 (cheaper on weekends). It's closed late June to early August.

Places to Eat

Valvet, on Allhelgona kyrkogata, near the arch, has good daily specials for Skr40.

Habanero (Kyrkogatan 21) is where local students go for an el cheapo Tex-Mex fill (weekday lunch Skr59). *Govindas i Lund (Bredgatan 28)* offers an all-you-can-eat vegetarian Indian deal for Skr50 (open 11.30 am to 5 pm Monday to Thursday, but closing 3 pm on Friday).

Self-caterers can stock up at the *ICA* supermarket on Bangatan, opposite the train station. The excellent bakery *Lundagård Konditori (Kyrkogatan 17)* sells bread, pastries and bagels. Filled baguettes cost from Skr19 to Skr24.

Getting There & Away

Lund is just 10 minutes by train (both Centralstationen and Pågatågen) from Malmö. All long-distance trains from Stockholm stop in Lund.

Buses leave from outside the train station.

TRELLEBORG
☎ 0410

The main reason to come here is to catch a ferry to/from Germany. The tourist office (☎ 53322) and the post office are both on Hamngatan, opposite the Scandlines ferry terminal.

The few medieval remnants in Trelleborg are complemented by **Trelleborgen**, a recreated Viking fortress off Bryggaregatan (free). The medieval **church** was renovated in the 19th century.

Night Stop (☎ 41070, Östergatan 59), diagonally opposite Trelleborgs Museum, has rooms with shared facilities for Skr199/299; breakfast is Skr40. For takeaways, try *Pizzeria Antonio's* on Algatan or *McDonald's* on CB Friisgatan.

Getting There & Away

Express bus No X146 travels every 15 to 60 minutes from Malmö (Skr40) to the bus station, some 500m from the ferry terminals.

There are two ferry terminals. Malmö-Berlin trains use the Scandlines terminal on the eastern side of the harbour. Scandlines ferries (☎ 65000) connect Trelleborg to Sassnitz (Germany) five times daily and Rostock (Germany) two or three times daily.

The western terminal is used by TT-Line (☎ 56200). Its ferries and catamarans shuttle between Trelleborg and Travemünde three to five times a day, and between Trelleborg and Rostock up to three times daily; rail pass holders get 50% discounts on both TT-Line services.

YSTAD
☎ 0411

This ferry-transport hub (for Denmark and Poland) has rambling cobbled streets and half-timbered houses. The friendly tourist office (☎ 77681), opposite the train station, provides a good town map. Don't miss the 16th-century Sankta Maria kyrka at Stortorget or the historical Ystads Stadsmuseum in the old monastery church of Gråbrådraklostret (open daily; Skr20).

Places to Stay & Eat
The central *SVIF Hostel* (☎ 577995), in the renovated railway building at Ystad's train station, charges Skr160 for beds. The *STF Hostel* (☎ 66566), 2km east of Ystad, has beds for Skr120. *Bäckagården* (☎ 19848, Dammgatan 36) charges from Skr395/565 for singles/doubles, and nearby *Tornväkteren* (☎ 12954, Stora Östergatan 33) has similar prices.

Most budget eating places are on Stora Östergatan, the main pedestrian street.

Getting There & Away
Pågatågen trains run hourly to/from Malmö (less on weekends). Buses depart from outside the train station.

The Unity Line (☎ 16010) ferry runs daily to/from Świnoujście in Poland; the terminal is within walking distance of Ystad's train station. The same terminal is used by ferries to/from Rønne on Bornholm (Denmark); ScanRail gives a 50% discount.

HELSINGBORG
☎ 042

The busy port of Helsingborg is perched on the Öresund coastline, which, at best, means it has a breezy seaside character and, at worst, means it's buffeted by strong winds. Architecturally it's a comely place, with some winding streets and elegant beachfront houses. Denmark is only 25 minutes away by ferry.

Information
The tourist office (☎ 104350), on Stortorget, is open daily in summer. Most other travel-related needs are met inside the vast Knutpunkten complex at the seafront, including

Forex (open daily). First Stop Sweden (☎ 126500), at Bredgatan 2 near the car-ferry ticket booths, has countrywide information.

The large public library, at Stadsparken (near Knutpunkten) and the Cyberspace Café, Karlsgatan 9, both offer Internet access.

Things to See
Kärnan, a square medieval tower, high above Stortorget's east end, dates back to the 14th century (Skr15). The historic Mariakyrkan on Mariatorget is worth a visit for its medieval countenance and its choral and organ concerts. The imposing 18th-century manor that houses Fredriksdals Friluftsmuseum is just off Hävertgatan, 2km north-east of the centre (open daily; Skr30). Summer performances are held in its baroque open-air theatre. The new city museum, in the area just north of the transport terminals, will open in 2001.

Places to Stay
The tourist office books *private rooms* from as little as Skr125 per person, but charges a fee of Skr70. The only hostel in the city centre, *Vandrarhem* (☎ 147881, Östra Vallagatan 11), certainly isn't Helsingborg's prettiest but it's good value with singles for Skr150.

SVIF's *Villa Thalassa* hostel (☎ 210384), 3km from the city centre, has beautiful gardens and beds in huts (from Skr125). Take bus No 7 or 44 to the bus stop at Pålsjöbaden and follow the path.

In the city, the budget hotel *Hotell Linnea* (☎ 214660, Prästgatan 4) has weekend and summer singles/doubles for Skr365/645.

Places to Eat
You can get a quick snack upstairs in the Knutpunkten complex. In the city centre, *Möllebackens våffelbruk*, up the stairs from Södra Storgatan, serves hot waffles with whipped cream and jam for Skr23. A good licensed restaurant is *Telegrafen* on Norra Storgatan. *Rhodos*, by the Continental Hotel on Möllegränden, serves takeaway pizzas from around Skr45, but you can also eat in. The best central supermarket is *OJ* on Karl Krooks gata.

Getting There & Away
The Knutpunkten complex on Järnvägsgatan has underground train platforms

SWEDEN

(both Centralstationen and Pågatågen) that serve Stockholm, Copenhagen, Oslo and nearby towns. Above ground and a bit south, but still inside the same complex, is the bus terminal.

Knutpunkten is also the terminal for Scandlines (☎ 186300) car ferries to Helsingør (Skr23, free with rail passes). Across the inner harbour, Sundsbussarna (☎ 216060) has a terminal with passenger-only ferries to Helsingør (Skr20, rail passes not valid). Frequent HH-Ferries (☎ 198000) services to Helsingør are the cheapest, both for cars (from Skr189) and individual passengers (Skr17, rail passes not valid). DFDS Seaways (☎ 241000) runs ferries every evening to Oslo (seats from around Skr600) from the Sunds terminal, a few hundred metres south-west of the Knutpunkten complex.

Götaland

GOTHENBURG
☎ 031
Gothenburg (Göteborg), with 460,000 residents, is wedded to its port and has a more Continental outlook than Stockholm. There's a lot more to Gothenburg than just the showpiece Kungsportsavenyn boulevard and Konstmuseet art museum. The Liseberg fun park, with its prominent Spaceport needle, is statistically Sweden's top attraction.

Orientation
Gothenburg has a network of old canals. From the centre of the city, Kungsportsavenyn crosses a large canal and leads up to Götaplatsen. The 'Avenyn' is the heart of the city, with restaurants, galleries, theatres and street cafes.

Information
Tourist Offices The main tourist office (☎ 612500, ✉ turistinfo@gbg-co.se), Kungsportsplatsen 2, is open daily year-round (except Sunday from mid-August to April). There's also a branch in the Nordstan shopping complex (open daily).

Göteborg Card The 24-hour Göteborgkortet (Skr75) allows free entry to six city museums and Liseberg, as well as free public transport. The card is available at the tourist offices, hotels and Pressbyrån newsagents.

Money There's a Forex exchange office at Centralstationen.

Post & Communications The central post office is at Drottningtorget 6, but the nearby Nordstan post office has longer hours. The Globe Internetcenter, Viktoriagatan 7, charges Skr30 per half-hour for Internet access.

Things to See & Do
Liseberg The spaceport-like tower dominates this fun park – don't miss the 83m ride to the top. The other amusements and rides seem tame by comparison. A day pass is Skr215, or pay for the rides individually (Skr10 to Skr40). General admission costs an extra Skr45 (free with Göteborg Card). Liseberg is open until 11 pm daily (to midnight on Friday and Saturday during midsummer) from mid-May to mid-August. Take tram No 5 from Brunnsparken.

Museums The Konstmuseet on Götaplatsen displays an impressive collection of photographs, as well as art works by Nordic and European masters such as Rubens, Van Gogh, Rembrandt and Picasso (closed Monday from September to April; Skr35).

The **Stadsmuseum** in Östindiska huset, west of Nordstan, has archaeological and historical collections, including Sweden's only Viking ship (closed Monday; Skr40).

The city's oldest secular building, **Kronhuset**, between Postgatan and Kronhusgatan, has temporary art exhibitions and occasional concerts and there are several artisan workshops nearby at **Kronhusbodarna**.

Göteborgs Maritima Centrum, which is off Götaleden, claims to be the world's largest maritime museum; it displays 15 historical ships, including the submarine *Nordkaparen* (Skr50, 50% off with Göteborg Card). The main museum of maritime history, **Sjöfartsmuseet**, Karl Johansgatan 1, near Stigbergstorget (Skr35/10 including the interesting attached aquarium). Take tram No 3, 4 or 9. **Klippan precinct** comprises 18th-century sailors' cottages and depicts waterfront life from the area's past; it's just off Oscarsleden and not far from the **old Älvsborg ruins**. Take the Älvsnabben ferry or bus No 64 from Brunnsparken.

Skansen Kronan, next to Skanstorget, is the last of the city's defensive towers in any

GOTHENBURG (GÖTEBORG)

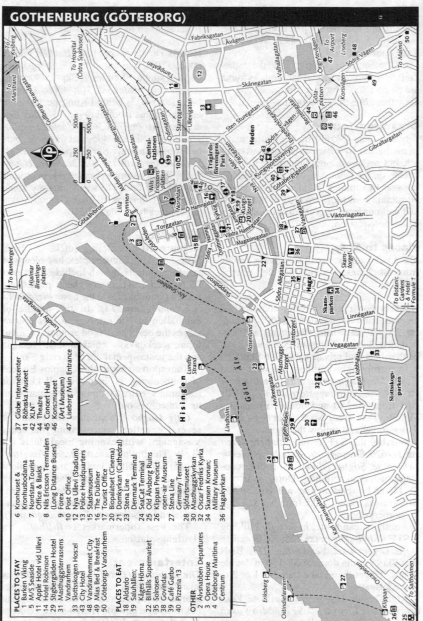

PLACES TO STAY
1 Barken Viking
5 M/S Seaside
11 Apple Hotel vid Ullevi
14 Hotel Robinson
29 Stigbergsliden Hostel
31 Masthuggsterrasens Vandrarhem
33 Slottsskogen Hostel
43 City Hotel
48 Vandrarhemmet City
49 Mias Bed & Breakfast
50 Göteborgs Vandrarhem

PLACES TO EAT
18 Aldardo
19 Saluhallen;
   Kåges Hörna
22 Billhälls Supermarket
35 Solrosen
38 Govindas
39 Café Garbo
40 Pizzeria 13

OTHER
3 Älvsnabben Departures
3 Opera House
4 Göteborgs Maritima Centrum
6 Kronhuset & Kronhusbodarna
7 Nordstan Tourist Office & Basks
8 Nils Ericsson Terminalen (Long Distance Buses)
9 Forex
10 Post Office
12 Nya Ullevi (Stadium)
13 Police Headquarters
15 Stadsmuseum
17 Tourist Office
20 Domkyrkan (Cathedral)
21 Biopalatset (Cinema)
23 Stena Line
24 Denmark Terminal
24 SeaCat Terminal
25 Old Älvsborg Ruins
26 Klippan Precinct
27 open-air Museum
27 Stena Line
   Germany Terminal
28 Sjöfartsmuseet
30 Masthuggskyrkan
32 Oscar Fredriks Kyrka
34 Skansen Kronan;
   Military Museum
36 Hagakyrkan
37 Globe Internetcenter
41 Röhska Museet
42 XLN
44 Theatre
45 Concert Hall
46 Konstmuseet (Art Museum)
47 Liseberg Main Entrance

state of repair and has fine views. There's a military museum here (open from noon to 3 pm daily April to September; Skr30/10). Take tram No 1 or 2.

Of the churches, **Domkyrkan** (the cathedral), **Hagakyrkan** and **Oscar Fredriks kyrka** are worth a look, but don't miss the superb view from **Masthuggskyrkan**.

Organised Tours

City bus tours (Skr80 for 1½ hours) leave from the tourist office at Kungsportsplatsen, but perhaps more popular are the boat cruises on the Göta Älv, or farther afield to the sea. In summer, Paddan runs frequent 50-minute boat tours (Skr75) of the canals and harbour from near the tourist office on Kungsportsplatsen.

Places to Stay

The tourist office arranges *private rooms* from Skr225/350 single/double, plus a Skr60 fee.

Hostels For a little novelty consider the moored and renovated *M/S Seaside* (☎ 105970, @ seaside@gmtc.se) at Packhuskajen. Beds are Skr100/175 in dorms/two-berth cabins, and private cabins are Skr250.

In a truly ugly building but with good views, *Masthuggsterrassens Vandrarhem* (☎ 424820, Masthuggsterrassen 8). Beds cost from Skr130 and double rooms are Skr350. Take tram No 3, 4 or 9 to Masthuggstorget and follow the signs.

Nearby, the STF hostel *Stigbergsliden* (☎ 241620, @ vandrarhem.stigbergsliden@ swipnet.se, Stigbergsliden 10) is in a renovated historical building. Dorm beds cost Skr110 and singles/doubles are Skr220/260. Breakfast is Skr40. Take tram No 3, 4 or 9 to Stigbergstorget.

Another clean hostel in an ugly building is STF's *Slottsskogen* (☎ 426520, @ mail@ slottsskogenvh.se, Vegagatan 21). Beds cost Skr95 in the dorm or Skr130 in double rooms. To get there, take tram No 1 or 2 to Olivedalsgatan.

Right beside Liseberg, the private *Vandrarhemmet City* (☎ 208977, Södra Vägen 60), is small but well run and charges Skr150 per bed.

Göteborgs Vandrarhem (☎ 401050, Mölndalsvägen 23) is just south of Liseberg in yet another large, unattractive building in

Beds are Skr150. Take tram No 4 from Brunnsparken to Getebergsäng.

Hotels The large boat hotel *Barken Viking* (☎ 635800) is moored by Gullbergskajen and has singles/doubles at Skr425/590 year round. *City Hotel* (☎ 708 4000, Lorensbergsgatan 6) is behind Kungsportsavenyn and has rooms from Skr495/695. *Mias Bed & Breakfast* (☎ 778 3692, Carlandersplatsen 3) costs Skr350/495, and three- or four-bed rooms are only Skr225 per person.

Hotel Robinson (☎ 802521, Södra Hamngatan 2) has summer and weekend rooms from Skr395/550. The small and cosy *Apple Hotel vid Ullevi* (☎ 802090, Folkungsgatan 16) charges from Skr395/540.

Places to Eat

If you need something quick, the huge Nordstan shopping complex has plenty of fast-food outlets, which include a 24-hour *McDonald's*. There are cheap pizzas and kebabs (from Skr35) at the basic *Pizzeria 13* (Chalmersgatan 13). In the middle of Saluhällen at Kungstorget, *Kåges Hörna* serves the best cheap food around (11 am to 6 pm, weekdays) – chicken salad, lasagne and the pasta special are each only Skr30.

Kungsportsavenyn, the Champs-Élysées of Gothenburg, is lined with all kinds of restaurants. Alfresco dining is popular when the sun comes out.

Café Garbo (Vasagatan 40) is one of several excellent places along the leafy Vasagatan, with evening meal deals for Skr49. The Italian cafe *Aldardo* (Kungstorget 12) has tortellini, lasagne and cannelloni dishes for Skr47. For good vibes and filling veggie victuals, visit *Govindas* (Viktoriagatan 2A). For more mainstream vegetarian, head for *Solrosen* (Karponjärgatan 4).

The best supermarket is *Billhälls*, on Hvitfeldtsplatsen.

Entertainment

The Dubliner (Östra Hamngatan 50B), is an authentic Irish pub. *XLNT*, east of Kungsportsavenyn, is a trendy club on Vasagatan (23 to 30 age group). The 10-screen cinema *Biopalatset* (☎ 174500) is on Kungstorget.

Getting There & Away

Bus The bus station (Nils Ericsson Terminalen) is right beside the train station. The

Swebus Express office (☎ 0200 218218) handles frequent buses to most major towns and also sells Eurolines bus tickets. Cheaper Säfflebussen (☎ 711 5460) runs services to Copenhagen (Skr150, four daily), Oslo (Skr150, four daily) and Stockholm (Skr260, once or twice daily).

Train Centralstationen (central train station) serves SJ and regional trains, with direct services to Copenhagen (Skr201), Malmö (Skr190), Oslo (Skr246) and Stockholm (Skr260), and night trains to the north. Direct trains to Stockholm depart approximately hourly, but budget travellers should avoid X2000s which incur a Skr50 supplement.

Boat Stena Line's (☎ 704 0000) terminal near Masthuggstorget (take tram No 3, 4 or 9) serves Frederikshavn in Denmark (50% discount for rail pass holders).

Faster SeaCat catamarans to Frederikshavn, depart from near Sjöfartsmuseet, but are more expensive. Take tram No 3 or 9 to Stigbergstorget. Farther west is the Stena Line car ferry terminal for Kiel (Germany). Take tram No 3 or 9 to Chapmans Torg.

DFDS Seaways sails twice weekly to Newcastle from Skandiahamnen on Hisingen; buses (Skr40) leave 1½ hours earlier from Nils Ericsson Terminalen.

Getting Around

The easiest way to cover lengthy distances in Gothenburg is by tram. There are nine lines, all converging near Brunnsparken, one block from the train station. Also convenient and fun are the Älvsnabben ferries, which run between Lilla Bommen and Klippan every 30 minutes or so.

Individual bus, tram and ferry tickets cost Skr16. Discount magnetic cards cost Skr100 (Skr50 or Skr100 from bus drivers). A 24-hour Dagkortet for the whole city area costs Skr40. All services are free with a Göteborg Card.

VARBERG
☎ 0340

The main attraction in this pleasant coastal town is the **medieval fortress**, with its superb museums. If you're game, brave the Nordic weather and swim in **Kallhusbadet**, built in Moorish style above the sea on stilts; a sauna bath here costs Skr37.

Places to Stay & Eat

The *SVIF Hostel (☎ 88788)* – one of the finest in Sweden – offers singles for Skr135 in old prison cells or larger rooms in other buildings for Skr150. Breakfast is good value at Skr45.

Most cheap restaurants are along the pedestrianised Kungsgatan, but the fortress *cafe* offers the best sea views.

Getting There & Away

Ferries from the Danish town of Grenå dock near the town centre. SJ trains between Gothenburg and Malmö stop regularly at the train station. Buses depart from outside the train station.

NORRKÖPING
☎ 011

From the late 19th century, large textile mills and factories sprang up along Norrköping's swift-flowing Motala ström. Today this industrial-revolution architecture, complete with canals, locks and waterfalls, is one of Sweden's most awesome urban sights.

Information

The tourist office (☎ 155000) is at Dalsgatan 16 (closed Sunday in winter). Ask about discount passes (Skr340) for entry to Kolmården zoo and other attractions.

Things to See & Do

Pedestrian walkways and bridges lead around the ingenious system of locks and canals along the riverside. The city's industrial past is on show at the free city museum, **Stadsmuseum**, Västgötegatan 19 (closed Monday). Sweden's only museum of work, the free **Arbetets Museum**, is also worth a look; it's just across the bridge from Stadsmuseum; open 11 am to 5 pm daily.

Norrköpings konstmuseum, a large art museum south of the centre at Kristinaplatsen, has many early 20th-century works (closed Monday; Skr30).

For a view of the city and out to Bråviken climb the **Rådhuset** tower, open in summer only (Skr20).

Kolmården Kolmården zoo is billed as the largest in Europe and has about 1000 animals from all climates and continents. Tickets cost Skr235/155 in summer/winter. The cable car (Skr60 return) around the park gives a better view of the forest than the animals. The zoo, open year-round, is on the northern shore of Bråviken and 25km northeast of Norrköping. To get there take bus No 432 or 433 (Skr42).

Places to Stay
The most central hostel, STF's *Turistgården* (☎ 101160, Ingelstagatan 31) has beds from Skr120 and singles/doubles for Skr210/260. It's closed Christmas and New Year.

The STF hostel *Abborreberg* (☎ 319344), open May to mid-September, is beautifully situated – take bus No 101 or 111 to Lindö and walk through the Abborreberg park. Beds cost Skr110.

The best budget hotel is the small *Hotell Isabell* (☎ 169082, Vattengränden 7) with singles/doubles for Skr450/550 all year.

Places to Eat
There are plenty of eateries along Drottninggatan. *Restaurang New Delhi*, on the corner of Trädgårdsgatan and Gamla Rådstugugatan, offers main courses from Skr60. *Olai Puben*, by the park on the corner of Skolgatan, offers a tasty mid-priced dinner. The *Rimi* supermarket is in the Spiralen centre.

Getting There & Away
The main bus station, opposite the train station, serves regional destinations and sends long-distance buses to Stockholm, Gothenburg, Jönköping and Kalmar.

Norrköping is on the main south-north railway line, and SJ trains stop hourly. Regional trains run south to Tranås and take bicycles.

LINKÖPING
☎ 013
Linköping is a modern city noted for its medieval cathedral and its widely assorted museums – it's worth a day or so if you're in the area, longer if you take a cruise on the Kinda Canal.

The tourist office (☎ 206835) is in Quality Hotel Ekoxen at Klostergatan 68. The central post office is at Kungsgatan 20.

Things to See & Do
The enormous **cathedral** with its 107m-tall spire is the main landmark of Linköping.

Just north of the cathedral, **Östergötlands länsmuseum** (County Museum) has a big collection by European painters, including Cranach's *Original Sin*, and Swedish art dating back to the Middle Ages (closed Monday; Skr20).

Some 2km west of the city is **Gamla Linköping**, one of the biggest living-museum villages in Sweden. Among the 60 houses there are 13 theme museums, many shops and a small chocolate factory. You can wander at will, for free, daily year-round. Take bus No 202, 213 or 232.

The nearby **Valla Fritidsområde**, just 300m through the forest, has more museums and many old houses.

Cruises on Linköping's 90km **Kinda Canal** run early May to late August down the canal to Rimforsa. The one-way trip on the *M/S Kind* (☎ 0141-233370) departs from the Tullbron dock on Wednesday, Friday and Sunday at 10 am (Skr245, including return by bus or train).

Places to Stay
The STF-associated hostel *Vandrarhem Linköping* (☎ 149090, Klostergatan 52A), is open all year and has beds from Skr150. A few hotel-style rooms cost from Skr300. In Valla Fritidsområde, *Mjellerumsgårdens Vandrarhem* (☎ 122730) has dorm beds for Skr120 and singles/doubles for Skr225/320. It doesn't have a kitchen for use but is open year-round.

In town, *Hotell Östergyllen* (☎ 102075, Hamngatan 2B) charges from Skr255/345 for a single/double.

Places to Eat
Marmaris on Tanneforsgatan offers the best budget burgers, kebabs and pizzas (from Skr45). *Linds*, on Stora Torget, has tasty pastries and *Överste Mörner* is an Irish-style pub/restaurant with something for the hungry and thirsty. The *Wärdshus* in the Valla area serves an inexpensive lunch.

Getting There & Away
Linköping is on the main north-south railway line and SJ trains arrive hourly. Regional and local buses stop next to the train station. Long-distance buses depart 500m north of the train station, but go to the railway office for Swebus Express tickets and timetables.

VADSTENA
☎ 0143

Beautiful Vadstena on Lake Vättern is perhaps one of the most pleasant spots in Sweden, complete with a brooding abbey and castle. You can also cycle to nearby Rök to inspect Rökstenen, Sweden's most impressive and famous rune stone.

The tourist office (☎ 31570) is inside Vadstena's castle and is open daily.

Things to See & Do
The Renaissance castle **Vadstena slott**, built by early Vasa kings, looks over the harbour and lake beyond. In the upper apartments are some items of period furniture and paintings. The castle and its chapel are open daily from May to September (Skr45).

The 15th-century **klosterkyrkan** (abbey) has a combination of Gothic and Renaissance features. Inside are the accumulated relics of St Birgitta, who established an order in Vadstena in 1370. **Bjälboättens palats** is a former royal residence that later became a convent. It's open daily from May to September (Skr35).

A series of ancient legends is connected with the 9th-century **Rökstenen** (rune stone). The sections that have been translated refer to the Ostrogothic hero-king Theodoric, who conquered Rome in the 6th century. The stone is at the church in Rök, just off the E4 on the road to Heda and Alvastra. There's a small tourist office at the site.

Places to Stay & Eat
A good camping ground is *Vätterviksbadet* (☎ *12730*), by the lake 2km north of town and open May to mid-September. Camp sites cost from Skr100 and cabins range from Skr300.

STF's *Vandrarhem Vadstena* hostel (☎ *10302, Skänningegatan 20*) is open year-round, but you must book ahead from late August to early June; beds cost Skr140. *Birgittasystrarnas gästhem* (☎ *10943*) is run by nuns of the town convent and has singles/doubles from Skr220/397; breakfast is Skr30 extra. The small *27:ans Nattlogi* (☎ *13447, Storgatan 27*) has a nice atmosphere and charges Skr370/490 for singles/doubles, including breakfast.

Pizzas from Skr45 are available from *Pizzeria Venezia (Klostergatan 2). Rådhuskällaren*, under the old town hall, has a

pleasant stone-and-timbered atmosphere and main courses from Skr69.

Getting There & Away
Only buses run to Vadstena – take bus No 650 or 661 to Mjölby (for trains to Linköping and Stockholm), or Swebus Express No 840 from Jönköping Örebro via Vadstena.

Småland

JÖNKÖPING
☎ 036

Jönköping, pleasantly situated at the south end of Lake Vättern, is a popular summer spot and the home of the safety match. It's the main centre of an urban strip stretching eastwards around the shore to Huskvarna.

The tourist office (☎ 105050) is in the Juneporten complex, near the train station (open daily in summer).

Things to See
The museum of the history of matches, **Tändsticksmuseet**, is west of the train station (open daily; Skr25). Nearby is the fairly interesting **Radio Museum** (Skr20).

The **Länsmuseum** collections, on Dag Hammarskjölds plats, cover local history and contemporary culture; don't miss the strangely haunting works of John Bauer (closed Monday; Skr20).

Stadsparken is above town to the west. Its curiosities include the 1458 mounted ornithological taxidermic masterpieces of **Fågelmuseet** (closed late August to April; Skr10). The park's **bell tower** has sweeping views of Lake Vättern.

Places to Stay & Eat
Rosenlunds Camping (☎ *122863*), on the lakeshore off Huskvarnavägen, 3km east of the town centre, has sites for Skr140. There are also cabins and rooms from Skr290.

Close to the train station, *Kulturhusets Härbärge* (☎ *190686, Svavelsticksgränd 7*), open mid-June to mid-August, has dorm beds for Skr100.

The *Grand Hotel* (☎ *719600*) on Hövrättstorget is the cheapest hotel in town, with discounted singles/doubles that cost from Skr390/490.

Most cheap eateries are on the pedestrian streets in the eastern part of the town centre.

Mäster Gudmunds Källare (Kapellgatan 2)
is a cellar restaurant with weekday lunch
specials for Skr56. Self-caterers should head
for the *supermarkets* in the A6 Center.

Getting There & Away

Swebus Express services from Jönköping
include Nos 830/831 to Gothenburg, No 831
to Stockholm and No 833 to Malmö.

The central train station serves Vättertåg
and regional trains and long-distance buses.
Vättertåg trains run roughly hourly to connect with SJ services on the main lines (in
Nässjö and Falköping).

EKSJÖ
☎ 0381

Eksjö partly dates from the 16th century
and many of its wooden buildings, as well
as most of its medieval street plan, have
been preserved.

Beds cost from Skr120 at the *STF Hostel (☎ 36180, ✉ vandrarhem@eksjo.se,
Österlånggatan 31)*, just five minutes walk
from the train station.

*Balkan Restaurang (Norra Storgatan
23)* is a combined Chinese, Swedish and
pizza place (pizzas from Skr33).

The rural surroundings of Eksjö deserve
a visit – hire a bicycle (Skr50 per day) from
the tourist office and tour the local villages
or visit the Skurugata cliff.

Getting There & Away

Take the tiny *länståg* train (rail passes accepted) or bus No 320 from Nässjö. The bus
station is beside the train station.

GLASRIKET

This area of Sweden with dense forests and
quaint red houses is popular among tourists
– it's the most visited area of the country
outside Stockholm and Gothenburg. The
'Kingdom of Crystal' has at least 16 glass
factories – look for 'glasbruk' signs – scattered around the wilderness. Factory outlets
that are open to the public offer substantial
discounts on seconds.

Despite the busloads of European and
American tourists, it's quite easy to escape
the crowds. The narrow, quiet roads are excellent for cycling, there are plenty of hostels and you can camp almost anywhere
except near the military area on the Kosta-
Orrefors road.

Nybro
☎ 0481

The eastern part of Glasriket boasts two
glass factories, but only **Pukeberg** is worth
a look. Nybro's tourist office (☎ 45215) is
on Stadshusplan. About 2.5km west of the
centre is the 200m-long kyrkstallarna building, the old church stables which now house
the excellent museum, **Madesjö Hemby-
dgsgård** (Skr20).

The *STF Hostel (☎ 10932, Vasagatan
22)*, south of the centre near Pukeberg, has
beds in small/large dorms for Skr175/130.
Nybro's upmarket *Stora Hotellet (☎ 51935)*
on Stadshusplan has rooms in summer for
Skr580/650.

SJ trains between Alvesta and Kalmar
stop in Nybro at least hourly, as do buses
to/from Kalmar.

Orrefors
☎ 0481

Founded in 1898, Orrefors is perhaps the
most famous of Sweden's glassworks. The
factory has a museum, glass blowing shows
and a shipping service in the shop. However, excepting the factory, Orrefors is
rather a boring little place.

Orranässjöns Camping (☎ 30414),
2km west of Orrefors, has summer-only
lakeside sites from Skr110. The *STF Hostel (☎ 30020)*, near the factory, has beds
from Skr110. Try *Pizzeria Alexandra* for
takeaways.

Kosta
☎ 0478

This is where Glasriket started in 1742. At
times it feels like the biggest tourist trap in
southern Sweden, but there are two good
museums, glass-blowing demonstrations
and the photogenic **old factory quarters**.
There are also plenty of discount shops.

Opposite the factory, *Kosta värdshus
(☎ 50006)* has singles/doubles for Skr400/
550 and serves inexpensive lunches (Skr51).
Kosta is served by bus from Växjö via
Lessebo.

OSKARSHAMN
☎ 0491

Oskarshamn isn't an immensely interesting
town, though it's useful for the boat connection to Visby (Gotland). Stora Torget is
the main square. At Hantverksgatan 18

you'll find the tourist office (☎ 88188, open daily), a good library and two **museums** (open daily in summer; combined entry Skr30) with maritime exhibits and wood-carvings by Döderhultaren. The bus station is also on Hantverksgatan.

Summer-only *Gunnarsö Camping* (☎ *13298*), 3km south-east from town, has seaside sites from Skr80. The pleasant *STF Hostel* (☎ *88198, Åsavägen 8*), a few hundred metres from the train station, offers beds from Skr75.

Blå Jungfrun National Park, a granite island rising 86m above sea level, was known as the 'Mountain of Witches' by sailors. In summer, boats run from the jetty at the head of the harbour in Oskarshamn (Skr150).

Getting There & Away
Länstrafik trains run from Linköping and Nässjö (rail passes valid).

The bus station displays easy-to-read timetables that list long-distance services. Boats to Visby (see Gotland later in this chapter) depart from near the train station daily year-round.

KALMAR
☎ 0480
The port of Kalmar was long the key to Baltic power and the short-lived Scandinavian Union of 1397 was signed at its castle. Today Kalmar's streets and impressive edifices retain much of their historical flavour.

The tourist office (☎ 15350) is at Larmgatan 6. Storgatan is the main street and has Dillbergs bookshop at No 18.

Things to See
The Renaissance castle **Kalmar slott**, by the sea, was vital to Sweden's defences until lands to the south were claimed from Denmark. The castle's highlights are the King Erik chamber, and the chamber with exhibits of punishment methods used on women in crueller times (open daily April to September; Skr60, students Skr30).

Kalmar länsmuseum is in the old steam mill by the harbour on Skeppsbrogatan. Its highlight is the ship *Kronan*, which sank off Öland (open daily in summer; Skr50). Aft and slightly to port is **Kalmar Sjöfartsmuseum**, a delightfully eccentric maritime museum at Södra Långgatan 81 (open daily in summer; Skr25).

Places to Stay & Eat
The tourist office books *private rooms* from Skr190/300, plus a Skr40 fee. The well-equipped STF hostel *Vandrarhem Svanen* (☎ *12928, Rappegatan 1*) is attached to *Kalmar Lågprishotell* (☎ *25560*), across the bridge to Ängö, 1km from town. Beds cost Skr150, with rooms from Skr300.

There are plenty of hotels in the city centre – *Frimurarhotellet* (☎ *15230, Larmtorget 2*) has singles/doubles for Skr480/645 in summer.

McDonald's and the *ICA supermarket* are in the Baronen Shopping Centre, near the tourist office. *Restaurang 4 Kök (Storgatan 21)* offers pizza, pasta and salad dishes for Skr45.

Getting There & Away
SJ trains run every hour or two between Kalmar and Alvesta (with connections to the main north-south line) and Gothenburg.

All regional and long-distance buses depart from the train station.

ÖLAND
☎ 0485
More windmills than Holland? The 137km-long island of Öland has 400, as well as lighthouses at the island's northern and southern tips. Öland can be reached from Kalmar via the 6km Ölandsbron (bridge), once the longest in Europe. Buses connect all main towns from Kalmar.

Borgholm
The 'capital' of Öland is a pleasant, small town with the immense ruins of **Borgholm castle**, shops, cafes and museums. The tourist office (☎ 89000) is at the bus station and the cybercafe ISSCO is on Råggatan.

Grönhags Camping (☎ *72116*), in Köpingsvik (4km north of Borgholm), has sites from Skr95. Just outside the town centre, the *STF Hostel* (☎ *10756*), in Rosenfors Manor, is open May to mid-September and has beds from Skr90. *Olssons rumsuthyrning* (☎ *77913, Tullgatan 12A*) has simple double rooms from Skr325/400 in winter/summer. *Mamma Rosa* on Södra Långgatan serves pizzas from Skr55.

Northern Öland
At **Sandvik**, about 30km north of Borgholm, you'll find the more familiar Dutch-style

windmill. In summer you can climb the eight storeys for a view back to the mainland (Skr15). There's also a *restaurant*.

The remains of the medieval fortified church **Källa ödekyrka**, at a little harbour off road 136, 36km north-east of Borgholm, are worth a look; a broken **rune stone** inside shows the Christian cross growing from the pagan tree of life.

Northern Öland has plenty of camping grounds. The *STF Hostel* (☎ 22038) in Böda is open May to August and charges from Skr110.

Färjestaden & Around

Färjestaden itself is not of much interest, but north of the bridge is **Ölands djurpark**, which is a zoo and amusement park (open daily in summer; Skr170).

Adjacent to the tourist office (☎ 560600), south of the bridge, **Historium** is worth a visit if you plan to tour the island's ancient sites (open daily; Skr40).

In the middle of the east coast at Långlöt, **Himmelsberga** is a farm village of the single-road type, and its quaint cottages have been grouped into a good summer-only museum (open daily in summer; Skr40). The **Isman-torp fortress**, with house remains and nine mysterious gates, is 5km west of the Himmelsberga museum.

The tourist office in Färjestaden books *rooms* (doubles from Skr250) and cabins in the area for a Skr75 fee. The STF hostel *Ölands Skogsby* (☎ 38395), 3km south-east of Färjestaden, charges from Skr75 per bed.

Southern Öland

The impressive reconstructed ring fort of **Eketorp**, 40km south of Färjestaden, has a museum to show what fortified villages of Öland must have been like during early medieval times. The fort is always open and the museum is open daily from May to mid-September (Skr50; bus No 103 from Kalmar).

Gotland

Gotland, the largest of the Baltic Islands, has the walled medieval trading town of Visby and an untold number of prehistoric sites. Nowhere else in northern Europe are there so many medieval churches in such a small area – there are 92 outside Visby and

over 70 have medieval frescoes. Most churches on Gotland are open 9 am to 6 pm daily, mid-May to August. Sometimes the key is hidden above the door. *The Key to the Churches in the Diocese of Visby* is a useful English-language brochure available free from tourist offices.

Gotland is also a major Scandinavian budget travel destination. Touring by bicycle is by far the best option, free camping in forests is easy and legal, most attractions are free and there are more than 30 hostels around the island.

VISBY
☎ 0498

The walled and cobbled medieval port of Visby is a living historical relic – more than 40 proud towers and the ruins of great churches attest to Visby's former eminence. Today it's a Unesco World Heritage-listed town that certainly leaves no tourist disappointed.

The tourist office, Gotlands Turistförening (☎ 201700, ✉ info@gtf.i.se), Hamngatan 4, is open daily in summer. From mid-May to mid-August cars are banned in the old town.

Gotlands Fornsal, Strandgatan 14, is one of the best regional museums in Sweden, with pre-Viking picture stones, silver treasures and medieval wooden sculptures (open daily in summer; Skr40).

Try to visit Visby during the first or second week of August when the Medieval Week festival is in full swing.

Places to Stay

The closest camping ground is *Snäcks* (☎ 211750), 6km north of town (Skr60 per tent). The *STF Hostel* (☎ 269842) off Lännavägen, south-east of the centre, is open mid-June to mid-August and has beds from Skr100. The *Old Jail Hostel* (☎ 206050, *Skeppsbron 1*) has beds in converted cells for Skr150.

Hamnhotellet (☎ 201250, *Färjeleden 3*), has rooms in summer for Skr495/690 (cheaper off-season). It also arranges *private rooms* from around Skr300/450 and rents bicycles.

Places to Eat

Most restaurants are around the old town squares or on Adelsgatan. Touristy places

Bustling Raekoja Plats, Tallinn, Estonia

The Oleviste tower, Tallinn, Estonia

St John's Church in Rīga's Old Town, Latvia

Soviet Sculpture Park in Grutas, Lithuania

Nightscape, Bergen, Norway

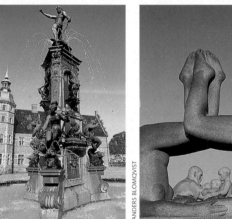

Frederiksborg Castle, Denmark

Sculpture, Vigeland Park, Norway

Statue, Copenhagen, Denmark

Summer crowds line the harbour in Nyhavn, Copenhagen, Denmark

Emergencies – Italian

Help!	Aiuto!
Call a doctor!	Chiama un dottore/ un medico!
Call the police!	Chiama la polizia!
Go away!	Vai via!
I'm lost.	Mi sono persoa. (m/f)

post office	la posta
the tourist office	l'ufficio di turismo

What time does it open/close?	A che ora (si) apre/chiude?

Accommodation

hotel	albergo
guesthouse	pensione
youth hostel	ostello per la gioventù
camping ground	campeggio

Do you have any rooms available?	Ha delle camere libere/ C'è una camera libera?
How much is it per night/per person?	Quanto costa per la notte/ciascuno?

a single room	una camera singola
a twin room	una camera doppia
a double room	una camera matrimoniale
for one night	per una notte
for two nights	per due notti

Time, Days & Numbers

What time is it?	Che ora è?/ Che ore sono?

today	oggi
tomorrow	domani
yesterday	ieri
morning	mattina
afternoon	pomeriggio

Monday	lunedì
Tuesday	martedì
Wednesday	mercoledì
Thursday	giovedì
Friday	venerdì
Saturday	sabato
Sunday	domenica

1	uno	7	sette	
2	due	8	otto	
3	tre	9	nove	
4	quattro	10	dieci	
5	cinque	100	cento	
6	sei	1000	mille	

one million	un milione

Latvian

Pronunciation

ā	as the 'a' in 'father'
ē	as the 'e' in 'there'
ī	as the 'i' in 'marine'
ū	as the 'u' in 'chute'
c	as the 'ts' in 'bits'
č	as the 'ch' in 'cheat'
g	always hard, as in 'get'
ģ	as the 'dy' sound in 'had you'
j	as the 'y' in 'yes'
ķ	as the 'tu' sound in 'tune'
ļ	as the 'lli' in 'billiards'
ņ	as the 'ni' in 'onion'
o	as the 'a' in 'water'
š	as the 'sh' in 'ship'
ž	as the 's' in 'pleasure'
ie	as in 'pier'

Basics

Hello.	Labdien. (polite)
	Sveiks. (informal)
Goodbye.	Uz redzēšanos. (polite)
	Atā. (informal)
Yes.	Jā.
No.	Nē.
Please.	Lūdzu.
Thank you.	Paldies.
You're welcome.	Laipne lūdzam.
Excuse me. (sorry)	Atvainojiet.
Do you speak English/Russian?	Vai jūs runājiet angliski/krievi?
How much is it?	Cik maksā?

Getting Around

What time is the next ... to ...?	Cikos attiet nākamis ... uz ...?
boat	kugis
bus	buss/autobuss
tram	tramvajs
train	vilciens

I'd like a ...	Es vēlos nopirkt ...
one-way ticket	vienvirziena biļete
return ticket	turpatpakaļ biļete

1st/2nd class	pirmā/otrē klase
left luggage	bagāžas glabātuve
timetable	saraksts
trolleybus stop	trolejbusa pietura
tram stop	tramvaja pietura
train station	vilcienu stacija
ferry terminal	vilcienu osta

Where can I hire a car/bicycle?	Kur es varu noīrēt mašīnu/velosipēdu?

Where is the ...?	*Kur atrodas ...?*
Is it far from here?	*Vai tas atrodas tālu?*
Go straight ahead.	*Uz priekšu.*
Turn left/right.	*Pa kreisi/labi.*

Around Town

bank	*banka*
chemist/pharmacy	*aptieka*
... embassy	*... vēstniecība*
market	*tirgus*
newsagent/	*rakstampiederumu*
stationer	*veikals*
post office	*pasts*
tourist office	*tūrisma agentūgra*

| What time does it open/close? | *Cikos ciet/atvērts?* |

Accommodation

hotel	*viesnīca*
guesthouse	*viesu māja*
youth hostel	*jauniešu kopmītne*
camping ground	*kempings*

| Do you have any rooms available? | *Vai jums ir brīvas istabas?* |
| How much is it per night? | *Cik maksā pa nakti?* |

I'd like a ... room.	*Es vēlos istabu ...*
single	*vienai personai*
double	*divām personām*

| one night | *vienu nakti* |
| two nights | *divas naktis* |

Time, Days & Numbers

What time is it?	*Cik ir pulkstenis?*
today	*šodien*
tomorrow	*ritdien*
yesterday	*vakar*
morning/afternoon	*rīts/pēcpusdiena*

Monday	*pirmdiena*
Tuesday	*otrdiena*
Wednesday	*trešdiena*
Thursday	*ceturtdiena*
Friday	*piektdiena*
Saturday	*sestdiena*
Sunday	*svētdiena*

1	*viens*	7	*septiņi*
2	*divi*	8	*astoņi*
3	*trīs*	9	*deviņi*
4	*četri*	10	*desmit*
5	*pieci*	100	*simts*
6	*seši*	1000	*tūkstotis*

| one million | *viens miljons* |

Lithuanian

Pronunciation

y	as the 'ea' in 'heat'
c	as the 'ts' in 'bits'
č	as the 'ch' 'church'
g	always hard, as in 'get'
š	as the 'sh' in 'ship'
ž	as the 's' in 'pleasure'
j	as the 'y' in 'yes'

Note that accents lengthen vowels.

Basics

Hello.	*Labas/Sveikas.*
Good day.	*Laba diena.*
Goodbye.	*Viso gero.*
Yes.	*Taip.*
No.	*Ne.*
Please.	*Prašau.*
Thank you.	*Ačiū.*
You're welcome.	*Sveiki atvykę.*
Excuse me. (sorry)	*Atsiprašau.*
Do you speak English?	*Ar kalbate angliškai?*
How much is it?	*Kiek kainuoja?*

Getting Around

| What time does the ... leave/arrive? | *Kada atvyksta/ išvyksta ...?* |

boat	laivas
bus	autobusas
tram	tramvajus
train	traukinys

I'd like a one-way/ return ticket.	Aš norėčiau bilietą į vieną/abi puses.
1st class	pirmos klasės
2nd class	antros klasės
left luggage	bagažo saugykla
timetable	tvarkaraštis
bus stop	autobusų stotelė
train station	geležinkelio stotis

Where can I hire a car/bicycle?	Kur aš galėčiau išnuomoti mašiną/ dviratį?
Where is the ...?	Kur yra ...?
Turn left.	Pasukti į kairę.
Turn right.	Pasukti į dešinę.
straight ahead	tiesiai
near/far	arti/toli

Around Town

bank	bankas
chemist/pharmacy	vaistinė
... embassy	... ambasada
market	turgus
newsagent	spaudos kioskas
post office	paštas
tourist office	turizmo informacijos centras

Accommodation

hotel	viešbutis
guesthouse	svečių namai
youth hostel	jaunimo viešbutis
camp site	stovyklavietės

I'd like a ...	Aš norėčiau ...
single room	vienviečio kambario
double room	dviviečio kambario

Do you have any rooms available?	Ar turite laisvų kambarių?
How much is it per night/per person?	Kiek kainuoja nakvynė/ nakčiai asmeniui?
one day/two days	vieną dieną/dvi dienas

Time, Days & Numbers

What time is it?	Kiek dabar valandų?
today	šiandien
tomorrow	rytoj
yesterday	vakar
morning	rytas
afternoon	popietė

Monday	pirmadienis
Tuesday	antradienis
Wednesday	trečiadienis
Thursday	ketvirtadienis
Friday	penktadienis
Saturday	šeštadienis
Sunday	sekmadienis

1	vienas	7	septyni
2	du	8	aštuoni
3	trys	9	devyni
4	keturi	10	dešimt
5	penki	100	šimtas
6	šeši	1000	tūkstantis

one million	vienas milijonas

Macedonian

Basics

Hello.	Zdravo.
Goodbye.	Priatno.
Yes.	Da.
No.	Ne.
Please.	Molam.
Thank you.	Blagodaram.
You're welcome.	Nema zošto/Milo mi e.
Excuse me.	Izvinete.
Sorry. (forgive me)	Oprostete ve molam.
Do you speak English?	Zboruvate li angliski?
How much is it?	Kolku čini toa?

Emergencies – Macedonian

Help!	Pomoš!
Call a doctor!	Povikajte lekar!
Call the police!	Viknete policija!
Go away!	Odete si!
I'm lost.	Jas zaginav.

Getting Around

What time does the next ... leave/arrive?	Koga doagja/zaminuva idniot ...?
boat	brod
bus (city)	avtobus (gradski)
bus (intercity)	avtobus (megjugradski)
train	voz

I'd like ...	Sakam ...
a one-way ticket	bilet vo eden pravec
a return ticket	povraten bilet
1st class	prva klasa
2nd class	vtora klasa

timetable	vozen red
bus stop	avtobuska stanica
train station	zheleznička stanica

Where is ...?	Kade je ...?
Go straight ahead.	Odete pravo napred.
Turn left/right.	Svrtete levo/desno.
near/far	blisku/daleku

I'd like to hire a car/bicycle.	Sakam da iznajmam kola/točak.

Around Town

bank	banka
chemist/pharmacy	apteka
the embassy	ambasadata
the market	pazarot
newsagent	kiosk za vesnici
the post office	poštata
the tourist office	turističkoto biro

What time does it open/close?	Koga se otvora/ zatvora?

Accommodation

Do you have any rooms available?	Dali imate slobodni sobi?
How much is it per night/per person?	Koja e cenata po noć/ po osoba?

hotel	hotel
guesthouse	privatno smetuvanje
youth hostel	mladinsko prenoćište
camping ground	kamping

a single room	soba so eden krevet
a double room	soba so bračen krevet
for one/two nights	za edna/dva večeri

Time, Days & Numbers

What time is it?	Kolku e časot?
today	denes
tomorrow	utre
yesterday	včera
morning	utro
afternoon	popladne

Monday	ponedelnik
Tuesday	vtornik
Wednesday	sreda
Thursday	četvrtok
Friday	petok
Saturday	sabota
Sunday	nedela

1	eden	7		sedum
2	dva	8		osum
3	tri	9		devet
4	četiri	10		deset
5	pet	100		sto
6	šest	1000		hilyada

one million	eden milion

Signs – Macedonian

Entrance	
Влез	**Vlez**
Exit	
Излез	**Izlez**
Open	
Отворено	**Otvoreno**
Closed	
Затворено	**Zatvoreno**
Information	
Информации	**Informacii**
Prohibited	
Забането	**Zabraneto**
Rooms Available	
Сози За Издавање	
	Sobi Za Izdavanje
Full/No Vacancies	
Полно/Нема Место	
	Polno/Nema Mesto
Police Station	
Полициска Станица	
	Policiska Stanica
Toilets (Men/Women)	
Клозети (Машки/Женски)	
	Klozeti (Maški/Enski)

Maltese

Pronunciation

ċ	as the 'ch' in child
g	as in good
ġ	'soft' as the 'j' in job
għ	silent; lengthens the preceding or following vowel
h	silent, as in 'hour'
ħ	as the 'h' in 'hand'
j	as the 'y' in 'yellow'
ij	as the 'igh' in 'high'
ej	as the 'ay' in 'day'
q	a glottal stop; like the missing 't' between the two syllables in 'bottle'
x	as the 'sh' in shop
z	as the 'ts' in 'bits'
ż	soft as in 'buzz'

Basics

Hello.	Merħba
Good morning/ Good day.	Bonġu.
Goodbye.	Saħħa.
Yes.	Iva.
No.	Le.
Please.	Jekk jogħġobok.
Thank you.	Grazzi.
Excuse me.	Skużani.
Do you speak English?	Titkellem bl-ingliż? (informal)
How much is it?	Kemm?

Getting Around

When does the boat leave/arrive?	Meta jitlaq/jasal il-vapur?
When does the bus leave/arrive?	Meta titlaq/jasal il-karozza?
I'd like a ... ticket.	Nixtieq biljett ...
one-way/return	'one-way/return'
1st/2nd class	'1st/2nd class'

Dhul	**Entrance**
Hruġ	**Exit**
Informazzjoni	**Information**
Miftuħ	**Open**
Magħluq	**Closed**
Tidħolx	**No Entry**
Pulizija	**Police**
Toilets	**Toilets**
Rġiel	**Men**
Nisá	**Women**

Help!	Ajjut!
Call a doctor!	Qibgħad ghat-tabib!
Police!	Pulizija!
I'm lost.	Ninsab mitluf.
hospital	sptar
ambulance	ambulans

left luggage	hallejt il-bagalji
bus/trolleybus stop	xarabank/coach

I'd like to hire a car/bicycle.	Nixtieq nikri karozza/rota.
Where is a/the ...?	Fejn hu ...?
Go straight ahead.	Mur dritt.
Turn left.	Dur fuq il-lemin.
Turn right.	Dur fuq ix-xellug.
near/far	il-viċin/-boghod

Around Town

the bank	il-bank
chemist/pharmacy	l-ispiżerija
the ... embassy	l'ambaxxata ...
the market	is-suq
the post office	il-posta
shop	ħanut
What time does it open/close?	Fix'ħin jiftaħ/jagħlaq?

Accommodation

Do you have a room available?	Għandek kamra jekk jogħġobok?
Do you have a room for one person/ two people?	Għandek kamra għal wieħed/ tnejn?
Do you have a room for one/two nights?	Għandek kamra għal lejl/żewġt iljieli?

Time, Days & Numbers

What's the time?	X'ħin hu?
today	illum
tomorrow	għada
yesterday	il-bieraħ
morning	fil-għodu
afternoon	nofs in-nhar

Monday	it-tnejn
Tuesday	it-tlieta
Wednesday	l-erbgħa
Thursday	il-ħamis
Friday	il-ġimgħa
Saturday	is-sibt
Sunday	il-ħadd

0	*xejn*	7	*sebgha*
1	*wiehed*	8	*tmienja*
2	*tnejn*	9	*disgha*
3	*tlieta*	10	*ghaxra*
4	*erbgha*	11	*ḥdax*
5	*ḥamsa*	100	*mija*
6	*sitta*	1000	*elf*

one million	*miljun*

Moroccan Arabic

Pronunciation

A stroke over a vowel ('macron') gives it a long sound.

a	as in 'had' (sometimes very short)
e	as in 'bet' (sometimes very short)
i	as in 'hit'
o	as in 'hot'
u	as the 'oo' in 'book'
aw	as the 'ow' in 'how'
ai	as the 'i' in 'high'
ei, ay	as the 'a' in 'cake'
j	more or less as the 'j' in 'John'
H	a strongly whispered 'h', almost like a sigh of relief
q	a strong guttural 'k' sound
kh	a slightly gurgling sound, like the 'ch' in Scottish 'loch'
sh	as in 'she'
z	as the 's' in pleasure
gh	called 'ghayn', similar to the French 'r', but more guttural

Glottal Stop (') The glottal stop is the sound you hear between the vowels in the expression 'oh oh!'. In Arabic it can occur anywhere in a word – at the beginning, middle or end. When the (') occurs before a vowel (eg, 'ayn), the vowel is 'growled' from the back of the throat. If it's before a consonant or at the end of a word, it sounds like a glottal stop.

Basics

Hello.	*as-salām 'alaykum*
Goodbye.	*ma' as-salāma*
Yes.	*īyeh*
No.	*la*
Please.	*'afak*
Thank you (very much).	*shukran (jazilan)*
You're welcome.	*la shukran, 'ala wajib*
Excuse me.	*smeH līya*
Do you speak English?	*wash kat'ref neglīzīya?*

I understand.	*fhemt*
I don't understand.	*mafhemtsh*
How much (is it)?	*bish-hal?*

Getting Around

What time does the ... leave/arrive?	*emta qiyam/wusūl ...*
boat	*al-babūr*
bus (city)	*al-otobīs*
bus (intercity)	*al-kar*
train	*al-mashīna*

1st/2nd class	*ddarazha llūla/ttanīya*
train station	*maHattat al-mashīna/ al-qitar*
bus stop	*mawqif al-otobis*

Where can I hire a car/bicycle?	*fein yimkin ana akra tomobīl/beshklīta?*
Where is (the) ...?	*fein ...?*
Go straight ahead.	*sīr nīshan*
Turn right.	*dor 'al līmen*
Turn left.	*dor 'al līser*

Around Town

the bank	*al-banka*
the embassy	*as-sifāra*
the market	*as-sūq*
the police station	*al-bolīs*
the post office	*al-bōsta, maktab al-barīd*
a toilet	*bayt al-ma, mirHad*

Accommodation

hotel	*al-otēl*
youth hostel	*dar shabbab*
camp site	*mukhaym*

Is there a room available?	*wash kayn shī bīt xawīya?*
How much is this room per night?	*bshaHal al-bayt liyal?*

Time, Dates & Numbers

What time is it?	*shHal fessa'a?*
today	*al-yūm*
tomorrow	*ghaddan*
yesterday	*al-bareh*
in the morning	*fis-sabaH*
in the evening	*fil-masa'*

Emergencies – Moroccan Arabic	
Help!	*'teqnī!*
Call a doctor!	*'eyyet at-tabīb!*
Call the police!	*'eyyet al-bolīs!*
Go away!	*sīr fHalek!*

Monday	(nhar) al-itnēn
Tuesday	(nhar) at-talata
Wednesday	(nhar) al-arba'
Thursday	(nhar) al-khamīs
Friday	(nhar) al-juma'
Saturday	(nhar) as-sabt
Sunday	(nhar) al-ahad

1	wāHid	7	saba'a
2	jūj or itnīn	8	tamanya
3	talata	9	tissa'
4	arba'a	10	'ashara
5	khamsa	100	miyya
6	sitta	1000	alf

| one million | melyūn |

Norwegian

Pronunciation

å	as the 'aw' in 'paw'
æ	as the 'a' in 'act'
ø	long, as the 'er' in 'fern'; short, as the 'a' in 'ago'
u, y	say 'ee' while pursing your lips
ai	as the word 'eye'
ei	as the 'ay' in 'day'
au	as the 'o' in 'note'
øy	as the 'oy' in 'toy'
d	at the end of a word, or between two vowels, it's often silent
g	as the 'g' in 'get'; as the 'y' in 'yard' before ei, i, j, øy, y
j	as the 'y' in 'yard'
k	as in 'kin'; as the 'ch' in 'chin' before ei, i, j, øy, and y
r	a trilled 'r'. The combination rs is pronounced as the 'sh' in 'fish'.
s	as in 'so' (never as in 'treasure'); as the 'sh' in 'ship' before ei, i, j, øy and y

Basics

Hello.	Goddag.
Goodbye.	Ha det.
Yes.	Ja.
No.	Nei.
Please.	Vær så snill.
Thank you.	Takk.
That's fine/You're welcome.	Ingen årsak.
Excuse me. (sorry)	Unnskyld.
Do you speak English?	Snakker du engelsk?
How much is it?	Hvor mye koster det?

Getting Around

What time does ... leave/arrive?	Når går/kommer ...?
the boat	båten
the (city) bus	(by)bussen
the intercity bus	linjebussen
the tram	trikken
the train	toget

I'd like ...	Jeg vil gjerne ha ...
a one-way ticket	enkeltbillett
a return ticket	tur-retur
1st class	første klasse
2nd class	annen klasse

left luggage	reisegods
timetable	ruteplan
bus stop	bussholdeplass
tram stop	trikkholdeplass
train station	jernbanestasjon
ferry terminal	ferjeleiet

Where can I rent a car/bicycle?	Hvor kan jeg leie en bil/sykkel?
Where is ...?	Hvor er ...?
Go straight ahead.	Det er rett fram.
Turn left.	Ta til venstre.
Turn right.	Ta til høyre.
near/far	nær/langt

Around Town

bank	banken
chemist/pharmacy	apotek
... embassy	... ambassade
market	torget
newsagent	kiosk
post office	postkontoret
telephone centre	televerket
tourist office	turistinformasjon

Accommodation

hotel	hotell
guesthouse	gjestgiveri/pensjonat
youth hostel	vandrerhjem
camping ground	kamping/leirplass

Signs – Norwegian

Inngang	Entrance
Utgang	Exit
Åpen	Open
Stengt	Closed
Forbudt	Prohibited
Opplysninger	Information
Politistasjon	Police Station
Toaletter	Toilets
Herrer	Men
Damer	Women

Emergencies – Norwegian

Help!	*Hjelp!*
Call a doctor!	*Ring en lege!*
Call the police!	*Ring politiet!*
Go away!	*Forsvinn!*
I'm lost.	*Jeg har gått meg vill.*

Do you have any rooms available?	*Har du ledige rom?*
How much is it per night/ per person?	*Hvor mye er det pr dag/ pr person?*
one day/two days	*en dag/to dager*
I'd like ...	*Jeg vil gjerne ha ...*
a single room	*et enkeltrom*
a double room	*et dobbeltrom*

Time, Days & Numbers

What time is it?	*Hva er klokka?*
today	*i dag*
tomorrow	*i morgen*
yesterday	*i går*
in the morning	*om formiddagen*
in the afternoon	*om ettermiddagen*

Monday	*mandag*
Tuesday	*tirsdag*
Wednesday	*onsdag*
Thursday	*torsdag*
Friday	*fredag*
Saturday	*lørdag*
Sunday	*søndag*

0	*null*	7	*sju*	
1	*en*	8	*åtte*	
2	*to*	9	*ni*	
3	*tre*	10	*ti*	
4	*fire*	11	*elleve*	
5	*fem*	100	*hundre*	
6	*seks*	1000	*tusen*	

one million	*en million*

Polish

Pronunciation

ą	a nasal vowel sound like the French *un*, similar to 'own' in 'sown'
ę	also nasalised, like the French *un*, but pronounced as **e** when word-final
y	similar to the 'i' in 'bit'
c	as the 'ts' in 'its'
ch	similar to the 'ch' in the Scottish *loch*
cz	as the 'ch' in 'church'
ć	much softer than Polish **c** (as 'tsi' before vowels)
dź	as **dz** but softer (as 'dzi' before vowels)
dż	as the 'j' in 'jam'
h	as **ch**
j	as the 'y' in 'yet'
ł	as the 'w' in 'wine'
ń	as the 'ny' in 'canyon' (as 'ni' before vowels)
rz	as the 's' in 'pleasure'
sz	as the 'sh' in 'show'
ś	as **s** but softer (as 'si' before vowels)
ź	softer version of **z** (as 'zi' before vowels)
ż	as **rz**

Basics

Hello. (informal)	*Cześć.*
Hello/Good morning.	*Dzień dobry.*
Goodbye.	*Do widzenia.*
Yes.	*Tak.*
No.	*Nie.*
Please.	*Proszę.*
Thank you.	*Dziękuję.*
Excuse me/ Forgive me.	*Przepraszam.*
I don't understand.	*Nie rozumiem.*
What is it called?	*Jak to się nazywa?*
How much is it?	*Ile to kosztuje?*

Getting Around

What time does the ... leave/arrive?	*O której godzinie przychodzi/odchodzi ...?*
boat	*statek*
bus	*autobus*
train	*pociąg*
tram	*tramwaj*
plane	*samolot*

arrival	*przyjazd*
departure	*odjazd*
timetable	*rozkład jazdy*

Signs – Polish

Wejście	**Entrance**
Wyjście	**Exit**
Informacja	**Information**
Otwarte	**Open**
Zamknięte	**Closed**
Wzbroniony	**Prohibited**
Posterunek Policji	**Police Station**
Toalety	**Toilets**
Panowie	**Men**
Panie	**Women**

1	jeden	7	siedem
2	dwa	8	osiem
3	trzy	9	dziewięć
4	cztery	10	dziesięć
5	pięć	100	sto
6	sześć	1000	tysiąc

one million   milion

Where is the bus stop?	Gdzie jest przystanek autobusowy?
Where is the station?	Gdzie jest stacja kolejowa?
Where is the left-luggage room?	Gdzie jest przechowalnia bagażu?
Please show me on the map.	Proszę pokazać mi to na mapie.
straight ahead	prosto
left	lewo
right	prawo

Around Town

the bank	bank
the chemist	apteka
the market	targ/bazar
the post office	poczta
the tourist office	informacja turystyczna

Accommodation

hotel	hotel
youth hostel	schronisko młodzieżowe
camping ground	kemping
private room	kwatera prywatna
Do you have any rooms available?	Czy są wolne pokoje?
How much is it?	Ile to kosztuje?
single room	pokój jednoosobowy
double room	pokój dwuosobowy

Time, Days & Numbers

What time is it?	Która jest godzina?
today	dzisiaj
tonight	dzisiaj wieczorem
tomorrow	jutro
yesterday	wczoraj
in the morning	rano
in the evening	wieczorem
Monday	poniedziałek
Tuesday	wtorek
Wednesday	środa
Thursday	czwartek
Friday	piątek
Saturday	sobota
Sunday	niedziela

Portuguese

Note that Portugese uses masculine and feminine word endings, usually '-o' and '-a' respectively – to say 'thank you', a man will therefore use obrigado, a woman, obrigada.

Nasal Vowels Nasalisation is represented by an 'n' or an 'm' after the vowel, or by a tilde over it, eg, ã. The nasal 'i' exists in English as the 'ing' in 'sing'.

ão	nasal 'ow' (owng)
ãe	nasal 'ay' (cing)
õe	nasal 'oy' (oing)
ui	similar to the 'uing' in 'ensuing'
é	short, as in 'bet'
ê	long, as the 'a' in 'gate'
ô	long, as in 'note'
c	as in 'cat' before a, o or u; as the 's' in 'sin' before e or i
ç	as the 'c' in 'celery'
g	as in 'go' before a, o or u; as the 's' in 'treasure' before e or i
h	never pronounced when word-initial
nh	as the 'ni' in 'onion'
lh	as the 'lli' in 'million'
j	as the 's' in 'treasure'
m	not pronounced when word-final – it simply nasalises the previous vowel, eg, um (oong), bom (bõ)
x	as the 'sh' in 'ship', as the 'z' in 'zeal', or as the 'x' in 'taxi'
z	as the 's' in 'treasure' before a consonant or at the end of a word

Basics

Hello.	Olá.
Goodbye.	Adeus/Ciao. (informal)
Yes.	Sim.
No.	Não.
Please.	Se faz favor.
Thank you.	Obrigado/a. (m/f)
You're welcome.	De nada.
Excuse me.	Com licença.
Sorry. (forgive me)	Desculpe.

Do you speak English?	*Fala Inglês?*
How much is it?	*Quanto custa?*

Getting Around

What time does the ... leave/arrive?	*A que horas parte/ chega ...?*
boat	*o barco*
bus (city)	*o autocarro*
bus (intercity)	*a camioneta*
tram	*o eléctrico*
train	*o combóio*

bus stop	*paragem de autocarro*
train station	*estação ferroviária*
timetable	*horário*

I'd like a ... ticket.	*Queria um bilhete ...*
one-way	*simples/de ida*
return	*de ida e volta*
1st class	*de primeira classe*
2nd class	*de segunda classe*

I'd like to hire ...	*Queria alugar ...*
a car	*um carro*
a bicycle	*uma bicicleta*

Where is ...?	*Onde é ...?*
Go straight ahead.	*Siga sempre a direito/ Siga sempre em frente.*
Turn left.	*Vire à esquerda.*
Turn right.	*Vire à direita.*
near/far	*perto/longe*

Around Town

a bank	*um banco*
the chemist/ pharmacy	*a farmácia*
the ... embassy	*a embaixada de ...*
the market	*o mercado*
the newsagent	*a papelaria*

the post office	*os correios*
the tourist office	*o (posto de) turismo*

What time does it open/close?	*A que horas abre/ fecha?*

Accommodation

hotel	*hotel*
guesthouse	*pensão*
youth hostel	*pousada da juventude*
camping ground	*parque de campismo*
Do you have any rooms available?	*Tem quartos livres?*
How much is it per night/per person?	*Quanto é por noite/ por pessoa?*

a single room	*um quarto individual*
a twin room	*um quarto duplo*
a double bed room	*um quarto de casal*
for one night	*para uma noite*
for two nights	*para duas noites*

Time, Days & Numbers

What time is it?	*Que horas são?*
today	*hoje*
tomorrow	*amanhã*
yesterday	*ontem*
morning	*manhã*
afternoon	*tarde*

Monday	*segunda-feira*
Tuesday	*terça-feira*
Wednesday	*quarta-feira*
Thursday	*quinta-feira*
Friday	*sexta-feira*
Saturday	*sábado*
Sunday	*domingo*

0	*zero*	7	*sete*
1	*um/uma*	8	*oito*
2	*dois/duas*	9	*nove*
3	*três*	10	*dez*
4	*quatro*	11	*onze*
5	*cinco*	100	*cem*
6	*seis*	1000	*mil*

one million	*um milhão*

Romanian

Pronunciation

ă	as the 'er' in 'brother'
î	as the 'i' in 'river'
c	as 'k', except before 'e' and 'i', when it's as the 'ch' in 'chip'
ch	always as the 'k' in 'king'
g	as in 'go', except before 'e' and 'i', when it's as in 'gentle'
gh	always as the 'g' in 'get'
ş	as 'sh'
ţ	as the 'tz'in 'tzar'

Basics

Hello.	Bună.
Goodbye.	La revedere.
Yes.	Da.
No.	Nu.
Please.	Vă rog.
Thank you.	Mulţumesc.
Sorry. (forgive me)	Iertaţi-mă.
Excuse me.	Scuzaţi-mă.
I don't understand.	Nu înţeleg.
What is it called?	Cum se cheamă?
How much is it?	Cît costă?

Getting Around

What time does the ... leave/arrive?	La ce oră pleacă/soseşte ...?
boat	vaporul
bus (city/intercity)	autobusul
train	trenul
tram	tramvaiul
plane	avionul

arrival	sosire
departure	plecare
timetable	mersul/orar

Where is the bus stop?	Unde este staţia de autobuz?
Where is the station?	Unde este gară?
Where is the left-luggage room?	Unde este biroul pentru bagaje de mînă?

Please show me on the map.	Vă rog arătaţi-mi pe hartă.
straight ahead	drept înainte
left	stînga
right	dreapta

Around Town

the bank	banca
the chemist	farmacistul
the ... embassy	ambasada ...
the market	piaţa
the post office	poşta
the tourist office	birou de informatii turistice

Accommodation

hotel	hotel
guesthouse	casa de oaspeţi
youth hostel	camin studentesc
camping ground	camping
private room	cameră particulară
single room	o cameră pentru o persoană
double room	o cameră pentru două persoane

Do you have any rooms available?	Aveţi camere libere?
How much is it?	Cît costă?

Time, Days & Numbers

What time is it?	Ce oră este?
today	azi
tonight	deseară
tomorrow	mîine
yesterday	Ieri
in the morning	dimineaţa
in the evening	seară

Monday	luni
Tuesday	marţi
Wednesday	miercuri
Thursday	joi
Friday	vineri
Saturday	sîmbătă
Sunday	duminică

1	*unu*	7	*şapte*
2	*doi*	8	*opt*
3	*trei*	9	*nouă*
4	*patru*	10	*zece*
5	*cinci*	100	*o sută*
6	*şase*	1000	*o mie*

one million   *milion*

Russian

Note that bold letters indicate word stress.

Basics

Hello.	*zdrastvuyte*
Good morning.	*dobraye utra*
Good afternoon.	*dobryy den'*
Good evening.	*dobryy vecher*
Goodbye.	*da svidaniya*
Goodbye.	*paka* (informal)
How are you?	*kak dila?*
Yes.	*dat*
No.	*net*
Please.	*pazhalsta*
Thank you (very much).	*(bal'shoye) spasiba*
Pardon me.	*prastite/pazhalsta*
No problem.	*nichevo* (lit: 'nothing')
Do you speak English?	*vy gavarite pa angliyski?*
How much is it?	*skol'ka stoit?*

Getting Around

What time does the ... leave?	*f katoram chasu pribyvaet ...?*
What time does the ... arrive?	*f katoram chasu atpravlyaetsa ...?*
bus	*aftobus*
fixed-route minibus	*marshrutnaye taksi*
steamship	*parakhot*
train	*poyezt*
tram	*tramvay*
trolleybus	*traleybus*
pier/quay	*prichal/pristan'*
train station	*zhilezna darozhnyy vagzal*
stop (bus/trolleybus/tram)	*astanofka*
one-way ticket	*bilet v adin kanets*
return ticket	*bilet v oba kantsa*
two tickets	*dva bilety*
soft or 1st-class (compartment)	*myahkiy*
hard or 2nd-class (compartment)	*kupeynyy*

reserved-place or 3rd-class (carriage)	*platskartnyy*
Where is ...?	*gde ...?*
to (on) the left	*naleva*
to (on) the right	*naprava*
straight on	*pryama*

Around Town

bank	*bank*
market	*rynak*
newsstand	*gazetnyy kiosk*
pharmacy	*apteka*
post office	*pochta*
telephone booth	*tilifonnaya budka*
open	*otkryta*
closed	*zakryta*

Accommodation

hotel	*gastinitsa*
room	*nomer*
breakfast	*zaftrak*
How much is a room?	*skol'ka stoit nomer?*

Time, Date & Numbers

What time is it?	*katoryy chas*
today	*sivodnya*
yesterday	*vchira*
tomorrow	*zaftra*
am/in the morning	*utra*
pm/in the afternoon	*dnya*
in the evening	*vechira*
Monday	*panidel'nik*
Tuesday	*ftornik*
Wednesday	*srida*
Thursday	*chitverk*
Friday	*pyatnitsa*
Saturday	*subota*
Sunday	*vaskrisen'e*

Signs – Russian

Вход	**Entrance**
Выход	**Exit**
Мест Нет	**No Vacancies**
Открыто	**Open**
Закрыто	**Closed**
Справки	**Information**
Касса	**Ticket Office**
Больница	**Hospital**
Милиция	**Police**
Туалет	**Toilets**
Мужской (М)	**Men**
Женский (Ж)	**Women**

Emergencies – Russian

Help!	na **pomashch'**!/ **pama**giti!
I'm sick.	ya **bo**lin (m) ya bal'**na** (f)
I need a doctor.	mne **nuzhin** vrach
hospital	bal'nitsa
police	militsiya
I'm lost.	a zablu**dil**sya (m) ya zabludilas' (f)

0	nol'	7	sem'
1	adin	8	vosim'
2	dva	9	devit'
3	tri	10	desit'
4	chityri	11	adinatsat'
5	pyat'	100	sto
6	shest'	1000	tysyacha

one million   (adin) milion

Slovak

Pronunciation

The 43 letters of the Slovak alphabet have similar pronunciation to those of Czech (refer to the Czech section in this guide).

Basics

Hello.	Ahoj.
Goodbye.	Dovidenia.
Yes.	Áno.
No.	Nie.
Please.	Prosím.
Thank you.	D'akujem.
Excuse me/ Forgive me.	Prepáčte mi/ Odpuste mi.
I'm sorry.	Ospravedlňujem sa.
I don't understand.	Nerozumiem.
How much is it?	Koľko to stojí?

Signs – Slovak

Vchod	Entrance
Východ	Exit
Informácie	Information
Otvorené	Open
Zatvorené	Closed
Zakázané	Prohibited
Polícia	Police Station
Telefón	Telephone
Záchody/WC/ Toalety	Toilets

Getting Around

What time does the ... leave/arrive?	Kedy odchádza/ prichádza ...?
boat	loč
bus (city)	(mestský) autobus
bus (intercity)	(medzimestský) autobus
plane	lietadlo
train	vlak
tram	električka
arrival	príchod
departure	odchod
timetable	cestovný poriadok
Where is the bus stop?	Kde je autobusová zastávka?
Where is the station?	Kde je vlaková stanica?
Where is the left-luggage room?	Kde je úschovňa batožín?
Please show me on the map.	Prosím, ukážte mi to na mape.
straight ahead	rovno
left	vľavo
right	vpravo

Around Town

the bank	banka
the chemist	lekárnik
the market	trh
the post office	pošta
the tourist office	turistické informačné centrum

Accommodation

hotel	hotel
guesthouse	penzion
youth hostel	mládežnícka ubytovňa
camping ground	kemping
private room	privat
Do you have any rooms available?	Máte voľné izby?
How much is it?	Koľko to stojí?
single room	jednolôžková izba
double room	dvojlôžková izba

Time, Days & Numbers

What time is it?	Koľko je hodín?
today	dnes
tonight	dnes večer
tomorrow	zajtra
yesterday	včera
in the morning	ráno
in the evening	večer

Emergencies – Slovak

Help!	Pomoc!
Call a doctor!	Zavolajte doktora/ lekára!
Call an ambulance!	Zavolajte záchranku!
Call the police!	Zavolajte políciu!
Go away!	Chod preč! (sg)/ Chodte preč! (pl)
I'm lost.	Nevyznám sa tu.

Monday	pondelok
Tuesday	utorok
Wednesday	streda
Thursday	štvrtok
Friday	piatok
Saturday	sobota
Sunday	nedeľa

1	jeden	7	sedem
2	dva	8	osem
3	tri	9	deväť
4	štyri	10	desať
5	päť	100	sto
6	šesť	1000	tisíc

one million	milión

Slovene

Pronunciation

c	as the 'ts' in 'its'
č	as the 'ch' in 'church'
ê	as the 'a' in 'apple'
e	as the 'er' in 'opera' (when unstressed)
é	as the 'ay' in 'day'
j	as the 'y' in 'yellow'
ó	as the 'o' in 'more'
ò	as the 'o' in 'soft'
r	a rolled 'r' sound
š	as the 'sh' in 'ship'
u	as the 'oo' in 'good'
ž	as the 's' in 'treasure'

Basics

Hello.	Pozdravljeni. (polite) Zdravo or Živio. (informal)
Good day.	Dober dan!
Goodbye.	Nasvidenje!
Yes.	Da. or Ja. (informal)
No.	Ne.
Please.	Prosim.
Thank you (very much).	Hvala (lepa).

You're welcome.	Prosim/Ni za kaj!
Excuse me.	Oprostite.

Getting Around

What time does ... leave/arrive?	Kdaj odpelje/ pripelje ...?
boat/ferry	ladja/trajekt
bus	avtobus
train	vlak

one-way (ticket)	enosmerna (vozovnica)
return (ticket)	povratna (vozovnica)

Around Town

Where is the/a ...?	Kje je ...?
bank/exchange	banka/menjalnica
embassy	konzulat/ambasada
post office	pošta
tourist office	turistični informa- cijski urad

Accommodation

hotel	hotel
guesthouse	gostišče
camping ground	kamping

Do you have a ...?	Ali imate prosto ...?
bed	posteljo
cheap room	poceni sobo
single room	enoposteljno sobo
double room	dvoposteljno sobo

How much is it per night?	Koliko stane za eno noč?
How much is it per person?	Koliko stane za eno osebo?
for one night	za eno noč
for two nights	za dve noči

Time, Days & Numbers

today	danes
tonight	nocoj
tomorrow	jutri
in the morning	zjutraj
in the evening	zvečer

Signs – Slovene

Vhod	**Entrance**
Izhod	**Exit**
Informacije	**Information**
Odprto	**Open**
Zaprto	**Closed**
Prepovedano	**Prohibited**
Stranišče	**Toilets**

Emergencies – Slovene	
Help!	*Na pomoč!*
Call a doctor!	*Pokličite zdravnika!*
Call the police!	*Pokličite policijo!*
Go away!	*Pojdite stran!*

Monday	*ponedeljek*
Tuesday	*torek*
Wednesday	*sreda*
Thursday	*četrtek*
Friday	*petek*
Saturday	*sobota*
Sunday	*nedelja*

1	*ena*	7	*sedem*
2	*dve*	8	*osem*
3	*tri*	9	*devet*
4	*štiri*	10	*deset*
5	*pet*	100	*sto*
6	*šest*	1000	*tisoč*

one million	*milijon*

Spanish

Basics

Hello/Goodbye.	*¡Hola!/¡Adiós!*
Yes.	*Sí.*
No.	*No.*
Please.	*Por favor.*
Thank you.	*Gracias.*
You're welcome.	*De nada.*
I'm sorry.	*Lo siento/Discúlpeme.*
(forgive me)	
Excuse me.	*Perdón/Perdoneme.*
Do you speak English?	*¿Habla inglés?*
How much is it?	*¿Cuánto cuesta?/ ¿Cuánto vale?*

Getting Around

What time does the next ... leave/arrive?	*¿A qué hora sale/ llega el próximo ...?*
boat	*barco*
bus (city)	*autobús, bus*
bus (intercity)	*autocar*
train	*tranvía*

I'd like a ... ticket.	*Quisiera un billete ...*
one-way	*sencillo/de sólo ida*
return	*de ida y vuelta*
1st class	*de primera clase*
2nd class	*de segunda clase*

left luggage	*consigna*
timetable	*horario*

bus stop	*parada de autobus*
train station	*estación de ferrocarril*

I'd like to hire ...	*Quisiera alquilar ...*
a car	*un coche*
a bicycle	*una bicicleta*

Where is ...?	*¿Dónde está ...?*
Go straight ahead.	*Siga/Vaya todo derecho.*
Turn left.	*Gire a la izquierda.*
Turn right.	*Gire a la derecha/recto.*
near/far	*cerca/lejos*

Around Town

a bank	*un banco*
the chemist	*la farmacia*
the ... embassy	*la embajada ...*
the market	*el mercado*
newsagent/ stationer	*papelería*
the post office	*los correos*
the tourist office	*la oficina de turismo*

What time does it open/close?	*¿A qué hora abren/ cierran?*

Accommodation

hotel	*hotel*
guesthouse	*pensión/casa de huéspedes*
youth hostel	*albergue juvenil*
camping ground	*camping*

Do you have any rooms available?	*¿Tiene habitaciones libres?*
How much is it per night/per person?	*¿Cuánto cuesta por noche/por persona?*

a single room	*una habitación individual*
a double room	*una habitación doble*

Signs – Spanish	
Entrada	**Entrance**
Salida	**Exit**
Habtaciones Libres	**Rooms Available**
Completo	**Full/No Vacancies**
Información	**Information**
Abierto	**Open**
Cerrado	**Closed**
Comisaría	**Police Station**
Prohibido	**Prohibited**
Servicios/Aseos	**Toilets**
Hombres	**Men**
Mujeres	**Women**

Emergencies – Spanish

Help!	¡Socorro!/¡Auxilio!
Call a doctor!	¡Llame a un doctor!
Call the police!	¡Llame a la policía!
Go away!	¡Váyase!
I'm lost.	Estoy perdido/a. (m/f)

a room with a double bed	una habitación con cama de matrimonio
for one night	para una noche
for two nights	para dos noches

Time, Days & Numbers

What time is it?	¿Qué hora es?
today	hoy
tomorrow	mañana
yesterday	ayer
morning	mañana
afternoon	tarde

Monday	lunes
Tuesday	martes
Wednesday	miércoles
Thursday	jueves
Friday	viernes
Saturday	sábado
Sunday	domingo

1	uno/una	10	diez
2	dos	11	once
3	tres	12	doce
4	cuatro	13	trece
5	cinco	14	catorce
6	seis	15	quince
7	siete	16	dieciéis
8	ocho	100	cien/ciento
9	nueve	1000	mil

one million	un millón

Basics

Hello.	Hej.
Goodbye.	Adjö/Hej då.
Yes.	Ja.
No.	Nej.
Please.	Snälla/Vänligen.
Thank you.	Tack.
That's fine/ You're welcome.	Det är bra/ Varsågod.
Excuse me. (sorry)	Ursäkta mig/Förlåt.
Do you speak English?	Talar du engelska?
How much is it?	Hur mycket kostar den?

Getting Around

What time does ... leave/arrive?	När avgår/kommer ...?
the boat	båten
the city bus	stadsbussen
the intercity bus	landsortsbussen
the tram	spårvagnen
the train	tåget

I'd like ...	Jag skulle vilja ha ...
a one-way ticket	en enkelbiljett
a return ticket	en returbiljett
1st class	första klass
2nd class	andra klass

left luggage	effektförvaring
timetable	tidtabell
bus stop	busshållplats
train station	tågstation

Where can I hire a car/bicycle?	Var kan jag hyra en bil/cykel?
Where is ...?	Var är ...?
Go straight ahead.	Gå rakt fram.
Turn left.	Sväng till vänster.
Turn right.	Sväng till höger.
near/far	nära/långt

Swedish

Pronunciation

å	long, as the word 'awe'; short as the 'o' in 'pot'
ä	as the 'a' in 'act'
ö	as the 'er' in 'fern', but without the 'r' sound
y	try saying 'ee' while pursing your lips
c	as the 's' in 'sit'
ck	as a double 'k'; shortens the preceding vowel
tj, rs	as the 'sh' in 'ship'
sj, ch	similar to the 'ch' in Scottish *loch*
g	as in 'get'; sometimes as the 'y' in 'yet'
lj	as the 'y' in 'yet'

Signs – Swedish

Ingång	**Entrance**
Utgång	**Exit**
Öppet	**Open**
Stängt	**Closed**
Förbjudet	**Prohibited**
Lediga Rum	**Rooms Available**
Fullt	**No Vacancies**
Information	**Information**
Polisstation	**Police Station**
Toalett	**Toilets**
Herrar	**Men**
Damer	**Women**

Around Town

bank	*bank*
chemist/pharmacy	*apotek*
... embassy	*... ambassaden*
market	*marknaden*
newsagent/	*nyhetsbyrå/*
stationer	* pappers handel*
post office	*postkontoret*
tourist office	*turistinformation*

What time does it	*När öppnar/*
open/close?	* stänger de?*

Accommodation

hotel	*hotell*
guesthouse	*gästhus*
youth hostel	*vandrarhem*
camping ground	*campingplats*

Do you have any	*Finns det några*
rooms available?	* lediga rum?*
How much is it	*Hur mycket kostar det*
per night/	* per natt/*
per person?	* per person?*
for one night	*i en natt*
for two nights	*i två nätter*

I'd like ...	*Jag skulle vilja ha ...*
a single room	* ett enkelrum*
a double room	* ett dubbelrum*

Time, Days & Numbers

What time is it?	*Vad är klockan?*
today	*idag*
tomorrow	*imorgon*
yesterday	*igår*
morning	*morgonen*
afternoon	*efter middagen*

Monday	*måndag*
Tuesday	*tisdag*
Wednesday	*onsdag*
Thursday	*torsdag*
Friday	*fredag*
Saturday	*lördag*
Sunday	*söndag*

0	*noll*	7	*sju*
1	*ett*	8	*åtta*
2	*två*	9	*nio*
3	*tre*	10	*tio*
4	*fyra*	11	*elva*
5	*fem*	100	*ett hundra*
6	*sex*	1000	*ett tusen*

one million	*en miljon*

Turkish

Pronunciation

A, a	as the 'ar' in 'art' or 'bar'
E, e	as in 'fell'
İ, i	as 'ee'
I, ı	as 'uh'
O, o	as in 'hot'
U, u	as the 'oo' in 'moo'
Ö, ö	as the 'ur' in 'fur'
Ü, ü	as the 'ew' in 'few'

Note that both **ö** and **ü** are pronounced with pursed lips.

Ç, ç	as the 'ch' in 'church'
C, c	as English 'j'
Ğ, ğ	not pronounced; draws out the preceding vowel a bit – ignore it!
J, j	as the 's' in 'treasure'
S, s	hard, as in 'stress'
Ş, ş	as the 'sh' in 'shoe'
V, v	as the 'w' in 'weather'

Basics

Hello.	*Merhaba.*
Goodbye.	*Allahaısmarladık/*
	* Güle güle.*
Yes.	*Evet.*
No.	*Hayır.*
Please.	*Lütfen.*
Thank you.	*Teşekkür ederim.*
That's fine/You're	*Bir şey değil.*
welcome.	
Excuse me.	*Affedersiniz.*
Sorry/Pardon.	*Pardon.*
Do you speak	*İngilizce biliyor*
English?	* musunuz?*
How much is it?	*Ne kadar?*

Getting Around

What time does the	*Gelecek ... ne zaman*
next ... leave/arrive?	*kalkar/gelir?*
ferry/boat	* feribot/vapur*
bus (city)	* şehir otobüsü*
bus (intercity)	* otobüs*
tram	* tramvay*
train	* tren*

Signs – Turkish

Giriş	Entrance
Çikiş	Exit
Açik/Kapali	Open/Closed
Danişma	Information
Boş Oda Var	Rooms Available
Dolu	Full/No Vacancies
Polis Karakolu/	Police Station
Emniyet Müdürlüğü	
Yasak(tir)	Prohibited
Tuvalet	Toilets

I'd like ...	... istiyorum
a one-way ticket	gidiş bileti
a return ticket	gidiş-dönüş bileti
1st/2nd class	birinci/ikinci mevkii
left luggage	emanetçi
timetable	tarife
bus/tram stop	otobüs/tramvay durağı
train station	gar/istasyon
boat/ship dock	iskele
I'd like to hire a	Araba/bisiklet kirala
car/bicycle.	mak istiyorum.
Where is a/the ...?	... nerede?
Go straight ahead.	Doğru gidin.
Turn left.	Sola dönün.
Turn right.	Sağa dönün.
near/far	yakın/uzak

Around Town

a bank	bir banka
a chemist/pharmacy	bir eczane
the ... embassy	... büyükelçiliği
the post office	postane
the market	çarşı
the tourist office	turizm danışma bürosu
What time does it	Ne zamam
open/close?	açılır/kapanır?

Accommodation

hotel	otel(i)
guesthouse	pansiyon
student hostel	öğrenci yurdu
camping ground	kampink
Do you have any	Boş oda var mı?
rooms available?	
How much is it per	Bir gecelik/Kişibaşına
night/per person?	kaç para?
a single room	tek kişilik oda
a double room	iki kişilik oda

Time, Days & Numbers

What time is it?	Saat kaç?
today	bugün
tomorrow	yarın
yesterday	dün
morning	sabah
afternoon	öğleden sonra
Monday	Pazartesi
Tuesday	Salı
Wednesday	Çarşamba
Thursday	Perşembe
Friday	Cuma
Saturday	Cumartesi
Sunday	Pazar
January	Ocak
February	Şubat
March	Mart
April	Nisan
May	Mayıs
June	Haziran
July	Temmuz
August	Ağustos
September	Eylül
October	Ekim
November	Kasım
December	Aralık

1	bir	8	sekiz
2	iki	9	dokuz
3	üç	10	on
4	dört	11	on bir
5	beş	12	on iki
6	altı	100	yüz
7	yedi	1000	bin

one million	bir milyon

Emergencies – Turkish

Help!/Emergency!	İmdat!
There's been an accident!	Bir kaza oldu!
(There's a) fire!	Yangın var!
Call a doctor!	Doktor çağırın!
Call the police!	Polis çağırın!
Could you help us please?	Bize yardım edebilir-misiniz lütfen?
Go away!	Gidin/Git!/Defol!
I'm lost.	Kayboldum.

LONELY PLANET

You already know that Lonely Planet produces more than this one guidebook, but you might not be aware of the other products we have on this region. Here is a selection of titles that you may want to check out as well:

Read This First Europe
Phrasebooks: Baltic States
          Central Europe
          Eastern Europe
          Europe
          Western Europe
World Food: France
          Italy
          Spain
          Turkey
Out To Eat: Paris
          London
Condensed: Amsterdam
          Crete
          Frankfurt
          London
          Paris
Cycling: Britain
          France
Walking in: Switzerland
          Britain
          France
          Ireland
          Italy
          Spain
Mediterranean Europe
Central Europe
Eastern Europe
Western Europe
Scandinavian & Baltic Europe
City Maps: Amsterdam
          Barcelona
          Berlin
          Brussels
          Dublin
          Istanbul
          London
          Paris
          Prague
          Rome
          St Petersburg
Travel Atlases: Portugal
          Turkey

Index

Abbreviations

Text

Bold indicates maps.

around Stora Torget include *Nunnan*, *Restaurang Rosengården* and the cellar restaurant *Gutekällaren*; there's also an ICA supermarket. *Effes*, an eerie bar built into the town wall, serves main courses (including vegetarian) from Skr70. *Clematis*, in a medieval house on Strandgatan, serves medieval lunches in July for only Skr80.

Getting There & Away
Air The airfield is 4km north of Visby and is served by buses. Flying Enterprise (☎ 020 691452) has the cheapest flights from Stockholm Bromma (around Skr700/1100 single/return). Visby is also served by SAS and Skyways from Stockholm Arlanda and Helsinki (Finland), and Air Express flies to Visby from Norrköping and Riga (Latvia). People under age 25 should ask about discounted stand-by fares.

Bus Kollektiv Trafiken (☎ 21411) runs buses from Visby to most corners of the island. The most expensive one-way ticket costs Skr42.

Boat From Visby, Destination Gotland (☎ 20102) runs daily car ferries and Sea-Cat catamarans to/from Nynäshamn and Oskarshamn (from Skr150 to Skr430 depending on the season; three to 6½ hours). Some overnight, evening and early morning sailings in summer have discount fares (Skr130/205 ferry/catamaran). Bicycles cost Skr35 to Skr75.

Getting Around
Bicycles can be hired for Skr55/275 per day/week at Österport.

Svealand

ÖREBRO ☎ 019

Örebro is an attractive city, another pleasant place to spend a day or two in fine weather. The main tourist office (☎ 21212) is in the castle and it's open daily.

The city's main attraction is Örebro slott, perhaps the most photogenic castle in Sweden. Entry costs Skr45, including a guided tour (in English at 2 pm, daily in summer). A little bit east is the free Wadköping museum village, which has craft workshops, a bakery and period buildings – a definite highlight (closed Monday).

Places to Stay & Eat
The *STF Hostel* (☎ 310240, *Fanjunkarevägen 5*), 600m north-east of the train station, has beds from Skr120. *Hotel Linden* (☎ 611 8711, *Köpmangatan 5*), just off the main square, has singles/doubles from Skr250/300.

Restaurang Lokus, on Näbbtorget, serves pizzas and kebabs from Skr40.

Getting There & Away
Swebus Express No 844 and 845 run to/from Karlstad (Skr150), and No 840 runs to/from Jönköping (Skr180). Direct buses run daily to Stockholm (Skr150) and Oslo (Skr260).

Direct SJ trains run to/from Stockholm (Skr130) every hour. To get to Gothenburg (Skr165), take a train to Hallsberg where you will have to change to another train.

UPPSALA ☎ 018

Uppsala is the fourth-largest city in Sweden, and one of its oldest. Gamla (Old) Uppsala flourished as early as the 6th century. The cathedral was consecrated in 1435 after 175 years of building and the castle was first built in the 1540s, although today's appearance belongs to the 18th century. The town focus is the sprawling university, Scandinavia's oldest (established in 1477).

Information
The main tourist office, Uppsala Turist och Kongress (☎ 274800, ☎ tb@utkab.se), is at Fyris torg 8 (closed Sunday in off-season). There are smaller tourist offices at the castle and the cathedral.

The main post office is upstairs in a shopping arcade at the corner of Bredgränd and Dragarbrunnsgatan. Net Zone at the corner of Sankt Persgatan and Salagatan charges Skr25 per hour for Internet access.

Things to See
The Gothic cathedral dominates the city, just as some of the dead who rest there dominated their country: St Erik, Gustav Vasa, Johan III and Carl von Linné (the inventor of the binomial system for naming species).

The **Gustavianum** museum, immediately west of the cathedral, has an excellent antiquities collection and features an old 'anatomical theatre' (open daily in summer; Skr40). The **Upland Museum**, in the old mill at Sankt Eriks gränd 10, houses county collections from the Middle Ages (closed Monday and Tuesday; Skr20).

The **Linnaeum Orangery** and excellent **Botanic Gardens** are below the castle. Don't confuse them with the **Linné Museum** (open June to mid-September; Skr20) and its garden (free) at Svartbäcksgatan 27. Just north of the Botanic Gardens, Carolina Rediviva (the old university library) displays the surviving half of the 6th-century Gothic-language manuscript Codex Argentus (Skr10).

Uppsala Slott The highlight of this castle, originally built by Gustav Vasa, is the state hall, where kings were enthroned and a queen abdicated. The castle is open daily in summer by guided tour only (in English at noon, 1.30 and 3 pm; Skr40). The **Vasa vignettes** wax museum in the dungeon illustrates the past intrigues of the castle (Skr35, Skr60 for combined ticket).

Gamla Uppsala Uppsala grew up around the three great grave mounds at Gamla Uppsala, 4km north of the modern city. The mounds, said to be the graves of legendary pre-Viking kings, lie in a cemetery of about 300 small mounds. A new museum exhibits ancient artefacts excavated from Gamla Uppsala.

Next to the flat-topped mound Tingshögen is the **Odinsborg Inn**, known for its horns of mead, although daintier refreshments are offered in summer. The nearby **Disagården museum village** is free and open daily from June to August.

To reach Gamla Uppsala, take bus No 2 from Stora Torget in Uppsala.

Organised Tours

From Östra Ågatan old steamers run to the baroque castle at Skokloster (from Skr70/105 one way/return), where there are connecting boats to Stockholm.

Places to Stay

Fyrishov Camping (☎ 274960), 2km north of the city and by the river at Fyrisfädern, offers sites from Skr145 and four-bed cabins with cooking facilities from Skr400. Take bus No 4, 24, 50 or 54.

STF's *Sunnersta Herrgård* hostel (☎ 324220, Sunnerstavägen 24), in a manor house about 6km south of the centre, has beds in small dorms for Skr170 and singles/doubles from Skr320/340. Take bus No 20 or 50.

The central *Basic Hotel* (☎ 480 5000, *Kungsgatan 27*) has self-contained dorms for six people for Skr150 (mid-June to mid-August only) and singles/doubles from Skr545/695. *Apartmenthotel Paprikan* (☎ 262929, Paprikagatan 14) has rooms with shared bath for Skr300/400.

A 15-minute bus ride (No 7 or 56) from Stora Torget is the *Hotell Arsta Gård* (☎ 253500, Jordgubbsgatan 14) with rooms for Skr445/575.

A local agency (☎ 42030) finds *private rooms* from Skr135.

Places to Eat

Saffer's, on Stora Torget, specialises in Tex-Mex fast food, but fish and chips are only Skr32. *Palmyra Restaurant*, opposite the Basic Hotel, has good cheap felafels (from Skr20), and kebabs with rice that cost about Skr45.

In the evenings, local students converge at the popular pub-restaurants, including *Svenssons taverna (Sysslomansgatan 14)*, at *Pavels*, at Pavel Snickares gränd and *Café katilin*, on Svartbäcksgatan.

The indoor produce market *Saluhallen* is at Sankt Eriks torg, between the cathedral and the river (closed Sunday). There's a *HemKöp* supermarket on Stora Torget.

Getting There & Away

There are frequent SJ trains from Stockholm (X2000 trains require a supplement). All SJ services to/from Gävle, Östersund and Mora stop in Uppsala.

The bus station is outside the train station.

SALA
☎ 0224

The sleepy town of Sala, 120km from Stockholm, is worth at least a day's visit. The silver mine was considered the treasury of Sweden in the 16th and 17th centuries. The channels that weave through and around town were once the source of power for the mines; the wooden bridges that cross them are now the town's symbols.

A stroll along the Gröna gången path takes you south-west through the parks to Sala silvergruva, the old silver mine area. The fascinating tour of the shafts (down to 60m) costs Skr75, including entry to the museum and information centre.

Places to Stay & Eat

The tourist office (☎ 13145) at Normanska gården, just off Stora Torget, books private rooms from Skr120 per night. The pleasant STF Vandrarhem & Camping Sofielund (☎ 12730), west of the town centre, has beds for Skr110 and, from mid-May to September, basic camp sites (Skr50). Walk 25 minutes along Gröna gången from the bus terminal, or take the Silverlinjen bus to the water tower.

Hotell Svea (☎ 10510, Vassbygatan 19), diagonally right from the train station, has rooms starting at Skr400/500, as well as some hostel-type beds for Skr150.

At Bergmästaren (Fredsgatan 23) a kebab with rice is Skr50, but burgers start at Skr30 and a la carte starts at Skr55.

Getting There & Away

Sala is on the main Stockholm-Mora railway line, with trains every two hours. There are also buses to Uppsala (Skr62) and Västerås (Skr44 to Skr58).

FALUN ☎ 023

Falun is synonymous with mining and with Stora, perhaps the world's oldest public company (first mentioned in 1288). You'll find the town's tourist office (☎ 83050) at Trotzgatan 10-12.

The Falu koppargruva copper mine was the world's most important by the 17th century, but it closed in 1992. The Stora museum describes the miners' wretched lives and work. It's open daily (Skr10), but admission is included in the excellent one-hour tour (Skr60) into the disused mines (take bus No 709 from Faluån). For local folk culture and art, visit Dalarnas museum (Skr20), by the bridge on Stigaregatan.

Three kilometres east of town is the STF hostel Hälsingården (☎ 10560, Vandrarvägen 3). Take bus No 701 from Vasagatan, then walk for 10 minutes. Beds cost Skr120.

Lilla Pizzerian (Slaggatan 10) does takeaway and eat-in pizzas from Skr40.

Getting There & Away

Falun isn't on the main railway lines – change at Borlänge when coming from Stockholm or Mora – but there are direct trains to/from Gävle (Skr100).

SÄRNA & AROUND ☎ 0253

Särna village, at the start of beautiful upland wilderness, is popular with hikers. The helpful tourist office (☎ 10205) is at Särnavägen 6.

For one of the best views in Sweden, drive or climb to the peak of Mickeltemplet (625m), 2km south of Särna. There's a ski-tow, two simple runs (up to 350m) and 20km of cross-country trails. For lessons or ski hire go to Halvarssons Alpin (☎ 10471).

The plateau Fulufjället, 25km south-west of Särna, feeds Njupeskär, Sweden's highest waterfall (93m). There's excellent hiking at Grövelsjön, 72km north-west of Särna.

STF's Turistgården hostel (☎ 10437, Sjukstugvägen 4), is open year-round and has beds for Skr110. Vårdshuset Gästis (☎ 10881), beside the tourist office, has rooms for Skr250 per person. Grövelsjön's STF Lodge (☎ 59880) has beds for Skr165 and singles/doubles from Skr265/360.

Getting There & Away

Dalatrafik bus No 170 runs from Mora to Särna (Skr88, two hours, daily) and onwards to Idre and Grövelsjön.

Norrland

GÄVLE ☎ 026

Gävle is the gateway to Norrland and probably the most pleasant of the northern cities thanks to its architecture and parks. The town comes alive during the three-day City Fest in early August.

Information

The helpful tourist office (☎ 147430) is at Drottninggatan 37. The central post office is at Drottninggatan 16, off Stortorget. The library, at Slottstorget 1 (near the castle), offers free Internet access.

Things to See & Do

The wooden old town of Gamla Gefle, south of the city centre, shows what Gävle was like before it burned in 1869. One of the houses, **Joe Hill-gården**, was the birth-place of the US union organiser who was executed in Utah in 1915.

The regional **Länsmuseum**, on Södra Strandgatan, has an excellent art collection and interesting historical exhibitions (closed Monday; Skr25). The oldest of the churches in Gävle is **Heliga Trefaldighets kyrka** at the western end of Drottninggatan; it has an 11th-century rune stone inside the church.

In summer there are daily boats (Skr30 one way) to the island of **Limön** (inquire at the tourist office). The island has a nature trail and a mass grave and memorial to the sailors of a ship lost in the early 19th century. Railway buffs should check out **Järnvägsmuseet** (the national rail museum), 2km south of the town centre on Rälsgatan (closed Monday in winter; Skr30).

The leisure park and zoo, **Furuvik**, is about 12km south-east of Gävle (closed September to mid-May; Skr95). From the train station, take bus No 838 (Skr20).

Places to Stay & Eat

The central STF *Gamla Gefle* hostel (☎ *621745, Södra Rådmansgatan 1*) is clean and quiet, with beds for Skr120. The cheapest hotel is *Nya Järnvägshotellet* (☎ *120990*), which is opposite the train station. Singles/doubles start at Skr300/450.

The *American Take Away* (*Nygatan 9*) serves pizzas from Skr33. The excellent *Delikatessen* (*Södra Kungsgatan 11*) serves home-made snacks and meals from Skr10 to Skr116.

Getting There & Away

All northbound trains from Stockholm (Skr130) go via Gävle, with X2000 services via Uppsala two to six times daily. There are also useful direct trains from Gävle to Falun (Skr100) and Örebro (Skr155).

The bus station behind the train station serves large towns and cities.

ÖSTERSUND
☎ 063

This pleasant town on Lake Storsjön (in whose chill waters lurks a seldom-sighted monster) has good budget accommodation and is worth a visit. Some attractions lie on the adjacent island of Frösön, where there's a winter-sports centre.

Information

The tourist office (☎ *144001*), opposite the town hall, is open daily. The budget card, Storsjökortet, valid for nine days (Skr110), gives discounts or free entry to many local attractions. The post office, at Storgatan 38, handles currency exchange until 6 pm (2 pm on Saturday). The public library opposite the bus station has free Internet access.

Things to See & Do

Don't miss **Jamtli**, 1km north of the town centre. Its village and regional museum are the highlight of Östersund (closed Monday in winter; Skr50/80 winter/summer). Lake cruises on the old S/S *Thomée* steamship cost from Skr55 to Skr110 (50% off with Storsjökortet).

Frösön This island is reached by road or footbridge from the middle of Östersund. It features the Frösöns djurpark animal park (open daily from mid-May to mid-August; Skr100, Storsjökortet not valid) and the old church Frösöns kyrka. For skiers, there are slalom and Nordic runs on the island at Östberget (lift cards Skr70 per day).

Places to Stay & Eat

The quaint STF *Vandrarhemmet Jamtli* (☎ *105984*), in the Jamtli museum precinct, is open all year and offers beds for Skr130. Centrally-located *Östersunds Vandrarhem* (☎ *101027, Postgränd 4*) charges Skr140/170 for dorm beds/singles. *Vandrarhemmet Kallaren* (☎ *132232, Bangårdsgatan 6*), by the train station, has dorm beds for Skr125 and singles/doubles for Skr170/290.

Most restaurants are on the pedestrianised Prästgatan, including *Volos* (*Prästgatan 38*) with pizzas from Skr40, and *Pavljong Thai Restaurang* at (*Prästgatan 50B*), where generous lunches starts at Skr60. The *Konsum* supermarket is on Kyrkgatan.

Getting There & Away

The train station is a short walk from the town centre. Trains run direct from Stockholm via Gävle, and some go on to Storlien.

Places to Stay & Eat

The clean and central *STF Hostel* (☎ 77 16 50, *Västra Esplanaden 10*), has beds from Skr110. Small *Tegs Hotell* (☎ 127700, *Verkstadsgatan 5*), just south of the river, has singles/doubles from Skr320/440. *Pizzeria Eldorado* (*Vasagatan 10*) serves pizzas (from Skr35), felafel and salads.

Getting There & Away

Bus The bus station is near the train station. Direct buses to Mo i Rana in Norway run once or twice daily (Skr196); other daily destinations include Östersund, Skellefteå and Luleå.

Train Only one train departs daily from Umeå. Vännäs is the nearest station on the main north-south line. Connecting SJ buses (see the timetable at the station) between Umeå and Vännäs accept all rail passes.

Boat Ferries to Vasa (Finland) depart from the harbour at Holmsund (Skr205 to Skr280); rail passes give a 50% discount. Buses to the dock (Skr30) leave from near the tourist office an hour before departure.

SKELLEFTEÅ ☎ 0910

Skellefteå is one of the most agreeable coastal towns in northern Sweden. The peripatetic summer tourist office (☎ 736020) moves around the town centre; in winter it relocates to Skellefteå Camping (☎ 736020), 1km north-east of the centre.

A short walk from the centre takes you to the Nordanå park, which includes the free Skellefteå museum (free) and several old houses. West of Nordanå is Bonnstan, a unique housing precinct with 392 17th-century houses. Farther west is the small island of Kyrkholmen; cross over on the Lejonströmsbron, Sweden's longest wooden bridge.

Places to Stay & Eat

Friendly *Skellefteå Camping* (☎ 18855), off the E4 1km north-east of town, charges from Skr120/210/280 for tents/rooms/cabins. Central *Hotell Stensborg* (☎ 10551), on Vinkelgränd, has single/double rooms starting at Skr300/400.

Max, on Kanalgatan, has burgers, chicken and vegetarian food. *Monaco* (*Nygatan 31*) serves good pizza from Skr35.

The main regional bus station is central on Gustav III Torg.

ÅRE ☎ 0647

Arguably Sweden's top mountain sports resort, Åre has 45 ski lifts that serve some 1000 vertical metres of skiable slopes, including a superb 6.5km-long downhill run (day passes Skr180 to Skr250). Åre also offers great summer outdoor recreation, including hiking, kayaking, rafting and mountain biking. The cable car (Skr80) runs until 4 pm daily to the upper station, half an hour below the panoramic summit of Åreskutan (1420m).

The tourist office (☎ 17720), on the central square, is open daily.

Places to Stay & Eat

In winter book rooms through Årefjällen Resor (☎ 17700). Summer bargains include *Café Villan* (☎ 50400, *Källvägen 10*), B&B for Skr195 (possibly closed June), and *Pensionat Bråta* (☎ 51140, *Totrvägen 12*), with singles/doubles for Skr375/600.

Typical Swedish junk food is available at *Åre Kiosk & Grill*, on the central square, but nearby *Liten Krog* and *Werséns* (both with dishes from Skr68) have more style.

Getting There & Away

Regular trains between Stockholm and Storlien, via Östersund, stop at Åre station (Skr110 from Östersund). Regional bus No 156 runs from Östersund (Skr100), and connects Åre to the nearby winter-sports centre of Duved.

UMEÅ ☎ 090

Umeå has a large university and a port with ferry connections to Finland. It's the fastest growing town in Sweden and has over 26,000 students. The tourist office (☎ 16161) is at Renmarkstorget 15.

Don't miss the Gammlia area, 1km north-east of the town centre. It consists of several free museums, including the regional Västerbottens Museum, the modern art museum Bildmuseet, the Maritime Museum and Friluftsmuseet, with old houses and staff wearing period clothes. The museums are open daily in summer (closed Monday in winter).

Getting There & Away

Bus Bus No 100 runs between Umeå and Luleå, via Skellefteå, every two to three hours. Bus No 200 runs via Arvidsjaur to Bodø in Norway daily except Saturday (Skr350). The nearest train station is Bastuträsk and bus No 260 goes there three times daily (Skr43).

LULEÅ
☎ 0920

Sweden's fourth-busiest airport lies just outside Luleå, the capital of Norrbotten.

The tourist office (☎ 293500) is at Storgatan 42, on Luleå's main pedestrian mall. The SAS office (☎ 587100) is opposite the bus station at Storgatan 61.

The free regional museum on Köpmangatan is worth a visit just for its section on the Sami. Luleå's other attractions are outside the centre – the most famous being Gammelstad (old town). This is the biggest of the region's restored 'church villages'; you can wander around its 15th-century stone church and 424 wooden houses (catch the hourly bus No 32 from Luleå; Skr 20). The open-air museum, Hägnan, and a nature reserve are nearby.

Places to Stay & Eat
The STF Hostel (☎ 252325, @ hotell@ orrviken.se, Orrviksvägen 87) is 3km west of town; catch bus No 6 and walk 400m. Beds cost from Skr100; there's a kitchen and restaurant. Park Hotell (☎ 211149, Kungsgatan 10) has simple singles/doubles for Skr250/400.

There are some good inexpensive restaurants along, or just off, Storgatan, including Velanders, at No 43, and Corsica, on Nygatan. The Domus supermarket is opposite the tourist office.

Getting There & Away
Air People under age 25 should inquire about discounted stand-by tickets to/from Stockholm. There are buses to Luleå's airport (Skr40) from the bus station or the SAS office.

Bus Bus No 100 runs to/from Umeå via Skellefteå every few hours. Bus No 28 runs frequently to/from Boden (Skr36). No 21 (via Boden and Alvsbyn) runs to Arvidsjaur (Skr15) and No 44 (via Boden and Vuollerim) runs to Jokkmokk (Skr130).

Train Direct Tågkompaniet trains from Stockholm and Gothenburg run at night only. Most trains from Narvik and Kiruna terminate at Luleå.

ARVIDSJAUR
☎ 0960

Welcome to Lappland. Lappstaden museum village, run by the Sami community, contains almost 100 buildings as well as forestry and reindeer-breeding concerns; it's open at all times (free; tours in English Skr25). The tourist office (☎ 17500), at Garvaregatan 4, books accommodation. Lappugglans Turiststation (☎ 12413), near the station, has hostel beds for Skr100. On Storgatan, Frasses serves burgers from Skr33 and friendly Athena offers small pizzas from Skr35.

Getting There & Away
Bus The Gällivare to Östersund bus (No 45) stops only at the bus station on Storgatan. Bus No 200 between Skellefteå and Bodö (Norway) runs via Arvidsjaur. The Inlandsbanan train goes north via Jokkmokk to Gällivare (Skr136). From early July to early August the old Ångloket steam train makes return evening trips to Slagnäs on Friday and Moskosel on Saturday (both Skr130).

JOKKMOKK
☎ 0971

The small town of Jokkmokk, reached by Inlandsbanan, is just north of the Arctic Circle and originated as a Sami market and mission. The town's main event is the three-day Sami winter fair, which starts on the first Thursday in February.

Information
The tourist office (☎ 12140), Stortorget 4, is open daily in summer. The public library, Föreningsgatan 8, offers Internet access.

Things to See
Ájtte, Kyrkogatan 3, gives the most thorough introduction to Sami culture of any museum in Sweden. It also offers exhaustive information on Lappland's mountain areas (open daily all year; Skr40).

Naturfoto, at the main Klockartorget intersection, exhibits and sells work by local wilderness photographer Edvin 'Sarek' Nilsson.

Places to Stay & Eat

Ask at the tourist office about *private rooms* from just Skr125/200 per single/double. STF's *Åsgården* hostel (☎ *55977, Åsgatan 20*) has beds from Skr110 and is open all year round. At *Jokkmokks Turistcenter* (☎ *12370*), 3km south-east of town, rooms cabins start at Skr290/475 and tent sites are from Skr80.

Opera on Storgatan is the liveliest restaurant (meals from Skr40). At the museum's *restaurant* you can try local fish or a sandwich with reindeer meat. The *Konsum* supermarket is on Storgatan.

Getting There & Away

Buses arrive and depart from the bus station on Klockarvägen. Bus Nos 44 and 45 run to/from Gällivare (Skr77) and No 45 runs to/from Arvidsjaur (Skr115).

The train station is only for railcars on Inlandsbanan: to meet SJ trains take No 94 to Murjek via Vuollerim or the No 44 bus to Boden (Skr105) and Luleå (Skr130).

GÄLLIVARE
☎ 0970

The town of Gällivare is surrounded by Nordic wilderness and dwarfed by the bald Dundret hill, which is a nature reserve. Gällivare's helpful tourist office (☎ *16660*), near the church at Storgatan 16, organises numerous wilderness excursions.

There are four Nordic courses and 10 ski runs on Dundret; day lift tickets cost Skr180. Halfway to the top, Sameläger-Repisvare exhibits Sami traditions and has reindeer (open daily from late June to late August).

In Malmberget, 5km north of Gällivare, *Kåkstan* is a 'shanty town' museum dating from the 1888 iron-ore rush. It's free and open daily from mid-June to mid-August. Bus No 1 to Malmberget (Skr13) departs from opposite Gällivare's church.

Places to Stay & Eat

Gällivare Camping (☎ *16545*), by the Vassara älv, open June to early September, has tent sites for Skr75 and cabins from Skr380. The *STF Hostel* (☎ *14380*), across the footbridges from the train station, is open year-round and charges Skr120/75 for beds in small/large dorms. Enjoy the sauna. Just south of the train station, *Lappgårbürget* (☎ *12534*) has dorm beds for Skr100, a kitchen and a TV room. *Hotell Dundret* (☎ *55040, Per Högströmsgatan 1*) offers singles/doubles from Skr250/350.

Sibyllagrillen (*Industrigatan 1*) is good for burgers and *MR's* (*Östra Kyrkallén 10*) charges from Skr55 for pizzas.

Getting There & Away

Skyways flies direct to the airport (7km from the town) from Stockholm.

Länstrafik i Norrbotten regional buses depart from the train station. Bus Nos 10 and 42 run daily to/from Kiruna, No 45 daily to/from Östersund and No 44 goes to/from Jokkmokk (Skr77).

Tågkompaniet trains come from Luleå and Stockholm (sometimes changing at Boden), and from Narvik in Norway. More exotic is the Inlandsbanan train which ends at Gällivare; the railcar from Östersund costs Skr320 (rail passes not valid).

ABISKO & KUNGSLEDEN
☎ 0980

Abisko National Park (75 sq km), on the southern shore of scenic Lake Torneträsk, is well served by trains and buses. It's less rugged and more accessible than most northern parks.

The *Naturum*, next to the STF lodge, has information and free film shows (open daily in summer). The Linbana chair lift (from Skr60/75 one-way/return) takes you to 900m on Njulla (1169m), where there's a cafe.

The 450km Kungsleden hiking route leads south from Abisko and offers detours to the summit of Kebnekaise or the magical Sarek national park. Waterproof boots are essential at any time of the year. July, August and September are the best months for hiking, although in July there's still some boggy ground. It can still get cold very quickly, despite the midnight sun.

Fill out the sheets and books provided at mountain huts with your details as you go. The 1:100,000 Fjällkartan maps (with pink covers) cost Skr98 each at the STF lodge. Tours are organised by STF, which maintains huts and several big mountain stations with excellent facilities and services.

A good alternative to the Kungsleden trail is the four-hour return hike to the former Sami sacrificial site Paddus, 4km south of Abisko Östra station. There's also a short route around Abisko canyon.

Places to Stay & Eat
Camp Abisko (☎ *40148*), near Abisko Östra train station, has beds from Skr125 and Swedish meals from Skr40. The STF lodge *Abisko Fjällstation* (☎ *40200*, @ *info@abisko.stfturist.se*), open from mid-February to mid-September, offers beds from Skr155 and singles/doubles from Skr495/870 (including dinner). Trekking gear can be hired here, and lunch/dinner costs Skr65/145.

There's an *ICA* supermarket in Abisko village for self-caterers.

Getting There & Away
Apart from trains (stations at Abisko Östra and Abisko Turiststation), bus Nos 91 and 95 run from Kiruna.

Switzerland

Switzerland (Schweiz, Suisse, Svizzera, Svizra) offers its share of clichés – irresistible chocolates, kitsch cuckoo clocks, yodelling Heidis, humourless bankers – but plenty of surprises too. Travellers will find flavours of Germany, France and Italy, always seasoned with a unique Swissness.

Goethe described Switzerland as a combination of 'the colossal and the well-ordered', a reference to the majestic Alpine terrain set against the tidy, efficient, watch-precision towns and cities.

Prices are high in Switzerland, so you may be tempted to get in and get out again as quickly as possible. You don't have to do it that way. Scenery and hiking cost nothing. So base yourself at a friendly hostel in the mountains, slow down, recharge your batteries, and enjoy some of the most spectacular landscapes Europe has to offer.

Facts about Switzerland

AT A GLANCE	
Capital:	Bern
Population:	7.1 million
Official Languages:	French, German & Italian
Currency:	1 Swiss franc (Sfr) = 100 centimes

HISTORY

The first inhabitants of the region were a Celtic tribe, the Helvetii. The Romans appeared on the scene in 107 BC by way of the Great St Bernard Pass. They were gradually driven back by the Germanic Alemanni tribe, which settled the region in the 5th century. The territory was united under the Holy Roman Empire in 1032 but central control was never very tight. That was all changed by the Germanic Habsburg family, spearheaded by Rudolph I, who gradually brought the squabbling nobles to heel.

Upon Rudolph's death, local leaders saw a chance to gain independence; the forest communities of Uri, Schwyz and Nidwalden thus formed an alliance on 1 August 1291. Their pact of mutual assistance is seen as the origin of the Swiss Confederation, and soon other communities joined: Lucerne (1332) was followed by Zürich (1351), Glarus and Zug (1352), and Bern (1353). The Swiss gained independence from Holy Roman Emperor Maximilian I after their victory at Dornach in 1499.

The French Republic invaded Switzerland in 1798 and established the Helvetic Republic. The Swiss vehemently resisted such centralised control, causing Napoleon to restore the former confederation of cantons in 1803. Following Napoleon's defeat by the British and Prussians at Waterloo, Switzerland gained independence and established its neutrality.

Throughout the gradual move towards one nation, each canton remained fiercely independent, even to the extent of controlling its own coinage and postal services. They lost these powers in 1848 when a new federal constitution was agreed upon, with Bern as the capital.

The Swiss have carefully guarded their neutrality in the 20th century. Their only involvement in WWI lay in organising units of the Red Cross (founded in Geneva in 1863). Despite some accidental bombing, WWII left Switzerland largely unscathed, and its territory proved a safe haven for escaping Allied prisoners.

To preserve its neutrality after WWII, Switzerland declined to become a member of both the United Nations (though it currently has observer status) and the North Atlantic Treaty Organisation (NATO). Switzerland's EU application has been frozen following a Swiss 1992 referendum, in which voters failed to endorse the federal government's strategy.

Switzerland's WWII record has come under critical scrutiny in recent years. Swiss

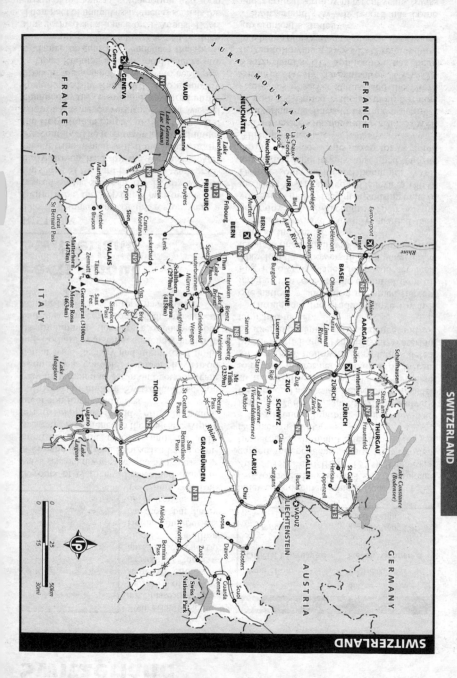

SWITZERLAND

banks were major conduits for Nazi plunder during WWII – at least US$400 million (US$3.8 billion in today's values) was deposited. The banks also held on to huge sums deposited by Jews who subsequently became victims of the Holocaust. In 1998, legal action prompted the banks to offer a US$1.25 billion settlement in respect of these deposits.

GEOGRAPHY

Mountains make up 70% of Switzerland's 41,285 sq km. The land is 45% meadow and pasture, 24% forest and 6% arable. Farming of cultivated land is intensive and cows graze on the upper slopes in the summer as soon as the retreating snow line permits.

The Alps occupy the central and southern regions of the country. The Dufour summit (4634m) of Monte Rosa is the highest point, although the Matterhorn (4478m) is more famous. Glaciers account for an area of 2000 sq km, most notably the Aletsch Glacier – which, at 169 sq km, is the largest valley glacier in Europe.

CLIMATE

Ticino in the south has a hot, Mediterranean climate, and Valais in the southwest is noted for being dry. Elsewhere the temperature is typically 20°C to 25°C in summer and 2°C to 6°C in winter, with spring and autumn hovering between 7°C and 14°C. Summer tends to bring a lot of sunshine, but also the most rain.

POPULATION & PEOPLE

With a population of 7.1 million, Switzerland averages 172 inhabitants per sq km. Zürich is the largest city (population 354,000), followed by Basel (177,000), Geneva (175,000) and Bern (132,000).

Despite its long-standing neutrality, Switzerland maintains a 400,000-strong civilian army. Every able-bodied male undergoes national service at age 20 and stays in the reserves for 22 years, all the while keeping his rifle and full kit at home.

SOCIETY & CONDUCT

In a few mountain regions such as Valais, people still wear traditional rural costumes, but dressing up is usually reserved for festivals. Yodelling and playing the alp horn are also part of the Alpine tradition, as is Swiss wrestling (a few too many beers may tempt you to try out such activities. Our advice: don't).

Always shake hands when being introduced to a Swiss, and again when leaving. Formal titles should also be used (in German – Herr for men and Frau for women). It is also customary to greet shopkeepers when entering shops. Public displays of affection are OK, but are more common in French and Italian Switzerland than in the slightly more formal German-speaking parts.

LANGUAGE

Switzerland has three official languages: German (spoken by 64% of the population), French (19%) and Italian (8%). A fourth language, Rhaeto-Romanic (or Romansch), is spoken by less than 1% of the population, mainly in the canton of Graubünden.

Though German-speaking Swiss have no trouble with standard High German, they use Swiss German (Schwyzertütsch) in private conversation.

English is widely understood in the German-speaking parts of Switzerland. However, it is simple courtesy to greet people with the Swiss-German Grüezi (Hello) and to inquire Sprechen sie Englisch? (Do you speak English?) before launching into English.

See the Language chapter at the back of this book for German, French and Italian pronunciation guidelines and useful words and phrases.

Facts for the Visitor

HIGHLIGHTS

The Jungfrau Region has magnificent hiking and scenery – the views from Schilthorn or its neighbour, Jungfrau, are unforgettable. Zermatt combines inspiring views of the Matterhorn and quality skiing. Be sure to take a boat trip: Lake Lugano reveals the sunny side of Switzerland's Italian canton, and Lake Thun offers snowcapped scenery and several castles. The Château de Chillon near Montreux is justifiably the most famous castle in Switzerland. Picturesque town centres include Bern, Lucerne and St Gallen. Zürich, Basel and Geneva are bursting with museums and art galleries.

SWITZERLAND

SUGGESTED ITINERARIES

Three days
Visit Geneva and take a trip on the lake. Don't miss Château de Chillon in Montreux.

One week
Visit Geneva and Montreux. En route to Lucerne, spend a few days exploring Interlaken and the Jungfrau Region.

Two weeks
As above, but spend longer in the mountains. Visit Bern, Basel and Zürich.

PLANNING

When to Go

Switzerland is visited throughout the year – December to April for winter sports, and May to October for general tourism and hiking. Alpine resorts all but close down in May and November.

TOURIST OFFICES

Tourist offices have plenty of literature, and somebody invariably speaks English. Local offices book hotel rooms (sometimes for a small fee) and organise excursions. Tourist offices also stock free city and regional maps.

Tourist Offices Abroad

A free-phone number for Switzerland Tourism that works worldwide (in countries with an office) is ☎ 00-800 100 200 30.

Canada (☎ 416-695 2090, fax 695 2774, @ storonto@switzerlandtourism.com) 926 The East Mall, Etobicoke, Toronto, Ontario M9B 6K1
UK (☎ 020-7734 1921, fax 7437 4577, @ slondon@switzerlandvacation.ch) Swiss Centre, Swiss Court, London W1V 8EE
USA (☎ 212-757 59 44, fax 262 61 16, @ stnewyork@switzerlandtourism.com) Swiss Center, 608 Fifth Ave, New York, NY 10020

EMBASSIES & CONSULATES

Swiss Embassies

Australia (☎ 02-6273 3977, fax 6273 3428, @ swissembcan@dynamite.com.au) 7 Melbourne Ave, Forrest, Canberra, ACT 2603
Canada (☎ 613-235 1837, fax 563 1394, @ swissmot@compuserve.com) 5 Marlborough Ave, Ottawa, Ontario K1N 8E6
New Zealand (☎ 04-472 1593, fax 472 1593) 22 Panama St, Wellington
UK (☎ 020-7616 6000, fax 7724 7001, @ vertretung@lon.rep.admin.ch) 16-18 Montague Place, London W1H 2BQ
USA (☎ 202-745 7900, fax 387 2564, @ vertretung@was.rep.admin.ch) 2900 Cathedral Ave NW, Washington, DC 20008-3499

Embassies & Consulates in Switzerland

All embassies are in Bern (area code ☎ 031):
Canada (☎ 357 32 00) Kirchenfeldstrasse 88
UK (☎ 359 77 00) Thunstrasse 50
USA (☎ 357 70 11) Jubiläumsstrasse 93

Foreign consulates include:
Australia (☎ 022-799 91 00) 2 Chemin des Fins, Geneva
Canada (☎ 022-919 92 00), 5 Ave de l'Ariana, Geneva
New Zealand (☎ 022-929 03 50) 2 Chemin des Fins, Geneva
UK (☎ 022-918 24 00), 37-39 Rue de Vermont, Geneva
USA (☎ 01-383 65 60) Minervastrasse 117, Zürich
(☎ 022-798 16 05) 29 Route de Pré-Bois, Geneva
(☎ 01-422 25 66) Dufourstrasse 101, Zürich

MONEY

Swiss francs (Sfr – written CHF locally) are made up of 100 centimes (called *Rappen* in German-speaking Switzerland). There are notes for 10, 20, 50, 100, 500 and 1000 francs, and coins for five, 10, 20 and 50 centimes, as well as for one, two and five francs.

All major travellers cheques and credit cards are accepted. Virtually all train stations have exchange facilities that are open daily. Commission is not usually charged for changing cash or cheques but it's gradually creeping in. ATMs (called 'Bancomat' in banks, 'Postomat' in post offices) are common everywhere, though some don't accept Visa cards for cash advances.

Exchange Rates

country	unit		swiss franc
Australia	A$1	=	Sfr0.99
Canada	C$1	=	Sfr1.16
euro	€1	=	Sfr1.55
France	1FF	=	Sfr0.24
Germany	DM1	=	Sfr0.79
Japan	¥100	=	Sfr1.58
New Zealand	NZ$1	=	Sfr0.77
UK	UK£1	=	Sfr2.58
USA	US$1	=	Sfr1.72

Costs

Prices are higher in Switzerland than anywhere else in Western Europe. Some travellers can scrimp by on about Sfr55 a day after buying a rail pass. This is survival level – camping or hostelling, self-catering when possible and allowing nothing for nonessentials. Minimum prices per person are around SFr22/38 in a hostel/hotel and SFr9/15 for lunch/dinner (excluding drinks). Taking cable cars is a major expense; if you're not fit enough, walk instead.

Tipping

Tipping is not strictly necessary as hotels, restaurants, bars and even some taxis are required by law to include a 15% service charge on bills.

POST & COMMUNICATIONS

Post

Postcards and letters to Europe cost SFr1.30/1.20 priority/economy; to elsewhere they cost SFr1.80/1.40. The term 'poste restante' is used nationwide, or you could use the German term, Postlagernde Briefe. Mail can be sent to any town with a post office and is held for 30 days; show your passport to collect mail.

Telephone & Fax

The country code for Switzerland is ☎ 41. Drop the initial zero on city area codes when dialling in from overseas.

The minimum charge to use Swisscom pay phones is a massive SFr0.60. For Swisscom, the normal rate for local/national calls (SFr0.07/0.12 per minute) applies 8 am to 5 pm Monday to Friday; the cheapest rate is from 10 pm to 6 am every night. For Swisscom international calls, rates are 20% lower on weekends.

A normal-rate call to USA/Australia/UK costs SFr0.58/0.78/0.78 per minute. The post office sells a range of budget prepaid cards. Swisscom phonecards (taxcard) are available for SFr5, SFr10 and SFr20. To send a fax at Swisscom offices costs SFr4, plus phone time.

Warning: Regional telephone codes in Switzerland will disappear before April 2002. Instead, the current regional code will form part of the subscriber number.

INTERNET RESOURCES

Most large towns have an Internet café. Occasionally you can find free places (eg, some post offices). Addresses/prices are quoted in this chapter, or ask at local tourist offices. The tourism authority's Web site is at www.myswitzerland.com has useful links, eg, to rail/Swissair timetables. The site at www.sri.ch has current news.

BOOKS

For more detail refer to Lonely Planet's Switzerland and Walking in Switzerland. Living and Working in Switzerland by David Hampshire is an excellent practical guide. Why Switzerland? by Jonathan Steinberg looks at the country's history and culture, and enthusiastically argues that Switzerland is not a boring country.

WOMEN TRAVELLERS

Women travellers should experience few problems with sexual harassment in Switzerland. However, Ticino males suffer from the same machismo leanings as their Italian counterparts, so advice given in the Italy chapter applies to some extent there too.

GAY & LESBIAN TRAVELLERS

Attitudes to homosexuality are reasonably tolerant. The age of consent is 16 years. The Cruiser magazine (☎ 01-261 82 00, e info@cruiser.ch, Postfach, Zürich CH-8025) has extensive listings of gay and lesbian organisations, bars and events in Switzerland (SFr4.50).

There are pride parades in Geneva (early July) and Zürich (mid-July).

DISABLED TRAVELLERS

Many hotels have disabled access, and most train stations have a mobile lift for boarding trains. The Swiss Invalid Association (☎ 062-212 12 62), or Schweizerischer Invalidenverband, is at Froburgstrasse 4, CH-4600 Olten. Web site: www.siv.ch.

DANGERS & ANNOYANCES

Crime rates may be low but don't neglect security. Some people might find congregations of young drug addicts in cities unsettling. Emergency telephone numbers are: police ☎ 117; fire brigade ☎ 118; and ambulance (most areas) ☎ 144. Take special care in the mountains: helicopter rescue (☎ 1414) is extremely expensive, so make sure your travel insurance covers Alpine sports.

BUSINESS HOURS

Most shops are open 8 am to 6.30 pm week-days (with a 90-minute or two-hour break for lunch at noon), and till 4 or 5 pm Saturday. Some towns have late opening on Thursday or Friday, and shops in large train stations may be open daily. Banks are open 8.30 am to 4.30 pm weekdays, with some local variations.

PUBLIC HOLIDAYS & SPECIAL EVENTS

National holidays are 1 January, Good Friday, Easter Monday, Ascension Day, Whit Monday, 1 August (National Day), and 25 and 26 December. Some cantons observe 2 January, 1 May (Labour Day), Corpus Christi and All Saints' Day.

Switzerland's liveliest festival is the Fasnacht Carnival in Basel and Lucerne in February. There's also the Montreux Jazz Festival in July, the onion market in Bern in November, and the Engadine ski marathon in March.

ACTIVITIES
Skiing

There are dozens of ski resorts throughout the Alps, the pre-Alps and the Jura. Equipment can always be hired at resorts; for one day you'll pay about SFr43/20 for downhill/cross-country gear. Ski passes (SFr35 to SFr60 per day) allow unlimited use of mountain transport.

Hiking & Mountaineering

For information contact the Swiss Alpine Club (SAC; ☎ 031-351 36 11), Helvetiaplatz 4, CH-3005 Bern. There are 50,000km of designated footpaths with refreshment stops en route. Yellow signs marking the trail make it difficult to get lost. White-red-white markers indicate the course of the more strenuous mountain paths.

ACCOMMODATION

Switzerland's 450 camping grounds are classified from one to five stars depending on amenities and convenience of location. Charges per night are around SFr7 per person plus SFr5 to SFr10 for a tent. Free camping is discouraged.

There are 60 official Swiss Youth Hostels (*Jugendherberge*, *auberge de jeunesse*, *alloggio per giovani*). Most include breakfast and sheets in the price and charge SFr2.50 less during the low season. Some have kitchens. HI membership is required; nonmembers pay a nightly SFr3 'guest fee', with six fees adding up to full international membership.

Hostels do get full, and telephone reservations are not accepted. Write, or ask your Swiss hostel to reserve ahead for your next one (SFr1 plus a SFr9 refundable deposit). Better yet, book on the association's Web site: www.youthhostel.ch. The Swiss Youth Hostel Association (SYHA), or Schweizer Jugendherbergen (☎ 01-360 14 14, fax 360 14 60, ⓔ bookingoffice@youthhostel.ch), is at Schaffhauserstrasse 14, Zürich CH-8042.

Independent 'backpacker hostels' are listed in *Swiss Backpacker News*, free from hostels and some tourist offices. Web site: www.backpacker.ch. Breakfast/sheets at these places are often extra, but they are less regulated than youth hostels and allow you to escape the hell of noisy school groups. Many offer double rooms and kitchens; some have a bar. Membership is not required.

'Hotel Garni' means a B&B establishment without a restaurant. Private houses in rural areas sometimes offer inexpensive rooms; look for signs saying *Zimmer frei* (room(s) vacant). Note that some hotels in mountain resorts have a cheap dormitory annexe (*Massenlager* or *dortoir*), and the Swiss Alpine Club maintains high-altitude dormitory huts.

FOOD & DRINKS

Basic restaurants and taverns (*Stübli*) provide simple but well-cooked food, although prices are generally high. Many budget travellers rely on picnic provisions from supermarkets, but even here prices can be a shock. The main supermarket chains (closed Sunday, except at some train stations) are Migros and Coop. Buffet-style restaurant chains, like Manora and Inova, offer good food at low prices.

The best value is a fixed-menu dish of the day (*Tagesteller*), *plat du jour* or *piatto del giorno*). Main meals are eaten at noon and cheaper restaurants (except pizzerias) tend to be fairly rigid about when they serve.

Cheeses form an important part of the Swiss diet. Emmental and Gruyère are combined with white wine to create *fondue*, which is served up in a pot and eaten with bread cubes. *Raclette* is another cheese dish, served with potatoes. *Rösti* (fried, shredded potatoes) is German Switzerland's national dish. *Bündnerfleisch* is dried beef, smoked and thinly sliced. There's also Switzerland's finest gift to the world – chocolate!

Alcohol is expensive in bars and clubs. Lager beer comes in 0.5L or 0.3L bottles, or on draught (vom *Fass* or *à la pression*).

Getting There & Away

The main entry points for flights are Zürich and Geneva.

Zürich has Eurolines buses to London via Basel (UK£53 one-way, 20 hours, one to three weekly) and Eastern Europe (see Zürich for details); Geneva has them to London (UK£59, three to six per week), Chamonix and Barcelona. Zürich and Geneva are also stops on Busabout routes (see the Getting Around chapter).

Zürich is the busiest international rail terminus in Switzerland. It has two direct day trains to Vienna (nine hours) and one night train (departs 10.33 pm). There are several trains a day to both Geneva and Lausanne from Paris; journey time is three to four hours by superfast TGV. Most connections from Germany pass though Zürich or Basel. Nearly all connections from Italy pass through Milan. Reservations on international trains are subject to a surcharge of SFr5 to SFr33, depending on the service.

Roads into Switzerland are good despite the difficulty of the terrain, but special care is needed when negotiating mountain passes. Upon entering Switzerland you will need to decide whether you wish to use the motorways. If so, there is a one-off charge of SFr40 to buy a sticker (called a *vignette*); it's valid for a year and must be displayed on the windscreen. You can buy a vignette in advance from Switzerland Tourism. Some Alpine tunnels incur additional tolls.

Getting Around

PASSES & DISCOUNTS

The Swiss Pass is valid for unlimited free travel on Swiss Federal Railways, boats, most Alpine postbuses and on trams and buses in 35 towns. Reductions of 25% apply on funiculars and mountain railways.

Passes are valid for four/eight days (SFr230/320), 15/21 days (SFr380/440) or one month (SFr500). Flexi versions are also available.

The Swiss Card allows a free return journey from your arrival point to any destination in Switzerland, 50% off rail, boat and bus excursions, and reductions on mountain railways. The cost is SFr150 for one month. The Half-Fare Card (SFr90 for one month) is a similar deal minus the free return trip. Buy it in Switzerland; the other passes are best purchased before arrival, from Switzerland Tourism or a travel agent.

Larger lakes are serviced by steamers, for which rail passes are usually valid (including Eurail; Inter-Rail often gets 50% off). A Swiss Navigation Boat Pass (SFr35) is good for 50% reductions.

BUS

Yellow postbuses are a supplement to the rail network, following postal routes and linking towns to the more inaccessible regions in the mountains. In all, routes cover some 8000km of terrain. They are extremely regular, and departures tie in with train arrivals. Postbus stations are next to train stations.

TRAIN

The Swiss rail network covers 5000km and is a combination of state-run and private lines. Trains are clean, reliable and frequent. Prices are high, though the travel passes mentioned earlier in this chapter will cut costs. All fares quoted are for 2nd class; 1st-class fares are about 65% higher. In general, Eurail passes are not valid for private lines and Inter-Rail gets 50% off. All major stations are connected by hourly departures. Services stop from around midnight to 6 am, but if you have a ticket, it's generally no problem to spend the night in a station waiting room.

Train stations store luggage at a counter (usually SFr5 per piece) or in 24-hour lockers (SFr2 to SFr5). Train information is on ☎ 0900-300 300 (SFr1.19 per minute), though you can get detailed and reliable information direct at train stations.

CAR & MOTORCYCLE

Be prepared for winding roads, high passes and long tunnels. Normal speed limits are

50km/h in towns, 120km/h on motorways, 100km/h on semi-motorways (rectangular pictograms show a white car on a green background) and 80km/h on other roads. Don't forget you need a vignette to use motorways and semi-motorways (see the Getting There & Away section). Some minor Alpine passes are closed from November to May – check with tourist offices or motoring organisations. The Swiss Touring Club (TCS; ☎ 022-417 27 27) is at 4 Chemin de Blandonnet, Case postale 820, CH-1214, Geneva. Web site: www.tcs.ch.

Ring ☎ 140 for the national 24-hour breakdown service. Switzerland is tough on drink-driving, so don't risk it; the BAC limit is 0.05%.

BICYCLE

Despite the hilly countryside, cycling is popular in Switzerland. Bicycles can be hired from most train stations; return your bike to a different station and you pay a surcharge of Sfr6. Rentals cost Sfr20/80 per day/week. Bikes can be transported on most trains; get a one-day bike pass for Sfr15. Bern, Basel, Geneva and Zürich offer free bike loans – see the city sections.

Bern

☎ 031

Founded in 1191 by Berchtold V, Bern (Berne in French) is Switzerland's capital and fourth-largest city. The story goes that the city was named for the bear (Bärn in local dialect) that was Berchtold's first kill when hunting in the area. Even today the bear remains the heraldic mascot of the city. Despite playing host to the nation's politicians, Bern retains a relaxed, small-town charm. A picturesque old town contains 6km of covered arcades and 11 historic fountains. The world's largest Paul Klee collection is housed in the Museum of Fine Arts.

Information

Bern Tourismus (☎ 328 12 12, ℮ info-res @bernetourism.ch) is in the train station, open 9 am to 8.30 pm daily (in winter: to 6.30 pm, 5 pm Sunday). Staff can make hotel reservations, or use the free hotel phone outside. There's an SBB exchange office in the lower level of the train station.

open 6.15 am to 8.45 pm (until 9.45 pm in summer) daily.

The main post office (Schanzenpost 3001) is on Schanzenstrasse. Free Internet terminals are at the Medienhaus, Zeughausgasse 14 (closed Sunday). The Loeb department store on Spitalgasse has an Internet café in the 2nd-level basement.

The budget and student travel agency SSR (☎ 302 03 12) has two offices: Falkenplatz 9 and Rathausgasse 64. They're open weekdays and Saturday morning.

The university hospital (☎ 632 21 11) is on Friburgstrasse. For help in locating a doctor or pharmacy, call ☎ 311 22 11.

Things to See

The free city map from the tourist office details a picturesque walk through the old town. The core of the walk is Marktgasse and Kramgasse with their covered arcades, colourful fountains, and cellars containing shops, bars and theatres. Check the ogre fountain, on Kornhausplatz, depicting a giant enjoying a repast of wriggling children. Nearby, the Zeitglockenturm is a clock tower on which revolving figures herald the chiming hour. Originally a city gate, the clock was installed in 1530.

The unmistakably Gothic 15th-century cathedral (Münster) is noted for its stained-glass windows and elaborate main portal. Just over the River Aare are the bear pits (Bärengraben). Bears have been at this site since 1857, although their ursine ancestors have been fed by the city since 1441. The adjoining Tourist Center has an informative, free multimedia show. Up the hill is the Rose Garden, which has 200 varieties of roses and an excellent view of the city.

Well worth a visit are the Bundeshäuser, home of the Swiss Federal Assembly. There are free daily tours when the parliament is not in session (watch from the public gallery when it is). Arrive early and reserve a place for later in the day.

An open-air produce market is at Bärenplatz on Tuesday and Saturday mornings, or daily in summer.

Museums There's no shortage of museums. The Kunstmuseum (Museum of Fine Arts), Hodlerstrasse 8-12, holds the Klee collection and an interesting mix of Italian masters, Swiss and modern art. It's open

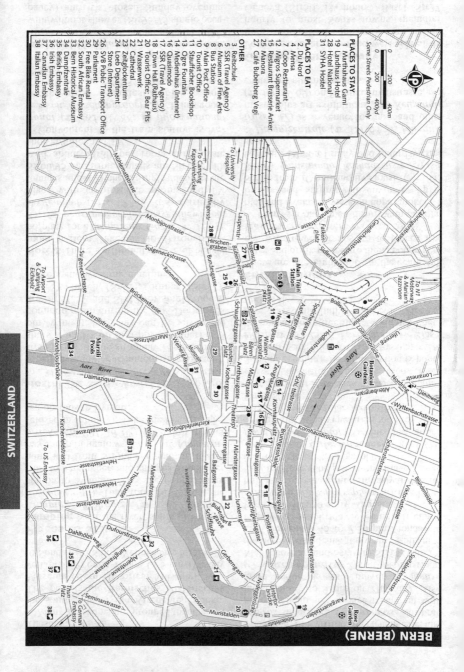

BERN (BERNE)

PLACES TO STAY
1 Marthahaus Garni
19 Landhaus Hotel
28 Hotel National
31 SYHA Hostel

PLACES TO EAT
2 Du Nord
4 Mensa
7 Coop Restaurant
12 Migros Supermarket
15 Restaurant Brasserie Anker
25 Manora
27 Café Bubenberg Vegi

OTHER
3 Reitschule
5 SSR (Travel Agency)
6 Museum of Fine Arts
8 Bus Station
9 Main Post Office
10 Tourist Office
11 Stauffacher Bookshop
13 Ogre Fountain
14 Quasimodo
16 Medienhaus (Internet)
17 SSR (Travel Agency)
18 Town Hall (Rathaus)
20 Tourist Office; Bear Pits
21 Wasserwerk
22 Cathedral
23 Zeitglockenturm
24 Loeb Department Store (Internet)
26 SVB Public Transport Office
29 Parliament
30 Free Bike Rental
32 South African Embassy
33 Bern Historical Museum
34 Dampfzentrale
35 British Embassy
36 Irish Embassy
37 Canadian Embassy
38 Italian Embassy

SWITZERLAND

10 am to 5 pm Tuesday to Sunday (to 9 pm Tuesday; SFr6/4).

Many museums are grouped together on the south side of the Kirchenfeldbrücke. The best is the **Bernisches Historisches Museum** (Bern Historical Museum), Helvetiaplatz 5, open 10 am to 5 pm Tuesday to Sunday (to 8 pm Wednesday; SFr5/3).

Places to Stay

Camping Near the river, south of town is *Camping Eichholz* (☎ 961 26 02, *Strandweg 49*). Take tram No 9 from the station to Wabern. The site is open from May to September, and charges SFr6.90 per adult and from SFr2.50 per tent/car. It also has cheap bungalows. *Camping Kappelenbrücke* (☎ 901 10 07) is slightly pricier (closed in January). Take the Hinterkappelen postbus to Eymatt.

Hostel The SYHA hostel (☎ 311 63 16, fax 312 52 40, *Weihergasse 4*) is in a good location below Parliament (signposted). It's usually full in summer. The reception shuts from 10 am to 3 pm (summer) or 5 pm (winter), but bags can be left in the common room during the day. Dorm beds are SFr27.25; add SFr13 for single rooms. There's lunch (SFr12), dinner (SFr11), lockers and washing machines.

Hotels There's a limited choice of budget rooms in Bern. Take bus No 20 from Bahnhofplatz for *Marthahaus Garni* (☎ 332 41 35, @ pension.marthahaus@bluewin.ch, *Wittenbachstrasse 22a*). It's a friendly place with comfortable rooms and TV lounges and a kitchen. Singles/doubles are SFr60/95 and triples/quads are SFr120/140. Add about SFr30 per room for private shower/toilet and TV.

Convenient to the train station is *National* (☎ 381 19 88, @ info@national-bern.ch, Hirschengraben 24). It has good-for-the-price singles/doubles from SFr60/100, or SFr85/130 with private shower and toilet.

Near the bear pits is *Landhaus Hotel* (☎ 331 41 66, @ landhaus@spectraweb.ch, Altenbergstrasse 4). Doubles are SFr140/110 with/without shower (SFr95/75 single occupancy) and it's closed Sunday evening. Dorms for SFr30 exclude bedding and breakfast (so use the kitchen).

Places to Eat

The *Coop*, in Ryfflihof on Neuengasse, and *Migros* supermarket (*Marktgasse 46*) both have a cheap self-service restaurant with late opening to 9 pm on Thursday. Also good value is the university *mensa* (*Gesellschaftsstrasse 2*), on the 1st floor. Meals cost around SFr10 to SFr14, with reductions for students. It is open 11.30 am to 1.45 pm and 5.45 to 7.30 pm Monday to Friday (closed Friday evening). It closes from mid-July to early August.

Manora (*Bubenbergplatz 5a*) is a busy, buffet-style restaurant with tasty dishes for SFr9 to SFr16. The pile-it-on-yourself salad is SFr4.20 to SFr8.90 per plate.

Nearby is *Café Bubenberg Vegi* (*1st floor, Bubenbergplatz 8*) which has terrace seating and good vegetarian food for SFr14 to SFr20, and regular Indian buffets from SFr23.80.

Restaurant Brasserie Anker (*Zeughausgasse 1*) has affordable Swiss food (closed Sunday evening). Its front section is popular with beer drinkers (SFr4 for 0.5L). *Du Nord* (☎ 332 23 38, *Lorrainestrasse 2*) is a bar-restaurant attracting a youngish clientele. Swiss and Italian food costs SFr14 to SFr35 (closed Wednesday).

Entertainment

There are late-night clubs in the centre but entry and drink prices are high. Young people with fewer francs go to places like *Wasserwerk* (*Wasserwerkgasse 5*).

There's a bar (open 8 pm) with pool tables and a relaxed view on dope smokers, a Friday and Saturday disco (entry up to SFr15; from 10 pm) and live music (SFr18 to SFr30). *Quasimodo* (*Rathausgasse 75*) is a bar with DJs on Friday and Saturday (free entry).

Dampfzentrale (☎ 311 63 37, *Marzilistrasse 47*) is a venue for jazz and other music, plus art exhibitions. The *Reitschule* (☎ 306 69 69) on Schützenmattstrasse, is a centre for alternative arts.

Getting There & Away

Postbuses depart from the west side of the train station. Rail connections are at least hourly to most Swiss towns, including Geneva (SFr50, 1¾ hours), Basel (SFr37, 70 minutes), Interlaken (SFr25, 50 minutes) and Zürich (SFr48, 70 minutes).

Getting Around

Bus and tram tickets cost Sfr1.50 (maximum six stops) or Sfr2.40. A day pass for the city and regional network is Sfr11.50. Buy single-journey tickets at stops and passes from the tourist office or SVB public transport office at Bubenbergplatz 5. Outside Loeb department store and on Casinoplatz are depots offering free bike loans in summer.

AROUND BERN

Neuchâtel
☎ 032

Neuchâtel (population 32,000) is inside the French-speaking region of Switzerland, on the north-west shore of the lake that shares its name. This relaxing town is worth a trip if you're not pressed for time. Nearby are the mountain areas of the Jura, where there's good cross-country skiing and hiking.

Orientation & Information The central pedestrian zone and Place Pury (the hub of local buses) are about 1km downhill from the train station. The nearby tourist office (☎ 689 68 90, ✉ tourisme.neuchatelois@ ne.ch) is in the main post office by the lake.

Things to See The centrepiece of the old town is the 12th-century castle, now housing cantonal offices, and the adjoining Collegiate Church, containing a 14th-century cenotaph. Nearby, the Prison Tower (Sfr0.50) offers a good view and has interesting models showing the town as it was in the 17th and 18th centuries.

One of several museums, the **Museum of Art and History** (Musée d'Art et d'Histoire), Esplanade Léopold Robert 2, is especially noted for three 18th-century clockwork figures, which are activated on the first Sunday of each month, but can be seen anytime. Entry is Sfr7 (Sfr4 for students; closed on Monday, free on Thursday).

Places to Stay & Eat *Oasis Neuchâtel* (☎ 731 31 90, *Rue du Suchiez 35*) is over 2km from the town centre; take bus No 1 to Vauseyon then follow the signs to Centre sportif. It is a small, pleasant independent hostel, with vegetarian evening meals and a kitchen. Check-in is from 5 to 9 pm. Dorms/doubles are Sfr24/30 and it closes from November to March. *Hôtel du Marché* (☎ 724 58 00, *Place des Halles 4*) is central and provides singles/doubles for Sfr70/100 with TV and hall showers.

Chauffage Compris (*Rue des Moulins 37*) is a place for drinks and good lunches (from Sfr13.50). A unique feature of Neuchâtel is its *restaurants de nuit*, open from around 9 pm to 6 am for eating, drinking and dancing. *Garbo Café* (*Rue des Chavannes 7*) is one such place (closed Monday).

Getting There & Away From Neuchâtel there are hourly fast trains to Bern (Sfr17.20, 35 minutes) and Geneva (Sfr42, 70 minutes).

Geneva
☎ 022

Geneva (Genève, Genf, Ginevra) is Switzerland's third-largest city, comfortably encamped on the shore of Lake Geneva (Lac Léman). Geneva belongs not so much to French-speaking Switzerland as to the whole world. Over 40% of residents are non-Swiss and many world organisations are based here, not least the European headquarters of the United Nations.

Geneva won respite from the Duke of Savoy in 1530, and was ripe for the teachings of John Calvin two years later. It soon became known as the Protestant Rome, during which time fun became frowned upon. Thankfully this legacy barely lingers and today Geneva offers a varied nightlife. By day, you can see some of the best Geneva has to offer by simply strolling along the lakeside.

Orientation

The Rhône River runs through the city, dividing it into *rive droite* (north of the Rhône) and *rive gauche* (the south). The main train station, Gare de Cornavin, is on the north side, while to the south lies the old part of town. In summer, Geneva's most visible landmark is the Jet d'Eau, a giant fountain on the southern shore.

Information

The tourist office (☎ 909 70 00, fax 909 70 11, ✉ info@geneve-tourisme.ch), 18 Rue du Mont-Blanc, is open to 6 pm Monday to Saturday (daily in summer). Hotel reservations cost SFr5. Youth-oriented information is dispensed from the CAR bus on Rue du Mont-Blanc, daily in summer.

The main post office, in the same building as the tourist office, is at 18 Rue du Mont-Blanc, 1211 Genève 1. Find Internet access at Club Videorom, 19 Rue des Alpes (SFr1/5 for 10/60 minutes; closed Sunday morning).

American Express (☎ 731 76 00) is at 7 Rue du Mont-Blanc. Bureau de Change Michel, 32 Rue de Zurich, has excellent exchange rates (closed Sunday). The budget and student travel agency SSR (☎ 329 97 34) is at 3 Rue Vignier.

The Cantonal Hospital (☎ 372 33 11) is at 24 Rue Micheli du Crest. Permanence Médico Chirurgicale (☎ 731 21 20), 1-3 Rue de Chantepoulet, is a private clinic, open 24 hours a day.

Things to See & Do

The city centre is so compact that it is easy to see many of the main sights on foot – start at the Île Rousseau, noted for a statue in honour of the celebrated free thinker. Turn right (west) along the south side of the Rhône until you reach the 13th-century Tour de l'Île, once part of the medieval city fortifications.

Walk south down the narrow, cobbled Rue de la Cité until it becomes Grand-Rue. Here at No 40 is Rousseau's birthplace. A short detour off Grand-Rue is the partially Romanesque, partially Gothic Cathédral St Pierre. John Calvin preached here from 1536 to 1564. There is a good view from the tower (SFr3; open daily o at least 5 pm). Grand-Rue terminates at Place du Bourg-de-Four, the site of a medieval marketplace that now has a fountain and touristy shops. Take Rue de la Fontaine to reach the lakeside. Anticlockwise round the shore is the Jet d'Eau. Calling this a fountain is something of an understatement. The water shoots up with incredible force (200km/h, 1360 horsepower) to create a 140m-high plume. At any one time, seven tonnes of water is in the air. It's not active in winter.

Parks & Gardens On the lakefront near the old town, the Jardin Anglais features a large clock composed of flowers. Further up Grand-Rue is Promenade des Bastions, with a massive Reformation Monument to Bèze, Calvin and other figures of the Reformation. Colourful flower gardens and the occasional statue line the promenade on the north shore of the lake, and lead to two peaceful parks, the Botanical Gardens and Parc Mon Repos.

Museums Geneva has plenty of museums, many of them free. The most important is the free Musée d'Art et d'Histoire (Museum of Art and History), 2 Rue Charles Galland, with a vast and varied collection including paintings, sculpture, weapons and archaeology (closed Monday).

By the UN is the International Red Cross & Red Crescent Museum, a vivid multimedia illustration of the history of those two humanitarian organisations. It's open 10 am to 5 pm (closed Tuesday; SFr10/5).

United Nations & CERN If you want to blow SFr8.50, take the so-so hour-long tour of the United Nations building at Place des Nations (passport required). However, if you're not one of the 3000 international civil servants who have a special reason to be there, hop instead on bus No 15 to CERN, a particle physics research laboratory near Meyrin. This was the first lab to create antimatter (in 1996). There's an interesting free exhibition (closed Sunday and Monday morning). Book well ahead (☎ 767 84 84, @ visits-service@cern.ch) for free Saturday tours of the 27km-long particle accelerator (take your passport).

Activities

Centre Sportif des Vernets (☎ 418 40 00), 4 Rue Hans Wilsdorf, has swimming and ice skating (closed Monday; SFr5 each). You can swim in Lake Geneva at Genève Plage (SFr7, including pool with waterslide) or at Bains des Pâquis (SFr2), which is also a great place to hang out on summer evenings.

Places to Stay

Camping Seven kilometres north-east of the city centre on the southern lakeshore is Camping Pointe à la Bise (☎ 752 12 96), Vesenaz. It costs SFr6 per person, plus from SFr9 for tents. Take bus E from Rive.

Hostels – North of the Rhône The SYHA hostel (☎ 732 62 60, 28-30 Rue Rothschild) is big, modern and busy. Dorms

SWITZERLAND

GENEVA (GENÈVE)

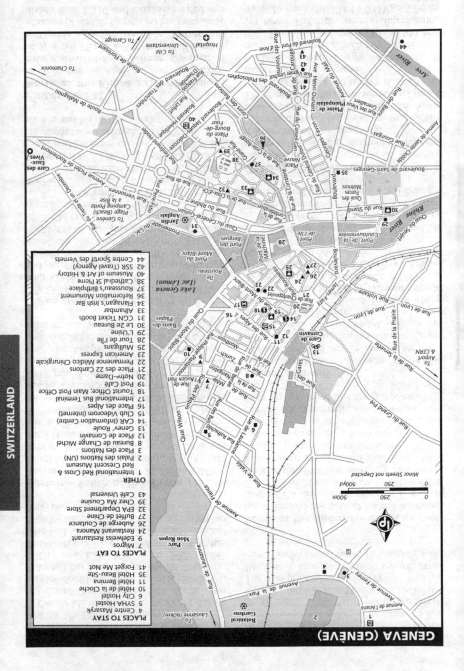

PLACES TO STAY
4 Centre Masaryk
5 SYHA Hostel
6 City Hostel
10 Hôtel de la Cloche
11 Hôtel Bernina
35 Hôtel Beau-Site
41 Forget Me Not

PLACES TO EAT
7 Migros
9 Edelweiss Restaurant
24 Restaurant Manora
26 Auberge de Coutance
27 Buffet de Chine
32 EPA Department Store
39 Chez Ma Cousine
43 Café Universal

OTHER
1 International Red Cross & Red Crescent Museum
2 Palais des Nations (UN)
3 Place des Nations
8 Bureau de Change Michel
12 Place de Cornavin
13 Genev' Roulé
14 CAR (Information Centre)
15 Club Videorom (Internet)
16 Place des Alpes
17 International Bus Terminal
18 Tourist Office; Main Post Office
19 Post Café
20 Notre-Dame
21 Place des 22 Cantons
22 Permanence Médico Chirurgicale
23 American Express
25 Mulligans
28 Tour de l'Île
29 L'Usine
30 Le Ze Bureau
31 CGN Ticket Booth
33 Alhambar
34 Flanagan's Irish Bar
36 Reformation Monument
37 Rousseau's Birthplace
38 Cathédral St Pierre
40 Museum of Art & History
42 SSR (Travel Agency)
44 Centre Sportif des Vernets

are SFr24, doubles are SFr65 and dinners are SFr12.50. The hostel is closed from 10 am to 4 pm (to 2 pm in summer).

Centre Masaryk (☎ 733 07 72, 11 Ave de la Paix) has dorms for SFr30 and singles/doubles/triples for SFr45/80/105. Take bus No 5 or 8 from Gare de Cornavin. The new *City Hostel (☎ 901 15 60, info@cityhostel.ch, 2 Rue Ferrier)* has four-bed dorms for SFr24 and singles/doubles for SFr50/70. There's a kitchen, no breakfast, and all-day reception.

Hostels – South of the Rhône The *Cité Universitaire (☎ 839 22 22, 46 Ave Miremont)* has many beds, but dorms (SFr17) are only available in July and August. Take bus No 3 from Gare de Cornavin to the terminus at Champel, south of the city centre. Singles/doubles cost SFr45/61, or SFr38/55 for students. Breakfast is SFr6. Reception is open 8 am to noon (9 to 11 am on Sunday) and 2 pm (6 pm on weekends) to 10 pm.

Forget Me Not (☎ 320 93 55, 8 Rue Vignier) has simple, student-style rooms with sink for SFr45/80. Dorms are SFr25 and there are kitchens but no breakfast.

Hotels *Hôtel Beau-Site (☎ 328 10 08, fax 329 23 64, 3 Place du Cirque)* is a good deal, with kitchen facilities, free tea and coffee, and sizeable, old-fashioned rooms with high ceilings and creaky wood floors. Singles/doubles/triples cost from SFr60/82/100, or SFr70/90/110 with private shower. *Hôtel de la Cloche (☎ 732 94 81, 6 Rue de la Cloche)* is small, old-fashioned, friendly and liable to be full unless you call ahead. Big singles/doubles using hall shower are SFr55/85; doubles with shower/toilet are SFr120. *Bernina (☎ 908 49 50, fax 908 49 51, 22 Place de Cornavin)* has renovated rooms with TV and telephone and charges SFr105/150/150 with shower and SFr80/105 without.

Places to Eat

North of the Rhône Explore the streets north of Rue des Alpes for inexpensive oriental and Asian food. *Migros* supermarket on Rue des Pâquis has a cheap self-service restaurant. The buffet-style *Restaurant Manora (4 Rue de Chavrin)* has tasty daily dishes from SFr10 and extensive salad and dessert bars. Opposite, *Auberge de Couvance (☎ 732 79 19)* is recommended

South of the Rhône For the cheapest eating in the old town, head for the restaurant in the EPA department store on Rue de la Croix d'Or. Meals are SFr8 to SFr14. *Chez Ma Cousine (6 Place du Bourg-de-Four)* is a tiny place offering just one dish – half-chicken, potatoes and salad for SFr12.90. It's closed Sunday. *Café Universal (26 Blvd du Pont d'Arve)* is atmospheric, French and smoky; prices are high, though lunches cost from SFr16 (closed Sunday and Monday).

for exquisite south-west France specialities from SFr25 (closed Sunday). A good option for Chinese food is *Buffet de Chine (5 Rue de Grenus)*, with daily plates for SFr10 (open 11 am to 9 pm, Monday to Saturday). The mid-priced *Edelweiss (☎ 731 36 58, 2 Place de la Navigation)* allows you to experience Swiss kitsch via its free nightly folklore show.

Entertainment

Geneva's expensive nightclubs, along with dance, music and theatre venues, are listed in *Genève Agenda*, free from the tourist office. *L'Usine (☎ 781 34 90, 4 Place des Volontaires)* is a centre for cinema, theatre and concerts, and has a bar and cheap restaurant. Nearby, *Le 2e Bureau (☎ 320 24 49, 9 Rue du Strand)* is a relaxed bar with free concerts (closed Sunday). *Alhambar (☎ 312 20 36, 1st floor, 10 Rue de la Rôtisserie)* is similar.

English-speakers head for *Post Café (7 Rue de Berne)*, with British sports on TV. *Mulligans (14 Rue Grenus)* or *Flanagan's Irish Bar* at Rue du Cheval-Blanc.

Getting There & Away

Geneva's Cointrin airport is an important transport hub and has frequent connections to every major European city.

International buses depart from Place Dorcière (☎ 732 02 30), off Rue des Alpes. There are four buses a week to London (SFr150, 17 hours) and several daily to Chamonix (SFr43, 1½ hours).

There are hourly train connections to most Swiss towns; Zürich takes three hours (SFr77), as does Interlaken Ost (SFr65), both via Bern. There are regular international trains to Paris (SFr103 by TGV, 3½ hours; reservations essential), Hamburg (SFr273, 10 hours), Milan (SFr81, four hours) and

Barcelona (Sfr100, 10 hours). Gare des Eaux-Vives is the station for Annecy and Chamonix. To get there from Gare de Cornavin, take any bus going to Bel Air and then tram No 12 or 16.

Compagnie Générale de Navigation (CGN; ☎ 312 52 23), on Quai du Mont-Blanc and by Jardin Anglais, operates a steamer service to all towns and major villages bordering Lake Geneva, including those in France. Most boats only operate between May and September, such as those to Lausanne (Sfr33, 3½ hours) and Montreux (Sfr38.80, 4½ hours). Eurail and Swiss passes are valid on CGN boats. CGN and other companies also do short circular excursions, from Sfr8 for 30 minutes.

Getting Around

Getting from Cointrin airport is easy with 200 trains a day into Gare de Cornavin (Sfr5, six minutes). Bus No 10 (Sfr2.20) does the same 5km trip.

There's bike rental at Gare de Cornavin, but from May to October Genev' Roule (☎ 740 13 43) has bikes free of charge, available at 17 Place de Montbrillant, Bains des Pâquis, Place du Rhône and Plaine de Plainpalais. Some ID and a Sfr50 deposit are required.

Lake Geneva Region

LAUSANNE

☎ 021

Capital of the canton of Vaud, this hilly city is Switzerland's fifth largest. Don't miss Musée de l'Art Brut, one of Europe's most unusual art collections.

Orientation & Information

The main tourist office (☎ 613 73 73), 4 Place de la Navigation, is in the Ouchy metro station, by the lake. It's open 9 am to 6 pm (8 pm in summer) daily. In the train station is another tourist office (open 9 am to 7 pm daily), bicycle rental and money-changing facilities. Opposite, behind McDonald's, is Quanta, with Internet access (Sfr4 for 30 minutes). The main post office (Poste Principale 1001) is by the station. The cathedral, shopping streets and Place St-François (the main hub for local transport) are up the hill to the north.

Things to See

The fine Gothic cathedral was built in the 12th and 13th centuries and has an impressive main portal and attractive stained-glass windows, not least the famous rose window. The church and its tower are open daily.

The Musée de l'Art Brut, 11 Ave de Bergières, is a fascinating amalgam of art created by untrained artists – the mentally unhinged, eccentrics and incarcerated criminals. Some of the images created are startling, others merely strange. Biographies and explanations are in English and the collection is open 11 am to 1 pm and 2 to 6 pm Tuesday to Sunday (Sfr6/4).

Lausanne is the headquarters of the International Olympic Committee, hence the lavish and impressive Musée Olympique (Olympic Museum), 1 Quai d'Ouchy. It's open daily (closed Monday in winter) and tells the Olympic story using videos, archive film, interactive computers and memorabilia (Sfr14/9).

The large Palais de Rumine contains several museums, covering natural history and other sciences. Its Fine Arts (Beaux-Arts) collection exhibits many works by Swiss artists (Sfr6; closed Monday).

Places to Stay

Year-round lakeside camping is available at Camping de Vidy (☎ 624 20 31, 3 Chemin du Camping), west of the centre (take bus No 2). Two-/four-person bungalows cost about Sfr55/90.

Nearby on the same bus route, the SYHA Jeunotel (☎ 626 02 22, @ jeunotel@ urbanet.ch, 36 Chemin du Bois-de-Vaux) is a hostel with hotel pretensions. It offers no-frills accommodation in dorms (Sfr25), singles/doubles (Sfr76/92 with shower and toilet, Sfr52/76 without), and triples/quads (Sfr87/116 without). The self-service restaurant serves cheap meals.

Pension Bon-Séjour (☎ 323 59 52, 10 Rue Caroline) is more central. Rooms cost Sfr40/66, some with shower; phone ahead.

Places to Eat

The buffet-style Manora (17 Place St François) has a good choice of vegetables, salad and fruit, and main dishes are around

SFr10. *Le Bleu Lézard (10 Rue Enning)* has inexpensive food, and a cellar bar with free live music or DJs most nights. Opposite is *Caroline Café*, which is a food hall in the Coop Centre with a range of cheap meals (closed Sunday).

Getting There & Away

There are three trains hourly to/from Geneva (SFr20, 50 minutes), and one or two hourly to Bern. Trains to Interlaken Ost cost SFr54 via Bern (two hours); the scenic route via Montreux/Zweisimmen is SFr58 (three hours).

MONTREUX
☎ 021

Centrepiece of the so-called Swiss Riviera, Montreux offers marvellous lakeside walks and access to the ever-popular Château de Chillon. Nearby Vevey is an equally good base.

Orientation & Information

The train station and main post office are on Ave des Alpes, which, down to the south, leads to Place de la Paix and the main streets of Grand-Rue and Ave du Casino. The tourist office (☎ 962 84 36, ☑ tourism@montreux.ch) is a few minutes away in the pavilion on the lakeshore (descend the stairs or lift, opposite the post office).

Things to See & Do

Montreux is known for the **Château de Chillon** (pronounced 'sheeyoh'), which receives more visitors than any other historical building in Switzerland. Occupying a stunning position right on Lake Geneva, the fortress caught the public imagination when Lord Byron wrote about the fate of Bonivard, a follower of the Reformation, who was chained to the fifth pillar in the dungeons for four years in the 16th century. Byron etched his own name on the third pillar. Allow at least two hours to tour the site. The castle is open from at least 10 am to 5 pm daily (SFr7.50/6). It's a pleasant 45-minute walk along the lakefront from Montreux (15 minutes from the hostel), or take the local train (stop: Veytaux-Chillon) or bus No 1 (SFr2.60; stop: Veytaux).

Montreux's other claim to fame is the **Jazz Festival** in early July. The program is announced in late April; inquire then for tickets on ☎ 963 82 82. Check their Web site at www.montreuxjazz.com.

Places to Stay & Eat

The SYHA **hostel** (☎ 963 49 34, 8 Passage de l'Auberge), in Territet, is a 30-minute walk along the lake clockwise from the tourist office (or take the local train to Territet, or bus No 1). It's near the waterfront, under the railway line, and is closed in December and January. Dorms are SFr29 and doubles (bunk beds) are SFr76.

A good alternative is the **Yoba Riviera Lodge** (☎ 923 80 40, fax 923 80 41, ☑ rivieralodge@bluewin.ch, 5 Grande-Place) in central Vevey. Beds are SFr25 in dorms or SFr35 in double rooms. Breakfast is SFr7, or use the kitchen. Reception is closed from noon to 4 pm.

Pension Wilhelm (☎ 963 14 31, fax 963 32 85, 13 Rue de Marché) charges SFr55/100 for rooms without shower in an old-fashioned, family-run hotel.

Paradise (58 Grand-Rue) has fast food but is best for its extensive salad buffet (SFr2.60 per 100g). Across the street is **Metropole**, with idyllic outside seating overlooking the lake. Meals, including pizzas, start at SFr14.

Getting There & Away

Hourly trains run to/from Geneva (SFr29, 70 minutes) and Lausanne (SFr9.40, 25 minutes). Interlaken can be reached via a scenic rail route, with changeovers at Zweisimmen and Spiez; rail passes are valid, though there is a SFr6 supplement on some trains.

VAUD ALPS

If you're in this region in late January, don't miss International Hot Air Balloon Week, a visually spectacular event in **Château d'Oex**, on the Montreux-Interlaken railway line. Contact the tourist office (☎ 924 25 25, ☑ chateau-doex@bluewin.ch).

To get off the beaten track, consider staying in quiet, untouristed **Gryon** (1130m). It is scenically situated, close to the Villars ski area and 30 minutes by train from Bex (on the Lausanne-Sion rail route). There are several cheap places to stay; ask at the tourist office (☎ 024-498 14 22). **Swiss Alp Retreat** (☎ 024-498 33 21), based in the Chalet Martin, is favoured by young backpackers. Beds cost SFr18 in dorms or from

SFr28 in doubles; add SFr13 for the first night. There's a kitchen (no breakfast) and check-in is from 9 am to 9 pm (phone ahead). Web site: www.gryon.com.

Leysin, accessible from Aigle on the Lausanne-Sion route, is a skiing and hiking centre. Stay at the *Hiking Sheep Guesthouse* (☎/fax 024-494 35 35, @ hsg1@omedia.ch) where there's a kitchen and friendly staff. Beds are SFr30/35 in dorms/doubles, without breakfast (reductions in the low season). Reception is closed from noon to 5 pm.

Valais

The dramatic Alpine landscape of Valais (Wallis in German) once made it one of Switzerland's most inaccessible regions. Nowadays the mountains and valleys have been opened up by an efficient network of roads, railways and cable cars. It is an area of great natural beauty and each impressive panorama has spawned its own resort. Skiing (47 listed centres) in the winter and hiking in the summer are primary pursuits.

Valais is also known for its Combats de Reines (Kuhkämpfe in German) – cow fights organised in villages to determine which beast is most suited to lead the herd up to the summer pastures. They usually take place on selected Sundays starting in late March. There is a grand final in Aproz round about Ascension Day (40 days after Easter), and the last meeting of the season is at the Martigny Fair in October.

SION
☎ 027

Sion, the capital of the Lower Valais, merits a brief perusal en route from Montreux to Zermatt (all trains stop here). Two ancient fortifications dominate the town, Tourbillon Castle and, on the neighbouring hill, the Valère church. Both provide a fine view of the Rhône Valley. The Valais regional museums are here too. If you want to stop over, there's a SYHA hostel (☎ 323 74 70, fax 323 74 38, Rue de l'Industrie 2), behind the station: exit left and turn left under the tracks.

ZERMATT
☎ 027

Skiing, hiking and mountaineering are the main attractions in this resort, all overseen by the most famous peak in the Alps, the Matterhorn (4478m), which stands sentinel at the head of the valley. Note that Zermatt is car-free except for electric taxis, and street names are rarely used.

Information
The tourist office (☎ 967 01 81, @ zermatt@ wallis.ch) is beside the train station. Next door is a travel agent that changes money. The Alpin Center (☎ 966 24 60) on the main street near the post office is another good information source.

Activities
Zermatt has many demanding slopes to test the experienced skier; beginners have fewer possibilities. February to April is peak time, though in early summer the snow is still good and the lifts are less busy. Ski shops open daily for rentals – one-day hire prices are SFr28 for skis and stocks and SFr15 for boots.

The Klein Matterhorn is topped by the highest cable station in Europe (3820m); it provides access to summer skiing slopes, as well as the ski route down to Cervinia in Italy (don't forget your passport). A day pass for all ski lifts, excluding Cervinia, costs SFr62.

Places to Stay & Eat
Camping Matterhorn (☎ 967 39 21), left of the train station, is open from June to early September.

The *SYHA hostel* (☎ 967 23 20) has an excellent view of the Matterhorn. Turn left at the church, cross the river and take the second right. Dorm beds at half-board are SFr46. The hostel is shut between seasons.

Nearby, *Matterhorn Hostel* (☎ 968 19 19, @ info@matterhornhostel.com) is open year-round. Dorms are SFr24/29 in low/high season, and basic doubles are SFr34/36 per person. Optional breakfast/dinner is SFr6/12. In both hostels, doors stay open during the day though check-in is from 4 pm.

Opposite the train station, and popular with mountaineers, is the renovated *Hotel Bahnhof* (☎ 967 24 06, @ hotel-bahnhof@hotmail.com) with 12-bed dorms for SFr30 and compact singles/doubles from SFr54/84. There's a kitchen but no break-fast. *Hotel Gabelhorn* (☎ 967 22 35), in the Hinter Dorf area of the village, is small and friendly, charging from SFr50/88.

SWITZERLAND

Beyond the church on the main street, *Restaurant Weisshorn* and the *Café du Pont* next door are both good places for food. *North Wall Bar*, near the hostel, is one of the cheapest and best bars in the village. It's closed between seasons, but otherwise it's open from 6 pm daily.

Getting There & Away
Hourly trains depart from Brig, calling at Visp en route. The steep and scenic journey costs Sfr37/63 one way/return and takes 80 minutes. Being a private railway, Eurail passes are not valid, Inter-Rail earns 50% off and the Swiss Pass gets free travel. See the St Moritz section for information on the *Glacier Express*.

As Zermatt is car-free, you need to park at Täsch (Sfr4.50 to Sfr11 per day) and take a train from there (Sfr7.40). Parking is free near Visp station if you take the Zermatt train.

OTHER RESORTS
The best-known resort in west Valais is **Verbier**, with 400km of ski runs. Ski passes cost Sfr56/318 per day/week. Lesser-known resorts can have perfectly adequate skiing yet be much cheaper – ski passes in **Leukerbad**, west of Brig, are Sfr41 (students Sfr34) for one day.

Ticino

Situated south of the Alps and enjoying a Mediterranean climate, Ticino (Tessin in German) gives more than just a taste of Italy – the cuisine, architecture and vegetation reflect that found farther south. Indeed, Ticino belonged to Italy until the Swiss Confederation seized it in 1512. Though many locals also speak French and German, you will find English less widely understood.

LOCARNO ☎ 091
Locarno lies at the northern end of Lake Maggiore. At 205m elevation, it's Switzerland's lowest town.

Orientation & Information
The centre of town is Piazza Grande. The tourist office (☎ 751 03 33, @ locarno@ticino.com) is nearby at Largo Zorzi, within the casino complex. A five-minute walk east is the train station. Pardo Bar, Via della Motta 3, has Internet access (Sfr4 for 20 minutes).

Things to See & Do
The principal attraction is the **Madonna del Sasso**, up on the hill with a good view of the lake and the town. It contains some 15th-century paintings, a small museum and several distinctive statue groups. There is a funicular, but the 20-minute walk up is easy (take Via al Sasso off Via Cappuccini). A few churches are worth a look, including the 17th-century **Chiesa Nuova** on Via Cittadella.

Locarno has more hours of sunshine than anywhere else in Switzerland – just right for strolls round the lake. **Giardini Jean Arp** is a small lakeside park, off Lungolago Motta, where sculptures by the surrealist artist are scattered among the palm trees and tulips.

Places to Stay & Eat
Pensione Città Vecchia (☎/fax 751 45 54, @ cittavecchia@datacomm.ch, Via Toretta 13), uphill from Piazza Grande's Innovazione, is an independent hostel without a curfew or daytime closing. Dorm beds are Sfr24, plus Sfr4.50 each if you require sheets or breakfast; both are provided in singles/doubles costing Sfr35/70 (open March to November). The SYHA hostel (☎ 756 15 00, Via Varenna 18) is another 500m west. Prices start at Sfr31 for dorms, Sfr57/66 for singles/doubles. Between the two, *Osteria Reginetta* (☎/fax 752 35 33, @ reginetta.locarno@bluewin.ch, Via della Motta 8) has singles/doubles/triples for Sfr42 per person, or Sfr49 including breakfast (closed in winter). *Inova* (*Via Stazione 1*), by the train station, has good self-service dishes from Sfr9.

Getting There & Away
There are trains every two hours from Brig, passing through Italy en route (Sfr50, three hours). You change trains at Domodossola across the border, so bring your passport. One-day travel passes for boats on Lake Maggiore cost Sfr11 to Sfr20. For more information contact Navigazione Lago Maggiore (NLM; ☎ 751 18 65). There is a regular boat and hydrofoil service from Italy (not in winter).

LUGANO
☎ 091

Switzerland's southernmost tourist town offers an excellent combination of lazy days, watery pursuits and hillside hikes. Winding alleyways, pedestrian-only piazzas and colourful parks make Lugano an ideal town for walking around.

Orientation & Information

The train station has money-exchange, bike rental and an Aperto supermarket, all open daily. The old town lies down the hill to the east (10 minutes' walk), where you'll find the tourist office (☎ 913 32 32, fax 922 76 53, e info@lugano-tourism.ch) on Riva G Albertolli, by Lake Lugano. Internet access is at City Disc, Via P Peri; charges are SFr4/8/10 for 20/40/60 minutes.

Things to See & Do

The Santa Maria degli Angioli church, Piazza Luini, has a vivid fresco of the Crucifixion by Bernardino Luini dating from 1529.

The Thyssen-Bornemisza Gallery, Villa Favorita, Castagnola, is a famous private art collection (SFr10/6). It covers every modern style from abstract to photorealism, and opens 10 am to 5 pm Friday to Sunday, from April to November only. The Cantonal Art Museum, Via Canova 10, also has a worthwhile modern selection (closed Monday; SFr7/5). Exhibitions cost extra at both.

The Lido, east of the Cassarate River, charges SFr7 for its swimming pool and sandy beaches; it's open daily from May to mid-September.

There are excellent hikes and views from Monte San Salvatore and Monte Brè. The funicular from Paradiso up Monte San Salvatore operates from mid-March to mid-November (SFr12/18 one way/return). To get up Monte Brè, you can take the year-round funicular from Cassarate (SFr13/19). A boat tour of Lake Lugano is a worthy excursion, especially to nearby Melide. This is noted for the Swissminiatur, which displays 1:25 scale models of national attractions (closed in winter; SFr11).

Places to Stay & Eat

The relaxed SYHA hostel (☎ 966 27 28, fax 968 23 63, Via Cantonale 13) is a hard 20-minute walk uphill from the train station (signposted), or take bus No 5 to Crocifisso (SFr1.20). Dorm beds are SFr23 and doubles are SFr56. Optional breakfast is SFr7, and reception is closed from 12.30 to 3 pm. The hostel closes from November to late March. Close to the train station is Hotel Montarina (☎ 966 72 72, e asbest@tinet.ch, Via Montarina 1), in two buildings with a garden, kitchen and swimming pool. Beds in large dorms are SFr20 (sheets SFr4) and singles/doubles start at SFr50/80. Prices exclude breakfast, and the hotel is closed from 31 October to pre-Easter.

Self-service food is at the EPA department store (Via Nassa 22) and at Ristorante Inova, up the stairs, on the northern side of Piazza Cioccaro.

Getting There & Away

In summer, postbuses run twice daily (thrice weekly in winter) from Lugano to St Moritz (SFr73, four hours). Reserve seats the day before at the bus station, the train information office or by phoning ☎ 807 85 20. Buses leave from the bus station on Via Serafino Balestra, though the St Moritz bus also calls at the train station.

Graubünden

Graubünden (Grisons, Grigioni, Grischun) has some of the most developed and best-known winter sports centres in the world, including Arosa, Davos, Klosters, Flims and, of course, St Moritz. Away from the international resorts, Graubünden is a relatively unspoiled region of rural villages, Alpine lakes and hill-top castles. It takes a while to reach here from other parts of Switzerland, so if you're short on time and money, you may want to skip this region.

CHUR
☎ 081

Chur is the canton's capital. Its compact old town is noted for 16th-century buildings, fountains, photogenic alleyways and an impressive 12th-century cathedral. Augusto Giacometti designed three of the windows in the 1491 Church of St Martin. The Kunstmuseum on Postplatz displays modern art, including many Giacomettis (by Alberto, Augusto and Giovanni), and sci-fi stuff by local artist HR Giger, creator of the Alien monster (closed Monday; SFr10).

Orientation & Information

From the train station, walk down Bahnhofstrasse and turn left for the tourist office (☎ 252 18 18, ℮ info@churtourismus.ch). The regional tourist office (☎ 254 24 24), Alexanderstrasse 24, has information on the canton (closed weekends).

Places to Stay & Eat

Camp Au (☎ 284 22 83), by the sports centre, is open year-round. Hotel Schweizerhaus (☎ 252 10 96, Kasernenstrasse 10) has dorms for SFr30, and singles/doubles for SFr55/110 with shower and SFr40/80 without. Breakfast is SFr5.

Speise Restaurant Zollhaus (Malixerstrasse 1) has two parts. Bierschwemme, the downstairs bar, serves hot meals from SFr12. Upstairs is the more cultured Bündnerstube, where there's a range of cheapish to mid-price meals.

Getting There & Away

Postbuses leave from the depot above the train station. There are rail connections to Davos, Klosters and Arosa, and fast trains to Sargans (the station for Liechtenstein, only 25 minutes away) and Zürich (SFr38, 90 minutes); Chur can be visited on the Glacier Express route (see St Moritz).

ST MORITZ
☎ 081

This playground for international jet-setters is great for people-watching and (expensive) sports. In the St Moritz region there are 350km of downhill runs, albeit with a limited choice for beginners. A one-day ski pass costs SFr55, and ski and boot rental is about SFr43 per day. There are also 160km of cross-country trails (equipment rental SFr20) and 120km of marked hiking paths.

Orientation & Information

The village centre is St Moritz Dorf. The train station is near the lake; just up the hill is the post office and five minutes farther on is the tourist office or Kurverein (☎ 837 33 33, ℮ information@stmoritz.ch) at Via Maistra 12 (closed Sunday). Around the lake, 2km south-west and accessible by bus, lies St Moritz Bad. Not much stays open in November, May and early June. Bobby's Pub, Via dal Bagn, has Internet access.

Places to Stay

The Olympiaschanze camping ground (☎ 833 40 90), 1km south-west of St Moritz Bad, is open late May to late September. The year-round SYHA Stille Hostel (☎ 833 39 69, Via Surpunt 60) is in eastern St Moritz Bad, back from Hotel Sonne (good pizzas!). Half-pension prices are SFr43.50 in four-bed dorms or SFr56 in double rooms. Reception is closed from 10 am to 4 pm. Bellaval (☎ 833 32 45, fax 833 04 06), by the train station, has bare singles/doubles using hall shower for SFr67/130.

Getting There & Away

To Lugano by postbus (see Lugano for schedules) you must reserve a seat the day before on ☎ 837 67 64. Nine daily trains travel south to Tirano in Italy, with connections to Milan. The famous Glacier Express connects St Moritz to Chur and Zermatt via the Oberalp Pass (2033m), taking 7½ hours to cover 290 scenic kilometres (SFr132, plus SFr9 reservation fee on some trains).

Zürich
☎ 01

Switzerland's most populous city offers an ambience of affluence and plenty of cultural diversions. Banks and art galleries will greet you at every turn, in a strange marriage of finance and aesthetics.

If you've got the money, there's plenty to do. At night, the pin-stripe brigade yields the streets to bar-hoppers and techno-party clubbers.

Zürich started life as a Roman customs post and graduated to the status of a free city under the Holy Roman Empire in 1218. It joined the Swiss Confederation in 1351. The city's long-standing reputation as a cultural and intellectual centre was given fresh impetus during WWI with the influx of luminaries such as Lenin, Trotsky and James Joyce, plus Tristan Tzara and Hans Arp, key figures in the founding of Dadaism in 1916 at the Cabaret Voltaire.

Orientation

Zürich is at the northern end of Lake Zürich (Zürichsee), and is split by the Limmat River. The main train station (Hauptbahnhof) is on the west (or left) bank of the river.

SWITZERLAND

Information

Tourist Offices The Tourist Service (☎ 215 40 00, ✉ information@zurich tourism.ch) in the train station's main hall is open till at least 6.30 pm, daily year-round. Staff charge for maps – get one free from one of the larger city banks instead.

Money You'll have no trouble locating a bank in Zürich. American Express (☎ 228 77 77), Uraniastrasse 14, is closed weekends.

Post The main post office is Sihlpost (☎ 296 21 11), Kasernenstrasse 95-97, 8021. There's another post office at the train station.

Email & Internet Access Stars Bistro, in the main hall of the train station, charges Sfr5 for 20 minutes (11 am to midnight daily). Datacomm, Badenerstrasse 29, is Sfr5/8 for 30/60 minutes.

Travel Agencies SSR (☎ 297 11 11) is a specialist in student, youth and budget fares. Branches are at Leonhardstrasse 10 and Bäckerstrasse 40. Globetrotter (☎ 211 77 80), Rennweg 35, also has budget fares.

Medical & Emergency Services For medical and dental help, ring ☎ 261 61 00. The Cantonal University Hospital (☎ 255 11 11), Rämistrasse 100, has a casualty department. There is a 24-hour chemist at Bellevue Apotheke (☎ 252 56 00), Theaterstrasse 14. The police (☎ 216 71 11) are at Bahnhofquai 3.

Things to See & Do

The pedestrian streets of the old town, on either side of the Limmat, contain most of the major sights. Features to take note of are winding alleyways, 16th- and 17th-century houses and guildhalls. Zürich has 1030 fountains and the locals insist the water is drinkable in them all.

The elegant Bahnhofstrasse was built on the site of the city walls, which were torn down 150 years ago. Underfoot are bank vaults crammed full of gold and silver. Zürich is one of the world's premier precious metals markets but the vaults (for some reason) aren't open to the public.

The 13th-century tower of St Peter's Church, St Peterhofstatt, has the largest clock face in Europe (8.7m in diameter). The Fraumünster Church nearby is noted for the distinctive stained-glass windows in the choir created by Marc Chagall. Augusto Giacometti also did a window here, as well as in the Grossmünster Cathedral across the river where Zwingli preached in the 16th century.

Museums The most important of many museums is the Kunsthaus (Museum of Fine Arts), Heimplatz 1. The large permanent collection ranges from 15th-century religious art to the various schools of modern art. It's open 10 am to 9 pm Tuesday to Thursday, 10 am to 5 pm Friday to Sunday (Sfr6/4; free on Sunday). The Schweizerisches Landesmuseum (Swiss National Museum), Museumstrasse 2, has a definitive section on church art, plus weapons, coins and more, housed in a pseudo-castle built in 1898. Opening hours are 10.30 am to 5 pm Tuesday to Sunday (Sfr5).

The Lindt & Sprüngli chocolate factory, Seestrasse 204, offers a museum, film and generous chocolate gift – all free. Take bus No 165 from Bürkliplatz to Schooren. It's open 10 am to noon and 1 to 4 pm Wednesday to Friday.

Zoo The large zoo has 2500 animals from around the world; it's open 8 am to 6 pm daily (5 pm November to February). Entry costs Sfr14/7 and you can get there by tram No 5 or 6. The zoo backs on to Zürichberg, a large wood ideal for walks.

Special Events

On the third Monday in April, Zürich holds its spring festival, **Sechseläuten**, when guild members parade the streets in historical costume and tour the guildhalls, playing music. A fireworks-filled 'snowman' (the Böögg) is ignited at 6 pm.

Fasnacht brings musicians and a large, costumed procession. The carnival commences with typical Swiss precision at 11.11 am on 11 November, though the biggest parades are in February. Less traditional is the techno **Street Parade** in August. A huge fairground takes over central Zürich during the **Züri Fäscht**, usually every third year (2001 etc) in early July. The **Zürcher festspiele**, mid-June to mid-July, concentrates on music and the arts, and the **Züri Jazz Woche** takes place in early September.

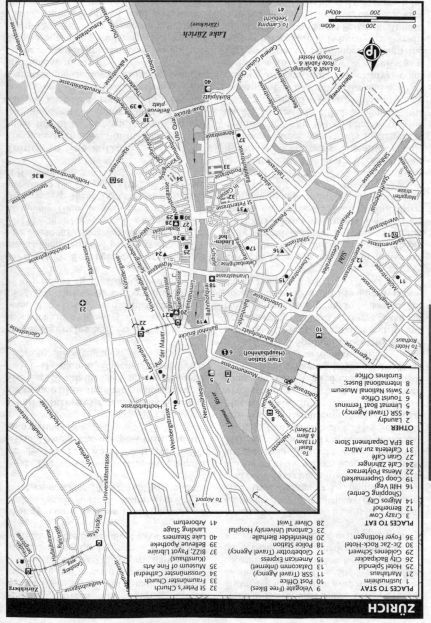

ZÜRICH

PLACES TO STAY
1 Justinusheim
3 Crazy Cow
12 Bremerhof
14 Migros City
(Shopping Centre)
16 Hill Vegi
19 Coop (Supermarket)
21 Marthahaus
25 Hotel Splendid
26 City Backpacker
29 Goldenes Schwert
30 zic-Zac Rock-Hotel
36 Foyer Hottingen

PLACES TO EAT
22 Mensa Polyterrace
24 Café Zähringer
27 Gran Café
31 Cafeteria zur Münz
38 EPA Department Store

OTHER
2 Laundry
4 SSR (Travel Agency)
5 Limmat Boat Terminus
6 Tourist Office
7 Swiss National Museum
8 International Buses;
Eurolines Office

9 Velogate (Free Bikes)
10 Post Office
11 SSR (Travel Agency)
13 Datacomm (Internet)
15 American Express
17 Globetrotter (Travel Agency)
18 Police Station
20 Rheinfelder Bierhalle
23 Cantonal University Hospital
28 Oliver Twist

32 St Peter's Church
33 Fraumünster Church
34 Grossmünster Cathedral
35 Museum of Fine Arts
(Kunsthaus)
37 BIZZ; Payot Librairie
39 Bellevue Apotheke
40 Lake Steamers
41 Arboretum

Lake Zürich
(Zürichsee)

To Camping
Seebucht 41

Central Quai/Quai Quai

To Lindt & Sprüngli;
Rote Fabrik &
Youth Hostel

To Basel
(113km) &
Bern (125km)

Places to Stay

Cheap accommodation can be hard to find, particularly from August to October. Book ahead if you can, or use the information board and free phone in the train station.

Camping Camping Seebucht (☎ 482 16 12, Seestrasse 559) is on the west shore of the lake, 4km from the city centre (signposted). Take bus No 161 or 165 from Bürkliplatz. It is open from around May to September and prices are Sfr8.50 per adult, Sfr12 for a tent.

Hostels The SYHA hostel (☎ 482 35 44, fax 480 17 27, Mutschellenstrasse 114), in Wollishofen, has four- or six-bed dorms for Sfr31. There's a restaurant and laundry facilities. Take tram No 7 to Morgental or the S-Bahn to Wollishofen. More central is City Backpacker (☎ 251 90 15, @ backpacker@ access.ch, Niederdorfstrasse 5), also known as Hotel Biber. Small dorms are Sfr29; singles/doubles are Sfr65/88 and triples/quads are Sfr120/156. There are kitchens but no breakfast. Reception is closed from noon to 3 pm.

Hotels Also central is Martahaus (☎ 251 45 50, @ info@martahaus.ch, Zähringer-strasse 36). Singles/doubles/triples cost Sfr70/98/120, and six-bed dorms with individual cubicles are Sfr35 per person.

Foyer Hottingen (☎ 256 19 19, @ reservation@foyer-hottingen.ch, Hottingerstrasse 31) has a calm ambience and kitchen facilities. Singles/doubles are Sfr70/110 and triples/quads are Sfr140/180. Women-only doms cost Sfr35.

Justinusheim (☎ 361 38 06, Freuden-bergstrasse 146) is a student home with beds available, particularly during student holidays. Singles/doubles are Sfr60/100 with shower or Sfr50/80 without. Take tram No 10 from the train station to Rigiplatz and then the frequent Seilbahn to the top.

Hotel Rothaus (☎ 241 24 51, @ uhk@swissonline.ch, Sihlhallenstrasse 1) is in a seedy part of town, but has good-value rooms with shower/toilet and TV. Prices start as low as Sfr60/98.

In the old town, Hotel Splendid (☎ 252 58 50, Rosengasse 5) has 43 beds. Singles/doubles/triples for Sfr56/93/123 are with hall showers. The optional breakfast is Sfr9.50 and there's live piano music nightly in the bar downstairs.

Nearby, the Zic-Zac Rock-Hotel (☎ 261 21 81, @ rockhotel.ch @ bluewin.ch, Marktgasse 17) is a theme hotel with singles/doubles for Sfr88/135 or Sfr68/116 without shower. Goldenes Schwert (☎ 266 18 18, fax 266 18 88, @ hotel@rainbow.ch, Marktgasse 14) has creatively decorated rooms for Sfr110/140 with private bath. It's a gay-friendly hotel and one floor has gay-themed rooms.

Places to Eat

The Zürich speciality, Geschnetzeltes Kalbsfleisch (thinly sliced veal in a cream sauce), generally costs above Sfr20. There are various affordable places in and around the main train station, especially in the underground Shopville, which has a Migros supermarket open till 8 pm daily. Above ground, by the station, the large Coop supermarket has a takeaway section serving hot food.

The large and busy Mensa Polyterrace (Leonhardstrasse 34) has good meals for Sfr10.50, including vegetarian options. It's open 11.15 am to 1.30 pm and 5.30 to 7.15 pm weekdays; from mid-July to around mid-October it's open for lunch only. Food is just as cheap at the self-service restaurants in EPA department store at Bellevueplatz and the Migros City shopping centre.

Bernerhof (Zeughausstrasse 1) is a typical, simple restaurant with satisfying, filling food. Several daily menus from Sfr12 (including soup) are available at midday and evening. Café Zähringer, on Spitalgasse, serves mostly organic food, from Sfr17. Try Gran Café (Limmatquai 66) for all-you-can-eat spaghetti for Sfr9.50.

Vegetarians will have a field day in the meat-free environment of Hiltl Vegi (☎ 227 70 00, Sihlstrasse 28). Varied meals cost from Sfr16.50 and the salad buffet is both extensive and expensive. Crazy Cow (Leonhardstrasse 1) is a popular, quirky place serving Swiss food from about Sfr6. Here you will find two things that many people believe don't exist: a written form of Swiss-German (on the menus), and examples of Swiss humour (bread is served in a slipper, the chicken wings in a toy supermarket trolley).

Zürich has numerous cafes where you can linger over a coffee. Try the entertaining

Cafeteria zur Münz (Münzplatz 3), which is closed Sunday.

Entertainment

Many late-night pubs, clubs and discos are in Niederdorfstrasse and adjoining streets in the old town. Try *Rheinfelder Bierhalle (Niederdorfstrasse 76)*, a cheap if rough-and-ready beer hall. English-speakers gravitate towards *Oliver Twist*, an Irish pub on Rindermarkt.

Rote Fabrik (☎ 481 91 21 for concert information, ☎ 482 42 12 for theatre, Seestrasse 395) has rock and jazz concerts, theatre, original-language films and a bar/restaurant; take bus No 161 or 165 from Bürkliplatz.

Getting There & Away

Kloten airport is 10km north of the city centre and has several daily flights to/from all major destinations.

Various buses head east to Budapest, Prague, Zagreb and elsewhere. The Eurolines office behind the train station is open 5.30 or 6 pm to 7.30 pm daily. For information, call ☎ 272 40 42.

The busy train station has direct trains to Stuttgart (Sfr62, three hours), Munich (Sfr97, 4½ hours), Innsbruck (Sfr69, four hours), Milan (Sfr75, four hours) and at least hourly departures to most Swiss towns including Lucerne (Sfr22, 50 minutes), Bern (Sfr48, 70 minutes) and Basel (Sfr31, 65 minutes).

Getting Around

Taxis to/from the airport cost around Sfr45, so take the train for Sfr5.40.

All tickets – good for bus, tram, inter-city S-Bahn and boats on the Limmat River – must be bought in advance from dispensers at stops. Short trips of about five stops are Sfr2.10. For the city of Zürich, a one-hour pass costs Sfr3.60 and a 24-hour pass is Sfr7.20.

Lake steamers depart from Bürkliplatz every 30 to 60 minutes from early April to late October (Swiss Pass and Eurail valid, Inter-Rail 50% discount). For boat information phone ☎ 487 13 33.

There's bicycle rental via SBB in the train station, but use of city bikes is free of charge from Velogate on platform 18, 7.30 am to 9.30 pm year-round. Bring photo ID and Sfr20 deposit.

Central Switzerland

This is the region which many visitors think of as the 'true' Switzerland, rich in typical Swiss features – mountains, lakes, tinkling cowbells, Alpine villages and ski resorts.

LUCERNE

☎ 041

Ideally situated in the historic and scenic heart of Switzerland, Lucerne (Luzern in German) is a great base for a variety of excursions. It also has plenty of charm in its own right, particularly the medieval town centre.

Orientation & Information

The old town centre is on the north bank of the River Reuss. The train station is nearby on the south bank. By platform 3 is the tourist office (☎ 227 17 17, @ luzern@luzern.org), Zentralstrasse 5, which is open daily.

In front of the train station is the boat landing stage, and close by is the main post office (Hauptpost, Luzern 1, 6000). The cheapest Internet access (Sfr2 for 30 minutes) is in the library (Stadtbibliothek), Löwenplatz 10 (closed Sunday).

Things to See

The picturesque old centre offers 15th-century buildings with painted facades, and the towers of the city walls. Some of these towers can be climbed for extensive views. Be sure to walk along the two covered bridges, **Kapellbrücke**, with its water tower that appears in just about every photograph of Lucerne, and **Spreuerbrücke**. Both contain a series of pictorial panels under the roof.

The poignant **Lion Monument**, carved out of natural rock in 1820, is dedicated to the Swiss soldiers who died in the French Revolution. Next to it is the fascinating **Gletschergarten** (Glacier Garden), Denkmalstrasse 4, where giant glacial potholes prove that, 20 million years ago, Lucerne was a subtropical palm beach. The potholes can be perused daily (except Monday in winter) for Sfr7. Also worth a look is the **Bourbaki Panorama**, Löwenstrasse 18, an 1100-sq-m circular painting of the Franco-Prussian War (Sfr6/5).

The town's widely acclaimed **Verkehrshaus** (Transport Museum), Lidostrasse 5,

Bleak highlands around Akureyri, seen from Mt Sulur, Iceland

DEANNA SWANEY

Kunstkammer, St Petersburg

GEORGI SHABLOVSKY

Contemplation, the Hermitage, St Petersburg

JOHN KING

Puffins, Iceland

DAVID CURL

Rock-climber, Kullaberg, Sweden

ANDERS BLOMQVIST

Sibelius Monument, Helsinki, Finland

JOHN BORTHWICK

Rape fields, Skåne, Sweden

ANDERS BLOMQVIST

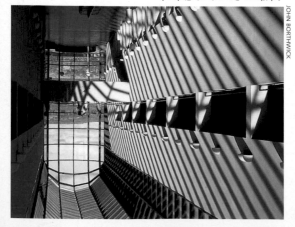

Arktikum, Rovaniemi, Finland

JOHN BORTHWICK

Björnriket, Sweden

CHRISTIAN ÅSLUND

contains trains, planes and automobiles (open daily). It's more fun than it sounds and costs SFr18 (rail pass/student reductions). Take bus No 2 from Bahnhofplatz.

Places to Stay

Camp Lido (☎ *370 21 46, Lidostrasse 8*), on the northern shore and east of the town, is open from 15 March to 31 October. It charges SFr1.70/3 per adult/tent and SFr13 for a bunk in a cabin.

The modern SYHA *hostel* (☎ *420 88 00, fax 420 56 16, Sedelstrasse 12*) is a 15-minute walk north of the city walls, or take bus No 18 from Bahnhofplatz. Dorm beds are SFr30.50, doubles cost from SFr75. Reception opens at 2 pm (4 pm in winter).

Backpackers Lucerne (☎ *360 04 20, Alpenquai 42*) is a friendly, independent hostel a 12-minute walk south-east of the station. It charges SFr21.50/26.50 per person in quads/doubles. Reception is closed from 10 am to 4 pm. *Hotel Löwengraben* (☎ *417 12 12*, e *hotel@loewengraben.ch, Löwengraben 18*) in the old town is a converted prison with literally 'cell-like' rooms. Dorms start from SFr20 and singles/doubles from SFr75/90, all without breakfast. Check-in is from 3 pm.

The small *Hotel Linde* (☎/*fax 410 31 93, Metzgerrainle 3*), off Weinmarkt, has basic singles/doubles for SFr44/88 without breakfast. Rooms are available from April to October only, and there's no check-in on Sunday.

Places to Eat

Look out for the local speciality, *Kügeli-pasteili*, a vol-au-vent stuffed with meat and mushrooms and served with a rich sauce. *Coop* and *Migros* have restaurants close together on Hertensteinstrasse. *EPA* department store, Mühlenplatz, has an excellent self-service restaurant with low prices. *Bistro du Theatre* (*Theaterstrasse 5*) is popular among young people for fairly inexpensive eating and drinking (closed lunchtime on weekends). *Jazzkantine* (*Grabengasse 8*) is a bar/restaurant with a Tagesteller for SFr12.50, vegetarian meals and jazz concerts (closed Sunday lunch).

Getting There & Away

Hourly trains connect Lucerne to Zürich (SFr22, 50 minutes), Interlaken (SFr27, two hours), Bern (SFr32, 1½ hours) and Lugano (SFr58, 2½ hours).

AROUND LUCERNE

There are a number of scenic cruises on Lake Lucerne. An excellent route is to take the lake steamer to Alpnachstad, the cog railway (closed in winter) up Mt Pilatus (2120m), the cable car down to Kriens and the bus back to Lucerne. The total cost for this jaunt is SFr77.60 (reductions with Eurail and Inter-Rail passes).

INTERLAKEN ☎ 033

Interlaken is flanked by Lake Thun and Lake Brienz and within striking distance of the mighty peaks of the Jungfrau, Mönch and Eiger. Though Interlaken is a great base for exploring the Bernese Oberland, the Jungfrau Region (see that section later) also has good accommodation options, and that's where the scenic wonders of Switzerland really come into their own.

Orientation & Information

Most of Interlaken is coupled between its two train stations – Interlaken West and Interlaken Ost. Each station offers bike rental and money-changing facilities, and behind each is a boat landing for lake services. The main shopping street, Höheweg, runs between the two stations. You can walk from one to the other in 20 minutes. The tourist office (☎ 822 21 21, e mail@InterlakenTourism.ch), Höheweg 37, nearer to the West station, is open Monday to Saturday year-round, and Sunday in summer. Internet access is at The Wave, Rosenstrasse 13, open daily.

Things to See & Do

Numerous hiking trails dot the area surrounding Interlaken, all with signposts giving average walking times. The funicular up to Harder Kulm (SFr21 return) yields an excellent panorama and further signposted paths. Boats go to several towns and villages around the lakes (Eurail valid, Inter-Rail 50% off). On Lake Thun, the towns of Spiez (SFr10.60 one way by steamer, SFr8.40 by train) and Thun (SFr15.60 by steamer, SFr13.20 by train) both have a castle. A short boat ride (SFr5.80) from Interlaken are the St Beatus Höhlen (caves), with some

tasty Swiss and vegetarian food (SFr12 to SFr38; closed Thursday). For Mexican food from SFr15 and free live music on Friday/Saturday nights, go to *El Azteca* (*Jungfraustrasse 30*). Hotel Metropole, by the tourist office, has a *panoramic café* on the 18th floor. It's worth a visit for the view, and the food is affordable.

Getting There & Away

Trains to Lucerne (SFr27, two hours) depart hourly from Interlaken Ost. Trains to Brig and to Montreux (via Bern or Zweisimmen) depart from both stations.

JUNGFRAU REGION
☎ 033

The views keep getting better the farther south you go from Interlaken, and it's an ideal playground for hiking, skiing and adventure sports. Don't miss this region. You'll probably end up staying here longer than you planned.

Grindelwald

Only 40 minutes by train from Interlaken Ost (SFr9.40 each way) is Grindelwald, a busy resort under the north face of the Eiger. In the First region there are 90km of hiking trails above 1200m. Of these, 48km stay open year-round. In winter, the First is also the main skiing area, with a variety of runs stretching from Oberjoch at 2486m, right down to the village at 1050m. The cable car from Grindelwald-Grund to Männlichen, where there are more good views and hikes, is the longest in Europe (SFr28 up, SFr46 return; non-skier reductions in winter). Grindelwald can be reached by road.

The tourist office (☎ 854 12 12, ⓔ *touristcenter@grindelwald.ch*) is in the centre at the Sportzentrum, 200m up from the train station. It's open daily in season (closed Sunday otherwise).

Places to Stay & Eat Grindelwald's SYHA *hostel* (☎ 853 10 09) is at Terrassenweg (great views), a 20-minute climb from the train station. Dorm beds cost SFr30.60, doubles SFr71.20. Reception is closed until 3 pm (5 pm on Sunday). Close to the hostel is the *Naturfreundehaus* (☎ 853 13 33), which has a kitchen and dorms from SFr30 without breakfast. Both hostels are closed between seasons.

impressive stalagmite formations (SFr14). The caves are open 9.30 am to 5 pm from Palm Sunday to late October.

Lake Brienz has a more rugged shoreline than its neighbour, and fewer resorts. Brienz itself (SFr12.40 by steamer, SFr6 by train) is the centre of the Swiss woodcarving industry and is close to the **Freilichtmuseum Ballenberg**, a huge open-air park displaying typical Swiss crafts and houses (SFr14/12). The park is open daily from mid-April to 1 November.

Places to Stay

One of many camping grounds is *Sackgut* (☎ 822 44 34), behind Interlaken Ost train station on Brienzstrasse. It costs SFr7.10 per adult and from SFr6 for a tent. It's open from April to October.

The SYHA *hostel* (☎ 822 43 53, *Aareweg 21, am See, Bönigen*) is a 20-minute walk round Lake Brienz from Interlaken Ost, or take bus No 1. Beds in large dorms are SFr26.60, there's a kitchen and check-in is from 4 pm. The hostel is closed from mid-November to late January. *Balmer's Herberge* (☎ 822 19 61, ⓔ *balmers@tcnet.ch, Hauptstrasse 23*) is a 15-minute walk (signposted) from either station. Excellent facilities include leisure/games rooms, kitchen, cellar bar and restaurant. Beds cost SFr24 in dorms; singles/doubles are SFr40/64 and triples/quads are SFr90/120. Sign for a bed during the day (facilities are open) and check in at 5 pm. Nearby, behind the Matterhorn Hotel on Hauptstrasse, is *Funny Farm* (☎ mobile/cellphone 079-652 61 27, ⓔ *James@funny-farm.ch*). This free-and-easy place has an Australasian ambience, party atmosphere, pool and bar. Accommodation is a bit basic (dorms from SFr25) but they have big plans for improvements. Nearer Höheweg is *Backpackers Villa Sonnenhof* (☎ 826 71 71, ⓔ *backpackers@villa.ch, Alpenstrasse 16*). This well-run, renovated villa has a kitchen and dorms/doubles for SFr29/37 per person. Reception is closed from 11 am to 4 pm.

Places to Eat

The cheapest food is at the supermarket restaurants opposite each station. A good, inexpensive place for Italian food is *Pizzeria Mercato*, on Postgasse, off Höheweg. *Anker Restaurant* (*Marktgasse 57*) has

In the village centre, just off the main street (signposted), is *Lehmann's Herberge* (☎ 853 31 41), with good-value rooms for one to six people costing SFr40 or SFr45 per person. For food, head east to *Onkel Tom's Hütte*, where pizzas cost from just SFr8.50 (closed Tuesday lunch and Monday).

Lauterbrunnen Valley

This valley is the other fork branching out from Interlaken into the mountains. The first village reached by car or rail is **Lauterbrunnen**, known mainly for the impressively powerful Trümmelbach Falls, 4km south (SFr10; open April to October). Find out more from the tourist office (☎ 855 19 55) on the main street.

Above the village (via funicular) is Grütschalp, where you switch to the train to **Mürren** (SFr9.40 total), a skiing and hiking resort. The ride yields tremendous unfolding views across the valley to the Jungfrau, Mönch and Eiger peaks. Mürren's tourist office (☎ 856 86 86) is in the sports centre. A 40-minute walk down the hill from Mürren is tiny **Gimmelwald**, relatively undisturbed by tourism.

Gimmelwald and Mürren can also be reached from the valley floor by the Stechelberg cable car, which runs all the way up to **Schilthorn** (2971m), where James Bond performed his stunts in *On Her Majesty's Secret Service*. The full return fare is a wallet-withering SFr89.

Places to Stay & Eat

Lauterbrunnen has some bargains for accommodation. *Camping Schützenbach* (☎ 855 12 68) and *Camping Jungfrau* (☎ 856 20 10) have cheap dorms and bungalows in addition to camping. *Matratzenlager Stöckli* (☎ 855 17 54) has a sociable atmosphere and dorm beds for SFr13. *Valley Hostel* (☎/fax 855 20 08, e valleyhostel@bluewin.ch) charges SFr21/25 per person in dorms/doubles. All the above places have free kitchens but no breakfast.

In Gimmelwald, the *Mountain Hostel* (☎ 855 17 04, e mountainhostel@tcnet.ch), close to the cable-car station, has a great view. Dorms without breakfast cost SFr16. It has kitchen facilities but bring your own food as the village has no shop. Next door is *Restaurant-Pension Gimmelwald* (☎/fax 855 17 30) with affordable accommodation and hot meals from SFr15.

Jungfraujoch

The trip to Jungfraujoch by railway (the highest in Europe) is excellent. Unfortunately, the price is as steep as the track and is hardly worth it unless you have very good weather – call ☎ 855 10 22 for forecasts. From Interlaken trains go via Grindelwald or Lauterbrunnen to Kleine Scheidegg. From here a 10km rail line powers through both the Eiger and the Mönch, with majestic views from two windows blasted in the mountainside, before terminating at Jungfraujoch (3454m).

On the summit there is the ice palace (exhibition rooms cut within the glacier; free entry), a self-service restaurant, great views from the terrace of the Sphinx Research Institute (a weather station), and walking, sliding or skiing on the glacier.

From Interlaken Ost, the journey is 2½ hours each way and the fare is SFr162 return (Eurail 25% off). Allow at least three hours at the site. There's a cheaper 'good morning ticket' (SFr125) if you take the 6.35 am train (in winter, also the 7.35 am train).

Northern Switzerland

BASEL
☎ 061

Basel (Bâle in French) joined the Swiss Confederation in 1501. Despite being a relatively large industrial city, it has an attractive old town, a handful of worthy museums, and a lively student-led nightlife. Basel's strategic position on the Rhine, at the dual border with France and Germany, has been instrumental in its development as a commercial centre.

Orientation & Information

On the north bank of the Rhine is Kleinbasel (Little Basel), surrounded by German territory. The pedestrianised old town and most of the sights are on the south bank in Grossbasel (Greater Basel).

The main tourist office (☎ 268 68 68, e office@baseltourismus.ch) is by the Mittlere Brücke at Schifflände 5 (closed Sunday). Less than 2km south is the main SBB Bahnhof (train station), which has a tourist office (☎ 271 36 84). Outside is a

but offering free bike loans in summer. Internet access costs SFr5/8 for 30/60 minutes at Datacomm, Steinentor Strasse 11 (closed Sunday morning).

Things to See & Do

The tourist office has leaflets on walks through the old town, taking in cobbled streets, colourful fountains and 16th-century buildings. The impressive rust-coloured **Rathaus** (town hall) has a frescoed court-yard. The 12th-century **Münster** (cathedral), restored in 1998, is another highlight with its Gothic spires and Romanesque St Gallus doorway.

Of the many museums, the most important is the **Kunstmuseum**, St Albangraben 16, with a good selection of religious, Swiss and modern art (notably Picasso). It's open 10 am to 5 pm Tuesday to Sunday (SFr7/5, free on the first Sunday of the month). Take a look at the **fountain** on Theaterplatz; it's a typical display by the Swiss sculptor Jean Tinguely, with madcap machinery playing water games with hoses. The **Tinguely Museum**, Grenzacherstrasse 210, is closed Monday and Tuesday.

Basel's **zoo**, open daily, is one of the best in Switzerland (SFr12/10). Basel is also a carnival town – on the Monday after Ash Wednesday look for Fasnacht, a three-day spectacle of parades and music, all starting at 4 am!

Places to Stay

Hotels are expensive and liable to be full during the numerous trade fairs and conventions. The tourist office in the SBB Bahnhof reserves rooms for SFr10 commission, compared to SFr5 in the main tourist office. Ask your accommodation for the free Mobility Card, good for free local transport.

Six kilometres south of the train station is **Camp Waldhort** (☎ 711 64 29, Heideweg 16, Reinach).

At the central SYHA **hostel** (☎ 272 05 72, fax 272 08 33, St Alban Kirchrain 10), dorm beds are SFr29 and double rooms are SFr98. Reception is closed from 10 am to 2 pm. Near the pedestrian zone is **Hotel Steinenschanze** (☎ 272 53 53, ✉ steinenschanze@datacomm.ch, Steinengraben 69) which has singles/doubles with private shower and toilet for SFr110/160 (SFr50/100

for students under 25). Uphill from Barfüsserplatz, **Hotel Brasserie au Violon** (☎ 269 87 11, ✉ auviolon@prolink.ch, Im Lohnhof 4), is a former prison. Singles/doubles with shower/toilet are SFr80/120, breakfast is SFr10.

Places to Eat

Cheap self-service restaurants are in the **EPA department store** (Gerbergasse 4) and **Migros supermarket** (Sternengasse 17). The pedestrian-only Steinenvorstadt has lots of affordable restaurants, including **Mr Wong** at No 1a for self-service Asian food, and **Café Gleich** at No 23 for vegetarian food (closed weekends). **Cedro am Barfi** (Streitgasse 20) has pizzas from SFr12 and set lunches for SFr16. For Basel specialities in a typical ambience, try **Weinstube Gifthüttli** (☎ 261 16 56, Schneidergasse 11). Meals start at SFr14.50.

Getting There & Away

Basel is a major European rail hub. For most international trains you clear customs in the station, so allow extra time. All trains to France leave from SBB Bahnhof; there are five or six daily to Paris (SFr70, five hours). Trains to Germany stop at Badischer Bahnhof (BBF) on the north bank. Main destinations along this route are Amsterdam (SFr179, eight hours), Frankfurt (SFr80, four hours), Hamburg (6½ hours) and Cologne (three hours). Services within Switzerland go from SBB: there are two fast trains an hour to both Geneva (SFr67, three hours; via Bern or Biel/Bienne) and Zürich (SFr30, 70 minutes).

SCHAFFHAUSEN
☎ 052

Schaffhausen is on the northern bank of the Rhine, surrounded by Germany. The attractive old town is bursting with oriel windows, painted façades and ornamental fountains. The best streets are Vordergasse and Vorstadt: they intersect at Fronwagplatz, where you'll find the tourist office (☎ 625 51 41, fax 625 51 43, ✉ tourist@swissworld.com). Get an overview of the town from the **Munot** fortress on the hill (open daily; free). The **Allerheiligen Museum**, by the cathedral on Klosterplatz, encompasses ancient bones and modern art (closed Monday; free).

The **Rhine Falls** (Rheinfall) can be reached by a 40-minute stroll westward along the river, or by bus No 1, 6 or 9 to Neuhausen. The largest waterfall in Europe drops 23m and makes a tremendous racket as 600 cubic metres of water crashes down every second.

Places to Stay & Eat

Schaffhausen can be visited on a day trip from Zürich, but there are a few options if you want to stay overnight, including a SYHA hostel (☎ 625 88 00, *Randenstrasse 65*) which is closed December to February. There's cheap eating in the centre at *Migros supermarket* and restaurant (*Vorstadt 39*), *China Town Take Away* (*Vorstadt 36*), *EPA department store* restaurant (*Vordergasse 69*), or at *Manora* in the Manor department store, by the tourist office.

Getting There & Away

Hourly trains run to Zürich (SFr16.40). Constance and Basel can be reached by either Swiss or (cheaper) German trains. Steamers travel to Constance several times daily in summer, and the trip takes four hours; they depart from Freier Platz (call ☎ 625 42 82 for information). Schaffhausen has good roads in all directions.

AROUND SCHAFFHAUSEN

The 45km of the Rhine from Schaffhausen to Constance is one of the river's most beautiful stretches, passing by meadows, castles and ancient villages, including picturesque Stein am Rhein, 20km to the east, where you could easily wear out your camera in Rathausplatz.

ST GALLEN ☎ 071

In 612, an itinerant Irish monk called Gallus fell into a briar. The venerable Gallus interpreted this clumsy act as a sign from God and decided to stay and build a hermitage. From this inauspicious beginning the town of St Gallen evolved and developed into an important medieval cultural centre.

Orientation & Information

The main post office (Bahnhofplatz, 9001) is opposite the train station. Two minutes away is the tourist office (☎ 227 37 37, @ info@stgallen-bodensee.ch) on Bahnhofplatz (closed Sunday). It has a free hotel booking service. A few minutes to the east is the pedestrian-only old town. Quanta, on Bohl, has Internet access.

Things to See

Several buildings in St Gallen have very distinctive oriel windows: the best are on Gallusplatz, Spisergasse and Kugelgasse. The twin-tower **cathedral** (1766) should not be missed. The ceiling frescoes are by Josef Wannenmacher; look out also for the pulpit, arches, statue groups and woodcarvings around the confessionals.

Adjoining the church is the **Stiftsbibliothek** (Abbey Library), containing some beautifully etched manuscripts from the Middle Ages and a splendidly opulent rococo interior. There's even an Egyptian mummy dating from 700 BC and as well preserved as the average grandparent. Entry is SFr7/5.

Places to Stay

The SYHA *hostel* (☎ 245 47 77, *Jüchstrasse 25*) is a signposted but tiring 15-minute walk east of the old town, so take the Trogenerbahn from outside the station to 'Schülerhaus' (SFr2.40). Beds are SFr24 in a dorm or SFr33 in a double room. The reception is closed from 10 am to 5 pm and the hostel closes mid-December to early March. *Weisses Kreuz* (☎/fax 223 28 43, *Engelgasse 9*) is central and good value. Singles/doubles with shower and toilet are SFr60/100. The reception is in the bar downstairs (closed 2 to 5 pm weekdays).

Getting There & Away

St Gallen is a short train ride from Lake Constance (Bodensee), upon which boats sail to Bregenz in Austria, and to Constance and Lindau in Germany (not in winter). There are also regular trains to Bregenz (SFr16, one hour), Constance (SFr16.40, one hour), Chur (SFr34, 90 minutes) and Zürich (SFr29, 70 minutes).

APPENZELL ☎ 071

Parochial Appenzellers, inherently resistant to change, are often the butt of Swiss jokes. Appenzell village reflects this conservatism and has an old-fashioned ambience that attracts plenty of tourists. It's a delight to

SWITZERLAND

wander around, with traditional old houses, painted facades and lush surrounding countryside. The streets are bedecked with flags and flowers on the last Sunday in April, when the locals vote on cantonal issues by a show of hands in the open-air parliament (Landsgemeinde). Everyone wears traditional dress for the occasion and many men carry swords as proof of citizenship.

Getting There & Away

There are hourly connections to Appenzell from St Gallen by narrow-gauge train (Swiss Pass and Eurail are valid; Inter-Rail gets half-price).

The route meanders along, mostly following the course of the road (40 minutes). There are two routes so you can make it a circular trip.

SWITZERLAND

Turkey

To use a hoary old travel cliche, 'Turkey is where west finally meets east, a country with one foot firmly planted in Europe while its body inclines towards Asia. One of the world's greatest cities, Istanbul, is popular with travellers on the way to/from Greece and Bulgaria, but Turkey also boasts 4000km of warm-water Mediterranean coastline. Although eastern Turkey is still relatively unspoilt by tourism, western Turkey, especially along the coast, is well and truly discovered, with ugly holiday villages now crowding the hundreds of ruined Greek and Roman cities for shore space.

The Turks are mostly very friendly, especially when you escape the resorts and head into the heartland, and prices are still low compared to Western Europe. Turkey makes for a relatively painless introduction to travelling in an Islamic country – unless you're a fair-skinned woman with long blonde hair, in which case, all bets are off.

Facts about Turkey

HISTORY
In 330 AD the Roman emperor Constantine founded a new imperial city at Byzantium (modern Istanbul). Renamed Constantinople, this strategic city became the capital of the Eastern Roman Empire and was the centre of the Byzantine Empire for 1000 years. During the European Dark Ages, when the glories of Greece were just a memory and Rome had been overrun by barbarians, the Byzantine Empire kept alive the flame of Western culture.

The beginning of the Byzantine Empire's decline came with the arrival of the Seljuk Turks, who had previously conquered Persia. In 1071 the Seljuk Turks defeated a Byzantine army near Lake Van and occupied most of Anatolia.

A Mongol invasion in the late 1200s put an end to Seljuk power, but new small Turkish states were born soon after in western Anatolia. One of these, headed by Osman (1258-1326), grew into the Ottoman Empire, and in 1453, Constantinople fell to the Ottoman sultan Mehmet II (the Conqueror).

A century later, under Süleyman the Magnificent, the Ottoman Empire reached the peak of its cultural brilliance and power, spreading deep into Europe, Asia and North Africa. Ottoman success was based on military expansion, not on industry or agriculture. When their march westwards was stalled at Vienna in 1683, the rot started. A succession of incompetent sultans hardly helped.

In the 19th century Turkey found itself with unruly populations in the Balkans. In 1829 the Greeks won their independence, followed by the Serbs, the Romanians, and in 1878, the Bulgarians. Italy took Tripolitania in North Africa in 1911, and after the 1912-13 Balkan War the Ottomans lost Albania and Macedonia.

Finally, the unfortunate Turks emerged from WWI stripped of their last non-Turkish provinces: Syria, Palestine, Iraq and Arabia. Most of Turkey (Anatolia) itself was to be parcelled out to the victorious Greeks, Italians, French and Russians, leaving the Turks with virtually nothing.

At this low point in Turkish history, Mustafa Kemal, the father of modern Turkey, took over. Atatürk, as he was later called, rallied the tattered remnants of the army, pushed the weak Ottoman rulers aside and out-manoeuvred the Allied forces in the Turkish War of Independence.

Final victory came in 1923 at Smyrna (modern İzmir), where invading Greek armies were literally pushed into the sea. This was followed by an exchange of populations similar to that which took place in India at the time of the India-Pakistan partition. Well

AT A GLANCE	
Capital:	Ankara
Population:	68 million
Official Language:	Turkish
Currency:	Turkish lira

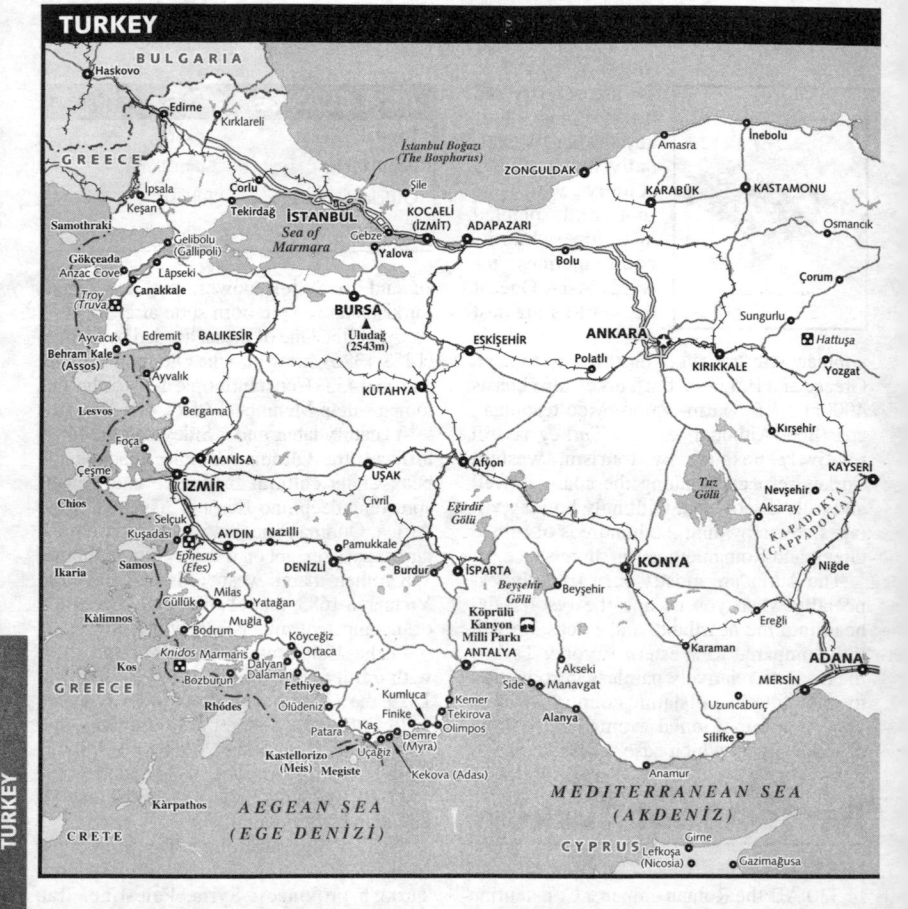

over a million Greeks left Turkey and nearly half a million Turks moved in. Relations with Greece improved markedly in 1930, but were soured again after WWII by conflict over Cyprus, particularly after the Turkish invasion of the island in 1974.

With Turkey reduced to smaller but more secure boundaries, Atatürk embarked on a rapid modernisation program by establishing a secular democracy, de-emphasising religion, introducing the Roman alphabet and European dress, and moving towards equal rights for women. In 1923 the capital was moved from 'decadent' İstanbul to Ankara.

Since Atatürk's death Turkey's history has been turbulent, with several military coups replacing elected governments, most recently in 1980. During the 1980s and 1990s the country was wracked by violence as the army struggled to suppress the demands of the Kurdistan Workers' Party (PKK) for an independent Kurdistan in south-eastern Turkey. In 1999, the arrest and sentencing to death of the PKK leader Abdullah Ocalan brought hope that a struggle which had claimed more than 30,000 lives could finally be drawing to a close.

Elections in 1999 resulted in unexpectedly high support for the MHP, the National Action Party, an overtly nationalist party. They formed a coalition government with the DSP (Social Democratic Party) and ANAP, the right-of-centre Motherland Party, with veteran political Bulent Ecevit as Prime Minister. The current president is former judge, Ahmet Necdet Sezer.

TURKEY

GEOGRAPHY

Turkey is divided into Asian and European parts by the Dardanelles, the Sea of Marmara and the Bosphorus. Thrace (European Turkey) comprises only 3% of the total 780,580 sq km land area. The remaining 97% is Anatolia, a vast plateau rising eastward towards the Caucasus Mountains. Turkey's coastline is over 6000km long.

CLIMATE

The Aegean and Mediterranean coasts have mild, rainy winters and hot, dry summers. In Istanbul, summer temperatures average around 28°C to 30°C; the winters are chilly but usually above freezing. Eastern Turkey can be snowbound from October through to the end of May.

POPULATION & PEOPLE

Turkey's population of nearly 68 million is 99% Muslim (mostly Sunni) and made up predominantly of Turks. Muslim Kurds make up a significant minority (perhaps 12 million) and there are small groups of Jews, Greeks, Armenians, Laz and Hemşin (Black Sea peoples), and Arabs. Its five biggest cities are Istanbul (16 million people), Ankara (4 million), Izmir (3 million), Adana (1.9 million) and Bursa (1.6 million).

SOCIETY & CONDUCT

Ottoman Turkey was ruled by the sharia (Islamic religious law), but Atatürk ensured that republican Turkey largely adapted to a modern, westernised lifestyle. Although many Turks drink alcohol (and don't mind

TURKEY

if you do either), it's as well to remember that they still revere the moral and spiritual teachings of their religion, and observe its customs, if somewhat loosely sometimes.

When visiting mosques, dress conservatively (no 'revealing' clothing like shorts or sleeveless shirts), remove your shoes, don't take flash photographs and be respectful. Women should cover their head, shoulders and arms to the elbow.

Never make disparaging remarks about Atatürk, the Turkish flag or the Turkish nation unless you want to get into a scrap.

LANGUAGE

Ottoman Turkish was written in Arabic script, but Atatürk decreed a change to Roman script in 1928. In big cities and tourist areas, many locals know at least some English and/or German. See the Language chapter at the back of this book for pronunciation guidelines and useful words and phrases.

Facts for the Visitor

HIGHLIGHTS

Istanbul, the Aegean and Mediterranean coasts and Cappadocia are the areas most people come to see.

The WWI battlefields of Gallipoli, on the Dardanelles, are particularly moving; however, if you visit over Anzac Day (25 April) make sure to book your accommodation months in advance. Many visitors find Troy disappointing, but not so Ephesus, the best-preserved classical city on the Mediterranean. Turkey's best beaches are at Ölüdeniz, Bodrum, Patara and Antalya. The improbable 'lunar' landscapes of Cappadocia remain the single most visually impressive feature in all Turkey, although the famed travertine ledges of Pamukkale are past their prime. Many people also like to take a side trip to see the great Commagenian heads on Nemrut Daği, widely touted as the 'Eighth Wonder of the World'.

SUGGESTED ITINERARIES

Three days
Explore Istanbul.

One week
See Istanbul and the Aegean coast to Bodrum or Marmaris.

Two weeks
Travel from Istanbul south and east along the Aegean and Mediterranean coasts as far as Antalya, then return to Istanbul via Cappadocia.

PLANNING

When to Go

In general, spring (April/May) and autumn (September/October) have the most pleasant weather for travelling. In July and August accommodation along the coast fills up and prices rise accordingly. Temperatures can also be pretty unbearable.

Maps

Tourist offices stock excellent free maps of Istanbul, Ankara, Izmir, Adana and Antalya. Otherwise check locally produced maps carefully before buying as they're often little more than sketches.

TOURIST OFFICES

Government tourist offices exist in every tourist-oriented town but they can rarely do much more than hand out glossy brochures. Ask for the Youth Travel Guide Book, which has lots of advice for budget travellers.

Turkish Tourist Offices Abroad

Australia (☎ 02-9223 3055, fax 02-9223 3204, @ turkish@ozemail.com.au) Room 17, Level 3, 428 George St, Sydney NSW 2000

Canada (☎ 613-230 8654, fax 613-230 3683) Constitution Square, 360 Albert St, Suite 801, Ottawa Ontario K1R 7X7

UK (☎ 020-7629 7771, fax 020-7491 0773, @ tio@cityscape.co.uk) 1st floor, 170-173 Piccadilly, London W1V 9DD

USA (☎ 212-687 2194, fax 212-599 7568, @ tourny@idt.net) 821 UN Plaza, New York, NY 10017

VISAS

Nationals of most Western European countries may enter free for visits of up to three months. Others must pay a visa fee in cash notes upon arrival: UK subjects pay UK£10, Australians US$20, US and Canadian citizens US$45, etc.

EMBASSIES & CONSULATES

Turkish Embassies Abroad

Australia (☎ 02-6295 0227, fax 6239 6592) 60 Mugga Way, Red Hill 2603 ACT

Canada (☎ 613-789 4044, fax 781 3442) 197 Wurtemburg St, Ottawa, Ontario K1N 8L9

TURKEY

UK (☎ 020-7393 0202, fax 7393 0066) 43 Belgrave Square, London SW1X 8PA
USA (☎ 202-659 8200, fax 659 0744) 1714 Massachusetts Ave NW, Washington, DC, 20036

Foreign Consulates in Turkey

Most embassies are in Ankara but the following consulates are all in Istanbul (area code ☎ 212):

Australia (☎ 257 7050, fax 257 7054) Tepecik Yolu 58, 80630 Etiler
Canada (☎ 272 5174) Büyükdere Caddesi 107/3, Bengün Han, 3rd floor, Gayrettepe
New Zealand (☎ 275 2989, fax 275 5008) Maya Akar Center, 24th floor, Büyükdere Caddesi 100/102, Esentepe 80280
UK (☎ 293 7545, fax 245 4989) Mesrutiyet Caddesi 34, Tepebaşı, Beyoğlu
USA (☎ 251 3602, fax 267 0057) Mesrutiyet Caddesi 104-108, Tepebaşı, Beyoğlu

MONEY

The Turkish lira (TL) comes in coins of 10,000, 25,000, 50,000 and 100,000 lira, and notes (bills) of 100,000, 250,000, 500,000, one million, five million and ten million lira

Because of Turkey's continuing inflation, prices in this chapter are quoted in more stable US dollars (US$). At the time of writing US$1 was equal to 600,000TL, and still rising although the government had pegged monthly exchange rates in a bid to check inflation.

Exchanging Money

Although Turkey has no black market, you can often spend US dollars or German marks (DM) in place of liras. Exchanging cash in major world currencies is fast and easy in most banks, exchange offices, post offices, shops and hotels.

Cashing travellers cheques is less easy (some places resist) and the exchange rate is usually slightly lower. Many places charge a *komisyon* (commission); ask first.

ATMs Turkey has an extensive, reliable network of ATMs linked to the MasterCard, Visa, Cirrus and Plus networks. The keypads only accept numeric PIN numbers so if you have an alpha-numeric PIN ... if you can get it changed.

Costs

Although prices are steadily rising, you can still travel on as little as US$15 to US$20 per person per day using buses, staying in pensions and eating one restaurant meal daily. For US$20 to US$35 per day you can stay in one and two-star hotels with private bath, and eat most meals in average restaurants. Costs are highest in Istanbul and the big coastal resorts.

Tipping & Bargaining

In mid-range restaurants, waiters appreciate a tip of 5% to 10% (15% in expensive places): barbers, hairdressers and Turkish baths attendants expect 10% to 15%. It's normal to round up taxi fares rather than actually tipping. It's never necessary to tip *dolmuş* (minibus) drivers.

It's wise to bargain for souvenirs. Even if the establishment has set prices, it's still worth trying if you're buying several items when shopping in the low season. In tourist areas hotel prices tend to be fixed; elsewhere it's worth bargaining if you visit between October and late May or plan to stay more than one night.

POST & COMMUNICATIONS

Turkish post offices are called *postanes*; look for the black-on-yellow (PTT) signs.

Turkey's public telephones, operated by Türk Telekom, take *telekart* (phonecards) sold at telephone centres, shops and by street vendors. A few older phones use *jeton* (tokens). If you get stuck, look for a shop with a *kontörlü* telephone. It's metered so you can pay as you go.

Turkey's country code is ☎ 90. A three-minute telekart call to the USA costs US$6 peak, US$4.50 off peak. To call from one city to another within Turkey, dial ☎ 0, then the city code and number.

It's much easier to send/receive faxes at a hotel or travel agency than to try and use the post office service.

Email and Internet access is sprouting up all over Turkey, and small hotels and pensions will often let you check and send email for a small fee.

INTERNET RESOURCES

The Turkey Home Page (www.turkey.org) has news, arts and cultural features, lists of upcoming events and links to dozens of

Turkey-related Web sites. The *Turkish Daily News* site (www.turkishdailynews.com) is useful for keeping up with what's going on in the country. For transportation details, try (www.neredennereye.com).

BOOKS

Lonely Planet's *Turkey* is a detailed guide to the entire country. LP also publishes the *Turkish phrasebook*, the *Turkey Travel Atlas* and *Istanbul to Cairo on a shoestring*, a guide to the classic overland route.

Jeremy Seal's *A Fez of the Heart* and Tim Kelsey's *Dervish* are very readable accounts of recent travels in Turkey. For a good factual account of the making of modern Turkey look for *Turkey Unveiled* by Nicole and Hugh Pope.

HEALTH

Travellers in Turkey may experience 'traveller's diarrhoea', so take precautions. Drink bottled water; make sure fruit is washed in clean water or peeled with clean hands; avoid raw or undercooked seafood and meat; and don't eat food that has been standing unrefrigerated.

Emergency medical and dental treatment is available at simple dispensaries (*sağlık ocağı*), clinics and government hospitals (*hastane*). Look for signs with a red crescent or big 'H'.

WOMEN TRAVELLERS

In traditional Turkish society, men and women have lives apart: the husband has his male friends, the wife her female friends. Younger Turks are slowly shedding these roles, and women now hold some positions of authority; there has even been a female prime minister.

Despite these advances foreign women are often hassled while travelling in Turkey. Men pinch, grab and make strange noises, which can become very tiresome; more serious assault is uncommon but possible. Travelling with a male improves matters, as does travelling with another female. Turkish women completely ignore men who speak to them in the street. Wearing a headscarf, a skirt that comes below the knees, a wedding ring and sunglasses makes you less conspicuous. Away from beach resorts you should certainly avoid skimpy tops and brief shorts.

GAY & LESBIAN TRAVELLERS

While not illegal, homosexuality is not generally socially acceptable in Turkey. It exists openly at a small number of gay bars and clubs in major cities and resorts but elsewhere you should be discreet. Lambda Istanbul (www.qrd.org/qrd/www/world/eu rope/turkey) is a Turkish gay and lesbian organisation with links to a 'Gay Turkey' guide.

DANGERS & ANNOYANCES

Although Turkey is considered one of Europe's safest countries, you must still take precautions. Wear a money belt under your clothing and beware of pickpockets and purse-snatchers in buses, markets and other crowded places. Exercise extra care while in Istanbul, especially when staying in hostels.

In Istanbul, single men often fall victim to a thinly veiled form of robbery: after being lured into a bar or nightclub (often one of those along İstiklal Caddesi) by new Turkish 'friends', they may be forced to pay an outrageous bar bill even if no drink passed their lips.

On intercity buses, there have been incidents of theft by drugging; a person (or persons) who has befriended you buys you a beverage (often ayran in a sealed container) at a rest stop, injects a drug into it and, as you sleep, makes off with your luggage. More commonly, the hard-sell tactics of carpet sellers can drive you to distraction; be warned that 'free' lifts and suspiciously cheap accommodation often come attached to near compulsory visits to carpet showrooms.

PUBLIC HOLIDAYS & SPECIAL EVENTS

National holidays include: 1 January, 23 April (National Sovereignty and Children's Day), 19 May (Youth & Sports Day), 30 August (Victory Day), 29 October (Republic Day).

Major holidays and events include:

Kurban Bayramı (Sacrifice Holiday) A four-day event commemorating Abraham's near-sacrifice of Isaac. It starts on 5 March 2001, 22 February 2002 and 11 February 2003. Plan ahead – almost everything closes.

International Istanbul Music Festival From early June to early July, world-class musicians perform in Istanbul.

TURKEY

Ramazan (Ramadan)

During the holy month of Ramazan, observant Muslims fast during daylight hours, feast after sunset, and go to mosque often. Ramazan runs from 27 November to 26 December 2001, from 16 November to 15 December 2002 and from 5 November to 4 December 2003. If you visit at this time you should do your best to avoid smoking, eating or drinking in public during the fasting hours.

ACCOMMODATION

Some hotels and pensions let you camp in their grounds and use their toilets and wash-rooms for a small fee. Well-equipped European-style camp sites are rare.

Turkey has plenty of cheap hotels, although the very cheapest are *very* basic and often not suitable for women travelling without men.

Only a few hostels are affiliated to Hostelling International (HI), and they're generally not much better (or cheaper) than budget hotels.

One and two-star hotels (US$20 to US$45 double) offer reasonable comfort and private bathrooms at moderate prices; three-star places can be quite luxurious.

FOOD & DRINKS

Turkish food, which is similar to Greek but more refined, is usually delicious and of high quality. *Şiş kebap* (shish kebab), lamb grilled on a skewer, is a Turkish invention, and you'll find *kebapçı*, cheap eateries specialising in roast lamb, everywhere. Try the ubiquitous *döner kebap* (lamb packed onto a vertical revolving spit and sliced off when done). The best cheap and tasty meal is *pide*, Turkish pizza.

A proper meal consists of a long procession of dishes. First come the *meze* (hors d'oeuvres), such as *beyaz peynir* (white sheep's-milk cheese), *börek* (pastry stuffed with white cheese and parsley) and *cacık* (yoghurt, cucumber and garlic). *Dolma* are vegetables (aubergine, zucchini, peppers, cabbage or vine leaves) stuffed with rice, currants and pine nuts, and served cold, or hot with lamb.

For dessert try *firın sütlaç* (baked rice pudding), *kazandibi* (caramelised pudding), *aşure* (fruit and nut pudding), *baklava* (pastry stuffed with walnuts or pistachios, soaked in honey), or *kadayıf* (shredded wheat with nuts in honey).

Beers, such as Tuborg lager or Efes Pilsen, supplement the familiar soft drinks. There's also good Turkish wine and fierce aniseed *rakı*, which is like Greek ouzo. Turkish *kahve* (coffee) is legendary; order your first cup *orta* (with middling sugar). Turkish *çay* (tea) is served in tiny glasses, sweet and without milk. A milder alternative is the wholly chemical *elma çay* (apple tea).

Getting There & Away

You can get in and out of Turkey by air, sea, rail and bus, across the borders of seven countries.

AIR

There are international airports at Adana, Ankara, Antalya, Bodrum, Dalaman, Istanbul and Izmir. Turkish Airlines has direct flights from Istanbul to two dozen European cities, New York and Chicago, the Middle East, North and South Africa, Central Asia, Bangkok, Karachi, Singapore, Tokyo and Osaka.

The major European airlines fly to Istanbul: British Airways, Lufthansa and the independent airline Istanbul Airlines have flights to Ankara, Antalya, Izmir and Dalaman as well. One-way full-fare tickets from London to Istanbul can cost as much as US$450, so it's usually advisable to buy an excursion ticket for around US$300 even if you don't plan to use the return portion.

Turkish Airlines flies nonstop to Istanbul from New York and Chicago, Delta nonstop from New York. The European airlines also fly one-stop services from many North American cities to Istanbul. Return fares range from US$500 to US$1200.

There are no direct flights from Australia or New Zealand to Turkey, but you can fly Qantas or British Airways to London, or Olympic to Athens, and get a connecting flight from these cities. You can also fly Qantas or Singapore Airlines from most Australian cities, or from Kuala Lumpur, to Singapore to connect with Turkish Airlines' thrice-weekly flights to Istanbul. Excursion fares start from around US$2200, which is almost as much as you would pay for a more versatile round-the-world (RTW) ticket.

TURKEY

Getting Around

AIR

Turkish Airlines (Türk Hava Yolları, THY) links all the country's major cities, including the busy Istanbul-Ankara corridor (US$90, 50 minutes).

Domestic flights tend to fill up fast, so try and book a few days ahead. On a few routes Istanbul Airlines offers cheaper flights with lower fares but less frequently. Smoking is prohibited on all domestic flights.

The network of domestic airports is growing fast and although flying is relatively expensive, given the size of Turkey taking one internal flight can be a good way to cut down the time spent on buses.

SEA

Turkish Maritime Lines (TML) runs car ferries between İzmir and Venice weekly, year-round. The one-way fare with reclining seat is US$215; or US$390 per person in a mid-price cabin.

There are daily services to Turkish Cyprus from Taşucu (near Silifke), and less frequent services from Antalya and Alanya. Private ferries run between Turkey's Aegean coast and the Greek islands, which are in turn linked by air or boat to Athens. Services are frequent (usually daily) in summer, several times weekly in spring and autumn, and infrequent (perhaps once a week) in winter.

The most reliable winter services are Chios-Çeşme, Rhodes-Marmaris and Samos-Kuşadası; other in-season services include Lesvos-Ayvalık, Lesvos-Dikili, Kos-Bodrum, Rhodes-Bodrum and Kastellorizo-Kaş.

LAND

The daily Balkan Express train links Budapest and Istanbul (31 hours), while the Bucharest-Istanbul Express links Bucharest and Istanbul (17 hours). Neither service is speedy, the trains are barely comfortable and theft is a problem.

Several Turkish bus lines, including Ulusoy and Varan/Bosfor, offer services between Istanbul and European cities such as Frankfurt, Munich, Vienna and Athens. A one-way ticket to Sofia costs just US$30, a ticket to Moscow US$90.

BUS

Comfortable modern buses go everywhere, frequently and cheaply (around US$3 to US$4 per hour or 100km). Kamil Koç, Metro, Ulusoy and Varan cost a bit more but have better safety records than most.

The bus station (otogar) is often on the outskirts of town, but the bigger bus companies usually offer free servises (minibuses) between the city-centre ticket office and the otogar.

Many of the larger otogars have left-luggage rooms (emanets) with a small charge. Don't leave valuables in unlocked luggage. If there's no emanet, leave luggage at the bus ticket office.

No smoking is allowed on the buses although the driver may (and usually does) smoke.

TRAIN

The Turkish State Railways' ageing rolling stock has a hard time competing with the long-distance buses for speed or comfort. Only on the special Istanbul-Ankara express trains such as the Fatih and Başkent can you get somewhere faster and more comfortably than by bus, at a comparable price.

Slower Ekspres and mototren services sometimes have one class only and are cheaper than the buses. If they have 2nd class it costs 30% less than 1st.

Student fares are 20% cheaper, as are return fares. On yolcu and posta trains you could grow old and die before reaching your destination. Trains east of Ankara are not as punctual or comfortable as those to the west.

Sleeping-car trains linking İstanbul and Ankara (US$25/35 single/double) are good value; the cheaper örtülü kuşetli carriages have four simple beds per compartment.

CAR & MOTORCYCLE

Turkey has a very high motor vehicle accident rate. Drive defensively, avoid driving at night and don't drink and drive.

An International Driving Permit may be handy if your licence is from a country likely to seem obscure to a Turkish police officer. Türkiye Turing ve Otomobil Kurumu (TTOK), the Turkish Touring & Automobile Association (☎ 212-282 8140, fax 282 8042), Oto Sanayi Sitesi Yanı, 4 Levent, İstanbul, can help with questions and problems.

BOAT

Car ferries depart from Istanbul on Friday year-round and arrive the next morning in İzmir. From İzmir departures are on Sunday afternoon. Fares, including meals, are US$16 (reclining seat) to US$100 (luxury cabin bed), and US$60 for a car.

In summer a ferry leaves Istanbul for Trabzon at 2 pm every Monday, returning from Trabzon at 8 pm on Wednesday. A Pullman seat costs US$17.50 or there are shared cabins starting from US$35 a berth.

Istanbul

☎ 212

With 3000 years of colourful history, Istanbul, formerly Constantinople, has plenty to show for itself. The 6th-century cistern, the 550-year-old labyrinthine bazaar, splendid Aya Sofya – these are mere introductions to Istanbul's remarkable sites. But this city is more than a step back in time. After dark, a plethora of bars and fine restaurants will satiate the most energetic of souls. Istanbul has theatre and galleries – it's also a shopper's paradise.

After the Roman emperor Constantine moved his capital in 330 AD from Rome to Byzantium (renamed Constantinople and later Istanbul), the sturdy city walls kept out barbarians for centuries. When Constantinople fell for the first time it was to the misguided Fourth Crusade in 1204. The Ottoman Turks' first attempt to take Constantinople was in 1314. Finally, in 1453, after a long and bitter siege, the walls were breached near Topkapı Gate on the west side of the city. Mehmet the Conqueror marched to Hagia Sofia (Aya Sofya) and converted the church to a mosque. The Byzantine Empire had ended.

As capital of the Ottoman Empire, the city entered a new golden age, especially during the glittering reign of Süleyman the Magnificent (1520-66). The empire's long and celebrated decline was accelerated by the capital's occupation by Allied forces after WWI. Istanbul's final conquest was a catalyst for Atatürk's armies to shape a new, republican state.

Orientation

The Bosphorus strait between the Black and Marmara seas divides Europe from Asia.

European Istanbul is divided by the Haliç (Golden Horn) estuary, into the 'newer' quarter of Beyoğlu in the north and Old Istanbul in the south; Galata Bridge spans the two.

Sultanahmet, the heart of Old Istanbul, has many tourist sites, cheap hotels and restaurants. The boulevard Divan Yolu runs west, through Sultanahmet, past the Grand Bazaar (Kapalı Çarşı) and Istanbul University to Aksaray, a major traffic intersection. Eminönü, north of Sultanahmet at the southern end of Galata Bridge, is a major transport hub, the terminus of a tram and many bus and ferry lines. Sirkeci train station, the terminus for the European train line, is 100m east of Eminönü.

Karaköy, at the northern end of Galata Bridge, is another ferry terminus. Up the hill from Karaköy is the southern end of Beyoğlu's pedestrian mall, İstiklal Caddesi. At the northern end of the street is Taksim Square ('Taksim Meydanı'), heart of 'modern' Istanbul with its fancy hotels and airline offices.

Information

Tourist Offices There are offices in the international arrivals hall at Atatürk airport (☎ 573 4136); in Sirkeci train station (☎ 511 5888); at the north-east end of the Hippodrome in Sultanahmet (☎ 518 8754); and on İstiklal Caddesi (☎ 245 6876), near Taksim Square.

Money Most banks exchange foreign currency and dispense Turkish liras from ATMs linked to the MasterCard, Visa, Plus and Cirrus networks. Private exchange offices are plentiful in Sultanahmet, Sirkeci and Beyoğlu. Most are open from 9 am to 9 pm.

Post & Communications The main post office (merkez postane) is just south-west of Sirkeci train station. There is a post office in the law courts near the Hippodrome, in Sultanahmet, and also on Taksim Square in Taksim, and in the departure areas at the airport. Istanbul has two telephone codes: ☎ 212 for the European side and ☎ 216 for the Asian. Assume phone numbers given here are ☎ 212 unless stated otherwise.

Email & Internet Access Internet cafes are popping up everywhere; many places to

TURKEY

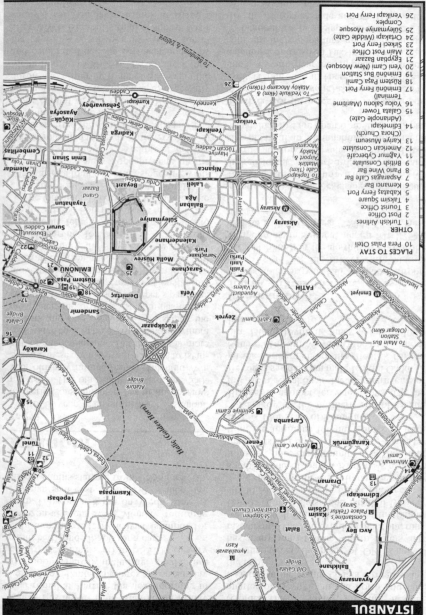

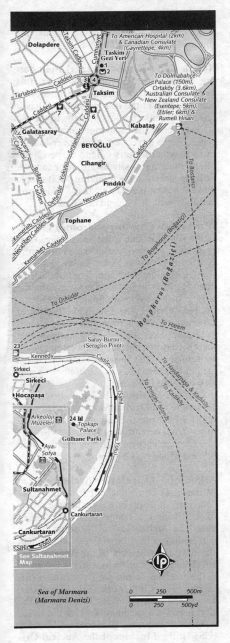

Sea of Marmara
(Marmara Denizi)

0   250   500m
0   250   500yd

stay also have facilities. In Sultanahmet try the Backpackers Internet Cafe opposite the Orient Youth Hostel.

Travel Agencies Sultanahmet has many small travel agencies, all of them selling transport tickets and tours, some offering foreign-exchange; shop around for the best deals. Midillis (☎ 458 0800, ✆ midillis@ fornet.net.tr), at Küçük Ayasofya Caddesi 21, has a good reputation. Beside the Orient Youth Hostel you'll find the Fez Travel Agent. Fez offers hop-on-hop-off bus tours of Turkey.

Laundry In Sultanahmet, dump your crusty clothes at the Star Laundry (☎ 638 2302), Akbıyık Caddesi 18, opposite the Orient Youth Hostel.

Medical & Emergency Services Try the tourist police (☎ 527 4503), Yerebatan Caddesi 6, Sultanahmet, across the street from the Sunken Palace Cistern.

The American Hospital (☎ 311 2000), at Güzelbahçe Sokak 20, Nişantaşı (2km north-east of Taksim Square) has a good reputation.

Things to See & Do
Head straight for Sultanahmet – all the major sites are within walking distance of the Hippodrome.

Aya Sofya The Church of the Holy Wisdom was begun under Emperor Justinian in 532 and was intended to be the most magnificent church in the world – for a thousand years it was certainly the largest. The interior, stunning even today, must have been overwhelming centuries ago when it was covered in gilded mosaics.

Climb up to the gallery to see the splendid surviving mosaics. After the Turkish conquest these mosaics were covered over, they were not revealed until the 1930s, when Atatürk declared Aya Sofya a museum. The minarets were added during the centuries when Aya Sofya functioned as a mosque (closed Monday, US$5).

Sultan Ahmet Camii (Blue Mosque) The Mosque of Sultan Ahmet I, just southwest of Aya Sofya, was built between 1609 and 1619. The exterior is notable for its six slender minarets and cascade of domes and half-domes. Inside, the tiled walls and painted dome create the luminous overall impression of blue that earns the mosque its name. You're expected to make a small donation when visiting the mosque; leave your shoes outside. There is a sound-and-light show here on summer evenings – different nights, different languages. A board outside lists which languages are on which night.

On the north-east side of the Blue Mosque, up the ramp, is the **Carpet & Kilim Textile Museum** (closed Sunday and Monday; US$1.30).

In the **Arasta** behind the Blue Mosque you'll find – between the carpet touts – the entrance to the **Great Palace Mosaic Museum** with exquisite portions of Byzantine pavements showing scenes from nature (closed Monday, US$1.30).

Topkapı Palace Just north-east of Aya Sofya is the fortified, sprawling Topkapı Sarayı, the opulent palace of the sultans from 1462 until they moved to Dolmabahçe Palace in the 18th century. Topkapı is not just a palace but a collection of courtyards, houses and libraries, with an intriguing 400-room harem.

Buy your ticket to the Second Court at the Ortakapı (middle gate).

Within the Second Court are exhibits of priceless porcelain, silverware and crystal, arms and calligraphy. Right beside the Kubbealtı, or Imperial Council Chamber, is the entrance to the **harem**, a succession of sumptuously decorated rooms which served as the sultan's family quarters.

In the Third Court are the sultan's ceremonial robes and the fabulous **treasury**. The **Shrine of the Holy Relics** holds a solid-gold casket containing the Prophet Mohammed's cloak and other Islamic relics.

In the Fourth Court, beautiful tiled kiosks have fine views of the city.

Topkapı is open 9 am to 4.30 pm daily (closed Tuesday; US$6). You'll pay an extra US$2.50 to visit the harem, which is open 9.30 am to 3.30 pm.

Yerebatan Sarnıcı (Sunken Palace Cistern) Across Divan Yolu, from the north-eastern end of the Hippodrome, is the entrance to the beautiful Yerebatan cistern. Built by Constantine and later enlarged by Justinian, this vast, columned cistern held water not only for summer use but also for times of siege (US$4.50).

Kapalı Çarşı (Grand Bazaar) Built during Mehmet the Conqueror's reign, this labyrinthine bazaar has a long history of selling. Only in the last few decades has it turned its focus on tourists; many of the old stalls are converted into modern, glassed-in shops. Some streets are given over to selling one type of touristy item: carpets, jewellery, clothing or silverware, for example. Still, 65 streets and a tempting 4400 shops, make it a great place to get lost – which you certainly will. It's closed on Sunday.

Atmeydanı (The Hippodrome) In front of the Blue Mosque is the 3rd-century Hippodrome, where chariot races and the Byzantine riots took place. Today, three ancient monuments remain. The **Obelisk of Theodosius** is an Egyptian column from the temple of Karnak, with pristine 3500-year-old hieroglyphs. The 10m-high **Obelisk of Constantine Porphyrogenitus** was covered in bronze plates (until the crusaders spotted them). Between these two monuments are the remains of the **Spiral Column**, erected at Delphi by the Greeks to celebrate their victory over the Persians.

On the west side of the Hippodrome, the **Turkish & Islamic Arts Museum** houses exhibits which run the gamut of Islamic history – from beautifully illuminated Korans to exquisite carpets and mosque furniture (closed Monday; US$2.50).

Arkeoloji Müzeleri (Archeological Museums) Down the hill from the outer courtyard of Topkapı Palace are the Arkeoloji Müzeleri, a complex of three museums. The **Archaeological Museum** has an outstanding collection of Greek and Roman statuary. The **Museum of the Ancient Orient** (Eski Şark Eserleri Müzesi) is dedicated to the pre-Islamic and pre-Byzantine civilisations. The **Çinili Köşk** (Tiled Pavilion), among the oldest Turkish buildings in the city, is now a museum of Turkish tile work.

The museums are all closed on Monday (US$4); the Museum of the Ancient Orient only opens Tuesday through Friday, and the Tiled Pavilion opens on Tuesday afternoon.

Süleymaniye Behind İstanbul University to the north-west rises the city's grandest mosque complex, the **Süleymaniye**. Construction was completed in 1557 on orders of Süleyman the Magnificent; he and his foreign-born wife Roxelana (Hürrem Sultan) are buried in **mausolea** behind the mosque to the south-east.

Byzantine Walls Stretching for 7km, from the Golden Horn to the Sea of Marmara, the walls date back to about 420 AD.

Near the **Edirnekapı** (Adrianople Gate) is the marvellous **Kariye Museum** (Chora Church), a Byzantine building with the best 14th-century mosaics east of Ravenna (closed Wednesday; US$3). To get there, take İETT bus No 28, 86 or 91 from Eminönü or a dolmuş along Fevzipaşa Caddesi.

Eminönü At Galata Bridge's southern end looms the large **Yeni Cami** (New Mosque), built between 1597 and 1663 – hardly new! Beside it the **Mısır Çarşısı** (Egyptian Bazaar), full of spice and food vendors, is worth wandering through. To the west is the **Rüstem Paşa Camii**, a small, richly tiled mosque designed by Sinan.

Beyoğlu Cross the Galata Bridge and head uphill towards the **Galata Tower**. In its present form this tower dates from 1216, when Galata was a Genoese trading colony. The observation deck charges US$2.50.

At the top of the hill is **İstiklal Caddesi**, once called the Grand Rue de Péra. At the other end, **Taksim Square** (Taksim Meydanı) is the hub of modern İstanbul.

The Bosphorus North from İstanbul, towards the Black Sea, are some beautiful Ottoman buildings, including the imposing **Dolmabahçe Palace**. You'll also find **Rumeli Hisarı**, the huge castle built by Mehmet the Conqueror, and many small and surprisingly peaceful villages.

The standard Bosphorus cruise departs from Eminönü's Boğaz Hattı dock at 10.35 am and 1.35 pm. The boat heads to Anadolu Kavağı where you can have lunch before returning. The trip takes 1½ hours each way and costs US$2.50 for the round trip.

The Princes' Isles Once the site of monasteries and a haven for pirates, this string of nine small islands is a popular summer getaway for İstanbul's middle class. With a few tiny beaches, some open woodland and transport by horse-drawn carriages, they make a pleasant escape from İstanbul's noise and hustle. Ferries (US$1.75) depart regularly from Sirkeci's Adalar İskelesi dock.

Ferry Cruising Enjoy İstanbul, by water, on a budget cruise across the Bosphorus. Board a ferry from Eminönü for Üsküdar or Kadıköy, or from Karaköy for Haydarpaşa or Kadıköy, then just come back (US$0.50 each way).

Turkish Baths İstanbul's historical baths are worth visiting, but they're also very touristy. A basic option is the **Kadırga Hamamı**, on Kadırga Hamamı Sokak, in Küçük Ayasofya; you'll clean up for US$8 (for the works). The **Çemberlitaş Hamamı**, off Divan Yolu, was designed by Sinan in 1584. It charges a whopping US$15 for all services. The famous and attractive **Cağaloğlu Hamamı**, at Kazım İsmail Gürkan Caddesi 34, costs a crazy US$20 for bath and massage.

Places to Stay

Camping In this big city, camping is not convenient, nor, at US$3 for a tent site plus US$4 per person, is it value for money. Try *Ataköy Mocamp* (☎ 559 6000) on the shore east of the airport. To get to Ataköy, take bus No 81 from Eminönü.

Hostels & Hotels South-east of Sultanahmet is Cankurtaran, an area of quiet streets and good, cheap and moderate hotels.

Sultanahmet A block along Yerebatan Caddesi, past the Sunken Palace Cistern, is the *Hotel Ema* (☎ 511 7166, Salkım Söğüt Sokak 18) with cheap dorm beds for US$5.

The *Yücelt Interyouth Hostel* (☎ 513 6150, ✉ info@yucelthostel.com, Caferiye Sokak 6/1) has dorm beds for US$6, doubles with toilet for US$18. Rooms are bland and you might need your earplugs, but there are heaps of services on offer.

Nestled against the Topkapı Palace walls, quaint *Coşkun Pension* (☎ 526 9854, ✉ chieko@atlas.net.tr, Soğukçeşme Sokak 40) has clean singles/doubles (with bathroom) for US$20 to US$45 depending on the room; book ahead.

TURKEY

Cankurtaran Many budget hotels are clustered around the out-of-our-league Four Seasons Hotel (US$320 per double), southeast of the fountain park between Aya Sofya and the Blue Mosque. Dry your tears and continue around the corner to Kutlugün Sokak. *Mavi Guesthouse* (☎ 516 5878, @ mavipans@hotmail.com), at No 3, has basic dorm beds for US$8, doubles for US$18; both prices include breakfast. Continue down the hill and around the corner to Akbıyık Caddesi where, at No 13, you can't miss the *Orient Youth Hostel* (☎ 518 0789, @ orienthostel@superonline.com). Dorm beds cost US$6, doubles US$14. The top-floor cafe has marvellous Bosphorus views and decent food. In high season, both these places offer rooftop mattresses for a dirt-cheap US$4.

Another option farther downhill is the friendly *Konya Pansiyon* (☎ 638 3638, @ aytekinelif@hotmail.com, Terbıyık Sokak 15), with dorm beds for US$5 and doubles for US$14. There's a shabby kitchen you can use.

Near the Four Seasons, the *Side Hotel & Pension* (☎ 517 6590, @ info@sidehotel .com, Utangaç Sokak 20) is good value. The pension rooms cost US$20/25 per single/double, US$30/35 with bathroom; the adjoining newer building has squeaky-clean rooms for US$40/50 with bathroom. The terrace has awesome Bosphorus views.

Places to Eat

For self caterers, pop into one of the seemingly ubiquitous *halk pazarı* (people's markets) and you'll find most things you're after. Akbıyık Caddesi, in Cankurtaran, has a *fruit and vegetable market* on Wednesday. In Eminönü, the Egyptian Bazaar and surrounding streets have dried fruit, pulses, fish and more.

For a cheap lunch, buy a filling fish sandwich from one of the boats near the Galata Bridge for just US$1.

At *Cennet (Divan Yolu 90)* you can watch *gözleme* (Turkish crepe) being made, try on Turkish traditional dress, or recline 'Ottoman-style' and listen to live musicians. It's as cheesy as it sounds. You'll pay about US$2 per *gözleme*.

Get a bargain feed at *Doy-Doy (Şifa Hamami Sokak 13)*, downhill off the southeastern end of the Hippodrome. Pides and

kebabs will set you back US$2 to US$3. Head north-west to *Yeni Birlik Lokantası (Peykhane Sokak 46)*, a restaurant serving delicious ready-made food (some vegetarian) and favoured by attorneys from the nearby law courts. Meals cost around US$5; open 11 am to 4 pm, Monday to Friday.

Once a legend among travellers, the *Pudding Shop* (or Lale Restaurant) nowadays is just one of a string of average, medium-priced restaurants along Divan Yolu – typical meals cost US$5 to US$7.

Entertainment

Bars & Clubs There are heaps of touristy bars in Sultanahmet and Cankurtaran; you'll pay around US$1 for a beer. Near the Sunken Palace Cistern you'll find a group of bars. Bunker-style *Bodrum* really fires up, *Gila* attracts *some* locals and has awesome views of Aya Sofya and *The Sultan Pub* is better for a quiet drink (and good for women travellers). The Orient and Yücelt hostels have popular, smoky *bars* frequented by the 'best belly dancer in İstanbul' – don't be fooled.

In Beyoğlu you'll see how some Turks spend their time and money (and at US$4 to US$6 per beer, they have plenty of it). Check out the buzzing *Pano* wine bar, opposite the British Consulate (ask for İngiliz Konsolosluğu Karşısı), approximately half way up İstiklal Caddesi. This place really knows how to wine and dine. Opposite the Nature & Peace restaurant, *Asparagas Cafe Bar*, on İstiklal Caddesi, has live Turkish rock every night while up the northern end of the street, *Kemancı (Sıraselviler Caddesi 69)* will satiate the headbangers among you.

Note: Beyoğlu can be seedy. Ignore touts who try to encourage you into their bar/club – it'll only end in tears.

Getting There & Away

Bus İstanbul's main bus station (☎ 658 0037) is at Esenler, about 10km north-west of Sultanahmet. Buses depart from here to all parts of Turkey and beyond. Get to it via the light railway from Aksaray; disembark at Otogar.

Train Sirkeci (☎ 527 0050) is the station for trains to Thrace (Trakya) and Europe. There are regular trains to Edirne. The nightly *İstanbul Express* goes to Munich.

TURKEY

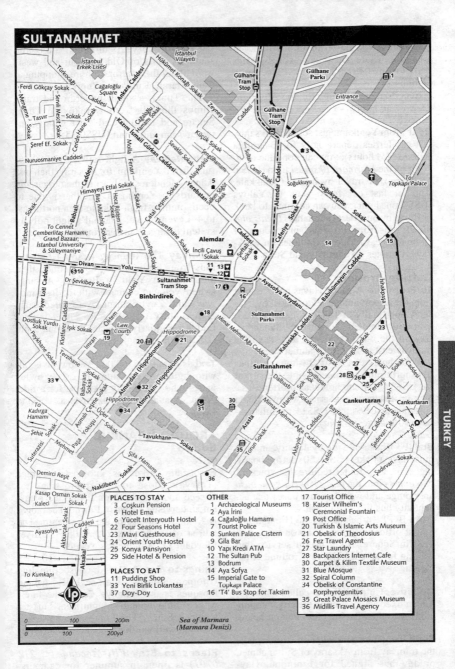

SULTANAHMET

TURKEY

PLACES TO STAY
3 Coşkun Pension
5 Hotel Ema
6 Yücelt Interyouth Hostel
22 Four Seasons Hotel
23 Mavi Guesthouse
24 Orient Youth Hostel
25 Konya Pansiyon
29 Side Hotel & Pension

PLACES TO EAT
11 Pudding Shop
33 Yeni Birlik Lokantası
37 Doy-Doy

OTHER
1 Archaeological Museums
2 Aya İrini
4 Cağaloğlu Hamamı
7 Tourist Police
8 Sunken Palace Cistern
9 Gila Bar
10 Yapı Kredi ATM
12 The Sultan Pub
13 Bodrum
14 Aya Sofya
15 Imperial Gate to
   Topkapı Palace
16 'T4' Bus Stop for Taksim

17 Tourist Office
18 Kaiser Wilhelm's
   Ceremonial Fountain
19 Post Office
20 Turkish & Islamic Arts Museum
21 Obelisk of Theodosius
26 Fez Travel Agent
27 Star Laundry
28 Backpackers Internet Cafe
30 Carpet & Kilim Textile Museum
31 Blue Mosque
32 Spiral Column
34 Obelisk of Constantine
   Porphyrogenitus
35 Great Palace Mosaics Museum
36 Midillis Travel Agency

Sea of Marmara
(Marmara Denizi)

0   100   200m
0   100   200yd

Haydarpaşa (☎ 216-336 0475), on the Asian shore, is the terminus for trains to Anatolia. There are seven express trains daily to Ankara (US$6 to US$12, seven to eight hours).

See Boat, following, for the *Marmara Ekspresi* to İzmir.

Boat From Yenikapı, just south of Aksaray, fast car ferries depart daily for Bandırma (US$11, 2½ hours); you can continue on to İzmir on the *Marmara Ekspresi* train (US$5, 6½ hours), or travel by bus to Çanakkale. Another fast car ferry goes to Yalova (US$7, one hour); you can continue to İznik or Bursa by bus. Fast catamarans *(deniz otobüsü)* run from Kabataş, just south of Dolmabahçe, to Yalova six times on weekdays, 11 times on Saturday and Sunday.

Getting Around
To/From the Airport Havaş buses depart from the airport and travel to Bakırköy, Aksaray and finally to Taksim Square (US$3, every 30 minutes). To get to Sultanahmet, stay on the bus to Aksaray and catch the tramvay east to the Sultanahmet stop.

Your hotel can book 24-hour minibus transport from your hotel door to the airport for US$3.50. Some hotels also offer a free pick-up and drop off service. An airport taxi costs about US$11 to US$14 to Sultanahmet (50% more at night).

Bus İETT buses are run by the city, and you must have a ticket (US$0.50) before boarding; some long routes require that you stuff two tickets into the box. *Özel Halk Otobüsü* are orange and white private buses that accept city bus tickets or cash.

An İETT T4 bus passes the Hippodrome tourist office in Sultanahmet on its way to Taksim Square. It's a useful service, but waiting for it will have you frothing at the mouth.

Dolmuşes Cute minibuses called dolmuşes run on fixed routes around the city charging a bit more than the bus fare. Pay on board.

Train To get to Sirkeci train station, take the tramvay from Aksaray or Sultanahmet, or any bus signed for Eminönü. Haydarpaşa train station is connected by ferry to Karaköy (US$0.60, at least every 30

minutes). Banliyö (suburban) trains run (US$0.50, every 20 minutes) along the southern walls of Old İstanbul and westward along the Marmara shore, stopping at Cankurtaran, Kumkapı, Yenikapı, etc.

The Tünel, a small underground train, climbs the hill from Karaköy to Tünel Square and İstiklal Caddesi regularly between 7 am and 9 pm (US$0.35).

Light Railway A light railway (US$0.45) runs from Yenikapı to Aksaray then via Adnan Menderes Bulvarı to the otogar and onwards to Yenibosna. Another is due to open, running from Taksim then north-east to 4. Levent. Note: İstanbul's light railway system is largely underground.

Tramvay The tramvay (tram; US$0.45) runs from Eminönü to Sultanahmet, then along Divan Yolu to Beyazıt, Aksaray (where you can connect with the light railway) and Zeytinburnu. A restored early 20th century tram trundles along İstiklal Caddesi regularly between 7 am and 9 pm (US$0.35).

Taxi İstanbul has 60,000 yellow taxis, all with digital meters; some are driven by lunatics who will really take you for a ride. From Sultanahmet to Taksim costs US$3 to US$4.

AROUND İSTANBUL
Edirne
☎ 284
European Turkey is known as Thrace (Trakya). Close to border crossings for Greece and Bulgaria you'll find the pleasant, undervisited town of Edirne. The otogar is 2.3km south-east of the town centre. The tourist office (☎/fax 213 9208), Hürriyet Meydanı 17, is in the town centre.

Things to See & Do Amongst crumbling Ottoman houses and several striking mosques is the **Selimiye Camii**, the finest work of Süleyman the Magnificent's master architect Sinan. The impressive **Beyazıt II Camii** is well worth a walk across the river.

Places to Stay *Fifi Mocamp* (☎ 212 0101) is open in summer for campers. Head south from the tourist office along Maarif Caddesi to the quaint *Hotel*

Aksaray (☎ *212 6035, Alipaşa Ortakapı Caddesi 8).* Basic singles/doubles cost US$7/12. The spotless *Efe Hotel* (☎ *213 6166),* next door, has beds for US$25/42 and two bars. It's a good, though pricey, option for women travellers.

Getting There & Away Buses run frequently to İstanbul (US$8, 2½ hours) and five times daily south to Çanakkale (US$6, 3½ hours).

Bursa
☎ 224
Bursa was the first Ottoman capital city; it retains several fine mosques and pretty neighbourhoods from its early Ottoman times. The big attraction, now and historically, is its mineral springs.

Orientation & Information Bursa's centre is along Atatürk Caddesi between the Ulu Cami (Grand Mosque) and the main square, Cumhuriyet Alanı, commonly called Heykel. Bursa's otogar is 10km north on the Yalova road, reached by grey buses marked 'Terminal' that leave from Heykel. Çekirge, with its mineral baths, is about 6km west of Heykel.

The tourist office (☎ 220 1848) is in the Orhangazi Altgeçidi subway, Ulu Cami Parkı 1, beside the belediye. Log on at Elite Internet Cafe near the Yeşil Türbe.

Things to See & Do The largest of Bursa's beautiful mosques is the 20-domed **Ulu Cami** (Grand Mosque) on Atatürk Caddesi in the city centre. About 1km east of Heykel, in a pretty pedestrian zone, are the early Ottoman **Yeşil Cami** (Green Mosque), its beautifully tiled **Yeşil Türbe** (Green Tomb) and the **Turkish & Islamic Arts Museum** (Türk İslam Eserleri Müzesi; closed Monday). Try the **mineral baths** at Eski Kaplıca in Çekirge.

Places to Stay & Eat Camp at *Çeltik Köyü Kamp* (☎ *253 0282)* on the road to Yalova.

South of the Ulu Cami, the friendly *Otel Güneş* (☎ *222 1404, İnebey Caddesi 75)* has waterless rooms for US$9/14; book ahead. The quaint *Öz Yeşil Yayla Termal Otel* (☎ *239 6496, Selvi Sokak 6),* in Çekirge, charges US$24 a double, with free mineral baths.

Bursa's speciality, İskender kebaps, will send your cholesterol levels rocketing but they're worth every sinful mouthful. *Adanur Hacıbey* (*Ünlü Caddesi 4),* just east of Heykel, is tacky but will grease you up with İskender for US$5. Self-caterers should head to the market streets north of Ulu Cami.

Getting There & Away The fastest way to/from İstanbul is by bus to Yalova (US$3, 70 minutes, every half-hour), then catch the fast (one hour) Yalova-İstanbul (Yenikapı) *deniz otobüsü* (catamaran; five a day), or the 'jet feribot' to Yenikapı, either for US$6. You can also book a *feribot ile* bus through to İstanbul. These buses use the Topçular-Eskihisar ferry and are quicker (US$7, 2½ hours) than the land route *(karayolu ile)* round the Marmara (US$9, four hours).

Buses leave frequently for Çanakkale (US$7, five hours), İzmir (US$7, six hours) and Ankara (US$12, 5½ hours).

The Aegean Coast

ÇANAKKALE
☎ 286
Laid-back Çanakkale is a base for transport to Troy and across the Dardanelles to Gallipoli. The defence of the straits during WWI led to a Turkish victory over Anzac forces on 18 March 1916, and placed this area on the map as a pilgrimage site for many Australians and New Zealanders.

The helpful tourist office (☎/fax 217 1187) and many cheap hotels are within a few blocks of the ferry pier, near the landmark clock tower. Micronet Internet Cafe is also near the tower.

Things to See & Do
The Ottoman **castle** built by Mehmet the Conqueror is now the **Army & Navy Museum**. Just over 2km south of the ferry pier, the **Archaeological Museum** holds artefacts found at Troy and Assos.

Places to Stay
Most accommodation is heavily booked in summer; the town is extremely crowded around Anzac Day, 25 April.

Camp at Güzelyalı Beach, 15km south by dolmuş, off the road to Troy; try *Mocamp Trova* (☎ *283 0061).*

TURKEY

Near the clock tower, *Kervansaray* (☎ 217 8192, *Fetvane Sokak 13)* has a gorgeous garden. You'll pay US$5/9 for singles/doubles with charm rather than cleanliness. *Hotel Efes* (☎ 217 3256, *Aralık Sokak 6)*, behind the clock tower, is run by a Turkish woman and has beds for US$8/14. Popular *Anzac House* (☎ 213 5969, **@** *has slefree@anzachouse.com, Cumhuriyet Meydanı 61)* offers dorm beds for US$5, sterile rooms for US$9/14 and heaps of services.

Places to Eat & Drink

Self-caterers will find a *supermarket* near the Army & Navy Museum. The *Gaziantep Aile Kebap ve Pide Salonu*, behind the clock tower, serves excellent, cheap pide and kebabs, as does *Trakya Restaurant*.

Women travellers will feel comfortable drinking at the jumping *TNT* by the clock tower, or the quieter *Yalı Hanı (Fetvane Sokak 28)*.

Getting There & Away

The Otogar is 1km east of the ferry pier, but many buses pick up and drop off near the bus company offices near the clock tower. Buses leave frequently for Bursa (US$7, five hours), Ayvalik (US$7.50, 3½ hours) and İstanbul (US$13, six hours).

GALLIPOLI

Although the Dardanelles had always been İstanbul's first line of defence, it was in WWI that they proved their worth. After an unsuccessful naval attempt on the strait by the British, on 25 April 1915, Allied forces were sent in to take Gallipoli peninsula. The Anzacs miscalculated and landed at Arı Burnu, a desolate beach lined by towering slopes. Mustafa Kemal (Atatürk) and his troops were soon waiting at the top – the Anzacs didn't stand a chance.

The easiest way to visit Gallipoli is to take one of the tours on offer. Several companies run six-hour minibus tours (around US$19) from Çanakkale, Eceabat and Gelibolu. Try Hassle Free (**@** hasslefree@anzachouse.com) at Anzac House, Çanakkale, or TJs Tours (**@** TJs–tours@excite.com). If you're a hiker, take a ferry from Çanakkale to Eceabat and a dolmuş to Kabatepe, and follow the trail around the sites described in a booklet sold at the visitor centre (Kabatepe Tanıtma Merkezi) there.

Turkish Maritime Lines' car ferries cross the straits hourly from Lapseki to Gelibolu and from Çanakkale to Eceabat (US$0.70). Small private ferries cross from Çanakkale (in front of the Hotel Bakır) to Kilitbahir.

TROY

Don't get excited – there's little of Troy (Truva) to be seen (and most people aren't thrilled with the tacky 'Trojan Horse'). It's estimated that nine successive cities have been built on this same site: Troy I goes right back to the Bronze Age; legendary Troy is thought to be Troy VI; most of the ruins you see are Roman ones from Troy IX (US$2.50).

Dolmuşes run the 30km from Çanakkale frequently for US$1.50. Walk straight inland from the ferry pier to Atatürk Caddesi, and turn right towards Troy; the dolmuş stop is at the bridge.

BEHRAMKALE (ASSOS)

☎ 286

Nineteen kilometres west of Ayvacık, Behramkale, once known as Assos, has the hill-top **Temple of Athena** looking across the water to Lesvos (Greece), and was considered one of the most beautiful cities of its time. It's still stunning, particularly the tiny port *(iskele)* 2km beyond the village. Dolmuşes depart from Ayvacık for Behramkale hourly in high summer. Off-season, Assos is a nightmare to get to; you may have to hitch.

Plaj Camping provides tent sites (US$7 per tent) and bungalows (US$30 for two) beside the water. On the heights, *Timur Pansiyon* (☎ 721 7449), near the top entrance to the Temple, has awesome views for US$25 per couple; the *Kale Restaurant* will feed you.

AYVALIK

☎ 266

Beautiful Ayvalık has winding cobbled streets, terracotta-tiled roofs and Greek Orthodox churches (now converted to mosques) from its time as an Ottoman Greek village. The main street, İnönü Caddesi, links the otogar, 1.5km north of the town centre, and the tourist office (☎ 312 2122), 1km south, opposite the yacht marina.

Offshore is **Alibey Adası** (island), with open-air restaurants (take the red Ayvalık Belediyesi bus north). Six kilometres south on a blue 'Sarımsaklı Belediyesi' bus is the 12km-long **Sarımsaklı Plaj** (beach), also called Plajlar.

Catch a boat to Lesvos for an outrageous US$50 one-way and US$65 same-day return (including taxes). Boats operate at least three days per week from early July to late September.

Places to Stay & Eat

Several camping grounds are on Alibey Adası outside the village. Down on the waterfront, on the street directly behind the post office, is *Yalı Pansiyon* (☎ 312 2423), a grand old house. Rooms are fairly basic but the house has a large garden lit with coloured lights, and its own jetty. Dorms go for US$5, doubles/triples/quads cost US$30/35/40 with breakfast. Don't miss the stunning *Taksiyarhis Pansiyon* (☎ 312 1494, Maraşal Çakmak Caddesi 71), which charges US$8 per bed; book ahead.

There's a *Migros supermarket* near the tourist office. The *Anadolu Pide ve Kebap Salonu*, on İnönü Caddesi, and the *Yeni Bahar Lokantası*, just off it, have decent cheap meals.

BERGAMA
☎ 232

From the 4th to the 2nd centuries BC, Bergama (Pergamum) was a powerful and cultured kingdom. A line of rulers beginning with a general under Alexander the Great ruled over this small but wealthy kingdom.

The tourist office (☎ 633 1862) is at İzmir Caddesi 54. Köse Internet is on the street north of the tourist office that heads up to the asclepion.

Things to See & Do

The star attractions here are the city's ruins, especially the **acropolis**, a hill-top site 6km from the city centre (US$2), an excellent **archaeology & ethnography museum** in the city centre (US$2), and the **asclepion** (medical school), 2.5km from the city centre, which grew famous during Alexander the Great's rule (US$2.50). Taxis wait at the tourist office and charge US$5 to the acropolis, US$12 total if they wait an hour and bring you back down. If you're feeling fit, follow the path down through the ruins instead. A tour of the acropolis, the asclepion and the museum costs US$22.

Places to Stay & Eat

Camp at *Hotel Berksoy* (☎ 633 2595), 2km south-west of town, on the main road to the highway to İzmir, just west of it, *Caravan Camping* have camp sites.

South of the otogar, you'll find the spotless, family-run *Böblingen Pension* (☎ 633 2153, Asklepion Caddesi 2), offering rooms with bathroom and breakfast for US$13/16. The *Nike Pension* (☎ 633 3901, Tabak Köprü Çıkmazı 2), a gorgeous 300-year-old Ottoman Greek house, offers doubles for US$17, including breakfast.

About 150m south-west of the old red basilica on the main street is a small square where you'll find the *Meydan Restaurant* charging about US$5 for a delicious feed. The nearby *Sarmaşık Lokantası* has no outdoor seating, but is cheaper.

Getting There & Away

Whether you approach Bergama from the north or south, check to see your bus will drop you *in* Bergama or you may find yourself twiddling your thumbs beside the highway. Buses to İzmir go every half-hour in summer (US$4, 1¾ hours). Five buses go to Ayvalık daily (US$2, 45 minutes).

İZMİR
☎ 232

Turkey's third-largest city is said to be the place where Homer was born in 700 BC. Today it's a transport hub and a good place to dodge.

Orientation & Information

Anafartalar Caddesi twists towards Konak, the commercial and government centre. Atatürk Caddesi, also called Birinci Kordon, runs north-east from Konak along the waterfront 1km to Cumhuriyet Meydanı. Here you'll find the main post office, the Büyük Efes Oteli, the tourist office (☎ 445 7390) and airline offices. İzmir's otogar is 3km north-east of the city centre.

Things to See & Do

If you do stay, İzmir does have some pluses: few tourists, the interesting **bazaar**, the 2nd-century **Roman agora**, the hill-top **Kadifekale fortress**, and the **archaeological and ethnographic museums**. You can get to the Greek island of Chios from Çeşme, 90km (two hours) west of İzmir.

TURKEY

Places to Stay

You can camp at *Oba Camping (☎ 234 2015)*, in Güzelbahçe, 15km south-west of İzmir.

İzmir has more than its fair share of seedy dives. Still keen? Head to Anafartalar Caddesi south-west of Basmane train station. Note: women may not feel comfortable in this area at night, but the three hotels recommended are suitable for women travellers.

Near the Hatuniye (or Kuşlu) Camii (mosque) is the *Otel Saray (☎ 483 6946, Anafartalar Caddesi 635)*, which has been popular with backpackers for years, and looks it. Single/double rooms go for US$4/8, with sink. If the *Saturday Night Fever* foyer doesn't scare you off, the nearby *Otel Hikmet (☎ 484 2672, 945 Sokak 26)* is better and charges US$7/13. The fancier *Otel Antik Han (☎ 489 2750, Anafartalar Caddesi 600)* charges US$20/30 with bathroom and breakfast.

Places to Eat

Anafartalar Caddesi is a self-caterer's paradise. On 1296 Sokak you'll find the good value *Güneydoğu Kebap Salonu*, where a kebab and a drink costs around US$3. At *Dört Mevsim Et Lokantası (1369 Sokak 51a)*, watch your meat cook on the *ocakbaşı* (fireside) grill. You'll be stuffed for US$5.

Getting There & Away

Many bus companies have ticket offices around Dokuz Eylül Meydanı, just north of Basmane train station. Ask about the free minibus to the otogar.

The evening *mavi tren* hauls sleeping and dining cars from Basmane station to Ankara (US$18, 14 hours). The evening *İzmir Ekspresi* to Ankara (15 hours) has 1st/2nd-class carriages for US$9/6.

For İstanbul, take the *Marmara Ekspresi* to Bandırma, then a car ferry to Yenikapı; in total the journey costs US$11. Four pokey but cheap trains go from Basmane to Selçuk/Ephesus (US$1.50, 2½ hours); three continue to Denizli (for Pamukkale; US$4, six hours).

Ferries to Chios depart from Çeşme, west of İzmir, daily in summer (US$30 one-way, including taxes). Catch any Güzelyalı, Altay Meydanı or Balçova bus or dolmuş from Konak and get out at Güzelyalı (Fahrettin)/

Altay Meydanı to board a Çeşme-bound bus (US$3, 1½ hours).

Getting Around

If you crawled into town you would probably get there before the city buses (look for 'Basmane' signs on the bus; US$0.50) which go from the otogar to Konak via the Basmane train station. Save your sanity and jump on the free minibus services *(şehiriçi servis)* to/from İzmir's otogar.

SELÇUK & EPHESUS
☎ 232

Selçuk has enough ruins, resident storks and an annual camel wrestling festival to entice most visitors, but this quaint town lives in the shadow of its neighbour – the splendid Roman ruins of Ephesus (Efes). In its Ionian heyday only Athens was more magnificent, and in Roman times this was Asia's capital.

Orientation & Information

On the east side of the main road (Atatürk Caddesi) are the otogar, restaurants, some hotels and the train station; on the west side, behind the museum, are many pensions. The tourist office (☎ 892 6328) is in the park on the west side of Atatürk Caddesi, across from the otogar. Namel Internet Cafe is on Siegburg Caddesi.

Ephesus is 3.5km west from the centre of Selçuk.

Things to See & Do

The excellent **Ephesus Museum** in Selçuk has a striking collection of artefacts from Ephesus (US$3.50).

Ephesus flourished as the centre for worship of the Anatolian goddess later identified with Diana/Artemis. The **Arcadian Way** through Ephesus was the main street to the port, which has long been silted up. The immense **Great Theatre** holds 24,000 people. The **Temple of Hadrian**, the **Celsus Library**, the **Marble Way** (where the rich lived) and the **Fountain of Trajan** are still in amazingly good shape, or under painstaking restoration.

Ephesus is open from 8 am to 5.30 pm daily (7 pm in summer) for US$5. It's a 3km, 35-minute walk west from Selçuk's otogar along a shady road – turn left (south) at the Tusan Motel. Frequent dolmuşes to Pamucak and Kuşadası pass the Ephesus turn-off (US$0.50).

Places to Stay & Eat

Garden Motel & Camping (☎ *892 2489*) is west of Ayasoluk; walk past the basilica, down the hill, then turn right at the İsabey Camii. Sites cost US$4 per person.

There are many pensions up the hill behind the Ephesus Museum, all charging about US$4 to US$8 per person. A good choice is the *Barım* (☎ *892 6923, Turgutreis Sokak 34*). The popular *Australia & New Zealand Pension* (☎ *892 6050,* ✉ *oznzpension@superonline.com, 1064 Sokak 12)* has dorm beds for US$4, as does *Artemis Guest House* or 'Jimmy's' (☎ *892 6191,* ✉ *jimmy@egenet.com.tr, 1012 Sokak 2)* near the train station.

For cheap eats (around US$2), try the *Artemis Pide Salonu*, near Jimmy's; *Hünkarım Pide Salonu* (*Kızılay Caddesi 16)* is similar. *Pink Bistro Cafe Bar* (*Siegburg Caddesi 24a)* livens up after dark.

Getting There & Away

Minibuses leave frequently for Kuşadası (US$1, 30 minutes) and Pamucak (US$0.80, 10 minutes).

You can make a day trip to Pamukkale (US$7 one-way, three hours) on direct buses leaving before 9 am and returning by 5 pm. Frequent buses and three cheap trains (US$3) go daily to Denizli, where you can get a dolmuş to Pamukkale. Buses leave regularly for Bodrum (US$5.50, three hours), Marmaris (US$10, 6½ hours) and İzmir (US$2, 1¼ hours).

KUŞADASI

☎ 256

Welcome to this cruise-ship port and cheerfully sleazy tourist trap. The main reason to visit is to catch a boat to the Greek island of Samos, though Kuşadası does have a pretty kaleiçi (old town) worth strolling through and its beaches are OK.

The tourist office (☎ 614 1103) is in the middle of town, right by the pier. The dolmuş station is on Adnan Menderes Bulvarı, 1km south-east of the tourist office; continue 500m to the otogar out on the highway. Kismet Internet Café is near the pier.

Boats to Samos (Sisam) sail daily in summer for US$30 one-way, US$35 same-day return, or US$63 open return, including Turkish and Greek port taxes; call Diana Travel (☎ 614 3859) for details.

Places to Stay & Eat

Camping at *Önder* (☎ *614 2413)*, north of town near the marina, costs US$9 for two.

Good, cheap lodgings are uphill behind the tourist office near or along Aslanlar Caddesi.

The pension-with-the-best-views award goes to the clean *Pension Golden Bed* (☎ *614 8708, Uğurlu 1 Çıkmazı 4*) off Aslanlar Caddesi. Dorm beds cost US$4, rooms US$10/16. *Hotel Sammy's Palace* (☎ *612 2588,* ✉ *sammy@superonline.com, Kıbrıs Caddesi 14)* gets mixed reviews from readers. The services, daily room cleaning, free bellydance shows and bed/food deals are decent value at US$5 for dorm beds, US$12/16 for singles/doubles.

The *Avlu Restaurant* (*Cephane Sokak 15)* has delicious, dirt-cheap food. In the late afternoon grab first-rate views and a coffee at *Ada Cafe* on Güvercin Adası (the little fort-topped island). When the sun goes down head to *İstanbul Meyhanesi* (*Kısla Sokak 7)*, in the kaleiçi district, with live music and meals for around US$7.

Getting There & Away

Dolmuşes leave frequently for Selçuk (US$1, 30 minutes), via Pamucak. Head to the otogar for far-flung destinations such as Bodrum (US$6.50, 3½ hours), Marmaris (US$11, seven hours) and İzmir (US$3, 1¾ hours).

PAMUKKALE

☎ 258

Pamukkale is famous for the hot, calcium-rich waters that flowed over a plateau edge and cooled to form brilliant white ledges. Today some visitors are disappointed: much of the water has been diverted, most of the terraces are dry and the days of wallowing in the water-filled ledges are over. However, for US$4.50 you can walk along a thin path through the site which allows you to see the terraces up close. You can still swim in the calcium-rich waters at Pamukkale Motel at the top of the ridge (US$5 for two hours).

Above and behind this natural wonder lie the extensive ruins of the Roman city of Hierapolis (US$5), an ancient spa.

Places to Stay & Eat

Beds at *Meltem Motel Backpackers Inn* (☎ *272 2413,* ✉ *meltemmotel@superonline .com.tr)* cost US$4 for dorms, US$5/10 for

TURKEY

rooms. There are videos and a comfy lounge but some of the rooms are dark. For super-friendly service and decent rooms, try the family-run *Kervansaray Pension (☎ 272 2209)*, US$12/18 a single/double with breakfast and a pool.

Taking meals in your pension or hotel is usually best here. Venture out and you'll pay US$3 per meal to be offended at *Mustafa's*, on the main drag. Munch on tasty food (some vegetarian) while he mimics foreigners; tally your bill carefully.

Getting There & Away
Heading to Pamukkale you might get dropped in Denizli otogar; you'll need to jump on one of the dolmuşes (US$0.70, 30 minutes) that shuttle to and from Pamukkale.

BODRUM
☎ 252
Don your designer sunglasses and take a stroll through the dazzling white lanes of this postcard-perfect yachting town. After dark, Bodrum has a thumping nightlife, come morning, revellers hide in the restaurants lining the bays, during the day they shop.

Orientation & Information
Below the castle lies the centre of town where you'll find the tourist office (☎ 316 1091) and Adliye Camii. Cevat Şakir Caddesi runs from Adliye Camii 500m inland to the otogar. Head north of Adliye Camii up Türkkuyusu Sokak to find the Neşe-i Muhabbet Internet Café.

Things to See & Do
Formerly Halicarnassus, Bodrum is the site of the **Mausoleum** (closed Monday; US$2.50), the monumental tomb of King Mausolus, one of the Seven Wonders of the World. Little remains of the Mausoleum, which was probably partially destroyed by an earthquake and finished off by the Knights of St John.

Placed between Bodrum's perfect twin bays is the medieval **Castle of St Peter**, built in 1402 and rebuilt in 1522 by the knights, using stones from the Mausoleum. It's now a **museum of underwater archaeology** and contains finds from the oldest shipwreck ever discovered (closed Monday; US$4.50).

Gümüşlük, to the far west of the Bodrum peninsula, is the best of the many smaller villages nearby. Dolmuşes run there every hour (US$1).

Places to Stay
Some villages on the peninsula, such as Bitez Yalısı and Ortakent Yalısı, have camp sites.

Head up Türkkuyusu Sokak, to the friendly *Şenlik Pansiyon (☎ 316 6382)* at No 115, single/doubles go for US$7/12. With balconies overlooking the marina, *Gurup Otel (☎ 316 1140, Karantina Sokak 3)* charges US$15 per person, with breakfast; check there's hot water.

Places to Eat & Drink
Self-caterers will find fruit and vegetables on Cevat Şakir Caddesi, on the way to the otogar. In the grid of small market streets just east of the Adliye Camii are several restaurants. One of the best is *Kardeşler Restaurant (Yeni Çarşı 6, Sokak 10)*, with tasty meat dishes for about US$5; beer costs US$1.

Try *Cafe-In Bar (Cumhuriyet Caddesi 84)* which opens onto the bay. Turkish cover songs are played here every night; it's a good spot for women travellers.

Join the queue, open the purse strings and release the ridiculous sum of US$17 to the noisy, brash and mega-fun *Halikarnas Night Club,* on the eastern bay at the end of Cumhuriyet Caddesi.

Getting There & Away
Bus services include: İzmir (US$12, four hours), Selçuk (US$5.50, three hours) and Marmaris (US$6, three hours).

Boats go to Kos (İstanköy) frequently in summer for US$16 one-way, US$20 same-day and US$30 open return; these prices include port taxes. In summer there are also boats to Datça, Dalyan, Didyma, Marmaris and Rhodes.

The Mediterranean Coast

MARMARİS
☎ 252
Primed for the package-holiday set, Marmaris has decent food, innumerable souvenirs and lascivious living after dark. If you're after something else it's time to move on.

Orientation & Information
Marmaris has a small castle overlooking the town centre. İskele Meydanı (the main square) and the tourist office (☎ 412 1035) are just north of the castle. Hacı Mustafa Sokak (or Bar Street) runs east from İskele Meydanı; the bazaar spreads northwards. In the bazaar you'll find the post office. Beside Netsel marina is the homely Marmaris Internet Cafe-Bar. The otogar is 1.5km north-east of the centre of town, on the way to Muğla.

Things to See & Do
There are daily boat trips in summer to **Paradise Island** (about US$15 a head) and farther afield to **Dalyan** and **Kaunos** (around US$25). **Datça**, a village on the peninsula, has been 'discovered' but is still a great place to visit; less spoilt are **Bozburun**, not as far west, and **Aktaş**, 4km east of Marmaris. At the tip of the peninsula are the ruins of the ancient port of **Knidos**, accessible by road or excursion boat.

Places to Stay
About 1km east of Marmaris is the Günlücek Reserve and basic *Dimet Camping* (☎ 412 5601). The spartan, but clean, *Interyouth Hostel* (☎ 412 3687, ✉ intery outh@turk.net, Tepe Mahallesi, 42 Sokak 45), in the bazaar, charges US$4.50 for a dorm bed, US$6/12 for singles/doubles. The quaint *Yılmaz Pansiyon* (☎ 412 3754, 7 Sokak 33) is just inland from the little park near the Turkish Airlines office on Atatürk Caddesi. Doubles/triples cost US$9/13.

Places to Eat & Drink
Head to 51 Sokak (the street with the post office). Try *Marmaris Lokantası* for a US$4 feed or the better (and pricier) *Yeni Liman Restaurant*, on İsmetpaşa Caddesi, around the corner. At Bar Street, you could be in for a long (and expensive) night. *Down Town* is decked out with windmills; you'll get lost in *Greenhouse*. *Le Petit Cafe* offers respite and jazz (and is a haven for women travellers) while *Sıla Türkü Bar* has live, traditional music.

Getting There & Away
Buses go regularly to all places in the region, including Antalya (US$12, seven hours), Bodrum (US$6, three hours) and Köyceğiz (US$3, one hour).

Small car ferries run to Rhodes daily in summer (less frequently in the off season) for US$35 one-way, US$40 same-day return, or US$70 open return; these fares include port taxes.

KÖYCEĞİZ & DALYAN
☎ 252
Köyceğiz, 75km east of Marmaris, nestles beside the enormous Köyceğiz Gölü (lake), surrounded by hills. It's becoming a popular choice with backpackers, and for good reasons: everything you can do at Dalyan you can do from Köyceğiz, it has decent places to stay, plenty of things to do, and (so far) it's relatively untouched by tourism.

However, while Köyceğiz has some drawcards, Dalyan has them all: a river meandering by, excellent fishing and, to the south at İztuzu, a beautiful **beach** which is the nesting ground of the *Carretta carretta*, or ancient sea turtle.

As if that were not enough, Dalyan has ruins: dramatic rock-cut **Lycian tombs** overlooking the town, and the ruined city of **Kaunos** easily visited by boat excursion downriver. Upriver there are mud baths; on the shores of Köyceğiz Gölü,at Sultaniye Kaplıcaları, are **hot springs**.

The local boaters' cooperative sets rates for river excursions. Daily tours taking in the mud baths, the ruins at Kaunos and 'turtle' beach cost about US$5 a head. Forty-minute (one-way) runs just to the beach cost US$2.50. From Köyceğiz, a day boat tour to 'turtle' beach and the mud baths will set you back US$10.

In Köyceğiz, there's camping at *Anatolia Camping* (☎ 262 2752), near the water. *Tango Pension* (☎ 262 2501, ✉ tangopen sion@superonline.com), on Alihsan Kalmaz Caddesi, gets rave reviews. Beds under the stars cost US$2.50, dorm beds US$5 and singles/doubles go for US$7/14.

In Dalyan, *Dalyan Camping* has tent sites for US$4. The family-run *Önder Pansiyon* (☎ 284 2605) charges US$12/17 for singles/doubles, including breakfast.

Inland, near the tourist office, *Narin* has good food for around US$4. For a drink, the *Sofra* cafe-bar has been well tested; the *Albatros* is good for dancing.

In summer there are morning buses from Dalyan to Marmaris, Fethiye and Muğla; if not, catch a dolmuş to Ortaca and change.

FETHİYE
☎ 252

Fethiye has superb beaches, cheap lodgings and plenty of nightlife; it's crowded in summer but worth the diversion off the road. This is the site of ancient **Telmessos**, with giant Lycian stone **sarcophagi** from 400 BC littered about.

The otogar is 2km east of the town centre. The tourist office (☎ 614 1527), next to the Dedeoğlu Otel, is near the yacht marina on the western side of town. Restaurants and bars are in, or around, the bazaar area, east of the tourist office.

Things to See & Do

Check out the rock-cut **Tomb of Amyntas** (US$1.50) looming from a cliff above the town. There's also a marked hiking trail over the hills to the beautiful Ottoman Greek ghost town of **Kayaköy**, or you can catch the dolmuş. Working up a sweat? Head to the beach at **Çalış**, or the gorgeous **Saklıkent Gorge**, which cuts 18km into the Akdağlar mountains. Next stop could be the **hammam** in the bazaar back in town.

A '12 Island Tour' boat excursion is a must. With its swimming, cruising and sightseeing, it may be your best day in Fethiye. Prices average around US$12 per person.

Places to Stay

Good options are up the hill, off Fevzi Çakmak Caddesi, west of the tourist office. The family-run *Tan Pansiyon* (☎ 614 1584, *Eski Karagözler Caddesi 89)* has clean rooms for US$5/10 and a huge tiled terrace. Farther up the hill, the popular *İdeal Pension* (☎/fax 614 1981, Zafer Caddesi 1) costs a few dollars more, but has a great terrace and muesli for breakfast.

Places to Eat & Drink

The *Özlem Kebap Salonu* on Çarşı Caddesi (the main market street) will fill you up for around US$2. Cross the road to find Tütün Sokak, where *Sedir Restaurant* serves delicious mains for around US$4, including a 'vegetarian surprise'. *The Duck Pond* (guess the gimmick), in the bazaar, has similar fare. Also in the bazaar, the *Car Cemetery Bar* and *Club Bananas* will get you dancing. Beside the Roman theatre, *Zeytin Cafe Bar* has live traditional music every night in summer.

Getting There & Away

If you're heading directly for Antalya, note that the *yayla* (inland) route is shorter (3½ hours) and cheaper (US$6) than the *sahil* (coastal) route (US$8, eight hours). Buses from the otogar also serve Kaş (US$4.50, 2½ hours) and Dalyan (US$2.50, one hour).

Minibuses depart from their own terminal, 600m west of the otogar toward the centre, on short hops to other points along the coast, like Patara (US$2.50, 1½ hours), Kınık (for Xanthos; US$2, 1½ hours) and Ölüdeniz (US$1.50, 15 minutes).

ÖLÜDENİZ & BUTTERFLY VALLEY
☎ 252

Ölüdeniz has (mostly) hidden from the monstrous hotels on the hills and is still a beautiful beach spot. There are moderately priced bungalows and camping areas; book ahead.

A boat ride (US$7 per person) away from Ölüdeniz is stunning **Butterfly Valley**, where you'll find serenity, your sanity, and butterflies (if you're there between May and September). Visit the waterfall or brave the hike (45 minutes) to the village above.

Places to Stay

Nestled beside Ölüdeniz Lagoon, *Ölüdeniz Camping* (☎ 617 0048, fax 617 0181) has bungalows with/without bathrooms for US$13/10 a double; camp for US$2 per person.

In the village above Butterfly Valley you'll find *George's Place* (☎ 642 1102). George offers no-frills bed, breakfast and dinner for US$6. Alternatively, you can doss in basic *treehouses* near the beach for US$10; all meals included.

KAŞ
☎ 242

Kaş has a picturesque quayside square, a big Friday **market**, Lycian stone **sarcophagi** dotted about its streets and rock-cut **tombs** in the cliffs above the town – it's a fine, laid-back place. Aside from enjoying the town's ambience and a few small pebble beaches, you can walk west a few hundred metres to the well preserved **theatre**. Or you could take one of the **boat excursions** to Kalkan, Patara, the Blue Cave, Saklıkent Gorge, Üçağız or Demre.

The Greek island of Kastellorizo (Meis in Turkish) is visible just a short distance across the water and can be reached by boat in summer (US$30 one-way, daily).

The otogar is 400m north-west of the main square and marina. The tourist office (☎ 836 1238) is on the main square; the post office and Net-House Internet Cafe are a short walk north.

Places to Stay
Kaş Camping (☎ 836 1050), in an olive grove 1km west of town, past the theatre, has tent sites and simple bungalows.

At the otogar you'll be accosted by pension-pushers. Yenicami Caddesi (or Recep Bilgin Caddesi), just south of the otogar, has lots of standard, clean places charging US$10/15 for singles/doubles, with breakfast. Try *Anı Motel* (☎ 836 1791) or *Melisa* (☎ 836 1068). At the southern end of the street near the mosque is the *Ay Pansiyon* (☎ 836 1562), where the front rooms have sea views.

Places to Eat & Drink
The *Corner Café*, at the post office end of İbrahim Serin Caddesi, serves yogurt with fruit and honey for US$2. The *Café Merhaba* across the street is good for cakes.

The *Eriş*, behind the tourist office, is a favourite, as much for its setting as for its food. Also popular is *Smiley's Restaurant* next door, where pizza or mains cost around US$4.

On the main square, *Noel Baba* is well placed to people watch. Lift the pace at trendy *Redpoint* or the outdoor *Full Moon Club*, a little out of town but right on the waterfront.

OLİMPOS & THE CHİMAERA
☎ 242
There are two roads off the main Kaş-Antalya highway to Olimpos. One you'll reach coming from Kumluca (from the west); the other as you come from Tekirova (from the east). If you're travelling by bus you'll get dropped off at the top of the eastern road. From here it's a dolmuş ride just over 8km down a winding road to the first of the string of pensions, and a farther 3.5km to the site of ancient Olimpos. Wild and abandoned, the Olimpos ruins peek out from forest copses and river banks. The pebble beach is magnificent.

According to legend, the **Chimaera** (Yanartaş), a natural eternal flame, was the hot breath of a subterranean monster. Easily sighted by mariners in ancient times, it's a mere glimmer of its former self now. To see the Chimaera – best visited at night – go 3km east from Çıralı down a neighbouring valley. It's a half-hour climb to the flame. Most of the pensions organise night-time 'romantic flame' tours.

Places to Stay
Olimpos's accommodation has had its fair share of criticism (and praise). Pensions offer comfy bungalow beds or a mattress on the floor in a treehouse; rates include breakfast and dinner. Security has been a big issue around here – none of the treehouses have locks but most of the pensions have safes you can use.

You must have heard the good/bad hype about *Kadir's* (☎ 892 1250, @ treehouse@superonline.com) – it's *the* place to stay. It has Internet access, a bar, vegetarian food and the highest treehouses – bungalows will set you back US$12 per person, treehouses US$7. *Sheriff* (☎ 892 1301) has good value, clean treehouses/bungalows for US$4/6 per person; you'll pay the same at friendly *Bayram's* (☎ 892 1243), which seems to attract Aussies and is set in an orange grove. *Orange Pansiyon* (☎ 892 1242) gets good reviews by readers and charges US$7/12, but has identical facilities to the others.

ANTALYA
☎ 242
Antalya, set against the Taurus mountains, has one of the most attractive harbour settings in the Mediterranean. Unfortunately, much of Antalya is ugly apartment blocks – its saving grace is Kaleiçi, the restored Ottoman town (now the yacht marina). The beaches are out of town: Konyaaltı Plajı, a long pebble beach to the west, and Lara Plajı, a sand beach to the east.

Orientation & Information
The otogar is 4km north of the centre reached by dolmuş along Güllük (Anafartalar) Caddesi. The city centre is at Kalekapısı, near Cumhuriyet Meydanı, with its dramatic equestrian statue of Atatürk. Kaleiçi, the old town, is south of Kalekapısı down the hill. Atatürk Caddesi, 100m east of Kalekapısı, goes south past Hadriyanüs

TURKEY

Kapısı (Hadrian's Gate). The tourist office (☎ 241 1747, Cumhuriyet Caddesi 2) is 500m west of Kalekapısı (look for the sign 'Antalya Devlet Tiyatrosu' on the right-hand side; it's in this building). Sanal Alem Net Cafe, 260m north of Kalekapısı, has Internet access.

Note: lone travellers should be careful after dark – Kaleiçi and around Kalekapısı can be sleazy.

Things to See & Do
Don't miss the Antalya Museum (closed Monday; US$4); it houses finds from Perge and some wonderful ethnographical exhibits. Hadriyanüs Kapısı (Hadrian's Gate) was built for the Roman emperor's visit in 130 AD. Near the clock tower is Antalya's graceful symbol, the Yivli Minare (Grooved Minaret), which rises above an old building, once a mosque and now a fine-arts gallery. In Kaleiçi, the Kesik Minare (Truncated Minaret) marks a ruined Roman temple.

Places to Stay & Eat
Try *Bambus Motel, Restaurant & Camping (☎ 321 5263)*, 300m west of the Hotel Dedeman on the one-way (eastbound) coast road to Lara Plajı.

In Kaleiçi the *Adler (☎ 241 7818, Civelek Sokak 16)* is grim but friendly; beds are US$5 a night. The *Erkal Pansiyon (☎ 244 0159, Kandiller Geçidi 5)* is good value, for a few dollars more. A good choice for women travellers is the *Senem Family Pansion (☎ 247 1752, Zeytin Geçidi Sokak 9)*. You'll pay US$12/18 for singles/doubles with the bonus of a terrace with views.

Eski Sebzeciler İçi Sokak, a short street just south-west of the junction of Cumhuriyet and Atatürk Caddesis, is filled with *open-air restaurants* where a kebab, salad and drink can cost as little as US$4. Try Antalya's own *tandır kebap* (mutton cooked in an earthenware pot).

Getting There & Away
Catch a dolmuş heading north on Güllük Caddesi to the Yeni Garaj (otogar) or to Vatan Kavşağı (roundabout at the intersection of Vatan and Gazi boulevards). Vatan Kavşağı serves as an informal bus station for regional traffic; take an 'Aksu' dolmuş for Perge (US$1), or a 'Manavgat' bus for Side (US$2). From Yeni Garaj buses depart every 20 minutes (in summer) for Alanya (US$3.50, two hours), Denizli (US$7.50, four hours), Kaş (US$5, four hours) and Nevşehir (for Cappadocia; US$12, eight hours).

Getting Around
The tramvay (US$0.30) trundles back and forward from Antalya Museum in the west, along Cumhuriyet Caddesi past Kalekapısı to Atatürk Caddesi and the stadium.

Central Anatolia

ANKARA
☎ 312
The capital of Turkey since 1923, Ankara is not an especially exciting city. However, because of its central location there's a good chance you'll pass through at least once.

Orientation & Information
Atatürk Bulvarı and Çankırı Caddesi serve as the city's north-south axis. AŞTİ, Ankara's mammoth otogar, is 6.5km southwest of Ulus (the historic centre) and Opera (or İtfaiye) Meydanı (with a concentration of cheap hotels), and 6km west of Kızılay, the modern centre. The Ankaray underground train connects AŞTİ, Tandoğan and Kızılay; change at Kızılay for the Metro which leads to Ulus.

The tourist office (☎ 231 5572) is at Gazi Mustafa Kemal Bulvarı 121, opposite the Maltepe Ankaray station. The main post office is on Atatürk Bulvarı just south of Ulus.

Things to See & Do
The Anatolian Civilisations Museum (Anadolu Medeniyetleri Müzesi) on Hisarparkı Caddesi is the most worthwhile attraction, with the world's richest collection of Hittite artefacts. It's uphill (south-west) from Ulus, and open from 8.30 am to 5 pm daily ('closed' on Monday in winter unless you pay double the US$3 entry fee).

The Anıt Kabir (Mausoleum of Atatürk), 2km west of Kızılay, is a monumental tomb and memorial to Atatürk. It's open from 9 am to 5 pm daily (free).

Places to Stay
In Ulus, along the east side of shabby Opera (or İtfaiye) Meydanı, are several cheap hotels: the very basic *Otel Fuar (☎ 312 3288,*

TURKEY

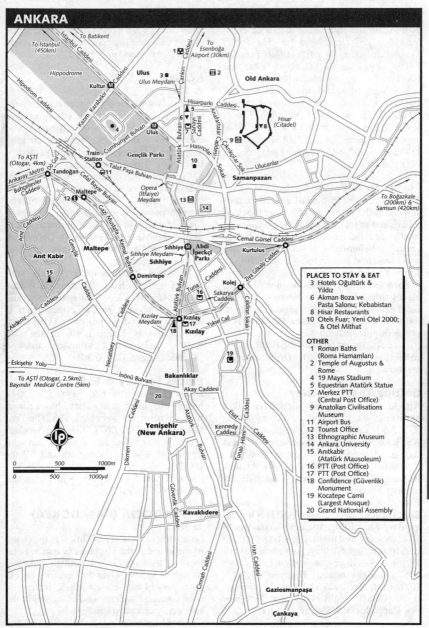

ANKARA

PLACES TO STAY & EAT
3 Hotels Oğultürk &
    Yıldız
6 Akman Boza ve
    Pasta Salonu; Kebabistan
8 Hisar Restaurants
10 Otels Fuar; Yeni Otel 2000;
    & Otel Mithat

OTHER
1 Roman Baths
    (Roma Hamamları)
2 Temple of Augustus &
    Rome
4 19 Mayıs Stadium
5 Equestrian Atatürk Statue
7 Merkez PTT
    (Central Post Office)
9 Anatolian Civilisations
    Museum
11 Airport Bus
12 Tourist Office
13 Ethnographic Museum
14 Ankara University
15 Anıtkabir
    (Atatürk Mausoleum)
16 PTT (Post Office)
17 PTT (Post Office)
18 Confidence (Güvenlik)
    Monument
19 Kocatepe Camii
    (Largest Mosque)
20 Grand National Assembly

Kosova Sokak 11), with waterless singles/doubles for US$6/12; and the more comfortable **Yeni Otel 2000** (☎ *311 0037, Kosova Sokak 3)* or **Otel Mithat** (☎ *311 5410, Tavus Sokak 2)*, both charging US$12/19 a single/double with bath.

North of Ulus and one street west of Çankırı Caddesi, the three-star **Hotel Oğultürk** (☎ *309 2900, Rüzgarlı Eşdost Sokak 6)* has rooms with TV for US$26/40 negotiable, breakfast included. The nearby **Yıldız** (☎ *312 7584, Rüzgarlı Eşdost Sokak 4)* is similar.

Places to Eat

Akman Boza ve Pasta Salonu *(Atatürk Bulvarı 3)*, in the courtyard of a huge block of offices and shops, serves pastries, omelettes, sandwiches and quick snacks. Immediately above is **Kebabistan**, a kebab place with good food and low prices – about US$3 to $5 for a full meal.

For a seemingly endless choice of cheap places to eat hop on the Metro to Kızılay and head into the pedestrianised streets to the east where every other building is a kebab or pide restaurant.

For a splash-out head for the Hisar and its collection of restored **Ottoman-style restaurants**.

Getting There & Away

Air Ankara's Esenboğa airport is 33km north of the city centre. Havaş buses (US$3.50) depart every 30 minutes from AŞTİ otogar, stopping at Ankara Garı train station; allow two hours to get to the airport.

Turkish Airlines (☎ 482 0200), Atatürk Bulvarı 154, Kavaklıdere, has daily flights to most Turkish cities.

Bus Ankara's huge otogar (AŞTİ) is the vehicular heart of the nation, with coaches to all places day and night. For İstanbul (from US$10, six hours) they go at least every 15 minutes. Other coaches go to Antalya (US$12, eight hours), Bodrum (US$12, 10 hours), Erzurum (US$18, 13 hours), İzmir (US$10, eight hours) and Nevşehir (for Cappadocia; US$8, five hours).

Train From the Ankara Garı station in Ulus, seven express trains connect Ankara and İstanbul (US$5 to US$35, 7½ to 11 hours); the *Ankara*, *Fatih* and *Başkent* express

trains are fastest and most expensive. The *İzmir Mavi Tren* (US$11, 14 hours) hauls dining and sleeping cars. A train to Kayseri (eight hours) need cost only US$3.

KONYA
☎ 332

Modern Konya, the Roman Iconium, is a religiously conservative place. It's also one of the world's oldest continually occupied cities and a showcase for some striking Seljuk architecture. This was the capital of the Seljuk Turks, and it was here, in the 13th century, that the poet Celaleddin Rumi (Mevlana) founded the whirling dervishes, one of Islam's major mystical orders. Atatürk put a stop to the whirling except as 'folk dance'; you can see it performed here during the Mevlana Festival in December, although performances in İstanbul are actually more enjoyable.

Mevlana's tomb is topped by the brilliant turquoise-tiled tower near the tourist office (☎ 351 1074) and hotel area; it's now the **Mevlana Müzesi**, open from at least 10 am to 5.30 pm daily (US$2.50). The otogar is 3.5km north of the city centre, linked by dolmuşes marked 'Konak-Otogar' (US$0.30).

Places to Stay & Eat

If you're staying, the **Ulusan** (☎ *351 5004)*, behind the main post office, has beds in rooms without showers for US$5. The **Yeni Köşk Otel** (☎ *352 0671, Yeni Aziziye Caddesi, Kadılar Sokak 28)* is good value with tidy doubles with private bath and TV for US$20.

For decent food, try the **Şifa Lokantası** *(Mevlana Caddesi 30)*.

CAPPADOCIA (KAPADOKYA)
☎ 384

South-east of Ankara and almost in the centre of the country, the Cappadocia region is famous for the fantastic rock formations dotting its remote valleys. Over the centuries people have carved houses, churches, fortresses, even complete underground cities, out of the soft, eerily eroded volcanic stone.

Travel agencies in İstanbul offer two and three-day tours to Cappadocia, which are OK if you're pressed for time and don't mind spending many hours in a cramped minibus, but pick carefully as some are very overpriced. It's better to take a bus to Göreme and spend a few leisurely days hiking in the valleys.

Nevşehir

A loud, unattractive provincial capital, Nevşehir is only good for information and transport connections. From outside the tourist office (☎ 213 3659) in the town centre there are frequent buses to Göreme, Avanos, Uçhisar and Ürgüp, and to the astonishing underground cities of **Derinkuyu** and **Kaymaklı** (US$1.25; open 8 am to at least 5.30 pm daily).

Göreme

The Göreme Valley is one of the most amazing sights in Turkey. Over the centuries a thick layer of volcanic tuff has been eroded into fantastic shapes, and many of the resulting tuff cones and cliffs have been carved (mostly by early Christians) into churches, stables and homes. Painted church murals date from as early as the 8th century, though the finest are from the 10th to 13th centuries. The best examples are in the **Göreme Open Air Museum** (Göreme Açık Hava Müzesi), which is open 8 am to at least 4.30 pm daily. Entry is US$5 with an extra US$6 to see the recently renovated **Karanlık (Dark) church**.

Three kilometres south-west of Göreme village is picturesque **Üçhisar**, a town built around and into a prominent peak. A room-by-room scramble through its rock citadel (US$1.25) leads to fine views from the summit.

You can walk to the above sights, or hire a bicycle or moped in Göreme village. Alternatively Göreme travel agencies offer daily tours which take in one of the underground cities and the Ihlara Valley as well as more local sites. Expect to pay around US$30.

Göreme's Nese Internet Café is on the main road through town, next to the Neşe Travel Agency.

Places to Stay You can camp at the *Dilek* and *Berlin* camping grounds, side by side amid rock formations on the road from Göreme village to the Open Air Museum. *Kaya Camping* is even better; to find it continue along the road past the museum towards Ortahisar.

Pensions in Göreme village charge similar rates: around US$4 for a dorm bed, US$5.50 in a waterless private room, and US$7 to $10 per bed in a private room with bath and/or toilet.

Favourites include *Köse* (☎ 271 2294), near the post office, with a swimming pool and good meals; *Kelebek* (☎ 271 2531), with cave rooms and spectacular views; *Flintstones* (☎ 271 2555), with a swimming pool; *Paradise* (☎ 271 2248); and *Peri* (☎ 271 2136), with an inviting cave bar.

Cave Hotel Melek (☎ 271 2463), high on the valley wall, has rock-cut double rooms with private bath and breakfast for US$25. The newer *Ottoman House* (☎ 271 2616) offers luxury rooms for US$15/30, plus US$5 for an excellent buffet breakfast and US$10 for a set dinner menu.

Places to Eat Of the restaurants along the main road the *SOS* tends to be cheapest but the *Sultan*, *Sedef* and *Tardelli* all serve up good standard Turkish fare. The *Orient*, on the road heading for Üçhisar, serves good food in a pleasing ambience. Across the road *Cafedoci@* serves a more westernised menu – big portions of burgers, etc. Other cheaper restaurants are clustered around the cone of rock called the Roma Kalesi. Or there's the friendly *Vegemite Café* at the start of the road to the Open Air Museum.

Ürgüp

Ürgüp is a very appealing old town, with crumbling sandstone buildings, cobbled streets and a stone hill riddled with rooms and passages. There are some delightful hotels and pensions in old restored houses if you can afford to splash out a bit.

You can go wine-tasting here; Cappadocia's best is bottled at wineries on Mustafapaşa Caddesi and at the top of the hill on the Nevşehir road.

The helpful tourist office (☎ 341 4059) is in the park, downhill from the main square.

Places to Stay & Eat One of the cheapest places to stay is the *Bahçe Hostel* (☎ 341 3314, fax 341 4878, ✉ bahce@altavista.net), across the road from the hammam, which has basic bathless rooms for US$4.50 a head and pension rooms with baths for US$7/13 per single/double. Up the hill a bit is the homy *Hotel Elvan* (☎ 341 4191, fax 341 3455,

TURKEY

İstiklal Caddesi, Barbaros Hayrettin Sokak 11), with nicer rooms arranged around a small courtyard and good views from the roof terrace.

Heading up İstiklal Caddesi on the right you'll see the fairly simple but friendly *Kemer Hotel (☎ 341 2168, Hamam Sokak 19)*, with similar prices. The *Şölen* and *Kardeşler* restaurants, behind the otogar, have good, cheap food. *Şömine*, right in the centre, is good for grills and *mezes*.

The Black Sea Coast

Steep and craggy, damp and lush, and isolated by the Pontic Mountains along most of its length, the Black Sea coastline is dramatically different from the rest of Turkey. Tourism hasn't penetrated far, though you'll find plenty of cheap hotels and camp sites. Prices are lower than on the Mediterranean coast. Partly because of heavy industry around Zonguldak, the coast west from Sinop to the Bosphorus is almost unknown to tourists, though the pretty fishing port of **Amasra**, with its Roman and Byzantine ruins, is worth a look.

The eastern end of the coastal Kaçkar mountain range is dominated by Kaçkar Dağı (3937m), inland from Rize. Around it are excellent opportunities for camping, wilderness treks and even white-water rafting on the Çoruh River. A good base for day hikes and trekking towards Kaçkar Dağı is the town of **Ayder**, 40km east of Rize and 40km inland, with hot springs as a bonus.

On your way to the coast, stop at **Amasya**, an old Ottoman town in a dramatic setting, or **Safranbolu**, famous for its wooden Ottoman houses.

TRABZON
☎ 462
Trabzon is the most interesting town on the Turkish Black Sea coast, with mild weather, good-natured people, lots of Byzantine architecture and the amazing Sumela Monastery nearby.

Orientation & Information
Modern Trabzon is centred on Atatürk Alanı (Atatürk Square), on a steep hill above the harbour. Uphill are Ulusoy and Metro bus ticket offices.

The long-distance otogar is 3km east of the port. The tourist office (☎ 321 4659) is south-east of Atatürk Alanı.

Things to See
Trabzon's medieval **old town**, with its timber houses and stone bridges, is a 30-minute walk west of Atatürk Alanı.

Of the many Byzantine churches, the best preserved is the 13th-century **Aya Sofya**, now a museum (closed Monday in winter; US$1); take a minibus from Atatürk Alanı. Among the town's more beautiful Ottoman mosques are the **Gülbahar Hatun Camii** west of the city walls and the **Çarşı Camii** (Osmanpaşa Camii) in the bazaar.

Forty-six kilometres south of Trabzon, the 14th-century **Sumela Monastery** is built into a cliff-face like a swallow's nest. It was inhabited until 1923 and has many fine murals and amazing views. In summer Ulusoy runs an 11 am bus (returning at 2 and 3 pm) from the town-centre terminal, just uphill from Atatürk Alanı. The 40-minute trip costs US$4. Taxis to the monastery depart from Atatürk Alanı and charge US$35 for up to five passengers, including a two-hour wait and the trip back. Entry to the monastery is US$1.50.

Places to Stay
Some hotels east of Atatürk Alanı, especially on Güzelhisar Caddesi and adjacent streets, are filled with traders and prostitutes from the former Soviet republics.

The aged *Hotel Benli (☎ 321 1022, Cami Çıkmazı 5)* is just off the eastern end of Atatürk Alanı, uphill behind the belediye. It looks as if nothing much has changed since the day it opened but beds could hardly be cheaper, at US$3.50 a head, plus US$1 for a hot shower. *Hotel Gözde (☎ 321 9579, Salih Yazıcı Sokak 7)*, just off Güzelhisar Caddesi, could do with a makeover but the rooms, at US$4.50 a head, are tolerable. *Hotel Anıl (☎ 326 7282, Güzelhisar Caddesi 10)* is a good choice with clean rooms with shower for US$12/20 a single/double, breakfast included.

Better than this is the nearby *Hotel Nur (☎ 321 2798, fax 321 9576, Cami Sokak 4)*, where clean singles/doubles cost US$12/20 with shower.

Travellers can also stay in the hostel of the **Sankta Maria Katolik Kilisesi** (☎ *321 2192, Sümer Sokak 26)*, a few blocks downhill (north) from Atatürk Alanı in exchange for a (realistic) donation.

Places to Eat

Atatürk Alanı is ringed with decent places to eat. Try *Derya Restaurant* or *Volkan 2* for a good selection of ready-made food, or *Murat Balık Salonu* for mackerel (US$3) or *hemsi*, a Black Sea winter delicacy. *Güloğlu Baklava ve Kebap Salonu* also serves a wide range of meals in cheerful surroundings.

Getting There & Away

Dolmuşes to the otogar ('Garajlar – Meydan') leave from Taksim Caddesi, just up the hill from Atatürk Alanı.

From the otogar, dolmuşes go every half hour to Rize (US$2.50, 1½ hours) and daily buses head to Erzurum (US$10, six hours).

Eastern Turkey

Turkey's eastern region is the harshest and hardest part of the country to travel in but rewards visitors with dramatic landscapes, like Turkey's highest mountain, Mt Ararat (5137m), the legendary resting place of Noah's Ark, and some unusual historical relics. In the winter, bitterly cold weather blows in from the Russian steppes; it's best to avoid travelling here from October to April.

ERZURUM

☎ 442

Eastern Turkey's main transport hub and a military centre, Erzurum is a fairly drab town, famous for its harsh climate but with some striking Seljuk buildings that justify staying a day or so.

Orientation & Information

The tourist office (☎ 218 5697) is on Cemal Gürsel Caddesi, the main street, just west of the Atatürk statue, although you may not find anyone there. The otogar is inconveniently located 3km from town on the airport road; catch bus No 2 into town from the otogar.

Things to See & Do

From the well-preserved walls of a 5th-century **Byzantine fortress** you get good views of the town's layout and the bleak plains that surround it. The **Çifte Minareli Medrese**, built in 1253, is a seminary famous for its Seljuk architecture. The oldest mosque, **Ulu Cami**, built in 1179, is next door.

Farther west along Cumhuriyet Caddesi, an open square marks the centre of town, with an Ottoman mosque and another seminary, the **Yakutiye Medresesi**, which now houses the Turkish and Islamic Arts and Ethnography Museum (closed Monday; US$1.25).

Places to Stay

Erzurum has lots of cheapies, although some of them are pretty dismal. *Örnek Otel* (☎ *218 1204, Kazım Karabekir Caddesi 8)* has basic rooms for US$9/12 per single/double.

The nearby *Otel Polat* (☎ *218 1623, Kazım Karabekir Caddesi 3)* is much better, with singles/doubles from US$13/21.

Around the corner, the *Hotel Sefer* (☎ *218 6714)*, on İstasyon Caddesi, charges US$15/25 per single/double with bath and TV, including breakfast. All three are conveniently situated between the train station and the town centre.

Highly recommended by readers is the *Yeni Hotel Çınar* (☎ *213 1050, Ayazpaşa Caddesi 18)*, which charges about the same as the Örnek. To find it, look for the Gürpınar Sineması (cinema) in the bazaar. The street opposite leads to the Çınar.

Places to Eat

There are several reasonable options along Cumhuriyet Caddesi near the Yakutiye Medresesi. *Güzelyurt Restorant*, although tarted up with tablecloths and uniformed waiters, is not that expensive. Try the house speciality *mantarlı güveç*, a delicious lamb stew. Meals cost US$7 to US$10.

Getting There & Away

Turkish Airlines (☎ 234 1516), Kazım Karabekir Caddesi, has two flights daily (US$65) to Ankara, with connections to İstanbul and İzmir. A taxi to the airport costs US$3.50.

From the otogar there are frequent buses to Ankara, İstanbul and Kars. Trains to/from Erzurum are slow and should be avoided.

TURKEY

KARS & ANI
☎ 474

About 260km north-east of Erzurum, Kars was much fought over and has a suitably massive fortress. The main reason to come here now is to see the ruins of ancient Ani.

There's not much to do in Kars itself, although the **museum**, north-east of the train station on Cumhuriyet Caddesi, has exhibits dating from the Bronze Age (admission US$1.25).

Ani, 44km east of Kars, was completely deserted in 1239 after a Mongol invasion but before that had been a major city and a capital of both the Urartian and Armenian kingdoms. Surrounded by huge walls, the ruins lie in fields overlooking the Arpaçay River, which forms the border with Armenia. The ghost city is extremely dramatic and there are several notable churches, including a cathedral built between 989 and 1010 that was the seat of the Armenian prelate.

To get permission to go to Ani, first go to the Kars tourist office (☎ 223 2300) in Aatürk Caddesi and fill out a form. Then take the form to the Emniyet Müdürglü for approval. Then go to Kars museum and buy your ticket. Taxi drivers know the procedure only too well and charge around US$30 for arranging the entire trip.

The best value place to stay is the *Güngören Oteli* (☎ 212 5630, fax 223 4821, Halit Paşa Caddesi, Millet Sokak 4), where spacious rooms cost US$15/25 per single/double.

DOĞUBAYAZIT
☎ 472

This drab frontier town, dramatically situated at the far side of a sweeping grass plain that runs to the foot of Mt Ararat, is where you come to cross into Iran. It doesn't take long to find your bearings, as everything is within a five-minute walk. Apart from spectacular views of **Mt Ararat**, there's an interesting palace-fort, the **İshak Paşa Sarayı** (open 8 am to 5 pm; US$2), perched romantically among rocky crags, 5km east of town. The occasional dolmuş passes nearby, but unless you want to walk you'll probably have to negotiate for a taxi (about US$5 there and back).

Getting permission to climb Mt Ararat can be time-consuming. Otherwise, there are excursions to a giant **meteor crater, Diyadin hot springs** and the supposed resting-place of **Noah's Ark**.

If you decide to stay, a good choice is the *Hotel Ararat* (☎ 312 4988), right beside the bazaar. Doubles with views go for US$15. The *Hotel İsfahan* (☎ 311 5159, Emniyet Caddesi 26) also has serviceable rooms for US$25/38 per single/double. Smaller hotels, like the nearby *Hotel Erzurum* (☎ 312 5080), on Belediye Caddesi, provide beds for US$5 to US$7.

NEMRUT DAĞI
☎ 416

North of Şanlıurfa and south of Malatya, pretty much in the middle of nowhere, stands Nemrut Dağı (Mt Nimrod), surmounted by a 2000-year-old **memorial sanctuary** to an obscure Commagene king. The heads of huge statues of gods and kings lie toppled by earthquakes and scattered on the ground.

Most people approach from the south side of the mountain where the **Kahta** tourist office (☎ 725 5007) is particularly helpful. The owners of Kahta's hotels, including the *Kommagene* (☎ 715 1092), *Mezopotamya* (☎ 725 5112) and *Zeus Camping* (☎ 725 5695), arrange tours to see the heads.

Three-day trips to Nemrut are also available from Göreme; they cost US$150 a head and take in lots of other sites along the way.

Yugoslavia (Југославија)

The Federal Republic of Yugoslavia, consisting of Serbia and Montenegro, is at the heart of the Balkan Peninsula. Beyond Belgrade, there are the gorges and beaches of Montenegro, the mystical Orthodox monasteries of southern Serbia and the imposing fortresses along the Danube.

Since the withdrawal of Croatia, Slovenia, Bosnia-Hercegovina and Macedonia in 1991, Yugoslavia (Jugoslavija) has become a mere 'Greater Serbia', with oppressed Hungarian, Slavic Muslim and Albanian minorities. The federal government in Belgrade has been punished by sanctions and bombing for its role in Bosnia and Kosovo. The NATO bombing campaign in response to Yugoslav ethnic cleansing in Kosovo ended with Kosovo becoming a UN-NATO protectorate.

AT A GLANCE	
Capital:	Belgrade
Population:	11.2 million (1999 est.)
Languages:	Serbia and Montenegro – Serbian (Serbo-Croatian) Kosovo – Albanian
Currency:	1 Yugoslav novi dinar (DIN) = 100 paras

Facts about Yugoslavia

HISTORY

In the middle of the 6th century, Slavic tribes (Serbs, Croats and Slovenes) occupied much of the Balkan Peninsula.

An independent Serbian kingdom appeared in 1217. Serbia had its 'Golden Age' during the reign of Stefan Dušan (1346–55), who built many frescoed Orthodox monasteries. After Stefan's death Serbia declined, and at the Battle of Kosovo on 28 June 1389 the Serbian army was defeated by the Ottoman Turks, ushering in 500 years of Islamic rule.

A revolt in 1815 led to de facto Serbian independence from the Turks. Autonomy was recognised in 1829 and complete Serbian independence was achieved in 1878.

On 28 June 1914, Austria-Hungary used the assassination of Archduke Ferdinand by a Serb nationalist as an excuse to invade Serbia, thus sparking WWI. After the war, Croatia, Slovenia and Vojvodina were united with Serbia, Montenegro and Macedonia to form the Kingdom of Serbs, Croats and Slovenes under the king of Serbia. In 1929 the name was changed to Yugoslavia.

On 25 March 1941, Yugoslavia joined the Tripartite Alliance, a fascist military pact supported by the Nazis. This sparked a military coup that installed Peter II as king, and Yugoslavia abruptly withdrew from the alliance. Livid, Hitler ordered an immediate invasion and the country was carved up between Germany, Italy, Hungary and Bulgaria.

Almost immediately the Communist Party, under Josip Broz Tito, declared an armed uprising, laying the basis for a future communist-led Yugoslavia under Tito.

Tito broke with Stalin in 1948 and, as a reward, received US$2 billion in economic and military aid from the USA and UK between 1950 and 1960. Growing regional inequalities led, however, to increased tension as Slovenia, Croatia and Kosovo demanded greater autonomy within the Yugoslav federation.

In 1986 the Serbian Academy of Sciences prepared a memorandum promoting Serbian nationalism. A year later Slobodan Milošević took over as Communist Party leader in Serbia. His vision of a 'Greater Serbia' horrified Slovenia and Croatia which declared their independence on 25 June 1991. In response the Yugoslav federal army invaded Slovenia. As punishment the European Community (EC), now the EU, imposed a weapons embargo on Yugoslavia.

On 15 January 1992, the EC recognised the independence of Croatia and Slovenia,

YUGOSLAVIA (JUGOSLAVIJA)

Note: At the time of publication the railway network in Kosovo was not operating

The Effects of War

The disruptions are now mainly economic, affecting the traveller mostly when changing money. However, visas for Yugoslavia (Serbia) are much more difficult to obtain and some embassies in Belgrade are closed. There seems to be no negative reaction towards Western travellers but caution is always advised.

prompting Macedonia and Bosnia-Hercegovina to demand recognition of their own independence. Montenegro alone voted to remain in Yugoslavia.

In Kosovo, economic neglect and discrimination led to resistance by the Albanian majority and the formation of the Kosovo Liberation Army (KLA). The Serbian response was to attack and clear out Albanian villages on the pretext of eradicating the KLA.

In March 1999, peace talks in Paris failed when Serbia rejected a US-brokered peace plan. In reply Serbian forces moved to clear the country of its Albanian population. Hundreds of thousands fleeing into Macedonia and Albania galvanised the US and NATO into a 78-day bombing campaign. On 12 June 1999 Serbian forces withdrew from Kosovo.

Following elections held in September 2000 president Slobodan Milošević was forced to concede defeat and relinquish power by popular demonstrations. At the time of writing Vojislav Kostunica holds the presidency, with further elections scheduled for December 2000.

GEOGRAPHY
Mountains and plateaus account for the lower half of 102,350-sq-km Yugoslavia. Its interior and southern mountains belong to the Balkan range, while the coastal range is an arm of the Dinaric Alps.

Most of the rivers flow north into the Danube, which runs through Yugoslavia for 588km.

CLIMATE
The north has a continental climate with cold winters and hot, humid summers. The coastal region has hot, dry summers and relatively cold winters with heavy snowfall inland.

POPULATION & PEOPLE
There have been no official revisions to the population total of 11 million since the 1991 census (1999 estimate is 11.21 million). Then the ethnic proportions were Serbs (including Montenegrins) (67.3%), Albanians (16.6%), Hungarians (3.3%) and Slavic Muslims (3.1%), plus Croats, Roma, Slovaks, Macedonians, Romanians, Bulgarians, Turks and Ukrainians. These figures will have changed especially as there are now some 600,000 war refugees in Serbia and Montenegro.

Population estimates in 2000 for Yugoslavia's largest cities are Belgrade (two million), Novi Sad (250,000), Niš (230,000), Prishtina (210,000) and Subotica (160,000). Nearly a quarter of Vojvodina's population is Hungarian and there are large Slavic Muslim and Albanian minorities in Montenegro and southern Serbia.

SOCIETY & CONDUCT
The Serbs are proud and hospitable people, despite their newly tarnished reputation. Respect should be shown for all religious establishments and customs. Learning some basic Serbian, Hungarian or Albanian will open doors and create smiles.

Be careful when discussing politics, as nationalist passions can be unpredictable. It's striking the way Serbs who seem to be reasonable people suddenly become tense when the subject of Kosovo comes up.

LANGUAGE
Serbian is the common language, though many Yugoslavs speak German and (to a lesser extent) French. Albanian is spoken in Kosovo.

Hungarians in Vojvodina and Albanians in Kosovo use the Latin alphabet. In Montenegro there's a mixture of Latin and Cyrillic, while in Serbia nearly everything is in Cyrillic. (For an explanation of the Cyrillic alphabet, see the Macedonian language section at the back of this book.)

Facts for the Visitor

HIGHLIGHTS
Yugoslavia has a wealth of castles, including the baroque Petrovaradin Citadel at Novi Sad. The old capital of Cetinje and the

UNESCO-listed walled town of Kotor, both in Montenegro, will please romantics. Of the beach resorts, Budva is chic but Ulcinj has more atmosphere and is cheaper. Montenegro's Tara Canyon will amaze nature lovers.

SUGGESTED ITINERARIES

Visit Serbia first and leave from Kosovo if you're going to both places. A Kosovo stamp in your passport may invalidate your Yugoslav visa.

Three days
  Visit either Serbia (Belgrade and Novi Sad) or Montenegro (Budva, Cetinje and Kotor) or Kosovo (Prizren).
One week
  Visit two of the above.
Two weeks
  Visit all areas covered in this chapter for two of the above.

PLANNING
When to Go

Avoid the July/August high season along the Montenegrin coast, when accommodation is more expensive and difficult to find, and public transport is crowded. For skiers the season in Mount Durmitor National Park is from December to March.

Maps

Freytag & Berndt produce a good map of all of former Yugoslavia with the new countries. The *Savezna Republika Jugoslavija Autokarta* map, showing the new borders, and the detailed Belgrade city map *Plan Grada Beograd* are both free from the Tourist Organisation of Belgrade.

TOURIST OFFICES

There are tourist offices in Belgrade, Novi Sad and Prizren. Commercial travel agencies such as Montenegroturist and Putnik will often provide local information.

VISAS & DOCUMENTS

Most visitors require a Yugoslav visa for Serbia; you don't need one for Montenegro or Kosovo. Allow at least six weeks for obtaining a visa. Australian citizens are charged A$50 and UK passport holders as much as UK£30 for a visa. You will need either a pre-arranged travel itinerary with confirmed hotel reservations or an invitation from a Yugoslav citizen (all in writing) before your application is considered. NATO-country passport holders may be refused a visa.

EMBASSIES & CONSULATES
Yugoslav Embassies & Consulates

In addition to those listed, Yugoslav embassies or consulates can also be found in its neighbours' capitals.

Australia (☎ 02-9362 3003, fax 9362 4555, ✉ yugcon@rosebay.matra.com.au) 12 Trelawney St, Woollahra, NSW 2025
Canada (☎ 613-233 6289) 17 Blackburn Ave, Ottawa, Ontario, K1N 8A2
France (☎ 01 40 72 24 24, fax 01 40 72 24 11) 54 rue Faisanderie 16e, Paris
Netherlands (☎ 070-363 2397, fax 360 2421) Groot Hertoginnelaan 30, 2517 EG, The Hague
UK (☎ 0171-370 6105, fax 370 3838) 5 Lexham Gardens, London, W8 5JJ
USA (☎ 202-462 6566) 2410 California St NW, Washington DC, 20008

Embassies & Consulates in Yugoslavia

Due to the war, the Canadian, UK and US embassies are closed. Visas are payable in US dollars or Deutschmarks, cash only. The following are in Belgrade.

Australia (☎ 624 655, fax 628 189) Cika Ljubina 13. Open 8.30 am to 4.30 pm weekdays.
Bulgaria (☎ 646 422) Birčaninova 26. Open 8 am to 3 pm weekdays.
Hungary (☎ 444 0472) Ivana Milutinovića 75. Open 9 to 11 am weekdays.
Romania (☎ 646 071) Kneza Miloša 70. Open 8 am to 3 pm weekdays.
Slovakia (☎ 311 1052) Bulevar Umetnosti 18, Novi Beograd. Open 8 to 11 am weekdays except Wednesday.

MONEY
Currency

Kosovo has adopted the Deutschmark (DM), which is also the de facto currency of Montenegro. Serbia clings to the dinar (DIN) out of national pride but people favour the Deutschmark as a hard currency.

Exchange Rates

country	unit		Deutschmark		dinar
Australia	A$1	=	DM1.27	=	6.88DIN
Canada	C$1	=	DM1.46	=	7.91DIN

euro	€1	=	DM1.96	=	10.59DIN
France	10FF	=	DM2.98	=	16.14DIN
Germany	DM1	=	–	=	5.41DIN
Japan	¥100	=	DM1.99	=	10.76DIN
NZ	NZ$1	=	DM0.97	=	5.25DIN
UK	£1	=	DM3.21	=	17.37DIN
USA	US$1	=	DM2.15	=	11.66DIN

Exchanging Money

Bring Deutschmarks in cash, as travellers cheques can be difficult to exchange. Banks change Deutschmarks at the unofficial rate of 22.5 DIN although your receipt will only show the official rate of 6 DIN to DM1. The street rate in Montenegro is 26 DIN to DM1. There are no ATMs in Yugoslavia.

POST & COMMUNICATIONS
Post

To mail a parcel, take it unsealed to a main post office for inspection. Allow plenty of time to check the repacking and complete the transaction.

You can receive mail at poste restantes in all towns for a small charge.

Telephone

Yugoslavia's country code is ☎ 381. Drop the initial zero from city codes when dialling from abroad.

International calls made from main post offices cost 42 DIN per minute to the USA and Australia. International calls from cardphones in Belgrade are possible but the limited value of the phonecards (50 DIN or 90 DIN) only allows a short call. The access code for outgoing international calls is ☎ 99.

Fax

Faxes can be sent from post offices or any large hotel, which will charge 139 DIN per page to Australia or the USA and 101 DIN to Europe.

Email & Internet Access

There are Internet cafes in most towns in this chapter (for details see under Information in relevant town sections).

INTERNET RESOURCES

The Tourist Organisation of Belgrade has a useful Web site (www.belgradetourism .org.yu). Check out www.montenet.org for information on Montenegro. Some of the information on both sites is out of date.

BOOKS

Recommended are *The Destruction of Yugoslavia* by Branka Magaš; *Yugoslavia: Death of a Nation* by Laura Silber and Allan Little; and *Blood and Vengeance* by Chuck Sudetic (Norton).

After Yugoslavia by Zoë Brân (Lonely Planet Journeys) retraces the author's 1978 trip through the now much-changed former Yugoslavia.

TOILETS

Restaurant and hotel toilets are a cleaner option than public toilets, which usually cost 2 DIN or 3 DIN in Belgrade.

WOMEN TRAVELLERS

Other than cursory interest shown by Yugoslav men towards solo women travellers, travel is hassle-free and easy. In Muslim areas it's a good idea to dress conservatively (ie, show as little skin as possible).

GAY & LESBIAN TRAVELLERS

Homosexuality has been legal in Yugoslavia since 1932. For more information, contact Arkadia, Brace Baruh 11, 11000 Belgrade.

DISABLED TRAVELLERS

Few public buildings or streets have facilities for wheelchairs. Access could be problematic in Belgrade with its numerous inclines.

DANGERS & ANNOYANCES

Travel in northern Serbia and Montenegro is safe but south-eastern Serbia around the Kosovo border should be avoided. (For travel in Kosovo, see the Kosovo section later in this chapter.) Belgrade is a remarkably safe city, perhaps because of the heavy police presence. Throughout Yugoslavia theft is rare.

Many Yugoslavs are chain-smokers who can't imagine that their habit might inconvenience nonsmokers, so choose your seat in public places carefully. The 'no smoking' signs are often ignored.

It's wise to avoid political discussions, and don't give police the impression that you are anything but a tourist. Do not photograph police or military-guarded buildings.

Travel in the Albanian parts of Kosovo is reasonably safe but there are many landmines and unexploded bombs in the countryside. Don't go to areas like Mitrovica where there is Albanian-Serb tension.

YUGOSLAVIA

LEGAL MATTERS

If you are visiting Serbia, it is sensible to register with your embassy in Belgrade in case of problems. Citizens of Canada, the UK and USA, whose Belgrade embassies are closed, should check about registration with their governments.

BUSINESS HOURS

Banks are open 7 am to 7 pm weekdays, until noon on Saturday. On weekdays shops open between 6 am and 8 am, many shops close for lunch from noon to 4 pm but stay open until 8 pm. Department stores, supermarkets and self-service restaurants generally stay open throughout the day. On Saturday, shops stay open until 2 or 3 pm.

PUBLIC HOLIDAYS & SPECIAL EVENTS

Public holidays include: 1 and 2 January (New Year), 6 and 7 January (Orthodox Christmas), 27 April (Day of the FR of Yugoslavia), 1 and 2 May (International Labour Days), 9 May (Victory Day) and 29 and 30 November (Republic Days). In addition, 28 March (Constitution Day) and 7 July (Uprising Day) are holidays in Serbia and 13 July is a holiday in Montenegro. If any of these should fall on a Sunday, then the following Monday or Tuesday is a holiday.

Many shops close during Orthodox Easter, which falls anywhere between one and three weeks after regular Easter.

Belgrade hosts a film festival in February, a jazz festival in August, an international theatre festival in September and a festival of classical music in October.

ACCOMMODATION

Accommodation is extremely expensive. In summer you can camp along the Montenegrin coast, though many camping grounds are closed due to the absence of tourists. There are summer-only branches of Hostelling International (HI) hostels in Kopaonik and Ulcinj. Yugoslavia's HI representative is Ferijalni Savez Beograd (☎ 011-324 8550, fax 322 0762), Makedonska 22, Belgrade.

FOOD

The cheapest breakfast is *burek*, a greasy layered pie made with *sir* (cheese) or *meso* (meat) or *Krompirusa* (potato).

Serbia is famous for grilled meats such as *evap ići* (mince-meat kebabs), *pljeskavica* (spicy hamburger steak) and *ražnjići* (pork or veal kebabs with onions and peppers). Serbian *duve* is grilled pork cutlets with spiced stewed peppers, zucchini and tomatoes in rice.

Other popular dishes are *musaka* (aubergine and potato baked in layers with minced meat), *sarma* (cabbage stuffed with minced meat and rice), *kapama* (stewed lamb, onions and spinach served with yoghurt) and *punjena tikvica* (zucchini stuffed with minced meat and rice).

Most restaurants serve the vegetarian *Švopska salata* (Serb salad – raw peppers, onions and tomatoes, with oil, vinegar and chilli). Other vegetarian options are *gibanica* (layered cheese pie) and *zeljanica* (cheese pie with spinach) or the ubiquitous pizza.

DRINKS

Pivo (beer) is always available. Yugoslav cognac (grape brandy) is called *vinjak*. Coffee is usually served Turkish-style, boiled in a small individual pot, though espresso is served in many cafes.

Getting There & Away

For most travellers the easiest access is by train (Inter-Rail passes are valid in Yugoslavia; Eurail passes are not). Reservations are usually required on international rail services. Services between Belgrade and Budapest take six hours and a ticket costs 1400 DIN, while trains to Vienna take 11 hours and cost 2200 DIN. Trains running to Vienna, Venice and Munich all go through Zagreb; the cost for the 12½-hour journey is 720 DIN. The fare for the overnight train to Bucharest is 1600 DIN.

The train to Greece terminates at Thessaloniki and the fare for the 16-hour journey is 1100 DIN. There are two trains running to Sofia (Bulgaria); the fare is 690 DIN and the trip takes nine hours. No trains run through Kosovo, and there are none to Turkey.

There are daily international buses from Belgrade, Podgorica and Prishtina to many European destinations. Journeys to/from Croatia require a change of bus at the border.

In summer, ferries operate from Bari and Ancona in Italy to Bar in Montenegro.

Getting Around

Though trains are generally the best way to get around, you'll need to use buses in Montenegro once you get to Bar. Apart from expensive taxis, buses are the only way to travel in Kosovo.

Jugoslovenske Železnice (JŽ) provides adequate rail services between Subotica and Novi Sad, Belgrade and Niš. A highly scenic line runs from Belgrade down to the coast at Bar. There are four classes of train: *ekspresni* (express), *poslovni* (rapid), *brzi* (fast) and *putnicki* (slow), so make sure you have the right ticket for your train.

Serbia

BELGRADE (БЕОГРАД)
☎ 011

Belgrade (Beograd) is strategically situated on the southern edge of the Carpathian basin, where the Sava River joins the Danube. Just east of the city is the Morava Valley, route of the famous 'Stamboul Road' from Turkey to Central Europe.

Destroyed and rebuilt 40 times in its 2300-year history, Belgrade has never quite managed to pick up all the pieces. It is nonetheless a vibrant city of almost two million people, with fine restaurants and cafes – an interesting place to explore.

Orientation

To reach town from the train station, walk east along Milovana Milovanovića for a block, then go straight up Balkanska to Terazije, the heart of modern Belgrade. Kneza Mihaila, Belgrade's lively pedestrian boulevard, runs north-west through Stari Grad from Terazije to the citadel in Kalemegdan Park.

Information

Tourist Offices The helpful Tourist Organisation of Belgrade (☎/fax 635 343) has an office in the underpass below the Jugoslovenska Knjiga bookshop on Terazije. Hours are 9 am to 8 pm weekdays and 9 am to 4 pm Saturday. The tourist office at the airport is open 8 am to 8 pm daily.

Money The JIK Banka across the park in front of the train station is open 8 am to 8 pm weekdays, and 8 am to 3 pm Saturday.

American Express travellers cheques can only be changed at the Astral Banka on the corner of Maršala Birjuzova and Pop Lukina; at the airport branch; and at the Komercijalna Banka on Trg Nikole Pašića.

There are a few private exchange offices in Belgrade. The very central VODR, near the tourist office, is open 9 am to 7 pm weekdays and 9 am to 3 pm Saturday. Another is near Zeleni Venac market, 300 metres north of the train station. Private kiosks (except those with Politika or Duvan signs) will change Deutschmarks.

Post & Communications The telephone centre at the main post office at Takovska 2 is open 7 am to 10 pm daily. Other telephone centres are at the more central post office on Zmaj Jovina (open 24 hours) and by the train station (open until at least 10 pm daily).

Note that Belgrade is still introducing seven-digit phone numbers.

Café Sezam (☎ 322 7231, @ info@sezampro.yu), 2nd floor, Skadarska 40c, is open 10 am to 11 pm. Another Internet cafe is on the ground floor of the Bioskop Doma Omladine cinema on Moše Pijade, where it costs about 40 DIN per hour.

Travel Agencies Putnik Travel Agency (☎ 330 669, fax 334 505), Terazije 27, sells domestic and international tickets. There's also another Putnik office adjacent to Turist Biro Lasta (☎ 641 251), another travel agency, which sells tickets for international buses. BS Tours (☎ 361 9616), Gavril Principa 46, also runs buses to Croatia.

Beograd Tours (☎ 641 258, fax 687 447), Milovana Milovanovića 5, books international train tickets and couchettes and sleepers within Yugoslavia.

Bookshops You can buy international magazines and newspapers at the Plato Bookshop, Vasina 17, or at The International Press Service Bookshop in the basement of Bilet Servis in the centre of Trg Republike.

Libraries The City Library is at the Kalemegdan end of Kneza Mihaila. Here you

CENTRAL BELGRADE

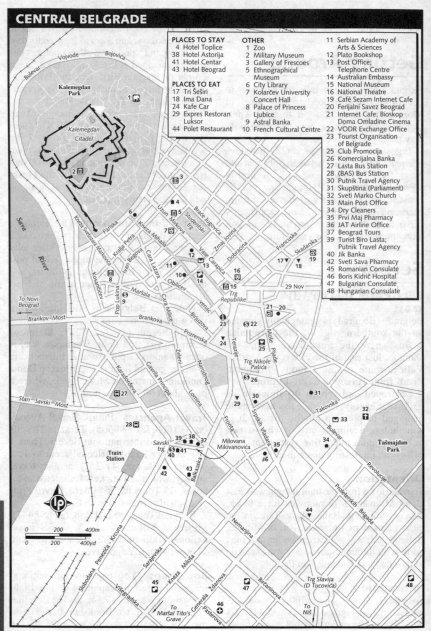

PLACES TO STAY
4 Hotel Toplice
38 Hotel Astorija
41 Hotel Centar
43 Hotel Beograd

PLACES TO EAT
17 Tri Šeširi
18 Ima Dana
24 Kafe Car
29 Expres Restoran Luksor
44 Polet Restaurant

OTHER
1 Zoo
2 Military Museum
3 Gallery of Frescoes
5 Ethnographical Museum
6 City Library
7 Kolarčev University Concert Hall
8 Palace of Princess Ljubice
9 Astral Banka
10 French Cultural Centre
11 Serbian Academy of Arts & Sciences
12 Plato Bookshop
13 Post Office; Telephone Centre
14 Australian Embassy
15 National Museum
16 National Theatre
19 Café Sezam Internet Cafe
20 Ferijalni Savez Beograd
21 Internet Cafe; Bioskop Doma Omladine Cinema
22 VODR Exchange Office
23 Tourist Organisation of Belgrade
25 Club Promocija
26 Komercijalna Banka
27 Lasta Bus Station
28 (BAS) Bus Station
30 Putnik Travel Agency
31 Skupština (Parliament)
32 Sveti Marko Church
33 Main Post Office
34 Dry Cleaners
35 Prvi Maj Pharmacy
36 JAT Airline Office
37 Beograd Tours
39 Turist Biro Lasta; Putnik Travel Agency
40 Jik Banka
42 Sveti Sava Pharmacy
45 Romanian Consulate
46 Boris Kidrič Hospital
47 Bulgarian Consulate
48 Hungarian Consulate

can do some photocopying, or have a coffee or a beer in the snack bar.

Laundry The dry cleaners at Resavska 6, just off Bulevar Revolucije, has a 24-hour service. It's open 7 am to 8 pm weekdays and 8 am to 3 pm Saturday.

Left Luggage The left-luggage office at the BAS bus station is open 6 am to 10 pm and costs 15 DIN per piece.

The train station's left-luggage office is at the end of track No 9 and is open 24 hours. Left luggage costs 10 DIN per piece. You'll need to show your passport at both places.

Medical Services The Boris Kidrič Hospital (☎ 361 9088), Pasterova 1, has a special clinic for foreigners, open 7 am to 1 pm Tuesday to Saturday (consultations cost 20 DIN).

Two 24-hour pharmacies are the Prvi Maj, Srpskih Vladara 9; and the Sveti Sava, Nemanjina 2.

Things to See
Unless otherwise noted, all museums are closed on Monday.

The **Kalemegdan Citadel**, a strategic hilltop fortress, has ancient gates, Orthodox churches, Muslim tombs and Turkish baths. Ivan Meštrović's *Monument of Gratitude to France* (1930) is at the citadel's entrance. The large **Military Museum** on the battlements presents a complete history of Yugoslavia in 53 rooms.

Next to Kalemegdan Citadel is **Stari Grad**, the oldest part of Belgrade. The best museums are here, especially the **National Museum**, Trg Republike, which has archaeological exhibits downstairs, paintings upstairs.

A few blocks away at Studentski trg 13 is the **Ethnographical Museum**, with an excellent collection of Serbian costumes and folk art. Not far away, at Cara Uroša 20, is the **Gallery of Frescoes**, with full-size replicas of paintings from remote churches in Serbia and Macedonia.

Belgrade's most memorable museum is the **Palace of Princess Ljubice**, on the corner of Kneza Svetozara Markovića and Kralja Petra. It's an authentic Balkan-style palace built in 1831, complete with period furnishings.

The marble **grave of Maršal Tito** is at his former residence on Bulevar Mira, a few

kilometres south of the centre; take trolleybus No 40 or 41 south from Kneza Miloša 64.

Escape the bustle of Belgrade on **Ada Ciganlija**, an island park in the Sava River, just upstream from the city. In summer you can swim in the river, rent a bicycle or stroll among the trees. Small cafes overlooking the beach sell cold beer at reasonable prices.

Places to Stay
Accommodation in Belgrade is very expensive. Although prices are in dinar, they reflect the street exchange rate for Deutschmarks, so expect prices to go up as the dinar depreciates. You can save money by overnight bus or train travel.

Hotels The cheapest central place is *Hotel Centar* (☎ 644 055, fax 657 838, Savski trg 7), opposite the train station. Basic doubles (no singles) are 440 DIN. *Hotel Toplice* (☎ 634 222, fax 626 459, Kralja Petra 56) charges 443/636 DIN for singles/doubles, including breakfast.

Hotel Beograd (☎ 645 199, fax 643 746, Nemanjina 6), visible from the train station, has time-worn rooms for 458/716 DIN, including breakfast. *Hotel Astorija* (☎ 645 422, fax 686 437, Milovana Milovanovića 1), has rooms with breakfast for 520/790 DIN.

Places to Eat
Expres Restoran Luksor (*Balkanska 7*) is the cheapest self-service place in town. A great spot for breakfast burek is the *Burek i Pecivo* (*Nemanjina 5*), just below Hotel Beograd. *Kafe Car* (*Terazije 4*), near the tourist office, is perfect for an espresso and croissant.

For inexpensive seafood try the *Polet Restaurant* (*Njegoševa 1*). Between 1 and 6 pm on weekdays there's a special set menu of *čorba* (spicy fish soup), salad, bread and a main dish of fish and vegetables.

Restaurants in the Bohemian quarter along Skadarska stage open-air folkloric performances with dinner – try *Tri Šeširi* or *Ima Dana*. Prices are a bit high, but the atmosphere is good. For cheaper eats, there are good *hamburger stands* at the bottom end of Skadarska.

Entertainment
During winter, opera performances are held at the elegant *National Theatre* on Trg Republike. Yugoslavs aren't pretentious about

YUGOSLAVIA

theatre dress – jeans are OK. For classical music try the concert hall at *Kolarčev University (Studentski trg 5)*. In October a festival of classical music is held here. The *Belgrade Philharmonia* is hidden away at Studentski trg 11, opposite the Ethnographical Museum. Concerts also take place in the hall of the *Serbian Academy of Arts & Sciences (Kneza Mihaila 35)*.

The Bilet Servis, Trg Republike 5, sells tickets to many events, and the staff speak English.

The disco *Club Promocija* is at the end of a dark lane at Nušićeva 8, just off Terazije; it's closed on Sunday.

Getting There & Away

There are overnight buses to destinations throughout Yugoslavia. Posted destinations are in Cyrillic only. When possible buy tickets in advance from a travel agency – it's easier.

For information on international trains to/from Belgrade, see the Getting There & Away section earlier in this chapter. Overnight domestic trains with couchettes or sleepers run from Belgrade to most major cities, including Bar (8½ hours) for between 80 DIN and 560 DIN, depending on class and number in the compartment. Add to that a ticket for 284/200 DIN for 1st/2nd class.

Getting Around

Private buses have joined Belgrade's buses, trams and trolleybuses. The 3 DIN fare is paid to the conductor.

Taxis charge 10 DIN at flag fall, and a trip around the centre should cost between 50 DIN and 60 DIN. Make sure the meter is being used.

VOJVODINA (ВОЈВОЛИНА)

Until Serbian nationalists took control of Vojvodina in 1990, the province's 345,000 Hungarians had fared better than Hungarian minorities in Romania and Slovakia. Since then the minority has come under increasing pressure; Serbs make up most of the region's population.

Novi Sad (Нови Сад)
☎ 021

Novi Sad, capital of Vojvodina, is a friendly, modern city situated at a strategic bend of the Danube. The city developed in the 18th century when a Habsburg fortress was built overlooking the river. Novi Sad remained part of the Austro-Hungarian empire until 1918 and, even today, retains a Hungarian flavour. The main sights can be covered in a couple of hours or you can make a leisurely day of it.

Orientation & Information The adjacent train and bus stations are at the end of Bulevar Oslobođenja, on the north-western side of the city centre. There is a tourist office to the right as you exit the train station.

It's a brisk 20 minutes' walk to the centre; otherwise catch bus No 4 from the station to Bulevar Mihajla Pupina, then ask directions to the tourist office at Dunavska 27, in a quaint old part of town. This office has brochures and maps of Novi Sad.

KSR Beograd Tours, on Svetozara Miletića, sells domestic and international train tickets.

Things to See The two branches of the Muzej Vojvodine (Vojvodina Museum) at Dunavska 35 and 39, near the tourist office, have exhibits on the Vojvodina region and are worth a visit. Entry is 3 DIN; closed Monday.

Walk across the old bridge to majestic **Petrovaradin Citadel**, the 'Gibraltar of the Danube', designed by French architect Vauban and built between 1699 and 1780. The stairs beside the large church in the lower town lead up to the fortress. The citadel has two small museums but the chief pleasure is simply to walk along the walls and enjoy the splendid views. From here you can also see the damage that NATO bombing did to the Danube bridges.

Places to Stay There's a large year-round *autocamp* (☎ 368 400) near the Danube at Ribarsko Ostrvo, with bungalows for 496 DIN. Bus No 4 runs frequently from the train station to Liman via the city centre; from the end of the line walk towards the river.

The most appealing of Novi Sad's six hotels is *Hotel Vojvodina* (☎ 622 122, fax 615 445), right on Trg Slobode. It has an attractive pastel facade but is expensive at 700/1000 DIN for singles/doubles, including breakfast.

Places to Eat *Sloboda Grill 11*, on Modene in the centre, is cheap and unassuming.

Atina Restaurant, next to the Catholic church on Trg Slobode, has a self-service section and a full-service restaurant at the back. It's nothing special.

Entertainment The *Red Cow* Irish pub is a trendy spot for Guinness (cans only) and for an evening out. Enter via an arched alleyway off Zmaj Jovina or from an alleyway off Dunavska.

Getting There & Away Novi Sad is on the main international train line to/from Yugoslavia (see the Getting There & Away section earlier in this chapter). Domestic trains to Subotica (1½ hours) and Belgrade (1¼ hours) run every two hours.

Subotica (Суботица)
☎ 024
Subotica is a large Hungarian-speaking city 10km from the Yugoslav-Hungarian border. Subotica is a useful transit point to/from Szeged (Hungary) and the train station is just a short walk from the centre of town.

Places to Stay & Eat The only hotel in Subotica is the seven-storey *Hotel Patria* (☎ *554 500, fax 551 762*) on Đure Đakovića, three blocks to the left as you exit the train station. Singles/doubles are 1212/1824 DIN with bath and breakfast.

There is a dearth of restaurants in the town centre. An exception is the *Boss Pizzeria (Engelsova 7)* off Borisa Kidriča, a relaxing spot for pizza and a beer.

Getting There & Away There are two local trains a day to/from Szeged, Hungary (115 DIN, 1¾ hours). A daily bus links Subotica to Szeged (DM5). Bus fares to Hungary must be paid for in Deutschmarks or Hungarian forints.

Subotica is on the main international train line between Belgrade and Budapest (see the Getting There & Away section earlier in this chapter).

Montenegro (Црна Гора)

The 13,812-sq-km Republic of Montenegro (Crna Gora) has impressive bare limestone mountains plummeting down to an Adriatic coastline. This is a very popular holiday spot with the rest of Yugoslavia, especially in July and August.

North of Podgorica, both railway and road run through the Morača Canyon, giving fantastic views of canyon walls and clear emerald waters, while 40km west of Mojkovac is the 1.3km deep Tara Canyon. Other striking features are the winding Bay of Kotor and the vast Lake Skadar shared with Albania. Of historical interest are the old towns of Budva, Cetinje and Kotor.

BAR (БАР)
☎ 085
Bar is a white apartment-block city fronting a bland commercial centre. It is, however, Yugoslavia's only port and the terminus of the railway from Belgrade. If you find a cheap private room, Bar makes a good base for day trips to Ulcinj, Cetinje, Kotor and Budva.

Orientation & Information
The ferry terminal is only a few hundred metres from the centre of town. The adjacent bus and train stations are 2km south-east.

Tourist information is very limited but your best bet is to try Montenegro Tourist by the ferry terminal. Ask for directions to the Lunar Café, which is opposite a handy Internet cafe.

Places to Stay
The Putnik Turist Biro (*☎/fax 313 621*), near the ferry terminal, arranges *private rooms* for around DM10 per person.

Hotel Topolica (☎ 311 244, fax 312 731, @ htpkorali@cg.yu), a crumbling four-storey relic by the beach, is the only hotel in town. Rooms are DM33/50 for a single/double.

Getting There & Away
Four trains a day (two with couchettes) travel to/from Belgrade (DM9.50, nine hours). There are buses to all destinations along the coast. There are ferries to Bari and Ancona (both in Italy), and starting from July 2000 to Corfu (Greece). The frequency of departures depends upon the season.

ULCINJ (УЛЦИЊ)
☎ 085
Ulcinj, 26km south-east of Bar, is a popular summer resort for Serbs. It gets very crowded in July and August.

The Turks held Bar and Ulcinj for over 300 years, and today there are many Muslim Albanians in Ulcinj. Many older women in this town still wear traditional Islamic dress, especially on market day (Friday).

Buses to/from Bar (DM2) run every few hours.

Orientation & Information

Mala Plaža is the small beach below the old town. Ulcinj's main drag is 26 Novembar.

Any travel agency should be able to help with tourist information. The telephone centre is in the main post office, at the foot of 26 Novembar.

Places to Stay

Montenegro Travel Agency (☎/fax 51 522, Bratstva Jedinstva), a few hundred metres from the bus stop, has *rooms* from DM4/8 for a single/double depending on the class of accommodation and the time of year.

BUDVA (БУДВА)
☎ 086

Budva is Yugoslavia's top beach resort, with a stunning walled citadel and high coastal mountains forming a magnificent backdrop. Budva is not cheap, but prices drop outside the high season.

Orientation & Information

The bus station is 1km from the old town. The main square is at the end of Mediteranska in the old town, by the harbour.

Staff at travel agencies and car rental offices will be able to help with tourist information.

Places to Stay

Autocamp Avala (☎ 51 205) is 2km southeast of town in Boreti. It's crowded with caravans, but at least it's near the beach. Avala is open from June to September.

The helpful Emona Globtour (☎ 51 020, fax 52 827, ☻ mpalic@cg.yu), Mediteranska 23, can arrange *private rooms*, or just look out for signs *sobe, zimmer* or *rooms*.

The modern *Hotel Mogren* (☎ 51 780, fax 51 750), just outside the northern gate of the old town, has rooms for DM80/130 in high season and DM60/90 at other times.

Getting There & Away

There are almost hourly buses to Podgorica (74km) via Cetinje (31km) and seven a day

to Bar (38km). Buses also go to Belgrade, Žvabljak and other parts of Yugoslavia.

If coming by train from Belgrade, get off at Podgorica and catch a bus to Budva. In the other direction it's probably best to take a bus from Budva to Bar and catch the train to Belgrade there, since many people board the train in Podgorica.

KOTOR
☎ 082

Kotor is something of a secret. Not only is the town at the head of southern Europe's longest and deepest fjord but it also has a walled medieval city.

There are frequent buses from Budva but it's enjoyable to stay within the old town. The Meridian Travel Agency (☎ 11 188, fax 11 226, ☻ travel@cg.yu) can arrange *private rooms* from DM10/20 for a single/double in the low season and DM15/30 in the high season.

CETINJE (ЦЕТИЊЕ)
☎ 086

Cetinje is the old capital of Montenegro, and the subject of songs and epic poems. Much remains of old Cetinje, from museums and palaces to mansions and monasteries. It's worth spending the night here if you can find an inexpensive place to stay.

Orientation & Information

The bus station is 500m from the main square, Balšića Pazar (walk left out of the station and take the first right).

Places to Stay

For *private rooms* ask at Intours (☎ 31 157), marked 'Vincom Duty Free Shop', next to the post office.

Getting There & Away

There are many buses a day between Cetinje and Podgorica (45km) and to Budva (31km). Cetinje is an easy day trip from Bar; catch an early train to Podgorica and then switch to a Cetinje-bound bus.

DURMITOR NATIONAL PARK
☎ 083

Montenegro's Durmitor National Park is a popular hiking and mountaineering area just west of Žabljak, a ski resort and the highest town in Yugoslavia.

Some 18 mountain lakes dot the slopes of the Durmitor Range south-west of Žabljak. You can walk around the largest lake, **Crno jezero** (Black Lake), 3km from Žabljak, in an hour or two, and swim in its waters in summer. The national park office next to Hotel Durmitor sells good maps of the park. Be prepared for changeable weather even in summer.

Durmitor's claim to fame is the 1.3km-deep **Tara Canyon**, which cuts dramatically into the mountain plateau for 80km. Čurevac is a good viewing place and is either a 17km return hike or DM7 taxi trip from Žabljak.

White-Water Rafting

There are rafting trips down the steep forested Tara Gorge, beginning at Splavište near the Đurđevića Tara bridge. For information, contact Ski Centar Durmitor (☎ 61 144, fax 61 579) in Žabljak, or the same organisation in Podgorica (☎/fax 081-242 387). One- and two-day raft trips depart from Žabljak every Tuesday and Friday between June and September.

Places to Stay

The English-speaking owner of the Sveti Đorđije tourist agency (☎/fax 61 367), just opposite the turn-off to Hotel Jezera, can arrange *private rooms* for DM10 per person.

The central *Hotel Žabljak (☎ 88 300)*, charges DM49 per person, including breakfast. Cheaper is the basic *Hotel Durmitor (☎ 61 278)*, at the entrance to the national park, a 15 minutes' walk from town. Rooms with half-board cost DM24/36 a single/double but there's no hot water.

Getting There & Away

From the north, take a bus from Belgrade to Pljevlja (334km), then one of two daily buses to Žabljak (57km). From the south, catch a bus from Podgorica or Budva to Žabljak. When you arrive in Žabljak, inquire at the bus station about booking onward buses.

Kosovo

Since June 1999, Kosovo (Kosova in Albanian) has been administered as a UN-NATO protectorate.

Before ethnic cleansing, an estimated two million people occupied Kosovo's 10,887 sq km, making it a densely populated region. Today it is a divided region, with the remaining Serbs living in ghettos.

The Albanians adopted Islam after the Turkish conquest and today the region has a definite Muslim air, from food and dress to the ubiquitous mosques.

History

Following their defeat in 1389 by the Turks, the Serbs abandoned the region to the Albanians, descendants of the Illyrians, the original inhabitants.

When the Turkish government pulled out in 1913, Serbia regained control apart from during WWII when Kosovo was incorporated into Italian-controlled Albania.

In early 1945, Kosovo became part of post-war Yugoslavia but incorporated into Serbia, which has always maintained a historic right to the region. The post-war history of Kosovo has been one of economic neglect and discrimination despite mineral and agricultural wealth. An autonomous province was created in 1974 but cancelled in 1981 as the Albanian Kosovars agitated for republic status.

The Kosovo Liberation Army (KLA) was formed in 1997 out of frustrated attempts to negotiate autonomy. Serbia increased its military presence, attacking and clearing out Albanian villages. Peace talks in March 1999 in Paris failed and Serbia stepped up its attacks on the KLA.

Nearly 850,000 Albanian Kosovars fled into Albania and Macedonia. Serbia ignored demands to desist and NATO unleashed its bombing campaign on 24 March 1999. On 12 June Serb forces withdrew and the Kosovo Force (KFOR), comprising NATO and Russian forces, took over.

Peace has not been easy. The UN has had to persuade the KLA to demilitarise and the Serb population to return to Kosovo. Continuing revenge attacks on the remaining Serbs have made them an isolated community protected by KFOR.

The properties of many Albanians and Serbs have been destroyed and Orthodox churches and monasteries are now guarded to prevent their destruction.

YUGOSLAVIA

Warning

The Current Situation

Kosovo's administration, under the UN, is starting from scratch. The information in this chapter was accurate at the time of writing but will change rapidly.

The railway is not operating and there's no postal system. The only functioning bank, the German Micro Enterprise Bank, has branches in Prishtina, Prizren and Peja. Bring sufficient cash, in Deutschmarks, for your stay.

In a process of Albanianisation, Serbian place names are no longer used and many streets have no names. In this section Albanian names are used with the Serbian ones in brackets.

Despite the presence of KFOR troops in Kosovo there are still dangers. Be aware that there are many landmines and unexploded bombs left in this recent war zone and avoid any places like Mitrovica where there are Albanian-Serb tensions. The main towns of Prishtina, Peja and Prizren, and the roads between, are relatively safe but it is essential to check with KFOR of the UN administration about travelling elsewhere and especially into the countryside. Do not be inquisitive about fenced-off areas where KFOR troops have authority to shoot if necessary.

Getting There & Away

Direct buses go from Skopje (Macedonia) to Prishtina (DM10) and Prizren (DM15) daily.

There are direct buses from Prishtina and Prizren to Istanbul, Sofia, Rome and Paris. From Montenegro or Serbia catch a bus stopping at Rožaje.

From there minibuses (DM10) or taxis (DM50) at the bus station can take you to Peja.

Getting Around

There are many buses linking Prizren, Prishtina and Peja with minibuses plying to smaller towns.

PRISHTINA (PRIŠTINA)
☎ 038

The capital has all the beauty and grace that Soviet-style excesses in concrete could bestow. Prishtina has little to offer and can be considered a jumping off point to the more interesting towns of Peja and Prizren.

Orientation & Information

Central Prishtina focuses on Mother Theresa and Ramiz Sadiku Sts. The bus station is in the south-western outskirts of Prishtina, and the airport is 17km to the south-west.

Ask at kiosks or bookshops along Mother Theresa St for a map of Prishtina. Travel agencies on the same street can be useful sources of information.

There's nowhere to change money at the airport. The Micro Enterprise Bank, off Mother Theresa St, cashes Deutschmark travellers cheques.

The telephone exchange is in the stylish copper-roofed building next to the National Theatre. The Internet@Click! Café is in a long arcade in the district of Dardania and is open 8.30 am to midnight.

Places to Stay & Eat

Book in advance if possible for the *Iliria* (☎ 24 042) on Mother Theresa St, the cheapest hotel in town at 70/140 DM for a single/double, including breakfast. Ask taxi drivers for information on *private rooms*, which will be less expensive.

There are many places to eat along Mother Theresa and Ramiz Sadiku Sts. Side streets abound with *cafes* selling burek and hamburgers for DM2 to DM3; pasta and pizza cafes charge up to DM5.

PEJA (PEŽ)
☎ 039

Peja was badly damaged by departing Yugoslav forces, many picturesque buildings are rubble and the roads are atrocious. However, the backdrop is superb with 2000m mountains towering above the town.

Orientation & Information

Both road and railway from Prishtina run into the northern part of town where the bus station is.

Peja is blessed with several private telephone centres. Look for the big yellow 'Telefon' sign; there's even one in the bus station. Just south of the bazaar is the Internet Caffe.

Things to See

Peja's mosques have been severely damaged and are locked awaiting restoration. However, the imposing dome of the

YUGOSLAVIA

15th-century **Bajrakli Mosque** rising above the colourful **bazaar** gives Peja an authentic Oriental air.

Also closed but worth seeing if you can get a pass from KFOR are the **Patrijaršija Monastery** and the impressive **Visoki Dečani Monastery** (1335).

About 4km west of town is the **Rugovo Gorge**, which is an excellent hiking area. Although there should be no problem, check with KFOR before doing anything adventurous.

Places to Stay & Eat

With *Kamp Karaga* and *Hotel Park* closed, *Hotel Dypon (☎/fax 31 593)* is the only hotel in town and charges DM100/170 for a single/double. Check whether any of the opposition have reopened before going to the Dypon.

There are plenty of cheap *burek* and *hamburger* joints around the bus station.

PRIZREN
☎ 029

Prizren was the medieval capital of 'Old Serbia' but the architectural influence is Turkish.

Now that Serbian oppression has ended, evenings here give the impression of Prizren being a party town, as people throng the many bars and cafes along the river and in Shadrvan.

Warning Prizren has a curfew, so be off the streets between 1 and 4 am.

Orientation & Information

The town centres around the river and Shadrvan, a cobblestoned plaza. The bus station is on the north-western side of town.

Try the Tourist Association of Prizren (☎ 32 843) for a city map. Its office is behind the Turkish restaurant, a few metres south-east of the main bridge.

The main post office, adjacent to the Theranda Hotel, is currently just a telephone centre. The UN runs a free Internet centre, behind the main post office, but book in advance.

Things to See

The Orthodox **Church of Bogorodica Lje-viška** (1307) and **Sveti Georgi** (1856) are closed and protected by soldiers and barbed wire. The **Sinan Pasha Mosque** (1561) beside the river dominates the centre and has a fine decorated high dome ceiling. Up the road from the Theranda Hotel are the **Gazi Mehmed Pasha Baths** (1563), now being restored.

Places to Stay & Eat

Accommodation in Prizren is limited. The faded *Theranda Hotel (☎ 22 292)*, in the centre of town, charges DM70/90 for a single/double with private bath and breakfast.

Hotel Prizren (☎ 41 552, fax 43 107), about a kilometre north-west of the centre, charges DM50/70 for a room with bath and breakfast.

There is an abundance of *cafes*, *bars* and *restaurants* around the central area.

Appendix I – Climate Charts

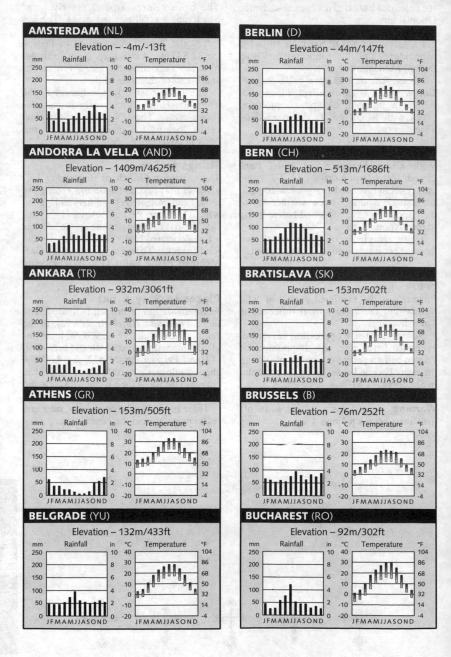

AMSTERDAM (NL)
Elevation – -4m/-13ft

BERLIN (D)
Elevation – 44m/147ft

ANDORRA LA VELLA (AND)
Elevation – 1409m/4625ft

BERN (CH)
Elevation – 513m/1686ft

ANKARA (TR)
Elevation – 932m/3061ft

BRATISLAVA (SK)
Elevation – 153m/502ft

ATHENS (GR)
Elevation – 153m/505ft

BRUSSELS (B)
Elevation – 76m/252ft

BELGRADE (YU)
Elevation – 132m/433ft

BUCHAREST (RO)
Elevation – 92m/302ft

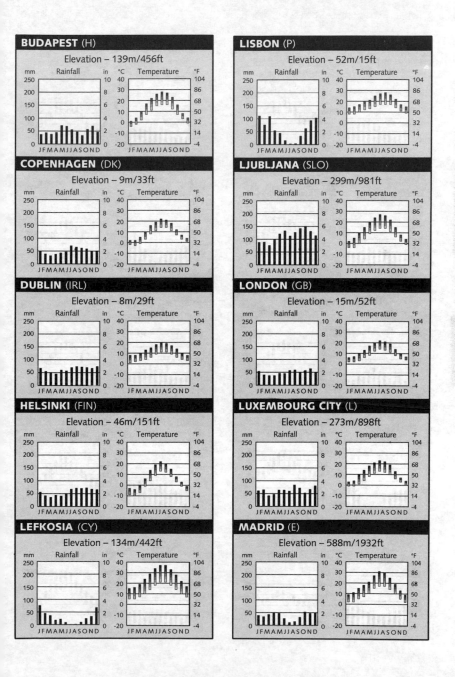

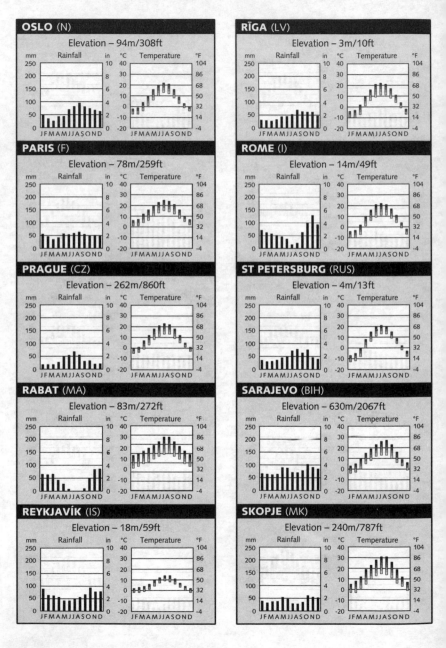

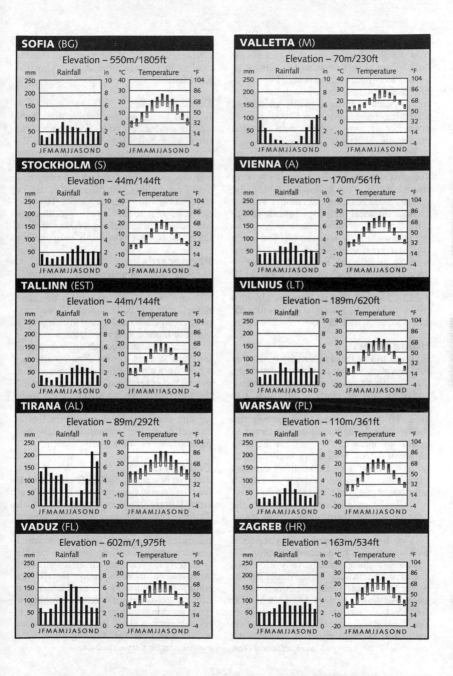

Appendix II – Telephones

Dial Direct

You can dial directly from public telephone boxes from almost anywhere in Europe to almost anywhere in the world. This is usually cheaper than going through the operator. In much of Europe, public telephones accepting phonecards are becoming the norm and in some countries coin-operated phones are difficult to find.

To call abroad you simply dial the international access code (IAC) for the country you are calling from (most commonly 00 in Europe but see the following table), the country code (CC) for the country you are calling, the local area code (usually dropping the leading zero if there is one) and then the number. If, for example, you are in Italy (international access code 00) and want to make a call to the USA (country code 1), San Francisco (area code 212), number ☎ 123 4567, then you dial ☎ 00-1-212-123 4567. To call from the UK (00) to Australia (61), Sydney (02), number ☎ 123 4567, you dial ☎ 00-61-2-1234 5678.

Home Direct

If you would rather have somebody else pay for the call, you can, from many countries, dial directly to your home country operator and then reverse charges; you can also charge the call to a phone company credit card. To do this, simply dial the relevant 'home direct' number to be connected to your own operator. For the USA there's a choice of AT&T, MCI or Sprint Global One home direct services. Home direct numbers vary from country to country – check with your telephone company before you leave, or with the international operator in the country you're ringing from. From phone boxes in some countries you may need a coin or local phonecard to be connected with the relevant home direct operator.

In some places (particularly airports), you may find dedicated home direct phones where you simply press the button labelled USA, Australia, Hong Kong or whatever for direct connection to the operator. Note that the home direct service does not operate to and from all countries, and that the call could be charged at operator rates,

which makes it expensive for the person paying. Placing a call on your phone credit card is more expensive than paying the local tariff.

Dialling Tones

In some countries, after you've dialled the international access code, you have to wait for a second dial tone before dialing the code for your target country and the number. Often the same applies when you ring from one city to another within these countries: wait for a dialling tone after you've dialled the area code for your target city. If you're not sure what to do, simply wait three or four seconds after dialling a code – if nothing happens, you can probably keep dialling.

Phonecards

In major locations phones may accept credit cards: simply swipe your card through the slot and the call is charged to the card, though rates can be very high. Phone-company credit cards can be used to charge calls via your home country operator.

Stored-value phonecards are now almost standard all over Europe. You usually buy a card from a post office, telephone centre, newsstand or retail outlet and simply insert the card into the phone each time you make a call. The card solves the problem of finding the correct coins for calls (or lots of correct coins for international calls) and generally gives you a small discount.

Call Costs

The cost of international calls varies widely from one country to another: a US$1.20 call from Britain could cost you US$6 from Turkey. The countries in the table opposite are rated from * (cheap) to *** (expensive), but rates can vary depending on which country you are calling to (for example, from Italy it's relatively cheap to call North America, but more expensive to call Australia). Reduced rates are available at certain times, usually from mid-evening to early morning, though it varies from country to country – check the local phone book or ask the operator. Calling from hotel rooms can be very expensive.

Telephone Codes & Costs

	CC	cost (see text)	IAC	IO
Albania	355	***		
Andorra	376	**	00	821111
Austria	43	*	00	09
Belgium	32	**	00	1224 (private phone)
				1223 (public phone)
Bosnia	387	**	00	901
Bulgaria	359	***	00	
Croatia	385	**	00	901
Cyprus	357	***	00	
Cyprus (Turkish)	90+392		00	
Czech Republic	420	***	00	0149
Denmark	45	**	00	141
Estonia	372	***	00	165
Finland	358	**	00, 990, 994, 999	020222
France	33	*	00(w)	12
Germany	49	*	00	11834
Gibraltar	350	***	00	100
Greece	30	*	00	161
Hungary	36	*	00(w)	199
Iceland	354	***	00	5335010
Ireland	353	*	00	114
Northern Ireland	44+28	*	00	155
Italy	39	**	00	15
Latvia	371	***	1(w)00	1(w)115
Liechtenstein	423	***	00	114
Lithuania	370	***	8(w)10	194/195
Luxembourg	352	**	00	0010
Macedonia	389	***	99	
Malta	356	**	00	194
Morocco	212	***	00(w)	12
Netherlands	31	**	00	0800-0410
Norway	47	**	00	181
Poland	48	**	0(w)0	901
Portugal	351	*	00	172
Romania	40	***	00	971
Russia	7	***	8(w)10	070
Slovakia	421	**	00	0149/0139
Slovenia	386	**	00	901
Spain	34	**	00(w)	025
Sweden	46	**	00	118119
Switzerland	41	**	00	114
Tunisia	216	**	00	
Turkey	90	***	00	115
UK	44	*	00	155
Yugoslavia	381	***	99	901

CC – Country Code (to call into that country)
IAC – International Access Code (to call abroad from that country)
IO – International Operator (to make enquiries)
(w) – wait for dialling tone

Other country codes include: Australia 61, Canada 1, Hong Kong 852, India 91, Indonesia 62, Israel 972, Japan 81, Macau 853, Malaysia 60, New Zealand 64, Singapore 65, South Africa 27, Thailand 66, USA 1

Home Direct

If you would rather have somebody else pay for the call, you can, from many countries, dial directly to an operator in your home country and then reverse charges; you can also charge the call to a phone company credit card. See the following Home Direct appendix.

Home direct services allow you to dial a toll-free number from many European countries that connect you to an operator in your home country. Home direct services are handy for reverse-charge and phonecard calls, especially in countries where English-speaking operators are rare.

Home direct numbers vary from country to country - we list many below, but check with your telephone company before leaving for number changes and/or new coverage, or with the international operator in the country you're ringing from. Remember that from phone boxes in some countries you may need a coin or local phonecard to be connected with the relevant home direct operator. Note that the home direct service does not operate to and from all countries, and that the call could be charged at operator rates, which makes it quite expensive for the person who's paying. In general, using a home direct service using your phone credit card is much more expensive than paying the local direct-dial tariff.

	USA	Canada (AT&T)	Australia (Telstra)	New Zealand (NZ Telecom)
Albania	00800-0010 (AT&T)	N/A	N/A	N/A
Andorra	N/A	N/A	N/A	N/A
Austria	0800-200288 (AT&T) 0800-200236 (Sprint) 0800-200235 (MCI)	0800-200245	0800-200202	0800-200222
Belgium	0800-10010 (AT&T) 0800-10014 (Sprint) 0800-10012 (MCI)	0800-10018	0800-10061	0800-10064
Bosnia	00800-0010 (AT&T)	N/A	N/A	N/A
Britain	0800-890011 (AT&T) 0800-890877 (Sprint) 0800-890222 (MCI)	0800-890216 0500-891999	0800-8566161	0800-890064
Bulgaria	00800-0010 (AT&T) 00800-1010 (Sprint) 00800-0001 (MCI)	00-800-0011	N/A	N/A
Croatia**	0800-220111 (AT&T) 0800-220113 (Sprint) 0800-220112 (MCI)	0800-220102	N/A	N/A
Cyprus	080-90010 (AT&T) 080-90001 (Sprint) 080-90000 (MCI)	080-90013	080-90061	080-90064
Czech Republic	0042-000101 (AT&T) 0042-087187 (Sprint) 0042-000112 (MCI)	0042-000159	0042-006101	N/A
Denmark	800-10010 (AT&T) 800-10877 (Sprint) 800-10022 (MCI)	808-880080	800-10061	800-10064
Estonia	800-8001001 (AT&T) 800-8001122 (MCI)	N/A	N/A	N/A
Finland	0800-110015 (AT&T) 0800-110284 (Sprint) 0800-110280 (MCI)	0800-110012	0800-110610	0800-110640

	USA	Canada (AT&T)	Australia (Telstra)	New Zealand (NZ Telecom)
France	0800-990011 (AT&T) 0800-990087 (Sprint) 0800-990019 (MCI)	0800-993016	0800-990061	0800-990064
Germany	0800-2255288 (AT&T) 0800-8880013 (Sprint) 0800-8888000 (MCI)	0800-080101	0800-0800061	0800-0800064
Greece	00800-1311 (AT&T) 00800-1411 (Sprint) 00800-1211 (MCI)	00800-017111	00800-6111	00800-6411
Hungary	06*800-01111 (AT&T) 06*800-01877 (Sprint) 06*800-01411 (MCI)	06*800-01214	06*800-06111	06*800-06411
Iceland	800-9001 (AT&T) 800-9003 (Sprint) 800-9002 (MCI)	800-9011	N/A	800-9064
Ireland	1800-550000 (AT&T) 1800-552001 (Sprint) 1800-551001 (MCI)	1800-550200	1800-550061	1800-550064
Italy	172-1011 (AT&T) 172-1877 (Sprint) 172-1022 (MCI)	172-1002	172-1061	172-1064
Latvia	7007007# (AT&T) 8*2-7007007## (AT&T) 800-8888 (MCI)	N/A	N/A	800-2100
Liechtenstein	809-2288 (AT&T) 809-8000 (MCI)	0800-555236	N/A	N/A
Lithuania	8*800-92800 (AT&T) 8*800-95877 (Sprint)	8*800-91005	N/A	N/A
Luxembourg	08002-0111 (AT&T) 0800-0115 (Sprint) 8002-0112 (MCI)	0800-0114	0800-0061	0800-0064
Macedonia	99800-4288 (AT&T) 99800-4266 (MCI)	99800-4276	N/A	N/A
Malta	0800-890110 (AT&T) 0800-890120 (MCI)	0800-890151	0800-890610	0800-890640
Morocco	002-110011 (AT&T) 002-110012 (MCI)	N/A	N/A	N/A
Netherlands	0800-0229111 (AT&T) 0800-0229119 (Sprint) 0800-0229122 (MCI)	0800-0229894	0800-0220061 0800-931818	0800-0224464
Norway	800-19011 (AT&T) 800-19877 (Sprint) 800-19912 (MCI)	800-19113	800-19961	800-19964
Poland**	00800-1111111 (AT&T) 00800-1113115 (Sprint) 00800-1112122 (MCI)	0*0800-1115133	00800-6111161	N/A

	USA	Canada (AT&T)	Australia (Telstra)	New Zealand (NZ Telecom)
Portugal	800-800128 (AT&T) 800-800187 (Sprint) 800-800123 (MCI)	800-800124	800-800610	800-800640
Romania**	01800-4288 (AT&T) 01800-0877 (Sprint) 01800-1800 (MCI)	01800-5010	N/A	N/A
St Petersburgž	325-5042 (AT&T) 8095-7473324 (Sprint) 346-802215161 (MCI)	N/A	N/A	810800-1101064
Slovakia	0042-100101 (AT&T) 0042-187187 (Sprint) 0800-100112 (MCI)	0800-100152	0800-006101	0800-006400
Slovenia	080-8808 (MCI)	N/A	N/A	N/A
Spain	900-990011 (AT&T) 900-990013 (Sprint) 900-990014 (MCI)	900-990016-611	900-990061	900-990064
Sweden	020-799111 (AT&T) 020-799011 (Sprint) 020-795922 (MCI)	020-799018	020-799061	020-799064
Switzerland	0800-890011 (AT&T) 0800-899777 (Sprint) 0800-890222 (MCI)	0800-555236	0800-555004	0800-556411
Turkey	00800-12277 (AT&T) 800-5504823 (Sprint) 00800-11177 (MCI)	00800-15577	00800-611177	N/A
Yugoslavia	N/A	N/A	N/A	N/A

Notes: N/A not available
* wait for second tone
** all services have limited availability
# within Rīga
outside Rīga
§ all services available only within St Petersburg (not greater Russia)

Appendix III – Alternative Place Names

The following abbreviations are used:

(Alb) Albanian
(Ara) Arabic
(Bas) Basque
(Bul) Bulgarian
(Cat) Catalan
(Cze) Czech
(Cro) Croatian
(Den) Danish
(Dut) Dutch/Flemish
(Eng) English
(Est) Estonian
(Far) Faroese
(Fre) French
(Fin) Finnish
(Fle) Flemish/Dutch
(Ger) German
(Gre) Greek
(Hun) Hungarian
(Iri) Irish
(Ita) Italian
(Lat) Latin
(Lav) Latvian
(Lit) Lithuanian
(Lux) Luxembourgian
(Mac) Macedonian
(Nor) Norwegian
(Pol) Polish
(Por) Portuguese
(Rom) Romanian
(Rsh) Romansch
(Rus) Russian
(Ser) Serbian
(Slk) Slovak
(Sle) Slovene
(Spa) Spanish
(Swe) Swedish
(Tur) Turkish

ALBANIA
Shqipëria
Durrës (Alb) – Durazzo (Ita), Epidamnos (Gre), Dyrrhachium (Lat)
Korçë (Alb) – Koritsa (Gre)
Lezha (Eng) – Lezhë (Alb), Alessio (Ita)
Saranda (Eng) – Sarandë (Alb)
Shkodra (Eng) – Shkodër (Alb), Scutari (Ita)
Tirana (Eng) – Tiranë (Alb)

AUSTRIA
Österreich
Carinthia (Eng) – Kärnten (Ger)
Danube (Eng) – Donau (Ger)
East Tirol (Eng) – Osttirol (Ger)
Lake Constance (Eng) – Bodensee (Ger)
Lower Austria (Eng) – Niederösterreich (Ger)
Upper Austria (Eng) – Oberösterreich (Ger)
Styria (Eng) – Steiermark (Ger)
Tirol (Eng, Ger) – Tyrol (Eng)
Vienna (Eng) – Wien (Ger)
Vienna Woods (Eng) – Wienerwald (Ger)

BELGIUM
België (Fle), Belgique (Fre)
Antwerp (Eng) – Antwerpen (Fle), Anvers (Fre)
Bruges (Eng, Fre) – Brugge (Fle)
Brussels (Eng) – Brussel (Fle), Bruxelles (Fre)
Courtrai (Eng, Fre) – Kortrijk (Fle)
Ghent (Eng) – Gent (Fle), Gand (Fre)
Liège (Eng, Fre) – Luik (Fle), Lüttich (Ger)
Louvain (Eng, Fre) – Leuven (Fle)
Mechlin (Eng) – Mechelen (Fle), Malines (Fre)
Meuse (River) (Eng, Fre) – Maas (Fle)
Mons (Eng, Fre) – Bergen (Fle)
Namur (Eng, Fre) – Namen (Fle)
Ostende (Eng) – Oostende (Fle), Ostende (Fre)
Scheldt (River) (Eng) – Schelde (Fle), Escaut (Fre)
Tournai (Eng, Fre) – Doornik (Fle)
Ypres (Eng, Fre) – Ieper (Fle)

BULGARIA
Bâlgariya
Bachkovo Monastery (Eng) – Bachkovski Manastir (Bul)
Balchik (Bul) – Krunoi (Gre), Dionysopolis (Lat)
Golden Sands (Eng) – Zlatni Pyasâtsi (Bul), Goldstrand (Ger)
Hisar (Tur) – Hisarya (Bul), Augusta (Lat)
Nesebâr (Bul) – Mesembria (Gre)
Plovdiv (Bul) – Philipopolis (Gre), Philibe (Tur)
Ruse (Bul) – Rouschouk (Tur)
Rila Monastery (Eng) – Rilski Manastir (Bul)
Shumen (Bul) – Chumla (Tur)
Sofia (Eng) – Sofiya (Bul), Serdica (Lat)
Sozopol (Bul) – Apollonia (Gre)
Stara Planina (Bul) – Balkan Mountains (Eng)
Sunny Beach (Eng) – Slânchev Bryag (Bul), Sonnenstrand (Ger)
Varna (Bul) – Odessos (Gre)
Vidin (Bul) – Bononia (Lat)

CROATIA
Hrvatska
Brač (Cro) – Brazza (Ita)
Brijuni (Cro) – Brioni (Ita)
Cres (Cro) – Cherso
Dalmatia (Eng) – Dalmacija (Cro)
Dubrovnik (Cro) – Ragusa (Ita)
Hvar (Cro) – Lesina (Ita)
Korčula – Curzola (Ita)
Krk (Cro) – Veglia (Ita)
Kvarner (Eng) – Quarnero (Ita)
Lošinj (Cro) – Lussino (Ita)
Mljet Island (Cro) – Melita (Ita)
Poreč (Cro) – Parenzo (Ita), Parentium (Lat)
Rab (Cro) – Arbe (Ger)
Rijeka (Cro) – Fiume (Ita), Reka (Sle)
Rovinj (Cro) – Rovigno (Ita)
Split (Cro) – Spalato (Ita)
Trogir (Cro) – Trau (Ger)
Zadar (Cro) – Zara (Ita), Iader (Lat)
Zagreb (Cro) – Agram (Ger)

CYPRUS
Kípros (Gre), Kibris (Tur)
Gazimağusa (Tur) – Famagusta (Gre), Ammo-
chostos (Gre)
Girne (Tur) – Kyrenia (Gre), Keryneia (Gre)
Lefkosia (Gre) – Lefkoşa (Tur), formerly Nicosia
(Gre)
Lemessos (Gre), formerly Limassol (Gre)

CZECH REPUBLIC
Česká republika
Brno (Cze) – Brünn (Ger)
České Budějovice (Cze) – Budweis (Ger)
Český Krumlov (Cze) – Krumau (Ger)
Cheb (Cze) – Eger (Ger)
Danube (Eng) – Dunáj (Cze), Donau (Ger)
Giant Mountains – (Eng)Krkonoše (Cze)
Hluboká nad Vltavou (Cze) – Frauenberg (Ger)
Karlovy Vary (Cze) – Karlsbad (Ger)
Labe (River) (Cze) – Elbe (Ger)
Mariánské Lázně (Cze) – Marienbad (Ger)
Ore Mountains (Eng) – Krušné Hory (Cze)
Plzeň (Cze) – Pilsen (Ger)
Prague (Eng) – Praha (Cze), Prag (Ger)
Telč (Cze) – Teltsch (Ger)
Vltava (River) (Cze) – Moldau (Ger)
Znojmo (Cze) – Znaim (Ger)

DENMARK
Danmark
Copenhagen (Eng) – København (Den), Kööpen-
hamina (Fin), Köpenhamn (Swe)
Elsinore (Eng) – Helsingør (Den)
Jutland (Eng) – Jylland (Den)
Funen (Eng) – Fyn (Den)
Zealand (Eng) – Sjælland (Den), occasionally Sea-
land (Eng)

ESTONIA
Eesti
Tallinn (Est) – Talinas (Lit), formerly Reval or Revel
Tartu (Est) – Tartto (Fin)
Saaremaa (Est) – Ösel (Swe)

FAROE ISLANDS
*Færoe Islands (Eng), Færøerne (Dan), Føroyar
(Far)*

FINLAND
Suomi
Åland (Swe) – Ahvenanmaa (Fin)
Hämeenlinna (Fin) – Tavastehus (Swe)
Helsinki (Fin) – Helsingfors (Swe)
Kokkola (Fin) – Karleby (Swe)
Lappeenranta (Fin) – Villmanstrand (Swe)
Lapland (Eng) – Lappi (Fin), Lappland (Swe)
Naantali (Fin) – Nådendal (Swe)
Oulu (Fin) – Uleåborg (Swe)
Pietarsaari (Fin) – Jakobstad (Swe)
Tampere (Fin) – Tammerfors (Swe)
Tornio (Fin) – Torneå (Swe)
Turku (Fin) – Åbo (Swe)
Vaasa (Fin) – Vasa (Swe)

FRANCE
Bayonne (Fre, Eng) – Baiona (Bas)
Basque Country (Eng) – Euskadi (Bas),
Pays Basque (Fre)
Burgundy (Eng) – Bourgogne (Fre)
Brittany (Eng) – Bretagne (Fre)
Corsica (Eng) – Corse (Fre)
French Riviera (Eng) – Côte d'Azur (Fre)
Dunkirk (Eng) – Dunkerque (Fre)
Channel Islands (Eng) – Îles Anglo-Normandes
(Fre)
English Channel (Eng) – La Manche (Fre)
Lake Geneva (Eng) – Lac Léman (Fre)
Lyons (Eng) – Lyon (Fre)
Marseilles (Eng) – Marseille (Fre)
Normandy (Eng) – Normandie (Fre)
Rheims (Eng) – Reims (Fre)
Rhine (River) (Eng) – Rhin (Fre), Rhein (Ger)
Saint Jean de Luz (Fre) – Donibane Lohizune (Bas)
Saint Jean Pied de Port (Fre) – Donibane
Garazi (Bas)
Sark (Channel Islands) (Eng) – Sercq (Fre)

GERMANY
Deutschland
Aachen (Eng, Ger) – Aix-la-Chapelle (Fre)
Baltic Sea (Eng) – Ostsee (Ger)
Bavaria (Eng) – Bayern (Ger)
Bavarian Alps (Eng) – Bayerische Alpen (Ger)
Bavarian Forest (Eng) – Bayerischer Wald (Ger)
Black Forest (Eng) – Schwarzwald (Ger)

Cologne (Eng) – Köln (Ger)
Constance (Eng) – Konstanz (Ger)
Danube (Eng) – Donau (Ger)
East Friesland (Eng) – Ostfriesland (Ger)
Federal Republic of Germany (Eng) – Bundes-
 republik Deutschland (abbrev BRD; Ger)
Franconia (Eng) – Franken (Ger)
Hamelin (Eng) – Hameln (Ger)
Hanover (Eng) – Hannover (Ger)
Harz Mountains (Eng) – Harzgebirge (Ger)
Hesse (Eng) – Hessen (Ger)
Lake Constance (Eng) – Bodensee (Ger)
Lower Saxony (Eng) – Niedersachsen (Ger)
Lüneburg Heath (Eng) – Lüneburger Heide (Ger)
Mecklenburg-Pomerania (Eng) – Mecklenburg-
 Vorpommern (Ger)
Munich (Eng) – München (Ger)
North Friesland (Eng) – Nordfriesland (Ger)
North Rhine-Westphalia (Eng) – Nordrhein-
 Westfalen (Ger)
Nuremberg (Eng) – Nürnberg (Ger)
Pomerania (Eng) – Pommern (Ger)
Prussia (Eng) – Preussen (Ger)
Rhine (Eng) – Rhein (Ger)
Rhineland-Palatinate (Eng) – Rheinland-Pfalz (Ger)
Romantic Road (Eng) – Romantische Strasse (Ger)
Saarbrücken (Eng, Ger) – Sarrebruck (Fre)
Saxon Switzerland (Eng) – Sachsische Schweiz
 (Ger)
Saxony (Eng) – Sachsen (Ger)
Swabia (Eng) – Schwaben (Ger)
Thuringia (Eng) – Thüringen (Ger)
Thuringian Forest (Eng) – Thüringer Wald (Ger)

GREECE
*Hellas (*or *Ellas)*
Athens (Eng) – Athina (Gre)
Corfu (Eng) – Kerkyra (Gre)
Crete (Eng) – Kriti (Gre)
Patras (Eng) – Patra (Gre)
Rhodes (Eng) – Rodos (Gre)
Salonica (Eng) – Thessaloniki (Gre)
Samothrace (Eng) – Samothraki (Gre)
Santorini (Eng, Ita) – Thira (Gre)

HUNGARY
Magyarország
(Lake) Balaton (Hun) – Plattensee (Ger)
Danube (Eng) – Duna (Hun), Donau (Ger)
Danube Bend (Eng) – Dunakanyar (Hun)
Debrecen (Hun) – Debrezin (Ger)
Eger (Hun) – Erlau (Ger)
Esztergom (Hun) – Gran (Ger)
Great Plain (Eng) – Nagyalföld (Hun)
Győr (Hun) – Raab (Ger)
Kőszeg (Hun) – Guns (Ger)
Lendva (Hun) – Lendava (Sle)
Little Plain (Eng) – Kisalföld (Hun)

Pécs (Hun) – Fünfkirchen (Ger)
Sopron (Hun) – Ödenburg (Ger)
Szeged (Hun) – Segedin (Ger)
Szombathely (Hun) – Steinamanger (Ger)
Transdanubia (Hun) – Dunántúl (Hun)
Vác (Hun) – Wartzen (Ger)
Vienna (Eng) – Bécs (Hun), Wien (Ger)

ICELAND
Ísland

IRELAND
Eire
Aran Islands (Eng) – Oileáin Árainn (Iri)
Athlone (Eng) – Baile Átha Luain (Iri)
Bantry (Eng) – Beanntraí (Iri)
Belfast (Eng) – Beál Feirste (Iri)
Cork (Eng) – Corcaigh (Iri)
Derry/Londonderry (Eng) – Doire (Iri)
Dingle (Eng) – An Daingean (Iri)
Donegal (Eng) – Dún na nGall (Iri)
Dublin (Eng) – Baile Átha Cliath (Iri)
Galway (Eng) – Gaillimh (Iri)
Kilkenny (Eng) – Cill Chainnigh (Iri)
Killarney (Eng) – Cill Áirne (Iri)
Kilronan (Eng) – Cill Ronáin (Iri)
Limerick (Eng) – Luimneach (Iri)
Roscommon (Eng) – Ros Comáin (Iri)
Rossaveal (Eng) – Ros an Mhil (Iri)
Shannon (Eng) – Sionann (Iri)
Tipperary (Eng) – Tiobraid Árann (Iri)
Waterford (Eng) – Port Láirge (Iri)
Wexford (Eng) – Loch Garman (Iri)

ITALY
Italia
Aeolian Islands (Eng) – Isole Eolie (Ita)
Apulia (Eng) – Puglia (Ita)
Florence (Eng) – Firenze (Ita)
Genoa (Eng) – Genova (Ita)
Herculaneum (Eng) – Ercolano (Ita)
Lombardy (Eng) – Lombardia (Ita)
Mantua (Eng) – Mantova (Ita)
Milan (Eng) – Milano (Ita)
Naples (Eng) – Napoli (Ita)
Padua (Eng) – Padova (Ita)
Rome (Eng) – Roma (Ita)
Sicily (Eng) – Sicilia (Ita)
Sardinia (Eng) – Sardegna (Ita)
Syracuse (Eng) – Siracusa (Ita)
Tiber (River) (Eng) – Tevere (Ita)
Venice (Eng) – Venezia (Ita)

LATVIA
Latvija
Cēsis (Lav) – formerly Wenden (Ger)
Kurzeme (Lav) – formerly Courland (Eng), Kurland
 (Ger)

Riga (Eng) – Rīga (Lav), Riika (Fin)
Sigulda (Lav) – formerly Segewold (Ger)

LITHUANIA
Lietuva
Kaunas (Lav) – Kowno (Pol)
Klaipėda (Lit) – formerly Memel (Ger)
Juodkrantė (Lit) – formerly Schwarzort (Ger)
Nida (Lit) – formerly Nidden (Ger)
Vilnius – Wilno (Pol)

LUXEMBOURG
Letzeburg (Lux), Luxemburg (Ger)

MACEDONIA
Makedonija
Ohrid (Mac) – Lihnidos (Lat)
Skopje (Mac) – Uskup (Tur), Scupi (Lat)

MOROCCO
Ceuta (Spa) – Sebta (Ara)
Casablanca (Fre) – Dar al-Beida (Ara)
Marrakesh (Eng) – Marrakech (Fre)
Tangier (Eng) – Tanger (Fre), Tanja (Ara)

THE NETHERLANDS
Nederland
Den Bosch (Eng, Dut) – 's-Hertogenbosch (Dut)
Flushing (Eng) – Vlissingen (Dut)
Hook of Holland (Eng) – Hoek van Holland (Dut)
Meuse (River; Eng, Fre) – Maas (Dut)
Rhine (River; Eng) – Rijn (Dut)
The Hague (Eng) – Den Haag (or 's-Gravenhage; Dut), La Haye (Fre)

NORWAY
Norge
Kirkenes (Nor) – Kirkkoniemi (Fin)
Lofoten (Nor) – Lofootit (Fin)
North Cape (Eng) – Nordkapp (Nor)
Tromsø (Nor) – Tromsö (Swe), Tromssa (Fin)
Vardø (Nor) – Vuoreija (Fin)

POLAND
Polska
Oświdcim (Pol) – Auschwitz (Ger)
Brzezinka (Pol) – Birkenau (Ger)
Bydgoszcz (Pol) – Bromberg (Ger)
Czdstochowa (Pol) – Tschenstochau (Ger)
Gdańsk (Pol) – Danzig (Ger)
Gdynia (Pol) – Gdingen (Ger)
Gniezno (Pol) – Gnesen (Ger)
Kołobrzeg (Pol) – Kolberg (Ger)
Kdtrzyn (Pol) – Rastenburg (Ger)
Kraków (Pol) – Krakau (Ger), Cracow (Eng)
Malbork (Pol) – Marienburg (Ger)
Małopolska (Pol) – Little Poland (Region) (Eng)
Nowy Sącz (Pol) – Neusandez (Ger)

Nysa (River; Pol) – Neisse (Ger)
Odra (River; Pol) – Oder (Ger)
Olsztyn (Pol) – Allenstein (Ger)
Opole (Pol) – Oppeln (Ger)
Poznań (Pol) – Posen (Ger)
Silesia (Eng) – Śląsk (Pol), Silesien (Ger)
Świnoujście (Pol) – Swinemünde (Ger)
Szczecin (Pol) – Stettin (Ger)
Sopot (Pol) – Zoppot (Ger)
Stdbark (Pol) – Tannenberg (Ger)
Toruń (Pol) – Thorn (Ger)
Vistula (River) (Eng) – Wisła (Pol), Weichsel (Ger)
Warsaw (Eng) – Warszawa (Pol), Warschau (Ger)
Wielkopolska (Pol) – Great Poland (Region) (Eng)
Wrocław (Pol) – Breslau (Ger)

PORTUGAL
Cape St Vincent (Eng) – Cabo de São Vicente (Por)
Lisbon (Eng) – Lisboa (Por)
Oporto (Eng) – Porto (Por)

ROMANIA
Romania
Alba Iulia (Rom) – Karlsburg/Weissenburg (Ger), Gyula Fehérvár (Hun), Apulum (Lat)
Baia Mare (Rom) – Nagybánya (Hun)
Braşov (Rom) – Kronstadt (G), Brassó (Hun)
Bucharest (Eng) – Bucureşti (Rom)
Cluj-Napoca (Rom) – Klausenburg (Ger), Kolozsvár (Hun), Napoca (Lat)
Constanţa (Rom) – Constantiana (Lat), Tomis (Gre), Küstendje (Tur)
Dobruja (Eng) – Dobrogea (Rom), Moesia Inferior (Lat)
Hunedoara (Rom) – Eisenmarkt (Ger)
Iaşi (Rom) – Jassy (Ger)
Mangalia (Rom) – Callatis (Lat)
Mediaş (Rom) – Mediasch (Ger)
Oradea (Rom) – Grosswardein (Ger), Nagyvárad (Hun)
Satu Mare (Rom) – Szatmárnémeti (Hun)
Sebeş (Rom) – Muhlbach (Ger)
Sibiu (Rom) – Hermannstadt (Ger), Cibinium (Lat), Nagyszében (Hun)
Sic (Rom) – Szék (Hun)
Sighişoara (Rom) – Schässburg (Ger), Szegesvár (Hun)
Suceava (Rom) – Soczow (Pol)
Timişoara (Rom) – Temeschburg (Ger), Temesvár (Hun)
Tirgu Mureş (Rom) – Marosvásárhely (Hun)
Transylvania (Rom) – Siebenbürgen (Ger), Erdély (Hun)

RUSSIA
Rossiya
Kaliningrad (Rus) – Królewiec (Pol), formerly Königsberg (Ger)

Moscow (Eng) – Moskva (Rus, Swe), Moskova (Fin)
St Petersburg – Pietari (Fin), formerly Leningrad (Rus)
Vyborg (Rus) – Viipuri (Fin)
Zelenogradsk (Rus) – Cranz (Ger)

SLOVAKIA
Slovensko
Banská Bystrica (Slk) – Neusohl (Ger)
Bratislava (Slk) – Pressburg (Ger), Pozsony (Hun)
Dunaj (Slk) – Danube (Eng)
Gerlachovský štít (Slk) – Mt Gerlach (Eng)
Košice (Slk) – Kaschau (Ger), Kassa (Hun)
Levoča (Slk) – Leutschau (Ger)
Lučenec (Slk) – Losonc (Hun)
Malá Fatra (Slk) – Little Fatra (Eng)
Nízke Tatry (Slk) – Low Tatras (Eng)
Prešov (Slk) – Preschau (Ger)
Rožnava (Slk) – Rozsnyó (Hun)
Slovenské rudohorie (Slk) – Slovak Ore Mountains (Eng)
Slovenský raj (Slk) – Slovak Paradise (Eng)
Spišský hrad (Castle) (Slk) – Zipser Burg (Ger)
Trnava (Slk) – Nagyszombat (Hun)
Vysoké Tatry (Slk) – High Tatras (Eng)
Zlaté piesky (Slk) – Golden Sands (Eng)
Zvolen (Slk) – Altsohl (Ger)

SLOVENIA
Slovenija
Koper (Sle) – Capodistria (Ita)
Ljubljana (Sle) – Laibach (Ger)
Piran (Sle) – Pireos (Gre), Pirano (Ita)
Postojna Cavc (Sle) – Adelsberger Grotten (Ger)
Vintgar Gorge (Eng) – Soteska Vintgar (Sle)

SPAIN
España
Andalusia (Eng) – Andalucía (Spa)
Balearic Islands (Eng) – Islas Baleares (Spa)
Basque Country (Eng) – Euskadi (Bas), País Vasco (Spa)
Catalonia (Eng) – Catalunya (Cat), Cataluña (Spa)
Cordova (Eng) – Córdoba (Spa)
Corunna (Eng) – La Coruña (Spa)
Majorca (Eng) – Mallorca (Spa)
Minorca (Eng) – Menorca (Spa)
Navarre (Eng) – Navarra (Spa)
San Sebastián (Eng, Spa) – Donostia (Bas)
Saragossa (Eng) – Zaragoza (Spa)
Seville (Eng) – Sevilla (Spa)

SWEDEN
Sverige
Gothenburg (Eng) – Göteberg (Swe)
Haparanda (Swe) – Haaparanta (Fin)
Stockholm (Swe) – Tukholma (Fin)

SWITZERLAND
Schweiz (Ger), Suisse (Fre), Svizzera (Ita), Svizzra (Rsh)
Basel (Eng, Ger) – Basle (Eng), Bâle (Fre), Basilea (Ita)
Bern (Eng, Ger) – Berne (Eng, Fre), Berna (Ita)
Fribourg (Eng, Fre) – Freiburg (Ger), Friburgo (Ita)
Geneva (Eng) – Genève (Fre), Genf (Ger), Ginevra (Ita)
Graubünden (Eng, Ger) – Grisons (Fre), Grigioni (Ita), Grishun – (Rsh)
Lake Constance (Eng) – Bodensee (Ger)
Lake Geneva (Eng) – Lac Léman (Fre)
Lake Maggiore (Eng) – Lago Maggiore (Ita)
Lucerne (Eng, Fre) – Luzern (Ger), Lucerna (Ita)
Neuchâtel (Eng, Fre) – Neuenburg (Ger)
Ticino (Eng, Ita) – Tessin (Ger, Fre)
Valais (Eng, Fre) – Wallis (Ger)
Zürich (Ger) – Zurich (Fre), Zurigo (Ita)

TURKEY
Türkiye
Cappadocia (Eng) – Kapadokya (Tur)
Ephesus (Eng) – Efes (Tur)
Euphrates River (Eng) – Firat (Tur)
Gallipoli (Eng) – Gelibolu (Tur)
İzmir (Tur) – Smyrna (Ger)
Mt Ararat (Eng) – Ağri Daği (Tur)
Mt Nimrod (Eng) – Nemrut Daği (Tur)
Thrace (Eng) – Trakya (Tur)
Tigris River (Eng) – Dicle (T)ur
Trebizond (Eng) – Trabzon (Tur)
Troy (Eng) – Truva (Tur)

YUGOSLAVIA
Jugoslavija
Bar (Ser) – Antivari (Ita)
Belgrade (Eng) – Beograd (Ser), Nándorfehérvar (Hun)
Deçan (Alb) – Dećani (Ser)
Kotor (Ser) – Cattaro (Ita)
Montenegro (Eng) – Crna Gora (Ser)
Novi Sad (Ser) – Neusatz (Ger)
Peja (Eng) – Pejë (Alb), Peć (Ser)
Prishtina (Eng) – Prishtinë (Alb), Priština (Ser)
Serbia (Eng) – Serbija (Ser)
Ulcinj (Ser) – Ulqin (Alb), Dulcigno (Ita)

Appendix IV – International Country Abbreviations

The following is a list of official abbreviations that you may encounter on motor vehicles in Europe. Other abbreviations are likely to be unofficial ones, often referring to a particular region, province or even city. A vehicle entering a foreign country must carry a sticker identifying its country of registration, though this rule is not always enforced.

A	–	Austria
AL	–	Albania
AND	–	Andorra
B	–	Belgium
BG	–	Bulgaria
BIH	–	Bosnia-Hercegovina
BY	–	Belarus
CDN	–	Canada
CH	–	Switzerland
CY	–	Cyprus
CZ	–	Czech Republic
D	–	Germany
DK	–	Denmark
DZ	–	Algeria
E	–	Spain
EST	–	Estonia
ET	–	Egypt
F	–	France
FIN	–	Finland
FL	–	Liechtenstein
FR	–	Faroe Islands
GB	–	Great Britain
GE	–	Georgia
GR	–	Greece
H	–	Hungary
HKJ	–	Jordan
HR	–	Croatia
I	–	Italy
IL	–	Israel
IRL	–	Ireland
IS	–	Iceland

L	–	Luxembourg
LAR	–	Libya
LT	–	Lithuania
LV	–	Latvia
M	–	Malta
MA	–	Morocco
MC	–	Monaco
MD	–	Moldavia
MK	–	Macedonia
N	–	Norway
NGR	–	Nigeria
NL	–	Netherlands
NZ	–	New Zealand
P	–	Portugal
PL	–	Poland
RL	–	Lebanon
RO	–	Romania
RSM	–	San Marino
RUS	–	Russia
S	–	Sweden
SK	–	Slovakia
SLO	–	Slovenia
SYR	–	Syria
TN	–	Tunisia
TR	–	Turkey
UA	–	Ukraine
USA	–	United States of America
V	–	Vatican City
YU	–	Yugoslavia
ZA	–	South Africa

OTHER

CC	–	Consular Corps
CD	–	Diplomatic Corps
GBA	–	Alderney
GBG	–	Guernsey
GBJ	–	Jersey
GBM	–	Isle of Man
GBZ	–	Gibraltar

Language

Albanian

Pronunciation

ë	often silent; at the beginning af a word it's like the 'a' in 'ago'
c	as the 'ts' in 'bits'
ç	as the 'ch' in 'church'
dh	as the 'th' in 'this'
gj	as the 'gy' in 'hogyard'
j	as the 'y' in 'yellow'
q	between 'ch' and 'ky', similar to the 'cu' in 'cure'
th	as in 'thistle'
x	as the 'dz' in 'adze'
xh	as the 'j' in 'jewel'
zh	as the 's' in 'pleasure'

Basics

Hello.	Tungjatjeta/Allo.
Goodbye.	Lamtumirë.
	Mirupafshim. (informal)
Yes.	Po.
No.	Jo.
Please.	Ju lutem.
Thank you.	Ju falem nderit.
That's fine.	Eshtë e mirë.
You're welcome.	S'ka përse.
Sorry. (excuse me, forgive me)	Më vjen keq/Më falni, ju lutem.
Excuse me.	Me falni.
Do you speak English?	A flisni anglisht?
How much is it?	Sa kushton?

Getting Around

What time does the ... leave/arrive?	Në ç'orë niset/ arrin ...?
boat	barka/lundra
bus	autobusi
tram	tramvaji
train	treni

I'd like ...	Dëshiroj ...
a one-way ticket	një biletë vajtje
a return ticket	një biletë kthimi

1st/2nd class	klas i parë/i dytë
timetable	orar
bus stop	stacion autobusi

Where is ...?	Ku është ...?
Go straight ahead.	Shko drejt.
Turn left/right.	Kthehu majtas/djathtas.
near/far	afër/larg

Around Town

a bank	një bankë
chemist/pharmacy	farmaci
the ... embassy	... ambasadën
the market	pazarin
the post office	postën
the telephone centre	centralin telefonik
the tourist office	zyrën e informimeve turistike

What time does it open/close?	Në ç'ore hapet/ mbyllet?

Accommodation

hotel	hotel
camping ground	kamp pushimi
a single room	një dhomë më një krevat
a double room	një dhomë më dy krevat

Do you have any rooms available?	A keni ndonjë dhomë të lirë?
How much is it per night/per person?	Sa kushton për një natë/ për një njeri?

Time, Days & Numbers

What time is it?	Sa është ora?
today	sot
tomorrow	nesër
yesterday	dje
in the morning	në mëngjes
in the afternoon	pas dreke

Monday	e hënë
Tuesday	e martë
Wednesday	e mërkurë
Thursday	e ënjte
Friday	e premte
Saturday	e shtunë
Sunday	e diel

Signs – Albanian

Albanian	English
Hyrje	Entrance
Dalje	Exit
Informim	Information
Hapur	Open
Mbyllur	Closed
E Ndaluar	Prohibited
Policia	Police
Nevojtorja	Toilets
Burra	Men
Gra	Women

Emergencies – Albanian

Help!	Ndihmë!
Call a doctor!	Thirrni doktorin!
Call the police!	Thirrni policinë!
Go away!	Zhduku!/Largohuni!
I'm lost.	Kam humbur rrugë.

1	një	7	shtatë
2	dy	8	tetë
3	tre	9	nëntë
4	katër	10	dhjetë
5	pesë	100	njëqind
6	gjashtë	1000	njëmijë

one million   një milion

Bosnian, Croatian & Serbian

Pronunciation

Bosnian and Croatian use a Roman alphabet – it's used here to cover Serbian as well (which normally uses the Cyrillic alphabet). Most letters are pronounced as in English – the following are some specific pronunciations.

c	as the 'ts' in 'cats'
ć	as the 'tch' sound in 'future'
č	as the 'ch' in 'chop'
đ	as the 'dy' sound in 'verdure'
dž	as the 'j' in 'just'
j	as the 'y' in 'young'
lj	as the 'lli' in 'million'
nj	as the 'ny' in 'canyon'
š	as the 'sh' in 'hush'
ž	as the 's' in 'pleasure'

In the following phraselist any differences in vocabulary are indicated with 'B' for Bosnian, 'C' for Croatian and 'S' for Serbian.

Basics

Hello.	Zdravo.
Goodbye.	Doviđenja.
Yes.	Da.
No.	Ne.
Please.	Molim.
Thank you.	Hvala.
That's fine/ You're welcome.	U redu je/ Nema na čemu.
Excuse me.	Oprostite.
Sorry. (excuse me, forgive me)	Pardon.
Do you speak English?	Govorite li engleski?
How much is it ...?	Koliko košta ...?

Getting Around

What time does the ... leave/arrive?	Kada ... polazi/dolazi?
boat	brod
citybus	autobus gradski
intercity bus	autobus međugradski
train	voz (S, B)/vlak (C)
tram	tramvaj

one-way ticket	kartu u jednom pravcu
return ticket	povratnu kartu
1st class	prvu klasu
2nd class	drugu klasu
Where is the ...?	Gde/Gdje je ...? (S/C)
Can you show me (on the map)?	Možete li mi pokazati (na karti)?
Go straight ahead.	Idite pravo napred (S)/ naprijed. (B, C)
Turn left.	Skrenite lijevo (B, C)/ levo. (S)
Turn right.	Skrenite desno.
near/far	blizu/daleko

Around Town

I'm looking for ...	Tražim ...
a bank	banku
the ... embassy	... ambasadu
my hotel	moj hotel
the market	pijacu
the post office	poštu

Signs

Entrance/Exit
Улаз/Излаз
Ulaz/Izlaz
Open/Closed
Отворено/Затворено
Otvoreno/Zatvoreno
Information
Информације
Informacije
Rooms Available
Слободне Собе
Slobodne Sobe
Full/No Vacancies
Нема Слободне Собе
Nema Slobodne Sobe
Police
Милиција
Milicija (S)/*Policija* (B, C)
Prohibited
Забрањено
Zabranjeno
Toilets
Тоалети
Toaleti (S, B)/*Zahodi* (C)

Emergencies

Help!	Upomoć!
Call a doctor!	Pozovite lekara! (B, S)/
	Pozovite liječnika! (C)
Call the police!	Pozovite miliciju! (S)
	Pozovite policiju! (C)
Go away!	Idite!
I'm lost.	
Izgubio/Izgubila sam se. (m/f) (B, S)	
Izgubljen/Izgubljena sam. (m/f) (C)	

the telephone centre	telefonsku centralu
the tourist office	turistički biro

Accommodation

hotel	hotel
guesthouse	privatno prenoćište
youth hostel	omladinsko prenoćište
camping ground	kamping

Do you have any rooms available?	Imate li slobodne sobe?
How much is it per night/per person?	Koliko košta za jednu noć/po osobi?

I'd like a ... room.	Želim ... sobu.
single	sa jednim krevetom
double	sa duplim krevetom

Time, Days & Numbers

What time is it?	Koliko je sati?
today	danas
tomorrow	sutra
yesterday	juče (S, B)/jučer (C)
in the morning	ujutro
in the afternoon	popodne

Monday	ponedeljak
Tuesday	utorak
Wednesday	sreda (S)/srijeda (B, C)
Thursday	četvrtak
Friday	petak
Saturday	subota
Sunday	nedelja (S)/ nedjelja (B, C)

1	jedan	7	sedam
2	dva	8	osam
3	tri	9	devet
4	četiri	10	deset
5	pet	100	sto
6	šest	1000	hiljada (B, S)/ tisuću (C)

one million	jedan milion (S)/ jedan milijun (B, C)

Bulgarian

Basics

Hello.	zdraveyte (polite)
	zdrasti (informal)
Goodbye.	dovizhdane (polite)
Goodbye.	chao (informal)
Yes.	da
No.	ne
Please.	molya
Thank you.	blagodarya
	mersi (informal)
I'm sorry. (forgive me)	sâzhalyavam (prostete)
Excuse me.	izvinete me
I don't understand.	az ne razbiram
How much is it?	kolko struva?

Getting Around

What time does the ... leave/arrive?	v kolko chasa zaminava/pristigha ...?
bus (city)	ghradskiyat avtobus
bus (intercity)	mezhdughradskiyat avtobus
plane	samolehtât
train	vlakât
tram	tramvayat

Where is the ...?	kâde e ...?
bus stop	avtobusnata spirka
train station	zhelezopâtnata gara
left-luggage room	garderobât

Please show me on the map.	molya pokazhete mi na kartata
straight ahead	napravo
left/right	lyavo/dyasno

Around Town

the bank	bankata
the hospital	bolnitsata
the market	pazara

Signs – Bulgarian

Вход	**Entrance**
Изход	**Exit**
Информация	**Information**
Отворено	**Open**
Затворено	**Closed**
Забранено	**Prohibited**
Полицейско Управление	**Police Station**
Тоалетни	**Toilets**
Мъже	**Men**
Жени	**Women**

Emergencies – Bulgarian

Help!	*pomosh!*
Call a doctor!	*povikayte lekar!*
Call the police!	*povikayte politsiya!*
Go away!	*mahayte se!*
I'm lost.	*zagubih se.*

the post office	*poshtata*
the tourist office	*byuroto za turisticheska informatsiya*

Accommodation

Do you have any rooms available?	*imateh li svobodni stai?*
How much is it?	*kolko struva?*

camping ground	*kâmping*
double room	*dvoyna staya*
guesthouse	*pansion*
hotel	*khotel*
private room	*stoya v chastna kvartira*
single room	*edinichna staya*
youth hostel	*obshtezhitie*

Time, Days & Numbers

What time is it?	*kolko e chasât?*
today	*dnes*
tonight	*dovechera*
tomorrow	*utre*
yesterday	*vchera*
in the morning	*sutrinta*
in the evening	*vecherta*

Monday	*ponedelnik*
Tuesday	*vtornik*
Wednesday	*sryada*
Thursday	*chetvârtâk*
Friday	*petâk*
Saturday	*sâbota*
Sunday	*nedelya*

1	*edno*	7	*sedem*
2	*dve*	8	*osem*
3	*tri*	9	*devet*
4	*chetiri*	10	*deset*
5	*pet*	100	*sto*
6	*shest*	1000	*hilyada*

one million	*edin milion*

Czech

Pronunciation

An accent lengthens a vowel. When consulting inxdexes on Czech maps, be aware that **ch** comes after **h**.

c	as the 'ts' in 'bits'
č	as the 'ch' in 'church'
ch	as in Scottish 'loch'
ď	as the 'd' in 'duty'
ě	as the 'ye' in 'yet'
j	as the 'y' in 'you'
ň	as the 'ni' in 'onion'
ř	as the sound 'rzh'
š	as the 'sh' in 'ship'
ť	as the 'te' in 'stew'
ž	as the 's' in 'pleasure'

Basics

Hello/Good day.	*Dobrý den.* (polite)
Hi.	*Ahoj.* (informal)
Goodbye.	*Na shledanou.*
Yes.	*Ano.*
No.	*Ne.*
Please.	*Prosím.*
Thank you.	*Děkuji.*
That's fine/You're welcome.	*Není zač/Prosím.*
Sorry. (Forgive me)	*Promiňte.*
I don't understand.	*Nerozumím.*
How much is it?	*Kolik to stojí?*

Getting Around

What time does the ... leave/arrive?	*Kdy odjíždí/přijíždí ...?*
boat	*loď*
bus (city)	*(městský) autobus*
bus (intercity)	*(meziměstský) autobus*
train	*vlak*
tram	*tramvaj*

arrival	*příjezdy*
departure	*odjezdy*
timetable	*jízdní řád*

Where is thc ...?	*Kde je ...?*
bus stop	*autobusová zastávka*
station	*nádraží*
left-luggage room	*úschovna zavazadel*

Signs – Czech

Vchod	**Entrance**
Východ	**Exit**
Informace	**Information**
Otevřeno	**Open**
Zavřeno	**Closed**
Zakázáno	**Prohibited**
Policie	**Police Station**
Telefon	**Telephone**
Záchody/WC/ Toalety	**Toilets**

Emergencies – Czech

Help!	Pomoc!
Call a doctor/	Zavolejte doktora/
ambulance/police!	sanitku/policii!
Go away!	Běžte pryč!
I'm lost.	Zabloudil jsem. (m)
	Zabloudila jsem. (f)

1	jeden	7	sedm
2	dva	8	osm
3	tři	9	devět
4	čtyři	10	deset
5	pět	100	sto
6	šest	1000	tisíc

one million	jeden milión

Please show me	Prosím, ukažte mi
on the map.	to na mapě.
left/right	vlevo/vpravo
straight ahead	rovně

Danish

Pronunciation

a	as in 'father'
a, æ	as in 'act'
o, å	
& u(n)	a long rounded 'a' as in 'walk'
e(g)	as in 'eye'
e, i	as the 'e' in 'bet'
i	as the 'e' in 'theme'
ø	as the 'er' in 'fern'
o, u	as the 'oo' in 'cool'
o	as in 'pot'
o(v)	as the 'ou' in 'out'
o(r)	as the 'or' in for' with less emphasis on the 'r'
u	as in 'pull'
y	say 'ee' while pursing your lips
sj	as in 'ship'
c	as in 'cell'
(o)d	a flat 'dh' sound, like the 'th' in 'these'
r	a rolling 'r' abruptly cut short
j	as the 'y' in 'yet'

Around Town

Where is it?	Kde je to?
the bank	banka
the chemist	lékárna
the church	kostel
the market	trh
the museum	muzeum
the post office	pošta
the tourist office	turistické informační
	centrum (středisko)
travel agency	cestovní kancelář

Accommodation

hotel	hotel
guesthouse	penzión
youth hostel	ubytovna
camping ground	kemping
private room	privát
single room	jednolůžkový pokoj
double room	dvoulůžkový pokoj

Do you have any	Máte volné pokoje?
rooms available?	
How much is it?	Kolik to je?

Time, Days & Numbers

What time is it?	Kolik je hodin?
today	dnes
tonight	dnes večer
tomorrow	zítra
yesterday	včera
in the morning	ráno
in the evening	večer

Monday	pondělí
Tuesday	úterý
Wednesday	středa
Thursday	čtvrtek
Friday	pátek
Saturday	sobota
Sunday	neděle

Basics

Hello.	Hallo.
	Hej. (informal)
Goodbye.	Farvel.
Yes.	Ja.
No.	Nej.
Please.	Må jeg bede/Værsgo.
Thank you.	Tak.
That's fine/	Det er i orden/
You're welcome.	Selv tak.
Excuse me. (sorry)	Undskyld.
Do you speak	Taler De engelsk?
English?	
How much is it?	Hvor meget koster det?

Getting Around

What time does ...	Hvornår går/
leave/arrive?	ankommer ...?
the boat	båden
the bus (city)	bussen
the bus (intercity)	rutebilen
the tram	sporvognen
the train	toget

I'd like ...   *Jeg vil gerne have ...*
  a one-way ticket   *en enkeltbillet*
  a return ticket   *en tur-retur billet*
  1st/2nd class   *første/anden klasse*

left luggage office   *reisegodsoppbevar-*
                          ingen
timetable   *køreplan*
bus stop   *bus holdeplads*
tram stop   *sporvogn holdeplads*
train station   *jernbanestation*
                          (banegård)

Where can I hire a   *Hvor kan jeg leje en*
  car/bicycle?   *bil/cykel?*
Where is ...?   *Hvor er ...?*
Go straight ahead.   *Gå ligefrem.*
Turn left/right.   *Drej til venstre/højre.*
near/far   *nær/fjern*

Around Town

a bank   *en bank*
a chemist/pharmacy   *et apotek*
the ... embassy   *den ... ambassade*
the market   *markedet*
a newsagent   *en aviskiosk*
the post office   *postkontoret*
the tourist office   *turistinformationen*

What time does it   *Hvornår åbner/*
  open/close?   *lukker det?*

Accommodation

hotel   *hotel*
guesthouse   *gæstgiveri*
hostel   *vandrerhjem*
camping ground   *campingplads*

Do you have any   *Har I ledige værelser?*
  rooms available?
How much is it   *Hvor meget koster det*
  per night/   *per nat/*
  per person?   *per person?*
one day/two days   *en nat/to nætter*

Signs – Danish	
Indgang	**Entrance**
Udgang	**Exit**
Åben	**Open**
Lukket	**Closed**
Forbudt	**Prohibited**
Information	**Information**
Politistation	**Police Station**
Toiletter	**Toilets**
Herrer	**Men**
Damer	**Women**

Emergencies – Danish	
Help!	*Hjælp!*
Call a doctor!	*Ring efter en læge!*
Call the police!	*Ring efter politiet!*
Go away!	*Forsvind!*
I'm lost.	*Jeg har gået vild.*

I'd like ...   *Jeg ønsker ...*
  a single room   *et enkeltværelse*
  a double room   *et dobbeltværelse*

Time, Days & Numbers

What time is it?   *Hvad er klokken?*
today   *i dag*
tomorrow   *i morgen*
yesterday   *i går*
morning   *morgenen*
afternoon   *eftermiddagen*

Monday   *mandag*
Tuesday   *tirsdag*
Wednesday   *onsdag*
Thursday   *torsdag*
Friday   *fredag*
Saturday   *lørdag*
Sunday   *søndag*

0	*nul*	7	*syv*
1	*en*	8	*otte*
2	*to*	9	*ni*
3	*tre*	10	*ti*
4	*fire*	11	*elve*
5	*fem*	100	*hundrede*
6	*seks*	1000	*tusind*

one million   *en million*

Dutch

Pronunciation

au, ou pronounced somewhere between the 'ow' in 'how' and the 'ow' in 'glow'

eu a tricky one; try saying 'eh' with rounded lips and the tongue forward, then slide the tongue back and down to make an 'oo' sound; it's similar to the 'eu' in French *couleur*

i, ie long, as the 'ee' in 'meet'

ij as the 'ey' in 'they'

oe as the 'oo' in 'zoo'

ui a very tricky one; pronounced somewhere between **au/ou** and **eu**; it's similar to the 'eui' in French *fauteuil*, without the slide to the 'i'

ch & g in the north, a hard 'kh' sound as in the Scottish *loch*; in the south, a softer, lisping sound

j as the 'y' in 'yes'; also as the 'j' or 'zh' sound in 'jam' or 'pleasure'

r in the south, a trilled sound; in the north it varies, often guttural

Basics

Hello.	*Dag/Hallo.*
Goodbye.	*Dag.*
Yes.	*Ja.*
No.	*Nee.*
Please.	*Alstublieft/Alsjeblieft.*
Thank you.	*Dank U/je (wel).*
You're welcome.	*Geen dank.*
Excuse me.	*Pardon.*
Sorry.	*Sorry.*
Do you speak English?	*Spreekt U/spreek je Engels?*
How much is it?	*Hoeveel kost het?*

Getting Around

What time does the ... leave/arrive?	*Hoe laat vertrekt/ arriveert de ...?*
(next)	*(volgende)*
boat	*boot*
bus/tram	*bus/tram*
train	*trein*
I'd like to hire a car/bicycle.	*Ik wil graag een auto/fiets huren.*
I'd like a one-way/ return ticket.	*Ik wil graag een enkele reis/een retour.*
1st/2nd class	*eerste/tweede klas*
left luggage locker	*bagagekluis*
bus/tram stop	*bushalte/tramhalte*
train station/ ferry terminal	*treinstation/ veerhaven*
Where is the ...?	*Waar is de ...?*
Go straight ahead.	*Ga rechtdoor.*

Emergencies – Dutch

Help!	*Help!*
Call a doctor!	*Haal een dokter!*
Call the police!	*Haal de politie!*
Go away!	*Ga weg!*
I'm lost.	*Ik ben de weg kwijt.*

Turn left/right.	*Ga linksaf/rechtsaf.*
far/near	*ver/dichtbij*

Around Town

a bank	*een bank*
the ... embassy	*de ... ambassade*
the market	*de markt*
the pharmacy	*de drogist*
the newsagent/ stationer	*de krantenwinkel/ kantoorboekhandel*
the post office	*het postkantoor*
the tourist office	*de VVV/het toeristenbureau*

What time does it open/close?	*Hoe laat opent/ sluit het?*

Accommodation

hotel	*hotel*
guesthouse	*pension*
youth hostel	*jeugdherberg*
camping ground	*camping*
Do you have any rooms available?	*Heeft U kamers vrij?*
single/double room	*eenpersoons/twee- persoons kamer*
one/two nights	*één nacht/twee nachten*
How much is it per night/ per person?	*Hoeveel is het per nacht/ per persoon?*

Time, Days & Numbers

What time is it?	*Hoe laat is het?*
today	*vandaag*
tomorrow	*morgen*
in the morning	*'s-morgens*
in the afternoon	*'s-middags*
Monday	*maandag*
Tuesday	*dinsdag*
Wednesday	*woensdag*
Thursday	*donderdag*
Friday	*vrijdag*
Saturday	*zaterdag*
Sunday	*zondag*

LANGUAGE

0	*nul*	7	*zeven*
1	*één*	8	*acht*
2	*twee*	9	*negen*
3	*drie*	10	*tien*
4	*vier*	11	*elf*
5	*vijf*	100	*honderd*
6	*zes*	1000	*duizend*

one million	*één miljoen*

Estonian

Pronunciation

ä   as the 'a' in 'cat'
õ   somewhere between the 'e' in 'bed' and the 'u' in 'fur'
ö   as the 'u' in 'fur' but with rounded lips
ü   as a short 'you'
j   as the 'y' in 'yes'

Basics

Hello.	*Tere.*
Goodbye.	*Nägemiseni.*
Yes.	*Jah.*
No.	*Ei.*
Please.	*Palun.*
Thank you.	*Tänan/Aitäh.*
You're welcome.	*Palun.*
Excuse me. (Sorry)	*Vabandage.*
Do you speak English?	*Kas te räägite inglise keelt?*
How much is it?	*Kui palju see maksab?*

Getting Around

What time does the ... leave/arrive?	*Mis kell lähels/ saabub ...?*
the boat	*paat*
the bus	*buss*
the tram	*tramm*
the train	*rong*

Where can I hire a car/bicycle?	*Kust ma saan laenu- tada auto/jalgratas?*
I'd like a one-way/ return ticket.	*Palun üks/edasi-tagasi pilet.*
left luggage	*pagasi hoiuruum*
timetable	*sošiduplaan*
bus station	*bussijaam*
train station	*rongijaam*
ferry terminal	*sadam*

Where is the ...?	*Kus on ...?*
Is it near/far?	*Kas see on lähedal/kaugel?*
Go straight ahead.	*Otse.*
Go left/right.	*Vasakule/Paremale.*

Around Town

bank	*pank*
chemist/pharmacy	*apteek*
... embassy	*... saatkond*
post office	*postkontor*
market	*turg*
the tourist office	*turismibüroo*

What time does it open/close?	*Mis kell see avatakse/suletakse?*

Accommodation

hotel	*hotelli*
youth hostel	*noorte hotell*
camping ground	*telkimis plats*

Do you have any rooms available?	*Kas teil kohti on?*
How much is it per night/person?	*Kui palju maksab ööpäev/voodikoht?*
one/two days	*üheks/kaheks päevaks*

I'd like a ...	*Ma tahaksin ... tuba.*
single room	*ühe voodiga*
double room	*kahe voodiga*

Time, Days & Numbers

What time is it?	*Mis kell on?*
today	*täna*
tomorrow	*homme*
yesterday	*eile*
morning	*hommikul*
evening	*õhtul*

Monday	*esmaspäev*
Tuesday	*teisipäev*
Wednesday	*kolmapäev*
Thursday	*neljapäev*
Friday	*reede*
Saturday	*laupäev*
Sunday	*pühapäev*

Signs – Estonian

Sissepääs	Entrance
Valjapääs	Exit
Avatud	Open
Suletud	Closed
On Vabu Kohti	Rooms Available
Kohad Kini	No Vacancies
Informatsioon	Information
Politseijaoskond	Police Station
Tualett (WC)	Toilets
Meestele	Men
Naistele	Women

Emergencies – Estonian

Help!	*Appi!*
Call a doctor!	*Kutsuge arst!*
Call the police!	*Helistage politseile!*
Go away!	*Minge ära!*
I'm lost.	*Ma olen eksinud.*

1	*üks*	7	*seitse*
2	*kaks*	8	*kaheksa*
3	*kolm*	9	*üheksa*
4	*neli*	10	*kümme*
5	*viis*	100	*sada*
6	*kuus*	1000	*tuhat*

one million   *üks miljon*

Finnish

Pronunciation

The final letters of the alphabet are **å**, **ä** and **ö** (important to know when looking for something in a telephone directory).

y	as the 'u' in 'pull' but with the lips stretched back (like the German 'ü')
å	as the 'oo' in 'poor'
ä	as the 'a' in 'act'
ö	as the 'e' in 'summer'
z	pronounced (and sometimes written) as 'ts'
v/w	as the 'v' in 'vain'
h	a weak sound, except at the end of a syllable, when it is almost as strong as 'ch' in German *ich*
j	as the 'y' in 'yellow'
r	a rolled 'r'

Basics

Hello.	*Hei/Terve.*
	Moi. (informal)
Goodbye.	*Näkemiin.*
	Moi. (informal)
Yes.	*Kyllä/Joo.*
No.	*Ei.* (pronounced 'ay')
Please.	*Kiitos.*
Thank you.	*Kiitos.*
That's fine/You're welcome.	*Ole hyvä.* or *Eipä kestä.* (informal)
Excuse me. (sorry)	*Anteeksi.*
Do you speak English?	*Puhutko englantia?*
How much is it?	*Paljonko se makasaa?*

Getting Around

What time does ... leave/arrive?	*Mihin aikaan ... lähtee/saapuu?*

the boat	*laiva*
the bus (city)	*bussi*
the bus (intercity)	*bussi/linja-auto*
the tram	*raitiovaunu/raitikka*
the train	*juna*

I'd like a one-way/ return ticket.	*Saanko menolipun/ menopaluulipun.*
Where can I hire a car?	*Mistä mina voisin vuokrata auton?*
Where can I hire a bicycle?	*Mistä mina voin vuokrata polkupyörän?*

1st class	*ensimmäinen luokka*
2nd class	*toinen luokka*
left luggage	*säilytys*
timetable	*aikataulu*
bus/tram stop	*pysäkki*
train station	*rautatieasema*
ferry terminal	*satamaterminaali*

Where is ...?	*Missä on ...?*
Go straight ahead.	*Kulje suoraan.*
Turn left.	*Käänny vasempaan.*
Turn right.	*Käänny oikeaan.*
near/far	*lähellä/kaukana*

Around Town

bank	*pankkia*
chemist/pharmacy	*apteekki*
... embassy	*... -n suurlähetystöä*
market	*toria*
newsagent	*lehtikioski*
post office	*postia*
tourist office	*matkailutoimistoa/ matkailutoimisto*

What time does it open/close?	*Milloin se aukeaan/ sul jetaan?*

Signs – Finnish

Sisään	**Entrance**
Ulos	**Exit**
Avoinna	**Open**
Suljettu	**Closed**
Kielletty	**Prohibited**
Huoneita	**Rooms Available**
Täynnä	**No Vacancies**
Opastus	**Information**
Poliisiasema	**Police Station**
WC	**Toilets**
Miehet	**Men**
Naiset	**Women**

Emergencies – Finnish

Help!	*Apua!*
Call a doctor!	*Kutsukaa lääkäri!*
Call the police!	*Soittakaa poliisi!*
Go away!	*Mene pois! (Häivy!)*
I'm lost.	*Minä olen eksynyt.*

Accommodation

hotel	*hotelli*
guesthouse	*matkustajakoti*
youth hostel	*retkeilymaja*
campground	*leirintäalue*

Do you have any rooms available?	*Onko teillä vapaata huonetta?*

How much is it ...?	*Paljonko se on ...?*
per night	*yöltä*
per person	*hengeltä*

I'd like ...	*Haluaisin ...*
a single room	*yhden hengen huoneen*
a double room	*kahden hengen huoneen*

one day	*yhden päivän*
two days	*kaksi päivää*

Time, Days & Numbers

What time is it?	*Paljonko kello on?*
today	*tänään*
tomorrow	*huomenna*
yesterday	*eilen*
morning	*aamulla*
afternoon	*iltapäivällä*

Monday	*maanantai*
Tuesday	*tiistai*
Wednesday	*keskiviikko*
Thursday	*torstai*
Friday	*perjantai*
Saturday	*lauantai*
Sunday	*sunnuntai*

0	*nolla*	7	*seitsemän*
1	*yksi*	8	*kahdeksan*
2	*kaksi*	9	*yhdeksän*
3	*kolme*	10	*kymmenen*
4	*neljä*	11	*yksitoista*
5	*viisi*	100	*sata*
6	*kuusi*	1000	*tuhat*

one million	*miljoona*

French

Basics

Hello.	*Bonjour.*
Goodbye.	*Au revoir.*
Yes.	*Oui.*
No.	*Non.*
Please.	*S'il vous plaît.*
Thank you.	*Merci.*
That's fine, you're welcome.	*Je vous en prie.*
Excuse me.	*Excusez-moi*
Sorry. (apology)	*Pardon*
Do you speak English?	*Parlez-vous anglais?*
How much is it?	*C'est combien?*

Getting Around

When does the next ... leave/arrive?	*À quelle heure part/ arrive le prochain ...?*
boat	*bateau*
bus (city)	*bus*
bus (intercity)	*car*
tram	*tramway*
train	*train*

left luggage (office)	*consigne*
timetable	*horaire*
bus stop	*arrêt d'autobus*
tram stop	*arrêt de tramway*
train station	*gare*
ferry terminal	*gare maritime*

I'd like a ... ticket.	*Je voudrais un billet ...*
one-way	*aller simple*
return	*aller retour*
1st class	*première classe*
2nd class	*deuxième classe*

I'd like to hire a car/bicycle.	*Je voudrais louer une voiture/un vélo.*

Signs – French

Entrée	**Entrance**
Sortie	**Exit**
Chambres Libres	**Rooms Available**
Complet	**Full/No Vacancies**
Renseignements	**Information**
Ouvert/Fermée	**Open/Closed**
(Commissariat de) Police	**Police Station**
Interdit	**Prohibited**
Toilettes, WC	**Toilets**
Hommes	**Men**
Femmes	**Women**

Where is ...?	*Où est ...?*
Go straight ahead.	*Continuez tout droit.*
Turn left.	*Tournez à gauche.*
Turn right.	*Tournez à droite.*
far/near	*loin/proche*

Around Town

a bank	*une banque*
chemist/pharmacy	*la pharmacie*
the ... embassy	*l'ambassade de ...*
market	*le marché*
newsagent	*l'agence de presse*
post office	*le bureau de poste*
the tourist office	*l'office de tourisme/ le syndicat d'initiative*

What time does it open/close?	*Quelle est l' heure de ouverture/fermeture?*

Accommodation

the hotel	*l'hôtel*
the youth hostel	*l'auberge de jeunesse*
the camping ground	*le camping*

Do you have any rooms available?	*Est-ce que vous avez des chambres libres?*
for one person	*pour une personne*
for two people	*deux personnes*
How much is it per night/ per person?	*Quel est le prix par nuit/ par personne?*

Time, Days & Numbers

What time is it?	*Quelle heure est-il?*
today	*aujourd'hui*
tomorrow	*demain*
yesterday	*hier*
morning	*matin*
afternoon	*après-midi*

Monday	*lundi*
Tuesday	*mardi*
Wednesday	*mercredi*
Thursday	*jeudi*
Friday	*vendredi*
Saturday	*samedi*
Sunday	*dimanche*

1	*un*	7	*sept*
2	*deux*	8	*huit*
3	*trois*	9	*neuf*
4	*quatre*	10	*dix*
5	*cinq*	100	*cent*
6	*six*	1000	*mille*

one million	*un million*

German

Pronunciation

au	as the 'ow' in 'vow'
ä	short, as in 'cat' or long, as in 'care'
äu	as the 'oy' in 'boy'
ei	as the 'ai' in 'aisle'
eu	as the 'oy' in 'boy'
ie	as the 'brief'
ö	as the 'er' in 'fern'
ü	similar to the 'u' in 'pull' but with lips stretched back
ch	as in Scottish *loch*
j	as the 'y' in 'yet'
qu	as 'k' plus 'v'
sch	as the 'sh' in 'ship'
sp, st	as 'shp' and 'sht' when word-initial
tion	the 't' is pronounced as the 'ts' in 'its'
v	as the 'f' in 'fan'
w	as the 'v' in 'van'
z	as the 'ts' in 'its'

Basics

Good day.	*Guten Tag.*
Hello. (in Bavaria and Austria)	*Grüss Gott.*
Goodbye.	*Auf Wiedersehen.*
Bye. (informal)	*Tschüss.*
Yes.	*Ja.*
No.	*Nein.*
Please.	*Bitte.*
Thank you.	*Danke.*
You're welcome.	*Bitte sehr.*
Sorry. (excuse me, forgive me)	*Entschuldigung.*
Do you speak English?	*Sprechen Sie Englisch?*
How much is it?	*Wieviel kostet es?*

Getting Around

What time does ... leave/arrive?	*Wann (fährt ... ab/ kommt ... an)?*
the boat	*das Boot*
the bus (city)	*der Bus*
the bus (intercity)	*der (überland) Bus*
the tram	*die Strassenbahn*
the train	*der Zug*

I'd like to hire a car/bicycle. — *Ich möchte ein Auto/ Fahrrad mieten.*
I'd like a one-way/ return ticket. — *Ich möchte eine Einzel- karte/Rückfahrkarte.*

1st/2nd class — *erste/zweite Klasse*
left luggage lockers — *Schliessfächer*
timetable — *Fahrplan*
bus stop — *Bushaltestelle*
tram stop — *Strassenbahnhaltestelle*
train station — *Bahnhof (Bf)*
ferry terminal — *Fährhafen*

Where is the ...? — *Wo ist die ...?*
Go straight ahead. — *Gehen Sie geradeaus.*
Turn left. — *Biegen Sie links ab.*
Turn right. — *Biegen Sie rechts ab.*
near/far — *nahe/weit*

Around Town
a bank — *eine Bank*
the ... embassy — *die ... Botschaft*
the market — *der Markt*
the newsagent — *der Zeitungshändler*
the pharmacy — *die Apotheke*
the post office — *das Postamt*
the tourist office — *das Verkehrsamt*

What time does it open/close? — *Um wieviel Uhr macht es auf/zu?*

Accommodation
hotel — *Hotel*
guesthouse — *Pension, Gästehaus*
youth hostel — *Jugendherberge*
camping ground — *Campingplatz*

Do you have any rooms available? — *Haben Sie noch freie Zimmer?*
a single room — *ein Einzelzimmer*
a double room — *ein Doppelzimmer*
How much is it per night/person? — *Wieviel kostet es pro Nacht/Person?*

Signs – German

Eingang	**Entrance**
Ausgang	**Exit**
Zimmer Frei	**Rooms Available**
Voll/Besetzt	**Full/No Vacancies**
Auskunft	**Information**
Offen	**Open**
Geschlossen	**Closed**
Polizeiwache	**Police Station**
Toiletten (WC)	**Toilets**
Herren	**Men**
Damen	**Women**

Emergencies – German

Help!	*Hilfe!*
Call a doctor!	*Holen Sie einen Arzt!*
Call the police!	*Rufen Sie die Polizei!*
I'm lost.	*Ich habe mich verirrt.*

Time, Days & Numbers
What time is it? — *Wie spät ist es?*
today — *heute*
tomorrow — *morgen*
yesterday — *gestern*
in the morning — *morgens*
in the afternoon — *nachmittags*

Monday — *Montag*
Tuesday — *Dienstag*
Wednesday — *Mittwoch*
Thursday — *Donnerstag*
Friday — *Freitag*
Saturday — *Samstag/Sonnabend*
Sunday — *Sonntag*

0	*null*	8	*acht*
1	*eins*	9	*neun*
2	*zwei/zwo*	10	*zehn*
3	*drei*	11	*elf*
4	*vier*	12	*zwölf*
5	*fünf*	13	*dreizehn*
6	*sechs*	100	*hundert*
7	*sieben*	1000	*tausend*

one million — *eine Million*

Greek

Basics
Hello. — *yasu* (informal) *yasas* (polite/plural)
Goodbye. — *andio*
Yes. — *ne*
No. — *okhi*
Please. — *sas parakalo*
Thank you. — *sas efharisto*
That's fine/ You're welcome. — *ine endaksi/parakalo*
Excuse me. (forgive me) — *signomi*
Do you speak English? — *milate anglika?*
How much is it? — *poso kani?*

Getting Around
What time does the ... leave/arrive? — *ti ora fevyi/apo horito ...?*
boat — *to plio*
bus (city) — *to leoforio (ya tin boli)*

bus (intercity)	to leoforio
	(ya ta proastia)
tram	to tram
train	to treno

I'd like a ... ticket.	tha ithela isitirio ...
one-way	horis epistrofi
return	met epistrois
1st class	proti thesi
2nd class	dhefteri thesi

left luggage	horos aspokevon
timetable	dhromologhio
bus stop	i stasi tu leoforiu

Go straight ahead.	pighenete efthia
Turn left.	stripste aristera
Turn right.	stripste dheksya

Around Town

a bank	mia trapeza
the ... embassy	i ... presvia
the market	i aghora
newsagent	efimeridhon
pharmacy	farmakio
the post office	to takhidhromio
the tourist office	to ghrafio turistikon
	pliroforion

| What time does it | ti ora aniyi/klini? |
| open/close? | |

Accommodation

a hotel	ena xenothohio
a youth hostel	enas xenonas neoitos
a camp site	ena kamping

I'd like a ... room.	thelo ena dhomatio ...
single	ya ena atomo
double	ya dhio atoma

How much is it ...?	poso kostizi ...?
per night	ya ena vradhi
per person	ya ena atomo

Emergencies – Greek

Help!	voithia!
Call a doctor!	fona kste ena yatro!
Call the police!	tilefoniste stin
	astinomia!
Go away!	fighe/dhromo!
I'm lost.	eho hathi

Time, Days & Numbers

What time is it?	ti ora ine?
today	simera
tomorrow	avrio
yesterday	hthes
in the morning	to proi
in the afternoon	to apoyevma

Monday	dheftera
Tuesday	triti
Wednesday	tetarti
Thursday	pempti
Friday	paraskevi
Saturday	savato
Sunday	kiryaki

1	ena	7	epta
2	dhio	8	okhto
3	tria	9	enea
4	tesera	10	dheka
5	pende	100	ekato
6	eksi	1000	khilya

| one million | ena ekatomirio |

Hungarian

The semantic difference between **a**, **e** or **o** with and without an accent mark is great. For example, *hát* means 'back' while *hat* means 'six'. The combinations **cs**, **zs**, **gy** and **sz** (consonant clusters) are separate letters in Hungarian and appear that way in telephone books and other alphabetical listings.

á	as in 'father'
é	as the 'e' in 'they' with no 'y' sound
í	as the 'i' in 'police'
ö	as the 'o' in 'worse' with no 'r' sound
ő	a longer version of **ö** above
ú	as the 'ue' in 'blue'
ü	similar to the 'u' in 'flute'; purse your lips tightly and say 'ee'
ű	a longer, breathier version of **ü** above
c	as the 'ts' in 'hats'
cs	as the 'ch' in 'church'
gy	as the 'j' in 'jury'

LANGUAGE

j	as the 'y' in 'yes'
ly	as the 'y' in 'yes'
ny	as the 'ni' in 'onion'
s	as the 'sh' in 'ship'
sz	as the 's' in 'set'
ty	as the 'tu' in 'tube' in British English
zs	as the 's' in 'pleasure'

Basics

Hello.	Jó napot kivánok. (pol)
	Szia/Szervusz. (inf)
Goodbye.	Viszontlátásra. (pol)
	Szia/Szervusz. (inf)
Yes.	Igen.
No.	Nem.
Please.	Kérem.
Thank you.	Köszönöm.
Sorry. (forgive me)	Sajnálom/Elnézést.
Excuse me.	Bocsánat.
I don't understand.	Nem értem.
Do you speak English?	Beszél angolul?
How much is it?	Mennyibe kerül?

Getting Around

What time does the ... leave/arrive?	Mikor indul/érkezik a ...?
boat/ferry	hajó/komp
bus (city)	helyi autóbusz
bus (intercity)	távolsági autóbusz
plane	repülőgép
train	vonat
tram	villamos

arrival	érkezés
departure	indulás
timetable	menetrend

Where is the bus stop?	Hol van az autóbuszmegálló?
Where is the station?	Hol van a pályaudvar?
Where is the left-luggage room?	Hol van a csomagmegőrző?

Please show me on the map.	Kérem, mutassa meg a térképen.
(Turn) left.	(Forduljon) balra.
(Turn) right.	(Forduljon) jobbra.
(Go) straight ahead	(Menyen) egyenesen előre.
near/far	közel/messze

Around Town

Where is ...?	Hol van ...?
a bank	bank
a chemist/pharmacy	gyógyszertár
the market	a piac
the post office	a posta
a tourist office	idegenforgalmi iroda

Accommodation

hotel	szálloda
guesthouse	fogadót
youth hostel	ifjúsági szálló
camping ground	kemping
private room	fizetővendég szoba

| Do you have rooms available? | Van szabad szobájuk? |
| How much is it per night/ per person? | Mennyibe kerül éjszakánként/ személyenként? |

| single room | egyágyas szoba |
| double room | kétágyas szoba |

Time, Days & Numbers

What time is it?	Hány óra?
today	ma
tonight	ma este
tomorrow	holnap
yesterday	tegnap
in the morning	reggel
in the evening	este

Monday	hétfő
Tuesday	kedd
Wednesday	szerda
Thursday	csütörtök
Friday	péntek
Saturday	szombat
Sunday	vasárnap

1	*egy*	7	*hét*
2	*kettő*	8	*nyolc*
3	*három*	9	*kilenc*
4	*négy*	10	*tíz*
5	*öt*	100	*száz*
6	*hat*	1000	*ezer*

one million   *millió*

Icelandic

Pronunciation

i, y	as the 'e' in 'pretty'
í, ý	as the 'e' in 'evil'
ú	as the 'o' in 'moon', or as the 'o' in 'woman'
ö	as the 'er' in 'fern', but without a trace of 'r'
á	as the 'ou' in 'out'
ei, ey	as the 'ay' in 'day'
ó	as the word 'owe'
æ	as the word 'eye'
au	as 'er' + 'ee' (as in French *oeil*)
é	as the 'y' in 'yet'
ð	as the 'th' in 'lather'
j	as the 'y' in 'yellow'
þ	as the 'th' in 'thin' or 'three'

Basics

Hello.	*Halló.*
Goodbye.	*Bless.*
Yes.	*Já.*
No.	*Nei.*
Please.	*Gjörðu svo vel.*
Thank you.	*Takk fyrir.*
That's fine/	*Allt í lagi/*
You're welcome.	*Ekkert að þakka.*
Excuse me. (Sorry)	*Afsakið.*
Do you speak English?	*Talar þú ensku?*
How much is it?	*Hvað kostar tað*

Getting Around

What time does ... leave/arrive?	*Hvenær fer/kemur ...?*
the boat	*báturinn*
the bus (city)	*vagninn*
the tram	*sporvagninn*

I'd like ...	*Gæti ég fengid ...*
a one-way ticket	*miða/aðra leiðina*
a return ticket	*miða/báðar leiðir*
1st class	*fyrsta farrými*
2nd class	*annað farrými*

timetable	*tímaáætlun*
bus stop	*biðstöð*
ferry terminal	*ferjuhöfn*

I'd like to hire a car/bicycle.	*Ég vil leigia bíl/reiðhjól.*
Where is ...?	*Hvar er ...?*
Go straight ahead.	*Farðu beint af áfram.*
Turn left.	*Beygðu til vinstri.*
Turn right.	*Beygðu til hægri.*
near/far	*nálægt/langt í burtu*

Around Town

bank	*banka*
chemist/pharmacy	*apótek*
... embassy	*... sendiráðinu*
market	*markaðnum*
newsagent/stationer	*blaðasala/bókabúð*
post office	*pósthúsinu*
tourist office	*upplýsingaþjónustu fyrir ferðafólk*

Accommodation

hotel	*hótel*
guesthouse	*gistiheimili*
youth hostel	*farfuglaheimili*
camping ground	*tjaldsvæði*

Do you have any rooms available?	*Eru herbergi laus?*
How much is it per night/per person?	*Hvað kostar nóttin fyrir manninn?*
one day	*einn dag*
two days	*tvo daga*

I'd like ...	*Gæti ég fengið ...*
a single room	*einstaklingsherbergi*
a double room	*tveggjamanna-herbergi*

Time, Days & Numbers

What time is it?	*Hvað er klukkan?*
today	*í dag*
tomorrow	*á morgun*
yesterday	*í gær*

Signs – Icelandic

Inngangur/Inn	**Entrance**
Útgangur/Út	**Exit**
Opið	**Open**
Lokað	**Closed**
Bannað	**Prohibited**
Full Bókað	**No Vacancies**
Upplýsingar	**Information**
Lögreglustöð	**Police Station**
Snyrting	**Toilets**
Karlar	**Men**
Konur	**Women**

Emergencies – Icelandic

Help!	Hjálp!
Call a doctor!	Náið í lækni!
Call the police!	Náið í lögregluna!
Go away!	Farðu!
I'm lost	Ég er villtur/villt. (m/f)

in the morning	að morgni
in the afternoon	eftir hádegi

Monday	mánudagur
Tuesday	þriðjudagur
Wednesday	miðvikudagur
Thursday	fimmtudagur
Friday	föstudagur
Saturday	laugardagur
Sunday	sunnudagur

0	núll	7	sjö
1	einn	8	átta
2	tveir	9	níu
3	þrír	10	tíu
4	fjórir	20	tuttugu
5	fimm	100	eitt hundrað
6	sex	1000	eitt þúsund

one million	ein milljón

Italian

Pronunciation

c	as 'k' before **a**, **o** and **u**; as the 'ch' in 'choose' before **e** and **i**
ch	a hard 'k' sound
g	as in 'get' before **a**, **o** and **u**; as in 'gem' before **e** and **i**
gh	as in 'get'
gli	as the 'lli' in 'million'
gn	as the 'ny' in 'canyon'
h	always silent
r	a rolled 'rrr' sound
sc	as the 'sh' in 'sheep' before **e** and **i**; a hard sound as in 'school' before **h, a, o** and **u**
z	as the 'ts' in 'lights' or as the 'ds' in 'beds'

Basics

Hello.	Buongiorno. (polite)
	Ciao. (informal)
Goodbye.	Arrivederci. (polite)
	Ciao. (informal)
Yes.	Sì.
No.	No.
Please.	Per favore/Per piacere.
Thank you.	Grazie.

That's fine/ You're welcome.	Prego.
Excuse me.	Mi scusi.
Sorry. (excuse me/ forgive me)	Mi scusi/Mi perdoni.
Do you speak English?	Parla inglese?
How much is it?	Quanto costa?

Getting Around

When does the ... leave/arrive?	A che ora parte/ arriva ...?
boat	la barca
ferry	il traghetto
bus	l'autobus
train	il treno

bus stop	fermata dell'autobus
train station	stazione
ferry terminal	stazione marittima
1st class	prima classe
2nd class	seconda classe
left luggage	deposito bagagli
timetable	orario

I'd like a one-way/ return ticket.	Vorrei un biglietto di solo andata/ di andata e ritorno.
I'd like to hire a car/bicycle.	Vorrei noleggiare una macchina/bicicletta.

Where is ...?	Dov'è ...?
Go straight ahead.	Si va sempre diritto.
Turn left/right.	Giri a sinistra/destra.
far/near	lontano/vicino

Around Town

a bank	una banca
chemist/pharmacy	la farmacia
the ... embassy	l'ambasciata di ...
the market	il mercato
newsagent	l'edicola

Signs – Italian

Ingresso/Entrata	Entrance
Uscita	Exit
Camere Libere	Rooms Available
Completo	Full/No Vacancies
Informazione	Information
Aperto	Open
Chiuso	Closed
Polizia/Carabinieri	Police
Questura	Police Station
Proibito/Vietato	Prohibited
Gabinetti/Bagni	Toilets
Uomini	Men
Donne	Women